20 years ago Costain Concrete started supporting trains.

Costain prestressed concrete sleepers
make tracks for the trains of today and tomorrow.

Costain Concrete Co. Ltd.,
Duncan House, Dolphin Square,
London SW1V 3PR, England.
Phone: 01-821 1581. Telex: 919858.

COSTAIN CONCRETE

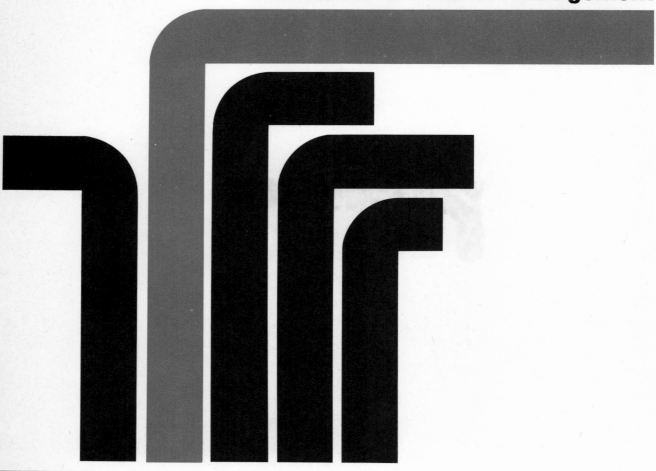

JANE'S
WORLD RAILWAYS
1978

A broad experience
at the service
of rail transport for public use

BREDA COSTRUZIONI FERROVIARIE S.p.A.
PISTOIA (ITALY)

Modern Rolling Stock

Newest lightweight suburban train of the Swiss Federal Railways
(15,000 V a.c.; length 100 m; tare 149 t; 272 seats; 3060 h.p.; 125 km/h)

COMFORT LONG LIFE ECONOMY

SWITZERLAND

Our production programme includes:
High-power motor coaches, luxury train sets, railway coaches of every kind and for all gauges, rack railcars, goods wagons, special wagons for heavy transports, bogies, etc.

 Swiss Industrial Company
Neuhausen Rhine Falls

 Swiss Car and Elevator
Manufacturing Corp., Ltd.
Schlieren-Zürich

Schindler Carriage and
Wagon Co., Ltd.
Pratteln

EXPORT ASSOCIATION OF SWISS ROLLING STOCK MANUFACTURERS

[3]

Alphabetical List of Advertisers

PRESTRESSED CONCRETE RAILWAY SLEEPERS

Monier is Australia's largest manufacturer of concrete products, with operations in many countries throughout the world.

Over the past two decades, continued research, development and technological innovation have enabled Monier to design and develop a highly efficient and economical method of producing prestressed concrete sleepers.

Monier's proven manufacturing systems are low in capital cost, utilise a minimum of labour and are flexible in capacity to meet varying demands.

For further information contact Concrete Industries (Monier) Ltd. for a copy of "Prestressed Concrete Railway Sleepers".

Operating for 125 years in the area of public transport

ANSALDO's production today:
Electrical equipment for electric and diesel-electric locomotives, railcars, multiple units, subway, tramway, trolleybus cars with conventional or thyristor control; ac and dc substations; signalling and train control equipment.

Power signalling apparatus, block signalling and token type instruments, track circuit equipment and accessories, automatic train control equipment, centralized traffic control and remote control systems, marshalling yard equipment including retarders.

1853·1978

Classified List of Advertisers

The companies advertising in this publication have informed us that they are involved in the fields of manufacture indicated below:—

Air brake equipment
Mitsubishi
Knorr-Bremse
Kolmex
Wabco Westinghouse

Air-conditioned carriages
Bre-Metro
Brown Boveri
Ganz Mavag
Hawker Siddeley Canada
SIG
Snia Viscosa

Air-conditioning equipment
Mitsubishi
Pintsch Bamag
Tokyo Shibaura Electric
Wabco Westinghouse

Air filters
Wabco Westinghouse

Air springs
Silentbloc

Audible signals and alarms
Pintsch Bamag
Wabco Westinghouse

Automatic couplers
Ateliers de Sécheron
GEC Traction
Knorr-Bremse
Voest-Alpine
Wabco Westinghouse

Automatic equipment for optimum train control with minimum energy consumption
Ateliers de Sécheron
GRS
Philips Telecommunicatie

Autopilots for trams, underground railways, etc.
GRS
Philips Telecommunicatie

Auxiliary motors
GEC Traction

Axle-box liner plates
Kolmex

Axle-boxes and bearings
Kolmex
Silentbloc

Axle drive for diesel hydraulic locomotives
Ganz Mavag
Krauss-Maffei
Fried. Krupp
Voith Getriebe

Axles, railway
Kolmex

Ballast cleaners
Plasser & Theurer

Ballast compactors
Plasser & Theurer

Ballast regulators
Plasser & Theurer

Ballast tampers
Plasser & Theurer

Ballast wagons
SNAV

Ballastless track
Robert McGregor

Battery locomotives
GEC Industrial Locomotives

Bearings, roller
Kolmex

Bogies
ASEA
Flug und Fahrzeugwerke
Ganz Mavag
GEC Traction
Hawker Siddeley Canada
Kolmex
Krauss—Maffei
Fried Krupp
MAN
SIG
Silentbloc
Societe Franco Belge
Sulzer Bros
Tokyo Shibaura Electric
Wabco Westinghouse
Waggonfabrik Uerdingen

Bogies—especially air suspension type
Ganz Mavag
Hawker Siddeley Canada
MAN
SIG

Boxes, battery
Flug-und Fahrzeugwerke
GEC Traction

Brake equipment
Breda
Kolmex
Miner
Mitsubishi
Wabco Westinghouse

Brake equipment (hydraulic disc)
Wabco Westinghouse

Brake equipment (hydrodynamic braking system)
Mitsubishi
Voith Getriebe
Wabco Westinghouse

Brake slack adjusters
Knorr-Bremse
Kolmex
SAB Industri
Wabco Westinghouse

Brake units for disc brakes
Knorr-Bremse
Krauss-Maffei
SAB Industri
Wabco Westinghouse

Brake units for tread brakes
Knorr-Bremse
SAB Industri
Wabco Westinghouse

Buffer Springs
Kolmex

Buffer friction
Miner
Waggonfabrick Uerdingen

Buffers, rubber
Krauss-Maffei
Silentbloc

What do Brazil, British Rail, Pakistan, South Africa and Taiwan have in common?

High voltage ac thyristor controlled locos from GEC Traction, world leaders in electric traction.

[9]

CLASSIFIED LIST OF ADVERTISERS

Car body tilting equipment
Knorr-Bremse
MAN
SIG

Cardan shafts
Voith Getriebe

Carriages and wagons
Flug und Fahrzeugwerke
Ganz Mavag
Hawker Siddeley Canada
Kolmex
MAN
Ortner
SIG
Snia Viscosa
Societe Franco Belge
Waggonfabrik Uerdingen

Castings, aluminium and aluminium alloy
Dresser
Ganz Mavag

Castings, iron
Dresser
Ganz Mavag
Italsider
Krauss-Maffei

Coach heaters
GEC Traction
Pintsch Bamag
Wabco Westinghouse

Coal wagons
Kolmex
Ortner
SIG
Societe Franco Belge
Waggonfabrik Uerdingen

Compressed air drying equipment
Wabco Westinghouse

Compressor motors
ASEA
Ganz Mavag
GEC Traction
Mitsubishi

Compressors
Brown Boveri
Ganz Mavag
Knorr-Bremse
Wabco Westinghouse

Computer controlled district control centres and marshalling yards
ASEA
Mitsubishi

Concrete slab track
Robert McGregor
Wabco Westinghouse

Concrete sleepers/manufacturing plant and equipment
Concrete Industries (Monier)
Costain Concrete
Dow-Mac

Concrete sleepers/ties
Concrete Industries (Monier)
Costain Concrete
Dow-Mac

Containers
Flug und Fahrzeugwerke
Interfrigo
Kolmex
SNAV
Snia Viscosa
Tokyo Shibaura Electric
Waggonfabrik Uerdingen

Control equipment, locomotive
Ansaldo
ASEA
Ateliers de Sécheron
Brown Boveri
Deuta Werke
GEC Traction
GRS
Holec
Krauss-Maffei
Mitsubishi
Wabco Westinghouse

Control equipment, Signal etc.
Ansaldo
GEC Traction
GRS
Mitsubishi
Philips Telecommunicatie
Silentbloc
Wabco Westinghouse

Conveyors for ballast
Plasser & Theurer

Cooling units
Voith Getriebe

Couplings
Dresser
Krauss-Maffei
Tokyo Shibaura Electric
Mitsubishi
Silentbloc
Voith Getriebe
Wabco Westinghouse

Crane carriers
SNAV

Cranes, electric
Brecknell, Willis
Holec
MAN

Crankshafts
Ganz Mavag
Italsider

Crossings
Dow-Mac
Elektro-Thermit
Voest-Alpine

Current collectors
Brecknell Willis
Brown Boveri
GEC Traction
Tokyo Shibaura Electric

DC high speed circuit breakers
Ateliers de Secheron

Diesel-electric locomotives
BRE-Metro
Brown Boveri
Fried. Krupp
Ganz Mavag
GEC Traction
Kolmex
Krauss Maffei
Mitsubishi
SIG
Sulzer Bros
Tokyo Shibaura Electric

Diesel-electric railcars
BRE-Metro
Brown Boveri
CIMT
GEC Traction
Hawker Siddeley Canada
MAN
SIG
Tokyo Shibaura Electric
Waggonfabrik Uerdingen

Diesel engine parts
Brown Boveri
Ganz Mavag
Kolmex
MAN

CLASSIFIED LIST OF ADVERTISERS

Diesel engines
Alsthom-Atlantique
Ganz Mavag
MAN
Motoren und Turbinen-Union
SAGM

Diesel-hydraulic coaches
Ganz Mavag
GEC Traction
MAN
Waggonfabrik Uerdingen

Diesel-hydraulic locomotives
Fried. Krupp

Diesel-hydraulic railcars
Ganz Mavag
MAN
Waggonfabrik Uerdingen

Diesel locomotives
Ganz Mavag
GEC Industrial Locomotives
GEC Traction
Kolmex
Krauss Maffei
Sulzer Bros

Diesel mechanical
GEC Industrial locomotives

Diesel mechanical railcars
Ganz Mavag
GEC Traction
MAN

Diesel passenger rail buses
GEC Traction
MAN
Waggonfabrik Uerdingen

Disc brake equipment for trams, locomotives, etc
ASEA
Knorr-Bremse
Krauss-Maffei
Wabco Westinghouse

Disc brakes
ASEA
Knorr-Bremse
Krauss-Maffei
Wabco Westinghouse

Door and window fittings
Kolmex
Pintsch Bamag
Snia Viscosa

Draught (draw) gears
Miner

Draw springs
Kolmex
Silentbloc

Draw and buffer device with rubber shock absorbers
Krauss-Maffei

Driver's safety and vigilance equipment
Ateliers de Sécheron
Deuta Werke
GEC Traction
Krauss-Maffei

Earthing brushes
Ateliers de Sécheron

Electric brake control
Ateliers de Sécheron

Electric locomotive equipment
Ansaldo
ASEA
Ateliers de Sécheron
Brecknell, Willis
Deuta-Werke
GEC Traction
Holec
Kolmex
Mitsubishi
Sulzer Bros
Tokyo Shibaura Electric

Electric couplers
Ateliers de Sécheron
Mitsubishi
Tokyo Shibaura Electric

Electric railcars
ASEA
CIMT
Flug und Fahrzeugwerke
Ganz Mavag
GEC Traction
Kolmex
MAN
Mitsubishi
SIG
Societe Franco Belge
Tokyo Shibaura Electric
Waggonfabrik Uerdingen

Electric tractors
SIG

Electric trailer cars
CIMT
Flug und Fahrzeugwerke
GEC Traction
Hawker Siddeley Canada
Kolmex
MAN
Mitsubishi
SIG
Waggonfabrik Uerdingen

Electrical equipment
Ansaldo
ASEA
Ateliers de Sécheron
GEC Traction
Holec
Mitsubishi
Pintsch Bamag
Tokyo Shibaura Electric
Wabco Westinghouse

Electromagnetic rail brakes
Ateliers de Sécheron
GEC Traction
Knorr-Bremse
SAB Industri
Wabco Westinghouse

Electronic control systems for diesel locomotives including adaptation for radio control
GEC Traction
Krauss-Maffei
Fried. Krupp
Mitsubishi

Electro pneumatic brake
Holec
Mitsubishi
Wabco Westinghouse

Electronic protection equipment for rail vehicles (slip and spin protection)
Ateliers de Sécheron
Deuta Werke
GEC Traction
Krauss Maffei
Mitsubishi

Electronic testing equipment
Mitsubishi
Pintsch Bamag

Engine parts, diesel
Ganz Mavag
MAN

Engine testing equipment
Deuta Werke

Engineers
Grant Lyon Eagre

Exhaust motors
GEC Traction

Explosion proof locomotive
Ganz Mavag
Wabco Westinghouse

CLASSIFIED LIST OF ADVERTISERS

Fail-safe warning systems
Deuta Werke
Mitsubishi
Wabco Westinghouse

Filters (air)
Wabco Westinghouse

Fixed target braking
Ateliers de Sécheron

Flameproof mining locomotives
GEC Industrial Locomotives
GEC Traction
Kolmex

Flexible couplings (Rubber)
Wabco Westinghouse

Fluorescent lighting
Brown Boveri
Pintsch Bamag
Wabco Westinghouse

Forgings, steel
Italsider

Freight cars
Bre-Metro
Hawker Siddeley Canada
MAN
Ortner
SIG
Snia Viscosa
SNAV
Societe Franco Belge
Waggonfabrik Uerdingen

Forgings—steel
Bre-Metro

Gears and gearboxes
ASEA
Ganz Mavag
GEC Traction
Mitsubishi
Sulzer Bros
Voith Getriebe

Generators
Ansaldo
ASEA
Brown Boveri
Deuta Werke
GEC Traction
Holec
Mitsubishi
Pintsch Bamag
Siemens

Generators, portable
ASEA
Plasser & Theurer
Siemens

Heating equipment (switch)
Elektro-Thermit
Pintsch Bamag

Hopper cars
Bre-Metro
GEC Traction
Kolmex
MAN
Ortner
SNAV
Snia Viscosa
Waggonfabrik Uerdingen

Hose and couplings
Wabco Westinghouse

Hydraulic pumps
Voith Getriebe

Information display units/indicators
Philips Telecommunicatie

Inspection, track
Plasser & Theurer

Instruments
Philips Telecommunicatie

Insulated rail joints
Elektro-Thermit

Insulation Electric
Elektro-Thermit

Intercommunication equipment
GEC Traction
Mitsubishi
SIG
Wabco Westinghouse

Interlocking signalling equipment
Wabco Westinghouse

Lifting jacks
Loc Manutention

Lighting equipment—locomotives
Brown Boveri
GEC Traction
Kolmex
Fried. Krupp
Pintsch Bamag

Lighting equipment, trains
Fried. Krupp
Pintsch Bamag
Tokyo Shibaura Electric
Wabco Westinghouse

Lighting equipment—station buildings
ASEA

Load braking devices
Knorr-Bremse
SAB Industrie
Wabco Westinghouse

Locomotive equipment
Ansaldo
ASEA
Brown Boveri
Ganz Mavag
GEC Industrial Locomotives
GEC Traction
Knorr-Bremse
Kolmex
Mitsubishi
Sulzer Bros
Tokyo Shibaura Electric
Wabco Westinghouse

Locomotive equipment electric
Ansaldo
ASEA
Ateliers de Sécheron
Brecknell, Willis
Brown Boveri
GEC Traction
Kolmex
Mitsubishi

Locomotive, industrial
ASEA
Ganz Mavag

Locomotives, diesel-electric
Bre-Metro
Brown Boveri
Fiat
Ganz Mavag
GEC Traction
Kolmex
Krauss-Maffei
Fried. Krupp
Mitsubishi
SIG
Sulzer Bros

Locomotives, diesel-hydraulic
Ganz Mavag
GEC Traction
Krauss Maffei
Fried. Krupp
Sulzer Bros

Locomotives, diesel-mechanical
Ganz Mavag
Kolmex
Sulzer Bros

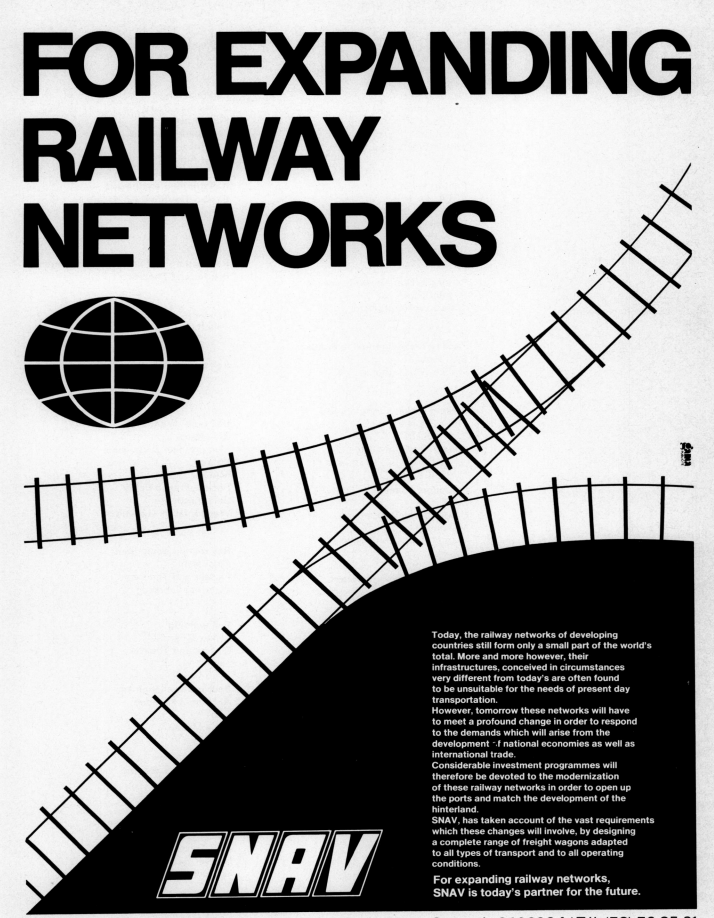

FOR EXPANDING RAILWAY NETWORKS

Today, the railway networks of developing countries still form only a small part of the world's total. More and more however, their infrastructures, conceived in circumstances very different from today's are often found to be unsuitable for the needs of present day transportation.
However, tomorrow these networks will have to meet a profound change in order to respond to the demands which will arise from the development of national economies as well as international trade.
Considerable investment programmes will therefore be devoted to the modernization of these railway networks in order to open up the ports and match the development of the hinterland.
SNAV, has taken account of the vast requirements which these changes will involve, by designing a complete range of freight wagons adapted to all types of transport and to all operating conditions.

For expanding railway networks, SNAV is today's partner for the future.

Chemin du Génie 69631 Vénissieux France / B.P. 4 – Télex : Snavenix 340603 f / Tél. (78) 72.85.21

CLASSIFIED LIST OF ADVERTISERS

Locomotives, electric
Ansaldo
Bre-Metro
Brown Boveri
Fiat
GEC Traction
Kolmex
Krauss Maffei
Fried. Krupp
Mitsubishi
Sulzer Bros

Locomotives, industrial and mining
Brown Boveri
GEC Traction
Kolmex
Mitsubishi
SIG

Locomotives, tilting body
Fiat

Materials handling equipment
ASEA
Brecknell, Willis
Plasser and Theurer
SIG

Metro cars
ASEA
CIMT
Flug und Fahzeugwerke
Ganz Mavag
GEC Traction
Hawker Siddeley Canada
MAN
Mitsubishi
Societe Franco Belge
Waggonfabrik Uerdingen

Motor car carriers
SNAV

Motor coaches
Ansaldo
ASEA
Bre-Metro
CIMT
Flug und Fahrzeugwerke
Ganz Mavag
MAN
Mitsubishi
SIG
Waggonfabrik Uerdingen

Motors, electric
ASEA
Ateliers de Sécheron
Brown Boveri
GEC Traction
Holec
Mitsubishi

Multi-axle heavy load vehicles
Fried. Krupp

Overhead line inspection vehicles
Plasser and Theurer
Waggonfabrik Uerdingen
Zweiweg-Fahrzeug

Overspeed protection systems
Ateliers de Sécheron
Deuta-Werke
GEC Traction
Krauss-Maffei
Mitsubishi
Wabco Westinghouse

Pantographs
ASEA
Ateliers de Sécheron
Brecknell, Willis
Brown Boveri
GEC Traction

Parking brake, electro-hydraulic
SAB Industri
Wabco Westinghouse

Parking brake, manual-hydraulic
SAB Industri
Wabco Westinghouse

Parking brake, spring applied
Knorr-Bremse
SAB Industri
Wabco Westinghouse

Passenger coaches
CIMT
Hawker Siddeley Canada
Mitsubishi
Waggonfabrik Uerdingen

Permanent way equipment
Elastic Rail Spike
Elektro-Thermit
Le Materiel de Voie
Pandrol
Plasser and Theurer
SATEBA
Voest-Alpine

Plastic sleepers
Voest-Alpine

Platform trucks
SIG
Zweiweg-Fahrzeug

Power transmission
ASEA
Ateliers de Sécheron
Ganz Mavag
GEC Traction
Mitsubishi

Pre-set speed controls
Ateliers de Sécheron

Radio remote control
GRS

Rail corrugation recording vehicle
Speno International

Rail fastening
Elastic Rail Spike
Kowa Kasei
Le Materiel de Voie
Pandrol
Voest-Alpine

Rail grinding equipment
Elektro-Thermit
Plasser and Theurer
Speno International

Rail loading and unloading equipment
Plasser and Theurer

Rail pads
Silentbloc

Rail spikes and chairs
Elastic Rail Spikes
Pandrol

Rail tank wagons
Bre-Metro
Flug und Fahrzeugwerke
Kolmex
MAN
Societe Franco Belge
Snia Viscosa
Waggonfabrik Uerdingen

Rail testing equipment
Mitsubishi
Plasser and Theurer
Zweiweg-Fahrzeug

Rail welding
Elektro-Thermit
Plasser and Theurer

Railcar diesel engines
Alsthom-Atlantique
CIMT
Ganz Mavag
MAN

Railcar trains, electric
ASEA
Bre-Metro
CIMT
Flug und Fahrzeugwerke
Ganz Mavag
GEC Traction
Hawker Siddeley Canada
Kolmex
MAN
Mitsubishi
SIG
Societe Franco Belge
Waggonfabrik Uerdingen

SERIES 331

There is no substitute

MTU is supplying rail traction engines throughout the world. At present the single engine output available for rail traction ranges up to 5000 hp UIC-rated power.

Employing modern design and the very latest in technological development MTU has produced a very compact diesel engine family — the series 331. Exceptional power-to-weight and power-to-space ratios, economical operation and long life make these engines the ideal choice for driving shunting- and industrial locomotives. Ruggedly built, they have proven themselves under extreme operating conditions.

The 6-, 8- and 12-cylinder high performance diesel engines offer a UIC-rated power range from 560 to 1115 hp single engine output for railway traction. A clear configuration, using a maximum number of identical parts, guarantees convenient accessibility to all engine components for easy servicing and maintenance.

To assure the highest possible degree of availability MTU offers exchange engines as well as exchange components for maximum performance and reliable operation. Service is available wherever MTU engines are in operation — from our world-wide sales and service network or directly from our main service center in Friedrichshafen.

mtu

Motoren- und Turbinen-Union
Friedrichshafen GmbH
M.A.N. Maybach Mercedes-Benz
7990 Friedrichshafen/W. Germany
P.O.Box 2040

CLASSIFIED LIST OF ADVERTISERS

Railcars, diesel powered
ASEA
CIMT
Flug und Fahrzeugwerke
Ganz Mavag
Hawker Siddeley Canada
MAN
SIG
Waggonfabrik Uerdingen

Railcars, electric
CIMT
Flug und Fahrzeugwerke
Ganz Mavag
GEC Traction
Hawker Siddeley Canada
MAN
Mitsubishi
SIG
Societe Franco Belge
Waggonfabrik Uerdingen

Rails
Le Materiel de Voie
Voest-Alpine

Railway carriage
Flug und Fahrzeugwerke
SIG
Wabco Westinghouse

Railway consultants
Flug und Fahrzeugwerke

Railway cranes
Fried. Krupp

Railway electrification
ASEA
Brecknell, Willis
Brown Boveri
GEC Traction
Mitsubishi

Railway snow clearing equipment
Beilhack

Railway wheels and axles
Italsider
Kolmex
Krauss-Maffei

Rapid transit control systems
GRS

Rectifiers
ASEA
Ateliers de Sécheron
Brown Boveri
GEC Traction
GRS
Mitsubishi

Rectifiers, silicon
ASEA
Ateliers de Sécheron
Brown Boveri
GEC Traction
Mitsubishi
Pintsch Bamag
Tokyo Shibaura Electric

Refrigerated equipment
Brown Boveri
Mitsubishi
Pintsch Bamag

Refrigerated wagons
Interfrigo
MAN
Societe Franco Belge
Snia Viscosa

Regulations, ballast
Plasser and Theurer

Remote control equipment
Brown Boveri
CSEE
GEC Traction
Mitsubishi
Tokyo Shibaura Electric
Wabco Westinghouse

Resilient wheels
SAB Industri
Wabco Westinghouse

Retarders
ASEA
Voith Getriebe

Roller bearing axle-boxes
CSEE
Ganz Mavag

Rolling stock, railway
Breda
CIMT
Ganz Mavag
Hawker Siddeley Canada
MAN
Mitsubishi
Ortner
SIG
SNAV
Societé Franco Belge
Snia Viscosa
Sulzer Bros
Tokyo Shibaura Electric
Waggonfabrik Uerdingen

Sanding devices
Ansaldo
Krauss-Maffei
Plasser and Theurer

Seats—passenger
Bre-Metro
Flug und Fahrzeugwerke
SIG
Snia Viscosa

Signalling systems and apparatus
Ansaldo
Deuta-Werke
GRS
Mitsubishi
Pintsch Bamag
Wabco Westinghouse

Sleepers
Concrete Industries (Monier)
Costain Concrete
Dow-Mac
Jarrah and Karri
Le Materiel de Voie
SATEBA

Sliding side wagons
Voest-Alpine
SNAV

Snow removers
Beilhack

Snow switch cleaners
Zweiweg-Fahrzeug

Solenoid valves
Ateliers de Sécheron

Special purpose self-propelled railway vehicles
Flug und Fahrzeugwerke
Hawker Siddeley Canada
Plasser and Theurer

Speed control devices
ASEA
Ateliers de Sécheron
Brown Boveri
Deuta-Werke
GEC Traction
Holec
Krauss-Maffei
Wabco Westinghouse
Mitsubishi

Speed indications
Deuta-Werke
GEC Traction
Mitsubishi

Standby diesel generators
MAN

Steel castings
Bre-Metro
Ganz Mavag
Italsider

Uerdingen Railcars

1926 India

1937 Greece

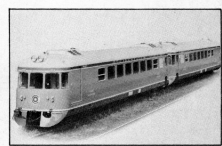

1958 Cuba

1962 RENFE

**1965
Danish Private Railways**

1969 Cambodia

1972 DB

1973 DB

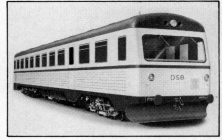

1978 DSB

Creative, capable and competent in design, engineering and manufacturing.

Waggonfabrik Uerdingen AG

Duisburger Strasse 145 · D-4150 Krefeld-Uerdingen (West-Germany) · Telephone 02151/4491 · Telex 0853845

CLASSIFIED LIST OF ADVERTISERS

Steel sleepers
Le Materiel de Voie
Voest-Alpine

Steel structures
MAN
SIG

Surface and underground battery and trolley locomotives
Bre-Metro
GEC Traction
Kolmex
SIG

Suspension components
Flug und Fahrzeugwerke
Krauss-Maffei
Silentbloc

Suspension systems
Silentbloc

Switchgear, electric
Ansaldo
ASEA
Ateliers de Sécheron
CSEE
Dueta-Werke
GEC Traction
Holec
Mitsubishi
Pintsch Bamag
Tokyo Shibaura Electric

Switch heaters
Brown Boveri
Elektro-Thermit
Pintsch Bamag

Switches, trackwork
Voest-Alpine

Tank cars
Bre-Metro
Flug und Fahrzeugwerke
Kolmex
MAN
SIG
Snia Viscosa
Societe Franco Belge
Waggonfabrik Uerdingen

Telecommunications
CSEE
Mitsubishi
Tokyo Shibaura Electric

Thyristors and thyristor equipment
AEG
Ansaldo
ASEA
Ateliers de Sécheron
Brown Boveri
GEC Traction
Mitsubishi
Tokyo Shibaura Electric

Ties
Costain Concrete
Jarrah and Karri
Le Materiel de Voie
SATEBA
Voest-Alpine

Toilets, flushing
SAB Industri

Torpedo cars for liquid iron transport
Fried. Krupp

Track analyser
Plasser and Theurer

Track/ballastless
Robert McGregor

Track/concrete slab
Robert McGregor

Track inspection cars
Plasser and Theurer

Track liners and levellers
Plasser and Theurer

Track maintenance equipment
Concrete Industries (Monier)
Elastic Rail Spike
Elektro-Thermit
Mitsubishi
Pandrol
Plasser and Theurer

Track measuring vehicle (cars & coaches)
Flug und Fahrzeugwerke
Plasser and Theurer

Track renewal train
Plasser and Theurer

Track undercutters
Plasser and Theurer

Trackwork
Elastic Rail Spike
Grant Lyon Eagre
Pandrol
Voest-Alpine

Traffic control systems
CSEE
Deuta-Werke
GRS
Mitsubishi
Philips Telecommunicatie
Pintsch Bamag
Tokyo Shibaura Electric
Wabco Westinghouse

Trailers
CIMT
Flug und Fahrzeugwerke
GEC Traction
MAN
SIG
Waggonfabrik Uerdingen

Tramcars
ASEA
Brown Boveri
CIMT
Flug und Fahrzeugwerke
GEC Traction
Hawker Siddeley Canada
Kolmex
MAN
Mitsubishi
SIG
Waggonfabrik Uerdingen

Transformers
ASEA
Ateliers de Sécheron
GEC Traction
GRS
Mitsubishi
Tokyo Shibaura Electric

Trucks
ASEA
Bre-Metro
Dresser
Flug und Fahrzeugwerke
GEC Traction
Hawker Siddeley Canada
MAN
SIG

Tunnel linings (tubbings)
Voest-Alpine

Turbo-chargers
Brown Boveri
Snecma Division Hispano Suiza

Turbo-generators
Siemens

Two-way vehicles
Plasser and Theurer
Siemens
Zweiweg-Fahrzeug

Tyres(railway)
Kolmex

Tyres (tramways)
Kolmex

Ultrasonic testing equipment
Plasser and Theurer

Korean Republic - Electric locomotive-BBB 5300 Hp.

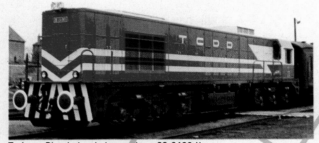

Turkey - Diesel electric locomotive - CC 2400 Hp

Portugal - Diesel electric railcar - 550 Hp.

France - S.N.C.F. - Very high speed Turbotrain TGV 001 - 300 Km/h.

RER-Paris - Regional express train

Mexico - metro

[21]

CLASSIFIED LIST OF ADVERTISERS

Underground supplies vehicles
ASEA
GEC Traction
Societe Franco Belge

Vacuum brake equipment
Knorr-Bremse
Tokyo Shibaura Electric
Wabco Westinghouse

Vacuum brake testing equipment
Wabco Westinghouse

Valves, pneumatic
Knorr-Bremse
SAB Industri
Wabco Westinghouse

Ventilation equipment
Brown Boveri

Mitsubishi
Voith Getriebe
Equip Rail
Wabco Westinghouse
Tokyo Shibaura Electric

Ventilators
Voith Getriebe
Siemens
Tokyo Shibaura Electric

Wagons and carriages
Bre-Metro
CIMT
Flug und Fahrzeugwerke
Hawker Siddeley Canada
Kolmex
MAN
Ortner
SIG
Societé Franco Belge
Snia Viscosa
Waggonfabrik Uerdingen

Welded fabrications
Flug und Fahrzeugwerke
Ganz Mavag
MAN

Wheels and axles
Italsider
Kolmex
Krauss-Maffei

Wheel and axle testing equipment
Mitsubishi

Wheel flange lubrication
Ateliers de Sécheron

Windscreen wipers
Knorr-Bremse
Wabco Westinghouse

The other landmark of Paris will be in aluminium.

Paris has always given technology a chance. This was not only demonstrated by the famous steel tower erected by Mr. Gustave Eiffel, but also by the decision of the Paris Metro to use aluminium for the first time for its new trains.
Everyone knows that aluminium weighs less than steel, but is more expensive. The Alusuisse consulting engineers therefore developed a new technology permitting the 1000 cars to be made from preformed elements – called extruded sections by the experts. These elements, with cross-sections up to 600 mm and each of 15 metres length, are welded together. This simplified assembly saves the French manufacturer, Société Franco-Belge de Matériel de Chemins de Fer, so much labour that the new trains can be produced more economically than conventional designs. Quite apart from the saving in driving power.
When, therefore, the new trains are running beneath the streets of Paris, it will be possible to say that the material has changed but the spirit has remained the same. The spirit which places technology at the service of mankind.

Aluminium is our business.

Swiss Aluminium Ltd.
Buckhauserstr. 11, CH-8048 Zurich, Tel. 01/54 22 41, Telex 52310

**Have you thought about
turning to us with your
railway vehicle problems?
You can rely on our experience
and know-how.**

*Diesel railcars and
Diesel trains with
hydraulic or mechanic
power transmission*

*Diesel-electric
locomotives from 600
to 3000 Hp
Diesel-hydraulic
locomotives from 400
to 1800 Hp*

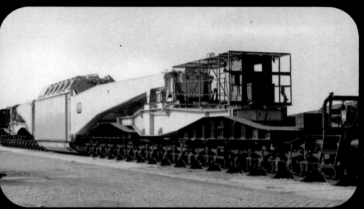

PLASSER & THEURER
serving progress for

1953 **25** years 1978

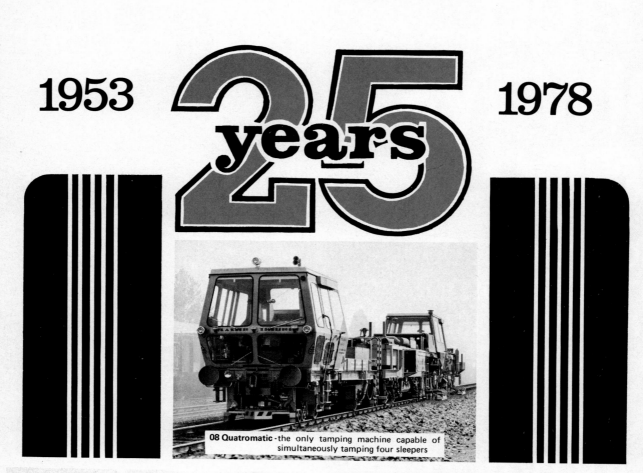

08 Quatromatic - the only tamping machine capable of simultaneously tamping four sleepers

SUZ-programm - the first track renewal trains working by the assembly line principle

RM 76-U - the only high-capacity ballast cleaning machine for **plain track and switches**

PLASSER & THEURER

Head Office: A - 1010 Vienna, Johannesgasse 3
Great Britain: Plasser Railway Machinery (G.B.) Ltd. Manor Road, West Ealing, London W 13

S.E.M.T. PIELSTICK
diesel locomotives engines
from 1000 to 7200 hp

French railway locomotive, fitted with a PA6-280 of 4800 HP. Has run in service for more than 500.000 km. Is now the world's most powerful single engined diesel locomotive.

33 differents types of S.E.M.T. Pielstick diesel locomotives are – to date –
in service in 17 different countries by 25 railways systems.
They use the well known S.E.M.T. Pielstick PA4 – 185 and PA4 – 200 ranging from 1000 to 3150 HP.
With the new S.E.M.T. Pielstick PA6 – 280, the world's most powerful unit for diesel locomotive,
the range of power offered extends now from 1000 to 7200 HP.

 **ALSTHOM-ATLANTIQUE DÉPARTEMENT MOTEURS**
2, quai de Seine, 93203 Saint-Denis - France - 820.61.91 - Télex 620 333 F Motla

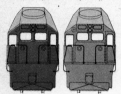
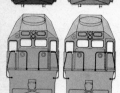

82 different overseas customers bought GM locomotives for the same reason.

They'd bought one before.

And they know that the only thing better than an old GM locomotive is a new GM locomotive.

It's no wonder.

We've been delivering locomotives outside the U.S. since 1946. To date, we've shipped over 6000 of them. In gauges ranging from 3 feet to 5 feet 6 inches. For either normal or light axle loading. And with ratings up to 3900 gross horsepower.

Much of the dependability that keeps customers coming back comes from GM's hard-working 645 engine. Parts are interchangeable with other GM locomotives to let you cut spare parts stocking.

We make certain every GM locomotive is rugged enough to give you many years of trouble-free service. That way, we know you'll be back.

For more information, contact Electro-Motive Division, General Motors Corporation, La Grange, IL 60525, U.S.A. Telex: 270041, McCook, IL, U.S.A., or cable ELMODIV, La Grange, IL, U.S.A.

ANOTHER ITALIAN HEAVYWEIGHT

Ercole Marelli
wise to the demands of public transport.

Complete electric traction systems.

Ercole Marelli (it means Hercules in Italian) has the power to get things moving.

His traction effort includes design and production of:
- complete electric equipment for electric and diesel-electric locomotives and train-sets; for suburban and urban transit systems including commuter trains, underground trains, trams and trolley-buses
- on-board auxiliary equipment
- converting substations
- electronic systems for automatic operation control and for training simulators. Get in touch for detailed data on the following recent developments:

Tilting body 3kV d.c. train-sets for FS and RENFE.

The electric equipment of these high-speed trains features an electronic system for stepless variation of the series excitation of the traction motors. This permits continuative operation within a wide field of efforts and speed as well as operation at preset speed, automatically regulated in accordance with the characteristics of the line.

Full chopper underground trains.

For the Milan underground system a series of 750 V d.c. full chopper electric motor coaches has been developed by Ercole Marelli. They have regenerative braking and offer the advantages of low maintenance costs, high reliability and low power consumption in both starting and braking.

Shunt chopper locomotives.

The electric equipment of two 3 kV d.c. locomotives of the E444 FS series has been designed with shunt chopper equipment, allowing a constant traction effort in starting and thus utilisation of higher adhesion coefficients.

Control is of the traditional type, or automatic with preset speed.

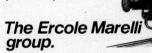

The Ercole Marelli group.

For almost half a century the Ercole Marelli group of operative divisions and associate companies has been producing components, motors and systems for traction. The group's technology has made itself felt worldwide, choosing to operate where it matters. Electronics, electromechanical, nuclear. And protection of the environment.

Front-line engineering; front-line products.

The driving plant of this modern railcar* too has been optimized by Voith!

It is not only the weight advantages to be gained when using Voith turbo transmissions —

It is not only the worldwide reputation of the reliability of Voith products —

It is to a large degree our know-how in respect of the power pack and transmission system as a whole which is of prime importance for railway companies:

We bring harmony into the interaction of engine, transmission, cardan shafts, axle drives and cooling unit!

We execute all necessary computations and torsional analyses and assist in the designing of the control system!

We understand the influences of the desert, the tropics, of ice-cold winters, high altitudes, and high speed stretches through flat country, and the characteristics of narrow-gauge railways!

* Manufacturer: Macosa, Barcelona (with M.A.N. licence). Built for Yugoslavia (ZTP Skopje). Equipped with Voith turbo transmissions T 211 r, axle drives V 13/15 and E 13/15, and Voith engine governor units.

Voith supply for railcars of all power classes
Turbo transmissions
Retarders
Cardan shafts
Axle drives
Engine governor units
Cooling units

G 7619 e /29

May we inform you of the latest state of engineering? Write to us to arrange an interview.

Voith Getriebe KG
D-7920 Heidenheim, P.O. Box 1920
Phone (0 73 21) 32 91, Telex 07 14 888

In railroading... in transit: the one name to know in signal & control is WABCO.

WABCO is 14,000 people, in 28 locations, 12 countries, around the world: the world's largest supplier of braking, signaling and communications systems, and on-board auxiliary services for rail transportation.

Signal and control equipment from WABCO helps railroads get increased productivity from their track and rolling stock investments, whether in the U.S., Brazil, or Turkey. And WABCO is at the wayside and aboard the cars of some of the world's most productive passenger transport systems: in New York, Sao Paulo, Italy and Spain.

WABCO has 96 years experience and can help you select the most efficient rail transportation signal and control systems, whether people or goods are being moved.

These resources are at your service, worldwide. Write for more information. Our Eastern Hemisphere Headquarters is: WABCO Westinghouse S.p.A., Via Pier Carlo Boggio 20, 10138 Torino, Italy. In the Western Hemisphere: WABCO, Union Switch & Signal Division, Swissvale, PA 15218, U.S.A.

WABCO

An **American-Standard** Company

Transportation from the word go.

High horsepower -high speed.

Three out of twenty NOHAB-GM type Mz diesel-electric 3900 HP locomotives for Denmark.

Another fifteen Mz locomotives with the GM turbocharged 20-cylinder, 3900 HP engine and new electronic control gear are now under delivery to the Danish State Railways. These locomotives are geared for 165 km/h and equipped with 500 kW, 1500 V, 50 Hz electric train heating powered from the main engine.

 **BOFORS**
NOHAB LOCOMOTIVE

AB BOFORS-NOHAB
S-461 01 TROLLHÄTTAN SWEDEN
Tel. 0520/180 00 Telex: 42084 Cables: NOHAB

[33]

Sweden

A technologically - advanced and highly - industrialized nation which looked abroad - to Italy - for some of the rolling stock it needed for its national railway network

Sweden is a country that is "near the top" not only geographically-speaking but also from the technological point of view.
So, if its Government decided to give Fiat an order for 100 highly-sophisticated railcars, it must have had a good reason.
And indeed: a first test held in May-June 1975 and a second one in  January-February 1976 gave extremely positive results. Winter trials were staged under savage environmental conditions - blizzards, ice, and temperatures reaching 40°C below zero.
Of course, Fiat was not alone in these trials: it had to compete with other leading rolling stock manufacturers.
A number of Swedish firms will be taking part as major suppliers in the order.
Italian engineering is crossing national boundaries and showing the world the advanced technological content of its diesel engines and mechanical rolling stock components.

Main railcar specifications:
Twin-engine diesel type unit. 294 kw. Weight, 42 tonnes
Seating capacity, 76. Max speed, 130 kph (over 80 mph)

SAB on all Continents

Rail history was made in October 1976 as British Railways brought into regular passenger service their new generation 'Inter-City 125' high-speed trains — the fastest diesel trains in the world.

The Inter-City trains are fitted with SAB Brake Cylinder Adjuster Units for disc brakes. The SAB Brake Units consist of compressed air brake cylinders with built-in rapid-acting slack adjusters for continuous brake slack adjustment.

The SAB Railway programme for main line, suburban, rapid transit and freight rolling stock includes brake regulators, block brake and disc brake units, load brake equipment, weighing valves, spring applied and hydraulic parking brake equipment, resilient wheels, vacuum operated train toilet system and overfill protection equipment.

SAB has supplied millions of brake equipment to Railways on all Continents and many of these Railways use and specify SAB products as standard equipment on their vehicles. As a result of the ever increasing demand for SAB products a world wide marketing and technical service organisation has developed.

Make use of it — ask SAB

Belgium: SAB Broms S.A. Nossegem (Bruxelles). **France:** Société SAB, Saint Cloud (Paris). **Great Britain:** SAB Brake Regulator Co. Ltd. Darlington. **Italy:** SAB Broms S.p.A. Caldine (Firenze). **Spain:** SAB Ibérica S.A. Madrid. **Sweden:** SAB Industri AB, Malmö. **Brazil:** Suecobras Indústria e Comércio S.A. Rio de Janeiro. **USA:** SAB Harmon Industries Inc. Grain Valley, Missouri 64029. Further 15 licensees and representatives on all continents.

Dependable Stock for Suburban Services

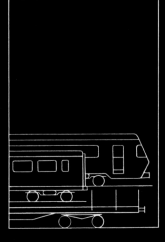

Toshiba is justifiably proud of its "air-conditioning" technology. And no wonder. We've put confortable, refreshing systems into thousands of buildings, factories, and homes. And we scored another "world first" by introducing unit cooling systems for rolling stock. Not only offering top performance, these systems also come in a wide variety of types and capacities to meet every demand.

- A line of unit cooling systems ranging from an underfloor concentration type to a ceiling-mounted, dispersed or concentration type are available in capacities as small as 2,250kcal/h to as large as 42,000kcal/h designed for commuter trains.
- An optimum type of a unit cooling system is selectable according to car size and installation restrictions for both newly built cars as well as for those already in operation.
- The electronic automatic temperature controller constantly maintains car interior temperature at the most comfortable cooling level.
- Toshiba unit cooler systems for about three hundreds of cars have been exported to the Philippines, Australia, Republic of Korea, United Arab, New Zealand, and elsewhere throughout the world.

Toshiba know-how ensures comfortably cool car interiors

Toshiba **TOSHIBA**

TOKYO SHIBAURA ELECTRIC CO., LTD.
1-6, Uchisaiwaicho 1-chome, Chiyoda-ku, Tokyo, 100 Japan
Cable: TOSHIBA TOKYO Telex: J22587 TOSHIBA Phone: (501) 5411

The wide range of Brown Boveri electrical traction equipment

gives you

Increased power
Improved adhesion
Prolonged intervals between overhauls
Enhanced safety
Still more comfort
Rationalization

Brown Boveri supply: Power equipment for all types of electric, diesel-electric and diesel-hydraulic locomotives including exhaust-gas turbochargers for diesel engines
Electronic equipment for stepless control systems, closed-loop control systems and automation
Equipment for transmission of data and telephony between track and train
Air conditioning, lighting and heating equipment

If you have traction problems, consult Brown Boveri. You will find manufacturing facilities and representatives all over the world.

BBC
BROWN BOVERI

Brown, Boveri & Company, Ltd., Baden/Switzerland

In Great Britain: British Brown-Boveri Ltd., Stag Place, London SW1 E 5 AG

153787.VI

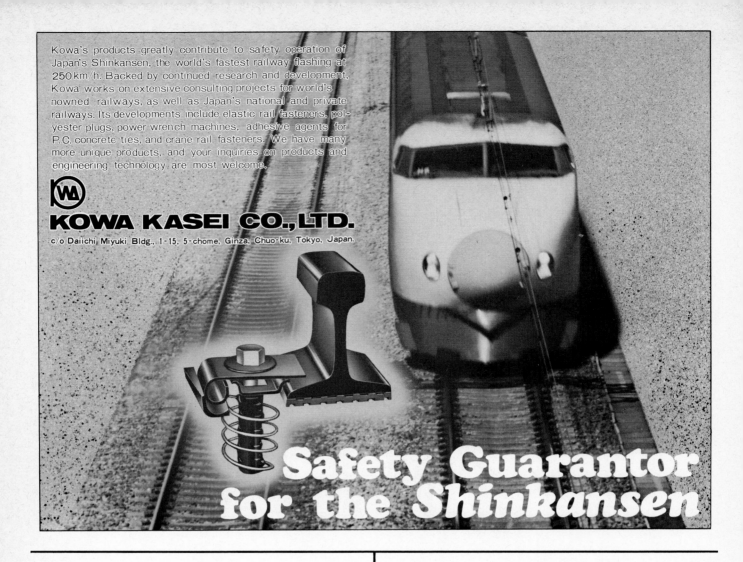
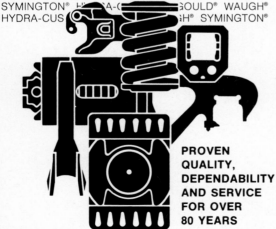

turbosuperchargers

[45]

[47]

A TOTAL TRACK ENGINEERING SERVICE

Grant Lyon Eagre's track engineering capability means track built to face the toughest conditions and to give the highest track performance anywhere.

We can supply a total package, from the manufacture in our extensive Workshops and modern Foundry of all types of switches and crossings together with the appropriate cast iron fittings, to the design, construction and servicing of a complete railway system, at home or abroad, for any main line requirement or industrial project.

Whether for passenger or industrial traffic, overground or underground, Grant Lyon Eagre have the Railway Engineering Specialists, the Surveyors and Engineers, the skills, the facilities and the work force to meet your particular project demands, fast.

Grant Lyon Eagre Limited, 80a Scotter Road, Scunthorpe, South Humberside, DN15 8EF. Telephone Scunthorpe (0724) 62131. Telex 527215.

GRANT LYON EAGRE
International Railway Engineers and Contractors

 A member of the Royal Bos Kalis Westminster Group N.V. Z32

HRS Elastic Rail Spikes for quick and safe connections

The first rule in rail traffic is safety. In this, the HRS Elastic Rail Spike plays an important part. More than 30 years ago, HRS experts discovered a paradox solution: Square elastic spikes for round holes. These elastic spikes don't come loose – friction keeps them in place. Since then, rails throughout the world have been fastened with HRS Elastic Rail Spikes. They guarantee frame rigidity and constant track alignment. Cheap to buy and place. No maintenance.

HRS engineers are at your disposal to pit their experience, expert knowledge and ingenuity against your rail fastening problems. Challenge them. Or just ask us for information.

A call or a postcard will do:
HOESCH ROTHE ERDE – SCHMIEDAG AG, Abt.: 34
Tremoniastr. 5 – 11,
4600 Dortmund 1,
Tel. 0231 – 1961,
FS-Nr. 822 245 hrs d.

HRS Elastic Rail Spikes

We would like to know more:
HRS drop forgings
HRS ductile iron
HRS cold extrusion parts
HRS elastic rail spikes
Rothe Erde large anti-friction bearings
Rothe Erde gear rings and ring forgings

VÖEST-ALPINE

RAILS, SWITCHES
PERMANENT WAY EQUIPMENT
such as fishplates, soleplates,
ribbed soleplates, screws
SLEEPERS
(steel and plastic)
AUTOMATIC COUPLER
TUBBINGS
(steel and cast)

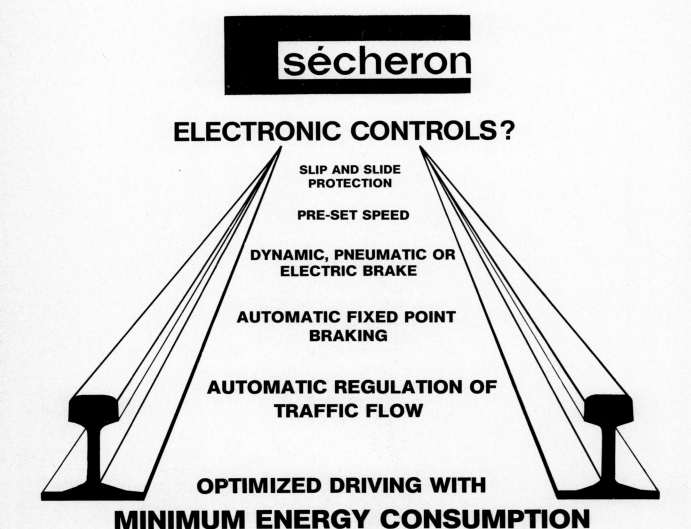
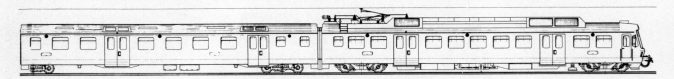

Safety
in railroading!

Fast trains need safe tracks. Take the crucial problem of level crossings.
Here precise reliability is a must. PINTSCH BAMAG traffic signaling with its unfailing
flash-light equipment, provides absolute safety 24 hours a day.
There are more than 1,000 installations e. g. of the Lo 1/57 type in actual service with the
German Federal Railways, privately-owned and industrial railway societies.
Write for descriptive literature.

Road Traffic

Pretimed and traffic-actuated roadway signalization, also for intersections near grade crossings (BÜSTRA) · Network coordination · Radar equipment for automatic actuation of the „Green"-phase for privileged road users („Green Wave") · Radar control equipment for optimum traffic flow (selection of phases, of lanes, and of traffic direction by radar recording of traffic density) · Pedestrian crossing protection signals · Identification beacons of the mirror- and 3-lens-type for privileged road users and for the industry

Rail Traffic

Electrical and electronic power supply, lighting, heating and air conditioning equipment for rail vehicles · Level crossing protection equipment with flash-lights and luminous signals, with barrier guarding and radar obstacle detectors · Contactless speed measurement of rail vehicles by DOPPLER radar · Electrical and propane-fuelled point heating equipment · Solid-state frost and snow detectors · Electric train preheating equipment · Test sets for electrical installations on rail vehicles

18

PINTSCH BAMAG
DINSLAKEN

PINTSCH BAMAG Antriebs- und Verkehrstechnik GmbH · Postfach 100 420 · D-4220 Dinslaken · Telefon (0 2134) 602-1* · Telex 08 551938

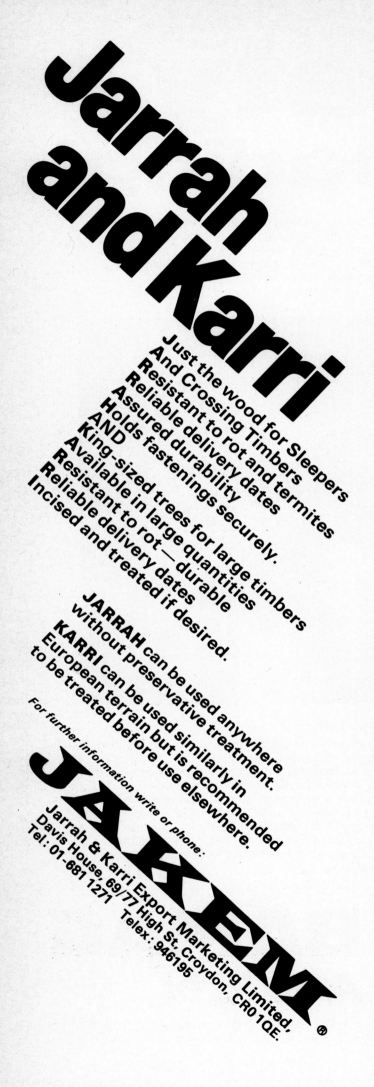

A fast train needs more than a strong motive power.

Proper braking systems allow this train to travel at speeds of 125 mph (200 km/h) and higher.

One of the braking systems is the Knorr electromagnetic rail brake. This produces a braking force independent of the adhesion between wheel and rail. Moreover, the sliding action of the magnet cleans the rail, thus improving the wheel-rail adhesion factor.

High speed operation requires two things:

High motive power.

High total braking effort.

<u>Let Knorr tell you more.</u>

Brake magnet with high suspension.
An example of our products for rail vehicles.

KNORR-BREMSE GMBH MUNICH

E 7470 e

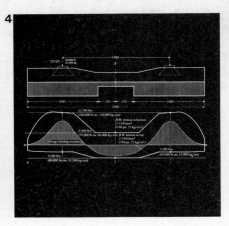

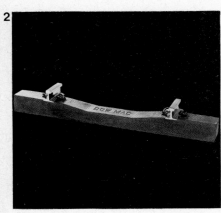

35 years of sleeper experience at your service

THE BACKGROUND

1. Production Capacity
Dow-Mac's main plant, one of three is the largest and most efficient in Europe.

2. Design and Development Experience
The current British Rail Monobloc pretensioned concrete F27 sleeper, fruit of 35 years development.

3. Production Experience
Over 10 million Dow-Mac sleepers are in the high speed tracks of British Rail.

THE SERVICE

4. Sleeper Design
Dow-Mac will design sleepers for any railway and advise on rail fastenings and costs.

5. Factory and Plant Design and Manufacture
Factory designs range from turnkey projects to the adaptation of existing plants. Specialised moulds and machinery are available for export.

6. Production Engineering
Dow-Mac have developed a range of manufacturing processes with varying degrees of sophistication to suit all circumstances.

7. Staff Training
Key personnel are trained at Dow-Mac's United Kingdom plants.

8. Other Products
Dow-Mac sleeper plants can be adapted for the manufacture of bridge beams and other building products.

TO SUM UP
Dow-Mac's services, ranging from technical assistance to the supply of specialised equipment and complete factory layouts, are available not only to railroads, but also to both established and potential manufacturers.

Terms are flexible to meet client's individual requirements and may include direct equity participation or licensing agreements on a royalty or lump sum fee basis.

Send for further information and an illustrated brochure.

SNIA
RAILWAY CONSTRUCTIONS

CONSTRUCTION AND REPAIR OF

- ☐ **PASSENGER, LUGGAGE AND MAIL CARS**
- ☐ **COOLING AND REFRIGERATING CARS**
- ☐ **COVERED AND UNCOVERED GOODS WAGGONS, FLAT AND SPECIAL WAGGONS AND TANK-CARS**

ENGINEERING DIVISION
VIA MONTEBELLO 18 - 20121 MILANO - TEL. 6332 - TELEX 34503

All commercial enterprises need to be guided by research into the fundamentals which determine their present and future role — otherwise unquestioning reliance on traditional products and methods leads eventually to diminished cost effectiveness and a consequently reduced share of markets. The transportation of passengers and goods is a highly competitive business and a major function of the Research and Development Division of British Railways is the investigation of all innovatory technology leading to improvements in railway operation ; these include the design, installation and maintenance of track, signalling and train control as well as vehicle dynamics, structures and systems. The benefits of this research are available to BRE-Metro customers.

BRE-Metro Ltd. is the joint export sales company of British Rail Engineering Ltd. and Metro-Cammell Ltd.

BRE·Metro
for research

BRE·Metro Limited
274/280 Bishopsgate,
London EC2M 4XQ
Tel : 01-247 5444/Telex :
885353 BREBIS G.

TWO WAYS MITSUBISHI MAKES RAIL TRAVEL COMFORTABLE.

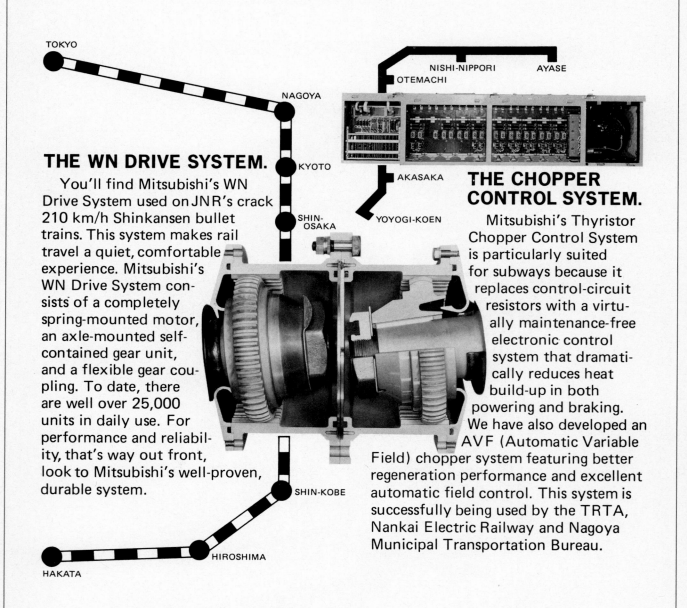

THE WN DRIVE SYSTEM.

You'll find Mitsubishi's WN Drive System used on JNR's crack 210 km/h Shinkansen bullet trains. This system makes rail travel a quiet, comfortable experience. Mitsubishi's WN Drive System consists of a completely spring-mounted motor, an axle-mounted self-contained gear unit, and a flexible gear coupling. To date, there are well over 25,000 units in daily use. For performance and reliability, that's way out front, look to Mitsubishi's well-proven, durable system.

THE CHOPPER CONTROL SYSTEM.

Mitsubishi's Thyristor Chopper Control System is particularly suited for subways because it replaces control-circuit resistors with a virtually maintenance-free electronic control system that dramatically reduces heat build-up in both powering and braking. We have also developed an AVF (Automatic Variable Field) chopper system featuring better regeneration performance and excellent automatic field control. This system is successfully being used by the TRTA, Nankai Electric Railway and Nagoya Municipal Transportation Bureau.

MITSUBISHI ELECTRIC CORPORATION

HEAD OFFICE: MITSUBISHI DENKI BLDG., MARUNOUCHI, TOKYO 100. TELEX: J24532 CABLE: MELCO TOKYO

7711-A01-A9-18

if you are looking for railway traction diesel engines........

here they are____

ID36 series from 300 to 1200 hp

diesel engines and complete railway power units

ID19 series 500 hp

Railway rolling stock
for passenger and freight

▲ First class VTU 75
SNCF coach

◄ Rolling stock for R.A.T.P.
(Paris Métro)
MF 77 Type

 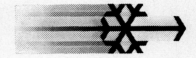

the racing snowflake
la flèche du froid
der kühle Pfeil
la freccia del freddo

The racing snowflake

It is known in all Europe, in the Middle East and in the Mediterranean Basin -it links the South with the North and the East with the West. It knows neither days nor seasons, neither frontiers nor obstacles.

It brings perishable goods fast and safe to their destination: in refrigerator wagons, in refrigerator containers and in mechanically refrigerated wagons -on the rails!

Interfrigo – International Railway-owned Company for Refrigerated Transport
General Management: Wettsteinplatz 1, CH-4005 Basle, Telephone: 26 33 33, Telex: 62231 + 63372

4-axle mechanically refrigerated wagons of Interfrigo on their way to Teheran

JANE'S

JANE'S ALL THE WORLD'S AIRCRAFT

Edited by John W. R. Taylor,
Fellow, Royal Historical Society,
Associate Fellow, Royal Aeronautical Society.

JANE'S FIGHTING SHIPS

Edited by Captain J. E. Moore, Royal Navy

JANE'S WEAPON SYSTEMS

Edited by Ronald Pretty

JANE'S INFANTRY WEAPONS

Edited by Denis H. R. Archer

JANE'S SURFACE SKIMMERS

Edited by Roy McLeavy

JANE'S OCEAN TECHNOLOGY

Edited by Robert L. Trillo

JANE'S FREIGHT CONTAINERS

Edited by Patrick Finlay

JANE'S WORLD RAILWAYS

Edited by Paul Goldsack

JANE'S MAJOR COMPANIES OF EUROPE

Edited by Jonathan Love

Convincing arguments for SLM motive power

Firstly, SLM designs are purpose-oriented. The employment of a low-level tractive device and axle-load compensation facilitate optimal adhesion utilization and the transmission of maximum tractive forces. The well-balanced lightweight construction means an increase in the specific power to locomotive weight

tain railways. The experts are well acquainted with the extremely stringent requirements for gear units and braking systems.

About 60% of the world's rack traction vehicles have been built by SLM. You will find them in the Swiss Alps, the Rocky Mountains, the High Tatras, in

Brazil, Chile, the Federal Republic of Germany and in France.

Fourthly, SLM railed vehicles are economical, ensure low maintenance costs and idle times of short duration, as well as low wear of rail and wheel. Irrespective of whether it concerns a line or shunting locomotive, railcar or railcar set, adhesion or rack-rail drive, electric or thermal operation, narrow, standard or wide gauge—the operating requirements of the railway are always fully considered. Our customers are aware of this. Licensees have acquired the rights to build complete vehicles, major assemblies and detail parts. A reflection of the confidence placed in SLM and its developments.

Finally, SLM is always at your disposal with expert advice and a world-wide network of contacts. Why not ask for our documentation or better still arrange a personal meeting?

ratio. The interbogie coupling, the lateral spring centering of the axle and, last but not least, correct selection of the axle arrangement result in optimal tracking and minimum horizontal forces between wheel and rail. Favourable matching of the spring suspension, damping devices and suitable arrangement of the running gear ensure excellent operating characteristics. These are only some aspects of SLM technology.

SLM®

Swiss Locomotive and Machine Works
CH-8401 Winterthur, Switzerland
Telephone 052 85 41 41
Telex 76131 slm ch

Member of the SULZER Group

80.24 e

Secondly, the quality and stringent testing of the materials, meticulous fabrication and continuous quality control provide SLM vehicles with their recognized ruggedness and ensure the durability needed for the exacting duties over a great many years, even in alpine regions.

Thirdly, safety and reliability have been the essential features of SLM products for over a century. This is demonstrated not only by the vehicles built for adhesion railways, but also very impressively by rack locomotives and railcars for moun-

In railroading... in transit: the one name to know in braking is WABCO.

Whether your rail system is transporting goods or people, WABCO has a century of experience in rail braking to help you. WABCO was the originator of the train air brake in 1869. And WABCO has continued to be the leader in rail braking innovations.

For example, WABCO can supply all modes of AAR or UIC train braking, for the heaviest locomotive or the lightest "goods-wagon." And for transit braking systems, WABCO makes a full line of disc, tread, and track brakes including all necessary pneumatic, electric and electronic controls. Experienced in all braking techniques, WABCO can help you select the most effective braking systems for your application.

WABCO serves the world's rail transportation systems from 28 locations in 12 countries. More than 14,000 people are ready to design, engineer, install—and service—WABCO products worldwide.

These resources are at your service. To see just how, write us today:
Eastern Hemisphere Headquarters: WABCO Westinghouse, 2 Boulevard Westinghouse, BP2, 93270 Sevran, France.

In the *Western Hemisphere:* WABCO, Three Gateway Center, Pittsburgh, PA 15222, U.S.A.

An **American-Standard** Company

Transportation from the word go.

A Chinese *Tungfeng* type *(East Wind)* diesel-electric locomotive built at the Talien Locomotive and Rolling Stock plant. *Tungfengs* are built in 2 000, 3 000 and 4 000 hp. The unit above is 3 000 hp

JANE'S WORLD RAILWAYS

TWENTIETH EDITION

EDITED BY
PAUL J. GOLDSACK

1978

ISBN 0 531 03285 X

JANE'S YEARBOOKS

FRANKLIN WATTS INC. NEW YORK

THE ALL-WEATHER RAIL FASTENING

The award-winning 'Pandrol' Rail Clip is in use today all over the world, coping with traffic and climatic conditions in countries as different as Nigeria and Norway, Australia and India, Canada and Taiwan. For some years now the standard fastening on British Rail, 'Pandrol' Rail Fastening Assemblies are equally suitable for wood, concrete and new and old steel sleepers. They can be driven simply with a hammer, though the 'Pandriver' we are now marketing makes the job even easier; they resist creep forces in both directions and so require no maintenance; while their working life can be expected to equal, at least, the life of the average rail. Switch now to 'Pandrol'; the all-weather rail fastening that's right for you.

PANDROL®

PANDROL LTD., 9 HOLBORN, LONDON, EC1N 2NE.
TELEPHONE: 01-242 5252 TELEX: 21474

CONTENTS

ORTNER
self-clearing railroad cars for coal, ores, aggreates

ORTNER is the designer and builder of various capacity RAPID DISCHARGE™ bottom unloading railroad cars with a proven door system that provides for fast, self-clearing unloading of coal, ores, aggregates.

An entire unit coal train of 75 Ortner RAPID DISCHARGE 100-ton cars can unload in 15 minutes. Cars of the RAPID DISCHARGE design also readily clear sticky base materials for the aggregate industry.

The design of the car allows for variations to meet individual capacity, unloading or transportation conditions. Worldwide inquiries invited.

ORTNER
FREIGHT CAR CO.

2652 Erie Avenue, Cincinnati, Ohio 45208, U.S.A.
Telephone (513) 871-2600.

FOREWORD

A lot of people have been talking energy conservation in recent years. Two British documents issued during 1977 added their considerable weight to the arguments surrounding the energy consumption of various modes of transport. The first was a paper issued by the British Advisory Council on Energy Conservation and covered short and medium-term considerations for passenger transport. The second was a Railway Engineers Forum discussion paper entitled Railway Design for Energy Consumption.

The Government-sponsored paper made interesting reading, albeit dismal stuff for rail devotees. It appears that railways are burning energy at a frightening rate. An electric locomotive-hauled train on British Rail's mainline to Bristol uses energy at the rate of one megajoule per passenger-km. As one megajoule equals 10^6 joules (with one joule equal to one watt second) that is a lot of energy: twice as much as a long-distance express bus travelling the same route.

If these statistics were not enough to send the highway lobby happy to their beds, there was worse to come. A double-deck bus seating 70 passengers, concluded the Advisory Council, burns 0.8 megajoules per passenger-km in urban service and a London Transport underground train burns 1.6 megajoules per passenger-km.

Given the available statistics and picking the statistic that best suits your purpose it is possible to prove just about anything. But even the most committed railway advocates would be hard pressed to manipulate the Advisory Council's findings to prove anything other than that rail transport costs more than competitive passenger modes. There are, of course, extenuating circumstances. By scrapping the train's traditional extra comforts of leg room, freedom to move about, WC facilities, buffets, restaurant cars and so on and refit them with seating at express bus densities energy consumption per seat could be cut to about 14 per cent of present levels. But, then, who would wish to pay the price for such austere intercity rail travel?

So what can railways do about the speed our trains are eating up existing energy resources? As it happens, a great deal. Even the loudest rail critics have to admit that railways have already made a considerable contribution to energy saving through the world-wide trend from steam to diesel to electric operations. British Rail's change from steam to diesel and electric traction between 1960 and 1972, for instance, cut energy consumption by 80 per cent. Further electrification would cut consumption even more.

But while numerous railway administrations throughout the world are actively pursuing far-reaching electrification policies, major systems in the western world, in Britain and North America, for example, are falling far behind. While France and the Federal Republic of Germany have each electrified about 10 000 route-km (approximately 6 200 miles) and are now converting lines of only secondary importance, British Rail has only one electrification project planned: a suburban scheme running 85 km between London and Bedford. In the USA, Amtrak is about to convert the 250 km (155 mile) line between New Haven and Boston but nothing, so far, has come of the dozen or so studies into the conversion of 50 000 km (31 000 miles) of the lines which carry about half of all freight traffic in North America.

There are signs in Britain, at least, that policies are due to change. A Government White Paper published in November 1977 hinted for the first time at a new rail electrification attitude, based on the need to find substitutes for oil in the years ahead. Full significance of the paper was not immediately obvious. Initially it seemed that the Government's statement was just yet another sop issued to pacify those pressing for greater energy consumption. Now, however, comes news that British Rail has actually been asked by the Government for firm proposals for a widesweeping programme of electrification. "What we are hoping to do," explained British Rail's Chairman Peter Parker, "is to explore the case for a rolling programme of core mainline electrification over perhaps 20 years—embracing anything up to 3 000 miles (4 828 km) of intercity routes—and we are working towards this objective now.

"If we aim to provide a railway which allows our successors to enjoy an economic transport system in the year 2000 and beyond, in the energy situation that will prevail then, we need to start work now to convert the nation's main public bulk transportation system to electric power by that time."

Financing, of course, is going to be a major obstacle. BR at present has an annual investment ceiling of around £ 300 million—and that sum will certainly not stretch to new electrification works.

At the moment, in fact, only a measly 5 per cent of total investments can be allocated towards system improvements. The remainder is divided up into 47.5 per cent for day-to-day maintenance and 47.5 per cent on renewal of existing assets. Obviously new electrification would have to be financed by the Government as a separate entity. Mr. Parker had a comment to make on the subject: "Traditional financial rules for investment appraisal create problems for electrification schemes in that the massive initial costs in the early years outweigh the discounted values of the benefits in the succeeding years. While we appreciate that the longer term economic advantages of further mainline electrification appear to be attractive, the short term difficulty is the financial justification for the scheme," he said. "Nevertheless, as this country moves towards an energy shortage at the end of the 1980s and the cost of fuel oil inevitably increases, the energy sums start to look different. If we add in the possibility of a more favourable discount rate, and the availability of capital for infrastructure investment from oil—then the picture for mainline electrification is transformed."

Strangely, the rising price of oil has not yet encouraged the USA in wholesale railway electrification. President Carter's April 1977 statement on energy policy was widely criticised as urging conservation and a switch from oil to coal without even mentioning railways, let alone electrification. It is a situation which, on the surface at least, is hard to understand. After all, the USA did pioneer mainline electrification in 1895 and by the early 1930s had 20 per cent of all the world's electrified mileage. But there the story ended.

For one thing, dieselisation came along—oil was plentiful and cheap. For another, the cost of electrification was too high for an industry hampered by Government over-regulation and subsidised competition.

Have you tougher tests than these for locomotives to pass?

We'd like to take them, too...

It happened in Austria. On the steep grades of the Tauernbahn in the Alps, in 1970, an ASEA Rc2 locomotive proved it could haul much heavier trains than any other design. Result: The first order for thyristor locomotives in Austria.

It happened again in Norway. On the mountainous line between Oslo and Bergen, in the winter of 1971, ASEA Rc2 locomotives were tested by "CP RAIL". Similar tests with Rc4 locomotives in 1976, this time in cooperation with the Norwegian State Railways gave the same answer. Result: The first order for thyristor locomotives in Norway.

It happened once more in the U.S.A. last fall. A modified Rc4 running on Amtrak's Northeast Corridor between New York and Washington proved it could stand up to the rigors of daily high-speed passenger service. Labelled X995, this distinctive locomotive maintained METROLINER schedules even during the worst winter in two hundred years.

The high power-to-weight ratio, low track forces, and good running characteristics of ASEA thyristor locomotives can help you increase train speeds and tighten up your schedules. Whether your need is heavy freight haulage or high-speed passenger service, it will pay you to contact ASEA.

An ASEA locomotive hauling Amfleet cars in METROLINER scheduled service.

ASEA
Transport Division
S-721 83 VÄSTERÅS
SWEDEN

ASEA Inc.
4 New King Street
WHITE PLAINS
New York 106 04 U.S.A.

ASEA

There are other possible hidden factors why the US has been reluctant to string up electrified catenaries. For instance, the nation's biggest motive power supplier (General Motors) is tooled up for diesels. And few American railway managements have been in favour of electrification due to the deep Government involvement which widespread conversion would imply. It now seems, however, that the establishment of the quasi-nationalised railroad agencies such as Amtrak and Conrail may be changing all that. As mentioned earlier, Amtrak has embarked on construction of a 25 kV overhead catenary line between New Haven and Boston. And in February 1978 came the news that Conrail is to undertake a major study into the feasibility of electrifying several sections of its system. Principal focus of the study will be on the route between Harrison, western terminus of Amtrak's electrified line from Philadelphia and Pittsburgh, Pennsylvania. This 480 km (300 mile) route carries the heaviest freight tonnage of any line in the United States. In addition, Conrail will be examining the feasibility of electrifying the former Reading line from Philadelphia to a connection with the former Lehigh Valley system at Manville, New Jersey.

The proposed electrification would be made possible by $ 200 million in Government-guaranteed loans, provisionally authorised in the 4R act of 1976.

Whether other railroads will be able to afford to follow Conrail's lead remains to be seen. The amount of investment involved would be formidable. Present estimates of US conversion costs, including catenary, substations, communications and signalling, are approximately $150 000 a track mile. Double track would cost $ 250 000 per mile. Assuming an average cost of $ 200 000 a route mile, the total cost of electrifying the 10 000 route miles (16 000 route km) carrying at least 40 million ton-miles a year would approximate $ 2 000 million. The declining fortunes of US railroads undoubtedly puts a big question mark over the future of electrification. A recent study by the First National City Bank (Citibank) projected that from 1976 to the end of 1985 Class I railroads would incur cash outlays of $ 21 100 million in excess of internal cash generation. Of this amount, Citibank estimated that $ 11 800 million could be raised through traditional equipment financing leaving a $ 10 000 million financing problem.

Against this background it is clearly unreasonable to expect the railroads to finance, from their own resources, the vast sums needed for a national programme of electrification. On the other hand, it would be possible for particular electrification projects to be financed by owner-railroads. An 800 km (500 mile) to 2 400 km (1 500 mile) route electrification scheme would cost $ 100 million to $ 300 million. There are railroads in a position to finance such sums. Whether they do so or not will depend principally on the projected return on investment and the possible advantages of electrification.

For this reason many railroad administrators are keeping a close watch on the Conrail studies which will help to determine whether the advantages of electrification are as substantial as its adherents allege. These include:

lower maintenance costs: the maintenance cost of electric locomotives is lower than for diesel locomotives, primarily because a diesel unit carries its own power plant. Electric locomotives, in contrast, receive power from remote sources: the electric utilities.

less possibility of failure: the electric locomotive has a smaller number of moving parts than diesel, which reduces possibility for failure.

flexibility power source: electric locomotives employ whichever fuel the utilities use to generate electricity, whether coal, oil, nuclear or hydro-electric whereas diesels, of course, must use fuel oil.

longer life expectancy of locomotives: electric locomotives generally have a life expectancy of 30 years or more while diesels last about 18 years.

While electrification alone will play a major role in saving energy, a world-wide trend in new rolling stock design and motive power technology is making an increasing contribution to the better use of available energy by railways. British Rail's new High Speed Train, for instance, is not only faster, more reliable and more comfortable than previous stock; it is cutting energy costs as well by providing much improved operations at 200 km/h (125 mph) for about the same energy consumption as a conventional 160 km/h (100 mph) locomotive-hauled train. And it is a fact that the new train's higher speeds are attracting new business, substantially cutting energy consumption per seat km to about 0.4 megajoules, equivalent to that of a much slower, less comfortable express bus.

In the light of these facts it is a useful exercise to consider exactly how much progress has been made by railways around the world in highspeed train operations. Leading, of course, is Japan where Shinkansen trains are now timetabled to cover the 174 km (108 miles) route between Nagoya and Sizouka in 59 minutes at an average speed of 177.5 km/h (103.7 mph). Other Shinkansen trains operate only slightly slower.

Next comes Britain with four trains timetabled to cover the 66 km (41 miles) distance between Swindon and Reading in 24 minutes at a speed of 166.2 km/h (103.2 mph). In fact, 59 of British Rail's trains are now advertised to operate at just over 150 km/h (93 mph).

The fastest French train is the *Etendard* which operates between St. Pierre des C. and Poitiers (101 km/63 miles) on the Paris-Bordeaux line which has now been passed for 200 km/h (124 mph) operating throughout. The *Etendard* is time-tabled to cover the journey in 37 minutes at a speed of 163.7 km/h (101.6 mph). Best time for the complete 579 km (360 mile) journey between Paris and Bordeaux is 230 minutes at an average speed of 151 km/h (93.8 mph).

In fourth place is the USA where Metroliner trains are operating over the 110.1 km (68.5 mile) Baltimore to Wilmington section at an advertised best of 44 minutes at an average speed of 150.1 km/h (93.4 mph).

Surprisingly, perhaps, the Federal Republic of Germany's fastest timetabled service at present is the 143.7 km/h (89 mph) run between Dortmund and Bielefeld (98.2 km/61 miles) by the *Nymphenburg*, while delays to high-speed improvements over the Moscow-Leningrad line in the Soviet Union means that the fastest train operated by Soviet Railways is the 135.1 km/h (83.9 mph) *Aurora* which completes the 331 km section between Moscow and Bologoe in 147 minutes.

While higher speeds help solve the problems of energy conservation other technological improvements are playing their roles, too, in cutting railway fuel costs. British Rail, for instance, expects to make substantial savings with introduction of the Advanced Passenger Train. Its lighter weight achieved through aluminium construction, recirculating toilets, low ambient air-conditioning and articulation will provide an energy saving of about 25 per cent, says the railway. Additionally the train's tilting ability through curves will further reduce energy consumption by reducing braking and acceleration.

Transit systems around the world are seeking similar technological improvements to conserve energy. In the USA rail transit continues to receive repeated criticisms from the Carter administration. In October 1977 the Congressional Budget Office released a study which claimed that metros consume more energy per passenger-mile than shared cars or urban buses. The obvious implication was that federal support for rail transit was a waste of money.

The alleged high consumption of energy by rail transit vehicles was based on the assumption that 70 per cent of passengers drive to the station in their own cars, burning considerable amounts of fuel en route. The figure is clearly incorrect. While the study assumed that only five per cent of rail passengers walk to the station, a previous survey proved conclusively that in Boston, at least, 50 per cent of rail commuters go on foot to the station.

The new administrator of the Urban Mass Transportation Administration, Richard S. Page, did not agree with the

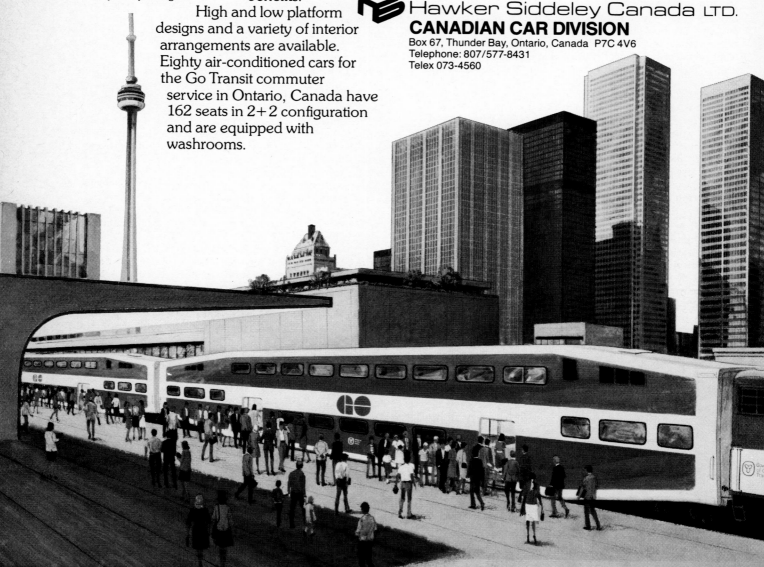

report's findings. "Most of it is a highly sophisticated exercise by some economists who have laid out, manipulated, tabulated and interpreted a great deal of data," he commented. "That's not the way we do our studies. We do them on a site-specific, corridor-by-corridor analysis. We examine alternatives, including light rail, heavy rail, surface and sub-surface, major bus and limited bus; and for those alternatives, we get capital and operating costs, patronage, cost per capita, cost per passenger and energy consumption.

"The critical problem facing the country, and what the President's programme is oriented to, is conservation of petroleum, half of which we import. The critical advantage of rail rapid transit is that it relies on electrical energy and not petroleum energy. Bus fleets, car pools, van pools are all heavy users of petroleum."

Generally, however, it is not so strange that rail transit is being criticised in the USA at present. A US Department of Transportation official was quoted as saying in 1977: "the projected costs of rail are scaring everybody" soon after a widely publicised March memorandum from President Carter commenting "many of the rapid transit systems are grossly over-designed."

It has to be admitted that the arithmetic used by US transit critics appears persuasive. The less informed merely point with alarm at escalating construction and operating costs. The more sophisticated calculate costs of a comparable trip by express bus or rail and arrive at the conclusion that bus is cheaper. There is no doubt that construction of rail transit is costly; but then all building work in city areas is expensive, whether of offices, highways or transit. Many rail advocates in the USA contend, in fact, that rail rapid transit is not overpriced. Louis J. Gambaccini, vice-president and general manager of the Port Authority Trans-Hudson Corporation, comments: "In Philadelphia the 1.5 mile rapid transit extension to Veterans Stadium and the Spectrum cost approximately $40 million. The total capital investment by the Port Authority of New York and New Jersey in its rail subsidiary, PATH, is $250 million—equivalent to but one mile of New York City's proposed Westway highway."

Yet it is the cost factor of transit construction and operation which continues to sway official agencies responsible for financing urban transport, a fact of life that has caused postponement of rail schemes throughout the world. S-Bahn and U-Bahn schemes in the Federal Republic of Germany have been set back, along with light rail and full-metro schemes throughout the USA and Canada. Work on all but one line of a major expansion programme for Montreal's metro system was cancelled due to a financial crisis precipitated by the Olympics. New light rail line plans for Vancouver and Toronto in Canada appear to have been shelved. In the USA Atlanta, Miami and Baltimore are finding money difficult to obtain which must be difficult for the city authorities to accept after the dramatic swing back to metros by the USA in the 1960s.

Washington has cut back construction plans from 160 km to 100 km despite public acclaim for the short section now open. The reason: rising costs and operating problems. The city has repeated many of the mistakes of San Francisco's Bart system which is still trying to solve the problem created by badly designed cars. Now, directly under the watchful eyes of the Carter administration, Washington's service reliability has slumped with brakes and doors jamming: faults caused by distortion of car bodies when fully laden.

No wonder, then, that North American cities are increasingly going elsewhere for their rolling stock. In late 1977 came the news that Cleveland is to buy new light rail cars from Italy's Breda Construsioni Ferroviaria. Breda will design and supervise construction of the cars, but about 40 per cent of components will be manufactured in the USA.

The Cleveland order came not long after the Massachusetts Bay Transportation Authority (MBTA) held a press conference to announce that it was refusing to take delivery of light rail vehicles. The 43 cars previously accepted by MBTA were said to have derailed 23 times in under ten months, availability was below 50 per cent, and the cars were absorbing four times as many man-hours per car as the elderly trams they were supposed to replace.

In Canada, both Edmonton and Calgary ordered new transit cars from Siemens and Duwag (Waggonfabrik-Uerdingen) of the Federal Republic of Germany: a move which would appear to lessen hopes that Canada is eventually to get a standard light rail vehicle. Two out of six prototypes intended to be the first of a standard family of light rail vehicles for Canada were completed during 1977 by SIG of Switzerland. The cars were ordered by Canada's Urban Transportation Development Corporation, which is to deliver 196 light rail vehicles to the Toronto Transit Commission. The balance of the order will be built by Hawker Siddeley Canada.

In March 1978 the first of 100 cars ordered by the Metropolitan Atlanta Rapid Transit Authority (MARTA of the USA) were out shopped from Societe Franco-Belge's plant at Raismes in northern France, part of the company's production which transit and railmen have dubbed the "aluminium revolution."

The revolution started in August 1975 when the Paris Transport Authority (RATP) ordered 1 000 new coaches for the metro. Four firms entered bids for the contract which was open to steel, stainless steel or alloy construction. Three of the firms put forward steel proposals, but the Ffr 1 200 million contract went to Franco-Belge for aluminium rolling stock. The contract was the first ever in which aluminium had underpriced steel construction in straight competition.

Full significance of the order was not immediately apparent. The French are noted for backing non-conventional solutions. Franco-Belge replied to those who said that the order was no more than a flash in the pan that the company would continue to undercut competitors by using aluminium construction methods which would save 500 man hours a vehicle and therefore undercut comparable finished steel costs by 30 per cent.

In April 1976 it became clear that Franco-Belge had meant what it said. The company won a second aluminium contract, in conjunction with technical consultants, Alusuisse, for the coaches of Atlanta (MARTA) in the USA. The company had undercut domestic builders by $100 000 a vehicle, a price which caused a number of US commentators to observe that the French Government must be backing the order. MARTA despatched a team to look at Franco-Belge's books. The assistant general manager of the Atlanta transit team reported back that the company "is positive in its intention to make a profit. We see no way that it will get a subsidy or any help from the French Government."

Then in September 1976 Franco-Belge won a Ffr 1 500 million contract for 750 vehicles needed for the Paris interconnection (RATP/French National Railways) services. Franco-Belge has certainly found one answer to a major problem facing railways: controlling the upward trend in the cost of capital equipment in relation to general inflation. There is evidence to show that in real terms railways are able to buy less and less for more and more cash. Take, for instance, the cost of a rail transit vehicle against that of a bus: metro cars today cost ten times more than a bus which was not so ten years ago. In the 1950s a freight wagon was frequently cheaper than a highway truck which is not so today.

Standardisation and volume production could provide one answer. But if, as it almost certainly does, that answer depends on an increase in international purchasing then it is not going to be simple to apply. Take what is happening now in the USA, for instance, where there is increasing talk about "buy American". Transportation Secretary Brock Adams has expressed concern about the 'intrusion' of foreign manufacturers into the United States rail transit car market and asked UMTA to look into the matter. Pullman-Standard is fighting in the courts to halt Breda building cars for Cleveland, while the chairman of Budd, Gilbert Richards, publicly protested early in 1978 about unfair foreign competition.

Budd set its case out in a letter to the Treasury Department,

pointing out that 372 of the 552 transit and commuter cars bought in the US during 1976 were foreign-built. The company complained that foreign suppliers are subsidised while tariff and other barriers prevent outsiders getting into foreign-owned railways or metros.

Concern by companies about international competition is understandable. But it would be a tragedy if US builders are to sit and wring their hands, complaining about unfair competition and subsidies or assistance or indirect aid, while losing the ability to build rapid transit cars. US builders must be prepared to learn from their own past mistakes and from the experiences of others better versed in the construction of modern transit equipment.

May 1978   Paul Goldsack

trains run on italsider steel

Track material and points
Italsider produces both double and single switches and crossings for any gauge, lenght and connection, as well as track accessories (joint bars, tie plates, rail anchors) according to any technical specification

MANUFACTURERS

LOCOMOTIVES AND ROLLING STOCK

ACEC
Ateliers de Constructions Electriques de Charleroi
(A member of the Westinghouse Electric Group)

Head Office: ACEC BP4 B-6000 Charleroi, Belgium

Products: Railway, tramway and metro electric equipment for locomotives, railcars and multiple unit stock.

President: A. Dubuisson
Director, Transport Division: G. Tanghe
Marketing Director: A. Leriche

Sales: 3 kV dc chopper railcar units; 20 delivered in 1975, 12 more for 1977 delivery and 38 more scheduled for 1979 delivery. Type 20 locomotives (3 kV dc with choppers rated at 7 000 hp); 15 delivered to Belgian State Railways (SNCB) in 1975; 10 more for delivery in 1977; orders carried out during 1977 for components for 50 electric locomotives ordered by FEPASA of Brazil (value BFr 1 000 million).

New equipment: 3 kV dc electric railcar units, composed of four permanently-coupled cars. Total rating: 1 372 kW. Maximum speed: 140 km/h. Operation by multiple units possible, with a maximum of 12 cars (combinations of quadruple or double railcar units).
Control of the motors by thyristor choppers (gradual variation of the voltage applied to the motors). Body and bogies designed and built by La Brugeoise et Nivelles, SA, Bruges, Belgium.
Electrical traction equipment arranged in two independent circuits, practically identical to those in the double railcar units, types 1970 to 1974. Each circuit consists of a thyristor chopper supplying four motors, permanently connected in series-parallel. Current collection by a single pantograph. General protection by single high-speed circuit-breaker. Field weakening of motors by purely ohmic shunts.
Operation in multiple units with a maximum of 12 cars (combinations of quadruple or double railcar units).

7 000 hp Co-Co 3 kV dc locomotive with ACEC choppers built for SNCB

ACF
ACF Industries, Incorporated
Amcar Division
Shippers Car Line Division

Head Office: 750 Third Avenue, New York, NY 10017, USA

Amcar Division: Main & Clark Streets, St. Charles, Missouri 63301, USA. Telephone: (314) 724 7850

Shippers Car Line Division: 620 N. Second Street, St. Charles, Missouri 63301, USA. Telephone: (314) 723 9600

Products: Amcar designs and builds freight cars for railroads, industrial shippers, and Shippers Car Line's lease fleet. Amcar also produces railway car parts, piggyback trailer hitches, ingot mould and mine cars, pressure vessels, mixing bowls, and storage tanks. Shippers Car Line leases and sells special purpose railroad freight and tank cars to industrial corporations and provides maintenance for cars in the service lease fleet at seven plants. As 1976 opened, there were more than 36 000 cars in Shipper's service lease fleet.

President: Henry A. Correa
Amcar General Manager: James C. O'Hara
Shippers Car Line General Manager: Bruce A. Gustafsen

New equipment: Centre Flow Cannonaide covered hopper car—utilises a unique compressed air system to dislodge and unload "problem" materials with blasts of air. Centre Flow Conditiontrol covered hopper car—uses an exterior layer of foam insulation that enables perishable commodities to be shipped in bulk.

AEBI
Robert Aebi AG

Head Office: Uraniastrasse 31-33, Postfach 8023, Zürich, Switzerland

Products: Diesel-hydraulic and diesel-mechanical locomotives.

Telegrams: AEBI, Zürich
Telephone: (01) 211 09 70
Telex: 53795

AECKERLE
Hugo Aeckerle

Head Office: 2000 Hamburg 66 (Ohlstedt), Bredenbekstrasse 12, German Federal Republic

Telegrams: UNILOK, Hamburg
Telephone: 6 05 01 69
Telex: 02-12359

Products: Unilok road/rail shunting locomotives.

AEG/TELEFUNKEN
Nachrichten-und Verkehrstechnik AG, Geschaeftsbereich Bahnen

Head Office: Hohenzollerndamm 150, D-1000 Berlin 33, German Federal Republic

Works: Gutleutstrasse 82, D-6000, Frankfurt (Main), German Federal Republic

Products: Electric equipment for locomotives, rail cars, multiple units, transit stock, suburban and underground railways, trams and trolley-buses.

Constitution: For more than 80 years AEG-Telefunken has been concerned with the development of generation, distribution, and consumption of electric power for all purposes. Manufacture of traction equipment started in 1889, and to date, more than 9 000 locomotives have been equipped by AEG-Telefunken.

Telegrams: ELEKTRON BAHNEN, Berlin
Telephone: (030) 828-1
Telex: 185 498

Sales: AEG-Telefunken delivered the electrical equipment for a series of 73 freight locomotives class 151 (16 2/3 Hz, 15 kV) for the German Federal Railways (DB) in cooperation with Krupp, Essen. Class 151 locomotive has a Co Co wheel arrangement, a nominal rating of 6 00 kW at 95 km/h and a maximum speed of 120 km/h.
Also delivered recently were 66 5 300-hp electric locomotives for Korean National Railways (KNR) built by AEG-Telefunken as a member of the 50 Hz Group.
Latest passenger equipment includes continuous train running control for the two-car electric trainset designed for the Amsterdam Metro.

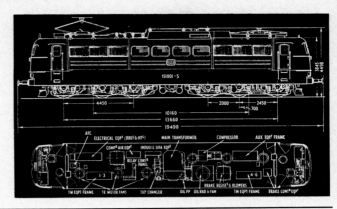

Class 151 locomotive designed by DB for high speed freight and built by AEG

AGV
AB Gävle Vagbverkstad

Telegrams: AGEVE, Gävle
Telephone: (026) 11 58 90
Telex: 811 06

Head Office: PO Box 497, S-801 06 Gävle, Sweden

Products: Freight wagons and mine locomotives.

New equipment: Range of special-purpose wagons now produced by AGV includes:

ore unit with loading capacity of 80 tons; Uahs tank wagon, capacity 50 tons, volume 63 m³; Qbo long-loader with capacity of 45 tons on a platform length of 22 m. Mine equipment includes two and four-axle tipping wagons and 18 types of locomotives. Battery, electric and diesel locomotives are available.

ALCAN
Alcan Canada Products.

Telegrams: ALCAN, Canada
Telephone: 416 366-7211

Head office: Box 269, Toronto-Dominion Centre, Toronto, Ontario, Canada

Products: Aluminium bodies for freight wagons and passenger coaches.

Sales: The LRC (Lightweight Rapid Comfortable) has been developed jointly by Alcan, Dofasco and MLW-Industries (NB no longer Worthington). Built with the financial backing of the Federal Department of Industry (Canada) which shared half the estimated cost of $C 2.5 million and extensively tested with the assistance of the Federal Transportation Development Agency, the LRC is designed to operate at high speeds as a push pull unit with up to 12 coaches and a locomotive at each end or as a shorter unit with a single locomotive. Lightness, low centre of gravity, diesel electric traction and a servo controlled body tilting suspension are the basics of the design.

New equipment: The LRC car body structure is a stressed skin design in which Alcan aluminium alloy sheet and extrusions have been combined. Length of the coach is 25.91 m (85 ft); height, 3.58 m; and maximum width 3.18 m. The centre sill is eliminated in the LRC coach, with horizontal loads being carried by large tubular side sills. Buffing and draft loads are transferred to the side sills by horizontal shear structures fabricated from plate and extrusions which join the side sills. Side frame consists of outside skin, side sill, waist rail, top of window stringer, side plate and side posts. Main longitudinal framing members are continuous over the length of the coach. Side plates consist of two continuous extrusions, one a modified channel shape and the other a modified zed section. Side posts are extruded channel shapes which form box section members spanning the area between the side sills and side plates. The roof is supported on extruded hat section roof bows, which span between the side plates, stiffened by extruded zed section intercostals.

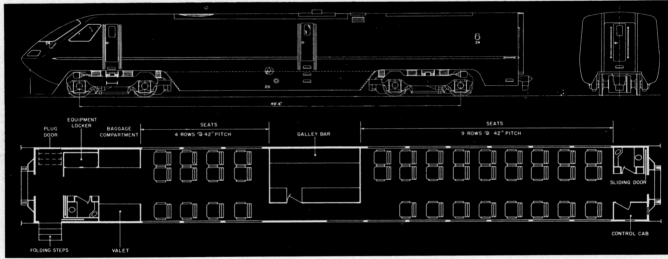

LRC train developed at a cost of $C 2.5 million

ALSTHOM
(Member of Traction Export)

Telegrams: ALSTHOM, Paris
Telephone: 502 14 13
Telex: 611 938

Head Office: 38 avenue Kléber, 75784 Paris, France

Products: Electric, diesel-electric, industrial and mining locomotives; electric, diesel and gas-turbine railcars; electric and diesel multiple units; passenger coaches; automatic couplers; electrical equipment and transmissions; railway electrification; signalling systems and apparatus.

Chairman: Pierre Loygue
General Director: Roger Chalvon Demersay
Export Sales Director: Paul De Lieven
Railway Division Manager: Franck Vaingnedroye
Counsellor to Management for Railway Matters: Jacques Bedel De Buzareingues

New Developments 1977: Alsthom and Société Franco-Belge de Materiel de Chemins de Fer agreed during 1977 to co-operate in the optimum utilisation of their manufacturing capacity, technical research and export marketing. In addition, Alsthom has taken a 12.5 per cent holding in the capital of Franco-Belge.

Sales: During 1977, Alsthom signed a new contract with Burma Railways for the supply

of 21 new locomotives valued — together with spares and miscellaneous workshop equipment — at Frs 73 million. Delivery of the locomotives, all rated at 1 600 hp, will bring the number of Alsthom-built motive power units in operation in Burma to 127. Also last year, French Railways (SNCF) confirmed the order placed with Alsthom-Francorail MTE in February for the 85 series production TGV trainsets for the projected new Paris — Sudest high-speed line. Delivery is due to begin in October 1979.
The company continues its activities in Africa. In mid-1977 an order was placed by Senegal Railways (Regie de Chemins de Fer du Senegal) with Alsthom for three type AD 18B diesel-electric locomotives valued at Frs 10 million. During the year, the company delivered six new diesel-electric locomotives to Gabon State Railways (OCT-RA). The locomotives are a B-B design with a nominal (UIC) output of 3 000 hp, although under Gabon's difficult climatic conditions the rating is reduced to 2 800 hp. Westinghouse air brakes act in conjunction with rheostatic braking. A single AGOV12DSHR diesel engine is installed which drives a three-phase alternator and rectifier set supplying dc to the two traction motors. Each locomotive weighs 92 tonnes and has a maximum speed of 85 km/h. The body is 15.8 m long and has air-conditioned cabs raked forward.

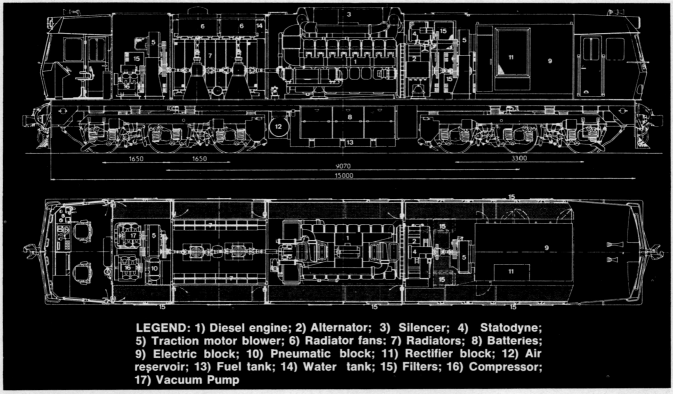

LEGEND: 1) Diesel engine; 2) Alternator; 3) Silencer; 4) Statodyne; 5) Traction motor blower; 6) Radiator fans; 7) Radiators; 8) Batteries; 9) Electric block; 10) Pneumatic block; 11) Rectifier block; 12) Air reservoir; 13) Fuel tank; 14) Water tank; 15) Filters; 16) Compressor; 17) Vacuum Pump

Details of the 2 250 hp diesel-electric locomotive built by Alsthom of which 54 have been exported to Thailand State Railways

ALTAI

Altai Wagon Works, Altai, USSR

Telephone: 1472177
Telex: 7565

Products: Freight wagons

Among new equipment recently built by Altai for Soviet Railways (SZD) is a four-axle

covered wagon with a capacity of 62 tonnes. Used by SZD for grain transports, the wagon has an inside body length of 12.8 m and an inside body width of 2,76 m. Height of the body over sidewall is 2.791 m.

AMMENDORF

VEB Waggonbau, Ammendorf, German Democratic Republic
(Member of Maschinen-export)

Telephone: 22050
Telex: 11 26 89

Products: Long distance passenger coaches and restaurant cars.

Sales: New equipment from the Ammendorf plant includes a four-axle long-distance passenger coach type WPW k/Kr. The coach is fully air-conditioned and is equipped with a hot water heating system and a boiler which can be operated with either coal or electric power. For overnight travel, the coach has berths for 36 passengers. Designed to operate at a maximum of 160 km/h, the coach has a service weight (with stores) of 56 tonnes. It is one of a long series being supplied by the company to the Soviet Railways (SZD). Also under construction at present for SZD is the SK/K long-distance restaurant car. Other stock built by Ammendorf for both SZD and Deutsch Reichsbahn includes

the type 47 K3k air conditioned coach and the SK/k dining car. Bodies of both are of all-welded, self-supporting steel construction. The outer longitudinal members, cross girders, two extensions and flanged floor situated between the main cross sections and rolled steel sections are used for the box framework. Shell plating consists of steel sheet with an addition of copper. Both coaches are fitted with type KWS-ZNII bogies — also supplied by the Ammendorf plant — with primary and secondary suspension operating through helical springs interacting with friction and hydraulic shock absorbers. Type SA-3 automatic central buffer couplings of Soviet design are fitted. Matrosov system automatic pneumatic brakes are adopted. The type 47 K/k coach has seats for 38 passengers in nine compartments; the type SK/k dining car seats 48 passengers in two compartments.

ANBEL

The Anbel Group

Telephone: 715/658-9995

Head Office: 602 Capital National Building, Houston, Tex 77002, USA

Products: Diesel-hydraulic locomotives, freight wagons.

ANF-INDUSTRIE

Société ANF-Frangeco

Telephone: 788 15 15/788 33 11
Telex: 610 817

Head Office: Tour Aurore, 92080 Paris-Defense, Cedex 5, France

Products: Turbotrains ETG and RTG; diesel trainsets; passenger coaches; freight wagons.

Chairman: André Pelabon
General Manager: Jean Pelabon

New equipment: The RTG-type turbotrains first went into service with French National Railways in May 1973. They are designed to run at 200 km/h and, compared with the earlier ETG sets—also built by ANF-Industrie, have a number of new features: five passenger cars per set with two turbopowered; 50 per cent boost in passenger capacity; higher speed potential; improved comfort standards. Each power car is propelled by an 850 kW nominal output Turbomeca Turmo IIIF turbo engine. Rate of output to weight is 7.5 kW/ton for a set of five coaches. Transmission is by an L411 or U Voith hydraulic transmission box with torque converter, coupler and reverser. Coupling between drive box and motor axle is through a cardan shaft. Powered bogies are Y223 type; both powered and non-powered bogies are equipped with four braking packages and two electro-magnetic rail-brake skids. In addition, non-powered bogies carry additional disc brakes plus one holding brake on every vehicle. A hydrodynamic brake is mounted on the transmission box. Auxiliary power is delivered by one generating set

per powered car, comprising an Astazou A Turbomeca turbo-motor driving a 50 Hz 220/380 v, 210 kVa alternator.

Sales: During 1977 SNCF received from ANF-Industrie 15 two-car diesel-electric 440 kW trainsets (shared with Creusot Loire); orders were placed by SNCF during the year for 12 stainless-steel trailers for operation on the *Stelyrail* service between Lyon and St. Etienne.
At the 1977 Leipzig Spring Fair, held March 13-20, ANF showed two new freight wagons—a bogie flat wagon and a tank wagon. The flat wagon was one of a series of 2 000 built for SNCF. It has a length of 20.09 m and a useful loading area of 50.5 m². The tank wagon, for liquefied gas, has a length of 18.96 m and a volume of 111.5 m². More than 500 of this type have been supplied to French industry by ANF.
ANF-INDUSTRIE has sold 70 gas turbine trains of the ETG or RTG type, four of them to the Iranian State Railways; six RTG trains to AMTRAK in USA and seven RTG trains intended for AMTRAK after being manufactured under licence in USA by ROHR.
The company also sold in 1974/75 to French National Railways (SNCF) 27 self-propelled elements of 330 kW and 660 kW making a total of 400 self-propelled elements supplied to the SNCF.
Together with the firm De Dietrich the company has won an order for 750 passenger coaches of the UIC type for the SNCF.
Furthermore ANF-INDUSTRIE is manufacturing 700 RILS wagons with mechanical sheeting for the SNCF and 1 450 wagons of different types for exportation.

ANSALDO

Head Office: Via Nicola Lorenzi 8, 16152 Genova-Cornigloano, Italy

Transportation Division: Via Bergognone 34, Milan, Italy

Products: Electrical equipment for electric and diesel-electric locomotives, railcars, mu's, subway cars, trams, trolley buses with conventional or thyristor control.

Telegrams: ANSALDO CORNIGLIANO LIGURE — ANSALDO MILANO
Telephone: Geonoa 010-4105/Milano 02 4244
Telex: 27098 Ansado Genova/39192 Ansal-MI Milano

Chairman: Renato de Leonardis
Chief Executive Officer: Daniele Luigi Milvio
Commercial Director: Piero Mortara
Manager, Transportation Division: Franco Fiocca

Sales: Among contracts won by Ansaldo from Italian State Railways (FS) is electrical equipment for 56 type E-656 electric locomotives and 50 per cent of the electric equipment for six 3 kV four-car trainsets ordered in 1975 from the GAI group of which Ansaldo is a member together with E. Marelli, TIBB, Fiat and Breda. The E-656 is FS's most recent addition to the locomotive fleet: a Bo-Bo-Bo unit based on the existing E-646 but with a higher continuous rating of 4 200 kW and a top speed of 160 km/h. Designed for heavy freight and passenger service, the locomotive has a length over buffers of 18.29 m, body length of 17.05 m, six type 82-400 traction motors and a service weight of 115 tonnes. By early 1977, FS had taken delivery of 40 of the locomotives. The 3 kV four-car trainsets (M + T + T + M) are designed for suburban service. The motor coaches have full shopper control with dynamic and regenerative braking. Continuous rating is 1 900 kW and capacity is for 800 passengers, 340 of which are seated.

Ansaldo also supplies the electric power transmission system for the E-444 *Tartuga* high-speed (200 km/h) Bo-Bo electric locomotive which first went into service with FS in 1971. Between that date and 1974 the railway took delivery of 110 units. A 3 kV, 80-tonne locomotive with conventional electrics, it has continuous output at wheel rim of 4 000 hp. Three E 444s have been fitted with additional electronic control equipment by Ansaldo. One, the E-444.005, has full chopper supply and control equipment. The four traction motors are supplied in parallel directly from the contact line through four interconnected choppers. These control motor tension from a minimum of 10 V in a multiple of 10 to a maximum of 1 800 V, whatever the catenary voltage. The new locomotive has a continuous rating of 4 800 kW, top speed of 200 km/h, continuous control of stress at the wheel rim, slide control, and a device for operation at pre-selected speeds. In addition, two locomotives—the E-444.056 and the E-444.057—have been fitted with shunt-chopper equipment.

ARAD
Arad Car and Carriage Building Works (Intreprindera de Vagoane)

Head Office: 29-31 Ave. Aurel Vlaicu, 2900-Arad, Romania

Products: Passenger coaches, freight wagons—open, covered, flat, self-discharge, ballast—up to 60 tonnes loading capacity. Special purpose wagons on up to 32 axles.

Chairman: Eng. Nicolae Iosif
Managing Director: Eng. Aurel Cioruga
Export Sales: Eng. Mihai Scorteanu

Telephone: 1 30 20/1 36 80/3 26 51/3 27 96
Telex: 036273/046256

Sales: Exports have been completed to Brazil (air conditioned first and second class coaches, electric power vans, vapour generator cars for train heating), Syria (air conditioned passenger coaches, electric power vans, vapour generator cars), Greece (air conditioned and non air conditioned coaches), Iran (ore transport and flat wagons), Algeria (various types of ore and phosphate wagons). At present under manufacture are passenger coaches for Gabon, Angola, Mozambique, Sri Lanka and a wide range of freight wagons for all East-European railway administrations.

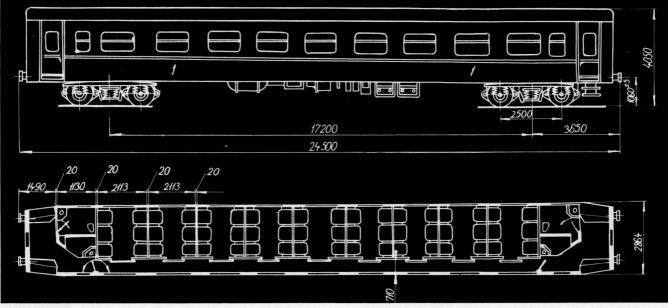

First-class passenger coach
Length over buffers 24.5 m; length between bogie pivot pitch 17.2 m; maximum body width 2.864 m; total height from rail 4.05 m; corridor width 710 mm; number of seats 54; number of compartments 9; maximum speed 160 km/h

Four axle tank wagon for transport of liquified gas
Pay volume 95 m³; tare weight 31 tonnes; maximum payload 49 tonnes; length over buffers 15.84 m; length of underframe 14.6m; length between bogie pivot pitch 9.8 m; brake type KE-GP 16; height of buffers (empty) 1.060 m; length of tank 14.150 m; loading pressure 26 atm; minimum curve radius 35 m; gauge 1.435 m; maximum speed 100 km/h

Special two-axle wagon for powder transports (right)
Length between buffers 9.190 m; length between bogie pivot pins 5 m; total height above rail 4.04 m; diameter of reservoir 3 m; payload 27 tonnes; tare weight 12.3 tonnes; discharge speed 7 m/sec; brake type Hildebrand Knorr 12; maximum speed 100 km/h; load capacity of reservoirs 2 × 12.5 m³.

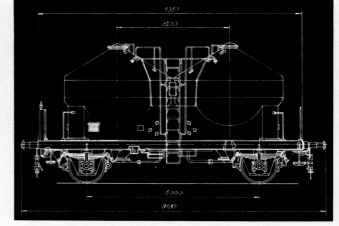

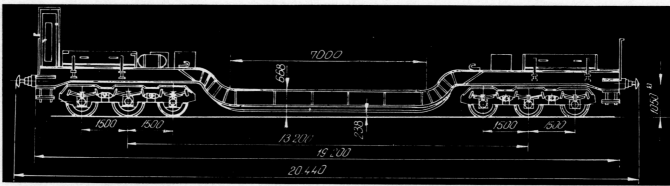

Six axle flat wagon with low floor platform
Length between front beams 19 m; distance between bogie pivot pins 13.2 m; serviceable length of low floor platform 7 m; width of underframe (maximum) 2.3 m; height of floor side (empty) 650 mm; height of platforms at the ends 1.635 m; maximum payload 70 tonnes.

ARBEL
Arbel Industrie

Telegrams: INDARBEL, Douai
Telephone: (20) 88 33 11
Telex: 130 036

Head Office: 194 boulevard Faidherbe, 59506 Douai, France

Products: Freight wagons; mining equipment; rolling-stock components.

Chairman: Paul Echalier
General Manager (Rolling Stock Department): Conrad Bernstein
Sales Director: Antoine Azais

Sales: Arbel-Industrie is producing more than 5 000 wagons a year at a rate of 20 to 35 wagons per day for French and foreign railways. Under construction in the Douai plants are:

For French National Railways (SNCF)—4 000 bogie covered wagons of high capacity of which 500 have an overall length of 21,500 m (Gabss type); 1 170 bogie wagons with sliding roofs for transport of coils (Shis type)— this wagon which is the model approved by UIC for the transport of coils. The central bearer cradle can support a coil of 45 tonnes maximum.
For export (recently supplied)—500 bogie hopper wagons of 66 m³ capacity to the German State Railways (DR); 900 bogie containers wagons to Intercontainer (Switzerland).

Type Shis telescopic bogie wagon for coil transports
Overall length 12.04 m; tare weight 22 tonnes; maximum load (20 t/axle) 58 tonnes; maximum load (22 t/axle) 66 tonnes; maximum mass weight on centre cradle 45 tonnes; maximum mass weight on inside cradles 17 tonnes; maximum mass weight on outside cradles 34 tonnes; automatic compressed air brake. Each covered section rests on four small bogies, suspended on a spiral spring.

Twin-hopper coal wagon
Among the numerous French built wagons at the 1977 Leipzig Spring Fair was the Arbel twin hopper coal wagon (type Fads) which incorporates the company's recently patented discharge system. Capacity is 70 m³, load 56.6 tonnes, against a tare of 23.4 tonnes. The two-leaf flap doors are opened mechanically and closed oleo-pneumatically using the energy generated by the coal thrust on the four doors during unloading. The body is made of E 36-2 steel, with side thickness ranging from 2 mm at the top through 3.5 mm at the vertical section, to 4.5 mm at the bottom inclination. End thickness is 4 mm. End panel inclination is 55 degrees. Overall length is 17.59 m.

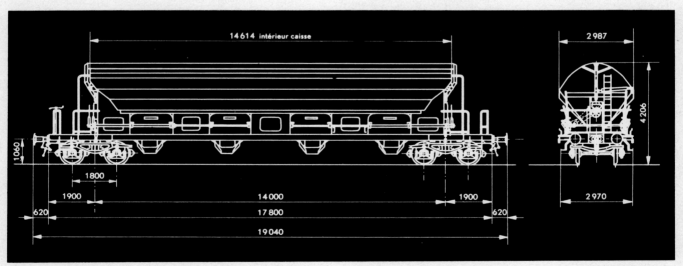

Type Tads 66 m³ bogie hopper freight wagon with bilateral adjustable roof
Capacity 66 m³; Tare 26.2 t; loading capacity for load per axle of 20 t; in S speed 54 t. The unloading is performed through eight openings provided at the lower part of the car and controlled by eight levers located on the two end platforms. Removable gutters are located under the unloading openings and are controlled by levers set on each side of car facings, so as to allow unloading away from track. The car is fitted with a roof with opening and closing performed by means of a mechanical device located on the platform, near by hand-brake lever. The frame of the car is designed to be eventually equipped with the automatic coupling system. The car is fitted with every required UIC regulation instruments. Length over headstocks 19 040 m; Length of the underframe 17 800 m; Distance between pins 14 000 m; overall height 4 220 m; capacity 66 m³; width of the unloading openings 480 × 1 500 mm; number of unloading openings four on each side; tare 26,2 t; loading capacity for load per axle of 20 t in S speed 54 t; bogie Y 25 Cs. 2; air brake; hand brake handled from the platform.

ASEA

Allmänna Svenska Elektriska Aktiebolaget

Telegrams: ASEA, Västeras
Telephone: (021) 10 00 00
Telex: 4720

Head Office: S-721 83 Västeras, Sweden

Products: Electric ac and dc locomotives; commuter and intercity trains with conventional, diode or thyristor control; subway cars with conventional or thyristor (chopper) control; electrical equipment for railway electrification and rolling stock; rotary and static convertors for ac and dc substations; marshalling yard equipment; mining and industrial equipment.

Chairman: Curt Nicolin
Managing Director: Torsten Lindström
Chief Sales Director: Arne Bennborn
General Manager, Transport Division: Åke Nilsson

Constitution: The company was founded in 1883 and built its first dc locomotive in 1891 and its first complete railway electrification project for 25 Hz single-phase was carried out in 1907. The first two diesel electric motor coaches in the world were supplied in 1912.

Sales: ASEA Group orders for transportation equipment—including railway equipment, military vehicles, materials handling equipment, marine turbines and equipment for merchant vessels—amounted to $US 130 million in 1976 compared with $US 175 million a year earlier. The decrease is largely attributable to the fact that in 1976 there was no order comparable to the contract for 40 class Rc 4 locomotives received from the Swedish State Railways in 1975. Sales during 1976 for railway motive power were restricted to an order for six thyristor locomotives from Norwegian State Railways (NSB) and delivery of the first of 16 ASEA 65-tonne mine locomotives with dc chopper control to LKAB. By mid-1977 it appeared that sales were due for a big improvement with successes announced on both the home and export markets. Order bookings over the first six months of 1977 increased from $US 70 million (in the first six months of 1976) to $US 100 million; a record order for 40 thyristor-controlled class Rc 4 locomotives placed by Swedish State Railways (SJ) represents just half the total value of first-half 1977 bookings. Orders now in hand for thyristor locomotives destined to go into operation with SJ, including the new contract, now amount to about 70 units. Also announced during 1977 was a contract placed by the Queensland Government of Australia with a consortium, Walkers-ASEA Pty Ltd, for the delivery of 39 electric passenger cars for Brisbane's electrification scheme. ASEA is to be responsible for the electric traction equipment as well as for the design of bogies and car bodies. Total order sum is about $A 20 million. The new passenger cars, which will incorporate ASEA's thyristor control system, will run in the Greater Brisbane area where diesel trains are now being used. The 39 cars on order will operate as 13 three-car units or 6 six-car trains with one spare unit. A three-car unit will comprise a driver motor car, a central motor car and a driver trailer car which will be unmotored. The two motor cars will each be powered by four 132 kW dc motors. The train crew will have radio/telephone contract with the train control centre. A three-car trainset will carry 248 seated passengers during normal operating with an increase up to over 500 passengers during peak periods. Trains will have a top speed of 120 km/h. Nominal voltage of the Brisbane rail network will be 25 kV, 50 Hz. Regular passenger services under the catenary are planned to begin mid-1979.

Also during 1977, the first in a series of six class Rm locomotives for hauling iron-ore trains was delivered by ASEA to the Swedish State Railways (SJ). The new locomotives are modified versions of the ASEA thyristor-controlled class Rc 4 locomotives. Main

modifications include electric rheostatic braking and greater axle load. Furthermore bogies are of special heavy-duty design similar to those developed by ASEA for its six-axle Bo-Bo-Bo locomotives. The Rm locomotives are fitted with automatic couplers, type SA 3. Three multiple-connected locomotives will be used to head each train. The driver's cab is fitted with extra heating facilities in view of the severe winter conditions likely to be encountered. A newly designed frequency converter for 16⅔ Hz/50 Hz replaces the MG set previously used over the Lulea-Kiruna-Narvik iron-ore line. With a rating of 7 200 kW the new class Rm locomotives are among the most powerful in the world.

Orders were placed with ASEA during 1976/77 for six additional chopper mine locomotives for the Henderson Mine in Colorado operated by the Climas Molybdenum Company of the United States—bringing the total number of locomotives ordered by the company from ASEA to 32. These 45 tonne dual voltage dc locomotives operate at a higher voltage and greater output than any previously built by ASEA. They are designed for single or multiple unit service and can be operated by remote automatic control by means of track signals or manually by a driver working from the master locomotive. Up to four units can be operated in m-u service. The electrical regenerative or rheostatic braking is used down to 8 km/h (5 mph) speed, when pneumatically operated disc brakes on all wheels take over. Rheostatic braking is automatically connected in only when the line cannot cope with brake power. Main Data: nominal speed at 1 400 V dc, 40 km/h (25 mph); nominal speed at 600 V dc, 24 km/h (15 mph); line voltages 1 400/600 V dc; gauge 1.067 m (3 ft 6 in); wheel arrangement, Bo; wheel diameter, new, 920 mm (3 ft 0¼ in); wheelbase 3.8 m (12 ft 5⅝ in); height pantograph down, 2.775 m (12 ft 1¼ in); maximum width over body 2.01 m (6 ft 7⅛ in); length over end frames 8.0 m (26 ft 3 in); length over couplers 8.84 m (29 ft) weight fully loaded 45 tonnes (50 short tons); axle load 22.5 tonnes (25 short tons); maximum horizontal curve radius (40 km/h) 210 m (700 ft); minimum horizontal curve radius, shunting 50 m (165 ft); number of traction motors 2; continuous rating 2 × 400 kW.

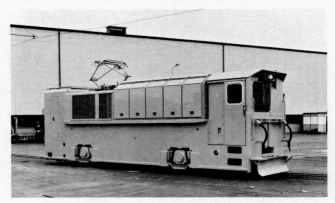

First of the new class Rm 7 200 kW electric locomotives delivered by ASEA to Swedish State Railways (SJ) during 1977. The new locomotives—modifications of the class Rc 4 thyristor-controlled locomotives—will operate on the Lulea-Kiruna-Narvik iron ore line and will supplement the triple-articulated class Dm locomotives delivered earlier by ASEA. Main data: maximum speed 100 km/h; length over buffers 15.57 m (including the automatic coupler); weight 92 tonnes; axle load 23 tonnes; number of traction motors, 4; gear ratio 38 : 164; traction motor control, thyristors; transmission ASEA hollow shaft motor drive; brakes, shoe with dynamic; continuous rating 3 600 kW; maximum starting effort 314 tonnes.

General Motors all-electric demonstrator locomotive model GM6C with ASEA thyristor control. First results of a new licensing agreement between General Motors of the United States and ASEA are two prototype locomotives, GM6C and GM10B equipped with ASEA built traction motors and ASEA designed bogies. Following a severe test programme in 1976, ASEA reports that the locomotives have passed all tests with extraordinary good results. The locomotives are now operating in revenue service with ConRail. Main data: maximum speed 117 km/h (73 mph); line frequency and voltage 25 Hz 11 kV, 60 Hz 12.5/25 kV; gauge 1.435 m (4 ft 8½ in); driving wheel diameter new 1.067 m (42 in); bogie wheel base 4.150 m (13 ft 7⅜ in); distance between bogie centres 13.259 m (43 ft 6 in); total wheelbase 17.304 m (56 ft 9¼ in); height over pantograph (down) 4.547 m (14 ft 11 in); length over couplers 20.980 m (68 ft 10 in); weight (total) 163 tonnes; maximum axle load 27.25 tonnes; number of fraction motors 6; gear ratio 76 : 18; continuous transformer rating excluding heating and auxiliaries 5 115 kVA; maximum starting effort 57.1 tonnes.

Under a contract signed in 1976, Amtrak of the United States, has leased from ASEA a modified class Rc 4 locomotive. The locomotive has been tested on daily passenger service between New York and Washington.

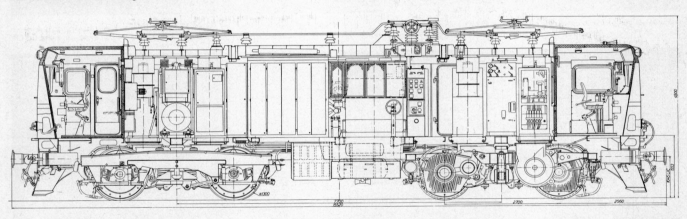

ASTARSA
Astilleros Argentinos Rio de la Plata SA

Telegrams: ASTARSA, Buenos Aires
Telephone: 40 3425/7014
Telex: 0121692

Head Office: Tucumán 1438, Buenos Aires, Argentina

Associated Company: General Motors Corporation

Licences: MTE and Alsthom, (France)

Products: Diesel-electric locomotives.

Sales: To accomplish negotiations completed in 1973 between the Argentine Railways (FA) and General Motors Interamerica Corporation, for the domestic production of 170 GM locomotives, ASTARSA is currently performing the construction of the underframe and cabins and the general assembly and final testing of the locomotives. For the same purpose, Siam provides traction motors and generators, Aceria Bragado supplies the bogies and Siemens Argentina is in charge of the electrical cabinet.

New equipment: Newest locomotive listed on the ASTARSA range is the G22-CU which has been designed for light rail application where axle loading is limited and heavy tonnages prevail. The locomotive is fitted with six-wheel bogies, its maximum speed being: 12 km/h; length: 14.173 m; height: 3.96 m; distance between bogie centres: 8.077 m; bogie wheelbase: 3 632 m and weight: 89.617 kg.

AT
Auxiliar de Transportes

Telegrams: Autrans, Madrid
Telephone: 2/22 04 14/232 35 47

Head Office: Avinida José Antonio 20, Apartado 358, Madrid 14, Spain.

Products: Diesel-hydraulic locomotives; passenger coaches; freight wagons.

ATEINSA
Aplicaciones Técnicas Industriales SA

Telegrams: ATEINSA-Madrid
Telephone: 419 95 50
Telex: 22055 ATIE

Head Office: PO Box 3276, Zurbano 70, Madrid 10, Spain

Works: Factoria de Villaverde, Carretera Villaverde, Vallecas 18, Madrid 21, Spain

Products: Locomotives: electric, diesel/electric. Railcars: diesel. Rolling stock: passenger carriages, goods wagons, mineral wagons, ballast wagons, special purpose freight cars for steel works and other industries.

President: Manuel Costales Gómez-Olea

Constitution: ATEINSA was set up in 1974/75 to takeover the railway rolling stock production of ASEA.

Sales: 400 high-sided wagons type XX and 1015 type ORE 1 wagons placed by Spanish National Railways (RENFE); 41 special ingot casting wagons placed by ENSIDESA; 147 iron ore wagons with automatic discharge placed by Vagones Frigorificos SA; 27 type PMM wagons ordered by Altos Hornos de Vizcaya.

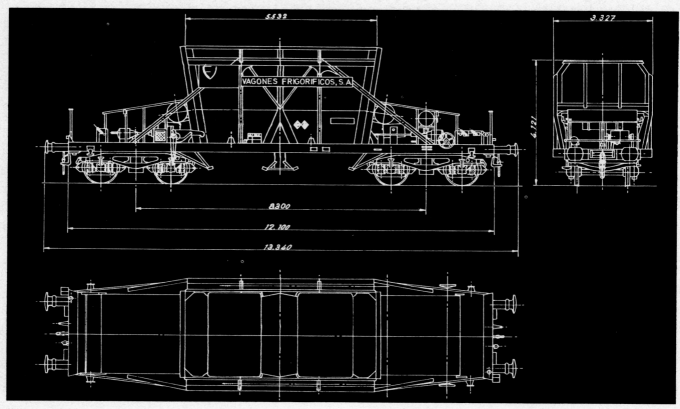

Hopper ore wagons with automatic discharge built by ATEINSA
Tare 23.8 Tm; maximum load 56.2 Tm; volume 41.5 m³; bogies Y-21 Ces; distance between pivots 8.300 mm; max height in tare 4.121 mm; width 3.327 mm; total length over the buffers 13.340 mm; vacuobrake—cylinders of 24″; air brake—cylinders of 12″.

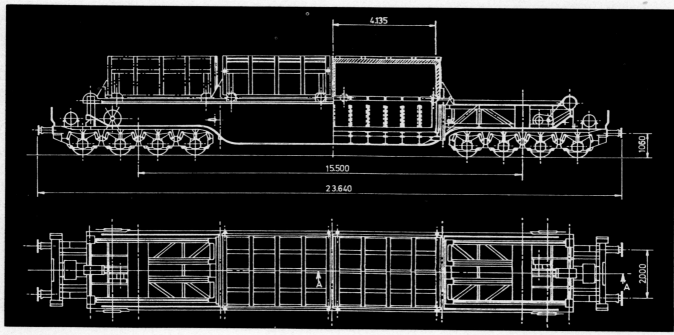

Ingot casting wagons by ATEINSA
Tare 130 Tm; load 110 Tm; wheel diameter 920 mm; axle load 30 Tm; total length 23 640 mm; distance between pivots 15 500 mm; four-axle bogies; air brake.

AUGUST, 23

"23 August" Works
(member of mecanoexportimport)

Telephone: 12 46 00
Telex: 10269

Address: 10 M. Eminesou St, Bucharest, Romania

Products: Diesel-hydraulic and diesel-electric locomotives. Constitution: The "23 August" plant is at present completing five new 1 500 hp diesel-electric locomotives to be used for shunting and secondary line duties in 1964, with turnover based on licences purchased from Sulzer, Alco, Maybach-Mercedes-Benz, Voith, Brown Boveri and Knorr-Bremse.

Sales: Apart from series orders being carried out for East-Europe railway administrations, the "23 August" plant is at present completing five new 1 500 hp diesel-electric locomotive for the Hedjaz Railway. Prime movers for the locomotives will be supplied by MTU, Friedrichshafen, German Federal Republic and will consist of MTU 12 V 652 TD 11 diesel engines with external air-change cooling equipment.
Locomotives produced by the plant include the LDH45 (450 hp BB), the LDH70 (700 hp

BB) and the LDH125 (1 250 hp BB)—all of which featured prominently at the 1976 Brno Fair. The full range of the company's diesel locomotives form an interesting example of efficient assembly. In the LDH45 unit, for instance, the MB836Bb six-cylinder turbo-charged 1 450 rpm diesel motor is manufactured under a Maybach-Mercedes licence, the turbo-blower is to a Brown Boveri design, the type TH1 turbo transmission and axle drive gears are built at Hidromechanica, Brasov, under licence from Voith, and brake equipment is to Knorr designs. Top speed of the LDH45 is 60 km/h in secondary freight or passenger line haul operations—30 km/h in shunting duty. Total length is 11.46 m with bogie centres spaces at 5.64 m and axles spaced at 2.5m.
A much larger locomotive is the LDH125 designed for heavy shunting, transfer and line duties. The unit features a Sulzer licenced type 6LDS28 direct injection six-cylinder diesel, built at the Resita works, which drives the axles through a TH2 Voith hydraulic transmission and an NE1200/2 Voith reversing reducer. Top speed on line duties is 100 km/h, total length is 13.7 m with a pivot base of 9.7 m and axles spaced at 2.5 m.

BABCOCK & WILCOX ESPAÑOLA

Sociedad Española de Construcciones Babcock & Wilcox

Telegrams: BABCOCK Bilbao
Telephone: Bilbao 41 14 50
Telex: 33776

Head Office: Alameda de Recalde, 27 Bilbao 9, Spain

Products: Electric, diesel-electric, diesel-hydraulic locomotives; electric and diesel railcars; industrial and mining locomotives; special freight wagons.

Managing Director: Gregorio Millán Barbany

BADONI

Telegrams: BADONI, Lecco
Telephone: 24306
Telex: 38086

Antonio Badoni SpA

Head Office: Corso Matteotti 7, 22053 Lecco, Italy

Products: Diesel-hydraulic shunting locomotives; hydrostatic transmissions.

Chairman: Dott. Emilio Walter

Managing Director: Ditt. Ing. Guiseppe Riccardo Kramer Badoni
Sales Director: Dott. Angelo Airoldi

BAGULEY-DREWRY

Telegrams: BAGULEY, Burton-on-Trent
Telephone: (0283) 66751

Head Office: Uxbridge Street, Burton-on-Trent, Staffordshire DE14 3JT, England

Products: Diesel-mechanical, diesel-hydraulic, diesel-electric, industrial and mining locomotives (battery and trolley); diesel-mechanical and diesel-hydraulic railcars.

Chairman: W. R. Souster

Sales: Major sales in 1976/77 included 12 seater standard-gauge railcars for the Ministry of Defence (UK) and diesel-hydraulic locomotives for Algeria, Zambia and the Royal Navy (UK) dockyards.

New 15 tonne diesel-hydraulic locomotive built by Baguley Drewry with a Perkins V8 diesel engine, torque converter, frame-mounted final drive unit and chain drive to axles.

BARCLAY

Telegrams: BARCLAYSON, Kilmarnock
Telephone: (0563) 23573/4/5/6
Telex: 778497

Andrew Barclay Sons & Co Ltd

Head Office: Caledonia Works, Kilmarnock, Scotland

Products: Diesel hydraulic, diesel-electric locomotives (30-hp to 1 000 hp); steam, fireless and crane locomotives; boilers and locomotive components; general engineering and fabrications.

Chairman: C. R. C. Fryers
Managing Director: S. E. H. Kewney

BARLOWS

Telegrams: SWIVEL, Benoni
Telephone: (011) 54-7511
Telex: 80559 SA

Barlows Heavy Engineering Ltd (Rolling Stock Division)

Head Office: Lincoln Road, Industrial Sites, Benoni 1500, Transvaal, South Africa
(PO Box 183, Benoni 1500, South Africa)

Products: Freight wagons; end-of-car and sliding sill hydraulic cushioning; underframes for locomotives and passenger coaches.

Chairman: K. C. Comins
Managing Director: A. L. Snell
Sales Manager (Rolling Stock Div): G. M. Kew

Constitution: Barlows Heavy Engineering Ltd—the major engineering subsidiary of the Barlow Group—is one of the largest companies of its kind in South Africa. The company was founded in 1889 when the original company of Wright Boag & Co was established in Johannesburg. In 1946 Wright Boag & Co merged with Head Wrightson & Co. In 1965 Thos. Barlow & Sons Ltd. bought the share capital of Wright Boag and was renamed Barlow Head Wrightson. This was followed by Barlows taking over the

Head Wrightson shareholdings, thus making it a wholly-owned South African subsidiary of the Barlow Group.

In October 1956 the company entered the rolling stock manufacturing field when the Rolling Stock Division was formed. During the past 21 years, nearly 17 000 wagons of various types have been built.

Sales: Major sales during 1976 included 1 000 Bogie Grain Wagons.

New Equipment: Railway equipment now being manufactured by Barlows includes Bogie Ballast Wagons. Centre sill cushioned bogie covered wagons, sulphuric acid tank wagons. Hydraulic end-of-car cushioning devices and centre sill cushioning devices are manufactured under licence. In the passenger coach field, the manufacturing programme includes the supply of all welded main line coach underframes.

BATIRUHR

Telegrams: BATIRUHR, Paris
Telephone: 531 87 49

Head Office: 54 rue Santos-Dumont, Paris 15, France

Products: Diesel-hydraulic, diesel-mechanical, mining and industrial locomotives; electric and diesel personnel coaches for industrial and mining operations.

Sales: Deliveries include diesel-electric locomotives for Morocco; diesel-hydraulic locomotives for French National Railways and Spanish National Railways.

BAUTISTA BURIASCO

Telephone: 214

Bautista Buriasco E Hijos Ltda SA

Head Office: 2445 Maria Juana, Province Santa Fe, Argentina

Products: Freight wagons.

Sales: Bautista is sharing in an order for 232 container flat wagons placed by Argentine Railways (FA) with four companies. Total value of the order is pesos 9 140 800.

BAUTZEN

VEB Waggonbau Bautzen

Head Office: DDR 86 Bautzen, Neuesche Promenade, German Democratic Republic

Products: Passenger coaches; freight wagons.

New equipment: Among latest products manufactured by Bautzen is a new Y four-axle dining car handed over for operation on CSD international services in the autumn of 1976. Fitted with two Gorlitz bogies—with axle and cradle type springs—the car has been built using lightweight construction methods. Main dimensions: length over buffers 24.5 m; width 2.883 m; height 4.230 m; distance between bogie centres 17.2 m; weight 45.5 tons; top speed 160 km/h; number of seats in dining compartments 48. The coach interior includes a lavatory, two dining compartments (one seating eight passengers and the larger, 40), two pantries, dish washing compartment, buffet, and kitchen.
Bautzen showed one of the 110 passenger coaches now being delivered to Egyptian State Railways at the 1977 Liepzig Spring Fair. Fully air-conditioned, the saloon-type coach has bar facilities in both first and second class versions. Seat arrangement is 2 + 2 in second class and 2 + 1 in first class. Seats are fully adjustable and can be swivelled according to the direction of travel. Bogies are Gorlitz V type. Braking is provided by indirect-acting compressed air brakes type KE-GPR with pressure controller and slide protection equipment. Design is for a maximum permitted speed of 120 km/h.
A new type Z2 composite-class coach was developed and built by VEB Waggonbau Bautzen during 1976. The major changes and improvements featured by the coach are:

—The length of the coach over buffers has been extended to 26.4 metres in compliance with the UIC leaflet 567-2;
—Empty weight: 40 tons;
—The vehicle's safe running and braking speed has been raised to 160 km/h;
—Passenger comfort has been improved thanks to the vehicle's good running properties, reduced noise level in the compartments, and modern upholstered seats fitted in either class; temperature and humidity are also kept at a comfortable level in both classes;
—A greater measure of safety has been achieved thanks to a central door closing and locking system;
—The power supply and ventilation systems require little maintenance;
—The interior has been designed to allow mechanical washing;
—Extensive standardisation.
The new coach is 4 050 mm high and 2 824 mm wide. The distance between bogie pins is 19 m. The height of 4 050 mm is in compliance with UIC leaflet 567-2.
New attractive high-speed intercity connections were introduced by Deutsche Reichsbahn towards the end of 1976 to supplement the country's existing network of fast intercity passenger rail services. The coaches employed were built by VEB Waggonbau Bautzen.
The coaches in the Y/B 70 series follow UIC specifications. The merits of the new vehicles are their reduced empty weight due to lightweight construction and the use of high-strength materials for parts that are subject to high static and dynamic stresses. The car body inclusive of the underframe is an all-welded lightweight steel structure. Smooth metal sheeting has been used for the body shell to simplify mechanical washing. The vehicles have an automatic door closing and locking system which

comes as a new feature on DR coaching stock. The coaches are carried on bogies of the Görlitz V type. Electric power is supplied by axle-mounted contactless three-phase generators (4.5 kW output) that require little maintenance.
Other features of the high-speed trains are:
—There are only six seats to the compartment, both first-class and second-class, and there is a reading light above each seat in either class.
—Each car has nine compartments and provides seating for altogether 54 passengers. There are two toilet compartments and a separate washing compartment, storerooms, and a side corridor.
—A through-connection has been provided to control the door closing system and the train lighting. The main air-reservoir pipe that serves the door closing system develops a pressure of 0.981 N/mm².
—Provision has been made for a two-duct air heating system using either steam or electricity (multiple-voltage operation, 40 kW) with automatic temperature control. The temperature inside the compartments is 22°C at an Accuracy of ±2°C. Ventilation is provided by the air heating system or by static fans.
—The washing water in the toilet compartments is warmed-up when the train's heating system is in operation.

The coaches are incorporated in the following high-speed intercity trains: Rennsteig-Express, from Meiningen via Suhl, Erfurt and Halle to Berlin; Elstertal-Express, from Gera via Leipzig to Berlin; Elbflorenz-Express, from Dresden to Berlin; Stolteraa-Express, from Rostock to Berlin; Sachsenring-Express, from Zwickau via Karl-Marx-Stadt to Berlin; Börde-Express, from Magdeburg to Berlin; and Petermännchen-Express, from Schwerin to Berlin.

Major technical data:

Length over buffers	24 500 mm
Width over body	2 881 mm
Height of body above rail top	4 230 mm
Bogie pivot pitch	17 200 mm
Bogie wheel base	2 500 mm
Rim dia.	920 mm
Floor height above rail top	1 250 mm
Top speed, cruising	160 km/h
Top speed, braking	140 km/h
Minimum radius curvature	90 m

BBC BROWN BOVERI

BBC Brown, Boveri & Company Ltd

Head Office: Postfach 85, CH - 5401 Baden, Switzerland

Associate companies
German Federal Republic
Brown, Boveri & Cie Aktiengesellschaft
Postfach 351, D - 8600 Mannheim,
Telegrams: Brownboveri Mannheim
Telephone: (0621) 381-1
Telex: 462411 120 bbd

France
Société de Traction CEM-Oerlikon
37, rue du rocher, F - 75383 Paris Cedex 08, France
Telegrams: Oerlik Paris
Telephone: (01) 522 8590
Telex: 650 663

Austria
Oesterreichische Brown Boveri-Werke AG
Postfach 184, A - 1101 Vienna, Austria
Telegrams: Brownboveri Wien
Telephone: (0222) 62810
Telex: 011 760 Oe BBWA

Brazil
Industria Elétrica Brown Boveri SA
CP 5528, 01000 São Paulo, Brazil
Telegrams: Brownboveri São Paulo
Telephone: (011) 227 1011
Telex: 1122275

Italy
Tecnomasio Italiano Brown Boveri SpA
Casella postale 3392, 1 - 20100 Milan, Italy
Telegrams: Tecnomasio Milano
Telephone: (02) 5797
Telex: 31153

Norway:
A/S Norsk Elektrisk & Brown Boveri

Postboks 429 Sentrum, N - Oslo 1, Norway
Telegrams: NEBB Oslo
Telephone: (02) 55 70 90
Telex: 11268

Spain
Brown Boveri de Espana SA
Apartado 12120, E - Barcelona 11, Spain
Telegrams: Brownboveri Barcelona
Telephone: (03) 321 6900/(03) 321 6950

Telegrams: BROWNBOVERI
Telephone: (056) 75 11 11
Telex: 52921, 53203

Products: Electrical equipment for all traction applications (Main-line, local and industrial railways, including systems for very high speeds. Local transport services, such as fast suburban and underground lines, trams and trolleybuses); rack railways and ropeways; new unconventional transport systems. Supply of components: electrical machines for traction and auxiliary duties for ac, dc and multisystem vehicles, thermo-electric and thermo-hydraulic vehicles as well as battery-fed vehicles. Equipment for conversion and distribution of electrical energy, such as transformers, static convertors, switchgear, resistors, etc. Protective and control systems for the traction and auxiliary circuits. Lighting, heating and air-conditioning equipment for railway coaches. Data transmission and processing systems for continuous train control. Contact-wire systems for all traction applications.

New equipment: Following tentative testing with an experimental three-phase electric locomotive since 1974, Deutsche Bundesbahn (DB) has now placed orders with Krauss Maffei, Krupp, Thyssen Henschel and BBC Brown Boveri for five new 15 kV 16²/3 Hz Bo-Bo electric locomotives—designated class E120— with a continuous rating of 4 400 kW and a 20-minute rating of 5 600 kW. Evaluation trials are due to start by the end of 1978 and series production is expected to follow before 1980. The advantages of three-phase motors for electric traction appear to be numerous. Those listed by BBC Brown Boveri as the most important are: 1) better use of available adhesion resulting in markedly higher traction forces at maximum speeds; 2) lighter bogies—the two bogies on the E120 unit will weigh only about 15 tonnes compared with 22 tonnes using conventional motors; 3) three-phase locomotives have all the characteristics needed to haul both passenger trains at a top speed of 160 km/h and heavy freight; 4) absence of slip rings, commutator and brushgear will result in lower maintenance costs; 5) electric braking is simplified. BBC Brown Boveri predicts that the three-phase brushless traction motor will prove universally applicable to all traction systems.

Electric locomotive E 444.005 of the Italian State Railways. One-hour rating 5 050 kW at 118 km/h, top speed 200 km/h. This locomotive is equipped with chopper control. Feeding System: 3 000 V dc. Electrical equipment was supplied by BBC Brown Boveri.

Four-axle heavy-duty class E 1200 locomotives with ac drive system. (Solid-state converter and asynchronous motors). Weight 88 tonne. Continuous rating 1 500 kW at 60 km/h

Thyristor-controlled locomotive of the 1 044 class of the Austrian Federal Railways. One-hour rating 5 100 kW at 90 km/h, top speed 160 km/h.

Two-part motor-coach train used for suburban services of the Netherlands Railways. One-hour rating 1 480 kW at 51 km/h (all axles driven), top speed 125 km/h. Feeding System 1 500 V dc.

BETHLEHEM STEEL

Bethlehem Steel Corporation

Telephone: (215) 694 2424

Head Office and Export sales: Bethlehem, Pennsylvania 18016, USA

Foreign agents: United Kingdom — Brettenham House, Lancaster Place, London WC2E 7EN, England

Products: Freight wagons; components; wheels and bogies; rails and track accessories.

Chairman: L. W. Foy
Vice-Chairmen: F. W. West Jr.
C. W. Ritterhoff
R. M. Smith
Sales: J. G. White, Jr.

BEML

Bharat Earth Movers Ltd (Railcoach Division)

Head Office: Unity Buildings, J. C. Road, Bangalore 560 002, India

Products: Freight wagons; passenger coaches.

Managing Director: O. M. Mani
General Manager: K. T. Sampathgopal
Factory Manager: H. Sreenivasiah

Senior Design Manager: K. S. Jagannatha

Constitution: The Railcoach Division of Bharat Earth Movers Ltd was the first factory in India to take up manufacture, in 1947, of all-metal broad-gauge railcoaches.

Sales: The Railcoach Division manufactures about 300 coaches annually for the Indian Railways. So far over 6 100 coaches have been supplied to the Railways. As a first step towards export drive, 50 broad gauge third class coaches have been delivered to Bangladesh Railways. Diversification of production is on hand and the manufacture of a 50 tonne, twelve twin-wheel low bed tank transporter and a 20 tonne low deck trailer has been taken up.

BEML's newly built bogie postal van for Indian Railways

BOEING

Boeing Aerospace Company

Telephone: A/C (206) 773 2816

Head Office: PO Box 3999, Seattle, Wash 98124, USA

Products: Automated transportation systems.

Sales: Associate contractor responsible for equipment and technical integration on Phase II of Personal Rapid Transit system at Morgantown, West Virginia, funded by US Department of Transportation. Phase II expands present Morgantown system, which

Morgantown (USA) personal rapid transit (PRT) car shown on Boeing's test track:
One of the 45 vehicles which comprise the Morgantown PRT fleet shown during a test run on Boeing's 0.8 km test track at Kent, Washington, prior to shipment to the West Virginia city. Each of the electrically powered, rubber-tyred vehicles carries up to 21 passengers at speeds of up to 48.3 km/h. Power is provided by a third rail on the guideway. Small follower wheels jutting out sideways near the ground steer the vehicle. The wheels run along a steering rail at the side of the guideway, directing the car into the proper lane as ordered by the computer system which controls its movements.

has been in public service since October 1975. System manager for Morgantown Phase I, and designer (for Kobe Steel, Ltd) of automated transit system which carried visitors at International Ocean Exposition, Okinawa, Japan, official 1975 World's Fair.

Boeing Vertol Company

Head Office: PO Box 16858, Philadelphia, Pennsylvania 19142, USA

Products: Rapid transit stock.

Sales: Production under way on 275 Light Rail Vehicles (streetcars) for Boston and San Francisco and 200 rapid rail cars for Chicago. Systems manager for US Department of Transportation's Urban Rapid Rail Vehicle & Systems programme, including development and demonstration of two State-of-the-Art (SOAC) cars, two Advanced Concept Train (ACT) vehicles, and Advanced Subsystem Development programme involving new-type propulsion system and new trucks.

BOFORS-NOHAB
AB Bofors-Nohab

Head Office: S-46101 Trollhättan, Sweden

Products: Diesel-electric, diesel-hydraulic and electric locomotives; snow clearing machines.

General Manager: H. de Verdier
Division Manager: L. B. Alin
Technical Manager: R. Olsson

Telephone: 0520/18000
Telex: 42084
Telegrams: NOHAB

Marketing Manager: H. Sörsdahl
Works Manager: H. Hugoson

Recent Sales: Deliveries and work in hand include 3 900, 3 300, 1 950, 1 650 and 1 425 hp diesel-electric locomotives in collaboration with General Motors, USA; electric locomotives of 3 300 hp, 4 900 hp and 10 000 hp in collaboration with ASEA.

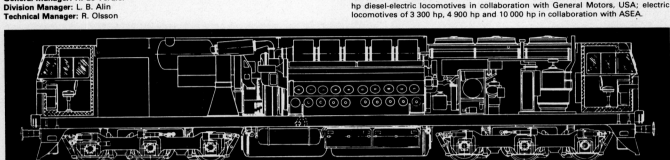

3 900 hp diesel-electric Co Co locomotive type Mz
Two-cab, full width, self-supporting on two three-axle motor bogies of flexi-coil type. A total of 46 have been delivered to Danish State Railways.

Type T46 3 900 hp locomotive

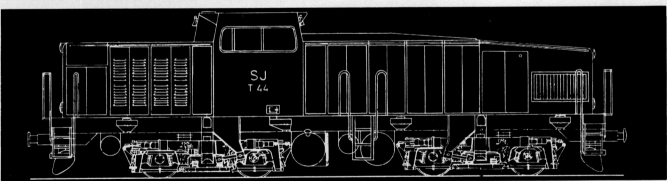

1 650 hp diesel-electric Bo Bo locomotive type T44. Designed for Swedish State Railways heavy shunting and freight haulage. Can be geared for speeds of between 105 and 143 km/h.

BRAINE-LE-COMTE
Usines de Braine-le-Comte SA

Head Office: Rue des Frères Dulait, Braine-le-Comte, B-7490 Belgium

Products: Freight wagons.

Managing Director: M. Lejeune

Telegrams: USINES, Braine-le-Comte
Telephone: (067) 55 31 07
Telex: 57458

BRAITHWAITE
Braithwaite & Co (India) Ltd

Head Office: Hide Road, Calcutta 700 043, India

Works: Clive Works, 5 Hide Road, Calcutta 700 043, India
Angus Works, Angus PO, Hooghly, West Bengal, India

Products: Freight wagons; pressed steel tanks; containers; wagon components.

Chairman: R. N. Sen
General Managers: R. L. Sengupta, A. N. Sarkar

Telegrams: BROMKIRK, Calcutta
Telephone: 45 9901
Telex: CA: 7910

Sales: Latest deliveries include tank wagons to Burma, Sri Lanka, Tanzania and Korea, covered wagons to Ghana and Taiwan, high-sided open wagons to Yugoslavia, freight wagons to Indian Railways, steel plants and port authorities. During early 1977 Braithwaite—in partnership with Texmaco—won a contract from Uganda for 250 freight wagons, 20 passengers coaches and spare parts valued at $US 9 million.

Bogie covered wagon built by Braithwaite for Ghana Railways

Prototype tank wagon for heavy oil products built by Braithwaite for Korean National Railways

BRATSTVO

Telegrams: VAGONI, Yugoslavia
Telephone: 23 762 5
Telex: 15138

Head Office: Preduzece Sinskih Vozila Subotica, Yugoslavia

Products: Freight wagons.

New equipment: The Bratstvo wagon plant is at present producing five types of wagon; 1a 13-m long flat wagon designed for carrying containers; types 1 and 2 two-axle covered wagons; a two-axle covered wagon ordered for operation over 1 000-mm gauge operation in Greece; and a bogie 1 000-mm gauge wagon also ordered by Greek Railways.

Last deliveries for domestic railways were three-axle coupled two-level wagon units for carrying automobiles. The unit accommodates 10 medium class passenger cars or 20 light cars or (maximum): 12 medium class cars or 28 light cars.

The running gear and brake equipment is suited for the speeds of 100 km/h or alternatively for 120 km/h.

For 1 000 mm gauge a number of four-axle covered freight cars have been delivered to the Brazilian Railways. The wagon, with bogies and automatic couplings, sides and roof from thin metal, is designed for carrying 60 tonne in tropical climate conditions.

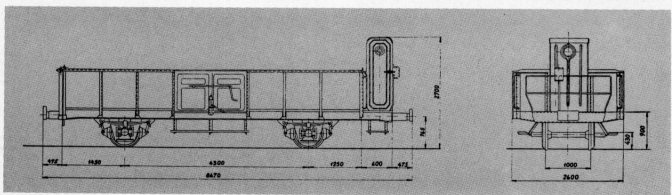

Two-axle open wagon 1 000 mm gauge

BREL

British Rail Engineering Ltd
(wholly-owned subsidiary of British Railways Board)

Telephone (London): (01)-247 5444
Telex (London): 885353 BREBIS-G
Telephone (Derby): (0332) 49211
Telex (Derby): 37367 RAILTK-G

Head Offices: 274/280 Bishopsgate, London EC2M 4XQ, England
Railway Technical Centre, London Road, Derby, DE2 8UP, England

Products: Diesel and electric locomotives and multiple units; passenger coaches; freight wagons; containers; steel, iron and non-ferrous castings; coil and laminated springs; crane machinery; railway equipment in glass reinforced plastic.

Chairman: I. M. Campbell
Managing Director: I. D. Gardiner
Engineering Director: J. J. C. Barker-Wyatt
Financial Director: J. B. Watts
Commercial Director: J. F. Thring

Constitution: The company was formed in January 1970 as a subsidiary of the British Railways Board to manage the thirteen main railway works. It undertakes all types of railway engineering work both for British Rail and private companies. Exports are handled by BRE-Metro Limited, the joint export sales company of British Rail Engineering Limited and Metro-Cammell Ltd.

Sales: High Speed Trains, comprising diesel electric power cars fitted with Paxman diesel engines giving an output of 1 680 kW and Mk III passenger coaches, for 200 km/h services; the Advanced Passenger Train comprising electric power cars and specially-designed trailers, capable of speeds up to 250 km/h; Mk III coaches for loco-hauled inter-city services; high density electric multiple unit stock for use on the newly electrified Great Northern Inner suburban line, (these units have the ability to utilise the 25 kV ac 50 Hz overhead power supply or the 750 V dc from third rail); electric multiple unit stock for Great Northern Outer suburban line; electrical multiple units for Taiwan Railway Administration; high capacity 2-axle coal wagons (45 tonnes GLW, 14 tonnes tare); 2-axle hopper wagons (46 tonnes GLW, tonnes tare); steel carrying wagons (100 tonnes GLW, 24 tonnes tare); two-axle covered vans (45 tonnes GLW, 15.8 and 16.2 tonnes tare); freightliner wagons (71.7 tonnes GLW, 19.7 tonnes tare and 72.2 tonnes GLW, 20.2 tonnes tare). Special purpose two-axle hopper wagons for British Steel Corporation (50.7 tonnes GLW, 13.7 tonnes tare); two-axle powdered cement carrying wagons for Associated Portland Cement Manufacturers Limited and Tiger Leasing Group (50.1 tonnes GLW, 13.1 tonnes tare), bogie phosphate carrying wagons for Aqaba Railway Corporation (62 tonnes GLW, 20 tonnes tare); freight containers for Bell Lines, Ocean Lines, Seatrain Inc.

Class 313 high density electric multiple unit built for British Rail's Great Northern Inner suburban electrification scheme.

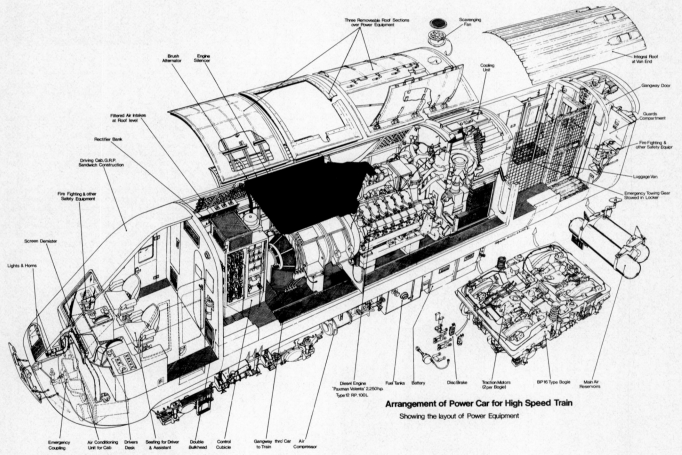

Three Removeable Roof Sections over Power Equipment

Scavenging Fan

Integral Roof at Van End

Gangway Door

Guards Compartment

Fire Fighting & other Safety Equipr

Luggage Van

Emergency Towing Gear Stowed in Locker

Cooling Unit

Brush Alternator

Engine Silencer

Filtered Air Intakes at Roof level

Rectifier Bank

Driving Cab. G.R.P. Sandwich Construction

Fire Fighting & other Safety Equipment

Screen Demister

Lights & Horns

Emergency Coupling

Air Conditioning Unit for Cab

Drivers Desk

Seating for Driver & Assistant

Double Bulkhead

Control Cubicle

Gangway thro' Car to Train

Air Compressor

Diesel Engine 'Paxman Valenta' 2,250 h.p. Type 12 RP.100L

Fuel Tanks

Battery

Disc Brake

Traction Motors (2 per Bogie)

BP 16 Type Bogie

Main Air Reservoirs

Arrangement of Power Car for High Speed Train
Showing the layout of Power Equipment

Power car for British Rail's High Speed Train

High capacity 45 tonne GLW coal wagon

BRE-METRO

(Export sales company of BRE and Metro-Cammell Ltd)

Telephone: (01) 247 5444
Telex: BR ENGHQ 885353

Head Office: 274/280 Bishopsgate, London EC2M 4XQ, England

Products: Diesel and electric locomotives; multiple-unit trains; passenger coaches; freight wagons; rapid transit stock.

Chairman: R. L. E. Lawrence
General Manager: F. D. Pinto
Senior Sales Engineer: R. W. Kelly
Contracts Manager: N. A. Brunt
Senior Contracts Engineer: D. A. Sandland

Sales: Contracts obtained/completed in the past five years have included 800 type gas wagons to Yugoslavia, 36 bogie bolster wagons to Ghana, 140 bogie phosphate hopper wagons for Aqaba, 1 160 bogie wagons for Kenya, 20 Hunslet shunting locomotives for Kenya and 65 emu cars for GEC (Taiwan).

The contract signed by BRE-Metro in Nairobi in March 1977 for the supply of 600 bogie wagons and 20 diesel-hydraulic shunters to Kenya Railways represents the biggest export contract ever negotiated by the export sales company. The two orders—which

together are worth approximately £40 million—was expected to bring the 1977 order intake of BREL (BRE-Metro's parent company) for customers outside British Rail to over £50 million—five times the company's previous best sales record. The order comprises 560 bogie covered freight wagons with hinged doors, 400 bogie low sided wagons, 100 bogie covered wagons with sliding roofs and 100 bogie covered freight wagons with sliding doors. In addition, the contract called for supply of 20 525-hp 0-8-0 diesel hydraulic shunters to be manufactured by Hunslet.

New equipment: With delivery of the APT production prototypes now well under way and passenger evaluation trials on London to Glasgow trains due to commence in 1978, BRE-Metro are apparently optimistic concerning the prospects of sales in overseas markets for this advanced technology product. The High Speed Trains are now well established in regular passenger service with BR and BRE-Metro hopes that a growing reputation of speed, reliability and comfort will aid sales of the HSTs abroad. Another unit which BRE-Metro considers a potential export winner is the BR class 313 Inner Suburban Electric Stock. Although initial quantity production was for 25 kV overhead line operation, variants have also been produced for 650/750 V third rail dc and for thyristor controlled 25 kV.

80 tonne glw type gas bogie wagon supplied to ZTP Zagreb of Yugoslavia

62 tonne glw bogie phosphate wagon as supplied to Aqaba Railway Corporation of Jordan

BREDA

Breda Costruzioni Ferroviarie SpA

Telegrams: FERBREDA Pistoia
Telephone: (0573) 33633/24371/37222
Telex: 57186 FERBREDA

Head Office: Via Ciliegiole, 51100 Pistoia, Italy

Products: Passenger coaches, light alloy or steel electric trainsets for long distances, for rapid transit of commuters and for underground lines.

Chairman: Dr. Eng. Franco de Gasperis
General Manager: Dr. Eng. Ugo Solone

Constitution: The San Giorgio Co was founded in 1907 in Pistoia as part of the company of the same name in Genova Sestri engaged in the repair of railway rolling stock. In 1914 this type of manufacturing was replaced by war production for the Army and Air Force. The production for the Air Force was later resumed in 1937. In 1949, after the firm split off from the San Giorgio Co, the trade name was changed into Officine

Meccaniche Ferroviarie Pistoiesi SpA. In the post-war period, in addition to the basic activity involving the construction of trailing and trailed railway rolling stock, the company began to manufacture public transportation vehicles like buses and trolley cars. In 1968, as a result of the reorganisation of the State participation firms operating in the railway sector into the EFIM and after the Officine Meccaniche Ferroviarie Pistoiesi was absorbed into the Breda Ferroviaria of Milan, the new company was given the trade name of "Ferroviaria Breda Pistoiesi". This trade name was then finally changed into Breda Costruzioni Ferroviarie with head office and works in Pistoia.

Recent sales: Deliveries in 1977 included 56 type Le 108 trailer coaches for new FS electric trainsets, 190 first-class passenger coaches for FS and 152 electric railcars for Rome Metro.

Trailer coach Le 108 type for suburban trains

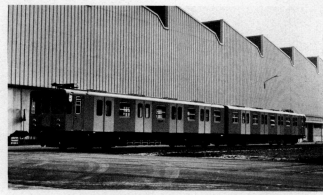

Light alloy electric driving cars for Rome underground

BRISSONNEAU ET LOTZ

SA Des Établissements Brissonneau et Lotz

Telegrams: ETABRIS, Paris
Telephone: (1) 727 35 79
Telex: 62-719F

Head Office: 8 rue Bellini, 75016 Paris, France

Products: Electric, diesel-electric, diesel-hydraulic, gas-turbine, mining and industrial locomotives; electric, diesel, gas-turbine railcars; electric and diesel multiple units; passenger coaches.

Constitution: The railway division was taken over by Alsthom in 1972 and merged with that company's Traction Division. The name of Brissonneau et Lotz is, however, still being used.

BREMER

Bremer Waggonbau GmbH

Telegrams: Bremer Waggonbau Bremen
Telephone: 45 40 11
Telex: 024 4423

Head Office: Postfach 110 109, Pfalzburger Strasse 251, 2800 Bremen 11, German Federal Republic

Products: Passenger coaches; freight wagons, in particular repair and renovation.

Managing Director: Peter Müller

Export Sales: Chr. Trahm

Constitution: The company was formed in December 1975. The works occupy the site of the former Hansa Waggon Ag.

BRIGGS & TURIVAS

Briggs & Turivas, Inc.

Telephone: (614) 922-5994

Head Office: Box 270, 310 Grant St, Dennison, Ohio 44621, USA

Products: Freight wagons.

BRITANNIA ENGINEERING

Britannia Engineering Works (Wagon Division)

Telephone: 51 Mokameh
Telegrams: BRITTANIA Mokameh

Head Office: PO Mokameh, Distt. Patna, Bihar 803302, India

Products: Bogie type BCX and BOXC wagons.

BROOKVILLE
Brookville Locomotive

Telephone: (814) 849 7321
Telegrams: BROLOC

Head Office: Brookville, Pennsylvania 15825, USA

Vice President (Marketing): Dalph S. McNeil
Sales Engineer: Robert R. Schreyer

Products: Four to 20 tonne diesel or gasoline locomotives with hydraulic torque converter or mechanical transmissions, designed for industrial, plantation, mining or yards.

Photographs (above) and blueprint drawings (below) show examples from Brookville's standard locomotive production line.

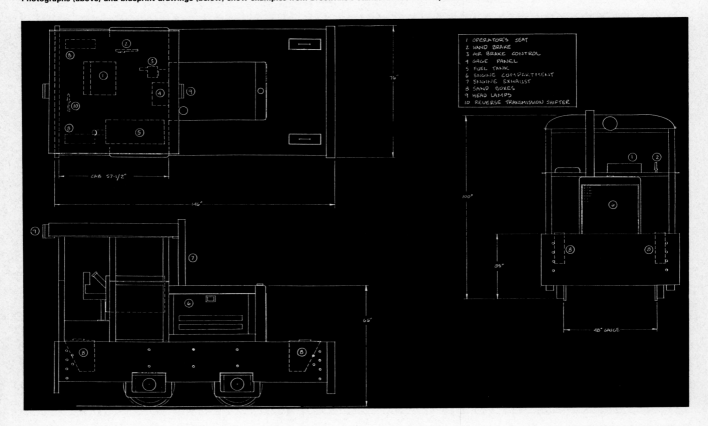

BRUSH

Brush Electrical Machines Ltd (Traction Division)
(Member of the Hawker Siddeley Group)

Telegrams: BRUSH, Loughborough
Telephone: (0509) 63131
Telex: 341091

Head Office: Falcon Works, Loughborough, Leicestershire, England

Products: Mainline diesel-electric and electric locomotives. Diesel electric transfer and shunting locomotives. Power equipments including alternators, generators, motors, and auxiliary machines, transformers, rectifiers, invertors, electronic and conventional control gear equipment for diesel-electric and electric locomotives, diesel rail cars, diesel and electric multiple unit trains.
Complete electrical propulsion equipment for rapid transit trains.

Chairman: Sir John Lidbury
Deputy Chairman and Managing Director: J. M. Durber
Traction Director: G. S. W. Calder
Special Director: F. H. Beasant
Executive Director (Engineering): W. G. Jowett
Commercial Manager: R. J. Gardener
Sales Manager: D. R. Minkley

Constitution: Brush Electrical Engineering Ltd was formed in 1889 with the acquisition of the Falcon Engine and Car Works in Loughborough, and the Company has been closely involved in electric traction since that time. Falcon Works' history of rail traction building began in 1875, with the manufacture of steam locomotives. Originally producing tram cars in large numbers, Brush entered the diesel-electric field in 1948 and since that date have built 2 000 diesel locomotives and power equipments and provided electrical equipment for over 2 500 power cars.

Sales: Four diesel electric shunting locomotives of 425 bhp for Tyne and Wear Passenger Transport Authority. Six 25 kV electrical power equipment sets for British Railways Class 314 thyristor controlled EMU trains operating on Clyderail PTE.
Thirty sets of electrical power equipment for British Railways Class 56 diesel electrical locomotives.
Seventy-five sets of electrical equipment for London Transport new District Line six-car trains.

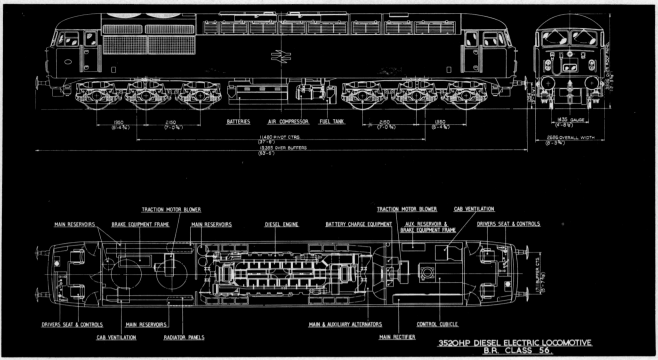

3520HP DIESEL ELECTRIC LOCOMOTIVE
B.R. CLASS 56.

New 3 520-hp diesel-electric for BR
Wheel arrangement Co-Co; Track gauge 4 ft 8½ in (1 435 mm); Wheel diameter 3 ft 9 in (1 143 mm); Overall length 63 ft 6 in (19 355 mm); Overall width 9 ft 2 in (2 794 mm); Overall height 12 ft 9⅜ in (3 896 mm): Minimum curve negotiable 80 m; Weight in working order 128 tonnes

Thyristor controlled three-car electric multiple unit class 314 operated by British Rail
Brush equipment is installed in the Clyderail Class 314 trainsets—a 25 kV/6.25 kV 50 Hz single-phase system operation; equipment supplied consists of a transformer mounted under the trailer pantograph car, an under-car mounted three arm assymetric bridge, two-stage control thyristor convertor and four dc series with axle suspended traction motors continuously rated at 410 V, 275 A (75% field), permanently connected in a series parallel configuration. Associated control and protection equipment is included.

BUDD

Telephone: (215) 673 1020

The Budd Company (Railway Division)

Head Office: Red Lion & Verree Roads, Philadelphia, Pennsylvania 19115, USA
Works: Red Lion Plant, Red Lion & Veree Roads, Philadelphia, Pennsylvania, 19115, USA (Telephone: 215-OR 3-1020; Cables: LIONRED)

Export Sales: International Activities, Philadelphia, Pennsylvania 19132, USA

Foreign Agent: *Europe*—9, rue de l'Industrie, 92 Courbevoie, France (Telephone: 333-58-60; Telex: 842-61061)

Products: Stainless-steel passenger coaches and components, fabricated passenger coach bogies and components.

Chairman: G. F. Richards
General Manager (Railway Division): N. W. Feshmire
Marketing Manager (Railway Division): S. W. Madeira

Recent sales: Deliveries completed in 1977 of 492 stainless-steel coaches for Amtrak; 72 stainless-steel suburban cars (50 for Chicago Regional Transportation Authority and 22 for Burlington Northern; 210 car sets of bogie components and engineering for Rio de Janeiro Metro; 108 car sets of bogie components for Sao Paulo Metro; 46 bogie car sets and stainless steel components for Delaware River Port Authority.

BURN STANDARD CO LTD

Telegram: 'BURN' CALCUTTA
Telephone: 44-1067, 1762, 1772, 1788
Telex: 'BURN' CAL CA2795

Head Office: Burn Standard Co Ltd, 10-C, Hungerford Street, Calcutta-700017, India

Works: Howrah, Burnpur, Raniganj, Durgapur, Ondal, Gulfarbari, Jabalpur, Niwar & Salem.
PO Box 191, Calcutta, India

Chairman and Managing Director: Shri N. R. Bhargava

Products: Railway Rolling Stock and Components; Centre Buffer Couplers and Components; Points and Crossings; Crossing Sleepers; Casting-Steel, Grey Iron, S G Iron and Alloy Steel; Forging, Stamping and Pressing; Railway Sleepers and Fishplates; Springs for Railway and Automotive Industry.

Constitution: Burn Standard Company Limited, a Government of India Undertaking, is successor to Burn and Co Ltd and The Indian Standard Wagon Co, Ltd. The Company has come into existence following the nationalisation of the undertakings of the two Companies by the President of India on 1 April, 1975. The Company has two Engineering Units located at Howrah and Burnpur in West Bengal and nine Refractory and Ceramic Units spread over different parts of the country.
Established in 1874, the Howrah Works of the Company was the first manufacturer of rolling stock in India and pioneers in foundry practice and structural steel fabrications of a wide range including bridge construction. The Works have extensive facilities for manufacture of Railroad equipment such as Crossing Sleepers, Switches and Crossings. The Burnpur Works manufactures prototype of almost all new types of wagons introduced by the Indian Railways and have guided the Railway Board in design and manufacture of wagons for use in the country and also for export. It specialises in production of Springs for coaches, locomotives, wagons and automobiles and for various other uses. The Burnpur Works also specialises in heavy die forgings, material handling structurals and equipment for the mining industry.

CAF

Telegrams: CAFAUXILIAR, Madrid
Telephone: 225 11 00
Telex: 23197

Construcciones y Auxiliar de Ferrocarriles SA
(Member of Servicio de Exportacion de Material Ferroviario)

Head Office: Padilla 17, Madrid 6, Spain

Products: Electric, diesel-electric and diesel-mechanical locomotives; electric and diesel-electric railcars; passenger coaches; rapid transit stock; freight wagons; rolling stock components.

President: José I. Cangas
Chairman: Pedro Ardaiz
General Manager: Juan José Anza

Constitution: The present company, Construccones y Auxiliar de Ferrocarriles, SA was formed by the merger of Material Movil y Construcciones, SA (MMC) into Compania Auxiliar de Ferrocarriles, SA (CAF) retaining the initials CAF. It is the largest manufacturer of railway rolling stock in Spain. Established in 1917 when deliveries started for RENFE.

New equipment: Among new equipment built by CAF is an experimental tilting train with Fiat equipment and to Fiat design which is now undergoing trials on difficult mountain routes in Spain. Also new by CAF are the bodies of 1.445 m-gauge two-car trainsets designated Series 300 which went into operation in June 1977 on Madrid Metro's Plaza Espana—Aluche route. Each two-car set is an autonomous unit with electrical equipment supplied by Westinghouse divided between the two cars to give even weight distribution. Stepless traction and rheostatic braking control is fitted. The bodies are of lightweight steel construction with three sets of double sliding doors on each side. Bogies, also supplied by CAF, feature Clouth primary suspension and secondary suspension consisting of helical springs resting on a pivoting cross-beam. Air operated disc brakes are fitted. Seating capacity in each 14.4 m long car is 36 with bench type seats arranged longitudinally. There is standing room for 144 passengers per car and loaded weight is 40 tonnes.

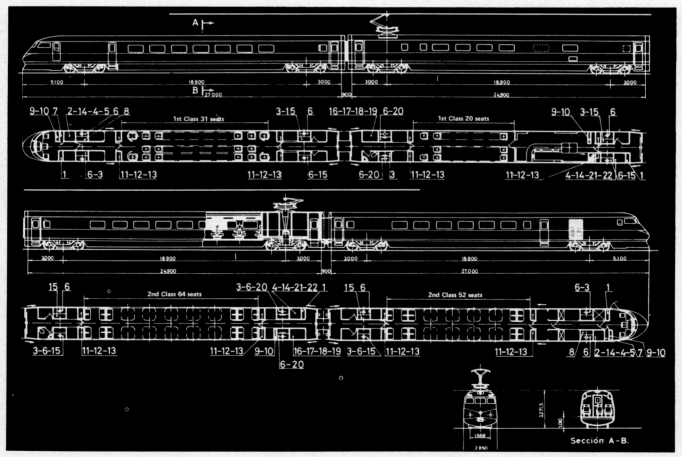

Sección A - B.

New equipment: RENFE's new experimental *Basculante* tilting train is based closely on Fiat's ETR 0160 design for Italian State Railways and consists of two head cars with two intermediate trailers. On straight sections the train is capable of top speeds of 180 km/h and through curves it can achieve speeds up to 105 km/h—35 per cent higher than RENFE's existing top speed trains. The pendulum suspension allows the train to rotate 8 degrees to each side around its own longitudinal axis. The pantograph is carried by a frame work which is supported on the swing bolster so that current collection is unaffected by tilting. To limit bogie weight, two motors are supported beneath the floor of each car. Motors are 220 kW output, producing a total of 1 760 kW. The train is designed for current collection at 3 000 V. The train has 51 first-class seats and 116 second class giving a high standard of comfort. Full air conditioning by Stone Iberia is provided. Doors are automatically controlled and will not open if the train is travelling above 5 km/h. RENFE officers predict the new train will make it possible to cut the journey time between Madrid and Gijon, for instance, from 7 hours 27 minutes to 5 hours 13 minutes.
Basculante train: 1) Auxiliary control panel; 2) Speed control panel; 3) Hydraulic controls for body rotation; 4) Electronic controls for body rotation; 5) Static convertor; 6) Hydraulic cylinder for body rotation; 7) Conductor's closet; 8) Speed regulator; 9-10) Control panels for air conditioning; 11-12-13) Air conditioning equipment; 14) Automatic rheostat; 15) WC waste tank; 16) Circuit breaker; 17) Pantograph controls; 18) Voltage relay and resistance for voltmeter; 19) Discharge condenser; 20) Pantograph and support; 21-22) Compressor and air tank for pantograph.

CADOUX
Établissements Cadoux

Telephone: 53 74 62

Head Office: 9 rue de Bassano, Paris 75016, France

Products: Freight wagons.

CANADIAN VICKERS
Canadian Vickers Ltd

Head Office: 5000 Notre Dame East, Montreal, Quebec H1V 2B4, Canada

Products: Rapid transit cars, commuter trains, double deck coaches, car bodies, fabricated shells and parts.

CALLEGARI
José Callegari E Hijos

Telephone: 2800/3228

Head Office: Rivadavia y Peru, Zarate, Pcia, Buenos Aires, Argentina

Production: Freight wagons.

President: Pablo A. A. Callegari
Director General: Clara Mandelli Vda. de Callegari

Sales Director: Ing. Eduardo Rivas
Export Director: Ing. Eduardo Rivas

Sales: Major sales have included 60 refrigerated wagons for Cuban Railways, and 464 tank containers for petroleum shipments to Argentine Railways. The company is sharing in a $US 110 million freight car order placed by Cuban Railways with three Argentine companies.

CANTON MOTIVE POWER
Canton Motive-Power Machinery Works

Works: Canton, Kwangtung, People's Republic of China

Products: Basically steam locomotives, but a trial 380-hp internal combustion narrow-gauge locomotive was produced in March 1975 and two others have been produced subsequently for local province operation.

CAREL FOUCHE-LANGUEPIN
Carel Fouché-Languepin SA

Telegrams: CARLANG, Paris 8
Telephone: 874 01 71
Telex: 290985F

Head Office: 55 rue d'Amsterdam, 75366 Paris Cedex 8, France

Works: Aubevoye; Le Mans; St. Denis; Saumur; Blois; Bluchy

Sales Organisation: FRANCORAIL-MTE

Products: Railway passenger cars of stainless steel (Budd system), and of conventional design.

President: P. Braudeau
General Manager: M. Mermet

Technical Manager: P. Foret
Commercial Manager: J. Porchez

Constitution: Carel Fouché has been building passenger cars for many years and, since 1935, has built under licence from Budd more than 2 000 cars. Early in 1954 the Budd Company acquired a large financial interest in this company. In 1968 Carel Fouché merged with La Soudure Électrique Languepin, the new company taking the name Carel Fouché-Languepin. In August 1973, together with the companies Creusot-Loire, De Dietrich, Jeumont-Schneider and MTE, Carel Fouché-Languepin created a "Groupement d'Intérêt Economique", under the name of FRANCORAIL-MTE.

Z 6400 suburban motor train built for French National Railways

CASARALTA
Officine di Casaralta

Telegrams: ROTABILI, Bologna
Telephone: 35 84 54
Telex: 52068

Head Office: Via Ferrarese 205, 40128 Bologna, Italy

Products: Electric locomotives and railcars; passenger coaches; freight wagons.

President: Rag. Aldo Farina
Chairman: Dott. Ing. Giorgio Regazzoni
General Manager: Dott. Ing. Carlo Farina
Commercial Manager: Geom. Sergio Nascetti

Sales: 1976 deliveries included 30 type E.656 electric locomotives for Italian State Railways (FS); 75 first and second-class passenger coaches, type UIC-X, for FS.

New equipment: The E.656 locomotive is a higher-powered modification of FS's E.646 unit. Traction motor design has been uprated utilising class H insulators for the field winding and class F for the stator windings. Increase in installed power has made it necessary to provide a more robust rheostat, and to improve ventilation.

Electric locomotive type E.656 for Italian State Railways built by Casaralta.

CAT

Compañia Auxiliar de Transportes

Head Office: Avenida José Antonio 20, Madrid 14, Spain

Products: Freight wagons.

President: D. Miguel Igartua Losa

Telegrams: AUTRANS, Madrid
Telephone: 232 35 47/231 69 12

Sales Director: D. José Ma Oteiza

Recent sales: Deliveries in 1975 included 60 wagons for Tunisia (SNCFT) and 88 wagons for Yugoslavia.

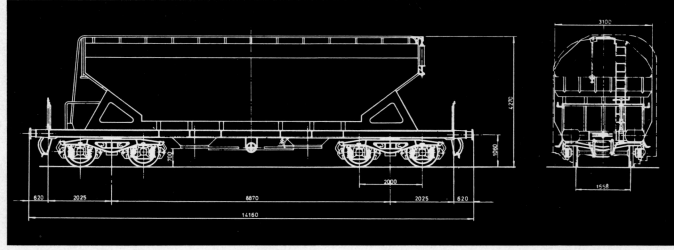

New hopper wagon for corn transport is fitted as standard with ORE-DB bogies but the units can also be equipped with Y-25, Y-21 Cs bogies. Approximate capacity 70 m³; load 55 tonnes; tare 25 tonnes

CATTANEO

Ferriere Cattaneo SA

Head Office: 6512 Giubiasco, Switzerland

Products: Freight wagons.

Managing Director: Rag. Fausto Cattaneo

Constitution: The company was established in 1870; considerable extensions were made to the works just before World War II. Among work in hand or recently delivered

Telegrams: FERRUM
Telephone: (092) 27 31 31/32/33/34
Telex: 79392

are various types of freight cars including special wagons for carrying cement and grain for Swiss Federal Railways and for private customers.

New equipment: Wagon range now includes a 58 m³ capacity cement tank wagon which consists of two separate tanks (2 × 29 m³). Tare weight is 24.2 tons; length over buffers, 13.2 m. Pneumatic loading and emptying is by the Cattaneo-Streblow system operating at a pressure of 2 atm.

CEGIELSKI

Cegielski Locomotive and Wagon Works
(Member of Kolmex)

Head Office: Zaklady Przemyslu Metalowego H. Cegielski, 61-485 Poznan ul. Dzier zynskiego 223/229, Poland

Exports: Mokotowska, 49.00-542, Warsaw, Poland

Telephone: 212-31
Telex: 0415343

Products: Electric locomotives. During 1977, Cegielski's plant at Poznan completed the first 4 000 kW production electric locomotive which are to enter operation with Polish State Railways (PKP) during 1978 as tandem units hauling primarily heavy freight trains.

CENTRAL CHINA PLANT
Central China Locomotive and Rolling Stock Plant

Works: Changsha, Hunan, People's Republic of China.

Products: Since 1969 has produced high-powered diesel-electric locomotives; also manufactures passenger coaches and freight wagons.

CESKA LIPA
Vagonka Ceska Lipa
(Member of Strojexport)

Head Office (Exports): Vaclabske nam 56, Prague 1, Czechoslovakia

Products: Freight wagons.

Telephone: Prague 248 851
Telex: Prague 171 208

Sales: During 1977 an order was placed by Kolmex of Poland for 500 doubledeck automobile carrying wagons with Ceska Lipa.

CID
Cid SA

Head Office: Calle 37, No 1005, Rosario, Argentina

Telephone: 33163/39

Products: Passenger coaches; freight wagons.

CFD
Compagnie de Chemins de Fer Départmentaux

Head Office: 10 avenue Friedland, 75008 Paris, France

Products: Diesel-hydraulic; diesel-mechanical locomotives; Asynchro hydro-mechanical transmission; railcars.

Telephone: 227 14 30
Telex: 660 955

President: M de Moussac
Director General: M. Grau

Sales: Contracts recently completed include metre-gauge railcars for Soc Gen de Chemins de Fer et de Transport Automobiles (CFTA).

CFMF
Compagnie Francais de Materiel Ferroviaire

Head Office: 4 rue de Ventadour, 75001 Paris, France

Telephone: 742 24-50/59

Products: Freight wagons.

CHANGCHOU DIESEL PLANT
Changchou Diesel Locomotive Plant

Works: Changchou, Kiangsu, People's Republic of China.

Products: Has produced diesel locomotives ranging from 60 to 120 hp since 1965; larger diesel-hydraulic locomotives up to 500 hp have been produced for mine and industrial service since 1968.

CHANGCHUN LOCOMOTIVE WORKS
Changchun Locomotive Works

Works: Changchun, Kirin, People's Republic of China

Products: Steam and electric locomotives; electric rapid transit trainsets Changchun has produced steam locomotives—including the Heping (Peace) freight locomo-

tive—since 1959. The locomotive has a top speed of 80 km/h, operates at 21 km/h on 0.6 degrees gradient. Also constructs 234 hp steam locomotives for mine operations. Latest equipment manufactured includes Peking Metro sets which first went into operation in October 1969: 19 m long cars designed to operate at a maximum of 80 km/h, accommodate 186 passengers (60 seated), operate over 750 V dc lines. Other products include passenger coaches and sleeping cars. The type YM-22 third-class sleeping coaches, first built in 1959 by Changchun, are still in operation: eight sleeping compartments; maximum speed 120 km/h.

CHANGCHUN PASSENGER CAR WORKS
Changchun Passenger Car Works

Works: Changchun, Kirin, People's Republic of China

Products: Lightweight passenger coaches for high-speed (160 km/h) operations.

CHARLEZ
Ateliers Charlez SA

Head Office: Quartier des Anglais, 7070 Houdeng-Goegnies, Belgium

Telegrams: CHARLEZ, Houdeng
Telephone: 064 225 44/242 91

The company ceased to trade in railway products in 1975.

CHICAGO FREIGHT CAR
Chicago Freight Car Co.

Head Office: Executive Plaza, Park Ridge, Ill 60068, USA

Products: Special and industrial freight wagons.

CHICHIHAERH CAR PLANT
Chichihaerh Railway Car Plant

Works: Chichihaerh, Heilungkiang, People's Republic of China.

Products: Freight wagons; latest reported product is a 370 tonne flat wagon for transport of complete machines and heavy equipment.

CHIANGAN ROLLING STOCK
Chiangen Rolling Stock Plant

Works: Chiangan, Wuhan, Hupei, People's Republic of China.

Products: Freight wagons and passenger coaches.

CHISHUYEN ROLLING STOCK
Chishuyen Rolling Stock Plant

Works: Changchou, Kiangsu, People's Republic of China

Products: Diesel-electric and diesel-hydraulic locomotives. Produced a 2 000 hp

locomotive with electric transmission in 1958. In 1975/76 produced the 5 000-hp diesel-hydraulic locomotive, Dongfanghong 4, after five years development. Tests were carried out through 1976 in mountainous territory in northwest China, and in service on the Shanghai—Nanking and Shanghai—Hangchow lines. The unit is reported to have over come earlier tortional vibrations which occurred when the high-output engine was operated at full load at 1 500 rpm.

CHUCHOU ROLLING STOCK WORKS

Works: Chuchou, Hunan, People's Republic of China

Products: Gondola wagons and all types of freight wagons. More recently development work on electric locomotives has started.

CIMMCO INTERNATIONAL

Head Office: 4D, Vandhana 11, Tolstoy Marg, New Delhi, India

Products: Flat, hopper, box, open high-sided, tank, covered, container and special purpose wagons.

Telegrams: CIMWAG NEW DELHI
Telephone: 44203/44204

General Manager: D. K. Goyal
Marketing Manager: S. K. Sharma

CIMT-LORRAINE

Compagnie Industrielle de Matériel de Transport

Telephone: 704 51 10
Telex: Cimtran 610 113F

Head Office: 42 avenue Raymond Poincaré, 75116 Paris, France

Products: Diesel-electric and electric trainsets; passenger coaches; freight wagons.

President: Roland Koch
Director General: Jean Colin
Commercial Manager: Jacques Smith

Constitution: Founded in 1918.

Sales: An order for 500 double-deck coaches for SNCF suburban services has been completed. Orders have been placed for new transit cars for Marseille and diesel-electric railcars for RAN (Abijdau-Niger Railway).

Double-deck coaches:
New 25 m double-deck coaches built by CIMT-Lorraine for French National Railways (SNCF) take 175 passengers seated and 132 standing. Normal consist is an eight coach train made up of four types of coach: Bxe—a second-class unit with driver's cab; Bde-second class with baggage compartment; BE-second class coach; and ABe-mixed first and second-class. Trains are locomotive hauled with the driver's cab in Bxe duplicating controls. Entrance doors at each end are 1.80 m wide to ensure swift boarding and dismounting.

Diesel electric railcar:
One of five built by CIMT-Lorraine for the Abijdan-Niger Railway (RAN). Delivered in 1975, the new railcars—together with 35 new passenger coaches also built by CIMT Lorraine—made an immediate impact on RAN operations. Operating as a single unit, the first railcar in service with RAN set a new record for African metre-gauge operations by running at a speed of 150 km/h. Operating as part of a seven-unit trainset (two railcars; five passenger coaches) a speed over straight track of 120 km/h was established. The railcar is powered by a SACM type MGO V 12 ASHR diesel engine. Electrical equipment was supplied by TCO and bogies by Creusot Loire. (For further information see the Railway System entry under Ivory Coast).

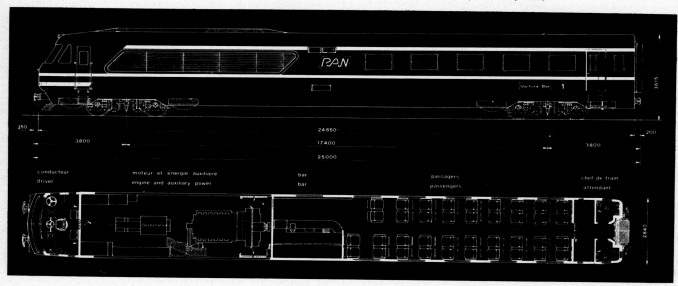

Mass transit cars built for Marseille Metro:
Train consists of three cars: two motor coaches with drivers cabin and one trailer. Length is 49 m, width 2.6 m, height 3.55 m. Number of passengers, seated 136; standing 216. Under normal load the train weighs 98 tonnes; bogies have pneumatic suspension, wheels are rubber tyred. Total power: 1 050 kW (750 V third rail). Maximum speed 80 km/h. Body structure is in aluminium with sliding double plug doors operated automatically. Forced ventilation is supplied together with public address system and radio telephone controls.

CKD

CKD Praha
(Member of Czechoslovakia's Pragoinvest diesel locomotive exporting group)

Head Office: U Kolbenky 159, Praha 9, Czechoslovakia

Export sales: Pragoinvest, Ceskomoravská, 23 Praha, Czechoslovakia

Telegrams: CKD, Praha
Telephone: 83 13 54
Telex: 01 1160/01 1229

Products: Diesel-electric locomotives; diesel engines.

Constitution: The company began steam locomotive production in 1900 and diesel locomotive production in 1927.

CLAYTON EQUIPMENT

Head Office: Clayton Works, Hatton, Derby DE6 5EB, England

Telegrams: Clayquip, DERBY
Telephone: 0283 88 2382
Telex: 341828

Products: Battery, trolley and diesel locomotives with electric, hydraulic or mechanical transmissions; electric and battery driven industrial and mining locomotives; special purpose internal combustion engined or electric rail vehicles.

General Manager: R. A. Baost

Constitution: The Clayton Equipment Co Ltd, now the Clayton Unit of Clarke Chapman Ltd's International Combustion Division, was incorporated in 1931 by Mr S. R. Devlin to carry on the manufacture of locomotives, rail cars, transfer cars and general engineering products.

In 1957 International Combustion (Holdings) Limited acquired the whole of the shareholding in the Company, but Clayton's continued to operate as an entirely self-contained and self-supporting unit.

In 1969 the company was fully integrated into International Combustion Limited which merged with Clarke Chapman Ltd in 1974. At this time the present Clayton Unit was formed to operate as an independent manufacturing and marketing organisation for Clayton Locomotives.

CLW

Chittaranjan Locomotive Works

Head Office: Chittaranjan, Burdwan District, West Bengal, India

General Manager: K. S. Ramaswamy

Products: Electric locomotives; diesel shunters; narrow-gauge diesel locomotive.

Constitution: This motive power plant, a production unit of Indian Railways started production in January 1950 and by the end of March 1977 had built a total of 3 253 locomotives—2 351 steam, 593 electric, and 309 diesel.

Sales: During 1976/77 a total of 44 electric and 32 diesel locomotives were delivered to Indian Railways.

New equipment: Currently, CLW is simultaneously manufacturing five types of locomotives—three types of electric and two types of diesel—all entirely designed and developed in the country by the Design Wing of the Research, Designs and Standards Organisation and the Chittaranjan Locomotive Works.

The first dual voltage (ac/dc) electric locomotive manufactured in India was turned out in January 1975 and series of production of this type of locomotive has been commenced. These locomotives are to be used to haul both high speed passenger trains and heavy goods trains between Bombay and Ahmedabad on the Western Railway. The section from Bombay Central to Virar was electrified at 1.5 kV dc during the period 1928-36, whereas electrification from Virar to Ahmedabad, recently completed, is on the modern system of 25 kV, 50 cycle, single-phase ac.

The manufacture of traction motors and traction equipments for electric locomotives was taken up in 1965. The largest traction motors, ever built in India, each with 1,580 hp, were manufactured by the CLW for use on ac freight type locomotives. CLW is now manufacturing type TAO-659 traction motors for ac mixed traffic (WAM-4) and ac/dc dual voltage locomotives (WCAM-1).

Telegrams: LOCOWORKS
Telephone: Asansol 2021/2022/2023

Class WCG-2 dc freight locomotive built by CLW for Indian Railways
Co-Co; 4 200 hp; axle load 22 tonnes; voltage supply 1 500 V dc; total weight 132 tonnes; maximum speed 120 km/h; braking, rheostatic.

Class WAM-4 mixed traffic electric locomotive of which 185 have been delivered by CLW to Indian Railways
Co-Co; axle load 18.8 tonnes; supply voltage 23 kV; total weight 112.8 tonnes; braking, rheostatic; maximum service speed 120 km/h; 3 640 hp.

CLW took up production of class WDS-4 diesel-hydraulic shunters for Indian Railways in 1968
Axle load, 2 000 kg; maximum speed, shunting, 27 km/h; maximum speed, mainline service, 65 km/h; weight 6 000 kg.

Class WCAM-1 ac/dc dual current mixed traffic locomotives, first built for Indian Railways by CLW in 1975
Co-Co; 3 640 hp at 60 km/h on ac; 2 930 hp at 35 km/h on dc; axle load 18.8 tonnes; supply voltages 25 kV ac and 1 500 V dc; total weight 112.8 tonnes; maximum speed 120 km/h.

CLYDE
The Clyde Engineering Company Pty Ltd

Telegrams: CYDEENGCO, Sydney
Telephone: 682 2111

Head Office: Factory Street, Granville, NSW, Australia

Branches (Workshops) in: Sydney Road, Bathurst, NSW, Australia. Neptune Terrace, Rosewater, South Australia. Links Avenue, Eagle Farm, Queensland, Australia.

Products: Diesel-electric and diesel-hydraulic locomotives; rapid transit stock.

Constitution: This company has from the early days built steam locomotives for Australian Railways. In 1951, by arrangement with General Motors Corporation, they started to build diesel-electric locomotives to GM design incorporating Electro-Motive power equipment.

Sales: Contracts in hand at June 1977: eight 3 300/3 3 000-hp diesel-electric locomotives for Australian National Railways; 10 3 300/3 000-hp diesel-electrics for Victorian Railways; 10 1 650/1 500-hp diesel-electrics for Queensland Railways; 14 1 650/1 5-00-hp diesel-electrics for Queensland Railways 35 1 650/1 500 hp diesel-electrics for New Zealand Railways (rebuild and modernisation).

CNCFSA
Constructora Nacional de Carros de Ferrocarril SA

Telegrams: CONCARRIL, Mexico City
Telephone: 575 55 17

Head Office: Av Universidad y Miguel Laurent No 803, Mexico 12, DF, Mexico

Products: Passenger coaches; freight wagons.

Director General: Lic. Francisco Javier Alejo

Export sales: Ing. César Mota Aguilar

Sales: Orders and deliveries handled in 1977 included 1 600 gondola cars of 100 tons capacity and tank wagons of 20 000 gallons capacity.

COBRASMA
Cobrasma SA

Telegrams: COBRASMA, São Paulo
Telephone: 478 8000/227 6711
Telex: 23145

Head Office and Works: Rue da Estacào, 523 Osaco, São Paulo, Brazil.

Products: Freight wagons; passenger coaches; 'Ride Control' bogies; rolling stock components.

President: Luis Eulalio de Bueno Vidigal
Vice-President: Luis Eulalio de Bueno Vidigal Filho
Director General: Marcos Vidigal Xavier da Silveira
Production Director: José Teixeira Beraldo
Export Sales: Eduardo Hubert Kirmaier Monteiro

Sales: In 1976 and 1977 the first fertiliser wagons were delivered to RFFSA (Federal Railroads Authority).
In 1977 the first all-door cars were delivered to FEPASA (São Paulo State Railroads) and CV Rio Doce.
Also in 1977 Rio's subway contract was signed with COBRASMA for the pioneer supply in Brazil of 68 articulated cars for the Rio Pre-Metro subway line.
COBRASMA is now manufacturing at its new and modern Sumaré plant 162 train units of three cars each (one motor and two trailers), of which 82 will go to FEPASA and 80 to RFFSA.

COCKERILL
SA Cockerill-Ougrée-Providence et Espérance- Longdoz

Telegrams: COCKERILL-OUGREE, Seraing
Telephone: Liège 34 08 10/34 28 10
Telex: 41225

Head Office: Avenue Adolphe Greiner 1, B-4100, Seraing, Belgium

Products: Diesel-hydraulic locomotives.

Managing Director: Charles Huriaux

Sales Manager: Roger Wolfers

Constitution: The present company was formed in 1970 by the merger of SA Cockerill-Ougrée-Providence and SA Métallurgique d'Espérance-Longdoz.

CODER
Établissements Coder

Telegrams: CODER, Marseilles
Telephone: 47 68 13
Telex: 42722

Head Office: Marseille-Saint-Marcel (Bouches-du-Rhone) 13, France

Products: Freight wagons.

COMENG

Comeng Holdings Ltd

Telegrams: COMHOLD, Sydney
Telephone: (02) 682 3677
Telex: AA24572

Head Office: 41 Berry Street, Granville, NSW 2142 Australia

Products: Locomotives; railcars; passenger coaches; freight wagons; containers.

Managing Director: K. P. McInerney.

Constitution: Comeng Holdings Limited and its Subsidiary Companies comprise the largest rolling stock manufacturing group in the Southern Hemisphere with manufacturing plants in all Australian mainland States, including: Commonwealth Engineering (NSW) Pty Limited; Commonwealth Engineering (Queensland) Pty Limited; Commonwealth Engineering (Victoria) Pty Limited; Comeng Western Australia.

Sales: Contracts received during 1976/77 included: Locomotives: 30 - 2 000-hp diesel-electric for Public Transport Commision of New South Wales (PTC-NSW); 4 - 3 600-hp diesel-electric for Hamersley Iron; 3 - 3 600-hp diesel-electric for Mt Newman Mining; 2 3 600-hp diesel-electric for Cliffs Robe River; 10 - 2 700-kw electric for PTC-NSW.
Passenger Cars: 150 double-deck suburban coaches for PTC-NSW: 30 double-deck Interurban coaches for PTC-NSW.
Freight Vehicles: Deliveries and orders have included;— 200 Stainless steel coal hopper wagons, code 'CHS'; 230 Aluminium wheat hopper wagons, code 'WTY'; and 100 Aluminium Air Discharge cement tank vehicles, code 'PRX' for PTC-NSW; 150 covered wagons for Australian National Railways; 33 woodchip wagons for Westrail; 125 aluminium coal wagons; 35 brake vans; 50 louvre vans and 30 refrigator vans for Queensland Railways.

New Equipment: The 10 Comeng 3 000-volt dc 2 700-kw mainline electric locomotives ordered by PTC-NSW weigh 120-tons and is the first contract let for electric locomotives designed and manufactured in Australia. They will have Co-Co wheel arrangement with axle-hung traction motors mounted on roller bearing suspension and the driver's cabs will be fully air-conditioned.

New Freight Wagons developed by Comeng include:
1. The stainless steel coal hopper wagons for PTC-NSW with tare weight 22-tons and gross weight 100-tons. All surfaces with which the coal may come into contact are stainless steel to avoid any problems with corrosion, wear etc.
2. The 76-ton aluminium cement hopper wagons with pressure and gravity discharge is the first of the type to be produced in Australia.
3. Woodchip Wagons for Westrail manufactured in 350-grade steel with gross weight of 76-tons with four large longitudinal bottom discharge doors which open in pairs for rapid discharge.
The new all stainless steel Interurban double-deck electric passenger coaches are designed for operation in two-car sets comprising one Motor and one Control Trailer Car and they are fully air-conditioned and will have PA system installed. Each two-car set will seat 182 passengers.

Stainless-steel double-deck inter-urban electric multiple unit air-conditioned coaches for PTC-NSW

The Prospector—a 90 ft long, 160 km/h air-conditioned diesel railcar built by Comeng for Westrail.

COMETAL

Cometal-Mometal Sarl

Telegrams: COMETAL, Maputo
Telephone: 752124/8

Head Office: PO Box 1401, Maputo, Mozambique

President: José Manuel Batista Silva
Director General: Eng. Armando Monteiro

Products: Freight wagons; inspection cars.

Sales: Major sales in 1977/78 included 100 tank wagons for South African Railways.

Bogie petrol tank wagons built by Cometal for South African Railways

Bogie covered wagons with sliding doors built for the Tanzam Railway

COMETARSA

Cometarsa SA

Head Office: L.N. Alem 619, 3°P, Buenos Aires, Argentina

Telegrams: COMETARSA, B. AIRES

Products: Diesel-electric, diesel-hydraulic locomotives; freight wagons.

COMMONWEALTH AIRCRAFT

Commonwealth Aircraft Corporation

Head Office: Port Melbourne, Australia

Products: Railway motive power, rolling stock and systems.

Constitution: The Commonwealth Aircraft Corporation began manufacture of railway rolling stock and systems during 1977 following completion of a licencing agreement with MAN of Germany. The agreement gives the Australian company access to all MAN's technical know-how and provides for MAN technicians to work at the corporation's Port Melbourne plant.

CONSTRUCTIONS FERROVIAIRES ET MÉTALLIQUES BN

Head Office: rue de Manage 61, B6548 Familleureux, Belgium

Products: Diesel-electric and diesel-hydraulic locomotives; passenger coaches; electric trainsets; freight wagons; rapid transit stock; containers.

Chairman: A. Dubuisson
Managing Director: O. J. Bronchart
General Manager: M. Simonart

Telegrams: BRUNIVEL, Brugge
Telephone: 050/33 07 21
Telex: 191 22

Constitution: With the merger on 1 July, 1977 of La Brugeoise et Nivelles SA and Constructions Ferroviaires du Centre SA, the new company, Constructions Ferroviaires et Métalliques BN was formed.

Sales: During the last five years, the company has won the following contracts: 128 articulated premetro cars for Brussels; 54 PCC tramcars for Ghent; 40 PCC tramcars for

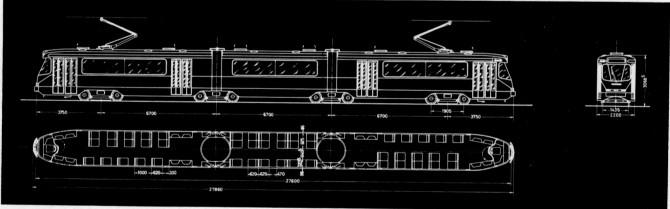

Two-car articulated semi-metro set for STIB of Brussels

Antwerp; 70 PCC tramcars for The Hague (Holland); 30 metrocar-units for Brussels; 60 double articulated premetro cars for Brussels of which 20 ordered and 40 still in negotiation; 100 articulated tramcars for Charleroi and for the line alongside the Belgian coast (in negotiation).

New equipment: The Brussels Metro Company's (STIB's) basic pre-metro operating unit is a traction unit or single set of two permanently-coupled cars. The traction and braking equipment being distributed over the two cars, the traction unit can only be separated in the workshops. Each car has a driver's cab, providing a traction unit with (length 36.400m and passenger capacity 420) a driver's cab at each end. Two or three single sets can be coupled to form a double set (four cars) to take 840 passengers, or a triple set (six cars) to take 1 260 passengers.

The car is of the total-adhesion "railway" type, using steel wheels running on steel rails. Overall length 18 200 m; overall width 2 700 m; overall height above rails 3 550 m; height of floor above rails 1 090 m; number of seated passengers 40; total number of passengers with 7 passengers/m² 210; with 4 passengers/m² 137; tare weight about 31 tonne.

The service brake is electrical: regenerative, when the system permits; rheostatic, automatically applied, when regenerative braking is not possible. When the electric brake is ineffective at a speed of less than 15 km/h or for any other reason, it is automatically replaced by the disc brake on the axle, operated by compressed air, but electrically remotely controlled. A single movement of the control handle operates the electric brake and, if this fails, the electrically-operated pneumatic brake, which takes over automatically. By moving the control handle (which has a wide range of braking positions) the driver can select the rate of deceleration of the car. There is thus a quite definite rate of deceleration for each position of the control handle, independently of the vehicle load.

By the same movement of the control handle the driver also "makes ready" the emergency brake which consists of a pneumatic control of the same axle disc brake. This pneumatic control is out of action as long as the electric control operates, but automatically and immediately comes into play if the electric control fails.

The safety brake consists of two brakes used simultaneously: the maximum braking obtainable by the pneumatically-operated discs on the axles; braking by electromagnetic shoes on the rails. This brake is operated either by turning the control handle to the appropriate position, by operating a special safety device known as a "coup de poing" (plunger), by the special automatic brake control linked with the signalling, or by means of the "dead man's handle".

Four-car electric trainset built for Belgian National Railways (SNCB)

Four-wheeled covered freight wagon built by CFetM BN for SNCB

High-sided bogie wagon now in service with SNCB

Two-car electric trainset in special airport service livery built by CFetM BN

COSTAMASNAGA

Officine di Costamasnaga SpA

Telephone: 031 85 51 92
Telex: 38184

Head Office: 22041 Costamasnaga (Como), Italy

Products: Freight wagons.

Chairman: Paolo Angelo Figliodoni
Managing Director: Luciano Trevisan
Sales Director: Ida Magni
Director (Exports): K. M. Glensy

Sales: Italian State Railways placed orders during 1977 with Costamasnaga for a series of four-axle ballast wagons. A prototype wagon was constructed and put through a rigorous test programme. With a capacity of 40 m³ the wagon is 12.24 m long and distance between centres of the type Y 25 Cs2 bogies is 7.20 m. The hopper discharges through four doors— two between the rails and the others just outside the track. Each door can be independently controlled from an operators platform at one end of the wagon. The frame is designed to accept automatic couplers at a later date. Maximum running speed is 120 km/h.

New type Eaos wagon—assembled on type Y25Cs2 bogies—built by Costamasnaga for Italian State Railways
Tare 20.7 tonnes; welded steel frame; frame suitable for future fitting of automatic coupler; non continuous traction with 1 Mn hook; 0.85 Mn coupling screw; great shock absorbing power buffers; bogies type Y25Cs2; roller bearing axle box type Tr.315; automatic air brake with 410 mm cylinder and V-C pneumatic device; body frame; walls and doors in steel plate; the wagon can run in curves of 35 mr; floor: larch wood—thickness 48 mm; loading area: 35.3 m²; volume 71.4 m³.

CREUSOT-LOIRE

Société Creusot-Loire (Traction Division)

Telephone: 776 41 62
Telex: 61425

Head Office: 31/32 quai National, 92806 Puteaux, France

Products: Diesel-electric, diesel-hydraulic locomotives and railcars, mechanical equipment; freight wagons; bogies.

President: M. Forgeot
Director: Henry Julien

Sales: A total of 15 two-car diesel-electric 440 kW trainsets were delivered by Creusot-Loire and ANF Industrie between April and September 1977.

New Equipment: The new Poma 2000 urban transit system was demonstrated at the French Transport-Expo 77 show held at Le Bourget in April 1977. Developed by Creusot-Loire in conjunction with Pomagalski, the system is suitable for operation at ground level, on an overhead track, or underground. It is automatic, essentially continuous, and has a capacity of up to 9 000 passengers hourly. The system consists of a succession of small cars, each with a maximum capacity of 30 passengers. The two-axle cars are spaced about 100 m apart and are hauled at speeds up to 33 km/h by cable mounted at track level. At each station entrance cars automatically disconnect from the cable and decelerate. They then move along the station platform at a speed of 300 mm a second making it possible to board or dismount safely.

CZECHOSLOVAK WAGON WORKS

Ceskoslovenské Vagonky Praha
(Member of Pragoinvest, Strojexport and Skoda)

Telegrams: EVIKAVAGON, Praha
Telephone: 542 513
Telex: 011218

Head Office: Kartpuzska 2, 150 21 Prague 5, Czechoslovakia

Products: Electric and diesel railcars; passenger coaches; freight wagons.

Chairman: Ing. Jiri Spevák
Managing Director: Ing. Oldrich Nepras
Sales Director: Ing. Ivo Dolezal

Sales: Orders and deliveries in 1974 included: 3 300 series Gbgs covered wagons for Hungarian State Railways (MAV); 1 000 series Fads coal wagons for Polish State Railways (PKP); 500 series Laas four-axle short-coupled flat wagon for a private German company; 300 series Les two-axle short-coupled automobile carriers for PKP; 850 air-operated side-tipping dump wagons for the Soviet Union; 700 series Hadgs covered multiple-purpose wagon for Czechoslovak State Railways (CSD); 165 type B passenger coach for CSD; and 700 series Fads coal wagons for CSD.

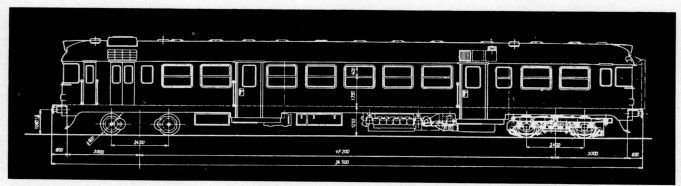

M474.0 power car
24.5 m long; weight 54,000 kg; top speed 100 km/h; seating capacity 72 passengers

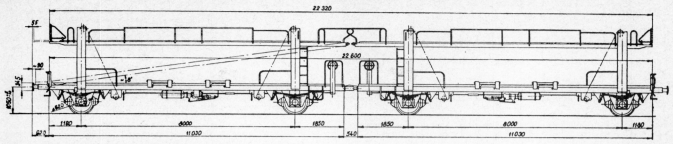

Series Laaes four-axle short-coupled car transporter

25 kV 50 Hz electric trainset built by Czechoslovak Wagon Works for CSD

DAVIS

W. H. Davis & Sons Ltd

Head Office: Langwith Junction, Nr. Mansfield, Nottingham, England

Products: Freight wagons; specialised stock for industry.

Telephone: (062 385) 2621
Telex: 37657

Chairman: W. H. T. Davis
Sales: D. Sharpe

50 tonne special purpose wagon designed and built by Davis for carrying steelworks scrap skip

50 tonne capacity palletised UKF fertilizer wagon
Stainless steel body, tare weight 24.4 tonnes, maximum speed 60 mph, *(96 km/h)*, overall length 15.239 m.

DE DIETRICH
De Dietrich & Cie

Telegrams: DIETRIWAGONS
Telephone: (88) 09 02 56
Telex: 870850 F

Head Office: 67, Reichshoffen, 67110 Niederbronn-les-Bains, France

Products: Passenger coaches; freight wagons; special wagons for steel shipments (torpedo ladle wagons).

Sales Organisation: Francorail-MTE (for railway rolling stock)
De Dietrich & Cie (for other equipment)

Constitution: Established in 1864, the company went into the construction of rolling stock during the middle of the 19th Century. In August 1973, the companies De Dietrich, Carel Fouche Languepin, Creusot-Loire, Jeumont-Schneider and MTE, created the Groupement d'Interel Economique 'Francorail-MTE'.

Currently the company is dealing with contracts covering high speed bogies, long UIC cars, and cars for the main lines of the French National Railways and other Railway Companies abroad. Besides rolling stock, the company makes and sells other equipment related to railways such as special wagons for the steel industry and points and crossings for the railways and underground networks.

Sales: Sales in 1977 included UIC mainline coaches ordered by SNCF, as well as special wagons for the steel industry.

Type B6D Second-class air passenger coach delivered to SNCF in 1977 by De Dietrich

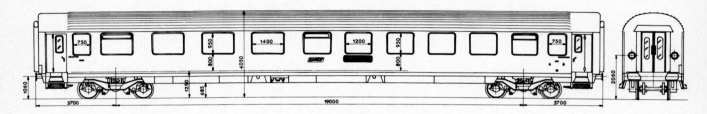

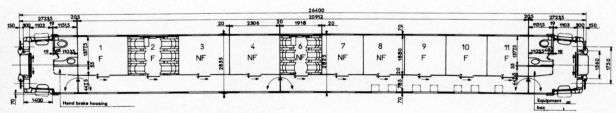

A4B6 passenger coach built by De Dietrich for French National Railways (SNCF)

Torpedo ladle wagon built by De Dietrich during 1977 for the French steel industry

DESSAU

Veb Waggonbau Dessau

Telegrams: WAGG DD
Telephone: 7510
Telex: 048841

Head Office: Joliot-Curie-Strasse 48, DDR 45 Dessau, German Democratic Republic

Products: Mechanically-refrigerated wagons and trains; ice-cooled wagons.

Sales: Major sales included sets of five refrigerated wagons for Soviet Railways, delivered in long series since 1965.

New equipment: Dessau's standard 19-m long four-axle refrigerated wagon has now been replaced by a 21-m design fitted with two independent diesel-driven Schkenditz refrigeration units—one at each end. Internal temperatures can be maintained at any level between +20 and −14°C.
Several years ago, the VEB Waggonbau Dessau started experimentally to use the

sandwich construction method in the production of refrigerator cars. This method consists of applying a core of polyurethane foam between the inner and outer skins, completely filling all cavities. This prevents condensation in the insulation—one of the main causes of the dreaded corrosion which normally sets in on the inner surfaces of the sheeting, especially in the lower sections of the wagon walls. Owing to its adhesive quality, the foamed material amalgamates with the walls, whilst the seamless, homogenous polyurethane foam core provides excellent insulating qualities which remain almost constant throughout the life of the wagon. Dimensions: length over head stocks 21 m, freight room width 2 784 mm, freight room length 17 365 mm. loading area 48.5², loading volume 114 m³, empty weight, ready for service 41.4 tons, effective load 42.6 tons.

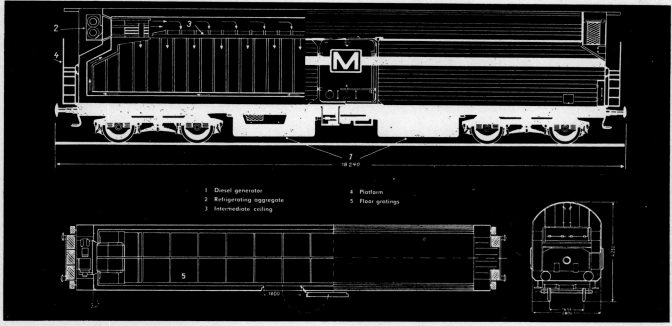

1 Diesel generator
2 Refrigerating aggregate
3 Intermediate ceiling
4 Platform
5 Floor gratings

Mechanical refrigerator wagon Type Mk 4

DIFCO

Difco Inc.

Telegrams: DIFCO, Findlay
Telephone: 419 422 0525

Head Office: PO Box 238, Findlay, Ohio 45840, USA

Products: Airside dump wagons.

Managing Director: Fred F. Flowers
Chief Sales Director: R. J. Ward

Constitution: Founded in 1915 for the production of heavy and light industrial railway rolling stock and mine haulage equipment.

Sales: 110 100 ton capacity air dump wagons for Southern Peru Copper Corp; 151 100 ton Airside dump wagons for US Steel; other purchases during 1977 included Texas Utilities, Seaboard Coastline RR, ATSF Ry.

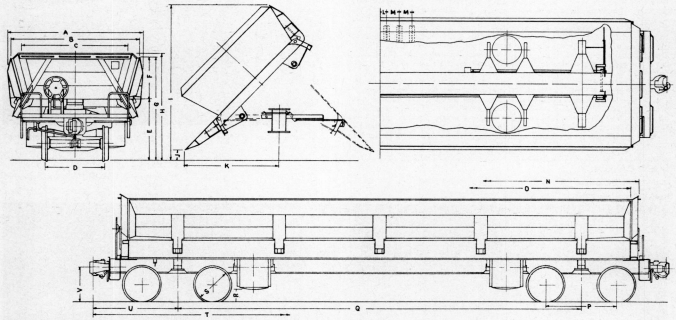

DIFCO wagons are made in various standard sizes ranging from 40 yds³ to 60 yds³

DIEMA

DIEMA Diepholzer Maschinenfabrik Fritz Schottler GmbH.

Telegrams: DIEMA DIEPHOLZ
Telephone: 05 441/3041-42
Telex: 09 41 222

Head Office and Works: Diemastrasse 11, 2840 Diepholz 1, German Federal Republic

Products: Standard and broad-gauge diesel shunting locomotives, narrow-gauge diesel mine locomotives, narrow-gauge industrial locomotives, hydraulic tippers.

Chairman: Dipl.-Ing. Karl Grebestein
Managing Director: Ing. Peter Benzien
Sales Director: Klaus Fuhrmann

Type DVL 150 diesel shunting locomotive: 250 hp; weight 24 tonnes; hydraulic power transmission; cardan shafts; bevel gear axle drive.

Narrow-gauge type DFL 90 diesel locomotive designed specifically for plantation operation overseas: 250 hp; weight 24 tonnes.

DORBYL

Dorman Long Vanderbijl Corporation Ltd

Telegrams: DORBYL
Telephone: 724 1441
Telex: 8-7539

Head Office: Dorbyl House, cnr. Jorissen & Reserve Streets, Braamfontein, South Africa.

Postal Address: PO Box 2997, Johannesburg, South Africa.

Products: Railway rolling stock, diesel-electric locomotives, industrial locomotives, cast steel wheels and axles.

Executive Chairman: C. D. Ellis
Managing Director: T. L. Roux
General Manager, Rolling Stock Division: C. R. L. Thorp
Manager, Export and Project Operations: R. E. Searle

Constitution: The Company, a subsidiary of International Pipe and Steel Association (IPSA), was established in South Africa as Wade & Dorman Limited, Structural Engineers in the year 1909. The manufacturer of rolling stock was begun in 1944.

Sales: Seven types of rolling stock for South African Railways are now being built at the Dorman Long Vanderbijl plant. Included are 104 double-deck automobile carriers, 30 steam-heating vehicles, 300 refrigerator wagons, 200 phosophoric-acid tank wagons, 25 LP gas tank wagons, 500 GZ 11 cattle wagons and 1400 gondola coal wagons. Dorman Long completed delivery of 425 sugar hopper wagons to SAR in 1976.
The automobile carriers (19.5 m long over headstocks) are designed to take four family saloons on each of the two decks. Mounted on two two-axle bogies, they have a rated maximum load of 16 tonnes. Tare weight is 26 tonnes. All will be fitted with air brakes. A number of existing automobile wagons were converted to dual air and vacuum brakes in SAR workshops recently. Delivery of the new wagons began in April 1977.
The refrigerator wagons have a 177 mm layer of polyurethane foam sandwiched between an outer skin of steel and an inner one of aluminium. Inner and outer body framing will be joined with high-density polypropylene material. Length of the wagon over headstocks is 17m. Delivery of these wagons also began in April this year.
The coal gondolas (CCRI type) are of 'bath-tub' bottom construction, to lower the centre of gravity and to accommodate a greater capacity than a standard flat-bottom car. They will be used for coal traffic on the Richards Bay line.
The LP gas tank wagons are of frameless design, built of mild steel plate approximately 16 mm thick for the cylindrical tanks, with thicker end discs. Built to AAR specification, they are fitted with vacuum brakes. Capacity is 550 hl. Dorman Long has supplied similar wagons to SAR under a previous order.
The phosophoric tank wagons are also of frameless design, but are being built in carbon steel and the tanks are lined with rubber. Total load capacity is 50 tonnes.
The GZ 11 cattle wagons are to be provided with insulated steel bodies. SAR already has a number of steel-bodied cattle wagons. Delivery of the new units began in September 1977 and continue at a rate of 60 units a month.
The steam-heat vehicles are being built at the Dorbyl associate yards of Swan Hunter, in Cape Town. Design is similar to earlier Dorman Long deliveries to SAR.
The Dorman Long-General Electric locomotive manufacturing consortium is now building 100 GE SG 10 B shunting locomotives for SAR, for marshalling yard hump duty and for inter-yard working. These will be used on the Natal network. An order for 50 GE U 15 C branch line locomotives (SAR class 35/400) has also been placed with the consortium, and these are now under construction. Diesel-electric units with a nominal

1 500-hp rating, they will be used in the Western Cape and the Orange Free State. Dorbyl has now delivered 1 750 gondola ore wagons ordered by South African Iron and Steel Corporation (ISCOR) for the new Sishen—Saldanha ore line. A building programme of five wagons a day started in April 1976. Two prototypes built by Dorbyl have been operating over the line fully loaded since April that year.
Built from unpainted Corten steel the new wagon has a capacity of 32.3 m³, a tare of 20 tonnes and payload capacity of 80 tonnes. Designed for tippler discharge, each wagon is fitted with a rotary coupler at one end and a fixed non-rotary coupler at the other, so that wagons are tippled in pairs. Originally, the wagons were to be built on heavy-duty Barber bogies. But following experiments with SAR's new cross-anchor bogie, designed by Herbert Scheffel ISCOR opted for the Scheffel bogie. This was designed for a 25-tonne axle-load. Scheffel was awarded the Shell Prize for Industrial Design last year, for his design of the new bogie. It has a self-steering action which reduces the wear of the rail and the wheel flange. And though the initial cost is higher than that of the Barber bogie, major economies are expected as a result of reduced hunting. The bogie also has greater stability at high speed than conventional bogies as a result of the cross-anchor design and damping provided by the rubber primary springs. Tests carried out at 110 km/h have shown stability in both loaded and empty conditions. Bogies are being supplied by Scaw Metals. The 36 in (944 mm) diameter wheels manufactured by Vecor, were treated in manufacture with a rim-quench to harden the skin. Composition brake-blocks, supplied by Metpro Development Corporation, are claimed to have ten times the life of cast-iron blocks and a higher friction co-efficient. The wagons are fitted with Cardwell Westinghouse air brakes, with a load detection device which decreases the braking action when the wagons are not loaded. Air pipe for the braking system is fitted to one side of the wagon only, to permit handling in the tippler.

U26C diesel-electric built by Dorbyl under licence from South African General Electric Company

DURO DAKOVIC

Duro Dakovic Industries

Head Office: Slavonski Brod, Yugoslavia

Telegrams: LOKOMOTIVE, Slavonski Brod
Telephone: 41 011
Telex: 28 521/102 155

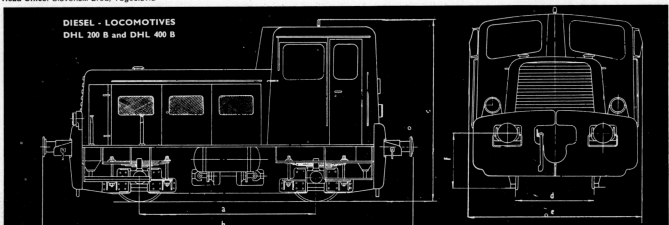

DHL 200B
(a) 3 200 mm; (b) 6 680 mm; (c) 3 302 mm; (d) 1 000-1 676 mm; (e) 3 030 mm; (f) 1 060 mm

Products: Diesel-electric, diesel-hydraulic and diesel-mechanical locomotives; electric locomotives; diesel railcars and trainsets; passenger coaches; freight wagons.

Constitution: Duro Dakovic was founded in 1921 as the first Yugoslavian locomotive and wagon manufacturer. Diesel locomotives have been produced since 1954.

ELECTROEXPORTIMPORT

(Romanian foreign trade company)

Head Office: Calea Victoriei nr. 133, Sector 1, Bucharest, Romania

Products: Romanian built electric and diesel -electric and locomotives for export.

General Manager: Ing. D. Suteu.
Deputy Manager: Ing. D. Togui.

Telegrams: ELECTROEXPORTIMPORT BUCHAREST
Telephone: 50.28.70
Telex: 11388

Sales: During 1976/77 30 diesel electric (3 500 hp) locomotives to Brush Electrical Machines of Britain; 58 5 100 kW electric locomotives to Investimport of Yugoslavia; 20 2 100-hp diesel-electric locomotives to China National Machinery Import and Export Corporation; 12 2 100-hp diesel-electric locomotives to Kolmex of Poland.

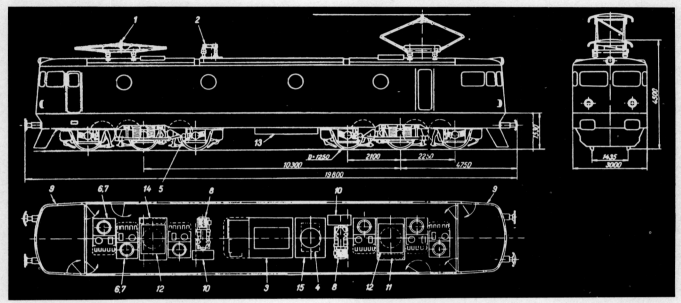

5 100 kW electric locomotive for Yugoslav Railways

During 1976/77, Electroexportimport delivered 58 new 5 100 kW electric locomotives to Yugoslav Railways (JZ). The 25 kV 50 Hz 5 100 kW electric unit is designed for haulage of either freight or passenger trains and may be used with single control or dual traction control. The locomotive is designed to operate at a minimum temperature of —35C and a maximum of +40C. The unit is equipped with rheostatic braking. Main data: wheel arrangement Co-Co; length over buffers 19.8 m; overall width 3.0 m; height, pantog-

raph down, 4.5 m; bogie centres 10.3 m; diameter of wheels (new) 1.25 m; diameter of wheels (half worn tyres) 1.21 m; total weight with ballast 126 tonnes; axle load with ballast 21 tonnes; maximum speed (gear ratio i = 2.74) 160 km/h. Equipment layout: 1) pantograph 2) main circuit breaker with isolators 3) transformer with tap changer 4) oil cooler with cooling fan 5) traction motor 6) fan and apparatus for the traction motor 7) silicon rectifiers with protections 8) air compressors for braking system 9) driver's cab 10) control cubicle 11) capacitors for phase splitting 12) resistor for rheostatic braking 13) storage batteries 14) pneumatic brake apparatus 15) smoothing choke.

ELECTROPUTERE

Electroputere, Craiova

Head Office: 7, Matei Millo St, Bucharest, Romania

Products: Diesel electric Co-Co locomotives from 2 100 to 2 500 hp; electric Co-Co locomotives of 7 350 hp

Telephone: 14 94 30
Telex: 216
Telegrams: MASEXPORT BUCHAREST

ENERGOMACHEXPORT

V/O Energomachexport

Head Office: 35 Mosfilmovskaya Ul, Moscow, Union of Soviet Socialist Republics

Products: Soviet exports of diesel and electric locomotives; electric trainsets; passenger coaches; freight wagons; railway interlocking equipment; signalling and block systems; subway stock.

Chairman: G. Sarubkin
Managing Director: N. Evteev
Sales Directors: V. Sunin, N. Lubin, V. Tubin

Constitution: The company was formed to handle all railway equipment exports from the Soviet Union. Principal partners include locomotive works: Ludinovo, Novocherkassk, and Voroshilvograd.

Diesel locomotive range designed for export:
TEM-2: The Model TEM-2 1200-hp diesel-electric locomotive with dc transmission designed for shunting, train and humping service on 1 435- and 1 524-mm railways.
TEM-4: The general-purpose Model TEM-4 1 000-hp diesel-electric locomotive is designed for shunting and main-line service both in countries with an ordinary climate and in countries with a dry or humid tropical climate.
TEM-6: The Model TEM-6 general-purpose 1 500-hp diesel-electric locomotive is designed for freight, passenger and shunting service on 1 524-mm railways.

Telegrams: ENERGOEXPORT
Telephone: 1472177
Telex: 7565

TGM-6A: The Model TGM-6A eight-wheel 1 200-hp shunting diesel-hydraulic locomotive is designed for shunting and transfer service on 1 524-mm railways.
TGM-3A: The Model TGM-3A 750-hp diesel-hydraulic shunting locomotive is designed for shunting service at railway yards and industrial enterprises having 1 524-mm tracks.
TGM-4: The Model TGM-4 750-hp diesel-hydraulic locomotive is designed for shunting service at railway yards and industrial enterprises with 1 524-mm tracks.
TGM-23B: The Model TGM-23B 500-hp diesel-hydraulic locomotive of the bonnet type is designed for shunting work on 1 524-mm tracks of railways and industrial enterprises.
TGM-25: The Model TGM-25 400-hp diesel-hydraulic locomotive is designed for shunting and light train service on 1 435-mm railway tracks of industrial enterprises.
TGM-8: The Model TGM-8 800-hp diesel-hydraulic locomotive is designed for shunting and transfer service.
TG-16: The Model TG-16 two-unit diesel-hydraulic locomotive is designed for freight and passenger service on 1 067- and 1 000-mm railways. It can also be manufactured for operation on 1 435-, 1 524-, 1 600- and 1 676-mm railways.
TU7: The Model TU7 400-hp diesel-hydraulic locomotive is designed for shunting and train service on railway lines, at yards, on the industrial tracks of timber-felling, peat-processing enterprises and quarries having 750-mm tracks.

EUSKALDUNA DE CONSTRUCTION

Euskalduna de Construction y Reparation de Buques SA Cia

Head Office: Bilbao, Spain

Products: Electric, steam, diesel-electric, diesel-mechanical, mining locomotives.

Telegrams: EUSKALDUNA, Bilbao
Telephone: 41 14 50
Telex: 33712

EXPORT ASSOCIATION OF SWISS ROLLING STOCK MANUFACTURERS

Member companies: SIG (Swiss Industrial Company); SWS (Swiss Car & Elevator Manufacturing Corp Ltd); SWP (Schindler Carriage & Wagon Co Ltd).

Products: Electric and diesel railcars; electric multiple units; diesel multiple units; passenger coaches; freight wagons.

FABLOK

Locomotive Works Fablok

Head Office: 32-500 Chrzanow ul. Fabryczna 10, Poland

Export sales: Kolmex, 49 Mokotowska, Warsaw, 00-542 Poland

Telegrams: FABLOK CHRZANOW
Telephone: 22-31
Telex: 032256

Products: Diesel-electric, diesel-hydraulic and diesel-mechanical locomotives; brake equipment.

800 hp diesel-electric. Weight 72 tonnes; length 14 240 m; top speed 90 km/h.

FAIRBANKS

Fairbanks Morse Engine Division of Colt Industries

Head Office: 701 Lawton Avenue, Beloit, Wisconsin 53511, USA

Products: Diesel-electric locomotives; diesel engines; railcars; generator sets; motors.

President: John Morgan
General Sales Manager: E. L. Fay, Jr

Telegrams: COLTIND
Telephone: (608) 364 4411

Constitution: The business started in 1830 as E. & T. Fairbanks, manufacturers of scales. Later the company manufactured windmills and, in 1893, shipped the first successful internal combustion engine produced in the US. This started them in the power business which covers diesel and gas engines, electric motors and generators, diesel-electric locomotives, pumps and hydraulic machinery.

FAUVET-GIREL

Établissements Fauvet-Girel

Head Office: 4, ter avenue Hoche, 75008 Paris, France

Products: Light rail shunters (300 to 1 600-hp); hopper wagons; tank wagons; special wagons; semi-trailers; containers.

President: Jacques Dambrine
General Manager: Hubert Foullon
Commercial Director: René Baldensperger

Constitution: The company was formed in 1918; now has three main wagon-building plants at Arras, Lille and Casablanca.

Telegrams: FAUVGIR
Telephone: 766 04 10
Telex: 650 337

Sales: Over the past five years, Fauvet Girel has built 10 000 wagons, notably 1 300 tank wagons for the transport of white petroleum products; 900 tank wagons for black petrol products; 600 wine and alcohol tank wagons; 700 chemical tank wagons; 1 100 liquefied gas wagons; and 4 150 hopper wagons. Approximately 50% of sales have been exported to: Belgian National Railways (SNCB); British Rail (BR); Italian State Railways (FS); Deutsche Bundesbahn (DB); Deutsche Reichsbahn (DR); Hungarian State Railways (MAV); Polish State Railways (PKP); Romanian Railways (CFR); Yugoslavia Railways (JZ); Cameroun Railways; Congo Railways; Moroccan National Railways (ONCF); Algerian National Railways (SNTF); Tunisian National Railways (SNCFT); Spanish Railways (RENFE); Syrian Railways (CS).

Four-bogie tank wagon
Capacity 130 000 litres; tare weight 45 700 tons; load 114 300 tons; GLW 160 000 tons.

A wagon of this type (see photograph above), exhibited at the Leipzig Fair won the gold medal.

FAVYS SAIC

Fabrica Argentina de Vagones y Silos

Head Office: Maipo 726, 3er piso, Buenos Aires, Argentina

Telephone: 392 2736

Products: Rolling stock.

FERROSTAAL
Ferrostaal AG

Telegrams: FERROSTAAL, Essen
Telephone: Essen 20141
Telex: 0857521

Head Office: PO Box 4, Huyssenallee 22-30, Essen, German Federal Republic

Products: Diesel-electric, diesel-hydraulic, diesel-mechanical, diesel mining locomotives; diesel railcars; railbuses; diesel multiple units; passenger coaches; freight wagons.

Directors: Dr Hans Singer
Wilhelm Haverkamp
Dr. Paul Lindemann
Wilhelm Lüttenberg
Dr. Klaus von Menges
Gerhard Thulmann

Ferrostaal-built lightweight diesel railcar designed for tourist service on the Cuzco-Machu Picchu line in Peru

---

FERROSUD
Ferrosud SpA

Telegrams: TF 22114 FERROSUD
Telephone: PBX 22114
Telex: 76025

Head Office: Via Appia Antica Km.13, Matera, Italy, PO Box 94

Products: Electric and diesel locomotives; railcars and trailers for electric and diesel trains; passenger coaches; freight wagons; bogies.

Chairman: Dr. Ing. Renato Piccoli
Vice-Chairman: Dr. Ing. Giuseppe Capuano
Managing Director: Dr. Ing. Angelo Mangone

Constitution: Ferrosud was set up in 1963 for the manufacture and marketing of

railway and tramway rolling stock. Production began in 1968. Export sales are handled through Fiat and Breda Costruzioni Ferroviarie.

Sales: Since 1969 the following sales to Italian State Railways have been recorded: 117 couchette coaches; 52 luggage vans; 1 050 box cars; 1 952 flat wagons; 48 three axle diesel-hydraulic locomotives; 9 124 bogies of various types; 35 postal vans; 19 railcars and 11 trailer coaches; and 174 type 402A flat wagons for private companies.

Mixed first and second-class couchette coach built by Ferrosud for Italian State Railways

Interior of second class compartment in Ferrosud's type AcBcz-x sleeper coach in night position

---

FFA
Flug-und Fahrzeugwerke AG

Telegrams: FFA Rorschach
Telephone: (071) 43 01 01
Telex: 77 230 FFA Altenrhein

Head Office and Works: Flug- & Fahrzeugwerke AG Altenrhein/Staad, German Federal Republic

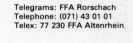

First class passenger coach for Swiss Federal Railways with light alloy body-structure, fully airconditioned

Products: Complete passenger wagons for all gauges, light weight steel and aluminium alloy design, normal carriages, traction carriages and pilot carriages, bogies for all types of carriages, street cars and tram bogies, postal, goods and container wagons.
Special constructions for all purposes, designs, understructure, modification and individual components and sub-assemblies.

Presidents (Board of Management): Dr. C. Caroni and Dr. L. Caroni

Managing Director: H. Eisenring
Commercial Director: H. Hutter
Director of Works: A. Kormann
Technical Deputy Manager: E. Erni

Constitution: The FFA developed from the original Dornier Works founded in 1925-1927.

Thyristor-controlled 3-car trainset for Rhätische Bahn (RhB)
Line current 10.5 kV 16.2/3 Hz. Metre gauge. Each set comprises a motor coach (Bo-Bo), an intermediate trailer, and a driving trailer. One-hour rating 1 000 hp. Weight 71 tonnes. Length over couplers 183 ft 1 in (55 800 mm). Total seating capacity 170. Max speed 56 mph (90 km/h)

FIAT
Fiat Ferroviaria Savigliano SpA

Head Office: Corso Ferrucci 122, 10141 Turin, Italy

Products: Electric, diesel-electric locomotives; electric and diesel railcars; multiple units; passenger coaches; freight wagons.

Chairman: Ing. Carlo De Benedetti
Managing Director: Ing. Renato Piccoli

Telephone: 332033
Telex: 22307 FIATDMFT

Constitution: The activity of FIAT in the field of railway rolling stock began in 1917 with the manufacture of passenger and freight cars. In 1926, in collaboration with Italian Brown Boveri, the first diesel-electric locomotives were built for Eritrea. In 1960 production of standardised light railcars, powered by petrol engines began, diesel engines having been introduced in 1934.
At the end of 1975 all the activities of FIAT concerning design and manufacture of railway rolling stock were entrusted to FIAT Ferroviaria Savigliano SpA.

Light Diesel Train for SNCFA (Algerian State Railways)
Power output 4 × 195 CV; weight 74 tons; max speed 130 km/h; wheel arrangement 1A—A1=1A—A1; seats 166; gauge 1 435 mm; multiple control.

Tilting-body electric train set
Power output 8 × 250 kW; weight 40 +40 + 41 + 40 tons; max speed 250 km/h; wheel arrangement 1A—A1; seats 49 + 49 + 24 + 49; gauge 1 435 mm; multiple control. On

straight sections, the train has a top speed of 250 km/h. On curves, FIAT engineers claim the new train will make it possible to raise speeds by at least 30% above the present maximum with conventional stock.

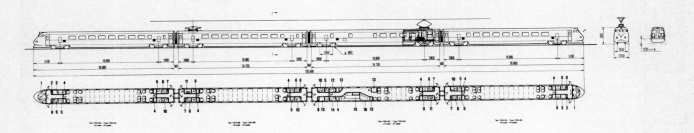

ETR Y 0160 tilt train

1. Driver's cab; 2. Personnel locker; 3. Instrument and signal repetition compartment; 4. Air-conditioning unit; 5. Body rotation actuator and instrument compartment; 6. Luggage compartment; 7. Control board and air-conditioning control; 8. Control board and auxiliaries control; 9. Body rotation actuator and pantograph replacement compartment; 10. Toilet; 11. Rapid circuit braker housing; 12. Chief-conductor's room; 13. Restaurant service closet; 14. Restaurant personnel room; 15. Galley; 16. Bar.

Italy's new tilting-body train, the prototype ETR Y 0160, has now carried out more than 50 000 km of test runs. Built by Fiat, it has been designed to operate over difficult mountainous routes at high speeds.

On straight sections, the train has a top speed of 250 km/h. On curves, Fiat engineers claim the new train will make it possible to raise speeds by at least 30% above the present maximum with conventional stock. This should make it possible to cut an hour and ten minutes off the present Bologna—Bari time; an hour from the run between Rome and Villa San Giovanni; and at least 25 minutes between Milan and Florence. The prototype train consists of two identical end cars, each with driver's cab, and two

intermediate cars. When fitted for passenger service the end cars will have seating for 49 passengers each; one of the intermediate cars will seat 49, while the other will seat 38 and will include a bar and kitchen. Each car will have its own air-conditioning unit, and windows will be non-opening double-glazed.

The pendulum suspension system allows the body to rotate around its own longitudinal axis. The pantograph is supported by a framework carried by the swing bolster, so that movement of the body does not affect current collection.

Motors—two to each car—are suspended beneath the floor to limit bogie weight. Output of each motor is 220 kW, giving a total installed power of 1 760 kW for the four-car prototype. Motors are paired and connected in series. Three types of braking system are installed—electrodynamic, mechanical electropneumatic (with two cast iron discs to each wheel set), and an electromagnetic system using a special system of brake shoes which act directly on the rail, independently of wheel adhesion.

Total length of the train is 103.7 m. Weight, with full load, would be 150 tons. Though the basic formation consists of four cars, trains can be increased to 6, 8 or 10 cars by interposing twinned pairs, so that power to weight ratio remains constant.

FIVES LILLE-CAIL

Telegrams: FIVCAIL, Paris
Telephone: 265 22 01

Société Fives Lille-Cail

Head Office: 7, rue Montalivet, Paris 8, France

Products: Rolling stock.

FIAT-CONCORD

Telegrams: CONCORDSA
Telephone: 35 3044
Telex: 012 1144

Fiat-Concord Saic (Division Productos Diversificados)

Head Office: Cerrito 740, Buenos Aires, Argentina

Products: Diesel-electric, diesel-hydraulic, diesel-mechanical locomotives; railcars; passenger coaches; freight wagons.

Constitution: Fiat-Concord began production of railway rolling stock in 1960.

Sales: To date, the company has delivered: (a) to Argentina Railways—over 2 000 passenger coaches; 339 multiple unit diesel railcars; 41 1 000 hp Bo-Bo diesel electric locomotives and 70 diesel engines to repower diesel electric locomotives. Also 280 diesel engines were delivered for 1 050/1 350 hp Co-Co diesel electric locomotives made in Argentina (b) Export area: to Uruguayan National Railways, 12 suburban passenger coaches; to Chilean Railways; 30 first class passenger coaches. Contracts have been signed to supply to Chilean Railways, 20 sets of electric (3 000 V dc) passenger trains and with Cuban Railways to supply 185 first class, air conditioned passenger coaches, 15 mail vans and 100 diesel hydraulic air conditioned railcars.

Travelling track gang coach

Specially built for Argentine Railways by Fiat-Concord for long-distance track inspection jobs.

1. Cabin No 1; 2. Conditioning air unit; 3. Power group room; 4. Motorman toilet; 5. Motormen bedroom with three beds; 6. Motorman closet; 7. Kitchen room with oven and gas irons; 8. Service corridor; 9. Engine air inlet; 10. Engine gases outlet; 11. Engine expansion water tank compartment; 12. Main toilet with bath; 13. Main living room; 14. Bedroom with two beds; 15. Toilet and shower bath; 16. Main corridor; 17. Hall; 18. Clean clothes and luggage closet; 19. Electrical rig case for engine control panel and auxiliary control panel; 20. Dinner room; 21. Closet; 22. Cabin No 2; 23. Electrical rig case for engine No 1 only on the upper part.

FMC

FMC Corp (Marine and Rail Equipment Division)

Telephone: (503) 228 9281
Telex: 36 0672

Head Office: 4700 NW Front Avenue, PO Box 3616, Portland, Oregon 97208, USA

Products: Freight wagons.
Chairman: C. Bruce Ward

Managing Director: C. Bruce Ward
Chief Sales Officer: William R. Galbraith

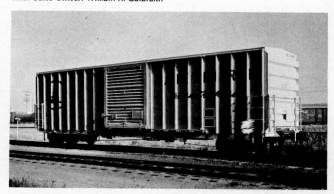

100-tonne capacity covered hopper wagon designed for a wide range of bulk commodities including grain and mineral products

70-tonne capacity wood products box wagon for a wide variety of lading; features include nailable steel decking, 10-ft sliding doors and cushioned underframe

100-tonne open top gondola wagon, designed for unit train operation utilising rotary dump service

FNV

Fabrica Nacional de Vagoes SA

Telegrams: FABRIVA
Telephone: (011) 239 3055
Telex: 01121901

Head Office: Praca Dom José Caspar 134-13° Andar, Sao Paulo, Brazil

Products: Freight wagons; passenger coaches; electric trainsets; Barber stabilised bogies; draft gears and couplers.

President: Aureliano Pires e Albuquerque
Industrial Director: Dr. Waldemar Fonseca
Sales Director: Dr. Leon Ravinowich
Sales Manager: Dr. Horst Muller Carioba

Constitution: The company was formed in 1943 to manufacture freight wagons. Today the plant covers an area of over 700 000 sq ft.

Sales: Major sales for Brazilian Federal Railways in 1975 included 170 closed hopper wagons (55 tonne capacity); 300 box wagons (54 tonne); 45 gondola wagons (75 tonne); 350 gondola wagons (95 tonne); 50 box wagons (72 tonne); 185 gondola wagons (55 tonne); 50 flat wagons (55 tonne); 5 flat wagons (70 tonne).

FRANCO-BELGE

Société Franco-Belge de Matériel de Chemins de Fer

Telegrams: LOCOMORAM, Paris
Telephone: 723 55 24
Telex: Herlicq No 290 060F

Head Office: 49 avenue George V, 75008 Paris, France

Products: Passenger cars for main line, suburban and underground railways; electric multiple unit; standard and special freight cars; standard and special bogies for passenger and freight cars.

President: Francois Herlicq

Assistant General Manager: Serge Fauconnet
Works Manager: André Rousset
Commercial Manager: Jean Nobilet

Constitution: The company came under the control of the Herlicq Group in 1962.

FRANCORAIL-MTE

Telephone: 292.05.10
Telex: 29638 F

Head Office: 2, rue de Léningrad, 75008 Paris, France

Managing Directors: P. Braudeau, President of Carel Fouché-Languepin
G. de Dietrich, President of De Dietrich & Cie
H. Jullien, General Manager of Société MTE
J. Lerebours-Pigeonnière, President of Société MTE
Secretary: André Gubi
Commercial Managers: H. Dhaussy
S. Bartmann
J. Y. Porchez

Constitution: The FRANCORAIL-MTE group, established in August 1973, pools the technological know-how, research and design capacities and means of production of five companies amongst the most important ones in France: Carel Fouché-Languepin, Creusot Loire, De Dietrich & Cie, Jeumont-Schneider, Société MTE.
FRANCORAIL-MTE coordinates the activities of these Railroad rolling stock manufacturers capable of supplying: main line electric and diesel-electric locomotives; shunting locomotives and other hauling stock; electric and diesel motor coach trains, railcars, metro cars; passenger coaches and other rolling stock; bogies; constituent sub-assemblies of the above-mentioned equipment; advanced vehicles and transport systems; metropolitan rapid transit systems; suburban transport systems.

Passenger coach supplied by Francorail-MTE being craned aboard ship for transport to the Abijdan-Niger Railway (RAN)

New 3 600 hp diesel-electric locomotive ordered from Francorail-MTE by Cameroun Railways being loaded on board ship during 1977

FRICHS

A/S Frichs

Telegrams: FRICHS, Aarhus
Telephone: Aarhus (06) 15 85 55
Telex: 64373

Head Office: Postbox 115, DK-8100 Aarhus C, Denmark

Products: Diesel locomotives and railcars; centrifugally cast cylinder liners for diesel engines.

Managing Director: B. Bigaard Soerensen

Constitution: Founded as a general engineering company in 1854; the manufacture of diesel locomotives started in 1925.

Sales: Work in hand includes electric railcars for suburban traffic and the bogies, underframe and superstructure of 3 300 and 3 900 hp diesel-electric locomotives for Danish State Railways.

New equipment: Only minor modifications are to be made to the eight-car trainset originally designed for DSB Copenhagen suburban line service and now the subject of new orders. The set consists of four two-car units each comprising a driving motorcar and trailer.

FRUEHAUF

Fruehauf Railcar Division

Telephone: (201) 779 1976

Head Office: 660 Van Houten Avenue, Clifton, New Jersey 07015, USA

Products: Freight wagons.

General Manager: H. W. Crank

General Sales Manager: R. S. Warntz

Constitution: The Division, successor to the Magor Corporation, was set up in 1964. Steel open wagons, box wagons, flat wagons, steel and aluminium covered hopper wagons, wood chip wagons, pulpwood wagons and dump wagons comprise the major part of production.

FSSA

Ferrovias y Siderugia SA

Telegrams: FERROVIAS
Telephone: 222 64 90

Head Office: Cedaceros 4, Madrid, Spain

Products: Railway rolling stock.

President: Guillermo Ed. Bernstein Diaz-Alvarez

General Manager: Luis Rios Sidro

Constitution: Founded in 1924, this company specialised originally in equipment for light railways, but recently extended its activities to supply equipment for Spanish National Railways (RENFE).

FUCHIN

Fuchin Rolling Stock Works

Works: Nanking, Kiangsu, China

Products: Passenger coaches, freight wagons, chilled cast wheels, shaft boxes, brake cylinders.

FUJI

Fuji Heavy Industries Ltd.

Head Office: 7-2 Nishi-Shinjuku 1-chome, Shinjuku-ku, Tokyo, Japan

President: Eiichi Ohara
Executive Director: Sukemitsu Irie
Director & General Manager: Yutaki Hasegawa
Manager, Rolling Stock Sales: Masami Suwabe

Products: Electric and diesel trainsets; passenger coaches; freight wagons.

Constitution: Fuji Heavy Industries stems from the Nakajima Aircraft Company and fully utilises the engineering experience, production facilities and business policies which made that company famous in aviation circles. The Nakajima Company was dissolved in 1945, but in 1953 it was reorganised as Fuji Heavy Industries. Specialising

Constitution: Originally a locomotive repair yard, facilities at present include nine shops.

Telegrams: FUJIHEAVY, Tokyo
Telephone: 347 2436
Telex: 0-232-2268

in building vehicles and aircraft for both civil and military purposes.

Sales: Sales for 1976 included: 25 passenger coaches; 45 sleeping cars; 105 electric cars; 115 track construction and maintenance machines; 40 tank cars and various freight wagons.

New equipment: Among recent exports were first and second class passenger coaches (type DCP), third class passenger coaches (type SP), and brake third class passenger coaches (type BSP) for the Nigerian Railways Corporation. Among the recent deliveries in this country were coaches and sleeping cars for limited expresses, diesel cars, and air-conditioned commuter trains for the private railway companies as well as the National Railways Corporation.

Limited Express Passenger Car for JNR (Model SUHAFU 14)

Diesel Rail Car for JNR (Model KIHA 66)

FUJI CAR

Fuji Car Manufacturers Co Ltd

Head Office: 383, Sayama-cho, Minamikawachi-gun, Osaka-Fu, Japan

Products: Electric locomotives; electric railcars; diesel locomotives; diesel railcars; passenger coaches; freight wagons; bogies.

Chairman: Toyozo Fujimoto
Managing Director: Takeomi Nishimura
Chief Sales Director: Takao Yamamoto
Export Sales: Hisashi Okumura

Telegrams: FUJICAR, Sakai
Telephone: 0722 36 5761
Telex: 5374-487

Constitution: The company was formed in 1924 by the Ishihara Brothers. In 1945 the name was changed in order to specialise mainly in the manufacture of rolling stock.

FUNKEY

C. H. Funkey & Co (Pty) Ltd

Head Office: Fuchs St, Alrode, Alberton, Transvaal, South Africa

Products: Diesel-hydraulic shunting locomotives; diesel mining locomotives; battery operated and trolley wire electric locomotives; track inspection railcars.

Telegrams: FUNKEYCO
Telephone: 864 2725
Telex: 8-4989

Chairman: J. P. Funkey
Managing Director: J. J. Galloway

GALLINARI

A. Gallinari SpA

Head Office: Viale Ramazzini 37, Reggio Emilia, Italy

Telegrams: GALLINARI, Reggio Emilia
Telephone: 31 641

Products: Passenger coaches; freight wagons.

GANZ ELECTRIC

Ganz Electric Works

Head Office: 1024 Budapest, Lövóház u. 39, Hungary

Telegrams: ALTERNO, Budapest
Telephone: 158 210
Telex: 22 5363

Products: Thyristor controlled and Silicon rectifier electric locomotives, thyristor controlled electric multiple unit trains, electric equipment for diesel-electric, diesel-hydraulic locomotives and railcars, trams and underground multiple units.

New equipment: Ganz Electric Works have developed a 5 000 hp six-axle thyristor-controlled electric locomotive, with a top speed of 120 km/h and 20 Mp maximum axle load. This new locomotive type is characterised by the extensive application of power electronics. The mechanical part has been manufactured by Ganz-Mavag, with electrics by the Ganz Electric Works. Its basic features are the fixed ratio transformer without tap changer, the semi-controlled thyristor rectifier in following control duty, the traction motors with compound excitation, the thyristor controlled auxiliaries and separate excitation. The speed regulation and the automatic continuous field weakening, with the help of an effective electronic anti-slip device simplify the driving of the

locomotive and result in an optimum energy utilisation.
Continuously adjustable 2 600 kW electric resistance brake is also installed.
In 1976 Ganz Electric Works began delivering 25 kV, 50 Hz three-car electric multiple unit trains of 1 200 kW continuous output with thyristor control for the Yugoslav Railways. The mechanical part is the construction of Ganz-Mavag. Thyristor rectifier and control equipment will be supplied by AEG-Telefunken. The unit consists of two driving trailers and one motorcoach in the middle. Three such units can be coupled by means of automatic couplers, and multiple control is ensured.
Maximum train speed is 120 km/h, the speed control occurs automatically and continuously by the control of the thyristor rectifier unit. The trains have effective electric resistance brake mainly for speed holding on longer slopes. The bogies assure excellent running qualities in the whole speed range.
The passenger compartments are uniformly second class.

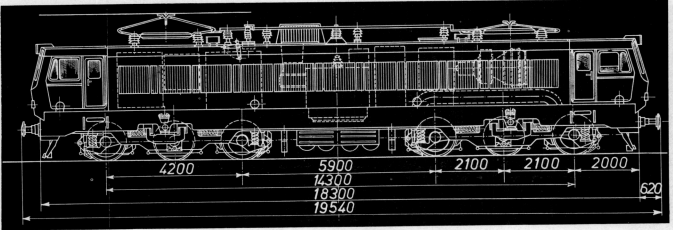

Type VM15 5 000 hp 50 Hz 16 kV thyristor rectifier locomotive built for Hungarian State Railways (MAV)

GANZ-MAVAG

Ganz-Mavag Locomotive and Railway Carriage Manufacturers Mechanical Engineers

Head Office: 1967 Budapest, PO Box 136, Hungary

Telegrams: GANZMAVAG Budapest
Telephone: 335 950/140 040
Telex: 22 5576/22 5575

Products; Diesel-electric, diesel-hydraulic locomotives (350 to 3 000 hp); diesel railcars and multiple units.

Chairman: Dr András Dunaiszki
Managing Director: Dr Antal Fleck
Sales Director: Tibor Trompler

Constitution: Ganz Railway Carriage Manufacturers and Mechanical Engineers, and Mavag Locomotive and Machine Works were merged in 1959 to form Ganz-Mavag.

New equipment: The diesel-electric locomotives of type DVM9 of 1 000 hp power manufactured for Cuba are improved variants of the DVM8 type units designed earlier for MAV. The parameters of the earlier and later types have much in common, but there are also some differences of importance. One of them is the class "F" insulation essential because of operation under tropical conditions, the rotary electric machines, the absence of a heating boiler, the application of larger brake compressors and of brake fittings of Soviet make. Another improvement against the DVBM type locomotives is type DVM11, of 1 000 hp, manufactured for the Egyptian Railways, of which 30 were delivered in 1972-1973. With consideration to desert service the locomotives had to be provided with special dustproofing. Air supply to the overpressure air space had

to be passed through a dynamic filter system. The penetration of dust into the machine compartments has been excluded, engine and power transmission, as well as all the other machinery and apparatus in operation are perfectly protected. The multiple-control locomotive of 74 tons weight is fit for line service and heavy shunting duty, too.
The factory started manufacturing Diesel-hydraulic locomotives in 1957. The first engine of this type was a shunting locomotive coded DHM1, of 400 hp power with rod drive, of C axle disposition. From this type 105 units were manufactured, 98 of them for the Egyptian Railways. The hydrodynamic drive powers the six coupled wheels through a blind-crank axle drive accommodated at the back of the locomotive and combined with the reversing gear. The final speed of the engine of 45 tons weight in shunting service is 30 km/h, on line service 60 km/h.
This type was later improved and gave the 450 hp locomotive type DHM2 designed for shunting service in Hungary. In the first few engines Voith L26/St type hydrodynamic drives were adopted.
In 1973 the factory brought out the DHM7 type locomotive of 1 800 hp power, B'-B' axle disposition and axle load not exceeding 16.5 tons. The locomotive is powered by a SEMT-Pielstick 12 PA4-185 type engine manufactured by the Ganz-Mavag factory under licence; the engine powers the Voith L720 rU2 type hydrodynamic drive integral with the reversing gear through a cardan shaft, and the axle driving gears through further cardan shafts.
The diesel-electric heavy shunting and mainline locomotives of type DVM11 (1 000 hp) are improved variants of the DVM8 units designed earlier for the Hungarian State

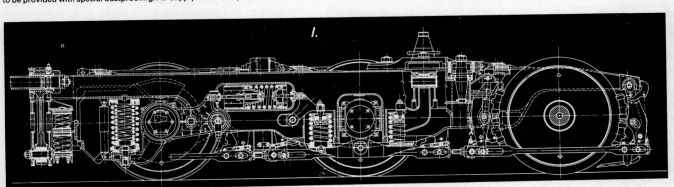

General assembly of the Ganz-Mavag three-axle bogie fitted to the DVM10

Railways (MÁV) and the DVM9 units delivered to Cuba. The DVM11 locos were specially manufactured for the Egyptian Railways.

The DHM7 type diesel-hydraulic locomotives (1 800 hp), are B'-B' axle arrangement and have an axle load of 16.5 Mp. These locomotives are equipped with a 1 500 V ac train-heating generator of 280 kW capacity.

The DVM10 type 3 000 hp mainline diesel-electric locomotive of Co'-Co' axle arrangement and an axle load of 20 Mp are also built with 1 500 V ac electric train heating equipment and 500 kW capacity. The DHM7 and DVM10 types are powered by SEMT-Pielstick PA4-185 type diesel engines (number of cylinders 12 and 18 respectively) built under licence agreement.

Recent deliveries in the diesel multiple-unit train field include: the three-unit standard-gauge express trains for the Hellenic Railway Organization (OSE) delivered in 1976. The trains consist of a power railcar—powered by a 1 140 hp SEMT-Pielstick 8PA4-185 type supercharged 8 cylinder diesel engine manufacturerd by Ganz-Mávag under licence, an intermediate trailer with buffet and a trailer with driver's cab. The power transmission is a two-converter hydrodynamical gearbox fitted by an additional hydraulical brake equipment for service in mountainous lines. The ac electrical energy

for the auxiliaries is supplied by an underframe mounted diesel-generating set. Similar trainsets were delivered to OSE for metre-gauge operation. The metre-gauge units have identical machinery and auxiliary equipment to the standard-gauge trains, but an additional second-class intermediate trailer was added. The top speed of the OSE diesel-trains is 140 km/h and 100 km/h respectively.

A total of 15 diesel trainsets were manufactured for the Uruguay State Railway Authority (AFE) in 1977. The composition of the trains is a power car with drivers' cabs on both ends, a second-class intermediate trailer and a first-class control trailer with bar compartment. The trainsets can be completed by an additional first-class intermediate trailer. The power cars are fitted with a 935 hp 12VFE 17/24-T type diesel engine and with a Hydro-Ganz type 3 speed hydromechanical gearbox of the factory's own construction. The control system is fully automatic by means of a patented control device of electronical elements. The standard-gauge trainsets have a maximum axle load of 12 tonnes and a top speed of 100 km/h.

Manufacture of the well-known Ganz-Mavag four-unit suburban diesel-trainsets for the Soviet Railways continues. From 1964 to 1976 a total of 400 of this type were delivered for SZD.

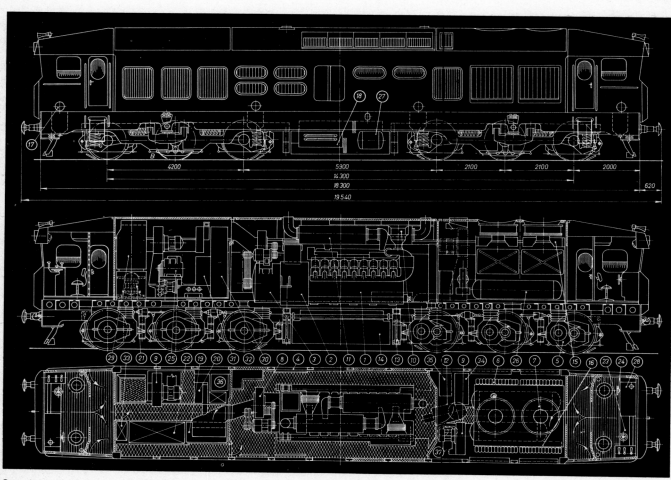

General arrangement of the type DVM10 diesel-electric locomotives: a 3 000 hp main line diesel-electric unit

Track gauge	1.435 mm
Loading gauge	ORE B13a and UIC 505
Axle arrangement	C'o-C'o
Min track curve radius	100 m
Weight in running order, with full supplies:	
Variant I	120 000 kp
Variant II	124 000 kp
Calculated average axle load:	
Variant I	20 000 kp
Variant II	20 700 kp
Fuel oil supply	4 260 kp (4 900 litres)
Water supply (for washing)	100 kp
Sand supply	600 kp
Top speed:	
Variant I	130 km/h
Variant II	160 km/h
Traction drive, gear ratio:	
Variant I	79:17 = 4 647
Variant II	76:21 = 3,62
Rated output of the Diesel engine	2 700 hp
Rated speed of the Diesel engine	1 500 rpm
Tractive effort on wheel rim on starting, with the electrical heating cut out:	
Variant I	40 000 kp
Variant II	31 500 kp

continuous rating:	
Variant I	21 700 kp (24,3 km/hr)
Variant II	16 920 kp (31,2 km/hr)
at top speed:	
Variant I	4 120 kp (130 km/hr)
Variant II	3 350 kp (160 km/hr)
Electrical train heating	1,5 kV, 50 c/s
Electrical dynamical brake:	
Variant I	active at 30-120 km/hr
Variant II	active at 40-160 km/hr

Legend
1. Diesel engine; 2. Main (traction) generator; 3. Heating and auxiliary generator; 4. Excitation generator; 5. Traction motor; 6. Radiator (water-cooled); 7. Radiator fan; 8. Fan to the main, heating and auxiliary generators; 9. Traction motor blower; 10. Diesel engine air cleaner; 11. Silencer; 12. Fan of the machinery room; 13. Bogie linkage structure (for Variant I only); 14. Fuel oil tank; 15. Cooling-water tank; 16. Wash-water tank; 17. Sander; 18. Storage battery; 19. Main (traction) rectifier box; 20. Auxiliary rectifier box; 21. Fan to the electrical brake and shunt resistors; 22. Control box; 23. Controller box; 24. Hand-brake; 25. Air compressor; 26. Main air reservoir; 27. Storage air reservoir; 28. Heater in the driver's cabin; 29. Electrical brake and shunt resistors; 30. Relay box; 31. Auxiliary voltage regulator; 32. Battery charger; 33. Power regulator; 34. Starter compressor; 35. Fuel oil feed pumps; 36. Carbonic acid (CO_2) bottles for fire-extinguishing; 37. Engine preheating equipment.

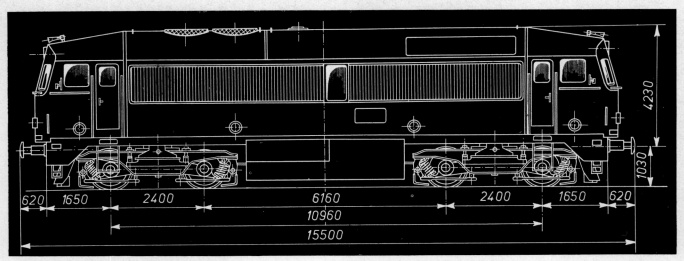

Type DHM7 diesel-hydraulic locomotive rated at 1 800 hp

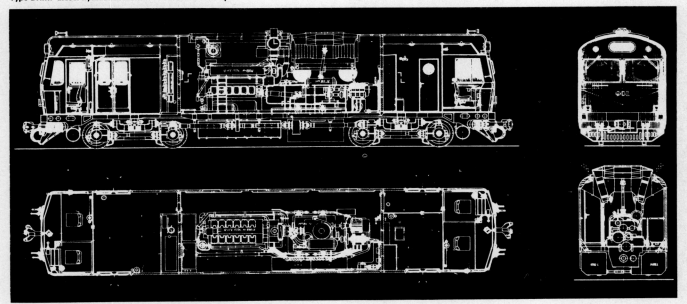

A total of 15 diesel trainsets were manufactured for **Uruguay State Railways (AFE) in 1977**
Power car (general arrangement drawing shown above) has a driver's cab at both ends,
is fitted with a 935-hp 12VFE 17/24-T diesel engine and Hydro-Ganz three-speed hydromechanical gearbox.

GARRETT

Garrett Airesearch

Head Office: Torrance, California, USA

Products: Rapid transit trainsets.

Constitution: Garrett joined the railway industry in 1974 when Boeing Vertol—acting on behalf of the US Department of Transportation—awarded a contract worth US$8 million to Garrett for construction of a two-car prototype Advanced Concept Train.

New equipment: The twin ACT prototype cars left Garrett's Torrance plant in Spring 1977 and are at present undergoing tests at DOT's Transportation Test Centre at Pueblo, Colorado.

GATX

General American Transportation Corp

Head Office: 120 S Riverside Plaza, Chicago, Illinois 60606, USA

Products: Freight wagons.

New equipment: General American Transportation Corporation has designed and developed a special-type open top hopper car known as the "Cascade" car. This is

Open top hopper car known as "Cascade" by GATX

primarily designed for the shipment of coal in unit trains where rapid unloading is a prerequisite. The car will be offered as a part of GATX's leasing facilities.

The car is a novel hopper car with two longitudinal hoppers each having a longitudinal single door, one on either side of the car's continuous, longitudinal centre sill. Each door provides a part of one of the hoppers. Each of the doors on the car is connected to an air cylinder that opens and closes the doors. Positive three point locking is provided for each door. End slope sheet can also be constructed to 50 degrees. The end slope sheets are 50 degrees and center ridge sheets are 60 degrees. The car is of rugged construction and meets or exceeds the latest AAR and FRA requirements. All materials in contact with the lading are of corrosion resistant steel to the ASTM A242 spec.

AAR class HTS; truck capacity 100 tons; light weight (approx) 66 000 lb; load limit (approx) 197 000 lb; length over strikers 52 ft 10½ in; length over pulling face of couplers 55 ft 6 in; length inside, at top, 50 ft 8 in; overall width 10 ft 6 in; width inside 9 ft 8½ in; extreme height 12 ft 9 in; door orientation longitudinal; number of doors two; number of clear openings four; size of clear openings 2 ft 5¾ in × 14 ft 5⅝ in; total square feet of openings 148 sq ft; cubic capacity level full 3 700 cu ft; cubic capacity 10 in average heap 4 110 cu ft.

The car can be loaded by any conventional means now being utilised to load open top hopper cars including a "flood" type loading arrangement from a tipple for unit coal trains while cars are in motion. The car clearance relates to AAR. Plate B, except in instances where current collectors, retractable and locked in during transit, are in operating position. It exceeds Plate B clearance then, with a dimension from the centreline of the car, of 5 ft 6 in.

Unloading of the car is accomplished through the opening of the two longitudinal doors, each of which is actuated by a power air cylinder. Actuation of the cylinders can be accomplished, automatically by use of car mounted current collectors, receiving 24V dc electrical current from a track-side elevated rail, or by manually operated air valves mounted at the AL corner of car. The "Cascade" car is designed to discharge the lading between the rails into a pit below the track. This car can be unloaded in motion and can discharge its lading in a matter of seconds from the time that the air cylinders are actuated. Auxiliary trainline air is stored in a separate reservoir and used to actuate the cylinders to open and close the doors.

In 1973 GATX unveiled a revolutionary concept with an inter-connected unit train that fills and empties as easily as a single tank car. A new GATX system of interconnects—flexible hoses and special valves—permits a string of 40 Tank Train cars to be loaded or unloaded from a connection at the centre of the train.

The system, which was three years in research and development, is simple in operation. One crewman connects the first car of each 20-car unit to the fluid supply and turns on a pump. A sensing device in the last car indicates when all cars are sufficiently filled, and can automatically shut down the pump. It eliminates the series of manual steps required under present methods of individual tank car handling.

GATX estimates that a two-man crew can fill or empty an 80-car Tank Train, broken into four 20-car strings, within an eight-hour shift. The system utilises pumps and compressed air or inert gas (depending on volatility of liquids) to achieve an average flow rate of 3 000 gallons per minute for loading or unloading with most viscosities.

Other advantages of the new system are increased safety and environmental acceptability. Two types of systems are available to handle the entire range of viscosities and volatilities of fluid products. The closed system captures vapours of volatile products, such as crude oil, for recycling or for release through a flare to the atmosphere. The open or simplified system vents vapours directly to the atmosphere and is used for fluids whose fumes are non-combustible, non-contaminant, and of no reusable value.

Extensive research and testing were required to perfect interconnect hoses that would maintain their flex under conditions involving corrosion, weather, and movement stress. The problem of refining the valving system presented equal difficulties.

The mechanism is a spring-loaded valve that is pneumatically operated. All valves on a Tank Train are opened and closed automatically, remaining open throughout filling or emptying operations, and remaining closed during transit. The closed valves isolate each car and its cargo from the next.

Tank Train eliminates the need for extensive terminal equipment, GATX officials point out. A conventional pump is all that is needed to move the liquid from a storage tank, or an ocean-going tanker. A minimum amount of track is necessary. No longer needed are terminal racks, manifold piping and below grade pits.

Tank Train cars can be loaded and unloaded in a conventional manner as each car has a top-load manway and may be fitted with a bottom outlet. Inter-connecting flexible hoses are removable.

GATX expects Tank Train applications for the petroleum industry to be vast, including transporting oil from new out-of-the way wells to refineries. The Tank Train is also being discussed as a possibility for transporting Alaskan oil from its entry point in the US to domestic distribution.

Spot shipments could be made via Tank Train to any plant or utility that has storage facilities and a rail spur.

GEC

GEC Traction Ltd

Head Office: Trafford Park, Manchester M17 1PR, England

UK Works: Manchester, Newton-le-Willows, Preston and Sheffield

Products: Complete electric, diesel electric, diesel hydraulic and diesel mechanical locomotives; multiple-unit trains, power cars and power equipments.
Industrial and mining locomotives and equipments. Traction alternators and generators, motors, auxiliary machines, transformer, rectifiers, inverters, electronic and conventional control gear; vigilance systems; special purpose apparatus, main drive gears.

Managing Director: J. Legg
Sales Director: D. R. Love
Contracts Director: K. Gunary
Technical Director: A. L. Fairbrother
Manufacturing Director: J. Harwood

Telegrams: ASSOCELECT, Manchester
Telephone: (061) 872 2431
Telex: 667152

Constitution: First constituent company established 1823—Robert Stephenson and Company.
Major constituents include traction interests of BTH, Dick, Kerr, English Electric, GEC, Metro-Vickers, AEI, Siemens (UK) and Vulcan Foundry Limited.
Britain's largest exporter to railways in 45 countries of the five continents, including locomotives and trains for main line, mixed traffic, commuter, heavy freight, industrial and mining applications, on narrow, standard and broad gauge systems with axle loads between 10 and 30 tons.

Sales: Major orders have included:

Portugese Railways (Estoril Line): 21 motor-coach power equipments for this 1 500 V dc line plus equipment on associated trailer cars;
Brazil: 180 tonne 25kV 60 Hz locomotives designed complete by GEC Traction;
London Transport: Propulsion control equipment for 300 power cars, type D78, for the District Line. Production is complete on the contract for 73 TS "Heathrow" tube

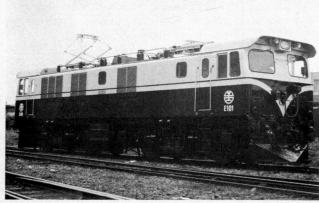

The first 25 kV electric locomotive to be delivered by GEC Traction to Taiwan.

Artist's impression of the new 180 tonne Co Co 25 kV 60 Hz locomotive ordered by Brazilian Federal Railways (RFFSA).

Artist's impression of one of the class 9E 50 kV locomotives being built for South Africa.

Diesel-electric 0-6-0 locomotive with cross equalisation suspension, in service at a UK steelworks.

stock equipment on the Piccadilly Line, including the cars with regenerative braking choppers, and is continuing on the contract for C77 surface stock;
British Rail: Thyristor controlled propulsion equipment for twenty 25/6. 25 kV 50 Hz power cars has been ordered for Clyderail. Deliveries of equipment for Merseyside's class 507 dc trains is well advanced although some trains may be delivered to the Southern Region and be redesignated class 508. The class 313 (25 kV/750 V) and 312 (25 kV and 25/6.25 kV) equipments for King's Cross Inner and Outer Suburban and for Liverpool Street services have now all been delivered;
South Africa: Manufacture is proceeding against further orders for 3000 V dc equipments for class 6E1 locomotives and for multiple unit trains. Following the transfer of the Sishen-Saldanha Line from ISCOR to South African Railways the 50 kV locomotives will now be delivered to SAR and will be known as class 9E.
They are expected to be the first production ac locomotives delivered to SAR;
Hong Kong: Production is well advanced on equipment for the first 140 cars;
Taiwan: Delivery of the thyristor controlled 25 kV 60 Hz locomotives is complete, and is well advanced for the 13 five car luxury train sets;

Industrial Locomotives: Orders for the 76 tonne diesel electric locomotives from British Steel Corporation and the National Coal Board now total 36. A large number are in service, with both customers, and the cross-equalisation suspension has demonstrated its ability to overcome wheelslip even under the worst adhesion conditions.

New development: The Company is continuing its work on the application of power electronics to traction which began some twenty years ago. GEC Traction is the only manufacturer in the world to have thyristor equipment in current production for all the world's standard electrification systems, namely:
(single phase, industrial frequency) 50 kV, 25 kV (and 6.25 kV) 50 and 60 Hz and dc at 3 000 V, 1 500 V, 750 and 600 V. Regenerative braking is included in the applications for Denmark (1 500 V) and London Transport (600 V).
For 50 kV applications the Company developed a new vacuum circuit breaker as there was none available for that rating on the world market. The equipment for the Glasgow Underground cars, whilst conventional in many ways, was specially developed to fit in the extremely small space below the floor level of these cars.

GEC AUSTRALIA

The General Electric Company of Australia Ltd

Head Office: Evans Rd, Rocklea, Queensland 4106, Australia

Products: Electric and diesel-electric locomotives; rolling stock; electric and diesel-electric traction power and control equipment.

Telegrams: GECHED, Brisbane
Telephone: (072) 47 1511
Telex: AA 40167

Recent sales: 1976 Sales of Type 1 970/1 455 kW Co-Co 1 067 mm 91.4 tonne diesel-electric locomotives are four to Queensland Railways bringing the total in service in Queensland to 16 units, and two to Tasmanian Railways increasing the total in service in Tasmania to 6 units.

GENERAL ELECTRIC

General Electric Company

Head Office: 2901 East Lake Rd, Erie, Pennsylvania 16531, USA

Export Office: International Sales Div., GE Co, 570 Lexington Ave., New York, NY 10022, USA

Products: Diesel-electric and electric locomotives; mining and industrial locomotives.

New developments: In 1977, GE extended the application of ac-dc transmission systems in its export locomotive line. The 8 cylinder engine powered U18C delivered to SNFA (Algeria) is equipped with the GTA-11 alternator and rectifiers, "CHEC" excitation system, and "CMR" wheelslip system to provide a lower powered version of the 12 cylinder engine powered U26C of which over 240 were supplied to South Africa, New Zealand and Kenya. This is the same transmission system which is standard in GE's line

Telegrams: INGECO, New York
Telephone: 212 750 2000

of domestic locomotives.
Both the U18C and U26C locomotive are provided with low weight transfer tandem bogies with all 6 traction motors in parallel. These features, together with the "CMR" wheel slip system optimise the adhesion characteristics of the locomotives.
CHEC, a Constant Horsepower Excitation Control System, is a modern electronic system of Traction Alternator Excitation introduced in 1974, after extensive field testing on large domestic diesel-electric locomotives built by the General Electric Co. It offers many advantages over previous systems, largely by use of new electronic technology not available for use in earlier systems.
The most important objective pursued in developing the CHEC System was to improve control of emissions from the diesel engine, to meet today's needs in improving man's environment.
Other very important objectives include providing higher locomotive reliability, mak-

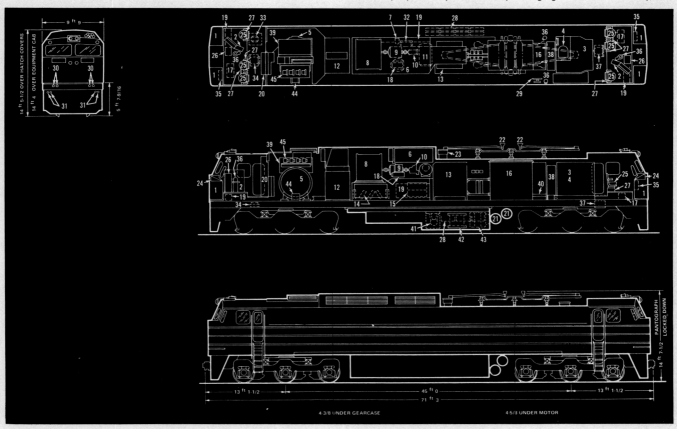

General Electric's model E60CP electric locomotive (6 000 hp), three of which have been supplied to the Black Mesa and Lake Powell Railroad.
General arrangement: 1. Sand Box; 2. Control Stand; 3. Control Compartment; 4. Toilet; 5. Motor Alternator Set; 6. Dynamic Braking Resistor; 7. Hand Pump; 8. Equipment Blower; 9. Blower & Comp. Motor; 10. Air Compressor; 11. Oil Sump; 12. Smoothing Reactor; 13. Rectifiers; 14. Equipment Air Filters; 15. Paper Filters; 16. Transformer; 17. Cab Heater; 18. Auxiliary Motor Smoothing Reactor; 19. Air Brake Equipment; 20. Relay Compartment; 21. Air Reservoir; 22. Pantograph; 23. Vacuum Circuit Breaker; 24. Sand Filler; 25. Cab Seat; 26. Refrigerator; 27. Cab Heater Register; 28. Battery; 29. Hand Brake; 30. MU Receptacle; 31. Power Receptacles; 32. Computor Control Panel; 33. Battery Charging Smoothing Reactor; 34. Battery Charging Transistor; 35. E.P. Air Brake Equipment; 36. Fire Extension; 37. Wheel Slip Transistor; 38. Telephone Interference Equipment; 39. M.A. Control Computor; 40. Compressor Cooler; 41. Auxiliary Blower; 42. Auto-Transformer; 43. M.A. Smoothing Reactor; 44. Control Transformer; 45. M.A. Rectifiers;

The new E60 locomotives, rated at 6 000 hp, were built at the Erie headquarters of GE at an approximate cost of US$500 000 each. The units will be totally automated and will be used to haul coal trains over 124 km from the Black Mesa coal mine to a 2 310 mW generating station at Navajo, Arizona.
Trains will be made up of as many as 83 122-ton-capacity bottom-dump coal wagons. A

single train will make three 248-km round trips daily.
The locomotives will be challenged by grades of 0.9 per cent with loaded wagons which will require special draft gear since drawbar pull on the first wagon will at times reach over 120 000 kg.
Each locomotive is capable of withstanding up to 450 000 kg of buffing force, while providing horsepower and tractive effort in excess of continuous ratings for varying periods of time.
The units are rectifier types, equipped with six dc traction motors, one geared to each driving axle. Thyristors will provide automatic voltage phase control for low maintenance operation.
If the power requirement changes, the thyristors automatically control tractive effort and maintain desired train speed.
The locomotives will operate from a single substation at one end of the railway rather than the three which would have been required on 25-kW operation. The railway claims that this amounts to a 20 per cent saving on the power system.
GE is supplying the substation equipment and complete automation, including control of automatic loading and unloading loops and speed control on the mainline, under a US$2.3 million package deal with the railway.
Although movement of the train will be automatically controlled during the journey to and from the mine, an operator will ride in the cab of the lead engine to assume manned control in case of a malfunction of the electronic gear.

ing the sytem easier to adjust, providing greater standardisation of sub-assemblies to permit their interchangeability throughout the entire line of large diesel-electric locomotives, and making improvements in testing techniques aimed at facilitating the investigation and correction of problems.

Where double end, box cab design is a railroad requirement, GE has developed the type UM22C of which 20 are in service in Sudan and six in Gabon. The problem of inaccessibility for maintenance generally associated with box cab design is minimised in the GE design with "lift-off" engine cabs and hinged side access panels.

In 1977, General Electric shipped the first of a new line of domestic locomotives. The New Series locomotives identified as model B-23-7, C-30-7 etc are the result of an intensive three year design and manufacturing programme to further improve locomotive quality. They include many improvements which have been included on an evolutionary basis and a new equipment arrangement.

When the New Series Locomotive was conceived, goals were established in the areas of maintenance cost, reliability and availability. The objective was to phase in devices and improvements which had been proved in service and which would result in a locomotive design of outstanding maintainability, reliability and availability. This objective has been fully achieved.

The 26 high performance E60CP electric locomotives supplied by General Electric are pulling high speed Amtrak passenger trains on the Northeast Corridor. These thyristor locomotives feature 9 800 hp for train acceleration and can operate on 11 kV at 25 Hz as well as 12.5 kV and 25 kV at 60 Hz. A double ended box cab is used with a stressed superstructure. Equipment features include; a vacuum circuit breaker, clean air system, rotary air compressor, automatic blending of air and dynamic braking, and head end power from a 750 kW 480 V 60 Hz three phase MA set.

General Electric has delivered 5 25 kV 60 Hz 2 500 hp thyristor locomotives to the Texas Utilities Services Incorporated for their coal haul operation. This E25B design features a full width operators' cab with a road switcher type equipment cab and is equipped with radio remote control and slow speed control for the automatic operation of the loading and unloading cycle. Two additional locomotives will be delivered in 1977.

General Electric has delivered 74 25 kV 60 Hz 4 200 hp E42C locomotives to the Taiwan Railway Administration. These lightweight six-axle units are the principle motive power for TRA's new electrified West Coast mainline. The double ended box cab design is supplied at 16 tonnes per axle. Freight and passenger service will be provided by the E42C with 35 of the 74 locomotives equipped with a 440 V, three-phase, 60 Hz MA set for head end power.

Three additional E60C's have been delivered to the Black Mesa & Lake Powell Railroad. These locomotives are essentially duplicates of the first three 50 kV 60 Hz locomotives delivered in 1973 except that air conditioning has been added to the operator's cab.

Export Models — Locomotive types

	U6B	U10B	U18C	U18C ac/dc	U22C	U26C ac/dc	UM22C BOX CAB
Gross hp	700	1 050	1 950	1 950	2 300	2 750	2 300
hp for Traction	640	950	1 820	1 820	2 150	2 600	2 150
Number of Axles	4	4	6	6	6	6	6
Track Gauge	All Gauges from 36 inches to 66 inches (914 mm to 1 676 mm) To suit railroad requirements						
Couplers							
Tractive Effort at Continuous Motor Rating							
lb	33 600	36 200	54 300	54 300	54 300	54 300	54 300
kg	15 200	16 400	24 630	24 630	24 630	24 630	24 630
Maximum Speed (93 : 18 Gear Ratio and 36 in (914 mm) wheels)							
mph	64	64	64	64	64	64	64
km/h	103	103	103	103	103	103	103
Minimum Weight							
lb	104 000	109 600	177 500	193 500	196 000	212 000	209 000
kg	47 300	49 800	80 500	87 760	88 900	96 161	94 600
Major Equipment							
Engine	Cat D379	Cat D398	GE FDL8	GE FDL8	GE FDL12	GE FDL12	GE FDL12
Traction Motor	GE 761	GE 761	GE 761	GE 761	GE 761	GE 761	GE 761
Generator	GT 601	GT 601	GE 581	GTA11	GT 581	GTA11	GT 581

ELECTRIC LOCOMOTIVES

Model	E60CP	E60C	E42	E25B
Rail hp—continuous	5 100	5 100	3 570	2 125
Rail hp—short time	9 800	NA	NA	NA
Voltage—kV	11/12·5/25	25/50	25	25
Frequency	25/60	50/60	60	60
Number of axles	6	6	6	4
Minimum weight				
lb	350 000	264 000	198 000	240 000
kg	159 100	120 000	90 000	109 100
Maximum speed				
mph	120	70	68	70
km/h	193	113	110	113
Continuous tractive effort				
lb	34 000	85 200	44 000	55 000
kg	15 455	38 700	20 000	25 000
Track gauges				
in	56·5/66	56·5/66	39·4/42	56·5/66
mm	1435/1676	1435/1676	1000/1067	1435/1676
Major Equipment				
Traction motors	GE780	GE780	GE761	GE780
Line breaker	Vacuum circuit breaker			
Transformer	Core-foam, forced oil cooled			
Power converter	Forced air cooled thyristors			
Ventilating system	Single blower, self cleaning filters			

Quantity	Description		Country
Export diesel-electric locomotives			
6	850 hp		New Zealand
26	2 600 hp		Kenya
3	3 600 hp		Australia (Hamersley)
1	1 500 hp		South Africa Manganese
49	1 800 hp		Indonesia
25	1 800 hp		Algeria
25	1 800 hp		Nigeria
3	1 800 hp		Jordan
9	600 hp		Tunisia
8	2 000 hp and		
9	950 hp	for	Bolivia
10	1 000 hp and		
10	1 400 hp	for	Philippines
60	2 000 hp		Brazil
Straight electric locomotives			
74	4 200 hp/25 kV/60 Hz		Taiwan Railway Administration
7	2 500 hp/25 kV/60 Hz		Texas utilities Service Inc
3	6 000 hp/50 kV/60 Hz		Black Mesa & Lake Powell RR
Domestic (USA) diesel-electric locomotives			
48	3 000 hp 4 axle		Atckison, Topeka & Santa Fe RR
14	2 300 hp 4 axle		Atckison, Topeka & Santa Fe RR
15	2 300 hp 4 axle		Southern Railway System
10	2 300 hp 4 axle		Missouri Pacific RR
55	3 000 hp 6 axle		Union Pacific RR
55	3 000 hp 6 axle		Burlington Northern
4	3 600 hp 4 axle		Consolidated Rail Corp
27	2 300 hp 4 axle		Consolidated Rail Corp
10	3 000 hp 6 axle		Consolidated Rail Corp
8	3 000 hp 4 axle		St Louis-San Francisco RR
24	3 000 hp 4 axle		Southern Pacific RR
10	3 000 hp 4 axle		Chessie System

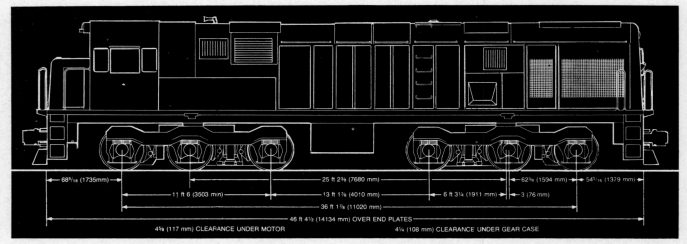

General Electric's model U18C diesel-electric locomotives have been delivered in quantity to Syrian Railways. For picture of the locomotive in SR livery see Syrian entry in the Railway section.

GENERAL ELECTRIC COMPANY
DOMESTIC (USA) DIESEL-ELECTRIC LOCOMOTIVE PRODUCT LINE

	A	B	C	D	E	F	G	H	I
Builder	GE	GE	GE	GE	GE	GE	GE	GE	GE
Model	B18-7	B23-7	C23-7	B26-7	C26-7	B30-7	C30-7	B36-7	C36-7
Service	General Purpose	General Purpose	General Purpose	General Purpose	General Purpose	General Purpose	General Purpose	General Purpose	General Purpose
Operating Cab & Controls	Yes	Yes	Yes	Yes	Yes	Yes	Yes	Yes	Yes
Wheel Arrangement	B-B or 0-4-4-0	B-B or 0-4-4-0	B-B or 0-6-6-0	B-B or 0-4-4-0	C-C or 0-6-6-0	B-B or 0-4-4-0	C-C or 0-6-6-0	B-B or 0-4-4-0	C-C or 0-6-6-0
Engine Data:									
A. Number of Engines	1	1	1	1	1	1	1	1	1
B. Horsepower of Engine	1800	2250	2250	2750	2750	3000	3000	3600	3600
C. Total Horsepower	1800	2250	2250	2750	2750	3000	3000	3600	3600
D. Number of Cylinders	8	12	12	12	12	16	16	16	16
E. Model	GE FDL-8	GE FDL-12	GE FDL-12	GE FDL-12	GE FDL-12	GE FDL-16	GE FDL-16	GE FDL-16	GE FDL-16
F. Bore and Stroke, Inches	9 x 10-1/2	9 x 10-1/2	9 x 10-1/2	9 x 10-1/2	9 x 10-1/2	9 x 10-1/2	9 x 10-1/2	9 x 10-1/2	9 x 10-1/2
G. R.P.M.	1050	1050	1050	1050	1050	1050	1050	1050	1050
H. Compression Ratio	12.7:1	12.7:1	12.7:1	12.7:1	12.7:1	12.7:1	12.7:1	12.7:1	12.7:1
I. Cycle	4	4	4	4	4	4	4	4	4
J. Turbocharged	Yes	Yes	Yes	Yes	Yes	Yes	Yes	Yes	Yes
K. Engine Cooling Fans	1	1	1	1	1	1	1	1	1
L. Engine Cooling Fan Drive	Engine	Engine	Engine	Engine	Engine	Engine	Engine	Engine	Engine
Traction Equipment:									
A. Main Generator	GTA-11	GTA-11	GTA-11	GTA-11	GTA-11	GTA-11	GTA-11	GTA-11	GTA-11
B. Traction Motor	4 - GE752	4 - GE752	6 - GE752	4 - GE752	6 - GE752	4 - GE752	6 - GE752	4 - GE752	6 - GE752
C. Traction Motor Blowers	1	1	1	1	1	1	1	1	1
D. Blower Drive	Engine	Engine	Engine	Engine	Engine	Engine	Engine	Engine	Engine
E. Wheelslip Correction	(1) Auto Sanding (2) Auto Unloading of Main Alternator	(1) Auto Sanding (2) Auto Unloading of Main Alternator	(1) Auto Sanding (2) Auto Unloading of Main Alternator	(1) Auto Sanding (2) Auto Unloading of Main Alternator	(1) Auto Sanding (2) Auto Unloading of Main Alternator	(1) Auto Sanding (2) Auto Unloading of Main Alternator	(1) Auto Sanding (2) Auto Unloading of Main Alternator	(1) Auto Sanding (2) Auto Unloading of Main Alternator	(1) Auto Sanding (2) Auto Unloading of Main Alternator
Air Brake Schedule	26L	26L	26L	26L	26L	26L	26L	26L	26L
Major Dimensions:									
A. Length	56' 8"	62' 2"	67' 3"	62' 2"	67' 3"	62' 2"	67' 3"	62' 2"	67' 3"
B. Height	14' 9-1/4"	14' 9-1/4"	15' 4-1/4"	14' 9-1/4"	15' 4-1/4"	14' 9-1/4"	15' 4-1/4"	14' 9-1/4"	15' 4-1/4"
C. Width	10' 3-1/4"	10' 3-1/4"	10' 3-1/4"	10' 3-1/4"	10' 3-1/4"	10' 3-1/4"	10' 3-1/4"	10' 3-1/4"	10' 3-1/4"
D. Bolster Centers	30' 8"	36' 2"	40' 11"	36' 2"	40' 11"	36' 2"	40' 11"	36' 2"	40' 11"
E. Truck Wheel Base	9' 0"	9' 0"	13' 7"	9' 0"	13' 7"	9' 0"	13' 7"	9' 0"	13' 7"
F. Minimum Track Curvature Rad. & Deg.									
(1) For Single Unit	150' or 39°	150' or 39°	273' or 21°	150' or 39°	273' or 21°	150' or 39°	273' or 21°	150' or 39°	273' or 21°
(2) For MU or Coupled To Train	250' or 23°	250' or 23°	273' or 21°	250' or 23°	273' or 21°	250' or 23°	273' or 21°	250' or 23°	273' or 21°
Driving Wheel Diameter	40"	40"	40"	40"	40"	40"	40"	40"	40"
Weight:									
A. On Drivers - # Min. & Max.	230,600/268,000	253,000/280,000	359,000/420,000	253,000/280,000	359,000/420,000	259,000/280,000	366,000/420,000	259,800/280,000	366,000/420,000
B. Total Minimum and Maximum	230,600/268,000	253,000/280,000	359,000/420,000	253,000/280,000	359,000/420,000	259,000/280,000	366,000/420,000	259,800/280,000	366,000/420,000
Tractive Effort:									
A. Starting at 25% Adhesion for Minimum & Maximum Weight	57,650/67,000	63,250/70,000	89,750/105,000	63,250/70,000	89,750/105,000	64,750/70,000	91,500/105,000	64,950/70,000	91,500/105,000
B. Cont. Tractive Effort & Speed MPH									
(1) For Smallest Pinion	61,000/8.4	61,000/10.7	91,500/6.7	61,000/10.6*	91,500/8.4	61,000/10.6*	91,500/9.5	61,000/10.6*	91,500/11.7
(2) For Largest Pinion	43,480/11.9	43,480/15.0	65,220/9.4	43,480/14.9*	65,220/11.8	43,480/14.9*	65,220/13.4	43,480/14.9*	65,220/16.4
Gear Ratio and Maximum Speed MPH:									
A. Smallest Pinion	83/20 - 70	83/20 - 70	83/20 - 70	83/20 - 70	83/20 - 70	83/20 - 70	83/20 - 70	83/20 - 70	83/20 - 70
B. Intermediate Pinion	80/23 - 79	80/23 - 79	80/23 - 79	80/23 - 79	80/23 - 79	80/23 - 79	80/23 - 79	80/23 - 79	80/23 - 79
C. Largest Pinion	77/26 - 93	77/26 - 93	77/26 - 93	77/26 - 93	77/26 - 93	77/26 - 93	77/26 - 93	77/26 - 93	77/26 - 93
Supplies:									
A. Fuel - Gal. - For Min. & Max. Tank	1200/2150	2150/3250	3250/4000	2150/3250	3250/4000	2150/3250	3250/4000	2150/3250	3250/4000
B. Coolant - Gallon	335	350	350	350	350	365	365	365	365
C. Lube Oil - Gallon	245	300	300	300	300	380	380	380	380
D. Sand - Cubic Feet	60	60	60	60	60	60	60	60	60
Compressor, Air CFM:									
A. Maximum Delivery	296	296	296	296	296	296	296	296	296
B. Delivery Idling	127	127	127	127	127	127	127	127	127
C. Type of Cooling	Water	Water	Water	Water	Water	Water	Water	Water	Water
Steam Generator									
A. Steam Capacity - LBS/HR	None	None	None	None	None	None	None	None	None
B. Water Capacity - Gallon									
Layover Protection	Optional	Optional	Optional	Optional	Optional	Optional	Optional	Optional	Optional
Dynamic Brakes	Standard	Standard	Standard	Standard	Standard	Standard	Standard	Standard	Standard
Draft Gear	MC-390 with Align. Control	MC-390 with Align. Control	MC-390 with Align. Control	MC-390 with Align. Control	MC-390 with Align. Control	MC-390 with Align. Control	MC-390 with Align. Control	MC-390 with Align. Control	MC-390 with Align. Control
Air Filtering Devices:									
A. Primary	Vortex Self Clean	Vortex Self Clean	Vortex Self Clean	Vortex Self Clean	Vortex Self Clean	Vortex Self Clean	Vortex Self Clean	Vortex Self Clean	Vortex Self Clean
B. Secondary Engine Air Intake	GE Paper	GE Paper	GE Paper	GE Paper	GE Paper	GE Paper	GE Paper	GE Paper	GE Paper
C. Engine Room Pressurized	Yes	Yes	Yes	Yes	Yes	Yes	Yes	Yes	Yes
D. Main Generator Pressurized	Yes	Yes	Yes	Yes	Yes	Yes	Yes	Yes	Yes
Head End Power Supply	—	—	—	—	—	—	—	—	—
Production Date	1977	1977	1977	1977	1977	1977	1977	1977	1977

*Power Match

NOTE: ALL UNITS EQUIPPED WITH ROLLER BEARING JOURNALS.

The first of a series of 13 model UM10B locomotives of 1 065 hp supplied to Greek State Railways

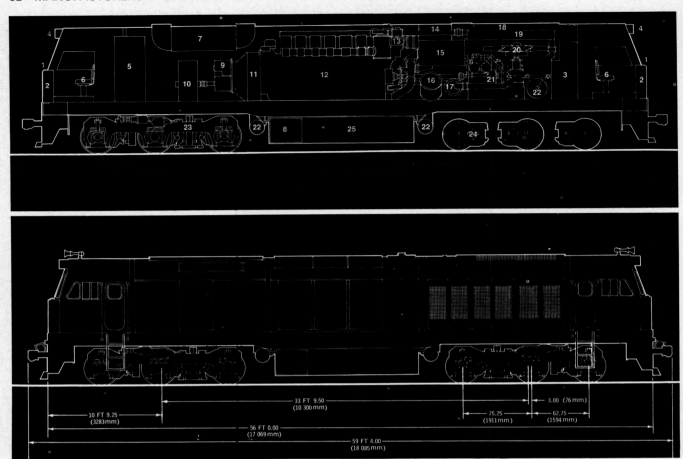

Among deliveries by General Electric during 1977 were six model UM22C diesel-electric locomotives for Gabon State Railways (OCTRA). The locomotives are almost flat-fronted and have a Co-Co wheel arrangement. They are rated at 2 200 hp and are powered by a 7FDL 12D25 series 265777 diesel-engine.

General arrangement: 1. Sand Box Fill; 2. Sand Box; 3. Air Brake Equipment; 4. Headlight; 5. Control Compartment; 6. Cab Seat; 7. Single Stack Dynamic Brake (if used); 8. Battery; 9. Battery Charging Generator; 10. Traction Motor Blower; 11. Traction Generator; 12. Engine; 13. Turbocharger; 14. Engine Water Tank; 15. Engine Inlet Air Filters; 16. Lubricating Oil Filter; 17. Lubricating Oil Cooler; 18. Radiator Shutter; 19. Radiator; 20. Radiator Fan; 21. Air Compressor; 22. Air Reservoir; 23. Floating Bolster Truck; 24. Traction Motor; 25. Fuel Tank

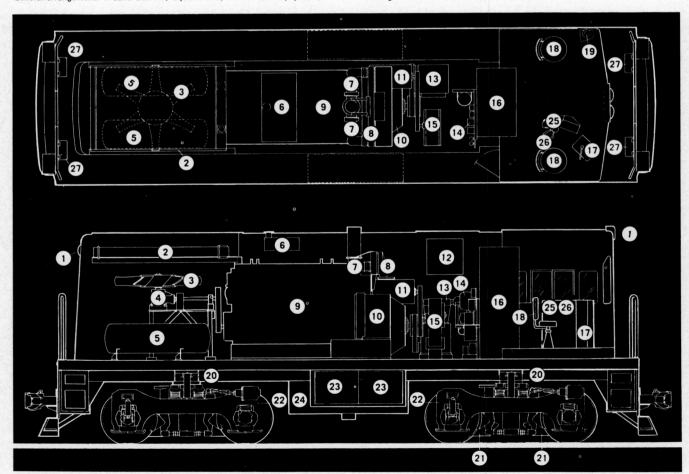

Among recent deliveries to the Philippines by General Electric were 10 model U10B locomotives rated at 1 050/950 hp and powered by Caterpillar D-398 diesel engines.
General arrangement: 1. Headlight; 2. Radiator; 3. Radiator Fan; 4. Radiator Fan Gear Box; 5. Main Air Reservoirs; 6. Expansion Tank; 7. Turbochargers; 8. Engine Air Intake Filter; 9. Diesel Engine; 10. Traction Generator; 11. Exciter-Battery Charging Generator; 12. Dynamic Brake (if used); 13. Air Compressor; 14. Air Brake Equipment; 15. Traction Motor Blower; 16. Control Compartment; 17. Controller; 18. Cab Seat; 19. Handbrake; 20. Jacking Pad and Lifting Lug; 21. Traction Motor; 22. Floating Bolster Truck; 23. Batteries; 24. Fuel Tank; 25. Gauge Panel; 26. Brake Valves; 27. Sand Box Fill.

GENERAL ELECTRIC DO BRAZIL
General Electric do Brazil S/A

Telephone: 34 9131
Telex: 011 24018

Head Offices: Rua Antonio de Godoy 88, Sao Paulo, Brazil

Telephone: 224 3312
Telex: 021 21694

Av Almirante Barroso 81, Rio de Janeiro, Brazil

Works: Bairro Boa Vista s/nº, PO Box 1150, Campinas, Brazil

Chairman: G. T. Smiley
President: T. Romanach

Telephone: 41 1944
Telex: 019 1168

Manager Locomotive Operation: C. W. Steenberge
Railroad Operation, Enterprise, Transportation and Electrification: Guilhermo Marin

Products: General Electric (USA) electric, diesel-electric locomotives

Sales: Locomotive orders completed or in hand at June 1977 included:

Client	Locomotive	Number	hp	Tonne	Gauge (m)	Type of Service	Year completed	Country
Companhia Siderúrgica Paulista (COSIPA)	Diesel-electric	4	500	91	1.60	Shunting	1966	Brazil
Companhia Paulista de Estrada de Ferro (Fepasa)	Electric-C-C (3 000 V-CC)	10	5 200	144	1.60	Line	1967	Brazil
Estrada de Ferro Sorocabana (Fepasa)	Electric B-B (3 000 V-CC)	30	2 200	73	1.00	Line	1967	Brazil
Companhia Docas de Santos (CDS)	Diesel-Electric 80 Tonne	20	570	73	1.60	Shunting	1970/72	Brazil
Rède Ferroviária Federal S/A (RFFSA)	Diesel-Electric U10B	80	1 000	60	1.00	Line	1971/72	Brazil
Administracion Nacional de Combustibles, Alcohol Y Portland (ANCAP)	Diesel-Electric 80 Tonne	1	570	73	1.435	Shunting	1971	Uruguay
Usinas Siderúrgicas de Minas Gerais S/A (Usiminas)	Diesel-Electric 80 Tonne	7	570	73	1.00	Shunting	1971/72/74	Brazil
Administração do Porto do Rio de Janeiro (APRJ)	Diesel-Electric 100 Tonne	2	670	100	1.60	Shunting	1972	Brazil
Rede Ferroviária Federal S/A (RFFA)	Diesel-Electric U23C	80	2 250	180	1.60	Line	1972/74	Brazil
Companhia Siderurgica Mannesmann (CSM)	Diesel-Electric 80 Tonne	1	570	73	1.60	Shunting	1974	Brazil
Companhia Siderurgica Nacional (CSN)	Diesel-Electric 80 Tonne	1	570	73	1.60	Shunting	1974	Brazil
Aços Anhanguera	Diesel-Electric 25 Tonne	1	145	25	1.60	Shunting	1974	Brazil
Ferrovias Paulista S/A (FEPASA)	Diesel-Electric U20C	136	2 000	108	1.00	Line	1974/80	Brazil
Companhia Siderúrgica Paulista (COSIPA)	Diesel-Electric 100 Tonne	5	670	91	1.60	Shunting	1975/76	Brazil
Companhia Siderúrgica Nacional (CSN)	Diesel-Electric 80 Tonne	2	570	73	1.00	Shunting	1975	Brazil
Companhia Siderúrgica Nacional (CSN)	Diesel-Electric UM 10B	11	1 050	100	1.60	Shunting	1975	Brazil
Rède Ferroviaria Federal S/A (RFFSA)	Diesel-Electric U20C	105	2 150	108	1.00	Line	1975/76/77	Brazil
Rède Ferroviaria Federal S/A (RFFSA)	Diesel-Electric U23C	90	2 500	165	1.60	Line	1975/76	Brazil
INACESA-Chile	Diesel-Electric 45 Tonne	1	300	45	1.00	Shunting	1977	Chile
Companhia Siderúrgica da Guanabara-(COSIGUA)	Diesel-Electric 100 Tonne	1	91	91	1.60	Shunting	1976	Brazil
Cia Docas da Guanabara	Diesel-Electric 100 Tonne	2	670	91	1.60	Shunting	1976	Brazil
Adm. Porto do Recife	Diesel-Electric 25 Tonne	1	166	22.5	1.00	Shunting	1977	Brazil
Cia Acero del Pacifico	Diesel-Electric 65 Tonne	2	570	65	1.676	Shunting	1977	Brazil
ENFE-Bolivia	Diesel-Electric U20C	8	2 150	100	1.00	Line	1976/77	Bolivia
ENFE-Bolivia	Diesel-Electric U10B	9	1 050	65	1.00	Shunting	1977	Bolivia
Cia Siderúrgica Nacional (CSN)	Diesel-Electric 80 Tonne	1	570	80	1.60	Shunting	1977	Brazil
ACESITA	Diesel-Electric 65 Tonne	2		65	1.00	Shunting	1977	Brazil
USIMINAS	Diesel-Electric 80 Tonne	5	570	80	1.00	Shunting	1977	Brazil
Cia Siderúrgica Paulista	Diesel-Electric 100 Tonne	9	670	100	1.60	Shunting	1977/78	Brazil
Cia Sid Mannesman	Diesel-Electric 80 Tonne	1	570	80	1.60	Shunting	1978	Brazil
Acesita	Diesel-Electric 45 Tonne	4	300	45	1.00	Shunting	1978	Brazil
SOMISA-Soc Mixta Sid Argentina	Diesel-Electric 65 Tonne	2	570	65	1.676	Shunting	1978	Argentina
							1966/67	

GENERAL MOTORS
Electro-Motive Division, La Grange, Illinois, USA

Telegrams: ELMODIV, La Grange, USA
Telephone: (312) 485-7000
Telex: 728304, La Grange, Il.,USA

Head Office: Detroit, Michigan, USA

Export Office: La Grange, Illinois, USA

General Manager: Peter K. Hoglund
Director of Sales and Service: Warren A. Fox
General Sales Manager, Domestic Locomotives and Associates: R. E. Hill
General Sales Manager, Export Locomotives: John L. Rose

Products: Diesel-electric locomotives.

DOMESTIC MODELS

		Road Switchers		B-B Locomotives			C-C Locomotives	
Model Number		SW1001	MP15	GP38-2	GP40-2	SD38/2	SD40-2	SD45-2
Engine Type		8-645E	12-645E	16-645E	16-645E	16-645E	16-645E3	20-645E3
Turbocharged		No	No	No	Yes	No	Yes	Yes
Rated hp		1 100/1 000	1 650/1 500	2 200/2 000	3 300/3 000	2 200/2 000	3 300/3 000	3 900/3 600
Wheel diameter and gear ratio		40 in 62:15	40 in 62:15	40 in 62:15	40 in 62:15	40 in 62:15	40 in 62:15	40 in 62:15
Continuous tractive	lb	41 700	46 800	55 400	55 400	83 400	83 100	83 100
	kg	18 910	21 228	25 130	25 130	37 830	37 690	37 690
Continuous speed	mph	6.7	9.3	10.8	11.3	6.8	11.1	11.3
	km/h	10.8	15.0	10.4	18.2	10.9	17.9	18.2
Maximum speed	mph	65	65	65	65	65	65	65
	km/h	105	105	105	105	105	105	105
Total weight	lb	230 000	248 000	250 000	256 000	356 000	368 000	368 000
	kg	104 330	112 490	113 400	116 120	161 480	166 920	166 920
Overall length	ft in	44 ft 8 in	47 ft 8 in	59 ft 2 in	59 ft 2 in	68 ft 10 in	68 ft 10 in	68 ft 10 in
	m	13.61	14.52	18.03	18.03	20.98	20.98	20.98
Overall height	ft in	14 ft 3 in	15 ft 0 in	15 ft 4 in	15 ft 4 in	15 ft 7 in	15 ft 7 in	15 ft 7 in
	m	4.34	4.57	4.67	4.67	4.75	4.75	4.75
Overall width	ft in	10 ft 0 in	10 ft 0 in	10 ft 4 in	10 ft 4 in	10 ft 0 in	10 ft 0 in	10 ft 0 in
	m	3.05	3.05	3.15	3.15	3.05	3.05	3.05

EXPORT MODELS

		B-B Locomotives		C-C Locomotives			
Model Number		G-18U	G-22U	G-22CW	G-26CW	GT-22CW	GT-26CW-2
Engine Type		8-654-E	12-645-E	12-645-E	16-645-E	12-645-E3	16-645-E3
Turbocharged		No	No	No	No	Yes	Yes
Rated hp		1 100/1 000	1 650/1 500	1 650/1 500	2 200/2 000	2 475/2 250	3 300/3 000
Wheel diameter and gear ratio		40 in 63:14	40 in 63:14	40 in 62:15	40 in 62:15	40 in 62:15	40 in 62:15
Continuous tractive	lb	33 600	33 360	58 200	57 960	57 840	67 220
	kg	*15 240*	*15 130*	*26 400*	*26 290*	*26 240*	*30 490*
Continuous speed	mph	8.6	13.5	7.2	10.3	12.1	14.1
	km/h	*13.8*	*21.7*	*11.6*	*16.6*	*19.5*	*22.7*
Maximum speed	mph	60	60	65	65	65	65
	km/h	*97*	*97*	*105*	*105*	*105*	*105*
Total weight	lb	143 800	163 560	196 800	209 400	219 750	255 400
	kg	*65 230*	*74 190*	*89 270*	*94 980*	*99 690*	*115 850*
Overall length	ft in	38 ft 0 in	46 ft 6 in	46 ft 6 in	51 ft 9 in	57 ft 0 in	64 ft 0 in
	m	*11.58*	*14.17*	*14.17*	*15.76*	*17.37*	*19.51*
Overall height	ft in	12 ft 3 in	12 ft 7 in	12 ft 7 in	12 ft 7 in	13 ft 3 in	13 ft 6 in
	m	*3.73*	*3.83*	*3.83*	*3.83*	*4.04*	*4.11*
Overall width	ft in	9 ft 8 in	9 ft 3 in	9 ft 3 in	9 ft 3 in	9 ft 3 in	9 ft 3 in
	m	*2.95*	*2.82*	*2.82*	*2.82*	*2.82*	*2.82*

GENERAL MOTORS OF CANADA

Diesel Division, General Motors of Canada Ltd.

Telegrams: GEMODIESEL
Telephone: (519) 452 5136
Telex: 064 7231

Head Office: PO Box 5160, London, Ontario N64 4 N5, Canada

Products: Diesel-electric locomotives ranging from 1 000 to 3 600 hp in four and six axle configurations for track gauges from 1m to 1.68m.

General Manager: A. G. Warner

General Sales Manager: P. G. Brewer
Export Manager: H. E. Mitchell

Sales: Major sales in 1975/76 included a contract for four 25 model GT 22 CWP locomotives and 15 model GT 26 CW locomotives for Algeria (SNTF).

Model GT 26 CWP diesel-electric locomotive for Algerian National Railways (SNTF)

GESTESA

Groupo Español Suizo de Trenes Electricos SA

Telegrams: GESTREN, Madrid
Telephone: 28 52 36

Head Office: Calle Felipe IV, 10-1° Dcha, Madrid, Spain

Products: Electric multiple units.

Constitution: This group comprises La Maquinista Terrestre y Maritima; Material y Construcciones SA; Industrias Aguirena SA.

GESTIONI

Gestioni Industriali SpA Soc

Telegrams: ROTABILI
Telephone: 72 918/72 787

Head Office: Via Adriano Cecchetti, 62012 Civitanova Marche (Macerata), Italy

Products: Diesel railcars; freight wagons; passenger coaches.

GLOUCESTER

Gloucester Railway Carriage & Wagon Co Ltd

Telegrams: WINGLOS
Telephone: 25 104/5
Telex: 43179

Head Office: Bristol Rd, Gloucester, England

Products: Freight wagons; railcars.

Chairman: A. D. Thomson
Managing Director: J. S. P. Phillips
Technical Director: J. F. G. Ash

General Sales Manager: R. A. Clark

Constitution: First known as the Gloucester Wagon Co Ltd, the company was formed in 1860 and two years later built the first iron wagon in Britain. Since 1969 the company has concentrated on the design of railway wagons and the design and manufacture of bogies and vehicle suspensions.

GMEINDER

Gmeinder & Co GmbH

Telegrams: GMEINDER, Mosbachbaden
Telephone: (06261) 4041
Telex: 04 66111

Head Office: Postfach 1260, 6950 Mosbach, Baden, German Federal Republic

Products: Diesel-electric and diesel-hydraulic locomotives up to 1 200 hp; special freight wagons.

Managing Director: Hans Kärcher
Export Sales: Friedrich Krone

GONINAN

A. Goninan & Co Ltd

Telegrams: PLATINUM
Telephone: 61 3811
Telex: 28061

Head Office: PO Box 21, Broadmeadow, NSW 2292, Australia

Products: Diesel-electric locomotives; freight wagons; passenger coaches.

General Manager: E. W. Eddy
Assistant. General Manager: J. G. Fitzgerald
Engineering Manager: A. Rice
Sales Manager: J. Nixon

Constitution: Engaged in the general engineering field for more than 76 years, this company recently extended its licence agreement with General Electric, USA for diesel electric locomotives, and entered a new licence agreement with Pullman Standard Division, USA, for rail passenger coaches.

Sales: Three C36-7 diesel-electric locomotives of 3 600 hp are currently being manufactured for Hamersley Iron Pty Ltd in Western Australia. A contract was recently obtained for 150 stainless steel double deck passenger cars from the Public Transport Commission of New South Wales. The order covers 80 motor cars and 70 trailer cars to be used on the Sydney suburban rail system.

Artist's impression of the type C36-7 diesel-electric locomotives being built by Goninan for Hamersley Iron

GOODWIN
A. E. Goodwin Ltd.

Telegrams: GOODWINENG
Telephone: Sydney 698 1163
Telex: AA 22656

Head Office: 863-871 Bourke St, Waterloo, NSW 2017, Australia

Chief Executive: D. W. Chambers

Products: Freight wagons; draft gear; track construction and equipment.

GORLITZ
Veb Waggonau Görlitz

Telegrams: WAGGONBAU, Görlitz
Telephone: 690
Telex: 286227

Head Office: DDR 89 Görlitz, Brunnenstrasse 11, German Democratic Republic

Products: Passenger coaches; sleeping cars; double-deck coaches; bogies.

New equipment: A redesign of the Görlitz standard double-deck car has recently been completed. Result is a general-purpose coach that can be run in mixed formations and can be added to any train needing extra capacity. The body is self-supporting framework of welded steel construction, with the underframe fabricated from 52-S steel sections and bodywork in 38 lightweight sections. All metal parts have been coated with a layer of bitumen-based noise-deadening compound, and thermal insulation is provided by glass-fibre material between inner and outer wall sections. Two-axle Görlitz type VI bogies with coil springs primary and secondary suspension are fitted. The bolster supports the body through pendular links. Automatic, inter-acting pneumatic disc brakes or shoe brakes with automatic load braking can be supplied.

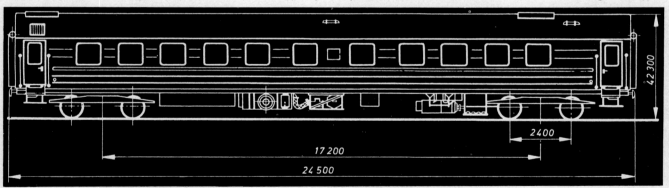

RIC sleeping coach, built for SZD gauges of 1 435 and 1 520 mm
Length, 24 500 mm; weight 52.5 tonnes; maximum speed 160 km/h; 18 berths; one service compartment; air-conditioning.

Type DBme double deck passenger coach

GOSA
Gosa Wagon and Steel Construction

Head Office: Smederevska Palanka, Poland

Products: Passenger coaches.

Sales: Gosa is building 90 railway coaches for Indonesia ordered in 1976. Value of the contract is put at US$ 22 million and delivery is due to be completed by 1979.

New equipment: Latest "Y" type passenger coach built by Gosa complies with UIC specification 567 for international services.

The car underframe is constructed of all-welded rolled and pressed sections. The underframe end construction allows the subsequent installation of automatic coupling without need for extensive reconstruction.

The car body is of steel, with posts and other components of pressed sheet metal and sheathing sheet metal. These elements are welded by electric arc. The roof consists of a number of roof arches made of pressed roof sheathing metal sheets joined by arc-welding.

The car is provided with two bogies of Wegmann type, or alternatively of Minchen-Deutz type. The wheel assemblies are designed in accordance with UIC Standard specification 813. The axle bearings are IKL or Pretis roller type, in compliance with UIC Standard specification 512. The bogies are made of welded rolled sections and pressed steel sheets which form box-like bolsters.

The draft gear is of end type to UIC 520 and 521 specifications, with a hook of 100 Mp capacity and a screw-type coupling of 85 Mp braking strength.

The buffer gear consists of four sleeve-type buffers all to UIC Standard, of 30 Mp strength as per UIC 528 and 567 specifications.

The car is provided with an automatic air-brake of large braking capacity, Oerlikon-Rapid type, in accordance with UIC 546 specifications. The brake leverage is provided with an automatic SAB DRV2 regulator. The brake head supports two brake shoes according to UIC 541 specification. Each compartment is provided with a brake handle to be used in case of emergency.

The hand-brake is in one of the end entrances and acts on one of the bogies independently on the air-brake. Each end of the car is provided with two terminal end tapes of the main line in accordance with UIC 541.

Electric lighting is designed in compliance with UIC standard specification No. 550 and 532. The car compartments are provided with standard light and blue light. The regulator is of Pintsch type. The generator is of 24—30 V, and 4.5 kW. Storage batteries are for 24 V, 2 × 240 Ah.

The car heating may be electrical or by steam. The installation for steam heating system is of low pressure, Fredmann type. The temperature of the heating elements must not exceed 95°C. They are located under the seats. Each compartment is provided with a handle for the regulation of temperature. The corridor, washroom and lavatory are each provided with heating elements, but with no temperature control devices. The electric heating is designed in accordance with UIC specifications 552 and 553. The water supplying system in the washroom and lavatory consists of a water tank, pipes, taps, and waste pipe. The water tank is filled through connectors, and is thermally insulated so that freezing is prevented during 12 hours at temperature of −10°C, provided that the initial temperature in the moment of switching-off of heating was +20°C.

The compartment ventilation is carried out by Kuckuck system, a device for natural aeration.

The closed-circuit broadcasting installation in the car is designed in compliance with UIC specifications 568.

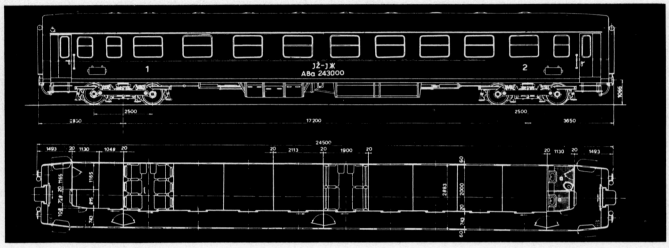

International "Y" type passenger coach
Gauge 1 435 mm; Overall length over buffers 24 500 mm; Length over underframe end sills 23 200 mm; Car body width 2 883 mm; Height from top of rails 4 050 mm; Bogie pivot centres 17 200 mm; Wheel taping line diameter 920 mm; Bogie wheel base 2 500 mm; Light weight 40 Mp; Maximum speed 160 km/h.

GRAAFF
Graaff Kommanditgesellschaft

Head Office: 321 Elze (Han), German Federal Republic

Products: Freight wagons; containers.

Managing Director: Dipl. Ing. Wolfgang Graff

Constitution: The works was founded in 1914.

Sales: Major sales include: six-axle flat wagons for heavy loads, three-axle articulated double-deck automobile carriers (type Laes 552) and type DDM 915 four-axle double-deck carriers for accompanied car-express service for Deutsche Bundesbahn.

New equipment: The three-axle Graaff Laes 547 double-deck car transporter consists

Telegrams: GRAFFWAGGON, Elze
Telephone: (051) 24 20 41
Telex: 0927168 graaf d.

of two sections connected by an articulated joint over the common centre axle. The underframe—arranged for automatic coupling—and the wagon body are welded in 52-3 steel. A KE-GP-A brake equipment with 10/12 in cylinders is fitted. The handbrake is operated by a handwheel at the lower loading level near the centre of the wagon. Another new development by Graaff is a four-axle wagon for the bulk transport of plastics granulate in four spherical tanks flattened at the bottom and equipped with hopper shaped discharge connections. The tanks are made of 52-3 steel and designed for an operating pressure of 2.5 kp/cm². Bogies are DB's standard type. Brakes are Knorr, Type KE-gp with 10 in brake cylinders. Two and four-axle stainless-steel tank wagons for the transport of various chemical products belong to the company's standard production programme.

Four-axle wagon for the bulk transport in spherical tanks

GREENBAT

Greenbat Ltd

Head Office and Works: Albion Works, Armley Rd, Leeds LS12 2TP, England

Products: Battery, trolley, trolley/battery and pantograph locomotives up to 30 tonnes in weight; coke car locomotives; motor transmission and control units.

Chairman: T. H. de Monte
Managing Director: A. H. Miller
Sales Director: E. P. Hartmann

Telegrams: GREENBAT LEEDS
Telephone: 442933
Telex: 55368

Sales: Battery locomotives to Nigeria; trolley/battery locomotives to Zambia Copper Mines; battery driven locomotives to be used for track laying on Hong Kong's Mass Transit Railway.

Licensing Agreement: Mining and Allied Machinery Corporation Ltd, West Bengal India.

GREENVILLE

Greenville Steel Car Company

Head Office: Greenville, Pennsylvania 16125, USA

Products: Freight Wagons.

Chairman: Edwin Hodge, Jr
President: A. F. Sarosdy
Executive Vice-President: D. F. Lewis
Vice President, Sales: G. C. Brecht

Constitution: Formed in 1910 as the Greenville Metal Products Co, the present name was adopted in 1914 when the company first undertook repair of freight wagons. In 1916 the first new wagons were built and this has been the major activity since, combined with extensive repair work and supply of replacement parts.

Sales: Major freight car orders completed in 1975: Southern Railroad 530 100 ton

Telegrams: GREENCAR
Telephone: 412 588 7000

woodchip hoppers; Atchison, Topeka and Santa Fe 100 100 ton woodchip hoppers; American Electric Power 500 100 ton triple hoppers; Southern Railway 50 100 ton ballast; Missouri Pacific 200 100 ton woodchip hoppers; Pittsburg & Shawmut 200 100 ton triple hoppers; St Louis-San Francisco 200 100 ton triple hoppers; Consol Coal 100 100 ton triple hoppers; Southern Railway 400 100 ton quad hoppers; Southern Railway 710 70 ton, 52 ft 6 in gondolas; Southern Railway 300 100 ton aggregate hoppers; Cleveland Electric 100 100 ton triple hoppers; Seaboard Coast Line 200 100 ton woodchip hoppers.

New equipment: New wagon announced by Greenville is the 'Bathtub' claimed to weigh about 13 000 lbs less than a conventional 100 tonne hopper wagon while carrying about 105.5 tonnes of coal within gross rail limits.

GREGG

NV Gregg Europe SA

Head Office: 53, Huysmanlaan, B-1660 Lot, Belgium

Products: Freight wagons; bogies.

President: Richard Gregg
Director General: Jean K. N. Ma
Commercial Manager: A. Timmerman

Telegrams: GREGGCAR, LOT
Telephone: Brussels 02376 20 10
Telex: B 21 357

Recent sales: Major sales in 1976 included equipment for Belgian National Railways, Sudan Railways, Saudi Government Railways, Caroni Ltd, West Indies. Following completion of 60 Gregg-built aluminium hopper wagons for carrying raw grains and cereal products on the Saudi Government Railway between Damman and Riyadh, a repeat order for 48 more was placed in 1977.

GRIVITA ROSIE

CFR Grivita Rosie Works

Head Office: 7, Matei Millo St, Bucharest, Romania

Exports: Mecanoexport, 10, Mihail Eminescu St, Bucharest, Romania

Telephone: 1494 30
Telex: 216

Products: Tank wagons up to 90 m³ capacity for oil products and derivatives, liquid and liquefied gas.

GSI

General Steel Industries Inc. Engineering Division

Head Office: 8400 Midland Blvd, St Louis, Missouri 63114, USA

Products: Design of cast steel rapid transit, coach and locomotive bogies.

Vice President and General Manager: Keith L. Jackson

Telephone: (314) 423 6500

Sales Manager: Thomas P. Taylor
Manager of Engineering: Eugene L. Benner

Constitution: GSI was founded in 1904 by General Steel Castings Corp and became Castings Division, GSI, in 1964, and Engineering Division in 1973.

GUNDERSON

Gunderson Inc

Head Office: 4700 NW Front Ave, Portland, Oregon 97208, USA

Products: Freight wagons.

President: C. Bruce Ward
Chief Engineer: W. H. Sample

Telephone: (503) 228 9281
Telex: 36 0672

Vice President, Sales: W. R. Galbraith

Constitution: Gunderson Bros. Engineering Corp. was founded in 1920 and has been building railway wagons since 1960. Became subsidiary of FMC Corporation in 1965. The company name was changed to Gunderson in 1971.

HANKOOK

Hankook Machine Industrial Co.
(Part of the Shunjin Motor Group)

Head Office: Inchon, South Korea

Products: Passenger coaches, freight wagons, multiple unit electric stock license to Nippon Sharyo of Japan.

HAWKER SIDDELEY

Hawker Siddeley Canada Ltd.

Head Office: 7, King Street East, Toronto, Ontario M5C 1A3, Canada

Sales Office: *(Freight Equipment):* Suite 1515, 800 Dorchester Blvd West, Montreal, Que H3B 1X9, Canada. *(Passenger Equipment):* P.O. Box 67, Station F, Thunder Bay, Ont P7C 4V6, Canada.

Products: Railway freight cars of all types; subway, rapid transit suburban and main-line passenger equipment.

Director of Marketing: R. L. McCallum
General Sales Manager, Railcars: A. F. Philbin
Sales and Service Manager:
  Freight Equipment: G. W. Smith
  Passenger Equipment: K. Chapman

Telegrams: HAWSIDCAN
Telephone: 362 2941
Telex: 06 21774

Constitution: The Eastern Car Company Ltd, the original predecessor of this company, started in the railway freight car business in 1913.
The Canadian Car Division of Hawker Siddeley Canada Ltd pioneered the long, light-weight rail car on the North American continent.

Developments: The first of 80 double-deck commuter cars were due to roll off the production lines in late 1977 at Thunder Bay, where the Canadian Car Division of Hawker Siddeley Canada is at present working on three major contracts. The double deckers are destined for Toronto's GO-Transit commuter routes. Other contracts at present underway include 138 rapid transit cars for Toronto Transit Commission and 200 mainline coaches for Mexican National Railways (NdeM). An order for 190 rapid transit cars for Boston was at the pre-production stage by mid-1977.

HÄGGLUNDS

AB Hägglund & Söner

Head Office: S891 01 Örnsköldsvik 6, Sweden

Products: Rapid Transit surface and underground cars; street (tram) cars; bogies; mining and construction equipment; heavy trucks; bus bodies; hydraulic motors.

Telegrams: HÄGGLUNDSÖNER
Telephone: (0660) 102 40
Telex: 6050 haegg s

Constitution: Hägglunds was founded in 1899 and is one of the largest engineering companies in northern Sweden. On 1 January 1972 it became a subsidiary company of ASEA of Västeras. On 1 January 1973 Hägglunds acquired the railcar and locomotive division of ASJ of Linköping and production was transferred to Örnsköldsvik.

Sales: Underground trains for Stockholm rapid transit system.

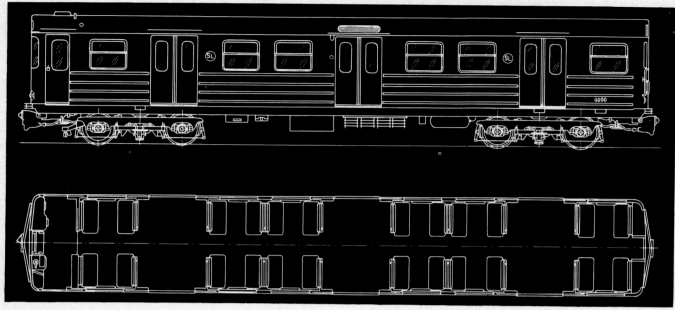

General arrangement drawing of the C6-type cars built for Stockholm by Hagglunds which the company is now rebuilding.

Wheel diameter (new) 864 mm; Distance between bogie centres 11 000 mm; Bogie wheelbase 2 300 mm; Height of floor from top of rail 1 170 mm max; Max width over body 2 800 mm; Overall length of ten-coach train 174 000 mm; Vehicle length over body 17 320 mm; Tare weight 23.5 tonnes; Seating capacity 48; Standing capacity 108; Number of traction motors 4; Number of starting steps 19; Rating, one-hour (750/2 V) $4 \times 110 = 440$ kW; Rating, continuous (750/2 V) $4 \times 100 = 440$ kW; Gear ratio 126.20; Transmission: Bogie-suspended motor and double gear coupling; Maximum acceleration on level tangent track (laden) 1.1 m/s².

Type C7-car also built for Stockholm by Hagglunds—basically the same design as the earlier C6 cars.

HEAD WRIGHTSON

Head Wrightson Teesdale Ltd

Telephone: (064 2) 62241

Head Office: Thornaby-on-Tees, England

Products: Wagons, coaches, special duty rolling stock.

Chairman: J. D. Eccles
Managing Director: R. J. Edwards

Constitution: Head Wrightson Teesdale Ltd, a subsidiary of Head Wrightson & Co Ltd, handles the design and manufacture of a large variety of equipment and components. The Wagon Department has for many years specialised in the production of standard main-line wagons and in the design and manufacture of special duty railway stock.

HEEMAF

Heemaf BV

The company ceased manufacturing railway equipment in 1975. It now operates under the name *Holec Machines & Systems*.

HENSCHEL
Thyssen Industrie AG, Henschel

Telegrams: Henschel Kassel
Telephone: (0561) 8011
Telex: 099791

Head Office: D-3500 Kassel 2, Henschelplatz 1, German Federal Republic

Products: Diesel-hydraulic, diesel-electric and electric locomotives; diesel engines for rail traction, marine and stationary duties.

General Manager (Locomotives): Dipl.-Wirtschaftsingenieur R. Jasper
Director, Sales and Service: Ing. M. Kunis
Chief Engineer: Dipl.-Ing. S. Kademann

Constitution: Henschel started manufacturing locomotives in 1848 and to date more than 32 000 locomotives have been supplied to railways around the world. In 1975, Thyssen Industrie AG became the new group name of the Rheinstahl companies.

Sales: Orders were received in 1976 from the following administrations: German Federal Railways; Egyptian Railways; Ghana; East African Railways; Indonesian State Railways; Swedish State Railways.

New developments: Following tests with an experimental three-phase electric locomotive since 1974, Deutsche Bundesbahn (DB) placed orders in 1977 with Thyssen Henschel, Krauss Maffei and Brown Boveri for five new 15 kV 16¼/3 Hz Bo-Bo electric locomotives—designated class E120—with a continuous rating of 4 400 kW and a 20-minute rating of 56 kW. Evaluation trials are due to start by the end of 1978 and series production is expected to follow before 1980. Meanwhile, a new three-phase locomotive from Thyssen Henschel went into service during 1977 with Netherlands Railways (NS). It has a 1 400 kW continuous rating and top speed of 140 km/h with a service weight of 84 tonnes. It is to be used as a test-bed for a future generation of mixed traffic locomotives with three-phase induction motors. The locomotive, in fact, began life as a diesel-electric prototype. The mechanical parts of the locomotive are virtually unchanged since its days as a diesel-powered unit. Electrical components available from previous tests were a current converter and a single QD646 squirrel-cage traction motor with a continuous output of 1 400 kW originally developed for DB's E120 design.

Also in the field of three-phase power at the end of June 1977, Eisenbahn & Häfen of Duisburg took delivery of six EDE 1 000/500 electro-diesel locomotives with three-phase transmission. Mechanical parts and the diesel engines were supplied by Thyssen-Henschel of Kassel and electrical components by Brown Boveri & Cie of Mannheim.

The Thyssen-Henschel type AA 22 T high-speed diesel-electric locomotive, has been in service with Egyptian Railways (ER) since 1975. It has a top speed of 120 km/h and a rated output of 2 475 hp with a service weight of 121.8 tonnes. Length over buffers is 20 900 mm; distance between bogie centres 13 100 mm and bogie wheelbases of 2 000 and 2 000 mm on Co-Co axle arrangement.

Ghana Railway and Port Authority has been using the class DHG 600 diesel-hydraulic locomotive since last year. Using a C axle-arrangement it has a top speed of 45 km/h. The engine turns out 660 hp and gives a tractive effort on starting of 14 050 kg. Service weight is 42.6 tonnes; length over buffer beams 8 600 mm; width 2 740 mm and height above railhead 3 700 mm.

The Henschel DHG 1 000 diesel-hydraulic mainline locomotive, as used by Indonesian State Railways since 1976, has a rated output of 1 150 hp and a maximum speed of 90 km/h. It has a service weight of 42.7 tonnes and tractive effort on starting of 14 100 kg. Statistics: length over buffer beams, 11 200 mm; maximum width, 2 800; height over railhead, 3 690 mm; distance between bogies (BB), 5 800 mm and bogie wheelbase 2 200 mm.

Class 61/62 - 1.0 m gauge BB locomotive of 1 000 hp; EAR Kenyan region have taken delivery of 66 units since 1972.

Type E1200 BB electric dual-current locomotive (16⅔ and 50 Hz, 15 kV) with BBC three-phase ac equipment (system Henschel-BBC DE 2500)—one of six units supplied to Ruhrkohle AG mining company in 1976/77

HITACHI
Hitachi Ltd

Telegrams: Hitachi Tokyo
Telephone: Tokyo (270) 2111
Telex: J22395, J22432, J24491, J26315

Head Office: 6-2, 2-chome, Otemachi, Chiyoda-ku, Tokyo 100, Japan

Products: Electric, diesel-electric, diesel-hydraulic locomotives; electric and diesel railcars; passenger and freight cars; industrial rolling stock.

Chairman: Kenichiro Komai
Chief Sales Director: Tadashi Ouchida
Export Sales: Masafumi Misu

HSIANGTAN
Hsiangtan Electric Generator Plant

Works: Hunan, People's Republic of China

Products: Electric locomotives. The plant produced China's first electric CC locomotives in the 1950's; a 4 900 hp unit based on the Soviet-designed N-60s; numbered 6-Y-1.

HUDSON (SOUTH AFRICA)
Robert Hudson & Sons (Pty) Ltd

Telegrams: Raletrux
Telephone: 836 9772/3
Telex: 43 0250

Head Office: PO Box 25259, Ferreirasdorp, Transvaal, South Africa

Products: Main line freight cars, narrow gauge mine and estate cars, electric locomotives for mines.
Chairman: W. R. Hudson

Managing Director: R. H. Wardrop

Construction: Manufacturing facilities established at Durban in 1927. To keep pace with increased demand, a further manufacturing plant was established at Benoni in 1948.

HUDSON (RALETRUX)
Robert Hudson (Raletrux) Limited

Head Office: PO Box 4, Morley, Leeds LS27 8TG, England

Products: Industrial rolling stock, including special cars for mine main haulages, quarries and estates. Complete narrow gauge railway systems for all applications.

Chairman: D. A. Norton

Telegrams: RALETRUX, Morley
Telephone: Morley 534931
Telex: 55133

Managing Director: G. Galletly
Sales Director: C. R. Whyte

Constitution: Manufacturing facilities established in 1865, currently exporting to hard-rock mining operations throughout the world. Robert Hudson (Raletrux) Ltd is now part of the Firsteel Group of companies.

HUDSWELL CLARKE
Hudswell Clarke & Co Ltd

Head Office: Hunslet Engine Works, Leeds LS10 1BT, England

Chairman: C. R. C. Fryers
Managing Director: P. J. O. Alcock

Telephone: (0532) 32261
Telex: 55237

Constitution: Hudswell Clarke was established at Jack Lane, Leeds, by William Hudswell and John Clarke, both of whom had been with Kitson & Co Locomotives had been built at the Railway Foundry since its founding in 1838, its previous occupants being the pioneer locomotive firm of E. B. Wilson & Co.

HUNGARIAN
Hungarian Railway Carriage and Machine Works

Head Office: 9002 Györ, PB 50, Hungary

Products: Passenger and freight cars; air-conditioning equipment (Stone licence) for passenger cars.

Constitution: This concern started building railway rolling stock in 1897 and two years later the thousandth wagon was completed, adding self-propelled railcars and motor-cars in the early 1900s. It has always been commissioned by the Hungarian State

Telegrams: Rába Györ
Telephone: 12 300
Telex: 02 4253

Railways to build rolling stock and to supply switches, track construction materials, cranes, etc, but export has always been a feature of the factory's activities since the earliest days.

Sales: Major sales in 1973 included 500 flat wagons for Iranian State Railways valued at US$6 million; container wagons for Czechoslovakia.

HUNSLET
The Hunslet Engine Company Ltd

Head Office: Hunslet Engine Works, Leeds LS10 1BT, England

Products: Diesel mechanical, diesel hydraulic and diesel electric, steam locomotives; fully flameproof surface and underground mines diesel locomotives; electric trolley and battery locomotives; flameproof diesel power packs and standard flameproof components; final drive and reverse gearboxes; diesel exhaust gas conditioners track and maintenance equipment.

Chairman: C. R. C. Fryers
Managing Director: P. J. O. Alcock

Constitution: The Hunslet Engine Company has been building locomotives since 1864; introduced diesel shunting locomotives in 1927 and pioneered the first flameproof diesel locomotive for coal mine working in 1939. The Hunslet Engine Company incorporates Kerr Stuart & Co, The Avonside Engine Company, Manning Wardle & Co,

Telegrams: Engine, Leeds
Telephone: (0532) 32261
Telex: 55237

Kitson & Co, and The Hunslet Group includes the Associate Companies Hudswell Clarke & Co Ltd, and Andrew Barclay Sons & Co Ltd.

Sales: Over the past year locomotives have been exported to Iran, Malaysia, New Guinea, Nigeria, Pakistan, Peru, Sudan and Zambia. At present orders in building include a batch of 35 diesel hydraulic locomotives for Kenya Railways, 562 hp locomotives designed to operate in tandem for South Korea and a large repeat order for narrow gauge locomotives for Bord-na-Mona in the Republic of Ireland. Orders are in hand for diesel electric industrial locomotives ranging from 1 562 hp to 1 124 hp generally designed for the Steel Industry. In addition to the standard Hunslet range of shunters for private Railways, specially protected locomotives for working in hazardous areas have been delivered in the past year mainly for working in petroleum and petro-chemical installations.

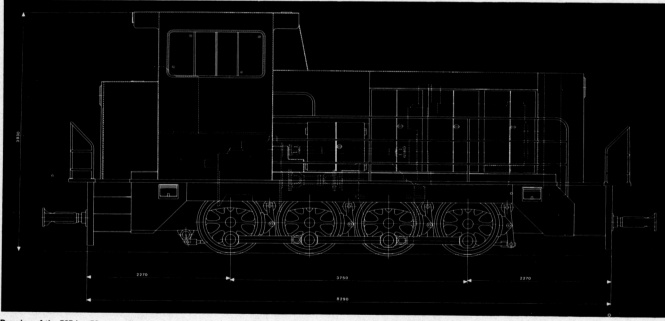

Drawing of the 525 hp, 53 tonne diesel-hydraulic locomotive—one of 35 now under construction by Hunslet for Kenya Railways.

HUNSLET TAYLOR
Hunslet Taylor Consolidated (Pty) Ltd

Postal Address: PO Box 178, Germiston, Transvaal, South Africa

Products: Electric locomotives; diesel-electric locomotives; diesel-mechanical and diesel-hydraulic locomotives for surface shunting and underground use in mines; electric trolley and battery locomotives; transfer cars; mine cars and a wide range of

Telegrams: HUNSLETCO, Germiston
Telephone: 825 1212
Telex: 8 0899 SA

mining equipment.

Chairman: J. S. Feek
Managing Director: G. van Est

ICF
The Integral Coach Factory

Head Office: Perambur, Madras 600038, India

Products: Passenger coaches.

General Manager: J. Matthan

Telegrams: RAILCOACH
Telephone: 661091
Telex: 7390

Constitution: This is a production unit under the Ministry of Railways, Government of India, and was set up during the first Five Year Plan in collaboration with Messrs Swiss Car & Elevator Manufacturing Corporation Ltd, Switzerland. Commencing production in 1955, the factory has turned out to July 1977 over 12 021 passenger coaches of 64 different types for the Indian Railways and has an installed capacity of 750 coaches per year.

Sales: Sales during 1976-77 include air-conditioned coaches of different types with self-generating power viz. deluxe, composite, 2-tier sleeper and electrical multiple units ac and dc types, pantry cars, and other types such as first class, second class etc. Recently ICF turned out special second class coaches with upholstered seats for the superfast metre gauge express.

113 all-welded light weight passenger coaches to Taiwan Railways, 4 inspection coaches and 2 caboose cars for Zambian Railways.

During the year 1975, two bogies have been shipped to Burma, 96 bogies to Taiwan and 30 economy cars have been delivered to the Philippine Railways. In the year 1976, 15 third class and two second class coaches were exported to Tanzanian Railways.

The ICF is the only manufacturing unit of its kind in Asia. The high standard of its products accounts for the increased orders as also repeat orders it receives from sister countries and the satisfaction it affords them.

New passenger coach for Tanzania being shipped from India in August 1976—one of 17 coaches ordered by Tanzania.

Second-class coach built by ICF for Indian Railways metre-gauge Superfast Express.

IGARRETA
Igarreta SA

Telephone: 28 3198/2660

Head Office: Avda Amancio Alcorta 2200, Buenos Aires, Argentina

Products: Electric subway coaches.

INARCO
Inarco SA

Telephone: 253 3788

Head Office: N Videla 666, Quilmes, Buenos Aires, Argentina

Products: Freight wagons.

INDEMDET
Industrielle de Materiel de Transport, Cie

Telegrams: CIMTRANS, Paris
Telephone: 704 51 10
Telex: 61 119 F

Head Office: 42 ave Raymond Poincaré, 75116 Paris, France

Products: Trolley locomotives; electric multiple units; passenger coaches; freight wagons.

INDIAN STANDARD
The Indian Standard Wagon Co Ltd

Telephone: Burnpur—7-421 & 7-422
Telex: 065-210
Answer Back Code: Standard—AL 210

Head Office: The Indian Standard Wagon Co Ltd, 10-C, Hungerford Street, Calcutta 17, India

Works: The Indian Standard Wagon Co Ltd, Santa Works, Burnpur PO, Dist. Burdwan, West Bengal, India

Products: Railway rolling stock; forgings; pressings; springs; structural fabrication and mining equipment.

Chairman: Sri R. C. Dutt,
Custodian and Executive Vice Chairman: Sri N. R. Bhargava
General Manager: Sri D. Roy

Constitution: The Company came into existence in 1918 as Designers and Manufacturers and assisted the Indian Railways in the development and supply of railway rolling stock and essential components. It has now been taken over by the government. The Company is also an established manufacturer of springs, forgings and pressings of all types for railway rolling stock, automobiles and other equipment. A large number of mining equipment have already been developed and are being supplied to various mines.

Sales: The Wagons manufactured include: 350 "EAS" wagons for Yugoslav Railways; 100 Nos of "covered bogie goods wagons" with sliding doors for East African Railways Community; four wheeler covered wagons and high sided bogie wagons for the Indian Railways.

INTERNATIONAL COMBUSTION

Head Office: Clayton Works, Hatton, Derby DE6 5EB, England

Telegrams: Clayquip
Telephone: 0283 88 2382
Telex: 37581

Products: Battery, trolley and diesel locomotives with electric, hydraulic or mechanical transmissions; electric and battery driven industrial and mining locomotives; special purpose internal combustion engined or electric rail vehicles.

General Manager: R. A. Boast

Constitution: The Clayton Equipment Co Ltd, now part of International Combustion Limited, was incorporated in 1931 by Mr S. R. Devlin to carry on the manufacture of locomotives, rail cars, transfer cars and general engineering products. Many types of locomotives and other equipment were made for export to various countries, eg Australia, New Zealand, Poland, and Korea and a number of diesel-electric locomotives were made for British Railways as they started their modernisation programme.

In 1957 International Combustion (Holdings) Limited acquired the whole of the shareholding in the Company, but Clayton's continued to operate as an entirely self-contained and self-supporting unit.

In 1969 the company was fully integrated into International Combustion Limited, and whilst retaining its original work site, it became absorbed into the Group operation.

Sales: The response from International Combustion indicates that no sales have been made recently.

INSINOORITOIMISTO
Insinooritoimisto Saalasti

Head Office: Arinatie 4, 00370 Helsinki 37, Finland

Telegrams: 12694 sf-insa
Telephone: 90-57 775

Products: Diesel shunting locomotives; rail repair locomotives; shunting couplings; snow ploughs.

Chairman: Eng. Tapio Saalasti

ITALSIDER
Italsider SpA

Head Office: Via Corsica 4, Genova, Italy

Telegrams: ITALSIDE GENOVA
Telephone: (010) 5999
Telex: 27690 Italsid

Products: Freight wagons (special purpose).

Chairman: Ambrogio Puri

Managing Director: Ing Mario Costa
Sales Director: Ing Sergio Magliola
Export Sales: Dr Ulisse Corsi

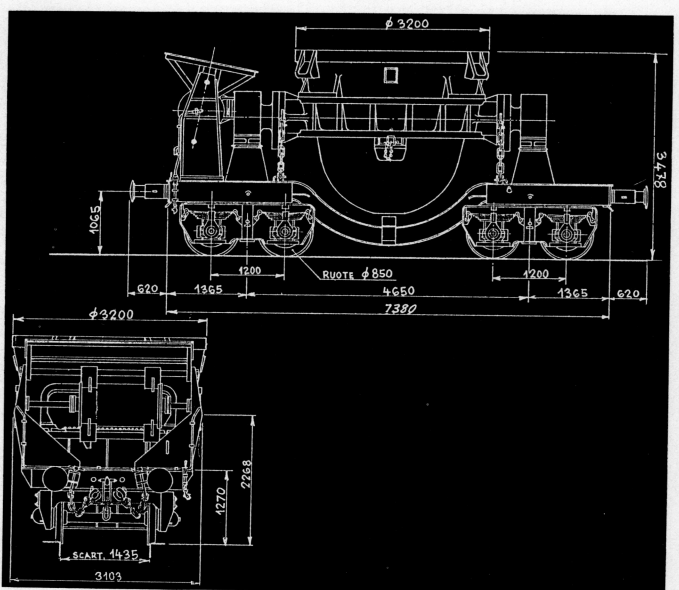

Tilting ladle wagon for carrying molten steel

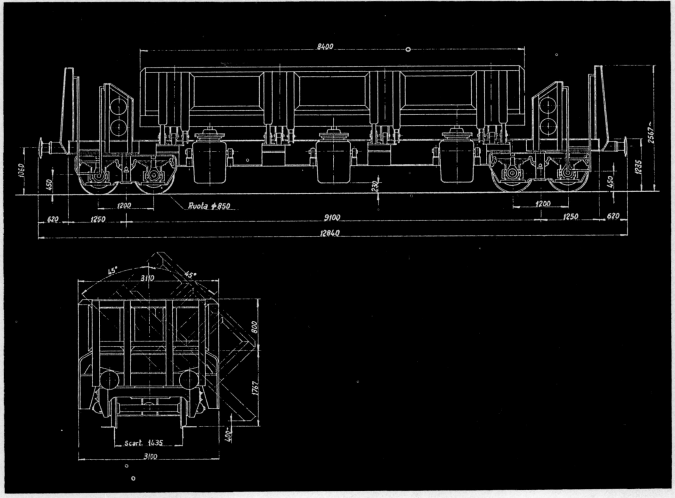

Four-axle 50 tonne side-tipping wagon; capacity 18 m³

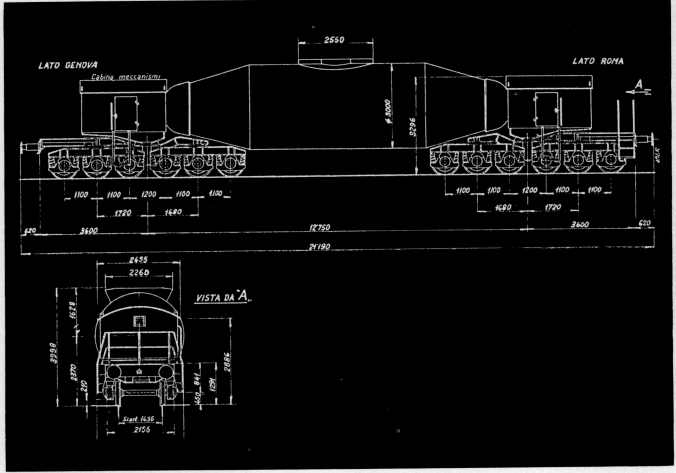

Special 12-axle 150 tonnes torpedo wagon: capacity 24 m³

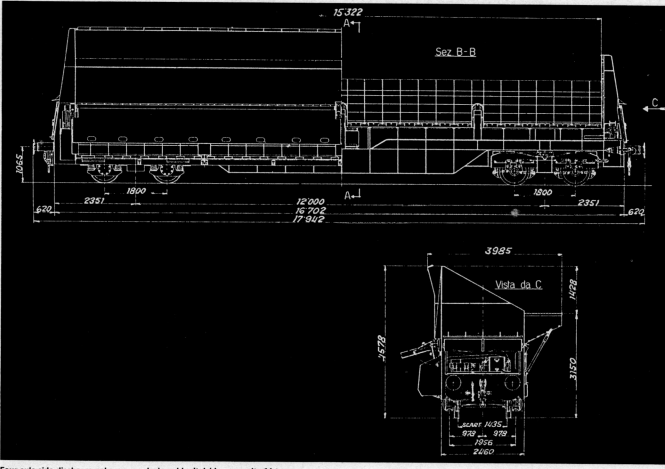

Four-axle side-discharge coke wagon designed by Italsider: capacity 14 tonnes

---

ITALTRAFO

Head Office: Via Nuova delle Brecce 260, 80147 Napoli, Italy

Telegrams: Italtrafo Napoli
Telephone: 266022
Telex: 71131 Itraf Na

Products: Complete electrical equipment for electric and diesel-electric locomotives, electric trains, trolley-buses, trams; distribution, power and special transformers of any size and voltage.

Constitution: ITALTRAFO is a new company incorporating four of the largest Italian electro-mechanical concerns:—the transformer department of ASGEN, OCREN, ALCE, and Breda Elettromeccanica. The company is concerned entirely with research,

engineering, manufacturing and servicing transformers of any type and rating and traction equipments.

Sales: In the traction field OCREN, ALCE and Breda have supplied electro-mechanical equipments to the Italian State Railways and a number of foreign customers for many years.

JANKO GREDELJ

Head Office: Zagreb, Yugoslavia

Telegrams: TEZEV ZAGREB
Telephone: 515 266

Products: Diesel-electric trainsets.

New equipment: Among latest equipment is an aluminium four-car diesel-electric trainset, comprising one motor car on each end of the coach, having 40 seats, a luggage compartment, and a power-unit compartment; one trailer with bar and 48 seats; one trailer with 64 seats.
The motor coaches are of a streamline design, capable of double-switching. Coach control is possible from either end by means of remote controls.
The bogies under the motor cars are of driving type. Each is provided with two electric traction motors, the power of which is transferred to axles through gears. The cars are coupled by a central draft-buffer gear. For reduced air friction the cars are coupled by telescopic concertina connection. The ends of the motor cars are provided with standard draft and buffer gear. By these, connection of the coaches at the end of standard gauge is possible. The motor coach is provided with two-winged doors opened and closed pneumatically.
The motor coach is provided with two diesel engines for driving an electric alternator. The electric alternator is manufactured by Raeezjocarof Zagreb, and is of 270 kV rating. The driving electric motor is produced by Rade Koncar, too, and has continuous rating of 81 kV at 1 530 rpm.

The control desks, accommodating all control instruments, for train operation, generator operation, and operation of driving and auxiliary diesel engines, are located in the driver's cab. By a special switch the remote control system is switched on for the diesel aggregate on the other end of train, or for an additional diesel train if operated jointly.
The air compressors are connected to the engine of the auxiliary aggregate. Capacity is satisfactory for requirements of air-brake, pneumatic opening of doors, horn and other pneumatic equipment. Speedometers are located in both driver's cabs; one of them is of registering type.
The "deadman's" provision is connected with pneumatic drive and electric controls. The driver's cabs are provided with telephone communication. At request, the train can be fitted with a closed-circuit broadcasting system to be used for giving information to passengers.
Heating of cars is effected by hot air. All the cars are provided with independent heating apparatus of Webasto type.
The ventilation of cars is performed by ventilators built in the car roof, enabling 14 complete exchanges of air in the passenger compartments.
Braking is by automatic air-brake, an electro-magnetic track brake, built on all bogies, and an electric brake through traction motors. Each car is provided with hand and auxiliary brakes.

JENBACHER

Jenbacher Werke AG

Telegrams: Motor Jenbach
Telephone: Jenbach 2291-5
Telex: 053756-7

Head Office: Jenbach, Tyrol, Austria

Products: Diesel-mechanical and diesel-hydraulic rail tractors and locomotives; passenger coaches; diesel engines; diesel compressors; diesel generator and pumping sets.

Managing Director: H. V. Pichler
Technical Director: Dr. Söllner
Sales Manager: B. Gerber

Constitution: The company was started in 1946 for the manufacture of diesel engines and combined units. It builds diesel-powered locomotives up to 1 500 hp.

Developments: The first Schlieren-designed passenger coach in an order for 40 being built by Jenbacher completed trials in 1977. All cars are due to be delivered at the end of 1978.

JEFFREY

Jeffrey Mining Machinery Division

Telegrams: JEFFREY
Telephone: (614) 421 3123
Telex: 245486

Head Office: PO Box 1879, Columbus, Ohio 43216, USA

Products: Underground mine electric, battery, trolley locomotives.

Constitution: A division of Dresser Industries, Inc.

Four-wheel locomotives—specifications

Model	27C	20A	20B	15A	15B	11A	11B	8A	6A	6B
Nominal Weight—tons	27	20	20	15	15	11	11	8	6	6
Actual Weight—tons	27	24	23	15	18	12	12	9	7	7
Voltage—dc	250	250	250	250	250	250	250	250	250	250
Total hp	360	300	300	190	190	100	120	80	60	60
Rated Drawbar Pull—lb	13 500	10 000	10 000	7 500	7 500	5 500	5 500	4 000	3 000	3 000
Speed at Rated Drawbar Pull—mph	10.8	10.2	10.2	8.3	9.4	5.9	6.9	6.5	6.7	6.9
Motor Type	MH 2340	MH 2411	MH 2411	MH 2409	MH 2409	MH 2313	MH 2328	MH 2100	MH 2186	MH 288
Gear Ratio	15/68	16/76	16/76	14/65	16/63	15/74	14/75	14/74	14/58	13/75
Track Gauge—in	42	42-48	42-48	42-44	42	42-48	42	42	42-44	24-30
Width—in	80	82	82	70	78	78	78	66	66	60
Length Over End Frames—ft	22.8	22.5	23.3	20.0	24.1	18.7	18.7	17.1	14.5	14.5
Height Over Frame—in	42	34	34	30	30	32	32	30	29	32
Height Over Locked-down Trolley Pole or Cable Reel—in	49	41	41	37	37	39	39	42	36	39
Wheel diameter—in	36	31	31	27	27	28	28	26	20	26

Eight-wheel locomotives-specifications

Model	50A	50B	37A	37B	37C	27A	27B
Nominal Weight—tons	50	50	37	37	37	27	27
Actual Weight—tons	52	60	44	44	40	33	33
Voltage—dc	250	250	250	250	250	250	250
Traction Motors—Number	4	4	4	4	4	4	4
Total hp	720	720	600	600	600	380	380
Rated Drawbar Pull—lb	25 000	25 000	18 500	18 500	18 500	13 500	13 500
Speed at Rated Drawbar Pull—mph	10.5	11.0	10.6	10.2	10.6	9.6	9.6
Track Gauge—in	42	42	36	42	42	42-48	42-44
Width—in	88	90	74	74	84	88	80
Length Over End Frames—ft	37.0	37.3	34.3	34.3	34.5	36.3	31.0
Height Over Frame—in	42	50	44	44	43½	38	41¾
Height Over Locked-down Trolley Pole—in	49	57	50	50	45½	45	48
Wheel Diameter—in	34	36	33	31	33	27	27
Motor Type	MH 2340	MH 2340	MH 2370	MH 2411	MH 2370	MH 2409	MH 2409
Gear Ratio	15/66	15/68	14/66	16/76	14/66	16/63	16/63

JESSOP

Jessop & Co Ltd, Calcutta

Telegrams: JESSOPS
Telephone: 22 (5041)/22-3426
Telex: 021-2135/021-7564

Head Office: 63, Netaji Subhas Road, Calcutta 1, India

Products: All types of rolling stock including electric multiple unit coaches, passenger coaches.

Chairman and Managing Director: R. J. Shahaney
Commercial Manager: P. Chakrabarti

Constitution: Jessop and Co was founded in 1788 and is one of the oldest engineering firms in India. The works at Dum Dum cover 80 acres comprising six separate units:—wagon, coach, structural, road roller, bogie and mechanical.
The project at Durgapur is built on 116 acres, for the manufacture of laminated and coil springs, and heavy duty iron castings.
Labour force consists of about 10 000 men. Annual output is about Rs40 crores, ie £23.5 million sterling.

Sales: 175 covered wagons for Yugoslavia. Orders in hand include 86 metre-gauge coaches and 24 EMUs.

JUNG

Arn. Jung., Lokomotivfabrik GmbH

Telegrams: Lokomotivfabrik Kirchen-Sieg
Telephone: Betzdorf (02741) 6831
Telex: 08 753 19

Head Office: D-5242 Jungenthal b. Kirchen, a.d. Sieg, German Federal Republic

Products: Electric and diesel locomotives.

Type RC 43 C diesel-hydraulic locomotive developed by Jung for shunting and branch-line duties
Designed as a three axle rigid frame locomotive, it is driven by an MTU four-stroke diesel engine and equipped with Voith hydrodynamic forward/reverse transmission. The axles are driven via cardan shafts and axle gear boxes. Axles are sprung by rubber springs and equipped with hydraulic shock absorbers. The driver's cab is designed for good all-round vision. Controls are electro-pneumatic. In service with Deutsche Bundesbahn the locomotive is frequently equipped with radio control equipment.

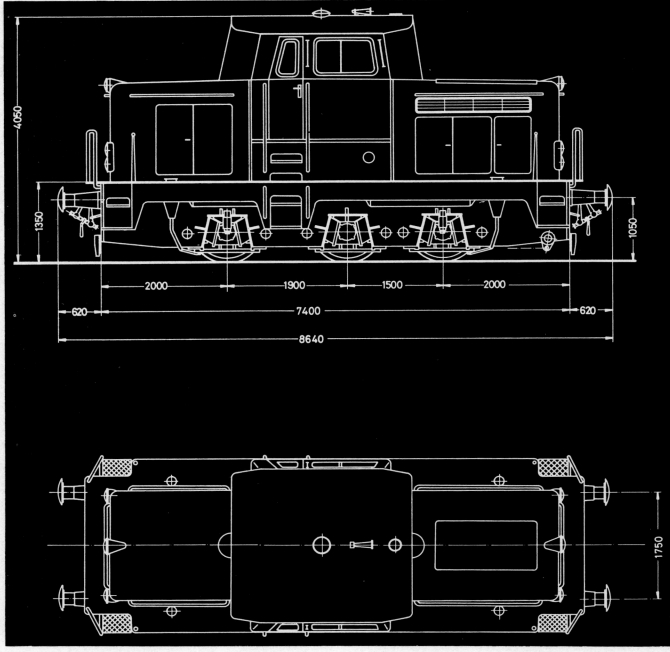

Type RC 43 C locomotive—basic data:

		Dimensions 405 kW version	580 kW version
Axle arrangement	—	0-6-0	0-6-0
Gauge	mm	1 435	1 435
Wheel base	mm	3 400	3 400
Length over buffer	mm	8 640	8 640
Smallest curve radius	m	60	60
Engine make	—	MTU	MTU
Power	kW	405	580
Engine rpm	1/min	2 100	2 100
Power transmission	—	hydro-dynamic	hydro-dynamic
Transmission type	—	Voith-forward reverse transmission L2r3z	Voith-forward reverse transmission L4r4U2
Wheel diameter	mm	950	950
Weight	t	48-60	48-60
Speed (normal)	km/h	0-20; 0-40	0-42

JEUMONT-SCHNEIDER
Jeumont-Schneider SA

Telephone: 776 43 23
Telex: 61 425 melec f.

Head Office: 31-32, quai National 92806 Puteaux, France

Product: Power equipment for electric locomotives.

See Société MTE and FRANCORAIL-MTE.

KALMAR
Kalmar Verkstads

Telegrams: KVAB, Kalmar
Telephone: Kalmar 0480/150 70
Telex: 43029

Head Office: Fack, S-381 01, Kalmar, Sweden

Products: Passenger coaches; freight wagons.

Sales: Deliveries in 1975-1977 included 20 couchettes and 30 passenger coaches for Swedish State Railways (SJ) as well as 160 freight wagons and 25 tank wagons for Zambia Railways.

New orders obtained: 25 passenger coaches for East African Railways, 150 passenger coaches for Swedish State Railways, 30 motor coaches (subcontractor to Fiat, Italy for Swedish State Railways).

Chairman: Olof Söderström
Managing Director: Sven Arnerius
Director, Railway Products: Hans Lönn

KARL MARX

VEB Lokomotivbau "Karl Marx"

Head Office: Bavelsberg, German Democratic Republic

Products: Diesel locomotives.

KAWASAKI

Kawasaki Heavy Industries Ltd, Rolling Stock Group

Head Office: Nissei-Kawasaki Bldg, 16-1 Nakamachi-Dori, 2-chome, Ikuta-ku, Kobe, Japan

Tokyo office: World Trade Centre Bldg, 4-1 2-chome, Hamamatsu-cho, Minato-ku, Tokyo, Japan

Works: *Hygo*—1/18, Wadayama-Dori 2-chome, Hyogo-ku, Kobe (Telephone: (078) 671 5021)
Utsunomiya (Freight wagons)—2857-2, Naka Okamoto, Kawachi-cho, Kawachi-Gun, Tochigi Pref (Telephone: 02867 3 0022)

Chairman: Kiyoshi Yotsumoto
President: Zenji Umeda
Executive Vice Presidents: Tsuneo Ando
Toraichi Imai
Managing Director (In charge of Rolling Stock): Akira Hoshi
Directors (In charge of Rolling Stock): Shigeru Mori
Masahiko Ishizawa

Telegrams: KAWASAKI HEAVY TOKYO
Telephone: Tokyo (03) 435-2589
Telex: J-22672, J-26888, (Domestic) 242-2851

Sales: (For JNR) 138 electric cars for Shinkansen, 255 super express and commuter cars, 227 diesel locomotives, 106 electric locomotives, 1 460 freight cars for public and private railways) 80 pneumatic tyred electric cars (for new line in Sapporo), 90 electric cars, 27 diesel locomotives, 519 tank cars; (for export) 39 subway cars for Korea, 12 baggage vans for Zambia, 37 passenger coaches for Nigeria (see entry under Nigeria), 6 passenger coaches for East Malaysia, 260 passenger coach bogies for Thailand, doors for 1 200 pallet wagons for Africa, 8 electric cars for Indonesia, 120 underframes for Gabon, 34 passenger coaches for Malaysia, 32 electric cars for Brazil. Besides, more than 800 various cars will soon be delivered for JNR, Public and Private railways and Foreign countries (Nigeria, Burma, Hong Kong, Vietnam, etc.).

Products: Electric, diesel-electric, diesel-hydraulic locomotives; electric railcars; diesel railcars; freight wagons; passenger coaches; containers.

Constitution: Kawasaki Heavy Industries Ltd, was formed on 1 April 1969 by the merger of Kawasaki Rolling Stock Manufacturing Company, Kawasaki Aircraft Company, and Kawasaki Dockyard Company Ltd. With effect from 1 April 1972, Kisha Seizo Kaisha Ltd was taken over and merged into Kawasaki Heavy Industries Ltd.

Third class passenger coach equipped with two lavatory compartments—one of 20 supplied to Malayan Railways by Kawasaki in 1976/77. Seating capacity 76 passengers, tare weight 32 800 kg, maximum speed 96 km/h, gauge 1.0 m length over coupling faces 22.084 m, length over headstocks 21.33 m, distance between bogie centres 14.63 m, coach body width 2.72 m, overall width 2.816 m, roof height from rail 3.614 m, maximum height 3.826 m, brake equipment: two 21 in vacuum brake cylinders, combined type/two brake regulators type DRV2A-450

Diesel electric trainset built by Kawasaki for New Zealand Railways' long-distance services. Manufactured as an ace train for NZR, the main power source is provided by a Caterpillar 1 010 hp engine. The train is formed by two cars (maximum of six) and is used for the Silver Fern express service between Wellington and Auckland (680 km). Main data:

Track gauge		1 067mm
Tare weight	DE 1	61tonne
	DE 2	43tonne
Passenger capacity Seating	DE 1	36
	DE 2	60
Length over coupler face		23 720mm

Overall width		2 743mm
Height to top of roof		3 759mm
Bogie center distance	DE 1	17 374mm
	DE 2	17 552mm
Wheel base		1 650 mm + 1 650mm
		2 200 mm
Wheel dia.		787mm
Diesel engine output		940mm
(at 1 300 rpm)		1 010ps
Max. speed		112km/h

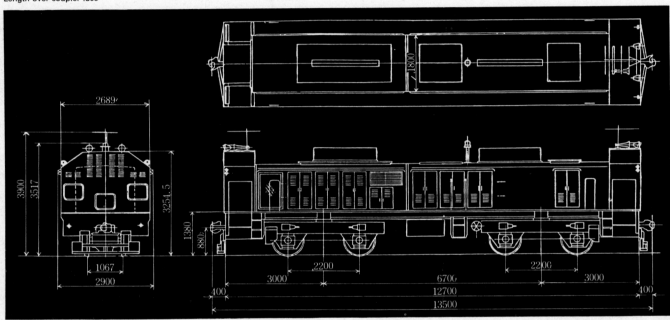

Radio controlled diesel hydraulic locomotive built by Kawasaki for the parent company steel corporation. No operating controls are fitted in keeping with the main design specification to build a purely remote-control locomotive.

Track gauge	1 067 mm
Weight in working order	70 tonne
Maximum tractive effort	21 000 kg
Maximum service speed	17.5 km/h
Diesel engine	
Model/Q'ty	DMF 31SI/1
Standard output	600 metric hp
Hydraulic transmission	

Model/Q'ty	Shinko DS1.35A/1
Gear ratio	12.287
Control system	Electro-magnetic, electro-pheumatic remote control by radio
Storage battery	
Voltage/capacity	dc 24V/400 Ah (20 hour rating)
Brake system	Air brake by electro-magnetic control and hand brake
Capacity of fuel tank	2 000 litres

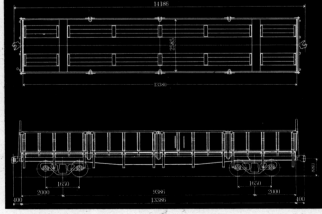

Two-axle bogie 30 tonne box wagon for JNR, built by Kawasaki. A type WAKI 1000 wagon, it had four sliding doors and can be partitioned into four compartments designed for carrying palletised freight. Main data:

Track gauge	1 067mm
Loading capacity	30tonne
Tare weight	22tonne
Useful floor area	35.9m²
Body capacity	89.6m³
Length over coupler face	15,650mm
Overall width	2 984mm
Height to top of roof	3 704mm
Bogie center distance	10 850mm
Wheel base	2 100mm
Wheel dia.	860mm
Max. speed	100km/h

Two-axle bogie 36 ton gondola wagon—latest type of JNR's general purpose open-top wagons. Main data:

Track gauge	1 067mm
Loading capacity	36tonne
Tare weight	16.8tonne
Useful floor area	34.6m²
Body capacity	79.6m³
Length over coupler face	14 186mm
Overall width	2 835mm
Height to top of side door	2 276mm
Bogie centre distance	9 386mm
Wheel base	1 650mm
Wheel dia.	860mm
Max. speed	75km/h

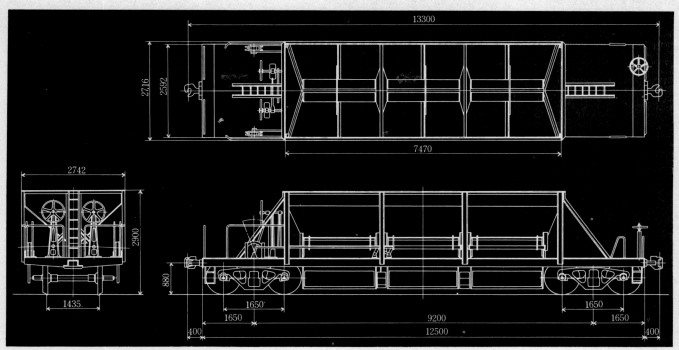

Two-axle bogie 30 ton ballast hopper wagon designed to scatter ballast on the track of JNR's Shinkansen. To regulate three-way scattering over the track bed a special scatter adjusting door is provided, operated by a handle on the deck at the end of each wagon. Main data:

Track gauge	1 435mm
Loading capacity	30tonne
Tare weight	19tonne
Body capacity	18m³
Length over coupler face	13 300mm
Overall width	2 742mm
Height to top of body	2 900mm
Bogie centre distance	9 200mm
Wheel base	1 650mm
Wheel dia.	860mm
Max. speed	75km/h

Series 500 electric car built by Kawasaki for Keihan Electric Railway. While normal seating is for 38 per car during off peak periods extra seats can be brought down from the ceiling to increase seating capacity to 54. To obtain maximum lightness, aluminium light-alloy construction was used throughout. Main data:

Track gauge	1 435mm
Electric system	dc 600V
Tare weight (Motor car)	32tonne
Passenger capacity (Motor car)	
Total	150
Seating	38or 54
Length over coupler face	18 700mm
Overall width	2 726mm
Height to top of roof	3 710mm
Bogie centre distance	12 000mm
Wheel base	2 100mm
Wheel dia.	860mm
One hour rating output	
(2 motor cars 1 unit)	1 040kw
Max. speed	120km/h

KIDRIC

Boris Kidric

Head Office: Maribor, Yugoslavia

Products: Passenger coaches.

New equipment: New B-type two-axle passenger coach is of all-welded rolled steel sections. The body sheathing is of 2 mm sheet steel, while that of the roof is 1.5 mm in thickness. The car floor is of 1.5 mm trapezoid shaped corrugated steel, welded by electric arc to the underframe.

The slides and ends are lined with a layer of 4–4 mm lesonite board, and over it a layer of lesomine board of the same thickness. The car ceiling is lined with two glued lesonite boards enamelled white.

The insulation of the sides, ends and roof is effected by means of modern insulating materials. The passenger space is divided into three compartments. Seats have soft backs and are upholstered in artificial leather. The car can be manufactured either with electric heating system or with Friedmann-of Wien steam-heating system.

Technical Particulars:

Body length	14 200 mm
Height from top of rails	4 145 mm
Number of seats	70
Speed permitted	80 km/h
Light weight	18.5 Mp

The A-type coach is constructed of all-welded steel rolled and pressed sections. The car sheathing is of 2 mm pickled sheet steel, while that of the roof is 1.5 mm in thickness. The floor is of 1.5 mm corrugated steel electrically welded to the underframe. A frame of oak billets is fastened over the floor, and then lined with waterproof panels. The insulation of sides, ends and roof is effected by contemporary insulation materials. The car is equipped with electrical heaters.

The car has five compartments, 1 780 × 2 155 mm, with eight seats in four compartments, and seven seats in the fifth, or a total of 39 seats. The seats and backs are soft. The car is provided with low-pressure steam heating system of Friedmann type.

Technical Particulars:

Height from top of rails	4 145 mm
Number of seats	39
Speed permitted	100 km/h
Light weight	19.3 Mp

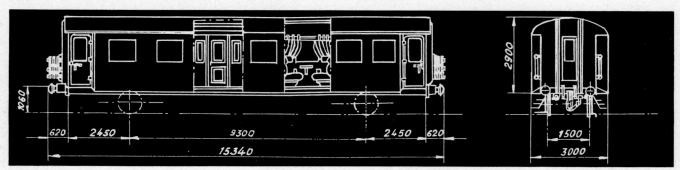

A-type coach

KINKI

Kinki Sharyo Co Ltd
(Kinki Rolling Stock Mfg Co, Ltd)

Head office: 1-1 Hashimoto, Higashi Osaka, Japan

Products: Electric and diesel railcars; tank cars; refrigerator cars; passenger and freight cars; industrial wagons and equipment.

President: Shoitch Hashimoto

Constitution: In 1920 a factory was started in Osaka for manufacture of rolling stock which in 1936 became the Tanaka Sharyo Co. In November 1945 the latter company

Telegrams: Kinsha Fuse
Telephone: Osaka (782) 1231

was taken over by the Kinki Nippon Railways Co, the largest private railway company in Japan, and the present company was formed.

The company was the first in Japan to build lightweight rolling stock and in 1953 came to an arrangement with Swiss Car and Elevator Corporation, Schlieren, to use their manufacturing techniques and to produce "Schlieren" type lightweight cars and bogies.

Sales: Kinki Sharyo is a member of a group (including Kawasaki and Sumitom) awarded contracts valued at Yen 4 070 million by Burma Railways in 1977. Kinki Sharyo is to supply 20 tank wagons and five refrigerated wagons.

KOLMEX

Head Office: Mokotowska, 49.00-542, Warsaw, Poland

Products: Electric and diesel locomotives; electric trainsets; passenger coaches; freight wagons.

Chairman: Eng. Włodzimierz Rachiborski
Managing Director: Władysław Kostuj
Chief Sales Director: Eng. Antoni Łukasiewicz

Constitution: Kolmex acts as the Foreign Trade Enterprise of TASKO and is the sole exporter of railway Motive power and passenger and freight stock manufactured in Poland. Members: Cegielski; Pafawag; Fablok; Konstal; Zastal; Swidnica.

Telegrams: KOLMEX
Telephone: 28 22 91
Telex: 813270/813714

Sales: Major orders in 1974 included: 250 passenger coaches; 30 mail vans; 6 electric locomotives; 21 diesel locomotives; 16 mining locomotives; 2 685 covered freight wagons; 1 985 self-discharge wagons; 1 156 tank wagons; 210 open wagons.

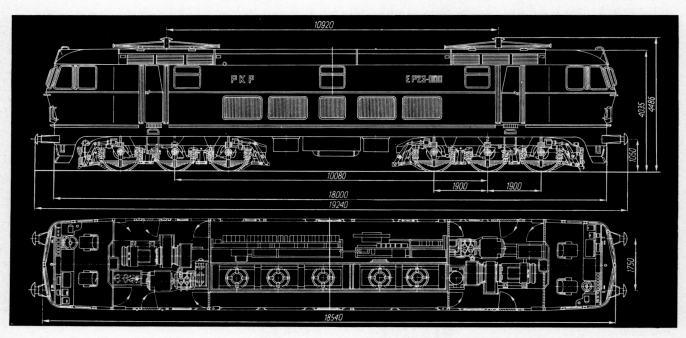

Universal type 201E electric locomotive designed for mainline freight and passenger haulage

Track gauge	1 435 mm
One-hour rating	3 120 kW (4 230 hp)
Continuous rating	3 000 kW
Axle arrangement	Co-Co
Weight in working order	120 Mg
Maximum speed	125 km/h
Continuous speed	56 km/h

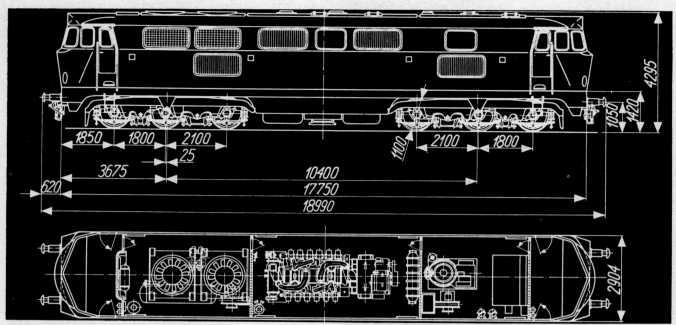

Type SZ 2 800 hp diesel-hydraulic locomotive

Track gauge	1 435 mm
Axle arrangement	Co-Co
Axle load of wheelset onto track	17 tonne
Narrowed limiting outline (clearance gauge)	to UIC 505
Running tread diameter	1 100 mm
Bogie wheel base	1 800 and 2 100 mm
Spacing of king pins (distance between)	10 400 mm
Length over buffers	18 990 mm
Width of locomotive body	2 904 mm
Height	4 295 mm
Minimum track curvature radius	100 m
Weight with full supplies	102 tonne
Maximum speed	120 km/h

KONSTAL

Steel Construction Works Konstal

Head Office: 41-500 Chorzow, ul. Metalowcow 7, Poland

Export Sales: Kolmex, 49 Mokotowska, 00-542 Warsaw, Poland

Products: Electric and storage battery mine locomotives; freight wagons; wheel sets.

Telegrams: KONSTAL, Chorzow
Telephone: 41-10-51
Telex: 0312451

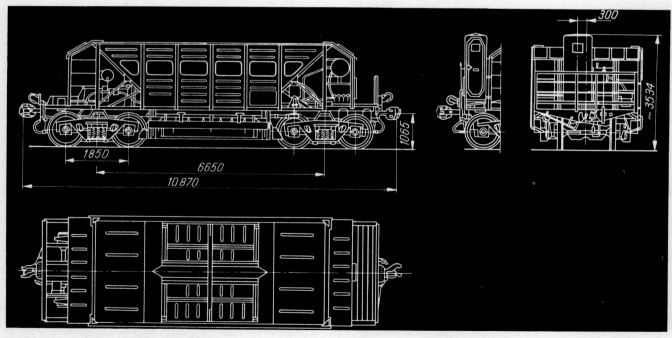

Hopper wagon type 902V designed for hauling ballast

Track gauge 1 524 mm; loading capacity 60 tonne; Car's own weight: with parking brake 23.6 tonne; with hand brake 23.7 tonne; Maximum axle load 21.0 tonne; Capacity (volume), with prism 40.0 m³; without prism 32.4 m³; Car length between automatic coupling axes 10 870 mm; Car width between farthest protruding parts 3 243 mm; Car length between bogie pivots 6 650 mm; Car height above top of rail 3 167 mm; Number of flaps, exterior hatches 2; interior hatches 2; Discharge opening dimensions of exterior flap 2 680 × 345 mm; of interior flap 2 680 × 330 mm; General clearance space of discharge openings 3.62 m²; vehicle gauge to GOST 9238-59 1-T.

KOREA SHIPBUILDING & ENGINEERING

Head Office: Pusan, South Korea

Products: Open, tank and container wagons, cast steel bogies, bolsters, couplers and wheels.

KRALJEVO

Kraljevo Car Factory

Head Office: Kraljevo, Yugoslavia

Products: Passenger coaches and freight wagons.

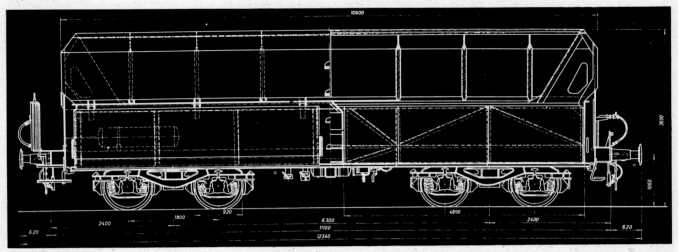

Four-axle iron-ore hopper wagon
Gauge 1 435 mm; overall length, 12.3 m; width, 2.86 m; height from top of rails, 3.6 m; bogie pin centres 6.4 m; bogie wheel base 1.8 m; hopper volume 60 m³; unladen weight 23 Mp; Load limit 57 Mp; Gross weight 80 Mp; Axle-loading 20 Mp.

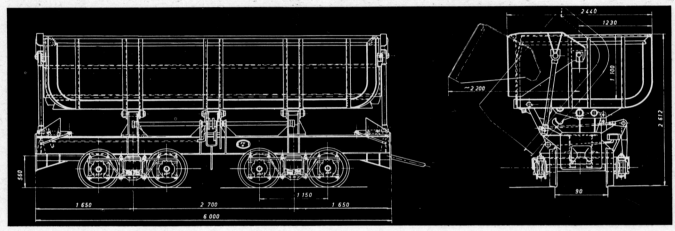

900 mm gauge four-axle wagon for coal haulage
Unloading can be performed on both sides directly into bunkers by means of mechanical devices for door opening. Door control is performed from the locomotive. In addition to pneumatic and remote-control door systems, they can be opened by hand.

The wagon is intended primarily for use in mines. Coupling is effected through a centrally located draft and buffering coupler, the cushioning being provided by worm springs.

KRAUSS-MAFFEI
Krauss-Maffei Aktiengesellschaft

Head Office: 8 München 50, Krauss-Maffei Strasse 2, German Federal Republic

Export Sales: Dept. GL, 8 München 50, Krauss-Maffei Strasse 2, German Federal Republic

Products: Diesel and electric locomotives; track-bound high speed systems with contact-free suspension and guidance.

Board of Directors: Dr rer pol Hans-Heinz Griesmeier
Dipl-Ing H.-D. v. Bernuth
Wolfgang Raether
Managing Director, Transportation Division: Dipl-Ing Hans-Dietrich von Bernuth

Telegrams: Kraussmaffei Müchenallach
Telephone: 089/88991
Telex: 05-23 163

Constitution: The present firm of Krauss-Maffei came into being by the fusion in 1931 of two locomotive builders, J. A. Maffei AG, founded in 1837, and Krauss & Co KG, founded in 1866. In 1935-37 a factory, replacing the former two plants, was erected at Allach, a suburb of Munich.

Sales: Work in hand or recently delivered includes diesel-hydraulic and diesel-electric locomotives for Brazil, Germany, India, Indonesia, Italy, Liberia, South Africa, Spain, Turkey and other countries; electric locomotives for the German Federal Railways and for Indian State Railways.

The new E 111, used for DB long and short-haul passenger trains and high-speed freight services.

Following successful operations with the first examples of the E 111 locomotive Deutsche Bundesbahn has now ordered 146 locomotives of this type from Krauss Maffei. Now Krauss Maffei has been chosen as the prime contractor for development of the new E 120 universal standard locomotive for both passenger and freight train service utilising new three-phase current technology. Five prototypes of the new class are to be built.

First tests started late in 1977 on Krauss Maffei's new test facility at Munich DB repair shop on which speeds of up to 500 km/h can be simulated. Purpose of the specially commissioned dynamic test stand is to explore the technical and economic limits of conventional rail technology.

In the sector of railway electronics, Krauss Maffei has developed new electronic antislip and antiglide equipment for locomotives. At present a modern electronic antislip device is being developed jointly with DB for use on passenger coaches. Series production is due to begin late in 1978.

Since 1976 Krauss Maffei has been supplying two types of electronic equipment for remote control of locomotives. One is for assembling trains from a portable transmitter; the other for automatic humping locomotives operated by a central processing computer.

The Transrapid magnetic levitation train with linear motor propulsion continues under development by Krauss Maffei and Messerschmitt Bolkow Blohm. In 1977 the Transrapid 04 test vehicle (see picture) achieved speeds of 206 km/h and is at present being retro-fitted for speeds to exceed 250 km/h. A speed of 401 km/h was set up by the unmanned test magnetic levitation vehicle Comet.

A public demonstration system in magnetic levitation technology developed by the two companies will be operational at the International Transport Exhibition to be held in Hamburg in 1979.

The Transrapid magnetic levitation train last year set up speeds of 206 km/h and is now being prepared for speeds of over 250 km/h.

KRUPP

Fried Krupp GmbH
Krupp Industrie-und Stahlbau, Railway Rolling Stock Division

Head Office and Works: Helenenstrass 149, 4300 Essen 1, German Federal Republic

Telephone: (0201) 31901
Telex: 08 57 9331

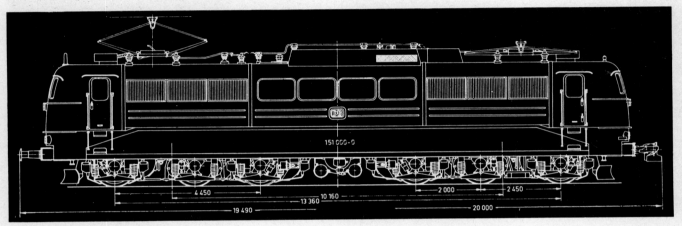

5 370 kW electric locomotive for DB

Built by Krupp, the unit is basically a repeat of the Class 150 six-axle freight locomotive. The new locomotive has a weight of 124 t, which is 2 t less than the earlier design. The hourly rating is 6 370 kW, which is substantially higher than the 4 500 kW of the Class 150. Also, the new locomotive has a maximum permitted speed of 120 km/h compared with the 100 km/h of the Class 150. The electrical equipment is made up of successful components from various locomotive series, transformer, thyristor-controlled 28-stage high-voltage switch and thyristor-controlled amplified electric brake. The extra weight is compensated by weight savings in the mechanical part. The bogie, bridge frame and removable engine-room cowls are similar to those on the Class 103 express locomotives.

Class BB 304 four-axle 1 270 kW diesel-hydraulic locomotive supplied to the Indonesian State Railways by Krupp: UIC nominal rating 1 270 kW; maximum speed 120 km/h; weight 52 tonnes; maximum tractive effort 170 tonnes; overall length 12.73 m.

Class 181.2 four-axle 3 300 kW dual frequency thyristor locomotive built by Krupp for Deutsche Bundesbahn: for 16⅔ Hz 15 kV and 50 Hz, 25 kV systems, starting power 5 000 kW; one hour rating 3 300 kW; maximum speed 160 km/h; maximum tractive effort 275 tonnes; length over buffers 17.940 m.

KUIBYSHEV
Kuibyshev Diesel Locomotive Works

Head Office: Kolomensk, USSR

Products: Diesel locomotives.

New equipment: Locomotives powered by 6 000 hp, 8 000 hp and 10 000 hp diesel engines have been designed for operation on the Baikul-Amur (BAM) Railway.

LEW
VeB Lokomotivbau-Elektrotechnische Werke Hans "Beimler"

Head Office: 1422 Hennigsdorf, German Democratic Republic

Products: Electric and diesel-hydraulic locomotives; multiple unit trains.

Telegrams: ELEKTROLOK
Telephone: Hennigsdorf 851
Telex: 015 8531

Constitution: Member of Transportmaschinen Export-Import.

Class 250 16⅔ Hz electric locomotive supplied by LEW to DeutscheReichsbalm: a six-axle unit with automated control and designed for low maintenance

Class 110 diesel-hydraulic locomotive for DR has a B-B wheel arrangement, is rated at 1 000 hp and capable of a top speed of 100 km/h in passenger service or 65 km/h in freight service

New narrow-profile trainset for East Berlin Metro service

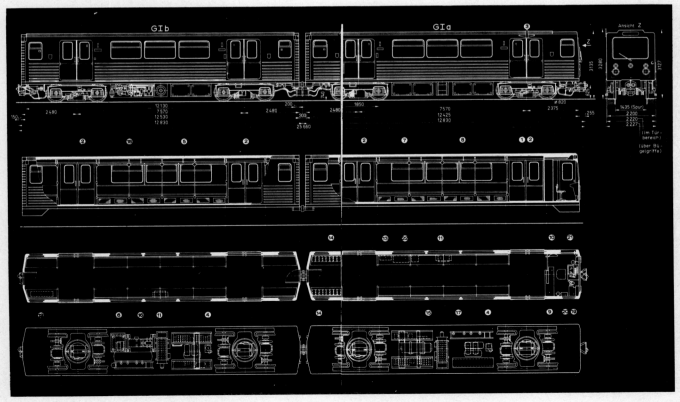

LINKE-HOFMANN-BUSCH

Linke-Hofmann-Busch Waggon-Fahrzeug-Maschinen GmbH

Head Office: Postfach 411160, D-3320 Salzgitter 41, German Federal Republic

Products: Passenger and freight cars of all kinds; electric and diesel railcars and trainsets; electric and diesel locomotives; underground railway cars; tramcars.

Technical Director: Dipl-Ing Heinz Alten

Commercial Director: Karl-Alfred Meier

Constitution: Established in 1839 at Breslau under the name of Carbuilding Workshops of Gottfried Linke; in 1912 the Company amalgamated with Gebruder Hofmann & Co to form Linke-Hofmann Werke AG, Breslau. In 1928 the Waggon & Maschinenfabrik AG vorm. Busch joined the company to form Linke-Hofmann-Busch. As a result of the war the company's works at Breslau had to be abandoned, but in 1949 L-H-B resumed their activities at Salzgitter-Watenstedt, near Braunschweig, and now have 130 year's experience of car building behind them.

Six-axled open self-discharging ore wagon (type Fad) for the steel mills of Stahlwerke Peine-Salzgitter AG. The wagon is destined for the transport of fine ore, lump ore and pellets. Four large side flaps in combination with a saddle bottom facilitate discharging into underground hoppers. The flaps are opened and closed by means of a crank gear with thumb shaft lock. The four side flaps can be simultaneously operated, but it is also possible to operate individually. The flaps are actuated by means of a handwheel arranged on the front wall.

Main data:

Type	Fad ore wagon
Average tare weight	34 000 kg
Length of loading opening	12 810 mm
Width of loading opening	1 950 mm
Loading space	60 m³
Maximum opening of side flaps in supported position:	
clear	abt 4 360 mm
full (100%)	abt 4 080 mm
half (60%)	abt 3 740 mm
Interior width of discharge opening	5 000 mm
Bogie acc. to drg.: 3-axled	0 Fwg 711.5.04.000.01
Type of wheelsets	BA.02 (22 t)
Max diameter on tread	920 mm

Minimum diameter on tread	870 mm
Journal distance	2 000 mm
Type of axle boxes	roller bearing
Laminated bearing springs:	
Extended length	1 200 mm
Number of spring leaves	9
Cross section of spring leaves	120 x 16 mm
Carrying height	164 mm
Carrying load	1 755 kg
Type of spring suspensions	long shackles
Type of brake	KE-GP
Number of brake cylinders	2
Diameter of brake cylinders	14 in
Type of control valve	KE 2a SL-L
Type of load braking	two-stage, pneumatic/ mechanical, manually operated
Automatic coupler	UIC-69e
Spring type	B 412 B ring spring
Max speed loaded/empty	80/100 km/h
Minimum radius of curves	75 m
First year of manufacture	1976

Type VT 2E twin car diesel-electric trainset (shown above) built by Linke-Hofmann-Busch for AKN Hamburg

The six-axled diesel-electric two-car unit of lightweight steel construction cannot be separated in operation, and is equipped with 2 two-axled motor bogies and one central carrying bogie. Each unit consists of two largely identical railcars with the same interior furnishing and uniform driver's cabins and mechanical equipment.

The VT 2E is equipped with a centre gangway which is protected between car A and car B by means of rubber tubes. Passenger compartments are closed by hinged doors. The car body shell construction is designed for a buffer force of 80 tons. The two-car units are equipped with full-automatic centre buffer couplers type Scharfenberg by means of which both pneumatic and electric lines are also coupled. Protection of the couplers carrier is by means of a shock absorption member responding at a pressure force of 50 Mp.

The two individual cars of one two-car unit have been provided with independent traction equipment, electric and pneumatic brake equipment and low voltage systems. In case of failure of one of these operation can be maintained although possibly with reduced capacity. For generation of compressed air a compressor, driven by an electric motor, has been provided in the A-car exclusively; energy for the compressor is, however, supplied from both the low voltage system of the A and B-cars.

For diesel-electric traction each individual car is provided with a diesel engine type MAN serving as drive motor and mounted underfloor, delivering the torque to a three-phase alternator supplying via rectifiers the two tractions motors which are arranged in the corresponding motor bogie.

Control of the vehicles has been designed so that it is possible to form a train consist of up to four two-car units. In case of failure the train consist can be extended to a maximum of eight two-car units.

The heat which is delivered from the diesel engine to the cooling water is carried-off by an elastically suspended underfloor mounted cooling system. The ventilator is driven hydrostatically.

Main data:

Year of construction	1976-1977
Mean acceleration v = 0 - 40 km/h	$a_1 = 0.8$ m/s²
Mean acceleration v = 40 - 80 km/h	$a_2 = 0.31$ m/s²
Total mean acceleration v = 0 - 80 km/h	$a_3 = 0.45$ m/s²
Mean deceleration of main brake	$a_4 = 0.8$ m/s²
Mean deceleration of through brake	$a_5 = 1.0$ m/s²
Permissible speed	80 km/h
Maximum number of units in train consist	4 units
Tare weight A-car	25 590 kg
Tare weight B-car	25 240 kg
Weight in running order, per unit	52 050 kg
Fully loaded weight, per unit	58 65; kg
Maximum axle load (overloaded)	12 130 kg

Technical Data:

Tare weight per gross basic area	593 kg/m¼
Wheel diameter on tread	870 - 800 mm
Minimum radius of curve	100 m
Diesel engine type MAN-D 3256 BTYUE	2 x 228 kW
Generator type BBC (rectified)	2 x 216 kW
Traction motor type BBC - 4 EKG 2422	4 x 78 kW
Axle gear transmission (wheel: pinion)	1:5.8235
Control current voltage	110 V -
Motor generators	2 x 127 V/30 kW
Lead starter batteries	2 x 110 V/140 Ah
Electric hot-air heating	
Seven diesel-electric running steps	

Seating capacity:

	A-car	B-car	per Unit
Seats	44	44	88
Standing capacity 0.15 m¼/person	86	86	172
Total capacity	130	130	260

MACOSA

Material y Construcciones, SA

Telegrams: Material Madrid
Telephone: 2 22-47-87
Telex: 22168 Mayco

Head Office: Plaza de la Independencia 8, Madrid, Spain

Products: Electric, diesel-electric and diesel hydraulic locomotives; passenger and freight cars.

President: Joaquin Reig Albiol
General Manager: Adolfo Pizcueta Alfonso
Vice-President: Eugenio Martin Antelo
General Secretary: Luis Cuñat Albiol
Commercial Manager: Ramón Trénor Trénor
Works Director, Barcelona: José Ma Ardévol Vidiella
Works Director, Valencia: Ildefonso Carrascosa Vallés

Constitution: This company was formed in 1947 by the merger of two concerns, Material para Ferrocarriles y Construcciones, SA of Barcelona and Construcciones Devis, SA of Valencia. The first was founded in 1895 by Girona Agrafel and made into a limited liability company in 1881. The second was started in Valencia in 1897 by Miguel Devis Pérez as a boiler works, became Construcciones Devis SA in 1929, and in 1941 opened the present factory at Alcázar de San Juan.

Recent sales: Orders placed by Spanish National Railways (RENFE) included: 50 diesel-electric GM26T 3 345-hp locomotives; 250 grain hopper wagons; 100 box wagons fitted with sliding roofs.
Orders placed by private companies during 1973 included: 350 tank wagons.

MAFERSA

Material Ferroviario SA

Telegrams: Mafersa
Telephone: 36-6371

Head Office: Avienda da Luz 220, São Paulo, Brazil

Products: Freight cars; passenger cars; stainless steel cars (Budd licence); wrought steel forged wheels; heavy forgings.

Director: J. P. Barbosa, Jnr

Constitution: Mafersa (Material Ferroviario SA), of Brazil is divided into three groups: passenger coach division, based in Sao Paulo; freight wagon division, based in Belo Horizonte; and wheel and axle division, based in Cacapava.

Main production items at the 18 500 m² Sao Paulo passenger coach plant are stainless-steel coaches built under Budd license. With a payroll of 842 employees at present and turnover of 144 coaches last year, the division has contracts in hand for the following deliveries during 1975/76: 198 power cars for Sao Paulo subway; 30 trainsets (power coach plus two trailers) for RFFSA; 30 four-car trainsets for FEPASA.

Sales: The freight wagon division has a production capacity of around 1 200 wagons annually. Contracts are in hand for 1 405 wagons: 1 100 open. covered, tank and hopper wagons for RFFSA; 305 tank and general purpose wagons for FEPASA.

MAK

MaK Maschinenbau GmbH

Telegrams: MaK Kiel
Telephone: 30111
Telex: mak d 02 99877/78

Head Office: Postfach 9009 23 Kiel 17, German Federal Republic

Products: Diesel-hydraulic locomotives from 275 hp up to highest power range and for all track gauges; diesel engines for rail traction.

Board of Directors: Dr. Holtmeier
　　　　　　　　　　Joseph Kempa
　　　　　　　　　　Dr. Lembcke

Constitution: MaK has continued the development of the products of the former Deutsche Werke Kiel AG (DWK) which started designing internal combustion engine railcars in 1918, and has constructed diesel locomotives since 1928.

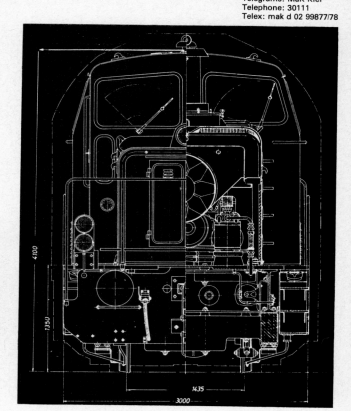

530/700 hp diesel-hydraulic locomotive
For shunting service and axle loads from 16 to 20 tons. Built by MaK. Powered by medium speed MaK diesel engine with Voith forward-reverse turbo transmission.

MAN

Maschinenfabrik Augsburg- Nürnberg AG
Railway Division

Telegrams: Manwerk Nürnberg
Telephone: 0911/181
Telex: 0622291

Head Office: Katzwanger Strasse 101, 8500 Nürnberg 1, German Federal Republic

Sales Office: 8500 Nürnberg, German Federal Republic

Products: Diesel-engined railcars and trainsets; electric railcars and multiple unit trains; rapid transit tube trains; tramcars for surface and sub-surface routes; passenger and freight cars, including high capacity flat and special purpose cars; diesel engines.

Chairman: Hans Moll
Executive Director: Alfred Roth
Divisional Manager (rolling stock): Heinz Raedeke

Constitution: The Numberg works of MAN, which was founded in 1841 took up the manufacture of railway rolling stock in 1850. Formerly known as Maschinenbau-

Aktiengesellschaft Nürnberg, the company merged with the Maschinenfabrik Augsburg in 1898 to form Maschinenfabrik Augsburg-Nürnberg Aktiengesellschaft, in short, MAN.

Sales: Series 614 Diesel trains for DB, electric twin-car units for Tunisia, passenger stock for DB, luggage van for DB, air-suspension bogies for ET 420, ET 403 and Amsterdam Metro, freight cars. An order worth DM 11 million was placed with MAN of Nürnberg for five electric two-car multiple train units for Tunis in 1977. The order follows a previous one for 13 train units. Electrical equipment is provided by Siemens with whom MAN cooperates under a consortium. Delivery of the units, 40 m long over buffers and weighing 68 tonnes, should be completed by mid-1978. The trains have a capacity of 604 passengers and will operate on the suburban line along the coast between Tunis and Le Marsa. They are powered by four 750V dc motors with a total output of 660 kW.

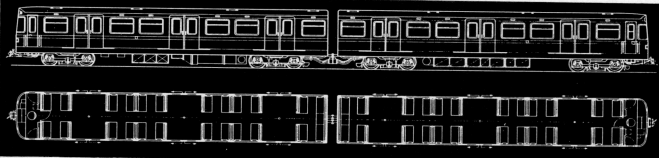

Underground railway twin railcars
The twin railcars by MAN for the Nürnberg underground railway are of the same design and construction as the vehicles for the Munich underground.
The smallest unit comprises two eight-wheel railcars of identical dimensions, layout and interior furnishing, equipped with common electric and pneumatic equipment. Depending upon traffic density, a number of twin railcars can be coupled to form a train-set.
The car shell is a modern fully welded aluminium alloy construction made up of extruded sections and sheet metal. The outer walls, roof and corrugated flooring provided with anti-drumming compound and insulated with sprayed cork. Fibre glass mats are also fitted in the outer walls. The PVC floor covering is welded and carried up the side walls. The side wall panelling is carried out with plastic sheets having a wood decor while the ceiling is made up of fibre glass reinforced plastic sheets. At the joints between the side wall and ceiling, strip lighting is provided at each side over the full length of the car. All windows are of safety glass. The upper sections of the side wall windows are hinged. The seat cushions and backrests are made up of preformed foamed rubberised hair with artificial leather covering.
For heating of the passenger compartment the heat from the traction and brake resistors is employed. With the help of a fan, air from the outside is blown over the resistors into the passenger compartment. A thermostat control device ensures uniform temperature. The spent air passes through eight roof ventilators to the atmosphere. During summer months ventilation is carried out in the opposite direction. All the electrical equipment is mounted in flexibly supported equipment boxes under the car and in cubicles in the driving position.
At each side of the car, three double-leaf flush-closing sliding doors allowing a clear width of 1 300 mm are provided. These doors are closed pneumatically from the driver's position and can be opened individually by the passenger, air-assisted, when

the interlocking system has been released by the railcar driver. The rheostatic braking system is supplemented by an electro-pneumatic disc brake. In the event of faults, the latter brake acts alone. A spring accumulator brake is employed for parking.

MARCROFT
Marcroft & Co Ltd

Telegrams: MARCROFT
Telephone: (07613) 3203

Head Office: Radstock Wagon Works, Radstock, Bath, Avon BA3 3QU, England

Products: Freight wagons.

MARELLI
Ercole Marelli & C SpA

Telegrams: VENTILATOR MILANO
Telephone: 2494
Telex: 31043 MILANO

Head Office and Works: Viale Edison, 50 Sesto San Giovanni, Milan CAP 20099, Italy

Products: Electric equipment for all types of electric traction and auxiliary equipment.

Managing Director: Umerto Di Capua
Plant and Systems Division, Energy: Giancarlo Lucchini
Traction Department Manager: Ferdinando Gambassi

Constitution: Ercole Marelli & C was founded in 1891 for the production of small electric motors and fans but quickly grew to become a large producer of electric machinery and equipment. Products for the railway industry now form an important part of the company's activities.

Sales: Shunt chopper locomotives class E 444 for Italian State Railways (FS); full chopper and traditional electric multiple unit trains for FS suburban services; electronic systems for the tilting body trainsets of both FS and RENFE; diesel-electric locomotives class D 345 for FS; full chopper motor coaches for Milan Metro; light transit system cars for Milan Municipal Transport Authority.

Full chopper motor-coach for Milan Metro

Shunt chopper locomotives class E 444 for Italian State Railways

EMU class ALe 801 train for Italian State Railways

MARINE INDUSTRIES

Marine Industries Ltd

Head Office: 1405 Peel St, Montreal, Quebec, Canada

Telegrams: MARINDUS, Quebec
Telephone: 743 3351
Telex: 01 26136

Products: Freight wagons.

MARTIN & KING

Martin & King Pty Ltd

Telegrams: MARKING, Melbourne
Telephone: 305 4160

Head Office: Somerton Road, Campbellfield, Victoria, Australia

Products: Electric, diesel railcars; electric multiple units; passenger coaches; freight wagons.

Constitution: An associate company of Clyde Industries Ltd.

New equipment: The six-car stainless steel trainsets, built by Martin & King for Melbourne's suburban system, were built to a basic design by Hitachi of Japan. The trains are designed for a maximum speed of 112.5 km/h. Acceleration on a level track will be 2.4 km/h per second to at least 32 km/h. Body framing is of mild steel externally sheathed with satin-finished stainless steel—plain on the roof and between doors and windows, and corrugated above and below window level. Jacking and lifting points have been provided on each side of the coaches and at each end near the transverse centreline of the bogie bolsters. The structure should be capable of withstanding a minimum static buffing force of 91 tonnes at the coupler centreline. Vertical anti-collision members are provided at each end of each car and are designed to carry a load of at least 54.5 tonnes, without failure at a point 1.65 m above rail level.
Passenger saloons have three doors each side. They are of two-section balanced sliding type fitted with Belmatic door engines. A sheathed sponge rubber seal section is

fitted to the leading edge of each door. Door control is by push button from each guard's compartment. Closed by power operation, they can be opened manually by passengers after power release by the guard. End walls of all coaches are fitted with a hinged inward opening door, glazed with clear glass in the upper part. Half-drop aluminium-framed windows are fitted in the passenger saloon area. All are glazed with toughened 5-mm-thick tinted glass and sealed by rubber extrusions. Side windows of driver's and guard's compartments are of full drop balance type with aluminium frame. These also have 5-mm-thick toughened glass, rubber sealed.
Rigid transverse wind barriers are fitted by the doors, and a 31-mm-diameter stainless steel handrail is fitted to the top of the barriers. Aluminium hand grips on reinforced leather straps are provided for standing passengers. Motor coaches have seating capacity for 86 passengers, driving trailers 90 passengers, and trailers 96 passengers. Motor coaches are equipped with a Westcode (Westinghouse Brake and Signal UK) load compensated electro-pneumatic brake and an automatic air standby and emergency brake. A rheostatic brake, continuously blended with the electro-pneumatic brake from speeds of 56.5 km/h, is integrated with the Westcode system. Driving trailers and ordinary trailers are fitted with Westcode load compensated electro-pneumatic self-lapping brake gear superimposed on an automatic air brake. Final stopping is by on-tread non-metallic or composition brake blocks. Mean retardation rate of coaches under all load conditions is 3.70 km/h per second.

MASCHINEN-EXPORT

Head Office: DDR-108 Berlin, Mohrenstr 53/54, German Democratic Republic

Telephone: 2240
Telex: 112461
Telegrams: MASCHEXPORT, Berlin

Products: Locomotives; freight wagons, passenger coaches.

Constitution: The exporter of motive power and rolling stock built in the German Democratic Republic.

MBB

Messerschmidt-Bölkow-Blohm GmbH
Rolling Stock Division

Telegrams: EMBEBE Donauwörth
Telephone: 0891 711
Telex: 51843 mbbvd

Head Office: Industriestrasse, 885 Donauwörth, German Federal Republic

Products: Light weight vehicles for underground and subway lines, passenger cars for suburban and long distance traffic, sleeping cars, dining cars, saloon cars, diesel and electric railcars, freight cars of all kinds, special cars.

Technical Director: Peter W. D. Schulz
Commercial Director: Hannes Völke

Constitution: Formerly Waggon- und Maschinenbau Donauwörth (WMB). Recent deliveries and work in hand includes rapid transit trainsets ET 420/421 for DB and ET472 for Hamburger S-Bahn; prototype coach for new Intercity ET 403.

Developments: A second-class coach with an aluminium body was constructed by MBB in 1977 to enable DB to evaluate the advantages or disadvantages of aluminium construction. Final decision whether or not to adopt aluminium for production coaches will depend to a great extent on durability since the new series—to be designated Bwnrzb 731—will be required to remain in service for at least 30 years. The prototype vehicles—six second class, three composite and two driving trailers—are being tested in two sets. The new coaches have wider entrances than existing stock and greater comfort for passengers has been achieved through an improved seating arrangement (88 passengers in a second-class coach compared with an average of 96 in existing local-service stock), better lighting and new bogies with superior riding characteristics.

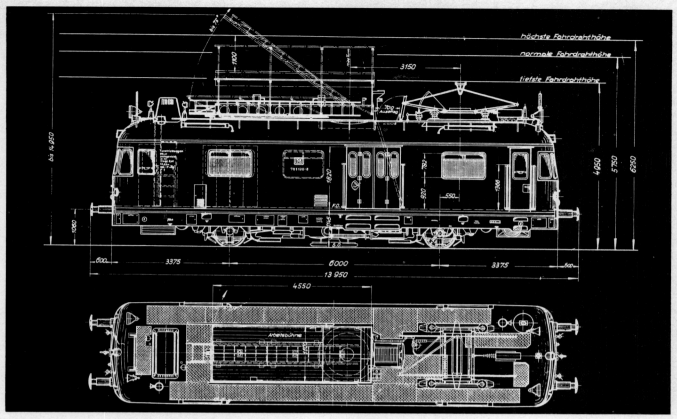

TVT maintenance car delivered to Norwegian State Railways (NSB) last year

MATERIAL

Material Movil y Construcciones SA

Head Office: San Vicente 112, Apartado 127, Spain

Telegrams: MATERIAL
Telephone: 21 73 61
Telex: 62452

Products: Diesel railcars; electric multiple units; passenger coaches; freight wagons.

MECHANOEXPORTIMPORT

Head Office: 10, Mihail Eminescn St, Bucharest, Romania

Telegrams: MECANEX BUCHAREST
Telephone: 12 46 00
Telex: 269

Products: Electric and diesel-electric locomotive railcars; passenger coaches; freight wagons.

Constitution: The Romanian railway rolling stock export/import enterprise.

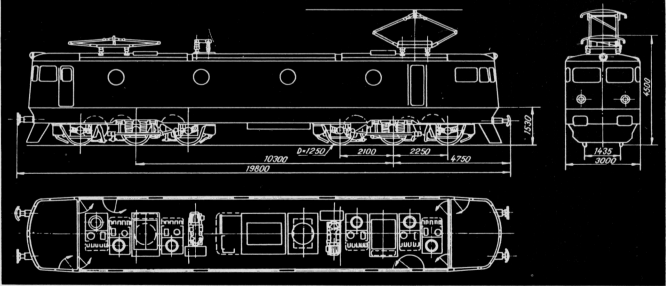

7 350 hp 25 kV 50 Hz electric locomotive

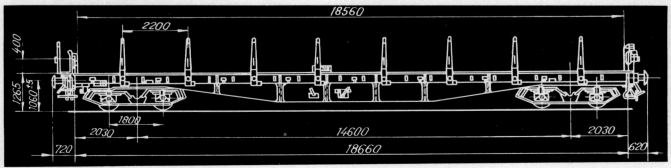

Four axle flat wagon

METALLURGIQUE
Cie. Francais de Products Metallurgique

Head Office: 4, rue de Ventadour, Paris ler, France

Telegrams: COMPAWAGON
Telephone: 742 24 50
Telex: 68 444

Products: Freight wagons.

METRO-CAMMELL
Metro-Cammell Ltd
(wholly owned subsidiary of Metropolitan Cammell Ltd.)

Head Office: PO Box 248, Leigh Road, Washwood Heath, Birmingham B8 2YJ, England

Export Sales: BRE-Metro Ltd. 274/280 Bishopsgate, London EC2M 4XQ, England

Telephone: (01) 247 5444
Telex: 885353

Telegrams: Metro Birmingham
Telephone: 021-327 4777
Telex: 337601

Products: Electric and diesel electric locos, rapid transit cars for surface, sub-surface and underground routes. Specialists in design and construction of cars for pre-metro and full metro and suburban rapid transit systems.

Chairman: A. H. Sansome, BComm
Director and General Manager: D. B. Whitehouse
Director and Chief Engineer: F. J. Bonneres, CEng, FIMechE

88 articulated two-car sets have been ordered by Tyne and Wear Metro

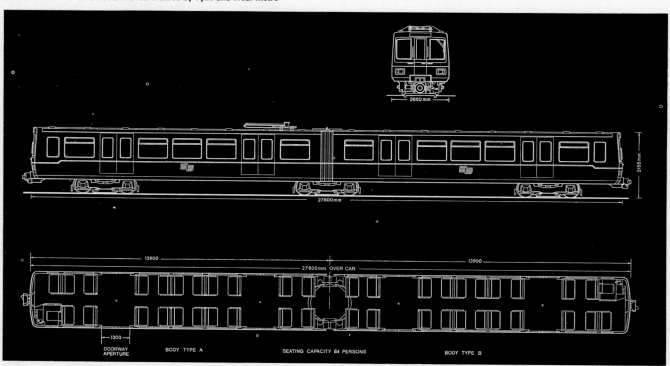

Rapid transit articulated car designed for adaption to specific requirements

Production Director: G. E. Canham, CEng, FIMechE
Financial Controller/Secretary: A. V. Tipper, ACMA
Sales Manager: W. J. Wright

Constitution: The Company originated from a coach builder's works in London operated by Joseph Wright, who owned most of the stage coaches running between London and Birmingham. He started building railway carriages in 1840, transferred the business to Birmingham in 1845 and within a few years the firm of Joseph Wright & Sons was building rolling stock for railways in Britain, Europe, Egypt, South America, India and Australia. In 1862 the Company became Metropolitan Railway Carriage & Wagon Co Ltd, and, over the years, having absorbed several other rolling-stock builders, the carriage building interests of Vickers Ltd and Cammell Laird & Co Ltd were merged in 1929 to form Metropolitan-Cammell Carriage & Wagon Co Ltd with the object of concentrating production in the Birmingham area.

In the latter part of 1966 Metropolitan-Cammell absorbed the railway rolling stock business of Cravens of Sheffield, thus consolidating their position still further in this field. As from January 1969 Vickers Ltd relinquished their 50 per cent shareholding and a new company was formed for railway matters under the style of Metro-Cammell Ltd.

Sales: For London Transport services, delivery has commenced on a contract for 66 surface stock cars for the Wimbledon section of the District Line following completion of 525 tube cars for the Piccadilly Line and a further contract has recently been recieved for 450 new design surface stock cars for the modernisation of the District Line. Other contracts currently in production are 88 articulated cars for Tyne and Wear Metro, 33 motor cars for Glasgow underground and 140 rapid transit cars for the new Hong Kong Mass Transit Railway.

MEYER
Josef Meyer AG

Telegrams: JOSEFMEYER, Rheinfelden
Telephone: (061) 88 12 41

Head Office: CH-4310 Rheinfelden, Switzerland

Products: Freight wagons.

MIN
Masinska Industrija Nis

Telegrams: MIN, Nis
Telephone: 65 129
Telex: 16187

Head Office: Sumadijcka 1, Nis, Yugoslavia

Products: Diesel-hydraulic locomotives; petrol railcars; electric multiple units; diesel multiple units; freight wagons.

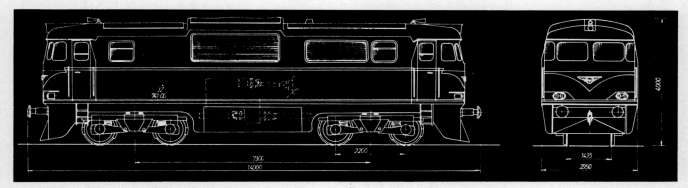

DHL 1500 diesel hydraulic locomotive built by MIN for Yugoslav Railways (JZ)

Gauge, 1 435 mm; Axle arrangement, B'B'; Driving axles, 4; Wheel taping line diameter, 920 mm; Truck wheel base, 2 200 mm; Truck pivot centre distance, 7 300 mm; Locomotive body width, 2 950 mm; Overall length over non-compressed buffers, 14 000 mm; Maximum height from top of rails, 4 000 mm; Rating to UIC at n = 1 500 rpm, 1 500 hp; Engine revolutions no.: maximum, 1 740 rpm; minimum, 640 rpm; Locomotive weight with full supplies, 64 Mp; Weight per linear meter of fully supplied locomotive, 4.57 Mp/m; Maximum axle weight 16 Mp; Maximum design speed, 120 km/h; Minimum continuous speed, 14 km/h; Maximum permitted constant speed, 110 km/h; Pulling force at minimum continuous speed of 14 km/h, 17 750 Kp; Pulling force on the wheel circumference (u = 0.33), 21 300 Kp; Fuel tank capacity 2 850 lit; Boiler firing fuel capacity, 650 lit; Boiler supply water, 4 000 lit; Sand, 240 kg; Minimum curve negotiable, 80 m.

M 360 JM diesel hydraulic locomotive

Gauge, 1 435 mm; axle arrangement, C; driving axles, 3; new wheel diameter, 1 000 mm; locomotive body width, 2 906 mm; overall length over non-compressed buffers, 10 560 mm; maximum height from top of rails, 4 170 mm; rating to UIC at n = 1 500 rpm, 600 hp; engine revolutions no: maximum, 1 500 rpm; minimum, 650 rpm; locomotive weight with full supplies, 48 Mp; maximum axle weight, 16 Mp; maximum design speed, 75 km/h; maximum permitted speed, 60 km/h minimum continuous speed, 4 km/h; pulling force at minimum continuous speed of 4 km/h, 10 600 kp; fuel tank capacity, 1 600 lit; Sand, 260 kp; minimum curve radius, 80 m.

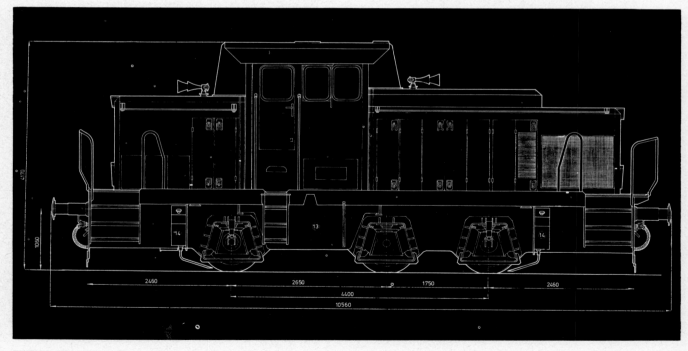

MISKIN CRNI
Vaso Miskin Crni

Telegrams: MISKIN CRNI SARAJEVO
Telephone: 41 222/41 234/41 343
Telex: 41119

Head Office and Works: Industrija Transportnih Sredstava 1 Masina, Sarajevo, Yugoslavia

Constitution: Vaso Miskin Crni was founded in 1890 and is ranked among the oldest manufacturers of railway vehicles in Yugoslavia.

Products: Freight wagons, passenger coaches.

MITSUBISHI
Mitsubishi Heavy Industries Ltd.
Rolling Stock and Physical Distribution Equipment Dept.

Telegrams: Hishiju Tokyo
Telephone: Tokyo (212) 3111
Telex: J22282; J22443

Head Office: No. 5-1, Marunouchi 2-chome, Chiyoda-ku, Tokyo, Japan

Products: Electric, diesel-electric, diesel-hydraulic and diesel-mechanical locomotives; freight and tank cars of all types; air-brakes. Traction diesel engines.

President: Gakuji Moriya
Executive Vice-President: Kazuo Naito
Managing Director: Kazuhisa Toshimitsu
Manager of Rolling Stock Section: Eikichi Kojima
General Manager of Mihara Machinery Works: Katsuzo Yasuda

Constitution: Founded in 1870, Mitsubishi Heavy Industries Ltd is now the largest heavy industry manufacturer in Japan, employing 82 000 people. Annual sales exceed 1 100 000 million Yen (US$ 3 700 million).

Recent sales: Major sales in 1974/75 included 731 freight wagons for New Zealand Railways; 130 freight wagons for Indonesian State Railways; 200 bogies for Hamersley Iron Pty Ltd; 38 electric locomotives for Spanish National Railways; 32 diesel and electric locomotives for Japanese National Railways.

New equipment: Three new types of locomotives have been developed over the past five years for export and domestic sales. For New Zealand Railways, Mitsubishi built a 1 050-hp diesel electric locomotive—weight in working order 63.5 tons; engine, Caterpillar D398TA; control, electro-pneumatic and magnetic multiple unit control; length, 13.106 m; width, 2.590 m; height, 3.530 m—for Zaire (KDL Railways), diesel-electric locomotive—weight in working order, 80 tons; engine, MAN type V6V 22/30 ATL; control, electro pneumatic and magnetic multiple unit control; length, 14.3 m; width, 2.950 m—for JNR, an electric locomotive—ac 20 kV 50 Hz/60 Hz and dc 1 500 V silicon rectifier.

Diesel electric locomotive built by Mitsubishi for Zaire
Wheel arrangement A1A-A1A; weight in working order 80 tonnes; entire type MAN V6V 22/30 ATL; output 1 870 hp; revolutions 925 rpm; main generator 920 kW × 1; control device electro-pneumatic and magnetic multiple unit control; gauge 1 067 mm.

1 050-hp diesel-electric locomotive for New Zealand Railways (above and below)
Wheel arrangement BBB; weight in working order 63.5 tonnes; engine type Caterpillar D398TA; output 1 050 hp; revolutions 1 300 rpm; main alternator 697 kW × 1; traction motor 100 kW × 6; control device electro-pneumatic and magnetic multiple unit control; gauge 1 067 mm.

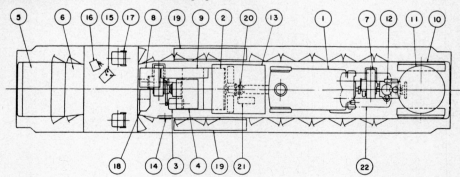

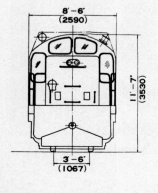

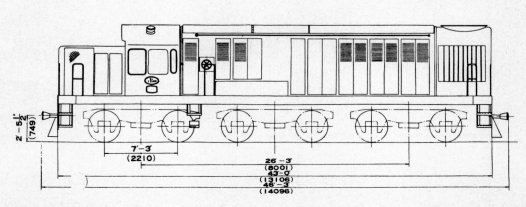

MITSUBISHI ELECTRIC

Mitsubishi Electric Corporation

Telegrams: MELCO, Tokyo
Telephone: 218 3404
Telex: J24532

Head Office: 2-3 Marunouchi 2-chome, Chiyoda-ku, Tokyo, Japan

Products: Electric, diesel-electric, industrial and mining electric battery and trolley locomotives; electric railcars; electric multiple units.

President: Sadakazu Shindo
General Manager (Overseas Marketing Department): Shinichi Yufu
Manager (Transportation Department of Itami Works): Takashi Kitaoka

Capital: Yen 58 928 million (approx. US$200 million)

Employees: 55 593

Constitution: A member of Mitsubishi Group.

Sales: Major sales in recent years included 186 series 279, 289, 269 electric locomotives, and 161 EMU for series 532, 440 railcars for RENFE; 132 EMU for suburban double-decker railcar. and 4 diesel electric locomotives for NSW PTC; 64 EMU for General Urquiza, Argentine Railways; 2 468 traction motors, 529 main transformers, 127 silicon rectifiers, 366 tap-changers, 54 ATC for JNR., Shinkansen Line; 80 electric locomotives for JNR (since 1970); 80 chopper controller for TRTA and the other Japanese municipal bureaus; etc.

New equipment: dc 1 500 V EMU included 135 kW continuous traction motors, 16 step cam controllers, 8 kW ac-dc converters, etc for 8 car trains for NSW PTC Australia: dc 3 000 V EMU included 1 500 V 290 kW continuous, WN drive traction motors and two phase chopper controls with regenerative braking applicable from 140 km/h to 15 km/h for RENFE; Noise proof electric freight locomotives dc 600 V Bo-Bo, 85 000 kg, 560 kW for Nippon Steel Corporation; "MATS" (Mitsubishi Automatic Transportation System), 3 550 V 50/60 Hz, centre guide, rubber tyre guideway bus system, tare weight 5 000 kg, 65 kW dc motor drive, 32 persons each, 1—10 buses coupled, minimum headway 60 second, full automatic operation (schedule and demand mode).

TRTA Chiyoda line ten car train (6M4T) equipped with Mitsubishi EMU; dc 1 500 V catenary; gauge 1 067 mm; maximum speed 100 km/h; traction motor 145 kW 1 hour rating with WN gear coupling; two phase chopper control system with regenerative braking; chopping frequency 660 hZ

Series 269 electric locomotive for RENFE; dc 3 000 V; rated output 3 100 kW; maximum speed 140 km/h; weight 88 tonnes; designed by Mitsubishi Electric

MLW INDUSTRIES
A Division of Bombardier-MLW Ltd.

Telegrams: MONLOCO, MONTREAL
Telephone: (514) 255 3681
Telex: 05 828841

Head Office: 1505 Dickson Street, Montreal, Quebec, Canada

Products: Diesel electric locomotives from 900 hp to 4 500 hp (with single engine), for passenger, freight and switching service; diesel engines, subway cars; freight cars; heat exchangers; pressure vessels; industrial machinery.

President and General Manager: R. L. Grassby
President (Transportation Marketing): H. Valle
Senior Vice President (Transportation Marketing): J. Byrne

Constitution: MLW Industries, (an all Canadian company and member of the Bombardier-MLW Group), one of three major locomotive builders in North America, has been manufacturing locomotives for 75 years. Since 1948 the company has built diesel electric units for Canadian railroads and for export to countries on six continents.

A Canadian consortium, comprising MLW Industries, Alcan Canada Products and Dominion Foundries and Steel, has designed, built and is marketing the LRC (light, rapid, comfortable) high-speed intercity passenger train.

Sales: MLW has recently received orders for locomotives from Venezuela, Iraq, Cuba, Jamaica, Greece, Mexico, Sri Lanka, the Canadian domestic market, and re-sales to Tunisia, Portugal and Bangladesh.

Equipment: MLW locomotives, available from 1 000 hp to 4 500 hp, meet most of the world's gauges, from 3 ft upwards; axle loads from 12 tonne and up and conform to international clearance outlines, including North American and UIC specifications. MLW Industries maintains extensive development facilities to keep abreast of and to pioneer world railroad technology.

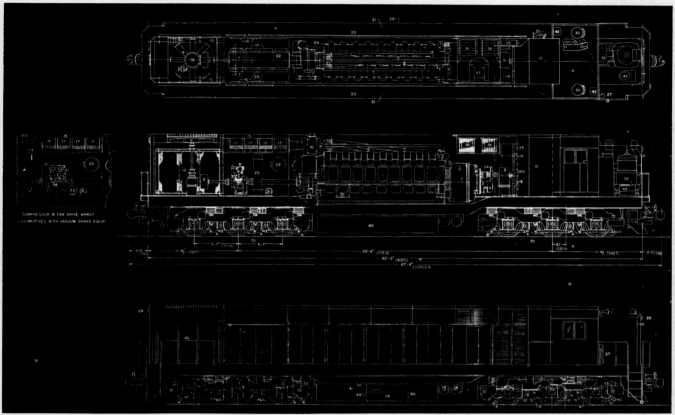

General arrangement of the standard Model M640 North American gauge locomotive built for CP Rail of Canada by MLW

1. Engine; 2. traction alternator; 3. exciter; 4. auxiliary generator; 5. traction motor blower; 6. traction motor; 7. compressor; 8. radiator fan clutch; 9. radiator fan; 10. radiator; 11. control stand; 12. control compartment; 13. brake stand; 14. main air reservoir; 15. cooling water expansion tank; 16. turbo supercharger; 17. engine air filters—secondary; 18. engine air filters—primary; 19. carbody filters; 20. fuel oil tank; 21. fuel oil filling connection; 22. lubricating oil filter; 23. lubricating oil cooler; 24. lubricating oil strainer; 25. rectifiers; 26. horn; 27. hand brake; 28. headlight; 29. batteries; 30. cab seat; 31. fuel oil filter; 32. sand box; 33. sand box fill; 34. engine room pressurising fan.

Modifications: 35. clasp brakes; 36. dynamic brake grids; 37. dynamic brake blower; 38. compressor—exhauster; 39. train heating steam generator; 40. train heating water tank; 41. water tank fill connection; 42. cab heater; 43. toilet; 44. water tank level gauge; 45. radiator shutters.

MOËS
Moteurs Moës, SA

Telegrams: MOTORMOES
Telephone: (019) 32 23 52
Telex: 41568

Head Office: 62 rue de Huy, 4370 Waremme, Belgium

Products: Narrow-gauge diesel-hydraulic, diesel-mechanical, diesel-mining locomotives.

Chairman: G. M. Den Bezemer
Managing Director: F. A. C. Haegeman
Sales Director: J. Antoine

Range of Moes mine locomotives awaiting delivery

MOUTY
Etablissements Jean Mouty

Telephone: 46 63 20
Telex: 82 178

Head Office: La Sentinelle (Nord), France

Products: Freight wagons.

MOYSE
Moyse, SA

Telephone: Paris 352 33 37/838 91 06
Telegrams: Locotrol-Paris
Telex: Locotrol 680765F

Head Office: 7 rue Pascale F, 93126 La Courneuve, France

Products: Diesel-electric and diesel-hydraulic 0-4-0, 0-6-0 and Bo-Bo locomotives from 100 to 1 400 hp and from 18 to 80 tonnes, for all track gauges. These units can be fitted with remote control, flame proof, double traction and low constant speed equipment.

President: G. Delille
Directors: A. Haffner
　　　　　　A. Justafré
　　　　　　J. C. Gimaray

Sales Manager: M. Audra
Export Sales: V. Bräunlich

Constitution: Founded by Gaston Moyse in 1922, the Company has specialised in the manufacture of diesel locomotives. The factory and offices, just to the north of Paris, were rebuilt and extended in 1954 and in 1965 additional capital was invested in the Company to increase production and to extend the product range. At the same time Moyse became a Private Limited Company with Gaston Moyse as Chairman and Managing Director.

MTE
Société MTE

Telephone: 776 41 62
Telex: 610 425F

Head Office: 32 quai National F, 92806 Puteaux, France

Works: Le Creusot, Jeumont, La Plaine St Denis, Champagne-sur-Seine, Lyons, France

Products: Electric, diesel-electric and diesel-hydraulic locomotives and railcars; industrial and mining locomotives; explosion-proof diesel shunting locomotives; railcars; motor coach trainsets; bogies and electrical equipment for high-speed trainsets used on urban and suburban rail transport networks.

Chairman: J. Lerebours-Pigeonniere
Managing Director: H. Jullien

Products: Design and engineering of any class of traction equipment and motive stock, incorporating the products of the traction divisions of Jeumont-Schneider and Creusot-Loire:

electric, diesel-electric, diesel-hydraulic locomotives, trainsets and railcars; electric multiple units for line or commuting service; bogies, main control and ancillary electric equipment for motive power units operating on urban and suburban networks.
Planning and achievement of traction policy and commercial strategy of the trading Group Francorail-MTE, incorporating the associated companies: Carel-Fouché-Languepin, Creusot-Loire, De Dietrich, Jeumont-Schneider and Société MTE.

Works at:
Le Creusot, Traction Unit (CL): power bogies for locomotives and railcars bogies for fast trainsets and metros.
Jeumont (JS): rotating machines, traction motors and ac generators.
Plaine St Denis: (JS): traction control equipment for dc-powered locomotive trainsets

2 400-hp (UIC) diesel-electric Co Co locomotive for Turkish State Railways (TCDD)
200 of this type of locomotive are operating on TCDD lines, supplied by MTE. In addition, 150 more are now being built in Turkey.

Timber wagon operating in the Congo Democratic Republic

and railcars, signalling equipment.
Champagne (JS): ac single-phase current control equipment, Auxiliary current converters.
Lyons (JS): Transformers for ac-powered locomotives trainsets and railcars.

Sales: One of the main suppliers of the French National Railways (SNCF) and the Paris Metro Transit Authority (RATP), Société MTE, whether on its own or as a member of the Francorail-MTE Group, partakes the manufacture of the major rolling and motive stocks for the French Railway systems.
MTE is now supplying the following equipment: three hundred electric locomotives of threefold class BB 7 200-15 000-22 200; the 87 TGV high speed electric trains; the

25 150 dual current electric locomotives; the two hundred MF 77 RATP five car trainsets; Z 2 class SNCF's inter-city electric trains; the Marseilles Metro System; the Interconnection of the RATP and SNCF networks in the Paris conurbation.
As a major French exporter, MTE has booked substantial orders from abroad.
In Africa expanding sales confirm the reliability of the diesel-electric locomotives of the series 2B, 3B and 4B, mainly operated in the Cameroons, Ivory Coast and Congo.
Co-operation with national industries of the partner countries is the actual style of business with Turkey and Brazil for the modernisation and development of the rolling and motive stock.
General network rehabilitation is also MTE business, as already well-advanced for the Guinea Railways.

BB 15 000 locomotive supplied in single phase 25 kv—50 Hz current, defined for a power of 4 499 kW (6 000 ch) and designed to run at 180 km/h

MTM
La Maquinista Terrestre y Maritima SA

Telegrams: MAQUINISTA
Telephone: 345 5700
Telex: 54539

Head Office: PO Box 94, Calle Fernando Junoy, 2 San Andrés, Barcelona 16, Spain

Products: Electric, diesel-electric, diesel-mechanical and diesel-mining locomotives; marine and stationary diesel engines; railway traction engines; steam generators; electric equipment for railway traction; electric generating units; electric, diesel railcars; passenger coaches; freight wagons

President of the Board of Directors: Alvaro Alvarez Lipkau
Managing Director: Adolfo Ramiro Fernandez
Secretary: Ricardo Fornesa Ribó

MYTISCHY
Mytischy Railway Car Works

Head Office: Mytischy, USSR

Products: Passenger coaches: subway cars.

Constitution: Member of Energomachexport.

NATIONAL STEEL CAR
National Steel Car Corporation Limited

Telegrams: Nasteel
Telephone: (514) 866 7461
Telex: 05 24488 NASTEEL MTL

Head Office: PO Box 450, Hamilton, Ontario, Canada

Sales Office: Suite 1011, 1155 Dorchester Boulevard West, Montreal, Quebec H3B 2J2, Canada

70 ton air-side dump wagon for the British Columbia Railway delivered in 1977 by National Steel Car

Products: Freight cars of all types; industrial cars.

President and Chief Executive Officer: T. F. Rahilly, Jr (Hamilton)
Vice President, Engineering: J. A. Aitken (Hamilton)
Vice President, Finance: R. W. Cooke (Hamilton)
Vice President, Purchases: L. G. Dornan (Hamilton)

Vice President, Sales: H. S. Ashby (Montreal)
Comptroller and Secretary: M. G. Nichols (Hamilton)
Works Manager: R. M. Lovell (Hamilton)

Constitution: National Steel Car Corporation was incorporated in 1919 and is now a wholly owned subsidiary of Dominion Foundries and Steel Limited, Hamilton, Ontario.

NIEDERSÄCHSISCHE

Niedersächsische Waggonfabrik Joseph Graaff GmbH

This company has been amalgamated with its associated company, *Niedersächsische*

Fahrzeugbau Joseph Graaff KG, to form a new company named **Graff Kommanditgesellschaft.**

NIESKY

VEB Waggonbau Niesky

Telephone: Niesky OL, Coll 661
Telex: 0198 621

Head Office: 892 Niesky, German Federal Republic

Products: Freight wagons, passenger coaches.

Constitution: Member of Transportmaschinen Export-Import.

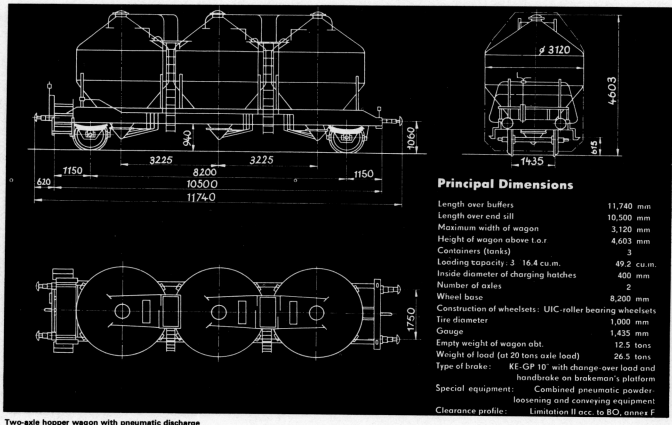

Principal Dimensions

Length over buffers	11,740 mm
Length over end sill	10,500 mm
Maximum width of wagon	3,120 mm
Height of wagon above t.o.r	4,603 mm
Containers (tanks)	3
Loading capacity: 3 16.4 cu.m.	49.2 cu.m.
Inside diameter of charging hatches	400 mm
Number of axles	2
Wheel base	8,200 mm
Construction of wheelsets: UIC-roller bearing wheelsets	
Tire diameter	1,000 mm
Gauge	1,435 mm
Empty weight of wagon abt.	12.5 tons
Weight of load (at 20 tons axle load)	26.5 tons
Type of brake:	KE-GP 10″ with change-over load and handbrake on brakeman's platform
Special equipment:	Combined pneumatic powder-loosening and conveying equipment
Clearance profile:	Limitation II acc. to BO, annex F

Two-axle hopper wagon with pneumatic discharge

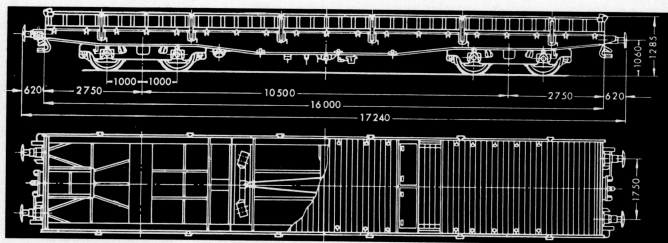

Four-axle universal platform wagon
Length 17 240 mm; Width 2 980 mm; Distance between bogie axles 2 000 mm; Empty weight 24.5 tons; Load weight 55.5 tons

NIIGATA

Niigata Engineering Co. Ltd.

Telegrams: Nite Tokyo
Telephone: Tokyo (03) 504 2111
Telex: 222 7111 NITETOJ

Head Office: 4-1, Kasumigaseki 1 chome, Chiyoda-ku, Tokyo 100, Japan

Managing Director: Mitsugu Shatari

Products: Electric and diesel railcars; diesel-hydraulic locomotives; passenger and freight cars; transit cars.

Constitution: In 1895 Niigata Engineering Co Ltd, was established at Niigata City as Niigata Iron Works of the Nippon Oil Co, Ltd, In 1910 Niigata Iron Works separated from

the Nippon Oil Co, Ltd, and became the present Niigata Engineering Co., Ltd., to manufacture a wide range of heavy industrial machinery. Since then, Niigata has expanded its business to keep pace with the rapidly increased demand of industry.

Sales: Work recently delivered or in hand includes: diesel railcars for Japanese National Railways: diesel-hydraulic locomotives, railcars, passenger and freight for national and private railways and industrial concerns.

Diesel-hydraulic railcar, type KIHA 66 for JNR. This type of car is designed and made for fast, general, commuter or express services

Main features:

Car body	
Length over couplers	21 300 mm
Max width	2 993 mm
Max height	4 077 mm
Distance between bogie centres	14 400 mm
Floor height	1 215 mm
Seating capacity	62
Standing capacity	36
Tare weight	40·7 ton
Type of bogie	
Driving bogie	DT43
Trailing bogie	TR226
Rigid wheel base	2 100 mm
Maximum service speed	95 km/h
Traction diesel engine	
Maker	Niigata Engineering Co Ltd
Type	DML30HSH
Continuous rating	440 PS/1 600 rpm
Hydraulic torque converter	
Maker	Niigata Converter Co Ltd
Type DW9	
Generating diesel engine	Type 4 VK
Continuous rating	90 PS/300 rpm
Brake system	CLE
Capacity of fuel tank	1 500 litres

Electric multiple-unit train, series 1 000 for suburban service.

Main features:

Electric system	1 500 dc
Train formation	M1C M2 TC
Max service speed	90 km/h
Traction motors	100 kw × 4 sets/M
Type of bogie	
Driving bogie	FS395
Trailing bogie	FS095
Rigid wheel base	2 200 mm
Car body	
Length over couplers	20 000 mm
Max width	2 869 mm
Max height	4 140 mm
Distance between bogie centres	13 800 mm
Floor height	1 200 mm

Type of cars	Seating capacity	Tare weight tons
KUMOHA 1000 (M1C)	66	37
MOHA 1200 (M2)	72	36
KUHA 1300 (TC)	66	28
Powering system	Rheostatic control with motor connection and field control	
Brake system	Dynamic brake and electro-magnetic straight air brake	

NIPPON SHARYO

Nippon Sharyo Seizo Kaisha Ltd

Telegrams: Nishiya Nagoya
Telephone: 052 882 3311

Head Office: 1-1, Sanbonmatsu-cho, Atsuta-ku, Nagoya, Japan

Products: Electric and diesel locomotives and railcars; passenger coaches; freight cars.

President: Shunichi Amano
Managing Director: Masakazu Yata

Constitution: The founding of this company in 1896 marked the start of railway rolling stock building in Japan.

Recent sales: Deliveries in 1974 included: 374 freight wagons, 296 electric cars, 74 passenger cars, 75 diesel locomotives for JNR; 7 diesel locomotives for Zaire; 6 diesel locomotives for China; 45 passenger cars for Zambian Railways; 39 electric cars for Korean National Railroad; 50 ammonia tank wagons for Korean General Chemical Corp.

Diesel-hydraulic locomotive for Iraqi Republic Railways
1 435 mm gauge; weight 50 tons

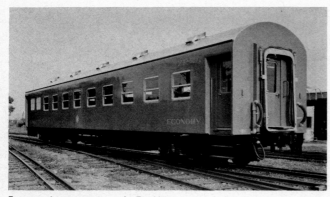

Economy class passenger car for Zambia
1 067 mm gauge; weight 30 tons; accommodation 90 seats

Electric multiple unit train for JNR
For limited express services on dc lines

NOVOCHERKASSK

The Novocherkassk Electric Locomotive Works

Telex: 7565

Sales Office: V/O Energomachexport, 35 Mosfilmovskaya ul, Moscow 117330, USSR

Products: Electric locomotives and railcars.

Recent sales: First batch of 22 electric locomotives ordered by Finnish State Railways was delivered in 1974.

New equipment: The SRI electric locomotive for Finland is designed for hauling freight trains weighing 1 500 to 1 800-tons and passenger trains weighing 600 to 900-tons on lines with upgrades of up to 12.5% with 35-kV, 50-Hz current supply. Operating on alternating current with a contact-line voltage of 22.5 kV, the locomotive develops, within four minutes, a tractive effort of 18 000 kg at a speed of 70 km/h, and 11 000 kg at 100 km/h, while at 140 km/h with no load the tractive effort will be 6 000 kg. Maximum speed of the unit is 140 km/h, though it can be increased to 160 km/h by changing the gear ratio which will bring about a corresponding change in the electric locomotive's tractive capacity. The power of the electric rheostat-type brake is not less than 2 000 kW. The pneumatic system of the brake is of the Knorr type.

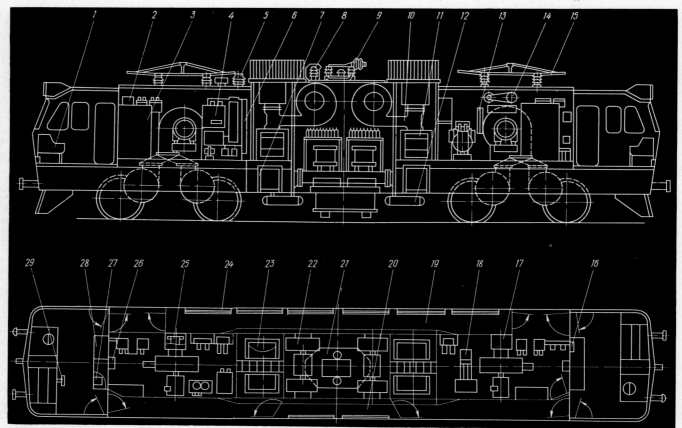

SRI electric locomotive for Finland
Arrangement of the SRI locomotive equipment: 1. control panel; 2. power equipment; 3. air braking equipment; 4. battery charging device; 5. measuring transformer; 6. control panel; 7. smoothing reactor; 8. discharger; 9. master switch; 10. air switch; 11. rectifier; 12. main air holder; 13. exciting rectifier; 14. auxiliary compressor; 15. current collector; 16. wash-basin; 17. centrifugal fan; 18. motor-compressor; 19. larger premix chamber; 20. smaller premix chamber; 21. power transformer; 22. centrifugal fans; 23. braking resistors; 24. air intake louvres; 25. induction shunt; 26. voltage converter for radio communication; 27. radio station; 28. wardrobe; 29. hand brake.
Specifications: Wheel arrangement 2'2'; Track gauge, 1 524 mm; Rated supply voltage 25 000 V; Power one hour of operation 3 280 kW; cruising 3 100 kW; Tractive effort: one hour of operation 15 200 kg; cruising 14 080 kg; Speed: one hour of operation 77.2 km/h; cruising 78.8 km/h; Maximum speed 140 km/h; Axle pressure on the rails 21.5 tons; Brakes pneumatic and electric (rheostat type); Weight 84-tons.

O & K
Orenstein & Koppel AG

Telegrams: RAILWAYS
Telephone: 0231 1921
Telex: 0822 222

Head Office: Karl-Funke-Strasse 30, 4600 Dortmund 1, German Federal Republic

Products: Diesel locomotives; diesel railcars; electric railcars; passenger and freight cars.

Directors:
Dr.-Ing. Helmut Heusler
Dr. Heinz-Günter Kohlen
Dr.-Ing. Alfred Welte

Constitution: The O&K Orenstein & Koppel AG was founded in 1876 at Berlin. The first product of the company was portable and narrow-gauge rail equipment. The manufacture of robust and inexpensive light railway locomotives was the next step. Before the turn of the century O&K began to manufacture standard-gauge locomotives for European and overseas state railways and a whole range of passenger railcars and special wagons for freight traffic. Around 1900 O&K's own construction division was laying railway lines in practically every continent. Between 1903 and 1906, the 600 km long Otavi Railway was planned, built and equipped with rolling stock.

By 1940, 24 000 locomotives had been produced by O&K, 14 000 of these being steam driven and 10 000 being IC-engine powered. Since 1949 the company has manufactured over 80 000 diesel locomotives of all sizes, 10 000 goods wagons, more than 1 000 passenger coaches and about 1 000 railcars for underground and fast suburban services.

Today O&K employs almost 11 000 people who every year produce and sell products worth more than DM 900 million. There are six factories in Germany and two factories abroad as well as 12 subsidiary companies and more than 200 agencies in Europe and overseas.

New Equipment:
Diesel locomotives: within the power range 60-2 200 hp; service ratings of 6-120 tonnes; equipped with diesel-hydraulic or diesel-electric power transmission; two, three, four or six sets of wheels; for all gauges; for shunting or mainline service.
Railcoaches for passenger traffic; diesel-engined railcars and train sets; electric railcars and multiple unit trains; rapid transit underground trains; passenger coaches; dining cars (also in quick pick design); sleeping cars; saloon cars; luggage vans; mail vans.
Wagons for goods traffic: Bottom-discharging wagons, large-body tipping wagons, ore wagons, wagons for steel works, tank wagons, bucket cars, tipping wagons, saddle-back wagons, container wagons, side discharging wagons.

Large saddle-back wagon built for the German Federal Railways, type Fad (00 t), capacity 98 yd³.

Diesel hydraulic locomotive MBB 1200 (720 HP) for shunting service, service weight 90 t, 4-axled B1/B1, built for steel works Hoogovens BV, IJmuiden.

Multiple-unit train for overhead and underground railways of Berlin Transport (BVG), short-coupled double units, made of light metal, service weight 38 t.

OMS
Officina Meccanica della Stanga

Telegrams: Officinastanga Padua
Telephone: Padua 76 04 88
Telex: 43218

Head Office and Works: Corso Stati Uniti, 35100 Padua, Italy

Products: Electric and diesel railcars and multiple unit trainsets; passenger cars; freight wagons.

Chairman: Dr Dino Marchiorello
Managing Director: Ing Aldo Iaia

Production Director: Dr Ing. Antonio Romano

Sales: Sales in 1973 included: 100 Taes wagons for Italian State Railways (FS); 85 Habis sliding side wagons for FS; 29 ABzx passenger coaches for FS; four narrow-gauge rail cars for the Circumetnea Railway; six axle wagons for Italsider.

ORTNER
Ortner Freight Car Company

Telephone: 871 2600

Head Office: 2652 Erie Avenue, Cincinnati, Ohio 45208, USA

Products: Freight wagons and components.

President: Robert C. Ortner

New equipment: In addition to building standard flat, open and covered gondola and

hopper cars, the Company designs and builds cars for special application. Recent deliveries of special cars have been primarily open top hopper cars with unique Rapid Discharge door arrangement for the unloading of difficult-to-clear bulk materials such as coal, wood chips, etc. The wood chip cars are built in various cubic capacities, up to 7 000 ft³ (198 m³). The coal cars are used in unit train service where quick turn-round is essential. Doors can be operated mechanically or can be equipped to be opened automatically upon wayside signal.

ORVAL
Ateliers de Matériel Ferroviaire d'Orval

Telephone: 870 82 50
Telex: 62645

Head Office: 53, ave Paul-Doumer, 75016 Paris, France

Products: Freight wagons.

President: Jacques Marret
General Manager: Jacques Lafin
Commercial Manager: Philippe Gautier

Constitution: Founded in 1945, the company designs and builds wagons for the transport and ease of loading and unloading of heavy products, powders, liquids, for the oil, chemical, food, forestry, steel and other industries—hopper and covered hopper cars, tank cars, open cars, flat cars, tippers, special cars. The company holds the licence for the Spitzer system of air discharge of powdered products.

PAFAWAG
P.F.W. Pafawag

Telephone: 340 61
Telex: 034431

Head Office: Panstwowa Fabryka Wagonow Pafawag 53-609 Wroclaw ul. Robotnicza 12, Poland

Constitution: Member of Kolmex Foreign Trade Enterprise.

Type 201E (EU22) standard-gauge electric locomotive
One-hour rating 3 120 kW (4 230 hp); Continuous rating 3 000 kW; Axle arrangement Co-Co; Weight in working order 120 Mg; Maximum speed 34,8 m/s (125 km/h); Continuous speed 56 km/h; Maximum starting tractive effort 41 160 daN (42 000 kg); Distance between bogie pivots 10 300 mm; Wheel diameter 1 250 mm; Length over buffers 19 240 mm; Height with lowered pantograph 4 456 mm; Traction motors Six motors Type EE 5416; Power transmission Unilateral gear drive; Motor suspension fully suspended; Gear ratio 79:18 = 4.39; Brake Oerlikon air-brake; Brake compressor Two 1 700 l/min compressor units: Heating and lighting electric.

PAKISTAN RAILWAY CARRIAGE
Pakistan Railway Carriage Factory

Telephone: 67256, 67260
Telegrams: CARFAC ISLAMABAD

Head Office: P.O. Box 286, Rawalpindi, Islamabad, Pakistan

Products: Passenger coaches; freight wagons.

Chairman: Crulzar Ahmed
Managing Director: M. Raschid
Sales Director: Z. I. Puri

PERRY
Perry Engineering Company Ltd.
(A member of Johns-Perry Group)

Telegrams: SPERRY, Adelaide
Telephone: 352 1777
Telex: AA 82493

Head Office: Railway Terrace, Mile End South, 5031 South Australia

Products: Railway rolling stock.

Chairman: D. H. Laidlaw
General Manager: L. G. Rowe

Constitution: In 1966, Perry Engineering Co. Ltd., merged with Johns and Waygood Holdings Ltd. of Melbourne, to form the Johns-Perry Group, and so became part of an Australia-wide structural, mechanical and electrical engineering business with over 5 000 employees.

PETRU GROZA

Telephone: 14 94 30
Telex: 216

Head Office: 7 Matei Millo St, Bucharest, Romania

Products: Mine wagons of 0.75-1 and 1.2 m³ capacity; tipping wagons of 0.36 and 0.4

m³ capacity; mineral wagons of 1.5 m³ capacity; self-discharge VA-3 wagons of 3 m³ capacity.

Rail tank wagon completed by Perry in 1977 for Australian petroleum transport
A chassis-less design, of steel construction, single compartment, 1.435 m gauge;
70 000 litres capacity, 76 tonnes gross.

PIAGGIO

Industrie Aeronautiche e Meccaniche Rinaldo Piaggio SpA
The Company stopped building railway equipment in December 1973.

PLYMOUTH

Plymouth Locomotive Works
A Banner Industries Inc Company

Head Office: Bell St, Plymouth, Ohio 44865, USA

Products: Diesel-hydraulic locomotives for heavy-duty hauling and switching ranging from 3-120 tons. "Mine-O-Motive" mining locomotive.

Managing Director: Miles W. Christian

Telegrams: Fateco
Telephone: (419) 687 4641
Telex: 810 491 2550

Sales Director: Beecher Caudill
Export Sales: John Dick

Equipment: "Mine-O-Motive" range of mines locomotive cover:— HSD series 1½-10 tons, F series 5-7½ tons, D series 8-16 tons, J series 12-35 tons, M series 25-45 tons.

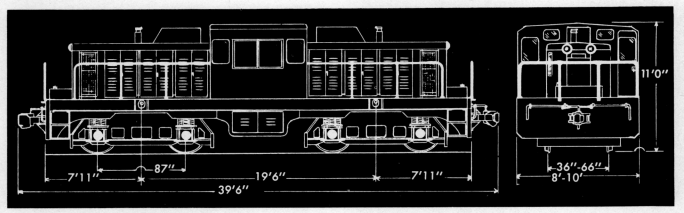

CR-8—45 to 65 tons—36 in to 66 in gauge
Plymouth's CR-8 model is an 8-wheel (double truck) diesel hydraulic locomotive with cardan shaft final drive. Dual engines power the 45 to 65 ton unit with total horsepower ranging from 400 to 1 000. The CR-8 can be built to operate on gauges 36 in to 66 in. (A separate CR-8XT Series is available in weights from 70 to 120 tons).

These locomotives can be built with various engine and drive component combinations, all of which effect speed, power and tractive effort. Haulage capacity is contingent upon locomotive weight, horsepower developed, adhesion factors, track and roadbed conditions.

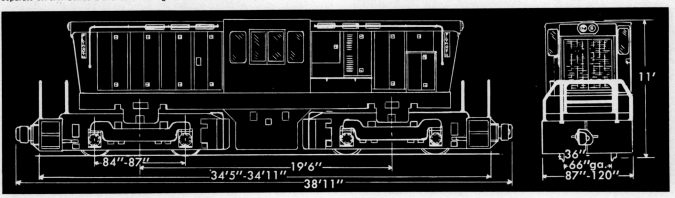

CR-8XT—70 to 120 tons—36 in to 66 in Gauge
The Plymouth CR-8XT with "XT" standing for "extra Tonnage"—"extra Power"—"extra Performance". This is the heavyweight in Plymouth's diversified line of locomotives. Weights from 70 to 120 tons; gauges 36 in to 66 in. The CR-8XT is a dual engine, 8-wheel (double truck), diesel hydraulic locomotive with cardan shaft final drive. The total horsepower range is from 650 to 1 400. (A separate CR-8 Series is

available in weights 45 to 65 tons).
These locomotives can be built with various engine and drive component combinations, all of which effect speed, power and tractive effort. Haulage capacity is contingent upon locomotive weight, horsepower developed, adhesion factors, track and roadbed conditions.

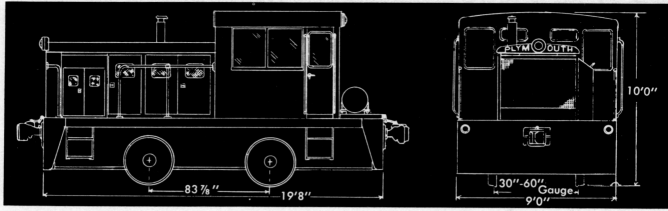

M-Series—25 to 45 tons—30 in to 66 in gauge

The Plymouth M-Series (4-wheel) and W-Series (6-wheel) locomotives are available in weights from 25 to 45 tons, gauges 30 in to 66 in. These units are very versatile and powerful enough for almost any type of industrial or similar application. They also have multiple unit capability as well as remote control operation if so desired.

These locomotives can be built with various engine and drive component combinations, all of which affect speed, power and tractive effort. Haulage capacity is contingent upon locomotive weight, horsepower developed and adhesion factors such as track and roadbed conditions.

PORTER

H. K. Porter-France SA
(The French subsidiary of Porter has ceased activities)

Telegrams: Aciemarpent Paris
Telephone: 359 55 79
Telex: Portmar Paris 29061

PRICE

A. & G. Price Ltd

Telegrams: PRICECO THAMES
Telephone: Thames 34
Telex: 2655

Head Office: Beach Road, Thames, New Zealand
Private Bag—Thames

Products: Diesel-hydraulic, diesel-mechanical and battery locomotives; freight wagons.

Managing Director: R. S. O'Hagan
Resident Manager: J. W. Wiseman

Constitution: This company stems from a foundry and workshop set up at Onehunga near Auckland in 1868 by two brothers, Alfred and George Price. Their first connection

with railways was the supply of undergear and carriage bodies for the new Auckland-Drury Railway in 1872. The Thames works was opened in 1870 and four years later the Onehunga works was closed down, all operations being concentrated at Thames. The first locomotive, a geared type, was built in 1883 for a gold mine, then in 1903, five years after the railway reached Thames, Price began building locomotives for the NZR and continued to do so until 1928 when their last order was completed following a decision by NZR to build all locomotives in Railway workshops.

Sales: In recent years the company has produced over 70 diesel-mechanical and diesel-hydraulic locomotives for NZR and private users.

PROCOR

Procor Limited, Rail Car Division

Telephone: Toronto (416) 362 2641
Telex: 06 98 2241

Head Office: 2001 Speers Rd., Oakville, Ontario L6J 5E1, Canada

Products: Freight wagons.

Chairman: S. H. Bonser
President and Chief Executive Officer: K. Jagger

Vice President, Sales: Gordon C. Mills

Constitution: Procor's Rail Car Division designs and manufactures tank cars and freight cars for a great variety of products, for lease to shippers in Canada and the UK. Procor operates and maintains the largest fleet of railway freight cars (well over 10 000) in Canada.

Vacuum pneumatic wagon for plastic pellet service.

This new Procor car will carry 5 838 ft³ of product. To ensure product purity, the car was designed so that no product would be trapped inside the car after unloading, and the interior was also sprayed with epoxy. Loading is completed through the ten top weather-tight hatch covers. The product is unloaded through the bottom of the four hoppers using a tube connector to a plant-based compressor. The compressor vacuums the pellets through this tube and then blows them into storage bins.

Dual flow wagon of unusual structural design
Will unload powdered products by either pressure discharge or air assisted gravity discharge. The car has a product carrying capacity of one hundred tons and will operate at a pressure of up to 30 psi.

PROCOR (UK) LIMITED

Telephone: (0924) 271881
Telex: Procor Horbury 556457

Head Office: Horbury Wagon Works, Horbury Junction, Wakefield, West Yorkshire, WF4 5QH, England

Products: Railway Freight Rolling Stock.

Managing Director: F. J. Swindell
Financial Controller: G. B. Reast
Director of Sales: J. K. Jagger

Constitution: Procor (UK) Limited, a wholly owned subsidiary of the Trans Union Corporation, Chicago designs, builds, sells, hires, leases, repairs and maintains all types of railway freight rolling stock. With a fleet of over 3 000 wagons, Procor is the largest wagon hiring company in the UK and has customers in the petroleum, chemical, food and construction Industries.

New Equipment: Two train sets of 102 tonne gross laden weight bogie tank wagons for Class 'A' petroleum products. The non cylindrical barrels mounted on cradles and stub underframes each have a gross capacity of over a 100 000 litres. Works vehicles for the Tyne and Wear Passenger Transport Executive comprising bogie flat and hopper ballast wagons. Liquified petroleum gas wagons with a payload of 40·7 tonnes of propane and 48·1 tonnes of butane.

83 ton gross laden weight liquified petroleum gas wagon

50 ton gross laden weight aggregate hopper wagon

50 ton gross laden weight pressure flow pressure discharge wagon

PULLMAN-STANDARD
Division of Pullman Incorporated

Telephone: (312) 322 7070

Head Office: 200 S. Michigan Ave, Chicago, Illinois 60604, USA

Products: Freight and passenger cars of all types.

President: J. A. McDivitt
Executive Vice President: E. T. Ahnquist
Executive Vice President and General Manager, Freight: R. A. Cumming
Executive Vice President and General Manager, Passenger: C. M. Parrish
Senior Vice President, Marketing, Freight: Stanley Brown
Vice President, Marketing, Passenger: T. W. Fenske
International Affairs: T. C. Nault (Freight)

Constitution: In 1867 George M. Pullman formed Pullman's Palace Car Company to build and operate sleeping cars, the name being changed to the Pullman Company in 1899. In 1921 the Haskell & Barker Car Company, founded in 1852, was acquired and three years later the various car-building activities were consolidated in a new company— Pullman Car & Manufacturing Corporation. In 1927 Pullman Incorporated was formed as the parent company with two main subsidiaries, The Pullman Company operating sleeping cars, and Pullman Car and Manufacturing Corp building cars. In 1934 the latter was merged with Standard Steel Car Company (acquired in 1930) to form Pullman-Standard Car Manufacturing Company. Then in 1959 this company merged into Pullman Incorporated as Pullman-Standard Division. Pursuant to a Federal Court order requiring separation of sleeping car operation and the manufacture of railroad cars, in 1947 Pullman Incorporated sold the Pullman Company to a group of railroads.

113 m³ (4 000 ft³) capacity triple hopper wagons

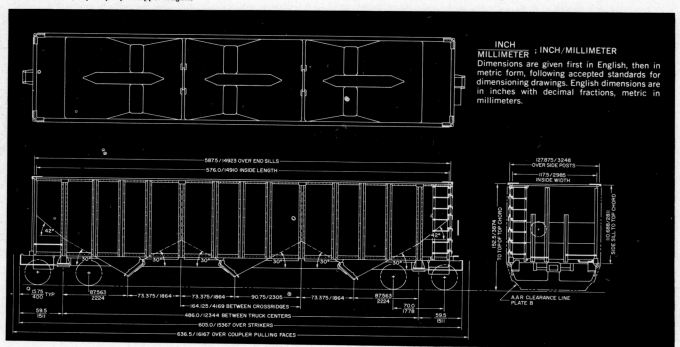

INCH/MILLIMETER
Dimensions are given first in English, then in metric form, following accepted standards for dimensioning drawings. English dimensions are in inches with decimal fractions, metric in millimeters.

100-ton capacity general service gondola (above and below)

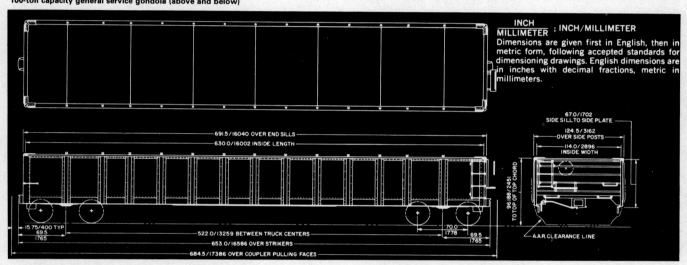

INCH/MILLIMETER ; INCH/MILLIMETER

Dimensions are given first in English, then in metric form, following accepted standards for dimensioning drawings. English dimensions are in inches with decimal fractions, metric in millimeters.

R-46 transit cars being built for subway and elevated services on the New York City Transit Authority Lines

RAMON MUGICA
Herederos de Ramon Mugica SA

Head Office: Barrio de Ventas, s/n Apartado No 14, Irun, Spain

Products: Special wagons to customer's requirements: tank cars, hopper cars, flat cars, bulk powder cars, low-bed type cars, etc.

Telegrams: HEREM
Telephone: 61 34 45
Telex: 36 195 Herem E

Chairman: Juan O. Ohlsson
Managing Director: Francisco Mauleón
Chief Mechanical Engineer: José R. Jusué
Assistant Manager: Inigo Saldāna

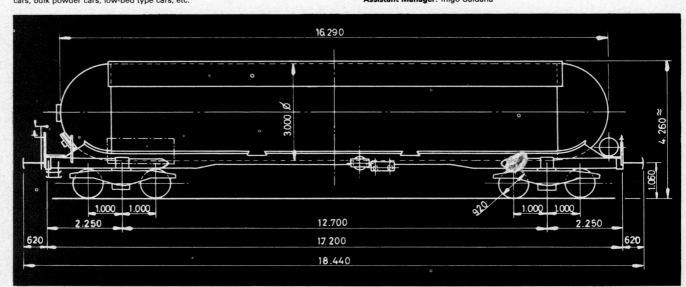

Tank wagon for anhydrous ammonia (above and below)
Tare weight 35 000 kg; maximum load 45 000 kg

RANZI
SpA Ranzi-Legnano

Head Office: Viale Cadorna 34-40, 20025 Legnano, Italy

Products: Diesel shunting and line service locomotives from 100 hp to 750 hp.

Telegrams: RANZI, Legnano
Telephone: 54 87 54

Sales: In addition to locomotives for Italy, 50 have been delivered to India, Central and South America.

REGGIANE
Officine Meccaniche Italiano SpA

Head Office: 27 Via Vasco Agosti, Reggio Emilia, Italy

Products: Electric, diesel-electric, diesel-hydraulic and diesel-mechanical locomotives, railcars, passenger, pilot, dining, sleeping, saloon cars; freight wagons rolling stock components.

Chairman: Avv. Prof Crisanto Moandrioli
Managing Director: Dr Ing. Pietro Fascione

Telegrams: Reggiane
Telephone: 41341, 41741
Telex: 51265 Reggiane

Administrative Manager: Rag. Gino Rovegno

Sales Manager: Dr Ing. Edmondo Del Cupolo

Constitution: Founded in 1904 to build rolling stock and, a few years later, steam locomotives. After being largely destroyed during the war the works were rebuilt and re-equipped.

REMAFER
Soc. de Construction et de Réparation de Matériel Ferroviaire

Head Office: 3 rue Christophe Colomb, 75008 Paris, France

Telephone: 29 04 71
Telex: (1) 723 76 51

Products: Rolling stock.

RESITA
Resita Machine Building Works

Head Office: 7, Matei Millo St, Bucharest, Romania

Telephone: 14 84 30
Telex: 216

Products: Diesel-electric and diesel-hydraulic locomotives.

RIGA
Riga Carriage Building Works

Head Office: Riga, USSR

Products: Motive power and rolling stock.

Constitution: Member of Energomachexport.

New equipment: The ER-200 built at the Riga Carriage Building Works, is designed for fast passenger transport between large Soviet industrial and administrative centres, primarily Moscow and Leningrad.
The basic formation of the electric train consists of six two-car power sets—provided

with a common traction unit and one current collector—with an unmotored head-end car at each end. Variations in the basic formation are possible using two to six two-car power units.

The development of a high-speed train designed for travelling at a speed of 200 km/h is a complicated task. It is therefore not surprising that specialists of many institutes, plants, construction and designing organisations took part in the creation of the first Soviet express.

Interior. The interior lay-out provides for one passenger saloon in each car, as well as the necessary auxiliary equipment. Motor car saloons seat 64 passengers and the head-end cars are fitted with a refreshment bar and passenger saloon accommodating 24 passengers. Saloons are furnished with soft two-seated chairs with collapsible backs which give the passenger a choice of three tilting positions. Seats are fitted with a swivel device to alter the direction of travel.

The cars are provided with air-conditioning and so, even if the temperature outside is 32 degrees C above zero, inside the car the mercury column will not rise above 20-22 degrees C. In winter the electrical heating automatically maintains a temperature of 18-20 degrees C in the passenger saloon while outside the air temperature is 40 degrees C below zero.

Adjustment of the braking force during braking from 200 km/h to train stoppage is attained firstly by a smooth increase of the motor excitation current, and then by gradual disconnection of the brake rheostat stages with smooth interstage regulation. During electrical braking energy is quenched in blowout resistances. In order to brake the train before stoppage, the electro-pneumatic disc brake is set on the rheostat brake at travel speed of approximately 35 km/h. At full service braking, which is carried out at a travel speed of 200 km/h with simultaneous action of the rheostat and disc brakes, a braking distance of 2 100 m is secured.

For emergency braking it is necessary to additionally switch in the magnetic rail brake, after which the braking distance for a speed of 200 km/h is reduced to 1 600 m. Starting and braking is controlled along train conductors leading from the head car cabin either directly by aid of the driver's controller or by the automatic 'autodriver' train control system which automates all train travel controls.

The 'Autodriver' consists of two devices each of which is set up in one of the head cars. For greater reliability both may be operated simultaneously, when the circuit excludes the possibility of issuing differing commands. After reception of information from the head car sensor on travel speed and passed distance, the 'Autodriver' maintains the prefixed speed with a precision of up to ±5 km/h and acts on the internal automatic system of the motor cars, for which purpose it automatically switches in traction brakes.

Braking is controlled by automatic cab signalling (ACS) which is the basic system providing traffic safety. In case of necessity, the ACS system cancels all commands issued by the driver or 'Autodriver' and brings into action train braking.

Driving car body design was result of extensive aerodynamic testing at the Moscow Institute of Mechanics

Technical details

Gauge	1.524 m
Top speed	200 km/h
Basic train formation	14 cars
Number of seats	816
Train tare weight	830 tons
Axle load	17 tons
Length of 14-car train	372 m
Length of car	26 m
Width of car	3.080 m
Distance between bogie centres	18.8 m
Bogie base	2.5 m
Power	10 320 kW

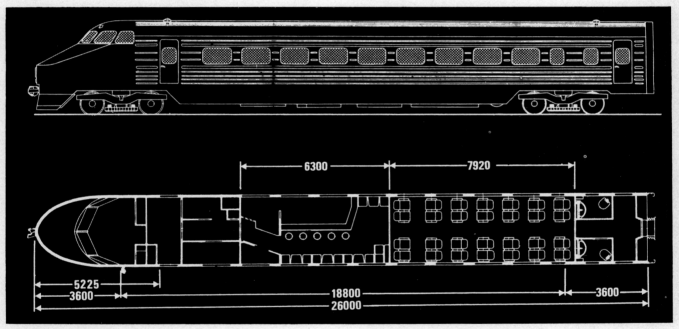

Driving car saloons seat 24 passengers

ROBERTS

Charles Roberts & Co Ltd

Head Office: Horbury Junction, Wakefield, England

Products: Railway wagons and tank wagons, and their components.

Subsidiary Companies: Blenheim Engineering Co, Ltd
S. J. Claye Ltd
Tank Rentals Ltd
R. Murfitt Ltd
W. P. Butterfield (Engineers) Ltd

Director and Group General Manager: A. D. Stark, C.A.
Secretary: A. Griffiths
Director and General Manager: F. Stothard
Technical Manager: G. L. Hart
Sales Manager: G. Purchon
Rail Chief Designer: J. England

Telegrams: Roberts, Horbury
Telephone: Horbury 4681
Telex: 55-242

Constitution: The Company was established in 1856, and has, over the ensuing period, designed and built wagons of all types for all parts of the world.

Sales: Recent deliveries and orders on hand include 100-ton GLW bogie hopper wagons, 90-ton LP gas cars, 50-ton hopper wagons, 50 ton Class A and cement wagons.

New equipment: 100-ton gross laden weight wagons marketed by Charles Roberts include four basic types; a bogie powder wagon; steam cooled and insulated bogie tank wagon; bogie tank for transport of nitric acid; and bogie tank for transport of liquefied oxygen and nitrogen.

The 60 ft (18.2 m) tank unit for hauling liquefied oxygen and nitrogen measures 8 ft 10 in wide (2.69 m); 12 ft 11 in high (3.95 m); has an unladen weight of 44 tons and capacity of 56 tons. Bogies are cast steel three-piece type, mark IV lightweight Gloucester units fitted with Timken axleboxes and Girling disc brakes. Also included are air-powered caliper sets actuated by Westinghouse compressed-air control gear.

ROHR

Rohr Industries Inc.

Head Office: Chula Vista, California 92012, USA

Products: Electric multiple units; rolling stock.
(Rohr has discontinued railway equipment manufacture)

Telephone: (714) 426 7111

Chairman: Burt F. Raynes
President: Fred W. Garry
Export Sales: William J. Bird

RUHRTHALER
Ruhrthaler Maschinenfabrik, Schwar & Dyckerhoff KG

Telegrams: RUHRTALOKO, Mülheimruhr
Telephone: 0208/44131
Telex: 0856710

Head Office: Scheffelstrasse 14-28, D-4330 Mülheim/Ruhr, German Federal Republic

Products: Diesel-hydraulic; diesel-mechanical locomotives; suspended monorail.

Hauling capacities and principal details of Ruhrthaler diesel mine locomotives

Type		G 22 H 2	G 30 H 2	G 40 H 2	G 50 H 2	G 50 H/St	G 70 H 2	G 70 HVE	G 100 HVE	G 150 HVE
Throttled capacity for underground operation	HP	23	28,5	40	58	55	70	70	100	134
	r p m	2600	3000	2800	2550	2400	2550	2400	2000	1800
Continuous capacity „B" DIN 6270 for surface operation	HP	30	30	45	64	64	105	105	158	158
	r p m	3000	3000	3000	2600	2600	2600	2600	1800	1800
Number of cylinders		2	2	3	4	4	6	6	6	6
Speed, infinitely variable	km/h	0...10,8	0...12,5	0...14	0...17,2	0...17,2	0...15,6	0...14,4	0...14,4	0...14,4
Draw bar pull	kp	970–395	1090–440	1330–515	1700–555	1700–550	2420–760	2420–880	3390–1300	3890–1790
Loads hauled, in tons / Rolling resistance 8 kp/ton (against a gradient of)	on the level 1:∞	121 – 49	136 – 55	166 – 64	212 – 70	212 – 69	302 – 95	302 – 110	423 – 162	484 – 212
	½% 1:400	91 – 36	103 – 41	125 – 48	160 – 51	160 – 50	228 – 70	228 – 81	320 – 120	365 – 165
	½% 1:200	73 – 29	82 – 32	100 – 37	127 – 40	127 – 40	182 – 55	182 – 64	255 – 94	291 – 130
	¾% 1:133⅓	60 – 23	66 – 26	83 – 30	106 – 32	106 – 32	151 – 44	151 – 52	211 – 77	242 – 107
	1% 1:100	51 – 19	58 – 22	71 – 25	90 – 27	90 – 27	129 – 37	129 – 43	180 – 64	206 – 90
Length over buffers	mm	3200	3200	3850	4000	4000	4650	4950	5500	5600
Min. length for transport approx.	mm	2800	2800	2450	2700	2700	3200	2800	3100	3115
Width	mm	850	850	900	900	900	1000	930	1050	1050
Height	mm	1400	1400	1500	1600	1600	1600	1650	1650	1650
Wheel base	mm	750	750	900	1000	1000	1100	1100	1350	1350
Radius of smallest curve	m	8	8	10	10	10	12	12	15	15
Service weight ± 5 %	kg	4000	4500	5500	7000	7000	10000	10000	14000	16000
Empty weight ± 5 %	kg	3850	4350	5300	6750	6750	9700	9700	13700	15700
Shipping weight ± 5%	kg	3950	4450	5400	6850	6850	9800	9800	13800	15800
Shipping dimensions	m	3,1x0,9x1,5	3,1x0,9x1,5	3,7x1x1,6	4x1x1,7	4x1x1,7	4,4x1,1x1,7	4,8x1x1,8	5,1x1,1x1,8	5,2x1,1x1,8

Type		D 24 H 2	D 30 H 2	D 45 H 2	D 60 H 2	D 60 H	D 100 H 2	D 150 H	D 175 HL
Continuous capacity „B" DIN 6270	HP	26	30	45	60	60	105	150	175
	r.p.m.	3000	3000	3000	3000	2250	2600	1800	1800
Number of cylinders		2	2	3	4	4	6	6	10V
Speed, infinitely variable	km/h	0...12,5	0...12,5	0...15	0...15	0...16,5	0...16,5	0...20	0...20
Draw bar pull	kp	970–390	1090–455	1330–560	1570–775	1700–650	2420–1230	3870–1420	3870–1650
Loads hauled, in tons / Rolling resistance 8 kp/ton (against a gradient of)	on the level 1:∞	121 – 49	136 – 57	166 – 70	196 – 96	212 – 82	302 – 154	484 – 178	484 – 206
	½% 1:200	73 – 28,5	82 – 33	100 – 41	118 – 57	128 – 48	182 – 91	292 – 103	292 – 121
	1% 1:100	51 – 19,5	58 – 23	71 – 28	83 – 39	90 – 32	129 – 63	206 – 70	206 – 83
	2% 1:50	33 – 11	36 – 13	43 – 16	51 – 23	56 – 18	79 – 37	127 – 39	127 – 48
	3% 1:33⅓	22 – 7	25 – 8	30 – 10	35 – 15	39 – 12	56 – 24	89 – 25	89 – 31
Length over buffers	mm	2900	3000	3600	3700	3700	4500	5300	5300
Width	mm	1200	1200	1200	1200	1200	1700	1700	1800
Height	mm	2000	2000	2200	2200	2200	2800	3000	3000
Wheel base	mm	750	750	1000	1000	1000	1100	1350	1350
Radius of smallest curve	m	8	8	15	15	15	15	15	15
Service weight ± 5 %	kg	4000	4500	5500	6500	7000	10000	16000	16000
Empty weight ± 5 %	kg	3800	4300	5300	6250	6750	9750	15750	15750
Shipping weight ± 5% kg		3900	4400	5400	6350	6850	9850	15850	15850
Shipping dimensions	m	2,7x1,2x2,1	2,7x1,2x2,1	3,3x1,2x2,3	3,4x1,2x2,3	3,4x1,2x2,3	4,3x1,7x2,9	4,9x1,7x3,1	4,9x1,8x3,1

Estimated co-efficient of friction between wheel and rail $\mu = 0,25$. Details for 600 mm track gauge

---

SANTA MATILDE
Cia Industrial Santa Matilde

Telephone: 252 6090
Telex: (021) 21042

Head Office: Rua Buenos Aires No 100-7° Rio de Janeiro, CP 1854, Brazil

Products: Passenger coaches; freight wagons; Containers.

Refrigerated wagon delivered to Fepasa of Brazil in 1976 by Santa Matilda: tare weight 27 300 kg; gauge 1.0 m

Tank wagon for cement transport. Client: Ciminas-Cimento Nacional de Minas. Gauge 1.60 m; capacity 65 m³; tare weight 25 530 kg

Box Wagon for Brazilian Federal Railways (RFFSA) supplied by Santa Matilde in 1977: gauge 1.60 m; capacity 100 tonnes; tare weight 28 000 kg

Special caboose wagon built for ICOMI of Brazil by Santa Matilde: tare weight 17 000 kg; gauge 1.435 m.

SCANDIA
Scandia-Randers A/S

Head Office: Udbyhøjvej 66, PO Box 200, DK-8900 Randers, Denmark

Telegrams: Scandia Randers
Telephone: Randers (06) 42 53 00
Telex: 65145 scanas dk

Products: Passenger and freight cars; electric railcars; railbuses.

SCHLIEREN
Swiss Car and Elevator Manufacturing Corp Ltd, Schlieren-Zürich, Switzerland

Head Office: CH-8952 Schlieren, Switzerland

President of Management: Hans Rudolf Haller
Director, Rolling Stock: Pierre Matthey
Director, Works: Max Gröbly

Constitution: The company was formed in 1899 for the manufacture of rolling stock, an elevator department being started in 1917.

Telegrams: SCHLIECO Schlieren
Telephone: 01/730 70 11
Telex: 52961 SWS ch

Products: Passenger coaches, motor coaches and driving trailers in all-welded steel light-weight and in light alloy design; day-cum-sleeper coaches; car transport vehicles, motor luggage cars; wagon bogies for freight liner trains, motor and trailer bogies for all types of rolling stock; streetcars, articulated twin streetcars; lifting jacks for rail- and road vehicles as well as for big containers.

Sales: Passenger coaches type RIC and trailer bogies for the Swiss Federal Railways; motor cars, passenger coaches, motor and trailer bogies for inland traffic; double motor car units for suburban lines; lifting jacks.

RIC railway passenger coach
Second class, type X, for international traffic, built for the Swiss Federal Railways (SBB) to UIC-specifications. With eleven compartments with six seats each

Track recording car A-461
For the Société Nationale de Transports Ferroviaires, Algeria; for standard gauge (1 435 mm); measuring equipment manufactured by Matisa SA (Canron Railgroup), Crissier, Switzerland, and lodged in separate compartment with optimal insulation

Articulated twin railcar Be 8/8
For the Forch Railway, Zurich (Switzerland); with two drivers' cabins and passenger compartments first and second class; with four motor bogies supplied by Schindler Carriage and Wagon Comp. Ltd, Pratteln, and electric traction equipment supplied by Brown Boveri & Co Ltd

Articulated twin streetcar, type Be 4/6
Of the Transport Authority of the City of Zurich. All-electric car. Electric traction equipment built by Brown Boveri & Co Ltd. Motor and trailer bogies supplied by Schindler Carriage and Wagon Co Ltd

SCHINDLER

Schindler Carriage & Wagon Co Ltd

Telegrams: SCHINDLERWAGON
Telephone: (061) 81 55 11
Telex: 62386

Head Office: CH-4133 Pratteln, near Basle, Switzerland

Products: Electric and diesel railcars; passenger and freight cars.

Managing Director: P. Piffaretti
Managers: H. Knecht
          M. Corneille
          K. Harnisch (Sales)

Sales: Recent deliveries and work in hand include 12 first and second class coaches for the Jamaica Railway Corp in stainless steel; 18 passenger coaches, airconditioned for the Saudi Government Railroad (8 second class; 4 first class; 3 dining cars; 3 power-luggage vans); express mail cars for the Mexican State Railways; motor bogies for electric trains for the Portuguese State Railways; electric trains for the Bex-Villars-Bretaye Railway (Switzerland); driving trailers for the CEV (Chemins de fer électriques Veveysans); articulated tramcars for the BLT (Baselland Transport AG); motor and trailer bogies to articulated tramcars for VBZ (Verkehrsbetriebe der Stadt Zürich); Flexicoil type trailer bogies for standard passenger cars for the Rhaetian Railways; luggage cars for Swiss Federal Railways; passenger car bogies type SWP-71 for different kinds of rolling stock for Swiss Federal Railways; Covered wagons with sliding sidewalls (two axled wagons).

SCHOMA

Christoph Schöttler Maschinenfabrik GmbH

Telegrams: SCHÖMA, Diepholz
Telephone: Diepholz (05441) 2047/2048
Telex: 09 41217

Head Office: Postfach 128, 2840 Diepholz 1, German Federal Republic, 128

Manager: Ing. Fritz Schöttler

Products: Shunting, narrow gauge and mining locomotives with hydrodynamic, hydrostatic or mechanical transmission; gang trolleys; trailers and diesel railcars.

Equipment: Schoma locomotives are powered by water or aircooled diesel engines of reputable manufacture. Hydrodynamic or hydrostatic transmission is used in most of the locomotives, while mechanical transmission can be supplied optionally for less-powerful narrow gauge, or mining locomotives, if required. Power is transmitted by propeller-shafts to the axle gears.
Final drive consists of: cast steel axle boxes with vertical torque supports, bevel gears and pinions with spiral teeth (Gleason or Klingelnberg system) running in anti-friction bearings. Oil seals, mounted on hard ground wear-rings fitted on the axles, or labyrinth packings are used. Lubrication is splash type. Oil levels are checked by sight glasses. The final drive, which is highly efficient, does not need any maintenance apart from oil changing.

Frame is of box type fabricated steel, reinforced with additional cross stays to counteract torsional effects. The front plates are strengthened to take bumping shocks. Inspection holes are cut into side plates to provide accessibility for maintenance and repair purposes. The frame is suspended either by laminated springs or by trapezoidally arranged rubber-metal springs. Mechanically or pneumatically operated sand gear is applied to the leading axle in both directions of travel. The sand boxes are fitted with water-proof covers. All locomotives can be fitted with closed cabins with rubber supported windows of security glass giving a good aspect in both directions. Heat and noise isolated cab can be provided if specified.
The main controls are dually arranged and all the other instruments are so arranged that they are within easy reach of the driver from any position. Remote controls can be supplied if required.
Light locomotives are provided with screw type brakes which act on all wheels. In locos with hydrostatic transmission the main braking is through the hydrostatic drive. In heavy locomotives a pressurised direct air brake system is provided. Indirect train air brake can be fitted if required.

Schoma cardan-shaft shunting locomotive (230 hp, 28 tonnes, 1.435 m gauge)

Schoma diesel mining locomotive

SECHERON

SA des Ateliers de Sécheron

Telegrams: Electricité Geneva
Telephone: (022) 32 67 50
Telex: 22130 SAAG CH

Head Office: 14 avenue de Sécheron, 1202 Geneva 21, Switzerland

Products: Complete electrical equipment for electric and diesel-electric locomotives, railcars, multiple-unit trainsets, trolleybuses and streetcars; wheel flange lubricators; earthing brushes; manual and automatic couplers; dc circuit breakers; complete dc substations.

General Manager: C. Rossier
Sales Manager: A. Reymond
Manager, Traction Division: H. Hintze
Deputy Manager, Traction Division: R. Germanier

Constitution: Member of the Brown Boveri Group. The company was founded as **A. de Meuron & Cuenod** for the manufacture of electrical equipment and in 1883 was awarded a diploma for a two-pole generator shown at the Swiss National Exhibition at Zurich. In 1884 the first power transmission was carried out, and by 1891 a total of 35 power transmission installations and 40 power stations had been completed. By this time the name had been changed to **Compagnie de l'Industrie Electrique et Mecanique.** In the traction field, the electrical equipment for a number of tramways and railways had been supplied when in 1903 the first application of high voltage to electric traction was effected to the metre-gauge St. Georges de Commiers-La Mure Railway (2 400 V).

Sales: Sécheron has recently supplied electrical thyristor equipment for 3 000 hp locomotives for the Swiss Federal Railways and the first thyristor equipments for the rack railway of Brig-Visp-Zermatt. In 1976 Sécheron supplied the electronic equipment for the new two-car Sprinters built by Waggonfabrik Talbot for Netherlands Railways (NS).

SEMAF

Société Générale Egyptienne de Matériel des Chemins de Fer

Telegrams: SEMAF, Cairo
Telephone: 38715
Telex: 2364 ORIP. U.N.

Head Office: Ein Helwan, Cairo, Egypt

Products: Railcar trailers; passenger coaches; freight wagons.

Chairman: Eng. F. Abu Zaghla

Technical Director: Eng. H. F. Babyoomy
Commercial Manager: Eng. F. El-Barkouky

SGI

Societá Gestioni Industriali SpA

Telephone: 72 918/72 787

Head Office: 62012 Civitanova Marche, Italy

Products: Passenger and freight cars of all types, pressure tank cars for compressed gas and acids; refrigerator cars; special tanks for motor vehicles.

Manager: dott. Giuseppe Manni
          dott. Ing. Giorgio Caputo

Constitution: In August 1957 SGI took over the business of **Costruzioni Meccaniche A. Cecchetti,** which had been wound up in the previous April after having been operating since 1892.

SIAM DI TELLA

Siam di Tella Ltda (Division Electromecanica)

Telegrams: SIAMLECTRI
Telephone: 651 0020/9
Telex: 012 1046

Head Office: Derqui 1868, San Justo, Buenos Aires, Argentina

Products: Electrical equipment for diesel and electric locomotives.

SIDERUGIA

Ferrovias y Siderurgia SA

Telegrams: FERROVIAS, Madrid
Telephone: 222 6490

Head Office: Cedaceros 4, Madrid 14, Spain

Products: Freight wagons.

President: Don Carlos Roeb Ungeheuer
Director General: Don Luis Rios Sidro

S-G-P
Simmering-Graz-Pauker AG

Telegrams: ESGEPE Vienna
Telephones: 02 22/93 35 35
Telex: 01 2574, and 01 2767

Head Office: Mariahilfer Strasse 32, 1071 Vienna, Austria

Products: Diesel and electric locomotives; diesel and electric railcars; passenger and freight rolling stock; special wagons.

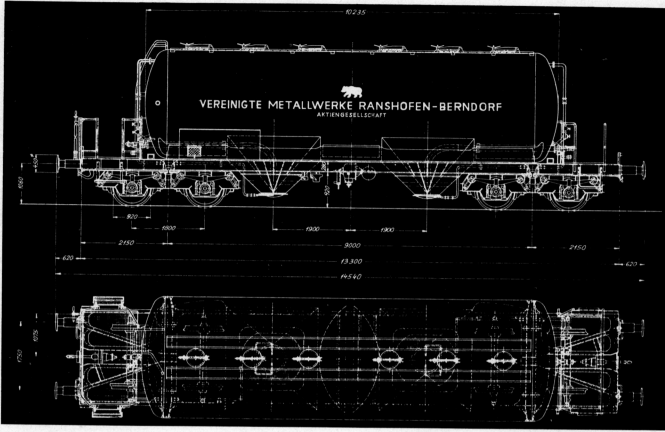

Four-axle tank wagon; capacity 64 m³

SIEMENS
Siemens Aktiengesellschaft

Power Engineering Group, Railway Department

Telegrams: SIEMENS erlangen
Telephone: (0 91 31) 71
Telex: 629 8259

Head Office: Werner-von-Siemens-Strasse 50, Postfach 3240 8520 Erlangen 2, German Federal Republic

Products: Electric and diesel-electric vehicles and associated electrical equipment for main-line, interurban, urban-rapid-transit, underground, narrow-gauge, industrial and mine railways, also for tramways and trolley bus systems. Power transmission and overhead contact wires including accessories and fittings, traction power supply equipment. Electrical equipment for railway stations and workshops.

President: Peter von Siemens
Chairman: Bernhard Plettner

Director of Rolling Stock Department: Karl Werner Seibert

Sales: Equipment for 146 Class 111 Locomotives Bo' Bo' with a continuous rating of 4 040 kW for inter-city and freight services of the German Federal Railways (DB). The electrical equipment of the locomotives with a top speed of 150 km/h have been developed by Siemens AG. The locomotives are based on the well proven E 110 Series keeping such main components as the traction motors, drives, tap changers etc, but also incorporating improvements resulting from experience gained in service and from technical advances in this field.

As member of the 50 c/s Group Siemens Aktiengesellschaft is participating in deliveries for numerous Railways eg South Korea, Portugal, India and Yugoslavia. Of special importance is an order of 100 thyristor-controlled freight traffic Co' Co' locomotives (Class 7E) for the South African Railways (SAR). Delivery starts early 1978.

SIG
Schweizerische Industrie-Gesellschaft
(Swiss Industrial Company)

Telegrams: SIG Neuhausenamrheinfall
Telephone: (053) 8 15 55
Telex: 7 68 02 sig ch

Head Office: CH-8212 Neuhausenam Rhein Falls, Switzerland

VBW/SZB commuter train

Products: Electric and diesel luxury trainsets (TEE trains); electric and diesel railcars and trailers; rapid transit stock; rack locomotives and railcars; shunting locomotives; passenger and freight cars; special transport cars for heavy and bulky loads; air-spring and other kinds of bogies; articulated tramcars; arc-welded integral all-steel light-weight constructions and all-welded integral aluminium coach designs.

Chairman of the Board: Fritz Halm
Managing Director: Wolfgang Gähwyler
Director, Coach Factory: Peter Gsell

Constitution: Founded in 1853 for the manufacture of railway rolling stock.

Sales: Recent deliveries and work in hand include: five 4-current electric Trans-Europe-Express trains, composed of five luxury trailer coaches and one 3 200 hp motor coach designed for operation on all European systems of electric traction, viz. 15 000 V ac 16⅔ cycles; 25 000 V ac 50 cycles; 1 500 V dc and 3 000 V dc; all the trailer coaches of the 2 300 hp diesel-electric TEE trains built for the Netherlands and Swiss Federal Railways; 3 000 V dc three-coach multiple units for Indian Railways; 3 000 hp electric high-speed intercity-traffic railcars and new type first and second class and mixed first and second class standard coaches for Swiss Federal Railways; 2 800 hp electric highspeed railcars for various private Railway Companies; 1 600 hp twin motor coaches and passenger cars for Bern-Loetschberg-Simplon Railway; electric twin railcar units for the Montreux-Oberland Bernois Railway; 360 hp diesel rack railcars for Monte Generoso Railway; electric rack line shuttle train units for Bex-Villars-Bretaye Railway; postal vans for Swiss PTT; torsion-bar power and trailer bogies, and special intercommunication equipment and entrance doors, for diesel-hydraulic 3-car high speed luxury trainsets for Finnish State Railways; freight cars and tank wagons for various companies; cabins for aerial cableways; all-welded integral light alloy (aluminium) passenger coaches of various classes for Swiss Federal Railways Brünig line, Bernese Oberland Railway and Brig-Visp-Zermatt Railway; 620 hp type Ee 2/2 electric dc shunting locomotives for Orbe-Chavornay Railway; four 1 500 hp electric ac 4-coach shuttle trainsets of all-welded integral aluminium design for Furka-Oberalp Railway; cross-overs for the new 15-coach Blue Trains of South African Railways; air-conditioned standard gauge high comfort passenger cars with all-welded integral light alloy structure, and light alloy cars of all-welded integral body design with air-sprung bogies for rapid suburban traffic, both types for Swiss Federal Railways. Commuter trains for VBW and SZB. Air-sprung power and trailer bogies for electric suburban trainsets for Netherlands Railways and for Finnish State Railways.

SIKORSKY

Surface Transportation Systems sub-division of Sikorsky Aircraft Division of United Aircraft Corporation

Head Office: Stratford, Connecticut 06602, USA

Telephone: 378-6361

Products: Light-weight high speed gas-turbine powered trains (TurboTrains).

Marketing Manager: C. J. Englehardt

SIMPLEX

Simplex Mechanical Handling Limited
(Subsidiary of The Wemyss Development Company Ltd)

Head Office: Simplex Works, Bedford, MK42 9LB, England

Sales Manager: J. P. Hulme

Products: Narrow gauge diesel-mechanical and diesel-hydraulic locomotives from 2 to 14 tons; fork lift truck attachments including bale and paper roll clamps and tipplers, rotating heads, sideshifters, mechanical drum handlers, container handling equipment.

Telegrams: SIMPLEX Bedford
Telephone: Bedford (0234) 56422
Telex: 82254 Simplex Bedford

Sales: In addition to the many Units in daily use in the home market, large numbers are in service overseas, particularly in Africa and the Far East, including approximately 1 000 in South Africa, 400 in East Africa, 300 in Malaysia.

Locomotive Range: 'G' Series 2¼-3 tons, 40S Series 2½-4½ tons, 60S Series 4-6 tons, 'U' Series 5-10 tons, 'T' Series 9-12½ tons.

SLM

Schweizerische Lokomotiv-und Maschinenfabrik

Head Office: CH-8401 Winterthur, Switzerland

Products: Electric and thermal main line and shunting vehicles for adhesion railways; electric and diesel traction units for rack railways, including traction units for combined rack and adhesion operation; special purpose rail vehicles; industrial gears; gears for special vehicles; light-metal castings.

President, Board of Management: Rudolph Schmid
General Manager: K. von Meyenburg
Technical Deputy Manager: Dr. H. Loosli
Commercial Deputy Manager: Dr. M. Knüsli

Telegrams: LOCOMOTIVE Winterthur
Telephone: (052) 85 41 41
Telex: 7 61 31 slm ch

Works Deputy Manager: Emil Lutz
Sales Deputy Manager: Charles Erzinger

Sales: 1975: Shunting locomotives Tm IV for Swiss Federal Railways; electric rack and adhesion railcar Beh 2/4 for Lyon Transport Authority, France; gears for army vehicles.

Deliveries: 1975: Re 6/6 electric locomotives for the Swiss Federal Railways; mechanical parts for locomotives of the Bern-Lötschberg-Simplon Railway, Switzerland; Tm IV shunting locomotives for Swiss Federal Railways; bogies for rack railcars of the Brig-Visp-Zermatt Railway, Switzerland.

SNAV

Société Nouvelle des Ateliers Venissieux

Head Office and Works: BP 4 Chemin du Genie, 69631-Venissieux, France

Products: Railway wagons; ISO containers; crane-carrier trucks; welded assemblies.

Chairman: P. Cacouault
General Manager: C. Louwet
Director, Finance: P. Andrevon
Director, Engineering: R. Dousset
Director, Sales: A. Serval

Constitution: Located in the south-east outskirts of Lyons, the works occupy an area of 42 acres (17 hectares) of which 15.5 acres (65 000 m²) are covered. The manufacture of railway equipment is the most important of the company's four activities, dating back to the formation of the company in 1949.

Telegrams: SNAVENIX
Telephone: 72 85 21/72 90 16
Telex: 340603

Sales: 1 265 hopper bogie ballast wagons for French National Railways (SNCF); 150 three-axle flat wagons with a two-element chassis for the transport of industrialised agricultural vehicles delivered to STVA—an SNCF affiliated company.

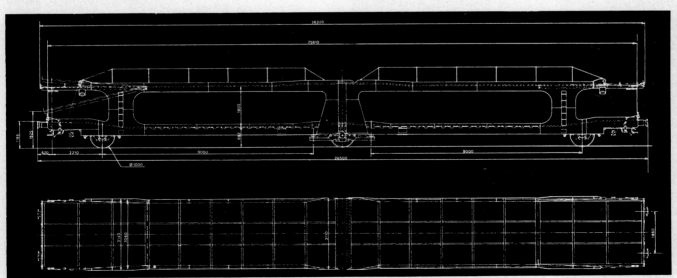

Three-axle double-deck articulated car-carrier

Three-axle double-deck articulated car-carrier

Three-axle articulated double element wagon, covered with sliding tarpaulin

SNIA
Divisione Ingegneria e Costruzioni Industriali

Telephone: 6332
Telex: 34503

Head Office: 20121 Milano, 18 via Montebello, Italy

Products: Electric-locomotives; suburban trainsets; passenger coaches; freight wagons; refrigerator wagons; containers.

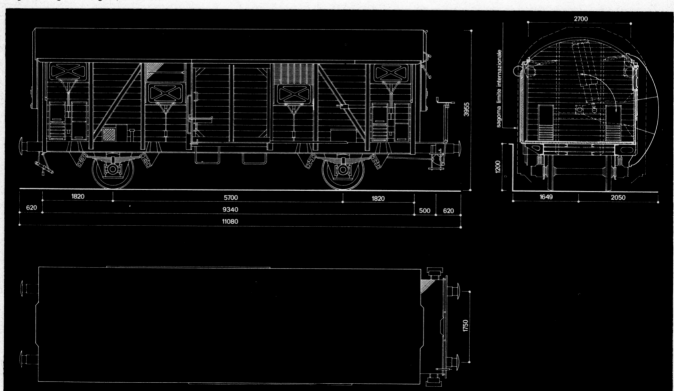

Series Tbs wagon with rotating roof built for Italian State Railways (FS)

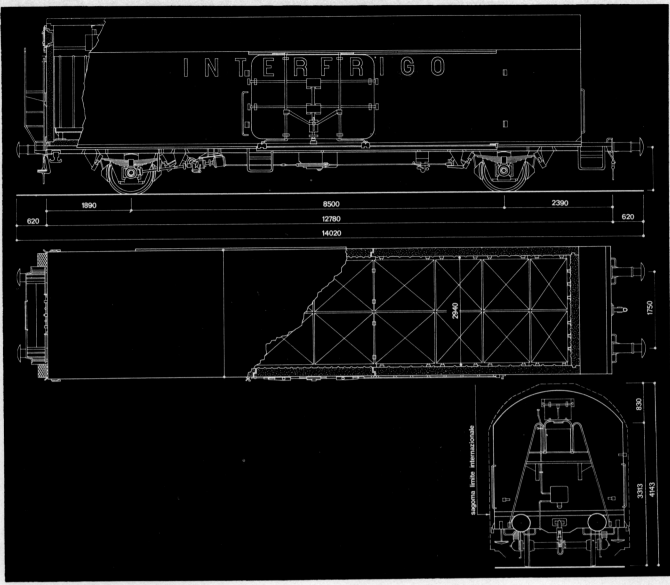

Continental gauge refrigerating waggon

Continental gauge, refrigeration by means of refrigerating plant fixed intermediate (small) walls. Useful inside dimensions: frame length 12 780 mm; refrigerator capacity 4 m³; length 10 610 mm; width 2 600 mm; height 1 875 mm; useful floor surface 27 500 m²; useful case volume 55 m³; width and height of door opening 2 725 × 1 900 mm; height of floor above rail flush-line 1 335 mm; "K"-co-efficient 0,13 Kcal/h m² °C; brake type W-U; tare 14.8 tonne; loading gauge-limits A 17.2; B C 21.2.

SOCIMI
Soc. Costruzioni Industriali Milano SpA

Head Office: Via S. Calimero 3, 20122 Milano, Italy

Telephone: (02) 54 65251/5

Products: Electric trainsets for suburban railways and transit systems.

SOFER
SOFER—Officine Ferroviere, SpA

Head Office: Pozzuoli (Naples)—Via Miliscola 33, Italy

Products: Electric, diesel-electric and diesel-hydraulic locomotives; electric and diesel trainsets; diesel and electric railcars; trailers; passenger coaches of all types and classes; luggage and mail vans; motor and carrying bogies for articulated electric trainsets.

Telegrams: SOFER-Pozzuoli
Telephone: 867 1200; 867 2522/3/4; 867 2543
Telex: 71048 SOFER

Chairman: Dr Ing. Franco De Gasperis
General Manager: Dr Ing. Vittorio Curcio

SOMA
Soma Equipamentos Industrias SA

Head Office: Parque Industrial Mariano Ferraz, Avienda Soma, 700 Sumaré, São Paulo, Brazil

São Paulo Office: Avienda Brigadeiro Faria Lima, 1709-7° andar conjumto A. CP 2321, São Paulo, Brazil

Products: Freight cars; tank cars; refrigerator cars; ore cars; ingot cars; hopper cars; car building, repairing, maintenance and leasing.

Constitution: This company was founded in 1929 and was the first company in South America to manufacture freight cars. It has specialised in the development of refrigerator cars and tank cars which are leased to various concerns for transportation purposes. In addition to the usual tank cars SOMA developed and built 32 large ones of a capacity of 70 000 litres in 1956, designed and built 18 units of 92 000 litres capacity for 1.600 m gauge in 1973, and more recently designed and built one 100 000 litre unit for delivery in 1974.

In addition to the Railroad Division, there is an Equipment Division whose products include: compressors and blowers; equipment for the cement industry; equipment for mining and processing industries.

Telegrams: SOMAFER
Telephone: 210 2218
210 2925

SOREFAME
Sociedades Reunidas de Fabricações Metálicas, SARL

Head Office: Rua Vice-Almirante Azevedo Coutinho, Amadora, Portugal

Works: Amadora, Portugal

Telegrams: SOREFAME AMADORA
Telephone: 97 60 51
Telex: 12 608 SOREFAM-P
16 101

Products: Passenger and freight cars; locomotives; electric trainsets; special wagons.

Board of Directors: Eng. Eduardo Abranches de Magalhães
Dr. Dominique M. G. Vincent Rousseau
Dr. Antunes da Silva
Rolling Stock Sales Manager: Eng. M. Andrade Gomes
Constitution: The company was established in 1943, and has supplied rolling stock for Portugal, Africa, North America and Brazil as well as electromechanical equipment for hydro-electric and thermal power stations (classical and nuclear), equipment for the chemical and petroleum industry, offshore equipment for oil exploration and production.

Sales: 58 vehicles and some spare equipment for the Estoril Line. The material will be supplied in collaboration with GEC Traction (England) for the related traction equipment; thirty 3 000 hp diesel locomotives to be supplied in consortium with Alsthom-Atlantique and EFACEC. All orders for the above equipment have been placed by the Portuguese National Railways. About 1 650 items of rolling stock have been delivered to the Portuguese Railways and to the Lisbon Underground. This figure includes items for export to Africa and USA.

Stainless steel three car electric trainset built by Sorefame for Portuguese National Railways.

SOULE

SA des Établissements Industriels D. SOULE

Head Office: BP-1, 65200 Bagnères-de-Bigorre, France

Products: Diesel railcars and trailers; passenger cars; insulated and mechanically refrigerated wagons and containers.

Chairman: André de Boysson
General Manager: Joseph Anglade
Sales Director: Dominique Outters

Telegrams: SOULÉ-Bagneres de Bigorre
Telephone: (62) 95 07 31
Telex: 530 179 Soulé bagnb

Constitution: Founded in 1862, the company has specialised in recent years in the manufacture of: metre gauge diesel-electric railcars and passenger cars; metre and standard gauge insulated and mechanically refrigerated wagons and containers; standard gauge postal cars for European systems.

Sales: Metric gauge railcars and passenger coaches for African railways; containers and refrigerated wagons for French National Railways; 400 postal vans for Postes Françaises.

New passenger coach supplied by Soule to OCTRA, Gabon

950 hp diesel-electric railcar for metre-gauge operation with Mali Railways

SOUTHERN IRON

Southern Iron & Equipment Company

Telephone: (404) 457 3716

Head Office: PO Box 81067, 5522 New Peachtree Road, Chamblee, Georgia 30 341 USA

Products: Freight cars, freight car leasing.

President: Tom C. Campbell
Executive Vice President: Hubert P. Hahn
Vice President, Sales: Jack Foster
Vice President, Manufacturing: J. A. Wilde

Constitution: Southern Iron was founded by Frank P. Kern in 1889 and is now a division of Evans Transportation Company, a wholly-owned subsidiary of Evans Products Company.

Sales: 485 rotary dump gondola wagons for unit train coal service, 1 000 box wagons, 400 bulkhead flat wagons, 100 flat wagons, 60 long log wagons, 50 covered gondolas for coil steel service.

5 ft 6 in 100 ton gondola

50 ft 70 ton bulkhead flat car for carrying pulpwood

New Southern Iron Auto-Train car

50ft 70 ton all door box car

52ft 6in 100-ton gondola car with high strength ends

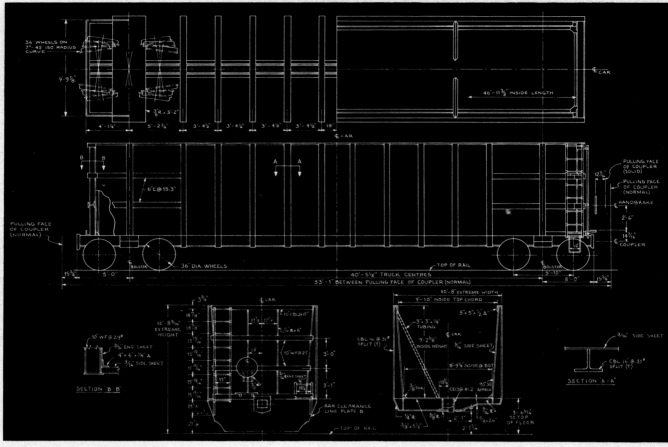

100 ton rotary dump gondola for unit train coal service

STAG
Stag Ltd

Telephone: 085 9 19 02
Telex: 7 42 69

Head Office: CH-7304 Maienféld, Switzerland

Products: Tank wagons.

STANDARD
The Standard Railway Wagon Co Ltd
A Mercantile Credit Company

Telegrams: WAGONS, Stockport
Telephone: (061) 480 4222/3
(061) 480 8916
Telex: 669056

Head Office: Roland Road, Reddish, Stockport SK5 6TJ, Cheshire, England

Products: Freight cars of all types.

Subsidiary: Railease Ltd—formed to supply wagons on hire throughout the UK.

Constitution: The L & Y Works at Heywood have been building railway wagons for over a century. The company designs and builds all types of 4-wheel and bogie freight rolling stock.

Sales: Recent deliveries include a high-capacity pressure discharge wagon for soda ash.

New high-capacity pressure discharge wagon built by Standard for soda ash transport is 50 tonnes gross laden weight and has a capacity of 45m³.

STEEL INDUSTRIES
K.T. Steel Industries Pvt, Ltd

Telegrams: METTICORAIL, Bombay
Telephone: 38 24 42
Telex: 011 2649

Head Office: Chattan, 9 SK Barodawalla Marg, PO Box 6517, Bombay 400 026, India

Products: Rolling stock.

STEELE
E. G. Steele & Co Ltd

Telegrams: MOUNTINGS Hamilton
Telephone: (069 82) 22601
Telex: 77454

Head Office: 25 Dalziel Street, Hamilton, Lanarkshire ML3 9AU, Scotland

Associated Companies: SA Ateliers de Construction de Jambes-Namur, Belgium
Noord-Nederlandse Machinefabriek BV, Winschoten,
The Netherlands

Products: Locopulsor shunting machines; wagon mountings.

Directors: E. G. Steele, Dipl. R.T.C., J.P.
M. S. Steele
J. G. Steele, B.Sc.

Constitution: E. G. Steele & Co. are rolling stock contractors, hirers, repairers, and suppliers of wagon mountings. They also supply purpose-built wagons for internal works traffic. They are the British manufacturers of the "Locopulsor" shunting machines, and the UK agents for the Trackmobile range of road/rail shunters.

STRÖMBERG
Oy Strömberg AB

Works
Telephone: 90-550045
Telex: 12405 strp sf

Head Office: PO Box 69, SF-65101 Vaasa 10, Finland

Main Works: Vaasa and in Helsinki
In Helsinki: Electric drives for rolling stock among others

Address: PO Box 118, SF-00101 Helsinki 10, Finland

Products: Electric drives, especially traction drives for trains, undergrounds, locomotives, trams and trolley buses.

STRÖMMENS

A/S Strömmens Vaerksted

Head Office: PO Box 83, N-2011 Strömmen, Norway

Telegrams: VERKSTEDET, Strömmen
Telephone: (022) 71 36 40
Telex: Oslo 11551 SVSTR N

Products: Electric trainsets; diesel railcars; passenger and freight cars of all types; tramcars and subway cars; containers.

Managing Director: T. W. Schöyen
Technical Director: H. S. Svendsen

Constitution: The company was established in 1873 for the manufacture of railway

rolling stock and is now the only car builder in Norway. It took over the rolling stock building activities of A/S SKABO in 1960 and A/S HÖKA in 1968.

Sales: Recent deliveries include: electric two-car suburban trains, bogie flat-wagons and tank wagons, passenger coaches for Norwegian State Railway; 45 electric cars for Oslo Underground; 10 hopper wagons for A/S Norcem, Norway.

STROJEXPORT

(Czechoslovak foreign trade corporation for the export and import of railway rolling stock)

Head Office: PO Box 662, 886 Václavské n 56, Prague 1, Czechoslovakia

Products: Strojexport handles all transactions for the export of passenger and freight rolling stock built by Czechoslovak Wagon Works.

Telegrams: STROJEXPORT Prague
Telephone: Prague 2131
Telex: Prague 121671

STUDÉNKA

Vagonka Studénka, np, Studénka, Czechoslovakia

Products: Passenger coaches, freight wagons, electrical components and motors.

Telegrams: VAGONKA STUDENKA
Telephone: 713 73/714 66

EM 488 electric trainset built for Czechoslovak State Railways (CSD) by Studénka

Class B1m railcar used for CSD branch line services; supplied by Studénka

Class M 151·0 railcar built by Studénka

Ra type tank wagon built by Studénka

SWIDNICA
Wagony-Swidnca Factory

Telephone: Centrala 29 83/29 89
Telex: 034222

Head Office: ul, Strzdinska 35, Swidinca, Poland 58-100

Products: Tank wagons, flat wagons; self-discharging wagons.

TALBOT
Waggonfabrik TALBOT

Telegrams: TALBOT Aachen
Telephone: Aachen (0241) 4681
Telex: 08 32 845 watal d

Talbot hopper wagon

Head Office: Jülicherstrasse 213-237, 51 Aachen, Postfach 1410, German Federal Republic

Products: Passenger and freight cars.

Constitution: This is the oldest German railway rolling stock manufacturer, being founded in 1938.

In addition to conventional stock, Talbot designs and builds freight cars with special features, including: self-discharging wagons able to empty to either side and between the rails; covered hopper wagon with swivelling roof; covered wagon with "telescopic" sliding-section body; "piggyback" flat with pocket for wheels of semi-trailer.

Four axle sliding wall wagon
Loading length 20·868 m; loading width 2·78 m; interior door height 2·50 m. Built by Talbot for hauling steel coils by Deutsche Bundesbahn.

THOMAS HILL

Thomas Hill (Rotherham) Limited
(Subsidiary of Rolls-Royce Motors Limited)

Telegrams: ENGINE, Rotherham
Telephone: Mexborough 2571
Telex: 54421

Head Office: Vanguard Works, Hooton Road, Kilnhurst, Nr. Rotherham, Yorkshire, England

Products: Industrial locomotives and railcars; diesel hydraulic, diesel electric and battery electric.

Chairman: G. R. Torrance
Managing Director: D. A. Harper
Sales Director: J. N. Capes
Secretary: R. L. Maxwell
Directors: T. W. Hill
B. B. Leverton

Constitution: The company was founded by Thomas A. Hill and between 1937 and 1956 collaborated with Sentinel Wagon Works (1936) Ltd (later Sentinel (Shrewsbury) Ltd) in connection with the maintenance and sales of Sentinel steam and diesel road vehicles and steam industrial locomotives. In 1956 Sentinel (Shrewsbury) Ltd was acquired by Rolls-Royce Ltd, to become the Headquarters for their Oil Engine Division. Production of steam locomotives ceased in 1958 and was replaced by Sentinel—Rolls-Royce diesel-hydraulic locomotives in 1959. A complementary range of Rolls-Royce powered locomotives was introduced under the registered trade name "VANGUARD", particularly to cater for "special applications" such as flameproofed locomotives for use in oil refineries and similar fire hazardous industries.

In 1963 Rolls-Royce Ltd acquired a controlling interest in the company. During 1970-71 the complete transfer of locomotive building from Rolls-Royce Ltd to Thomas Hill (Rotherham) Ltd at Vanguard Works, Kilnhurst took place.

New equipment: Rubber suspension with hydraulic dampers (Shock Absorbers) is offered at extra cost as an alternative to standard conventional laminated springs. Power transmission is by combination of cardan shaft, coupling rods and/or roller chain drive as may be appropriate having regard to the weight and power of individual locomotives. The combination of suspension and transmission systems provides exceptionally good qualities of adhesion and smooth power application.
The standard types are:—
Rigid Frame: Diesel-hydraulic or diesel-electric 0-4-0, 0-6-0, 0-8-0.
Articulated: locomotives of 0-4-0+0-4-0.
Power Range: 170 to 800 bhp gross per locomotive. Multiple operation of up to 3 locomotives or locomotives with power tenders can be arranged to be operated from one driving cab by one man.
Weight Range: 20 to 75 tons per locomotive or power tender
Flameproof Locomotive: Locomotives can be built with flameproof equipment including water quenched or dry spark arrester exhaust systems and electrical systems protected to BS4683 and BS229.
Rail Gauges catered for: 3 ft 0 in to 5 ft 6 in.

Vanguard 740 hp 75 ton 0-6-0 Diesel Hydraulic Locomotive
Powered by two Rolls-Royce C8T Diesel Engines

THRALL
Thrall Car Manufacturing Company

Head Office: PO Box 218, Chicago Heights, Illinois 60411, USA

President: R. L. Duchossois
Executive Vice President: J. A. Thrall
Executive Vice President: C. H. Wright

Telephone: (312) 757 5900

Vice President, Sales: J. P. Lynch
Vice President, Finance: S. D. Christianson

Products: Freight cars.

Constitution: The company was founded in 1916 by Mr A. J. Thrall, the present Chairman of the Board.

Centre-beam car
Inward sloping deck forms 90 degrees angle with centre beam. Usable for both high and low density cargoes. Load carrying capacity 200 000 lb.

100-ton gondola car for Rock Island

Bulkhead flat wagon for timber and building materials shipments

THUNE
Thune-Eureka A/S

Head Office: Joseph Kellers vei

Postal Address: PO Box 38, N-3401 Lierbyen, Norway

Products: Locomotives, electric and diesel hydraulic.
Director: K. Lofstad

Telegrams: THUNE, Drammen
Telephone: 83 80 50
Telex: 18608 Thune N

Chief Engineer, Industrial Division: P. Lassen

Constitution: Thunes Mekaniske Voerksted was founded in 1815 becoming a limited company in 1902. In 1969 the company merged with Eureka Mekaniske Verksted to form Thune-Eureka A/S.

TIBB
Tecnomasio Italiano Brown Boveri

Head Office: Piazzale Lodi 3, 20137 Milano, Italy

Telegrams: TECNOMASIO Milan
Telephone: 5797

Products: Electric, diesel-electric and industrial locomotives; electric trailers; turbo-chargers for traction diesel motors; equipments and bogies for railway and subway cars, trams and trolleybuses; complete electrical plants for all kinds of industrial installations; electrical machinery and apparatus for the production and distribution of electric power.

TOKYU
Tokyu Car Corporation

Head Office: 1 Kamariya-cho, Kanazawa-ku, Yokohama, Japan

Sales and Export Department: 7, 5-chome, Yaesu, Chuo-ku, Tokyo

Products: Electric and diesel railcars; stainless steel cars of various types; passenger cars.

Chairman: Toshiji Yoshitsugu
President: Ihaho Takahashi

Telegrams: TOKYUCARCORP TOK
Telephone: Tokyo 272 8091
Telex: 0222 2020 TCCTOK J

Executive Vice-President: Ichiro Kato
Export Manager: Kenichiro Tanimoto

Constitution: This company was formed in 1948, its predecessors being the Yokohama Plant of the Tokyo Electric Express Railway Co. It has grown rapidly and built the first stainless steel trainset in Japan following technical agreement with the Budd Company of USA in 1960. Merging Teikoku Car & Manufacturing Co of Osaka into its organisation in March 1968, the company is now the largest Japanese supplier of rolling stock to home and overseas railways.

TOMLINSON
Tomlinson Steel Limited

Head Office: Planet Street, Carlisle, Western Australia, Australia

Postal Address: GPO P1223, Perth, Western Australia 6001, Australia

Products: Freight cars.

Chairman: E. E. Tomlinson

Telegrams: TOMLINSONS Perth
Telex: 92230

General Manager: A. Moredoundt
Secretary: R. H. Dobbin

Constitution: The company was founded in Perth, Western Australia in 1892 as Tomlinson Bros. and was formed into a public company in 1951 with its present name. Recent deliveries and work in hand include iron ore trucks for mining companies.

TOSHIBA
Tokyo Shibaura Electric Co Ltd

Head Office: 1-1, Uchisaiwai-cho, Chiyoda-ku, Tokyo, Japan

Products: Electric, diesel-electric and diesel-hydraulic locomotives; electric and diesel railcars; trolley buses; electric traction equipment; coach air-conditioner.

Director, General Manager of Producer Goods Export Division: Haruhiko Takasaki

Constitution: Established in 1875, the company has steadily expanded and its range of

Telegrams: TOSHIBA Tokyo
Telephone: (501) 5411
Telex: J2 2587 Toshiba

products now covers almost everything electrical and electronic from power stations to electronic computers.

Sales: Railway equipment has recently been supplied to Algeria, Argentina, Australia, Brazil, Chile, Egypt, India, Korea, New Zealand, Philippines, South Africa, Thailand, Zaire and Zambia, as well as Japanese National Railways and Japanese private railways.

TOYO
Toyo Denki Seizo KK
(Toyo Electric Mfg Co, Ltd)

Head Office: Yaesu Mitsui Bldg., No. 7, Yaesu, 5-chome, Chuo-ku, Tokyo, Japan

Products: Electric locomotives; diesel-electric locomotives; trolley buses; airslide cars; traction motors and electric machinery and apparatus for railway vehicles.

President: Eiichi Ishii

Constitution: Established in 1918, this company produces traction motors and control equipment etc. for home and export. It was responsible for the axle drive with cardan

Telephone: (272) 4211
Telegrams: YOHDEN Tokyo
Telex: 2224666

shaft and steel blade coupling which is used as standard equipment by the Japanese National Railways and by many of the private railways in Japan.

Sales: Numerous railway rolling stock and equipment have been delivered to JNR; numerous Japanese private railways; Korean National Railroad; Soeul Metropolitan Government Railway; Chilian State Railways; Argentine Railways; Panama Canal Co; Indian Railways; Public Transport Commission of New South Wales; Tasmanian Government Railways; Queensland Government Railways; Victorian Railways; etc.

TRACTION—EXPORT
Société Francaise d'Exportation de Matériel de Traction

Head Office: 3 avenue Victor Hugo, 75116 Paris, France

Products: Electric locomotives, diesel-electric locomotives, diesel-hydraulic locomotives, railcars, motor coaches and trailers for city underground and suburban rapid transit systems.

Telegrams: Tractionex
Telephone: (1) 500-90-01
Telex: 270105F (ref 594)

Constitution: Traction-Export is a subsidiary organisation of Alsthom and MTE, created to develop the export of rail traction equipment manufactured by **Alsthom; Brissonneau; Creusot-Loire;** and **Jeumont-Schneider.**

TRANSPORTMASCHINEN EXPORT-IMPORT
Volkseigener Aussenhandelsbetrieb- der Deutschen Demokratischen Republik

Head Office: Taubenstrasse 11/13, DDR-108 Berlin, German Democratic Republic

Constitution: Transportmaschinen Export-Import is a member of **Vereinigter**

Telegrams: TRANSMASCH
Telephone: 22050
Telex: 11 26 89

Schienenfahrzeugbau der DDR, e.V (United Rolling Stock Manufacturers of the German Democratic Republic) and is the sole exporter for the products of locomotive and coach and wagon factories.

TURNU-SEVERIN
Turnu-Severin Wagon Works

Head Office: 7, Matei Millo St, Bucharest, Romania

Products: Freight wagons.

UERDINGEN
Waggonfabrik Uerdingen AG

Head Office: 415 Krefeld 11, Duisburger Strasse 145, German Federal Republic

Products: Passenger cars; electric, diesel-hydraulic and diesel-electric multiple-unit trains; tank cars; freight cars of all types; bogies; tramway cars; subway cars; containers.

Directors: Kurt Bredehorst
Dr. D. G. Meyer-Ohlert
Dr. Ch. Stiefel

Telegrams: WAGGONFABRIK
Telephone: Krefeld 4491
Telex: 08 53 845 wague d

Sales: Recent deliveries and work in hand include: 15 type ET 420 trainsets to DB; 30 type VT 628 trainsets to DSB; 735 type Habis-wagons to DB; 220 type Habis-wagons to private companies; 160 type Remms 665 wagons to DB; 60 pressure tank cars to private companies; 100 pressure tank cars for USSR.

VT 2
Sitzplätze   76

VT 1
Sitzplätze   60

Commuter train type VT 628
Total length over coupling of the double-unit train 44 350 mm; length of the car bodies 21 700 mm; maximum width of the cars over sheets 2 883 mm; height of floor above top of rail 1 220 mm; wheel base of the bogies 1 900 mm; centre pivot distance 15 100 mm; diameter of tread of the wheels 760 mm; control: multiple control 110 V; maximum speed 120 km/h; seats: 136.

UNIKON
Fabryka Urzadzen Wagonowych UNIKON

Head Office: 70-893 Szczecin, Poland

Products: Freight wagons.

Telephone: 61271
Telex: 042221

UNIO
Unio-Satu Mare

Head Office: 7 Matei Millo St, Bucharest, Romania

Products: Diesel, electric and battery mine locomotives; forestry wagons; mine wagons; freight wagons.

UNION CARRIAGE
Union Carriage & Wagon Co (Pty) Ltd

Works & Registered Office: Marievale Road, Vorsterkroon, Nigel, Transvaal, South Africa

Products: All metal rolling stock; mainline and industrial locomotives.

Chairman: Dr W. J. de Villiers
Managing Director: Mr J. Clarke

Constitution: General Mining and Finance Corp, Anglo-American Corp and Comeng Holdings are the principal shareholders of this company. Less than 25% in value of all the contracts received is spent overseas, mostly on electrical traction equipment which is not obtainable from South African sources.

Sales: Over 1 400-3 000 V dc electric locomotives; nearly 3 500 electric MU suburban coaches; over 3 500 sleeping, sitting and staff cars of various types; approximately 40 special coaches, including lounge, kitchen, dining and buffet cars; the two world famous "Blue Trains"; over 400 specialised freight vehicles.

The material and equipment for these vehicles are primarily from South African sources with it being necessary to import only limited quantities of specialised equipment.

Telegrams: 'UNICARWAG'
Telephone: 739 2411
Telex: 8 6328 SA

When the SAR decided to introduce 25kV ac locomotives, the initial order for 100 locomotives was awarded to the 50 Cycle Group with Union Carriage as the locomotive builder, as a sub-contractor to the 50 Cycle Group.
In a similar manner UCW are building the 50kV ac electric locomotives for the Sishen/Saldanha Railway, in this instance as a sub-contractor to GEC Traction of the United Kingdom. These locomotives weigh 168 tons and have a rating of over 3 600 kW, which places them amongst the highest axle load and kW rating of 1 065 mm gauge locomotives in operation throughout the world.
Export contracts awarded to the company in recent years comprise 20 mainline coaches for Luanda Railways, 12 mainline coaches for Benguela Railways, 10 mainline coaches for Malawi Railways and 20 Thyristor controlled 25kV ac Bo-Bo electric locomotives for Taiwan, which contract was executed as a sub-contractor of GEC Traction Limited, United Kingdom.
The company is the leader in the field of the industrial locomotive manufacture in the Republic of South Africa, having supplied in recent years over 100 diesel hydraulic and diesel electric locomotives. These locomotives are in the 30 tonne to 75 tonne weight range, and vary between 250 and 1 000 kW output.
The covered works area is approximately 56 000 m² situated on a total area of 36.4 hectares. The current weekly production rate is 10 passenger cars and 5 locomotives per week, total plant capacity being considerably in excess of this.

UNION TANK
Union Tank Car Company

Head Office: 111 West Jackson Boulevard, Chicago, Illinois 60604, USA

Products: Steel, stainless steel, and aluminium tank cars carrying liquids, compressed gases, and granular solids.

Equipment: Union Tank Car Company has developed a number of modern tank car designs to meet the needs of shippers in the chemical, petroleum, food, and fertiliser

Telephone: (312) 431 3100

industries. A recent innovation has been Funnel-Flow sloping tank design for fast, complete unloading of liquids. Union Tank has also developed the Sandwich car for superphosphoric acid, polyglycols, and food products—temperature control is provided by urethane foam insulation with no metal-to-metal contact. For granular solids such as cement, the company's pneumatically-operated Pressure-Flow cars unloads quickly. For anhydrous ammonia and liquefied petroleum gas, Union Tank has introduced pressure cars in 30 000 and 33 800 gallon sizes.
The company owns and operates a fleet of 43 000 tank cars which are leased to shippers.

VALMET
Valmet Oy Tampere Works

Head Office: Punanotkonkatu 2, Helsinki, Finland

Products: Diesel-hydraulic locomotives; electric multiple unit trains; rapid transit cars; articulated tramcars; coaches for special purposes.

President: Jaako Ihamuotila
Manager, Railways Division: Leo Lahtinen

Recent sales: For Finnish State Railways: All-aluminium 720 kW electric 2-car trainsets

Telegrams: VALMET, Helsinki
Telephone: 931 65 3322
Telex: 22112 vallesf

(motor coach and driving trailer) with seats for 204 and max speed of 75 mph *(120 km/h);* 1 400 hp BoBo diesel-hydraulic general purpose locomotives; 355 hp B diesel-hydraulic shunting locomotives.
For the Rapid Transit Office of the City of Helsinki: All-aluminium 1 000 kW rapid transit 2-car units with seats for 134 and max speed of 56 mph *(90 km/h).*
For Finnish and Swedish industry: 545 hp and 970 hp C diesel-hydraulic shunting locomotives.

VOROSHILOVGRAD
Voroshilovgrad Diesel Locomotive Works

Head Office: Voroshilovgrad, USSR

Products: Diesel locomotives.

Constitution: Member of Energomachexport.

New equipment: The new Soviet 3 000 hp diesel locomotive can be seen in a number of European countries. Exports of Soviet diesel locomotives started in 1958 with a delivery of 750 hp shunting units. The development of 2 000 hp mainline diesel locomotives specially for use on European railways was an important milestone in promoting this line. Deliveries began in 1965.
These locomotives, designated M-62 in Hungary, 120 in the GDR, T-679.1 and T-679.5 in Czechoslovakia, CT-44 in Poland and K-62 in the Korean People's Democratic Republic, are handling a considerable proportion of the freight and passenger transport there. Experience gained during the operation of the 2 000 hp units was taken into account

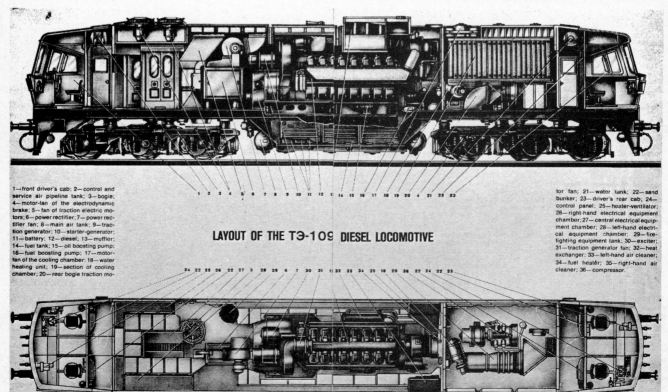

1—front driver's cab; 2—control and service air pipeline tank; 3—bogie; 4—motor-fan of the electrodynamic brake; 5—fan of traction electric motors; 6—power rectifier; 7—power rectifier fan; 8—main air tank; 9—traction generator; 10—starter-generator; 11—battery; 12—diesel; 13—muffler; 14—fuel tank; 15—oil boosting pump; 16—fuel boosting pump; 17—motor-fan of the cooling chamber; 18—water heating unit; 19—section of cooling chamber; 20—rear bogie traction mo-

LAYOUT OF THE TƏ-109 DIESEL LOCOMOTIVE

tor fan; 21—water tank; 22—sand bunker; 23—driver's rear cab; 24—control panel; 25—heater-ventilator; 26—right-hand electrical equipment chamber; 27—central electrical equipment chamber; 28—left-hand electrical equipment chamber; 29—fire-fighting equipment tank; 30—exciter; 31—traction generator fan; 32—heat exchanger; 33—left-hand air cleaner; 34—fuel heater; 35—right-hand air cleaner; 36—compressor.

when the T-109 was designed and constructed. The prototypes of this locomotive have been subjected to extensive trials on Soviet railways. Certain improvements were introduced into its design at the request of foreign customers.

In 1970, V/O Energomachexport began to export these locomotives. The new locomotive was designated "130" in the GDR, 07 in Bulgaria and T-679.2 in Czechoslovakia. The unit is a powerful six-axle main line diesel locomotive with a trailing weight of 120 tons. At the customer's request, it can come in a freight or passenger version for 1 435 mm or 1 524 mm track gauge. In the passenger version the maximum speed is 140 kph. An important feature of the locomotive's design is the ac/dc electrical transmission with a silicon rectifier. The use of this type of drive has made it possible to equip the locomotive with a light compact ac diesel generator and dc electric motors with the most suitable traction features.

The locomotive is provided with a 16 cylinder four-stroke V-type diesel engine with gas-turbine super-charging. The engine runs at 1 000 rpm. It is started electrically, from a starter-generator. Fuel consumption is 151 gr/bhp/hr. Oil consumption is 2.5 gr/bhp/hr. The cooling water and oil temperature in the diesel is maintained automatically. Automatic controls keep the cooling water at a constant temperature, maintain the temperature and pressure of the oil, and pressure in the braking system.

The main generator of the locomotive is a 12 pole ac synchronous machine. This makes it possible to use lightweight and simple commutatorless ac motors for driving the auxiliary mechanisms. In accordance with requests from customers in the GDR, 600 kW units rated at 16⅔ Hz have been installed in the last batches of 3 000 hp diesel locomotives to heat the passenger coaches electrically.

The locomotive has two six-wheel bogies with separate drives of the wheel sets. The arrangement of the traction motors on one side considerably improves the coefficient of utilisation of the trailing weight. Fastening of the axle boxes prevents friction and wear on the fastenings. The axle boxes are equipped with antifriction bearings. The rubber shock-absorbers and friction oscillation dampers ensure the smooth running of the locomotive. The passenger version of the locomotive is equipped with electro-dynamic brakes.

The light-weight strong locomotive body is designed to withstand compressive and tensile forces of up to 250-tons. The arrangement of the locomotive's units and assemblies makes for easy maintenance and repair. Due to the detachable roof the diesel, the generator and other units can easily be installed and dismounted. The diesel locomotive has two control cabs, so it can be controlled from each of them. The instruments and controls in the cabs are logically placed. The cabs are light and spacious and very convenient for the drivers. They have excellent sound proofing and an efficient heating and ventilation system.

V/O Energomachexport at the 1973 Leipzig Spring Fair agreed to deliver 279 locomotives of this type to the German Democratic Republic in 1974-75.

WAGGON UNION
Waggon Union GmbH

Offices: P.B. 2240, 5902 Netphen 2

Products: Freight cars of all types, covered, open, mineral, tank, refrigerated, and for transport of road vehicles and containers; electric and diesel-powered railcars, railbuses, and multiple-unit trainsets; passenger cars.

Management: Heinrich König
Dipl-Ing. Rolf Kramer
Dr Hermann J. Oelmann
Prof Dr-Ing. Walter Döpper

Telegrams: WAGGONUNION Siegen
Telephone: Siegen (0271) 702-1
Telex: 08-72843 wusi d

Constitution: This company was formed on 1 April 1971 as a result of the merger between **SEAG Waggonbau** (of Rheinstahl Transporttechnik) and **DWM Deutsche Waggon- und Maschinenfabrik GmbH.**

WALKERS
Walkers Limited

Head Office: Bowen Street, Maryborough, Queensland 4650, Australia

Products: Diesel-hydraulic locomotives from 250 to 1 200 hp; passenger and freight rolling stock.

Chairman: T. Braddock
Managing Director: Dr. W. L. Hughes
Secretary: M. F. Dittmann

Constitution: The company was started at Ballarat, Victoria, in 1864 by John Walker as

Telegrams: ITOLZAK
Telephone: 21 2321
Telex: 49718

The Union Foundry, to build mining machinery for the newly-opened goldfields, and the works at Maryborough were opened on the present site in 1868. In 1884 a public company was formed with the name John Walker & Co Ltd, later changed to Walkers Limited.

In addition to general engineering, sugar mills and ships, Walkers Ltd have been producing steam, diesel mechanical, diesel electric and diesel hydraulic locomotives since 1896. In recent years the company has specialised in the production of a standard range of diesel hydraulic locomotives which are available in a power range from 250 to 1 200 hp.

WEGMANN
Wegmann & Co

Head Office: Wolfhagerstr 77/79, D-35 Kassel, German Federal Republic

Works: Kassel-Rothenditmold (rolling stock construction).
Kassel-Bettenhausen (fittings, frames and castings)

Products: Passenger and freight cars of all types, including lightweight construction; railcars; electric trainsets; air-conditioned units; freight cars of all kinds; tramcars; "München-Kassel" motor and trailer bogies; containers.

Telegrams: WEGMANN, Kassel
Telephone: 19411
Telex: 99 859

Directors: Dipl. Ing. F. Bode
Dr E. Bode

Constitution: This company was established in 1876 and has specialised in passenger and freight car building.

Sales: Recent deliveries include: a Royal train for Iran; saloon coaches for Yugoslavia and Guinea; passenger coaches for Ghana, Denmark, Luxembourg, Spain and Germany; goods wagons with opening roofs for Ghana and German railways.

WESTINGHOUSE SA
(Formerly CENEMESA)

Head Office: Avda José Antonio 10, Madrid 14, Spain

Products: Electric locomotives, electric railcars.

President: D. Santiago Foncillas Casaus

Telephone: (2) 31 72 00
Telex: 22430

General Manager: D. Carlos Alvarez de Toledo

Constitution: Member of the Westinghouse Electric group of companies.

65 emu's series 5000 rated at 180 × 4 kW 600 V dc have been delivered by Westinghouse SA to Madrid Metro

WHITEHEAD & KALES
Whitehead & Kales International Inc

Head Office: 58 Haltiner St, River Rouge, Michigan 48218, USA

Products: Freight cars of all types, car components and underframes, shipping racks,

Telephone: Area Code 313 849-1200

containers, and special dunnage and cushioning devices.

President: Walter W. Borland
Sales Director: A. F. Debicki

WHITING
Whiting Corporation

Telephone: (Aera code 312) Interocean 8-9400

Head Office: Harvey, Illinois 60426, USA

Products: "Trackmobile" road-rail switcher; remote control car-movers; car washing equipment; transfer tables; rip jacks.

New equipment: The 4TM "trackmobile" is a 43 hp diesel-powered switcher (shunter) with a T.E. of 7 400 lb *(3 368 kg)* at 1.5 mph *(2.4 km/h)* in first gear. Having moved

wagons to the desired position the 4TM is quickly raised clear of the track, driven on its road wheels to another location and lowered to the track in 30 seconds ready for its next task, provided that the road surface is roughly level with the top of the rails as in industrial plants, or can be temporarily built up with planks.
Weight transfer from loaded wagon to Trackmobile is effected by the two projecting arms of the hydraulic jacking coupler. The Trackmobile can be fitted for operation with automatic couplers or with European-type centre-hook and buffers.

WICKHAM
D. Wickham & Company Limited

Telegrams: WICKHAM, Ware
Telephone: Ware 2491
Telex: 81340

Head Office: Crane Mead, Ware, Hertfordshire, SG12 9QA, England

Products: Diesel railcars and rail buses, gang trolleys, inspection cars, overhead line maintenance and inspection cars, crane trolleys, small trailers, self propelled special purpose vehicles, vehicle washing equipment.

Chairman and Managing Director: James Cooper
Sales Director: J. F. Atkinson
Chief Designer: K. J. F. Bishop

Constitution: D. Wickham & Company, which was incorporated as a private limited company in 1912, has been building railway vehicles since 1922. The company pioneered the use of roller bearing axle boxes, welded steel frames, underslung springs and all steel bodies, using solid drawn square steel tubing to eliminate the conventional underframe and produce cars with a high power/weight ratio for operating under arduous mountain conditions. The company specialises in track maintenance and inspection vehicles and offers a wide range of equipment for this purpose.

Sales: Recent deliveries have included a number of type 42 Senior Officers' Inspection Cars to Nigerian Railways, Sudan Railways, Tanzanian Railways and Onatra (Zaire). Also delivered have been a batch of 41 Type IV Inspection Cars to Indonesian Railways and the first of a long series of type 37D gang trolleys for Greek Railways.

New equipment: Among the range of new equipment the company is now offering are special vehicles for the inspection of overhead catenary systems, heavy duty crane trolleys and overhead line maintenance vehicles. Introduction of the type 37 trolley has made available a basic vehicle which can be finished as an inspection car, gang trolley or rail ambulance with a petrol or diesel engine.
The Wickham self-propelled overhead line inspection car is designed to provide a high powered maintenance inspection unit for overhead line equipment. It is basically a two axle, short wheelbase vehicle, powered by a diesel engine, with driving controls at both ends. The car is divided into an upper and lower compartment. The upper compartment is reached by steps and forms an observation cabin for inspectors surveying the overhead line. A pantograph is fitted to the roof of the vehicle so that it is under full observation by the inspectors in the upper compartment. The vehicle is also designed to tow a special trailer car which provides accommodation for maintenance crews and on which is mounted an elevating platform for carrying out maintenance to the overhead lines and gantries.
The new Type IV inspection car, as supplied to Indonesian Railways, is a lightweight, but very rugged trolley for general purpose work. Despite being light enough to be off-tracked and turned round by its crew it is nevertheless capable of carrying seven

people and towing a trailer loaded to 2 000 lbs. The trolley is available in three versions; Open, with panelled end frames only, Open with a front windscreen and Semi-open with front and rear windscreens and canvas hood. The engine is a single cylinder, 4 stroke Bernard petrol unit of about 10 hp with centrifugal clutch. Transmission is by cardan shaft to a two-speed, two direction box mounted on the driving axle.

Semi-open version of the new type IV Inspection Car

Type 42 Inspection Car, fitted with a roof mounted air conditioning plant for Onatra of Zaire

Ambulance version of the type 37 trolley supplied to Malayan Railways

---

YALE & TOWNE
Yale & Towne Inc
A subsidiary of Eaton Yale & Towne Inc.

Works: Trojan Division, Batavia, Illinois, USA

Products: Pneumatic tyred switching tractors; materials handling equipment; earth moving equipment.

Equipment: Although it does not run on rails, the Trojan 254R tractor operates as a yard

switching (shunting) locomotive, with the additional facility that, on completion of one duty, it can quickly and easily travel across intervening tracks to its next duty without having to be switched around the lines. Its low-pressure rubber tyred wheels straddle the rail track and enable it to operate on cross ties and to cross tails, drainage trenches, and uneven surfaces generally.
The tractor is equipped with standard couplers at front and rear; coupling and uncoupling is effected by the driver operating a lever in the cab. It also has its own 35 ft³/min compressed air system with connecting hoses for operation, when necessary, of the air brakes on the cars being moved.
The Trojan 254R weighs 31 500 lb *(14 300 kg)* and can push or pull up to 1 500 tons of rolling stock.

ZASTAL
Z.Z.P.M. Zastal Zelona Gora

Telegrams: ZASTAL-ZIELONA GORA
Telephone: 4411
Telex: 043201

Head Office: Zaodrzanskie Zaklady Przemyslu Metalowego "Zastal", 65-114 Zielona Gora, ul. Towarowa 10, Poland

Products: Freight wagons.

ZWEIWEG-FAHRZEUG

Telephone: (08031) 15031
Telex: 525 731

Head Office: Vertriebs KG, Kufsteiner Strasse 12, D-8200 Rosenheim, German Federal Republic

Products: Interesting novelties in the field of rail and road operations are manufactured by Zweiweg-Fahrzeug. The track-keeping device, comprising articulated track-keeping rollers, which are adapted to the Daimler-Benz Unimog, has been supplied by Zweiweg for many years. These rollers turn the well known road vehicle into a valuable rail vehicle—admitted by all railway administrations. Besides its use as a shunting unit—its tractive power equals about that of a 20 ton locomotive—the track-keeping device ZW-82S also permits to use the Unimog on rails as a working unit, equipped with various supplementary equipment.

A Zweiweg Unimog model ZW-82S provided with a steam-jet equipment for points cleaning (in use in Switzerland for example), another unit equipped with a loading crane—and at the same time as a shunting unit—it pulls up to 25 fully laden waggons. Another one has been equipped as auxiliary vehicle (in operation with the German Federal Railways). For winter operation a rotary snow plough or a drum-type snow plough can be fitted, permitting effective snow removal on rails as well as on the road.

Two special units are available for the construction and maintenance of the aerial lines: a Zweiweg Unimog with hydraulic lifting platform and a new special vehicle, the Zweiweg road-railer with working platform which was initially constructed for the Dutch State Railways. This equipment proved a great success so that several units were ordered subsequently.

The Zweiweg Unimog vehicles are also available for broad gauge lines.

The Trenkle all-purpose vehicle Model A-52S equipped with track-keeping device ZW-52S is available for demonstrations on narrow gauge lines.

Director: Adolf Löw

Constitution: It is ten years since the firm of Zweiweg-Fahrzeug GmbH & Co, Vertriebs-KG in Rosenheim was founded. Mr Adolf Löw was appointed Director and has been in charge of the management up to this day. The organisation and extension of the enterprise to its present leading position on the market is entirely due to him. The firm's track-holding device enables road vehicles to be operated on the rail.

The bulk of the vehicles supplied during the past ten years has been in the following sequence: Daimler-Benz Unimog, Ford-Transit and the Trenkle all-purpose vehicle A-52S for narrow gauge lines.

Zweiweg Unimog model ZW-82 for points cleaning

DIESEL ENGINES
FOR RAIL TRACTION

ABC

Anglo Belgian Company
43 Wiedauwkaai, Gand, Belgium

Formed in 1912, to take over the SA des Anciens Ateliers Onghena which had been building gas engines since 1904, the company manufactures four-stroke diesel engines for marine, industrial and rail traction services.

DXS and DXC Series

Type: 6 and 8 cylinder vertical in-line, 4-cycle turbocharged and charge air cooled (DXC), water cooled.
Cylinders: Bore 9.53 in *(242 mm)*. Stroke 12.6 in *(320 mm)*. Swept volume 14.72 litres per cylinder. Compression ratio 12.05:1. Cast iron wet type cylinder liners with two rubber seal rings. Cast iron cylinder heads secured by studs.

Model		DXS		DXC	
Turbo-charged		Yes	Yes	Yes	Yes
No of cylinders		6	8	6	8
bhp continuous		630	840	900	1 200
Max engine speed	rpm	750		750	
Bmep continuous	lb/sq in	121.8		170	
	(kg/cm²)	*(8.56)*		*(12.22)*	
Bmep maximum	lb/sq in	134.1		187	
	(kg/cm²)	*(9.43)*		*(13.4)*	
Weight (dry without flywheel) lb		16 710	22 490	17 710	22 490
	(kg)	*(8 035)*	*(10 200)*	*(8 035)*	*(10 200)*
Length	in	130	159	130	159
	(mm)	*(3 320)*	*(4 030)*	*(3 320)*	*(4 030)*
Width	in	44		44	
	(mm)	*(1 120)*		*(1 120)*	
Height	in	74		74	
	(mm)	*(1 890)*		*(1 890)*	
Consumption Fuel	lb/hp/hr	0.354		0.354	
	(gr/hp/hr)	*(160)*		*(160)*	
Lube oil		0.5% fuel consumption			

Rated output: DIN specification

Pistons: Aluminium alloy with four compression rings (first ring chrome-plated) and one oil control ring with expander. Fully floating gudgeon pin.
Connecting rods: Heat treated alloy steel drop forged "H" section. Steel bearing shells lined with copper lead. Phosphor bronze bushes.
Crankshaft: Forged alloy steel crankshaft with copper lead lined steel bearing shells.
Crankcase: Cast iron.
Valve gear: One inlet and one exhaust silichrome steel overhead valve per cylinder. Valve seat insert in cylinder head. Gear-driven camshaft located inside the cylinder block.
Fuel injection: Direct injectors with one pump per cylinder.
Supercharger: Exhaust gas turbo-blower.
Lubrication: Forged feed with one lubricating and one scavenging gear pump.
Cooling system: Panel radiator with one centrifugal pump.
Starting: Electric or compressed air.

Model 8DXC 8-cylinder turbocharged and charge air cooled engine developing 1 200 hp at 750 rpm

ALCO POWER INC

100 Orchard Street, Auburn, NY 13021, USA

Although they have ceased manufacturing diesel-electric locomotives, ALCO continue to manufacture their diesel engines for both stationary and marine applications and for locomotives, and through licensees in various parts of the world including Canada, Argentina, Australia, India, Romania and Spain. They also continue to supply renewal parts and rebuilding components on a world-wide basis.
ALCO was the first manufacturer in the US to introduce turbo-supercharging for a diesel engine. The 12 and 16 cylinder V-type 244 model was introduced in the 1940s. First rated at 1 580 hp at 1 000 rpm, it was developed to give 1 760 hp at the same speed. The V16 model gave 2 360 hp. The 251 series with the same bore and stroke supersedes these with many improvements in design, and research work continues to obtain even higher specific outputs.

251 Series

6 cylinder in-line, 8, 12, 16 and 18 cylinder Vee, 4-cycle high pressure turbocharged with charge air cooling.
Cylinders: Bore 9 in *(228 mm)*. Stroke 10½ in *(267 mm)*. Swept volume 668 cu in per cylinder. Compression ratio 11.5 : 1. Cast iron water cooled heat treated cylinder liners, chrome plated on inner surface. Cast iron-nickel alloy cylinder heads.
Pistons: Forged aluminium body with steel cap, embodying ring grooves, bolted on. Pistons cooled by pressure-circulated oil, and piston pins are full-floating type.
Connecting rods: Drop-forged steel in an "H" beam cross-section. Piston-pin end has pressed steel-backed bronze bushing. Crank-pin bearing is grooveless in the load-carrying area.
Crankshaft: Alloy-steel forging, precision machined and heat-treated for hardness. Fully counter-balanced. Rifle-drilled oil passages through crankshafts.

Crankcase: Fabricated steel.
Valve gear: Air and exhaust valves are of wear-resistant alloy and are completely interchangeable. Cast iron valve guides are replaceable, and cylinder-head wear is reduced by use of replaceable stellite valve-seat inserts in the head. Two camshafts, one for each bank, located inside engine block, gear driven from crankshaft.
Fuel injection: Designed for flat fuel-consumption curves. System is high-pressure, with fuel supplied to cylinders by individual single-acting plunger pumps.
Turbocharger: High pressure ratio exhaust gas driven turbo-charger. ALCO designed and built with replaceable blades on the turbine wheel. Water cooled charge air cooler.
Fuel: ASTM specification 2-D. Other fuels can be used (heavy oils, natural gas, crudes, etc) with suitable standard modifications to fuel injection equipment and governing apparatus.
Lubrication: Forced feed with one gear driven pump.
Cooling System: Varies with type, locomotive or other installation. One ALCO pump, gear driven from engine.
Starting: Motored main generator, or air.
Mounting: 4-point.

251 Series

No of cylinders		6 in line	8V	12V	16V	18V
Turbocharged		Yes	Yes	Yes	Yes	Yes
Continuous rating	bhp	1 500	1 820	3 000	3 900	4 500
Engine speed	rpm	1 100	1 000	1 100	1 100	1 100
Max Bmep	lb/sq in	269	252	269	269	269
	(kg/cm²)	*(18.9)*	*(17.7)*	*(18.9)*	*(18.9)*	*(18.9)*
Engine weight (dry)	lb	24 700	26 400	32 300	42 500	49 000
	(kg)	*(11 200)*	*(12 000)*	*(14 700)*	*(19 300)*	*(22 200)*

CATERPILLAR

Caterpillar Tractor Co
Industrial Division, Peoria, Illinois 61602, USA
and
Caterpillar Overseas SA
118 rue du Rhône, 1211 Geneva 3, Switzerland

Caterpillar builds a range of diesel engines with outputs from 85 hp to 1 300 hp. These engines are designed for a wide range of industrial and railway applications.

Specification for all models

Cylinders: Removable wet type cylinder liners of hardened cast iron. Alloy cast iron cylinder heads with water directors and removable precombustion chambers.
Pistons: Aluminium alloy with cast in iron ring band, stainless steel heat plug, and chrome-faced rings.
Connecting rods: Forged of "Boron" steel and shot peened.
Crankshaft: Total hardened crankshaft, superfinished and dynamically balanced.
Crankcase: Strongly reinforced, one-piece alloy cast iron with large inspection plates,
Fuel injection: Gear-type transfer pumps, replaceable full-flow filter elements, individual fuel injection pumps and single orifice injection valves. Designed and built by Caterpillar.
Fuel: No 2 fuel oil (ASTM Specifications D396-48T). Premium quality diesel fuel can be used, but it is not required.
Lubrication: Full pressure system. Includes gear-type pump, efficient filter elements and water-cooled oil cooler.
Cooling system: Built-in, centrifugal-type circulating pump. Thermostatic water temperature control.
Starting: Air, electric or hydraulic.

Caterpillar Model D399 16-cylinder Vee engine

		D399	D398	D379	D353	D349	D348	3412	3408	3406	3306	3304
Bore & Stroke	in	6.25 × 8				5.4 × 6.5		5.4 × 6		5.4 × 6.5	4.75 × 6	
	(mm)	(159 × 203)				(137 × 165)		(137 × 152)		(137 × 165)	(112 × 152)	
No of cylinders		V-16	V-12	V-8	1-6	V-16	V-12	V-12	V-8	1-6	1-6	1-5
Turbocharged		Yes	Yes	Yes	Yes	Yes	Yes	Yes	Yes	Yes	Yes	Yes
Aftercooled		Yes	Yes	Yes	Yes	Yes	Yes	Yes	Yes	Yes	No	No
Locomotive rating												
bhp*		1 300	975	650	490	1 130	850	750	475	375	250	165
	rpm	1 300	1 300	1 300	1 300	2 000	2 000	2 100	2 100	2 100	2 200	2 200
Weight (dry)	lb	15 000	11 800	9 000	6 180	9 900	8 100	1 955	1 474	2 890	1 960	1 628
	(kg)	(6 800)	(5 350)	(4 080)	(2 800)	(4 490)	(3 675)	(1 955)	(1 474)	(1 323)	(890)	(738)
Length	in	128.34	105.6	83.50	80.4	100.71	85.55	77.05	61.08	64.88	50.62	38.92
	(mm)	(3 260)	(2 682)	(2 120.1)	(2 042)	(2 558)	(2 172.9)	(1 952)	(1 551.4)	(1 647.9)	(1 285.7)	(988.6)
Width	in	59.3	59.3	59.3	46.83	60.12	60.12	58.4	25.62	35.5	29.71	29.71
	(mm)	(1 505.7)	(1 505.7)	(1 505.7)	(1 189.48)	(1 527)	(1 527)	(1 483.4)	(673.6)	(902.2)	(754.6)	(754.6)
Height	in	78.8	78.8	75.36	65.8	65.28	65.28	53.9	54.2	51.6	43.5	39.4
	(mm)	(2 001)	(2 001)	(1 914)	(1 671)	(1 658)	(1 658)	(1 496)	(1 376)	(1 311)	(1 104)	(1 101)

* Consult factory for applicable ratings dependant on service.

Also TA version

COCKERILL

SA Cockerill-Ougrée-Providence et Esperance-Longdoz
Seraing, Belgium

The present firm of SA ''Cockerill'' was formed in 1970 by a merger of the two companies SA Cockerill-Ougrée-Providence and SA Metallurgique d'Esperance-Longdoz. Their first diesel engine was built in 1913 with assistance from its inventor Rudolph Diesel.

Series 240CO
Type: 6 and 8 cylinders in line, 12, 16 and 18 cylinders in Vee, 4 cycle water cooled.
Cylinders: Bore 9.5 in *(241.3 mm)*. Stroke 12.0 in *(304.8 mm)*. Swept volume 13.92 litres per cylinder. Cast iron wet cylinder liners, separate cast iron cylinder heads, direct injection combustion chambers.
Pistons: Oil-cooled pistons made of aluminium alloy.
Connecting rods: Drop forged.
Crankshaft: Forged, very strong, with hardened journals.
Crankcase: One piece cylinder block.
Valve gear: Two inlet and two exhaust valves per cylinder.
Fuel injection: Mechanical pumps and nozzles.
Lubrication: One pressure pump.
Cooling system: One centrifugal water pump.

				240 CO Series		
Model		6TR	8TR	V12TR	V16TR	V18TR
No of cylinders		6	8	12	16	18
Turbo charged		Yes	Yes	Yes	Yes	Yes
Charge air cooled		Yes	Yes	Yes	Yes	Yes
Continuous power	CV	1 650	2 200	3 300	4 400	4 950
Engine speed	rpm	1 000	1 000	1 000	1 000	1 000
Bmep	lb/sq in	253	253	253	253	253
	(kg/cm²)	(17.80)	(17.80)	(17.80)	(17.80)	(17.80)
Piston speed	ft/min	1 999	1 999	1 999	1 999	1 999
	(m/sec)	(10.16)	(10.16)	(10.16)	(10.16)	(10.16)
Weight (dry)	lb	18 722	24 230	34 580	45 815	51 542
	(kg)	(8 500)	(11 000)	(15 700)	(20 800)	(23 400)
Length	in	129.92	156.93	174.35	221.97	255.83
	(mm)	(3 300)	(3 986)	(4 403)	(5 638)	(6 498)
Width	in	47.64	48.03	86.62	84.25	84.25
	(mm)	(1 210)	(1 220)	(2 200)	(2 140)	(2 140)
Height	in	104.73	104.73	102.00	105.79	102.00
	(mm)	(2 660)	(2 660)	(2 591)	(2 687)	(2 591)
Fuel consumption	lb/hp/hr	0.353	0.353	0.353	0.355	0.353
	(gr/cv/hr)	(158)	(158)	(158)	(159)	(158)

CREUSOT-LOIRE

Société Creusot-Loire, Traction Division
31-32 quai National, 92806-Puteaux, France

This company has been manufacturing diesel engines for over 50 years. They hold licenses to manufacture the designs of several companies including, since 1957, engines for rail traction of Adolf Saurer Ltd, Switzerland. Nearly a thousand engines have been built to date, and a special workshop has been equipped for serial production of the ''S'' series engine, developed for mounting beneath the floor of railcars.

CL. SAURER type SDHR six-cylinder horizontal engine

Very special efforts have been made regarding the design and development of the 6 cylinder horizontal versions of this engine to meet the requirements of under-floor-engined railcars.
More than 400 SDHR engines have been mounted in new SNCF railcars and give full satisfaction. Some of these engines have more than 310 000 miles *(500 000 km)* of running to their credit.
The SDHR engine, equipped with oil cooled pistons, has passed acceptance tests, in accordance with UIC regulations, at 550 nominal hp at a 1 500 rpm rated speed. It is now possible to increase this power output to 600 hp with the SIOHR.
The power ratings, according to UIC regulations, of the ''S'' series CL. SAURER engines are as follows:

		Power ratings in metric hp at 1 500 rpm
SD	6 normally aspirated vertical cylinders	315
SDH	6 normally aspirated horizontal cylinders	315
SDL	6 turbocharged vertical cylinders	450
SDHL	6 turbocharged horizontal cylinders	450
SDR	6 turbocharged vertical cylinders with air cooling	550/600
SDHR	6 turbocharged horizontal cylinders with air cooling	550/600
SEV	12 normally aspirated Vee arranged cylinders	630
SEH	12 normally aspirated horizontal cylinders	630
SEVL	12 turbocharged Vee arranged cylinders	900
SEHL	12 turbocharged horizontal cylinders	900
SEVR	12 turbocharged Vee arranged cylinders with air cooling	1 100/1 200
SFV	16 normally aspirated Vee arranged cylinders	840
SFVL	16 turbocharged Vee arranged cylinders	1 200
SFVR	16 turbocharged Vee arranged cylinders with air cooling	1 400/1 600

The normally aspirated SD315 hp 6-cylinder engine is mounted in light rail tractors.

Mention must also be made of developments covering the 16-cylinder Vee engine in the field of stationary power generating sets.

CUMMINS

Cummins Engine Company, Inc
Columbus, Indiana 47201, USA

Cummins Engine Company manufactures a range of diesel engines from 175 to 1 200 hp for a wide variety of applications. Experience in industrial and railway installations covers a span of 40 years. Over 2 000 sales and service outlets are located throughout the world. Cummins design features are listed below for the ''K'' series.

General Specification
Bearings: Precision type, steel backed inserts. 7 main bearings, 6.5 in *((165 mm)* diameter. Connecting rod—4.25 in *(108 mm)* diameter.
Camshaft: Dual camshafts control all valve and injector movement. Induction hardened alloy steel with gear drive.
Camshaft Followers: Roller type for long cam and follower life.
Connecting Rods: Drop forged 11.4 in *(290 mm)* centre to centre length. Rifle drilled for pressure lubrication of piston pin. Taper piston pin end reduces unit pressures.
Crankshaft: High tensile strength steel forging. Bearing journals are induction hardened.
Cylinder Block: Alloy cast iron with removable, wet liners.
Cylinder Heads: Individual cylinder heads. Drilled fuel supply and return lines. Corrosion resistant inserts on intake and exhaust valve seats.
Fuel System: Cummins PT (TM) self adjusting system with integral flyball type governor. Camshaft actuated injectors.
Gear Train: Heavy duty, induction hardened, located at front of cylinder block.
Lubrication: Force feed to all bearings, gear type pump. All lubrication lines are drilled passages, except pan to pump suction line.
Pistons: Aluminium, cam ground, with two compression and one oil ring. Oil cooled.

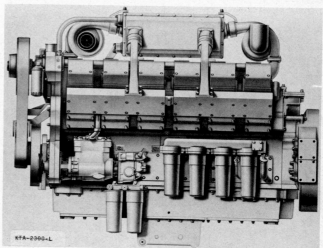

Cummins KTA-2300-L engine

Piston Pins: 2.4 in *(61 mm)* diameter, full floating.
Turbocharger: Scroll diffuser, top mounted.

Valves: Dual intake and exhaust each cylinder. Each valve 2.22 in *(56 mm)* diameter. Heat and corrosion resistant face on exhaust valves.

Engine	Intermittent Traction rating BS 2953: 1958 hp at rpm		Continuous Traction rating UIC and BS 2953: 1958 hp at rpm		Displacement Cubic Inches (litres)	Bore and Stroke Inches (mm)	Number of Cylinders	Aspiration	Net Weight lb (kg)
Locomotives Engines									
N-855-L3	235	2 100	200	1 900	855	5½×6	6	N	2 590
			210	2 100	*(14.0)*	*(140 × 152)*			*(1 175)*
NT-855-L4	335	2 100	275	1 900	855	,,	6	T	2 625
			285	2 100	*(14.0)*				*(1 191)*
NTA-855-L3	400	2 100	335	1 900	855	,,	6	T/A	2 750
			340	2 100	*(14.0)*				*(1 247)*
VTA-1710-L1	700	2 100	560	1 900	1 710	,,	12	T/A	5 780
			595	2 100	*(28.0)*				*(2 621)*
VTA-1710-L2	800	2 100	640	1 900	1 710	,,	12	T/A	5 780
			680	2 100	*(28.0)*				*(2 621)*
KT-1150-L	450	2 100	370	1 900	1 150	6¼ × 6¼	6	T	3 450
			380	2 100	*(18.8)*	*(159 × 159)*			*(1 565)*
KTA-1150-L	600	2 100	490	1 900	1 150	,,	6	T/A	3 500
			510	2 100	*(18.8)*				*(1 588)*
KT-2300-L	900	2 100	725	1 900	2 300	,,	12	T	7 750
			765	2 100	*(37.6)*				*(3 315)*
*KTA-2300-L	1 200	2 100	975	1 900	2 300	,,	12	T/A	8 000
			1 020	2 100	*(37.6)*				*(3 629)*
Railcar Engines									
N-855-R2	235	2 100	210	2 100	855	5½ × 6	6	N	2 600
					(14.0)	*(140 × 152)*			*(1 185)*
NT-855-R4	335	2 100	285	2 100	855	,,	6	T	2 700
					(14.0)				*(1 200)*
NTA-855-R	400	2 100	340	2 100	855	,,	6	T/A	2 800
					(14.0)				*(1 255)*

*Certified to BS 2953: 1958 BSI Certificate No. 36791

DEUTZ

Klöckner-Humboldt-Deutz AG
D-5000 Köln-Deutz, Postfach 800509, German Federal Republic

The Deutz Engine Works is the oldest internal combustion engine factory in the world. Started in 1864 as N. A. Otto & Co., it soon became Gasmotorenfabrik Deutz AG The first engine working on the "OTTO" or 4-stroke cycle, invented by N. A. Otto, was built in 1876.
Deutz diesel engines range from 3-9 680 hp (2-7 120 kW) for industrial, marine, rail, traction and automotive applications. They are all four-stroke, air-cooled (3-500 hp) or water-cooled (270-9 680 hp). For rail traction series B/FL 413F, BAM 816 and PAGV 280 are used.

Series B/FL 413F
Type: 6, 8, 10 and 12 cylinder Vee 4-stroke, air-cooled, direct injection or two-stage combustion.
Cylinders: Bore 4.92 in *(125 mm)*, stroke 5.12 *(130 mm)*, swept volume 1.59 litres per cylinder. Compression ratio 18 : 1 (naturally aspirated), 16.5 : 1 (turbo-charged).

Series BAM 816
Type: 6 and 8 cylinder-in-line, 12 and 16 cylinder Vee, 4-stroke, water-cooled, two-stage combustion system.
Cylinders: Bore 5.59 in *(142 mm)*, stroke 6.30 in *(160 mm)*. Swept volume 2.53 litres per cylinder. Compression ratio 16.1:1.

Deutz F12L 413F 12-cylinder air-cooled engine
Output (UIC) 246 kW (335 hp) at 2 500 rpm.

Deutz BA16M 816 16-cylinder water-cooled engine
Output (UIC) up to 830 kW *(1 130 hp)* at 1 800 rpm.

Series PA6V 280		12PA6V	14PA6V	16PA6V	18PA6V
No of cylinders		12V	14V	16V	18V
Turbocharged		Yes	Yes	Yes	Yes
Charge air cooled		Yes	Yes	Yes	Yes
Output (UIC)	kW	3 533	4 122	4 710	5 299
	hp	4 800	5 600	6 400	7 200
Engine speed	rpm	1 050	1 050	1 050	1 050
Length	in	152³/₈	171¹/₄	189³/₈	207¹/₂
	(mm)	*3 870*	*4 350*	*4 810*	*5 270*
Width	in	70¹/₁₆	70¹/₁₆	70¹/₁₆	70¹/₁₆
	(mm)	*1 780*	*1 780*	*1 780*	*1 780*
Height	in	97⁵/₈	97⁵/₈	97⁵/₈	97⁵/₈
	(mm)	*2 480*	*2 480*	*2 480*	*2 480*
Weight	lb	42 500	50 040	55 780	60 510
	(kg)	*(19 300)*	*(22 700)*	*(25 300)*	*(27 450)*

Series B/FL 413F		F6L	BF6L	F8L	BF8L	F10L	BF10L	F12L	BF12L
No of Cylinders		6V	6V	8V	8V	10V	10V	12V	12V
Turbocharged			Yes		Yes		Yes		Yes
Output (UIC)	kW	123	157	165	210	206	262	246	315
	hp	167	214	225	286	280	356	335	428
Engine speed	rpm	2 500	2 500	2 500	2 500	2 500	2 500	2 500	2 500
Length	in	41¹/₄	44³/₁₆	47¹¹/₁₆	50¹¹/₁₆	55⁹/₁₆	56⁵/₁₆	62	62¹³/₁₆
	(mm)	*(1 047)*	*(1 123)*	*(1 211)*	*(1 288)*	*(1 412)*	*(1 430)*	*(1 575)*	*(1 595)*
Width	in	40⁷/₈	41³/₄	40⁷/₈	41³/₄	40⁷/₈	44	40⁷/₈	46¹⁵/₁₆
	(mm)	*(1 038)*	*(1 060)*	*(1 038)*	*(1 060)*	*(1 038)*	*(1 118)*	*(1 038)*	*(1 192)*
Height	in	35³/₄	34¹/₄	33⁷/₈	34¹/₄	37¹⁵/₁₆	41⁵/₁₆	37¹⁵/₁₆	41⁵/₁₆
	(mm)	*(908)*	*(870)*	*(860)*	*(870)*	*(963)*	*(1 050)*	*(963)*	*(1 050)*
Weight	lb	1 335	1 500	1 700	1 985	2 070	2 425	2 470	2 755
	(kg)	*(605)*	*(680)*	*(770)*	*(900)*	*(940)*	*(1 100)*	*(1 120)*	*(1 250)*

Series BAM 816		BA6M LLK U	BA6M LLK W	BA8M LLK U	BA8M LLK W	BA12M LLK U	BA12M LLK W	BA16M LLK U	BA16M LLK W
No of cylinders		6	6	8	8	12	12	16	16
Turbocharged		Yes	Yes	Yes	Yes	Yes	Yes	Yes	Yes
Charge air cooled		Yes	Yes	Yes	Yes	Yes	Yes	Yes	Yes
Output (UIC)	kW	285	310	370	415	570	620	740	830
	hp	390	420	505	565	780	840	1 010	1 130
Engine speed	rpm	1 800	1 800	1 800	1 800	1 800	1 800	1 800	1 800
Length	in	72		84 7/8		76 13/16		97 1/8	
	(mm)	1 829		2 156		1 951		2 467	
Width	in	38 3/4		37 1/2		64		64	
	(mm)	984		952		1 626		1 626	
Height	in	56 11/16		58		52 15/16		52 15/16	
	(mm)	1 440		1 473		1 345		1 345	
Weight	lb	3 540		4 520		6 395		7 980	
	(kg)	1 605		2 050		2 900		3 620	

ENERGOMACHEXPORT

Moscow V-330, Mosfilmovskaja 35, USSR

Model D49 16-cylinder Vee engine
Turbocharged and charge air cooled. Output 3 000 hp at 1 000 rpm. Built by Kolomna Diesel Works.

Series		D100				D40	D45
Type		2-stroke, opposed piston				2-stroke Vee	2-stroke Vee
Bore	in	8.15				9.06	9.06
	(mm)	(207)				(230)	(230)
Stroke	in	10.0				11.8/11.98	11.8/11.98
	(mm)	(254)				(300/304.3)	(300/304.3)
Model		6D100	2D100	10D100	9D100-F	1D40	11D45
No. of cylinders		8	10	10	12	12	16
Output	hp	2 000	2 000	3 000	4 000	2 000	3 000
Engine speed	rpm	850	850	850	900	750	750
Piston speed	ft/min	1 417	1 417	1 417	1 496	1 476	1 476
	(m/sec)	(7.2)	(7.2)	(7.2)	(7.6)	(7.5)	(7.5)
Bmep	lb/sq in	111	88	132	108	115	129
	(kg/cm²)	(7.8)	(6.2)	(9.3)	(7.6)	(8.1)	(9.1)
Weight	lb	34 200	42 750	46 300	50 700	23 100	30 400
	(kg)	(15 500)	(19 400)	(21 000)	(23 000)	(10 500)	(13 800)
Length	in	238.3	240.7	243.3	260.6	145.7	158.3
	(mm)	(6 052)	(6 115)	(6 180)	(6 620)	(3 700)	(4 020)
Width	in	66.5	56.7	68.1	59.1	69.7	66.9
	(mm)	(1 690)	(1 440)	(1 730)	(1 500)	(1 770)	(1 700)
Height	in	118.6	127.6	126.4	124.0	95.3	97.2
	(mm)	(3 013)	(3 240)	(3 210)	(3 150)	(2 421)	(2 470)

Series		D49				D50			D70				M		1D
Type		4-stroke Vee				4-stroke in line			4-stroke Vee				4-stroke Vee		4-stroke Vee
Bore	in	10.24				12.5			9.45				7.09		5.9
	(mm)	(260)				(318)			(240)				(180)		(150)
Stroke	in	10.24				13.0			10.63				7.88/8.26		7.09/7.35
	(mm)	(260)				(330)			(270)				(200/208.8)		(180/186.7)
Model		4D49	12D49	D49-V16	D49-F	D50	D50M	11D1M	8D70	12D70	D70	D70F	M753	M756	1D12
No of cylinders		6	12	16	16	6	6	6	8	12	16	16	12	12	12
Output	hp	1 200	2 000	3 000	4 000	1 000	1 000	1 200	1 200	2 000	3 000	4 000	750	1 000	400
Engine speed	rpm	1 000	1 000	1 000	1 000	740	740	750	1 000	1 000	1 000	1 000	1 400	1 500	1 600
Piston speed	ft/min	1 713	1 713	1 713	1 713	1 604	1 604	1 624	1 772	1 772	1 772	1 772	1 837/1 929	2 087/2 205	1 890
	(m/sec)	(8.7)	(8.7)	(8.7)	(8.7)	(8.15)	(8.15)	(8.25)	(9.0)	(9.0)	(9.0)	(9.0)	(9.3/9.8)	(10.6/11.2)	(9.6)
Bmep	lb/sq in	188	156	174	232	110	110	131	196	175	196	262	105	131	82.5
	(kg/cm²)	(13.2)	(11.0)	(12.2)	(16.3)	(7.7)	(7.7)	(9.2)	(13.8)	(12.3)	(13.8)	(18.4)	(7.4)	(9.2)	(5.8)
Weight	lb	14 300	24 200	30 900	30 900		39 700		24 700	31 300	37 500	37 500	35 300	39 700	41 900
	(kg)	(6 500)	(11 000)	(14 000)	(14 000)		(18 000)		(11 200)	(14 200)	(17 000)	(17 000)	(16 000)	(18 000)	(19 000)
Length	in	96	142	170	170		205		157	181	217	220	89.4	95.3	61.4
	(mm)	(2 400)	(3 600)	(4 300)	(4 300)		(5 200)		(4 000)	(4 600)	(5 500)	(5 600)	(2 270)	(2 420)	(1 560)
Width	in	55	63	63	63		59		63	63	63	63	42.7	44.1	33.7
	(mm)	(1 400)	(1 600)	(1 600)	(1 600)		(1 500)		(1 600)	(1 600)	(1 600)	(1 600)	(1 085)	(1 120)	(856)
Height	in	90	102	110	110		98		110	114	118	118	47.3	58.3	42.3
	(mm)	(2 300)	(2 600)	(2 800)	(2 800)		(2 500)		(2 800)	(2 900)	(3 000)	(3 000)	(1 200)	(1 480)	(1 075)

GE

General Electric Company
Transportation Systems Business Division,
2910 East Lake Road, Erie, Pennsylvania 16531, USA

Series FDL (8, 12 and 16 cylinder 45° Vee)
Type: 4 cycle turbocharged with water cooled charge air cooler.
Cylinders: Bore 9 in (229 mm). Stroke 10-½ in (267 mm). Swept volume of 668 cu in per cylinder. Individual unitised cast cylinder with renewable liner and head. Compression ratio 12.7:1.
Pistons: Current-production engines use two-piece pistons. The steel crown, contoured on the top to form the combustion chamber and on the bottom to form cooling-oil passages, is bolted to an aluminium-alloy skirt.

Pistons used in older engines were one-piece, cast-iron pistons, with six, and later four, rings. Current-production engines also use four rings—three compression rings and one oil-control ring.
Crankcase: Main frame of high strength cast iron.
Valve gear: Roller type cam followers, push rods and rockers, 4 valves per cylinder. Gear driven sectionalised camshaft on each side of engine.
Fuel injection: Individual injectors and fuel pumps.
Turbocharger: One, exhaust driven (no gear drive to crankshaft).
Lubrication: Forced full flow filtered oil to all bearings and pistons, gear type engine driven pump.
Cooling system: Forced circulation water cooling of cylinders, turbocharger, and intercoolers. The water passages are—external of the crankcase and main frame.

General Electric 3 940 hp (UIC) 16-cylinder Vee engine

Current Design Engine Specifications

Model	7FDL8	7FDL12	7FDL16
No of cylinders	8	12	16
Output (UIC) standard	1 970	2 960	3 940
Stroke cycle	4	4	4
Cylinder arrangement	45-degree V	45-degree V	45-degree V
Bore	9 in (228.6 mm)	9 in (228.6 mm)	9 in (228.6 mm)
Stroke	10½ in (266.7 mm)	10½ in (266.7 mm)	10½ in (266.7 mm)
Compression ratio	12.7-1	12.7-1	12.7-1
Idle speed	450 rpm	450 rpm	450 rpm
Full-rated speed	1 050 rpm	1 050 rpm	1 050 rpm
Firing order	1R-1L-2R-2L-4R-4L-3R-3L	1R-1L-5R-5L-5L-3R-3I-6R 6L-2R-2L-4R-4L	1R-1L-3R-3L-7R-7L-4R-4L 8R-8L-6R-6L-2R-2L-5R-5L
Turbocharger	Single	Single	Single
Engine Dimensions:			
Height (excluding stack)	86¼ in (2 191 mm)	90⅛ in (2 289 mm)*	9⅛ in (2 289 mm)
Length (over-all)	128½ in (3 264 mm)	159½ in (4 051 mm)	193 in (4 902 mm)
Width (over-all)	68¼ in (1 734 mm)	68⅜ in (1 740 mm)	68⅜ in (1 740 mm)
Weight (dry)	27 000 lb (12 200 kg)	35 000 lb (15 900 kg)	43 500 lb (19 700 kg)

*Note: This dimension is for domestic (USA) type engines. The export model has a lower water header (86¼ in—2 191 mm)

GEC DIESELS

GEC Diesels Limited
Vulcan Works, Newton-le-Willows, Merseyside WA12 8RU, England

GEC Diesels Ltd is the parent company of **Ruston Diesels Ltd, Paxman Diesels Ltd** and **Dorman Diesels Ltd.**

Engine range	Company	Location
Dorman	Dorman Diesels Ltd	Tixall Road, Stafford
English Electric	Ruston Diesels Ltd	Newton-le-Willows, Merseyside
Paxman	Paxman Diesels Ltd	Colchester, Essex
Deltic	Paxman Diesels Ltd	Colchester, Essex

DELTIC ENGINES

The Deltic is an opposed piston engine with the cylinders arranged in three banks, each bank forming one side of an inverted equilateral triangle with a crankshaft at each apex. Power from the three crankshafts is transmitted through phasing gears to a single central output shaft.

Specification

Type: 18 cylinder. Opposed piston. 2-stroke cycle. Compression-ignition, liquid cooled. The cylinders are arranged in three banks each forming one side of an inverted equilateral triangle with crankshaft on each apex. Power from the three crankshafts is transmitted through phasing gearing to a single output shaft.

Cylinders: Bore 5.125 in (130.17 mm). Stroke 7.25 in (184.15 mm) × 2. Swept volume 299m³ (4.91 litres) per cylinder. Compression 16:1 (13.8:1 CT18-52B). Cylinder blocks are identical light alloy castings of monobloc construction. Open ended wet type cylinder liners machined from hollow steel forgings, chromium plated in bore.

Pistons: Aluminium alloy body with copper-alloy crown, oil cooled, with three compression rings and three oil control rings. Fully floating hardened steel gudgeon pin.

Connecting rods: Each crankpin carries two high-tensile, alloy steel, forged connecting rods, one plain and one forked. The forked rod, to which the exhaust piston is attached, is reinforced at the big end by a nitrided steel sleeve which has a thin wall bearing on the inside and, on the outside, provides a journal for the big end of the plain rod to which the inlet piston is attached.

Crankshaft: Nitrided steel with hollow crank pins statically balanced. The top crankshafts are identical and rotate clockwise; the bottom crankshaft has opposite-handed throws and rotates anti-clockwise. Thin-wall, lead-bronze, lead-plated, indium-infused main bearings.

Crankcase: Three crankcases are arranged between adjacent cylinder blocks to form the triangular engine assembly, the six separate castings being secured together by high-tensile bolts. The two upper crankcases are identical but the lower one is deepened in section to provide effective oil drainage for the dry sump lubrication system.

Valve gear: None. Inlet and exhaust ports are provided in each cylinder.

Fuel injection: CAV inward opening valve injectors, one per cylinder, with CAV individual jerk type pumps.

Scavenge air blower: Double sided single-stage centrifugal blower, mounted on the free end of the engine. Mechanically driven from top crankshafts. Provides complete scavenging and a degree of supercharge.

Turbo-blower: Exhaust gas driven and mechanically coupled to the engine. The unit consists of a centrifugal air compressor and a single stage axial flow turbine. On the CT 18-528 engine the charge-air coolers are integral with the blower unit.

Fuel: To BS 2869: 1970 Class AI and A2 diesel fuel.

Lubrication: Dry sump system. Pressure fed to all bearings and gear trains, with one pressure pump and one scavenge pump.

Cooling system: Forced draught radiator with engine driven centrifugal pump. On charge-cooled engines, the coolers are fed by an independent system comprising a radiator and engine-driven pump.

Starting system: Electric or compressed air.

Mounting: 4-point.

The Deltic can be either mechanically blown or turbocharged, the turbocharged engines being available with or without charge-air cooling. British Railways 3 300 hp Type 5 diesel electric locomotives in service on Eastern region are powered by two

Deltic 18-25 mechanically blown engine

mechanically blown Deltic engines.
Several of these have now completed 2 million miles (3.2 million km) in under 12 years service, and others are approaching this total.

		Type 18-25B Mechanically blown	Type T18-27B Turbocharged	Type CT18-52B Charge air cooled Turbocharged
Length	in	94	123	126
	(mm)	(2 388)	(3 124)	(3 200)
Width	in	70	70	70
	(mm)	(1 778)	(1 778)	(1 778)
Height	in	90	90	90
	(mm)	(2 286)	(2 286)	(2 286)
Weight (dry):		10 850 lb	11 600 lb	13 600 lb
		(4 920 kg)	(5 260 kg)	(6 170 kg)
Engine speed rpm		1 500	1 600	1 600
Power ratings:				
Intermittent		1 825 bhp	2 300 bhp	2 750 bhp
Continuous:		1 750 bhp	2 200 bhp	2 625 bhp
Fuel consumption:				
Intermittent:		0.350 lb/bhp	0.365 lb/bhp/hr	0.358 lb/bhp/hr
Continuous:		0.350 lb/bhp	0.368 lb/bhp/hr	0.358 lb/bhp/hr

Rated output on all Deltic engines is based on BS 2953

DORMAN ENGINES

Special features of the Dorman series of diesel engines are the wide speed range of 800 to 2 600 rpm on the water cooled engines, and 1 000 to 2 500 rpm on the air cooled engines; their compact and robust design and excellent power to weight ratio, standard cylinder sizes, maximum standardisation and parts interchangeability throughout each series. Fuel consumption is extremely economical.

DA Series: 4 and 6 cylinders in line, 8 cylinder Vee, air cooled
L   ,,   6 cylinders in line, water cooled
Q   ,,   6 cylinders in line, 8 and 12 cylinder Vee, water cooled
J   ,,   8 and 12 cylinder Vee, water cooled

	Bore	Stroke
DA Series	4.134 in (105 mm)	4.724 in (120 mm)
L ,,	5.000 in (127 mm)	5.118 in (130 mm)
Q ,,	6.250 in (159 mm)	6.500 in (165 mm)
J ,,	5.118 in (130 mm)	5.921 in (125 mm)
S ,,	6.250 in (159 mm)	7.500 in (190 mm)

Connecting Rods: DA, L and 6Q, Alloy steel H section stampings. 8Q, 8J, 12Q and 12S, H section alloy steel stampings, side by side on common crankpin.
Crankshafts: Dynamically balanced, hardened steel crankshaft.

Bearings: Steel backed lined with reticular tin.
Crankcase: Rigid cast-iron structure, Monobloc in the case of water cooled engines and with separate barrels in the case of air cooled engines.
Cylinder heads: Water cooled engines; high grade iron castings. Air cooled engines die cast light alloy.
Pistons: Aluminium Alloy with toroidal combustion chamber.
  S, Q and DA series have three pressure rings and two oil control rings
  L series have two pressure rings and two oil control rings
  J series has two pressure rings and one oil control ring
Starting: Air, electric or hydraulic.

Dorman 12 QTCW engine generator unit
Turbocharged and air-to-water charge cooled. 572 kW at 1 800 rpm

Dorman 8J 8-cylinder Vee engine
234 hp at 2 200 rpm

		L Series					
Model	6LD	6LDT	6LDTCA	6LDTCW	6LE	6LET	6LETCA
No of cylinders	6	6	6	6	6	6	6
Turbocharged	No	Yes	Yes	Yes	No	Yes	Yes
Charge air cooled	No	No	Air to air	Air to water	No	No	Air to air
bhp continuous	162	216	227	227	186	224	250
Engine speed rpm	2 400	1 800	1 800	1 800	2 200	1 800	1 800

							Q Series						
Model	6Q	6QT	6QTCA	6QTCW	8Q	8QT	8QTCA	8QTCW	12Q	12QT	12QTCA	12QTCW	12QBTCA	12BQTCW
No of cylinders	6	6	6	6	8	8	8	8	12	12	12	12	12	12
Turbocharged	No	Yes	Yes	Yes	No	Yes	Yes	Yes	No	Yes	Yes	Yes	Yes	Yes
Charge air cooled	No	No	Air to air	Air to water	No	No	Air to air	Air to water	No	No	Air to air	Air to water	Air to air	Air to water
bhp continuous	250	345	385	414	318	540	575	570	477	691	769	827	825	760
Engine speed rpm	1 800	1 800	1 800	1 800	1 800	1 800	1 800	1 800	1 800	1 800	1 800	1 800	1 800	1 500

		J Series		S Series		DA Series		
Model	8J	8JT	12JAT	12ST	4DA	6DA	8DA	6DAT
No of cylinders	8	8	12	12	4	6	8	6
Turbocharged	No	Yes	Yes	Yes	No	No	No	Yes
Charge air cooled	No	No	No	No	No	No	No	No
bhp continuous	234	330	450	760	68	103	134	95
Engine speed rpm	2 200	2 200	2 000	1 500	2 500	2 500	2 500	1 800

ENGLISH ELECTRIC ENGINES

English Electric "RK" series
English Electric rail traction engines, proved by many years of intensive service in locomotive applications throughout the world, are available in turbocharged and charge-air cooled versions. Medium speed engines with cylinder dimensions of 10 in (254 mm) bore and 12 in (305 mm) stroke throughout the range, they offer long periods between overhauls with a high degree of interchangeability of components.

RK3XT   Turbocharged
RK3CT   Turbocharged and charge-air cooled.

Type: Four-stroke, water cooled.
Cylinders: Bore 10 in (254 mm). Stroke 12 in (305 mm). Swept volume 942.5 in³ (15.45 litres) per cylinder. Compression ratio 11.53:1. Renewable wet type alloy cast iron cylinder liners secured by cylinder head. Separate alloy cast iron cylinder heads secured by 6 studs.
Pistons: Oil cooled trunk type aluminium alloy pistons with four compression and two oil control rings, one above and one below fully floating gudgeon pins.
Connecting rods: Solid forged carbon steel. Lead bronze lined bearing shells.
Crankshaft: Fully machined CGF forged alloy steel. Lead bronze lined main bearing shells.
Crankcase: Monobloc alloy iron casting.
Valve gear: Two inlet and two exhaust silicon chrome steel poppet-type valves. High grade cast iron insert valve seats, press fit in cylinder head. Gear driven camshaft.
Fuel injection: Bryce multi-hole type injectors, with one Bryce constant stroke pump per cylinder.
Supercharger: Napier exhaust gas driven turbo chargers.
Lubrication: Forced feed to all bearing surfaces. Gear-type pumps.
Cooling system: Centrifugal type pumps. Forced draught cooled radiator. Water cooled charge cooler, where fitted.
Starting: Electric or air starting appropriate to application.

English Electric 8RK3CT 8-cylinder Vee engine
Turbocharged and charge air cooled, developing 1 760 bhp at 900 rpm.

Mounting: Suitable for flange-mounted generator and 3 or 4 point mounting of power unit.

PAXMAN ENGINES

Paxman engines were first introduced into railway traction in 1930. The Paxman engines in the present range are of compact design while providing maximum accessibility for maintenance. They combine high power-to-weight ratio with the rugged construction necessary for reliable traction service.

British Railways high speed train now entering public service is powered by two 12 cylinder RP200 engines. Two years of exhaustive testing proved the performance and reliability of the train which achieved a speed of 143 mph *(229 km/h)*, a world record for diesel traction. 141 engine sets are on order for British Railways.

Following the successful operation of Paxman 12RPHXL engines since 1951, the Sri Lanka Railway are operating a total of 82 Ventura 8YJXL, 12YJXL and 16YJXL engines. These engines are now in service operating in every kind of geographical environment at a high degree of availability.

Recent orders include a repeat for 21 8RPHXL engines for the Nigerian Railway Corporation in addition to the 22 sets of diesel-electric shunting locomotives already in service.

The Company continues to receive orders for engines to power steel works shunters from existing owners of Paxman engined locomotives.

RPH, YH, YK, YJ and RP200 Series

Type: Four cycle, water-cooled 60° Vee (in line 6 YK), normally-aspirated, pressure-charged (Suffix 'X' to engine type number) or pressure-charged and intercooled (Suffix 'C'). All RP200 engines are pressure-charged and intercooled.

Housing: Cast iron (RPH, YH, YK and YJ), fabricated (RP200 and alternatively 8, 12 and 16YJ). Cast cylinder blocks mounted on top of housing with cast iron liners (YK, YJ and RP200). Wet liners chromium plated on water side and in bore (YJ and RP200 engines only).

Crankshaft and main bearings: Underslung forged steel crankshaft drilled for large end lubrication. YJ and RP200 crankshafts nitride and YK induction hardened. Steel bearing shells tin aluminium lined.

Connecting rods and bearings: Fork and blade machined steel stampings drilled for small end lubrication and piston cooling (YK side-by-side rods). Large end (forked rod) tin aluminium lined, large end (blade rod) steel shells lined with copper-lead (RPH and YH); lead-bronze (YJ and RP200) and flashed with lead (RPH and YH), lead-tin (YJ and RP200). Small end bushes nickel gunmetal, lead bronze YK engines.

Pistons: Aluminium alloy, oil cooled with three compression and one oil control ring (except YJ which has one scraper ring). Iron insert for top chrome-faced pressure ring (plain ring YJ and RP200).

Cylinder heads and valve gear: Two-unit head 8RPH, three-unit head 6RPH, single-unit head all other engines. Replaceable valve seat inserts. Heads accommodate spherical antechambers of Comet Mk III combustion system (RPH). One inlet and exhaust hardened valve per cylinder (RPH); direct injection of fuel with two inlet and exhaust valves (YH, YK, YJ and RP200). Pressure-lubricated rocker gear.

Camshaft and drive: Gear-driven camshaft for valve gear (valve and injection pumps YK).

Fuel injection equipment: Gear-driven monobloc pumps (one on 6RPH; two on 8 and 12RPH, YH, 6, 8 and 12 YJ; four on 16YJ). Single unit pumps on YK and RP200. Injectors single-hole, pintle or pintaux type (RPH); multi-hole type (YH, YJ, YK and RP200).

Paxman 8RPHXL turbocharged diesel engine with torque converter drive

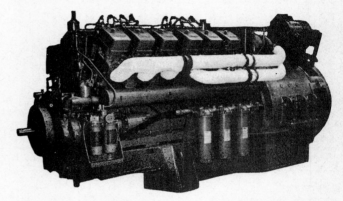

Paxman 12YHXL turbocharged diesel engine with generator

Engine Type	Turbo charged	No of Cylinders	Cont-Traction Rating (bhp)	Engine Speed rpm	Bmep lb/in² (kg/cm²)	Piston Speed ft/min (m/sec)	Full Load Fuel Consumption lb/bhp/h (gr/bhp/h)	Bore in (mm)	Stroke in (mm)	Displacement in³ (litres)	Compression Ratio	Length	Width	Height	Crankcase Centre Line Height	Approx Dry Weight lb (kg)
6RPHL	No	6	274*	1 500	81 (5.7)	1937 (9.84)	0.417 (189)	7.0 (178)	7.75 (197)	1 790 (29.3)	17.25 : 1	56.5 (1 435)	49 (1 245)	63 (1 600)	19.25 (490)	5 240 (2 376)
6RPHXL	Yes	6	304*	,,	90 (6.33)	,,	0.430 (195)	,,	,,	1 790 (29.3)	15.5 : 1	63.5 (1 613)	49 (1 245)	62 (1 575)	19.25 (490)	5 340 (2 422)
6RPHCL	Yes	6	375*	,,	110 (7.7)	,,	0.424 (192)	,,	,,	1 790 (29.3)	15.5 : 1	64.5 (1 638)	49 (1 245)	69 (1 753)	19.25 (490)	5 445 (2 469)
8RPHL	No	8	366*	,,	81 (5.7)	,,	0.418 (190)	,,	,,	2 380 (39.0)	17.25 : 1	69 (1 727)	49 (1 245)	63 (1 600)	19.25 (490)	6 550 (2 970)
8RPHXL	Yes	8	406*	,,	90 (6.33)	,,	0.417 (189)	,,	,,	2 386 (39.0)	15.5 : 1	74 (1 880)	49 (1 245)	62 (1 575)	19.25 (490)	6 650 (3 016)
8RPHCL	Yes	8	500*	,,	110 (7.7)	,,	0.424 (192)	,,	,,	2.386 (39.0)	15.5 : 1	74 (1 880)	49 (1 245)	69 (1 755)	19.25 (490)	6 750 (3 061)
12RPHL	No	12	562*	,,	83 (5.84)	,,	0.410 (186)	,,	,,	3 580 (58.7)	17.25 : 1	91 (2 310)	51 (1 295)	71 (1 805)	27 (686)	9 400 (4 263)
12RPHXL	Yes	12	610*	,,	90 (6.33)	,,	0.407 (184)	,,	,,	3 580 (58.7)	15.5 : 1	100 (2 540)	59 (1 500)	73 (1 854)	27 (686)	9 700 (4 400)
12RPHCL	Yes	12	750*	,,	110 (7.7)	,,	0.392 (178)	,,	,,	3 580 (58.7)	15.5 : 1	100 (2 540)	59 (1 500)	79 (2 007)	27 (686)	9 860 (4 472)
12YHXL	Yes	12	900	,,	133 (9.35)	,,	0.374 (170)	,,	,,	3 580 (58.7)	13.0 : 1	100 (2 540)	62.5 (1 588)	75 (1 905)	27 (686)	10 800 (4 898)
12YHCL	Yes	12	1 050	,,	155 (10.9)	,,	0.374 (170)	,,	,,	3 580 (58.7)	,,	100 (2 540)	62.5 (1 588)	77 (1 955)	27 (686)	11 100 (5 034)
6YKCL	Yes	6	900	1 800	230 (16.2)	2 184 (11.09)	0.365 (166)	7.09 (180)	7.28 (185)	1 724 (28.3)	13.1 : 1	1 155 (2 934)	47.5 (1 207)	87 (2 210)	29.5 (750)	10 700 (4 853)
8YKCL	Yes	8	1 200	,,	230 (16.2)	,,	0.365 (166)	,,	,,	2 300 (37.7)	,,	114.5 (2 910)	57 (1 448)	80.75 (2 051)	29.5 (750)	12 200 (5 533)
12YKCL	Yes	12	1 800	,,	230 (16.2)	,,	0.365 (166)	,,	,,	3 448 (56.6)	,,	147.25 (3 740)	57 (1 448)	85.75 (2 178)	29.5 (750)	16 860 (7 646)
6YJXL	Yes	6	650	1 500	143 (10.2)	2 125 (10.80)	0.375 (170)	7.75 (197)	8.5 (216)	2 405 (39.4)	13.0 : 1	63 (1 600)	56 (1 420)	70 (1 780)	21 (535)	7 075 (3 209)
6YJCL	Yes	6	750	,,	165 (11.8)	,,	0.375 (170)	,,	,,	2 405 (39.4)	,,	63 (1 600)	56 (1 420)	70 (1 780)	21 (535)	7 320 (3 320)
8YJXL	Yes	8	900	,,	148 (10.6)	,,	0.375 (170)	,,	,,	3 207 (52.6)	,,	67 (1 700)	52.5 (1 335)	83 (2 110)	23 (585)	8 250 (3 742)
8YJCL	Yes	8	1 000	,,	165 (11.8)	,,	0.363 (165)	,,	,,	3 207 (52.6)	,,	67 (1 700)	52.5 (1 335)	83 (2 110)	23 (585)	8 500 (3 855)
12YJXL	Yes	12	1 350	,,	148 (10.6)	,,	0.375 (170)	,,	,,	4 811 (78.9)	,,	81 (2 060)	52.5 (1 335)	79 (2 010)	23 (585)	10 650 (4 830)
12YJCL	Yes	12	1 500	,,	165 (11.8)	,,	0.363 (165)	,,	,,	4 811 (78.9)	,,	81 (2 060)	52.5 (1 335)	79 (2 010)	23 (585)	11 270 (5 111)
16YJXL	Yes	16	1 800	,,	148 (10.6)	,,	0.377 (171)	,,	,,	6 415 (105.1)	,,	105 (2 670)	52.5 (1 335)	81 (2 060)	23 (585)	14 360 (6 513)
16YJCL	Yes	16	2 000	,,	165 (11.8)	,,	0.365 (166)	,,	,,	6 415 (105.1)	,,	105 (2 670)	52.5 (1 335)	81 (2 060)	23 (585)	14 970 (6 789)
8RP200L	Yes	8	1 500	,,	247 (17.3)	,,	0.353 (160)	,,	,,	3 207 (52.6)	,,	76.25 (1 936)	57.5 (1 460)	92.5 (2 350)	29 (740)	9 325 (4 229)
12RP200L	Yes	12	2 250	,,	247 (17.3)	,,	0.353 (160)	,,	,,	4 811 (78.9)	,,	96.75 (2 458)	57.5 (1 460)	90.75 (2 305)	29 (740)	15 050 (6 825)
16RP200L	Yes	16	3 000	,,	247 (17.3)	,,	0.353 (160)	,,	,,	6 415 (105.1)	,,	117.5 (2 980)	57.5 (1 460)	92.5 (2 350)	29 (740)	19 600 (8,889)
18RP200L	Yes	18	3 380	,,	247 (17.3)	,,	0.353 (160)	,,	,,	7 217 (118.3)	,,	126.25 (3 207)	57.5 (1 460)	89.0 (2 260)	29 (740)	21 750 (9 864)

Paxman Valenta 12RP200L engine and alternator set

The Rp 200 Valenta introduced in 1971 incorporates many of the features of the Paxman Ventura but has been extensively redesigned to increase its continuous power to 3 000 bhp, whilst retaining almost the same physical dimensions of the YJ engine. The Valenta has been chosen by British Rail for powering its 200 km/h *(125 mph)* inter-city high speed train sets.

Governor: Regulators 1100 series hydraulic servo type for mechanical, electric or pneumatic control (all engines).
Pressure charging: ('X' and 'C' engines). Exhaust gas driven, air-cooled (RPH, YH and 6YK) water-cooled (YJ, 8 and 12YK and RP200) turbo-blower.
Intercooling: ('C' engines and RP200). Air to water cooler.
Lubrication: Pressure lubrication to all bearings by engine driven gear type pumps separate pump for cooling system (not YK and RP200). Engine mounted oil filters (RPH and YH), independently mounted (YJ, YK and RP200). Integral oil cooler (YJ and RP200). Cooling by engine jacket water (YJ), radiator-cooled (other engines).
Cooling: Centrifugal, gear-driven pump.
Starting: Electric, air or hydraulic starter motors, motoring by main generator or dynastarter.
Rotation: Anti-clockwise, looking on flywheel.

Paxman Ventura 16JXL turbocharged engine

Fuel: To BS 2869: 1970 Class A1, A2 or B1 (RPH, YH and YK), Class B2 (RPH and YK) or Class A1 or A2 (YJ and RP200), or as may be agreed.

Notes
Engine ratings: Continuous traction rating corrected for altitude of 500 ft *(150 m)*, air temperature of 85°F *(30°C)* and ('C' engines and RP 200) water temperature to intercooler 113°F *(45°C)*.
*Engines marked with an asterisk can be offered with an intermittent rating 10 per cent higher for shunting duty.
Dimensions: These are for engines with standard equipment.
Engine weights: These include fuel and lubricating oil filters, oil cooler (YJ and RP 200), damper and sump, but exclude flywheel, air filters, and mounting. Those for 8, 12 and 16 YJ include fabricated housing.

GMT

Grandi Motori Trieste SpA
(FIAT-ANSALDO-CRDA)
Corso Cavour, 1—Trieste, Italy

Grandi Motori Trieste build diesel engines for railway traction, marine and industrial applications. For rail traction their locomotive engine range includes: series A210 and A230 from 750 to 4 500 hp.

Series A210
Type: 4-stroke, turbocharged, with charge air cooling.
Cylinders: Bore 8.27 in *(210 mm)*. Stroke 9.05 in *(230 mm)*.

Series A230
Type: 4-stroke, turbocharged with charge air cooling.
Cylinders: Bore 9.05 in *(230 mm)*. Stroke 10.62 in *(270 mm)*.

The other main characteristics, common to the two types of engines are as follows:
Cylinder liners: Wet type removable liners of special cast iron.
Cylinder heads: One per cylinder, in alloyed cast, iron; each has two inlet and two exhaust valves and the fuel injector in the centre.
Pistons: Aluminium alloy, oil cooled. They have three compression rings and one oil scraper ring.
Crankshaft: Of highly alloyed forged steel. The surface of the pins is hardened by electric induction process. Thin walled three metal bearings.
Frame: Cast iron.
Valve gear: One or two camshaft for in-line and Vee engines respectively driven at flywheel side. The two inlet and two exhaust valves are driven by rollers—push rods—rocker arms through a transverse piece.
Turbocharging: Achieved by means of exhaust gas turbo-blowers operating with pulse systems. The air is then cooled in suitable coolers.

Fuel injection pumps: Of plunger type with a spiral groove. The fuel injection is controlled by rotating the plunger by means of a transversal rack.
Fuel: Gas oil.
Lubrication: Forced fed by directly driven gear pump.
Cooling system: Fresh water fed by two centrifugal pumps, one for the engine, one for the oil and air cooling system.

GMT four-stroke diesel engine type A230.20, turbocharged with aftercooling; 4 500 bhp at 1 100 rpm

Engine type	Data	Version	Cyls No	Output bhp (UIC)	Weight kg	Length mm	Width mm	Height mm
A 210								
Output	187.5 bhp/Cyl	A 210.4	4 V	750	4 400	1 700	1 770	1 570
Bore	210 mm	A 210.6	6 V	1 125	5 500	2 000	1 770	1 570
Stroke	230 mm	A 210.8	8 V	1 500	7 000	2 250	1 820	1 930
Speed	1 500 rpm	A 210.12	12 V	2 250	9 500	2 835	1 820	2 020
MEP	14,1 KG/cm²	A 210.16	16 V	3 000	11 800	3 690	1 820	1 980
MPS	11.5 m/sec	A 210.18	18 V	3 375	13 000	4 010	1 820	2 080

Length: at crankshaft—*Width:* overall—*Height:* from underside of feet

Fuel consumption: 158 gr/hp/hr
Lubricating oil: 1.7

Engine type	Data	Version	Cyl-inder	Output bhp (UIC)	Weight kg	Length (mm)	Width (mm)	Height (mm)
B 230								
		B 230.4	4 L	1 000	5 700	2 755	1 120	2 000
		B 230.6	6 L	1 500	7 900	3 440	1 120	2 000
Output	250 bhp/Cyl	B 230.8	8 V	2 000	9 500	3 055	1 720	1 800
Bore	230 mm	B 230.12	12 V	3 000	14 500	4 195	1 720	1 800
Stroke	270 mm	B 230.16	16 V	4 000	18 000	5 000	1 720	2 340
Speed	1 200 rpm	B 230.18	18 V	4 500	21 000	5 380	1 720	2 340
MEP	16.71 kg/cm²	B 230.20	20 V	5 000	23 500	5 840	1 720	2 340
MPS	10.8 m/sec							

Length: at crankshaft—*Width:* overall—*Height:* from underside of feet

Fuel consumption: 160 gr/hp/hr
Lubricating oil: 1.7

GMT four-stroke diesel engine type A210.8, turbocharged with aftercooling; 1 500 bhp at 1 500 rpm

GANZ-MÁVAG

H-1967 Budapest, Könyves Kálmán körut 76, Hungary

Ganz-Mávag Works build various diesel engines, mainly for their own makes of locomotives and railcars. Here is a brief description of two typical engines in these ranges.

Type: SEMT-PIELSTICK 12PA4-V-185 VG/made under licence from Alsthom-Atlantique, France

General: 12 cylinders in Vee, 4 stroke with "Variable Geometry" combustion chamber, turbocharged and intercooled.
Cylinders: Bore 185 mm, stroke 210 mm. Swept volume 5.65 litre per cylinder. Individual cylinder heads and separate cast-iron water jackets with wet liners. Nodular graphite iron pistons with internal oil cooling.
Connecting rods: Side-by-side type.
Crankcase: Tunnel type, with integral oil sump of arc-welded steel castings and steel plates.
Fuel injection: Conventional type injection pump and pintle type injectors.
Valve gear: Single camshaft in the Vee, with push-rods and rockers.
Output: Nominal power rating 1 472 kW/2 000 hp/at 1 500 rpm.
Dry weight: About 6 700 kg/complete with all accessories.

Type 12 VFE 17/24-T
General: 12 cylinders in Vee, 4 stroke with prechamber, turbocharged and intercooled.
Cylinders: Bore 170 mm, stroke 240 mm. Swept volume 5.45 litre per cylinder. Individual cylinder heads, wet liners and light metal oil cooled pistons.
Connecting rods: Fork-and-blade type.
Crankcase: Light alloy casting with separate oil sump.
Fuel injection: "Jendrassik" type spring injection pump and semi-open injectors.
Valve gears: Single camshaft in the Vee, with push-rods and rockers.
Output: Nominal power rating: 736 kW/1 000 hp/at 1 250 rpm.
Dry weight: About 5 000 kg/complete with accessories.

PA4 engine range comprise also 6, 8 and 18 cylinder models. 17/24 range comprises also 6 and 8 cylinder models.

Ganz Mavag 16VFE 17/24 16-cylinder Vee
1 000 hp at 1 200 rpm

Ganz-Mavag-Pielstick 12 PA4V-185 engine
12-cylinder Vee, turbocharged and charge-air cooled, developing 1 800 hp at 1 500 rpm
(UIC rating)

GARDNER

L. Gardner & Sons Ltd
Barton Hall Engine Works, Patricroft, Eccles, Manchester M30 7WA, England

Started by the Gardner brothers in 1898 as a general engineering works on the present site, employing 80 men, the works to-day cover nearly 20 times the original area and has 2 800 employees. In 1901 a limited company, L. Gardner & Sons Ltd, was formed, and this is now the parent company of Gardner Engines (Sales) Ltd. Hot air engines and horizontal gas engines were built at first and development of the compression ignition engine followed at an early stage in its growth. For example, a 6-cylinder Gardner engine powered what is claimed to be the first diesel rail traction unit in the British Isles; this was a 52-seat railcar built by County Donegal Railways in 1931.
Current production comprises automotive, rail traction, marine and industrial engines. For rail traction the main types are L3B, 8LXB, and 6LXB from 180 to 260 hp. They are fitted in locomotives and railcars produced by numerous builders including Barclay, Baguley-Drewry, Hunslet, Hudswell Badger, etc. The National Coal Board (GB) uses LW type engines in flame-proof underground locomotives, and British Rail operates a large number of small diesel mechanical shunting locomotives powered by the larger Gardner engines. Overseas, Gardner-powered railcars and locomotives are in service in countries throughout the world.

6LXB, (vertical) and 6HLXB (horizontal)
Type: 6 and 8 cylinder, 4-cycle, vertical, in-line, water cooled.
Cylinders: Bore 4¾ in (120.6 mm). Stroke 6 in (152.4 mm). Swept volume 1.7 litres per cylinder. Compression ratio 14 : 1. High tensile cast iron cylinder blocks with dry type renewable liners. Detachable cast iron cylinder heads in two 3-bore units, secured with HT studs and nuts with indented steel (corrojoint) cylinder head packing.
Pistons: Medium silicon aluminium alloy with combustion chamber in crown. Two compression rings and one oil control ring, fully floating hollow gudgeon pin.
Connecting rods: Chrome molybdenum steel H section stampings machined all over. Pre-finished steel shell bearings lined with copper lead overlay plated for big-ends and bronze bushes for small ends.
Crankshaft: Solid one piece chrome molybdenum steel die stamping with hollow main and crankpin journals. Pre-finished steel shell main bearings lined with copper lead overlay plated.
Crankcase: Aluminium alloy with separate detachable cast iron single cylinder block fitted with renewable dry liners.
Valve gear: One exhaust and one inlet alloy steel overhead valve per cylinder. Press fit renewable stellite faced valve seats. Camshaft in crankcase driven by triplex bush roller chain.
Fuel injection: Multi-hole non-adjustable Gardner injectors with twin CAV type BPF (3 Ram) pumps.
Fuel: High speed diesel fuel oil.
Lubrication: Pressure feed throughout with one gear-type pump. Additional pump and oil cooling radiator as required.
Cooling System: Gardner centrifugal type pump with spherical carbon gland. Gardner multi-tube radiator and fan or proprietary make.
Starting System: 24 V electric starter.
Starting System: 24 V CAV or Simms axial motor.

8L3B
Type: 8 cylinder, 4-cycle, vertical in-line, water cooled.
Cylinders: Bore 5½ in (140 mm). Stroke 7¾ in (197 mm). Swept volume 3.0 litres per cylinder. Compression ratio 12 : 1. Detachable cast iron wet liners with renewable dry type liners. Detachable individual cast iron cylinder heads secured with studs and nuts. Metal to metal joint with no packing.

Pistons: Low expansion medium silicon aluminium alloy with combustion chamber in crown. Two compression rings and one oil control ring, fully floating hollow gudgeon pin.
Connecting rods: Chrome molybdenum steel stampings machined all over. Pre-finished steel shell bearings lined with copper lead overlay plated for big ends and

Gardner 6HLXB 6-cylinder Horizontal Diesel Engine

Gardner 8L3B 8-cylinder diesel engine

bronze bushes for small ends.

Crankshaft: Solid one piece chrome molybdenum steel die stamping with hollow main and crankpin journals. Pre-finished steel shell main bearings lined with copper lead overlay plated.

Crankcase: Upper and lower half type cast iron crankcase with detachable cast iron cylinder blocks.

Valve gear: One exhaust and one inlet alloy steel overhead valves per cylinder. Press fit renewable hardened alloy iron valve seats. Camshaft in crankcase driven by triplex bush roller chain.

Fuel injection: Multi hole non-adjustable Gardner injectors with CAV type BPF pumps.

Fuel: High speed diesel oil fuel.

Lubrication: Pressure feed throughout with one gear type pump. Additional pump and oil cooling radiator as required.

Cooling system: Gardner centrifugal type pump with spherical carbon gland. Gardner multi-tube radiator and fan, or proprietary make.

Starting system: 24 or 32 V electric starter.

Mounting: 6 point.

Model		8 L3B	LXB	HLXB	8LXB
No of cylinders		8	6	6	8
Max bhp		260	180	180	240
Engine speed	rpm	1 300	1 850	1 850	1 850
Weight approx	lb	5 523	1 560	1 707	2 045
	(kg)	(2 505)	(707.6)	(774.3)	(927.6)
Length	in	97¾	55	55	64
	(mm)	(2 483)	(1 397)	(1 397)	(1 626)
Width	in	34½	26¼	55	27
	(mm)	(807)	(667)	(1 397)	(686)
Height	in	50¾	45¼	26	50
	(mm)	(1 276)	(1 149)	(660)	(1 270)

All the above engines are normal aspiration. BS AU 141A Ratings are: 6LXB HLXB 188 bhp; 8LXB 250 bhp.
Road Vehicles only.

GENERAL MOTORS

General Motors Overseas Operations
767 Fifth Ave, New York, New York 10022, USA

The Electro-Motive Division of General Motors first developed the Model 567 diesel engine in 1938 when it began locomotive manufacture at La Grange, Illinois, USA.
To provide increased horsepower and greater efficiency, the Model 645 engine was introduced in mid-1965. The major change in the Model 645 over the 567 is the increase in cylinder liner bore from 8½ in (216 mm) to 9¹/₁₆ in (230 mm), the stroke remaining at 10 in (254 mm).
The Model 645 engine, either mechanically supercharged (Roots blown) or turbocharged, is standard for US domestic type locomotives and is also available for export.

Model 645E Series		Roots Blown			Turbocharged	
No of cylinders		8	12	16	16	20
Traction Rating	hp (SAE)	1 000	1 500	2 000	3 000	3 600
Engine rpm		900	900	900	900	900
Max Bmep	lb/sq in	94	94	94	141	133
	(kg/mm)	(69.2)	(69.2)	(69.2)	(99.1)	(93.5)
Max piston speed	ft/min	1 500	1 500	1 500	1 500	1 500
	(m/sec)	(7.63)	(7.63)	(7.63)	(7.63)	(7.63)
Weight (dry)	lb	18 700	25 000	33 400	34 500	41 100
	(kg)	(8 480)	(11 340)	(15 150)	(15 650)	(18 640)
Length	in	142	176	215	215	248
	(mm)	(3 607)	(4 470)	(5 461)	(5 461)	(6 299)
Width	in	63	65	63	67	67
	(mm)	(1 600)	(1 651)	(1 600)	(1 702)	(1 702)
Height	in	89	89	89	98	98
	(mm)	(2 260)	(2 260)	(2 260)	(2 489)	(2 489)

GM model 20-645E3

GM model 16-645E

GROSSOL

Société Grossol
BP 104, 14 rue Chaptal, 92303 Levallois-Perret, France

After many years research into the problems of diesel engine design, construction and utilisation, Société Grossol was formed by the two engineers concerned, Messrs Grosshans and Ollier, comprising a bureau of continuous study and research as well as a commercial service to users. Manufacture of their designs of engine has been taken up by three famous French engineering firms: Société Surgérienne de Constructions Mécanique (Poyaud series); Société Alsacienne de Constructions Mécanique (MGO

and AGO series); and Société Alsthom (agricultural machinery and industrial applications).

MGO: The initials of the three people concerned in the original engine design— S. N. Marep, F. Ollier, and J. Grosshans.

AGO: Following the success of the MGO engines manufactured under licence by SACM (Société Alsacienne de Constructions Mécanique) that company joined with the Société Grossol to design engines with a higher output, these are the AGO range.

F.A. ISOTTA FRASCHINI-BREDA

Fabbrica Automobili Isotta Fraschini e Motori Breda, SpA
Via Milano 7, Saronno (VA)—Italy

Telephone: (02) 960.3252/2/3
Telex: 39403

Isotta Fraschini-Breda build diesel engines for rail and road traction, marine and industrial applications.
Rail and road traction: Locomotives, railcars, special railroad vehicles, earth moving equipments.
For rail traction the locomotive engine range includes: series ID 19 from 450 to 680 hp, series ID 26 from 400 to 1 100 hp and series ID 36 from 300 to 1 100 hp.

F.A. Isotta Fraschini-Breda ID 19 series
12 cylinder horizontally opposed, 4-stroke, direct injection, water cooled.
Cylinders: Bore 5.71 in (145 mm). Stroke 7.09 in (180 mm). Swept volume 35.67 litres. The output is based on UIC specification.

F.A. Isotta Fraschini-Breda ID 26 series
6, 8 and 12 cylinders, 60° Vee, 4-stroke, direct injection, water cooled.
Cylinders: Bore 7.09 in (180 mm). Stroke 7.48 in (190 mm). Swept volume 4.833 litres per cylinder. The output is based on BS specifications.

F.A. Isotta Fraschini-Breda ID 36 series
6, 8 and 12 cylinders, 90° Vee, 4-stroke, direct injection, water cooled.
Cylinders: Bore 6.69 in (170 mm). Stroke 6.69 in (170 mm). Swept volume 3.858 litres per cylinder. The output is based on UIC specifications. Engine speed maximum 2 000 rpm.

		D19 Series			D26 Series								
Model		N12P	S12P	SS12P	N6V	S6V	SS6V	N8V	S8V	SS8V	N12V	S12V	SS12V
No of cylinders		12	12	12	6	6	6	8	8	8	12	12	12
Turbo-charged		—	Yes	Yes	—	Yes	Yes	—	Yes	Yes	—	Yes	Yes
Charge air cooled		—	—	Yes	—	—	Yes	—	—	Yes	—	—	Yes
bhp (UIC)		450	600	680	300	460	550	400	610	735	600	960	1 100
Engine speed	rpm	1 650	1 650	1 650	1 650	1 650	1 650	1 650	1 650	1 650	1 650	1 650	1 650
Weight (dry)	lb	7 616	7 947	8 278	3 311	3 421	3 532	4 415	4 591	4 746	6 291	6 622	6 843
	(kg)	(3 450)	(3 600)	(3 750)	(1 500)	(1 550)	(1 600)	(2 000)	(2 080)	(2 150)	(2 850)	(3 000)	(3 100)
Length (*) max	in	89.37	99.21	99.21	53.15			63			88.55		
	(mm)	(2 270)	(2 520)	(2 520)	(*) (1 350)			(*) (1 600)			(*) (2 250)		
Width (*) max	in	68.89	75	75	47.24			47.24			47.24		
	(mm)	(1 750)	(1 905)	(1 905)	(*) (1 350)			(*) (1 600)			(*) (2 250)		
Height (*) max	in	37	37	42.51	47.24			49.60			58.26		
	(mm)	(940)	(940)	(1 080)	(*) (1 200)			(*) (1 260)			(*) (1 480)		
Fuel consumption All models					Normally aspirated	0.386 lb/hp/hr (175 gr/hp/hr)			Turbo-charged	0.375 lb/hp/hr (170 gr/hp/hr)			

Notes: N = Naturally aspirated. S = Turbocharged. SS = Turbocharged and intercooled.

ID 1912P series diesel engine for railway traction from 450 up to 680 bhp at 1 650 rpm.

ID 36 series diesel engine for railway traction from 300 up to 1 100 bhp at 1 650 rpm.

JW

Jenbacher Werke AG
A-6200 Jenbach, Tirol, Austria

Formed in 1946, this company builds diesel locomotives and diesel engines for industrial and marine purposes up to 3 000 hp

Jenbacher LM1500 12-cylinder engine
1 500 hp at 1 000 rpm

LM Series

Type: 4, 6, 8 and 12 cylinder 90 degree V, two stroke, water cooled, direct injection.
Cylinders: Bore 9.45 in *(240 mm)* stroke 9.84 in *(250 mm)* swept volume 11.3 litres per cylinder. Cast iron cylinder block and crankcase with centrifugally cast wet cylinder liners. Individual cylinder heads.
Pistons: Light alloy coated, with tin, oil cooled. Four compression rings, the top one chrome plated, and two oil control rings.
Connecting rods: Separate side by side drop forged with lead-bronze big end bearings, and fixed gudgeon pin.
Crankshaft: Drop forged, carried in lead-bronze main bearings. Viscous damper.
Fuel injector: Gear-driven from flywheel end of crankshaft.
Scavenge blower: Centrifugal pump driven from flywheel end of crankshaft.
Lubrication: Pressure pump driven by V belts from the forward end of the crankshaft.
Starting: Electric or compressed air.

Model		LM500	LM750	LM1000	LM1500
No of Cylinders		4	6	8	12
Output	bhp	500	750	1 000	1 500
Speed	rpm	1 000	1 000	1 000	1 000
Weight (dry)	lb	9 480	11 025	15 000	20 950
	(kg)	*(4 300)*	*(5 000)*	*(6 800)*	*(9 500)*
Length	in			141.7	
	(mm)			*(3 600)*	
Width	in			66.93	
	(mm)			*(1 700)*	
Height	in			67.03	
	(mm)			*(1 705)*	
Fuel consumption	lb/hp/hr	0.39	0.39	0.39	0.38
	(gr/hp/hr)	*(178)*	*(176)*	*(175)*	*(172)*

MAK

MaK Maschinenbau GmbH Kiel
Kiel-Friedrichsort, German Federal Republic

Before the 1939-45 war Deutsche Werke Kiel produced diesel locomotives and railcars. MaK was formed after the war to continue this programme, concentrating engine production on the slow running type M 300. The original output was 60 hp per cylinder at 750 rpm which was increased to 125 hp with high pressure supercharging. By increasing the engine speed to 900 rpm an output of 150 hp per cylinder was attained. The new rail traction engine M282 is a result of continuous search for product improvement, and retains the best features of the previous designs, the M300 and M 301. It is of compact and modern design, a medium speed unit with high performance and extended overhaul periods.

Series M 282
Type: 6 and 8 cylinders in-line, 12 cylinder Vee, 4-stroke-cycle, water cooled.

Combustion method: All M 282 series engines have direct injection.
Cylinders: Bore 9.44 in *(240 mm)*. Stroke 11.02 in *(280 mm)*. Swept volume 12.66 litres per cylinder. Compression ratio 12.2:1. Removable wet type cast iron liners; individual cast iron cylinder heads bolted to cylinder block.
Pistons: A depression in the crown of the piston in conjunction with the cylinder head forms the combustion chamber. The material used for the piston is a heat-resisting light-metal alloy with the best heat conducting quality. Four self-tightening elastic piston rings are fitted on the piston. One oil control ring is arranged above the gudgeon pin.
Connecting rods: Drop forged steel.
Crankshaft: Solid forged steel.
Constructional features: Closed engine housing with hanging bearings and underhung sump. Main and big-end bearings of the bronze-lined steel shell type, with lead-tin bearing surface. The bearings can be exchanged without removing the crankshaft.
Valve gear: Each cylinder head carries two inlet and two exhaust valves. Gear train driven camshaft in cylinder block.

Model			6M282				8M282		12M282		
		A	A(k)	A(k)	Ak	A(k)	A(k)	AK	A(k)	A(k)	AK
No of cylinders		6	6	6	6	6	8	8	12	12	12
Turbocharger, BBC		—	VTR 200	VTR 200	VTR 250	VTR 250	VTR 250	VTR 250	2 × VTR 200	2 × VTR 250	2 × VTR 250
Charge air cooled		—	—	single circuit	single circuit	double circuit	single circuit	double circuit	single circuit	single circuit	double circuit
Max bhp (UIC)		530	700	900	1 000	1 200	1 200	1 600	1 800	2 000	2 400
Engine speed	rpm	1 050	1 000	1 000	1 000	1 000	1 000	1 000	1 000	1 000	1 000
Max Bmep	lb/sq/in	83.9	118.0	150.7	167.8	201.9	150.7	201.9	151.4	168.4	201.9
	(kg/cm²)	*(5.9)*	*(8.3)*	*(10.6)*	*(11.8)*	*(14.2)*	*(10.6)*	*(14.2)*	*(10.65)*	*(11.84)*	*(14.2)*
Max piston speed	ft/min	1 929	1 840	1 840	1 840	1 840	1 840	1 840	1 840	1 840	1 840
	(m/sec)	*(9.6)*	*(9.35)*	*(9.35)*	*(9.35)*	*(9.35)*	*(9.35)*	*(9.35)*	*(9.35)*	*(9.35)*	*(9.35)*
Weight (dry)	lb	14 770	15 200	15 670	16 000	16 200	20 200	20 300	25 360	26 000	26 000
	(kg)	*(6 700)*	*(6 900)*	*(7 100)*	*(7 250)*	*(7 350)*	*(9 150)*	*(9 200)*	*(11 500)*	*(11 800)*	*(11 800)*
Length	in	113	113	113	113	115.5	139	139	111.5	111.5	111.5
	(mm)	*(2 876)*	*(2 876)*	*(2 876)*	*(2 876)*	*(2 934)*	*(3 530)*	*(3 530)*	*(2 831)*	*(2 831)*	*(2 831)*
Width	in	53.5	55	55	61	61	61	61	65	65	65
	(mm)	*(1 360)*	*(1 400)*	*(1 400)*	*(1 550)*	*(1 550)*	*(1 550)*	*(1 550)*	*(1 650)*	*(1 650)*	*(1 650)*
Height	in	79	79	80	80	80	80	80	86.5	86.5	86.5
	(mm)	*(2 006)*	*(2 006)*	*(2 035)*	*(2 035)*	*(2 035)*	*(2 035)*	*(2 035)*	*(2 196)*	*(2 196)*	*(2 196)*
Fuel consumption	lb/hp/hr	0.372	0.358	0.354	0.349	0.338	0.354	0.352	0.354	0.349	0.338
	kg/hp/hr	*(166)*	*(160)*	*(158)*	*(156)*	*(151)*	*(158)*	*(157)*	*(158)*	*(156)*	*(151)*

Fuel injection: Bosch injectors with individual Bosch pumps.
Supercharger: Exhaust gas turbo-blower, Brown Boveri.
Starting: Electric, compressed air alternatively.
Mounting: Elastic suspension by metal bonded rubber elements.

MaK model 12 M 282 AK 12-cylinder engine

MAN
Maschinenfabrik Augsburg-Nürnberg AG
8500 Nürnberg, Katzwangerstrasse 101, German Federal Republic

The world's first diesel engine was built at Augsburg—between 1893 and 1897 by Maschinenfabrik Augsburg AG established in 1840. Shortly afterwards a merger with Maschinenbau AG, Nürnberg, produced MAN

The range of diesel engines produced by the Nuremberg Division includes a number of underfloor engines for railway applications. The engines incorporate MAN's "M" or "HM" system of combustion which provides controlled diesel combustion for low engine stress levels and low noise level. Dubbed the "whisper engine", these units are noted for their flexibility permitting fast load acceptance. Direct injection confers efficient fuel utilisation and fuel economies. High unit ratings and good power weight ratios permit installation in a minimum of space. Little maintenance is needed, and low stress levels throughout the engine ensure reliability in service.

MAN Horizontal engines
Model D3256 BTY UE/310
Type: 6 cylinder horizontal, 4-stroke, water cooled, direct injection, turbocharged
Cylinders: Bore 5.197 in *(132 mm)*, stroke 5.906 in *(150 mm)*, swept volume 52 in³ *(12.32 litres)*, compression ratio 15 : 1
Output: UIC rating 310 hp at 2 100 rpm
Torque, max: 1 180 NM at 1 400 rpm
Fuel consumption: 0.348 lb *(155 g)*/hp/h at 1 600 rpm
Length: 53.65 in *(1 363 mm)*
Width: 48.70 in *(1 237 mm)*
Height: 24.37 in *(619 mm)*
Weight: 2 340 lb *(1 060 kg)*

Model D3650 HM5U 12-cylinder horizontal engine
As power unit of heating generator set for installation in locomotives.

Series D 3650
Three (Models D 3650 and HM12U) are railcar underfloor engines, and one (Model D 3650 HM5U) is used as heating generator set.
Type: 12 cylinder horizontally opposed, 4-cycle, water cooled, "HM" combustion system, normally aspirated.
Cylinders: Bore 5.354 in *(136 mm)*, stroke 6.102 in *(155 mm)*, swept volume 1 649 in³ *(27.02 litres)*, compression ratio 16 : 1.
Rated output:
HM5U: 512 hp (UIC), 500 hp (service), at 1 950 rpm
HM12U: 512 hp (UIC), 500 hp (service), at 1 950 rpm
Torque, max:
HM12U: 1 418 ft lbf *(196 mkgf)* at 1 400 rpm
HM5U: 1 418 ft lbf *(196 mkgf)* at 1 400 rpm
Fuel consumption:
HM12U: 0.379 lb *(172 g)*/hp/h at 1 950 rpm
HM5U: 0.373 lb *(169 g)*/hp/h at 1 950 rpm
Length: HM5U: 90.55 in *(2 300 mm)*; others 90.55 in *(2 300 mm)*
Width: HM5U: 70.87 in *(1 800 mm)*; others 109.06 in *(2 770 mm)*
Height: HM5U: 64.96 in *(1 650 mm)*; others 34.25 in *(870 mm)*
Weight:
HM12U: 6 170 lb *(2 800 kg)*
HM5U: 6 600 lb *(3 000 kg)* without generator

Model D 3650 HM12U 12-cylinder horizontal engine
For underfloor mounting in railcars.

MTU
Motoren- und Turbinen-Union Friedrichshafen GmbH
D-779 Friedrichshafen, German Federal Republic

The manufacturing programme of MTU Friedrichshafen for rail traction application includes quick-running diesel engines; hydro-dynamic Mekydro transmissions; and spiral bevel gear axle drive.

Quick-running MTU Friedrichshafen diesel engines are equally suitable for diesel-hydraulic or diesel-electric drive. If diesel-hydraulic drive is specified MTU Friedrichshafen is in a position to offer a complete propulsion system consisting of engine, transmission and axle drives. In diesel-electric applications the light-weight, quick-running engines can be combined with a light-weight generator for maximum performance on low axle loads.

MTU model 12V 331

Country	Series	MTU diesel engines in rail service Locomotive type	Engine type
Belgium	237	260	GTO 6/GTO 6A
Bulgaria	240	DHG 1200	12 V 493
Denmark	246 Bild	power car	12 V 538
	246	MT 151—167	12 V 493
Finland	249	Hr 11	6 R 538
Germany (DB)	263	V 210	12 V 956 + Gasturbine
	263	V 232	2 × 16 V 652
	263	V 220	2 × 12 V 538 or 2 × 12 V 493
	263	V 221	2 × 12 V 652
	263	V 216	16 V 652 16 V 538
	263	V 215	16 V 652
	263	V 211	12 V 956 12 V 538 12 V 493
	263	V 212	12 V 652
Germany	263	V 290	12 V 652
	263	V 260	GTO 6/GTO 6A 12 V 493
	263	V 219	16 V 538 + Gasturbine
	263	V 218	12 V 956 12 C 956
	263	V 213	12 V 652
Greece	274	DE 2000	16 V 538
	274 Bild	A 401—A 410 Esslingen-Triebwagen	GTO 6A
	274 Bild	Esslingen-Triebwagen	6 R 493
		V 260	GTO 6A
Ireland	278	E 401—419 E 421—434	4 R 538
	278	B 233 + 234	12 V 538
Italy	283	D.343	2 × 8 V 538
	283	D.342	8 V 538
	283	D.341	12 V 538
	283	D.442	2 × 12 V 538
Romania	298	Schneeschleuder	12 V 493
Spain	301	ML 3000	2 × 12 V 538
	301	ML 4000	2 × 12 V 538

Country	Series	MTU diesel engines in rail service Locomotive type	Engine type
	301	ML 2000	2 × 12 V 538
	301	Talgo	6 R 538
United Kingdom	320	D 803—829 D 866—87	2 × 12 V 538
	320	D 7000—7100	16 V 538 (Lizenzmotoren)
	320	D 1000—1073	2 × 12 V 538 (Lizenzmotoren)
	320	Falcon Lok	2 × 12 V 538
Yugoslavia	337	D 66 001—003	2 × 12 V 538
	337	DHL 1500	12 V 538
Brazil	474	ML 4000	2 × 16 V 538
Angola	501	M 1500	12 V 538
Congo Otraco	505	Toshiba-Loks	6 R 493
CFL	505	HL 220 + 221 HL 230 — 233	12 V 538
CFL	505	HL 210 + 211	2 × 8 V 538
Mozambique	520	ML 1100	12 V 493
South Africa Iscor	533	700	GTO 6A
Sudan	535	1600	12 V 538
Togo	536	DHG 1101 + 02	12 V 493
Tunisia	537	MAN-Triebwagen	12 V 493
Union of Burma	550	DD 1501—1528	12 V 538
Ceylon	552	S2 Triebwagen	8 V 538
	552	S3 Triebwagen S4 Triebwagen Lok 630—674	
	552	V 150	
China	553	DHG 4000	2 × 16 V 652
India	560	WDS 3	8 V 538
	560	ZDM 2	8 V 538
	560	WDM 3	20 V 538
Indonesia	562	BB 300	12 V 493
	562	D 300	6 R 493
	562	D 301	6 R 493
	562	BB 301	12 V 538
	562	C 300	6 R 493
	562	BB 302	12 V 493
Japan	573	Mitsubishi-Lok	16 V 538
Malaysia	581	KSK 21 100	12 V 493
	581	KSK 21 200	12 V 493
Pakistan	583	550 C	8 V 538
Thailand	589	3001—3027	12 V 493
	589	3101—3130	12 V 652
Turkey	592	ML 2700	12 V 538
	592	DH 6500	GTO 6A

NIIGATA

Niigata Engineering Co Ltd
4-1, Kasumigaseki 1-Chiyoda-ku, Tokyo, Japan

Founded in 1895, one of Japan's leading engineering manufacturers, Niigata build diesel engines for marine and industrial use up to 20 000 hp and for rail traction up to 2 000 hp.

DMP81Z
16-cylinder Vee, water cooled, 4-stroke, turbo-charged and charge air cooled. Bore 7.09 in *(180 mm)*. Stroke 7.87 in *(200 mm)*. Swept volume 311 m³ *(5.09 litres)* per cylinder.

DMF31ZN
6-cylinder vertical in-line, water cooled, 4-stroke turbo-charged and charge air cooled. Bore 7.09 in *(180 mm)*. Stroke 7.87 in *(200 mm)*. Swept volume 311 m³ *(5.09 litres)* per cylinder.
General specifications for both models.
Cylinders: Monobloc cast iron cylinder block and crank case, removable cast iron liners with integral water jacket. Cast iron cylinder heads secured by studs.
Pistons: Oil-cooled two piece pistons with three compression rings and two oil control rings; fully floating gudgeon pins.
Connecting rods: Ni-Cr steel drop forged.
Crankshaft: Alloy steel forging, copper-lead lined steel shell bearing (DMF31ZN), roller bearing (DMP81Z).
Valve: Two inlet and two exhaust steel valves per cylinder.
Fuel injection: Bosch type injectors and Bosch type pump.

Turbo-charger: Niigata-Napier type turbo-blower. Two for DMP81Z, one for DMF31ZN.
Lubrication: Forced feed.
Starting: Electric starter.

Model		DMP81Z	DMF31ZN
Turbocharged		Yes	Yes
Charge air cooled		Yes	Yes
No of Cylinders		16V	6
Power rating (max)	hp	2 000	700
Engine speed	rpm	1 500	1 500
Bmep (max)	lb/sq in	209	167.5
	(kg/cm²)	*(14.73)*	*(13.74)*
Piston speed	ft/min	1 970	1 970
	(m/sec)	*(10.0)*	*(10.0)*
Weight (dry)	lb	19 600	7 280
	(kg)	*(8 900)*	*(3 300)*
Length	in	170	129
	(mm)	*(4 322)*	*(3 280)*
Width	in	74	51.6
	(mm)	*(1 880)*	*(1 310)*
Height	in	78	70.7
	(mm)	*(1 978)*	*(1 795)*
Fuel consumption	lb/hp/hr	0.370	0.375
	(gr/hp/hr)	*(168)*	*(170)*

Niigata DML 30H SH 12 cylinder engine

Niigata DMF 15 HSA

PERKINS

Perkins Engines Ltd
Perkins Engines Group, Peterborough, England

The Perkins Engines Group has its international headquarters in Peterborough. Founded in 1932, the Group can boast of a growth rate equalled by few companies anywhere in the world. In four decades, it has grown from a small firm to an international organisation whose high performance engines are now operating in every country in the world.

The main factory at Eastfield, Peterborough, was opened in 1947 and now has a production capacity of 1 500 engines a day. The company employs more than 9 000 people.

Perkins engines are available to manufacturers and operators anywhere in the world. Internationally known manufacturers are using locally produced Perkins engines in automotive, agricultural, industrial and marine applications in North and South America, Africa, Europe, Asia and Australia.

World production of Perkins engines from all sources in 1975 totalled 511 100. Over 85 per cent of the 225 000 complete engines produced in the UK factories were exported. Perkins three, four, six and V-eight cylinder industrial diesels power locomotives, rail cars, cranes, compressor sets, hydraulic test rigs, road rollers, welding sets, excavators, tractor shovels and a wide range of industrial plant.

Perkins T6.354 turbocharged 6-cylinder engine

Perkins V8.540 diesel engine

Engine type	Turbo-charged	No of cylinders	Bore in (mm)	Stroke in³ (mm)	Swept volume in³ (litre)	Com-pression ratio	Continuous Rating to BS 649 : 1958 bhp (kW)	eng speed rpm	Max Intermittent Rating to BS AU 141a : 1971 bhp (kW)	eng speed rpm	Max Gross Torque lbf ft (kgf)	Engine speed rpm	Length in (mm)	Width in (mm)	Height in (mm)	Bare engine dry weight lb (kg)
D3.152	No	3	3.6 (91.4)	5.0 (127.0)	152.7 (2.50)	18.5:1	39 (29.0)	2 250	49 (36.5)	2 500	118 (160)	1 400	24.0 (610)	20.7 (526)	31.1 (791)	458 (208)
4.108	No	4	3.125 (79.4)	3.5 (88.9)	107.4 (1.76)	22:1	38 (28.0)	3 000	45 (33.5)	3 000	83 (113)	2 300	23.2 (590)	19.1 (485)	25.7 (653)	330 (150)
4.165	No	4	3.622 (92.0)	4.0 (101.6)	164.9 (2.70)	21:1	52 (39.0)	3 000	62 (46.0)	3 000	113 (153)	2 100	25.8 (655)	25.7 (653)	32.7 (830)	442 (201)
4.203	No	4	3.6 (91.4)	5.0 (127.0)	203.6 (3.34)	17.4:1	50 (37.0)	2 250	61 (45.5)	2 400	152 (206)	1 350	28.2 (715)	19.4 (493)	29.4 (746)	484 (220)
4.236	No	4	3.875 (98.4)	5.0 (127.0)	235.9 (3.86)	16:1	64 (48.0)	2 250	81 (60.5)	2 600	197 (267)	1 350	28.8 (721)	20.7 (525)	32.1 (816)	594 (270)
4.248	No	4	3.975 (101.0)	5.0 (127.0)	248.2 (4.07)	16:1	66 (49.0)	2 250	84 (63.0)	2 500	194 (263)	1 400	30.6 (778)	20.4 (519)	28.4 (722)	548 (249)
6.3544	No	6	3.875 (98.4)	5.0 (127.0)	353.8 (5.80)	16:1	94 (70.0)	2 250	122 (91.0)	2 600	283 (384)	1 400	38.0 (965)	25.1 (637)	35.4 (900)	957 (435)
T6.3544	Yes	6	3.875 (98.4)	5.0 (127.0)	353.8 (5.80)	16:1	117 (87.0)	2 250	145 (108.0)	2 600	346 (469)	1 600	36.8 (935)	29.3 (743)	30.7 (780)	979 (445)
V8.540	No	8	4.25 (108.0)	4.75 (120.7)	539.1 (8.83)	16.5:1	148 (110.0)	2 250	192 (143.0)	2 600	410 (556)	1 700	36.7 (933)	32.7 (830)	35.5 (902)	1 338 (608)
V8.640	No	8	4.63 (117.6)	4.75 (120.7)	639.8 (10.48)	16.2:1	165 (123.0)	2 250	215 (160.0)	2 600	485 (658)	1 650	40.6 (1 030)	32.7 (830)	39.1 (992)	1 604 (729)
TV8.640	Yes	8	4.63 (117.6)	4.75 (120.7)	639.8 (10.48)	15.0:1	208 (155.0)	2 250	255 (190.0)	2 600	602 (816)	1 700	41.3 (1 070)	32.8 (832)	38.6 (980)	1 659 (754)

ROLLS-ROYCE

Rolls-Royce Motors Limited
Diesel Division, Shrewsbury, Salop SY1 4DP, England

Rolls-Royce manufacture a range of rationalised high-speed diesel engines for rail traction available as vertical or vee types. The engines are also used in automotive, earth moving, generating, industrial and marine applications.

In rail traction applications complete installations—engines, transmissions and controls—tailored to customers' requirements are supplied and the Company deals directly with railway builders and operators in all countries.

Rolls-Royce diesel engines for rail traction can be classified under two headings.

'C' Range
Comprising 4-stroke, direct injection, normally aspirated, or turbocharged, vertical, in-line engines with outputs varying from 100 to 400 bhp. For all normally aspirated turbocharged versions, the engine has two cylinder heads, each covering half the total number of cylinders and having one inlet and one exhaust valve per cylinder.
Type: In-line, 4-stroke, water cooled direct injection.
Bore: 5.125 in (130.175 mm) all models.
Stroke: 6 in (152.4 mm) all models.
Capacity: 6 cylinder 742.64 in³ (12.13 litres); 8 cylinder 990.19 in³ (16.2 litres).
Compression ratio: Normally aspirated 16 : 1. Turbocharged 14 : 1.
Mean piston speed: 1 800 ft/min at 1 800 rpm.
Crankcase and cylinders: Monobloc integral construction in close grained cast iron with brass push fit core plugs and differentially hardened wet-type cylinder liners.
Crankshaft: Forged chrome molybdenum steel, nitride hardened, dynamically balanced with 7 or 9 main bearings.
Connecting rods: Forged chrome molybdenum steel, drilled for lubrication to gudgeon pins and cross drilled for cylinder lubrication.
Bearings: Pre-finished lead-bronze steel-backed shell-type; lead indium bearing surfaces.
Pistons: Tin plated aluminium alloy with straight sided toroidal cavity combustion chambers. Molybdenum inlayed top compression rings carried in "Ni-resist" inserts. Spring backed conformable type oil control rings. Fully floating nickel-chrome case-hardened gudgeon pins.
Valve gear: Overhead; in nickel chrome steel with stellited stem-tips and valve seats. Valve rockers are drilled for lubrication, and are operated by pushrods and chilled cast iron tappets.

Telegrams: Roycar, Shrewsbury
Telephone: (0743) 52262
Telex: 35171/2.

Rolls-Royce DV8T 90 degree Vee-type 8 cylinder engine

Camshaft: Forged chrome-molybdenum steel, nitride hardened, 7 or 9 lead-bronze bearings.
Lubrication: Pressure feed to all bearings wheelcase gears, rocker arms and compressor when engine mounted. Engine mounted oil-coolant heat exchanger.
Fuel injection: Jerk-type pump with hydraulic or mechanical governor. Multi-hole injectors and engine mounted filters.

Cooling: Gear driven circulating pump; thermostat control and heat exchanger for lubricating oil. Engine or radiator mounted multi-belt driven fans for vertical engines. Shaft, Hydrostatic or electric driven fans for horizontal engines.
Starting: Axial-type electric starter motor.
Mounting: 4-point; engine front and fly-wheel housing.
Output: Fly-wheel and fly-wheel housing to suit hydraulic, electric or mechanical transmission.

	Continuous Traction Rating to BS 2953 : 1958	Intermittent Traction Rating to BS 2953 : 1958	Maximum rating for yard shunting locomotives
Max Bmep	lb/sq in (kg/sq cm)	lb/sq in (kg/sq cm)	lb/sq in (kg/sq cm)
Normally aspirated	101 (7.1)	106 (7.45)	112 (7.87)
Turbocharged	140 (9.8)	156 (10.97)	164 (11.53)

'D' Range
Comprising 90 degree V-type, 4-stroke, direct injection, normally aspirated or tur-

bocharged, with or without charge air cooling, 8-cylinder engines with outputs ranging from 423 to 750 bhp.
Type: 8-cylinder, 90 degree Vee, 4-stroke, liquid-cooled.
Combustion system: Direct injection with toroidal cavity pistons.
Bore: 6.625 in (168.275 mm).
Stroke: 7.25 in (184.150 mm).
Capacity (swept volume): 2 000 m³ (32.776 litres).
Maximum governed rpm: 1 800.
Mean piston speed: 2 174 ft/min (11.11 m/sec) at 1 800 rpm
Compression ratio: Naturally aspirated 15.5 : 1. Turbocharged 13.5 : 1.
Rotation: Anti-clockwise viewed on flywheel.
Hydraulic transmission equipment: Three stage hydro-kinetic torque converter of Lysholm-Smith type, manufactured by Rolls-Royce under licence from Twin Disc Clutch Company. The operating fluid is diesel fuel oil or other approved fluids, cooled by a shell and tube heat exchanger in the engine coolant circuit. Various designs are available to suit all Rolls-Royce engines and rail traction applications.
Reversing gearboxes:
(a) Rolls Royce-type CG 100, air operated, coupled direct to torque converter ratio 1 : 1.
(b) Rolls-Royce type CGF 310, axle mounted final drive air operated, ratios from 2 : 1 to 4.44 : 1.

Model designation	bhp rating (BS 2953) Intermittent rating B	Max governed speed rpm	Engine form	2 or 4 stroke	No. of cylinders	Valves per cylinder	A B	Cylinder bore in (mm)	Piston stroke in (mm)	Full-load Bmep lb/in² (kg/cm²)	Piston speed max rpm ft/min (m/sec)	Full-load fuel consumption lb/bhp-h (g/bhp-h)	Starting system	Complete engine weight (dry) lb (kg)	Overall length in (mm)	Overall width in (mm)	Overall height in (mm)
C6NFL	179	1 800	V	4	6	2	—	5.125 (130.175)	6 (152.4)	106 (7.455)	1 800 (9.14)	0.379 (172)	E	2 499 (1 133)	57.07 (1 449)	29.12 (740)	41.30 (1 039)
C6TFL	262	1 800	V	4	6	2	A	5.125 (130.175)	6 (152.4)	155.2 (10.91)	1 800 (9.14)	0.360 (163.3)	E	2 613 (1 185)	61.43 (1 560)	33.80 (858)	50.97 (1 295)
C8NFL	239	1 800	V	4	8	2	—	5.125 (130.175)	6 (152.4)	106.2 (7.466)	1 800 (9.14)	0.390 (177)	E	3 079 (1 396)	70.74 (1 797)	31.00 (787)	41.30 (1 039)
C8TFL	350	1 800	V	4	8	2	A	5.125 (130.175)	6 (152.4)	155.5 (10.93)	1 800 (9.14)	0.370 (168)	E	3 242 (1 470)	70.74 (1 797)	33.30 (836)	49.30 (1 252)
DV8N	445	1 800	90° Vee	4	8	4	—	6.625 (186.275)	7.25 (184.150)	97.92 (6.884)	2 174 (11.11)	0.381 (173)	E	7 700 (3 493)	70.95 (1 802)	60.35 (1 533)	63.20 (1 605)
DV8T	534	1 800	90° Vee	4	8	4	A	6.625 (168.275)	7.25 (184.150)	117.5 (8.261)	2 174 (11.11)	0.410 (186)	E	7 860 (3 565)	75.90 (1 927)	60.35 (1 533)	67.55 (1 716)
DV8TCE	618	1 800	90° Vee	4	8	4	A & B	6 625 (168.275)	7.25 (184.150)	136 (9.562)	2 174 (11.1)	0.380 (172.4)	E	8 060 (1 656)	75.90 (1 927)	60.35 (1 533)	67.55 (1 716)
DV8—TCA	707	1 800	90° Vee	4	8	4	A & B	6.625 (168.275)	7.25 (184.150)	155.6 (10.94)	2 174 (11.11)	0.384 (174.2)	E	8 060 (1 656)	75.90 (1 927)	60.35 (1 533)	67.55 (1 716)

Engine Form:	V	Vertical	Starting:	E	Electrical
	90°	Vee configuration			
	A	Pressure charged			
	B	Charge cooled			

SACM
Société Alsacienne de Constructions Mécanique de Mulhouse
1 rue de la Fonderie, 68 Mulhouse, France

175 Series
Type: 8, 12 and 16 cylinder Vee, 4-cycle, water cooled.
Cylinders: Bore 6.89 in (175 mm). Stroke 7.08/7.56 in (180/192 mm). Swept volume 275 in³ (4.5 litres) per cylinder. Compression ratio 15:1. Centrifugal cast iron cylinder liners. Individual cast iron cylinder heads with 4 valves.
Pistons: Aluminium alloy with combustion chamber in crown. Four compression rings (one chromium plated) and two oil control rings.
Connecting rods: The rods are articulated, giving each bank of cylinders a different

piston stroke. The knuckle of the articulated rod is located in the big end cap of the master rod.
Crankshaft: Heat treated chrome-molybdenum steel. Steel shell bearings lined with copper-lead alloy.
Valve gears: Two inlet and two exhaust valves per cylinder. Separate camshaft for each cylinder bank operating rocker arm.
Fuel injection: Injection pumps Bosch or CAV located between cylinder banks.
Fuel: Normal diesel fuel.
Supercharger: Brown-Boveri, Hispano or Holset exhaust gas turbo-blowers.
Lubrication: Pressure feed with one geared pump. Water cooled heat exchanger.
Cooling system: Heat exchanger or honeycomb type radiator with centrifugal pump.
Starting: Compressed air or electric starter.

175 Type

Model		V8A	V8ASH	V8ASHR	V8BSHR	V12ASH	V12ASHR	V12BZSHR	V16BSHR	V16BZSHR
No of Cylinders		8	8	8	8	12	12	12	16	16
Turbocharged		No	Yes	Yes	Yes	Yes	Yes	Yes	Yes	Yes
Charge air cooled		No	No	Yes	Yes	Yes	No	Yes	Yes	Yes
bhp cont (UIC)		400	500	600	800	825	950	1 200	1 400	1 600
Engine speed	rpm	1 500	1 500	1 500	1 500	1 500	1 500	1 500	1 500	1 500
Mean piston speed	ft/min (m/sec)	1 772/1 890 (9.0/9.6)	1 772/1 890 (9.0/9.6)	1 772/1 890 (9.0/9.6)	1 772/1 890 (9.0/9.6)	1 772/1 890 (9.0/9.6)	1 772/1 890 (9.0/9.6)	1 772/1 890 (9.0/9.6)	1 772/1 890 (9.0/9.6)	1 772/1 890 (9.0/9.6)
Bmep	lb/sq in (kg/cm²)	95 (6.66)	119 (8.40)	142 (10.0)	190 (13.30)	131 (9.19)	149 (10.47)	190 (13.30)	165 (11.66)	190 (13.30)
Weight (dry)	lb (kg)	6 220 (2 820)	6 680 (3 030)	7 100 (3 220)	7 720 (3 500)	9 500 (4 300)	9 940 (4 500)	10 600 (4 800)	13 450 (6 100)	13 670 (6 200)
Length	in (mm)	60 (1 520)	73.6 (1 870)	73.6 (1 870)	73.6 (1 870)	87.5 (2 220)	87.5 (2 220)	87.5 (2 220)	102 (2 590)	102 (2 590)
Width	in (mm)	52 (1 320)	52 (1 320)	52 (1 320)	52 (1 320)	50.4 (1 280)	52.3 (1 330)	52.3 (1 330)	52 (1 320)	52.3 (1 330)
Height	in (mm)	58.5 (1 486)	69.3 (1 760)	69.8 (1 774)	69.8 (1 774)	69.1 (1 755)	69.1 (1 755)	69.1 (1 755)	68 (1 727)	68 (1 727)
Fuel consumption	lb/hp/hr (gr/hp/hr)	0.353 (160)	0.346 (157)	0.346 (157)	0.346 (157)	0.346 (157)	0.346 (157)	0.346 (157)	0.340 (154)	0.340 (154)

195 and 240 Type

Model		195 Type			240 Type		
		V12CSHR	V16CSHR	V12DSHR	V16ESHR	V20ESHR	V20E2SHR
No of cylinders		V12	V16	V12	V16	V20	V20
bhp continuous	(UIC)	1 800	2 400	3 300	4 400	5 500	6 000
Engine speed	rpm	1 500	1 500	1 350	1 350	1 350	1 350
Bmep	lb/sq in (kg/cm²)	232 (16.3)	232 (16.3)	257 (18)	257 (18)	257 (18)	280 (19.6)
Mean piston speed	ft/min (ft/sec)	1 764/1 890 (9.0/9.6)	1 764/1 890 (9.0/9.6)	1 944/2 646 (9.9/10.35)	1 944/2 646 (9.9/10.35)	1 944/2 646 (9.9/10.35)	1 944/2 646 (9.9/10.35)
Weight (dry)	lb (kg)	11 000 (5 000)	15 400 (7 000)	26 450 (12 000)	33 070 (15 000)	39 700 (18 000)	44 100 (20 000)
Length	in (mm)	98.4 (2 500)	118.1 (3 000)	137 (3 480)	165 (4 190)	220 (5 588)	220 (5 588)
Width	in (mm)	57.5 (1 460)	57.5 (1 460)	69 (1 752)	69 (1 752)	71 (1 803)	71 (1 803)
Height	in (mm)	76.4 (1 938)	77.2 (1 961)	102.8 (2 610)	102.8 (2 610)	102.8 (2 610)	102.8 (2 610)
Fuel consumption	lb/hp/hr (gr/hp/hr)	0.353 (153)	0.353 (153)	0.353 (153)	0.353 (153)	0.353 (153)	0.353 (153)

195 and 240 Series

Generally similar in construction to the 175 engines these are available as 12, 16 and 20 cylinders Vee, and in two cylinder sizes:

195—Bore 7.68 in *(195 mm)*, stroke 7.09 in *(180 mm)* (articulated rod in V engines stroke 7.56 in) *(192 mm)*. Swept volume approx. 5.6 litres per cylinder.

240—Bore 9.45 in *(240 mm)*, stroke 8.66 in *(220 mm)*, (articulated rod in V engines stroke 9.055 in) *(230 mm)*. Swept volume approx 9.3 litres per cylinder.

SACM-AGO Type V20EZSHR engine
Output 6 000 hp at 1 350 rpm

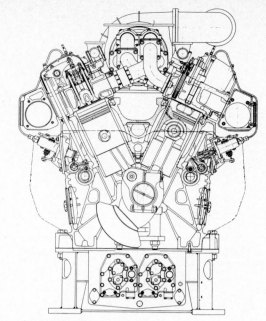

Cross section of 240 Vee-type engine

SEMT

Société d'Etudes de Machines Thermiques
2, Quai de Seine, 93203-St. Denis, France

The Société d'Etudes de Machines Thermiques (SEMT), formed in 1947 to develop diesel engines, is a subsidiary company of the Alsthom Atlantique. It has successfully designed and developed diesel engines in the high speed range.

SEMT-Pielstick PA series of engines are used for rail traction, generating plants, drilling and pumping sets, and for submarine and fast ship propulsion. More than 2 300 PA engines are in service around the world, manufactured by SEMT licensees.
The PA series includes the following models:—
  PA4-185 developing 150 hp per cylinder at 1 500 rpm
  PA4-200 developing 192.5/250 hp per cylinder at 1 500 rpm
  PA6-280 developing 400 hp per cylinder at 1 050 rpm

ALSTHOM ATLANTIQUE

2, quai de Seine, 93-St. Denis, France

SEMT-Pielstick PA4-185 Series

Type: 6 cylinder in line horizontal; 6 and 8 cylinders in line vertical; 6, 8, 12, 16 and 18 cylinders Vee (90 degrees), 4-cycle, water cooled.

Cylinders: Bore 7.28 in *(185 mm)*. Stroke 8.25 in *(210 mm)*. Swept volume 345 in³ *(5.65 litres)* per cylinder. Wet liners, individual cast iron cylinder heads. Central pre-combustion chamber fitted with pintle type injectors.

Pistons: Cast iron pistons cooled by pressure lubricating oil fed through connecting rod and piston pin into an annular chamber level with top compression ring.

Connecting rods: Identical for both banks of cylinders and arranged side by side on crankpins. Thin wall steel backed copper lead lined bearings for big end.

Crankshaft: Steel alloy with induction hardened journals. Balance weights bolted to circular webs. Power can be taken off from either end of engine.

Crankcase: Tunnel type frame unit, with integral timing gear case, is enclosed by the sump.

Valve gear: Two inlet and two exhaust valves with pressed in valve inserts. Valves operated through roller type followers by a single camshaft located between cylinder banks.

Fuel injection: Pintle type injectors fitted to pre-combustion chambers. Monobloc injection pump located inside Vee, controlled by hydraulic governor.

Superchargers: Exhaust gas turbo-chargers, one for 6 and 8 cylinder engines, one or two for 12 cylinders and two for 16 and 18 cylinders are located between cylinder banks. Air coolers arranged on timing gear side.

Lubrication: Pressure feed throughout with pumps in sump below oil level.

Cooling: Water pumps fitted on timing gear end of frame.

Starting: Either electrically or by compressed air.

SEMT-Pielstick PA6-280 Series

Type: 6, 8 and 9 cylinders in line, 12, 14, 16, 18 and 20 cylinder Vee—supercharged, water cooled.

Cylinders: Bore 11 in *(280 mm)*. Stroke 11.40 in *(290 mm)*. Swept volume 1 090 in³ *(17.85 litres)* per cylinder. Wet liners directly mounted in the crankcase, without cooling jackets. Individual cast iron cylinder heads. Single combustion chamber—Direct injection.

Pistons: Pistons made of light alloy, with inserted head, cooled by lubricating oil circulating in an annular chamber; oil is delivered by the connecting rod to the piston pin.

Connecting rods: Identical for both cylinder banks, arranged side by side on the crankpins. Notched connecting rod big end bevel cut. Screwed cap. Cupro-lead shell on thin steel backing for the big end, babbitted steel bushing for the small end.

Crankshaft: Made of alloy steel, high frequency treated. Power can be taken off on either end of the shaft.

Crankcase: One piece, of Mechanite special, iron cast with crankshaft underslung bearings. Inlet air box integrated on top.

Valves: Two inlet valves and two exhaust valves per cylinder head, with inserted seats. Valves operated through rocking levers and cam followers from two camshafts (one per cylinder bank), housed in the crankcase, outside the Vee.

Fuel injection: Direct injection by means of injectors of the multi-hole type. Individual injecting pump housed in the crankcase, directly controlled by the camshafts. Injection controlled by hydraulic speed governor.

Turbochargers: Two per engine, driven by a turbine on the exhaust gas, and housed in the centre line of the engine above each end of the crankcase.
Air cooler at supercharger outlets, housed above the middle of the crankcase, and crossed by a special water line.

Lubrication: Two pumps of the gear type, driven by a timing gear train sunk into the sump.

Cooling: Two water pumps of the centrifugal type, driven by the timing train, one for jacket and cylinder head line, the other for air-cooler and lube-oil line.

Starting: Compressed air.

360-hour UIC test

The first 18-cylinder 18PA6V-280 engine has officially run its 360-hour UIC locomotive test in accordance with ORE regulations.

SEMT-Pielstick PA4-200 Series

Type: 8, 12, 16 and 18 cylinders Vee (90 degree) 4 cycles, water cooled.
Three models:
  DI—Direct Injection
  VG—Variable geometry pre-combustion chamber
  VG, DS VG + two—stage turbo-charging

SEMT-Pielstick 16PA4V-185 engine
UIC rating 2 400 hp at 1 500 rpm

SEMT-Pielstick 18PA4V-200 engine
UIC rating 3 150 hp at 1 500 rpm

Cylinders: Bore 7.88 in *(200mm)*. Stroke 8.25 in *(210 mm)*. Swept volume 403 in³ *(6.6 litres)* per cylinder. Wet liners, individual cast iron cylinder heads.

Pistons: Cast iron pistons cooled by pressure lubricating oil fed through connecting rod and piston pin into an annular chamber level with top compression ring.

Connecting rods: Identical for both banks of cylinders and arranged side by side on crankpins. Thin wall steel backed copper lead lined bearings for big end.

Crankshaft: Steel alloy with induction hardened journals. Balance weights bolted to circular webs. Power can be taken off from either end of engine.

Crankcase: Tunnel type frame unit, with integral timing gear case, is enclosed by the sump.

Valve gear: Two inlet and two exhaust valves with pressed in valve inserts. Valves operated through roller type followers by single camshaft located between cylinder banks.

Fuel Injection: Monobloc injection pump located inside the Vee, controlled by hydraulic governor.
DI—Direct system—spray type injectors
VG—Variable geometry pre-combustion
VG, DS—chamber

Superchargers: Exhaust gas turbo-chargers, one for 8 cylinder engine, two for 12, 16 and 18 cylinders are located between cylinder banks. Air coolers arranged on timing gear side.

Lubrication: Pressure feed throughout with pumps in sump below oil level.

Cooling: Water pumps fitted on timing gear end of frame.

Starting: Either electrically or by compressed air.

SEMT-Pielstick 18PA6V-280 engine
UIC rating 1 200 hp at 1 050 rpm

	IN-LINE					VEE		
	6 PA6L	8PA6L	9PA6L	12PA6V	14PA6V	16PA6V	18PA6V	20PA6V
No of cylinders	6	8	9	12	14	16	18	20
Supercharged	Yes	Yes	Yes	Yes	Yes	Yes	Yes	Yes
Charge air cooled	Yes	Yes	Yes	Yes	Yes	Yes	Yes	Yes
Power rating (UIC)	2 400	3 200	3 600	4 800	5 600	6 400	7 200	8 000
Engine speed	1 050	1 050	1 050	1 050	1 050	1 050	1 050	1 050
Piston speed	1 015	1 015	1 015	1 015	1 015	1 015	1 015	1 015
Bmep	2 030	2 030	2 030	2 030	2 030	2 030	2 030	2 030
Weight (dry)	11 200	14 400	16 000	18 800	21 500	24 100	26 200	28 500
Length	3 860	4 700	5 120	3 675	4 135	4 595	5 055	5 515
Width	1 425	1 425	1 425	1 780	1 780	1 780	1 780	1 780
Height	2 630	2 670	2 670	2 480	2 480	2 480	2 480	2 480

	PA4 200 VG				PA4 200 VG DS			
No of cylinders	8	12	16	18	8	12	16	18
Turbo charged	yes	yes	yes	yes	yes	yes	yes	yes
Charge air cooled	yes	yes	yes	yes	yes	yes	yes	yes
Power rating	1 540	2 310	3 080	3 465	1 920	2 880	3 840	4 320
Bmep	17.3	17.3	17.3	17.3	23	23	23	23
Weight (dry)	4 500	6 200	7 900	8 800	5 300	7 200	9 300	10 200
Length	2 090	2 530	3 130	3 430	1 878	2 975	3 078	3 378
Width	1 580	1 450	1 700	1 700	1 450	1 450	1 850	1 850
Height	1 865	1 800	1 865	1 865	2 226	2 285	2 225	2 225

Model		6PA4H 185	6PA4L 185	8PA4L 185	6PA4V 185	8PA4V 185	12PA4V 185	16PA4V 185	18PA4V 185	8PV4V 200	PA4 200 Di 12PA4V 200	16PA4V 200	18PA4V 200
No of cylinders		6 horiz	6 line	8 line	6 Vee	8 Vee	12 Vee	16 Vee	18 Vee	8	12	16	18
Turbocharged		Yes	Yes	Yes	Yes	Yes	Yes	Yes	Yes	Yes	Yes	Yes	Yes
Charge air cooled		Yes	Yes	Yes	Yes	Yes	Yes	Yes	Yes	Yes	Yes	Yes	Yes
Power rating (UIC)	hp	1 000	1 000	1 335	1 000	1 335	2 000	2 670	3 000	1 400	2 100	2 800	3 150
	rpm					1 500					1 500		
Piston speed	ft/min					1 968					1 968		
	(m/sec)					(10.5)					(10.5)		
Bmep	lb/sq in					227					227		
	(kg/cm²)					(16.0)					(16.0)		
Weight dry	lb	7 500	7 500	9 700	7 100	8 530	12 390	15 700	17 700	9 500	13 200	17 000	19 000
	(kg)	(3 400)	(3 400)	(4 400)	(3 220)	(3 870)	(5 620)	(7 120)	(7 970)	(4 300)	(6 000)	(7 720)	(8 620)
Length	in	117.3	120.2	143.8	63.8	75.8	99.4	123.1	134.9	75.8	99.4	123.1	134.9
	(mm)	(2 980)	(3 054)	(3 654)	(1 626)	(1 926)	(2 526)	(3 126)	(3 426)	(1 926)	(2 526)	(3 126)	(3 426)
Width	in	68.9	33.9	33.9	57.1	57.1	57.1	57.1	67.0	62.0	57.1	66.9	66.9
	(mm)	(1 750)	(860)	(860)	(1 450)	(1 450)	(1 450)	(1 450)	(1 702)	(1 575)	(1 450)	(1 700)	(1 700)
Height	in	33.5	65.4	65.4	73.3	73.3	75.6	73.3	73.3	73.4	75.6	73.4	73.6
	(mm)	(850)	(1 660)	(1 660)	(1 863)	(1 863)	(1 921)	(1 863)	(1 863)	(1 865)	(1 920)	(1 865)	(1 920)

SSCM

Société Surgérienne de Constructions Mécanique
Surgères, Charente Maritime, France

POYAUD SERIES

Series PZ: 2, 3, 4 or 6-cylinder vertical in-line engines.
Series 150: 6 cylinder in-line, 12-cylinder Vee.
Prefix: A=vertical engine, **C**=horizontal engine.
Suffix: S=supercharged (Turbocharged), **Sr**=Supercharged with temperature water intercooling (charge air cooling), **SR**=Supercharged with low temperature intercooling (Charge air cooling), **SrH**=Supercharged with high temperature water intercooling (Charge air cooling) and piston cooling.
All are water cooled.

Cylinders: Bore 5.9 in *(150 mm)*. Stroke 7.1 in *(180 mm)*. Swept volume 3.18 litres per cylinder. Compression ratio: normally aspirated, 15.1 : 1, supercharged 14.4 : 1. Removable wet type cast iron cylinder liners. Individual cast iron cylinder heads. Special alloy removable valve seats.

Pistons: Aluminium alloy pistons with three compression rings (the top one chromium plated) and one oil control ring. Combustion chamber in crown. Case hardened gudgeon pin.

Connecting rods: Die casting of special hardened steel.

Crankshaft: Solid forging of chrome molybdenum steel. Steel bearing shells with lead-copper lining, interchangeable for either crankshaft main bearings or connecting rod bearings.

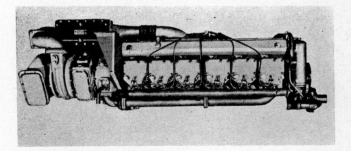

Poyaud C 6150 SrH 6-cylinder horizontal engine
Turbocharged and charge air cooled 375 hp at 1 800 rpm

Crankcase: Monobloc iron casting, strongly ribbed with a crankshaft bearing between each cylinder. Access doors on each side.

Valve gear: Two admission and two exhaust valves per cylinder. Gear driven camshaft.

Fuel injection: Bosch or Sigma multiple hole injectors. Bosch type P fuel pump or SIGMA DM fuel pump.

Supercharger: Holset exhaust gas-driven turbo-charger.
Lubrication: Forced feed throughout by gear-type feed pump.
Cooling system: Centrifugal circulating pump.
Starting: Electric; compressed air; Berger "hydraulic".

*Dimensions of horizontal engines as follows:
  Length; C6150 72.8 in *(1 850 mm)*, others 92.5 in *(2 350 mm)*
  Width; all engines 66.1 in *(1 680 mm)*
  Height; all engines 30.1 in *(765 mm)*

Series 520: 6 cylinder vertical in line, 8 and 12 cylinder Vee 4-stroke cycle, water cooled, combustion chamber in cylinder head.
Suffix: NS=naturally aspirated; SI=turbocharged; S2=turbocharged and charge air cooled.
Cylinders: Bore 5.315 in *(135 mm)*. Stroke 4.803 in *(122 mm)*. Swept volume per cylinder 106.5 in³ *(1.745 litres)*.

Poyaud V12 SI 12-cylinder Vee engine
Turbocharged 480 hp at 2 500 rpm

Series 150		A4150	A6150 C6150	A6150S C6150S	A6150Sr C6150Sr	A6150SR C6150SR	A6150SrH C6150SrH	A8150	A8150S	A8150Sr	A8150SR	A12150	A12150S	A12150Sr	A12150SR	A12150SrH
No of cylinders		4	6	6	6	6	6	8V	8V	8V	8V	12V	12V	12V	12V	12V
Turbocharged		No	No	Yes	Yes	Yes	Yes	No	Yes	Yes	Yes	No	Yes	Yes	Yes	Yes
Charge air cooled		No	No	No	Yes	Yes	Yes	No	No	Yes	Yes	No	No	Yes	Yes	Yes
bhp continuous		160	240	340	375	420	450	276	400	440	480	480	680	750	840	900
Engine speed	rpm	1 800	1 800	1 800	1 800	1 800	1 800	1 500	1 500	1 500	1 500	1 800	1 800	1 800	1 800	1 800
Mean piston speed	ft/min	2 124	2 124	2 124	2 124	2 124	2 124	1 772	1 772	1 772	1 772	2 124	2 124	2 124	2 124	2 124
	(m/sec)	*(10.8)*	*(10.8)*	*(10.8)*	*(10.8)*	*(10.8)*	*(10.8)*	*(9.0)*	*(9.0)*	*(9.0)*	*(9.0)*	*(10.8)*	*(10.8)*	*(10.8)*	*(10.8)*	*(10.8)*
Bmep	lb/sq in	92.5	92.5	128	139	154	154	92.5	135	148	161	92.5	128	139	154	154
	(kg/cm²)	*(6.5)*	*(6.5)*	*(9.0)*	*(9.8)*	*(10.8)*	*(10.8)*	*(6.5)*	*(9.5)*	*(10.4)*	*(11.3)*	*(6.5)*	*(9.0)*	*(9.8)*	*(10.8)*	*(10.8)*
Weight (dry)	lb	2 866	3 968	4 409	4 960	4 960	4 960	5 181	6 173	6 283	6 283	6 614	7 275	7 937	7 937	7 937
	(kg)	*(1 300)*	*(1 800)*	*(2 000)*	*(2 250)*	*(2 250)*	*(2 350)*	*(2 350)*	*(2 800)*	*(2 850)*	*(2 850)*	*(3 000)*	*(3 300)*	*(3 600)*	*(3 600)*	*(3 600)*
Length	in	49.6	65.4*	92.5*	92.5*	92.5*	92.5*	61.0	77.6	77.6	77.6	81.1	84.6	84.6	96.9	96.9
	(mm)	*(1 260)*	*(1 600)*	*(2 350)*	*(2 350)*	*(2 350)*	*(2 350)*	*(1 548)*	*(1 969)*	*(1 969)*	*(1 969)*	*(2 056)*	*(2 151)*	*(2 151)*	*(2 459)*	*(2 459)*
Width	in	33.5	33.5*	33.5*	33.5*	33.5*	33.5*	42.9	42.9	42.9	42.9	42.9	42.9	42.9	43.7	43.7
	(mm)	*(850)*	*(850)*	*(850)*	*(850)*	*(850)*	*(850)*	*(1 087)*	*(1 087)*	*(1 087)*	*(1 087)*	*(1 087)*	*(1 087)*	*(1 087)*	*(1 110)*	*(1 110)*
Height	in	57.1	57.1*	58.3*	58.3*	58.3*	58.3*	54.7	66.1	66.1	67.1	54.7	67.3	67.3	67.3	67.3
	(mm)	*(1 450)*	*(1 450)*	*(1 480)*	*(1 480)*	*(1 480)*	*(1 480)*	*(1 390)*	*(1 675)*	*(1 675)*	*(1 705)*	*(1 390)*	*(1 710)*	*(1 710)*	*(1 710)*	*(1 710)*

Series 520		6L NS	6L S1	6L S2	V8 NS	V8 S1	V8 S2	V12 NS	V12 S1	V12 S2
No of cylinders		6	6	6	8V	8V	8V	12V	12V	12V
Turbocharged		—	Yes	Yes	—	Yes	Yes	—	Yes	Yes
Charge air cooled		—	—	Yes	—	—	Yes	—	—	Yes
bhp continuous		170	230	290	220	310	400	360	480	600
Engine speed	rpm					2 500				
Weight (dry)	lb	2 140	2 195	2 290	2 625	2 690	2 845	3 640	3 725	3 900
	(kg)	*(970)*	*(995)*	*(1 040)*	*(1 190)*	*(1 220)*	*(1 290)*	*(1 650)*	*(1 690)*	*(1 770)*
Length	in	57.5	57.5	57.5	50.4	53.2	53.2	69.8	73.5	73.5
	(mm)	*(1 460)*	*(1 460)*	*(1 460)*	*(1 279)*	*(1 351)*	*(1 351)*	*(1 767)*	*(1 866)*	*(1 866)*
Width	in	28.0	31.9	31.9	43.3	46.5	46.5	40.9	46.2	46.2
	(mm)	*(710)*	*(810)*	*(810)*	*(1 098)*	*(1 181)*	*(1 181)*	*(1 038)*	*(1 174)*	*(1 174)*
Height	in	42.7	45.6	45.9	36.8	36.8	42.7	36.8	36.8	42.7
	(mm)	*(1 085)*	*(1 158)*	*(1 166)*	*(935)*	*(935)*	*(1 084)*	*(935)*	*(935)*	*(1 084)*

SCANIA

Saab-Scania Division
Södertälje, Sweden

This company, which produced its first internal combustion engine in 1897 and its first diesel engine in 1936, specializes in high-speed engines.

Types D8, DS8, D11, DS11
6 cylinder in-line, 4-stroke, water cooled.
Cylinders: Bore and stroke. D8 and DS8 4.53 × 4.92 in *(115 × 125 mm)*. D11 and DS11 5.0 × 5.71 in *(127 × 145 mm.)* Wet type centrifugal cast iron cylinder liners, the outer surfaces directly flushed by cooling water. Alloy cast iron cylinder heads, each covering two cylinders (D8 and DS8), or three cylinders (D11, DS11).

Type D14 and DS14
8 cylinder Vee, 4-stroke, water cooled.
Cylinders: Bore and stroke 5.0 × 5.51 in *(127 × 140 mm)*. Alloyed cast iron cylinder heads, one for each cylinder.
Pistons: Aluminium silicon alloy castings with three compression rings and two oil control rings (DS14, one oil control ring). Case hardened chrome nickel steel fully floating gudgeon pins.
Connecting rods: Heat treated special alloy steel "H" section stampings with steel backed indium-coated thin-wall type big end bearings, and bronze bushes.
Crankshaft: Alloy steel one piece stamping, statically and dynamically balanced, carried in steel backed indium-coated thin-wall type bearings. Individual bearings can be exchanged without dismounting crankshaft.
Crankcase: Cylinder block and crankcase integrally cast of cast iron alloy. The main

Scania DS14 turbocharged 8-cylinder engine

Model	D8	DS8	D11	DS11	DS111	D14	DS14	DSI14
No of cylinders	6	6	6	6	6	V8	V8	V8
Bore	115	115	127	127	127	127	127	127
Stroke	125	125	145	145	145	140	140	140
Displacement, litres	7.8	7.8	11.0	11.0	11.0	14.2	14.2	14.2
Continous output, light duty								
bhp DIN/revs	142/2 000	173/2 000	203/2 000	262/1 800	300/1 800	237/1 900	316/1 900	347/1 900
kW/revs	105/2 000	128/2 000	149/2 000	193/1 800	221/1 800	175/1 900	234/1 900	257/1 900
Continuous output, heavy duty								
bhp DIN/revs	128/2 000	156/2 000	182/2 000	236/1 800	270/1 800	213/1 900	286/1 900	314/1 900
kW/revs	95/2 000	115/2 000	134/2 000	174/1 800	199/1 800	157/1 900	211/1 900	232/1 900
Max torque, light duty								
kpm/revs	53/1 500	65/1 500	78/1 400	110/1 500	128/1 400	94/1 400	125/1 400	133/1 750
Nm/revs	500/1 500	637/1 500	764/1 400	1 078/1 500	1 254/1 400	921/1 400	1 225/1 400	1 303/1 750
Max torque, heavy duty								
kpm/revs	48/1 500	58/1 500	71/1 400	100/1 500	115/1 800	85/1 400	112/1 400	120/1 750
Nm/revs	470/1 500	568/1 500	696/1 400	980/1 500	1 127/1 800	833/1 400	1 097/1 400	1 176/1 750
Spec. fuel consumption at 100% load								
g/bhph at 1 500 rpm	165	165	165	159	156	165	160	160
g/kWh at 1 500 rpm	224	224	224	216	212	224	218	218
Weight, excl oil, water and gear, kg	850	875	1 080	1 110	1 135	1 175	1 275	1 350
Length, excl gear, etc	1 270	1 270	1 548	1 548	1 548	1 442	1 442	1 442

bearing caps are steel forgings.

Valve gear: One inlet and one exhaust valve per cylinder, of stellite faced heat resisting steel with chromium plated stems. Heat resistant alloy replaceable valve seats. Hardened steel forging camshaft.

Fuel injection: Multi-hole type injectors with special cold starting device. Helical gear driven injection pump.

Turbocharger: Exhaust gas turbo-charger.

Fuel: Diesel fuel.

Lubrication: Forced feed to all bearings and gear trains with intermittent oil supply to the valve rocker mechanism. One gear-type pump.

Cooling system: One centrifugal type water pump driven from the crankshaft through vee-belts (DS14 through gear chain). Thermostatic control for low temperature operation.

Starter: Electric.

SHINKO

Shinko Engineering Co Ltd

This is a subsidiary of Kobe Steel Company Ltd. Manufacture of high speed diesel engines for rail traction began in 1950 and their present range is from 140 hp to 2 000 hp. They also build hydraulic torque converters under an agreement with Svenska Rotor Maskiner AB (SRM).

Vertical in-line watercooled 4-cycle

DMF 13C	6-cylinder normally aspirated
DMH 17C	8-cylinder normally aspirated
DMH 17S	8-cylinder turbo-charged
DMH 17SB	8-cylinder turbo-charged
DMF 31SB	6-cylinder turbo-charged
DMF 31SI	6-cylinder turbo-charged and charge air cooled
DMF 31ZB	6-cylinder turbo-charged and charge air cooled
DMH 41S	8-cylinder turbo-charged
DMH 41Z	8-cylinder turbo-charged and charge air cooled
DMH 41ZB	8-cylinder turbo-charged and charge air cooled

Horizontal in-line watercooled 4-cycle

DMH 17H	8-cylinder normally aspirated
DMH 17HS	8-cylinder turbocharged
DMF 15HS	8-cylinder turbocharged
DML 30HSE	12-cylinder turbocharged

Vee-type watercooled 4-cycle

DML 61S	12-cylinder turbocharged
DMH 61Z	12-cylinder turbocharged and charge air cooled
DML 61ZA	12-cylinder turbocharged and charge air cooled
DML 61ZB	12-cylinder turbocharged and charge air cooled
DMP 81Z	16-cylinder turbocharged and charge air cooled

Vertical in-line

Model		DMF13C	DMH17C	DMF31SB	DMF31Z	DMF31S1	DMF31ZB	DMH41S	DMH41Z	DMH41ZB
Bore	in	5.12	5.12	7.09	7.09	7.09	7.09	7.09	7.09	7.09
	(mm)	(130)	(130)	(180)	(180)	(180)	(180)	(180)	(180)	(180)
Stroke	in	6.30	6.30	7.87	7.87	7.87	7.87	7.87	7.87	7.87
	(mm)	(160)	(160)	(200)	(200)	(200)	(200)	(200)	(200)	(200)
No. of cylinders		6	8	6	6	6	6	8	8	8
Displacement	in³	777	1 036	1 864	1 864	1 864	1 864	2 483	2 483	2 483
	(litres)	(12.74)	(16.98)	(30.55)	(30.55)	(30.55)	(30.55)	(40.7)	(40.7)	(40.7)
Turbocharged		—	—	Yes	Yes	Yes	Yes	Yes	Yes	Yes
Charge air cooled		—	—	—	Yes	Yes	Yes	—	Yes	Yes
Power rating continuous	hp	140	180	500	550	600	750	700	800	1 000
Engine speed	rpm	1 500	1 500	1 500	1 500	1 500	1 500	1 500	1 500	1 500
Bmep	lb/sq in	93.7	90.5	139.8	153.6	167.8	209.0	146.5	167.8	209.0
	(kg/cm²)	(6.59)	(6.36)	(9.83)	(10.8)	(11.8)	(14.7)	(10.3)	(11.8)	(14.7)
Piston speed	ft/min	1 576	1 576	1 970	1 970	1 970	1 970	1 970	1 970	1 970
	(m/sec)	(8.0)	(8.0)	(10.0)	(10.0)	(10.0)	(10.0)	(10.0)	(10.0)	(10.0)
Weight, dry	lb	2 430	3 090	6 830	7 055	7 276	7 716	9 921	9 987	10 031
	(kg)	(1 100)	(1 400)	(3 100)	(3 200)	(3 300)	(3 500)	(4 500)	(4 500)	(4 550)
Length	in	65.4	79.2	105.2	105.4	109.1	105	126.6	126.6	126.6
	(mm)	(1 661)	(2 011)	(2 672)	(2 677)	(2 772.6)	(2 667)	(3 210)	(3 217)	(3 216)
Width	in	44.5	44.5	37.8	49.9	51.2	49.9	42.0	41.9	41.9
	(mm)	(1 131)	(1 131)	(961)	(1 269)	(1 300)	(1 268)	(1 066.5)	(1 066)	(1 066)
Height	in	38.9	38.9	78.6	66.7	66.7	66.7	71.0	70.9	70.9
	(mm)	(987)	(987)	(1 995)	(1 695)	(1 695)	(1 695)	(1 803.5)	(1 803)	(1 803)
Fuel consumption	lb/hp/hr	0.419	0.419	0.397	0.397	0.386	0.386	0.397	0.397	0.386
	(gr/hp/hr)	(190)	(190)	(180)	(180)	(175)	(175)	(180)	(180)	(175)

Horizontal / Vee-type

Model		DMH17H	DMH17HS	DMF15HS	DML30HS	DML61S	DML61Z	DML61ZA	DML61ZB	DMP81Z
Bore	in	5.12	5.12			7.09	7.09	7.09	7.09	7.09
	(mm)	(130)	(130)	(140)	(140)	(180)	(180)	(180)	(180)	(180)
Stroke	in	6.30	6.30			7.87	7.87	7.87	7.87	7.87
	(mm)	(160)	(160)	(160)	(160)	(200)	(200)	(200)	(200)	(200)
No of cylinders		8	8	6	12	12	12	12	12	16
Displacement	in³	1 036	1 036	901	1 803	3 728	3 728	3 728	3 728	4 970
	(litres)	(16.98)	(16.98)	(14.78)	(29.56)	(61.10)	(61.10)	(61.10)	(61.10)	(81.5)
Turbocharged		—	Yes	Yes	Yes	Yes	Yes	Yes	Yes	Yes
Charge air cooled		—	—	—	—	—	Yes	Yes	Yes	Yes
Power rating continuous	hp	180	250	250	500	1 000	1 100	1 250	1 500	2 000
Engine speed	rpm	1 500	1 500	1 600	1 600	1 500	1 500	1 500	1 550	1 500
Bmep	lb/sq in	90.5	125.6	135.1	135.1	139.8	153.6	174.9	203.3	209.0
	(kg/cm²)	(6.36)	(8.83)	(9.5)	(9.5)	(9.83)	(10.8)	(12.3)	(14.3)	(14.7)
Piston speed	ft/min	1 576	1 576	1 674.5	1 674.5	1 970	1 970	1 970	2 035	1 970
	(m/sec)	(8.0)	(8.0)	(8.5)	(8.5)	(10.0)	(10.0)	(10.0)	(10.33)	(10.0)
Weight dry	lb	2 420	2 420	3 968	7 495	12 130	12 240	12 346	14 330	19 842
	(kg)	(1 550)	(1 550)	(1 800)	(3 400)	(5 500)	(5 550)	(5 600)	(6 500)	(9 000)
Length	in	93.2	105.9	64.8	97.5	108.1	108.1	108.9	108.9	141
	(mm)	(2 392)	(2 691)	(2 149.5)	(2 477)	(2 746)	(2 746)	(2 768)	(2 768)	(3 582)
Width	in	53.7	48.2	61.4	76.5	65.0	72.4	72.4	74.0	74.0
	(mm)	(1 363)	(1 225)	(1 561)	(1 944)	(1 652)	(1 840)	(1 840)	(1 880)	(1 880)
Height	in	29.6	29.5	28.2	37.6	36.9	36.9	72.2	72.2	72.6
	(mm)	(753)	(750)	(716)	(955)	(936)	(936)	(1 833)	(1 833)	(1 844)
Fuel consumption	lb/hp/hr	0.419	0.408	0.397	0.386	0.397	0.397	0.386	0.395	0.395
	(gr/hp/hr)	(190)	(185)	(180)	(180)	(180)	(180)	(175)	(170)	(170)

TAMPELLA

Oy Tampella Ab
Engineering Works, 33101 Tampere 10, Finland

Formerly known as the Tampere Linen and Iron Company, this company was formed in 1861 by the merger of an engineering works founded in 1842 and a linen mill built in 1856. Later, wood pulp mills, paper mills and a cotton mill were added, and the company has considerable interests in hydro-electric schemes. The company com-menced the manufacture of diesel engines in the early 1930s and supplied the first diesel engines to the Finnish State Railways.

Since 1955 the company has made MAN WV 22/30 (now RV 22/30) and VV 22/30 engines on licence, and from 1960, MGO V engines of *175 mm* bore. The engines built to date total about 500 000 hp

In developing engines special consideration has been given to the requirements imposed on engines by the severe Finnish winters.

The following types are available, output quoted being in accordance with the UIC 623 Form.

Model		MAN 22|30 turbocharged						
	R6VAT	R8VAT	R6VATL	R8VATL	V6VAT	V8VAT	V6VATL	V8VATL
Type	Vertical	Vertical	Vertical	Vertical	"V"	"V"	"V"	"V"
No of cylinders	6	8	6	8	12	16	12	16
Charge air cooled	—	—	Yes	Yes	—	—	Yes	Yes
Metric hp	790	1 050	935	1 250	1 460	1 950	1 800	2 400
Engine speed rpm	950	950	950	950	925	925	925	925

Model			MGO "V" Type			
	V12A	V12ASH	V12BSHR	V16A	V16ASH	V16BSHR
No of cylinders	12	12	12	16	16	16
Normally aspirated	Yes	—	—	Yes	—	—
Turbocharged	—	Yes	Yes	—	Yes	Yes
Charge air cooled	—	—	Yes	—	—	Yes
Metric hp	600	825	1 050	800	1 100	1 400
Engine speed rpm	1 500	1 500	1 500	1 500	1 500	1 500

Tampella-MGO V16BSHR engine
Turbocharged and charge air cooled, 1 400 bhp at 1 500 rpm

THYSSEN HENSCHEL

Rheinstahl AG Transporttechnik
HENSCHEL Dieselmotoren, Henschelplatz 1, 3500 Kassel, German Federal Republic

Since 1958, HENSCHEL has manufactured high speed locomotive diesel engines with or without turbocharging. These engines, operating on the direct injection system, have been developed as a result of more than 35 years experience in the design and manufacture of diesel engines. The present output ranges from 240 to 3 000 hp, 4-stroke, water cooled, for rail traction and industrial and marine applications.

Series 1516
Type: 6 cylinders in line, 8 and 12 cylinders in Vee form, 4-stroke, watercooled, turbocharged. Bore *5.71 in* (145 mm), stroke *6.10 in* (155 mm).

Series 2423
Type: 12-cylinder Vee 4-stroke, watercooled, turbocharged and intercooled. Bore *9.45 in* (240 mm), stroke *9.06 in* (230 mm).
Cylinder frame and crankcase: A monobloc of cast iron.

Individual cylinder heads: Cast iron, 2 inlet, 2 exhaust valves.
Cylinder liners: Centrifugal cast iron, wet type, easily replaceable.
Pistons: Light alloy with combustion chambers in crown, (series 2423; oil-cooled by annular chamber, shaker effect).
Connecting rods: Die-forged steel, double T-cross section.
Crankshaft: Forged steel with induction-hardened journals.
Bearings: Three-material type.
Valve gear: Gear driven camshaft (series 1516 one per engine; series 2423 one camshaft for each cylinder bank), push rods and rocker arms.
Supercharging: With turbocharger; series 1516 intercooling possible; series 2423 intercooled.
Fuel injection: Bosch multi-hole nozzles, Bosch block-injector pumps.
Lubricating system: Forced feed by gear pump, water-cooled oil cooler and micro-filters in the main system, centrifugal-filters in the secondary system.
Cooling system: One separate circulation system each for cylinder and charge-air cooling.
Starting: Compressed air.
Mountings: Multi-point suspension using rubber-metal pads.

Model		6R1516A	8V1516A	12V1516A	12V2423Aa
No of cylinders		6 inline	8 Vee	12 Vee	12 Vee
Turbocharged		Yes	Yes	Yes	Yes
Power output range (a)	bhp	330 to 388	440 to 517	660 to 782	2 500 to 3 000
Engine speed	rpm	1 800	1 800	1 800	1 500
Bmep	lb/sq in	154 to 179	154 to 179	154 to 180	171 to 205
	(kg/cm²)	(10.8 to 12.6)	(10.8 to 12.6)	(10.8 to 12.7)	(12.0 to 14.4)
Mean piston speed	ft/min	1 836	1 836	1 836	2 264
	(m/sec)	(9.3)	(9.3)	(9.3)	(11.5)
Weight	lb	3 645	4 273	5 616	24 230
	(kg)	(1 655)	(1 940)	(2 550)	(11 000)
Length	in	82.64	67.72	83.66	122.24
	(mm)	(2 098)	(1 720)	(2 125)	(3 105)
Width	in	33.39	47.64	48.82	69.29
	(mm)	(848)	(1 210)	(1 240)	(1 760)
Height	in	50.59	51.77	54.13	88.98
	(mm)	(1 285)	(1 315)	(1 375)	(2 260)
Fuel consumption	lb/hp/h	pme62	0.360	0.362	0.358
	(gr/PS/h)	(162)	(161)	(162)	(160)

(a) Continuous output B according to DIN 6270 corresponding approx to UIC conditions depending upon applications   without fan

HENSCHEL model 12V 1516A turbocharged and intercooled engine

HENSCHEL model 12V 2423Aa turbocharged and intercooled engine

TRANSMISSION SYSTEMS

ACEC
(Ateliers de Constructions Electriques de Charleroi)

Head Office and Works: BP 4, B 6000 Charleroi, Belgium

Telephone: (07) 36 20 20.
Telex: 51 227

Products: Electrical transmission for diesel-electric locomotives and railcars.

Constitution: A member of the Westinghouse Electric Group

ASEA
Allmänna Svenska Elektriska AB

Head Office and Works: S-721, Vasteras, Sweden

Telephone: Västerås (021) 10 00 00
Telex: 40720

Products: Entire electrical transmissions for 150 hp stock and above.

ALSTHOM
Soc. Générale de Constructions Electriques & Mechaniques Alsthom

Head Office: 38 avenue Kleber Paris 75016, France

Telephone: 727 77 79
Telex: 27672

Works: Belfort Telephone: (84) 28 12 31; Tarbes Telephone: (62) 93 02 97.

Products: Complete electrical transmissions. The actual production power range with main dc generators is up to 2 800 hp and with alternators up to 5 000 hp.

BRISSONNEAU & LOTZ
Brissonneau & Lotz Chaudronnerie, SA

Head Office: 15, rue Bellier, 44000 Nantes, France

Products: Electric transmissions with main generators of up to 2 400 hp

BROWN BOVERI (BBC)
Brown, Boveri & Cie

Head Office and Works: Haxelstr, CH-5401. Baden Switzerland.

Telephone: (056) 75 11 11
Telex: 52921 and 53 203.

Works: Baden, Birr, Turgi Zurich-Oerlikon, Switzerland

Associated Companies: Brown Boveri & Cie. AG, Mannheim, Germany; Cie, Electro-Mécanique, Paris, France; Tecnomasio Italiano Brown Boveri SA, Milan, Italy. Oesterreichische Brown Boveri-Werke AG, Vienna, Austria; A/S Norsk Elektrisk & Brown Boveri, Oslo, Norway; Industria Eletrica Brown Boveri SA, Osasco, São Paulo, Brazil; Hindustan Brown Boveri Ltd, Bombay, India.

Products: Complete electric transmissions for railcars and locomotives.

BRUSH
Brush Electrical Machines Ltd. (Traction Division)

Head Office and Works: PO Box 18, Loughborough, Leics., England

Telegrams: BRUSH LOUGHBOROUGH
Telephone: (050) 93 63131
Telex: 341091

Products: Electric transmission systems of up to 6 000 hp

Constitution: A Hawker Siddeley company

CANADIAN GENERAL ELECTRIC
Canadian General Electric Co Ltd

Head Office: 214 King St West, Toronto, Ontario M5H 1K7, Canada

Telephone: (416) 366 7311.
Telex: 022 052

Works: 107, Park St North, Peterborough, Ontario K9 7B5, Canada

Telephone: (705) 742 7711
Telex: 029 826

Associated Company: General Electric Co Ltd, USA

Products: Diesel-electric traction systems 600 to 4 000 hp per single unit; rapid transit propulsion systems.

ELEKTRO-MECHANIK
Elektro-Mechanik GmbH

Head Office and Works: Wendenerhütte 596 OLPE, Postfach 40, German Federal Republic

Telephone: 02762 1631
Telex: 0876 616

Products: Hydraulic and hydro-mechanical transmissions 150/600 hp (AEG-EMG system), cardan shaft axle drives.

ERCOLE MARELLI
Ercole Marelli & C.SpA

Head Office: Via Borgonuovo 24, Milan, Italy

Telephone: Milan 65 22 51

Works: Sesto San Giovanni, Milan

Telephone: Milan 2494
Telex: 34575 31043 33348

Products: Complete electric transmissions for locomotives and railcars.

FIAT
Fiat SpA (Railway Rolling Stock Division)

Head Office: Corso Ferrucci 22, 10141 Turin, Italy

Telephone: 33 20 33
Telex: 21056

Works: 15, Via Rivalta, Turin, Italy

Telephone: Turin 596784

Products: Hydro-mechanical, hydraulic and mechanical transmissions of up to 500 hp axle drives.

GANZ MAVAG
Ganz-Mavag

Head Office and Works: Könyves Kálmán Krt 76 Budapest VIII, Hungary

Telephone: Budapest 335 950, 141 040
Telex: 22 55 75 22 55 76

Products: Ganz mechanical change-speed transmissions up to 620 hp; in conjunction with co-operating company electric transmissions of 550/3 000 hp per unit; hydraulic and hydro-mechanical transmission 350-1 800 hp.

G E
General Electric Co (USA)

Head Office: 570 Lexington Ave, New York, NY 10022, USA

Telephone: (212) 750 2000

Works: 2901, East Lake Rd, Erie, Pennsylvania 16531, USA

Telephone: (814) 455 5466

Products: Complete electric transmissions.

GEC TRACTION
GEC Traction Ltd

Head Office and Works: Trafford Park, Manchester, M17 1PR, England

Telegrams: ASSOCIATED MANCHESTER
Telephone: (061) 872 2431
Telex: 667152

Products: Gearboxes; main drive gears; electric and hydraulic transmissions; alternators of up to 5 000 hp, dc generators of up to 2 700 hp, main and auxiliary equipment, transformers, rectifiers, and inverters.

GENERAL ELECTRIC (BRAZIL)
General Electric do Brazil SA

Offices and Works: Estrada Campinas-Monte Mor km 103-13 100, Campinas, SP

Telephone: 2 1011
Telex: 025819

Associated Company: General Electric Co (USA)

Products: Electrical transmission 1 000-2 400 hp axle hung motor

GM
General Motors Corporation
(Detroit Diesel Allison Division)

Head Office: Detroit Diesel Allison Division International Operations, 252, Telegraph Ru, Southfield, Michigan 48075, USA

Telephone: (313) 424 4800

Works: Detroit Diesel Allison Division GMC, J5A, PO Box 894, Indianapolis, Indiana, 46206 USA

Telephone: (317) 243 1874

Products: Hydraulic "Torqmatic" transmissions, of 80 to 1 000 hp

GMEINDER
Gmeinder & Co GmbH

Head Office and Works: 695, Mosbach/Baden PO Box 1260, German Federal Republic

Telephone: (06261) 4041
Telex: 04 66111

Products: Mechanical gears; axle drives; alternate-speed and reduction gears for hydraulic transmissions with jackshaft, cardan shaft and chain drives.

GOTHA
Getriebewerk Gotha

Head Office and Works: 58 Gotha, Karl-Liebknecht-Str 26, German Federal Republic

Products: Axle drives for diesel powered vehicles.

HEEMAF
Heemaf BV

Head Office and Works: Bornsestraat 5, PO Box 4, Hengelo, Netherlands

Telephone: 05400 51234
Telex: 44307

Products: Electrotechnical project engineering, Industrial electrical machinery and systems.

HUNSLET
Hunslet Precision Engineering Ltd

Head Office and Works: Hunslet Engine Works, Leeds, LS10 1BT, England

Telegrams: "ENGINE LEEDS TELEX"
Telephone: (0532) 32261
Telex: 55237

Products: Hydraulic locomotives and railcars, main transmission gears forward and reverse and final drives, axle drive units for diesel-mechanical, mechanical change-speed, hydraulic and hydro-mechanical transmissions, of up to 1 000 hp tractor gearing for electrical transmissions.

HURTH
Carl Hurth Maschinen-und Zahnrad Fabrik

Head Office and Works: Holz-strasse 19, 8000 Munich 5, German Federal Republic

Telephone: (089) 23 70 21
Telex: 05 29322

Products: Jackshaft gears, hollow shaft and bevel gear axle drive units, cardanic axle couplings, mechanical change-speed gears: alternate-speed and reverse-reduction gears of up to 500/600 hp.

KAWASAKI
Kawasaki Electric Mfg Co Ltd

Head Office: 1-2, chome, Wadayama-dari, Hyogo-ku, Kobe, Japan

Telephone: Kobe 581 6291
Telex: 356 28

Products: Complete control equipment and electric transmissions.

MAK
MaK Maschinenbau GmbH

Head Office and Works: 2300 Kiel 17, German Federal Republic

Telephone: Kiel 0431 301 11
Telex: 0299877

Products: Axle drives.

MECANOEXPORT EXPORT—IMPORT
Mecanoexport Export—Import

Head Office: 10, Milhail Eminescu St, Bucharest, Romania

Telephone: 12 46 00
Telex: 269

Works: Hidromecanica Works, 78 Blvd Lenin, Brasov, Romania

Telephone: 6153

Products: Hydraulic transmissions.

MONTMIRAIL
Ateliers de Montmirail

Head Office: 10 ave de Friedland, 75008 Paris, France

Telephone: 227 14 30
Telex: 66 0955

Works: Montmirail (Marne).
Telephone: Montmirail (Marne) 26 42 21 90

Parent Company: Cie. de Chemins de fer Departmentaux.

Products: Asynchro mechanical change-speed transmission with cardan-shaft drive, from 200 to 3 000 hp.

MPM
Meccanica Padana Monteverde SpA

Head Office: Viale dell 'Industria N° 46/48, 35100 Padova, Italy

Telegrams: INGRANAGGI PADOVA
Telephone: (049) 655566
Telex: 43320 Mongears

Products: Traction gears, special gearboxes, special axle drives.

Sales Director: Giovanni Compiani

MTE
Société MTE

Head Office: 31-32 quai National, 92806 Puteaux, France

Telephone: 776 41 62
Telex: 61425

Works: Société Creusot-Loire Le Creusot (S & L); Jeumont Schneider—Usines de Jeumont (Nord) de la Plaine Saint Denis (Seine); de Champagne-sur-Seine (S & M) Lyon (Rhone)

Products: Full range of electric transmissions.

MTU
Motoren-und Turbinen-Union Friedrichshafen GmbH

Head Office and Works: 799 Friedrichshafen, German Federal Republic

Telephone: (07541) 207
Telex: 0734 360

Products: Axle drives; Mekydro hydraulic transmissions 500 to 2 500 hp.

OM
OM SpA

Head Office: Piazza San Ambrogio 6, Milan, Italy

Telephone: Milan 898351

Works: Via Pompeo Leoni 18, Milan

Telephone: Milan 53 14 61

Products: Reverse reduction gears; OM/SRM hydraulic and hydro-mechanical transmissions built under licence; axle drives

ROCKWELL INTERNATIONAL
Rockwell International (Mass Transit Sales, Automotive Operations)

Head Office: 2135 W. Maple Rd, Troy, Michigan 48084, USA

Products: Gear boxes and couplings for subway stock.

SCG
Self-Changing Gears Ltd

Head Office and Works: Lythalls Lane, Coventry, W. Midlands, CV6 6FY, England

Telegrams: "SELFCHANGE, COVTELEX"
Telephone: (0203) 88881
Telex: 31644

Products: SCG final drives for heavy-duty locomotives and railcars.

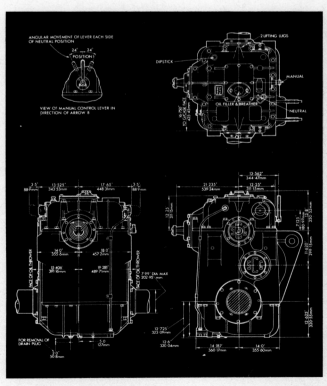

Basic installation details of the SCG type RF11 final drive for locomotives; data—ratios, 5.03:1 up to 15.32:1 reduction; maximum imput torque variable up to a maximum 1 300 kgf/m² (9 400 lbf/ft²); operation, pneumatic 3.5-5.6 ATU (50-80 lb); weight with oil 2 000 kg (41.5 cwt)

SECMAFER
Secmafer SA

Head Office and Works: Chemin des Meuniers Buchelay, 78203 Mantes, France

Telephone: 092 40 00
Telex: 600815

Products: Axle drives. Hydrostatic transmissions for up to 8 000 hp.

SHINKO
Shinko Engineering Co Ltd

Head Office and Works: 1682, Motoima-Cho, Ogaki, Japan 503

Telephone: Ogaki (0584) 89 3121
Telex: 4793 624

Products: Cardan shaft drive hydro-mechanical transmissions of up to 1 600 hp, Shinko torque converters, and, under licence, Shinko SRM torque converters and transmissions.

SIEMENS
Siemens Aktiengesellschafft

Head Office: Werner-von-Siemens-Str. 50, Erlangen, German Federal Republic

Telephone: 09131 71
Telex: 629871

Products: Entire electric transmissions of up to 4 000 hp

SRM
SRM Hydromekanik AB

Head Office and Works: Skattegardsvägen 120, 162 26 Vällingby-Stockholm, Sweden

Telephone: Stockholm 38 02 30
Telex: 174 12

Products: SRM hydraulic transmission of 30 to 2 000 hp and SRM hydrostatic clutch. Licensees: Fiat SpA (Italy) Kobe Steel Ltd (Japan), Shinko Engineering Co Ltd (Japan). GKN Transmissions Ltd, United Kingdom, Oy Tampella AB (Finland), Zahnraderfabrik Renk AG (Germany, DBR), and CKD Praha (Czechoslavakia).

STROMUNGSMASCHINEN
VEB Strömungsmaschinen

Head Office: 83, Pirma Sonnenstein, Postschliebfach 64, Dresden, German Democratic Republic

Works: Otto-Buchwitz-Strasse 96, 806 Dresden, German Democratic Republic

Products: Hydraulic couplings, hydraulic and hydrodynamic transmissions, flow converters.

TWIN DISC
Twin Disc Incorporated

Head Office and Works: 1328 Racine St, Racine, Wisconsin 53403, USA

Telephone: (414) 634 1981
Telex: 264432

Associated Companies: Twin Disc International SA Chaussee de Namur 54, 1400 Nivelles, Belgium
Telephone: (067) 2249 41
Telex: 57 414

British Twin Disc Ltd, Knight Rd, Rochester, Kent ME2 2A7 England
Telephone: Medway/778/55
Telex: 96182

Twin Disc (Pacific) Pty Ltd, Union Road, PO Box 126, Lavington, New South Wales 2641, Australia
Telephone: 25 2577
Telex: 56473

Twin Disc (South Africa) Ltd, PO Box 75140, 2047 Gardenview, Transvaal, South Africa
Telephone: 616 4300

Affiliated Company: Niigata Converter Co Ltd, Nambu Building 27-9, Sendagaya 5-Chome, Shibuyaku, Tokyo 151, Japan
Telephone: 3547111
Telex: 2323105 Nicoto J

Products: Universal joints, gas turbine starting drives, power take-offs, mechanical, hydraulic and pneumatic clutches, axles and control systems. Hydraulic torque converters, power-shift transmissions.

VOITH
Voith Getriebe KG

Head Office and Wokrs: Heidenheim/Brenz, German Federal Republic

Telephone: Heidenheim 3291
Telex: 7 14888

Products: Fluid couplings; axle drives; cooling units, hydrodynamic brakes, hydrostatic equipment, mechanical gearboxes, Voith hydraulic transmissions (turbo transmissions); torque converters; DIWA and DIWA-matic hydro-mechanical transmissions.

ZAHNRADFABRIK VELBERT
Zahnradfabrik Velbert

Head Office and Works: D-562 Velbert, Postfach 926, German Federal Republic

Products: Reining transmissions including flexible steel main wheel for the transmission of ac electric locomotives, type SWP-CEV multiple transmission supplied to the Vevey-Bloney-Le Pleiades mountain railway (combination of spur wheel stages with cyclo-palloid-toothed bevel wheel stage), single motor bogie drive type K520 specially developed for high-speed suburban and local service trains with a speed reduction ratio of 5.83:1 a maximum speed of 2 800 rpm and an input torque of 950 Nm, and the type CC-2400 coupling with spur wheel and hollow shaft for electric locomotives.

BRAKES AND DRAWGEAR

ABEX
Abex Corporation (Railroad Products Group)

Head Office: Valley Road, Mahwah, NJ 07430, USA

Telephone: (041) 529-3450

Products: Metal and composition brake shoes, disc brake pads.

European Works and Sales Office: Parc Industrial Des Hauts-Sarts, B-4400 Herstal (Liege), Belgium

Telegrams: ABEX LIEGE
Telephone: (041) 64.55-55/64.55.45
Telex: 41430

AIRESEARCH
Airesearch Manufacturing Co of California

Head Office: 2525 West 190th St, Torrance, Cal 90509, USA

Telephone: (213) 323-9500

Products: Brake equipment.

AJAX
Ajax Consolidated Co

Head Office: 4615 West 20th St, Chicago, Ill 60650, USA

Telephone: (312) 242 0940

Products: Brake equipment including power hand brakes.

ASF
American Steel Foundries

Head Office: 1005 Prudential Plaza, Chicago, Ill 60601, USA

Telephone: (312) 645 1746
Telex: 25 4187

Products: Automatic couplers and yokes.

Constitution: A member of Amsted Industries.

AVON
Avon Industrial Polymers Ltd

Head Office: Bradford-on-Avon, Wiltshire BA15 1AA, England

Telegrams: INDUSTRIAL BRADFORD/ON/AVON
Telephone: 02216-3911
Telex: 44856

Products: Draftgear, drawgear, buffers, air-brake hose.

AZBEST
Head Office: Ploce, Yugoslavia

Products: Composition brake linings built under licence from Jurid Werke of the German Federal Republic.

BLAIR
Geo Blair & Co (Sales) Ltd

Head Office: Pottery Lane, Forth, Newcastle upon Tyne, England

Telephone: 610711/6
Telex: 53464

Products: Extensive range of steel castings and assemblies for railway rolling stock including automatic couplers.

BRADKEN
Bradken Consolidated Ltd

Head Office: 22 O'Riordan St, Alexandria, Sydney, NSW, Australia

Products: Friction draftgear.

BREMSENWERK
VEB Berliner Bremsenwerk

Head Office and Works: Hirschberger Strasse 4, 1134 Berlin, German Democratic Republic.

Telephone: 55740
Telex: 0112408

Products: Braking equipment.

BSI
Bergische Stahl-Industrie

Office and Works: Papenberger Strasse 38, PO Box 10 07 40, D-5630 Remscheld German Federal Republic

Telephone: (02191) 364
Telex: 8513858

Products: Brake systems and equipment, disc brakes with high thermal capacity and cooling by self-ventilitation, tread brakes, automatic centre buffer couplers, shunting couplers, cast steel castings for the railway industry, brake control equipment.

BUFFALO BRAKE BEAM
Buffalo Brake Beam Co

Head Office: 400 Ingham Ave, Buffalo, NY 14218, USA

Products: Brake Beams

Agent: Canada-Davanac Industries Ltd, 155 Montpellier Blvd, Montreal, Quebec H4N 2G3, Canada.

Telephone: (716) 283-4200

CARDWELL WESTINGHOUSE
Cardwell Westinghouse Company

Head Office: 332 S. Michigan Ave, Chicago, Ill 60604, USA

Telegrams: CARDWELL CHICAGO
Telephone: (312) 427 5051
Telex: 25 4210

Products: Friction draftgear.

Export Sales: J. L. Karrigan.

Licence Agreements
South Africa: Sturrock (South Africa) Ltd, 91 Commissioner Street, PO Box 2863, Johannesburg
Australia: Vickers Hadwa Division, 123 Railway Parade, Bassendean, Western Australia, 6054
Bradken Consolidated Limited, 22 O'Riordan Street, Alexandria, Sydney, NSW
Brazil: Cobrasma SA Caixa Postal 8225-ZP-1, Sao Paulo
Portugal: Engenharia E. Comercio Lda, Rua da Alegria, 61 R/C, Lisbon 2
Belgium: Acieries de Haine-Saint-Pierre & Lesquin, 7160 Haine Saint Pierre

CARRIER KHEOPS
Carrier-Kheops SA

Head Office: 12 villa d'Este, 75643 Paris Cedex 13, France

Telephone: 583-90-01
Telex: 200 800F

Products: Electro-pneumatic braking systems.

COBRA
Cobra Railroad Friction Products Corporation

Head Office: Wilmerding, Pa 15148, USA

Products: Composition brake shoes.

Agents: Cobra Friction Products Ltd, Hamilton, Ontario L8N 3T5, Canada.

COBRASMA
Cobrasma SA Industria E Comercio

Head Office: Rua da Estacao, 523 Osasco, Sao Paulo, Brazil

Telegrams: COBRASMA SAO PAULO
Telephone: 478 8000/227 6711
Telex: 23145

Products: Brake equipment and friction draftgear.

COBREQ
Cia Brasileira de Equipamentos

Head Office: Rua 1° De Marco, 112, Caixa Postal 422-ZC-00, Rio de Janeiro, Brazil

Telegrams: COBREQ
Telephone: 223-1760
Telex: 21632

Products: Non-metallic composition brake shoes.

COMMONWEALTH ENGINEERING
Commonwealth Engineering (NSW) Pty Ltd

Head Office: 11 Berry St, Granville, NSW 2142, Australia

Telegrams: COMENG SYDNEY
Telephone: 637 0166

Products: Miner RF-361 draftgear.

CZECHOSLOVAK WAGON WORKS
Ceskoslovehske Vagonky Praha

Head Office: Kartouzska 2, 150 21 Prague 5, Czechoslavakia

Telegrams: EVIKAVAGON PRAHA
Telephone: 549251
Telex: 121418

Products: Automatic couplers.

DAVANAC
Davanac Industries Ltd

Head Office: 155 Monpelier Blvd, Montreal, Quebec H4N 2G3, Canada

Products: Brake beams under licence to Buffalo Brake Beam Co, USA.

DAVIES AND METCALFE
Davies and Metcalfe Ltd

Head Office and Works: Injector Works, Romiley Nr Stockport, Cheshire SK6 3AE, England

Telegrams: EXHAUST ROMILEY
Telephone: 061-430 4272
Telex: 668801

Products: Air brakes, electro-pneumatic braking, overspeed protection equipment, automatic couplers, two-stage air compressors, disc brakes, wheel slip detection and correction equipment. The company offers a range of products specifically developed for rapid transit systems, including:
Type EBC/5 electro-pneumatic brake system–supplied with a fully variable (anologue) or stepped (digital) control;
Two-stage air compressors–with flange-mounted ac or dc electric motors and an integral intercooler with forced air cooling to ensure effective performance;
Metcalfe-BSI Compact coupler–fully automatic with wide coupling capacity in all planes to carry up to 140 electrical connections and two through pneumatic circuits (this device also provides buffing and draft gear functions);
Spring parking brake–a spring applied air released mechanism controlled from any of the driving positions;
Metcalfe-BSI disc brake sets–fully ventilated patented construction (both axle and wheel mounted sets, together with actuators and release indicator systems are available).

Subsidiaries: *Australia*—Davies & Metcalfe Engineering Ltd, 22 George St, Granville, NSW, Australia 2142

An important licence agreement was concluded between Davies & Metcalfe and Bergische Stahl-Industrie of Ramscheld, German Federal Republic, in 1977.
The agreement gives Davies & Metcalfe exclusive rights to a range of railway products developed by Bergische Stahl-Industrie (BSI) comprising railway disc brake systems, multi-function automatic couplers for rail vehicles, electro magnetic rail brakes and other equipment. In addition to the UK market Davies & Metcalfe have exclusive rights for all Commonwealth countries and some other territories.
Davies & Metcalfe (Oswestry) Ltd, a subsidiary of the parent company will specialise in the BSI range of products in addition to equipment specially designed for rapid transit applications. Already this has led to important contracts won against international competition: 190 "Compact" type automatic couplers and 400 sets of disc brake equipment for the 95 articulated cars being built for the Tyne & Wear Metro. The Metcalfe-BSI couplers are also specified for the 140 rapid transit cars being built by Metro-Cammell for the Hong Kong Metro.
Thirty sets of electro-pneumatic brake equipment for the New South Wales double-deck inter-urban cars are being supplied by Davies and Metcalfe Engineering Ltd, the Australian subsidiary Co. Davies & Metcalfe brake equipment has also recently been fitted to coaches being built in India for Tanzania. The company has also received an order for sixteen sets of locomotive brakes and vigilance control equipment for locomotives being built in India for Tanzania.

DAVIS BRAKE BEAM
Davis Brake Beam Co

Head Office: Johnstown, Pa, USA

Products: Solid-truss brake beams and bogie-mounted braking system manufactured under the trade-name, TRU-PAC.

Telephone: (814) 535-1595

DIMETAL
Dimetal SA

Head Office and Works: Km 18 800 de la Antigua Carretera de Madrid a Barcelona, Torrejon de Ardoz, Madrid, Spain

Telegrams: WABCO MADRID
Telephone: 6-75-11-00
Telex: 22332

Products: Brake equipment built under licenses from Westinghouse Air Brake of the United States, Westinghouse Brake & Signal.

DOWSON & DOBSON
Head Office: 29 Webber St, Selby, PO Box 7764, Johannesburg 2000, S Africa

Telephone: 836 1301
Telex: 8-7717SA

Products: Miner RF-361 draftgear under licence.

DRESSER
Dresser Industries Inc (Transportation Equipment Division)

Head Office: 2 Main St, Depew, NY 14043, USA

Telephone: (716) 683-6000

Products: Automatic couplers.

ELLCON-NATIONAL
Ellcon-National Inc

Head Office: 30 King Road, Totowa, NJ 07512, USA

Telephone: (201) 256-7110

Products: Geared hand brakes, automatic double-acting slack adjusters, empty/load devices.

Licensees:
South Africa—Conbrako Ltd, Tedstone Rd, Wadeville, Transvaal
Canada—Beclawat Ltd, 1128 Berlier St, Laval, Quebec
Mexico—Dinamica SA, Avenida Madero 40, Mexio 1 DF

EMILE HENRICOT
Usines Emile Henricot SA

Head Office: 1490 Court-Saint-Etienne, Belgium

Products: Draft gears, buffers, snubbers, handbrakes.

ENERGOMACHEXPORT
v/o Energomachexport

Head Office: 35 Mosfllmovskaya Ul, Moscow, USSR

Telegrams: ENERGOEXPORT MOSCOW
Telephone: 1472177
Telex: 7565

Products: Matrosov system automatic pneumatic brakes, drawgear including the type SA-3 automatic central buffer couplings.

FABRIKA VAGONA KRALJEVO

Head Office: Postanski FAH 90, Kraljevo, Yugoslavia

Products: Draftgears, buffers under licence from Miner, brake equipment, automatic couplers.

FERMAT
La Societe Fermat

Head Office: 19 quai du Moulin, 92230 De Cage, Gennevilliers, France

Telephone: 793 4544

Products: Oerlikon braking systems.

FERODO
Societe Anonyme Francaise du Ferodo

Head Office: 64 avenue de la Grande Armee, 75017 Paris, France

Telegrams: FERODO PARIS
Telephone: 380-56-50
Telex: 20053 IF

Products: Brake shoes.

FIAT
Fiat (Division Ferroviaria)

Head Office: Corso Fermucci, 122 Turin, Italy

Products: Brake equipment, draftgear, buffers, couplers, snubbers.

Telephone: 332033
Telex: 22307 FIATDMFT

FNV
Fabrica Nacional de Vagoes SA

Head Office: Praca DOM Jose Caspar 134, Caixa Postal Number 9797, Sao Paulo, Brazil

Telegrams: FABRIVA SAO PAULO
Telephone: 011 239 3055
Telex: 01121901

Products: Draft gears and couplers.

FORGES DE FRESNES
Forges de Fresnes

Head Office: 80 rue Pasteur, 59970 Fresnes Sur Escaug, France

Telephone: 474222

Products: Braking mechanisms including release gear.

FORJA
Forja Argentina SA

Head Office: San Jose 317, 8° p, Buenos Aires, Argentina

Telephone: 37-9833/38-8474/9453
Telex: 122573AR FORJA

Works: Calle 1 N° 171, Barrio Talleres (E), Cordoba, Argentina

Telephone: 71-2898/5468/9905

Products: Screw and chain couplings, drawgear rings, rolled forgings (see also entry under Bogies and Suspension Systems).

FREIGHTMASTER
(A Halliburton Company)

Head Office: 8600 Will Rogers Blvd, Fort Worth, Tex, 76140 USA

Telephone: (817) 293-4220
Telex: 75 8284

Products: End-of-car cushioning units.

President: O. E. Seay
Sales Director: P. D. Howard

FRESINBRA
Fresinbra Industrial SA

Head Office: Rua Primeiro de Marco 112, Rio de Janeiro, Brazil

Telegrams: FREINDUS
Telephone: (021) 233-2122

Works: Rua Lauriano Fernandes Jr 10, SAO Paulo, Brazil

Telephone: 011 260-3122)

Products: Automotive brake components under licence of WABCO-Westinghouse GmbH, couplers.

Constitution: The company is a joint venture of Fonseca Almeida of Brazil and Westinghouse Air Brake (Wabco) of the United States. Equipment supplied includes AB and ABD air brakes for locomotives and couplers for mass transit vehicles.

GIRLING
Girling Ltd

Head Office: Railway Product Group, Abelson House, 2297 Coventry Rd, Sheldon, Birmingham B26 3PR, England

Telephone: 021-742-2323
Telex: 339464

Works: Thermal Rd, Bromborough, Cheshire, England
Kings Rd, Tyseley, Birmingham, England

Products: Wheel-mounted disc brakes, transmission disc brakes, axle-mounted disc brakes, wheel slide prevention equipment.

Girling wheel-mounted disc brakes consist of air-operated caliper assemblies which operate on discs mounted on both sides of the vehicle wheel. Axle and transmission-mounted disc brakes are identical in operation to wheel-mounted equipment with the exception that the discs are mounted either on the axle or transmission and are capable of operating at speeds in excess of 3000 rpm. Wheelslide prevention equipment marketed by the company consists basically of two individual units—one, the sensing device attached to the axle box and the other an electro pneumatic valve which, when energised, momentarily releases the brake on the axle from which excessive deceleration has been sensed.

Products Group Manager: P. L. Quinn
Sales Manager (UK and N America): E. A. Leason
Sales Manager (Europe): M. D. Gorridge

Agents:
Portugal—Conde Barao, Avenida 24 De Julho, 62-64, Largo do Conde Barao, Lisbao 2
Belgium—Etablissement Jos Buhlmann, Rue des Coteaux 249, 1030 Bruxelles
Finland—Oy Elektro Diesel AB, Lonnrotinkatu 45, SF-00180, Helsinki 18
Sweden—Helge Meuller AB, Bredgrand 2, 11130 Stockholm
Denmark—Axel Ketner, 23 Frabriksparken, DK 2600, Glostrup
The Netherlands—Transmark BV, Handelmaatschappij, PO Box 30, Bussum
France—Freins Girling SA, 2/4 Ave. Albert Einstein, 93155 Le Blanc Mesnil

Sales: Since 1958 when Girling first designed railway disc brakes, over 18,000 vehicle sets have been supplied to British Rail (BR). Major sales to BR in 1976/77 included wheel mounted disc brakes for multiple unit stock, freight wagons and mainline passenger coaches including the HST; axle-mounted disc brakes for multiple units and freight wagons; and wheelslide prevention equipment for multiple units and mainline coaches.
The company's disc braking was first introduced into Europe in 1967 when new transit cars for Rotterdam subway were fitted with Girling disc brakes as an integral part of the transmission system. Since that time, sales abroad have included wheelslide prevention equipment for Denmark's S-Train stock.

GODWIN
Godwin Warren Engineering

Head Office and Works: Emery Rd, Bristol BS4 5PW, England

Telephone: 778399
Telex: 449375

Products: Friction stop buffers (see also entry under Signalling, Computer and Control Equipment)

Chairman: M. B. Derbyshire
Managing Director: D. A. Ball
Marketing Director: M. T. Roberts
Export Sales Director: G. D. Soames

GRESHAM & CRAVEN
Gresham and Craven Ltd

Head Office and Works: Chippenham, Wiltshire, SN15 1JD, England

Telegrams: BRAKE, CHIPPENHAM
Telephone: Chippenham 4141 Ext. 374
Telex: 449411/12

Products: Complete vacuum brake equipment and systems; exhauster equipment for locomotives together with portable and fixed installation test sets; air control equipment for hopper door, engine speed control etc.

Chairman: D. Pollock
Managing Director: J. R. C. Boulding
Sales Director: S. J. Pursey

Agents:
Australia & Tasmania—Westinghouse Brake & Signal Co (Australia) Pty Limited, Railway Brake & Industrial Products Division, PO Box 21, Burwood, NSW 2134
Austria; Bulgaria; Czechoslavakia; Hungary; Romania; Yugoslavia—WABCO Westinghouse GesmbH, 1205 Vienna 20, Hochstadtplatz 4, Postfach 49, Austria
Bangladesh—Purbachal Commercial Agencies, PO Box No 28, 1167 Dacca Trunk Road, Kadamtali, Chittagong
Belgium—Auxicom SPRL, 58 Rue des Deportes, 6510 Morlsnwelz
Brazil— Norton Megaw & Co Limited, Avenida Presidente Wilson, 165-30, Caiza No 34, Rio de Janeiro
France (North)—Auxicom SPRL, 58 Rue des Deportes, 6510 Morlanwelz, Belgium
Germany (DBR)—WABCO Westinghouse GmbH, 3000 Hannover 91, Postfach 911280
Ghana—Goodwill Associates Limited, PO Box 10630, Accra North
Iraq—Hakim's Bros Company, Alwiyah Andalus Sq, PO Box 2089, Alwiyah, Baghdad
Italy—WABCO Westinghouse, Divisione Equipaggiamenti, Veicoli Ferroviari, Via Pier Carlo Boggio 20, 10138 Torino
Japan—Jardine Matheson (Japan) Limited, Nissoki Honkan Central, PO Box 282, Tokyo
Nigeria—Nigerian Technical Equipment, Services Limited, 125A Apapa Road, PO Box 359, Apapa, Lagos
Pakistan—Flecbon Corporation, Lloyds Bank Building, 3rd Floor, Merewether Tower, II Chundrigar Road, Karachi 2
Portugal—Sociedade Victor Limitada, Rua Filipe Folque, 5-1° DTO, Lisboa 1
Rhodesia—Bellamy & Lambie (Pty) Limited, PO Box 3101, Hermes Road, Southerton, Salisbury
South Africa; Angola; Botswana; Lesoth; Mauritius; Mozambique; Namibia; Swaziland; Zambia—Westinghouse Bellambi (Pty) Limited, PO Box 453, Johannesburg, 2000
Spain—Dimetal SA, Plomo 10, Madrid 5
Sri Lanka—P. Rajagopal, 18A Alfred Place, Colombo 3
Sudan—National Engineering Co Limited, PO Box 208, Khartoum
Sweden—WABCO Westinghouse, Idunsgatan 26, 21446 Malmo
Switzerland—WABCO Westinghouse AG, 3018 Bern, Freiburgstrasse 384
Thailand—Yip In Tsoi & Jacks Limited, 523 Mahaprutharam Road, PO Box 2611, Bangkok
Zaire—Alexicom SPRL, 58 rue des Deportes, 6510 Morlanwelz

GRESHAM AND CRAVEN OF INDIA
Gresham & Craven of India (Private) Ltd

Head Office and Works: 22, Gobra Rd, Calcutta 700 014, India

Telegrams: CYLVAC CALCUTTA
Telephone: 44-1754

Products: Vacuum brake equipment, rotary exhausters, air brake valves and reservoirs.

Constitution: A state-owned company.

GREYSHAM
Greysham & Co

Office and Works: 7249, Roop Nagar, Delhi 110007, India

Telegrams: GREYSHAMCO
Telephone: 22316/225914
Telex: 031 3872

Products: Brake equipment.

HAINE/SAINT/PIERRE
Acieries de Haine-Saint-Pierre & Lesquin

Head Office: 7160 Haine-Saint-Pierre, Belgium

Products: Brakes and drawgear equipment.

HURST AIRHEART
Hurst Airheart Products

Head Office: 20235 Bahama St, Chatsworth, Cal 91311, USA

Telephone: (213) 882 6600

Products: Disc brakes.

JURID
Jurid Werke GmbH

Head Office and Works: Postfach 1249, 2057 Reinbek/Hamburg, German Federal Republic

Telegrams: JURIDAG HAMBURG
Telephone: Hamburg 72711
Telex: Jurid hmb 0217834

Products: Composition brake blocks, disc brake linings, friction plates. Main product line is plastic friction linings for block disc brakes made of one piece for friction sizes up to 300 cm¼ and in two pieces for friction area sizes over 300 cm¼.

Chairman: Dr Schroiff
Managing Director: Hr Glanz
Sales Director: Dr Ehlers

Licensees: Azbest Ploce, Yugoslavia

KNORR-BREMSE
Knorr-Bremse GmbH

Head Office and Works: Moosacher Strasse 80.8 Munich 40, German Federal Republic

Telephone: (089) 3505-1
Telex: 0524228

Products: Air brake systems and equipment, disc brakes, electro-magnetic brake equipment, slip prevention devices, automatic central buffer couplings.

New equipment: New modular brake units developed by Knorr-Bremse provide a simplified method of interconnection thereby saving on labour costs in the installation of piping, maintenance and overhaul. In the design of the modular units three basic types have been evolved: 1) with bored manifold plate for small basic units: 2) with laminated layer manifold plate for medium-sized units where limited space is available; 3) the panel unit for medium and large units which can be manufactured economically even in small series. In the plate of the bored manifold the air connections are provided for in the form of holes bored in co-ordinated right angles through the plate. The laminated layer manifold consists of a control plate, in which the air connection channels have been machined, and a mounting plate in which all the necessary tappings and connecting elements have been drilled. The two panels are laminated together and glued—a sealing gasket providing air tightness and mechanical strength. In the panel unit the manifold is a fully sealed off sheet metal cabinet in which copper tubing and adapter nipples are used to form the air connections. The modular units are bolt connected to pre-rivetted nuts on the panel front. The air connections to the piping system are made through the use of sealing rings.
Knorr-Bremse's axle-mounted disc brake consists of a grey cast-iron friction ring and a cast steel hub, connected by radially-arranged elastic resilient sleeves. The friction ring is manufactured as a solid component or in a split version when the two halves are held together by two tight-fit screws. Splitting the disc, Knorr points out, permits easy renewal without the additional expenditure involved in having to press the wheel off the axle.
Among the range of braking equipment manufactured by Knorr-Bremse is the type PK7S pneumatic block brake which has been designed for installation in the generally limited space available on bogies. The unit comprises a CK7S brake cylinder, a hanger, a brake block and brake block insert. Built into the brake block is a single-acting slack adjuster which ensures automatic compensation of the wear on the block. Used in conjuction with a disc brake, the PK7S exerts a cleaning action on the wheel, thereby improving the coefficient of friction between wheel and rail.

KOLMEX
Head Office: Mokotowska 49, 00-542 Warsaw 1, PO Box 236, 00 950, Poland

Telegrams: KOLMEX WARSZAWA
Telephone: 28-22-91/29-92-41
Telex: 813270/813714

Products: Brake equipment and components.

LDA
Engenharia e Comercio LDA

Head Office: Rua da Alegria, 61 R/C, Lisbon 2, Portugal

Products: Brake equipment and friction draftgear.

LLOYD
F. H. Lloyd & Co Ltd (ABC Coupler Division)

Head Office and Works: James Bridge Steel Works: Wednesbury, West Midlands WS10 9SD, England

Telephone: 021-526-3121
Telex: 337538

Products: Automatic couplers, semi rigid bar couplers, draftgear, side buffers, carbon and alloy steel castings for the railway industry

Chairman: F. Clymer
Managing Director: A. D. Harris
Sales Director: D. A. Silcox
Export Sales Manager: D. C. Lloyd

Agents:
Bangladesh–James Finlay & Co Ltd, Finlay House, PO Box 118, Chittagong
India–James Finlay & Co Ltd, 2 Netaji Subhas Rd, PO Box 209, Calcutta 1
Japan–Jardine, Matheson & Co (Japan) Ltd, 3-12 Nisseki Honkan, Nishi Shimbashi-1-chome, Minato-ku, CPO Box 282, Tokyo 105
South Africa–Conbrako (Pty) Ltd, PO Box 14010, 167 Tedstone Rd, Wadeville, Transvaal

MACHINE TOOL WORKS
Machine Tool Works Oerlikon-Burhle Ltd

Head Office and Works: Birchstrasse 155, CH-8050, Zurich, Switzerland

Telegrams: OUTIL ZURICH
Telephone: 01-463610
Telex: 52147

Products: Air brakes for automatic and manual systems, anti-wheel slip equipment, electro-pneumatic controls.

MACLEAN FOGG
Maclean Fogg (Railroad Division)

Head Office: 332 South Michigan Ave, Chicago, Ill 60604, USA

Telephone: (312) 427 7294

Products: Brake equipment.

MACOSA
Material y Construcciones SA

Head Office: Ausias March, 26, Barcelona, Spain

Products: Draftgears, buffers, snubbers, handbrakes.

McCONWAY & TORLEY
McConway & Torley Corp

Head Office: Pittsburgh, Pennsylvania 15201

Telephone: (412) 682 4700

Products: Couplers, yokes and related components

Vice President (Marketing): T. R. Gerosky

MECANOEXPORTIMPORT
Head Office: 10 Mihail Eminescu St, Bucharest, Romania

Telegrams: MECANEX
Telephone: 124600
Telex: 269

Products: Brakes built under licence from Knorr-Bremse and drawgear equipment for locomotives and rolling stock.

MINER
Miner Enterprises Inc (International Division)

Head Office: 1001 East 87th St, Chicago, Ill 60619, USA

Telegrams: MINER CHICAGO
Telephone: (312) 374 7400
Telex: 253724

Products: Draft gears, buffers, snubbers, handbrakes.

President: G. A. Withall
Vice President (Engineering): J. R. Fuenzalida
General Sales Manager: R. J. Bredin

Foreign Sales Offices:

Colombia–Quinteros Limitada Apartado Aereo 4308, Bogota
Peru–Albino Boggiano Delaude, Casilla 2500, Lima 1
Chile–Alfredo Campaña T, Casilla de Correo 2080, Santiago
Argentina–D. G. Cormick SRL, Casilla de Correo 5260, Buenos Aires
Bolivia–Mercantil Sudamericana Ltds, Casilla de Correo, 1185 La Paz
Egypt–Misr Import & Export Company, PO Box 1688, Cairo
Iran–Aftab-Shargh Techanical & Trading Corp, Aftab-Shargh Building Avenue Ferdowssi, Teheran
Turkey–Industrial Equipment and Supply Company, Nenehatun Caddesi No 124, Cankaya, Ankara
Pakistan–Willcox & Islam Ltd, PO Box 23 Karachi, 2 Pakistan
Thailand–Anglo-Thai Engineering Ltd, GPO Box 18, Bangkok
German Federal Republic–Knorr Bremse GmbH, Postfach 40-1060, 8000 Munich 40, West Germany (For "Comecon" countries only)
Zambia–Fairway Engineering Limited, PO Box 348, Kitwe
Kenya
Spain–Tecnicom, SA, Ayala, 120 Madrid

MINER Y MENDEZ
Miner y Mendez de Mexico SA

Head Office: Avenida Coyoacan No 912, Mexico 12, DF, Mexico

Products: Miner draft gears, buffers, snubbers, brake equipment built under licence.

MITSUBISHI
Misubishi Heavy Industries

Head Offices: 3-2 Marunouchi 2 chome, Chiyoda-ku, Tokyo, 100 Japan

Telegrams: MELCO TOKYO
Telephone: 03-218-2111
Telex: MELCO J2 4532

Products: Air brakes.

NEW YORK AIR BRAKE
New York Air Brake Co
(Member of the General Signal group)

Head Office: Starbuck Ave, Watertown, NY, USA

Telephone: 315-782-7000

Products: Pneumatic and electro-pneumatic air brakes and compressors.

NIPPON AIR BRAKE
The Nippon Air Brake Co Ltd

Head Office: Sannomiya Bldg, Nishikan, 1-12, Goko-dori 7 chome, Fukiai-ku, Kobe, 651, Japan

Telegrams: NABCO KOGE
Telephone: 078-251-8101
Telex: 5622-143

Works: Kobe, Seishin, Konan, Yokosuka, Tokyo

Products: Air brakes, NABCO composition Brake shoes, automatic slack adjusters.

OHIO BRASS
Ohio Brass Co

Head Office: 380 N. Main Street, Mansfield, Ohio, USA

Telephone: (312) 239-4200

Products: Automatic couplers.

Sales: Ohio Brass couplers have been supplied for the new Advanced Concept Train (ACT-1) built by Garrett for the Urban Mass Transportation Administration.

OLEO
Oleo Pneumatics Ltd

Head Office and Works: Blackdown, Leamington Spa, Warks, England

Telephone: 0926 21116/7

Products: Hydraulic buffing equipment. Oleo uses hollow extrusions with integral ends in its hydraulic buffers. The use of one-piece components provides higher strength than fabrication while reducing machining operations and cost, says the supplier. The two extrusions are used for the main cylinder of the buffer body and the plunger. Performance of the buffer is controlled by metering oil from the cylinder into the plunger through an orifice. Even energy absorption requires precise metering of the oil which is achieved by a complex series of oilways around the plunger orifice.

PAULSTRA

Head Office: 61, rue Marius Aufan, BP 164, F9230 Levallois-Perret, France

Telephone: (1) 757 3114
Telex: 620 898 Paulval

Products: Buffers, shock absorbers for UIC automatic couplings.

PHOENIX
Phoenix Gummiwerke AG

Head Office: 21 Hamburg 90, PO Box 90 11 40, German Federal Republic

Telegrams: PHOENIXPARA HAMBURG
Telephone: (040) 76 67-1
Telex: 02 17571 pshh d

Products: Vacuum brake hose.

PLOERMEL
Acieries de Ploermel

Head Office: 2, rue Alfred-de-Vigny, 75008 Paris, France

Telephone: (1) 227.98.85
Telex: 21311F

Products: Steel castings for railways including buffing equipment.

PURDY
Purdy Co

Head Office; 2400 West 95th St, Chicago, Ill 60642. USA

Telephone: (312) 239 4200

Products: Brake equipment.

RESERVOIR, LE
La Societe le Reservoir

Head Office: Rue Jean Henri Fabre 03103 Montlucon, France

Telephone: 05 3974

Products: Brake reservoirs and cylinders.

RINGFEDER
Ringfeder GmbH

Head Office and Works: 4150, Krefeld-Uerdingen, Duisberger Strasse 145, Postfach 486, German Federal Republic

Telegrams: RINGFEDER
Telephone: Krefeld 4491
Telex: 0853846

Products: Side buffers, draw and buffing gear for automatic central coupling, draw gear.

ROCKWELL
Rockwell International
(Mass Transit Sales)

Head Office: 2135 W. Maple Rd, Troy, Mich 48084, USA

Products: Heavy-duty braking systems—wedgem, cam, disc or spring brakes actuated by air or hydraulic pressure.

REUNERT & LENZ
Reunert & Lenz Ltd

Head Office: PO Box 92, Johannesburg, S Africa

Products: Brake regulators, disc brakes, parking brake equipment, load brake equipment, weighing valves.

SAB
SAB Bromsregulator

Head Office: Adelgatan 5 Malmo c, PO Box 306, S-201 23 Malmo 1, Sweden

Telegrams: BROMSREGULATOR MALMO
Telephone: (040) 738 80
Telex: 32413 SABROMS S

Works: SAB Thulinverken, Fack, S-261 02 Landskrona 2, Sweden.

Products: Double-acting, rapid working brake regulators for automatic brake slack adjustment; tread brake and disc brake units; electro-hydraulic, electro-pneumatic spring parking brake equipment with mechanical, quick release lever brake; load brake equipment for automatic adjustment of braking force; weighing valves.

Chairman: Alf Luning
Managing Director: Hans Wallgren
Sales Director (Sweden): Knut Sorensson
International Sales Director: Lennart Nilsson

Subsidiaries:
Belgium–SAB Broms SA, Walenstraat 30, B-3072 Nossegem
Telephone: (02) 759 79 12
France–Société SAB, 305, Bureaux de la Colline, F-92 213 Saint Cloud
Telegrams: Régleursab St Cloud
Telephone: (1) 602 05 47
Telex: 250935F
Germany–SAB Bremstechnik GmbH, Landskronstrasse 46, D-6100 Darmstadt
Telephone: (6151) 662 366
United Kingdom–SAB Brake Regulator Co Ltd, Aycliffe Industrial Estate, Darlington, Durham DL5 6HR
Telegrams: Britsab Darlington
Telephone: (32571) 2666
Telex: 58416 Britsab Ayclif
Italy–SAB Broms SpA, Via Faentina 218, 1-500 10 Caldine
Telephone: (55) 58 04 76
Spain–SAB Ibérica SA, Calle Andrés Mellado, 31 Madrid-15
Telegrams: Sabiberica Madrid
Telephone: (1) 449 46 62
Sweden–SAB Thulinverken, Fack, S-261 02 Landskrona 2
Telegrams: Thulinverken Landskrona
Telephone: (0418) 162 80
Telex: 72416 teve S
USA–American SAB Company, Inc, 2443 Crescent Drive, Broadview, Ill 60153
Telegrams: Americansab Broadviewill
Telephone: (312) 344-6130 (Chicago)
Telex: 721412 AMSAB BRDV
Brazil–Suecobras Indústria e Comércio SA, Rua Cachambi 713 ZC-16, Rio de Janeiro—GB
Telegrams: Suecobras Riodejaneiro
Telephone: 281-8285
Telex: 2123702 Suic BR

SAB BROMS
SAB Broms SA

Head Office: Walenstraat 30, B-3072 Nossegem, Belgium

Products: SAB brake equipment.

SAMBRE ET MEUSE
Usines et Acieries de Sambre et Meuse

Head Office: Tour Aurore-Cedex N° 5, 92080 Paris-Defense, France

Telephone: 788.15.15
Telex: 620.161

Products: Drawgear, disc brakes, shoe insert holders. Couplers include UIC type, and Miner RF4-29 drawgear built under licence.

Chairman: Pierre Boissier
Sales Director: Gilbert Labadie
Major sales: Drawgear equipment in 1976/77 was manufactured for French National Railways (SNCF), Iranian State Railways (RAI) and Italian State Railways (FS).

SCHINDLER
Schindler Waggon AG

Head Office: 4133 Pratteln, Switzerland

Telegrams: SCHINDLERWAGON
Telephone: (061) 815511
Telex: 62386

Products: Full range of braking equipment.

SECHERON
Des Ateliers de Secheron SA

Head Office and Works: 14 Avenue de Secheron, 1202 Geneva, Switzerland

Telegrams: ELECTRICITE
Telephone: (022) 32 67 50
Telex: 22 130

Products: Automatic couplers.

SKF ARGENTINA
Compania SKF Argentina SA

Head Office: Casilla de Correo 197, Buenos Aires, Argentina

Products: Brake regulators, disc brakes, parking brake equipment, load brake equipment, weighing valves.

SOCMI
Societa Costruzioni Industriali Milano SpA

Head Office: 20122 Milano—Via S. Calimero 3, Italy

Telephone: (02) 54 65 251
Telex: 31331

Products: Disc brakes under BSI licence.

STABEG
Stabeg Apparatengesellschaft GmbH

Head Office: Reinlgasse 5-9, Vienna XIV, Austria

Products: Brake regulators, disc brakes, load brake equipment, weighing valves, parking brake equipment.

STONE
J. Stone & Co (India) Ltd

Head Office: PO Box 16731, Calcutta 53, India

Products: Brake regulators, disc brakes, parking brake equipment, load brake equipment, weighing valves.

STURROCK
Sturrock (South Africa) Ltd

Head Office: 91 Commissioner St, PO Box 2863, Johannesburg, S Africa

Products: Friction draftgear.

SUECOBRAS
Suecobras Industria e Comercio SA

Head Office: Rua Cachambi, 713 ZC-16, Rio de Janeiro, Brazil

Products: Brake regulators, disc brakes, parking brake equipment, load brake equipment, weighing valves.

SUMITOMO
Sumitomo Metal Industries Ltd

Head Office: 3-2, Maranouchi 1 chome, Chiyoda-ku, Tokyo, X100 Japan

Telegrams: SUMITOMOMETAL TOKYO
Telephone: 03-282-6111
Telex: J 22865

Products: Couplers, draft gear and steel castings for the railway industry.

TECHNIKA
Head Office: 10 Graf Ignatiev St, Sofia, Bulgaria

Products: Brake regulators, disc brakes, parking brake equipment load brake equipment, weighing valves.

TITO
Metalski Zavod Tito

Head Office: Postfach 216, Skopje, Yugoslavia

Products: Brake regulators, disc brakes, parking brake equipment, load brake equipment, weighing valves.

TOKYU CAR
Tokyu Car Corporation

Head Office: 1, Kamariyacho, Kanazawa ku, Yokohama, 236 Japan

Telegrams: TOKYUCARCORP YOH
Telephone: 045-701-5151
Telex: 3822-392

Products: Disc brakes.

UNIVERSAL
Universal Railway Devices Company

Head Office: 332 South Michigan Ave, Chicago, Ill 60604

Telephone: (312) 427 7775

Products: Automatic slack adjusters.

UZINEXPORTIMPORT
Head Office: Calea Victoriei 133, Bucharest, Romania

Products: Brake regulators, disc brakes, parking brake equipment, load brake equipment, weighing valves.

VALTIONRAUTATIET
Head Office: Rautatiehallitus, Box 10488, SF-00101, Helsinki, Finland

Products: Brake regulators, disc brakes, parking brake equipment, weighing valves.

VICKERS HADWA
Vickers Hadwa Division

Head Office: 123 Railway Parade, Bassendean, Western Australia, Australia 6054

Products: Friction draftgear.

VOEST/ALPINE
Vereinigte Osterreichische Eisen-Und/Stahlwerke-Alpine Montan AG

Head Office: A-1040 Vienna, Prinz-Eugen/Strasse 8-10, Austria

Telegrams: VOEST ALPINE VIENNA
Telephone: 65 67 11
Telex: 1-2683

Products: Draftgears, buffers, snubbers, handbrakes, automatic couplers.

WABCO
Westinghouse Air Brake Division (Westinghouse Air Brake Co)

General Offices and plant: Wilmerding, Pa 15148, USA

Telegrams: WESTINGHOUSE WILLMERDING
Telephone: (412) 271-1490
Telex: 866467

Products: Freight wagon air-brake control equipment (including control valve—type ABDW—, brake cylinder, retaining valve, combined dirt collector and cut-out cock and angle cocks; high friction composition brake shoes—, the Cobra high friction composition brake shoe—, bogie mounted freight brake equipment — the WABCOPAC brake assembly offered as an alternative to the conventional car body mounted lever arrangements); locomotive brake equipment (including air brake control equipment—including engineer's brake valve, control valve, relay valves, safety control valves and brake cylinders), air compressors; mass transit car brake equipment (including control equipment)—both pneumatic and electro-pneumatic, bogie mounted brake equipment, and various transit car devices including automatic couplers, air compressor units and air spring levelling valves.

Affiliated Companies:

Belgium—WABCO Westinghouse, Av Van Volxem 164-166, 1190 Brussels
Federal Republic of Germany—WABCO Westinghouse, PO Box 91 12 80, D-3000 Hannover 91
The Netherlands—WABCO Westinghouse, Mient 12-16, Postbus 26, Capelle Ald Ijssel
Switzerland—WABCO Westinghouse, 384 Freiburgstrasse, Bumplitz, 3018 Berne
South Africa—WABCO Westinghouse (Railway Brake) (Pty) Ltd, PO Box 2863, Johannesburg 2000
France—WABCO Westinghouse, Boite Postal No 2, 93270 Freinville-Sevran
Italy—WABCO Westinghouse, Via Pier Carlo Boggio, 20 10138 Torino
Sweden—WABCO Westinghouse, NYA Agnes Fridsvagen 190, 213 75 Malmo
Austria—WABCO Westinghouse, Hochstadtplatz 4, Postfach 48, 1205 Vienna
Brazil—Fresinbra Industrial, SA, Caixa Postal 8776, 01236 Sao Paulo, SP

International Offices:

Argentina—Westinghouse Air Brake Trade Corp, Tucuari 147-4°, 1071 Buenos Aires
Mexico—Westinghouse Air Brake Trade Corp, EDIFICIO AZTLAN, Desp 506, Avenida Juarez 76, Mexico 1, DF

Wabco Licences:

Argentina—SIAM Di Tella Ltda, Division Electromecanica, Derqui 1868, San Justo, -Prov de Buenos Aires
Australia—Westinghouse Brake & Signal Co, (Australia) Ltd Pty, Railway Brake & Industrial Products Co, PO Box 120, Concord West, NSW 2138
Japan—Nippon Air Brake Co, Ltd, Sannomiya Bldg, Nishikan 1-12, Goko-Dori, 7-Chome, Fukiai-Ku, Kobe 651
Japan—Mittsubishi Electric Corp, 2-2-3 Marunouchi, Chiyoda-Ku, 2 Chome, Tokyo 100

WALTON
Walton Products Inc

Head Office: 868 Sussex Boulevard, Broomall, Pa 19008, USA

Telephone: (215) 544 8410
Telex: WALTON BROO 831/765

Products: Automatic couplers, including mechanical coupler assemblies, electro-pneumatic system, designed and manufactured by the wholly-owned subsidiary, Walton Electric Coupler Inc.

Chairman: G. Gobrecht
Managing Director: D. Murphy
Chief Sales Director: R. Dethloff

The company has no licencing agreements abroad but seeks inquiries from foreign suppliers of coupling assemblies and sales agents.

WESTINGHOUSE BRAKE AND SIGNAL
Westinghouse Brake and Signal Co Ltd and Works

Sales Office and Works: Chippenham, Wiltshire, England

Telephone: 0249 4141
Telex: 449411

Products: Air and vacuum brake equipment, electro-pneumatic brake equipment, E Weslake slack adjusters, 'Westcode' brake control system (See also entries under Signalling; Passenger coach equipment).

WILDE
Wilde, SAICI

Head Office: Monte 521, Buenos Aires, Argentina

Products: Draft gears, buffers, snubbers, handbrakes built under Miner licence.

BOGIES AND SUSPENSION SYSTEMS, WHEELS AND AXLES

ADIRONDACK
Adirondack Steel Casting Co, Inc

Head Office: Watervliet, NY 12189, USA

Products: One piece, cast steel bogies.

AMMENDORF
VEB Waggonbau
(Member of Maschinen-export)

Ammendorf, German Democratic Republic

Telephone: 22050
Telex: 11 26 89

Products: Bogies (including the type KWS-ZNII) now being fitted to latest long distance coaches for Soviet Railways; primary and secondary suspension systems, wheels, wheelsets.

ANF/INDUSTRIE
Societe ANF Frangeco

Head Office: Tour Aurore, 75092 Paris-Defense Cedex 5, France

Telephone: 788 1515
Telex: 610 817

Products: Power and trailer bogies for passenger stock, including rubber-tyred bogies for transit vehicles

ASEA
Allmanna Svenska Elektriska Aktiebolaget

Head Office: S-721 83, Vasteras, Sweden

Telegrams: ASEA Vasteras
Telephone: (021) 10 00 00
Telex: 40720 aseava s

Products: Special bogies incorporating rubber suspension.

ASF
American Steel Foundries

Head Office: 1005 Prudential Plaza, Chicago, Ill 60601

Products: Ride control bogies. The ASF Ride Control bogie snubbing system is a built-in design that maintains constant control of spring action. The ASF Side Frames and Bolsters exceed AAR strength requirements and can be furnished either as grade "B" or grade "C" steel castings. The pressure between the friction shoes and the Side Frame friction plates provides the necessary loadings to exercise optimum control. This pressure is generated by the Ride Control springs which force the friction shoes up the inclined ledges and outwardly against the friction plates. These Ride Control springs are compressed during assembly, and this amount of compression is not changed by varying Bolster loads or truck spring movements.

AVON
Avon Industrial Polymers Ltd

Head Office: Bradford-on-Avon, Wiltshire, England

Telephone: 02216 3911
Telex: 44856

Products: Rubber suspension systems and air springs

Commercial Manager: D. A. Washbrook
Sales Manager: B. O'Meara
Sales Offices:

Canada: Westcode Ltd, 3688 Nashua Drive, Mississauga, Ontario L4V 1M5, Canada
USA: Westcode Inc, 620 Allendale Road, King of Prussia Pa. 19406
Belgium: J. S. Oury Place Albert Leemans 1050 Brussels
Sweden, Norway and Denmark: Ulinco Industrial Agency AB, Kungsgatan 38-40, S 411 19 Goteborg Sweden
Finland: Oy Interco AB, 00121 Helsinki 12, P1 179 PB
Spain: Promar, SA P1 Duque de Medinaceli, 5 Barcelona (2)
Portugal: Unilock SARL, Aven de Republica 52-8°, Lisbon
Egypt: The Mechanical Tools Company, 62 Gamhouria Street, Cairo
Sudan: National Engineering Company Ltd, PO Box 208, Khartoum
Kenya: Avon Rubber Co Ltd, PO Box 18270, Nairobi
Zaire: Armand Duty & Co Ltd, Claridge House, 32 Davies Street, London W1
South Africa: Conbrako (Pty) Ltd, Tedstone Road, Wadeville , Transvaal
Korea: Paterson, Simons & Co Ltd, 67 Upper Thames Street, London EC4V 3 AH
Japan: Matheson & Co Ltd, Matheson House, 142 Minories, London EC3N 1QL
Australia: Spencer Moulton Pty Ltd, GPO Box 1649 N, Melbourne, 3001

BETHLEHEM
Bethlehem Steel Corporation

Head Office: Bethlehem, Pa 18016, USA

Products: Wheels and axles to AAR standards including mounted sets with or without roller bearings.

BRAINE-LE COMTE
Usines de Braine-le Comte SA

Head Office: Rue des Freres Dulait, Braine-le Comte, Belgium

Telegrams: USINES BRAINE-LE-COMTE
Telephone: (067) 553107
Telex: 57458

Products: Bogies

Managing Director: M. Lejeune

BREL
British Rail Engineering Ltd

Head Offices: Railway Technical Centre, London Rd, Derby DE2 8UP, England

Telephone: (0332) 49211 Ext 3795
Telex: 37367

Products: Production at BREL's specialised bogie facilities at present includes four basic types: the BT10 bogie for British Rail's 200 km/h Intercity 125 coaches, the BP14 bogie for class 312 outer suburban multiple unit stock, BX1 bogies for class 313 inner suburban multiple unit trains, and the FBT6 freight bogie.

BRITISH STEEL
British Steel Corp, Special Steels Division
(Forges, Foundries & Engineering Works Group)

Head Office: Brightside Lane, PO Box 99, Sheffield SR9 2RX, England

Telephone: 07 42 49071
Telex: 54185

Products: Bogies.

(Carbon Steels Works Group)

Head Office: PO Box 50, Sheffield Rd, Rotherham, S. Yorks, S60 1DW, England

Products: Tyres, wheels and axles.

BRITISH VITA
British Vita Co Ltd

Head Office: Middleton, Manchester, England

Telephone: (061) 653 6800
Telex: MR 667722

Products: Rubber mouldings for locomotive and rolling stock underframe construction.

BUCKEYE
Buckeye Steel Castings

Head Office: 2211 Parsons Ave, Columbus, Ohio 43207, USA

Telephone: (614) 444-2121

Products: Six, eight, ten and twelve-wheel bogies. Buckeye six-wheel Elasto-Cushion Trucks, with equalised design, introduce controlled lateral movement to cars with modern anti-friction bearings, thus reducing wear to truck and underframe assemblies. Draft arms attached to eight-, ten-, and twelve-wheel truck span bolsters have been used with cars of relatively long overhang to enable them to negotiate curves of short radii with standard coupler and draft gear arrangements.

CANADIAN STEEL WHEEL
Canadian Steel Wheel Division
(Member of Hawker Siddeley Canada Ltd)

Head Office: 1900 Dickson St, Montreal, Quebec H1N 2H9 Canada

Telephone: 514 255-3605
Telex: 05 828603

Products: Wrought carbon steel wheels.

CARDWELL WESTINGHOUSE

Head Office: 332 So. Michigan Ave, Chicago Ill, 60604, USA

Products: AAR standard and alternate standard coil springs.

CANADIAN STEEL WHEEL
Canadian Steel Wheel Division
(Member of Hawker Siddeley Canada Ltd)

Head Office: 1900 Dickson St, Montreal, Quebec H1N 2H9 Canada

Telephone: 514 255-3605
Telex: 05 828603

Products: Wrought carbon steel wheels.

COMETNA
Societe Cometna

Head Office: Case Postale 2402, Lisbon, Portugal

Products: Sambre et Meuse type bogies under licence.

DORBYL
Dorman Long Vanderbijl Corporation Ltd

Head Office: PO Box 229, 1460 Boksburg, S Africa

Telegrams: DORBYL
Telephone: 724 1441
Telex: 87539

Products: Sambre et Meuse type bogies under licence.

DRESSER
Transportation Equipment Division, Dresser Industries, Inc

Head Office and Works: 2 Main Street, Depew, NY 14043, USA

Telephone: (716) 683-6000
Telex: 91-277

Products: Caboose cushioning and cushion underframe components including Hydra-cushion underframe equipment; Symington XL bogies.

Marketing Director: W. F. Greenwood

DUNLOP
Dunlop Ltd, Polymer Engineering Division

Head Office: Evington Valley Rd, Leicester, LE5 5LY, England

Telegrams: POLYENG LEICESTER
Telephone: 0533-730281
Telex: 34397

Products: Rubber-bonded-to-metal springs for primary and secondary suspension systems, anti-vibration mountings, flexible bearings

Sales Offices:
North America: Metalastik Canada, 11 Curity Avenue, Toronto, Ontario M4B 1X5 Canada (Telephone (416) 755-77871)
India: Dunlop India Limited, Dunlop House, 57B Mirza Ghalib Street, Calcutta 700016 PO Box No 9023 (Telephone 24 9641)
Australia: Dunlop Automotive & Industrial Group, Industrial & Aviation Division, 838 Mountain Highway Bayswater, Victoria 3153 PO Box 41 (Telephone 729 6411)
Belgium: Dunlop Limited, Polymer Engineering Division, 31 Rue du Sel Bruxelles 1070 (Telephone (02) 21.00.10-22.79.21-22.79.22)
Denmark: P Otterstrom's EFTF, Trading & Engineering Company, 64 Tietgensgade Copenhagen V Telephone (01) 21 67 11
Finland: Ab Axel von Knorrings Tekniska Byra, SF-00381 Schliessfach, Helsinki 38 (Telephone 554488)
Germany: D-7581 Buehl Vimbusch Tullastrasse 30 (Telephone (07223) 24486)
Netherlands: Dunlop Nederland BV Polymer Engineering Division Schiedamsedijk 55a, Rotterdam 3001 (Telephone (010) 83 28 44)
Norway: Per-Kr Askim A/S Tollbodgt 28 Oslo 1 (Telephone 41 00 16)
Portugal: Turbomar Comercio E Tecnica De Maquinas LDA LINDA-A-VELHA (Telephone PPC 2190006)
Spain: Productos Pirelli SA Avda Jose Antonio 612-614, Barcelona (7) (Telephone CORNELLA 277 09 54)
Sweden: Metalastik Sweden Division of Svenska Dunlop AB Kopmangatan 7 15136 Sodertalje (Telephone (0755) 344 90)
Switzerland: Dunlop (Suisse) SA Polymer Engineering Division Haumuhlestrasse 5 8424 Embrach—ZH (Telephone Zurich 80 01 82)
Yugoslavia: Jugohemija Beograd Gen Zdanova 31, PO Box 441 (Telephone 341-141)

ENERGOMACHEXPORT
V/O Energomachexport

Head Office: 35 Mosfilmovskaya Ui, Moscow, USSR

Telegrams: ENERGOEXPORT MOSCOW
Telephone: 1472177
Telex: 7565

Products: Full range of bogies, primary and secondary suspension units, wheels wheelsets.

FORJA
Forja Argentina SA

Head Office: San Jose 317, 8° p, Buenos Aires, Argentina

Telephone: 37-9833
Telex: 122573AR FORJA

Works: Calle 1 N° 171, Barrio Talleres (3), Cordoba, Argentina

Products: Wheels and wheelsets.

FRANCO/BELGE
Societe Franco-Belge de Materiel de Chemins de Fer

Head Office: 49 Avenue George V, 75008 Paris, France

Telegrams: LOCOMORAM PARIS
Telephone: 723 55 24
Telex: 290 060F

Products: Standard and special bogies for passenger coaches and freight wagons.

FREIGHTMASTER
(A Halliburton Company)

Head Office: 8600 Will Rogers Blvd, Fort Worth, Texas 76140 USA

Products: Hydraulic cushioning units.

GLOUCESTER
Gloucester Railway Carriage & Wagon Co Ltd

Head Office: Bristol Rd, Gloucester, England

Telegrams: RAILCAR GLOUCESTER
Telephone: (0452) 25104/5
Telex: 43179

Products: Bogies and suspension systems.

GRESHAM & CRAVEN
Gresham & Craven Ltd

Head Office: Chippenham, Wiltshire SN15 1JD, England

Telegrams: BRAKE CHIPPENHAM
Telephone: Chippenham 4141 Ext 374
Telex: 449411/12

Products: Air suspension equipment

Sales Director: S. J. Pursey.

GRIFFIN
Griffin Wheel Company

Head Office: 200 W. Monroe St, Chicago, Ill 60606, USA

Products: Wheels available in the following sizes: 28", 33", 36", 38", 40".

HANSENS
Hansens Gummi & Packungs-Werke KG

Head Office: 3 Hannover 27 m PB 27 01 20, German Federal Republic

Products: Rubber shock absorbers for all types of rolling stock and motive power.

HIGH DUTY ALLOYS
High Duty Alloys Forgins Ltd
(A Hawker Siddeley company)

Head Office: Windsor Road, Redditch, Worcs, England B97 6EF

Telephone: Redditch 64211
Telex: 337773

Products: Die and hard-forged components for lightweight bogie side-frames, axlebox yokes and suspension tubes largely for transit operation.

HOLLAND
Holland Company, Freight Equipment Division

Head Office: 747 East Roosevelt Rd, Lombard, Ill 60148, USA

Telephone: (312) 629 8500

Products: Volute anti-roll device

Sales Director: H. B. Nordstrom

ICF
Integral Coach Factory

Head Office: Perambur, Madras 600 038, India

Telegrams: RAILCOACH MADRAS
Telephone: 661091
Telex: 7390

Products: Passenger coach bogies. ICF has exported 66 bogies to Burma, 100 to Taiwan, 45 to Thailand in addition to producing prototype high-speed units to RDSO design.

ITALISIDER
Italsider spa

Head Office: Via Corsica 4, 16128 Genoa, Italy

Telephone: (010) 5999
Telex: 27.039 Italsid

Products: Freight wagon bogies, wheels and wheelsets.

KNORR-BREMSE
Knorr-Bremse GmbH

Head Office: Moosacher Strasse 80, 8 Munich 40, German Federal Republic

Telephone: (089) 3505-1
Telex: 0524228

Products: Sambre et Meuse bogies under licence.

KONI
Koni BV

Head Office: Langeweg 1 (PO Box 1014), Oud-Beijerland, The Netherlands

Telegrams: KONI OUDBEIJERLAND
Telephone: 01860 2500
Telex: 21181

Products: Primary and secondary dampers.

Chairman: M. de Koning
Managing Director: M. de Koning
Chief Sales Director: G. E. Seckel

Major Agents:
German Federal Republic: De Koning GmbH, Industriegebiet, 5431 Ebernhahn/Uww (Telephone: 02623-3068 Telex: 863104)
France: Koni France SARL, 41, Rue Bayen, Paris 17-c (Telephone: 17557575 Telex: 290518)
United Kingdom: B. & M. Stork, 695 A London Road, North Cheam, Surrey (Telephone: 13303505 Telex: 918778)
Austria: Siems & Klein KG, Fach 126, 1015 Wien (Telephone: (0222) 521 631 Telex: 01; 2885)

LEW
Veb Lokomotivbau-Elektrotechnische Werke Hans Beimler

Head Office: 1422 Henigsdorf, German Democratic Republic

Telegrams: ELEKTROLOK HENIGSDORF
Telephone: Henigsdorf 851
Telex: 015 8531

Products: Power and trailer bogies for passenger stock and locomotives. Among latest developments by LEW is a Series 277 powered bogie for use with electric multiple units. With slight modifications the same bogie can be used for non-powered applications.

LORD
Lord Kinematics (Vehicle Products Group)

Head Office: Erie, Pa 16512, USA

Products: Bogie springs and adapter mountings; LC Pads for use between adapter and sideframe; V-Springs; Lastosphere springs.

MAFERSA
Material Ferroviario SA Mafersa

Head Office: Ave. Raimundo Pereira de Magalhaes 220, (CEP 05092) Sao Paulo, SP, Brazil

Telegrams: MAFERSA SAO PAULO
Telephone: 260 4591

Products: Forged and rolled steel wheels and wheelsets.

MAN
Maschinenfabrik Augsburg-Nurnberg AG Railway Division

Head Office: Katzwanger Strasse 101, 8500 Nurnberg 1, German Federal Republic

Telegrams: MANWERK NURNBERG
Telephone: 0911/18-1
Telex: 0622291

Products: Bogies and air suspension equipment.

NIKEX
Nikex Hungarian Trading Company

Head Office: 1016 Budapest, Meszaros utca 48-54, Hungary

Telegrams: NIKEXPORT BUDAPEST
Telephone: 851 122/852 111
Telex: 224971 nikex h

Products: Tyres and tyred wheelsets
Chairman: L. Varga
Managing Director: H. Szucs
Sales Director: I Minya
Export Sales: Z. P. Szadvary.

PAULSTRA
Societe Paulstra

Head Office: 61 rue Marius Aufan BP 164, F 92305 Levallois-Perret, France

Telephone: (1) 757.31.14
Telex: 620 898 Paulval

Products: Rubber/elastomer suspension systems.

PHOENIX
Phoenix Gummiwerke AG

Head Office: 21 Hamburg 90, PO Box 90 11 40, German Federal Republic

Telegrams: PHOENIXPARA, Hamburg
Telephone: (040) 76 67-1
Telex: 02 17571 phh d

Products: Rubber/metal axle springs.

PIONEER
Pioneer Springs (Pioneer Export Division)

Head Office: 23 George Street, Homebush, NSW, Australia 2140

Telegrams: PIOSPRING HOMEBUSH

Products: Springs for railway suspension units

Associated Companies: *Ethiopia:* Grima W. Giorgis, PO Box 577, Addis Ababa
Ethiopa: Girma W. Giorgis, PO Box 577, Addis Ababa
Hong Kong: Fuda & Co, PO Box 1130, Hong Kong
Indonesia: E, Herman, Jalan Mangga Besat, IV-P 58A Jakarta
Malaysia: Yew P. Ong P/L, 302 Hardware Hse, 400 Jalan Tuanku Abdul Rahman, Kuala Lumpur
Singapore: Yew P. Ong & Co, Queen St, PO Box 3
Iran: T. Sarhang Pour, 3/90 Iranshahr St, Teheran
West Indes: Auto and Gen, PO Box 702, Port of Spain, Trinidad
Kenya: E. Auto Spares Ltd, PO Box 1439, Nairobi
New Zealand: Fox & Gunn, PO Box 1537, Wellington 1
Pakistan: Overseas Distributing, PO Box 7342, Karachi 3
Philippines: Allenco Steel Corp, PO Box 2266, Manila
Sri Lanka: Milhuisen & Hock, 47/19 Galla Rd, Colomba 3
Sudan: Sudanese Autospares Co, PO Box 2396, Khartoum (Railway)
Thailand: Kayha Wat Co. Ltd, 461 Nakorm Swan Rd, Tavakum Bridge, Bangkok

ROCKWELL
Rockwell International
(Transport Equipment Division)

Head Office: 2100 W. Maple Rd, Troy, Mich 48084, USA

Products: Complete bogies and components for locomotives, freight wagons, transit and commuter passenger stock.

RUHFUS NEUSS
A. Ruhfus Neuss

Head Office: D 404 Neuss, Budericher Strasse 7, PO Box 980, German Federal Republic

Telephone: (02101) 26116
Telex: 08 517807

Products: Leaf springs, buffer springs and helical springs.

R. W. MAC
R. W. Mac Company

Head Office: 525 Craig Ave, Crete, Ill 60417, USA

Telephone: (312) 672-6376

Products: Car-Safe bogie bolster supports for 50-90 tonne wagons.

SAB
SAB Bromsregulator

Head Office: Adelgatan 5 Malmo c, PO Box 306, S-201 23 Malmo 1, Sweden

Telegrams: BROMSREGULATOR MALMO
Telephone: 040/738 80
Telex: 32413 SABROMS S

Works: SAB Thulinverken, Fack S-261 01 Landskrona 2, Sweden

Products: Resilient wheels.

SAMBRE ET MEUSE
Sambre et Meuse

Head Offices: Tour Aurore, 92080 Paris-Defense, Cedex 5, France

Telephone: 788 15 15
Telex: 620 161

Products: Design, testing and manufacturing of bogies for all gauges, including the UIC Y25 type and its derivatives; wheels and wheelsets. The Sambre et Meuse design of sprung bolster is made to AAR, British Rail and Crown Agents specifications.

Managing Director: Pierre Boissier

Sales Director: Gilbert Labadie

SCHINDLER
Schindler Carraige & Wagon Co Ltd

Head Office: Pratteln, near Basle, Switzerland

Telegrams: SCHINDLERWAGON PRATTELN
Telephone: (061) 815511
Telex: 62386

Products: Passenger stock and freight wagon bogies.

SCHLIEREN
Swiss Car and Elevator Manufacturing Corp Ltd

Head Office: CH-8952 Schlieren, Switzerland

Telegrams: SCHLIECO SCHLIEREN
Telephone: 01/730 70 11
Telex: 52961 SWS ch

Products: Motor and trailer bogies for all types of rolling stock.

SCULLIN
Scullin Steel Co

Head Office: 6700 Manchester Ave, St. Louis, Mo 63139, USA

Telephone: (314) 645-0400

Products: Castings for freight wagon bogies.

SOCMI
Societa Construzioni Industriali Milano SpA

Head Office: Via S. Calimero 3, 20122 Milan, Italy

Telephone: (02) 54.65. 251/5
Telex: 31331

Products: Bogies under license to Duwag.

STANDARD
Standard Car Truck Co

Head Office: 332 S. Michigan Avenue, Chicago, Ill 60604, USA

Telegrams: CARTRUCKS

Products: Barber stabilised bogies. The Barber load-sensitive variable damping system includes a friction shoe (iron-alloy casting with large bearing areas), hardened steel wear plate bolted and/or welded to the side frame column, and preloaded spring which provides actuating support for the friction casting.

Telephone: (312) 427-1466
Telex: 25-6140

Associated companies: Barber products designed and engineered by Standard are available under license in Australia, Belgium, Brazil, Canada, Japan, Mexico and South Africa.

STUCKI
A. Stucki Co

Head Office: 2600 Neville Rd, Pittsburgh, Pa 15225, USA

Telephone: 412 771 7300

Products: Freight wagon suspension systems including the types HS-6 and HS-7 Stabilisers designed to control harmonic rocking and vertical bounce in 50, 70 and 100-tonne freight wagons; side bearings.

SUMITOMO
Sumitomo Metal Industries Ltd

Head Office: New Sumitomo Bldg, 1-3-2, Marunouchi, Chiyoda-ku, Tokyo, Japan

Telephone: 03-282-6111
Telex: J22865 SMIMETAL

Products: Bogies, suspension systems, wheels and wheelsets

General Manager, Sales: H. Tanabe
Manager, Export Section: H. Nakata

UNION SPRING
Union Spring and Manufacturing Co

Head Office: New Kensington, Pa 15068, USA

Telephone: (412) 337-4571

Products: Suspension systems including Everlast springs, spring plates, undercushion springs, journal box lids, wear plates and pedestal liners.

UNITY
Unity Railway Supply Co, Inc

Head Office: 332 S. Michigan Avenue, Chicago, Ill 60604, USA

Telephone: 312 939 3438

Products: No-Sway locomotive stabilisers, wheels, axles.

VALDUNES
Valdunes (Creusot Loire-Usinor)

Head Office: 12, rue de la Rochefoucauld, 75428 Paris, France

Telephone: (1) 280 65 77
Telex: CLLAR 650 802 F

Products: Wrought solid wheels, straight axles, mounted wheelsets

Managing Director: Philippe Kessler
Chief Sales Director: Jean Cambuzat

Constitution: Valdunes represents the combined resources of Usinor and Creusot Loire.

VANGUARD
Vanguard Corp.

Head Office: PO Box 525, Highland Park, Ill 60035, USA

Telephone: (312) 432-2425

Products: Trioid side bearings: model 173 for all types of freight wagon; model 190 for cabooses; model 1002-1 replacement for existing single solid steel roller, model 1002-2 replacement for double solid steel rollers on 90, 100 and 125 tonne wagons.

WOODHEAD
Jonas Woodhead Ltd

Head Office: Walbottle Rd, Newburn, Newcastle-upon-Tyne NE15 9UD, England

Telephone: Lemington 674141/513/142

Products: Laminated springs for locomotives, wagons, mine cars; solid eye and rolled forged main plates; solid and welded type buckles; conventional, featherlite and minimum leaf parabolic tapers; telescopic shock absorbers; coil springs.

Chairman: T. S. Richardson
Manager: N. T. Crosby
Chief Sales Manager: G. C. Redican
Export Sales Manager: R. Thomlinson

YUSOKI KOGYO
Yusoki Kogyo K.K

Head Office: 102, Kamihamacho, Handa, Aichi 475 Japan

Telephone: 0569 21 3311
Telex: 4563 605

Products: Passenger coach and freight wagon bogies.

BEARING MANUFACTURERS

ABEX

Abex Corporation (Railroad Products Group)

Head Office: Valley Road, Mahwah, NJ 07430, USA

Products: Standard steeple back bearings; alternate standard Hi-Hat bearings; roller bearing adapters—to AAR standards.

AMERICAN KOYO

American Koyo Corp

Head Office: 29570 Clemens Rd, PO Box 45028, Westlake, Ohio 44145, USA

Telephone: (216) 835 1000

Products: ABU type journal roller bearings.

BRENCO

Brenco Inc

Head Office: PO Box 389, Petersburg, Virginia 23803, USA

Telephone: (804) 732-0202

Products: Roller bearings.

COMET

Comet Industries Inc

Head Office: 4800 Deramus Ave, Kansas City, Missouri 64120, USA

Telephone: (816) 483 3757

Products: Roller bearings.

FAG

FAG Bearings Corporation

Head Office: Stamford, Connecticut 06904, USA

Products: Journal roller bearings.

FUJIKOSHI

Fujikoshi Ltd

Head Office: World Trade Centre Bldg, 4-1 Hamamatsucho 2 chome, Minato-ku Tokyo 105, Japan

Telegrams: NACHI TOKYO
Telephone: 03-435 5111
Telex: J 24327

Products: Ball bearings, roller bearings, linear ball bearings.

GARRETT

Garrett Railroad Car and Equipment Inc

Head Office: PO Box 2208, Newcastle, Pennsylvania 16102, USA

Telephone: (412) 658 9061

Products: Roller bearings.

GRIFFIN

Griffin Wheel Co

Head Office: 200 W Monroe, Chicago, Ill 60606, USA

Telephone: (312) 346 3300

Products: Journal bearings (brass).

ILLINOIS RAILWAY EQUIPMENT COMPANY

Head Office: 80E Jackson Blvd, Chicago, Ill 60604, USA

Products: 'Economy' journal centering guides; 'Mobil' insert-type journal stops.

KOYO SEIKO

Koyo Seiko Co Ltd

Head Office: 9-2, Sueyoshibashi 3 chome, Minami-ku, Osaka, 542 Japan

Telegrams: KOYOBRG OSAKA
Telephone: 06-271 8451
Telex: 5222240 KOYOOS J

Products: Axle box, grease-sealed journal bearing (ABU type), roller bearing, ball bearing, needle roller bearing, pillow block.

ISNR

(Subsidiary of Renault)

Head Office: 75783 Paris, Cedex 16, France

Products: Roller-bearing axle boxes.

KUGELFISCHER

Kugelfischer Georg Schafer

Head Office: Schweinfurt, German Federal Republic

Products: FAG journal bearings with light metal housings.

MAGNUS PRODUCTS

(NL Industries, Bearings Division)

Head Office: 5461 Southwyck Blvd, Toledo, Ohio 43614, USA

Telephone: (419) 385 9911

Products: Roller bearings, solid and flat back journal bearings.

MULTI-SERVICE SUPPLY

Multi-Service Supply Inc
(Subsidiary of the Buncher Co)

Head Office: 1080 Third St, PO Box 149, North Versailles, Pennsylvania 15137, USA

Telephone: (412) 824 3630

Products: Roller bearings.

NIPPON SEIKO

Nippon Seiko KK

Head Office: Mita Kokusai Bldg, 4-28 Mita 1 chome, Minato-ku, Tokyo 108, Japan

Telegrams: NSKBEARING TOKYO
Telephone: 03-454 8011
Telex: 02224280 NSKBRG J

Products: Axle box, tapered roller bearing and package unit for rolling stock, ball bearing, roller bearing, ball recirculating type steering gear, ball screw pillow block, liner ball bearing.

NL INDUSTRIES

NL Industries Inc (Bearings Division)

Head Office: 5461 Southwick Blvd, Toledo, Ohio 43614, USA

Products: Solid and roller bearings.

NTN BEARING CORP

NTN Bearing Corp of America

Head Office: 31 E Oakton St, Des Plaines, Ill 60018, USA

Products: Journal rolling bearings, including the new NTN Titan—a self-contained, doublerow RCT bearing and housing unit.

NTN TOYO

NTN Toyo Bearing Co Ltd

Head Office: 3-17, chome, Kyomachibori, Nishi-ku, Osaka, Japan

Telegrams: TOYOBEAR OSAKA
Telephone: 06 (443) 5001

Tokyo Office: 17-22, 7 Nishigoranda, Shinagawa-ku, Tokyo, Japan

Telegrams: TOYOBEAR TOKYO
Telephone: 03 (494) 5861

Products: Journal roller bearings.

RAILKO

Railko Ltd (A BBA Group Co)

Head Office: Loudwater, High Wycombe, Bucks HP10 9QU, England

Telephone: (062-85) 22551
Telex: 848406

Products: Plastics bearings, including the Railko centre pivot liner developed to replace greased metal on UIC-Y25C type bogies.

SKF

SKF Svenska Kullagerfabriken
Head Office: Sweden
Products: Roller bearings.

TIMKEN

The Timken Company

Head Offices: Canton, Ohio 44706, USA (US sales)
British Timken, Duston, Northampton, England

Subsidiaries: Manufacturing plants in Australia, Brazil, Canada, France, South Africa, UK and the USA

Products: Tapered roller bearings.

UNITY

Unity Railway Supply Co Inc

Head Office: 332 S Michigan Ave, Chicago, Ill 60604, USA

Telephone: 312-939 3438

Products: Journal package including: No-Sway side-bearing stabiliser; journal box rear seal; journal stop for use in rib or non-rib types; Easy-ply lid seal.

VANDERVELL

Vandervell Products Ltd

Head Office: Maidenhead, Berkshire, England

Products: Roller bearings.

PASSENGER COACH EQUIPMENT

ADAMS & WESTLAKE

Adams and Westlake Co

Head Office: 1025 N Michigan St, Elkhart, Ind 46514, USA

Telephone: (219) 264 1141

Products: Windows and lighting equipment.

AIR INDUSTRIE

(Subsidiary of the Saint-Gobain-Pont A-Mousson Group)

Sales Office: 75783 Paris, Cedex 16, France

Products: Air conditioning equipment.

AIRSCEW HOWDEN

Head Office: Weybridge, Surrey, England

Products: Ventilation fans.

ALNA KOKI

Alna Koko Co Ltd

Head Office: 4-5 Higashi Naniwacho 1 chome, Amagasaki, Hyogo, 660 Japan

Telegrams: ALNA AMAGASAKI
Telephone: 06 401 7281
Telex: 524 2782

Products: Aluminium window sash for electric railcars and passenger coaches.

BBC

Brown Boveri & Cie Aktiengesellschaft

Head Office: Mannheim, German Federal Republic

Products: Air conditioning systems.

BECKETT, LAYCOCK & WATKINSON

Beckett, Laycock & Watkinson Ltd

Head Office: Acton Lane, London NW10, England

Telephone: 01 965 5403
Telex: 261770

Products: Beclawat windows, door systems and route indicators.

BELZ

August Belz Apparatebau GmbH

Head Office: Postfach 12 25, D-7990 Friedrichshafen, German Federal Republic

Products: Sapor soap dispensers supplied to nine European railway companies.

CLEMANCON

Societe Clemancon

Sales Office: 75783 Paris, Cedex 16, France

Products: Heating and regulation equipment, lighting systems.

DEANS AND LIGHTALLOYS

Deans & Lightalloys Ltd

Head Office: PO Box 8, Beverly, Yorkshire HU17 0JL, England

Telephone: 883171

Products: Doors, seats, windows and general fittings including complete sliding doors and pneumatically-operated equipment.

ELLCON/NATIONAL

Ellcon-National Inc

Head Office: 30 King Rd, Totowa, NJ 07512, USA

Telephone: (201) 256 7110

Products: Window and door gear.

ERCOLE MARELLI

Ercole Marelli & C SpA

Head Office: Via Borgonuovo 24, Milan, Italy

Telegrams: VENTILATOR MILANO
Telephone: 2494
Telex: 31043

Products: Air conditioning systems and equipment.

FAIVELEY

Faiveley SA

Head Office: 93, rue du Docteur Bauer, BP 151, 93494 Saint-Ouen Cedex, France

Telephone: 076 12 60
Telex: 290653

Products: Manually operated doors; electro-pneumatic doors and door gear; electric and electro-pneumatic door control fittings, electric and electronic control fittings for heating equipment; miscellaneous electronic equipment. To date about 80,000 door equipments have been supplied to a number of railways, including: Montreal Metro (access door suspension and coordinating mechanism); Mexico Metro (automatic access door equipment including door leaves and mechanism); Santiago Metro (automatic access doors); Rio Metro (access door controls); Madrid Metro (access door controls); Barcelona Metro (access door controls) Paris Metro (access door equipment). Mainline railways using Faiveley door equipment include: Danish State Railways, Italian State Railways, French National Railways, Romanian State Railways, South African Railways, Australian Railways, Iranian State Railways.

GRAHAM WHITE

Graham White Sales Corp

Head Office: 1209 Colorado St, Salem, Virginia 24153, USA

Telephone: (703) 389 2305

Products: Windows.

HITACHI

Hitachi Ltd

Head Office: 6-2, 2 chome Otemachi, Chiyoda-ku, Tokyo, 100 Japan

Telephone: 03 270 2111
Telex: J 22395, J 22432, J 24491

Products: Air conditioning equipment.

	Roof-mounted Type
Unit cooler	
Model	FTUR-550-202
Dimensions	
(length×width×height)	4 030 mm × 1 780 mm × 390 mm
Weight	900 kg
Cooling capacity per coach	40 000 kcal/h
Evaporator inlet air temperature	DB 28°C—WB 22.9°C
Condenser inlet air temperature	DB 33°C
Heating capacity per coach	
Heating device	
Refrigerant	R-22
Power source	
Main power source	ac 3ø 440V or 220 V 60 Hz
Control power source	ac 2ø 100 V 60 Hz
Compressor	
Type	Hitachi hermetic type 750FH4
Motor	5.5 kW
Number of unit used	2
Condenser	Air-cooled multipath fin-and-tube type
Evaporator	Direct expansion multipath fin-and-tube type
Blower for condenser	
Type	Centrifugal fan
Air flow rate per coach	170 m³/min × 2
Motor	1.5 kW
Blower for evaporator	
Type	Tandem type double-suction multiblade fan
Air flow rate per coach	120 m³/min
Motor	2.2 kW
Throttling	Capillary tubes
Cycle protective device	
Temperature control	Two-stage type thermostat

	Floor-mounted Type
Unit cooler	
Model	FTUF-550-201
Dimensions	
(length×width×height)	1 450 mm × 850 mm × 1 850 mm
Weight	1 515 kg
Cooling capacity per coach	30 300 kcal/h
Evaporator inlet air temperature	DB 26.7°C—WB 19.4°C
Condenser inlet air temperature	DB 36.7°C
Heating capacity per coach	8 600 kcal/h
Heating device	Sheathed wire with fins
Refrigerant	R-12
Power source	
Main power source	ac 3ø 440 V 60 Hz
Control power source	ac 2ø 100 V 60 Hz
Compressor	
Type	Copelametic semi-sealed type 9RC1-0760-TFD
Motor	5.5 kW
Number of unit used	2
Condenser	Air-cooled multipath fin-and-tube type
Evaporator	Direct expansion multipath fin-and-tube type
Blower for condenser	
Type	Centrifugal fan
Air flow rate per coach	300 m³/min × 3
Motor	1 kW
Blower for evaporator	
Type	Tandem type double-suction multiblade fan
Air flow rate per coach	128 m³/min
Motor	1.5 kW
Throttling	Temperature type automatic expansion valve
Cycle protective device	High-and low-pressure switches
Temperature control	Thermostat × 3

	Underfloor-mounted Type
Unit cooler	
Model	FTU-750-101
Dimensions	
(length×width×height)	3 290 mm × 1 170 mm × 772 mm
Weight	1 450 kg
Cooling capacity per coach	40 000 kcal/h
Evaporator inlet air temperature	DB 28°C—WB 21.2°C
Condenser inlet air temperature	DB 40°C
Heating capacity per coach	
Heating device	
Refrigerant	R-500
Power source	
Main power source	ac 3ø 220 V 50 Hz
Control power source	ac 2ø 200 V 50 Hz
Compressor	
Type	Hitachi semi-sealed type 1000FSVW6-A
Motor	7.5 kW
Number of unit used	1 × 2
Condenser	Air-cooled multipath fin-and-tube type
Evaporator	Direct expansion multipath fin-and-tube type
Blower for condenser	
Type	Double suction multiblade fan
Air flow rate per coach	200 m³/min × 2
Motor	3.75 kW
Blower for evaporator	
Type	Single-suction multiblade fan
Air flow rate per coach	120 m³/min
Motor	1.5 kW
Throttling	Temperature type automatic expansion valve
Cycle protective device	High-and low-pressure switches
Temperature control	Thermostat

HIRST ELECTRIC

Hirst Electric Industries Ltd

Head Office: Gatwick Rd, Crawley, Sussex RH10 2SA, England

Telegrams: HIRSTELEC CRAWLEY
Telephone: (0293) 25721
Telex: 87424

Products: Microwave ovens, coffee pot warmers supplied to British Rail for use in the catering vehicles of High Speed Trains, the APT and Intercity trains.

Agents: *France:* CLEA, 48 Avenue Gabriel Peri, 78630 Montesson; *Germany:* (a) HO & Technical, Burger Eisenwerke AG, 6348 Herborn, Postfach 1120; (b) Senkingwerk GmbH, 32 Hildesheim 1, Postfach 86; *Norway:* K E Gleditsch, Radhusgt 30, Oslo 1; *Sweden:* Maskinkonstruktioner AB, Klangfargsgatan 8, 421 52 Vastra Frolunda; *Denmark:* Oluf Brønnum & Co A/S, Holbergsgade 8, 1057 Copenhagen K; *Holland:* Marja International BV, Koningsweg 4, Utrecht, Postbus 2381; *Switzerland:* CORY AG, CH 8703 Erlenbach, Drusbergstrasse 1; *Australia exc SA:* Luke Equipment, 30 Queens Parade, North Fitzroy, Victoria 3068; *South Australia:* Commonwealth Industrial Gases, PO Box 305, Cowandilla, SA 5033; *Eire:* Masser Irish Food Machines Ltd, Precision Works, Kylemore Road, Dublin 10; *N Ireland:* GKS Supplies, 100 University Avenue, Belfast BT7 1GY; *Monaco:* Sam's Place Restaurant, Palais de la Scala, 1 Ave Henri Dunant, Monte Carlo; *Italy:* Solisa snc, Via B Bouzzi 12/2, 40067 Rastignano, Bologna.

HUTTMANN

Richard Huttmann

Head Office: D-3575 Kirchhaib 1, German Federal Republic

Products: 24 V dc special aero fans for roof and wall mounting.

KISMOTOR ÉS-GEPGYAR

Head Office: Budapest XI, Fehervari ut 44 (RB), Hungary

Telephone: 452-150
Telex: 4 384

Products: Door and window gear.

KLEIN

Georg Klein

Sales Office: Equip Rail, 75783 Paris, Cedex 16, France

Products: Hera type window balancing and operating devices; windows.

KUCKUCK

Kuckuck Bau stromungstechnischer Apparate

Head Office: Bremen, An der Weide 29/40, German Federal Republic

Telephone: 32 43 73
Telex: 02 44479

Products: Exhaust fans.

LUWA

Luwa GmbH

Head Office: Frankfurt, German Federal Republic

Products: Air conditioning and air heating systems.

MEALSTREAM CATERING

Mealstream Catering Systems

Head Office: 24 Cornwall Rd, London SE1 8TW

Products: On-board railway catering equipment.

MONOGRAM INDUSTRIES

Monogram Industries Inc (Venic Division)

Head Office: 3226 Thatcher Ave, Venic, Cal 90291, USA

Telephone: (213) 870 8772
Telex: 65-2447

Products: On-board waste handling and sewage treatment systems; self-contained retention toilet equipment. Systems marketed worldwide include: Model 12952-001 Chemical Recirculating System used on French National Railways' (SNCF) RTG/TGV trainsets; Model 28000 On-Board Waste Handling System designed for Amtrak of the United States; Model 20000-001/002 Centralised Waste Treatment System designed for Amtrak and also installed in new bi-level passenger coaches manufactured by Pullman Standard; Models 55000-002 and 15000-001 Self-Contained Flushing Toilets installed as standard production units by Armtrak, Canadian National, Swedish State Railways (SJ), Swiss Federal Railways (SBB), Finnish Railways (VR) Norwegian State Railways (NSB).

Agents: *German Federal Republic:* Gebr Happich GmbH, 56 Wuppertal-Elberfeld, Neuenteich 62-76; *Scandinavia:* Monomatic Sanitation Sys AB, 421 32 V Frolunda, Frotallsgatan 30; *France:* Materiels & Constructions, 44 Rue Paul Valery, F-75 Paris; *Belgium, Netherlands, Luxembourg:* I Auerhaan & Zonen, Spuistraat 36-38, NL Amsterdam-C, The Netherlands; *Spain:* Ercesa SA, Alcala 29, E-Madrid 14; *South America:* Marcopolo SA, Carrocerias E Onibus, Rua Marcopolo 280, 95100 Caxias do Sul-RS Brazil; *Thailand, Burma, Malaysia, Singapore, Laos:* Satchawatana, 486-488 Mahajak, (Klong Thom Wattuk), Bangkok, Thailand; *Switzerland:* Dr Ing Koenig AG, Lagerstrasse 10, 8953 Dietkon; *Finland:* Oy Finncall AB, Fredrikinkatu 33B, SF-00120 Helsinki 12; *USA, Canada:* Vapor Corporation, 6420 W Howard St, Chicago, Illinois 60648

PHOENIX

Phoenix Gummiwerke AG

Head Office: 21 Hamburg 90, PO Box 90 11 40 German Federal Republic

Telegrams: PHOENIXPARA HAMBOURG
Telephone: (040) 76 67 1
Telex: 02 17571 pxhh d

Products: Rubber sealing profiles for windows and doors, rubber floor coverings.

PLC ENGINEERING

PLC Engineering Co Ltd
(Peters Door Gear Division)

Head Office: Pasadena Close, Bilton Way, Hayes, Middlesex UB3 SNS, England

Telephone: 01 573 6172

Products: Door power and control equipment.

RESEARCH PRODUCTS

Head Office: 2639 Andjon St, Dallas, Tex 75220, USA

Telephone: 214/358 4238
Telex: 730 16

Products: Model S electric incinerating toilet.

SAB

SAB Bromsregulator

Head Office: Malmo, Sweden

Products: Electrolux vacuum-operated train toilets.

SABLE

Sable International

Head Office: 22, rue du Pré St-Gervais 93507, Pantin, France

Telephone: 843 61 91

Products: Seating for SNCF Corail and TGV stock.

SCHALTBAU

Head Office: 8 Munchen 90, Hohenwaldeckstr 1, German Federal Republic

Telephone: (098) 62 32 - 1
Telex: 05 23 156

Products: Heating, control and lighting equipment for passenger coaches.

STANRAY CORPORATION

Standard Railway Equipment Division

Head Office: 200 South Michigan Avenue, Chicago, Ill 60604, USA

Telephone: (312) 922 8480

Products: Cooling and refrigeration units for cold storage.

STONE-PLATT

Stone-Platt Electrical Ltd (Electrical division of Stone-Platt Industries)

Head Office: PO Box 5, Gatwick Rd, Crawley, West Sussex RH10 2RN, England

Telegrams: TOSTONES CRAWLEY
Telephone: Crawley (0293) 27711
Telex: 877481

Products: Air conditioning, pressure ventilation, train lighting equipment, alternators, water equipment.

Chairman: R. F. Taverner
Sales Director: R. A. Scott

Divisional manufacturing and marketing companies: *Spain:* Stone Iberica SA, Antonio Maura 8, Madrid 14, Tel: 231 3907 Telex: 23245; *Canada:* Stone-Platt Electrical (Canada) Limited, 165 Steelcase Road, Markham, Ontario L3R 1G1, Tel: 416 495 1500 Telex 219899; *India:* Stone-Platt Electrical (India) Limited PO Box 16731, Calcutta 700053, Tel: 45-2891 Telex: 7249; *Australia:* Stone-Platt Electrical (McColl) Pty Limited, PO Box 31, Springvale 3171, Victoria, Tel: 546 8622 Telex: 32365; *Pakistan:* Stone-Platt Electrical (Pakistan) Limited, PO Box 4943 Karachi 2, Tel: Karachi 201486 Cables: Stonecoy Karachi; *Republic of South Africa:* Stone-Platt Electrical (Stamcor) (Pty) Limited, PO Box 50292, Randburg, 2125, Tel: Randburg 48 1150 Telex: 8-0931; *USA:* Safety Electrical Equipment Corporation, PO Box 798, Wallingford, Conn. 06492, Tel: 203 265 7131 Telex: 963454

STONE PLATT ELECTRICAL (INDIA)

Head Office: 16, Taratalla Rd, Calcutta-700 053, India

Telegrams: STONECO CALCUTTA
Telephone: 45-2891
Telex: 021 7249

Products: Air conditioning and refrigeration equipment, trainlighting equipment.

STUART TURNER

Stuart Turner Ltd

Head Office: Henley-on-Thames, England

Products: Pressurised water system for passenger coaches.

TEMPERATURE LTD

Head Office: 192-206 York Rd, London SW11 3SS, England

Telegrams: TEMTUR LONDON TELEX
Telephone: 01 223 0511
Telex: 28228

Products: Unit air conditioning for all passenger stock, drivers cabs, kitchen cars, dining cars, crew cabins and guards' vans; heating and ventilation units for multiple unit stock.

TOKYO SHIBAURA

Tokyo Shibaura Electric Co Ltd

Head Office: 1-6, Uchisaiwaicho 1 chome, Chiyoda-ku, X Tokyo, 100 Japan

Telegrams: TOSHIBA TOKYO
Telephone: 03 401 5411
Telex: J 22587, J 24344, J 24576 TOSHIBA

Products: Lighting, air conditioning, blower and heating equipment and systems.

TOYO DENKI

Toyo Denki Seizo KK

Head Office: 7, Yaesu 5 chome, Chuo-ku, Tokyo, 104 Japan

Telegrams: YOHDEN TOKYO
Telephone: 03 272 4211
Telex: X TOK (0) 222 4666/7

Products: Door operating equipment.

VAPOR

Vapor Corporation (Transportation Systems Division)

Head Office: 6420 West Howard St, Chicago, Ill 60648, USA

Products: Automatic 'Slim-Line' door control units; self-contained Newmatic toilets.

YOUNG WINDOWS

Young Windows Ltd

Head Office: Claydon Works, Wishaw, Scotland

Products: Windows.

YUSOKI KOGYO

Yusoki Kogyo KK

Head Office: 102, Kamihamacho, Handa, Aichi, 475 Japan

Telephone: 0569 21 3311
Telex: 4563 605

Products: Door panels.

SIGNALLING, COMPUTER AND CONTROL EQUIPMENT

ACEC
Ateliers de Constructions Electriques de Charleroi SA

Head Office: PO Box 4, B6000, Charleroi, Belgium

Telegrams: Ventacec, Charleroi
Telephone: 07/36.20.20 (Internal).   07/36.20.20 (International)
Telex: 051.227—ACEC Charleroi

Products: Station interlocking; automatic block signalling; centralised traffic control; level crossing protection (all-relay and static style); automatic stop equipment; automatic train control equipment, etc.

ACI
ACI Systems Corporation

Head Office: 16950 Westview, So. Holland, Ill 60473 USA

Products: Track circuit equipment and accessories; marshalling yard equipment.

AEG-TELEFUNKEN
AEG-Telefunken Nachrichten-und Verkehrstechnik A.G.

Head Office: Hohenzollerndamm 150, D-1000 Berlin 33, German Federal Republic

Telegrams: ELEKTRONBAHNEN BERLIN
Telephone: (030) 828-1
Telex: 1 85 498

Products: Signalling equipment; automatic block systems; mobile radio equipment; centralised computer controlled traffic control; continuous automatic train control; electronic axle counters; train detection devices; process computer-controlled information display, marshalling yard equipment, control panels and desks, point machines.

ALKMAAR
Nederlandse Machinefabriek Alkmaar BV

Head Office: PO Box 50, 1800 Alkmaar, Netherlands

Telegrams: Nemal
Telephone: 072-127070
Telex: 57213

Director: Ir. A. Brouwer

Products: Level crossing protection; flashing light installations;.light signals; electric point machines; electric point detectors; electric point blocks.

ALSTHOM-ATLANTIQUE
Société Genérale de Constructions Electriques at Mécaniques Alsthom

Head Office and Works: Transport Division, Signalling Department, 25, rue des Bateliers, 93403 Saint-Ouen, Paris 15e, France

Telegrams: ALSTHOMSIG
Telephone: 257 12.34
Telex: 290.317

Products: Point machines ac and dc; luminous signals; all types of track circuits, particularly jointless track circuits for railways and metros; manual block system; automatic block system (single or double track) wireless type; electric level crossing equipments with half barriers (2 or 4) and signals; electric signalling systems for all stations (individual or route type); entrance-exit type with or without presetting; remote control for signalling installations; parking electric mechanism.

AMALGAMATED WIRELESS
Amalgamated Wireless (Australasia) Ltd

Works: 422, Lane Cove Rd, North Ryde, NSW 2113, Australia

Telephone: 02-888-811
Telex: 20623

Products: Power signalling equipment, electrical indicating and describing equipment, level crossing gates and warning signals, automatic train control equipment and train stops, centralised traffic control and remote control systems.

AMF-SASIB
AMF-Sasib SpA

Head Office: Via Di Corticella 87, 40128, Bologna, Italy

Parent Company: American Machine & Foundry Inc., 777 Westchester Avenue, White Plains (10604), New York, USA

Products: Mechanical and power signalling apparatus; block signalling apparatus; track circuiting equipment and accessories including jointless overlay track circuits, electrical indicating and train describing equipment; level crossing gates, barriers and warning signals, automatic train control equipment and train-stops, centralised traffic control and remote control systems; marshalling yard equipment and retarders (conventionally and computer controlled, process computers for operation control); rapid transit control systems.

ANSALDO

Head Office and Works: Via Nicola Lorenzi 8, Genoa, Italy

Telephone: Genova 010-4105
Telex: 27098 Ansaldo Genova

Products: Power signalling apparatus, block signalling and token type instruments, track circuit equipment and accessories, automatic train control equipment and train

stops, centralised traffic control and remote control systems, marshalling yard equipment including retarders.

ASI
Algemene Sein Industrie BV
(GRS—Standard Electric)

Head Office: Croeselaan 28, Utrecht, Netherlands

Telegrams: genrasig utrecht
Telephone: (030) 94 26 46
Telex: 47455 grasi nl

Works: PO Box 1013, The Hague, Netherlands

Manager: P. J. van Dijk

Parent Companies: General Railway Signal Co., Rochester, NY, USA; Nederlandsche Standard Electric Mij BV, The Hague, Netherlands

Products: Power and block signalling apparatus, electrical indicating and train describing equipment, track circuit apparatus and accessories, level crossing barriers and warning signals, automatic train control and train stops, centralised traffic and remote control systems (including radio control of locomotives), marshalling yard equipment and retarders, computerised traffic control systems, etc.

Work recently completed or in hand: Several centralised traffic control installations, relay interlocking equipment, automatic block equipment, automatic level crossing protection and automatic train control with cab signalling, computerised traffic control systems, for the Netherlands Railways.

BENDIX
Bendix Corp (Transportation Systems)

Works: 3621, S. State Rd, Ann Arbor, Mich 48107, USA

Products: Power signalling, block signalling, automatic train control, centralised traffic control.

BROWN BOVERI
Brown, Boveri & Company, Limited

Head Office and Main Works: Baden, Switzerland

Telegrams: Brownboveri Badenschweiz
Telephone: (056) 75 11 11

Products: Linear transmission of information between track and train and vice-versa; radio remote control of shunting locomotives; automatic motoring and braking control of traction vehicles; speed control to set reference value; automatic fixed-point braking; stored running programme, etc.

Switzerland: BBC Brown, Boveri & Company Ltd, Postfach 85, CH - 5401 Baden
Telephone: (056) 75′11′11. Telex: 52921, 53203. Telegrams: Brownboveri
German Federal Republic: Brown, Boveri & Cie, AG, Postfach 351, D - 8600 Mannheim
Telephone: (0621) 381-1. Telex: 462411 120 bbd. Telegrams: Brownboveri Mannheim
France: Société de Traction CEM-Oerlikon 37, rue du rocher, F - 75383 Paris Cedex 08
Telephone: (01) 522 8590. Telex: 650 663. Telegrams: Oerlik Paris
Austria: Oesterreichische Brown Boveri-Werke AG, Postfach 184, A - 1101 Vienna
Telephone: (0222) 62810. Telex: 011 760 Oe BBWA. Telegrams: Brownboveri Vienna
Brazil: Industria Elétrica Brown Boveri SA, Caixa Postal 5528, 01000 São Paulo
Telephone: (011) 227 1011. Telex: 1122275. Telegrams: Brownboveri São Paulo
Italy: Tecnomasio Italiano Brown Boveri Spa, Casella postale 3392, I - 20100 Milan
Telephone: (02) 5797. Telex: 31153. Telegrams: Tecnomasio Milano
Norway: A/S Norsk Elektrisk & Brown Boveri, Postboks 429 Sentrum, N - Oslo 1
Telephone: (02) 55 70 90. Telex: 11268. Telegrams: NEBB Oslo
Spain: Brown Boveri de Espana SA, Apartado 12120, E - Barcelona 11
Telephone: (03) 321 6900, (03) 321 6950. Telegrams: Brownboveri Barcelona
Other countries: Brown Boveri International, Postfach 85, CH - 5401 Baden, Switzerland
Telephone: (056) 75′11′11. Telex: 54 595 bbci ch, 59 634 bbci ch. Telegrams: Brown-Boveri Baden

Works recently completed: LZB-ORE Continuous Automatic Train Control System—Installation on the Turgi-Koblenz line of Swiss Federal Railways. Automatic Fixed-Point Braking for Multiple-Unit Trains on Milan Underground Railway.

CANADIAN GENERAL ELECTRIC
Canadian General Electric Co. Ltd.

Head Office: PO Box 417, Commerce Court North, Toronto, Ontario, M5L W2, Canada.

Works: 107, Park Street, North, Peterborough, Ontario, K9J 7B5, Canada.

International Sales Office: 1900, Eglinton Avenue East, Scarborough, Ontario, MIL 2M1, Canada.

Products: Automatic train control and train stops.

CARRIER-KHEOPS
Carrier-Kheops SA

Head Office: 12, villa d'Este, 75643 Paris Cedex 13, France

Telephone: 583-90-61
Telex: 200 800F

Sales Director: C. Derenemesnil

Products: Signalling equipment.

CIVEL CONSTRUÇÃO
Civel Construção Industria Viacão e Engenharia SA

Head Office: Rua de Lapa 180, 11° e 12° Andares, Rio de Janeiro 20000, Brazil

Products: Wireless networks, transmission and distribution lines, installation of fixed and movable stations.

COBRASMA
Cobrasma SA Ind e Com.

Offices: Rua da Estação 523, Osasco, São Paulo, PO Box 8225, São Paulo, Brazil

Products: All kinds of signalling apparatus.

CONTROL CHIEF
Control Chief Corp

Head Office: PO Box 141, Bradford, Pa 16701, USA

Telephone: (814) 368-4131

Products: Automatic train control equipment.

CLAVIER
Clavier Corp.

Head Office: 743 Park Ave., Huntingdon, NY 11743, USA

Telephone: (516) 423-5850

Products: Automatic train controls.

CLYDE ENGINEERING
Clyde Engineering Co. Pty. Ltd.
(A member of Clyde Industries Group)

Head Office and Works: 140, Arthur Street North, Sydney, New South Wales 2060. PO Box 923, Australia
Telegrams: CLYDEENGCO
Telephone: 439 6655
Telex: 20742

Products: Railway signal equipment (under licence from GRS International, Rochester, New York, USA).

C.S.E.E.
Compagnie de Signaux et d'Entreprises Electriques

Head Office: 2-8 rue Caroline, 75850 Paris Cedex 17, France

Telegrams: Sigtay Paris
Telephone: (331) 3873929
Telex: 650519

Works: C.S.E.E., 15, ave Archon-Despérouses, 63200 RIOM, Telephone: (33 73) 38176 and C.S.E.E., Z.I. Périgueux Boulazac, 24000 PERIGUEUX-USINEX, Telephone: (33 53) 536426

Affiliated Companies: S.A.T., 41, rue Cantagrel, 75013 Paris and SAGEM, 6, avenue d'Iéna, 75016 Paris

Products: Mechanical and power signalling, electronic remote control and centralised traffic control systems, automatic block control, jointless track circuits, cab-signalling equipment, level crossing barriers and warning signals, automatic train stops and train control, marshalling yard equipment, hot box detectors, electronic treadles, safety relays.

DIMETAL
Dimetal SA

Head Office and Works: San Fernando de Henares, Apartado Correos 14.485, Madrid 5, Spain
Telephone: 294 6000

President: Don Frederico Escario y Nuñez del Pino

Products: Electric interlockings, electronic CTC; automatic traffic control and marshalling yard control signalling equipment; level crossing protection and radio telephone equipment, as licensees of the WABCO group of Westinghouse Companies.

Recent Installations: Electric signalling on 134 stations, relay interlocking at 43 stations, automatic block on 372 miles *(600 km)*, electronic single line block on 136 miles *(219 km)*, five CTC installations on 200 miles *(325 km)*.

Work in Hand: Vicalvaro marshalling yard control and retarders, and CTC on 304 miles *(490 km)*, as major contract.

DSI
Dansk Signal Industri A/S

Head Office: Stamholmen 175, Avedore Holme, DK-2650 Hvidovre, Denmark

Managing Director: F. Loell

Products: Relay interlockings, automatic block systems, level crossing signals and lifting gates.

Work completed: Relay interlockings on approximately 100 stations, including geographical systems for Copenhagen Main, Korsor, Roskilde, and Aalborg stations and 10 stations on Copenhagen suburban lines. 400 level crossings installations for DSB and road authorities in Denmark. Relay interlockings and audio frequency CTC on some 55 stations for DSB and private railways.

Work in Hand: Geographical systems for interlockings and automatic blocks and an ATC system for Copenhagen suburban lines. CTC for Copenhagen suburban lines based on electronic components in association with L.M. Ericsson of Stockholm.

ELECTRO PNEUMATIC
Electro Pneumatic Corp

Head Office: 2525 Kansas Ave, Riverside, California 92507, USA

Telephone: (714) 784-0410

Products: Automatic block signalling apparatus.

ERICO
Erico Products Inc.

Head Office: 34600 Solon Rd., Solon, OH 44139, USA

Telephone: (216) 248 0100

Products: Power signalling, track circuit equipment.

ERICSSON
Telefonaktiebolaget L. M. Ericsson

Head Office: Box 42015, S-126 12 Stockholm 42, Sweden

Telegrams: Ellemsignal
Telephone: 08-1900 90
Telex: 10442 LMEMI S

Chief of Department: B. Nilsson

Associated Companies: Member of the Ericsson group, with representatives in most countries.

Products: Relay and computer based interlockings, automatic and tokenless block systems automatic train control, centralised traffic control with such adjuncts as train describers with or without automatic route setting features, internal train control and marshalling yard equipment.

Work completed: Centralised traffic control on 3 800 km of Swedish State Railways lines with some 430 field stations and 12 central offices and on a further 2 700 km in Europe and Asia.
Among installations taken into service and continuously extended are electronic CTC for the Stockholm Area (Swedish State Railways), Copenhagen Suburban Network (Danish State Railways), the line Zaragoza-San Vicente (Spanish State Railways), the latter presently operating 32 stations.
The installations at Stockholm and Copenhagen are computer based and include train describer and automatic routing systems. The Stockholm installation has about 60 stations and 400 km of track and Copenhagen some 50 stations along 125 km in service. Electronic CTC for Barcelona Metro and Lisbon Metro.

Work in Hand: Electronic CTC and ATC for 30 stations for the Taiwan Railway Administration. Re-signalling of earlier installations on Taiwan in connection with installation of electric traction system. Marshalling yard Pipri in Pakistan with 48 sorting tracks and reception and departure yards. Electronic CTC and traingraph installation for 25 stations along 160 km in Bosnia in Yugoslavia. Computer based interlocking system for the Gothenburg and Malmö areas developed in cooperation with the Swedish State Railways. Automatic train control system for the Swedish State Railways to be commissioned for the complete Stockholm Area Commuter Service in 1979 and successively installed on the entire network. Computer based control system for the Oslo Area on the Norwegian State Railways and the Barcelona Area of the Spanish National Railways.

L. M. ERICSSON SA
L. M. Ericsson SA

Head Office: Paseo Felipe Calleja 6, Getafe, Spain

Managing Director: Lennart Nilsson
Sales Manager, Signalling Equipment: H. M. Zalote

Products: Relay interlockings, automatic block systems, level crossing signals.

Work completed: Relay interlockings on approximately 100 stations, including a geographical system for Copenhagen Main Station, automatic block, and level crossing installations for DSB.

Work in hand: Relay interlockings, automatic block, including geographical systems and block for Copenhagen suburban lines (about 80 stations), and level crossing installations, for DSB.

FRENOS CEFALACCION Y SENALES
Soc Espanola de Frenos Cefalaccion y Senales

Works: Nicolas Fuster 2, Pinto, Madrid, Spain

Telephone: 6910054

Products: Mechanical and power signalling equipment.

FRESINBRA
Fresinbra Industrial SA

Head Office: Rua Primeiro de Marco 112, Rio de Janeiro, Brazil

Telegrams: FREINDUS
Telephone: (021) 233-2122

Works: Rua Lauriano Fernandes Jr. 10 São Paulo, Brazil

Telephone: (011) 260.3122

Products: Railway signalling and braking systems, under license of Westinghouse Air Brake Co.; electro-pneumatic door operating mechanism; air compressors.

Work in hand: This company, in which the Westinghouse Air Brake Company of Pittsburg, Pa., USA, is the majority stockholder, is supplying its products to the Brazilian National Railway network, the São Paulo State Railways, the Companhia Vale de Rio Dôce (iron ore railway) and several railway vehicle builders. At present its activities are limited to the territory of Brazil.

FUJITSU
Fujitsu Limited

Head Office: 6-1, Marunouchi 2-chome, Chiyodaku, Tokyo, Japan

Telegrams: "FUJITSULIMITED TOKYO"
Telephone: (Tokyo) 216-3211
Telex: J22 833

President: Taiyu Kobayashi

Products: Telephone exchange, carrier transmission and radio communication equipment; telegraph and data communication equipment; electronic computers and peripheral equipment (FACOM); remote control and telemetering equipment; electronic components.

Works: Kawasaki, Suzaka, Oyama, Nagano, Kobe, Akashi, Aizu

Related Companies: Fuji Electric Co., Ltd.

Work in hand: Fujitsu manufactures all forms of communications and electronics equipment. In the railway field it supplies Japanese National Railways (JNR) with radio communications equipment, telephone exchange equipment, carrier transmission equipment, electronic computer systems and especially group control system of machine tools.

GEC - GENERAL SIGNAL
GEC-General Signal Limited

Head Office: Elstree Way, Borehamwood, Herts WD6 1RX, England

Telegrams: Railsigko Borehamwood
Telephone: 01-953 8211
Telex: 22777

Managing Director: T. P. Cunningham

Products: Power signalling apparatus (including route-relay interlocking, geographical circuitry and electro-mechanical points machines), electronic control indicating and train describing equipment, track circuit equipment and accessories, level crossing equipment, automatic train control, centralised traffic and remote control systems for mainline and industrial railways, rapid transit and personalised rapid transit systems.

Work recently completed:

Scottish Region—BR	Resignalling on West Coast mainline, including train describer systems at Glasgow and Motherwell.
Southern Region—BR	Train describer system at Feltham, and London Bridge.
London Transport Executive	Computer control system equipment for the Northern and Victoria Lines.
Hoogovens Estel, Holland	Signalling and control system.
Mt Newman Mining Co	Centralised control system for 415 km of track from mine to Port Resig.
Eastern Region—BR	Resignalling of Kings Cross Station and the Great Northern Line as far as Sandy and including the Hertford Loop. Resignalling of East Coast mainline between Kings Cross and Stoke (Grantham), a distance of 122 route miles *(195 km)*.

Work in hand:

Scottish Region—BR	Signalling and control systems for Edinburgh and East Coast mainline modernisation. Signalling of new underground rail link to Glasgow city centre.
Southern Region—BR	Train Describer System at Three Bridges. London—Victoria area re-signalling.
RFFSA—Brazil	Signalling of steel railroad from Belo Horizonte to Volta Redonda.

GENERAL ELECTRIC
General Electric Co (Transportation Systems)

Head Office: 2901 E. Lake Rd, Erie, Pa 16531

Telephone: (814) 455-5466

Products: Automatic train control equipment.

GRS
General Railway Signal Company

Head Office: Rochester, NY 14602, USA

Telegrams: Genrasig, Rochester, NY
Telephone: (617) 436 2020
Telex: 978317 GENRASIG

President of GRS Company: G. E. Collins
President of GRS International: J. W. Porter

Products: Centralised traffic control, route-type interlockings, automatic block signalling, level crossing warning signals and gates, overlay track circuits, hot journal detection systems, automatic gravity marshalling yard systems, radio remote control of locomotives, automatic train control, train stops and rapid transit control systems.

Offices of Affiliates and Associates:
GEC-General Signal Ltd., Boreham Wood, Herts, England
Algemeine Sein Industrie BV Utrecht, Netherlands
GRS de Mexico SA, Guadalajara, Jalisco, Mexico
General Railway Signal Co. de Argentina SAIC, Buenos Aires
GRS Trading Corporation, Rochester, New York

GRS (AGENTINA)
General Railway Signal Co de Argentina SAIL

Works: Aréralo 3070, 1426 Buenos Aires, Argentina

Telephone: 772-9542

Products: Automatic signalling; level crossing equipment.

HARMON
Harmon Industries Inc

Head Office: RRI, Grain Valley, MO 64029, USA

Telephone: (816) 249-3112

Products: Power signalling; track circuit equipment; CTC.

HARRIS
Harris Corporation (Controls Division)

Head Office: P.O. Box 430, Melbourne, Florida 3290, USA

Telephone: (305) 727 5764

Products: Locotrol remote control train equipment.

HUDSWELL
Hudswell, Clarke & Co., Ltd.

Head Office and Works: 125, Jack Lane, Hunslet, Leeds LS10 1BT, England

Products: Marshalling yard equipment.

HWD
Henry Williams Limited

Head Office: Darlington, Co. Durham, England

Telegrams: Williams Darlington
Telephone: Darlington 62 722
Telex: 58421

Managing Director: O. M. Williams
Electrical Division Manager: R. A. Thompson

Products: Control panels; treadles; road/rail barrier schemes.

IBERICA
Iberica de Construcciones Electricas, Soc

Head Office: Zurbano 14, Madrid, Spain

Works: Ave de Burgos 16, Madrid

Products: Mechanical, power and block signalling apparatus; electrical indicating and train describing equipment; track circuit equipment; level crossing barriers and warning signals; automatic train control and train stops; centralised traffic control and remote control systems

INTEGRA
Integra Ltd Zürich

Head Office: Industriestrasse 42, CH-8304 Wallisellen, Zürich, Switzerland

Telegrams: Integra Wallisellen
Telephone: Zürich 93.19.15
Telex: 56022 tegra CH

President: Dr. Ing. K. Oehler

Products: Signal lamp unit for railway signals and a special wide/short range asymmetric type for level crossing signals; safety relays for packaged circuits and as individual plug-in units; DOMINO* unit construction panels for all railway purposes including marshalling yards and for any application as monitoring and control panels; electric point motors and trailable type point locks; jointless electronic overlay track circuits for treadle functions; electronic track circuits, electronic axle counting system and last vehicle detection for automatic block purposes; all relay and mixed electronic relay remote control; all electronic 10 000 Baud remote control.

Systems: DOMINO* all-relay signalling schemes incorporating a packaged geographical circuit technique; RAB all-relay block systems with manual control (tokenless block) or automatic control with track circuiting, axle counting or checkout device; automatic level crossing protection with flashing lights and half barriers; centralised traffic control with automatic crossing loops and remote supervision of line; automatic train control, intermittent type multi-aspect ATC with or without speed control, and the A.W.D.—Approach Warning Device—system as a simplified form of ATC; an electronic train describer system for display of train numbers and for automatic train routing.
*DOMINO and INTEGRA are registered trade names of Integra Ltd. Zürich.

ITT BUSINESS SYSTEMS
(Data Systems Division)

Works: Progress Way, Enfield, Middx, England

Products: Remote control systems.

JEUMONT-SCHNEIDER
Jeumont Schneider SA
Division Appareillage Traction Signalisation

Office and Works: BP No. 51, 93212-La Plaine St-Denis, France

Telegrams: Apparjeumont Paris
Telephone: 752 21 90
Telex: 620 387 MECALEC PLDNI

Division Manager: Michel Gillet

Products: Automatic block system; CTC and remote control; tokenless block, all-relay interlockings; points and signal machines; safety relays; solid state safety relays; electronic track circuits, mechanical, electromechanical and electronic operation of all safety and signalling equipment; centralised control and monitoring; teletransmissions.

KYOSAN

Kyosan Electric Manufacturing Co Ltd

Head Office: 4-2, Marunouchi 3-chome, Chiyoda-Ku, Tokyo, Japan

Works: Tsurumi Factory, 29, 2-chome, Heiancho, Tsurumi-Ku, Yokohama City, Japan

Products: Total traffic control equipment; train describers; programmed train control equipment; relay interlocking equipment; automatic block signalling equipment; tokenless block instruments; power switch machines and relays; cab signal and cab alarm equipment; automatic train control equipment; marshalling yard control equipment; car retarders; automatic route setting; highway crossing signal and crossing gates; automatic control device for diesel engine starter; ac and dc automatic voltage regulators; silicon and selenium rectifiers.

LAMP

Lamp Manufacturing & Railway Supplies Ltd

Head Office: 1 Curtis Rd, Industrial Estate, Dorking, Surrey, RH4 1XB, England

Telephone: (0306) 4411

Products: Mechanical signalling equipment, power signalling apparatus, block and token instruments, level crossing gates, barriers, warning signals.

ML ENGINEERING

ML Engineering (Plymouth) Ltd

Head Office: Burrington Way, Plymouth, Devon, PL5 3NB, England

Products: Power signalling apparatus.

MODERN INDUSTRIES

Modern Industries Inc

Head Office: 101 Outer Loop, PO Box 14287, Louisville, Kentucky, USA

Telephone: (502) 361-1113

Products: Power signalling, level crossing equipment; CTC; marshalling yard equipment.

NATIONAL ELECTRIC

National Electric Control Co

Head Office: 2931 Higgins Rd, Elk Grove Village, Ill 60007, USA

Products: Level crossing gates and warning signals.

NIPPON SIGNAL

Nippon Signal Co Ltd

Head Office: 3-1, Marunouchi, 3-chome, Chiyoda-Ku, Tokyo, Japan

Telephone: (Tokyo) 212-8371
Telex: 2222 178 SIGNALJ

Works: Yono Factory, 13-1, chome, Kamikizaki, Urawa City, Japan
Utsunomiya Factory, 2-11 Hiraide Kougyo Danchi, Utsunomiya City, Japan

Associated Companies: Nisshin Industrial Co Ltd, Nisshin Electrical Installation Co Ltd

Products: Centralised traffic control, automatic transit control, relay interlocking, automatic block signalling, level crossing signals and automatic gates, overlay track circuits, automatic gravity marshalling yard equipments, traffic signalling systems, automatic revenue control systems, synthetic brake block, fire alarm equipment.

NORD

Nord Instruments Co Inc

Head Office: 5457 JAE Valley Road, Roanoke, VA 24014, USA

Products: Automatic train control equipment, remote control systems.

ORLIANS

Orlians & Co, NV

Head Office: Populierendreef 35, 2800 Mechelen, Belgium

Telephone: 015 2185 85

Products: Warning signals for crossing gates, signal lanterns for electric railways.

PHILIPS

Philips Telecommunicatie Industrie BV

Head Office: PO Box 32, Hilversum, Netherlands

Telegrams: Signal Hilversum
Telephone: (02150) 99111
Telex: 11274

Products: Telecommunications (carrier, telephone and telegraph), exchanges, data systems, mobile radio, radio relay, transceivers.

Other Products in the Philips Group:

Intercommunication and public address systems;	N.V. Philips
Fire alarm and electric clock systems;	Gloeilampenfabrieken,
Message repeater system;	Eindhoven
High frequency heating;	
Interlocking signalling systems;	
Automatic block systems;	TRT
Centralised traffic control systems;	Paris
Wagon and train identification systems;	
Telemetering equipment;	MBLE, Brussels
Traffic automation systems	Spoorweg Sein Industrie

PINTSCH BAMAG

Pintsch Bamag Antriebs- und Verkehrstechnik GmbH

Head Office: D-422 Dinslaken, Postfach 10 04 20, German Federal Republic

Telegrams: PINTSCHBAMAG-DINSLAKEN
Telephone: (0 21 34) 602-1
Telex: 8551938

Directors: Dr. Ing. Dieter Böhm
Dr. rer. pol. Gerhard Kummer

Products: Electrical and electronic power supply, lighting, heating and air conditioning equipment for rail vehicles; level crossing protection equipment (hand-operated or rail-actuated) with flashlights and luminous signals, with barrier guarding and radar obstacle detection; train approach indicator for gang warning; electrical and gas-operated infra-red compact-type point heating equipment; solid-state snow detectors; train preheating equipment; test sets for electrical installations on rail vehicles.

PLESSEY

Plessey Controls Ltd

Head Office: Sopers Lane, Poole, Dorset, BH17 7ER, England

Telephone: (02013) 5161
Telex: 41272

Chairman: Dr B. F. Willetts
Managing Director: E. Clark
Chief Sales Manager: A. H. Taylor

Products: Train-to-track data systems, positive train identification, wagon identification, monitoring on-train equipment, in cab displays, centralised remote control equipment.

ROBOT

Robot Industries Inc

Head Office: 7041 Orchard Ave, Dearborn, Mich 48126, USA

Telephone: (313) 846-2623

Products: Power signalling apparatus, level crossing gates, barriers and warning signals, centralised traffic control and remote control systems.

SAFETRAIN

Safetrain Systems Corporation

Head Office: 7721 National Turnpike, Louisville, Ky 40214, USA
Telephone: (502) 361 1691
Works: Railroad Accessories Co., Division of Safetrain Systems Corporation, 7721 National Turnpike, Louisville, Kentucky 40214; 4650 Main Street, NE, Minneapolis, Minnesota 55421; Marquardt Industrial Products Co., 9271 Arrow Highway, Cucamonga, California 91730

Products: Power signalling apparatus, track equipment and accessories, level crossing gates and warning equipment, centralised traffic control equipment.

SAXBY

Saxby

Head Office: 40 Rue de l'Orillon, 75011 Paris, France

Telegrams: SAXBY SA PARIS
Telephone: 357 65 30
Telex: 220554F

Products: Route relay interlocking; automatic block systems; centralised traffic control; automatic level crossing barriers; marshalling yard equipment and retarders; passenger information systems.

SCHEIDT

Scheidt & Bachmann GmbH

Offices and Works: 132 Breite Str., D4070 Rheydt, Rhineland, German Federal Republic

Telephone: Rheydt 4531
Telex: 0852818

Products: Power signalling apparatus, level crossing gates, barriers and warning signals, mechanical signalling equipment and accessories, automatic train control equipment and train-stops, centralised traffic control and remote control systems.

SEL

Standard Elektrik Lorenz AG

Head Office: Hellmuth-Hirth-Strasse 42, 7000 Stuttgart-Zuffenhausen, German Federal Republic

Telegrams: Stanlor, Stuttgart
Telephone: (0711) 8211
Telex: 7 211-0

Works: At 22 locations in West Germany

Associated Companies: SEL has 27 associate companies outside Germany (the name of the majority incorporating the word Standard); and utilises its association with the International Telephone and Telegraph Corporation (ITT) in providing local manufacture in many parts of the world.

Products: Geographic relay interlocking system; computer controlled traffic control systems and continuous train control systems; electronic axle counters; automatic humping control; control panels and desks; relays; signalling equipment; switch machines; train detection devices; centralised traffic control; automatic block equipment, automatic train control; train describers and indicating systems, mobile radio equipment, cables; etc.

SIEMENS
Siemens Aktiengesellschaft
Railway Signalling Division

Head Office and Works: Ackerstrasse 22, 33 Brunswick (Braunschweig), German Federal Republic

Telegrams: "Stellwerk Braunschweig"
Telephone: Braunschweig 706-1
Telex: 9 52 495

President: Peter von Siemens
Chairman: Bernhard Plettner
General Manager of railway signalling division: Horst Girke

Products: Power signalling (all-relay interlocking) and block systems; geographical circuitry "Spoorplan" interlockings; central operation control by data processing electrical indicating and train describing equipment; track circuit and axle counter equipment; scanner and indicator equipment for automatic vehicle identification and train control and locating; marshalling yard equipment and retarders; level crossing gates, barriers and warning signals; remote control and supervisory systems; centralised traffic control (CTC); automatic train control (ATC) and train stops; continuous automatic train control (CATC) for high speed transportation and rapid transit; equipment for underground railway signalling systems; data processing equipment for operative scheduling, seat reservation and statistical problems.

SIGNAUX ET D'ENTERPRISES ELECTRIQUES CIE

Head Office: 2-8 rue Caroline, 75850, Paris Cedex 17, France

Telephone: 387-39-29
Telex: 650519

Products: Mechanical and power signalling equipment; automatic train control; centralized traffic control; train indicating and describing equipment.

SILEC
Soc Industrielle de Liaisous Electriques (SILEC)

Head Office: 69, rue Ampere, 75017, Paris, France

Telephone: 267.20.60
Telex: 28748 SILECSI

Chairman: R. Thibault
Managing Director: P. Loisel
Sales Director: R. Le Bail

Products: Electro-mechanical treadles, safety relays, punctual data transmission.

SERVO
Servo Corporation of America

Head Office: 111 New South Rd, Hicksville, NY 11802, USA
Telephone: (516) 938-970

Marketing Manager: C. A. Gallagher

Products: Kartrak automatic car identification system.

SYLVANIA
Sylvania Electric Product Inc.
(Commercial Electronics Division)

Head Office: 730 Third Avenue, New York, NY, 10017, USA

Telephone: (217) 617 275

Sales Office and Works: PO Box 268, Burlington Road, Bedford, Massachusetts 01730, USA

Products: Electronic systems for transportation control, including automatic vehicle identification and closed circuit television equipment.

Parent Company: The General Telephone & Electronics Corporation.

President: Gene K. Beare
Transportation Control Systems Manager: J. W. Barriger
Sales Manager, Vehicle Identification Systems: Robert Shallow

Agency Abroad: Sylvania International, Division of General Telephones & Electronics International, 40 rue du Rhône, Geneva, Switzerland

Vice-President: H. P. Bryers

Constitution: Sylvania was founded in 1901 as a small concern in Massachusetts producing light bulbs. It entered into the radio tube field in the 1920s and in 1931 became Sylvania Electric Products Inc. In March 1959 Sylvania merged into the General Telephone & Electronics Corporation with Sylvania funtioning as a wholly owned subsidiary. The Sylvania Automatic Vehicle Identification System was designed, developed and produced by Sylvania in 1963 after more than three years of field tests proved it ready to give railroads new speed and efficiency in car identification and utilisation. In 1967 the Association of American Railroads accepted Sylvania's Kartrack system as AAR's standard automatic car identification for the USA and Canada.

Systems: The Kartrack scanner sends out beams of white light and receives coloured reflected light from strips of special material attached to each car. The strips form a colour code representing the number of each car and its weight when empty. The information read by the scanner is transmitted to a central point. The coloured strips may be seen on the wagon sides above the second axle boxes.

TOKYO SHIBAURA
Tokyo Shibaura Electric Co. Ltd.

Offices: 1-1 Uchisaiwai-cho, Chiyoda-ku, Tokyo, Japan

Works: Fuchu Works, 1, Toshiba-machi, Fuchu-shi, Tokyo, Japan

Products: Automatic train control equipment, automatic train stop equipment, electrical indicating and train describing equipment, centralised traffic control and remote control systems, marshalling yard equipment, including retarders, etc.

TRANSCONTROL
Transcontrol Corporation

Head Office: 2 Yennicock Avenue, Port Washington, NY 11050, USA

Products: Power signalling apparatus, automatic train control equipment, centralised traffic control equipment, marshalling yard equipment, track circuit equipment and accessories, level crossing gates, barriers and warning signals.

TRANSPORTATION TECHNOLOGY
Transportation Technology

Head Office: PO Box 7293, Denver, Colo 80209, USA

Products: Automatic train control equipment.

TRW
TRW Inc

Head Office: One Space Park, Building R4/2128, Redondo Beach, Cal 90278, USA

Products: Train control system, automatic train control equipment, central traffic control equipment.

TRT
Telecommunications Radioelectriques et Telephoniques

Head Office: 88, rue Brillat-Savarin, Paris 13, France

Telephone: 707 7779

Products: Electronic railway signalling equipment.

WABCO
Union Switch & Signal Division, Westinghouse Air Brake Company
(An American Standard Company)

Head Office: Swissvale, Pittsburgh, Pa. 15218, USA
Telegrams: Uniswitch, Pittsburgh
Telephone: (412) 273-4000
Telex: 866-448

Products: Electronic car or train detection and identification; automatic train control; mechanical, power, and block signalling and switching; highway crossing barriers and warning signals; automatic train stops; remote control systems; centralised traffic control; track circuit apparatus; two-way railway radio; classification yard equipment and retarders; computerised dispatching systems for control, indication and information; etc.

Branch Offices: Chicago, Montreal, New York, San Francisco, Philadelphia, St. Louis, St. Paul, Jacksonville

Vice-President and General Manager: G. E. Stinson
Vice-President, International Sales: G. Lombardi

WABCO WESTINGHOUSE
Executive Offices: 207 blvd du Souverain, B1160 Brussels, Belgium

Telephone: 73 60 53

Vice-President and Group Executive: Richard W. Foxen

Products: Automatic train control; block signalling; level crossing barriers and warning signals; automatic train stops; remote control systems; centralised traffic control; train describers; track circuit apparatus; cab signalling system of both intermittent and continuous type; two-way railway radio; marshalling yard equipment and retarders, etc.
Complete systems and devices for all aspects of motive power control, locomotive and train braking, and passenger car lighting, heating and air-conditioning.
Grouped under the marketing identity of Wabco Westinghouse, the Westinghouse Air Brake companies have designed and manufactured railway signalling and braking equipment since the turn of the century. Current developments include advanced magnetic track brake systems, air and electric converters for automatic car couplers, motive power control devices for gas turbine powered vehicles, radar for speed assessment and computerised retarder actuation in marshalling yards, etc.
The manufacturing companies in the Wabco Westinghouse group are as follows:—

Austria	**Westinghouse Bremsen- und Apparatebau GmbH** Hochstadplatz 4, 1205 Vienna XX, Austria
Belgium	**International Brake and Rectifier, SA** Rue des Anciens Etangs 6, 1190 Brussels, Belgium
France	**Compagnie des Freins et Signaux Westinghouse** POB 2, 93 Freinville-Servan, France
Germany	**Westinghouse Bremsen- und Apparatebau GmbH,** PO Box 21-280, 3 Hannover-Linden, German Federal Republic
Italy	**Compagnia Italiana Westinghouse Freni e Segnali,** Via Pier Carlo Boggio 20, 10138 Turin, Italy
Netherlands	**Westinghouse Remmen en Apparatuur NV,** Postbus 29, Capelle a/d Ijssel, The Netherlands
Spain	**Dimetal SA,** Apartado de Correos 14.485, Madrid, Spain
Sweden	**Westinghouse Broms- och Regleteknik AB** Idungsatan 26, 214 46 Malmö, Sweden
Switzerland	**Westinghouse Bremsen- und Signale AG** 384 Freiburgstrasse, 3018 Bern Bumplitz, Switzerland

WESTERN-CULLEN-DIVISION

Western-Cullen-Division
(Federal Sign & Signal Corp.)

Head Office and Works: 2700, West 36th Place, Chicago, Ill 60632, USA

Products: Track circuiting equipment and accessories, level crossing barriers and warning lights, marshalling yard equipment, including retarders, etc.

WESTERN INDUSTRIES

Western Industries (Pty) Ltd.

Head Office: 41-43 Troye Street, Johannesburg, PO Box 10554, South Africa

Works: 7 Bankfield Rd, Industria North, Johannesburg, South Africa

Products: Power signalling apparatus; track circuit equipment and accessories

WESTINGHOUSE-BELLAMBIE

Westinghouse Bellambie (Pty) Ltd

Head Office and Works: PO Box 453, Johannesburg, 112 Clark St, North Ahode, Alberton, Transvaal, South Africa

Telegrams: Bellambie, Johannesburg
Telephone: 864 2150
Telex: 8-8223

Works: Clark St North, Alberton, Transvaal, South Africa

Products: General railway signalling equipment and systems design, remote control, centralised traffic control, telecontrol schemes.

Associated Companies: Westinghouse Brake & Signal Co Ltd London, Roberts Construction Co Ltd

Directors: J. E. Cheetham (Chairman), A. G. Jansen (Managing)

WESTINGHOUSE

Westinghouse Brake and Signal Co Ltd

Head Office: 3 John Street, London WC1N 2ER, England

Works and Sales Office: Chippenham, Wiltshire, England

Telephone: Chippenham 4141
Telex: 449411

Products: Signalling equipment; remote control systems; air, electro-pneumatic and vacuum brake equipment, level crossing protection, marshalling yard equipment, traction rectifiers; computer-based train description; automatic train operation; automatic fare collection; railway door equipment; electricity power control supervision systems.

Managing Director: D. Pollock
Divisional Manager, Signals: H. Duckitt
Divisional Manager, Brakes: J. R. C. Boulding

Work in hand and recently completed: Contracts in Chile, South Africa, Spain, South Korea, Pakistan, Australia, New Zealand, USA, Hong Kong and for British Railways.

Subsidiary Companies:
England: Gresham & Craven Ltd; Douglas (Sales & Service) Ltd; Partridge Wilson Ltd.
Australia: Westinghouse Brake (Australasia) Pty Ltd; Westinghouse Road Brake Co Pty Ltd; Westinghouse—McKenzie—Holland Pty Ltd; Westinghouse Track & Engineering Pty Ltd.

New Zealand: McKenzie & Holland (New Zealand) Ltd.
France: Westingred SA
Canada: Westcode Ltd.
USA: Westcode Inc.

Associated Companies:
England: Bendix Westinghouse Ltd; Partridge Wilson & Co Ltd.
South Africa: Westinghouse Bellambie (Pty) Ltd.

WILLIAMS

Henry Williams Ltd

Head Office: Dodsworth St, Darlington, Durham, England

Telegrams: WILLIAMS DARLINGTON
Telephone: (0325) 2722
Telex: 58421

Products: Mechanical and electronic signalling equipment, level crossing protection systems; control panels; Silec electro-mechanical rail treadles.

WOODINGS

Woodings Canada Ltd.

Head Office: 220 Brunswick Boulevard, Pointe Claire 730, Quebec, Canada

Products: Power signalling apparatus, level crossing equipment.

WSF

Westinghouse Saxby Farmer Limited

Head Office: 17 Convent Road, Calcutta 14, India

Telegrams: Interlock, Calcutta
Telephone: 24-7161 (7 lines)

Products: Mechanical and electrical signalling equipment, point layouts and mechanism, relays, point and signal machines, ball and tablet token instruments, reversers, electric control panels and illuminated diagrams, colour light signals and route indicators, wagon retarders, hump yard equipment, vacuum and air brake equipment for wagons, coaches, locomotives compressors and slack adjusters.

Works: At above address and at 24 Canal South Road, Calcutta 15.

Managing Director: P. C. Sen
Financial Adviser & Chief Accounts Officer: S. Chakravorti
Chief Executive (Marketing Electrical): R. N. Sengupta
Chief Executive (Marketing Mechanical): S. N. Mukherji
Chief Executive (Manufacturing): Dr. K. Roychoudhury

Westinghouse Saxby Farmer Ltd is a joint enterprise of Westinghouse Brake & Signal Co. Ltd. of London, England, and the State Government of West Bengal, India.

ZONE CONTROLS LTD

Zone Controls Ltd

Office and Works: PO Box 22, Building 39, Pensnett Trading Estate, Brierley Hill, Staffs., DY6 7PN, England

Telegrams: CONTROLS BRIHILL
Telephone: (038 44) 70171
Telex: 338359

Products: Signalling equipment.

COMMUNICATIONS SYSTEMS AND EQUIPMENT

AEG/TELEFUNKEN

AEG/Telefunken

Head Offices: Hohenzollerndamm 150, D-100 Berlin 33, German Federal Republic
Works: D-6000 Franfurt 70, AEG-Hochaus, German Federal Republic

Telephones: Berlin 6281/Frankfurt (0611) 6001
Telex: 183581/411076

Products: Telecommunications, radio-telephone and data processing equipment. Due to the increasing overloading of the frequencies available for remote-control AEG-Telefunken has developed a new radio system which enables operation of a large number of remote-control installations upon one high-frequency channel (simplex) independent of the site control and of each other. If the new system is used for control of shunting operations, it can be adapted for at least 10 locomotives on one channel. The system consists of two components arranged in pairs: transmitter unit and mobile installation. Operation is by selective calling and data transmission on one simplex channel in the frequency range of 160-460 MHz at a data transmission speed of 2400 bites/s. Instructions are transmitted by means of short remote-control messages automatically emitted quasi-periodically. An error correction code is used to ensure reliable transmission. 'Due to the reliability of the system,' says the supplier, 'an acknowledgement of the executive signal is not necessary.' A maximum of 16 separate remote-control commands, independent of each other, may be transmitted in one remote-control message.

ANTENNA SPECIALISTS

Antenna Specialists Co

Head Office: 12435 Euclid Ave, Cleveland, Ohio 44106, USA

Export Sales: 2200 Shames Drive, Westbury, L.I. New York 11590, USA

Products: Two-way communications systems.

AUTOPHON

Autophon (Sales Management and International Sales Division)

Office: CH-8036 Zurich, Steinstr. 21, Switzerland

Telephone: 01 35 85 35
Telex: 53838

Products: The Swiss-based Autophon company has supplied radio communication systems over the past 15 years to railways in Switzerland, France, Finland, Norway, The Netherlands and Sweden. The company markets four basic systems: 1) the Suba, designed for branch-line operations; 2) the Palyma—adopted by French National Railways (SNCF)— for mainlines requiring practically total radio coverage: 3) the Safra developed for mainlines with high traffic density; 4) radio communication for shunting operations. In addition, Autophon supplies the Informatic Display System for station platforms.
The Suba system was developed for branch and private lines needing radio communications between operator and trains as well as train-to -train. The system consists of a base station, a remote control unit and mobile transceivers in the trains. By adding portable units to the basic system, Suba can also be adopted for use in shunting operations.
The Palyma system consists of three basic elements: base transceivers, station centres and mobile on-board equipment. All section base stations are connected to a line installed parallel to the track. The system operates on the frequency diversity principle with three successive stations working on different frequencies. It is possible to replace the wire transmission with radio links with the link between base stations controlled from a radio centre.
The Safra system for mainlines is a development of the basic Palyma. With its greater flexibility of communication and control Safra is able to cope with a quick succession of trains, optimally adapted speeds and ensures high traffic safety.

BAYLY ENGINEERING

Bayly Engineering Ltd

Head Office: 167 Hunt St, Ajax, Ontario L1S 1P6, Canada

Products: Bayly 5260 wayside radio control unit

BICC

BICC Ltd (Formerly British Insulated Callender's Cables)

Head Office: 21 Bloomsbury St, London WC1B 3QN, England

Telegrams: BICALBEST LONDON
Telephone: 01-637 1300
Telex: 23463/28624

Products: Communications cables of all types

CARRIER KHEOPS

Carrier Kheops

Head Office: 12, Villa d'Este (23, Avenue d'Ivry), 75013 Paris, France

Telephone: 583 90 01
Telex: 200800 F

Products: On-train public address systems.

CGE

Compagnie Generale d'Electricite

Head Office: 54 Rue La Boetie, 75382 Paris Cedex 08, France

Telegrams: ELECTRICITE PARIS 8
Telephone: 266 54 60
Telex: 28.953

Products: Telecommunications equipment and systems

CIT/ALCATEL

Compagnie Industrielle des Telecommunications

Head Office: 12 Rue de la Baume, 75 Paris 8e, France

Telephone: 577 10 10
Telex: 25 927

Products: Electronics and telecommunications equipment and systems.

DRALLIM TELECOMMUNICATIONS

Drallim Telecommunications Ltd

Head Office and Works: Brett Drive, Bexhill-on-Sea, East Sussex TN402JR, England

Telegrams: DRALLIMIND BEXHILL
Telephone: (0424) 221144
Telex: 95285

Products: Gas pressurisation systems for telephone cables.

Executive Director (Sales): J. R. Tickner

ERICSSON

LME Telefonaktiebolaget LM Ericsson

Head Office: Telefonplan, S-126, 25 Stockholm, Sweden

Telegrams: TELEFONBOLAGET STOCKHOLM
Telephone: 08-719 00 00
Telex: 174 40

Products: Designs, manufactures, markets and installs all kinds of telecommunications systems and products including telephone telex and data communication systems intercom systems, transmission equipment, radio communications equipment, cables and wires.

F & G

Felten & Guilleaume Carlswerke AG

Head Office: D-5000 Koln-80, Schanzenstrasse 24, Postfach 80 50 01, German Federal Republic

Telegrams: CARLSWERK KOLN
Telephone: (0221) 676-1
Telex: 08 873 261 fug d

Products: Wires and cables, switchgear, telecommunications equipment.

FERRANTI

Ferranti Ltd

Head Office: Hollinwood, Lancashire, 019 7JS, England

Telegrams: FERRANTI HOLLINWOOD
Telephone: 061 681 2000
Telex: 667044

Products: Information displays and telecommunications equipment, microwave links.

FUJITSU

Fujitsu Ltd

Head Office: 6-1, Marunouchi 2 chome, Chiyodaku, Tokyo, Japan

Telegrams: FUJITSULIMITED TOKYO
Telephone: (Tokyo) 216-3211
Telex: J22 833

Products: Telephone exchange, carrier transmission and radio communication equipment, telegraph and data communication equipment.

President: Taiyu Kobayashi

GEC TELECOMMUNICATIONS

GEC Telecommunications Ltd

Head Office: 1 Stanhope Gate, London W1A 1EH, England

Telegrams: POLYPHASE LONDON
Telephone: (01) 493 8484
Telex: 22451

Products: Telecommunications equipment: GEC Telecommunications received an order from British Rail during 1977 for 30-channel pulse-code modulation (PCM) equipment. It will be used to expand the capacity of the existing BR communications link between Euston and St Pancras. With PCM, 30 high-quality speech-bandwidth circuits, carrying telephone and data signals, can be provided by two pairs in an ordinary telephone cable which would normally carry only two circuits. The signals are transmitted as a digital pulse code. Repeaters at intervals along the cable regenerate the signal and eliminate interference. The first commercial 30-channel PCM communications system in the UK was supplied by GEC to BR to link Birmingham New Street and Birmingham stations. The latest installation will use the special interface units, developed by GEC for the initial contract, which allow remote users to operate over the PCM link directly into a central automatic exchange.

GRS

General Railway Signal Company

Head Office: Rochester, NY 14602, USA

Telegrams: GENRASIG ROCHESTER NY
Telephone: (617) 436 2020
Telex: 978317 Genrasig

Products: Radio remote control systems.

GTE LENKURT

GTE Lenkurt Inc

Head Office: Dept C134, 1105 County Rd, San Carlos, Cal 94070, USA

Telephone: (415) 591 8461

Products: Type 36A2 multiplex radio system with 614 channels. A new 208B compatible 4800-bits-per-second data set offered by GTE Lenkurt, Inc enables dial-up direct access to the switched (DDD) telephone network for data transmission. The 262B (208B) Data Set transmits and receives synchronous serial binary data in either simplex or half-duplex modes of operation over two-wire lines. End-to-end compatibility and electrical interchangeability are provided with the Western Electric type 208B Data Set, which also conforms to EIA Standard RS-232-C and to CCITT Recommendations V.24. Automatic adaptive equalisations continuously compensates for delay and amplitude distortion introduced by the transmission facility. Training time to achieve equalisation is less than 50 milliseconds. Switch selection provides automatic answering of incoming calls. Alternate voice/data operation and automatic call origination can be provided when the unit is used with an Automatic Electric type 186 Key Telephone Unit and type 801 calling equipment, respectively. Built-in test and diagnostic facilities permit rapid pinpointing of the cause of the problems between terminal equipment, the local or remote data set, and the transmission facility.

HARRIS

Harris Corporation (RF Communications Division)

Head Office: 1680 University Ave, Rochester, NY 14610, USA

Telephone: (716) 244-5830

Products: Two-way radio systems.

KRAUSS-MAFFEI

Krauss-Maffei Aktiengellschaft

Head Office: 8000 München 50, Krauss-Maffei-Str 2, German Federal Republic

Telegrams: KRAUSSMAFFEI, Munchenallach
Telephone: (089) 8899551
Telex: 05-23 163

Products: Two-way radio specially developed for hump locomotives at Deutsche Bundesbahn's Mannheim yard.

KRUPP

Krupp Industrie- und Stahlbau

Head Office: 4100 Duisburg-Rheinhausen, German Federal Republic

Products: Radio communications. Krupp is now offering a transmitter/ receiver capable of 16 function commands for radio remote control of shunting locomotives. The transmitter/receiver weighs 2.5 kg.Commands are given in the form of a remote control telegram which is transmitted quasi-periodically. Faultless transmission is ensured by use of an error detecting code. The electric power unit which serves as an adapter between the receiver and the running and brake control system in the form of a printed circuit card which is protected against shock and vibration by metal-rubber isolators and wired through flat plug connectors. A pneumatic control unit is used as the link to the traction and braking equipment.

LARRY McGEE

Larry McGee Co

Head Office: 4937 Fullerton Ave, Chicago, Ill 60639, USA

Telephone: (312) 237-7000

Products: Loudspeaker and telephone communicating systems for yards, shops, freight stations, dispatcher offices, way stations, terminals; radio control systems.

LMT

Le Materiel Telephonique

Head Office: 46/47 Quai Alphonse Le Gallo, 92103 Boulogne-Billancourt (Hauts-de-Seine), France

Telegrams: MICROPHON PARIS
Telephone: 604 81 00
Telex: 20.972

Products: Electro-mechanical and electronic telephone circuit switching equipment.

MOTOROLA

Motorola Communications and Electronics Inc

Head Office: Dept 708, 1301 East Algonquin Rd, Schaumburg, Ill 60172, USA

Telephone: (312) 576 2099

Products: Railway communications equipment including the Micor two-way radio now used by more than 95 US railroads.

NELSON TANSLEY

Nelson Tansley Limited

Head Office: 10, Sheperds Bush Road, London W6 7PJ, England

Telegrams: Thectron London W6
Telephone: (01) 749 1393

Chief Design Engineer, Rail Division: M. Millett
Sales Director, Rail Division: G. N. Bowling

Products: Communications and control equipment for railway and rapid transit networks; remote-controlled inter-station public address; standard time system (centralised clock); in-train passenger address system; inter-train radio; end-to-end train crew intercommunication; etc. The trade name "ENTEL" covers certain products.

Work completed: Work in hand and recently completed includes installation of inter-station public address system for British Rail; ENTEL 390 end-to-end driver/guard telephone inter-communication, and ENTEL 378 in-train public address system to all passenger cars (6 loudspeakers per car), radio-telephone communications between driving cabs of two closely-following trains of up to 16 multi-unit cars per train for London Transport.
A recent development and production contract will provide driver/guard and passenger address equipment for the new Piccadilly Line stock for London Transport.

NEUMANN

Neumann Elektronik AG

Head Office and Works: Mulheim-Ruhr, German Federal Republic

Products: Radio communications systems, Intercom equipment for direct speech links between control centres and men working in marshalling yards and similar locations. Sealed reed switches are used to ensure high reliability and resistance to corrosion.

PIRELLI

Pirelli SpA

Head Office: Centro Pirelli, 5 Piazza Duca Aosta, Milan, Italy

Telegrams: GOMMA MILANO
Telephone: 6222
Telex: 31135 Pirelli

Products: Power and telecommunications cables. Pirelli has recently introduced low-smoke, low-toxity, non-flame propagating cable designs for signalling and communications purposes. The new cables have been named Losmoke and are specifically designed for railway subway systems. Losmoke cables were developed in close collaboration with London Transport with full testing carried out on the London underground. During tests, the behaviour of the cables was monitored under artificially-induced fire conditions in a disused section of line.

PHILIPS

NV Philips

Head Office: Eindhoven, The Netherlands

Telegrams: PHILIPS EINDHOVEN
Telephone: (040) 791111
Telex: 51121 PHTC NL

Products: Telecommunications and radio communication systems.

PLESSEY

The Plessey Company Ltd

Head Office: 2-60 Vicarage Lane, Ilford, Essex, IG1 4AQ, England

Telegrams: PLESSEY ILFORD
Telephone: 01 478 3040
Telex: 23166

Products: Telecommunications systems.

RACAL

Racal Electronics Ltd

Head Office: Western Rd, Bracknell, Berkshire RG12 IRG, England

Telegrams: RACAL BRACKNELL
Telephone: 0344 3244
Telex: 848166

Products: Radio communication systems, data communications.

REDIFON TELECOMMUNICATIONS

Redifon Telecommunications Ltd

Head Office: Broomhill Rd, Wandsworth, London SW18 4JQ, England

Telephone: 01 874 7281

Products: Telecommunications equipment. The first passenger train to use train radio in Britain was inaugurated on 28 May 1977 when the 381 mm gauge Ravenglass & Eskdale Railway ran a special train to mark the event. Supplied by Redifon Telecommunications Ltd, the Ravenglass & Eskdale Railways's VHF FM two-way voice communication system eliminates the need for conventional signalling although this has been retained at Ravenglass. A solid-state MRT12 12-channel mobile station is fitted in the cab of each of the eight motive power units. Drivers report to the line controller via a single fixed BRT12 station which is linked to a RTC12 remote control unit over two-wire 600 ohm lines. The line controller can communicate simultaneously with all drivers, but a selective calling facility is provided. Under present Ravenglass & Eskdale operating procedure the controller speaks to each driver and plots the movement of each train on a graph. All drivers can hear the controller but only the driver to whom he is speaking is allowed to reply.
A special feature of this installation, which is designed for two-frequency simplex or duplex operation, is provision of data interface. A transmitter time-out facility prevents unduly prolonged or accidental transmission. Power supply is from a nominal 12 V or 24 V dc source.

RIPPER

Ripper Systems Limited

Head Office: Cranfield Institute of Technology, Cranfield, Bedford MK 43 0AL, England

Telegrams: Ripper Cranfield Bedford
Telephone: Bedford 750123
Telex: Cranfield 825072

Directors: F. V. Waller
R. A. Ripper *(Managing)*

Products: Communications and public address systems for mobile and static railway applications.

The Company designs and builds to customers' specific requirements or can offer a standard range of equipment, for main line and rapid transit surface and underground rail services. Typical products are:—

driver to guard telephone links
conductor to passenger public address systems
driver to control communications
information tape broadcasting systems
emergency talk back systems between passenger and driver
audible alarms for use in driving cabs

Currently on order or being supplied to British and other railways are: Audio and FM public address, crew communication equipment, emergency passenger to driver communication system and through train engine control systems.

Systems: The Company specialises in communications systems using through train wires also used for other functions such as 1 000 V heating wires, lighting and pantograph control etc. Also by using special circuitry several communication links can be achieved by using only one pair of existing wires.

SAFETRAN

Safetran Systems Corp

Head Office: 7721 National Turnpike, Louisville, Kentucky 40214, USA

Telephone: (502) 361-1691

Products: Mobile radio access system; centralised dispatcher radio control system; dispatcher call decoder; communications control console; yard paging systems; intercoms; speakers.

SEL

Standard Elektrik Lorenz AG

Head Office: D-7000 Stuttgart 40 (Zuffenhausen), Hellmuth-Hirth Strasse 42 Postfach 40 07 49, German Federal Republic

Telegrams: STANLOR STUTTGART
Telephone: (0711) 8211
Telex: 72110

Products: Telecommunications equipment, mobile radio systems.

SIEMENS

Siemens Aktiengesellschaft

Head Office: D-8000 Munchen 2, Wittelsbacherplatz 2, Postfach 103, German Federal Republic

Telegrams: SIEMENSDIR MUENCHEN
Telephone: (089) 23 41
Telex: 523 121

Products: Telecommunications equipment.

SOLAR POWER

Solar Power Corp

Head Office: Braintree, Massachusetts, USA

Products: Solar electric generator module designed for remote power applications such as radio repeater stations, microwave links, signalling devices. Following tests with a solar energy unit near Montreal CP Rail has installed an experimental solar unit at Silver Creek in British Columbia. In this application the solar energy is used for communications. A panel of silicon solar cells is mounted in a fixed position on Mount Cotterell. The energy generated by the cells is used to charge a battery housed in an adjacent building. The battery powers a radio repeater for transmission of conversations between CP track maintenance personnel. Until now the Silver Creek radio installation has been powered by electricity supplied from two diesel-powered generators located in a valley. CP Rail hopes that use of solar power will eliminate fuelling of remote generators and allow an important reduction in maintenance requirements.

STC

Standard Telephones and Cables Limited

Head Office: 190 Strand, London, WC2R 1DU, England

Telegrams: RELAY, London W.C.2
Telephone: (01) 836 8055
Telex: 22385

Works: At 155 locations in the United Kingdom

Related Companies: Many subsidiary and associated companies within the United Kingdom. Associated companies abroad within the International Telephone and Telegraph Corporation (ITT).

Managing Director: K. G. Corfield
Marketing Director: R. T. Soper

Products: Coaxial line systems, pulse code modulation equipment and frequency division multiplex equipment for railway communication networks; telephone exchanges and instruments, office intercom systems, public address and loudspeaker systems; telephone instruments, remote control and telemetry systems; teleprinters and message swithing systems for teleprinter network, data terminal and modems; control and communication cables.

Work in hand or recently completed: Communication systems to carry speech, telex and data provided for part of BR's main line electrification schemes for the West Coast route in Scotland. Coaxial line systems, multiplex equipment and coaxial codes have been supplied for use in British Rail's National Telecommunication Plan (NTP) and Total Operations Processing System (TOPS).

TELEPHONE CABLES

Telephone Cables Ltd

Head Office: Dagenham, Essex, England

Telegrams: DRYCORE DAGENHAM
Telephone: 01 592 6611
Telex: 896216

Products: Cables for telecommunications systems.

THOMSON/CSF

Thomson-CSF

Head Office: 173 Boulevard Haussmann, 75360, Paris Cedex 08, France

Telephone: 256 96 00

Products: Telecommunications, audiovisual communications, rail control systems.

TRT

Telecommunications Radioelectriques et Telephoniques

Head Office: 88, Rue Brillat Savarin, 75640 Paris Cedex 13, France

Telegrams: TERATEL PARIS
Telephone: 589 69 45
Telex: 25.828 F

Products: Electronic and telecommunications equipment including rail control systems. As one of the first French companies to develop a ground-train radio link in cooperation with SNCF, TRT has created a series of systems which conform with UIC requirements. The company is supplying ground/train communications systems to both the SNCF and Algerian National Railways (SNCFA). Each ground/train link consists of:
1) A mobile transceiver which includes UHF transmission and reception functions, the AF signalling facilities necessary for operating, and an automatic frequency search device. The transceiver is controlled by a synthesiser allowing its use as a service duplex link.
2) A mobile operating desk which includes all the specific operating controls for a mainline network. It can be used for either simple telephone communication or equipped with auxiliary devices, for digital data transmission.
3) A fixed station including a telephone line interconnection device. Where telephone links are not available a two-way amplification repeater equipment is used.
4) Radiation device. Transceiver radiation is accomplished by means of omnidirectional or directional antennae, or by radiating-slot cables, arranged to fit the topographical requirements of the system.
5) Controller's desk with all monitoring and control elements.

WABCO

WABCO Union Switch and Signals Division

Head Office: SwissRale, Pittsburgh, Pa 15218, USA

Telephone: (412) 242-5000
Telex: 866-448

Products: Two-way voice radio equipment.

WESTERN CULLEN

Western Cullen Division, Federal Signal Corp

Head Office: 2700 West 36th Place, Chicago, Ill 60632, USA

Telephone: (312) 254-9600
Telex: 25-3206

Products: Voice Patrol II radio.

ELECTRIFICATION EQUIPMENT

ACEC

Ateliers de Construction Electriques de Charleroi

Head Office: BP4 B6000 Charleroi, Belgium

Telegrams: Transportation Division Charleroi
Telephone: (071) 36 20 20
Telex: 51227

Products: Railway electrification equipment.

ALSTHOM

Soc Generale de Constructions Electriques & Mecaniques

Head Office: 38 Avenue Kleber, Paris 16, France

Telegrams: ALSTHOM PARIS
Telephone: 727 77-79
Telex: 27672

Products: Generators, alternators and traction motors.

ANSALDO

Ansaldo Societa Generale Elettromeccanica SpA

Head Office: Via Nicola Lorenzi 8, 16152 Genoa, Cornigliano, Italy

Telegrams: ASGEN CORNIGLIANO
Telephone: 4105
Telex: 27098

Products: Fixed power equipment for electrified railways and sub stations.

ASEA AB

Head Office: Vasteras, Sweden

Telegrams: ASEA VASTERAS
Telephone: Vasteras 021-10-00-00

Products: Railway electrification systems.

BALFOUR BEATTY

Balfour Beatty Power Construction Ltd

Head Office: PO Box 12 Acornfield Road, Kirkby, Liverpool L33 & UG, England

Telegrams: BICALCON KIRKBY TELEX
Telephone: 051-546-5681
Telex: 62749

Products: Complete electrification equipment for railway provision and erection.

BBC

Aktiengesellschaft Brown Bouverie & Cie

Head Office: Haselstr CH 5401, Baden, Switzerland

Telegrams: BROWN BOVERIE, BADEN SCHWEIZ
Telephone: (056) 75 11 11
Telex: 52921 and 53 203

Products: Generators and traction motors.

BRECKNELL, WILLIS

Brecknell, Willis & Co Ltd
(A member of the Beyer Peacock Group)

Head Office: Chard, Somerset TA20 2AA, England

Telegrams: PROGRESS CHARD
Telephone: 04606 2246
Telex: CHARD 46289

Products: Range of overhead line fittings, pantographs, third rail shoe gear and complete current collector systems. The company also offers a consultancy service for current collection requirements.

New equipment: The company has pioneered Brecktrank—a new safety covered conductor rail system together with new design of the single arm Highreach pantograph for electrically propelled rapid transit vehicles.

BRISSONNEAU AND LOTZ CHAUDRONNERIE SA

Head Office: 15 rue Bellier, 44000, Nantes, France

Products: Traction and generator motors.

BRUSH

Brush Electrical Machines Co Ltd

Head Office: Falcon Works, Loughborough, Leicestershire, England

Telegrams: BRUSH LOUGHBOROUGH TELEX
Telephone: 050-93-63131
Telex: 341091

Products: Complete electrical propulsion systems and traction motors.

CEM/OERLIKON

Head Office: 37 Rue Du Rocher, 75008, Paris

Telephone: 522. 85. 90/74.61
Telex: 650663

Products: Subway electric and electronic equipment.

DEARMEDELEC

Dearmedelec SAIC

Head Office: Juramento 4182/86, 1430 Buenos Aires, Argentina

Telephone: 52-6766/3409/7036

Products: Static exciting systems, traction motor transition systems, battery charge regulator.

DELTA

Delta Enfield Cables Ltd

Head Office: Millmarsh Lane, Brimsdowne, Enfield Middlesex, England

Telephone: 01-804-2468
Telex: 261749

Products: Accessories, power cables, rubber cables plastic cables and specialised equipment.

ELECTROTRACK

Electrotrack Inc

Head Office: 2414 Morris Avenue, Union NJ, USA
Parent Companies General Cable (USA), Balfour Beatty Group of BICC Ltd (Great Britain)

Products: Power supply for signalling for railway electrification projects; engineering and project management of catenary systems.

ERCOLE MARELLI

Ercole Marelli & C SpA

Head Office: Via Borgonuovo 24 Milan, Italy

Telephone: Milan 65.22.51
Telex: 27098

Products: Electric transmissions for locomotives and railcars.

EVR

Electronique des vehicules et des reseaux

Head Office: 11 rue de la Nouvelle, 93301 Aubervillers, France

Telephone: 833 23 45
Telex: 680075

Products: Statodyne equipment.

FUJI ELECTRIC

Head Office: New Yurakucho Building 12-1, Yurakucho 1 Chome, Chiyoda-ku, Topko 100, Japan

Telephone: 211-7111
Telex: J22331

Products: Diesel and axle generating sets, traction motors, main controllers and motor generators.

GEC

GEC Rectifiers Ltd

Head Office: Stafford, England

Telephone: 0785 51222
Telex: 35206

Products: Power electronics, rectifiers for dc power supply and instrumentation and control.

GEC TRANSPORTATION PROJECTS

Head Office: Elstree Way, Borehamwood, Herts, England

Telephone: (419) 522-7111
Telex: 22777

Products: Complete provision of railway installation and equipment.

GENERAL DI ELECTRICITA

Head Office: Via Bergognone 34, Milan, Italy

Telegrams: "Cogenel, Milan"
Telephone: Milan 4242
Telex: 31092

Products: Electric transmissions.

GENERAL ELECTRIC (CANADA)

Head Office: 214 King Street West, Toronto, Ontario M5H IK7, Canada.

Telephone: (416) 366-7311
Telex: 022-052

Products: Automation equipment for substation and locomotive equipment.

GENERAL ELECTRIC CO (USA)

Head Office: 570 Lexington Avenue, New York, NY 10022, USA

Telegrams: Ingeco New York
Telephone: 212-750 2000

Products: Locomotives, substation equipment and automation.

GENERAL ELECTRIC SA

Head Office: Campinas, Sao Paulo, Brazil

Telegrams: INGENETRIC CAMPINAS
Telephone: 31-9144
Telex: 025189

Products: Traction equipment for electric locomotives.

GROUPEMENT 50 HZ

(50 cycle Group)

Head Office: Postfacht 605 CH 8021, Zurich 1, Switzerland

Products: Provision and erection of complete railway electrification equipment.

HEEMAF BV

(now operating as HOLEC SYSTEMS)

Head Office: Bornestraat 5, Postbox 4, Heneglo, Netherlands

Telegrams: HEEMAF HENGELO
Telephone: 054000-51234
Telex: 4307

Products: Stationary electrical equipment for long distance and urban railways.

MTE

Head Office: 31-32 Quai National, 92806, France

Telephone: 776.41.62
Telex: 61425

Products: Conventional control aparatus, generators, alternators, traction motors, transformers and rectifiers.

OHIO BRASS CO

Head Office: 380n Main Street, Mansfield OH 44902, USA

Telephone: (419) 522-7111

Products: Catenary overhead equipment, third rail current collectors and insulators.

PIRELLI

Construction and Co Ltd

Head Office: PO Box Leigh Road, Eastleigh, Hampshire, England

Telephone: 042-126-2261
Telex: 477525

Products: Railway overhead electrification equipment, provision and erection.

SECHERON

SA Des Ateliers de Secheron

Head Office: Case Postale 40, CH 1211, Geneva 21, Switzerland

Telephone: (022) 32 67 50
Telex: 22130

Products: Transformers for railway electrification, dc traction substations traction motors, rectifiers and circuit breakers.

SIEMENS

Head Office: Werner-von-Siemens Str 50, Erlangen, German Federal Republic

Telepone: 09131.71
Telex: 629871

Products: Railway electrification equipment.

TECNOMASIO ITALIANO BROWN BOVERI SpA

Head Office: Piazzle Lodi, Milan, Italy

Telegrams: "Tecnomasio, Milan"
Telephone: (02) 57-97
Telex: 31153

Products: Generators and traction motors.

TOKYO SHIBAURA ELECTRIC CO LTD

Head Office: 1-6 Uchisaiwaicho 1 chome, Chiyada-Ku, Tokyo 100, Japan

Telegrams: Toshiba Tokyo
Telephone: 03-501-5411
Telex: J22587 J24344 J24576

Products: Electric railcard, control equipment.

TOYO DENKI KK

Head Office: 7 Yaesu 5 chome, Chuo -ku Tokyo 104, Japan

Telegrams: YOHDEN TOKYO
Telephone: 03-272-4211
Telex: TOK (0) 222/4666/7

Products: Locomotives electric, control equipment, pantograph.

WICKHAM

Head Office: Crane Mead, Ware, Herts, England

Telephone: 0920 2491
Telex: 81340

Products: Overhead line inspection cars.

PERMANENT WAY EQUIPMENT

AEBI
Robert Aebi AG

Head Office: Uraniastrasse 31-33, Postfach 8023, Zürich, Switzerland

Telegrams: AEBI, Zürich
Telephone: 01-2110970
Telex: 53795

Products: Rotary snow ploughs.

A.I. WELDERS
A.I. Welders Ltd

Head Office: Academy Street, Inverness, Scotland

Telegrams: 'Aiwelds. Invss'.
Telephone: 0463-39381

Products: Rail welding machines, rail stripping machines, ancillary equipment for rail welding plants.

A new development in automatic flash welding control for the production of long welded rail has been marketed by A.I. Welders. System 80 is a composite control system, controlling and monitoring the movement of switching functions of the welder platen, using five closed servo loops: (1) a current feed-back loop which permits the use of low secondary voltages for flashing and eliminates any chance of premature butt up; (2) a velocity feed-back loop which gives complete compensation for any changes in hydraulic pressure, temperature or slide friction; (3) a pressure feed-back loop which allows strict control of interface pressure to be pre-set and maintained during welding; (4) a power feed-back loop which ensures total usage of the energy pre-set and also acts as an overall monitor of total energy input; (5) a positional control loop through which the main welding parameters are preset on electronic dial settings. The system is designed to give platen positional movements to repeat accuracies of +0.0250 mm.

ALDON
The Aldon Co

Head Office: 3410 Sunset Ave, Waukegan, III 60085, USA

Telephone: (312) 623 8800

Products: Lightweight straddle-type rerailers.

A & K
A & K Railroad Materials Inc

Head Office: PO Box 1276, Bldg 12, Freeport Center, Clearfield, UT 84016, USA

Telephone: (801) 773 3236
Telex: 389 406

Manager: B. R. Bateman

Products: Complete switches, frogs, anchors, bolts, spikes, lockwashers, gauge rods, sleepers, hand track tools.

ARNEKE
Arneke & Co, Heinrick

Head Office: Seelze, Hanòver, German Federal Republic

Telephone: 05137 818

Products: Sleeper placing machines and track laying equipment.

ALUMINOTHERMIQUE
L'Aluminothermique

Head Office: 15, rue de Chabrol, 75010 Paris, France

Products: Rail welding equipment.

ATLANTIC TRACK
Atlantic Track and Turnout Co

Head Office: 149 Nichol Ave, McKees Rocks, Pa 15136, USA

Telephone: (412) 771 5008

Products: Trac-Grip gauge rods.

ATLAS
Atlas Engineering Co

Head Office: 84 Lillie Road, London SW6 1TN, Great Britain

Telegrams: 'Fabricants, London SW6'
Telephone: 01-385 9323
Telex: 895 1847

Products: Jacks, screwing machines, underfloor wheel truing machines, double wheel lathes, hydraulic wheel presses.

ATLAS COPCO
Atlas Copco (Great Britain) Ltd

Head Office: PO Box 79, Swallowdale Lane, Hemel Hempstead, Herts HP2 7HA, England

Telegrams: 'Atlascopco'
Telephone: (0442) 61201

Products: Self-contained power tamper/drill, and pneumatic equipment, pumps, tampers.

BEILHACK
Martin Beilhack GmbH

Head Office: 82 Rosenheim, Postfach 160, German Federal Republic

Telephone: 4033
Telex: 05.25840

Products: Snow clearing machinery, mechanical shovels and hammers.
Beilhack rotary snow ploughs are in service on railways in Austria, Germany, Finland, Norway, Spain, Sweden, Switzerland, Yugoslavia.
A new PB-600 snow plough has been added to Beilhack's range. The plough unit can be extended to a total clearing width of 6 m. The front-mounted plough has been designed so that both side wings can be rotated around a heavy central bolt. This permits its use as a side or wedge-type plough. The hydraulic rotating cylinders are operated by push buttons. Clearing height is controlled from the driver's seat. In 1974, an order for 14 of these new units was delivered to Deutsche Bundesbahn.

BETHLEHEM
Bethlehem Steel Corp

Head Office: Bethlehem, Pa 18016, USA

Telephone: (215) 694 2424

Sales Manager: W. T. Anthony

Products: Rails, switch stands, trackwork, switches, spikes, frog bolts, switch bolts, spikes, track bolts.

BOFORS
AB Bofors-Nohab

Head Office: Trollhättan, S-461 01, Sweden

Telegrams: 'Nohab Trollhättan'
Telephone: 0520 18000
Telex: 42084

Products: Snow clearing equipment.

BOC
BOC Ltd

Head Office: Hammersmith House, London W6 9DX, Great Britain

Telegrams: 'Britoxygen', London W.6
Telephone: 01 748 2020
Telex: 264664

Products: Hand and machine gas cutting equipment, gas and electric welding equipment.

BRITISH VITA
British Vita Co Ltd

Head Office: Middleton, Manchester, M24 2DB

Telephone: 061-653 6800

Products: Resilient rubber/RBC rail pads, oil point heater hoses, chair pads, plugs.

CANRON
Canron Railgroup
(Formed by merger of Tamper and Matisa)
(Division of Canron Ltd)

Head Office and Plant: 2401 Edmund Road, West Columbia, South Carolina 29169, USA

Telephone: 514 637 5531
Telex: 012715

Division Headquarters:
Canada: 171 Eastern Avenue, Toronto, M5A AH7
Australia: PO Box 150, Niddrie, Victoria 3042
Switzerland: Case Postale, CH-1001, Lausanne
Italy: Matema SpA, Via Quintino sella n.8, 1-00187 Roma
France: 39, rue d'Amsterdam, F-75 Paris
Great Britain: 14, Elstow Road, Bedford MK42 9LA
Germany: Markgrafenstrasse 1, D-48 Bielefeld-BRD
Spain: c/Alcala No 65, Madrid-14
Japan: PO Box 1058, Tokyo 100-91

Parts Depot: 1902 University Avenue, St. Paul, Minn. 55104, USA
Telephone: 612-645-5055

Agents: Argentina, Bolivia, Brazil, Chile, Colombia, Costa Rica, Ecuador, El Salvador, Guatemala, Honduras, Jamaica, Mexico, Peru, Trinidad, Uruguay, Venezuela.
Canron Railgroup, is further represented in most other countries. The names of representatives in the above and other countries can be obtained by contacting the head office.

Products: Canron Railgroup manufactures a complete range of railway track maintenance of way equipment including: Ballast cleaning and dressing machines, bolting machines, brush cutters and attachments, track lubricators, frog and switch point grinders, track gauges, mobile generator sets, inspection and recording cars, spike drivers, spike pullers, production tampers, switch tampers, spot tampers, tie inserters and removers, track levelling and lining equipment, rail saws, rail drills, rail bolting machines, snow blowers and a complete contracting service.

CEMAFER
Cemafer Gleisbaumaschinen und Gerate GmbH

Head Office: 7814 Breisach, Ihringer Landstr, 3 Postfach 1327, Germany

Telephone: 07667/585
Telex: 7722524

Products: Power wrenches, coach-screwing machines, rail drills, rail saws, sleeper drills, sleeper adzing and drilling machines, rail grinding equipment, rail benders, light tampers, inspection trolleys, trailers, portal cranes, hand tools, electric generators (portable), gauges, jacks, rail cutting machines, rail stripping machines, sleeper boring machines, sleeper placing machines, spanners, spike drivers and extractors, track laying equipment, wrenches.

CGM
CGM Sté Anonyme Compagnie Générale de Manutention

Levage et Conditionnement SA

Head Office: 27 Boulevard General Jacques, Brussels, Belgium

Telegrams: 'Cegeham Brussels'
Telephone: 48.65.62 3 47.01.43
Telex: 22365

Products: Ballast cleaners, ballast excavators, ballast regulators, cranes, drilling machines, rail anchor tighteners, rail benders, rail cutting machines, rail de-hoggers, rail de-stressers, rail grinding machines, rail lifting barrows, rail saws, rail stripping machines, spike drivers and extractors, trenching machines.

CHEMETRON
Chemetron Corporation, Railway Products Division

Head Office: 111 E. Wacker Drive, Chicago, Illinois 60601, USA

Telegrams: Chemrail
Telephone: (312) 565 5000
Telex: 25-4383

Products: Contract welding of continuous rail of 39 ft lengths into quarter-mile lengths; portable abrasive rail cutters; portable multiple spindle rail drills; dual rail pusher cars; rail welding units.
Formerly known as The National Cylinder Gas Division of Chemetron Corporation the present name was taken on 1 January 1970 following a reorganisation of operations.

CLARKE-CHAPMAN
Clarke Chapman John Thompson Ltd., Crane and Bridge Division

Head Office: Rodley, Leeds LS13 1HN, England

Telegrams: Cranes Rodley
Telephone: 09735 79001
Telex: 55159

Products: Heavy diesel breakdown cranes, turntables, track laying machines, hydraulic railway equipment.

COLES CRANES
Coles Cranes Ltd

Head Office: Crown Works, Sunderland, SLA 6BR, Great Britain

Sales: Harefield, Uxbridge, Middlesex UB9 6QG, England

Telephone: (089 582) 377
Telex: 2169

Products: Diesel-electric, diesel-hydraulic, mobile truck-mounted, tower cranes, diesel mechanical cranes and excavators.

CONSTAIN
Constain Concrete Co Ltd

Head Office: Duncan House, Dolphin Square, London SW1V 3PR

Telephone: 01 821 1581
Telex: 919858 G

Products: Prestressed concrete sleepers.

DEHE
Soc des Entreprises A. Dehe et Cie

Head Office: 40, quai de l'Ecluse, 78290 Croissy-sur-Seine, France

Products: Track construction and maintenance equipment.

DELACHAUX
C. Delachaux SA

Head Office: 119, ave Louis-Roche, 92231, Gennevilliers, France

Telephone: 790 61 20
Telex: DECHO 620 118F

Products: Aluminothermique rail welding equipment.

DESQUENNE ET GIRAIL
Soc Desquenne et Girail

Head Office: 26, rue Lalo, 75016 Paris, France

Products: Track maintenance equipment.

DONELLI
Donelli, SpA

Head Office: Via Romana 69, 42028 Poviglio, Reggio Emilia, Italy

Telegrams: 'Donelli Poviglio'
Telephone: (0522) 689119/689129
Telex: 53320

Products: Ballast regulators, hydraulic cranes, jacks, sleeper placing machines, track aligners, track laying equipment, track lining machines.
Donelli offers gantry equipment as part of a complete package of track relaying machinery: gantries, rail threaders, sleeper positioners, hydraulic track lifters and slewers. The two motorised gantries combine with a lifting beam to form a 36-m track panel lifter and sleeper laying unit. Straddling the track on which it is working, the equipment is capable of renewing 300 m/h. Auxiliary rails used for operation of the unit are later turned onto the new sleepers to provide the final track rail. The gantries are hydraulically operated.
The rail-threader and sleeper positioner works in conjunction with the gantry. It automatically spaces and aligns sleepers as it threads on the new rail. The unit is diesel powered and all operations are hydraulic. With outputs of up to 2 000 m/h, the supplier claims big savings in time and manpower.
For lifting the track during new construction and relaying, Donelli markets a hydraulic track lifter and slewer which jacks the track out of the ballast. Hydraulic rail clamps grip the rail while the lifting jacks are extended onto the ballast. After lifting the machine and track, jack cylinders are tilted to displace or slew the track laterally.

DOW MAC
Dow Mac Concrete

Head Office: Tallington, Stamford, Lincs, England
Telephone: Market Deeping 2301

Works: Eaglescliffe, Teeside, England
Telephone: Eaglescliffe 781811

London Office: 110/112 The Strand, London WC2, England
Telephone: 01/836 8918

Products: Dow Mac prestressed concrete sleepers.

DROUARD
Soc Drouard Frères

Head Office: 153, rue de la Pompe, 75 782 Paris Cedex 16, France

ELASTIC RAIL SPIKE
Elastic Rail Spike Co Ltd

Head Office: 7 Rolls Buildings, Fetter Lane, London EC4A 1JB, England

Telephone: 01 242 5252
Telex: 21474

Products: Rail spikes.

ELEKTRO-THERMIT
Elektro-Thermit GmbH

Head Office and Works: 43 Essen 1, Gerlingstr. 65, German Federal Republic

Telegrams: ELEKTROTHERMIT ESSEN
Telephone: (0201) 173-1
Telex: 0857-727

Products: Thermit railwelding equipment and materials, rail de-stressers, rail grinding machines, glued insulated rail joints.

ENERGOMACHEXPORT
V/O Energomachexport
Export company for all USSR-built railway products

Head Office: Moscow, V-330, Mosfilmovskaya 35, USSR

Telegrams: Moscow Energoexport
Telephone: 147 21 77
Telex: 255

Products: Ballast cleaning machines; tamper-leveller-liner machines; track laying cranes and gantries; snow ploughs; snow clearing and removal equipment; rail welding equipment; portable powered machines for tamping, rail cutting-drilling-grinding and spike driving-pulling; electronic and ultrasonic fault finding equipment; inspection cars; gang and maintenance railcars and trailers.

ERNEST HOLMES
(A Dover Corporation Division)

Head Office: 2505 East 43rd Street, Chattanooga, Tennessee 37407, USA

Telephone: (615) 867 2142

Products: Wrecking cranes.

EXORS OF JAMES MILLS
Exors of James Mills Ltd

Head Office: Bredbury Steel Works, Woodley, Nr Stockport, England

Products: Resilient fastenings; switch heaters; lubricators for rail and wheel flanges.

FAIRMONT
Fairmont Railway Motors, Inc

Head Office: Fairmont, Minnesota 56031, USA

Works: Fairmont, Minnesota 56031, USA, and 6230 NW Drive (Toronto) Malton, Ontario, Canada

Telex: 910 565-2122
Telegrams: Fairmotor
Telephone: (507) 235 3361

Export Manager: K. J. Nelson

Products: Inspection cars; section and gang cars; hy-rail equipment for road or rail movement; motor car engines; push cars and trailers; wheels, axles and bearings; derrick cars; ballast maintenance cars; weed control equipment; track liners; tie sprayers and tie and rail renewal equipment.
The company was founded in 1909 and has been a manufacturer of railway track machinery during this time. Its products are used around the world by the railways of some 70 countries.
Latest product from Fairmont is the W119-A tie inserter which inserts, levels and squares new sleepers tight under the rail at the rate of 3 sleepers/minute. No respotting or additional handling of the units are required, says the supplier. All functions, including the inserting force of 4 020 kg, are hydraulically powered and electronically controlled with very little operator effort. A three-section telescoping boom provides a reach of 4.25 m from track centre-line, with a lift of 450 kg when fully extended. The machine will handle both timber and concrete sleepers.

FAMATEX
Famatex SRL

Head Office: Aviendia San Martin 7910, San Martin, Province of Buenos Aires, Argentina

Telephone: 755 0352

Products: Inspection cars, light and heavy gangers' trollies.

FRUEHAUF
Fruehauf Division, Fruehauf Corporation

Head Office: 10900 Harper Avenue, Detroit, Michigan 48232, USA

Telegrams: Fruco Detroit
Telephone: 921-2410

Products: On-track/off-track service vehicles; highway trailers; containers.

FINDLAY, IRVINE
Findlay, Irvine Ltd

Head Office and Works: Bog Road, Penicuik, Midlothian, Scotland

Telegrams: AUTRONICS PENICUIK
Telephone: (0968) 72111
Telex: 727502

Products: Points heating controller; thermostats.

Chairman: James S. Findlay
Managing Director: John A. Irvine
Sales Manager: W. C. Taylor

Products: The Icelert Model 162 points heating controller is suitable for controlling electric or gas points heating and a special temperature and moisture probe assembly has been designed for this particular application. It controls on a temperature and moisture detection basis and only when the temperature set point (usually 1°C) is reached and moisture is detected at the probes will a relay be activated. This gives a better degree of control than the normal thermostat working on a temperature basis only. Another control knob is provided to enable the selection of a second operating point at a number of degrees below the normal operating level. The heaters will be switched on when the ambient temperature falls to this level and moisture and snow is not detected.

FOSTER
L. B. Foster Co

Head Office: Foster Bldg, 415 Holidag Drive, Pittsburgh, Pa 15220, USA

Telephone: (412) 928 3400

Manager: J. L. Foster

Products: Track bolts, braces, tools, gauges, levels, liners, pads, trackwork.

GTG
Greenside Hydraulics Ltd

Head Office: Chapeltown, Sheffield S30 4RY, England

Telephone: Ecclesfield (07415) 4971
Telex: 54118

Products: Rail tensors for tensioning continuous welded rail; rail support arms and rollers; rail welding jigs; track lifting machines; rail joint straightening machines; rail manipulators; rail lifting bars; lightweight trolleys; rail curving machines.

GEISMAR
Société des Anciens Etablissements L. Geismar

Head Office: 113 bis Avenue Charles de Gaulle, 92200-Neuilly sur Seine, France

Telephone: (1) 475500
Telex: Fermar NLLSN 620700

Works: 5, rue d'Altkirch, 68 Colmar, France Tel: (1) 7475500. Telex: Fermar NLLSN 620700

Products: Rail saws; rail drills; coachscrewing machines; fishbolt fastening machines; rail profile grinding machines; rail butt grinding machines; sleeper drilling machines; chamfering machines; sleeper adzing machines; lightweight ballast tampers; illumination plants; track warning devices; hydraulic rail benders; hydraulic rail joint straighteners; rail lubricators; trolleys (1 to 200 tons); inspection trolleys; rail loaders; rail pullers; rail changers; sleeper loading machines; tamping and slewing jacks; complete range of hand tools; self propelled track laying gantries; thermit weld shears; hydraulic rail tensors; heavy-duty sleeper changing machine; spike drivers and pullers; combination track gauge and level; in-plant sleeper adzing-drilling-sawing machine; track-slewing and lining machines; electronic train warning device; for gangs working on the track; electronic train loading gauge control device, etc.
Geismar markets a comprehensive range of track relaying equipment, which includes hydraulic portal cranes with hoisting capacities of 16, 24 and 30 tons. These machines lay or relay track at a rate of about 1 000 ft/h. A recent addition to Geismar equipment is a self-propelled hydraulic rail threader designed to move rail lengths to and from the track position. The machine is able to remove old rails before threading new rails into fixing and welding. Operation is by one man and all lifting and transferring movements are made hydraulically.

GEMCO
George Moss Pty Ltd

Head Office: 10-14 Woolwich St, Leederville, Perth, Western Australia

Telephone: 81 2033
Telex: 92645
Telegrams: ROCKDRILL PERTH

Products: Hydraulic controlled track machines for sleeper extraction and replacement, track lifting, levelling, ballast scarifying, sleeper boring, spike pulling and bolt renewal. Also Australian agents for Geisman rail maintenance machines.

GEORGE COOPER
George Cooper (Sheffield) Ltd

Head Office: Sheffield Rd, Tinsley, Sheffield S9 1RS, England

Telephone: (0742) 441026
Telex: 547092

Products: Fish bolts, track bolts, screw spikes, crossing bolts, frog bolts.

GRANT LYON EAGRE
Grant Lyon Eagre Ltd

Head Office: 80A Scotter Road, Scunthorpe, South Humberside DN15 8EF, England

Telephone: Scunthorpe 62131
Telex: 527215

Products: Switches and crossings, cast iron baseplates, blocks, collector shoes.

Managing Director: D. W. Schafer
Director: J. W. Woodford
    R. F. M. Grant

GRINAKER PRECAST
Grinaker Precast (Pty) Ltd

Head Office: 77 Lemmer Rd, Vulcania Ext. 2, Brakpan 1540, South Africa

Telephone: 55-9340
Telex: 82322

Chairman: J. R. Ellis
Managing Director: E. J. Sadie
Chief Sales Director: A. S. Taylor

Products: Prestressed concrete sleepers.

GRUNDY
Grundy and Partners Ltd

Head Office: Bond's Mill, Stonehouse, Glos. GL10 3RG, England

Telephone: Stonehouse 3611
Telex: 43484

Chairman: S. W. Grundy
Managing Director: C. G. Burcher
Product Manager: H. R. Stocken

Products: Traklink mobile stud and pin brazing equipment.

HANOMAG
Rheinstahl Hanomag

Head Office: 3000 Hanover, German Federal Republic

Telegrams: 'Hanomag, Hanover'
Telephone: 44491

Products: Ballast regulators.

HENRY BOOT
Henry Boot Engineering Ltd

Head Office: Dronfield, Sheffield S18 6XZ, England

Telephone: 0246 414615
Telex: 547079

Chairman: E. H. Boot
Managing Director: D. H. Boot
General Manager, Contracting Division: G. A. Jarrett
General Manager, General Engineering Division: J. M. Stevenson
Marketing and Sales Manager: J. Newby

Products: Railway switches and crossings; lever boxes and ancillary equipment; construction and maintenance of railway track.

HOLLAND
Holland Co (Railweld Division)

Head Office: 1020 Washington Ave, Chicago Hts, Ill 60411, USA

Telephone: (312) 756-0650/468 6566

Products: Rail welding equipment.

HRS
Hoesch Rothe Erde-Schmiedag AG

Head Office: Tremoniastrasses 5-11, D-4600 Dortmund 1, German Federal Republic

Telephone: 0231 1961
Telex: 8 22 245 hrs d

Products: Rail spikes.

HUNSLET
The Hunslet Engine Company Ltd

Head Office: Hunslet Engine Works, Leeds LS10 1BT, England

Telegrams: Engine Leeds
Telephone: 32261 (10 lines)
Telex: 55237

Products: Self-propelled six-foot and shoulder ballast cleaning machines; rail mounted drainage trenchers.

IRVINE
J. E. Irvine & Co. Ltd

Head Office: Knoll Road, Camberley, Surrey, England

Telephone: 0276 5069/21419

Products: Sleeper placing machines and track laying equipments inc. wagon-mounted cranes for rail handling. (In association with Heinrick Arneke & Co., Hanover).

ITALSIDER
Italsider SpA

Head Office: Via Corsica 4, Geneva, Italy

Telephone: 5999
Telex: 27696
Telegrams: ITALSIDER GENOVA

Products: Permanent way equipment including baseplates, fishplates, clips, switches and crossings.

ITS
International Track Systems, Inc

Head Office: 620 West 32nd Street, Ashtabula, Ohio 44004, USA

Telephone: 216-992-9206/216-993-8076

Managing Director: Alfred E. Carey
Sales Director: L. L. Corbissero

Products: Rubber products for railway track such as butyl rubber shock barriers for use between the base of rails and steel tie plates and between the plates and sleepers.

JACKSON
Jackson Vibrators Inc.

General Sales Office: 1905 Bernice Road, Lansing, Illinois 60438, USA

Telegrams: Jaktamp
Telephone: (312) 895-0100

Factory: Ludington, Michigan

Vice-President, Sales: J. H. Bush
Marketing Manager: Allan McCarthy

Products: Complete line of tie tampers, automatic with or without liners (curve and tangent one unit); non-automatic switch tampers; surfacing light beam fits all manufacturers tampers; hand tampers; Jackson/Jordon spreader-ditcher-snow plough.

JAMBES-NAMUR
Jambes-Namur, SA Des Ateliers de Construction de

Head Office: B-5100 Jambes, Belgium

Telegrams: 'Jamur, Jambes'
Telephone: 081-318.51
Telex: 59127

Products: Vibrators for testing of sleepers and rail fixing devices; vibrators for ballast cars unloading.

JARRAH
Jarrah & Karri Export Marketing Ltd.

Head Office: Davis House, Croydon, Surrey CR0 1QE, England

Telephone: 01 681 1271
Telex: 946195

Products: Sleepers.

KANGO
Kango Electric Hammers Ltd

Head Office: Lombard Road, South Wimbledon, London SW19 3XA, England

Telegrams: Kangolim London SW19
Telephone: 01-542 8544
Telex: 261789

Depots: Leyton, London E10 7JQ; East Dulwich, London SE22 9AN; West Bromwich, West Midlands; Colwick, Nottingham; Coventry, Warwicks; Prestwich, Manchester; Kirkby, Liverpool; Preston, Lancs; East Kilbride, Scotland.
Kango Ballast Tamping Equipment is in use in Australia, Belgium, Brazil, Canada, Chile, France, Greece, Holland, Hong Kong, Hungary, India, Malaysia, Norway, South Africa, South Korea, Sweden, Thailand, Yugoslavia, and the United Kingdom.

Products: Kango electric ballast tampers and power generators.

KERSHAW
The Kershaw Companies Inc

Head Office and Works: 2205 West Fairview Avenue, Montgomery, Alabama 36108, USA. PO Box 9328

Telephone: (205) 263 5581
Telex: 59-3416

Managing Director, International Operations: Peter H. Deckert

Products: Complete range of self-propelled machines for mechanised track, switch and yard maintenance: ballast regulator and ballast broom—snow switch cleaner—brush cutter attachment; track patrol with attachments; brush type kribber; track broom; yard cleaner; dual tie saw and end remover; tie bed scarifier and tie inserter; tie end remover; tie injector; tie, bridge and bundle cranes; crawler adzer; snow switch cleaner; track and switch liner; clear way brush cutter and snow blower; super jack all; Railroader trailer; undercutter and ballast cleaner; portable set off.

Affiliated Companies:
Kershaw Manufacturing Canada Ltd, 2062 Chartier Avenue Dorval, Quebec, Canada
Royce Kershaw Company, Inc, Montgomery, Alabama 36108, USA
Evans Deakin Industries Ltd., 12 Boundary Street, South Brisbane, Queensland 4101, Australia

KOEHRING
Koehring GmbH—Bomag Division

Head Office: 5407 Boppard/Rhein, Postfach 180, German Federal Republic

Telegrams: Bomag Boppard
Telephone: (06742) 2051
Telex: 04 263 16

Products: Tamping compactors, reversing vibratory plate compactors, trench compactors, double vibratory rollers, single drum vibratory rollers, double vibratory slope compactors, tandem vibratory rollers, single drum vibratory rollers, towed vibratory rollers, sheepsfoot rollers, refuse compactors.

KRAUTKRAMER
Krautkrämer GmbH

Head Office: 5 Köln-Klettenberg, Luxemburger Str 449, German Federal Republic

Telegrams: Impulsschall, Koeln
Telephone: 44 60 61

Products: Stationary rail testing installations, rail testers, rail test cars.

Affiliated Company: Wells Krautkramer Ltd, Blackhorse, Letchworth, Herts, England
This equipment is in use in Belgium, France, Germany, Greece, Hungary, Ireland, Italy, Japan, Luxembourg, Sweden, Switzerland, UK, USA.

LESTEEL
Lesteel Spring Co (Pty) Ltd

Head Office: PO Box 261, Luipaardsvlei 1743, Transvaal, South Africa

Telephone: 664-6005/6

Products: FIST/BTR concrete rail fastenings.

LIFTEC
Liftec Engineering Limited

Technical and Sales Office: PO Box 8, Berkhamsted, Herts, England

Telephone: Berkhamsted 4060

Head Office and Works: Long Rock, Penzance, Cornwall, England

Telephone: Penzance 5228

Products: Special purpose platforms in standard designs or to customer's requirements; universal viaduct inspection unit for British Rail.

Chairman: A. J. Stancomb
Directors: J. M. Harrison *(Managing)*
R. F. Kempe *(Sales)*
R. T. N. Bowen
K. W. J. Bradford
D. L. Coller
S. M. Wills

LORAM
Loram Maintenance of Way, Inc

Head Office: 3900 Arrowhead Drive, Hamel, Minnesota 55340, USA

Telegrams: Mannix
Telephone: 545 0411

Marketing Manager: J. E. Gavin

Products: Autotrack, single track ploughs, double track ploughs, ballast sleds, winch carts, multi-purpose machines (undercutters), autosleds, rail grinders, shoulder ballast cleaners and sleeper inserters.

MATEMA
Matema Materiali Meccanici SpA

Head Office: Via Ardeatina Km 21,00040 S. Palomba (Rome), Italy

Telegrams: 'Matistal Pomezia'
Telephone: 919112
Telex: 68150

Products: Track recording trolleys; automatic track levelling, tamping, and lining machines; ballast cleaners; ballast regulators; heavy and light gang cars; sleeper boring machines; rail power saws; wrenches and drills; continuous-rail welding machines and grinding machines; electric generators (portable); gauges; handfacing equipment; jacks; screwing machines; sleeper placing machines; spike drivers and extractors; track laying equipment.

MATISA
Matériel Industriel SA

Head Office: MATISA Matériel Industriel SA, Arc-en-Ciel 2, Crissier near Lausanne, Switzerland, PO Box, CH-1001 Lausanne.

Works: Renens and Crissier (Lausanne), Santa Palomba (Rome)

Associated Companies:
German Federal Republic: Matisa, Maschinen GmbH, Markgrafenstrasse 1, D-48 Bielefeld.
UK: Matisa (UK) Limited, Elstow Road 14, Bedford MK42 9LA.
Spain: Matisa Española, C/Alcalá 65, Madrid-1.
Italy: Matema Materiali, Meccanici SpA, Via Ardeatina KM 21, 1-00040 S. Palomba.
Japan: Matisa Japan, Co., Ltd., Inose Building 6th floor, 16-6 Chiba 5-chome, Minato-ku Tokyo.
France: Matisa, Agence en France, Rue d'Amsterdam 39, F-75009 Paris.

Products: Automatic tamper-leveller-liners; universal switch tamper-leveller-liners; medium tamper-leveller-liners; light tampers; ballast cleaners; ballast regulators; and hopper wagons; ballast crusher wagons; ballast compactors; track recording trolleys; rail cars and coaches; track measuring and analysing equipment; curve calculators and curve correctors; track renewal train; power wrenches; rail saws and rail drills; sleeper drills; sleeper adzing; and drilling machines; portable rail grinders; rail scooters; and length gang trolleys.

LATEST EQUIPMENT

B 200
Tamper-leveller-liners
Modular design providing a choice of nine models:
—single workhead for tamping in open track
—double workheads for tamping in open track
—single workhead for tamping in open track with check rail where obstacles are present.
Each type can be fitted with:
—2 axles: 3-point suspension, UIC standard
—3 axles: front axle and rear bogie, 3-point suspension UIC standard
—4 axles: 2 railway type bogies with primary steel coil spring suspension, anti-yaw dampeners.

B 133
Universal Tamper-leveller-liner:
"Regelfahrzeug" train formation vehicle for switches and plain track
80 km/h self-propelled
100km/h in train formation
Production speed on plain track: 500 m/h
Complete treatment of:
simple switch: 20 min.
double switch: 30 min.
cross-over: 40 min.
cross-over/junction: 60 min.

B 124
Tamper-leveller-liner:
"Regelfahrzeug" train formation vehicle for plain track high output
80 km/h self-propelled
100 km/h in train formation.
Production speed: 1 200 m/h.

B 85
Tamper-leveller-liner
of proven reliability.
easy to use and maintain.
model M with double tools: 1 000 m/h
model N with single tools: 600 m/h
New lining device on the axle.

LCR 04
Tamper-liner
for all gauges from 700 mm, restricted structure gauges, special adaptations for mine railways, steelworks, urban and metro lines.

BL 09
Light Ballast Tamper
Single head and double head.
Single or double head, motorised, for gradients up to 60 o/oo, for loop lines, sidings, etc.

C 330
Ballast Cleaner
Very high output.
for worksites where advance is extra rapid
Production: 600 m³/h

C 311
Universal Ballast Cleaner
with lifting and track holding device, for difficult, sinuous, uneven tracks of restricted gauge with various fixed obstacles.
Production: 350 m³/h

12 CB 8
Ballast Cleaner
High output, proven reliability
Production: 450 m³/h

R 7 D + WB 1
Ballast Regulator with Ballast Hopper
for all transfers
Working speed:
from 2 to 20 km/h in either direction
Travel speed: 80 km/h
Optional equipment: excavator-loader arm

D 912
Crib and Shoulder Compactors-Production Speed 900 m/h
Optional equipment: ploughs and brush for finishing in one pass

P 811
Track Renewal Train Valditerra System
for all types of rails and sleepers
Length: 67 m
Length of cut: 4 m
Personnel: 14
Production speed: 500 m/hr
Worksite start-up time: 18 min.
Worksite clearance time: 12 min.
Economic operation even during the shortest track occupations.

PV 6
Track Recording Trolley
with Matisa analyser AV 521 for numerical values of the 7 parameters
Recording speed: 30 km/h

M 422
Track Recording Railcar
with Matisa analyser AV 522 for numerical values of the 7 parameters
Recording speed: 80 km/h

A 461
Track Recording Coach
with Matisa analyses AV 522 for the numerical value of 10 parameters.
Recording speed: 160 km/h
Coach layout including a recording compartment, a conference room, a two-berth sleeping compartment, kitchen and toilets, as well as small workshop with generator for independent power supply of the coach and its equipment.

AV—521/522

MATIX-INDUSTRIES
Soc Matix Industries

Head Office: 59, rue Saint-Lazare, 75009 Paris, France

Products: Track maintenance machinery including inspection cars.

McGREGOR
Robert McGregor & Sons Ltd

Head Office: Turnoaks Lane, Birdholme, Chesterfield, Derbyshire S40 2HB, England

Telephone: 0246 76971
Telex: 547467
Telegrams: McGREGORS CHESTERFIELD

Directors: R. R. McGregor
M. McGregor
W. J. McGregor
F. D. Lebish
R. F. P. David
L. Yates
H. Breedan
H. Whelan

Products: In collaboration with British Rail's Research and Development Division, Robert McGregor developed PACT—the Paved Concrete Track system. PACT was developed as an alternative to classical track of steel rails, sleepers and ballast to reduce expenditure involved in maintenance. The system consists essentially of continuously welded rails laid on a continuously reinforced concrete slab, designed to ensure that the track geometry remains within tolerance over long periods, with negligible maintenance. Resilient rail fastenings locate the rails on the slab and resilient pads are interposed between the rail foot and slab surface.

Several versions of PACT have been constructed, both in Britain and overseas. An essential feature of PACT is the provision of custom-made slip form pavers, which can be used to construct the concrete track bed on a single width right-of-way. Associated with the pavers is machinery which dispenses and places the slab reinforcement, and carried the concrete into the paver—ensuring a continuous progress of slab construction.

MECANOPLASS

Mecanoplass (Subsidiary of Plasser & Theurer, Austria).

Head Office: 90, rue de la Gare 57, Bening-les-St-Avold, France

Telephone: (87) 045454
Telex: 8602N3

Products: Automatic track leveliing, tamping and lining machines, ballast cleaners, ballast regulators, hydraulic power track wrenches.

MONIER

Concrete Industries (Monier) Limited

Head Office: PO Box 295, Chatswood, NSW 2067 Australia

Telegrams: Monier, Sydney
Telephone: (02) 411 1122
Telex: AA 26673

Products: Concrete sleepers; plant and equipment for manufacture of prestressed concrete sleepers.
Monier have developed a highly efficient and economical method of producing prestressed concrete sleepers, with plant capacities from 480 to 1 920 sleepers per day.

NCM

Nederlandse Constructiebdrijven en Machinefabrieken NV

Head Office: Schieweg 2, Delft, PO Box 10, Netherlands

Telegrams: 'NECEM, Delft'
Telephone: 015-569244
Telex: 31031

Products: Rails and accessories, switches, crossings and turntables, trackmobiles.

ORTON

Orton McCullough Crane Company

Head Office: Oakbrook Executive Plaza, 1211 West 22nd Street, Oakbrook, Illinois 60521, USA

Telegrams: ORCRANE
Telephone: (312) 654 1695

Products: Cranes and heavy lifting gear.

PANDROL
Pandrol Ltd

Head Office: 7 Rolls Buildings, Fetter Lane, London EC4A 1JB, England

Telephone: 01 242 5252
Telex: 21474

Products: Resilient rail fastenings.

PERSONER
Personer Spårteknik AB

Head Office: S-27100 Ystad, Sweden

Telephone: 0411-13800
Telex: 33235 pst s

Products: Heavy-duty point lock.

PINTASCH BAMAG
Pintsch Bamag Antriebs-und Verkehrstechnik GmbH

Head Office: Postfach 100420, D-4220 Dinslaken, German Federal Republic

Telephone: (02134) 602-1
Telex: 08551938

Products: Automatic propane-fuelled infra-red point heating equipment.

PLASSER
Plasser & Theurer

Head Office: Johannesgasse 3, 1010 Vienna, Austria

Telegrams: Bahnbau Vienna
Telephone: 52 49 51
Telex: 02/1178

Factory: Pummererstraße 5, 4020 Linz, Austria

Subsidiary Companies:
Australia: Plasser Australia, Pty Ltd, PO Box 84, Toongabbie, NSW 2146

Brazil: Plasser do Brasil Ltda, Comercio, Industria e Representacoes, Avenida Marechal Camara, 271—Grupo 1.201, Castelo (ZC-39), 20.000—Rio de Janeiro, GB
Canada: Plasser Canadian Corporation Ltd, 2705 Marcel Street, Montreal 9, Que.
France: Mecanoplass SA 90, rue de la Gare, 57801 Beeningles-St. Avold
German Federal Republic: Deutsche Plasser Bahnbaumaschinen GmbH, Works: D-8228 Freilassing, Industriestraße 31—Spare Parts Depot and Customer Service: D-8 München 81, Friedr. Eckart-Straße 35
Great Britain: Plasser Railway Machinery (GB) Ltd, Manor Road, West Ealing, London W13
India: Plasser & Theurer Railway Machinery Manufacturers, B/52 Greater Kailash, New Delhi-48
Italy: Plasser Italiana Srl, Via Gaeta 16, 00185 Rome, Sales Department, Service, Workshop, Spare Parts: Piazzale Stazione F.S., 00049 Velletri (Rom)
Japan: Nippon Plasser K.K., 26—11, Kasuga, 2-Chome Bunkyoku, Tokyo
South Africa: Plasser Railway Machinery (South Africa), Pty Ltd, PO Box 10494, Johannesburg
Spain: Plasser Espanola SA Posterior Occidental 8, Madrid
USA: Plasser American Corporation, 2001 Myers Road 23324, Chesapeake, Virginia

Products: Automatic track tamping, surfacing and lining machines; universal points and crossing tamping machines; ballast consolidating machines; ballast regulators; ballast cleaning machines; track relaying trains and machines; mobile rail welding machines; track recording cars, railway motor vehicles; railway cranes and light weight equipment for track maintenance
The Plasser & Theurer 07 and 08 Series of tamping machines covers a range of machines for the most different conditions and demands. The latest equipment is the 08-Quatromatic which tamps, levels and lines 4 sleepers at a time, which guarantees highest output.
Outstanding features of the 07-275 points and crossing tamping machines are the lateral moveable tamping heads, the sidewards tiltable tamping tools and the operators cabin which is situated immediately in front of the working units.
The ballast regulators PBR 103 and SSP 90 have an x-shaped centre plough which enlarges their working capability.
The dynamic track stabiliser DGS applies lateral vibration and horizontal pressure to the track, thus stabilising it immediately after the tamping operation.
The RM 76 U is the first undercutter ballast cleaner, which besides of plain track also can undercut and clean switches and crossings.
The assembly line principle was applied to track relaying by Plasser & Theurer in 1968 with the development of the track relaying train SUZ 2000. Today the series SUZ 350 and SUZ 500 are manufactured, which can be adapted for any railway conditions.
The self propelled track recording and analysing car EM 80 works with electronic track measuring systems which have proven their reliability under most severe conditions from extreme cold weather to tropic and desert conditions.
With the K 355 PT the flash butt welding principle—which up to now had been used stationary only—became mobile and flash but welding can be carried out on track now.
For the demands of customers additionally a wide range of special machines for track maintenance and track works is supplied, including all kinds of motor vehicles and one-or twin-jib heavy railway cranes as well as light weight track maintenance equipment.

PLASTICA
Plastica Kunststoffwerk GmbH

Head Office: Postfach 2165, 5828 Ennepetal 1, German Federal Republic

Telephone: 02333-7821/92
Telex: 0823 382 Plku

Products: Resilient rail fastenings and insulating elements.

PLUTO
Société d Exploitation des Poutres de Levage Universelles et Traveleuses Oleopneumatiques

Head Office: BP 63; Les Mureaux (78), France

Telephone: 097 881 3442
Telegrams: 'Tracman-Wrexham

Products: Track laying and replacement wagon.

PORTEC INC
Portec Inc (Transportation Products)

Head Office: 300 Windsor Drive, Oak Brook, III 60521

Telephone: (312) 325-6300

Products: Rail anchors, insulated rail joints, rail and flange lubricators, rail joint heater, sleepers, track machines, tampers, snow blowers, rail laying equipment.

PORTEC (UK)
Portec (UK) Ltd
Head Office: Vauxhall Industrial Estate, Ruabon, Wrexham, Clwyd, LL14 6UY

Telephone: (097) 881-3442

Products: Rail anchors, rail and flange lubricators, maxi-mu adhesion fluid applicators, track swith protectors and two way rail benders.
Rail and flange lubrication as a method of saving rail wear is becoming more and more important as the cost of materials and labour spirals upwards. The Portec range of track-mounted lubricators—marketed under the old company name of P&M—includes the well-tried Model C4, which bolts to the rail, and the Pammek series.Latest addition to the range is the Tramway Lubricator for the lubrication of grooved, rails laid within paved or tarmacadam areas.

POUGET
Pouget Etablissements SA

Head Office: 190 Bis, Ave de Stalingrad, 93240 Stains, France

Telegrams: 'Motovoi Puget-Stains'
Telephone: 826 62 12

Products: Track laying gantries, coach screwing machines, sleeper drills, rail saws, rail drills, portable vibrating tampers, rail grinding machines, rail loaders, sleeper adzing and drilling machines, jacks, hand tools, light ballast cleaner.

PRORAIL
(Group consisting of STEDEF, FREYSSINET INTERNATIONAL and Sateba)

Head Office: 16 Blvd République 92200, Boulogne, France

Telephone: 603 54 00
Telex: 200 888

Products: Pre-stressed and dou block sleepers; rail fastenings.

RACINE
Racine Railroad Products Inc

Head Office and Works: 1524 Frederick Street, Racine, Wisconsin 53404, USA

Telephone: 414 637 9681

Chairman/Chief Executive Officer: G. W. Christiansen, Sr
President & Treasurer: Robert C. Schrimpf
Executive Vice President & Secretary: George W. Christiansen, Jr
Service Engineer: R. L. Turner

Products: Portable rail saws; drills and cut-off machines; rail clip applicators and adjusters; electronic gaugers; cribbers; brooms; vibrators; rail polishers; hydraulic power packages; wrenches; spike drivers; spike hole filling material and applicators.

RAILS CO
The Rails Company

Head Office: 187 Maplewood Ave, Maplewood, NJ 07040, USA

Telephone: (201) 763 4320
Telex: 138 206

President: G. N. Burwell

Products: Rail anchors, switch point locks, switch heaters (propane and natural gas), snow detectors.

REXNORD
Nordberg Division of Rex Chainbelt Inc, (Railway Equipment Division)

Head Office: 3073, South Chase Avenue, Milwaukee, Wisconsin 53201, USA

Export Sales: American Equipment Co, 150 E. Palmetto Park Rd, Boca Raton, Florida 33432, USA

Licensee: Noyes Bros Pty Ltd, Frederick Street, St. Leonard's NSW, Australia

Products: Trackliners, switchliners, self propelled adzers, rail drills, surf-rail grinders, heavy duty rail grinders, utility grinders, spike hammers, hydraulic spike pullers, spike straighteners, tie drills, self propelled spike pullers, hydraulic power jacks, dun-rite gauging machines, hydra-spiker, line indicator, plate placer, tie spacer, rail gang spiker, X-level indicator.

RMC
Portec Inc., RMC Division

Head Office: PO Box 1888, Pittsburgh, Pennsylvania 15230, USA

Telegrams: Ramaco Pittsburg
Telephone: (412) 782 1000
Telex: 86-6145

Export Sales Office: Portec International, 300 Windsor Drive, Oak Brook, Illinois, 60521

General Sales: E. J. Powell (Pittsburgh)

Associated Companies:
IEC-Holden Ltd., Railway Division, 8180 Cote de Liesse Road, Montreal H4T 1G8, PQ, Canada.

Products: RMC Hydramatic 16-Tool Tamper, 8-Tool Tamper, 4-Tool Switch/Spot Tamper, Tie Master, Line Master, Tie Spacer, Spike Master, Auto-Spiker, Bolt Master, Rail and Joint Straightener, Anchor Master, Tie Unloader, Surfacing and Lining Devices, Ballast Distributor and Ballast Distributor/Cleaner, Brush Cutter, Snow Blowers Typhoon Model (delivers 165 mph wind blast—Hurricane Jet Engine Model delivers 650 mph blast), Concrete Tie Clip Machine, Anchor Distributing Cart, Spike Distributing Cart, Equipment for Laying Rail and Welded Rail, Tie Plate Broom, Track Broom, Rail End-Hardening Machine, Rail and Fastener Spray Machine, Spot Car Repair Systems and components for freight car and locomotive repair, Anchor adjuster, Zapper railgang spiker, Zapper tie gang spiker, RMC sand blower, RMC lime measuring device.

ROBEL
Robel GmbH & Co

Head Office and Works: Thalkirchnerstrasse 210, 8000 München 75, German Federal Republic

Telegrams: robelco muenchen
Telephone: 7233011
Telex: 05-23012

General Managers: W. Hentzen, Jr
　　　　　　　　　W. Mueller
Sales Manager: G. Eibler

Products: Powered ganger's trolleys with hydraulic tipping platform and crane, trailers, stationary and mobile machines for processing sleepers and rails, equipment for loading and unloading long-welded rails, rail drilling machines, rail saws, power wrenches, rail grinders, hydraulic rail benders, ratchet track jacks and spanners, gauges, automatic track lining machines, portal cranes and so on.

ROLBA
Rolba Co Ltd

Head Office: Barengasse 29, CH-8039, Zurich, Switzerland

Products: Rotary snowploughs from 10 to 1 000 hp.

RS
Roger P. Sonneville

Head Office: Tour Maine-Montparnasse, 33 ave du Maine, 75755 Paris Cedex 15, France

Telephone: 538 73 20/538 74 62

Products: Steel and reinforced two block sleepers, elastic insulated fastenings.

RT-W
The Railway Track-Work Company

Head Office: 2381 Philmont Ave, Bethayres, Pennsylvania, USA

Telephone: 215/947-7100

Products: Tie handlers, cross grinders, rail drills.
Equipment has been supplied to practically all the railways in the United States and Canada, to The Danish Railways and to the US Government.

SATEBA

Head Office: 262 Blvd St-Germain 75007 Paris, France

Telephone: 551 59 19/551 67 51
Telex: 200 800 F

Products: Vagneux type prestressed concrete sleepers.

SCHLATTER
Schlatter AG HA

Head Office: Bandstrasse CH 8952, Schlieren, Switzerland

Telegrams: 'Elektropunkt Schlieren'
Telephone: 01 730 0951
Telex: 53054

Products: Rail welding equipment, Rectifier rail welding and burr-removing machine.

SECEM
Soc d'Essais de Constructions Electriques, Mécaniques et Métallurgiques

Head Office: 15, rue Chabrol, 75010 Paris, France

Products: Track maintenance and inspection equipment.

SECMAFER
Secmafer SA

Head Office and Works: Chemin des Meuniers, Buchelay—78203 MANTES France

Telephone: 092 40 00
Telex: 600815

Managing Director: Jean-Jacques BOYER

Agents Abroad: Agents and after sales service throughout the world.

Products: Complete track relaying trains for mechanised track maintenance and construction; fully automatic relaying gantries; ballast regulators; track assembly and lining machines; fully automatic ballast cleaning and levelling machines; shunting locomotives, etc.
For 20 years Secmafer has been marketing beam and gantry systems for mechanised track maintenance and rehabilitation, consisting of two mobile gantries connected by a longitudinal beam. Power is supplied by 80 hp diesel engines. The gantries are telescopic, allowing work to be carried out beneath overhead wires and in confined areas such as tunnels. The machines can position new track (prefabricated panels or single ties) at a rate of 350 m per hour.
Early in 1975 Secmafer built a new type of gantry/beam system which—sold to Iran and Skandinavia—increases track relaying speeds to 600 m/h. The 216 M10 gantries and 401 BR beam form a monoblock assembly about 18 m long. As in previous models, they simultaneously dismantle two old track panels of 18 to 24 m in length, and on a second pass relay the corresponding number of new sleepers.
Main differences between the new and old models is that motive power consisting of two diesel-air engines rated at 250 hp each, is installed on the beam instead of the gantry. This, says the maker, leaves two solid but streamlined gantries with all wheels driven—"giving increased adherence to the running rails and a firm guarantee against derailment".

SKYHI
C. F. Taylor (Skyhi) Limited
(A member of the Weir Group of Companies)

Head Office: Molly Millars Lane, Wokingham, Berks, England

Telephone: 0734 782500
Telex: 848478

Works: Wokingham

Telephone: (01) 588 7621
Telegrams: Kenitracom London

Products: Track and wagon hydraulic jacks; jack test rigs; rail benders; rail hole broach units (hand or power operated); Air-draulic power packs.

Directors: C. F. Taylor, OBE, DL
　　　　　　 G. J. Dupree
　　　　　　 M. J. Page
　　　　　　 P. D. Smith
　　　　　　 P. F. Drewitt
Sales Manager: F. E. Bing

SOCADER

Head Office: 2, rue de Leningrad, 75008 Paris, France

Telephone: 293 5610
Telex: 641217 SOCADER

Products: Points and crossings.

SOLA

Ing Guido Scheyer

Head Office: A-6840 Gotzis, Postfach 36, Austria

Products: Track measuring equipment.

SPENO

Speno International SA

Head Office: 22-24 Parc Chateau-Banquet, 1211 Geneva, Switzerland

Telephone: 022 31 81 41
32 04 48
32 84 04
Telex: 23 921

Products: In-track rectification and reprofiling units; wave formation recording car.

SPERRY

Sperry Rail Service
Division of Automation Industries Inc

Head Office: Shelter Rock Road, Danbury, Connecticut 06810, USA

Telephone: (203) 748 9243

Australian Office: Automation Sperry Ltd, Rydalmere, NSW, Australia

Sperry started rail testing in 1928 and since then have inspected more than 6 400 000 miles of track and detected over 3 500 000 rail defects.
They own and operate a fleet of 26 Induction-Ultrasonic Cars and two All Ultrasonic Cars
Sperry services has been used by more than 100 North American Railroads as well as many in Europe and Australia.

SPIE BATIGNOLLES

Soc S.P.I.E. Batignolles (Service Voies Ferrées)

Head Office: 6-8, rue du Quatre Septembre, 92130 Issy-les-Moulineux, France

Products: Track construction and maintenance equipment.

SRS

Swedish Rail System AB SRS

Head Office: Framnasbacken 18, PO Box 1031, S-171 21 Solna, Sweden

Telegrams: RAILSYSTEM STOCKHOLM
Telephone: 08-830660
Telex: 104 06 rail s

Managing Director: Ingvar Svensson

Products: Concrete sleepers; Hambo rail fastenings; FIST rail fastenings; machines developed for the mechanical mounting of sleepers and fastenings.

STEDEF

Head Office: 16/18 de la Republique, 92 100 Boulogne, France

Telephone: (1) 620 54 00
Telex: Rail 200 888 F

Products: Track materials and equipment including elastic fastenings.

STIRAIL

Stirail

Head Office: 8 Rue Daru, PO Box 795-08, Paris 8

Telephone: 924 07 29
Telegraphic: RSORNOR
Telex: USIDARU F 650515

Products: Rail spikes.

TAMPER

Tamper Division of Canron Limited

Head Office and Plant: 2401 Edmund Road, West Columbia, South Carolina 29169, USA

Telegrams: 610-422-3843
Telephone: 514-637-5531
Telex: 0525738

Plant and Offices: 160 St. Joseph Blvd., Lachine (Montreal), Quebec, Canada
5119 Main Street, Vancouver, BC, Canada
18 Maplehurst Rd., Winnipeg, Man., Canada
13448-113th St., Edmonton, Alberta, Canada
18 Earl Street, Airport West, Melbourne, Victoria 3042, Australia

Parts Depot: 1902 University Ave., St. Paul, Minn. 55104, USA
Telephone: 612-645-5055

Plant, Sales, Service and Parts: Tamper (Australia) Pty., Ltd., 15-19 Marshall Rd., Airport West Melbourne, Victoria 3042, Australia. Telephone: 338-3911

Agents: Argentina, Brazil, Chile, Columbia, Ecuador, France, India, Mexico, Mozambique, Peru, Uruguay, Venezuela, Spain, Sweden, Indonesia, Japan, Pakistan, Philippines, Turkey.
Tamper Inc. is further represented in most other countries. The names of representatives in the above and other countries can be obtained by contracting the head office.

Products: Automatic track levelling, tamping and lining machine, autojack electromatic tamper, autoliner, junior electromatic tamper, switch electromatic tamper, points and crossing tampers, electric hand tampers, tamping jack, ballast equaliser, independent track lifting and linking equipment for medium tampers, spike driver-spike puller, tie renewer-spike puller, switch and yard cleaning snow blower, rail and flange lubricators, universal autojack, power wrenches, rail saw, rail drill, rail bolting machine, gangers trolleys, heavy duty brush cutters, various track motor and inspection cars, push cars and trailers, light weight utility cars, universal portable set-off assembly and take off rails and a complete line of track gauges and levels, track laying equipment, track recorder analysis equipment.
Tamper Inc. manufacture a complete range of railway track maintenance of way equipment including heavy duty ballast tampers, track liners and ballast equalisers. Medium range tampers and switch tampers. Also machines for removing and inserting ties, drilling and bolting rail, pulling and driving spikes.
Effective 30 April 1969, Tamper Inc. acquired the Railway Products Division of Kalamazoo Manufacturing Company, and have taken over the manufacture and marketing of the Kalamazoo range of track maintenance equipment.

TAYLOR

Taylor Bros. (Sandicore) Ltd

Telephone: (0602) 395252

Head Office: Midland Foundry, Sandacre, Nottingham, England

Chairman: W. J. Smith
Managing Director: P. B. Dodson
Technical Director: D. V. Adams

Products: Prefabricated railway layouts, cast iron chairs, baseplates, blocks, pressed and machined junction fishplates, lever boxes and stretcher bars, insulated soleplates and joints.

THERMIT WELDING

Thermit Welding (GB) Ltd

Head Office: Ferry Lane, Rainham, Essex RM13 9DP, England

Telegrams: THERMIT DAGENHAM
Telephone: Rainham 53322
Telex: 896296/7

Products: Portable rail welding equipment; welding consumables; insulated rail joints.

TREC

Tempered Railway Equipment Co

Head Office: PO Box 20, Park Works, Foley St, Sheffield S4 7YU, England

Telephone: (0742) 20031
Telex: 54103

Products: KTG resilient rail clips.

UNIT RAIL ANCHOR

Unit Rail Anchor Company

Head Office: 2 N. Riverside Plaza 2336, Chicago Ill. 60606, USA

Telephone: 312-454-1813
Telex: 28-3407

President: J. C. Cosgrove

Products: Rail anchors, spring washers.

VÖEST-ALPINE

Vereinigte-Österreichische Eisen-Und Stahlwerke-Alpine Montan AG

Head Office: A1040 Vienna, Prinz-Eugen-Str 8-10, Austria

Telephone: 656711
Telex: 1-2683

Products: Rails, switches, fishplates, soleplates, steel and plastic sleepers.

VON ROLL

Von Roll Ltd

Head Office: Gerlafingen Works, CH4563 Gerlafingen, Switzerland

Products: Rail fastenings, points, crossings.

VOSSLOH-WERKE

Vossloh-Werke GmbH

Head Office: Postfach 1860, 5980 Werdohl 1, Austria

Telegrams: VOSSLOHWERKE
Telephone: 02392-521
Telex: 08 26 444 vauwe d

Products: Resilient rail fastenings including: Tension Clamp Skl 1 on concrete sleepers with lateral angled guide plates; Tension Clamp Skl 3 on timber sleepers with ribber plates.

WESTERN-CULLEN

Western-Cullen Division
Federal Sign and Signal Corporation

Head Office: 2700 West 36th Place, Chicago, Illinois 60632, USA

Telegrams: Wesrailsup Chicago
Telephone: (312) 254-9600

Vice-President and General Manager: R. L. Tannehill
Sales Director: R. E. Deasey

Products: "Burro" locomotive cranes, rail tongs and threaders, panel track lifters; multiple rail lifters, derails, track liners, rail benders, power drills, hand drills; "Western" (formerly Buda) hydraulic, journal and mechanical jacks, 100 models from 3 to 100 tons capacity; bumping posts, derails, vehicle warning lights.
Western-Cullen is a consolidation of the Western Railroad Supply Co., the Cullen-Friestedt Co. and the Hayes Track Appliance Co.

WICKHAM

D. Wickham & Company Ltd.

Head Office and Works: Ware, Hertfordshire, England

Telephone: Ware 2491-7
Telex: 81340

Products: A range of self-propelled railway track and overhead line inspection cars, maintenance gang trolleys, and other special purpose vehicles; also hand and push cars and track tools.

Agencies Abroad: World wide; addresses available from the company.

Countries Supplied: Angola, Argentine, Australia, Bolivia, Brazil, Burma, Cambodia, Cameroun, Canada, Chile, China, Colombia, Congo, Republic Costa Rica, Egypt, Guyana, Honduras, India, Indonesia, Iran, Ivory Coast, Jamaica, Kenya, Lebanon, Malawi, New Zealand, Nigeria, Pakistan, Paraguay, Peru, Portugal, Mozambique, Rhodesia, Sabah, South Africa, Sudan, Swaziland, Taiwan, Thailand, Trinidad, Uruguay, United Kingdom, Venezuela.

AUTOMATIC FARE SYSTEMS

ALMEX

AB Almex

Head Office: Sankt Goransgatan 160B, S-112 51 Stockholm, Sweden

Telegrams: MEXAL STOCKHOLM
Telephone: Domestic— (08) 54 02 20
International— 468 5402 20
Telex: 10646 Almex S

Products: Ticket machines, ticket cancellors, ticket vending machines, data recording ticket machines.

Chairman: S. Gustafsson
Managing Director: Per Wejke
Marketing Manager, operative: Jan-Patrik Reutersward
Marketing Manager, admin: Dan Erik Goransson

AUTOMATIC SYSTEMS

Automatic Sytems Ltd

Head Office: Brussels, Belgium

Products: Full range of gates, turnstiles and special electro-mechanical barriers, card readers, ticket dispensers.

CGA

Compagnie Generale d'Automatisme
(Consortium including Camp, Crouzet, Klein)

Head Office: 75783 Paris Cedex 16, France

Products: Automatic fare equipment based on the use of microprocessors and using multimode magnetically coded tickets; turnstile gates; automatic ticket vendors.

CONTROL SYSTEMS

Control Systems Ltd

Head Office: The Island, Uxbridge, Middlesex UBB 2UT, England

Telegrams: CONTROL SYSTEMS
Telephone: Uxbridge 51255
Telex: 22225

Products: Electronically-controlled ticket issuing systems assembled from standard modules in configurations designed for individual requirements.

Chairman: E. W. Pattle
Managing Director: E. H. Mude
Chief Sales Manager: M. C. S. Moore

Export Sales Manager: J. B. C. de Jager

CUBIC WESTERN

Cubic Western Data

Head Office: 5650 Kearny Mesa Rd, San Diego, Cal 92111, USA

Telephone: (714) 279 7400
Telex: 910 335 1550

Products: Automatic fare collection equipment including entry and exit only barriers, reversible barriers, ticket vendors, change makers, addfare machines (excess fares), ticket analysers, sorter/encoders, coin sorter/counters, control/monitor units, central audit units.

HASLER

Hasler Ltd

Head Office: Belpstrasse 23, CH-3000 Berne 14, Switzerland

Telephone: 031 652111
Telex: 32413 hawe ch

Products: Automatic ticket and money changing machines.

LANDIS & GYR

Landis & Gyr Ltd

Head Office: Victoria Rd, North Acton, London W3 6XS, England

Products: Automatic ticket vending machines based on microprocessor control logic systems working in conjunction with a needle printer.

LAAKMANN

H Laakmann K G Kartonfabrik

Head Office: 5620 Velbert-11-Langenberg, Bonsfelderstri 1-4, German Federal Republic

Telegrams: LAAKMANN LANGENBERGRHEINLAND
Telephone: 02127-3016
Telex: 08516863

Products: Tickets for automatic machines

Export Sales: R. Mollenkott

Chairman: H. W. Laakmann
Managing Director: Dr W. R. Roloff
Chief Sales Director: E. Junkersfeld

OMRON

Omron Tateisi Electronics Co

Head Office: Osaka Center Bldg, 9F, 68, 4-chome, Kita-Kyutaro-cho Higashi-ku, Osaka, Japan

Telephone: (06) 253 0481
Telex: 522 9413

Products: Automatic fare collection system including money changers, ticket vendors, ticket checking and collecting gates, ticket issuing machines, automatic fare adjuster, season ticket issuing machines.

TOSHIBA

Tokyo Shibaura Electric Co Ltd

Head Office: 1-6, Uchisaiwaicho 1 chome, Chiyoda-ku, Tokyo, 100 Japan

Telephone: 03 501 5411
Telex: J 22587, J24344, J 24576 TOSHIBA

Products: Automatic fare collection systems.

TOYO DENKI

Toyo Denki Seizo

Head Office: 7, Yaesu 5 chome, Shuo-ku, Tokyo, 104 Japan

Telegrams: YOHDEN TOKYO
Telephone: 03 272 4211
Telex: YOK (0) 222-4666/7

Products: Season ticket issuing machine, automatic ticket gate equipment.

TILTMAN LANGLEY

Head Office: Redhill Aerodrome, Redhill, Surrey RH1 5LA, England

Products: Automatic turnstile gates and associated equipment.

YARD AND TERMINAL EQUIPMENT

AABACAS

Aabacas Engineering Co Ltd

Head Office: Kelvin Road, Wallasey, Merseyside L44 7DN, England

Telegrams: Aabacas Wallasey
Telephone: 051-638-5932

Products: Double girder four point lift cranes, suitable for container terminals, manufactured in spans ranging from 25 ft to 80 ft and in safe working load capacities from 10 tons to 20 tons.

ABEX

Abex Corporation (Railroad Products Group)

Head Office: Valley Rd, Mahwah, NJ 07430, USA

Telephone: (201) 529 3450
Telex: 133335

Products: Yard control systems.

ACEC

Ateliers de Constructions Electriques de Charleroi SA

Head Office: PO Box 4, B6000 Charleroi, Belgium

Telegrams: VENTACEC CHARLEROI
Telephone: 07/36.20.20
Telex: 051.227—ACEC Charleroi

Products: Yard control systems.

ACI

ACI Systems Corporation

Head Office: 16950 Westview, So Holland, Ill 60473, USA

Products: Yard control systems including retarders.

AEG/TELEFUNKEN

AEG/Telefunken Nachrichten— und Verkehrstechnik AG Geschaeftsbereich Bahnen

Head Office: Hohenzollerndamm 150, D-1000 Berlin 33, German Federal Republic

Telegrams: ELEKTRONBAHNEN BERLIN
Telephone: (030) 828-1
Telex: 1 85 498

Products: Marshalling yard equipment; automatic humping control; control panels and desks; point machines.

AIP

American Identification Products Inc

Head Office: 143-145 58th St, Brooklyn, NY 11220, USA

Products: Yard control equipment.

ALLIS CHALMERS

Allis Chalmers

Head Office: Industrial Truck Division, 218000 S. Cicero Ave, Matteson, Illinois 60443, USA

Telephone: 312 7475151

Products: Heavy duty sideloaders and front loading forklift trucks suitable for container handling.

ALLEN

Allen Cranes (Northampton) Ltd

Head Office: Spencer Bridge Works, Northampton NN5 7DT, England

Telephone: (0604) 52242
Telex: 311264

Products: Goliath type rail mounted container cranes. Capacity up to 40 tons.

AMERICAN HOIST

American Hoist and Derrick Co

Head Office: 63 S Robert St, St Paul, Minnesota 55107, USA

Telephone: (612) 228 4321

Products: Yard mobile wagon cranes.

AMF-SASIB

AMF-Sasib SpA

Head Office: Via Di Corticella 87, 40128 Bologna, Italy

Products: Yard control equipment and retarders (conventional and computer controlled).

ANSALDO

Societa Generale Elettromeccanica SpA

Telephone: Genova 010-4105
Telex: 27098 Ansaldo Genova

Head Office: Via Nicola Lorenzi 8, Genoa, Italy

Products: Yard control equipment including retarders.

ASCHE

Asche

Head Office: Botany Estate, Soverign Way, Tonbridge, Kent, England

Telegrams: CONJACK TONBRIDGE
Telephone: 63377/8/9
Telex: 95516

Products: Terminal tractors trailer systems, container handling equipment for lifting and transporting of containers and stuffing of containers.

ASEA

ASEA Mechanical Products Division

Head Office: Fack, S-251 01 Helsingborg, Sweden

Telegrams: ASEA Helsingborg
Telephone: Helsingborg (042) 13 93 00
Telex: 72330 (ASEAHA)

Products: Railway terminal gantry cranes for container handling; yard conveyance systems.

ASI

Algemene Sein Industrie BV

Head Office: Croeselaan 28, Utrecht, Netherlands

Telegrams: GENRASIG UTRECHT
Telephone: (030) 94 26 46
Telex: 47455 grasi nl

Products: Yard control equipment and retarders.

BABCOCK & WILCOX

Babcock & Wilcox Espanola

Head Office: Alda de Recalde 27, Bilbao 9, Spain

Telephone: 415700
Telex: 33776

Products: Container handling cranes with 50 tonnes lift capacity above the spreader.

BASF WYANDOTTE

BASF Wyandotte Corporation (Chemical Specialities Div)

Head Office: 1532 Biddle Ave Wyandotte, Missouri 48192, USA

Telephone: (313) 282 3300

Products: Rolling stock cleaning equipment.

BATTIONI & PAGANI

BP—Battioni & Pagani SpA

Head Office: Localita Croce, 43058 Sorbolo, Parma, Italy

Telephone: 69157
Telex: 53081

Products: A complete range of side loaders including container handling machines up to 45 ton capacity equipped with telescopic spreaders.

BROWN BOVERI

Brown, Boveri & Company Ltd

Head Office and Works: Baden, Switzerland

Telegrams: BROWNBOVERI BADENSCHWEIZ
Telephone: (056) 75 11 11

Products: Radio remote control of shunting locomotives.

CLARK CHAPMAN

Clark Chapman Ltd

Head Office: Crane & Bridge Division, Woodeson House, Rodley, Leeds LS13 1HN, England

Telegrams: Cranes Rodley
Telephone: Pudsey 79001
Telex: 55159 Cranes Rodley

Products: Container transporter cranes, Goliath transporter cranes, all types of bridge cranes and other cranes.

CLYDE
Clyde Engineering Co Pty Ltd

Head Office: Factory St, Granville, NSW 2142, PO Box 73, Australia

Telephone: 682 2111
Telex: 21647

Products: Yard control equipment, including retarders.

CONLIFT
Conlift Container Hebegerate GmbH & Co

Head Office: D 6982 Freudenberg, 3 Josef Haamann Strasse, German Federal Republic

Telephone: 09375 333
Telex: 689224

Products: Container handling straddle carriers; jacks and stilts and mobile gantries.

COLES
Coles Cranes Ltd

Head Office: Harefield, Uxbridge, Middlesex UB9 6QG, England

Telephone: Harefield 3777
Telex: 21619

Products: Coles mobile port tower and mobile port cranes equipped with appropriate spreaders for handling freight containers in ports, rail yards and inland container terminals.

CONRAD/STORK
Conrad-Stork BV
(Member of VMF-Stork Group)

Head Office: Waaderweg 80, PO Box 134, Haarlem, Netherlands

Telephone: (023) 319170
Telex: 41048

Products: Ship-shore container cranes, bridge type container stacking cranes and multi-purpose cranes.

COSTAMASNAGA
Costamasnaga SpA

Head Office: 22041 Costamasnaga (Como) Italy

Telephone: 85.51.92
Telex: 38184

Products: Container handling crane for rail and sea terminals.

DICKERTMANN
Gebr Dickertmann Hebezeugfabrik AG

Head Office: PO Box 2109, Hakenort 47, 4800 Bielefeld 1, German Federal Republic

Telegrams: GEDI D
Telephone: 0521/323021
Telex: 09 32 750 gedi d

Products: Gedi shunting winch type 289; screw jacks type 370 for lifting locomotives, wagons and other heavy loads; lifting equipment for complete trains.

DIMETAL
Dimetal SA

Head Office: San Fernando de Henares, Apartado Correos 14.485, Madrid 5, Spain

Telephone: 294 6000

Products: Yard control signalling equipment.

ELLCON/NATIONAL
Ellcon-National Inc

Head Office: 30 King Rd, Totowa, NJ 07512, USA

Telephone: (201) 256 7110

Products: Rolling stock washing equipment.

ERICSSON
Telefonaktietbolaget L.M. Ericsson

Telegrams: ELLEMSIGNAL

Telephone: 08 1900 90
Telex: 10442 LMEMI S

Products: Yard communications and signalling control equipment.

ERNEST HOLMES
Ernest Holmes Division (Dover Corporation)

Head Office: Railroad Crane Dept, 2505 E 43rd St, Chattanooga, TN 37407, USA

Telephone: (615) 867 2142

Products: Yard cranes.

FERGUSSON
Alex C. Fergusson Company

Head Office: Spring Mill Dr, Frazer, Pennsylvania 19355, USA

Telephone: (215) 647 3300

Products: Whistlclean rolling stock cleaning equipment.

GRAEMROSS
Graemross Plant and Equipment Ltd

Head Office: Automation House, Rosebery Rd, Anstey, Leicester LE7 7EJ, England

Telephone: Anstey (053 721) 4248
Telex: 35694

Products: Equipment for wagon handling including wagon controllers, Hydrabrakes, automatic wheel and buffer stops and sqeezer retarders.

GODWIN WARREN
Godwin Warren Engineering Ltd

Head Office: Emery Rd, Bristol BS4 5PN, England

Telephone: 0272 778399
Telex: 449375

Products: Yard control and signalling equipment.

GRS
General Railway Signal Co

Head Office: PO Box 600, Rochester, NY 14602, USA

Telephone: (716) 436 2020

Products: Yard control systems.

HAUHINCO
Hauhinco Maschinenfabrik G. Hausherr Jochums GmbH & Co KG

Head Office: Zweigertstr 28/30, PO Box 639, D-4300 Essen, German Federal Republic

Telegrams: HAUINCO ESSEN
Telephone: 0201 771071
Telex: 857 834 hinco d

Products: Wagon shunting equipment for classification and sorting tracks at marshalling yards and industrial sites; the Hauhinco Handling System 73, adopted in Deutsche Bundesbahn's new high capacity Maschen yard, comprises two basic conveying units: 1) a clearance conveyor which keeps tracks free for further shunting; 2) linking unit which accepts incoming wagons and links them in sets for coupling.

HUDSWELL
Hudswell, Clarke & Co Ltd

Head Office: Darlington, Co Durham, England

Telegrams: WILLIAMS DARLINGTON
Telephone: Darlington 2722
Telex: 58421

Products: Yard control equipment.

HUNGARIAN SHIPYARDS
Hungarian Shipyards

Head Office: Budapest, XIII, Vaci ut 202, Hungary

Telephone: 200-800
Telex: 22 5047

Products: Container gantry cranes.

HYSTER
Hyster Europe Ltd

Head Office: PO Box 54, Berk House, Basing View, Basingstoke, Hants RG21 2HQ, England

Telephone: Basingstoke 61171
Telex: Basingstoke 858384

Products: Lift Trucks for handling 20 ft, 30 ft and 40 ft ISO containers.

IHI
Ishikawajima-Harima Heavy Industries Co Ltd

Head Office: New Ohtemachi Building, 2-chome 2-1 Ohtemachi, Chiyoda-ku, Tokyo 100, Japan

Cables: IHICO TOKYO
Telephone: (03) 244-6496
Telex: J22232

Products: Standard dockside container crane; Multipurpose dockside container crane (IHI's Universe); Speed Tainer System.

INTEGRA

Integra Ltd Zurich

Head Office: Industriestrasse 42, Ch 8304 Wallisellen, Zurich, Switzerland

Telegrams: INTEGRA WALLISELLEN
Telephone: Zurich 931915
Telex: 56022 tegra CH

Products: DOMINO unit construction panels for marshalling yard control systems.

JAMBES/NAMUR

Ateliers de Construction de Jambes-Namur SA

Head Office: B-5100 Jambes, Belgium

Products: Shunting machine "Locopulseur Pulso"; transporters; elevators; trucks.

Managing Director: Jean Md.
Chief of sales: André Riquette

Telephone: (081) 318.51
Telegrams: Jamur-Jambes
Telex: 59127 Jamur-Jambes

Recent sales: During the last two years, Locopulseur Pulso machines were sold to Spanish National Railways (RENFE), French National Railways (SNCF), Kolmex, Poland, Algerian steel companies, Jeumont Schneider, Belgian National Railways (SNCB), Italian State Railways (FS).
Equipment: The Locopulseur Pulso shunting machine is a single-wheel vehicle capable of moving freight cars weighing 160-200 tons on straight level track. It can also move cars in curves, split a line of cars and handle a car on a turntable. Power is supplied by a 490 cc (29.9 cu in) Lombardini single-cylinder 4-stroke petrol engine (tyres 602 L and 602 LH) or by a 510 cc Lombardini single-cylinder 4-stroke Diesel engine (types 602 LD, 602 LDex, 602 LHD, 602 LHDex). The types LDex and LHDex are explosion proof. The engine is controlled with automatic throttle regulator. The driving wheel has a special profile high-pressure pneumatic tyre to fit over and grip the rail. The 4-speed gearbox is pre-selective; a Fr:27 planetry reduction gear is fitted in the wheel hub. Two small side-wheels allow easy handling. The machine is designed to provide, through the driving wheel, the grip and power necessary for propulsion.
On the types 602 L, LD and LDex, the "pushing head" is raised into position by a hand-operated mechanical device. The types 602 LH, LHD and LHDex, incorporate a hydraulic system for raising the head, involving no operator effort. A special version of the "H" series includes more powerful hydraulic equipment acting on a 5 hp hydraulic motor. From 1977, the Belgian made machines can be fitted with a compressor to actuate the compressed air brakes of the shunted wagons and also to inflate the Locopulsor tyre at the correct pressure. Type 602 L weighs 440 lb (200 kg); type 602 LH weight 480 lb (220 kg). Consumption: 3½ pints of petrol or gas oil per hour.

JONES

Jones Cranes Limited

Head Office: PO Box 13, Letchworth, Herts SG6 1LU, England

Telegrams: Jones, Letchworth
Telephone: Letchworth (04626) 2360
Telex: 82112

Products: Mobile, crawler tracked and truck-mounted cranes with lifting capacities up to 45 tons.

KONE

Kone Oy Crane Division, Hyvinkää, Finland

Head Office: Munkkiniemen Kartan, Helsinki 33, Finland

Telegrams: Kone
Telephone: Hyvinkää 13700
Telex: 15-122 or 12-466

Products: Container handling dockside cranes, multipurpose cranes, twin container cranes, railway terminal gantry cranes, cargo and container handling gantry cranes, container storage cranes, overhead travelling cranes for containers and other loads.

KYOSAN

Kyosan Electric Manufacturing Co Ltd

Head Office: 4-2 Marunouchi 3-chome, Chiyoda-Ku, Tokyo, Japan

Products: Yard control equipment.

LETOURNEAU

Marathon Letourneau Company
(Subsidiary of Marathon Manufacturing Company, Longview Division)

Head Office: PO Box 2307, Longview, Texas 75601, USA

Telephone: 214 753-4411
Telex: MARLET LGV 730 371

Products: Gantry Cranes and the 'Letro Porter' handling equipment for containers and piggyback trailers.

LIEBHERR

Liebherr Container Cranes Ltd

Head Office: Killarney, Co Kerry, Republic of Ireland

Telephone: 31511
Telex: 6946

Products: Liebherr manufactures ship to shore cranes with wide spans. Span to outreach is approximately 1 : 1. Typically 100 ft (30 m) with optional outreach over the water of up to 115 ft (35 m).
Rail terminal cranes have spans between 34 ft (11 m)-140 ft (44 m) and travel speeds up to 300 ft/min (100 m/min), with or without overhang on either side.

MARINE ELECTRIC

Marine Electric Railway Products Div, Inc

Head Office: 166 National Rd, Edison, NJ 08817, USA

Telephone: (201) 287 2810
Telex: 833351

Products: Marshalling yard communication systems

MODERN INDUSTRIES

Modern Industries Inc

Head Office: 101 Outer Loop, PO Box 14287, Louisville, Kentucky, USA

Products: Yard control equipment.

MITSUBISHI

Mitsubishi Heavy Industries Ltd

Head Office: 5-1 Marunouchi 2 chome, Chiyoda Ku, Tokyo, Japan

Telephone: (03) 212 3111
Telex: J22443 (HISHISU)
Products: Straddle carrier, gantry cranes and skeletal semi-trailers.

NIPPON SIGNAL

Nippon Signal Co Ltd

Head Office: 3-1 Marunouchi, 3-chome, Chiyoda-Ku, Tokyo, Japan

Products: Yard control equipment including retarders; remote control radio communication equipment.

NOORD/NEDERLANDSCHE

Noord-Nederlandsche Machinefabriek BV

Head Office: ST Vitusstraat 81, PO Box 171, Winschoten, Netherlands

Telephone: 05970 9223
Telex: 53096

Products: Road/rail range of Trackmobile shunting units.

PACECO

Paceco, a Division of Fruehauf Corp

Headquarters: 2350 Blanding Avenue, Alameda, California, 94501 USA

Telephone: (415) 522-6100
Telex: 335-399

Products: Rubber-tyred and railmounted Transtainers for handling loads up to 50 tons; Universal lifting spreaders; Shiptainer cranes; Portainer pierside handling crane.

PEINER

Peiner Maschinen-und Schraubenwerke AG

Head Office: 315 Peine, PO Box 1649, German Federal Republic

Telegrams: Peinerag Peiner
Telephone: (05171) 431
Telex: 09 2662/63 peined

Products: Peiner container cranes; PPH32D 325 and 335 straddle carriers; spreaders, harbour and wharf cranes, grabs, scaffolding equipment, nuts and bolts.

PENETONE

Penetone Corporation

Head Office: 74 Hudson Ave, Tenafly NJ 07670, USA

Telephone: (800) 631 1652

Products: Rolling stock cleaning equipment.

ROSS AND WHITE

The Ross and White Company

Head Office: 50 W Dundee Rd, Wheeling, Ill 60090, USA

Telephone: (312) 537 0060

Products: Railway sand handling equipment including cleaning, drying, storage and delivery of sand to locomotives; Buck Cyclone Cleaners for rail passenger coach interiors incorporating high-pressure, high volume hand guns; brush scrubbing systems for passenger coach exteriors; pressure washing equipment for locomotives.

RUBERY OWEN

Rubery Owen Conveyancer Ltd

Head Office: PO Box 24, Thornton Road, Warrington WA5 1QT, England

Telegrams: Rocon/Warrington
Telephone: (0925) 35922
Telex: 62375

Products: Straddle carriers and mobile gantry cranes for container handling.

SAFETRAN
Safetran Systems Corporation

Head Office: 7721 National Turnpike, Louisville, Kentucky 40214

Telephone: (502) 361 1691

Products: Marshalling yard communication systems.

SAXBY
Saxby

Head Office: 40 Rue de l'Orillon, 75011 Paris, France

Telephone: 357 65 30
Telex: 220554F

Products: Yard control equipment and retarders.

SEL
Standard ELEKTRIK Lorenz AG

Head Office: Hellmuth-Hirth-Str 42, 7000 Stuttgart-Zuffenhausen, German Federal Republic

Telephone: (0711) 8211
Telex: 7 211-0

Products: Mobile radio equipment; automatic humping control; yard control equipment.

SERVO
Servo Corporation of America

Head Office: 111 New South Rd, Hicksville, NY 11802, USA

Telephone: (516) 938 9700

Products: Marshalling yard communication systems.

SIEMENS
Siemens Aktiengesellschaft

Head Office: Ackerstrasse 22, 33 Brunswick, German Federal Republic

Telephone: 706-1
Telex: 9 52 858

Products: Yard control equipment and retarders.

SIGNAUX ET D'ENTERPRISES ELECTRIQUE CIE DE
Head Office: 2-8 Rue Caroline, 75850, Paris Cedex 17, France

Telephone: 387 39 29
Telex: 650519

Products: Yard control equipment.

SMITH BROS & WEBB
Smith Bros & Webb Ltd

Head Office: Brittannia Works, Arden Forest, Industrial Estate, Alcester, Warwickshire, England

Products: Train washing systems including the Britannia fully-automatic train washer.

STEELE
E. G. Steele & Co Ltd

Head Office: 25 Dalziel St, Hamilton, Lanarkshire, Scotland

Telegrams: MOUNTINGS HAMILTON
Telephone: Hamilton 22601
Telex: 77454

Associated Company: SA Ateliers de Construction de Jambes-Namur, Belgium; Noord-Nederlandsche Machinefabriek BV, Winschoten, The Netherlands.

Products: Locopulsor shunting machines; Trackmobiles; wagon mountings.

STOTHERT & PITT LTD
Head Office: PO Box 25, Bath, BA2 3DJ

Telegrams: Stothert, Bath, England
Telephone: Bath 63401
Telex: 44311

Products: Telescopic spreader beams, twin lift spreader beams, automatic or manual fixed length spreader beams. Goliath cranes for container marshalling and for loading on road/rail transport. Quayside transporter cranes for loading container vessels. Jib cranes for container handling.

TAKRAF
VVB Takraf

Head Office: 701 Leipzig, German Democratic Republic

Telephone: 7 92 20
Telex: 051577

Products: Container transporters and stackers. Side-loading inter transport transfer devices. Railway wrecking and general purpose cranes.

TOKYO SHIBUARA
Tokyo Shibuara Electric Co Ltd

Head Office: 1-1 Uchisaiwai-cho, Chiyoda-ku, Tokyo, Japan

Products: Yard control equipment including retarders.

TRANSCONTROL
Transcontrol Corp

Head Office: 68 Sintsink Dr E PO Box 389, Port Washington, NY 11050, USA

Telephone: (516) 883 6900

Products: Yard control systems.

TYSOL
Tysol Products Inc

Head Office: 200 E Walton Place, Chicago, III 60611, USA

Telephone: (312) 642 4823

Products: Rolling stock cleaning equipment.

UNILOKOMOTIVE
Unilokomotive Ltd (International Division)

Head Office: 46-49 Upper O'Connell St, Dublin 1, Republic of Ireland

Telegrams: LOCOMOTIVE DUBLIN
Telephone: 744953, 744958, 743576
Telex: 31128, 20559

Production and international sales were taken over from the Hugo Aeckerle Co of Hamburg in 1976 and all sales and production are now controlled from Dublin.

Products: Unilok road/rail switching locomotives for industrial and railway siding work: 17 sizes with tractive effort beginning at 5000 kg and rising to 15 000 kg for loads ranging from 400 tonnes to 2 500 tonnes. Uniloks are built for all gauges and all coupler systems. The machines are now in rail service with 55 countries.

VALMET
Valmet Oy

Head Office: Tampere Works, 33101 Tampere 10 Helsinki, Finland

Telephone: (931) 653 322
Telex: 22-112 valle sf

Products: Straddle carriers of standard and special design and forklift trucks suitable for container handling.

VOLLERT
Hermann Vollert KG Maschinenfabrik

Head Office: 7102 Weinsberg/Wurtt, German Federal Republic

Telephone: 0728/736

Products: Shunting robot offering radio control and high tractive power.

WABCO/UNION SWITCH
WABCO/Union Switch & Signal Division

Head Office: 3 Gateway Center, Pittsburgh, PA 15222, USA

Telephone: (412) 471 3241

Products: Yard control systems and retarders.

WABCO WESTINGHOUSE
Head Office: 207 Boulevard de Souverain, B1160, Brussels, Belgium

Telephone: 73.60.53

Products: Two-way radio equipment; yard control systems and retarders.

WESTERN/CULLEN
Western-Cullen Division (Federal Sign and Signal Corp)

Head Office: 2 700, West 36th Place, Chicago, III 60632, USA

Products: Yard control equipment including retarders.

WESTERN INDUSTRIES
Western Industries (Pty) Ltd

Head Office: 41-43 Troye St, Johannesburg, PO Box 10554, South Africa

Telephone: 22-0716
Telex: 8-0074

Products: Yard control equipment, including retarders.

WESTINGHOUSE

Westinghouse Brake and Signal Co Ltd

Sales Office: Chippenham, Wiltshire, England

Telephone: Chippenham 4141
Telex: 44941

Products: Yard control equipment.

WHITING

Whiting Corporation

Head Office: 15621 Lathrop Ave, Harvey, III 60426, USA

Telephone: (312) 331 4000

Products: Yard control systems; jacks; Hydrabrake car speed retarder; train washing systems; Trackmobile wagon movers; transfer table with remote car movers.

ZAGRO

Zagro Bahn— und Baumaschinen GmbH

Head Office: D 6927 Bad Rappenau-Grombach, Muhlstr 13 German Federal Republic

Telegrams: ZAGRO
Telephone: 07266/458
Telex: 782381

Products: Yard shunting system incorporating special rail mounted chassis powered by an unmodified fork-lift truck.

ZONE CONTROLS

Zone Controls Ltd

Head Office: PO Box 22, Building 39, Pensnett Trading Estate, Brierley Hill, Staffs, DY6 7PN, England

Telephone: 038 44 70171
Telex: 338359

Products: Yard control equipment.

WORKSHOP EQUIPMENT

ALZMETALL

Machine Tool Factory and Foundry Friedrich & Co

Head Office: D-8226 Altenmarkt/Alz, German Federal Republic

Telephone: 08621/881
Telex: 05 63124

Products: Drilling machines, boring mills.

BAHCO VENTILATION

Bahco Ventilation Ltd

Head Office: Bahco House, Beaumont Rd, Banbury, Oxon OX 16 7TB, England

Telephone (0295) 57461
Telex: 837567

Products: Workshop heating systems.

CAM INDUSTRIES

Cam Industries Inc
(Peerless Tool Division)

Head Office: 215 Philadelphia St, PO Box 227, Hanover, PA 17331, USA

Telegrams: CAM
Telephone: 717 637 5988
Telex: 840-470

Products: Workshop equipment for electric motor and generator repair shop.

Managing Director: Charles A. McGough

DICKERTMANN

Gebr Dickertmann Hebzeugfabrik AG

Head Office: 48 Bielefeld, German Federal Republic

Telephone: 6 80 05
Telex: 09 32 750

Products: Spindle lifting Jacks, underfloor elevators, bogie lifting platforms, various types of hoist.

HEGENSCHEIDT

W. Hegenscheidt

Head Office: 514 Erkelenz/Brd, Postfach 2109, 4800 Bielefeld 1, German Federal Republic

Telephone: (02431) 6011

Products: Wheel set reconditioning and wheel boring machinery including a full wheel set reconditioning line.

PROBAT

Probat-Werke

Head Office: Emmerich/Rhein, German Federal Republic

Telegrams: PROBAT EMMERICH
Telephone: 25 61
Telex: 8 125 154

Products: Spring testing machines.

WAGNER

Gustav Wagner Maschinenfabrik

Head Office: Postfach 113, 741 Reutlingen, German Federal Republic

Telephone: 07121/2081
Telex: 0729846

Products: Rail sawing and drilling machines.

YVAC

Yvac Company Inc

Head Office: 1 World Trade Center, New York, NY 10048, Suite 1713, USA

Telegrams: YVACCOMP
Telephone: 432 0192

Products: Designers and builders of railroad shop facilities.

CONTAINER MANUFACTURERS

ACKERMAN / FRUEHAUF GMBH

Head Office: 5600 Wuppertal-Vohwinkel, Ludwig-Richter-Str 1-9, Postfach 110 117, German Federal Republic

Telephone: (02121) 73 20 81
Telex: 0859 1754

Products: Containers for the transport of standard European railway pallets; part of a demountable body system known as Eurotainers.

ADAMSON CONTAINERS LTD

Head Office: Station Rd, Reddish, Stockport, Cheshire, England

Telephone: (061) 432 0211
Telex: 668174

Products: All-steel, all-welded freight containers constructed to ISO standards and conforming to UIC regulations.

BEHALTER und APPARATEBAU ERICH WOLFF GMBH & CO

Head Office: 7100 Heilbronn/Neckar, Lichtenberger Str 24, German Federal Republic

Telephone: (07131) 10981

Products: ISO tank containers.

BRAIDESI

Costruzioni Meccaniche Braidesi SpA
Via XXIV, Maggio 10, 12042 BRA (Cunero), Italy
Telephone: 43611
Telex: 21366

Products: Open and tilt type steel dry freight containers.

BREMER

Bremer Waggonbau

Head Office: Pfalzburger Str 251, PO Box 110 109, 2800 Bremen, German Federal Republic
Telephone: (0421) 454011
Products: Dry freight and insulated ISO containers.

BRUGEOISE

SA La Brugeoise et Nivelles

Head Office: B 8 201, Saint-Michiels, Belgium

Telephone: 050 330721-51
Telex: 811.22 BNBRGE

Products: General purpose, insulated and refrigerated containers.

BUDD

The Budd Company

Head Office: Trailer Division Headquarters, Dowington, Pa 19335, USA

Telephone: 458 5301

Products: Aluminium and plastic/plywood, refrigerated and insulated containers.

BUTTERFIELD

W. P. Butterfield Ltd

Head Office: PO Box 38, Shipley, Yorks, England

Telephone: (0274) 52244.
Telex: 51583

Products: 20 and 30 ft ISO tank containers.

BREL

British Rail Engineering Ltd

Head Office: 274/280 Bishopsgate, London EC2 4XQ, England

Telephone: (01) 247 5444
Telex: 885353 BREBIS-G

Products: Full Range of all-steel dry freight containers.

BSL

Bignier Schmid-Laurent

Head Office: 25, quai Marcel Boyer, BP 205, 94201 Ivry S/Seine, France

Products: 20, 30 and 40 ft stainless-steel tank containers supplied for Transcontainer Express and Eurotainer services.

COMET

Comet Corporation

Head Office: N 3808 Sullivan Rd, Spokane, Washington 99216, USA

Telephone: (509) 924 4800
Telex: 510 773 2143

Products: Dry freight and refrigerated containers supplied to Alaska Railroad.

CONTAINER SAFE

Container Safe AB

Head Office: PO Box 5031, S 42105 Vastra Frolunda, Gothenburg, Sweden

Telephone: 292 130
Telex: 21085

Products: 20 and 40 ft ISO containers supplied to Swedish State Railways.

CRANE FRUEHAUF

Crane Fruehauf Containers Ltd

Head Office: Cromer Rd, North Walsham, Norfolk, England

Telephone: (06924) 3411
Telex: 97366

Products: Dry freight, insulated and refrigerated containers; Tilt-tainers, container tanks, hopper container tanks to ISO, TIR, Lloyds, ABS and UIC standards.

CRAVEN TASKER

Craven Tasker (Sheffield) Ltd

Head Office: Staniforth Rd, Darnall, Sheffield S9411, England

Telephone: (0742) 99301
Telex: 54281

Products: Standard containers.

DAVIS

W. H. Davis & Sons Ltd
St Annes Building, 349 Clifton Drive North, St Annes-on-Sea, Lancs FY8 2NA, England
Telephone: (0253) 729912
Telex: 67641

Products: Multistack 20, 30 and 40 ft dry freight containers.

DORSEY

Dorsey Trailers

Head Office: Elba, Alabama 36323, USA

Telephone: (205) 897 2241
Telex: 810 744 3110

Products: Dry freight and refrigerated containers.

DURAMIN

Duramin Engineering Co Ltd

Head Office: Harbour Rd, Lydney, Glos GL15 4EN, England

Telephone: (05944) 2371-8
Telex: 43289

Products: Insulated refrigerated, temperature controlled, semi-insulated dry freight containers; principal users include British Rail.

EIMAR

Constructora de Equipos Industriales y Marinos, SA

Head Office: Poligono Industrial de Malpica, Calles A-D, Zaragoza, Spain

Telephone: 299350
Telex: 58163

Products: ISO steel dry freight containers.

FINSAM

Finsam A/S

Head Office: PO Box 3064, Elinesberg, Oslo 2, Norway

Telephone: (02) 441860
Telex: 18050

Products: Containers and refrigerating systems.

FREIGHT BONALLACK

Freight Bonallack Ltd

Head Office: Fifers Lane, Norwich, Norfolk NR6 6ET, England

Telephone: (0603) 49241
Telex: 97117

Products: Insulated and refrigerated containers.

FREIGHTER

Freighter Industries Ltd

Head Office: 409 St Kilda Rd, Melbourne 3004, Victoria 3004, Australia

Telephone: (03) 267 3888
Telex: Escor AA 31148

Products: 20 ft and 40 ft all steel containers designed for Australian inter-road/rail transport; principal owners include Australian National Railways.

FRIGOR
Frigor Koleanlaeg, Tage W. Nielsen A/S

Head Office: Hvam, DK, 8620 Kjellerup, Denmark

Telephone: (06) 667300
Telex: 6 62 09

Products: ISO insulated containers with all-welded steel frames.

FRUEHAUF
Fruehauf Division

Head Office: 10900 Harper Ave, Detroit, Michigan 48232, USA

Telephone: (313) 267 1000
Telex: 23 5351

Products: All sizes and types of dry freight, insulated and refrigerated tank, platform and open top containers.

FRUEHAUF FRANCE

Head Office: 2 Ave de L'Aunette, 91 Ris-Orange (Essonne), France

Telephone: 906 12 94
Telex: Fruehauf Risor 69967

Products: Steel, aluminium alloy and GRP plywood and GRP plastic containers in addition to tank units, refrigerated units and flat and tilt containers.

GRAAFF
Graaff Kommanditgesellschaft

Head Office: Postfach 160-180, 3210 Elze (Han), German Federal Republic

Telephone: (05124) 2041
Telex: 0927168

Products: Dry freight, insulated, refrigerated, top loading and tank containers.

GRANGES GRAVER
SA Granges Graver BV

Head Office: Molenweg 107, B-2660 Willebroek, Belgium

Telephone: 031 86 71 11
Telex: 31 293

Products: 20, 30 and 40 ft aluminium tilt containers for transporting dry chemicals.

GREAT DANE
Great Dane Trailers Inc

Head Office: PO Box 67, Savannah, Georgia 31402, USA

Telephone: (912) 232 4471

Products: Refrigerated containers.

HANSA
Hansa Waggonbau GmbH

Head Office: 2800 Bremen 11, Pfalzburger Str 251, Postfach 110 109, German Federal Republic

Telephone: 45 40 11
Telex: 0244423

Products: Dry freight plastics/plywood ISO containers.

HUNGARIAN SHIPYARDS
Hungarian Shipyards and Crane Factory

Head Office: Budapest XIII, Vaci ut 202, Hungary

Telephone: 200-800
Telex: 22-5047

Products: 20 ft all steel containers and 20 ft tank containers built to ISO, UIC and TIR standards; production is approved by the Hungarian State Railways (MAV).

LUCHAIRE
Lunchaire SA

Head Office: Department Conteneurs, 180 blvd Haussman 75382 Paris, Cedex 08, France

Telephone: 924 6344
Telex: 650312

Products: 20 ft ISO containers; French National Railways (SNCF) are among the principal users.

LUTHER-WERKE
Luther-werke GmbH & Co

Head Office: Containertechnik GmbH & Co, 2000 Hamburg, 2 Heilwigstr 75, German Federal Republic

Telephone: 460 2031
Telex: 213571 1whh

Products: Tank containers, standard and non-standard dry freight containers.

McARDLE
Thomas McArdle Ltd

Head Office: Industrial Estate, Coe's Rd, Dundalk, Republic of Ireland

Telephone: (042) 35533
Telex: 4572

Products: Full range of containers to ISO standards and conforming to UIC requirements.

MITSUBISHI
Mitsubishi Heavy Industries Ltd

Head Office: 5-1 Marunouchi 2 chome, Chiyoda-ku, Tokyo, Japan

Telephone: (03) 213 3111
Telex: 52282

Products: Aluminium, plywood and steel dry freight containers.

MORTEO SOPREFIN
Morteo Soprefin SpA

Head Office: Corso Andrea Podesta 8, 16128 Genoa, Italy

Telephone: 593261
Telex: 27570 Morteo

Products: Dry freight and refrigerated all steel containers to ISO and UIC standards.

PACTON
Pacton BV

Head Office: PO Box 50, Strangeweg 1, Ommen, Netherlands

Telephone: (05) 291 15 0 0
Telex: 42199

Products: Dry freight, tank and special-purpose containers.

SNAV
Societe Nouvelle des Ateliers de Venissieux

Head Office: Chemin du Genie, 69631 Venissieux, PO Box 4, France

Telephone: (78) 72851
Telex: 340603F

Products: Steel, aluminium, plywood containers to ISO, UIC and TIR standards.

SOUTH AFRICAN RAILWAYS

Head Office: Paul Kruger Building, Wolmarans St, Johannesburg, South Africa

Products: ISO type three and six-metre containers for dry freight.

STEADMAN
Steadman Container Ltd

Head Office: 150 Glidden Rd, Brampton, Ont L6W 3L2, Canada

Telephone: (416) 457 9700
Telex: 05-97536

Products: 20 and 40 ft steel and aluminium containers, insulated units, heated and tank containers.

STRICK
Strick Corporation

Head Office: US Highway No 1, Fiarless Hills, Pa 19030, USA

Telephone: (215) 949 3600
Telex: 84-3412

Products: Full range of dry freight containers together with insulated and refrigerated units.

THYSSEN

Thyssen Behalter und Logertechnik

Head Office: Postfach 20, 5758 Frondenberg-Langschede, German Federal Republic

Telephone: (02378) 3031 821
Telex: 0 858 7965

Products: Full range of dry freight, refrigerated and insulated containers conforming to ISA, ASA, UIC, TIR and DIN standards.

TOKYU

Tokyu Car Corporation

Head Office: Container sales, Yaesu-Mitsui Bldg, 7-5 Chome, Yaesu, Chuo-Ku, Tokyo, Japan

Telephone: 272 7051
Telex: 0222 2220

Products: Steel and GRP/plywood dry freight and refrigerated containers.

TRAILOR

Trailor SA

Head Office: 3 Route No. 10, Coignieres 78, France

Telephone: 050 61 26
Telex: 69.896f trailco coigns

Products: Dry freight 20, 30 and 40 ft containers to UIC standards.

WEW

Westerwalder Eisenwerk Gerhard GmbH

Head Office: 5241 Weitefeld/Sieg, German Federal Republic

Telephone: (02747) 2171
Telex: 0875323

Products: Tank containers for the transport of hazardous and non-hazardous liquids, granula bulk solids and gases.

YORK

York Trailer Co Ltd

Head Office: Northallerton, Yorkshire, England

Telephone: (0609) 3155
Telex: 58600

Products: All-steel containers.

TABULATED DATA

NAME OF COMPANY ADDRESS	Gauge ft. in. (metres)	Route length incl. E=Electrified miles (km.)	Track length incl. E=Electrified miles (km.)	Elect. system and type of conductor	Loco-motives L=Line S=Shunt Steam Electric Diesel De=elec. Dh=hyd.	Rail-cars Electric Diesel Trailer Railbus Multiple Unit set	Pass. train cars	Freight train cars Con-tainers	Freight movement Total Volume carried. Thous-ands of tonnes	Av'ge haul per ton miles (km.)	Av'ge net train load tonnes	Max. trailing load tonnes	Passengers Total number carried in 1 000's	Aver-age jour-ney miles (km.)

ALBANIA
**Albanian State Railways
Hekurudha e Shqiërisë, Tirana — Gauge 4' 8½" (1·435)

ALGERIA
**Société Nationale Chemins de Fer Algériens (SNCFA)
21-23 blvd Mohamed V, Algiers
Gauge 4' 8½" (1·435); Route length 2 429 (3 912); Track length E 185 (299); Elect. 3 000 V dc; Locos E 37, De 165; Railcars D 37, T 69; Total Volume carried 6 400; Av'ge haul 173 000 ton-km; Total number carried 10 220

C.F. de Tebessa à Djebel-Onk
Bir-el-Ater
(Operated by SNCFA) — Route length 67 (107)

ANGOLA
**Caminho de Ferro de Benguela
(Benguela Railway Company)
C.P. 32, Lobito
Gauge 3' 6" (1·067); Route 810 (1 304); Track (1 664); Locos SL 95, DeL 10, SS 12, DhS 6; Pass. train cars 54; Freight train cars 1 838; Total Volume 2 383·7; Av'ge haul 2 427 738 ton-km; Average journey 1·9

Caminho de Ferro do Amboim
Avenido Infante Santo,
Lisbon, Portugal
Local office: Porto Amboim
Gauge 1' 11⅝" (0·600); Route 77 (123); Track 78 (126); Locos SL 5, DS 2; Railcars D 4; Pass. train cars 6; Freight train cars 73; Total Volume 8·0; Av'ge haul 598 218 383 ton-km; Average journey 34·2

Direcção dos Servicos de Portos, Caminhos de Ferro e Transportes
Gauge 3' 6" (1·067) / 1' 11⅝" (0·600); Route 558 (899); Locos DeL 37, DhL 19, DhS 10; Railcars D 5; Pass. train cars 18; Freight train cars 25; Total Volume 6 408·5; Av'ge haul 563 343 824 ton-km; Average journey 394·1

Caminhos de Ferro de Luanda
Caixa Postal 1229
Luanda
Gauge 3' 6" (1·067) / 1' 11⅝" (0·600); Route 263 (424) / 19 (31); Track 324 (521); Locos SL 23, DeS 8, DhS 11; Railcars D 6, DT 3; Pass. train cars 38; Freight train cars 569; Max. trailing load 1 100; Total number carried 728·3

Caminho de Ferro de Moçamedes
Caixa Postal 130, Sá da Bandeira
Gauge 3' 6" (1·067); Route 536 (863); Track 623 (1 003); Locos De 37, Dh 17, Dm 9; Railcars D 5; Pass. train cars 16; Freight train cars 1 377; Total Volume 6 302·5; Av'ge haul 325·6 (524·1); Max. trailing load 3 316; Total number carried 272·1; Average journey 83·3 (134·1)

ARGENTINA
**Ferrocarriles Argentinos
Argentine Railways
Avenida Ramos Mejia 1302,
Buenos Aires
The former 6 separate railways have been re-formed into 4 regional systems

Región Noroeste (Northwest)
Avenida Maipu No. 4, Buenos Aires
Formerly: FC Gen. Belgrano
Gauge 2' 5½" (0·75) / 3' 3⅜" (1·00); Route 48 (77) / 8 358 (13 451); Track 377 (607) / 9 870 (15 885); Locos S 124, D 45; Railcars D 107, E 95; Pass. train cars 349; Freight train cars 3 592; Max. trailing load 291; Total number carried 630

Región Centro (Central)
Avenida Ramos Mejia 1302,
Buenos Aires
Formerly: FC Gen. Mitre and FC Gen. San Martin
Gauge 5' 6" (1·676); Route 6 774 (10 902) / E 36 (58); Track 7 331 (11 798) / E 94 (115); Elect. 800 V dc 3 R; Locos S 306, D 516; Railcars E 386, D 167, T 126; Pass. train cars 1 372; Freight train cars 23 166

Región Suroeste (South-West)
Plaza Constitución, Buenos Aires
Formerly: FC Gen. Roca and FC Gen. Sarmienta
Gauge 5' 6" (1·676) / 2' 5½" (0·75); Route 7 808 (12 656) / E 26 (42) / 250 (403); Track 8 219 (13 228) / E 82 (132) / 250 (403); Elect. 800 V dc 3R; Locos S 450, D 630, E 4; Railcars E 312, D 219; Pass. train cars 1 387; Freight train cars 18 895; Max. trailing load 390

Región Noreste (North-East)
Rivadavia 456, Concordia, Entre Rios
Formerly: FC Gen. Urquiza
Gauge 4' 8½" (1·435) / 1' 11⅝" (0·60); Route 1 920 (3 091) / E 14 (23) / 130 (209); Track 2 238 (3 603) / E 28 (45) / 137 (221); Elect. 600 V dc OH; Locos SL 108, SS 32, DeL 45, E 10; Railcars E 88, D 53, EMU 16; Pass. train cars 181; Freight train cars 3 646; Max. trailing load 346; Total number carried 650

AUSTRALIA
**Australian National Railways
325 Collins St, Melbourne, Vic 3000

NEW SOUTH WALES
**Public Transport Commission of New South Wales
19 York St, Sydney, NSW 2000

QUEENSLAND
**Queensland Government Railways
305 Edward St, Brisbane

Colonial Sugar Refining Co Ltd
1-7 O'Connell St., Sydney, NSW
Operates four sugar mills in Queensland
Gauge 2' 0" (0·610); Track 320 (515); Locos SL 9, DmS 21, DhL 25; Freight train cars 8 000; Total Volume 3 000·0; Av'ge haul 10 (16); Av'ge net train load 200; Max. trailing load 300

SOUTH AUSTRALIA
**South Australian Railways
PO Box 2351, Adelaide — SA 5001
Gauge 5' 3" (1·60) / 3' 6" (1·067) / 4' 8½" (1·435); Route 1 572 (2 531) / 598 (963) / 245 (395); Track 2 010 (3 235) / 671 (1 035) / 290 (470); Locos SL 4, DeL 105, DeS 46; Railcars D 125, DT 44, DMU 37; Pass. train cars 198; Freight train cars 7 132; Total Volume 6 183.8; Av'ge haul 1 686 571 425 ton-km; Total number carried 12 672·1

The Emu Bay Railway Co Ltd
PO Box 82, Burnie, Tas 7320
Gauge 3' 6" (1·067); Route 83 (133); Track 89 (143); Locos DhL 11, DS 1, DhS 1; Pass. train cars 2; Freight train cars 123; Total Volume 501·7; Av'ge haul 60 259 736 ton-km; Average journey 1·3

** See main entry

Average Speeds: Freight Train mph *(km/hr)*	Average Speeds: Pass. Train mph *(km/hr)*	Average Speeds: Speed max. mph *(km/hr)*	Financial Data: Revenue Expenses in 1 000's	Braking (continuous)	Couplers: Type and Height above rail ins *(mm)*	Buffers: Centres and Height above rail ins *(mm)*	Rails: Weight lb. per yd *(kg/m)*	Sleepers (crossties): Type and thickness ins *(mm)*	Sleepers (crossties): Spacing Number per mile *(per km)* or centres ins *(mm)*	Curvature max.	Gradient max. (**U**=not compensated)	Axle load max. tonnes	Altitude max. feet *(m)*	Staff employed. Total no. (inclu. workshop)	Names of officials. Extended lists can be found at the end of the individual country in the report section immediately following
							86 *(43)*					21			
		74 *(120)*	DA 375 000		Screw Semi-Auto	Air	91/110 *(45/54)*	Wood Conc. & Steel		218 ft *(200 m)*	3·0%	22		12 380	Dir. Gen: Benmechdjonba
21 *(34)*	25 *(40)*	43 *(70)*	Escudos 1 273·4 978·7	Vac. Gresham & Craven	Auto Henricot 34⅝ *(880)*		90/60 *(45/30)*	Wood and steel	2 655 *(1 650)*	1 020 ft *(310 m)*	2·5% 2·0% **U**	15·0	5 413 *(1 650)*	12 800 *(1 312)*	Gen. Man: Eng. L. Lama de Oliveira
12·5 *(20)*	22 *(36)*	Freight 16 *(25)*	Escudos 1 429·3 4 621·0	Vac. Jourd. Monn; Davies & Metcalfe	Chain 20 *(510)*	Central 20 *(510)*	40/35 *(20/17)*	Wood 4¾ *(120)*	18″ *(460)*	246 ft *(75 m)*	3·8% **U**	7	3 358 *(1 054)*	400 *(65)*	Director: Gabriel Aguiar dos Santos
			$ 679 161·0 333 513·8												Director: Eng. Agostinho A. S. de Almeida
25 *(40)*	37 *(60)*	50 *(80)*		Vac. Gresham	Atlas Auto 35¼ *(896)*		130/30 *(65/15)*	Metal	2 260 *(1 450)*	361 ft *(110 m)*	3·1% **U**	14	3 806 *(1 160)*	2 158 *(470)*	Eng. Luis H. E. Abreu Eng. B. L. Almeida Eng. J. P. Duarte
23·9 *(38·5)*	24·8 *(40·0)*	40 *(65)*	Escudos 563 378·7 279 540·0	Vac. Gresham	Atlas IR & 2 38·7 *(983)*		90/60 *(43/30)*	Metal & wood 5½ *(140)*	Metal 2 250 *(1 400)* Wood 2 575 *(1 600)*	377 ft *(115 m)*	2·8%	16	6 266 *(1 910)*	4 591 *(877)*	Eng. Maria Augosto de Paiva Neto
															President: Gen. Emiliano A. S. Flouret
		56 *(90)*		Air W'hse	Auto 31¼ *(795)*		80/50 *(40/25)*	Wood 4¾ *(120)* and Metal	2 320 *(1 450)*	295 ft *(90 m)*	3·19% Rack 6·0%	6·8	2 780 *(4 475)*	50 009 *(7 977)*	
				Air W'hse	Screw *(1 065/950)*	Crs. 77 *(1 950)* Ht. *(1 065/950)*	100/60 *(50/30)*	Wood 4¾ *(120)* Some Steel	2 160 *(1 350)*	656 ft *(200 m)*	2·4%	10·4		55 000	
							90/70 *(45/35)*	Wood 4¾ *(120)*	2 240 *(1 400)*	5·0°	2·5% 1·5%	10 *(8·52)*		31 131	
							100/60 *(50/30)*	Wood 4¾ *(120)*	2 160 *(1 350)*	7·0°	3·8%	9·69		12 528	
				Air W'hse			80/50 *(40/25)*	Wood 4¾ *(120)*	2 240 *(1 400)*	5·8°	1·31%	15		11 562 *(1 541)*	
10 *(16)*							60/45 *(30/22)*	Wood 4 *(102)* & Conc.	24″ *(610)*	100 ft *(30·5 m)*	2·0% **U**	6	200 *(61)*		Gen. Man: Sir James Vernon
			$A 50 098·6 84 778·7											7 949	Gen. Man: J. M. Doyle
18 *(29)*		28 *(45)*		Vac G & C	Screw 30½ *(775)*	57 *(1 448)* 30½ *(775)*	82/63 *(31/41)*	Wood 5 *(127)*	24″ *(610)*	330 ft *(100 m)*	3·0% 2·5% **U**	14·25	2 201 *(671)*	180	Man: B. P. Fagan

NAME OF COMPANY ADDRESS	Gauge ft. in. (metres)	Route length incl. E=Electrified miles (km.)	Track length incl. E=Electrified miles (km.)	Elect. system and type of conductor	Loco-motives L=Line S=Shunt Steam Electric Diesel De=elec. Dh=hyd.	Rail-cars Electric Diesel Trailer Railbus Multiple Unit set	Pass. train cars	Freight train cars Con-tainers	Total Volume carried. Thous-ands of tonnes	Av'ge haul per ton miles (km.)	Av'ge net train load tonnes	Max. trailing load tonnes	Total number carried in 1 000's	Average journey miles (km.)

AUSTRALIA (contd.)

VICTORIA
**Victorian Railways
67 Spencer St, Melbourne,
Vic 3000

WESTERN AUSTRALIA
**Westrail
Bank of New South Wales
Building, cnr. Williams and
Murray St, Perth, WA 6000

Hammersley Railways — Hamersley Iron Pty Ltd, Box 21, Dampier, WA 6713 — Gauge 4' 8½" (1·435); Route 240 (382); Track 365 (588); Locomotives DeL 40, DeS 1; Pass. train cars 1; Freight train cars 2 237; Total Volume carried 34 821; 11 509 000 000 ton-km

Goldsworthy Railway — Goldsworthy Mining Ltd., Box 84, Port Hedland, WA 6721 — Gauge 4' 8½" (1·435); Route 113 (179); Track 121 (195); Locomotives DeL 6, DeS 2; Freight train cars 257; Total Volume carried 7 300

**Mt Newman Railroad — Mt Newman Mining Co Pty Ltd, 200 St Georges Terrace, Perth, WA 6001 — Gauge 4' 8½" (1·435); Route 265 (426); Track 324 (521); Locomotives De 51; Pass. train cars 1; Freight train cars 2 083; Total Volume carried 20 120; 12 575 000 000 tonne-km

AUSTRIA

**Austrian Federal Railways OBB (Österreichische Bundesbahnen), Elisabethstrasse 9, A-1010 Vienna —
Gauge 4' 8½" (1·435); Route 3 361 (5 418) E I 702 (2 744); Track 6 062 (9 756) E 3 678 (5 913); Elect. 15 000 V 16²/₃ OH; Locomotives SL 111, EL 597, DeL 51, DhL 165, DhS 276, ES 43, DeS 2; Rail-cars D 51, DT 266, EMU 97; Pass. train cars 3 404; Freight train cars 35 858; Total Volume carried 46 358·0; 10 547 877 ton-km; Total number carried 168 172·0; Average journey 24·8 (39·7)
Gauge 3' 3⅜" (1·00); Route 9 (15); Track 319 (513); Elect. 6 500 V OH
Gauge 2' 6" (0·76); Route 273 (439) E 57; Track E 60 (97); Elect. 25 OH; Locomotives DeS 2
Route 91

Achenseebahn AG — Jenbach, Tirol — Gauge 3' 3⅜" (1·0); Route 4·3 (6·8); Track 4·6 (7·4); Locomotives S 3; Pass. train cars 6; Freight train cars 3; Max. trailing load 51; Total number carried 64·861

Graz-Köflacher Eisenbahn und Bergbau-gesellschaft — Grazbachstrasse 39, A-8010 Graz — Gauge 4' 8½" (1·435); Route 59 (95); Track 90 (145); Locomotives SL 12, SS 3, DeL 3, DhS 2; Rail-cars D 8, T 18; Pass. train cars 34; Freight train cars 695; Total Volume carried 1 700·0; Av'ge haul 31 (50); Av'ge net train load 800; Max. trailing load 1 600; Total number carried 3 041·0; Average journey 16 (26)

Montafonerbahn AG — A-6780 Schruns (Vorariberg) — Gauge 4' 8½" (1·435); Route E 8 (13); Track E 9 (14); Elect. 15 kV 16²/₃ OH; Locomotives S 1, De 1; Rail-cars R 2, E 3, DT 1, ET 1; Pass. train cars 6; Freight train cars 4; Total Volume carried 153·1; Av'ge haul 3·5 (5); Max. trailing load 500; Total number carried 825·2; Average journey 5·6 (9)

Reisseck-Kreuzeck Höhenbahnen — Österr. Draukraftwerke AG, A 9020 Klagenfurt, Anzengruberstr 50 — Gauge 1' 11⅝" (0·60); Route 2·0 (3·3); Track 2·2 (3·6); Locomotives D 2, Dh 1*; Pass. train cars 2; Freight train cars 7; Total Volume carried 1·2; Av'ge haul 2·0 (3·3); Max. trailing load 13; Total number carried 121·9; Average journey 2·0 (3·3)

Raab-Oedenburg-Ebenfurter Eisenbahn† — Vienna 1 — Gauge 4' 8½" (1·435); Route 39‡ (64); Track 50 (81); Locomotives S 27, D 4; Rail-cars D 12; Pass. train cars 104; Freight train cars 540; Total Volume carried 1 680·1; Av'ge haul 15·5 (25); Total number carried 315·4; Average journey 14 (22)

Salzburger Stadtwerke Verkehrsbetriebe-Lokalbahn — A-5020 Salzburg, Kaiserschützenstr 26 — Gauge 4' 8½" (1·435); Route E 15 (25); Track E 20 (32); Elect. 1 000 V dc OH; Locomotives EL 2, ES 2; Rail-cars E 10; Pass. train cars 15; Freight train cars 16; Total Volume carried 319·5; Total number carried 1 318·6; Average journey 8 (13)

Steiermärkische Landesbahnen — A-8011 Radetzkystr 31, Graz, Postfach 553 (Operates following 8 lines): — Gauge 4' 8½" (1·435) Route 121 590 (195 681) Track 140 106 (225 479) Elect. DhS 2; Gauge 2' 6" (0·76) Route E 19 349 (31 279) Track E 20 191 (32 497) Elect. DmS 2; Locomotives SL 9, EL 1, DeL 8, DhL 3; Rail-cars E 5, ET 1; Pass. train cars 35; Freight train cars 388; Total Volume carried 497·3; 7 201 129 ton-km; Total number carried 890·1

Feldbach-Bad Gleichenberg — A-8330 Feldbach — Gauge 4' 8½" (1·435); Route E 13 (21); Track E 14 (22); Elect. 1 800 V dc OH; Locomotives E 1; Rail-cars E 2; Freight train cars 8; Total Volume carried 129·6; 684 927 tonne-km; Max. trailing load 120; Total number carried 40·8; Average journey 10·5 (17·0)

Gleisdorf-Weiz — Local office: A-8160 Weiz — Gauge 4' 8½" (1·435); Route 9 (15); Track 11 (18); Locomotives S 1, De 2; Pass. train cars 5; Freight train cars 6; Total Volume carried 132·7; 1 824 403 tonne-km; Max. trailing load 172·5; Total number carried 176·5; Average journey 8·2 (13·1)

Kapfenberg-Seebach-Turnau — Local office: A-8605 Kapfenberg — Gauge 2' 6" (0·76); Route 12 (20); Track 15 (25); Locomotives Dh 1, SL 1, De 1; Freight train cars 134; Total Volume carried 128·6; 1 514 402 tonne-km; Max. trailing load 160

Lokalbahn Mixnitz — Localbahn Mixnitz-St. Erhard AG, Local office: A-8131 Mixnitz — Gauge 2' 6" (0·76); Route E 6·2 (10); Track E 7·4 (12); Elect. 800 V dc OH; Locomotives ES 2, EL 2, DeS 1, DhS 1; Freight train cars 42; Total Volume carried 54·7; 601 161 tonne-km; Average journey 5·4 (8·6)

Peggau-Übelbach — A-8124 Ubelbach — Gauge 4' 8½" (1·435); Route E 7 (11); Track E 8 (13); Elect. 15 kV 1/16²/₃ OH; Rail-cars E 3, T 1; Freight train cars 1; Total Volume carried 6·1; 46 892 tonne-km; Max. trailing load 214·0; Total number carried 203·8

Preding-Wieselsdorf-Stainz — A-8510, Stainz — Gauge 2' 6" (0·76); Route 7 (11); Track 7·5 (12); Locomotives S 1, DhS 2; Pass. train cars 4; Freight train cars 23; Total Volume carried 7·5; 89 376 tonne-km; Max. trailing load 170; Average journey 13·7 (22·0)

Murtalbahn-Unzmarkt-Mauterndorf — A-8850 Murau — Gauge 2' 6" (0·76); Route 48 (76); Track 53 (85); Locomotives SL 4, DeL 3, DmS 1; Pass. train cars 17; Freight train cars 132; Total Volume carried 47·1; 2 195 881 tonne-km; Max. trailing load 240; Total number carried 456·5; Average journey 17·5 (25)

Feistritztalbahn Weiz-Ratten — A-8160 Weiz — Gauge 2' 6" (0·76); Route 27 (43); Track 31 (50); Locomotives S 2, De 2, DhS 1; Pass. train cars 8; Freight train cars 84; Total Volume carried 45·8; 845 208 tonne-km; Max. trailing load 240; Total number carried 12·6; Average journey 6·2 (10·0)

Stern & Hafferl Lokalbahn Betriebe — Postfach 3, A-4810, Gmunden (Operates 7 railways, 6 of which it owns):

Lokalbahn Lambach-Vorchdorf-Eggenberg — Lambach — Gauge 4' 8½" (1·435); Route E 7 (12); Track E 8 (13); Elect. 750 V dc OH; Locomotives E-D 1; Rail-cars E 2; Pass. train cars 3; Freight train cars 7; Av'ge haul 8·4 (13·5); Av'ge net train load 35; Max. trailing load 180

**   See main entry
*   Snow-clearing locomotives
†   Details for Austrian section only. Extends into Hungary as Györ-Sopron Ebenfurt
‡   Includes figures pertaining to Neusiedlerseebahn AG

	Average Speeds		Financial Data		Couplers	Buffers	Rails	Sleepers (crossties)							
Freight Train	Pass. Train	Speed max.	Revenue Expenses	Braking (continuous)	Type and Height above rail	Centres and Height above rail	Weight	Type and thickness	Spacing Number per mile (per km) or centres	Curvature max.	Gradient max. (U=not compensated)	Axle load max.	Altitude max.	Staff employed. Total no. (inclu. workshop)	Names of officials. Extended lists can be found at the end of the individual country in the report section immediately following
mph (km/hr)	mph (km/hr)	mph (km/hr)	in 1 000's		ins (mm)	ins (mm)	lb. per yd (kg/m)	ins (mm)	ins (mm)		sated)	tonnes	feet (m)	shop)	
30 (48)	40 (64)	$A 28 497·0	Air W'hse ABD/W	Type F 35½ (902)		136/119 (67/59)	Wood Conc. 6 (152)	19½" (495)	1 300 ft (396 m)	2·0% U 1·92%	30	2 500 (762)	955	Man: M. S. Purcell
26 (42)	35 (56)		Air W'hse	Alliance 35 (889)		101 (50)	Wood 5 (127)	24 (610)	1 900 ft (579 m)	1·0% U 1·04%	23·5	442 (135)	161 (50)	Rly. Supt: J. R. O'Farrell Asst. Supt: J. G. Fitzgerald
	Loaded 35 (56) Empty 40 (64)		Vac W'hse	Type F 34½ (876)		132 (65·5)	Jarrah 6 (152)	21" (533)	1 900 ft (579 m)	1·5%	30	1 680 (512)	924	RR Man: R. S. Murphy
	Main 87 (140) Second 37 (60) Narrow 25 (40)	Schillings 13 487 000 17 399 000	Air Oerlikon (under licence) (940)	Standard Screw Max 41¾ (1 065) Min F.37 P 38½ (980)	68⅞ (1 750) Height as for Coupler	130/99 (64·3/ 49·4) 5⅛ (130)	Wood Standard gauge 6½ (160) Narrow (650/700) Conc 8 (200) 7 (180)	25½ (650) 25½/27½ 18·2°	6·5° N: 25·5% N.	Std: Main 2·97% Other 4·0% Rack Narrow 4·0%	Std: 20 12	Std: 5 773 (1 796)	71 274 (9 182)	Gen. Dir.: Dr. Wolfgang Pycha
	9 (14)	13 (20)		Central 29½ (750)		46 (23)	Iron & Wood 5½ (140)	33½ (850)	13·0°	16% (rack)	10	3 182 (970)	19	
19 (30)	30 (50)	56 (90)		Air Hardy; Knorr	Standard Railcar Scharff	Standard	98/53 (49/26)	Form I, II & III	2 400 (1 500)	7·3°	1·57%	16	1 476 (450)	1 060	Dr. Edward Prochaska
19 (30)	30 (50)	47 (75)	S.32 163·9 31 816	Air Oerlikon	Standard Railbus Scharff	Standard	67 (33)	Wood 6 (152)	25½ (650)	10·0°	2·5%	20	2 231 (680)	58	Gen. Man.: Guntram Juen
3 (5)	9 (14)	10 (15)			Buffer coupler		36·5 (18·3)	Wood	2 010 (1 250)	38·0°	3·9%	2	7 375 (2 248)	7	
										5·8°	0·8%			175	
20 (33)	22 (35)	37 (60)		Vac Hardy	Auto 23⅝ (600)		67 (33)			7·5°	2·1%	18		121	Man.: Dipl. Ing B. Robenhaupt
			Schillings 34 926·6 86 355·9											269	Gen. Man.: Dr. Jur. W. Zauhar
19 (30)	25 (40)	28 (45)	Schillings 5 144·8 7 949·5							11·7°	4·1%	16	1 280 (390)	26	
19 (30)	28 (45)	37 (50)	Schillings 8 769·7 15 333·6							8·7°	1·5%	18	1 499 (457)	56	
		15·5 (25)	Schillings 6 583·4 10 713·4							22·0°	3·0%	10	2 352 (717)	31	
12·5 (20)		12·5 (20)	Schillings 2 827·8							29·0°	3·0%	10	2 031 (619)	12	
19 (30)	19 (30)	25 (40)	Schillings 2 325·7 3 070·8	Standard Air Oerlikon Narrow Vac. Hardy	Standard European Narrow Buffer-Coupler	Standard European Narrow 22½ (570)	Standard 72/52 (36/26) Narrow 52/36 (26/18)	Wood 5½ (140)	28 (710)	9·7°	3·2%	16	1 673 (510)	11	
9 (14)		9·5 (15)	Schillings 688·1 1 948·6							17·5°	1·1%	12	1 070	8 (326)	
19 (30)		28 (45)	Schillings 9 293·9 34 035·6							22·0°	2·0%	6·5	3 652 (739)	105	
15·5 (25)	19 (30)	19 (30)	Schillings 3 523·3 12 760·2							29·0°	2·5%	6·5	2 424 (739)	32	
															Dipl. Ing Ingobert Stern
25 (40)	25 (40)	31 (50)					61 (30)	Wood 6 (150)		6·0°	1·5%	16	1 381 (421)		

NAME OF COMPANY ADDRESS	Gauge ft. in. (metres)	Route length incl. E=Electrified miles (km.)	Track length incl. E=Electrified miles (km.)	Elect. system and type of conductor	Loco-motives L=Line S=Shunt Steam Electric Diesel De=elec. Dh=hyd.	Rail-cars Electric Diesel Trailer Railbus Multiple Unit set	Pass. train cars	Freight train cars Con-tainers	Total Volume carried. Thous-ands of tonnes	Av'ge haul per ton miles (km.)	Av'ge net train load tonnes	Max. trailing load tonnes	Total number carried in 1 000's	Aver-age jour-ney miles (km.)
AUSTRIA *(contd.)*														
Linzer Localbahn AG (Linz-Eferding-Waizenkirchen) A-4020 Linz	4' 8½'' *(1·435)*	E 27 *(43)*	E 29 *(47)*	750 V dc OH	EL 5 ES 1	E 7	10	10		9·3 *(15)*	260			9·3 *(15)*
Lokalbahn Neumarkt-Waizen-kirchen-Peuerbach AG *Local office:* Waizenkirchen	4' 8½'' *(1·435)*	E 10 *(16)*	E 11 *(18)*	750 V dc OH		E 3	3	3	324·9	4 448 400 ton-km			2 322·2	5 *(8)*
Burmoos-Trimmelkam Trimmelkam, Upper Austria	4' 8½'' *(1·435)*	E 6 *(9)*	E 8 *(13)*	1 000 V dc OH	EL 2	E 2		0		5·3 *(8·5)*		450		4·3 *(7)*
Lambach-Haaga/Hausruck	4' 8½'' *(1·435)*	E 17 *(27)*	E 20 *(32)*	750 V dc OH	EL 1	E 2	2	3		6·2 *(10)*				8 *(13)*
Lokalbahn Gmunden-Vorchdorf AG Postfach 2, 4810 Gmunden	3' 3⅜'' *(1·00)*	E 9 *(15)*	E 10 *(16)*	750 V dc OH		E 4	6	5	2·7	30 116 ton-km			597	5 *(8)*
Lokalbahn Volkermarkt-Attesee AG Postfach 2, 4810 Gmunden	3' 3⅜'' *(1·00)*	E 8 *(13)*	E 9 *(15)*	750 V dc OH		E 5	6	24	7					5 *(8)*
Stubaitalbahn AG Klostergasse 2, A-6010 Innsbruck	3' 3⅜'' *(1·00)*	E 11 *(18)*	E 12 *(20)*	3 000 V ac		E 4	7	12	6·0	6 *(10)*			700·0	6 *(9)*
Wiener Lokalbahn AG Eichenstr 1, Vienna XII	4' 8½'' *(1·435)*	19 *(29)* E 16 *(26)*	38 *(62)* E 33 *(54)*	850 V dc OH	ES 1 DhL 2	E 26 T 6	35	31	103·1	3 113 200 ton-km	1 000		4 232·6	6·8 *(11)*
Zillertalbahn Zillertaler Verkehrsbetriebe AG Austr 1, A-6200 Jenbach	2' 6'' *(0·760)*	20 *(32)*	24 *(38)*		SL 4 DeS 1 DhL 2 DhS 3	D 2	19	74	81·4	15·5 *(25)*	120	394	842·7	10 *(16)*
BANGLADESH **Bangladesh Railways** Central Railway Buildings Chittagong														
BELGIUM **Soc. Nat des C. F. Belges (S.N.C.B.)** 21 Rue de Louvain, 1000 Brussels														
Soc. Nat. des C.F. Vicinaux (SNCV) 14 Rue de la Science, 1040 Brussels	3' 3⅜'' *(1·00)*	137 *(221)* E 134 *(216)*	*(334)* *(329)*	600 V dc OH	SL 5	E 178 D 9	139						23 068	4·5 *(7·3)*
BENIN **Organisation Commune Benin-Niger des Chemins de Fer et des Transports (O.C.D.N.)** B.P. 16, Cotonou	3' 3⅜'' *(1·00)*	359 *(579)*	395 *(635)*		DeL 11	D 4 T 5	29	387 C 23	281·4	110 721 402 ton-km			1 291·0	39 *(63)*
BOLIVIA **Empresa Nacional de Ferrocarriles** Calle Bolivar 72 4, La Paz	3' 3⅜'' *(1·00)*	2 080 *(3 348)*	2 125 *(3 427)*		SS 17 SL 54 DeL 21 DhL 5 DhS 4 EL 1 ES 2 DmS 1	D 5 DMU 10 E 2	132	1 147	1 141·0	465 449 000 ton-km			309 615 000 pass-km	147 *(237)*
Guaqui-La Paz Railway Casilla 280, La Paz	3' 3⅜'' *(1·00)*	54 *(87)* E 5½ *(9)*	61 *(98)* E 8 *(13)*											
F.C. Uyuni—Pulacayo Pulacayo	2' 6'' *(0·762)*	20 *(32)*	24 *(39)* E 8 *(13)*		S 5 E 11 D 1			47						
F.C. Machacamarca-Uncia Corporacion Minera de Bolivia Machacamarca	3' 3⅜'' *(1·00)*	65 *(105)*	74 *(119)*		SL 1 SS 1 DeL 1 DS 2	D 2 R 5	12	84	765·6				17·8	31 *(50)*
BRAZIL **Rede Ferroviaria Federal SA (RFFSA)** Praça Duque de Caixas 86, Rio de Janeiro *Formed into 4 Regions sub-divided into Divisions*	2' 6'' *(0·762)* 3' 3⅜'' *(1·00)* 5' 3'' *(1·60)*	125 *(202)* 14 088 *(22 671)* 1 039 *(1 673)* E 678 *(1 092)*			S 85 E 62 D 1 083	D 26 E 293	2 519	30 075 C 29	30 226·0	239 *(384)*		321	5 000 *Main* 35 801·0 *Suburb* 229 646·0	47·6 *(76·6)* 12·3 *(19·8)*
Systema Regional Nordeste Ave Marquês de Olinda 262, Recife, PE	3' 3⅜'' *(1·00)*	4 502 *(7 245)*			De 167		247	3 617	2 789				13 617	

** See main entry

Average Speeds: Freight Train mph (km/hr)	Average Speeds: Pass. Train mph (km/hr)	Average Speeds: Speed max. mph (km/hr)	Financial Data: Revenue Expenses in 1 000's	Braking (continuous)	Couplers: Type and Height above rail ins (mm)	Buffers: Centres and Height above rail ins (mm)	Rails: Weight lb. per yd (kg/m)	Sleepers (crossties): Type and thickness ins (mm)	Sleepers (crossties): Spacing Number per mile (per km) or centres ins (mm)	Curvature max.	Gradient max. (U=not compensated)	Axle load max. tonnes	Altitude max. feet (m)	Staff employed. Total no. (inclu. workshop)	Names of officials. Extended lists can be found at the end of the individual country in the report section immediately following
19 (30)	28 (45)	31 (50)								7·6°	2·7%	20	1 283 (391)		
19 (30)	25 (40)	31 (50)	S.46 624 50 987	Freight W'hse Air Pass. Hardy Vac	Standard	Standard (33)	66 5 (140)	Wood		6·0°	1·6%	16 (384)	1 260	190	
25 (40)	25 (40)	31 (50)					66 (33)	Wood 6 (150)		6·7°	1·5%	18			
19 (30)	25 (40)	31 (50)					61 (31)	Wood 6 (150)		7·6°	2·8%	18			
	25 (40)	31 (50)	S.461 900 448 600	Vac			48/36 (24/18)	Wood 5 (140)		11·5°	4·0%	8·5	1 763 (557·5)	35	
22 (35)	22 (35)	31 (50)		Vac			44/36 (22/18)	Wood 5 (140)		28·0°	4·7%	7·5	1 866 (569)		
		16 (25)	Revenue S.3 600·0	Air	Buffer Coupler	21⅞ (555)	53/38 (26·5/ 18·7)	Wood	1 930 (1 200)	44·0°	4·5%	6·0	3 304 (1 007)	46	
12 (20)	21 (33·8)	31 (50)	S.34·685 46 552	Vac Hardy	B.S.I. Compakt 20⅝ (525)	Centre Buffer Coupler	66·6 (33)	Wood 6¼ (160)	26 (650)	57·0°	5·0%**U**	18	755 (230)	296 (91)	Gen. Man.: Dipl. Ing E. Hübner
16 (25)	28 (45)	31 (50)	S.13 685·0 14 450·0	Vac Hardy Air W'hse	Centre Buffer Coupler 22⅜ (570)	Centre Buffer Coupler	53/36 (26·2/) 17·9)	Wood 5½ (140)	28⅜"-31⅞" (700-810)	0·25°	1·6%**U** 1·5%	12·5	2 058 (627)	102 (30)	Dir.: Dipl. Ing Erich Heiss
Steam 19 (30)	Town 12 (19) Country 14 (23)	*	FR. 216 300 461 800	Air and Vac W'hse Oil Pieper	18⅛ (460)	Crs. 26⅜ (671) Ht. 25⅝ (650)	64·5 (32)	Wood 7¾ (200) 4¾ (120)	1 780- 2 220 (1 110- 1 390)	58°F 95°P	*Diesel* 6% *Steam lines* 3%				Dir. Gen: M. C. Henrard
20 (33)	33 (53)	50 (80)	CFA 1 175 628·4 1 168 957·6	Vac Wh'se Jourdain Monn	Willison Auto & unified type 55/70 tons 30 (760)	Crs. 15¾ (400) Ht. 30 (760)	60/40 (30/22)	Metal	2 400 (1 500)	525 ft (160 m)	2·3%	13	1 276 (389)	1 588 (418)	Gen. Man: M. A. Boittiaux
15 (25)	22 (35)	37 (60)	$b 28 550 25 800	Air W'hse	Henricot Auto 342 (792)		80/50 (40/25)	Wood 4¾ (120)	2 400 (1 500)	Rad 252 ft (76·6 m)	3·09%	15	15 702 (4 787)	6 457 (502)	Gen. Man: Ing. Gustavo A. Méndez T.
19 (30)				Air W'hse	"Visco" Alliance Engl: St:		60 (30)	Wood 6 (150) Conc. 5½ (140)	23⅝ (600)	17·5°	6% **U**	11	13 416 (4 069)	679 (100)	Gen. Man: J. G. Lances
							35 (17·3)	Wood 6 (150)	3 200 (2 000)	17·0°	3·28%	14			Gen. Man: Samuel Fernandez C.
		25 (40)		Air W'hse	Centre Buffer Coupler	29½ (750)	60/50 (30/25)	Wood 4¾ (120)	31·5" (800)	14·5°	2·5% 3·5% **U**	12	14 436 (4 400)	234 (67)	Gen. Man: Ricardo M. Bayá B
11·2 (18·0)	19·3 (31·0)	62 (100)	$C 1 103 000 1 836 000	Air	Cobrasma Auto 29½ (750) BG 39 (990)		115/90 (57/45)	Wood 6¼ (160)	21⅝-23⅝ (550-600)		MG 3·3% **U** BG 2·0% **U**	MG 17 BG 27	4 518 (1 377)	115 338	President: Gen. Antonio Adolfo Manta
			$Cr. 118 567·2 319 798·8												

* In towns trains must come to a standstill in 98 ft *(30 m)* and to 393 ft *(120 m)* in the country

NAME OF COMPANY ADDRESS	Gauge ft. in. *(metres)*	Route length incl. E=Electrified miles *(km.)*	Track length incl. E=Electrified miles *(km.)*	Elect. system and type of conductor	Locomotives L=Line S=Shunt **S**team **E**lectric **D**iesel **D**e=elec. **D**h=hyd.	Railcars **E**lectric **D**iesel **T**railer **R**ailbus **M**ultiple **U**nit set	Pass. train cars	Freight train cars Containers	Freight movement: Total Volume carried. Thousands of tonnes	Freight movement: Av'ge haul per ton miles *(km.)*	Freight movement: Av'ge net train load tonnes	Freight movement: Max. trailing load tonnes	Passengers: Total number carried in 1 000's	Passengers: Average journey miles *(km.)*
BRAZIL *(contd.)*														
Systema Regional Centro Pça Cristiana Otoni, S/No, Rio, GB	5′ 3″ *(1·60)* 3′ 3⅜″ *(1·00)* 2′ 6″ *(0·76)*	937 *(1 508)* 4 288 *(6 901)* 125 *(202)*												
Systema Regional Centro-Sul CP 8064, ZC 01120 São Paulo SP	5′ 3″ *(1·60)*	105 *(170)* **E** 105 *(170)*	325 *(523)* **E** 217 *(350)*	3 kV dc OH	**S** 19 **E** 24 **De** 59	**E** 30 **De** 3	186	4 181	6 065·4	46·6 *(75)*	350	4 000	*Main* 7 314·2 *Suburb* 54 493·1	31 *(50)* 8·7 *(14)*
	3′ 3⅜″ *(1·00)*	1 000 *(1 609)*	1 135 *(1 827)*		**De** 71	**De** 7	148	3 921	1 067·9	467 *(752)*	323	350	4 383·3	117 *(188)*
Systema Regional Sul Palácio do Comércio, Porto Algere, RS	3′ 3⅜″ *(1·00)*	4 297 *(6 916)*												
Ferrovia Paulista SA (FEPASA) Rua Libero Badaró 39, 01009 São Paulo, SP *Formed into 3 divisions*	5′ 3″ *(1·60)*	1 030 *(1 657)* **E** 306 *(492)*	4 206 *(6 769)*	3 000 V dc	**EL** 165 **DeL** 329 **DhS** 20 **DS** 4	*Metre* **E** 34 **ET** 68 **D** 8 **DT** 16	*Broad* 418 *Metre* 661	*Broad* 5 727 *Metre* 11 689	10 564·0	198·0 *(318·6)*		1 500	45 698·5	44·2 *(71·1)*
	3′ 3⅜″ *(1·00)*	2 234 *(3 595)* **E** 498 *(802)*												
1a Divisão Rua Libero Baderó 39, São Paulo, SP *(Formerly Paulista and Araraquara)*	5′ 3″ *(1·60)*	1 030 *(1 657)* **E** 306 *(492)*												
2a Divisão Praça Julio Prestes 148, São Paulo, SP *(Formerly Sorocabana)*	3′ 3⅜″ *(1·00)*	1 253 *(2 016)* **E** 498 *(802)*												
3a Divasão Rua Visconde do Rio Branca 148, Campinas, SP *(Formerly Mogiana and São Paulo-Minas)*	3′ 3⅝″ *(1·00)*	981 *(1 579)*												
Estrado de Ferro do Amapá Box 396, 66000 Belem, Para, SP	4′ 8½″ *(1·435)*	121 *(194)*	129 *(207)*		**De** 5		6	139	1 338·8	158·9 *(225·8)*		2 900	130·3	106·9 *(172·0)*
Estràdo de Ferro Campos do Jordão Pindamonhangaba, SP	3′ 3⅜″ *(1·00)*	**E** 29 *(47)*	**E** 30 *(49)*	1 500 V dc OH		**E** 13	7	5	7·0	23·1 *(37·2)*			533·9	8·5 *(13·7)*
Estràdo de Ferro Vitória a Minas (EFVM) Ave Governador Bley 236 Vitória, Espirito Santo, Brazil	3′ 3⅜″ *(1·00)*	438 *(705)*	807 *(1 300)*		**DeL** 136 **DeL** 25 **DhL** 16		49	9 000	66 385·7	35 244 873 044 ton-km			1 871·6	83 *(134)*
Estràdo de Ferro Votorantim Votorantim, SP	3′ 3⅜″ *(1·00)*	**E** 9 *(14)*		600 V dc OH					520·4	9 *(14)*			*Suburb* 2 480	9 *(14)*
BULGARIA														
****Bulgarian State Railways** Sofia														
BURMA														
****Union of Burma Railways** PO Box 118, Rangoon	3′ 3⅜″ *(1·00)*	1 949·25 *(3 127)*	2 701 *(4 347)*		**SL** 179 **SS** 50 **DeL** 79 **DeS** 15 **DhL** 72	**D** 23	1 228	9 527	1 675·3	242 492 812 ton-miles				
CAMEROON														
****Régie Nationale des C.F. du Cameroon** Boite Postale 304, Douala	3′ 3⅜″ *(1·00)*	521 *(839)*	727 *(1 172)*		**DeL** 49 **DeS** 32	**D** 11	80	1 243	1 168·8	400 163 798 tonne-km		750	1 956·3	64 *(103)*
Office du F.C. Trancameronnais Yaoundé, PO Box 625 *(To take charge of Trans-Cameroon Railway–Yaoundé to Ngaounderé)*														
CANADA														
Algoma Central Railway PO Box 7000, Sault Ste. Marie, Ont P6A5P6	4′ 8½″ *(1·435)*	322 *(518)*	422 *(680)*		**DeL** 32 **DeS** 2		55	1 853	3 749·0	1 043 984 000 ton-km			207·0	108·6 *(174·8)*
Alma and Jonquiere Rly Co Alma, Lac St. Jean, Que.	4′ 8½″ *(1·435)*	10 *(16·0)*	27 *(43)*		**DeLS** 2			6	1 200·0	10 *(16)*	600	1 800		
BCH Railway British Columbia and Power Authority 260-12th Street New Westminister, BC V39 4H3	4′ 8½″ *(1·435)*	103 *(166)*	193 *(311)*		**DeL** 21 **DeS** 4			14	2 558·0		1 500	4 500		
****British Columbia Railway** 1095 W. Pender St, Vancouver 1, B.C. *(Formerly Pacific Great Eastern Railway)*	4′ 8½″ *(1·435)*	1 248 *(1 845)*	1 616 *(2 607)*		**DeL** 119 **DeS** 3	**D** 6		8 851	6 173·0	3 200 000 000 ton-km			66·1	
Burlington Northern (Manitoba) Ltd. 963, Lindsay St., Winnepeg, Man R3N IX6 *(Formerly Midland Railway Co of Manitoba)*	4′ 8½″ *(1·435)*	73·3 *(117·4)*	95·74 *(159)*		**DeS** 1			1	850 000	83 *(134)*				

** See main entry

Average Speeds			Financial Data	Braking (con-tinuous)	Couplers	Buffers	Rails	Sleepers (crossties)		Curva-ture max.	Gradient max. (U=not compen-sated)	Axle load max.	Alti-tude max.	Staff em-ployed. Total no. (inclu. work-shop)	Names of officials. Extended lists can be found at the end of the individual country in the report section immediately following
Freight Train	Pass. Train	Speed max.	Revenue Expenses		Type and Height above rail	Centres and Height above rail	Weight	Type and thick-ness	Spacing Number per mile or centres ins						
mph (km/hr)	mph (km/hr)	mph (km/hr)	in 1 000's		ins (mm)	ins (mm)	lb. per yd (kg/m)	ins (mm)	(mm)			tonnes	feet (m)		
		F 37 (60) P 56 (90)					115/64 (57/32)	Wood 6¾ (170)	2 950 (1 833)	1 148 ft (350 m)		25	2 740 (835)	7 140	Supt. Eng: Frederico Guilherme de Castro Braga Operations: Ing. Ildo Bertucci
		F 37 (60) P 47 (75)					91/50 (45/25)	Wood 6¼ (160)	2 950 (1 833)	984 ft (300 m)		20 (641)	2 103 Ing.	6 311	Engineering: Ruben Muller
Broad 18 (29) Metre 14 (23)	Broad 37 (60) Metre 30 (48)	75 (120)	$Cr 288 914·8 472 131·7	Air	Alliance Cobrasma 29½ (750)		115/60 (57/30)	Wood 6¾ (170) Conc Steel	Wood 2 575 (1 600) Conc 2 414 (1 500)	492 ft (150 m)	2·0%	25	4 068 (1 240)	29 104 (4 642)	President: Sr. J. Pires de Castro
		34 (55)	$Cr. 45·1 5 367·1	Air W'hse	Type E		129/88 (64/44)	Wood 6¾ (170)		1 066 ft (325 m)	0·35% 1·5% U		400 (122)	128	Gen. Man: Antonio José de Castro Lyra Porto
8·6 (14)	27 (44)	38 (62)	$Cr * 358 774 871 228	Air W'hse	Interlock F 29½ (750)	29½ (750)	115 (57)	Wood 6¼ (160)	2 640 (1 640)	8·7° up 12·2° down	1·0% up 0·5% down	24	2 723 (830)	5 593 (1 093)	Gen. Man: Eng. Joao Christostomo Belesa
			Kyats 198 813·6 223 650·1											29 223	
18 (30)	25 (40)	37 (60)	Fr CFA 5 339 007·3 6 498 345·9	Vac W'hse (Jourdain Monn-eret)	Willison Auto 33½ (850)		72/40 (36/20)	Metal Metal & conc	2 400-2 800 (1 500-1 750)	394 ft (120 m)	2·1% U 1·7%	13	2 625 (860)	3 094 (1 000)	Pres; Gen. Man.: Gilbert Ntang
20 (32)	21 (34)	P 50 (80) F 45 (72)	$ 19 146·0 17 589·0	W'hse AB	Type E 34½ (876)		100/80 (50/40)	Wood 7 (178)	22" (559)	13·5°	Sth. 2·5% Nth. 1·5%		1 511 (461)	690	Gen. Man (Rail): S. A. Black
20 (32)		55 (40)		W'hse AB	AAR 27 (686)		100/85 (50/43)	Wood 6 (153)	2 900 (1 800)	5·0°		110 Per car	400 (122)	25 (2)	Gen. Supt.: J. R. Gosselin
20 (32)		35 (56)		W'hse Air	AAR 34½ (876)		115/60 (57/30)	Wood 6 (153)	22" (559)	Mn. 15° Sid. 23°	3·0% 3·0% U	33	433 (132)	320	Man.: G. I. Stevenson
17 (27)	32 (51)	F 40 (64) P 50 (80)	$C 68 377 76 194	W'hse Air	AAR 34 (880)		85/115 (42/57)	Wood 7 (178)	1970/km	Rad. 145 m	2·2%	33	433 (132)	3 000	Man: N. A. MacPherson
		50 (80)					90/68 (45/34)	Wood (7 178)						24 (1)	Pres.: N. M. Lorentzsen Supt.: J. A. Lowry

* Excludes iron ore receipts which are credited to the Cio Vale Rio Doce, owners of EFVM

NAME OF COMPANY ADDRESS	Gauge ft. in. (metres)	Route length incl. E=Electrified miles (km.)	Track length incl. E=Electrified miles (km.)	Elect. system and type of conductor	Loco-motives L=Line S=Shunt Steam Electric Diesel De=elec. Dh=hyd.	Rail-cars Electric Diesel Trailer Railbus Multiple Unit set	Pass. train cars	Freight train cars Con-tainers	Total Volume carried. Thous-ands of tonnes	Av'ge haul per ton miles (km.)	Av'ge net train load tonnes	Max. trailing load tonnes	Total number carried in 1 000's	Aver-age jour-ney miles (km.)
CANADA *(contd.)*														
Canada and Gulf Terminal Rly. PO Box 578, Mont Joli, Que G5H 3LB	4' 8½'' *(1·435)*	36 *(58)*	41 *(67)*		DeS 2			*	242·5	4 709 803 ton-miles			32	*(51·4)*
Canadian National Railways 935 Lagauchetiere St West, (PO Box 8100) Montreal H3C 3N4, Que														
**CP Rail Canadian Pacific Limited Windsor Station, Montreal, Que H3C 3E4														
Cumberland Railway Sydney & Louisburg Division PO Box 2500 Sydney, NS	4' 8½'' *(1·435)*	39 *(63)*	101 *(162)*		DeS 15			1 100	3 258·9	10·0 *(16)*	1 641	2 500		
Esquimalt and Nanaimo Railway Co Cordova & Granville St, Vancouver 2, BC *(Division of CP Rail)*	4' 8½'' *(1·435)*	196 *(316)*	253 *(407)*		DeL 11 DeS 1 (all CPR)	D 1			†		1 200	3 200		
Essex Terminal Railway Co. 1070 University Ave, Windsor Ontario N9A 554	4' 8½'' *(1·435)*	23 *(37)*	54 *(85)*		De 6			4	1 734 000 ton-miles					
Greater Winnipeg Water District Rly. 598 Plinquet St., St. Boniface, Man	4' 8½'' *(1·435)*	92 *(148)*	120 *(193)*		DeL 4	D 1 De 1	3	118	724·1	50 912 ton-km			4·4	75 *(121)*
Napierville Junction Railway Co. 1117 St. Catherine St. West, Montreal 2	4' 8½'' *(1·435)*	42 *(68)*	82 *(132)*		D 2				1 988·8	27·0 *(43·4)*			218·5	40·0 *(64·3)*
Northern Alberta Railways Co 13025 St. Albert Trail, Edmonton, Alta T5L 4L4 *(Jointly owned by CNR and CPR)*	4' 8½'' *(1·435)*	922 *(1 484)*	1 064 *(1 701)*		DeL 21		2	279	2 695·0	1 092 000 000 ton-km			7·9 *(143·5)*	890 292
Ontario Northland Railway 195 Regina St., North Bay, Ont P1B 8L3	4' 8½'' *(1·435)*	753 *(1 212)*			DeL 34	DMU 4	33	997	5 191·6	896 090 065 ton-km			127·8	22 059·0 17
Quebec Cartier Mining Co., Ltd Port Cartier, G5B 2H3 Saguenay County	4' 8½'' *(1·435)*	193 *(310)*	226 *(364)*		Dh 54			12 1 779	24 657·6	2 750 197 ton-km	13 000	16 400 *(306)*	7 776	190
Quebec Central Railway Sherbrooke, Que.	4' 8½'' *(1·435)*	355 *(571)*	426 *(686)*		De 9		8	341						
Quebec North Shore and Labrador Railway Company PO Box 1000, Sept-Iles, Que, G4R 4L5	4' 8½'' *(1·435)*	391 *(629)*	422 *(680)*		DeL 83		26	4 500	30 626	38 339 094 000 ton-km			20·8 *(325)*	202
Roberval and Saguenay Rly Co PO Box 277, Arvida, Que	4' 8½'' *(1·435)*	56 *(90)*	102 *(164)*		DhL 12 DhS 2			452	5 803					
Toronto, Hamilton and Buffalo Rly Co 36 Hunter St E, Hamilton, Ont L8N IMI	4' 8½'' *(1·435)*	106 *(170)*	158 *(250)*		DeL 10 DeS 8			1 179	2 613·7	5 729 260 ton-km				37·6 *(60·7)*
White Pass & Yukon Route‡ 17th Floor IBM Tower, Pacific Centre, 701, West Georgia St, PO Box 10140, Vancouver, BC V7Y IE6 *Comprises:* Pacific and Artic Rly and Nav Co British Columbia-Yukon Rly Co The British Yukon Rly Co The British Yukon Nav Co Ltd														
CHILE **Antofagasta (Chile) and Bolivia Rly Co Ltd** *Head office:* 1 Broad St. Place, London, E.C.2 *Local office:* Antofagasta	3' 3⅜'' *(1·00)*	438 *(704)*	449 *(722)*		DeL 15 DeS 4		96	2 619	1 322·0	319 969 000 tonne-km			47·0	71 *(114)*
F.C. Rancagua al Teniente *Sociedad Minera El Teniente SA* Milan 1040, Rancagua	2' 6'' *(0·762)*	42 *(68)*	61 *(98·7)*		DeS 1 DeL 13	R 11 D 3	37	297		33 *(53)*	60	170	960·2	43 *(65)*
**Ferrocarriles del Estado (FFCCE) *(Chilean State Railways)* Avenida Bernardo O'Higgins, No. 924 Casilla 134-D, Santiago *Comprising:*														
F.C. Arica-La Paz *(Chilean Section)*	3' 3⅜'' *(1·00)*	129 *(207)*	152 *(244)*											
Red Norte *(Northern Network)*	3' 3⅜'' *(1·00)*	920 *(1 481)*	1 210 *(1 630)*											
Red Sur *(Southern Network)*	5' 6'' *(1·676)* 3' 3⅜'' *(1·00)* 1' 11⅝'' *(0·600)*	2 086 *(3 357)* E 499 *(803)* 177 *(285)* 22 *(35)*	2 711 *(4 363)* E 795 *(1 280)* 203 *(327)* 24 *(38)*											

** See main entry
* All freight cars on hire basis from CP Rail
† All operational data embodied in figures for CP Rail
‡ See entry for British Columbia Railway in Railway Systems section

Average Speeds			Financial Data	Braking	Couplers	Buffers	Rails	Sleepers (crossties)		Curvature max.	Gradient max. (U=not compensated)	Axle load max.	Altitude max.	Staff employed. Total no. (inclu. workshop)	Names of officials. Extended lists can be found at the end of the individual country in the report section immediately following
Freight Train	Pass. Train	Speed max.	Revenue Expenses in 1 000's	(continuous)	Type and Height above rail	Centres and Height above rail	Weight lb. per yd	Type and thickness	Spacing Number per mile (per km) or centres ins (mm)						
mph (km/hr)	mph (km/hr)	mph (km/hr)			ins (mm)	ins (mm)	(kg/m)	ins (mm)				tonnes	feet (m)		
30 (48)	30 (48)	35 (56)	$ 705·1 641·5	Clasp	Type E 34 (864)		80 (40)	Wood 7 (178)	20"	5·0°	1·5	39	60 (18)	29	Gen. Man.: J. B. Quimper
15·0 (24)		25 (40)		W'hse AB	Type E 34½ (876)		100/85 (50/42)	Wood 6 (153)	30" (762)	4·40°	1·5% U	30	140 (43)	345 (43)	Gen. Man.: H. S. Haslam
13 (20·9)		F 52 P 45		W'hse	E 50		85/65 (42/32)	Wood 8 (203)	20" (508)	14·0°	2·2% 1·74% U		1 285 (392)	266 (59)	Pres.: J. N. Fraine
10 (16)		35 (65)		K-1 W'hse	Droppin Sharron West Simplex		100/85 (50/42)	Wood 6 (153)	3 000 (1 864)	18·0°	1·00% U	31		90	Gen. Man: M. A. Elder
25 (40)	35 (56)	50 (80)		W'hse Air	Type K		85/60 (42/30)	Wood 6 (153)	3 500 (2 174)	6°	4·5% U	20	1 060 (322)	24 (15)	Dir.: A. Penman Supt: J. Nielsen
30 (48)	55 (88)						132/127 (65/63)	Wood 7 (178)	2 970 (1 845)	7°	0·58%				
19 (30)	38 (61)	P 50 (80) F 35 (56)		W'hse Air	Type E and D 34½ (876)		100/60 (50/30)	Pine 7 (178) and 6 (153)	2 111 (534)	12°	2·4%	32·8	2 660 (811)	653 (87)	Gen. Man.: K. R. Perry
30 (48)	35 (56)	60 (97)	$49 853·6 38 902·8	W'hse Air	Type E 34½ (986)		115/80 (57/40)	Wood 7 (178)	22" (559)	M. 6·5° B. 12°	1·5% U	32·8	1 289	1 683 (350)	Chairman: I. W. Hollingsworth Gen. Man: F. S. Clifford
25 (40·2)	35 (56)	F. 40 (64) P. 50 (80)		W'hse Air	33½ (851) E& F Nat. Mall. Steel Co.		132 (66)	Wood 7 (178)		7°	loaded 0·4% empty 1·35%	32·5	1 970 (600)		Pres.: L. J. Patterson
							100/75 (50/37)	Wood 7 (178)	20" (508)	10·0°	2·67%	62·5			
34·5 (55)	34 (59·5)	F. 30 (55) P. 60 (97)	$ 58 400 61 500	W'hse AB	Nat. Mall. Can Car. Type F		132 (65/5)	Wood 7 (178)	20" (508)	8·0°	1·32%	32	2 066 (628)	1 084 (309)	Pres.: W. J. Bennett
30 (48)	No limit		$ 5 092 5 819	W'hse AB	Standard		100 (49·6)	Wood 6 (153)	2 900 (1 800)	10·0°	1·25%	32·5	400 (122)	250	Supt. of Railway Operations: Raymond J. Girard
40 (64)	50 (80)	F. 60 (96) P. 65 (104)	$8 183·5 7 805·4	W'hse	AAR 34½ (876)	105/80		Wood 19·5" 6 (153)		6°	1·04% U	31	525 482 (100)	400	Gen. Man.: J. A. Hill
		31 (50)		W'hse Air	Henricot Auto 30 (762)		75/65 (37/32)	Wood		246 ft (75 m)	3·0%	15	14 396 (4 388)	1 563	Gen. Man: E. J. Barrie Ops. Man: J. L. Hill
8·6 (14)	8·6 (14)	18·6 (30)	$ 10·2 4 428·4	W'hse Air	Alliance ACF 27 (686)		75/60 (37/30)	Wood 6 (152)	3 200 (1 987)		4·39% 5·36% U	16	6 933 (2 113)	800	Supt: R. T. Patton

NAME OF COMPANY ADDRESS	Gauge ft. in. (metres)	Route length incl. E=Electrified miles (km.)	Track length incl. E=Electrified miles (km.)	Elect. system and type of conductor	Loco-motives L=Line S=Shunt Steam Electric Diesel De=elec. Dh=hyd.	Rail-cars Electric Diesel Trailer Railbus Multiple Unit set	Pass. train cars	Freight train cars Con-tainers	Freight movement Total Volume carried. Thousands of tonnes	Av'ge haul per ton miles (km.)	Av'ge net train load tonnes	Max. trailing load tonnes	Passengers Total number carried in 1000's	Average journey miles (km.)
CHILE *(contd.)*														
F.C. Iquique (See footnote)	Combined *(1·00/ 1·435)* 4′ 8½″ *(1·435)* 3′ 3⅜″ *(1·00)*	† 70 * *(113)* 84 *(135)* 657 *(1 057)*	78 * *(126)* 155 *(250)* 710 *(1 143)*											
F.C. Transandino por Los Andes *(Chilean Transandine)*	3′ 3⅜″ *(1·00)*	E 44‡ *(71)*	52 *(83)*	3 000 V dc OH										
F.C. Mineral de Chuquicamata *(Ceased operations)*														
F.C. de Concepcion a Curanilahue Apart 141, Coronel	5′ 6″ *(1·676)*	80 *(128)*			30			43	807					
F.C. Electrico Cruz Grande el Tofo Box 19D, La Serena *(Ceased operations)*														
F.C. Potrerillos Potrerillos *(Owned by Andes Copper Mining Co.)*	3′ 3⅜″ *(1·00)*	61 § *(98)*	64 *(103)*		SS 3 DeL 6 DeS 2			4	175	557·5	43·5 *(70)*	320	Up 750 Down 1 150	1·5	43·5 *(70)*
F.C. Militar de Puente Alto a El Volcan Regimiento de Ingenieros de Ferrocarriles No. 7, Puento Alto	1′ 11⅝″ *(0·600)*	37 *(60)*	43 *(70)*		DL 6	D 5	10	52 C 2	21·4	155 *(250)*	90	120	113·0	18 *(29)*
F.C. Tocopilla al Toco (Soc Quimica y Minera de Chile SA) Casilla 2098, Tocopilla *Also operates:*	3′ 6″ *(1·067)* E 35 *(57)*	73 *(117)*	106 *(170)* E 50 *(80)*	1 500 V dc OH	EL 7 DeL 5 DeS 7		8	853	889·7	59·8 *(96·2)*	400		3·1	30·4 *(48·9)*
Maria Elena Mine Railway *(Industrial Line)*	3′ 6″ *(1·067)*		E 68 *(109)*	550 V dc	B 22 E 13		8	506						
Pedro de Valdivia Mine Railway *(Industrial Line)*	3′ 6″ *(1·067)*		E 88 *(141)*	550 V dc	B 28 E 13		14	533						
F.C. Salitrero de Taltal (Soc. Quimica y Minera de Chile SA) O' Higgins Station, PO Box E, Taltal	3′ 6″ *(1·067)*	65 *(104)*	79 *(127)*		D 5		3	350						
CHINA **Chinese People's Republic Railways** Ministry of Railways, Peking														
Hong Kong **Kowloon-Canton Railway** *(British Section)* Tsim Sha Tsui, Kowloon, Hong Kong														
COLOMBIA **Ferrocarriles Nacionales de Colombia** Edif, Estacion de la Sabena calle 13, No. 18-24, Bogotá	3′ 0″ *(0·914)*	2 135 *(3 436)*			S 30 DeL 128 DeS 18	D 32	336	7 664 C 2	2 731·0	272·7 *(438·9)*	293	519	4 263·0	58·0 *(93·3)*
Consists of the following lines: **Division Central**		850 *(1 368)*												
División Santander		249 *(400)*												
División Magdalena		264 *(425)*												
División Pacifico		561 *(903)*												
División Antioquia		211 *(340)*												
CONGO **C.F. Congo-Océan** B. P. 651, Pointe-Niore	3′ 6″ *(1·067)*	320 *(515)*	392 ‖ *(640)*		DeL 34 DeS 7 DhS 16	D 7	58	1 165 C 62	3 612·0	207 *(333)*	631	1 250	1 220·5	71 *(114)*
C.F. Comilog Compagnie, Miniére de l'Ogooué, Moando, Gabon *Local office:* Makabana	3′ 6″ *(1·067)*	177 *(285)*	193 *(311)*		DeL 16 DS 4	R 9		374	1 511·6	302 *(485)*	2 000	3 600	0	
COSTA RICA **Chiriqui Land Company** *(Extensions only of United Fruit Co's lines in Panama)*	3′ 0″ *(0·914)*	30 *(48)*												
Ferrocarril del Sur la Cra Cia, Bananero de Costa Rica, Golfito Costa Rica, Provincia de Puntavenas	3′ 6″ *(1·067)*	91 *(147)*	184 *(297)*		SL 1 DeL 14	D 16	18	415	312·6	56 *(90)*	1 000	1 440	110·0	30 *(48)*
Ferrocarril Nacional Al Atlántic Apartado 10096, San José	3′ 6″ *(1·067)*	281 *(453)*	361 *(581)*		DeL 19 DeS 17 DhL 12	R 2	58	650	1 560·0			Level 400 5% gr. 200	1 900·0	

** See main entry
* Combined 1·00/1·435 metre gauge incorporates a third rail
† Formed by a merger of standard-gauge F. C. Salitero de Tarapaca (formerly owned by Nitrate Co of London) and metre-gauge F.C. de la Provincia de Tarapaca (F.C. Iquiqui-Pintados)
‡ Including rack-rail section
§ Operates trains over 43 miles *(68 km)* of Chilean State Railway between Pueblo Hundido and Chanaral, in addition to its own 58 miles *(94 km)* of main line
‖ Congo-Océan provides a public service over the 280 km COMILOG line between Mont-Belo station M'Bunda

Average Speeds			Financial Data	Braking (continuous)	Couplers	Buffers	Rails	Sleepers (crossties)		Curvature max.	Gradient max. (U=not compensated)	Axle load max.	Altitude max.	Staff employed. Total no. (inclu. workshop)	Names of officials. Extended lists can be found at the end of the individual country in the report section immediately following
Freight Train	Pass. Train	Speed max.	Revenue Expenses		Type and Height above rail	Centres and Height above rail	Weight	Type and thickness	Spacing Number per mile or centres						
mph (km/hr)	mph (km/hr)	mph (km/hr)	in 1 000's		ins (mm)	ins (mm)	lb. per yd (kg/m)	ins (mm)	ins (mm)			tonnes	feet (m)		
							50 (25)	Oak		476 ft (145 m)	1·62%				
16 (26)	18 (30)	37 (60)		W'hse	Type E 30 (762)		70 (35)	Oak 7 (175)	2 720 (1 690)	279 ft (85 m)	3·5% U	13·5	9 449 (2 880)	350 (62)	Gen. Man: L. O. Fines
18·6 (30)	21·8 (35)	25 (40)		Air W'hse	Hook & Chain 19⅝ (500)	Crs. 15¾ (400) Ht. 19⅝ (500)	82 (37)	Oak 6 (150)	19⅝ (500)	197 ft (60 m)	5·5% 1·2% U		4 593 (1 400)	84	
22 (35)	22 (35)	25 (40)		Air W'hse	Alliance 30 (762)		80/60 (40/30)	Oak 6 (150)	24½" (620)	180 ft (55 m)	1·51% 4·1% U	18·2	4 900 (1 493)	389 (284)	Gen. Man: Miguel Alvarez A.
9 (15)		16 (25)		Manual	Chain 32½ (825)	Central 32½" (825)	Steel 56/40 (28/20)	Wood 8 (200)	2 414 (1 500)	230 ft (70 m)	4·19% 3·25% U	10	7 169 (2 185)	147 (69)	Gen. Man: P. S. Dias Martinez
12·6 (20·3)	12·6 (20·3)	47 (75)	535 409·0 758 807·0	Air W'hse	Auto 24 (610)		75/50 (37/25)	Wood 6 (153)	2 720 (1 700)	262 ft (80 m)	3·8%	10	9 512 (2 900)	11 291 (2 300)	Gen. Man.: Marco Tulio Lora Borrero
23 (37)	34 (60)	50 (80)	Francs C.F.A. 3 347 718·3 3 109 743·9	Vac Jourdain Monn-eret	Willison auto. 34¼ (870)	Buffer-coupler	72/60 (36/30)	Metal 4¾ (120)	2 816 (1 750)	492 ft (150 m)	2·2%	16	1 578 (481)	3 086 (1 172)	Gen. Man.: S. R. Tchichelle
14 (23)		34 (55)	Francs C.F.A. No revenue	Vac J.M.R. & Gresham	Willison auto. 34¼ (870)	Crs 34¾ (884) Ht. 34¾ (870)	60·4 (30)	Metal 7 (178)	22½" (570)		2·5% 2·3% U	16	2 142 (653)	1 234 (242)	Gen. Man.: M. Lauraint (Moanda) A. Brittiaux (Makaban)
20 (32)	18 (29)	30 (48)		Air W'hse	Magor & Pullman 25 (635)		70 (35)	Pine Wood 6 (153)	2 900 (1 800)	Rad. 470 ft (143 m)	Loaded 0·65% Empty 1·0%	Coopers E. 40	265 (81)	205 (21)	Pres: W.W. Booth
10 (16)	18 (29)	30 (48)	$41 843·0 50 599·8	Air W'hse & Lee Neville	Tower 29 (737)		70/50 (35/25)	Wood (Some steel) 6 (153)	2 640 (1 620)	Rad. 164 ft (40 m)	5·0% U	13	5 074 (1 547)	2 200 (455)	Pres. and Gen. Man.: Donald Z. van Hart

NAME OF COMPANY ADDRESS	Gauge ft. in. (metres)	Route length incl. E=Electrified miles (km.)	Track length incl. E=Electrified miles (km.)	Elect. system and type of conductor	Loco-motives L=Line S=Shunt Steam Electric Diesel De=elec. Dh=hyd.	Rail-cars Electric Diesel Trailer Railbus Multiple Unit set	Pass. train cars	Freight train cars Containers	Total Volume carried. Thousands of tonnes	Av'ge haul per ton miles (km.)	Av'ge net train load tonnes	Max. trailing load tonnes	Total number carried in 1 000's	Average journey miles (km.)

CUBA
Cuba Nacional Railways
FF.CC. Nacionales de Cuba
Ministry of Transportation
Havana

Western Region	4' 8½" (1·435)	1 220 (1 963) E 11 (17)												
(Narrow gauges are 3' 0" (1·067 m) and 2' 6" (0·762 m))	Narrow	70 (113)												
Camaguey Region	4' 8½" (1·435)	1 270 (2 044)							10 765·9				17 912·2	
Guantanamo Region	4' 8½" (1·435)	81 (130)												
Camilo Cienfuegos Region	4' 8½" (1·435) 3' 0" (0·914)	208 (335)												

CZECHOSLOVAKIA
Czechoslovak State Railways CSD
Prague

DENMARK
Danish State Railways DSB
Sølvgade 40, DK-1349 Copenhagen K

Amagerbanen (AB) DK-2770, Kastrup	4' 8½" (1·435)	3 (5)	6 (7)		Dh 1				118·9					
Gribskovbanen (GDS) DK-3400 Hilleröd, Sjaelland	4' 8½" (1·435)		26 (42)		DeL 1 DhL 2 D 1	R 2 DMU 10	2		7·1				687	11·6 (18·4)
									128 054 ton-km					
Hads-Ning Herreders Jernbane (HHJ) DK-8300 Ödder, Jutland	4' 8½" (1·435)	22 (35)	23 (36)		DL 2 DeL 2 DS 1	R 3 RT 2 DMU 4	6	8	62·3				346·0	
									937 680 ton-km					
Helsingoer-Hornbaek-Gilleleje Jernbane (HHGB) DK-3000 Helsingoer	4' 8½" (1·435)	15 (25)	19 (31)		D 5	R 3 RT 3 DMU 4		2	2·2	8·6 (13·8)			351·1	8·1 (13·0)
Hilleroed-Frederiksvaerk-Hundested Jernbane (HFHJ) DK-3400 Hilleröd, Sjaelland	4' 8½" (1·435)	24 (39)	29 (47)		DeL 5 DhL 2 DS 3	DMU 10* R 1	10	5	201·4				1 059·6	13·7 (22·0)
									5 242 366 ton-km					
Hjørring Privatbaner (HP) Banegardspladsen 6¹, DK 9800 Hjørring	4' 8½" (1·435)	11 (18)	12 (20)		DeL 1 DhL 2	DMU 3	7	1	41·7	739 047 ton-km			170·9	9·5 (15·3)
Høng-Tølløse Jernbane (HTJ) Holbaek, Sjaelland	4' 8½" (1·435)	32 (51)			SL 2 DeL 1	D 1 R 3 RT 2	7 5	28	7·7	14·4 (23·1)			277·9	8·6 (13·9)
A/S Lollandsbanen 4930 Maribo Lollandske Jernbane (LJ) DK-4930, Maribo	4' 8½" (1·435)	49 (77·5)			DeS 1 DeL 5 Dh 6 Dh 1 D 3	D 1 R 3	9	27	154·1				606·1	16 (25)
									5 976 450 ton-km					
Lyngby-Naerum Jernbane (LNJ) Firskovvej 28, 2800 Lyngby, Sjölland	4' 8½" (1·435)	5 (8)	5 (8)			D 4	2						873·3	3·7 (5·9)
Odsherreds Jernbane (OHJ) DK-4300 Holbaek, Sjaelland	4' 8½" (1·435)	31 (50)	35 (56)		SL 2 D 8	D 2 RT 6 R 5	9	20	31·1	18·8 (30·4)			498·2	13·4 (21·6)
Ostsjaellandske Østbanen 4652 Haarlev, Sjaelland	4' 8½" (1·435)	29 (46)	37 (59)		DeL 2 D 1	D 3 R 7 RT 8		20	54·9	16·5 (26·8)			269·4	12·0 (19·3)
Skagensbanen (SB) DK-9990 Skagen, Jutland	4' 8½" (1·435)	25 (40)	28 (46)		DeL 3 DS 2	DMU 4	4	8	11·1				229·0	16·2 (26·0)
									405 100 ton-km		500		
Varde-Nörre Nebel Jernbane (VNJ) Varde, Jutland	4' 8½" (1·435)	24 (38)	31 (50)		S 2 DeL 2	R 3 RT 3	7	6	43·7	11·7 (18·8)			181·4	11·6 (18·7)
Vemb-Lemvig-Thyboron Jernbane (VLTJ) 7620 Lemvig, Jutland	4' 8½" (1·435)	37 (60)	42 (68)		SL 2 DeL 1 DS 2	D 11 R 6 RT 5	2	5	1 275·5			180	205·2	27·4 (44·1)
									1 322 528 ton-km					

DOMINICAN REPUBLIC

F.C. Central Rio Haina Apartado 1258, Haina	4' 8½" (1·435)	70 (113)	128 (206)		D 13				800					
F.C. de Central Romana La Romana	4' 8½" (1·435)		220 (354)		De 11 S† 1 DL 3 DS 1		None	970	3 000	20 (32)	1 200	2 000		
F.C. Unidos Dominicanos (Ceased operation)	2' 6" (0·76) 3' 6" (1·067)	65 (105) 72 (116)												

EAST AFRICA
KENYA, TANZANIA, UGANDA

East African Railways Corporation PO Box 30121, Nairobi, Kenya	3' 3⅜" (1·00)	3 663 (5 894)	4 340 (6 985)		SL 213 SS 22 DeL 100 DhS 74 DS 18		536	16 099	5 989·5	3 998 231 986 ton-km			5 750·4	127 (204)

** See main entry
 * Owned jointly with GDS
 † Fireless

Average Speeds			Financial Data	Braking (continuous)	Couplers	Buffers	Rails	Sleepers (crossties)		Curvature max.	Gradient max. (U=not compensated)	Axle load max.	Altitude max.	Staff employed. Total no. (inclu. workshop)	Names of officials. Extended lists can be found at the end of the individual country in the report section immediately following
Freight Train	Pass. Train	Speed max.	Revenue Expenses		Type and Height above rail	Centres and Height above rail	Weight	Type and thickness	Spacing Number per mile or centres ins (mm)						
mph (km/hr)	mph (km/hr)	mph (km/hr)	in 1 000's		ins (mm)	ins (mm)	lb. per yd (kg/m)	ins (mm)				tonnes	feet (m)		
				W'hse Air	Auto		100/200 (99/120)	Wood 6 (153) 7 (178)		459 ft (195 m)	2·0%	20			
				Knorr Air			90/74 (45/37)								
37 (60)	43 (70)	43 (70)	Kr 4 804·2 7 405·3	Knorr Air	Standard	Standard	74 (37)	Wood 6 (150)	2 400 (1 500)	7·0°	1·4%	15·4			Dir: M. Krusen-stjerna-Hafstrøm
		43 (70)	Kr 4 593·1 7 711·1	Air	Standard	Standard (37/22)	74/45 6 (150)	Wood 6 (150)	2 000 (1 250)	4·7°	1·25%	14			Dir: Aagard Frandsen
		47 (75)	Kr 1 173·1 2 859·2	Knorr Air	Scharff (760)	Buffer Coupler	74 (37)	Wood 6 (150)		3·5°		10		57	Man. Dir: K. Sørensen
44 (70)	47 (75)	47 (75)	Kr 9 896·4 11 514·4	Knorr Air	Standard *	Standard	74/67 (37/33·4)	Wood 6 (150)	2 400 (1 500)	7·25°	1·25%	20			Gen. Man: K. Hafstrom
37 (60)	47 (75)	47 (75)	Kr 5 621 6 382	Knorr Air	Standard (1 060)	Standard (1 750)	74 (37)	Wood		3·7°	5·0%	20		73	Gen. Man: Aage Velling
		43 (70)		Knorr Air	Standard	Standard	90/74 (45/37)	Wood 4¾ (120)	29½" (750)	4·1°	1·0%	16·3	161 (49)	20	Gen. Man:: N. D. Andersen
50 (80)	62 (100)	62 (100)	Kr 12 005·1 18 503·7		Standard	Standard (32/24½)	64/49 5 (125)	Pine (1 560)	2 500	2·8°	0·5%	14·3		158	Dir: Sven Panhen
			Kr 2 209·5 3 975·9		BSI 29½ (750)	69/42 (1 750)	81 (37)	Wood 6 (125)	(790)	7·0°	1·25%	18		39	Dir: H. Grundsøe
		43 (70)		Knorr Air	Standard *	Standard	55·5/ 74 (27·6/ 37)	Beech 5⅛ (130)	27½"/29½" (700/750)	3·7°	1·25%	16·3	164 (50)	69	
					Standard	Standard	56 (28)	Wood 5½ (140)		7·0°	1·0%	14·3			Dir: F. E. Nielsen
37 (60)	47 (75)	47 (75)	Kr 2 266·0 3 304·0	Knorr Air	Standard	Standard	74 (37)	Wood 5½ (140)	25¾" (650)	2·5°	4·5%U	20		49	Gen. Man: J. V. Petersen
				Air	Standard	Standard (27·5)	55 5½ (140)	Pine (1 335)	2 150	5·8°	1·25%	16			
37 (60)	43 (70)		Kr 2 917·9 4 754·6	Knorr Air	Standard	Standard	110/90 (55/45)	Pine 6 (150)		4·6°	0·67%	16·5			Gen Man: O. Olsson
				W'hse			80/60 (40/30)	Wood 8 (203)	20" (510)	640 ft (140)	1·5% U				
40 (40)	50 (80)			W'hse Air	Type E 28½ (725)		80/60 (40/30)	Wood 7-8" (610)	24" (610)	476 ft (145 m)	1·5%	17·5	300 (91)	425 (30)	Gen. Man: Dr. T. Rosell
19 (30)	20 (32)	45 (72)	£30 200 28 200	Air Metcalf-Oerlikon W'hse.	MCA, F. H. Lloyd Co Ltd	Buffer-coupler 23 (584)	95/45 (47/22)	Steel Timber at turn-outs, 5" (127)	2 300 (1 430)	358 ft (109 m)	Main 1·5% (some 2·0%) Branch 3·5% U	21 on 95 lb track only	Kenya, Uganda 9 136 Tanzania 4 350	43 539 (4 500)	Dir. Gen.: Dr. E. N. Gakuo

* Railcars have Scharffenburg couplers, no buffers.

NAME OF COMPANY ADDRESS	Gauge ft. in. (metres)	Route length incl. E=Electrified miles (km.)	Track length incl. E=Electrified miles (km.)	Elect. system and type of conductor	Loco-motives L=Line S=Shunt Steam Electric Diesel De=elec. Dh=hyd.		Rail-cars Electric Diesel Trailer Railbus Multiple Unit set		Pass. train cars	Freight train cars Con-tainers	Freight movement — Total Volume carried. Thousands of tonnes	Av'ge haul per ton miles (km.)	Av'ge net train load tonnes	Max. trailing load tonnes	Passengers — Total number carried in 1 000's	Average journey miles (km.)
ECUADOR																
**Empresa de Ferrocarriles del Estado Bolivar 443, Quito *Operates following railways:*	3' 6" (1·067) 2' 5½" (0·750)	600 (966) 96 (155)	726 (1 169)		S DeL	53 14	D	10	46	430	589·0	140 (225)		1 000	1 687·0	38·5 (62)
F.C. de Bahia a Chone	2' 5½" (0·750)	50 (80)														
F.C. de Puerto Bolivar a Pasaje	3' 6" (1·067)	15 (25)														
F.C. de Puerto Bolivar a Piedras	2' 5½" (0·750)	46 (75)														
F.C. de Guayaquil a Quito	3' 6" (1·067)	281 (452)														
F.C. Quito a San Lorenzo	3' 6" (1·067)	232 (373)														
F.C. de Sibamba a Azogues	3' 6" (1·067)	72 (116)														
EGYPT																
**Egyptian Railways Rameses Square, Cairo																
Basse Egypt Railway Mansura	3' 3⅜" (1·000)	157 (253)			S	23		20	54	371						
Egyptian Delta Light Railway Cairo *(Being replaced by road services)*	2' 5½" (0·75)															
EL SALVADOR																
International Railways of Central America Head office: 15 Exchange Place, Jersey City, New Jersey, USA Local office: San Salvador *(Connects with the I.R.C.A. lines in Guatemala)*	3' 0" (0·914)	285 (459)	316 (509)		S D	36 2			57	513	560·1	96·6 (160)	70	1 200	2 216·5	27 (43·4)
FC de El Salvador San Salvador *(Former Salvador Railway Co Ltd, taken over by the State 11 October, 1962)*	3' 0" (0·914)	100 (161)	116 (187)		S	17	D	11	28	234						
ETHIOPIA																
**Cie du C.F. Franco-Éthiopien de Djibouti a Addis-Ababa PO Box 1051, Addis Ababa																
Northern Ethiopia Railway PO Box 218, Asmara	3' 1⅜" (0·95)	191 (306)	221 (355)		DhL SL SS DS	3 8 10 3	D	5	19	565	109·0	82·1 (132·1)			215·0	33·7 (54·3)
FIJI																
The Fuji Sugar Corporation Ltd PO Box 283, Suva	2' 0" (0·610)	400 (644)	420 (676)		S Dm	7 41			5	* 7 000	1 750·0	15 (24)	200	360	N.A. Free travel	15 (24)
FINLAND																
Valtionrautatiet VR Finnish State Railways Vilhonkatu 13, 00100 Helsinki																
Jokioisten Rautatie Forssa	2' 5½" (0·75)	14 (23)	16 (25·5)		SL DL	1 3				90	50·0	11 (18)		250		
Karhulan-Sunilan Rautatie Oy 48600 Karhula	5' 0" (1·524)	4·1 (6·4)	6·5 (10·7)		DhL	2				751		4 806 000 ton-km	1 800			
FRANCE																
**Société Nationale des Chemins de fer Française (SNCF) 88 rue Saint-Lazare, 75436 Paris, Cedex 09																
C.F. de Chamonix au Montenvers Mer de Glace, Chamonix, Ht. Savoie *(Rack railway)*	3' 3⅜" (1·00)	E 3·7 (6)	E 4·3 (7)	11 000 V 1/50 OH	SL Dh	3 1	E	5	7	3		3·7 (6)			200·0	3·7 (6)
Cie C.F. Départementaux 10 avenue de Friedland, Paris	4' 8¹¹/₁₆" (1·440) 3' 3⅜" (1·00)	77 (124) 189 (304)														
Soc. Gen. de Chemins de Fer et de Transport Automobiles (CFTA) Cité de Londres 4, Paris, 9e	4' 8½" (1·435) 3' 3⅜" (1·00)	488 (746) 323 (520)			S D S D	38 16 29 7	D D	24 26	78 95	1 427 1 178						
C.F. de L'est de Lyon 86 rue du Dauphiné, Lyon	4' 8½" (1·435)	45 (70)			D	11				300	1 100·0			1 100		
Regie du C.F. de Mamers à St. Calais 1 rue Hauréau, 72000 Le Mans, Sarthe *(Ceased operations 1 January, 1978)*	4' 8½" (1·435)	62 (100)			Dd DeL Dm	1 1 3	R†	3		31		73 341 ton-km	450			
Chemin de Fer de la Provence 52 rue Dabray, 06000 Nice	3' 3⅜" (1·00)	94 (151)	104 (168)		D	5	D T	12 6		11					220	80

** See main entry
* Capacity or 2·5·3 tons of Sugar Cane
† Railcars in store, no passenger service operated

Average Speeds			Financial Data		Couplers	Buffers	Rails	Sleepers (crossties)							
Freight Train mph *(km/hr)*	Pass. Train mph *(km/hr)*	Speed max. mph *(km/hr)*	Revenue Expenses in 1 000's	Braking (continuous)	Type and Height above rail ins *(mm)*	Centres and Height above rail ins *(mm)*	Weight lb. per yd *(kg/m)*	Type and thickness ins *(mm)*	Spacing Number per mile *(per km)* or centres ins *(mm)*	Curvature max.	Gradient max. (**U**=not compensated)	Axle load max. tonnes	Altitude max. feet *(m)*	Staff employed. Total no. (inclu. workshop)	Names of officials. Extended lists can be found at the end of the individual country in the report section immediately following
15·5 *(25)*	18·6 *(30)*			Air W'hse	Gould X-E 31 *(788)*		70/45 ASCE	Wood 6 *(150)*	24" *(610)*	197 ft *(60 m)*	5·5%	15·4			
							60/35 *(30/17)*				3·0%				
							43/35 *(21/17)*				2·5%				
							70/55 *(35/27)*				5·5%				
				Triple K-Kl- Kll-F- H. W'hse	Auto: Tower; Sheran; Alliance Atlas 26 *(660)*		70/54 *(35/27)*	Wood 6 *(150)*	Average 2 900 *(1 800)*	361 ft *(110 m)*	3·9% 4·0% **U**	15			
							60/54 *(30/27)*	Wood 6 *(150)*		377 ft *(115 m)*	4·5%				
			E.$1 980·7 2 557·2	Nil	Buffer- coupler 32⅞ *(605)*		56/50 *(28/25)*	Metal	1 955- 2 310 *(1 222- 1 444)*	230 ft *(70 m)*	3·5%	12·5			
7-10 *(11-16)*	7-10 *(11-16)*			Air and manual			61/35 *(31/17)*	Steel, conc. 4 *(102)*	28" *(711)*	Rad. 460 ft *(140 m)*	0·33%	7	400 *(122)*	700 *(100)*	Ch'man: A.S. Hermes Gen. Man: G. M. R. Day
28 *(35)*		34 *(55)*			23⅝" *(600)*	Buffer Couplers	44 *(22)*	6 *(150)*	27½ *(700)*	394 ft *(120 m)*	1·6%	8	328 *(100)*	20 *(2)*	Gen. Man: Ahti Haapakoski
15·5 *(25)*		25 *(40)*	Kr. 1 686·1 1 802·3	W'hse Air	Auto Vapit	Crs 72" *(1 830)* Ht 41·3" *(1 060)*	60 *(30)*	Pine 6½ *(165)*	27½ *(700)*	541 ft *(165 m)*	1·0%	7		38	Gen. Man: Jouko Punnonen
9 *(15)*	9 *(15)*	12 *(20)*				Centre buffer- coupler	40 *(20)*	Metal		17·5°	20%		6 276 *(1 913)*	50	Dir: P. Bayle
							1·44 g *(46/24)* 1·0 g *(30/20)*	Oak 4¾/5½ *(120/140)*	*(700/ 850)*	1·44 g 5·8° 1·0 g 8·7°	3·3%	1·44 g 18 1·0 g 11	1 575 *(480)*		
		28 *(45)*		W'hse Air	Standard	Standard	93/61 *(46/30)*	Oak 5½ *(140)*	26" *(660)*	11·0°	1·6% **U**	15	1 112 *(339)*	43 *(2)*	Pres: R. Baratier
15·5 *(25)*		43 *(70)*	Francs 980·1 1 707·9	Air W'hse	Screw and Automatic 39⅜" *(1 000)*	68⅞" *(1 750)* 39⅜" *(1 000)*	84/60 *(42/30)*	Oak 4⅜ *(120)* Metal	31½" *(800)*	3·8°	1·5%	19	577 *(176·5)*	40	Gen. Man: G. Dauxerre
	25 *(40)*	53 *(85)*		W'hse Air	Buffer- coupler	31½ *(800)*	50·5 *(25)*	Oak 4¾ *(120)*	31½ *(800)*	11·6°	3·0%	11	3 340 *(1 018)*	140	Dir: P. Saracino

NAME OF COMPANY ADDRESS	Gauge ft. in. (metres)	Route length incl. E=Electrified miles (km.)	Track length incl. E=Electrified miles (km.)	Elect. system and type of conductor	Loco-motives L=Line S=Shunt Steam Electric Diesel De=elec. Dh=hyd.		Rail-cars Electric Diesel Trailer Railbus Multiple Unit set		Pass. train cars	Freight train cars Containers	Freight movement Total Volume carried. Thousands of tonnes	Av'ge haul per ton miles (km.)	Av'ge net train load tonnes	Max. trailing load tonnes	Passengers Total number carried in 1 000's	Average journey miles (km.)

FRANCE *(contd.)*

NAME OF COMPANY ADDRESS	Gauge	Route length	Track length	Elect.	Locos		Railcars		Pass	Freight	Total Vol	Av'ge haul	Av'ge load	Max. load	Passengers	Avg journey
C.F. de la Banlieue de Reims 11 rue Gosset, 51100 Reims	4' 8¹¹/₁₆'' (1·440)	8 (13)			DeS	4					866·8	1·2 (2)	600	800		
C.F. de Somain à Anzin et à Vieux-Condé Place Roger Salengro, 59410 Anzin	4' 8¹¹/₁₆'' (1·440)	20 (33) E 0·5 (0·9)	158 (255)	25 000 V dc 1/50 OH	De Dh	17 6				2 103	5 420·8	5·5 (8·9)	1 000	1 700		
C.F. de Super Lagnères Luchon, Hte. Garonne	3' 3⅜'' (1·00)	E 3·5 (5·6)	3·8 (6·1) E 3·7 (5·9)	3 000 V ac 3-phase	EL	4	EMU	4	8	6			10			7·0 (11·2)

GERMANY, Democratic Republic
**Deutsche Reichsbahn
Ministerium für Verkehrswesen
DDR-108 Berlin, Voss Str 33

GERMANY, Federal Republic
**Deutsche Bundesbahn
German Federal Railway
Central Administration
Friedrich-Ebert-Anlage 43-45
6 Frankfurt (Main)

NAME OF COMPANY ADDRESS	Gauge	Route length	Track length	Elect.	Locos		Railcars		Pass	Freight	Total Vol	Av'ge haul	Av'ge load	Max. load	Passengers	Avg journey
Nebenbahn Aalen-Dillingen (Härtsfeldbahn) *(Ceased operation 1972)*	3' 3⅜'' (1·00)	35 (56)														
Nebenbahn Achern-Ottenhöfen *(Operated by Südwestdeutsche Eb.AG)*	4' 8½'' (1·435)	6 (10)	9 (14)		SL DL	1 1	D T	1 3	5	1	69·0	4·5 (7·2)			458·6	4·1 (6·6)
Ahaus-Enscheder Eisenbahn 4442 Bentheim Bahnhofstr 24 *(Operated by Bentheimer Eb.AG)*	4' 8½'' (1·435)	6 (9)	8 (12)								30·9	3·4 (5·5)				
Albtalbahn Albtal-Verkehrs GmbH Tullastrasse 71, 7500 Karlsruhe	4' 8½'' (1·435)	E 27 (43)	E 39 (63)	720 V dc OH	DhS	2	E	26			64·0	353 000 ton-km			7 377·0	3·9 (6·2)
Alsternordbahn (ANB) 2 Hamburg 1, Steinstr 20	4' 8½'' (1·435)	6 (10)	8 (13)				D T	4 3							1 169·5	3·7 (5·9)
Altona-Kaltenkirchen-Neumünster Eisenbahn-Ges D-2000 Hamburg 1, Steinstr 20 *(Also operates* Alsternordbahn; and Elmshorn-Barmstedt-Odelsloer)	4' 8½'' (1·435)	60 (97)	115 (185)		DhL DhS	4 10	D T M	12 9 9			1 036·2	10 289 700 ton-km			3 761·3	8·2 (13·2)
Nebenbahn Amstetten-Gerstetten Württembergische Eb GmbH 7 Stuttgart 1, Konigstr 1B	4' 8½'' (1·435)	12·5 (20)	13·5 (22)				D	1	2		22·8	9·6 (15·5)		500	110·2	4·8 (7·7)
Nebenbahn Amstetten-Laichingen Württembergische Eb GmbH 7 Stuttgart 1, Konigstr 1B	3' 3⅜'' (1·00)	12 (19)	14 (22·5)				D T	3 4	2	3	18·2	9·5 (15·4)		165	220·0	5·9 (9·4)
Ankum-Bersenbrücker Eisenbahn 4559 Ankum, Bersenbrücker Str *(Operated by Bentheimer Eb)*	4' 8½'' (1·435)	3 (5)	4 (6)								10·6	3·1 (5·0)				
Augsburger Localbahn 8900 Augsburg, Friedburger str 41	4' 8½'' (1·435)	18 (29)	50·4 (80·1)		DS	5					485·1	6 306 300 ton-km				
Bad Orber Kleinbahn Kreiswerke Gelnhausen GmbH 646 Gelnhausen, Barbarossastr 28	4' 8½'' (1·435)	4 (7)	5 (8)		D	2			1	2	3·4	4·3 (7·0)			491·5	4·3 (7·0)
Bayerische Zugspitzbahn AG D 8100 Garmisch-Partenkirchen Olympiastr 27 Part adhesion (A); Part rack (R)	3' 3⅜'' (1·00)	(A) E 4·7 (7·5) (R) E 6·9 (11·1)		1 650 V dc OH	(A) E (R) E	6 4 6	E (R)	6	17	6	1·4	2 032 300 ton-km			836·1	10 (16)
Bentheimer Eisenbahn AG Bentheim, Bahnhofstr 24 *Operates 5 other lines:* Ahaus-Enscheder Ankum-Bersenbrücker Ihrhove-Westrhauderfehn Meppen-Haselünner Wittlager-Kreisbahn	4' 8½'' (1·435)	47 (76)	58 (94)		Dh	10	D T	2 5	10	12	488·7	20·1 (32·4)			325·0	10 (17)
Nebenbahn Biberach-Oberharmersbach *(Operated by Sudwestdeutsche Eb. AG)*	4' 8½'' (1·435)	7 (11)	8 (13)				D	2	2		11·3	2·9 (4·6)			323·6	5·0 (8·1)
Birkenfelder Eisenbahn GmbH 6588 Birkenfeld (Nahe)	4' 8½'' (1·435)	3 (5)	4 (7)		D	1				1	30·2	3·7 (6·0)				
Borkumer Kleinbahn und Dampfschiffahrt GmbH Am Georg Schutte Platz 2972 Borkum	2' 11½'' (0·90)	4 (7·4)	9 (15·7)		De Dh	1 2	D	1	17		ton-km	3 214 000		70	440·4	4·5 (7·3)
Hafenbetriebsges Braunschweig GmbH 33 Braunschweig-Veltenhof, Hafenstr 14	4' 8½'' (1·435)	2·2 (3·5)	9 (15)		SL D	1 2				7	263·1	2·2 (3·5)				
Bregtalbahn *(Operated by Südwestdeutsche Eb. AG)*	4' 8½'' (1·435)	19 (30)	22 (36)		SL DhL	1 1	D	2	9	2	33·3	10·7 (17·2)			283·0	7·7 (12·4)

** See main entry

Average Speeds			Financial Data		Couplers	Buffers	Rails	Sleepers (crossties)							
Freight Train mph (km/hr)	Pass. Train mph (km/hr)	Speed max. mph (km/hr)	Revenue Expenses in 1 000's	Braking (continuous)	Type and Height above rail ins (mm)	Centres and Height above rail ins (mm)	Weight lb. per yd (kg/m)	Type and thickness ins (mm)	Spacing Number per mile (per km) or centres ins (mm)	Curvature max.	Gradient max. (U=not compensated)	Axle load max. tonnes	Altitude max. feet (m)	Staff employed. Total no. (inclu. workshop)	Names of officials. Extended lists can be found at the end of the individual country in the report section immediately following
7 (10)		16 (25)	1 457·8	Air W'hse	Standard		92/82 (46/41)	Wood 6 (150)	2 400 (1 500)	7·5°	2·0%	21	262 (80)	21 (2)	Dir: Lucien Beauchard
19 (30)		25 (40)		W'hse Air	Type V (940- 1 065)	68⅞" (1 750) Ht. 40¾" (1 035)	100/70 (50/35)	Wood 5⅜ (135)	2 400 (1 500)	5·8°	1·3%U	18·4			Tfc. Supt: N. Brunot Op. Supt: M. Cochoise
5·1 (8·2)	5·1 (8·2)						40 (20)	Metal	31½" (800)	25·0°	25·5%	9	5 906 (1 800)	24 (5)	Gen. Man: A. Nérou
		31 (50)		Knorr Air	Standard	Standard	66 (33)	Wood 5½ (140)	(700- 800)	7·3°	3·3%U	18	978 (298)	24 (2)	Gen. Man: A. Deissler
															Man: Heinrich Heijnk
19 (30)	25 (40)	31 (50)	DM 14 350·3 11 900·0	Knorr S 75/0	Compakt		70/82·6	Wood Conc	(1 500)	Rad 80 m.	3·50%	20	1 155 (352)	251	Gen. Man: Dipl. Ing. Kurt Stengel
20 (32)	31 (50)			Knorr Air	Standard	Standard	110/108 (55/54)	Wood 6 (150)	25½ (650)	7·0°	1·0%	20	125 (38)	23	Gen. Man: Dipl. Ing. H. Wittenbecher
15 (25)	25 (40)	37 (60)	DM 19 082 26 275	Knorr Air	Standard Draw- hook Scharff- enberg	Standard 68⅞	100 (50)	Wood	(1 539)	7·0°	2·1%	20	138 (42)	376	Gen. Man: Dipl. Ing. Hans Wittenbecher
		31 (50)		W'hse Knorr			67·4 (33·4)	Wood 6 (150)	25½" (650)	8·7°	2·5%	18	2 257 (688)	17	Gen. Man: Franz Grossrubatscher
		25 (40)		W'hse Knorr			49·2 (24·4)	Wood 5½ (140)	26¼" (666)	12·5°	2·86%	18	2 427 (740)	23	Gen. Man: Werner Morlok
16 (25)		19 (30)	DM 150·3 143·9		Standard	Standard		Wood 5½ (140)	937 (1 500)	2·5°	1·6%			2	
9·3 (15)		12·5 (20)		Standard	Standard	Standard	98/66 (49/33)	Wood St. conc.	24⅝" (625)	9·7°	0·98% 2·2% U	20	1 621 (494)	63 (17)	Gen. Man: Dr. Max Keller
														25	Gen. Man: Ing. Hans Malkmes
A. 25 (40) R. 6 (9)	A. 25 (40) R. 11 (18)	A. 25 (40) R. 13 (20)	DM 4 640·5 3 533·9	Locos. A.E.G. Railcar S.L.M.	Scharff- enberg 19¼-20 (490-508)		A. 68 (34) R. 61 (30·2)	A. Wood 5½ (140) R. Metal	31½" (800)	22·0°	A. 3·7% R. 25·0%	15	8 694 (2 650)	92	Gen. Man: Dipl. Ing. P. Hirt
21 (35)	31 (50)	37 (60)		Knorr W'hse Air	Standard	Standard	82·6 (41)	Wood 6 (150)	2 400 (1 500)	5·7°	1·33%	20		209	
		25 (40)		Knorr Air	Standard	Standard	66/48 (33/24)	Wood 5½ (140)	(650-850) 850)	8·7°	2·0% U	18	1 027 (313)	16	Gen. Man: Edmund Lutz
														17	Gen. Man: Walter Kunz
15·5 (25)	15·5 (25)	19 (30)			23·6 (600)		48 (24)	Wood 6·2 (16)	27½" (700)	251 ft (80 m)	0·6%	8·0	2 (0·9)	43	Gen. Man: M. Graff von Spee
		25 (40)		Air	Standard	Standard	67/49 (33/24)	Wood 5½ (140)	25 (650)	5·8°	1·6% U	20	164 (50)	54 (4)	Gen. Man: Arthur Kraatz
22 (35·4)	25·1 (40·5)	31 (50)		Knorr Air	Standard 39⅜ (1 000)	Standard	67/49 (33/24)	Wood 6 (150) Steel	23½" (600)	9·2°	1·0%U	18	2 812 (857)	37	Gen. Man: Wilhelm Lust

GERMANY, FEDERAL REPUBLIC (contd.)

NAME OF COMPANY ADDRESS	Gauge ft. in. (metres)	Route length incl. E=Elec- trified miles (km.)	Track length incl. E=Elec- trified miles (km.)	Elect. system and type of con- ductor	Loco- motives L=Line S=Shunt Steam Electric Diesel De=elec. Dh=hyd.	Rail- cars Electric Diesel Trailer Railbus Multiple Unit set	Pass. train cars	Freight train cars Con- tainers	Total Volume carried. Thous- ands of tonnes	Av'ge haul per ton miles (km.)	Av'ge net train load tonnes	Max. trailing load tonnes	Total number carried in 1 000's	Aver- age jour- ney miles (km.)
Bremervörde-Osterholzer Eisenbahn GmbH Am Bahnof Süd 3, Bremervörde *(Operated by Osthannoversche Eb)*	4' 8½" (1·435)	30 (48)	37 (59)		D 3	D 5	5	4	96·7	17·9 (28·8)			491·4	8·7 (14·0)
Brohltal Eisenbahn GmbH 5474 Brohl-Lützing 1, Bahnhofstr 11	3' 3⅜" (1·00)	16* (26)	19 (31)		Dh 4			135	167·5	7·4 (11·9)		450		
Nebenbahn Bruschsal-Hilsbach-Menzingen *(Operated by Sudwestdeutsche Eb.AG)*	4' 8½" (1·435)	21 (34)	24 (39)			D 6 T 1	6	1	38·4	9·0 (14·5)			977·4	6·3 (10·1)
Buxtehude-Harsefelder Eisenbahn 215 Buxtehude, Kleinbahnhof *(Operated by Osthannoversche Eb)*	4' 8½" (1·435)	9 (15)	12 (19)		DhL 1 DS 1	D 1 T 2		†	57·7	6·1 (9·9)		900	‡	
Delmenhorst-Harpstedter Eisenbahn GmbH Bahnof, 2833 Harpstedt Bez Bremen	4' 8½" (1·435)	14 (23)	15 (24)		D 1	D 1	2		85·3	7·1 (11·4)				
Deutsche Eisenbahn-Ges Frankfurt/Main Mainzerlandstr 41 *Operates 11 lines:* Farge-Vegesacker Frankfurt (M)-Konigstein Geilenkirchener Kb. Jülicher Kreisbahn Kassel-Naumberg Kiel-Schönberg Moselbahn Neheim-Hüsten-Sundern Reinheim-Gross Bieberau Rinteln-Stadthangener Teutoburger Wald Eb														
Dortmunder Eisenbahn Dortmunder Hafen und Eisenbahn AG 46 Dortmund, Speichstr. 23	4' 8½" (1·435)	11 (18)	43 (69)		DhL 10 DhS 5			369	13 094·6	7·6 (12·3)	900	1 500		
Durener Kreisbahn GmbH *(Ceased operations 1 March 1970)*	4' 8½"	7·7												
Nebenbahn Ebingen-Onstmettingen Tailfingen Würtembergische Eisenbahn GmbH 7000 Stuttgart 1, Konigstr 1B	4' 8½" (1·435)	5 (8)	7 (11)			D 1 T 2	2	2	28·5	4·0 (6·5)		500	83·0	3·5 (5·7)
Elmshorn-Barmstedt-Oldesloer Eisenbahn *(Eis.-Ges. Altona-Kaltenkirchen-Neumunster)*	4' 8½" (1·435)	32 (52)	37 (59)		D 1	D 6 T 4		1	168·4	21·7 (35·0)			1 025·9	5·6 (9·1)
Euskirchener Kreisbahnen Kölner str 75, 535 Euskirchen	4' 8½" (1·435)	2 (3)	3 (5)						101·5	3 (5)				
Extertalbahn AG 4923 Extertal	4' 8½" (1·435)	E 15 (24)	E 17 (28)	1 500 V dc OH	E 2			2	46·4	9·4 (15·1)		350		
Farge-Vegesacker Eisenbanh *(Operated by Deutsche Eb.G)*	4' 8½" (1·535)	6 (10)	9 (15)		SL 2 DhL 1		1	8	788·4	5·8 (9·4)				
Filderbahn Hauptstätterstrasse 153, 7 Stuttgart	3' 3⅜" (1·00)	E 17§ (48)	E 30 (49)	OH	E 2	E 15		9	102·0	2·8 (4·5)			5 654·1	3·4 (5·4)
Kleinbahn AG Frankfurt (M)-Königstein *(Operated by Deutsche Eb.G)*	4' 8½" (1·435)	10 (16)	14 (22)		DL 1	D 6 DT 5	6	3	19·6	5·5 (8·8)			2 114·6	5·5 (8·9)
Nebenbahn Gaildorf-Untergröningen Untergröningen *(Operated by Württembergische Eb.G)*	4' 8½" (1·435)	12 (19)	13 (21)			D 1 T 1	3	1	49·0	4·7 (7·6)			185·9	5·2 (8·3)
Geilenkirchener Kreisbahnen *(Operated by Deutsche Eb.G)*	3' 3⅜" (1·00)	7 (11)	7·5 (12)		DhS 2	D 1		1	25·2	6·3 (10·1)				
Kreiswerke Gelnhausen 646 Gelnhausen, Barbarossastr. 28 *Operates bus services and one rail line:–* Bad-Orber Kleinbahn														
Georgsmarienhütten Eisenbahn Georgsmarienhütte bei Osnabrück	4' 8½" (1·435)	8 (13)	39 (63)		SS 2 DL 3 DS 7	D 2 T 2	1	387	2 393·8	4·5 (7·3)			220·2	4·0 (6·5)
Eisenbahn Gittelde-Bad Grund GmbH Laubhütterweg 30, Bad Grund (Harz.) *(Operated by Osthannoversche Eb.)*	4' 8½" (1·435)	3 (4)	4 (6)		D 1			1	44·8	3·1 (5·0)				
Gross Bieberau-Reinheimer Eisenbahn *(Operated by Deutsche Eb. GmbH)*	4' 8½" (1·435)	2·5 (4)	3 (5)		D 1				42·3	2·5 (4)				
Nebenbahn Haltingen-Kandern *(Operated by Sudwestdeutsche Eb.AG)*	4' 8½" (1·435)	8 (13)	9 (15)			D 2 T 1		1	21·5	6·5 (10·5)			190·7	3 (7·0)
Hersfelder Kreisbahn 643 Bad Hersfeld Heinrich Börnerstr 10	4' 8½" (1·435)	16 (26)	22 (36)		Dh 3	D 4	9	1	931·8	3·6 (10·2)			613·2	8·1 (13·8)
Hildesheim-Peiner Kreiseisenbahn *(Ceased railway operations)*	4' 8½" (1·435)	3·4 (5·5)												

* Of which 1·3 miles has a third rail for standard gauge vehicles
† Freight cars of German Federal Railway used
‡ Passenger traffic discontinued 1 June, 1969
§ Of which 6·6 miles has a third rail for standard gauge vehicles

Average Speeds: Freight Train mph *(km/hr)*	Pass. Train mph *(km/hr)*	Speed max. mph *(km/hr)*	Financial Data: Revenue Expenses in 1 000's	Braking (continuous)	Couplers: Type and Height above rail ins *(mm)*	Buffers: Centres and Height above rail ins *(mm)*	Rails: Weight lb. per yd *(kg/m)*	Sleepers (crossties): Type and thickness ins *(mm)*	Spacing Number per mile *(per km)* or centres ins *(mm)*	Curvature max.	Gradient max. (U=not compensated)	Axle load max. tonnes	Altitude max. feet *(m)*	Staff employed. Total no. (inclu. workshop)	Names of officials. Extended lists can be found at the end of the individual country in the report section immediately following
														55	Gen. Man: Hermann Ehlen
12 *(20)*			DM 1 146 1 310	Hardy W'hse	Standard	Standard					1·2	12		39	Gen. Man: J. Annen
12·4 *(20·0)*	16·0 *(26·0)*	31 *(50)*		Knorr Air	Standard	Standard	66/48 *(33/24)*	Wood 5½ *(140)*	*(650-850)*	9·7°	2·5%**U**	18	801 *(244)*	49	Gen Man: Werner Lehmann
19 *(30)*		28 *(50)*		Knorr Air	Screw	Standard	56 *(27·5)*	Wood 6 *(160)*	*(580-680)*	9·0°	1·4% 1·4%**U**	20	60 *(18)*	7	Gen. Man: Harm Kliege
19 *(30)*		25 *(40)*		Knorr Air	Standard	Standard	98/83 *(49/41)*	Wood Types I & II	25½" *(650)*	9·25°	1·60%	30	417 *(127)*	304	Dir: W. Schürmann
		31 *(50)*		W'hse Knorr			67·4 *(33·4)*	Wood 6 *(150)*	25½" *(650)*	11·6°	2·5%	18	2 627 *(801)*	19	Gen. Man: Adolf Weiss
12 *(20)*	20 *(33)*	31 *(50)*		Knorr Air	Screw	Standard	(92/108) *(45/54)*	Wood 5½ *(140)*	25½" *(650)*	8·8°	1·0%	20	164 *(50)*	58	Man: Dipl. Ing. H. Wittenbecher
				Kunze-Knorr	21 *(530)*	480 *(750)*	66/44 *(33/22)*	Wood 5½ *(140)*	27½" *(700)*	35·0°	3·0%	9		5	Man: Johann Krosch
4·7 *(7·6)*		25 *(40)*		Bosch air/elec	Albert *(450)*	Buffer-coupler	117/60 *(58/30)*	Wood 8½ *(220)*	25½" *(650)*	8·7°	2·5%	20	840 *(256)*	40 *(15)*	Man: Ing. Bernd Rehm
		25 *(40)*		Knorr Air	Standard	Standard	99/83 *(49/41)*	Wood 6¼ *(160)*	25½" *(650)*	6·5°	1·1% **U**	20	8 621 *(2 625)*	46 *(10)*	Dr: jur. Frank Niethammer Dipl. Ing: Herbert Güldner
														132	Man: Otto Neef
7 *(11)*	22 *(35)*	37 *(60)*		Air	Standard	Standard	99/67 *(49/33)*	Wood 5½ *(140)*	27/28 *(670/700)*	8·7°	1·4% **U**	20	11·5 *(340)*	37	Dir: Dr. E. Paul
		25 *(40)*		W'hse Knorr			67·4 *(33·4)*	Wood 6 *(150)*	25½" *(650)*	9·7°	1·0%	18	1 158 *(353)*	15	Man: Willi Kunz
		19 *(30)*		Air	Buffer-coupler *(750)*		49·2 *(24·4)*	Wood 5½ *(140)*	2 360 *(1 470)*	17·5°	2·0% **U**	16	567 *(173)*	7	Dr: jur. Frank Niethammer Dipl. Ing. Herbert Güldner
31 *(50)*	31 *(50)*			Air Knorr	Screw 41½ *(1 060)*	Crs. 68⅞ *(1 750)* Ht. 41½ *(1 060)*	99 *(49)*	Wood 6¼ *(160)*	27½" *(700)*	2·50	0·9%	20	407 *(407)*	255 (3)	Gen. Man: H. Rodrian Frt. Man: C. Suendorf
														7	Gen. Man: Hans Orf
														7	Man: Dr. Karlheinz Geuckler
	17·4 *(28)*	31 *(50)*		W'hse Knorr Air	Standard	Standard	66/48 *(33/24)*	Wood 5½ *(140)*	*(650-850)*	13·5°	1·50% **U**	16	1 135 *(346)*	53	Gen. Man: Karl Fischer
				Knorr Air	Screw 17¾ *(450)*	*(1 750)* *(940)*	83·5 *(41·4)*	Wood 6 *(150)*	24¾" *(630)*	8·75°	2·0%		1 169 *(357)*	63	Man: Hans Stuckhardt

GERMANY, FEDERAL REPUBLIC (contd.)

NAME OF COMPANY ADDRESS	Gauge ft. in. (metres)	Route length incl. E=Electrified miles (km.)	Track length incl. E=Electrified miles (km.)	Elect. system and type of conductor	Loco-motives L=Line S=Shunt Steam Electric Diesel De=elec. Dh=hyd.		Rail-cars Electric Diesel Trailer Railbus Multiple Unit set		Pass. train cars	Freight train cars Con-tainers	Total Volume carried. Thousands of tonnes	Av'ge haul per ton miles (km.)	Av'ge net train load tonnes	Max. trailing load tonnes	Total number carried in 1 000's	Average journey miles (km.)
Hohenlimburger Kleinbahn AG Muhlenteichstr 8, 585 Hohenlimburg	3′ 3⅜″ (1·00)	2 (3)	7 (12)		D	5				45	161·7	1·5 (2·4)				
Hohenzollerische Landesbahn AG Hofgartenstr 39, Hechingen	4′ 8½″ (1·435)	67 (107)	71 (115)		D	6	D T R	7 2 1	15	13	415·6	4·1 (6·6)			1 196·0	7·7 (12·4)
VB Grafschaft Hoya GmbH 3092 Hoya/Weser	4′ 8½″ (1·435) 3′ 3⅜″ (1·00)	4 (6) 25 (40)	5 (9) 30 (49)		D	5	D T	4 2			94·2	13·7 (22·1)			329·1	11·6 (18·6)
Hummlinger Kreisbahn 4476 Werlte	4′ 8½″ (1·435)	16 (25)	19 (30)		D	3	D	2	2	5	74·6	12 (20)				
Kb Ihrhove-Westrhauderfehn 2953 Westrhauderfehn, Bahnofstr 4 (Bentheimer Eb. AG)	4′ 8½″ (1·435)	7 (11)	8 (12)								27·3	4·5 (7·2)				
Ilmebahn Ges. AG 3352 Einbeck, Langer Wall 14	4′ 8½″ (1·435)	8 (13)	10 (16)		S D	1 2				3 5	136·6	2·4 (3·8)			417·3	2·5 (4·0)
Nebenbahn Jagstfeld-Ohrnberg (Operated by Württembergische Eb.G)	4′ 8½″ (1·435)	14 (22)	16 (26)				D	1	1		28·9	6·6 (10·7)		400	109·1	3·8 (6·1)
Jülicher Kreisbahn (Operated by Deutsche Eb. G)	4′ 8½″ (1·435)	9 (15)	11 (18)		D	1	D	1	1	2	91·6	4·7 (7·5)			53·7	5·5 (8·9)
Juister Inselbahn 2981 Norddeich	3′ 3⅜″ (1·00)	2 (3)	3 (4)		D	2	D	4	12	22	21·1	1·9 (3·0)			230·8	1·9 (3·0)
Kahlgrund Eisenbahn Schöllkrippen Landkreis Alzenau	4′ 8½″ (1·435)	14 (23)	16 (26)				D	5	10		25·2	7·5 (12·1)			744·3	7·4 (11·9)
Kaiserstuhlbahn (Operated by Südwestdeutsche Eb.AG)	4′ 8½″ (1·435)	25 (40)	30 (49)		DhL	1	D T	5 2	10	4	68·4	10·9 (17·6)			754·4	5·2 (8·3)
Kleinbahn Kassel-Naumberg AG (Operated by Deutsche Eb.G)	4′ 8½″ (1·435)	21 (33)	25 (41)		DL	3	D T	1 1	8	5	911·2	5·0 (8·1)			219·1	8·8 (14·2)
Kerkerbachbahn AG 6251 Runkel/Kerkerbach	4′ 8½″ (1·435)	2·4 (3·8)	4·3 (7·0)		D	2				1	204·2	1·9 (3·1)				
Kiel-Schonberger Eisenbahn (Operated by Deutsche Eb.G)	4′ 8½″ (1·435)	15 (24)	18 (29)		D	2	D	2	5	4	270·4	4·8 (7·7)		600	463·4	8·3 (13·3)
Köln-Bonner Eisenbahnen AG Am Weidenbach 12-14, Postfach 101128, D-5000 Köln 1	4′ 8½″ (1·435)	62·8 (101·4) E 45·9 (74·8)	142·2 (229·1) E 78 (127·2)	1 200 V dc OH	DeL DeS	13 12	E T EMU	4 9 20		522	5 207·1		54 807 698 ton-km	1 800	9 651·1	7·2 (11·6)
Kleinbahn Köln Deutz-Porz-Zündorf Bayenstr 2, Koln	4′ 8½″ (1·435)	10 (16)	13 (21)		Dh	3				10	640·4	3·1 (5·0)				
Köln-Frechen-Benzelrather Eisenbahn Kölner Verkehrs-Betriebe AG Scheidtweilerstr 38, 5000 Köln 41	4′ 8½″ (1·435) E 8 (13)	23·8 (38·1)	63 (102) E 9·3 (15)	800 V dc OH	DeL	14			12	54	3 839·0		38 010 000 ton-km		3 234	5·6 (9)
Nebenbahn Korntal-Weissach (Operated by Württembergische Nb.AG)	4′ 8½″ (1·435)	14 (22)	16 (26)				D T	5 2	8		38·9	7·9 (12·7)		160	449·2	6·9 (11·2)
Städtische Eisenbahn Krefeld 4150 Krefeld-Uerdingen, Oberstr 13	4′ 8½″ (1·435)	12 (19)	28 (45)		Dl	5				148	1 027·6	1·9 (3·0)		575	1 200	
Krefelder Eisenbahn-Gesellschaft 4150 Krefeld, St. Töniser Str. 270	4′ 8½″ (1·435)	18 (29)	24 (39)		DS	4				3	190·7					
Nebenbahn Krozingen-Münstertal-Sulzburg (Operated by Sudwestdeutsche Eb.AG)	4′ 8½″ (1·435)	10 (17)	12 (19)				D	2	1	1	31·7	3·0 (4·8)			414·8	4·2 (6·7)
AG Lokalbahn Lam-Kötzting 8496 Lam, Eisenbahnweg 1	4′ 8½″ (1·435)	11 (18)	13 (20)		DhL DhS	2 2	D T	4 6		1	17·5	6·7 (10·8)		300	356·9	6·3 (10·2)
Langenfeld-Monheim-Hitdorf (See Bahnen de Stadt Monheim GmbH)																
Inselbahn Langeoog Schiffahrt der Inselgemeinde Langeoog 2941 Langeoog	3′ 3⅜″ (1·00)	1·6 (2·6)	2·4 (3·8)		DhL DmL	2 1	D TD	2 2	7	1	23·0				358·2	1·6 (2·6)
Marburger Kreisbahn (Operated by Deutsche Eb)	4′ 8½″ (1·435)	10 (17)	14 (22)		D	2				23	126·7	7·8 (12·5)				
Meppen-Haselunner Eisenbahn Bahnhofstr 24, Bentheim (Operated by Bentheimer Eb)	4′ 8½″ (1·435)	19 (31)	22 (35)		D	4				2	121·6	8·0 (12·9)				
Merzig-Büschfelder Eisenbahn Losheimerstr 1, 664 Merzig	4′ 8½″ (1·435)	14 (23)	18 (29)		D	2				18	151·0	3·0 (4·8)				
Mindener Kreisbahnen 495 Minden (Westfalen)	4′ 8½″ (1·435)	55 (88)	69 (111)		D	12	D	3	13	28	1 147·0	5·3 (8·5)		1 253	231	7·0 (11·2)
Mittelbadische Eisenbahnen AG Friedrichstr 59, Lahr (Schwarzwald) (Operated by Südwestdeutsche Eb.AG)	3′ 3⅜″ (1·00) 4′ 8½″ (1·435)	25 (41)	31 (50)		D	2	D	2	2	46	139·2	6·2 (10·0)			372·7	5·6 (9·1)

Average Speeds — Freight Train mph (km/hr)	Pass. Train mph (km/hr)	Speed max. mph (km/hr)	Financial Data — Revenue Expenses in 1 000's	Braking (continuous)	Couplers — Type and Height above rail ins (mm)	Buffers — Centres and Height above rail ins (mm)	Rails — Weight lb. per yd (kg/m)	Sleepers — Type and thickness ins (mm)	Spacing Number per mile (per km) or centres ins (mm)	Curvature max.	Gradient max. (U=not compensated)	Axle load max. tonnes	Altitude max. feet (m)	Staff employed. Total no. (inclu. workshop)	Names of officials. Extended lists can be found at the end of the individual country in the report section immediately following
														28	Man: Otto Muchon
				W'hse & Knorr Air	39⅜ (1 000)	(1 750) (1 000)	67/51 (33·4/25)	Wood 6 (150)		11·0°	2·8%	18	2 398 (731)	224	Dir: Stirsel
														33	Dir: Wilhelm Leder
25 (40)				Knorr Air	Standard	Standard	99/67 (49/33)	Wood 6 (150)	30¾" (680)	5·7°	1·0%	20	112 (34)	16	Dir: Joseph Kimmann
															Dir: Peter Elster
														29	Dir: Heinrich Dietrich
		31 (50)		W'hse Knorr			67·4 (33·4)	Wood 6 (150)	25½" (650)	9·7°	1·11%	18	584 (178)	22	Gen. Man: Karl Volz
		25 (40)		Air	Standard	Standard	67/49 (33/24)	Wood 5½ (140)	28" (700)	8·7°	1·18% U	16		12	Dir: Dr. Innecken
														25	Dir: Walter Stegmann
				Kunze-Knorr Air	Standard	Standard	67·4 (33·4)	Wood 5½ (140)	30" (760)	8·8°	1·0%	16	668 (204)	38	Man: Hans Lux
18·6 (29·9)	22·7 (36·6)	31 (50)	DM 786·3 823·5	Knorr Air	Standard 39⅜ (1 000)	Standard 39⅜ (1 000)	67 (33·4)	Steel 5/16 (9)	23½" (600)	8·70	1·1%	18	627 (191)	51	Man: Richard Riesch
25 (40)	25 (40)	37 (60)		Air	Standard	Standard	67/55 (33/27)	Wood 5½ (140)	27/28" (680/700)	8·7°	1·3%	20	1 322 (403)	70 (9)	Dir: Dr. Edgar Paul
				Knorr	Joch Kuppl 22½ (570)	19⅝ (500) 29½ (750)	68·6 (34)	Wood 5½ (140)	23" (580)	22·0°	2·0%	18		35	Dir: Richard Kuhn
15 (25)	23 (37)	31 (50)		W'hse Air	Standard	Standard	67/49 (33/24)	Wood 5½ (140)	2 110 (1 320)	8·25°	1·6%	20	1 575 (480)	18 (7)	Dr. Oskar Sommer
28 (45)	22/37 (35/60)	53/68 (85/110)	DM 39 259·0 58 619·0	Air Knorr	Standard *	Standard *	110-99 (54·5/49)	Wood 6¼ (160) & Conc	25½" (650)	9·2°	2·5%	20	445 (136)	1 097	A. Scheib J. Prinz F. Brock
			DM 675·0 1 203·0											37	Dir: A. Causemann
18·6 (30)	14·8 (23·8)	Pass 37 (60) Frt 25 (40)	DM 16 428·0 28 633·0	Knorr Air	Standard *	Standard *	99 (49)	Oak 6-6¼ (150-160)	25½" (650)	9·7°	1·66%	20	322	485	Dir: Dipl. Ing. J. Prinz
		31 (50)		Knorr W'hse	42 (1 065)	68⅞ (1 750) 41⅞ (1 065)	67·4 (33·4)	Wood 6 (150)	25½" (650)	8·7°	2·0%	18	1 312 (400)	19	Gen. Man: Hans Schweizer
9 (5)				Screw		Standard	95/66 (47/33)	Wood 6 (150)	26⅜" (670)	11·3°	2·0%	20	111 (34)	94	Man: Oskar Märkisch
18 (30)		25 (40)	DM 3 651 3 843	Knorr W'hse	Standard	Standard	98 (49)	Wood 6 (150)		8·7°	1·18%	20		61	Gen. Man: Dr. Franz Brendgen
9·3 (15·0)	16·2 (26·0)	31 (50)		Knorr Air	Standard	Standard	66/48 (33/24)	Wood 5½ (140)	(650-850)	8·7°	2·2% U	18	1 217 (371)	35	Man: Bruno Weber
15·5 (25)	22 (35)	31 (50)	DM 717·5 773·5	Knorr Air	Standard	Standard	66·8 (33·4)	Wood 5½/6 (140/150) and concrete	23½ (600)	9·7°	1·2% U	16		38 (10)	Dir: Dipl. Ing. Max Janker
		16 (25)	DM 1 016·5 1 077·5	Knorr Air	Scharfenberg	Central	80 (40)	Wood	23½" (600)	11·3°		6	17		Gen. Man: A. Schmidt
				Knorr W'hse	Standard	Standard	67·2 (33·3)	Steel Wood	23¾" (620)	9·0°	2·13%	18	902 (275)	25	Man: Gotthard Dinter
15·5 (25)	22 (35)	25 (40)		Knorr W'hse	Standard	Standard	67·4 (33·4)	Wood 6 (150)	25½" (650)	5·7°	1·0%			30	Man: Ewald Schómaker
														30	Man: Edmund Lux
18 (30)		31 (50)		Knorr	Standard	Standard (1 750)	82/67 (33/41)	Wood 5½ (140)	25½-30¾" (650-780)	12·5°	2·78%	18/20	15 (4·6)	153	Gen. Man: Pfefferkorn
														54	Gen. Man: Klaus Helbling

* Passenger cars have Schaffenberg couplers

GERMANY, FEDERAL REPUBLIC (contd.)

NAME OF COMPANY ADDRESS	Gauge ft. in. (metres)	Route length incl. E=Electrified miles (km.)	Track length incl. E=Electrified miles (km.)	Elect. system and type of conductor	Loco-motives L=Line S=Shunt Steam Electric Diesel De=elec. Dh=hyd.		Rail-cars Electric Diesel Trailer Railbus Multiple Unit set		Pass. train cars	Freight train cars Con-tainers	Total Volume carried. Thous-ands of tonnes	Av'ge haul per ton miles (km.)	Av'ge net train load tonnes	Max. trailing load tonnes	Total number carried in 1 000's	Aver-age jour-ney miles (km.)
Nebenbahn Möckmühl-Dörzbach (Operated by Sudwestdeutsche Eb.AG)	2' 5½'' (750)	24 (39)	27 (43)		D	3	D	2	6	30	42·9	15 (25)			76·8	6·2 (9·9)
Bahnen der Stadt Monheim Heinsetr 2, 4019 Monheim	4' 8½'' (1·435)	E 8 (12)	E 10 (17)		E	3				2	175·4	3·7 (5·9)				
Moselbahn (Operated by Deutsche Eb.G)	4' 8½'' (1·435)	2·4 (4)	6 (10)		D	2				1	113·2	2·5 (4·0)				15 (25)
Nebenbahn Neckarbischofsheim-Hüffenhardt (Operated by Sudwestdeutsch Eb.AG)	4' 8½'' (1·435)	10 (17)	13 (20)				D	3	3	1	32·2	8·5 (13·6)			348·5	3·9 (6·3)
Kleinbahn Niebüll-Dagebüll Nordfriesische Verehrsbetriebe AG Bahnhofstr 6, 2260 Niebüll	4' 8½'' (1·435)	9 (14)	11 (17)				D	2	2	6	5·7	8·4 (13·5)			206·0	7·5 (12·1)
Eb. Neheim Hüsten-Sundern (Operated by Deutsche Eb.)	4' 8½'' (1·435)	9 (14)	13 (21)		D	1	D T	1 2		3	79·0	5·8 (9·3)			65·6	5·5 (8·8)
Neukölln Mittenwalder Eb-Ges Gottlieb Dunkelstr 47, Berlin 42	4' 8½'' (1·435)	10 (16)	22 (36)		D	5					569·1	4·2 (6·8)				
Neusser Eisenbahn Hammer Landstr 3a, 404 Neuss/Rh	4' 8½'' (1·435)	7 (11)	30 (49)		DhS Dm	5 1				7	1 429·7	5 718 800 ton-km		1 200		
Niederrheinische Verkehrsbetriebe AG (NIAG) Hombergerstr 113, 4130 Moers	4' 8½'' (1·435)	22 (36)	33 (54)		DhL	4	RD T MU	1 2 1		106	2 370	23 050 019 ton-km			2·1	7·7 (12·4)
Nebenbahn Nürtingen-Neuffen Neuffen (Operated by Württembergische Eb.G)	4' 8½'' (1·435)	5·5 (9)	6·2 (10)				D T	5 1	8	12	570·7	5·4 (8·7)		800	762·0	4 (6·4)
Oberrheinische Eisenbahn-Gesellschaft AG 68 Mannheim, Käfertalerstr 9-11	3' 3⅜'' (1·00)	37 (60·9)	61·7 (99·4) E 76 (129)	1 200 V dc OH	EL DmS	3 1	E ET	38 34	55	3	14·0		187 200 ton-km	150	14 509	5·6 (9·1)
Osterwieck Wasserlebener-Eisenbahn Brannlage Harz Bahnhof	4' 8½'' (1·435)	3·7 (6)	5 (8)		Dh	1	D T	4 3	1		3·5	3·2 (5·1)			77·0	3·1 (5·0)
Kreisbahn Osterode am Harz-Kreniesen Am Bahnhof 6, Osterode (Harz) 336	4' 8½'' (1·435)	5 (8)			DhL	1					18·3	5·0 (8·0)				
Osthannoversche Eisenbahnen AG Biermannstr 33, 3100 Celle 1 Also operates: Bremervörde-Osterholzer Eb Buxtehude-Hansefelder Eb Gittelde-Bad Grund Eb Steinhuder Meer-Bahn Wilstedt-Zeven-Tostedter Eb	4' 8½'' (1·435)	202 (326)	247 (399)		DL DhL	2 30	D R	10 1	27	39	2 220·4	127 908 725 tonne-km		1 800	716·3	
Osthavelländische Eisenbahn Bahnhof, Johahnesstift, Berlin, Spandau	4' 8½'' (1·435)	9 (15)	14 (22)		D	4			2	10	804·0	5·3 (8·6)				
Peiner Eisenbahn Am Hillenholz 28	4' 8½'' (1·435)	33 (54)	84 (136)		D Dm	74 10	D	1		1 500	39 232	274 354 000 ton-km		1 400	612	4 (6·4)
Eisenbahn Gross Ilsede-Broistedt	4' 8½'' (1·435)	8 (13)	11 (18)		D	3				57·	1 615·7	8·6 (13·9)				
Hafenbahn Regensburg Linzer Str 6 D-8400 Regensburg	4' 8½'' (1·435)	2·4 (3·5)	32 (52)		DhS	7				3	2 800·8			1 500		
Regentalbahn 8374 Vietach, Bahnhofsplatz 1	4' 8½'' (1·435)	27 (44)	31 (50)		S D	4 2	D DT	4 1	8		88·7	12·4 (20·0)			203·3	5·8 (9·4)
Eisenbahn Reinheim-Gross Bieberau (Operated by Deutsche Eb. G)	4' 8½'' (1·435)	2·4 (4·0)	2·6 (2·4)		D	2				2						
Nebenbahn Reutlingen-Gönningen Reutlingen (Operated by Württembergische Nb.AG)	4' 8½'' (1·435)	10 (16)	12·4 (19·5)				D	1			25·6	5·2 (8·4)		130	5·8	5·5 (9·0)
Rhein-Haardtbahn GmbH 6800 Mannheim, Augartenstr 130	3' 3⅜'' (1·00)	E 11 (17)	E 21 (33)	750 V. dc OH	E	2	E ET	12 17	10							
Rhein-Sieg Kreis Eisenbahn Verkehrsbetriebe des Rhein-Siegkreises, 521 Troisdorf, Postfach 4026	4' 8½'' (1·435)	25 (41)	39 (63)		D	9				1	257·1	8·3 (13·3)			2 167·3	6·0 (9·7)
Rinteln-Stadthagener Eisenbahn (Operated by Deutsche Eb.G)	4' 8½'' 1·435)	12 (20)	22 (35)		DhL	3			1	8	446·6	7·6 (12·2)				
A.G. Ruhr-Lippe Eisenbahnen Brüderstr 65A, 477 Soest/Westf	4' 8½'' (1·435)	23 (37)	33 (53)		Dh	6				13	519·5	6 276 700 ton-km				
*Salzgitter Eisenbahn Verkehrsbetriebe Peine-Salzgitter GmbH Am Hillenholz 28, Postfach 100670, 3320 Salzgitterl	4' 8½'' (1·435)	24 (39) 74 (119)	82 (132) 197 (318)		Dh Dm	62 13	D	1	9	1 346	39 232	274 354 000 ton-km		2 600	612	5·9 (9·5)
Schleswiger Kriesbahn Verkhersbetriebe des Kreises Schleswig 238 Schleswig, Konigstr 1	4' 8½'' (1·435)	47 (76)	65 (104)		D	5	D	3	5	5	229·6	6·2 (10·0)		500	232·7	7·9 (12·8)
Siegener Kreisbahn GmbH 59 Siegen, Friedrichstr 47	4' 8½'' (1·435)	25 (41)	39 (63)		D	9				1	1 274·6	3·4 (5·5)				
Söhrebahn GmbH Closed down																
Stammbahn Closed down																
Steinhuder Meer-Bahn GmbH 3050 Wunstorf, Hindenburgstr 49 (Operated by Osthannoversche Eb)	4' 8½'' (1·435)	4 (6)	5 (8)		D	2					145·8					

* Operated jointly with Reiner Eisenbahn

Average Speeds			Financial Data	Braking (continuous)	Couplers	Buffers	Rails	Sleepers (crossties)		Curvature max.	Gradient max. (U=not compensated)	Axle load max.	Altitude max.	Staff employed. Total no. (inclu. workshop)	Names of officials. Extended lists can be found at the end of the individual country in the report section immediately following
Freight Train	Pass. Train	Speed max.	Revenue Expenses		Type and Height above rail	Centres and Height above rail	Weight	Type and thickness	Spacing Number per mile (per km) or centres						
mph (km/hr)	mph (km/hr)	mph (km/hr)	in 1 000's		ins (mm)	ins (mm)	lb. per yd (kg/m)	ins (mm)	ins (mm)			tonnes	feet (m)		
6·8 (11)		16 (25)		Knorr Air	Chain	Central	48/40 (24/20)	Wood 5½ (140)	(650-850)	22·0°	1·0% U	16	784 (239)	34	
														16	
		25 (40)		Air W'hse	Standard	Standard	170/67 (84/33)	Wood 5½ (140)	25½ (650)	9·7°	1·09%	20	449 (137)	8 (1)	
		22 (35)		Knorr Air	Standard	Standard	66/48 (33/24)	Wood 5½ (140)	(700-850)	8·7°	1·67% U	18	974 (297)	22	Man: Anton Bott
														34	
				Knorr W'hse	Standard	Standard								14	Dr. jur: Frank Niethammer
														54	Dir: Werner Britze
9 (15)		12 (20)	DM 4 221·1 6 094·9	Knorr Air	Standard	Standard	100 (49·4)	Wood (5 150)	26 (660)	11·5°	2·22%	20		59	Dir: Ludwigron Hartz
10 (16)	20 (32)	32 (50)	DM 8 322 6 524	Knorr Kunze	Standard	Standard	108/92 (54/46)	Oak 6½ (160)	25½'' (650)	1·1°	1·47% U	20		75	Gen. Man: Josef Fenger
		31 (50)		W'hse Knorr			100 (49·4)	Wood 6 (150)	23⅝'' (600)	8·7°	2·0%	18	1 293 (394)	18	Gen. Man: Horst Bell
15·5 (25)	28 (45)	43·5 (70)	DM 11 029·0 22 758·0	W'hse Knorr	Scharffenberg 18¾ (475)	Central 24¼ (615)	192/76 (95/38)	Steel Sl 9 (250) Wood 6 (150)	27½'' (700)	17·5° Tram track 44·0°	1·7% 3·3% U	11	374 (114)	434 (164)	Gen. Man: Dipl. Ing. Carl Hartwig
				Air W'hse Knorr	Standard	Standard	130/90 (54/44)	Wood 6 (150)		3·5°	0·3%	20		19	Ewald Weishof
		24·9 (40)	DM 25·9 28·9	Air W'hse Knorr	Screws 23⅝ (600)	Ht. 23⅝ (600)	82/40 (41/20)	Wood	26'' (650)	22°	2·5% 3·1% U	11		6	Dipl. Ing. Bernhard Pohlig
28 (45)	26 (42·5)	37 (60)	DM 28 400·0 32 400·0	Air W'hse Knorr	Standard	Standard	100/80 (49/40)	Wood Metal	24·4'' (620)	8·2°	1·67%	20		634	Gen. Man: Dr. Jur. H. W. Wolff
														36	Gen. Man: Gunter Wrietz
25 (40)		37 (60)		Air Knorr	Scharffenberg	Plunger	100/130 (49/54)	Wood 6¼ (160)	26'' (650)	5·8°	0·41%	30	426 (130)	1 600	Dir: D. Werner Jurisch
														29	,, ,,
		15 (25)					99 (49)	Wood 6¼ (160)	1 550 km	6·0°	1·3% 2·66% U	20	1 109 (338)	70	Ludwig von Hartz
														26	Dipl. Ing. Hans Reinfelder
				Knorr W'hse	Standard	Standard									
		25 (40)		W'hse Knorr			49·2 (24·4)	Wood 6 (150)	25½'' (650)	9·7°	2·63%	18	1 703 (519)	11	Gen. Man: Jakob Schwenkglenks
	23 (37)	31 (50)		Siemens Electric	Scharffenberg 17⅞ (450)	27⅞ (710)	80 (41)	Wood 6 (150)	25½ (650)	13·5°	2·0%	7·5	10 449 (3 185)	50 (10)	Dir: Dipl. Ing. O. Dietrich Tr. Man: Dipl. Ing. Norkauer
														13	Dipl. Ing. Werner Kumpe
		20 (32)		Air Knorr	Standard	Standard	100/83 (49/41)	Wood 6¼ (160)	26'' (650)	5·8°	1·4% U	20	443 (135)	34 (2)	Dr. jur: Frank Niethemmer
		20 (32)	DM 17 446 17 284	W'hse Knorr	Standard	Standard	99/79 (49/39)	Wood 6 (150)	28⅜'' (670)	7·8°	1·25	15		60 (6)	Dir: H. Helmutelliger
25 (40)		37 (60)		W'hse Knorr Air	Scharffenberg	Standard	99 (49·4)	Wood 6 (150)	26'' (650)	9·2°	2·5%	35	426 (130)	1 600	D. Werner Jurisch
				Kunze Knorr Air	Screw 37¾ (960)	(1 750) (1 040)	A.99 (49) B.47 (23)	Wood 5½ (140)	30¾'' (780)	9·7°	2·08%	A.18 B.14	159 (49)	60	Gen. Man: Gustav Wode
														143	Man. Heinz Krämer
														15	Gen. Man: Oskar Tramitz

NAME OF COMPANY ADDRESS	Gauge ft. in. (metres)	Route length incl. E=Electrified miles (km.)	Track length incl. E=Electrified miles (km.)	Elect. system and type of conductor	Loco-motives L=Line S=Shunt Steam Electric Diesel De=elec. Dh=hyd.		Rail-cars Electric Diesel Trailer Railbus Multiple Unit set		Pass. train cars	Freight train cars Con-tainers	Freight movement Total Volume carried. Thousands of tonnes	Av'ge haul per ton miles (km.)	Av'ge net train load tonnes	Max. trailing load tonnes	Passengers Total number carried in 1 000's	Average journey miles (km.)

GERMANY, FEDERAL REPUBLIC (contd.)

Sudwestdeutsche Eisenbahnen AG
7630 Lahr/Schwarzwald, Friedrichstr 59
Operates 12 lines:
 Achern-Ottenhöfen
 Biberach-Oberharmersbach
 Bruchsal-Hilsbach-Menzingen
 Haltingen-Kandern
 Krozingen-Munstertal-Sulzburg
 Möckmuhl-Dörzbach
 Neckerbischofsheim-Huffenhardt
 Wiesloch-Schattausen-Waldengelloch
 Bregtalbahn
 Kaiserstuhlbahn
 Mittelbadische Eisenbahnen
 Mülheim-Badenweiler

Company	Gauge	Route	Track	Elect	Locos	Railcars	Pass	Freight	Vol	Haul	Net	Max	Pass carried	Journey
Taunusbahnen Stadtwerke Frankfurt a. Main 6 Frankfurt a. Main 1, Dominikanerplatz 3	4' 8½'' (1·435)	E 12 (20)	E 24 (39)		E 2 D 1			3	46·7	4·8 (7·6)				
Tecklenburger Nordbahn 44 Münster (Westf), Koslinerstr 11	4' 8½'' (1·435)	30 (49)	39 (63)		D 3			2	117·1	148·8 (23·8)				
Tegernsee-Bahn AG 8180 Tegernsee, Bahnhofsplatz 5	4' 8½'' (1·435)	7 (12)	9 (15)		SL 1 Dh 2		5		9·1	81 700 ton-km		220	518·1	6·0 (9·6)
Teutoburger Wald Eisenbahn (Operated by Deutsche Eb.G)	4' 8½'' (1·435)	63 (102)	76 (123)		DhL 8 DS 2	D 3 T 2	5	27	519·0	25·7 (41·3)			65·6	7·5 (12·0)
Uetersener Eisenbahn AG 2082 Uetersen, Bahnstr 15	4' 8½'' (1·435)	3 (5)	6 (10)		D 2				73·0	3·1 (5·0)				
Nebenbahn Vaihingen- Enzweihingen Vaihingen (Enz) (Operated by Württembergische Eb.G)	4' 8½'' (1·435)	4·5 (7·2)	5·0 (8·2)			D 1 T 1			67·2	3·4 (5·7)		300	62·3	3·0 (5·0)
Verden-Walsroder Eisenbahn 309 Berden (Aller), Bahnhof Verden-Süd	4' 8½'' (1·435)	16 (25)	20 (32)		D 4				221·7	3·0 (4·8)				
Vorwohle-Emmerthaler Verkersbetriebe GmbH 3452 Bodenwerder	4' 8½'' (1·435)	20 (32)			D 3	D 1	2	6	98·9	2 069 200 ton-km			28·5	9·3 (15·0)
Bahngesellschaft Waldhof Sandoferstr 176, Mannheim-Waldhof	4' 8½'' (1·435)	3 (5)	4 (7)		D 3			19	558·1	1·3 (2·1)				
Wanne-Herner Eisenbahn Am Westhafen 27, 4690 Herne 2	4' 8½'' (1·435)	9 (14)	23 (37)		DhL 9			394	7 426·1	33 776 158 ton-km				
Wendelsteinbahn GmbH (6 km rack) D8204 Brannenburg, Rosenheimerstr 88	3' 3⅜'' (1·00)	E 4 (7)	E 5 (8)	1 500 V. d.c. OH	E 4		8	4	1·3	1 500 ton-km			142·8	4·4 (7·1)
Werne-Bockum-Höveler Eisenbahn 4618 Kamen, Lünenerstr 219	4'8½'' (1·435)	8 (12)	11 (17)		S 1			1	470·6	5 647 300 ton-km			0·4	
Wesel-Rees-Emmerich (Closed down)														
Westerwaldbahn D5241 Bindweide über Betzdorf/Sieg	4' 8½'' (1·435)	16 (26)	20 (33)		DhL 4				259·9	6·8 (11·0)		2 400		
Westfälische Landes-Eisenbahn AG 478 Lippstadt, Südertor 6 (Operates 6 lines): Lippstadt-Warstein Lippstadt-Neubeckum Soest-Brilon Stadt Neubeckum-Westkirchen Neubeckum-Munster (Westf) Borken (Westf)-Burgsteinfurt	4' 8½'' (1·435)	127 (205)	199 (320)		SL 1 DhL 12 DeL 3 SS 1 DhS 5 DS 2	D 3 T 4	15	152	20 051·0	21·7 (35·0)		1 500	1 578·0	9·3 (15)
Nebenbahn Wiesloch- Schatthausen-Waldangelloch (Operated by Sudwestdeutsche Eb.AG)	4' 8½'' (1·435)	12 (20)	15 (25)		DL 1	D 4	5		62·4	3·7 (6·1)			731·2	3·5 (5·7)
Wilstedt-Zeven Tostedter- Eisenbahn 2148 Zeven, Bahnhofstr 67	4' 8½'' (1·435)	40 (64)	48 (77)		D 4	D 2 T 1	2	6	289·5	19·9 (32·0)			129·6	7·8 (12·5)
Wittlager Kreisbahn AG 4508 Bohmte (Operated by Bentheimer)	4' 8½'' (1·435)	24 (39)	25 (41)		D 2	D 2 T 1	2	8	84·6	7·5 (12·0)				

Württembergische Eisenbahn-Ges
7000 Stuttgart 1, Königstr 1 B
Operates 7 lines:

	Gauge	Route	Track						Vol			Max		
Amstetten-Gerstetten		(20)	(23)						24·6			80·5		
Amstetten-Laichingen		(20)	(23)						14·9			216·9		
Gaildorf-Untergröningen	4' 8½'' (1·435)	(16·5)	(18·5)						64·6			190·0		
Ebingen-Onstmettingen		(8·2)	(11)						22·1			112·7		
Jagstfeld-Ohrnberg		(22·6)	(25)						55·2			124·3		
Nürtingen-Neuffen		(8·9)	(10)						624·0			778·6		
Vaihingen-Enzweihingen		(7·2)	(8)						62·5			49·6		

Württembergische Nebenbahnen GmbH
7000 Stuttgart 1, Königstr 1 B
Operates 2 lines:

	Gauge	Route	Track						Vol			Max		
Korntal-Weissach	4' 8½'' (1·435)	(22·3)	(25)						50			427·9		
Reutlingen-Gönningen		(16·5)	(19)						16·6			1·8		

| **Nebenbahn Zell—Todtnau** (Operated by Mittelbadische Eb) | 3' 3⅜'' (1·00) | 12 (19) | 14·3 (23) | | SL 3 | D 1 | 8 | 10 | 11·7 | 7·3 (11·8) | | 19 310 | 360·1 | 5·8 (9·4) |

Average Speeds			Financial Data		Couplers	Buffers	Rails	Sleepers (crossties)		Curvature max.	Gradient max. (U=not compensated)	Axle load max.	Altitude max.	Staff employed. Total no. (inclu. workshop)	Names of officials. Extended lists can be found at the end of the individual country in the report section immediately following
Freight Train	Pass. Train	Speed max.	Revenue Expenses	Braking (continuous)	Type and Height above rail	Centres and Height above rail	Weight	Type and thickness	Spacing Number per mile (per km) or centres						
mph (km/hr)	mph (km/hr)	mph (km/hr)	in 1 000's		ins (mm)	ins (mm)	lb. per yd (kg/m)	ins (mm)	ins (mm)			tonnes	feet (m)		
														9	Gen. Man: Helmut Österling
														32	Gen. Man: Werner Otte
18·6 (30)	25 (40)	37 (60)	DM 2 278·6 2 226·5	Knorr W'hse	Screw (1 200) (1 100)	(1 200) (850)	S41, S49	Pine	25½'' (650)	7·7°	3·0%	18	2 722 (830)	43	Gen. Man: Dr. P. F. Von Aretin
	25 (40)			Air	Standard	Standard	99/60 (49/30)	Wood 5½ (140)	2 350 (1 470)	7·0°	1·25% U	20/18		153	Gen. Man: Dr. K-H. Geuckler
				Knorr Air	Standard	Standard	99/68·6 (49/34)	Wood 6 (150)	26⅜'' (670)	17·5°	0·92%	18		15	Gen. Man: Gerhard Knorr
		31 (50)		W'hse. Knorr	Standard	Standard	67·4 (33·4)	Wood 6 (150)	25½'' (650)	8·7	2·0%	18	843 (257)	11	Dipl. Ing. Ständebach
														37	Gen. Man: K-H. Sievers
														27	Gen. Man: Kurt Santelman
9·3 (15)		12·5 (20)					Type 8	Wood	27½'' (700)	9·7°		25	325 (99)	20	Gen. Man: Luthar Reiss
21·7 (35)		24·9 (40)		Knorr Air	Standard	Standard 39⅜ (1 000)	99/87 (49/43)	Oak 6¼ (160)	26'' (660)	9·7°	0·8% 1·4%U	22·5	180 (55)	224	Gen. Man: Dipl. Kfm R. Görl
Rk. 6 (9) Ord 9·5 (15)	Rk. 6 (9) Ord 9·5 (15)	Rk. 6·5 (10) Ord 9·5 (15)		W'hse Air	26¾ (680)	Centre (500)	48/40 (24/20)	Wood Steel	W. (800) St. (700)	25·0°	23·7%	10·2	5 653 (1 723)	31	Gen. Man: Ing Rüdigen Dietrich
		18·6 (30)		Kunze Knorr	Standard	Standard	(99/83) (49/44)	Wood		9·75°	3·0%	20		49	Dipl. Ing. Heinz Stolle
		18·6 (30)		Air	Standard	Standard	Type F6	Type 2B	27½'' (700)	8·7°	2·5%	20	1 860 (567)	26 (4)	Dipl. Ing. Ständebach
19 (30)	25 (40)	37 (60)		Air Knorr; W'hse	Standard	Crs.68⅞'' (1 750) Ht. 41¼'' (1 050)	109/67 (54/33)	Wood 6 (150)	25½'' (650)	13°	2·0%	20	1 404 (428)	615 (100)	Directors: Dipl-Kfm Wienand Dr. Ing Müller
8·7 (14·0)	15·5 (25·0)	31 (50)		Knorr Air	Standard	Standard	66/48 (33/24)	Wood 5½ (140)	(650-850)	9·7°	1·67% U	18	578 (176)	118	Gen. Man: Siegfried Funk
														47	Gen. Man: Hermann Ehlen
15·5 (25)		31 (50)		Knorr Air		Ht. 37'' (940) and 41⅞'' (1 065)		Wood 5½ (140)	937 (1 500)	8·7°		20	40 (4)	38 (13)	Gen. Man: Diedrich Vagt
															Gen. Man: Josef Sowa
10·4 (16·8)	18·4 (29·6)	31 (50)		Hardy-Vac	Bolt (650)	Central (650)	67/49 (33/24)	Steel	23½'' (600)	25·0°	2·9% U	18	2 106 (642)	37 (3)	

NAME OF COMPANY ADDRESS	Gauge ft. in. (metres)	Route length incl. E=Electrified miles (km.)	Track length incl. E=Electrified miles (km.)	Elect. system and type of conductor	Loco-motives L=Line S=Shunt Steam Electric Diesel De=elec. Dh=hyd.	Rail-cars Electric Diesel Trailer Railbus Multiple Unit set	Pass. train cars	Freight train cars Con-tainers	Total Volume carried. Thousands of tonnes	Av'ge haul per ton miles (km.)	Av'ge net train load tonnes	Max. trailing load tonnes	Total number carried in 1 000's	Average journey miles (km.)
GHANA **Ghana Railway and Ports Authority** PO Box 251, Takoradi	3' 6" (1·067)	592 (953)	801 (1 289)		* SL 84 * SS 26 DeL 70 DeS 15 DhS 10		259	3 689	1 626·0	110 (177)	130	1 200	7 273·3	28·4 (45·7)
GREECE **Hellenic Railways Organisation Ltd (CH)** Organisme des Chemins de Fer Helléniques SA 31 Rue El. Venizelou, Athens	4' 8½" (1·435)	1 596 (2 572)	1 661 (2 672)		D 188		522	10 170	930 667 000 tonne-km				12 466	72 (115)
Rack	3' 3⅜" (1.00) 2' 5½" (0.75) 1' 11⅝" (0.60)	597 (961) 13 (22) 18 (29)	672 (1 078) 14 (23) 19 (30)											
Athens-Piraeus Electric Railway (Ceased operation 23 March 1977)														
Hellenic Electric Railway 67 Athinas Street, Athens	4' 8½" (1·435)	22 (36) E 22 (26)		600 V Third Rail	E 5 P 7	E 58 ET 77								
GUATEMALA **Ferrocarriles Guatamaltecos (FEGUA)** 18 Calle y 10a avenida, Zona 1, Guatemala	3' 0" (0·914)	509 (819)	595 (958)		S 90 D 17	D 2	153	2 155	1 219·4	155·7 (250·6)	99	1 085	3 463·6	50 (80)
Verapez Railway Livingston, Izabal	3' 0" (0·914)	30 (48)												
Cia. Agricola de Guatemala (United Fruit Company) Cia de Desarrollo, Tiquisate Baranero de Guatemala	3' 0" (0·914)		74 (119)		S 44 D 7			612						
United Fruit Company Railways Bananera, Izabal	3' 0" (0·914)	56 (90)	94 (151)		DeL 7 DhS 4	D 5 R 16	16	22		22 (35)	250	300	350·0	28 (45)
GUINEA **C.F. de la Guinea														
PO Box 581, Conakry														
C.F. Conakry-Fria Compagnie Friguia BP 554, Conakry	3' 3⅜" (1 000)	90 (144)	96 (155)		De 5	D 2		53 C 15				1 000	1 900	
C.F. de la Cie. miniero du Conakry Conakry	4' 8½" (1·435)	9 (14)			De 2			12						
C.F. de Boke (Under construction)														
GUYANA **Demba Railroad** Demerara Bauxite Co Linden	3' 0" (0·914)	50 (80)			DL 18 DS 19		12	646	754	25 (40)	400	550	18·5	10 (16)
HAITI **National Railroad Company of Haiti** (Ceased operation)														
Cie. des C.F. de La Plaine du Cul-de-Sac (Ceased operation)					S 3 E 2 D 5			371						
HONDURAS **F.C. Nacional de Honduras** 1a Calle No. 2, San Pedro Sula	3' 6" (1·067)	79 (127)	126 (203)		DeL 8 SS 2	RD 3	16	517	382·9	30 234 400 ton-km	460	1 200	130·1	31·8 (51·2)
Standard Fruit Company's Railway Head Office: PO Box 50830, 2 Canal St., International Trade Mart, New Orleans, La., USA Local office: Apart. 96 and 101, La Ceiba	3' 0" (0·914)		258 (458)		EL 16 De 5		26	718			390	390		
Tela Railroad Co. (United Fruit Co., 80 Federal Street, Boston, Mass., USA) La Lima	3' 6" (1·067)	103 (166)	217 (350)		DeL 13 DhS 12	R 21	22	1 584	1 420·0	44·7 (72·0)		1 500	1 350·0	29·8 (48·0)
HUNGARY **Hungarian State Railways** **Magyar Allamvasutak (MAV)** Budapest VI, Népköztársaság Utja 73-75	5' 0" (1·524) 4' 8½" (1·435) 2' 6" (0·76)	4 934 (7 550) E 621 (1 196)	7 960 (12 523) E 1 760 (3 211)	16 000 V and 25 000 1/50	NA	NA	NA	NA C 3 607	121 700	22 818 000 000 ton-km			335 700	25 (40)

** See main entry
* All steam locomotives are in store

Average Speeds Freight Train mph (km/hr)	Pass. Train mph (km/hr)	Speed max. mph (km/hr)	Financial Data Revenue Expenses in 1 000's	Braking (continuous)	Couplers Type and Height above rail ins (mm)	Buffers Centres and Height above rail ins (mm)	Rails Weight lb. per yd (kg/m)	Sleepers Type and thickness ins (mm)	Spacing Number per mile or centres ins (mm)	Curvature max.	Gradient max. (U=not compensated)	Axle load max. tonnes	Altitude max. feet (m)	Staff employed. Total no. (inclu. workshop)	Names of officials. Extended lists can be found at the end of the individual country in the report section immediately following
12 (19)	28 (45)	Frt. 35 (56) Pass 40 (64)	NC 9 684.3 13 815.2	Vac Brake Co	Auto. Central Buffer-coupling 34½ (876)	E.S. Co Alliance	80/60 (40/30)	Wood 5 (127); Steel	2 200 (1 370)	660 ft. (201 m)	1.0%	16	938 (286)	15 524 (12 499)	Gen. Man: P. O. Aggrey
25 (40)	32.3 (52)	62 (100)		W'hse Hilde-brand Knorr Knorr Hardy	Standard European 21.7 (550) 20.9 (530)	Standard European / Central 750 mm / Central 530 mm	93 (46) / 65 (32) / 40 (20) / 32 (16)	Steel / Wood / Wood / Wood	23⅝ (600) (600/750)	5.8° / 14.6° / 38° / 44°	2.7% 2.5% U / 3.0% 2.5% U / 3.4% / 3.0%	20 / 13.5 / 4.5 / 6.0	2 523 (769) / 2 671 (814) / 2 362 (720) / 951 (290)	12 901 (3 202)	Gen. Dirs: S. Keramidas I. Kazantzoglou
	22 (35)	43.5 (70)		Knorr Air	Schafen-berg 36⅝ (930)	Crs. 68⅞ (1 750) Ht. 39⅜ (1 000)	104/78 (52/39)	Wood 6¼ (160)	27½' (700)	7.2	3.0%U 2.7%U	18	162 (269)	203 (103)	Gen. Mans: N. Vlangalis and S. Andreadis
				Triple K-KI-KII-F-H. W'hse	Auto: Tower; Sheran; Alliance Atlas 26 (660)		75/60 (37/30)	Wood 6 (152)	Average 2 900 (1 800)	279 ft (85 m)	3.7%	15			
						70/54 (35/27)	Wood 6 (153)		2 600 (1 615)	4.0°	2.0%	14			
20 (32)	17 (27)	25 (40)	185.4 498.3	Air W'hse	Gregg Standard 30 (762)		60/40 (30/20)	Pine 6 (153)	24" (608)	18.0°	1.1% U	10	230 (70)	197 (72)	Gen. Man: B. E. Taylor
17 (37)	34 (55)			Vac W'hse	Willison auto 29½ (750)		93 (46) / 102 (50)	Metal 2 400 (1 500) / Metal 2 400 (1 500)		984 ft. (300 m)	1.2%	17	722 (220)	80	Gen. Man: Lancei Traorè
12 (19)	15 (24)	25 (40)		W'hse Air	Greggs 23¼		90/60 (45/30)	Hard-wood (Mora) 4 (100)	26" (660)	722 ft (220 m)	1.0° U	15	260 (79)	157 (30)	Gen. Man: J. V. Rabbeck
21.7 (35)	31.0 (50)		$ 5 192.3 5 237.9	W'hse Air	AAR Autos 24 (610)		75/60 (37/30)	Wood 6 (150)	20" (508)	886 ft (270 m)	1.5%		769 (213)	223	Gen. Man: Ing. D. Panting Mena
15 (25)	22 (35)	37 (60)		W'hse	Knuckle	22 (560)	76/50 (37/25)	Wood 8 (200)	2 800 (1 750)	886 ft (270 m)	1.0% 0.72% U	15	142 (43)	528 (100)	Gen. Man: H. H. Lacombe
11.6 (16.4)	22.6 (36.6)	75 (120)	Forint 26 246 000 24 280 000	Air Hilde-brand-Knorr	U.I.C.	Crs. 67⅞ (1 750) Ht. 39⅜ (1 000)	108/96 (54/48)	Wood Conc 7½ (190)	23⅝ (600)	4.3°	4.0%	23	1 345 (410)	126 346 (18 585)	Gen. Man: Zoltan Szucs

NAME OF COMPANY ADDRESS	Gauge ft. in. (metres)	Route length incl. E=Electrified miles (km.)	Track length incl. E=Electrified miles (km.)	Elect. system and type of conductor	Locomotives L=Line S=Shunt Steam Electric Diesel De=elec. Dh=hyd.	Rail-cars Electric Diesel Trailer Railbus Multiple Unit set	Pass. train cars	Freight train cars Containers	Total Volume carried. Thousands of tonnes	Av'ge haul per ton miles (km.)	Av'ge net train load tonnes	Max. trailing load tonnes	Total number carried in 1 000's	Average journey miles (km.)

HUNGARY (contd.)

Györ-Sopron-Ebenfurti-Vasut *
Szilagyi Deszsö-ter, 1, Budapest 1
(Operates 2 lines):

| Györ-Csorna-Fertöszentmiklos-Sopron Offices: Györ | 4' 8½" (1 435) | 53 (85) | | | S 21 De 13 | | | | | | | | | |
| Celldömölk-Fertöszentmiklos-Mekszikopuszta (for Fertö-videki Helyiérdeku Vasut) Offices: Sopron | 4' 8½" (1-435) | 39 (63) | | | | | | | | | | | | |

Budapest Suburban Railway
Budapesti Helyi Erdekü Vasut
Akácfa v. 15, Budapest VII
(Now part of the Budapest Traffic Board: Budapesti Közlekedési Vállalat)
(Operates the following lines):

	4' 8½" (1 435)	10 (17) E 63 (101)	179 (289)	1 000 V dc OH Fischer-Jellinek	E 41 De 13	E 162 D 3	353	420	1 598·0				163 210·0	
Zsigmond tér-Szentendre	4' 8½" (1 435)	E 2 (3)		1 000 V dc OH F-J										
Vágóhid-Rákeve (Electric only to Tököl)	4' 8½" (1 435)	10 (17) E 15 (24)		1 000 V dc OH F-J										
Gyártelep-Taksony	4' 8½" (1 435)	E 5 (8)		1 000 V dc OH F-J										
Borároster-Csepel Tanacshaz tér (Rapid line)	4' 8½" (1 435)	E 4 (7)		MAV-Kando										
Csepel-Pesterzsébet Határút	4' 8½" (1 435)	E 2 (4)		1 000 V dc OH F-J										
Ors vezér ter-Gödöllö	4' 8½" (1 435)	E 18 (29)		1 000 V dc OH F-J										
Cinkota-Csömör Beke tér		E 3 (5)		1 000 V dc OH F-J										

INDIA

Indian Government Railways Ministry of Railways (Railway Board), Rail Bhavan, New Delhi 1	5' 6" (1·676)	18 667 (30 041) E 2 497 (4 025)	26 532 (42 755) E 6 130 (9 865)	1 500 V 3 000 V dc OH 25 000 V 1/50	S 5 475 De 864 Dh 102 E 619	D 26 DT 6 E 525 ET 1 189	15 443		33 900 000 000 tonne-km				148 916 000	29·3 (47·4)
	3' 3⅜" (1·00)	15 876 (25 550) E 103 (166)	21 690 (34 907) E 183 (294)	1 500 V dc OH	S 3 355 De 257 Dh 27 E 20	D 45 DT 6 E 43 ET 129	12 176							
Narrow gauges are 2' 6" (762) and 2' 0" (610)	Narrow	2 781 (4 476)	3 125 (5 028)		S 392 Dh 38	D 19 DT 12	1 547							
	Total all gauges	37 324 (60 067) E 2 456 (3 952)	62 018 (99 808) E 6 313 (10 160)		S 9 222 De 1 121 Dh 167 E 639	D 90 DT 24 E 568 ET 1 318	29 166							

Non-Government owned railways:

Arrah-Sasaram Light Railway Calcutta	2' 6" (0·762)	60 (97)	66 (107)		S 12 D 2		39	147	29·0	32·2 (51·9)			3 106·0	17·0 (27·0)
Bombay Port Trust Ramjibhai Kamami Marg, Ballard Estate, Bombay-400 038	5' 6" (1·676)	7 (11)	133 (214)		SS 18 Dm 17 Dm 3			330	3 857·3	21 472 350 tonne-km				
Calcutta Port Trust 15, Strand Rd, Calcutta 700 001, West Bengal	5' 6" (1 676)	22 (36) E (1·75)	221 (356) E (44)	2 500 V. ac 50Hz	S 33 Dh 29			850	4 520					
Dehri-Rohtas Light Railway	2' 6" (0·762)	42 (67)	64 (103)		S 27	D 3 Pet 2	18	752	779·0	34·9 (56·2)			472·0	16·7 (26·9)
Fatwah-Islampur Railway 12 Mission Row, Calcutta 700001	2' 6" (0·762)	27 (43)	29 (47)		S 4		18	33	20·0	19·3 (31·0)			1 886·0	12·4 (19·9)
Madras Port Trust Railway South Beach Road, Madras	5' 6" (1·676) 3' 3⅜" (1·00 m)		11 (18) 29 (46)		SS 11 DhS 22				3 017·3					
Visakhapatnam Port Trust Andhra Pradesh	5' 6" (1 676) 2' 6" (0·672)		75 (120) 5·5 (9)		De 6 Dm 11 S 4 D 2				7 403·8	10 (16)		1 000		
Bhilai Steel Plant Bhilai-1 (M.P.)	5' 6" (1·676)		91 (146)		SL 5 SS 4 DeS 41 DS 6 Oth 2			565	8 323	2·5 (4)	1 500	3 200		

* Details for Hungarian section only. Extends into Austria as Raab-Oedenburg-Ebenfurter

Average Speeds — Freight Train mph (km/hr)	Pass. Train mph (km/hr)	Speed max. mph (km/hr)	Financial Data — Revenue Expenses in 1 000's	Braking (continuous)	Couplers — Type and Height above rail ins (mm)	Buffers — Centres and Height above rail ins (mm)	Rails — Weight lb. per yd (kg/m)	Sleepers (crossties) — Type and thickness ins (mm)	Spacing Number per mile (per km) or centres (mm)	Curvature max.	Gradient max. (U=not compensated)	Axle load max. tonnes	Altitude max. feet (m)	Staff employed. Total no. (inclu. workshop)	Names of officials. Extended lists can be found at the end of the individual country in the report section immediately following
		43 (70)			Auto	95·5/67 (48/34) 67 (23)					3·5%	20			
		50 (80)													
S. 7·5 (12·0) D. 14·2 (22·9) E. 15·6 (25·2)	20·4 (32·9)	62 (100)	(Crores) 1 767·01 1 609·62	Air and Vac	Screw; also AAR 43½–41 (1 105–1 040)	Crs. 77 (1 956) Ht (1 105–1 040)	105/90 (52/45) C.I. and	Wood 5 (127) (680) steel conc	Main 26·8″ Branch 33″ (840)	574 ft (175 m)	2·94%	22·9			Chairman: G. P. Worrier
S. 8·1 (13·1) D. 11·6 (18·7) E. 11·7 (18·9)	17·1 (27·5)	47 (75)		Air and Vac	ABC 23 (584)		75/60 (37/30) C.I. and steel	Wood 4½ (114)	Main 26·3″ (670) Branch 33″ (840)	358 ft (109 m)	2·70% (Rack section 8·15%)	12·2			
S. 7·9 (12·7) D. 8·4 (13·5)	11·7 (18·9)	31 (50)		Air and Vac	ABC		60/30 (30/15)	Wood 4 (102)	2′ 6″ g 112 ft (34 m) 2′ 0″ g 43 ft (13 m)				Varies with weight of rail 7 407 (2 258)	1 391 000 (414 000)	
														576	Gen. Man: C. S. Mehta
		25 (40)	Rs. 17 667·4 33 189·8	Air & Vac W'hse			90/75 (45/37)	Wood 6 (150)			22·5		Sea level	1 895 (308)	Manager: Shri N. P. Bapat
4 (6)	6 (10)		Lakhs 300 447				90/75 (43/37)	Wood 5 (127)		14°		20	20 (6)		Rly Supt: Shiri A. Shukla
														827	Sec: J. K. Jain
														233	Chf. Eng. B. B. Mukherjee
3 (5)	5 (8)	10 (16)	Rs. 9 227·1 10 625·1				90/75 (44·6/37)	Wood 5 (127)		14°	0·25%	22·5		643 (112)	Gen. Man: Shri K. N. Chennabassappa
5 (8)		9 (15)		Vac and Air	Screw; Henricot Auto		90/75 (44·6/37) 40/30 (20/15)	Wood 5 (127) Steel	N+3	8·0°	0·67%	BG 20 NG 7·5		635	Traffic Manager: K. Sridharan
		4 (7)		Comp-ressed Air	41⅜ (1 050)	Central 76⅞ (1 956) Ht. 43½ (1 105)	105/86 (52/43)	5 (127)		10·0°	15%	40	1 020 (316)	642	

NAME OF COMPANY ADDRESS	Gauge ft. in. (metres)	Route length incl. E=Electrified miles (km.)	Track length incl. E=Electrified miles (km.)	Elect. system and type of conductor	Locomotives L=Line S=Shunt Steam Electric Diesel De=elec. Dh=hyd.	Rail-cars Electric Diesel Trailer Railbus Multiple Unit set	Pass. train cars	Freight train cars Containers	Total Volume carried. Thousands of tonnes	Av'ge haul per ton miles (km.)	Av'ge net train load tonnes	Max. trailing load tonnes	Total number carried in 1 000's	Average journey miles (km.)
INDONESIA **Indonesian State Railways** Perusahaan Jawatan Kereta Api Jalan Geredja 1, Bandung, Java	3' 6" (1·067) 2' 5½" (0·750) 1' 11⅝" (0·600)	3 970 (6 389) E 48 (77) 314 (505) 65 (105)	4 500 (7 246) E 63 (101) 326 (525) 57 (92)	1 500 V dc OH	SL 202 EL 4 DeL 75 DhL 84 DhS 137	D 10	2 423	22 279	4 679·9	706 000 000 ton-km			19 978	49·3 (79·3)
IRAN **Iranian State Railways** Teheran	4' 8½" (1·435) 5' 6" (1·676)	2 802 (4 525) 57 (92)	2 962 (4 766)		DeL 226 DeS 33 DhS 2 DmS 44		343	7 999	6 347·1	5 309 188 849 ton-km			6 457·5	314·4 (506)
IRAQ **Iraqi Republic Railways** Baghdad	4' 8½" (1·435)	767 (1 235)			S 19 De 163		240	3 280		1 853 000 000 tonne-km				
IRELAND **Coras lompair Eireann** Heuston Station, Dublin 8	5' 3" (1·60)	1 361 (2 190)	1 930 (3 106)		DeL 196 DhS 33	D 57	485	6 519 C 1 197	3 477	585 189 257 tonne-km			13 607	35 (56)
ISRAEL **Israel Railways** Central Station PO Box 44, Haifa	4' 8½" (1·435)	462 (647)	550 (886)		DeL 35 DhS 22		114	2 095	3 650	462 000 000 tonne-km			3 040	54·7 (88)
ITALY **Italian State Railways** **(Ferrovie dello Stato-Italia)** Piazza della Croce Rossa, 00161 Roma	4' 8½" (1·435) 3' 1⅝" (0·95)	9 950 (16 014) E 4 919 (7 916)	18 051 (29 070) E 11 140 (17 928)	3 600 V 3/16⅔ and 3 000 V dc OH	SL 691 SS 233 EL 1 798 ES 70 DeL 231 DeS 84 DhL 21 DhS 517 DmS 227 *Narrow* SL 15 DdS 2	E 434 ET 310 D 1 068 DT 187 EM 23 DM 8 *Narrow* D 24 DT 5	10 031	118 261 C 31 820	48 433	16 375 000 000 ton-km			390 070	58·8 (94·6)
Ferrovie Alta Valtellina Tirano	4' 8½" (1·435)	E 16 (26)	E 21 (34)	3 600 V 3/16⅔	S 2 E 4		17	22	37·2				945·3	
Ferrovia dell' Alto-Pistoiese S. Marello Pistoiese	3' 1½" (0·95)	E 10 (17)	E 11 (18)	1 200 V dc OH	E 2	E 3	5	16	3·7				432·2	
Ferrovie Biella-Novara Piazza Lombardia 6, Biella	4' 8½" (1·435)	32 (52)	40 (64)		S 5	D 7	3	15	12·2	16 (26)	80	310	669·6	
Ferrovie Calabro-Lucane Via Nizza 35, Rome	3' 1½" (0·95)		339 (545)		SL 3 SS 7 DeL 7 DhL 72	D 32 T 89	84	540	21·1	553 456 ton-km	70	480	7 630·5	13·7 (20·3)
Ferrovia Circumvestnea Catania 330141-330704	3' 1½" (0·95)	71 (114)	75 (120)		S 1 De 3 DS 9	D 3	9	59						
Ferrovia Circumvesuviana Strade Ferrate Secondarie Meridionali, Corso Garibaldi 387, Naples 80142	3' 1½" (0·95)	E 80 (128)	E 93 (150)	1 200 V dc OH	DhL 2 DhS 1 Other 1	E 70 R 4	47						43 086	10·6 (17·1)
Ferrovia Cumana (SEPSA) Naples 44 Via Cisterna dell Olio	4' 8⅞" (1·445)	E 16 (26)		3 000 V dc OH	D 2 E 1 De 3 Dh 1	E 11		31			77	110	11 000·0	6·2 (10)
Ferrovia delle Dolomiti *(Ceased operation)*	3' 1½" (0·95)	E 41 (66)												
Società Emiliana Ferrovie, Tramvie ed Automobili (SEFTA) Piazza Manzoni, Medena	4' 8½" (1·435)	E 25 (41)	E 38 (61)	3 000 V dc OH	EL 4 DS 1	E 10	29	80 C 98	100·0	15·2 (24·5)	500	580	1 191·5	11·0 (17·5)
Gestione Governativa Ferrovie Padane Via Foro Boario 27, C.A.P. 44100 Ferrara	4' 8¹¹/₁₆" (1·445)	32 (52)	39 (62)		Dm 3	D 9	9	28	13·2	424 443 ton-km	600		770·1	16·9 (27·3)
S.A. La Ferroviaria Italiana Arezzo	4' 8½" (1·435)	E 52 (84)	E 60 (96)	3 000 V dc	E 2	E 3	10	28	21·7				1 788·0	
S.A. It. Ferrot amviaria Via Napoli 161, Bari	4' 8½" (1·435)	E 5 (8)	E 5 (8)	1 200 V dc	D 1	E 2	4	10	1·3				311·1	
Ferrovia Genova-Casella Genoa	3' 3⅜" (1·00)	E 15 (25)		2 600 V dc OH	E 3	E 3	5	16	1·4	5·4 (8·7)			433·3	
Guidovia Santuario della Guardia Genova S. Quirico	3' 3⅜" (1·00)	7 (11)	7 (11)		De 11 DhS 2			2					158·6	

	Average Speeds			Financial Data		Couplers	Buffers	Rails	Sleepers (crossties)		Curvature max.	Gradient max. (U=not compensated)	Axle load max.	Altitude max.	Staff employed. Total no. (inclu. workshop)	Names of officials. Extended lists can be found at the end of the individual country in the report section immediately following
	Freight Train	Pass. Train	Speed max.	Revenue Expenses	Braking (continuous)	Type and Height above rail	Centres and Height above rail	Weight	Type and thickness	Spacing Number per mile (per km) or centres ins (mm)						
	mph (km/hr)	mph (km/hr)	mph (km/hr)	in 1 000's		ins (mm)	ins (mm)	lb. per yd (kg/m)	ins (mm)				tonnes	feet (m)		
	17·4 (28)	43 (70)	62 (100)	Rs. 22 222 23 103	W'hse Air and Vac	Henricot Sumitomo	30 (760)	1 067 g 85/52 *Narrow* 33/25 (16/12·4)	Teak 4¾ (120) (42/56) Some metal	*Main* 26⅞'' (680) *Branch* 31½'' (800)	*Main* 492 ft (680) *Branch* 328 ft (100 m)	4·0% *Rack* (150 m) 8·0%	*Main* 13·5 8·0% *Branch* 8-10	Java 4 088 Sumatra 3 788	70 795 (6 178) (1 246)	Chief Dir: R. Soemali
	25 (40)	32 (51)	50 (80)	Rials 10 249 129 10 700 568	Air Knorr W'hse	Screw and auto 41¾ (1 060)	Crs 68⅞ (1 750) Ht as coupler	101/79 (50/38)	Conc Steel; Wood 6 (150)	23⅝'' (600)	722 ft (220 m)	2·8%	20	6 946 (2 177)	29 693	Pres: F. Mahmoodian
	St 31 (50)	St 37 (60)	St 50 (80)		W'hse Air Vac	Auto & Screw 41¾ (1 060) 23 (584)	68⅞ Crs (1 750)	90/75 (45/37) 75/60 (37/30)	Wood 5 (127) Wood 4½ (114)	N+4 N+3	*Standard* 4° 34' *Metre* 5°	0·8% 0·5%	17 12	1 377		Director General: Ibrahim Mahmoud
	13 (21)	Main 39 (63) Suburb 23 (37)	75 (121)	£ 23 262 44 960	Vac G. & C.	P. Screw Fr. 3-link 42 (1 067)	75 (1 905) 42 (1 067)	*Main* 101/85 (50/42)	Wood 5 (127) and Concrete	32½'' (826)	275 ft (84 m)	2·0% 1·67% **U**	20	630 (192)	9 123 (2 050)	Gen Man: J. F. Higgins
	17 (27)	32 (52)	65 (105)	£ls	Air Knorr W'hse	Standard UIC 41¾ (1 060)	Crs 68⅞ (1 750) Ht 41¾ (1 060)	101/76 (50/37·5)	Wood 6 (150) conc Steel	2 680 (1 670)	13·1°	2·0% **U** 2·5%	21	2 625 (800)	1 837 (637)	Gen. Man: Zvi Tsafriri
	28 (45)	57 (92)	112 (180)	L. 1 864 638 000 2 740 420 000	Air Breda W'hse	Standard UIC	Standard UIC	121/101/ 99 (60/50/ 49)	Wood 6 (150) Conc 6/7½ (150/190)	60 kg RI (1 666) 50 kg RI (1 445- 1 666) 49 kg RI (1 390- 1 430)	Radius 820 ft (250 m)	3·1%	20	1 503 (1 375)	159 693 (28 492)	Dir Gen: Doff Ercole Semenza
											7·0°	2·4%				
								50·4 (25)			50·0°	4·2%				
					W'hse Air	Standard	Standard	73 (36·1)	Wood 5½ (140)	30'' (770)	5·7°	2·0%	16			
	20 (40)	25 (40)	43 (70)		W'hse Air	Screw 24½ (620)	Central Crs. 33½ (855)	55/50 (27/25)	Wood 5½ (140)	29½'' (750)	17·5°	10% **U** 6·0%	11	(1 406)	3 200	Dir. Gen: J. Bari
	15 (25)	22 (35)	72 (45)		W'hse Air			55 (27·3)			9·2°	2·3%	10	3 202 (976)	382 (80)	
		25 (40)	56 (90)	L. 4 141 18 329	W'hse Air	Auto 32·6 (829)	Central 34·2 (870)	73 (36)	Oak 5½ (140)	29'' (630)	11·5°	3·0%	12		1 223 (332)	Gen. Man: Dott. Ing. U. Paci
	18·6 (30)	49·7 (80)	55·9 (90)		W'hse Air		41⁵/₁₆ (1 050)	92 (46)	Wood 5½ (140)	2 000 (1 250)	11·3°	1·35%	18	141 (43)	290 (100)	Gen. Man: Dott. Ing Angelo Brofferio
	25 (40)	34 (55)	37 (60)	L. 192 601·1 520 760·4	W'hse Air	Standard	Standard	55 (27·3)	Wood 4¾ (120)	32¾'' (833)	8·75°	1·2%	15	397 (121)	167 (65)	Pres: Sig Y. Morselli
	25 (40)	43 (70)	56 (90)	L. 343 188·5 1 413 359·2	W'hse Air	Standard Bagnara	Standard	55 (27·3)	Oak 7 (180)	29½'' (750)	7·7°	0·6%	18	30 (9)	177	Dir: Dr Paolo Fiorini
								56·5 (28)			5·8°	1·7%				
								54·5 (27)			17·5°	2·9%				
					W'hse Air	24½ (620)	Central 33½ (855)	55 (27·3)	Wood 4¾ (120)	2 140 (1 330)	29·0°	4·5%	8			
								18·2 (9)			70·0°	8·3%				

NAME OF COMPANY ADDRESS	Gauge ft. in. (metres)	Route length incl. E=Electrified miles (km.)	Track length incl. E=Electrified miles (km.)	Elect. system and type of conductor	Loco-motives L=Line S=Shunt / Steam Electric Diesel De=elec. Dh=hyd.		Rail-cars Electric Diesel Trailer Railbus Multiple Unit set		Pass. train cars	Freight train cars / Containers	Total Volume carried. Thousands of tonnes	Av'ge haul per ton miles (km.)	Av'ge net train load tonnes	Max. trailing load tonnes	Total number carried in 1 000's	Average journey miles (km.)
ITALY *(contd.)*																
Ferrovia Napoli-Piedimonte Matese Cia delle Ferrovie del Mezzogiorno d'Italia 80137 Naples, Piazza Carlo 3 *(Operates 2 lines):*																
Napoli-S. Maria C.V. (S. Andrea)	3' 1½" (0·95)	E 24 (39)	E 25 (41)	11 000 V 1/25	E	2	E	9	13	22						
S. Maria C.V. (F.S.)— Piedemonte	4' 8½" (1·435)	25 (40)	28 (46)		Dh	2	D T	5 4		22						
Società Nazionale Ferrovie e Tranvie Iseo *(Operates 2 lines):* Brescio-Iseo-Edolo, and Iseo-Rovato)	4' 8½" (1·435)	68 (109)	79 (127)		S D	12 1	D	12	39	105	286·3				1 516·5	
Ferrovie Nord Milano Piazzale Luogi Cadorna 14, 20123 Milan	4' 8½" (1·435)	135 (218) E 124 (200)	230 (370) E 216 (348)	3 000 V dc OH Copper	SL EL DeL DeS	1 9 3 2	E ET	49 93	109	297	587·6	9·0 (14·5)	46	800	27 791·6	12·9 (20·8)
Societa Romana per le Ferrovie del Nord Via di Villa Ruffo 5, Rome	4' 8½" (1·435)	E 63 (102)	E 76 (123)	3 300 V dc OH	E	14	E	10	32	93	0·8		100	220	1 946·5	10·7 (17·2)
Ferrovie Reggiane V. Trento Trieste 9, Reggio Emilia	4' 8½" (1·445)	47 (76)	54 (86)		S D	4 2						10·7 (17·3)				
Ferrovia del Renon Balzano *(4·2 km. Rack rail)*	3' 3⅜" (1·00)	E 7 (12)		800 V dc	E	4	E	5	2	10	5·6				352·8	
Società Ferrovie Elettriche di Roma (STEFER) Via dei Radiotelegrafisti 44, Rome *(Operates 3 railways):*																
Ferrovie Roma-Fiuggi-Alatri	3' 1½" (0·95)	E 59 (96)		1 500 V dc OH	E	3	E EMU	2 34	3	60	0·4			58	165	14 116·5	17 (27·3)
Metropolitana Termini-Laurentina	4' 8½" (1·435)	E 7 (11)	E 17 (27·5)	1 500 V dc OH			E T	40 8							23 152·0	
Ferrovie Roma-Lido	4' 8¼" (1·435)	E 18 (29)	E 40 (65)	1 500 V dc OH	EL DS	9 2	E	4	48	34	8·3	12·4 (19·9)		500	10 055·9	11·8 (19·1)
Ferrovia Sangritana Soc. per le Ferrovie Adriatico-Appennino, Lanciano	4' 8½" (1·435)	E 68 (100)	E 74 (119)	3 200 V dc	E	3	E	9	6	14	6·8				1 162·3	
Società Ferrovie Complementari Della Sardegna Cagliari	3' 1½" (0·95)	319 (513)			S D	58 3	D	26	89	327	30·2				524·4	
Strade Ferrate Sarde SA Via Sicilia 20, Sassari	3' 1½" (0·95)	139 (224)	148 (238)		S	19	D	11	84	159	7·1				876·2	
Ferrovie Meridionali Sarde Iglesias (Cagliari)	3' 1½" (0·95)	70 (113)	90 (145)		SL	32	D	10	15	330	267·0	9 (15)	440	760	520·0	14 (22)
Società Subalpina di Imprese Ferroviarie P.O.B. 60, Domodossola *Operates 2 lines:* Domodossola-Swiss Border (1·0 m) Spoleta-Norcia (0·95 m)	3' 3⅜" (1·00) 3' 1½" (0·95)	E 21 (33) E 32 (51)	E 22 (36) E 34 (55)	1 500 V dc OH 3 000 V dc OH	E D EMU E	6 2 7 5	10 7	32 34	1·7	13 719 ton-km	488·6 105·5					
Ferrovie del Sud-est, SpA Via Ravenna 14, Rome *Local Office:* 70122 Bari	4' 8½" (1·435)	294 (473)	342 (550)		DeL DhL DhS	13 1 5	D T	42 24	30	279	170·3	23·2 (37·3)	82	900	7 160·5	15·1 (24·4)
Ferrovia Suzzara-Ferrara Corso Porta Reno 65, Ferrara	4' 8¹¹⁄₁₆" (1·440)	51 (81)	59 (95)		DhL DhS	2 2	D T	20 7		22	57·1	18·6 (30)	50	800	937·9	28 (45)
Ferrovie Torino Nord Corso Giulio Cesare 15, Turin	4' 8⅞" (1·445)	55 (88) E 27 (43)	68 (110) E 35 (56)	4 000 V dc	S E	14 5	E D	2 5	32	50	157·4				5 332·4	
Ferrovia Elettrica Transatesina Corso Italia 30, Bolzano	4' 8½" (1·435)	E 8 (13)	E 10 (16)	1 350 V dc			E	4	8	11	14·4				699·1	
SM Strade Ferrate Umbro Aretine Largo Cacciatori delle Alpi, Perugia	4' 8½" (1·435)	E 59 (95)	E 67 (107)	3 000 V dc	S De	12 1	E ET	2 9	13	78	72·5		3 187 308 ton-km		5 907·2 *	10 (16)
Ferrovia Elettrica Val di Fiemme Bolzano	3' 3⅜" (1·00)	E 31 (50)	E 37 (59)	2 400 V dc	E	3	E	3	6	92	8·0				183·5	
Ferrovia Valle Caudina Soc. Italiana Strade Ferrate Sovvenzionate, Benevento	4' 8½" (1·435)	30 (48)	32 (51)		S D	4 1	D	8	16	38	7·5				983·2	
Società Autoferrovie Bergamo *(Closed down, replaced by bus service)*																
Società Veneta per Ferrovie Secondarie Italiane Via Enrico degli Scrovegni 1, Padova *Operates 5 lines:*																
Udine	4' 8½" (1·435)	22 (36)	24 (39)		SL DeL	5 1	D	3	7	9	39·8	9·3 (15)	60	380	697·4	8·7 (14)
Piovene Rocchette	4' 8½" (1·435)	12 (19)	14 (22)		SL DL	1 1	D	4	2	10	10·6	10·6 (17)	50	250	299·3	6·2 (10)
Parma	4' 8½" (1·435)	27 (44)	31 (50)		SL DeL	2 2	D DT	4 4	5	26	11·2	13 (21)	40	380	747·4	10·2 (16·6)

* Totals for combined rail and bus services

Average Speeds: Freight Train mph (km/hr)	Average Speeds: Pass. Train mph (km/hr)	Speed max. mph (km/hr)	Financial Data: Revenue Expenses in 1 000's	Braking (continuous)	Couplers: Type and Height above rail ins (mm)	Buffers: Centres and Height above rail ins (mm)	Rails: Weight lb. per yd (kg/m)	Sleepers (crossties): Type and thickness ins (mm)	Sleepers (crossties): Spacing Number per mile (per km) or centres ins (mm)	Curvature max.	Gradient max. (U=not compensated)	Axle load max. tonnes	Altitude max. feet (m)	Staff employed. Total no. (inclu. workshop)	Names of officials. Extended lists can be found at the end of the individual country in the report section immediately following
															Dr. Ing. Marcello Rossetti
	19 *(30)*	37 *(60)*	L. 79 239·6 1 397 731·4	W'hse Air			60/44 *(30/22)*	Wood 5½ *(140)*		22·0°	3·6%			182 *(35)*	
	43 *(70)*	50 *(80)*	L. 101 018·5 796 205·4	Air			72·5 *(36)*	Wood 5½ *(140)*		5·8°	2·5%			93 *(16)*	
				W'hse	Standard	Standard	72·6 *(36)*	Wood 5⅛ *(130)*	29½" *(750)*	7·0°	2·4% 2·2% **U**	18			
10 *(16)*	26 *(42)*	50 *(80)*	L. 4 800 717·9 14 387 425·9	W'hse. Air	Draw- hook 42" *(1 065)*	69 *(1 750)* 42 *(1 065)*	93/60 *(46/30)*	Wood 5⅛/5½ *(130/140)* Conc.	24-28½" *(600-725)*	4·6°	3·0%	16	1 266 *(386)*	2 270 *(330)*	Op. Man: Dott. Ing. Carlo Gaifami
72 *(45)*	88 *(55)*	43 *(70)*	L. 253 579·8 1 709 117·8	W'hse Air	Draw- hook 41¼ *(1 050)*	67½ *(1 720)* 41¼ *(1 050)*	72/60 *(36/30)*	Wood 5⅛ *(130)*	31½" *(800)*	17·5°	3·0%	15	1 476 *(450)*	401 *(66)*	Gen Man: Dr. Ing. Piero Dionisi Vici
				W'hse	Standard	Standard	72/60 *(36·30)*	Wood 5½ *(140)*	31½" *(800)*		1·2%	14·5			
										35·0°					
	21·9 *(35·3)*	43 *(70)*	L. 742 443·0 4 883 626·0	Air W'hse	33½" *(850)*	Buffer- Coupler	72/56 *(36/28)*	Wood 5⅛ *(130)*	25⅛ *(640)*	35·0°	6·0%**U**	10	213 *(700)*	803 *(185)*	Ing. L. Catanoso
	24 *(38)*	50 *(80)*	L. 1 108 180·0 2 254 611·0	Air W'hse	29" *(740)*		93 *(46·3)*	Wood 6 *(150)*	25⅛" *(640)*	8·7°	3·5%**U**		151 *(46)*	194	Ing. L. Catanoso
	30 *(49)*	53 *(85)*	L. 951 988·0 3 209 018·0	Air W'hse			93 *(46·3)*	Wood 6 *(150)*	25⅛ *(640)*	6·3°	1·9%**U**	16	132 *(40)*	609 *(191)*	Ing. L. Catanoso
								55·4 *(28)*		17·5	4·0%				
							55/42 *(27/21)*			22·0°	3·0%				
							55/42 *(27/21)*			17·5°	2·5%				
12 *(20)*	28 *(45)*	50 *(80)*		W'hse Air	21 *(530)*	Central 31 *(785)*	55/50 *(27/25)*	Wood 5½ *(140)*	29½" *(750)*	17·5°	2·5%	10	984 *(300)*	532 *(94)*	
28 *(45)*	37 *(60)*	37 *(60)*	L. 305 155·8 1 219 886·3	W'hse Air	23 *(600)*	23 *(600)*	55/50·4 *(27·3/25)*	Wood 5⅛ *(130)*	27½" *(700)*	35·0°	6·0%	4·9	2 723 *(830)*	107	Gen. Man: Dr. Z. Paolo
							50·4 *(25)*			25·0°	4·5%				
15·5 *(25)*	30 *(50)*	56 *(90)*		Air W'hse Breda	Standard	Standard	73/55 *(36/27)*	Wood 5½ *(140)*	29½" *(750)*	7·0°	1·3% 2·4% **U**		1 486 *(453)*	2 500 *(250)*	Ing. Renato De Marco Ing. Guglielmo Zoldester
15·5 *(25)*	32 *(52)*	56 *(90)*	L. 533 934·0 1 024 000·7	W'hse Air	Standard	Standard	101/55 *(50/27·6)*	Wood 5½ *(140)* Conc.	29½" *(750)*	3·8°	1·0%	14·5	80 *(24·5)*	149 *(35)*	Dr. Ing. Luciano Puccetti
										8·7°	**E** 3·5% **S** 1·8%				
										14·5°	6·2%				
19 *(31)*	25 *(41)*	31 *(50)*	L. 4 978 821·1 5 167 231·8 *	W'hse Air	Standard	Standard	73/55	Oak 5½ *(140)*	28¼ *(720)*	5·9°	0·8% 0·2% **U**	16	1 380 *(420)*	460 *(195)*	Ing. Raffaele Roasali Ing. Carlo Simoncelli
							44·4 *(22)*			29·5°	4·4%				
							72·6 *(36)*			5·8°	2·0%				
															Gen. Man: Dott. M. Fabro
		43 *(70)*		W'hse Air	Standard	Standard	60 *(30)*	Wood *(140)*	31½" *(800)*	7·0°	1·6% **U**	15	1 191 *(363)*	63 *(26)*	
		37 *(60)*		W'hse Air	Standard	Standard	55 *(27·6)*	Wood *(140)*	35⅞" *(910)*	11·7°	2·6% **U**	15	1 168 *(356)*	35 *(19)*	
		37 *(60)*		W'hse Air	Standard	Standard	55 *(27·6)*	Wood *(140)*	28¾" *(730)*	5·8°	0·94% **U**	14·5	171 *(52)*	82 *(26)*	

* Totals for combined rail and bus services

NAME OF COMPANY ADDRESS	Gauge ft. in. (metres)	Route length incl. E=Electrified miles (km.)	Track length incl. E=Electrified miles (km.)	Elect. system and type of conductor	Loco-motives L=Line S=Shunt / Steam Electric Diesel De=elec. Dh=hyd.		Rail-cars Electric Diesel Trailer Railbus Multiple Unit set		Pass. train cars	Freight train cars / Containers	Freight movement Total Volume carried. Thousands of tonnes	Av'ge haul per ton miles (km.)	Av'ge net train load tonnes	Max. trailing load tonnes	Passengers Total number carried in 1 000's	Average journey miles (km.)
ITALY *(contd.)*																
Piove di Sacco	4' 8½" (1·435)	36 (58)	42 (67)		SL 2 DeL 3		D	5	20	44	40·5	6·8 (11)	100	380	1 170·8	12·4 (20)
Bologna	4' 8½" (1·435)	46 (74)	55 (89)		SL 3 DL 1 DeL 3		D DT	6 3	21	59	81·3	11·2 (18)	150	380	1 031·0	11·2 (18)
IVORY COAST Regie des Chemins de Fer Abidjan-Niger	3' 3⅜" (1·000)	730 (1 173)	817 (1 318)		D	63	D T	18 33	87	1 247	962		200-650	1 800	2 828	63 (102)
JAMAICA Jamaica Railway Corporation PO Box 489, 142 Barry Street, Kingston	4' 8½" (1·435)	205 (330)	228 (367)		DeL 23 Dh 2		D T	6 11	23	382	4 009·5				1 106·0	29 (46)
Kaiser Bauxite Company Discovery Bay	4' 8½" (1·435)	16 (25)	23 (37)		DeL 3 DeS 1					88	5 000·0	11 (18)	1 700			
Alpart Railway Alumina Partners of Jamaica Spur Tree	4' 8½" (1·435)	11 (18)	13 (21)		DeL 4 DeS 1					343	1 500·0	11 (18)	1 200			
JAPAN Japanese National Railways 1-6-5 Marunouchi, Chiyoda-ku, Tokyo	3' 6" (1·067)	13 180 (21 272) E 4 855 (7 813)	24 854 (40 039) E 11 888 (19 132)	20 000 V 1/50 & 1/60; 600 V & 1 500 V dc OH	E 1 918 D 1 793		E D	13 918 5 426	7 757	135 912 C 39 916	142 000		46 000 000 000 ton-km		7 048 000	15·5 (24·9)
Hanshin Electric Railway Co Ltd 8 Umeda-cho, Kita-Ku, Osaka	4' 8½" (1·435)	E 45 (72)	E 105 (169)	600 V dc OH			E T EMU	265 45 28		7					226 129·4	6·6 (10·6)
Jozankei Railway Co 108, 9-chome, 3-Jou, Toyohira, Sapporo City	3' 6" (1·067)	E 17 (27)	E 67 (108)	1 500 V dc OH			E	2	24	29	52·2	7·3 (4·3)		510	1 752·6	7 (12)
Kei-Hin Electric Railway Co Tenmabashi, Higashi-ku, Osaka	4' 8½" (1·435)	E 55 (88)	E 124 (200)	600 V dc OH			E ET	324 312	402						172 529·8	7·8 (12·6)
Hankyu Corporation 41 Kakuta-cho, Kitaku, Osaka	4' 8½" (1·435)	E 88 (141)	E 171 (276)	1 500 dc OH	EL	2	E ET	630 411		28					693 761·1	8·4 (13·6)
Keihin Electric Express Railway Co 17 Shiba Takanawa-Minami-cho, Minato-ku, Tokyo	4' 8½" (1·435)	E 50 (80)	E 114 (183)	1 500 V dc OH			E	120	443	24					173 565·0	7 (12)
Kei-Sei Electric Railway Co Gojo-machi, Taito-ku, Tokyo	4' 6" (1·372)	E 52 (83)			E	2	E T	103 155		16						
Kinki Nippon Railway Company (Kintetsu Corporation) 581, 6-chome, Uehommachi, Tennoji-ku, Osaka 543	4' 8½" (1·435) 3' 6" (1·067) 2' 6" (0·762)	E 364 (586)	E 711 (1 129)	750 & 1 500 V dc OH	E	13	E T	865 725		94	325·5		18 705 889 ton-km		727 071·1	
Nagano Electric Railway Gondo-cho 2201, Nagano City Nagano	3' 6" (1·067)	E 44 (71)	E 58 (94)	1 500 V dc OH	E	3	E ET EMU	30 8 4	50	358	15·6 (25·1)			400	17 457·4	9·3 (15)
Nagoya Railroad Co 1-223, Sasashima-cho, Nakamura-ku, Nagoya City	3' 6" (1·067)	E 325 (523)	487 (785)	600 & 1 500 V dc OH	EL 14 ES 2 DhS 5		E D ET	521 12 171		75	539·2		7 358 037 ton-km		369 692·8	9·8 (15·8)
Nara Electric Railway Co 184 Mikanomija Monzen, Fushimi-ky, Kyoto	4' 8½" (1·435)	E 35 (56)		600 V dc OH												
Nishi Nippon Railroad Co 11-17 Tenjin 1-chome, Fukuoka City, Fukuoka	4' 8½" (1·435) 3' 6" (1·067)	E 59 (95) E 13 (21)	E 122 (196)	1 500 V and 600 V dc	ES	1	E T	163 88							106 000·0	
Odakyu Electric Railway Co 2-28-12, Yoyogi, Shibuya-ku, Tokyo	3' 6" (1·067)	E 69 (111)	E 160 (257)	1 500 V dc OH	EL 4 ES 1		E T	400 212		33	1 410·7	18·9 (30·4)	660		400 137·0	10·1 (16·1)
Oita Transportation Co Seike, Oita City	3' 6" (1·067)	58 (94) E 12 (19)	59 (95)	600 V dc OH	S 8 D 6		E D	37 14	39	65	155·6	5 (7)			17 422·6	7 (12)

Average Speeds			Financial Data		Couplers	Buffers	Rails	Sleepers (crossties)			Curvature max.	Gradient max. (U=not compensated)	Axle load max.	Altitude max.	Staff employed. Total no. (inclu. workshop)	Names of officials. Extended lists can be found at the end of the individual country in the report section immediately following
Freight Train	Pass. Train	Speed max.	Revenue Expenses	Braking (continuous)	Type and Height above rail	Centres and Height above rail	Weight	Type and thickness	Spacing Number per mile (per km) or centres ins (mm)							
mph (km/hr)	mph (km/hr)	mph (km/hr)	in 1 000's		ins (mm)	ins (mm)	lb. per yd (kg/m)	ins (mm)					tonnes	feet (m)		
	43 (70)			W'hse Air	Standard	Standard	60 (30)	Wood (140)	33⅞" (860)		5·8°	1·2% U	15	16 (5)	137 (49)	
	47 (75)			W'hse Air	Standard	Standard	60 (30)	Wood (140)	33½" (850)		11·7°	1·0% U	15	171 (52)	50 (38)	
			F. 6 170 000 6 060 000	Willison auto All 29¾ (755)								A. 1·0 B. 2·5	A. 15 B. 13			
	23 (37)	40 (25)	$J 6 262·0 7 296·0	W'hse Air	AAR 34½ (876)		80/60 (40/30)	Wood & Conc. 6 (153)	26" (660)		300 ft (92 m)	3·0% U	17	1 705 (443)	1 454 (235)	Chairman: John Allgrove Gen. Man: A. B. Tapper
20 (32)		25 (40)		Air W'hse	Type F AAR Standard		115 (57)	Wood 7 (178)	22" (560)		886 ft (270 m)	3·0%	32	1 600 (488)		
15 (24)		20 (32)		Air W'hse	Type E AAR 34½ (876)		106/90 (53/45)	Wood 7 (178)	22" (560)		886 ft (270 m)	2·2%	31·5	700 (213)	36	Gen. Man: F. J. Haydel
Express 41 (67) Local 24 (39)	Express 49 (79) Local 32 (51)	75 (120)	Yen 1 833 200 000 2 747 900 000	Air; Nippon ABC; Mitsubishi Electric	Auto 34⅝ (880)	None	101·8/60·6 (50/40) 30·4/30·1	Wood 5½ (140) Conc 6½ (170)	Track Class (1) 22⅞ (580) (2) 26 (660) (3) 26 (660) (4) 27⅛ (690)	Track Class (1) 2·25 (2) 2·9 (3) 4·25 (4) 5·75	Track Class (1) 1·0% (2) 1·0% (3) 2·5% (4) 3·5%	18	4 511 (1 375)	450 338 (33 998)	President: Famio Takagi
	100·9 (162·2)	130 (210)		Air	Auto 33⅜ (1 000)		123/107 (60·8/53·8)	Conc 7½ (190)	2 780 (1 725)	8 200 ft (2 500 m)	1·5%	16	571 (174)		
*		68 (110)	Yen 10 778 619·3 8 652 990·8	Air Electro Magnet	Van Dorn 25⅜ (645)		101/60 (50/30)	Wood 6 (150) & Conc	2 480/2 400 (1 540/1 490)		11·0°	3·03%	13	62 (19)	3 291 (557)	Gen. Man: Chuziro Noda
16·2 (26·1)	24 (39)	43 (70)	Yen 124 406·0 300 738·0	Air Mitsubishi	(Sibata) 32 (830)		60 (30)	Wood 8¼ 322	26¼" (690)		11·0°	3·3%	14·4	912 (278)	904 (150)	Gen. Man: Tadao Ebina
	Express 33 (54) Local 25 (41)	Keihan 62 (100) Oten Line 37 (60)		Air	Auto 31 (790)		100/60 (50/30)	Wood 6 (150) Conc	(1 680-1 800)	Keihan 14·3° Oten 56·0°	Keihan 3·3% Oten 6·67%	15·5	626 (191)	3 142 (433)	Gen. Man: Shiro Muraoka
	46 (74)	68 (110)	Yen 46 890 000 38 687 000	Air	Auto 34¼ (880)		60/112 (30/60)	Wood 6 (150) Conc	2 560 (1 600)		17·5°	4·0%	17·78	368 (112)	5 894	Pres: Kaoru Mori
34 (55)	27 † (43)	65 (105)	Yen 8 429 031·1 6 179 036·1	Air AMM Elec HSCD	NCB 34¼ (870)	Crs 54 (1 435) Ht. 43 (70)	101 (50)	Wood 5½ (140)	23" (580)		15·9°	2·0% 3·05% U	12	312 (96)	5 300 (600)	Gen. Man: Haruo Sato
				Air	Auto		101 (50)	Wood 6 (150)	27½" (700)		14·6°	4·0%				
	46 (75)	68 (110)	Yen 101 921 808 81 443 928	Air AMA NAB	Sumitomo Tightlock 340 (880)		101/75 (50/37)	Wood 6 (150)	19⅝" (500)		11·5°	3·5% 3·3% U	18	1 187 (362)	12 600	Chairman: Isamu Saheki President: Eizo Imazato
21 (33)	Express 33 (53) Local 25 (40)	56 (90)		Air dynamic	Auto 34⅝ (880)		80/60 (40/30)	Wood 5½ (140)	30⅜"/15 (770/380)		8·75°	4·0%	13	2 129 (649)	1 794 (69)	
21·1 (34)	Express 46 (74) Local 25 (40)	68 (110)	Yen 34 884 573·0 29 515 904·0	Air dynamic	Auto 34⅝ (880)		100 (50)	Wood 5½ (140)	19⅝" (500)		10·9°	3·5%	13		4 107	President: Kotaro Takeda
		59 (95)	Yen 5 086 000·0 4 784 000·0	W'hse AMAR-D AMM-R	Tomlinson Tightlock (648/880)		101/60 (50/30)	Wood 5½ (140) Conc	26" (660)		Rad 558 ft (170 m)	3·3% U	12		1 075 (146)	President: Hirotsugu Yoshimoto
20 (32)	Express 42·5 (68·4)	Express 68 (110) Local 53 (85)	Yen 16 229 000·0 13 080 000·0	Air dynamic regen	Auto (880)		100 (50)	Wood 5½ (140) Conc 6¼ (160)	2 640 (1 640)		8·75°	2·5%	15	564 (171·9)	3 592 (420)	Pres: Soh Hirota Man. Dirs: Y. Hayashi H. Miki
					Auto (880)		60 (30)	Wood 6 (150)			44·0°	2·1%				

* Limited Express 50 mph (80 km/h)
Express 43 mph (70 km/h)
Local trains 31 mph (50 km/h)
† Excludes special express trains: 38 mph (61 km/h) and ordinary express trains: 32 mph (52 km/h)

NAME OF COMPANY ADDRESS	Gauge ft. in. *(metres)*	Route length incl. E=Electrified miles *(km.)*	Track length incl. E=Electrified miles *(km.)*	Elect. system and type of conductor	Locomotives L=Line S=Shunt Steam Electric Diesel De=elec. Dh=hyd.	Railcars Electric Diesel Trailer Railbus Multiple Unit set	Pass. train cars	Freight train cars Containers	Freight movement: Total Volume carried. Thousands of tonnes	Freight movement: Av'ge haul per ton miles *(km.)*	Freight movement: Av'ge net train load tonnes	Freight movement: Max. trailing load tonnes	Passengers: Total number carried in 1 000's	Passengers: Average journey miles *(km.)*
JAPAN *(contd.)*														
Seibu Railway Co 16-15, 1-chome, Minami-Ikebukuro, Toshima-ku, Tokyo 171	3' 6" *(1·067)*	111 *(179)* E 109 *(175)*	227 *(366)* E 224 *(361)*	1 500 V dc OH	EL 15 DS 1 Bat 6	E 349 T 343	25	308	1 231·0	25 *(40)*	300	600	471 192·0	7·1 *(11·4)*
Takamatsu Kotohira Electric RR Co 320 Sakuramachi, Takamatsu City	4' 8½" *(1·435)*	E 37 *(66)*	E 42 *(68)*	1 500 & 600 V dc OH		E 51							12 717·9	6 *(9)*
Tobu Railway Co. 2/1, 1-chome, Oshiage, Sumida-ku, Tokyo	3' 6" *(1·067)*	301 *(485)* E 295 *(474)*	593 *(955)* E 587 *(945)*	1 500 V dc OH	E 43	E 613 ET 442 D 3		784	6 638·0	25 *(40)*	140	500	568 832·0	8·7 *(14)*
Tokyu Corporation 26-20 Sakuragoka- Cho, Shibuya-ku, Tokyo 150	3' 6" *(1·067)*	E 55 *(88)*	E 113 *(182)*	1 500 V dc		E 683 T							59 664 894 pass-km	
JORDAN														
Hedjaz Jordan Railway PO Box 582, Amman *Note: This is the Jordanian section of the Hedjaz Railway which runs from Damascus (Syria) to Ma'an. The continuation from Ma'an to Medina (Saudi Arabia) is being rebuilt.*	3' 5⅜" *(1·050)*	310 *(500)*	350 *(550)*		SL 13 SS 2 DeL 5	D 2 T 24	6	330	56·0	28 210 800 ton-km			7·0	
KAMPUCHEA	3' 3⅜" *(1·00)*	*(1 800)*	403 *(649)*		SL 24 DeL 13 DeS 10		67	688	117·4	11 512 900 ton-km			1 027	
KOREA														
Korean National Railroad 3, 1-ka, Doding, Chungku, Seoul *Operates all lines in South Korea; no information available regarding railways in North Korea.*	4' 8½" *(1·435)* 2' 6" *(0·762)*	2 323 *(3 744)* 125 *(78)*	2 448 *(3 822)*		S 68 De 306 E 90	D 122 E 171	1 785	16 208	31 550·9	7 841 000 000 ton-km			131 001·0	45 *(72)*
LEBANON														
C.F. de l'Etat Libanais PO Box 109, Souk el Arwam, Beirut *(All Lebanese railways became State-owned in 1960)*	4' 8½" *(1·435)* 3' 5¼" *(1·050)*	208 *(335)* 51* *(82)*	300 *(483)*		SL 14 SS 18 DeL 6		15	881	659·8	45 *(72)*	350		72·6	71 *(114)*
LIBERIA														
Lamco J. V. Operating Co Roberts International Airport	4' 8½" *(1·435)*	167 *(270)*	205 *(330)*		DeL 14 DeS 10	D 5		591	10 701·2	2 719 433 000 000 ton-km		8 100		168 *(270)*
Bong Mining Co PO Box 538, Monrovia	4' 8½" *(1·435)*	48 *(78)*	57 *(92)*		DeL 4 DhS 5	D 2		219	6 253·7	80 175 000 ton-km	3 250	3 200		
LIBYA														
Cyrenaica Government Railway Benghazi *(Ceased operation)*	3' 1 7/16" *(0·95)*	108 *(174)*												
LUXEMBOURG														
Soc. Nat. des C.F. Luxembourgeois 9, Place de la Gare, Luxembourg	4' 8½" *(1·435)*	168 *(271)* E 86 *(138)*	415 *(668)* E 213 *(344)*	3 000 V dc OH and 25 000 V 1/50 OH	EL 19 DeL 151 DhL 16	D 17 DMU 9	77	3 419 C 207		865 993 000 ton-km			13 391·6	12·4 *(19·9)*
MADAGASCAR														
** **Reseau National des C.F. Malgaches** Gare Soarano, Antananarivo														
MALAWI														
Malawi Railways Ltd., Central Africa Railway Co. Ltd. PO Box 5144, Limbe, Malawi	3' 6" *(1·067)*	352 *(566)*	374 *(601)*		DeL 14 DhS 5 DhL 11	D 2	23	649	1 105·2	225 4 475 000 ton-km			1 079	45·8 *(73·7)*
MALAYSIA														
** **Malaysian Railway** PO Box No. 1, Kuala Lumpur	3' 3⅜" *(1·00)*	1 035 *(1 665)*	1 338 *(2 153)*		SL 84 DL 91 DS 41	D 26 T 15	375	6 450	4 500	1 164 200 000 ton-km			598 700 000 pass-km	66·2 *(106·5)*
Rompin Mining Company Ltd. Kuala Rompin, Pahang	3' 3⅜" *(1·00)*	50 *(80)*	55 *(89)*		De 3 Dh 4	R 8 D 2	3	116	2 524·0	50 *(80)*	1 400	2 160	84·0	50 *(80)*
MALI														
** **Regie du C.F. du Mali** BP 260, Bamako Mali	3' 3⅜" *(1·000)*	399 *(642)*	426 *(685)*		DeL 15 DeS 7	D 3 T 28	24	330	291·5	299 *(481)*	250	800	624·3	78 *(126)*

** See main entry
* 51 miles, of which 20 miles *(32 km)* are rack-rail ABT system

Average Speeds			Financial Data	Braking (continuous)	Couplers	Buffers	Rails	Sleepers (crossties)		Curvature max.	Gradient max. (U=not compensated)	Axle load max.	Altitude max.	Staff employed. Total no. (inclu. workshop)	Names of officials. Extended lists can be found at the end of the individual country in the report section immediately following
Freight Train	Pass. Train	Speed max.	Revenue Expenses		Type and Height above rail	Centres and Height above rail	Weight	Type and thickness	Spacing Number per mile (per km) or centres ins (mm)						
mph (km/hr)	mph (km/hr)	mph (km/hr)	in 1 000's		ins (mm)	ins (mm)	lb. per yd (kg/m)	ins (mm)				tonnes	feet (m)		
20 (32)	Express 33 (54) Other 29 (47)	56 (90)	Yen 15 630 000·0 12 380 000·0	Air Tokorozawa	Auto 34⅝ (880)		101/75 (50/37)	Wood 5½ (140)	28" (710)	11·0°	2·5% U 3·5%	12	377 (115)	3 631	President: Shojiro-Kojima
					Auto (880)		60 (30)	Wood 5½ (140)	2 570 (1 600)	22·0°	2·5% U	9			
20 (32)	40 (65)	68 (110)	Yen 20 278 251·0 20 802 039·0	Air Nippon A.B. Co	Auto 34⅝ (880)		100/60 (50/30)	Wood 5½ (140) Conc	29½/24" (750/620)	19·1°	2·5% 3·3% U	12·7	1 772 (540)	16 712	Gen. Man: Kaichiro Nezu
	Express (51) Slow (41)	Express (90) Slow (85)	Yen 25 395 000 23 093 000	Air Nippon AMA & HSC	Auto 34⅝ (880)		100 (50)	Wood 5½ (140) Conc	22" (575)	525 ft (160 m)	3·5%	15·5	226 (69)	2 934 (319)	Gen. Man: Seija Egawa
19 (30)	25 (40)	31 (50)	JD 368 881 369 745	Vac	Screw 29 (740)	Centre 29 (740)	43 (21·5)	Steel	27½" (700)	328 ft (100 m)	1·7% 2·0% U	10·5	5 059 (1 542)	686 (196)	Gen. Man: Mohammad R. Qoseini
			$C 265 118 411 966												Pres: In Nhel
16 (25)	25 (40)	68 (110)	Won 33 514 33 514	Air	Auto 34⅝ (880)	AAR	101/60 (50/30)	Wood 7 (180) 6 (150) Conc 7¼ (185)	Wood 22" (560) Conc 25" (630)	4·25°	2·5% U	18·0	2 319 (707)	39 776 (32 348)	Director General: Kim, Jai Hyun
23 (45)	23 (45)	34 (55)		Air & Vac. Oerlikon Knorr, Jourdain Monneret	Jourdain Monneret		75/60 (37/30)	Conc. 82 (220) Wood 5 (130) Metal 138 (223)		8·0% (1 435 m) 17·5% (1·05 m)	7·0% (Rack) 2·0% U	16 (1 435 m) 13 (1·05 m)	4 879 (1 487)	1 305	Dir. Gen: M. Antoine Barouki
Loaded 30 (49) Empty 33·6 (54)	50 (80)	Loaded 37 (60) Empty 43 (70)		Knorr Air	Type F AAR 36 (914)		132 (65·5)	Wood 7 (180)	21½" (545)	1 640 ft (500 m)	Loaded 0·5% Empty 1·7%	30	1 853 (565)	608	Man: H. N. Bas Koenen Chief Eng. (Operations): Brian R. Hughes Chief Eng. (Maintenance: Björn Ekrem
19 (30)		43 (70)		Knorr Air	Scharfenberg rotary		98 (49)	Wood 6¼ (160) Steel	25" (630)	3 280 ft (1 000 m)	0·25% 1·0% U	25	492 (150)	100	Gen. Man: Carl Enneker
37 (60)	50 (80)	68 (110)	Fr. 4 220 220·5 4 377 325·7	Air W'hse Knorr Oerlikon	Standard	Standard	108/92 (54/46)	Wood 6 (150) Conc 8¼ (210)	24½/25½" (620/650)	Main 984 ft (300 m) Branch 820 ft (230 m)	1·5%	22	1 640 (500)	4 323 (934)	Gen. Man: Justin Kohl
24 (38)	24 (38)	35 (56)	MK 7 573 6 244	Vac D & M	Auto AAR E.S.C. 34 (864)		80/40 (40/20)	Wood 5 (127); steel; conc.	32½" (826)	363 ft (111 m)	2·5% U	16·5	3 805 (1 160)	3 597 (693)	Gen. Man: G. G. Geddes
	45 (72)	60 (96)	$M 75 540 000 84 150 000	W'hse Vac	Type M.C.A. 22¾ (578)	Buffercoupler	80/60 (40/30)	Wood 5 (127)	30" (762)	11·1°	1·75% U	16	412 (126)	13 386 (2 193)	Gen. Man: Waad bin Jamaluddin
24 (38)	24 (38)	30 (48)		Air W'hse	Auto. Sharon 10-A 34⅝ (880)		110/90/ 80 (54/45/ 40)	Wood 6 (150)	21" (534)	5·0°	0·5% U	14	300 (91)	384 (74)	Gen. Man: D. T. Woods
15 (24)	28 (46)	46 (75)	F.M. 3 771 000 3 478 000	Air W'hse	Unic Oferom	Crs. 49¼ (1 250) Ht. 29¾ (755)	60 (30)	Metal	2 400 (1 500)	948 ft (300 m)	2·4% 2·6% U	15	1 463 (446)	1 605 (360)	Gen. Man: Djibril Diallo

NAME OF COMPANY ADDRESS	Gauge ft. in. (metres)	Route length incl. E=Electrified miles (km.)	Track length incl. E=Electrified miles (km.)	Elect. system and type of conductor	Loco-motives L=Line S=Shunt Steam Electric Diesel De=elec. Dh=hyd.	Rail-cars Electric Diesel Trailer Railbus Multiple Unit set	Pass. train cars	Freight train cars Con-tainers	Freight movement Total Volume carried. Thousands of tonnes	Av'ge haul per ton miles (km.)	Av'ge net train load tonnes	Max. trailing load tonnes	Passengers Total number carried in 1 000's	Average journey miles (km.)
MAURITANIA **C.F. Miferma** *Head office:* SA des Mines de Fer de Mauritanie Rue La Boëtie 87, Paris 8e, France *Local office:* PO Box 42, F'derik, Republique Islamique de Mauritanie	4' 8½'' (1·435)	404 (650)	454 (730)		DeL 26 DeS 11			1 084	8 750·0	401 (645)	13 400	18 500		
MEXICO **F.C. Chihuahua al Pacifico, SA de CV** PO Box 46, Chihuahua, Chih.	4' 8½'' (1·435)	941 (1 515)	1 083 (1 742)		DeL 54 DeS 5	D 13	65	2 057	2 510·0	228 (367)	570		602·0	137 (221)
F.C. Coahuila y Zacatecas, AG Apartado 116, Saltillo, Coah.	3' 0'' (0·914)	101 (162)	120 (193)		De 3		6	164						
Cia. del F.C. Inter-California Mexicali, B. CFA	4' 8½'' (1·435)	52 (84)	72 (116)		D 2									
F.C. Mexicano del Pacifico PO Box 14, Los Mochis, Sinaloa	4' 8½'' (1·435)	10 (16)	10 (16)		S 3			13						
****F.C. Nacionales de Mexico** Avenida Central No. 140 Col. Guerrero, Mexico DF3														
F.C. Occidental de Mexico Culiacan, Sinaloa	4' 8½'' (1·435)	19 (31)	24 (38)		S* 2			40						
F.C. del Pacifico, SA de CV 15-M, Guadalajara, Jalisco	4' 8½'' (1·435)	1 359 (2 279)	1 699 (2 733)		De 102		220	2 971	4 710·0	395 (640)	1 005	1 984	860·0	449 (722)
F.C. Industrial el Potosi y Chihuahua AP 13, Chihuahua, Chih	4' 8⅜'' (1·435)	E 14 (22)	E 17 (27)	600 V dc OH	EL 5	E 110		12		9 (14·5)	180	300		
F.C. Sonora-Baja California Ulises Irigoyen Final, Mexicali, BC,	4' 8½'' (1·435)	376 (605)	437 (703)		DEL 16		34	109	713	294 959 733 ton-km			513	164 (264)
F.C. del Sureste Merged into F.C. Unidos del Sureste, September 1968														
F.C. Unidos del Sureste Av. Colon 212, Coatzacacos, Veracruz	4' 8½'' (1·435) 3' 0'' (0·914)	576 (927) 262 (422)	628 (1 011) 272 (438)		DeL 18 DeS 6 DeL 6 DeS 3	De 1	68 42	848 136	839·0	236 (380)	929	3 000	2 348·5	61·9 (99·6)
F.C. Unidos de Yucatan Merged into F.C. Unidos del Sureste, Sept. 1968	4' 8½'' (1·435) 3' 0'' (0·914)													
MONGOLIA **Mongolian State Railways** Ulan-Bator	5' 0'' (1·524) 4' 8½'' (1·435) }	} 868 (1 397)												
MOROCCO **Office National des CF du Maroc** 19 Avenue Allal Ben Abdallah, Rabat	4' 8½'' (1·435) E 440 (708)	1 091 (1 756)		3 000 V dc OH	EL 57 DeL 82 DS 46	DMU 4	221		3 143 175 000 ton-km		1 090	4 000	4 128·0	87·9 (141·5)
Also operates: **Cie. Franco-Espanole des C.F. de Tanger a Fez**					Included in C. F. du Maroc									
C.F. de la Mediterranee au Niger	4' 8½'' (1·435)	170 (273)			D 5	D		300						
MOZAMBIQUE **Caminhos de Ferro de Mozambique** C.P. No. 276, Maputo	3' 6'' (1·067) 2' 5½'' (0·75)	1 857 (2 999) 92 (148)	2 355 (3 791)		S 84 DeL 32 DhL 5 DhS 6	D 11	188				1 000	2 200	4 746	32 (52)
Trans-Zambesia Railway Co., Ltd. C.P. 61, Beira	3' 6'' (1·067)	180 (289)	195 (316)		SL 9 DeL 15 DhS 3	D 2	11	459	1 510·6	147 (236)	642	1 900	437·7	83·3 (134)
NEPAL **Nepal Government Railway** Birganj, PO Raxaul, Dist. Champaran (via India)	2' 6'' (0·762)	6·2 (10)	32 (51)		S 4		1	18	50·0	29 (46)	130	200	250·0	25 (40)
Nepal Jaynagar-Janakpur Railway Jaynagar (Darbhanga) via India	2' 6'' (0·762)	33 (53)	40 (64)		SL 9		15	60	9·1		100	250	306·0	11·5 (18·5)
NETHERLANDS **N.V. Nederlandse Spoorwegen NS** Moreelsepark, Utrecht	4' 8½'' (1·435) E 1 023 (1 646)	1 758 (2 825)	4 440 (7 146) E 2 368 (3 812)	1 500 V dc OH	EL 113 DeL 269 DeS 231	E 35 De 30 EMU 503 DMU 103	381	14 237 C 575	23 600	2 696 000 000 ton-km			183 800·0	26·4 (42·5)

** Effective 17 January, 1977 all railways in Mexico were merged with F.C. Nationales
* These are oil-burning

Freight Train mph (km/hr)	Pass. Train mph (km/hr)	Speed max. mph (km/hr)	Revenue Expenses in 1 000's	Braking (continuous)	Couplers Type and Height above rail ins (mm)	Buffers Centres and Height above rail ins (mm)	Rails Weight lb. per yd (kg/m)	Sleepers Type and thickness ins (mm)	Sleepers Spacing Number per mile (per km) or centres ins (mm)	Curvature max.	Gradient max. (U=not compensated)	Axle load max. tonnes	Altitude max. feet (m)	Staff employed. Total no. (inclu. workshop)	Names of officials. Extended lists can be found at the end of the individual country in the report section immediately following
24 (38)	Loaded 31 (50) Empty 37 (60)			Knorr Air	Willison Auto. 36 (920)		109 (54)	Steel UIC28 Wood 6 (150)	23⅝" (600)	3 280 ft (1 000 m)	0·5% (loaded) 1·0% U (empty)	25	1 148 (350)	1 240 (500)	Man: Jean Audibert
22 (35)	31 (50)	37 (60)		W'hse	AAR		60/40 (30/20)	Wood 6 (153)	20" (508)	10·3°	4·0%				Gen. Man: Ing. Alfredo Magallanes R
							90/62 (45/31)	Wood 7 (178)	22" (559)	7·5°		31			
							60/56 (30/28)	Wood 6 (153)			1·5%			15	Pres: Ing. Mario Zamora Cortes
								Wood 8 (203)	20" (508)	2·3°	0·5%				Pres: E. Batiz
21 (34)	32 (52)	59 (95)	$ Mex 518 055 819 712	W'hse Air	Type E 34½ (876)		112/100 (56/50)	Wood 7 (178)	21½" (546)	8·0°	2·6%	11	5 268 (1 606)	9 416 (1 388)	Gen. Man: Luis Gomez Zepeda
9 (15)		11 (18)		W'hse Air	Auto 18 (457)		45 (22·3)	Wood 6 (153)	24" (610)	58·0°	3·77% U	15	6 138 (1 871)	25 (6)	Gen. Man: John A. Engstrom
29·1 (46·9)	38·2 (61·5)	P. 43 (70) F. 56 (90)	$ Mex 87 327·0 141 559·0	W'hse Air	AAR 34½" (876)		90/80 (45/40)	Wood 7 (178)	20" (508)	6·0°	0·7% 1·3% U		2 345 (715)	1 374 (366)	Gen. Man: Ing. R. I. Hernandez
17·7 (28·5)	32·7 (52·6)	53 (85)		W'hse Air	AAR 34½" (876)		90/70 (45/35)	Wood 7 (178)	3 200 (2 000)	8·0°	1·12%	30	459 (140)	3 373 (532)	Gen. Man: Ing. Gelasio Luna y Luna
25 (40)	45 (72)	DMU 72 (115)	(DH millions) 302·52 349·15	Air W'hse	Standard European	Standard European	111/73 (55/36)	Wood 6 (150) Metal conc	1 880- 2 770 (1 166- 1 722)	984 ft (300 m)	1·23% 1·5% U	22	4 288 (1 306)	8 455	Dir. General: Moussa Moussaoui
25 (40)	37 (60)	50 (80)		Vac W'hse	Atlas and Alliance	35¼ (896)	90/60 (45/30)	Wood 5⅛ (130)	2 400 (1 500)	984 ft (300 m)	2·0% 1·8% U	18	4 468 (1 362)	34 275	Gen. Man: Eng. L. M. Alcantara Santos
24 (39)	33 (54)	50 (80)	Esc. 2 351 286 1 454 297	Vac W'hse	Alliance English Steel Co. 33½ (850)		75/40 (37/20)	Wood 5 (127) steel	2 350- 2 080 (1 460- 1 300)	800 ft (244 m)	1·1% U	16	1 188 (362)	1 764 (313)	Exec. Man. (Beira): Eng Fernando Teixeira
					A.B.C. 19½- 21½		30 (15)	Wood 4½ (115)	(860)	16·0°	1·0% U	14			
10 (16)	15 (24)	20 (32)			A.B.C. 19½- 21½	Buffer- coupler	30 (15/12)	Wood 4½ (115)	(925)	4·0°	1·0%	14	1 000 (305)	171 (41)	Gen. Man: Bhuban Bahadur Pradhan
40 (65)	78 (125)	87 (140)	Hfl 1 797 153 1 797 153	Air Auto	Standard except trainsets Auto Multi- Servo	Central 68·8 (1 750) Ht 41·6 (1 060)	127/93 (63/46)	Wood 6 (150) and Conc 11½ (290)	Main (2 680) (1 666) Branch 2 150 (1 333) Conc (1 433)	900 ft (275 m)	2·0% 1·43% U	20	597 (182)	27 886 (4 929)	Pres: M. G. de Bruin

NAME OF COMPANY ADDRESS	Gauge ft. in. (metres)	Route length incl. E=Electrified miles (km.)	Track length incl. E=Electrified miles (km.)	Elect. system and type of conductor	Locomotives L=Line S=Shunt; Steam Electric Diesel De=elec. Dh=hyd.	Railcars Electric Diesel Trailer Railbus Multiple Unit set	Pass. train cars	Freight train cars / Containers	Total Volume carried. Thousands of tonnes	Av'ge haul per ton miles (km.)	Av'ge net train load tonnes	Max. trailing load tonnes	Total number carried in 1 000's	Average journey miles (km.)
NETHERLANDS (contd.)														
Hoogorens Steel Works Koninklijke Nederlandsche Hoogovens en Staalfabrieken NV Hoogovens, Ijmuiden	4' 8½" (1·435)	104 (167)	132 * (214)		S 2 DS 49		5	1 146	26 000·0	45 000 000 ton-km				
NEW ZEALAND **New Zealand Government Railways** Bunny Street, Wellington	3' 6" (1·067)	2 982 (4 799) E 62 (100)	4 290 (6 904) E 151 (243)	1 500 V dc OH	S 2 EL 14 DeL 285 DeS 90 DhS 65 DS 36	E 49 ET 79 D 136	412	29 530 C 720	13 193·0	8 638 392 000 ton-km			20 035·3	16·4 (26·4)
NZ Forest Products Ltd. **Whakatane Board Mills Division** Private Bag, Whakatane	3' 6" (1·067)	7 (11)	14 (22)		DmL 2			NZR Stock	135·0	12 290 000				
Kaitangata Coal Co. Ltd. Kaitangata to Stirling		4 (7)												
Ohai Railway Board PO Wairio	3' 6" (1·067)	9 (14)	10 (16)		DL		2	300		8 (13)	500	800	3·0	8 (13)
Stuart Chapman Ltd. Ross to Duffers Creek		15 (24)												
NICARAGUA F.C. del Pacifico de Nicaragua Apartado Postal No. 5-Managua	3' 6" (1·067)	217 (350)	240 (387)		DeL 9	D 1	1	185	65·7	9 209 321 tonne-km			537·4	18·6 (30)
NIGERIA **Nigerian Railway Corporation** Ebute Metta, Lagos	3' 6" (1·067)	2 178 (3 505)	2 680 (4 313) (3 523)		SL 133 SS 43 DeL 130 DeS 39 DhL 8 DhS 2	D 2	515	5 738	1 717	1 349 796 ton-km			5 819·4	45 (72·5)
NORWAY **Norwegian State Railways** Norges Statsbaner (NSB) Storgt. 33, Oslo 1	4' 8½" (1·435)	2 635 (4 240) E 1 516 (2 440)	2 106 (3 397) E 1 954 (3 144)	15 000 V 1/16⅔ OH	EL 141 Es 17 DeL 35 DhS 135	E 94 D 50 ET 217 DT 40 EMU 29	654	8 929 C 1 207	25 061·5	2 560 800 000 tonne-km			33 500	34 (55)
Hydro Transport a.s., Rjukanbanen 3661, Rjukan	4' 8½" (1·435)	E 10 (16)	E 14 (22)	15 000 V 1/16⅔ OH	EL 4 DhS 3			209	200·9	3 200 000 tonne-km		650		
PAKISTAN **Pakistan Railway** Shara-e-Sheikh Abdul Hameed Bin Badees, Lahore	5' 6" (1·676)	4 665 (7 507) E 178 (286)	6 798 (10 940) E 321 (516)	25 000 V 1/50	S 623 D 337 E 29	D 71 DT 117	2 815	35 893			464	2 000		
	3' 3⅜" (1·00)	277 (446)	343 (552)		S 46		158	1 073	11 924·8	388·4 (626·7)	74	875	131 861·7	46·9 (75·5)
	2' 6" (0·762)	380 (612)	453 (729)		S 41		160	564			50	265		
PANAMA **Chiriqui Land Company Railways** Puerto Armuelles Div, Chiriqui *(Subsid of United Brands Co)*	3' 0" (0·914)	82 (130)	84 (135)		De 14 Dh 2 D 1	D 9	11	650	27·7	691 900 ton-km			331·0	
Bocas Division Changuinola	3' 0" (0·914)	60 (96)	160 (257)		DeL 14 DeS 10	D 22	13	508					297·6	
Armuelles Division Puerto Armuelles, Chiriqui	3' 0" (0·914)	78 (126)	104 (167)		De 13 Dm 3	D 3	6	788	4·8	14·1 (22·7)				
F.C. Nacional de Chiriqui Apartado 12-B, David, Chiriqui	3' 0" (0·914)	78 (125)	81 (130)		Dh 2 Dm 3	D 4	6	130	14·6				543·6	
Panama Railroad Division of Panama Canal Company Box 5067, Cristobal, Canal Zone	5' 0" (1·524)	47 (75)	117 (188)		DeL 3 DeS 3		24	391	231 000				864 000	
PARAGUAY **F.C. Presidente Carlos Antonio Lopez** PO Box 453, Calle Mexico 145, Asuncion	4' 8½" (1·435)	273 (440)	274 (441)		SL 17 SS 5	10	13	196	144·3	32 503 998 ton-km			207·6	12·7 (20·4)
F.C. del Norte Villa Concepcion	3' 3⅜" (1·00)	35 (56)			S 4		3	29						
Industrial Railways Christopherson	2' 0" (0·610)	11 (18)												

* Includes 835 switches

Average Speeds			Financial Data		Couplers	Buffers	Rails	Sleepers (crossties)							
Freight Train mph (km/hr)	Pass. Train mph (km/hr)	Speed max. mph (km/hr)	Revenue Expenses in 1 000's	Braking (continuous)	Type and Height above rail ins (mm)	Centres and Height above rail ins (mm)	Weight lb. per yd (kg/m)	Type and thickness ins (mm)	Spacing Number per mile (per km) or centres ins (mm)	Curvature max.	Gradient max. (U=not compensated)	Axle load max. tonnes	Altitude max. feet (m)	Staff employed. Total no. (inclu. workshop)	Names of officials. Extended lists can be found at the end of the individual country in the report section immediately following
9 (15)		19 (30)		Air W'hse.	Atlas (880) SA-3 (1 100)	Crs. 68¾" (1 750) Ht. 42⅜" (1 080)	128/98 (64/49)	Oak 6 (150)	21½" (550)	312 ft (95 m)	2·38%	60	sea level	400	Man Harbours and Transport: T. Ensink Sup Rail Transport: W. A. Salverda
16·70 (26·27)	28·71 (46·19)	Freight Bogie 55 (88) 4-wh. 35 (56) Passenger Train 55 (88) Railcar 60 (96)	$ 170 206·6 233 160·1 †	W'hse. Air	Buffer-coupler 30 (762) Mainly "Norwegian" some Alliance auto.		100/55 (50/28) New rail 91 (45)	Wood Hard 4½ (114) Soft 6 (153) conc. 7 (190)	Main Wood 2 600 (1 625) Conc. 2 112 (1 320) Branch 2 400 (1 500)	Rad. 460 ft (140 m)	Main 3·0% Branch 4·1%	14·5 up to 16 for special wagons, locos	2 671 (814)	20 899 (3 937)	Gen. Man: T. M. Hayward
15 (25)		25 (40)	$ 0 116·0	W'hse. Air	NZR standard 25 (648)	25 (648)	55 (27)	Wood 6 (150)	24" (610)	Rad. 321 ft. (98 m)	1·5%	10	50 (15)	15	Gen. Man: R. C. Sparrow
25 (40)		30 (48)		W'hse. Air	30 (760)	30 (760)	70 (35)	Wood 5 (127)	2 386	230 ft (70 m)	0·66%	14	600 (183)	12 (2)	Directors: R. G. Stark F. J. Gaitt
12 (20)	R'car 28 (46) DeL 22 (35)	R'car 31 (50) DeL 26 (42)	Cordobas 4·3 6·6	Air W'hse.	Type E 28 (711)		60/40 (30/20)	Wood 7 (178)	22" (560)	Main 10·0° Branch 15·0°	Main 2·8% Branch 3·0% U	12	1 914 (583)	820	Dir. Gen: A. Somoza D.
11·4 (18·3)	12·0 (19·3)	40 (64)	$N 20 860 52 542	Vac	ABC Buffer-coupler 34 (864)		80/60 (40/30)	Wood, steel, Conc	2 336- 2 112	575 ft (175 m)	2·0%	Locos 18 Wagons 20	4 496 (1 370)	29 731	Gen. Man.: T. I. O. Nzegwu
37 (60)	40 (64)	75 P (120) 56 F (90)	Kroner 1 251 900 1 570 700	Air Knorr KE Hildebrand Knorr (Hik)	Standard European 41⅜ (1 050)	Standard European 41⅞ (1 065)	Main 128/72 (64/35) Branch 72/50 (35/25)	Wood 5½ (140) and Conc 6¼ (160)		Main 590 ft (180 m)	Main 2·5% Branch 5·5%	18 (25 on Ofoten line)	4 265 (1 300)	18 052 (2 228)	Gen. Man: R. F. Nordén
27 (43)		34 (55)	Kroner 3 695·5 3 265·1	Air Hik KF	Standard	Standard	99 (49)	Wood 5⅛ (130)	2 576 (1 600)	590 ft (180 m)	1·8%	18	995 (303)	51	Ch. Eng: H. Thorbjornsen
10 (16) 8 (13) 10 (16)	 19 (30)	65 (104) 35 (56) 25 (40)	Rs 726 422·2 513 596·8	Vac	BG Screw MG Buffer-Coupler 42½ (1 080)	BG Crs. 77 (1 702) Ht 43½" (1 105)	100/60 (50/30)	Wood; BG 5" M & NG 4½" metal; conc	N+1 to N+8	BG = 10·42° MG = 6·0° NG 2·4°	BG 4·0% MG 0·8% NG 3·5%	BG 22·5 MG 10 NG 7·6	6 398 (1 950) 210 (64) 7 291 (2 222)	134 887	Chairman: A. H. Akhoond Vice-Chairman: K. T. Kidwai
15 (25)	15 (25)	20 (32)	Guavanies 247 669·4 209 056·9	K-14F	Type E 25⅝ (645)	55/70	(27/35)	Wood 6 (150)	(1 600)					142	Manager: Dr. Modesto Ali
15 (24)	15 (24)	40 (64)			AAR Type 10A 25 (635)		75/45 (37/22)	Wood 7 (178)	2 320 (1 440)	1·2% U		17·5	98 (30)	246 (36)	Gen. Man: B. D. Walker
		30 (48)		Air W'hse	AAR 25 (635)		70/55 (35/27)	Wood 6 (150)	2 600 (1 615)	10·0°	0·75%	14		203	Gen. Man: Victor Heyl
9 (15)	22 (35)	25 (40)					70/55 (35/27)	Wood		12·0°	3·0%				
40 (64)	45 (72)	50 (80)	$3 381 000 3 231 000	W'hse	AAR D. & E.		100/90 (50/45)	Wood 8 (203)	20 (508)	7·0°	1·25%	15	273 (83)	232 (48)	Pres: Col. R. Hunt Man: F. R. Call
			$C 247 669·3 209 056·9				60·8 (31)	Wood 5 (127)		4·0°	2·0%			915 (150)	Gen. Man: Dr. Modesto Ali

† Excluding revenue and expenses from road, ferries and other services

NAME OF COMPANY ADDRESS	Gauge ft. in. (metres)	Route length incl. E=Electrified miles (km.)	Track length incl. E=Electrified miles (km.)	Elect. system and type of conductor	Loco-motives L=Line S=Shunt Steam Electric Diesel De=elec. Dh=hyd.	Rail-cars Electric Diesel Trailer Railbus Multiple Unit set	Pass. train cars	Freight train cars Containers	Total Volume carried. Thousands of tonnes	Av'ge haul per ton miles (km.)	Av'ge net train load tonnes	Max. trailing load tonnes	Total number carried in 1 000's	Average journey miles (km.)

PARAGUAY (contd.)

NAME OF COMPANY ADDRESS	Gauge	Route length	Track length	Elect.	Loco-motives	Rail-cars	Pass.	Freight	Total Volume	Av'ge haul	Av'ge net	Max. trail.	Total no. carried	Av'ge journey
Fassardi Ltda.	2' 5½" (0·750)	21 (34)												
Puerto Guarani	2' 5⅞" (0·760)	57 (92)												
International Products	3' 3⅜" (1·00)	59 (95)												
La Azucarera	2' 6" (0·762)	25 (40)												
Puerto Ibapoba	2' 6" (0·762)	20 (32)												
Puerto Sastre	2' 5½" (0·75)	56 (91)												
Puerto Casado	2' 6" (0·762)	99 (159)												

PERU

Empresa Nacional de Ferrocarriles del Peru (ENAFER-PERU)
Direction General, Lima, Peru
Formed on 1 December 1972 to operated on behalf of the Government, the lines formerly owned by the Peruvian Corporation and the Peruvian State Railways. The integrated railways are formed into the following two operating groups:-

NAME OF COMPANY ADDRESS	Gauge	Route length	Track length	Elect.	Loco-motives	Rail-cars	Pass.	Freight	Total Volume	Av'ge haul	Av'ge net	Max. trail.	Total no. carried	Av'ge journey
Empresa Nacional de Ferrocarriles del Peru (ENAFER-PERU)					SL 4 / SS 3 / DeL 32 / DeS 1 / DhS 3		77	855 / C 71	812 607				807·5	
Ferrocarril del Centro Jr. Ancash 201, Estaciòn Desamparados Lima	4' 8½" (1·435) / 3' 0" (0·94)	238 (384) / 80 (129)	303 (488) / 84 (136)		SL 1 / SS 3 / DeL 17 / Dm 5	D 5	39	1 084	1 400·2	269 417 962 ton-km			310·1	
Ferrocarril del Sur Apartado 194, Arequipa	4' 8½" (1·435)	574 (924)	688 (1 108)		SL 4 / SS 6 / DeL 28 / DeS 1 / DhS 3	R 5	68	726 / C 71				125		
Empresa Minera del Centro del Peru Augusto N, Wiese 891, Lima	4' 8½" (1·435)	132 (212)	150 (242)		SL 2 / DeL 7 / DeS 3		13	588	998·8	107 440 086 ton-km		1 500	498·2	46·5 (74·9)
Ilo-Toquepala Railway Southern Peru Copper Corp., Casilla 2640 Lima	4' 8½" (1·435)	177 (189)	119 (192)		De 8			233	722·7	117 (189)		4 286		
F.C. Pimental-Pomaico Pimental, Chicago (Cia del F.C. y Muelle de Pimental)	3' 0" (0·914)	43·5 (70)			SL 10 / SS 5		5	425	342·6	31·0 (50)		300	3·7	8 (13)
F.C. Eten-Chichayo-Patapo (Empresa del Ferrocarril y Muelle de Eten.) Puerto de Eten	4' 8½" (1·435)	42 (67)	46 (74)		S 8		14	105	81·4	18·3 (29·4)			738·6	7·2 (11·6)
F.C. Supe-Barranca-Alpas Barranca, Supe	1' 11⅝" (0·60)	29 (46)			S 5			20						
Empresa Agricola Chicama Casilla 678, Lima	3' 0" (0·914)	75 (122)	131 (211)		S 18 / D 1		3	1 155						

(Industrial road)

PHILIPPINES

NAME OF COMPANY ADDRESS	Gauge	Route length	Track length	Elect.	Loco-motives	Rail-cars	Pass.	Freight	Total Volume	Av'ge haul	Av'ge net	Max. trail.	Total no. carried	Av'ge journey
Philippine National Railways 943 Claro M. Recto Ave., Manila	3' 6" (1·067)	658 (1 060)	730 (1 175)		DeL 53 / DeS 20 / DhS 3	D 37 / DT 34	238	1 723	790·8	70 199 188 ton-km			9 674·6	73 (110·7)
Phividec Railways Inc PO Box 300, Ioilo City	3' 6" (1·067)	73 (117)	92 (148)		De 8 / Dh 1	R 11	19	326	165 201·2	6 (10)	52·1	600	3 189·4	170 (274)

POLAND

NAME OF COMPANY ADDRESS	Gauge	Route length	Track length	Elect.	Loco-motives	Rail-cars	Pass.	Freight	Total Volume	Av'ge haul	Av'ge net	Max. trail.	Total no. carried	Av'ge journey
Polish State Railways (Polskie Koleje Panstwowe—P.K.P.) Ministry of Transport, Chalubinskiego 4, Warsaw *Narrow gauges in operation*	4' 8½" (1·435)	14 553 (23 421) E 2 492 (4 010)		3 000 V dc OH			8 283	198 524	398 105·0	167 (269)	634	2 700	1 066 380	21·9 (35·3)
600, 750, 785, 800 and 1 000 mm	Narrow	1 993 (3 207)							13 219				19 699·0	

PORTUGAL

NAME OF COMPANY ADDRESS	Gauge	Route length	Track length	Elect.	Loco-motives	Rail-cars	Pass.	Freight	Total Volume	Av'ge haul	Av'ge net	Max. trail.	Total no. carried	Av'ge journey
Companhia dos Caminhos de Ferro Portugueses (CP) Calcada do Duque, 20 Lisbon	5' 5·55" (1·665) / 3' 3⅜" (1·00)	1 744 (2 807) E 252 (406) / 472 (760)	2 386 (3 841) E 520 (837) / 524 (843)	25 000 V 1/50 OH	SL 55 / EL 35 / DeL 131 / DeS 30 / DhS 36 / DmS 6 / *Metre* S 66	E 81 / ET 162 / D 64 / DT 45 / *Metre* D 12 / DT 7 / *Metre* 13	433 / *Metre* 70	8 019 / *Metre* 735	4 403·0				110 338·0	16·8 (27)

Average Speeds			Financial Data	Braking (continuous)	Couplers	Buffers	Rails	Sleepers (crossties)		Curvature max.	Gradient max. (U=not compensated)	Axle load max.	Altitude max.	Staff employed. Total no. (inclu. workshop)	Names of officials. Extended lists can be found at the end of the individual country in the report section immediately following
Freight Train	Pass. Train	Speed max.	Revenue Expenses		Type and Height above rail	Centres and Height above rail	Weight	Type and thickness	Spacing Number per mile (per km) or centres ins (mm)						
mph (km/hr)	mph (km/hr)	mph (km/hr)	in 1 000's		ins (mm)	ins (mm)	lb. per yd (kg/m)	ins (mm)				tonnes	feet (m)		
			397 122·4 448 320·0												Director-Gen de FFCC Ing. Luis Praeli
19 (30)	22 (36)	Standard 47 (75) Narrow 37 (60)	363 032·9 357 020·6	W'hse Air	Type E 34 (864)		St. 80/70 (40/35) N 75/50 (37/25)	St. Wood 6 (153) * N. 25" Wood 6 (153)	St. 26" (660) N. 25" (635)	St. rad. 330 ft (100 m) N. rad. 246 ft (75 m)	St. 4·37% N. 3·5%	18·5	† 15 806 (4 818)	1 782	Manager: Jose Baigorria P.
18 (28)	24 (38)	F. 37 (60) P. 50 (80)		Air W'hse	Alliance 34 (864) Narrow 24½ (620)		St. 80/60 (40/30) N. 75/5 (37/25)	Wood 6 (150) Conc 6 (150)	23⅝" (600)	St. rad. 330 ft. (100 m) N. rad. 295 ft (90 m)	St. 4·9% U N. 4·0% U	St. 18·3 N. 14	14 685 (4 476)	2 662 (290)	Dep. Gen. Man: Verner C. Foulkes
M'line 24 (40)	31 (50)	44 (70)	120 736·9 119 807·3	Air W'hse	Sharon AAR 10A 33 (839)		90/70 (45/35)	Wood 6 (150) & Conc	21⅝" (550)	10·5°	4·73% 4·15% U	10·5	15 190 (4 630)	368	Ciro A. Odiaga
20 (32)	45 (72)			Air W'hse	Type E		90 (45)	Wood 6 (150)	22" (560)	20°	3%	35	9 500 (2 896)	135 (38)	
24·9 (40)	24·9 (40)						45 (22·3)	Wood 6 (150)	2 640 (1 650)	11·5°	0·5%		820 (250)	180 (53)	
						60 (30)	Wood 6 (150)	2 250 (1 400)	9·7°	0·6%	9				
							20/18 (10/9)	Wood 6 (150)	2 640 (1 650)	63·0°	3·0%				
16 (25)	34 (54)	45 (72)		Air W'hse and Nippon	AAR Nikko and Shibata		75/65 (37/32)	Wood 5 (127)	22·8 (580)	9·2°	2·6% 2·6% U	35·0	522 (159)	6 049	Gen. Man: Col. N. T. Jimenez
18·6 (30)	25 (40)	31 (50)	P. 9 282·0 7 548·1	Air W'hse	Junior-Major 33½ (851)	35 (889)	75/70 (37/35)	Wood 5 (127)	18 (458)	5·0°	·5%	13·0	275 (84)	480	Gen. Man: A. T. Viray
23·7 (38·1)	29·7 (47·8)	68 (110)	Revenue zlotys 35 545 538·0	Air W'hse LUV Oerlikon	Screw and Scharfenberg 41½ (1 050)	Standard European Crs 66⅛ (1 750) Ht 37-41½ (940-1 065)	98/84 (49/42)	Wood 6 (150) and Conc 7⅞ (200)	25⅝" (650)	590 ft (180 m)	6%	21	2 736 (834)	361 200	Minister of Communications: Mieczyslaw Zajfryd, MTS
12 (20)	24 (40)	B.G. 75 (120) N.G. 43 (70)	Escudos 2 733 905·5 3 479 618·2	Vac Clayton Air W'hse	UIC 41¾ (1 060) Scharfenberg	Crs 78¾ (2 000) Ht 41¾ (1 060)	Broad 111/40 (55/20) Metre 73/40 (36/20)	Broad Wood 5⅛ (130) Metre Wood 4¾ (120)	Broad 23⅝" (600) Metre 29½" (750)	Broad 984 ft (300 m) Metre 197 ft (60 m)	Broad 2·0% 1·8% U Metre 2·8% 2·5% U	Broad 20 Metre 14	Broad 2 667 (813) Metre 2 789 (850)	24 267 (7 796)	President: Eng Emilcar Marques

* Also twin-block concrete sleepers on standard gauge lines
† At a siding: maximum altitude on main line is 15 688 ft (4 782 m)

NAME OF COMPANY ADDRESS	Gauge ft. in. (metres)	Route length incl. E=Electrified miles (km.)	Track length incl. E=Electrified miles (km.)	Elect. system and type of conductor	Loco-motives L=Line S=Shunt Steam Electric Diesel De=elec. Dh=hyd.	Rail-cars Electric Diesel Trailer Railbus Multiple Unit set	Pass. train cars	Freight train cars Con-tainers	Freight movement — Total Volume carried. Thous-ands of tonnes	Av'ge haul per ton miles (km.)	Av'ge net train load tonnes	Max. trailing load tonnes	Passengers — Total number carried in 1 000's	Aver-age jour-ney miles (km.)
PORTUGAL *(contd.)*														
Sociedade "Estoril" Estação do Cais do Sodré, Lisbon	5' 5·55" *(1·665)*	E 16 *(26)*	E 34 *(63)*	1 500 V dc OH	EL 3	EMU 31	6	26·0	7·5 *(12·0)*		300	43 380·8	11·2 *(18·0)*
PUERTO RICO **Ponce and Guayama Railroad** Aguirre, Puerto Rico, 00608	3' 3⅜" *(1·00)*	60 *(92)*	81 *(132)*		DeL 3 DhL 11 DhS 2 DS 6			1 280	562·0	7 357 073 tonne-km		1 100	
RHODESIA **Rhodesia Railways** PO Box 782, Metcalfe Square, Bulawayo	3' 6" *(1·067)*	2 013 *(3 240)*			S 189 Dh 6 DeL 79		601	14 458 C 4	12 644	6 190 000 000 ton-km		3 010	
ROMANIA **Romanian State Railways (Caile Ferate Române) (CFR)** Calea Grivitei 193 B, Bucuresti 12	5' 0" *(1·524)* 4' 8½" *(1·435)* E *(560)* Narrow gauges	21 *(34)* 6 424 *(10 340)* E 348 393 *(632)*	11 818 *(19 019)* E 889 *(1 431)*	25 kV 1/50					193 740·0	153·9 *(247·7)*			361 467·0	34·7 *(55·8)*
SABAH **Sabah State Railways** PO Box 118, Kolta Kinabalu, Sabah, East Malaysia	3' 3⅜" *(1·00)*	86 *(138)*	92 *(148)*		DhL 8 DhS 4 DS 3	R 11 DMU 6	22	148	84·6	3 170 529 ton-km		825·5	22·8 *(36·7)*
SAUDI ARABIA **Saudi Government Railroad** Dammam	4' 8½" *(1·435)*	357 *(575)*	455 *(733)*		DeL 9 DeS 17	D 4	25	1 144	1 307·6	191 887 488 ton-km		132·6	222·8 *(385·5)*
SENEGAL **C.F. du Sénégal** Cité Ballabey, Thies	3' 3⅜" *(1·00)*	641 *(1 032)*	736 *(1 184)*		De 33 DeS 4 DhL 4 DhS 17	D 10 T 21	86	1 051	1 806·0	326 240 000 ton-km		3 825·3	49 *(78)*
SIERRA LEONE **Sierra Leone Railways** Cline Town, Sierra Leone *(Closed 30 June, 1977)*													
Marampa-Pepel Mineral Railway Sierra Leone Development Ltd. Co. Brook House, Chertsey Road, Working, Surrey, GU21 5BJ, England	3' 6" *(1·067)*	52 *(84)*	60 *(92)*		DeL 4 DeS 2 DhS 2 Dh 2 D 2	D 2		200	2 750·0	169 124 000 ton-km			
SOUTH AFRICA **South African Railways & Harbours Administration** Paul Kruger Building, Wolmarans St., Johannesburg-2001	3' 6" *(1·067)* E 3 051 *(4 913)* 2' 0" *(0·610)*	13 918 *(22 426)*	20 381 *(32 868)* E 6 524 *(10 528·8)*	3 000 V dc OH			5 610	169 412	128 012·0	68 190 712 000 tonne-km		632 889·0	
South African Iron & Steel Industrial Corp. Ltd. PO Box 450, Pretoria *(Steelworks: Pretoria and Vanderbijlpark)*	3' 6" *(1·067)*	536 *(864)*	627 *(1 013)*										
Iscor Private Siding 1143 PO Box 19, Pretoria 0001	3' 6" *(1·067)* E 1·3 *(2·0)*	6 *(10)*	120 *(193)* E 1·3 *(2·0)*	3 000 V dc OH	DeS 11 DhS 22 * 9			618		16 500 ton-km	200	950	
Iscor Private Siding 1414 PO Box 2 Vanderbijlpark	3' 6" *(1·067)*	8 *(13)*	180 *(289)*		DeS 54 DmS 2			1 137	151 000	3·0 *(4·8)*	900	3 000	
Iscor Private Siding 2227 PO Box 2, Newcastle	3' 6" *(1·067)* E 4·3 *(7)*	9 *(14)* E 10 *(17)*	30 *(210)*	3 000 V dc OH	DeS 18 †			150	8 487·3	135 797 482 ton-km			
Union Lime Company Ltd. PO Box 6810, Johannesburg	3' 6" *(1·067)*	5 *(8)*	10 *(16)*		De 2								
SPAIN **Red Nacional de Los Ferrocarriles Españoles (RENFE)** Plaza de los Sagrados Corazones, 7, Madrid-16	5' 5·67" *(1·668)* E 2 274 *(3 665)*	8 326 *(13 497)*	12 365 *(19 927)* E 4 231 *(6 816)*	1 350 V 1 500 V & 3 000 V dc 6 000 V 3/25	EL 391 DeL 343 DeS 307 DhL 42 DhS 14 DmS 46	R 212 D 68 DT 231 EMU 349 DMU 59	2 126	36 897	37 000·0	10 693 000 000 tonne-km		199 600·0	50·3 *(80·9)*
Ferrocarril de las Minas de Aznal-collar al Guadalquiver Av. Queipo de Llano No. 15, Seville	3' 3⅜" *(1·00)*	27 *(43)*	30 *(48)*		S 6		10	175	83·9	15·5 *(25)*	260	450	

‡ Fireless locomotives
† Also six Trackmobiles

	Average Speeds			Financial Data		Couplers	Buffers	Rails	Sleepers (crossties)							
	Freight Train	Pass. Train	Speed max.	Revenue Expenses	Braking (continuous)	Type and Height above rail	Centres and Height above rail	Weight	Type and thickness	Spacing Number per mile (per km) or centres	Curvature max.	Gradient max. (U=not compensated)	Axle load max.	Altitude max.	Staff employed. Total no. (inclu. workshop)	Names of officials. Extended lists can be found at the end of the individual country in the report section immediately following
	mph (km/hr)	mph (km/hr)	mph (km/hr)	in 1 000's		ins (mm)	ins (mm)	lb. per yd (kg/m)	ins (mm)	ins (mm)			tonnes	feet (m)		
	19 (30)	37 (60)	56 (90)	Es. 111 986·7 64 557·9	Air Jourd. Monneret	Scharf 39 (990)	Crs. 76¾ (1 950) Ht. 41⅜ (1 050)	98/80 (49/40)	Conc. Type RS 7⅞ (200)	24½" (620)	1 066 ft (325 m)	1·24%	18	92 (28)	677 (110)	Gen. Man: Duate M. A. Bello
			19 (30)		Air W'hse.	Gould Type V		60/75 (30/37)	Wood 6 (150)	22" (560)	13·5°	0·75% U	12	100 (30)	170 (37)	Gen. Man: J. M. Mitchelhill
	18·2 (29·3)	25·5 (41·0)	56 (90)	R$ 63 003 56 664	Air Vac	Auto Alliance and Atlas 35¼ (896)		91/60 (45/30)	Steel; Conc Wood 5 (127)	2 348-2 112 (1 460-1 305)	880 ft (268 m)	2·5%	18·6	5 538 (1 688)	21 430 (2 600)	Ch'man: W. N. Wells Gen. Man: T. A. Wright
		14·0 (22·5)	24·9 (40·1)									1·3%			237 522 (16 158)	Head of Railway Dept: Ionel Diaconescu
	16 (27)	25 (40)	45 (72)	M$ 2 768·1 4 590·5	Vac Air	Alliance 34¾ (883)		60/30 (30/15)	Wood 4½ (114)	30" (762)	330 ft (101 m)	2·0% 3·0% U	12	650 (198)	750	Gen. Man: Datuk Wong Len Hin
	31 (50)	50 (80)	62 (100)	44 541·4 53 281·6	W'hse air	Type E 34½ (876)		115/80 (57/40)	Wood 6 (150)	2 980 (1 850)	3·0°	1·0%	29	1 900 (579)	1 521 (507)	Gen. Man: Omar A. Fakieh
	38 (45)	38 (60)	50 (80)		Vac Jordain Monn	29¾ (755)	Crs. 49½ (1 250) Ht. 29¾ (755)	72/40 (36/20)	Metal Conc 6⅞ (175)	2 520-2 220 (1 566-1 375)	984 ft (300 m)	1·0%	15	236 (72)	4 028 (1 591)	Gen. Man: Khalilou Sall
	25 (40)		30 (48)		Vac	Auto AP type F 34½ (876)		80/65 (40/32)	Steel, Pandrol clips	24½" (622)	820 ft (250 m)	Loaded 0·80% Empty 1·75%	17	350 (107)	320	Technical Director: S. D. M. Robertson
	13-24 (21-39)	27-38 (44-62)	Main 56 (90) *	R 1 120 569·7 972 636·2	Vac S.A.R.	Auto 35¼ (895)		115/61 (57/30) Min. on N. gauge 44 (22)	Conc Steel: Wood 5 (127)	27¼" (700) Existing Branch 31½ (800)	Min rad Existing 300 ft (91·4 m) New 550 ft (167·6 m)	Existing 3·3% New 2·0%	†	6 871 (2 094)	227 820 (32 020)	Gen. Man: J. G. H. Loubser
	7 (11)	25 (40)		Expenses 1976: R 5 768·1	Vac W'hse	Atlas; Alliance 32 (813)	32 (813)	96/81 (48/40)	Steel; Wood 5 (127)	32" (813)	330 ft (100 m)	1·33% 2·5% U	30	4 550 (1 387)	600	Man: P. Leroux
	10 (16)	15 (24)			Vac W'hse	Atlas 29½ (749)		96 (48)	Steel; Wood 5 (127)	32" (813)	330 ft (100 m)	4·16% 1·43% U	20	4 909 (1 496)	551 (60)	Gen. Wks. Man: D. W. Lamont
	25 (40)	25 (40)		R 982·1	Vac W'hse	Bell 35 (889)		96/80 (48/40)	Wood 5 (127)	32 (813)	300 ft (92 m)	1·0% 1·43% U	15	3 890 (1 186)	150	Gen. Wks. Man: F. P. Kotzee
																Chairman: H. Byland Admin. Man: M. G. McGlashan
	15·0 (24·1)	29·2 (47·0)	87 (140)	Pesetas 38 100·0 44 200·0	Air W'hse Knorr and Vac Jourd Monn-eret	Screw 41¾ (1 060)	Crs. 78¾ (2 000) Ht. 41¾ (1 060)	*Main* (54/45) *Branch* (42·5/32)	Wood 5½ (140) and conc	23⅝" (600)	820 ft (250 m)	1·6%	25		77 820	
	12·4 (20)				None	Hook & chain	Central 29½ (750)	62/59 (31/28)	Oak 4¾ (120)	23⅝" (600)	328 ft (100 m)	0·25%	7·5			

* Maximum speed is 56 mph *(90 km/h)* over main lines, and 47 mph *(75 km/h)* over certain secondary main lines. On the Johannesburg-Pretoria route motorcoach trains are allocated to travel at 62 mph *(100 km/h)*
† 22·5 tonnes on 57 and 48 kg/m rail
  18·5 tonnes on 40 kg/m rail
  14·0 tonnes on 30 kg/m rail
  10·5 tonnes on 20 kg/m rail

SPAIN *(contd.)*

Name of Company / Address	Gauge ft. in. (metres)	Route length incl. E=Electrified miles (km.)	Track length incl. E=Electrified miles (km.)	Elect. system and type of conductor	Locomotives L=Line S=Shunt Steam/Electric/Diesel De=elec. Dh=hyd.	Rail-cars Electric/Diesel/Trailer/Railbus/Multiple Unit set	Pass. train cars	Freight train cars / Containers	Total Volume carried. Thousands of tonnes	Av'ge haul per ton miles (km.)	Av'ge net train load tonnes	Max. trailing load tonnes	Total number carried in 1 000's	Average journey miles (km.)
Compañia F.C. Estratégicos Secundarios de Alicante — Av. Villajoyosa, Alicante	3' 3⅜" (1·00)	60 (97)	60 (97)		S 9	2	38	116	21·9	37 (60)			497·2	19 (30)
Ferrocarril de Astillero a Ontaneda — Santander	3' 3⅜" (1·00)	22 (35)			S 5	2	12	64	36·1				381·9	
Ferrocarriles Económicos de Asturias — Avda. Santander, Oviëdo	3' 3⅜" (1·00)	71 (115)			S 29	D 2, T	46	975	603·7	50 (80)	300	430	1 723·1	16·8 (27)
Ferrocarriles del Bidasoa — Irun	3' 3⅜" (1·00)	32 (52)			S 7	3 / 7	58	14·3					116·3	
Ferrocarriles Y Transportes Surburbanos de Bilbao SA — Bilbao	3' 3⅜" (1·00)	E 37 (59)	E 47 (67)	1 500 V dc OH	S 3	E 18, EMU 10	50	172	206·9				15 658·0	6·5 (10·4)
Ferrocarril de Minas de Cala — Bailen 9, Bilbao	3' 3⅜" (1·00)	91 (146)												
Ferrocarril del Cantabrico — Plaza de las Estaciones, Santander	3' 3⅜" (1·000)	65 (105)	88 (141)		S 26, D 1	D 2, T 3	56	818	880·8	32·3 (52)	260	300	1 852·5	13·7 (22)
Ferrocarril de Carreño — Marques de San Estaban 2, Gijon	3' 3⅜" (1·00)	E 12 (20)	14 (23)	650 V dc	D 1	E 9, T 14	7	56	172·9	5·7 (9·2)	24	127	4 001·3	6·8 (11)
Cia. Gen. de Ferrocarriles Catalanes SA — Calle de la Diputacion 239-3, Barcelona	3' 3⅜" (1·00)	124 (200), E 35 (56)	93 (150), E 37 (60)	1 500 V dc OH	EL 4, DL 24, DS 4, Dh 1	E 33, ET 24, D 15, DT 3	50	864	626	44 (71)	200	600	12 350	8 (13)
Manresa a Olván — Santa Isobel 44, Madrid	3' 3⅜" (1·00)	31 (50)	32 (52)		S 13, D 3	D 3		178	791·0	(16)			305·1	(17·8)
Ferrocarriles de Cataluña S.A. — F.C. de Sarriá a Barcelona — Plaza de Cataluña No. 1, Barcelona 2	4' 8½" (1·435)	E 25 (41)	E 39 (63)	1 300 V dc OH		E 62, T 13		1	1·1				46 355·1	4 (7)
Explotacion de Ferrocarriles por El Estado — Ferrocarriles de Via Estrecha (FEVE) — General Rodrigo 6, Madrid — *Operates the following narrow-gauge lines:*		1 087 (1 757), E 238 (384)		1 200 V dc OH, 600 V dc OH, 1 500 V dc OH					5 298·6				56 323·7	
Alicante-Gandia — Avenida Villajoyosa, 2, Alicante	3' 3⅜" (1·00)	78 (125)	99 (160)		DhL 4, DhS 1	D 14, T 7							892·1	15·5 (24·9)
Amorebieta-Guernica-Bermeo — Estacion F.C. Guernica, Vizcaya	3' 3⅜" (1·00)	19 (30)	21 (34)		DeL 3, DhS 1	D 3, T 2	15						1 090·5	8·5 (13·7)
Cartagena-Los Blancos — Estación F. C. Cartagena	3' 5¾" (1·06)	10 (16)	14 (22)			D 6, T 2							793·7 / 8·1	5·0
Ferrocarril Gijon — Estación F.C. El Ferrol del Caudillo — Estación F.C. Muros de Nalón (Asturias)	3' 3⅜" (1·00)	187 (301)	199 (321)		DhL 3, DhS 2	D 27, T 18							1 578·4	16·1 (26·0)
F.C. de Mallorca — Estación F.C., Palma de Mallorca	3' 0" (0·914)	67 (107)	85 (136)		DhL 2	D 8, T 7							1 288·1	15·7 (25·3)
Santander-Bilbao — Calle Bailén 5, Bilbao	3' 3⅜" (1·00)	111 (179)	117 (188)		DeL 4, DhL 11, DhS	D 26, T 19	55	825	112·6	42·2 (67·9)			4 441·2	14·4 (23·1)
Ferrocarriles de Valencia — Cronista Rivelles 1, Valencia	3' 3⅜" (1·00)	E 71 (115)	E 85 (136)	600 V dc OH	EL 12	E 50, T 74							30 606·1	4·2 (6·7)
Ferrocarril Secundario de Guardiola a Castellar d'en Huch — *(Ceased operation)*	1' 11⅝" (0·60)	8 (12)												
Ferrocarril Secundario de Haroa a Ezcaray — Haro (Logrono)	3' 3⅜" (1·00)	21 (34)			S 3		13	61						
Ferrocarril de Langreo en Asturias — Av. Menendez Pelayo 67, Madrid	4' 8½" (1·435)	40 (64)	43 (70)		S 27		36	2 024	2 841·7				2 630·6	
F.C. Estragetico de Leon a Matallana — *(Operated by F.C. de la Robla)*														
Ferrocarriles Suburbanos de Málaga — Plaza de Queipo de Llana 1, Málaga	3' 3⅜" (1·00)	65 (105)	80 (130)		S 11	R 3, T 3	25	182	156·2	6·4 (10·3)	13·9	160	539·6	10·6 (17·0)
F.C. de Montaña a Grandes Pendientes — Paseo de Gracia 36, Barcelona 6 — *Routes:* Ribas-Caralps-Nuria (Rack), Montserrat-San Juan (Funicular), Montserrat-San Cueva (Funicular)	3' 3⅜" (1·00)	E 7·5 (12)	8 (13)	1 500 V dc OH	E 4		150	14	0·7	8 (13)			177·3	7 (11·5)
F.C. de Ponferrada a Villablino — Minero Siderurgica de Ponferrada, SA — Ruiz de Alarcon, 11 Madrid-14	3' 3⅜" (1·00)	40 (64)	56 (91)		SL 20, SS 2		21	637*	1 782·4	86 763 445 tonne-km		650	95·4	22·7 (36·6)
F.C. E. de Reus a Salou — Carreterra Salou, Reus	3' 3⅜" (1·00)	5 (9)	6 (10)		S 4		20		3·9		17		229·9	
Les Minas de Union Explosives Rio Tinto SA — Minas de Rio Tinto, Huelva	3' 6" (1 067)	57 (92)	202 (326)		SL 7, SS 70, DhS 1, De 4		20	65	1 200·0	33·4 (53·8)	116	2 324	5·0	50 (80)
Ferrocarriles de la Robla — Bailen 5, Bilbao	3' 3⅜" (1·00)	211 (340)	242 (390)		SL 35, SS 8, DeL 18, DhS 8		82	1 084	773·0	76 (122·3)	170	900	932·0	29 (50)

* Of which 302 are privately owned

Average Speeds			Financial Data	Braking (continuous)	Couplers	Buffers	Rails	Sleepers (crossties)		Curvature max.	Gradient max. (U=not compensated)	Axle load max.	Altitude max.	Staff employed. Total no. (inclu. workshop)	Names of officials. Extended lists can be found at the end of the individual country in the report section immediately following
Freight Train	Pass. Train	Speed max.	Revenue Expenses		Type and Height above rail	Centres and Height above rail	Weight	Type and thickness	Spacing Number per mile (per km) or centres ins (mm)						
mph (km/hr)	mph (km/hr)	mph (km/hr)	in 1 000's		ins (mm)	ins (mm)	lb. per yd (kg/m)	ins (mm)				tonnes	feet (m)		
					Buffer coupler	29½ (750)	70/60 (35/30)	Wood 4¾ (120)	(600-750)	492 ft (150 m)	2·0%	10			
11 (18)	21·7 (35)				Buffer coupler	Central 29½ (750)	71/61 (35/30)	Oak 5⅛ (130)	25½" (650)	328 ft (100 m)	1·8%	10			
				Vac & Air	Screw 29½ (750)		71/91 (35/45)	Wood 4¾ (120)	27½" (700)	328 ft (100 m)	2·2%	12			
18·6 (30)	31 (50)			W'hse	21 (530)	29¾ (755)	90/60 (45/30)	Wood 5⅛ (130)	23⅝" (600)	328 ft (100 m)	2·0%	12			
12·4 (20)	22 (20)	(35)		W'hse Air			90/70 (45/35)	Wood 5⅛ (130)	27½" (700)	328 ft (100 m)	26·5%	13			
19 (30)	31 (50)	43 (70)		W'hse Air	35⅜ (900)	Central 41⅜ (105)	90/60 (45/30)	Oak 4¾ (120)	23⅝" (600)	328 ft. (100 m)	2·5%	14	2 365 (721)	677 (195)	Gen. Man: Don Joaquin de Tord
					26½ (675)	34 (875)	70·6 (35)	Wood 5 (130)	25½" (650)	328 ft. (100 m)	2·96%	11			
	25 (40)	56 (90)	P. 268 142·2 221 739·4	W'hse Air	Tomlinson 25⅝ (650)	Central 43⅜ (1 100)	110 (54)	Oak 5½ (140)	24" (600)	492 ft (150 m)	0·44%	12	971 (296)	800 (280)	Gen Man: Don Ramón Montagut y de Miquel
			P. 985 670·2 1 586 861·5												Director: D. Mariano Pascual Laguna
	30 (48)	43 (70)	P. 133 042·0 205 925·0	W'hse Air	Willison 26 (660)		70/60 (35/30)	5" (130)	26" (660)	9·5°	1·9%	5	597 (182)	226	Evilio Portillo
	31 (50)	37 (60)	P. 10 872·0 30 177·0	Vac	17⅝ (550)		70·6 (35)	Oak 4¾ (120)	26" (660)	7·6°	2·25%	12	485 (148)	67	Alfonso Martinez Alvarez
	30 (48)	43 (70)	P. 5 889·0 14 393·0	Air	Willison 29½ (747)		85 (32·5)	Oak 5 (130)	25½" (650)	6·75°	3·6%	5	462 (141)	60	Evilio Portillo
	29 (47)	50 (80)	P. 30 546·0 49 227·0	Knorr Air	Scharf. 27½ (700)		109/85 (54/42)	Wood 4¾ (120)	2 740 (1 700)	7·6°	2·0%	8	843 (257)	148	José Ma López Martin
	30 (48)	43 (70)	P. 28 026·0 63 961·0	Knorr Air	Scharf. 27½ (700)		65 (32·5)	4¾ (120)	26" (660)	3·9°	1·2%	8	502 (153)	244	Sebastian Alvear Criado
25 (40)	34 (55)	40 (65)	P. 88 809·0 147 518·0	Vac	21·7 (550)		91/85 (45/42)	5 (130)	26" (660)	7·6°	2·0%	8	879 (268)	571	G. Pérez Cossio Regato
	25 (40)	31 (50)	P. 133 042·0 205 925·0	W'hse Air	29·5 (750)		91/65 (45/32)	Oak 5½ (140)	26" (660)	7·6°	1·8%	8	482 (147)	938	Evelio Portillo Hernández
9·3 (15)	12·4 (20)			W'hse Air	Screw 15¾ (400)	Central 23 (580)	70/46 (35/23)	Wood 5½ (140)	30¼" (770)	17·5°	1·5%	11			
Pass and Frt 18 (30) Rack 8 (13) Funicular			P. 6 116·6 5 709·8	Air			40 (20) Rack 30 (15) Funicular			22·0°	8% 15%U		6 442 (1 964)	34	
16 (25)	25 (40)	29 (45)	P. 143 804·1 197 732·4	W'hse Air	Buffer-coupler	Central 29½ (750)	108/91 (54/45)	Oak 5 (130)	27½/24¾ (700/630)	19·5°	1·88% U	12·5	3 159 (963)	566 (65)	Antonio Pachón Ruiz
				None	Central	None	64·6 (32)	Oak 6 (150)	25½" (650)	19·5°	2·3% U	7			
15·5 (25)	15·5 (25)	30 (48)		Vac Gr. & Cl.	Central 27½ (700)	Buffer coupler	90/65 (45/32)	Wood 5⅛ (130)	27½/31½" (700/800)	17·5°	2·0%	13	1 319 (420)	597	Gen. Man: Don Antonio de Torres Espinosa
18 (28)	26 (42)	43·5 (70)	P. 111 228·0 113 592·0	Clayton Vac	Buffer coupler 29½ (750)	Central 29½ (750)	109/70 (54/35)	Oak 5⅛ (130)	20/30" (500/700)	14·5°	2·6% 2·3% U	16	3 904 (1 190)	1 009 (171)	Gen. Man: A. Zurita

NAME OF COMPANY ADDRESS	Gauge ft. in. *(metres)*	Route length incl. E=Electrified miles *(km.)*	Track length incl. E=Electrified miles *(km.)*	Elect. system and type of conductor	Locomotives L=Line S=Shunt **S**team **E**lectric **D**iesel **De**=elec. **Dh**=hyd.	Railcars **E**lectric **D**iesel **T**railer **R**ailbus **M**ultiple **U**nit set	Pass. train cars	Freight train cars Containers	Freight movement: Total Volume carried. Thousands of tonnes	Freight movement: Av'ge haul per ton miles *(km.)*	Freight movement: Av'ge net train load tonnes	Freight movement: Max. trailing load tonnes	Passengers: Total number carried in 1 000's	Passengers: Average journey miles *(km.)*
SPAIN *(contd.)*														
Ferrocarril Secundario de Sadaba a Gallur Gallur, Zaragozo	3' 3⅜" *(1·00)*	35 *(56)*			**S** 5	2	9	96	58·4				118·0	
Ferrocarril de San Feliu de Guixols a Gerona *(Ceased operations)*														
Sociedad Explotadora de Ferrocarrarriles y Tranvias (S.E.F.T) Peñaflorida 6, San Sebastian	3' 3⅜" *(1·00)*	**E** 13 *(21)*	**E** 19 *(31)*	500 V dc OH	**EL** 2	**E** 10	30	6	0·4	14 *(23)*		150	3 263·5	4·1 *(6·6)*
Ferrocarril del Tajuna, SA Avenida Mendendez Pelayo 67, Madrid 9	3' 3⅜" *(1·00)*	27 *(44)*	32 *(52)*		**DeL** 6 **DeS** 1	**D** 3	0	158	1 204·5	19·8 *(32)*	200	600		
Ferrocarril de Tharsis a Rio Odiel Cia. de Azufre y Cobre de Tharsis Ltda. Minas de Tharsis, Huelva	4' 0" *(1·219)*	28 *(46)*	48 *(80)*		**DhS** 5 **DL** 5	**R** 2		80	900	27 *(43)*	600			
Urola (Ferrocarril de Zumarraga a Zumaya) Palcio Diputacion Provincial, San Sebastian	3' 3⅜" *(1·00)*	**E** 23 *(37)*	**E** 27 *(44)*	1 600 V dc OH		**E*** 10	20	120	38·3	14 *(22·6)*	59	320	898·0	7·2 *(11·6)*
Ferrocarriles Vasco-Asturiana Jovellanos 17, Ovieda	3' 3⅜" *(1·00)*	65 *(105)*	84 *(135)*		**S** 38		53	1 663	1 859·7	36 *(57·9)*	117	5 209	2 929·0	10·8 *(17·5)*
Ferrocarriles Vascongados Achuri 8, Bilbao	3' 3⅜" *(1·00)*	**E** 98 *(158)*	**E** 105 *(169)*		**S** 7 **E** 17	**E** 18 **D** 2	136	895	537·1				7 947·1	
F.C. Electrico de Vigo a La Ramallosa Tranvias Electricos de Vigo, SA Ave. de la Florida 2, Vigo (Pontevedra)	3' 3⅜" *(1·00)*	**E** 13 *(21)*				**E** 10	10	10						
Ferrocarril de Soller, SA Castañer 7, Soller, Majorca A=Palma Section B=Puertode Soller Section	3' 0" *(0·914)*	**E** 20 *(32)*	**E** 22 *(35)*	1 200 V dc OH	**E** 1	**E** 8	17	0·5	2·6	16·8 *(27·1)*			A.640·9 B.735·6	A.16·0 *(25·7)* B.2·9 *(4·6)*
SRI LANKA														
Sri Lanka Railways PO Box 355 Colombo 10	5' 6" *(1·676)*	925 *(1 496)*	1 153 *(1 856)*		**DeL** 39 **DhL** 66 **DeS** 9 **DhS** 34	**D** 18	BG 916 NG 99	BG 3 895 NG 199	1 941·7	39 046 100 ton-km			68 460·5	20·8 *(33·5)*
SUDAN														
Sudan Railways PO Box 43 Atbara	3' 6" *(1·067)*	2 970 *(4 780)*	3 379 *(5 441)*		**SL** 96 **SS** 31 **DeL** 102 **DeS** 5 **DhS** 54 **DhL** 1	**D** 6 **TD** 3	392	5 577	2 380·2	2 389 336 000 ton-km			2 541 851	501 *(806)*
SURINAM														
Surinam Government Railways Oneverwacht, Paramaribo	3' 3⅜" *(1·00)*	53 *(86)*			**S** 8	**D** 3 **T** 6	16	58						
SWAZILAND														
Swaziland Railways PO Box 475, Mbabane	3' 6" *(1·067)*	136 *(219)*	139 *(224)*					703	2 947·3	489 513 000 ton-km				
SWEDEN														
Swedish State Railways (Statens Järnvägar) **(S.J.)** S-105 50 Stockholm	Total all gauges	7 059 *(11 361)* **E** 4 324 *(6 959)*	11,297 *(18 180)* **E** 6 794 *(10 934)*		**EL** 653 **ES** 134 **DeL** 101 **DhL** 96 **DhS** 430 **DmS** 27 **Mu** 137	**E** 50 **D** 211 **ET** 42 **DT** 158	1 725	Cont *small* 8 174 *large* *683*	47 714	14 762 000 000 ton-km			66 000	44·7 *(72·0)*
	4' 8½" *(1·435)*	6 946 *(11 179)* **E** 4 324 *(6 959)*	10 845 *(17 453)* **E** 6 794 *(10 934)*	16 kV 1/16⅔ OH										
	3' 6" *(1·067)*		*23* *(37)*											
	2' 11" *(0·891)*	113 *(182)*	429 *(690)*											
Gränges TGOJ Fack, S-631 01 Eskilstuna	4' 8½" *(1·435)*	**E** 186 *(300)*	343 *(552)* **E** 312 *(503)*	16 000 V. 1/16⅔ OH	**EL** 27 **ES** 5 **DhS** 15 **DS** 5	**D** 13	8	2 064	5 597·0	107 *(172)*	2 100	2 700	1 085·0	15 *(24)*
Nora Bergslags Järnväg Box 29, 571300, Nora Stad	4' 8½" *(1·435)*	104 *(168)*	107 *(173)*		**DhL** 6 **DS** 9			301	402·0	17 261 348 ton-km				
Nordmark-Klarälvens Järnvägar S-683 01 Hagfors	2' 11¹/₁₆" *(0·891)*	**E** 68 *(110)*		16 000 V 1/16⅔ OH	**EL** 6 **ES** 3 **DhS** 4			475	590·1	31 248 136 ton-km				

* 7 passenger, 3 freight

Average Speeds			Financial Data		Couplers	Buffers	Rails	Sleepers (crossties)							
Freight Train mph *(km/hr)*	Pass. Train mph *(km/hr)*	Speed max. mph *(km/hr)*	Revenue Expenses in 1 000's	Braking (continuous)	Type and Height above rail ins *(mm)*	Centres and Height above rail Ins *(mm)*	Weight lb. per yd *(kg/m)*	Type and thickness ins *(mm)*	Spacing Number per mile *(per km)* or centres ins *(mm)*	Curvature max.	Gradient max. (U=not compensated)	Axle load max. tonnes	Altitude max. feet *(m)*	Staff employed. Total no. (inclu. workshop)	Names of officials. Extended lists can be found at the end of the individual country in the report section immediately following
16 *(25)*	17 *(27)*	22 *(35)*		Air	Chain and hook 30⅜ *(770)*	Ht. 29½″ *(750)*	90/70 *(45/35)*	Wood 4¾ *(120)*	25½″ *(650)*	17·5°	1·2%	5		121 *(21)*	Gen. Man: Don Francisco Allende Ordorica
19 *(30)*			P. 34 394·6 33 479·0	W'hse. Vac	Henricot Auto 29½ *(750)*		90 *(45)*	Oak 7⅞ *(200)*	23½″ *(600)*	11·5°	2·6% **U**	15	2 296 *(700)*	95 *(23)*	Gen. Man: Don Enrique Zamacola Urtizberea
18 *(30)*		22 *(35)*		W'hse Vac	Link 30 *(762)*	Crs. 35½ *(900)* Ht. 29½ *(750)*	90/70 *(45/35)*	Pine and Oak 6 *(150)*	27½″ *(700)*	12·5°	2·86%	14	761 *(232)*	226	
12·4 *(20)*	21·4 *(34·5)*			Vac			65 *(32·2)*	Oak 5½ *(140)*	2 400 *(1 500)*	17·5°	2·9%	12			
					29½ *(750)*	Buffer coupler	71/60 *(35/30)*	Oak 5⅛ *(130)*	27½″ *(700)*	11·6°	1·6% **U**	12	1 696 *(517)*		
A. 21·7 *(35)* B. 9·3 *(15)*	A. 21·7 *(35)* B. 9·3 *(15)*	37 *(60)*	P. 38 670·2 38 606·0	Vac	Screw 19⅝″ *(500)*	Central 27½ *(700)*	70/45 *(35/22·5)*	Pine & oak 4¾ *(120)*	23⅝″ *(600)*	6·4°	2·3% **U**	9	784 *(239)*	106 *(23)*	President: D. Jose Puig Morell Dir. Gen: D. Miguel Colom Rullán
20 *(48)*	35 *(56)*	Steam 50 *(80)*		Air and Vac W'hse	Alliance 41½ *(1 060)*	Crs. 77 *(1 956)* Ht. 45″ *(1 153)* BG 34½″ *(877)* NG	88/80 *(44/39)* *Narrow* 46 *(23)*	Wood 5 *(127)* *Narrow* 4½ *(114)*	2 480 *(1 441)* *Narrow* 2 112 *(1 305)*	*Broad* 17·5° *Narrow* 25·0°	*Broad* 2·3% **U** *Narrow* 3·45% **U**	18	6 226 *(1 898)*	4 064	Gen. Man: V. T. Navaratne
31 *(50)*	31 *(50)*	37 *(60)* Expenses 50 *(80)* Railcars	$S 25 441 038 29 529 449	Vac Gr & Cr	Auto Alliance 35 *(889)*	Buffer-coupler 35 *(889)*	90/50 *(45/25)*	Wood: 6 *(153)*	2 100 *(1 300)*	1 452 ft *(443 m)*	1·0%	16·5 (75 lb) 12·5 (50 lb)	3 038 *(926)*	41 099 *(8 548)*	Gen. Man: Mohamed Al Rahman Wasfi
18 *(29)*		43 *(70)*	R. 5 429 5 561	Vac	Alliance 36 *(914)*		81 *(40)*	Wood 5 *(127)*	30″ *(762)*	690 ft *(210 m)*	2·0%	18	4 525 *(1 379)*	852	Ch. Exec. Officer: A. L. Weidemann
(a) 28 *(45)* (b) 37 *(60)*	(a) 34) *(55)* (b) 56 *(90)*	80 *(130)*	Kroner 3 657 000 3 540 000	Air Knorr	Standard *except railcars* Scharff Ht. 40¾ *(1 040)* Railcars 19½″ *(500)*	Standard	101/86 *(50/43·2)*	Wood 6 *(150)* and conc *type 101* 8¼ *(210)* *type LS* 5¼ *(133)*	Crs. Main 25½″ *(650)* Secondary 29½″ *(750)* Ore Line 19⅝″ *(500)*	Main 3 280 ft *(1 000 m)* Secondary 1 968 ft *(600 m)* Other lines 984 ft *(300 m)*	High speed lines 1·0% **U** *(1·25%U)* Med. speed lines 1·6% **U** *(2·0%U)*	20 (25 on Kiruna-Riksgränsen line)	1 971 *(601)*	40 028 *(2 966)*	Gen. Man: Lars Peterson
43 *(70)* ore 31 *(50)*	55 *(90)*	62 *(100)*	Kr. 76 500·0 62 800·0	Air Knorr W'hse	Standard except railcars Scharff 19⅝ *(500)*	Standard	101/87 *(50/43)*	Wood 6½ *(165)*	30⅜″ *(770)*	4·0°	1·7%	20	945 *(288)*	907 *(147)*	Gen. Man: A. Karlstrom
28 *(45)*		31 *(50)*	Kr. 9 954·9 9 650·1	Air Knorr	Screw 41 *(1 040)*	68⅞ *(1 750)* 41 *(1 040)*	87/66 *(43/33)*	Pine 6¼ *(160)*	31½-34″ *(800-865)*	7·25°	2·08%	18		100	Gen. Man: K. Hermansson
25 *(40)*		50 *(80)*	Kr. 9 011·9 9 393·9	Air	Automatic 29 *(735)*		83/50 *(41/25)*	Wood 6/6½ *(150/165)*	27½-33 *(710-830)*			10		105	Gen. Man: Einar Severin

SWITZERLAND

NAME OF COMPANY ADDRESS	Gauge ft. in. (metres)	Route length incl. E=Electrified miles (km.)	Track length incl. E=Electrified miles (km.)	Elect. system and type of conductor	Loco-motives L=Line S=Shunt Steam Electric Diesel De=elec. Dh=hyd.	Rail-cars Electric Diesel Trailer Railbus Multiple Unit set	Pass. train cars	Freight train cars Con-tainers	Total Volume carried. Thousands of tonnes	Av'ge haul per ton miles (km.)	Av'ge net train load tonnes	Max. trailing load tonnes	Total number carried in 1 000's	Average journey miles (km.)
Swiss Federal Railways (Schweizerische Bundesbahnen) (SBB) (Chemins de Fer Fédéraux Suisses) (CFF)	4' 8½" (1·435)	4 684 (2 913) E 4 684 (2 913)	11 089 (6 893) E 11 089 (2 913)	15 000 V 1/16⅔ OH	EL 714 ES 171 DeS 103	E 181	3 607	37 780	47 640 000	7 140 000 000 ton-km			223 900	23·0 (37·0)
(Ferrovie Federali Svizzere) (FFS) Hochschulstr 6, CH-3000 Bern	3' 3⅜" (1·00)	E 46 (74) E 58 (93)	63 (102)		EL 2	E 16	115	220						
Aarau-Schöftland-Bahn *(Merged with Wynentalbahn)*														
C.F. Aigle-Leysin (AL) Avenue de la Gare 38, CH 1860 Aigle *(Part ABT Rack)*	3' 3⅜" (1·00)	E 4 (6)	E 5·5 (8·8)	1 300 V dc	EL 3 ES 1	E 5	4	25	3·6	(6·0)			306·5	3·5 (5·5)
C.F. Aigle-Ollon-Monthey Champery (Morgins) (AOMC) Place de la Gare 6, Aigle *(Strub rack rail on 2 miles)*	3' 3⅜" (1·00)	E 14 (23)	E 15 (25)	750 V dc OH		E 8 ET 6		2	3·7	7·7 (12·3)		70	650·0	4·4 (7·1)
C.F. Aigle-Sepey-Diablerets (ASD) Avenue de la Gare, 38, CH 1860 Aigle	3' 3⅜" (1·00)	E 14 (22)	E 15 (24)	1 300 V dc		E 5	5	18	3·2	12·3 (19·8)			189·2	11·1 (17·9)
Appenzeller-Bahn (AB) Bahnhofareal 5, CH-9100, Herisau. 1.	3' 3⅜" (1·00)	E 20 (32)	E 27 (43)	1 500 V dc	ES 1 Dh 1 SL 1	E 9 D 1 T 2	32	52	7·9	139 027 ton-km			1 326·2	
Arth-Rigi Bahn (ARB) Postfach 32 CH-6410 Goldau *(Riggenback rack)*	4' 8½" (1·435)	E 5·3 (8·6)	E 5·8 (9·3)	1 500 V dc	E 1	E 6	8	8	1·5	1 796 ton-km			338·4	5·3 (8·5)
C.F. des Alpes Bernoises Bern-Lötschberg-Simplon (BLS) 11 Genfergasse, 3001 Berne *Also operates C.F. Berne-Neuchâtel; Gürbetal-Berne-Schwarzenburg-Bahn: and Simmentalbahn*	4' 8½" (1·435)	E 71 (115)	E 142 (228)	15 000 V 1/16⅔ OH	EL 43 ES 8 DeS 9	ER 3 EMU 7 DhS 11	124	308	4 777·3	233 040 992 ton-km			8 040·3	13·7 (22·0)
Vereinigte Bern-Worb Bahnen (VBW) Postfach 28, 3048 Worblaufen	3' 3⅜" (1·00)	E 16 (25)	E.*18 (29)	800 V dc OH	EL 3	E 14 T 7	16	2 plus 23 tonne	135	(5·09)	40	240	4 073	3·9 (6·2)
C.F. Berne-Neuerburg (BN) *(See Bern-Lötschberg-Simplon)*	4' 8½" (1·435)	E 27 (43)	E 33 (54)	15 000 V 1/16⅔ OH	EL 4 EeS 3 DhS 2	E 2 EMU 6	12	31	643·9	13 247 612 ton-km		2 000	3 428·3	(17·1)
Berner Oberland-Bahnen (BOB) Hoheweg 3800 Interlaken A=adhesion, R=Riggenbach rack	3' 3⅜" (1·00)	E 15 (24)	E 22 (35)	1 500 V dc OH	ES 5 DmS 1	E 8	45	34	17·6	254 659 ton-km			1 388·7	8·8 (13·8)
C.F. Biasca-Acquarossa (BA) Biasca	3' 3⅜" (1·00)	E 9 (14)		1 200 V dc		E 4	2	13						
Biel-Täuffelen-Ins Bahn (BTI) Tauffelen	3' 3⅜" (1·00)	E 14 (22)	E 15 (25)	1 300 V dc OH	E 10	E 9 ET 7	18	10	15	5·7 (9·0)		100	900	6·0 (9·7)
C.F. Bière-Apples-Morges (BAM) Apples, Vaud	3' 3⅜" (1·00)	E 19 (30)	E 22 (35)	15 000 V 1/16⅔OH		E 5	9	23	29	11·0 (17·8)		70	318	9·3 (15)
Birsigthalbahn A.G. (BTB) Weidenstr 27, CH-4142, Münchenstein	3' 3⅜" (1·00)	E 10 (16)	E 13 (21)	940 V dc		E 9 ET 7	8						3 081·7	4·3 (7·0)
Bodensee-Toggenburg-Bahn (BT) Bahnhofplatz la, CH-9001 St. Gallen	4' 8½" (1·435)	E 41 (66)	E 45 (73)	15 000 V 1/16⅔	S 1 E 6 D 1	E 8	57		479·4	6 798 136 ton-km		600	4 792·9	8·6 (13·9)
Bremgarten-Dietikon-Bahn (BD) CH-5620 Bremgarten *Also operates: Wohlen-Meisterschwanden-B*	4' 8½" (1·435)	E 11·7 (18·8)	E 10 (17)	1 200 V dc	DeL 2 DeS 1	E 11		14	17·2	150 944 ton-km		240	1 174·8	5·7 (9·3)
Brienz-Rothorn-Bahn (BRB) CH-3855, Brienz, Bernese Oberland *Abt rack system; line climbs 5 525 ft (1 846 m) in 4·7 miles (7·6 km)*	2' 7½" (0·80)	4·7 (7·6)	5·3 (8·6)		D 3 S 7		50	4	326·3	2·5 (4)			153·3	4·3 (7)
C.F. Brig-Visp-Zermatt (BVZ) CH-3900 Brig *(Part Abt rack)*	3' 3⅜" (1·00)	E 26 (43)	31 (51)	11 000 V 1/16⅔OH	SL 1 EL 6 DeS 2 Dm 2	E 5 T 4	55	80	61·8	1 914 379 tonne-km			1 952·9	
Emmental-Burgdorf-Thun-Bahn (EBT) Bucherstr 1 CH-3400 Burgdorf *(Also operates Solothurn-Münster-Bahn and Vereinigte Huttwil-Bahnen)*	4' 8½" (1·435)	E 47 (76)	E 80 (128)	15 000V 1/16⅔	EL 10 ES 14 D 4	E 9 M 9	37		1 551·9	21 575 105 ton-km			4 659·6	6·3 (10·2)
Forchbahn (FB) Postfach 8023 Zurich 1	3' 3⅜" (1·00)	E 9·5 (15)	E 11 (17)	600/1 200 V dc† OH		E 12 ET 8	3		2·1	29 734 ton-km			2 212·5	
Frauenfeld-Wil-Bahn (FW) CH-8570 Weinfelden	3' 3⅜" (1·00)	E 11 (18)	E 13 (20)	1 300 V dc OH	E 1	E 3	7	43	24·1	275 383 ton-km		140	717·6	5·4 (8·6)
C.F. Fribourgeois (GFM) Perolles 3, 1700 Fribourg *(Operates 3 lines)*														
Gruyère	3' 3⅜" (1·00)	E 31 (49)	E 36 (59)	900 V dc	E 4	E 11 EMU 3	26	113	} 610	} 83 000 000 ton-km			} 1 900	} 6 (9·7)
Fribourg-Morat-Anet	4' 8½" (1·435)	E 21 (33)	E 21 (33)	15 000 V 1/16⅔		E 9								
Bulle-Romont	4' 8½" (1·435)	E 11 (18)	E 13 (21)	15 000 V 1/16⅔	E 3	EMU 3	9	35						

* Includes 2·8 miles *(4·5 km)* of dual gauge (metre and standard)
† 600 V in Zurich, 1 200 V outside

Average Speeds: Freight Train mph (km/hr)	Average Speeds: Pass. Train mph (km/hr)	Speed max. mph (km/hr)	Financial Data: Revenue Expenses in 1 000's	Braking (continuous)	Couplers: Type and Height above rail ins (mm)	Buffers: Centres and Height above rail ins (mm)	Rails: Weight lb. per yd (kg/m)	Sleepers (crossties): Type and thickness ins (mm)	Sleepers (crossties): Spacing Number per mile (per km) or centres ins (mm)	Curvature max.	Gradient max. (**U**=not compensated)	Axle load max. tonnes	Altitude max. feet (m)	Staff employed. Total no. (inclu. workshop)	Names of officials. Extended lists can be found at the end of the individual country in the report section immediately following
		TEE 87 *(140)* *Main line* 78 *(125)*	Fr. 2 224 700 2 242 400	Air Oerlikon Charmilles	Standard	Standard	108/72 *(54/46)*	Wood, 5·9 *(150)* Concrete 8·6 *(220)* Steel 3·5 *(90)*	25½" *(650)*	*Main line* 656 ft *(200 m)* *Narrow* 377 ft *(115 m)*	*Main line* 3·8% *Narrow* 12·0%	20	3 747 *(1 142)*	41 561	Pres: Ing Roger Desponds
4·7 *(7·5)*	8·7 *(14)*	9·3 *(15)*	F. 1 569 1 559	W'hse Air	Central 19⅝ *(500)*	Central	117/50 *(58/25)*	Metal	29½" *(750)*	18·5°	23·0%	8	4 767 *(1 453)*	38 *(10)*	Gen. Man: P. Jotterand
16 *(25)*	17 *(28)*	37 *(60)*	F. 1 375·0 1 930·0	W'hse Charmilles	Central 29½ *(750)*	Central 29½ *(750)*	120/60 *(58/30)*	Wood & Metal	27½" *(700)*	30·0°	6·5% (Rack 13·5%)	14	3 445 *(1 050)*	51 *(5)*	Gen. Man: Jean Kuhni
	18·6 *(30)*	22 *(35)*	F. 1 015 1 379	W'hse Air	Central 29½ *(750)*	Central	60 *(30)*	Metal	29½" *(750)*	18·5°	6·0%	8	3 773 *(1 154)*	38 *(6)*	Dir: M. P. Jotterand
		40 *(65)*	F. 3 471·2 5 364·2	Oerlikon Air	Buffer coupler	Central 29½ *(750)*	72/61 *(36/30·1)*	Wood 6 *(150)* & Metal	24¾" *(630)*	7·5°	3·7%	10	2 959 *(902)*	100 *(15)*	Dir: J. Hordegger
		Up *(14)* Down *(17)*	F. 2 479·4 2 144·9	SLM	G.F. Auto	Central 29½ *(750)*	52·4 *(26)*	Metal	29½" *(750)*	10·9°	20·0%	11	5 895 *(1 797)*	45 *(16)*	Gen. Man: Joseph Jütz
		71 *(115)*	F. 145 413·2 142 206·7	Oerlikon Air and Rheost	Standard	Standard	108/92 *(54/46)*	Wood 6 *(150)* and steel	23⅝" *(600)*	7·9°	2·7%	20	4 067 *(1 240)*	1 931 ¶	Gen. Man: Dr. F. Anliker
22 *(35)*	31 *(50)*	40 *(65)*	F. 4 195 6 248	Air Charm. Hardy	S.I.G. Centre 19⅝ *(500)*		72/50 *(36/25)*	Wood 6" *(150)* Steel	23⅝" *(600)*	Rad. 98 ft *(30 m)*	3·6%**U**	10	2 021 *(616)*	122 *(32)*	Gen Man: Dr J. Fahm Com Man: H. Gerber
		78 *(125)*	F. 11 273·9 16 965·6	Air Rheost	Standard	Standard	92 *(46)*	Wood/Steel 6 *(150)*/3½ *(90)*	23⅝" *(600)*	6·1°	1·8%	20	1 903 *(580)*		Gen Man: Dr. F. Anliker
		A. 40 *(65)* R. 20 *(32)*	F. 10 369·9 13 033·8	Air Charmilles	G.F. Auto	Central *(650)*	90/60 *(45/30)*	Metal; Wood	35½ *(900)*	19·5°	R. 12·0% A. 3·4%	12	3 392 *(1 034)*	272	Dir: Dr. Roland Hirni
											17·0%		1 750 *(538)*		
19 *(30)*	19 *(30)*	37 *(60)*	F. 1 160 2 550	Vac Hardy	Fischer Auto	18½ *(470)*	72·5 *(36)*	Wood 7⅛ *(182)*	28⅝" *(600)*	25·0°	4·8%	12	1 644 *(501)*	35	Gen Man: J. Mathys
			F. 1 171 1 581	W'hse Air	G.F. Auto	24½ *(620)*	40/60/72 *(23/30/36)*	Wood 6 *(150)*	26" *(660)*	17·5°	3·5%	28	2 339 *(713)*	126	
	16 *(25)*	40 *(65)*	F. 7 798·1 10 095·9	Charmilles Air	Buffer Coupler 23⅜ *(600)*		60/50 *(30/25)*	Wood 7 *(180)*	25⅝ *(640)*	35·0°	2·8%	8·5	1 293 *(394)*	80	Dir: P. E. Matzinger
43 *(70)*	50 *(80)*	62 *(100)*	F. 15 939·9 18 735·3	Oerlikon Air	Standard	Standard	92 *(46)*	Wood & Metal	25⅛" *(640)*	600 ft. *(30 m)*	2·4%	20	2 618 *(798)*	270	Gen. Man: Dr. W. Kesselring
34 *(55)*	34 *(55)*	43 *(70)*	2 651·3 4 360·3	Air W'hse	Buffer Coupler *(560)*		60/90 *(30/45)*	Wood & Metal	23⅝ *(600)*	98 ft *(30 m)*	5·3%	20	1 804 *(550)*	67	Dir: W. Zurcher
		5·6 *(9)*	F. 1 463·0 1 446·7			Central 17¾ *(450)*	40 *(20)*	Metal	31½" *(800)*	29·5°	25·0%	6·5	7 386 *(2 252)*	40	Man: P. Cosandier
25 *(40)*	28 *(45)*	31 *(50)*	F. 18 838·3 15 782·1	Air W'hse and Hardy	Screw Hook	Central 24½ *(630)*	72/30 *(36/30)*	Steel Concrete Wood	A 28¼ *(720)* R 26 *(660)*	22·0°	A 2·5% R 12·5%	13	5 266 *(1 605)*	219	Dir: R. Perren
25 *(40)*	37 *(60)*	62 *(100)*	F. 24 355 27 710	Oerlikon Air	Standard	Standard	93/73 *(46/36)*	Steel Wood 6 *(150)*	23½" *(600)*	7·0°	2·5%	20	2 516 *(767)*	473 *(90)*	Gen. Man: Dr Ch Kellerhals
		37 *(60)*	F. 2 581·7 4 838·8	Air Charmilles	G.F. Semi-Auto.	None	72·4 *(35·9)*	Metal	28¼" *(720)*	20·0°	7·0%	9	2 250 *(686)*	44	Gen. Man: H. Hartmann
	21 *(34)*	34 *(55)*	SwF. 1 519·7 1 882·6	Vac	G.F. Auto	19⅝ *(500)*	50·4 *(24·8)*	Oak	26⅜" *(680)*	50·0°	4·6%	9	1 873 *(571)*	45 *(7)*	Dir: Dr. R. Sax Dir: A. Welter
			10 000 12 200												Gen. Man: Dr. G. Dreyer
		40 *(65)*		Vac			60/48 *(30/24)*	Metal	29½" *(750)*	19·5°	5·0%	11	2 815 *(858)*		
				W'hse Oerlikon Air	Standard	Standard	92/72 *(46/36)*	Metal	24⅞/27½" *(630/700)*	8·75	3·0%	20	2 743 *(836)*	267	
		56 *(90)*						Metal							

NAME OF COMPANY ADDRESS	Gauge ft. in. (metres)	Route length incl. E=Electrified miles (km.)	Track length incl. E=Electrified miles (km.)	Elect. system and type of conductor	Loco-motives L=Line S=Shunt Steam Electric Diesel De=elec. Dh=hyd.	Rail-cars Electric Diesel Trailer Railbus Multiple Unit set	Pass. train cars	Freight train cars Con-tainers	Total Volume carried. Thous-ands of tonnes	Av'ge haul per ton miles (km.)	Av'ge net train load tonnes	Max. trailing load tonnes	Total number carried in 1 000's	Aver-age jour-ney miles (km.)

SWITZERLAND *(contd.)*

NAME OF COMPANY ADDRESS	Gauge	Route length	Track length	Elect.	Loco-motives	Rail-cars	Pass.	Freight	Total Volume	Av'ge haul	Av'ge net load	Max. load	Total carried	Av. journey
Furka-Oberalp-Bahn P.B. 97, 3900 Brig (Valais) *(Part ABT rack)* **(FO)**	3' 3⅜" *(1·00)*	E 62 *(100)*	E 71 *(114·4)*	12 000 V 1/16⅔ OH	SL 1 EL 11 ES 1 DeL 2 DS 1	E 4	39	89	201·89	16 *(26·9)*		*100	1 298·3	10 *(17·7)*
C.F. Glion-Rochers de Naye Rue du Lac 36, 1815, Clarens **(GN)**	2' 7½" *(0·800)*	E 4·5 *(7·6)*	E 5 *(8)*	850 V dc OH	E 2	E 8	5	11	880	1 249 959 ton-km			299·9	3 *(4·5)*
Gornergrat-Bahn PO Box 254, CH-3900, Brig *(Abt rack system)* **(GGB)**	3' 3⅜" *(1·00)*	E 5·8 *(9·3)*	E 9 *(14·6)*	725 V 3/50	EL 3	E 16		4	2·8				2 167·7	
Gürbetal-Bern-Schwarzenburg-Bahn *(Operated by Bern-Lötschberg-Simplon.)* **(GBS)**	4' 8½" *(1·435)*	E 32 *(52)*	E 38 *(61)*	15 000 V 1/16⅔ OH	EL 5 DhS 1	E 1 EMU 5	10	40	374·2	6 298 040 ton-km		2 000	3 068·3	*(13·8)*
Vereingte Huttwil-Bahnen *(Operated by Emmental-Burgdorf-Thun-Bahn.)* **(VHB)**	4' 8½" *(1·435)*	E 41 *(67)*	E 42 *(68)*	15 000 V 1/16⅔ OH	ES 2 DS 5	E 5 M 3			407	13 261 406 ton-km			1 839	6·0 *(9·8)*
Jungfrau-Bahn 38000 Interlarken *(Operated by BOB)* *(Strub rack system)* **(JB)**	3' 3⅜" *(1·00)*	E 5·6 *(9)*	E 7 *(12)*	1 100 V 3/50 OH	E 5	E 10	19	15	0·342		2 908 ton-km		766·8	
C.F. du Jura 1 rue Général Voirol, 2710 Tavannes **(CJ)**	4' 8½" *(1·435)*	E 7 *(11)*	E 8 *(13)*	15 000 V 1/16⅔	DS 2	} 11	{ 26	68·0	7·3 *(11·7)*	747 949 ton-km	469	873·9	8·1 *(13·1)*	
	3' 3⅜" *(1·00)*	E 45 *(74)*	E 50 *(81)*	1 500 V dc	EL 14 D 1									
Kriens Luzern Bahn Verkehrsbetrieb der Stadt Luzern Tribschenstr 65, 6000 Lucerne 12 **(KLB)**	4' 8½" *(1·435)*	3 *(4·3)*	4 *(5·6)*		D 1				64·6		224 175 ton-km			
Oberaargau-Jura Bahn Grubenstr 12, CH-4900 Langenthal **(OJB)**	3' 3⅜" *(1·00)*	E 15 *(25)*	E 16 *(26)*	1 200 V dc	EL 2 ES 4	R 18 E 6 T 2	2	8	31·9		150 201 ton-km	230	504·4	4·3 *(7)*
C.F. Lausanne-Echallens-Bercher CH 1040 Echallens **(LEB)**	3' 3⅜" *(1·00)*	E 14 *(23)*	E 16 *(26)*	1 500 V dc OH		E 6	9						1 180·5	8·0 *(12·8)*
C.F. de Lausanne à Ouchy CP568, CH-1001 Lausanne *(Abt rack system)* **(LO)**	4' 8½" *(1·435)*	E 1·7 *(2·8)*	E 3 *(5)*	†	E 5‡	E 4 (rack)	5		31·0	0·6 *(1·0)*			8 000	
Bergbahn Lauterbrunnen-Mürren *(Operated by Berner Oberland)* **(BLM)**	3' 3⅜" *(1·00)*	E 2 *(3)* E 1 *(1·5)*	=cable	550 V dc		E 4	2§	4 2§	5·2	3·7 *(6·1)*			395·4	3·5 *(5·7)*
Leuk-Lukerbadbahn *(Operating omnibuses only since 1967)* **(LLB)**														
Ferrovia Lugano-Ponte Tresa 6900 Lugano **(FL)**	3' 3⅜" *(1·00)*	E 8 *(12)*		1 200 V dc		E 6	5	4	3·0	6·2 *(10)*			1 181	5·5 *(8·9)*
Ferrovia Lugano-Tesserete *(Operating omnibuses only since 1967)* **(LT)**														
C.F. de Martigny au-Châtelard Martigny *(Part Strub rack rail)* **(MC)**	3' 3⅜" *(1·00)*	E 12 *(19)*	E 14 *(21)*	830 V dc OH 3R		E 10 T 9	19	18	19·7	274 525 ton-km			350·2	4·3 *(6·9)*
C.F. Martigny-Orsières Martigny-Ville **(MO)**	4' 8½" *(1·435)*	E 16 *(25)*		15 000 V 1/16⅔ OH		E 9		2	43·5	11·6 *(18·7)*			466·7	10·7 *(17·3)*
Mittel-Thurgau Bahn 8570 Weinfelden **(MThB)**	4' 8½" *(1·435)*	E 26 *(42)*	E 28 *(45)*	15 000 V 16⅔	D 1 S 2 E 1 De 1	D 2 E 3 EM 2	3		385·4	7 130 897 ton-km		2 000	1 010	9·5 *(15·2)*
Cie des C.F. des Montagnes Neuchâteloises La Chaux-de-Fonds **(CMN)**	3' 3⅜" *(1·00)*	E 12½ *(20)*		1 500 V dc	S 1	E 5	4	24	1·6	*(12·8)*			551·7	4·2 *(6·8)*
Ferrovia Del Monte Generoso 6825 Capolago, Nt. Lugano *(Abt rack system)* **(MG)**	2' 7½" *(0·80)*	6 *(9)*			DhL 1 DL 2	D 4	6 *(3)*	3		6 *(9)*	1·0	16	113·1	6 *(9)*
Münster-Lengnau-Bahn *(Operated by B.L.S.)* **(MLB)**	4' 8½" *(1·435)*													
C.F. Montreux-Oberland Bernois Rue du Lac 36, 1815 Clarens *(Operates Montreaux-Glion and Glion aux Rochers de Naye)* **(MOB)**	3' 3⅜" *(1·00)*	E 47 *(75)*	E 55 *(89)*	900 V dc OH	EL 2	E 20	36	120	25·8	62 767 602 tonne-km			1 626·9	11·4 *(18·3)*
C.F. Nyon-St. Cergue-Morez Chemin de Bourgogne 16, 1260 Nyon **(NSé-CM)**	3' 3⅜" *(1·00)*	E 17 *(27)*	E 18·6 *(30·6)*	2 200 V dc	E 7	T 7	13	27	3·9		64 930 ton-km		280	9 *(14·9)*
Oensingen-Balsthalbahn Balsthal **(OeBB)**	4' 8½" *(1·435)*	E 3 *(4)*		15 000 V 1/16⅔	E 2 S 2	E 2	9		79		278 026 ton-km		450	
C.F. Orbe-Chavornay 1350 Orbe **(OC)**	4' 8½" *(1·435)*	E 3 *(4)*	E 3·2 *(5·2)*	750 V dc OH	E 2	E 5	3		140	1·9 *(3·0)*		600	180	3 *(4)*
Pilatus-Bahn Grendelstr 2, 6002 Lucerne *(Locher rack)* **(PB)**	2' 7½" *(0·50)*	E 2·9 *(4·6)*	E 3·2 *(5·2)*	1 550 V dc OH		E 10			0·259	2·6 *(4·2)*			236·9	2·6 *(4·2)*
Cie du C.F. Pont-Brassus rue de la Gare 8 1347 Le Sentier **(PB)**	4' 8½" *(1·435)*	E 11·8 *(19)*	E 9 *(13)*	15 000 V 1/16⅔	§	§			14·5	164 551 ton-km			223·5	4·5 *(7·3)*
Rhätische Bahn Bahnhofstr 25, CH-7000 Chur **(RhB)**	3' 3⅜" *(1·00)*	E 308·8 *(391)*	E 242 *(497)*	11 000 V 1/16⅔ OH ‖	SL 3 EL 51 DeL 2 DeS 4	E 35 MU 4	261	990	719·8	36 409 381 ton-km			7 332·7	13·8 *(22·2)*

* Up to 11% gradients
† 700 V dc Lausanne-Quchy: 1·5 km
  700 V dc Lausanne-Gare Flon: 0·3 km
  15 kV 16⅔ Hz: Flon-Sébeillon: 1·0 km
‡ 3 rack, 2 adhesion
§ Provided by SBB
‖ Except for V 2 400 dc Chur Aroso, 16 miles *(26 km)* 1 500 V dc Castione-Mesocco, 19 miles *(31 km)* 1 000 V dc St. Moritz-Tirano, 38 miles *(61 km)*

Average Speeds			Financial Data		Couplers	Buffers	Rails	Sleepers (crossties)							
Freight Train mph *(km/hr)*	Pass. Train mph *(km/hr)*	Speed max. mph *(km/hr)*	Revenue Expenses in 1 000's	Braking (continuous)	Type and Height above rail ins *(mm)*	Centres and Height above rail ins *(mm)*	Weight lb. per yd *(kg/m)*	Type and thickness ins *(mm)*	Spacing Number per mile *(per km)* or centres ins *(mm)*	Curvature max.	Gradient max. (U=not compensated)	Axle load max. tonnes	Altitude max. feet *(m)*	Staff employed. Total no. (inclu. workshop)	Names of officials. Extended lists can be found at the end of the individual country in the report section immediately following
		34 *(55)*	F. 5 834·9 8 155·4	Vac Hardy	Screw S.L.M. 23½ *(605)*	Central 17⅞ *(450)* Ht. 23½	70 *(35)*	Metal	25⁵⁄₁₆″ *(650)*	22·0°	11·0% **U** 17·9% *	12	7 085 *(2 160)*	220 *(44)*	Gen. Man: Dr. S. Zehnder
	6·8 *(11)*	11 *(17·5)*.		Electric	19½″ *(500)*	19½″ *(500)*	Abt. rack system		35½ *(900)*	29·0°	22·0%	5·0	6 801 *(1 973)*	20 *(5)*	Gen. Man: R. Widmer
5 *(8)*	10 *(16)*	10 *(16)*	F. 8 854·2 7 716·2	Regen	Buffer coupler	Ht. 24⅞ *(630)*	60/40 *(30/20)*	Metal	25⅞/35½ *(660/900)*	22·0°	20·0%	6·75	10 132 *(3 089)*	96	Dir: R. Perren
		59 *(95)*	F.10 900 16 634	Air Rheost	Standard	Standard	93/73 *(46/36)*	Wood 6 *(150)*	24⅞″ *(630)*	9·8°	3·5%	20	2 598 *(792)*		Gen. Man: Dr. F. Anliker
25 *(40)*	37 *(60)*	56 *(90)*	F. 8 481·2 11 644·5	Air Oerlikon	Standard	Standard	93/73 *(46/36)* Type V	Metal & Wood 6 *(150)*	23½″ *(600)*	9·5°	2·8%	20	2 444 *(745)*	173 *(5)*	Gen. Man: Dr. Ch. Kellerhals
		39 *(63)*	F.8 779·9 8 044·9	Regen	Buffer-Coupler	Central *(520)*	41·6 *(20·6)*	Metal	39⅜″ *(1 000)*	17·5	25·0%	8	11 333 *(3 454)*	123	Gen. Man: Dr. Roland Hirni
22 *(35)*	28 *(45)*	43 *(70)*	F. 3 085 6 558	W'hse Charmilles	Screw *(1 050)* Semi-auto. 23⅛ *(600)*	Crs. 56½ *(1 435)* Central *(600)*	72/40 *(36/20)*	Metal & Wood 6 *(150)*	28⅜″ *(720)*	29·5°	5·0%	St. 20 M. 14	3 517 *(1 072)*	118	Gen. Man: J. von Kaenel
		19 *(30)*	F. 553·0 519·9				60/90 *(30/45)*	Metal & Wood	31⅞″ *(800)*	17·5°	3·4%	16	1 604 *(489)*	6	Dir: Dipl. Ing. Max Goll
11 *(18)*	17 *(28)*	37 *(60)*	F. 1 642 3 078	Air Oerlikon	G.F. Auto. 19½ *(500)*		72/48 *(36/24)*	Metal Wood	26″ *(670)*	25·4°	6·5%	20	1 722 *(524)*	59	Dir: J. Mathys
37 *(30)*			F. 1 543·5 3 027·9		G.F. Auto.	20½ *(520)*	60·2 *(30)*	Metal	31⅞″ *(800)*	4·4°	4·0%	8		36	
13 *(20)*	19 *(30)*		F. 3 108·1 2 756·4	Charmilles Air	G.F. Auto.		72·6 *(36)*	Metal & Wood 6 *(150)*	35½″ *(900)*	3·6°	12·0%	16	1 575 *(480)*	79 *(10)*	Gen. Man: J. Perret
				Air							5·0% 60·6%¶		4 859 *(1 481)*	42	Gen. Man: Dr. Roland Hirni
															Pres: Aw. Dott Demetrio Balestra
										29·0°					
			F. 2 130 2 253	Charmilles W'hse	Scharff. 28⅜ *(720)*	†	51 *(36)*	Oak 5½ *(140)*	2 280 *(1 416)*	10·0°	7·0% 20·0%		4 028 *(1 228)*	58	
			F. 191·3 187·5							7·3°	4·0%		2 959 *(902)*	63	
24·8 *(40)*	31·0 *(50)*	49·7 *(80)*	F. 5 864·9 5 338·8	W'hse	Standard	Standard	90/73 *(45/36)*	Wood 6/9½ *(150/240)*	24⅞″ *(630)*	7·2°	20%	20	1 873 *(571)*	99	Dir: Dr. R. Sax
							72/40 *(36/20)*				4·0%		3 657 *(1 115)*		
9 *(14)*	9 *(14)*	9 *(14)*	F. 675 0 1 002·9	W'hse Air	MG 24 *(620)*		36 *(18)*			22°	120%	5	5 315 *(1 620)*	11	Ch. H. Hochstrasser
11 *(18)*	25 *(40)*	47 *(75)*	F. 6 395·2 8 601·7	Hardy Vac	Screw 19⅝ *(500)*	Central 29½ *(750)*	61/48 *(30/24)*	Wood 6 *(150)* Concrete 8½ *(220)* *& Metal*	25½″ *(650)*	22°	7·2%	11	4 183 *(1 275)*	226 *(35)*	Eng: E. Styger
24·8 *(40)*	24·8 *(40)*	24·8 *(40)*	F. 1 000·9 1 763·7	Air W'hse	19⅜ *(500)*	Central 23·6 *(650)*	40/72 *(20/26)*		1 200 km	45 m	6·0%		4 044 *(1 233)*	35	Dir: Dr. F. Girard
			F. 1 371 1 361·7								12·0%		1 614 *(492)*		D. Müller
17 *(30)*	22 *(35)*	31 *(50)*	F.907 888	Oerlikon			101/73 *(50/36)*		*(1 500)*	11·6°	3·0%	20	1 552 *(473)*	18 *(3)*	
		Down 5·6 *(9)* Up 7·5 *(12)*	F. 2 441·2 2 441·2	Electric			Locher Rack System			2·0°	48%		6 791 *(2 070)*	38	Gen. Man: H. Janwyl
37 *(60)*	37 *(60)*	40 *(60)*	F. 711 1 040	Air	39·3 *(1 000)*		92 *(46)*	SBB 1 SBB 2 steel	*(1 666)*	17·5°	2·8%		3 445 *(1 050)*	15	Dir: R. Armand
23 *(37)*	28 *(45)*	56 *(90)*	F. 86 529·8 95 614·9	Vac Hardy	Screw 24⅜″ *(620)*	Centre 24⅜ *(620)*	60/50 *(30/25)*	Oak 6 *(150)* Metal	26¾-32¼ *(680-820)*	39·0°	‡	12	7 405 *(2,257)*	1 450	Dir: Dr. O. Wieland

* 11% Brig-Disentis. 17·9% is Göschenen-Andermatt
† Old stock has screw coupling 23⅝ in *(600 mm)* with central buffer 31½ in *(800 mm)*
‡ Maximum gradients: St. Moritz-Tirano: 7·0% over 17 miles *(27 km)*. Chur-Aroso: 6·0%. Bellinzona-Mecocco: 6·0%. Klostes-Davos: 4·5%. Filisur-Preda: 3·50%

NAME OF COMPANY ADDRESS	Gauge ft. in. (metres)	Route length incl. E=Electrified miles (km.)	Track length incl. E=Electrified miles (km.)	Elect. system and type of conductor	Loco-motives L=Line S=Shunt Steam Electric Diesel De=elec. Dh=hyd.	Rail-cars Electric Diesel Trailer Railbus Multiple Unit set	Pass. train cars	Freight train cars Containers	Total Volume carried. Thousands of tonnes	Av'ge haul per ton miles (km.)	Av'ge net train load tonnes	Max. trailing load tonnes	Total number carried in 1 000's	Average journey miles (km.)

SWITZERLAND *(contd.)*

NAME OF COMPANY ADDRESS	Gauge	Route length	Track length	Elect. system	Locomotives	Rail-cars	Pass.	Freight	Total Vol.	Av'ge haul	Av'ge net	Max. trailing	Total no.	Av. journey
Rheinech-Walzenhausen-Bahn (RhW) Walzenhausen *(part Riggenbach rack)*	3′ 11¼″ (1·200)	E 1·2 (2)				E 1								
Rigi-Bahn *(See Arth-Rigi-Bahn)*														
Rorschach-Heiden-Bahn (RHB) Heiden *(Riggenbach rack system)*	4′ 8½″ (1·435)	E 4 (6)		15 000 V 1/16⅔		E 3	13	14						
St. Gallen-Gais-Appenzell-Alstätten-Bahn (SGA) 9053 Teufen, Appenzell 9053 A=adhesion, R=rack.	3′ 3⅜″ (1·00)	12 (19·48)†		1 700 V dc OH		E 9	25	54	7·2		109 468 ton-km		1 396	5·1 (8·3)
St. Gallen-Speicher-Trogen (TB) 9042 Speicher, AR	3′ 3⅜″ (1·00)	E 6 (10)	8 (13)	1 000 V dc		E 8	12	17	4·7	5 (8·6)	6·5	29	850·0	5·0 (8·1)
Schöllenenbahn (SB) *(Merged into Furka-Oberalp-Bahn)*														
Schweizerische Südostbahn (SOB) CH-8820 Wadenswil	4′ 8½″ (1·435)	E 30 (49)	E 36 (58)	15 000 V 1/16⅔	EL 1 ES 1	E 11	21	23	3·2				2 694	5·4 (8·7)
Schynige Platte-Bahn (SPB) *(Operated by Berner Oberland Bahnen.) (Riggenbach rack system.)*	2′ 7½″ (0·80)	E 4·5 (7·2)	E 5·3 (8·5)	1 500 V dc	S 1 E 11		26	8						
Sensetalbahn (STB) 3177 Laupen B.E.	4′ 8½″ (1·435)	E 7 (11)	9·3 (15)	15 000 V 1/16⅔ OH	S 1 D 1	E 3	4		73·1	2·7 (4·3)			370·0	3·3 (5·3)
Simmentalbahn (SEZ) *(Spiez-Erlenbach-Zweisimmen) (Operated by Bern-Lötschberg-Simplon)*	4′ 8½″ (1·435)	E 22 (35)	E 27 (43)	15 000 V 1/16⅔ OH	EL 1 DhS 1	EMU 4	8	14	68·8		1 642 112 ton-km	2 000	976·6	12 (20)
Solothurn-Münster-Bahn (SMB) *(Operated by Emmental-Burgdorf-Thun-Bahn.)*	4′ 8½″ (1·435)	E 14 (22)	E 16 (26)	15 000 V 1/16⅔	EL 2 OS 1	E 2 M 1			109·5		2 245 536 ton-km		596	4·9 (8·1)
Solothurn-Niederbipp-Bahn (SNB) Grubenstr 12, CH-4900 Langenthal	3′ 3⅜″ (1·00)	E 10 (16)	E 11 (17)	1 200 V dc	EL 2 ES 1	R 17 E 5 T 2	2	6	43·0		131 712 ton-km	300	577·1	4·7 (7·5)
Solothurn-Zollikofen-Bern-Bahn (SZB) Postfach 28, 3048 Worblaufen	3′ 3⅜″ (1·00)	E 23 (37)	E 34 (54)	1 250 V dc	EL 3 DeS 2	E 15 ET 13	16	13‡	212·8	5·1 (8·2)	24	240	6 303·9	6·5 (10·5)
Luzern-Stans-Engelberg Bahn § (LSE) CH-6362 Stansstad. *(Riggenback rack)*	3′ 3⅜″ (1·00)	E 16 (25) Rack (1·5)	E 17 (28)	15 000 V 1/16⅔ OH	DhS 3 DS 1	E 7 ET 7	11	4	34·5		235 186 ton-km	450	1 336·8	6·2 (10)
Ferrovie Autolinee Regionali Ticinesi (FART) 6601 Locarno	3′ 3⅜″ (1·00)	E 12 (20)	E 14 (23)	1 300 V		E 4	8	17	3·9	3·0 (4·8)	12	40	745	8·0 (12·8)
Sihltal-Zürich-Uetliberg-Bahn (SZU) Sihlamstr 5, CH-8039 Zürich Selnau	4′ 8½″ (1·435)	E 16·7 (27)	E 17·3 (30)	15 000 V 1/16⅔ OH	SL 1 EL 2 DeL 2 DhL 1 DmL 1	E 13 T 2	21	4	172·9		864 352 ton-km		3 963·1	5·1 (8·2)
Sursee-Triengen-Bahn (ST) Betriebsleitung, 6234 Triengen	4′ 8½″ (1·435)	5·6 (9)			SL 2 DeL 1		22	2	250	4·5 (7·1)	61	100	161	4·5 (7·2)
Uetlibergbahn (BZUe) Postfach, 0839 Zürich *(Owned and operated by Sihltalbahn)*	4′ 8½″ (1·435)	E 5·6 (9)	E 6·5 (10·2)	1 200 V dc OH		E 4 T 3	9	3	0·8	5·0 (8·5)			915·2	4·2 (6·8)
C.F. Régional du val de Travers (RVT) Fleurier (Neuchâtel)	4′ 8½″ (1·435)	E 9 (14)		15 000 V 1/16⅔ OH	E 1 D 1	E 2 D 1	10	21	78·6	4·9 (7·9)			989·1	3·5 (5·7)
C.F. Electriques Veveysans (CEV) 4 avenue de Gilamont, 1800 Vevey *(Stub rack)*	3′ 3⅜″ (1·00)	E 7 (11)	E 8 (13)	800 V dc OH	EL 3	R 10	15	10	0·795		4 543 ton-km		723·6	3·6 (5·8)
Waldenburgerbahn AG (WB) 4437 Waldenburg	2′ 5½″ (0·75)	E 8 (13)	E 10 (16)	1 500 V dc OH	SL 1 E 3		10	20	2·6		32 260 ton-km		679·5	5·8 (9·3)
Wengernalp-Bahn (WAB) Interlaken *(Operated by BOB) (Riggenbach rack system.)*	2′ 7½″ (0·800)	E 12 (19)	E 17 (28)	1 500 V dc	EL 8	E 24	40	54	31·6		143 608 ton-km		2 576·2	4·8 (7·7)
Wohlen-Meisterschwanden-Bahn (WM) 5620 Bremgarten *(Operated by Bremgarten-Dietikon-B)*	4′ 8½″ (1·435)	E 5 (8)	E 7 (11)	15 000 V dc	DeS 2 Other	E 2	2		94		311 883 ton-km		300·8	3·5 (5·7)
Wynental-und Suhrentalbahn (WSB) Hintere Bahnhofstr 85, Aarau	3′ 3⅜″ (1·00)	E 21 (33)	E 25 (40)	750 V dc OH		E 19	21	27	71·8	6·8 (10·9)	88	165	3 991·7	4·2 (6·8)
C.F. d'Yverdon — Ste. Croix Quai de la Thièle 32, CH-1400, Yverdon	3′ 3⅜″ (1·00)	E 15 (24)	E 14·9 (24)	15 000 V 1/16⅔ OH		E 5	28	2	12·1		199 394 ton-km	402·4	401·4	9 (14·2)

SYRIA

NAME OF COMPANY ADDRESS	Gauge	Route length	Track length	Elect. system	Locomotives	Rail-cars	Pass.	Freight	Total Vol.	Av'ge haul	Av'ge net	Max. trailing	Total no.	Av. journey
Syrian Railways Chemins de Fer Syriens BP 182, Aleppo	4′ 8½″ (1·435)	565 (910)			SL 34 SS 2 DL 10	D 11	123	1 106	687·5		303 229 000 ton-km		519·2	

† 2·7 miles *(4·4 km)* Riggenbach rack on St. Gallen-Gais-Appenzell line
 2·0 miles *(3·3 km)* Strub rack on Appenzell-Altstätten line
 Motive power by SBB
‡ Plus 30 specials for transport of standard gauge rail wagons
§ Conversion of Former Stansstad-Engelberg-Bahn. Re-opened 1964

Average Speeds			Financial Data		Couplers	Buffers	Rails	Sleepers (crossties)		Curvature max.	Gradient max. (U=not compensated)	Axle load max.	Altitude max.	Staff employed. Total no. (inclu. workshop)	Names of officials. Extended lists can be found at the end of the individual country in the report section immediately following
Freight Train	Pass. Train	Speed max.	Revenue Expenses	Braking (continuous)	Type and Height above rail	Centres and Height above rail	Weight	Type and thickness	Spacing Number per mile or centres						
mph (km/hr)	mph (km/hr)	mph (km/hr)	in 1 000's		ins (mm)	ins (mm)	lb. per yd (kg/m)	ins (mm)	ins (mm)			tonnes	feet (m)		
											25%				
										14·5°	9·0%		2 605 (794)		
			F. 3 511·7 5 114·5							59·0°	R.16·0% A. 5·9%		3 054 (931)		Pres: E. Vitzthum
	16 (25)	31 (50)		Charmilles Air	Screw 17' 7" (450)	Centre 27½ (700)		Metal	26½" (680)	58·0°	7·5%		3 136 (956)	48 (16)	Gen. Man: D. Brugger
	28 (45)	50 (80)	F. 9 284 9 169	Air Oerlikon			93 (46)	Wood Metal & Conc.		8·2°	5·0%	20	3 035 (925)	139 (23)	Dir: E. A. Gross
	6·8 (11·0)							Metal			26·0%		6 453 (1 967)	incl. in BOB	Dr. Roland Hirni
18·6 (30)	22·3 (36)	47 (75)		Air W'hse	R.J.V. (1 060)	41¾ (1 060)	90/60 (45/30)	Wood Metal	(550-650)	9·7°	3·6%	20	1 811 (552)	35 (5)	Gen. Man: Hans Spring Pres: Dr. Willi Marki
		47 (75)	F. 5 736·1 8 526·5	Vac Rheost	Standard	Standard	94/74 (46/36)	Wood 6 (150)	26¼" (666)	8·7°	2·5%	20	3 090 (942)		Gen. Man: Dr. F. Anliker
25 (40)	37 (60)	50 (80)	F. 2 364·1 3 722·6	Oerlikon	Standard	Standard	93/73 (46/36) Type V.	Metal Wood 6 (150)	23½ (600)	6·25°	2·8%	16	2 359 (719)	35 (15)	Gen. Man: Dr. Ch. Kellerhals
15 (25)	19 (31)	37 (60)	F. 1 045 1 903	Air	Central 19⅝ (500)		60/50 (30/25)	Metal Wood	35½" (900)	25·5°	4·5%	20	4 757 (1 450)	27	Gen. Man: J. Mathys
22 (35)	37 (60)	47 (75)	F. 8 254·7 10 953·5	Charmilles Air	G.F. Auto 19⅝ (500)		72/60 (36/30)	Metal Wood & Conc.	23⅝" (600)	Rad. 295 ft (90 m)	2·7%*	12	1 837 (560)	242 (45)	Gen. Man: Dr. J. Fahm Com. Man: H. Haltiner
22 (35)	28 (45)	47 (75)	F. 5 222·5 5 219·9	Charmilles Air	Auto Fischer 25⅝ (650)		73/60 (35/30)	Metal & Wood 6 (150)	24⅞" (630)	25·0°	5% U 25% U Rack	16	3 287 (1 002)	77 (6)	Gen. Man: J. Neuhaus
	25 (40)	37 (60)	F. 2 234 3 162	Air	Buffer-Coupler	23⅝ (600)	61/48 (30/24)	Wood 7⅞ (200)	2 240 (1 400)	29·5°	6·1%	10	1 801 (549)	95 (41)	Gen. Man: Marco Pessi
37 (60)	37 (70)	43 (70)	F. 7 534·8 11 478·9	Oerlikon Air	Standard (1 050)		92/72 (46/36)	Wood 6 (150)	24½" (620)	7·7°	2·8%	20	1 690 (515)	150	Gen. Man: H. Tempelmann
		31 (50)	F. 369·3 771·6	W'hse Air	Standard		72·6 (36)		1 035 (1 666)	8·25°	1·5%	20	1476 (450)	17 (2)	Gen. Man: B. Jakob
		28 (45)	F. 1 474·8 1 565·0	Knorr W'hse Air	G.F. Auto (400)		72 (36)	Wood 6 (150)	25½" (650)	8·5°	7·0%	20	2 667 (813)	18 (2)	Gen. Man: W. Stricker
							72·5 (36)			11·6°	1·7%		2 522 (769)		
		22 (35)	F. 1 235·9 2 417·9	Vac Hardy	MOB 29 (750)		50/83 (25/41·8)			29·5°	5·0% 20·0 rack	12	4 450 (1 356)	39	Gen. Man: E. Lehmann
27 (45)	34 (55)	34 (55)	F. 1 220·0 1 386·9	Charmilles Air	G.F. 15¼ (388)	17⅞ (440)	61/50 (25/30)			25·0	3·0%	7·5	1 082 (330)	29	Pres: Dr. Roland Straumann
6·8 (11)	13 (21)	46 (74)	F. 16 736·8 14 917·4	SLM type	Buffer-Coupler	Central (530)	51/40 (20/25·5)	Metal	39⅜" (1 000)	29·0°	25·0%	8	6 762 (2 061)	222	Dr. Roland Hirni
31 (50)	22 (35)	40 (65)		Air Oerlikon	4 (104)	7·2 (185)	92 (46)	Wood & Metal	23⅝" (600)	14·5°	4·2%	20	1 765 (538)	30 (7)	Dir: W. Zurcher Gen. Man: W. Fink
		40 (65)		Air Charmilles	G.F. auto. (600)		72/60 (36/30)	Metal CTU	27½" (700)	65·0°	3·7%	10	1 798 (548)	170	Dir: Dipl. El.-Ing. P. Diem
(37·5)	(37·5)	31 (50)	F. 1 634·7 2 553·6	Air	Central 10⅛ (260)		60 (30)	Steel & Wood 7 (180)		17·5°	4·4%		3 508 (1 069)	62	Dir: Chevalley Marcel
21·7 (35)	21·7 (35)	N. Line 37 (60) S. Line 31 (50)	£S 12 000·0 14 000·0	Air W'hse Knorr	UIC	UIC	74/60 (37/30)	Metal (7/14 mm)	N. (1 249) S. (1 257) 1 152	N. Line 4·35° S. Line 5·8°	N. Line 2·5% U S. Line 2·0% U	N. 16·7 S. 15·0°	N. 2 024 (617) S. 1 762 (526)	1 452 (346)	Gen. Man: Ing. Ing Abdel Jabbar Koundakji

* Maximum gradient 2·7% except tunnel entrance Berne 4·5%

NAME OF COMPANY ADDRESS	Gauge ft. in. (metres)	Route length incl. E=Electrified miles (km.)	Track length incl. E=Electrified miles (km.)	Elect. system and type of conductor	Loco-motives L=Line S=Shunt Steam Electric Diesel De=elec. Dh=hyd.	Rail-cars Electric Diesel Trailer Railbus Multiple Unit set	Pass. train cars	Freight train cars Con-tainers	Freight movement Total Volume carried. Thousands of tonnes	Av'ge haul per ton miles (km.)	Av'ge net train load tonnes	Max. trailing load tonnes	Passengers Total number carried in 1 000's	Average journey miles (km.)

SYRIA *(contd.)*

Hedjaz Railway Administration
Direction Général des C.F. du Hedjaz
PO Box 134, Damascus

Operates two railways

| Hedjaz Railway | 3′ 5¼″ (1·050) | 157 (253) | 173 (279) | | SL 26 SS 9 | R 4 | 24 | 313 | 101·5 | 82·4 (136) | 165 | 275 | 311·0 | 30 (48) |
| Damascus-Serghaya Railway | 3′ 5¼″ (1·050) | 42 (67) | 45 (72) | | SL 9 SS 1 | | 24 | 139 | 74·5 | 37 (62) | 84 | 140 | 232·3 | 22 (35) |

TAIWAN
Taiwan Railway
Taiwan Ry. Administration,
2 Yenping Rd. North, Taipei

| | 3′ 6″ (1·067) 2′ 6″ (0·762) | 512 (824) 109 (176) | 1 193 (1 926·5) 149 (240) | | De 161 SL 141 | D 63 T 10 MUD 42 | 1 150 | 7 172 C 1 619 | 16 264 | 2 700 080 323 ton-km | | | | |

TANZANIA
Tanzania Zambia Railway Authority (TAZARA)
PO Box 2834, Dar-es-Salaam
(Responsible for the Tanzam Railway)

THAILAND
State Railway of Thailand
Krung Kasem Rd, Bangkok

| | 3′ 3⅜″ (1·00) | 2 392 (3 855) | 2 746 (4 428) | | SL 220 SS 21 DeL 138 DhL 67 DhS 2 | D 45 DT 45 | 962 | 9 398 | 5 116·7 | 2 504 583 616 ton-km | | | 61 408·5 | 52·7 (84·9) |

TOGO
Réseau des Chemins de Fer du Wharf du Togo
PO Box 340, Lomé

| | 3′ 3⅜″ (1·00) | 275 (442) | 310 (499) | | DeL 11 DhL 2 DhS 2 Dm 6 | R 5 D 5 | 63 | 378 C 2 | | 5 368 000 000 tonne-km | | | 77 502 000 pass-km | 31 (50) |

TUNISIA
Societe Nationale des Chemins de Fer Tunisiens (S.N.C.F.T.)
67 Avenue Farhat Hached, Tunis

| | 4′ 8½″ (1·435) 3′ 3⅜″ (1·00) | 1 200 (1 928) | 1 292 (2 089) | | De 122 | D 60 T 10 | 111 | 5 387 C 283 | 7 367·4 | 1 521 783 960 ton-km | | | 18 783·5 | 18·7 (30·1) |

Chemin de fer de Gafsa
(Incorporated into SNCFT)

TURKEY
Turkish State Railways (TCDD)
Türkiye Cumhuriyeti Devlet
Demiryollar
TCDD Isletmesi, Genel Müdürlügü,
Ankara

| | 4′ 8½″ (1·435) E 68 (109) | 5 128 (8 253) E 157 (253) | 6 109 (9 831) | 25 000 V 1/50 OH | SL 719 SS 100 EL 12 DeL 122 DhL 9 DhS 61 | E 30 D 14 DMU 27 R 25 | 1 175 | 19 168 | 17 041·8 | 7 932 271 000 ton-km | | | 112 956·6 | 29·4 (47·2) |

UGANDA
(See East Africa)

USSR
Soviet Railways
Ministry of Railway Transport of USSR
Moscow 107104
Novo Basmannaia 2

| | 4′ 11⅞″ (1·520) 4′ 8½″ (1·435) 3′ 6″ (1·067) 1′ 11⅝″- 3′ 3⅜″ (0·60- 1·0) | 84 700 (136 300) E 22 475 (36 170) | | 25 000V 1/50 OH 1 500 V dc OH 3 000 V dc OH | | | | | 3 329 400 | 3 236 500 000 ton-km | | | 3 306 400 | 56 (90) |

UK
British Rail
British Railways Board
222 Marylebone Road,
London NW1 6JJ

| | 4′ 8½″ (1·435) E 2 365 (3 800) 1′ 11½″ (0·597) | 11 326 (18 190) 12 (19) | 29 387 (47 153) | 25 kV 1/50 OH 1·5 kV dc OH 1·2 kV dc 3R 650/750 Vdc 3R 630/650 Vdc 4R | S 3 EL 333 DeL 2 444 DeS 985 DhL 73 DhS 3 DmS 134 | D 28 EM 7 173 DM 3 440 ET 4 514 DT 1 424 | 7 168 | 248 682 C 5 039 | 195 820 | | | | 728 270 | |

| Bluebell Railway Ltd. Sheffield Park Stn, Uckfield, Sussex | 4′ 8½″ (1·435) | 5 (8) | 10 (16) | | SL 18 PS 1 SS 2 | | 30 | 20 | | | | | 306·4 | 8 (13) |

| British Steel Corporation 33 Grosvenor Place, London SW1 | 4′ 8½″ (1·435) | | | | | | | | | | | | | |

Average Speeds			Financial Data	Braking (continuous)	Couplers	Buffers	Rails	Sleepers (crossties)		Curvature max.	Gradient max. (U=not compensated)	Axle load max.	Altitude max.	Staff employed. Total no. (inclu. workshop)	Names of officials. Extended lists can be found at the end of the individual country in the report section immediately following
Freight Train	Pass. Train	Speed max.	Revenue Expenses		Type and Height above rail	Centres and Height above rail	Weight	Type and thickness	Spacing Number per mile (per km) or centres						
mph (km/hr)	mph (km/hr)	mph (km/hr)	in 1 000's		ins (mm)	ins (mm)	lb. per yd (kg/m)	ins (mm)	ins (mm)			tonnes	feet (m)		
															Gen. Man: Fahmi Kosara
22 (35)	25 (40)	31 (50)		Vac Hardy	Air 31 (800)	Air 31 (800)	50/43 (25/21·5)	Metal	27½" (700)	17·5°	2·4% 2·0%U	10·5	2 428 (740)	865 (488)	Gen. Man: Fahmi Kossara
12 (30)	15 (25)	22 (35)		Vac Hardy	UIC 31 (800)	UIC 31 (800)	55 (27·6)	Metal	35½" (900)	17·5°	3·4% 3·0%U	11·5	4 609 (1 405)		
			US$ 171 280·8 151 287·4	Semi-auto 34⅝ (880)			W 10/75 (50/37) E 44 (22)	W Wood 5½ (140) Conc E 4 (100)	2 785 (1 732)	W 5·8° E 17·5°	W 2·31% E 3·04%	Coopers E 33			Man. Director: J. Fan
		P 50 (80) F 37 (60)	Baht 1 395 308 1 436 690	R'cars Air Trains Vac	Auto US Type 33½ (850)		80/50 (40/25)	Wood 6 (150) and Conc	25½/27½ (650/700)	590 ft (180 m)	2·3% 2·6% U	Diesel loco 13·75 Steam 10·5 R'stock 12·0	1 886 (575)	33 976 (6 212)	Gen. Man: Sanga Navicharern
28 (45)	28 (45)	44 (70)		Vac Jordain Monneret	Willison	Central Buffer Coupler	66/40 (33/20)	Metal	2 400 (1 490)	8·7°; in yards 22·0°	1%	12·5	1 083 (330)	1 072	Gen. Man: W. Eiden
25 (40)	37 (60)	68 (110)	D 16 541·5 17 964·9	Air W'hse Vac	Screw St. 41 (1 040) M. Ht. 30" (775)	Standard (1 720) (1 050) M. Central (800)	94/60 (46/30)	Oak (120-140) Conc. (190) Steel	22½-29½" (575-750)	Standard 9·75° Metre 11·3° 11·75°	2·0%	Standard 21 Metre 18	1 066 (325)	7 239 (1 217)	Gen. Man: Mohamed Ali Soussi
19 (30)	39 (63)	78 (125)	T.L. 7 004 039 7 197 462	Oerlikon Knorr air	Standard	Standard	109/90 (54/45)	Wood 6¼ (160) Conc B 55	2 575 (1 600)	Min rad 656 ft (200 m)	2·9% 2·75% U but general 2·5%	20	7 402 (2 256)	63 502 (36 774)	Gen. Director: Orhan Acartar
20·9 (33·7)	28·7 (46·2)	100 (160)	Milliard Roubles 15·6 8·8	Air	SA-Z Auto 42⅛ (1 070)		151/104 (75/51·6) mainly 104 (51·6)	Wood 6¼ (160) 7 (180) Conc.	3 013 (1 872)	Main Line 2 132 ft (650 m) general some 1 148 ft (350 m)	Class I and II 1·5% Class III 2·0% Class IV 3·0%	23		2 031 200	Min of Communications: Boris Pavlovich Beschev
		100 (161)		Vac Air on diesel and electric locos and MU trains	P Main Buckeye P Sub Screw F Fast Screw or Instanter F Slow 3-link or Instanter Ht 41¼ (1 048)	Crs 68¼ (1 734) Ht 41¼ (1 048)	Main 110 (55)	Wood 5 (127) Conc 5½" (140) at centre 8" (203) at rails	30" (762)	Main 2 640 ft (805 m)	Main 2·70%	22·5	1 484 (452)	196 635 (33 001)	Chairman: Peter Parker MVO
10 (16)	20 (32)	25 (40)	£97·3 83·5	Vac	Screw		Bullhead	Wood Conc.	2 112 (1 312)	2·2°	1·75%	17		7*	Supt: B. J. Holden
															Head of Transport: P. A. Thompson

* The railway is principally operated on a voluntary basis by members of the Bluebell Railway Preservation Society

UK (contd.)

NAME OF COMPANY / ADDRESS	Gauge ft. in. (metres)	Route length incl. E=Electrified miles (km.)	Track length incl. E=Electrified miles (km.)	Elect. system and type of conductor	Locomotives L=Line S=Shunt / Steam Electric Diesel De=elec. Dh=hyd.	Railcars Electric Diesel Trailer Railbus Multiple Unit set	Pass. train cars	Freight train cars Containers	Total Volume carried. Thousands of tonnes	Av'ge haul per ton miles (km.)	Av'ge net train load tonnes	Max. trailing load tonnes	Total number carried in 1 000's	Average journey miles (km.)
Scunthorpe Division														
Scunthorpe Works	4' 8½" (1·435)		248 (399)		DE / DH	69 / 16		2 600						
Shelton Works			26 (42)		DE / DH	8 / 4		569						
Monks Hall Work			1 (1·8)		DE	2		4						
Warrington Works			1 (1·8)		DE	3								
Irlam Works			4 (6)		DE	4		16						
Sheffield Division														
River Don Works	4' 8½" (1·435)	0·5 (0·8)	8 (13)		DM / DH	8 / 4		78						
Grimesthorpe Works		0·5 (0·8)	2 (3·2)		DM	1		10						
Cyclops Works			1 (1·8)		DM	1		1						
Stocksbridge Works		1 (1·8)	19 (30·5)		DE	10		450						
Stocksbridge Railway		2 (3·2)	8 (13)		DE	1		44						
Tinsley Park Works		3 (4·8)	16 (26)		DM / DH / DE	2 / 4 / 1		196						
Panteg Works		1 (1·8)	6 (9·6)		DE / DH	1 / 3		100						
Shepcote Lane Works			1 (1·8)		DM	1								
Bilston Works		5 (8)	22 (35)		DE	15		634						
Wolverhampton Works		—	1 (1·8)		DE	1								
Craigneuk Foundry Works		—	3 (4·8)		DE	2		22						
Fullwood Works		—	1 (1·8)		DE / DM	1 / 1		13						
Distington Works		4 (6·4)	5 (8)		DE	2		72						
Dowlais Works		1 (1·8)	2 (3·2)		DM	2		35						
Landore Works		2 (3·2)	3 (4·8)		DH	3		41						
Rotherham: Templeborough Works		2 (3·2)	50 (80)		DE	16		787						
Rotherham: Aldwarke Works		4 (6·4)	50 (80)		DE / DH	14 / 3		382						
Trafford Park Works		1 (1·8)	10 (16)		DH	2		45						
Teesside Division														
Barrow Works	4' 8½" (1·435)	4 (6·4)	7 (11·2)		DE	2		192						
Consett Works		25 (40)	38 (61)		DH / DE	25 / 1		502						
Hartlepool Works		16 (25)	40 (64)		DH / DE	21 / 2		678						
Jarrow Works			2 (3·2)		DM	2		4						
Skinningrove Works		5 (8)	8 (12·8)		DH	3		12						
South Teesside Works		118 (174)	152 (245)		DH	65		1 818						
Workington Works		38 (61)	44 (71)		DH / DE	10 / 12		755						
Scottish Division														
Ravenscraig Works	4' 8½" (1·435)		50 (86)		DH	22		230						
Dalzell Works		2 (3·2)	10 (16)		DH / DE	4 / 3		478						
Clydebridge Works		5 (8)	13 (21)		DE	7		221						
Glengarnock Works		4 (6·4)	18 (29)		DH / DE	3 / 4		200						
Lanarkshire Works		1 (1·6)	12 (19)		DH / DE	3 / 2		267						
Victoria Works		0·5 (·8)	1 (1·6)		DE	2								
Hallside Works					DE	2								
Welsh Division														
Shotton Works	4' 8½" (1·435)		68 (109)		DE / DH / DM	1 / 23 / 3		1 581						
Llanwern Works			50 (86)		DH / DE	15 / 5		253						
Port Talbot Works			111 (179)		DE	28		1 002						
Orb Works			4 (6·4)		DE / DM	1 / 1								
Whiteheads Works			5 (8)		DE / DH	2 / 2		25						
Ebbw Vale Works			55 (88)		DH	17		260						
Trostre			4 (6·4)		DE	2		9						
Velindre			3 (4·8)		DE	2		—						
East Moors					DH	18								

Average Speeds			Financial Data			Couplers	Buffers	Rails	Sleepers (crossties)							
Freight Train	Pass. Train	Speed max.	Revenue Expenses	Braking (con-tinuous)		Type and Height above rail	Centres and Height above rail	Weight	Type and thick-ness	Spacing Number per mile (per km) or centres	Curva-ture max.	Gradient max. (U=not compen-sated)	Axle load max.	Alti-tude max.	Staff em-ployed. Total no. (inclu. work-shop)	Names of officials. Extended lists can be found at the end of the individual country in the report section immediately following
mph (km/hr)	mph (km/hr)	mph (km/hr)	in 1 000's			ins (mm)	ins (mm)	lb. per yd (kg/m)	ins (mm)	ins (mm)			tonnes	feet (m)		

Average Speeds			Financial Data			Couplers	Buffers	Rails	Sleepers (crossties)							
Freight Train	Pass. Train	Speed max.	Revenue Expenses	Braking (con-tinuous)		Type and Height above rail	Centres and Height above rail	Weight	Type and thick-ness	Spacing Number per mile (per km) or centres	Curva-ture max.	Gradient max. (U=not compen-sated)	Axle load max.	Alti-tude max.	Staff em-ployed. Total no. (inclu. work-shop)	Names of officials. Extended lists can be found at the end of the individual country in the report section immediately following
mph (km/hr)	mph (km/hr)	mph (km/hr)	in 1 000's			ins (mm)	ins (mm)	lb. per yd (kg/m)	ins (mm)	ins (mm)			tonnes	feet (m)		

NAME OF COMPANY ADDRESS	Gauge ft. in. (metres)	Route length incl. E=Electrified miles (km.)	Track length incl. E=Electrified miles (km.)	Elect. system and type of conductor	Locomotives L=Line S=Shunt / Steam Electric Diesel De=elec. Dh=hyd.	Rail-cars Electric Diesel Trailer Railbus Multiple Unit set	Pass. train cars	Freight train cars / Containers	Total Volume carried. Thousands of tonnes	Av'ge haul per ton miles (km.)	Av'ge net train load tonnes	Max. trailing load tonnes	Total number carried in 1000's	Average journey miles (km.)
UK (contd.)														
Tubes Division British Works	4' 8½" (1·435)	0·5 (·8)	2 (3·2)											
Calder Works		0·5 (·8)	2 (3·2)					2						
Clydesdale Works		3 (4·8)	14 (22)		D 3 DE 3			53						
Imperial Works		0·5 (·8)	2 (3·2)		D 2									
Tollcross Works		0·5 (·8)	2 (3·2)											
Bromford Works		0·5 (·8)	2 (3·2)		DE 3			33						
Stanton Works		2·5 (4)	25 (40)		DH 12			940						
Staveley Works		5·5 (8·8)	17 (27)		DE 7			505						
Holwell Works		1 (1·6)	7 (11)		DH 3			140						
Corby Works			152 (245)		DH 52			2 912						
BSC (Chemicals) Ltd Orgreave and Brookhouse Works, Sheffield Clarence Works, Middlesbrough	4' 8½" (1·435)		9 (14)		DE 4			422						
British Steel Service Centres Meadow Hall Works, Sheffield	4' 8½" (1·435)		2 (3·2)		DM 1			—						
Greenwich Works, London			1 (1·6)		DM 1			—						
Scottish Division Ravenscraig	4' 8½" (1·435)		50 (80)		D 24			230						
Dalzell		2 (3·2)	10 (16)		DH 4 DE 3			478						
Clydebridge		5 (8)	13 (20)		DH 5 DE 1			221						
Glengarnock		4 (6·4)	18 (29)		DH 3 DE 4			200						
Lanarkshire		1 (1·6)	12 (19)		DH 3			267						
Victoria		·5 (·8)	11 (18)		Nil			Nil						
Mossend Eng		1 (1·6)	4·1/4 (6·6)		DE 2			12						
Clyde Iron		7 (11·2)	15 (24)		DH 4 DE 3			Nil						
Gartcosh		2 (3·2)	5.1/2 (8·8)		DE 3			Nil						
Briton Ferry Steel Company Ltd. PO Box 15, Briton Ferry, Neath, West Glamorgan	4' 8½" (1·435)	5½ (8·5)	7 (11)		S 1 D 3 Dh 3									
Brown Bayley Steels Ltd. *Incorporating* Rotherham-Tinsley Steel Ltd. Leeds Rd, Sheffield S9 3TT	4' 8½" (1·435)		3 (4·8)		S 3 DS 1									
Central Electricity Generating Board *Southern Division* *(Swindon and Earley power stations)* Swindon Power Station, Purton Rd, Swindon, Wilts.	4' 8½" (1·435)		1 (1·6)		Batt 1									
Darlington & Simpson Rolling Mills Ltd PO Box 9, Rise Carr Rolling Mills, Darlington, Co Durham	4' 8½" (1·435)		3 (5)		Dh 2									
Derwent Valley Railway Co Layerthorpe Station, Yorks.	4' 8½" (1·435)	4·2 (6·8)	6 (10)		D 2 DL 1*		3*		58·0					
Esso Petroleum Co Ltd Victoria St, London SW1 24 refineries plants and depots with private sidings	4' 8½" (1·435)		21 (34)		DhS 9			3 200† C 20	4 000	90 (145)	450	1 300		
Felixtowe Dock & Rly Co The Dock, Felixtowe, Suffolk IP11 8SY	4' 8½" (1·435)	1·5 (2·5)	6 (10)		DeS 1				49·1					
Festiniog Railway Portmadoc, Gwynedd	1' 11½" (600)	14 (21)	17 (27)		SL 6 DhL 2 DS 5		30	175					390	9 (12·8)
Firth Brown Ltd PO Box 114, Atlas Works, Sheffield S4 7US and Canklon Sidings, Rotherham	4' 8½" (1·435)		11 (18)		DhS 5 DS 2			259	411·8	0·5 (0·8)	75	671		
Firth Vickers Stainless Steels Ltd Staybrite Works, Weedon St, Sheffield 9, Yorks	4' 8½" (1·435)	·75 (1·2)	1·25 (2)		DS 1									
Shepcote Lane Works, Shepcote Lane, Sheffield 9, Yorks	4' 8½" (1·435)	·37 (0·6)	0·5 (0·8)		D 1									
Fishguard and Rosslare Railways and Harbours 163/203 Eversholt St, London NW1 1BG	Wales: 4' 8½" Eire: 5' 3"		1 (1·6) 75 (120)	Operated in Wales by British Railways and in Ireland by Coras Iompair Eireann.										
Ford Motor Co Ltd Dagenham, Essex	4' 8½" (1·435)	6 (9·6)	23 (32)		DhS 6			400			300			

* On loan for passenger services commencing 4 May 1977
† 2 100 owned, 1 100 hired

Average Speeds			Financial Data		Couplers	Buffers	Rails	Sleepers (crossties)							
Freight Train	Pass. Train	Speed max.	Revenue Expenses	Braking (continuous)	Type and Height above rail	Centres and Height above rail	Weight	Type and thickness	Spacing Number per mile (per km) or centres	Curvature max.	Gradient max. (U=not compensated)	Axle load max.	Altitude max.	Staff employed. Total no. (inclu. workshop)	Names of officials. Extended lists can be found at the end of the individual country in the report section immediately following
mph (km/hr)	mph (km/hr)	mph (km/hr)	in 1 000's		ins (mm)	ins (mm)	lb. per yd (kg/m)	ins (mm)	ins (mm)			tonnes	feet (m)		
														42 (2)	Gen. Man: D. J. D. Unwin
							95 (47)	Wood Standard							
								Wood 9" (228)	30" (762)						
20 (32)	25 (40)		£41·0 37·7	Air			B.H. 80 (40)	Wood 5 (127)	42" (1 067)	1·45°	0·67%	12		8	Gen. Man: J. Acklam
22 (35)		60 (96)		Vac G & C	Screw 41½ (1 060)	Crs. 68 (1 750) Ht. 41½ (1 060)	98 (48)	Wood 10 (250)	30 (762)	29°		25			
		15 (25)		Air W'hse		Various	75 (37)	Wood 5 (127)	28" (712)	14·5°	Nil	25	12 (3·6)		Man. Dir: J. G. Parker
	13 (30)	20 (32)		Vac G & C	Norweg 18 (457)	Central Buffer	75/50 (37/25)	Wood 5 (127)	29" (737)	49·0°	1·25%	6	800 (244)	55	Gen. Man: A. G. W. Garraway
4·5 (7)	5 (8)				Standard	Standard	B.H. 95 (42)	Wood 5 (127)	30" (762)	11·5°	2·6%	50	140 (42)	64	Traffic Man: J. P. Bishop
12 (19·3)				Air Langs	3-link 36½ (928)	Crs. 70 (1 788) Ht. 39 (1 880)	80 (40)	Wood 6 (153)	33"	72·0°	6·6%			2	
12 (19·3)				Air Langs	3-link 36½ (928)	Crs. 70 (1 788) Ht. 39 (1 880)	95 (47)	Wood 6 (153)	33"	66·0°	5·0%			2	
12 (19·3)				Air	3-link 10½ (267)	Crs. 68 (1 750) Ht. 42 (1 069)	95 (47)	Weed 6 (153)	30	62·0°	5·0%			4	
5 (8)	10 (17)				3-link	Standard	F.B. 98/75 (49/37)	Wood 4½ (115)	30" (800)	65·0°	1·0%	25		46 (16)	Man: M. R. Vale

NAME OF COMPANY ADDRESS	Gauge ft. in. (metres)	Route length incl. E=Electrified miles (km.)	Track length incl. E=Electrified miles (km.)	Elect. system and type of conductor	Locomotives L=Line S=Shunt Steam Electric Diesel De=elec. Dh=hyd.		Railcars Electric Diesel Trailer Railbus Multiple Unit set		Pass. train cars	Freight train cars Containers	Total Volume carried. Thousands of tonnes	Av'ge haul per ton miles (km.)	Av'ge net train load tonnes	Max. trailing load tonnes	Total number carried in 1 000's	Average journey miles (km.)

Freight movement spans Total Volume carried, Av'ge haul per ton, Av'ge net train load, Max. trailing load columns. **Passengers** spans Total number carried, Average journey.

UK (contd.)

Gas Boards

NAME OF COMPANY ADDRESS	Gauge	Route length	Track length	Elect.	Locomotives		Railcars		Pass.	Freight	Total Volume	Av'ge haul	Av'ge net	Max. trailing	Total number	Average journey
East Midland Gas Board	4' 8½" (1·435)															
North Eastern Gas Board	4' 8½" (1·435)															
Tingley Works Wakefield, West Yorks	4' 8½" (1·435)		2 (3)													
Scottish Gas Board Provan Works, 100 Provan Rd, Glasgow	4' 8½" (1·435)	2·7 (4·3)	2·7 (4·3)													
West Midlands Gas Board																
Guest Keen & Nettlefolds (South Wales) Ltd. PO Box 40, Castle Works, East Moors Rd, Cardiff CF1 1TQ	4' 8½" (1·435)	4·5 (7·2)	25 (40·2)		DeS	14				430	1 000					
Imperial Chemical Industries Ltd																
Agricultural Division Severnside Works, Halen, Bristol	4' 8½" (1·435)		4 (6)		DeS	2										
Alkali Division PO Box 7, Winnington, Northwich Cheshire	4' 8½" (1·435)	3·5 (5·6)	41 (66)		DS	12				488	610·8	0·8 (1·3)	700	1 000		
Aricultural Division PO Box 8, Billingham, Durham	4' 8½" (1·435)	12 (19)	36 (58)		DeS	4				255	778·2	2 (3·2)	250	600		
Wilton Works Middlesbrough, Cleveland	4' 8½" (1·435)	6 (10)	16 (25)		DeS DS	2 1	D	1						700		
Isle of Man Railway Co Douglas Station, Douglas, IoM	3' 0" (0·914)	16* (25)			SL	5	D	2	28					150		10 (16)
Kent & East Sussex Railway (Operator Tenterten Railway Co Ltd) Tenterten Town Station, Tenterten, Kent TN30 6ME	4' 8½" (1·435)	4 (6·5)	4·5 (7·5)		SL SS DmS DhS	7 1 1 1	D	1	10						80·0	
Leighton Buzzard Light Railway Pages Park Station, Billington Rd, Leighton Buzzard, Beds LU7 8TN	2' 0" (0·61)	3·5 (5·6)	7 (11)		S† Dm Petrol	6 9 1			7						9·8	3 (4·8)
Lincolnshire Coast Light Rly. North Sea Lane Station, Humberston, Grimsby, Lincs DN36 4EP	1' 11⅝" (0·60)	1 (1·6)	1·25 (2)		S D	1 1			4	6					50·0	1 (1·6)
Manchester Ship Canal Railway Ship Canal House, King St, Manchester M2 4WX	4' 8½" (1·435)		50 (80)		De Dh D	2 8 5					1 311·9	5 (8)	200	1 000		
Manx Electric Rly Board 1 Strathallan Crescent, Douglas, IoM	3' 0" (0·914) 3' 6" (1·067)	E 18 (29) E 5 (8)	E 36 (58) E 10 (16)	560 V dc OH			E T	16 16							250·0	
Middleton Railway Middleton Railway Trust Garnet Rd, Leeds LS11 5JY	4' 8½" (1·435)		2 (3)		SS DS	8 4				5	1·0	1 100 ton-km			8·0	2·0 (3·2)
Ministry of Defence Royal Dockyards Portsmouth, Hants	4' 8½" (1·435) 3' 3⅜" (1·00)		38 (61) 5 (8)		SS DS DS	15 71 4										
Armament Supply Depots	Broad Narrow		81 (130) 61 (98)		SS DS DS	3 31 61										
National Coal Board Hobart House, Grosvenor Place, London SW1																
Northumberland Area Ashington, Northumberland	4' 8½" (1·435)		110 (177)		S De Dh	18 12 23										
North East Area Coalhouse, Team Valley, Gateshead, Tyne and Wear	4' 8½" (1·435)	37 (60)	130 (209)		S E De Dh D	1 10 9 38 15										
North Durham Area Whitburn, Co. Durham	4' 8½" (1·435)		165 (265)		S E Dm	3 12 25										
South Durham Area Spennymoor, Co. Durham	4' 8½" (1·435)		78 (126)		S Dh Dm	11 5 20										
Northern Ireland Railways 1 York Road, Belfast BT15 Ing.	5' 3" (1·60)	203 (327)	355 (571)		DeL DhL	3 3	D T	87 54	13	31				720	7 000	
The Ravenglass and Eskdale Railway Co Ltd Ravenglass, Cumbria	1' 3" (0·381)	7 (11)	8 (13)		SL DhL D	4 1 2	D T	1 2	41	12					300·0	6·5 (10·2)

* The remaining 30 miles (48 km) closed to traffic
† The 5 steam locomotives are preserved and include one 0-4-0 de Winton vertical boilered and 4 tank locomotives

Average Speeds			Financial Data	Braking (continuous)	Couplers	Buffers	Rails	Sleepers (crossties)		Curvature max.	Gradient max. (U=not compensated)	Axle load max.	Altitude max.	Staff employed. Total no. (inclu. workshop)	Names of officials. Extended lists can be found at the end of the individual country in the report section immediately following
Freight Train	Pass. Train	Speed max.	Revenue Expenses		Type and Height above rail	Centres and Height above rail	Weight	Type and thickness	Spacing Number per mile (per km) or centres						
mph (km/hr)	mph (km/hr)	mph (km/hr)	in 1 000's		ins (mm)	ins (mm)	lb. per yd (kg/m)	ins (mm)	ins (mm)			tonnes	feet (m)		
15 (24)		20 (32)	£ 8·0	Vac	3-link 36½ (928)	Ht. 54 (1 372)	95 (47)	Wood Conc. (228)	(1 094)			100			F. Armstrong
6 (9·9)		10 (17)			as BR	as BR		Wood 5 (130)		58°	Level	25	77	100	Traffic Man: R. W. Cockram
		20 (32)					95 (47)	Wood 5 (130)	30″ (762)	17·5°	1·5%	18		3	
10 (16)		12 (19)		Vac.	Standard	Standard	95 (47)	Wood 5 (130)	31″ (787)	17·5°	2·1%	18	125 (38)	70 (37)	Rail Trans. Man: C. Bennet
10 (16)		20 (32)	Expenses only £383·4	None	as BR	as BR	95 (42)	Wood 5 (130)	26″ (662)	43°	2·3% U	22·5	40 (12)	96 (45)	Trans. Op. Man: J. F. R. Moddrel
		10 (16)			as BR	as BR	95 (47)	Wood 5 (130)	31″ (787)	12·5°	2·03%	22·5		5 (2)	
	18 (29)	25 (40)	£30·4 34·2	Vac	Norwegian 27 (686)	Buffer-couplers	60 (30)	Wood 5 (130)	36″ (915)	8·75°	1·5%	7	210 (64)	27 (6)	Gen. Man: William Lambden
	19 (30)	25 (40)	£41·0 35·0	Vac	Buckeye Standard	Standard	95/91¼ (47/45)	Wood & Steel	29″ (737)	10·5°	2·0%	10	250 (76)	23	Chairman: S. G. N. Bennett
	4 (6)	10 (16)	£6·6 5·5		Centre Hudsons 18 (985)		40 (20)	Wood Standard	30″ (762)	40°	3·3%	3·5	350 (107)	All Volunteers	Chairman: A. P. Tomknis Traffic. Man: R. W. Hughes
	10 (16)	12 (19)	£1·6 0·9			Buffer-Coupler 18″ (458)	25/20 (13/10)	Wood	24″-36″ (610-915)	30°	None	2·5	Sea level	1	Man. Dir: W. Woolhouse
5 (8)		10 (16)		Air	Standard	Standard	95/110 (47/55)	Wood 5 (127)	31″ (787)	25·0°	2·5%	25		43	Railway Supt: B. Valentine
				Air and Ratchet			62/50 (31/25)						1 950 (594)	100	Gen. Man: H. Gilmore
5 (8)	8 (13)	10 (16)			Standard 3-link	Standard	95 (47)	Wood 5 (127)	30″ (762)	17·5°	3·0%	16		All voluntary	Chairman: J. K. Lee Sec: J. D. Edwards
							98 (49)	Wood 5 (127)	30 (762)	12·5°	2·8%	15	204 (56)		
		70 (113)		Air & Vac. W'hse	P. Screw F. 3-link 41 (1 041)	75 (1 905) 41 (1 041)	92/85 (46/42)	Wood 5 (127)	30″ (760)	1 370 ft (418 m)	1·33%	18	375 (114)	1 229 (181)	Man. Dir: H. Waring
15 (25)	30 (48)	20 (32)	£88·8 88·8	Air W'hse	Link & Pin	9½ (241)	30/35 (15/18)	Wood 5 (127)	36″ (914)		2·77%		170 (51)	20	Gen. Man: D. M. E. Ferreira Ch. Eng: I. Smith

NAME OF COMPANY ADDRESS	Gauge ft. in. (metres)	Route length incl. E=Electrified miles (km.)	Track length incl. E=Electrified miles (km.)	Elect. system and type of conductor	Loco-motives L=Line S=Shunt Steam Electric Diesel De=elec. Dh=hyd.	Rail-cars Electric Diesel Trailer Railbus Multiple Unit set	Pass. train cars	Freight train cars Containers	Total Volume carried. Thousands of tonnes	Av'ge haul per ton miles (km.)	Av'ge net train load tonnes	Max. trailing load tonnes	Total number carried in 1 000's	Average journey miles (km.)
UK *(contd.)*														
Sittingbourne and Kemsley Light Railway	2' 6" (0·762)	2 (3)	3 (5)		SL 7 Dh 1 Dm 1		8	50					13·0	4 (6·4)
Romney, Hythe and Dymchurch Light Rly Co New Romney, Kent	1' 3" (0·138)	13 (21)	23 (37)		SL 10 DS 1		70	35				40	289·4	8 (13)
Snowdon Mountain Railway Ltd Llanberis, Gwynedd, Wales	2' 7½" (0·800)	4·6 (7·4) Abt rack	5 (8)		SL 7		7	2					89·0	8 (13)
Shell UK Ltd Shell Centre, London SE1 7NA														
Ardrossan Refinery	4' 8½" (1·435)		1 (1·6)		D 1									
Stanlow Refinery	4' 8½" (1·435)		17 (22)		D 8									
Shell Haven Refinery	4' 8½" (1·435)		12 (13)		D 6									
Teesport Refinery	4' 8½" (1·435)		8 (7)		D 3									
Southend Pier Railway Southend-on-Sea, Essex	3' 6" (1·067)	E 1·2 (1·6)	E 1·2 (1·6)	600 V. dc 3rd rail		E 8 T 6							1 500·3	2·3 (3·7)
Talyllyn Railway Co Wharf Station, Tywyn, Gwynedd LL3L 9EY	2' 3" (0·686)	7 (11)	8 (13)		SL 6 DhL 1 DmL 1 DmS 1		20	45					180·2	
Trafford Park Company Estate Office, Trafford Park, Manchester M17 1AU *(Operated by Manchester Ship Canal Co)*	4' 8½" (1·435)		6 (10)		D 5*				146·8					
Tyne Tees Steam Shipping Co Ltd PO Box No. 41, Vulcan St, Middlesbrough, Cleveland	4' 8½" (1·435)		6·5 (8)		D 7									
Lever Brothers & Associates Ltd Port Sunlight, Wirrell, Merseyside	4' 8½" (1·435)	5 (8)	7 (11)		D 2				25·0		120	250		
Volks Railway 285 Madeira Drive, Brighton, East Sussex	2' 8½" (0·82)	E 1·25 (2·1)	E 1·5 (2·4)	3rd† rail		E 9 T 1 M 4	9						328·4	2·5 (4)
Welshpool and Llanfair Light Railway Preservation Co Ltd Llanfair Caereinion Station, Powys, Wales	2' 6" (0·76)	5·5 (8·8)	6 (9)		SL 6 SS 1 DL 1 DS 1		14	21					24·7	6 (10)
USA														
Aberdeen & Rockfish Railroad Co PO Box 917 Aberdeen, NC 28315	4' 8½" (1·435)	47 (76)	62 (100)		S‡ 1 De 3			1	1 065·5					
Abilene & Southern Railway Co *(Subsidiary of Missouri Pacific)*	4' 8½" (1·435)	39 (63)												
Ahnapee & Western Railway Co PO Box 91, Algoma, WI 54201	4' 8½" (1·435)	14 (23)	18 (29)											
Akron & Barberton Belt RR Co PO Box 712, 43 2nd St NW Barberton, Ohio 44203	4' 8½" (1·435)	23 (37)	43 (69)		DeS 2				35 157 loads					
Akron, Canton & Youngstown RR 8 N. Jefferson St, Roanoke, Va 24042	4' 8½" (1·435)	171 (275)	229 (368)		DeL 15		0	1 756	3 425	293 111 ton miles			0	
Alabama Great Southern RR *(Included on Southern Railway System)*	4' 8½" (1·435)	327 (527)	773 (1 244)		DeL 71 DeS 26		23	3 517	8 289·1	156 (251)	2 100		111·8	160 (257)
Alameda Belt Line PO Box 24352, Oakland, Cal, 94623	4' 8½" (1·435)	3·5 (5·6)	19 (30·5)		DeS 1			4	12 500 carloads					
Alaska Railroad The Alaska Railroad, Pouch 7-2111, Anchorage, Alaska 99510	4' 8½" (1·435)	478 (769)	526 (847)		DeL 32 DeS 22		38	1 613	2 131·6	529 917 000 ton-miles		6 000	84·5	162·9 (262)
Alexander Railroad Co PO Box 277, 145 2nd ave NE. Taylorsville, NC 28681	4' 8½" (1·435)	19 (31)	20 (32)		DeS 3				155·9	10 (16)		400		
Algers, Winslow & Western Ry Co PO Box 188, Oakland City, Ind 47660	4' 8½" (1·435)	16 (26)	24 (39)		D 6									
Aliquippa and Southern R.R. Co. PO Box 280, Aliquippa, Pa 15001	4' 8½" (1·435)	47 (76)			DeS 19			891	15 140·8					

* Owned by the Manchester Ship Canal Company
† 400 V mains input, rectified to 15 V dc to track
‡ In reserve

Average Speeds: Freight Train mph (km/hr)	Pass. Train mph (km/hr)	Speed max. mph (km/hr)	Financial Data: Revenue Expenses in 1000's	Braking (continuous)	Couplers Type and Height above rail ins (mm)	Buffers Centres and Height above rail ins (mm)	Rails Weight lb. per yd (kg/m)	Sleepers (crossties) Type and thickness ins (mm)	Spacing Number per mile (per km) or centres ins (mm)	Curvature max.	Gradient max. (U=not compensated)	Axle load max. tonnes	Altitude max. feet (m)	Staff employed. Total no. (inclu. workshop)	Names of officials.
12 (20)	15 (24)		£7·0 6·0		Central buffer & hook		60 (30)	Wood 6 (152)	24 (600)	82°		6	20 (6)	All Volunteers	Sec: G. Stickler Lite Hjem, Woodlands Estate, Blean, near Canterbury, Kent
12 (19)	25 (40)		£158·5 148·2	Vac V.B. Co	Instanta 13 (360)	23½ (597) 14½ (369)	F.B. 24 (11·8)	Wood 4½ (115)	22	12·5°	0·67%	2	Sea Level	27/45	Gen. Man: P. C. Hawkins
5 (8)	5 (8)			SLM Abt type			39·75 (19·7)	Steel	36" (914)	24·0°	18·2%	6	3 560 (1 075)	40	Gen. Man: G. C. Nicholas
															Works Man: Clifford C. Williams
															Man: F. W. A. Paterson
															Man: S. J. Gallacher
															Man: F. E. Hixon
															Man: G. G. Rose
16 (26)	18 (28)		$ 70 000 140 000	Air and Elec	Type AB 24 (610)	Centre 11 (250)	45 (22·5)	Wood 4½ (115)				2·5	Sea Level	23	Foreshore Off: D. Tyler
11 (16)	15 (24)		£57·9 52·7	Nil	Screw 18 (457)	Centre 36 (915) Ht. 18 (457)	40/61 (20/31)	Wood 5 (127)	33" (838)	22·0°	1·67U	5	230 (70)	18	Traf. Man: D. Woodhouse Ch Eng: J. L. H. Bate Man Dir: W. H. D. Faulkner
	10 (16)		£12·7 52·1		BR	BR	95/75 (47/37)	Wood 5 (127)	30" (762)	29·2°		16		5	Dir: N. G. Westbrook (Chairman) Gen Man: A. D. Lennie Eng: J. Carnley
9 (14·5)	15 (24)				Standard	Standard	95/90 (47/45)	Wood 5 (127)	33" (838)	67·0°	1·1%	25	50 (15)		
	12 (20)			Hand	Own	17·4 (444)	50 (25)	Wood & Conc 5 (127)	36" (914)	17·5°		7·5	Sea Level	20 (3)	Dir: A. J. Hewison
9 (14)	15 (24)		£10·9		Link & Pin		45 (23)	Wood 5 (127)	27" (686)	29·0°	3·1% 3·5%U	8	600 (183)		Gen. Man: R. T. Russell Sec: J. Dickenson
35 (56)	40 (64)		$ 778·5 572·7	Air			90/70 (45/35)	Wood		10°	3·5%			65 (5)	Pres: W. Formyduval
15 (25)				Air			70 (35)	Wood 6 (153)	2 880 (1 790)					20	Pres: C. T. Hester
6 (9·5)	25 (41)			W'hse			100 (49·6)	Oak 6 (153)	22" (560)	11·8°	2·28% U			70 (16)	Pres: R. W. Coffey
16 (26)	50 (79)		$ 8 931·2 7 341·0	Air	Type E 33" (839)		115/90 (57/45)	Wood 6 (153)	22" (560)	5·3°	East 0·63% West 0·56%	30·0		352 (61)	Pres and Gen Man: J. L. Cowan
			$ 12 676 8 769												
				W'hse	AAR Standard		110/70 (54/35)	Fir (Imp.) 7 (178)	20" (508)	17·3°	0·6%	20	Sea Level	29 (14)	Pres: R. W. Walker
34 (55)	30·8 (49·5)	49 (79)	$ 29 337·9 32 051·5	W'hse NYAB	Type E 28½" (724)	Cr. 42¾ (1 086) Ht. 50 (1 270)	115/70 (57/35)	Impreg. Fir & Hemlock 7 (178)	19½" (495)	14·0°	3·0% (S) 2·2% (N)	30	2 363 (720)	825 (190)	Gen. Man: W. L. Dorie
20 (32)	25 (40)		$ 389·7 185·4	Air			85/60 (42/30)	Wood 7 (178)	27" (690)				1 250 (381)	11 (1)	Pres: S. J. Zachary
							90 (44·6)	Wood 6 (153)	22½" (572)	12·0°	2·0%	25			Pres: L. S. Crause
							115 (57)	Wood 7 (178)	22" (560)	28·7°	0·74% 3·7% U			565	Gen. Supt: J. J. Deyak

NAME OF COMPANY ADDRESS	Gauge ft. in. (metres)	Route length incl. E=Electrified miles (km.)	Track length incl. E=Electrified miles (km.)	Elect. system and type of conductor	Locomotives L=Line S=Shunt Steam Electric Diesel De=elec. Dh=hyd.		Rail-cars Electric Diesel Trailer Railbus Multiple Unit set		Pass. train cars	Freight train cars Containers	Total Volume carried. Thousands of tonnes	Av'ge haul per ton miles (km.)	Av'ge net train load tonnes	Max. trailing load tonnes	Total number carried in 1 000's	Average journey miles (km.)
USA *(contd.)*																
Almanor Railroad Co. 909 Terminal Sales Bldg, Portland, Oreg 97205	4' 8½" *(1·435)*	13 *(21)*	16 *(25)*		De	1					94·6	14 *(20)*	280			
Alton and Southern Railway Co 1000 S 22nd St E Louis, Ill 62207	4' 8½" *(1·435)*	32 *(53)*	130 *(209)*		DeS	20				390	1 390·0					
Amador Central Railway Co PO Box 8498, San Francisco, Cal 94119	4' 8½" *(1·435)*	12 *(19)*	15 *(25)*		DeL	2				3	98 100	12 *(19)*	140	340		
Amtrak National Railroad Passenger Corp 400 North Capitol St, Washington, DC 20024	4' 8½" *(1·435)*	26 144* *(42 073)* E 401 *(645)*		1 100 V 25 Hz	EL 66 DeL 310 DeS 13		RD 11 ER 61 Turbo 79		2 057						18 614 510	
Angelina & Neches River RR Co PO Box 1328, Lufkin, Tex 75901	4' 8½" *(1·435)*	12 *(20)*			De	2				109	530·9	5 *(8)*	737	2 100		
Ann Arbor Railroad Co PO Box 30050, Lansing, Mich 48909	4' 8½" *(1·435)*	299 *(481)*	412 *(663)*		DeL 15 DeS 2					273	4 800·8	195 *(314)*	2 356			
Apache Railway Co. PO Drawer E, Snowflake, Ariz 85937	4' 8½" *(1·435)*	74 *(119)*	90 *(144·8)*		DeL 6 DeS 2				0	613	1 186·6					
Apalachicola Northern Railroad Co PO Box 250, Port St. Joe, Fla 32456	4' 8½" *(1·435)*	96 *(154)*	123 *(198)*		DeL	11				131	1 647·0	96 *(154)*				
Arcade & Attica Railroad Corp 278 Main St, Arcade, NY 14009	4' 8½" *(1·435)*	15 *(24)*	17 *(27)*		SL 2 DeL 2				7	22		5 *(8)*			41·0	15 *(24)*
Arcata & Mad River Railroad Co PO Box 368, Blue Lake, Cal 95525	4' 8½" *(1·435)*	7·5 *(12)*	9·4 *(15)*		DeL	3				20	7 000 cars	6·1 *(9·8)*				
Arkansas & Louisiana Missouri Ry Co PO Box 1653, Monroe, La 71201	4' 8½" *(1·435)*	55 *(88)*	64 *(103)*		DL 3 DeS 1					31						
Arkansas Western Rly Co 114 W 11th St, Kansas City, Mo 64105 *(Subsidiary of KCS Rly Co)*	4' 8½" *(1·435)*	35 *(56)*														
Aroostook Valley Railroad Co. *(Canadian Pacific Railway)* PO Box 509, Presque Isle, Mont 04769	4' 8½" *(1·435)*	32 *(51)*	45 *(72)*		DeS	3					98·7	11·5 *(18·5)*	500	2 100		
Ashley, Drew & Northern Railway Co. Box 757, Crossett, Ark 71635	4' 8½" *(1·435)*	41 *(66)*	53 *(85)*		DeS	5			1	818	1 404·6	23 *(37)*	4 000	8 300		
Atchison, Topeka & Santa Fe Rly Co 80 East Jackson Blvd, Chicago, Ill 60604	4' 8½" *(1·435)*	12 321 *(19 800)*	21 506 *(34 611)*		DeL 1 598 DS 93					68 939	90 000					
Atlanta & Saint Andrews Bay Rly 514 E Main St, PO Box 729, Dothan, Ala 36301	4' 8½" *(1·435)*	88 *(142)*	138 *(222)*		DeL 7 DeS 7					365	2 648·4	187 364 211 ton-miles				
Atlanta and West Point RR Co 1590 Marietta Blvd NW, Atlanta Ga 30318	4' 8½" *(1·435)*	225 *(362)*			DL 11 DS 13					1 209	6 154·6	71·5 *(115)*				
Atlanta Terminal Co PO Box 1808, Washington DC 20013	4' 8½" *(1·435)*		5·3 *(8·6)*													
Atlanta Stone Mountain and Lithonia RR Co 717 5th Ave, New York, NY 10022	4' 8½" *(1·435)*	4·3 *(6·6)*			DeL	1										
Atlantic & Danville Railway Co *(See Norfolk, Franklin and Danville Rly)*																
Atlantic & East Carolina Rly Co PO Box 1808, Washington DC 20013	4' 8½" *(1·435)*	94 *(151)*	128 *(206)*		D	7				220						
Atlantic & Western Railway Co PO Box 1208, Sandford, NC 27330	4' 8½" *(1·435)*	4 *(6·4)*	3 *(5)*		DeS	2				387	30·8					
Atlantic Coast Line Railroad Co *(See Seaboard Coast Line RR)*																
Augusta & Summerville Railroad Co. † 1590 Marietta Blvd NW, Atlanta Ga 30318	4' 8½" *(1·435)*	2·7 *(4·7)*	5 *(8)*													
Aurora Elgin & Fox River Electric Co. PO Box 44 So., Elgin, Ill 60177	4' 8½" *(1·435)*	1·3 *(2·1)*	5 *(8)*		De	1										
Auto Train Corp 1801 K St, NW, Washington DC 20005	4' 8½" *(1 438)*	1 685 *(2 710)*			DeL 11 DeS 4				89	83						
Baltimore & Annapolis RR Co 801 Baltimore-Annapolis, Blvd, Glen Burnie, Md 21061	4' 8½" *(1·435)*	28 *(45)*	30 *(48)*		De	1										
Baltimore & Eastern Railroad Co *(See Conrail)*	4' 8½" *(1·435)*	62 *(100)*														
Baltimore & Ohio Chicago Terminal R.R. Co. 2 N. Charles St, Baltimore Md. 21201 *(Subsidiary of Baltimore and Ohio)*	4' 8½" *(1·435)*	350 *(563)*	356 *(573)*													

* Track owned by Amtrak totals 1 661 miles *(2 687 km)*, remainder is the track over which operations are carried out
† Terminal switching line with track only

Average Speeds			Financial Data	Braking (continuous)	Couplers	Buffers	Rails	Sleepers (crossties)		Curvature max.	Gradient max. (U=not compensated)	Axle load max.	Altitude max.	Staff employed. Total no. (inclu. workshop)	Names of officials. Extended lists can be found at the end of the individual country in the report section immediately following
Freight Train	Pass. Train	Speed max.	Revenue Expenses		Type and Height above rail	Centres and Height above rail	Weight	Type and thickness	Spacing Number per mile or centres ins						
mph (km/hr)	mph (km/hr)	mph (km/hr)	in 1 000's		ins (mm)	ins (mm)	lb. per yd (kg/m)	ins (mm)	(mm)			tonnes	feet (m)		
15 (24)				Air BW	Standard	None							4 700 (1 439)		Pres: A. C. Goudy
20 (32)		35 (56)		Air W'hse			115/85 (57/42)	Oak 7 (178)	21″ (533)	12·5°	3·55%	31·5		623 (50)	Pres: R. L. King
10 (16)		12 (19)		Air W'hse	Type E 33½″ (851)		80/40 (40/20)	Wood 6 (153)	20″ (508)	20·0°	4·5%U	30	1 535 (468)	10 (1)	Gen. Man: Russel Evitt
	47 (76)	105 (169)	$ 278 000 719 000	Air E. Pneu	F & H		59/76 (119/152)	Wood 7 (178)	1932/km	8·0°	1·34%	25		20 000	Pres: Paul Reistrup
15 (24)							75/70 (37/35)	Wood 6 (153)	10″ (254)		3·0%				Pres: N. E. Kurth
		45 (73)	$ 10 542 10 318	Air W'hse	Type E		115/85 (57/42)	Wood 6 (153)	19½″ (495)	10·2°	1·6% 1·4%U		1 382 (421)	459 (75)	Gen Man: B. L. Strohl
25 (40)		35 (57)	$3 201·4 2 460·2	Air W'hse	Type E		131/110 (65/54·6)	Wood 6 (153)	20″ (508)	7·0°	2·4% 2·1%U	17·5	7 300 (2 225)	58	Pres and Chief Exec: Flake Willis
				Air W'hse	Type E		132/90 (65·5/45)	Wood 7 (178)	18″ (457)	4·0°	1·5%U			90 (18)	Pres: E. Ball
		15 (24)		Air W'hse			70 (35)	Wood 6 (153)	24″ (610)			25	1 900 (579)	17 (2)	Pres: J. A. Yansiels
15 (24)							70 (35)	Fir 6 (153)		25·0°	1·0%			18	Pres: G. L. Oswald
25 (40)		35 (56)		W'hse Air	Auto		90/60 (45/30)	Wood 7 (178)	20″ (508)	16°	1·0%			87 (9)	Pres: J. L. Keller
15 (24)		30 (48)	$ 215·0 204·0	NY AB			85/70 (42/35)	Wood 6 (153)	1 165 (2 600)	12·0°	2·0%U	30	648 (198)	17 (2)	Pres: G. E. Benoit
15 (24)		40 (64)		Air W'hse	AAR	AAR Standard	90/85 (45/42)	Oak & Pine 7 (178)	21″ (533)	10·0°	4·0%	35	165 (50)	75	Pres: S. R. Tedder Supt: J. H. Richards
27·7 (44)	51·5 (83)		$ 1 432·2 1 250·3				136/90 (68/45)	Wood 7 (178)	3 200 (2 000)					39 740	Pres. and Chief Exec: John S. Reed
		49 (79)	$ 6 634·2 4 045·4	Air W'hse	Type E 34″ (867)	Standard	115/90 (57/45)	Wood 7 (178)	3 200 (2 000)	4·0°	1·0%U	36·0	356 (108)	167	Pres. and Chief Exec: A. V. Hooks
							100 (50)	Oak 7 (178)	20″ (508)	3·0°	1·0%				Pres: M. S. Jones
															Pres: C. L. Davidson Jr
															Pres: L. S. Crane
							85 (42)	Wood 7 (178)		8·67°	0·5%	26			
			$ 51·6 55·9	Air			70/50 (35/20)	Oak 7 (178)	2 640 (1 650)					8 (1)	Pres: T. G. Proctor, Jr
															Pres: M. S. Jones Jr
15 (24)															Pres: F. D. Lonnes
															Pres: E. K. Garfield
		25 (40)													Pres. and Gen. Man: E. J. Jubb
															Pres: A. M. Schofield
															Gen. Supt: M. O. Benson

NAME OF COMPANY ADDRESS	Gauge ft. in. (metres)	Route length incl. E=Electrified miles (km.)	Track length incl. E=Electrified miles (km.)	Elect. system and type of conductor	Loco-motives L=Line S=Shunt Steam Electric Diesel De=elec. Dh=hyd.	Rail-cars Electric Diesel Trailer Railbus Multiple Unit set	Pass. train cars	Freight train cars Con-tainers	Freight movement Total Volume carried. Thous-ands of tonnes	Av'ge haul per ton miles (km.)	Av'ge net train load tonnes	Max. trailing load tonnes	Passengers Total number carried in 1 000's	Aver-age jour-ney miles (km.)
USA *(contd.)*														
Baltimore & Ohio Railroad Co B & O Building, 2 North Charles St, Baltimore, Md 21201 *(See Chessie)*	4' 8½'' *(1·435)*	5 433 *(8 730)*	10 229 *(16 623)*		DeL 790 DeS 243		6	52 157	110 778·1	225 *(410)*	1 837	20 000		
Bangor & Aroostook Railroad Co. Northern Maine Junction Park, RR2 Bangor, Maine 04401	4' 8½'' *(1·435)*	543 *(874)*	790 *(1 271)*		DeL 45			4 808	4 032·5					
Bath & Hammondsport Railroad Co Water St, Hammondsport, NY, 14840	4' 8½'' *(1·435)*	9 *(14)*	11 *(18)*		DeL 2			1	55	8 *(13)*	106			
Bauxite & Northern Railway Co PO Box 138, Bauxite, Ark 72011	4' 8½'' *(1·435)*	3 *(4·8)*	19 *(30)*		De 2									
Beaufort & Morehead Railroad Co PO Box 300, 16 Broad St, Beaufort, NC 28516	4' 8½'' *(1·435)*	4° *(6)*	17 *(27)*		DL 3			2	190	4 *(6)*	1 200			
Beech Mountain RR PO Box 1319, Maryville, Tenn 37801	4' 8½'' *(1·435)*	8 *(13)*	8 *(13)*		DeL 1				364·1					
Belfast & Moosehead Lake RR Co 11 Water St, Belfast, Maine 04915	4' 8½'' *(1·435)*	33 *(53)*	37 *(59)*		DeL 4			3	182·6	4 766·6 ton-miles *(7 016 ton-km)*				
Bellefonte Central Railroad Co 116 N Spring St Bellefonte, Pa 16823	4' 8½'' *(1·435)*	5 *(8)*	7 *(12)*		DeS 2				165·0	825·0 ton-miles				
†**Belt Railway Co of Chicago** 6900 S Cent Ave Chicago, Ill 60638	4' 8½'' *(1·435)*	27 *(43)*	430 *(692)*		DeL 35			29						
Belton RR Co PO Box 836, Denison, Tex 75020	4' 8½'' *(1·435)*	7 *(11)*	7 *(11)*		De 1									
Bessemer & Lake Erie RR Co Albion, Pa 16401	4' 8½'' *(1·435)*	205 *(330)*			DeL 71 DeS 2			9 781	28 600·0	8·55 *(137·5)*				
Bevier & Southern Railroad Co PO Box 51, Bevier, Macon County, Miss 63532	4' 8½'' *(1·435)*	10 *(16)*	15 *(24)*		DeL 1				858·6	10 *(16)*	1 500	2 000		
Birmingham Southern Railroad Co PO Box 579, Fairfield, Ala 35064	4' 8½'' *(1·435)*	91 *(146)*	91 *(146)*		DeS 26			1 147	6 576·0					
Black Hills Central Railroad Hill City, SD 57745	4' 8½'' *(1·435)* 3' 0'' *(916)*	32 *(51)*	32 *(51)*		S 6 Pet 7		23	13						
Black River and Western Corp PO Box 83, Ringoes, NJ 08551	4' 8½'' *(1·435)*	19 *(30)*	19 *(30)*		S 1	DeS 4		14	6					
Bonhomie & Hattiesburg Southern RR Co PO Box 1546, Hattiesburg, Miss 39401 *(See Illinois Central Gulf)*	4' 8½'' *(1·435)*	27 *(43)*	30 *(49)*		DeL 2		0					2 700	0	
Boston & Maine Corporation 150 Causeway St, Boston, Mass 02114	4' 8½'' *(1·435)*	1 529 *(2 461)*	2 696 *(4 339)*		DeL 9 DeS 67	D	84	3 543	12 748·4	5 393 057 000 ton-miles			4 248·5	
Brooklyn Eastern District Terminal 86 Kent Ave, Brooklyn, NY 11211	4' 8½'' *(1·435)*	11 *(18)*	14 ‡ *(23)*		DeS 6			8	1 000·0					
Buffalo Creek Railroad PO Box 2046 Buffalo 5, NY *(See ConRail)*	4' 8½'' *(1·435)*	6 *(10)*	35 *(56)*		DeS 7			1 240						
Burlington Northern Inc (Merger of CB & Q, GD, NP, and SP & S) 176 E Fifth Street, St Paul Minn 55101	4' 8½'' *(1·435)*	23 103 *(37 230)*	35 081		DeL 1 754 DeS 382		587	109 106	137 603·5	122 *(083 256·0)*	21 000	12 098	94 318·4 *(29)*	
Butte, Anaconda & Pacific Rly Co PO Box 1421, 300 West Commercial Ave, Anaconda, Mont 59711	4' 8½'' *(1·435)*	56 *(90)*	108 *(174)*		DeL 9 DeS 9	R	1	677	2 124·8	86 552 197 ton-km				
Cadiz Railroad Co. Box B, Cadiz, Ky 42211	4' 8½'' *(1·435)*	10 *(16)*	12 *(20)*		DeS 2			100						
California Western Railroad Foot of Laurel St, Fort Bragg, Cal 95437	4' 8½'' *(1·435)*	40 *(64)*	49 *(79)*		SL 2 DeL 4	D	2	10	92·9	36 *(63)*	800	1 700	110·7	39·1 *(63)*
Camas Prairie Railroad Co PO Box 815, 13th & Main St, Lewiston, Idaho 83501 *(Operating Co for NP and UP)*	4' 8½'' *(1·435)*	256 *(411)*	315 *(507)*		DeL 16 DeS 4									
Cambria & Indiana Railroad Co. 1275 Daly Ave, Bethlehem, Pa 18015	4' 8½'' *(1·435)*	38 *(61)*	62 *(99)*		DeS 19			912						
Camino, Placerville & Lake Tahoe RR Co PO Box L, Camino, Cal 95709	4' 8½'' *(1·435)*	9 *(15)*			DeS 2			1	80·0	8 *(13)*	155			
Campbell's Creek Railroad Co. Port Amherst, Charleston, W Va	4' 8½'' *(1·435)*	14 *(22)*	20 *(32)*		D 1			110						
CP Rail Canadian Pacific Ltd. *(Lines in Maine)*	4' 8½'' *(1·435)*	234 *(376)*												

* Two miles over water
† ConRail became official owner 1 April 1976
‡ Plus 26 miles over water with 2 tugs and 10 car floats

Average Speeds			Financial Data	Braking (continuous)	Couplers	Buffers	Rails	Sleepers (crossties)		Curvature max.	Gradient max. (U=not compensated)	Axle load max.	Altitude max.	Staff employed. Total no. (inclu. workshop)	Names of officials. Extended lists can be found at the end of the individual country in the report section immediately following
Freight Train	Pass. Train	Speed max.	Revenue Expenses		Type and Height above rail	Centres and Height above rail	Weight	Type and thickness	Spacing Number per mile (per km) or centres ins (mm)						
mph (km/hr)	mph (km/hr)	mph (km/hr)	in 1 000's		ins (mm)	ins (mm)	lb. per yd (kg/m)	ins (mm)				tonnes	feet (m)		
18·6 (29·9)	28·7 (46·2)	Freight 60 (96) Pass. 70 (113)	$ 648·383 444 661	W'hse & NYAB Air	AAR Types E & F 34½" (867)		140/90 (70/45)	Wood 7 (178)	22" (560)	Main 12·0° Branch 22·0°	2·84% 3·0%U		2 694 (821)	20 000 (5 800)	Pres. and Chief Exec Officer: H. T. Watkins, Jr
16 (25)		49 (79)	$ 15 691·9 16 813·0	W'hse Air	Type E 34½" (876)		115/70 (57/35)	Wood 6 (153)	3 000 (1 865)	10·0°		33	748 (228)	783 (220)	Pres: W. E. Travis Chairman: W. J. Strout
			$ 179·2 162·7				90/60 (45/30)	Wood 7 (178)		22·0°					Pres: K. M. Honeyman
20 (32·1)		35 (56)					115/85 (57/42)	Oak 7 (178)	21" (533)	9·4°	2·05%	31·5		35	Pres: W. Murray
5 (8)		10 (16)					30 (15)								Leasee: A. T. Leary
5 (8)		8 (13)	$ 181·1 343·7	Air	AAR Standard		85 (42)			Rad 15 m	5%	25	2 600 (792)	8	Pres: D. C. Semonite
10 (16)		10 (16)	$ 593·0 611·5	W'hse Air	AAR Standard		90/67 (45/33)	Cedar 6 (153)	14" (360)	14·0°	2·2% U	32·8	498 (152)	30 (13)	Pres: H. H. Hutchings Jr Gen. Man. and Auditor: W. I. Hall
15 (24)		20 (32)	$ 112·0 110·0	N. York AB Co Air	Standard 34" (864)		130/100 (64·5/50)	Oak 6 (153)	21" (686)	11·0°	2·4%		1 179 (359)	5 (1)	Ex. VP & Gen Man: Harold R. Ammerman
25 (40)		30 (48)	$ 18 701·3 22 705·5	W'hse Air	Type E 34½" (877)		115 (57·5)	Oak 7 (178)	19½" (495)	8·0°	2·5% U	36·0	630 (192)	1 200 (185)	Pres & G. M.: R. E. Dowdy Vice Pres: R. G. Rubino
															Pres. F. H. Guffy
			$ 53 998 36 353												Gen. Man: M. S. Toon
25 (40)			$ 341·7 291·8	W'hse AB	Type E		90 (45)	Pine 6 (153)	20" (510)	30·0°	1·5%			30 (4)	Pres: Mrs C. F. Agee
				W'hse AB	Type E Nat. Mall		100 (49·6)	Oak 7 (178)	21" (533)	12·0°	1·5%	30			Pres: M. S. Toon
															Pres. and Gen. Man: W. B. Heckman
25 (40)	25 (40)			Air			75/85 (37/42·5)	Wood 6 & 7						20 (3)	Gen. Man: T. J. Pittman
15·7 (25·2)			$ 99 977·0 86 095·0	N York AB Co	Types E & H		131/85 (65/42)	Wood 7 (178)	20" (508)	18·0°	1·38% U	31		3 000	Trustee: B. H. Lacy
				W'hse	M.C.B.		159/60 (79/30)	Wood 7 (178)		38·0°	7·0% on float bridges			150	Pres. and Gen. Man: F. F. Dayton
															Gen. Man: J. L. Morey
22·2 (35·7)	34·6 (56)	79 (127)	$1 320 960·0 1 066 668·0	Air W'hse	Types E.F.H.		140/56 (69/28)	Wood 7 (178)	19·5-22 (496-559)	12·3°	2·2%	33	6 323 (1 927)	48 699	Chairman and Chief Executive Officer: Louis W. Menk Vice Chairman and Chief Operating Officer: Robert W. Downing
25 (40)		35 (56)	$ 4 657·2 3 908·7	Air W'hse			115/75 (57/37)	Wood 7 (178)	22" (560)	10·0°	1·0%	30	6 205 (1 891)	20	Pres. and Gen. Man: L. V. Kelly
10 (16)		25 (40)	$ 100·0 83·6	Air			85/60 (42/30)	Oak 6 (153)	21"					10	Pres. and Gen. Man: H. S. White
13 (21)	20 (32)	25 (40)	$ 772·6 1 009·5	Air W'hse	AAR		112/75 (56/37)	Wood 6/7 (153/180)	22" (560)	22·0°	3·0%	25	1 740 (530)	55 (8)	Pres. and Dir: R. B. Pamplin
15 (24)		40 (64)		W'hse Air	Type E 33½" (851)	Crs. 36½	90 (45)	Wood 7 (178)	14 (356)	16·0°	3·0% U		3 720 (1 200)	251 (120)	Pres: J. W. Wicks
															Gen. Man: R. N. Young
							60 (60)	Fir 6 (153)	20" (508)	16·0°	3·5%				Pres: V. S. Lindgren
				Air W'hse	Type E		131/70 (65/30)	Wood 7 (178)	22" (560)	16·0°	3·25%	30			
			$ 9 506 8 375												

NAME OF COMPANY ADDRESS	Gauge ft. in. (metres)	Route length incl. E=Electrified miles (km.)	Track length incl. E=Electrified miles (km.)	Elect. system and type of conductor	Loco-motives L=Line S=Shunt Steam Electric Diesel De=elec. Dh=hyd.		Rail-cars Electric Diesel Trailer Railbus Multiple Unit set	Pass. train cars	Freight train cars Con-tainers	Total Volume carried. Thous-ands of tonnes	Av'ge haul per ton miles (km.)	Av'ge net train load tonnes	Max. trailing load tonnes	Total number carried in 1 000's	Aver-age jour-ney miles (km.)
USA (contd.)															
Cananea Con Copper Cos R Cananea, Sonora, Tex	4' 8½" (1·435) 3' 0" (0·914)	32 (51)	32 (51)		DeS	2			137						
Canton Railroad Co PO Box 447, Baltimore, Md 21203	4' 8½" (1·435)	5·5 (10)	40·4 (64)		DeS	9				1 936·9				2 450	
Cape Fear Railways Inc PO Box 70, Fort Bragg, NC 28307	4' 8½" (1·435)	5·910 (10)	34		DeL	2			2	99·2					
Carbon County Railway Co PO Box 1007, E. Carbon Utah 84520	4' 8½" (1·435)	11 (18)			D	2			125						
Carrollton Railroad PO Box 116, Carrollton, Ky 41008	4' 8½" (1·435)	16 (25)			DeS	4				150·0	8·8 (14·16)				
Castle Valley RR Co Suite 670, 3333 So Bannock St, Englewood, Colo 80110	4' 8½" (1·435)	65 (105)	65 (105)												
Cedar Rapids & Iowa City Ry Co PO Box 351, Cedar Rapids, Iowa 52406	4' 8½" (1·435)	25 (40)	54 (86)	•	DeS	6			59	1 330·6	25 (40)			3 600	
Central California Traction Co 526 Mission St, San Francisco, Cal 94105	4' 8½" (1·435)	52 (84)	72 (116)		De	4					23 (37)				
Central Indiana Railway Co PO Box 993, Anderson, Ind (See Conrail)	4' 8½" (1·435)	27 (43)													
Central of Georgia Railway Co 99 Spring St, SW Atlanta, Ga 30303 (Southern Railway System)	4' 8½" (1·435)	2 208 (3 553)			DeL DeS	114 23				4 160					
Central Romana RR (Ferrocarrilles de Centrale Romana) PO Box 1329, Vero Beach, Fla 32960	4' 8½" (1·435)	235 (378)			DeL DhL D	11 3 1				950					
Central Vermont Railway Inc 2 Federal St, St Albans, Vt 05478 (Canadian National)	4' 8½" (1·435)	381 (590)	509 (817)		DeL DeS	14 1			1 061	2 232·6	270 067 000 ton-miles				0·322
Chattahoochee Indus RR POB 253, Cedar Springs, Ga 31732	4' 8½" (1·435)	15 (24)			DeS	6			722						
Chattahoochee Valley Railway Co PO Box 111, West Point, Ga 31833	4' 8½" (1·435)	10 (16)	10 (16)		DeS	2				259·5	10 (16)	235	1 300		
Chesapeake & Ohio Railway Co Terminal Tower, Cleveland, Ohio 44101 (See Chessie)	4' 8½" (1·435)	4 086 (6 576)	10 059 (16 000)		DeL DeS	885 100			72 411	111 884·4	258 (415)	2 364	24 000		
Chesapeake Western Railway PO Box 231, 141 W Bruce St, Harrisonburg, Va 22801	4' 8½" (1·435)	53 (85)	54 (87)		DeS	2				301·58	23·4 (37·6)				
Chessie System The Terminal Tower, Cleveland, Ohio 44101	4' 8½" (1·435)	11 000 (17 700)													
Chestnut Ridge Railway Co Palmerton, Pa. 18071	4' 8½" (1·435)	11 (18)	14 (23)		DeS	1									
*Chicago & Eastern Illinois RR Co 72 West Adams St, Chicago, Ill 60603 (Owned 45·2% by Missouri Pacific)	4' 8½" (1·435)	643 (1 035)	872 (1 403)		DeL DeS	36 6		42	3 314 C 24	15 652·2	184·5 (296)	1 955			234 (377)
Chicago Heights Terminal Transfer RR (Chicago & E. Illinois RR) 72 West Adams St, Chicago, Ill 60603	4' 8½" (1·435)	7 (11)	32 (52)		DeS	2			2 223	134·4					
Chicago & Illinois Midland Ry Co PO Box 139, Springfield, Ill 62707	4' 8½" (1·435)	121 (195)	175 (281)		DeL DeS	15 6			837	9 549·9			13 000		
Chicago & Illinois Western RR 233 N. Michigan Ave, Chicago, Ill 60601 (Illinois Central Railroad)	4' 8½" (1·435)	12 (19)	36 (58)		DS	4									
Chicago, Milwaukee, St Paul & Pacific RR Co 516 W. Jackson Blvd, Chicago, Ill 60606	4' 8½" (1·435)	10 200 (16 410) E 662 (966)		3 000 V dc OH	EL DeL DeS	38 264 232		69	30 125	42 640·3		1 569			
The Chicago & North Western Transportation Company 400 W. Madison St, Chicago, Ill 60606	4' 8½" (1·435)	10 168 (16 430)	14 864 (24 000)		DeL DeS	796 154		282	34 776				3 500	24 942	
Chicago River & Indiana Railroad Co. 680 Union Station, Chicago, Ill 60606	4' 8½" (1·435)	15 (25)	138 (220)		DeS	17									
Chicago, Rock Island & Pacific RR La Salle St Station, Chicago, Ill 60605	4' 8½" (1·435)	7 385 (11 870)	11 070 (17 816)*		DeL DeS	452 157		132	25 818 C 58	49 125·0	420 (675)				
Chicago Short Line Railway Co 9746 Avenue N, Chicago, Ill 60617	4' 8½" (1·435)	29 (47)	35 (56)		D	4			67						

* Merged into the Missouri Pacific 15 October 1976

Average Speeds			Financial Data	Braking (continuous)	Couplers	Buffers	Rails	Sleepers (crossties)		Curvature max.	Gradient max. (U=not compensated)	Axle load max.	Altitude max.	Staff employed. Total no. (inclu. workshop)	Names of officials. Extended lists can be found at the end of the individual country in the report section immediately following
Freight Train	Pass. Train	Speed max.	Revenue Expenses		Type and Height above rail	Centres and Height above rail	Weight	Type and thickness	Spacing Number per mile (per km) or centres ins (mm)						
mph (km/hr)	mph (km/hr)	mph (km/hr)	in 1 000's		ins (mm)	ins (mm)	lb. per yd (kg/m)	ins (mm)				tonnes	feet (m)		
6 (10)		10 (16)	$ 3 454·4 3 274·8	Air W'hse	Type E		90 (44·6)	Oak 7 (178)	22″ (560)	20·0°	1·5% 2·0%U		70 (22)	203 (14)	Pres: R. W. Dale, Jr
														22	Pres: J. Ostrom
							90 (44·6)	Wood 7 (178)		12·0°	1·67% 0·5%U				Pres: M. S. Toon
25 (40·2)							101 (50·1)	Oak 7″ (177·8)	20″ (508)	9°	3·0%U			7	Gen Man: R. D. Tigar
															Pres: W. Teel
12 (19)	35 (56)		$ 1 660·3 823·0	W'hse Air	AAR 32½″ (825)		100/90 (50/45)	Oak 6 (153)	21″ (533)	6·0°	1·5%	40	685 (209)	69 (9)	Gen. Man: D. Arnold
							75/70 (37/35)	Wood 6 (153)	22″ (559)	6·0°	0·7%				Pres: R. W. Walker
															Pres: J. E. Martin
17·5 (28·2)	57 (92)	79 (127)	$ 81 266 53 969	N York AB	AAR 34½ (876)		132/56 (66/28)	Wood 7 (178)	20″ (508)	6·0°	2·21% 2·05%U	32	1 070 (326)	1 253 (77)	Pres: R. E. Franklin
															Pres: A. Carta
35 (56)	50 (80)	55 (88)	$ 11 490 10 757	AB-ABD	E 32½ (825)		90/115 (45/57)	Wood 7 (178)	3 200		1·9%	25	1 008 (303)	420	Pres and Chairman: R. A. Bandeen Gen Man: P. C. Larson
															Pres: B. P. Ellen
12 (19)		20 (32)	$ 409·4 403·0	W'hse	Type E Beth'm		80/70 (40/35)	Oak 7 (178)	22″ (560)	11·0°	2·0%	30	600 (183)	29 (4)	Pres: G. W. Neal
17·7 (38·6)	42·2 (67·9)	F. 60 (97) P. 70 (113)	$ 568 830 415 650	W'hse NYAB	Types E & F 34½ (876)		140/85 (69·4/42)	Wood 7 (178)	21″ (538)	Main 10·0° Branch 18·0°	Main 2·76% Branch 4·3%U	39·3	Main 2 082 Branch 3 408	23 000 (5 000)	Chairman of Board and Chief Exec. Officer: Hays T. Watkins
20 (32·18)		20 (32·18)		W'hse	Standard		80/85 (40/42)	Wood 6 (153)	3 168 (1 980)	6·0°	6·0%			31 (10)	Pres: R. F. Dunlap
							80 (40)	Wood 7 (178)	22″ (560)	10·0°	3·0%				Gen. Man: A. F. Halmi
22 (35)	47 (75)	79 (127)	$ 44 367 32 484	N York AB Co	Type E & H Tightlock 34½ (876)		115/90 (57/45)	Wood 6 (153)	20″ (508)	8°	0·9%	30	769 (234)		Pres: J. H. Lloyd
				N York AB Co	Type E		112/90 (56/45)	Wood 6 (150)	20″ (508)	12°	1%	30	620 (204)	24 (0)	
25 (40)	40 (64)		$ 13 826·0 12 171·0	W'hse N York Air	Type E AAR 33½ (851)		132/75 (65·5/37)	Wood 6 (153) 7 (178)	3 000 (1 860)	10°	1·64%U	26·3	616 (188)	482	Pres: Carl D. Forth Vice Pres and Gen Man: William G. Harvey
				AB N York	Type E		90 (45)	Oak 6 (153)	24″ (610)	8·0°	0·61%				Pres: J. F. Palmer
21·8 (35)	45·0 (72·4)	100 (160)	$ 392 842·0 416 487·0	Air	AAR		132/115 (66/57)	Wood 7 (178)	3 250 (2 030)	15·33°	1·0% Electric 2·2%		6 317 (1 925)	16 470 (6 012)	Pres: W. L. Smith Chairman of Board and Chief Executive Officer William J. Quinn
17 (27·4)	34·9 (56·2)		$ 458 990·0 455 983·0	Air W'hse. N York AB Co	Types D.E.F. 32½/34½ (825/876)		115/60 (57/30)	Wood 6/7 (153/178)	20½/23 (520/585)	Main 3·0° Branch 6·0°	Main 1·35% Branch 2·5% U	33·5	6 028 (1 837)	15 252 (6 220)	Pres: J. R. Wolfe
			$ 4 394 3 601·5	Air			105 (52)	Wood 8 (203)	23″ (585)			23	16 (5)	258 (21)	Pres: K. E. Smith
21·5 (34·6)	43·4 (69·8)	90 (145)	$ 384 835 650 660	Air AB	Types E.F.H. and Tightlock 34½ (876)		136/60 (68/30)	Wood 7 (178)	21″ (530)	12·2°	Main 1·0% Branch 3·6%	Coopers E 60	6 880 (2 097)	14 354 (2 765)	Pres: William J. Dixon
							90 (45)	Oak 6 (153)	21″ (533)						Trustee: William M. Gibbons Pres. and Chief Ext. Officer: John W. Ingran

USA (contd.)

NAME OF COMPANY / ADDRESS	Gauge ft. in. (metres)	Route length incl. E=Electrified miles (km.)	Track length incl. E=Electrified miles (km.)	Elect. system and type of conductor	Locomotives L=Line S=Shunt / Steam Electric Diesel De=elec. Dh=hyd.	Rail-cars Electric Diesel Trailer Railbus Multiple Unit set	Pass. train cars	Freight train cars / Containers	Freight movement — Total Volume carried. Thousands of tonnes	Av'ge haul per ton miles (km.)	Av'ge net train load tonnes	Max. trailing load tonnes	Passengers — Total number carried in 1 000's	Average journey miles (km.)
Chicago South Shore & South Bend RR North Carroll Ave., Michigan City, Ind 46360	4' 8½" (1·435)	E 73·8 (117)	E 93·6 (149)	1 500 V dc OH	EL 3, DeL 8	E 49, T 6	57	60	5 675·4	148 827 974 ton-miles			1 768·3	31 (50)
Chicago & Western Indiana RR Co 80 E. Jackson Blvd, Chicago 5, Ill 60604	4' 8½" (1·435)	27 (43)	137 (220)											
Chicago, West Pullman & Southern RR Co 2728 E 104th St, Chicago, Ill 60617	4' 8½" (1·435)	30 (48)	31 (50)		DeS 10			396						
Cincinnati, New Orleans & Texas Pacific Rly Co (Southern Rly System)	4' 8½" (1·435)	337 (542)	817 (1 315)		DL 124, DS 48		46	8 098	14 360·2	184 (296)	1 690		137·8	256 (412)
City of Prineville Railway 10th and Main Sts, PO Box 338, Prineville, Oreg 97754	4' 8½" (1·435)	18 (29)	27 (43)		DeL 3			202*	389·1	7 135 305 ton-km				
Claremont and Concord Rly Co 100 Federal St, Boston, Ma 02110, Claremont, NH	4' 8½" (1·435)	14 (23)			DeS 2			10						
Clarendon & Pittsford RR Co 267 Battery St, Burlington, Vt 05401	4' 8½" (1·435)	20 (32)	23 (37)		De 1			60	100·8	5·1 (8·0)	325			
Cliffside Railroad Co Cliffside, NC 28024	4' 8½" (1·435)	4 (6)			S 2									
Clinchfield Railroad Co 229 Nolichucky Ave, Erwin, Tenn 37650 (Subsidiary of Seaboard Coast Line RR)	4' 8½" (1·435)	275 (442)	490 (788)		DeL 91, DeS 12, S 1			5 683			2 347			
Colorado & Southern Railway Co 1405 Curtis St, Denver, Colo 80202 (Subsidiary of BN)	4' 8½" (1·435)	683 (1 099)	1 103 (1 791)		DeL 94, DeS 10			2 878	9 326·6	2 516 637 ton-km				
Colorado & Wyoming Railway Co PO Box 316, Pueblo, Colo. 81002	4' 8½" (1·435)	39 (63)	117 (188)		DeL 6, DeS 13			799	4 745·1	7·7 (12·4)				
Columbia & Cowlitz Railway Co PO Box 188, Longview, Wash 98632	4' 8½" (1·435)	8 (13)	15 (24)		DeL 2			78	704·3	6·5 (10·5)				
Columbia, Newberry & Laurens R. R. Co. 500 Water St, Jacksonville, Fla 32202	4' 8½" (1·435)	75 (121)	88 (142)		DeL 5			1	1 660·0	61·3 (98·7)	1 117	1 830		
Columbus & Greenville Railway Co 1302 Main St, Columbus Miss 39701 (Merged into Illinois Central Gulf in Sept 1972)	4' 8½" (1·435)	168 (270)	225 (351)		DeL 12, DeS 8			345			3 000	6 000		
Condon, Kinzua & Southern RR Co Kinzua, Ore 97849	4' 8½" (1·435)	24 (39)			D 1									
Conemaugh & Black Lick Railroad Co 1275 Daly Ave, Bethlehem, Pa 18015	4' 8½" (1·435)	9 (14)	47 (76)		DeS 27			25						
†ConRail Consolidated Rail Corp 1040 Six Penn Center Plaza, Philadelphia, Pa 19104	4' 8½" (1·435)	17 000 (27 358) E 822 (1 322)	34 000 (54 717) E 2 962 (4 760)		D 4 507, E 148				151 614	79 500 000 000 ton-miles			360·0‡	
Conway Scenic RR Inc Norcross Circle, N Conway, NH 03860	4' 8½" (1·435)	7·5 (12)			SS 2, De 1		10	4						
Coopers Town and Charlotte Valley R Corp 1 Railroad Ave, Cooperstown, NY 13326	4' 8½" (1·435)	16 (26)			SL 1, DeL 1		6	23						
Corinth & Counce RR Co PO Box 128, Highway 57, Counce, Tenn 38326	4' 8½" (1·435)	26 (40)	26 (40)		DeS 3			437	1 382·5	221 121 344 ton-km				
Curtis Milburn & Eastern RR PO Box 540, Cheholis, Wash 98532														
Cuyahoga Valley Railway Co 315 Clark Ave, Cleveland, Ohio 44101	4' 8½" (1·435)	10 (16)	15 (24)		DeS 14			215	5 500·0					
Dansville & Mount Morris RR Co Dansville, NY 14437	4' 8½" (1·435)	10 (16)	12·2 (19)		DeL 2			0	58·6	10 (16)		1 000		
Dardanelle & Russellville RR Co 101 Sth Front St, PO Box 150, Dardenelle, Ark 72834	4' 8½" (1·435)	5 (8)	7 (11)		DeL 3, Dh 1				214·0	2·4 (4)	611			
Davenport, Rock Island & North-Western Rly Co 1025, Harrison St, Davenport, Iowa 52801	4' 8½" (1·435)	48 (76)			DeS 7			10						
Delaware & Hudson Railway Corp Delaware & Hudson Bldg, 40 Beaver St, Albany, NY 12207	4' 8½" (1·435)	1 400 (2 253)			DeL 178		24	6 034			1 997			
Delray Connecting Railroad Co PO Box 266, Detroit, Mich 48232	4' 8½" (1·435)	4·1 (6·5)	18·5 (29)		DeS 3			160	975·8	3·0 (4·8)		1 050		
Delta Valley & Southern Railway 1 Park St, Wilson, Ark 72395	4' 8½" (1·435)	2 (3)	4 (6)		DeL 1		0	0	75·0	1·5 (2·4)	450			

* 200 freight cars leased
† ConRail took over portions of six bankrupt carriers on 1 April 1976: Penn Central; Reading; Central of New Jersey; Erie Lackawana; Lehigh Valley; and Lehigh and Hudson River
‡ Daily average

Average Speeds			Financial Data	Braking	Couplers	Buffers	Rails	Sleepers (crossties)		Curvature	Gradient	Axle	Altitude	Staff	Names of officials
Freight Train	Pass. Train	Speed max.	Revenue Expenses	(continuous)	Type and Height above rail	Centres and Height above rail	Weight	Type and thickness	Spacing Number per mile (per km) or centres ins (mm)	max.	max. (U=not compensated)	load max.	max.	employed Total no. (inclu. workshop)	Extended lists can be found at the end of the individual country in the report section immediately following
mph (km/hr)	mph (km/hr)	mph (km/hr)	in 1 000's		ins (mm)	ins (mm)	lb. per yd (kg/m)	ins (mm)				tonnes	feet (m)		
40 (64)	60 (96)	79 (128)	$ 12 118·0 386·2	Air W'hse	AAR 33 (874)		115/100 (57/50)	Oak 6 (153)	3 250 (2 030)	14·4%	2·5%		826 (252)	413 (45)	Pres. and Gen. Man: A. W. Dudley
	60 (96)						115/80 (57/40)	Wood 7 (178)	20" (508)	13·5	2·4%	36	580 (177)	732 (115)	Pres: J. H. Park
														200	Pres. and Gen. Man: J. E. Rice
			$ 76 265 47 725	W'hse 14 E.L.											Man: G. S. Gray
15 (24)	20 (32)		$ 896 647	W'hse	Type E 32½ (825)		90/60 (45/30)	Fir 6 (153)	22" (559)	10·0°	3·5%	25	2 800 (850)	25	Pres: Riley L. Allen
															Vice Pres: K. H. Lemnah
	30 (48)			Air W'hse 14 EL	Type E Nat. Mal.		80/70 (40/35)	Wood 6 (153)	18" (458)	18·0°	4·5%	33·5	600 (183)	10	Pres: H. T. Filskov
															Pres: P. C. Gratale
20 (32)		55 (86)	$ 39 225 24 833	Air W'hse	31½/34½ (800/876)		132/115 (126/57)	Wood 7 (180)	19½ (500)	14°	1·2% 1·5% U	36	2 630 (802)	1 207 (225)	Gen. Man: T. D. Moore
21·5 (34·6)		49 (79)	$ 29 323·9 29 323·6	W'hse Air	Tightlock 34½ (876)		112/90 (56/45)	Wood 7 (178)	Main 3 168 (1 910) Branch 2 756 (1 660)	15·0°	2·0% U	31	11 320 (3 450)	874 (89)	Pres: G. F. Defiel
								Wood 7/9 (178/229)		10·0°	2·0%	33·4			Pres: F. H. Jones
20 (32)			$ 1 918·3 1 589·9	Air 26 L			90/85/112 (45/42/56)	Wood 7 (178)	(3 000)	14°	2·5%	30		24	Pres: J. H. Wilkinson Vice Pres. and Gen. Man Tom S. Brace
14 (22·5)	40 (64)			Air W'hse	Auto 34½ (876)		115/75 (51/37)	Wood 7 (178) 6 (153)	19½" (495)	6°	1·3%	30		46 (0)	Pres: P. F. Osborn
30 (48·2)	45 (72)			W'hse N York	Type E 34½ (876)		85/60 (42/30)	Wood 8 (203)	24" (610)	12·0°	1·6%	19	447 (136)	175	Pres: H. C. Bitner
							80/60 (40/30)	Wood 7 (178)	20" (508)	12·0°	1·67%	26·25			Gen. Man: H. W. Stuchell
														534	Pres: R. J. Kent
			$ 2 447 292·0 2 614 137·0											95 742	Chairman and Chief Exec: E. G. Jordan
															Pres: D. A. Smith
															Pres: W. G. Rich
25 (32)	25 (40)		$ 2 504 900·8	Air Ny-6BL	AAR Type E 34" (860)		115/85 (57/42)	Wood 6 (153) 7 (180)	20" (508)	8·0°	1·5%	32·8	496 (151)	37	Pres: C. W. Byrd
															Pres: J. R. Callaghan
6 (9·7)							115 (57)								Pres: L. E. Smith
5 (8)	35 (58)		$ 241·5 120·5	Air W'hse	Type D BSC		90/60 (45/30)	Wood 7" (178)	2 820 (1 762)	22°	2·0%	33		13 (3)	Gen Man: R. F. Hart
10 (16)	20 (32)		$ 166·0 156·0	Air	Standard		75/65 (37/33)	Wood 6 (150)	24" (610)			33		16 (2)	Pres: D. C. Phelps
															Gen Man: B. A. Webster
17·1 (27·5)	32·5 (52·3)		$ 44 415 35 526	N York AB Co			132/80 (66/40)	Wood 7 (178)	20" (508)	14·0°	0·88% 1·36%U			2 136	Pres: C. B. Sterzing
5 (8)				Air W'hse	Type E 34½ (876)		115/80 (57/40)	Wood 6 (153)	22" (559)			25		59 (25)	Pres: Chas. A. O'Brien
15 (24)				Air W'hse			75/56 (37/28)	Wood 7 (178)					220 (67)	8	Gen Man: M. A. Davisor

USA (contd.)

NAME OF COMPANY / ADDRESS	Gauge ft. in. (metres)	Route length incl. E=Electrified miles (km.)	Track length incl. E=Electrified miles (km.)	Elect. system and type of conductor	Locomotives L=Line S=Shunt (De=elec. Dh=hyd.)	Rail-cars (R=Railbus)	Pass. train cars	Freight train cars / Containers	Total Volume carried. Thousands of tonnes	Av'ge haul per ton miles (km.)	Av'ge net train load tonnes	Max. trailing load tonnes	Total number carried in 1 000's	Average journey miles (km.)
Denver & Rio Grande Western RR Co PO Box 5482, 1515 Arapahoe St, Denver, Colo 80217	4' 8½" (1·435) Narrow gauge	1 811 (3 025) 45 (72)	3 166 (5 085)		DeL 235 DeS 20 SL 3*		19	8 742	29 127·8	336·2 (531·0)	1 780	12 000	250	65·1 (104·8)
Denver Union Terminal Rly Co 233 Union St, Denver, Colo 80202	4' 8½" (1·435)		6 (10)											
Des Moines Terminal Co 205 Hubbell Bldg, Des Moines, Iowa 50309	4' 8½" (1·435)		9 294 (14 980)											
Des Moines Union Railway Co 902 Walnut Street, Des Moines, Iowa 50309 (CMSt P & P and N & W own 50% each)	4' 8½" (1·435)	6 021 (10)	39·6 (68)		DeS 4									
Detroit and Mackinac Railway 120 Oak St, Tawas City, Mich 48763	4' 8½" (1·435)	398 (641)	453 (729)		DeL 10		5	964	2 476·0		294 407 000 ton-km		0	
Detroit Terminal Railroad Co Detroit 12, Mich	4' 8½" (1·435)	18 (29)	158 (254)		DeS 13			11						
Detroit. Toledo & Ironton RR Co One Park Lane Blvd, Dearborn, Mich 48126	4' 8½" (1·435)	476 (766)	758 (1 220)		DeL 69			4 237	13 070·4	110 (177)	1 377			
Detroit & Toledo Shore Line 131 W. Lafayette Ave, Detroit 26, Mich	4' 8½" (1·435)	59 (95)	174 (280)		DeL 10 DeS 6			841	4 944·4	46 (74)	963·9	9 000		
Duluth, Missabe & Iron Range Rly Co Missabe Bdg, Duluth, Minn 55802	4' 8½" (1·435)	462 (744)	599 (970)					8 559						
Duluth & North-Eastern RR Co Ave C & Arch St, Cloquet, Minn 55720	4' 8½" (1·435)	11 (18)	18 (29)		DeS 3 DeL 1					420·2	11 (18)			
Duluth, Winnepeg & Pacific Rly (Canadian National) 131 W. Lafayette Blvd, Detroit, Mich 48226	4' 8½" (1·435)	43 (69)			DeS 3			32						
Durham & Southern Rly Co PO Box 451, Durham, NC 27702	4' 8½" (1·435)	59 (95)		DeL 4			50							
East Camden & Highland RR Box 7305, Erie, Pa 16510	4' 8½" (1·435)	25 (40)												
East Erie Commercial Railroad 1030 Lawrence Parkway, Erie, Pa 16510 (General Electric Co.)	4' 8½"† (1·435)	12½ (20) E 3 (5)	12½ (20) E 3 (5)	Catenary and third rail	DeS 3			60	23·0					
East Jersey Railroad & Terminal Co. East 22nd St, Bayonne, NJ	4' 8½" (1·435)	3 (5)			DeS 2									
East St. Louis Junction RR Co National Stockyards, Ill 62071	4' 8½" (1·435)		16 (26)		D 2				12 265 Cars					
East Tennessee & Western North Carolina RR Co 132 Legion St., Johnson City, Tenn 37601	4' 8½" (1·435)	11 (17)	22 (35)		DeL 2				388·0	8 (13)		1 500		
East Washington Railway Co 6701, Geo Palmer Highway, Seat Pleasant, Md 20027	4' 8½" (1·435)	4 (6)	5 (8)		DeS 1	R 2								
Edgmoor & Manetta Railway	4' 8½" (1·435)	3 (5)			De 1									
El Dorado & Wesson Railway Co PO Box 46, El Dorado, Ark 71730	4' 8½" (1·435)	6 (10)	12 (20)		D 3			2						
Elgin, Joliet & Eastern Ry Co PO Box 899, Gary, Ind 46401	4' 8½" (1·435)	200 (320)	1 000 (1 600)		DeL 44 DeS 59			11 242			1 376			
‡**Erie Lackawanna Railway Co** Buffalo, NY 14206	4' 8½" (1·435)	3 029 (4 860)												
Escanaba & Lake Superior RR Co 827 Wells Bldg, Milwaukee, Wis 53202	4' 8½" (1·435)	63 (101)	87 (135)		DeS 5			79	192·0					
El Paso Union Passenger Dept Co Rm 2, Union Depot, El Paso, Tex 79901	4' 8½" (1·435)	3·25 (5·2)	3·25 (5·2)											
Everett Railroad Co. PO Box 96, Everett, Pa 15537	4' 8½" (1·435)	3·6 (5·6)	4·9 (8·1)		DeL 1									
Fairport, Painesville & Eastern Rly. Co. PO Box 229, Painesville, Ohio 44077	4' 8½" (1·435)	20 (32)			DeS 8			85						
Feliciana Eastern RR Co PO Box 47127, Dallas, Tx 75247	4' 8½" (1·435)	0·5 (0·8)			DeL 2									
Ferdinand Railroad Co. PO Box 47127, Dallas, Tex 75247	4' 8½" (1·435)	6 (10)	7 (11)		DeL 1				24·2	14 (12)	130			
Fernwood, Columbia & Gulf RR Co Fernwood, Miss 39635 (Acquired by ICG in September, 1972)	4' 8½" (1·435)	44 (71)	47 (72·4)		DeL 2								0	
Florida East Coast Railway Co Suite 395, 2220 Parklake Dr, NE Atlanta, Ga 30345	4' 8½" (1·435)	530 (680)	1 029 (1 640)		DL 53 DS 4			1 490	6 828·7	197 (317)				

* Narrow gauge
† 7 other gauges used for locomotives testing. Electrified line is used for this purpose only.
‡ Taken over by ConRail 1 April 1976

Average Speeds			Financial Data		Couplers	Buffers	Rails	Sleepers (crossties)							
Freight Train	Pass. Train	Speed max.	Revenue Expenses	Braking (con-tinuous)	Type and Height above rail	Centres and Height above rail	Weight	Type and thick-ness	Spacing Number per mile (per km) or centres	Curva-ture max.	Gradient max. (U=not compen-sated)	Axle load max.	Alti-tude max.	Staff em-ployed. Total no. (inclu. work-shop)	Names of officials. Extended lists can be found at the end of the individual country in the report section immediately following
mph (km/hr)	mph (km/hr)	mph (km/hr)	in 1 000's		ins (mm)	ins (mm)	lb. per yd (kg/m)	ins (mm)	ins (mm)			tonnes	feet (m)		
26·6 (42·8)	38 (61)	P. 70 (113) F. 70 (113)	$ 168 503·0 125 762·0	Air W'hse.	Types E and P		136/112 (67/56)	Wood 8 (203) 9 (229)	19½" (495)	12·8°	3·0%	36	10 221 (3 115)	3 502 (654)	Chief Exec.: G. B. Aydelott
															Pres: W. J. Hottman
															Pres: R. G. Beers
			$ 1 162·6 1 735·6	Air	AAR		115/75 (57/37)	Oak 7 (178)	16" (407)					109 (15)	Pres: M. Garelick
25 (41)	35 (56)		$ 4 828·0 3 967·0	Air	AAR		100/85 (50/42)	Wood 6 (150)	20" (508)	1·0°	1·0%U			150	Chr: C. A. Pinkerton Jr
15 (24·14)							100/30 (50/40)	Wood 6"(153)	21½" (547)	4°	0·8%U	35			Pres: L. A. Baggerly
10 (16)	49 (79)		$ 45 213·0 36 322·0	N York AB Co W'hse.	Type E 34½ (876)		140/85 (69·4/ 42·5)	Wood 7 (178)	22" (559)	16·0°	1·8%U	38	1 217 (371)	1 623 (484)	Pres: R. A. Sharp
20 (32)	49 (79)		$ 7 062 6 286	Air	Auto. 34½ (876)		100 (50)	Wood 7 (178)	18" (460)	4·3°	0·33%	35	599 (183)	360 (70)	Pres: R. F. Dunlap
			$ 59 674 38 013	W'hse	Type E		115 (57)	Wood 7 (178)	21" (533)	6·0°	0·6%			1 602	Pres: M. S. Toon
15 (24)	25 (40)		$ 949·2 557·3	Air W'hse			80/60 (40/30)	Wood 7 (178)	22" (559)					38 (18)	Pres and Gen. Man: R. N. Congreve
			$ 14 789 9 115												Pres: J. H. Burdakin
															Pres: G. W. Hill
															Pres: R. S. O'Connor
		80 (129)	$ 486	Air Various	AAR Standard 34" (860)		100 (50)	Oak 7 (178)	22" (559)	19°	2·5%U	33	750 (229)	24 (9)	Pres and Gen Man: D. E. Sheeran
															Pres: T. P. Connelly
5 (8)				W'hse	Type E Am. Steel		90/80 (45/40)	Oak 6 (153)	21" (533)	16·0°	Level	17			Pres: G. Novotny
10 (16)			$ 563·0 488·4				112/70 (56/35)	Wood 6 (153)	2 400 (1 500)				1 600 (488)	24 (5)	Gen. Man: K. E. Wilhoit
			$ 158·2 92·9				80 (40)								Pres: W. V. Hodges
															Pres: W. Heath
															Pres: H. D. Reynolds
		45 (72)	$ 90 471 61 040				131/80 (65/40)	Wood 6 (153)	3 200 (2 000)	Main 3·0°	1·2%	32·5		3 000 (500)	Pres: M. S. Toon
			241 414				140/112 (60/56)	Wood	3 250 (2 050)	9·0°	1·3%				
25 (40)	35 (56)		$ 545·8 493·7	W'hse	Type E		90/75 (45/37)	Wood 6 (153)	3 000 (1 870)	6·0°		30	1 397 (426)	26 (6)	Pres: N. A. Lemke Vice Pres. & Gen. Man: L. L. Hamilton
															Pres: R. O. Coltrin
5 (8)	10 (16)	20 (32)	$ 23 626·9 19 902·4		Standard		100/70 (50/35)	Wood 6 (153)	24"	6·0°	2·08%				Pres: Donald S. Laher
															Pres: A. P. Ford
							90/75 (45/37)	Wood 6 (153)	21" (530)	4·0°	2·75% U				Pres: R. O. Evans
13 (21)	20 (32)		$ 42·3 33·5	Air NYBL			56 (28)	Woood 6 (150)	18" (457)		4·0%	33		4	Gen. Man: L. R. Greaves
30 (32)				Air			60 (30)	Wood 6" & 7"	21" (530)					51 (4)	Gen. Man: T. J. Pittman
		60 (96)	$ 47 612 27 618	Air	Auto		132/90 (65/45)	Wood Conc. 7 (178)	21"/24"	8·5°	3·17%	65	42 13)	1 030 (201)	Pres: W. L. Thornton

NAME OF COMPANY ADDRESS	Gauge ft. in. (metres)	Route length incl. E=Electrified miles (km.)	Track length incl. E=Electrified miles (km.)	Elect. system and type of conductor	Loco-motives L=Line S=Shunt Steam Electric Diesel De=elec. Dh=hyd.		Rail-cars Electric Diesel Trailer Railbus Multiple Unit set	Pass. train cars	Freight train cars Con-tainers	Freight movement Total Volume carried. Thous-ands of tonnes	Av'ge haul per ton miles (km.)	Av'ge net train load tonnes	Max. trailing load tonnes	Passengers Total number carried in 1 000's	Aver-age jour-ney miles (km.)

USA *(contd.)*

NAME OF COMPANY ADDRESS	Gauge	Route length	Track length	Elect.	Loco L/S		Rail-cars	Pass.	Freight	Total Vol.	Av'ge haul	Av'ge load	Max. load	Passengers	Av journey
Fonda, Johnstown & Gloversville RR 111 W. Fulton St., Gloversville, NY 12078	4' 8½" (1·435)	20 (32)	31 (50)		DeL 2				260	73·0	11 (18)	250			
Fordyce & Princeton R.R. Co. PO Box 660, Fordyce, Ark 71742	4' 8½" (1·435)	1·5 (2)	2·4 (4)		DeS 1							300	400		
Fore River Railroad Corp. 145 East Howard S., Quincy, Mass 02169	4' 8½" (1·435)		3 (5)		DeS 2										
Fort Smith & Van Buren Rly. Co. 114 W. Eleventh St, Kansas City, Mo 64105	4' 8½" (1·435)	21 (24)													
Fort Worth Belt Railway Co. North Fort Worth, Tex *(Subsidiary of Missouri Pacific)*	4' 8½" (1·435)	3 (5)	18 (29)		D 1										
Fort Worth & Denver Railway Co PO Box 943, Fort Worth, Tex 76101	4' 8½" (1·435)	1 241 (2 001)			DL 12 DS 8				1 370						
Frankfort & Cincinnati RR Co Union Passenger Depot, Frankfort, Ky 40601	4' 8½" (1·435)	7 (11)			DeS 4										
Gainesville Midland Railroad Co 3600 W. Broad St, Richmond, Va 23230	4' 8½" (1·435)	42 (68)	51 (82)		DeS 1				1						
Galveston, Houston & Henderson RR Co PO Box 28, Galveston, Tex 77550	4' 8½" (1·435)	49 (79)	105 (169)												
Galveston Wharves PO Box 328, Galveston, Tex 77553 *(Owned by City of Galveston)*	4' 8½" (1·435)	45 (72)	50 (80)		DeS 6										
Garden City Western Railway Co PO Box 597, Garden City, Kans 67846	4' 8½" (1·435)	14 (23)	17 (27)		DeL 2					164·4	8 (12·9)				
Genesee and Wyoming RR Co 3846 Retsof Road, NY 14539	4' 8½" (1·435)	12 (19)	23 (37)		DeL 4 DeS 2		1		208	1 700	11 (18)	5 000			
Georgia Railroad 1590 Marietta Blvd, NW Atlanta, Ga 30318 *(Subsidiary of Seaboard Coast Line RR)*	4' 8½" (1·435)	331 (533)	521 (838)		DL 18 DS 15		2		1 407						
Georgia Northern Railway Co PO Box 152, Moultrie, Ga 31768	4' 8½" (1·435)	68 (109)			DeS 1										
Georgia, Southern & Florida Ry Co *(Southern Railway System)*	4' 8½" (1·435)	397 (639)	565 (909)		DL 44 DS 4				46			1 041			
Gettysburg RR Co Box 631, Gettysburg, Pa 17325	4' 8½" (1·435)	23 (37)			DeL 4			5	4						
Grafton & Upton Railroad Co Depot St, Hopedale, Mass 01747	4' 8½" (1·435)	15 (24)			DeL 1 DeS 1										
Graham County Railroad Co Oil City, Pa	4' 8½" (1·435)	12 (19)			D 1				2						
Grand Trunk Western RR Co *(Subsidiary of Grand Trunk Corp)* 131 W. Lafayette Blvd., Detroit, Mich. 48226	4' 8½" (1·435)	1 235 (1 979)	1 939 (3 110)		DeL 122 DeS 73		17 *		10 183	81 259·6	8 162 641 000 ton-miles			331·4	14 (23)
Graysonia, Nashville & Ashdown RR Co 210 S. Front St, Nashville, Ark 71852	4' 8½" (1·435)	32 (51)	50 (80)		DeS 3				14	523	7 846 321 ton-km				
Great Southwest RR Inc 1169 109th St, Grand Prairie, Tex 75050	4' 8½" (1·435)		22 (35)		DeS 2										
Great Western Railway Co PO Box 5308, Terminal Annex, Denver, Colo 80217	4' 8½" (1·435)	58 (93)	77 (124)		DeL 5				226	600·4					
† **Green Bay & Western Railroad Co** PO Box 2507, Green Bay, Wis 54306	4' 8½" (1·435)	255 (410)	305 (526)		DeL 16				1 450	2 492·2	284 565 000 ton-miles				
Green Mountain Railroad Corp PO Box 57, Chester Depot, Vt, 05144	4' 8½" (1·435)	52 (80)	56 (90)		DeL 6		2		16	109·0 (61)	38	515	850	33·9	11 (18)
Greenville & Northern Railway Co Depot Sq, Barre, Ut 05641	4' 8½" (1·435)	14 (22)	16 (26)		DeS 3				10						
Gulf, Mobile & Ohio Railroad Co 104 St. Francis St., Mobile, Ala 36602 *(Merged with Illinois Central RR)*	4' 8½" (1·435)	2 240 (3 604)			DL 167 DS 91	D 3 T 3	3		12 487	497 000 car-loadings					
Hampton & Branchville RR Co PO Box 56, Hampton, SC 29924	4' 8½" (1·435)	17 (27)	49 (79)		DeL 4	D 1									
Harbor Belt Line Railroad 340 Water St., Wilmington, Cal 9074 *(Terminal Switching Line for Atchison Topeka and Santa Fe Ry Co)*	4' 8½" (1·435)		120 (193)		D 3										
Hartford and Slocomb RR PO Box 2243, Dothan, Ala 36301	4' 8½" (1·435)	20 (32)	24 (38)		DeL 2				100	63 124	18 (29)	5 000			
Hartwell Railway Co Box 429, Hartwell, Ga 30643	4' 8½" (1·435)	10 (16)	11 (18)		DeS 2										

* Owned by SEMTA
† Including Kewaunee, Green Bay and Western RR Co, forming a through line from Kewaunee, Wisconsin (on Lake Michigan) via Green Bay to Winona, Minnesota

Freight Train mph (km/hr)	Pass. Train mph (km/hr)	Speed max. mph (km/hr)	Revenue Expenses in 1 000's	Braking (continuous)	Couplers Type and Height above rail ins (mm)	Buffers Centres and Height above rail ins (mm)	Rails Weight lb. per yd (kg/m)	Sleepers Type and thickness ins (mm)	Spacing Number per mile or centres ins (mm)	Curvature max.	Gradient max. (U=not compensated)	Axle load max. tonnes	Altitude max. feet (m)	Staff employed. Total no. (inclu. workshop)	Names of officials. Extended lists can be found at the end of the individual country in the report section immediately following
15 (26)							80/60 (40/30)	Wood 6 (153)	21" (533)	14.0°	2.75%	Coopers E-60	850 (259)	26 (3)	Pres: W. Rich
6 (10)	15 (24)		$ 43.9 41.8	Air W'hse	AAR	AAR	60/85 (30/42)	Wood 7 (178)	21" (534)	12°	1.0% U	27.5		3	Pres: R. Tedder Supt: Tom Branch
							85 (42)	Wood 9 (229)							Pres: C. L. Hartshorn
			$ 36 849 27 462												Pres: G. F. Defiel
															Gen. Man: B. A. Raine
															Pres: W. T. Rice
25 (40)							115/90 (57/45)	Pine 7 (178)	19½" (495)	4.0°	0.75%	Coopers E-52	53 (16)	67 (8)	Gen. Man: J. M. Bynum
			$ 1 146 825 1 382 111				112/70 (56/35)	Wood 8 (203)	14" (356)	20.0°	1.0% 1.0% U			430 (13)	Chairman Board of Trustees: J. Yarborough Gen. Man: C. S. Devoy
15 (24)		30 (48)					85/70 (42/35)	Wood 6 (153)	20" (508)					5	Pres: W. F. Stoeckly
30 (48)	40 (64)		$ 1 984.5 1 697.2	Air W'hse	Standard 30½ (775)		130/80 (64/40)	Wood 6 (153)	21" (534)	12.0°	1.12% 1.12% U	33	763 (233)	52 (11)	Pres: M. B. Fuller
			$ 11 258 10 100				100 (50)	Oak 7 (173)	20" (508)	3.0°	1.0%				Gen. Man: M. S. Jones Jnr.
															Pres: W. L. Pippin
			$ 21 943 12 858	W'hse.											Gen. Man: S. Cornell
															Gen. Man: F. H. Abbott
															Oper. Man: H. E. Chandler
20.6 (33.2)	23.7 (38)	84 (135)	$ 152 600.0 148 500.0	W'hse	E.F.H. 34½ (876)		132/100 (65/50)	Oak 8 (203)	18" (457)	14.3°	0.5% U	33	1 023 (312)	4 200	Pres: J. H. Burdakin Exec. Asst. & Corp. Sec: E. G. Fontaine
							85 (42)	Pine 6 (153)	21" (533)		1%		40		Pres: A. F. Backus
															Gen. Man: J. F. Robinson
		40 (64)	$ 995.5 641.8	W'hse			100/60 (50/30)	Wood 6 (153)	20" (508)	8.0°	1.82%	31.25	5 280 (1 609)	78	Ex. Vice Pres: R. E. Monroe
45 (72)		49 (78)	$ 11 047.9 9 439.2	Air W'hse	E' Type 33½ (851)		90 (45)	Wood 9 (228)	22"	7.0°	0.98%	33	1 186 (362)	405 (80)	Pres: H. Weldon McGee Sec. and Tres: Robert Goethe
30 (48)	30 (48)	45 (72)		Air W'hse	Janney 34½ (876)		105/80 (52/40)	Wood 7 (178)	21" (533)	4°	2.6% 1.9% U	35	1 278 (390)	15 (3)	Pres and Supt: R. W. Adams
20 (32)	30 (48)	45 P (72)	$ 146.8 110.3				70/56 (35/28)	Wood 7 (178)	18-24"	10.0°	1.9%			11	Gen. Man: C. M. Ledford
			$ 106 127.0 81 047.0				115/90 (57/45)	Wood 7 (178)	2 700 (1 680)	M: 7.9° B: 12.0°	M: 2.12% B: 1.57%				Vice Pres and Gen. Man: B. V. Bodie
															Pres: E. O. Lightsey
															Gen. Man: D. R. Stanton
20 (32)		60 (96)		Air W'hse			70 (35)	Oak 7 (178)	22" (560)					9	Pres: G. F. Fischer
							85/56 (42/28)	Wood 6 & 7	24" (610)			18		5 (2)	Pres: M. G. Pfaender

NAME OF COMPANY ADDRESS	Gauge ft. in. (metres)	Route length incl. E=Electrified miles (km.)	Track length incl. E=Electrified miles (km.)	Elect. system and type of conductor	Locomotives L=Line S=Shunt / Steam Electric Diesel De=elec. Dh=hyd.	Rail-cars Electric Diesel Trailer Railbus Multiple Unit set	Pass. train cars	Freight train cars	Freight movement: Total Volume carried. Containers Thousands of tonnes	Av'ge haul per ton miles (km.)	Av'ge net train load tonnes	Max. trailing load tonnes	Passengers: Total number carried in 1 000's	Average journey miles (km.)
USA *(contd.)*														
Helena Southwestern Railroad Co PO Box 2517, West Helena, Ark 72390	4' 8½" (1-435)	5 (8)	5 (8)		DeS 1			12	Yard Switching only					
High Point, Thomasville & Denton RR Co PO Box 1855, High Point. NC 27260	4' 8½" (1-435)	34 (55)				4								
Hillsboro & Northeastern RR Co Hillsboro, Wis	4' 8½" (1-435)	5 (8)			DeL 2									
Hillsdale County Rly Co 50 Monroe St, Hillsdale, Mich 49242	4' 8½" (1-435)	59 (95)			DeL 2			65						
Hollis & Eastern RR Co PO Drawer C, Duke, Ok 73532	4' 8½" (1-435)	14 (22)			DeL 1									
Holton Inter-Urban Railway Co. *(Southern Pacific System)*	4' 8½" (1-435)	10 (16)												
Houston Belt & Terminal Railway Co 202 Union Station, Houston, Tex 77002 *(Subsidiary of Missouri Pacific)*	4' 8½" (1-435)	53 (85)	234 (376)		DeS 23				switching service only					
Hutchinson & Northern Railway Co 1800 E Carey Blvd, Hutchinson, Kans 67501	4' 8½" (1-435)	E 5 (10)	E 6½ (11)	OH 600 V dc	DeL 2									
Illinois Central Gulf Railroad / Illinois Central Industries 233 N Michgan ave, Chicago, Ill 60601 *(Merged with GM & O RR)*	4' 8½" (1-435)	9 159 (10 472) E 38 (61)	14 532 (23 350) E 127 (204)	1 500 V. dc OH	DeL 895 DeS 156	5		47 723	95 160·8					
Illinois Northern Railway 2610 South Western Avenue, Chicago 8, Ill 60608 *(Merged with Atchison, Topeka and Santa Fe Railway Co)*	4' 8½" (1-435)	27 (27)	19 (31)		DS 5			1						
Illinois Terminal Railroad Co PO Box 7282 St Louis, Mo 63177	4' 8½" (1-435)	387 (620)	547 (880)		DeL 16 DeS 20			2 662	6 469·1	71·6 (115·2)	2 121			
Indiana Harbor Belt RR Co *(New York Central System)*	4' 8½" (1-435)	114 (183)	566 (911)		DeS 103			83						
Indianapolis Union Rly Co 31 E. Georgia St, Indianapolis, Ind 46204	4' 8½" (1-435)	16 (26)	65 (105)		DS 12									
Jacksonville Terminal Co * PO Box 2319, Jacksonville, Fla. 32202	4' 8½" (1-435)		51 (82)											
Johnstown & Stony Creek RR Co PO Box 536, Johnstown, Pa 15230	4' 8½" (1-435)	3 (5)	6 (10)		DeS 3									
Joplin Union Depot Co 114 West 11th St, Kansas City, Mo 64105	4' 8½" (1-435)		5 (8)											
Kanawha Central Railway Co Charleston, W Va *(Ceased operations during 1977)*	4' 8½" (1-435)	5 (8)			D									
Kansas City Southern Lines 114 West 11th St, Kansas City, Mo 64105 *(Consists of:)*														
† **Kansas City Southern Ry. Co.** 114 West 11th St., Kansas City, Mo 64105	4' 8½" (1-435)	1 618 (2 640)			DeL 146 DeS 97			8 440	27 755·8		2 788	6 877 087 000		
Kansas City Connecting RR Co 1600 Genesee St, Kansas City, Mo, 64102	4' 8½" (1-435)	1·9 (3·1)	11 (18)											
Kansas City Terminal Railway Co 207 Union Station Building, Kansas City, Mo, 64108 *(Switching and Terminal Co)*	4' 8½" (1-435)	10·8 (17·5)	131 (210)		DeS 10			11						
Kansas & Missouri Rly & Terminal Co 1709 Minnesota ave, Kansas City, Kans 66102 *(Kansas City Southern System)*	4' 8½" (1-435)	E 5 (8)	E 11 (18)											
Kansas City Public Service Freight Operation 8641 Highland ave, Kansas City, Mo 64131	4' 8½" (1-435)	10 (16)			DeS 2									
Kansas, Oklahoma & Gulf Railway Co *(Subsidiary of Missouri Pacific)*	4' 8½" (1-435)	327 (526)	368 (592)		De 15									
Kelly's Creek & Northwestern RR Co 700 Westgate Tower, Cleveland, Ohio 44116 *(Owned by Valley Camp Coal Co)*	4' 8½" (1-435)	7 (11)			DeS 4			127						
Kentucky & Indiana Terminal RR Co 2910 Northwestern Parkway, Louisville, Ky 40212	4' 8½" (1-435)	8 (13)	131 (211)		DeS 16			2						
Kentucky & Tennessee Railway Stearns, McCreary County, Ky 42647	4' 8½" (1-435)	10 (16)	17 (28)		DeL 4			4	571·0	10 (16)	800	1 500		

* Owned by Seaboard Coast Line, Florida East Coast Railway and Southern Railway
† Incorporates Louisiana and Arkansas Rly Co

Freight Train mph (km/hr)	Pass. Train mph (km/hr)	Speed max. mph (km/hr)	Revenue Expenses in 1 000's	Braking (continuous)	Couplers Type and Height above rail ins (mm)	Buffers Centres and Height above rail ins (mm)	Rails Weight lb. per yd (kg/m)	Sleepers Type and thickness ins (mm)	Sleepers Spacing Number per mile or centres ins (mm)	Curvature max.	Gradient max. (U=not compensated)	Axle load max. tonnes	Altitude max. feet (m)	Staff employed. Total no. (inclu. workshop)	Names of officials. Extended lists can be found at the end of the individual country in the report section immediately following
				Air			85/56 (42/28)	Oak 7 (178)	3 168 (1 968)	None	Level			4 (1)	Vice Pres and Gen. Man: R. Rich
															Pres: J. P. Fishwick
															Pres: H. D. Anderson
															Pres: J. H. Marino
															Pres: P. Simpson
															Pres: R. L. King
							115/75 (57/37)	Wood 6 (153) 9 (225)	18-22"	Negligable	1·75%				Pres and Gen. Man: L. B. Griffin
		10 (16)	$ 99·5 84·4	Air W'hse.	AAR		90/70 (45/35)	Wood 6 (153)	24" (610)	16·0°	Level		25 (8)	8 (1)	Pres: C. N. Bowler
60 (96)	90 (145)		$ 626 878 633 330	ABDW	E & F 34½ (875)		90 (45)	Wood 6 (153) 9 (225)	3 259/km	10°	2%	18		20 435	Pres. and Chief Operating Officer: William J. Taylor
															Pres: L. Cena
			$ 14 632·0 11 749·0	Air			90 (45)	Wood 6 (153)	20" (508)	18·5°	1·25% U	32	516 (93)		Pres: E. B. Wilson Vice Pres and Gen. Man D. E. Visney
															Gen. Man: A. B. Cravens
															Pres: L. S. Crane
														425	Pres: D. C. Hastings
							115/70 (57/35)	Wood 7 (178)							Pres: M. S. Toon
															Pres: T. S. Carter
			$ 48 135 33 952												Vice Pres. and Gen. Man: R. J. Blair
35 (56)		40 (64)	$ 147 392·6 113 058·9	AB	Type E		146/85 (67/42)	Oak 6 & 7	.19½" (496)	10·0°	1·8%	30	1 650 (503)	3 161	Pres: T. S. Carter
							90/80 (45/40)	Wood 7 (178)						17	Pres, A. W. Letzig Jr
25 (40)		45 (72)	$ 5 916·1 5 895·5	W'hse AB	Type		131/90 (65/45)	Oak 7 (178)	3 140 (1 950)	17·15°	2·0% U *	33	855 (261)	1 000	Pres. and Gen Man: V. E. Coe
							85 (42)	Wood 6 (153)	1 718 (2 750)					2	Gen. Man: D. W. Henry
															Tfc Man: J. G. Ashley
				Air	Type E		115/75 (57/37)	Oak 6 & 7	22" (559)	7·0°	1·0%				
															Pres: H. S. Richey
				Air W'hse	Type E 34½" (876)		100 (50)	Wood 7 (178)	22" (559)	13·0°	1·24%	35	489 (149)	696 (170)	Pres. and Gen. Man: J. J. Gaynor
15 (24)		25 (40)	$ 242·0 185·0	Air W'hse	AAR 32		90/80 (45/40)	Wood 9 (229)	2 600 (1 620)	22·0°	3·0%	36	900 (274)	19 (4)	Gen. Man: E. R. Tindle

* 2·0% sidings, 1·43% through tracks

NAME OF COMPANY ADDRESS	Gauge ft. in. *(metres)*	Route length incl. E=Electrified miles *(km.)*	Track length incl. E=Electrified miles *(km.)*	Elect. system and type of conductor	Locomotives L=Line S=Shunt Steam Electric Diesel De=elec. Dh=hyd.	Railcars Electric Diesel Trailer Railbus Multiple Unit set	Pass. train cars	Freight train cars Containers	Freight movement: Total Volume carried. Thousands of tonnes	Freight movement: Av'ge haul per ton miles *(km.)*	Freight movement: Av'ge net train load tonnes	Freight movement: Max. trailing load tonnes	Passengers: Total number carried in 1 000's	Passengers: Average journey miles *(km.)*
USA *(contd.)*														
La Salle & Bureau County RR Co PO Box 497, La Salle, Ill 61301	4' 8½" *(1·435)*	10 *(16)*	15 *(24)*		**De**L**S** 2			51	225	5 *(7)*	700			
***Lackawanna & Wyoming Valley RR Co** Scranton, Pa 18053	4' 8½" *(1·435)*	19 *(31)*	23 *(37)*		**D** 1 (leased from Erie Lacka)									
Lake Erie & Eastern Railroad Co P & LE Ter. Bdg., Pittsburgh, Pa. 15219 *(Owned jointly by Pittsburgh and Lake Erie RR and Mahoning Coal RR, operated by P. and L. E. with P. and L. E. equipment)*	4' 8½" *(1·435)*	15 *(24)*	130 *(209)*											
Lake Erie and Fort Wayne RR Co 8N. Jefferson St, Roanoake, Va 24011	4' 8½" *(1·435)*	4 *(6)*	4 *(6)*							1·4 *(2·2)*				
Lake Erie, Franklin & Clarion RR Co PO Box 430, East Wood St, Clarion, Pa 16214	4' 8½" *(1·435)*	15 *(24)*	24 *(39)*		**De**S 3			50	8·452	5 *(8·5)*				
Lakefront Dock & RR Terminal Co Two North Charles St, Baltimore Md 21201 *(Owned jointly by Penn Central and Baltimore and Ohio)*	4' 8½" *(1·435)*	3 *(5)*	63 *(101)*											
Lake Superior Terminal & Transfer Rly Co of the State of Winconsin 933, Oakes Ave, Superior, Wis 54880	4' 8½" *(1·435)*	5 *(8)*	24 *(38·6)*		**De**S 6			5						
Lake Superior & Ishpeming RR Co 105, E. Washington St., Marquette, Mich 49855	*4' 8⅝"* *(1·435)*	*98* *(157)*			**De**L 16			2 409						
Lake Terminal Railroad Co PO Box 536, Pittsburgh, Pa 15230	4' 8½" *(1·435)*	4 *(6·4)*	22 *(35)*		**De**S 14			329	2 684·5					
Lancaster & Chester Railway Co PO B 230, Lancaster, SC 29720	4' 8½" *(1·435)*	29 *(47)*	37 *(60)*		**De** 2			48	168·1					
Laona & Northern Railway PO B 126-Laona, Wis 54541	4' 8½" *(1·435)*	8 *(13)*	12 *(19)*		**S**L 1 **De**L 2		3	23	61·9	7·5 (12)	200	300		
Laurinburg & Southern RR Co PO Box 546, Laurinburg, NC 28352	4' 8½" *(1·435)*	28 *(45)*	39 *(63)*		**De**L 6 **Dh** 1			31	341·1	1 309 133 ton-miles				
†**Lehigh & Hudson River Railway Co** PO Drawer F, Warwick, NY 10990	4' 8½" *(1·435)*	90 *(145)*	130 *(209)*											
†**Lehigh Valley Railroad Co.** 415 Brighton St, Bethlehem, Pa 18015	4' 8½" *(1·435)*	503 *(809)*	1 591 *(2 414)*		**De**L 71 **De**S 76		Nil	3 966 **C** 193	19 438		360 *(260)*		3 292	
Little Rock Port Railroad 1500 Lindsey Rd, Little Rock, Ark 72206	4' 8½" *(1·435)*	9·7 *(15·9)*			**De**S 1									
Live Oak Perry & South Georgia Railroad Co McPherson Sq, Washington 5, DC	4' 8½" *(1·435)*	58 *(93)*	73 *(117)*		**De**L 2 **De**S 1		0	3	428·6		11 *(18)*		105	
Livonia Avon & Lakeside R.R. Corp 3401 Rochester Rd, Lakeville, New York NY 14480	4' 8½" *(1·435)*	13 *(21)*			**De** 2 **S**L 1		6	1						
Long Island Railroad Co Jamaica Station, Jamaica, NY 11435	4' 8½" *(1·435)*	321 *(516)* **E** 133 *(214)*	494 *(795)* **E** 331 *(532)*	700 V dc Third rail	**De**L 59 **De**S 10	**E** 764 **DT** 264†	1 036		2 421·2	28 860 000 ton-miles			67 363	26 *(42)*
Longview, Portland & Northern Ry Co PO Box 579, Longview, Wash 98632	4' 8½" *(1·435)*	42 *(68)*			**De**L 4									
Los Angeles Junction Railway Co. 4521 Produce Plaza, Los Angeles, Cal 90058	4' 8½" *(1·435)*	28 *(45)*	58 *(93)*		**De**S 5									
§**Los Angeles Union Passenger Terminal** 800 N Alameda St, Los Angeles, Cal 90012	4' 8½" *(1·435)*		7 *(11)*											
Louisiana & Arkansas Railway Co *(See Kansas City Southern Lines)*	4' 8½" *(1·435)*	746 *(1 200)*												
Louisiana Eastern RR PO Box 742, Amite, La 70422	4' 8½" *(1·435)*	6 *(9·5)*	8 *(13)*		**De**L 1 **De**S 2				600	55				
Louisiana & North West RR Co Homer, La 71040	4' 8½" *(1·435)*	62 *(100)*			**De**L 5			10						
Louisiana & Pine Bluff Railway Co *(See Arkansas and Louisiana Missouri Rly)* PO Box 1653, Monroe, La 71201	4' 8½" *(1·435)*	3 *(5)*			**De**L 2	**P** 1			3					
Louisiana Southern Railway Co *(Southern Railway System)*	4' 8½" *(1·435)*	16 *(26)*			**D** 2									
Louisville, New Albany & Corydon RR Co Box 10 Corydon, Ind 47112	4' 8½" *(1·435)*	8 *(13)*	10 *(16)*		**De**L 1			842	10·9	8·6 *(13·8)*	315			

* Incorporated into ConRail
† Taken over by ConRail 1 April 1977
‡ Including eight gas-turbine railcars
§ Operating agency of Southern Pacific, Santa Fe and Union Pacific

Average Speeds			Financial Data		Couplers	Buffers	Rails	Sleepers (crossties)							
Freight Train	Pass. Train	Speed max.	Revenue Expenses	Braking (continuous)	Type and Height above rail	Centres and Height above rail	Weight	Type and thickness	Spacing Number per mile or centres	Curvature max.	Gradient max. (U=not compensated)	Axle load max.	Altitude max.	Staff employed. Total no. (inclu. workshop)	Names of officials. Extended lists can be found at the end of the individual country in the report section immediately following
mph (km/hr)	mph (km/hr)	mph (km/hr)	in 1 000's		ins (mm)	ins (mm)	lb. per yd (kg/m)	ins (mm)	ins (mm)		sated)	tonnes	feet (m)		
20 (32)			$ 201·0 186·9				100/85 (50/42)	Oak 6 (153)	2 600 (1 620)	14·0°	1·5%		300 (91)	16 (3)	Gen. Man: E. T. Barnes Jr.
			$ 130·9 112·5				90 (45)	Wood 6 (153)	24'' (610)	26·0°	2·5%			11	Gen. Man: H. J. Fawley
16 (26)		20 (32)	$ 1 426·4 1 506·1				132/131 (65·5/65)	Oak 7 (178)	19½'' (495)	4·0°	0·30% 0·25% U	33	888 (271)		
			$ 68·0 49·0	Air W'hse			90/85 (45/42)	Wood 6 (153)	22'' (560)					4	Pres: R. F. Dunlap
12 (19)		25 (40)	$ 570·5 351·9	Air W'hse			115/80 (57/40)	Oak 7 (178)	2 728 (1 705)		2·4%			30 (4)	Pres: J. F. Miller
								Wood	21¼'' (533)	12·0°	0·3%			31	Pres: J. T. Colinson
		20 (32)	$ 351·7 1 201·8	Air W'hse	Standard		115/75 (57/37)	Wood 8 (204)	3 052 (1 907)	16·0°	0·5%		641 (195)	125 (3)	Pres: W. S. Burn
12·5 (19·5)		35 (56)	$ 6 341 5 766	Air W'hse	Type E Nat. Mal. Cast. Co.		132/80 (66/40)	Wood 7 (178)	3 000 (1 860)	12·3°	1·9% U	27·5	1 500 (457)	259 (68)	Pres. and Gen. Man: J. J. Scullion
			$ 446·7 440·7	AB			115 (57)	Wood 7 (178)	17'' (431·8)	32·0°	2·5% U				Pres: M. S. Toon
			$ 568·0 444·5				112/60 (56/30)	Wood 6 (153)	22'' (560)					26 (7)	Pres: J. B. Bethea
6 (9·7)		20 (32)		Air W'hse	Type E ACF		75/56 (37/23)	Wood 6 (153)	23'' (585)	6·0°	2·5%	12·5	1 000 (305)	7 (1)	Gen. Man: J. S. Mason
15 (24)		25 (40)	$ 759·3 678·7	Air			90/56 (45/28)	Wood 8 (204)	21'' (533)			32·8		24	Vice Pres. and Gen. Man: W. S. Jones
25 (40)		35 (56)		W'hse			131/100 (65/50)	Wood 7 (178)	21'' (533)	8·0°	0·53% 1·18% U	33	601 (183)		
45 (72)		60 (96)	$ 73 295·7 80 991·6	Air W'hse	Type E 34½'' (876)		136/55 (67/28)	Wood 7 (168)	19''M (428) 21''B (535)	Main 13·0° Branch 20·0°	2·2% 1·8% U	32	1 739 (530)	2 670 (513)	Trustee: Robert C. Haldeman
															Agent: M. J. Rayney
			$ 539·6 275·4	Air			100/90 (50/40)	Wood 7 (178)	22'' (560)	5·0°	2·0%			31	
															Pres: C. A. Haak
35 (56)	45 (72)	80 (128)	$ 131 370 226 144	W'hse Air	Mod. Sharon No. 10D 34½ (876)		100 (50)	Wood 8 (200)	21'' (535)	7·5°	2·0%	Coopers E 72	238 (72·5)	6 700 (2 344)	Pres: R. K. Pattison
							110/60 (55/30)	Fir 7 (178)							Pres: B. H. Wills
															Pres: R. W. Walker
															Supt: R. L. Pfister
			$ 30 487 20 567												Chairman: W. N. Derams
25 (40)				Air W'hse			90 (45)	Wood 8 (203)	26'' (660)					10 (2)	Pres: A. E. Morse
							75 (37)	Wood 6 (153)	3 200 (2 000)	2·8°					Pres: M. M. Salzberg
															Pres: J. D. Mullins
15 (24)		30 (48)	$ 237 483·9 207 894·6				90/65 (45/32)	Wood 7 (178)	24'' (610)	12·0°	3·2% 1·8% U			14	Chairman: W. Buchanan Gen. Man: W. Saulman

Name of Company / Address	Gauge ft. in. (metres)	Route length incl. E miles (km.)	Track length incl. E miles (km.)	Elect. system	Locomotives L=Line S=Shunt	Rail-cars	Pass. train cars	Freight train cars / Containers	Total Volume carried. Thousands of tonnes	Av'ge haul per ton miles (km.)	Av'ge net train load tonnes	Max. trailing load tonnes	Total number carried in 1 000's	Average journey miles (km.)
Louisville & Nashville RR Co 908 West Broadway, Louisville, Ky 40201 (98% owned by Seaboard Coast Line RR)	4' 8½" (1-435)	6 574 (10 579)	10 076 (16 216)		DeL 877 DeS 164			65 873	122 338·2	265 (426)				
Louisville & Wadley RR Co 416 E. Broad St, Louisville, Ga 30434	4' 8½" (1-435)	10 (16)						50						
Lowville & Beaver River RR Co 111 Shady ave, Lowville, NY	4' 8½" (1-435)	11 (18)	14 (23)		De 2			1	42·3	9 (14)	6 cars	13 cars		
Ludington & Northern Rly 2840 Bay Rd, Saginaw, Mich 48603	4' 8½" (1-435)	4 (7)			DeL 1									
McCloud River Railroad Co Drawer A. McCloud, Cal 96057	4' 8½" (1-435)	94 (151)	111 (179)		DeL 4		2	7	532·6					
McKeesport Connecting Railroad PO Box 536, Pittsburgh, Pa 15230	4' 8½" (1-435)	5 (8)	16 (26)		DeS 5			159						
Magma Arizona Railroad Co PO Box 37, Superior, Ariz 85273	4' 8½" (1-435)	28 (45)	35 (56)		DeL 3				91·6	28 (45)				
Maine Central Railroad Co 242 St. John St, Portland, Maine 04102	4' 8½" (1-435)	850 (1 367)	1 043 (1 740)		DeL 45 DeS 21			4 363	6 975·5	812 767 565 ton-km	2 380			
Manitou & Pike's Peak Railway Co PO Box 1329, Colorado Springs, Colo 80901 (Abt system rack railway)	4' 8½" (1-435)	9 (14)	10 (16)		DeL 3 Dh 1		3	1					14·0	9 (14)
Manufacturers' Junction Rly Co 2335 S Cicero ave, Cicero, Ill 60650	4' 8½" (1-435)	2 (3)	11 (18)		DeS 2			62						
Manufacturers' Railway Co 2850 S Broadway, St. Louis, Mo 63118	4' 8½" (1-435)	42 (67)			DeS 11			1 225						
Marinette, Tomahawk & Western RR Co PO Box 315, Tomahawk, Wis 54487	4' 8½" (1-435)	14 (22)			DeL 2			3						
Maryland & Penna RR Co 490 E. Market St, York, Pa 17403	4' 8½" (1-435)	90 (145)			DeS 6			1 371	120·0	26 (42)				
Massena Terminal Railroad Co 410 One Allegheny Sq, Pittsburg, Pa 15212	4' 8½" (1-435)	2 (3)	9 (14)		DeS 2									
Meridian & Bigbee River Railroad PO Box 551, Meridian, Miss 39301	4' 8½" (1-435)	51 (82)	57 (92)		DeL 4			126						
Michigan Northern Rly Co PO Box 869, Cadillac, Mich 49601	4' 8½" (1-435)	248 (399)			De 3									
Middletown & Hummelstown RR Co PO Box G, Hummelstown, Pa 17036	4' 8½" (1-435)	6·5 (10·4)												
Middletown & New Jersey Rly Co 140 East Main St, Middletown, NY 10940	4' 8½" (1-435)	15 (24)	17 (27)		DeS 2									
Midland Valley Railroad Co (Subsidiary of Texas & Pacific)	4' 8½" (1-435)													
Minneapolis Eastern Railway Co 325, South First St, Minneapolis, Minn 55401	4' 8½" (1-435)	2 (3)			DeS 1									
Minneapolis, Northfield & Southern Rly 911 Hennepin ave, Minneapolis, Minn 55403	4' 8½" (1-435)	77 (123)			DeL 12 DeS 2			546	1 664·5	48·9	1 342·5	6 000		
Minnesota, Dakota & Western Rly Co PO Box 7747, Boise, Idaho 83707	4' 8½" (1-435)	4 (6)	17 (27)		DeS 5			639	876·6	3 (5)				
Minnesota Transfer Railway Co 2071 University Ave, St Paul, Minn 55104 (Switching Line only)	4' 8½" (1-435)	13 (21)	75 (121)		DeS 5									
Mississippi & Skuna Valley RR Co PO Box 265, Bruce, Miss 38915	4' 8½" (1-435)	22 (35)	26 (42)		DeL 2		None	8·2	147·0	22 (35·4)	249·3			
Mississippian Railway PO Box 446, Amory, Miss 38821	4' 8½" (1-435)		24 (39)		De 2									
Missouri & Illinois Bridge & Belt RR Co (C.B. & Q. and Mo. Pac.)	4' 8½" (1-435)	3 (5)	5 (8)											
Missouri-Illinois Railroad Co (Subsidiary of Missouri Pacific)	4' 8½" (1-435)	324 (522)												
Missouri-Kansas-Texas RR Co 101 E Main St, Denison, Tex 75020	4' 7" (1-435)	2 223 (3 576)	1 909 (5 015)		DeL 131 DeS 37			8 108		315 (507)				
Missouri Pacific Railroad 210 N. 13th St, St Louis, Miss 63103	4' 8½" (1-435)	11 674 (18 788)	17 189 (27 663)		DeL 983 DeS 196			55 822	141 574·4	31 237 236 761 ton-km				
Mobile & Gulf Railroad Co 409 Commonwealth Bldg, Louisville, Ky	4' 8½" (1-435)	11 (18)	15 (24)		DL 1					11 (18)	100			

Average Speeds			Financial Data		Couplers	Buffers	Rails	Sleepers (crossties)							Names of officials. Extended lists can be found at the end of the individual country in the report section immediately following
Freight Train	Pass. Train	Speed max.	Revenue Expenses	Braking (continuous)	Type and Height above rail	Centres and Height above rail	Weight	Type and thickness	Spacing Number per mile (per km) or centres	Curvature max.	Gradient max. (U=not compensated)	Axle load max.	Altitude max.	Staff employed. Total no. (inclu. workshop)	
mph (km/hr)	mph (km/hr)	mph (km/hr)	in 1 000's		ins (mm)	ins (mm)	lb. per yd (kg/m)	ins (mm)	ins (mm)			tonnes	feet (m)		
20·3 (32·7)		60 (96)	$ 504 687 384 304	Air W'hse	Type E 33¼ (851)		130/75 (64/37)	Wood 7 (178)	3 100 (1 930)	17·3%	2·5%U	33	2 150 (655)		Pres: Prime F. Osborn
															Pres: B. D. Gibson
							80/60 (40/30)	Wood 6 (153)	2 800 (1 740)	6·0°	2·5%				Pres: A. J. Turnbull
															Pres: Miss M. L. Sargent
10 (16)	35 (56)		$ 2 004·1 1 299·7	Air W'hse	Type E Miner 33½ (851)		90/70 (45/35)	Fir 8 (204)	3 100 (1 930)	13·0°	4·0%	30	4 600 (1 398)	65 (9)	Pres: Carl T. Hester
10 (16)			$ 2 204 1 381	AB W'hse	AAR Type E		130/100 (65/50)	Wood 7 (178)	22″ (560)	41·0°	Level	21		102 (82)	Pres: M. S. Toon
15 (24)	20 (32)			Air W'hse	Standard		70 (35)	Wood 6 (153)	18″ (460)	13·5°	3·7%		2 800 (853)		Pres: R. B. Wright
13·2 (21·2)		60 (96)	$ 37 209·8 33 039·4	Air W'hse	AAR Type E 34½ (876)		115/75 (57/37)	Wood 6 & 7 (153/4)	21″ (533)	Main 9·0° Branch 15·0°	2·85%U	32·8	1 893 (577)	1 402 (206)	Pres and Chairman: E. Spencer Miller
7·5 (12·0)	10 (16)			Electro-dynamic	Roller G.E. 27½ (699)		40 (20)	Wood 7 (178)	20″ (508)	16·0°	25·0%	12	14 110 (4 300)	60	Gen Man and Vice Pres: Martin Frick
			$ 529·7 288·0	Air	AAR Type E		90/80 (45/40)	Wood 6 (153)	20″ (508)					16 (2)	Pres: M. C. Kirby
															Pres: R. W. Chapman
															Pres: P. J. Fluge
15 (24)	20 (32)		$ 421·9 309·0	Air	Type E		90/70 (45/35)	Wood 7 (178)	22″ (560)	20·0°	2·5% 3·5%U	30	700 (213)	27 (6)	Pres: H. Lazarus
20 (32)	35 (56)						15/85 (57/42)	Oak 6 (153)	21″ (533)	10°	0·5%	31·5		10	Pres: W. Murray
40 (64)				NY 6 BL	Type E		110/90 (55/45)	Oak 7 (178)	21″ (533)	6·0°	1·0%	37·5			Pres: J. W. Bard
															Pres: Elizabeth Andrus
															Pres: W. J. Dillinger
							80/70 (40/35)	Wood 6 (153)		4·0°	2·3%				Pres: R. T. Rasmussen
															Pres: T. P. Heffelfinger
30 (48)	45 (72)		$ 5 214·9 4 454·1	Air W'hse	Type E 32½″ (825)		100/80 (50/40)	Wood 7 (178)	21¼″ (540)	Main 10° Branch 20°	Main 2% Branch 3·5%	28	1 038 (317)	195 (20)	Pres: H. E. Pence
10 (16)	20 (32)		$ 1 397·4 1 244·4	Air W'hse	Various		100/60 (50/30)	Wood 8 (200)	18″ (460)	Main 8° Secondary 20°				85 (20)	Pres: Robert H. Schwarz Vice Pres: J. S. Gendron
10 (16)	30 (48)						115/85 (57/42)	Wood 6 (153)	22″ (560)	3·0°	1·0%			150 (14)	Pres: M. Garelick Supt: W. S. Hammond
20 (32)	25 (40)		$ 162·5 136·4	Air W'hse			90/70 (45/35)	Wood 7 (178)	20″ (508)				600 (183)	22 (1)	Pres: R. C. Allen
															Pres: R. W. Wetherby
			$ 6 949 6 928												
33 (53)			$ 96 500·0 —	W'hse	Types E, F		119/52 (59/26)	Wood 7 (178)	3 200 (2 000)	8·0°	1·4%	32	1 106 (337)	2 834 (440)	Pres: R. N. Whitman
22·4 (36)			$ 8 013 668·1 747 241·6	Air W'hse	AAR 34½″ (876)		Up to 131	Wood 7 (178)		20°	2·9%	30		21 945	Pres: J. H. Lloyd
10 (16)	15 (24)			Air										7	

NAME OF COMPANY ADDRESS	Gauge ft. in. (metres)	Route length incl. E=Electrified miles (km.)	Track length incl. E=Electrified miles (km.)	Elect. system and type of conductor	Locomotives L=Line S=Shunt Steam Electric Diesel De=elec. Dh=hyd.	Rail-cars Electric Diesel Trailer Railbus Multiple Unit set	Pass. train cars	Freight train cars Containers	Total Volume carried. Thousands of tonnes	Av'ge haul per ton miles (km.)	Av'ge net train load tonnes	Max. trailing load tonnes	Total number carried in 1000's	Average journey miles (km.)
Modesto & Empire Traction Co PO Box 3106, Modesto, Cal 95353	4' 8½" (1·435)	5 (8)	28 (45)		DeS 7				1 250·3	5 (8)				
Monongahela Connecting Railroad 3540 Second ave, Pittsburgh, Pa 15219	4' 8½" (1·435)		47 (76)		DeS 22			643	15 000·0					
Monongahela Railway Co 53 Market St, Brownsville, Pa 15417	4' 8½" (1·435)	171 (275)	254 (408)		DeL 11				7 178·1	54 (87)		19 000		
Montour Railroad Co (Owned by P.C. and Pitts. and L. Erie RR) 1 429 Fourth Ave, Coraopolis, Pa 15108	4' 8½" (1·435)	50·6 (81·4)	79 (127)		DeS 14			343						
Montpelier & Barre RR PO Box 314, Barre, Vt	4' 8½" (1·435)	14 (22)			D 5			40						
Morristown & Erie Railroad Co PO Box 2206-R, Morriston, NJ, 07960	4' 8½" (1·435)	11 (18)	15 (24)		DeL 2 DeS 1		3	1	864·8	4 (6)	8 000			
Moscow, Camden & San Augustine Railroad PO Box 77, Camden, Tex	4' 8½" (1·435)	7 (11)	7·8 (12·6)		DeS 1		1						3·9	7 (11)
Moshassuck Valley Railroad Co Saylesville, RI	4' 8½" (1·435)	2 (3)	5 (8)		DeL 1 DeS 1			15						
*Mount Hope Mineral Railroad Co (C.R.R. of N.J. Terminal) Jersey City, NJ	4' 8½" (1·435)	3·4 (5·5)	3·7 (6)		†									
Muncie & Western Railroad Co 1425 E 12th St, Muncie, Ind 47302	4' 8½" (1·435)		4·2 (7·0)		DeS 2									
Narragansett Pier Railroad Co Inc 1, Railroad St, Peace Dale, RI	4' 8½" (1·435)	6 (10)	7 (11)		DeL 2		1	25	400	5 (8)			400	0·2
Natchez & Southern Railway Co MP Freight Station, Natchez, Miss. (Subsidiary of Missouri Pacific)	4' 8½" (1·435)	4 (6)												
National Railroad Passenger Corp (See under Amtrak)														
Nevada Northern Railway Co PO Box 476, East Ely, Nev 89315	4' 8½" (1·435)	162 (260)	190 (306)		DeL 2 S 1			23	361	121 (198)	2 600	8 000		
Newburgh & South Shore Railway Co PO Box 536 Pittsburgh, Pa 15230	4' 8½" (1·435)	5 (8)	42 (68)		DS 11			298						
New Jersey, Indiana & Illinois RR Co 8 N Jefferson St, Roanoke, Va 24011	4' 8½" (1·435)	11 (18)	31 (50)		DeL		0	515		11 (18)				
New Orleans & Lower Coast RR Co (Missouri Pacific) New Orleans, La 7014 (Subsidiary of Missouri Pacific)	4' 8½" (1·435)	60 (97)	73 (117)											
New Orleans & Northeastern RR Co. (Southern Railway System)	4' 8½" (1·435)	203 (326)	368 (592)		DL 15 DS 5		15	1 821	5 119·9	157 (253)	1 830		77·1	174
New Orleans Public Belt Railroad 1247 International Trade Mart Buildings New Orleans, La, 70130	4' 8½" (1·435)	24 (35)	153 (246)		DeS 11			4	64 811 revenue cars handled					
‡ New Orleans Union Passenger Terminal 1001 Loyola Ave, New Orleans, La 70113 (Subsidiary of Southern Rly)	4' 8½" (1·435)	6 (10)	25 (40)		DS 2		None	None						
New York Dock Railway 34 Furman St, Brooklyn, NY 1120	4' 8½" (1·435)		8 (13)		DeS 4				6 075 Cars					
‡ New York & Long Branch Railroad Co. 1100 Raymond Blvd, Newark, NJ 07102 (Owned by CRR of NJ and Penn Cen.)	4' 8½" (1·435)	38 (61) E§ 3·5 (5)	65 (105) E 11 (18)	ac	II								4 000·0	22 (35)
‡ New York, New Haven & Hartford RR Co 54 Meadow St, New Haven, Conn 06506	4' 8½" (1·435)	1 546 (2 488) E 83 (133)	3 343 (5 379) E 531 (854)	11 000 V 1/25 OH	EL 21 DeL 227 DeS 84	E 132 ET 56 D 45	663	4 000¶	18 187·3	161 (259)	2 804		23 938·8	39·8 (62·7)
New York, Susquehanna & Western RR Co One River Road, Edgewater, NJ 07020	4' 8½" (1·435)	65 (105)	65 (105)		DeL 15		1	26	5 794·2	16 (26)				
Nezperce Railroad Co Nezperce, Idaho	4' 8½" (1·435)	14 (23)	15·3 (24·6)		DeL 4					14 (23)	250			
‡ Niagara Junction Railway Co Box 341, Niagara Falls, NY 14302	4' 8½" (1·435)	E 5 (8)	E 50 (80)	600 V dc OH										
Norfolk & Portsmouth Belt Line RR Co Terminal Bldg, Norfolk 10, Va	4' 8½" (1·435)	27 (43)	82 (132)		D 15									
Norfolk & Western Railway Co 8 North Jefferson St Roanoke, Va 24042	4' 8½" (1·435)	7 659 (12 450)	14 868 (22 529)		DeS 110 DeL 1 389 Others 20		18	96 684	30 404·9	142 844 357 ton-km			402·9	

* Incorporated into ConRail
† Owns no equipment; CRR of NJ uses track and pays for occupation time
‡ Incorporated into ConRail
§ Electrified between Perth Amboy and South Amboy 1·79 miles for PRR
‖ Owns no rolling stock
¶ Includes 183 cabooses

Freight Train mph (km/hr)	Pass. Train mph (km/hr)	Speed max. mph (km/hr)	Revenue Expenses in 1 000's	Braking (continuous)	Couplers Type and Height above rail ins (mm)	Buffers Centres and Height above rail ins (mm)	Rails Weight lb. per yd (kg/m)	Sleepers Type and thickness ins (mm)	Spacing Number per mile (per km) or centres ins (mm)	Curvature max.	Gradient max. (U=not compensated)	Axle load max. tonnes	Altitude max. feet (m)	Staff employed. Total no. (inclu. workshop)	Names of officials. Extended lists can be found at the end of the individual country in the report section immediately following
10 (16)		20 (32)	3 978.3 3 162.0	Air W'hse	AAR 34½ (876)		160/50 (79/24)	Wood 6 (153)	22" (560)	12·3°	1·0%		125 (38)	66	Pres: R. F. Olsen
5 (8)		12 (19)	$ 7 468 4 951	Air W'hse	Type E 34½ (876)		115 (57)	Oak 7 (178)	21" (533)	48·0°	2·25% 2·0%U	35	800 (244)	798 (239)	Gen Super: R. L. McCombs
		35 (56)	$ 10 291·6 7 402·7	W'hse AB	Types D & E		140/85 (70/41)	Wood 6 & 7	22" (560)	Main 10·0° Branch 20·0°	Main 0·5% Branch 2·18%	30	1 207 (368)	240 (43)	Pres: H. G. Allyn Jr
15 (24·1)		25 (40)	$ 3 123·0 2 555·2	6 BL W'hse	AAR 34½" (876)		132/90 (65/45)	Oak 7 (178)	20" (508)	11·3°	M: 1·2% Br: 2·44	26	1 225 (373)		Pres: L. E. Smith
															Gen. Man: R. Coxon
15 (24)		20 (32)	$ 445·6 350·8	Air W'hse	AAR T peE 33½ (851)		100/80 (50/40)	Wood 7 (150)	24" (610)	18·0°				40	Pres: Andrew L. Cobb
15 (24)		15 (24)	$ 57·9 64·2	Air	Auto	Standard	50 (25)	Oak 6 (150)	3 334 (2 080)	10·0°	3·0%		322 (98·1)	9	Pres: N. C. T. Hester
															Pres: P. J. O'Toole
							100/76 (50/38)	Wood	2 622 (1 630)						
10 (16)				Air	Yoke		100/70 (50/35)	Wood 6 (153)	2 640 (1 640)				927 (283)	6	Pres: A. M. Bracken
15 (24)	20 (32)	30 (48)	$ 0·48 0·42	Air W'hse	AAR Standard		70/60 (35/30)	Wood 6 (153)	3 000 (1 870)	4·0°	2·5%	25	380 (116)	2	Pres: Dr. P. J. Miller Jr
							60 (30)	Wood 7 (178)							
22 (35)		30 (48)	$ 1 068 977	W'hse Air	National Type E 32½ (825)		115/60 (57/30)	Fir 8 (206)	22" (560)	12·0°	3·0%	28	7 000 (2 133)	95 (28)	Pres: H. H. Kremmer
			$ 3 125·1 2 404·1	W'hse Air			115/90 (57/45)	Wood 6 & 7	22"-24" (560-610)	20·0°	1·18% U	35		210 (57)	Gen. Man: J. W. Read
15 (24)		45 (72)	$ 508·8 730·3	W'hse Air	Type E 30½ (775)		90/80 (45/40)	Wood 7 (178)	24" (616)	5·0°	1·29% U	33	884 (269)	24 (4)	Pres: R. F. Dunlap
20 (32·2)				AAR	AAR		112/75 (56/37)	Wood 7 (178)	20" (508)	9·0°	0·2%				Pres: J. H. Lloyd
			$ 13 011·0 10 218·0	W'hse											
15 (24)		25 (40)		Air W'hse	AAR Type E 32½/34 (825/864)		115/80 (57/40)	Wood 6 (153)	20" (508)	13°	1·25%	30	284		Gen. Man: P. A. Webb Jnr.
		30 (48)					115/90 (57/45)	Wood 7 (178)	21" (533)	10·0°	1·0%			150	
							159/70 (79/35)	Oak 6 (150)	2 900 (1 800)	5·0°	0·87% U	38·8	112 (48)	48 (8)	Pres: O. Carey
	33 (53)	60 (96)					140/100 (70/50)	Wood 7 (178)	22 (559)	5·0°	0·8%U	33	111 (34)	246	Gen Man: S. R. Jones Compt: C. S. Hill
Through 22 (35) Local 8·6 (13)	38·5 (61)	Pass. 79 (127) Frt. 50 (80)	$ 121 002 119 216	Air W'hse	EFH 34½ (876)		174/70 (87/35)	Wood 6 & 7 (153 & 178)	22½" (572)	9·0°	2·0%	37·5		9 191 (2 291)	Vice Pres Ops: B. W. Tyler
8 (13)		40 (64)	$2 679·2 2 574·0	Air NYAB	Type E 33½ (851)		112/80 (56/40)	Wood 6 (153)	22" (559)	7·3°	2·0%	30	1 024 (311)	85	Pres: I. Maidman
		15 (24)					60/50 (30/25)	Wood 8 (200)	20" (510)					6 (0)	Pres: J. Lux
							131/70 (65/35)	Wood 6 & 7	22" (559)	14·0°	0·5%				Pres: F. S. Morrison
18 (29)	40 (64)	78 (125)	$ 1 255 179·0 1 123 576·0	Air W'hse	E. 34½ (876)		132/115 (78/42)	Wood 7 (178)	19½" (495)	18·2°	1·4% 1·9% U	32·8	3 577 (1 090)	27 668	Pres: J. P. Fishwick

USA (contd.)

NAME OF COMPANY ADDRESS	Gauge ft. in. (metres)	Route length incl. E=Electrified miles (km.)	Track length incl. E=Electrified miles (km.)	Elect. system and type of conductor	Loco-motives L=Line S=Shunt	Rail-cars	Pass. train cars	Freight train cars / Containers	Total Volume carried. Thousands of tonnes	Av'ge haul per ton miles (km.)	Av'ge net train load tonnes	Max. trailing load tonnes	Total number carried in 1 000's	Average journey miles (km.)
Norfolk, Franklin & Danville Rly Co 181 South Main St, Suffolk, Va 23434 *(Subsidiary of Norfolk & Western)*	4' 8½" (1·435)	207 (333)	233 (375)		DeL 6			233	1 614·3	60 (96)	646			
Norfolk Southern Railway Co PO Box 2210, Raleigh, NC	4' 8½" (1·435)	592 (953)	750 (1 207)		DL 29 DS 8		None	2 353	5 163·3	120 (193)	873			
North Louisiana & Gulf RR Co PO Drawer 550, Hodge, La 71247	4' 8½" (1·435)	40 (64)	44 (71)		DeS 4			50	749·5	40 (64)				
Northwestern Pacific Railroad Co PO Box 629, Willits, Cal 95490 *(Subsidiary of Southern Pacific Co)*	4' 8½" (1·435)	273 (440)	409 (650)		DeL 41 DeS 11				2 819			11 200		
Oakland Terminal Railway 1925 Sherman St, Alameda, Cal	4' 8½" (1·435)		26 (42)		DeS 1				11 700 carloads					
Ogden Union Railway & Depot Co 198 West 28th St, Ogden, Utah	4' 8½" (1·435)	5 (2)	116 (186)											
Okmulgee Northern Railway Co PO Box 2271, Okmulgee, Okl	4' 8½" (1·435)	10 (16)	13 (21)		D 2									
Omaha, Lincoln & Beatrice Rly Co Box 80268, 1815 Y St., Lincoln, Nebr 68501	4' 8½" (1·435)	4 (7)	6 (10)		DeS 2					12·6 cars switched				
Oregon & Northwestern RR Co PO Box 557, Hines, Oreg 97738	4' 8½" (1·435)	51 (82)	51 (82)		DeL 4			146			780	2 200		
Oregon, Pacific & Eastern Rly Co Cottage Grove, Oreg	4' 8½" (1·435)	24 (39)	30 (48)		De 2									
Paducah & Illinois RR Co *(Illinois Central Railroad)*	4' 8½" (1·435)	15 (24)												
Patapsco & Back Rivers Railroad Co Sparrows Point Bvd, Sparrows Point, Md 21219	4' 8½" (1·435)		103 (166)		DeS 55			100						
Pearl River Valley Railroad Co Picayune, Miss	4' 8½" (1·435)	5 (8)	6 (10)		DeS 1			6	101·2	5 (8)				
Pecos Valley Southern Railway Co PO Box 349, Pecos, Texas	4' 8½" (1·435)	40 (64)	48 (77)		DeS 2			2	172·4	12 (19·3)	678	1 500		
***Pennsylvania & Atlantic RR Co** New Egypt, NJ	4' 8½" (1·435)	19 (31)												
†Penn Central Co Pennsylvania New York Central Transportation Company Penn Center, Philadelphia, Pa. 19104	4' 8½" (1·435)	19 211 (30 890) E 822 (1 322)	36 572 (58 740) E 2 962 (4 760)	600 V dc and 11 000 V										
† Pennsylvania-Reading Seashore Lines 22 Federal St, Camden, NJ 08103	4' 8½" (1·435)	318 (512)	428 (689)		DeL 15 DeS 11	D 10		0	4 927·0	24·2 (39·0)			117·3	48·1 (77·4)
†Peoria & Eastern Railway Co *(New York Central)*	4' 8½" (1·435)	202 (325)												
Peoria & Pekin Union Rly Co Peoria, Ill 61607	4' 8½" (1·435)	12 (19)	147 (236)		DeS 14			29	444·4 cars				0	
Peoria Terminal Company *(Chicago, Rock Island Pacific RR)*	4' 8½" (1·435)	10 (16)	29 (47)											
Petaluma & Santa Rosa Railroad Co *(Subsidiary of Southern Pacific)* PO Box 629, Willits, Cal 95490	4' 8½" (1·435)	26·4 (42)	31·9 (51)					6	32·8			3 000		
Philadelphia, Bethlehem & New England Railroad Co 1275 Daly Avenue, Bethlehem, Pa 18015	4' 8½" (1·435)	3 (5)	61 (98)		DeS 24			51						
Philadelphia Suburban Transportation Co Red Arrow Division	5' 2¼" (1·579)												
Pickens Railroad Co 402 Cedar Rock St, Pickens, SC 29671	4' 8½" (1·435)	9 (14)	10 (16)		De 1			1 066	29·7		291 600 ton-km	325		
Piedmont & Northern Railway Co PO Box 480, Charlotte, NC 28201 *(Subsidiary of Seaboard Coast Line)*	4' 8½" (1·435)	150 (241)	164 (263)		DeL 12 DeS 6			16		39·5 (64)				
Pioneer & Fayette Railroad Co 414, E. Main St, Fayette, Ohio 43521	4' 8½" (1·435)	0·5 (0·8)			DeS 1									
Pittsburgh, Allegheny & McKees Rocks RR Co 180 Nichol Ave, McKees Rocks, Pa.	4' 8½" (1·435)		13 (21)		D 2			2						
Pittsburgh, Chartiers & Youghiogheny Ry Co McKees Rocks, Pa 15136	4' 8½" (1·435)	13·5 (21·8)	29 (46)		DeS 4			3				9 600		
Pittsburgh & Lake Erie Railroad Co P. and L.E. Ter. Bldg, Pittsburgh, Pa 15219	4' 8½" (1·435)	211 (340)	758 (1 220)		DeL 28 DeS 70		5	18 094						
Pittsburgh & Ohio Valley Rly Co Neville Island, Pittsburgh, Pa 15225	4' 8½" (1·435)	7 (11)	20·7 (82·9)		DeS 2				1 210·9					
Pittsburgh & Shawmut Railroad Co RD 2-Middle St, Brookville, Pa 15825	4' 8½" (1·435)	88 (142)	137 (220)		DeL 9			1 873	2 500·0	48 (77)	4 000	10 000		
Pittsburgh & West Virginia Rly Co *(Leased to Norfolk and Western)*	4' 8½" (1·435)	132 (212)	207 (333)			0	0							

* Incorporated into ConRail
† Taken over by ConRail 1 April 1977

Average Speeds			Financial Data		Couplers	Buffers	Rails	Sleepers (crossties)		Curvature max.	Gradient max. (U=not compensated)	Axle load max.	Altitude max.	Staff employed. Total no. (inclu. workshop)	Names of officials. Extended lists can be found at the end of the individual country in the report section immediately following
Freight Train	Pass. Train	Speed max.	Revenue Expenses	Braking (continuous)	Type and Height above rail	Centres and Height above rail	Weight	Type and thickness	Spacing Number per mile (per km) or centres						
mph (km/hr)	mph (km/hr)	mph (km/hr)	in 1 000's		ins (mm)	ins (mm)	lb. per yd (kg/m)	ins (mm)	ins (mm)			tonnes	feet (m)		
35 (56)			$ 2 164·0 2 083·0	Air W'hse	Type E 34½ (876)		85/70 (42/35)	Wood 7 (178)	20″ (508)	5·0°	1·92%	31·25		111	Gen Man: F. K. Turner
		40 (64)	$16 186 14 004				100 (50)	Wood 7 (178)	20″ (508)	8·0°	2·9%	25		765	Pres: Henry Oeljen
18 (29)		30 (48)		Air Various	AAR Standard		90/65 (45/32)	Wood 7 (178)	3 200 (2 000)					51 (8)	Pres: J. Hannigan
12 (20)		45 (72)	$ 12 792 9 539				136/90 (67/45)	Wood 6 (153)	19½″ (495)	15°	3·04%	25		471	Pres: R. L. King
8 (12·9)				W'hse	AAR Standard		110/70 (55/35)	Imp. Fir. 7 (178)	20″ (508)	17·3°	0·6%	40	20 (6)	30 (3)	Pres: R. G. Flannery
														1 032 (42)	Supt: R. O. Bills
5-10 (8-16)		35 (56)					100/75 (50/37)	Wood 6 (153)	24″ (610)	30·0°			1 918 (365)	3 (0)	Pres: J. W. Hewitt
25 (40)		35 (57)		W'hse Air	Type E		90/70 (45/35)	Fir 7 (178)	3 000 (1 870)	12·0°	2·5%	22·5	4 800 (1 463)	19	Pres: H. H. Howard Supt: R. L. Roy
							80/75 (40/37)								Pres: W. B. Kyle
							115/112 (57/42)	Wood 7 (178)	18″ (508)	7·3°	0·97% U	33	397 (457)		Supt: L. Hogan
															Gen. Man: J. A. Emery
20 (32)		30 (48)		N York AB			85 (42)	Wood 6 (153)	24″ (610)	3·0°	Level			25 (2)	Pres: T. L. Crosby
15 (24)		20 (32)		W'hse			110/40 (55/20)	Wood 8 (203)	24″ (610)	12·5°	1·4%	30	2 960 (902)	28 (2)	Gen. Man: H. L. Cox
				Air	D.E. & Tightlock 34½″ (876)	28″ (711) 50″ (1 270)	140/100 (70/50)	Wood 7 (178)	19½″ (495)	12°	2·9% 2·6% U	33	2 195 (6 430)		
35 (56)	60 (96)	70 (112)	$ 9 828 11 478	Air W'hse NYAB	AAR Type E 34½ (876)		133/70 (66/35)	Wood 7 (178) 9 (228)	19½″ (495)	7·0°	3·0% 3·0% U	32·8	167 (51)	511	Gen. Man: R. E. Blosser
		35 (56)	$ 2 788·7 2 473·5				90 (45)	Wood 6 & 7		10·0°	1·0%	33		414 (30)	Pres: F. J. Duggan
							100/66 (50/33)	Wood 6 (153)	3 020 (1 880)	13·75°	1·42%	22·5			
6 (10)		15 (24)	$ 166 151				90/70 (45/35)	Wood 6 (153)	19½″ (495)	30°	3·04%	22·5			Pres: R. L. King
														671	Vice Pres. and Supt: R. N. Henning
15 (24)		15 (24)	$ 5 105·7 4 169·4	Air W'hse	AAR Type E		100/85 (50/42)	Wood 7 (178)	2 600 (1 615)		3·0%			7	Pres: Jane Gillespie
		49 (79)	$ 6 694 3 704											355 (37)	Gen. Man: F. Sellers
															Pres: R. C. Repp
							90 (45)	Wood 6 (153)	22″ (560)						Pres: W. H. Moser
15 (24)		20 (32)	$ 1 707 1 187	W'hse	Type E		115 (57)	Oak 7 (178)	22″ (560)	17·5°	1·85% U	30·8			Pres: H. G. Pike
28 (45)	30 (48)	50 (80) F 65 (105) P	$ 52 752·5 47 383·6	Air W'hse	AAR 34½ (876)		132/100 (66/50)	Oak 7 (178)	20″ (508)	10·0°	0·6% 0·3% U	39	916 (279)	2 970 (740)	Pres: H. G. Allyn
		15 (24)	$ 862·6 501·1	Air W'hse	AAR 34½ Type D		130/80 (65/40)	Wood 7 (178)	21/24″ (533/610)	18·0°	0·75%	33	735 (224)	33	Pres: T. H. Connolly
30 (48)		40 (64)	$ 3 715·0	W'hse	Type E		131/85 (65/42)	Wood 7 (178)	21″ (533)	9·0°	1·0%	31·0	1 642 (501)	140 (61)	Chair: A. G. Dustin Pres: W. R. Weaver

NAME OF COMPANY ADDRESS	Gauge ft. in. (metres)	Route length incl. E=Electrified miles (km.)	Track length incl. E=Electrified miles (km.)	Elect. system and type of conductor	Locomotives L=Line S=Shunt; Steam Electric Diesel De=elec. Dh=hyd.	Rail-cars Electric Diesel Trailer Railbus Multiple Unit set	Pass. train cars	Freight train cars Containers	Total Volume carried. Thousands of tonnes	Av'ge haul per ton miles (km.)	Av'ge net train load tonnes	Max. trailing load tonnes	Total number carried in 1 000's	Average journey miles (km.)
Point Comfort & Northern Railroad 410 One Allegheny Sq, Pittsburgh, Pa 15212	4' 8½" (1·435)	13 (21)	16 (25)		DeL 3									
Port Huron & Detroit Railroad Co 2100 Thirty-Second St, Port Huron, Mich	4' 8½" (1·435)	20 (32)	30 (48)		D 2				342·2	10 (16)	2 100			
Portland Terminal Company (Switching Terminal for Maine Central) 242 St John St, Portland, Maine 04102	4' 8½" (1·435)	*23 (37)	99 (159)		DeS 14			50						
Portland Traction Company Portland 14, Oreg 97204	4' 8½" (1·435)	37 (60) E 25 (40)	65 (105) E 39 (63)	600 V dc OH	E 2 D 2	E 16		87	426·7				447·4	
Port Terminal Railroad Assn. PO Box 9504, Houston, Tex 77011	4' 8½" (1·435)	31·6 (50·6)	156 (251)		DeS 16									
Port Townsend Railroad Joshua Green Bldg, Seattle 1, Wash	4' 8½" (1·435)	12 (19)			D 2									
Prattsburgh Railway Corporation Prattsburgh, Steuben Co, NY	4' 8½" (1·439)	12 (19)	13 (21)											
Prescott & Northwestern RR Co PO Box 579, Prescott, Ark 71857	4' 8½" (1·435)	32 (51)	38 (61)		DeL 3				168·8	18 (29)	800			
Quincy Railroad Co Inc PO Box 420, Quincy, Cal 95971	4' 8½" (1·435)	4 (5)	4 (7)		DeL 2				63·9	3 (5)	150			
Rahway Valley Co Blvd & Market St, Kenilworth, NJ 07033	4' 8½" (1·435)	11 (18)	15 (24)		D 2				118·8	2·7 (4·3)				
Raritan River Railroad Co 170 John St, South Amboy, NJ	4' 8½" (1·435)	17 (27)	34 (55)		DeS 6				904·3	6 (10)	500			
Reader Railroad PO Box 9, Malvern, Ark 72104	4' 8½" (1·435)	24 (39)	27 (43)		SL 1									
† The Reading Company 12th & Market St, Philadelphia, Pa 19107	4' 8½" (1·435)	1 120 (1 802) E 92 (148)	2 536 (4 071) E 193 (310)	12 000 V. 1/25 OH										
Richmond, Fredricksburg & Potomac RR Co PO Box 11281, Richmond, Va 23230	4' 8½" (1·435)	113‡ (182)	473 (761)		DeL 26 DeS 14			1 329	10 134·0	102·4 (164·8)	2 217	8 350	524·3	106·3 (171·1)
Richmond Terminal Railway Co Broad St Station, Richmond, Va 23220	4' 8½" (1·435)	1·5 (2·5)	8 (13)		DeS 1									
River Terminal Railway Co 3100 East 45th St, Cleveland, Ohio	4' 8½" (1·435)		27 (43)		D 18			244						
Rockdale, Sandow & Southern RR 410 One Allegheny Sq, Pittsburg, Pa 15212	4' 8½" (1·435)	6 (10)	8 (12)		De 2									
Roscoe, Snyder & Pacific Rly Co PO Box 68, Roscoe, Tex 79545	4' 8½" (1·435)	30 (48)	39 (57)		DeL 2			766	665·2	0·63 (1·1)	625	4·92		
St Johnsbury & Lamoille County RR Stratford St, Morrisville, Vt 05661	4' 8½" (1·435)	98 (154)	98 (174)		DeL 2									
St Joseph Belt Railway Co South St. Joseph, Mo (Subsidiary of Missouri Pacific)	4' 8½" (1·435)	2 (3)	18 (29)		D 3		None	None						
St Joseph Terminal Railroad Co 803 South 4th St, St. Joseph, Mo	4' 8½" (1·435)		9 (14)		DS 2		None	None						
St Louis-San Francisco Railway Co ("Frisco" Lines including QA & P) 906 Olive St, St Louis, Mo 63101	4' 8½" (1·435)	4 736 (7 616)	6 850 (11 020)		DeL 339 DeS 92			15 706	20 108·6	34 139 270 000 ton-miles				
St Louis Southwestern Railway Lines 408 Pine St, St. Louis, Mo 63162 (Southern Pacific)	4' 8½" (1·435)	1 441 (2 318)	2 240 (3 605)		DeL 190 DeS 53			19 085						
St Mary's Railroad Co PO Box 528, St. Marys, Ga	4' 8½" (1·435)	11 (18)	20 (32)		D 3			56	8 824·3	11 (18)	1 800	5 800		
St Paul Union Depot Co 2071 University Ave, St Paul Minn 55104 (Switching line)	4' 8½" (1·435)	1·54 (2·3)												
Sacramento Northern Railway (In conjunction with Tidewater Southern RR) 526 Mission St, San Francisco, Cal	4' 8½" (1·435)	349 (583)	470 (785)	600 V dc OH	De 13		None	233	949·4	50 (80)	445			
Salt Lake, Garfield & Western Rly Co 11th West and South Temple, Salt Lake City, Utah 84116	4' 8½" (1·435)	17 (27)	20 (32)		DeL 3		5	3	106·0	9 (15)	350	840	3·5	30 (48)
Sandersville Railroad Co PO Box 269, Sandersville, Ga	4' 8½" (1·435)	(14)	22 (35)		DeS 3			248	400·0	5 (8)	2 000			
San Diego & Arizona Eastern Ry Co (Subsidiary of Southern Pacific) 45 12th St, San Diego	4' 8½" (1·435)	138 (222)	166 (267)		DeS 5			16						

* Includes mainline leased from BN
† Taken over by ConRail 1 April 1976
‡ Only 109 miles (175 km) operated

Freight Train mph (km/hr)	Pass. Train mph (km/hr)	Speed max. mph (km/hr)	Revenue Expenses in 1 000's	Braking (continuous)	Couplers Type and Height above rail ins (mm)	Buffers Centres and Height above rail ins (mm)	Rails Weight lb. per yd (kg/m)	Sleepers Type and thickness ins (mm)	Spacing Number per mile or centres ins (mm)	Curvature max.	Gradient max. (U=not compensated)	Axle load max. tonnes	Altitude max. feet (m)	Staff employed. Total no. (inclu. workshop)	Names of officials.
20 (32)		35 (56)					115/85 (57/42)	Oak 6 (153)	21" (533)	6·5°	0·47%	31·5	40 (12·2)	32	Pres: W. Murray
				W'hse			80 (40)	Wood 6 (153)	24" (610)	9·0°	3·0%	30·5			Pres: G. Y. Duffy
10 (16)		40 (64)		Air W'hse	AAR Type E 34½ (876)		115/75 (57/37)	Wood 6 & 7	21" (533)	15·0°	1·5% **U**	32·8	111 (33·8)	322 (64)	Pres: E. Spencer Miller
	15·6 25·1)						90/70 (45/35)	Wood 7 (178)	22½" (570)	100·0°	3·0%				Pres: T. P. Rogers
		30 (48)					115/75 (57/37)	Oak 6 (153)	19½" (495)	9·1°	1·04% 0·86% **U**	32·8	40 (12·2)	400 (80)	
12 (19)			$ 320·5 234·3				85/56 (42/27)	Wood 6 (153)	22" (560)	6·0°	1·6%	35	250 (76)	21 (4)	Gen Man: H. B. Graham
5 (8)	10 (16)		$113·1 73·6	Air W'hse			75/45 (37/22)	Fir 6 (153)	22" (560)	14·0°			3 550 (1 082)	4	Pres: A. A. Emerson
10 (16)	25 (40)		$ 192·5 166·7	Air			70 (36)	Oak					175 (53)	14	Pres and Gen Man: B. J. Cahill
		20 (33)		W'hse			100 (50)	Wood 7 (178)	24" (610)	12·0°	1·82%	33		57 (5)	Vice Pres: Robert G. Kipp
12 (19)	12 (19)	25 (40)		Air			85/52 (42/26)	Wood						21 (3)	Gen Man: R. A. Grigsby
17·1 (27)	32 (50)	75 (121)					140/79 (70/39)	Wood 7 (178)	2 960 (1 840)	Main 2·0° Br. 12·7°	3·3%	32·0	1 468 (447)		
		70 (112)	$ 30 910·9 18 102·8	Air W'hse NYAB	Tightlock Nat. Mal. 34½ (876)		140/100 (70/50)	Oak 7 (178)	20" (508)	4·0°	0·8%	30	225 (68)	1 253 (405)	Pres: Stuart Shumate
			$ 22·6 555·5				131/100 (65/50)	Oak 7 (178)	20" (508)	12°	0·5%	30	197 (60)	28	Pres: Stuart Shumate
							115/85 (57/42)	Wood 7 (178)	20" (508)						Gen. Man: T. E. Malloy
20 (32)		35 (56)					115/85 (57/42)	Oak 6 (153)	21" (533)	5·1°	1·6%	31·5	537	16	Pres: W. Murray
25 (40)	45 (72)		$ 1 812·1 1 408·6	Air W'hse	AAR Standard Type E		75/56 (37/27)	Wood 6 (155)	22" (560)	12·0°			22 (7)	51 (1)	Pres: R. B. Mize
18 (29·0)			$ 475 107 439 588	Air			85/67 (42/33)	Wood 6 & 7	22" (560)	14·0°	2·%	25			Pres & Gen Man: Bruno A. Loati
							90 (45)	Wood 6 (153)	25" (635)	20·0°	0·54%U				Pres: K. D. Hestes
							90 (45)	Wood		18·0°				65	Supt: H. T. Hinman
21·4 (34·4)	65 (105)		$ 321 512·4 244 935·2	Air	AAR Standard AB		132/90 (66/45)	Wood 7 (178)	3 250 (2 030)	10·4°	2·35% 2·15%U	39	3 195 (1 228)	8 300	Chairman of Board and Pres: R. C. Grayson
		70 (112)	$ 163 405 123 258				136/80 (68/40)	Wood 7 (178)	20" (508)	4·0°	1·0% 1·0% U	32·5	860 (262)		Pres: D. K. McNear
		40 (64)		Air W'hse			90 (45)	Wood 7 (178)	21" (533)	8·0°	0·5%			31 (4)	Vice Pres. and Man: R. W. Chaplin
										15·0°					Pres: C. R. Hussey Gen Man: J. A. Lehn
		30 (48)	$ 3 228·5 1 815·7	Air W'hse	Type E & F 34½ (876)		100/60 (50/30)	Wood 6 (153) 7 (178)	2 880 (1 790)	20·0° *	1·3% 1·1%U *	27·5	200 (61)	123	Pres: R. G. Flannery
30 (48)	35 (56)	40 (64)		Air W'hse	AAR		60 (29·8)	Fir 7 (178)	20" (508)	10·0°	1·0%	33	4 235 (1 292)	10	Vice Pres. and Gen Man: Rex N. Firth
							90 (45)	Wood 7 (178)	22" (559)						Gen Man: B. J. Tarbutton Jr
		30 (48)					90/75 (45/37)	Wood 6 (153)	22" (559)	20·0°	2·2%	26·2	3 360 (1 200)		Pres: R. L. King

* On Arthur Sub near MP 476

NAME OF COMPANY ADDRESS	Gauge ft. in. (metres)	Route length incl. E=Electrified miles (km.)	Track length incl. E=Electrified miles (km.)	Elect. system and type of conductor	Loco-motives L=Line S=Shunt Steam Electric Diesel De=elec. Dh=hyd.	Rail-cars Electric Diesel Trailer Railbus Multiple Unit set	Pass. train cars	Freight train cars Containers	Total Volume carried. Thousands of tonnes	Av'ge haul per ton miles (km.)	Av'ge net train load tonnes	Max. trailing load tonnes	Total number carried in 1 000's	Average journey miles (km.)
USA (contd.)														
San Francisco Belt Railroad Ferry Bdg., San Francisco, Cal 94111	4' 8½" (1·435)	8·5 (14)	60 (96)		DeS 4				5 742 cars					
San Luis Central Railroad Co PO Box 1249, Evanston, Ill 60204	4' 8½" (1·435)	13 (21)	16 (26)		DeS 1			452	57·7	714 335 ton-miles				
San Manuel Arizona Railroad Co San Manuel, Ariz 85631	4' 8½" (1·435)	30 (48)	30 (48)		DeL 6			4	1 030·8	29·4 (46·8)			3 000	
Sand Springs Railway Box 427, Sand Springs, Okla	4' 8½" (1·435)	8 (13)			D 3			4						
Santa Maria Valley RR Co PO Box 340, Santa Maria, Cal 93454	4' 8½" (1·435)	18 (29)	28 (45)		DeL 8			3	1 460·4	7 935·186				
Savannah & Atlanta Railway Co *(Merged into Southern Railway System)*	4' 8½" (1·435)	168 (270)												
Seaboard Coast Line Railroad Co 3600 West Broad St, Richmond, Va 23230 *(part of The Family Lines System)*	4' 8½" (1·435)	9 028 (14 514)	9 380 (15 106)		DeL 1 135* DeS 191			63 449 (C 3 546)	146 895	51 037 942 000 ton-km				
Sierra Railroad Company 781 S. Washington St, Sonora, Cal 95370	4' 8½" (1·435)	56 (92)	67 (124)		S 2 DeL 3		15	23	484·1	45·7 (73)		900	1 200	
Sioux City Terminal Railway Co 340 Livestock Exch Bldg, Sioux City, Iowa 51107	4' 8½" (1·435)	2·5 (4)	12 (19)		DeS 3									
Skaneateles Short Line Railroad Corp 32 Fennell St, Skaneateles, NY	4' 8½" (1·435)	5 (8)	6 (10)		DL 2			2	87·7	2 (3·2)				
Soo Line RR Company 800 Soo Line Building, Minneapolis, Box 530, Minn 55440	4' 8½" (1·435)	4 589 (7 370)	6 103 (9 822)		DeL 196 DeS 30			12 100	21 060·0	105 591 000 000				
South Brooklyn Railway Co 990 Third ave, Brooklyn, NY 11232	4' 8½" (1·435)	6 (10)	12 (20)		DL 2									
South Buffalo Railway Co 2558 Hamburg Turnpike, Lackawanna 18, NY	4' 8½" (1·435)	30 (48)	75 (121)		DeS 46		0	69	24 000·0	3 (4·8)		2 000	7 500	
South Carolina State Ports Authority PO Box 874, Charleston SC 29402 *Operates the following two railroads:*														
Port Utilities Commission	4' 8½" (1·435)		10 (16)		D 5									
Port Terminal Railway	4' 8½" (1·435)		8 (13)											
South Georgia Railway Co Atlanta 3, Ga	4' 8½" (1·435)	77 (124)			D 1			1						
South Omaha Terminal Railway Co 920 Livestock Exchange Bldg, Omaha, Nebr 68107	4' 8½" (1·435)	26 (42)			DeS 1			3	Switching only					
Southern Industrial Railroad Inc PO Box 358, Centreville, Iowa 52544	4' 8½" (1·435)	15 (24)	20 (32)		D 2									
Southern New York Railway Inc 22 Morgan Ave, West Oneonta, NY	4' 8½" (1·435)	2 (3)	3 (5)		D 2									
Southern Railway System 920 15th St, NW, Washington DC 2005	4' 8½" (1·435)	10 494 (16 732)	17 282 (27 537)		DeL1 115 DeS 193		129	76 721	140 439·9 ton-km	45 743 147	1 809	18 000	217·9	382 (507)
Southern Pacific Transportation Company One Market Plaza, San Francisco, Cal 94105	4' 8½" (1·435)	13 601 (21 762)	21 300 (34 200)		DeL 559 DeS 1 405		103	87 445	112 992·5	591 (951)			NA	
Southern San Luis Valley Railroad PO Box 98, Blanca, Colo 81123	4' 8½" (1·435)	1·3 (2·1)	2·6 (4·2)		DhS 1				13·8	0·9 (1·4)	100	300		
Spokane International Railroad Co 1416 Dodge St, Omaha, Nebr 68102	4' 8½" (1·435)	150 (241)						85	2 516·9	511 285 084 ton miles				
Springfield Terminal Railway Co Clinton St, Springfield, Vt 05156	4' 8½" (1·435)	6 (10)	7·5 (12)		DeS 1				Switching only					
Staten Island Rapid Transit Ry Co 25 Broadway, New York, NY 10004 *(Subsidiary of Baltimore & Ohio Railroad)*	4' 8½" (1·435)	27 (43) E 14 (23)	145 (233) E 29 (47)	600 V dc 3 rail	DeS 8		55		1 509·9	10·6 (17)	1 217		4 839·2	6·5 (10·6)
Steelton & Highspire Railroad Co Steelton, Pa 17113	4' 8½" (1·435)	3	28 (55)		DeS 8									
Stewartstown Railroad Co Stewartstown, Pa	4' 8½" (1·435)	7 (11)			D 1 Pet 1									
Stockton Terminal & Eastern RR PO Box 1410, Stockton, Cal 95201	4' 8½" (1·435)	14 (22)	19 (30)		DeL 3				606·0			1 800		
Strasburg Railroad Co. PO Box 96, Strasburg, Pa 17579	4' 8½" (1·435)	4·5 (7·2)	5 (8)		S 5 De 1 Gas 1		14	4	600·1				363·2	
Strouds Creek and Muddlety RR Grafton, W Va	4' 8½" (1·435)	23 (37)			D 1									

* Includes 129 owned by SCL and leased to L&N

Average Speeds			Financial Data		Couplers	Buffers	Rails	Sleepers (crossties)							
Freight Train	Pass. Train	Speed max.	Revenue Expenses	Braking (continuous)	Type and Height above rail	Centres and Height above rail	Weight	Type and thickness	Spacing Number per mile (per km) or centres	Curvature max.	Gradient max. (U=not compensated)	Axle load max.	Altitude max.	Staff employed. Total no. (inclu. workshop)	Names of officials. Extended lists can be found at the end of the individual country in the report section immediately following
mph (km/hr)	mph (km/hr)	mph (km/hr)	in 1 000's		ins (mm)	ins (mm)	lb. per yd (kg/m)	ins (mm)	ins (mm)			tonnes	feet (m)		
6 (10)		10 (16)	$ 187·3 485·4	Air W'hse	Type D 33 (850)		174/85 (86/42)	Wood 7 (178)	2 285 (1 420)	25·0°	5·0%			24 (11)	Pres: W. B. Kyle
10 (16)		10 (16)	$ 607 287 589 407	Air W'hse			56 (28)	Wood 6 (153)	22" (559)	1·0°	0·1%	26	7 650 (2 332)	7	Pres: G. G. Betke, Jr.
20 (32)		35 (56)		Air W'hse			90 (45)	Wood 8 (204)	21" (534)	6°	2·0% U	35	3 200 (975)	44	Pres: W. L. Parks
			$ 1 898·9 949·1				90/75 (45/37)	Fir 7 (178)	3 168 (1 970)					46	Pres: Marian H. Barry Vice Pres: Sue J. Ford
60 (96)		79 (127)	$ 728 485 549 107	Air W'hse NY Co	E 34½" (876)		100/131 (49/65)	Wood 7 (178)	2 960 (1 850)	10·0°	1·8%	24		19 882	Pres. and Chief Executive Officer: Prime F. Osborn III
15 (24)	25 (40)	35 (56)	$ 474·6 310·0	Air W'hse			110/90 (55/45)	Fir 7 (178)	21" (534)	18·0°	3·0%	19	1 769 (547)	25 (14)	Pres: Charles Crocker Gen. Man: D. J. Franco
							90/85 (45/42)	Oak 6 (153)	18" (457)	26·0°	4·0%	20	1 135 (346)	35	Pres: Ray. A. Rodeen
30 (48)				Air W'hse			70 (34·7)	Wood 7 (178)	18" (457)					7	Pres: G. A. Coffenberg
21 (34)		40 (64)	$ 161 155·0 125 694·0	Air	E & F 35½" (902)		131/52 (65/26)	Wood 6/7	20-22	6·0°	2·9% 3·2% U	32	2 550 (777)	5 110 (1 200)	Pres: L. H. Murray
															Pres: J. G. de Roos
6 (9·6)		25 (40)	$ 11 420·0 8 802·5		34 (864)		115/105 (57/52)	Wood 7 (178)	22" (559)	38·0°	2·0% 2·0% U	30	611 (983)	1 200 (65)	Pres: R. J. Kent
			$ 542·2 552·9	Air AB	Type E 33 (840)		75 (37)	Oak 6 (153)	22" (559)	10·0°	2·5%	33	14 (4)	40 (4)	Pres: W. W. Kratville
							141/100 (70/50)	Wood 7 (178)	20" (508)	6·0°					Pres: L. S. Crane
20·8 (33·5)	44 (71)	79 (127)	$ 1 052 785·6 914 605·0	Air W'hse	Types E & F		132/70 (66/35)	Wood 7 (178)	3 250 (2 030)	6·0°	4·36% 4·21% U	35	3 360 (1 024)	21 569	Pres: L. S. Crane
25 (40)		79 (127)	$ 1 447·5 89 577	Air AB	AAR Type E		136/113 (67/53)	Wood 9 (229)	19½" (497)	14·0°	2·8%	35	7 032 (2 143)	43 900	Pres. & Chief Ex. Off: B. F. Biaggini Vice Pres: L. E. Hoyt
8 (13)		13 (22)	$ 17·3 15·2	Air			65 (32)	Wood 7 (180)	30" (672)		2·0%		7 820 (2 384)		Pres. and Gen. Man: George M. Oringdulph
16 (26)				Air	AAR		131/72 (65/36)	Wood						124	Pres: J. C. Kenefick
10 (16)		30 (48)		Air W'hse	34½" (878)		85/70 (42/35)		15" (381)					12 (3)	Tres: W. O. Moeser
12·5 (20)	20 (32)			W'hse	H2A W'hse		100 (49·6)	Wood 7 (178)	22" (559)	16·0°	1·86%	25			Exec. Vice Pres: J. T. Collinson
															Pres: R. J. Kent
															Pres: J. H. Anderson
5 (8)		10 (16)		W'hse	AAR		90/60 (45/30)	Pine 8 (203)	24" (610)	24·0°	2·0%	20	Sea level	51 (1)	Gen Man: L. Hardaway Jr
29 (47)	29 (47)	29 (47)	$ 665·9 489·4	Air W'hse	AAR		85/90 (42/45)	Wood 6 (153)	22" (599)	18·0°	2·0%U	30·0	345 (105)	50	Pres: W. M. Moedinger
															Man: J. E. Sell

NAME OF COMPANY ADDRESS	Gauge ft. in. (metres)	Route length incl. E=Electrified miles (km.)	Track length incl. E=Electrified miles (km.)	Elect. system and type of conductor	Loco-motives L=Line S=Shunt Steam Electric Diesel De=elec. Dh=hyd.	Rail-cars Electric Diesel Trailer Railbus Multiple Unit set	Pass. train cars	Freight train cars Con-tainers	Total Volume carried. Thous-ands of tonnes	Av'ge haul per ton miles (km.)	Av'ge net train load tonnes	Max. trailing load tonnes	Total number carried in 1 000's	Average journey miles (km.)
Sumter & Choctaw Railway Co Bellamy, Ala 36901	4' 8½" (1·435)	4 (6)	4·9		De 1*			24		92	170			
Sunset Railway Co (Southern Pacific Affiliated Co)	4' 8½" (1·435)	51 (82)												
Sylvania Central Railway Co Dublin, Ga.	4' 8½" (1·435)	25 (40)												
Tacoma Municipal Belt Line Railway PO Box 11007, Tacoma, Wash 98424	4' 8½" (1·435)		33 (53)		DeS 6				60 000 carloads					
Tavares & Gulf Railroad Co Box 1007, Tavares, Fla	4' 8½" (1·435)	38 (61)												
Tennessee, Alabama & Georgia Rly Co 1478 Market St, PO Box 6508, Sta "B" Chattanooga, Tenn 37408	4' 8½" (1·435)	93 (150)	104 (167)		DeLS 4			115	1 279·1	80 (129)	1 728			
Tennessee Railroad Co PO Box 498, Oneida, Tenn 37841	4' 8½" (1·435)	57 (92)	71 (114)		D 6				940·4	30·5 (49·0)	3 200	6 500		
Terminal Railroad Assn of St. Louis 18th & Market St, St. Louis, Mo 63103	4' 8½" (1·435)	53 (87)	378 (608)		DeS 93			75	740 033 carloads					
Terminal Railway of the Alabama State Docks Department Box 1588, Mobile, Ala 36601	4' 8½" (1·435)		75 (121)		DeS 11				111 344 carloads	6 (10)				
Texas City Terminal Railway Co PO Box 591, Texas City, Tex 77590 (Subsidiary of Missouri Pacific)	4' 8½" (1·435)	32 (53)	32 (53)		DeS 3				36 381 carloads					
Texas Mexican Railway Co 1200 Washington St, PO Box 519, Laredo, Tex (Subsidiary of Nat. Rlys of Mexico)	4' 8½" (1·435)	162 (261)	240 (386)		DeL 11 DeS 2			141	2 222·0					
Texas, Oklahoma & Eastern RR Co PO Box 1060, Hot Springs, Ark 71901	4' 8½" (1·435)	40 (64)	46 (74)						697·2	38·8	3 400			
Texas Pacific-Missouri Pacific Terminal RR of New Orleans New Orleans 13, La (Subsidiary of Missouri Pacific)	4' 8½" (1·435)	60 (96)	155 (249)		D 4									
Texas South-Eastern RR Co Diboll, Tex	4' 8½" (1·435)	21 (34)	27 (43)		DeS 3			1	225·1	13·5 (21·7)	722			
Tidewater Southern Railway Co 1025 19th St, Sacramento, Cal (In conjunction with Sacramento Northern)	4' 8½" (1·435)	57 (92)	70 (113)		DeL 3			93						
Toledo, Angola & Western Rly Co PO Box 307, Sylvania, Ohio 43560	4' 8½" (1·435)	8 (13)	10 (16)		DeS 1				200·0	8 (12·8)	400	20 Cars		
Toledo, Peoria & Western RR Co ("The Peoria Road") 2000 E. Washington St, East Peoria, Ill 61611	4' 8½" (1·435)	239 (385)	323 (520)		DeL 19 DeS 2			611	5 806·0	107·5 (172·5)	2 944		26	37 (59·5)
Toledo Terminal Railroad Co 3648 Hoffman Rd, PO Box 5148, Toledo, Ohio 43611	4' 8½" (1·435)	29 (47)	88 (142)		De 7									
Tooele Valley Railway Co 35 Nth, Broadway, Tooele, Utah 84074	4' 8½" (1·435)	7 (11)	9 (14)		DeLS 2				171·8	7 (11)	750	900		
Trona Railway Co Box 427, Trona, Cal 93562	4' 8½" (1·435)	31 (50)	34 (55)		DeL 4			1	1 176·9			125		
Troy Union Railroad Co (New York Central)	4' 8½" (1·435)	2 (3)												
Tucson, Cornelia & Gila Bend RR Co. Box 400, Ajo, Ariz	4' 8½" (1·435)	44 (71)	48 (77)		De 2		1	13	219·5					
Tulsa Sapulpa Union Railway PO Box 520 Sapulpa, Okla 74066	4' 8½" (1·435)	10 (16)	12 (19)		De 3				170·8	5 (8)	576	900		
Union Belt of Detroit (Track owned by PRR, C & O and Wabash RR) (Switching only)	4' 8½" (1·435)	115 (185)												
Union Pacific Corporation 1416 Dodge St, Omaha, Nebr 6817	4' 8½" (1·435)	9 432 (15 176)	15 836 (25 430)		DeL 1 318 DeS 140		T 1 500	71 798	89 679·9	659·3 (1 060)	1 876			
Union Railroad Co 600 Grant St, PO Box 536, Pittsburgh, Pa 15230	4' 8½" (1·435)	31·3 (49)	280 (451)		DeS 110			1 635						
Union Railway Co (Memphis) (Subsidiary of Missouri Pacific)	4' 8½" (1·435)	18 (29)												
Union Terminal Co (Dallas) 400 S Houston St, Dallas, Tex 75202	4' 8½" (1·435)	2 (3)	14·3 (22)											
Upper Merion & Plymouth RR Co PO Box 112, Conshohocken, Pa 19428	4' 8½" (1·435)	16 (26)	16 (26)		DeS 9			126						
Utah Railway Co 1770, University Club Bldg, 136 East S Temple, Salt Lake City, Utah 84111	4' 8½" (1·435)	94 (151)			DeL 14			194		1 266 278 ton-km				

* Diesel locos rented from Seaboard Air Line system

Average Speeds			Financial Data		Couplers	Buffers	Rails	Sleepers (crossties)							
Freight Train	Pass. Train	Speed max.	Revenue Expenses	Braking (continuous)	Type and Height above rail	Centres and Height above rail	Weight	Type and thickness	Spacing Number per mile or centres	Curvature max.	Gradient max. (U=not compensated)	Axle load max.	Altitude max.	Staff employed. Total no. (inclu. workshop)	Names of officials. Extended lists can be found at the end of the individual country in the report section immediately following
mph (km/hr)	mph (km/hr)	mph (km/hr)	in 1 000's		ins (mm)	ins (mm)	lb. per yd (kg/m)	ins (mm)	ins (mm)			tonnes	feet (m)		
6 (8)	10 (16)		$ 67 834 66 337	Air	AAR		85/56 (42/28)	Wood 7 (178)	18" (458)			66		3	Pres: J. W. Bard
															Pres: R. L. King
				Air W'hse	Type E 34" (860)		100/60 (50/30)	Wood 8 (200)	22" (560)	12°	level	33	Sea level	50 (2)	Gen Man: Donald E. Carlson
		40 (64)					100 (50)	Wood 7 (178)	21" (533)	8·5°	1·3%	30	954 (291)	85	
20 (32)	25 (40)		$ 582·4 493·1	Air W'hse	F National		112/70 (55/35)	Wood 7 (178)	18" (458)	16°	3·5%U	30	1 510 (460)	81 (4)	Gen Man & Co-Receiver: Tom Gentry
25 (40)				Air W'hse	AAR 33" (850)		115/100 (57/50)	Wood 6 & 7	21" (533)		2·6%	32·8	621 (189)	1 965 (100)	VP & Gen Man: O. R. Bailey Jr
10 (16)	30 (48)		$ 2 600·9 2 442·0	Air NYAB 14 KL	AAR		90/100 (45/50)	Wood 6 (153)	21" (553)	9°	1·0%	Coopers 72K	30 (9)	175 (18)	Gen Man: A. B. McKenzie
5 (8)			$ 2 194·0 2 028·6		AAR		112/60 (56/30)	Wood 6 (153)	2 600 (1 615)	17·0°			20 (6)	95 (12)	Gen Man: J. B. Wimberley
			$ 10 870·0 7 375·0		AAR		100/90 (50/45)	Wood 7 (178)	3 168 (1 930)	6·0°	0·75%		800 (244)		Pres. and Gen Man: B. F. Wright Jr
	35 (56)		$ 527·6 233·3				90/75 (45/37)	Wood 6 (153)	22" (560)	6·0°			480 (146)	23	
20 (32)							75/60 (37/30)	Wood 6 (153)	20" (508)	10·0°	1·5%				
		30 (48)		Air W'hse. NYAB			141/56 (70/28)	Wood 6 & 7	2 880 (1 790)	10·0°	1·0%	27	117 (36)	30 (0)	VP and Gen Man: L. D. Michelson
15 (24)			$ 118 000 113 000		AAR		75 (37)	Oak 6 (153)	22" (560)	15·0°	2·0%		660 (210)	9	
		49 (79)	$ 15 250·0 11 610·0	W'hse	AAR		131/80 (65/40)	Oak 6 (153)	20" (508)	6·0°	1·3%U	33	770 (1 239)	422 (80)	Pres: C. L. Pattison Chairman: J. Russel Coulter
							112/100 (56/50)	Oak 6 (153) 7 (178)	21" (533)	6·0°	0·83%	Coopers E-70		136	
6 (9·7)	18 (29)		$ 121·5 167·7	Air W'hse	Type E 34½ (876)		85 (42)	Wood 7 (178)	15" (381)	14·0°	2·4%	31	4 950 (1 509)	23 (2)	VP: E. W. Steinbeck
14 (22·5)	25 (40)		$ 1 466·0 843·3	Air W'hse	Type F 32 (813)		112/75 (56/37)	Wood 7 (178)	18" (458)	30·5°	1·85%	2·5	3 248 (990)	52	Pres: J. S. Latham
			$ 671·7 484·1												
10 (16)	15 (24)		$ 209·0 208·3	Air W'hse			90/60 (45/30)	Oak 8 (203)	18" (457)		2·0%			19 (9)	Gen. Man: E. M. Grosvener
32 (51·5)	52·2 (84)		$ 1 174 600·0 849 000·0	Air W'hse	Type E		133/75 (66/37)	Wood 7 (178)			2·21%		8 240 (2 511)	29 362	Pres: J. C. Kenefick
			$ 36 636·9 28 337·9	Air W'hse									2 186 (865)		Pres: M. S. Toon
		25 (40)		Air			100/90 (50/45)	Wood 6 (153)	25" (635)	12·0°	0·54% U		424 (129)	108 (1)	Gen. Man: D. E. Walker
6 (9)	10 (16)		$ 2 526·7 2 124·1	Air			115/90 (57/45)	Wood	2 344 (1 465)					116 (24)	Pres: W. F. Finley Gen. Supt: V. P. Perone
			$ 2 447·7 2 407·7				115/75 (57/37)	Wood 7 (178)	22" (560)	8·0° Br. 12·0°	2·0% Br. 3·9%	31·5		8	Pres: O. K. Curtis

NAME OF COMPANY ADDRESS	Gauge ft. in. (metres)	Route length incl. E=Electrified miles (km.)	Track length incl. E=Electrified miles (km.)	Elect. system and type of conductor	Locomotives L=Line S=Shunt Steam Electric Diesel De=elec. Dh=hyd.	Rail-cars Electric Diesel Trailer Railbus Multiple Unit set	Pass. train cars	Freight train cars Containers	Total Volume carried. Thousands of tonnes	Av'ge haul per ton miles (km.)	Av'ge net train load tonnes	Max. trailing load tonnes	Total number carried in 1 000's	Average journey miles (km.)
Valdosta Southern RR PO Box 1147, Valdosta, Ga 31601	4' 8½" (1-435)	28 (45)			D 2									
Ventura County Railroad Co PO Box 432, Oxnard, Cal 93030	4' 8½" (1-435)	10 (16)	12 (19)		D 3			2	350·0	10·7 (16)				
Virginia Blue Ridge Railway Piney River, Va 22964	4' 8½" (1-435)	10 (16)	11 (17)		DeL 2			3	59·9	8 (13)	75			
Virginia Central Railway PO Box 239, Fredericksburg, Va 22401	4' 8½" (1-435)	1 (1-6)	2 (3-2)				1		20·0	1 (1-6)	50	50		
Visalia Electric Railroad Co (Southern Pacific Affiliated Co)	4' 8½" (1-435)	34 (55)	45 (72)											
Wabash Railroad Company St. Louis, Miss (Leased to Norfolk and Western October 1964)	4' 8½" (1-435)													
Waco, Beaumont, Trinity & Sabine Railway Co Trinity, Tex	4' 8½" (1-435)	14 (22)												
Walla Walla Valley Railway Co 176 E. Fifth St, St Paul, Minn 55101	4' 8½" (1-435)	19 (30)	28 (45)		DeS 2				83·6	8 (13)				
Ware Shoals Railroad Co Ware Shoals, SC	4' 8½" (1-435)	5 (8)			D 1									
Warren & Ouachita Valley Rly Co 325 West Cedar St, PO Box 150, Warren, Ark 71671	4' 8½" (1-435)	16 (26)	17 (28)		DeL 1				185·5	15 (24)				
Warren & Saline River Railroad Co PO Box 390, Warren, Ark 71671	4' 8½" (1-435)	16 (25-7)	17 (27-3)		DeS 2	R 2 T 2		1	70·5	2-2 (3-5)				
Warrenton Railroad Co PO Box 518, Warrenton, NC 27589	4' 8½" (1-435)	3 (5)	3-8 (7-2)		DeL 2				6·5					
Warwick Railway Co Box 2262, Edgewood 5, RI	4' 8½" (1-435)	1 (2)			D 2									
Washington, Idaho & Montana Rly Co Lewiston, Idaho	4' 8½" (1-435)	50 (80)	64 (103)											
Washington Terminal Co Union Station, Washington, DC	4' 8½" (1-435)	52 (84)	50 (80) E 17 (27)		DeS 7									
Waterloo Railroad Co Waterloo, Iowa (ICGR)	4' 8½" (1-435)	67 (108)	92 (148)		DeS 4			8						
Wellsville, Addison & Galeton RR Galeton, Pa	4' 8½" (1-435)	80 (129)	133 (214)		D 4			135						
Western Railway of Alabama (See Atlanta & West Point RR Co)														
West Pittston-Exeter Railroad Co 901 Hamilton St, Allentown, Pa 18101 (Acquired by the Lehigh Valley Railroad in 1973)	4' 8½" (1-435)	3 (5)	4-4 (6)		DeL 1									
West Virginia Northern Railroad Co PO Box 458, Kingswood, W Va	4' 8½" (1-435)	17 (27)	22 (35)		DeS 3									
Western Maryland Railway Co 2 N Charles St, Baltimore, Md 21201	4' 8½" (1-435)	860 (1 181)	1 380 (2 247)		DeL 115 DeS 4									
Western Pacific Railroad Co 526 Mission St, San Francisco, Cal	4' 8½" (1-435)	1 187 (1 910)	1 695 (2 727)	OH	DeL 138 DeS 15		9	5 943 C 274	11 794·6	555 (893)	1 650			
White Sulphur Springs & Yellowstone Park Railway Co Box 30, White Sulphur Springs, Mont 59645	4' 8½" (1-435)	23 (37)	48 (37)		De 1 S 1			5						
Wichita Union Terminal Rly 1537 Barwise, Wichita, Kans 67214	4' 8½" (1-435)	9 (15)												
Wilkes-Barre Connecting RR Co Hudson, Pa	4' 8½" (1-435)	9 (14)												
Winchester & Western Railroad Co Piccadilly and Kent Sts, PO Box 264, Winchester, Va 22601	4' 8½" (1-435)	18 (29)	18 (29)		DeL 1				118·5	18 (29)	600	1 200		
Winfield Railroad Co Cabot, Penn 16023	4' 8½" (1-435)	9 (14)	10-95 (17-7)		DeL 1				17·7	9 (14)	300	950		
Winifrede Railroad Co Winifrede, W Va	4' 8½" (1-435)	7 (11)	12 (19)		DeL 1			75	916·6	7 (11)	1 300			
Winston-Salem Southbound Ry Co PO Box 205, Winston-Salem, NC	4' 8½" (1-435)	99 (159)			D 4			42						
Woodward Iron Co's Railroad Woodward, Ala 33189	4' 8½" (1-435)	20 (32)	60 (95)		DeLS 9			548	8 760·0	10 (16)	2 500	70		
Wrightsville & Tennille RR Co Tennille, Ga (Subsidiary of Central of Georgia)	4' 8½" (1-435)	36 (58)			S 1			5						

Average Speeds			Financial Data		Braking (con- tinuous)	Couplers	Buffers	Rails	Sleepers (crossties)		Curva- ture max.	Gradient max. (U=not compen- sated)	Axle load max.	Alti- tude max.	Staff em- ployed. Total no. (inclu. work- shop)	Names of officials. Extended lists can be found at the end of the individual country in the report section immediately following
Freight Train	Pass. Train	Speed max.	Revenue Expenses			Type and Height above rail	Centres and Height above rail	Weight	Type and thick- ness	Spacing Number per mile (per km) or centres ins (mm)						
mph (km/hr)	mph (km/hr)	mph (km/hr)	in 1 000's			ins (mm)	ins (mm)	lb. per yd (kg/m)	ins (mm)				tonnes	feet (m)		
10 (16)		15 (24)						90/60 (45/30)	Wood 6 & 8	22'' (560)	13·0°	1·0% U				Gen. Man: C. C. O'Hara Cont: W. Graf
15 (24)		20 (32)	$ 216·6 154·3					80/75 (40/37)	Wood 9 (229)	2 600 (1 600)					14 (1)	Gen. Supt: J. M. Drumheller
10 (16)		15 (24)	$ 19·5 27·3	W'hse	AAR 32½'' (877)			100/60 (50/30)	Wood 6 (153)	21'' (534)	20·0°	40% U	35	96 (26)	3	Gen. Man: F. Freeman Funk
								80/60 (40/30)	Fir 6 (153)	18'' (457)	13·0°	1·0% U				
12 (19)		20 (32)	$ 173·0 177·9		Standard			100/56 (50/28)	Wood 6 (153)	2 816 (1 760)	14·0°	1·0%		1 000 (305)	18 (2)	Gen. Man: K. E. Schneidmiller
10 (16)															8	Pres: R. J. Lane
5 (8)		20 (32)	$ 115·5 137·7	NY Air				75/60 (37/30)	Wood 6 (153)	3 000 (1 875)	3·0°	1·6%	25	Sea level	11 (1)	Gen. Man: H. B. Graham
		20 (32)	$ 17·5 18·1	Air				70/60 (35/30)	Wood 6 (153)	2 640 (1 640)					2	Pres: E. Clayton Jnr.
								70 (35)	Wood 7 (178)	18'' (457)						
		30 (48)						140/100 (70/50)	Wood 7 (178)	20-24'' (508/610)						Gen Man: C. W. Shaw Jr
																Sen VP: J. C. Humbert
15 (24)				W'hse Air	AAR			100 (49·6)	Wood 7 (178)	24'' (610)					4	VP: W. U. Baum
15 (24)		25 (40)		N.York AB	Auto			115/85 (57/42)	Wood 7''/9'' (178/229)	22'' (560)	29·0°			2 300 (702)	15 (3)	Gen Man: J. D. Everly
10 (16)		55 (89)	$74 165 000 49 551 000	Air W'hse	Type E, F and H 34½'' (876)			132/115 (66/57)	Oak 7 (178)	21'' (533)	30·0°	1·75% 3·75%U	Coopers E-72	4 066 (1 233)	2 730	Pres: W. P. Coliton
29·9 (48·2)	52·8 (86·6)	79 (127)	$ 89 578 74 474	Air	Type E 34¼'' (876)			136/75 (68/37)	Wood 7 (178)	3 250 (2 020)	10·0°	1·0%	35	5 903 (1 799)	3 051 (632)	Chairman: H. A. Newman
		12 (19)		Air				85/65 (42/32)	Fir 7 (178)	20'' (508)	12·0°	1·25%			5	Pres: K. Willson
																Pres: H. C. Bitner Vice Pres: W. C. Hoenig
10 (16)		35 (56)	$ 180·6 206·7	Air W'hse	AAR			100/65 (50/32)	Oak 6 (153)	2 800 (1 750)	15°	2·0%	33	945 (288)	10 (5)	Pres: Lemvel W. Brown
5 (8)		8 (13)	$ 25 960·00 50 924·00	Air W'hse	BSC Co.			100/85 (50/42)	Oak 6 (153)		14·0°	1·0%	33	965 (294)	2	Pres: Jerome Castle
15 (24)		25 (40)		Air W'hse	AAR 34½ (876)			100 (50)	Oak 7 (178)	22'' (559)	25·0°	7·0%	35	1 060 (323)	20 (3)	
15 (24)		25 (40)		Air W'hse	AAR			100/90 (49/44)	Wood 8 (203)	21'' (533)	10·0°			509 (155)	225	Gen Man: C. W. Lewis

NAME OF COMPANY ADDRESS	Gauge ft. in. (metres)	Route length incl. E=Electrified miles (km.)	Track length incl. E=Electrified miles (km.)	Elect. system and type of conductor	Locomotives L=Line S=Shunt Steam Electric Diesel De=elec. Dh=hyd.	Rail-cars Electric Diesel Trailer Railbus Multiple Unit set	Pass. train cars	Freight train cars Con-tainers	Total Volume carried Thousands of tonnes	Av'ge haul per ton miles (km.)	Av'ge net train load tonnes	Max. trailing load tonnes	Total number carried in 1000's	Average journey miles (km.)
Wyandotte Southern RR 4655 Biddle Ave, Wyandotte, Mich 48192 *(Switching only)*	4' 8½" *(1·435)*	4 *(6·4)*	4 *(6·4)*		DeS 1									
Wyandotte Terminal Railroad Co 43 Perry Place, Wyandotte, Mich 48192	4' 8½" *(1·435)*	9 *(14)*	12 *(19)*		DeS 5			35	588·4					
Yakima Valley Transportation Co 104 West Yakima Ave, Yakima Wash 98902	4' 8½" *(1·435)*	E 21 *(34)*	E 27 *(43)*	d.c.	EL 2									
Yancey Railroad Co. Box 547, Burnsville, NC 28714	4' 8½" *(1·435)*	13 *(21)*	15 *(24)*		DeL 2				37·0	12 *(19)*				
Youngstown & Northern Railroad Co. 1131 Waverley St, Youngstown, Ohio	4' 8½" *(1·435)*	5 *(8)*	8 *(13)*		DeS 10			345						
Youngstown & Southern Railway Co. *(Subsidiary of Montour RR Co)* 7891 Southern Blvd, Youngstown, Ohio 44512	4' 8½" *(1·435)*	49 *(79)*	60 *(96)*											
Yreka Western Railroad Co 300 E. Miner St, Yreka, Cal 96097	4' 8½" *(1·435)*	9 *(15)*	11 *(18)*		S 2 DeL 2					9 *(15)*	675	12		
URUGUAY **Administración de Ferrocarriles del Estado** La Paz 1095, Montevideo	4' 8½" *(1·435)*	1 866 *(3 008)*	2 047 *(3 294)*		S 156 DeL 75 DeS 28	D 21 T 3	186	3 560	2 039·5	137 *(221)*	352		8 581·1	35·8 *(57·6)*
Administración Nacional de Puertos Montevideo	4' 8½" *(1·435)*		19 *(31)*		S 5 D 2			143						
VENEZUELA **Venezuelan State Railways** Instituto Autonomo Administración de Ferrocarriles del Estado Ave Principal los Ruices, Edif Stemo, Pisos 1/3, Caracas	4' 8½" *(1·435)*	107 *(173)*	164 *(264)*		DeL 8 DeS 3	R 5 T 10	6	221	116·2	13 652 109 ton-km			381·7	
VIET-NAM **Viet-Nam Railway System** Regie des CF du Viêt-Nam 2, Công-Truòng, Diên-Hông, Ho Chu Minh City *(Part Rack rail)*	3' 3⅜" *(1·00)*	872 *(1 404)* (a)	879 *(1 415)*		S 7 DeL 35 DhS 10 DmS 2	D 1	106	660 C 1 230	35·1				3 945·7	18·6 *(30)*
North Viet-Nam Railways No official information Unofficial reports assess route length between 450 and 500 miles *(725-800 km)*	3' 3⅜" *(1·00)*													
YUGOSLAVIA **Yugoslav Railways** General Management, Nemanjina 6, Belgrade	4' 8" *(1·435)* 3' 3⅜" *(1·00)* 2' 6" *(0·76)* 1' 11⅝" *(0·60)*	7 367 *11 856)* E 938 *(1 510)*	9 433 *(15 181)* E 981 *(1 605)*	3 000 V dc OH and 25 000 V 1/50 dc OH	SL 1 432 E 162 De 280 Dh 74	R 266 E 2 D 4 TD 1 EMU 24 EMD 9	4 0002	63 300 70 198		156·5 *(252)*	184 *(296)*	Stand-ard 742 Nar-row 225·9	63 217·0	40 *(64)*
ZAÏRE **Compagnie des Chemins de fer Kinshasa-Dilolo-Lubumbashi** (KDL) B.P. 297, Lubumbashi	3' 6" *(1·067)*	1 628 *(2 620)* E 533 *(858)*	1 965 *(3 162)* E 643 *(1 035)*	25 000 V. 1/50 OH	SL 23 SS 3 EL 56 ES 5 DeL 52 DeS 16 DhS 25		187	4 888	5 920·0	2 645 087 ton-km			1 426·6	131·7 *(212)*
Office Zairois des C.F. des Grands Lacs PO Box 230, Kalemie	3' 6" *(1·067)* 3' 3⅜" *(1·00)*	596 *(959)* 78 *(125)*	657 *(1 058)* 87 *(140)*		SL 7 SS 15 DhL 13 DhS 8 SL 6 SS 8 DhS 2		52 20	487 83	2 192 14 183		227·1 280	690	472·7	
C.F. de Matadi a Kinshasa Office National des Transports (ONATRA) Boulevard du 30 juin, 98, Kinshasa	3' 6" *(1·067)*	254 *(409)*	418 *(673)*		De 27 DeS 20 DhS 12 DS 4	D 3	63	2 940	1 629·7		300	500	1 290·1	71·5 *(115)*
C.F. du Mayumbe ONATRA Zone du Mayumbe a Boma	2' 0¼" *(615)*	85 *(136)*	93 *(150)*		DeL 4 DhL 4 DS 6			370	120·4	47 (75) Up 42 (68) Down				
Ste. des C.F. Vicinaux du Zaire Aketi, Province Orientale	1' 11⅝" *(0·60)*	521 *(839)*	541 *(871)*		S 29 DL 10 DS 5		19	350	304·5	146 *(235)*			93·2	129 *(207)*
ZAMBIA **Zambia Railways** PO Box 935, Kabwe	3' 6" *(1·067)*	649 *(1 044)*	1 000 *(1 609)*		DeL 79 DhS 18		86	128	26 486	919 401 000 ton-km			1 014·0	

Average Speeds			Financial Data		Couplers	Buffers	Rails	Sleepers (crossties)							
Freight Train mph *(km/hr)*	Pass. Train mph *(km/hr)*	Speed max. mph *(km/hr)*	Revenue Expenses in 1 000's	Braking (continuous)	Type and Height above rail ins *(mm)*	Centres and Height above rail ins *(mm)*	Weight lb. per yd *(kg/m)*	Type and thickness ins *(mm)*	Spacing Number per mile *(per km)* or centres ins *(mm)*	Curvature max.	Gradient max. (U=not compensated)	Axle load max. tonnes	Altitude max. feet *(m)*	Staff employed. Total no. (inclu. workshop)	Names of officials. Extended lists can be found at the end of the individual country in the report section immediately following
6 *(9·6)*		6 *(9·6)*		Air W'hse	Auto 27 *(684)*		105/90 *(52/45)*	Wood 6 *(153)*	12″ *(305)*	19·0°	Level	50	579 *(176)*	15	Pres: H. J. Withers Vice Pres: N. E. Sylvander
5 *(8)*		10 *(16)*	$ 1 682·0 1 295·0											35	Pres: Earl F. Schuknecht
30 *(49)*		35 *(56)*					60/75 *(30/37)*	Wood 7 *(180)*	18″ *(457)*	52°				10 *(1)*	Man: J. L. Price Supt: R. B. Hardin Ch Eng: G. W. McDonald
		15 *(24)*					60 *(30)*	Wood 6 *(153)*	18″ *(457)*					10 *(8)*	Pres: W. H. Banks
															Pres: Edward J. Bernard Jr
20 *(32)*				Air			100/90 *(49/44)*	Wood 7 *(178)*	20″ *(508)*	8°	2%		1 240 *(378)*	36	Man: R. A. Weller
20 *(32)*		40 *(64)*	$ 175·0 169·7	Air W'hse	Auto		75 *(37)*	Fir 6 *(153)*	18″ *(457)*	16·0°	2·2%		2 620 *(799)*	15 *(None)*	Gen Man: L. Cecil
16·3 *(26·1)*	27·8 *(44·8)*			W'hse Vac. except railcars air	Screw 41 *(1 040)* except railcars auto: 34½ *(877)*	Crs. 68 *(1 725)* Ht. 41 *(1 040)*	80/56 *(40/28)*	Wood 4¾ *(120)* Some metal and conc	2 100- 2 400 *(1 300-* *1 500)*	8·75°	2·17%	4		9 985	Gen. Man: Ing. Delfino Fros Torres
				Steam Vac *Diesel* air	33 *(990)*	Crs. 67⅜ *(1 710* Ht. 33 *(990)*	80 *(39·7)*						12		
25 *(40)*	25 *(40)*	62 *(100)*	Bs 8 812·0 19 864·0	Air W'hse K/AB/ ABD	Auto 34½ *(877)*		100 *(50)*	Wood 7 *(180)* *(1 723)*	23½″ *(800)*	5·8°	10%	31·75	1 938	741 *(591)*	Gen. Man: Roberto Agostini
19 *(30)*	19 *(30)*	44 *(70)*		Vac Jourdain- Monn W'hse	Auto & Draw- hook 22½/34½ *(570/876)*	Central 32½ *(825)*	60/50 *(30/25)*	Steel; pre-str Conc	28¾″ *(730)*	984 ft *(300 m)*	Adhes 1·5% Rack 11·5%	13	2 750 *(838)*		Gen. Man:
12 *(19·1)*	25 *(40)*	74·5 *(120)*	Dinars 5 204 000·0 2 811 000·0		Standard 41¾ *(1 060)*	Cr. 68¼ *(1 750)* Ht. 41¾ *(1 060)*	98/70 *(49/35)*	Wood & Conc	600 *(750)*	820 ft *(250 m)*	3·0% 2·5% **U**	20	2 854 *(870)*		Gen. Man: Nikola Filipovic
13·7 *(22·0)*	13·9 *(22·3)*	*Elec.* 32 *(52)* *other* 28 *(45)*	Zaires 39 557·0 38 191·2	Vac Jourdain Monn (Air on el locs)	Henricot Atlas 34⅝ *(880)*		80·6/59 *(40/29)*	Metal and Wood	2′400 *(1 500)*	656ft *(200 m)*	1·25% (Special cases to 2·3%)	15; Special cases 20	5 295 *(1 614)*	16 500	Dir. Gen: Gaston Goor
28 *(45)*	31 *(50)*	37 *(60)*		Vac and air	Henricot Atlas 34⅝ *(880)*		59/49 *(29·3/* *24·4)*	Metal & wood 5⅛ *(130)*	2 400- 2 100 *(1 500-* *1 300)*	328 ft *(100 m)*	1·25% 2·0% **U**	15	3 510 *(1 070)*	4 538 *(1 348)*	Dir. Gen: R. Cherrier Man: G. Mugana Tech. Dir: J. Stas
		31 *(50)*									2·0% **U**	12·5			
18 *(29)*	20 *(32)*	37 *(60)*		Vac W'hse	Henricot Atlas 34⅝ *(880)*	Ht 34⅝ *(880)*	80·6/67 *(40/33·4)*	Metal	2 800- 2 400 *(1 750-* *1 500)*	508 ft *(155 m)*	1·7% **U**	16·5	2 444 *(745)*		Gen. Man: Kanyama Kanana
		22 *(35)*			Hook 12 5/16 *(312)*		36·4 *(18)*	Metal	2 250 *(1 400)*	98 ft *(30 m)*	3·2% **U**	8			Gen. Man: J. F. Iyeki
		28 *(45)*		W'hse Oer- likon	Buffer- coupler	19⅝ *(500)*	66/20 *(33/10)*	Metal	2 400 *(1 500)*	656 ft *(200 m)*	1·5%	8	2 756 *(840)*	3 471	
15 *(24)*	30 *(48)*	55 *(88)*		Vac Gresham and Craven	Alliance 35¼ *(900)*		91/80 *(44·6/* *39·7)*	Wood Metal 5 *(127)*	2 240 *(1 392)*	656 ft *(200 m)*	1·6%	17	4 527 *(1 380)*	7 800 *(525)*	Gen. Man: H. J. Fast

INTERNATIONAL
RAILWAY ASSOCIATIONS AND AGENCIES

INTERNATIONAL UNION OF RAILWAYS (UIC)
Union International des Chemins de Fer

Offices: 14-16 rue Jean Rey, 75 015 Paris 15e, France

Telephone: 273 01 20
Telex: 27035

Directors and Officers
President (Vice-Minister German State Railways): Dr V. Winkler
Secretary General: B. H. de Fontgalland
Chief Executive Officer: P. Ballet
Vice-Presidents: P. Gentil, France
W. Vaerst, German Federal Railways
R. L. E. Lawrence, Great Britain
L. Mayer, Italy
J. Raczkowski, Poland

The UIC was founded in 1922. The object is the standardisation and improvement of railway equipment and operating methods, in particular international traffic. All principal European railways are members and also a considerable number of non-European countries. The UIC has a number of specialist agencies: the Office for Research and Experiments (ORE) for the pooling of technical research; a publicity centre for preparing publicity campaigns; the Public Relations Centre, for ensuring that the railways' interests are maintained; the Documentation Bureau, for the exchange of information between railways (publishes 10 times a year "A Selection of International Railway Documentation" in English, French, German and Spanish, jointly with the International Railway Congress Association); the Statistics Bureau, which publishes "Annual Summary of Monthly Statistics"; the Railway Film Bureau, enabling information to be exchanged in this field and the Central Clearing House in Brussels, which is responsible for settling accounts between railways.

Office de Recherches et d'essais—ORE
Oudenaard 60, 3513 EV Utrecht, The Netherlands (Tel: 314646)

Bureau centrale de compensation—BCC
B-1060 Brussels, 49A ave Fonsny, Section 31, Belgium

Bureau Internationale du film du chemin de fer—BFC
F-75009 Paris, 88 rue Saint-Lazare, France

Bureau de documentation—BD
Chemins de fer de l'Etat tchécoslovaque, Na prikopé 33, Prague, Czechoslovakia

Bureau de stalistiques—BS
Generaldirektion ÖBB; A-1010, Vienna, Elisabethstr 9, Austria

AFRICAN UNION OF RAILWAYS

Offices: Avenue Tombalbaye, 869, Kinshasa, Zaire.
Executive Council: Representatives from Central, East, North and West Africa
Secretary General: Adama Diagne

The first general assembly of the Union was held in 1973. The objectives of the Union is to seek to bring about the unification, development and improvement of the railway services of the members of the Union with a view to linking their networks, and other transportation services which connect Africa with the rest of the world.
Major railway projects under study include the proposed new links from Maidguri, to N'Djamena, Chad; Parakou, Benin to Niamey, Nigeria; Ouangolodougou, Ivory Coast to Sikasso, Mali, and in Mali itself a link between Bamako, Diola, Bobo Ansongo and Ouagadougou.
In North Africa the section of the Trans-Maghrebin line between Algiers and Tunis was opened in June 1975, and the section from Casa to Algiers in 1976. Projected is a further extension from Tunis to Tripoli.
Sudan Railways plans links with other countries—Nyala—Ceneina (320 km); Ed Aen Hufrat Enanaus (425 km) also links with Malawi, Ethiopia, Zaire, Uganda, and with Egypt at the Aswan Dam.

INTERNATIONAL RAILWAY CONGRESS ASSOCIATION
(Association Internationale du Congres Des Chemins de Fer)

Offices: 85 rue de France 1070, Brussels, Belgium

Telephone: 522 62 83

Management Committee
President: G. Vanhee, Director General Belgian National Railways Company
Vice-Presidents: T. L. Bagley, Deputy Secretary, Department of Environment Transport Industries, United Kingdom, A. D. Karetnikov, Director of the Railway Scientific Research Institute of the USSR
Secretary General: R. Squilbin, Chief Engineer, Deputy Director of Belgian National Railways Company

Established in 1885 the IRCA exists to promote the development of railway transport by all means possible. It holds periodic Congresses and general or specialised meetings: supplying information on specific problems to it's members and publishing technical reviews.
The Associations bulletins are published in English, French, German, Russian and Spanish.

INTERNATIONAL UNION OF PUBLIC TRANSPORT (UITP)

Head Office: 19 avenue de l'Uruguay, B-1050, Brussels, Belgium

Telephone: 673 33 25 and 673 04 66

Officers: R. Belin, Paris
K. N. Andersen, Copenhagen
M. Cirenei, Milan
M. Hansen, Brussels
K. Klopotov, USSR
S. J. B. Skyrme, London
H. Tappert, Hamburg
General Secretary: Andre J. Jacobs

This association established in 1885 pools information and experience of urban and interurban public transport undertakings, operating buses tramways, trolleybuses, metropolitan and light railways for joint study and research and promotes the technical and economic development of the industry.
Publications include the reports of congresses, technical papers, and a periodic review and a bibliographical card index. They are published in English, French and German.

INTERNATIONAL SLEEPING CAR COMPANY (CIWLT)
(Cie Internationale Des Wagons—Lits et Du Tourisime)

Head Office: 40 rue de l'Arcade, Paris, France
Telegrams: 'Wagolits'
Telephone: 265 4280/3709
Telex: 65233

Officers
Administrator Director General: Jacques Bernard Dupont
Director General (Joint): Francois Boyaux
Director of Administrative Services: Claude Savary
Director of Railways: Francoise Rupied
Director of Hotels: Louis Besseyre des Horts
Financial Director: Andre Frandeboeuf
Personnel Director: Jean Pierre Mayet
Director of Tourism: Michel Tondeur

Director of Catering Services: Emilio Naegeli
Representative of the Director General (Brussels): Jacques De Meeus d'Argenteuil

Founded in 1876 in Brussels the company's vehicles and trains were known all over Europe by 1914 and further extended in 1919.
Since 1971, most of CIWLT sleeping cars and dining cars have been taken over by various national and international railway systems under the "Trains Euro Nuit" (TEN). CIWLT merely staffs, furnishes victuals and maintains the sleeping and dining cars on behalf of the various railways.

CENTRAL OFFICE FOR INTERNATIONAL RAILWAY TRANSPORT (OCTI)

Office: Gryphenhübeliweg 30, 3000, Berne, Switzerland

Telegrams: 'OCTI Berne'
Telephone: (031) 43.17.62

Chairman of Administrative Committee: Alfred Schaller
Director: John Favre
Vice-Director: Roger Gratreau

EUROPEAN COMPANY FOR THE FINANCING OF RAILROAD ROLLING STOCK (EUROFIMA)

Offices: Rittergasse 20, CH-4001 Basel, Switzerland

Telephone: 22.33.40

General Manager: Heinz Weber

EUROPEAN CONFERENCE OF MINISTERS OF TRANSPORT (ECMT)

Offices: 33, rue de Franqueville, 75775, Paris, Cedex 16, France

Telegrams: 'Comitrans, Paris'
Telephone: 524-82-00
Telex: 20.999 Paris

Chairman: E. Lanc, *Federal Minister of Transport (Austria)*
First Vice-Chairman: K. Damsgaard, *Minister of Public Works (Denmark)*
Second Vice-Chairman: A. Achille-Fould, *Secretary of State in Charge of Transport (France)*

EUROPEAN DIESEL AND ELECTRIC LOCOMOTIVE MANUFAC-TURERS' ASSOCIATION
(Constructeurs Européens de Locomotives Thermiques et Electriques—Celte)

Offices: 12, rue Bixio, Paris 75007, France

Telegrams: 'Interwagon, Paris'
Telephone: 705 36 62

President: Klaus Von Meyenburg (Swiss)
Delegate General: X. Allain-Dupré (French)

EUROPEAN GOODS TIMETABLE CONFERENCE

Offices: Czechoslovak State Railways, Na Prikopé 33, Prague, Czechoslovakia

Telegrams: 'Domini Praha CEM/EGK'
Telephone: Praha 2122/3287
Telex: 005966

President: Ing Frantisek Kotora
Secretary: Josef Basta

EUROPEAN PASSENGER TIMETABLE & THROUGH CARRIAGE CONFERENCE
Conference Européenne Des Horaires des Trains de Voyageurs et des Services Directs (CEH)

Offices: c/o Direction générale des Chemins de fer fédéraux suisses, Hochschulstrasse 6, CH-3000 Berne, Switzerland

Telephone: (031) 60 11 11
Telex: 32500

President: K. Wellinger *(General Manager, Swiss Federal Railways)*

EUROPEAN WAGON POOL (EUROP AGREEMENT)
Communauté d'Exploitation des Wagons Europ (Convention Europ)

Offices: c/o Swiss Federal Railways, Hochschulstrasse 6, CH-3000 Berne, Switzerland

Telephone: (031) 60 11 11
Telex: 32500

INTERCONTAINER

Company for International Transport by Transcontainers
(Société Internationale pour le Transport par Transcontainers)

CH-4010 Basle, Hirschgässlein 11, Switzerland

Telephone: 22 25 25
Telegrams: Transcofer Basle
Telex: 62 298

General Manager: G. Fléchon
Manager, Operating Dept.: R. Bouvry
Manager, Finance and General Affairs: M. Bussy
Manager, Commercial Service: W. Nitsche
Manager, Technical Service: G. Sempio
Manager, Marketing Services: H. W. H. Welters
Manager, Organisation and Data Processing Department: Février

GENERAL

The national railway administration of the following twenty-three European countries are participating in the Company for International Transport by Transcontainers known as INTERCONTAINER:
Austria, Belgium, Bulgaria, Czechoslovakia, Denmark, Finland, France, Germany (DB), Germany (DR), Greece, Hungary, Ireland, Italy, Luxembourg, Netherlands, Norway, Poland, Portugal, Spain, Sweden, Switzerland, United Kingdom, Yugoslavia.

SCOPE OF OPERATIONS

As common commercial agency of its member railways, Intercontainer's task is to market international container transportation. Essentially, this consists of grouping consignments to form large, regular traffic flows. Individual railways can then reduce their unit costs, which in turn results in keener prices for Intercontainer. The price advantage is passed on by Intercontainer to its customers in proportion to the scale and regularity of their traffic.
For the first time in their history, the European railways have granted a jointly-owned subsidiary far-reaching commercial powers. A first step has thus been achieved towards a "European Railway".
Intercontainer is represented in each country, either by the relevant railway itself or through a firm appointed by it.

RAIL CONTAINER SERVICES

The transportation services provided by Intercontainer fall into two categories:
1. Movement of containers individually, or in small groups by TEEM- and TEC-Services.
2. Specialised container trains.

Individual container movements

The facilities provided are extremely diverse. All the specialised container terminals, of which nearly 700 are already operational throughout the European rail network, can be served, the concentration of traffic upon these terminals being the key to the improvement of service quality. So, while the majority of freight stations and private sidings throughout Europe are open to Intercontainer consignments, preference is naturally given to development of the flows between the natural centres of concentration.
Within the catchment area of each terminal, Intercontainer can usually provide a range of road collection and delivery services, either with vehicles of its local representative or of the national railway concerned. Customers, too, have direct access to the terminals with their own road vehicles.
To obtain the best possible transit times, individual container consignments and small groups are normally carried on the widely developed network of TEEM (Trans-Europ-Express Marchandises) and TEC (Transports Européens Combinés) trains.

SPECIALISED CONTAINER TRAINS (TECE):

These services operate along routes with a regular large scale volume of traffic. They offer the following advantages:
—rapid, regular and reliable transit, by direct terminal—terminal container trains,
—no shunting, the transit-time being therefore considerably reduced,
—often no formalities at frontiers,
—mainly customs clearance at the terminals,
—movement between well equipped terminals where Intercontainer road-services are available, when required,
—competitive rates.

At present, the following trains of this type are regularly in operation:
—Amsterdam/Rotterdam/Basle/Milan and vice versa.
—Zeebrugge/Antwerp-Basle and vice versa.
—Antwerp-Turin-Novara-Rivalta Scrivia-Milan and vice versa.
—Dunkirk-Turin-Milan-Rivalta Scrivia and vice versa, 5 times a week.
—Paris-Novara and vice versa.
—Amsterdam-Rotterdam-Antwerp-Zeebrugge and vice versa.

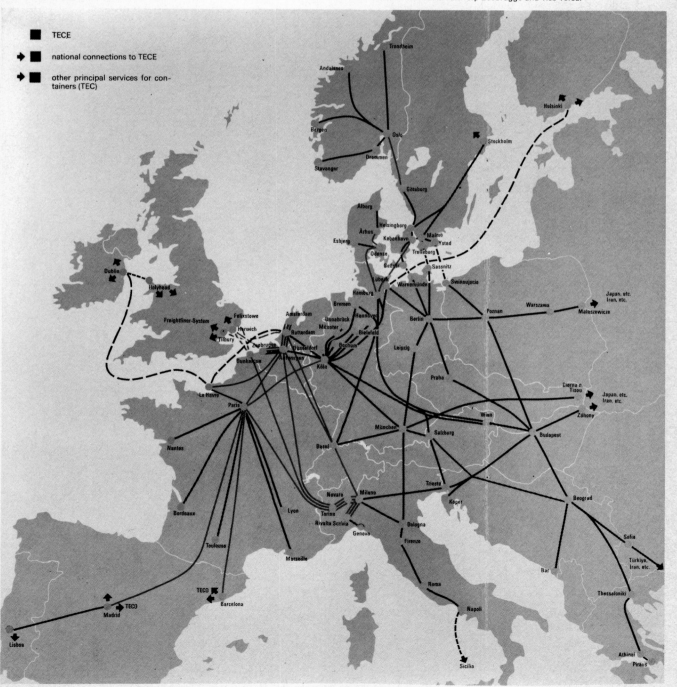

—Paris-Madrid and vice versa.
—Paris-Barcelona and vice versa.
—Hamburg-Copenhagen and vice versa.
—Hamburg-Jutland and vice versa.
—Paris-Köln-Düsseldorf and vice versa, connections to Hannover, Bielefeld, Hamburg etc on the German side, on the French side to Nantes, Bordeaux, Toulouse, Marseilles, Lyons etc.
—Paris-Antwerp/Rotterdam and vice versa, both services with connections to Nantes, Bordeaux, Toulouse, Marseilles, Lyons etc.
—Paris-Turin-Novara-Milan and vice versa, 5 times a week.
—Göteborg-Oslo and vice versa, with connections to Western Norway.
—Rotterdam-Le Havre, and vice versa.

These services form a basic network of special container trains, connecting the most important industrial centres in Europe.

TERMINALS
Intercontainer does not operate its own terminals, but uses those run by railways or private companies, of which over 400 are now in operation.

CONTAINERS AND WAGONS
The containers with which Intercontainer are primarily concerned are 8 ft × 8 ft × 20 ft-30 ft-40 ft standard ISO types. Others varying somewhat from these sizes, such as the 8 ft wide maritime containers 8 ft 6 in high × 35 ft long, can also be accommodated. Intercontainer does not own any containers at the moment, but on some routes for example, Western Germany-Spain, it places a number of hired containers at the disposal of its customers in order to develop its traffic in the pure continental market. Also some of its representatives have containers available, under interchange agreements for international traffic.
Intercontainer owns 1 352 specialised 60 ft (18.5 m) wagons built for its own use and 100 80 ft articulated wagons of a completely new type.

TRAFFIC
The Intercontainer traffic has increased progressively since the Company began operations in May 1968, as is shown by the following table:

Year	Number of containers in TEU (20 ft equivalent units)	Compared to the year before
1972	327 969	+ 28%
1973	435 865	+ 23%
1974	456 511	+ 5%
1975	414 753	− 9%
1976	493 022	+ 19%

REFRIGERATED CONTAINER TRAFFIC:
It is appropriate to mention the very close cooperation established between Intercontainer and Interfrigo. The latter is entrusted with the organisation and development of international, controlled temperature transports. It is owned by 23 railway companies and is a founder member of Intercontainer.
Under the policy adopted between the two companies Interfrigo maintains both commercial and technical management of all controlled-temperature container transport, since this traffic is of a kind involving services differing from those of pure and simple carriage. Interfrigo supplies ventilated or refrigerated transcontainers and services these regularly.

REPRESENTATIVES

Austria
Generaldirektion der Oesterreichischen Bundesbahnen (OeBB)
Kommerzielle Direktion, Abteilung IV/3, Gauermanngasse 4, A-1010 Vienna
Telephone: (222) 5650 ext 5823, 5329
Telex: 12104

Belgium
Société Anonyme Interferry
Zomerweg 26, B-2030 Antwerp
Telephone: (31) 416950
Telex: 32529

Bulgaria
Bulgarische Staatseisenbahnen (BDZ)
ul. Iwan Wazow 3, BG-Sofia
Telephone: 843 43 34, 843 44 34
Telex: 22423

Czechoslovakia
SKD-Intrans
Perucka 5
CS-Praha 2
Telephone: 21 24
Telex: 121486

Denmark
Danske Statsbaner (DSB)
Generaldirektoratet Godssalgskontoret, Sølvgade 40, DK-1349 Copenhagen K
Telephone: 14 04 00 Ext 3429
Telex: 22225

Finland
Valtionrautatiet Rautatiehallitus (VR)
Betriebsabteilung, Vilhonkatu 13, SF-00101 Helsinki 10
Telephone: 717711
Telex: 1230151

France
Compagnie Nouvelle de Cadres (CNC)
BP No. 55, 20, rue Hector Malot, F-75560 Paris Cédex 12
Telephone: (1) 345 32 20 — (1) 346 12 05
Telex: 22500 — 21494

Germany (DB)
Transfracht GmbH
Gutleutstrasse 160/164, D-6 Frankfurt (Main)
Telephone: (611) 23 03 51
Telex: 41 45 45

Germany (DR)
Deutsche Reichsbahn DDR-Cont
Otto-Grotewohl-Strasse 25, DDR-108 Berlin
Telephone: (31) 220 01 21
Telex: 173 096

Greece
Org. des Chemins de fer Hélléniques SA(CH) Direction Commerciale
Bureau de représentation Intercontainer, 1 rue Karolou GR-Athens 107
Telephone: (21) 524 4822
Telex: 215 187

Hungary
Mavtrans-MAV
Szállitmànyozasi Iroda, Deak Fernc-ùtca, 23, H/Budapest V
Telephone: 38 23 24
Telex: 225343

Ireland
Coras Iompair Eireann (CIE)
Office of the Commercial Manager,
Transport House, Dublin 1
Telephone: 741857
Telex: 5695

Iran
Perse Transport Bar (PTB)
International Forwarding Co Ltd
165 Takhte Tavous Ave, PO Box 1197
Telephone: 859 050 51 52
Telex: 212 626

Italy
INT
Via Savoia 19, I-00198 Rome
Telephone: (6) 861 851

Luxembourg
Société Nationale des Chemins de fer Luxembourgeois (CFL)
Service Commercial, Place de la Gare 9, L-Luxembourg
Telephone: (352) 49901
Telex: 288

Netherlands
NV Nederlandse Spoorwegen (NS)
Dienst van Commerciele Zaken
Ie Afdeling, Sectie Containers, Moreelsepark 1, NL-Utrecht
Telephone: (30) 35 45 52
Telex: 70 131

Norway
Norges Statsbaner (NSB)
Hovedadministrasjonen, Salsavdelingen, Storgaten, 33, N-Oslo 1
Telephone: (2) 20 95 50 ext 2147
Telex: 11168

Poland
Przedsiebiorstwo Spedycji Krajowej Zarzad (PSK)
ul. Ordona 2a, PL-01237 Warszawa
Telephone: 36 69 23

Portugal
Companhia dos Caminhos de Ferro Portugueses (CP)
Commercial Department, Gabinete do Trafego de Contentores,
Rua Vitor Cordon 45, P-Lisbon 2
Telephone: 366935, 367236
Telex: 12382

Spain
RENFE
Trafico Intermodales
Direccion Comercial, Paseo del Rey 32, E-Madrid 8
Telephone: 247 67 52, 248 02 71
Telex: 27632

Sweden
Statens Järnvägar
Commercial Dept., Mäster Samuelsgatan 70, S-10550 Stockholm C
Telephone: (8) 226420 ext. 4316
Telex: 1410

Switzerland
Chemins de fer Fédéraux Suisses
Service Commercial, Trafic Marchandises, Mittelstrasse 43, CH-3000 Berne
Telephone: (31) 60 11 11
Telex: 32500

United Kingdom
(Harwich Terminal)
British Railways Board
Shipping & Int. Services Division
163-203 Evershopt Street, London NW 11BG
Telephone: (1) 387 4776, ext 2029
Telex: 269 295

(Freightliner Terminals)
Freightliners Ltd.
43 Cardington Street, London NW1
Telephone: 01-388 0611, ext 3324
Telex: 24743

Yugoslavia
Zajednica Jugoslovenskih Zeleznica (JZ)
Zastupnistvo Intercontainera, Nemanjina 6/II YU-11000 Beograd

INTERFRIGO

International Railway-owned Company for Refrigerated Transport

General Management:
Wettsteinplatz 1, PO Box 341, CH-4005 Basle, Switzerland

Telegrams: Interfroid Basle
Telephone: 26 33 33
Telex: 62 231 and 63 372

Board of Directors:
Chairman, General Manager (rtd) of Belgian State Railways: Mr. Lataire
Vice-Chairman
General Manager of Italian State Railways: Mr. Mayer
Chairman of German Federal Railways: Mr. Kalb
Commercial Manager of The Netherlands Railways Company (from 24 February 1976): Mr. Boender
Members:
    Manager of the Economic Department of Danish State Railways: Mr. Jenstrup
    General Manager, British Rail, Shipping and Internal Services Division: Mr. Kirby
    General Manager, Swiss Federal Railways: Mr. Wellinger
    Deputy General Manager, French National Railways: Mr. Dupuy
Secretary
    Legal Adviser to Belgian State Railways: Mr. Demanche
Auditors
    Financial Manager of Swiss Federal Railways: Mr. Diemant
    Minsterial Adviser to the General Management of German Federal Railways: Mr. Eiermann

Chief Financial Inspector of Belgian State Railways: Mr. Duchêne
Manager of the Construction Department of Italian State Railways: Mr. Monopoli
Deputy Financial Manager of Hungarian State Railways: Mr. Varga
General Management
   General Manager: Mr. Naud
   Operating Manager: Mr. Bense
   Administrative Manager: Mr. Biesold
   Organisation and Methods Manager: Mr. Carlier
   Technical Manager: Mr. Cresti
   Commercial Manager: Mr. Klaassen
   Head of Personnel and Financial Department: Mr. Isler

Registered Office: 85, rue de France—Brussels
General Management: 1, Wettsteinplatz—Basle

In 1976 the total number of "ton-kms", the yardstick best illustrating the development of traffic, was 4 054 million. This figure is 5 per cent lower than in 1975.
In 1976, after having achieved highly satisfactory results with a steady upward trend in the first 24 years of its existence, INTERFRIGO, which was founded 27 years ago on 24 October 1949, again experienced a decline in its total traffic volume.

Year	Ton-kms loaded (in millions)	Percentage change in relation to preceding year	Index (1974 = 100)
1967	2 957	+ 7.7%	68.6
1968	3 106	+ 5.0%	72.1
1969	3 518	+ 13.3%	81.6
1970	3 967	+12.8%	92.0
1971	4 209	+6.1%	97.7
1972	4 294	+2.0%	99.6
1973	4 468	+ 4.1%	103.7
1974	4 310	− 3.5%	100.0
1975	4 266	− 1.0%	99.0
1976	4 054	− 5.0%	94.1

This decline relates to refrigerator wagon traffic, the mainstay of the Company's activity. However, this loss of traffic was slightly offset by special shipments which, although productive, are not apparent in the relevant statistics. This concerns seasonal domestic traffic in refrigerator wagons on long-term rental to railway administrations. While there was a notable increase in traffic in mechanically refrigerated wagons and transcontainers, the decline in refrigerator wagon traffic can be attributed to a combination of the following factors:
—The general economic recession, together with the aggravating effects of keen competition for regular traffic (fresh and frozen meat, preserves).
—Above all, the detrimental effect upon traffic of the extremely unfavourable weather in a number of countries of origin during the second half of the year (reduction of agricultural production by drought in Hungary and Romania, severe diminution of Italian grape exports due to excessive rainfall in Apulia).
It is gratifying to note that in the first quarter of 1977 refrigerated wagon traffic showed an increase of 10 per cent over the same period in the preceding year.
As a result of the reforms that came into force on 1 July 1975 with the agreement of the member administrations, satisfactory financial results were achieved in 1976 despite the drop in traffic.

Traffic in refrigerated wagons
General remarks
The number of ton-kms loaded, which in 1976 was 3 968 million as against 4 203 million in 1975, showed a decline of 5.6 per cent in actual traffic. There were further diminutions in the number of refrigerator wagons loaded, which fell from 253 228 in 1975 to 235 649 in 1976, and in the number of tons carried, which fell from 3 077 008 in 1975 to 2 972 514 in 1976.
On the other hand the average load per wagon increased by 3.3 per cent from 12.2 to 12.6 tons.
Finally the average distance travelled per load decreased slightly from 1 347 km in 1975 to 1 325 km in 1976.
When evaluating the results for 1976, allowance should be made for the productive activity of the wagons on long-term rental for seasonal domestic transport, which amounted to 39 150 days of use and is not apparent in the statistics for 1976.

	1973	1974	1975	1976
Number of shipments	291 014	264 159	253 228	235 649
Average distance travelled per shipment (km)	1 278	1 310	1 347	1 325
Total number of tons carried (thousands)	3 410	3 194	3 077	2 973
Average load carried per wagon (tons)	11.7	12.1	12.2	12.6
Total number of ton-kms (million)	4 385	4 230	4 203	3 968

Variations in traffic at point of departure
a. Traffic on the increase (number of tons carried)

France	+ 97 149 =	+ 33.9%	(Peaches, apples and pears, grapes, apricots, fresh fruit, tomatoes, misc. fresh vegetables, potatoes)
Germany (GFR)	+ 13 085 =	+ 5.0%	(Potatoes, fresh dairy products, fresh and frozen fish, frozen meat)
Belgium	+ 12 725 =	+ 23.3%	(Bananas, frozen meat)
Italy	+ 11 292 =	+ 1.1%	(Citrus fruits, berries, misc. vegetables and fresh dairy products)
Spain	+ 9 154 =	+ 22.5%	(Plums, grapes and tomatoes)

Increases were also experienced in traffic from Austria with + 7 026 tons (potatoes), Poland with + 3 474 tons (misc. foods), Yugoslavia with + 2 933 tons (potatoes) and Great Britain with + 1 322 tons (misc. foods).

b. Traffic on the decrease (number of tons carried)

Greece	− 92 766 =	−43.3%	(Peaches, fresh vegetables)
Romania	− 63 447 =	− 24.1%	(Peaches, misc. fresh vegetables, foodstuffs)
Hungary	− 52 160 =	− 20.0%	(Apples and pears, potatoes, fresh vegetables, fresh meat products)
Bulgaria	− 22 865 =	− 8.0%	(Peaches, misc. fresh vegetables, fresh dairy products, beverages)
Denmark	− 11 319 =	− 11.6%	(Fresh and frozen meat, frozen fish)
Switzerland	− 7 604 =	− 22.1%	(Potatoes, cheese, frozen meat)
Germany (GDR)	− 5 505 =	− 12.4%	(Butter, preserves)
Netherlands	− 3 182 =	− 2.2%	(Bananas, potatoes, fresh meat products)
Sweden	− 2 707 =	− 21.9%	(Fresh butter, frozen meat)

There was also a fall in the traffic from Norway with − 971 tons (fresh and frozen meat).

Variations in the nature of the goods carried
a The main increases were observed in the following types of goods (number of tons carried):

Frozen products	+ 27 479 =	+ 15.4%	(Meat and Poultry)
Potatoes	+ 16 042 =	+ 12.3%	
Misc. products	+ 12 710 =	+ 4.1%	(Beverages, industrial products)
Sea products	+ 8 509 =	+ 28.1%	(Fresh fish)

B. Decreases were observed principally in the following types of goods (number of tons carried):

Fresh fruit	− 76 152 =	− 5.6%	(Apricots, peaches, apples and pears, plums, grapes)
Meat products	− 47 792 =	− 38.6%	(Fresh meat and poultry)
Dairy products	− 19 923 =	− 20.2%	(Butter, eggs, cheese)
Fresh vegetables	− 14 610 =	− 1.9%	(Cauliflower, salads, misc. vegetables)
Foodstuffs	− 10 757 =	− 13.6%	(Preserves, misc. foodstuffs)

Traffic in mechanically refrigerated wagons
In 1976 almost the whole of this traffic was carried in INTERFRIGO-owned mechanically refrigerated wagons.
The number of ton-kms loaded was 63 millions in 1976 as against 40 million in 1975, thus representing an increase of 57.5 per cent.

Supercapacity bogie mechanically refrigerated wagons crossing Lake Van (Eastern)

The number of shipments increased from 1 567 in 1975 to 1 832 in 1976. The average distance travelled per load increased from 1 261 km in 1975 to 1 506 km in 1976. This development is due to the expansion of transport to the Middle East in mechanically refrigerated train sets (237 wagons in 1976 as against 182 in 1975). The average load per wagon was 21.9 tons in 1976 compared with 20.1 tons in 1975.

Traffic in mechanically refrigerated transcontainers
Traffic "per journey"
The rail transport of privately owned mechanically refrigerated transcontainers in Europe showed an appreciable increase over 1975, particularly in overseas traffic. The decline in traffic "per journey" in INTERFRIGO-owned mechanically refrigerated transcontainers is principally due to the reduction of the container stock employed in this field of activity.

	1975	1976
Number of units carried:		
—Private containers (P), including IF		
containers on long-term rental	2 126	3 726
—INTERFRIGO containers (IF)		
"per journey"	4 071	3 087
—Total (P + IF)	6 197	6 813
Average distance travelled per shipment (km)	638	499
Total number of tons carried (thousands)	36	45
Average load carried per unit (tons)	12.4	13.2
Total number of ton-kilometres (millions)	23	23

Traffic in containers on long-term rental
This transport service, which is greatly appreciated by the international shipping companies, showed a favourable development in 1976. More than half the INTER-FRIGO mechanically refrigerated transcontainer stock is now rented on the basis of long-term agreements.

Number of INTERFRIGO-owned mechanically refrigerated transcontainers	20'	40'	TEU (equiv to 20')
A = total	241	170	581
B = "on long-term rental"	170	90	350
Percentage 100 B / A	70.5%	52.9%	60.2%

Commercial
The delay in the normalisation of the world economic situation that was expected in 1976 prevented a resumption of the growth in traffic, which had shown a steady expansion until 1973.
However, total INTERFRIGO traffic in terms of ton-kms was only 5 per cent lower than in 1975.
In 1976 INTERFRIGO took part in the following functions:
—1st International Food and Beverages Fair in Saloniki (4 to 11.4.1976)
—28th International Fair in Trieste (17 to 29.6.1976)
—International Autumn Fair in Budapest (22 to 30.9.1976)
—3rd International Transport Fair in Belgrade (25 to 30.10.1976)
—International Transport Exhibition (IVA) in Hamburg (16 to 20.11.1976)
INTERFRIGO rolling stock was also shown in an exhibition train which was used by the SNCB in September/October 1976 on the 25th anniversary of its foundation and at the opening of the SNCB container terminal in Brussels on 28.11.1976.

Refrigerated wagons
In terms of ton-kilometres the traffic in refrigerator wagons fell by 5.6 per cent in 1976. This is due to a large reduction in traffic from certain countries (in particular Greece, Hungary and Romania) which was not fully offset by an increase in traffic from other countries (principally France and Spain).
It should again be pointed out that in 1975 the French peach harvest was severely affected by frost and that the resultant deficiency was covered largely by Greek exports. This situation did not occur again in 1976. The decline in fruit and vegatable exports from Hungary and Romania in mainly due to the drought that affected the whole of Europe but had particularly severe consequences for agricultural production in south-eastern Europe. Conversly, the marketing and export of Italian grapes were considerably diminished as a result of excessive rainfall in Apulia.
In 1976 charges for refrigerated wagons were maintained at the same general level. The only exception was for shipments from countries in which the charges in terms of local currency had to be adjusted to allow for the depreciation of the currency in question.

Mechanically refrigerated wagons
In terms of the number of shipments and ton-kms, traffic in mechanically refrigerated wagons increased by 17 and 57 per cent respectively. Special mention should be made of the development of traffic to the Middle East and in particular the transport of more than 3 000 tons of fresh eggs from the Netherlands to Baghdad. The fulfilment of this contract involved the use of 11 train sets each consisting of 14 mechanically refrigerated wagons and one dormitory car for technical personnel. The accompanying technicians supervise the operation of the machinery over a distance of more than 5 000 km.
Traffic in Europe is also showing a progressive revival. In this connection mention should be made primarily of the promising banana traffic, which has been captured from the road, between Hamburg and various stations in Norway.
Traffic in 1976 was so heavy that it was sometimes difficult to meet all requests for mechanically refrigerated wagons. As a consequence, refrigerator wagons with dry ice sometimes had to be used in order to overcome the shortage of mechanically refrigerated wagons. In this way INTERFRIGO was able to obtain contracts for the shipment of considerable amounts of frozen meat from France to Bulgaria and Poland.

Mechanically refrigerated transcontainers
The number of shipments transported in mechanically refrigerated transcontainers increased by 10 per cent from 6 197 in 1975 to 6 813 in 1976; 55 per cent of this figure was accounted for by containers which are owned by shipping companies or owned by INTERFRIGO and rented to shipping companies on a long-term basis, and 45 per cent by containers which are owned by INTERFRIGO and used principally in "per journey" traffic from Morocco.
As a result of sales promotion efforts directed at international shipping companies, 77 per cent of the INTERFRIGO stock was rented on a long-term basis at the end of 1976.

INTERFRIGO rolling stock in service
The company's total rolling stock decreased from 7 899 units at the end of 1975 to 7 662 units at the end of 1976 as a result of:
—Scrapping of 262 old wagons including:
   210 normal-capacity wagons
   50 large-capacity wagons
   2 supercapacity wagons
—Delivery of 25 mechanically refrigerated bogie wagons of the 14th series
—Conversion of:
   2 refrigerator and 7 mechanically refrigerated wagons to insulated wagons
   1 refrigerator wagon to a mechanically refrigerated wagon.
Annual average stock available diminished from 7 996 units in 1975 to 7 750 units in 1976, representing a decline of 3.1 per cent.
111 581 journeys were made with the total stock (108 494 in wagons, 3 087 in transcontainers) in 1976, compared with 118 450 (114 379 in wagons, 4 071 in transcontainers) in the preceding year, a decline of 5.8 per cent.

The share of total wagon traffic accounted for by INTERFRIGO wagons increased from 44.9 per cent in 1975 to 45.7 per cent in 1976.

Type of stock	In service on 31.12.1976
1. **Refrigerator wagons**	
GC (Continental loading gauge)	1 851
GC (British loading gauge)	1 323
TGC	3 805
SC	121
Total	7 100
2. **Insulated wagons**	
GC (Continental loading gauge)	10
GC (British loading gauge)	9
SC	1
Total	20
3. **Liquid nitrogen wagons**	
GC (Continental loading gauge)	1
GC (British loading gauge)	5
Total	6
4. **Mechanically refrigerated wagons**	
2-axle	69
Bogie	51
Total	120
5. **Mechanically refrigerated transcontainers**	
20-foot	241
40-foot	170
Total	411
6. **Crew Dormitory Cars**	5
Grand total	7 662

The suspension of new construction due to the present decline in traffic provided the Company with an opportunity to give close attention to the optimisation of its rolling stock. This has been effected principally by means of the following measures:
—Faster scrapping of old wagons;
—Increased technical adaptations to improve commercial performance;
—The establishment, on the basis of existing and foreseeable commercial requirements, of an accurate catalogue of technical characteristics enabling a rapid choice to be made in accordance with the service required;
—The creation of suitable managerial instruments.
All these measures are part of an overall plan which has been elaborated by the Company in order to adjust its general policy to the altered requirements of its customers and to present and future railway transport conditions, particularly with regard to investments and the use of rolling stock.

Rolling stock owned by the Railway Administrations and specialised companies
As a result of scrappings and restricted construction programmes in accordance with the recommendations of INTERFRIGO, the insulated, refrigerator and mechanically refrigerated wagons hired by INTERFRIGO in international traffic diminished from 18 305 units at the end of 1975 to 17 590 units at the end of 1976.
However, the Company believes that in the present situation the endeavours to reduce investment programmes and increase the scrapping of old wagons must be stepped up. For this reason a joint plan has been submitted to the railway administrations for the attainment of this objective and in order to effect a synthesis of administative and investment problems with the aim of optimising the community policy of the member Administrations.
Rolling stock hired by INTERFRIGO from member administrations and specialised companies completed 128 987 journeys in 1976 as against 140 416 journeys in 1975; this corresponds to 54.3 per cent of the total wagon traffic, compared with 55.1 per cent in the preceding year.

Traffic conditions
During 1976 the operating conditions of refrigerator wagon traffic were characterised principally by the following factors:
—Greater fluidity of traffic as a whole, with a reduction in the average turn-round time from 14.11 days in 1975 to 13.78 days despite the persistence of local difficulties, particularly at the crossing of frontiers.
—A decline in the overall productivity of the jointly owned rolling stock, whose utilisation declined by 5.8 per cent while the average available rolling stock diminished only by about 2 per cent.
The shortening of the average distance travelled is due largely to a reduction in exports from peripheral countries (Greece, Romania, Hungary, Bulgaria). Although this is principally a result of import restrictions imposed by the Common Market and a fall in consumption, it is also partly due to the joint efforts to improve operations.
The loss of traffic was not completely cancelled out by traffic from other exporting countries. As a consequence there was an appreciable fall in demand for INTERFRIGO rolling stock, which normally is fully utilised in the course of the summer campaigns.

Operational development
The steps initiated at the operational level relate to the following fields:
—*General field,* for the consolidation of the relevant regulations by two submissions to the European Goods Timetable Conference (CEM) which are of a fundamental nature and give official priority to the traffic administered by INTERFRIGO.
—*Cooperation* in order to directly involve the Company in the joint efforts at research and the improvement of the instruments used by UIC for the acceleration of transports.
—*Local measures* in order to create and consolidate the operational bases for the establishment of the organisation required for the orderly operation of new services in train units and of traffic which has been captured from competitors and needs to be specially cultivated.
—*Future development* with the purpose of bringing about a progressive concrete improvement in routings and preparing the introduction of "programmed routings" in collaboration with the relevant railway administrations.
At the same time the Company continued its systematic analysis of each load movement, railway by railway, in order to locate and eliminate routing anomalies.
Finally, considerable progress was made with the study for the trial of real time management of goods traffic which the UIC has entrusted to INTERFRIGO. This is likely to lead to an experiment that is of benefit to the whole railway community.
The financial results for the 1976 business year show a profit of FB 4 218 025, including FB 83 341 carried forward from the preceding year. In accordance with Article 32 of the Company Statutes, the Board of Directors proposes to the Annual General Meeting the following distribution of profits:

Dividend	FB 4 122 000
Carried forward to new account	FB 96 025

The profit distributed to the owners of the Company as dividends—FB 4 122 000—represents 12 per cent of the value of the shares forming the company's registered capital. After deduction at source of taxes payable by shareholders, the net dividend received by them will be approximately 10 per cent.

Assets
On 31 December 1976 the gross fixed assets showed a reduction of FB 52.3 million in relation to 31 December 1975; this decline is due in particular to the scrapping of 262 transport units.
The other fixed assets show a diminution of FB 10.4 million due to security issue expenses (—FB 10.4 million depreciation).

Operating assets, which are accounted for by spare parts and stocks of material, show an increase of FB 1.8 million.

The diminution of FB 218.9 million in liquid or easily realisable assets is due principally to short-term funds deposited with banks and earmarked for the repayment of a loan. Accounts receivable, which showed a decrease of FB 94.3 million, had largely been settled by 31 March 1977.

Liabilities
The increase in "Capital and Reserves" (+FB 5 000) is due to the allocation to the legal reserve of a sum from the profit for the 1975 business year.
Long-term liabilities diminished by FB 552.6 million.
Short-term liabilities diminished by FB 2.3 million, mainly due to the settlement of credit guarantees.

Non-balance sheet items
On 31 December 1976 the amount of guarantees secured by the founder organisations in application of Article 30 of the Statutes was FB 3 033.4 million (FB 150.5 million less than on 31 December 1975). This corresponds in effect to the items "Borrowings and loans" shown under Liabilities on the balance sheet.
The ceiling for guarantees which the founding organisations are able to provide is at present FB 4 000 million.

Trading account
The gross trading profit of FB 691.3 million (FB 71.3 million more than in the 1975 business year) is made up as follows:
—Revenue: FB 1 779.9 million (+FB 65.4 million compared with 1975),
—Expenditure: FB 1 088.6 million (−FB 5.9 million compared with 1975)
The main revenue items are:
—Refrigeration charges for the normal customer uses of stock, totalling FB 1 035.4 million as against FB 976.8 million in 1975;
—Kilometric/time and RIV rentals paid by the railway administrations, amounting to FB 710.1 million as against FB 696.2 million in 1975;
—Demurrage charges relating to loading and unloading delays, which amount to FB 25.4 million compared with FB 38.7 million in 1975.
The most significant item of expenditure is represented by hire charges paid to owners of wagons, i.e. FB 461.2 million compared with FB 489.2 million in 1975. The items "Maintenance" and "Trials and Research" together amount to FB 238.6 million as against FB 292.2 million in 1975.

Profit and loss account
Total revenue, which amounts to FB 706.4 million compared with FB 637.9 million in 1975 includes, in addition to the gross operating profit of FB 691.3 million, financial income of FB 15.1 million (FB 2.8 million less than in 1975) arising mainly from interest on investments.
Expenditure totalled FB 702.3 million as against FB 633.8 million in 1975, and includes in particular:
—overhead expenses of FB 31.9 million
—depreciation of FB 363.8 million, calculated at 8.3 per cent of the purchase price of the refrigerator wagons and 12.5 per cent of the purchase price of refrigerating machinery and equipment
—financial charges of FB 250.4 million
—exchange rate losses of FB 51.5 million.
The net profit for the business year is FB 4.1 million.

THE REPRESENTATIVES OF INTERFRIGO
Austria
Oesterreichische Bundesbahnen (OeBB)
Verkaufsdirektion—Abt IV/3, Gauermanngasse 4, A-1010 Vienna
Tel: (0222) 5650/5329
Telex: 12104

Belgium
NV Interferry
Zomerweg 26, B-2030 Antwerpen
Tel: 41 69 50
Telex: 32529

Bulgaria
UEE—"BDZ"—Eisenbahnkühltransporte INTERFRIGO-Zentralbüro
Sofia, Moskowska-Strasse 17
Tel: 843 43 69
Telex: 22423

Czechoslovakia
"CSKD Intrans"/Skupina INTERFRIGO
CS-12000 Praha 2, Perucka 5
Tel: 83 05 19 or 2124 (ext 4953)
Telex: 121 486

Denmark
Danske Statsbaner (DSB)
DK-1349 Copenhagen K, Sølvgade 40
Tel: (01) 140400
Telex: 27054

Finland
Valtionrautatiet (VR)
Rautatiehallitus, PB 488, SF-00101 Helsinki 10
Tel: 90 717 711
Telex: 12-30151 VRSF

France
Stef, 93 bd Malesherbes, F-75008 Paris
Tel: 522 8894
Telex: 280969

Germany (GDR)
Deutsche Reichsbahn—Ministerium für Verkehrswesen
INTERFRIGO-Büro DDR-1086 Berlin 8, Voss-Strasse 33
Tel: 530201
Telex: 112250

Germany (GFR)
Operating representation:
Deutsche Bundesbahn, Zentrale Transportleitung—Abteilung VW
D-65 Mainz 1, Kaiserstrasse 3
Tel: (06131) 15 58 47 or 15 58 25
Telex: 04187732

Commercial representation:
Transthermos GmbH, D-28 Bremen 1 Parkstrasse 123, Postfach 100929
Tel: (0421) 340 21
Telex: 244457 or 245518

Greece
Hellenic Railways Organisation Ltd
Athens (107), Karolou Street 1/3
Tel: 54 25 84
Telex: 215187

Hungary
Magyar Allamvasutak (MAV), Vezérigazgatósága 8B,
INTERFRIGO-Vezérkepviselet, H-1940 Budapest VI, Népköztársaság Utja 73
Tel: 428-575 or 220-660/183
Telex: 224342

Iran
Iranian State Railways (RAI)
49 West Takhte Jamshid Avenue, Teheran
Tel: 525121-28
Telex: 213103

Ireland
Coras lompair Eireann (CIE)
Office of the Commercial Manager, 35 Lower Abbey Street, Dublin 1
Tel: 30 07 77
Telex: 5695

Italy
Ferrovie Italiane dello Stato
Direzione Generale (for transports in refrigerator wagons)
1-00161 Roma, Piazza della Croce Rossa
Servizio Movimento
Tel: 8490/2136
Telex: 61089
Servizio Commerciale e del Traffico
Tel: 8490/2329-33625
Telex: 61089
Istituto Nazionale Trasporti
(for transports in mechanically refrigerated wagons and transcontainers)
1-00198 Roma, Via Savoia 19
Tel: 861 851
Telex: 68504 FERRINT

Luxemburg
Chemins de fer Luxembourgeois
Service commercial
9 place de la Gare, Luxembourg
Tel: 49901
Telex: 2288

Netherlands
NV Nederlandse Spoorwegen (NS)
Dienst van Commerciële Zaken, 1e Afdeling
NL-2501 Utrecht, Katreinetoren
Tel: (030) 35 45 52
Telex: 70131

Norway
Norges Statsbaner (NSB)
Hovedadministrasjonen, N-Oslo 1, Storgaten 33
Tel: 20 95 50
Telex: 11168

Portugal
Companhia dos Caminhos de ferro Portugueses (CP)
Departamento Comercial
Largo dos Caminhos de Ferro, Lisboa-2
Tel: 86 41 81-86 61 01/8
Telex: 12382

Romania
Caile Ferate Române (CFR)
Service INTERFRIGO
Bucuresti 7, Bulevardul Dinicu Golescu 38
Tel: 17 20 60
Telex: 11553

Spain
Transfesa
Madrid (3), Bravo Murillo No 38-2°, Apartado 3225
Tel: 448 89 00
Telex: 27745 or 22632

Sweden
Statens Järnvägar (SJ)
Centralförvaltningen-Trafikavdelningen, S-105 50 Stockholm
Tel: 22 64 20
Telex: 19410

Switzerland
Frigosuisse (National Representation)—Schweizerische Bundesbahnen
—Kommerzieller Dienst Güterverkehr
CH-3000 Bern, Mittelstrasse 43
Tel: (031) 60 32 81
Telex: 69144

Betriebsabteilung-Sektion 6
CH-3000 Bern, Schwarztorstrasse 57
Tel: (031) 60 27 11
Telex: 69121

Bahnhofkühlhaus AG, Münchensteinerstrasse 93
CH-4002 Basel, Postfach 111
Tel: (061) 35 55 90
Telex: 62271

Société de Gares Frigorifiques et Ports Francs de Genève
CH-1227 Carouge, rue Blavignac 5, Case postale 88
Tel: (022) 43 87 60
Telex: 28177

Marco Celoria SA
Fabrique de glace, CH-6830 Chiasso
Tel: (091) 44 26 02

United Kingdom
General Operating Representation (wagons):
British Railways Board
Executive Director, Systems and Operations, Freight Rolling Stock Officer, 222
Marylebone Road, London NW1 6JJ
Tel: 01-262-3232 (ext. 5619)
Telex: 24678

General Commercial Representation:
British Rail—Shipping and International Services Division
(for all traffic in refrigerator wagons, mechanically refrigerated wagons and transcontainers originating from or destined for Harwich)
163-203, Eversholt St, London NW1 1BG
Tel: 01-387-1234
Telex: 269295

Operating and Commercial Representation:
Freightliners Ltd
(for international transports in mechanically refrigerated transcontainers originating from or destined for the inland Freightliner terminals other than Harwich)
43 Cardington Street, London NW1 2LR
Tel: 01-387-9400 (ext 3326)
Telex: 24743

Turkey
Türkiye Cumhuriyeti Devlet Demiryollari (TCDD)
Hareket Dairesi Baskanligi, Ankara
Tel: 24 12 20 (ext. 205)
Telex: 42571

Yugoslavia
Zajednica Jugoslovenskih Zeleznica (JZ)
Zastupnistvo INTERFRIGA i Intercontainera (1-4)
YU-11000 Beograd, Nemanjina 6/11
Tel: 682-525
Telex: 11166

INTERNATIONAL ASSOCIATION OF ROLLING STOCK BUILDERS

(Association Internationale des Constructeurs de Matériel Roulant—AICMR)

Offices: 12, rue Bixio, 75007, Paris, France

Telegrams: 'Interwagon, Paris'
Telephone: 705 36 62

President: Baron P. van der Rest (Belgian)
Delegate General: X. Allain-Dupré (French)

INTERNATIONAL CARRIAGE & VAN UNION (RIC UNION)

Union Internationale des Voitures et Fourgons (Union RIC)

Offices: c/o Swiss Federal Railways, Hochschulstrasse 6, CH-3000, Berne, Switzerland

Telephone: (031) 60 11 11
Telex: 32500

INTERNATIONAL CONTAINER BUREAU (ICB)

Offices: 38, Cours Albert 1, Paris 8, France

Telephone: 359-05-92

President: J. Martial

INTERNATIONAL FEDERATION OF RAILWAY ADVERTISING COMPANIES

Offices: Orell Füssli Expo AG, Bahnhof-u, Aussenwerbung, Buhlstrasse 1, 8125 Zollikerberg, Switzerland

Telephone: 63 96 40

Secretary: H. Menti

INTERNATIONAL ORGANISATION FOR STANDARDISATION (ISO)

(Organisation internationale de Normalisation)

Offices: Case postale 56,1 rue de Varembé, 1211, Geneva 20, Switzerland

Telephone: 34 12 40
Telex: 23887

Officers
President: Dr. Ake T. Vrethem (Sweden)
Vice-President: R. L. Henessy (Canada)
Treasurer: Léopold Borel
Secretary General: Olle Sturen
Assistants: R. Marechal and Robert Middleton

INTERNATIONAL UNION OF PRIVATE RAILWAY TRUCK OWNERS' ASSOCIATIONS

Offices: General Secretary 2, rue Fendt, PO Box 877, CH-1211 Geneva 1, Switzerland

Telegrams: 'Genefert, Geneve'
Telephone: 34 88 00 (022)
Telex: 22 139

Secretary General: E. J. Fert, 2, rue Fendt, CH-1211 Geneva 1

INTERNATIONAL RAIL TRANSPORT COMMITTEE (CIT)

Offices: Managing Railway: General Management of the Swiss Federal Railways, Hochschulstr 6, CH-3000 Berne, Switzerland

Telephone: 60 25 65 or 60 27 94

President and Chairman: Desponds
Secretary: Bertherin

INTERNATIONAL UNION OF RAILWAY MEDICAL SERVICES (UIMC)

Offices: 85, rue de France, 1070, Brussels, Belgium

Telephone: 02/23.80.80-2561

Treasurer: Dr J. Dufaux
Secretary General: Dr C. T. Newnham, Medical Department, First Floor General Offices, Paddington Station, London W2 1HA
Tel: 01-723 7000
Assistant Secretary General: Dr J. Gorissen

INTERNATIONAL WAGON UNION (RIV UNION)

Union Internationale des Wagons (Union RIV)

Offices: c/o Swiss Federal Railways, Hochschulstrasse 6, CH-3000, Berne, Switzerland

Telephone: (031) 60 11 11
Telex: 32500

LATIN AMERICAN RAILWAY ASSOCIATION

Head Office: Florida 783, Ier.Piso 1005 Buenos Aires, Argentina

Telephones: 31 9463 and 32 5151

Officers:
General Secretary: Emiliano A. S. Flouret
Administrative Secretary: Felipe Muniain

The Association was founded at a meeting of Latin-American Railway representatives in Argentina in 1964. Principal objectives are the creation of transcontinental routes; settling of traffic interchange problems; development and integration of Latin-American railways elimination of frontier and customs difficulties; the exchange of technical, information and the sale, loan or exchange of railway material between members; co-ordination of railway industries in Latin America and the creation of a code of standards for Latin-American built railway equipment and the formation of a Latin-American Railway Bank.

PAN AMERICAN RAILWAY CONGRESS ASSOCIATION

Offices: Av. 9 de Julio 1925, Piso 13,1332 Buenos Aires, Argentina

Telephone: 38 4625

Officers:
President: Juan Carlos De Marchi
Vice Presidents: Roberto Agostini Centeno and Dr. Pedro Chiriboga Founes
General Secretary: Cayetano Marletta Rainieri
Treasurer: José Luis de Pabón

Inaugurated in 1907 at the celebrations of the 50th anniversary of the first Argentinian railway the association was originally made up of Latin-American countries. Originally the United States was limited to sending observers to congresses but now all the 21 American Republics are members and the main aims of the association is to promote the development and progress of railways in the Western Hemisphere.

TEE
TRANS-EUROP-EXPRESS

Administration: Netherlands Railways, 3500 HA Utrecht, Moreelsepark 1, The Netherlands

It was in 1954, following a proposition put forward by Mr. Den Hollender, then President of the Netherlands Railways, that the railway administration of Belgium, France, West Germany, Italy, Luxembourg, The Netherlands and Switzerland decided to form the Trans-Europ-Express Group, having the object of connecting the major European centres of population and industry by a network of very fast and very comfortable trains. Two more countries, Austria and Spain, have since joined.
The Managing Administration of the TEE-Group, with offices at the Headquarters of the Netherlands Railways in Utrecht, is charged with coordinating the TEE activities of the member administrations, and with studying the possibilities of improving existing services and developing others. The TEE group is not a railway system as such; it is an organisation of studies and direction.
All the motive power units and rolling stock are owned and operated by the various railway administrations in the Group. However all the trains carry the emblem "TEE" and have to satisfy certain minimum specifications as to speed and comfort.
For accountancy purposes, because each country has its own currency, the money basis adopted is the gold franc. The tariff applicable to TEE trains consists of the first class fare in force in each of the countries in which they operate, plus a supplement fixed uniformly at 2 gold centimes per km.
In order to reduce the length of, or to eliminate, stops at frontiers, arrangements are made for customs and security controls to be effected during the journey; and the use of multi-current electric locomotives and trainsets gives smooth change-over, without stopping, from one system of electrification to another, irrespective of country.
Since it commenced on 2 June 1957, the Trans-Europ-Express train-service has gone from strength to strength. Today it covers nine countries: *Austria, Belgium, France, Germany, Italy, Luxembourg, The Netherlands, Spain* and *Switzerland.* It now has 28

Name of Train	Route	Distance		Booked time	Inter-mediate stops	Average speed	
		miles	km	hr min		mph	kmlh
Adriatico	Milano-Bari	540	869	8 35	13	63	101
Aquitaine	Paris Austerlitz-Bordeaux	361	581	4 00	—	90	145
l'Arbalète	Paris Est-Zürich	382	614	5 43	4	66	107
Bavaria	Zürich-München	221	365	4 12	6	53	85
van Beethoven	Frankfurt (Main)- Amsterdam-Bonn	295	475	4 52	9	61	98
Blauer Enzian	Hamburg Altona- Klagenfurt	743	1 195	13 11	19	56	91
Brabant	Paris Nord- Bruxelles Midi	193	311	2 23	—	81	130
Le Capitole du matin	Paris Austerlitz-Toulouse	443	713	5 56	4	75	120
Le Capitole du soir	Paris Austerlitz-Toulouse	443	713	5 56	4	75	120
Le Catalan/Talgo	Barcelona-Genève	537	864	9 43	15	55	89
Cisalpin	Paris Lyon-Milano	510	821	7 44	5	66	106
Cycnus	Ventimiglia-Milano	191	307	3 46	7	51	82
Diamant	Köln-Bruxelles Midi	142	228	2 24	4	59	95
Edelweiss	Zürich-Amsterdam	560	902	9 33	14	58	94
Erasmus	Den Haag-München	568	914	9 19	12	61	98
Etendard	Hendaye-Paris Austerlitz-Irun	507	816	6 20	6	80	129
Etoile du Nord	Amsterdam-Paris Nord	336	540	5 00	6	67	108
Goethe	Paris Est-Frankfurt (Main)	403	649	5 52	6	69	111
Gottardo	Basel SBB-Milano-Zürich	237	381	5 00	3	47	76
Helvetia	Hamburg-Altona-Zürich	599	964	9 28	12	63	102
Ile de France	Paris-Nord-Amsterdam	336	540	5 05	6	66	106
Kléber	Paris Est-Strasbourg	313	504	3 48	1	83	133
Lemano	Genève-Milano	232	373	3 53	4	60	96
Ligure	Avignon-Milano	426	686	7 28	12	57	92
Le Lyonnais	Paris Lyon-Lyon	318	512	3 50	—	83	134
Mediolanum	München-Milano	369	594	6 48	7	54	87
Le Mistral	Paris Lyon-Nice	676	1 088	9 03	9	75	120
Molière	Paris Nord-Düsseldorf	330	531	5 14	7	63	101
Oiseau Bleu	Bruxelles Nord-Paris Nord	197	317	2 36	3	76	122
Parsifal	Paris Nord-Hamburg Altona	602	969	9 15	17	65	105
Prinz Eugen	Bremen-Wien	688	1 107	10 45	9	64	103
Rembrandt	München-Amsterdam	549	884	9 06	14	60	97
Rheingold	Genève-Amsterdam/Hoek van Holland	644	1 037	10 52	16	59	95
Le Rhodanien	Paris Lyon-Marseille	536	863	6 34	3	81	131
Roland	Bremen-Milano	730	1 174	12 40	15	58	93
Saphir	Nürnberg-Bruxelles Midi-Frankfurt (Main)	432	696	7 22	11	58	94
Stanislas	Paris Est-Strasbourg	313	504	3 47	1	83	133
Ticino	Zürich-Milano	182	293	3 49	2	48	77
Vesuvio	Milano-Napoli	526	846	7 35	3	70	112

different routes, which are served by 39 trains stopping at over 190 stations, carrying some 5.0 million passengers annually. TEE-trains are first class only. Seat reservation (supplementary charge) is not essential but is strongly recommended. Seats can be reserved up to three months in advance and can be reserved for both outward and homeward journeys at the same time.

TEE-trains provide maximum comfort such as individual reclining seats, fluorescent lighting, cloakrooms, luggage-racks, air-conditioning and soundproofing. Amongst normal facilities a loudspeaker-system can be mentioned, used for announcing stations, passport-control or other relevant messages. Special facilities include the vista-dome-cars of the *Rheingold* from Hoek van Holland to Genève and the *Erasmus* from Den Haag to München; and in France the *Mistral*, *Lyonnais* and *Rhodanien* have a bar-car in their train composition with bookstall, secretarial offices and hairdressing saloon. Paris-bound trains offer an extra facility which avoids delay on arrival; during the journey passengers are able to reserve taxis by paying an amount which covers the first kilometre plus a small reservation-fee. These reserved taxis wait at a special lane near the station exit.

The first TEE-trains were diesel multiple-unit trainsets with a maximum speed of 87 mph *(140 kmlh)*. Capacity varied from 81 to 163 seats. In 1961 the Swiss Federal Railways introduced four five-coach multi-current electric trainsets (still running) on the Milan-Paris and Milan-Zurich routes. In 1967 the capacity was adjusted to the increased demand by adding a sixth coach to the units which brought capacity up to 168 seats, apart from the restaurant capacity.

In 1964 France and Belgium formed a pool of 36 stainless steel coaches hauled by multi-current electric locomotives. This made it possible to vary the seating capacity to adjust for the peaks of the day and of the week. On Monday mornings and Friday nights TEE trains composed of 15 coaches carrying 550 passengers are no exception.

In 1965 the *Helvetia* was electrified with air-conditioned rolling stock of German type. Other German locomotive-hauled trains followed and replaced the diesel-stock.

The Italian diesel trainsets have been replaced by electric locomotive-hauled coaches of special Fiat design. *Lemano*, *Ligure* and *Mediolanum* run with this new stock, as well as the three new TEE trains in Italian internal traffic: Adriatica, Cycnus and Vesuvio.

Arbalète, *Bavaria*, *Catalan-Talgo* and *Edelweiss* are today the only diesel-hauled trains.

The *Catalan-Talgo* tightens Spain to the TEE-network by means of a special design of wheel-adjustment, to compensate for gauge difference, which came into operation in 1969.

In general, speeds have increased in the 1957-1971 period; for example the average speed of the *Ile de France* the *Etoile du Nord* and the *Brabant* between Brussels and Paris is now 83 mph *(133 kmlh)*. In Germany and France some trains are run at a top speed of 124 mph *(200 kmlh)*, where the track has been upgraded and special modifications of signals have been arranged.

The *Blauer Enzian* does so on the Munich-Augsberg and Hanover-Hamburg sections, as do the *Etendard* and *Aquitaine* on the Paris-Bordeaux 581 km route of which roughly half is available for this speed. The *Aquitaine* has the highest average speed 90 mph *(145 kmlh)* on the longest non-stop journey of all the TEE trains.

London is on the TEE-teleprinter network, but the nearest connection is the Hook of Holland where the *Rheingold* starts to Germany, Switzerland and Italy. The linking of British Rail with the TEE-network, should the Channel tunnel be built, is on the planning-table. Timings of 4½ hours from London to Paris (city centre to city centre)

would be possible. The night-Ferry—once called "The only train leaving the country"—may someday be one of a series of common (market) daily practice.

TEEM

TRANS-EUROP-EXPRESS-MARCHANDISES

The importance of the creation of fast timings, particularly with transit traffic, between the large centres of production and consumption, led to the eventual creation of TEEM by the European railway administrations.

The timings had originally been decided by bilateral agreements between the administrations concerned. In 1961 the idea of creating a network of fast goods trains arose which, by analogy with what had been done for passengers with the TEE trains, received the designation of Trans-Europ-Express-Marchandises or, in brief, TEEM.

The first TEEM trains were introduced in May 1961. The reductions in transit times they made possible from the moment of their introduction were quite considerable; for example, the Bologna to London time fell from 60 to 38 hours.

Since 1961, however, the network of TEEM connections has steadily been improved and extended. There now exist 126 connections between 20 countries. Apart from the normal TEEM trains operating during the whole year there are several season connections assuring the transport of perishable goods between the agricultural areas and the regions of consumption.

TEEM routes have been established for Spanish fruit to the other countries of Western Europe, for French vegetables from Brittany to Belgium, Holland and Germany, and most of the transport of fruit in refrigerator wagons from the Balkans is executed by TEEM trains. The rapidity and the regularity of the transits provided by them make it possible to present a solid front against road competition and to promote international trade between the centres of production and consumption.

The development of the Common Market has contributed to accelerate the traffic by simplifying the customs formalities. The stops at the frontiers have been reduced to a minimum.

Another significant factor of TEEM is that its network reaches into eastern Europe, for its advantages are apparent to all European countries.

Co-ordinated by the Czechoslovak Railways, the managing administration of TEEM, the European railways are continually aiming at improvements to this system.

Stops of minimum duration are made at all frontier stations for customs and other formalities. A certain number of stops are also made at intermediate stations, some of which provide rail connections to and from other destinations.

TEEM trains operate at maximum speeds of 53-62 mph *(85-100 kmlh)*, and are restricted to wagons carrying the international marking S which indicates that they are capable of safe operation at 100 km/h the only other restrictions are (a) wagons to and from Spain must be fitted for interchangeable axles because of the difference in gauge, and (b) only ferry-boat wagons can be used for through traffic by train-ferry to and from England. The TEEM network provides the essential long-distance international routes linking the railway systems of all European countries west of the USSR and Finland. It is intended for the rapid transport of perishables and other products requiring speedy transit, excluding very heavy freight such as coal, stone, metals etc. There are no supplementary charges for transport by TEEM trains.

Representative TEEM trains

Train No.	Route		Distance		Inter-mediate stops	Time hours	Average speed	
			miles	km			mph	kmlh
101	Alicante (Spain)	Dunkerque (France)	1 270	2 043	1	51	25	40
111	Marseille (France)	Bruxelles (Belgium)	742	1 195	4	26	28	46
129	St. Pol-de-Léon (France)	München Ost (Germany)	957	1 540	6	30	32	51
151	Sagunto (Spain)	Genève (Switzerland)	751	1 209	2	33	23	37
301	Bologna (Italy)	Zeebrugge (Belgium)	895	1 441	6	34	26	42
302	Rotterdam (Neth.)	Basel Bad. (Switzerland)	470	757	1	13	36	58
338(a)	Stockholm (Sweden)	Salzburg (Germany)	1 251	2 013	10	53	23	38
350	Amsterdam (Neth.)	Nürnberg (Germany)	446	718	3	16	28	45
354	Hannover (Germany)	Wien (Austria)	606	975	4	19	32	51
408	Praha (Czechoslovakia)	Budapest (Hungary)	375	603	1	11	34	55
413(b)	Budapest (Hungary)	København (Denmark)	944	1 520	7	44	21	35
631	Thessaloniki (Greece)	München (Germany)	1 051	1 692	7	43	24	39
740	Warszawa (Poland)	Hannover (Germany)	569	915	6	21	27	44
759(c)	Hamburg (Germany)	Oslo (Norway)	711	1 145	6	38	19	30

(a) via 2 train ferries:— Hälsingborg (Sweden)-Helsingør (Denmark) and Rødby F. (Denmark)-Puttgarden (W. Ger.)
(b) via 1 train ferry:— Warnemünde (E Ger.)-Gedser (Denmark).
(c) via 1 train ferry:— Sassnitz Hafen (E Ger.)-Trelleborg (Sweden)

UNION OF EUROPEAN RAILWAY INDUSTRIES

(Union des Industries Ferroviaires Européennes—UNIFE)

Offices: 12, rue Bixio, 75007 Paris, France

Telegrams: 'Interwagon, Paris'
Telephone: 705-36-62

President: Baron P. Van der Rest (Belgian)
Secretary General: X. Allain-Dupre (French)

UNITED NATIONS ECONOMIC COMMISSION FOR EUROPE

Offices: Palais des Nations, Geneva, Switzerland

Telephone: 34 60 11

Officers:
Executive Secretary: J. Stanovnik
Deputy Executive Secretary: A. I. Alexandrov
Director Transport Division: H. G. Halbertsma

Established in 1947 to advise and help with the reconstruction of Europe. It has three main working parties for rail, road and inland water transport.
In the rail transport field it deals with customs, frontier formalities for passengers and goods; the exchange of transport equipment; the introduction of automatic coupling; the unification and standardisation of rolling stock; the adoption of a standard type of electro-pneumatic brakes and measurers for achieving high speed in rail transport.

ASSOCIATIONS AND GOVERNMENT AGENCIES (CANADA)

MINISTRY OF TRANSPORT

Tower C, Place de Ville, Ottawa, Ontario K1A ON5

Telephone: (613) 996 7501

Minister: O. Lang
Deputy Minister: S. Cloutier
Asst Deputy Minister, Operations: G. A. Scott
Sr Asst Deputy Minister, Planning: D. W. Kirkwood
Surface Transport, Admin: S. Cameroun
Transport Development Agency: P. H. Aykroyd
President, Canadian Transport Commission: E. J. Benson
Railway Transportation Directorate
Director General: R. Bechamp
Freight Capacity Development: E. Gilliatt
Railway Relocation & Crossing: J. H. Galvin
Railway Planning: K. Henderson
Railway Passenger Development: R. Taborek
Grain Transportation: A. W. Burges

CANADIAN TRANSPORT COMMISSION (RAILWAY TRANSPORT COMMITTEE)

275 Slater St, Ottawa, Ontario K1A ON9

Telephone: (613) 996 4468

Chairman: D. H. Jones
Commissioners: M. D. Armstrong
Mrs. A. Carver
E. H. La Borde
G. F. Lafferty
J. A. D. Magee
J. B. G. Thomson
J. M. Woodward
Executive Director Railway Transport Committee: J. d'Avignon
Director Safety & Standards: A. G. Hibbard
Director Rail Systems Development: E. W. Eastman
Director Rail Economic Analysis: M. C. Tosh

ASSOCIATIONS AND GOVERNMENT AGENCIES (UNITED KINGDOM)

DEPARTMENT OF THE ENVIRONMENT

2 Marsham St, London SW1P 3EB

Telephone: (01) 212 3434

Minister of Transport: Dr John Gilbert

Railways
Under-Secretary: W. J. Sharp
Assistant Secretaries: R. G. S. Johnston
K. Peter
Railway Inspectorate,
Chief Inspecting Officer: Lt Col I. K. A. McNaughton
Inspecting Officers: Major P. M. Oliver
Major A. G. B. King
Major C. F. Rose
Lt Col A. G. Townsend Rose
Senior Railway Employment Inspector: C. H. Hewison

CROWN AGENTS FOR OVERSEAS GOVERNMENT AND ADMINISTRATIONS

4 Millbank, London SW1P 3JD

Telephone: (01) 222 7730
Telex: 916205
Telegrams: CROWN LONDON SW1

Chairman: J. G. Cuckney
Crown Agents: J. F. Goble
J. G. D. Gordon
H. L. Kirkley
Mrs. E. H. Boothroyd
H. S. Hoff
J. Jack
Executive Board:
Technical Services: M. J. Cotton; N. Hewins
Financial Services: S. A. W. Eburne
Financial Controller: A. H. N. Molesworth
Engineering Services: E. A. Kirkby
Personnel & Organisation: H. T. Eaton
Supplies: R. Newman
Head of Railway Division: K. F. Douglas

Overseas Offices:
North America: 3100 Massachusetts Ave, NW, Washington, DC 2008. Telephone: (202) 462 1340
Far East: 7th Floor, Tokyo Chamber of Commerce and Industry Building, 2-2, 3-chome, Marunouchi, Chiyoda-ku, Tokyo 100, Japan. Telephone: 211 5035. Telex: Tokyo 22946
Mid-East: 3rd Floor, Al Moayyed Building North, PO Box 531, Manama, Bahrain, Arabian Gulf. Telephone: 54672. Telex: GJ 8307
East Africa: 2nd Floor, IPS Building, Kimathi St, PO Box 47246, Nairobi, Kenya. Telephone: 25524/26917. Telex: 22536
West Africa: Western House, 8/10 Broad St, PO Box 583, Lagos, Nigeria. Telephone: 21241. Telex: 21416
South-East Asia: 6th Floor, Chartered Bank Building, 2, Jalan Ampang, Kuala Lumpur, 01-16 Malaysia. Telephone: 21538/21545
Australia: 9th Floor, IAC Building, 54-62, Carrington St, Sydney, NSW 2000. Telephone: 290 2266. Telex: 22461
Caribbean: Barclays Bank Building, Roebuck St, PO Box 82, Bridgetown, Barbados. Telephone: 60458
Singapore: Suite 707, Cathay Building, Mount Sophia, Singapore 9. Telephone: 321167. Telex: RS 22171
Indonesia: Pexamin Pacific Inc 2nd Floor, PPM Building, Jalan Menteng, Raya 9, Jakarta. Telephone: 357310. Telex: 46377

ASSOCIATED SOCIETY OF LOCOMOTIVE ENGINEERS & FIREMEN

9 Arkwright Rd, London NW3 6AB

Telephone: 01 435 6300

General Secretary: R. W. Buckton

ASSOCIATION OF BRITISH RAILWAY CARRIAGE & WAGON MANUFACTURERS

7 Ludgate, Broadway, London EC4V 6DX

Chairman: T. Roland Bell
Secretaries: Peat, Marwick, Mitchell & Co.

ASSOCIATION OF MINOR RAILWAY COMPANIES

Offices of Derwent Valley Railway, Layerthorpe Station, York YO3 7XS

Telephone: 0904 58981

Chairman: A. G. W. Garraway (Festiniog Rly)
Vice-Chairman: D. Ferreira (Ravenglass & Eskdale Rly)
Secretary: J. Acklam

ASSOCIATION OF CONSULTING ENGINEERS

Hancock House, 87 Vincent Square, London SW1P 2PH

Telephone: 01 222 6557

Chairman: Sir Ralph Freeman
Secretary: Major-General M. W. Prynne
Assistant Secretary: A. H. Trembath

ASSOCIATION OF PRIVATE RAILWAY WAGON OWNERS

18 Great Marlborough St, London W1V 2NJ

Telephone: 01 629 S434

Secretary: J. M. B. Gotch

BRITISH TRANSPORT OFFICERS' GUILD

Room 307, West Side Offices, King's Cross Station, London N1 9AX

Telephone: 01 837 0782

CHARTERED INSTITUTE OF TRANSPORT

80 Portland Place, London W1N 4DP

Telephone: 01 580 5216

President: J. Morris Gifford
Secretary: L. F. Aldbridge

COUNCIL OF ENGINEERING INSTITUTIONS
2 Little Smith St, London SW1 P3DL

Telephone: 01 799 2912

Secretary: M. W. Leonard

DIESEL ENGINEERS AND USERS ASSOCIATION
18 London St, London EC3R 7JR

Telephone: 01 481 2393

FEDERATION OF CIVIL ENGINEERING CONTRACTORS
Romney House, Tufton St, London SW1P 3DU

Telephone: 01 222 2544

INSTITUTION OF CIVIL ENGINEERS
Great George St, London SW1P 3AA

Telephone: 01 839 3611

President: J. W. Baxter
Secretary: J. G. Watson

INSTITUTION OF BRITISH ENGINEERS
Regency House, 3 Marlborough Place, Brighton BN1 1UB

Telephone: (0273) 61399

Secretary: Dorothy Henry

INSTITUTION OF ELECTRICAL ENGINEERS
Savoy Place, London WC2R 0BL

Telephone: 01 240 1871

President: R. J. Clayton
Secretary: Dr G. F. Gainsborough

INSTITUTION OF MECHANICAL ENGINEERS RAILWAY DIVISION
1 Birdcage Walk, London SW1

Chairman: F. H. Beasant
Secretary: Miss J. M. Johnson

INSTITUTION OF RAILWAY SIGNAL ENGINEERS
Hon General Secretary: R. L. Weedon, 21 Avalon Rd, Early, Reading, Berks

LOCOMOTIVE & CARRIAGE INSTITUTION
General Secretary: D. Kirkland, 208A Chapter Rd, Willesden, London NW2 5NB

Telephone: 01 459 5326

NATIONAL COUNCIL OF INLAND TRANSPORT
Hon Secretary: Roger Calvert, Woodside House, High Rd, London N22 4LJ

NATIONAL UNION OF RAILWAYMEN
Unity House, Euston Rd, London NWL 2BL

Telephone: 01 387 4771

General Secretary: S. Weighell

PERMANENT WAY INSTITUTION
27 Lea Wood Rd, Fleet, Hants GU13 8AN

Hon General Secretary: L. J. Harris

RAILWAY DEVELOPMENT ASSOCIATION
Hon Secretaries: A. W. T. Daniel (London Area), The Old Vicarage, Piddinghoe, Newhaven, Sussex BN9 9AP and A. Bevan (Midland Area), 12 Morris Field Croft, Birmingham B28 0RN

RAILWAY INDUSTRY ASSOCIATION OF GREAT BRITAIN
9 Catherine Place, London SW1E 6DX

Telephone: 01 834 1426

Director: G. R. Curry

TRANSPORT & GENERAL WORKERS UNION
Transport House, Smith Square, London SW1P 3JB

Telephone: 01 828 7788

TRANSPORT SALARIED STAFFS' ASSOCIATION
Walkden House, 10 Melton St, London NW1 2EJ

Telephone: 01 387 2101

General Secreatry: D. A. Mackenzie

ASSOCIATIONS AND GOVERNMENT AGENCIES (UNITED STATES)

ASSOCIATION OF AMERICAN RAILROADS
American Railroads Bldg., 1920 "L" St., NW, Washington, DC 20036

Telephone: 202-293 4000

Chicago Office: 59 East Van Buren St., Chicago, Ill. 60605. Telephone: 312-939 0770
New York Office: Room 2177, Two Pennsylvania Plaza, New York, NY 10001. Telephone: 212-563 2710
Research Centre: 3140 South Federal St., Chicago, Ill. 60616. Telephone: 312-567 3575

President and Chief Executive Officer: W. H. Dempsey
Senior Vice President: C. V. Lyon
Vice President—Assistant to President: J. E. Murray
Assistant to President—Staff Studies: A. S. Lang
Vice President and General Counsel: H. J. Breithaupt, Jr
General Solicitor: P. F. Welsh
Vice President (Economics and Public Affairs): R. E. Briggs
Vice President (Operations and Maintenance): J. E. Martin
Vice President (Research & Test): W. J. Harris, Jr
Vice President (Legislative): E. F. Waldrop, Jr
Vice President (Management Systems): H. W. Meetze
General Attorney and Secretary: H. G. Duensing
Treasurer: C. P. Safrit
Chief Accountant: J. C. Slattery

THE AMERICAN SHORT LINE RAILROAD ASSOCIATION
2000 Massachusetts Ave., NW, Washington, DC 20036

Telephone: 202-785 2250

President and Treasurer: P. H. Croft
Vice-President and General Counsel: C. H. Johns
Traffic Managers:
  Atlanta: S. D. Austin
  Chicago: J. C. Johnson
  Washington: J. S. Dow
Regional Vice-Presidents:
  Baltimore, Md: R. W. Dale
  Yreka, Ca: W. B. Kyle
  Moultrie, Ga: W. L. Pippin
  Roscoe, Tx: G. E. Pitts
  Chicago, Ill: J. E. Rice

INTERSTATE COMMERCE COMMISSION
12th & Constitution Ave., NW, Washington, DC 20423

Telephone: 202-275 7000

Chairman: A. Daniel O'Neal
Commissioners: Rupert L. Murphy
  Virginia Mae Brown
  Dale W. Hardin
  Robert L. Gresham
  Alfred T. MacFarland
  G. M. Stafford
  Charles L. Clapp
  Betty Jo Christian
Rail Services Planning Officer: Alan M. Fitzwater
Dir Bar of Investigations & Enforcement: P. M. Shannon
Secretary: R. L. Oswald
Managing Director, Vacant: J. P. Kratzke (Acting)
General Counsel: M. L. Evans
Director Bureau of Accounts: J. Grady
Director Bureau of Economics: Ernest R. Olson
Director Bureau of Operations: J. E. Burns
Director Bureau of Traffic: M. Foley
Public Information Officer: D. Baldwin

DEPARTMENT OF TRANSPORTATION
400 7th St. SW, Washington, DC 20590
Secretary: B. Adams
Under Secretary: A. A. Butchman
Deputy Under Secretary: M. L. Downey
Executive Secretary: Linda Smith
General Councillor: Linda Heller Kamm
Assistant Secretary for Policy and International Affairs: C. Davenport
Assistant Secretary for Systems of Development and Technology: W. D. Owens
Assistant Secretary for Congressional and Inter Governmental Affairs: T. L. Bracy
Assistant Secretary for Administration: E. W. Scott
Director of Public Affairs, Office of Secretary: D. A. Jewell
Administrator of Federal Aviation Administration: L. M. Bond
Acting Administrator of Federal Highway Administration: W. M. Cox
Federal Railroad Administrator: J. M. Sullivan
Administrator of Urban Mass Transportation: R. McManus

FEDERAL RAILROAD ADMINISTRATION
400 7th St, SW Washington, DC 20590

Telephone: 202-426 4000

Eastern Office: 434 Walnut St, Rm 1020, Philadelphia, Pa 19106. Telephone: 215-597 0750
Southern Office: 1568 Willingham Dr, Suite 216B, College Park, Ga 30337. Telephone: 404-526 7801
Southwestern Office: 819 Taylor St, Rm 11A23, Ft Worth, Tx 76102. Telephone: 817-334 3601
Western Office: Two Embarcadero Center, Suite 630, San Francisco, California 94111. Telephone: 415-556 6411

Administrator: J. M. Sullivan
Chief Counsel: R. K. James
Associate Administrator for Administration: F. G. Bremer
Acting Associate Administrator, Office of Safety: D. W. Bennett
Acting General Manager, Alaska RR: W. L. Dorcy
Associate Administrator for Research and Development: R. E. Parsons
Public Affairs Officer: D. Umansky
Associate Administrator, Federal Assistance: C. Swinburn

NATIONAL TRANSPORTATION SAFETY BOARD
800 Independence Avenue, SW Washington DC 20591

Chairman: Webster B. Todd Jr.
Member: W. R. Haley
Member: Philip A. Hogue
Member: I. A. Burgess
Member: F. H. McAdams
General Counsel: F. L. Puls
General Manager: Harry Zink
Chief Hearing Examiner: Robert R. Boyd
Director of Public Affairs: E. E. Slattery Jr.

URBAN MASS TRANSPORTATION ADMINISTRATION
Department of Transportation, 400 7th St
SW Washington DC 20590

Administrator: R. E. Patricelli
Deputy Administrator: C. F. Bingman
Special Assistant: P. Ehrhardt
Director of Office of Civil Rights and Service Development: H. B. Williams
Associate Administrator of Office of Administration: W. H. Boswell
Chief Counsel of Office of Chief Counsel: J. M. Christian
Associate Administrator of Office of Research and Development: G. J. Pastor
Associate Administrator of Office of Transportation Management and Demonstrations: R. J. McManus
Associate Administrator, Office of Transit Assistance: J. C. Premo
Director, Office of Public Affairs: L. Schwalb
Associate Administrator Office for Policy & Programme Development: K. C. Orski
Associate Administrator for Transportation Planning: R. Gallamore

NATIONAL MEDIATION BOARD
1425 K St, NW, Suite 910
Washington, DC 20572

Chairman: David H. Stowe
Member: G. S. Ives
Member: Kay McMurray
Executive Secreary: Rowland K. Quinn, Jr
Staff Mediation Director: E. B. Meredith
General Counsel: Wm. E. Fredenberger, Jr
Hearing Officer: Ronald M. Etters
Research Analyst: Michael Cimini
Mediators: C. R. Barnes
            H. D. Bickford
            C. H. Callahan
            J. W. Cassle
            R. J. Cerjan
            S. J. Cognata
            R. T. Colliander
            F. J. Dooley
            R. J. Finnegan
            E. F. Hampton
            T. B. Ingles
            T. C. Kinsella
            W. S. Lane
            R. B. Martin
            C. A. Peacock
            W. L. Phipps
            W. H. Pierce
            T. H. Roadley
            Alfred Smith
            Joseph Smith
            J. B. Willits

RAILROAD RETIREMENT BOARD
844 Rush Street, Chicago, Ill 60611

Telephone: 312-751 4500

Chairman: J. L. Cowen
Member: N. P. Spiers
Secretary of the Board: R. F. Butler
Chief Executive Officer: K. J. Nolan

AMERICAN ASSOCIATION OF RAILROAD SUPERINTENDENTS
18154 Harwood Ave, Homewood, Ill 60430

Telephone: 312-799 4650

President: F. F. Dayton
Secretary: Mrs A. Wilson

AMERICAN RAILROAD TRUCK LINES ASSOCIATION
516 West Jackson Blvd, Chicago, Ill 60606

Telephone: 312-236 7600

President: D. H. Bergmann (Manager, Intermodal Ops, N&W Rly)

AMERICAN RAILWAY CAR INSTITUTE
11E 44th St, New York, NY 10017

Telephone: 212-867 6577

Chairman: J. Salathe (Pacific Car & Foundry)
President, Secretary and Treasurer: W. A. Renz
Vice-Presidents: W. T. Anthony (Bethlehem Steel Corp, Railroad Products)
                 R. C. Ortner (Ortner Freight Car Co)

AMERICAN RAILWAY DEVELOPMENT ASSOCIATION
8 No Jefferson St, Roanoke, Va 24011

President: C. S. Catlett
Secretary: D. A. Cox

AMERICAN RAILWAY ENGINEERING ASSOCIATION
59 East Van Buren St, Chicago, Ill 60605

Telephone: 312-939 0780

President: B. J. Worley

AMERICAN SOCIETY OF MECHANICAL ENGINEERS — RAIL TRANSPORTATION DIVISION
1000 West Shore Dr, Culver, In 46511

Telephone: 219-842 3989

Chairman: N. E. Bateson
Secretary: W. H. Chidley

ASSOCIATION OF RAILROAD ADVERTISING MANAGERS

President: R. G. Nelson (East Adv Manager, Union Pacific)
Executive Secretary: J. D. Singer

ASSOCIATION OF RAILROAD EDITORS
1920 L St, NW, Washington, DC 20036

Telephone: 202-293 4200

President: R. W. Sprague

ASSOCIATION OF SOUTHEASTERN RAILROADS
1920 L St, NW, Washington DC 20036

Telephone: 202-293 3140

Chairman: P. F. Osborn
Assoc Secretary: H. W. Hird

CENTRAL RAILWAY CLUB OF BUFFALO
39 Paul Place, Buffalo, NY 14210

President: P. A. Mastrolio
Executive Secretary: C. M. Voll

LOCOMOTIVE MAINTENANCE OFFICERS' ASSOCIATION
3144 Brereton Ct, Huntington, Wv 25705

Telephone: 304-523 7276

President: T. A. Tennyson
Secretary: J. J. T. Koerner

NATIONAL RAILROAD ADJUSTMENT BOARD
220 South State St, Chicago, Ill 60604

Chairman: G. L. Naylor

NATIONAL RAILROAD PIGGYBACK ASSOCIATION
210 N 13th St, St Louis, Mo 63103

President: G. A. Volkers (Dir Operations and Equipment, TOFC/COFC, Chessie)
Vice-President: E. W. Frey (General Manager TOFC, Santa Fe)
Secretary: T. A. Holzmann (Director TOFC, MoPac)

NATIONAL RAILWAY LABOR CONFERENCE
1225 Connecticut Ave, NW Washington, DC 20036

Telephone: 202-656 9320

Chairman: C. I. Hopkins

RAILROAD CONSTRUCTION AND MAINTENANCE ASSOCIATION

3001 West Soffell Ave, Melrose Park, Ill 60160

President: R. Deprizio
Secretary: D. Timony
Executive Director: L. Shields

RAILROAD PERSONNEL ASSOCIATION

American Railroads Bldg, Washington, DC 20036

Telephone: 202-293 4137

President: R. C. Prophater
Secretary: H. S. Dewhurst

RAILROAD PUBLIC RELATIONS ASSOCIATION

American Railroads Bldg, Washington, DC 20036

Telephone: 202-293 4191

President: R. W. Sprague
Secretary: J. N. Ragsdale

RAILWAY ENGINEERING—MAINTENANCE SUPPLIERS ASSOCIATION INC

332 So Michigan Ave, Chicago, Ill 60604

Telephone: 312-922-3373/922-7686

President: J. H. Hines (Pandrol)
Secretary: G. Barrett (Railway Track Work)
Executive Secretary: L. D. McGuan

RAILWAY PROGRESS INSTITUTE

700 No Fairfax St, Alexandria, Va 22314

Telephone: 703-836 2332

Chairman: W. T. Anthony
Vice-President: R. A. Matthews
Treasurer: R. F. Griffin

RAILWAY SUPPLY ASSOCIATION

332 S Michigan Ave, Suite 1540, Chicago, Ill 60604

Telephone: 312-939 4478

President: W. J. Burrows (Vapor Co)
Vice President: P. O. Williams (New York Air Brake Co)
Executive Secretary: A. Schiffers, Jr

RAILWAY SYSTEMS SUPPLIERS, INC

Rm 120 A, 401 Seventh Ave, New York, NY 10001

Telephone: 212-239 7038

Chairman and President: E. H. Cole
Executive Vice President: G. Harmon
Executive Director and Secretary: F. Aikman, Jr

ROADMASTERS AND MAINTENANCE WAY ASSOCIATION OF AMERICA

Cary Bldg, 18154 Harwood Ave, Homewood, Ill 60430

Telephone: 312-799 4650

President: W. J. Cruse
Secretary: Mrs A. Wilson

TRAFFIC CLUBS INTERNATIONAL

1040 Woodcock Rd, Orlando, Florida 32803

Chairman of Board: J. M. Beaupre
Secreatary: Althea B. Erikson
Executive Director: C. T. Harper

CONSULTANCY SERVICES

AMERICAN TRANSIT CORPORATION

120 South Central ave, St Louis, Mo 63105, USA

Telephone: (314) 726 5330

Vice-President Administration: H. C. Ashby

AMMAN & WHITNEY

World Trade Centre, Ste 1700, New York, NY 10048, USA

Telephone: (212) 938 8200

Partner: Allen M. Custen

PROJECTS
Relocation of two track rapid transit line including stations, tunnel and viaducts ($38 million) for Pa Dept of Transportation (Penndot); Design rapid transit station and ancillary modal-split facilities ($20 million) for Metropolitan Atlanta Rapid Transit Authority (MARTA).

ARTHUR ANDERSEN & CO

1666K St NW, Washington DC 20006, USA

Telephone:(202) 785 9510

Partner: Michael E. Simon

PROJECTS
Management system plan for Central New York Regional Transportation Authority and its three subsidiaries in the Syracuse area; Design general ledger, financial management reporting and accounting system for New York City Transit Authority (NYCTA).

WS ATKINS & PARTNERS

Woodcote Grove, Ashley Road, Epsom, Surrey KT18 5BW, England

Telephone: Epsom 26140
Telex: 23497
Cables: Kinsopar Epsom

Principal officers
Director of WS Atkins & Partners, Transportation Engineering Division F. L. Johnson BSc (Hons), CEng, MICE, FICE
R. A. Long OBE, FCIT, FRSA
H. Ormiston MBE, BSc, CEng, FCIT, FPWI

CAPABILITIES
As a major subsidiary of the WS Atkins Group of planning, engineering and management consultants, WS Atkins & Partners have experience in railway projects in various parts of the world. Their overall capability includes feasibility studies, traffic forecasts, cost estimates, detailed design of trackwork and structures, and supervision of construction. Studies devoted to the socio-economic aspects of a project, route assessment, environmental impact analyses, rationalisation of services, operating methods, future strategy, inventories of facilities and asset valuations are also undertaken.
WS Atkins & Partners frequently work with Henderson, Hughes & Busby.

PROJECTS
Integrated steelworks in Venezuela (with study of comparative costs of rail link); in Morocco (with study for rail link to coast; in another North African country (with study for rail link for work force); and in Sheffield, UK, for Drax power station and Selby coalfield.*

Suburban modal interchanges in Melbourne.
Land use and traffic forecast in East Sussex, UK.
Rapid transit in Cardiff-Llantrisant, UK.
Container terminal feasibility, Melbourne.
Multi-modal facilities in Tasmania.
Route selection and environmental impact analyses for Channel Tunnel rail link.
Signal and telecommunication etc, services maintenance rationalisation for British Rail.
Suburban rail service feasibility in Venezuela.
Railway workshop modernisation in New South Wales.
Valuation of entire steelworks railway system in Sweden.

* current.

MICHAEL BAKER JR INC

4301 Dutch Ridge Rd, Beaver Pa 15009, USA

Telephone: (412) 495 7711

Partner: Edgar C. Richardson

PROJECTS
South Busway ($20 million) and exclusive bus roadway ($65 million) for Port Authority of Allegheny County (PAT).

R. L. BANKS & ASSOCIATES

900 17th St, NW, Washington DC 20006, USA

Telephone: (202) 296 6700

Partner: Robert L. Banks

PROJECTS
Deficit allocation study for Washington Metropolitan Area Transit Authority (WMATA); Commuter service subsidies for the Interstate Commerce Commission, Rail Service Planning Office.

HAROLD BARTHOLOMEW AND ASSOCIATES

188 Jefferson ave, Memphis, Tenn 38103, USA

Telephone: (901) 527 3521

PROJECTS
Transit technical study at Savannah Ga, for Chatham County Metropolitan Planning Commission; Southeast Florida transit corridor study (Miami region) for Florida Department of Transportation (DOT).

BARTON-ASCHMAN ASSOCIATES, INC

820 Davis St, Evanston, Ill 60201, USA

Telephone: (312) 491 1000

Senior Vice-President: Michael A. Powills Jr

PROJECTS
Study of equity in transit service ($65 000) for Urban Mass Transportation Administration (UMTA); East corridor transit study ($136 000) for Regional Transportation District (RTD).

BECHTEL INCORPORATED
(Hydro & Community Facilities Division)

50 Beale Street, San Francisco, Cal 94119, USA

Telephone: (415) 768-7219
Cable: WATEKA- SF, CA
Int'l Telex: 470195
Dom TWX: 910-372-7961
Dom Telex: 34783

Associated companies:
Bechtel Corporation and Bechtel Power Corporation, (same address).

CAPABILITIES
Started in 1898, Bechtel's headquarters are located in San Francisco, California, with worldwide regional offices. The staff totals nearly 30 000 permanent employees, over half of which are graduate engineers and technical personnel.
Rail projects are the responsibility of Bechtel's Hydro and Community Facilities Division, headquartered in San Francisco, California, USA. The Rail Projects Department in this division is staffed with railway specialists, planners, engineers, and project managers covering all principal railroad disciplines. Bechtel performs railway services in terms of techno-economic feasibility studies, master planning, preliminary and final engineering, procurement services, construction engineering, and construction, or a combination of these. When called upon to handle complete packages Bechtel also offers assistance in securing required financing.
Bechtel's experience in railroad projects dates back to 1898 when the founder of the company, Warren A. Bechtel, started building railroads in what is now Oklahoma. Bechtel's comprehensive railroad construction activities started in 1920, with work on the realignment of Southern Pacific's Overland Route and the building of other parts of that system, as well as the original construction of the Western Pacific and the Northwestern Pacific. Experience increased worldwide over the following five decades.

PROJECTS

Assignment	Completion Date
Coronado Railroad—Engineering, procurement and construction of a coal hauling railroad using 8 000 metric ton trains.	Ongoing
Northeast Corridor IHSR—Develop improvement plans and feasibility for the establishment of High-Speed passenger Rail service to Northeast Corridor from Washington, DC, to Boston, Massachusetts.	Ongoing
Regional Railroad Reorganisation Inventory—Co-ordinate and perform inventory and costs of rehabilitation of all bankrupt railroads in the Northeast and Midwest United States.	1974-1975
Navajo Mine—Design of 16 km railroad from mine to power plant. Prepared car and locomotive specifications.	1973
Big Stone Plant—Assistance in arranging unit coal transportation, including freight rates, tariffs, design of 13 km of mine and plant trackage and development of "flip-top" covered gondola.	1969-1974
Robe River 167 km railroad to handle iron ore. Design, construction management, procurement, and operating procedures, including selection of rolling stock.	1969-1970
Mt. Newman 432 km railroad to handle iron ore. Construction management and procurement of rolling stock and other items.	1969-1970
MBR 644 km railroad to handle iron ore. Consultation on expansion and modernisation of existing line to haul additional 135 million metric tons per year.	1970-1973
Maryland and Pennsylvania Railroad—Final design of physical improvements to rehabilitate a 56 km section of line to carry 153 metric tons nuclear fuel cars. Includes 35 bridges.	Ongoing
Labadie—Assistance in unit coal train arrangements. Designed 10 km of track to plant.	1967-1972
Hope Creek Station—Logistical and site access study; comparison of rail, highway, and barge transport.	1974
Mildred Lake Project—Study of alternate methods of railroad transportation of tar sands from a moving loading area to extraction plant.	1972-1974
ISUA Iron Ore Project—148 km railroad to handle iron ore. Feasibility study of railroad from a point at the edge of the ice cap to the coast.	1971-1972
Sulawesi—Comparison of 60 km railroad and truck operations to handle lateric nickel. Study included equipment, roadbeds, manning, operations, and maintenance.	1971
Sishen-West Coast Railway—900 km railroad to handle iron ore. Conceptual engineering to haul 13.5 million metric tons per year.	1969
Edwin I. Hatch Plant—20 km railroad access to nuclear plant.	1968
Cerro Bolivar Mine—Field engineering and construction management for 145 km, heavy-duty iron ore railway, including terminal and support facilities.	1952

Assignment	Completion Date
Roy Nelson Station—Feasibility study of unit coal trains from Rocky Mountain areas. Assisted in arranging unit train transportation including size trackage.	1973
Eastalco—Assistance in freight rate negotiations, freight car specifications, and plant trackage design for shipment of aluminia and aluminium.	1968-1969
Pilgrim I—Site access study; rail, highway, or water handling.	1967
Pilgrim II—Preparation of transport portions of environmental impact reports.	1972
Evaluation of iron ore unit trains or special trains for hauling taconite tailings to alternate disposal sites.	1969
St. Louis Area Rail/Barge Terminal—Assistance in evaluating railroad capabilities and track capacities, unloading options, and terminal facilities.	1974
Queensland Phosphates—690 km railroad to handle phosphates. Preliminary design and specification study.	1969
Wyoming Coal Conversion Project—Economic feasibility studies of coal shuttle trains between mine and gasification plant.	1973-1974
Centralia Power Plant—Design, engineering, and construction management of 8 km access railroad.	1968-1970
Sterling Power Plant—Transportation and site access study. Evaluation of coal transportation alternatives; all-rail versus rail-water.	1973-1974
Bowling Point—Transportation and site access study, including shipment of spent fuel.	1968
Muskogee Station—Assistance in arranging unit coal transportation from Wyoming, including freight rates, tariffs, and freight car specifications.	1972-1973
Susquehanna—Evaluation of rail access to nuclear power plant. Design of 5 km of track to plant.	Ongoing
Amarillo Copper Refinery—Analysis of plant switching of rail cars to yard design purposes and design of access spur.	1973
Houston Site Study—Preliminary analysis of unit coal train transportation from Rocky Mountain areas.	1973
Limerick—Analysis of probability and magnitude of potential train accidents with nuclear fuel.	1971-1973

BLAUVELT ENGINEERING CO

1 Park ave, New York, NY 10016, USA

Telephone: (212) 481 1600

Partner: Francis M. Fuerst

PROJECTS
Vienna Line ($40 million) for Washington Metropolitan Area Transit Authority (WMATA).

BOGEN JENAL ENGINEERS

983 Willis ave, Albertson, NY 11507, USA

Telephone: (516) 747-4220

Vice-President: Joseph R. Jenal, PE

PROJECTS
Section D-6, final M/E design ($45 million) and Section E-I final M/E design ($85 million) for Washington Metropolitan Area Transit Authority (WMATA).

BOLT BERANEK AND NEWMAN INC

50 Moulton St, Cambridge, Mass 02138, USA

Telephone: (617) 491 1850

Department Manager: David N. Keast

PROJECTS
Vehicle noise control consulting engineering for New York City Transit Authority (NYCTA); environmental analysis and preliminary engineering on the Boston south-west corridor for Massachusetts Bay Transportation Authority (MBTA).

CANAC CONSULTANTS LTD
(A subsidiary of Canadian National Railways)

935 Lagauchetiere St W, Montreal, Quebec, Canada

Postal address: PO Box 8100, Montreal, Canada H3C 3N4

Telephone: (514) 877 4816
Telex: 01-20250
Telegrams: CONDIV MONTREAL

President: J. W. G. MacDougall

CAPABILITIES
This multimodal arm of Canadian National Railways and Air Canada has carried out transportation consultancy projects in Africa, Asia, the Caribbean and North and South America. Services offered include: market and economic surveys; organisation and management studies; management and personnel training and development programmes; route reconnaissance and construction supervision; motive power and rolling stock evaluation; signal system studies.

CANADIAN PACIFIC CONSULTING SERVICES LTD.

Room 171, Windsor Station, Montreal, Quebec H3C 3E4, Canada

Telephone: (514) 861 6811
Telex: 055-60147

Associated Companies: Transource Inc. One World Trade Centre, Suite 5075, New York, NY 10048, USA
Canadian Energy Projects Ltd, PO Box 777, Place Bonaventure, Montreal, Quebec, Canada

Parent Company: Canadian Pacific Limited

OFFICERS
Chairman of the Board: J. A. McDonald
President and Chief Executive Officer: H. M. Romoff
Vice-President & General Manager: G. T. Fisher
Vice-President Business Development: J. Denis Bélisle
Vice-President: W. J. Riley
Director: A. F. Joplin
J. Fox
K. Campbell
R. Klein
P. A. Nepveu
R. T. Riley
L. M. Riopel

CAPABILITIES
Canadian Pacific Consulting Services is the international consulting arm of Canadian Pacific. Canadian Pacific was incorporated in 1881 and today has assets of over $6 000 m (Cdn) with extensive interests in railroad, water, road, and air transport, real estate development, oil and gas, mining, metals, chemicals, and timberlands.
CP Rail operates 26 600 km of track across Canada and controls another 16 000 km in the United States. Its equipment includes approximately 77 500 freight cars, 1 300 locomotives, 380 passenger coaches and six coastal vessels and barges. The railway has played a pioneer role in the development of sophisticated unit train systems and pricing techniques for transporting bulk commodities such as coal, sulphur, and grain.
Canadian Pacific group CPCS is able to call upon the professional, technical and the latest methods of interfacing rail, truck and ship traffic, and the ability to provide cost-benefit studies using computer-oriented financial analysis programmes for any given present and foreseeable traffic requirements, places it in a unique position to optimise any conceivable transportation investment. Through its affiliation with the Canadian Pacific group, CPCS is able to call upon the professional, technical and operating personnel of any of the group's member companies to meet specific engineering, research, economic, marketing or supervisory requirements of individual projects anywhere in the world.

PROJECTS
Railway clients served by Canadian Pacific Consulting Services Ltd. include the following:
Turkish State Railways; Korean National Railroad; Tunisian National Railways; Congo-Ocean Railway; Egyptian Railways; Mozambique Railways; Honduran National Railways; Venezuelan National Railways; Rede Ferroviaria Federal S.A. of Brazil; Malayan State Railways; Bangladesh Railway; Indonesian State Railways; Western Australian Government Railways; Quebec North Shore and Labrador Railway; British Columbia Railway; Togo Railway.
Ghana Railway; East African Railways Corp; State Railway of Thailand; Mt. Newman Railway (Australia); Hamersley Iron Ore Railway (Australia); Quebec Cartier Mining Railway (Canada); Peruvian National Railways; Sri Lanka Railway; Nicaraguan Pacific Railway; National Cameroon Railways; South African Railways; Panama Railroad.

Projects completed or still underway during the 1976/77 period included the following:
Canada—Railroad Orientation Programme for Shell Coal Int'l Ltd: For Shell Coal International Ltd, a railway personnel orientation programme on Canadian Pacific Limited's operating railway, CP Rail, to provide an insight into railway operating and railway maintenance problems. Completed 1976.

Congo—Ocean Railway Construction Phase: CPCS was retained by a major Canadian engineering consulting firm to supervise the reconstruction of large segments of the Congo-Ocean Railway. Completed 1976.

South Africa—Shell Coal, South African Railway Study: CPCS was commissioned by Shell Coal South Africa (Pty) Limited to review the capacity of the South Africa Railway related to bulk coal movements; including recommendations for improvement in volume carryings. Completed 1976.

Training Assistance in Cameroon for the Railway: CPCS was retained by the Canadian International Development Agency to assess personnel and training requirements of the Cameroon State Railway (Regifercam) including recommendations for a complete human resources inventory and training programme. Completed 1976.

Mozambique Port & Railway Re-organisation: Sponsored by the United Nations Development Programme, CPCS was retained to undertake a study of the country's railway system and ports network for the Mozambique department of transport. Completed 1976.

Egypt—Railway Cost Accounting System: CPCS participated in the introduction of a costing system for the Egyptian Railways. Completed 1976.

Canada—Saskatchewan Power Corp. Rail Line Construction: Provision of Consulting Services for railway construction on behalf of the Saskatchewan Power Corporation. Completed 1976.

Bureau of Transit Services, BC—Commuter Service Coquitlam-Vancouver: For the British Columbia Bureau of Transit Services, the study and costing of a rail commuter service from Vancouver to Port Moody and Coquitlam. Completed 1976.

Quebec Cartier Mining—Electrification Study: A railway electrification study for the Quebec Carier Mining Co. Completed 1976.

Peru—Railway Project: Contracted by a Canadian management consulting firm to evaluate present rail operations of the Peruvian railways to make recommendations for improvements. Completed 1976.

Brazil—RFFSA Project: CPCS was retained by Rede Ferroviaria Federal SA to participate in the design, engineering and supervision of the construction of new locomotive and freight car repair shops in Jaceaba. Completed 1976.

Korea—AAR Certification for Dae Woo Car Plan: At the request of Dae Woo International Company, CPCS studied their plant and recommended modifications required to obtain American Association of Railroads certification.

Sri Lanka—Track Specialist: CPCS was retained by the Canadian International Development Agency to assess damage to rails of the Sri Lanka Railway, to determine causes thereof, and recommend solutions for the prevention of further damage. Completed 1976.

TDA–Bills of Lading Study: Commissioned by the Canadian Transport Development Agency, a study of the practices and requirements of bills of lading, waybills and similar shipping documents used in domestic and international trade. The study was aimed at the development of a standard intermodal through-bill-of-lading. Completed 1977.

Nicaragua–Rehabilitation Nicaragua Pacific Railroad: CPCS was retained by the Government of Nicaragua to study the feasibility of rehabilitating the Nicaragua Pacific Railway. Completed 1977.

TDA–High Speed Passenger Service Montreal–Quebec: A preliminary evaluation of a high-speed inter-city rail service for the Canadian Ministry of Transport. Completed 1977.

Canada–BCR Repair Shops: Examination of and recommendation for repair shop programmes for the British Columbia Railway. Due for completion late 1977.

Thailand State Railways Study: The work entails setting up an Operations Control Centre, assessing manpower requirements of shops, assisting the marketing section, providing management information system advice and assisting in the preparation of calculation of losses of two branchlines to provide a basis for subsidy or abandonment. Completed 1977.

Malaysia Railways General Transport/Railway Study: A general transportation and railway study funded by the World Bank which will serve as a basis for the overall transportation plan of the country. Completed 1977.

Indonesian Railway Technical Assistance Project: A consortium led by CPCS was retained by the Indonesian State Railways to undertake a two-year technical assistance programme in the fields of operating and planning procedures, maintenance programming, marketing, tariff development and information systems. The project was funded by the World Bank. Completed 1977.

Indonesia–Sumatra Coal Project: CPCS undertook a railway transportation economic study of Bukit Asam coal in South Sumatra on behalf of the Indonesian State Railways. Completed 1977.

Inspection of Canadian Wheat Board, Hopper cars, Phase II: Engineering, design, purchasing phase and physical inspection of components and finished cars at builders' plants for 2 000 grain covered hopper cars. Completed 1977.

Railway Study for Algoma Steel Corp: Analyse distribution system from Sault Ste. Marie, Ontario to Southern Ontario and recommend action to improve speed and consistency of delivery to customers at minimum distribution costs. Due for completion late 1977.

Railway Study, British Columbia Railway: A Study to determine requirements for information systems for cost reporting and management control from the point of view of using the existing working systems rather than developing new ones. Completed 1977.

Indonesia–North Sumatra Intermodal Study: Retained by the World Bank to provide the assistance of a physical distribution planning advisor to look into intermodal and alternate modes of shipping plantation products from North Sumatra. Completed 1977.

T.D.A.–Rail Passenger Seat Development Programme, Canada: A comprehensive review of all aspects of detail seating requirements and compliance standards for rail passenger travel. Completed 1977.

Thailand Government, railway feasibility study: Railway transportation portion of a feasibility study for a rock salt/soda ash project involving such aspects as economics, railway facilities and equipment, marketing. Due to run until 1978.

Korea–Repair Shops (World Bank): CPCS was retained by the Korean National Railroad to devise and supervise the implementation of efficient rail car repair shop procedures. This two-year project was funded by the World Bank. Due for completion during 1978.

Sri Lanka–Railway Technical Assistance: At the request of the Canadian International Development Agency, CPCS has provided technical assistance to improve the productivity and efficiency of the Sri Lanka Railway in the area of stores and purchasing management, railway operations and diesel locomotive maintenance. Due to be completed during 1978.

CAN DEUB FLEISSIG AND ASSOCIATES

11 Hill St, Newark, NJ 07102, USA

Telephone: (201) 643 3919

Vice-President: Burton R. Cohen

PROJECTS
Environmental Impact Statement ($975 000) for New Jersey Department of Transportation (DOT).

CAPITAL CONSULTANTS

5508 Wilson Lane, Bethesda, Md 20014, USA

Telephone: (301) 656 1180

Principal Partner: Edwin L. Mueller

PROJECTS
Automated transit guideway survey (under $10 000).

CE MAQUIRE INC

31 Canal St, Providence, RI 02903, USA

Telephone: (401) 272 6000

Executive Vice-President: Vincent M. Cangiano

PROJECTS
Red Line extension tunnel design ($110 million) for Massachusetts Bay Transportation Authority (MBTA); Section 2 tunnel design ($38 million) for Washington Metropolitan Area Transit Authority (AMATA).

CENTURY ENGINEERING INC

32 West Rd, Towson Md, 21204, USA

Telephone: (301) 823 8070

Assistant Vice-President: Robert G. James

PROJECTS
Glebe Road station section design ($31 million) for Washington Metropolitan Area Transit Authority (WMATA).

CHASE, ROSEN & WALLACE, INC

901 North Washington St, Alexandria, Va USA

Telephone: (703) 836 7120

Vice-President: Stanley B. Rosen

PROJECTS
Improved services for handicapped and demonstration development based on survey for Urban Mass Transportation Administration (UMTA); Microfiche-based information system for transit information agents for Chicago Transit Authority (CTA).

CITIES CORPORATION

102 Mount Auburn St, Cambridge, Mass 02138, USA

Telephone: (617) 491 8007

Director of Transit Mapping: Barbara Petersen

PROJECTS
System map design projects for Rhode Island Public Transit Authority (RIPTA) and Metro Regional Transit Authority, Akron, Ohio.

TERENCE J COLLINS ASSOCIATES, INC

703 Huntington Lane, Schaumburg, Ill 60193, USA

Telephone: (312) 529 8187

President: Terry Collins

PROJECTS
Radio, data communication system, supervisory system, control centre complex ($5 million) for Chicago Transit Authority (CTA); Two-way radio data communication system including control centre ($600 000) for Indianapolis Public Transportation Corp.

COMSUL LTD.

417 Montgomery St, San Francisco, Cal, 94104, USA

Telephone: (415) 989 6700

Vice-President: Colin W. Halford

PROJECTS
Providing engineering services in the planning, design, testing and review of the combined communications network for San Francisco Municipal Railway.

DALTON-DALTON-LITTLE-NEWPORT INC

3605 Warrensville Center Rd., Cleveland, Ohio 44122, USA

Telephone: (216) 283-4000

Vice-President: Frederick J. Richardson

PROJECTS
Baltimore Phase II transit study; cost/demand forecasting; construction guidelines for Maryland MTA; Ashby Street station, subway and at-grade construction; station; branch line study ($50 million) for MARTA.

DANIEL, MANN, JOHNSON & MENDENHALL

3250 Wilshire Blvd, Los Angeles, Calf 90010, USA

Telephone: (213) 381 3663

Vice-President/Transportation: Richard J. Bouchard

PROJECTS
Design of Baltimore rapid transit system ($600 million) for Maryland Mass Transit Administration (MTA); Design of Honolulu rapid transit system ($500 million) for City and County of Honolulu.

DAY & ZIMMERMANN, INC

1818 Market St, Philadelphia, Pa 19103, USA

Telephone: (215) 299 8000

Vice-President: John E. Kennedy

PROJECTS
Systems design ($1.9 million) for Niagara Frontier Transportation Authority; Construction and systems design of Mid-Town Tunnel ($57 million) for Southeastern Pennsylvania Transportation Authority (SEPTA).

DECONSULT
Deutsche Eisenbahn Consulting GmbH

Postfach 700 476, 6000 Frankfurt /M. 70, German Federal Republic

Telephone: (0611) 6050-1
Telegrams: DECONSULT FRANKFURTMAIN
Telex: 4 14 516 decond

Supervisory Board: Dr jur. E. Schneider
Dr-Ing. E. h. H. Delvendahl
Dr rer. pol. S. Eichler
General Manager: Dr-Ing. R. Janousch
F. W. Möller
Project Division Managers: General—Hr. Wendt
Germany—Hr. Wendt
Africa and Iran—Dr Ing. Haucke
Middle and Far East: Hr. Kabisch
America—Hr. Müller
Europe, Iraq, Turkey—Hr. Müller-Hande

CAPABILITIES
DECONSULT—an international consulting enterprise—carries out planning and consultancy work in the transportation sector all over the world. The main accents in such activities are placed upon national and municipal railway networks. The firm was founded in 1966 by the Federal German Railways and the Deutsche Bank AG, which are today still the only shareholders.
At present, DECONSULT employs about 200 engineers and economists. As DECONSULT operates a staff exchange scheme with the Federal German Railways, both the home office staff and the expert teams working abroad can be quickly supplemented to meet current requirements.

Associated Offices: DECONSULT has offices in:
Algiers, Algeria; Aqaba, Jordan; Baghdad, Iraq; Jakarta/Bandung, Indonesia; Lisbon, Portugal; Sao Paulo, Brazil; Taipei, Taiwan; Tehran/Esfahan, Iran.

PROJECTS
DECONSULT has executed or is at present executing projects in the following countries:
Algeria, Argentina, Brazil, Burma, Cameroon, Costa Rica, Federal Republic of Germany, Ivory Coast, Ghana, Greece, Guinea, India, Indonesia, Iran, Iraq, Jordan, Malaysia, Pakistan, Paraguay, Peru, Portugal, South Korea, Sudan, Taiwan, Thailand, Togo, Upper Volta, Venezuela, Vietnam, Zaire.

PROJECTS (CIVIL ENGINEERING)

Country	Client	Description of Project	Date of Completion
Algeria	SNTF	Preliminary project for the construction of the station of Oran	1977
Algeria	SNTF	Preparation for supervision of construction of new line Touggourt-Ghardaia	1977
Algeria	SNTF	Preliminary and final design, tendering for track-doubling of the El Harrach/Thenia railway line incl. structures, signalling and telecommunications systems	1977
Algeria	SNTF	Study, improvements and extensions of the railway and mass-transit network of the Metropolitan Area of Algiers	1978
Brazil	Ferrovia Paulista SA (FEPASA)	Advisory services, organisation and instruction of the FEPASA in the field of tracks	1978
Brazil	Ferrovia Paulista SA (FEPASA)	Continuation of supervision of construction as regards the new line of the FEPASA in the Vale do Ribeira	1976
Brazil	Companhia Metropolitana Rio de Janeiro	Advisory services in the fields of construction, direct rail support, power supply, operation, signalling	1977
Germany (FDR)	Deutsche Bundesbahn Research Office Minden	Draught for regulation "structure gauge"	1977
Germany (FDR)	Bundesbahn Frankfurt	Assistance when planning new lines and extending existing ones	1977
Iran	Iranian State Railways (RAI)	Detailed project for both track doubling and electrification of the lines Qom-Isfahan-Riz and Sagzi-Kerman	1978
Portugal	Portuguese State Railways (CP)	Modernisation of the suburban service in the region of Lisbon	1976
Portugal	Metropolitano de Lisboa, Empresa Nacionalizada	Metro Lisbon Underground railway junction Rotunda	1977
Venezuela	Deutsche Gesellschaft für technische Zusammenarbeit (GTZ)	Assistance to the Venezuelan State Railways (IAAFE) when elaborating tender documents for a new railway line	1976

PROJECTS (MECHANICAL)

Country	Client	Description of Project	Date of Completion
Brazil	Ferrovia Paulista SA (FEPASA)	Final acceptance of 155 saddle wagons and 75 sliding door wagons at Waggonunion in Siegen	1976
Germany (FDR)	Osthannoversche Eisenbahnen AG, Celle	Expertise for improvement of the maintenance system	1977
Germany (FDR)	Bergbau-Forschung GmbH Essen	New design of special freight wagons for pit coal underground working	1977
Indonesia	Department of Transport, Communication and Tourism	Consulting services for rehabilitation of maintenance of diesel locomotives	1977
Iran	Iranian State Railways (RAI)	Assistance when wagons were based by DB to RAI	1976
Liberia	Bong Mining Comp.	Acceptance of tank wagons, hopper wagons and bogies	1976

PROJECTS (SIGNALLING/ELECTROTECHNIQUES)

Country	Client	Description of Project	Date of Completion
Germany (FDR)	Deutsche Bundesbahn München	Planning of signalling systems	1978
Germany (FDR)	Deutsche Bundesbahn (DB)—ZTL	Investigations for new high speed railway lines comprising tele control engineering, power supply, and standardised substations	1977
Indonesia	Department of Transport, Communication and Tourism	Supervision of construction of the telecommunication system	1978
Korea	Korean National Railroad (KNR)	Supervision of assembly of signalling equipment within the main area of Seoul	1977

TRANSPORTATION STUDIES

Country	Client	Description of Project	Date of Completion
Brazil	RFFSA	Economic studies on the construction of a 170 km long railway line connecting the cement works at Barroso	1976
Germany (FDR)	Transnuklear GmbH, Hanau	Transportation study on heavy traffic container "Kalkar"	1976
Indonesia	Deutsche Gesellschaft für Technische Zusammenarbeit (GTZ)	Completion project "Train dispatching". Advisory services to the Indonesian State Railways (PJKA) on technical and economic fields	1977
Iraq	Ministry of Transport, Baghdad	Baghdad Rapid Transit System (BRTS) (Study on preliminary project)	1977

MISCELLANEOUS

Country	Client	Description of Project	Date of Completion
Iran	Ministry of Roads	Trainings project for Iranian State Railways (RAI)	1978
Iran	Ministry of Roads	Training of Iranian Railwaymen at schools of the German Federal Railway (DB)	1978
Iran	Knight Wegenstein Consultants	Reorganisation of the Iranian State Railways (RAI)	1976
Zaire	Office des Routes	Preparation of tender documents for ferries including economic evaluations	1976

DE LEUW, CATHER & COMPANY (DCCO)

165 West Wacker Drive, Chicago, Ill 60601, USA

Telephone: (312) 346 0424
Cable: DELCAC CHICAGO, USA
Telex: 9102215842

Offices: Chicago, Anchorage, Atlanta, Boston, Buffalo, Denver, Houston, Los Angeles, Newark, New York City, Philadelphia, San Francisco, Seattle, Tallahassee, and District of Columbia.

Associate Companies: De Leuw, Cather International Inc. (Chicago); De Leuw, Cather of Australia Pty. Ltd. (North Sydney, NSW and Canberra, ACT); De Leuw, Cather & Company of New York, Inc; De Leuw, Cather & Company of Michigan, De Leuw, Cather & Company of Virginia; and De Leuw, Cather Professional Corporation.

Parent Company: TRW Inc.—23555 Euclid Avenue, Cleveland, Ohio 44117, USA

OFFICERS
Chairman & Vice-President: R. B. Richards
Executive Vice-President & Secretary: J. E. Linden
Vice-President: J. A. Caywood
Senior Vice-Presidents: H. T. Boyd
L. A. Dondanville
I. Gilboa
V. P. Lamb
G. M. Randich
D. W. Cather
R. S. O'Neil
Staff Vice-Presidents: W. A. Barry
J. S. Collins
E. S. Diamant
W. G. Horn
R. P. Howell
R. S. Nielsen
M. F. Rupp
J. B. Saag
J. W. Schmidt
Vice-Presidents: D. M. Anderson
D. M. Harlan
L. D. Hazzard
R. W. Kessmann
J. W. Mullaney Jr
H. A. Quinn Jr
P. H. Strahm
H. D. Stubing
I. Bali
K. G. Cook
D. Kolodne
W. Kudlick
G. A. R. Meier
R. H. Meyer
N. J. Pointner II
W. R. Preece
A. L. Sams
R. Simon
Treasurer & Controller: L. Alvarez

CAPABILITIES
Services undertaken by DCCO include: feasibility studies, preliminary and final design, site development, surveys, soils investigations, specifications and cost estimates, contract documents, construction supervision, construction management.

PROJECTS
DCCO, in a joint venture with The Ralph M. Parsons Company, is currently responsible for the management of the Northeast Corridor Improvement Project. This Federal Railroad Administration programme to rehabilitate the 744 km (456 mile) rail line and facilities between Washington DC, and Boston will allow Amtrak passenger and Con-Rail service to operate at speeds up to 120 mph.

Main Line Relocations, Extensions, Consolidations, and Improvements: Major projects have been completed in California, Georgia, Illinois, Indiana, Iowa, Massachusetts, Michigan, Minnesota, Nebraska, Nevada, New Jersey, Pennsylvania, Texas, and Wisconsin as well as Canada, Indonesia, and Turkey.

Railroad Grade Separations and Related Studies: Assignments involving a variety of disciplines have been completed in 15 states, Australia, and Jordan.

Railroad Appraisals, Inventories, and Operational Studies: Engineering and economic analyses; revenue studies; operational studies; valuation appraisals; and condition reports for major railroad facilities in the United States, Canada, and the Philippines.

Railroad Signalling and Communications: Projects have included automatic interlocking circuits; remote control interlocking; electrification; design of signal and communication systems or modifications to existing facilities; and automatic crossing protection.

Yards, Shops, and Terminal Facilities: Modernisation of existing facilities or construction of new facilities in 13 states, Thailand, and Venezuela.

DUBIN, DUBIN, BLACK AND MOUTOUSSAMY

55 West Wacker Dr, Chicago, Ill 60601, USA

Telephone: (312) 641 0700

Architect: Arthur D. Dubin

PROJECTS
Modernisation of Loyola station ($2.1 million) for Chicago Transit Authority (CTA).

EDWARDS AND KELCEY

8 Park Place, Newark, NJ 07102, USA

Planning, environmental studies, design and construction management for rail and bus transit systems, railroads, terminals, tunnels, bridges, parking and utilities.

THOMAS K DYER, INC

1762 Massachusetts Ave, Lexington, Mass 02173, USA

Telephone: (617) 862 2075

Executive Vice-President: W. K. Hale

PROJECTS
Upgrading track and signals Dorchester Branch ($16 million) and Red Line extension to South Braintree for Massachusetts Bay Transportation Authority (MBTA).

FORD, BACON & DAVIS

600 North Jackson St, Media, Pa 19063, USA

Telephone: (215) 565 5115

Manager/Transportation Division: Dale N. Worfel

PROJECTS
New Jersey public transportation study for New Jersey Department of Transportation (DOT); Plan commuter rail line operations for Southwestern Pennsylvania Regional Planning Commission (SPRPC).

FOSTER ENGINEERING, INC

120 Howard St, Suite 670, San Francisco, Cal 94105, USA

Telephone: (415) 543 1193

President: H. A. Foster

PROJECTS
Construction administration and inspection of underground rapid transit station ($15 million) and design and preparation of contract documents for service and inspection facilities at Richmond and Concord Yards ($1.2 million) for Bay Area Rapid Transit District (BART).

FREEMAN FOX & PARTNERS

25 Victoria Street (South Block), Westminster, London SW1H 0EX, England

Telephone: (01) 222 8050
Telex: 916018 FOXVIC G
Telegraph: Traction London SW1

Associated Firms (in respect of railway work):
Freeman Fox & Partners (Far East), 42-46 Gloucester Road, Hong Kong
Telephone: 5-272127 Telex: 73868 FRFOX HX
Freeman Fox International Limited, 42-46 Gloucester Road, Hong Kong
Telephone: 5-272127 Telex: 73868 FRFOX HX
Halcrow Fox and Associates, 28 Grosvenor Gardens, London SW1W 0DY
Telephone: (01) 730 4500 Telex: 8811763 HALFOX G

Parent Firm:
Freeman Fox & Partners

Officers:
Sir Ralph Freeman, CVO CBE MA FICE FCIT FASCE MCONSE
J. T. Edwards BSc ACGI FICE FCIT MCONSE
W. T. F. Austin BSc FICE FIStrutE FIHE MASCE MCONSE
B. P. Wex BSc ACGI FICE FIHE MCONSE
W. C. Brown OBE BSc DIC PHD MICE
J. C. A. Roseveare DSO BSc FICE FIWES MCIT MCONSE
M. F. Parsons BSc FICE FIStrutE MCONSE
D. A. Meyers BSc(Eng) MICE FBCS
N. J. Dallard FICE FIHE MASCE
D. R. Wolstenholme BSc FICE FIHE
C. R. Coulson BA FICE MCIT FHKIE
D. A. Morris BSc DIC FICE FIStrutE FHKIE

Chief Railway Engineer: A. J. S. Blanchfield BSc(Eng) FICE FPWI

Partners:
Sir Ralph Freeman CVO CBE MA FICE FCIT FASCE MCONSE
J. T. Edwards BSc ACGI FICE FCIT MCONSE
B. P. Wex BSc ACGI FICE FIHE MCONSE
J. C. A. Roseveare DSO BSc FICE FIWES MCIT MCONSE
C. R. Coulson BA FICE MCIT FHKIE
D. A. Morris BSc DIC FICE FIStrutE FHKIE

HALCROW FOX AND ASSOCIATES
Directors:
F. A. Sharman BSc ACGI FICE FIHE FRGS
J. O. Tresidder MEng FICE FIHE MCIT
J. T. Edwards BSc ACGI FICE FCIT MCONSE
A. M. Muir Wood MA FICE FGS
D. A. Meyers BSc(Eng) MICE FBCS
B. K. Hartshorne MA MSc FICE FIHE
D. S. Kennedy BSc MICE MITE MIHE

CAPABILITIES
Freeman Fox & Partners were founded in 1857 by Sir Charles Fox who, with his two sons, established an international engineering consultancy practice primarily concerned with railway work. In the early years, the firm were responsible for railways in Britain, the Americas, Africa and India. In Southern Africa, the firm were responsible for over 8 000 km of railway and continued as consulting engineers for the Rhodesian and Benguela Railways to within the last decade. This work for the African railways included, in addition to civil engineering, specification and inspection during manufacture of all kinds of rolling stock, signalling and communication equipment etc.
During the 1950's, following the war, the firm designed three major bridges that were re-built for the Royal Thailand State Railway and, for the Indian Ministry of Railways, designed two major road/rail bridges for crossings of the Rivers Ganga and Brahmaputra.
During the last decade the firm's work for main line railways, in addition to the projects listed below, has been principally concerned with the design, specification and inspection during manufacture of rolling stock, including double-deck motor car transporter wagons, refrigerator wagons, freight wagon bogies and the development of a new large-capacity hopper wagon for carrying ores.
During the 1960s the firm entered the field of traffic and transportation engineering, this work being undertaken by Freeman Fox and Associates. A large number of national and regional studies have been completed, many of them related to railway operations. From 1 May 1977 this part of the Freeman Fox Group became jointly owned by Freeman Fox & Partners and Sir William Halcrow & Partners, and was re-named Halcrow Fox and Associates.
In earlier days, Freeman Fox & Partners had been concerned with sections of the London Underground system (particularly the Charing Cross-Hampstead section of the present Northern Line) and, in the 1960s, the firm returned to this field when it commenced studies for the Hong Kong Mass Transit Railway now being built at a cost of £500 million.

PROJECTS
Principal railway projects undertaken by the Freeman Fox Group during the last ten years are as follows:

Hong Kong Mass Transit Railway: This is the major railway project for which the firm is currently responsible. Work commenced in 1967 with the Hong Kong Transport Study which required:
a) study of all forms of transport and an evaluation of their potential in the changing conditions of Hong Kong;
b) evaluation of alternative routes for the potentially most attractive systems;
c) estimates of short-term and long-term travel demands;
d) proposals for long-term public transport development.

The firm then undertook further studies which led to the recommendation of a mass transit railway consisting of 4 separate lines with a combined route length of 64 km and 50 stations. Associated with Freeman Fox in this work were a number of specialist consultants including Kennedy & Donkin, Design Research Unit, Charles Haswell & Partners and Per Hall Associates. The firm were also required to specify the Initial System which should be put in hand first in order to provide maximum benefit to the community.
In 1972 Freeman Fox & Partners (Far East) began detailed design for the Initial System and have been responsible for evaluation of tenders and programming of contract activities. Construction on a multi-contract basis began in November 1975 and the first trains will operate on a limited section in late 1979 and the Initial System will be completed in 1980. In August 1977 authorisation was given for a start to be made on design of the second part of the full system so that construction could continue as resources became available on completion of the Initial System. By the mid-1980's when the whole system is in operation, the Hong Kong Metro will be carrying 2.7 million passengers daily with an average trip length of 5 km, making it possibly the most heavily used system in the world.

Taiwan Railway Electrification: In association with Kennedy & Donkin and China Engineering Consultants Inc. the firm worked on an electrification study of the 500 km of double-track narrow gauge line from Keelung in the north, through the capital Taipei, to Kaohsiung in the south. The study required a forecast of future traffic; engineering plans for handling the traffic by either electrical or diesel traction; and estimates of the capital and operating costs of electrical and diesel traction, with cost benefit comparisons of the alternatives. The report was submitted in 1971.

Metropolitan Rapid Transit System for Guadalajara: This study, which was undertaken in association with Kennedy & Donkin, was commissioned to prepare an outline plan for the first stage of a metropolitan underground railway for the City of Guadalajara. The consultants were required to recommend the type of metropolitan railway to be adopted and to provide layouts showing provisional alignments, type of construction, station locations, depots etc. The report was submitted in 1970.

Elevated Railway in Taipei City: The purpose of this study was to evaluate the economic and technical aspects of alternative schemes for improving the railway and road transport of the Taipei-Keelung metropolitan area. In particular, the study called for evaluation of elevating the railway through the urban area of Taipei (to eliminate the numerous level crossings existing) and build a new high-level ten-track station. The report was submitted in 1969.

Hovertrain Studies: The firm were retained in 1971 by the UK Department of Trade and Industry to assess the feasibility and cost of constructing and operating two high-speed Hovertrain routes, one operating at 240 km per hour, the other at 400 km per hour. A detailed engineering study was also made to ascertain an economic overhead structure able to accommodate the forces and speeds involved.

Reconstruction of Grosvenor bridge: This bridge carried all nine approach tracks over London's River Thames into Victoria Station, one of the most intensely used commuter stations in the world. The firm had previously been concerned with earlier widenings of the bridge in 1865 and 1901.
The bridge was completely re-built to provide ten tracks instead of the previous nine. The entire project was carried through with eight tracks always available for railway operations and without interference to either the main waterways of the River or road traffic under the approach span. Reconstruction was completed in 1969.

Reconstruction of Cannon Street station: This London commuter terminus, with eight platforms, was re-built to accommodate ten and twelve car trains instead of eight car trains. The station was partially re-roofed and a podium provided to support a multi-storey office block above the concourse and tracks, and the bridge carrying the tracks out of the station was re-built to allow the road below to be widened. The station was maintained in full operation during the daily peak periods throughout the work which was completed in 1965.

Railway yards for British power stations: Freeman Fox & Partners were consulting engineers to the Central Electricity Generating Board for civil engineering for three major coal-fired power stations in Britain: Castle Donington (600 MW), High Marnhan (1 000 MW) and Aberthaw B (1 500 MW). Each of these power stations required extensive rail sidings to main-line standards. The largest, for High Marnham, included 65 turnouts with a comprehensive electrical control and signalling system. At Aberthaw, the trains operate on a 'merry-go-round' principle, handling over 3 million tons of coal annually.

GANNETT FLEMING CORDDRY AND CARPENTER INC

PO Box 1963, Harrisburg, Pa 17105, USA

Telephone: (717) 238 0451

Chief/Mass Transit: Robert J. Dietz PE

PROJECTS
Detroit regional transit alternatives analysis ($1.6 thousand million) for Southeastern Michigan Transportation Authority (SEMTA); feasibility and preliminary engineering for DPM systems ($90 and $60 million) for Georgia Department of Transportation (DOT) and SEMTA.

GIBBS & HILL

Gibbs & Hill, Inc.

393 Seventh Avenue-New York, NY 10001, USA

Telephone: (212) 760-4000
Cables: GIBBSHILL NEW YORK
Telex: 127636
Teletype: 710/581-5535

Branch and Subsidiary Offices:
Gibbs & Hill, Inc., 50 Clinton Street, Hempstead, NY 11550 (Telephone: (516) 538 2500)

Gibbs & Hill, Inc., 8420 West Dodge Road, Omaha, Neb. 68114 (Telephone: (402) 391 0330 Telex: 9106220294)

Gibbs Hill Lockwood Greene, 1776 Peachtree Road, NW, Atlanta, Ga 30309 (Telephone: (404) 873 3261)

Gibbs & Hill, Inc., 1801 K Street, NW, Washington, DC 20006 (Telephone: (202) 785 1901)

Gibbs & Hill International, Inc., Square Vanak, Brezil Avenue, Narenj Alley, No. 15, Tehran, Iran (Telephone: 681190 Telex: 212798 Tehran)

Gibbs & Hill Espanola, SA, Magallanes, 3 Planta 9, Madrid 15, Spain (Telephone: 447 4800 Cable: GANDHESA MADRID)

Parent Company:
Dravo Corporation, Pittsburgh, Pennsylvania

Chairman: P. H. Smith
President and Chief Executive Officer: A. Matiuk
Executive Vice President and Chief Engineer: F. Mele
Vice President, Power Division: R. H. Gordon
Vice President, Power Engineering: F. D. Hutchinson
Vice President, Power Projects: K. L. Schepple
Vice President, Power Projects: T. R. Cuerou
Vice President, Project Services: J. E. Styles
Managing Director, Ghesa-Madrid: R. Safier
Vice President, International: D. P. Davis
Vice President, Transportation and Transmission Division: E. P. Foley
Vice President, Arch/Urban Development Division: R. W. Yokom

CAPABILITIES
Gibbs & Hill was founded in 1911 to provide engineering and design services for the then new field of railway electrification. The company has designed the electrification systems for over 70 per cent of all ac rail systems in the United States.
Following incorporation in 1923, the firm began diversifying into a number of related fields, including power engineering, now the major source of company business.
In 1965, Gibbs & Hill became a wholly owned subsidiary of Dravo Corporation, expanding the capabilities of both companies.
Overall, the company has a staff of more than 2 300 professional and support personnel, providing a variety of vital services.
The Transportation and Transmission Division operates as an integrated group with a permanent technical staff of over 100, together with all necessary supporting personnel. Assignments in the transportation field have comprised: engineering and economic feasibility reports; system planning studies; alternative transportation mode studies (bus, rail, private car); preliminary design and cost estimates; environmental impact studies and reports; preparation of project loan applications; site and right-of-way investigations; comprehensive investigations and appraisals of available hardware and rolling stock. Additionally, actual detailed engineering and design services have been furnished for: railroad and rapid transit electrification, including traction power supply and transmission facilities, substations, and overhead catenary or third rail distribution systems; signaling and train control; communications; automation; operations analysis and computer simulation; shops, yards and terminals; waste treatment and disposal facilities; steam generation; and all ancillary and supporting facilities.

PROJECTS
Texas Utilities Services, Inc. Dallas, Texas: Engineering and design services for a complete 25-kV, 60-Hz catenary-type distribution system including several configurations of wood and steel supporting structures, together with all necessary catenary arrangements, insulator assemblies and hardware. This system has been developed for the electrification of two lignite haulage railroads in eastern Texas. The first project, for the Martin Lake Electric Station near Tatum, involves the electrification of approximately 17.6 km (11 single-track miles) including two loading stations, a central shop and storage yard, and the unloading facilities for two lignite consists, at the powerplant. In addition to the electrification facilities, a three-phase, 25 kV distribution line was engineered and designed. This line parallels the railroad and is supported from the electrification structures, and provides power to the loading stations, the drag-line erection site, as well as for the ctc signal system.
The second project, for the Monticello Electric Station near Mount Pleasant, involves the electrification of approximately 10 single-track miles *(16.0 km)* and includes one loading station, a central shop, and the dumping facilities at the powerplant.
Extensions of approximately 10 single-track miles *(16.0 km)* are planned for both projects as the demand for lignite increases.

Port Authority of Allegheny County, Pittsburgh, Pennsylvania: General architectural and engineering services for design of all facilities required for implementation of the Authority's Transportation Implementation Programme, Stage I—Light Rail Transit System. A major portion of the work will be applied to the development of the Final System Design Specification (FSDS), the master document on which all subsequent design will be based. The FSDS will include appropriate treatment of the following: system description; overall system requirements; passenger vehicles; right-of-way and support structures; switches and transfer mechanisms; platforms and stations; maintenance, storage, and shop and yard areas; control system; communications system; traction power and distribution system; maintenance provisions.
Gibbs & Hill's participation will be principally with respect to system definition, electrification, traction power, signals and train control, communications, and value capture analysis. Work performed in Joint Venture with Parsons, Brinckerhoff, Quade & Douglas.

Hetch Hetchy Water and Power Company, San Francisco, California: Engineering and design services to provide both new and improved electric-traction power distribution facilities to serve the expanding requirements of the San Francisco Municipal Railway System, and to make appropriate provisions for the operation of a fleet of new Light-Rail Vehicles. These services included design and rehabilitation of the existing overhead trolley wire system on surface lines, the design of a new catenary system in the Twin Peak Tunnel required because of the projected increase in electric loads as a result of planned use of up to four-car trains of Light-Rail Vehicles. The design of the installation of gap breaker stations for sectionalising and fault isolation and positive and negative feeder cable installation was also included as a part of the services. In the design of these facilities electrolytic corrosion mitigative measures were provided for the steel-ring tunnel sections under Market Street. Work performed as part of a joint venture with PBQ & D.

New Jersey Department of Transportation, Trenton, New Jersey: A major project comprising the comprehensive physical rehabilitation and electrification of the New York and Long Branch Railroad between South Amboy and Red Bank, a distance of about 15 miles *(24 km)* Gibbs & Hill's portion of the work includes the design of all electrification facilities, as well as all signals, communications and controls. The work is being done under subcontract to Edwards & Kelcey.

Maryland Mass Transit Administration, Baltimore, Maryland: Engineering services as electric utility rate consultant to the Administration in connection with the Baltimore Subway Project. Gibbs & Hill will perform research, analyse and prepare data and presentation materials for a power rate schedule to be used by the Administration in their negotiations with the local utility company.

New Jersey Department of Transportation, Trenton, New Jersey: Engineering and design services for a major modernisation and rehabilitation programme of the Erie-Lackawanna Railway, an important link in the New York suburban area commuter network. The project includes the following assignments: (1) Conversion of the existing 3 kV, dc traction power system to 25 kV, 60 Hz; (2) Rehabilitation and reconstruction, where necessary, of 58 route miles *(92.8 km)* of overhead catenary system; (3) Extension of electrification system from Dover to Netcong, a distance of 10 route miles *(16 km)*; (4) Modifications to signal and communication systems to ensure compatibility with the ac traction power system; (5) Modification of existing heavy repair shops to accommodate new self-propelled rolling stock; (6) Provision of substantial additions to car storage facilities; (7) Siting and architectural design of three new passenger stations; (8) All necessary related modifications to existing facilities, auxiliary apparatus and systems.

Newmont Mining Corporation, New York: Comparative study of the power and ventilation requirements under electric and diesel traction in an 11 mile *(17.6 km)* railroad tunnel connecting the minemouth to the concentrator of the GranDuc Mining Company in British Columbia, Canada. Subsequent design of the electrification system, preparation of the specifications for and recommendations for the selection of electric locomotives specially designed for the reduced clearances and the traffic requirements in the tunnel. Design of an automatic train stop system to ensure operational safety at the concentrator end of the tunnel, should the operator fail to have the train under control when it approaches the end of its run.

Metropolitan Transportation Authority, New York: Engineering services for studies, design and supervision of construction in connection with the $200 million plus rehabilitation programme of the Long Island Rail Road which has the highest density commuter traffic of any railroad in the world. The plan involves extension of the electrification system, purchase of new rolling stock, design of 60 new traction-power substations, new central supervisory control system, increase of wayside electric traction system to permit train operation at speeds of up to 100 mph *(160 km/h)*, improved track alignment, and potential connections with New York City's rapid transit systems. Preparation of preliminary plans, long-lead item specifications and cost estimates for the proposed extension of third-rail electrification and necessary improvements on the Main Line from Hicksville to Ronkonkoma, and on the Port Jefferson Branch from Huntington to Port Jefferson. New electrification facilities, including substations, will be required for 46.2 additional track miles *(74.4 km)*. This work performed by Parsons, Brinkerhoff-Gibbs & Hill, with Gibbs & Hill responsible for all electrical engineering.

GREINER ENGINEERING SCIENCES INC

PO Box 23646, Tampa, Fla 33632, USA

Telephone: (813) 879-1711

Vice-President: T. Wallace Hawkes, P.E.

PROJECTS
Five mile rapid transit extension study ($100 million) for Massachusetts Bay Transportation Authority (MBTA).

HAMBURG-CONSULT
Gesellschaft für Verkehrsberatung und Verfahrenstechniken mbH (GVV)

Steinstrasse 20, 2000 Hamburg 1, German Federal Republic

Telephone: (040) 32 10 41
Telex: 02-161 858 hha-d
Telegraphic address: HOCHBAHN GVV

Parent company: Hamburger Hochbahn Aktiengesellschaft (Hamburg Public Transport Company)

Managing Directors: Dipl.-Volksw. Josef Hoffstadt
Dr.-Ing. Fritz Pampel
Dr.-Ing. Martin Runkel
Vice Directors: Dipl.-Ing. Peter Lenke
Dr.-Ing Peter Kirchhoff
Dipl.-Ing. Arnold Mies

CAPABILITIES
HAMBURG-CONSULT is a subsidiary of the public transport company, the Hamburger Hochbahn, and works in close connection with the management of the parent company as well as other affiliated local railroad companies.
Activities comprise consultancy services and advice in all fields of public short distance transport systems: electric suburban railways, underground railways (RTS), modern light railways and streetcars, unconventional public transport: (such as automated cabin taxis and monorails), bus and ferry services.

PROJECTS
Projected Amsterdam underground railway (1970-74): Preparation of timetables with the simulation of various operating conditions; selection of rail section and types of switches and crossings; design of track layouts; selection of train safety devices and operating control; ventilation of tunnel sections; acoustic measures; protective measures for foreign ducts and cables in the vicinity of tunnels; fire precaution measures. Siting, formation and design of stations; criteria for escalators at station entry and exit points; set-up of the electrical power supply; insurance cover during underground railway construction; suggestions for rolling stock construction; preparing and carrying through running-in operations; basic principles of rolling stock maintenance; designs for the workshops.

Projected Helsinki underground railway (1970-75): Preparation of basic technical and economic principles for rolling stock and operations: investigations into rolling stock/route layout systems up to and including the draft timetable using an analogue data processing unit: basic planning principles for operational layouts, tracks and stations as well as workshops and sidings; management techniques for operations and operating control, models for decentralised and centralised operating control and for automatic operations; technical components of the automation system, continuous train-running control equipment, passenger information, passenger handling and ticket machines; results of automatic trial operations; suggestions for draft tender specifications; recommendations for track current supply and live rail feed control; expert opinion on trial driving car, preparation of tender specifications for purchasing rolling stock in series production.

Other rapid transit studies completed include: radiotelephone system for Berlin in conjunction with AEG-Telefunken; planning Dusseldorf U-Bahn; optimum routing for Munich tunnel sections; construction advice on Vienna Metro; wheel rail investigations for Lisbon Metro; Helsinki rolling stock studies; fire investigations on the rubber-tyred Montreal Metro.

DELON HAMPTON & ASSOCIATES

8701 Georgia Ave, Ste 800, Silver Spring, Md 20910, USA

Telephone: (301) 589 5555

President: Delon Hampton

PROJECTS
Design of two transit car inspection, maintenance and repair shops for Washington Area Transit Authority (WATA); Provision of structural engineering consulting and design for Metropolitan Atlanta Rapid Transit Authority (MARTA).

HARBRIDGE HOUSE INC

11 Arlington St, Boston, Mass 0211, USA

Telephone: (617) 267 6410

Vice-President: Joseph E. Connolly

PROJECTS
Organisation studies, grants and project administration for Regional Transportation Authority, Greater Chicago Area; organisational studies and feasibility analysis for Chicago Transit Authority (CTA).

FREDERIC R HARRIS INC

268 Atlantic St, Stamford, Conn 06901, USA

Telephone: (203) 327 0240

Vice-President: Frank Lopresti

PROJECTS
Designing the joint venture of one mile of track and traction substation and West Lake station ($11 million) for MARTA; Constructional design of Section 2 of the Orange Line relocation project ($180 million) for MBTA.

HARZA ENGINEERING COMPANY

150 South Wacker Dr, Chicago III 60606, USA

Telephone: (312) 855 7000

Vice-President: Dr Ramon S. Larusso

PROJECTS
Section A-6 Rockville route, two miles rock tunnels and three stations ($100 million) for WMATA.

HENDERSON HUGHES AND BUSBY

16 St. John Street, London EC1M 4AY, England

Telephone: (01) 251 2051
Cables: Engecon London EC1
Telex: 28726 a/b ENGCON G

Partners: Andrew B. Henderson MA CEng FICE FIMechE MConsE
Robert H. Busby ERD CEng FICE MInstHE MConsE
C. W. H. Hay CEng FICE FIStructE
T. H. Rosbotham BSc (Eng)
Consultants: G. A. Hughes BA FCIT
D. McClure-Fisher FRICS FIArb
E. T. Williams CMG CEng MICE
G. A. Wilmot BA FCIT
W. G. Rhodes CEng MIMechE FIMarE
H. G. Kidner CEng FIEE
H. F. Dennison FIRSE
B. M. E. O'Mahoney CEng FICE FCIT
R. Stockings CEng MIMechE

CAPABILITIES & PROJECTS
The firm was founded for Railway Consultancy work in 1862. Some of the projects recently carried out are as follows:
—Design of modernisation and electrification of the Tehran-Tabriz line, Iran.
—Management and technical advice on rehabilitation and realignment of Ma'an—El Hassa Railway, Jordan.
—Design and operation of large sugar cane wagon yard, Mozambique.
—Survey and detailed report with advice on rehabilitation on Guayaquil—Quito Railway, Ecuador.
—Supervision railway rehabilitation in Zaire.
—Feasibility Study and outline design of Baghdad-Kut-Um Qasr standard gauge railway, Iraq.
—Technical survey and design of alignment with economic study of Tanzam Railway, Tanzania and Zambia.
—Coal transportation by rail, Colombia.
—Advisers on all railway technical work, Benguela Railways, Angola; Malawi Railways, Malawi; Antofagasta (Chili) and Bolivia Railway, Chile.
—Advising on diesel locomotives and rolling stock, 22 railways throughout the world.
—Survey study and design on strengthening for 500 railway bridges in Thailand.
—Design and supervision of construction of Eccleston Bridge, UK.
—National Rail Investment Study for Irish Republic Railways.

HENNINGSON, DURHAM AND RICHARDSON INC

8404 Indian Hills Dr, Omaha, Neb 68114, USA

Telephone: (402) 399 1000

Vice-President: Robert A. Rohling

PROJECTS
Plans and specifications for 8 500 ft of line and one station ($25 million), for Metropolitan Atlanta Rapid Transit Authority (MARTA); Plans and specifications, 2.5 miles of line; two stations ($30 million) for Washington Metropolitan Rapid Transit Authority (WMATA).

I.B.I. GROUP/INTERBASE INCORPORATED

1629 K St NW Washington, DC 20006, USA

Telephone: (202) 223 2082

Regional Manager: Andrew C. Kanen

PROJECTS
Route performance assessment ($30 000) for City of Windsor, Ontario, Canada; Integrated urban transportation control systems study ($80 000) for Transportation Development Agency.

INSTITUTION OF PUBLIC ADMINISTRATION

1717 Massachusetts Ave, NW Washington DC 20036, USA

Telephone: (202) 667 6551

Dir Transport-Technology: Sumner Myers

PROJECT
Technical assistance to service and method demonstration programme ($184 000); study of alternative means of financing mass transportation systems ($135 000) for Urban Mass Transportation Administration (UMTA).

JARTS
Japan Railway Technical Service)

Kishimoto Bldg, 2-2-1 Marunouchi Chiyoda-ku, Tokyo, Japan

Telephone: (03) 212 4972
Telex: J25254
Telegrams: RAILWAYTECHS TOKYO

Jarts was set up to cooperate with overseas countries in the development of mainline, suburban and transit railways; operating under the guidance of Japan's Ministry of Transport and in co-operation with Japanese National Railways. Fields of activity include: studies surveys and projects relating to land transportation (railway, subway, monorail), construction of new lines, modernisation and improvement of railway track, electrification, dieselisation, modernisation of rolling stock, automatic train control and centralised traffic control, seat reservation systems, marshalling yard automation.

KAISER ENGINEERS INC

300 Lakeside Drive, Oakland, Cal 94666, USA

Telephone: (415) 271 2211

Vice-President/Transportation: Herbert A. Thomas Jr

PROJECTS
General consultant, design phase (joint venture with DMJM)—$55 million—for Maryland Mass Transit Administration (MTA); General consultant on design phase—joint venture with other firms ($15 155 million) for Metropolitan Dade County Transit Agency, Miami.

KAMPSAX INTERNATIONAL A/S

Dagmarhus, Raadhuspladsen DK-1553 Copenhagen V., Denmark

Telephone: (01) 14 14 90
Telex: 15508 kmpsx dk
Telegraphic Address: KAMPSAX COPENHAGEN

Subsidiary and Associate Companies:
Iran-KAMPSAX Ltd, PO Box 11, Tehran, Iran.
KAMPSAX (Nigeria) Ltd, PO Box 5810, Lagos, Nigeria.
Geoplan A/S (Aerial photography and mapping), Dagmarhus, DK-1553 Copenhagen V, Denmark.
Geodan (Soils survey, geotechnical engineering), Gribskovvej 2, DK-2100 Copenhagen Ø, Denmark.
Geodata A/S, (Computer services), Dagmarhus, DK-1553 Copenhagen V, Denmark.

Parent Company:
KAMPSAX A/S, Dagmarhus, DK-1553 Copenhagen V., Denmark

OFFICERS
Managing Directors: Mogens Kierulff
Niels Brockenhuus-Schack
Erik Norsk
Svend Østrup
Senior Railway Engineer: A. Carlsen
Chief Engineer, in charge of overseas acquisition: E. Gejel-Hansen

CAPABILITIES & PROJECTS
KAMPSAX was founded in 1917 as a general Danish civil engineering firm by the three civil engineers Per Kampmann, Otto Kierulff and Jørgen Saxild. Ten years later, the firm entered the international market as consulting engineers. In Denmark, the firm still provides complete engineering services including construction, and through this activity the company has been able to apply much practical experience on its consulting activities abroad.
As Consultants, the company has the capacity and experience to undertake a wide range of projects, a range which continually expands. Transport and communications have been the most important KAMPSAX activity, and the company has undertaken major projects within all modes of transport. One of the earliest tasks was the consulting services related to the Trans-Iranian Railway, a major international engineering undertaking between World War I and II. Railways continue to be important, and the company now acts as Consultants in electrification and expansion of the Iranian railway system.
The company undertakes design and supervision, and covers planning, maintenance, and training activities as well. In recent years KAMPSAX has been involved with preliminary investigations, preparation of country-wide and regional long-term transport development and investment programme, and project feasibility studies, and has provided technical assistance for improvement of maintenance, and for administration and management of public sector transport agencies.
In 1966 Malawi entrusted KAMPSAX with the detailed planning and design of a new 100 km railway line linking an existing line with the railway system of neighbouring Mozambique. The firm subsequently supervised the construction of this new railway during 1968-70. In 1970, the firm was retained to carry out further railway studies in Malawi: rehabilitation of some 160 km of existing line, and appraisal of alternative alignments for a 120 km extension to the new capital, Lilongwe.
In 1972 the firm conducted a pre-feasibility study for a new railway in Iran between the port of Bandar Abbas and Kerman and Bafq on the existing railway, as well as for a line between Kerman and Zahedan. In 1974, the local subsidiary company IRAN-KAMPSAX was awarded a contract for final studies, complete design, and construction supervision of the 900 km Bandar Abbas—Kerman/Bafq electrified double-track railway.
Late in 1974 KAMPSAX was further called upon by the Iranian Government to furnish railway expertise for evaluating projects to increase the capacity of the existing line between Tehran and Bandar Shahpour on the Gulf. This 1 000 km section of the Trans-Iranian Railway was to be provided with a second track, to be electrified and modernised to handle 21 million tons of cargo yearly by the end of 1978. Subsequently KAMPSAX was awarded the assignment of establishing the necessary specifications, design criteria and terms of reference for this huge task, and eventually also of undertaking a selection study of a new alignment for 250 km of the railway through mountainous country to replace a part of the existing line.
The firm has been entrusted with the preparation of a new complete design manual, to be used for future railway construction in Iran. The manual deals with the principles of electrification of new and existing lines, and signalling and telecommunications systems in order to achieve uniformity in the entire network.
KAMPSAX has been engaged by the Iranian Government to draw up technical specifications and establish a procurement programme for electric locomotives for the entire 6 000 km rail network in Iran.

A. T. KEARNEY INC

100, South Wacker Dr, Chicago, Ill, USA

Telephone: (312) 782 2868

Vice-President Transportation: Lester K. Kloss

PROJECTS
Planning for goods movement in auto restricted zones for US Department of Transportation (DOT).

KENNEDY & DONKIN

Premier House, Woking, Surrey GU21 1DG, England

Telephone: (048) 62 5900
Telex: 859123
Telegrams: KINEMATIC WOKING

The firm's head office is in Woking and district offices are situated in Manchester (Generation Department), Manchester (Inspection Department), Glasgow, Linz, Dusseldorf, Varese (Italy), Baden, Iran, Amman, Qatar, Dubai, Sharjah, Nairobi, Bengazi, Derna, Tobruk, Tripoli, Blantyre, Hong Kong, Bogota, Rio de Janeiro, Santiego, Mexico City, Caracas.
Kennedy & Donkin is an independent partnership founded in 1889 from which date it has provided engineering services on electrical and mechanical engineering continuously. The firm is a member of the Association of Consulting Engineers. The current staff level exceeds 750 of whom 450 are professionally qualified. Activities cover generation, transmission, distribution and utilisation of electric power.
Alexander Kennedy BSc, MIMechE, MIEE is the partner in charge of transportation work and is supported by consultants who have held senior posts in transport undertakings such as British Rail and London Transport.
These include:
E. G. Brentnall OBE MEng, MICE, MIMechE, FIEE, FIRSE
A. Bull CBE, CStJ, MA, FCIT
A. H. Cantrell OBE, ERD, BSc (Eng), FICE
A. R. Dunbar CBE, FCIT, FRSA
Brigadier C. A. Langley CB, CBE, MC, FCIT
E. A. Rogers MBE, MIEE, FIRSE

The transportation department of the firm is staffed with engineers who have wide experience, either of railway organisations or with manufacturers.
These include:
Chief Engineer: G. G. Kibblewhite BSc (Eng), FIMechE, FIEE
Deputy Chief Engineer: H. B. Calverley BSc (Eng), FIMechE, FIEE
Rolling Stock: N. D. Ball MIMechE, MIEE
Power Supply: M. J. Woodmore MIEE
Telecommunications: R. J. Burke MIERE, AMIEE
Overhead Catenary Systems: J. W. Butler MIEE
Partner (Kennedy & Donkin Far East): Dr R. K. Edgley MSc (Eng), PhD, FIEE
Project Engineer Hong Kong Mass Transit: E. T. Bostock BEng, FIMechE, FIEE

PROJECTS
The engineering services provided include the preparation of feasibility and economic reports, project reports with preliminary designs and cost estimates; the preparation and issue of technical specifications, conditions of contract and enquiry documents; tendering procedures and the subsequent preparation of contract documents; the supervision of engineering design, plant manufacture, installation and the control of contract accounts. The firm in addition can provide comprehensive progressing and works inspection throughout the world, and site staff for the supervision of plant installation and of final commissioning tests.
Services for railway adminstrations and rapid transit authorities cover railway organisation, motive power, rolling stock, signalling and train control, power supply, telecommunications, permanent way, ventilation, escalators, ticketing machines and all other related mechanical and electrical equipment.

Major projects with which the firm has recently, or is currently, concerned include the following:

Hong Kong Mass Transit Railway: All the electrical and mechanical equipment for this large project currently under construction comprising 15 km of double track railway, mostly underground, which will carry extremely heavy traffic in an environmentally difficult climate.

Taiwan Railway Electrification Feasibility Study: financed by the International Bank for Reconstruction and Development. This major report estimated the economic benefit to the country of electrification of the 400 km West Coast main line and electrification is now being carried out.

East African Railway Study: (financed by the IBRD).

Australia: Urban Passenger Train Feasibility Study and Design in association with Maunsells
Perth Central City Railway Study (electrification aspects)

Brazil: Specifications for motive power and power supply for electrification of the Sao Paulo—Rio de Janeiro railway line (in association with Hidroservice).

Guadalajara rapid transits: 1970: Sponsored by the UK Ministry of Overseas Development, Kennedy & Donkin reported to the Mexican Government on the projected rail rapid transit system for the city of Guadalajara. The firm was responsible for the complete study and arranged for the civil engineering costs to be assesed by a Mexican firm to general designs prepared by Freeman Fox & Partners, and for the traffic analysis and proposals for fare structures to be prepared by Freeman Fox & Associates. The report recommended a three line system of 33 route km for completion by 1978. Further work, including a detailed investigation of the capabilities of Mexican industry in the rapid transit field was undertaken in 1971 in order to determine the extent to which the equipment required for the system could be manufactured in Mexico.

Taiwan Railway electrification: 1970: Financed by the International Bank for Reconstruction and Development (IBRD), Kennedy & Donkin carried out an economic feasibility study for the Taiwan Railway Administration of the electrification of the trunk lines of the Taiwan Railway. Various development programmes and associated traffic forecasts for the next 20 years were prepared based on the alternative use of electric and diesel traction on the trunk lines in order to determine the programme most beneficial to the Taiwan economy. In this study Kennedy & Donkin led a team assisted by China Engineering Consultants, Freeman Fox & Partners and Freeman Fox & Associates.

Australia: 1973: Perth Central City Railway feasibility study: Kennedy & Donkin collaborated with Wilbur Smith and Associates, MacDonald, Wagner & Priddle Pty Ltd, and other consultants in the feasibility study to electrify and place underground the urban railway in Perth, Australia. The firm was responsible for advising on electrification aspects such as traction system, power supplies, signalling and telecommunications.
1973: Tasmanian Government Railways-Signalling: In response to a request from Maunsell & Partners, Kennedy & Donkin prepared a report with recommendations on the rehabilitation of signalling for the Tasmanian Government Railways.
1974: Australia Urban Passenger Train: Also in associated with Maunsell & Partners, Kennedy & Donkin were appointed by the Department of Transport, Canberra, to undertake a feasibility study to determine the viability and consequential advantages of constructing a standardised Urban Passenger Train for all urban rail systems in Australia.
The recommendations of this study were accepted by the Department of Transport and the firm was then later retained to carry out the complete design study and full detailed specifications of such a vehicle.

Brazil: Railway Electrification: 1975: In collaboration with the Brazilian consulting engineering firm, Hidroservice, Kennedy & Donkin are responsible to Rede Ferroviaria Federal SA for determining all technical parameters associated with the proposed electrification of the main line railway between Rio de Janeiro and Sao Paulo (Barra Mansa—Manoel Feio). This responsibility includes the preparation of all detailed technical specifications associated with the project.

This project is of special interest since the suburban sections at both ends of the main line are already electrified at 3 000 volts dc and compatibility of these systems with the eventual main line electrification parameters is obviously one of the principal considerations.

Canada: Urban Rail Vehicle Design: 1974: Kennedy & Donkin took part in a design study of metro vehicle construction by Canadair Ltd, Montreal.

East African Railways Study: 1972: Kennedy & Donkin (Africa) were appointed by the East African Railways in association with Freeman Fox & Associates and Cooper Brothers and Co, to study and make recommendations to the Railway and the three Governments concerned in the future operation of passenger services over the whole system and freight and passenger services on some branch lines.

This study provided information on the effect of closing certain branch lines found to be uneconomical and of curtailing passenger traffic, and devised procedures for recovering costs of such lines required to remain open for social or communication purposes.

Taiwan: Interference Aspects of Electrified Railways: 1975: Kennedy & Donkin have been appointed to advise Taiwan Telecommunications Authority on the levels of interference to be expected in their communication systems due to the electrification being carried out on the Taiwan Railway network. They will also be responsible for recommending methods to reduce this interference to a safe and acceptable level.

Underground Amenity Study: 1972: Kennedy & Donkin carried out a detailed investigation into the noise and vibration caused by tube railways and their effect upon the structure and amenities of buildings within the immediate vicinity of a proposed extension to the London Underground network.

UK: Personal Rapid Transit Power Distribution Study: 1974: Kennedy & Donkin have been appointed to advise Hawker Siddeley Dynamics Ltd, in connection with power supplies distribution for a project definition study of a minitram system which they are carrying out for the Department of the Environment with particular reference to the City of Sheffield.

USA: North-East Corridor Railroad Electrification: 1974: Kennedy & Donkin have been appointed to advise Bechtel Corporation, under their contract with the US Federal Railroad Administration, on specialised technical aspects relating to the possible future electrification of the North-East Corridor railway in the United States of America.

LARAMORE, DOUGLASS AND POPHAM

332 South Michigan ave, Chicago, Ill 60604, USA

Telephone: (312) 427 8486

Vice-President: Richard T. Spada

PROJECTS
Power supply and substation improvements ($60 million) for Massachusetts Bay Transportation Authority (MBTA); substation modernisation ($100 million) for Chicago Transit Authority (CTA).

J. W. LEAS AND ASSOCIATES, INC

910 Potts Lane, Byrn, Mawr, Pa 19010, USA

Telephone: (215) 525 1952

President: J. Wesley Leas

PROJECTS
Specifications for fare collection equipment for Parsons Brinckerhoff/Metropolitan Atlanta Rapid Transit Authority (MARTA); system study for future fare collection and revenue control system for Toronto Transit Commission (TTC).

ARTHUR D. LITTLE INC

1 Maritime Plaza, San Francisco, Cal 94111, USA

Telephone: (415) 981 2500

Manager San Francisco Office: David Hurley

LONDON TRANSPORT INTERNATIONAL SERVICES LIMITED

Address: 55 Broadway, Westminster, London. SW1H 0BD, England

Telephone: (01) 222 5600
Telex: 8812227 Intran
Telegraphic Address: Passengers London

London Transport International is a wholly owned subsidiary of London Transport Executive.

OFFICERS:
Chairman: Ralph Bennett, CEng, FIMechE, FCIT
Managing Director: A. O. Knight, MCIT
Board Members: R. M. Robbins, CBE, FCIT
J. G. Glendinning, OBE, FCIT
W. W. Maxwell MA, CEng, FIMechE, FIEE, FCIT, FIRSE
J. C. F. Cameron, CEng, MICE, FIPM, FCIT
Dr. D. A. Quarmby, BA, PhD, FCIT
Secretary: P. E. Garbutt, MBE, FCIT, FIL
Consultancy Services Manager: D. H. Coombs, MCIT
Assistant Consultancy Services Manager: L. W. Rowe, MCIT

PROJECTS
Bombay (1972): A short term study was carried out in Bombay to identify the most suitable and economic corridors for a mass transit system for Bombay and to suggest a basis for a subsequent techno-economic feasibility study.

Cairo (1972): A report was prepared for the Governor of Cairo and the Cairo Public Transport Authority on the possible construction of an underground railway for Cairo.

Caracas (1977 and subsequently): A team of senior London Transport officials is resident in Caracas to advise the authorities on the formation of a proposed Metropolitan Transit Authority which will include the operation of the new Metro within its overall responsibilities for public transport in Caracas. The advice to be given by London Transport will also include staff training in advance of the commissioning of the new line.

Caracas (1971): An evaluation of rolling stock and signalling specifications for the Caracas Metro was carried out on behalf of the International Bank for Reconstruction and Development.

Chicago (1974): Advice was given to the Illinois Department of Transportation on the railway implications for a Preliminary Regional Operations Plan for Chicago. This required a study to be made of the existing commuter railroad operations in the Chicago area with suggestions for rationalisation of the terminal facilities, revised timetables with through running via Union Station, improvement of passenger facilities and maintenance arrangements.

Glasgow (1974): An assessment of rolling stock specifications for the modernisation of the Glasgow Subway was carried out on behalf of the Greater Glasgow PTE.

Helsinki (1971 and subsequently): Advice was given to Helsinki Rapid Transit Office on system layout, traffic estimates and rolling stock design for the Helsinki Metro.

Hong Kong: London Transport has been associated with the Hong Kong Mass Transit Railway project since the planning days and has formed part of a consortium lead by Freeman Fox and Partners which has served as adviser to the Hong Kong Government and the Mass Transit Railway Corporation. Apart from general operating and planning advice, London Transport has undertaken training for the Mass Transit Railway staff and is responsible for technical inspection work in respect of rolling stock, signalling equipment and lifts and escalators being manufactured in the United Kingdom and in West Germany. London Transport has also provided expertise to the Mass Transit Railway Corporation by seconding serving London Transport staff to work in Hong Kong during the commissioning period for the new railway.

Isle of Man (1976-77): Following a request from the Manx Electric Railway Board for London Transport to carry out design work on proposed new bogies and traction equipment for the Snaefell Mountain Railway, some secondhand tramway vehicles were acquired from West Germany and their motors, control equipment and certain bogie components were used to modernise the Isle of Man cars. Car No. 1 was completed as a prototype during the early months of 1977 and a decision on the remaining five cars is currently awaited from the Manx Electric Railway Board.

Johannesburg (1971): A report was submitted on the feasibility of a rapid transit system for the City of Johannesburg.

Madrid (1975): An appreciation was carried out of the project for a new maintenance and overhaul workshop for the Cia Metropolitano de Madrid.

Melbourne (1971): Advice was given to the Melbourne Underground Railway Loop Authority on operational and signalling aspects of the Melbourne Loop scheme.

Rio de Janeiro (1977): An assessment of training requirements has been prepared for the Rio Metro authorities and arrangements made for the attachment of a senior London Transport official to Rio de Janeiro for a period of one year to assist with training in advance of the completion of the new Metro line.

San Francisco (1974): Advice was given to the Bechtel Corporation on concrete tunnel lining development work being undertaken by Bechtel for the United States Federal Department of Transportation.

Sao Paulo (1976-77): A senior railway operating official of London Transport has been seconded to the Cia Metropolitano de Sao Paulo for a period of one year to assist with operating advice following the opening of the new Metro system.

Toronto (1971): Advice was given to Toronto Transit Commission on alignment problems faced on the northern extension of the Yonge Street Subway.

Tunis (1972 and subsequently): An evaluation was carried out for the International Bank for Reconstruction and Development of proposals made to the Bank for improvements in the Tunis—La Marsa railway.

Tyneside (1973): Assistance was given to Tyneside PTE in regard to legal aspects of land acquisition, estates matters and operational features for the new Tyneside rapid transit system.

United States of America (1975): Advice was given to US Consulting firms on certain aspects of the Disruptive Effects of Tunnelling, on subway maintenance procedures and on station design and construction.

Washington (1972): Assistance was given to Control Data Corporation, Rockville, Maryland, with technical advice for the automatic fare collection system for the proposed Washington Subway.

LOUIS T. KLAUDER AND ASSOCIATES

2100 Philadelphia National Bank Building, Philadelphia, Penn 19107, USA

Telephone: (215) 563 2570
Telex: 83-4783
Telegraphic Address: LTKlauder PHA

OFFICERS:
Partners: Louis T. Klauder, Sr.
Paul D. Dohan
John R. Vollmar
John A. Bailey
David H. Cushwa
Louis T. Klauder, Jr
Robert G. Stacy
Albert N. Ferrari
John W. Irvin
Associates: Richard F. Miller
Henry T. Raudenbush
Robert G. Schwab
Rush D. Touton, Jr.
Robert B. Watson
John J. Wilkins

CAPABILITIES

Louis T. Klauder and Associates, Consulting Engineers, offers a wide variety of engineering, managerial and planning services designed specifically for the transportation field. Based in Philadelphia, Pennsylvania, since its founding on 15 March, 1921, the firm has provided professional and technical assistance to numerous clients throughout the United States and Canada, as well as in Australia, Brazil, Japan, New Zealand and Spain.

The firm was established by Louis Tobias Klauder, former Construction Engineer of the Philadelphia Rapid Transit Company. During its early years, the firm concentrated its energies almost entirely in the field of electric utilities, providing engineering services for reports, appraisals, economic feasibility studies, and design and supervision of construction.

In 1935 Mr Klauder was named electrical engineer for the design of the rapid transit line over the Benjamin Franklin Bridge between Philadelphia, Pennsylvania and Camden, New Jersey. The firm's activities in the transit and railroad field have steadily increased since that time. In recent years, the firm's clients have been composed predominantly of public agencies operating bus, light rail, rapid transit, railroad and people mover systems, both domestically and overseas.

At the death of its founder in 1945, the firm was changed from sole proprietorship to a partnership headed by his son, Louis Thornton Klauder. In addition to Mr Klauder, the partnership at present consists of Paul D. Dohan, John R. Vollmar, John A. Bailey, David H. Cushwa, Louis T. Klauder, Jr, Robert G. Stacy, Albert N. Ferrari, Richard F. Miller and John W. Irvin. Associates are Robert M. Price, Henry T. Raudenbush, Rush D. Touton, Jr, Robert B. Watson, John J. Wilkins, and Robert G. Schwab. There are 75 other men and women on the professional and technical staff, of whom 45 hold at least one degree in engineering or other allied fields. Including supporting staff, the total number of personnel is approximately 130.

PROJECTS

Latest assignments undertaken by Louis T. Klauder during the past three years include assistance of the following electric rolling stock purchases.

Year	No of Cars	Car Type*	Owner
1975	270	Transit	Companhia do Metropolitano do Rio de Janeiro, Brazil
1975	230	Commuter	New Jersey Department of Transportation (Cars for ConRail's former Erie Lackawanna and North Jersey Coast electrified lines).
1976	46	Transit	Delaware River Port Authority (Lindenwold High Speed Line).
1977	190	Transit	Massachusetts Bay Transportation Authority (70 No. 4 Blue Line Cars and 120 No. 12 Orange Line Cars).

Advice on purchase of non-electric commuter cars during 1975/77 includes.

Year	Number	Type	Owner
1976	8	Push-Pull	Metropolitan Transportation Authority of the State of New York (for Erie Lackawanna push-pull trains).

The firm has assisted in the purchase of 776 locomotive-hauled passenger cars, 65 multiple-unit electric cars and 2 three-unit articulated gas turbine trains for inter-city passenger services since 1965.

Year	No of Cars	Car Type	Owner
1965	50	Metro	United States Department of Commerce (for New York-Washington service).
1965	2	Turbo	(United States Department of Commerce (for New York-Boston service).
1965	4	Test	United States Department of Commerce (for Trenton-New Brunswick high speed test track).
1966	11	Metro	Pennsylvania Department of Commerce and Southeastern Pennsylvania Transportation Authority.
1973 (492 fleet cars).	492	Locomotive	National Railroad Passenger Corporation (Amtrak's Amf-hauled
1974	284	Locomotive hauled	National Railroad Passenger Corporation (Amtrak's Bi-level cars).

Latest experience of Louis T. Klauder with electric and diesel-electric locomotives is as follows:

Federal Railroad Administration 1976: As subcontractor to Unified Industries, Incorporated, technical assistance in the evaluation of domestic and foreign locomotives as part of the FRA's Improved Passenger Equipment Evaluation Programme (IPEEP).

Federal Railroad Administration 1976: As subcontractor to DeLeuw Cather/Parsons Associates, engineering and technical support in the modification of existing electric locomotives (both freight and passenger) as part of the Northeast Corridor Railroad Improvement Programme (NECIP) to permit their operation at 25 000 V, 60 Hz, as well as at the present 11 000 V, 25 Hz catenary supply.

Metropolitan Transportation Authority of the State of New York 1977: Preparation of plans and specifications for the rehabilitation and equipping for push-pull service of approximately 40 FL-9 type diesel-electric/straight electric locomotives used on the Harlem and Hudson lines in commuter service operated by the Consolidated Rail Corporation (ConRail) for the MTA.

Southeastern Michigan Transportation Authority (SEMTA) 1976: Evaluation of available diesel-electric locomotives for use in the Detroit-area commuter service, including locomotive characteristics and design feature comparisons, train performance simulation, energy and fuel consumption, etc.

Miscellaneous projects undertaken by the firm include the following assignments:

Brisbane Metropolitan Transit Project Board, Queensland, Australia 1977: As subcontractor to P. G. Pak-Poy and Associates, Pty, Ltd, assistance with the Brisbane-to-Gold Coast Corridor Transit Study.

City and County of Honolulu, Hawaii 1977: Assistance to the Director of Transportation Services concerning the Honolulu fixed guideway rapid transit system.

City of Calgary, Alberta 1976: As a subcontractor to DeLeuw Cather, Canada, Ltd, provide engineering services in the areas of light rail vehicles, signal systems, and electrification in connection with a study of transit improvements for the City of Calgary.

City of Cincinnati, Ohio 1977: Assist the Public Utilities Department with transportation planning and policy matters.

County of Los Angeles, California 1976: Preliminary Operations feasibility study of the proposed Sunset Coast Line rail rapid transit system.

Federal Railroad Administration 1976: As subcontractors to Dalton, Dalton, Little, Newport, assistance in assessing the preliminary environmental impact of proposed railroad improvements in the Northeast Corridor.

Florida Department of Transportation 1976: As subcontractor to Harland Bartholomew and Associates, assistance in a study of alternatives for improving public transportation between Miami and North Palm Beach as part of the Southeast Florida Transit Corridor Study.

Greater Cleveland Regional Transit Authority 1976: Assistance in evaluating 20 bid proposals received from 10 domestic and foreign firms competing for an order of light rail vehicles (not to exceed 68) providing at least 4 000 seats.

Massachusetts Bay Transportation Authority 1976: As subcontractors to Sverdrup & Parcel and Associates, preliminary engineering for signals and communication, on the Red Line Extension from Davis Square to Alewife Brook Parkway, including information collection, signal and communication analysis and preliminary engineering, cost estimates, review of special problems and project management.

Memphis Area Transit Authority 1977: Pre-aware evaluation of a recording fare collection system designed for use on buses.

Metropolitan Suburban Bus Authority 1976: Computation of revenue yield from alternative possible revisions of fares.

Metropolitan Transportation Authority of the State of New York 1977: Technical study of a fully-automated fare collection system for passenger stations of the Long Island Rail Road.

Michigan State Department of Highways and Transportation 1977: Preliminary engineering investigation of the feasibility and cost of retrofitting commuter rail coaches of the Southeastern Michigan Transportation Authority to accommodate elderly and handicapped passengers.

Murphy Engineering Inc., (Chicago, Illinois) 1976: Supporting services for a study of public policy questions for the Regional Transit Authority of New Orleans, Louisiana.

New York City Transit Authority 1976: Implementation of Transit Police Major Crime Information System (MCIS).

New York City Transit Authority 1977: Systems analysis and programming services in connection with the Inventory Control System and allied applications.

Port Authority of Allegheny County 1977: As subcontractor to Parsons Brinckerhoff-Gibbs & Hill, evaluate vehicle alternatives, estimate cost of fleet and prepare draft specifications and bidding documents for light rail vehicles required for Stage I of the Pittsburgh Light Rail Transit (LRT) Programme. In addition, analyse and evaluate fare collection systems for above with special emphasis on interface with proposed vehicles and stations and impact upon existing bus/streetcar system.

Port Authority of Allegheny County 1977: As subcontractor to Parsons Brinckerhoff-Gibbs & Hill, analyse and evaluate fare collection systems for Stage I of the Pittsburgh Light Rail Transit (LRT) Programme. Special emphasis required in this assignment on interface with proposed vehicles and stations and impact on existing bus/streetcar system.

Port Authority of Allegheny County 1977: As subcontractor to Parsons Brinckerhoff-Gibbs and Hill, evaluate vehicle alternatives, including determination of design modifications required to accommodate non-ambulatory handicapped passengers, estimate cost and prepare draft specifications and bidding documents for light rail vehicles required for State I of the Pittsburgh Light Rail Transit (LRT) Programme.

Port Authority Transit Corporation of Pennsylvania and New Jersey (PATCO) 1976: Assistance in meeting Project FARE accounting system reporting requirements.

Regional Transportation District in Colorado 1976: Pre-award survey of the production capabilities and ability to make promised delivery of a manufacturer of recording fare collection equipment designed for use on buses.

Regional Transportation District in Colorado 1977: Engineering and Quality Assurance services during the manufacture and installation of wheelchair lifts of 18 transit coaches being built by the Flexible Company.

San Mateo County Transit District 1977: Engineering and Quality Assurance services during the manufacture by Transportation Design and Technology of wheelchair lifts to be installed in 24 transit coaches being built by AM General Corporation.

Southeastern Michigan Transportation Authority 1976: Operations planning and other engineering services in connection with the evaluation of proposed commuter railroad service improvements for six transportation corridors serving Detroit and its suburbs.

Southeastern Michigan Transportation Authority 1976: Operations planning and other engineering services in connection with the evaluation of proposed commuter railroad service improvements for six transportation corridors serving Detroit and its suburbs.

Southern California Rapid Transit District 1976: Technical analysis and evaluation of wheelchair lifts being manufactured by Transportation Design and Technology for installation on 200 transit coaches being built by AM General Corporation.

Trustees of the Penn Central Transportation Company 1977: Systems and programming services in support of operating cost model and related studies.

Trustees of the Penn Central Transportation Company 1976: Assist in the identification of Penn Central branch lines that would have value as public transportation routes.

Trustees of the Penn Central Transportation Company 1976: Assist in the identification of Penn Central branch lines that would have value as public transportation routes.

Unified Industries, Inc. 1976: Assistance to the Federal Railroad Administration in railroad passenger systems and equipment research.

A. A. MATTHEWS INC.

11900 Parklawn Dr, Rockville, Md 20852, USA

Telephone: (301) 881 6300

Senior-Vice President: Dr James E. Monsees

PROJECTS
Engineering consultants for Washington Metropolitan Area Transit Authority (WMA-TA).

MARTIN AND VOORHEES

Martin and Voorhees Associates Transportation and Planning Consultants.

112 Strand, London WC2R 0AA, England

Telephone: (01) 836 0871
Telex: 27200 Logica Ltd.
Telegraphic Address: Martinvor London WC2

Directors: Brian Martin BSc
Alan Powell MSc
David Hollings BA
Brian Large MSc
Martin Richards MSc

CAPABILITIES
The company has been commissioned for over 70 projects either exclusively or partially concerned with railways. These cover a wide range including rail investment, planning, operation and marketing.
The Consultancy is a British company concerned with transportation and planning. The company undertakes a comprehensive range of projects concerned with the planning of transport systems covering urban, regional, corridor and rural areas. These projects are concerned with the short term issues of marketing, operation and management as well as the larger term issues of investment policy. The consultancy was originally formed in 1969 as a subsidiary of AMV Inc. with whom it still continues to have an association.

Clients for rail and rail related studies in the United Kingdom have included: British Rail; Northern Ireland Railways; London Transport; Greater Manchester Passenger Transport Executive; Tyne and Wear Passenger Transport Executive; West Midlands Passenger Transport Executive; Mid and South Glamorgan County Council; South Yorkshire County Council; Tyne and Wear County Council; West Yorkshire County Council; Highlands and Islands Development Board; Peak Park Planning Board; Redditch Development Corporation.

International clients include: Union Internationale des Chemins de Fer (UIC); Coras Iompair Eireann (Ireland); Public Works Authority, Hong Kong; Urbanisticki Zavod Grada Beograda (Yugoslavia); West Pakistan Government; Ministry of Communications, Libya; Ministry of Transport, Victoria, Australia; EYSER (Madrid) for Commission for Planning, Valencia Region.

Project Experience
The Consultancy undertakes railway projects at many different levels including strategic studies (investment, operating and marketing), transport planning and co-ordination, and studies concerned with short term issues in respect of facilities such as catering and reservations or pricing and promotion.
Set out below are some short project descriptions together with listings of similar or related projects.

Corridor Studies
Such studies are normally concerned with forecasting future demand for transport and examining the role and capacity requirements for the railway given different levels of investment in railway facilities and in other modes. Economics and financial factors are evaluated together, in some cases, with a full cost benefit analysis. Clients are typically rail operators or national or regional transport administrations.

Local Rail or Area Studies
The Consultancy has undertaken a number of planning studies concerned with optimisation or rationalisation of such networks of urban railway networks.
In Wales, the Counties of Mid and South Glamorgan commissioned a study to assess how the rail infrastructure could contribute to planning objectives and overall transport responsibilities. Within the project a wide range of options were costed and evaluated for technical feasibility, financial return, and economic and social value. The options included network extensions or rationalisation, the opening, re-siting and closing of stations, alternative forms of traction and changes in speed and frequency. Mathematical modelling techniques were developed to forecast future traffic and indicate the loadings on the various parts of the network in many different circumstances.

Rail Rapid Transit Studies
The Consultancy has substantial experience in the evaluation and planning of rapid transit rail systems.
In its original Land Use and Transportation Study for the Tyne-Wear Region it was concluded that a rail rapid transit system should be included in the recommended plan. This was followed by a detailed study of alignments and an evaluation of the forms of the system concluding with a recommendation for an LRT version. Finally a cost benefit analysis was conducted comparing the rail rapid transit with all bus and 'busway' alternatives. This last study supported the successful application for Parliamentary Authority to proceed with construction.

Other rapid transit studies have included: Rapid transit feasibility study for Urbanisticki Zavod Grada Beograda (Belgrade); Dublin rapid transit study for Coras Iompair Eireann (Ireland); Island corridor study for Public Works Authority Hong Kong.

Special Projects
Many studies have been concerned with the design orientation of railway stock, stations and facilities towards rail user requirements. One major study related to the commercial justification for investment in new Inter-City rolling stock for British Rail. This study, based upon extensive engineering, physiological and psychological research, demonstrated conclusively the economic case for new rolling stock and for air conditioning.
In another, the modernisation of main line stations was examined using a combination of economic and attitudinal research techniques in conjunction with observational studies. The results, which related to station rationalisation as well as investment, were incorporated into the British Railways' station investment programme.
Many studies have been conducted concerned with pricing and fares structures covering short and medium timescales. Commuter and main line fares elasticities have been analysed. Projects for British Rail have ranged from the evaluation of the national fares policy through detailed studies for individual routes to the evaluation of many different forms of low fare offers.
Studies have been conducted in Britain, Ireland, and Australia for rail and other

transport clients of various forms of rail inter-change facilities. Forecasts have been produced of car parking requirements for commuters and main line travellers. Economic justifications for such facilities have been assessed and advice given on user charges.
Evaluations have been made of user reactions to different forms of design of station and on train catering facilities.
Reservations systems have been studied in respect of different categories of rail passengers and the costs involved.
Booking and information system studies conducted for British Rail have covered a wide range of issues ranging from the best method of disseminating information about late or irregular running through to the provision of preferential booking systems for business travellers. The role of Travel Agents has also been assessed.
Numerous studies have analysed the relationship between railway staff and the public and many recommendations have been formulated and adopted.

Marketing Railway Services
In the United Kingdom most rail services are confronted with competition from bus or coach and the private car and many inter-urban services are confronted with air competition. The Consultancy has continuously undertaken marketing studies in support of British Rail and its advertising agents. There have been specific studies for local services in seventeen different locations and a comparable number conducted at different times over the Inter-City network. The studies normally consist of the objective analysis of catchment area data, a comparative evaluation of rail and competing modes surveys to determine user profiles and market segmentation. This is supported by a series of attitudinal studies concerned to establish knowledge, awareness and motivations towards rail and the attractions it serves. Advice is given to the rail operator in respect of possible service changes, pricing variations and potential innovations in respect of facilities. Additionally promotional recommendations are formulated concerning target markets and advertising themes.

MAUNSELL CONSULTANTS LTD

Yeoman House, 63 Croydon Rd, Penge, London SE20 7TP, England

Telephone: 01-778 6060
Cables MAUNCIVIL LONDON SE20
Telex: 946171

Senior Partner: J. W. Baxter, CBE, BSc, FCGI, FICE, FIEAust, FInstPet, MSocCEF, FIHE, MConsE, MConsEAust.
Managing Partner: J. B. Laurie BE, FICE, FIEAust, MConsEAust.
Partners: L. M. Ramage, BSc, FICE, FIStructE, MIHE, MConsE, MConsEAust.
D. J. Lee, BScTech, DIC, FICE, FIStructE, FIHE, MConsE, PrEng, PEng.
P. G. Sands, BSc, ACGI, FICE, FIEAust, MConsE, MConsEAust.
G. N. Fernie, BE, MICE, MIEAust, MConsEAust.
D. M. A. Hook, MA, FICE, FIStructE, FIHE, MConsE.
J. W. Downer, BE, FICE, FIEAust, MIES, MConsE, MConsEAust.
J. G. Clayton, BE, MICE, MIEAust, MConsEAust.
J. A. Leslie, BE, FICE, FIEAust, MConsEAust.
C. J. Price, MBE, BE, FIEAust, MConsEAust
P. H. N. Norman, FACQS

Maunsell Consultants Asia
In addition to the Partners of Maunsell Consultants:—
Partners: Chan Chee Wah, BE, ME, FICE, FIES, FIEM, FIEAust, MConsESing, PEng
P. H. Gray, MA, MSc, MS, MICE, MITE, MIHE.
R. C. T. Ho, PhD, BSc, MICE, MIStructE.
R. Thomas, BSc, FICE, MIWE

Associates:
A. A. Wilkinson, BE, FIEAust, FASCE.
R. K. Grieve, BE, MIEAust.
A. Cameron-Smith, BSc, MICE, MIEAust, MIHE.
B. W. Choy, BE, MICE, MIEAust.
R. J. Garrett, MA, MICE.

Consultants to the Group
G. T. Bingham, BSc, ACGI, DIC, FICE, FIEAust, FWeldI, MConsE.
L. P. Hill, BA, BAI, FICE, FIHE, FIEI.
J. B. Holt, BScTech, MICE, FGS.
E. P. C. Hughes, OBE, BSc, FICE, FIEAust, MConsE, MConsEAust.
A. A. Osborne, MBE, TD, FICE, MRTPI, FIHE, MConsE.

ASSOCIATED COMPANIES:
Maunsell & Partners Pty Ltd
Melbourne, Australia
Contact:
Managing Director: J. B. Laurie
277, William Street, Melbourne, Victoria 3000, Australia
Also at: Perth, Sydney, Canberra, Adelaide, Hobart, Brisbane and Albury
Telephone: 60 1135
Telex: 31067
Cable: Mauncivil, Melbourne

Maunsell Consultants
Melbourne, Australia
Contact:
Managing Partner: J. B. Laurie
277, William Street, Melbourne, Victoria 3000, Australia
Also at: Perth, Sydney, Canberra, Adelaide, Hobart, Brisbane and Albury
Telephone: 60 1135
Telex: 31067
Cable: Mauncivil, Melbourne

Maunsell Consultants Asia
Kowloon, Hong Kong
Contact:
Senior Resident Partner: J. W. Downer
14th Floor, 1, Kowloon Park Drive, Tsim Sha Tsui, Kowloon, Hong Kong
Also at: Singapore, Kuala Lumpur, Jakarta and Bangkok.
Telephone: 3-940223
Telex: HX 74458
Cables: Mauncivil, Hong Kong

Al-Kubaisi and Partner
Baghdad, Iraq
Contact:
Resident Partner: S.I. Al-Kubaisi
PO Box 615 Baghdad, Iraq
Telephone: 93734
Cables PL 615 Baghdad

Maunsell Ibironke Consultants Ltd.
Lagos, Nigeria
Contact:
Managing Director: E. V. Jenkins
13/17 Breadfruit Street, PO Box 5382, Lagos, Nigeria
Telephone: 27023 27443
Cables: Com Eng Cons Lagos

Waad Maunsell Associates
Kuala Lumpur, Malaysia
Contact:
Resident Partner: R. K. Grieve
Wisma Perdana, Jalan Dungan, Damansara Heights, Kuala Lumpur 23-05, Malaysia
Telephone: 945811, 945866
Cable: Mauncivil Kuala Lumpur

Sindhu Maunsell Consultants
Bangkok, Thailand
Contact:
Partner: Sindhu Pulsirivong
Chongkolee Building, 56 Suriwong Road, Bangkok, Thailand

Telephone: 37956-9, 31307-9, 31300, 35239, 38344
Telex: Wepress BK 2549

Ingentra Maunsell Consultants
Munich, Germany Federal Republic
Contact:
Managing Director: Josef Jares
8000 Munchen 21, Maria-Birnbaum-Strasse 12, Germany Federal Republic
Telephone: (0.89) 575460/576833
Telex: 525281

C. H. Teoh Jan Rakan
Kuala Lumpur, Malaysia
Contact:
Managing Partner: C. H. Teoh
Tinkat 4, Bangunan, M.C.A. Jalan Ampang, Kuala Lumpur, 01-17, Malaysia
Telephone: 87052

Maunsell P.N.G. Pty Ltd
Port Moresby, Papua New Guinea
PO Box 484, Port Moresby, Papua New Guinea

Chan Chee Wah Maunsell & Partners
Singapore
Contact:
Managing Partner: Chan Chee Wah
9F/G Asia Insurance Buildings, Finlayson Green, Singapore 1
Telephone: 910644
Telex: RS 24297
Cable: Mauncivil Singapore

CAPABILITIES

The firm of G. Maunsell & Partners was established in London by the late Mr G. A. Maunsell to provide civil engineering consultancy services both in the British Isles and overseas. A branch office was established in Melbourne and this was later made a separate firm which was named Maunsell & Partners. The Australian partnership became an incorporated company and now practices under the name of Maunsell & Partners Pty Ltd.
The British firm is based in London with branch offices in Birmingham, Glasgow and Swansea.
The Australian firm is based in Melbourne with branch offices in Canberra, Sydney, Perth, Adelaide, Hobart, Brisbane and Albury.
Following a re-organisation of the activities of the firms designed to improve world-wide operations, the international partnership of Maunsell Consultants was formed. This international partnership comprises the partners of G. Maunsell & Partners and the directors of Maunsell & Partners Pty Ltd, and normally undertakes assignments in all parts of the world other than England and Australasia, which are served by the appropriate constituent firms.
Al-Kubaisi and Partner was formed to undertake the assignments in Iraq.
Maunsell Ibironke Consultants Limited was formed to undertake assignments in Nigeria and other West African countries.
Waad Maunsell Associates was formed to operate as a local partnership in Malaysia with a prime interest in those areas of engineering concerned with the improvement and protection of the environment.

The group is operating in many parts of the world and is registered with bodies concerned with world-wide developments, such as the International Bank for Reconstruction and Development, the United Nations Industrial Development Organisation, the Asian Development Bank, etc.
Some of the wide range of services offered are:

Engineering
The group can provide co-ordinated planning and control of a project from its inception to final completion. Particular aspects of this work are:
Feasibility studies and report estimates.
Detailed design, preparation of working drawings, contract documents, etc.
Evaluation of tenders and placing of contracts.
Supervision of construction and certification of interim and final payments to contractors.
Full Contract Management Services, with computer back up for major multi-discipline engineering contracts.

Land Survey
A comprehensive and fully experienced land survey section, employing the latest techniques and equipment is available to undertake work anywhere in the world. Electronic equipment is available to facilitate accurate linear measurement over any terrain.

Ground Exploration
The group employs qualified personnel fully experienced in soil mechanics, foundation engineering and geology and it arranges and supervises contracts for ground exploration.

Transportation Studies
A traffic engineering department was established in 1963 and is able to undertake transportation studies of all kinds together with the associated economic and cost benefit analyses, route location, traffic management and studies of environmental effects.

Town and Regional Planning
One of the individual consultants in the group is a past president of the Town Planning Institute and additionally, there are strong links with architects, landscape architects, building quantity surveyors and others so that the group is able to handle assignments involving town or regional planning.

Environmental and Health Engineering
The Health Engineering section designs and supervises the construction and installation of water supply systems, sewage treatment plants and solid waste disposal facilities. The group has been particularly active in the field of solid waste disposal and undertakes comprehensive studies which cover economic appraisal and management aspects. The group is well equipped to advise on liquid waste disposal problems. Expansion of the Group's activities in the fields of irrigation and major water supply schemes has been recently accomplished.
The organisation is active in the field of environmental engineering and carries out surveys to evaluate and appraise pollution of all forms including noise and gaseous emissions.

Economic Studies
When the scope of the work so demands, the group associates with various specialist firms or individuals who are experts in the field of economics.

Computing
Comprehensive computer facilities are available for the solution of problems in engineering design, traffic engineering, and land and marine surveying while specialised programmes for use with the foregoing have been developed by the group's engineers and applied mathematicians.
The Maunsell firms which employ over 600 staff, have dealt with outstanding engineering projects in many parts of the world and some indication of the scope of their activities is given in the accompanying brochure.

PROJECTS 1975/77

Completion Date	Project	Country	Client	Value $US (When Built)
in hand	Mass Transit Railway (2 stations and 1 100 m tunnel)	Hong Kong	Paul Y Construction Ltd.	69 000 000
in hand	Mount Newman Railway (30 km new route and duplication of 58 km railway and sidings)	Australia	Mount Newman Mining Company	21 500 000
1975	Railway Crossing Accidents Study	Australia	Commonwealth Department of Transport	
1975	Australian Urban Passenger Train Studies	Australia	Commonwealth Department of Transport	
1975	Diversion of Adelaide to Melbourne Railway	Australia	Monarto Development Commission	
1976	Survey of passengers using Railway Stations in Melbourne	Australia	With Transmark for Ministry of Transport, Victoria	
1976	Kowloon—Canton Railway	Hong Kong	With Transmark	
1976	State Railway System—Tasmania Master Plan	Australia	Tasmanian Government Railways	

Upgrading of Tasmanian Government Railways: Client: Transport Commission of Tasmania; work started in 1974 and is continuing. The advent of considerable increased traffic both from wood chipping operations, general industrial expansion and from the rising importance of the port of Bell Bay made necessary the complete upgrading of the Tasmanian Railway System. This system consisting of some 788 km of railway was very run down as a result of years of under-expenditure on maintenance and no capital works.
A complete appraisal of the system and recommendations for upgrading was prepared in 1973 and a ten year programme of work was prepared. The total cost was estimated (at 1973 prices) to be some $US 88 million.
The work of design, contract preparation, supervision and co-ordination with all parties is now proceeding. Detailed reports of requirements for each year's programme are under preparation.

Mount Newman Railway, Western Australia: Client: Mount Newman Mining Co Pty Ltd; Work started in 1976. Expansion of heavy iron ore railway currently handling in excess of 30 million tonnes per year. Maunsell undertaking complete engineering design and documentation leading to supervision of construction for the regrading of 30 km of the route, the duplication of 58 km of the railway and additional sidings. Total estimated value of work around $US 50 million.

Mass Transit Railway, Hong Kong: The Mass Transit Railway Corporation, which is to provide and then run the colony's first underground railway, has recently awarded the first series of design and construct contracts for stations and lengths of tunnel. Initially the system will cover a length of 15.6 km at an estimated cost of $US 160 million including land acquisition. Maunsell's, in conjunction with a local firm of contractors, have won four of the major contracts against international competition. The contracts are for the construction of two stations and two lengths of tunnels linking them.

Choi Hung Station: This station comprises a two tier underground structure with a passenger concourse at the upper level and two platforms served by three tracks at the lower level. The plan dimensions are approximately 300 × 30 m and the depth to track level is 8.50 m below ground level. The ground, in which the station is constructed, is decomposed granite rock. The construction includes main walls built by the diaphragm method and a combination of king plates and jack arches.

Diamond Hill Station: This is generally similar to Choi Hung Station but has a central platform serving two tracks. A particular feature includes provision for later widening by removal and reconstruction of the main outer walls to permit five tracks to be served by four platforms.

Tunnels: One length of tunnel serving two and three tracks will be constructed by cut and cover methods in decomposed granite rock with extensive use of sheet piling. The length of tunnel included in this contract is approximately 800 m and the depth of track slab level is 8.50 m below ground. A wide variation of cross sections is necessary to accommodate track turnouts and connections. The second length of tunnel comprises four separate bored tunnels passing through solid granite and decomposed granite rock for a nett length of 300 m. The tunnels serve both running lines and lines leading to the main depot.

Ermelo Marshalling Yard, South Africa: Client: South African Railways; Work started in 1974. Design of a new hump marshalling yard including a locomotive depot to cater for both steam and diesel motive power, carriage and wagon maintenance depots and all ancillary buildings and services associated with such a yard. Stage 1 under construction involves some 50 km of track and 175 turnouts and has a construction cost of $US 4 million. Completion to final stage will involve total expenditure of around $US 10 million.

Main line Railway, Venezuela: The first phase of construction of a standard gauge railway network for Venezuela is a 700 km line between Cuidad Guyana and San Juan de los Morros, including a spur line through difficult mountainous country to Tuy Medio. Maunsells were retained by a consortium of contractors preparing a tender for the construction work. Visits were made to investigate ground conditions along the route and to asses the availability of suitable construction materials. Outline designs were prepared for significant structures including a range of standard designs. Construction methods were established so that costs could be estimated.

MCDONALD & GREFE, INC

303 Sacremento St, San Francisco, Calif 94111, USA

Telephone: (415) 956 7670

Vice-President: Richard Grefe

PROJECTS
Economic impacts of transit alternatives ($110 000) for Southeastern Michigan Transportation Authority (SEMTA); economics and finance project BART impact Programme ($190 000) for Metropolitan Transportation Authority (MTC), Berkeley, Calif.

MODJESKI & MASTERS

PO Box 2345, Harrisburg, Pa 17105, USA

Telephone: (717) 761 1891

Partner: R. E. Felsburg

PROJECTS
L'Enfant Plaza-Pentagon section, Potomac Bridge ($15 million) for Washington Metropolitan Area Transit Authority (WMATA); second Newburg—Beacon Bridge ($90 million) for New York State Bridge Authority (NYSBA).

MORRISON/KNUDSEN COMPANY INC

One Morrison-Knudsen Plaza, PO Box 7808, Boise, Idaho 83729, USA

Telephone: (208) 345-5000
Telex: 368439

Consultancy subsidiary company: International Engineering Company Inc (IECO)

220 Montgomery St, San Francisco, Cal 94104, USA

Railroad Division Manager: Joseph G. Fearon

CAPABILITIES

Morrison-Knudsen ranks as one of the largest and most widely experienced railroad construction operations in the world. Since the Company's first railroad project in 1915, Morrison-Knudsen forces have built thousands of miles of new railroad grade; erected bridges; bored tunnels, crushed countless carloads of ballast; performed emergency repairs after storms, floods and earthquakes; and laid many miles of new track. This work has been performed in the continental United States and Alaska, Mexico, Canada, Australia, Peru, Brazil and many other countries.
Design/engineering work for the railroad industry is performed by International Engineering Company Inc (IECO), Morrison-Knudsen's San Francisco-based subsidiary. International Engineering Company has been engaged in the design of various heavy civil engineering projects, including railroads and their associated facilities for over 25 years. Comprehensive programme for increasing the safety, speed and economy of railroad services are a result of extensive studies and economic evaluations determining the size, capacity, location and disposition of various elements making up a railroad system.
In the design of railroads and maintenance facilities a partial inventory of IECO's railroad engineering accomplishments totals well over 19 200 km of overland railways.

Union Pacific Railroad Diesel Running Repair Facilities: The Union Pacific Railroad began operating a newly constructed Diesel Running Repair Facility at North Platte, Nebraska in April 1971. This facility was designed by IECO and constructed by Morrison-Knudsen Company. The UP facility is the largest and most modern running repair facility in the United States, capable of maintaining a fleet of over 600 locomotives. Scheduled repair and inspections are completed on over 400 locomotives per month by handling forty locomotives simultaneously inside the shop building. The facility requires a total staff of over 300 for around-the-clock operations. An adjacent washing facility, also designed by IECO, is capable of washing 200 locomotives per day in temperatures ranging from minus 20° F to plus 110° F.

Locomotive Repair Ship–Tubarao, Brazil: IECO has recently completed engineering designs for a Locomotive Repair Shop Complex at Tubarao, Espirito Santo, Brazil for Companhia Vale Do Rio Doce. This complex, now under construction, is designed to maintain a fleet of 200 locomotives with provisions in the facility for expansion to a fleet of 300 locomotives. Fuelling, sanding and washing facilities were provided for in the design. IECO also prepared the engineering design for an earlier maintenance shop at Tubarao, as part of an overall terminal complex for CVRD.

Locomotive Running Repair and Service Facilities–Pacatello, Idaho: IECO prepared the preliminary engineering designs, quantity and cost estimates for a locomotive running repair and servicing facility for the Union Pacific Railroad at Pocatello, Idaho. This installation now services 60 assigned switch locomotives and road locomotives as the need arises.

Muni Metro Rail Center–San Francisco, California: Presently under construction, this facility was designed by IECO for the maintenance, storage and terminal facilities of a new fleet of 110 standard light-weight rail vehicles being acquired by the San Francisco Municipal Railway. Washing and sanding facilities are provided for in the design.

Study for Rolling Stock Maintenance–RFFSA, Brazil: This current project involves managing a study team to review, update, and, as necessary, supplement the design of the Maintenance Shop Plans as these items relate to the system-wide "Five Year Plan of Action and Investment" of Rede Ferroviaria Federal SA (RFFSA), the national railroad of Brazil.

Remanufacturing Facilities–Morrison-Knudsen Co Inc: IECO also performed the mechanical design for the Morrison-Knudsen Company locomotive remanufacturing facilities in Boise, Idaho. This specially equipped facility for major locomotive rebuilding and overhaul is capable of accommodating 11 locomotives simultaneously.
IECO, together with its parent company, Morrison-Knudsen Company Inc, has performed numerous other railroad engineering and construction projects within the US and abroad. The total value of these projects is estimated at more than $2.2 thousand million. Following is a comprehensive listing of project locations and services performed by International Engineering Company, Inc.

| | Basic IECO Services | | | | Estimated |
Location and Project	Reconn. Study/ Planning	Feas Study/ Preliminary Design	Final Design	Length km	Project Cost ($ million)
AUSTRALIA					
Cooke Point Terminal					
Facilities	◆	◆		N/A	12
BRAZIL					
Aguas Claras	◆	◆	◆	18	4.2
Pico-Congonhas	◆	◆		47	12
Aguas Claras-Ibirite	◆	◆		23	5.5
Fabrica-Congonhas	◆	◆	◆	15	2
Vitoria Port Terminal	◆	◆	◆	40	N/A
Fabrica-Alegria	◆	◆	◆	95	16
Jangada Spur Line	◆	◆	◆	11	2.6
Tubarao Port Terminal					
and Connection Line	◆	◆	◆	15	5.6
EFVM Electrification	◆			550	160
Locomotive Repair					
Shop Complex		◆	◆	N/A	10
Teresa Cristina Electrification	◆			150	40
CANADA					
Elk River	◆	◆		73	20
ENGLAND-FRANCE					
Channel Tunnel	◆	◆		51	235
IVORY COAST					
Iron Ore Haul Railroad	◆			375	57
SAUDI ARABIA					
Riyadh-Jeddah	◆	◆		1 600	135
SOUTH KOREA					
Railroad Survey	◆			160	16
ZAIRE					
Matadi Bridge	◆	◆		N/A	N/A
UNITED STATES					
Arizona					
Black Mesa & Lake Powell	◆	◆	◆	125	50
SRP Coronado Station R.R.	◆	◆		80	30
California					
Norden Tunnel Ventilation	◆	◆		2	0.2
Western Pacific Relocation	◆	◆		45	20
Eel River Bridges					
Rehabilitation	◆	◆	◆	N/A	4
Eel River Line Relocation	◆	◆		140	140
Metro Railway Shop					
and Terminal	◆	◆	◆	N/A	15
Port of Oakland			◆	N/A	0.5
Colorado					
Fountain Creek Bridge	◆	◆	◆	N/A	0.2
Chacra-Glenwood					
Relocation	◆	◆	◆	13	1.4
W.R. Grace Railway	◆	◆	◆	35	16
Idaho					
Huntington Bridge					
& Relocation	◆	◆	◆	N/A	2
Ballard Mine	◆	◆	◆	8	N/A
Idaho-Washington					
Camaras					
Prairie Relocation			◆	21	14
Indiana					
Tunnel Enlargement	◆	◆	◆	1.5	3
Kansas to California					
Railroad Electrification	◆	◆		2 700	200
Montana					
Libby Line Change	◆	◆		143	60
Nebraska					
Diesel Locomotive					
Repair Facilities			◆	N/A	11
Oregon					
John Day Relocation			◆	4	1
Tennessee					
Tunnel Enlargement	◆	◆	◆	1	3
Utah					
Great Salt Lake Crossing	◆	◆	◆	20	45
Spur Line Location Survey	◆			N/A	N/A
D & RGW Tunnel		◆	◆	2	6
Washington					
Cascade Tunnel Ventilation	◆	◆		13	0.4
Rocky Reach Line Change	◆	◆		71	10
Wyoming					
Crow Lease Spur		◆	◆	29	18
TOTAL				over 6 670 km	over $1 370 million

The following examples are representative of the type and complexity of railroad construction projects performed by Morrison-Knudsen in recent years.

Great Salt Lake Causeway: One of the most significant railroad projects Morrison-Knudsen has completed was the design and construction of the Great Salt Lake Causeway in Utah. The causeway rises from a dredged foundation trench ranging from 175 to 600 ft in width and rises to a maximum height of 97 ft. Over 45 000 000 yds^3 of fill material was handled in three and a half years of earthmoving. The causeway, which replaced an old wooden trestle, was completed nine months ahead of schedule.

Australian Port-to-Mine Railroads: Another significant railroad project completed in 1973 was the construction of pioneer port-to-mine railroads to transport iron ore from deposits in the outback of Western Australia to the coast along the Indian Ocean. A total of 699 miles of track was constructed from the four roads using continuous-welded rail. Track laying operations included a record day in which 4.35 miles of track were laid, spiked and anchored in 11 hrs 40 mins, and a top month in which 49.7 miles of track were completed.

Black Mesa and Lake Powell Railroad: The world's first 50 kV electrified railway was designed, built and equipped by Morrison-Knudsen and IECO, under a "turnkey" programme. Known as the Black Mesa and Lake Powell Railroad, the all new line is an automated coal transportation route reaching 78 miles across Navajo Indian lands in northern Arizona. Train loading and unloading are all automatically regulated by an extensive "Rail-safe" automation system which stops the train in the event of any malfunction in the train or control system.

Railroad Operations: Congruent with railroad construction, Morrison-Knudsen is also experienced in railroad operations. All railroad construction operations are operated on an operating railroad basis under standard railroad operating rules and procedures. In addition, Morrison-Knudsen has operated several newly constructed railroads while training personnel for the client. These include the Black Mesa-Lake Powell Railroad in Arizona; the Hammersley Iron Railroad, the Mount Newman Railroad and the Robe River Railroad, all in Australia and all built by Morrison-Knudsen; the Quebec North Shore and Labrador Railroad in Canada; the Orinoco Railroad in Venezuela; the Southern Peru Copper Railroad in Peru; and the Burlington Northern Railroad at Libby, Montana.

Currently, the Vermont Northern Railroad Company, a subsidiary of Morrison-Knudsen Company Inc is under contract with the State of Vermont to operate and maintain the Swanton, Vermont, to St. Johnsbury, Vermont, rail line (formerly the St. Johnsbury and Lamoille County Railroad). The contract, awarded in October, 1976, required the rehabilitation of the trackage to FRA Class I standards as well as operating and management services. Upon award of the contract, Morrison-Knudsen personnel conducted a track study and at the request of the State of Vermont, compiled and submitted a report with recommendations to upgrade the trackage to a higher FRA classification and ultimately provide faster and more economical service to the area.

RAILROAD MAINTENANCE
The following is a sample of other Morrison-Knudsen-built projects involving railroad maintenance:

At North Platte, Nebraska, Morrison-Knudsen built a highly automated equipment maintenance plant to enable the Union Pacific to perform inspections and running repairs on 200 giant diesel locomotives a day. Capable of accommodating as many as 25 units simultaneously, it has reduced the time required for heavy running repairs, even the exchange of engines, from a matter of days to a maximum of 24 hours. Construction as well as design of the 140 000 ft² shop and an adjacent 200-locomotive-per-day wash facility were completed under a "Turnkey" contract awarded Morrison-Knudsen by the Union Pacific Railroad Company. Morrison-Knudsen performed construction, while design was carried out by Morrison-Knudsen's San Francisco-based subsidiary, International Engineering Company, Inc.

• Another facility for the railway industry was a 350 000 ft² commuter car assembly plant designed and built by Morrison-Knudsen near Erie, Pennsylvania, for the General Electric Company. GE uses the plant to assemble high-speed rapid transit cars. First production from the plant was delivered to agencies of New York and Connecticut for use on the New Haven Line.

• Morrison-Knudsen has also participated in the design, engineering, and construction of other maintenance and locomotive remanufacturing shops in the United States and several facilities in Australia. Morrison-Knudsen has designed, engineered and constructed numerous "loop" loadout rail facilities for mining projects in both North and South American as well as other areas of the world.

MOTT, HAY & ANDERSON

Head Office Address: 20/26 Wellesley Road, Croydon, Surrey CR9 2UL, England

Telephone: 01-686 5041
Telex: 917241
Cables: LYDONIST-CROYDON

Associated Companies: Mott, Hay and Anderson International Limited, Consulting Engineers, Croydon, UK
Mott, Hay, Preece Cardew, Railway and Rapid Transit Consultants, Croydon and Brighton, UK.
John Connell-Mott, Hay and Anderson Pty. Limited, Consulting Engineers, 60 Albert Road, South Melbourne 3205, Victoria, Australia.
Girec SA, 430 Avenue Louise, Boite No. 5, 1050 Brussels, Belgium.
Transit and Tunnel Consultants Inc., Suite 811, The Rand Building, 14 Lafayette Square, Buffalo, New York State, 14203, USA

CAPABILITIES
The Mott, Hay & Anderson group operates throughout the world as engineering and project management consultants.
Mott, Hay & Anderson was founded in 1902. During the last ten years the group has operated in over 40 countries and, in order to give clients the best service, taking into account the need to consider local problems, a number of permanent links have been established with consulting engineering practices in other countries.
The group is linked by a degree of common ownership. Each member of the group is independent and controlled by its own board of directors.
The group deploys a staff of about 1 200 professional and technical personnel.

DIRECTORS
J. R. Prosser BSc FICE
J. V. Bartlett CBE MA FICE FIEAust FASCE
C. D. Brown BSC FICE
A. J. Holland FCA
S. G. Tough BSc FICE FGS
B. L. Bubbers BSc FICE
J. W. Connell CEng FIStructE FIEAust MASCE (Australia)
E. M. T. Powell BSc FIMechE FIEE FIHVE
T. D. Wilson BSc FICE FIStructE FIMunE FIHE
F. P. D. Stables FICE MSAICE
J. A. Turnbull FICE MIMunE FIHE
R. Beresford BEng MICE
J. M. Whitefield BSc MICE FIHE MASCE
E. A. Cruddas BSc FICE MIStructE FIHE
J. B. Field MA FICE

PROJECTS 1976/77

Name of Project	Year Completed	Approx. Const. Cost	Details of Project
Caracas Metro	1976	£50.0m	Advice on section of underground railway
Mersey Railway Extensions	1977	£23.0m	Design and supervision of civil engineering works
Toronto Subway Extensions	1977	£21.5m	Design and supervision of tunnelling lengths
Baltimore Regional Rapid Transit Scheme	1977	£450.0m	Advice on tunnelling and construction
Caracas Metro	1977	£40.0m	Design assistance and advice

Name of Project	Year Completed	Approx. Const. Cost	Details of Project
Fleet Line— Underground Railway	—	£16.7m	Design of civil engineering work
Brussels Metro— Section 4F	—	£6.0m	Feasibility study, design and supervision of construction
Brussels Semi-Metro Troncon G6	—	£8.2m	Addition to metro, part underground, part surface railway
Melbourne Underground Rail Loop	—	£1110.0m	Study, design and supervision of construction
Helsinki Metro	—	£8.4m	Design and supervision of running tunnels and advice on ancillary works
Tyne and Wear Metro	—	£160.0m	Planning, design and supervision of construction
Manchester Urban Railway Scheme	—	£50.0m	Study of alternative routes
Buffalo Light Rail Rapid Transit	—	£197.6m	Design of sections of underground railway
The River Line	—	—	Advice on extension of London underground
Tehran-Tabriz	—	£1 000.0m	Design of new electrified railway
Dublin Suburban Railway	—	£8.0m	Design of electrification system for 45 km of railway
Antwerp Semi-Metro	—	£4.6m	Station and tunnel design for second phase of underground network
Caracas	1977	—	Evaluation of a Turnkey proposal for a rapid transit system between Caracas and the coast

Tehran (Shahyad)-Tabriz Railway Project, Iran:
In 1976 Mott, Hay & Anderson International Ltd were appointed to assist Transmark Ltd (British Rail's export consultancy) in the design of a new electrified railway between Tehran and Tabriz. The existing diesel operated single line railway follows a route of some 740 km. The prime requirements for the new railway is a main-line twintrack 630 km railway between the Iranian capital and its principal links to the Russian and Turkish frontiers. This railway will provide a high speed passenger service between Tehran and Tabriz as well as a major freight connection to deal with the increasing import/export requirement.
For the initial 440 km from Tehran westwards as far as Mianeh, the route generally follows the existing line and about two-thirds of this length will be constructed by widening the existing embankment. The remainder will be realigned to give improved running speeds. From Mianeh to Tabriz a completely new direct route through mountainous terrain is being planned. This line will be more than 100 km shorter than the existing route via Maragheh. Many major structures will be required including bridges, tunnels, viaducts and earthworks. In addition the existing 300 km route (Mianeh-Maragheh-Tabriz) will be upgraded. The project involves track length in excess of 1 500 km in total.
Mott, Hay & Anderson under the directions of the Chief Civil Engineer, British Railways Board are preparing the design of all earthworks, drainage, river training works, bridge works and tunnels together with the associated contract documents required for the civil engineering construction of the entire project.
This has required close collaboration with British Rail engineers to determine railway criteria to be adopted in design and consultation with others engaged on route selection and the geometric layout of the railway.
Fieldwork as part of the Transmark engineering team in Iran includes the supervision of soil investigations carried out by the client, geotechnical studies, structure surveys and hydrological studies to assist in the determination of the design criteria to be adopted.

Client: Transmark Ltd for the Ministry of Roads and Transportation, Iran
Capital cost of engineering works: £1 000 m

PETER MULLER-MUNK ASSOCIATES
(Division of Wilbur Smith & Associates)

1720 Four Gateway Center, Pittsburg Pa 15222, USA

Telephone: (412) 261 5161

Director: Paul Karlen

PROJECTS
Advanced concept train (ACT-1) for AiResearch/Urban Mass Transit administration (UMTA); Transit marketing for City of Montgomery, Ala.

NATIONAL CITY MANAGEMENT RAPID TRANSIT LINES

9720 Town Park Dr Ste 109, Houston, Tex, USA

Telephone: (713) 772 1272

President/General Manager: Stan Gates Jr.

PROJECTS
Management contracts with Rhode Island Public Transit Authority; Connecticut Department of Transportation; West Palm Beach, Fla; Central Ohio Transit Authority; Central Arkansas Transit, Little Rock; Shreveport, La; Colorado Springs, Colo; Spokane Transit System, Spokane, Wash.

NATIONAL INSTITUTE FOR COMMUNITY DEVELOPMENT INC

2021 K Street NW, Washington, DC 20006, USA

Telephone: (202) 872 1590

Senior Associate: Edward T. Herlihy

PROJECTS
Census data processing for the urban planning system for Urban Mass Transportation Administration (UMTA).

PARSONS BRINCKERHOFF QUADE & DOUGLAS INC

1 Penn Plaza, New York, NY 10001, USA

Telephone: (212) 239 7900

Senior Vice-President: W. O. Salter

PROJECTS
General consultant, planning, design, construction management ($1 200 million) for Metropolitan Atlanta Rapid Transit Authority (MARTA); Rail system, general consultant, design and construction management ($150 million) for Ministry of Public Works, Caracas, Venezuela.

THE RALPH M PARSONS COMPANY

100 West Walnut, Pasadena, Cal 91746, USA

Telephone: (213) 440 2000

Vice-President: Forrest C. Six

PROJECTS
Station and line design (two contracts)—$4.5 million—for Washington Metropolitan Area Transit Authority (WMATA); station and line design, North Avenue Station (Approx. $2 million) for Metropolitan Atlanta Rapid Transit Authority (MARTA).

PEAT, MARWICK, MITCHELL & CO

1025 Connecticut ave, NW, Washington DC 20036, USA

Telephone: (202) 223 9525

Principals: D. M. Hill, C. Macdorman

PROJECTS
Alternatives analysis restudy for Metropolitan Washington Council; alternatives analysis study for Southeastern Michigan Transportation Authority (SEMTA).

PEREGRINE AND PARTNERS

PO Box 3, Royston, Hertfordshire SG8 7BU, England

Telephone: (0763) 42384

US Associates: H. K. Friedland and Associates, PO Box 893, Cal 92075, USA
Telephone: (714) 481 9339

Established in 1950, the firm has an international practice in mechanical engineering design, manufacture and commissioning of prototypes and working machinery for Governments, Universities, Consulting Firms and major industry.

CAPABILITIES
1 Road, Track and Seagoing Prime Movers and accessories
Transmissions Gears
Turbomachinery
Combustion
Test Rigs
Civil Engineering Equipment
Process Machinery
System Studies and Appraisals
Marketing and Purchasing Support.

Jubilee Line, London, England: Following the successful completion of the Victoria Line, London Transport are constructing a new underground railway line across the central area of London—the Jubilee Line.
To the north the line will incorporate the Stanmore branch of the existing Bakerloo Line. At the southern end of this branch, the line will continue in new deep level twin tube tunnels from Baker Street to Fenchurch Street with intermediate stations at Bond Street, Green Park, Strand, Aldwych, Ludgate Circus and Cannon Street. Among its major benefits the new route will relieve serious overcrowding of the Bakerloo Line and contribute to the relief of the existing Central and District Lines. It will also link London's north west suburbs directly with the West end and City, and eventually extend to the eastern or south eastern suburbs of the metropolis.
Mott, Hay & Anderson have been appointed consulting engineers for the design and supervision of approximately half the civil engineering works of the new line. Construction work is now nearing completion on the first phase between Bond Street and Admiralty Arch. Detail design work is proceeding on the second section between Cannon Street and Fenchurch Street with preliminary mapping and route investigation contracts for the remaining phases of the project. The vertical geometry of the running and station tunnels on the first phase allows the drives to be carried out mostly within the London clay, except at Bond Street where the drives enter the Woolwich and Reading beds. The ticket hall at Bond Street station is being built beneath the busiest thoroughfare in the West End, involving construction from very small sites with limited access, and the diversion or strengthening of numerous underground services. The new tunnels cross the Central Line at right angles at this station and interchange passages will be provided between platforms. At Green Park a new subway-escalator connection will allow passenger interchange with the Piccadilly and Victoria Lines. Between Cannon Street and Fenchurch Street the tunnels are to be driven beneath multi-storey buildings in the heart of the City of London. Due to office development along the line of the future railway it has been necessary to protect the route. This necessitated in some cases fixing the track and tunnel setting out data accurately in relation to the surface topography and inspecting deep level foundations during construction to ensure compatibility with the proposed new tunnels. Assessment and modification of structural designs to minimise the subsequent effect of railway construction have also been carried out and any additional costs estimated. The new ticket hall at Fenchurch Street is being designed as an integral part of a new eleven-storey office block. At this station, interchange with the British Rail terminus will be provided, whilst at Cannon Street escalators will give access to the District Line. The stock, traction and signalling will be similar to that operating on the Victoria Line.
Client: London Transport Executive
Construction period of first phase: 1973-1977
Civil engineering cost for first phase: £16.71 m
Estimated civil engineering cost for the second phase: £16 m

Brussels Metro, Belgium: The transport authorities in Brussels, faced with increasing traffic congestion which is causing serious delays to trams on their existing network are carrying out a two stage plan for the construction of a comprehensive metro system. The first stage is a semi-metro in which the tunnels and stations are constructed to accommodate conventional standard gauge metro stock, but which in this stage are required for the operation of a tram system. The existing tram layout is connected to the tunnels by temporary ramps.
The sections that have been completed since the construction programme started in 1965 include parts of an inner circle, outer circle and north-south and east-west crossroutes. In 1976 the east-west line was converted to full metro-operation, the second stage in the development of the system.
Construction started in 1975 of the extension westward of the east-west line from its present terminal at St Catherine to a new temporary terminal at Place des Etangs Noirs. Mott, Hay & Anderson are in association with Frederick R. Harris (Belgium) NV as consulting engineers for this extension of the system which is some 1.3 km in length. The first stage comprised site investigations, route appraisal, comparative assessment of methods of construction and outline design of station and track layouts. Estimates of the cost of construction by alternative methods including costs of land acquisition and diversions of vehicular traffic, sewers and public utilities were also made. After assistance in the selection of the contractor, working drawings and assistance in supervision are being provided by the group.
The group's firm in Brussels, GIREC, has been appointed to provide similar consulting services for the Arts-Loi station, Yser station and an extension of the east-west line eastwards. Arts-Loi station which has already been constructed is at a two level junction of the east-west and inner circle lines. Yser station for which the preliminary design has so far been prepared by GIREC is to be constructed so as to incorporate the foundations of a major existing highway structure. The extension eastwards which makes use of existing railway alignment in open cut but includes as well a section of tunnel and a station underground, is also at the preliminary design stage in 1977.
Client: Société des Transports Intercommunaux
Estimated capital cost of work presently under construction on the Etangs Noirs extension: £14.9 m.

Tyne and Wear Metro, England: The metro will provide a 55 km long rapid transit facility to serve the major population centres of the area and will be operated by the Tyne and Wear Passenger Transport Executive. The system is based on 42 km of existing British Rail track serving both banks of the River Tyne connected by new underground routes through Gateshead and Newcastle and a new bridge over the river.
Prototypes of the articulated twin car metro vehicles, powered from a 1 500 V dc overhead supply, are being tested on a 2.4 km long test track in North Tyneside. The vehicles will be operated either singly or in trains of two or three units to provide a 7½ minute service in outlying areas and a 2½ minute service in the city centre.
Mott, Hay & Anderson have been entrusted with the design and supervision of construction of the tunnels and stations in the central areas of Newcastle and Gateshead which comprise the underground core of the system. The 4.75 m diameter running tunnels in Newcastle pass through glacial drift consisting mostly of boulder clay and are shield driven using boom type tunnelling machines. According to ground conditions the tunnels are lined with bolted pre-cast concrete or cast iron segments. The 7 m diameter station tunnel enlargements and crossovers up to 10 m diameter utilise high strength nodular cast iron linings. Low pressure compressed air is used to limit the undesirable effects of waterbearing and/or weak strata.
In order to stabilise the honeycomb of old coal workings along the Gateshead route a preliminary contract to explore and fill the cavities was let. The arched section tunnels, 5 m wide × 6.9 m high, are supported initially with steel ribs prior to construction of an *in situ* concrete lining. At the portals short lengths of the tunnels are built in *in situ* concrete using a cut-and-cover technique.
There are seven stations within the underground portion of the system, some presenting complex problems of construction. The technique of excavation beneath a preconstructed roof slab supported by piles is being employed to minimise disruption at some locations. Main electrical and mechanical services for the underground stations are being designed by the firms' associated Mechanical and Electrical group.
Construction of the metro started in October 1974 and the work is programmed so that the system will become operational in phases, reaching completion in 1981. The group is also fulfilling a project management role which includes coordination, programming and cost monitoring of all project elements through commissioning to operation.
Client: Tyne and Wear Passenger Transport Executive
Estimated cost of work for which the firm is responsible: £60 m.

Dublin Suburban Railway Electrification, Ireland: Early in 1977 Coras Iompair Eireann decided to proceed with the electrification of the existing suburban railway line between Howth and Greystones, a distance of approximately 45 kms, as a first stage of the Dublin Rail Rapid Transit Project. The firm was appointed to design the electrification system which is to be at 1 500 V dc with overhead current collection. Preece, Cardew & Rider are collaborating in this work.
The firm was also appointed to design the alterations to the layout and equipment of the existing diesel maintenance workshops at Fairview, which are to be adapted for the cleaning and maintenance of the new electric trains.
The firm has also been asked to assist in an assessment of the work required to alter certain bridges and station canopies to accommodate the overhead electrification equipment.
Client: Coras Iompair Eireann
Estimated cost of engineering works: £8 million.

PICKERING-WOOTEN-SMITH-WEISS INC

5909 Shelby Oaks Dr, Memphis, Tenn 38134, USA

Telephone: (901) 382 2350

Vice-President: Robert L. Haynie

PROJECTS
Transit planning southern corridor for Shelby County, Tenn

WM S POLLARD CONSULTING INC

1395 Madison ave, Memphis, Tenn 38104, USA

Telephone: (901) 726 6300

President: William S. Pollard

PROJECTS
Environmental impact assessment, Wilmington Outer Loop (approx $167 000) for North Carolina Department of Transportation (DOT).

PORTER AND RIPA ASSOCIATES INC

200 Madison ave, Morristown NJ 07960, USA

Telephone: (201) 267 8800

Senior Vice-President: Michael J. Dillon

PROJECTS
State airport system plan report for New Jersey Department of Transportation (DOT); Transportation centre (multi-modal)—$60 million—for Essex County (NJ).

R. H. PRATT ASSOCIATES INC

10400 Connecticut ave, Kensington, Md 20795, USA

Telephone: (301) 942 0332

President: Richard H. Pratt

PROJECTS
Transportation control strategy implementation ($100.258) for Metropolitan Washington Council; Western Prince George's County transportation alternatives study ($91 000) for Maryland Department of Transportation.

PRC RAILWAY SYSTEMS

7798 Old Springhouse Road, McLean, Va 22101, USA

Telephone: (703) 893 4310
Telex: 899105
Cable: AMVOR, McLean

Associated Companies:
Alan M. Voorhees & Associates, Inc.
Martin and Voorhees Associates
Frederic R. Harris, Inc.
Economic Research Associates
H. B. Maynard International
Logica

Parent Company
Planning Research Corporation
1850 K Street, NW, Washington DC 20036, USA

Officers:
Vice-President: Malcolm O. Laughlin
Principal: Richard H. Wiersema

Services Offered:
Consultancy services in railroad management planning and engineering.

CAPABILITIES
Planning Research Corporation is a diversified consulting firm working in many areas of transportation. PRC Railway Systems is the unit of Planning Research Corporation responsible for coordinating PRC services involving railroads.

PROJECTS
US Agency for International Development: Feasibility study of railway passenger car production plant.

Delaware River Port Authority: Design and construction supervision of a rapid transit line (Lindenwold line).

Association of American Railroads: Feasibility study of a centralised car location message system.

United States Railway Association: Development of techniques for projecting rolling stock requirements.

Federal Railway Administration: Development of an intermodal management information system.

Danish Railways: Design of workshops for emu cars.

Spanish Railways: Design of locomotive workshop.

RAIL INDIA TECHNICAL & ECONOMIC SERVICES LTD.

27, Barakhamba Road, New Delhi House, New Delhi-110001, India

Telephones: 44915/45362/44945
Telex: 031-4143 and 031-3996
Telegraphic Address: RITESRAIL NEW DELHI (INDIA)

Parent Company: Wholly owned by the Government of India.

OFFICERS
Chairman: G. P. Warrier
Managing Director: A. B. Ribeiro
Director Technical: C. M. Malik
Director Finance: S. R. Srinivasan
Chief Manager: K. Rangachari
Chief Engineer: S. Ponnuswamy
Chief Project Manager: T. N. Tandon

PROJECTS COMPLETED
1 Preliminary feasibility-cum-cost study of a 325 km long new standard-gauge line in Iran.
2 Preliminary feasibility-cum-cost study together with economic study of three new lines in Syria, aggregating to about 450 km.
3 Study of an existing broad-gauge line in Iran (92 km) and suggesting measures for its strengthening and rehabilitation for carrying a higher level of traffic.
4 System study of Ghana Railways suggesting measures for improving the maintenance of rolling stock.
5 Consultancy to Sri Lanka Railways in regard to improvements to workshops, sheds and sick lines.
6 Assistance to Malaysia International Consultants in the study of bridges on the Malaysian Railways.
7 Techno-economic feasibility study for standard gauge on the Nigerian Railways for the Nigerian Railway Corporation.

PROJECTS UNDER WAY:
1 Loaning 12 experts from different railway disciplines and providing necessary back-up services to the Zairean Railways.
2 Consultancy to the Philippine National Railway for rehabilitation of the Manila-Legaspi section and overall improvement to the entire railway system.
3 Consultancy to the Ghana Railways regarding new facilities for maintenance of rolling stock and training of personnel.
4 Survey of a 2 km long road bridge across the Brahmaputra river in Eastern India.
5 Consultancy to National Thermal Projects Corporation (India) for a Merry-Go-Round Railway Transport System, for moving coal from pitheads to the super-thermal power station.
6 Study for the transport of fertilisers and fertiliser raw-materials in India—a World Bank aided project.
7 Feasibility study for inland water transport in the Eastern Region of India.
8 Consultancy regarding planning and provision of rail facilities for a large steel plant in Southern India.

REAL ESTATE RESEARCH CORP

1101 17th st, NW, Washington DC 20036, USA

Telephone: (202) 223 4500

Vice-President: C. H. Broley

PROJECTS
People movers for US Department of Transportation.

RENDEL PALMER & TRITTON

Address: 61 Southwark Street, London SE1 1SA, England

Telephone: (01)-928-8999
Telex: 919553 a/b RENDEL G.
Cables: RENDELS LONDON SE1

Associate Firms:—
RTP Economic Studies Group
28 Maiden Lane, London WC2 7JS
Telephone: (01)-240 2054. Telex: 919553
Rendell & Partners
PO Box 62, 166 Albert Road, South Melbourne, Victoria 3205, Australia
PO Box 288, Toowong, Brisbane, 4066 Queensland, Australia
43 Ventnor Avenue, West Perth, 6005 Western Australia, Australia
118-122 Queen Street, Woollahra 2025, New South Wales, Australia
Irendco
PO Box 2588, Tehran, Iran
RPL Engenharia e Consultoria Ltda.,
Rua Costa Ferreira 106, Rio de Janiero, Brazil.

Partners: F. Irwin-Childs FICE
P. A. Cox, FICE
J. C. Munro, FICE
D. M. S. Fairweather, FIMechE
R. Downham, FRINA, FIMarE
J. A. N. Dennis, FICE
F. A. Fisher, FICE
B. J. Luxton, FICE
P. J. Clark, FICE
L. W. Hinch, FICE
Consultant: J. L. Koffman, DipIng, FIMechE

PROJECTS:
Railway Consultancy projects completed during the last ten years or at present under way include:
Northern Ireland Railways
Redevelopment of York Road terminal and Workshops, Belfast.
New freight yard at Adelaide, Belfast.
Reconstruction of Belfast Central railway and new Central Station.
Review of motive power and rolling stock.

British Rail
Channel Tunnel rail link—preliminary plans for 27 kms of route.
Design of 23 bridges and erection schemes for Eastern Region.
Reports and preliminary design of 11 bridges.

Australia
Investigation and report on Burragorong-Scarborough railway (60 kms.)
Goldsworthy-Kennedy Gap railway—design of 96 kms. of new railway.
Mt. Newman Mining Co.—reporting and advising on locomotives and track maintenance problems.

Malaysia
Investigation, report and outline relocation plan for Port Dickson railway.

Jordan
Survey, design and construction of El Hasa-Manzil extension (25 kms).
Report and preparation of tender documents for new rolling stock.
Transport study for carriage by road and rail of imports and exports.

Sudan
Comparative study of road and rail transport for agricultural products.

Iran
Transportation study, rail-road-sea for oil and gas fields development.

India
Report to Indian Railways Board on riding qualities of locomotives.

KENNETH ROBERTS & ASSOCIATES INC

10560 Main Street, Suite 515, Fairfax, Va 22030, USA

Telephone: (703) 591 6008

President: Kenneth R. Roberts

PROJECTS
Studies for Cleveland Regional Transit Authority and Washington Metropolitan Area Transit Authority.

RUMMEL, KLEPPER & KAHL

1035 North Calvert St, Baltimore, Md 21202, USA

Telephone: (301) 685 3105

Partner: A. L. Deen Jr

PROJECTS
Shady Grove extension of Rockville route, 2.7 miles ($35 million) for Metropolitan Area Transit Authority (WMATA).

S & S SYSTEMS INC

8585 North Stemmons Fwy, Dallas, Tex 75247, USA

Telephone: (214) 630 2287

President: J. G. Srygley

PROJECTS
Control system simulation for Metropolitan Atlanta Rapid Transit Authority (MARTA).

STV INC

Griffith Towers Building, Pottstown, Pa 19464, USA

Telephone: (215) 326 4600

Vice-President: Stewart F. Taylor

PROJECTS
Commuter rolling stock upgrading ($263,000) for Massachusetts Bay Transportation Authority (MBTA); Atlantic Terminal Project ($406 million) for Metropolitan Transportation Authority (MTA), NY.

SCHIMPELER CORRADINO ASSOCIATES

1429 South Third St, Louisville, Ky 40208, USA

Telephone: (502) 636 3555

Principal: Joseph C. Corradine

PROJECTS
Rapid transit implementation ($1 million/year) for Metropolitan Dade County Transit Agency, Miami; Corridor analysis ($60 million) for Ann Arbor-Ypsilanti Transportation Study.

SHERIDAN ASSOCIATES

575 Lexington Ave, New York, NY 10022, USA

Telephone: (212) 750 6960

President: James J. Sheridan

PROJECTS
ACT-1 vehicle design for General Electric Corp.

SIMPSON AND CURTIN

Division of Booz, Allen & Hamilton, Inc

1346 Chestnut St, Philadelphia, Pa 19107, USA

Telephone: (215) 545 8000

President: Michael G. Ferreri

PROJECTS
Statewide organisation and finance of public transportation for New Jersey Department of Transportation (DOT); Litigation assistance in Conrail reorganisation for US DOT, Office of the Secretary.

FRANK C. SMITH & ASSOCIATES

8585 Stemmons Freeway, Dallas, Tex 75247, USA

Telephone: (214) 630 4716

Principal: Frank C. Smith PE

PROJECTS
System availability studies in support of UMTA programme for Urban Mass Transportation Administration (UMTA).

SMITH AND LOCKE ASSOCIATES INC

500 12th St SW Ste 808, Washington DC 20024, USA

Telephone: (202) 554 2040

Partners: Irving P. Smith/Barry Locke

PROJECTS
Study of transportation for the elderly and handicapped ($60 000) for Urban Mass Transportation Administration (UMTA) also National mass transit marketing project for UMTA.

WILBUR SMITH AND ASSOCIATES

155 Whitney Ave, New Haven, Conn 06507, USA

Telephone: (203) 865 2191

Chairman: Wilbur S. Smith

PROJECTS
Corridor environmental impact study for State of Rhode Island; Transportation programme management for Tri-County Metropolitan Transportation District of Oregon (Tri-Met).

SOFRERAIL
(Societe Francaise d'Etudes et des Realisations Ferroviaries)

3 avenue Hoch, Paris 8e, France

Telephone: (755) 97 08/(766) 55 22

Sofrerail has carried out numerous railway studies throughout the world.

SOFRETU
(Societe Francaise d'Etudes et de Realisations de Transports Urbains)

Tour Gamma D, 195 rue de Bercy, 75012 Paris, France

Sofretu was set up specifically to deal with transit consultancy projects.

SUNDBERG-FERAR INC

Box 116, Southfield, Mich 48037, USA

Telephone: (313) 356 8600

President: Richard A. Heck

PROJECTS
Follow-up vehicle designs for Metropolitan Atlanta Rapid Transit Authority (MARTA) and Washington Metropolitan Area Transit Authority (WMATA).

SVERDRUP CORPORATION

800 North 12th Blvd, St Louis Mo 63101, USA

Telephone: (314) 436 7600

Vice-President: George H. Andrews

PROJECTS
Red line extension cut-and-cover tunnel and two stations ($100 million) for Massachusetts Bay Transportation Authority (MB.TA).

SYNERGY

PO Box 199, Northridge, Cal 91328, USA

Telephone: (213) 993 0926

Project co-ordinator: Dennis Cannon

PROJECTS
Planned fully accessible transit system and district headquarters for Southern California Rapid Transit District (SCRTD).

SYSTEMS CONSULTANTS INC

1054 31st St NW, Washington DC 20007, USA

Telephone: (202) 333 6800

Senior programme engineer: William V. Garvey

PROJECTS
Analysis and specification for automated information system ($80 000) for Washington Metropolitan Area Transit Auth. (WMATA); Designed/implemented automated information dissemination system ($95 million) for Southeastern Pennsylvania Transit Auth (SEPTA).

TIPPETTS-ABBETT-McCARTHY-STRATTON

345 Park ave, New York, NY 10022, USA

Telephone: (212) 755 2000

Partner: Austin E. Brant, Jr

PROJECTS
Long Island Railroad East Midtown Terminal and Third Avenue Line for Metropolitan Transportation Authority (MTA) NY.

THE TRANSIT SYSTEMS GROUP

44 King St, East, Toronto, Ontario, Canada.

Telephone: (416) 864 9696

Directors: Ian Moore, Peter Hildyard

PROJECTS
Automated scheduling implementation ($40 000) for Maryland Mass transit Administration (MTA) and Massachusetts Bay Transportation Authority (MBTA).

TRANSIT AND TUNNEL CONSULTANTS INC

14 Lafayette Sq, Suite 8II, Buffalo, NY 14203, USA

Telephone: (716) 822 5200

President: Richard W. Wilson

PROJECTS
Buffalo light rail rapid transit 3.5 mile twin rock tunnel including five stations ($360 million) for Niagara Frontier Transportation Authority.

TRANSMARK
Transportation Systems & Market Research Limited

23 Dorset Square, London NW1 6QT, England

Telephone: 01-402 5501 (5 lines)
Telegraphic No: Transmark London NW1
Telex: 24678 BR HQ LN

Parent Company: British Railways Board, BR HQ, 222 Marylebone Road, London NW1 6JJ, England

Directors and Consultants
Managing Director: K. V. Smith
Deputy Managing Director: D. M. Howes
Director: D. R. Meek
Principal Consultant: J. E. Todd
Principal Consultant: J. A. Houlder
Principal Consultant: A. B. Englert
Principal Consultant: N. J. B. Alexander
Special Consultant: A. W. McMurdo
Special Consultant: A. E. Robson
Special Consultant: J. F. H. Tyler
Senior Consultant: I. B. H. Murray
Senior Consultant: D. Doling
Senior Consultant: I. C. Cowe
Senior Consultant: W. A. C. Trethewey

PROJECTS AT PRESENT UNDERWAY

Country	Client	Project Description
Australia	Hamersley Iron: W. Australia	Testing of S & T Relays
Australia	Brisbane M.T.A.	Optimisation of suburban train schedules
Australia	Transport Commission of NSW	NSW Pack Track: feasibility
Australia	Transport Commission of NSW	Technical advice following Granville derailment
Bangladesh	Asian Development Bank	Technical assistance to Bangladesh Railways
Bangladesh	Ministry of Overseas Devel	Advice on setting up Training Institute for Ban. Railways
Brazil	GEC	Electrification of Belo Horizonte Railways: a) Technical Consultancy b) Staff Training
Canada	Daniel Arbour & Associates	Transport Advice
Canada	Hawker Siddley Limited	Assistance with rolling stock design
Costa Rica	Ministry of Overseas Devel.	Rail Transportation Study for Banana Industry
Guinea (W. Africa)	Nifergui-Nimba	Railway facilities for iron ore transport
Hong Kong	Hong Kong Government	Traffic Assessment feasibility study on Kowloon-Canton Electrification
Isle of Man	Isle of Man Government	Financial appraisal of Tramway museum services
Iraq	ICL Overseas	Advice on computer systems
Jamaica	Jamaican Railway Corporation	Civil Engineering advice
Kuwait	Team Consultants: Cairo	Kuwait-Shuaiba Port Study
Liberia	LAMCO	Rule book revision
Netherlands	NVI	EEC Freight forecasting study
N. Ireland	N. Ireland Railways	N.I. Signalling/Design studies
Pakistan	PRACS	Advice on stores
Spain	Renfe	Planning phase for introduction of TOPS on Renfe operation
Taiwan	GEC Transportation	Technical assistance to GEC
Taiwan	Balfour Beatty	Technical assistance to BB
USA	Chessie	Preliminary Feasibility Study: Management Information Systems for Track Maintenance

PROJECTS COMPLETED 1976

Country	Client	Project Description
Australia	Transport Commission of NSW	Productivity and cost control review of workshops with some training content
Brazil	EPC Limited	Electrification advice
Brazil	British Electricity Int. Ltd.	Training course for SEMIG engineer
Canada	Transport Canada	Canadian coach design study
Canada	Transport Canada	Passenger planning study of relationship between Govt. and railroad
Iraq	Wimpey International	Tender evaluations for signalling

County	Client	Project Description
Libya	Libyan Government	2nd opinion of proposals by other consultants
Liberia	LAMCO	Tokadeh station design and resignalling
Liberia	LAMCO	Train performance calculations
Madagascar	Booker McConnell	Sugar estates: railway study
Malaysia	MINCO	Railway bridge study
N. Ireland	N. Ireland Railways	Aid with EEC regulations
Nigeria	DGI	Railway staff training
Sri Lanka	Asian Development Bank	Study of the potentiality of improving railway
Swaziland	Swaziland Railways	Operating Study
Turkey	ELMS	Points & Crossings study
Thailand	BCEOM (Paris)	Transport planning study
USA	AMSTED	Bogie dynamic evaluation
USA	Turpin Industries	Los Angeles locomotive simulator
Venezuela	AVRAIL	Preparation of proposal for Venezuela Railway Project

THE TRANSPO GROUP

23 148th Ave SE, Suite 3, Bellvue, Wash 98007, USA

Principal Affiliate: James W. Macisaac

PROJECTS
Seattle transit operations plan for Municipal of Metropolitan Seattle; plan for future development of city transport for Nairobi City Council, Kenya.

TRANSPORT MANAGEMENT SERVICES LTD

Stratton House, Piccadilly, London W1X 6DD, England

Telephone: (01) 629 8886

Chief Executive: E. W. A. Butcher

PROJECTS
Plan for future development of city transport for Nairobi City Council, Kenya.

TRANSPORTATION DEVELOPMENT ASSOCIATES INC

316 Second Ave South Seattle, Wash 98104, USA

Telephone: 206/682 4750

PROJECTS
Long range transit plan for Seattle; transportation improvement programme for City of Boulder, Colo.

TUDOR ENGINEERING CO

149 New Montgomerey St, San Francisco, Cal 94105, USA

Telephone: (415) 982 8338

President: Louis W. Riggs

PROJECTS
Rapid transit system ($1 100 million) for MARTA; rapid transit system planning for Metro de Caracas, Venezuela ($1 000 million).

TREVOR CROCKER & PARTNERS

Drive House, 323/339 London Road, Mitchum, Surrey. CR4 4BE, England

Telephone: (01) 640 1981
Telex: 942153 Expert G

CAPABILITIES
Trevor Crocker & Partners carry out feasibility and economic studies for new railway facilities, transportation and traffic studies, route location studies, bridges, railways, workshops and ancillary facilities, preparation of specifications and tender documents, supervision of construction.

PROJECTS
Australia
Tom Price-Paraburdoo Railway
Hamersley Railway

Iraq
Baghdad-Erbil-Mosul High-Speed Railway
Assessment of alternative sleeper designs

UK
Feasibility studies for British Rail on Reconstruction of Liverpool Street Station
Reconstruction of London Bridge Station
Gatwick Airport Station
Railway Workshops
15 Rail over Motorway bridges
Bridgeworks for London-Bedford Electrification
40 Underline and Overline bridges.

URS/MADIGAN-PRAEGER INC

150 East 2nd St, New York, NY 10017, USA

Telephone: (212) 953 8600

President: Charles D. Morrissey

PROJECTS
Rail transit design for Washington Metropolitan Area Transit Authority (WMATA).

UNIMARK INTERNATIONAL CORP

2 North Riverside Plaza, Chicago, Ill 60606, USA

Telephone: (312) 782 5850

General Manager: Anthony Spadaro

PROJECTS
Northeast Corridor rail improvement programme in a joint venture with De Leuw Cather/Parsons for the Federal Railroad Administration.

URBAN ENGINEERS INC

19th St and Delancey Place, Philadelphia, Pa 19103, USA

Telephone: (215) 546 3222

Vice-President: K. Yervant Terzian

PROJECTS
Surface section, light rail transit line ($12 million) for Niagara Frontier Transportation Authority; airport high speed rail line ($70 million) for the City of Philadelphia.

URBITRAN ADDOSIATES

101 Park Ave, New York, NY 10017, USA

Telephone: (212) 689 6487

Partner: Dr. Edmund J. Cantilli

PROJECTS
Evaluation of automated guideway transit alternative analyses ($83 000) for UMTA.

VTN CONSOLIDATED INC

2301 Campus Drive, Irvine, Cal 92713, USA

Telephone: (714) 833 2450

Direction Transportation: J. Peter Cunliffe

PROJECTS
Master plan including all transportation modes for the Port of Los Angeles.

ALAN M. VOORHEES & ASSOCIATES INC

7798 Old Springhouse Rd, McLean, Va 22101, USA

Telephone: (703) 893 4310

Senior Vice-President: Thomas B. Deen

PROJECTS
Future transit requirements study for UMTA ($202 000).

WALLACE, McHARG, ROBERTS AND TODD

1737 Chestnut St, Philadelphia, Pa 19103, USA

Telephone: (215) 564-2611

Partner: David A. Wallace

PROJECTS
Baltimore Metro Phase II transportation plan and systemwide environmental impact and route selection studies ($1.4 million) for the Washington Metropolitan Area Transit Authority.

HARRY WEESE & ASSOCIATES

600 Fifth St, NW Washington, DC 20001, USA

Telephone: (202) 637 1761

Senior Vice-President: Stanley Allan

PROJECTS
Architectural studies for 100 mile, 86 station rail system for Washington Metro ($5 000 million); 16 mile, 20 station all aerial system plus two additional 16 mile lines for Metropolitan Dade County ($600 million).

WESTENHOFF AND NOVICK
(Division of Envirodyne Engineers)

222 West Adams St, Chicago, Ill 60606, USA

Vice-President: Charles F. May

Telephone: (312) 263 0114

PROJECTS
Supervising consulting engineers for Chicago Urban Transportation District.

RAILWAY SYSTEMS

AFGHANISTAN
AFGHANISTAN RAILWAYS

Proposed gauge: 1.435 m
Proposed route length: 1 815 km

The Afghanistan Government approved plans drawn up by Sofrerail for a 1 815 km network to be constructed during the seventh Afghanistan national plan (1976-80). A feasibility study designed to bring Afghanistan into the railway age was completed in August 1977 by the French company Sofrerail. Rail development is listed as one of the most important ventures in the seven-year economic and social development plan which started last year but doubts have already been expressed about the country's ability to generate sufficient traffic to keep a rail system going. Total cost will be in the region of $US2 000 million. Similar to the proposals prepared by Indian consultants the network, 1.435 m gauge, will link the Afghan capital Kabul with the cities of Kandahar and Herat. Other links will be with Iran at Islam Qala in the northwest, at Tarakun in the southwest, and with Pakistan at Chaman in the southeast. From Islam Qala an Iranian State Railways' line will run to Mashhad (Teheran), giving access via Tabriz or Djulfa to Western Europe. The link through Tarakun will join the planned Kerman-Zahedan line and give access to the Iranian port of Bandar Abbas, while the Pakistan link will allow traffic to reach the Arabian Sea at Karachi.

About 75% of the Afghan network will be laid out with a maximum gradient of 1.0 per cent and minimum curve radius of 2 000 m. The remaining 25 per cent will have gradients up to 1.5 per cent allowing speeds of 100 km/h. Initially maximum speed will be 160 km/h, but the proposals envisage 200 km/h running with high-speed lightweight trainsets at a later stage. Track will be continuously-welded UIC 45 kg/m rail laid on tied-block sleepers. Signalling installations will be backed by a train radio system.

At Kandahar there will be a traffic control centre, together with a motive power depot, workshop facilities and marshalling yard. Staff requirements were for 2 400 in 1975, rising to 3 300 with eventual expansion of the network. Motive power will be provided initially by 40 diesel locomotives of 2 400 hp with provision for an additional 65 units. Because of rarified atmosphere at high altitudes, power output losses of up to 22.5 per cent are expected.

Finance for the network is being provided by Iran. Initial forecasts are for 1 300 million passenger-km and 1 300 million tonne-km by 1985. Of major significance is the massive iron ore deposit at Hajigak in the Hindu-Kouch mountain range; ore will be transported by cableway from the deposit to a railhead 100 km away, and thence to steelworks in Iran.

ALBANIA
ALBANIAN STATE RAILWAYS
Hekurudhae Shqiperisë, Tirana

Gauge: 1.435 m
Route length: 292 km

The railways of Albania have no physical connection with the European railway network—and for many years will remain isolated from the major railways of the continent. "Hekurudhae ë Shqiperisë"—Albanian Railways—have now 292 route-km of standard gauge single track lines, fanning out from the port of Durrës (Durazzo) to the country's capital of Tirana, the important city of Elbasan and newly-built industrial centres. Motive power consists mainly of diesel-electric locomotives from CKD Praha, but some Polish steam locomotives remain in service.

After completion of the present Sixth Five-Year National Plan in 1980, railway traffic in Albania should be about 62 per cent above the present level, Prime Minister Mehmet Shehu told the 7th Party Congress meeting in Tirana early in 1977. Railway share of total freight transport in Albania will then be about 38 per cent, Congress was told. The first common carrier railway line, opened to traffic on 7 November 1947, was between the Adriatic port of Durrës (Durazzo) and Pequin, 27 miles (44 km) long. This was extended from Pequin to Elbasan in 1950 and subsequently a number of branch lines have been built:—Kashar—Yzberisht; Paper—Cerrik; a link line from Elbasan to the "Nako Spiro" timber combine; Elbasan—Kraste. The Tirana-Durres line, on which work started in 1948, was opened on 23 February 1949.

In 1963 the line from Vorë to Lac was completed and opened to traffic; and on 12 October 1968 a ceremony was held to celebrate the opening of the line from Rrogozhine to Fier, 34 miles (54 km) long.

NEW LINES
A new rail link between Elbasan and Prenjas was completed late in 1973 and went into operation in March 1974.

Infrastructure and track laying on a new 29.1-km line from Fier to Ballsh were completed early in January 1975—bringing the total route length of Albanian State Railways (Hekurudhae e Sqiperise) to about 292 km.

A new direct connection between the ASR system and Yugoslavia's Belgrade—Bar line is now under consideration. Main Albanian interest would be in faster freight shipments through the Adriatic port of Bar.

Work was put in hand during 1976 on an extension of the Durres—Elbasan—Librazhd line to provide an outlet for ore deposits located near Lake Pogradec.

Construction of the long projected—and once started—line between Fier and Vlonë has been included in the present Five-Year Plan.

TRACK
Most lines are laid with rails weighing 86.7 lb per yd (43 kg/m) imported from Czechoslovakia. Maximum axle load is 21 tonnes.

There are six tunnels varying in length from 761 ft (232 m) to 2 460 ft (750 m); and ten concrete bridges from 200 ft (60 m) to 720 ft (220 m).

LOCOMOTIVES AND ROLLING STOCK
Albania has no railway industry, therefore all equipment, especially rolling stock and motive power, must be imported. A first batch of steam locomotives came from Chrzanow works in Poland, those engines were similar to PKP's Tkt-48 class standard general purpose superheated 1D1 (2-8-2) tank type. Some secondhand engines seem to have found their way from Poland to Albania too. In 1958, Albanian Railways followed the world-wide trend to dieselisation and bought their first two diesel-mechanical class BN 150 shunting locomotives from CKD Praha, followed by two more of the same type and two 750 hp BoBo dieselectric road locomotives of CSD's T 435.0 class in the next year. Two other T 435.0 went to Albania in 1961 and three of the same class in 1962. Four more dieselelectrics of the slightly heavier T 458.1 class were delivered in 1967, DVM-2 BoBo diesel-electric locomotive from MÁVAG Budapest had no followers.

Passenger cars are mostly two-axled from the railways of East Germany, Hungary and Czechoslovakia, but an increasing number of bogie coaches are being put into service. Freight cars generally are older 15-tonne 2-axle types; the latest ar modern bogie cars with a capacity of 45 tonnes, built in Czechoslovakia, Hungary, and China.

TRAFFIC
Freight traffic is mainly bulk transport with nickel and chrome ore, asphalt, wood coal and cement being the main commodities. Passenger traffic shows the same rising trend as freight traffic: The mere 30 million passenger-km in 1950 went up to 110 millions in 1964, whereas the 8.5 million km-tonnes in 1950 augmented to 90 million in 1964. Train-km in the same years were 0.7 million and 2.9 millions. Since 1964 no more traffic details have been released, but under the general economic condition of the country the growth must have continued same as before.

HISTORY
The first lines built in Albania were the 168 km 600 mm and 336 km 700 mm gauge military lines constructed by Austrian army engineers in the final stage of World War I. These were, however, completely destroyed by the retreating Austrian troops in 1918. It was a 12-km industrial railway of 950 mm gauge, built around 1930 by an Italian firm exploiting the asphalt mines of Selenicë and Mavrovë near the port of Vlorë (Valona), which formed the country's first lasting railway.

During the Italian occupation of Albania the first plans for a public railway from Durrës to Tirana were drawn up and some minor construction work carried out. But full construction was not completed until after World War II when the new Communist Party government of Albania undertook a vast industrialisation programme, calling for extensive railway building. The first section of Albanian Railways from Durrës to Peqin (41 km) was opened on 7 November 1946 and this line was extended 30 km to Elbasan on 22 December 1950. In the meantime, another line from Durrës to Tirane, 38 km long, was completed on 23 February 1949. Building then continued at a much slower pace. In 1964 a 29 km spur from Vorë on the Tirana line to the superphosphate fertiliser plant at Laç was opened for traffic and one year later an industrial spur line east of Elbasan was completed.

A 54 km line from Rrogozhina on the Elbasan branch to a second fertiliser factory at Fier was completed in 1969.

INDUSTRIAL LINE
There is a short length of narrow gauge industrial line which is not operated by the Albanian State Railways. This 950 mm gauge runs from Vlonë, on the Adriatic, 5 miles (8 km) to the bitumen mine at Selenicë with a 2.5 mile (4 km) branch to Mavrove.

ALGERIA
ALGERIAN NATIONAL RAILWAYS
Société Nationale des Transports Ferroviaires (SNTF) 21-23 boulevard Mohamed V, Algiers

Director General: Benmehdjouba Saddek
Commercial Director: Bouifrou Tahar
Transport Director: Rabhi Rachid
Director of Technical/Economic Studies and Planning: Budin Karim
Director of Personnel and General Administration: Merouani Ahmed
Director of Material: Arris Mustapha
Director of General Installations: Touri Ali
Director of Equipment: Hadji Abdenour
Director of Finances: Smala Mohamed

Gauge: 1.435 m; Cape; 1.00 m
Route length: 3 890 km

Algerian National Railways (SNTF) planned for freight and passenger traffic on its 3 942 km *(2 450-mile)* network to more than double during the period of the country's second four-year plan (1973-77). The continued industrial expansion provided for by the plan led the SNTF to draw up a programme of investments which were to absorb an increase in passenger traffic from 944 million passenger-km in 1973 to 2 540 million passenger-km in 1977, and a corresponding increase in freight from 670 million tonnes to 210 million tonnes. The major flows are iron ores from Ouenza and phosphates from Djebel Onk.

Since Algeria gained independence in 1962, the economic importance of the railways has gradually increased in accordance with the country's industrialisation programme. Whereas then the main freight flows were still raw materials and agricultural produce for export, the network is now equally important for developing industries in the large industrial zones at Annaba, Skikda, Arzew and Algiers, as well as for isolated industrial sites throughout the country, many of which were provided with new rail links during the first Four-Year Development Plan (1969-73).

TRAFFIC
After a climb from 1962 to 1968, general traffic (other than minerals and phosphate) increased sharply in 1971 and showed a further rise in tonnage in 1972. Mineral and phosphate traffic—at 3 164 401 tons in 1971—rose in 1972 to a record 3 576 220 tons. Under the Four-Year Plan, the ton/km figure for goods other than minerals and phosphate rose from 709 million to 1 730 million by 1976 but was far short of the original plan forecast figure of 2 185 million expected by the end of 1977. Ton/km of phosphates and iron ore is likely to be more than double the 1972 figure.

In 1963, SNTF carried 3 489 073 passengers (421 million passenger/km). By 1971 the figure had reached 7 893 135 (1 097 passenger/km). There was a slight fall in 1972. Though the total number of passengers fell, revenues from passenger fares showed a steep increase, from about 58 million dinars (1971) to more than 80 million. In 1976, SNTF carried 10 220 000 passengers and recorded 1 370 000 passenger km.

	1975	1976
Total freight tonne-km	1 740 000 000	1 730 000 000
Total freight tonnage	717 000 000	640 000 000
Total passenger-km	1 130 000 000	1 370 000 000
Total passenger journeys	869 000 000	1 022 000 000

FINANCIAL	1975	1976
	(Dinar 'millions)	
Revenues	306	375

DEVELOPMENTS
A new development programme, to cost 1 800 million Algerian Dinars was completed in 1977. Main projects included:
—construction of a new standard-gauge line between Tebessa, Ain-Beida and Ouled-Rhamoun;
—studies for a new line running from Djebel Onk through Touggourt to Bechar Abadla;
—studies for a line running from Tebessa via Ain-Oussera to Sidi-Bel Abbes;
—double tracking of the mineral lines between El-Ghourzi and El Kroubs and from Ramdane Djamel to Constantine;
—double-tracking from Reghaia to Thenia (27 km) and introduction of automatic block with colour-light signalling on the Algiers suburban line from El Harrach to Thenia.
In August 1976, SNTF called for pre-qualification bids for doubling the line between Constantine and Ramdane Djamal and between El Gourzi and El Kroub.
During 1975, the Biskra—Touggourt line was converted to standard gauge and a new passenger service is now running.

ELECTRIFICATION
Total electrified route length on December 31, 1976: 299 km.
System of electrification: 3 000V.

MOTIVE POWER AND ROLLING STOCK
SNTF has already made considerable progress in replacing old locomotives and rolling stock in recent years. Purchases have included 29 diesel-electric locomotives of 3 300 hp (type GT 26 CW) bought from General Motors in 1971; and 32 3 000V electric locomotives, each with an output of 2 800 hp, from the LEW plant, Hennigsdorf (GDR), LEW also supplied 20 diesel-hydraulic shunters, 10 in 1971 and 10 in 1972.

Sliding-top cereal wagon built by Arbel: four axles; 14.96 m long over buffers; tare weight 23.5 tonnes.

Diesel mechanical railcar; eight axles; 46.99 m long overall; 74.2 tonnes; builder Fiat

Stainless-steel passenger coach built by Francorail: 24.5 m long over buffers; maximum speed 140 km/h

Passenger stock purchases have included 33 Fiat railcars. And an order for 1 000 freight wagons of various types was placed with the Algerian company SN Metal.

SNTF has also been increasing its fleet of flat wagons—100 of 50-ton capacity were ordered from ANF (France) in 1969. And in 1972, 100 flat wagons were fitted with exchangeable bogies at SN Metal, for SNTF.

Purchases under the 1973/77 plan included:
—40 diesel-electric locomotives of 1 500 hp
—20 straight electric locomotives of 2 000 kW output
—160 passenger coaches for long-distance transport

In addition, the plan provides for purchases of materials handling equipment and new machine tools for SNTF workshops.

NEW ORDERS

In 1975 the MTE-Francorail group of French companies won a contract for delivery of 165 passenger coaches and 34 baggage cars to SNTF. Deliveries were completed in 1976 at a cost of FFrs 205 million. Meanwhile, the railway awaits supply of 450 wagons, of which 100 are tank wagons, 70 are for grain transport, 90 are for cable-drum transport, 40 are for coke and 30 for sugar.

TRACK

The total length of track laid with welded rail is 921 miles *(1 482 km)*—standard gauge 788 miles *(1 269 km)* and narrow gauge 132 miles *(212 km)*.

Rail used is generally Type S33 weighing 92.8 lb per yard *(46 kg/m)* in 50 ft *(18 m)* bars, welded in depot into *72 m (4× 18 m)* lengths. These are laid on metal sleepers and secured by standard clips and bolts.

A certain amount of in situ welding has been done to provide long-welded rail—up to 1 500 m in tunnel and 1 200 m in open track.

DIESEL LOCOMOTIVES

Class	Axle Arrange-ment	Trans-mission	Rated Power hp	Max kg	Tractive Effort Continuous at kg	km/h	Max Speed km/h	Wheel Dia. mm	Axle Load Tons	Total Weight Tons	Length mm	No. Built	Year first Built	Builders: Mechanical Parts	Engine	Transmission
Standard Gauge:																
040DA	A1AA1A	Elec.	1 520	24 700	19 414	16.9	96	1 066	21.3	124.6	17 700	15	1946	Baldwin	Baldwin	Westinghouse
040DB	A1AA1A	Elec.	1 520	25 200	14 060	23.3	130	1 066	21.3	124.6	17 700	25	1947	Baldwin	Baldwin	Westinghouse
040DC	A1AA1A	Elec.	1014	22 800	14 700	15.2	85	1 066	17.4	103.1	16 175	20	1948	Baldwin	Baldwin	Westinghouse
040DD	A1AA1A	Elec.	1 520	21 400	17 000	20.0	120	1 016	19.5	110.7	16 896	5	1950	Alco	Alco	GE
040DG	A1AA1A	Elec.	1 622	21 500			120	1 016	19.8	113.8	17 050	5	1951	Alco	Alco	GE
060DB	CoCo	Elec.	1 315	16 800	12 600	15.0	120	950	14.5	87.0	17 200	10	1956	Schneider	Baldwin	Schneider
060DC	CoCo	Elec.	1 840	30 000	15 500		120	1 050	18.9	113.4	19 814	37	1957	Alsthom	SACM	Alsthom
060DD	CoCo	Elec.	3 300		26 020	26.6	124	1 016	20.0	120.0	20 745	29	1971	GM	GM	GM
060DF	CoCo	Elec.	3 300		26 020	26.6	124	1 016	20.0	120.0	20 745	25	1973	GM	GM	GM
40EA	B	Mech.	40				12	900	5.3	10.6	5 610	3	1955	Moyse	Renault	
80DA	B	Mech.	80				17	950	10.4	20.8	6 770	23	1955	Moyse	Renault	
150DEA	B	Elec.	150				25	950	15.9	31.8	6 770	5	1952	Moyse	Ricardo	
150DEB	B	Elec.	150				60	1 050	16.9	33.8	8 900	8	1956	Decauville	Poyaud	Oerlikon
200DA	C	Mech.	200				29	1 016	11.0	32.5	7 930	14	1948	Hunslet	Gardner	
200DB	B	Mech.	200				29	1 050	16.0	32.0	8 180	5	1955	Billard	Willème	
200DC	B	Mech.	200				29	1 050	16.0	32.0	8 170	1	1957	Billard	Willème	
400DA	B	Hydr.	400				55	1 050	17.3	34.6	9 360	16	1956	ANF	Saurer	Voith
400DB	B	Hydr.	400				55	1 050	18.4	36.7	9 360	8	1960	Billard	Saurer	Voith
400DC	B	Hydr.	400				50	1 050	17.3	34.6	9 360	4	1962	DeDietrich	Saurer	Voith
600DA	D	Hydr.	600				60	1 100	15.4	61.4	10 920	10	1971	LEW	LEW	LEW
600DB	D	Hydr.	600				60	1 100	15.4	61.4	10 920	10	1972	LEW	LEW	LEW
1 055 mm Gauge																
060YDA	CoCo	Elec.	960		14 800	20.0	85	914	12.0	72.0	18 550	10	1953	DeDietrich	Sulzer	Oerlikon
060YDB	BoBoBo	Elec.	920	16 000	9 200	18.0	80	920	10.0	59.0	13 360	10	1958	Alsthom	SACM	Alsthom
060YDC	BoBoBo	Elec.	935	18 500	10 000	19.0	80	920	12.0	72.0	14 396	6	1961	Alsthom	SACM	Alsthom
Y80DA	B	Mech.	80				17	950	10.1	20.2	7 060	2	1959	Moyse	Berliet	
Y150DA	C	Hydr.	150		6 160	4.8	22	860	9.9	29.6	7 340	10	1951	LLD	Willème	
Y200DA	B	Mech.	200				29	1 050	12.0	24.0	8 070	1	1957	Billard	Willème	
1 000 mm Gauge																
XZZDN	BoBo	Elec.	600				90	860	9.6	38.4	16 200	5	1938	DeDietrich	Saurer	Oerlikon
X200DA	B	Mech.	200				29	1 050	12.0	24.0	8 290	4	1957	Billard	Willème	

ELECTRIC LOCOMOTIVES

Class	Axle Arrange-ment	Line Current kV Type	Rated Power hp	Max kg	Tractive Effort Continuous at kg	km/h	Max Speed km/h	Wheel Dia. mm	Weight tonnes	Length mm	No. Built	First Built	Builders Mechanical Parts	Electrical Equipment
6BE	CoCo	3 dc	3 120		22 500	37.5	80	1 250	134.1	18 922	8	1958	Alsthom	Alsthom
6CE	CoCo	3 dc	2 700		24 600	30.0	80	1 350	130.0	18 640	32	1972	LEW	Skoda

ANGOLA
BENGUELA RAILWAY
Caminho de Ferro de Benguela, CP 32, Lobito

Gauge:1.067 m
Route length: 1 304 km

OFFICERS
General Manager: Eng. L. Lamas de Oliveira
Deputy General Manager: Eng. F. Melo Sampaio
Assistant General Manager: Dr. F. Fuso
Personnel Manager: J. Rocha
Mechanical Engineering Manager: Position vacant at present
Operations Manager: Dr. J. Teixeira de Sousa
Track and Civil Engineering Manager: Eng. Tec. M. Monteiro
Administrative Manager: Dr. G. Pratas
Commercial Manager: J. Avelar
Planning and Organisation Manager: A. Guedes

Due to continued hostilities in Angola, numerous railway services have been severely disrupted throughout 1976/77, making operating details and development news difficult to accumulate. The Benguela Railway virtually ceased operations during 1977 while the 968 km Caminho de Ferro de Moçâmedes in the south suspended all services between Entroncamento (east of Sade Bandeira) and Serpa Pinto by mid-77 due to damage to track and bridges on the line.
The Benguela Railway, 810 miles *(1 304 km)* route length of 3 ft 6 in *(1.067 m)* gauge, serves an extensive area of the Angola territory and connects the port of Lobito with Zaire and Zambia.
The traffic carried is mainly of minerals and ores from Zaire and Zambia, for shipping from Lobito. In the upward direction, the traffic consists essentially of machinery, petrol and oils, coal, coke and general merchandise.
Construction of an alternative alignment known as the "Cubal Variant" has been completed. 101 miles *(163 km)* long, it cost approximately £12.5 million including the purchase of new diesel locomotives. Track was laid with BS 90A flat bottom rail welded in 45 metre lengths. The Variant reduces the distance between Lobito and Cubal by 22 miles *(35 km)* on a minimum radius of curvature of 1 017 ft *(310 m)* with gradients not exceeding 1.25 per cent.

FINANCIAL RESULTS	1970	1971	1972	1973	1974
		(Thousands of Escudos)			
Revenue	802 056	869 026	873 080	1 211 862	1 273 361
Expenses	640 389	682 988	612 352	683 120	968 753
Operating ratio (%)	79.8	78.6	70.1	—	—

OPERATIONS		1971	1972	1973	1974
Freight tonne-kms	(000's)	1 896 000	1 772 805	2 309 209	2 427 738
Total tonnes carried	(000's)	2 061	1 900.6	2 566.7	2 383.7
Tonnes originating	(000's)	—	—	—	—
Tonnes in transit	(000's)	—	—	—	—
Passenger kms	(000's)	116 590	—	152 047.8	205 721
Total passengers carried	(000's)	1 214	1 412.6	1 587.7	1 983

NEW LINE
Construction of an alternative alignment known as the Cubal Variant was completed in 1974 at a cost of 907 million Escudos (approximately £12.5 million including the cost of locomotives). Track was laid with BS 90A flat bottom rail welded in 45-m lengths. The variant reduces the distance between Lobito and Cubal by 35 km and has a minimum radius of 310 m and gradients of less than 1.25 per cent.

MOTIVE POWER
The railway took delivery at the end of January 1975 of 12 type U20C diesel-electric locomotives from US General Electric. These will enable complete dieselisation of the line between Lobito and Silva Porto. Other locomotives in operation include 10 type General Electric U 20 C diesel-electric locomotives; two Andrew Barclay diesel-hydraulic locomotives powered by Paxman 8RPHXL engines and four North British diesel-hydraulic locomotives.

ARGENTINA
ARGENTINE RAILWAYS
Ferrocarriles Argentinos EFA Avienda Ramos, Meijia 1302, Buenos Aires

Gauges: 1.00; 1.435; 1.676 m
Route Length: 39 787 km

President: Gral. de Brigada (R.E.) D. Tomás J. Caballero
General Co-ordinator: Alberto B. Abadia
Director of Traffic: Ing. Emilio B. Nastri
Commercial Director (freight): Ing. Cayetano Marletta Rainieri
Inspector General: Ing. Angel Ceci
Director of Economic Studies: Ctdor. Horacio M. Allemand
Financial Director: Ctdor. Carlos F. Martin
Mechanical Director: Ing. Jorge A. Bilotti
Director, Way and Works: Ing Victor Gilardoni
Director, Planning: Ing. Alfredo Fernández
Director, Special Studies: Ing. Antonio P. Estévez
Chief of Public Relations: Mayor (R.E.) D. Jorge A.V. Mastropietro
Regional Directors:
F.C. Gral. Roca: Ing. Roberto Pedernera
F.C. Gral. Belgrano: Ing. Osvaldo Garau
F.C. Gral. Urquiza: Ing. Angel S. Butti
F.C. Gral. San Martin: Ing. Luis Donzelli
F.C. Gral. Mitre: Sr. Natalio D. Viola
F.C. D.F. Sarmiento: Ing. Hugo Berro

Regions	Gauge (metres)	Length of lines In service 1973	In service 1975
Roca	1.676	8,159	8,159
	0.750	403	403
		8,562	8,562
Mitre	1.676	6,241	6,174
San Martin	1.676	4,625	4,625
Sarmiento	1.676	3,830	3,830
Urquiza	1.435	3,086	3,086
Belgrano	1.000	13,461	13,461
Total Empresa		39,805	39,738

A new military administration took over control of FA in April 1976. During the first six months of operations (April-September 1976) the railway's fortunes—which had fallen to a very low level in 1975—improved substantially.

FREIGHT TRAFFIC
Between April and September 1976 FA transported 11 269 900 tonnes of freight—an improvement of 828 400 tonnes over the equivalent period of 1975. The railway's share of national grain shipments alone increased from 42.6% to 53.6%, up 673 500 tonnes.

PASSENGER TRAFFIC
During the April-September 1976 period the railway carried 273 277 000 passengers—an increase of 11 358 000 journeys.

	1974	1975
Total freight tonne-km	12 357 288 000	10 676 190 000
Total freight tonnage	19 122 200	16 337 700
Total passenger-km	14 103 176 000	14 366 749 000
Total passengers carried	422 836 000	436 459 000

New locomotives for South American railways at the Fiat Concord Argentina plant in Córdoba; the Fiat 1 500-hp unit at left is awaiting delivery to FA; the 2 000-hp unit at right is destined for Bolivia.

FINANCES

At his first press conference in June 1976 the new Comptroller of FA said that the present railway financial loss was totalling about $US 2 million daily. He confirmed that over half of the total diesel-electric locomotive fleet was at present out of service awaiting the arrival of spare parts. But he added that a number of locomotives were working services which were uneconomical and indicated that these might soon be cancelled so that locomotives could be transferred to more important lines.

TRACK RENEWAL

Most urgent of the problems facing new FA administrators is track renewal. Plans for upgrading and renewing 4 109 km of track were, in fact, unveiled in 1974, but were inevitably delayed following FA's worsening operating situation. Now, it seems, the plans may soon be put in hand.

The project is scheduled for completion by 1978/79 at a cost of $Arg 2 859 million. A total of 1 912 km will be completely renewed and 2 197 km will be upgraded. In addition, track improvements are to be carried out over 1 860 km during the next three years.

During the first six months of 1976 90 km of track was completely renewed and 274 km fully repaired.

The new plan is designed to replace the track improvement programme which formed a major part of the non-starting 1971-75 Medium Term Plan. Track projects under that plan were to have included complete reconstruction of 3 050 km of track and major improvement of 3 800 km. It is now expected that the newly-announced 1974-75 project will form the first stage of a similar track programme designed to create a "super-network" of mainlines. By 1980 it is hoped that maximum train speeds over many of FA's 1.676-m gauge lines will be increased to 160 km/h.

1. Renewal of track over 1 912 km using 198,800 tons of new rail, 39 500 tons of rail joints and accessories, 5.3 million tons of new ballast, and 308 300 tons of new wooden sleepers. Cost of track renewals will work out at around $Arg 1 941 million.

2. Track upgrading over 2 197 km using 66,900 tons of new rail, 13,190 tons of rail joints and accessories, 3.3 million tons of new ballast, and 168 200 tons of new wooden sleepers.

3. Simultaneously, track improvements are to be undertaken over 1 860 km of track involving installation of new sleepers, rail spikes and ballast. Cost of this work is estimated at $Arg 117.7 million. Under the programme FA is to purchase 175 000 new wooden sleepers, 1.6 million new rail spikes, and 673,000 tons of ballast. Four Matisa tampers will be used during improvement works.

FA has already placed orders with the Argentine company Somisa for a total of 265 700 tons of rails. No suppliers have yet been named for rail joints or accessories. Targets for 1980 are: 5 299 km (13 per cent) of very good track; 18 288 km (44 per cent) good; 14 736 km (35 per cent) adequate; and 3 369 km (8 per cent) poor. By the end of the plan period, trains will be able to operate over some sections of track at maximum speeds of: 160 km/h over 1.676-m gauge; 150 km/h over 1.435-m gauge; and 110 km/h over 1-m gauge.

ELECTRIFICATION

The total electrified route at the end of 1975 was 259 km, out of a total route length of 39 782 km. Lines now under electrification include the 8-km urban line of the Urquiza. The Roca suburban system totalling 125 route km is planned but has already been subjected to repeated postponements.

MOTIVE POWER

During April-September 1976, FA took delivery of five 1 500 hp General Motors locomotives built under licence in Argentina for the Belgrano Railroad.

ROLLING STOCK

Between April and September 1976, the railway placed 500 new hopper wagons in operation: 23 broad-gauge and 50 standard-gauge box-hopper wagons; 334 broad-gauge and 38 narrow-gauge ballast hoppers; 5 broad-gauge grain hoppers.

Locomotives in service	Line haul	Shunting (Switching)
Number of locomotives in steam	401	89
Number of locomotives in electric	—	6
Number of locomotives in diesel-electric	663	35
Number of locomotives in diesel-hydraulic	—	1
Number of locomotives in diesel-mechanical	—	10
Number of railcars, electric	440	
Number of railcars, diesel	131	
Number of trailer cars, electric	45	
Number of trailer cars, diesel	157	
Number of passenger train coaches	2 841	
Number of freight train wagons	43 016	
Number of containers for door-to-door service	552	

Cereal wagon designed to transport 65 tons.

Open top ballast hopper wagon built for FA by Bautista Buriasco e Hijos.

Fiat-type 7164 diesel-electric in FA livery.

New FA baggage/mail vans built by Fiat Concord.

Fiat diesel railcars.

AUSTRALIA

AUSTRALIAN NATIONAL RAILWAYS
Norwich Centre, 55 King William Road, North Adelaide, South Australia 5006

Telex: 31109
Telephone: 62 3621
Telegrams: AUSrail Melbourne

Gauge: 1.435 m; 1.067 m
Route length: 2 215 km; 1 380 km (SAR route-km is not included)

HEAD OFFICE, ADELAIDE
Chairman: K. A. Smith O.B.E.
Acting General Manager: V. H. Dyason M.B.E.
Assistant General Manager, Admin and Operations: A. Maddock
Assistant General Manager, Engineering and Planning: Dr. D. G. Williams
Executive Officer: J. D. Harris
Public Relations Officer: N. F. Travers
Industrial Officer: A. E. Edwards
Acting Comptroller: B. N. Walkom

COMERCIAL DIVISION, ADELAIDE
Acting Commercial Manager: R. D. Wickstein

OPERATING, PORT AUGUSTA
Mechanical
Chief Mechanical Engineer: J. M. Dudley
Assistant Chief Mechanical Engineer: J. W. Charter

Way and Works
Chief Civil Engineer: J. R. A. Walker
Assistant Chief Civil Engineer: G. Ryan
Acting Assistant Chief Civil Engineer (Construction): D. P. Smith
Senior Engineer (Maintenance): D. R. Green
Design Engineer (Civil): R. J. Dixon

TRAFFIC
Chief Traffic Manager: A. R. Polmear

Computer Information Services Manager: D. Sickles

Stores and Accounts
Stores Controller: H. R. Brown
Accounts and Audit Officer: E. J. R. Woodhams

Australian Capital Territory Railway
Superintendent: C. L. Bartram (Canberra, A.C.T.)

The Australian Government assumed responsibility for the Tasmanian Government Railways and the non-urban sections of the South Australian Railways on July 1, 1975. The non-metropolitan sections of SAR were transferred to the Australian National Railways Commission on March 1, 1978.
The following railways at present form the Commonwealth Railways section of Australian National Railways:
   Trans-Australian Railway (Port Pirie to Kalgoorlie and Port Augusta to Whyalla)
   Stirling North—Marree Railway
   Central Australia Railway (Marree to Alice Springs)
   North Australia Railway (Darwin to Birdum—effective railhead Larrimah)
   Australian Capital Territory Railway (Queanbeyan to Canberra)
   Tasmanian Government Railways
   South Australian Railways

NOTE
By the end of 1977, the ANR had not released the 1976/77 financial year report containing financial details required for this edition of JWR. The lengthy delay in releasing the details has resulted from the pending amalgamation of the South Australian non-metropolitan system and the Tasmanian Government Railways into the ANR system.

FINANCIAL	1975	1976
Total freight tonne-km	7 007 850 438	7 410 138 242
Total freight tonnage	996 003	1 081 336
Total passenger-km	1 312 793 512	1 324 571 481
Total passengers journeys	145 732	135 474

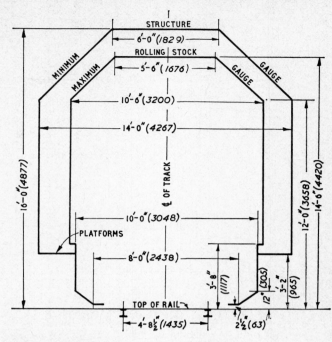

ANR 1.435 m-gauge (the former Commonwealth Railways)

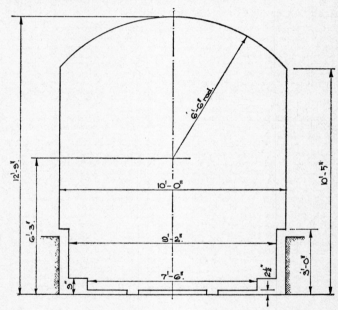

ANR 1.067 m-gauge lines in the Tasmania region (former Tasmanian Government Railways)

ANR has taken delivery of its eighth and final AL class locomotive from Clyde Engineering; the fleet of AL locomotives, each 3 300 hp, are in service on the Trans-Australian and Stirling North-Marree Railways.

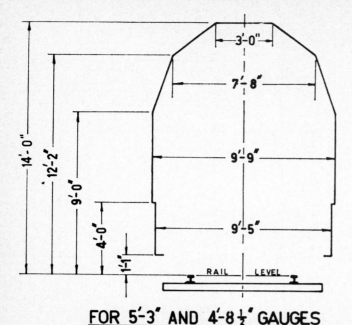

FOR 5'-3" AND 4'-8½" GAUGES

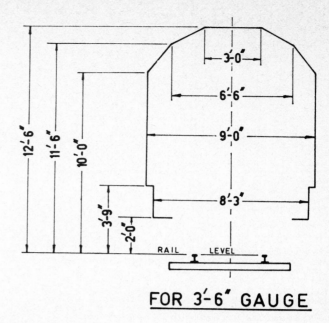

FOR 3'-6" GAUGE

ANR loading gauge for former South Australian Railways 1.6 m and 1.435 m lines (left) and 1.067 m lines (right)

TARCOOLA-ALICE SPRINGS RAILWAY

On April 12, 1975 construction began on the Tarcoola-Alice Springs railway at an estimated cost of $A 145 million. The railway is scheduled for completion by 1981. The railway will be a single track, standard gauge line of 831 km route length to connect Alice Springs to the Australian standard gauge railway network at Tarcoola on the Trans-Australian Railway, 400 km westwards from Port Augusta. It is to replace the existing narrow gauge (1 067 mm) gauge line which links Alice Springs to Marree, 300 km north of Port Augusta. This is a light 'pioneer' railway which can no longer cope with the traffic demands and which, because of its location in the Lake Eyre drainage basin, is prone to frequent flooding and washaway damage.

The new route is approximately 150 km west of the existing narrow gauge line, generally outside or near the edge of the Lake Eyre basin, avoiding many of the streams presently causing trouble and crossing others near their headwaters rather than in their flat lower reaches.

The railway will carry general freight to serve the whole of the Northern Territory. Present inwards traffic is approximately evenly divided between that required in Alice Springs and its surrounding areas and that for onward transit on the long road haul northwards to Darwin. Tourist traffic to the scenic areas of Central Australia forms the bulk of passenger movements. Outwards traffic at present, is mainly livestock. One potential source of bulk traffic lies on the route of the new railway, at Lake Phillipson, about 150 km north of Tarcoola, where a large deposit of steaming coal has been proved and is the subject of a current feasibility study for development.

Principal construction problems on the new railway will be those due to the remoteness and aridity of the area. Except for the opal mining settlement of Coober Pedy (about 40 km off the line) the area between Tarcoola and Alice Springs is occupied only by scattered pastoral properties and there are no towns or centres of habitation. Most of the materials and supplies will have to come thousands of kilometres from the industrial areas in or near the Capital cities of the Australian seaboard. All manpower must be similarly imported, and must have all facilities provided. The country is arid "semi-desert". Although occasional unpredictable and erratic heavy storms cause flooding, surface water is virtually non-existant, and potable water from underground sources is scarce. Shade temperature in mid summer frequently exceeds 50°C.

Design Standard: Ruling gradient is 8°/oo (1 in 125) in both directions, compensated on curves according to the formula C = 14/R where C is compensation in m/20 m and R is radius of curve in metres.

Parabolic vertical curves are inserted where net change of grade exceeds 2°/oo. Rate of change of grade in vertical curves is up to 1°/oo per 20 m on a summit, and 0.5°/oo per 20 m in a sag.

Minimum horizontal curve radius is generally 1 200 m, although two curves are of 1 000 m radius. For small total deflection angles, curves are of 3 000 and 4 000 m radius. A standard 60 m length cubic parabola transition is used for curves of all radii. Half of the 110 curves on the route have deflection angles of 10° or less.

Bridges and structures are being designed for Cooper's E-50 loading. There are no tunnels, and all overhead structures will provide at least 4.25 m clear width to a height of 6 m above rail level. Track centres on running lines will be 5 m and sidings will be 10 m clear of running lines.

Earthwork: The terrain is generally flat, with ill-defined watercourses and drainage lines. Cuttings are relatively few, and earthworks will mainly comprise long and fairly low embankments to provide the necessary headroom for bridges and culverts. Total volume of earthworks for the 831 km route will be approximately 7 000 000 m³.

Water supply bores are being drilled to depths of up to 150 m to provide water for compaction of earthworks. In some areas, water of any quality is difficult to obtain and even in sections where supplies are adequate, salinity is, in some cases, up to twice that of sea water.

Formation width for the single track is 7·5 m to 9 m on embankments (increasing with height), and 9 m minimum in cuttings. Much of the earthfill is from the sandy 'residual soil' which can be subject to wind erosion, and selected stable material has to be won to provide a top layer and protective blanket against deflation.

Bulk earthfill is being compacted to 80 per cent modified A.A.S.H.O. density, with a transition section to 85 per cent, and the top layer of selected material is being compacted to 90 per cent modified A.A.S.H.O. density.

Bridges and culverts: There will be no bridges on the first 160 km of the route northwards from Tarcoola, and a total of 52 bridges on the remainder, aggregating in length some 4 000 m.

Design of bridges is complicated by the complete lack of reliable hydrographic data, the erratic and unpredictable nature of the rainfall, and the fact that most of the streams to be crossed are wide and flat 'braided' steams with multiple channels. Some bridges will be quite short, but the typical ones will be long and comparatively low. Several will be 250 to 300 m in length and only 3 to 4 m high. The biggest bridge will be that over the Finke River, some 400 m long over a 150 m river channel and a 250 m wide flood plain. Most of the bridges will consist of multiple 11 m and 16 m steel girder spans. The two major bridges, over the Finke and Hugh Rivers, will be of longer spans for which design

Year	Km. Line	No. of Passengers	Tonnage of Goods and Livestock	Earnings from Goods and Livestock Traffic	All Other Earnings	Total Earnings
				$	$	$
Trans-Australian Railway						
1963-64	1 784	236 354	496 925	7 092 386	2 864 122	9 956 508
1964-65	1 784	237 637	590 431	8 327 718	3 238 132	11 565 850
1965-66	1 784	233 237	570 990	8 531 971	3 409 780	11 941 751
1966-67	1 784	261 645	560 881	9 063 742	3 759 924	12 823 666
1967-68	1 784	238 046	666 366	10 509 167	3 917 514	14 426 681
1968-69	1 784	195 595	895 517	11 981 717	4 249 868	16 231 585
1969-70	1 784	139 624	1 006 994	12 987 652	4 401 100	17 388 752
1970-71	1 784	144 107	1 108 192	13 900 257	4 803 307	18 703 564
1971-72	1 784	130 761	1 026 047	14 183 021	5 225 270	19 408 291
1972-73	1 859	147 260	1 137 204	15 059 051	5 496 831	20 555 882
1973-74	1 857	185 476	1 388 007	19 085 842	7 105 189	26 191 031
1974-75	1 857	175 132	1 437 444	21 965 876	7 845 148	29 811 024
Central Australia Railway						
1963-64	1 323	24 351	1 821 635	4 336 734	432 976	4 769 710
1964-65	1 323	25 605	2 136 735	4 802 668	516 796	5 319 464
1965-66	1 323	23 902	2 178 572	4 956 105	547 458	5 503 563
1966-67	1 317	22 242	2 247 494	5 298 866	555 189	5 854 055
1967-68	1 317	22 047	2 318 132	5 745 134	579 687	6 324 821
1968-69	1 317	23 142	2 431 910	6 385 404	659 898	7 045 302
1969-70	1 317	25 554	2 425 146	6 812 156	698 253	7 510 409
1970-71	1 317	26 996	1 899 767	6 618 504	792 675	7 411 179
1971-72	1 219	23 035	1 788 720	6 414 094	818 102	7 232 196
1972-73	1 219	23 863	1 836 484	6 887 057	948 552	7 835 609
1973-74	1 219	22 789	1 767 743	6 540 101	875 374	7 415 475
1974-75	1 219	21 794	2 062 811	8 864 873	972 429	9 837 302
North Australia Railway						
1963-64	511	733	29 209	314 080	33 204	347 284
1964-65	511	389	36 600	359 022	38 048	397 070
1965-66	511	327	49 375	467 852	32 311	500 163
1966-67	511	221	131 302	547 698	36 015	583 713
1967-68	511	89	465 747	1 220 606	48 157	1 268 763
1968-69	511	163	892 570	1 810 022	41 216	1 851 238
1969-70	511	121	1 176 888	2 430 281	48 125	2 478 406
1970-71	511	772	1 148 933	2 518 162	65 694	2 583 856
1971-72	511	593	1 015 927	2 241 067	66 905	2 307 972
1972-73	511	305	960 965	2 501 104	73 476	2 574 580
1973-74	511	329	802 636	3 227 499	74 518	3 302 017
1974-75	511	128	323 606	1 389 470	56 993	1 446 463
Australian Capital Territory Railway						
1963-64	8	76 976	169 639	88 374	31 398	119 772
1964-65	8	83 117	202 193	103 740	33 408	137 148
1965-66	8	84 376	224 442	113 621	31 702	145 323
1966-67	8	87 344	231 476	126 757	40 282	167 039
1967-68	8	86 673	234 950	167 347	45 795	213 142
1968-69	8	79 465	251 367	188 607	54 558	243 165
1969-70	8	78 647	292 331	212 942	58 054	270 996
1970-71	8	86 724	294 900	218 325	62 225	280 550
1971-72	8	52 992	287 715	207 187	51 907	259 094
1972-73	8	51 067	320 550	227 620	47 077	274 697
1973-74	8	54 637	311 471	240 023	68 866	308 889
1974-75	8	41 369	278 455	211 045	61 448	272 493
Commonwealth Railways						
1963-64	3 626	338 414	2 517 408	11 831 574	3 361 700	15 193 274
1964-65	3 626	335 671	2 853 893	13 593 148	3 826 384	17 419 532
1965-66	3 626	332 311	2 912 730	14 069 549	4 021 251	18 090 800
1966-67	3 620	361 515	3 058 652	15 037 063	4 391 410	19 428 473
1967-68	3 620	337 451	3 553 166	17 642 254	4 591 153	22 233 407
1968-69	3 620	287 834	4 280 412	20 365 750	5 005 540	25 371 290
1969-70	3 620	236 922	4 678 179	22 443 031	5 205 532	27 648 563
1970-71	3 620	247 372	4 217 433	23 255 248	5 723 901	28 979 149
1971-72	3 522	198 281	3 911 173	23 045 369	6 162 184	29 207 553
1972-73	3 597	213 351	4 040 277	24 674 832	6 565 936	31 240 768
1973-74	3 595	253 962	4 020 228	29 093 464	8 123 948	37 217 412
1974-75	3 595	230 695	3 857 500	31 994 893	9 372 389	41 367 282

has not yet been finalised. Bridges will be of both ballasted deck and open deck types. Ballasted deck bridges will have steel decking in some areas where concrete aggregates are very difficult to obtain, and in these sections steel trestle type piers will be used to further reduce requirements for concrete materials.

Culverts will consist of reinforced concrete pipes varying from 600 m to 2 100 m diameter, and 3 m span rail decked culverts (similar to concrete box culverts but with roof section of reclaimed rail decking at formation level).

Gypsum deposits and areas of gypseous soil are common, and accordingly, all in-situ concrete in bridges and culverts, and all reinforced concrete culvert pipes are to be manufactured using sulphate-resisting cement.

Track: The main line track structure will consist of:
—53 and 47 kg Australian Standard rails
—prestressed concrete sleepers.
—Pandrol fastenings.
—200 mm crushed stone ballast under sleepers.
Sidings will generally comprise reclaimed 47 kg and 40 kg rails on timber sleepers and 150 mm depth of ballast.
Main line turnouts will be 1:10 with rail-bound manganese steel cast frogs to suit 53 kg rail. Siding turnouts will be 1:10 and 1:8 fabricated from 47 kg rail.
Rails are being delivered to Port Augusta in 13·7 m lengths and there flash butt welded into 137 m lengths. Welding into continuous lengths of up to 80 km, from one siding to the next, is being done by the "Thermit" process as the rails are laid. All rail ends are blank (no fishbolt holes) and temporary clamped joints are installed pending continuous welding.
Pretensioned monoblock sleepers type CR2 (similar to the British F.27) are being

manufactured under contract at Port Augusta and transported by train 400 km to Tarcoola and thence to the rail head. "Geismar" gantries and sleeper laying beam will be used in the tracklaying procedure.

Ballast is graded in size from 40 mm to 8 mm, and will be produced from deposits of rhyolite, quartzite and dolerite. There will be four quarry sites along the route and a total quantity of some 1 600 000 m³ of crushed stone ballast is to be produced.

Facilities at stations: The principal station will be the terminal at Alice Springs which will provide for a complete road/rail interchange of freight (especially with container handling equipment), local goods and livestock, and a passenger terminal.
Intermediate sidings between Tarcoola and Alice Springs will be placed at an average spacing of 65 km approximately, providing train crossing points together with appropriate facilities for the handling at each of the small amount of local freight and livestock traffic.

Communications: The communications system will comprise an integrated microwave—VHF system with 72-channel capacity, of which 24 channels will be used initially. In addition to direct Tarcoola to Alice Springs communication and links to intermediate siding locations, the system will provide VHF communication to and from a moving train at any point on the line and will enable locomotive and brakevan crews and track maintenance gangs to have continuous communication with the train control and other supervisory centres and with each other.
28 microwave towers are to be built and equipped along the route, from 45 m to 75 m in height and at an average spacing of 30 km. The batteries providing power for the equipment at each tower will be recharged by solar cells.

DIESEL RAILCARS

Class	Axle Arrangement	Transmission	Rated Power hp	Max lb (kg)	Tractive Effort Continuous at lb (kg)	@	mph (km/h)	Max Speed mph (km/h)	Wheel Dia. in (mm)	Total Weight Tons	Length ft in (mm)	No. Built	Year first Built	Builders: Mechanical Parts	Engine & Type	Transmission
*CB.1, 2	1A-A1	Allison	275	3 626	907	@	137	137	838	49.25	25 100	3	1951	Budd Co. Philadelphia, USA	GM6/110 6 cyl (2 No.)	Allison USA
*CB.3	1A-A1	Allison	255	3 626	907	@	137	137	838	49.25	25 100		1971	Budd Co. Philadelphia USA	Rolls Royce C6TFH Mk 4 (2 No.)	Allison USA

*NOTE CB.1, CB.2 remain as built, CB.3 Refitted with Rolls Royce engines (see below).

DIESEL LOCOMOTIVES

Class	Axle Arrangement	Transmission	Power Rated hp	Tractive Effort Max kg	Continuous at kg @	km/h	Max Speed km/h	Wheel Dia. mm	Total Weight Tonnes	Length Over Headstocks Metres	No. Built	Year First Built	Builders Mechanical Parts	Engine & Type	Transmission
GM Nos 1-11	A1A-A1A	Traction Motors EMD-D27 (4 No.)	1 625/ 1 500	18 802	13 430 @	24	143	1 016	108	17.9	11	1951	Clyde Engineering New South Wales, Sydney, Australia	EMD 567B 16 cyl.	EMD, La Grange, Illinois, USA
GM Nos 12-47	Co-Co	Traction Motors (6 No.) EMD-D37	1 950/ 1 750	29 628	22 459 @15		143	1 016	116	17.9	36	1955	„	EMD 567C 16 cyl.	„
CL	Co-Co	6 No. Traction Motors EMD-D77	3 300/ 3 000	44 782	27 510 @	24	155	1 016	128	19.6	17	1970	„	EMD 645E3 16 cyl.	„
AL	Co-Co	6 No. Traction Motors EMD-D77	3 300/ 3 000	44 782	27 510 @	24	155	1 016	132	19.8	To Date 4	1976	Clyde Engineering New South Wales Rosewater, South Australia	EMD 645E 3 16 cyl.	„
DE	Bo-Bo	Traction Motors 4 No. GE 733	380/ 350	11 933	5 898 @	12	56	0 838	45	9	2	1943	General Electric USA	Caterpillar D17000 (2 No.) 8 cyl.	General Electric USA
DR	B	Hydraulic SLM	150	6 170			32	978	28.4	6.5	1	1957	Ruston Hornsby, England	Ruston 6VPHL 6 cyl.	S.L.L. Switzerland
NSU	A1A-A1A	Traction Motors (4) CP 170	955/ 850	10 163	6 942 @	25	80	Driven 915 Idler 762	62	12.75	14	1965	Birmingham Carriage & Wagon Works, England	Sulzer 6LDA28 6 cyl	Crompton Parkinson England
NT	Co-Co	Traction Motors (6) AEI-253AZ	1 400/ 1 300	21 552	18 149 @	16	80	940	70	14.2	13	1965	Tulloch Ltd Rhodes, NSW	Sulzer 6LDA 28-C 6 cyl.	Associated Electrical Industries, England
NJ	Co-Co	Traction Motors (6) Clyde CD36	1 650/ 1 500	1 769	16 180 @	20	80	953	67	13.9	6	1971	Clyde Engineering NSW, Sydney Australia	EMD 645 E 12 cyl.	Clyde Engineering NSW, Sydney, Australia
NB	C	Allison 600	140	4 574			32	915	18.3	5.74	1	1957	Commonwealth Railways	GM 6/71 6 cyl.	Allison USA
NC	0-6-0	Allison CRT 5 630	275	7 713			56	1 016	27.4	6.46	2	1956	Clyde Engineering NSW, Sydney Australia	GM 6/110 6 cyl.	Allison USA

GENERAL STATISTICAL INFORMATION

	Trans-Australian Railway		Central Australia Railway		North Australia Railway		Australian Capital Territory Railway		Total	
	Year ended 30 June		Year ended 30 June		Year ended 30 June		Year ended 30 June		Year ended 30 June	
	1975	1974	1975	1974	1975	1974	1975	1974	1975	1974
Average Kilometres of single track open including Sidings	2 069 929	2 068.333	1 330.802	1 329.961	561.528	561.528	29.403	29.226	3 991.662	3 989.
Average Kilometres open for Traffic	1 857	1 857	1 219	1 219	511	511	8	8	3 595	3
Train Kilometres										
Passenger	1 430 253	1 508 443	187 813	141 865	2 671	3 072	12 136	18 936	1 632 873	1 672
Goods	2 670 201	2 707 098	1 462 140	1 284 413	158 075	290 111	12 472	12 000	4 302 888	4 293
Passenger Journeys										
First Class	57 602	64 830	8 326	8 720	—	—	7 776	13 001	70 657	83
Economy Class	117 106	120 381	13 766	13 917	128	329	33 593	41 636	159 462	170
Season Tickets										
First Class	424	265	152	152	—	—	—	—	576	
Gross Tonne Kilometres										
Passenger	1 189 952 132	1 199 025 918	136 391 212	106 124 050	1 999 498	2 198 877	1 937 133	3 214 707	1 330 279 975	1 310 563
Goods	4 853 749 716	4 795 051 814	1 906 063 079	1 671 419 776	195 424 157	406 694 245	6 192 703	6 374 433	6 961 429 655	6 879 540
TONNES OF FREIGHT										
General Goods	1 288 409	1 308 256	155 611	176 208	31 743	34 962	278 390	311 399	1 594 190	1 645
Wool	3 638	4 627	7	14	1	—	—	65	3 704	4
Livestock	41 073	44 833	40 148	44 008	11	1 672	—	58	45 619	51
Coal, Coke, Shale	4 787	2 031	1 797 785	1 488 987	—	10	—	—	1 802 465	1 491
Other Minerals	99 537	28 260	69 260	58 526	291 851	765 992	—	14	411 522	826
TOTAL	1 437 444	1 388 007	2 062 811	1 767 ure	323 606	802 636	278 455	311 471	3 857 500	4 020

PUBLIC TRANSPORT COMMISSION OF NEW SOUTH WALES
11-31 York Street, Sydney, NSW 2000

Telephone: 219 8888

Gauge: 1.435 m
Route length: 9 756 km

Chief Commissioner: Alan S. Reiher
Deputy Chief Commissioner: J. Trimmer
Commissioner: E. R. Gordon
Nominated Commissioners: Hon. R. B. Marsh OBE
E. L. Byrne
Director of Operations: A. T. Griffith
Director of Personnel: W. J. McLatchie
Director of Planning: I. P. Arthur
Director of Finance: G. L. Corkill
Director of Marketing: K. W. Newton
Secretary: A. R. Coleman
General Manager Way & Works Branch: R. D. Christie
General Manager Workshops Branch: B. T. Richards
General Manager Electrical Equipment Branch: E. M. Bullock
General Manager Mechanical Branch: J. Bannister
General Manager Signals & Communications: J. Rees
General Manager Trading & Catering Services: E. M. Braithwaite
Operations Manager (Rail): E. A. Young
Operations Manager (Locomotive): F. A. Godfrey

The Public Transport Commission administers all public government rail and bus services in New South Wales. All statistical information quoted below refers to rail only.

HISTORY
During the early years of life in the colony of New South Wales, the problems of transport and communications were ever present in the minds of the settlers. As the settlement spread out to the west, north and south, the idea of distance assumed more and more significance. With the explorers leading the urge to see what was beyond the horizon, there followed the free settlers, the emancipists, the squatters, and then, with the discovery of gold in the central west, the diggers with their stampedes from one reported strike to another. That railways were necessary to New South Wales was only too apparent. They were an obvious solution to the inconvenience of travel by horseback or coach where the poor state of roads made every journey a hazardous experience, and freight transport was slow and expensive.
Thus, on 3 July, 1850, the 'first sod' was turned for construction of the colony's railway. Five years of toil were to elapse before the official opening of the first section of track between Sydney and Parramatta—on 26 September, 1855. From this first modest 23 kilometres, the railway system in New South Wales had grown to 4 524 kilometres by 1900.
At the turn of century, main lines radiated out from Sydney . . . north to Wallangarra and Moree, south to Nowra, Cooma, Albury, Finley and Hay and west to Condobolin, Cobar and Bourke. By 1900, the railways operated 1 131 passenger vehicles and 12 000 freight wagons which were hauled by 52 steam locomotives. About 27 million passenger journeys were made in that year, whilst five and a half million tonnes of freight were carried.

Developments since 1900: Since the turn of the century, the rail system has reached out to most parts of the State, providing an extensive 9 750 kilometre network serving all sectors of commerce and industry.
Electrification of Sydney's suburban train lines started on 1 March, 1926, with the running of the first electric train between Oatley and Sydney. Other lines were progressively electrified until today electric trains operate on 446 route kilometres extending north to Gosford, south to Campbelltown and The Royal National Park and west to Lithgow.
A milestone was reached in the history of railways in September 1937 when the 'Silver City Comet' went into service between Parkes and Broken Hill. This was the first diesel-powered air-conditioned train in Australia. From 1948 onwards, the fleet of air-conditioned trains was increased until the stage has now been reached where about 350 air-conditioned services operate each week, serving country and interstate locations. Foremost of the interstate expresses is 'The Indian Pacific'—the world-famous train which operates between Sydney and Perth three times weekly in both directions.
The advent of more efficient diesel traction in 1944 marked a new era with the progressive replacement of the steam locomotive fleet. Diesel locomotives provide greater capacity at higher operating speeds, lower maintenance costs, reduced fuel costs, and the ability to run high mileage with little running attention.
To this more productive form of motive power was harnessed progressively modern freight vans and wagons, equipped with passenger type bogies to enable maximum speeds. These include long flat cars for hauling containers; bi-level wagons for motor vehicles; sealed, louvred vans for fruit, vegetables and general merchandise, and aluminium-bodied wagons for ores, grains and minerals.
Other innovations over the years included the operation of 'unit' or 'block' trains; containerisation and palletisation; and better materials handling equipment. Standardisation of rail gauges between Sydney and Perth, together with bogie exchange facilities at Wodonga, Melbourne, Port Pirie and Peterborough, gave NSW and, ultimately Australian railways the flexibility that break-of-gaugehead previously denied them for so long.
In recent years, the introduction of double-deck carriages on suburban lines, with air-conditioned double-deck cars on the Gosford and Blue Mountains services, brought added comfort and extra seating capacity for commuters. Many additional improvements were effected, such as in the signalling, communications and other technological fields.

FREIGHT TRAFFIC
Total freight tonne-km in 1976 was 8 566 910 000 compared with 8 791 696 000 tonne-km in 1975. Tonnage carried was 31 179 000 tonnes in 1976 compared with 33 504 000 tonnes in 1975.

General Freight	Wagons Loaded	
	1976	1975
Bulk loading	153 097	158 955
Cement	23 216	36 977
Fertilizer	9 122	12 134
Flour	10 694	10 067
Fodder	4 236	5 370
General	289 322	300 528
Grain (other than wheat)	31 722	38 541
Interstate traffic	169 877	156 411
Ores	90 469	116 060
Perishables	75 014	74 378
Sand and gravel	23 715	28 013

Highspeed unit grain train: 5.3 million tonnes of grain was hauled in NSW during 1976/77.

General Freight (continued)

	Wagons Loaded	
	1976	*1975*
Steel	106 058	111 136
Timber	12 898	12 480
Wheat	148 954	139 883
Wool	18 534	19 014
	1 166 928	1 219 947

Coal and Coke

Coal	570 480	689 909
Coke	6 111	9 252
	576 591	699 161

Livestock

Cattle	24,645	17 522
Sheep	12 274	10 971
	36 919	28 493
Total	1 780 438	1 947 601
Number of bogie wagons included in total	703 301	714 500

PASSENGER TRAFFIC

For the year ended 30.6.76 a total of 2 935 000 passenger journeys were made on country and interstate services and 179 475 000 journeys on the suburban services.
In the year ending 30.6.77 revenue from country passenger journeys showed an 8 per cent increase and suburban services showed an increase of 3.2 per cent for number of passengers carried.
These increases reflect upon the 20 per cent reduction in all fares introduced in June 1976 and for the first time in 10 years the downward trend of passenger travel was arrested.
The Commission is continuing to update passenger services by progressively introducing new rolling stock and a variety of concessions for rail users—Concessions available in NSW include:
1. Day ROVER tickets—One day unlimited suburban travel by train, bus & ferry
2. NURAIL PASSES—14 day ticket available throughout NSW
3. Minifares—Off peak travel concession tickets.
4. Family Fares—Discounts for large families where adults and two children only pay fares, the other children travel free of charge.
5. Awayday Sunday tickets offering substantial discounts for Sunday travellers to the Outer Metropolitan area.
6. Discounts for pensioners and students and children.
7. Weekly and Quarterly ticket concessions for commuters.
The Commission also operates a large range of one-day and extended holiday, rail/coach tours.

FINANCIAL

	1976	*1975*	*1974*
	$A	$A	$A
	('000)	('000)	('000)
Revenue	323 562	296 059	307 083
Expenditure	472 188	415 234	413 148
Operating loss	148 626	119 175	106 065
Interest on loans	55 246	47 764	45 939
Total Loss	203 872	166 939	152 004

ROLLING STOCK IMPROVEMENTS

At 30.6.77, 364 of the total of 1 195 suburban and interurban electric carriages were double deck. Current contracts allow a further 50 double-deck suburban carriages and these will be followed by an additional 150 suburban cars under a new $44 million contract. 30 more double-deck air-conditioned interurban electric cars are also presently being built.
Tenders have been called for the manufacture of 40 new loco haul mainline air-conditioned carriages for country trains consisting of 10 economy class, 8 economy class with power compartment, 8 first class with buffet, 2 first class with staff compartment, and 6 twinette and 6 roomette sleeping cars.
Plans are now being prepared for the purchase of a further 32 self-propelled diesel passenger cars for use on the non-electrified suburban services.
Present contracts costing about $38 million provide for 1 530 new high speed bogie freight wagons of various types—many of these are now in service.

LOCOMOTIVES

A $31 million contract has been let for the manufacture of thirty 2 000 hp diesel electric locomotives and ten 3 600 hp all-electric locomotives.
All rolling stock and locomotives are being built in Australia, primarily within New South Wales.

TRACK UPGRADING

During 1977 the Commission started work on an extensive five year programme of track upgrading for which the New South Wales Government has allocated $A200 million. This will result in railway track throughout the entire State being upgraded to higher standards.
Maintenance of rail tracks in NSW is extremely difficult because of the various geographical features peculiar to the State. Sharp curves, steep grades, deep cuttings, poor soil for drainage, desert plains—are all in stark contrast to the ideal conditions on which to operate and maintain a railway.
Over 500 additional staff have already been employed exclusively for track maintenance work and the upgrading programme is being operated at a pace never before attempted in New South Wales.
Modern machinery, such as ballast cleaners capable of cleaning 550m³/hr are being used, other machines include ballast regulators, tamping machines, shoulder and crib compactors and sleeper removing and inserting equipment.
The $A 200 million being spent over 5 years is in addition to the normal allocation of approximately $A 80 per year for track maintenance.

When present orders are completed more than 50% of Sydney's electric trains will be double-deck

Plasser + Theurer ballast cleaner (right) meets up with a Tamper-built tamping unit (left)

The Woolloomooloo viaduct Eastern Suburbs Railway under construction

ELECTRIFICATION

By early 1977 electrified route distance totalled 446 km and total electrified track distance 1 251 km, out of a total system route distance of 9 756 km and total track distance of 11 185 km. Now projected is the electrification of the 10 km Erskineville City—Bondi Junction line.

EASTERN SUBURBS RAILWAY

The Eastern Suburbs Railway, one of the largest engineering projects undertaken by the NSW Government in recent times, will extend the operations of the existing Metropolitan rail network to serve the densly populated eastern suburbs of Sydney.

The section from Erskineville to and/including the new Central Station is being built by the Commission's own staff. From Central to Bondi Junction private contractors have been employed for stations, tunnels and viaducts.

A number of consultants have been engaged by the Commission to provide the necessary engineering and architectural design work. All track laying, signalling, substation installation and overhead wiring is being carried out by the Commission.

From a connection with the existing metropolitan rail network at Erskineville on the Illawarra line, the new railway will extend to Bondi Junction via Redfern, Central, Town Hall, Martin Place, Kings Cross and Edgecliff.

The line will be all double track running completely underground except for the Woolloomooloo and Rushcutters Bay viaducts. The route distance from Erskineville to Bondi Junction is 10 km.

At September 1977 60 per cent of track laying was complete—station construction was well advanced and overhead wiring signalling and communications systems progressing well. It is expected that the first section of the railway viz between Central and Bondi Junction will commence operating in 1979 and within another 12 months trains will operate through to Erskineville where the connection with the existing network is made.

NEW SIGNALLING EQUIPMENT

Remote Control Systems

Cabramatta Junction—A double line junction at Cabramatta on the suburban section of the Southern line was equipped with a remotely controlled route setting interlocking in September 1976.

The installation is controlled via a direct wire remote control system from Liverpool Signal Box, 3.8 km beyond the junction. Electrically operated points, electro-hydraulic train stops and high frequency jointless track circuits have been provided.

Gymea–Caringbah and Revesby—Existing power signalled crossing loops at Gymea and Caringbah on the Sutherland–Cronulla suburban line and at Revesby on the Tempe—East Hills suburban line have been equipped for remotely controlled operation.

The Gymea and Caringbah loops are now controlled from Sutherland Signal Box at the junction while the loop at Revesby is controlled from Riverwood signal box, 3.5 km away at the end of double line. In both cases, new time division multiplex remote control equipment has been installed to control the existing signalling equipment.

Level Crossings: Flashing light highway signals were provided at ten level crossings, and highway signals with half boom barriers were provided at one level crossing during 1976.

Supply and Installation of equipment—Suppliers of signalling equipment for new works were as follows:

(a) *Signals:* Westinghouse Brake and Signal Co (Aust) Pty Ltd and Commission Workshops.

(b) *Point Mechanisms:* Nippon Signal Co.

(c) *Relays:* Westinghouse Brake and Signal Co (Aust) Pty Ltd; CSEE (Western Industries Ltd).

(d) *Level Crossing Equipment:* Westinghouse Brake and Signal Co (Aust) Pty Ltd and

Western Cullen Division of Federal Sign and Signal Corporation.

(e) *TDM Remote Control Equipment:* Cutler Hammer (Aust) Pty Ltd.

CONTAINERS

The Commission operates the following containers:

40	Side loading (SL)
500	Modified side loading (MSL)
40	Open ISO containers for dry cargo
6	Louvred ISO
500	General Cargo (GC)
500	Ventilated Cargo (VC)
160	Refrigerated (LRC)

Two maritime container terminals, served by rail, are located at Sydney. The Balmain or White Bay Terminal which, owned by the Maritime Services Board, is operated under lease by Seatainer Terminals Ltd, and the Glebe Island Terminal also owned by the Maritime Services Board, is operated as a "common user" terminal under lease by a consortium—Glebe Island Terminals Pty Ltd. Each is also served by road.

A third Sydney terminal is located at Mort Bay, handling both container and roll on-roll off vessels between Australia and Japan and Australian coastal vessels. This terminal is not serviced by rail being located approximately two kilometres from the railhead at Rozelle.

At Newcastle, container ships call at No. 1 Throsby Wharf and No. 4 Western Basin Wharf, each of which is serviced by rail.

Container consolidation depots in the Sydney area are located at Chullora and Leightonfield, 18 km and 24 km respectively from the Balmain/Glebe Island Terminals. These depots are served by captive container trains on a 24-hour, seven days a week, basis.

Further rail served container complexes are located at Homebush 26 km and Yennora 29 km from Balmain/Glebe Island specialising mainly in containerisation of export wool.

Approximately 75 000 (TEU) containers are handled per annum on the captive container trains operating between the terminals and depots.

TRACK

Main Lines: Generally 8.7° = minimum radius of 201 m, but at two locations curvature is 10.85° = minimim radius of 161 m.

Branch Lines: 10.85° = minimum radius of 161 m, but there are three lines in difficult terrain where curvature is 17.4° = minimum radius of 101 m.

Minimum curvature:

Max gradient, compensated:

Main Line: 3.3% = 1 in 30 (electric traction on City Railway). 1.5% = 1 in 66 elsewhere.

Branch Line: 4.4% = 1 in 25 and 3.3% = 1 in 30.

Max gradient, uncompensated:

Main Line: 2.5% = 1 in 40, but there is a 30.5 km electrified length of 1 in 30 to 1 in 33 on the Blue Mountains.

Branch Lines: 3.3% = 1 in 30 and 2.5% = 1 in 40.

Longest continuous uniform gradient: Werris Creek to Binnaway Branch, 13 kms of 1% grade, 75% curved with radii varying from 282 m to 1 207 m (6.2° to 1.45°) with average of 503 m (3.5°). Compensated grade, single track, no tunnels.

Worst combination of curvature and gradient: On Batlow Line: radius of 90 m (19.3° curve) on 4% (1 in 25) compensated grade.

Max altitude: 377 m on main Northern Line, 645 kms from Sydney.

Standard rail: Rolled steel, flat bottom; 60, 71½, 80, 90, 94, 100, 103, 107 and 109 lb per yd *(29.8, 35.5, 39.7, 44.6, 46.6, 49.6, 51.1, 53.1, 54.1 kg/m)*. All rails are flash-butt welded at depot before laying. See "Welded Rail".

Main Lines: Adopted 1963: 107 and 94 lb per yd *(53.2 and 46.7 kg/m)* in 45 ft lengths.

All rails are flash-butt welded at depot before laying. See "Welded Rail". Older sections, 90 and 100 lb *(44.6* and *49.6 kg/m)* exist in 30 and 45 ft lengths; being replaced.
Branch Lines: 60, 71½, 80, 90 and 94 lb per yd *(29.8, 35.5, 39.7 44.6* and *46.7 kg/m).*
Rail joints: 4-hole bar type fishplate on some lines, General Main Line standard 6-hole bar type.
Cross ties (sleepers): Australian hardwood, 9 in × 4½ in × 8 ft 0 in *(228 × 114 × 2 438 mm)* (larger size 230 × 130 × 2 440 mm recently introduced), spaced 24 in *(160 mm)* centre to centre, except at rail joints 18 to 20 in. Where track is being reconstructed a closer spacing of 20 to 22 in is being introduced.
Concrete 12 in × 8 in × 8 ft 0 in *(305 × 203 × 2 438 m).* Test section only.
Rail fastenings: "Pandrol" rail fastenings and dog spikes with double shouldered rolled steel sleeper plates secured to wood sleepers with "Lockspikes", composition pad between rail seatings and sleeper plates—Departmental design.
Pads under rails: 9 in × 5¾ in *(299 × 146 mm)* Neoprene bonded cord ³/₁₆ in *(5 mm)* thick and composition pads as above locally manufactured to departmental specification on concrete sleeper test section only.
Filling (ballast):
Main Lines: Broken basalt 65.40 mm, 270 mm below sleepers.
Branch Lines: Basalt, ashes, gravel, sand, earth, or quarry dust, 5½ in *(140 mm)* below sleeper.
Max curvature:
Main Lines: Generally 8.7° = minimum radius of 660 ft *(201 m),* but at two locations curvature is 10.85° = minimim radius of 528 ft *(161 m).*
Branch Lines: 10.85° = minimum radius of 528 ft *(161 m),* but there are three lines in difficult terrain where curvature is 17.4° = minimum radius of 330 ft *(101 m).*
Max gradient, compensated:
Main Line: 3.3% = 1 in 30 (electric traction on City Railway). 1.5% = 1 in 66 elsewhere.
Branch Line: 4.0% = 1 in 25 and 3.3% = 1 in 30.
Max gradient, uncompensated:
Main Line: 2.5% = 1 in 40, but there is a 19-mile electrified length of 1 in 30 to 1 in 33 on the Blue Mountains.
Branch Lines: 3.3% = 1 in 30 and 2.5% = 1 in 40.
Longest continuous uniform gradient: Werris Creek to Binnaway Branch, 8.12 miles

(5.03 km) of 1% grade, 75% curved with radii varying from 924 ft to 3 960 ft (6.2° to 1.45°) with average of 1 650 ft (3.5°). Compensated grade, single track, no tunnels.
Worst combination of curvature and gradient: On Batlow Line: radius of 297 ft *(90 m)* (19.3° curve) on 4% (1 in 25) compensated grade.
Gauge widening on curves:
Main Lines: No widening.
Branch Lines: No widening on curves of 528 ft *(161 m)* radius (10.85° curve). Up to ³/₈ in *(9.5 mm)* on curves of 330 ft *(101 m)* (17.4° curve).
Super-elevation on sharpest grade:
Main Lines: 140 mm if maximum allowable speed can be obtained.
Branch Lines: 50 mm.
Rate of slope of super-elevation: Where S = mean speed on the particular curve, ramp varies between 1 in 10S and 1 in 16S, with a maximum steepness of 1 in 300.
Max altitude: 4 517 ft *(1 377 m)* on main Northern Line, 400 miles from Sydney.
Max axle load: 19 tonnes unrestricted; 25 tonnes restricted, special loads.
Max bridge loading: Coopers E60 plus impact.
Maximum permitted speed:
Main Line: Passenger: 115 km/h. Freight: 100 km/h Bogie; 70 km/h Four(4) Wheel.
Branch Line: Passenger: 80 km/h; Freight: 50 km/h.

Welded rail: At the end of 1975 the total length of track with welded rail was 6 540 km of which 300 km was laid during the year. The longest length of welded rail is 73 km. Rails used are 107 lb *(53 kg)* and 94 lb *(47 kg)* Australian Standard in 45 ft *(13.7 m)* bars. Flash-butt welded in depot into 360 ft *(8 × 45 ft)* lengths; Thermit welded after laying into 4 × 360 ft = 1 440 ft *(440 m)* length or longer. The 1 440 ft lengths are used where curves are not sharper than 924 ft radius (6.2 degrees). Below this the rail lengths are progressively reduced down to 80 ft for curves of 528 ft radius.
Current practice of fastening welded rail on heavy traffic lines and on all sharp curves is to use double shoulder sole plates with 1 in 20 cant on standard wooden sleeper, with two dog spikes on to the rail flanges and two "Lockspikes" for outside square hole of plate. "Fair" type rail anchors and Australian standard fishplates and bolts are used. "Pandrol" fastenings are used with "Dowmac" concrete sleepers.

Review in Brief
by Alan S. Reiher, Chief Commissioner

An increase of over 8.8 per cent in earnings from its rail and bus operations enabled the Public Transport Commission's revenue in 1976 to reach $369 million – the highest so far recorded. However, any enthusiasm on achieving this result was quickly dispelled by an even greater increase of 12.5 per cent in expenditure which amounted to $554 million. After meeting capital debt charges, the net deficiency was $244 million as compared to $204 million the previous year.
In the Commission's last Annual Report mention was made of the difficulties which would be encountered during 1975/1976. Regrettably, the truth of these predictions was reflected in the large deficit which was incurred. Such financial losses, of course, are not peculiar to New South Wales, but have been experienced by other Australian and most overseas public transport systems. Severe inflationary costs in this highly labour intensive industry, coupled to a shortage of modern rolling stock and other types of equipment have prevented or delayed the Commission from arresting the crippling operating losses at a time when capital debt repayments are also steadily rising.
During the year $122 million was made available to the Commission to upgrade the New South Wales Public Transport system. This was 50 per cent more than the previous year's allocation and was indicative, not only of community demand for increased spending on public passenger transport facilities, but also a recognition by Government that the railway infrastructure is capable of contributing to greater economies in overall transport costs. Important as it is to receive increased allocations for capital works programmes, it is an inescapable fact that the money made available has progressively less actual purchasing power in such severe inflationary times.

Passenger improvements
As from June 27, 1976 all passenger fares were reduced by an average of 20%. With recent completion of a contract for 106 new double-deck suburban carriages, one quarter of the Commission's suburban train fleet now consists of double-deck carriages which have proved very popular with commuters. A further 50 double-deck carriages for use on the Sydney suburban network are on order under a $12 million contract, and the Commission is negotiating the purchase of another 100 similar carriages. For the long distance commuter service between Sydney/Gosford (81 km) and Sydney/Lithgow (156 km), the Commission has ordered 30 double-deck airconditioned carriages of similar design to those already in service, costing approximately $18 million. Completion of a $0.5 million project of enlarging a tunnel at Glenbrook has enabled the Commission to operate these double-deck units on the Main Western line.
The external appearance of the Commission's extensive electric train fleet will be greatly improved with the installation of four automated car washing plants for which tenders have been called. Each unit will be capable of washing over 300 carriages per day, and this improved efficiency will allow the Commission to schedule all suburban and interurban trains for daily external cleaning.
Other improvements carried out to assist Sydney suburban passengers have included the installation of improved public address systems at stations incorporating pre-recorded cassette announcements; provision of clear back-lift station and route indicators; and the free issue of detailed rail/bus/ferry route guides and pocket timetables.
Whilst emphasis has been placed on improving present and future services, the 50th Anniversary of electric trains in Sydney was not overlooked, and an appropriate ceremony and display were arranged to commemorate this historic event.

Long distance travel
Improvements to long distance trains included increased frequency of the 'Indian-Pacific' and introduction of refurbished air-conditioned carriages featuring new seating. The demand for accomodation on the world-ranking 'Indian-Pacific', which provides the 3 961 km Sydney/Perth service, influenced

the commission, in conjunction with the other owning systems, to run an extra service in both directions bringing the total number of services to four return journeys each week.
'Brisbane Limited' and 'Gold Coast MotoRail Express' services were greatly improved with the acquisition of refurbished carriages featuring modern decor and comfortable 'Day-Niter' aircraft-type seats. Over 1 000 of these new seats are on order at a cost of over $1 million and will be installed in other carriages which are being progressively modernised.

Freight operations
A serious downturn in the demand for export coal was the main reason for the drop in freight hauled from 33.5 million tonnes in 1974/1975 to 31.2 million tonnes this year. Although vigorous marketing activities gained new business, including some of the more profitable freight previously hauled by other modes, it was not sufficient to offset the severe loss in the coal traffic which is the Commission's biggest single income earner.
With every confidence of increased coal exports in the future, the Commission is currently engaged in a number of projects involving expenditure of at least $27 million in the Newcastle area alone.
In the Newcastle area, the project includes facilities at Port Waratah which will increase export coal handling capacity from the present 7 million tonnes annually to 20 million tones; improved track installations at Carrington Basin, and a new 10 km coal line costing $6 million which will link Mt. Thorley with the Main Northern line at Whittingham.
Five hundred new 100-tonne coal wagons are being manufactured under current contracts and these include 200 which are believed to be the world's first rail freight wagons to be built of stainless steel. Tenders for a further 500 coal wagons are under consideration, which would result in 1 000 new wagons being available within the next five years to handle coal traffic.
That the Commission is determined to improve its freight carrying facilities is confirmed by the current investment programme which provides for the manufacturer, mainly by outside contractors, of a total of 1 524 new freight wagons, 1 660 containers and 3 670 high speed bogies.
The Commission has been priveleged to receive the 'SE Pike Memorial Trophy' from the Australian Institute of Materials Handling for the second year in succession. The most recent award was for the Commission's development of RACE (Railways of Australia Container Express system) which enables it to provide a rapid freight service incorporating the maximum use of the inter-modal unit load exchange system. The previous year's Award was for the design and installation of a magnet crane for handling steel at Cooks River Goods Yard.
Other important developments in freight and parcels operations included the opening of a new direct rail-served fruit and vegatable markets complex at Flemington; a 'Land-Bridge' service linking Sydney and Perth on the 3 961 km standard gauge line; introduction of 'Blue Spot', a fast and economical parcels service to NSW stations and interstate to Brisbane and Melbourne; and further progress on construction and planning of the Tamworth Freight Centre and other regional freight depots.

Future improvements
The Commission's plans for re-equipment and modernisation to ensure that NSW has an efficient and modern public transport system cover a very wide field.
The funds necessary for such a programme are considerable, and the Commission is endeavouring to ensure that sufficent finance is available so that it can meet its planned objectives. Without major improvements to productivity and without the equipment to take advantage of more business obtained by its marketing activities, the deficit can only continue to rise rapidly.
The Commission sees an extension of its rail freight business, continuation of the investment programme to increase its capability and reliability, the co-operation of staff through the trade union movement to substantially increase its productivity through new equipment and methods of operation, and the continued development of a strong customer service attitude as essential to the control of its rapidly rising deficit.

Class 442 diesel-electric locomotive: builder A. E. Goodwin and Comeng; class numbers 44201—44240; first in service 1971

DIESEL LOCOMOTIVES

Class	Axle Arrangement	Transmission	Rated Power hp	Max. lbs (kg)	Tractive Effort Continuous at lbs (kg)	mph (km/h)	Max. Speed mph (km/h)	Wheel Dia. ins (mm)	Total Weight Tons	Length ft ins (mm)	No. Built	Year first Built	Builders: Mechanical Parts	Engine & Type	Transmission
42	Co-Co	Elec.	1 900	80 500 (36 500)	61 250 (27 780)	9 (14.5)	71 (113)	40 (1 016)	120	60' 10'' (18 542)	6	1955	Clyde Eng. Co.	GM 16-567C	Clyde
421	,,	,,	1 950	72 576 (32 209)	70 920 (32 170)	6.9 (11.1)	,,	,,	108	62' 0¾'' (18 911)	10	1965	,,	,,	,,
422	Co-Co	,,	2 200	72 760 (33 000)	70 920 (31 170)	77 (124)		,,	,,	60' 6'' (18 440)	20	1969/70	Clyde Eng. Co.	GM645E EMD	,,
43	,,	,,	1 750	71 000 (32 200)	42 900 (19 460)	11 (17.6)	,,	,,	105	56' 8¼'' (17 278)	6	1956	Goninons	Alco 244	G.E.
44 see note (a)	,,	,,	1 950	75 300 (34 150)	47 000 (21 300)	11.5 (18.5)	80 (129)	,,	112	58' 5'' (17 805)	11	1957	Goodwin	Alco 251B	G.E.
44 see note (b)	,,	,,	1 950	71 500 (32 400)	40 200 (18 200)	13.7 (22)	75 (121)	,,	106	,,	47	1957	,,	,,	G.E. & A.E.I.
44 see note (c)	,,	,,	1 950	74 021 (33 575)	44 000 (20 000)	12.9 (20.8)	80 (129)	,,	110	,,	42	1965/67	,,	Alco 251C	A.E.I.
442	,,	,,	2 150	75 900 (34 400)	52 000 (23 600)		70 (113)	40 (1 067)	113	61' 3'' (13 669)	24	1971/72	,,	Alco 251B	A.E.I.
45	,,	,,	1 950	74 250 (33 780)	68 000 (30 800)	7.4 (11.9)	75 (120)	,,	110.5	58' 8'' (17 881)	40	1962	,,	Alco 251C	G.E. & A.E.I.
47	,,	,,	1 125	56 400 (25 580)	38 460 (17 540)		70 (113)	,,	84	50' 0¾'' (15 260)	12	1972	Hitachi	Caterpillar D 299	Hitachi
48 see note (d)	,,	,,	975	49 700 (22 500)	40 200 (18 200)	5.8 (9.2)	,,	,,	74	48' 5'' (14 757)	45	1959	,,	Alco 251B	G.E.
48 see note (d)	,,	,,	1 050	,,	,,	,,	,,	,,	,,	,,	40	1964	,,	,,	G.E. & A.E.I.
48 see note (b)	,,	,,	1 050	51 500 (23 360)	42 500 (19 300)	6.5 (10.5)	,,	,,	76.6	,,	80	1966/71	,,	,,	A.E.I.
49	,,	,,	950	53 760 (24 385)	37 200 (16 875)	6.3 (10)	77 (124)	,,	80	50' 4¼'' (15 348)	18	1960	Clyde Eng. Co.	G.M.8/567C	Clyde
70	C	Hyd.	580	32 200 (14 600)	25 600 (11 600)	6 (9.6)	45 (72)	48 (1 219)	48	33' 4'' (10 160)	10	1960	Com. Eng. Ltd.	Caterpillar D397	Voith L37zUC Deutsche-Getribe GmbH
73	B-B	Hyd.	700/670	33 000 (15 000)	25 000 (11 340)	5.4 (8.7)	40 (64)	40 (1 016)	49	39' 4'' (11 989)	45	1970/72	Walkers Ltd.	Caterpillar D379 Series B	Voith L4r4U2

Notes: (a) Fitted with G.E. 731 Traction Motors. (b) Fitted with A.E.I. 253 Traction Motors. (c) Fitted with A.E.I. 254 Traction Motors. (d) Fitted with G.E. 761 Traction Motors. (e) 8 units supplied by A. Goninan in 1974.

NEW SOUTH WALES RAILWAYS—MAIN LINE ELECTRIC LOCOMOTIVES

Class	Axle Arrangement	Line Current	Rated Output hp	Max. lbs (kg)	Tractive Effort (Full Field) Continuous at lb (kg)	mph (km/hr)	Max. Speed mph (km/hr)	Wheel dia. ins (mm)	Weight tonnes	Length ft in (mm)	No. Built	Year Built	Builders Mechanical Parts	Electrical Equipment
46	Co+Co	1 500 V. d.c.	3 780	60 500 (27 450)	40 800 (18 500)	34.5 (55.5)	70 (112)	45 (1 143)	108	53' 11¼'' (16 440)	40	1956	Beyer Peacock	Metropolitan-Vickers
71	Co+Co	,,	2 700	60 000 (27 200)	28 000 (12 700)	28 (45)	70 (112)	48 (1 219)	108	55' 4'' (16 866)	1	1952	N.S.W.G.R.	Metropolitan-Vickers

QUEENSLAND GOVERNMENT RAILWAYS

305 Edward St., Brisbane, Queensland 4000

Telephone: 225 0211

Guage: 1.435 m; 1.067 m
Route length: 111 km; 9 685 km

Commissioner for Railways: P. J. Goldston
Deputy Commissioner and Secretary: A. J. Neeson
Assistant Commissioner (Electrification): D. V. Mendoza
Chief Engineer (Civil): H. N. Walker
Chief Mechanical Engineer and Workshops Superintendent: J. F. Jeffcoat
Chief Accountant: R. T. Sheehy
Chief Railway Auditor: C. A. Murray
General Manager, Brisbane: C. J. Kelso
General Manager, Toowoomba: W. L. Fraser
General Manager, Rockhampton: T. K. Keating
General Manager, Townsville: C. V. Walton
Comptroller of stores: J. J. Williamson

HISTORY

Queensland's first Railway line was opened on July 31, 1865. It extended for 35 km (21½ miles) from Ipswich to Bigge's Camp (now known as Grandchester). From its start, the Railway was a Government-owned 1 067 mm gauge system, and has remained so ever since.

The first four locomotives imported for the Queensland Railway System were built by the Avonside Engine Company of Bristol, England. Burning firewood, they weighed 22.5 tonnes and could haul a load of 70 tonnes.

The opening of the Ipswich-Bigge's Camp section touched off what has been described as an epidemic of railway fever throughout the colony, and four more sections of line between Ipswich and Toowoomba had been constructed by the end of 1867.

The first section of what was then known as the Great Northern Railway, between Rockhampton and Westwood, a distance of 53 km, was completed on September 17, 1867.

The section of the Ipswich-Brisbane Railway was opened as far as Oxley Point in February, 1875, and the first passenger train left Brisbane for Ipswich on June 14th that year.

The Indooroopilly Railway bridge, which formed the last link in the Southern and Western Railway between Brisbane and the West, was opened in July, 1876.

In the late seventies, a decision was taken to build a new railway line west of Townsville, and the first 137 km section to Charters Towers was opened on December 14, 1882.

On September 24, 1921, the planned North-South rail link was opened as far as Mackay, and in 1924 work was completed on the system between Cairns and Brisbane to provide Australia's longest unbroken Railway at that time.

Work on the Queensland section of the Interstate uniform 1 435 mm gauge line from South Brisbane to Richmond Gap was started in 1926 and was completed in mid-1930. The South Brisbane-Kyogle (New South Wales line) link opened to traffic on September 27, 1930.

With the advent of the Second World War, the gigantic task of carrying the materials necessary to maintain the Queensland-based war machine fell on the railways.

After the war and as a result of successful operations overseas, Queensland placed its first order for the new diesel locomotives in 1951.

The intervening years have seen the introduction of air-conditioned long-distance passenger trains; modern freight wagons; the modernisation of the Brisbane Suburban network, including the introduction of stainless steel carriages; the rebuilding and modernising of railway Workshops; the operation of unit trains hauling minerals and grain in bulk wagons, with three and four locomotives operating in multiple; and the acquistion of new mechanised equipment for work on permanent way maintenance and replacement.

TRAFFIC	1975	1976
Total freight tonne-km	9 117 994 540	10 101 210 389
Total freight tonnage	30 208 127	33 117 597
Total passenger-km	Not recorded	Not recorded
Total passengers journeys	36 632 414	34 278 244

FINANCIAL RESULTS	1972 $A	1973 $A	1974 $A	1975 $A	1976 $A
Revenue (000's)	121 749	134 258	149 843	183 686	230 491
Expenses (000's)	115 742	129 285	161 922	227 924	265 661
Operating ratio	95.1	—	—	—	—

DIESEL LOCOMOTIVES

Class	Axle Arrangement	Trans-mission	Rated Power hp	Max. lb (kg)	Tractive Effort Continuous at lb (kg)	mph (km/h)	Max Speed mph (km/h)	Wheel Dia. in (mm)	Total Weight Tons	Length ft in (mm)	No. Built	Year first Built	Builders: Mechanical Parts	Engine & Type	Transmission
1150	Co-Co	Elec.	1 100	59,200 (26 850)	31 000 (14 100)	10.5 (16.9)	50 (80)	36 (914)	89	56' 0⅞'' (17 091)	13	1952	General Electric (USA) and Australian Electrical Industries	Cooper Bessemer (USA) FVL-12T	General Electric (USA and) Australian Electrical Industries
1170	A-1-A+ A-1-A	,,	640	26 880 (12 200)	19 750 (8 960)	9.6 (15.4)	,,	,,	60	41' 6'' (12 649)	12	1956	Walkers (Aust.)	Cooper Bessemer (USA) FWA-6T	Australian Electrical Industries
1200	Co-Co	,,	1 280	60 000 (27 200)	30 500 (13 850)	12.7 (20.4)	,,	37.5 (952)	90	54' 10⅜'' (16 722)	10	1953	Vulcan Foundry (Gt. Britain)	English Electric (Gt. Britain) 12-SVT	English Electric (Gt. Britain)
1250 (Locos 1250-54)	Co-Co	,,	1 440	,,	41 500 (18 800)	10.3 (16.6)	,,	,,	85.7	52' 11'' (16 129)	5	1959	English Electric (Aust.)	,,	,,
1250 (Locos 1255-66)	Co-Co	,,	1 440	,,	,,	,,	,,	,,	87.3	,,	12	1960	,,	,,	English Electric (Aust.) and Gt. Britain
1270 (1270-81)	Co-Co	,,	1 440	,,	,,	,,	,,	,,	84.9	,,	16	1964	,,	,,	,,
(1282-99)	,,	,,	,,	,,	47 500 (21 500)	8.7 (14)	,,	,,	,,	,,	14	1966			
1300	Co-Co	,,	1 795	,,	50 400 (22 860)	10.8 (17.4)	,,	,,	88	51' 5'' (15 672)	42	1967/ 71	English Electric (Aust.)	English Electric 12-CSVT	English Electric
1400	A-1-A+ A-1-A	,,	1 310	36 288 (16 400)	28 000 (12 700)	14.7 (23.7)	,,	Drivers 40 (1 016) Idlers 30 (762)	76 (Fab Bogie) 78.8 (C.S. Bogie)	47' 10⅜'' (14 590)	13	1955	Clyde Eng. (Aust.)	General Motors EMD (USA) 12-567C	General Motors EMD (USA)
1450	Co-Co	,,	1 310	54 432 (24 700)	42 000 (19 050)	9.5 (15.3)	,,	40 (1 016)	90	52' 8⅜'' (16 062)	10	1957	,,	,,	,,
1460 (1460-1501)	Co-Co	,,	1 310	,,	50 820 (23 050)	7.5 (12.1)	,,	,,	,,	53' 4'' (16 256)	42	1964	Commonwealth Eng. (under sub-contract to Clyde Eng	,,	General Motors EMD (USA) & Clyde Eng. (Aust.)
(1502 on)	,,	,,	1 500	,,	,,	8.8 (14.1)	,,	,,	,,	,,	23 6	1967 1969	,,	General Motors 12-645 E	,,
Co-Co	,,	1 500	60 480 (27 430)	50 820 (23 050)	8.8	,,	,,	90	59' 2¼''	9	1972	,,	,,	,,
1600	Co-Co	,,	838	41 500 (18 800)	30 000 (13 600)	7.8 (12.6)	,,	37.5 (952)	61.5	44' 2'' (13 462)	18	1963	English Electric (Aust.)	English Electric (Gt. Britain) 6-CSRKT	English Electric (Aust.) and Gt. Britain)
1620	,,	,,	862	,,	,,	,,	,,	,,	62.5	45' 5'' (13 843)	28 6	1967 1969	,,	,,	,,
1700	Co-Co	,,	875	39 650 (18 000)	33 600 (15 250)	7.1 (11.4)	,,	,,	59	43' 10'' (13 360)	12	1963	Commonwealth Eng. (under sub-contract to Clyde Eng	General Motors EMD (USA) 8-567CR	General Motors EMD (USA) Clyde Eng. (Aust.)
1720	Co-Co	,,	1 000	,,	,,	8.4 (13.5)	,,	,,	62.5	43' 11⅜'' (13 395)	56	1966/ 1970	,,	General Motors EMD (USA) 8-645E	Clyde Eng. (Aust)
2100	Co-Co	,,	2 000	58 060 (26 390)	50 820 (23 050)	11.5 (18.5)	,,	40 (1 016)	96	59' 2¼'' (18 040)	30	1970/ 72	,,	General Motors EMD (USA) 16-645E	General Motors EMD (USA) Clyde Eng. (Aust.)
Dh	B-B	Hyd.	465	25 000 (11 350)	18 000 (8 150)	6 (9.7)	,,	36 (914)	40	36' 5'' (11,100)	70	1968 1970	Walkers Ltd. (Aust.)	Caterpillar D355 Series E	Voith L42 or U2 (Germany)

Note: 1250 Class locomotives numbered 1250 to 1254 have been upgraded from original 1 290 hp to 1 440 hp.

Class	Arrange- ment	Trans- mission	Rated Power (kN)	Max (kN)	Tractive Effort Continuous (kN)	At (km/h)	Max Speed (km/h)	Wheel Dia mm	Number 1975	1976	Built 1977	Total Weight Tonne	Length mm	Number Built	Year First Built	Builders Mechanical Parts	Engine and Type	Transmission
1 550	Co-Co	Electric	1 119	269	226	at 14	- 80	1 016	5	16	7	88.5	18 040	32 (To 30th June '77)	1972	Commonwealth Engineering under Sub-Contract to Clyde Engineering	General Motors EMD (USA) 12-645 E	General Motors EMD-Clyde Engineering Australia
2 370	Co-Co	Electric	1 753	224	224	at 23	80	952	4	—	—	88.5	17 120	4	1975	English Electric Australia	English Electric 12 CSVT. Mk III	English Electric
2 130	Co-Co	Electric	1 491	239	226	at 18	80	1 016	3	—	—	94.5	18 040	11	1974	English Electric Australia	General Motors EMD (USA) 16-645 E	General Motors EMD (USA)— Clyde Engineering Australia

2 400 (1 550 Class) Details included in 1 550 Class above.

NEW TRACK WORK
Lines completed in 1976 included: Phosphate Hill—Flynn (66 km). New lines proposed include the Norwich Park line—an extension of the Saraji line (50 km) and the 65 km Gregory branch off the existing Central line.

TRACK CONSTRUCTION DETAILS
Standard rail: Flat bottom 94, 82, 80, 63, 61 and 60 lb per yd (47, 41, 40, 31 and 30 kg/m), in lengths of 40 ft (12.2 m). On certain branch lines, 42 lb (20 kg).
107 lb (53 kg) rail was used on the Goonyella Line, secured by 19 mm dog spikes in lieu of the normal 16 mm spike.
Joints: 4- and 6-hole angle and bar fishplates.
Welding: See "Welded Rail".
Cross ties (sleepers): Mostly unimpregnated local timber 9 in × 4½ in × 7 ft 0 in (230 × 115 × 2 150 mm), 6 in (150 mm) thick on mineral lines.
Spacing: 2 640 per mile (1 650 per km) on main lines.
Rail fastening: Normal standard was 16 mm and 14 mm dog spikes, but in recent years Elastic Rail Spikes have been used, mainly with welded track. 19 mm dogspikes used on the Goonyella Line. The use of elastic spikes has now been discontinued.
Ballast: Mainly broken stone. River gravel is used on many branch lines.
Max curvature: Generally 17.3° = radius of 330 ft (100 m), with a few curves down to 21.8° = 264 ft (80 m).
Max gradient: 3% = 1 in 33 uncompensated, but generally does not exceed 2.0% (1 in 50).
Longest continuous gradient: Between Brisbane and Gympie, ruling grade is 1 in 75 with 2 sections (one being 3.2 km long) of 1 in 50.
Max altitude: 3 035 ft (925 m) near Cairns.
Max permitted speed:
Freight: 35 mph (60 km/hr)
Passenger: 45 mph (70 km/hr) but on certain selected sections where track conditions, alignments, etc. are favourable, speed boards indicate speeds up to 50 mph (80 km/hr) maximum for passenger trains and express freight trains.
Max axle load: 19.8 tonnes.
Bridge loading: All bridges on important lines can carry loading equivalent to Coopers E25-E30. Many are equivalent to Coopers E35 and most new construction is to this standard. New mineral lines eg, to Moura, Goonyella, Greenvale and Phosphate Hill have their bridges built to carry Cooper's E50 loading.

Welded rail: The total length of track laid with welded rail is 4 064 km. Normal future programme is to be between 80 and 100 miles (130-160 km) per year.
Rail used weighs 53, 47, 41 and 31 kg/m in 22.2 m bars, which are flashbutt welded at depot into 61 m and 110 m lengths. The longest lengths of welded rail in track are 110 m (depot welded) and 244 m (4 × 61 m) thermit welded at site; but consideration is being given to increase rail length by site welding to form CWR (continuous welded rail). Sleepers are wood 2 150 × 230 × 150 or 115 m thick to which the rails are secured by elastic spikes or dogspikes.
Standard method of laying is by mechanised gang using a Pettibone Mullken crane. Because of the increasing shortage of timber, the adoption of concrete sleepers is being considered.
Rail fastenings: Elastic spikes or dogspikes, depending on conditions, are standard but the use of elastic spikes has now been discontinued.

NEW SIGNALLING INSTALLATIONS
CTC and power signalling has been installed over the 119 km route between Port Curtis Jm. and Toolooa. Equipment was supplied by Page Communications. To facilitate the movement of trains over one of the most densely trafficked sections of single track in the State modern signalling systems have been installed between Port Curtis (Rockhampton) and Toolooa, 11 kilometres south of Gladstone.
The work was carried out under contract by Page Communications Ltd, at a cost of $3 400 000.00. Centralised Traffic Control installed between Port Curtis and Callemondah just north of Gladstone is operated by the Rockhampton Signal Cabin while a new Signal Cabin at Gladstone controls operations by a remote control centralised signalling system over the 25 kilometre section of track between Gladstone and Toolooa.

MARSHALLING YARDS
New yard under construction is at Willowburn (Toowoomba) which will be a conventional yard with capacity for 1 200 metric units daily on the 28 track layout.

CONTAINER OPERATIONS
The railway owns 28 containers:—
4 20 ft × 8 ft × 8 ft	power pack containers
24 4 ft × 4 ft × 6 ft 4 in high	non-insulated containers

Terminals: Container Terminals integrated with other railway freight handling facilities at South Brisbane (Interstate), Clapham (Interstate), Roma Street, Hamilton (Privately operated container Terminals), Toowoomba, Gladstone, Rockhampton, Port Alma (Private), Mackay, Townsville and Mt. Isa.

VICTORIAN RAILWAYS (VicRail)
67 Spencer Street, Melbourne, Victoria 3000

Telegrams: Railways, Melbourne
Telephone: 6 1001

Victorian Railways Board
Chairman: A. G. Gibbs
General Manager: I. G. Hodges
Members: J. J. Brown
R. W. Ellis
L. M. Perrott
F. R. G. Strickland
J. G. W. Urbans
N. G. Wilson
Assistant General Manager (Technical) and Deputy General Manager: L. A. McCallum
Assistant General Manager (Operations): A. J. Nicholson
Assistant General Manager (Finance & Administration): N. H. Rashleigh
Secretary for Railways: A. Augustine
Heads and Assistant Heads of Branches:
Chief Traffic Manager: M. W. B. Ronald
Deputy Chief Traffic Manager: R. T. Barden
Chief Freight Manager: L. A. Krausgrill
Deputy Chief Freight Manager: J. S. Bell
Chief Civil Engineer: D. D. Wade
Assistant Chief Civil Engineer: J. K. Brodie
Chief Mechanical Engineer: S. F. Keane
Assistant Chief Mechanical Engineer: L. C. Rolls
Chief Electrical Engineer: A. Firth
Assistant Chief Electrical Engineer: E. W. Rudolph
Director of Personnel: V. A. Winter
Assistant Director of Personnel: R. A. Smith
Comptroller of Accounts: J. K. McGowan
Assistant Comptroller of Accounts: P. J. Stow
Chief Marketing Manager: A. W. Weeks
Deputy Chief Marketing Manager: A. T. Bewry
Comptroller of Stores: M. L. G. McKenzie
Assistant Comptroller of Stores: J. H. Judd
Manager, Trading & Catering Services: K. J. Feltscheer
Director of Planning: R. J. Gallacher
Director, Management Controls: P. E. Stuart

Gauge: 1.6 m; 1.435 m; 762 mm.
Route length: 6 645 km; 332 km; 13 km.

TRAFFIC
	1975	1976
Total freight ton-km	3 091 439 393	3 071 373 278
Total freight tonnage	11 056 834	10 802 692
Total passenger-km	2 400 411 699	2 327 852 262
Total passengers carried (Railways)	117 719 511	109 669 067
Total passengers carried (Road Motors)	792 952	790 070

FINANCIAL
Compared with the previous year, revenue in 1976 increased by $17.4 million, of which $8.2 million was derived from passengers and parcels; $8.5 million from freight and livestock, and the balance from trading and catering operations and rental. These increases were attained by imposing higher charges which resulted in an average fare increase of 19.8 per cent per passenger km for suburban passengers and 19.9 per cent for country passengers, and an average increase of 9.9 per cent per tonne km for freight and livestock.
Expenditure during the year increased by $28.6 million compared with 1974/75. During the same period costs were boosted to the extent of nearly $37 million by salary and wage awards and other labour-associated expenses, higher prices of materials and services, and an increased transfer of revenue to the Melbourne Underground Rail Loop Authority.

	1975	1976
Revenues	130 087 339	147 449 945
Expenses	256 373 369	286 770 710
(Includes Interest Charges)	12 594 526	14 375 661

FREIGHT TRAFFIC	1973-74	1974-75	1975-76
Total goods and livestock tonnes	11 370 162	11 056 834	10 802 692
Average haul per tonne of goods (kms)	275	280	284
Total net tonne kms (goods and livestock) in millions	3 126	3 091	3 071
Average kms per wagon per day	56.76	58.06	57.86
Average daily wagon output (net tonne kms)	655	647	663
Average net wagon load (tonnes)	16.89	16.67	17.07
Average tonne kms (net) per goods train	6 854	6 785	6 965
Average net train load (tonnes)	301	300	308
Standing time (hours) per 1 000 train kms	5.73	6.20	6.43

Freight business in 1976 generally was adversely affected by economic conditions during the year and, compared with the 1973-74 figure of 3 126 million tonne-kms, the total freight traffic task performed fell by 1.1 per cent. A marked decline was reflected in all classes of industrial traffic, together with superphosphate which experienced a particularly heavy fall in the second half of the year following withdrawal of the Commonwealth bounty, and the effect would have been much more serious had it not been for a substantial increase in wheat railings.

CAPITAL EXPENDITURE
Expenditure on Works and Services during the year ending June 30, 1976 amounted to $A38.6 million, allocated as follows:-

	$A	$A
Capital Works		
Fixed Assets		14 684 631
Renewals and Replacements		
Fixed assets	1 055 565	
Rolling stock	22 894 404	23 949 969
		38 634 600

URBAN DEVELOPMENTS
Under the urban transport programme a new station at Kananook (between Seaford

and Frankston) was brought into service with temporary buildings on September 5, 1975; the erection of permanent buildings was in course during 1975/76. Buildings at existing stations were reconstructed at Glenbervie, Glenroy, Macaulay and West Footscray.

Progress on major urban works was limited owing to the reduced funds made available for urban public transport in the August, 1975, Commonwealth Budget, and no such works were completed during 1975/76. Works in progress were—

Glen Waverley line: Upgrading project
South Kensington—Footscray: Quadruplication of line
Sunshine—Deer Park West: Duplication of line
Caulfield—Mordialloc: Third track
Macleod—Greensborough: Duplication of line
Ringwood—Bayswater: Duplication of line
Ringwood—Croydon: Duplication of line
Automatic power signalling between Bayswater—Fern Tree Gully and Mordialloc—Frankston
Amalgamation of signal boxes in the Newport area
Reconstruction of station buildings at Bayswater

Works continued in the Jolimont, Spencer Street and North Melbourne areas during the year in connection with construction of the Melbourne Underground Rail Loop. In this context the most significant event was the commissioning, in February, 1975, of the new consolidated 'E' signal box at Jolimont Junction, representing the first step in installation of a single operating and control centre—"Metrol"—at Batman Avenue which will initially control the inner metropolitan zone and the underground loops but eventually the whole suburban network.

Car parks at nine suburban locations were added to or redeveloped, and at the end of the year 14 526 car spaces were available for commuter car parking at stations within the Melbourne Metropolitan Study area.

Work proceeded both by contractors and within departmental work shops on production of 50 six-carriage stainless steel suburban electric trains, and during the year 61 new carriages were placed in service. Specifications were in course of preparation for a further 50 trains to follow the current order, with a view to tenders being invited later in 1976. Fifty-four obsolete wooden-bodied carriages were withdrawn from service and scrapped. Continued replacement, as rapidly as practicable, of the remaining obsolete wooden-bodied suburban rolling stock is a matter of vital importance if the suburban system is to fulfil its role of maintaining patronage as well as attracting passengers away from travel by private car. As at June 30, 1976, the total number of carriages comprising the electric suburban fleet was 1 134, made up as follows:—

Stainless steel 161; Blue 433; Red 540

The 540 wooden-bodied red carriages still in service at June 30 represent the equivalent of a fleet of 77 stainless steel trains. Although 10 new stainless steel trains per annum are currently coming into service, the requirements for additional trains to cope with the extended running on outer suburban lines (including lines to be electrified during the next ten years), where traffic growth is taking place, amount to an average of at least two trains per annum, and consequently the effective annual rate of replacement of obsolete trains would not be more than eight.

Contracts were let for new diesel locomotive maintenance depots at Ballarat and Geelong and for the erection of new staff amenities and classrooms at the Dynon Diesel Maintenance Workshops. The construction of improved office accommodation and amenities for yard staff at North Geelong was well advanced at the end of the year, and major building operations were carried out at No. 2 Shed, Melbourne Goods Depot, to provide for establishment of an office for the new Freight Accounting System referred to elsewhere in this Report.

SIGNALLING

At Horsham, track rearrangements and signalling works to meet present and foreseeable requirements were carried out during 75/76. The signalling works include a relay interlocked crossing loop, 1.2 km in length operated at this stage from a control panel located in the station building but suitable for subsequent incorporation into the proposed centralised traffic control system to cover the Ararat—Serviceton section.

MOTIVE POWER AND ROLLING STOCK

During 75/76 ten 2 200 hp 'X' class diesel-electric locomotives for main line freight and passenger services were placed in service. In a ceremony at Spencer Street station on November 14, 1975, the first of these units was named "Edgar H. Brownbill" in honour of a former Chairman of Commissioners who retired in 1967.

A further 10 locomotives of 3 300 hp ('C' class)—the most powerful units to be introduced on the Victorian system to date—were ordered, and deliveries commenced early in 1977.

Two 1 500 hp 'GM' class locomotives, which had been on hire from the Australian National Railways, were returned to that system.

Wagon construction in departmental workshops proceeded during the year to the limit of the funds available, and the following new bogie vehicles, 184 in all, were placed in service—

22 'FCF' Container wagons   16 'JX' Cement hopper wagons
79 'FQX' Container wagons   67 'VSX' Louvre vans

634 obsolete freight vehicles and 25 unserviceable brake vans were withdrawn from service and scrapped. The total capacity of the wagon fleet increased by 13 778 tonnes, or 3 per cent.

TRACK DETAILS

Standard rail: Flat bottomed 94 lb and 107 lb per yard *(46.6 kg* and *53.1 kg* per *m)* in 45 ft rolled lengths.

Cross Ties (Sleepers): Non-impregnated Australian hardwood *254 × 127 mm* cross section in *2 743 mm* lengths for *1.60 m* gauge and *2 591 mm* lengths for *1.435 m* gauge. At insulated joints, sleepers of *304 × 153 mm* are used. There is a current contract for the pressure treatment of 50 000 hardwood sleepers with creosote and oil.

Spacing: 2 420 per mile *(1 513 per km)*.

Rail Fastening: Dogspikes; double shoulder sleeper plates 4-hole angle and bar type fishplates; Fair rail anchors. No pads are used in conjunction with sleeper plates. A 6-hole bar fishplate is now used as the standard for 94 and 107 lb per yard rail rolled by BHP Australia.

Ballast: Generally broken stone or gravel 12 in thick under sleepers for track with welded rail in lengths over 180 ft; 10 in thick for all other first class track; 6 in thick on second class track and non-welded rail.

Max curvature: 11 ft = radius of 28 ft *(161 m)* × *(150 m)* 492R.

Max gradient:
  Main line: 2.08% = 1 in 48
  Branch line: 3.33% = 1 in 30.

Longest continuous gradient: 16.7 miles of 1 in 42 (0.24%) grade with 0.72% curves = radius of 7 920 ft *(2 414 m)* 9.24 miles of 1 in 40 (2.08%) grade with 2.48° curves = radius of 2 310 ft *(704 m)*.

Max altitude: 2 562 ft *(781 m)* near Shelley on Wodonga-Cudgewa line.

First of VicRail's ten new C class locomotives built by Clyde-GM.

Max axle load: (standard and broad gauges) 18.75 tons.

Welded Rail: Standard 45 ft new rail and serviceable rails are welded into lengths between 90 ft and 270 ft at the central Flash Butt Welding Depot.
Rails in the track are welded into continuous lengths between insulated joints or crossing work and distressed to be stress-free between rail temperatures of 32°C and 36°C.

SIGNAL AND TRAIN CONTROL INSTALLATIONS 1975/76

Horsham: Provision of a relay interlocking for long crossing loop and regional freight centre to replace a 64 lever mechanical interlocking machine with provision for future CTC operation. Design and installation by VR.

VICTORIA RAILWAYS—MAIN LINE DIESEL LOCOMOTIVES

Class	Axle Arrangement	Transmission	Rated Power hp	Max. lbs (kg)	Tractive Effort Continuous at lbs (kg)	mph (km/h)	Max. Speed mph (km/h)	Wheel Dia. ins (mm)	Total Weight Tons	Length ft ins (mm)	No. Built	Year first Built	Builders: Mechanical Parts	Engine & Type	Transmission
B	Co-Co	Elec.	1 500	60 000 (27 200)	40 000 (18 150)	11.0 (17.7)	83 (134)	40 (1 016)	111.6	60' 10'' (18 542)	26	1952	Clyde—G.M.	G.M. 567B	G.M.
F	C	,,	350	33 000 (15 000)	11 000 (5 000)	7.25 (11.7)	20 (32)	48½ (1 232)	49.5	29' 3'' (8 915)	16	1951	English Electric	English Electric 6 KT	E.E.
H	Bo-Bo	,,	1 050	44 800 (20 320)	33 380 (15 140)		60 (97)	40 (1 016)	80	43' 11'' (13 386)	5	1969	Clyde—G.M.	G.M. 8-645	G.M.
L	Co-Co	,,	2 400	47 000 (21 300)	25 200 (11 400)	30.0 (48.3)	75 (120)	40 (1 016)	93	59' 0'' (17 983)	25	1952	,,		,,
S	Co-Co	,,	1 800	63 800 (28 940)	53 500 (24 270)	9.5 (15.3)	83 (134)	,,	114	60' 11'' (18 567)	16	1957	Clyde—G.M.	G.M. 567C	G.M.
T	Bo-Bo	,,	950	38 080 (17 275)	28 000 (12 700)	,,	62 (100)	,,	68	47' 9'' (14 554)	28	1955	,,	,,	,,
			950		33 880 (15 370)	7.5 (12.1)	,,		,,	43' 11'' (13 386)	52	1959	,,	G.M. 8-567CR	,,
			1 050	,,	,,	8.8 (14.1)	,,		,,	,,	2	1966	,,	G.M. 8-645	,,
											12	1968	,,	,,	,,
W	C	Hyd.	650	32 250 (14 630)	29 200 (13 240)		40 (64)	48½ (1 232)	48	30' 1'' (9 169)	27	1959	Tulloch	Mercedes-Benz MB82OB	Krupp
X	Co-Co	Elec.	1 800	64 000 (29 030)	53 700 (24 360)	9.5 (15.3)	83 (134)	40 (1 016)	112	60' 3'' (18 364)	20	1966	Clyde—G.M.	G.M. 16-567E	G.M.
			2 000									1970	,,	G.M. 16-645E	Clyde-G.M.
Y	Bo-Bo	,,	750	35 800 (16 240)	17 550 (7 960)	10 (16.1)	40 (64)	42 (1 067)	64	43' 7'' (13 284)	50	1963	,,	G.M. 567	G.M.
											25	1968	,,	G.M. 645E	
C	Co-Co	,,	3 000	85 000 (38 548)			83 (134)	40 (1 016)	132	66' (20 117)	2	1977	,,	G.M. (645E3)	G.M.

Flinders Street 'E' Signal Box: Provision of push button route setting control panel and interlocking using geographical circuit system for vital circuits and electronic integrated circuit system for non-vital route setting controls and indication circuits. The illuminated track diagram uses light emmitting diodes for all indications. The installation comprises 141 routes. Point machines are electro-pneumatically operated clamp locks (149 No.) and signal are searchlight type (49 No.) and train stops are electro-pneumatic. Provision has been made for remote control from a future Metropolitan Train Control Center. Design and Installation by VR.

Oakleigh: Provision of a route setting control panel and interlocking using a geographical circuit system for vital circuits and an electronic integrated circuit system for non-vital route setting controls and indication circuits. The illuminated track diagram uses light emmitting diodes for all indications.

The installation comprises 47 routes and replaces two mechanical signal boxes. Point machines are electro-pneumatically operated clamp lock type (12 No.) and signals are searchlight type (19 No). Design and installation by VR.

Springvale: Provision of a relay interlocking for 9 No. electrically operated points, 24 searchlight signals and a boom barrier installation controlled from individual levers to replace a mechanical installation. Design and installation by VR.

Glenhuntly-Bentleigh: Provision of automatic signalling and boom barriers at 2 level crossings to replace mechanical signalling, 3 No. mechanical interlocking machines and double line manual block working on 3 km of the double track electrified suburban system.
Design and Installation by VR.

Ringwood-Croydon and Ringwood-Bayswater: Provision of automatic signalling to replace mechanical signalling and single line electric staff (token system) on 2 No. 5 km single line sections on the electrified suburban system.
Design and Installation by V.R.

Melbourne-Geelong Main Line: Provision of relay interlockings at Werribee (26 levers) Lara (25 levers) and Geelong-Maitland St Sidings (8 levers) using electrically operated dual control point machines and searchlight signals to replace mechanical interlocking machines.

Major Equipment Suppliers: Westinghouse Brake and Signal Co (Aust) Pty Ltd signals electric point machines, electro-pneumatic train stops, relays, level crossing apparatus.

Comp Air (Asia) Ltd—Electro Pneumatic equipment for point operation.

W. Tolson & Co PL—Control Panel for Flinders Street 'E'.

VR Workshops—Clamp Lock points machines.

STATE TRANSPORT AUTHORITY RAIL DIVISION (SOUTH AUSTRALIA)

GPO Box 2351, Adelaide, South Australia 5001

Telephone: 51 0231

General Manager: J. M. Doyle
Secretary: J. L. Hazeal
General Traffic Manager: P. E. Shearer
Chief Mechanical Engineer: W. D. Saunders
Chief Engineer: L. H. A. McLean
Signal and Telegraph Engineer: R. T. Carmichael
Comptroller: E. J. Hughes

Gauge: 1.6 m; 1.435 m; 1.067 m
Route length: 2 531 km; 395 km; 963 km

The former South Australian Railways was fully amalgamated into the Australian National Railways Commission on March 1, 1978.

TRAFFIC

	1974	1975	1976
Freight tonne-km	1 753 067 788	1 756 929 598	1 686 571 425
Freight tonnes	6 655 039	6 783 303	6 183 781
Passenger-km	337 166 247	332 484 601	328 405 182
Passenger journeys	13 597 271	12 696 685	12 672 027

FINANCE

	1974	1975	1976
	$A	$A	$A
Revenues	39 827 216	48 314 664	50 098 656
Expenses	56 241 130	74 963 769	84 778 677

MOTIVE POWER

	Line Haul	Switching
Locomotives in steam	4 (stored)	—
Diesel-electric locomotives	105	46
Diesel railcars	125	—

ROLLING STOCK

Passenger train coaches: 198 units, including 51 vehicles jointly owned with Victorian Railways and 52 (Indian Pacific) coaches of which South Australian Railways equity is approximately 10 per cent.

Number of freight wagons: 7 132.

Number of containers: 593.

TRACK WORK 1976

New line laid: Track doubling was completed between Brighton and Christie Downs (15 km).

New lines projected: Planning and surveying is in hand for the projected 191 km standard gauge line from Adelaide to Crystal Brook.

Line closures: No lines were closed.

Rail types and weights: 1 600 mm main lines—53 and 47 kg/m; 1 600 mm branch lines—41 and 31 kg-m; 1 435 mm main lines—47 kg/m; 1 067 mm main lines—40, 31 and 25 kg/m.

Sleepers: 1 600 mm gauge—local hardwood and creosoted pine, 254 mm × 127 mm × 2 600 mm spaced 760 mm. Also some steel sleepers. 1 435 mm gauge—local hardwood 254 mm × 127 mm × 2 600 mm spaced 760 mm. 1 067 mm gauge—local hardwood 203 mm × 115 mm × 980 mm spaced 670 mm.

Rail fastenings: 19 mm square dogspikes.

Welded Rail: 1.47 route km of new and 45.85 route km of second hand welded rail was laid, mostly in 73 metre lengths, making a total of 1 949 route km of welded rail, all welded by the flashbutt process at a central depot. Of this length a further 88 km was continuously welded in the field by the Thermit process making a total of 410 route km of continuous welded rail.

SIGNAL AND TRAIN CONTROL INSTALLATIONS

New relay interlockings have been installed at Brighton, Port Stanvac and Lonsdale, working in conjunction with the extension of the Port Stanvac line to Christie Downs. Signalling on the line has been installed to provide for future CTC control and electrification.

A further relay interlocking has been installed in preparation for CTC working between Belair and Tailem Bend, and the data transmission equipment for this section will be delivered and installed shortly.

CONTAINERS

The fleet of containers owned by the Railways consist of twenty-four 11.3 m trays complete with sides and gates, nine insulated containers of 22.4 m³ capacity and twenty 6.1 m ISO insulated containers which use liquid CO_2 as the refrigerant ("snow shooting"). They have polyurethane insulation 102 mm thick on the bottom and walls, and 127 mm thick on top. This insulation reduces the heat loss to a negligible 70 kilo Joules per hour per degree Kelvin (equal to 37 BTU's per hour per degree Fahrenheit). The containers are clad in aluminium with an aluminium T-bar floor and stainless steel interior. Further twenty containers of similar design and performance, but with a steel frame and fibreglass exterior cladding, are now being put into traffic.

A number of smaller containers, ranging from 6.5 m³ to 21.7 m³ and suitable for the transportation of a variety of dry goods, are also in service.

HANDLING EQUIPMENT

The two principle city freight depots—Mile End and Port Adelaide—have the following equipment for handling containers:-

Mile End
- 1 × 30 tonne gantry crane
- 1 × 20 tonne gantry crane
- 1 × 10 tonne mobile crane
- 1 × 8 tonne mobile crane
- 2 × 6 tonne mobile crane
- 2 × 10 tonne forklift

Port Adelaide
- 1 × 11.5 tonne mobile crane
- 1 × 6.5 tonne mobile crane
- 1 × 10 tonne forklift

DIESEL ELECTRIC LOCOMOTIVES

Class	Axle Arrangement	Trans-mission	Rated Power hp	Max. lbs (kg)	Tractive Effort Continuous at lbs (kg)	mph (km/h)	Max. Speed mph (km/h)	Wheel Dia. ins (mm)	Total Weight Tons	Length ft ins (mm)	No. Built	Year first Built	Builders: Mechanical Parts	Engine & Type	Transmission
350	Bo.Bo	Elec.	350	23 400	8 800	11	45	36	49.5	35'	2	1949	Islington Workshops SA with English Electric equipment	E.E. 6KT	E.E.C. 505D
500	Bo-Bo	Elec.	550	42 000	30 000	4.3	40	36	56	38' 6''	34	1964-1969	Islington Workshops SA with English Electric equipment	E.E. 4SRKT	E.E.C. 548
600	Co-Co	Elec.	1 950	83 000	69 600	—	70	40	111	54' 6''	7	1965-1970	A. E. Goodwin Ltd Alco 251		G.E. 752 (2 locomotives) A.E.I. 165 (5 locomotives)
700	Co-Co	Elec.	2 150	82 000	69 600	7	70	40	110	61' 3''	6	1971-1972	A. E. Goodwin Ltd Alco 251		A.E.I. 165
800	Bo-Bo	Elec.	750	43 000	23 500	6	60	42	72	42'	10	1956-1957	English Electric Co.	E. E. 6SRKT	E.E.C. 526
830	Co-Co	Elec.	975	52 000	40 200	6	60	40	70.5	44' 3''	45	1959-1970	A. E. Goodwin Ltd Alco 251		(17) G. E. 761; (15) G.E. 761; (13) A.E.I. 253 or A.E.I. 253
900	A1A-A1A	Elec.	1 760	60 000	34 000	15	70	42	126	63' 4''	10	1951-1953	Islington Workshops SA with English Electric equipment	E.E. 16SVT	E.E.C. 523
930	Co-Co	Elec.	1 750	77 500	43 900	11.3	70	40	102 single ended 104 double ended	55' 10''	37	1955-1967	A. E. Goodwin Ltd Alco 251		G.E. 761

DIESEL HYDRAULIC RAIL CARS

Class	Axle Arrangement	Transmission	Rated Power hp	Max. lbs (kg)	Tractive Effort Continuous at lbs (kg)	Tractive Effort Continuous at mph (km/h)	Max. Speed mph (km/h)	Wheel Dia. ins (mm)	Total Weight Tons	Length ft ins (mm)	No. Built	Year first Built	Builders: Mechanical Parts	Builders: Engine & Type	Builders: Transmission
250	1A-A1	Hyd.	300	—	—	—	70	36	60	78' 3''	11	1954-1959	Islington Workshops SA Railways	Cummins NT-855-R2	D.F.F.R. Torque converter with 303 Reverser
280	1A-A1	Hyd.	300	—	—	—	70	36	52	70' 3''	3	1958-1959	Islington Workshops SA Railways	Cummins NT-855-R2	D.F.F.R. Torque converter with 303 Reverser
300 G-M	1A-A1	Hyd.	219 each engine	—	—	—	55	36	40 42	65'	74	1955-1970	Islington Workshops SA Railways	54 cars— G-M 6.71	42 cars—D.F.R. converter with 300 Reverser 12 cars—T.D.D.F.R. converter with 303 Reverser
300 R-R		Hyd.	229 each engine (20 cars)	—	—	—								20 cars—R-R C.6.S.F.L.H.	Rolls D.F.R. Torque converter Rolls CG. CG.100 Reverser (20 cars)
400 G-M	1A-A1	Hyd.	219 each engine	—	—	—	55	36	42	65'	37	1959-1971	Islington Workshops SA Railways	G-M 6.71	D.F.F.R. Torque converter with 303 Reverser (20 cars) T.D.D.F.R. Torque converter with 303 Reverser (17 cars)

ROLLING STOCK ISSUED TO SERVICE DURING 1976

Class	Type	Dimensions (mm) Wheel & Axle	Dimensions (mm) Over Couplers	Dimensions (mm) Height	Dimensions (mm) Width	Mass (tonnes) Tare	Mass (tonnes) Load	Number of Units Issued	Builder
Freight Vehicles—1 600 mm Gauge									
'FQX'	Flat wagon carry (3) containers	2-four wheel bogies	20 085	1 100	2 510	19.3	55.0	23	Islington Workshops (S.T.A.) Rail Division South Australia
'OBF'	Open wagon	four wheel	7 580	2 550	3 005	9.0	21.3	36	Islington Workshops (S.T.A.) Rail Division South Australia
Service vehicles—1 435 mm Gauge									
'SH'	Ballast hopper wagons	2-four wheel bogies	10 310	3 300	3 045	17.4	55.9	2	Islington Workshops (S.T.A.) Rail Division South Australia

CONTAINER RAIL WAGONS AS AT 31.12.76

Class	Type	Dimensions (mm) Wheel & Axle	Dimensions (mm) Over Couplers	Dimensions (mm) Floor Height	Dimensions (mm) Width	Tare	Mass (tonnes) Load	No. of Units in Service	Builder
'FCS'	Flat Wagon	2 four-wheel bogies	10 970 over end sills	1 260	2 850	14.0	22.4	70	S.A. Railways
'SFCW'	Flat Wagon	2 four-wheel bogies	25 730	1 020	2 620	23.2	51.0	16	,,
'FQX'	Flat Wagon	2 four-wheel bogies	20 090	1 110	2 760	19.3	55.9	120	,,
'SFQX'	Flat Wagon	2 four-wheel bogies	16 510	1 230	2 670	15.2	40.6	3	,,
'SFKX'	Flat Wagon	2 four-wheel bogies	23 740	1 110	2 760	23.6	52.5	18	,,
'FWC'	Flat Wagon	2 four-wheel bogies	13 970	1 220	2 820	15.1	44.7	3	,,
'FBR'	Flat Wagon	2 four-wheel bogies	13 970	1 260	2 840	17.8	40.6	5	,,

WESTERN AUSTRALIAN GOVERNMENT RAILWAYS (WESTRAIL)

Westrail Centre, West Parade, East Perth, Western Australia

Telephone: 28 7777

Gauge: 1.067 m; 1.435 m; Dual gauge.
Route length: 4 750 km; 1 227 km; 127 km.

Commissioner of Railways: R. J. Pascoe
Assistant Commissioner: W. I. McCullough
Secretary for Railways: A. E. Williams
Chief Traffic Manager: I. J. Kinshela
Chief Civil Engineer: A. B. Holm
Chief Mechanical Engineer: L. Pitsikas
Commercial Manager: B. W. E. Copley
Comptroller of Accounts and Audit: R. L. Denison
Comptroller of Stores: W. T. Tobin
Director, Management Services Bureau: Dr. P. R. Grimwood

TRAFFIC

	1975	1976
Total freight tonne-km	4 269 270 279	4 532 000 000
Total freight tonnage	16 570 153	19 000 000
Total passenger-km	177 289 872	—
Total passengers carried (country only)	543 032	103 000

FINANCES

	1974	1975	1976
Revenues	$A79 860 962	$A108 309 240	$A138 000 000
Expenses	$A96 429 348	$A119 984 942	$A134 000 000

Westrail faced escalating labour and material costs during 1976/7 and experienced the effects of drought which hit some areas of the State's grain-growing belt.
Despite the problems record tonnages were moved during the financial year ended June 30 1976 and freight figures rose to 19 million tonnes, a healthy increase of 1.2 million on the previous year's haulage.Tonne-km fell only slightly to 4 532 million.
The trend of the past decade in which rail traffic has increased at a rate equivalent to 9 per cent per annum was continued despite the down-turn in grain haulage to 3.4 million tonnes due to the effects of drought and lack of shipping as well as a reduction in tonnage of iron ore railed from Koolyanobbing.
That a less favourable result was achieved (a loss of roundly $11.1 million after interest payments and other charges as compared with $3.1 million in 1975/76) was principally due to the State Government's decision to hold gazetted rail charges at the July 1975 level for a further 12 months. During the two-year period in which charges were pegged general costs increased by about 30 per cent.
With construction of harbour facilities at Bunbury an increasing tonnage of alumina is now being handled at this port instead of Kwinana and railed direct from Alcoa's second refinery at Pinjarra. This financial year over 820 000 tonnes was hauled to Bunbury and 1.2 million tonnes to their Kwinana installation.

FREIGHT

Bauxite has always been a steady bulk commodity for Westrail, but in 1976 movement

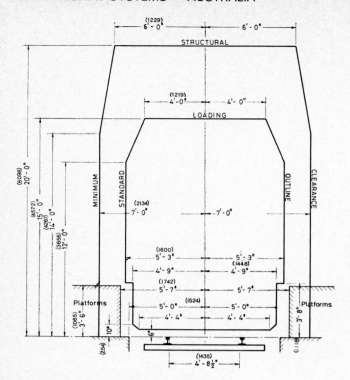

Westrail's 1.435 m loading and structural gauge

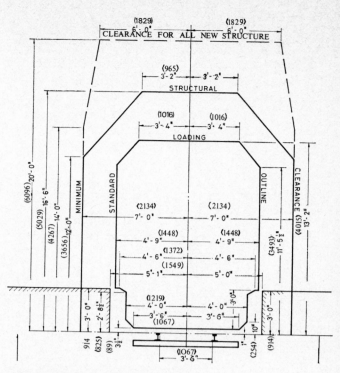

Westrail's 1.067 m loading and structural gauge

rose to 4.4 million from the mines at Jarrahdale in the Darling Ranges to the Alcoa refinery at the Kwinana industrial area south of Fremantle.

Movement of mineral sands increased to 713 000 tonnes, assisted by Western Titanium's introduction to the industry at Eneabba. They are railing direct to Geraldton for shipment overseas and to their Capel refinery south of Perth.

Railing of woodchips from Manjimup also accelerated to 424 000 tonnes in the first full year of operation, despite a halt to shipping at Bunbury.

Coal, from the State's coalfield at Collie, topped one million tonnes for the second year in succession, eclipsing last year's figure by 30 000 tonnes.

Coal is continuing to play an important role in Westrail's bulk commodity haulage and it seems it will continue to do so in future years.

The State Energy Commission has converted several power stations from oil to coal fuel and two new units at the Kwinana power station are expected to start using coal during 1980.

Industry is also maintaining an interest in coal as a power source and roundly 250 000 tonnes annually are being hauled from Collie to Bunbury and the metropolitan area.

The movement of salt from Lake Lefroy to the port of Esperance in the south east of the State fluctuates as the overseas demand by industry waxes and wanes. This financial year the demand rose and a total of 196 000 tonnes was hauled from the plant to the coast.

The largest drop in Westrail's haulage of bulk commodities last year was in the movement of iron ore. This traffic from Koolyanobbing to the rolling mills at Kwinana fell to 1.8 million tonnes.

NEW FACILITIES

Sophisticated freight handling facilities at Westrail's Kewdale Freight Terminal and Forrestfield Marshalling Yards, fast standard gauge trains operating on a daily basis between West and Eastern Australia, and a decline in coastal shipping around the country have all combined to produce an increasing volume of rail freight.

Since 1968 traffic has more than trebled topping the millionth tonne for the first time in 1976.

With reduction of the interstate shipping service from 1975 and subsequent transfer to rail, weekly handling of containers has also risen sharply to 2 000 during peak periods, both east and west-bound.

The Forrestfield Marshalling Yard, one of the most modern installations of its kind in Australia, has also been busy and during the latter part of this financial year recorded the second millionth wagon marshalled across the fully-automated hump since its introduction in 1973.

The 56 km railway line between Collie and Brunswick Junction, 155 kms south of Perth, is being upgraded to allow block coal trains to operate between the mines and the main south west line with 19 tonne axle loads.

Two new bridges were constructed and 12 deviations made on the route eliminating some of the 120 curves on the old line.

Planning for the upgrading of the standard gauge railway between Kwinana and Koolyanobbing is in hand. Concrete sleepers manufactured locally are to be used on this line for the first time in Western Australia.

The new 60 kg/m Australian standard rail will be used in rerailing. The first shipment rolled by BHP in Australia has arrived at Westrail's Midland Workshops to allow points and crossings to be constructed before work on the line starts.

Over 800 staff moved into Westrail's new $9.5 million "home" in East Perth on October 19 1975. The six storey Westrail Centre fulfills two major functions—a permanent terminal for interstate and intrastate rail and bus passengers and a combined office facility for Westrail's headquarters staff.

It has replaced a temporary structure which was in use as a station terminal since the interstate standard gauge services were inaugurated in 1969.

A new centre has been commissioned at Midland to handle four centralised traffic control sections. The total distance of CTC signalling now under control from Midland is 274 km and ranges from Coolup in the south to the industrial area of Kwinana and through the Avon Valley east of Perth.

MOTIVE POWER AND ROLLING STOCK

The first of 11 new narrow gauge locomotives was under construction over the 1975/76 financial year. They are being built by Commonwealth Engineering at Bassendean, with bogies cast at Westrail's Workshops, and will be the most powerful locomotives in service on the State's narrow gauge network.

A standard gauge double-deck car carrier was also converted at Midland to take an additional tier. A prototype operated successfully on a trial run between Port Augusta and North Fremantle and it is anticipated more of the double-deck carriers will be converted in due course.

Demands and attitudes towards public transport have changed over the years and a need for speedy efficient transport grows continuously.

Fast "Prospector" railcars operating between Perth, Merredin and Kalgoorlie have

Class L 2386/3—2 162 kW Co-Co diesel-electric main line locomotive

Class RA 1454—1 342 kW Co-Co diesel-electric main line locomotive

attracted increasing numbers of passengers and a fleet of modern buses covers the rest of the system with a web of regular services.

Passenger bus services are being complemented by a fleet of 12 new tourist-style coaches. They are fully air conditioned and feature airline-type interior decor. The first bus was scheduled to be introduced during October 1977, marking the first step in a progressive replacement of Westrail's present fleet.

TRACK

New track built:

Narrow Gauge (Single)   Dongara-Eneabba   52 km
                                                        46.6 kg rail

A three-tier automobile carrier built at Westrail's workshops

Type XW narrow-gauge wheat hopper wagon used to transport grain from country silos to transfer depots at major centres for onward haulage to coast-based silos.

MAIN LINE DIESEL LOCOMOTIVES

Gauge mm	Class	Axle Arrangement	Transmission	Rated Power kW	Max. kN	Tractive Effort Continuous at kN	kmlh	Max Speed kmlh	Wheel dia. mm	Total Mass tonnes	Length mm	No. Built	Year First Built	Builders Mechanical Parts	Engine & Type	Transmission
1.067	A	Co-Co	Elec.	1 063/977	240	226	12	100	1 016	89.16	15 036	12	1960	Clyde. Eng. Co.	EMD 12-567C	EMD D25-D29
,,	AA	,,	,,	1 230/1 120	240	226	14	100	1 016	90.51	15 036	5	1967	Clyde Eng. Co.	EMD 12-645E	EMD D25-D29
,,	AB	,,	,,	1 230/1 120	240	226	14	100	1 016	96.00	15 494	6	1969	Clyde Eng. Co.	EMD 12-645E	EMD D32-D29
,,	C	,,	,,	1 145/1 035	240	200	14.5	96	1 016	90.42	15 033	3	1962	English Electric	English Electric 12 SVT	EE 822 6C-548
,,	D	,,	,,	1 640/1 490	310	245.3	18	90	1 016	107.85	17 044	5	1971	Clyde Eng. Co.	EMD 16-645E	EMD D32-D29
,,	DA	,,	,,	1 640/1 490	310	245.3	18	90	1 016	96.72	17 044	7	1972	Clyde Eng. Co.	EMD 16-645E	EMD D32-D29
,,	F	AIA-AIA	,,	560/510	163.7	99.6	15.3	80	952	64.92	12 800	7	1958	English Electric	English Electric 6 SRKT	EE 827/4C-525
,,	G	Co-Co	,,	768/708	240	191.2	9.5	90	952	76.20	12 496	2	1963	,,	English Electric 8 SVT	EE 819/7E-548
,,	R	,,	,,	1 454/1 338	275	226.9	17.5	96	952	94.05	15 240	5	1968	,,	English Electric 12 CSVT	EE 822/16J-548
,,	RA	,,	,,	1 454/1 342	298	226.9	17.5	96	952	96.00	16 306	10	1969	,,	,,	EE 822/16J-548
,,	X, XA, XB	2-DO-2	,,	824/779	124.5	53.3	39	88	800	79.00	14 630	46	1954	Metro-Vickers	Crossley HST V8	MV TG 4203-136
,,	B	0-6-0	Hyd.	396/353	102.3	80	10	42	1 016	38.96	7 785	10	1962	Comm. Eng. Co.	Cummins VT-12-B	Twin Disc-Wiseman
,,	E	0-6-0	,,	186	80	—	—	40	915	26.42	5 588	1	1957	Comm. Eng. Co.	Rolls Royce C6SFL	Twin Disc-DF 11 500
,,	M	B-B	,,	522/484	—	109	9.6	53	1 016	49.66	10 961	2	1972	Walkers Ltd.	Cummins VTA 1710-L	Voith L4r4U2-G
,,	MA	B-B	,,	522/484	—	109	9.6	53	1 016	44.8	10 955	3	1973	Walkers Ltd.	Caterpiller D379B	Voith L4r4U2-G
,,	T	0-6-0	Elec.	492/447	111.2	69	18.6	65	1 016	37.35	75.69	5	1967	Tulloch	Cummins VT-12-825	Brush TG 78-43 TM 68-46
,,	TA	0-6-0	,,	492/447	111.2	69	18.6	65	1 016	38.10	7 569	10	1970	,,	Cummins VTA-1710-L	Brush TG-43 TM 68-46
,,	Y	Bo-Bo	,,	306/280	102.3	40	18.5	72	915	38.80	10 020	18	1953	British Thompson Houston	Paxman 12 RPHI	RTB 8944-B.T.H. 124 PV
,,	Z	0-6-0	Mech.	106/96	37.8	—	—	28	800	15.14	5 752	3	1953	Drewry Car Co.	Gardner 8 LW	Wilson Epicyclic
1.435	K	Co-Co	Elec.	1 454/1 388	298	189	19	130	1 016	117.3	16 764	9	1966	English Electric	English Electric 12 CSVT	EE 822/16L-538
*1.435	KA	Co-Co	Elec.	1 454/1 342	293	226.9	17.5	96	952	99	16 306	7	1969	English Electric	English Electric 12 CSVT	EE 822/161 548
,,	L	,,	,,	2 386/2 162	337.2	311.4	21	135	1 016	137.16	19 355	23	1967	Clyde Eng. Co.	EMD 16-645E3	EMD AR1O-D77
,,	H	Bo-Bo	,,	708/641	240	167.7	10	100	1 016	72.38	12 952	5	1965	English Electric	English Electric 6 CSRKT	EE 819/8F-538
,,	J	,,	,,	485/447	159.2	117.8	11.2	100	1 016	66.64	13 004	5	1966	Clyde Eng. Co.	EMD 6-567C	EMD D25-D29

DIESEL RAILCARS

Gauge mm	Class	Axle Arrangement	Transmission	Rated Power kW	Max. kN	Tractive Effort Continuous at kN	kmlh	Max Speed kmlh	Wheel dia. mm	Total Mass tonnes	Length mm	No. Built	Year First Built	Builders Mechanical Parts	Engine & Type	Transmission
1 067	ADG	1A-A1	Hyd.	90				80	800	30.99	19 050	18	1954	Cravens	AEC A 219	Voith DIWA 501
1 067	ADX	1A-A1	Mech.	112				80	800	33.53	19 050	10	1960	Westrail	AEC A 220	B.U.T. R 14
1 067	ADH	1A-A1	Hyd.	90				80	800	30.99	19 050	4	1963	Cravens	A.E.C. A 219	Voith DIWA 501
1 067	ADK	1A-A1	,,	195				85	800	33.28	20 254	10	1968	Comm. Eng. Co.	Cummina NHHTO-6-B1	Voith DIWA 501
1 435	WCA	1A-A1	,,	283				144	940	68.22	27 076	5	1972	Comm. Eng. Co.	M.A.N. D 3650 HM6U	Voith T113R

Future Work
Planning is in hand to upgrade the Standard Gauge line between Kwinana and Koolyanobbing (490 km) using 60 kg/m rail and concrete sleepers.

New Rail Laid

46.6 kg	18.5 km
40.6 kg	15.0 km

Rail Fastenings
19 mm square dogspikes.

Pads under rails
Double shoulder sleeper plates 13 mm thick made by B.H.P.

Welded Rail (Standard Gauge & New Works)
Length of track in route kilometres at December 31 1976.

Double Dual Gauge	Perth Terminal-Avon	113 km
	Woodbridge-Forrestfield	9 km
	Woodbridge-Triangle	2.5 km
	Woodbridge-Midland	2 km
Single Dual Gauge	Cockburn Jct.-Kwinana	13 km
Single N.G. and	Leighton-Cockburn Jct.	14.5 km
Single S.G.	Forrestfield-Kenwick	6.5 km
	Avon-East Northam	5 km
Single Narrow Gauge	Jarrahdale extension	6.5 km
	Dongarra-Eneabba	95 km
	Dongara-Walkaway	32 km
	Picton Jct.-Northcliffe	149 km
	Brunswick-Collie	20 km
	Claisebrook-Picton Jct.	177 km
	Kwinana-Mundijong	26 km
Single Standard Gauge	Kenwick-Cockburn Jct.	19 km
	East Northam-Kalgoorlie	538 km
	Kwinana Loop Railway	4 km
	Kalgoorlie-Esperance	312 km
Standard Method of Welding	Flashbutt to 109.75 m	
	Field Welding-Thermit	

TRACK DETAILS
Standard Rail: Flat bottom in 13.72 m length, weighing 46.6 kg/m and 40.61 kg/m (94 lb/yd and 82 lb/yd) and older rail of varying weights. New rail is 60 kg/m.
Joints: Fishplates; but in relaying the lengths are flashbutt welded to 109.75 m then Thermit Welded at into 439 m lengths or into continuous rail.
Rail fastenings: Dogspikes.
Cross ties (sleepers): Local hardwood, Jarrah, Wandoo etc. Standard & Dual Gauge: 2.5 m × 225 mm × 130 mm. Narrow Gauge: 2.1 m × 225 mm × 115 mm
Spacing: Standard Gauge: 1 640 km. Narrow Gauge: 1 310 km
Ballast: 38 mm granite ballast on main lines. Iron stone gravel on branch lines.
Curves, min radius: Main lines: 242 m = 7.25° curve. Branch lines: 141 m = 12.5° curve
Max gradient: 1 in 40 = 2½%
Max altitude: 520 m Meekatharra
Axle Loading: 1 067 mm gauge; Main lines 19 tonnes, Branch lines 11 tonnes. 1 435 mm gauge; Main lines 24 tonnes, Branch lines 16 tonnes

SIGNAL & TRAIN CONTROL INSTALLATIONS—1976

Description	Route Length	Location	Position of Control	Supplier
Bunbury Inner Harbour power signalling	4 km	Bunbury	Picton	WB & S (Aust.) Installed by Westrail.
Pinjarra Triangle power signalling	4.7 km	Pinjarra	Midland	WB & S (Aust.) Installed by Westrail.
Transfer of CTC control from Perth to Midland	115 km (existing CTC system)	Armadale —Kwinana —Coolup	Midland	WB & S (Aust.) Installed by Westrail
Transfer of CTC control from Perth to Midland	101 km (existing CTC system)	Bellevue —Avon Yard	Midland	WB & S (Aust.)
Train electric staff working Yornup to Lambert	33 km	Picton— Northcliffe Branch	Yornup, Manjimup, Lambert	
New relay room and equipment provided	—	Perth Terminal	Claisebrook	WB & S (Aust.) Installed by Westrail.
Kalgoorlie power signalling	5 km	Kalgoorlie	West Kalgoorlie	WB & S (Aust.) Installed by Westrail.

Flashlight & Boomgate Installations

3 level crossings with boomgate protection	—	—	—	WB & S (Aust.) Installed by Westrail
12 level crossings with flashlight protection	—	—	—	WB & S (Aust.) Installed by Westrail

AUSTRIA
AUSTRIAN FEDERAL RAILWAYS
Österreichische Bundesbahnen (ÖBB), Elisabethstrasse 9, A-1010 Vienna

Telephone: 5650
Telegrams: Genbandion

General Manager: Dr. Wolfgang Pycha
Deputy General Manager: Dr. Otto Seidelmann
Director, Managing Board: Dr. Friedrich Herzog
Director, Managing Board: Dipl. Ing. Dr. techn. Roman Jaworski
Board of Directors:
  President: Dkfm. Dr. Alfred Weiser
  Vice-President: Hermann Thalhammer
Staff Office, Data Processing and Cybernetics: Seilerstätte 1, 1010 Vienna
  Manager: Dipl. Ing. Rudolf Waitzer
Staff Office, Management and Audit: Hegelgasse 7, 1010 Vienna
  Manager: Dipl. Ing. Günther Winkler
General Secretariat:
  Secretary General: Dr. Johann Pregant
Administrative Directorate:
  Administrative Manager: Dr. Max Posch
Personnel Directorate:
  Personnel Manager: Dr. Herbert Schartl
Financial Directorate:
  Financial Manager: Dipl.Ing. Johann Mlinek
Operational Directorate:
  Operational Manager: Dr. Josef Pucher
Sales Directorate: Gauermanngasse 2-4, 1010 Vienna
Sales Manager: Dr. Karl Zach
Machinery Directorate: Langauergasse 1, 1150 Vienna
  Machinery Directorate: Dipl. Ing. Viktor Köttner
Building Directorate: Elisabethstrasse 18, 1010 Vienna
  Building Manager: Dipl. Ing. Walter Tschepper
Purchasing Directorate: Operngasse 24, 1010 Vienna
  Purchasing Manager: Dr. Wilhelm Marhold
Electronics Directorate: Daffingerstrasse 4, 1030 Vienna
  Electronics Manager: Dipl. Ing. Leo Mimmler
Motor Vehicles Servicing Section: Gauermanngasse 2-4, 1010 Vienna
  Manager: Alfred Tomschy
Chief Public Health Officers Section: Springergasse 5, 1020 Vienna
  Chief Public Health Officer: Dr. Richard Sasse
Vienna Federal Railways Directorate: Nordbahnstasse 50, 1020 Vienna
  President: Dr. Erhard d'Aron
Linz Federal Railways Directorate: Bahnhofstrasse 3, 4020 Linz
  President: Dipl. Ing. Wilhelm Haager
Innsbruck Federal Railways Directorate: Claudiastrasse 2, 6020 Innsbruck
  President: Dr. Adolf Rauch
Villach Federal Railways Directorate: Strasse des 10, Oktober 20, 9501 Villach
  President: Dipl. Ing. Franz Bachler

Gauge: 1.435 m
Route length: 5 409 km

First major job to be tackled by ÖBB's new board of directors, appointed in 1974 with the remit to sort out system finances which have been steadily deteriorating, was the development of a basic management policy programme. Lack of such a programme was one of the reasons why Transport Minister E. Lanc said he was not prepared to renew contracts of former Board members.
Heading the team is the new director-general Dr. Wolfgang Pycha, former director of operations and recognised as a leading Austrian marketing specialist. His deputy is Dr. O. Seidelmann, former director of administration. Remaining members are: Dr. F. Herzog, former director of finances; and, Dr.-Ing. R. Jaworski, former chief planning officer.
Among the jobs to be tackled by the new board immediately, Dr. Pycha referred to the need to speed up freight traffic movements, in particular by creating a network of overnight freight express trains linking Austria's economic centres. Sweeping changes alone could not improve the railway system overnight. Dr. Pycha called on the Government to stop investing in highway development at the expense of the railways. In 1973, he said, the state had spent 16,300 million Schillings on new highways, and only 2,725 million Schillings on the railways. "Railways" he said, "are entitled to get a bigger share of Government funds as we are still carrying 50 per cent of all national freight traffic".

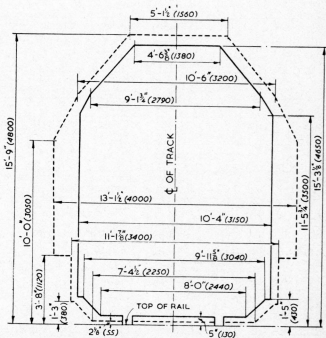

OBB structure and clearance gauge

Providing OBB gets the funds it needs then steps will be taken immediately to modernise the Tauern and Arlberg trunk line across the Alps, now nearing saturation. Double tracking will be carried out wherever possible. Several marshalling yards will be built and others reconstructed. Some particularly heavily burdened lines must be doubled or even quadrupled to cope with increasing traffic. Tariffs and timetables will be made more efficient. Departure times of passenger trains are to be standardised by introducing rigid timetable structures with trains departing at fixed time intervals.

In 1976, Austrian Federal Railways was expected to add to an initial deficit of 3 thousand million schillings by as much as "several hundred million". However, the basic question should be asked "whether railways in the west should be run profitably", declared Managing Director Wolfgang Pycha in a widely reported interview.

The effects of organisational changes and investments have meant that the establishment ie. the highest acceptable number of employees by the Federal Government, could be reduced by 950 in 1977. Within the framework of the planned investment programme, and consequently the staff policy, it is intended to reduce the workforce by another 880 each year.

There should be an improved passenger service with the running of twice daily connections (one connection each day and night) with big cities. At the moment, Austrian Federal Railways offer services *to Rome* on the trains "Romulus" and "Remus", *to Paris* with "Mozart" and "Orient Express" and *to Basle* with the trains "Transalpin" and "Wiener Waltzer". In the future all night connections will be sleepers and couchettes only.

But even with additional receipts and rationalisation the deficit cannot be checked. On this, Pycha says "over the last ten years, the European railway authorities have been faced with the task of reassessing their policies yet those railways which have striven for profits now face a loss. The Germans made a loss of 30 thousand million schilling in 1975, against 20 thousand million in 1974; the Swiss are 5 thousand million schilling in the red and the Dutch too have made a heavy loss".

Managing Director Pycha sees as one of the main reasons for this the preference shown to car and lorry traffic considering the costs of the infrastructure. The railway has both to build and calculate the costs of its own infrastructure, while individual transport does not. This inbalance in costs is particularly true with lorries and road freight traffic which bear 67 per cent of the costs compared to the motor car's 150 per cent.

However, Pycha at present sees no chance of a reasonably profitable rail transport of road trailers. Even on the experimental Austrian stretch between Salzburg and Spielfeld, where the work of a project team has been carrying out practical tests, the costs of such a service have been excessively high. Pycha, who insists that there should be no new lorry tax, says that time is on the side of the railways, "when the building of roads is no longer able to keep up with the number of cars being built, when traffic jams increase and fuel gets very expensive, then lorry traffic would have to take second place.

ELECTRIC LOCOMOTIVES

Class	Axle Arrange-ment	Line Current	Rated Output hp	Tractive Effort (Full Field) Max. lbs (kg)	Continuous at lb (kg)	mph (km/hr)	Max. Speed mph (km/hr)	Wheel dia. ins (mm)	Weight tonnes	Length ft in (mm)	No. Built	Year Built	Builders: Mechanical Parts	Electrical Equipment
1010	Co-Co	15 kV. 1/16⅔	5 400	57 300 *(26 000)*	26 500 *(12 000)*	62 *(99)*	81 *(130)*	51⅛ *(1 300)*	110*	58′ 7″ *(17 860)*	20	1955	S.G.P.	A.B.E.S.
1110	Co-Co	15 kV. 1/16⅔	5 400	61 700 *(28 000)*	30 900 *(14 000)*	53 *(85)*	68 *(110)*	51⅛ *(1 300)*	110	58′ 7″ *(17 860)*	30	1956	S.G.P.	A.B.E.S.
1020	Co-Co	15 kV. 1/16⅔	4 350	65 300 *(29 600)*	33 000 *(15 000)*	44 *(71)*	56 *(90)*	49¼ *(1 250)*	120	61′ 0″ *(18 600)*	47	1941	Krauss/Lofag	A.E.G./Ö.S.S.W.
1040	Bo-Bo	15 kV. 1/16⅔	3 200	44 000 *(20 000)*	22 500 *(10 200)*	44 *(71)*	50 *(80)*	53⅛ *(1 350)*	80	42′ 5″ *(12 920)*	16	1950	Lofag	A.B.E.S.
1041	Bo-Bo	15 kV. 1/16⅔	3 200	57 300 *(20 600)*	22 500 *(10 200)*	44 *(71)*	50 *(80)*	53⅛ *(1 350)*	83	50′ 3″ *(15 320)*	25	1952	S.G.P.	A.B.E.S.
1042	Bo-Bo	15 kV. 1/16⅔	4 770	46 296 *(21 000)*	26 455 *(12 000)*	57 *(91)*	80 *(130)*	49¼ *(1 250)*	84	53′ 2″ *(16 220)*	58	1963	S.G.P.	B.E.S.
1042-500	Bo-Bo	15 kV. 1/16⅔	5 360	46 296 *(21 000)*	24 900 *(11 300)*	63 *(102)*	93 *(150)*	49¼ *(1 250)*	84	53′ 2″ *(16 220)*	176	1967	S.G.P.	B.E.S.
1043	Bo-Bo	15 kV. 1/16⅔	4 830	66 100 *(30 000)*	37 000 *(16 800)*	48 *(78)*	84 *(135)*	49⅛ *(1 260)*	77.4 ‡	51′ 1½″ *(15 580)*	10	1971/72	ASEA	ASEA
1044	Bo-Bo	15 kV. 1/16⅔	5 400	—	—	160	*(160)*	*(1 300)*	83	*(16 000)*	2	1974	S.G.P.	B.E.S.
1141	Bo-Bo	15 kV. 1/16⅔	3 400	48 500 *(22 000)*	20 000 *(9 040)*	53 *(85)*	68 *(110)*	51⅛ *(1 300)*	80	46′ 9½″ *(14 260)*	30	1955	S.G.P.	A.B.E.S.
1046	Bo-Bo	15 kV. 1/16⅔	2 200	26 500 *(12 000)*	11 350 *(5 150)*	58.7 *(94.5)*	78 *(125)*	41 *(1 040)*	67	53′ 7″ *(16 330)*	25	1956	Lofag	A.B.E.S.
1062	D	15 kV. 1/16⅔	870	41 900 *(19 000)*	11 900 *(5 400)*	30 *(49)*	31 *(50)*	44⅞ *(1 140)*	68	35′ 6″ *(10 820)*	12	1955	Lofag	A.B.E.S.
1018	1-D-1	15 kV. 1/16⅔	4 400	42 900 *(19 450)*	24 900 *(11 300)*	65 *(105)*	80 *(130)*	63 *(1 600)*	110	55′ 6″ *(16 920)*	8	1939	Lofag	A.E.G.; Siemens
1161	D	15 kV. 1/16⅔	980	30 900 *(14 000)*	12 300 *(5 570)*	22 *(36)*	25 *(40)*	44⅞ *(1 140)*	56	34′ 5½″ *(10 500)*	21	1928	Lofag	A.E.G.
1245	Bo-Bo	15 kV. 1/16⅔	2 400	45 750 *(20 750)*	22 900 *(10 400)*	36 *(58)*	50 *(80)*	53 *(1 350)*	82	42′ 8″ *(12 920)*	38	1934	Lofag	A.B.E.S.
1670	1A-B-A1	15 kV. 1/16⅔	3 100	40 800 *(18 500)*	22 500 *(10 200)*	47 *(75)*	62 *(100)*	53 *(1 350)*	107	47′ 5½″ *(14 460)*	26	1928	Lofag/Krauss	Siemens

‡Nos. 1043-01, 02, 03 (1971) = 77 tonnes
No 1043-04 (1972) = 82 tonnes.

DIESEL LOCOMOTIVES

Class	Axle Arrange-ment	Trans-mission	Rated Power hp	Tractive Effort Max. lbs (kg)	Continuous at lbs (kg)	mph (km/h)	Max. Speed mph (km/h)	Wheel Dia. ins (mm)	Total Weight Tons	Length ft ins (mm)	No. Built	Year first Built	Builders: Mechanical Parts	Engine & Type	Transmission
2020	B-B	Hyd.	2 200	52 150 *(23 640)*	37 300 *(16 950)*	12.5 *(20)*	68 *(110)*	39⅜ *(1 000)*	75.4	59′ 10″ *(18 240)*	1	1960	S.G.P.	2×SGP T 12b	Voith
2043	B-B	Hyd.	1 500	45 182 *(20 500)*	30 636 *(13 900)*	30.5 *(19)*	62 *(100)*	37⅜ *(950)*	67.2 67.7	48′ 5″ *(14 760)* 51′ 8½″ *(15 760)*	76	1964	Jenbach	JW 1500	Voith
2045	Bo-Bo	Elec.	1 000	34 200 *(15 500)*	13 450 *(6 100)*	20.6 *(33.2)*	56 *(90)*	39⅜ *(1 000)*	71	48′ 6¾″ *(14 800)*	18	1952	S.G.P.	2×S.G.P. S 12a	ELIN/ÖBBW
2050	Bo-Bo	Elec.	1 520	40 100 *(18 200)*	32 700 *(14 850)*	13.1 *(21.1)*	62 *(100)*	41 *(1 040)*	75.5	58′ 2½″ *(17 740)*	18	1958	Henschel	G.M. 12-567C	G.M.
2060	B	Hyd.	196	22 500/ 11 300 *(10 200/* *5 130)*	15 200/ 7 700 *(6 900/* *3 500)*	2.2/4.3 *(3.5/6.9)*	19/37 *(30/60)*	37 *(940)*	27.4	22′ 0″ *(6 700)*	100	1954	Jenbach	Jenbach JW200	Voith
2062	B	Hyd.	390	27 000 18 400 *(12 270/* *8 350)*	17 600/ 12 000 *(8 000/* *5 450)*	4.7/7.0 *(7.6/* *11.2)*	25/37 *(40/60)*	37 *(940)*	32	26′ 3″ *(8 000)*	45 20	1958 1965	Jenbach	JW 400	Voith
2067	C	Hyd.	600	33 070 *(15 000)*	26 500 *(12 000)*	4.3 *(7.0)*	40 *(65)*	44⅞ *(1 140)*	49.1	33′ 11″ *(10 340)*	63	1959/ 64	S.G.P.	S.G.P. S 12a	Voith
2095	B-B	Hyd.	600	21 200 *(9 600)*	16 700 *(7 600)*	7.5 *(12.0)*	37 *(60)*	35½ *(900)*	32	34′ 1½″ *(40 400)*	10 5	1961 1962	S.G.P.	S.G.P. S 12a	Voith
2143	B-B	Hyd.	1 500	42 757 *(19 400)*	29 754 *(13 500)*	11 *(18)*	62 *(100)*	37⅜ *(950)*	65.4	51′ 6″ *(15 760)*	33	1965	S.G.P.	T12c	Voith

TRAFFIC

During the financial year 1976 Austrian Federal Railways (OBB) enjoyed the first fruits of the post-recession upturn in Europe's industrial activity. Total freight tonnage rose to 49.9 million tonnes with tonne-km reaching 10 548 million, which was 1 169 million more than in 1975.

The higher carryings partly resulted from the two-month closure to inland shipping of the Danube following the collapse of the Reichsbrücke in Vienna, but the only traffic to reach pre-1975 levels was the fast sundries service.

Passenger-km rose slightly from 6 470 million in 1976 to 6 499 million, but the number of passengers carried dropped from 169.3 million to 168.2 million. Second-class traffic continued to show the downward trend of previous years, but first-class gained slightly.

FINANCES

Revenues in 1976 totalled 14,942 million schillings while expenses were 18 734 million schillings. (1975: Revenue 13,114 million schillings, expenses 20,138 million schillings).

INVESTMENTS

One of ÖBB's most important needs at present is increasing investments to buy stock and facilities. The 10-year investment programme of the management policy predicts investments of approximately 51,9 thousand million schillings. The main points of the programme are maintaining the integrity of the installations and the modernisation and rationalisation.

In 1975 and 1976 the ÖBB took delivery of a total of: 45 electric locomotives, 34 diesel locomotives, 7 electric engines, 94 passenger coaches and 1 793 goods wagons.

As far as can be seen at present the following rolling stock will be ordered in 1977: 24—electric locomotives 1 044,27-50

    20—express coaches 4 020,21-40
    50—long distance passenger coaches
    40—inland passenger trains (with guards van)
    500—4-axle covered goods wagons
1 000—2-axle flat wagons
    10—diesel shunters

ELECTRIFICATION

At the end of 1976 the electrified route length was 2 727 km on standard gauge and 91 km on narrow gauge. By the end of 1977 the total electrified route length was 2 861 km. The lines, representing 48.8 per cent of the network, carrying nearly 90 per cent of ÖBB traffic.

Sections electrified since 1974 include: Stadlau—Breitenlee Nord, Leopoldau—Breitenlee Nord, Breitenlee—Nord—Sussenbrunn, Kledering—Gramatneusiedl—Wampersdorf, Kledering—Kleinschwechat, Inzersdorf Ort—Wr. Neustadt, Linz—Summerau, Gramatneusiedl—State border by Nickelsdorf (Hegyeshalom), Linz—Spital a. Pyhrn and Ganserndorf—State border by Bernhardsthal.

Stretches to be electrified during 1978 include: Wien FJB—Tulln, Tulln—Absdorf—Hippersdorf—Stockerau and Stockerau—Hollabrunn.

PERSONNEL

The previously strained personnel situation has been eased due to the overall change in the employment market situation. The number of personnel employed by ÖBB during 1976 was 70,702 ie. 299 or 0.4% less personnel employed than in 1975.

MARSHALLING YARDS

It is intended to erect a central marshalling yard in Sud Villach in the Furntiz area which will deal with the trains crossing the borders into Italy and Yugoslavia and also local traffic in the Villach area, which is intended to bring about a considerable speeding up of the freight traffic.

MOTIVE POWER

At 31.12.76 the ÖBB had 111 steam locomotives on their lists. Of these, 26 were no longer in operation and 38 had been put aside for conservation so that only 47 locomotives were left, that in 1976 made up 0.6 per cent of the train km and 0.3 per cent of the gross ton-km.

Altogether 1 321 electric and diesel powered locomotives make up 99.4 per cent of the train km and 99.7 of the gross ton-km. The stock of locomotives at 31.12.1976 was:
111 Steam locomotives
640 Electric locomotives
488 Diesel locomotives, 53 with electric transmission and 435 with hydraulic transmission.

In 1974 and 75 both prototypes of the class 1044 Thyristor electric were in operation, with axle arrangement Bo'Bo, a maximum speed of 160 km/h, weight 83 tons and length over buffers of 16 000 mm. The motive power is 337 kN, and tractive effort is 5 400 kW.

The following *passenger vehicles* are in operation.
76 multiple unit electrics for cummuter service.
21 multiple unit electrics for long distances (Inter-City)
16 multiple unit diesels
51 4-axle diesel railcars
29 2-axle diesel railcars (railbuses)

ROLLING STOCK STRENGTH

At 31.12.76 there were 3 670 passenger trains in use and 35 858 freight wagons.

WAY AND WORKS

New Rail Laid (end 1976)
Type S 64 rail weighing 129.6 lb/yd *(64.29 kg/km)* laid on 30.07 km
Type B rail weighing 99.7 lb/yd *(49.43 kg/km)* laid on 4 361.81 km
Type C rail weighing 108.5 lb/yd *(53.81 kg/km)* laid on 587.75 km

TRACK CONSTRUCTION DETAILS

Standard Rail:
Standard gauge: 108.5, 99.7 89.5 lb/yd *(53.81, 49.43, 44.35 kg)*
  Narrow gauge: 50.7 lb/yd *(26.15 kg/m)*
Length:
  Standard Gauge: 98.4 ft and 196.8 ft *(30m and 60m)*
  Narrow Gauge: 65.6 ft *(20 m)*
Cross Ties (sleepers):
  Standard Gauge: Impregnated wood 8 ft 6⅜ in × 10¼ in × 6¼ in *(2 600 × 260 × 160 mm)*
  also steel and concrete
  Narrow gauge: Impregnated wood 5 ft 3 in × 7 in × 5⅛ in *(1 600 × 200 × 130 mm)*
Cross ties spacing:
  Standard gauge: 600—700 mm *(1 540 per km)* 2 480 per mile
  Narrow gauge: 810 mm *(1 235 per km)* 1 970 per mile
Rail fastening:
  Standard gauge: Resilient fastening, ribbed slabs, clips and bolts, keyed plates and bolts, Pandrol (spring U-bolt) and Macbeth (spring grip spike)
  Narrow gauge: base plates and spikes
Filling:
  Standard gauge: broken stone ballast
  Narrow gauge: broken stone ballast

Thickness under sleepers:
  Standard gauge: 8 to 12 in *(200-300 mm)*
  Narrow gauge: 6 in *(150 mm)*
Minimum or sharpest curvature:
  Standard gauge: 9.7 = min rad of 590 ft *(180 m)*
  Narrow gauge: 29.1 = min rad of 197 ft *(60 m)*
Maximum gradient compensated:
  Standard gauge: 1 in 22 *(4.6%)*
  Narrow gauge: 1 in 40 *(2.5%)*
Maximum gradient uncompensated:
  Standard gauge: 7.4%
Maximum combination of gradient and curvature:
  Standard gauge: 1:46 with 125 m curve radius
  Narrow gauge: 1:40 with 100m radius
Gauge width with maximum curvature:
  Standard gauge: 20 mm
  Narrow gauge: 20 mm
Maximum super elevation:
  Standard gauge: 160 mm
  Narrow gauge: 60 mm
Maximum axle load:
  Standard gauge: 20 tonnes
  Narrow gauge: 12 tonnes
Maximum permitted speeds:
  Passenger trains on standard gauge: 140 km/h
  narrow gauge: 50 km/h
  Freight trains on standard gauge: 120 km/h
  narrow gauge: 40 km/h

Unbroken welded rail: at the end of 1976 the total length of welded track was 3 779 km of which 392 km had been laid during the year. The longest individual length of continuous welded rail is 18.3 km.

ROLLING STOCK STRENGTH

Rail types most used are Form B *(49.43 kg/m)* and Form C *(53.81 kg/m)* in 30m or 60 m lengths. Sleepers are wood, steel or concrete. Ribbed slabs, Pandrol or Macbeth fastenings are used.

BANGLADESH

BANGLADESH RAILWAY
Railway Building, Chittagong

Telephone: Chittagong 86011
Telegrams: Eprail

Chairman, Railway Board: Maqbul Ahmad
Member, Administration, Planning and Development: M. Asjad Ali
Member, Engineering: M. M. Haque
Member, Operation and Commercial: Mahmud Hasan
Member, Finance: Hamed Shafiul Islam
Secretary, Railway Board: A. K. M. Zainul Abedin
Chief Electrical Engineer: M. N. Karim
Chief Controller of Stores: M. H. Bhuiyan
Chief Planning Officer: M. N. Shukuruddin
Project Manager (Project): I. A. Chowdhury
Chief Engineer (Project): K. A. Chowdhury
Chief Mechanical Engineer: Raisuddin Ahmed
Chief Signal and Tele-Communication Engineer: S. A. B. M. Karimushan
Principal Railway Training Academy and Director of Training: M. Matiur Rahman
Chief Commercial Manager: M. Nazmul Haque
Chief Operating Superintendent: Md Mostaque Ahmed Chowdhury
Chief Engineer: A. H. M. R. Islam Bhuiyan
Chief Commandant, Railway Nirapatta Bahini and Deputy Inspector General of Police: A. R. Khondaker
Financial Adviser and Chief Accounts Officer: A. Z. M. Abdul Ali
Chief Medical Officer: M. A. Chowdhury
Chief Personnel Officer: M. T. Hussain
Engineer-in-Chief: M. A. Matin
Divisional Superintendent, Chittagong: A. K. M. Amanul Islam Chowdhury
Divisional Superintendent, Dacca: A. M. Z. Mahmud
Divisional Superintendent, Paksey: A. H. Khan
Divisional Superintendent, Lalmonirhat: A. B. M. Shamsuddain Ahmed

Gauge: 1.676 m; 1.0 m
Total route length: 1 786.22 miles *(2 874 km)*
Total track length: 2 797.49 miles *(4 510 km)*

One of Bangladesh's four diesel railcar units hauls a five-car consist out of Chittagong.

HISTORY
It required sustained efforts for over a century to build the railway network. The story dates back to 1862, when the first section of 53 km *(33 miles)* of broad-gauge line was opened to traffic on November 15 that year between Darsana and Jagati. The next railway connection opened to traffic was between Dacca and Narayanganj, a distance of 14.8 km *(9.31 miles)* on January 4, 1885. Gradually these lines were extended and new sections were constructed to cover more areas. In 1891, construction of the Assam Bengal Railway was taken up with British Government assistance, this was later taken over by the Assam Bengal Railway Company. On July 1, 1895, two sections of metre gauge lines were opened betwen Chittagong and Comilla, a length of 150 km (93.14 miles) and between Laksam and Chandpur, a length of 50 km *(31.62 miles)*.
The construction and operation of these sections in the middle and late 19th century were handled by British-based railway companies. Their primary objective was to operate the lines on purely commercial considerations. Later, the British Government of India took over statutory control and regulations for operation and management of the railway.
On January 1, 1942 the Assam Bengal Railway was amalgamated with the Eastern Bengal Railway under the name Bengal and Assam Railway. At the time of partition of India in 1947, the Bengal and Assam Railway was split up and the portion of the system which fell within the boundary of East Pakistan (2 603 km/1 618 miles) was named Eastern Bengal Railway with control remaining with the central Government of Pakistan. Later, with effect from February 1, 1961, the Eastern Bengal Railway was renamed Pakistan Eastern Railway. In the year 1962 the control of Pakistan Eastern Railway was transferred from the Central Government by the Presidential order to the Government of the East Pakistan province, and placed under the management of a Railway Board with effect from the Financial year 1962-63. With the independence of Bangladesh on December 16, 1971, Pakistan Eastern Railway naturally became "Bangladesh Railway".

Bangladesh Railway is the principal transportation organisation of the country. It serves a population of about 80 million living in an area of 88 715 km² *(55 126 miles²)*. The railway has always played a vital role in the development of the country and in the expansion of trade, commerce and industry. Bulk of the export and import traffic is still rail-borne, with the railway feeding industry with raw materials and subsequently shipping finished products at an economical cost. The railway moves food grains, fertilizers and consumer goods to all parts of the country at reasonably high speed and at comparatively low cost.
At the end of 1976-77, Bangladesh Railway had a total of 483 stations spread over 2 874 km *(1 786.02 route miles)* consisting of two gauges, broad (5'-6") and metre gauge (3'-3⅜"). In 1976-77, the railway operated with a fleet of 445 locomotives, 1 192 passenger carriages, 358 other coaching vehicles and 16 925 freight wagons.

ORGANISATION
Bangladesh Railway is a State-owned and State managed organisation. Until June 30, 1976, the General Manager was the Chief Executive of the Railway. With effect from July 1, 1976, there as been a major change in its organisational set-up. A Railway Board comprising of a Chairman and four Members has been set up, with responsibility for management and development vested in Bangladesh Railway Board. The Board functions under the administrative control of the Ministry of Communications (Railways, Roads, Highways and Road Transport Division-Railway Wing) of the Government of the People's Republic of Bangladesh.

TRAFFIC	1973	1974	1975	1976
Total freight ton-km (in millions)	408	391	610	730
Total freight tonnage (in thousands)	2 830	2 768	2 900	3 330
Total passenger-km (in millions)	1 740	2 070	4 038	4 436
Total passengers carried (in thousands)	63 655	72 936	82 600	93 800

FINANCES	1974	1975	1976
Revenues (thousands)	278 300	403 000	505 000
Expenses	354 000	410 000	494 000

MOTIVE POWER AND ROLLING STOCK
Number of locomotives in service (1976/77) included:
(1) Steam—104 broad-gauge line haul; 92 broad-gauge shunters; 192 metre-gauge line haul; 181 metre-gauge shunters.
(2) diesel-electric—32 broad-gauge line haul; 32 broad-gauge shunters; 151 metre-gauge line haul; 141 metre gauge shunters.
Rail buses in service include four diesel metre-gauge and eight trailers.
Number of passenger train coaches total 286 broad gauge and 868 metre gauge.
Freight train-wagons operating during 1977 totalled (four-wheel equivalents): 4 797 broad-gauge and 14 270 metre gauge.

The railway at present operates 337 steam locomotives.

Shortage of serviceable locomotives and rolling stock is among the railway's most pressing problems. Between 1970 and 1975 the number of locomotives in service fell from 412 (190 steam and 99 diesel in metre-gauge service; 106 steam and 17 diesel in broad-gauge service to 211 (72 steam and 90 diesel in metregauge; 26 steam and 23 diesel in broad-gauge service). Purchases in 1975 and 1976 has brought the total number in operation up to 569 but the railway is still short of motive power capacity. Calculated on a probable increase in passenger traffic of 2.5 per cent annually, and approximately 5 per cent in freight demand, the railway estimates that it will need to purchase additional locomotives, 949 passenger coaches and 8 469 freight wagons. In 1976, BR purchased 18 metre-gauge and 12 broad-gauge diesel-electric locomotives expected to cost in foreign exchange about £4.3 million. Tenders were received from MLW for the supply of 1 000-1 400 hp type 12DL-535A locomotives and from General Motors (Canada) for types GL18 and GL22 locomotives to be paid for under a loan from the Canadian International Development Agency. Also on the railway's purchase list are 22 new metre-gauge railcars and 58 trailers together with 11 broad-gauge railcars and trailers. Cost is estimated at £3.3 million.
Locomotives and rolling stock put into service during 1973 and 1974.
Newest passenger coaches to enter service are 26 metre-gauge units built by the Hungarian Railway Carriage and Machine Works and 13 units built by Linke-Hofmann-Busch of Germany, all of which were delivered in 1976. Now on order are 50 third-class coaches being constructed by Bharat Earth Moving Machines of India at a cost of Taka 1.5 million, and 77 coaches ordered from Turkish State Railways (TCDD) prior to 1971.

Also on order are 500 new four-wheel covered freight wagons to be supplied by Texmaco of India at an approximate cost of Taka 80 million. Provision for 500 metre-gauge wagons costing £2.1 million and 682 special purpose wagons costing £12.96 million has been included in the railway's plans.

TRACK

Work is already underway on extensive track upgrading plans expected to be carried out under a loan of $US 24.4 million from the Asian Development Bank. Most of the money is expected to be spent on upgrading the track and bridges along the metre-gauge Dacca-Chittagong line—the country's principal rail artery. Generally, existing 30 kg/m rail on all metre-gauge lines is to be replaced with 37 kg/m welded rails laid on new semi-hard Gojou timber sleepers which are expected to last up to 20 years. Studies are now underway into the economics of concrete sleepers. Broad-gauge lines are laid with 45 kg/m rails and it is proposed to keep the same weight rail on newly-welded broad-gauge sections.

Under the improvement programme, five lines have been selected for extensive upgrading at a total cost of £10 million: Akhaura-Chhatak; Bhairab Bazar-Bahadurabad; Khulna-Darsana; Dacca-Mymensingh; Sirajganj-Ishuradi-Abdulpur-Amnura.

A new line is planned from Faridpur to Barisal at a cost of Taka 44.2 million. So far 16 km has been completed linking Faridpur with Talma and work is underway on the next 16 km section as far as Bhanga.

Following completion of track doubling between Pahartali and Mirsarai, embankments and bridges between Laksam and Hasanpur have been constructed.

Work is continuing on track doubling between Chittagong and Sholashahar. This is due for completion when yard remodelling is concluded at Sholashahar and Jhaytala.

Meanwhile, preliminary engineering and detailed traffic surveys have been carried out on proposed new lines from Laksam to Dacca, Bagerhat to Perojpur, Jessore to Kamarkhali, Kishoreganj to Tangail, and Madaripur to Khulna.

In addition a proposal for construction of a new line from Khulna to Mongla—to include a major new bridge over the Rupsa river—has been submitted to the government for approval.

Rail types and weights: 75 lbs 'A' 90 lbs 'A' FF BSS rails, 50 lbs 'R' 60 lbs 'R' 90 lbs 'R' FF BSS rails, 50 NS, 50 ISR & 80 lbs.

Sleepers (cross ties) type:

Thickness: (a) wooden sleeper BG 5'', (b) steel through sleeper BG ½'', (c) cast iron CST/9 block, (d) wooden sleeper MG 4½'', (e) steel through sleeper MG ¹¹/₃₂'', (f) cast iron sleeper CST/9 (block).

Spacing: N+1, N+2, N+3, N+4, and N+5.

Rail fastenings (types used): Fish Plates, Fish Boxes, Dog Spikes, Bearing Plates, Anchor Bearing Plates, Round Spikes, Steel Keys and Steel Jaws and Rail Anchors of different sizes.

Signal and train control installations

Type: (i) Relay interlocking (ii) (iii) Mechanical interlocking mechanical interlocking

RAILWAY-OWNER SHIPPING SERVICES, TRAIN AND ROAD VEHICLE FERRIES

Routes served:

(i) Jagannathganj-Serajganj ghat (passenger ferry services)

(ii) Bahadurabad-Tistamukh ghat (passenger and wagon ferry services)

Description of vessels: 1 Steamer, 6 Tugs, 9 Barges.

Type and volume of traffic: 1973: Passengers carried 519 979. Tons carried 185 720. 1974: Passengers carried 536 749. Tons carried 158 652.

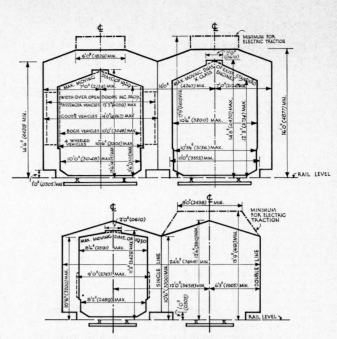

Loading and structure gauge diagrams for Bangladesh Railways showing (top) for broad-gauge tracks and (bottom) for metre gauge.

Class MLW-20 diesel-electric, built by MLW of Canada, hauling a food grain special.

DIESEL LOCOMOTIVES

Class	Axle Arrangement	Transmission	Rated Power hp	Max. lbs (kg)	Tractive Effort Continuous at lbs (kg)	mph (km/h)	Max. Speed mph (km/h)	Wheel Dia. ins (mm)	Total Weight Tons	Length ft ins (mm)	No. Built	Year first Built	Builders: Mechanical Parts	Engine & Type	Transmission
METRE GAUGE															
DE-1 & DE-2	AIA-AIA (AAR)	Elec.	1 125		28 000		60	3' 4''	70.5	49' 0¾''	40	1953/ 1954	G. Motors Corp, USA	EID 12-567B & 12-567C	
GMU-10	AIA-AIA (AAR)	Elec.	875		33 880		62	3' 4''	61.44	40' 4¾''	41	1960/ 1963	G. Motors, USA	EID 567-CR	
GMU-14	Co-Co	Elec.	1 300		42 900		71	3' 4''	70.5	48' 4¾''	10	1964	M/s International Gen Co, USA	7F-DL 8 AG	
MLU-14	Co-Co	Elec.	1 245		40 000		60	3' 4''	70.5	49' 6''	24	1969	M/s MLW Worthing Ton/Canada	ALCO 251-D	
ADE-1	Bo-Bo	Elec.	355		14 700			3' 0½''	40.4	36' 8⁹/₁₆''	11	1956	Baume Marpett Morlanwelz Belgium	Two Caterpillar D.17000	
ELU-6	Bo-Bo	Elec.	500		13 500		35	3' 0''	40.4	28' 0''	26	1971	M/s English ELEC. AE-1 England	Model No. 4 SRKT	
BROAD GAUGE															
ALU-20	00-00	Elec.	2000		42 540		66	3' 4''	106.5	58' 4½''	18	1966	M/s ALCO Production Newyark	Model No. 251-C	
MLU-20	00-00	Elec.	2 000		42 540		66	3' 4''	106.5	58' 4½''	16	1970	M/s MLW Worthing Ton/Canada	Model No. 251-C	
DIESEL RAILCARS (METRE GAUGE)															
	Bogie	Hyd	180				50	2' 4½''	32.98	68' 7⅝''	4	1963	M/s LHB	Bussing Diesel Engine-U.11/200	

BELGIUM

SOCIÉTÉ NATIONALE DES CHEMINS DE FER BELGES (SNCB)

17-21 Rue de Louvain, Brussels 1

Telephone: 523 80 80
Telegrams: Railbel

General Manager: G. Vanhee
Assistant General Manager: R. Weber
General Manager's Office:
Manager: R. Squilbin
Chief Engineer, Assistant to Manager: J. Neruez
Chief Legal Adviser, Assistant to Manager: M. Demanche
Chief Engineer: L. Verberckt
Press and Public Relations Officer; W. Van Gestel
Operating department:
Manager: A. Soete
Chief Engineers: P. Fransen
D. Demonie
L. Gueret
A. Guillaume
Chief Inspector: F. De Mesel
Equipment department:
Assistant General Manager: G. Deprez
Chief Engineer, Assistant to Manager: K. Suls
Chief Engineers: M. De Wulf
R. Verboven
H. Malengreau
H. Van Poucke
Chief Inspector: J. Van den Torren
Permanent Way Department:
Manager: O. Debaize
Chief Engineer, Assistant to Manager: P. Stordiau
Chief Engineers: L. Dogniez
L. Franssen
T. Bibauw
A. Couvreur
G. Gunst
E. Lallemand
Financial directorate:
Manager: L. De Smet
Chief Inspectors: A. Duchene
M. Hendrickx
Commercial department:
Manager: F. De Haeck
Chief Inspectors: C. Lokker
R. Boonen
E. Marnef
Personnel and Social Services Department:
Manager: E. Arys
Chief Medical Officer, Assistant to Manager: J. Bouckaert
Chief Inspector, Assistant to Manager: J. Roolant
Chief Medical Officer: J. Dufaux, G. David, F. Javaux, R. Van Roy
Chief Inspectors: M. Mahu
L. Rigaux
Purchasing directorate:
Manager: J. Carlier
Chief Engineer: M. Van Maele
Electricity and signalling department:
Manager: L. Maenhaut
Chief Engineer, Assistant to Manager: M. Gochet
Chief Engineers: A. Duquesne
F. Lauwers
H. De Sutter
A. Plenevaux
Data Processing department:
Manager: M. Colle
Chief Engineers: Y. Van der Veken
G. Van Dessel
Active services:
Divisional Chiefs:
Antwerp: H. Eeckels
Brussels: A. Houwen
Charleroi: P. Rossignol
Ghent: C. Van de Velde
Hasselt: B. Dhaenens
Liège: F. Melet
Mons: R. Ducobu
Namur: X
Central workshops:
Cuesmes: J. Rivière—Lorphèvre
Gentbrugge: R. Strobbe
Louvain: R. Willemans
Luttre: H. Bertrand
Malines: H. Verbeek
Salzinnes: J. Daivier

All standard gauge lines in the country are operated by the Société Nationale des Chemins de Fer Belges (SNCB), and all metre gauge light railways by the Société Nationale des Chemins de Fer Vicinaux (SNCV).
At the end of 1976, SNCB operated a route length of 3 998 km of which about 1 300 km are electrified at 3 kV dc with diesel traction on the remainder. Freight traffic is carried over the whole system; passenger traffic on 2 926 km.

TRAFFIC
Total freight ton-km carried in 1976 was 6 648.3 million ton-km compared with 6 757.5 million ton-km in 1975. Passenger-km in 1976 totalled 615.8 million compared with 607.8 million in 1975, while passengers carried: (1976) 54.4 million; (1975) 54.5 million.

FINANCES
Total revenues in 1976 were B.Frs 34 482 million compared with B.Frs 31 050 million in 1975. Expenses totalled B.Frs 36 577.1 million in 1976 compared with 32 120.3 million in 1975.

INVESTMENTS
Additional government support requested by Belgian National Railways (SNCB) in 1977 has been reduced by BFr4·88 billion. In return SNCB has pressed the Government for a reply to its request for annual credit of BFr 6 000 million (in 1974 money) for the period to 1980. Over the five years to 1975, total government investment in transport was BFr141 billions for road and BFr8.2 billions for the railways. In 1976, the expenditure was BFr29.7 billion road and BFr3.585 billion rail.

ELECTRIC LOCOMOTIVES

Class	*Axle Arrange-ment*	*Line Current*	*Rated Output* hp	*Max.* lbs *(kg)*	*Tractive Effort (Full Field) Continuous at* lb *(kg)*	mph *(km/hr)*	*Max. Speed* mph *(km/hr)*	*Wheel dia.* ins *(mm)*	*Weight* tonnes	*Length* ft in *(mm)*	*No. Built*	*Year Built*	*Builders* *Mechanical Parts*	*Electrical Equipment*
20	Bo-Bo	3 000 V dc	2 200	44 000 *(20 000)*	21 600 *(9 800)*	30 *(49)*	62 *(100)*	53⅛ *(1 350)*	81.5	42′ 3½″ *(12 890)*	20	1949	Baume-Marpent	ACEC Charleroi et SEM Gand.
20	Co-Co	3 000 V dc	7 000	70 100 *(32 000)*	52 100 *(23 600)*	50 *(80)*	100 *(160)*	49¼ *(1 250)*	111	63′ 11¾″ *(19 500)*	15	1975	Brugeoise et Nivelles	ACEC Charleroi
22	Bo-Bo dual-current	3 000/ 1 500 V dc	2 560	44 000 *(20 000)*	27 600 *(11 500)*	32 *(51)*	81 *(130)*	49⅝ *(1 262)*	87	59′ 0¾″ *(18 000)*	50	1954	Brugeoise et Nivelles	ACEC Charleroi et SEM Gand.
23	Bo-Bo	3 000 V dc	2 560	44 000 *(20 000)*	27 600 *(12 000)*	32 *(51)*	81 *(130)*	,,	93.3	59′ 0¾″ *(18 000)*	82	1955	Atel Metallurgiques de Nivelles	ACEC Charleroi et SEM Gand.
24	Bo-Bo	3 000 V dc	2 560	44 000 *(20 000)*	27 600 *(12 500)*	32 *(51)*	81 *(130)*	,,	93.3	59′ 0¾″ *(18 000)*	1	1955	Atel Metallurgiques de Nivelles	ACEC Charleroi et SEM Gand.
25	Bo-Bo	3 000 V dc	2 560	44 000 *(20 000)*	27 600 *(12 500)*	32 *(51)*	81 *(130)*	,,	83.9	59′ 0¾″ *(18 000)*	22	1960	Brugeoise et Nivelles	ACEC Charleroi et SEM Gand.
25.5	Bo-Bo dual current	3 000 V 1 500 dc	,,	,,	,,	,,	,,	,,	,,	,,	8	modi-fied 1973	Brugeoise et Nivelles	ACEC Charleroi and SEM Gent
26	B-B Mono-motor Bogies	3 000 V dc	3 070	58 200 *(26 400)*	34 400 *(15 600)*	30.7 *(49.5)*	100 *(160)*	45¼ *(1 150)*	82.4	56′ 5″ *(17 280)*	48	1963/73	Brugeoise et Nivelles	ACEC Charleroi
28	Bo-Bo	3 000 V d.c.	2 700	44 000 *(20 000)*	25 600 *(11 600)*	32 *(51)*	81 *(130)*	49⅝ *(1 262)*	85	56′ 4½″ *(17 180)*	3	1949	Baume-Marpent	ACEC Charleroi and SEM Gent
15	Bo-Bo triple-current	25 kV 1/50 3 000 V. dc 1 500 V dc	3 600	38 400 *(17 400)*	22 000 *(10 000)*	56 *(91)*	93 *(150)*	49¼ *(1 250)*	77.7	58′ 3″ *(17 750)*	5	1962	Brugeoise et Nivelles	ACEC Charleroi
16	Bo-Bo quadri-current	25 000 V 50 Hz 15 000 V 16 Hz. 3 000 V dc 1 500V	3 780	44 000 *(20 000)*			100 *(160)*		84	54′ 7¾″ *(16 650)*	8	1966	Brugeoise et	ACEC Charleroi Siemens
18	C-C quadri current	R 5 000 V-50 HZ 15 000 V-16 ⅝ HZ 3 000 V dc 1 500 V dc	6 050	37 300 *(17 000)*	26 500 *(12 000)*	81 *(130)*	112 *(180)*	43⅓ *(1 100)*	113	72′ 5⅓″ *(22 080)*	6	1973	Brugeoise et Nivelles	Alsthom

TEN YEAR PLAN

For the remainder of the ten-year plan period (1975-79) the railway wants government approval to spend B.Frs 13 400 million annually on improvement projects. The board of directors has asked for:

(1)   An endowment increase to B.Frs 6 400 million (compared with B.Frs 5 500 million in 1973) for the renewal of installations and rolling stock;

(2)   A new programme of annual investment totalling B.Frs 6 000 million yearly to be charged to the Ministry of Communications;

(3)   Approval for the railway to spend B.Frs 6 000 million annually—a sum to be raised through the issue of loan bonds.

Approval for SNCB's new cash plan must be given, says the board of directors, if the railway is to make good the delays already encountered in completing projects listed under the ten-year plan. Badly hit through lack of cash are the following priority projects:

—renewal of lines, including tunnel reconstruction and station rebuilding;

—renewal of passenger rolling stock (only one order for 80 international coaches has been placed since 1970 instead of the 255 coaches projected during the 1970-75 period);

—electrification works (out of B.Frs 1 500 million originally approved for electrification works, the railway has so far been authorised to spend only B.Frs 91 million);

DIESEL LOCOMOTIVES

Class	Axle Arrange-ment	Trans-mission	Rated Power hp	Max. lbs (kg)	Tractive Effort Continuous at lbs (kg)	mph (km/h)	Max. Speed mph (km/h)	Wheel Dia. ins (mm)	Total Weight Tons	Length ft ins (mm)	No. Built	Year first Built	Builders: Mechanical Parts	Engine & Type	Transmission
51	Co-Co	Elec.	2 150	61 200 (27 750)	37 250 (16 900)		75 (120)	39¾ (1 010)	117	66' 1¾'' (20 160)	93	1961	Cockerill-Ougrée	Cockerill-Ougrée	ACEC-SEM
59	Bo-Bo	Elec.	1 750	44 000 (20 000)	37 500 (17 000)		75 (120)	44 (1 118)	87	53' 1'' (16 180)	55	1955	Cockerill; Baume et Marp.	Cockerill (licence Baldwin)	ACEC (licence Westinghouse)
52-53	Co-Co	Elec.	1 720	55 000 (25 000)	35 500 (16 100)		75 (120)	39¾ (1 010)	108	61' 10'' (18 850)	13 19	1955	Anglo-Franco-Belge	GM (USA)	GM (USA) Smit
54	Co-Co	Elec.	1 900	55 000 (25 000)	27 500 (12 500)		87 (140)	,,	108	,,	8	1957	Anglo-Franco-Belge	GM (USA)	GM (USA); Smit
55	Co-Co	Elec.	1 950	61 200 (27 750)	38 000 (17 250)		75 (120)	,,	110	64' 2⅜'' (19 550)	42	1961	Brugeoise et Nivelles	GM (USA)	ACEC-SEM licence GM
60	Bo-Bo	Elec.	1 400	44 000 (20 000)	24 250 (11 000)		75 (120)	,,	85.4	56' 11'' (17 350)	106	1961	Cockerill-Ougrée	Cockerill (licence Baldwin)	ACEC
64	Bo-Bo	Hyd.	1 400	45 200 (20 500)	(P)25 350 (11 500) (F)37 500 (17 000)		(P)75 (120) (F)51 (82)	44 (1 118)	82	57' 5'' (17 500)	6	1962	Ateliers Belges Réunis; A.B.R.	Cockerill-Ougrée	Voith
62 Bogie Flexicoil	Bo-Bo	Elec.	1 425	47 600 (21 600)	24 250 (11 000)		75 (120)	39¾ (1 010)	80	55' 1'' (16 790)	136	1961	Brugeoise et Nivelles	GM (USA)	GM (USA)
62 Bogie BN	Bo-Bo	Elec.	1 425	47 600 (21 600)	24 250 (11 000)		75 (120)	,,	81.6	,,	3	1961	Brugeoise et Nivelles	,,	ACEC lic. GM
62 Bogie BN	Bo-Bo	Elec.	1 425	47 600 (21 600)	24 250 (11 000)		75 (120)	,,		,,	35	1962	Brugeoise et Nivelles	,,	ACEC lic. GM
65	B-B	Hyd.	1 460	42 978 (19 500)	(P)25 350 (11 500) (p)27 500 (17 000)		(P)75 (120) (F)51 (82)	44 (1 118)	76 79	,, ,,	6 6	1963 1965/6	Brugeoise et Nivelles	GMC 2-speed Type 12-567DI	Voith
66	B-B	Hyd.	950	39 700 (18 000)	(P)27 500 (12 500) (F)46 300 (21 000)		(P)50 (80) (F)31 (50)	39¾ (1 010)	72	43' 9½'' (13 350)	3	1962	A.B.R.	ACEC (licence MAN)	Voith L.217
90	B	Hyd.	245	21 800 (9 900)	16 000 (7 250) 7 500 (3 400)		(1g)13 (21) (2g)28 (45)	36¼ (920)	35.4	21' 9'' (6 625)	60	1961	Cockerill-Ougrée	Cockerill-Ougrée	Cockerill-Ougrée
91	B	Hyd.	335	22 000 (10 000)	(S)21 560 (9 800) (L)10 340 (4 700)		13 (21) 28 (45)	49⅝ (1 262)	36	21' 9'' (6 625)	60	1961	Cockerill Brugeoise et Nivelles ABC	GM HM	Twin-Disc + Cockerill
92	C	Hyd.	350	(S)33 000 (15 000) (L)20 700 (9 400)			(S)17 (28) (L)28 (45)	49⅝ (1 262)	50.55	34' 1½'' (10 400)	24	1960	Brugeoise et Nivelles	S.E.M.	Voith
84	C	Hyd.	550	(S)35 300 (16 000) (L)33 000 (15 000)			(S)20 (33) (L)31 (50)	,,	55.8	34' 11¼'' (10 650) 33' 3½'' (10 150)	35 25 10	1963 1955 1959	A.B.R.; Baume et Marpent	Anglo-Belgian Company	Voith L 37U
85	C	Hyd.	550	,,			,,	,,	58.5	32' 10'' (10 000)	25	1956	Forges, Usines et Fonderies Haine St. Pierre	S.E.M.	Turbo-transmission Voith L37U Invers.-reduct. SEMt.B.122
83	C	Hyd.	550	,,			,,	,,	57	35' 3¼'' (10 750)	25	1956	Cockerill-Ougrée	Cockerill-Ougrée (lic. Hamilton) 695 SA	Turbo-transmission Voith L37U Invers.-réduct
80	C	Hyd.	650	(S)38 800 (17 600) (L)28 400 (12 900)			(lg)24 (38) (2g)49 (78)	49¼ (1 250)	52.1	34' 0'' (10 360)	69	1960	Brugeoise et Nivelles; A.B.R.	Maybach	Voith
70	Bo-Bo	Elec.	700	44 000 (20 000)	34 000 (15 400)		31 (50)	42⅛ (1 070)	83	39' 10¼'' (12 150)	6	1954	Baume et Marpent	Anglo-Belgian Company	ACEC (licence Westinghouse)
71	D	Hyd.	750	52 900 (24 000)			31 (50)	49⅝ (1 262)	90	37' 8'' (11 480)	5	1956	Baume et Marpent	S.E.M.	Turbo-transmission Voith L217A Invers.-reduct.
72	D	Hyd.	750	(S)48 500 (22 000) (L)43 600 (19 800)			(S)20 (33) (L)31 (50)	,,	80	39' 7½'' (12 080)	15	1956	Brugeoise et Nivelles	S.E.M.	Voith L37Z
82	C	Hyd.	650	42 978 (19 500)			37 (60)	49⅝ (1 262)	57	36' 7¾'' (11 170)	75	1965/6	Brugoise et Nivelles; Atel Belges Réunis	Anglo-Belgian Company Type DXS 6 cyl	Voith L217U
73	C	Hyd.	750	47 386 (21 500)			37 (60)	49⅝ (1 262)	56	36' 7¾'' (11 170)	75	1965/8		Cockerill-Ougrée Type T695A 6-cyl	Voith L217U
74	C	Hyd.	750	47 386 (21 000)			37 (60)	49⅝'' (1 262)	59	36' 7¾'' (11 170)	10	1977	Brugeoise et Nivelles	Anglo Belgian Company 6 DXC	Voith L217V

—track upgrading for high-speed operation (nothing has been done on this vital project, says the board);
—improvement of rail links with France and Britain in preparation for construction of the Channel tunnel ("No initiative has been taken to this date," says the report);
—improvement of line capacities on routes serving large cities (only B.Frs 257 million out of B.Frs 3 530 million originally approved for the 1970-75 period have so far been obtained).

The board's report stresses the need for increased railway funds by spotlighting the imbalance of spending on highways, waterways and rail since 1963. Annual expenditure on new highways in 1963 totalled B.Frs 4 400 million. By 1974 the sum had increased to B.Frs 34 000 million annually. Spending on waterways during the same period went up from B.Frs 2 700 million in 1963 to B.Frs 12 million in 1974. But investments on railways had grown far more modestly—from B.Frs 1 100 million in 1963 to B.Frs 2 400 million in 1974.

ELECTRIFICATION

The Belgian Minister of Transport has given Belgian National Railways (SNCB) the go-ahead to electrify five lines by 1985. Scheduled for electrification are: Luttre—Manage—Braine-le-Comte by 1979; Manage-La Louviere-Mons by 1980; Antwerp-Aarschot-Leuwen by 1980; Marchienne-Pieton-La Louviere by 1982; and Ottignies-Charleroi by 1984/85. At the same time the Ministry of Transport has agreed to SNCB plans to increase speeds from a present maximum of 140 km/h to 160 km/h over five lines: Essen-Antwerp; Brussels-Quevy; Ostend-Gent; Brussels-Liege; Gent-Kortrijk.

TRACK DETAILS

Standard rail: Flat bottom, 100.8 lb per yd *(50 kg/m)*.
Length: 88.68 ft *(27.028 m)*.
Joints: 4-hole and 6-hole fishplates.
Rail fastenings: Soleplates and screws for wood sleepers. Type RN flexible fastenings on RS concrete sleepers; rigid clips on FB concrete sleepers. Pads are inserted under the rail when concrete sleepers are used. "Pandrol" fastenings are used in tunnels.
Sleeper (crossties): Generally oak, 11 in × 5½ in × 8 ft 6⅜ in *(280 × 140 × 2 600 mm)*. Two types of concrete sleeper are used:— Type RS (two blocks joined by a steel bar) with Type RN flexible rail fastenings, and Type F.B. pre-stressed concrete with rigid fastenings.
Rail fastenings: Soleplates and screws. "Pandrol" fastening is used in tunnels.
Cross ties (sleepers): Generally oak, 11 in × 5½ in × 8 ft 6⅜ in *(280 × 140 × 2 600 mm)*. Sections of welded-rail track have been laid with two types of concrete sleepers: Type RS (two blocks joined by a steel bar) with Type RN flexible rail fastenings, and Type F.F. (two blocks and a tie) with rigid fastenings.
Spacing: 2 670 to 2 190 per mile *(1 665 to 1 370 per km)*.
Filling: Broken stone or slag.
Max curvature:
  Main line: 2.18° = radius of 2 625 ft *(800 m)*.
  Secondary line 3.5° = radius of 1 640 ft *(500 m)*.
  Running lines 8.75° = radius of 656 ft *(200 m)*.
  Sidings   11.7° = radius of 492 ft *(150 m)*.
Max gradient: 1.8% = 1 in 55½; except 2 sections of 3.5% = 1 in 28½.
Max altitude: 1 759 ft *(536 m)* at Hockai on the Pepinster-Trois Ponts line.
Max permitted speed: 87 mph *(140 km/h)* on major main lines. 75 mph *(120 km/h)* on all other main lines.
Max axle load: Certain locomotives have axle load of 24 tons. Except for certain bridges they can operate anywhere on the system, subject to speed restriction.

Welded rail: On 1 Jan 1974 the total length of track with welded rail was 1 621 km of which 57 km had been laid in 1974. Rail used (type 50R) weighs 101 lb/yd *(50 kg/m)* in bars 88 ft 7 in *(27 m)* long. These are flash-butt welded at depot into 708 ft 8 in *(8 × 27 m)* lengths and, after laying, the joints are Thermit welded to form continuous rail. The longest individual length is 3.5 miles *(5.7 km)*.

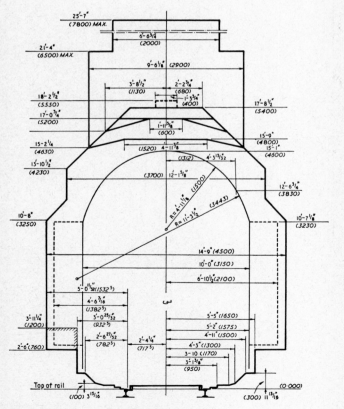

SNCB loading and structure gauge diagram

BENIN

ORGANISATION COMMUNE BENIN-NIGER DES CHEMINS DE FER ET DES TRANSPORTS (OCBN)
Boite Postale 16, Cotonou

Telephone: 31 33 80
Telegrams: Orcodani Cotonou
Telex: 210

President: Moudour Zakara
Director General: M. Do Rego
Chief of Planning: K. Romeuf

Gauge: 1.00 m.
Route length: 578 km.

OCBN operates, on behalf of the two Republics of Niger and Benin, a total route length of 359 miles *(578 km)* of single track metre gauge railway consisting of:—

Northern Line	fom Cotonou to Parakou via Pahou	272 miles	*438 km*
Eastern Line	from Cotonou to Pobè	66 miles	*107 km*
Western Line	from Pahou to Ségboroué	21 miles	*33 km*

From Parakou freight traffic is transported by road.

A future project is the extension of the Northern Line from Parakou to Dosso a distance of 300 miles *(480 km)*. An agreement was signed in 1976 between Niger and Benin for the construction of a rail link between Parakou and Niamey to give Niger access to the sea at Cotonou.

TRAFFIC

During 1975 OCBN recorded significant traffic increases in both passengers and freight:

		1973	1974	1975
Passengers	Journeys	1 372 964	1 500 523	1 563 364
	Pass-km	93 419 081	101 092 723	96 746 234
Baggage traffic	Tons	2 178	2 225	2 148
	Ton-km	290 614	293 910	268 141
Parcels	Tons	4 196	4 757	4 212
	Ton-km	1 198 519	1 302 981	1 099 470
Wagon freight	Tons	278 894	304 144	298 865
	Ton-km	113 305 128	126 928 894	125 179 134
Total freight	Tons	285 268	311 126	305 225
	Ton-km	114 894 261	128 525 785	126 546 745

MOTIVE POWER

Number of locomotives in operation at the end of 1975 totalled 11 diesel-electrics, 9 shunting tractors. Railcars totalled 5 diesel-electric and 6 diesel.

ROLLING STOCK

In operation are 8 passenger coaches, 20 railcar trailers and 341 freight wagons.

TRAFFIC PROSPECTS

From the **Republic of Niger:**—Because of the increase in imports of about 5 per cent per year and the outward movement of Ground Nut (peanut) traffic it is estimated that the probable annual traffic will be of the order of 150 000 tonnes. To this figure must be added the tonnage anticipated when the uranium deposit at Arlit is in full operation—10 000 tonnes of fuel and 20 000 tonnes of chemical products.
From **Nigeria:**—This future traffic from Northern Nigeria is being negotiated following agreement between the authorities of Nigeria, Niger, and Benin. It is anticipated that some 200 00 tonnes of Ground Nuts per year will be loaded on train at Parakou—60 000 tonnes from the Sokoto region via Gaya and Malanville, and 140 000 tonnes from the Kainji region via Yashikera and Nikki.

INTERNAL TRAFFIC

The maintenance of the tariff policy followed since 1967, and the expansion of industry in the middle and north of the country, particularly the increase in cotton production, should bring to the rail in the near future some 70 000 tonnes per year.

TRACK WORK

General: Within the limits of the OCDN budget and with aid from FAC subventions, track is being upgraded. Work in progress includes the complete renewal of track using rail weighing 60.5 lb per yard *(30 kg/m)* in place of the existing 42.4 lb *(22 kg)* rail; closer sleeper spacing under 22 kg rail, 1 770 sleepers per km in place of the existing 1 330; and ballast renewals.
Rail used weighs 60.5 lb per yd *(30 kg/m)* in 46 ft *(14 m)* bars, Thermit welded into 505 ft *(154 m)* lengths. After laying in track the joints are Thermit welded in situ from station to station.
The rails are secured by clips and bolts to "Cameroun" type metal sleepers 5 ft 9 in *(1 750 mm)* long and 9⅛ in *(232 mm)* wide.

CONTAINER OPERATION

Present stock consists of 15 of 3 m³ and 20 of 8.8 m³ for domestic use and 8 independently owned transcontainers 35 ft × 8 ft × 8 ft 6 in for service between France and Niger via OCDN.

Containers

Type	3m³	8.8 m³
Number	6	10
Length	6 ft 5 in *(1.96 m)*	6 ft 11 in *(2.10 m)*
Width	3 ft 9 in *(1.14 m)*	6 ft 11 in *(2.10 m)*
Height	5 ft 10 in *(1.78 m)*	8 ft 2½ in *(2.50 m)*
Capacity	106 ft³ *(3.0 m³)*	282 ft³ *(8.8 m³)*
Load	1.104 tonnes	4.25 tonnes
Tare	0.396 tonnes	0.75 tonnes
Total weight	1.5 tonnes	5.00 tonnes
Method of lifting	2 rings at the top	4 rings, one at each top corner
Access	1 side door	2 side doors
Owned by	OCDN	OCDN

The 8 large containers owned by the Société de Transit SO.CO.PAO of Cotonou, for shipment to and from France and carried through Benin into Niger by rail and road, are 35 ft 0 in *(10 668 mm)* long, 8 ft 0 in *(2 435 mm)* wide, 8 ft 6 in *(2 590 mm)* high; capacity 2 040 ft³ *(57.75 m³)*; load 23 tonnes, tare 2.84 tonnes.

Lifting equipment
1 20 tonne fixed crane which can lift 26 tonnes (at Parakou)
3 Hyster 5 tonne cranes
1 Pinguelly 10 tonne crane
1 Weitz 10 tonne mobile crane on pneumatic tyres
1 5 tonne fork lift truck
2 1.5 tonne fork lift trucks

BOLIVIA

BOLIVIAN NATIONAL RAILWAYS

Empresa Nacional de Ferrocarriles, Casilla 428, La Paz

Telephone: 27401 54756
Telegrams: ENFE, La Paz

Director General: Ing. Gustavo A. Méndez T.
Director, Operations: Ing. Carlos Azurduy T.
Director, Administration: Ing. Serafin Olmos R.
Heads of Departments
Financing: Lic. Valentin Quiroga
Commercial: Sr. Angel Peñaloza A.
Traffic and Operations: Sr. Cantalico Arce D.
Traction: Ing. Rafael Echazú B.
Purchases and Stores: Sr. Jorge Rada P.
Superintendent, Eastern Lines: Ing. Luis Bravo Hurtado
Chief of Operations, Eastern Lines: Ing. Jorge Mirabal M.

Gauge: 1.00 m.
Route length: 3 323 km.

As Bolivia is a landlocked country the railways are of major importance, because they constitute the principal means of access to ports on the Pacific and Atlantic Oceans via the neighbouring countries. These essential international railway connections are as follows:—
    with **Chile** to the Pacific ports of Arica and Antofagasta;
    with **Argentina** to the Atlantic ports of Rosario and Buenos Aires;
    with **Brazil** to the Atlantic port of Santos;
    with **Peru** (by ship across Lake Titicaca to Puno) to the Pacific port of Matarani.
The Empresa Nacional de Ferrocarriles (ENFE) consists of two separate rail systems:—Western, operating 1 305 miles *(2 101 km)* of route; and Eastern, operating 760 miles *(1 222 km)* of route. There is no connection between them as yet, but a link line is planned between Aiquile—Santa Cruz and Zudañez—Santa Cruz.
A total of $US32m was earmarked in fiscal 1976 for track upgrading and rolling stock purchases to improve services on Bolivian National Railways' principal routes. $US8.7m will be spent on track works, including rail replacement, while $US8.1m will finance purchase of 300 wagons and five passenger coaches.
The remainder of the money will provide spare parts, new workshop equipment, and technical assistance from Sofrerail.

TRAFFIC

Tonne-km rose in 1976 by 11 per cent, from 465 million to 518 million. Freight tonnage, on the other hand, fell from 1 141 041 in 1975 to 1 080 087 in 1976.
Passenger journeys remained fairly steady: 1 246 000 in 1976 compared with 1 230 000 in 1970. A substantial rise in passenger-km was noted: from 270 million in 1970 to 367 million in 1976.

MODERNISATION

With the aid of World Bank loans and other financial assistance, ENFE has been carrying out a modernisation plan since 1972. Second phase of the programme was launched in 1975, backed by a World Bank loan of $US 32 million—although this was subsequently reduced to $US 28.7 million when the railway failed to take up an allocation of $US 3.3 million for the purchase of diesel locomotives.
Major tasks for the next phase of the programme to be completed in 1981 has now been set out and ENFE hopes to raise a further World Bank loan of $US 45 million. Preference is to be given to track modernisation, purchase of materials and equipment for the construction of new station facilities at Santa Cruz, Oruro and Alto de La Paz, purchase of additional freight wagons, and workshop improvements. Bolivian Government assistance for this stage of the plan is expected to be Pesos 141 million.

TRACK IMPROVEMENTS

Track improvements completed in 1976 included: (1) construction of special embankment protections on the Oruro—Cochabamba section of the Western Andean network; (2) modernisation of track on the Oruro—Viacha section, including ballasting, sleeper replacement and rail welding; (3) replacement of 30 bridges with metal structures (six

more bridges were due to be replaced in 1977); (4) reconstruction of the Robore—Naranjos section of the Santa Cruz—Corumba line on the Eastern network, including reballasting, installation of new sleepers and heavier rail (track was welded in 1977).
New construction planned or already underway in 1976/77 includes initial engineeering studies for the Trans-continental railway connection of the Eastern and Western networks. The new line will run from Santa Cruz to Aiquile. Work is under control of joint Bolivian and Brazilian commissions.

Route of trans-continental railway

	miles	km	miles	km
BRAZIL				
Santos—Pto Esperanca	1 107	1 782		
Pto Esperanca—Corumba	58	93		
Corumba—Frontier	5	8		
Total in Brazil			1 170	1 883 = 47.64%
BOLIVIA				
Frontier—Santa Cruz	400	643		
Santa Cruz—Florida	57	92		
Florida—Aiquile	**186**	**300**	*(projected link line)*	
Aquile—Mizque	22	36		
Mizque—Cochabamba	112	180		
Cochabamba—Viacha	250	402		
Viacha—Frontier	131	211		
Total in Bolivia			1 158	1 864 = 47.17%
CHILE				
Frontier—Arica	127	205		
Total in Chile			127	205 = 5.19%
Distance from Santos to Arica			2 455	3 952 100%

Construction of the new Santa Cruz—Rio Mamore—Trinidad line is continuing under a joint Bolivian/Argentine commission; an agreement for the handing over of the Santa Cruz—Santa Rosa section to the Government of Bolivia was signed in 1976 making the Government responsible for all infrastructure and superstructure on the 104 km section. At the insistence of the World Bank, financial records for the line are to be kept separately from ENFE's other accounts.

MOTIVE POWER AND ROLLING STOCK

Purchase of 16 diesel-electric locomotives in 1976 (eight from Hitachi and eight from Mitsubishi Heavy Industries) fitted with 2 000 hp engines, has made it possible for ENFE to retire the last of its steam locomotives. The locomotives are fitted with electro-pneumatic and magnetic multiple controls and weigh 90 tonnes in working order.
Orders were placed during fiscal 1976/77 for eight U20C 2 150 hp and nine 1 000 hp diesel locomotives with General Electric do Brasil. Total value of the order, with spares, is $US 7.7 million.
Also purchased during 1976/77 were five new two-car diesel trainsets from Ferrostaal. Freight stock orders placed in 1976 included one for 280 wagons of 55 tonne capacity placed with Companhia Comercio e Construcoes (CCC) of Brazil, and one for 40 flat wagons and ten tank wagons.
Passenger stock ordered during 1976 included 12 coaches and three dining cars; during the year eight passenger coaches were rebuilt in railway workshops.

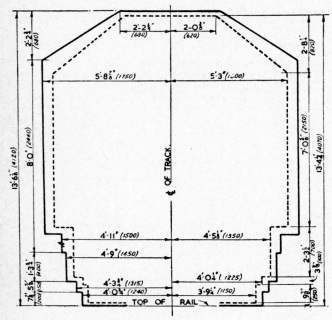

ENFE loading and structure gauge

BRAZIL

REDE FERROVIARIA FEDERAL SA (RFFSA)

Praca Duque de Caxias 86, Rio de Janeiro

President: Colonel Stanley Forks Baptista
Assistants: Eng. Fernando Limeira França
Col. João Monteiro de Lima Melo
Chief of Cabinet: Eng. Geraldo Costa Guimarães
Public Relations: Enio Amaral
Directors: Eng. Geraldo Soares Berford
Cel. Eng. Carlos Aloysio Weber
Admistrative and Financial Director: Eng. Alvaro Gomes Barbosa
Director of Engineering: Eng. Domingos Daré
Director of Personnel: Dr. Geraldo Jose de Oliveira
Director of Special Projects: Eng. José Himério da Silva Oliveira
Director of Planning: Eng. Mauro Rolf Fernandes Knudsen
Director of Operations: Eng. Napoleão Goretti
Commercial Director: Eng. René Fernandes Schoppa
Regional Superintendents:
Rio de Janeiro: Eng. Antonio Geral Soares Berford—Ed. D. Pedro 11-10° andar—Rio de Janeiro
São Paulo: Eng. José Teófilo dos Santos—Praça da Luz n° 1-Sạo Paulo
Belo Horizonte: Eng. Clovis Vaz da Costa—Rua Sapucai 571-Belo Horizonte—Minas Gerais
Curitiba: Eng. Renato Meister—Rua João Negrão 940-Curitiba-Paraná
Recife: Eng. Emerson Loureiro Jatobá—Praça da Central s/n°-Recife-Pernanmbuco
Porto Alegre: Eng. Plauto Adroaldo dos Santos Facin Largo Visconde de Cairu 17-3° andar-Porto Alegre-RS

Gauge: 1.60 m; 1.00 m; 0.762.
Route length: 24 491 km.

RFFSA routes now total 78.7 per cent of all track-km in Brazil, with a route length of 24 491 km. In addition to the 13 Federal-owned lines there are several other railways in operation, some owned by autonomous Federal departments, some by State governments, and some privately. RFFSA is now administered by five regional authorities and one commuter railway division (Rio de Janeiro). Brief descriptions of each regions follows:
The railways owned by the State of São Paulo have been combined into one central organisation called Ferrovia Paulista SA (FEPASA), divided into three divisions.
The Central Regional System is undoubtedly the most profitable of the regional systems. Extending for 8 300 kms it serves the most developed states of Brazil—Minas Gerais, Espirito Santo, Rio de Janeiro, Sao Paulo, Goias and the Federal District of Brasilia—and provides the RFFSA with one third of its total revenue. The railway is an important link in supplying industries with essential raw materials and in transporting exports to the ports of Rio de Janeiro and Angra dos Reis. Coffee is carried from the states of Sao Paulo, Minas Gerais and Espirito Santo and sugar and cement from the states of Sao Paulo and Rio de Janeiro. In 1973 the Central Regional System carried 67 per cent of the passengers, 59 per cent of the goods, 26 per cent of the baggage and parcels and 15.6 per cent of the livestock carried by the entire RFFSA network.
The most prestigious project in the RFFSA's new development plan will be undertaken in the Central Regional System. This is the Belo Horizonte-Itutinga-Volta Redonda line, or the 'Steel Line', as it has been nicknamed. A total of $US 3 500 million will be spent on improvements to this line so that it can increase its present cargo capacity from 20 million tons of iron a year in 1975 to 45 million tons a year by 1978. Originally this project was allocated only $US 400 million but difficulties in electrifying the line have increased the cost and made this project the most important and the most expensive of all.
A further project, costing 710 million cruzeiros, aims to improve the Rio-Sao Paulo transport corridor. A rail connection is to be built from Japeri to Barra do Pirai, to provide a more economical method of transport than the Rio-Sao Paulo highway. An integral part of this programme will be the installation of a new traffic control system (CTC) between Rio de Janeiro and Sao Paulo to allow high speed traffic to operate on the line.
The states of Rio Grande do Norte, Paraiba, Pernambuco, Alagoas, Maranhao, Sergipe, Piaul, Ceara and Bahia are served by the **North-Eastern Regional System.** The 7 361 kms of track cross an area which is economically dependent on sugar cultivation and vegetable farming. In 1973, the North Eastern regional lines transported 29 per cent of the baggage and parcels, 8.5 per cent of the passengers, 8 per cent of the goods, and 3.5 per cent of the cattle carried by the RFFSA network. The North East was not included in the original railway plan but the reappraisal in 1976 led to 2 700 million cruzeiros being allocated for the improvement of its tracks, railway stations and terminals.
The North West railway runs through a densely populated region of the State of Sao Paulo, and extends as far as Santa Cruz de la Sierra in Bolivia. The line between Bauru and Santa Cruz de la Sierra is operated jointly by Bolivian and Brazilian crews, and provides an important trade link with Bolivia. The railway is primarily concerned with the transport of cement, clinker, fertilisers, timber (both sawn and in log form), petroleum products and cattle within Brazil and with the export of steel tubes, cars, lorries and cattle to Bolivia. In 1973, 27 575 tons of products were imported and 5 234 tons were exported via this rail network. It is hoped shortly to increase trade with Paraguay via the Ponta Pora branch line. The system will be included in the general modernisation plans for the railways.
The Centre-South regional system consists of 1 779 kilometres of track serving the states of Sao Paulo and Mato Grosso with lines extending to Bolivia and Paraguay. Included in this system is the Santos-Jundiai railway, perhaps the most important of Brazil's railways, linking as it does Latin America's largest industrial centre with the port of Santos. A rack-rail system has replaced the funicular used previously to ascend the 800 m Serra do Mar range. Further improvements are planned along this stretch of track, which supplies oil to the Presidente Bernardes and Union Carbide refineries at Cubatao and Capuaba. The importance of this system is shown by the fact that in 1973 it carried 63 per cent of the cattle, 25 per cent of the baggage and parcels, 19 per cent of the passengers and 8.5 per cent of the goods carried in total by the entire RFFSA. It will be included in the general modernisation plans, and a further 1 272 million cruzeiros will be spent improving the Santos export corridor to enable the direct transport of dolomite and iron ore to the COSIPA steel plant. This will involve building an extension of the line from Paratinga to Piassaguera.
The Southern regional system, with 6 789 kms of track, serves the states of Parana, Santa Catarina and Rio Grande do Sul where the economy is based on agriculture and cattle raising. The railway transports wheat and soya, the wheat to other areas of Brazil, the soya to the ports of Rio Grande, Porto Alegre and Pelotas for export. Coal is transported from the mines of Santa Catarina to the ports of Imbituba and Laguna to be shipped to the Volta Redonda steel plant, while petroleum products from the Pasqualini refinery are transported to Curitiba via the Porto Alegre-Ponta Grossa railroad. Under the railway development plan the Rio Grande export corridor and the Paranagua export corridors will be improved. To enable agricultural goods such as soya, maize and wheat to be exported from the Upper Uruguay, Missoes, Central Plateau and the north eastern regions of Rio Grande do Sul to the port of Rio Grande, 1 880 million cruzeiros will be spent on improving and modernising the Rio Grande export corridor. A similar project to enable agricultural produce from the states of Parana, Santa Catarina and south Mato Grosso to be exported via the port of Parana will cost 1 648 million cruzeiros.

General Electric diesel electric locomotive 60 tonne; 900/810 hp.

All stainless-steel passenger/buffet self-propelled rail diesel car unloading from a Brazilian freighter for operation with RFFSA.

The railway development plan will also include two railways not under direct control of the RFFSA. The State of Sao Paulo Railways (FEPASA), was formed in November, 1971 when five companies were merged. Three lines under the control of RFFSA (Sao Paulo-Rio de Janeiro, Santos-Jundiai and Bauru-Corumba) connect with the FEPASA network. Its most important lines are those that link the industrial areas of the state and the state capital with the residential suburbs of Santo Andre, Sao Bernardo do Campo and Sao Caetāno do Sul and towns like Jundiai, Sorocaba, Campinas and Piracicaba. As the richest and most industrialised state in Brazil, Sao Paulo provides the railway with considerable traffic. In 1972 FEPASA carried 3 522 million tons of cargo.
The Companhia Vale do Rio Doce, the largest mining concern in Brazil, owns the most important lines that are still outside the direct control of RFFSA. The railway traffic consists mainly of iron ore transported along the Vitoria-Minas railway. The table below analyses the cargo carried on this line together with the company's projections for 1980:

Types of Cargo	*Net tons (m)*		*Ton km* $\times 10^9$	
	1973	*1980*	*1973*	*1980*
Ores	45	149	41	102
Agricultural products	6	24	2	12
Cement and clinker	4	15	2	5
Coal	3	7	—	1
Petroleum by-products	4	10	2	5
Sugar	4	7	1	2
Iron and steel products and pig iron	2	9	1	5
Fertilisers and composts	2	13	1	5
Limestone, timber, salt livestock, lime, paper and others	11	22	4	8

RECENT HISTORY

After the war, the Brazilian government acquired most of the foreign-owned railway companies and eventually, in 1957, 18 of the 22 railways were incorporated into one stock company, the Rede Ferroviaria Federal SA (The Federal Railway network). The Rio Grande do Sul and the Santa Catarina railways were first leased to their two respective state administrations and were later incorporated into the stock company, while the remaining two railways continued under special administrations. This rationlisation of the railway system enabled the government to concentrate on the construction of links to connect lateral east-west railways with one another and on the electrification of those lines serving the densely populated areas and the industrial centres. Uneconomical branch lines were closed and the railway deficit was slowly reduced. Brazil itself began to produce the materials it needed for the railways; most of the material for the extension of the line to Brasilia, completed in 1968, came from domestic plants. But the railways continued to lose passengers and although the carriage of general freight increased, it was not enough to make the lines profitable. From 1967 to 1974 the number of passengers carried by rail declined by 3.2 per cent each year while freight, due principally to growing iron ore exports, increased by 16.3 per cent each year.
This result was disappointing but typical of what was happening to railways all over the world. In Brazil old equipment, poor and overdue maintenance and archaic operating systems combined to make things worse, and the problems were exacerbated by the variety of different gauges employed by the different lines. Almost 90 per cent of the existing track is one metre gauge, 11 per cent is one metre sixty 0.7 per cent is less than one metre gauge. The table below gives the total extent of the railways in Brazil today and shows the disparity of gauges on existing tracks.
The railway might have continued to decline if the energy crisis in 1973 had not encouraged the government to take a fresh look at the system. At that time, Brazil was importing almost 80 per cent of the oil it needed and began to look for ways of reducing the enormous foreign exchange cost. The result of the reappraisal was a decision to undertake a huge programme of investment in railway development and modernisation. Costing 30 500 million cruzeiros ($US 3 050 million), the programme would form part of the Second National Development Plan and would cover the period 1975 to 1979. To reduce oil consumption, tracks would be electrified. Gauges would be standardised, more than 3 800 kms of track would be built and 10 800 kms improved, and 20 000 wagons, 300 locomotives and 140 passenger cars would be bought. According to the plan, this programme would triple the amount of cargo being carried by the railways from its present level of 15 per cent of the national traffic to 45 per cent by 1980.

INVESTMENTS

The effect on the Brazilian economy of the world slump in 1975 has forced a reappraisal of the programme in January 1976. While the aims of modernisation and expansion remain unchanged, the new proposals spread the programme over a longer period and in the initial stages more emphasis will be placed on improving existing lines than on building new ones. The total investment is now likely to be far smaller. Under latest spending plans published in June, 1977, the railway has called for total investments of Cr 67 059 million between 1977 and 1980. For track improvements and new line construction alone, RFFSA has allocated Cr 51 356 million. According, however to a JWR correspondent in Brazil, future investments up to 1980 are likely to be far smaller than the amount originally specified. RFFSA has proposed a budget of 24 000 million cruzeiros ($US 1 603 million) for 1978. This will cover only operating expenses and financial charges. Future investments will no longer be made through loans but through Government grants.

FINANCIAL

RFFSA President, Col Eng Stanley Baptista, reported in late 1977 that the railways' current total debt was about 20 000 million cruzeiros. Operating deficit in 1977 is expected to drop from the 1976 level of 6 100 million cruzeiros to about 4 680 million cruzeiros. Addition of interest and depreciation charges, however, will increase the total deficit in 1977 to 8 000 million cruzeiros, compared with 9 300 million cruzeiros in 1976.

Financial statistics for 1976 are not strictly comparable with 1975 by virtue of a 41 per cent devaluation of the cruzeiro. Income from all sources in 1976 was Cr$3 782 m, but there was a further dramatic rise in expenditure to Cr$9 844 m. After payment of interest and other charges, deficit for the year was Cr$6 061. This figure is almost double the unadjusted loss for 1975.

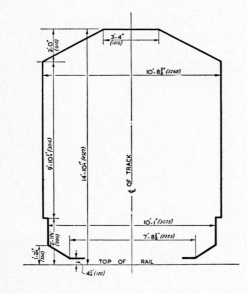

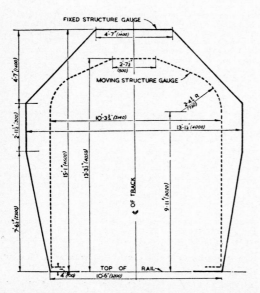

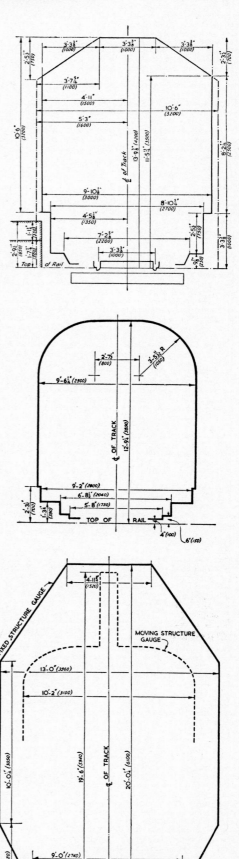

Six types of loading and structural gauge are encountered over Brazil's railway lines.

FREIGHT TRAFFIC

Both freight and passenger traffic climbed significantly during 1976 with the trend all set to continue through 1977. Freight carried during 1976 increased to 55.1 million tonnes, compared with 46.4 million tonnes in 1975, while the tonne-km figure increased from 19 732 million to 23 549 million. Most significant increase was in the movement of iron ore with 10.9 million tonne-km hauled in 1976 compared with 9.976 million tonne-km in 1975. Iron ore now accounts for 35 per cent of all freight carried by the railway, cement for 9.3 per cent, petroleum products 6.3 per cent, steel products 7.3 per cent, and soya 2.6 per cent. Of major importance to RFFSA in 1976 were increases of soya production in Rio Grande do Sul and Parana which have turned the cereal into the railway's fifth largest traffic. Shipments have increased from 67 000 tonnes in 1964 to 1.4 million in 1976. Improved freight traffic productivity is being achieved by more effective use of both locomotives and rolling stock. Last year, for instance, each wagon in service accounted for 581 500 tonne-km compared with 526 000 in 1975 and 361 000 in 1972.

PASSENGER TRAFFIC

An increase in passenger traffic—up from 7 628 million in 1975 to 8 744.9 million in 1976—reversed the downward trend experienced over the past few years. But two basic problems remain: (1) deteriorating facilities have resulted in big financial losses on long-distance passenger services: (2) the huge growth of suburban traffic (up from 5 101.4 million passenger/km in 1975 to 6 069.2 million in 1976) has created numerous operating difficulties.

The railway told a Government committee in 1976 that its services are no longer competitive in the longer-distance passenger market. A few examples bear this out. The Rio—Campos overnight express, for instance, now takes eight hours on a journey that was once handled by a similar train in six hours; hourly Rio—Campos bus services complete the same journey in four-and-a-half hours. The Rio—Sao Paulo daylight express—that once took about seven-and-a-half hours on the run—now takes nearly nine hours while a ten-minute interval bus service completes the journey in six-and-a-half hours.

COMMUTER TRAFFIC

RFFSA is taking measures to improve commuter services into Rio and Sao Paulo—a move which has resulted in even more frequent delays to intercity expresses operating into the cities. Commuter services into Rio, for instance, now takes complete precedence over all trains. A big improvement to Rio's commuter service was expected by late 1977 when all 30 of the new four-car electric trainsets built by a Japanese consortium led by Mitsui are expected to have been put into operation.

Existing three-car sets—built between 1937 and 1941 have been rebuilt to go back into service by late 1977 as four-car sets with two powered motor cars and two trailers. To cope with future traffic growth in the Rio area, RFFSA has ordered 140 new metre-gauge commuter cars from Pidner of Brazil. The cars will be used in the suburbs of Rio on the former British-built Leopoldina Railway.

Effective last July, RFFSA introduced a new commuter timetable for Sao Paulo, based on the introduction of 15 new three-car Mafersa-built commuter sets. Trains on the 35-km Pirituba—Maua line now operate at ten minute intervals during peak-periods and every 20 minutes during the remainder of the day. Further improvements are planned on the line when a double-track project between Maua and Ribeirao Pires is completed sometime in the future.

	1974	1975	1976
Total freight ton km	18 248 355 000	19 850 685 000	23 549 000 000
Total freight tonnage	43 292 000	46 446 000	55 000 000
Total passenger km	7 814 000 000	7 628 092 000	8 744 900 000
Total passengers carried	258 000 000	242 985 000	—

MOTIVE POWER AND ROLLING STOCK

New rolling stock is vital to expand the system's capacity, and deliveries continued at a high level in 1976/77 with 6 220 wagons, 87 locomotives and 17 electric multiple-units entering service during the year.

A total of 80 diesel-electric locomotives, rated at 2 300 hp, have been ordered by RFFSA from General Electric for operation over the Aguas Claras ore line.

FERROVIA PAULISTA SA (FEPASA)
Rua Libera Badaró 39, São Paulo

President: Walter Pedro Bodoni
Director, Administrative: Walfrido de Carvalho
Director, Commercial: Calim Eid
Director, Financial: Econ, Jarbas Maranhão
Director; Operations: Eng. Chafic Jacob
Director, Public Relations: Claudio de Asumpção Cardoso
Director, Technical: Eng. Oliver H. Salles de Lima
Director, Assistant to President: Eng. Ascelino Lopes de Morais
Director, Personnel: Prof. Ary Baddini Tavares

Departmental Heads:
Planning: Sergio de Azevedo Marques
Mechanical Engineering: Eng. Carlos Augusto Bandeiro de Mello
Civil Engineering: Eng. Guido Luciano A. Toselo
Permanent Way: Eng. Antonio Carlos C. de Camargo
Electrical Engineering: Eng. Cassio Penteado Serro
Systems: Eng. Mariano H. Aranho Domingues
Operations: Eng. Francisco de Paula R. Pesso Neto
Traction: Eng. Carlos Adolpho Mariante
Stations: Eng. Wilson De Bello
Supplies: Eng. José Carlos A. Fusaro
Commercial: Eng. Reynaldo José B. Nunes Sumares
Finance: Econ. Oscar Fernando S. Villas Boas
Economics: Econ. Carlos Alberto Lüders.

Gauge: 1.60 m; 1.00 m.
Route length: 1 647 km; 3 649 km.

FEPASA was formed in 1970 to consolidate the operation of five railways owned by the State of São Paulo. There are three divisions: First (the former Paulista and Araraquara); Second (the former Sorocabana); Third (the former Morgiana and São Paulo—Minas). In December 1977, the World Bank agreed in principle to grant a loan equivalent to Cr$850 m to Fepasa for construction of key freight lines. Boosting freight capacity is one of the main objectives of Fepasa's 1975-79 modernisation plan. Construction work will go ahead on the 173 km Uberaba—Ribeirao Preto route in the states of Sao Paulo and Minas Gerais, on the 23 km Piacaguera—Paratinga line, as well as on the Guedes to Mato Seco route which includes a major bridge over the Mogi Guacu river. Part of the loan will help finance construction of a bulk cargo handling terminal near Campinas. The World Bank loan forms part of Fepasa's 1978 budget which envisages expenditure of Cr 1 300 million. Much of this is being spent on upgrading and rehabilitation of Sao Paulo's suburban network.

TRAFFIC

	1973	1974
Total freight ton-km	3 589 161 000	4 190 615 000
Total freight tonnage	11 064 987	12 087 966
Total passenger-km	2 543 467 000	2 548 839 000
Total passenger journeys	46 185 183	45 116 486

FINANCIAL
Revenues in 1974 totalled Cr$ 668 641 700 compared with Cr$ 521 478 700 in 1973. Expenses in 1974 were Cr$ 845 476 200, compared with Cr$ 722 277 600 in 1973.

MOTIVE POWER
Number of locomotives in service in 1974 (with 1973 figures in brackets) were: 155 (165) electrics; 333 diesel-electrics (329); 10 (21) diesel-hydraulics; 2 (2) diesel mechanical units.

ROLLING STOCK
Passenger coaches in service in 1974 totalled 930 compared with 1 001 in 1973. Freight wagon totals have gone up from 16 738 in 1973 to 16 768 in 1974.

NEW LINE CONSTRUCTION
During 1974 the following lines were added to the basic system: 32 km at Apai; 23 km between Boa Vista and Helvetta. At present a total of 541 km are under construction—119 km of completely new lines and 422 km of replacement tracks.

SIGNALLING
New signalling installations projected include CTC over 106.5 km and ATC over the 24 km Jurubatuba—Sao Bernardo line.

Six-axle 4 000 hp diesel-hydraulic locomotive—one of 12 built by Krauss Maffei for operation over the Victoria Minas lines.

BULGARIA

BULGARIAN STATE RAILWAYS (BDZ)
Ministry of Transport, Sofia

Gauge: 1.435 m; 750 mm
Route length: 4 045 km; 245 km

General Manager: Ing. Iosiff Smilov

Structurally, the railway network is basically complete. In recent years, only a few sections of lines have been built which rationalise the transport system and create transport facilities for some new industrial objectives and sources of raw materials: Dulovo-Silistra, Zlataritza—Elena, Tscherven brajag—Zlatna Panega, etc. The systematic development of the different modes of transport, including railway transport, and the rational distribution of goods between these modes is the responsibility of the national Transport Authority which combines all the modes, including road transport; this ensures a high degree of efficiency in railway transport.

The rapid economic development of the country during the last 25 to 30 years has led to a considerable increase in the volume of goods and passenger traffic. In 1975, goods traffic had increased by 40% and passenger traffic by 17.8% compared with 1965 or, expressed in absolute figures, by 22.8 million tonnes of goods and more than 16 million passengers.

To enable the railway to cope with the offered volume of goods and passenger traffic, a technical reconstruction and modernisation of all the railway equipment (locomotives, vehicles, permanent way, stations, remote control installations, etc.) has been carried out in recent years. Priority is being given to highly effective measures which ensure a rapid increase in line and processing capacity.

The accelerated introduction of diesel traction enabled BDZ in 1977, to increase the share of electric and diesel traction in the total traction programme to more than 85 per cent—an increase that has taken place within a period of 12 to 14 years.

BDZ began taking delivery during 1977 of 70 class ER25 ac electric trainsets from the Soviet Union works at Riga.

The structure of the wagon fleet has been greatly improved by the modernisation of existing wagons and the introduction of heavy-duty and specialised goods wagons for carrying a variety of goods at speeds of 100 to 120 km/h.

The exacting demands for a better passenger service have led to a rapid renewal of the fleet of passenger coaches and to the additional introduction of coaches offering a higher level of travelling comfort and suitable for speeds ranging from 140 to 160 km/h.

SIGNALLING
At an ever increasing rate, new remote control instalations are being introduced, especially those which safeguard the train working on the open line and in the stations.

TRAFFIC
It is predicted that the railways will have to carry 110 million tonnes of goods and 118 million passengers in 1980, and 180 million tonnes of goods and 155 million passengers in 1990.
Total tonnage carried in 1975 was 79 000 000 tons (17 500 000 ton-km).
Number of passenger journeys in 1975 was 104 000 000. Number of passenger-km: 7 500 million.

DEVELOPMENT PLAN
BDZ is to spend 1 381.5 million Leva during the seventh (1976-80) five year plan on capital improvements, more than double the investments in the sixth five-year plan period.

ELECTRIFICATION
By the end of 1970, steam still accounted for 39 per cent of all BDZ traction. At the end of 1975, electric traction and diesel units were hauling 86.6 per cent of tonne-km—reducing steam traction to 13.4 per cent of the total.
Electrification of most of the principal railway lines has now been completed, using single-phase ac with voltage of 25 kV and 50 Hz frequency.
For the first electrified sections, 3 000 kW, four-axle series 41.0 electric locomotives were supplied by Skoda, Czechoslovakia. First batch of diesel locomotives were purchased from Simmering-Graz-Pauker, Austria.
Included in the new locomotives taken into service during the present plan period are: mainline electrics from Skoda; 3 000-hp diesels from the Soviet Union; 2 200-hp diesels from Romania.
Under the seventh plan (1976-80) about 900 km is scheduled for electrification: included will be sections Sofia-Mezdra; Plovdiv-Simnitsa; Gorna Orehovitza-Sindel;

Sofia-Dimitrovgrad South; Tulovo-Stara Zagora; Plovdiv-Svilengrad.
Proportion of electrified lines is planned to reach about 50 per cent of the total network by 1980. This will permit a 40 per cent increase of throughput and carrying capacity. At the same time the speed of freight and passenger trains will increase and there will be a sharp reduction in environmental pollution.
Introduction of new electric services will enable the railway to increase the gross weight of freight and passenger trains over lines at present restricted to low weights by nature of Bulgaria's terrain.

TRACK
Measures have been taken for continuous improvement of track. Over 36 per cent of the network has now been equipped with 49 kg/m rails. The proportion of continuous welded rails is now 24.3 per cent of the total length of running track. These measures have permitted train speeds to be increased to 100-120 km/h on some sections of line. Until now track doubling has been carried out relatively slowly. By 1973, only 253 km had been doubled—less than 6 per cent of the total network. Doubling is now planned during the seventh plan over 800 km: from Sofia to Plovdiv; Plovdiv to Zimnitsa; Mezdra via Gorna Orehovitza to Ruse; and Gorna Orehovitza to Sindel. In 1976 a total of 35 km was doubled and 120 km electrified. During 1977 track doubling and electrification was authorised for two routes totalling 725 km: Gorna Oryakhovitsa to Sindel and Plovdiv to Zimnitsa via Stara Zagora.

TRACK IMPROVEMENTS
Growing traffic is to be met, together with the increase in running speeds on individual railway lines, by double-tracking the single-track main lines and reconstructing them to a standard permitting a speed of 160 km/h. It is planned to introduce speeds ranging from 140 to 160 km/h for passenger trains and from 100 to 120 km/h for freight trains by perfecting vehicle design, permanent way and signalling techniques.
Associated with the double-tracking of the main lines is an extensive programme for improving the horizontal and vertical alignment of the permanent way and increasing its capacity through the introduction of rails with a metre weight of 54 and 60 kg. Also associated with the double-tracking of the lines is the reconstruction of stations with a view to lengthening tracks.
As a result of the double-tracking of about 780 route kilometres during the years 1976-1980, the share of double-track sections in the total route mileage will be raised to about 25 per cent.

SIGNALLING
There is to be increased application of automation and telemechanisation. Route-relay centralisation is to be installed at 65 stations and all electrified lines and mainline electric locomotives are to be equipped with semi-automatic cab signalling. By 1980, a total of 621 km will be equipped with semi-automatic relay blocking, and 400 level crossings will be fitted with automatic crossing devices.
Up to 1980, some 1 000 route kms of open lines will be equipped for central traffic control, and some 70 per cent of all locomotives will be equipped for automatic train control. All stations on the principal lines are being equipped with modern relay-type signal cabins.
Marshalling operations are being concentrated at the major marshalling yards which are equipped for the remote control of the marshalling process, making the most of the facilities provided by electronic data processing plants and other automatic equipment. The development of these key yards, capable of dealing with 500 to 600 wagons in 24 hours, is accompanied by that of auxiliary yards of lower capacity which handle, the traffic of a number of minor yards in the same area.

MARSHALLING YARDS
Two marshalling yards have been equipped with automatic humps, and 89 stations have been fitted with route re-lay centralisation.
As part of plans to speed delivery of freight and coordinate the operations of rail and road transport, loading and unloading will be concentrated at 100 to 150 terminals. This will help create conditions for full mechanisation of freight handling operations, with more efficient use of containers, pallets and packages.
BDZ's target is to mechanise 92 per cent of all freight handling operations by 1980. This will mean total elimination of manual labour, considerable qualitative changes in the material/technical base of the whole freight industry, and significant improvement in the organisation and management of rail transport.

TRANSIT TRAFFIC
Co-operation between Bulgaria and Greece on rail transit traffic under the 1964 agreements is making good progress. Transit freight traffic in 1976 was 30 per cent up on the previous year, and there are good prospects for increasing passenger traffic. The Kulata-Promahon line is to be rebuilt to increase its capacity allowing more traffic from Greece to be handled. Passenger services will be improved with a daily diesel railcar service between Sofia and Salonika and more of these units will be used on the Sofia-Athens line.

3 200 kW diesel-electric locomotive built by Skoda.

BURMA
UNION OF BURMA RAILWAYS
PO Box 118, Bogyoke Aung San Street, Rangoon

Telephone: 14455
Telegrams: Rheostat

Chairman, Management Board; Colonel Sein Ya
Managing Director: Colonel Sein Ya
General Manager: U Aye Pe
Deputy General Manager: U Kyaw Myint
Chief Traffic Manager: U Tun Aung
Chief Mechanical and Electrical Engineer: U Saw Clyde
Chief Engineer: U Tin Ohn
Controller of Railway Accounts: U Bo Lay
Controller of Stores: U Kyaw Hlaing

Gauge: 1.00 m
Route length: 3 130 km

Burma has a metre-gauge network comprising a main section and two short isolated sections of railway. The most important line connects the two principal cities, Rangoon the capital, and Mandalay 619 km to the north. Three passenger trains daily run in each direction, the fastest taking a scheduled 12 hours to cover the journey. Two classes of travel—upper and lower class—are offered.
A crash programme was announced in 1976 to upgrade services and track. Aim was to improve train speeds and frequencies by early 1977. A total of 34 additional freight trains were due to go into service together with 12 extra passenger services.

TRAFFIC

	1975/76	1976/77
Total freight tonne-miles	237 251 365	242 492 812
Total freight tonnage	1 619 888	1 675 369
Total passenger-miles	21 554 302 320	17 282 439 937
Total passenger journeys	49 055 360	32 053 102

FINANCES

	1975/76	1976/77
	(Kyats '000)	
Revenues	181 066.96	198 813.07
Expenses	196 204.37	223 650.17

MOTIVE POWER AND ROLLING STOCK
Alsthom, of France, signed a new contract with Burma Railways in 1977 for the supply of 21 new locomotives valued-together with spares—at Frs 73 million. Delivery of the locomotives, all rated at 1 600 hp, will bring the number of Alsthom-built motive power units in operation by the railway to 127.
Also during 1977, the railway awarded contracts worth Yen 4 070 million to a Japanese consortium for locomotives, coaches and wagons. The group, comprising Sumitomo Shoji, Kawasaki and Kinki Sharyo, is to supply five diesel-hydraulic locos of 500 hp, 12 first and 60 second-class passenger coaches, 20 tank wagons for petroleum products and five refrigerated wagons.

Number of locomotives in service	Line haul	Shunting (switching)
Steam	179	50
Diesel electric	79	15
Diesel hydraulic	72	—

Number of diesel trainsets	21 sets (3 car sets)
	2 sets (4 car sets)
Number of passenger train coaches	1 228
Freight train wagons	9 527
Containers for door-to-door service	Nil

TRACK CONSTRUCTION DETAILS
Standard rail: Flat bottom B.S.
  Main line: 75 and 60 lb *(37.2* and *29.8 kg)* in 39 ft lengths.
  Main branches: 60 lb *(29.8 kg).*
  Other branches and sidings: 50 lb *(24.9 kg).*
Joints: Suspended; joint sleepers 14 in centres. Rails are joined by fishplates and bolts.
Welded track: 117 ft *(35.7 m)* lengths. Thermit welded in situ.
Cross ties (sleepers): Hardwood (Xylia Dolabriformis) and creosoted soft wood, 8 in × 4½ in × 6 ft *(203 × 115 × 1 829 mm).*
Spacing:
  Main line: N + 3.
  Branch line: N + 2.
  (N = length of rail in linear yards).
Rail fastening: Dog spikes. Elastic Rail Spikes (Elastic Rail Spike Co, Ltd, London). Macbeth Rail Spikes (Exors. of James Mills Ltd, Cheshire, England) are under experimental use.
Filling (ballast): Broken stone, 2 in to ¾ in, shingle on branch lines.
Thickness under sleeper: 6 in *(150 mm).*
Max. curvature:
  Main line: 6° = radius of 955 ft *(291 m).*
  Branch line: 17° = radius of 338 ft *(103 mm).*
Max. gradient:
  Main line: 0.5% = in 200 compensated.
  Branch line: 4.0% = 1 in 25 compensated.
Max permitted speed:
  Main line: 30 mph *(48 km/hr)*.
  Branch line: 20 mph *(32 km/hr).*
Max axle load: 12 tons on 75 and 60 lb rail.
Bridge loading: Indian Railway Standard ML.

Class DD 900 diesel-hydraulic locomotive, rated at 960 hp, built for Burma in 1969; a total of six are still in service with the railway

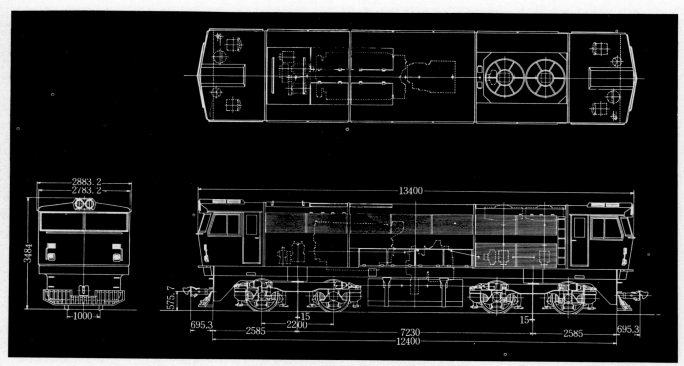

Type DD 1500 diesel-hydraulic locomotive built for Burma by Kawasaki for steep grade mainline service

CAMBODIA (KAMPUCHEA)

Phnom-Penh, Kampuchea

Telephone: 25156
Telegrams: FERCAM Phnom-Penh

Gauge: 1.0 m.
Route length: 649 km.

HISTORY

The 385-km line from Phnom-Penh, the capital, to Poipet where connection is made with the State Railway of Thailand, was built in two sections in 1930/32 and 1939/40 when the entire area was known as French Indo-China. The first section, to Mongkolborey, was built and worked by the Compagnie des Chemins de Fer du Sud de l'Indochine. This was purchased in 1936 by the Chemin de Fer Non Concedes de l'Indochine. In July 1952, all lines within Cambodia were formed into the Chemins de Fer du Cambodge.

The metre gauge Cambodian Railways has a total route length of 649 km of which only 33% is at present in operation. The newest line on the system, between Phnom-Penh and Kompong Som (264 km), opened in 1969, and has been closed to traffic since 1970 owing to damage caused during hostilities in the region. This is the country's only rail outlet to the sea, other than via Thailand to Bangkok. The Phnom-Penh—Poipet line is at present cut off between Phnom-Penh and Pyrsat.

TRAFFIC

	1972	1973
Total freight ton-km	9 769 343	11 512 900
Total freight tonnage	89 911	117 460
Total passenger-km	50 555 046	55 064 745
Total passenger journeys	902 813	1 027 317

FINANCIAL

	1962	1963	1965	1966	1969
		(millions of Riels)			
Revenue	74.9	91.9	126.6	81.8	122.4
Expenses	89.6	89.0	106.3	108.0	139.5
Operating ratio	119.6	96.8	83.9	132	113.9

MOTIVE POWER

Majority of the railway's present traction requirements are being met by 13 diesel-electric locomotives and a large number of steam locomotives. Backbone of the diesel electric fleet are the Alsthom-built BB 1 200 hp units fitted with MGO-V12 BZSHR which were delivered in 1966/67. Due to lack of spares, however, the workshops department experienced difficulties over the 1975/76 period in keeping these locomotives in operation.

NEW LINE

A line linking Phnom-Penh and Saigon has been projected for a number of years but consistently cancelled owing to hostilities. The line would fill one of the missing links in the Transasian Railway Project.

CAMEROON
REGIE DES CHEMINS DE FER DU CAMEROUN (REGIFERCAM)
PO Box 304, Douala

Telephone: 42-60-45
Telegrams: REGIFERCAM-DOUALA
Telex: 5607

President and General Manager: Gilbert Ntang
Technical Adviser: Samuel Minko
Assistant General Manager—Management: René Kamo
Assistant General Manager—Studies: Henri Leyrat
Administrative Manager: Eitel Ndedi-Mpacho
Assistant Administrative Manager: Jean Marie Omog-Samnick
Information Service: Samuel Evengue-Nsomoto
Judicial and Litigations Department: Janvier Bessala-Ngono
Financial Manager: Alfred Tamfu-Nchoko
Assistant Financial Manager: Jean Calvin Nana
Operations Department: Justin Teulale
Motive power and Rolling Stock Department: Paul Djoko Moyo
Track and Building Department: Gaston Monayong
Supply Department: Jean Trouslard

Gauge: 1.00 m
Total track length: 1 168 km

The new Transcameroonian Railway between Yaounde and Ngaoundére, which went into operation in February 1974, was officially inaugurated by the Cameroonian Chief of State on December 10, 1974. The ceremony was held in the new station at Ngaoundére, 623 km from Yaounde.
Cost of the line was Frs CFA 26 226.5 million with financing coming from United States (Frs 5 169.3 million), France (Frs CFA 4 038.9 million), German Federal Republic (Frs 1 088.7 million), Cameroon (Frs 3 691.6 million), and CEE (Frs 12 238 million).
During 1976, main projects undertaken by Regifercam included laying heavier rail between Otelé and Yaoundé and preliminary work on the Douala-Yaoundé realignment.

FINANCIAL

Total receipts for 1976 were FrCFA 6 425.6 m, about 26 per cent more than in the previous year. Expenditure rose to FrCFA 6 085.2 m, leaving an operating profit of FrCFA 340.4 m.

	1975	1976
	Frs CFA	
Revenues	5 339 007 290	6 425 600 000
Subvention (State)	1 182 382 558	—
Expenses	6 498 345 921	6 085 200 000

TRAFFIC

Freight traffic carried by Cameroon National Railways Authority in the financial year 1975-76 totalled 437·3 million tonne-km compared with 400·2 million tonne-km in the previous year. This satisfactory performance was nevertheless 16 per cent below the traffic forecast for the year; the shortfall is largely blamed on poor availability of motive power units. Wood, coffee, cotton and sugar traffics increased, but cocoa and metal products were lower than in 1974-75.
A drop in passenger traffic was 3 per cent more than forecast with passenger-km totalling 260·8 million compared with 282·0 million in 1974-75. The average journey of the 1·86 million passengers carried was 140·4 km.

FREIGHT

The following tonnage figures are reported for 1971-1976:

	West line	Trans cam line	Total
1971/1972	122 811	948 239	1 071 050
1972/1973	126 795	974 651	1 101 446
1973/1974	150 525	1 111 620	1 262 145
1974/1975	141 877	1 026 920	1 168 797
1975/1976 (both lines)	—	—	1 298 347

For the same period the following ton-km was carried:

	West line	Trans cam line	Total
1971/1972	14 825 222	288 216 033	303 041 255
1972/1973	15 441 848	310 807 630	326 249 478
1973/1974	18 720 510	386 603 943	405 324 453
1974/1975	17 942 445	382 221 353	400 163 798
1975/1976 (both lines)	—	—	438 189 000

PASSENGER

	West line	Trans cam line	Total
1971/1972 (Journeys)	711 902	1 167 254	1 879 156
1972/1973 ,,	670 818	1 046 803	1 717 621
1973/1974 ,,	600 459	1 082 532	1 682 991
1974/1975 ,,	551 209	1 405 032	1 956 301
1975/1976 ,,	—	—	1 857 398

MOTIVE POWER

Four mainline locomotives of 3 600 hp were added to the motive power fleet in 1976, together with three 900 hp shunters.

Type	Weight (tons)	Power (kw)	Number
Locomotives			
CEM AGO 4B 3 600	127	2 650	9
Alsthom AGO CC 2 400	86	1 250	5
Alsthom MGO BB 1 200	56	720	12
Alsthom MGO BB 300/500	54	415	17
Alsthom Sulzer BB 200	52	380	2
Total			45
Railcars			
Billard/Soulé/MGO ZE 10	45	315	7
Soulé/CEM/Poyaud ZE 100	47	500	4
Total			11
Locotractors			
CEM/MGO YE	30	215	32
Total			32

INVESTMENTS

During 1977, Regifercam invested a total of CFA Frs 539 million on track improvements (CFA Frs 169 million), new bridges and buildings (CFA Frs 140 million), yards and terminal facilities (CFA Frs 160 million) and repair facilities (CFA Frs 70 million). During 1977 a $US 2.3 million loan from the World Bank was used to finance studies for station reconstruction at Douala and for a new marshalling yard project.

CANADA

BRITISH COLUMBIA RAILWAY

1095 West Pender St, Vancouver, BC V6E 2N6

Telephone: 681 3131

Vice-President: M. C. Norris
Public Relations Manager: H. D. Armstrong
Administration Manager: G. L. Ritchie
Chief Mechanical Officer: G. L. Kelly
Operations and Maintenance Manager: N. A. McPherson
Controller: J. Pasowysty
Chief Engineer, Maintenance-of-way: A. G. Richmond
Chief of Engineering Services: V. W. Shtenko
Manager, Sales and Marketing: A. C. Sturgeon
Chief Financial Officer: P. D. Nelson
Chief of Communications: C. D. Marlatt
Chief of Transportation: A. T. Shannon
Labour Relations Manager: T. Teichman

Gauge: 1.435 m.
Route length: 1 387 km.

The British Columbia Railway's main track is geographically segregated into two operating divisions; the Cariboo and Peace River—Omineca Division. Within each of these lie the following subdivisions.
Cariboo Division: The Squamish subdivision is the southernmost on the Railway, running from Mile 0.0 at North Vancouver, to Mile 157.5 (Lillooet). It is followed by the Lillooet Sub-division which runs from Mile 157.5 to Mile 312.7, (Williams Lake) and the Prince George Subdivision, which extends from Mile 312.7 to Mile 462.5 (Prince George).
Peace River—Omineca Division: The Peace River portion runs from Prince George, over the Chetwynd Subdivision from Mile 462.5 to Mile 659.3 (Chetwynd). The Fort St John Subdivision is next, running from Mile 659.3 to Mile 816.5 (Beatton). The railway's northernmost Subdivision, the Fort Nelson, follows, extending from Mile 816.5 to Mile 979.4 (Fort Nelson). It should be noted that the 21.1 Mile Mackenzie Industrial Lead and the 61.1 Mile Dawson Creek Subdivision are also included in the Peace River Division. The Omineca portion begins at Odell, which lies in the Chetwynd Subdivision. It is composed of the Stuart Subdivision, which runs from Mile 0.0 at Odel to Mile 151.5, and the Takla Subdivision, which extends from Mile 151.5 to Mile 336.0. Beyond Lovell, which is situated at Mile 197.0, this line is considered to be under construction, as it has not yet been certified operational by the British Columbia Ministry of Energy, Transport and Communications. Effective April 5, 1977, work on this extension has been suspended.

FINANCES

The financial statements for the British Columbia Railway for 1973 and prior years indicated that the railway had been operating on substantially a break-even basis after absorption of both depreciation and interest on all borrowed funds. Two separate reports made public in 1973, questioned these financial statements and the general statements in these two reports were confirmed when the audited financial statements for 1974 were released in June of 1975. The previously accumulated deficit of $3.7 million as at December 31, 1973 was increased to a deficit of $66.1 million after restatement of the accounts to give effect to accounting principles generally accepted as appropriate for Canadian railways. The principal changes to previously issued operating results related to the provision of depreciation on the roadbed and the methods of accounting for track maintenance labour and interest capitalised on new rail lines.
The restated financial results showed almost steadily increasing net losses from 1957 to 1973, including steadily increasing depreciation charges and interest expense, none of which was apparent from the originally issued financial statements. In these years the Railway did, however, produce substantial cash flows from its operations. It was not until 1974 that the first operating cash loss was sustained, representing a change from the previous year of some $12 million. This was followed by successive cash losses in 1975 and 1976. These cash losses were incurred principally as the result of extension lines becoming operational for the first time in 1972 and 1974 with low traffic volumes, higher than normal maintenance costs and the interest on funds used to construct these lines no longer being capitalised. Other factors contributing to higher operating costs in the last three years were interruptions due to labour unrest, higher wage settlements and higher fuel costs not being offset with increased freight revenues.

	Fiscal year ended		
	1974	1975	1976
	$C	$C	$C
Operating revenues	48 983	57 765	66 998
Operating expenses			
Transportation	29 323	33 548	37 008
Road maintenance	12 091	19 772	20 172
Equipment maintenance	8 760	10 007	11 529
Depreciation	9 467	10 237	11 860
Other	3 160	6 507	7 485
	62 801	80 071	88 054
Operating loss	13 818	22 306	21 056
Other expenses			
Interest and dept expense	19 531	25 126	33 726
Less other income	1 107	1 561	1 379
	18 424	23 565	32 347
Net loss	32 242	45 871	53 403

TRAFFIC

In 1976, forest products represented almost 80 per cent of all car loadings on the British Columbia Railway. Of that, Eastern rail lumber, (including plywood and veneer), comprised 35.4 per cent of total carloadings. In 1975, 20 per cent of Eastern rail lumber was shipped to Canadian destinations; 80 per cent was shipped to destinations in the United States; 75 per cent of lumber shipped to all Eastern rail destinations was handled through North Vancouver; the remainder was interchanged through Prince George.

CARLOADINGS 1976

Commodity Group	Number of Carloads	Percentage of Total Carloads	Number of Tons	Percentage of Total Tons
Grain	2 891	2.4	176 698	2.6
Other Agricultural Products	44	—	565	—
Lumber	49 341	41.3	2 359 457	35.1
Other Forest Products	44 515	37.3	3 089 066	45.9
Products of Mines	2 973	2.5	276 476	4.1
Merchandise L.C.L.	3 985	3.3	16 394	0.2
Manufactures and Other	7 047	5.9	476 484	7.1
Piggyback	5 699	4.8	145 406	2.2
Received from Connections	2 985	2.5	186 042	2.8
Total	119 480	100.0	6 726 588	100.0

MOTIVE POWER AND ROLLING STOCK

To augment its growing power and car fleets the Railway during 1975/76 acquired eight 2 000 hp locomotives, specially designed for remote control use, 650 box cars, 70 bulkhead flat cars and 40 piggyback double flat cars. In addition, 247 wood chip cars had been delivered to the Railway by year-end from the rail car manufacturing plant at Squamish.
Four used RDC self-propelled Budd Cars, delivered early in 1976, were acquired from Amtrak at Reading, Pennsylvania. These cars, obtained for the Railway by the provincial Bureau of Transit, will be used both to expand the present fleet of five cars and to provide parts for the overall operating passenger fleet.
In 1976, the British Columbia Railway owned 119 diesel units. At year end 1976, the railway utilised the following equipment in revenue freight service:

FREIGHT CARS

	Cars
Box	3 190
Flat	3 493
Gondola	1 491
Hopper—Open top	135
Covered	59
Refrigerator	427
Stock	14
Tank	42
	8 851

MLW type M420 diesel locomotive built for British Columbia Railway; rated at 2 000 hp and used in road service.

CANADIAN NATIONAL RAILWAYS

PO Box 8100, Montreal, Quebec H3C 3N4

Telephone: 877 5430
Telegrams: CANANATIONAL MONTREAL

Chairman of the Board: P. Taschereau, Q.C.
President & Chief Executive Officer: Dr. R. A. Bandeen
Corporate Vice-President: W. D. Piggott
Corporate Vice-President: J. H. Spicer
Executive Vice-President: J. W. G. Macdougall, Q.C.
Senior Vice-President: J. H. Richer
Senior Vice-President: A. H. Hart, Q.C.
Vice-President and Senior Executive Officer, CN Rail: R. R. Latimer
Vice-President, CN Marine: J. Gratwick
Vice-President, Passenger Services and Hotels and Secretary of the Company: G. Lach
Vice-President, CN Trucking & Express: Y. H. Masse
Vice-President, Purchases & Stores: W. H. Bailey
Vice-President, Passenger Marketing: G. C. Campbell
Vice-President, Operations: J. L. Cann
Vice-President, Public Relations: J. G. Cormier
Vice-President: W. R. Corner
Vice-President, Law: J. M. Duncan
Vice-President, Strategic Rail Group: J. C. Gardiner
Vice-President, Industrial Relations & Organisation: K. E. Hunt
Vice-President, Freight Marketing: R. E. Lawless
Vice-President: J. L. Toole
Treasurer: J. Cunningham
Chief of Motive Power and Car Equipment: W. H. Cyr
Chief Engineer: G. A. van de Water

Gauge	4′ 8½″ *(1.435 m)* *miles*	3′ 6″ *(1.067 m)* *miles*	*Total* *miles*
Route length: 1st Main Tk	22 784.07	711.88	23 495.95
Track length:			
Main Tracks	23 718.68	711.88	24 430.56
Sidings	8 768.08	121.41	8 889.49
Total	32 486.76	833.29	33 320.05

ELECTRIFICATION
Total electrified route length on 31 December 1975: 27 miles ±
Total electrified track length on 31 December 1975: 46 miles ±

TRAFFIC	*1973*	*1974*	*1975*
Total freight (million ton miles)	67 662	74 142	72 729
Total freight tonnage	115 955 530	119 074 989	108 154 572
Total passenger miles (millions)	1 194.1	1 340.1	1 329.1
Total passengers carried (000)	10 138	11 984	10 286

FINANCIAL	*1973*	*1974* $C'000	*1975*
Revenues	1 400 840	1 725 985	1 812 615
Expenses	1 385 200	1 709 148	1 903 904

CAPITAL EXPENDITURES
CP capital spending in 1975 totalled $C363.8 million compared with $C211.9 million the previous year. The total included expenditure of $C135.7 million for rolling stock ordered in previous years and delivered during 1975. A total of 3 838 freight cars was delivered to Canadian Rail in 1975. Of these 2 709 were purchased and 1 129 were leased. This was exclusive of 672 covered hoppers for the carriage of grain which were provided by the federal government. A total of 140 new locomotives was added to the fleet of which 103 were purchased and 37 leased. Capital expenditures also included $C185.2 million for improvements to track and other railway facilities, mainly to take care of the increasing traffic in Western Canada. Expenditure on road property included $C62.5 million for the laying of 658 miles of new rail; $C23.8 million for tie and ballasting programmes; $C8.4 million for double-tracking the main line between Winnipeg and Portage la Prairie; $C1.3 million for the Edson Subdivision between Bissell and Spruce Grove, Alta; $C2.7 million for yard expansion at Port Mann, BC; $C1.2 million for improvement to the Winnipeg diesel shops and $C3.1 million for new car shops at Melville, Sask.

Passenger Equipment December 31st, 1975
Number of locomotives in service: 2 425; Line haul 2 061; Shunting (Switching) 364
Number of locomotives (Electric): 14-68 coaches
Number of locomotives (Diesel-electric): 2 411
Number of passenger train coaches: 431
Number of freight train cars: 112 653

TRACK WORK 1975
New lines projected (length, location): Total of 480 miles between now and 1985. Line north from Terrace, British Columbia, will be about 270 miles; lines to carry iron ore are projected in northern Quebec (100 miles) and northern Ontario (80 miles); a 10 mile line is projected in northern Ontario to serve proposed pulp and paper mill; in northern Manitoba a 20 mile line is projected to serve a Nelson River power development.
Rail, types and weights: Current sections being bought are 132 RE (2 564 miles in track); 115 RE (4 055 miles in track); and 100 ARA-A (7 556 miles in track). Balance is 31 different older sections 130 to 50 lbs/yard.

Sleepers cross ties type:	**Wood** Main lines	Branch lines	**Concrete (CN 60A)** Main lines
Thickness:	7″ or 6″	6″	8″ at rail seat
Spacing:	3 110 per mile	2 840 per mile	2 640 per mile
Rail fastenings types used:	6″ or 5½″ × ⅝″	track spikes	Pandrol fastenings

Welded rail:
Total length of track laid 31 December 1975: 4 324.42 CWR*; 1 752.47 SWR†; total 6 076.89.
Length laid in 1975 during year: 660.45 mi CWR, 3.68 mi SWR, total 664.13.
Notes: *CWR Continuous Welded Rail (over 400 ft long).
†SWR Short Welded Rail (sections less than 400 ft long).
Standard method of welding: Rails are electric pressure flash butt welded into lengths of about 1 170 ft in central plants, and after laying are field welded into longer lengths by alumino thermic process.

SIGNAL AND TRAIN CONTROL INSTALLATIONS
New signal installations:
Type: Centralised Traffic Control (CTC)
Route length: 53 miles (addition to existing system)
Location: Province of Ontario
Supplier: GRS Company

MARSHALLING YARDS
NEW OR REBUILT YARDS
St. Lawrence Region—Riviere des Prairies, Quebec: Construction of this new classification and storage yard was completed in 1975. The classification and storage yards hold 600 and 412 cars, respectively. It will reduce the workload at Montreal Yard as traffic to and from the Lake St. John area will be handled through the yard.
Ste-Cecile (Valleyfield), Quebec: Construction of two yard tracks, a switching lead and necessary lighting was completed. This additional trackage serving as a support yard for Valleyfield, is necessary in order to continue to serve the growing industrial activity of this area in an efficient and economic manner.
Senneterre, Quebec: During 1975 work began on a four year project to revise and expand Senneterre Yard with the construction of new storage and light repair trackage. Future work will involve the construction of an additional eight classification tracks. Completion of this project will see Senneterre Yard expand from 14 classification tracks and 3 receiving and departure tracks to 29 classification tracks and 6 receiving and departure tracks.
Great Lakes Region—Oshawa, Ontario: Construction of three additional yard tracks and an independent switching lead was completed in 1975. This work was necessary to provide better handling of the unanticipated increases in traffic volumes at Oshawa Yard.
Hamilton, Ontario: The expansion and upgrading of Stuart St. Yard in Hamilton was completed in 1975 as the last year of a five year project. Work involved additional classification tracks, improving switching leads, providing adequately sized receiving and departure tracks, developing a container yard and extending the existing freight shed.
Oakville, Ontario: Work began on a two year project intended to provide 10 additional tracks to support Ford Motor Co's loading operation at Oakville. The project will also involve the relocation and upgrading of car repair facilities in the yard. It is anticipated that this work will be completed in 1976.
Malport, Ontario: Unbated industrial expansion in the Malport Industrial Zone made it necessary to expand Malport Industrial Support Yard by constructing two additional yard tracks in 1975.
Kitchener, Ontario: Three yard tracks were extended at Kitchener to facilitate the handling of traffic and to eliminate delays in train performance.
Toronto, Ontario: Work continued on the extension of the diesel shop at MacMillan Yard, formerly Toronto Yard. Construction will continue in 1976.
Fort Erie, Ontario: Work continued on the construction of new car department facilities including cleaning tracks, upgrade ramp, covered repair shop and associated trackage at Fort Erie Yard. The new facilities will greatly improve the repair operation and decrease the out of service times for bad ordered cars. The project will be completed in 1976.
Hornepayne, Ontario: Pre-engineering work began for the reconstruction of Hornepayne Yard which is planned over a four year period. Hornepayne's strategic and remote location on the Montreal/Toronto—Winnipeg section of the transcontinental route and its unique role, are the basic factors in the selection of this project. Hornepayne experiences the greatest concentration of train delays due to meets and overtakes on the route between Toronto/Montreal and Winnipeg.
Four receiving and departure tracks will be constructed, double track sections approaches east and west of Hornepayne, reconstruct a 400 car capacity classification yard to accommodate industrial support functions, provide journal oiling, pollution control facilities, and construct necessary building to accommodate improved dispatching and control equipment.
Prairie Region—Winnipeg, Manitoba: A new intermodal terminal is being constructed in Winnipeg as the first step in the development of a complex which will ultimately accommodate carload freight and related operations relocated from other areas. Work is expected to continue during 1976.
Canora, Saskatchewan: Construction of 5 holding tracks to handle traffic destined north of Canora and other traffic set-off on east-west trains was commenced at Canora. Three tracks were completed in 1975 and the remaining two are scheduled for 1976.
Mountain Region—Edmonton, Alberta: The extension of hump tracks 1 to 4 in Calder Yard was completed in 1975. This will permit increased yard flexibility, better engine utilisation and an increased ability to absorb new traffic.
Vancouver, British Columbia: Major expansion and revision of the Port Mann Yard continued during 1975. Work was begun on the connection for the western half of the mainline by-pass, the construction of ancillary trackage, continuation of the removal of surcharge from the maintenance of way yard and further work involving the utilities, roadways and environmental work.
Construction of a Servocentre and yard tower was completed. Other work associated with the Port Mann Yard expansion involved the start of preloading of the proposed surge yard.
Work also began on the new Motive Power and Car Equipment building. It is expected that the building will be in operation in 1976.

NEW EQUIPMENT DELIVERED 1975
Locomotive Equipment

102	Diesel Electric Road Freight	3 000 (GM)	9531-9632
38	Diesel Electric Road Freight	3 000 (GM)	5241-5278

Freight Equipment
(Canadian Lines (owned)

No. of Cars	*Type of Equipment*	*Ton Cap.*	*Series*
1	Well Flat	100	CN 670002
53	Gondola	100	CN 137550-137849
206	Bulkhead Flat	70	CN 603025-603324
33	Caboose	50	CN 79685-79759
135	Trailer Flat	70	CN 682164-682298
125	Flat	100	CN 667411-667510
			CN 667925-667949
1 108	Covered Hopper	100	CN 369000-369999
			CN 371600-371999
21	Container Flat	100	CN 639445-639465
100	Covered Hopper	100	CN 375126-375225
50	Covered Hopper	100	CN 374050-374099
4	Well Flat	100	CN 670100-670103
500	Woodchip	70	CN 879250-879749
500	Gondola	100	CN 136600-136999
			CN 137850-137949
147	Ore Hopper	100	CN 346554-346700
50	Caboose	50	CN 79760-79837
330	Trailer Flat	70	CN 682299-682568
			CN 682940-682999
350	Flat	100	CN 668000-668299
			CN 639850-639999
61	Bi-Level Flat	70	CN 710400-710499
3 774			
Canadian Lines (leased)			
274	Gondola	100	CN 199294-199567
Canadian Lines (Gov of Canada)			
672	Covered Hopper	70	CNWX 106000-107599
Canadian Lines Freight: Total 4 720			
Grand Trunk Western (leased)			
6	Covered Hopper	50	GTW 316015-316020
100	Covered Hopper	100	GTW 54200-54299
106			
Grand Trunk Western (Owned)			
1	Caboose	50	GTW 75050

VIA RAIL
Via Rail Canada Ltd

PO Box 8116, Montreal, Quebec H3C 3N3

Directors: R. A. Bandeen
J. F. Roberts
G. A. Scott
J. Maurice LeClair

Via Rail took over all Canadian passenger operations on April 1, 1978. The new company was incorporated on January 12, 1977 as a subsidiary of Canadian National, although it is neither comprised in CN's railway operation nor consolidated in its accounts. To meet Government objectives under the new railway passenger policy announced by Transport Minister Otto Lang on January 29, 1976, Via Rail Canada was set up to manage all railway passenger services in Canada including services operated "over railway lines and services substituting for an ancillary to passenger services operating over railway lines but excluding commuter rail services and the carriage of goods." The company will contract with the Canadian Government for the provision of rail passenger services to be specified by the Minister. It will contract with any railway company for the operation of such services and is able to contract with non-railway enterprises for freight and services incidental to passenger haulage and non-railway transport firms for the provision of services such as bus operation in substitution of rail passenger lines. It will manage all passenger services within plans and budgets approved by the Government.

The company is to acquire or lease rolling stock and facilities required to provide passenger services and is to prepare programmes for the modification or acquisition of new equipment and facilities.

It will be Via's reponsibility to develop recommendations for new or revised routes, schedules and services to meet the Government's objectives, to recommend a pricing programme for transport and on-board services and to arrange for the transfer of CN and CP Rail officers to the company's administration.

MOTIVE POWER
Transport Minister Otto Lang announced on November 2, 1977, that the Canadian government had ordered 10 LRC trainsets from Bombardier-MLW for use by Via Rail on several routes in eastern and western Canada. The $60 m order covers 50 lightweight tilting-body coaches and 22 diesel power cars with a gross rating of 3 700 hp (2 700 hp for traction). The first sets will be introduced in 1980 between Montreal and Quebec after a $30 million programme of track improvements has been completed. Elimination of level crossings on parts of the line should allow the LRC's to reach their design speed of 200 km/h.

C P RAIL
Canadian Pacific Limited
Windsor Station, Montreal, Quebec H3C 3E4

Telephone: 861 6811
Telegrams: CANPACRY

Chairman and Chief Executive Officer: I. D. Sinclair
President: F. S. Burbridge
Vice-President: K. Campbell
Secretary: J. C. Ames
Vice-President, Adminstration: R. T. Riley
Vice-President, Telecommunications: J. G. Sutherland
Vice-President, Corporate Development: J. A. McDonald

Law Department
Vice-President and General Counsel: D. S. Maxwell, Q.C.

Finance and Accounting
Vice-President, Finance and Accounting: P. A. Nepveu
Assistant Vice-President, Finance and Accounting: J. P. T. Clough
Assistant Vice-President, Finance and Accounting: R. S. Demone
Treasurer: D. E. Sloan
Comptroller: J. D. Kenny

Investigation
Chief of Investagation: J. C. Machan

Medical Services
Chief of Medical Services: Dr. W. L. May

Public Relations and Advertising
General Manager: I. B. Scott
Assistant General Manager (Public Relations): R. A. Rice
Senior Manager, Advertising: J. M. Dowie

Research
Manager, Research: R. Klein

CP Air
President: Ian Gray

CP Hotels
Chairman, President and Chief Executive Officer: D. W. Curtis

CP Rail
Senior-Executive Officer: K. Campbell
Vice-President, Operations and Maintenance: W. W. Stinson
Vice-President, Industrial Relations: J. C. Anderson
Vice-President, Purchases and Stores: J. M. Bentham
Vice-President, Marketing and Sales: R. C. Gilmore
Senior Regional Vice-President, Pacific Region: L. R. Smith
Vice-President, Prairie Region: J. W. Malcolm
Vice-President, Atlantic Region: G. E. Benoit
Vice-President, Eastern Region: R. S. Allison
Director of Accounting: J. F. Hankinson
General Manager, Coastal Marine Operations: B. D. Margetts
General Manager, Freight Sales: C. C. Watson
General Manager, Intermodal Services: A. E. Jenner
General Manager, Pricing: A. Ferguson
General Manager, Pricing Economics: W. G. Scott
General Manager, Marketing: D. C. Coleman
General Manager, Overseas Trade: G. H. Creighton
General Manager, Passenger Services: A. R. Campbell
Chief of Transportation: G. H. Geddis
Chief Engineer: J. Fox
Chief Mechanical Officer: C. R. Pike

CP Ships
Chairman and Managing Director: R. Y. Pritchard
General Manager Operations: L. M. Charlton
General Manager Container Services: D. R. Newbery
General Manager Special Projects: M. W. Pudden
Asst. General Manager N. America: W. J. Ryan
Regional Manager UK: J. F. Davies
Regional Manager Container Services Continent: L. N. J. Smet

CP (Bermuda) Ltd
Chairman: W. R. Kempe
President and Chief Executive Officer: A. F. Joplin
Vice-President: The Hon. Sir Dudley Spurling
Vice-President, Special Duties: R. F. Lynch
Vice-President, Finance: G. B. Wilson
General Manager: R. K. Gamey
Manager, Marine Services: G. W. J. Bateman
Treasurer/Comptroller: B. S. Russel
Secretary: Mrs M. D. Smith

The title "Canadian Pacific Limited" is used to identify an integrated multimodal transportation enterprise which includes operation of trains, trucks, ships, aeroplanes and telecommunications, as well as hotels and resource development undertakings through Canadian Pacific Investments Ltd.

The railway system operates a total of 16 365.3 route miles, with a main line linking the Atlantic and Pacific coasts of Canada.

In addition to this, controlled companies in the US are the 32-mile Aroostook Valley RR, and the Soo Line of 4 590 route miles. Canadian Pacific Ltd has also recently acquired the Toronto, Hamilton and Buffalo Railway.

DIVERSIFICATION
Canadian Pacific is a widely diversified company with more than \$C6 000 million worth of assests in land, sea and air transportation, telecommunications, natural resources, hotels, real estate and manufacturing.

The company was incorporated on February 16, 1881, to build a transcontinental railway linking eastern Canada with the Pacific coast. The construction of the main line between Montreal and Port Moody, BC was completed on November 7, 1885.

Ever since, Canadian Pacific has been providing Canadians with vital transportation services. This is an important job in a country as large as Canada with its relatively small population and a vast store of natural resources which must be transported long distances to reach their markets.

The company's transportation system includes approximately 100 000 miles of rail, truck, ship and air lines plus related telecommunications facilities.

Today, however, Canadian Pacific is much more than a transportation system. Through Canadian Pacific Investments Limited, formed in 1962 to manage the company's expanding interests in non-transportation activities, Canadian Pacific has substantial investments in oil and gas, coal, lead, zinc and other mining properties, real estate, hotels, timberlands, pipelines, steel manufacturing, equipment leasing and waste disposal.

Canadian Pacific's transportation, telecommunications and hotel operations are linked by a common set of international names—CP Rail, CP Air, CP Ships, CP Transport, CP Telecommunications, CP Hotels—and a common symbol.

The symbol is a combination of part of a square to represent stability, a segment of a circle to suggest global activities and a triangle to denote motion or direction. The various operations are distinguished by different colours.

TRANSPORTATION SERVICES
Rail: CP Rail operates 16 365.3 miles of track extending from the Maritimes to the Pacific coast and controls another 4 700 miles in the United States. Its equipment includes more than 72 000 freight cars, 1 300 diesel locomotives and more than 300 pieces of passenger equipment.

The railway has developed sophisticated unit train systems for moving bulk commodities such as coal and sulphur; has one of North America's most advanced automated freight classification yards at Calgary to handle rapidly-increasing freight shipments to and from the Pacific coast; provides piggyback service (the movement of highway trailers on railway flatcars) and domestic container service across the country as well as transcontinental, inter-city and commuter passenger train services.

CP Rail has played a leading role in the development of container traffic in Canada. The railway is a joint owner of Brunterm Limited, a $4 million container terminal at Saint John, NB, and has an investment in CP Ships' container terminal at Quebec City. CP Rail and CP Ships have spent more than \$C4 million developing the Quebec City terminal to permit 1 600 containers to move through it weekly in each direction.

Shipping: CP Ships was begun at the end of the 19th century to provide passenger and freight business for the new railway. Today, CP Ships controls a land-ocean container shipping system which provides regular service between Quebec City, London, Rotterdam and Le Havre.

Three 16 000 dwt, 20 knot container ships, CP Trader, CP Voyageur and CP Discoverer, entered service in 1970 and 1971. Built at a total cost of \$C20 million, each ice-strengthened vessel carries 777 containers.

Canadian Pacific (Bermuda) owns and operates a diversified fleet of 29 vessels with a total capacity of more than two million dwt. The company has another three geared bulk carriers on order for delivery in 1978. Of the total of 32 vessels already built or on order, five are crude tankers (with three of those being VLCC's), eight are sophisticated product tankers, seven are gearless bulk carriers ranging in size from 57 000 dwt to 123 000 dwt, and 12 are geared bulk carriers ranging in size from 16 000 dwt to 35 000 dwt. Average age of ships in the CP (Bermuda) fleet is less than five years.

CanPac International Freight Services Limited groups under one financial and general management. Canadian Pacific is active in the warehousing, customs brokerage, international freight forwarding, ship agency, ship brokerage and terminal operating fields.

CP RAIL LINES AND TERRITORIES
The Canadian Pacific Railways' network of lines stretches from coast to coast with important extensions in USA in the states of Illinois, Wisconsin, Minnesota and North Dakota (Soo Line). Ownership of an extension into the state of New York via the Toronto, Hamilton & Buffalo Railway was formally acquired by CP Rail in 1977, with conclusion of a purchase agreement on April 19.

In many areas they are parallel and competitive with, the lines of the Canadian National Railways.

CP RAIL DEVELOPMENTS
Net income from CP Rail in 1976 was \$C51.1 million, an increase of $19.4 million from $31.7 million in 1975. The increase was primarily due to a reduction in labour disputes, an increase in freight charges, more remunerative traffic carried, improved operating efficiency and productivity gains in equipment and track maintenance. Canadian economic growth and a moderation in the rate of inflation also contributed to improved earnings. Rates of increase in costs were lower than in 1975. Wage rates were up 11 per

cent in 1976, pensions increased by 23 per cent, diesel fuel went up by 11 per cent and prices of other railway materials increased by 7 per cent.
The Snavely Commission on the costs of transporting grain by rail released its report in 1976, concluding that the railways suffer substantial losses carrying export grain, even on a variable cost basis. Now that an independent authority has established a basis for determining the size of the losses, it remains for the Government to decide the manner in which the railways are to recover them.
The Government announced during 1976 that it intends to pay the full cost of inter-city passenger losses once the basic inter-city passenger network is in place. At present, losses on such services are borne 80 per cent by the Government and 20 per cent by the companies.
Early in 1977 an Act to amend the National Transportation Act and the Railway Act was introduced in Parliament. Among other things, this Act sets some new objectives for transportation policy in Canada and establishes a wholly new concept of maximum rates. Both changes lead in the direction of rejecting the market mechanism and substituting it for rate-making by government.
CP Rail leased the first production model in 1976 of a computerised system for training engine men. The Train Dynamics Analyser helps enginemen analyse train handling problems of the heavy, fast supertrains carrying freight. Further development work in mobile operations of the TDA was carried out in 1977.
Since January, 1977, CP Rail has placed orders for 453 pieces of rolling stock worth more than $14.5-million with National Steel Car and has ordered 24 diesel locomotives valued at $15-million from General Motors Diesel Division, London, Ont.
Solar power, which was harnessed on an experimental basis in 1976 to operate track circuits and a highway crossing warning system, saw further development in 1977 in the form of a solar activated generator for use in railway communications. The generator, located in the mountains of British Columbia, converts the sun's rays to operate an automatic radio repeater. It is the first of its type in the CP Rail communications system.
Other developments in 1977 include the construction of a $3 million rail car repair shop at Thunder Bay, Ont.; track improvement projects on the main line between Calgary and Vancouver worth $45 million, and on the main line between Megantic, Que. and Saint John, N.B. worth $10 million; and $32 million on railway reconstruction and replacement projects in Saskatchewan.

RAIL REVENUE

	1975 (in thousands)	1976
Freight revenue	$C887 666	$C1 006 624
Passenger service	21 497	21 708
Other railway	26 188	29 862
Coastal steamships	16 486	16 690
Government payments	70 116	88 062
	$C1 021 953	$C1 162 946

TRAFFIC

	1974	1975
Total freight ton-km	86 092 666 460	84 095 792 875
Total freight tonnage	91 068 068	86 987 476
Total passenger-km	563 127 849	462 547 042
Total passengers carried	4 996 393	4 704 392

LOCOMOTIVES AND CARS

CP Rail's fleet of diesel-electric locomotives comprise 1 056 road units and 249 switchers. The road units range from 1 500 hp to 4 000 hp, built by MLW-Worthington and General Motors. The railroad operates approximately 315 pieces of passenger equipment. The freight car fleet comprises approximately 76 000 cars.
In the spring of 1977, CP Rail ordered 24 new 3 000 hp locomotives from the diesel division of General Motors of Canada Ltd.
The SD40-2 six-axle diesel electric units are valued at more than half a million dollars each, and have become the backbone of CP Rail's motive power fleet. The 70-ft, 197-ton locomotives have been instrumental in increasing the railway's freight handling capacity.
An operations nerve centre at the railway's Montreal headquarters plays an important role in increased locomotive utilisation. The system operations centre keeps tabs on all train movements and provides information for planning future operations.
CP Rail's network—covering 16 406 route miles and with 23 231 miles actual track length—is schematically represented on a 36 ft magnetic board at the operations centre. Routings of trains are planned and monitored along the board 24 hours a day, seven days a week.
Knowing what trains will arrive where and when, enables transportation specialists to plan subsequent uses for locomotives. There is less idle time for locomotives and strings of freight cars do not wait so long for the power to move them.
Train positions on all main and branch lines are constantly updated through open-line communications with dispatch points across Canada. In turn, dispatchers are in radio contact with locomotives as they move through key sectors of the system.
In March of 1976, a CP Rail engineman drove the experimental LRC (light, rapid, comfortable) train of a Canadian railway speed record of 129 mph. The previous speed record of 112 miles an hour, had been set by a CP Rail steam locomotive in 1936.
The speed run was part of a month-long programme of tests by CP Rail under the federal government's LRC development project. Actual construction of the prototype was a joint venture of Alcan Canada Products of Toronto, Dominion Foundries and Steel of Hamilton, and Bombardier-MLW of Montreal.
The testing also provided important information for a study of improved passenger rail service over the Montreal-Quebec City portion of eastern Canada's industrial corridor. CP Rail has been chosen to implement a new service between those two points, with federal government financing of 30 million dollars.
CP Rail's fleet of 72 213 (Aug 1977) freight cars includes more than 30 different types of specialised equipment. There are two and three-level auto transporters with longitudinally cushioned ("floating") superstructures; slurry cars for mineral concentrates in semi-liquid form; container and piggyback flatcars; insulated boxcars for the protection of cargo from Canada's harsh climate; bulkhead-end flatcars for durable goods such as building products; covered hopper cars for weather-sensitive dry bulk commodities; and gondola cars for unit trains which load and unload on the move.

INTERMODAL SERVICES

One of the familiar names in Canadian transportation circles, CP Rail Piggyback Services has become known as CP Rail Intermodal Services, combining the railway's piggyback and container handling operations.
In addition to the line haul movement of highway trailers, the railway's Intermodal Services group has responsibility for the handling of containers between Canada's east and west coast ports and a network of inland terminals across the country, as well as responsibility for the development and operation of the inland terminals themselves.
Upon arrival at any of CP Rail's 52 TOFC (piggyback) or 17 container handling facilities, containers are transferred to local delivery trucks which make final deliveries to customers and pick up new traffic.
Intermodal Services handled 122 000 trailers and 166 000 TEU containers in 1976. The 2 500 000th trailer was handled in March 1977.
In 1975, a total of 109 252 containers were handled, compared with 129 614 in 1974.
Trailers moved in 1975 totalled 119 242 in the railway's fleet of flatcars, compared to 144 437 trailers carried in 1974.
The movement of import and export containers grew from 74 283 TEUs in 1972, when Intermodal Services took over, to 165 000 TEUs in 1976—an increase of 122 per cent.
Domestic containerisation, a natural outgrowth of trailer-on-flatcar movements within Canada, is a comparatively new aspect of Intermodal Services. An example of how domestic containerisation works, and the ability of Intermodal Services to develop systems for specific needs, is the method employed to ship copper concentrate from the Umex Corporation mine at Pickle Lake, northern Ontario, 1 200 miles to smelters in Noranda, Que.
The copper concentrate is loaded into containers and carried on trailers down the highway from Pickle Lake 200 miles to Ignace. There the containers are transferred to flatcars. They make the 1 000-mile journey by rail to Noranda, where the containers stay on the flatcars and are emptied mechanically.
To move 90 000 tons a year of concentrate, Intermodal Services ordered 237 containers built to a special design, and had CP Rail's Angus Shops modify 41 flatcars to handle them. The top-lifter used at Ignace for the transfer of containers also had to be specially designed and constructed.
CP Rail has also developed 81 ft container flatcars with cushioned couplers that can carry four 20 ft or two 40 ft containers, all loaded to maximum weight.

TOFC (Piggyback)

Intermodal Services has established a coast-to-coast network of 52 TOFC terminals from which it is possible to serve any location in Canada with highway access and, via connections with US railways, to virtually any point in North America.
Terminal to terminal TOFC service is provided for motor common carriers and private industry semi-trailers. Door-to-door trailer service is provided in railway-owned semi-trailers. The most-used TOFC service, one which involves shipping goods in railway-owned trailers, has grown 700 per cent since 1967.
The TOFC side of Intermodal Services has five basic plans:

Plan 1: CP Rail supplies the flatcar and handles a trailer of a "for-hire" common motor carrier containing truck-billed traffic. The rail movement is on a ramp-to-ramp basis, confined to points between which the motor carrier has authority to operate by highway.

Plan 2: The railway handles traffic directly from the shipper to the consignee on rail billing and uses railway-owned trailers and flatcars.

Plan 3: The railway supplies the flatcars for movement of trailers owned by private shippers, not common motor carriers.

Plan 4: The shipper supplies the trailer and flatcar. The railway provides only the motive power.

Plan 5: A system of joint rail/truck rates. The rates serve to extend the territory of each carrier into that of the other and permit them to handle shipments originating in, or destined to, the territory of the other.
Another type of piggyback movement, to which no plan number has been assigned, is the handling of new or used empty semi-trailers on piggyback flatcars. These are mostly new trailers being shipped by the trailer manufacturers to the purchaser.

Trucking: Canadian Pacific is Canada's largest trucking operator and one of the biggest in North America. CP Express, CP Transport and the Smith Transport group of companies haul freight from coast to coast with approximately 6 000 units of modern road equipment.
CP Express specialises in the distribution of small package shipments and also functions as a freight forwarder, combining small shipments into full carloads for transportation and distribution. Sorting and distribution of containers is an important part of CP Express business.
Smith Transport, also active in the container field, hauls highway freight in eastern Canada and connects with other carriers to move goods anywhere in North America.
In western Canada, CP Transport specialises in heavy and bulk haul contract movements and has developed a number of distribution systems tailored to the needs of specific customers. The company has specially-designed trailers for hauling commodities such as sulphuric acid, liquid sulphur,edible oils, fertilizers, potatoes and fruit.

Air: CP Air's 80 000 km international route network radiates from the airline's headquarters city of Vancouver to link five continents. The airline also operates 12 350 kilometres of routes within Canada, serving principal Canadian cities.
International routes connect Hong Kong, Tokyo and Sydney with Honolulu, Vancouver and points across Canada, with connections to Amsterdam and the major cities of Southern Europe including Lisbon, Milan, Rome and Athens.
CP Air connects Montreal, Toronto and Vancouver with cities in south America such as Lima, Santiago and Buenos Aires. Los Angeles and San Francisco are connected to the CP Air system through Vancouver.
The CP Air fleet of 25 aircraft includes four Boeing 747s, 12 Douglas DC-8s (five of which are so-called stretch DC-8s), two Boeing 727s, and seven 737s. Utilisation of the fleet has been increased through revised maintenance programmes and improved loading and turn-around procedures.

Telecommunications: CP Telecommunications, which is a department within Canadian Pacific Limited, and CN Telecommunications which is a division of the Canadian National Railways Company, operate together as CNCP Telecommunications. CNCP is a pioneer in business communications, and among the services it has introduced to Canadians are:
—Telex, a written message system that now has more than 30 000 subscribers in Canada who have access to 847 000 telex subscribers in 197 other countries around the world;
—Telenet, a network that uses a computer to route messages to their destinations;
—Broadband that carries the spoken word, transmits messages and pictures, and sends high-speed data to and from computers;
—Infodat, a network for transmission of digital data. Digital data cuts transmission costs by up to 90 per cent, and increases the speed and accuracy of transmission.
CNCP implemented in 1977 a publicly accessible computer-switched digital network, called Infoswitch, that made communications economically available to a wider range of users in the business community.
CNCP leases local telephone company circuits for in-city transmission of data coming in from the CNCP trans-Canada microwave network.
In addition, CNCP operates large numbers of private networks for individual companies and for government departments, airlines, and banks. CNCP also provides teletype services to news wires, and broadcast services to radio and television stations. Telegram service is also available anywhere in Canada through CNCP Telecommunications.

Pipelines: ShelPac Research and Development Limited, owned jointly by Canadian Pacific and Shell Canada, engages in research and development work for solids pipelines projects.

CANADIAN PACIFIC INVESTMENTS LIMITED

The non-transportation companies wholly-owned or controlled by Canadian Pacific Investments Limited include CP Hotels, Marathon Realty Company Limited, Commandant Properties Limited, PanCanadian Petroleum Limited, CanPac Minerals Limited, Pacific Logging Company Limited, The Great Lakes Paper Company Limited, Cominco

Ltd, Fording Coal Limited, The Algoma Steel Corporation, Limited, Canadian Pacific Securities Limited and CanPac AgriProducts Limited. CPI also has an extensive portfolio of investments in companies in the energy, metals, chemicals and forest products industries.

Hotels: CP Hotels operates 18 hotels in Canada, two in Mexico, two in West Germany, one in Israel and one in Curacao. It also operates four airline catering facilities in Canada and one in Mexico City. The company owns the Niagara International Centre complex in Niagara Falls, Ont., and manages restaurant facilities at the Calgary Tower and Vancouver's Granville Square office complex.

Real Estate: Marathon Realty is one of Canada's largest developers and managers of industrial, commercial and residential real estate. Its properties include residential and office buildings, shopping centres, industrial parks, large office and commercial complexes, agricultural lands and miscellaneous interests in livestock markets, grain elevators and cold storage facilities.

Oil and Gas: PanCanadian Petroleum is Canada's largest hydrocarbon producer with working interest holdings in petroleum and natural gas rights in approximately 30.3 million gross acres in Canada, the Arctic islands, the United States, the North Sea, Iran, Greenland and Indonesia. The company is engaged in exploration for and production of petroleum, natural gas and related hydrocarbons.
PanCanadian Gas Products Ltd, a subsidiary, carries on petroleum exploration and production in western Canada and has a 50 per cent interest in a natural gas liquids extraction plant and related facilities for transporting and marketing liquified petroleum gases.

Mining: Cominco, in which CPI has a 54 per cent interest, is a major producer of lead, zinc and other metals, fertilizers and industrial chemicals.
Cominco's major exploration efforts are concentrated in Canada, the United States, Mexico, Australia, Spain, The Central African Republic and South Africa. The company produces lead, zinc, gold, mercury, copper, tin, coal, potash and phosphate rock ores in such places as British Columbia, the Northwest Territories, Saskatchewan, the United States, Greenland, Spain and Australia.

Forest Products: Great Lakes Paper, controlled by CPI, manufactures newsprint paper, bleached kraft pulp, unbleached sulphite pulp, stud lumber, particleboard and waferboard.
Pacific Logging, a wholly-owned CPI subsidiary, is engaged in logging and lumber operations on Vancouver Island.

Finance: Canadian Pacific Securities assists in the financing of capital projects and in meeting the working capital requirements of affiliated companies.

Waste Disposal: CanPac AgriProducts Limited is engaged in the recycling and disposal of waste products. The company has acquired all the outstanding shares of Rothsay Concentrates Co. Limited an Ontario-based company whose major business is the conversion of animal and vegetable waste products into valuable animal feed ingredients. CanPac AgriProducts also has an interest in Steirian Rendering Company of Austria.

CONSULTING SERVICES
Canadian Pacific Consulting Services Limited is a broadly-based engineering, transportation and economic consultant to governments and business around the world. The company can call on professional, technical and operating personnel in the Canadian Pacific group to meet the specific engineering, research, economic, marketing or supervisory requirements of projects anywhere in the world.
Since its formation in 1969, CPCS has carried out major projects in Canada, Australia, Indonesia, Malayasia, Tunisia, the Congo, Venezuela, Ghana, Togo, Panama, Zambia, Nigeria, Turkey, Egypt, Brazil, Algeria and Thailand.

CHILE
CHILEAN STATE RAILWAYS
Empresa de Los Ferrocarriles Del Estado
Alameda Bernardo O'Higgins, 924 Santiago

Telephone: 89116

Director General: Col. Ing. A. P. M. Juan E. Ossa Gatica
Subdirector (operations): Ing. Juan E. Ortiz Navarro
Subdirector (administration): Abogado Santiago Santa Cruz
Department Heads:
 Planning: Ing. Victor Celis Celis
 Finances: Ing. Antun Domic Bezic
 Traction (maintenance and production): Ing. Anibal Gajardo
 Traffic: Ing. Guido Fregonara Costa
 Chief Engineer: Ing. Guillermo Zenteno P.
Personnel: Sr. Pedro Javier Moreno G.

Gauge:	1.676 m	1.435 m	1.00 m
Track length:	4 223 km	243.1 km	3 432 km
Route length:	3 125 km	134.7 km	3 114 km

The complete system consists of:—
Red Norte (Northern Network): Extends from La Calera, near Valparaiso, change-of-gauge junction with Southern section, northward to Pueblo Hundido. It is completely dieselised.

Red Sur (Southern Network): Extends from Puerto Montt northward through Santiago to Valparaiso. The main line is electrified between Santiago and Concepcion, north from Santiago and west to Valparaiso and east to Los Andes. All branch lines on this section are diesel-operated.

FC Arica: Extends from Arica, on the coast close to Peruvian border, to Visvir where it connects with Bolivian section to La Paz. A 24 mile *(39 km)* section is operated by rack system.

FC Iquique-Pueblo Hundido: Extends southwards from Iquique on the coast to connection with Red Norte at Pueblo Hundido. All metre-gauge except for 155 miles *(250 km)* of 4 ft 8½ in *(1.435 m)* gauge, and a 3-rail combined gauge section of 79 miles *(126 km)*.

FC Transandino: Extends from Los Andes at the foot of the Andes Mountains to Caracoles on the Chile-Argentina border, connecting with Argentine State Railways (Northwest Region). Electrified; part rack rail.

Augusts Victoria-Socompa Line: Connects at Socompa with Argentine State Railways (Northwest Region), giving through service to Buenos Aires. Operated by FC Iquique-Hundido.

TRAFFIC
(figures in thousands)

Year	No. of passengers	Passenger kms	Goods carried (tonnes)	Tonnes/ kms
1961	20 158	1 738 567	8 280	1 506 590
1968	20 879	2 071 193	13 478	2 186 789
1969	21 684	2 209 600	13 522	2 173 000
1971	20 750	2 706 000	14 128	2 250 000
1972	24 900	3 028 000	12 381	2 167 000
1973	28 193	3 467 190	12 485	2 175 030
1974	26 877	2 815 596	12 873	1 929 068
1975	20 554	2 095 588	11 086	1 472 562
1976	21 800	2 356 100	10 700	1 650 900

FINANCIAL
Revenues

	1974	1975 (Pesos)	1976
Revenues (millions)	129 420 907	369 919 970	1 081 653 246
Expenses (millions)	109 160 131	526 082 377	1 342 980 296

Petroleum block train awaiting unloading in the Concepción region, 600 km south of Santiago

ELECTRIFICATION

Route length of electrification at December 31, 1976: 1 103 km.
Lines planned for electrification include: Laja—Temuco (189 km); Alameda—Cartagena (117.7 km).

MOTIVE POWER AND ROLLING STOCK

Locomotives in service (1976)

steam	307
electric	133
diesel electric	231
Number of electric railcars	32
Number of diesel railcars	16
Number of passenger coaches	749
Number of freight wagons	9 981
Number of containers	134

During 1976 FFCCE took delivery of 24 electric locomotives and the first eight of 20 electric railcar sets ordered from Fiat Concord of Argentina. The two-car (M + T) permanently-coupled sets have a total length of 52.9 m and capacity for 200 passengers.
Government approval was sought during 1977 for acquisition of three rack locomotives and clearing equipment for the international Trans-Andes Railway.

SIGNAL AND TRAIN CONTROL INSTALLATIONS

Existing signalling between Valparaiso and Talca is being changed to electric block and colour light signals. Total route length is 273 miles *(440 km)*.
Supplier: Union Switch and Signal, USA.
Centralised Traffic Control (CTC) has been installed between Talca and Puerta Montt. The line is divided into 5 sections. The first 3 sections, Talca-Chillán, Chillán-Concepcion, and San Rosendo-Temuco, are controlled from Concepcion. The other 2 sections, Temuco-Valdivia and Antilhue-Puerto Moutt, are controlled from Valdivia. Total route length is 510 miles *(820 km)*. The work will be completed in 1974.
Supplier: Westinghouse Brake & Signal Co. Ltd., England.

TRACK DETAILS

Standard rail: Type K, 119 lb/yd *(59 kg/m)*; Type Z, 100.9 lb *(50 kg)*; Type Y, 80.7 lb *(40 kg)*; Type U, 64.5 lb *(32 kg/m)*; Type F, 60.5 lb *(30 kg)*; Type P, 51.4 lb *(25.5 kg)*; Type L, 50.4 lb *(25 kg)*; and older rail of varying weights.
1.676 m gauge: Types K, Z, Y; 76.6 lb *(38 kg)*.
1.435 m gauge: Type F; also 85 lb *(42.16 kg)*.
1.000 m gauge: Types Y, U, L, P; also 70.6 lb *(35 kg)*, 55.7 lb *(27.5 kg)*, and 54.4 lb *(27 kg)*.
0.600 m gauge: 50.4 lb *(25 kg)* and 30.3 lb *(15 kg)*.
Sleepers (cross ties): Wood, 5.9 in *(15 cm)* deep × 7.9 in *(20 cm)* wide; except on rack rail section of FC Transandino:—metal.
Spacing, main lines: 3 025 per mile *(1 880 per km)*.
Spacing, branch lines: 2 415 per mile *(1 500 per km)*.
Spacing, rack rail: 1 835 to 3 100 per mile *(1 140-1 930 per km)*.

NEW CONSTRUCTION

A number of proposals for line renewal have been put to the Government for approval. These include:— line renewal in the North and South networks involving a total of 281 km with rail type K (119 RE) over 190 km; type Z (100 RA) over 66 km and type Y (80 AS) over 25 km; and line renewal over 155 km of the international railway from Arica to La Paz including renewal of signalling and communications over the whole of the Chilean section (206 km) and the acquisition of locomotives.
Several new lines are projected for future construction, including: Santiago—Valparaiso (108 km); Angol—Pidina (38 km); Hualqui—Cabrero (53 km); Curanilahue—Los Alamos (21 km); Nos—Puente Alto (17 km).

Suburban electric trainset, built in Argentina for FFCEE for service between Valparaiso and Peña Blanca

ARICA—LA PAZ RAILWAY (FCALP)

Ferrocarril de Arica a la Paz
Casilla 9-D, Arica

Director General: Juan Ossa G.
Administrator (delegate): Fernando Ipinza M.
Secretary: Manuel Avendaño L.
Chief of Traction and Workshops: Gustavo Moya R.
Chief of Way and Works: Manuel Castillo D.
Chief of Transport: Sergio Leal L.
Chief of Accounting: Carlos Diáz D.
Chief of Personnel: Victor Cisternas Z.

Gauge: 1.00 m.
Route length: 206 km (Chile section).

For more than half a century the Arica to La Paz Railway, belonging to the Chilean State Railways, has been railing freight and passengers between Chile and Bolivia. Its origin goes back to the years following the end of the War of the Pacific (1883) and its building was provided in the Peace and Friendship Treaty subscribed by the Chilean and Bolivian governments in 1904. The Chilean government financed the construction of the complete network of the line.
Because of its difficult mounting route, FCALP reflects one of the most remarkable examples of railway engineering. In turn, it represents "the shortest route from the Pacific to Bolivia", (its own slogan), covering 440 km between the port of Arica in Chile to the Bolivian capital city of La Paz. The difficulties arising out of its ascending layout to the Bolivian plateau and its high operational and maintenance costs are the main reasons for its low profitability.

MOTIVE POWER

The Arica to La Paz Railway operates 8 General Electric diesel-electric, 1 320 hp locomotives; 3 General Electric 600 hp locomotives and 3 General Electric—3 000, 270 hp locomotives.

New electric switch board panel at Curico, 180 km south of Santiago

Santiago's Mapocho station—new point of departure for rapid trainset services between the Chilean capital and Concepcion

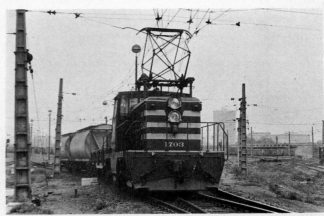

One of 24 new electric locomotives built under license from Fiat of Italy in 1976. The locomotives are rated at 1 715 hp

For its passenger service, FCALP operates 2 Schindler 360 hp saloon motor-coaches and 1 Schindler 360 hp first class motor-coach.
In 1969, the old rack-rail steam locomotives used up and down the line between Central and Puquios stations, were replaced by the GE locomotives. The haulage capacity in this difficult sector is of 300 t per train pulled by two locomotives.

ROLLING STOCK

Freight stock consists of 420 wagons: 313 BCt and DGt boxcars; 113 LMt, P5Ct and PCt flatcars; 10 double-deck motor vehicle carrying cars; 17 CCt container cars.

FREIGHT TRAFFIC	1975	1976
Total freight tonne-km	24 511 879	17 404 645
Total freight tonnage	120 063	85 679
Total passenger-km	8 505 573	9 219 433
Total passenger journeys	43 363	41 781

STREAMLINE PLAN

A plan to streamline operations, established 10 years ago, contemplates the up-dating of infrastructure, particularly a full renewal of the railtrack. About 70 km of the former 27.5 kg/plm rail on a 206 km section of the Chilean section have been replaced to date with Japanese 39.82 kg/plm Y track. Financing is being procured to purchase 3 new up-to-date saloon motorcoaches of a greater capacity to cover the passenger-tourist traffic in place of the existing stock which has already outrun its useful life.

ATLANTIC—PACIFIC LINK

The final studies entrusted to the Brazilian GEIPOT transport organisation with a view to completing the inter-continental rail network link between Arica (Chile) on the Pacific and Santos (Brazil) on the Atlantic, are now underway. The Government of Brazil has allocated the sum of $US 6 000 000 as its contribution to complete studies on the railroad layout connecting Aiguile and Santa Cruz. This represents approximately 300 km of track in Bolivian territory, which is the only missing connection in the Atlantic—Pacific intercontinental railway link. Work has been started by a Brazilian consulting firm with the cooperation of the Ministry of Transport of Bolivia. It is estimated that this new route will be completed and inaugurated by 1980.

CHINA

CHINESE PEOPLE'S REPUBLIC RAILWAYS

Ministry of Railways, Peking

Gauge: mainly 1.435 m
Track length: 88 000 km

ORGANISATION

The Ministry of Railways at present administers 20 railway bureaus and 16 sub-bureaus throughout China, as well as most of China's 33 locomotive and rolling stock factories via the Locomotive and Rolling Stock Factories Department.

Following successful completion of the 1971-75 fourth Five Year Plan, the Chinese People's Republic Railways (CPRR) is going ahead with projects listed under the fifth plan (1975-79). Major objectives include construction of new railway lines in the far west provinces of Tibet and Xinjiang which have so far been untapped by rail because of difficulty of access.

Delays in the plan occurred during 1976 due to civil disturbances following exposure of the 'Gang of Four', sacking the now-disgraced former Railway Minister Wan Li by Tuan Chun-yi, and virtual takeover of the railway administration by party and army. This grasping of control by the party indicates just how serious were railway disruptions in 1976. At the vital Chengchow junction—standing at the meeting of China's east-west and north-south lines, rioting in April 1976 was serious, cutting the Chengchow Railway Bureau's volume of coal transported by 12 million tonnes in 1976. Early in 1977, Peking transferred senior officers from the army's railway and engineering corps to run the Chengchow Bureau, since when the situation is reported to have improved significantly.

Chengchow was by no means the only place to be affected. Other troubled provinces include Kweichow, Anhwei, Kwangtung and Inner Mongolia.

During the fourth plan, a total of 10 000 km of new railway lines was built, bringing the length of the CPRR system to over 55 000 km. All the nation's provinces—with the exception of Tibet—are now linked by rail. During the last plan period, efforts were concentrated on extending the system into the mountainous regions of the south and south-west. Engineering difficulties posed by the geographical conditions in both regions were numerous. For instance, the new Chengdu (capital of Sichuan province) to Kunming (capital of Yunnan province) line—completed in 1972—involved construction of 427 tunnels and 653 bridges along the 1 085 km route.

With motive power still composed largely of steam locomotives, CPRR is keen to speed dieselisation and introduce electrification on major routes. The system's first 676 km electrified line was opened early 1975 between Baoji (Shenxi province) and Chengdu (Sichuan province) at 27 500 v single-phase ac; extension of China's first electrified line between Paochi and Fenghsien. In 1977, reports were received that China's second electrified line—the 365 km Yangpingkuan—Ankang in southern Shensi—had opened to traffic. Electrification is now planned between Datong and Dayuan.

MOTIVE POWER

China's modern locomotive park was originally based on Soviet-built stock, delivered between 1956 and 1959. Among the most significant of Soviet deliveries were about 1 000 of second-hand FD 2-102 class steam units. These relatively new and powerful locomotives represented a considerable upgrading of China's fleet of aging pre-war Consolidations, Mikados and so on. They were converted to Chinese gauge at Changchun and dubbed the 'Friendship' class. Soviet specialists also helped the Chinese to build the Heping ('Peace' steam locomotive—a more powerful 2-10-2 very similar to the Soviet LV 1-5-1 which was then just going out of production in the Soviet Union. The first prototype was assembled at Talien in 1956 and the Heping was in serial production by 1959.

European and Japanese locomotive builders entered the Chinese railway scene after 1960. (for details see table).

The first Chinese-built locomotive was a 2-8-2 constructed at Tsingtao in 1952. A 4-6-2 for passenger service and the Heping 2-10-2 for freight followed soon after. It was a practical move for the Chinese to build steam locomotives at a time when much of the rest of the world was moving over to diesel, bearing in mind the plentiful coal supplies available. In the late 1950s and early 1960s, however, a few prototypes of electric, diesel-electric and diesel-hydraulic designs were built. By the mid-1960s the Chinese had set up production line facilities for the 'Giant Dragon' and 'East Wind' series of locomotives. By 1975 China was producing about 530 locomotives annually—about 275 of which were diesel and 250 steam.

By 1975 it is thought China was producing about 530 locomotives a year, about 275 of which were diesel and 250 steam. Inventory was about 8 300 units. Production of locomotives increased about 16% during the Fourth Five-Year Plan (1971-1975) while rail-freight turnover rose by 30% to 458 billion ton-kms. At the same rate, the PRC's production will be about 610-620 units by 1980, when steam output should be minimal, and turnover will be about 595 billion ton-kms.

Output of freight cars rose from 14 000 in 1971 to 18 500 in 1975, according to US Government estimates, a rise of 32% Inventory in 1975 was about 237 000 units. By 1980 annual production should be about 24 000 units.

During the 1971-75 plan China's laid track increased by 12% to 52 280 km; at the same rate China's total track should reach 58 000 km by 1980.

To serve newly-electrified lines, Chinese builders have supplied new Shaoshan-type electric locomotives and orders were placed in 1974 with the Hans Beimler works of the German Democratic Republic for 30 type EL2 electric locomotives.

There are at present five Chinese plants building locomotives: at Dalian in Liaoning province; Datong in Shanxi province, building exclusively steam locomotives; in Sichuan and Guizhou provinces where new factories were set up in 1973.

At the start of the fourth plan, CPRR was operating a motive power fleet consisting of 12% diesel-electric and diesel-hydraulic locomotives and 88% of steam locomotives. Since 1971 a total of 50 diesel locomotives have been purchased from Alsthom, France, each rated at 4 000 hp. In addition, six 24 ton diesel shunters were purchased from Japan in 1975 at a cost of $US 500 000 per unit.

ROLLING STOCK

At the end of the 1971-75 plan a total of 200 000 freight wagons were in operation. Of these, 100 000 are hopper or open type and 40 000 are tank wagons. Practically all the wagon fleet have a bogie capacity of 50 tonnes. Annual wagon production in China is 140 000 units.

TRAFFIC

Freight traffic over the past five years has developed mainly between the industrial centres of the north-east and the port of Dalian. Increasing rail freight movements have also been recorded between northern and southern regions over routes which in the past have been traditionally served by maritime operators.

Track upgrading during the fourth plan period together with rolling stock modernisation have resulted in a big increase in freight train capacities. In 1975, the average train freight loading was 2 300 tonnes compared with 1 900 tonnes in 1958 and 1 100 tonnes in 1950.

FREIGHT TRAFFIC

By the end of the first Five Year Plan (1953-57) the railway accounted for 63 per cent of all freight hauled, 77·8 per cent of tonne-km and 73 per cent of passenger-km. The railway now carries a slightly lesser proportion, hauling 945 million tonnes in 1975—59 per cent of the 1 598 million tonnes of freight moved by all modes.

According to the last available official figures, in 1958 the average daily run per freight locomotive was 391 km; the average gross weight hauled per freight locomotive was 1 704 tonnes; the average daily efficiency per freight locomotive was 600 000 tonne-km; the average turn-round distance per freight wagon was 703·6 km; the average daily run per freight wagon was 255·6 km; the average stopping time per freight wagon per run was 10·4 hours; the average speed per freight train, including halts, was 25·7 km/h; average load per freight wagon was 37·5 tonnes; and the average daily efficiency per freight wagon was 6 596 tonne-km.

A Henschel diesel-hydraulic locomotive for the Chinese railways.

The efficiency of the Chinese railway system has almost certainly improved significantly since then.

Railways are still the dominant mode of freight transport in China. Even a light-traffic frontier line like the Kweiyang-Kunming carries an annual traffic of more than 3 million tonne-km per route-km. On such key lines as the Peking-Shenyang and the Peking-Wuhan, traffic densities have reportedly exceeded 25 million tonne-km per route-km.

Main reason for the poor freight results of 1950 was the inadequately-developed railway network. Over a total land area of 9.6 million km² there were 20 000 km of mainly single-track railway lines—10 000 km of which were concentrated in Manchuria alone.

Because of this, 20 per cent of China's expenditure on economic reconstruction of the country's resources and facilities since 1950 have been spent on railway developments. During the first five-year plan (1953-57), 15 per cent of total national development went into transport—two thirds of which was for railways.

During the first plan period two major trunk lines were constructed: Peking-Ouroumtsi and Baoji-Chendu. At the same time, two lesser lines were built: Sichuan-Tibet and Xinjiang-Tibet.

By 1966, on the eve of China's cultural revolution, the railway system totalled 36 500 km of lines of which 5 500 km were double tracked.

Since 1970, the ageing railway network has been given a marked push with expanded routes, new equipment and the addition of Peking's suburban underground system, which transports more than 70,000 commuters daily.

PASSENGER TRAFFIC

China's railways are critical links for passenger transport between major cities. The volume of passengers handled is immense. Even in 1958, the last year for which official data is available, approximately 346 million Chinese paid to travel by train. Between 1949 and 1958, the number of rail passengers increased by 236 per cent. Observers calculate that at present the railway is annually carrying between 450 and 500 million passengers.

NETWORK

Length of the Chinese People's Republic Railways in 1975 was 46 500 km—double the length reported in 1949. About 1 000 km of new track is being added, on average, every year; in 1970 more than 2 700 km was laid.

For the first few years after 1949, the new government of China concentrated on restoring the existing network to a more serviceable condition, although the construction of new lines also began rather quickly. The remote but populous interior province of Szechwan saw its first railroad in 1952, when the Chengtu-Chungking was completed. The mid-1950's brought the completion of the Yingtan-Amoy on the coast opposite Taiwan, the mountainous Paoki-Chengtu, and the trans-Mongolian railway which shortened the train trip from Peking to Moscow by about 700 miles. Also, 1956 saw the building of the first railway bridge across the Yangtze River, at Wuhan. In the late 1950's the desert line from Paotow to Lanchow was completed, and then carried in two directions to Sining and Urumchi. Another bridge across the Yangtze, at Chungking, was also built at the close of the decade.

During the 1960's, despite the severe economic difficulties of the early years, several additional lines were opened to traffic. Among these were the Chungking-Kweiyang (1965) and the Kweiyang-Kunming (1966). A third bridge across the Yangtze, at Nanking, was finished in 1968—its double tracks greatly expediting traffic between Shanghai and Peking. In 1976, officials indicated 120 trains used this bridge daily.

The 1970's have been a period of substantial further construction, beginning with the Chiaotso-Chihkiang and the Chengtu-Kunming lines in 1970. The Hunan-Kweichow was finished in 1972. And the Nenlin Railway through Manchuria's frigid Greater Khingan Mountains was opened to traffic in 1974.

Supplementing China's standard-gauge railroads is a system of lightweight, narrow-gauge lines. Information on this system is scanty, but the pattern in Honan province is revealing. In 1973 the Honan network was about 600 miles in length and reached into thirty counties. The gauge is described as half that of an ordinary railroad, and is therefore probably 750 mm.

A supplementary Shanghai-Nanking railway line was opened to traffic on June 29, 1976. It is 291.5 km long and required the expansion and building of 41 railway stations, the laying of more than 300 km of rails on the main line and more than 270 km of rails on branch lines. Natural difficulties meant slow progress in construction. There are many lakes and rivers and streams along the route. There is quick sand present and the geological structure is complex. This posed difficulties for the design and construction of bridges.

The 1 805-km Chengtu-Kunming railway line which passes through three of China's richest southwest provinces—Szechwan, Kweichow and Yunnan—had also been successfully completed. Reportedly with 427 tunnels and 653 bridges, the link passes through extremely rugged terrain typical of the area. It was expected to alter the industrial deployment of the area it serves.

Expansion of border trade, particularly with Pakistan, is difficult without rail links. Plans to build a line from Urumchi in Sinkiang to join the feeder service to the Soviet and Mongolia collapsed along with the Sino-Soviet dispute. But despite political and border differences of opinion, there was more emphasis on Sino-Soviet rail links, with two-way trade, mostly carried by rail, expected to pass $US 330 million this year.

DOUBLE TRACKING

The 1 300 km Tientsin-Shanghai Railway, a trunk line in east China running from Tientsin in the north to Shanghai in the south through Hopei, Shantung, Anhwei and

Alsthom 7 300-hp electric locomotive.

Kiangsu Provinces, has been double-tracked. Joined with the double-tracked Peking-Tientsin line, it forms an important link between the capital and east China. Double-tracking the line will help greatly to develop industry and agriculture in the coastal areas, facilitate construction in China's hinterland and consolidate its national defence. The old Tientsin-Shanghai line was of poor quality and its installations and equipment were obsolete. Construction of the second track began in 1958. The project, however, virtually stopped in 1960. Work was resumed during the cultural revolution.

Apart from professional builders, local people along the line turned out in large numbers to help. Progress quickened in the second half of 1975. A year's hard work since then included the moving of 9 140 000 cubic metres of earth and stone for the roadbed and the building of more than 400 big and small bridges including a 5.7 kilometre long one with 163 arches which spans the Yellow River at Tsinan. The double-tracking was completed ahead of schedule recently.

ELECTRIFICATION

Two lines have now been electrified: (1) Baoji—Chengdu (676 km); (2) Yangping-kuan—Ankang (365 km). Peking-Tatung-Paotow, 570 miles *(920 km)* and Tatung-Yangku-Tungkwan, 500 miles *(800 km).*

The system employed is 25 000 V, single phase, 50-cycles, with overhead conductor. The French electrical industry has assisted in the development of 50-cycle electrification in China and technical assistance has also been made available by the USSR.

FREIGHT TRAFFIC

	Total	Rail-roads	High-ways	Inland and Coastal Waterways
1953	211	161	30	20
1954	266	193	44	29
1955	280	194	50	36
1956	372	246	79	47
1957	429	274	101	54
1958	633	381	176	76
1959	864	520	230	114
1960	842	510	220	112
1961	565	340	150	75
1962	582	350	155	77
1963	634	380	170	84
1964	668	400	180	88
1965	737	440	200	97
1966	823	490	225	108
1967	690	410	190	90
1968	730	430	205	95
1969	872	510	250	112
1970	1 050	615	300	135
1971	1 229	725	344	160
1972	1 295	770	356	169
1973	1 398	830	385	183
1974	1 459	865	404	190
1975	1 598	945	445	208

SALES OF FOREIGN LOCOMOTIVES TO CHINA (1949-1976)

1958-1960 USSR
1 050 used Felix Dzherzhinskys (FDs) 2-10-2 steam locos, 12-wheel tenders, spoked "drivers", built 1931-41, valued at about $85.6 million.

1960 Alsthom—MTE, France
25 Co-Co, 139 ton, 6 000 kw electric locos for 4 400 kw DC op. with ignition rectifiers and energy recovery brakes; max speed 100 km/h; hauling capacity exceeding 32 tons at 47 km/h; energy recovery when braking of 3 500 kw for two units, 3 600 kw for 38; in multiple units could haul 1 500 tons up to 0.3 grade at 50 km/h. Numbered 6-Y-2 by Chinese; to work freight at —40° to +40°C.

1965 Japan
31 small electric locos.

1966 Sweden
17 small electric locos.

1966-67 Henschel (Rheinstahl), Germany
4 diesel hydraulic CC, 180-ton, 4 000-hp locos; max speed 160 km/hr; with Voith L830rU turbo-transmission; for freight and passenger hauling; each with two MB839B6 Maybach-Mercedes-Benz 16-cyl engines; dev. 2 000 bhp at 1 500 rpm; designed to operate from —40°C to +40°C; Behr cooling equipment. Khorr airbrakes; gauge 1 435 mm; NY5 class.

1968-72 Henschel
30 diesel-hydraulic CC 138 ton locos; max speed 120 km/h; length 23 610 mm; width 3 120 mm; height 4 570 mm; tractive effort (starting) 45 500 kg; Voith L820 hydro-

dynamic drives; gauge 1 435 mm; comprise ten NY6 4 600 hp (UIC), site rating 4 300 hp; with two MB16V652 diesel engines by MTU, and twenty NY7 5 400 hp. (UIC), site rating 5 000 hp, with two MA 12V 956 engines by MTU; bodies and cabs acoustically and thermally insulated, plus comprehensive heating system with Henschel WK200 boiler to keep engine, transmission oils and fuels warm; Behr cooling system; tank capacity 10 000 litres for 2 000 km range due to limited fuelling points.

1970-73 Alsthom—MTE
40 Co-Co, 7 300 hp electric locos for 5 400 km dc op. with silicon semi-conductors; for 25 kv/50hz system; hauling capacity exceeding 36 tons at 4.5 km/hr; energy recovery when braking 4 300 kw; numbered 6G 51-90; 138 tons; max speed 112 km/hr; rated tractive effort of 353 kN at 55 km/h continuous; provision for multiple working on very heavy freight trains; gauge 1 435 mm.

1971-74 Alsthom—MTE
50 Co-Co, 4 000 hp diesel-electric 138 ton locos with single-C motor trucks; 3-phase continuous ac/dc transmission; max speed 100 km/h single; AGO V-16 ESHR motor by SACM; supplying 3 650 hp at 30°C, towing at 1 350 rpm; withstand —40°C without anti-freeze; able to maintain traction performance at 30 km/hr with two engines coupled in multiple units tracking in one-way 5-km tunnels; freight use; numbered ND 4 1-50 by Chinese; tractive effort (starting) 48 000 kg; 23 020 mm long; width 3 290 mm; height 4 500 mm; gauge 1 435 mm; separate heating system; fuel capacity of 10 000 litres gives range of 2 000 km, two days normal use; large resistance banks provide dynamic braking at 4 000 hp; designed, when double-headed, to haul 5 000 ton freight train at 80 km/h on level, maintain 24 km/h hp and 25 km/h down 1.0 per cent gradient; also to haul 2 000 tons up 2.5 per cent grade and maintain 30-40 km/h down 2.5 per cent incline.

Early 70s East Germany
Heavy industrial electric locos 150 ton EL-1, 1 500 V dc overhead line op; 100-ton EL-2, with alternative 1 200-2 400 V dc rating; used in opencast mines, number unknown.

1973 Henschel
36 diesel locos, 5 500 hp, valued at $8 million.

1974 Nippon Sharyo Seizo Kaisha, Japan
Six 24 ton diesel locos valued at about $500 000; deal arranged via Nichimen.

1975 Electroputere, Romania
20 diesel-electric locos, 2 100 hp.

CHINA: ESTIMATED PRODUCTION OF LOCOMOTIVES AND FREIGHT CARS 1949-1975

	Mainline Locomotives (Units)				Freight Cars (Units)
	Total	Steam	Diesel	Electric	
1949	—	—	—	—	3 155
1950	—	—	—	—	696
1951	—	—	—	—	2 882
1952	20	20	—	—	5 792
1953	10	10	—	—	4 501
1954	52	52	—	—	5 446
1955	98	98	—	—	9 258
1956	184	184	—	—	7 122
1957	167	167	—	—	7 300
1958	350	346	2	2	11 000
1959	533	530	3	—	17 000
1960	602	600	—	2	23 000
1961	100	100	—	—	3 000
1962	25	25	—	—	4 000
1963	27	25	—	2	5 900
1964	27	25	2	—	5 700
1965	50	20	30	—	6 600
1966	220	150	70	—	7 500
1967	300	200	100	—	6 900
1968	340	200	140	—	8 700
1969	391	230	160	1	11 000
1970	435	250	180	5	12 000
1971	455	250	200	5	14 000
1972	475	250	220	5	15 000
1973	495	250	240	5	16 000
1974	505	250	250	5	16 800
1975	530	250	275	5	18 500

CHINESE MADE LOCOMOTIVES

Aiming to the Sun, (Shang Yan) (SY), Tangshan. Construction, (Jian She) (JS), Tsing-tao/Peking 2-7. 2-8-2 steam loco, trip and branch line work. 1952, 1958 steam 2-8-2 2 270 hp; 56 175 lbs TE; 54" WD; 54 mph; Cyls: 22.8" × 28"; BP: 220 psi; wgt: 201 317 lbs; TW: 70 600*.

East is Red, (Dong Hang Fong) (DFH), Tsingtao. (Dong Fang Hong 4), Chishuyen. 1968, 2 000 hp diesel hydraulic. 1976, 3 000 hp diesel hydraulic. 102 1 000 hp and 2 000 hp diesels shipped to Tanzania/Zambia.

East Wind, (Dong Feng W), Talien. 1 800 hp diesel loco remodeled in "design of a foreign diesel locomotive," used in Chengchow south locomotive section. According to NCNA "Most diesel locos used on major railways are of the "Dongfeng W" type for passenger services." In 1966, 2 000, 3 000 and 4 000 hp diesel electric versions noted.

(Dong Feng 4), Talien. Spring 1974, model at Canton Fair, with ac/dc electric transmission; 4 000 hp, 1 hr rating of diesel; 3 600 hp continuous rating.

Forward, (Qian Jin) (QJ), Tatung. 1965 (?), 2 .10 .2, 2 980 hp; 73 405 lbs TE; 59" WD; 50 mph; Cyls: 25.6" × 31.5"; BP: 220 psi; wft: 262 400 lbs; TW: 65 000.

Giant Dragon, (Ju Lung) (JL), Talien. 1963, series production 1965, 278 000 lbs, CC unit. Two 2 000 hp opposed piston diesel engines operate 1 350 kw dc generator. Traction capacity said to be 3 500 mt at 100 kw/hr.

Liberation, (Jie Fang) (JF), ?. 2-8-2, 1 545 hp, 52 985 lbs TE; 54" WD; 54 mph; Cyls: 22.8" × 28"; BP: 206 psi; wgt: 207 500 lbs; TW: 63 900.

Mao Tse-tung, Tsingtao. 2-8-0 or 2-8-2. Single steam loco rebuilt from foreign loco in 1946, had done 3 million miles by 1976.

Peace, (Heping) (HP), Changchun. Talien. 1956, 2-10-2 prototype 2 780 hp. 1959, max. 3 154 hp, 80 km/h. Total prod: 100 pa thru 1971. "Chinese designers borrowed heavily from the blueprints of the Soviet L-class 2-10-2 and threw in the best features of locomotives from other countries. The cylinder cocks were an American design; the blower was adapted from a Belgian design; and the self-adjusting wedges were Japanese. The Heping was given a mechanical stoker and lubricator, pneumatic rocking grates, and any other modern labour-saving device the Chinese could design. Crew comfort was a primary consideration. Inside the all-weather cabs are a small stove for tea and snacks, small changing room with a mirror and even a heater for keeping the engineer's feet warm. The Heping allegedly can haul 80 per cent more than the Construction 2-8-2 on an 0.4 per cent grade at 25 mph, while burning 12 per cent less coal. No thought was given to making the Heping an oil burner because China had massive coal deposits. (Sizable petroleum reserves were not discovered and exploited until fairly recently). The Heping is estimated to weigh between 330 000 and 485 000 lbs." (Trains 11.72).

Peking (Beijing) (BJ), Peking. 1958, steam loco. Also 3 000 hp diesels trial produced 1969.

Peking (Subway), (Beijing), Changchun. 1969, electric 750-V dc, 19 m cars; max speed: 80 km/h.

People, (Renmin) (RM), ?. Pre-1956, 4-6-2 steam loco, 1 900 hp, 39 800 lbs TE: 70" WD; 68 mph; Cyls: 22.4" × 26"; BP: 220 psi; wgt: 198 000 lbs; TW: 70 600 lbs.

Red Flag (Hungqi) (HQ);, Talien. 1958, steam, freight.

Rocket, Changchun. 1960, small steam loco, 234 hp, wgt 54 426 lbs; rural and small mine use.

Satellite, (Wei Xing) (WX), Tsingtao. 1959, 1960, 1 000 hp diesel hydraulic, 2 000 hp version, wgt; 188 000 lbs; BB, speed to 85 mph.

Shaoshan, (Shaoshan) (SS), Tienhsin. 1969, 5 200 hp electric for 25 000 V 50 cycle, single phase ac system.

Victory, (Shengli) (SL), ?. 4-6-2 steam passenger loco, 1 600 hp, 37 220 lbs TE; 70" WB; 68 mph; Cyls: 22.4" × 26"; BP: 206 psi; wgt: 195 600 lbs; TW: 61 500 lbs.

OTHERS

NA, Canton. 1975, 380 hp steam loco, narrow-gauge.

NA, Tsingtao. 1959, 2 000 hp hydraulic transmission internal combustion loco.

T-6, Tsingtao. 1960, 1 500 hp steam passenger loco.

288, Tsingtao. Steam loco.

NA, Chuchou. Electric locos.

NA, Hsiangtan. 150 ton electric locos.

NA, Peking Feb. 7. 3 000 and 6 000 hp diesel hydraulic locos.

"2-8-2", Talien. 1956, 1 544 hp steam freight loco.

NA, Talien. 1959, 4 000 hp freight diesel; 2 000 hp diesel electric with electric transmission.

NA, Tatung. Gas turbine loco.

NA, Tientsin. Internal Combustion loco.

NA, Shenyang. Internal Combustion loco.

CHINESE LOCOMOTIVE WEIGHTS AND LENGTHS

Locomotive Type	Total Weight of Locomotive With Coal and Water Cars (Tons)	Length of Locomotive With Coal and Water Cars (Metres)
XK2	48	11.0
MG4, 5, 6	66	17.6
DB1	66	14.3
JF8	69	19.8
KD5	71	18.7
ET1, 8	74	14.3
DB2	78	14.3
Dong-Fang-Hong (East is Red)	82	17.6
PL2, 9	86	20.9
KD6, 9	89	20.9
SL9	95	22.0
KD2	98	23.1
JF3, 5, 7, 12	99	22.0
JF6, 9, 10, 11, 13	102	23.1
DK1	102	23.1
SL3	104	23.1
DK2	105	23.1
Dong-Feng2 (East Wind)	106	16.5
SL12, 13, 14, 15	109	24.2
KD7	111	22.0
Dong-Feng (DF) (East Wind)	118	16.5
Sheng-Li (SL) (Victory)	120	25.3
Ren-Min (RM) (People's)	122	24.2
SL5	123	25.3
Jien-She (JS) (Construction)	126	24.2
Jie-Fang (JF) (Liberation)	127	24.2
Shao-Shan*	138	17.6
6Y2	138	23.1
SL7, 8	140	27.2
JF2, 4	140	25.3
KF1	144	30.8
Qian-Jin (QJ) (Forward)	154	29.7
FD	178	29.7

Source: Table in *Railroad Yards,* Prepared by the North China College of Communications, Transportation Division; Published by the People's Communications Press, Peking, September 1973. 18 000 copies known printed in two separate printings. Second in October 1974.

*Chairman Mao's birthplace, Hunan.

COLOMBIA

NATIONAL RAILWAYS OF COLOMBIA
Ferrocarriles Nacionales de Colombia (FCN), Calle 13, No 18-24 Bogotá

Telephone: 775577
Telegrams: FERROCARRILES

BOARD
President: Minister of Public Works—Humberto Salcedo Collantes
Principal Members of the Board: Jorge Marmorek Rojas
Sabas Pretelt de la Vega
Gustavo de Greiff Restrepo
Sinforiano Restrepo

General Manager: Marco Tulio Lora Borrero
Financial Manager: Jaime Fernandez Parada
Technical Manager: James Yepez Londoño
Administrative Manager: Ingrid Paulsen de Quintero
Commercial Manager: Antonio Carom Habib
Technical Advisors: Jorge Sossa Beltran
Jorge E. Bravo R.
Jaime Ucros Barros
Eduardo Rodriguez A.

Departmental Heads:
Workshops: Hector Osorio
Telecommunications: Fabio Roldan
Transportation: Carlos Blanco
Permanent Way: Hernan Garcia Martinez
Personnel: Jesus A. Carrizosa
Marketing: Juan Gongora Diaz
Accountancy and Control: Mario Romero Ospina
Real Estate: Marciano Puche
Medical: Pablo J. Mora

Gauge: 914 mm
Route length: 3 403 km

Columbia's seventh railway plan was launched in 1978 under a $US 70 million improvement programme. Major investments will include:
(1) $US 27 million for updating the infrastructure and fixed installations; (2) $US 22 613 000 for new motive power, passenger coaches, freight wagons and containers, and towards modernisation of existing stock.; (3) $US 10 878 000 for new workshop equipment; (4) $US 7 766 000 for yard and station improvements; (5) $US 2 503 000 for training and consultancy fees.

	miles	km
Division Pacifico		
Buenaventura to: Popoyan, A. Lopez, Manizales	561	903
Division Central		
Bogota to: Neiva, Ibague, Grecia, Barbosa, Belencito	850	1 368
Division Magdalena		
Santa Marta to: Garmarra	264	425
Division Santander		
Gamarra to: Grecia, Bucaramanga, Puerto Wilches	249	400
Division Antioquia		
Grecia to: A. Lopez	211	340
Total route length	2 135	3 436

Several studies have been initiated by FCN on proposed new lines. These were begun in 1974 and should be completed by the end of 1975/76 in time for consideration by the Government for an early start on construction by the end of 1976.

TRAFFIC	1973	1974	1976
Freight ton-km	2 140 000	2 124 000	1 221 000
Freight tons	2 760	2 899	2 990
Passenger km	427 378	482 502	510 000
Passenger journeys	4 287	4 552	4 050

FINANCES	1973	1974
	$'000s	
Revenue	658 023	892 601
Expenses	857 621	1 314 378

Operating deficit in 1976 reached Pesos 426 936 950 on a total income of Pesos 1 230 327 138.

MOTIVE POWER
Number of locomotives in service at the end of 1974 was: five mainline steam units and 174 diesel-hydraulic units. During 1974/75 a total of 28 new General Electric type GE-U-10-B units were taken into service.
Number of petrol-powered railcars in service was 22; number of diesel railcars, 5 931.

ROLLING STOCK
Total number of passenger train coaches: 306; freight wagons, 5 625.

LINE PROJECTS
A £2 million contract for rails was completed by British Steel in April 1977. The shipment is to be used for line upgrading projects over 54 km. A total of four new lines are under study. The most important proposed new link is likely to be between Barbosa and Puerto Berrio, designed to replace the uneconomic service between La Dorada and Facatativa. Steep gradients and narrow curves mean that trains travelling between the coast and the Mexican border have to be split up. From preliminary investigations it seems likely that the possible variant will run from a point located between Saboya and Garavito at approximately 182 km from Bogota. It would continue through easy mountainous terrain over 90 km to Landazuri where the line would descend to the plains before reaching Las Mulas (42 km north of Puerto Berrio). Mountainous sections would have a maximum gradient of 2% and the cost would be approximately $360 million. A line between Bogota and the port of Buenaventura was started in 1913 and abandoned in 1930 when the railhead had reached midway point on the Ibague—Armenia section of the line. Now an alternative route is under consideration which would replace the entire 109 682-m Ibague—Armenia section with a 11 600 m tunnel cut-off. Other lines under study would provide direct rail connections to the regions of the Carribean, Barranquilla and Cartenga at an estimated cost of $660 million.

INVESTMENTS
Spending on capital equipment and works in 1977 totalled $Colombian 52 293 700, with principal purchases as follows: line welding ($C 5 178 700); track improvements over 54 km ($11 700 000) and infrastructure improvements ($C 18 951 000).

CONGO
CHEMIN DE FER CONGO-OCÉAN
PO Box 651, Pointe Noire

Telephone: 94-05-63
Telegrams: CONGO OCEAN

General Manager: S. R. Tchichelle
Motive Power and Rolling Stock: M. Mazaleyrat
Way and Works: J. Duvic
Operations: P. Freudenreich

Gauge: 1.067 m
Route length: 515 km—running from the port of Pointe Noire to Brazzaville.

The People's Republic of the Congo is served by the Congo-Ocean Railway which extends from Pointe-Noire to Brazzaville; a 280 km branch line, built by the Compagnie Miniere de i'Ogooue (Comilog) connects Mont-Belo station (200 km from Pointe Noire) with M'Binda and public service over this line is now provided by the Congo-Ocean Railway. A major realignment of 100 km between Holle and Monte Belo was started in late 1976 but subsequently delayed during 1977 by an attack on a tunnel construction site by exiled dissidents from across the border with Cabinda. The attack put the Frs CFA 33 000 million project in danger of abandonment when the Franco-Italian consortium carrying out the work demanded financial compensation and military protection.

TRAFFIC	1973	1974	1975
		(First 10 months)	
Passenger journeys	1 103 200	1 315 600	1 608 000
Passenger-km	144 600 000	166 315 600	222 868 000
Tons carried	1 516 700	1 477 000	1 592 861
Ton km	438 000 000	440 900 000	445 350 000

FINANCES
During 1976 revenues totalled Frs CFA 589 566 000 million compared with Frs CFA 511 800 000 in 1974. Expenses in 1975 totalled 4 743 million.

MOTIVE POWER AND ROLLING STOCK
CFCO's traction park in 1976 included 41 diesel locomotives, 30 locotractors and 10 diesel railcars. Rolling stock included 24 coaches, 42 railcar trailers, 82 baggage vans, 1 518 wagons and 176 work vehicles.

STUDIES
Between mileage points 0 and 200 the Congo-Océan Railway consists of a single track line carrying uniform traffic, without any converging lines. There are increasingly signs of traffic saturation due to the developing economies of the region. A recent study was carried out over the route to determine future investment priorities. Pertinent facts are:
Alignment
Curves: 45 per cent of the length of the 110 km bottleneck consists of curves, 15 per cent of the length consists of curves of 100 to 140 m radius;
Gradients: 25 per cent canted in the zone of the principal block sections.
Track
Gauge: 1.067 m;
Ballast: 0.9 m³ per linear metre of track. Ballast uncleaned by renewal since 1930;
Rails: 36 kg/m ordinary welded quality between stations. UIC grade B semi-hard rail on curves (service life: two years on curves of 100 m radius);
Sleepers: 40 kg metal sleepers. Poor condition following repeated derailments. 1 750 sleepers per km of track;
Quality: mediocre. There is distortion of more than 4 mm/m for 5 km of track; 2 per cent of the length is subject to a temporary speed restriction of 20 or 30 km/h;
Speed: limited to 40 km/h for freight traffic and 50 km/h for passenger traffic. Limited to 30 km/h on the principal section;
Derailments: very frequent, 1 for every 200 trains approximately.
Stations
Spacing: average, 9 km; maximum, 13 km;
Usable length: minimum 500 m. 80 per cent of stations have been increased to 750 m following the work carried out in 1974. The principal section between stations of 750 m is 25 km long.
Locomotives
Type: Diesel-electric 1 000 to 3 300 hp with high adhesion. Possibility of multiple units;
Maintenance: high rate of failures during running, with a total number of cases of breakdowns and shortage of power of 200 per million kms.
Wagons
Axle load: 17 and 18 t;
Average load:
—timber traffic: 15 m wagons; 30 t; 22 m wagons: 60 t;
—hydrocarbons traffic: 15 m wagons: 43 t;
—manganese ore: 8.8 m wagons: 46 t;
Type: bogie;
Braking: vacuum, train of maximum 600 m. Can be improved by accelerating valves;
Coupling: Willison automatic. The permitted effort is 115 t for 35 per cent of the stock, and 37 t for 65 per cent of the stock.
Signalling: Electric single line token. Fixed warning signals. Home signals and points operated on the spot and not interlocked.
Regulations: Simultaneous station entry prohibited. The first crossing train is halted outside. The home stop signals are duplicated with manually placed detonators.
Telecommunications: Overhead of medium reliability.
Train control: Centralised.
Traffic:
Timber: 700 000 t/year, with rapidly increasing demand; hydrocarbons: 215 000 t/year; Manganese ore: 2 000 000 t/year, the demand being 2 500 000 t/year; miscellaneous: 550 000 t/year;
Regularity of the traffic demand: good.

COSTA RICA
SOC FERROCARRILES DE COSTA RICA
Apartado 543, San Jose

Telephone: 26-11-53/26-11-86

General Manager: J. Vargas
Auditor: R. Barboza
Railway Division Manager: Stanley Peralta Arias
Secretary: Julieta Casal B.
Chief Engineer: Ing. A. Rodriquez S.
Departmental Heads:
  Maintenance: Ing. C. Voljo
  Electromechanical Design: Ing. Alvaro A. Rodriguez Salazar
  Traffic: M. T. Alvarado
      I. Solano
  Commercial and Public Relations: Juan Bta. Vargas Soto
  Accounts: Alvaro Salas González
  Maintenance of way: A. Cruz
Purchasing Agent: Gilberto Rodriguez Villalobos
Electric Plant Officer: Alberto Gómez Lobo
Master Mechanic: Humberto Zapparolli Arroyo

Gauge: 1.067 m
Route length: 116 km—running from the port of Puntarenas inland to San José with a branch from Ciruelas to Alajuela.

The country's two principal railways, the National Atlantic and the Pacific were merged under the title of Ferrocarriles de Costa Rica in 1977. A total of 500 million Colons has been allocated for modernisation and extension of the Pacific's electrified network.

TRAFFIC
In 1976, freight traffic on the Pacific Railway totalled 393 905 tonnes. A total of 967 781 passenger journeys were recorded. The National Railway carried 1 234 822 tonnes of freight in 1976 and 1 177 771 passengers.

FINANCES
Total revenue on the Pacific Railway in 1976 was Colons 22 333 503. Income on the National Railway was Colons 89 250 851.

MOTIVE POWER
Fde CR purchased in 1977 all locomotives and rolling stock of the defunct Central Newfoundland Railway.
Most recent new purchases of locomotives was made with Faur of Romania for a total of four 1 000-hp diesel hydraulic locomotives. There are now proposals for locomotive purchases during 1975 or 1976.

Number of electric locomotives:	14
Number of diesel locomotives:	77
Number of railcars:	57
Number of passenger coaches:	108
Number of freight wagons:	1 716

ROLLING STOCK
In an attempt to solve the problem of wagon shortages, the Costa Rican Government was negotiating with the Agency for International Development in 1977 for financing for 50 covered wagons, 25 flat wagons and 25 dump wagons.

ELECTRIFICATION
A total of 127 km of track on the former Pacific Railway are electrified. Tenders were called in July 1977 for equipment to electrify the San Jose—Paraiso line. Tenders for electrification of the Puntarenas—Colorado de Abangares line were also expected to be announced during late-1977. Meanwhile the railway was negotiating terms for a new 52 km electrified line between Puntarenas and a cement factory at Colorado de Abangares.

PROPOSALS
F de CR called for tenders in 1977 for upgrading the 106 km line between Limon and Rio Frio.
A project is under study for total modernisation of the railway based on studies carried out by Firm Electroproyectos of Brazil. Construction of a 50 km branch line to serve a new cement factory at Colorado de Abangares has been proposed. Production of the plant will total 1 500 tons daily.
A new 4-km branch line is to be built to serve the new port of Calders now under construction and due for completion by 1976/77.
It was announced in March 1975 that an Arab bank is to provide a loan of $US million for the development of the railways in Costa Rica and construction of sugar mills.

COMPANIA BANANERA DE COSTA RICA
(Ferrocarril del Sur)
Golfito

Gauge: 1.067 m.
Route length: 317 km.

President and Chief Executive: W. W. Booth
General Manager: V. C. Heyl
General Passenger Agent: R. Ortega

CZECHOSLOVAKIA

CZECHOSLOVAK STATE RAILWAYS

Ceskoslovenské Státni Dráhy (CSD), Prague 1

Ministry of Transport
110 05 Prahal, Na prikope 33

Telephone: 2122
Telex: 121096 Domi C
Telegrams: DOMINI PRAHA

Minister of Transport: Ing V. Blazek
First Vice-Minister: Ing J. Lajciak
Vice-Ministers: Ing L. Blazek
    Ing J. Filinsky
    K. Kapr
    J. Dykast
Department Directors:
Finance: Ing Z. Slezak
International: Ing R. Schrötter
Personnel: K. Vajc
Movement and Traffic: Ing F. Kotora
Traction: Ing V. Farbula
Track: Ing J. Simůnek
Telecommunications and signalling: R. Farbula
Material: Ing J. Hlavác
Research: Ing Z. Holub
Public Relations: M. Kozák

		Totals
Railway route length,	miles	8 153
	km	13 186
Electrified route length,	miles	1 682
	km	2 174
Number of personnel		185 508
Length of State roads,	miles	45 303
	km	72 908

The change-over from steam to electric and diesel traction is proceeding rapidly and by 1975 steam accounted for less than 2 per cent, compared with 11 per cent of the total in 1973 and 96.9 per cent in 1950. Electrification is scheduled for 795 miles *(1 280 km)* of 25 000 V ac and 1 243 miles *(1 840 km)* of 3 000 V dc, a total of 2 038 miles *(3 280 km)* which is 25 per cent of the present route length.

HISTORY

The Czechoslovak railway transport has a very long tradition. 150 years ago (in 1825) the construction of the first railway line was started from Ceské Budejovice to Linz in Austria. 130 years ago (in 1845) the first railway station (today Praha Stred) was built and in the same year the first steam driven train arrived in Prague from Vienna via Olomouc. At the end of the nineteenth century the railway net of Bohemia, Moravia and Slovakia had about the same extent as today.

A lot has been achieved by Czechoslovak railwaymen since the end of the war. Approximately 50 per cent of the railway network was damaged and the rest was not properly maintained during the 6 years of occupation.
More than half of the locomotion means was destroyed or carried away by the occupants and the remainder was in a bad state. A similar situation existed as regards freight and passenger trains.

RAILWAY ORGANISATION

Overall responsibility for all forms of transport throughout the country—railways, road, urban, waterways, internal airlines—is vested in the Ministry of Transport.
The CSD system is divided into four administrative regions each of which is largely autonomous being responsible for traffic and for management and control of all

installations and equipment in its area:—

Name of Railway	Headquarters
Eastern	Bratislava
Midland	Olomouc
North-Eastern	Prague
South-Western	Pilsen

During the last 20 years the Czechoslovak railways have been in a state of technical reconstruction including the construction and reconstruction of railway stations and border stations as well as the reconstruction of important railway junctions (Praha, Brno, Bratislava).
During 20 years the Czechoslovak state invested more than 75 milliards of Ksc in the development of the railway traffic (including the planned expenses for the current year).
Basically the principle is followed to ensure a sufficient capacity and quality of railway transport for inland and foreign carriers including the increased transit service.

TRAFFIC

Czechoslovakia's national economic plan anticipates relatively small annual increases in freight traffic volume for the remainder of the 1970s. In 1973, for instance, CSD carried a volume of 258 500 000—only 2.5 million tons more than in 1972, a modest rise of less than one per cent. For most of the past decade, freight volume has increased by about 6 per cent a year.

	1976
Freight tonne-km	64 335 000 000
Passenger-km	17 908 000 000

TRACK WORK

In order to meet the demands of the increasing freight traffic and the heavier and faster trains being put into service, a programme of track strengthening and additional track laying is in hand.

SIGNALLING AND TRAIN CONTROL INSTALLATIONS

Automatic block system is installed on 524 miles *(843 km)* of line. Automatic train warning/stop system is in service on 258 miles *(415 km)* of line with cab signalling apparatus on about 715 locomotives. Remote control of switch points and signals by all-relay installations in operation at 45 major centres.
A contract was signed in 1977 with the Soviet Union for delivery of new signalling installations including a central control desk at the Bratislava railway centre and a central control panel for the Bratislava—Sturovo and Bratislava—Brelav lines.

ELECTRIFICATION

Considerable extension of the ac system is scheduled for the next few years. By 1975 the position was:—

	miles	km
3 000 V dc	1 243	31 840
25 000 V ac	795	1 280
	2 038	3 120

The increase in ore traffic has necessitated the electrification of the Vrutky-Cierna to Tisou line, which connects with the USSR railway network at Cop. A new broad gauge line, 55 miles *(88 km)*, was opened from Uzhgorod (USSR) to the VSZ iron works near Barca in Czechoslovakia.
Main electrification work underway in 1977 was continuation of the Haniska—Soviet border conversion project. For the past ten years the line has carried iron ore from the Soviet Union to the East Slovak Iron and Steel Works. CSD officers estimate that electric locomotives will haul 4 200 tonne gross trains, compared with existing 3 200 tonne trainloads now hauled by diesel stock.

CONTAINERS

CSD aims to invest heavily in containers, wagons and terminals during the next 12 years. With preliminary planning about completed, the first major works are being carried out. Containerisation is planned in three overlapping stages— 1973-78, 1976-82 and 1980-85. Construction of 21 terminals by 1985 will cost 19 000 million crowns (at present values). CSD spent 6 000 million crowns by 1976 on equipment—containers, cranes, and other terminals machinery, and special container wagons. Containers will carry about 30 per cent of total freight volume. Savings could average about 100 crowns a ton.

E669 electric locomotive shown hauling freight over the CSD 3 000V dc line along the foot of the High Tatras. The locomotive has a top speed of 90 km/h and output of 3 000 kW.

CUBA
CUBAN NATIONAL RAILWAYS
Ferrocarriles de Cuba
Ave Independencia y Tulipan, Havana

Vice-Minister for Railways: Manuel Alepuz Llansana
Director Western Division: Pedro Madruga Bello
Director Central Division: Pablo Figueroa Campos
Director East-Central Division: Alvaro Mentero Pasamonde
Director Eastern Division: Ramón López Vázquez
Director of Locomotives: Julio Fernandez Moreno
Director of Track and Bridges: Otto González Peniché
Director of Track Construction: Emilio Lluveras Martinez
Director of Safety: Michel Deverceaux Czaby
Director of Movements: Manuel Ferradas Acosta

Gauge: 1.435 m
Route length: 5 201.5 km

The Cuban Government is to invest Pesos 650 million in railway modernisation during the present Five-Year Plan (1976-80) under an integrated development programme for railway, highway and maritime transport. Main emphasis for railway improvements will be on renewing the 900-km mainline between Havana and Santiago. Reconstruction of the line began in 1975 and by the end of 1976, 114 km of new rail had been laid and extensive renewal of the railbed carried out. Upgrading on the route is due for completion by 1980 when traffic capacity will be substantially increased and operating speeds increased to 140 km for passenger trains and 100 km/h for freight.
Cuba, the largest island in the West Indies, with an area of 44 210 miles² (114 425 km²) is roughly 780 miles (1 255 km²) long and 55 miles (88 km²) wide, and lies about 100 miles (161 km²) south of Florida. Cuba's economy is mainly based on agriculture, sugar and tobacco being the principal products.
All the public service railways in the country are operated by the FF.CC. Nacionales. The system is being progressively rationalised, uneconomic lines being closed down and replaced by road transport.
At present the tracks are being renewed with USSR rails, wooden bridges are being replaced by concrete ones and some unprofitable branch lines are being closed down and replaced by road transport. For the first time Cuba has introduced an express inter-city service (imported and air-conditioned Pullman restaurant and entertainment cars)

ELECTRIFICATION
Route-km of electrified lines at the end of 1976 totalled 150.1 km.

TRAFFIC
	1975	1976
Freight tonne-km	1 762 800 000	1 847 900 000
Freight tonnes carried	10 862 400	11 277 200
Passenger-km	667 900 000	766 000 000
Passenger journeys	11 216 700	12 610 500

FINANCES
	1975	1976
	(1 000 Pesos)	
Income	61 628.0	66 795.0
Expenses	45 512.3	53 920.0

MOTIVE POWER AND ROLLING STOCK
Orders were placed in 1975 with MLW-Worthington for 20 diesel locomotives valued at $C 10 million. Deliveries were completed in 1976.
Following delivery of first-class coaches and mail vans to Cuban Railways in 1975, Fiat Concord Argentina delivered the first of 100 diesel railcars and trailers, and 20 air-conditioned restaurant cars to Havana in 1976.
Each of the diesel railcars is powered by two Fiat 6-cylinder (in-line) diesel engines developing 280 hp at 2 000 rpm. Engines are mounted between the bogies. For auxiliary circuits a 24 V generator is coupled to the traction motor. Braking is Westinghouse type SM.2 air-brake self-regulated and automatic for multiple-unit operation. Compressors are Marelli type AC.77.A, one for each diesel engine. A cab and control desk is provided at each end of the car. All controls are illuminated by ultra-violet light. Each motor coach is equipped with a bar and small kitchen for snacks. Distance between couplers (for both motor coaches and trailers) is 25 700 mm; between bogie centres 17 800 mm; between rail and roof 4 073.5 mm. Weight of the motor coach is 50 tonnes, of the trailer 42.3 tonnes. The motor coach seats 60 passengers, the trailer 72.
Each of the restaurant coaches is fitted with 25 tables. The service kitchen is provided with two cookers, refrigerator and other equipment. In addition there is a bar section with refrigerator, soft-drinks machine and coffee machine. The cars are fitted with Westinghouse U-type air brakes with an emergency valve in each car. Length between coupler heads is 25 560 mm; distance between bogie centres 18 300 mm; height from railhead to roof 407.3 mm; and width 3 140 mm. Diesel sets and restaurant cars are built of sheet steel treated to prevent corrosion. Bogies are Fiat, with helical spring suspension and hydraulic shock absorbers. Bogie frame is H-type. Automatic couplers are Alliance AAR 10, supplied by Miner Argentina. All cars have taped music with roof-mounted loudspeakers.

Number of locomotives in service:
	1975	1976
Steam	1	—
Electric	12	12
Diesel electric	234	300
Diesel hydraulic	74	74
Number of two-axle railcars:		
Electric	15	15
Diesel	69	65
Diesel trailers	62	62
Number of passenger coaches:	209	
Number of freight wagons:	6 256	6 315

Sugar Railways
The railways serving the sugar plantations and factories total about 6 200 miles (10 000 km) of which some 65 per cent are standard gauge.
The rolling stock on the sugar industry railway is only used during the sugar cane harvest (100 days). Cuba intends to increase its sugar production to 10 million tons in the next few years and modernise the railway network simultaneously, as well as using it for the transport of other agricultural products and minerals.

DENMARK
DANISH STATE RAILWAYS
Danske Statsbaner (DSB), 40 Sølvgade, 1349-Copenhagen K

General Manager: Povl Hjelt
Directors:
Way and Works: K. A. H. Gulstad
Mechanical Engineering: E. Risbjerg Thomsen
Commercial and Transport: E. Rolsted Jensen
Economy: S. A. Jenstrup
Affiliated Concern Activities: S. T. Thomasen

Gauge: 1 435 mm
Total route length: 1 999.1 km
Total track length: 4 640.4 km

ELECTRIFICATION
Total electrified route length on 31 December 1976: 103 km.
Total electrified track length on 31 December 1976: 243 km.
System of electrification: 1 500 V dc
Lines now under electrification: Length 22 km; location Hareskovbanen; completion date September 1977.
Line now under construction:
Length: 10.6 km
Location: Hundige—Solrød
Completion: September 1979
Electrification projected: Length 15 km; location Solrød—Køge, Tåstrup—Høje-Tåstrup; Ballerup—Måløv about 1983.

TRAFFIC
	1973/74	1974/75	1975/76
Total freight ton-km	1 957 651 000	1 765 394 000	1 591 806 000
Total freight tonnage	8 818 000	7 981 000	7 209 000
Total passenger-km	3 307 036 000	3 333 440 000	3 299 664 000
Total passengers carried	108 921 000	106 366 000	99 703 000

FINANCES
	1973/74	1974/75	1975/76
	(Kroner)	(Kroner)	(Kroner)
Revenues	1 445 030 000	1 661 997 000	1 865 752 000
Expenses	2 040 241 000	2 468 357 000	2 689 706 000

MOTIVE POWER AND ROLLING STOCK
Type		Put into service in 1975	Total 1.4.77
	Multicar trains electric		279
MM	7803-7806	4	
MU	8519-8541	23	
	(MM-MU + FS-FU)		
FS	7303-7306	4	
FU	8001-8018	23	
	Passenger train coaches		969
Bno	20 84 788-794	7	
Bn	20 84 827-843	17	
WLABm	75 80 460-461	2	
Bns	29 84 530-544	15	
	Freight train cars		9 098
Hbis	211 5 420-529	109	
Hbis-t	211 5 530-629	100	
Fds	946 0 811-879	69	

	01-04-1976	Line haul	Shunting
MZ-MY- MV-MX	Number of locomotives diesel-electric	150	17
MH	Number of locomotives diesel-hydraulic		120
MO	Number of railcars diesel	94	
MA	Number of multicars train diesel	11	

New type MZ diesel-electric locomotives, of which 150 units went into service in 1975

New MV Dronning Margrethe II rail ferry.

TRACK DETAILS

Standard rail: Flat bottom, 121 to 45.4 lb per yd *(60 to 22.5 kg/m).*

Joints: 4-hole flat or angle fishplates and bolts.

Rail fastenings: The rail is secured to wood sleepers by type RN and to concrete sleepers by type RS double flexible fastenings. In both cases a 4.5 mm thick chevron-grooved rubber pad is inserted between rail and sleeper. In switch points and sharp curves the rail sits on 16 mm steel sole plates on wood sleepers and is secured by "K" type fastenings.

Cross ties (sleepers): Creosoted beech or pine.
6 ft 8 in × 6¼ in × 10¼ in *(2 600 × 160 × 260 mm)* on all main tracks.
6 ft 8 in × 5½ in × 9½ in *(2 600 × 140 × 240 mm)* on branch lines.

Filling: Generally broken stone 1⅛-2¾ in *(30-70 mm).*

Curves: Min. radius varies from 787 to 3 281 ft *(240 to 1 000 m)* = max. curvature of 7.3° to 1.75° except between Aarhus H and Aarhus Ö where min. radius is 328 ft *(100 m)* = max curvature of 17.6°.

Gradients: Max gradients are 0.5%, 0.67%, 1% and 1.25%. Approximately 26% of lines are level.

Gauge widening on sharpest curve: 0.59 in *(15 mm).*

Super-elevation: 6.3 in *(160 mm)* on 902 ft *(275 m)* curve.

Rate of slope of super-elevation: Between 0.083 and 0.25% (1 in 1 200 and 1 in 400).

Max. permitted speed: 87 mph *(140 km/h)*

Max axle loading:
On 45 and 60 kg rail: 20 metric tonne.
On 37 kg rail: 16-18 metric tonne.
On 32 kg rail: 14 metric tonne.

Snow fences: Protection is given each year to 348 miles *(560 km)* of line.

NEW CONSTRUCTION

Work on new lines and line extensions has been going on in the Copenhagen area for some time. The Vallensbaek-Hundige section will be open for traffic by September 1976. Cost will be about 75 million Dkr. A continuation to Koge and the line extensions Tåstrup—Høje Tåstrup and Ballerup—Måløv has been agreed by Parliament with expected completion at 1981. An old single-track line from Ryparken to Farum is being doubled and electrified. Work was started some years ago but delayed by lack of funds. Now a deadline of September 1977 has been set for completion. Total cost of the work is likely to exceed 290 million Dkr. DSB officers are hoping for a Parliamentary decision on the planned Elsinore-Helsingborg tunnel under the Sound. The line would be single-track. There would be a 3-km approach on the Danish side and a similar extension on the Swedish side, with a 4.3-km tunnel. It will be state-financed. Each country would bear the approach costs on its own side, and the cost of the tunnel would be split down the middle. At 1972 prices, total cost was put at 920 million Dkr—with the Danes liable to bear a cost of 450 million Dkr. DSB engineers estimate that preparatory work would take three years, and actual building four to five years.

FERRY SERVICES

		Miles	km
Korsør-Nyborg	rail and car ferries	16	26
Halsskov-Knudshoved	passenger- and car-ferries	12	19
Kalundborg-Århus	passenger- and car-ferries	58	94
Bøjden-Fynshav	passenger- and car-ferries	9	14
Helsingø-Helsingborg (Sweden)	rail- and car-ferries	3	5
København-Malmö (Sweden)	rail- and car-ferries	19	30
Rødby Faerge-Puttgarden (W. Germany)	rail- and car-ferries	12	19
Gedser-Warnemünde (E. Germany)	rail- and car-ferries	30	48
København-Malmö (Sweden)	passenger- and car-ferries	22	36
Dragør-Limhamn	passenger- and car-ferries	11	17

The services are operated by 29 DSB ferries, 1 ship, 4 hydrofoils, and 8 foreign ferries or ships.

REPRESENTATIVE DSB FERRIES

Vessel	Engines max. hp	Routes	Service	Length of rail tracks	Number of Auto-mobiles	Number of Passen-gers
MV Romsø (1973) (5 603 tons, 17 knots)	2 diesel 12 000	Halsskov-Knudshoved	B		440 on 3 decks	1 500
MV Dronning Margrete II (1973) (5 623 tons, 17 knots)	2 diesel 12 000	Korsør-Nyborg	A	320.7 m in 3 tracks		1 500
MV Prins Henrik (1974) (5 623 tons, 17 knots)	4 diesel 11 500	Korsør-Nyborg	A	320.7 m in 3 tracks		1 500
MV Holger Danske (1976) (1 667 tons, 11 knots)	4 diesel 3 200	Helsingør-Helsingborg	A+B	80 m in one track or 70 cars		800

DIESEL LOCOMOTIVES

Class	Axle Arrange-ment	Trans-mission	Rated Power hp	Max. lbs (kg)	Tractive Effort Continuous at lbs (kg)	mph (km/h)	Max. Speed mph (km/h)	Wheel Dia. ins (mm)	Total Weight Tons	Length ft ins (mm)	No. Built	Year first Built	Builders: Mechanical Parts	Engine & Type	Transmission
MZ 1401-1426	Co-Co	Elec.	3 300	66 000 (27 480)	44 000 (20 000)	15 (24)	89 (143)	40 (1 015)	120	68' 3" (20 800)	26	1967	Nydqvist & Holm; Firchs	GM 16-645-E3	A/S Thrige
1427-1446	Co-Co	Elec.	3 900				103 (165)		121-126		20	1972	,,	,,	GM
MX 1001-1045	A1A-A1A	Elec.	1 425	35 300 (16 000)	28 700 (13 000)	13.7 (22)	83 (133)	40 (1 015) and 37½ (950)	89.0	60' 0½" (18 300)	45	1960	Nydqvist & Holm, Frichs	GM-567C and D, 12 cyl.	A/S Thrige, Odense, Denmark
MV 1101-1105	A1A-A1A	Elec.	1 700	39 700 (18 000)	32 000 (14 500)	14.6 (23.5)	83 (133)	40 (1 015)	98.6	62' 0" (18 900)	5	1954	Nydqvist & Holm, Frichs	GM-657B 16 cyl.	GM
MY 1106-1159	A1A-A1A	Elec.	1 950	39 700 (18 000)	35 500 (16 100)	14.6 (23.5)	83 (133)	40 (1 015)	101.6	62' 0" (18 900)	54	1956	Nydqvist & Holm, Frichs	GM-567C 16 cyl.	GM & Thrige
MT 151-157	B-B	Elec.	400	26 500 (12 000)	13 250 (6 000)	7.5 (12)	43 (70)	39⅜ (1 000)	52.1	41' 0" (12 490)	17	1958	A/S Frichs	MTU MB12V 493 AZ 10	A/S TITAN
MH 301-420	C	Hyd.	440	26 900 (12 200) and 29 750 (13 500)	25 800 (11 700)	2.5 (4)	37/18.5 (60/30)	45¼ (1 150)	40.5 and 45.0	31' 0" (9 440)	117	1960	A/S Frichs	MAN 8 cyl.	Voith
MH 201-203	C	Hydr.	440	26 900 (12 200)	25 800 (11 700)	2.5 (4)	37/18.5 (60/30)	45¼ (1 150)	40.5	31' 0" (9 440)	3	1957	Henschel	MAN 8 cyl.	Voith

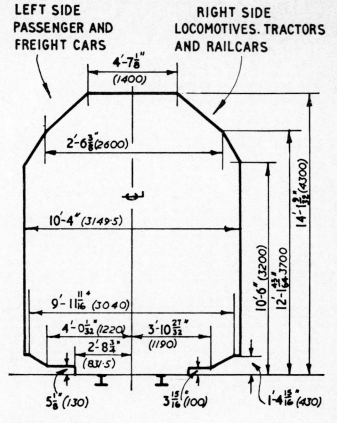

LEFT SIDE PASSENGER AND FREIGHT CARS

RIGHT SIDE LOCOMOTIVES. TRACTORS AND RAILCARS

4'-7⅛" (1400)
2'-6⅜" (2600)
10'-4" (3149·5)
9'-11¹¹⁄₁₆ (3040)
4'-0¹⁄₃₂ (1220)
3'-10²⁷⁄₃₂ (1190)
2'-8¾" (831·5)
5⅛" (130)
3¹⁵⁄₁₆" (100)
1'-4¹⁵⁄₁₆" (430)
14'-1²⁄₃₂ (4300)
10'-6" (3200)
12'-1⁴²⁄₆₄ 3700

DSB load clearance diagram

DSB operates three hydrofoil services for passengers.

MV Danmark (1968) 6 352 tons, 16 knots)	2 diesel 12 000	Rodby Faerge-Puttgarden	A	1 22 ft (342 m) in 3 tracks		1 500
			B		310 on 2 decks	1 500

Notes: A—as train ferry
B—as passenger and car ferry

ECUADOR

STATE RAILWAYS OF ECUADOR
Empresa de los Ferrocarriles del Estado, Bolivar 443, Quito

General Manager: Ing V. Pace Merizalda
Traffic Manager: René Cevallos
Workshop Manager: Ing Luis Barragán
Motive Power Superintendent: Eduardo Alban
Permanent Way Engineer: Ing Jorge Cifuentes
Chief Technical Dept: Ing H. Remache

Gauge: 1.067 m; 0.750 m
Route length: 697 km

The Republic of Ecuador, 106 178 miles^2 in area, is bordered by the Pacific Ocean on the west, Colombia on the north, and Peru on the south and east. There are 3 public service railways including the Ferrocarril Guayaquil-Quito, the Ferrocarril Quito-Ibarra-San Lorenzo and the Ramal Austral Sibambe-Cuenca all owned and operated by the Government, and several industrial railways.
The Quito plateau is about 9 375 ft *(2 867 m)* above sea level. In 49 miles *(79 km)* the F.C. de Guayaquil á Quito climbs 9 650 ft *(2 942 m)*.
The railways comprising the State system are:—

Railway	Gauge	Route length miles	km
F.C. Guayaquil-Quito	3 ft 6 in *(1.067 m)*	281	452
*F.C. Quito-San Lorenzo	,,	232	373
F.C. Sibambe-Azogues	,,	72	116
F.C. Puerto Bolivar-Pasaje	,,	16	25
F.C. Puerto Bolivar-Piedras	2 ft 5½ in *(0.750 m)*	46	75
F.C. Bahia-Chone	,,	50	80
		697	1 121

*The F.C. Quito-San Lorenzo is operated as a separate railway.

The major railway system in Ecuador is laid to 1.067 m (3 ft 6 in) gauge, and is operated by the Empresa de los Ferrocarriles del Estado, whose headquarters are in the capital, Quito.
The principal line, 452 km long, connects Guayaquil, the main port and largest city of the country, with Quito, which lies at some 2 800 m altitude in the Sierra of the Andes. From Duran, the terminus for Guayaquil, the line runs across low lying plains for 87 km to Bucay, at the foot of the western slopes of the Andes. Over the next 79 km the line climbs no less than 2 944 m, an average grade over the whole section of 3.7 per cent (1 in 27). The line contains many sharp curves, and several stretches are laid on a grade of 5.5 per cent (1 in 18), including a double reversing zig-zag which was required to negotiate a particularly awkward mountain outcrop known as the Nariz del Diablo (Devil's Nose). Once the summit of this section is reached at Palmira, 3 238 m in altitude and 166 km from Duràn, the line remains in the high Sierra, never falling below 2 500 m, and rising to 3 609 m at the overall summit of Urbina, 264 km from Duràn.
Riobamba, 230 km from Duràn, is the major intermediate station on the line, and the terminus of the daily mixed train from Duràn. Between Duràn and Bucay, on the coastal section, mixed trains are operated by both steam locomotives and diesels of a fleet of Spanish built Eskalduna Alco type Co-Co general purpose locomotives, which have been introduced in recent years. In addition, there is a supplementary service of small passenger railcars which operate from Duràn to intermediate stations on this section. Beyond Bucay freight is handled mainly by Baldwin built 2-8-0 steam locomotives, the most recent of which date from the 1950s. Trains worked over this steeply graded section have to be split into very short sections, and there is an additional operating problem due to landslides and river flood damage caused during the rainy seasons.
Between Riobamba and Quito there is a diesel hauled service of freight trains, and in addition a service of modern railcars operates three times a week in each direction between Duràn and Quito, taking some 12 hours over the journey.
The two remaining lines of the system are Quito with San Lorenzo, on the northwest coast of Ecuador near the Colombian border; and Sibambe, 131 km from Duràn on the main line, with Cuenca, an important provincial capital in the southern part of the country. The San Lorenzo line is 373 km long and was finally completed, with the aid of French backing, in 1957. Regrettably, San Lorenzo has failed to show the promise as a thriving port that was originally expected of it. Freight services are operated on this line by diesel locomotives, with the Cuenca line small railcars providing a passenger service. The Cuenca line is operated mainly by steam locomotives and small railcars, and is 148 km long.
The Guayaquil to Quito line was built in sections between 1873 and 1908, the major work on the western slopes of the Andes being carried out at the turn of the century. Originally operated by a private company with capital from the United States and England, the railway was taken into State control in 1944. Road competition is keenly flat, particularly between Riobamba and Quito where line is paralleled by the Pan American Highway, and much of the equipment in operation shows signs of considerable age.

MOTIVE POWER AND ROLLING STOCK

Number of locomotives in service (diesel-electric):	13
(steam):	9
Number of railcars in service:	30
Number of passenger coaches:	22
Number of freight wagons:	499

STUDIES
Several studies of the railway system have been carried out by overseas Consultants in recent years, and a French Team was in the country during 1975 making a further report on the economics and viability of the whole system, which is subsidised at present to the order of 50 million Sucres annually, according to the local press.
In 1966 it was announced that the State Railways were to be rehabilitated and 102 million Sucres would be spent during the next six years with authorisation to obtain loans up to 20.2 million Sucres from abroad for railway modernisation. The project, however, was largely abandoned.
The poor condition of rolling stock and of the permanent way, left without renewal during the past twenty years, gives rise to a permanent national problem. To remedy the situation a programme of rehabilitation and reorganisation of the State Railways is long overdue.
Studies have been carried out by Parsons, Brickerhoff, Quade Douglas of USA in 1963 on behalf of the World Bank. These were used as a basis for the development policy adopted in the Plan of Development.
Studies by Livesey Henderson of Great Britain on behalf of the Ecuador government in 1964 recommended, as the first step, the rehabilitation of the railway from Guayaquil-Quito-Cuenca, showing that it is essential to maintain rail services on this line in order to assist the commercial, industrial, agricultural, social and cultural development of the country. The closure of this railway would cost the Government more than rehabilitation.
Under Decree No. 180 on Railway Rehabilitation, work should have begun immediately on the modernisation and rehabilitation of the Guayaquil-Quito-Cuenca line. A first allocation of 10 million Sucres was made in 1966 for the Quito-Ibarra-San Lorenzo railway.

EGYPT

EGYPTIAN RAILWAYS
Ramses Square, Cairo

Chairman: Eng. Abd el Moniem Hashmat Gado
Deputy Chairmen: Eng. Zoul Hemma el Sharkaway
Eng. Mohmoud Adel Bahget
Heads of Departments:
Finance: Hassan Louty El-Boureiny
Administration: Eng. Abu El-Ela Gaballa
Fixed structures: Eng. Mohammed Anwar Yousef
Central Region: Eng. Aly Hassein Abboud
Planning: Eng. Mohammed Refaat Shafik
Operations: Eng. Zo El-Hemma
Mechanical and Electrical: Eng. Aly El-Nakib

Gauge: 1.435 m; 0.750 m
Route length: 4 510 km; 347 km

The railways in Egypt are mainly confined to the more fertile area of the Nile Delta, with a line following the course of the Nile southward to Shâllal, just below Assuan.
The Egyptian Republic Railways, which forms the largest system in the country, extends from the Mediterranean down the Nile Valley, serving the Nile Delta, Cairo, Alexandria, Port Said, Ismailia, Suez and connecting at Shâllal, its southernmost point, with the river steamers of Sudan Railways. From El Quantara, on Port Said-Ismailia line, a branch runs east following the coast and connects with Israeli Railways.
The first section was between Alexandria and Cairo, opened to traffic in 1854. Incidentally, this was the first railway in Africa.
The World Bank agreed in 1976 to lend $US 37 million for the foreign exchange costs of financing the second stage of ER's development plan. This will involve the introduction of automatic signalling and other improvements to increase traffic capacity. Minister of Transport and Communications, Abdel-Fateh Abdullah, indicated that the larger part of the loan will be used to replace antiquated equipment.
Plans are in hand for important extensions of the railway, including the 313 mile long line from Shâllal to Wadi Halfa, to connect with the Sudan Railways system.
A new line about 216 *(348 km)* long is being built from Helwan south west to Bahariya Oasis.
During 1977 it was announced that a new line between Qena and Safaga *(560 km)* is to be built for phosphate shipments from Abu Tartour.
Also in 1977 it was announced that a new line is to be built for agricultural traffic between Ifyai el Barud and Alexandria.
After reopening the Ismailia—Port Said line in October 1976, the railway decided in 1977 to build another line from Port Said to the inland town of El Mansoura. About 95 km of track are involved and cost will be £E 26 million.

PLANS
Work was carried out on a Five Year (1972-76) modernisation and development programme which cost about £E137 million:
1. Relaying of about 1 000 km of mainline track with 52 kg/m rail and about 250 km with reconditioned rail;
2. Completion of electric signalling and automatic block installation on several lines: Cairo—Qualyab; Cairo/Kobri—El Leimoun—El Marg—Gabal El Asfar; Cairo—Giza—Ausim; Qualyab—Benha; Alexandria—Sidi Gaber.
3. Installation of CTC on the Sohag (near Baliana)—Nag Hammadi (north of Luxor) section;
4. Purchase of 45 diesel locomotives rated at 2 200 hp; 25 rated at 1 000 hp; 25 rated at 400 hp; 25 electric railcar sets; and about 750 passenger coaches;
5. Installation of air brakes on about 1 000 freight wagons;
6. Modernisation of marshalling yards and remodelling of several station facilities and yards;
7. Reconstruction of ER's passenger coach repair shop at Bulaq and the freight wagon repair shop at Gabal El Zeitoum; modernisation of the main locomotive workshop at Bulaq; reconstruction and improvement of running sheds for passenger coaches at Abu Ghatis and rail cars at Korbi-El Leimoun and construction of a new running shed for diesel trains at El Fatz;

Henschel-built 2 510 hp diesel locomotive in ER livery.

8.   Purchase of road vehicles; reorganisation of stores and facilities and augmentation of stocks of essential stores, including spares; improvement of electric power supplies on the Helwan electrified line; new training centre facilities; training abroad of key personnel; and employment of consultants for introducing modern accounting techniques.

The World Bank has agreed to lend $37 million for the foreign exchange costs of financing the second stage of the railway development plan. This involves the introduction of automated signalling and other improvements to increase traffic capacity. Minister of Transport & Communications Abdel-Fateh Abdullah indicated that the larger part of the loan will be used in replacing antiquated equipment.

TRAFFIC
There was a sudden drop in ER's freight traffic in 1973/74, caused mainly by increased importation of highway trucks. Most of the traffic taken by the truckers consisted of less-than-carload short-haul traffic. ER still has a lot of less-than-carload traffic—about 30 per cent of total traffic. Long-haul traffic still belonged, basically, to the railways. Last year it increased by about 6 per cent. About 1.8 million tons of ore is scheduled for shipment from the new ore mine at Bahariya Oasis, and this is to increase within a year or two to 3.4 million tons—about 25 per cent of ER's existing traffic.

FINANCES	1972	1975
	££ (000)	
Income	52 562.9	49 736.7
Expenses	54 345.2	44 369.4

MOTIVE POWER
Shortage of modern motive power was partially solved in 1973 by a series of 2 200 hp diesels from General Motors (type G 26 CW).

Credits from the Soviet Union also made possible purchase of 23 diesels rated at 2 600 hp in 1975. Built at the Voroshilovgrad locomotive works, the Soviet locomotives (type TE 114) were specially developed for operation in hot climates.

Hungary is to supply $14 million for the purchase of four six-coach diesel express trains, which are to be built by Ganz-Mavag of Hungary. The money is part of a $25 million loan Hungary has agreed to extend to Egypt. It has a 5 per cent coupon and is repayable over 5 to 10 years.

Number of locomotives (diesel-electric):	434
Number of locomotives (steam):	39
Number of locomotives (electric):	50

ROLLING STOCK
A lot of equipment has reached Egypt from the GDR in recent years, and more may already be on the way. In 1974 Waggonbau Bautzen supplied 125 third-class coaches and 45 second-class. During 1977 ER took delivery of 110 air-conditioned passenger coaches built by East German suppliers. Freight equipment has also been imported from the German Democratic Republic, particularly from Waggonbau Niesky. Now Egypt's own SEMAF plant, at Helwan, is able to supply most of ER's needs—though braking equipment has been delivered in quantity to SEMAF from VEB Berliner Bremsenwerk in the GDR.

Five West European nations were chasing a possible contract to supply passenger coaches to Egyptian Republic Railways in 1977. The new rolling stock is urgently required to up-grade sleeping car and catering facilities for tourists, particularly on the Cairo-Luxor line. It has been suggested that a joint stock company to manufacture the new rolling stock is to be established by Egyptian Republic Railways and the successful foreign supplier. The precise form of such a scheme has not been made public. The countries involved are France, West Germany, Italy, Switzerland and Britain.

Number of passenger coaches: 1 362
Number of freight wagons: 17 717

ELECTRIFICATION
Total length of electrified line is 25 km.

SIGNALLING
Signal projects: Improvements to signalling, particularly on lines to and from Cairo, are considered vitally important if increased traffic is to be kept moving. One project—between Cairo and Qualyub—was completed in 1973. Another—from Cairo to Giza—is in progress. Installation of electric signalling on the Cairo-Qualyub section was carried out by VEB Werk für Signal- und Sicherungstechnik Berlin (WSSB). Introduction of automatic block has made it possible to operate at three-minute intervals. And by making effective use of all aspects of the installation, says the supplier, train intervals could be cut to one minute in peak hours. Capacity of the line has been increased from 260 to 400 trains a day, all with increased speeds. Automatic level crossings are controlled from the trains. Every main signal and level crossing has its own direct telephone connection with the main signalbox.

The work now being carried out, by L. M. Ericsson (Sweden), covers two main sections: Cairo to Giza-Ausim (25 km) and Kobri El Leimoun to El Gabal El Asfar (30 km). Installations include relay interlocking, etc, train describer, train graph and telephone systems. Both sections are heavily used suburban lines.

TRACK WORK
New construction: ER has a big programme of track improvements in hand. Track relaying has been going on for some years, with 52 kg/m rails replacing old 47 kg/m rails. An average of 250 km is changed each year, though in 1973, because of the October war, only 208 km was replaced. Where timber sleepers need renewal, they are being exchanged for concrete. At the beginning of this year about 285 km of track had been laid with concrete sleepers, 1 552 km was with steel sleepers and 2 235 km with timber sleepers.

Work is preceeding on the construction of the 216 mile *(340 km)* Helwan Bahariya Oasis line.

An agreement was signed in Cairo early in 1975 between the Egyptian and Sudanese Governments, for the construction of a new railway line between Egypt and the Sudan although work is still to be put in hand. A joint Sudanese/Egyptian team, however, completed surveys in 1977 in the border area of the proposed 410 km Wadi Halfa—Aswan link.

Welded rail: Total length of track with welded rail is 792 km, of which 56 km was laid in 1975. The longest individual length of continuous welded rail is 1.0 mile *(1.6 km)*. Standard rail used weighs 105 lb per yard *(52 kg/m)* in 59 ft *(18 m)* lengths. Prefabricated track panels are carried to site, the rail joints being Thermit welded in position.

Three types of fastening are used with *52 kg* rail:
(a) to steel sleepers with standard clips and bolts;
(b) to concrete sleepers with resilient clips and bolts;
(c) to concrete sleepers with rigid clips and screw spikes.

For the future, it is intended to extend the use of welded rail, using resilient fastenings on both wood, steel and concrete sleepers.

Suburban train in foreground on line between Cairo and Helwan. Freight train behind is hauling rubble to new line construction site at Shallal.

EL SALVADOR

EL SALVADOR NATIONAL RAILWAYS
(Ferrocarriles Nacionales de El Salvador—FENADESAL)
Final Avenida Peralta, Contiguo Colegio Don Bosco, San Salvador

President: L. A. Ruiz
General Manager: J. A. Nunez
Director Operations: F. J. Zepeda
Director Planning: H. R. Paz
Chief Transportation: U. Escobar
Chief Traffic: A. Escoto
Chief Equipment: R. Fratti
Chief Maintenance of Way: S. Huids

Gauge: 0.914 m
Route length: 602 km

Ferrocarriles Nacionales de El Salvador (FENADESAL) was formed from two railways which were formerly the property of overseas companies: The Salvador Railway, which passed to the state on October 11, 1965 under the name of Ferrocarril de El Salvador (FES); and the International Railway of Central America—a railway undertaking which includes the railway system and port at Cutuco—which was nationalised on October 3, 1974 under the name of Ferrocarril Nacional de El Salvador (FENASAL). The two undertakings were merged under state control on May 22, 1975, and renamed Ferrocarriles Nacionales de El Salvador.
Between January and December 1974, freight traffic carried by FES totalled 58 435 tons (4 614 422 ton-km). Passenger traffic totalled 695 397 journeys and 14 962 882 passenger-km. Operating revenue was 707 770 Colon and expenses 1 931 951 Colons—leaving a deficit of 1 224 180 Colons covered by subsidies from the government. During the same period, FENASAL carried 433 144 tons of freight, earning revenue of 6 138 127 Colons, and 1 232 014 passengers, earning revenue of 682 105 Colons. Total receipts (including miscellaneous revenue) were 7 285 380, and operating expenses 9 205 265—resulting in a loss of 1 919 884 Colons.
Following full nationalisation of the railways of El Salvador, officers of the newly-formed Ferrocarriles Nacionales de El Salvador (FENADESAL) drew up plans for cutting operating costs and modernising the 620 route-km system. Immediate moves to cut operating costs included reduction of the pay-roll in December 1974 by 112 employees, bringing the total number of staff working on the railways to 1928. Next in the pipeline is a plan to replace the existing 53 steam locomotives with a smaller diesel-electric locomotive fleet—although it is intended to retain some steam on lines popular with tourists. "This will help cut our costs considerably." said Juan Augustin Nunez Barillas, FENADESAL General Manager.
Under the 1975/76 investment programme the railway hoped to spend about one-million Colons on new locomotives, approximately 1.8 million Colons on freight stock, and 900 000 Colons on passenger coaches.
Biggest investment under the year's programme was for track equipment: 2.3 million Colons on new 32.2 kg/m and 35 kg/m rails; 565 000 Colons on sleepers; 240 000 Colons on ballast; 1.6 million Colons on rail accessories; and 75 000 Colons on new switches.

FINANCES
	1975
Revenue	8 268 300
Expenses	9 967 600
Deficit	1 699 300

TRAFFIC
Total freight traffic moved by the railways in 1974 was 432 113 tonnes. Passenger traffic totals were: Passenger journeys 1 628 493.

MOTIVE POWER AND ROLLING STOCK
Number of diesel-electric locomotives:	20
Number of diesel railcars:	5
Number of passenger coaches:	59
Number of freight wagons:	634

LINE DEVELOPMENT
The track of the railways (FES and FENASAL) has a gauge of 0.914 m and a length of 602 km, distributed in three districts:
District No. 1 which comprises San Salvador (Capital of the Republic) to the port of Cutuco, Department of La Union, (East Zone of the country) (252 km).
District No. 2 which runs from San Salvador to the frontier of El Salvador with Guatemala (West Zone) comprising 146 km and a Texis Juntion branch to Ahuachapan, in the West of the country with 60 km.
District No. 3 which leaves from San Salvador to the port of Acajutla, on the Pacific Ocean, comprising 104 km, and a branch from Sitio del Nino to Santa Ana in the west of the Republic with 40 km.
At present, renovation of the principal line on District 3 is under way, where mainly rails of 44 and 54 lb/yd are laid.
Rails of 65 and 70 lb/yd are now being relaid for future diesel operations. Complete renovation of 67 km is planned for which orders are being programmed for rails and accessories.

ETHIOPIA

DJIBOUTI-ADDIS ABABA RAILWAY
Compagnie du Chemin de Fer Franco-Ethiopian de Djibouti a Addis-Ababa
PO Box 1051, Addis-Ababa

Director General: M. Bekele Geleta
Assistant Director General: Ato Guerma Weldeyes
Technical Director: M. Max Rosso
Chief of Material and Traction Division: M. Wolde Guiorguis Assefa
Chief of Track Division: Ato Techome Wolde Guiorguis
Chief of Commercial Transport Division: M. Tchiane Tamerou
Chief of Financial Division: Mme Frehiwet Asrat
Chief of Administrative Division: M. Engueda Guebre Medhin
Chief of Planning and Research Division: M. Yohannes Kassa
Chief of Stores and Supplies Division: Ato Selechi Chifferaou

Gauge: 1.00 m.
Route length: 781 km.

There are two separate railways:—the larger is the metre gauge CFE Railway running from the port of Djibouti in the French Territory of Affars and Issas (TFAI) to Addis-Ababa, a route length of 485 miles (781 km) of which 62 miles (100 km) is in TFAI; the other is the 3 ft 1⅜ in (0.95 m) gauge Northern Ethiopia Railway, 191 miles (306 km) long running from the Red Sea port of Massawa inland to Agordat.

FINANCIAL
	1969/70	1970/71	1971/72	1972/73	1973/74	1975/76
					Thousands of Birr	
Revenue	15 614	17 416	16 704	17 209	21 406	25 298.3
Expenses	12 731	14 064	14 807	15 861	22 970	20 978.6

TRAFFIC
	1972/73	1973/74	1974/75	1975/76
Total freight ton-km ('000)	223 217	243 611	243 697	260 075
Total freight tonnage ('000)	405	444	453	470.6
Total passenger-km ('000)	78 733	95 164	107 681	131 955
Total passenger journeys ('000)	367	502.9	613.3	770.5

DIESEL LOCOMOTIVES
No. of units	Type	Builder year	Engine type	Rated Power CV	Trans- mission	Total weight Tonnes	Max speed mph (km/h)
9	Bo-Bo	SLM 1950/51	SLM 6VO25	580	Elec	48	43 (70)
6	Bo-Bo	Alsthom 1955	MGO V12SHR	675	Elec	48	43 (70)
3	Bo-Bo	Alsthom 1963	MGO V12BSHR	840	Elec	50	43 (70)
2	Co-Co	Alsthom 1965	Pielstick 16PA4	1 850	Elec	78	37 (60)
2	Co-Co	Alsthom 1968	Pielstick 16PA4	1 850	Elec	78	56 (90)
6	C	Coferna 1955	Poyand 6PX1	180	Hyd	26	16 (25)
4	C	Billard 1955	Poyaud 6VPX1	205	Hyd	33	19 (30)
4	Bo-Bo	Alsthom 1973		1 200	Elec	52	50 (70)

These railcars, hauling three light weight trailer cars, are in service on the 294 mile (473 km) route between Dire Daoua and Addis Ababa.

Rolling Stock
Number of passenger coaches	56
Number of freight wagons	872

TRACK WORK
Improved methods of maintenance are being adopted. Track rebuilding and strengthening is proceeding.
Rail type	20 kg, 25 kg, 30 kg
Sleepers	Metalbloc
Fastenings	Clips and bolts

Rail Laying: On average, depending on Planning and Investment programmes, 17 miles (13 km) of track is relaid with 60.5 lb/yd (30 kg/m) rail per year.

Welded rail: About 160 miles (200 km) of Thermit welded track has been laid, of which 10 miles (16 km) was laid in 1972/73. The longest continuous length is 5.40 miles (8 687 m). Rail used weighs 60.5 lb per yd (30 kg/m) in bars 49 ft 3 in (15 m) long, Rail is laid on steel sleepers 5 ft 11 in (1 800 mm) long, secured by clips.

INVESTMENTS
Capital expenditure in 1975/76 totalled Birr 1 231 589 with expenditure divided as follows: 4 diesel-electric mainline locomotives (Birr 417 425 part payment of Birr 3.02 million); 2 passenger coaches (Birr 341 564 part payment of Birr 735 000); 3 railcars (Birr 86 004 part payment of Birr 2 650 000); 50 freight wagons (Birr 172 253 part payment of Birr 1 550 000); 100 bogies (Birr 110 086 part payment of Birr 710 000); miscellaneous (Birr 104,257).

FINLAND
FINNISH STATE RAILWAYS
Valtionrautatiet (VR), Helsinki

Director General: Paul Paavela
Director in Chief and Director of Traffic: Herbert Römer
Technical Director in Chief: Eero Lamminpää
Director of Adminstration: Eero Jaakkola
Director of Economy: Panu Haapala
Director of Way & Works: Pertti Lattunen
Director of Rolling Stock: Jaakko Toivanen
Director of Purchases and Stores: Pentti Ohtonen

Gauge: 1.524 m
Route length: 6 010 km

The year 1976 proved capricious for the operation of the Finnish State Railways. After a slow start in the early part of the year, there followed a marked recovery in spring and in summer. However, the targets set were not reached, as the transport figures dropped again towards the end of the year. It can, however, be noted with satisfaction that the traffic volume of the previous year was exceeded and the deficit too could be somewhat reduced.

A positive achievement was the completion of certain major projects. The construction of the Kostamus mine line was a real challenge for the builders because of the difficult topographical conditions and the tight work schedule. Successful performance of the work presupposed unprejudiced use of modern technology and building methods. The opening of the new line to regular traffic depends on the outcome of the negotiations on the Kostamus project between Finland and the USSR. The reorganisation of part-load traffic is a step towards reassessment of traffic operation. The development of a terminal network and the implementation of tariff reforms create the preconditions for improving the low profitability of part-load traffic. The implementation of the cost responsibility principle, recommended by the Parliamentary Traffic Committee, will involve price adjustments, at times considerable. The aim of the reform, which will be carried through stepwise is to improve the quality of service—to increase transport speed and transport reliability—in a way that the new tariff policy will prove justified and legitimate.

In the field of personnel policy, the launching of the management-by-objectives project was a new step forward. By means of the MBO system, the aim is to improve cooperation and interaction in all sectors and at all levels of the railway administration. By setting a target for work, work becomes meaningful and provides a channel for one's creativeness and spirit of enterprise.

THE NETWORK
The railway network was shaped for a large part in the last century, when the railways were the most important form of transport in long-distance traffic. Only a few lines have been built since the Second World War, during the period of rapid changes in the economy and the social structure of the country. In the last few decades, the railway network has been considerably improved, so that traffic with 20-ton axle loads is now permissible almost on the whole of it. The maximum admissible speed for passenger trains is 120 km/h and the average speed approx. 80 km/h.

With the population concentrating in large centres, the number of railway stations in the thinly populated areas has diminished in recent years and various operations connected with traffic are being centred at the larger stations. For that reason, the main purpose in improving the railway network in recent years has been to renew the present system and to complete it with new lines, creating fast connections between large population centres and improving mass transport around them.

TRAFFIC
Goods Traffic: The development of goods traffic was variable in 1976. During the first months of the year, the volume of transport was 10 per cent smaller than the year before. The summer and the beginning of the autumn were a period of marked recovery: industrial production began to rise after a recession of more than a year, and with this rise the volume of railway goods traffic increased by 15 per cent. In the last months of the year, the growth of industrial production slackened. Besides, railway traffic was stopped for six days in November because of a strike. For these reasons, goods traffic increased by only about 5 per cent in the last four months of the year.

International Goods Exchange Traffic: Railway exchange traffic with the USSR runs via Vainikkala, Niirala and Imatrankoski railway operating points. Of them, Vainikkala is by far the most important. Most export and import traffic went through it, the total volume being somewhat over 4.5 million tons. The volume of transport via Niirala in 1975 for the first time exceeded the one-million-ton limit.

Transit traffic from the USSR via Finland to Western Europe grew vigorously. In 1976, the volume of transit transport amounted to 70 000 tons, in 1976, however, to as much as 490 000 tons. The main transit goods were various chemical products, natural petrol and ammonia.

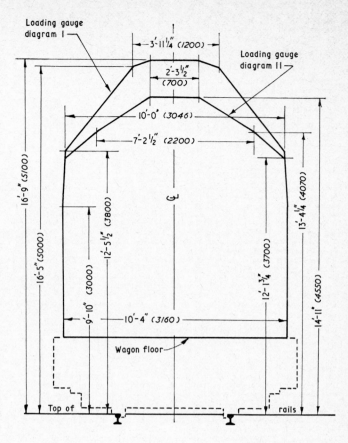

Newly completed line from Kontiomäki to Vartius

DIESEL LOCOMOTIVES

Class	Axle Arrange- ment	Trans- mission	Rated Power hp	Max. lbs (kg)	Tractive Effort Continuous at lbs (kg)	mph (km/h)	Max. Speed mph (km/h)	Wheel Dia. ins (mm)	Total Weight Tons	Length ft ins (mm)	No. Built	Year first Built	Builders: Mechanical Parts	Engine & Type	Transmission
Dr 12	Co-Co	Elec.	1 900	28 000	12 800	30	120	1 180	121.8	18 560	42	1959- 1963	Lokomo Oy, Valmet Oy	Tampella-MAN V8V 22/30 m.A.u.L.	Strömberg-BBC
Dr 13	Co-Co	Elec.	2 800	28 300	19 400	30	140	950	98.1	18 576	52	1962- 1966	Alsthom, Kokomo Oy, Valmet Oy under licence by Alsthom	Tampella-MGO V 16 BSHR (two engines)	Strömberg- Alsthom
Dv 12	B-B	Hydr	1 360	17 000	12 600	20	125	1 000	60.8	14 000	68	1964- 1966	Lokomo Oy, Valmet Oy	Tampella-MGO V 16 BSHR	Voith L 216 rs
Dv 12	B-B	Hydr	1 360	17 000	12 000	20	125	1 000	64.0	14 000	91	1974- 1975	Valmet Oy	Tampella-MGO V 16 BSHR	Voith L 216 rs
Dr 12	B-B	Hydr	1 360	18 700	12 600	20	125	1 000	65.6	14 000	42	1965- 1968, 1971- 1972	Lokomo Oy, Valmet Oy	Tampella-MGO V 16 BSHR	Voith L 216 rs
Dv 15	D	Hyd.	840	18 800	14 300	10	75	1 180	60.0	11 930	58	1958- 1961	Lokomo Oy, Valmet Oy	Tampella-MAN W8V 22/30 AmA	Voith L 217 U
Dv 16	D	Hyd.	950	18 800	14 850	10	85	1 270	60.0	11 930	28	1962- 1963	Lokomo Oy, Valmet Oy	Tampella-MAN W8V 22/30 AmAuL	Voith L 217 U
Dv 11	D	Hyd./ Mec.	840	16 500	12 000	10	75	1 180	56.0	11 930	16	1958- 1959	Lokomo Oy, Valmet Oy	Tampella-MAN W8V 22/30 AmA	Tampella-SRM D S 1,2
Dr 14	B-B	Hyd.	1 190	24 100	21 900	5	75	1 050	86.0	14 000	24	1969- 1972	Lokomo Oy	Tampella-MAN R8V 22/30 ATL	Voith L 206 rsb

Passenger Traffic: The growth of railway passenger traffic continued in 1976. The growth resulted, however, entirely from the increase in the number of journeys in the Helsinki commuter traffic area. On the other hand, Inter-City passenger traffic slightly decreased from 1975, due to the recession.

Because of the vigorous growth of the number of short journeys and the decrease in the number of long-distance journeys, the number of passenger-kms did not increase, though nearly 6 per cent more journeys were made in 1976 than the year before. According to preliminary data, the number of journeys amounted in 1976 to about 37.6 million and that of passenger-kms to nearly 3.1 thousand million.

Railway passenger traffic has grown vigorously in the 70s. The increase in demand has largely been a consequence of the improved quality of service.

Passenger traffic by electric railcars began on a trial basis between Helsinki and Tampere at the end of May, when the summer timetable came into force. Traffic is operated by two pairs of trains, departing from each end station in the morning and in the afternoon.

In 1976, 10 034 Inter-Rail cards were sold, which is 52 per cent more than in 1975. A new train announcement sy tem, taken into use in 1977, was built at Helsinki Central Station. The telephone information service operating at Helsinki Central Station was completed by an automatic night service.

FINANCES

Receipts: In 1976, the railway tariffs were raised twice. The aim of the rises was to make the prices correspond better to the cost responsibility principle and to implement thus the recommendation of the Parliamentary Traffic Committee.

From the beginning of 1976, both the railway passenger and goods tariffs were raised by 24 per cent on average. In passenger traffic, the rises varied according to distance and type of ticket from 20 to 40 per cent. As for goods traffic, the transport charges of wagon-load consignment were raised by 21.7 per cent on average. To improve low profitability of express and wagon-load consignments. Tariffs were raised more than on average—by 34 per cent.

The second rise in tariffs took effect as from the beginning of October. Passenger tariffs were then raised by 17.4 per cent and part-load tariffs by about 26 per cent. The rise in part-load tariffs was connected with the introduction of a new terminal and tariff system for part-load traffic, in use since 1 October 1976.

In 1976, the receipts amounted to 1 177 million marks, which is 213 million marks—22.1 per cent—more than the year before. Owing to the rises in tariffs, the growth of receipts was faster in 1976 than in 1971—1975, when the receipts grew 14.3 per cent a year on average.

Expenditures: The operating expenditures of the railways totalled 1 529 million marks in 1976, which is 197 million marks—14.8 per cent—more than the previous year. The growth of the expenditures was markedly slower than in the two previous years, when it was about 25 per cent a year.

Cost development varied according to the sector of activity. The material and energy costs grew 5 per cent, owing mainly to the price stop in February-June 1976. Wages and other personnel costs grew most—over 16 per cent. Wages were raised on 1 February by an average of 7 per cent. As the wage increases that had come into force on 1 April and 1 September 1975 also influenced the wage costs in 1976, the wage level in 1976 was 15 per cent higher than in 1975.

The growth of costs was almost entirely due to the rise in the wage and price level. By means of strict saving policy, it was possible to maintain the volume of operation at the level of the previous year. The growth of the size of operation staff, which in 1974 and 1975 was 4 per cent a year, slowed down during the first and second four-month period of the year. In the last months of the year, the size of staff diminished.

Financial Result: When preparing in December 1975 the budget for 1976, it was expected that the traffic would grow 6 per cent, which, together with the 24 per cent rise in tariffs, would have increased the receipts of the railways to 1 224 million marks. Since the economic recovery was slower than predicted, the target was not reached and the receipts grew 47 million marks less than expected.

The estimate of expenditures for 1976 was drawn up assuming that the operating expenditures would grow 16 per cent on average. Owing to the price stop and the strict saving policy, the costs grew less than predicted, which means a saving of 15 million marks compared to the estimate.

The financial result predicted in the budget for 1976 showed a deficit of 320 million marks. As the measures taken to cut down the costs did not fully compensate for the loss of receipts, the final deficit totalled 352 million marks. In 1975, the deficit totalled 368 million marks, so that it was reduced in 1976 by 16 million marks. Before that, a reduction in deficit was last booked in 1972.

INVESTMENTS

In 1976, the investments amounted to 750 million marks. Though less was spent on building new lines than in 1975, it was still considerably more than in 1970—1974. This was due to the building of the Kostamus line, for which about 55 million marks was used in 1976 (in 1975 about 78 million marks). A total of 88 million marks was spent on new lines. 243 million marks was used for renewal of tracks and 71 million marks for electrification of lines.

About 248 million marks was spent in 1976 on rolling stock, of which the largest part was on building new wagons and passenger cars. A total of 12 million marks was invested in traffic control and safety equipment and 29 million marks in buildings. The total of investments rose from 1975 to 1976 only 11 per cent. As the price level of investments rose in 1976 14 per cent, the real value of investments was lower than in 1975.

ROLLING STOCK

Both the size and output of rolling stock increased in 1976. At the end of the year, the railways had the following tractive stock:

Type of locomotive	Number	Output MW
Diesel locomotives	379	411
Electric locomotives	39	121
Diesel railcars	24	18
Electric railcars	72	57
Railbuses	168	22
Light tractive stock	251	37
Total	933	666

In 1976, ten general-purpose diesel-hydraulic locomotives of the Dv 12 series and ten electric railcar sets were ordered from Valmet Oy Lentokonetehdas. The deliveries were to begin in November 1977 at the rate of one unit per month.

In passenger traffic, ten new self-service dining-cars were placed in service, increasing thus the fleet of these cars to twenty. In addition to the six 2nd class compartment coaches already delivered, the Pasila workshop built a further 18 coaches of this type. The prototype of the Fh series was completed at the end of the year. The Fh cars, which are intended for use as guard vans in work and shunting trains, consist of a box mounted on a wagon frame.

At the end of 1976, the number of wagons in commercial traffic totalled 21 778, of which more than half were open wagons.

Type of wagon	Number	Capacity 1 000 tons
Covered wagons	7 514	187
Open wagons	13 177	379
Tank wagons	1 081	51
High-capacity wagons	6	1
Total	21 778	618

Class Dr 12 diesel-electric passenger and freight locomotive

Axle arrangement Co-Co; Transmission electric; Rated power 1 900 hp; Tractive effort Max 28 000 kg; Continuous 12 800 kg at 30 km/h; Maximum speed 120 km/h; Wheel dia. 1 180 mm; Axle load max 20.3 tons; Total weight 121.8 tons; Length 18 560 mm; Number of units in VR service 42; Builders Mechanical parts Lokomo Oy, Valmet Oy, Engine Tampella-MAN (V8V 22/30), Transmission Stromberg-BBC.

Dv 12 all purpose diesel-hydraulic locomotive

Axle arrangement B-B; Rated power 1 360 hp; Max speed 125 km/h; Weight 60.7 tonnes; Length 14 000 mm; Number of units in service 148; Builders Lokomo Oy (64), Valmet Oy (84).

Dr 14 diesel-hydraulic shunting locomotive

Axle arrangement B-B; Rated power 1 190 hp; Max speed 75 km/h; Weight 86 tonnes; Length 14 000 mm; Number of units in service 24; Builder Lokomo Oy.

Class Sr 1 electric passenger and freight locomotive

Axle arrangement Bo-Bo; Transmission electric; Rated power 4 460 hp; 3 100 kW; Max speed 140 km/h; Wheel dia. 1 250 mm; Axle load max 21.5 tons; Total weight 84.0 tons; Length 18 960 mm; Number of units 4 (January 1, 1974); Builders Mechanical parts Novocherkassk Works USSR, Electrical equipment Stromberg; System of electrification 25 kV, 50 Hz. 37 locomotives being built by Novocherkassk Works USSR.

Sm 2 electric multiple unit
Overall length 53 250 mm; Overall width 3 074 mm; Motor output 4 × 155 kW; Loaded weight 77 tonnes; Max speed 120 km/h; Max acceleration 1.2 m/s²; Seating capacity

204; Number of units 1.1.1976 10; Sets on order 30. Principal innovations of the Sm 2 design are aluminium alloy bodies and air suspension. Built since 1975.

At the end of the year, five wagons of a new series for the transport of bulk freight were placed in trial service. The rest of the 50 wagons on order will be completed by next autumn. The manufacture of prototype wagons for the transport of goods in powder form began in 1976. These wagons have been ordered from a private firm, which will build 25 wagons in all, of two different types. The wagons will be unloaded by compressed air.

25 wagons for the transport of peat and woodchippings were ordered from the Pasila workshop. These wagons are due to be completed during 1977. The tight financial situation of the State has made it necessary to reduce the production of new wagons since 1975. In 1976, only 771 wagons were built, as compared to 1 203 in 1975.

STAFF
Oversupply and unemployment continued on the labour market in 1976. As demand for transport services did not essentially increase from the previous year, the need for new staff on the railways was small. By pursuing the strict expense-cutting policy prescribed by the State, the growth of the size of staff, which in 1974 and 1975 was 4 per cent on average, could be stopped. Following the increase in unemployment relief work, the size of investment staff grew by a few hundred persons in 1976. The size of operation staff remained at the level of the previous year.

Staff employed at the end of 1976

Operation	24 232
Investment	5 008
Total	29 240

ELECTRIFICATION
System of electrification is 25 kV 50 Hz. On 31st December 1976 the total route length of electrified lines was 393 km.

Electrified lines	km	completion
Helsinki—Kirkkonummi	38	1969
Helsinki—Kerava	29	1970
Kerava—Riihimäki	42	1972
Riihimäki—Iittala	58	1973
Iittala—Toijala	18	1974
Toijala—Seinäjoki	199	1975
Huopalahti—Martinlaakso	9	1975
Total	393	
Work in progress		
Riihimäki—Kouvola	121	1976
Kouvola—Vainikkala	91	1978
Total	212	
Future electrification		
Luumäki—Imatra	67	1978
Seinäjoki—Oulu	334	1981
Kotka—Pieksämäki	235	1982
Hamina—Inkeroinen	26	1982
Pieksämäki—Iisalmi	174	1983
Imatra—Joensuu	191	1985
Pieksämäki—Jyväskylä—Tampere	234	1985

SIGNAL & TRAIN CONTROL
At the end of 1976 the Finnish State Railways had 115 all-relay interlocking boxes, of which two boxes were installed during that year. (Supplier: Siemens and WSSB). Automatic block signalling is in operation on the following lines:

	km
Pasila—Kirkkonummi	35
Huopalahti—Martinlaakso	9
Helsinki—Tampere	186
Riihimäki—Lappeenranta	206
Kouvola—Pieksämäki	184
Parikkala—Joensuu	130
Lielahti—Seinäjoki	155
Total	905

The two latter lines mentioned above are equipped with axle counters. CTC is in service on the following lines:

Kouvola—Pieksämäki	184
Luumäki—Lappeentanta	27
Parikkala—Joensuu	130
Lielahti—Seinäjoki	155
Huopalahti—Martinlaakso	9
Total	505

CTC is under construction on the following lines:

Helsinki—Oulunkylä	7
Tampere—Lielahti	6
Total	13

Plans for future conversion into CTC:

Helsinki—Kirkkonummi	38
Oulunkylä—Riihimäki	64
Pieksämäki—Kuopio	89
Total	191

These two lines are located in the area of Helsinki.
The central control plant in Helsinki, for the traffic area Helsinki—Oulunkylä was completed in 1975. Tampere, Seinäjoki and Pieksämäki will have similar equipment in the future.
On the line Tampere—Parkano—Seinäjoki, all the necessary interstation connections (including axle counting) as well as the circuits between the stations and the CTC-centre are arranged with radio links. For communication to and from the traction units there is a line radio system.
Line radio systems are in operation on the following main lines:

	km
Helsinki—Kirkkonummi	38
Helsinki—Parkano—Tornio—Kolari	994
Tampere—Haapamäki—Seinäjoki	232
Tampere—Rauma	144
Peipohja—Pori	38
Riihimäki—Kouvola—Parikkala—Joensuu	437
Hamina—Inkeroinen	26
Kotka—Kouvola—Kontiomäki—Oulu	684
Kontiomäki—Vartius	94
Jyväskylä—Pieksämäki	80
Total	2 767

Line radio system under construction:

Haapamäki—Jyväskylä	78
Jyväskylä—Jämsänkoski	53
Total	131

Marshalling yard radio systems comprise altogether 142 relaying base stations and several hundred portable radios. All diesel and electric locomotives are equipped with radio telephones, which are able to use both line radio and marshalling yard radio systems.

AUTOMATIC SEAT RESERVATION
The first stage comprises 24 booking terminals at 14 stations, and it was put into use in February 1975. The second stage shall extend the network to 50 terminals at 35 stations and went into operation in Autumn 1976.
The system is based upon the use of mini and micro computers and it uses different transmission speeds on various lines in VR's telecommunication network.

TRACK WORK 1976

Under construction	km	
Jämsänkoski—Jyväskylä	53	shorter route
Mynttilä—Ristiina	22	industrial line

Completed		
Kontiomäki—Vartius	94	

New self-service restaurant car Designation Rkt

The central control plant in Helsinki, for the traffic area Helsinki—Oulunkylä

Welded rail: At the end of 1976 the total length of track laid with continuous welded rail was 2 098 km of which 204 km were laid during the year. The longest individual section of continuous welded rail is 19 miles *(31 km).*

UIC rail weighing 54.45 kg/m is electric resistance welded in workshops into 492 ft *(150 m)* lengths. After laying at site these are Thermit welded into continuous lengths. Both wood and concrete sleepers are used, the latter being either German prestressed type of Swedish two-piece type.

Rails are secured to wood sleepers by Hey-Back fastenings, and to concrete sleepers by Pandrol fastenings.

Future programme is to lay continuous welded rail at a rate of about 163 miles *(250 km)* of track per year.

FERRY SERVICE

A ferry service is run between Helsinki and Lübeck, Germany, but rail wagons are not carried on this route, which provides an international container service to central and southern Europe.

There is also a train ferry service between Hank, Finland, and Travemünde, Germany, operated by a company Oy Railship Ab. The new route was opened in February 1975. The Hanko—Travemünde route is operated with a three-deck train ferry. For rail transports the company has a number of flat wagons and covered wagons with changeable wheelsets (gauges 1 435 mm and 1 524 mm).

CONTAINERS 1976

The Finnish State Railways (VR) has 40 ISO 20 ft containers, code marked VR 90001-90040.

The railway system has 60 cranes of 20 to 40 tonnes lifting capacity capable of handling containers at various locations. In different parts of the country there are 19 terminals with cranes for handling containers; this is done by gantry cranes and rail trucks at ports. Länsisatama, a port of Helsinki, is equipped with a 40-ton container crane.

The total number of ports capable of handling containers is seven: Helsinki, Hanko, Naantali, Turku, Kotka, Hamina and Mäntyluoto. There are several agents with their own terminals to which foreign containers are delivered.

In 1976 the Finnish State Railways handled about 13 500 containers. Due to recession, the total volume of container traffic is not expected to grow in 1977.

The railway system has four-axled bogie wagons capable of carrying three 20ft containers. The two-axled type of wagon can take either two 20 ft containers or one 40 ft container.

The officer concerned with container traffic is:

Raimo Piirilä, Assistant Traffic Manager,
Marketing Bureau, Finnish State Railways,
Vilhonkatu 13, SF-00100 Helsinki 10

In eastward exchange traffic, the volume of container transport increased by 19 per cent. The sharpest increase occurred in export traffic to Iran. Quite new export countries were India, Sri Lanka, the Philippines, Yugoslavia and Hungary. All import transport came from Japan.

FRANCE

FRENCH NATIONAL RAILWAYS

Société Nationales des Chemins de Fer Français, 88 rue Saint-Lazare, 75436 Paris Cedex 9
Chairman of the Board: Jacques Pelissier
General Manager: Paul Gentil
Assistant General Managers: Jean Dupuy
                                    Louis Lacost
                                    Marc Pieffort
Secretary General: Jean Jacques Burgard
Press Officer: Claude Roche

Personnel Department
Personnel Manager: André Beynet
Assistant Manager: Maurice Grimault

Operations Department
Operating Manager: André Leclerc du Sablon
Assistant Manager: Guy Carenco
  Passenger Operating: Jean Toubeau
  Freight Operating: André Bosc
  Safety: Jean Huet
  Transport Studies: Jean Plantureux
  Traction and Circulation: Robert Vagner

Commercial Goods Department
Director Commercial Goods: Jean Luc Flinois
Assistant Director Commercial Goods: Jean Querleux
Marketing Department: Henris Estournet
Sales Department: Maurice Auroy

Commercial Travel Department
Director of Travel: Jean Ravel
International Fares: Andre Poupazdin
Marketing: Maurice Poinsignon
Traffic: Yves Chenel
Publicity: Roger Bouygues
General Affaires and Personnel Department: Francois Chalot

Rolling Stock and Traction Department
Manager, Rolling Stock and Traction: Jean Bouley
Assistant Manager: Andre Portefaix
  Administration: Rene Perraud
  Traction Equipment Maintenance: Daniel Lebigre
  Rolling Stock Maintenance: Yves Roussier
  Department of Construction: Raymond Garde
  Department of Testing: Pierre Romestain
  Department of Investment: Maurice Gaide
  Laboratories: André Révillon

Way and Works Department
Manager, Way and Works: Jean Alias
Assistant Manager: Andre Prudhomme
  Administration: Robert Flauw
  Maintenance: Maxime Cexus
Track Design and Research: Georges Janin
Signalling: Philippe Roumeguere
Electrical Installations: Rene Delavergne
Works: Andre Guilmard
  Buildings: Robert Humbertjean
  Bridges and Tunnels: Etienne Chambron
  New Lines: Guy Verrier

Supplies and Purchasing Department
Manager, Supplies and Purchasing: Pierre Gauthier
Administration: Henri Soullier
  Purchasing Section No. 1: Maurice Papot
  Purchasing Section No. 2: Yves Segretain
  Purchasing Section No. 3: Pierre Boissel
  Fabrication Control: Maurice Jubin

Legal and Claims Department
Head of Department: Raymond Bronner

Accounts and Finance Department
Chief Accountant and Financial Manager: Pierre Bonneau
Assistant to Chief Accountant and Financial Manager: Jean Bornet

Regional Managers
  Eastern Region: Marcel Tessier
  Northern Region: Pierre Detappe
  Western Region: Pierre Ravenet
  South-Western Region: Charles Vignier
  South-Eastern Region: Etienne Alfassa

Gauge : 1.437 m
Route length: 34 717 km

Several factors have contributed to a renewal of confidence in the future of French National Railways (SNCF): 1) a renewed flow of traffic back to the railway following the falls of 1975 is causing SNCF officers to view the future with optimism; 2) Financing has been guaranteed for the new high-speed passenger line between Paris and the South-east, confirming that government, too, believes in the future of the railway.

Following the record traffics of 1974, freight movements on SNCF during 1975 fell by almost 17.5 per cent to 59 790 million tonne-km (compared with 72 400 million tonne-km in 1974). But in 1976 there was an increase of 7 per cent in total tonne-km with the final figure for the year rising to 63 970 million tonne-km.

There was no fall in passenger traffic during 1975: passenger-km rose from 40 200 million in 1974 to 43 400 million in 1975. Another increase during 1976 took the passenger-km figure for that year to 43 900 million. Passenger journeys over the same period rose from 231 million in 1974 to 240 million in 1975 and 239 million in 1976. Receipts from passenger business during 1976 added up to Frs 6 135 million—compared with Frs 6 150 million in 1975 and Frs 5 768 million in 1974.

While traffic has been rising the number of employees on SNCF payroll has dropped significantly over the past three years. In 1974 the railway employed 286 600; in 1975 this dropped to 276 000 and was down again by the end of 1976 to 271 920. So, in the final analysis, during 1976 SNCF once again succeeded in maintaining its set target of a 5 per cent annual rise in traffic—a figure that had taken a sharp setback during 1975. In terms of traffic units handled (passenger-km plus freight tonne-km), the railway reports a rise from 114 900 in 1975 to 120 200 in 1976.

TRAFFIC

	1974	1975	1976
Freight ton-km (million)	77 100	64 000	68 500
Freight tons carried (million)	266	219	227
Passenger-km (million)	47 300	50 700	51 500
Passenger journeys (million)	642	658	675

FINANCES

	1973	1974	1975	1976
		(Frs millions)		
Revenues	18 100	20 849	22 959	24 139
Expenses	18 373	20 929	24 142	25 255

MOTIVE POWER

The only diesel motive power purchase announced in 1977 was for a series of 300 hp Moyse shunters, as the railway maintained its policy to update the fleet of electric locomotives. Orders for 41 new 4 600 kW units were placed during 1977 with Alsthom and Francorail-MTE. With a maximum speed of 180 km/h, the locomotives are being supplied in three versions: the 88 tonne BB 15 000 ac type which SNCF has been using successfully since 1971; the 84 tonne BB 7 200 dc type; and the dual-current 89 tonne BB 22 200 type. Since 1971 a total of 50 class BB 15 000 units have been delivered and 15 more were due to go into operation by September 1977. They have been based at Strasbourg to serve the eastern region of SNCF. Also delivered during last year were 12 class BB 7 200 and the first of the dual-current series. Orders were placed during 1977 for six BB 7 200 dc units and 35 dual-current BB 22 200 units.

Total investment for motive power and rolling stock in 1977 was Fr 638 million which in addition to locomotives also covered purchase of 15 new electric trainsets for the new Paris-Southeast line, 49 electric trainsets, 25 railbuses, 450 Corail passenger coaches, 70 luggage vans and 48 stainless steel coaches.

The new trainsets for the high speed line are to be based closely on the experimental gas-turbined TGV 001. The railway is due to take delivery of two prototype electric sets before series production begins. A complete series of 85 trainsets is forecast. Though the Paris-Southeast line is to be electrified at 25kV 50Hz, it will correct at each end with lines already electrified at 1.5kV dc, so the new sets are to be equipped with a dual-current system making it possible to work over both types of electrification. Building the sets are Alsthom and Francorail-MTE. Each set will consist of a motor-coach at each end with eight intermediate trailers. Total length will be 200.12 m. Maximum speed for the initial sets will be 260 km/h. Each of the motor coaches will be mounted on two motored bogies, with one motored bogie beneath the immediately adjacent trailers. The remaining trailers will be linked by supporting trailer bogies. The two experimental sets are scheduled for delivery during 1978 and it is expected that the 85 series-built sets will be delivered from 1979 through 1983.

Other dual-system sets ordered during 1977 include the new Z2 two-car emus which will also be built in ac and dc versions. An order for 14 sets has been placed with Francorail-MTE and ANF Industrie. Designed for stopping services on lines now being served by old m-u sets or locomotive-hauled trains, they will have 68 seats (plus four folding seats) in the motor coach and 84 seats (plus eight folding) in the trailer. Total weight of the dc set is 107 tonnes. The dual-system set will weigh 114 tonnes. The ac set 111 tonnes. Motored bogies will be type M1, trailer bogies type Y 32 G. Maximum speed will be 160 km/h for all three types.

An order for ten more Z6400 four-car electric ac sets was also placed in 1977. They are to be built by Francorail-MTE with equipment from Alsthom and TCO. The first 15 type Z6400 sets, built by Carel Fouche, have been operating on the new line between Paris and Roissy airport since the end of May, 1976. During last year, 27 sets were delivered for service on the Paris-St. Lazare to Versailles line; leaving 23 more sets to be delivered under the original order. The four car sets (M + T + T + M) were designed to set a new standard of comfort for suburban passengers, providing individual seats for both first class and second class passengers. Bodies are of stainless steel with the two side sills in Corten steel. Headstock of the powered cars are fitted with integral Schaffenberg automatic coupling at the cab ends. Total train length is 92.33 m, total tare weight 189.4 tonnes. Total output is 2 360 kW, maximum speed 120 km/h. Acceleration is 1 m/s². The train has normal seating for 262 passengers. Maximum capacity with 447 standing passengers is 773.

Only purchases for the railway's diesel fleet announced during 1977 were for a new 440 kW diesel railbus which will have sufficient power to haul a trailer when necessary.

PASSENGER ROLLING STOCK

During 1976 SNCF took delivery of 629 new express passenger coaches—most of them part of the new Corail VTU 75 fleet for domestic services and VU 75 for international services. Included in the VU 75 deliveries were the first of a new type of second class couchette car which corresponds with European standards. Other passenger equipment delivered during the year included 13 type 72 sleeping cars. Now in service with SNCF are 1 800 VTU and 800 VU Corail coaches. During 1977, an additional 450 were ordered: the VTU type from Alsthom and Franco-Belge and the VU type from Francorail-MTE and ANF Industries. Included in the order was 95 couchette cars. SNCF has also ordered 311 baggage vans from Francorail—MTE and ANF Industrie and 48 stainless steel coaches for use on the Paris—Montparnasse suburban lines.

FREIGHT ROLLING STOCK

During 1976 SNCF took delivery of 2 000 new freight wagons including 1 200 covered

Series BB 1 500 locomotive

Series BB 17 000 25kV electric locomotive

Series BB 9 200v dc electric locomotive

wagons and 200 flat wagons fitted with a mechanically-operated sheeting system, and ten flat wagons with telescopic hoods for coil transport. In the same year a total of 12 000 old wagons were scrapped. Wagon orders during 1977 totalled 1 500, including 1 100 new type of reinforced high-sided wagon for iron and steel scrap.

Locomotives in service at 31.12.76	
Electric	2 306
Diesel	2 217
Locotractors	1 358

TGV-001 prototype turbotrain which will form the basic design for new trainsets to operate planned high-speed service over the new Paris-Lyon line.

ELECTRIFICATION

There are two main systems of electrification in France:—25 000 volts, 50 cycles ac and 1 500 V dc. There are however shorter lengths of different voltages, the total electrified route length at the end of 1974 being made up as follows:—

	km
25 000 volts single phase, 50 cycles	4 389
1 500 V, dc	4 826
850 V, dc	63
650/700 V, dc	62
600 V, dc	34
	9 327

Lines electrified in 1976 included:

Aulnay S/Bois—Roissy New Line	14 km

Lines under electrification in 1976/77 included:

Bordeaux—Montauban	206 km
Cerbere (Port-Bou)—Narbonne	104 km
Villeneuve—les-Avignon—Nimes	43 km
Givors—Avignon	221 km
Avignon—Miramas	66 km
Plaisir-Grignon—Epone-Mezieres	20 km
Lyon—Grenoble—Chambery	172 km

SNCF has adopted a programme of electrification to cost Frs 400 million annually (at 1977 prices) over the next ten years. Under the programme, the bypass route leading north to south around Paris is to be electrified, followed by conversion of the line southwest from Amiens to Rouen, providing a bypass route just north of Rouen to ensure free access to Le Havre. Also due for early electrification is the major freight route from Nantes through Anvers, Tours, Clermond-Ferrand and Lyon.

In 1977, SNCF spent Fr382 million, excluding work on the Paris—Southeast line (which has a separate investment budget). Of this total, Fr235 million was for actual electrification work, Fr20 million for expansion and reinforcement of substations to improve the power supply, and Fr127 million on signalling, telecommunications and cables.

Major works now in hand include the route along the right bank of the Rhone—from Miramas to Avignon, via Cavaillon (due to be switched on in October this year); Avignon to Givers (completion 1979); Nimes to Villeneuve-les-Avignon (1980). The line from Bordeaux to Montauban should also be energised by 1980. The Rhone bank electrification will be at 25kV. But the section from Plaisir-Grignon to Epône-Mézières, near Paris—which should also be ready for electric operation later this year—is being electrified at 25kV 50Hz. Reason for conversion is to facilitate exchange of freight traffic between the Paris—Rouen and Paris—Le Mans lines.

Considerable investment is being made in the Paris region on modernisation of existing electrified lines. On the important Paris—St. Lazare to Versailles line, with the branch to St. Nom-la-Bretéche, which carries 130 000 passengers a day, work is continuing on conversion from 750dc to 25kV operation.

The section from Paris to St. Cloud came into operation under 25kV catenary in September 1976; and the section from St. Cloud to Versailles was switched on at the new voltage by the end of 1977. Work on the St Cloud to St Nom-la-Bretèche section should be completed in 1978.

Also to be modernised at 25kV is the Paris-St-Lazare to Nanterre University section of the former Paris—St German line, which will be included in the route to serve the new town of Cergy.

The Paris-Invalides to Versailles Left Bank Line, which is being completely updated as part of the Orsay—Invalides link, is being converted from 750Vdc to 1.5kVdc to match adjacent Paris suburban lines.

TRACK

Annually, SNCF is renewing about 1 000 km of track at a cost of Fr 478 000/km. Complete renewals are being carried out mainly on high capacity, UIC classes 1 to 5, tracks. These groups comprise about 30 000 track-km of SNCF's 58 000 km of mainline tracks. Standards adopted for all track renewals includes adoption of 60 kg/m rails where the track carried at least 25 000 gross tonnes daily, and 50 kg/m in other cases. Rails are continuous welded, mounted on RS-type sleepers.

In addition to the renewal programme, the railway is carrying out continuous work on maintaining and improving the existing track. Maintenance consists primarily of mechanical tamping. Programme for 1977 included 5 000 km of mechanical tamping and 5 000 km of continuous shovel packing.

During 1976/77 SNCF placed increasing emphasis on rail welding, and by the end of 1976 a total of 17 700 track-km had been equipped with continuous welded rail (cwr). About 8 277 km of of welded rail is on concrete sleepers. Present policy calls for increasing the length of cwr track by up to 850 km annually, to produce a total cwr track length of about 30 000 track km by 1 990.

SNCF now has a total of more than 6 780 km of automatic block—6 600 km on the Block Automatique Lumineux-permissif (BAL) system and the remainder on Block Automatique A Permissivite Restreinte. During the past two years a total of 463 km of double track has been fitted with automatic block signalling—401 km with BAL and 62 km with BAPR. Now, BAL is being installed at the rate of about 220 route-km annually.

During 1976/77, a total of 37 PRS (poste tout relais a transit souple) boxes have been installed to control a total of 1 277 routes—including 690 sets of motorised points and 616 signals. In addition, SNCF has installed one new PRMI box (all relay interlocking installation with individual locks), one PELI power signal box, four PMV all relay boxes with track locks, and two PEMU electro mechanical unified signal boxes as well as one PM 45 mechanical signal box. The railway now has 430 electric signal boxes in operation, of which 284 are of the PRS type.

The new signal box opened at Versailles-Chantiers in February 1977 replaces seven existing boxes on the 17 km section between Sevres RG and St. Quentin-en-Yve lines. Later the control area of the box is to be extended to Ram-bouillet in the south, to Plaisir-Grignon and Noisy le Roi and Argenteuil. The computer-controlled box incorporates the first large-scale automatic train describer taken into operation by SBCF. A similar system may now be developed for control of the Paris-Southeast line, with all signalling controlled over the double track route between Paris and Lyon from a single box. The line will also be equipped with a track to train cab signalling system with automatic override if speed control commands are not obeyed.

For the Paris suburban network and as part of the Paris SNCF-Metro inter connection scheme, studies are being made for introduction of automatic train operation. The system could be put into operation by 1982.

PARIS-SOUTHEAST LINE

Preliminary work on the 388 km new high-speed line between Paris and Lyon has been in hand since mid 1976. During 1977, SNCF allocated Fr 937 million for work on the line: Fr 194 million for land purchase and Fr 743 million for civil engineering works. All right of way for the 270 km Florentin—Lyon section had been purchased by the end of 1977. Civil engineering works including tunnels, cuttings and bridges, should be completed by the end of 1979. Track laying and signalling should be completed by mid-1981 and the section should be in service by October 1981.

Work on the remainder of the line, up to Combs-la-Ville (Paris) should be completed by mid-1983 to permit high-speed operations to start up over the complete route by October 1983.

Design speed of the new line—which will be for passenger trains only—is 260-270 km/h, to be raised later to 300 km/h. Minimum curve radius is 4 000 m and maximum gradient 35 mm/m.

Series BB 67 000 diesel-electric locomotive

Series CC 6 500 locomotive rated at 5 900 kW—SNCF's most powerful

Series CC 72 000 diesel locomotive

Total cost of the line (in 1977 values) is expected to top Fr 3 854 million. Cost of rolling stock will be about Fr 2 680 million.

PARIS SUBURBAN

Among most important developments for SNCF's Paris Suburban services has been the 1977 competition of the Paris Metro's RER (Regional Express) line to link the city centre from Auber to Nation. Another Metro line, from St Remy will connect with the RER line running from the northwest of Paris through to the Gare St. Lazare. Already SNCF tracks to the northwest run close to the RER line, and the connection would be relatively inexpensive.

SNCF is also working on a direct connection between its northern region, now terminating at the Gare d'Orsay, and the southeast region terminating at Invalides. Cost of connecting the two terminals will be about Fr545 million. The line down from Invalides is at present electrified at 750V dc with third rail collection, and will have to be modernised to meet the 1 500V dc overhead collection of the northern region. Work should be completed in 1979. Operation will be at 60-second headways on the most congested lines, and new types of signalling are being designed to keep traffic moving. The through working will also make it possible for SNCF to increase its capacity on outer suburban lines.

To enable SNCF to operate on RATP lines, 150 special fourcar (M+T+T+M) sets have been ordered—65 by SNCF and 85 by RATP. The new cars will be built from aluminium by Société Franco-Belge, with traction equipment by Traction CEM Oerlikon (TCO) and bogies from ANF-Industrie. Main differences from normal suburban stock will be the special clearance gauge and provision for automatic operation. The new cars are also likely to provide a greater degree of comfort than normal suburban or metro trains. They will also provide SNCF with its first real service experience of aluminium car bodies. The new trains will be dual current, providing automatic changeover between 1 500V dc and 25kV 50Hz. Crush capacity of the four-car set will be 811 passengers, 312 of them seated. For use in non-peak periods, there will be 118 fold-down seats. The trains will have chopper control and regenerative braking. Acceleration will be 0.9m/s². Four prototypes will be delivered in November 1979, and from then on deliveries will be at a minimum of 30 sets a year.

ELECTRIC LOCOMOTIVES

Class	Axle Arrange-ment	Line Current	Rated Output hp	Tractive Effort (Full Field) Max. lb *(kg)*	Tractive Effort (Full Field) Continuous at lb *(kg)*	Tractive Effort (Full Field) Continuous at mph *(km/hr)*	Max. Speed mph *(km/hr)*	Wheel dia. ins *(mm)*	Weight tonnes	Length ft in *(mm)*	No. Built	Year Built	Builders: Mechanical Parts	Builders: Electrical Equipment
2D2-9100	2-Do-2	1 500 V dc	5 010	61 700 *(28 000)*	41 200 *(18 700)*	44 *(70.5)*	87 *(140)*	39⅜ *(1 000)* 68⅞ *(1 750)*	144	59′ 4″ *(18 080)*	31	1950	Fives-Lille-Cail	Cie. Electro-Mécanique
BB-8100	Bo-Bo	,,	2 850	67 000 *(30 400)*	36 000 *(16 300)*	25.8 *(41.5)*	65 *(105)*	55⅛ *(1 400)*	92	42′ 5″ *(12 930)*	171	1949	Alsthom	Alsthom
BB-8500 (2 gear ratios)	B-B	,,	4 000	44 300 *(20 100)* 73 850 *(33 000)*	28 200 *(12 800)* 46 700 *(21 200)*	51.3 *(82.5)* 30.6 *(49.2)*	93 *(150)* 56 *(90)*	43¼″ *(1 100)*	79	48′ 3″ *(14 700)*	146	1965	Alsthom	Alsthom
BB-7200	B-B	1 500 V dc	4 000		30 400 *(13 800)*	60 *(97)*	112 *(180)*	49 7/32 *(1 250)*	86	57′ 4 7/32″ *(17 480)*	35 (75 on order)	1973	Francorail-MTE-Alsthom	Francorail-MTE-Alsthom
BB-9001-2	Bo-Bo	,,	4 850	47 500 *(21 500)*	30 300 *(13 750)*	55.5 *(89)*	87 *(140)*	51⅛ *(1 300)*	80	50′ 6″ *(15 400)*	2	1953	S.L.M.	Brown-Boveri
BB-9003	Bo-Bo	,,	4 320	48 000 *(21 800)*	30 800 *(14 000)*	50.5 *(81)*	87 *(140)*	49¼ *(1 250)*	80	53′ 2″ *(16 200)*	1	1952	S.F.A.C.	F.A.C.E.J.: Oerlikon
BB-9004	Bo-Bo	,,	4 050	45 200 *(20 500)*	23 600 *(10 700)*	61.5 *(99)*	87 *(140)*	49¼ *(1 250)*	83	53′ 2″ *(16 200)*	1	1954	M.T.E.	M.T.E.
BB-9200 BB-9300	Bo-Bo	,,	5 230	58 500 *(26 500)*	32 600 *(14 800)*	58 *(93)*	100 *(160)*	49¼ *(1 250)*	82	53′ 2″ *(16 200)*	129	1958	M.T.E.	M.T.E.-C.E.M.
BB-9400	B-B	,,	3 000	60 600 *(27 500)*	34 800 *(15 800)*	31 *(50)*	81 *(130)*	40⅛ *(1 020)*	60	47′ 3″ *(14 400)*	132	1959	Fives-Lille-Cail	M.T.E.
CC 6500 (2 gear ratios)	C-C	,,	5 880				62 *(100)* 137 *(220)*	45″ *(1 140)*	116	66′ 3″ *(20.190)*	74	1969		
CC-7100	Co-Co	,,	4 740	58 500 *(26 500)*	34 600 *(15 700)*	49.5 *(79.5)*	93 *(150)*	49¼ *(1 250)*	107	62′ 1″ *(18 922)*	58	1950	Alsthom	Alsthom
BB-12000	Bo-Bo	25 kV 1/50	3 350	79 400 *(36 000)*	41 900 *(19 000)*	29.5 *(47.5)*	75 *(120)*	49¼ *(1 250)*	83	49′ 10½″ *(15 200)*	147	1954	M.T.E.	M.T.E.
BB-13000	Bo-Bo	,,	2 720	55 100 *(25 000)*	26 000 *(11 800)*	40.5 *(65)*	75 *(120)*	49¼ *(1 250)*	85	49′ 10½″ *(15 200)*	49	1954	M.T.E.	M.T.E.
BB-16000	Bo-Bo	,,	4 130	69 500 *(31 500)*	33 500 *(15 200)*	53 *(85)*	100 *(160)*	49¼ *(1 250)*	85	53′ 2″ *(16 200)*	61	1958	M.T.E.	M.T.E.
BB-15000	B-B	,,	4 650	64 000 *(29 000)*	33 000 *(15 000)*	62 *(100)*	112 *(180)*	49½ *(1 260)*	88	57′ 4¼″ *(17 480)*	48	1971	Alsthom	Alsthom
BB-16500 (2 gear ratios)	B-B	,,	3 500	72 700 *(33 000)*	24 900 *(11 300)* 42 300 *(19 200)*	51 *(82)* 30 *(48)*	93 *(150)* 56 *(90)*	43¼ *(1 100)*	74	47′ 3″ *(14 400)*	293	1958	Alsthom	Alsthom
BB-17000 (2 gear ratios)	B-B	,,	4 000	44 300 *(20 100)* 73 850 *(33 000)*	28 200 *(12 800)* 46 700 *(21 200)*	51.3 *(82.5)* 30.6 *(49.2)*	93 *(150)* 56 *(90)*	43¼″ *(1 100)*	79	48′ 3″ *(14 700)*	105	1965	Alsthom	Alsthom
CC-14000	Co-Co	,,	3 590	99 200 *(45 000)*	51 100 *(23 200)*	17.7 *(28.5)*	37 *(60)*	43¼ *(1 100)*	123	62′ 0″ *(18 890)*	11	1955	Batignolles-Chatillon	Oerlikon
CC-14100	Co-Co	,,	2 520	94 700 *(43 000)*	51 200 *(23 200)*	17.7 *(28.5)*	37 *(60)*	43¼ *(1 100)*	127	62′ 0″ *(18 890)*	93	1954	Alsthom	Alsthom
BB-20200 (2-current) (2 gear ratios)	B-B	25 kV 1/50 15 kV 16⅔	2 900 1 630				93 *(150)* 56 *(90)*				13	1971	Alsthom	Alsthom
CC-21000 (2-current) (2-gear ratios)	C-C	25 kV/50 1.5 kV dc	5 900				62 *(100)* 137 *(220)*	45″ *(1 140)*	122	66′ 3″ *(20 190)*	3	1969	Alsthom-M.T.E.	
BB-22200 (2-current)	B-B	25 kV/50 and 1 500 V dc	4 000		30 400 *(13 800)*	60 *(97)*	112 *(180)*	49 7/32″ *(1 250)*	90	57′ 4 7/32″ *(17 480)*	22 (128 on order)	1973	Francorail-MTE-Alsthom	Francorail-MTE-Alsthom
BB-25100 (2-current) 4 600	Bo-Bo	25 kV/50 and 1 500 V dc	5 600	81 600 *(37 000)*	39 000 *(17 700)*	52 *(83.5)*	81 *(130)*	49¼ *(1 250)*	84	53′ 3″ *(16 200)*	59	1964	M.T.E.	M.T.E.
BB-25200 (2-current)	Bo-Bo	25 kV/50 and 1 500 V dc	5 600 4 600	68 300 *(31 000)*	32 600 *(14 800)*	62 *(99.5)*	99 *(160)*	49¼ *(1 250)*	85	53′ 2″ *(16 200)*	49	1964	M.T.E.	M.T.E.
BB-25500 (2-current) (2 gear ratios)	B-B	25 kV/50 and 1 500 V dc	 4 460	44 300 *(20 100)* 73 850 *(33 600)*	25 100 *(11 400)* 41 900 *(19 000)*	51 *(82)* 30 *(48)*	93 *(150)* 56 *(90)*	43¼″ *(1 100)*	76	53′ 3″ *(14 700)*	193	1964	Alsthom	Alsthom
CC-25000 (2-current)	Co-Co	25 kV ac 1 500 V dc	4 140 410	53 500 *(24 300)*	35 300 *(16 000)*	42.3 *(68)*	62 *(100)*	55⅛ *(1 400)*	106	56′ 7″ *(17 250)*	2	1952	Batignolles	Oerlikon
BB-30,000 (3-current) (2 gear ratios)	B-B	25 kV/50 3 kV dc 1,5 kV dc	2 930	39 700 *(18 000)*	22 700 *(10 300)*	46 *(74)*	62 *(100)* 93 *(150)*	43½ *(1 010)*	69	47′ 3″ *(14 400)*	1	1961	Fives-Lille	M.T.E.-C.E.M.
CC-40100 (4-current) (2 gear ratios)	C-C	25 kV/50 15 kV/16⅔ 3 000 V dc 1 500 V dc	 5 040	32 000 *(14 500)* 44 500 *(20 200)*	19 000 8 600 27 000 *(12 000)*	95.4 *(153.5)* 68 *(110)*	149 *(240)* 99 *(160)*	42½″ *(1 080)*	107	72′ 3¼″ *(22 030)*	10	1964	Alsthom	Alsthom

SNAV double-deck automobile-carrying wagon.

SNCF central computer room now handling freight management throughout the network.

DOOR-TO-DOOR SERVICES

In addition to palletised freight carried in covered rail wagons, French Railways deal with the transport of unitised freight by (a) the use of containers and (b) the long-distance conveyance of highway semi-trailers.

CONTAINER OPERATIONS

Compagnie Nouvelle de Cadres (CNC)
20 boulevard Diderot, Paris 12e
Telephone: 345-32-20
Telegrams: Cadroferdir Paris
Telex: 22500-Cadrofer Paris

Chairman and General Manager: Jean Daudemard-Gregnac
Operating Manager: Henri Megoeuil
Chief Rolling Stock Manager: Gilbert Braud
Chief commercial Manager: Jean Jacques

To facilitate the development of container traffic through groupage, and the provision of lifting equipment and of terminal haulage (road delivery and collection), in 1948, the SNCF, in association with private interests, set up an organisation called the *Compagnie Nouvelle de Cadres* (CNC). In France CNC operates in more than 50 towns, arranges road collection and delivery, and offers assistance to provide the most suitable transport facilities at the best rates.

DIESEL LOCOMOTIVES

Class	Axle Arrange-ment	Trans-mission	Rated Power hp	Max. lbs (kg)	Tractive Effort Continuous at lbs (kg)	mph (km/h)	Max. Speed mph (km/h)	Wheel Dia. ins (mm)	Total Weight Tons	Length ft ins (mm)	No. Built	Year first Built	Builders: Mechanical Parts	Engine & Type	Transmission
AIA-AIA 62000	AIA-AIA	Elec.	380	32 200 (14 600)	27 800 (12 600)		60 (96)	42⅛ (1 070)	110	58' 1" (17 700)	100	1946	Baldwin	Baldwin 606 HA	Westinghouse
AIA-AIA 68000 et 685000	AIA-AIA	Elec.	1 660	67 000 (30 400)	39 700 (18 000)	19 (30.6)	81 (130)	49⁷/₃₂ (1 250)	106	58' 8½" (17 920)	109	1963	C.A.F.L. Fives-Lille	Sulzer 12LVA 24 or SAMC-AGO V12-DSHR	C.E.M.
CC65500	Co-Co	Elec.	1 190	80 700 (36 600)	47 800 (21 700)		47 (75)	47¼ (1 200)	122	63' 8½" (19 420)	35	1955	C.A.F.L.	Sulzer 12LDA28	C.E.M.
CC65000	Co-Co	Elec.	970	56 200 (25 000) 37 500 (17 000)	32 800 (14 900) 19 000 (8 600)		75 (120)	41¼ (1 050)	112	65' 0" (19 810)	20	1956	Alsthom C.A.F.L.	SACM MGO V12SHR	Alsthom
CC70000 mono-motor bogies (2 gears)	C-C	Elec.	3 000	50 700 (23 000) 75 000 (34 000)	29 750 at 50 (13 500 at 80) 44 500 at 33 (20 200 at 53)		87 (140)	43¼ (1 100)	117	74' 7" (22 730)	1	1966	Alsthom	2 × SEMT 16PA4	Alsthom
CC72000 mono-motor bogies (2 gears)	C-C	Elec.	2 250	48 500 (22 000) 81 600 (37 000)	30 900 at 34.7 (14 000 at 57.5) 51 800 at 21.5 (23 500 at 34.5)		87 (140) 53 (85)	44⅞ (1 140)	110	66' 3¼" (20 200)	92	1967	Alsthom	SACM-AGO V16 ESHR	Alsthom
BB63000	Bo-Bo	Elec.	355	37 500 (17 000)	23 100 (10 500)	6 (10)	50 (80)	41¼ (1 050)	68	48' 2" (14 680)	108	1953	Brissonneau et Lotz	Sulzer 6LDA22C	Brissonneau et Lotz
			435	37 500 (17 000)	24 200 (11 000)	8 (13)	50 (80)	41¼ (1 050)	68	48' 2" (14 680)	142	1957	Brissonneau et Lotz	Sulzer 6LDA22D	Brissonneau et Lotz
BB63500	Bo-Bo	Elec.	450	37 700 (17 100)	28 400 (12 900)	7.5 (12)	50 (80)	41¼ (1 050)	68	48' 2" (14 680)	602	1956	Brissonneau et Lotz	SACM MGO V12 SH	Brissonneau et Lotz
BB66000	Bo-Bo	Elec.	830	44 000 (20 000)	28 700 (13 000)	13.7 (22)	65 (105)	43¼ (1 100)	70	48' 10½" (14 898)	434	1959	Alsthom, CAFL Fives-Lille, SACM	SACM MGO V16BSHR	Alsthom, C.E.M.
BB67000 mono-motor bogies (2 gears)	B-B	Elec.	1 525	45 400 (20 600) 68 300 (31 000)	26 500 at 26 (12 000 at 42) 39 700 at 17.4 (18 000 at 28)		87 (140)	45¼ (1 150)	80	56' 1" (17 090)	422	1963	Brissonneau et Lotz M.T.E.	SEMT-Pielstick 16PA4	M.T.E. Oerlikon
BB69000	B-B	Hyd.	2 620	61 300 (27 800)			87 (140)		84	62' 4" (19 000)	2	1963	Cruesot	SEMT-Pielstick 2 × 16 PA4 (de-rated)	Voith-Creusot
BB71000	B-B	Mech.	400	37 500 (17 000)			50 (80)	34 (860)	55	38' 10½" (11 850)	30	1965	Fives-Lille	Poyaud	Asynchro
C61000	C	Elec.	285	35 250 (16 000)	18 300 (8 300)		37 (60)	55⅛ (1 400)	53	31' 2" (9 500)	48	1950	C.A.F.L.	Sulzer 6LDA22A	C.A.F.L.
Y 7100	B	Hyd.	129	16 300 (7 400)			34 (54)	41¼ (1 050)	32	29' 4" (8,940)	209	1958	Billiard	Poyaud 6PYT	Voith
Y 7400	B										488				

As the SNCF Container Tariff is based on wagon loading, ie. the rate per tonne is lower for a full load than for a part load, the CNC, by organising the grouping in wagon loads of containers from various consignors, can offer each of them lower rates than they individually might obtain from direct use of the railway tariffs.

The CNC is the representative in France of INTERCONTAINER, the international railway container organisation with operational headquarters in Basle, Switzerland. It has 36 terminals with special lift facilities for 20 ft containers; at 30 of these equipment similar to that at British Railways Freightliner terminals is installed.

The company owns about 5 000 small and medium containers for domestic and international service, and by the end of 1975 will have approximately 4 000 standard ISO 20 ft and 2 000 standard ISO 30 ft containers.

Although it has close contacts with the railways and is associated with all container transport development CNC is an independent entity with its own technical and commercial organisation. In 1974 the company was responsible for some 2.77 million tonnes of container freight transport.

Containers—Medium and small size: These containers have played a major role over the years, primarily in domestic services, both as a type of unit load for consignments less than the full capacity of a rail wagon, and as an intermodal door-to-door transport medium.

French Railways container tariff 106 has several main features:
1 Privately owned containers, of approved type, travel free when loaded;
2 Their return empty, where the traffic is not balanced, is effected at a cheap rate;
3 For commodities for which a minimum tonnage per wagon is required to obtain the lowest transport rate, the minimum tonnage figure is reduced by 20 per cent when containers are used.
4 The tariff generally is calculated on the basis of wagon loading and not per container, so that by groupage of unit loads, ie. carrying several containers on one rail wagon, lower freight rates apply to each unit.

There are a number of special containers, mostly privately owned for carrying a variety of products—wine, chemicals, radio active materials, cement, granulated or powdered plastics materials, zinc sheets, etc. For ordinary traffic, box containers ranging in capacity up to 300 ft³ (8 m³) are generally available, although there are also a number of 400 ft³ (11 m³) units. The SNCF owns some 19 000 of these domestic containers; the CNC has about 5 000.

Containers—Large size: Known in Europe as "Transcontainers", to distinguish them from the smaller containers which have been in use for many years, these are the units built to internationally agreed sizes with outside dimensions of 8 ft wide × 8 ft high, in three lengths of 20 ft, 30 ft and 40 ft.

There is a distinction in the SNCF Transportation Tariff between (a) overland transport only, and (b) combined land and sea transport.

For (a) rates are expressed per tonne, with minimums of 10 tonnes per 20 ft transcontainer, 15 tonnes per 30 ft, and 20 tonnes per 40 ft.

(b) rates are expressed as an overall figure, and take into account the length of journey, the size of the units and the weight of the contents. For any given distance there are three possible rates for each size of container, according to the load carried:—20 ft long, up to 8 tonnes, 8 to 13 tonnes, over 13 tonnes; 30 ft long, up to 10 T, 10 to 16 T, over 16 T; 40 ft long, up to 12 T, 12 to 20 T, over 20 T.

As in the case of small containers, a groupage rate applies so that two 20 ft. transcontainers together on a rail wagon are charged as one 40 ft with the total load; and cheap rates are granted for the empty return of transcontainers when a balanced traffic cannot be achieved.

For transcontainers in transit through France the International Transcontainer Tariff, jointly agreed by European railway administrations, is applicable. This gives an all-in rate expressed in Gold Francs, for traffic between certain North Sea and Channel ports and a number of specified towns in different European countries. This Tariff is concerned only with length of the transcontainer—20 ft, 30 ft, and 40 ft—weight is not taken into account.

Container trains: Regular services of container trains, known as "Container Express", are operating in both directions on the following routes:—

Paris—Bordeaux	Marseille—Bordeaux
Paris—Lyon	Marseille—Lyon
Paris—Marseille	Marseille—Strasbourg
Paris—Metz	Marseille—Toulouse
Paris—Strasbourg	
Paris—Toulouse	Bordeaux—Toulouse
Paris—Nantes	

Individual transcontainers: Where the traffic does not justify the operation of a block container train, the container wagons are forwarded by the most suitable fast freight train. However, because of the time spent in marshalling yards or sidings, the commercial speed is lower than that of a block container train and the transport charges higher.

Block-train wagons: The SNCF has wagons capable of carrying 8 ft 6 in high transcontainers in 60 ft lengths (10 ft lengths in any combination). These are of skeleton design, without floors, and are provided with ordinary couplings, as well as with devices enabling the transcontainers to be secured rapidly by means of their bottom corner castings.

Individual wagons: The SNCF has 60 ft flat wagons, capable of carrying 8 ft high transcontainers in any combination of 10 ft lengths.

Transcontainer depots: The first depots came into operation early in 1969; all depots are provided with modern handling equipment.

Each depot is equipped with at least one gantry crane, straddling a minimum of one railway track and one road (2 roads in the majority of cases) over a length of between 200 and 400 m. Areas are provided for the garaging and maintenance of road semi-trailers and tractors, as well as for offices, container storage, etc.

Consideration is being given to the optimum number of depots, which may be between 60 and 80, some 20 of which would be capable of handling one or more block trains.

Handling equipment: The SNCF has decided to make use of all-metal, rail-mounted, electric gantry cranes, with hydraulically operated locks and grabs, whose characteristics are set out below:—

Lifting power:	50 tonnes.
Span:	(a) 27 ft 3 in (8.30 m)
	(b) 40 ft 4 in (12.30 m)
	(c) 59 ft 1 in (18.0)
Height under hooks:	(a) and (b) 22 ft 4 in (6.80 m)
	(c) 27 ft 3 in (8.30 m)

The clearance for (c) will enable 8 ft 6 in (2.59 m) containers to be stacked three high

Time taken for transhipment:	between 3 and 4 minutes

To begin with, Paris has three depots, each equipped with two gantry cranes.

GABON

GABON STATE RAILWAYS
Le Chemin De Fer Du Gabon
Office Du Chemin De Fer Transgabonais (OCTRA)
PO Box 2198, Libreville

Telephone: 244 78/209 74
Telex: 5307

Director General: L. Vion
Secretary: Paul Moukambi

The Gabonese Government announced the decision to construct the first section of the Transgabonese Railways (gauge: 1.435 m) from Libreville/Owendo to Booué (328 km) in 1972. Construction work started in 1974. Estimated traffic capacity of the line is 1 200 000 tons annually, mainly timber. Completion is scheduled for 1978. Estimated cost of construction is Frs CFA 36 million, raised through international loans.

CONSTRUCTION
Some civil engineering work was completed in 1974/75 and track laid at Owendo docks, while a 10-km length of trackbed on the plains section is also ready. Other work included construction of offices and workshops at Owendo for OCTRA, the Trans Gabon Railway Authority.

A major change has been announced in the OCTRA plans, which originally called for construction first of the main Owendo-Booué section, and later extensions south to Franceville and north to iron ore fields at Belinga. However, the economic case for simultaneous construction of the Booué-Franceville line was found to be overwhelming, as there are large deposits of manganese at Moanda in the Haut-Ogooué as well as extensive reserves of timber. The present manganese output of only two million tonnes a year is transported from Moanda by a 75-km aerial ropeway across the border into the Congo at M'Binda, and thence by the Comilog and Congo-Ocean railways to Pointe-Noire for export. The Franceville extension will enable production to be expanded over 10 or 15 years to five million tonnes.

Contracts were signed November 1974 with Eurotag, a consortium of European civil engineers and manufacturers, for building the entire 695-km Owendo-Franceville line over a six-year period at a cost of FrCFA 160 000 m. Members of Eurotrag are: Spie-Batignolles, Razel, Fougerolie-SOFRARATP, SFEDTP, and Imprefer (France); Impresit, Salini Construttori, and Astaldi Estero (Italy); Stirling Astaldi (Britain); Philip Holzmann and Grün & Bulfinger (West Germany); Entreprises Industrielles (Belgium); and Interbéton (Netherlands).

It is likely that the 332-km section to Booué, which will form the Trans-Gabon trunk line, will be ready for service in 1978, while the extension to Franceville will follow in 1980. The 230-km branch northwards to Belinga, where vast iron ore deposits are awaiting exploitation will be financed by the Somifer (a consortium formed by Bethlehem Steel and several European mining companies). There seems little doubt that the branch will be built eventually, but the present world recession in the steel industry makes development of the Belinga ore fields less urgent.

Similar track standards have been devised for both sections of the Trans-Gabon. Rail will be 50 kg/m throughout, laid on 1 670 wood sleepers per km in 25 cm of ballast; maximum axle-load will be 23 tonnes. Steepest gradient against coast-bound trains will be 1 per cent between Franceville and Booué, and 0.5 per cent onwards to Owendo. Eastbound, the maximum grade is 1.5 per cent throughout. Several major river crossings are required, and standard steel spans are being designed for these. There is only one tunnel on the line—of 280 m at Junckville.

MOTIVE POWER AND ROLLING STOCK
OCTRA's first 12 locomotives (six built by Alsthom-Atlantique and six by General Electric) were delivered during 1977. The Alsthom units are B-B design with a nominal (UIC) rating of 3 000 hp, although under Gabon's severe climatic conditions the rating is reduced to 2 800 hp. A single AGOV12DSHR diesel engine is fitted which drives a three-phase alternator and rectifier set supplying dc to the two traction motors. Each locomotive weighs 92 tonnes and has a top speed of 85 km/h. The body is 15.8 m long. In contrast the UM22C General Electric locomotives have a Co-Co wheel arrangement. They are rated at 2 200 hp and are powered by a 7FDL12D25 series 265777 diesel engine. Weight is 108 tonnes.

Orders placed by OCTRA for rolling stock during 1976/77 include a series of passenger coaches and two railcars from Soule, 260 flat wagons from Kawasaki and Itoh, and 30 ballast hoppers of 80 tonnes from Ssangyong Trading of South Korea.

80-ton Bo Bo diesel-electric locomotive delivered to Gabon by Traction Export.

GERMANY (Democratic Republic)

GERMAN STATE RAILWAY

Deutsche Reichsbahn, Voss Strasse 33, DDR 106 Berlin

Telephone: 43 002 16
Telex: 112 250

Minister of Transport and General Manager of the German State Railway: Ing. O. Arndt
Deputy Minister and Assistant General Manager: Dr. rer. oec. V. Winkler
Deputy Minister and 1st Assistant General Manager: Dr. Ing. H. Schmidt
Assistant General Manager: Dipl. Ing. oec. G. Knobloch
Assistant General Manager: Dipl. Ing. D. Weiss
Assistant General Manager and Chief Departmental Manager: Dipl. rer. oec. E. Grahl
Chief Departmental Manager: Dipl. jur. H. Gerber
Manager of the International Department: Dipl. Ing. oec. C. König
Chief Finance Officer: Dr. rer. oec. D. Schwarzer
Chief Legal Adviser: Dr. jur. E. Thiele
Chief Operating and Traffic Manager: Ing. oec. R. Becker
Chief Rolling Stock Manager: Ing. G. Klotz
Chief Mechanical and Electrical Engineer: Ing. R. Wagner
Chief Permanent Way Engineer: Dipl. Ing. K. Sobotta
Chief Signal and Telecommunications Engineer: Dipl. Ing. H. Klemm
Chief Management and Operations Officer: Dipl. Ing. oec. H. Krüger
Chief Accountant: Dipl. Ing. oec. Dipl. jur. E. Ramlow
Chief Medical Officer: Dr. med. J. Stein
Chief Tariff Officer: Dr. Victor Kolloch
Manager of the Automatic Centre-Buffer Coupling Development and Research Centre: Dipl. Ing. W. Rehnert

Gauge: 1.435 m.
Route length: 14 289 km.

Public transport in the German Democratic Republic was expected to carry about 55 million passengers more in 1977 compared with 1976, as well as 1 000 million tonnes of freight. Deutsche Reichsbahn (DR) was scheduled to carry 7 000 000 tonnes more in 1977 than the previous year in order to keep pace with the demands of the building industry, ore mining, metallurgy and potash industries. This means that on average the railways handled around 703 000 tonnes daily. The railway was to get 40 per cent of all available transport investment during 1977, with only 19 per cent scheduled for highway development and modernisation; 17 per cent was allocated to marine transport and harbour management.

Between 1970 and 1976—despite the growing use of the motor car in the GDR—the number of people travelling by train rose by about 8 million. Between 1977 and 1980 a further increase of more than double that number is expected.

The same characteristics and development trends apply in the freight traffic sector; between 1970 and 1975 the volume of traffic went up by about 10 per cent (26 million tonnes).

Between 1970 and 1976, productivity per year per km of line rose from about 18 000 tonnes to 20 000 tonnes and the performance per double axle went up from about 1 700 tonnes to 1 800 tonnes over the same period.

The average freight wagon load per double axle also rose from approximately 18.5 tonnes to 19.3 tonnes and the average wagon turnround time dropped from 4.04 days/double axle to 3.89 for the period between 1970 and 1975.

TRAFFIC

Freight tonnage and ton-km is climbing steadily: from 128.5 million tons (15 064 million ton-km) in 1950 to 286.3 million tons (49 184 million ton-km) in 1974. Compared with 1970, DR carried 30 million tons more freight in 1975 (up 11 per cent) and six million more passengers (up 1 per cent). Freight tonne-km in 1976 totalled 50 811 million; passenger-km was 21 957 million. Total train-km in 1976 was 283 532 million. Passenger traffic stood at 18 576 million passenger-km in 1950; rose to 22 905 million in 1955; fell steadily to 17 446 million in 1965; but rose to 20 764 million passenger-km in 1974.

INVESTMENT PLANS

In addition to doubling about 720 km of route—about the same amount as in the previous five year plan—investments up to 1980 will go towards extensive renewal of existing track, installation of modern signalling equipment, and partial automation of major marshalling yards.

MOTIVE POWER

By the end of 1976 a total of 1 483 route-km had been electrified. Electrification under the new plan will be concentrated on completion of the Dresden—Schona conversion and extension of some other partially electrified routes. Target is elimination of steam traction by the early 1980s—with the main stress on dieselisation rather than on electrification. Major additions to the motive power fleet in the 1970-75 plan included purchase of 1 433 new locomotives—many of them Soviet-built series 120 and 130 to 132 series diesel locomotives, and series 211 and 242 electric built in the German Democratic Republic.

PASSENGER DEVELOPMENTS

The German State Railway (DR) extended its *Stadteschnellverkehr* network during the last quarter of 1976 starting with the 'Rennsteig' on the Meiningen Suhl-Erfurt-Halle-Berlin route on October 25. The Bautzen rolling stock works is building 103 train-sets for the services. Other new services are the 'Elstertal' (Gera-Leipzig-Berlin), 'Soltera' (Rostock-Berlin), 'Sachsenring' (Zwickau-Karl Marx Stadt-Berlin), 'Börde' (Magdeburg-Berlin) and 'Petermännchen' (Schwerin-Berlin). The trains run to Berlin in the morning and return in the afternoon. As part of the development of the island of Rügen as a winter-holiday resort, a new daily service has also been introduced between Berlin and Binz. The daily service between Leipzig and Binz is also continuing through the winter.

With the 1976 winter timetable, passenger trains between Hamburg and Berlin are now entering West Berlin through the new frontier post at Staaken. The route used is from Nauen (on the former main line) to Wustermark (on the former main line from Berlin to Hannover via Stendal) and then to Staaken. In West Berlin the route is Spandau, Ruhleben and Heerstresse to the Stadtbahn at Charlottenburg. On the East German side of the border at Staaken extensive frontier facilities have been provided. The line from Staaken to Charlottenburg completely relaid. Work is also in progress on the modernisation on Spandau Hbf where Hamburg trains now call. On the DR section of the route the Hamburg trains are hauled by Soviet built Class 132 diesels. The Line between Witlenberge and Nauen is entirely single, but with the loops signalled for reversible working. The speed limit is 120 km/h.

1 000 hp B-B diesel-hydraulic general-purpose locomotive Type 110 (old V100). Built by VEB LEW Hand Beimler, Hennigsdorf.

Double-deck coach train hauled by a V180 diesel locomotive

ROLLING STOCK
By the end of the 1970-75 plan over 31 000 new freight wagons had been put into service, with average capacity of new wagons 25 tonnes per double-axle. Proportion of four axle units has now reached 21.9 per cent of the total freight fleet. Systematic modernisation of the wagon fleet, with the purchase of a number of new special-purpose wagons for petroleum and chemical products will continue during the present plan period. By 1980, it is expected that 90 per cent of DR wagons will conform to RIV regulations and 72 per cent will be suitable for speeds of 100 km/h. Average load capacity will be increased to 26.7 tonnes per double-axle by 1980.

CONTAINERS
DR operated its first container train in October 1968. By 1974 total containerised freight moved by rail totalled 1 753 000 annually. During 1975 DR expected to move about 280 000 ISO containers, with about 400 special container trains operating weekly. The railway now intends to extend container transport to meet domestic and international demand.

TRACK
A target of 700 km of track doubling was set for the 1970-75 period; in fact, by mid-1975 a total of 720 km had been laid.
Types S49 and R65 rail in 82 ft (25 m) lengths are flash butt welded in the workshop and after laying, are thermit welded into continuous lengths.
Rails are seated on rubber pads 0.24 in (6 mm) thick or wood (poplar) 0.2 in (5 mm) thick, and are secured by "K" type fastenings to either 6.3 in (160 mm) thick wood sleepers or 7.9 in (200 mm) thick concrete sleepers.

Class 120 (old V200) Co-Co diesel locomotive
2 000 hp. Max speed 63 mph. Built by Voroshilovgrad Works, USSR.

Double-deck Passenger cars for Suburban Service

ELECTRIC LOCOMOTIVES

Class	Axle Arrangement	Line Current	Rated Output hp	Max. lbs (kg)	Tractive Effort (Full Field) Continuous at lb (kg)	mph (km/hr)	Max. Speed mph (km/hr)	Wheel dia. ins (mm)	Weight tonnes	Length ft in (mm)	No. Built	Year Built	Builders Mechanical Parts	Electrical Equipment
211 (E 11)	Bo-Bo	15 kV 16⅔ Hz	2 290	49 383 (22 400)	20 276 (9 200)	—	74.5 (120)	53.0 (1 350)	83	53' 4" (16 260)	—	1960	VEB Lokomotivbau-Elektrotechnische Werke 'Hans Beimler' Hennigsdorf, Berlin	
218 (E 18)	1—Do—1	,,	3 040	46 284 (21 000)	25 346 (11 500)	—	93.2 (150)	62.9 (1 600)	109	55' 6" (16 920)	—	1935	AEG; Krupp	AEG
242 (E 42)	Bo-Bo	,,	2 920	67 883 (30 800)	27 990 (12 700)	—	62 (100)	53.0 (1 350)	83	53' 4" (16 260)	—	1963	VEB Lokomotivbau-Elektrotechnische Werke 'Hans Beimler' Hennigsdorf, Berlin	
244 (E 44)	Bo-Bo	,,	2 200	44 080 (20 000)	26 007 (11 800)	—	56 (90)	49.1 (1 250)	77	50' 2" (15 290)	—	1933	Henschel; Krauss-Maffei	SSW
254 (E 94)	Co-Co	,,	3 300	81 548 (37 000)	56 863 (25 800)	—	56 (90)	49.1 (1 250)	119	61' 0¼" (18 600)	—	1940	AEG; Krupp; Henschel; Krauss-Maffei	AEG; SSW; BBC
251 (E251)	Co-Co	25 kV 50 Hz	3 660	85 074 (38 600)	3 967 (27 600)	—	49 (80)	53.0 (1 350)	126	61' 2" (18 640)	—	1965	VEB Lokomotivbau-Elektrotechnische Werke 'Hans Beimler' Hennigsdorf, Berlin	

DIESEL LOCOMOTIVES

Class	Axle Arrangement	Transmission	Rated Power hp	Max. lbs (kg)	Tractive Effort Continuous at lbs (kg)	mph (km/h)	Max. Speed mph (km/h)	Wheel Dia. ins (mm)	Total Weight Tons	Length ft ins (mm)	No. Built	Year first Built	Builders: Mechanical Parts	Engine & Type	Transmission
106 (V 60)	D	Hyd.	650	38 570 (17 500) 27 770 (12 600)	36 145 (16 400) 20 280 (9 200)	7 (4.5) 14 (9.0)	19 (30) 38 (60)	43.2 (1 100) (60)	60	35' 8½" (10 880)		1960	VEB Lokomotivbau-Elektrotechnische Werke "Hans Beimler" Hennigsdorf Berlin	12 kV D 18/21	VEB Strömungsmaschinen Pirna
107 (V 75)	B-B	Elec.	750	45 400 (20 600)	22 920 (10 400)	9 (14)	38 (60)	39.3 (1 000)	63	41' 2½" (12 560)		1962	CKD Praha	6 S 310 DR	
110 (V 100)	B-B	Hyd.	1 000	46 300 (21 000) 33 060 (15 000)	33 060 (15 000) 20 720 (9 400)	7 (11) 11 (17)	63 (100)	39.3 (1 000)	64	45' 9" (13 940)		1966	VEB Lokomotivbau-Elektrotechnische Werke "Hans Beimler" Hennigsdorf, Berlin	12 kV D 18/21 A-II	VEB Strömungsmaschinen Pirna
118 (V 180)	B-B	Hyd.	1 800 2 000	47 400 (21 500) 57 300 (26 000)	27 330 (12 400) 35 700 (16 200)	13 (21)	75 (120)	39.3 (1 000)	78	63' 10" (19 460)		1962	VEB-Lokomotivebau "Karl Marx" Babelsberg	12 kV D 18/21 A-1 12 kV D 18/21 A-II	VEB Strömungsmaschinen Pirna; Voith
118 (V 180)	C-C	Hyd.	2 000	57 300 (26 000)	35 700 (16 200)	13 (21)	75 (120)	39.3 (1 000)	90	63' 10" (19 460)		1966	VEB Lokomotivbau "Karl Marx" Babelsberg	12 kV D 18/21 A-II	VEB Strömungsmaschinen Pirna; Voith
120 (V 200)	Co-Co	Elec.	2 000	84 440 (38 300)	54 900 (24 900)	9.5 (15.1)	63 (100)	41.3 (1 050)	116	57' 7" (17 550)		1966	Vorovshilovgrad USSR	14 D40	Charkov Works USSR
130 (V 300)	Co-Co	Elec.	3 000	66 100 (30 200)	38 800 (17 600)	21.4 (34.5)	87 (140)	41.3 (1 050)	120	67' 8" (20 620)		1969	Vorovshilovgrad USSR	6 D49	Charkov Works USSR

GERMANY (Federal Republic)

GERMAN FEDERAL RAILWAY

Deutsche Bundesbahn (DB), Friedrich-Ebert-Anlage 43-45, Frankfurt (Main)

Telephone: 26 51
Telex: 04 414 087

Chairman of the Board: Dr. Hermann J. Abs
President: Dr. Wolfgang Vaerst
Vice-Chairman: Franz Eichinger
              Dipl. Ing. Friedrich Laemmerhold
              Helmut Stukenberg
Personnel: Dr. jur. Josef Fries
Traction and Rolling Stock: Prof. Dr.-Ing. Alfred Kniffler
Operating: Dipl.-Ing. Walter Völker
Civil Engineering: Dipl-Ing. Karl Friedrich Kümmell
Traffic and Tariffs: Kurt Samtleben
Finance: Alois Meyer
Legal and International: Dr. jur. Werner Hennig
Planning: Hans Kalb
Operating Economics: Dr.Ing. Willi Effmert
Purchases and Stores: Dr. rer. pol. Kurt Crusius
Federal Railway Central Office, Minden (Westphalia): Dr.-Ing. Heinrich Lehmann
Federal Railway Central Office, Munich: Dr.-Ing. Heinrich Lehmann
Federal Railway Social Dept., Frankfurt a.M.: Dr. jur. Walter Sieglaff
Headquarters Press Department: Dr. jur. Hans Glaser
              Franz Müller-Scherf

Gauge: 1.435 m.
Route length: 28 686 km.

Legislation passed by the Federal Republic of Germany, on April 27, 1977 charges German Federal Railway with the task of progressively reducing the annual operating loss, currently DM4 000 m, so that it is eliminated by 1985. A wide range of rationalisation measures including line closures is specified in a programme *(Leistungsauftrag)* drawn up by the Ministry of Transport. Subsidies at present totalling DM8 000 m, which include compensation for lossmaking suburban passenger traffic as well as pension payments, will continue to be paid from the Federal budget under EEC rules. The main points of the rationalisation programme are:

1. Rural passenger traffic on 6 000 km of the present passenger network of 23 500 km is to be replaced by bus services by 1981. The Federal Government and the *Länder* will decide jointly which routes are affected.
2. Freight traffic will be withdrawn from 3 000 km by 1981. This will effectively reduce the total network size to 25 500 km.
3. Staff numbers are to be reduced from the present figure of 370 000 to 315 000 by 1981; this is to be achieved by natural wastage and by increasing job mobility.
4. Inter-city passenger traffic is to be more market-orientated and must cover its own cost.
5. Wagonload freight traffic must cover its own costs, but subsidies will be paid on loss-making access lines which the Ministry requires to remain open because of their economic importance as feeder routes and because they will minimise the need to construct new roads.
6. Suburban passenger traffic is to be operated to standards set by the Ministry of Transport with costs being covered as far as possible from fares.
7. DB organisation is to be restructured so that it can be run more on the lines of private industry; this will necessitate a change in the basic railway law *(Bundesbahngesetz)*. In future members of the four-man Directorate *(Vorstand)* will be responsible for specific areas, and an additional position will be created at Directorate level to handle personnel matters.
8. Sales and marketing to be intensified with special attention paid to staff motivation and modern business methods.
9. Priority to be given to rationalisation measures which do not require capital investment.
10. Only those investments showing a good rate of return will be approved, but orders will be placed as far as possible as a rolling programme to give an even workload.

TRAFFIC

Following the slump of 1975, DB is striving to recover from freight traffic losses. Total freight fell from 68 127 million tonne-km in 1974 to 54 172 million tonne-km—a loss of more than 20 per cent in a single year. In 1976 the railway regained some, if not all, the ground it had lost with freight traffic rising to 58 267 million and total tonnages up from 286.7 million in 1975 (compared with 351.2 in 1974) to 298.3 million tonnes in 1976. The recovery was expected to continue through 1977 with total tonnages up to 307 million tonnes by the end of the year and a total of 325 million tonnes predicted for 1978.

Backbone of DB's freight operations are coal, iron and steel shipments. In 1976 coal produced 25 per cent of DB revenues, followed closely by iron and steel with 20 per cent. Building materials and mineral oil products each account for 9 per cent while iron ore shipments yield 7 per cent of the annual freight total revenue.

The total passenger market in the Federal Republic has risen steadily in recent years. From 1972 to 1975 the total number of passenger journeys increased by 1 800 million and the number of passenger-km by 25 100 million. But by the end of 1975 DB was carrying only 3.4 per cent of all passengers and accounting for only 6.5 per cent of passenger km. Total number of rail passenger journeys (including S-Bahn traffic) in 1976 was 974.8 million, compared with 1 059.5 million in 1974. Total passenger-km was 37 477 million, compared with 41 607 million. Forecast for 1977 was for a slight increase in demand with total passenger-km reaching 38 850.2 million. For 1978, DB expects a substantial increase in S-Bahn traffic and a further decline in long-distance traffic to produce a total passenger-km figure of 38 629.7 million.

MOTIVE POWER

Since scrapping its final steam locomotive on October 26, 1977, DB is now to invest heavily in new electric and diesel traction following the trend set up in 1974/75.

Electric locomotives delivered in 1975/76 included six class BR 181.2 units from Thyssen-Henschel, with electrical components by AEG-Telefunken; 67 class BR 111 units from Krupp, with electrics by Brown Boveri; and 69 class BR 151s from Krauss-Maffei with electrics by Siemens. By the beginning of 1977 the electric locomotive fleet totalled 2 700 units.

Electric locomotives now on order, in addition to the five prototype class E120s, include 76 class BR 111 units and 34 class BR 151 locomotives. The BR 111 is comparatively new, having first entered service in 1976. It has proved itself a worthy successor to the class E110 which it will eventually replace on long-distance and suburban passenger services. Principal specifications of the Bo-Bo class E111 are: hourly output, 3 700 kW; starting tractive force, 28 tonnes; braking force of the electric resistance brake at 150 to 160 km/h, 9 tonnes; maximum speed, 150 km/h; service weight (with automatic central buffer coupling) 84 tonnes; length over buffers, 16 750 mm; minimum negotiable curve radius, 100 m; axle load 20 tonnes.

The class E151 locomotive, designed to haul freight trains of 1 000 tonnes at 120 km/h is gradually helping DB to phase out existing class 150 locomotives which are proving inadequate for present-day requirements. The E151 weighs 181 tonnes for a continuous rating of 6 000 kW and a top speed of 120 km/h—compared with 198.6 tonnes, continuous rating of 4 400 kW and maximum speed of 100 km/h for class 150.

With the delivery during 1975/76 of 24 class ET 420 and 27 class ET 472 units, DB's fleet

A modified series 601 diesel fitted with gas turbine/diesel power

of electric trainsets now totals 1 124. In 1977 the railway decided to halt further purchases of the three-car ET 472—at least for the present—and concentrate trainset investments on purchases of 121 class ET 420s. Designed for S-Bahn services, the 420 has each axle powered, giving a total output of 3 700 kW for a four-car set. Speeds of up to 120 km/h can be reached in 37 seconds.

Strength of the railway's diesel-traction fleet—following deliveries during 1975/76 of 170 locomotives (86 class BR 218 units and 52 class BR 219 units from MaK; 40 class Köf 333 from Krupp, Thyssen Henschel, Krauss-Maffei, Arnold Jung and Gmeinder)—now stands at 4 719 locomotives. Orders placed in 1977 included: 70 class BR 218 locomotives; 36 class BR291 locomotives and 28 class Köf locomotives.

There were no purchases of diesel trainsets following delivery in 1976 of 20 new class VT 614 three-car sets supplied by Uerdingen, Orenstein & Koppel and MAN. The 614 has a top speed of 140 km/h and is 79.46 m long. Control cars back and front.

DEVELOPMENT PLANS

A major investment programme to 1985 was first outlined by DB in 1971. It called for investment of DM 31 000 million over 15 years, with the Federal Government putting up more than 50 per cent of the cost.

Major proposals included:
—Construction of 950 km of new 300 km/h lines
—Upgrading of 1 250 km of existing track for speeds of up to 200 km/h
—Electrification of 3 000 km
—Construction of four new marshalling yards
—Elimination of grade crossings throughout the system

Federal investment in all forms of transport rose from DM 1 000 million in 1950 to DM 15 600 million in 1970. But during that period railway share of the total declined from 35 per cent to less than 10 per cent of the annual allocation.

Given the money for overall system development, DB planners forecast a surge of new traffic towards the railways. By 1985, they say, total passenger-km could reach 79 000 million—more than twice the 1972 total of 37 000 million. And of the 1985 total, more than 47 000 million passenger/km are likely to be on the longer distance routes.

Anticipated increase in wagonload freight traffic is from 60 700 million ton/km in 1972 to around 97 500 million ton/km by 1985.

So by 1985 traffic revenues should yield DM 19 610 million. Federal subsidies for loss-making passenger services, track equalisation costs claimed by DB could yield DM 4 900 million. Operating costs are estimated at DM 21 470 million. Net result: operating surplus of DM 3 040 million.

If the programme is not developed DB believes there could then be a traffic growth across the board of just about 10 per cent. Receipts would rise only marginally, from the 1972 figure of DM 12 260 million to DM 13 370 million. Expenditures would go up from DM 18 590 million to DM 20 570 million. Subsidies would be at about the same level—DM 3 963 million. Result of DM 3 237 million.

HIGH SPEED PLANS

Important improvements in passenger train speeds will come when DB has been able to construct its planned high-speed links, suitable for operation to 300 km/h. Seven new links are planned, and in a blue-paper published in June 1973, Bonn promised cash for four of them: Mannheim—Stuttgart (105 km) at a cost of DM 900 million; Hanover—Gemunden (280 km), at a cost of DM 4200: Aschaffenburg—Wurzburg (65 km) at a cost of DM 1 200 million; and Cologne—Cross Gerau (180 km) at a cost of about DM 3 000 million.

The other three high-speed lines DB would like to build are Stuttgart—Munich (220 km; cost, DM 2 900 million); Rastatt—Offenburg (50 km; cost DM 330 million); and Kaiserslautern—Ludwigshafen (50 km; cost. DM 670 million).

Work started on construction of the Hanover—Kassel—Gemunden line during 1973.

Automatic train control: A total of some 7 087 motive-power units has now been equipped for automatic train control.

Telecommunications: After extensive studies, radio communication with trains was introduced on the DB, for the first time, between Lübeck and Puttgarden. Communication is maintained between the operating staff on the ground and 50 locomotives already equipped with radio, and the results have proved to be satisfactory.

In general, DB has made use of radio for a long time, and the number of sets employed was further increased by an additional 3 000 two-way radio, and other transmitting and receiving sets, to give a total of some 14 000.

Use of Computers: The "Electronic Seat Reservation Centre" in Frankfurt (Main), which came into operation on 1 February 1971, deals with the reservation of all accommodation in TEE, Intercity and through trains. It is the largest in Europe using real-time data-processing methods and is connected with the Austrian, Belgian, Luxembourg and Danish Railways.

Work is continuing, inter alia, on the development of computer programmes for the preparation of timetables, the economic turn-round of coaches used for holiday traffic, and duty rosters.

Local Transport: Some 25 per cent of DB's total building investments were in local transport in conurbations, including the Munich S-Bahn system and the airport line at Frankfurt (Main), although work on other S-Bahn projects, at Frankfurt (Main), Hamburg, and in the Ruhr, was delayed, largely because of increasing costs. New S-Bahn projects in Stuttgart and Cologne were begun in 1971 and 1972, respectively.

Marshalling Yards: Work on the future Maschen marshalling yard, to the South of Hamburg, continued actively, in order to complete the planning of the North-South system, and the preparation of the Jesteburg-Maschen arrival line, having a length of some 8 miles (13 km). 46 bridges are to be built over the lines, and 19 miles (30 km) of track and 60 sets of points were laid.

Having regard to the satisfactory experience obtained with the first fully-automatic hump used in Seelze marshalling yard, a commencement was made in the Mannheim marshalling yard with the provision, in an East-West direction, of installations for the automatic adjustment of the speed of shunted wagons.

Work on the Marshalling yards in Hamm (Westph.), Hagen-Vorhalle, Kornwestheim and Saarbrücken is proceeding according to plan.

Containers: The new container transhipment depot in Göttingen came into operation, the existing depots in Mannheim, Basle, and Wuppertal-Langerfeld were extended, and a second container crane was installed in the depot at Ludwigsburg.

At the beginning of 1972, the number of containers transported by the DB was as below:

Small containers:	
Railway-owned	109 896
Privately-owned	6 879
Medium-sized containers	
Railway-owned	23 393
Privately-owned	10 865
Large containers	
Railway-owned	1 267
Privately-owned	14 993

Track details

Standard rail: Type S49, weighing 99 lb per yard (49.5 kg/m), type S54, 109.8 lb per yd (54.5 kg/m) and type S64, 130.3 lb per yd (64.9 kg/m). Lengths are generally 30 to 120 m.

Type of rail joints: 4- and 6-hole fishplates.

Welded rail joints: See paragraph below

Cross ties (sleepers): Wood; steel; reinforced concrete.

Wood sleepers are impregnated beech, fir or oak, 8 ft 6⅜ in × 10¼ in × 6¼ in (2,600 × 260 × 160 mm)

Steel, 8 ft 6⅜ in long of 9 mm thickness, weighing 190 lb (86.3 kg)

The latest type of RC sleeper (Spannbetonschwelle B58) weighs 518 lb (235 kg), is 7 ft 11 in (2,400 mm) long, 7½ in (190 mm) thick under rails, 11 in (280 mm) wide at bottom and 5⅜ in (136 mm) at top.

Spacing: 25 in (650 mm) to 31½ in (800 mm)

Series 403 high-speed trainset

Rail fastenings: Baseplates and bolts, clips and spring washers with thin rubber or wood (poplar) pad between rail and plate; resilient rail spikes with wood and concrete sleepers and resilient rail clips with steel sleepers.

Max gradient: Main lines: 2.5% = 1 in 40.
Secondary lines: 6.6% = 1 in 16.5.

Max curvature: Main lines: 9.7° = min rad of 590 ft *(180 m)*
Secondary lines: 17.5° = min rad of 328 ft *(100 m)*

Gauge widening on curves: Radius over 984 ft *(300 m)* widening is *0 mm*
Radius 984-656 ft *(300-200 m)* widening is *5 mm*
Radius 656-492 ft *(200-150 m)* widening is *10 mm*
Radius 492-394 ft *(150-120 m)* widening is *15 mm*
Radius 394-328 ft *(120-100 m)* widening is *20 mm*

Max super-elevation: 5.9 in *(150 mm)* on curves of 590 ft *(180 m)* radius and under.

Rate of slope of super elevation: Generally 1: 10V (V = speed in *m/hr)*. On occasion this may be increased to 1: 8V up to 1 in 400. On reverse curves the permissible limit is 1: 4V up to 1 in 400.

Max altitude: Main Line: 3 172 ft *(967 m)* between Klais and Mittenwald. Highest station is Klais, 3 061 ft *(933 m)*
Secondary Line: 3 179 ft, *(969 m)* between Bärenthal and Aha on the Titisee-Seebrugg Line.

Max axle loading: 20 metric tons.

Welded rail: At the end of 1974 the total length of track laid with welded rails was 32 311 miles *(53 000 km.)*

Track Work: Considerable work was carried out on track renewal and maintenance, involving the extensive use both of wood and concrete sleepers, and UIC-60 rail (weighing *60.3 kg/m),* provision having been made for the laying of this rail in the proportion of 45 per cent The complete mechanisation of this work was facilitated by the use of the new track-renewal train UP 2.
The length of continuously welded rail increased to 79.3 per cent of the total rail laid on all tracks, and the number of welded points to 79.2 per cent of the total number. Research was carried out into the laying of track without sleepers, and track simplification continued, with the result that the number of points has been reduced, since 1960, by some 42 700.
The heating of points, principally by electricity, continued and now covers more than 15 000 sets.

Bridges and other structures: 160 new railway bridges, and 121 new road bridges, were opened together with 25 new, and 11 re-built, rail underpasses.
Joint work on structures in Hanover, Munich and Frankfurt (Main), continued actively, under the reorganisation of the DB, as did work on the railway buildings in Hanover, Frankfurt (Main), and Munich, and on S-Bahn buildings in the Hamburg, Rhine-Ruhr, Rhine-Main, and Munich conurbations.

Signalling and Telecommunications: 137 old-type signal boxes were replaced by 45 signal boxes with push-button geographical circuitry, to which 1 290 sets of points are connected. The DB has built a total of 1 061 signal boxes with geographical circuitry (of which 1 033 are in operation), to which 27 302 sets of points and derailers are connected, and which enabled 2 551 old-type mechanical and electro-mechanical signal boxes to be removed. The largest-signal boxes with geographical circuitry are those at the stations in Fürth (Bavaria), Buchholz (Kr. Harburg), Kirchweyhe, and Lauda.
The network of single and double track lines equipped with automatic block now covers a distance of 3 362 miles *(5 410 km)* including, installed recently, Bassum-Sagehorn, Altenbeken-Warburg (Westph.), Gemünden (Main)-Waigolshausen-Schweinfurt, and Gauting-Starnberg.

Level Crossings: 187 flashing-light and colour-light installations, with and without half-barriers, 38 other barriers, and 81 colour-light signals on barriers, were installed, and connections between barriers and protective railway signals were provided at 77 level crossings.

CONTAINER OPERATIONS: Container operations, domestic and international, are operated on behalf of the DB by:
TRANSFRACHT GmbH
Gutleutstrasse 160-164, 6 Frankfurt (Main)
Telephone: (611) 23 03 51
Telex: 41.45.45

General: The DB owns and operates some 23 700 containers of approximately 5.5 tonnes load capacity for domestic door-to-door service including collection and delivery by road. There are 12 main types, suitable for a variety of products.

Large DB-Containers for European International Service: These new 20 ft and 40 ft DB-containers, larger in width and height than Transcontainers, are intended for inland service in Germany and certain other European countries whose Loading Gauge permits. They conform to ISO standards in every other respect, including type and location of corner castings.

GHANA

GHANA RAILWAY AND PORTS ADMINISTRATION
PO Box 251, Takoradi

Telephone: 2181

General Manager, Ghana Railway & Ports Authority: Edward Moore
Solicitor: I. G. Carson
Training & Manpower Planning Manager: J. B. Yorke
Administrative Officer: J. R. Holdbrooke
Personnel Manager: F. A. Amissah
Engineering:
  Chief Engineer: S. Oduro
  Deputy Chief Engineers: J. Owusu
                                A. Ababio

Traffic:
Deputy Traffic Manager: G. L. Yamuah
  Assistant Traffic Manager: J. M. W. Aggrey
Locomotive:
  Chief Mechanical Engineer: F. G. Asamoah
Deputy Chief Mechanical Engineers: K. M. Amuah, J. A. K. Baidoo
  Senior Mechanical Engineer: J. J. Thompson
Accounts:
  Chief Accountant: B. K. Dadzie
  Deputy Chief Accountant: J. E. Sagoe
  Principal Accountants: K. Asoku
                              A. A. Amuah
                              D. A. Annan
Internal Audit:
  Chief Internal Auditor: P. A. Cudjoe
Port Management:
  Chief Ports Manager, Tema: D. A. Minta
  Port Manager, Takoradi: J. B. Kofie
  Port Manager, Tema: L. C. O. Cobblah
  Senior Port Superintendents: E. E. Thompson
                                     H. C. Ogoe
Electrical:
  Senior Electrical Engineer: J. K. Ankomah
Stores:
  Chief Stores Superintendent: G. A. Sey
  Principal Stores Superintendent: M. B. B. Wilson
  Senior Stores Superintendents: J. K. Hammond
                                       A. Entsua-Mensah
                                       Albert Ocran

Gauge: 1.067 m
Route length: 953 km

A multi-million pound facelift for Ghana Railways was announced by the Commissioner for Transport and Communications at the end of 1976. Under the programme priority is to be given to the realignment of the Takoradi-Hunt Valley line including double tracking.
During 1977 it was announced that Rail India Technical and Economic Services is to carry out consultancy and feasibility studies for the railway under a $US 1.7 million agreement signed in February.
Towards the end of 1977 World Bank officials travelled to Accra to discuss a possible $US 10 million loan to the railway for track upgrading and purchase of locomotives and rolling stock.
Under the railway's current Five-Year Development Plan (1975-79) rail services are to be extended 153 km from Awaso to Sunyani, capital of the Brong Ahafo region. Another extension will take the railway from Bosuso to Kibi in the eastern region. The railway is also considering the extension of rail facilities from the existing Shai Hills network to link with lake transport at Akosombo to provide an alternative means of cheap bulk transport for the heavy rice and livestock traffic originating in the north.

NEW LINE AND TRACK PROJECTS
The current proposal to extend the railway from Awaso to Sunyani is not new. Engineering and traffic surveys were first carried out in 1953 by Rendel Palmer and Tritton (UK). In 1963 another traffic survey was carried out by the railway itself. And in 1969 the Ministry of Economic Affairs submitted a report on the cost benefit of the scheme. But even though traffic potential in the area to be served has increased year by year, the project has never yet got off the ground, mainly because inflation has increased investment costs and interest charges. Now, however, the Ministry of Communications has allocated funds to meet the cost of feasibility studies—expected to reach Cedis 300 000. Actual construction cost is estimated at Cedis 35 million.
Ghana's railway network has excessive curvature in several sections, and this tends to increase line occupation and reduce line capacity. For example, between Kumasi and Takoradi there are 504 curves in a section of 270.48 km. Also there are several areas with excessively sharp curves—on the 12.88-km section between Kasi and Eduadin, for instance, there are 24 sharp curves, about two curves per km. Realignment of the permanent way on these sections will be aimed at increasing minimum curve radius to 335 m—improving train speeds and lessening the risk of derailments and damage to property.
One major realignment project involving nine sharp curves has already been completed on the Nsawam-Pakro section of the Eastern Line, and work on realignment of the section between Insu and Kuranti on the Western Line is also in hand. Total cost of all the realignment projects, covering the entire system, is expected to reach Cedis 25 833 500.
Track renewal, some track relaying, and installation of many new switches and crossings. Also included in the plan is: existing 39.7 kg/m rail to be replaced by 45 kg/m rail. A ballasting programme to provide for a depth of 15.7 cm of ballast on existing track and 23.6 cm on track which is to be relaid; this will involve laying 63,000 tonnes of ballast a year, and should result in a minimum of 15.7 cm beneath sleepers on all tracks after 12 years.

SIGNALLING
A separate project aimed at providing a centralised traffic and telecommunications system which will rely heavily on radio-telephone links is underway. The cost is estimated at Cedis 5 million. Most important features of the project are:
1. Extension of the trunk dialling telephone system.
2. Radio-telephone communication between control post and cab.
3. Automatic train reporting.
4. Centralised message centre, with telegraph/teleprinter system.
5. Takoradi region traffic control.
6. Centralised traffic control feasibility studies.

OTHER IMPROVEMENTS

Railway electrification, especially in such traffic intensive areas as the Western Line route and from Huni Valley to Takoradi where traffic density is highest, is believed to be vital. Feasibility studies into an electrification programme are to be carried out, with detailed examination of the engineering and economic aspects of the proposal. Technical and feasibility studies are also to be made into track doubling on the Western Line. The studies will examine:

a)   The present and anticipated future passenger and freight traffic volume, to determine when saturation would make it essential to double certain sections.

b)   The comparative costs of equipment to improve train safety, improve performance and increase line capacity, as an alternative to track doubling.

c)   A cost-benefit study of the project as a whole.

MOTIVE POWER AND ROLLING STOCK

	Line haul	Shunting (Switching)
Locomotives in steam	37	55
Locomotives in diesel-electric	66	12
Locomotives in diesel-hydraulic	—	22
Number of railcars, diesel	4	
Number of passenger train coaches	182	
Number of freight train cars	3 289	

TRACK CONSTRUCTION DETAILS

Standard rail, type and weight:
 Sekondi-Nsuta—RBS 81 lb per yd *(40.2 kg/m)*
 Nsuta-Obuasi—ARA 80 lb per yd *(39.7 kg/m)*
 Obuasi-Kumasi—RBS 80 lb per yd *(39.7 kg/m)*
 Kumasi-Tafo—BS 60 lb per yd *(29.8 kg/m)*
 Tafo-Accra—RBS 60 lb per yd *(29.8 kg/m)*
 Prestea branch—RBS 60 lb per yd *(29.8 kg/m)*
 Cen. Prov. Rly.—BS 60 lb per yd *(29.8 kg/m)*
 Awaso Branch—ASCE 75 lb per yd *(37.2 kg/m)*

Joints: 4-hole fishplates.

Cross ties (sleepers): Standard steel; and wood 5 in × 10 in × 6 ft 6 in *(127 × 254 × 1 981 mm)*

Spacing: 2 200 per mile *(1 365 per km)*

Rail fastenings:
 wood sleepers: Dog spikes, Macbeth spike anchors, Elastic rail spikes. Tests are being made with Lockspikes (England) and single shank spring spikes (Germany).
 steel sleepers: Keys, 1 and 0 clips, ARA clips, ABK clips.

Filling: Mainly crushed granite, some gravel.

Max Curvature: Sekondi-Kumasi 8° 40′=rad of 663 ft *(202 m)*
 Kumasi-Accra 8° 40′= rad of 663 ft *(202 m)*
 Cent. Prov. Rly. 8° 40′=rad of 663 ft *(202 m)*
 Prestea Branch 17° = rad of 338 ft *(103 m)*
 Awaso Branch 6° = rad of 955 ft *(291 m)*

Max gradient: 1.25% = 1 in 80; except Prestea Branch 2.5% = 1 in 40.

Longest continuous gradient: 6.2 miles with ruling grade of 1.25% and max curves of 8° 40′.

Max altitude: 938 ft *(286 m)* near Kumasi.

Permitted speeds:
 Freight trains 35 mph *(56 km/h)*
 Passenger trains 40 mph *(64 km/h)*
 Except Prestea branch:
 Freight trains 18 mph *(29 km/h)*
 Passenger trains 25 mph *(40 km/h)*

Axle loading:
 Sekondi-Kumasi-Accra 16 tons
 Central Province Railway 12½ tons
 Prestea Branch 13½ tons
 Awaso Branch 16 tons

Gauge widening on sharpest curve: 1 in

Super-elevation on sharpest curve: 3½ in

Rate of slope of superelevation: ½ in per rail length.

GREECE

HELLENIC RAILWAYS ORGANISATION

Organisme Des Chemins De Fer Hellenique SA,
1-3 Karolou Street, Athens—107

Telephone: 541 510
Telex: 215187

Governor and President of Administrative Board: Constantine Papageorghiou
Vice-Governor: M. Fikioris
General Directors: S. Keramidas
           I. Kazantzoglou
Central Administration:
 Personnel: P. Karakostas
 Operation: I. Lambros
 Traction: N. Bardis
 Track: N. Karagiorgas
 Organisation Design and Planning: C. Kohilas
 Commercial: C. Archondakis
 Supplies: A. Apergis
 Finance: Ch. Verriopoulos
 Audit: Th. Vouvopoulos
Regional Management:
 Athens: Th. Kounoupis, 1-3 Karolou St, Athens 107
 Thessaloniki: J. Karantzoglou, Dodekanissou 15, Thessaloniki
 Peloponnesus: V. Papageorgiou
 Workshops Manager: G. Charamis

Gauge: Various—see tabulated data.
Route length: 35 668 km

In 1975, CH-Railways reformed and unified their previously drawn-up long-term programmes and drew up a new modernisation and development plan; revising the 15 year one elaborated three years before. The new plan, will involve expenditure of 37 billion Drachmae.

During the next few years exclusive priority will be given to track renewal and curvature improvement, wherever possible. In the mean-time SOFRERAIL, the French consulting group, which was scheduled to stay in Athens up to the end of 1975, as Counselor of the Greek state and CH on railway matters, will continue giving advice up to the end of 1977.

Greek Railways (CH) are to invest 6 200 million drachmas (about 800 million French francs) between now and 1982 to modernise the railway network.

Mr John Lambros, CH Chairman, considers that this investment has two major objectives: firstly, it will increase the capacity of existing lines and, secondly, it will shorten journey times on certain routes.

A ferry-boat service is also being planned between the ports of Volos or Salonica and Latakia in Syria, following an agreement signed early in February by the Greek and Syrian Governments.

A new international service between Paris and Athens was introduced on 23 June 1977, which shortens the journey between the two capitals from 57 to 50 hours. The route followed is: Lausanne, Milan, Ancona, Bari, Brindisi, and by ferry to Patras.

The Governments of Greece and Syria signed an important agreement in Damascus early in February on the development of shipping links between their two countries. This document gives special priority to setting up a wagon ferry service between the ports of Volos or Salonica and Latakia or Tartus, a distance of about 1 500 km. This will provide an alternative route to the present single-track railway line via Istanbul for traffic towards the Middle East.

Aspects of modernisation stressed by the new plan include:

1.   Renewal of all old rails and sleepers on the lines linking Athens with Thessaloniki and on to Idomeni, and from Thessaloniki to Alexandroupolis.

2.   Important realignments to permit higher commercial speeds, particularly on the Athens-Thessaloniki and Thessaloniki-Alexandroupolis lines.

3.   Signalling improvements and resignalling throughout the network and installation of CTC on the Tithorea-Domokos line.

4.   Construction of more industrial sidings, extension of sidings at stations and improvements to station buildings.

5.   Modernisation of the railway's telecommunication system.

6.   Purchase of new locomotives and rolling stock.

In addition to the railway's direct investments, Dr.1100 million is being allocated for various works from the Public Investment Budget. These investments will be controlled by the Ministry of Public Works.

In 1977 CH purchased new locomotives, new passenger coaches and new freight wagons—all for standard-gauge operation.

FERRY SERVICES

CH is also studying a UIC proposal for the creation of a rail ferry service between Greece and a middle-east port. First proposals were for a service between a Greek port and Turkey. Due to continued congestion of Turkish railway routes, CH officers are reported to favour a ferry link with Latakia, Syria. Most likely Greece port to be selected as a ferry terminal would be Volos, which has capacity for more traffic (unlike Piraeus and

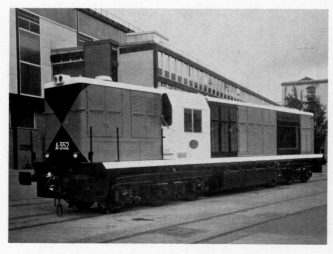

Alsthom CC diesel electric rated at 2 100 hp for a top speed of 105 km/h; fitted with SEMT 16 PA 4 diesel engine.

Thessaloniki) and is connected to the main north-south standard-gauge trunk line. There is space for a large marshalling yard close to the port area, and sufficient water depth for a ferry pier. A preliminary study on rail connections for the port and construction of the pier has already been completed. Under the UIC proposal, operation of the ferry service is to be mutually agreed between the two countries concerned.

A new international service being offered by CH this year will run from Athens to Paris via the Greek port of Patras and a ferry link with Brindisi. The existing direct Athens-Paris service via Yugoslavia is being phased out, and the new service will start on June 23. Using the Greece-Italy sea link, journey time will be cut from 57 hours (three nights) to 50 hours (two nights). The service from Paris will be via Lausanne, Milan, Ancona, Bari and Brindisi.

SUBURBAN PASSENGER SERVICES

Some Athens-Piraeus suburban services are still being handled independently by the Piraeus Electric Railway, in spite of a new law which puts control of all railways in Greece in the hands of CH. The line was taken over by the state early in 1976, but still has a separate management.

Mr Lambros, Chairman, said: "The Government has not yet decided which organisation will operate the Piraeus Electric Railway—though we know it is to be considerably extended.

"Ever since the establishment of CH, one of our fundamental aims has been to improve rail services in the Greater Athens area, in combination with the Metro. In association with Sofrerail experts we have elaborated plans which cannot yet be put into effect—because they are connected with the master plan for development of the Greater Athens area."

Contract for the preliminary study for a 17-km underground line in central Athens has gone to a consortium of three French companies. Value of the contract is put at Dr.157 million.

TRAFFIC

During 1974 and 1975 CH-Railways carried the following traffic:

	1974	1975
Transported tons of goods (in thousands)	3 955	4 034
Ton/kms (in thousands)	901 956	930 667
Transported passengers (in thousands)	12 468	12 466
Passenger/kms (in thousands)	1 594 173	1 552 706

MOTIVE POWER AND ROLLING STOCK

After delivery of new rolling stock in 1975, fleet figures are as follows:

Diesel-locomotives	Standard gauge	145
	Narrow gauge	43
Rail-cars	Standard gauge	52
	Narrow gauge	53
Passenger coaches	Standard gauge	344
	Narrow gauge	178
Freight wagons	Standard gauge	8 268
	Narrow gauge	1 902
Containers-tank wagons	Standard gauge	329

SIGNALLING AND TRAIN CONTROL

New signalling installations included automatic signalling over the Athens-Inoi and Thessaloniki-Plati routes which operates by colour lights through short isolated sections of track. Supplier was Spoorweg Sein Industrie.

A total of 330 grade crossings have been earmarked for automatic barriers by Westinghouse.

Three-car Esslingen diesel trainset built by Ferrostaal.

2 150-hp Co-Co Alco diesel-electric heading the Hellas-Balkan express.

Diesel-mechanical railcar built by Dusseldorf Wagonfabrik equipped with a 210-hp MAN engine hauling a trailer coach.

GUINEA

CHEMIN DE FER DE LA GUINÉE
PO Box 581, Conakry

Director: Diane Pierre

Gauge: 1.00 m
Route length: 662 km

The railway from Conakry to the River Niger joins the limits of navigability of the Upper Niger (Kouroussa) with the sea port of Conakry on the coast of Guinea. The railway was opened from Conakry as far as Kouroussa in 1910. In 1914, it was extended as far as Kankan, on the River Milo, a tributary of the Niger. Guinea produces an abundance of palm oil and rubber, and also ground nuts. There is, moreover, an extensive export trade in hides. The independent republic of Guinea was proclaimed on October 2, 1958, after the territory of French Guinea had decided at the referendum of September 28, to leave the French Community.

Studies have been completed and initial earthworks started on a new 1 400 km Trans-Guinea line which will link new bauxite deposits at Tongue and Dabola and the agricultural region of Nimba with the port of Conakry.

The new line, to be built to metre-gauge standards, will partly replace the existing Conakry-Kouroussa railway, as much of the present track is too lightly laid and gradients are too steep to handle growing traffic. Maximum gradient at present is 15 per cent compensated and maximum axle loading 13 tonnes. Existing 20 kg/m rails are to be replaced by 30 kg/m sections.

The present motive power fleet includes 27 mainline diesel locomotives, five diesel shunters and eight diesel railcars. Rolling stock includes 23 passenger coaches and 483 freight wagons.

Latest purchases include two model GL 22C diesel-electric 1 500-hp main-line diesels from General Motors which went into service earlier this year.

The Trans-Guinea (as it it is to be called) will in part replace the lightly-laid 600 km metre-gauge track built in 1900-14 to link navigable parts of the Niger river system with the sea at Conakry. Its basic function is to link bauxite deposits at Tougue and Dabola and iron ore mines at Simondou as well as Nimba with Conakry, but as the main line and branches will penetrate large tracts of the country hitherto unexploited, it will also boost agricultural, forestry and industrial development. Construction was scheduled to begin during 1975.

INDUSTRIAL RAILWAYS

There are three other lines in operation, all serving mineral deposits.

The **CF de Fria**, opened in 1960, carries the products of the bauxite mine and aluminium plant at Fria to the port of Conakry. It is of metre gauge, 89 miles *(143 km)* long single track, laid with 92.7 lb per yd *(46 kg/m)* continuous welded rail on metal sleepers. Three Alsthom 1 100 hp diesel-electric locomotives hauling 50-tonne load wagons transport some 500 000 tonnes of export per year.

The **CF de la Compagnie Minière de Conakry** is a 4 ft 8½ in × 3 *(1.435 m)* gauge line 9 miles *(14 km)* long, running between an iron ore mine on the outskirts of Conakry and the port. About 800 000 tonnes per year are carried to the port using two Alsthom 700 hp diesel-electric locomotives.

The **Boke Railway** is a mineral ore line, running 145 km inland from Port Kamsar on the coast of Guinea. Built by a consortium of European contractors, the line was inaugurated in mid-1973 and has, since then, been operated by Canac Consultants on behalf of the Guinea government and the railway administration, Office d'Amenagement de Boke. Canac was initially contracted to manage the operation of the line and to train Guinean staff for eventual self management by 1976. The contract has now, however, been extended for a further two years.

The first half of the line runs through the coastal sea plain while the upper half reaches into the foothills of the Fouta Djalon mountains. The line is standard gauge with 60 kg/m continuously welded UIC profile rail laid entirely on steel sleepers. The line has a capacity of 12 million tonnes annually with ore moving in European built wagons hauled by US-built rolling stock. In 1975 a passenger operation was started up and Canac reports that ridership is increasing.

HONG KONG

KOWLOON-CANTON RAILWAY (BRITISH SECTION)
Hung Hom, Kowloon

Telephone: K3-646321

General Manager: R. E. Gregory, J.P.
Assistant General Manager (Planning/Administration): U. L. Wong
Assistant General Manager (Traffic): —
Treasury Accountant: C. K. Woo
Project Manager: S. S. Choi
Departmental Secretary: H. Singh
Assistant Departmental Secretary: Raymond P. C. Kan
Traffic Controller i/c: T. L. Ma
Traffic Controller: Y. H. Choi
Assistant Traffic Controller: K. Y. Ngan
Way & Works Engineer i/c: K. S. Chung
Way & Works Engineer: M. R. Elvy
Railway Workshops Engineer i/c: Clement B. T. Chiu
Railway Workshops Engineer: Chang Yu-hong

Gauge: 4' 8½''
Route length: 33.5 km

Work is in progress on the construction of a new loop line and station near the Railway Workshops at Ho Tung Lau (Shau Tin) to service the new racecourse in Sha Tin. It is expected to be completed by September, 1978, in time for the opening of the new racecourse in October, 1978.

International tenders have been called to construct a new tunnel through Beacon Hill which will accommodate two railway tracks with lower approach gradients. The tunnel is two kilometres long. Tenders are also being called for remodelling of Mongkok and Sha Tin Stations.

Existing semaphore signals are being replaced by modern colour light signalling. A central train control room is to be provided at Hung Hom to monitor train movements along the whole line.

In January, 1977, Transportation System and Market Research Ltd (Transmark), a subsidiary of British Railways, was appointed to carry out a study of the electrification of the line and the viability of the following extensions: from Hung Hom to Tsim Sha Tsui, Tai Wai to Kwai Chung, Beacon Hill Tunnel (North Portal) to Sha Tin Racecourse Station via Yuen Chau Kok, Tai Po Market to Tai Po Industrial Estate and from a connecting point near Tai Po Market to Tuen Mun via Yuen Long. A report on their findings was submitted to Hong Kong Government in September, 1977.

Two new diesel electric locomotives, each of 2,000 hp, arrived in March, 1977 and both have been put into service.

Six rapid ticket issuing machines were installed at the booking office of Kowloon Station in April, 1977, each capable of issuing 200 tickets per minute.

TRAFFIC	1975/76	1976/77
Total freight ton-km	53 358 788	46 142 100
Total freight tonnage	1 538 958	1 386 865
Total passenger-km	275 419 895	244 732 600
Total passengers carried	13 398 244	12 210 985

FINANCES	1975/76	1976/77
Revenue	HK$38 656 650	HK$34 845 185(*)
Expenses	HK$26 916 362	HK$30 818 614(*)

(Note: K.C.R.'s financial year ends on 31st March. (*) Subject to audit).

MOTIVE POWER
KCR operates 12 line-haul diesel electric locomotives.

TRACK IMPROVEMENTS

Work on double tracking the line from Hung Hom to Sha Tin (excluding the Beacon Hill tunnel) commenced in October, 1975 and was completed at the end of 1977, it gives an additional daily capacity of 16,000 passengers in each direction.

The double tracking of the second third of the line from Sha Tin to Tai Po Market has recently been approved by the Hong Kong Government and work commenced in January, 1978. It is expected to be completed in the middle of 1979.

Two sidings at Fo Tan (near Sha Tin) were completed in July, 1977. One, an oil siding, was opened to traffic in May 1977 for unloading rail-borne petroleum products from China.

A marshalling Yard at Lo Wu, which will consist of 7 tracks with an overall trackage of 10,300 ft, will be partially in use in September 1977 and be completed in mid 1980.

Ballasting the existing track to a greater depth will start in September 1977. Heavier UIC 54 rails with concrete sleepers and long welded sections are being introduced progressively to replace 95 lb per yard rail on wooden sleepers.

Three new 2 000 hp locomotives delivered by General Electric between 1974 and 1977

The new Kowloon station in Hung Hom

HUNGARY
HUNGARIAN STATE RAILWAYS
Magyar Allamvasutak (M.A.V.), Népköztársaság Utja 75, Budapest VI

General Manager: Zoltán Szücs
Assistant General Managers: László Oroszváry
                                     János Gulyás
                                     Béla Szabó
Chief of Secretariat: Jenó Toppantó
Chief of International Section: Dénes Gazdi
Departmental Managers:
  Planning and Development: Dr. Lajos Holló
  Personnel and Education: Gyula Bálint
  General Administration: Dr. Imre Ács
  Labour: Dr. László Rimóczi
  Financial: Károly Jándi
  Construction and Track Maintenance: Dr János Telek
  Engineering and Traction: Béla Maráz
  Operations: Dr. Ferenc Géringer
  Telecommunications and Signalling: Sándor Urbán
  Workshops: Tibor Kardos
  Commercial: Miklós Juhász
  Control of materials: Alajos Horváth

Gauge: 1.435 m.
Total route length: 7 550 km.
Total track length: 12 523 km.

More than 40 000 million forints will be spent on railway modernisation in Hungary under the present 1976-80 Five-Year Plan. The programme includes upgrading of over 1 600 km of track and the installation of 800 light-protected or half-barrier level-crossings. A further 175 km of track will be electrified, including the 155-km line from Budapest to Kelebia. This will bring the total electrified length of track to 1 351 km or 58 per cent of the mainline system. Electrified trackage at present carries 60 per cent of traffic on MAV.
More than 70 railway yards are to be fitted with Integra-Domino safety equipment to bring about 80 per cent of the network up to modern standards. The reloading area at Zahony station on the Hungarian-Russian border is to be fully modernised; the marshalling yard at Budapest-Kelenfoeld is to be rebuilt; new joint border stations are to be established—with Yugoslav State Railways at Murakeresztur and with Romanian State Railways at Biharkerestes—while the existing station at Hegyeshalom on the Austrian border is to be completely renovated.
By 1980 it is expected that 92-96 per cent of all trains will be electric or diesel hauled and 85-90 per cent of shunting will be carried out by diesel locomotives.
Rolling stock is to be increased by the purchase of 750 new passenger coaches and 9 000 large-capacity freight wagons.

ELECTRIFICATION
Major projects to be carried out during 1977/78 include track improvements over 300 km and further electrification between Budapest and Kelebia. To accelerate work on the Budapest-Kelebia electrification project, MAV has signed a 5-million rouble ($US 6 700 000) credit agreement with the Comecon international investment bank. Cost of electrification will be 1 000 million forints. The new loan will make is possible for MAV to switch over to electric haulage on the line by July 1979 instead of the originally scheduled December 1979.

Total electrified route length on 31 December 1976: 1 196 km.
Total electrified track length on 31 December 1976: 3 211 km.
System of electrification: 25 000 V, 50 Hz.
Lines electrified during 1975:
  Length: 73 km.
  Location: Hatvan-Ujsreise, Füresabony-Eger
  Completion Dates: December 1975.

TRAFFIC		1974	1975	1976
Total freight ton-km	million	22 793	23 245	22 818
Total freight tonnage	million	128.8	130.8	130.7
Total passenger-km	million	15 128	14 557	14 341
Total passengers carried	million	356.3	342.8	335.7

FINANCIAL	1974	1975	1976
		(Million Ft)	
Revenues	22 366	24 034	26 246
Expenses	21 000	22 565	24 280

DIESEL LOCOMOTIVES

Class	Axle Arrangement	Transmission	Rated Power hp	Max kg	Tractive Effort Continuous at kg	Tractive Effort Continuous at kmlh	Max Speed kmlh	Wheel Dia. mm	Axle Load Tons	Total Weight Tons	Length mm	No. Built	Year first Built	Builders: Mechanical Parts	Builders: Engine	Builders: Transmission
M28	B	Mech.	135	5 490	5 250	5.0	30	950	10.0	20.0	7 390		1955	MVG	Ganz	MVG
M31	C	Hyd.	450	15 700	9 600	7.0	60	1 232	15.0	45.0	9 830		1958	MAVAG	Ganz	Voith
M32	C	Hyd.	350				60	920	12.0	36.0	9 510		1973	MAVAG	Ganz	Ganz
M38	C	Hyd.	350	11 000	7 000	5.0	60	920	10.6	32.0	8 850		1960	MVG	MVG	UVA
M40	BoBo	Elec.	1 000	24 300	13 600	13.7	100	1 040	18.9	75.6	13 590		1966	MAVAG	Ganz	Ganz
M41.20	BB	Hyd.	1 800	19 740	12 700	20.0	100	1 100	16.5	66.0	16 500		1973	MAVAG	Pielstick	Voith
M41.21	BB	Hyd.	1 200	25 400	15 200	14.00	100	920	15.7	62.6	13 940		1969	MAVAG	Pielstick	
M44	BoBo	Elec.	600	18 600	12 030	8.3	80	1 040	15.5	62.0	11 290		1956	MAVAG	Ganz	MVG
M46.0	BB	Hyd.	610	11 400	7 400	12.0	60	920	11.9	47.6	12 090		1964	MAVAG	Ganz	Ganz
M46.2	BB	Hyd.	760	13 050	7 900	13.0	65	920	12.0	48.0	11 840		1964	MAVAG	Ganz	Ganz
Mk48	BB	Mech.	135	4 740	4 480	5.0	50	700	4.4	17.6	8 965		1960	MVG	Ganz	MVG
Mk49	BB	Hyd.	270	8 000	7 800	5.0	50	700	6.8	27.0	11 060		1968	MVG	MVG	UVA
M61	CoCo	Elec.	1 950		21 000	19.2	100	1 040	18.5	108.0	18 900		1963	NOHAB	GM	GM
M62	CoCo	Elec.	2 000		20 000	20.0	100	1 050	20.0	120.0	17 560		1965	Lugansk	Kolomna	Charkow
M63	CoCo	Elec.	2 700	40 000	21 700		130	1 250	20.0	120.0	19 540		1971	MAVAG	Pielstick	MVG
MDa	BB	Hyd.	800				100		10.5	41.0	15 520			Mavag	Pielstick	Ganz
M43	BB	Hyd.	450	14 000	11 000	5.0	60	920	12	48.0	11 460		1974	Aug 23	Aug 23	
M47	BB	Hyd.	700	15 000	11 500	5.0	70	920	12	48.0	11 460		1974	Aug 23	Aug 23	

Mk48, Mk49: 760 mm Gauge.

ELECTRIC LOCOMOTIVES

Class	Axle Arrangement	Line Current kV	Type	Rated Power hp	Max kg	Tractive Effort Continuous at kg	Tractive Effort Continuous at kmlh	Max Speed kmlh	Wheel Dia. mm	Weight tonnes	Length mm	No. Built	Year First Built	Builders Mechanical Parts	Builders Electrical Equipment
V41	BoBo	25	50 ac	1 390		14 600	65.0	80	1 040	73.0	12 290	30	1958	MAVAG	Ganz
V42	BoBo	25	50 ac	1 650		15 500	70.0	80	1 040	74.0	12 290	42	1960	MAVAG	Ganz
V43	B B	25	50 ac	3 000		15 000	52.5	130	1 180	78.0	15 700	205	1963	MAVAG	Ganz
V63	CoCo	25	50 ac	5 000				120		116.0	19 540	2	1975	MAVAG	Ganz

INDIA
INDIAN GOVERNMENT RAILWAYS
MINISTRY OF RAILWAYS (RAILWAY BOARD)
Rail Bhavan, New Delhi 1

Minister for Railways: Madhu Dandavate
Railway Board
  Chairman: Shri G. P. Warrier
  Financial Commissioner: Shri P. N. Jain
  Member, Traffic: Shri B. M. Kaul
  Member, Mechanical: Shri P. N. Kaul
  Member, Staff: Shri V. P. Sawhney
  Member, Finance: K. T. Mirchandani
  Member, Health: Dr. S. S. Verma
  Member, Electrical Engineering: R. L. Mitra
  Member, Traffic: S. G. Samant
  Member, Mechanical: B. B. Lal
  Member, Vigilance: B. S. Lal
  Member, Works: Krishan Chandra
General Managers
  Central Railway: Shri A. L. Gupta
  Eastern Railway: Shri E. J. Simoes
  Northern Railway: Shri S. C. Misra
  North Eastern Railway: Shri P. R. Pusalkar
  Northeast Frontier Railway: G. H. Keswani
  Southern Railway: Shri R. M. Sambamoorthi
  South Central Railway: Shri K. S. Rajan
  South Eastern Railway: Shri M. Menezes
  Western Railway: M. G. Punoose
  Metropolitan Transport Project, (Railways), Calcutta: Shri A. K. Chakravarti
  Construction Organisation, Southern Railway: Shri T. V. Joseph
Manufacturing Units
  Chittaranjan Locomotive Works: Shri K. S. Ramaswamy
  Diesel Locomotive Works: K. P. Jayaram
  Integral Coach Factory: L. R. Gosain
Research, Design and Standards Organisation
  Director General: Shri G. N. Bhattacharjee

1976-77 was the third year of the Railways' fifth Five Year Plan of development which has been drawn up in keeping with the national Five Year Plan.

Tha main objective of the fifth Plan is to provide the capacity for increased freight and passenger traffic anticipated during the fifth Plan period with flexibility to meet any sudden changes in the pattern of traffic or any unforseen demands. The Plan now envisages development expenditure of over Rs. 2 200 crores* for this purpose inclusive of Rs. 50 crores for Metropolitan Transit Schemes. While finalising this provision, emphasis has been laid on better utilisation of existing track and rolling stock capacity by maximising movement in block rakes and reducing turn-round time.

Inclusive of an expenditure of Rs. 393 crores in 1975-76, the expenditure for the first two years of the Plan amounted to Rs. 739.5 crores; an outlay of Rs. 1 439 crores is proposed for the remaining years.

By 1978-79, the railways will be equipped to carry an estimated originating freight traffic of 250 to 260 million tonnes, of which the largest single commodity would be 98 million tonnes of coal. Against this, the railways moved 223.3 million tonnes, including 80.5 millions of coal, in the second year of the Plan. These figures include the railways own traffic.

The table below shows the progress made in the movement of freight traffic in block rakes and reducing wagon turn-round time in the first two years of the plan period:

		1974-75		1975-76	
	Unit	BG	MG	BG	MG
Ratio of loaded wagons hauled by block rakes	per cent	60.8	23.0	60.8	24.9
Wagon turn-round time	days	14.6	12.0	13.5	11.6

In regard to passenger traffic, it is now anticipated that the railways would be required to handle a 17 per cent increase in non-suburban and 25 per cent growth in suburban passenger traffic, in terms of passenger km, over 1973-74—the last year of the fourth Five Year Plan. An increase of eight per cent in non-suburban traffic and 17 per cent in suburban traffic had already taken place by the end of the second year of the Plan.

* Crore = 10 million rupees

FIFTH PLAN EXPENDITURE

	(Rs. Crores)		
Programme	Actual expenditure	Outlay as approved by Planning Commission	
	1974-76	1976-77	1977-79
Rolling Stock	374.8	185.2	500.0
New Lines, electrification & other line capacity works	189.2	96.3	230.0
Track & Bridges	79.8	49.0	129.0
Workshops/Sheds & Machinery & Plants	34.7	24.5	60.0
Signalling & Safety	28.4	13.0	32.0
Staff Quarters & Staff Welfare	13.9	10.0	22.0
Others	18.7	33.0	55.0
	739.5	411.0	1 028.0

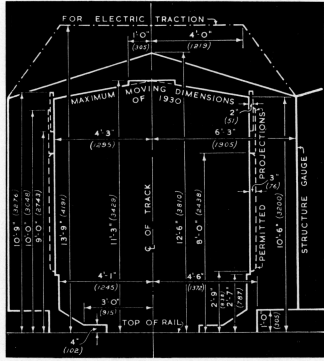

Medium Gauge

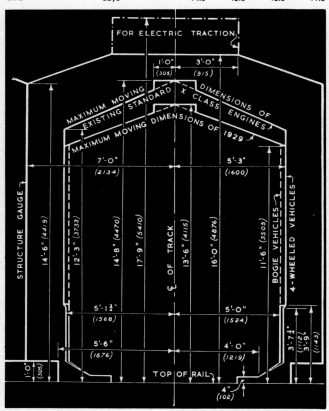

Broad Gauge

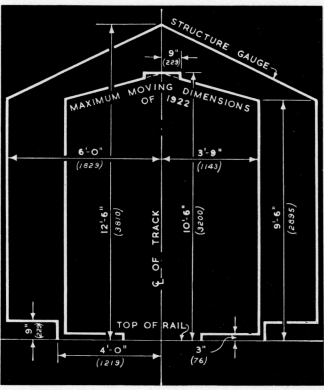

Narrow Gauge

Passenger traffic: Both passenger receipts and volume of passenger traffic increased in 1975-76 to an all time record. At Rs. 514.13 crores, the receipts were 24.6 per cent over the previous year; passenger journeys added up to 2 946 millions, 21.3 per cent more than the previous year's total.
Mail and Express earnings of Rs. 283 crores (Rs 225 crores in 1974-75) again indicated the growing popularity and importance of these services. Revenue from Ordinary stopping services amounting to Rs. 181 crores (Rs. 146 crores in 1974-75), and suburban traffic totalling Rs. 50 crores (Rs. 41 crores in 1974-75), increased at a slower pace and continued to contribute relatively less to the total.
The average passenger travelled 50.5 km in 1975-76 (52.0 km in 1974-75) and paid Rs. 1.74 for this transportation (Rs. 1.70 in 1974-75). The fare realised per passenger-km averaged to 3.45 Paise (3.27 Paise in 1974-75; the increase reflected the full year's effect of the revision of fares effected in September 1974, as also variations in the proportion of journeys performed at concessional rates and change in the average distance travelled.)

	1971-72	*1972-73*	*1973-74*	*1974-75*	*1975-76*
Passenger Earnings (Rs. 10 000 000)	320.1	343.8	367.1	412.6	514.1
Passenger Journeys (millions)	2 536	2 653	2 654	2 429	2 946
Passenger km (millions)	125 329	133 527	135 664	126 254	148 916
Average distance travelled (km)	49.4	50.3	51.1	52.0	50.5

Frequency and speed of long distance passenger trains were increased further during 1975-76, providing greater capacity and comfort for inter-city passengers.
56 new trains were introduced. These included six Janata Express trains and 26 other express trains. The run of 44 trains was extended and the frequency of six trains was increased. In all, 182 trains were speeded up during the year—21 by an hour or more and 161 by 15 minutes or more. There was also a remarkable improvement in passenger operations particularly on the broad gauge. The average speed of Mail and Express broad gauge trains increased to 46.4 km/h from 44.9 km/h in the previous year, and of all B.G. trains to 33.9 km from 33.1 km. 85 per cent of the trains arrived at their destination on time against 72 per cent in the previous year. There was also an improvement in the number of misuses of alarm chain apparatus; the average number of cases of alarm chain pulling per day declined to 446, 47 per cent less than in the previous year.
After a successful experiment in advanced booking, it was decided to permit reservations to be made six months in advance for all classes by all trains and at all stations. Further, additional booking windows, reservation counters, etc, were opened at important stations to cater for reservations.
Separate quotas of accommodation on important trains were provided for reservation for foreign tourists. 81 special trains (64 in 1974-75) were run for tourists and 8 756 reserved coaches (7 736 in 1974-75) provided for them during 1975-76.
A sum of Rs. 3.50 crores was spent in 1975-76 on provision of additional passenger amenities at stations. Electric water coolers were added at 43 stations and 103 more stations were electrified, bringing the total to 4 835 and 1 147 respectively. New retiring rooms were built at eight stations, raising the total to 261 stations. A significant improvement was also made in the proper operation of fans and lights, cleanliness of stations and coaches and in water supply arrangements.
Freight traffic: With the resurgence of the economy, revenue earning freight traffic in 1975-76 amounted to 196.8 million tonnes, an increase of 13.3 per cent over the previous year's total and, despite a slight drop of 14 kms (to 685 kms) in the average distance hauled, revenue tonne-kms reached an all-time high of 135 billion, 11.1 per cent over the previous year's figure. Reflecting the record volume of traffic, and generally higher rates, receipts from the freight business in 1975-76 amounted to 1 096 crores, 26.1 per cent over the previous year's income.
All principal commodity groups registered an increase in traffic, led by coal which rose by nine million tonnes or 16.2 per cent over the previous year. The substantially higher level of coal loading helped large consumers, particularly steel plants, power houses and cement factories, to stock-pile coal up to 25-40 days' requirements. The rail carrying of ores increased by 14.4 per cent, foodgrains by 8.2 per cent, cement and mineral oil by 5.9 per cent each, iron and steel by 5.5 per cent, limestone and dolomite by 4.2 per cent, fertilisers by 3.6 per cent and other stones by 2.4 per cent. The share of these commodities, mass transported in bulk, in the Railways' total revenue freight volume increased further by 1.5 per cent to 82.8 per cent, continuing the long range-trend of the Railways use for bulk carrying.
Average tonne-kilometre revenue in 1975-76 amounted to 8.12 Paise, 13.4 per cent more than previous year's average of 7.16 Paise. The improvement reflected the effect of the increase in rates made in September 1974. Changes in the composition of traffic and slight fall in the average haul also illustrated thus.
Revenue realised per tonne-kilometre from the carriage of coal (6.53 Paise) and foodgrains (5.51 Paise), the two most important commodities in the Railways freight business, was much less than the overall average of 8.12 Paise. In fact, the receipts from these were less than the cost of carriage; the loss on their carriage amounted to Rs. 22.45 crores (Rs. 4.44 crores coal and Rs. 26.89 crores foodgrains). Certain other low rated commodities were also carried at less than cost and the loss on these totalled Rs. 33.85 crores. These included fodder (Rs. 7.59 crores), salt for edible use (Rs. 6.61 crores), oilseeds (Rs. 3.06 crores), fruits and vegatables (Rs. 4.96 crores), gur, shakker and jaggery (Rs. 2.29 crores), etc. In addition, the Railways incurred a loss of Rs. 2.16 crores on carriage of live stock.

	1971-72	*1972-73*	*1973-74*	*1974-75*	*1975-76*
Freight earnings (Rs. crores)	665.7	695.9	644.2	868.9	1 095.7
Net tonne-km (millions)	116 894	121 164	109 391	121 374	134 874
Tonnes originating (millions)	170.1	175.3	162.1	173.6	196.8
Average lead (km)	687	691	675	699	685

There was a great improvement in the freight operations during the year. The net tonne-kms per goods engine hour, an overall index of efficiency reflecting utilisation of both wagons and locomotives, recorded an increase of 4.5 per cent on the broad gauge as compared with the previous year. With the improvement in freight operation, the capacity of the Railways to carry freight traffic generally outstripped the demand. All quotas and restrictions on movement of traffic were lifted over all the routes and in respect of traffic via break-of-gauge transhipment points as well. There was also a breakthrough in the movement of traffic to stations in Assam and other North-Eastern States. Demand for movement of essential commodities, such as foodgrains, salt, sugar, cement, to these States were met on a current basis and in total.
Both container service and 'freight forwarder' gained further popularity during the year. Container service was operated on 12 routes as in the previous year, but the number of containers loaded increased by 21.8 per cent to 36 939 and earnings therefrom by 33.5 per cent to Rs. 2.71 crores. The 'freight forwarder' scheme was introduced between another seven pairs of stations, raising the total to 73.
Apart from reduction in wagon delivery time, there was considerable reduction in loss and damage en-route. The number of loss and damage claims received during the year (632 973) was 5.37 per cent less than in the previous year (668 896). Claims for compensation were settled somewhat faster—on an average within 50 days against 51 days in the preceding year. The compensation paid in 1975-76, however, amounted to Rs. 15.25 crores against Rs. 14.65 crores in the previous year; the increase reflected mainly the higher price levels. At the year-end, 132 000 claims were outstanding against 141 000 in the previous year.

Commodity Group	*Tonnes Originating (Millions)* 1974-75	1975-76	*Tonne Kms (Billions)* 1974-75	1975-76	*Revenue (Rs. crores)* 1974-75	1975-76
Coal	55.3	64.3	32.9	37.7	193.0	246.0
Ores	24.0	28.3	9.0	11.3	69.8	96.3
Foodgrains	13.7	16.2	15.1	15.5	57.3	85.2
Mineral oils	10.8	11.7	6.9	7.1	72.3	86.1
Cement	9.2	11.6	6.1	8.6	46.3	72.7
Iron & Steel	9.8	10.7	10.5	10.8	100.4	118.4
Lime stone & dolomite	7.9	8.3	2.3	2.3	18.5	21.3
Fertilisers	6.0	7.2	4.8	6.2	37.5	52.2
Other stones	4.4	4.6	1.5	1.5	12.1	14.2
Total bulk	14.1	162.9	89.1	101.0	607.2	792.4
Other goods	32.5	33.9	32.3	33.9	261.7	303.3
All commodities	173.6	196.8	121.4	134.9	868.9	1 095.7

Finances
The Railways incurred a large deficit once again in 1975-76, despite record volume of business and the effect of fare and rate adjustments, due mainly to increase in staff costs as a result of backpayment of allowances to employees. The net revenue for the year amounted to Rs. 137.03 crores, producing a rate of return of only 3.15 per cent on the Capital-at-Charge of Rs. 4 354.78 crores. After payment of the obligatory dividend of Rs. 198.14 crores, the year-end deficit amounted to Rs. 61.11 crores.
The following is a brief summary of the Railways' financial position in 1975-76 as compared with 1974-75.

	(Rs. crores) *1975-76*		*Variation over* *1974-75*
Gross traffic receipts:	1 767.01	+	358.82
Working expenses:	1 609.62	+	292.33
Net traffic receipts:	157.39	+	66.49
Miscellaneous transactions:	20.36	+	3.10
Net revenue:	137.03	+	63.39
Dividend:	198.14	+	10.67
Deficit for the year:	61.11	−	52.72
	Percentage		
Working expenses to gross traffic receipts (Operating Ratio)	91.09	−	2.45
Net revenue to capital-at-charge:	3.15	+	1.36

The deficit of Rs. 61.11 crores in revenues for payment of the obligatory dividend was made good by borrowing from the General Revenues. In addition, the Railways had to borrow Rs. 22.34 crores to meet the expenditure on essential non-profitable works which are financed from the revenue surplus and a *net* amount of Rs. 7.25 crores, to pay interest, etc., on previous borrowings. Such borrowings on current account (together with the interest thereon) outstanding at the year-end totalled Rs. 460 crores.
Revenue rose by 25.5 per cent (Rs. 358.82 crores) in 1975-76 over 1974-75 to a new high of Rs. 1 767.01 crores.
A comparative summary of the receipts in 1975-76 and 1974-75 by major sources follows:

	(Rs. crores) *1975-76*		*variation over* *1974-75*
Passenger earnings:	514.13	+	101.58
Other coaching earnings:	89.42	+	20.21
Goods earnings:	1 150.27	+	232.77
Sundry other earnings:	50.04	+	11.02
Suspense (bills receivable):	− 36.85	−	6.76
	1 767.01		+358.82

87 per cent of the passenger earnings were received from full fare paying journeys; the remaining 13 per cent was paid by passengers travelling on season tickets or otherwise on reduced fares. Of the goods earnings, 72.3 per cent was derived from carriage of goods hauled in bulk (22.5 per cent coal and 49.8 per cent foodgrains, ores, fertilisers, mineral oils, iron and steel, cement, limestone and dolomite and stones); only the remaining 27.7 per cent was earned from carrying general merchandise.
As in the previous few years, increase in the revenues was substantially off-set by rise in the working expenses. The total working expenses climbed by 22.2 per cent (Rs. 292.33 crores) during the year to Rs. 1 609.62 crores, due mainly to one escalation in wage and price levels and partly to one increase in the level of operations.
The following is a comparative statement of working expenses for 1975-76 and 1974-75 by major categories:—

	(Rs. crores) *1975-76*		*variation over* *1974-75*
Administration	155.89	+	26.76
Repairs and maintenance	557.62	+	104.88
Operating staff	312.33	+	47.42
Operation (Fuel)	254.52	+	57.50
Operation other than staff and fuel	84.58	+	23.45
Miscellaneous expenses	54.36	+	4.35
Labour welfare	52.60	+	9.20
Suspense (bills payable)	− 1.73	+	10.33
Ordinary working expenses	1 470.17	+	283.89
Appropriation to Depreciation Reserve Fund	115.00		—
Appropriation to Pension Fund	24.25	+	8.40
Payment to worked lines	0.20	+	0.04
Total working expenses	1 609.62	+	292.33

Mainly because of the back payment of allowances during the year, the staff costs advanced sharply once again. The wage bill for the year (Rs. 878.77 crores) constituted 59.8 per cent of the ordinary working expenses. The price of fuel and other materials also rose during the year. The expenditure of Rs. 254.52 crores on fuel accounted for 17.3 per cent of ordinary working expenses. The remaining Rs. 336.88 crores of the ordinary working expenses, representing 22.9 per cent of the total, was spent on other materials, services and supplies.

MOTIVE POWER AND ROLLING STOCK

The motive power and rolling stock fleet was increased during 1975/76 by the addition of new stock and replacement of overaged units. New stock put into service included: 97 diesel locomotives; 76 electric locomotives; 8 668 freight wagons; 176 emu's; 939 passenger coaches; and 202 miscellaneous coaching vehicles.

Modern diesel and electric locomotives are gradually replacing the railway's steam fleet. Production of steam locomotives was halted in 1971. At the end of 1976, the motive power fleet comprised 11 095 locomotives— 8 496 steam locomotives, 1 803 diesel locomotives and 797 electric locomotives.

Diesel and electric locomotives now dominate the motive power scene for freight haulage. A total of 78.3 per cent of freight traffic in terms of gross tonne-km was hauled during 1975/76 by diesel and electric motive power—an increase of 2.3 per cent over the previous year. Passenger trains are, however, still largely worked by steam, although the proportion of passenger train-km hauled by diesel and electric locomotives increased from 32.8 per cent in 1974/75 to 34.7 per cent in 1975/76. All diesel and electric locomotives taken into service in 1976 were built in the railways' two locomotive workshops. The diesel Locomotive Works built 84 diesel locomotives—67 for the railways' own use, 11 for the public sector and six for export. Chittaranjan Locomotive Works built 54 electric locomotives and 17 diesel hydraulics for the railways. Electric locomotives produced during 1976 included four ac/dc units for use between Bombay Central and Ahmadabad.

TRACK

At the beginning of 1975-1976, approved new rail links including those under construction totalled a length of 1 798 km. A new broad gauge railway line from Sabarmati to Gandhinagar covering a distance of 27.85 km was completed and opened to goods traffic in January, 1976. The 36.25 km long metre gauge rail link between Pratapganj and Forbesganj was also restored to traffic in October, 1975. Construction of a section of 14 km from Hirdagarh to Damua was approved during 1975-76. At the end of the year work on new rail links and the restoration of dismantled lines totalling 1 748 km was underway.

Of the 2 264 km length of metre gauge lines conversion into broad gauge which had been approved earlier, the Ernakulam-Quilon section (155 km) forming part of Ernakulam-Trivandrum project and the Muzaffarpur-Sonepur section (59 km) forming part of Muzaffarpur-Barabanki conversion, were completed and opened to traffic in the year. No new conversion project was sanctioned during the year.

A number of major line capacity works and remodelling of yards were approved during 1975-76, the more important ones being—

i Remodelling of yard and provision of ancillary line capacity works at Katrasgarh;
ii Provision of additional loops at two stations on Bandel-Barddhaman section;
iii Augmentation of sectional capacity on Garwa Road-Son Nagar section-Phase 1.

In order to provide more capacity, the work of construction of 3rd line on the North East Ghat section of the Central Railway between Kasara and Igatpuri, including augmentation of power supply and distribution system, was taken up at a cost of Rs. 17.50 crores. Doubling of the track of 144.77 km was completed during the year and the doubling of another 31 km was approved. At the year-end, 937 km in all were being doubled on different Railways.

Permanent way: On the trunk routes connecting metropolitan cities and other important towns, track is being strengthened and modernised to meet the increasing demands of both freight and passenger traffic. The modernisation programme aims at re-inforcing the track structure and adoption of improved maintenance practices with a view to minimise both maintenance and operating costs.

During the year, 858 track km of trunk routes were relaid with heavier new rails and 1 191 track kms with new sleepers. On the broad gauge, 52 kg/m and 60 kg/m rails are now used for trunk routes and 37 kg/m on important metre gauge routes. The broad gauge track laid with 52 kg/m or heavier rails increased from 12 395 to 13 276 km at the end of the year. On the metre gauge, 37 kg/m track, increased from 2 766 to 2 880 km. Special wear-resistant rails have been used in sections on steep gradients and curves. All new rails laid on the track are now welded either in short welded panels or long lengths of one km or more. During the year, over 2 570 km of rails were welded, out of which 863 km were long welded. The total welded rail kilometrage stood at 28 710 at the end of the year, including 2 755 km of long welded rails. Reduction in the number of rail joints in this process has improved riding comfort of passengers, reduced fuel consumption, maintenance costs of track and rolling stock and at the same time has increased the life of rails and sleepers.

A start has been made with the use of prestressed mono-block concrete sleepers. 58 km of track were relaid with these sleepers in 1975-76.

On the heavy density and high speed routes, track is now being increasingly maintained mechanically with automatic 'On-track' tie tampers. Improved methods of maintenance viz., 'Directed track maintenance' and 'Measured showel packing' were also extended. 40 automatic 'On track' tie tampers were in use on the seven broad gauge Railways for tamping of over 4 000 km of track. 'Directed track maintenance' was being done on about 7 000 track km and it is programmed to extend this further. The running characteristics of track and track parameters were regularly monitored on important routes of broad and metre gauges, by eight track recording cars and two oscillograph cars. Large sections of track on heavy density and high speed routes was tested with 41 ultrasonic rail flaw detectors to detect the flaws of rails in track, not visible to the naked eye.

Bridges: There were 9 121 major and 101 217 other bridges on the Railways in 1975-76. During the year, regirdering, strengthening, rebuilding, raising and extension, etc, were done on 614 bridges and protection works such as spurs, guide bunds, drop walls, pucca flooring, pitching etc, were completed on another 251 bridges.

Level crossings and grade separation: On 31st March, 1976, there were 41 167 level crossings and 377 canal crossings on the Railways:—

Special Class	—	251
'A' Class	—	1 203
'B' Class	—	3 667
'C' Class		
Manned	—	9 289
Unmanned	—	22 449
'D' Class	—	4 308

During the year, 25 unmanned level crossings were raised to the level of being manned and 189 level crossings were upgraded. 60 level crossings were provided with lifting type barriers. 12 road over-under bridges in replacement of the existing level crossings were completed and 66 were under progress.

Electrification: Work continued on the electrification of heavy density routes or sections with a difficult profile although some what slowly due to lack of resources. During the year, Durgachak-Haldia section, the remaining portion of the electrification project of the Panskura-Haldia section on the South Eastern Railway, and Tundla-Ghaziabad alongwith Aligarh-Harduaganj section on the Northern Railway, were energised. At the yearend, electric trains were working on 4 649 route km.

Electrification works were in progress on 1 010 route km comprising Ghaziabad-Delhi/New Delhi (Ghaziabad-New Delhi section via the Goods Avoiding Line since it was energised in August, 1976) on the Northern Railway, Madras-Gudur and Madras-Tiruvallur sections on the Southern Railway, Vijayawada-Gudur section on the South Central Railway and Waltair-Kirandul section on the South Eastern Railway.

Cost-cum-feasibility surveys for electrification of Vadodara-Ratlam and Godhra-Anand sections on the Western Railway, and Arkonam-Erode and Jolarpettai-Bangalore sections on the Southern Railway, are in progress. The project report for the electrification of Madras-Guntakal-Hospet, Guntur-Renigunta-Tirupati East and Tornagallu-Ranjitpura were received during the year.

Rail, types and weight:

	Type/specification	Weight per metre
Flat bottom 65 kg steel rails	Gost 8160 & 8161-56	65 kg
Wear resistant rails 60 kg/metre	UIC 860/0 grade 'C'	60 kg
Wear resistant rails 52 kg/metre	UIC 860/0 grade 'B'	52 kg
Medium Manganese Flat bottom Rails 52 kg/metre	IRS speen T 12	52 kg
,, BS90R	,,	44.61 kg
,, BS75R	,,	37.13 kg
,, BS60R	,,	29.76 kg
,, BS50R	,,	24.80 kg

Sleepers: Wooden, cast iron and steel sleepers. A start has also been made with the use of concrete sleepers.

Thickness (dimensions):
Concrete sleepers: Mono block concrete sleepers, Thickness at rail level 196.25 mm, Length 2 750 mm. With Pandrol Rail clips, Thickness at rail level 210.00 mm, Length 2 750 mm. Two block concrete sleepers, Thickness at rail level 215.50 mm, Length 722 mm each with M.S. angle iron tie bar of 75 × 75 × 10 mm.

Domestic-built WAM4 class ACMT electric locomotive by Chittaranjan.

Wooden sleepers:
Broad Gauge 2 750 mm × 250 mm × 130 mm
Metre Gauge 1 800 mm × 200 mm × 115 mm
Narrow Gauge 1 500 mm × 180 mm × 115 mm

Spacing: 1 540 sleepers are provided per km.

Rail fastenings:
1. Fish plates and bolts and nuts to suit the type of rails viz. 65 kg, 60 kg, 52 kg, 44.61 kg, 37.13 kg, 27.76 kg and 24.80 kg rails.
2. Fittings for concrete sleepers:
   (a) For monoblock concrete sleepers

	Drawing No.
Pandrol clips	PR 401
Nylon liners	RDSO/T-383
Grooved Rubber pads	RDSO/T-382
Inserts	RDSO/T-381

(b) For twin—block concrete sleepers:

Grooved Rubber pads	RDSO/T-476
Clips and clamps	IRN 202 RDSO/T-465
Liners	RDSO/T-466
Bolts and nuts	RDSO/T-477
Rubber Heel Pads	RDSO/T-479

3. Fillings for steel trough sleepers:

Spring steel loose jaws	IRS spn. T.12
M.S. keys	Drg. No. T. 405 (m), IRS spn. T-8
(For high speed tracks)	
Modified loose jaws	RDSO/T-1801
Grooved Rubber pads	RDSO/T-382
Pandrol clips	PR/401

Fittings for wooden sleepers:

Mild steel or cast iron bearing plates	IRS Spen T.7
Screw spikes, Round spikes or Dog spikes or Rail screws	IRS Spen T.4.66
Keys B.G. Drg. No. T405 (M) & MG T413(M)	
Rail Anchors	
(For high speed tracks)	
C.I. Bearing plates	RDSO/T-646
Screw spikes	RDSO/T-650
Pandrol clips	PR-401
Grooved Rubber Pads	RDSO/647

Fittings for cast iron sleepers:
Tie bars, B.G. Drg. No. T.404(M), M.G. Drg. No. T.433(M).

Welded rails—Total:
Length of track laid up to 31.3.1974: 24 550 track kms.
Length laid during 1973-74: 2 228 running track kms.

Standard method of welding:
New rail is flash butt welded in workshops into 3 or 5 rail bar lengths, carried to site on specially designed wagons then alumino-thermic welded into LWR lengths after laying in position.

SIGNALLING
The following major works were provided and/or completed during the year 1975-76:—
Five non-interlocked stations were provided with inter-locking, bringing the total of interlocked stations to 5 039, out of 6 166 block stations on the Railways. In addition, five stations were provided with rudimentary interlocking, bringing the total of such stations to 860.
Token system of block working was provided on 30 single line block sections, lock and block working on 12 double line block sections and tokenless method of working on 42 block sections, thus bringing the total to 4 293 single line sections with token working, 1 698 with lock and block working on double line sections and 589 with tokenless working.
Track circuiting of run-through and reception lines was provided at 121 stations bringing the total to 1 637 stations.
The standard of interlocking was upgraded at 25 stations in keeping with the general policy of steadily improving the interlocking standards to cater for higher speeds and greater safety. Out of 5 039 interlocked stations 3 263 stations were interlocked to standard III, 101 to standard II and 1 675 to standard I.
Route-relay interlocking was commissioned at seven stations. 66 stations have so far been provided with route-relay interlocking.
Panel interlocking was provided at 33 stations. This brings the total of such stations to 199.
Replacement of two-aspect signalling by multi-aspect signalling was extended further. 29 stations were equipped with multi-aspect upper quadrant signalling and 39 more stations with multi-aspect colour light signalling. With this, a total of 1 335 stations have been equipped with multi-aspect upper quadrant signalling and 869 stations with multi-aspect colour light signalling.
Automatic block signalling was installed in 14.36 track kms raising the track kms of automatic block signalling to 1 190.

TELECOMMUNICATIONS
The setting up of microwave links in the communication net-work connecting important Railway operational centres progressed satisfactorily during the year. Microwave links commissioned during the year (1 140 route-km) consisted of Bombay-Bhusawal-Nagpur-Itarsi (1 010 km) on the Central Railway and Gorakhpur-Ahalyapur (130 km) on the North Eastern Railway. The total microwave coverage on the Indian Railways was 10 154 route-km at the end of the year.
Provision during the year of ACSR (Aluminium Conductor Steel Reinforced) overhead wires on 574 route km, on various vulnerable sections where the efficiency of circuits was not satisfactory and copper wire thefts were frequent, brings the total of such departmental alignment to 7 451 route km.

INDONESIA
INDONESIAN STATE RAILWAYS
Perusahaan Jawatan Kerata Api (PJKA)
Jalan Geraja, 1, Bandung

Principal Officers:
Chief Director: R. Soemali
Director Personnel: Aswasmarmo
Director Finance: Imam Rustadi
Director Civil Engineering: R. Moerhadi
Director Mechanical Engineering: Pantiarso
Director Transportation: Chaidir Nien Latief
Managing Secretary: Hersubno
Chief Planning: Sandjojo
Chief Research & Development: Partosiswojo
Chief Audit: Soedharmoen Pintodihardjo

Regional Managers:
East Java Region, Surabaya: Soeparto
Central Java Region, Semarang: Soeharso
West Java Region, Jakarta: Soetarno
South Sumatra Region, Palembang: Sugiarto
West Sumatra Region, Padang: Soekirian
North Sumatra Region, Medan: Asmanu

Gauge: 1.067 m; 0.75 m; 0.60 m.
Route length: 6 389 km; 505 km; 78 km.

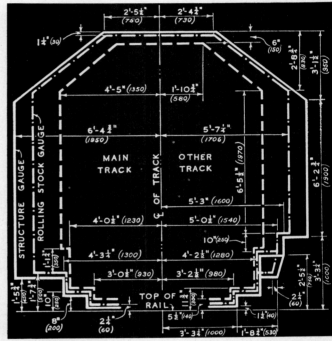

Loading gauge: main lines

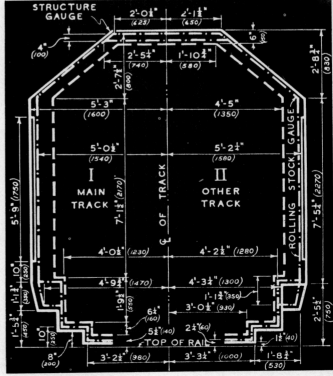

Loading gauge: secondary lines

Indonesia started its railways in the second half of the last century, when the first line was opened on June 17, 1868 between Kemijen (Semarang) and Tanggung in Central Java, a distance of about 28 km. The Indonesian State Railways operate a total route of 6 389 track km. Up to 1945 the railways in Indonesia consisted of privately owned railways. There were about twelve private railways systems with four types of gauges: 1.435 mm, 1.067 mm, 750 mm and 600 mm.
The Japanese abolished the 1.435 mm gauge between Semarang and Yogyakarta during their occupation in Java.
Rehabilitation of the PJKA system was carried out within the framework of the first National Five-Year Plan (1969-74), and a further development programme has been prepared for the government's second Five-Year (1974-79) Plan.
Improvement of PJKA's network will be continued during the second five-year plan, by the end of which the railway is expected to meet all its administrative and operating expenses out of revenues.

TRAFFIC

		1975	1976
Total freight ton-km	(000's)	980 000 000	706 000 000
Total freight tonnage	(000's)	3 999 000	3 268 300
Total passenger-km	(000's)	3 535 000 000	3 300 700 000
Total passengers carried	(000's)	23 851 000	19 978 400

FINANCES

Revenues (million)	Rp.21 217 000 000	Rp.22 222 000 000
Expenses (million)	Rp.27 271 000 000	Rp.23 103 000 000

MOTIVE POWER

PJKA's motive power fleet consists of 202 steam locomotives (including 37 shunting), 140 diesels (including 69 shunting), four electrics and ten diesel railcars. Under the plan, steam traction will be phased out, and more diesels acquired. All main line services in Java will have been dieselised by 1979, resulting in withdrawal of steam

locomotives. At the same time, the steam fleet in Sumatra will be reduced to about 70. The plan provides not only for rehabilitation of existing railcars, but also for purchase of ten two-car electric multiple-units and 12 two-car diesel railcars. The new railcars will operate between Jakarta and Bogor (electric), Jakarta and Cirebon, and Jakarta and Merak.

ROLLING STOCK

The passenger fleet consists of 698 coaches. The number of freight wagons in 1976 was 12 475.
Requirements for additional stock by 1979 will be 300 bogie wagons, including 120 ballast hoppers. In addition 7 500 wagons purchased since 1957 are to be fitted with air brakes.

ELECTRIFICATION

	Single track	Gauge 1.067 m Double track	Total
Total electrified route length on 31 December 1976	45 km	32 km	77 km
Total electrified track length on 31 December 1976	45 km	56 km	101 km

System of electrification=Catenary system, 1 500 V dc, with four sub-stations

TRACK

Approval has been granted for relaying the North line from Jakarta to Surabaya, totalling 725 km, with R14A rail weighing 42 kg/m on wooden sleepers. Additional ballast is to be provided to make the entire route suitable for speeds up to 100 km/h. Bridges are also to be strengthened. Part of the scheme, between Jakarta and Cirebon (207 km), has already been completed. The plan also provides for rehabilitation of the following sections of the main line in Java: Cirebon-Yogjakarta-Surabaya; Bandung-Kroya; Jakarta-Merak; Kalisat-Banyuwangi; and Malang-Blitar.

DIESEL LOCOMOTIVES

Class	Axle Arrangement	Transmission	Rated Power hp	Max. lbs (kg)	Tractive Effort Continuous at lbs (kg)	mph (km/h)	Max. Speed mph (km/h)	Wheel Dia. ins (mm)	Total Weight Tons	Length ft ins (mm)	No. Built	Year first Built	Builders: Mechanical Parts	Engine & Type	Transmission
CC200	C-2-C	DE	1 600	21 623	4 074	—	99.68	908	96	17 070	01-27	1951		12V.244E GE	
BB200	AIA-AIA	DE	875				120	1 016	74.8	14 006	01-35	1956		B.567CR GM	
BB 201	AIA-AIA	DE	1 310	21 810		15	120	1 016	78	14 026	01-11	1964		G12,567C GM	
BB202	AIA-AIA	DE	1 100	21 810		12,7	100	1 016	65	12 900	01-08	1968		GL8 645E GM	
BB300	B-B	DH	680	10 100			75	909	36	11 890	01-30	1956		MB820B	
BB301	B-B	DH	1 500	15 800	11 700	19	120	904	52	13 380	01-45 51-55	1962/ 63		MD655/MD12V 538TB10	L630 VU2
BB302	B-B	DH	1 100	14 520	12 500	15	80	904	44	12 810	01-06	1969		MB820	L520 rU 2
BB303	B-B	DH	1 150	14 100	11 500	15	90	904	42,8	12 320	01-21	1971		MB12V,493TZ	L520rU 2
BB304	B-B	DH	1 500			20	120	904	52	13 380	01-11	1974		MTU12U652TB11	L720 rU 2
CC201	C-C	DE	1 950		1 825			952	848	14 133	01-28	1976		7FDL8	
C 300	C	DH	350	9 800	9 250	4,5	30	904	30	8 020	01-20	1964		MB.836B	L203U
C301	C	DH	260		5 750	6,5	30	877	14,5	5 240	01-8	1969		BV71 N60	DBG115
D300	D	DH	340	10 200		5	50	904	34	9 279	01-30	1956		MB836B	2WIL1.15
D301	D	DH	340	8 400		5	50	904	28	8980	01-80	1960		MB8368/2	2WIL1.15 Krupp

ELECTRIC LOCOMOTIVES

Class	Axle Arrangement	Line Current	Rated Output hp	Max. lbs (kg)	Tractive Effort (Full Field) Continuous at lb (kg)	mph (km/hr)	Max. Speed mph (km/hr)	Wheel dia. ins (mm)	Weight tonnes	Length ft in (mm)	No. Built	Year Built	Builders Mechanical Parts	Electrical Equipment
BBC	IAA-AAI		1 130		300 000	25	90	1 500	69,2	12 530	1-4	1924		
WH	IAA-AAI		880		300 000	59	75	1 350	72	15 050	1-5	1924		
AEG	IB-IB		1 200		300 000	70,5	90	1 350	79	14 100	101; 102; 301	1023		

DIESEL RAILCARS

Class	Axle Arrangement	Transmission	Rated Power hp	Max. lbs (kg)	Tractive Effort Continuous at lbs (kg)	mph (km/h)	Max. Speed mph (km/h)	Wheel Dia. ins (mm)	Total Weight Tons	Length ft ins (mm)	No. Built	Year first Built	Builders: Mechanical Parts	Engine & Type	Transmission
MBW/ MADW	D	DH	215	200			90	784	36	19 640	01-071 01-03	1964		BV-71	DIWABUS U + S
MCW	IA-2	DH	180				90	774	42	20 000	01-24	1976		DMH 17	TC-2A

ELECTRIC RAILCARS

Class	Axle Arrangement	Line Current	Rated Output hp	Max. lbs (kg)	Tractive Effort (Full Field) Continuous at lb (kg)	mph (km/hr)	Max. Speed mph (km/hr)	Wheel dia. ins (mm)	Weight tonnes	Length ft in (mm)	No. Built	Year Built	Builders Mechanical Parts	Electrical Equipment
MCW	AA-AA		160				100	860	49,4	20 000	501-510	1976		HS-836
VCW											801-810			

Replacement of unserviceable sleepers and track fittings on main lines in Java, and North and South Sumatra will continue. Broadly, the plan provides for renewal of about 102 km of rail, 1.35 million sleepers, provision of new fastenings for 1 670 km of track, laying of 2.8 million m³ of ballast, and reconstruction of 262 turnouts.

Besides equipping track gangs with a full complement of tools for mechanised maintenance of permanent way, a track repair workshop is to be set up at Mediun, equipped with plant for carrying out repairs to points and crossings; cropping, strengthening and welding of rail; and repairs to steel sleepers.

TRACK CONSTRUCTION DETAILS
Standard rail:
  1.067 m gauge: R14A 86 lb/yd *(43.59 kg/m)*; R3 67 lb/yd *(33.4 kg/m)*; R2 52 lb/yd *(25.75 kg/m)*.
  0.750 m gauge: R10 33 lb/yd *(16.4 kg/m)*.   *0.600 m* gauge ID 25 lb/yd *(12.38 kg/m)*.
Type of joints: Fishplates and bolts; welding is also used.
Cross ties (sleepers): Mainly untreated teak, 6 ft 6¾ in × 8⅝ in × 4¾ in *(2 000 × 220 × 120 mm)*; some metal. Cross ties spacing: Main line, 27 in *(690 mm)*; Branch line, 31½ in *(800 mm)*
Rail fastening: Base plates, spikes and screws, elastic fastenings.
Filling (ballast): Stone ballast, 2-2¾ in *(50-70 mm)*
Thickness under sleeper:
  Main Line: 8.75° = min rad of 656 ft *(200 m)*
  Branch Line: 11.6° = min rad of 492 ft *(150 m)*
Max gradient: 4% = 1 in 25.
Gauge widening on sharpest curve: 0.787 in *(20 mm)*
Super elevation on sharpest curve: 4.33 in *(110 mm)*
Rate of slope of super-elevation: 1 in 450 to 1 in 1 200.
Max altitude: 4 088 ft *(1 246 m)* near Garut, Java.
Max axle loading:
  Main line: 13½ tons.
  Branch line: 8 to 10 tons.
Max bridge loading:
  Main line: 8.75 T. per lineal metre.
  Branch line: 5.56 T. per lineal metre.
Max permitted speed:
  Main line:
    Passenger trains, 62 mph *(100 km/h)*
    Freight trains, 43½ mph *(70 km/h)*
  Branch line:
    Passenger trains 37 mph *(59 km/h)*
    Freight trains 37 mph *(45 km/h)*

SIGNALLING
Except for the Jakarta-Bogor, Cikampek-Bandung, and Surabaya-Malang routes and the Jakarta area, where train services are frequent, PJKA's main lines are equipped with obsolete signalling. The plan provides for installing Siemens-Halske mechanical tokenless block system on the main lines of Java and some sections in Sumatra. Much of the equipment for this can be manufactured locally using imported materials. Improved signalling will be provided at 157 stations on Java main lines and at 33 stations in Sumatra.

IRAN
IRANIAN STATE RAILWAYS
49, West Takhte-Djamshid Ave, Tehran

Minister of Roads and Transportation: M. Salehi
President: F. Mahmoodian
Technical Vice-President: M. Badii
Financial Vice-President: N. Nakhai
Planning and Studies Vice-President: E. Nurzad
Administrative Vice-President: A. H. Guiti
Director, Administration: A. H. Guiti
Director, Confidential Affairs: D. J. Vaziri Nejad
Director, Traction Department: T. Bolandhemmat
Director, Track Department: M. Zandjany Nassab
Director, Operating: A. Assadi
Director, Electric Department: S. Hamed
Director, Telecommunications and Electrical Signalling: A. Sepahi
Director, Accounting Department: Tahbaz
Director, Personnel Department: M. Mousavi
Director, Legal Office: A. Fardaad
Deputy Director, Purchase Department: K. H. Zarandarz
Director, Assets Department: T. Afrashteh
Superintendent, Buffet and Restaurant Services: A. Aslanian
Director, Training Department: H. Rezapur
Chief, Railway Police Department: M. Parivar
Director, Planning and Studies Department: M. Behzadi
Director, Public Relations and Social Services Office: Hadj Alilu
LORESTAN DIVISION
Head Office: Andimeshk
Director of Division: Rezai
ARAK DIVISION
Head Office: Arak
Director of Division: M. Yahyavi
ESFAHAN DIVISION
Head Office: Esfahan
Director of Division: A. Tahmassebi
TEHRAN DIVISION
Head Office: Tehran
Deputy Director of Division: A. Niruzad
NORTH DIVISION
Head Office: Saari
Director of Division: G. H. Malek
SOUTH DIVISION
Head Office: Ahwaz
Director of Division: G. H. Hendizadeh
YAZD DIVISION
Head Office: Yazd
Director of Division: Aramesh
NORTH-EAST DIVISION
Head Office: Shahrood
Director of Division: G. H. Malek
KHORASSAN DIVISION
Head Office: Mashad
Director of Division: K. H. Bozorgmehr
NORTH-WEST DIVISION
Head Office: Zandjan
Director of Division: R. Anoshirvani
AZARBAYJAN DIVISION
Head Office: Tabriz
Director of Division: M. Khorrami

Gauge: 1.435 m.
Route length: 4 525 km.

The Iran State Railways is working on one of the world's largest expansion programmes to modernise and extend the country's rail network to link all major urban and industrial centres. The multi-billion rail programme provides for the creation of 10 000 kms of new tracks and the electrification of existing lines and changing them from single to double tracks.

The first phase provides for improvement of the existing facilities and services. Iran's existing rail network is generally out-dated and cannot answer the country's requirements. The Tehran-Gorgan, Tehran-Abadan and Tehran-Tabriz tracks are old and full of technical problems while the Tehran-Mashad roadbed has not been constructed to accommodate the high-speed turbotrains that run on the route. The increase in the number of passengers and cargo handled by the state railways during the past twelve months alone, and the need for faster freight and passenger trains has placed the country's railwork under great pressure. In order to ease this pressure and boost the railway's capacity the state railways recently started work on electrification of most of the existing lines.

The first project provides for the electrification of the Bandar Shahpur-Andimeshk-Tehran line and the construction of a double set of tracks along this route. Due to the expansion of port facilities at Bandar Shapur, which will become Iran's largest port over the next few years, the Tehran-Andimeshk-Bandar Shahpur project has been given top priority and construction work is to begin as soon as the necessary funds, already approved by the Government, are allocated.

The western tracks, connecting Tehran with Turkey via Tabriz will also be electrified and will be transformed from single to double tracks starting in 1977. New tracks are also to be laid between Mianeh and Tabriz to shorten the Tehran-Tabriz line by 110 kms. A similar project is planned for the Tehran-Isfahan-Zarand line and construction work on the 80 km stretch between Zarand and Kerman was expected to be completed in 1977.

The existing Tehran-Mashad line will be modified to handle electric trains at speeds of up to 240 km/h. Another set of rails will be established alongside the existing tracks to enable two-way traffic.

Railway experts have also been working on another set of plans, studies on which have already begun, to extend the existing network. These projects, provide for construction of 700 kms of track to connect Bandar Abbas with Baft via Gol Gowhar linking the Persian Gulf port with the nation-wide network. Pakdaman said that the project has already been offered to tenders and construction work would begin as soon as the necessary funds are allocated over the next few months.

The next project will connect the railway network to Pakistan by construction of 560 kms of track from Kerman to the border.

Other projects provide for the creation of lines from Isfahan to the Soviet border, a line along the Caspian coast an Isfahan-Shiraz-Bushehr line and a Bandar Pahlavi-Qazvin, Qom-Qasr-e-Shirin (Iraq border), Andimeshk-Kermanshah-Sanandaj-Maragheh, Mashad-Zahedan-Chahbahar and Persian Gulf coastal tracks to connect Bandar Abbas with Bandar Shahpour.

With the completion of these projects the country's total track will be increased from 4 500 kms to more than 14 000 kms, connecting all major Iranian urban and industrial centres and linking the country's rail network to the Soviet Union, Pakistan, Afghanistan, Turkey and Iraq.

Meanwhile the State Railways is working on the creation of a number of railway stations, three in Tehran, Shahyad Square, Aramghah, south Tehran and Qasre Firuz in east Tehran, and other stations in various cities.

The railways have also been working to improve the ticket sales and reservation system which will be completed in twelve days. Mechanisation of ticket sales and reservations, the creation of ticket stalls throughout Tehran and arrangements for the sale of tickets at travel agencies are other projects already underway.

TRAFFIC

	1975	1976
Freight ton-km	4 916 679 276	5 309 188 849
Tonnage	8 829 163	7 950 514
Passenger-km	2 266 458 233	3 484 646 317
Passenger journeys	4 535 313	6 457 502

FINANCES

	1975 Rials	1976 Rials
Revenue	8 251 456 328	10 249 129 385
Expenses	6 253 432 460	10 700 568 897

DEVELOPMENT PLANS

The present plan involves only the first stage in Iran's railway development programme. A 20-year plan calls for the construction of several completely new lines and new links with several neighbouring countries. Following the doubling and electrification projects for existing lines, a 550-km line is to be built between Kerman and Zahedan, terminus of the existing Pakistan Railways line projecting into Iran. A bogie-changing station will also be built at Zahedan.

During the Seventh and Eighth Plan periods the network will be extended from Shahrud to Bandar Shah and along the Caspian coastal strip to form a tourist route right up to the Soviet border at Astara.

During the Sixth and Seventh Plan periods the network will be extended 366 km up from Tehran to Bandar Pahlavi on the Caspian coast and up to Astara on the Soviet border. Then the railway will be continued eastwards along the Caspian coast through Lahijan, Rudsar, Shahsavar, Nowshahr, Amol and Sari, a distance of about 430 km. Also during the Seventh Plan (beginning in 1988), the programme provides for the existing Tehran-Mashad line to be extended up to Gorgan, from Shahrud. The line will also be extended from Mashad to provide another link with Soviet Railways at Sarakhs—giving RAI a much closer connection with the Trans-Siberian railway—and to Kal-Kaleh on the Afghanistan border. RAI also plans to offer technical and economic assistance to Afghanistan to construct a railway through to Kabul.

The line to Isfahan is to be extended 500 km to Shiraz, and then on for a further 140 km to Firuzabad. From there the line will continue 580 km to Bandar Abbas. About 330 km of new track will link Isfahan with Bebahan, in the southwest. The line will then turn northwest to Aghajari (88 km) and a further 150 km to Ahvaz. A connecting line will be built along the 410-km route from Firuzabad to Behbahan.

Other projected lines will run from Isfahan to Azna, on the existing south line, and from Qom, on the south line, to link with Iraqi Railways at Qasr-e-Shirin.

MOTIVE POWER

At the end of 1976 RAI's motive power fleet consisted of: 300 diesel-electric line haul units; 53 diesel-electric shunters.

Standard diesel locomotives operated by RAI were provided by General Motors. During the past three years 134 GM 3 300-hp locomotives have been delivered and orders were placed for 54 type GT 26 CW 3 000-hp units and 20 type G22 1 500-hp units with General Motors.

Introduction of four turbotrains from ANF Frangeco, at a cost of 500 million rials each, have substantially reduced transit time between Tehran, Mashad and Isfahan. However, it was reported during 1976 that RAI had dropped its option on 18 other turbotrains.

For heavy shunting, RAI has recently taken delivery of 28 Hitachi locomotives with an output of 1 050 hp, continuous tractive effort of 12 420 kg, Bo-Bo axle arrangement and top speed of 100 km/h.

ROLLING STOCK

At the end of 1976 RAI had a fleet of 13 556 freight wagons. A total of 606 passenger coaches were in operation during 1977.

TRACK CONSTRUCTION DETAILS

Standard rail:
  Main line:
  Type U33, 92.8 lb per yd *(46 kg/m)*
  Type IIA, 77 lb per yd *(38.4 kg/m)* in *12.5 m* lengths.
  Type III, 67 lb per yd *(33.5 kg/m)* in *12.0 m* lengths.
  Branch line:
  Type IV, 62 lb per yd *(30.9 kg/m)* in *12.8 m* lengths.
  American, 70 lb per yd *(34.7 kg/m)* in *10.0 m* lengths.
Rail joints: 4 and 6-hole fishplates; and welding (see below).
Cross ties (sleepers): Creosote impregnated hardwood, steel and concrete. Wood, 8 ft 6⅜ in × 9⅞ in × 6 in *(2 600 × 250 × 150 mm)*. Steel 7 ft 10½ in × 11⅞ in × 2¾ in *(2 400 × 300 × 70 mm)*. Concrete sleepers under welded rail.
Cross ties spacing: Wood sleepers, 2 180 per mile *(1 360 per km)*. Steel sleepers: 2 320 per mile *(1 450 per km)*.
Rail fastenings: Wood sleepers: Sole plates, screws and bolts. Steel sleepers: Clips and bolts.
Filling: Part broken stone, and part river ballast; min of 7⅞ in *(200 mm)* under sleepers.
Max curvature: 7.9° = min rad of 722 ft *(220 m)*.
Longest continuous gradient: 10 miles *(16 km)* of 2.8% (1 in 36) grade between Firouzkouh and Gadouk.
Max gauge widening: 0.95 in *(24 mm)* on 7.9° curves.
Max super-elevation: 3.94 in *(100 mm)* on 7.9° curves.
Max altitude: 7 273 ft *(2 177 m)* near Nourabad station.
Max axle loading: 25 tons.
Max permitted speed:
  Freight trains: 28 mph *(55 km/h)*.
  Passenger trains: 40 mph *(80 km/h)*.

SIGNALLING

New semi-automatic signalling was installed during 1974/75 over the 816-km south line by a group of Japanese companies.

Tehran station with Hitachi Bo-Bo locomotive on station pilot duties.

First-class passenger coach delivered to RAI in 1976 by Linke-Hofmann-Busch.

A G16 diesel electric locomotive.

General Motors Co-Co No 90-802.

IRAQ

IRAQI REPUBLICAN RAILWAYS
Bagdad

Director General: Ibrahim Mahmoud
Assistant Director General: Abdul Karen Nada
Chief Technical Inspector: Mohamed Haba
Chief Engineer: Abdul Razzak Mahmoud
Chief Mechanical Engineer: Paulus Abdul Messih
Chief Electrical and Signalling Engineer: Ahmed Al-Maliaka

Gauge: 1.435 m; 1.00 m.
Route length: 1 235 km; 1 294 km.

TRAFFIC

Most important traffics are oil products (about 940 000 tons last year), cement (600 000 tons), sugar (225 000), wheat and barley (113 000 tons). Total ton/km handled in 1972 was nearly 1 123 215 000—compared with about 1 032 140 000 in the previous year. By 1975 tonne-km carried had risen to 1 853 million, while passenger-km had gone up from 444 million in 1965 to 643 million in 1975. Already, increased sulphur production in Iraq is testing IRR facilities to the full. One extraction plant near Kirkuk is now railing nearly 200 000 tons/year of sulphur to Basra. But the toughest of new freighting jobs will come about when new sulphur mines near Mosul in the north-west go into operation in about 1977. IRR expects to be hauling up to 2 000 000 tons of production from this mine a year—"250 000 tons in the first year; 500 000 tons in the second year; and 2 000 000 in the third year" explains Al-Ani.

FINANCIAL RESULTS

| | 1961 | 1965 | *Year ending 31 st March* | | | |
			1967	1968	1970	1972
			(000's of Dinars)			
Revenue	4 721.1	6 906.3	6 001.4	6 770.8	66 633.4	6 821.3
Expenses	5 572.7	6 379.0	6 291.5	6 887.7	7 320.6	8 961.2
Operating ratio	118.0	92.4	105	88.4	110.5	—

MOTIVE POWER

New locomotives delivered in 1976 included 31 diesel-electrics rated at 2 000 hp built by MLW at a cost of $C 19.8 million.
The new locomotives will supplement earlier MLW units and 20 diesel-electric locomotives purchased in 1972 from Traction-Export, France.

ROLLING STOCK

During 1977, the railway took delivery of the first 50 of an order for 84 passenger coaches supplied by Maschinen-Export of the German Democratic Republic. In March 1977, Maschinen-Export won an IRR order for 250 freight wagons.

NEW LINE PLANS

The UK firm of consulting engineers, Henderson, Hughes & Busby were awarded a contract mid-75 for the feasibility, study, design and construction supervision of a new high-speed standard-gauge line in the Tigris valley linking Baghdad with Basra and Um-Qasr. Supplementing the existing lines following the Euphrates, the new line would be about 850-km long and would be expected to cost in the region of £ (Sterling) 200 million. It was announced in October 1977 that work is to start soon on the 242 km Al Mussayid (120 km south of Baghdad) to Samawa loop line off the Baghdad-Basra standard gauge route. Route of the loop will run through Kerbala cement works, Kufa and Najaf.
It was announced in 1974 that a credit of 70 million dinars had been made available for the beginning of work on construction of a standard-gauge line from Baghdad towards the Syrian border. The layout will be designed for a speed of 140 km/h and the line will link up with the Syrian Railway Line from Lattaqué to Deir-ez-Zor (via Aleppo) when the planned extension of the line along the Euphrates as far as Abou-Kenral is completed.
The new line may be built by Indian Railway engineers following a meeting in New Delhi in 1975 between Dr. Fakhri Quadouri, from Iraq, and K. Hanumanthaiya, Indian Railway Minister. India is believed to have agreed to build the line in return for an Iraqi offer of crude oil.
Plans for a 555 km railway from Baghdad to Al-Qaim with a branch to the phosphate mines at Akashat are also being drawn up. The Akashat to Al-Qaim spur will be needed to move phosphate rock to the fertilizer complex being built at Al-Qaim by Sybetra of Belgium. Passenger trains will average 150 km/h on the line and freight trains 100 km/h brahim Mahmoud, director general of the central area railways administration, said the Baghdad to Maqal railway should soon be completed and 14 stations will be opened. He has also announced that preliminary studies are under way for a standard gauge railway from Baghdad to Baquba, Kirkuk and Mosul and for a line from Baghdad to Kut and Amara.

SIGNALLING

A semi-automatic block system has been installed on the 585-km Baghdad-Mosul-Rabia line, using materials and technical assistance supplied by the German Democratic Republic. The installation was completed in 1974.

TRACK CONSTRUCTION DETAILS

Standard rail:
  Standard gauge: 90 lb. *(446.0 kg.)* on new line. 75 lb. *(37.2 kg.)* BSR, and German type.
  Metre, main: 75 lb. *(38.8 kg.)* USA, 75 lb. BS, BSR, RBS, USA.
  Metre, branch: 75 lb. BS and BSR, 60 lb. R, and 50 lb. BS and RBS.

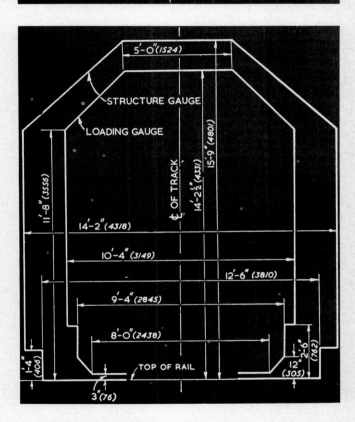

A Model MXS620, 2 000 hp, 4 ft 8½ in gauge locomotive built by MLW for Iraqi Republican Railways service.

IRELAND

CORAS IOMPAIR EIREANN

Irish Transport Company, Heuston Station, Dublin 8

Chairman of the Board: Dr. Liam St. John Devlin
Members: J. A. Bristow
                B. Connaughton
                E. Farrell
                W. J. Fitzpatrick
                E. Larkin
                E. Markey
General Manager: J. F. Higgins
Assistant General Manager, (Engineering Projects): L. Collins
Assistant General Manager, (Marketing): C. Finegan
Assistant General Manager, (Railways): M. J. Devereux
Assistant General Manager, (Personnel): P. Murphy
Assistant General Manager, (Finance): M. Grace
Assistant General Manager, (Operations): P. J. Darmody
Secretary: M. J. Hayes
Solicitor: M. J. Kenny
Purchasing Officer: J. Leonard
Mechanical Engineer (Rail): R. P. Grainger
Chief Civil Engineer: T. C. Yates
Area Manager:
  Dublin: E. O'Connor
  Cork: C. F. Clune
  Galway: C. MacGiolla Ri
  Limerick: E. B. Kehoe
  Waterford: J. A. O'Connor
Staff Relations Manager: M. J. Maguire
Manager, Public Relations & Publicity Department: S. J. White
Computer Services Manager: F. J. Curtin
Manager, Road Passenger Planning Group: K. G. Brady
Manager, Road Freight Planning Group: M. Flannery
Manager, Dublin City Services: B. J. Fitzgerald

Gauge: 1.600 m.
Route length: 2 189 km.

Development plans for the Irish Railways, adopted in 1971, have made steady progress and it is anticipated that they will be fully implemented within the target date of 1980. Developments on the passenger side call for the provision of a total fleet of Air conditioned rolling stock, and this with the recent purchase of 18 class 071 locomotives will provide more comfortable service and faster journey times between all major locations.
Freight operations are being concentrated on a lesser number of highly utilised depots, the conventional loose coupled train being replaced by high speed vacuumed braked liner or block trains, with all loading and discharge being effected by mechanical means.
Track improvements and upgrading to permit higher speeds and loads, and the modernisation of the Signalling and Communications networks will provide a highly efficient rail system to meet the challenges of the future.

TRAFFIC

	1975	1976
Total Freight ton kms (incl livestock)	559 081 571	585 189 257
Total Freight tonnage (incl livestock)	3 385 266	3 477 899
Total Passenger kms	898 620 547	787 626 256
Total passenger carried	13 891 145	13 607 724

FINANCES

	1975 £	1976 £
Revenues	20 270 940	23 262 004
Expenses (operating)	38 412 539	44 960 231

PLANS

The most important of plans is the Railways Development Plan which is a precise blue-print for the development of the railways up to 1980. Aimed at containing the rising railway deficit, the plan involves modernisation of stations and depots, introduction of new equipment and handling methods and redeployment of manpower. The plan will take six years to implement and will cost £27 m by present calculations which is £10 m above the normal capital requirements over the same period.
Progress was also made during 1973/74 in the preparation of plans for improving Dublin City transportation. The Government approved in principle the recommendations in the Dublin Transportation Study in relation to the suburban rail system. CIE personnel are now at work on the detailed designs. CIE has also employed Alan M. Voorhess and Company as consultants to examine the feasibility of building an underground rail system in Dublin. This also follows one of the recommendations of the Dublin Transportation Study.

MOTIVE POWER

The motive-power fleet at the end of 1976 totalled 190 mainline diesel-electric locomotives; 33 diesel-hydraulic shunters.

General Motors diesel-electric locomotive 071 class 2 250 hp built 1976 and placed in service in 1977. There are 18 units in this class—pictured at CIE's Inchicore Works

A block train of palletised fertiliser is loaded at the NET fertiliser factory at Shelton Abbey, near Arklow. The bogie wagons for this traffic were specially designed by CIE and built at Inchicore Works

Mainline passenger train composed of modern air conditioned coaches—built by British Rail Derby 1972—and hauled by latest 071 class General Motors 2 250 hp loco built 1976, on the main line between Dublin and Cork

A block train of dolomite ore en route from Bennetsbridge to Ballinacourty

ROLLING STOCK

Passenger stock includes 485 coaches and freight stock 6 519 wagons. New wagons taken into operation were as follows:

Classification	Bogie Fertiliser Wagons	Bulk Cement Hopper	22 foot Flat
Wheel/Axle Arrangements	Bogie	2 axle	2 axle
Max speed	50 mph	50 mph	50 mph
Dimensions			
Lt. over Headstock	42'—9''	20'—0''	22'—5''
Lt. over Buffers	46'—9''	23'—6¼''	26'—7''
Width	9'—0''	9'—0''	8'—0''
Height	13'—0''	12'—2''	3'—9''
Bogie Wheel Base	6'—6¾''	12'—0''	Wheel base 14'—0''
Weight	21T.—8C	10T.—5C	7T.—5C

TRACK DETAILS

Standard rail:
Main line: Flat bottom; 113 lb per yd *(50 kg/m)*, 95 and 92 lb per yd Bullhead; 90 and 87 lb per yd.
Branch line: Flat bottom; 85, 83, 80 and 74 lb per yd Bullhead; 85 lb per yd.

Length of rail:
Main line: 60 ft and 45 ft
Branch line: 45 ft and 30 ft
Joints: 4-hole fishplates, some welding.
Cross ties (sleepers), broad gauge: Wood, 8 ft 6 in × 10 in × 5 in *(2 600 × 260 × 130 mm)* Prestressed concrete.
Spacing: 1 970 per mile *(1 230 per km)* 2 112 per mile (timber), 2 146 per mile (concrete).
Rail fastenings: Wood sleepers—bolts: Concrete sleepers—H-M & Pandrol fastenings.
Filling: Stone ballast, min of 100 mm under sleeper.
Max curvature:
Main line (Dublin to Cork): 9° 40'.
Principal lines: 12° 25'.
Secondary lines: 21° 44'.
Max gradient:
Main line: 1.66% (1 in 60) for 1⅜ miles.
Other lines: 2.0% (1 in 50) for 2 miles.
Longest continuous gradient: 5¼ miles, with 1% (1 in 100) ruling gradient.
Max altitude: 630 ft. *(192 m)* at Barnagh, Co. Kerry.
Max permitted speed: 75 mph *(120 km/hr)*.
Max axle loads:
Principal lines: 16½ tons for locomotives, 15½ tons for wagons.
Secondary lines: 16½ tons for locomotives, 15½ tons for wagons.
Branch lines: 16½ tons for locomotives, 15½ tons for wagons
Bridge loading: 20 b.s. units for all renewals.

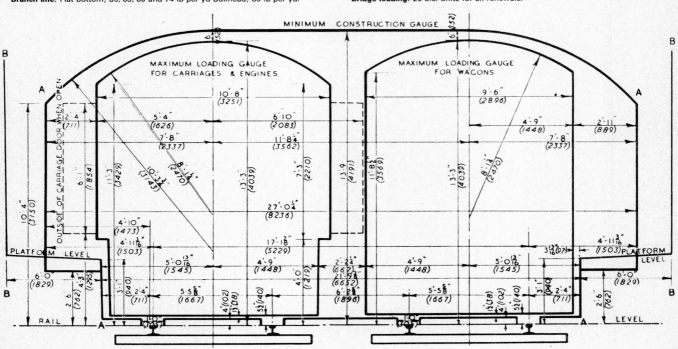

NOTE

AA Minimum distance for all works along line including signal boxes, signal posts, lamps etc.

BB Minimum distance for all station works above platform level. Level of passenger platforms only may be inside the construction gauge.

A liner freight train of B + I Line containers for shipping en route from Cork to Dublin, passing Cherryville Junction, Co. Kildare, where the Main Line from Cork is joined by the branch line from Waterford. Motive power is 001 class diesel electric, built by Metro-Vickers in 1955 and rebuilt by CIE with General Motors engine post-1968

A train of bulk cement tankers hauled by General Motors 181 class locomotive built 1966

A Plasser and Theurer Track Inspection and Recording Car placed in service in 1976

DIESEL LOCOMOTIVES

Class	Axle Arrangement	Transmission	Rated Power hp	Max. lb (kg)	Tractive Effort Continuous at lb (kg)	mph (km/h)	Max Speed mph (km/h)	Wheel Dia. in (mm)	Total Weight Tons	Length ft ins (mm)	No. Built	Year first Built	Builders: Mechanical Parts	Builders: Engine & Type	Builders: Transmission
071	Co-Co	Elec.	2 475/ 2 250		43 264	16.4	89	40″	99	57′ 0″	18	1976	GM	GM12-645 E3	Elec
AR	Co-Co	,,	1 375/ 1 250		18 000	21.5	75	38″	82	51′ 0″	51	1955/ 56	METRO/CAM	GM12-645 E	,,
AR	Co-Co	,,	1 650/ 1 500				75	38″	82	51′ 0″	9	1956/ 56	,,	,,	,,
B	AIA-AIA	,,	960/ 890		16 900	17.0	75	37½″	75	45′ 0″	12	1961/ 62	BC & W Co	Sulzer 6LDA 28	,,
121	Bo-Bo	,,	950/ 875		30 400	8.0	77	40″	64	39′ 10″	15	1961	GM	GM 567C	,,
141	Bo-Bo	,,	950/ 875		27 500	9.0	77	40″	67	44′ 0½″	37	1962	GM	GM 567 CR	,,
181	Bo-Bo	,,	1 100/ 1 000		26 400	11.0	89	40″	67	44′ 0½″	12	1966	GM	GM 8-645E	,,
CR	Bo-Bo	,,	1 100/ 1 040		14 200	22.2	75	38″	61½	42′ 0″	32	1957	Metro/Cam	GM8-645E	,,
E	0-6-0	D/Hyd	400					38″	42.8	31′ 4¼″	33	1957/ 62		Maybach MD650	Hyd
G	0-4-0	,,	130					38″	18.0	21′ 0″	3	1960	Brown-Boveri	Deutz	,,
G	0-4-0	,,	160/ 155		9 408	3.75		37⅜″	22.0	21′ 0″	7	1962	,,	,,	,,

ISRAEL

ISRAEL RAILWAYS
PO Box 44, Haifa

General Manager: Zvi Tsafriri
Deputy General Manager: I. Bar-Ilan
Traffic and Commercial Manager: E. Inbal
Chief Mechanical Engineer: A. Micsel
Chief Engineer: K. Slutzker
Chief Accountant: S. Klayer
Head, Supply and Stores Department: O. Trichter
Chief Signalling and Telecommunications Engineer: M. Lozar
Principal Assistant to the General Manager: D. Guy
Personnel Manager: Ch. Shadmi
Legal Adviser: H. Cassel
Public Relations and Publicity Officer: M. Gabrieli
Management Secretary: B. Z. Balila
Economic Adviser: I. Falkov
Deputy General Manager (Administration): L. Heyman
Head of Research and Development: A. Golan
Accidents investigation Officer: N. Gruenberg

Gauge: 1.435 m.
Route length: 647 km.

Israel Railways operate a total route length of 647 km, including the reconnected Yad Mordekhay-Gaza line opened to El-Arish in Sinai, 58 miles *(98 km)*. The railways are entirely diesel powered.

TRAFFIC	1976
Freight tonnage	3 650 000
Tonne-km	462 000 000
Passenger journeys	3 040 000
Passenger km	261 000 000

MOTIVE POWER
Number of diesel locomotives in mainline service total 35; number in shunting duties, 22.

ROLLING STOCK
Number of freight wagons in operation at the end of 1976 totalled 2 095, including 475 flat wagons, 412 grain hopper wagons, 261 for mineral transport, 174 for liquid transport and 773 miscellaneous general duty wagons. Number of passenger coaches in service (including buffet cars) totalled 114.
Eight second-hand 62-seat modern passenger coaches were bought in Britain by Israel Railways during 1977. IR's general manager Zvi Tsafriri visited London to negotiate the purchase, from Trans Eastern Ltd. Total price of the coaches—to be used on 'special-class' passenger services between Tel Aviv and Haifa—was £500 000. In 1976 IR cancelled an order with Fiat for 10 self-propelled railcars because the railway felt unable to provide adequate maintenance facilities. The Trans-Eastern coaches, originally manufactured for BR, will be used to attract passenger business. More passengers, say Tsafriri, could help reduce the annual deficit, currently running at an annual £170 million (app. $US 7 668 000). About 85 per cent of IP's expenses are covered by freight income.

NEW CONSTRUCTION
A new line between Oron and Har-Zin was officially opened in December 1977. This line will in fact constitute a section of the Trans-Israelian which is to extend as far as Eilath, near the Gulf of Akaba, 180 km to the south of Hor Hahar. Scheduled completion date is 1982. During 1977, the Transport Minister announced plans for construction of a direct line between Jerusalem, Lod and Tel Aviv, by-passing the present circuitous route.

LOCOMOTIVES IN SERVICE DECEMBER 1976

Series	Numbers	Builder	Power	Year first taken into service	Number in service
G 12 (Bo-Bo)	101-103	Franco-Belge	1 125	1952	3
	104-130	General Motors	1 425	1954-1961	24
G 16 (Bo-Bo)	161-163	General Motors	1 950	1960-1961	3
G 26 (CoCo)	601-604	General Motors	2 200 hp	1971-1974	4
G 8	201-25	General Motors Maybach Deutz	various	1956-1958	22

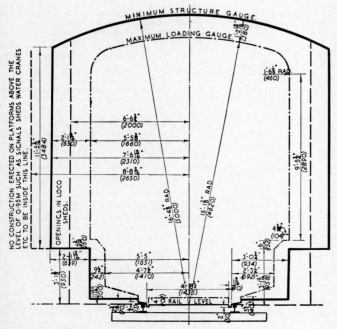

Structure and loading gauge for 1.435 m standard-gauge track

ITALY

ITALIAN STATE RAILWAYS
(Ferrovie dello Stato Italia) (FS)
Direzione Generale delle Ferrovie dello Stato,
Piazza della Croce Rossa, 00100 Rome

Director General: Dott. Ercole Semenza
Heads of Departments:
  Operations: Ing. Antonio Piciocchi
  Commercial and Traffic: Dott. Mauro Ferretti
  Motive Power and Rolling Stock: Ing. Paolino Camposano
  Personnel: Dott. Aldo Bonforti
  Electrical Installations: Ing. Enrico Bianco
  Maintenance and Construction: Ing. Francesco Monopoli
  General Business: Dott. Alberto Allegra
  Financial: Prof. Carlo Rolandi
  Supplies and Stores: Dott. Luca Campenni
  Medical: Prof. Mario Monti
  Research Institute: Ing. Giulio Giovanardi
Divisional Managers:
  Ancona: Ing. Aristide Loria
  Bari: Dott. Pietro Buccarelli
  Bologna: Ing. Domenico Muzzioli
  Cagliari: Ing. Calogero Augello
  Florence: Ing. Tullio Grimaldi
  Genoa: Ing. Francesco Melis
  Milan: Ing. Armando Sottile
  Naples: Ing. Luigi Frunzio
  Palermo: Ing. Armando Colombo
  Reggio Calibria: Ing. Antonino Bitto
  Rome: Ing. Lorenzo Scardia
  Turin: Ing. Eduardo Oliva
  Trieste: Ing. Gerardo Sangineto
  Venice: Ing. Quirido Castellani
  Verona: Ing. Salvatore Puccio
Public Relations: Dott. Alberto Ciambricco

Gauge: 1.435 m.
Route length: 16 014 km.

FS is now embarked on the 1975-79 Five-Year Programme under which the railway is to spend Lira 2 000 000 million on new motive power and rolling stock. During this period the Ministry of Public Works is to cover expenditure on new lines such as the 30 km cut-off through Savona on the Genoa-Ventimiglia route, a new line from Bari to Altamura, and one from Caltagirone to Gela in Sicily. In addition the building of the new Rome-Florence *Direttissima* line is separately financed.

TRAFFIC
After the disappointing results of the previous year the Italian State Railways (FS) achieved a slight but welcome improvement in 1976. Total receipts rose by 17 per cent, although comparison with 1975 is not truly significant because of subsequent rate and fare increases. Passenger-journeys increased by about 4 per cent to 392 million and the average journey increased to 101.9 km. Passenger-km amounted to 39 900 million. Freight traffic rose by about 10 per cent and 52.5 million tonnes were carried during the year, of which just under 8 per cent were for departmental purposes. Revenue tonne-km amounted to 16 600 million and two-thirds of the revenue tonnage was import and export traffic.
Steam locomotive-km dropped 40 per cent compared with the previous year and the average journey of the remaining 250 locomotives available to traffic each day during 1976 was only 13 km. This compares with 395 km for EMUs, 360 km for electric locomotives, 256 km for diesel locomotives and 300 km for diesel railcars.

	1974	1975	1976
Freight ton-km (million)	18 500	14 667	16 375
Freight tonnage	60 200 000	42 666	48 433
Passenger-km (million)	38 700.0	36 332	39 118
Passenger journeys (million)	390.0	370 115	390 070

FINANCIAL	1974 (Lira)	1975 (Lira)	1976 (Lira)
Revenues (millions)	1 307 287	1 465 526	1 864 638
Expenses	2 081 498	2 278 239	2 740 420

MOTIVE POWER
Motive power and rolling stock will absorb 750 000 m lira under the 1975-79 plan. On December 17, 1976, the Board of Italian State Railways (FS) placed an order with Italian industry for construction of five 3 kV Class E656 Bo-Bo-Bo locomotives with chopper control. The order follows studies involving FS Tecnomasio Italiano Brown Boveri and Fiat. The locomotives will be supplied with spare bogies and will cost 9 700m lira. The most notable item under the motive power procurement plan is the 180 electric Bo-Bo-Bo locomotives of the new Class E656 which has a 4 800 kW hourly rating for main line use. The design is based on the existing E646 class, but with improved traction motors to allow a greater output and a maximum speed of 160 km/h instead of 145 km/h. Estimated weight in working order will be 115 tonnes. The driver's controller will provide for running speeds to be selected and held automatically, and the auxiliary generator will supply 450 V 60 Hz. As these locomotives come into service the old Bo-Bo-Bo E626 class dating from before the second world war can be withdrawn.
In addition, four prototype E666 Class Co-Co locomotives will be built. These have a 6 400 kW hourly rating and a maximum speed of 200 km/h for service on the new Rome-Florence *Direttissima*. Other locomotives to be ordered are of existing types: 40 of the D345 class which is a 1 350 hp B-B diesel-electric, 75 of the 245 class 500 hp three-axle diesel-hydraulic shunters, and 50 of the 140 hp two-axle 214 class diesel-hydraulic shunting tractors.

ROLLING STOCK
Two prototype electric multiple-unit four coach trains are to be built under the new Five-Year Plan. The first will consist of an Ale 801 motor coach, two Le18 trailers, and an ALe 940 motor coach. Each motor coach will have an hourly rating of 1 020 kW with a maximum speed of 150 km/h, and both classes have an estimated weight in working order of 68 tonnes. The train will provide 420 seats and have a maximum capacity of 810 passengers.
A similar prototype train will have two ALe800 motor coaches rated at 1 800 kW hourly and with full chopper control, but each motor coach will be 2 tonnes heavier and the train will have 376 seats only. After trials, 42 trains will be ordered to replace EMUs dating from 1932 now in service around Milan and Naples. For local services elsewhere 100 diesel railcars of Class ALn668 will be purchased.
Locomotive-hauled rolling stock to be purchased in the five-year period includes 590 coaching stock vehicles and 8 050 freight wagons, and a train ferry will be ordered for the route to Sardinia. There is no specific provision for the purchase of high speed train sets, either the ALe481 railcars (formerly ALe541) being designed to run up to 300 km/h on the Rome-Florence *Direttissima* or the tilting-body coaches developed by Fiat for lines with numerous curves.

Ale electric power car and Le 803 trailer.

Class D445 diesel locomotive.

TRACK

The Italian Minister of Transport, Mr. Attilio Ruffini opened the first section (Rome-Città della Pieve, 122 km) of the new Rome-Florence highspeed rail link on 24 February 1977. The new line is being built to increase traffic capacity over this main route. Construction began in 1970 and completion of the whole line is scheduled for 1982. The new line will be more direct, cutting the rail distance between these two cities from 314 to 254 km; with high-speed trains, the journey will take 1½ hours instead of the present 3 hours.

The new line will not replace the old one which was no longer capable of ensuring a smooth flow of traffic for a daily throughput of more than 200 trains in peak periods; instead, it will be linked to it at eight different points so that trains can cross over from one line to the other. The end result will be a system of four tracks with two-way working, thereby increasing capacity and providing greater operating flexibility on a route that will be able to handle 600 trains daily.

Considerable geological and orographical difficulties occurred during construction of this first section, which involved building 17 tunnels, 37 viaducts and 304 other structures.

Quadrupling the Rome-Florence line will have significant positive effects at national level, particularly for freight traffic, and this is part of a larger programme for gradually reinforcing the main North-South rail route from Milan to Reggio di Calibria and the lines branching off to the Simplon Pass, Chiasso and the Brennner Pass to the North and towards Sicily in the South.

The technical and financial efforts made for the construction of the new Rome-Florence line are proportional to the importance this line will have in the overall rail system since it will contribute to bringing the farthermost ends of the country closer together.

To mark the inaugural run, Mr. Mayer, Director General of the Italian State Railways, described the new high-speed line to some one hundred journalists from the international press at Rome Central Station on 23 February. He also pointed out the many advantages of the new line for both passenger and freight traffic.

The UIC Secretary General, Mr. de Fontgalland, recalled that the *Direttissima* had a European background in that it formed an integral part of the UIC Master Plan, which had been presented to the international press on 22 November 1973 in Florence.

The programme of high-speed lines for European Railways had since made significant progress, as shown by the opening of a 143 km section of the Silesia-Baltic trunk line in

September 1974, the start of work on the Mannheim-Stuttgart line in August 1976, and on the Paris-Lyons line in December 1976.

After reminding his audience that the railways were the most energy-efficient of all transport modes, the UIC Secretary General stressed that high speeds were not a prestige operation: they were dictated by economic and social considerations, because they attracted new traffic due to the improved customer services, and enabled rolling stock to be used more efficiently. As a result, the railways bring progress in all its forms (including less travel fatigue) to the community.

During 1977 FS has brought into service a 14 km cut-off from Nocera Inferiore to Salerno on the main line from Naples to Sicily; it includes the 10 km Santa Lucia tunnel, and will allow important cuts in journey times, as well as eventual segregation of freight services.

FS is concentrating on upgrading secondary routes for freight traffic so as to leave existing main lines clear for faster passenger services. Between Naples and Rome, the inland Caserta to Cassino line has been electrified and work is proceeding northward to Rome. When completed the route will relieve the existing line of much through freight traffic, as well as selected passenger trains such as the Milan-Salerno services.

Further south double-tracking is in hand on the Cancello to Nola branch, landward of Mount Vesuvius, and double-tracking is to commence shortly over the 28 km on to Sarno. The remaining 13 km to Nocera Inferiore is across difficult terrain, and it is planned to build a new double-track railway to connect with the Santa Lucia cut-off between Nocera and Salerno. When the route is complete freight trains to and from southern Italy will be able to avoid the Naples area altogether by travelling from Salerno through Cancello and Caserta and then up the electrified Caserta-Rome line. On the east coast double-tracking has now been completed on the 20 km section from Osturi to Fasano between Brindisi and Bari. Work is now in progress on the 35 km section on to Mola di Bari.

ELECTRIFICATION

Electrification will absorb Lire 96 000 million under the 1975-79 programme, a quarter to be spent on strengthening the catenary and providing new or remodelled substations to allow heavier and faster trains. Aims of the new programme are partly to ease the difficulties caused by the energy crisis, partly to improve operations on several

ELECTRIC LOCOMOTIVES

Class	Axle Arrangement	Line Current	Rated Output hp	Max lb (kg)	Tractive Effort (Full Field) lb (kg) Continuous at	mph (km/h)	Max Speed mph (km/h)	Wheel Dia. in (mm)	Weight tons tonnes	Length ft in (mm)	No. Built	Year First Built	Builders Mechanical Parts	Electrical Equipment
E.626	Bo-Bo-Bo	3 000 V dc	2 100	50 300 (22 800) 57 800 (26 200)	26 000 (11 800) 30 200 (13 700)	32 (52) 28 (45)	59 (95)	49¼ (1 250)	93	49' 1" (14 950)	448	1928	Savigliano; CGE; Brown Boveri; Elettromeccaniche; Saronno; Breda; OM; Ansaldo; CENSA Saronno; Reggiane; FIAT	Marelli; Savigliano CGE; Brown Boveri; Elettro-meccaniche Saronno; Breda; OM; Ansaldo; CENSA Saronno
E.428	2-Bo-Bo-2	,,	2 800	44 000 (20 000) 48 500 (22 000)	23 000 (10 500) 25 300 (11 500)	48 (77) 44 (71)	80 (130)	74 (1 880)	135	62' 4" (19 000)	241	1934	Breda; Ansaldo; Reggiane; FIAT; Brown Boveri	Breda; Ansaldo; Marelli; Brown Boveri
E.424	Bo-Bo	,,	1 660	43 000 (19 500)	20 900 (9 500)	34 (55)	62 (100)	49¼ (1 250)	72.4	50' 10" (15 500)	158	1943	Breda; Savigliano; Ansaldo; Reggiane; Brown Boveri; OM	Breda; Savigliano; Ansaldo; Marelli; Brown Boveri; CGE
E.444	Bo-Bo	,,	4 020	44 500 (20 200)	25 400 (11 500)	56 (91)	112 (180)	49¼ (1 250)	79	55' 3" (16 840)	44	1967	Savigliano; Breda; Casaralta; Fiat	OCREN; Asgen; Savigliano
E.636	Bo-Bo-Bo	,,	2 100	48 500 (22 000)	25 300 (11 500)	32.3 (52)	75 (120)	49¼ (1 250)	101	59' 10½" (18 250)	469	1940	Breda; Brown Boveri; Savigliano; OM; Reggiane; Pistoiesi	Breda; Brown Boveri; Savigliano; CGE; Ansaldo S. Giorgio
E.645	Bo-Bo-Bo	,,	4 320	64 400 (29 200)	37 000 (16 800)	44.7 (72)	75 (120)	49¼ (1 250)	112	60' 0" (18 290)	93	1964	Breda; Brown Boveri; Savigliano; OM; Reggiane; Pistoiesi; IMAM	Breda; Brown Boveri; Savigliano; CGE; Marelli; Ansaldo S. Giorgio; OCREN
E.646	Bo-Bo-Bo	,,	4 320	52 500 (23 800)	29 750 (13 500)	57 (92)	93 (150)	49¼ (1 250)	110	59' 10½" (18 250)	203	1958	Breda; Brown Boveri; Savigliano; OM; Reggiane; Pistoiesi; IMAM	Breda; Brown Boveri; Savigliano; CGE; Marelli; Ansaldo S. Giorgio; OCREN
E.321	C(0-3-0)	,,	325	19 850 (9 000)	11 000 (5 000)	12.7 (20.5)	31 (50)	51½	36	30' 5½" (9 280)	50	1960	FS; Verona	Brown Boveri
E.444	Bo-Bo	3 000 V		23 600	12 800	105	200		82		117	1967	Savigliano; Breda; Casaralta; Fiat	OCREM Asgen; Savigliano
E321	C	3 000 V	190	9 000	5 000	20, 5	50	1 310	36	9 280	40	1961	Officine FS Verona (Transformte de loc)	TIBB
E.322	C	3 000 V	190	9 000	5 000	20, 5	50	1 310	36	9 280	20	1961	835	
E.323	C	3 000 V	190	11 700	8 400	11	65	1 040	46	9 240	30	1966	TIBB	TIBB
E.324	C	3 000 V	190	11 700	8 400	11	65	1 040	45	9 240	10	1966	TIBB	TIBB
E.656	Bo-Bo-Bo	3 000 V	4 200	24 900	13 100	103	160	1 250	120	18 290	61	1975	TIBB	TIBB

important routes by providing alternative electrified track.
Included in the new programme is:
—Rome-Caserta (Naples), a 211-km double-track line which is being modernised to take more freight traffic from the South to Rome and the Italian central Northern area. This will ease traffic on the Rome-Naples direct express route, which is at present near to saturation.
—Treviglio-Cremona-Codogno, 83 km of single track which carries heavy commuter traffic in the Milan area.
—Ferrara-Ravenna-Rimini, 124 km of single track. Electrification should strengthen the direct link between the Northeast and the Adriatic.
—Treviso-Vicenza, 60 km of single track. This work will involve modernisation of the connection between Milan and Verano and Northeast Italy without affecting the Venice Mestre junction.
—Bari-Taranto, a 111-km single-track line which will involve modernisation of the link with Taranto, important for the steel industry of the area.
In the new electrification, substations will be sited every 20-25 km. Each will be equipped with at least one silicon rectifier set with a nominal output of 3 600 kVa. Catenary consists of a double contact wire with support cables, together with automatic regulation, for a total section of 320 mm². A similar system has been used on the Sae-Milan, Luzi-Rome, Siette-Florence and Cariboni-Lecco lines, all recent conversions.
Operations with three-phase current at 3 600-V 16⅔ Hz, begun in 1902, came to an end on May 25, 1976, when the last two lines still working with this system were converted to 3 000 V dc. They were the Alessandria-Acqui-S. Giuseppe di Cairo (to Savona) and the Acqui-Asti lines.
First experiments with 16⅔ Hz traction were carried out on the Valtellina line, and the system reached its maximum development with a stretch of 200 km in the thirties. No more conversion to ac current was carried out after 1937.

SIGNALLING

Nearly one-third of the Lire 106 000 million five-year S & T budget will be absorbed by the extension of automatic signalling and coded track circuit cab signalling installations. Major main lines will be equipped with hot box detectors, a CTC installation for the Parma-Bologna-Prato route will be completed, and operations in the Bologna San Donato marshalling yard will be automated.
The most interesting signalling job will be the installation of non-continuous cab signalling based on transponders throughout the 237 km Verona-Brennero line; part of this route has been so equipped for more than a year. The circuitry of the transponders in the four-foot is varied according to the aspect of the associated signal; after interrogation by a passing locomotive, the transponders return the correct signal aspect back on board for display in the cab.
Italian State Railways (FS) has begun operation of two important all-electric interlocking installations at Parma (on the Bologna-Milan line) and at Venice St. Lucia. The two installations have route control and separate handling for routing. The Parma installation, with two-way working, completes the updating of installations on the Bologna-Milan line. All stations now have electrical interlocking installations for routing, with automatic two-way coded current block sections, with continuous cab signalling. The Parma installation, controlled from a central box at the station, replaces a number of signal boxes and manual points handling. It controls 82 colour-light signals, 114 electrically operated points, 157 track circuits, and 81 shunting signals. There are 8 000 relays. The equipment was built by AMF-Sasib, at a cost of Lire 1 680 million. The Venice St. Lucia installation, which replaces outdated electrical interlocking with individual levers, completes the signalling modernisation in connection with the quadrupling of the track to Venice Mestre, now nearing completion. The installation at Venice St. Lucia controls 64 colour-light signals, 93 shunting signals, 117 electrically operated points and 183 track circuits. It has 5 000 relays. Built by Societe Parisini of Bologna, the installation cost Lire 1 200 million.

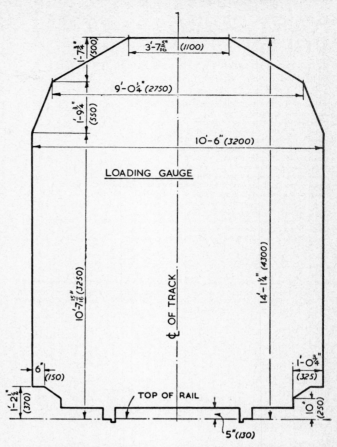

LOADING GAUGE

The minimum lateral clearance between Loading Gauge (diagram above) and Fixed Structure Gauge varies according to the radius of curvature, e.g.:

Radius of curve		inside of curve		Clearance outside of curve	
feet	metres	ins	mm	ins	mm
820	250	5.9	150	5.9	150
656	200	7.9	200	8.3	210
492	150	11.1	283	12.2	310
328	100	26.6	676	27.8	706
230	70	44.0	1 177	47.7	1 211

DIESEL LOCOMOTIVES

Class	Axle Arrangement	Transmission	Rated Power hp	Max. lbs (kg)	Tractive Effort Continuous at lbs (kg)	mph (km/h)	Max. Speed mph (km/h)	Wheel Dia. ins (mm)	Total Weight Tons	Length ft ins (mm)	No. Built	Year first Built	Builders: Mechanical Parts	Engine & Type	Transmission
D.341	Bo-Bo	Elec.	1 400	40 800 (18 500)	17 300 (7 850)	16 (26)	68 (110)	41 (1 040)	64	47' 6" (14 480)	68	1957	Fiat	Fiat 3212.SF or Breda-Paxman 12 YLX	Brown Boveri; OCREN
D.342	B-B	Hyd.	1 600	45 850 (20 800)	32 000 (14 500)	11.8 (19)	87 (140)	41 (1 040)	63	47' 7" (14 500)	20	1957	Ansaldo	2 Ansaldo-Maybach MD435	Maybach Mekydro C 32
D.343	B-B (monomotor bogies)	Elec.	1 500	41 900 (19 000)	24 250 (11 000)		81 (130)	41 (1 040)	59.5	43' 5¾" (13 240)	75		Fiat; O.M.	Fiat 218 SSF or Breda-Paxman 12YJC	TIBB generator; 2 traction motors Breda-Elettromeccanica; OCREN
D.443	B-B (monomotor bogies)	Elec.	2 000	48 500 (22 000)	30 900 (14 000)		81 (130)		69.5	47' 3" (14 400)	50	1967	Fiat; OM	Fiat 2312 SSF or Breda-Paxman 12 YLC	ASG generator; 2 traction motors Breda-Elettromeccanica; OCREN
D.235	C	Hyd.	350	32 200 (14 600)	19 800 (9 000)	4.6 (7.4)	25 Sw. (40) 34 Line (55)	42⅛ (1 070)	39	31' 4½" (9 540)	45	1961	Badoni; Jenbach; OM	Carraro; Jenbach; OM	Hydrotitan; Voith; OM
D.234	C	Hyd.	400	29 750 (13 500)	15 650 (7 100)	5.6 (9)	25 Sw. (40) 37 Line (60)	51½ (1 310)	36	30' 8" (9 340)	37	1961	Breda; OM	Breda; OM	O.M.
D.225	B	Hyd.	250	21 600 (9 800)	15 400 (7 000)	2.6 (4.2)	19 Sw. (30) 34 Line (55)	35½ (900)	28	27' 4½" (8 322)	97	1956	Breda; Jenbach; Greco	Breda; Jenbach; Deutz	Breda; Voith
D.141	Bo-Bo	Elec.	700	41 900 (19 000)	26 500 (12 000)	6.2 (10)	50 (80)	41 (1 040)	62	43' 5¼" (13 240)	3	1962	T.I.B.B.; Reggiane	FIAT MB	Brown Boveri
D.345	B-B	Elec.	1 350	19 000	11 270	25, 1	130	1 040	61	13 240	145	1970	Breda Pist; Sofer Savigliano	218SSF G.M.T.	TIBB; Marelli Italtrofo
D.445	B-B	Elec.	2 120	22 000	14 500	23, 5	130	1 040	72	14 100	35	1970	Savigliano	2112SSF G.M.T.	Asgen
2435	C	Hyd.	500	14 000	11 000	6, 5	60	1 040	48	9 240	312	1962	Reggione OM CNTR	MB820- Frot Gas D26N12V BRIF JW 600 CNTR	OM-SRM BRIF-Voith L24
214	B	Hyd.	130	5 700	4 000	4	35	910	22	7 158	175	1963	Badoni; Greco; Simm CNTR	8217-02,001 Fiat	BRIF-Voith L33

IVORY COAST — UPPER VOLTA

REGIE DES CHEMINS DE FER ABIDJAN-NIGER (R.A.N.)
PO Box 1394, Abidjan, Cote d'Ivoire

General Manager: Lancina Konate
Inspector General for Technical Affairs: Bony Aboh
Administrative Director: Ibrahima Coulibaly
Director Rolling Stock and Traction: Ousseyni Diarra
Director Track and Structure: Noël Privat
Director Studies and New Projects: N'Da Ezoa
Financial Director: Christopher Yesso
Commercial Director: Gbon Coulibaly
Improvements Director: André Balma
Head of Personnel and Social Affairs Service: Média Kone
Head of the Supplies and Shops Service: Mélindji Kacou
Head of the Sleeping Car and Tourism Service: Pierre Mariotti
Head of the Professional Services: Auguste Pruvost
Head of the Information Service: Aby Abagnilin
Head of the Telecommunication and Signalling Service: Nabilébié Bazie
Head of the Documentation Service: Bahi Kohirime
Head of the Press and External Affairs Office: Bernard Combes

Gauge: 1.00 m.
Route length: 1 173 km.

The railway comprises a principal line of 713 miles *(1 147 km)* which connects Abidjan, capital of Ivory Coast, with Ouagadougou, capital of Upper Volta, and two branches, one of 7.5 miles *(12 km)* from Abidjan to the oil port of Vridi and the other of 9 miles *(14 km)* from Azaguie *(41 km)* to Ake-Befiat.

TRAFFIC	1974	1975	1976
Freight ton-km	528 819 576	443 218 305	559 000 000
Freight tonnage	795 040	725 370	866 000
Passenger-km	918 135 021	945 736 974	1 040 000 000
Passenger journeys	2 931 344	3 006 736	3 254 000

FINANCES	1973	1974	1975	1976
		(F. CFA million)		
Revenue	6 497	7 473	8 423	11 751
Expenses	6 379	7 470	8 960	9 968

ROLLING STOCK (1976)

	Total
Passenger coaches	128
Freight wagons	645
Flat wagons	185
Tipping wagons	192
Special wagons	51
Service cars	11
Service wagons	74
Miscellaneous wagons	27
Tank wagons	114
TOTAL	1 427

MOTIVE POWER AND ROLLING STOCK
At present RAN operates 139 passenger coaches, 16 vans and 1 675 freight wagons, including 93 tankers owned by oil shippers. Motive power includes 127 locomotives for mainline operation, 110 rail cars and 25 shunters.
Motive power units and passenger coaches are serviced in the RAN shops at Abidjan. Maintenance shops for freight stock are at Bobo-Dioulasso, in Upper Volta.
Most recent motive power deliveries to RAN consisted of eight diesel-hydraulic locomotives, series DHG 400 B, from Rheinstahl Henschel, German Federal Republic.

TRACK
A major programme of track improvement is being pushed through. The swift growth of traffic has caused a number of operating problems, because of the relatively light structure, steep gradients and narrow curves. From Abidjan to Tafire (488 km) the track had gradients of up to 25 per cent and many curve radii as low as 200 m. Rails were only 25 kg/m. Beyond Tafire and up to Ougadougou the track was laid with 30 kg/m rails, with a maximum gradient of 10 per cent and minimum curve radius of 500 m. Modernisation began as soon as it was realised that the line would be unable to cope with the increased traffic. New 30 kg/m rails were laid between Abidjan and Agboville (82 km), and the track was substantially realigned by 1959.
Between 1970 and 1973 track was realigned between Agboville and Dimbokro (183 km) and 36 kg/m rail, welded from station to station, was laid. As a part of this work, track was doubled between Cechi and Anoumaba.
During the same period re-ballasting of the line was begun and a major programme of rail welding was launched. By the end of 1976 length of welded track totalled 875 km, while track reballasted with granite was 1 065 km.
Realignment is being carried out north of Dimbokro, and work should be completed as far as Tafire by 1978.
RAN announced in 1974 that it is to spend a further FrCFA15 000 m on track-doubling and other infrastructure works between 1977 and 1980. This is in addition to the ongoing rail replacement programme. Four more sections of double track are now to be laid between Abidjan and Bouaké at a cost of FrCFA10 000 m. These will bring considerable operating benefits and a further cut in journey time from Ouagadougou to the coast.
FrCFA 4 000 m has been allocated to several small realignment and bridge construction schemes on the line northwards from Tafire to Ouagadougou, and to miscellaneous rerailing with 36 kg/m rail. Total expenditure on infrastructure planned by RAN during the 1977-80 period is FrCFA 26 000 m.
Meanwhile, feasibility studies are to be carried out shortly for a 325-km railway to link iron ore deposits at Mt. Klahoyo near Man with the port of San Pedro.
An interesting outcome of RAN's upgrading project was high-speed trials run in 1974 with a Soulé/Alsthom ZE162 diesel-electric railcar on the newly-completed 36 kg/m track between Agboville and Dimbokro. The top speed of 130 km/h reached by the railcar demonstrated that high speeds are not the prerogative of standard gauge railways. Once realignment has been completed, a fast railcar service to Bouaké is planned and RAN engineers believe that only the limitations of existing motive power prevent speeds of 150 km/h being achieved on the new permanent way.

SIGNALLING AND COMMUNICATIONS
Modernisation of RAN's signalling and telecommunications is also going ahead. Negotiations are in progress with the African Development Nlent Bank for a grant to cover part of the FrCFA3 000 m cost of installing CTC throughout the main line and Sofrerail is providing consultancy assistance. There is already a 15-km double-track section between Checi and Anoumaba, just south of Dimbokro, which has considerably eased operation.

JAMAICA

JAMAICA RAILWAY CORPORATION
PO Box 489, 142 Barry Street, Kingston

Chairman: Brian Mair
General Manager: A. B. Tapper
Chief of Transportation: E. Shirley
Chief Civil Engineer: R. Nevers
Chief Mechanical Engineer: G. Mitchell
Financial Controller: E. Philp
Warehouse Supervisor: A. Henry

Gauge: 1.435 m
Route Length: 330 km

FINANCIAL DETAILS

	1972	1973	1974	1975
	J$	J$	J$	J$
Revenue	3,148,000	3,712,000	5,237,000	6,262,000
Expenses	3,488,000	4,514,000	6,352,000	7,296,000

TRAFFIC

	1975
Total Freight Tonnage	4,009,531
Total Passengers carried	1,106,002

MOTIVE POWER AND ROLLING STOCK (1975)

	Line Haul	Shunting
Number of locomotives in service		
Diesel-electric	22	3

Number of railcars, diesel: 6
Number of trailers: 3 Wickham
               14 Rolls Royce
Number of passenger train coaches: 6
Number of Freight train cars (JRC): 208; (ALCAN) 113; (ALCOA) 40; (REVERE) 21

TRACK WORK (1975)
New Construction: Nil
New rail laid: 80 lb/yd (39.7 kg/m) BS and ARA rail was laid on 9.4 miles.
New Sleepers laid: 27 804

KAISER BAUXITE COMPANY RAILROAD
Discovery Bay

Vice-President and General Manager: E. J. Coyne

The company is engaged in bauxite mining and the railway transports some 5 million short tons per year. It is a standard gauge line 16 miles *(35 km)* long.

JAPAN

JAPANESE NATIONAL RAILWAYS

6-5, Marunouchi 1-chome, Chiyoda-ku, Tokyo

Board of Directors:
Chairman: Fumio Takagi
Vice-Chairman: Masaji Amasaka
Members: Masaru Ibuka   Kōji Takahashi
Seija Kaya   Osamu Shinohara
Shigeo Yamaguchi   Masanori Ozeki
Mamoru Takiyama   Yoshiro Tomii
Michio Taguchi   Kazumasa Nawatari
Masaoki Kobayashi   Hiromasa Kittaka
Hideaki Suzuki   Kazuo Maruo
Shin-ichi Kimigafukuro   Hideo Yoshitake
Yoshio Shinohara
President: Fumio Takagi
Vice-President, Executive: Masaji Amasaka
Vice-President, Engineering: Mamoru Takiyama
General Manager, Affiliated Enterprises: Shigeo Yamaguchi
Advisory Directors:
 Head Office: Michio Taguchi
 Head Office: Masaoki Kobayashi
 Shinkansen Administration: Shin-ichi Kimigafukuro
 Hokkaido Region: Hideaki Suzuki
 Osaka Region: Yoshio Shinohara
 Head Office: Kōji Takahashi
 Nagoya Region: Osamu Shinohara
 Head Office: Masanori Ozeki
 Tokyo Metropolitan Sphere HQ: Yoshiro Tomii
 Head Office: Kazumasa Mawatari
 Head Office, Staff Relations: Hiromasa Kittaka
 Kyushu Region: Kazuo Maruo
 Sendai Region: Hideo Yoshitake
Directors of Departments:
 Director, Public Relations Dept: Takao Ishida
 Director, International Dept: Norio Tejima
 Director, Inspection & Audit Dept: Yoshiaki Kawagoe
 Director, Corporate Planning Dept: Tomoo Kagayama
 Director, Local Line Countermeasures Dept: Kazumasa Mawatari
 Directors, Technical Development Dept: Mitsuaki Ishiyama
             Yoshihiro Kyotani
             Masayuki Nishida
             Masaaki Yokoi
             Hisomu Katase
             Misao Sugawara
 Director, Staff Relations Dept: Hiromasa Kittaka
 Director, Finance & Accounting Dept: Hiroshi Yoshii
 Director, Purchasing & Stores Dept: Nobuto Takeda
 Director, Information Systems Dept: Akira Kurata
 Director, Environmental Preservation Dept: Hisashi Yoshimura
 Director, Passenger Dept: Kohei Hata
 Director, Freight Dept: Tadamasa Yamasaki
 Director, Train Operation Dept: Yoshito Fujita
 Director, Construction Dept: Tatsuo Okabe
 Director, Shinkansen Construction Dept: Hisashi Yoshimura
 Director, Track & Structure Dept: Hikaru Murayama
 Director, Electrical Engineering Dept: Tatsuya Ishihara
 Director, Rolling Stock & Mechancial Engineering Dept: Seihei Katayama
 Director, Motor Transportation Dept: Tomoaki Fujii
 Director, Ferry Service Dept: Sadahiko Shimoyama
 Director, Diversification Dept: Osamu Shinohara
 Director, Development Dept: Tetsuo Hanya
 Director, Railway Police Dept: Hayao Ikeda
 Director, Mutual Aid Association Secretariat: Takumi Hamada
 Director, Inquiry & Audit Board Secretariat: Yoshizo Yasui
 Director, Railway Technical Research Institute: Hiroshi Murayama
 Director, Railway Labour Science Research Institute: Yuji Iiyama
 Superintendent, Central Railway Training School: Fumio Tejima
 Director, Rolling Stock Design Office: Seihei Katayama
 Director, Structure Design Office: Fujio Ikeda
 Superintendent, Central Railway Hospital: Hideo Ueda
 Superintendent, Central Health Supervision Office: Hachiro Otake
 Director, Overseas Office:
  Hotsumi Harada (New York)
  Michitaro Yamaoka (Paris)
 Director, Work Costing System Office: Tatsuo Okabe
 Director, Information Systems Management Center: Tetsuya Yamamoto

Key Statistics	1975
Railway Route Length (km)	21 272
Double- and Multi-tracked Sections	5 447
	(25.6%)
Electrified Sections	7 813
	(36.7%)
Narrow Gauge Lines	
dc	4 603
ac	3 210
Shinkansen	
ac	1 177
Railway Stations	5 286
Passenger and Freight	1 542
Passenger	3 652
Freight	92
Total Length of Bridges (km)	2 174
Total Length of Tunnels (km)	1 779
Train-km (thousands)	694 719
Railway Traffic Volume (millions)	
Passengers Carried	7 048
Tons Carried	142
Passenger-km	215 289
Ton-km	46 600
Number of Employees	430 051
Total Revenues & Expenses (million yen)	
Revenues	1 833 200
Expenses	2 747 900

Notwithstanding the Government's economic policy for 1975 aimed at stabilisation of commodity prices and recovery of business activity, the protracted recession worsened, and the year ended with an unusually low rate of economic growth.
The total domestic traffic of all modes of transport, as compared with the preceding year, registered a gain of only 3 per cent in passenger-km and a loss of 4 per cent in freight ton-km. Taking JNR alone, passenger-km remained at about the same level, but

ton-km showed a 10 per cent decline largely due to the business recession, and in addition, to the frequent disruption of service caused by labour disputes.
Consequently, JNR's share in the total domestic traffic shrank to 30 per cent in passenger and 13 per cent in freight.
In the operating revenues, the extension of the Shinkansen down to Hakata and the revision of passenger charges in November were expected to bring about a notable gain in passenger revenue, but the increase registered was only 16 per cent; while there was almost no gain in the revenue from freight. The operating expenses, on the other hand, rose by 23 per cent on account of the rising personnel expense and interest payment.
The passenger-km in 1975 was 215 300 million, about the same as in the preceding year. Of this, 139 300 million was for non-commuters, almost the same as in the year before, and 76 000 million for commuters, a loss of 1 per cent. Of the non-commuters, the Shinkansen, which was opened down to Hakata on March 10, 1975, accounted for 53 300 million passenger-km, an appreciable gain of 31 per cent, but the narrow-gauge lines showed a loss of 13 per cent, accounting for only 86 000 million.
Accountable mainly for the standstill in total passenger-km are the four factors—the worsening of the protracted business recession, the frequent labour disputes, the obstruction of service on the Joetsu Line and the Hakodate Main Line due to landslides and collapse of embankment from heavy rains, and the 32 per cent rise in passenger charge effected in November.
In the major city spheres a notable improvement was made in services, particularly for the transportation of commuters.
For the promotion of sales, the ticket reservation system was expanded with various new and attractive features incorporated.

(1) Shinkansen

The Shinkansen carried 157.2 million passengers, an increase of 18 per cent over 1974, and the passenger-km reached 53 318 million, an increase of 31 per cent. The number of trains operated per day as of July 1976 averaged 275, that is, 132 HIKARIs (limited stop) and 143 KODAMAs.
In July 1976, the transport capacity of the Shinkansen west of Osaka down to Hakata was raised to meet the new traffic conditions and increased demand activated by the opening of the line from Okayama to Hakata.

(2) Narrow Gauge Lines

The number of trains operated per day on the narrow gauge lines averaged 18 178 as of July 1976, of which 534 were limited expresses, 1 082 ordinary expresses and 16 562 local trains.
The passenger-km by limited express was 32 112 million, a decrease of 11 per cent from 1974.
Intercity service in northern Japan was improved in 1975 by the electrification of the Ou Line between Uzen-Chitose and Akita, introduction of new limited express trains in Hokkaido and by coupling more cars on to limited express trains.
In July 1976, when electrification of the Nagasaki and Sasebo lines was completed, the transport capacity in Kyushu was brought up at the same time, mainly by putting a greater number of limited express trains into service. In October in Tokyo, the underground rail line between Tokyo Station and Shinagawa Station was completed for the extended operation of Sobu Line trains from Tokyo down to Shinagawa.

Passenger-Kilometers

(million)

			Narrow gauge lines					
Year	Shinkansen		Express train		Local train		Total	
1965	10 651	100	39 522	100	123 841	100	174 014	100
1970	27 890	262	54 626	138	107 210	87	189 726	109
1971	26 795	252	56 336	143	107 191	87	190 321	109
1972	33 835	318	57 978	147	106 017	86	197 829	114
1973	38 989	366	61 105	155	108 003	87	208 097	120
1974	40 671	382	63 921	161	110 952	90	215 544	124
1975	53 318	501	52 990	134	108 981	88	215 289	124

Note: Express train denotes limited express and ordinary express trains.

(3) Traffic in Major City Spheres

For the Tokyo and Osaka Spheres, efforts were made to improve the service during the commuting hours and the time in between and to strengthen the transport capacity of the lines in the peripheral districts where the traffic demand had been growing. Congestion of traffic during the commuting hours, however, still persists.
In some principal cities, traffic congestions of commuters are growing worse, and in the Sapporo and Niigata areas, more trains were operated and more cars coupled on to each train to ease the congestion.

(4) Computerised Seat Reservation System

MARS (Magnetic-electronic Automatic Reservation System) 105 has been at work since 1972 for individual reservation of accommodations on trains, buses and ferries, and the number of reservations made has come to reach 645 000 in all per day. For party and group travelers, MARS 201 had been in use. But as the demand for reserved accommodation grew along with the increasing number of limited and ordinary express trains, use of MARS 202 began in May 1975 replacing MARS 201, and the reservation capacity was almost doubled, from 320 000 to 600 000 spaces per day.
As of May 1975, MARS, with 1 857 terminal sets located at 758 places, is processing as many as 1 111 120 spaces a day.
Along with the opening of the Shinkansen down to Hakata in March 1975, a new system of reservation making by customer-computer dialog through push-button phones direct from offices and homes was introduced.

Pendulum emu Limited Express Series 381
Series 381 is high-speed electric railcars of natural pendulum type, light in weight, low in the center of gravity, with the pendulum structure of the body and the running capacity of the bogie improved. A train of Series 381 cars runs at the top speed of 120 km/h on the Chuo Line which abounds with curves.

FREIGHT SERVICE

In 1975 freight traffic totalled 141 939 000 tons and 46 577 million ton-km, both dwindling by 10 per cent from the figures for the year before.

Accountable for this decline are the tardiness of JNR in modernising its freight service in meeting the great changes taking place in the mechanism of freight transportation, the lack of flexibility in coping with seasonal fluctuations in transport demand, the rigidity of the tariff system, the aggravating business recession, and the frequent ocurrence of labour disputes.

FREIGHT TRAFFIC

Year	Tons carried (millions)	Index	Tons-kms (thousand millions)	Index	Average distance of haul/ton (km)
1965	200	100	56.4	100	282.2
1970	199	100	62.4	111	313.6
1971	193	97	61.3	109	317.6
1972	182	91	58.6	104	322.0
1973	176	88	57.4	102	326.1
1974	158	79	51.6	91	326.6
1975	142	71	46.6	83	328.2

(1) Container Service

Container goods carried amounted to 12 114 000 tons, 5 per cent less than the preceding year, and to 9 378 million ton-km, less 4 per cent.

For freightliners, trucking operators were encouraged to use their private-owned 10-ton containers in those sections where there was heavy demand.

The total marine containers carried, included in the table, numbered 2 627.

The total sea-borne containers carried, not included in the table, numbered 5 812.

CONTAINER TRAFFIC

Year	Tons carried (thousands)	Ton-kms (millions)
1965	1 906	1 197
1970	8 715	6 301
	(2 030)	(1 280)
1971	10 292	7 626
	(3 768)	(2 662)
1972	12 394	9 419
	(6 243)	(4 609)
1973	13 843	10 422
	(7 347)	(5 467)
1974	12 812	9 754
	(6 856)	(5 171)
1975	12 114	9 378
	(6 543)	(4 908)

Notes
1 The figures in parentheses denote the part of the total carried by freightliner.
2 Marine container traffic has been accounted for as container traffic since October 1974, before which, such was treated as carload traffic.

(2) Service Improvement and Effective Use of Transport Capacity

In March 1976 when all the Musashino Line was opened, about half of the freight trains that had been operating on the Yamanote Loop Line were shifted on to this new line. The freightliner service operating in the Tokyo Metropolitan Sphere was also improved with additional tracks laid between the Tsurumi Station and Shiohama Marshalling Yard on the Tokaido Line, the facilities in the Tokyo Freight Terminal Station built up, and the container bases thinned out to be integrated with main bases. Furthermore, efforts were made for more effective use of transport capacity by wider adoption of the system for suspension of service on certain days of the week in accordance with the fluctuations in transport demand.

(3) Base Stations and Yards

As for the base stations, 19 stations were successively built up, with the Chiba and Kajigaya freight terminal stations and the Nabeshima Freight Station newly established and the Sapporo, Tokyo, Koriyama and other freight terminal stations expanded. As for yards, work on the electrification of the Musashino Marshalling Yard is now almost completed, and the handling capacity was raised. Work to automate the Kitakami and Suita Marshalling Yards and the Suo Tonda Station was continued from the preceding year.

(4) Industrial Sidings

At the end of 1975, industrial sidings numbered 2 594 in all. The outgoing tonnage from these sidings for the year was 79 950 000 tons and the arriving tonnage 73 570 000 tons.

ac Electric Locomotive Type ED75

ED75 is the standard type of ac electric locomotives. Of all the types, ED75 locomotives are produced in the greatest number and used all over Japan, in Hokkaido in the North, with cold proofing done, and in Kyushu in the South

ROLLING STOCK AND TRAIN OPERATION
(1) Number of Rolling Stock

The use of a greater number of electric and diesel rolling stock has enabled JNR to increase train speed and improve its service.

Changes in the number of Rolling Stock

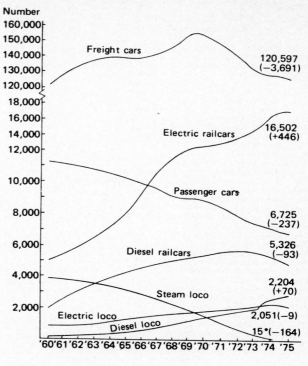

Notes
1 Increase or decrease compared with the previous year.
2 Denotes the number reserved in operable condition at Unekoji Engine Shed.

(2) Number of Electric Railcars

There has been a remarkable increase in electric railcars in recent years, as is seen in the following figure.

Changes in the Number of Electric Railcars

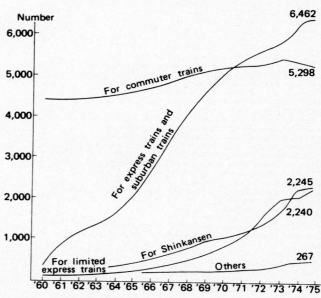

(3) Number and Kinds of Freight Cars

Wooden box cars	66 904	Container cars	7 291
Brake box cars	3 047	Auto cars	934
Steel box cars	650	Well cars	43
Refrigerator cars	2 378	Flat cars	1 862
Ventilated cars	332	Hopper cars	2 624
Stock cars	18	Coal cars	4 213
Earthenware cars	135	Tank cars	16
Caboose cars	2 740	Water tank cars	26
Gondola cars	26 693		
Ballast cars	54	Others	238

(4) Electrification and Dieselisation

As of October 1975, 36.7 per cent or 7 813 km of the total route length of JNR was electrified. Steam locomotives were all withdrawn from service in March 1976.

Year	Route length ac/dc electrified (km)		Percentage to the total route length
1971	6 239.3	(2 416.8)	29.9%
1972	6 684.8	(2 629.1)	31.9%
1973	6 961.4	(2 629.1)	33.0%
1974	7 374.8	(2 829.3)	34.9%
1975	7 628.1	(3 036.1)	35.9%
1976 (Oct)	7 813.0	(3 210.2)	36.7%

Note: The figures in parentheses indicate the route length ac electrified.

Train-Km by Type of Traction
(Daily average in thousands)

Passenger trains

(As of July 1976)

Electric loco	Electric railcar	Diesel loco and railcar
127	841	448
(9.0%)	(59.4%)	(31.6%)

Freight trains

	Electric loco	Diesel loco
	413	133
	(75.6%)	(24.4%)

FINANCES

	1975	1976
	(million Yen)	
Revenues	1 833 200	2 005 200
Expenses	2 747 900	2 919 300

(1) Rolling Stock

Major repairs of rolling stock are done at one of 19 workshops, located at vital points all over the country, and minor routine repairs and inspections at various depots. The repair and inspection work is now simplified through mechanisation and automation and the inspection intervals prolonged.
The system called KICS (Kosaku Information Control System), using computers for modernisation of management and operations at workshops, is proving quite effective in raising efficiency.

(2) Track

Labour saving and mechanisation of the inspection work are featured in modernising track maintenance work. Maintenance-free slab tracks, heavier rails and PC sleepers as well as machinery are used for labour saving and high-speed track measuring cars are operated on the Shinkansen once every ten days, and on the other lines two to six times a year depending upon the need.

(3) ATS

All the trains and lines have been operated under the Automatic Train Stop system since 1966, owing to which, accidents from violation of signals have been eliminated.

(4) ATC

The Automatic Train Control system, in which the brake works automatically, is adopted on the Shinkensan and some subway lines in Tokyo. Wider use is expected.

(5) CTC

In 1975 the Centralised Traffic Control system was put to work on three sections extending over 309 km, bringing up the lines under CTC to 3 897 km.

Year	Lines under CTC (km)	Percentage to total route length
1965	574	3
1971	2 392.6	12
1972	2 860.1	14
1973	3 335.1	16
1974	3 588.2	17
1975	3 896.9	18

(6) Automatic Signals

Automatic signals were installed on 142 km of lines in 1975 bringing up the percentage of lines with such signals to 47 per cent.

Year	Single track (km)	Double track (km)	Total (km)	Percentage to total route length
1965	2 270	3 548	5 818	28
1971	4 140	5 028	9 168	44
1972	4 237	5 110	9 347	45
1973	4 460	5 273	9 733	46
1974	4 538	5 376	9 914	47
1975	4 585	5 472	10 057	47

FINANCIAL REHABILITATION MEASURES

JNR was compelled to rewrite the Ten-Year Plan for Financial Rehabilitation drawn up under the Law for Special Measures for the Promotion of JNR Financial Rehabilitation. This was cause by the long delay of the National Diet in sanctioning the much needed tariff rate revision, leading to a large decrease in projected revenue, and by the swelling of expenditures from rising prices and labour costs. Besides, JNR was not fully capable of meeting the economic upheavals which were unanticipated at the time the plan was drawn up.
A new plan in the form of an "Outline of the Measures for JNR Financial Rehabilitation," was thus brought forth, and this was approved of by the Cabinet in December 1975 and passed the 78th Extraordinary Session of the Diet. The plan aimed to bring about a balance between revenue and expenditure in two fiscal years, 1976 and 1977, and sound finance thereafter.
The Law for Special Measures for the Promotion of JNR Financial Rehabilitation was abolished at the same time.
The main points of the Outline of the Measures for JNR Financial Rehabilitation are as follows:
Measures for the Recovery of Financial Balance

ELECTRIC LOCOMOTIVES

Class	Axle Arrangement	Line Current	Rated Output kW	Max lb (kg)	Tractive Effort (Full Field) Continuous at lb (kg)	mph (km/h)	Max Speed mph (km/h)	Wheel Dia. ins (mm)	Weight tonnes	Length ft in (mm)	No. Built as of 23/8/77	Year Built	Builders (abbreviations) M: (Mitsubishi Electric Co, Mitsubishi Heavy Industries). T: Tokyo Shibaura Elec. Co. H: Hitachi Mfg Co. K: Kawasaki Heavy Industries. To: Toyo Elec. Co. N: Nippon Sharyo Seizo Ltd.
ED 71	B-B	20 kV 1/50	1 900		35 270 (16 00)	26.5 (42.4)	59 (95)	44 (1 120)	67	47' 3" (14 400)	52	1959	M. T. H.
ED 72	B-2-B	20 kV 1/60	1 900		31 100 (14 100)	30.5 (49.1)	62 (100)	44 (1 120)	87	57' 1" (17 400)	20	1961	T.
ED 73	B-B	20 kV 1/60	1 900		31 100 (14 100)	30.5 (49.1)	62 (100)	44 (1 120)	67.2	47' 3" (14 400)	22	1962	T.
ED 74	B-B	20 kV 1/60	1 900		31 100 (14 100)	30.5 (49.1)	62 (100)	44 (1 120)	67.2	46' 11" (14 300)	6	1962	M.
ED 75	B-B	20 kV 1/50	1 900		31 100 (14 100)	30.5 (49.1)	62 (100)	44 (1 120)	67.2	60' 4½" (18 300)	301	1963	M. H. T.
ED 76	B-2-B	20 kV 1/50 or 60	1 900		31 100 (14 100)	30.5 (49.1)	62 (100)	44 (1 120)	90.5	60' 4½" (18 400)	130	1965	H. M. T.
ED 77	B-2-B	20 kV 1/50	1 900		31 100 (14 100)	30.5 (49.1)	62 (100)	44 (1 200)	75	51' 10" (15 800)	16	1965	H. M .T.
ED 78	B-2-B	20 kV 1/50	1 900		31 100 (14 100)	30.5 (49.1)	62 (100)	44 (1 120)	81.5	58' 9" (17 900)	12	1968	H.
EF 59	2C + C2	1 500 V dc	1 350		26 000 (11 800)	26 (42)	56 (90)	49¼ (1 250)	106.6	65' 4¼" (19 920)	24	1963	JNR. (R. B)
EF 62	C-C	1 500 V dc	2 550		51 600 (23 400)	24.2 (39)	62 (100)	44 (1 120)	96	59' 1" (18 000)	52	1962	K. T. To.
EF 63	B-B-B	1 500 V dc	2 550		51 600 (23 400)	24.2 (39)	62 (100)	44 (1 120)	108	59' 3" (18 050)	23	1962	T. M. K.
EF 64	B-B-B	1 500 V dc	2 550		44 850 (20 350)	28 (45)	71 (115)	44 (1 120)	96	58' 9" (17 900)	79	1964	T. K. To.
EF 65	B-B-B	1 500 V dc	2 550		44 850 (2 350)	28 (45)	71 (115)	44 (1 120)	96	54' 2" (16 500)	237	1964	K. To. T. N.
EF 66	B-B-B	1 500 V dc	3 900		43 200 (19 590)	44.9 (72.2)	75 (120)	44 (1 120)	100	59' 8½" (18 200)	56	1968	K. To.
EF 70	B-B-B	20 kV 1/60	2 300		42 990 (19 500)	26.1 (42.0)	62 (105)	44 (1 120)	96	54' 11½" (16 750)	81	1961	H. M.
EF 71	B-B-B	20 kV 1/50	2 700		46 500 (21 100)	28.6 (46.1)	62 (100)	44 (1 120)	100.8	60' 8" (18 500)	15	1968	M. T.
EF 30 Dual current	B+B+B	1.5 Vdc 20 kV 1/60	1 800		30 420 (13 800)	29.0 (46.7)	53 (85)	39⅜ (1 000)	96	54' 4" (16 560)	22	1960	H. M. T.
EF 81 Dual current	B--B-B	1.5 kVdc 20 kV 1/50, 1/00	2 550		44 050 (19 980)	28.4 (45.7)	62 (115)	44 (1 120)	100.8	61' 0" (18 600)	140	1968	H. M.
EF 80 Dual current	B-B-B	1.5 kVdc 20 kV 1/50	1 950		31 970 (14 500)	29.8 (48)	62 (105)	44 (1 120)	96	57' 5" (17 500)	63	1962	H. M.

DIESEL LOCOMOTIVES

Class	Axle Arrangement	Transmission	Rated Power hp	Max lbs (kg)	Tractive Effort Continuous at lbs (kg)	mph (km/h)	Max Speed mph (km/h)	Wheel Dia. ins (mm)	Total Weight Tons	Length ft ins (mm)	No. Built as of 31/3/76	Year first Built	Builders	Engine & Type	Transmission Type
DD 51	B-2-B	Hyd.	2 200		39 680 (18 00)		59 (95)	33¹³/₁₆ (860)	84	59' 1" (18 000)	626	1962	H. M. K.	2×1 100 hp DML 61Z	DW2A DW 2A
DD 53	B-2-B	Hyd.	2 200		39 680 (18 000)		59 (95)	,,	81	53' 2" (16 200)	3	1964	K.	2×1 100 hp DML 6182	DW 2AR DW 2AR
DD 54	B-1-B	Hyd.	1 820		37 040 (16 800)		59 (95)	,,	70	50' 2½" (15 300)	18	1966	M.	DMP 86Z	DW 5
DD 13	B-B	Hyd.	1 000		37 040 (16 800)		44 (70)	33¹³/₁₆ (860)	56	44' 7½" (13 600)	395	1957	K. M. N. H.	2 × 500 hp DMF 31SB	DS 12/135
DD 14	B-B	Hyd.	1 000		(18 540)		44 (70)	33¹³/₁₅ (860)	58	47' 0" (14 325)	36	1960	K.	2 × 500 hp DMF 31 SBR	,,
DD 15	B-B	Hyd.	1 000		36 380 (16 500)		44 (70)	33¹³/₁₆ (860)	55	44' 7½" (*⅓ †??(	50	1961	N.	,,	,,
DD 16	B-B	Hyd.	800		31 750 (14 400)		47 (75)	,,	49	38' 10" (11 840)	65	1972	J. N. R. N. k.	DML 61Z	DW 2A
DE 10	AAA-B	Hyd.	1 350		43 000 (19 500)		53 (85)	33¹³/₁₆ (860)	65	46' 5" (14 150)	692	1966	K. N. H.	DML61ZA, B	DWA
DE 11	,,	,,	,,		46 300 (21 000)		,,	,,	70	,,	112	1968	K. N.	,,	,,
DE 15	,,	,,	,,		43 000 (19 500)		,,	,,	65	,,	44	1967	N.	,,	,,
DF 50	B-B-B	Elec.	1 200		27 550 (12 500)	(17.5)	56 (90)	39⅜ (1 000) (85.7)	109	53' 10" (16 400)	109	1965	K. N. T. H.	MANV6V22/30mA Sulzer 8LDA25	
Shinkansen 911	B-B-B	Hyd.	2 200		59 500 (27 000)	100	35⅞ (160)	90 (910)	3	63' 8" (19 400)	3	1964	N.	2 × 1 100 hp DWZB DML61Z	
Shinkansen 912	B-B	Hyd.	740		(14 000)		44 (70)	33¹³/₁₆ (860)	56	44' 7¼" (13 600)	20	1959	N.	2 × 370 hp DMF 31S	DS 12/135

Names of lines	Sections between	Electrified route length dc km	ac km	Total km	Sum-up of electrified R.L. dc km 4 592.0	ac km 3 036.1	Total km 7 628.1	Completion Date	System
Lines electrified during 1976 (FY) (From 1 April 1976 to 31 March 1977)	Okata — Kitano-masuzuka & Sintoyoda	10.8		10.8				26 April 1976	dc1500V
	Nagasaki — Tosu & Nagasaki		125.3	125.3				1 July 1976	ac20KV60Hz
	Sasebo — Hizen-yamaguchi & Sasebo		48.8	48.8				1 July 1976	ac20KV60Hz
Total		10.8	174.1	184.9	4 602.8	3 210.2	7 813.0		
Lines now under electrification	Fukuchiyama — Amagasaki & Takasazuka	17.8		17.8					dc 1 500V
	Kisei — Shingu & Wakayama	200.7		00.7					dc 1 500V
	Tazawako — Mozioka & Omagasi		75.6	75.6					ac 20KV 50 Hz
	Sakurai — Nasa & Takada	29.4		29.4					dc 1 500 V
	Wakayama — Oji & Gojó	35.8		35.8					dc 1 500 V
	Kusatsu — Tsuge & Kusatsu	36.7		36.7					dc 1 500 V
	Hakubi — Kurashiki & Hoki-daisen	139.6		139.6					dc 1 500 V
	San-in — Hoki-daisen & Izumoshi	66.4		66.4					dc 1 500 V
	Nippo — Minami-Miyazaki & Kagoshima		120.1	120.1					ac 20kV 60 Hz
	Kamsai — Nagoya & Kameyama	59.9		59.9					dc 1 500 V
Total		586.3	195.7	782.0					
Electrification projected	Oito — Minami-Otari & Itoigawa	35.3		35.3					dc 1 500 V
	Kawagoe — Omiya & Komagawa	30.6		30.6					dc 1 500 V
	Chitose — Naebo & Numanohata		60.2	60.2					ac 20 kV 50 Hz
	Muroran — Numanohata & Naebo		74.9	74.9					ac 20 kV 50 Hz
Total		65.9	135.1	201.0					

1 Removal of Factors Oppressing JNR Finance
(1) Government subsidisation of interest payment on that part of the loans outstanding, 2 540 000 million yen in amount, equivalent to the greater part of the accumulated deficit, with such subsidisation calculated on the basis of redemption of principal and interest in equal amounts in 20 years; and Government loan of the principal to be so redeemed, without interest.
(2) Revision of Tariff Rates
Revision of tariff rates (nominal increase, 50 per cent) in order to raise the revenue by 37 per cent in 1976.
2 Measures for Maintenance of Sound Management
() Rationalisation of Management
 a Reduction in personnel by 50 000 by 1980
 b Study and determination of the measures to be taken regarding local unremunerative lines, by JNR initiative and with Government aid.
 c Adoption of necessary measures for modernisation and rationalisation of freight service so that by 1980 a balance may be attained between costs directly attributable to freight service and revenue therefrom, while maintaining current transport functions.
 d Greater utilisation of JNR assets and disposal of idle and unneeded assets and adoption of measures to increase the revenues from its subsidiary activities.
(2) Greater Flexibility in Rate-fixing.
Initiation of studies on the present system of determining rates through Diet legislation, and thereby securing an early conclusion on the means for attaining greater flexibility in rate-fixing, with the aim of strengthening the self-supporting capability of JNR.
Greater Efficiency of Investment on Facilities
Full consideration of their efficiency in making investments on facilities and equipment, and continuation of the present system of construction cost subsidisation to lighten the interest burden of construction financing.

NATIONWIDE SHINKANSEN NETWORK

The Law for Construction of Nationwide High-speed Railways was enacted in May 1970 to materialise the sound growth of the national economy and well-balanced development of the land aimed at in the New Comprehensive National Development Plan of 1969 and the New Economic and Social Development Plan of 1970.
Decided for construction under the law are three Shinkansen lines: the Tohoku (Tokyo—Morioka), the Joetsu (Omiya—Nigata) and the Narita (Tokyo—Narita Airport). The construction of these three lines is under way, mainly on the tunnels and long bridges at the present. The lines are expected to be completed, at the earliest, in 1979. The Shinkansen section between Okayama and Hakata, on which construction started before the enactment of the law, was opened in March 1975.
With a general survey completed for five other Shinkansen lines, the plans to construct these were decided in November 1973. They are the Tohoku (Morioka—Aomori), the Hokkaido (Aomori—Sapporo), the Hokuriku (Tokyo—Osaka via Toyama), the Kyushu (Hakata—Kagoshima) and the Nagasaki (Hakata—Nagasaki), and detailed plans for them are under study.
Contemplated for construction are twelve more Shinkansen lines, and preliminary surveys on some of them are now under way.
Under the plan for construction of a Nationwide Shinkansen Network, the islands of Honshu and Hokkaido are to be connected this time with an undersea railway tunnel, and Honshu and Shikoku with suspension bridges.

Seikan Undersea Tunnel between Honshu and Hokkaido
Length: 58.83 km (23.3 km undersea)
Maximum depth under sea level: 240 m
Construction period: About 10 years, completion set at 1982 at the earliest
Construction cost: About 355 400 million yen

Suspension bridges between Honshu and Shikoku
Bridges on the Kobe-Naruto Roue: (Approx 980 000 million yen)
Bridges on the Kojima-Sakaide Route: (Approx 690 000 million yen)

For the construction of these bridges, the Honshu-Shikoku Bridge Authority was established in July 1970, and construction work on the Onaruto Bridge, one of the two main bridges on the Kobe-Naruto Route started in July 1976.

TECHNICAL DEVELOPMENT PLAN
The Technical Development Department in the Head Office drafts an overall plan for technical development in line with JNR's Long-term Management Plan. It also studies and produces measures to cope with imporant current technical problems.
Each year a selection is made of important development themes and these are taken up as "Technical Themes" for research and development.
In 1976 weight was put on the technical development of the following:

1 Higher safety and reliability of service
2 Labour and cost saving
3 Preservation of environment
4 Build up of Nationwide Shikansen Network
5 Magnetic levitation linear motor railway

The main technical themes related to the above are:

1 Raising the operational safety of freight cars
2 Prevention of overhead wiring and pantograph trouble
3 Higher reliability of rolling stock, track and electric facilities
4 Improvement of data processing system
5 Technical development needed on forming a Nationwide Shinkansen Network
6 Studies on magnetic levitation linear motor railway
7 Mechanisation and automation of operations and job performance
8 Studies on structure designing and work execution methods
9 Betterment of services
10 Prevention of noise and vibration on the Shinkansen

Magnetic Levitation Linear Motor Railway
Progress has been made in the study of the basic approach to the magnetic levitation linear motor railway, and its potential has been technically ascerted. A 7 km long experimental track is presently under construction to ascertain the technical aspects in attaining speeds up to 500 km/h.
The guideway structures, suspension system, magnetic-guide and emergency brake system also will be studied.

JORDAN

HEDJAZ JORDAN RAILWAY
PO Box 582, Amman

General Manager: M. R. Qoseini
Assistant to General Manager: Walied Abu Laban
Departmental Heads:
　Finance: Ibrhim Qanah
　Operating and Mechanical: Z. M. Ali
　Traffic: Fauzi Rasheed
　Permanent Way: M. A. Sa'ad Eng.
　Engineering: M. K. Emad Eldein
　Stores and Supplies: I. Abu Taha
General Inspector: B. S. Nuseir
Chief Accountant: Kh. Y. Shukri
Asst. Chief Mechanical Sect.: Eng. S. Y. Sunia
Chief of Workshops: Eng. U. S. Khreishi

Gauge: 1.050 m.
Route length: 595 km.

Jordan began carting rock phosphate from its mines at Al-Hassa to the Port of Aqaba in 1976 over 161 miles (260kms) of new and rebuilt rail lines. The line should not only speed up the export of Jordan's phosphates—its most important foreign exchange earner—but it might also signal the start of a new effort to revive the Hedjaz railway. The railway gained fame during World War I through the attempts of Col. T. E. Lawrence to dismantle it. It runs south from Turkey through Damascus and Amman and on to the Holy City of Medina in the Hedjaz. Since then, the line has fallen into nearly complete disuse. Some of the trains derailed by Lawrence can still be seen lying next to the tracks.
About 74 miles (120 kms) of the new route—Hettiya west to Aqaba, which was never before connected to the line—is completely new; the rest, from Hettiya north to Al-Hassa, is the original Hedjaz line, newly strengthened and repaired.
The entire project, carried out by the West German contractors Held & Francke, cost JD 25 million ($US80.6 million). As part of the improvement scheme, the Jordanians have also purchased ten new 1 800 hp locomotives, built by General Electric, and 140 new hoppers. According to officials at the Jordanian Ministry of Transport, the new system will be able to handle 1.6 million tons of phosphate a year—equal to Jordan's phosphate exports in 1974.
The Hedjaz Jordan Railway called for pre-qualification bids in 1977 from contractors to reconstruct the railway from Al-Hasa to Menzil. In addition to reconstruction of 21 km of existing track, contractors have been asked to bid on construction of 3.5 km of new track to the phosphate mine at Al-Hasa and erection of a new station at Menzil.
Meanwhile, Jordanian and Syrian Transport Ministries have asked an international consultant to conduct economic and feasibility studies to standardize the existing narrow-gauge railway between Amman and Damascus. It will form part of the reconstruction of the 1 300 m Hedjaz railway linking Medina in Saudi Arabia with Western Europe. Cost of the Amman-Damascus section is estimated at $200 million. Sofrerail of France has completed studies for standardization of the line between Amman and the Syrian border.
Phosphate Plan: Although Jordan's future phosphate production goals will not be set until the new five-year plan, scheduled to start in January, is put in final form, it is certain that production will be substantially increased over the next few years. To meet the higher levels, Jordan will have to build more sidings and stations and, strengthen some bridges.
One of the most curious—and to some extent troubling—aspects of the Hedjaz railway and its new Hettiya-Aqaba branch is that it is one of the few remaining narrow gauge rail lines in the world: its rails are 41.3 ins (105 cms) apart while those of a standard gauge line are 56.2 ins (143 cms). The track-laying equipment as well as the locomotives and hoppers had to be specially designed and built. Even more serious problems would arise, however, if the Jordanians, Syrians and Saudis ever decided to put the entire line back in service.
Narrow Gauge Problems. The goal of a collaborative effort would be to give the Jordanians and Saudis a Mediterranean port—an export centre for Jordanian phosphates and an import centre for Saudi Arabia's equipment needs. Eventually it could provide all three countries with a direct link to Europe by rail, although rail service through Turkey and especially across the Bosporus is now slow. In the early 1960's the Jordanians and the Saudis coordinated efforts to repair the Hedjaz railwy all the way from Ma'an in northern Jordan to a point some 24.8 miles (40 kms) inside Saudi Arabia. Then, in 1971, the project came to an abrupt halt. The Syrians, in the meantime, have begun rebuilding several sections in the line with standard gauge track, including, for example the Damascus-Homs line. Recent press reports from Saudi Arabia have also talked of Saudi plans to rebuild their section of the line, also with standard gauge track.

TRAFFIC	1973	1974	1975	1976
Total freight km	28 210 815	7 693 539	14 299 948	89 934 096
Total freight tonnage	56 067	89 488	95 475	352 541
Total passenger-km	1 521 930	5 714 885	7 718 796	6 920 047
Total passenger journeys	7 021	80 125	94 815	96 649

FINANCIAL	1973	1974	175	1976
Revenues	JD368 881	421 363	465 000	661 881
Expenses	JD369 745	409 787	465 000	811 454

MOTIVE POWER AND ROLLING STOCK
Present stock consists of 9 steam line locomotives, 5 passenger cars and 464 freight cars.

SIGNALLING AND TRAIN CONTROL INSTALLATIONS
Type: semi automatic; Route length: 265 km; Location: Aqaba-El Hasa; Supplier: ML Engineering (Plymouth) England.
Originally designed to meet the need for a railway signalling tokenless block system for operation over a radio link where the environment is potentially noisy, the new system style 20, developed by ML Engineering of Britain, has been installed on the El Hasa-Aqaba Railway. Ultra high-frequency radio is being used in Jordan to provide communications links between drivers and to control block sections. In addition to the system, ML has equipped the 17 stations between El Hasa and Aqaba with local control consoles for conventional point operation through route-relay interlocking. Passing loop switches are power operated, and through train movements are supervised from the main traffic control room. Station areas are fully trac-circuited, and ML colour-light signals are used throughout, equipped with filament changeover relays arranged to indicate main filament failures.
The fail-safe Style 20 FDM equipment, which forms the heart of the system, allows block signalling from station to station, using UHF radio, and if speech is required over the same circuit, 16 individual channels are available within the carrier frequency 2000 Hz to 3400 Hz, allowing up to 2000 Hz for speech. The system operates on a frequency shift principle with both carrier frequencies being detected independently. Each channel can transmit one out of six bits of information at any given time.

KAMPUCHEA — SEE CAMBODIA

KENYA

KENYA RAILWAYS
PO Box 30121, Nairobi

Chairman: James King'ang'i Njoroge
Managing Director: Davidson Karundi Ngini
Deputy Managing Director: Patrick Joel Mwangola
Directors: Peter Mburu Echaria
        Jafeth Kimanthi Ilako
        Charles Ngari Kebuchi
Chief Traffic Manager: Brown Waweru
Chief Civil Engineer: Joel Mudhune
Chief Mechanical Engineer: Julius Mimano
Chief Administrative Secretary: Benjamin Edward Ombuoro
Chief Personnel Manager: Aaron Kimosop Kandie
Chief Accountant: Zadock Baraza Kambogo Shimba
Chief Supplies Officer: James Karanja

Gauge: 1.0 metre
Route length: 2 084 km

The break up of the East African Railways Corporation came about in August 1976 as a result of considerable financial and other allied problems and strains which for a long time faced the Railways Headquarters in Nairobi—mainly due to the failure by the partner states to remit funds to the headquarters for its maintenance. This break-up gave rise to the creation of three seperate railways systems and the birth of Kenya Railways in January 1977 as one of them with its headquarters situated in Nairobi. Kenya Railways is a state Corporation run by a board of Directors. The Board in the interim comprises of a Chairman and five directors amongst whom is the Managing Director who is the Chief Executive.

The Kenya Railways operates a total of 2 084 route-km of metre gauge line consisting of the main line from Mombasa through Nairobi, Nakuru and Eldoret to the border of Kenya with Uganda and the branch line joining the Lake Victoria town of Kisumu to the farming centre of Nakuru. The rest are branch lines linking Nairobi to Nanyuki near Mt Kenya, Gilgil to Nyahururu, Voi to Taveta, Kisumu to Butere, Konza to Magadi and Rongai to Solai.

The former East African Railways when originally developed had no other competitive modes of transport. To-day Kenya Railways is not only faced with severe road competition parallel to its routes, but also the white oil pipeline which will, as from February 1978 take all its white petroleum products. Despite the competition, the railway remains the main transportation mode for the bulk goods most of which are agricultural inputs, industrial and mining products. As a development tool, it is still expected to assist agriculture, industry and mining. It is however, expected that the Government which has been very interested in the future of the organisation, will continue to make sure of the survival of the railways. Indeed this has been amply demonstrated by the orders for locomotives and wagons placed recently by the Kenya Government for and on behalf of the Kenya Railways.

The Kenya Government is currently looking into ways of harmonising transportation efforts throughout the country in order to avoid undue competition between roads and railways and it is hoped that a realistic road licensing policy will follow, giving the railways (in which the Government has invested so heavily) a chance of existing viably without much dependence on government subsidy, a situation which may otherwise arise.

The Kenya Railways has recently submitted a draft development plan to the Government for inclusion into the 1979/83 National Development Plan of the Republic. It is hoped that the Government will provide funds either from its own resources or through external loans to finance some of the projects.

Emphasis in the development plan has been placed on improvement of the track, provision of locomotives and wagons (the whole requirement of which is now on order by the Kenya Government) and coaching stock either to replace worn out stock or to cater for anticipated growth both in the goods and passenger traffic. With continued Government interest and support, enlightened and dynamic management and with the problems of the former ailing East African Railways Corporation left behind and forgotten, it can be stated that the future augurs well for the Kenya Railways.

29 class 2-8-2 No. 2930 'Tiriki' having motion checked following overhaul

DIESEL LOCOMOTIVES

Class	Axle Arrange-ment	Trans-mission	Rated Power hp	Max. lbs (kg)	Tractive Effort Continuous at lbs (kg)	Tractive Effort Continuous at mph (km/h)	Max. Speed mph (km/h)	Wheel Dia. ins (mm)	Total Weight Tons	Length ft ins (mm)	No. Built	Year first Built	Builders: Mechanical Parts	Builders: Engine & Type	Builders: Transmission
92	1Co-Co1	Elec.	2 550	77 000 (35 000)	43 500 (19 730)	16.5 (26.4)	45 (72)	37½ (953)	114	59' 1¼" (18 015)	15	1971	MLW Ind	Alco 251F	GE Canada
87 (90)	1Co-Co1	Elec.	1 840	51 600 (23 300)	44 500 (20 180)	11.7 (18.8)	45 (72)	37½ (953)	101.5 (79.3) (Adhe-sive)	55' 7¼" (16 948)	10 14 20	1960 1964 1967/8	English Electric	E.E. 12 CSVT	E.E.
72	1Bo-Bo1	Elec.	1 240	40 000 (18 150)	32 500 (14 750)	10.7 (17.2)	45 (72)	37½ (953)	70.1	43' 9¼" (13 341)	10	1972	GEC Traction	EE 8CSVT	GEC
71 (91)	1Bo-Bo1	Elec.	1 240	40 000 (18 150)	32 000 (14 400)	10.5	45 (72)	37½ (953)	69 (13 341)	43' 9¼"	10	1967	English Electric	EE 8CSVT	EE
62	B-B	Hyd.	760	27 750 (12 500)	21 825 (9 900)	7.8 (12.3)	45 (72)	37½ (953)	38	37' 5" (11 404)	20	1972	Rheinstahl AG	MTU 493TZ(10) MTU 396TC(10)	Voith L520-U2
46 (86)	D	Hyd.	606 (2×203)	32 900 (14 900)			20 (32)	39½ (1 003)	48	36' 1¼" (11 007)	22	1967	Andrew Barclay	2 × Cummins	British Twin Disc CF 11500
45 (85)	D	Hyd.	855	35 000 (15 880)			22 (35)	45 (1 156)	52	34' 11" (10 643)	10	1957	N.B.L.	M.A.N. WBV 22/30A	N.B.L./Voith L 37zV
44 (84)	D	Hyd.	510	33 300 (15 102)			High 35 (56) Low 20 (32)	39½ (1 003)	52	33' 0¼" (10 065)	3	1956	N.B.L.	Davey Paxman 12PRHXL Ser. 2	N.B.L.-Voith L24V
43 (83)	D	Hyd.	312	20 000 (9 070)			High 35 (56) Low 20 (32)	39½ (1 003)	42	31' 11¼" (9 734)	14	1955	N.B.L.	Davey Paxman 8 RPHL Ser. S	N.B.L.-Voith L24V
35	C	Hyd.	300	24 460 (11 100)	20 000 (9 070)	3.8 (6.1)	17 (27)	39½ (1 003)	36	29' 7¼" (9 023)	15	1972	Andrew Barclay	Paxman 8 RPHL	Voith L320V
33 (81)	C	Mech-Hyd.	194	15 800 (7 166)			26.2 (42.2)	39½ (1 003)	29.4	26' 5¾" (8 071)	6	1950	Drewry Car Co.	Norris Henty & Gardner Gardner 8L3	Type 23 Vulcan Sinclair Hyd. C CAJ Wilson-Drewry-Gearbox
32 (80)	C	Mech.	80	6 850 (3 107)			15 (24)	28 (711)	18.5	23' 5½" (7 150)	6	1950	John Fowler	J. & H. McLaren McLaren Kk. 3	Fowler

English Electric locomotive awaiting urgent overhaul in Nairobi during 1975

While diesel motive power spent a high percentage of time in sheds during 1974/75 due mainly to lack of spares, remaining steam locomotives increased annual working proportionately. The 59 class Garratt ('Mount Suswa') above is pictured pulling up to the water tower at Athi River with a Nairobi-boundfreight consist from Mombassa

Nairobi carriage sidings—July 1975

MOTIVE POWER AND ROLLING STOCK

Orders placed during 1976 include 26 large main line diesel electric locomotives, 46 General purpose diesel-hydraulic locomotives, and 35 diesel-hydraulic shunting locomotives. Another 8 General purpose diesel-hydraulic locomotives are also expected from West Germany through a West German loan of DM 31 million offered to the defunct East African Community. These orders will help to complete the dieselisation programme of the Kenya Railways, and later for any possible additional requirement and or traffic expansion in the next five or so years.

The Kenya Government has also placed orders for 2 400 units of bogie wagons comprising of 1 120 units of covered goods bogie wagons, 880 units of low-sided bogie wagons, 200 units of covered goods bogie wagons with opening sides and 200 units of high sided bogie wagons. These will also cater for replacement of worn out stock, expected traffic growth and bring the wagon standage to a normal requirement level.

BRE-Metro of Britain won an order during 1977 for 35 shunters and 1 200 wagons. The first wagon deliveries were begun in February 1978 by BR Engineering (BREL). First part of the contract called for 440 low-sided wagons and when these have been completed, BREL will build 100 covered vans with sliding roofs, followed by 100 covered vans with sliding doors and, finally, 560 covered vans with hinged doors.

Apart from the above orders, Kenya Railways will also require 7 first class, 9 second class, and 28 third class bogie coaches, 2 twin unit restaurant cars and 2 composite buffet coaches. It is hoped that these will be acquired when funds become available. Sweden however will provide between 12-15 third class coaches through a Swedish Government Grant, leaving a total requirement of between 13-16 third class bogie coaches.

KOREA, Republic

KOREAN NATIONAL RAILROAD
168 Bongrae-dong 2ka, Jung-ku, Seoul

Director General: Kim, Jai Hyun
Deputy Director General: Lee, Yong Shik
Planning Co-ordinator: Im, Kyu Jai
Director of Business Management: Hwang Sung Yeun
Director of Material Management: Sin, Young Kook
Director of Transportation Bureau: Choi, Hyun Soo
Director of Engineering Bureau: Ham, Kiel
Director of Rolling Stock Bureau: Im, Young Tack
Director of Electrical Bureau: Hwang, Hae Joong
Director of Finance & Accounting Bureau: Kim, Yong Kwan
Chief of General Affairs Section: Lee, Yong Seoung
Public Information Officer: Kang, Jae Tack
Director of Busan Regional Railway: Lee, Weon Jeon
Director of Seoul Regional Railway: Jeong, Tae Yong
Director of Suncheon Regional Railway: Ahn, Chang Hwa
Director of Yeongju Regional Railway: Lee, Yak Woo

Gauge: 1.435 m.
Route length: 3 744.5 km.

When Korea was partitioned along the 38th parallel in 1945, the territory south of that line became the Republic of Korea, with a railway route length of 1 590 miles *(2 558 km)*. Rehabilitation and new construction was interrupted by the Korean War of 1950 during which severe damage and destruction of various facilities and equipment was experienced.

Following a period of reconstruction and new building, the government put in hand the First Five Year (1962-1966) Economic Development Plan, during which the Korean National Railroad invested a total of 18 300 million won (equivalent of $US 64 million). In the Second (1967-71) Plan, of which the basic objective was "to promote the modernisation of the industrial structure and to build the foundations for a self-supporting economy", a total of 92 000 million won was invested in the construction of new lines, increase in station and line capacity, reinforcement of the motive power and rolling stock, improvement of way and structures, etc. The Third (1972-76) Plan, aimed at increasing freight traffic capacity.

The backbone of the system is the 444-km double track Kyongbu Line, running between the nation's two principal cities, Pusan on the southeast coast across the Tsushima Straits from Japan and the capital city of Seoul in the northwest. Principal intermediate cities reached by this route include Taegu and Taejon. While it constitutes less than 15 per cent of total KNR route-km, the Kyongbu Line accounts for nearly half of the system's operating revenues. A second north-south route, and a revenue source second only to the Kyongbu Line, is afforded by the Chungang (Central) and Tonghaenambu lines. Diverging to the southwest from the Kyongbu Line at Taejon, the Honam Line reaches into the rich agricultural plain of North and South Cholla provinces and the important southwestern port of Mokpo. Branching from the Honam Line at Iri is the Cholla Line, which extends southward to Yosu, an important southern port and the site of a major oil refinery.

Linking these two lines across the south coast of Korea with the Kyongbu Line near Pusan is one of KNR's newest routes, the Kyongchon Line, which was completed in 1968.

The Yongdong Line, which links the east coast with the Chngang Line at Yongju, was completed in 1955, and was extended northward to the major east coast city of Kangnung in 1962. KNR's second route to the east coast was completed through the heart of the Taebaek Mountain range late in 1973.

FINANCES
Revenue

(P/L Account)	1977	1976	Difference
Passenger Revenue	55 604	47 282	8 322
Freight Revenue	66 256	47 693	18 563
Other Operating Revenue	6 895	6 595	300
Non-Operating Revenue	27 611	21 282	6 329
Sub-Total	156 366	122 852	33 514
(Capital Account)			
Long-term Borrowing	36 935	28 984	8 851
Foreign Loan	32 483	56 872	24 389
Depreciation & Other	23 293	17 275	6 018
Sub-Total	92 711	102 231	9 520
TOTAL	249 077	225 083	23 994

Expenditure

(P/L Account)	1977	1976	Difference
Personnel Expense	58 585	45 741	12 844
Fuel Expense	16 260	15 281	979
Maintenance	28 346	22 943	5 403
Interest	20 105	14 531	5 574
Material & Other	33 070	24 356	8 714
Sub-Total	156 366	122 852	33 514
(Capital Account)			
Investment	70 934	83 632	12 698
Repayment of Debt	15 201	12 060	3 141
Stores	6 576	6 539	37
Sub-Total	92 711	102 231	9 520
TOTAL	249 077	225 083	23 994

* 485 Won = 1 US $

MOTIVE POWER AND ROLLING STOCK
Locomotives

Type	Number
Diesel Elect Loco	386
Elect Loco	90
Elect Railcar	171
Diesel Railcar	122
Steam Loco	68
Diesel Loco	2
Total	839

Passenger Coaches

Type	Number
High Class Coach	628
Ordinary Coach	949
Other Dining, Baggage, etc	208
Total	1 785

GM built 3 000 hp diesel loco hauling limited express coaches at the east coast near Gangreung

European 50 C/S Group locomotive near Chiag station on Jungang Line

Freight Wagons

Type		Number
Box-Car		5 056
Gondola-Car		6 956
Tank-Car		2 476
Other Flat, Ref, Caboose		1 720
	Total	16 208

FACILITIES
Track

	km
Total trackage	5 618.8
Service	3 144.2
Main Line (double track)	4 149.8
Sidings	1 469

Rail

Type of Rail	Length	Percentage
50 kg/m	3 117.0 km	53
37 kg/m	2049.9 km	37
30 kg/m	451.9 km	10

Sleepers

Type	Number	Percentage
Wooden Ties	7 000	80
Pre-stressed Concrete Ties	1 700	20
Total	8 700	100

Tunnel and Bridge

Tunnel	Number	
	Longest Tunnel	4 505 m
Bridge	Number	2 388
	Longest Bridge	1 112m

Curvature

Main line/Radius	Tangent	400 m	Under 600 m	Over 600 m
(100%)	(66)	(8)	(13)	(13)
4 149	2 697 km	350 km	546 km	556 km

Gradient

Total	Level	Less than 10/1 000	Less than 20/1 000	More than 20/1 000
(100%)	(37)	(32)	(25)	(6)
4 149 km	1 543 km	1 346 km	1 019 km	241 km

SIGNALLING

Type	Line	Location	Route Length	Number of Station	Supplier
CTC	Jung Ang Line	Mangu-Bongyang	48.1 km	32	Westinghouse (British)
	Seoul Metropolitan Area	Seoul-Incheon	38.9 km	11	Siemens (W. Germany)
		Yeongdeungpo-Suweon	32.3 km	6	,,
		Yongsan-Seongbug	18.2 km	4	,,
		Seoul-Susaeg	8.5 kg	3	,,
	Total		246.5 km	56	
Relay	Tae Baeg Line	Jecheon-Baegsan		18	50 C/S Group (Europe)
Inter-locking System	Yeong Dong Line	Cheolam-Bogpyeong		14	,,
	Gyeong Bu Line	Saeryu-Sojeongri		9	Local
	Total			41	
ABS	Gyeong Bu Line	Seoul-Busan	444.5 km	Local	

DIESEL LOCOMOTIVES

Class (Series)	Axle Arrangement	Rated power (hp)	Max Speed (km/h)	Wheel Dia. (mm)	Total Weight (Tons)	Length (mm)	No Built	Year First Built	Mechanical parts	Engine & Type
SW 8 (2000)	Bo-Bo	800	105	1 016	94.5	13 420	13	1957	GMC (USA)	8-567 BC
SW 1001 (2100)	Bo-Bo	1 000	105	1 016	87.0	13 610	28	1969	,,	8-645 E
G8 (3000)	Bo-Bo	875	105	1 016	75.0	14 325	52	1959	,,	8-567 CR
ALCO (3100)	Bo-Bo	950	105	914	71.5	14 650	48	1967	ALCO (USA)	6-251 B
G12 (4000)	Bo-Bo	1 310	105	1 016	78.5	14 325	15	1963	GMC (USA)	12-567 C
G12 (4100)	Bo-Bo	1 310	105	1 016	85.0	14 325	10	1966	,,	12-567 C
G22 (4200)	Bo-Bo	1 310	105	1 016	88.0	14 170	22	1967	,,	12-567 E
SD9 (5000)	Co-Co	1 750	105	1 016	141.0	18 500	29	1957	,,	16-567 C
SD18 (6000)	Co-Co	1 800	105	1 016	147.0	18 500	14	1963	,,	16-567 D
SDP28 (6100)	Co-Co	1 800	105	1 016	147.0	18 500	6	1966	,,	16-567 E
SDP38 (6200)	Co-Co	1 800	105	1 016	147.0	18 500	16	1967	,,	16.567 E
SDP38 (6300)	Co-Co	1 800	105	1 016	148.0	18 500	23	1967	,,	16.567 E
G26CW (7000)	Co-Co	2 000	105	1 016	99.0	15 765	10	1969	,,	16-645 E
GT26CW (7500)	Co-Co	3 000	105	1 016	132.0	19 650	90	1971	,,	16-645 E3
GT26CW (7100)	Co-Co	3 000	120	1 016	132.0	19 650	10	1975	,,	16-645 E3

Type	Line	Location	Route Length	Number of Station	Supplier
ATS	Jung Ang Line	Cheongryangri-Gyeongju	382.7 km		Local
	Ho Nam Line	Daejeon-Mogpu	260.4 km		"
	Jeon Ra Line	Iri-Yeosu	198.3 km		"
	Tae Baeg Line	Jecheon-Baegsan	103.7 km		"
	Yeong Dong Line	Cheolam-Bugpyeong	61.8 km		"
	Jang Hang Line	Cheonan-Janghand	143.5 km		"
	Gyeong Weon Line	Yongsan-Seongbug	18.2 km		"
	Gyeong In Line	Seoul-Incheon	38.9 km		"
	Gyeong Eui Line	Seoul-Susaeg	8.5 km		"
	Ham Baeg Line	Yemi-Jodong	9.7 km		"
	Gyeong Bu Line	Seoul-Busan	444.5 km		"
	Gyeong Bug Line	Gimcheon-Yeongju	115.2 km		"
	Yeong Dong Line	Yeongju-Cheolam	86.4 km		"
	Total		1 829.1 km		

ELECTRIC LOCOMOTIVES

KNR Series	Axle Arrangement	Line Current	Rated Output (hp)	Tractive Effort Continuous Tons	at (km/h)	Max speed (km/h)	Wheel Dia. (mm)	Weight (tons)	Length (mm)	No Built	Year First Built	Builders Mechanical part	Electrical part
8 000	Bo-Bo-Bo	ac, 1ø, 25 kV (60 HZ)	5 300	31.3	46	85	1 250	132	20 730	90	1972	Alstom MTE	AEG ACEC

DIESEL RAILCAR

KNR Series	Axle Arrangement	Trans-Mission	Rated Power (hp)	Max Speed (km/h)	Wheel Dia. (mm)	Total Weight (tons)	Length (mm)	No. Built	Year Built	Builders Mechanical part	Engine Type
600	Bo-Bo	Hydraulic Converter	420	105	864	51	21 500	11	1962	NIGATA (Japan)	N-855-R (Cummins USA)
"	"	"	"	"	"	"	"	33	1963	KINKI (Japan)	"
"	"	"	"	"	"	"	"	37	1966	KAWASAKI (Japan)	"
7-12	"	"	360	"	"	"	"	9	1963	NIGATA (Japan)	DMH 17 (Japan)
700	"	"	420	"	"	"	"	12	1966	"	N-855-R (Cummins)
"	"	"	360	"	"	"	"	8	1966	"	DMH 17 H (Japan)
550	"	"	680	"	914	76	25 690	2	1969	"	VTA1710 (Japan)
160	"	"	210	"	711	25	14 750	6	1965	KNR	N-855-R (Cummins)
100	"	"	360	"	914	33.9	10 400	2	1969	NIGATA (Japan)	DMH17C (Japan)
510	"	"	210	"	"	51	21 500	2	1975	"	N-855-R (Cummins)

ELECTRIC RAILCAR

Axle Arrangement	Line Current	Rated Output (hp)	Max Speed (km/h)	Wheel Dia. (mm)	Weight (tons)	Length (mm)	No. Built	Year Built	Builders Mechanical Part	Electrical parts
Bo-Bo	ac, 1ø, 25 kv (60 Hz)	1287 (120 kwx 8)	110	860	TC: 33.3 M: 42.1 M: 46.1	20 000	126	1974	Hitachi (Japan)	Hitachi (Japan)
"	"	"	"	"	"	"	45	1977	Daewoo (Korea)	Hitachi (Japan)

LEBANON
CHEMINS DE FER DE L'ETAT LIBANAIS

Director General: Antoine Barouki

The state took over the railways in January 1961. They constitute 208 miles *(335 km)* standard track and 51 miles *(82 km)* 3 ft 5½ in *(1.050 m)* track of which 20 miles *(32 km)* are ABT system rack rail, on 7 per cent gradient.

MOTIVE POWER TREND
Proportion total train-km operated by:

		1969	1970	1977
Steam traction	%	41	39	50
Diesel traction	%	59	61	50

SPENDING
Major planned expenditure in 1974 was £L 2 million for three mainline diesel-electric locomotives. In 1975 the railway planned to purchase 18 containers, track maintenance machinery, new signalling equipment at a total cost of £L 4.5 million.

TRACK DETAILS
Max axle load: 15 tonnes on standard gauge lines; 13 tonnes on narrow gauge lines.
Rail types:

	Weight		Length laid	
	lb per yd	kg/m	miles	km
USA	75.0	37.2	51	82
BH	85.0	42.2	70	112
BD	55.7	27.62	51	82
RA	60.6	30.0	56	90
HT	60.6	30.0	29	47

Sleepers (cross ties):

	miles	km
Wood	79	127
Concrete (RS type)	39	63
Metal	139	223

Sleeper spacing: 28 to 35½ in *(710 to 900 mm)*
Curves, min radius: 4 ft 8½ in *(1.435 m)* gauge—715 ft *(218 m)*; 3 ft 5½ in *(1.050 m)* gauge—328 ft *(100 m)*
Gradient, max: 2.0% uncompensated. 7.0% on rack rail section.
Altitude, max: 4 879 ft *(1 487 m)*

Welded rail: At the end of 1973, the total length of track laid with welded rail was 21.3 miles *(34.2 km)*, the longest length being some 165 ft *(50 m)*
Rail used is 75 lb *(37.2 km)* USA in 33 ft *(10.06 m)* lengths welded by Alumino-thermic process. Rails are laid on RS type concrete sleepers and secured by RS type fastenings.

LUXEMBOURG
LUXEMBOURG RAILWAYS (CFL)
Société Nationale Des Chemins De Fer Luxembourgeois, Place De La Gare

President: M. René Logelin
General Manager: Justin Kohl
Secretary General, Finance and Personnel: M. Emile Schlesser
General Technical Inspector, General Technical Department: M. Marcel Conter
Chief Officer, Claims and International Relations: M. Georges Thorn
Chief Officer, Commercial Department: Emile Kamphaus
Chief Officer, Fixed Installations: Ernest Junck
Chief Officer, Personnel: Romain Kugener
Chief Officer, Development: Gilbert Schmit

Gauge: 1.435 m
Route length: 271 km

TRAFFIC	1973	1974
Total freight ton-km	786 100 000	865 993 000
Total freight tonnage	22 534 000	23 098 000
Total passenger-km	269 964 836	288 888 000
Total passengers carried	13 391 646	13 768 000

FINANCES	1974	1975
	(Frs)	(Frs)
Revenues	3 668 359 544	4 220 220 500
Expenses	3 756 362 573	4 377 325 783

MOTIVE POWER
During 1975 CFL operated 19 electric locomotives, 51 diesel-electric and 15 diesel-hydraulic units. Number of railcars in service totalled 17.

ROLLING STOCK
In service at the end of 1974 were 85 passenger coaches and 3 421 freight wagons

TRACKWORK 1974
Renewal of track in UIC 54 rail laid on wooden sleepers was completed over the Belval-Pétange line in 1974 together with renewal over the Berchem to Oetrange line (total length renewed: 19.9 km).
Rails, types and weights: UIC 60, 54 and S33.
Sleepers: wood.
   Thickness: 15 cm
   Spacing: 1 435 mm
Rail fastenings: 'K' fastenings.
Welded rail: Total length of track laid up to the end of December 1974 was 216.2 km. Length of cwr laid in 1974 was 11.6 km.

Signal and train control installations: All-relay interlocking signal boxes with illuminated diagram and push button control on 72 miles *(116 km)* route length. Supplied by Siemens and Integra.

	miles	km
Luxembourg—Wasserbillig	23.0	37
Berchem—Oetrange	7.5	12
Luxembourg—Kleinbettingen	11.2	18
Bettembourg—Rodange	18.0	29
Luxembourg—Pétange	12.4	20

Hybrid installations consisting of electronic circuits and relay switching, frequency control, automatic colour light signalling for two-way working. Suppliers: Jeumont Schneider, Siemens, Integra.

	miles	km
Luxembourg—Wasserbillig	23.0	37
Berchem—Oetrange	7.5	12
Bettembourg—Berchem	2.5	4

MALAWI
MALAWI RAILWAYS LTD.
PO Box 5144, Limbe

Executive Chairman: D. R. Katengeza
Deputy Chairman: S. B. Somanje
Directors: J. A. A. Henderson
R. G . Zanda
Chief Timbili
E. F. W. MacPherson
A. W. Mwafulirwa
General Manager: G. G. Geddes
Deputy General Manager: G. Ellis
Secretary: P. B. Galafa
Lake Service Manager: T. F. Goodanew
Chief Civil Engineer: C. J. R. Cobbett
Management Accountant: G. H. Woodcock
Works Manager: W. W. Gordon
Chief Traffic Manager: P. T. K. Nyasulu
Chief Diesel Engineer: J. R. P. McCrindle
Telecommunications Engineer: T. N. Bomford
Commercial Superintendent: J. Sanderson
Chief Personnel Officer: W. I. Banda
Internal Auditor: P. K. Hounsham
Stores Superintendent: P. A. Ridgeway
Road Transport Superintendent: A. T. Jones
Data Processing Manager: A. F. Morgan
Works Study Officer: D. A. Foster
Financial Accountant: L. F. Sheppard

Gauge: 1.067 m
Route length: 566 km

The total route length of 3 ft 6 in (1.067 km) gauge railway operated by Malawi Railways Ltd is 352 miles (566 km) including 16 miles (26 km) of its wholly owned subsidiary, The Central Africa Railway Company. The administration also operates passenger and cargo services on Lake Malawi and trunk road haulage services throughout the Central and Northern Region of the country.

TRAFFIC	1974	1975	1976
Total freight ton-km (000's)	225 475	246 567	203 760
Total freight tonnage	1 105 211	1 252 801	1 073 631
Total passenger-km (000's)	76 316	88 490	61 572
Total passengers carried	1 079 350	1 211 172	953 560

The total tonnage of goods traffic carried in 1976 dropped compared with previous years following the closure of the Rhodesia/Mozambique border in March and in which in turn closed the direct all rail route for imports and exports between Malawi and Southern Africa.

FINANCES	1974	1975	1976 (Provisional)
Malawi Kwacha (000's)			
Revenues	7 638	9 336	9 907
Expenses (operating)	6 583	7 604	8 557

MOTIVE POWER
The diesel fleet consists of 18 Main Line diesel electrics (including 4 on hire), 11 diesel hydraulic Main Line locomotives, 8 diesel hydraulic Shunters and 2 Diesel Rail Cars. The eleven diesel hydraulic locomotives now used on the Main Line will eventually revert to shunting duties when the track improvements on the Northern Extension now in hand are completed and additional diesel electric locomotives are received.

ROLLING STOCK
At the end of 1976 the fleet consisted of 712 goods wagons, (including tank cars), 33 passenger coaches, 55 service vehicles and 21 vans.

DEVELOPMENT
Under the five-year Capital Development Programme rehabilitation of the permanent way continued and with Canadian Aid funds the whole of the track from Mile 440 to Salima was rerailed with heavier rail section to permit heavier axle loads. The stone ballasting of this section also continued with some 7½ miles being completed during the year. On the section between Balaka and Southern Border a further 12 miles of resleepering was carried out and 4½ miles of stone ballasting.
Work on the new 68 mile extension from Salima to Lilongwe continues under the direction of a team of Canadian Engineers. Earthworks have been substantially completed over 63 miles and track laying has advanced to Mile 45. Three road over rail and four major railway bridges have been completed. Skeleton track is expected to reach Lilongwe by October 1977 enabling trains to be run to Lilongwe under construction conditions by December 1977.
Construction work on the further 73 mile extension from Lilongwe to the Zambia border which has already been surveyed and designed is due to commence in January 1978 and to be completed by 1980.

LAKE SERVICE
Development of Chipoka Harbour, the Southern terminal and rail/Lake transhipment point of the Lake Service, is to be financed as part of the World Bank sponsored Karonga Rural Development Project. All design work has been completed and construction is programmed to commence in October 1977.

SIGNALLING AND COMMUNICATIONS
Reconstruction of the overhead telephone trunk route between Border and Limbe was completed and brought into use early in 1977. A new 320 line PABX telephone exchange was commissioned at Limbe in June 1977.
Construction of an overhead telecommunications route from Salima to Lilongwe was started in November 1976 and is expected to be completed by February 1978.

TRACK CONSTRUCTION DETAILS
Standard rail: 80 lb and 60 lb per yd
Cross ties (sleepers): Steel trough, 5 ft 8½ in (1 750 mm) long and hardwood 6 ft 6 in × 5 in × 10 in. Concrete 6 ft 6 in (1 980 mm) × 9 in (226 mm) base
Spacing: 12 per 33 ft rail
15 per 39 ft rail
Rail fastening: Clip and steel key, elastic spikes, Pandrol clips with concrete sleepers.
Filling: Broken stone and earth
Max curvature: 15.8° = radius of 363 ft (111 m)
Max gradient: 2.27% = 1 in 44
Max axle load: 16½ tons (of 2 000 lb)
Max permitted speed: 35 mph, restricted in hill section to 15 mph
Max altitude: 3 840 ft (1 107 m)

Class	Axle Arrangement	Transmission	Rated Power hp	Tractive Effort Max kg	Tractive Effort Continuous at lb	Tractive Effort Continuous at (mph)	Max Speed (km/h)	Wheel Dia. in	Total Weight Tons	Length ft ins	No. Built	Year First Built	Builders Mechanical Parts	Builders Engine and Type	Builders Transmission
DIESEL LOCOMOTIVES															
Shunter	0-6-0	Hyd.	340	20 200			24	40	40.5	25' 6''	2	1962	Bagnall	R.R. C8-Tel-IV	Twin Disc
Shunter	0-6-0	Hyd.	355	21 800			25	41	43.0	24' 0''	2	1967	A. Barclay	Cummins NT 400	Twin Disc
Shunter	0-6-0	Hyd.	388	33 800			16	43	40.0	25' 4''	4	1975	Hunslet (UK)	Cummins NT 400	Twin Disc
Transfer	Bo-Bo	Hyd.	525	23 000			35	33	38.0	32' 4''	7	1969	Hunslet (SA)	Cummins VT 12	Niigata
Main Line	Bo-Bo	Hyd.	492	20 350			35	34	38.0	34' 6''	4	1968	N. Sharyo	Cummins NTA 380	Niigata
Main Line	Co-Co	Elec.	1 200	50 000	40 000	8	50	36	81.0	46' 3''	14	1963	M. Cammell	Sulzer	AEI
Main Line	Co-Co	Elec.	1 500	72 000	60 500	10	64	36	86.0	57' 7''	4	1973	MLW	Alco 8-251-E	GE
DIESEL RAILCARS															
PRC	Ao-Io	Hyd.	200	33 000			50	34	33		2	1952	Drewry	Leyland Re-902	V. Sinclair 550

MADAGASCAR

RESEAU NATIONALE DES CHEMINS DE FER MALAGASY
Gare Soarano, Antananarivo

General Manager: Adolphe Rakotoarivony
Rolling Stock Department: Jeannot Rakotondranaivo
Track and Building Department: Gilbert Rananjason M.
Operating Department: Samuel Razanamapisa
Planning Department: André Andriamampianina
Administration: Ranaivojaona
Warehousing and Victualling Department: Nicola Rakotoniaina

Gauge: 1.00 m.
Route length: 883 km.

The Malagasy system of 559 miles *(883 km)* metre gauge route length consists of:-

	miles	km
Line Antananarivo-Alarobia (TWS)	3	5
Line Tamatave-Antananarivo (TCE)	231	371
Line Moramanga-Ambatosoratra(MLA)	104	167
Branch Vohidiala-Mororano	12	19
Line Antananarivo-Antsirabe (TA)	98	158
Line Fianarantsoa-Manakara (FCE)	101	163

TRAFFIC	1971	1972	1973	1974	1975
Passengers carried (000's)	2 586	2 587	2 951	3 351	3 841
Passengers km (000's)	200 029	191 820	208 614	223 038	248 585
Freight tons carried (000's)	884	755	807	740	882
Tons-km (000's)	296 399	247 531	196 620	195 621	286 677

FINANCES	1971	1972	1973	1974	1975
Operating revenues	3 093	2 666	2 683	3 470	2 980
Operating expenses	2 803	2 647	2 675	2 900	2 331

INVESTMENTS
Following capital expenditure improvements totalling Frs MG 2 065 457 000 in 1974, the railway planned to spend Frs MG 3 900 million in 1975. Purchases were to have included: five diesel-electric shunting locomotives (cost: Frs 330 million); four mainline diesel-electric locomotives (cost: Frs 580 million); four passenger coaches (cost: Frs 185 million); two trainsets (two power cars plus eight trailers, cost: Frs 370 million); 125 freight wagons (cost: Frs 820 million); track renewals over 21.5 km (cost: Frs 380 million). The total spending is likely to be spread over the four year 1973-77 modernisation programme period. In addition, the railway is to spend Frs M 290 million on management modernisation.

DEVELOPMENT
In 1975 the main financial and technical efforts were concentrated on the following:—
1. Continuing the deviation work on the line TCE between Brickaville and Ambila-Lemaitso and achievement deviation and bridge 90 m long between KmP.164-3 and 165-5. Work on the difficult sinuous section between Brickaville and Ambila-Lemaitso was completed in 1975. The new deviation from KmP. 164-3 was opened to the circulation on May 1974. The old line with two narrow tunnels and curves of 50 m radius was abandoned.
2. Studies were continued on the projected new line, 176 miles *(283 km)* long between Antsirabe and Fianarantsoa to link the TA and FCE lines.
A line 3 miles *(4-8 km)* long, built in 1972 to serve the industrial zone south of Antsirabe is in effect the beginning of the projected link line.
3. The acquisition of:
    2 locomotives 1 200 hp Alsthom BB diesel-electric.
    41 flat cars
    6 tip wagons
    50 box cars
    100 points and crossings
    130 km rails
    20 000 m³ ballast
    20 passenger coaches
    miscellaneous materials and equipment:
    1 tamper
    1 automatic barrier
    1 crane
    2 bulldozers
    1 tractor
    4 tracks 8.5 tons
    1 loader

Moramanga-Lac Alaotra: 167 km, built 1914-1923
Minimum curve radius: 125 m
Max gradient: 1.5%
107 bridges, total length: 956 m
On about 20 km, rails 37 kg/m, 11 m length, laid in 1970-73; remaining rails 25-26 kg/m 10-12 m length laid in 1923.
On about 128 km, timber sleepers 1 250-1 500 per km laid between 1923-1971; on about 37 km, steel sleepers 1 200-1 250 per km laid in 1923.
Stone ballast, 500-600 l/m.

Fianarantsoa-Manakara, 163 km, built 1926-36
Minimum curve radius: 50 m
Max gradient: 3.5%
59 bridges, total length: 2 046 m
56 tunnels, total length: 5 788 m
Rails mainly 28-31 kg/m, 9-11 m length, laid in 1932-1936 (used rails from 1900). Mainly steel sleepers, 1 350 per km laid in 1927-1936.
Stone ballast, 600 l/m.

MALAYSIA

MALAYAN RAILWAY ADMINISTRATION
Pertadbiran Keretapi Tanah Melayu (PKTM)
PO Box 1, Kuala Lumpur

General Manager: Datuk Ishak Tadin
Deputy General Manager:
  Finance and Commerce: Abdul Hai bin Abdul Hadi KMN
  Operating and Engineering: K. Kularatnam KMN
  Staff: Mohd. Noor bin Abu Osman
Chief Civil Engineer: J. Patrick Lowe AMN
Traffic Manager: G. L. Rodrigo
Chief Accountant: Zahar bin Mohd Shariff
Stores Superintendent: Abdul Hamid bin Mohd. Shariff
Chief Mechanical Engineer: Tang Ying Woun

Gauge: 1.00 m.
Route length: 1 665 km.

PKTM has completed a $M85.7 million Five-Year (1971-75) Plan aimed at reaching commercial viability by 1978. The plan consisted of eight principal points.
1. Improvement of operations through dieselisation and replacement of out of date rolling stock.
2. Improvement of facilities such as telecommunications and signalling throughout the network; realignment of the heavily used Port Dickson line to meet an anticipated growth in petroleum traffic; expansion and modernisation of the Kuala Lumpur freight yard and station; and track doubling on the Kuala Lumpur-Salak South line.
3. Improvement of train services, aimed at cutting operating costs through an increase in freight train lengths and weights, strengthening of couplers, and lengthening of loops at major stations;
4. Introduction of new commercial methods, supported by revision of the costing and accounting system;
5. Reorganisation of all administrative departments and methods to meet changing requirements;
6. Improved training and retraining methods;
7. Introduction of labour motivation and productivity awards as part of improved management/labour relations;
8. Redressing of the economic imbalance between races through training, career development and commercial programmes.
The total investment during the Five-Year Plan period reached $M 85.7 million, with financing provided by the World Bank ($US 16 million), internally generated funds, suppliers' credits and bilateral aid from Britain, and a Malaysian Government loan. The World Bank loan—the first for railway development in Malaysia—permits a five-year grace within a repayment period of 25 years at 7.25 per cent interest.
The Malayan Railway had a profit of M$184 286 (US$74 010.44) for the first half of 1976, representing a big turnabout from 1975's operating deficit of more than M$1.4 million (US$562 249), it was reported on August 13 (F,3953). Freight traffic netted M$21.9 million (US$8.79 million) up to 24 per cent, while passengers' traffic went up by 200 000 to 2.6 million with earnings totalling M$15.2 million (US$6.10 million), up M$1.4 million (US$562 249).
For the whole of 1976, Malayan Railway forecasts that revenues from freight traffic would reach M$48 million (US$19.28 million), passengers' traffic M$40 million (US$16.06 million), parcel and mail traffic M$5 million (US$2.01 million) and for other services M$6 million (US$2.41 million).
The company anticipates carrying 3.6 million tons of freight for the period. This is estimated to reach 4.7 million worth M$68.2 million (US$27.39 million) at the end of 1980, based on an annual compounded growth rate of 5.5 per cent in traffic and 7.5 per cent in revenue over the five-year period beginning 1976. Earnings from passenger traffic are also expected to rise by 19.5 per cent to more than M$48 million (US$19.28 million) during 1976-80.

TRAFFIC	1967	1969	1971	1973	1974
Freight tons carried (000's)	3 694.0	3 687.5	3 328.0	3 416	3 251
Ton miles (millions)	657.7	—	—	665.3	602.7
Passengers carried (000's)	5 312.0	5 101.8	5 272.9	5 449.9	5 967
Passenger miles (millions)	352.0	—	—	495.6	592.6

FINANCES
Following the appointment last year of Datuk Ishak as General Manager of the Malayan Railway, the system reported profits of $M 184 286 for the first six months of 1976, representing a big turnaround from 1975's operating deficit of more than $M 1.4 million. The railway eventually made an operating surplus of $M 19 million in 1976 on earnings of $M 103 million—first surplus for 14 years. Future financial results are expected to be even better, predicted General Manager, Datuk Ishak Tadin, who announced plans to increase track capacity. At present only 70 per cent of the system's 1 659 km of track is being used; plans are in hand to increase this to 90 per cent within five years. The railway is also seeking financing to provide faster services and to increase freight movements. The return to profitable operations follows ten years of losses which had added up to a cumulative $M 12 million by the end of 1975.
Freight traffic during the first six months of 1976 netted $M 21.9 million—up 24 per cent—and passenger traffic went up by 200 000 journeys to 2.6 million with earnings totalling $M 15.2 million—up $M 1.4 million.
For the whole of 1976, the railway forecast that revenues from freight traffic would reach $M 48 million, passenger traffic $M 40 million, parcel and mail traffic $M 5 million, and miscellaneous services $M 6 million.
The railway anticipated carrying 3.6 million tonnes of freight during 1976. With a number of plans now in hand to win new freight business. MR expects to be handling about 4.8 million tonnes of freight annually by 1980, based on an annual compounded growth rate of 5.5 per cent. Earnings from passenger traffic are also expected to rise to more than $M 48 million during the 1976-80 period.
Additional revenue is expected from new container traffic.

MOTIVE POWER
No new motive power was taken into service in 1974. The fleet now includes: 47 steam locomotives; 91 mainline diesel-electric locomotives; 23 diesel-electric shunters; 25 diesel-hydraulic shunting units; and 22 diesel railcars.

ROLLING STOCK
The passenger fleet at the end of 1974 totalled 325 coaches. Freight wagons totalled 5 479 units.

INVESTMENTS
A loan of $US 1.8 million will be used by Malayan Railways to finance purchase of a new telecommunications and signalling equipment, as part of an $US 80 million, five-year (1976-80) programme to modernise railways in Malaysia. During the plan period about 40 per cent of passenger coaches will be replaced by 34 air-conditioned luxury class coaches and 53 economy-class (non-air-conditioned) coaches, to improve passenger services and reduce operating costs. Passenger terminal facilities at major stations are to be rebuilt or modernised. Freight stock purchases will include 341 bogie oil tank wagons, 117 latex tank wagons, 139 bulk hopper wagons, 122 palm oil tank wagons,

100 container flat wagons, 50 cattle wagons and 150 bogie underframes. About $US 12.153 million will be spent on track renewals and realignments, $US 6.382 million on new diesel mainline locomotives, $US 4 million on diesel shunters, and nearly $US 6 million on signalling and telecommunications.

TRACK

Under a bilateral agreement on economic co-operation signed in 1975 between the USSR and Malaysia. Soviet engineers have drawn up a plan for a cross-Malaysia railway linking the east and west coasts. Outline government approval has already been given for the scheme.

The Malayan Railway (MR) has set aside $M 24 million (approximately $US 9.64 million) for construction of a new 28.9 km line between Pasir Gudang and a railway terminal to be built 9.6 km from Johore Bahru. The new line, to be completed by about 1980, will handle a total of approximately 300 000 tonnes of freight annually and will help ease anticipated future freight bottlenecks between the hinterland and Pasir Gudang.

Standard rail: Flat bottom in 30 ft and 40 ft lengths.
  Main line;80 lb/yd *(39.7 kg/m)*
  Branch lines: 60 lb *(29.8 kg/m)*
Joints: 4-hole flat or angle fishplates and welding.
Rail fastening: Elastic Spikes used on main lines. Dog spikes on other lines and sidings.
Cross ties (sleepers): Malayan secondary hardwoods impregnated with 50/50 mixture of creosote and diesel fuel oil; primary hardwoods on bridges. 10 in × 5 in × 6 ft 6 in *(254 × 127 × 1 981 mm)*. In accordance with ECAFE recommendations for SE Asia, all new supplies are 9 in × 4½ in × 6 ft 6 in-7 ft 0 in *(229 × 114 × 1 981-2 134 mm)*
Spacing: 2 ft 6 in *(762 mm)*
Filling: 2¼ in limestone ballast to a depth of 6 in under sleepers.
Max curvature: 3° = radius of 1 910 ft *(582 m)*; except in the hill sections where there are some curves of 9° = radius of 637 ft *(194 m)* and 12.25° = radius of 467 ft *(142 m)*
Ruling gradient: 1% = 1 in 100; except Taiping Pass 1.25% = 1 in 80.
Longest cont. gradient: 5.1 miles *(8.2 km)* on Prai-Singapore main line, with 1.25% (1 in 80) grade, the sharpest curve being 12.25° *(467 ft radius)* for a length of 1 050 ft *(320 m)*
Gauge widening on curves: Nil down to 6.5° curve = radius of 880 ft *(268 m)*
  ¼ in *(6.4 mm):* 6.5° to 9° curve = radius of 880 ft *(268 m)* to 636 ft *(194 m)*
  ¾ in *(9.5 mm);* 9° to 13° curve = radius of 636 ft *(194 m)* to 440 ft *(134 m)*
  ½ in *(12.7 mm):* below 13°.
Super-elevation on sharpest curve: 3½ in *(89 mm)*
Rate of slope of super-elevation: Steepest permissible gradient 1 : 300 or 11 times max permissible speed of section in mph.
Max altitude: 450 ft *(137 m)* near Taiping.
Max axle load: 16 tons.
Max permitted speed: Passenger trains, Main Line and Kedah Line: 45 mph *(72 km/h)* East Coast Line and other branch lines: 40 mph *(64 km/h)*. Diesel railcars 50 mph *(80 km/h)*. Freight trains 35 to 40 mph *(56 to 64 km/h)*.

Welded rail: Total length of track laid with welded rail is 625 miles *(1 005 km)*. Rails used are 80 lb in 40 ft lengths flashbutt welded at depot into 480 ft lengths. After laying these are sometimes Thermit welded into 960 ft continuous lengths.
Welded rails are secured by Elastic Rail Spikes to wood sleepers.

MALI

CHEMINS DE FER DU MALI
BP 260, Bamako

Director: Djibril Diallo
Deputy Director: Noumoucounda Savane
Finance: Almany Saounera
Administration: Cheick N'Diaye
Operations: Yamadou Diallo
Way and Works: Mamadou Bah
Stores: Lassana Sanoko
Equipment and Traction: Mamadou Sidibe

Gauge: 1.00 m.
Route length: 641 km.

Approval for a World Bank loan of $10.5 m to Mali Railways to help finance a $28 m rehabilitation project was granted in June, 1977.
A tranche of $7.3 m has been allocated for bridge repairs and $3.8 m is to be spent on track upgrading, including relaying of points and crossings.
Rolling stock is another major item with $6.2 m allowed for purchase of main-line locomotives, shunters and railcars, $1.6 m for passenger coaches and $1.9 m for freight wagons, including some rebuilding of existing vehicles. Also included in the project is installation of telecommunications equipment, as well as staff training.
Track renewals and ballasting are to be in the hands of Mali Railways' own staff, but bridgework is to be carried out by an outside firm supervised by the French consultants Sofrerail.
The former Dakar—Niger Railway starts at Dakar in Senegal and runs inland via Kayes to the River Niger. The present C.F. du Mali is that portion of the line inside its territory, the remainder being the C.F. du Senegal. A new line linking Bamako, capital of Mali, with Conakry, capital of Guinea is planned to give Mali an alternative outlet to the Atlantic route length of 500 miles *(800 km)*, of which 373 miles *(600 km)* will be in Guinea.
Under a Canadian Government grant work began in 1975 on modernisation and restructuring of the enterprise with the aid of CANAC.

TRAFFIC	1974	1976
Total tonnage	373 840	349 680
Tonne-km	162 180 000	153 390 000
Passenger journeys	500 683	401 600
Passenger-km	98 260 000	102 714 000

FINANCES	1976
	FISCFA ('000)
Revenues	6 127 449
Expenses	5 508 775

MOTIVE POWER
CFM operated during 1976 a total of 17 diesel locomotives, 8 loco-tractors and two railcars.
During 1977, Soule of France delivered two new 950 hp diesel-electric railcar to CFM.

ROLLING STOCK
The 1976 rolling stock fleet included 20 passenger coaches, 8 railcar trailers, 12 baggage vans, 324 freight wagons and 41 service vehicles.

MAURITANIA

CHEMINS DE FER MIFERMA
SA Des Mines De Fer De Mauritanie
PO Box 42, F'Derik
Administration: 87 rue L Boetie, Paris 8e, France

General Manager: J. Audibert *(Paris)*
Assistant General Manager: A. Nicolas *(Paris)*
Deputy Manager: R. Hervouet *(Nouadhibou)*
Director Railway and Harbour: R. Guittard *(Nouadhibou)*

Gauge: 1.435 m.
Route length: 650 km.

This 4 ft 8½ in *(1.435)* line, 404 miles *(650 km)* long, was completed in 1963. It runs from Nouadhibou (ex-Port Etienne) to Akjoujit for the transport of iron ore from the mines at F'Derik (ex-Fort Gouraud). The maximum gradient against loaded trains is 0.5 per cent (1 in 200) and against empty trains 1.0 per cent (1 in 100). The minimum radius of curves is 3 280 ft *(1 000 m)*.
During 1973 a total of 12.1 million tonnes of ore was moved 401 miles *(645 km)* from mine to port. The equipment used consisted of 21 diesel-electric line haul locomotives, 10 shunting locomotives and 860 ore cars. The average net train load was 12 800 tonnes of ore, and the average speed was 24 mph *(38 kmlh)*. Triple-locomotive trains have a gross hauled load of some 13 500 tonnes, and quadruple-locomotive trains 18 500 tones.

TRACK CONSTRUCTION DETAILS
Standard Rail: 108.9 lb per yd *(54 kglm)* UIC
Welded Joints: Practically the whole line was laid with long-welded rail. 8 × 18 m railbars were flash-butt welded at the depot into 472 ft *(144 m)* lengths, which after laying were Thermit welded into continuous rail. The longest individual length of welded rail is 50 miles *(80 km)*.
Sleepers (crossties): Type U28 steel weighing 165 lb *(75 kg)*.
Spacing: 23⅝ in *(60 cm)*.
Rail Fastening: Clips and bolts to metal sleepers.
Max Curvature: 1.75° = min. radius of 3 280 ft *(1 000 m)*.
Max Gradient: 0.5% (1 in 200) against loaded trains.
1.0% (1 in 100) against empty trains.
Max Altitude: 1 148 ft *(350 m)*.
Max Axle Load: 25 tonnes.
Max Speed: Loaded trains 31 mph *(50 kmlh)*; empty 37 mph *(60 kmlh)*.

MEXICO

FERROCARRILES NACIONALES DE MEXICO
Avenida Central 140, Colonia Guerrero, Mexico 3, DF

President: Emilio Múgica Montoya
General Manager: Luis Gómez Zepeda
Assistant to General Manager: Alfredo Suarez Rábago
Assistant to General Manager—MP and RS: Luis Garcia Barrientos
Assistant to General Manager—Traffic: Eduardo A. Cota
Assistant to General Manager—Finances: Pedro C. García Treviño
Assistant to General Manager—Purchases: Guillermo Hernández Tapia
Assistant to General Manager—Administration: Jorge Sanchez Curiel
General Controller: Adolfo González Arellano
Director Public Relations: Luis Solana Salcedo

Gauge: mainly 1.435 m.
Route length: 14 174 km.

On January 17, 1977, Lic Jose Lopez Portillo, Constitutional President of Mexico, ordered the merger of all Mexican railway enterprises—Pacific Railway, SA de CV; Chihuahua-Pacific Railway, SA de CV; Sonora-Baja California Railway, SA de CV; Southeastern United Railways, SA de CV—with the National Railways of Mexico, under the Management of Luis Gomez Z.

The Mexican Railway Network, now consists of:

	Track km	No. of Employees	(Millions) Ton-km Net-1974	Percentage Total Freight Traffic
Nation Rys of Mexico	14 151.3	60 125	26 303.0	82.4
Pacific Ry	2 314.6	7 267	3 776.0	11.9
Chihuahua-Pacific Railway	1 515.5	2 836	903.0	2.8
Southwestern United Railways	1 359.8	3 051	601.0	1.9
Sonora-Baja California Ry	607.0	1 558	303.0	1.0
	19 948.2	74 837	31 736.0	100.00

FERROCARRILES NACIONALES DE MEXICO
Ferrocarriles Nacionales de Mexico (NdeM) was constituted as a decentralised firm by presidential decree on December 30, 1948. It extends from the northern border with the United States from the cities of Matamoros and Nuevo Laredo, Tamaulipas, from Piedras Negras and Ciudad Acuña, Coahuila and from Ciudad Juarez, Chihuahua to the southern border with Guatemala at Ciudad Hidalgo, Chiapas.
On the Gulf of Mexico, it connects with the ports of Coatzacoalcos, Veracruz, and Tampico. On the Pacific Ocean, it connects with the ports of Puerto Madero, Salina Cruz, and with Manzanillo.
In the interior, it connects the important cities of Mexico City, Queretaro, Leon, Aguascalientes, Zacatecas, Durango, Torreon, Chihuahua, San Luis Potosi, Saltillo, Monterrey, Ciudad Frontera (Coahuila), Morelia, Guadalajara, Colima, Pueblo, Oaxaco, Jalapa and Orizaba.
It interchanges in Coatzacoalcos with the Ferrocarriles Unidos del Sureste, in Guadalajara with the Ferrocarril del Pacifico and in Chihuahua and Ciudad Juarez with the Ferrocarril Chihuahua al Pacifico.
This railroad began in 1873 with the former Ferrocarril Mexicano (presently called the Mexican Division), which went from Mexico City to Veracruz via Orizaba and Córdoba. Afterwards, and through the construction of various lines, of which the most important were the Ferrocarril Central, the Ferrocarril Nacional, the Internacional, the Interoceanico, the Nacional de Tehuantepec, and the Panamericano, the current rail network was formed.
The railroad has 70 000 employees, distributed among 17 divisions with 107 operating districts. The main shop for locomotive repair is in San Luis Potosi and for rolling stock is in Aguascalientes. There are also 47 secondary shops, of which the most important are in Valle de Mexico (Pantaco, DF), Torreon, Monterrey, Ciudad Frontera (Coahuila), Puebla, Tierra Blanca (Veracruz) and Matias Romero (Oaxaca). The office of the General Manager and his deputy, as well as the Assistant Managers of Track and Structures, of Motor Power and Rolling Stock, of Operations, of Planning and Organisation, of Administration, of Finances, of Purchasing, and of Telecommunications, Signals and Electricity are all in Mexico City. Personnel of these departments and personnel in charge of programmed track maintenance are located in smaller offices along the line.
The 17 divisions with the number of operating districts within them are as follows:

Division	Districts
Cárdenas	5
Centro	8
Golfo	4
Guadalajara	6
Jalapa	4
Mexicano	3
México	9
Monclova	8
Monterrey	4
Pacifico	6
Pueblo	10
Querétaro	10
San Luis	6
Sureste V.C.I.	8
Sureste N.T.	3
Sureste P.A.	3
Torreón	10

In November 1974, NdeM established four regions as follows: (1) Western region headquarters in Torreón comprised of the Torreón and Centro divisions; (2) Eastern Region, headquartered in Monterrey, with the Monclová, Golfo, Monterrey, San Luis and Cárdenas divisions; (3) the Central Region, headquartered in Mexico City, with the Queretaro, Mexico, Pacifico and Guadalajara divisions; and (4) the Southeast Region, headquartered in Veracruz, comprising the Puebla, Mexicano, Jalapa, Sureste V.C.I., N.T. and P.A. divisions.
The regional manager is the authority within his region, reporting to the Deputy General Manager, and is responsible for the general operating administration of his region.
In some of the lines, operation of the trains is difficult and costly due to the governing grades, of which the most important are:

Line	Governing Grade	Between	Length
B	2.00%	Encantada-Agua Nueva	13 km
B	2.13%	Soledad-Higuéras	27 km
I	2.00%	Colima-Cdad. Guzmán	97 km
I	3.00%	Quemada-Nicolás	7 km
S	2.50%	Sumidero-Fortin	6 km

Nok M locomotive 9 100 purchased in 1973 from GE of the United States

Line	Governing Grade	Between	Length
S	4.10%	Encinas-Boca del Monte	31 km
V	2.56%	Tamarindo-Jalapa	78 km
V	2.88%	Jalapa-Las Vigas	53 km
V	2.12%	Rubin-Cruz Blanca	5 km
G	2.34%	Achotal-Angostura	24 km
G	2.27%	Azueta-B. Juárez	42 km
G	2.80%	Refugio-Cuichapa	35 km
G	2.33%	Rodriguez Clara-Colorado	41 km
G	2.30%	B. Juárez-Rodriguez Clara	78 km
G	2.35%	Tezonapa-Refugio	4 km

The railroad carries more than 45 million tons of cargo annually, of which the principal are: mineral, industrial, agricultural, petroleum and petroleum derivatives and inorganic products. In 1974 it carried 8 500 000 tons of cargo and 20 023 128 passengers.

FINANCES
Total operating revenue in 1976 amounted to $4 656.7 million (pesos). Total operating expenses amounted to 9 649.2 million (pesos), resulting in a deficit of $4 992.5 million (pesos).

TRAFFIC

	1975	1976
Total freight tonne-km (millions)	27 046.5	26 838.8
Total freight tonnage	52 250 412	51 322 262
Total passenger-km (millions)	2 612.7	2 507.6
Total passenger journeys	19 513 511	19 107 092

MOTIVE POWER AND ROLLING STOCK
On December 31st, 1975, the National Railways of Mexico's motive power and rolling stock, was as follows:

Motive Power	Units
Diesel-electric locomotives	1 112
Freight cars	32 783
Passenger train cars	1 244

FERROCARRIL SONORA—BAJA CALIFORNIA SA de CV
The Ferrocarril Sonora-Baja California, SA de CV was formed by presidential decree on June 24, 1972 and covers the desert area of the states of Sonora and Baja California Norte with 684 km of main and secondary track between the towns of Benjamin Hill, Sonora, and Mexicali, BC with a branch between Tijuana and Tecate, BC.
The railway began operating in 1938 and functioned as a part of the Secretariat of Communications and Transportation until June 24, 1972, when it was constituted as a corporation with the Federal Government as sole owner.
The Ferrocarril Sonora-Baja California operated under the control of a board of directors of which the Secretary of Communications and Transportation is the president with members being representatives of the Secretariats of Treasury, National Patrimony, Industry and Commerce, the Union of Railroad Workers of the Mexican Republic and the Director General of Operating Railroads.
The operation is on level terrain except for two short grades of 1.29 per cent and 1.31 per cent of 32 km in length between López Collada and Torres B.
It has the following equipment: 16 diesel electric locomotives with a total output of 36 200 hp. to operate four daily scheduled passenger trains and four daily scheduled freight trains, with necessary switching yards at Mexicali and Benjamin Hill.
Also, it has 309 freight cars: boxcars, gondolas, flatcars, open freight cars, etc. Furthermore, it has 87 passenger cars.
The system carries annually more than 600 000 tonnes of various products, of which the main ones are: industrial, agricultural, petroleum and derivatives, forest products, animals and animal products. Passenger traffic averaged 450 000 per year.

FINANCES
In order to evaluate the economic development of this railroad and consider its impact on regional development, it is helpful to review the results of its operation over the past 15 years:

		Total Operational	
Year	Income*	Expenses*	Profit (Loss)*
1960	3.12	3.28	(0.16)
1965	3.36	4.08	(0.72)
1969	4.80	4.80	0
1970	4.88	4.72	0.16
1971	5.28	5.28	0
1972	5.04	6.20	(1.16)
1973	5.84	8.84	(3.0)
1974	6.80	9.84	(3.04)

* in millions of US dollars

Rotation of freight equipment is: 3.7 days as a general average for a cycle of cargo with average distance travelled per ton of 427 km. Utilisation of motor power-locomotives is 87 per cent daily.

FERROCARRILES UNIDOS DEL SURESTE SA de CV
The Ferrocarriles Unidos del Sureste, SA de CV, was formed by presidential decree on August 29, 1968 by combining the Ferrocarriles Unidos de Yucatán, which was privately owned, with the Ferrocarril del Sureste, operated by the Secretariat of Communications and Transportation. As its name indicates, it covers the southeastern

The new Morelia passenger stations opened in 1976

region of Mexico, beginning in the port of Coatzacoalcos, Veracruz, crossing the same river and proceeding to Tancochapa, Tabasco; Pichucalco, Chiapas; Teapa, Tabasco; Tenosique, Tabasco; Escárcega, Campeche; Campeche, Campeche; Mérida, Yucatán; and Progreso, Yucatán, with 1 043 km of broad guage (143.5 cm) track. There is also 455 km of narrow guage (91.5 cm) track which connects Mérida with Tizimin, Valladolid, Sotuta and Peto.
The Ferrocarriles Unidos de Yucatán began operating with the Mérida-Progreso section in 1881. The Ferrocarril del Sureste began operating as a unit in 1950, but some sections had existed prior to this time such as Campeche-Tenosique and Allende-Teapa.
With the decreee of August 29, 1968 one corporation was formed out of both railroads with the Federal Government as majority stockholder.
The operation is on level terrain, with short compensated grades of 1 per cent, throughout its system.
The railway has the following equipment: 35 diesel electric locomotives with a capacity of 52 700 hp to operate 22 trains: four are passenger and six are freight between Coatzacoalcos-Mérida-Progreso; and 12 are mixed in the narrow gauge branches.
Also, it has 827 freight cars: boxcars, gondolas, flatcars, open freight cars, etc. Furthermore, it has 69 passenger cars: coaches of first and second class, express cars and mail cars.
Ferrocarriles Unidos del Sureste carried annually more than 1.0 million tons of various products, of which the main ones are: industrial, petroleum and derivatives, agricultural, inorganic and mineral.

FINANCES

		Total Operational	Profit
Year	Income*	Expenses*	(Loss)*
1960	3.1	5.4	(2.3)
1965	3.9	7.1	(3.2)
1969	3.8	9.8	(6.0)
1970	4.1	11.1	(7.0)
1971	4.3	12.2	(7.9)
1972	4.8	13.4	(8.6)
1973	5.3	16.0	(10.7)
1974	6.8	16.8	(10.0)

* in millions of US dollars

Rotation of freight equipment is: 12.9 days as a general average for a cycle of cargo with average distance travelled per ton of 333 km. Utilisation of motor power in locomotive-days is 67.3 per cent on the average.

FERROCARRIL CHIHUAHUA AL PACIFICO, SA de CV
Ferrocarril Chihuahua al Pacifico, SA de CV was formed by the fusion of the former Kansas City, Mexico and East and the Northwest Mexico rail systems through the section of new construction which linked the present system in 1960. The Federal Government acquired the Kansas City, Mexico and East Railroad in 1940 and the Northwest Mexico in 1952 and they were administered until January 12, 1955, by the Secretariat of Communications and Transportation. On that date the Ferrocarril Chihuahua al Pacifico was created by presidential decree.
The railroad is located in the states of Chihuahua and Sinaloa, uniting the northern border in the terminal at Ojinaga with the capital of the state of Chihuahua and continuing to La Junta. From there, after crossing the Sierre Madre Occidental it descends until it crosses the El Fuerte river where the level part of the state of Sinaloa begins. It continues to the town of Sufragio where it crosses the Ferrocarril del Pacifico and it terminates in the port of Topolobampo. A branch from La Junta, Chihuahua to the north connects the towns of Madera, Mata Ortiz, and Casas Grandes, terminating at the border at Ciudad Juarez. Its lines extend for 1 762 km using broad guage of 143.5 cm.
The line between Ojinaga, La Junta and Topolobampo is called Line A and is 941 km long. The portion between the stations of Agua Caliente and Creel has a continuous grade of 2.5 per cent for 214 km which makes operation costly and difficult. The branch between La Junta and Ciudad Juarez is called Line B and is 570 km long. It has grades of 2 per cent between the stations of Rincón and Las Varas for a distance of 12 km, and between the stations of Chico and Cumbre for a distance of 9 km. Between Caballo and Cumbre there is a 3 per cent grade for 11 km.
The railway has the following equipment: 44 diesel electric locomotives with a capacity of 87 400 hp to operate daily 10 passenger trains, 22 freight trains and 6 mixed. Also, it has 2 354 freight cars: boxcars, gondolas, flatcars, open freight cars, etc. Furthermore, it has 62 passenger cars: coaches of first and second class, express cars and mail cars, as well as 13 self propelled cars (autovias).
The railroad annually carries more than 2 000 000 tonnes of various products, of which the main ones are: forest, industrial, agricultural, mineral and petroleum and petroleum derivatives. Passenger traffic has averaged 500 000 per year. In 1974 542 256 persons were carried.

FINANCES

		Total Operational	Profit
Year	Income*	Expenses*	(Loss)*
1960	3.3	4.5	(1.2)
1965	8.4	8.8	(0.4)
1969	9.9	12.9	(3.0)
1970	9.8	15.1	(5.3)
1971	9.6	15.6	(6.0)
1972	10.2	18.0	(7.8)
1973	10.2	20.2	(10.0)
1974	11.8	23.4	(12.6)

* in millions US dollars

Rotation of freight equipment is: 12 days as a general average for a cycle of cargo with average distance travelled per ton of 368 km. Utilisation of motor power in locomotive—days is 63 per cent on the average.

FERROCARRIL DEL PACIFICO SA de CV

The Ferrocarril del Pacifico SA de CV, was formed as such by presidential decree on March 8, 1952. It runs through the states of Sonora, Sinaloa, Nayarit and Jalisco. Leaving from Nogales it crosses the state of Sonora headed south, passing through the cities of Hermosillo, Guaymas, Ciudad Obregón and Navojoa. In the state of Sinaloa it follows the Pacific coast connecting the cities of Sufragio, Culiacán and Mazatlán. In the state of Nayarit it touches the city of Tepic and terminates in Guadalajara. From Nogales to the west the railroad has a branch that connects with the towns of Cananea, Naco, Agua Prieta and Nacozari. There are also branches from Orendain to Ameca and to Etzatlán, Jalisco; Quila el Torito, Sinaloa and Navajoa Huatabampo, Sonora.

In the station at Benjamin Hill it interchanges with the Sonora-Baja California Railroad and at Sufragio, Sinoloa, it interchanges with the Chihuahua al Pacifico Railroad.

Upon becoming a separate corporation, the Federal Government acquired the majority of shares and the states of Sonora and Sinaloa the rest. It operates under the control of a board of directors of which the Secretary of Communications and Transportation is the president with members being representatives of the Secretariats of Treasury, National Patrimony, Industry and Commerce, and of the Director General of Operating Railroads, the Union of Railroad Workers of the Mexican Republic and the governments of the states of Sonora and Sinaloa.

The railroad has approximately 7 000 employees. The main repair and maintenance shops for locomotives and rolling stock are in Empalme, Sonora. Secondary shops are in Nogales, Mazatlán, Tepic and Guadalajara. The general offices are in Guadalajara, as are the departments of transportation, motor power, track, administration and accounting. Personnel of these departments and personnel in charge of programmed track maintenance are located in smaller offices along the line.

In this railroad there are two divisions—Sonora and Sinaloa. The Sonora division is divided into five operating districts and the Sinaloa has six. The trains operate on a flat plain, except on the Roseta slope, which is 53 km to Tepic and has a grade of 2.4 per cent. In Empalme Oredain there is also a slope of 2 per cent over a 22 km stretch. Towards the north between the stations of Agua Sarca and Encinas there is a grade of 2 per cent for 9 km, and between Guadalajara and La Venta there is a governing grade of 1.56 per cent for 19 km.

The railway has the following equipment: 93 diesel electric locomotives with a total capacity of 195 000 hp to operate four daily passenger trains, 46 freight trains and 6 mixed passenger/freight trains.

It has 3 700 freight cars: boxcars, gondolas, flatcars, Piggyback flat cars, tank cars, trailers with and without refrigeration, refrigeration cars, etc. Furthermore, it has 155 passenger cars: coaches of first and second class, express cars and mail cars.

The Ferrocarril del Pacifico carries annually an average of 5 000 000 tonnes of various products, of which the main ones are: a very high percentage of agricultural products, industrial, petroleum and its derivatives as well as mineral products. Passenger traffic has averaged 1 000 000 annually, a figure which has been maintained in the last four years.

FINANCES

Year	Income*	Total Operational Expenses*	Profit (Loss)*
1960	26.3	29.1	(2.8)
1965	31.8	38.7	(6.9)
1969	36.7	43.3	(6.6)
1970	35.6	44.5	(8.9)
1971	33.7	49.1	(15.4)
1972	33.7	52.4	(18.7)
1973	39.2	57.9	(18.7)
1974	44.6	74.0	(29.4)

* in millions US dollars

Rotation of freight equipment is: 12.4 days as a general average for a cycle of cargo, with average distance travelled per ton of 713 km. Utilisation of motor power in locomotive-days is 80.66 per cent.

FN de M DIESEL LOCOMOTIVES

Series	Class	Builder	hp	Date of Construction	Number in Service	Wheel arrangement
801	DE-28	EMD	800	7-31-71	3	B-B
5001	DE- 1	ALCO	600	8-10-44	1	B-B
5100	DE- 2	GE	600	10-18-62	3	B-B
5300	DE- 3	ALCO	900	1-25-56	1	B-B
5400	DE-28	EMD	800	10-12-64	16	B-B
5504	DE- 5	ALCO	1 000	9- -44	7	B-B
5602	DE- 6	ALCO	1 000	2- -50	45	B-B
5800	DE-18	EMD	1 310	1- 9-56	76	B-B
5900	DE- 4	ALCO-MLW	1 200	2-20-63	5	C-C
6201-A	DE-10	EMD	1 300	8- -46	4	B-B
6203-B	DE-10	EMD	1 300	1- -50	3	B-B
6300-A	DE-11	EMD	1 500	1- -52	15	B-B
6319-B	DE-11	EMD	1 500	12- -51	3	B-B
6507-A	DE-13	ALCO-MLW	1 600	8- -51	4	B-B
6516-B	DE-13	CONV	1 600	8- -51	1	B-B
6600	DE-14	EMD	1 500	4- -52	2	B-B
6701	DE-15	ALCO	1 600	9- -52	4	B-B
6801	DE-16	BLH	1 600	3- -54	15	C-C
6901	DE-19	ALCO	1 600	11-21-55	1	C-C
7000-A	DE-17	EMD	1 750	2- -54	26	B-B
7001-B	DE-17	EMD	1 750	2- -54	8	B-B
7100	DE-21	EMD	1 750	11-17-56	7	B-B
7108	DE-21	SLP-6	1 750	11- -65	1	B-B
7200	DE-22	ALCO	1 800	1- 4-57	14	B-B
7219	DE-22	MLW	1 800	7- 3-63	65	B-B
7294	DE-22	SLP-2	1 800	5-31-63	1	B-B
7300	DE-23	EMD	1 800	10- 4-58	22	C-C
7400	DE-24	ALCO	1 800	9-12-58	69	C-C
7473	DE-24	SLP-5	1 800	10-13-64	1	C-C
7500	DE-25	EMD	1 800	6-26-61	36	B-B
8100	DE-26	ALCO	2 400	7- 4-64	44	B-B
8200	DE-27	EMD	2 500	9- 8-64	54	B-B
8300	DE-29	ALCO	2 750	3-14-67	32	C-C
8400	DE-30	EMD	3 000	6-13-67	10	B-B
8500	DE-31	EMD	3 000	6-12-68	83	C-C
8522	DE-31	EMD	3 000	7-18-72	2	C-C
8600	DE-32	MLW	3 000	7- 7-72	20	C-C
8700	DE-33	EMD	3 000	10- 6-72	56 + 12	C-C
8800	DE-34	EMD	1 500	6-10-73	60	B-B
8900	DE-35	GE	3 500	7-28-73	87	C-C
9000	DE-36	GE	1 800	2-13-74	45	B-B
9100	DE-37	GE	2 250	4- 4-75	30	B-B
9200	DE-38	EMD	2 000	6-20-75	20	B-B
9300	DE-35	GE	3 600	3-19-75	17	C-C
9400	DE-38	EMD	2 000		81	B-B

(104 of them switcher units)

MOROCCO

MOROCCAN RAILWAYS

Office National Des Chemins De Fer Du Maroc (ONCFM)
ave Allal Ben Abdallah 19, Rabat

General Manager: Moussa Moussaoui
Chief Engineers: A. Benjelloun
                    M. Temri
                    D. Kanouni
Heads of Departments:
Operations: Y. Durand-Gasselin
Motive Power and Rolling Stock: A. Bouamri
Permanent Way and Works: M. El Aichaoui
Administration: A. Benali

Gauge: 1.435 m.
Route length: 1 756 km.

Of a total railway route length of 1 091 miles *(1 756 km)* of standard gauge, 440 miles *(708 km)* is electrified at 3 000 V dc with overhead wire conductor. The electrified lines run from Casablanca eastwards to Fes, south to Marrakech, and southeast to Oued-Zem and Beni Idir.

TRAFFIC		1975	1976
Total freight tonne-km ('000)		2 890 302	3 143 175
Total freight tonnage ('000)		18 973	20 198
Total passenger-km ('000)		835 123	827 818
Total passenger journeys ('000)		5 610	5 786

FINANCES	1975	1976
	(DH millions)	
Revenues	352.83	302.52
Expenses	293.83	349.15

DEVELOPMENT

At the end of 1973 a new five-year plan was launched at an estimated cost of 450 million dirham. Major projects completed by 1977 include:
   Renewal of the line between Casablanca and Marrakech
   Renewal of track between Casablanca and Sidi Kacem and between Tangier and Fez
   Renewal of track between Youssoufia and Safi
Motive power and rolling stock purchases include:
   20 electric locomotives
   12 mainline diesel-electric locomotives
   15 shunting locomotives
   45 passenger coaches
   200 hopper wagons for phosphate transport
   1 000 wagons of various types

Additional facilities are to be provided for the development of phosphate traffic, including additional track, a new station building. Equipment for phosphate traffic will include two diesel-electric line locomotives, one shunter, 125 hopper wagons and 32 tank wagons—all intended for a new phosphate line.

An additional programme provides for a service to the new phosphate centre of Benguerir; renewal of the section between Sidi Daoui and Khouribga; purchases of 352 phosphate wagons; and purchase of eight passenger coaches.

Cost of the phosphate programme, put at 109.3 million dirham, will be met entirely by the State. Cost of the eight coaches—about 7.7 million dirham—will be met from ONCFM funds.

ONCFM will also meet about 90 million dirham of the cost of the main programme, with the remainder coming from the State. And financial charges—a total of 30 million, with 18 million falling due during the plan period—will also come from railway funds.

TRACK

New Rail: For all track renewals the rail laid is Type S 33 weighing 90.8 lb per yd *(46 kgm).*

Rail fastenings: The rails are secured to sleepers by elastic fastenings supplied by *Les Ressorts du Nord.* Rubber seating pads 5 mm. thick are supplied by *Soc. Marocaine Berrionneau.*

Welded rail: The total length of track with welded rail is 76 miles *(123 km),* the longest individual length being 8.7 miles *(14 km).* Type S33 rail *(46 kg/m),* in 59 ft *(18 m)* bars is Thermit welded. Elastic fastenings secure the rail to reinforced concrete sleepers. A further 58 miles *(94 km)* of track was to be dealt with before 1972.

SIGNALLING AND TRAIN CONTROL

Automatic block with colour light signals was installed on 7 miles *(11 km)* of route from Casablanca Port to Beaulieu Junction, with control centre at Casablanca Nord. The equipment was supplied by *Cie de Signeaux et d'Enterprises Electriques.*

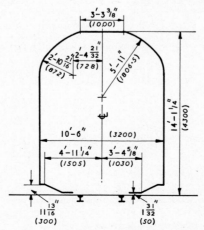

Cie. des C.F. du Maroc

Alsthom-built type DF-101 diesel-electric locomotive powered by an AGo-U-16 ESHR engine and rated at 2 650 kW; weight 108 tonnes; maximum speed 130 km/h.

Levelling and lining unit in operation following line renewal between Fes and Taza.

MOZAMBIQUE

MOZAMBIQUE HARBOURS AND RAILWAYS
(Direccao Nacional Dos Portoe Caminhos de Ferro)
CP No 276 Maputo

General Manager: Eng. L. M. Alcantara Santos
Railway Systems and Harbours Directors:
  Maputo: A. E. Castro
           A. E. Lopes
  Beira: Eng. J. Caldeira Pinto
  Nampula: Eng. D. M. Rocha Vaz
  Quelimane: Antonio Américo Batista (Inspector)
  Inhambane e Gaza: Custodio Carmo de Almeida (Inspector)
Technical Division: Eng. A. J. De Sousa Lafe
Works and Studies Division: J. Da Silva Pinta
                Eng. Artur Raul de Silva Marques

Gauge: 1.067 m.
Route length: 2 999 km.

Mozambique's Minister of Development & Economic Planning Dr Marcelino dos Santos announced in 1977 that the 31 km section of line between Moambo and Machava is to be doubled to increase capacity for export traffic from South Africa. South African exports through the Mozambique port of Maputo are expected to double by mid-1978. The Minister's decision to double the Moambo—Machava section means that a major bottleneck on the 600 km Witwatersrand to Maputo route will be eliminated. It results from a study carried out earlier by a team of South African railway experts led by SAR's General Manager Mr K Loubser. Concrete sleepers for the line will be supplied from South Africa.

Mozambique Railways consists of three main and two small lines, not connected to each other, running inland from ports on the Indian Ocean. From north to south of the country these are:

Mozambique Division
Gauge: 3 ft 6 in *(1.067 m)*
Route length: 680 miles *(979 km)*

This line runs from the port of Nacala, with a branch to Mozambique, westward to Nova Freixa and Vila Cabral. From Nova Freixa a new line has been built connecting at the border with Malawi Railways new link line giving Malawi rail access to the port of Nacala.

Quelimane Division
Gauge: 3 ft 6 in *(1.067 m)*
Route length: 590 miles *(950 km)*

From the port of Beira the line runs eastwards to connect with Rhodesia Railways at Machipanda. From Dondo Junction 18 miles *(29 km)*, from Beira, a line runs northward to connect with Malawi Railways with an extension from D. Ana to Moatize. The section from Dondo to Sena, 181 miles *(291 km)* is owned by the Trans-Zambesia Railway Co Ltd (see separate entry). A new line 52 miles *(83 km)* long was built from Inhamitango to Marromeu to replace the old 3 ft 0 in *(0.915 m)* gauge length.

Inhambane and Gaza Division
This consists of two isolated lines:
1. Joao Belo to Mauéle, with a branch from Manjacaze to Chicomo 2 ft 5½ in *(0.750 m)* gauge; 96 miles *(154 km)* route length.

Maputo
Gauge: 3 ft 6 in *(1.067 m)*
Route length: 479 miles *(771 km)*

From the port of Maputo lines run west to connect with South African Railways at Kamatipoort; north to Malvernia and southwest to connect with Swaziland Railways at Goba. A new line 47 miles *(75 km)* is being built from Umpala, on the Goba line to Salamanga.
In the South, having the port of Maputo (ex-Lourenço Marques) as railhead, there are four railway lines totalling 844 kms:

Goba Line (to the border of Swaziland)	64 km
Ressano Garcia Line (to the border of South Africa)	88 km
Limpopo Line (to the border of Rhodesia, at Chicualacuala)	528 km
Xinavane Line (domestic service)	93 km
Branch Lines (domestic service)	71 km

The first, joins up at the border of Swaziland with the Swaziland Railway, which connects the Umbovu Ridge iron-ore complex at Kadake with the port of Maputo. The second continues into the Republic of South Africa, and it carries a considerable portion of traffic from the Witwatersrand in the South Africa to this port—its natural outlet. In the upward direction liquid fuels and general cargo reach the highest figures, and in the downward direction, coal, maize, citrus and mineral ores predominate. The third goes through Rhodesia to Zambia, Botswana and the South East Zaire and conveys hundreds of thousands of tons of cargo per annum. Motor vehicles, chemicals, fertilizers and general cargo comprise the main upward traffic. Copper, mineral ores, and maize are the biggest commodities of the downward traffic. This line also, in effect, serves the Limpopo Valley. The fourth is the natural outlet for the sugar-cane producting region of Xinavane and cattle and dairy products of the Gaza province.
In the centre, having the port of Beira as railhead, there are three lines totalling 995 kms in length:

The Beira line (from Beira to Machipanda, on the Rhodesian border)	318 km
The Trans-Zambesia Railway (from Dondo to Sena)	291 km
The line from Sena to Vila Nova da Fronteira, on the Malawi border, including the branch line from Inhamitanga to Marromeu	132 km
Tete Line (from Dona Ana to Moatize)	254 km

The first continues through Rhodesia and serves the Rhodesia, Botswana, Zambia and the South East Zaire. It handles a considerable amount of traffic because it is the traditional gateway to these countries. In the downward direction it conveys mainly copper, minerals, tobacco, tea, refrigerated beef, etc. and in the upward traffic, machinery, fertilizers, timber and general cargo, etc.
The second which meets the above at Donda, 33 kms from Beira, is, one of the gateways to Malawi. Therefore it conveys the export and import traffic of that country in addition to the forest and sugar producing regions served specifically the Inhamitanga-Marromeu branchline.
The third meets the second at Dona Ana, on the left bank of the Zambezi River, and carries domestic traffic, made up mainly of coal and agricultural products bound for the coast. Liquid fuels and general cargo are conveyed in the upward traffic, to Cahora Bassa and to Zambia by road.
In the North, having the port of Nacala as railhead, there is a railway network which is 920 kms long and is known as the:

Moçambique Line to Lichinga (Vila Cabral) and the Eastern regions of Lake Nyasa	800 km
Branchline from Cuamba (Nova Freixo) to the Malawi frontier	78 km
Branchline from Lumbo to Monapo	42 km

NEPAL

NEPAL GOVERNMENT RAILWAY
Birganj

Ministry of Works & Transport: Babar Mahul, Katmandu
Minister: Hon Beleran G. Mager
Acting Manager: Devendra Singh
Acting Traffic Officer: Pratap Bahadur

Gauge: 750 mm
Route length: 10 km

There are only two short railways within the Himalayan kingdom of Nepal, operating in the Terai—a fertile and level strip adjacent to the border with India. The Janakpur Railway (JR) runs from Jaynagar in Bihar State, India, across the Nepal border north and west to Janakpurdam (32 km) and on to Bizulpra (21 km).
The Nepal Government Railway (NR) runs from Raxaul in Bihar State across the Nepal border to Birganj (9 km). The line was originally built as a key link in the railway-road-ropeway transport system that supplied the mountain-locked valley of Katmandu—closed to the outside world until the early 1950s.
The line, now terminating at Birganj, formerly continued north to the base of the Siwalik Hills at Amlekhganj.

DEVELOPMENT
The Government is now undertaking to develop Hetauda into a new industrial centre. As part of the scheme, preliminary feasibility studies are being made for the construction of a new rail line from Raxaul to Hetauda.
At the request of the Nepal Government, Indian Railways has made two studies of possible railway extensions from Raxaul to Hetauda. The first was for a metre-gauge line which would essentially follow the existing rail route. The second calls for an entirely new alignment for a broad-gauge line which would pass to the east of Birganj. The first scheme, in fact, has been virtually abandoned due to curvatures and grades necessary. The second, which includes extensive tunnelling through the Siwalik Hills, is now under study.
The broad-gauge scheme could be undertaken in three stages: 1) construction of metre-gauge line—built to broad-gauge engineering standards—to a terminal either on the north side of Birganj or the newly-completed east-west highway further north; 2) extension to Hetauda which would involve difficult mountain work; and 3) conversion to broad gauge when India extends broad-gauge operations to the border.

JANAKPUR RAILWAY
Khajuri

Manager: D. Singh Khatry
Operations Engineer: Dr. Pratish Chandra Bandopadhyay
Traffic Assistant: Krishna Shresth

Gaugé: 750 mm
Route length: 53 km

The Janakpur Railway (JR) was originally built as a timber line designed to open the virgin jungle to the north of Janakpurdam. As the forest has long since been cut, the railway now operates primarily to provide access in an area with few roads. Passengers are the main source of revenue with pilgrims to the temples of Janakpurdam forming the bulk of traffic.
In recent years JR officers have been upgrading track by laying new sleepers and second-hand 16 kg/m rail to replace existing 12.5 kg/m profile. Locomotives (including two Garrats) and wagons released from the Nepal Railway have been rebuilt and pressed into service.
A recent railway mission to Nepal from the Economic Commission for Asia and the Far East (ECAFE) suggested the possible use of diesel rail buses in place of existing steam-hauled trains.

NETHERLANDS

NETHERLANDS RAILWAYS
N.V. Nederlandse Spoorwegen (NS), Moreelsepark, Utrecht

Chairman of the Board: M. G. de Bruin
Secretary General and Manager Research and Planning Department: P. R. Leopold
Manager, Commercial Department: P. Boender
Manager, Operating Department: D. C. Hasselman
Manager, Finance and Audit Department: J. Walter
Manager, Staff Department: L. W. Wansink
Chief Civil Engineer: J. C. W. Jong
Public Relations Officer: C. P. van Strien

Gauge: 1.435 m
Route length: 2 825 km

For NS, 1976 proved a difficult year. Passenger traffic, for instance, fell by 3 per cent while freight traffic remained at practically the same level as in 1975. However, NS chiefs believe that, providing the country passes through a period of general economic revival, NS can look forward to hauling 24 million tonnes of freight annually—a considerable improvement on the 17.8 million tonnes railed in 1976. Several steps are to be taken immediately to ensure that NS finds the traffic it needs to ensure economic survival. During 1976 the decision was taken to reorganise the production system in freight business—a decision based on the assumption that by about 1980 the new marshalling yard at Kijfhoek near Rotterdam is to be open to service.

FINANCES
During 1976 the accumulated loss (over the period 1962-1975) was converted into a claim on the State of the Netherlands. This claim has partly been paid at once and the remainder will be cleared off within a period of 20 years.
The State also paid the cost that NS made for financing this loss (eg interest on loans). In 1976 a government grant for goods transport was received for the first time.
Total revenues amounted to Hfl. 1 797 million (+ Hfl. 318 million). Of this amount Hfl. 626 million is included as a grant for the continuation of obligations of social services in passenger transport under the EEC-regulation Nr. 1191/69. Costs increased to Hfl. 1 789 million (+ Hfl. 91 million); staff cost increased by Hfl. 103 million to Hfl. 1 175 million.
The total amount of investments amounted to Hfl. 342 million, of which Hfl. 135 million was for the construction of new lines and the purchase of new trainsets for short distance traffic in urban areas (the so-called 'Sprinter') and for Intercitytrains.
In connection with the financing of the new lines the government enlarged the share-capital by Hfl. 56 million to an amount of Hfl. 409 million.

	1975	1976
	Hfl.	
Revenues	1 479 136	1 797 153
Expenses	1 766 510	1 797 153

PASSENGER TRAFFIC
The volume of passenger traffic decreased by about 3 per cent to 8.2 thousand million passenger-km in 1976. The major reasons were: rise of the tariff-rates, the unfavourable economic situation—in particular the slight increase of the national revenue per head and the high level of unemployment—as well as the sharp rise of the number of private cars.
Above all the decrease was remarkable in the field of single and return journeys. On the other hand international transport increased slightly.

FREIGHT TRAFFIC
Because the expected economic recovery failed, the volume of freight carried in 1976 (17.8 million tons) was nearly the same as in 1975. But as a result of the rise of the tariff-rates the revenues increased by Hfl. 15 million to Hfl. 235 million.
Container-transport, set back by the recession in 1975, attained the high level of 1974. The number of transported containers amounted to about 145 000 in 1976.
Huckepacktransport (combined transport rail/road) showed an increase. Every month about 700 trailers were transported from the new transhipment-station of Rotterdam-Noord towards Germany, Switzerland and Italy. In the mean time Bâle is to be connected to the Huckepack-network as an arrival- and departure-station, and a further extension with Salzburg and Verona is considered. As a consequence of the unfavourable economic situation especially transport in block trains decreased by 9 per cent. Transport of household refuse showed an increase (12 per cent).

TRAFFIC TOTALS
	1975	1976
Total freight tonne-km (millions)	2 721	2 696
Total freight tonnage ('000)	17 696	17 681
Total passenger-km (millions)	8 501	8 218.4
Total passenger journeys (millions)	176.3	171.6

MOTIVE POWER
Number of locomotives in service during 1976 totalled 589, of which 112 were electric main line, 251 diesel electric line, and 226 electric shunters. Number of railcars totalled 30 diesel; number of emu's 550; and diesel trainsets 87.
During 1977, the railway took delivery of a BBC-Thyssen Henschel experimental three-phase locomotive for use as a testbed for a future generation of mixed-traffic locomotives with three-phase induction motors. The locomotive has been converted to accept 1.5 kV dc as an autonomous machine from its previous role as a 15 kV 16⅔ Hz testbed married temporarily to a DB laboratory coach. Its designation is 1 600 P.
NS requires replacement locomotives for a large part of its 1.5 kV fleet. One candidate was the SNCF prototype chopper dc locomotive BB 7003, with which two series of tests have been carried out on NS territory. It is now up to the German machine to prove the suitability and economy of three-phase power conditioning from a 1.5 kV supply. BBC Mannheim has carried out the 1 600 P conversion in close collaboration with NS and Thyssen Henschel.
After research the NS has decided that the life of its elderly Class 1 100 Bo-Bo electric locomotives can be economically prolonged to at least 1985 by some modest modifications. In essence the changes affect the suspension and bogies, which are to be equipped with roller bearings. The whole class is to be treated by the end of 1978.
Delivery on February 28 1977, of Netherlands Railways first 160 km/h trainset from Talbot of West Germany marked an important step forward in development of Dutch rolling stock. Designed to offer faster journey times and higher standards of comfort, the seven prototype trainsets are the forerunners of a future generation of rolling stock for NS *Intercity* services. First passenger service trials commenced on May 22, date of introduction of the summer timetable. All seven trainsets were delivered by the end of August.
The decision to revert to three-car sets for NS was based on a number of considerations. In particular a three-car set capable of running at 160 km/h with moderate acceleration can have a single power car with virtually all traction equipment mounted underfloor, whereas a four-car set would require two. The capacity of a two-car set is too low to justify provision of refreshment facilities, which is considered an essential service on NS *Intercity* routes. Future standardisation on three cars per set for these services will simplify maintenance procedures and still allow considerable operating flexibility.

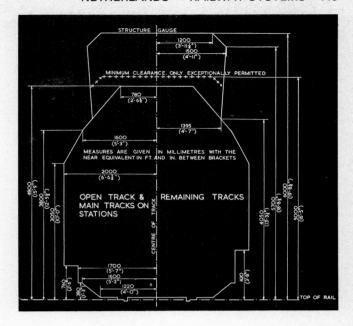

Ex-BR EM2 class 2 490-hp Co-Co locomotive hauling train out of Rotterdam for Mönchengladbach and Cologne

'Sprinter' Two-car electric trainset for high density traffic in urban areas

On the new IC-III the traditional bulbous nose with no end gangway has been abandoned. Instead the front end was designed with a through gangway that still affords the driver a high degree of protection in the event of a collision on a level crossing. Through gangways will allow a reduction in the number of catering staff and at the same time give passengers greater freedom of movement along the whole length of a train. In particular passengers will be able to walk to the correct part of a train which is to be split later for various destinations.
Besides the need for new *Intercity* electric multiple-units, NS has a parallel requirement for a number of locomotive-hauled coaches. About 60 are necessary for the Zandvoort-Maastricht/Heerlen line, which does not lend itself to being operated economically with multiple-units. A further 60 loco-hauled coaches would cover requirements for operating international services to Brussels and Köln, replacing obsolete stock.
It is planned to develop the centre car of the IC-III for loco-hauled use on these routes; it was for this reason that, as far as possible, on-train services have been concentrated on the power car. In the meantime NS is investigating the possibility of purchasing off-the-peg vehicles such as the *Corail* coaches recently introduced on a large number of services in France. The final decision will be made after evaluation of the overall cost; although an off-the-peg coach may be cheaper on first cost, it might require relatively high expenditure on maintenance facilities.
The Netherlands Railways (NS) is experimenting with closed-circuit TV on its 'Sprinter' electric multiple-units in conjunction with trial installations at two stations, Driemanspolder and Geldermalsen. Cameras on the platform transmit to a small receiver screen at the right-hand side of the emu's driving console, so that the driver—the only crewman—can monitor passenger movement and time train-door closure safely. Effects on the transmission of the traction current and train traction equipment are being studied.

Standard rail, weights:
  Main lines: 94 and 127 lb per yd *(46.9 and 63 kg/m)*
  Branch lines: 76.6 and 92.7 lb per yd *(38 and 46 kg/m)*
Standard rail, lengths:
  Main lines: 24 and 30 m
  Branch lines: 15 and 18 m
Rail joints: 4-hole fishplates and bolts; and some welding.
Cross ties (sleepers): Hard and soft wood, 10 in × 6 in × 8 ft 6½ in *(250 × 150 × 2 600 mm)*
Cross ties spacing:
  Main lines: 2 680 per mile *(1 666 per km)*
  Branch lines: 2 145 per mile *(1 333 per km)*
Rail fastenings: Coach screws (on hard wood), coach screws and soleplates (on soft wood), Ribbed soleplates and bolts, Ribbed soleplates and curved stirrups of spring steel. Elastic fastening with curved stirrups for both wood and concrete sleepers, the clips fitting into a cast iron housing having two pins glued into concrete sleeper or pressed into wood. Cast iron chairs and bolts. Pads under rails are grooved rubber 4 mm thick or wooden wearing plates 4 mm thick.
  Experimental sections laid with "Zig-zag" concrete block and steel tube track construction
Filling: Gravel or broken stone, ⅜ in to 3⅛ in *(10 to 80 mm)*
Minimum thickness under sleeper: 7⅛ in *(200 mm)*
Max curvature: 5.8° = min rad of 984 ft *(300 m)*
Max gradient, compensated: 2% = 1 in 50 (on Sittard-Hertzogenrath line)
Max gradient, uncompensated: 1.43% = 1 in 70 (on Sittard-Hertzogenrath line)
Longest continuous gradient: 5.5 miles *(8.85 km)* of 1 in 300 grade with three curves of 4 921 ft *(1 500 m)* radius.
Worst combination of gradient and curvature: 1 in 175 (0.57%) gradient with curves of 984 ft *(300 m)* radius.
Gauge widening on sharpest curve: 7mm.
Super elevation on sharpest curve: 4.72 in *(120 mm)* on track in gravel. 5.90 in *(150 mm)* on track in broken stone.
Rate of slope of super elevation:
  Speed higher than V 105 km/h: 1 in 8V.
  Speed 105 km/h or less: 1 in 1 100 with minimum of 1 in 600.
Altitude, max: 596 ft *(181.7 m)* on Simpelveld-German Frontier section.
Max axle loading: 21 tons.
Max permitted speed:
  Passenger trains: 87 mph *(140 km/h)*.
  Freight trains: 37 mph *(60 km/h)*.
  Fast freight trains: 56 mph *(90 km/h)*.

NEW LINE CONSTRUCTION

Netherlands railways' has approved 13 recommendations for engineering design of the 27 km Schipol airport-Leiden section of the Schipol line. The recommendations were contained in a report entitled 'Realisering Schiphollijn' drawn up by a joint government/NS committee in 1977.

Crude oil train from Schoomebeck oilfield hauled by double Alsthom diesel-electric locomotives with total output of 1 700 hp

Four-car electric trainset nicknamed 'Hondekop' (Dogshead) used for intercity services

DIESEL LOCOMOTIVES

Class	Axle Arrangement	Transmission	Rated Power hp	Max. lbs (kg)	Tractive Effort Continuous at lbs (kg)	mph (km/h)	Max. Speed mph (km/h)	Wheel Dia. ins (mm)	Total Weight Tons	Length ft ins (mm)	No. Built	Year first Built	Builders: Mechanical Parts	Engine & Type	Transmission
2400 2500	Bo-Bo	Elec.	850	36 400 (16 500)	12 830 (8 090)	12 (20)	50 (80)	39⅜ (1 000)	60	41' 1" (12 520)	129	1954	Alsthom	SACM, V 12 SHR	Alsthom
2200 2300	Bo-Bo	Elec.	900	40 800 (18 500)	27 000 (12 250)	8.7 (14)	62 (100)	37⅜ (950)	74	45' 11½" (14 010)	150	1955	Allan Schneider	Stork, Schneider (lic Superior) 40 C-LX-8	Heemaf Westinghouse
451-460	C	Elec.	330	19 000 (8 600)	11 902 (5 400)	6 (10)	37 (60)	43¼ (1 100)	38	29' 2½" (8 900)	6	1956	Werkspoor	Thomassen, 6 Fe	Westinghouse, Schneider-Westinghouse
501-545 601-665 701-715	C	Elec.	400	32 100 (14 600)	14 436 (6 550)	6 (10)	(30)	48⅜ (1 230)	47	29' 9" (9 070)	35	1949	English Electric	EEC, 6 KT	EEC
200-300	Bo	Elec.	72				60 (98)	39⅜ (1 000)	21	23' 7½" (7 220)	148	1934-1951	Schneider-Werkspoor	Stork, Henhelo	Heemaf: E.T.I.; Hengelo or Slikkerveer

ELECTRIC LOCOMOTIVES AND RAILCARS

Class	Axle Arrangement	Line Current	Rated Output hp	Max. lbs (kg)	Tractive Effort (Full Field) Continuous at lb (kg)	mph (km/hr)	Max. Speed mph (km/hr)	Wheel dia. ins (mm)	Weight tonnes	Length ft in (mm)	No. Built	Year Built	Builders Mechanical Parts	Electrical Equipment
1500	Co-Co	1 500 V dc OH	3 220	45 000 (20 400)	20 000 (9 100)	44.2 (78)	84 (135)	43 (1 092)	69	59' 0" (17 983)	6	1954	BR	
1300	Co-Co	1 500 V dc OH	3 870	51 000 (23 100)	28 600 (13 000)	31 (50)	84 (135)	49¼ (1 250)	111	62' 2" (18 950)	15	1952	Alsthom	Alsthom
1200	Co-Co	1 500 V dc OH	3 000	43 500 (19 700)	22 400 (10 200)	31 (50)	84 (135)	43¼ (1 100)	108	59' 4" (18 080)	25	1951	Werkspoor-Baldwin	Heemaf-Westinghouse
1100	Bo-Bo	1 500 V dc OH	2 580	34 200 (15 500)	14 300 (6 500)	31 (50)	84 (135)	49¼ (1 250)	80	42' 7½" (12 980)	58	1950	Alsthom	Alsthom
1000	(IA) -Bo (AI)	1 500 V dc OH	3 800	36 500 (16 600)	22 600 (19 300)	31 (50)	84 (135)	61 (1 550)	100	52' 2½" (16 220)	9	1948	S.L.M.; Werkspoor	Oerlikon; Heemaf Smit
3001/3035 (MP)	Bo-Bo	1 500 V dc OH					87 (140)		52	86' 4" (26 400)	35	1965	Werkspoor	Werkspoor
Electric Railcars 401-438 441-483 801-965 (EL2)	(2-Bo)+ (Bo-2)	1 500 V dc OH					86 (140)		85	170' 3" (52 140)	117	1966/71	Werkspoor Talbot	Heemaf/Smit
502/531 (ELD4)	(2-2)+ (Bo-Bo)+ (Bo-Bo)	1 500 V dc OH					86 (140)		168	331' 7" (101 240)	30	1964/65	Werkspoor	Heemaf/Smit
SGM (EL2) 2001-2015	Bo-Bo Bo-Bo	1 500 V dc OH	1 720			(950)	80 (125)		106	(52 200)	15	1975/76	Talbot SIG	Oerlikon Holec
ICI 111 4001-4007	Bo-Bo (2-2)+ (2-2)	1 500 V dc OH							114	80 600	7	1977	Talbot Wegmann	Heemaf/Smit TCO

Between Leiden and Warmond, where the Schipol line leaves the Den Haag-Haarlem route, there will be four tracks; the inner two will be reserved for Schipol services and will cross the existing Leiden to Haarlem track on a flyover. Maximum speed of the Leiden-Schipol airport section, due to open in 1981, will be 160 km/h and initially no freight trains will use the line; plans nevertheless envisage container trains running to a future terminal at the airport. Stations will be built to serve Hoofddorp and Nieuw Vennep. Hoofddorp will become a turnround point for stopping trains from Amsterdam at a later stage.

Main service on the Schipol line will consist of four trains per hour formed of 160 km/h IC-III stock with a journey time between Leiden and Schipol of 13 min.

Automatic block signalling and standard NS automatic train control with continuous cab signalling will be installed. Sound barriers will be built at selected locations where the line passes close to housing developments.

The Amsterdam-Schipol airport section of the line is due to open in December 1978. The cost of the whole work, estimated at 590 million florins in 1972, is necessarily influenced by increases in wages and prices. There may be modifications in the programme of conditions imposed from outside such as, for example, new requirements with regard to the fitting of the railway track into the countryside. For this reason, the budget is reviewed each year and submitted for approval to the Ministry of Communications and Highways. At the end of 1975 this budget was 742 million florins, based on prices at the beginning of 1974. This total comprises: 485 million for the section from the south end of the tunnel to the Museumplein, 215 million for the part from the tunnel to Leiden and 42 million for the work at The Hague. No decision has yet been taken concerning financing; provisionally 50 per cent are imputed to the State and 50 per cent to the NS.

On March 28, 1977, Netherlands Minister of Transport Mr T. E. Westerterp granted approval for construction of the *Sneltram* route from the city centre of Utrecht to Nieuwegein, a group of developing towns southwest of the city. Completion of the project is planned for 1981.

The route starts at NS' Utrecht Central station and runs through the southern part of Utrecht before crossing the Amsterdam-Rhine canal on a new 130 m bridge in a short section of line in relatively open country. It continues southwest to Nieuwegein Stadscentrum where it divides, one route serving new housing developments around the old town of Vreeswijk and the other running to IJsselstein where similar dormitory housing is springing up. There will be 21 stations or halts on the route.

Initial construction work will begin in Nieuwegein and the first section of track completed will be used as a test section to try out all components as well as rolling stock. Work on the Amsterdam-Rhine canal bridge will begin next year. Other major civil engineering works will be a bridge over the A2 Utrecht-Den Bosch motorway which divides the centre of Nieuwegein from IJsselstein, and the Leidsevertunnel. NS will be responsible for construction and will hand over the completed line for operation by the Westnederland bus company.

Rolling stock for the line is still under study but the West German Stadtbahnwagen B remains a likely choice.

The Netherlands Government has approved the construction of a new railway line between Amsterdam, Almere and Lelystad, two new towns in the former Zuider Zee. This line will be 50 km long.

Purchase of land will begin in 1978 and work will start in 1980.

The line will be completed as far as Almere by 1985 and will reach Lelystad in 1990. Cost of the line is estimated at 306 million guilders.

New three-car inter-city trainset—one of seven prototypes delivered by Talbot in 1976.

Dutch-Belgian push-pull unit for passenger-service Amsterdam—Brussels vv, suited for 1 500 and 3 000 V dc

Two-car electric trainset type 'plan V' used for stopping trains in densely populated areas. Max speed 140 km/h

NEW ZEALAND
NEW ZEALAND GOVERNMENT RAILWAYS
Bunny Street, Wellington

General Manager: T. M. Hayward
Deputy General Manager: L. G. Keys
Assistant General Manager, Finance and Administration: F. D. Daly
Assistant General Manager, Operating and Commercial: R. W. D. Thompson
Assistant General Manager, Personnel: I. E. Trask
Chief Mechanical Engineer: K. M. Frederic
Chief Civil Engineer: J. S. Berry
Chief Traffic Manager: B. B. McKeown
Director, Finance and Accounts Branch: A. J. Whitburn
Director, Management Services: A. E. McQueen
Director, Economic Planning and Research: J. G. Beckett
Director, Stores Branch: J. D. M. Lundie
Director, Road Services Branch: F. H. Marvelly
Commercial Manager: R. G. Cragg
Publicity and Advertising Manager: I. G. Holland
Director, Land Division: L. S. Harding
Director, Catering Services: P. W. Burton

Gauge: 1.067 m.
Route length: 4 716 km.

TRAFFIC	31 March 1977	31 March 1976
Total freight		
Gross tonne-km	8 922 137 000	8 638 392 000
Total freight tonnage	13 601 372	13 193 019
Total passenger		
Gross tonne-km	1 000 998 000	1 089 042 000

Long-distance passenger journeys decreased by 31.7 per cent to 1 288 593, while suburban journeys decreased by 5.3 per cent to 1 718 954. Long-distance passenger revenue increased from $5 589 421 to $5 577 086. Suburban passenger revenue increased from $3 409 371 to $4 348 100.

Freight revenue for the year increased by $64 027 488 to $189 211 283 due to the increase in traffic and tariff. Freight tonnage carried during the year rose by 405 353 tonnes to 13 601 372 tonnes.

FINANCES	31 March 1977	31 March 1976
Revenues	$248 068 785	$170 206 584
Expenses	$260 072 954	$233 160 088

Gross revenue earned by New Zealand Railways rose by 45.7 per cent to $248 069 785. Gross expenditure exceeded the previous year's figure by $29 912 866 (11.5 per cent)—the result of dearer fuel, higher wages, stores and material costs.

Final operating loss for the year was $12 003 169. After adding interest charges on loans from the International Bank for reconstruction and development and on overseas credits for capital equipment the net loss for the year was, on the whole undertaking $17 200 618.

LOCOMOTIVE POWER AND ROLLING STOCK
Locomotives
Number of locomotives in service at 31 March 1977:

	Line-haul	Shunting
Steam	2	—
Electric	14	—
Diesel-electric	314	90
Diesel-hydraulic	—	65
Diesel-mechanical	—	36

(Diesel tractors under 200 hp are not included in the above list).

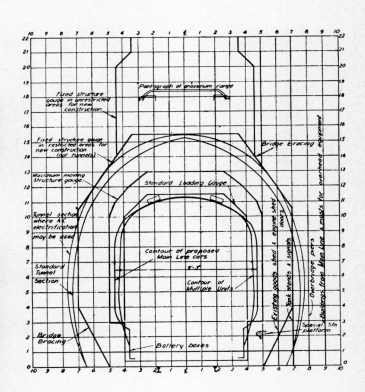

Number of railcars, electric: 49 (multiple units).
Number of railcars, diesel: 17 (14 being converted to passenger cars).
Number of trailer cars, electric: 79 (multiple units).
Number of passenger train coaches: 375.
Number of freight cars: 30 379 (also 4 mail vans, 4 generator vans, and 290 brake vans).
Number of containers (in service and on order)
Bulk liquid: 10
Thermal liquid: 28
General box: 32
Bulk flour: 56
General open: 2
Thermal box: 722
Bulk line: 25

SIGNAL AND TRAIN CONTROL INSTALLATIONS

New Signalling Installations: In the North Island loop extensions and resignalling was carried out on some loops on the North Island main trunk and the Stratford-Okahukura line. Resignalling of the Kereone-Putaruru section of the Kinleith Branch was completed. This section is now controlled by a new CTC machine in Hamilton replacing a CTC machine in Morrinsville.

In the South Island Spring Creek, on the main north line, was resignalled and is now operated by remote control from Blemheim. Studholme on the main south line was connected to power interlocking in preparation for CTC control from Christchurch. During the year 15 new level crossing warning devices, consisting of 4 half arm barriers and 11 flashing lights and bells, giving a total of 725 level crossings throughout the country protected by these warning devices.

ELECTRIFICATION

Plans for the electrification of NZR's North Island main trunk line were revived in 1977. Electrification was previously considered in the 1950s but advocates of dieselization won the argument for the best replacement for steam traction. Now, because of problems caused by the oil crisis, a committee has been formed to reconsider electrifying the 685 km line. Cost is expected to be about $NZ 100 million. NZR is known to want to electrify the Taumarunui to Taihape section as soon as possible. It is the most tortuous section of the line and includes the well-known Raurimu Spiral.

CONTAINER AND SEMI-TRAILER OPERATIONS

Rail facilities have been geared to handle all containers of ISO specifications, including refrigerated and insulated containers, and large numbers are now carried by rail. These containers, when loaded on normal flat-top wagons, can travel throughout the New Zealand railways system except on a few secondary lines with restricted overhead clearance where special bogie wagons have been constructed to permit the transport of ISO containers.

Many special container wagons are now in service or on order. There has been a considerable increase in the volume of container traffic handled, including regular daily services of freight consolidator containers between Auckland, Wellington and Christchurch, Dunedin and Invercargill.

NZ Railways operates four roll-on roll-off ferry vessels between Wellington in the North Island and Picton in the South Island. This sea service facilitates the movement of containers between the two Islands.

TERMINALS

There are no special rail container terminals but gantry-type lifting appliances are provided at Auckland, Huntly, Cambridge, Rotorua, Wanganui, Marton, Ahuriri (Napier), Gisborne, Ngauranga (Wellington), Spring Creek (Blenheim), Christchurch, Dunedin and Invercargill to facilitate the road/rail transfer of containers. Gantries are to be installed at Hamilton and Mangatainoka during 1976.

A new colour scheme is planned for NZR locomotives: picture shows a Dx locomotive in its new colours at the head of a mixed freight train.

NZR Silver Star sleeper express hauled by a Dx class locomotive arriving in Wellington at the end of its overnight journey from Auckland.

NZR freight train hauled by a Da class locomotive.

Wellington—Napier 'Endeavour' daylight express train, headed by a 1 425-hp Da class A1A-A1A General Motors diesel-electric locomotive, at Eaipukurau.

Wellington—Auckland express freight of Zp class covered wagons and containers travels north near Te Kuiti headed by a 2 750-hp Dx class Co-Co General Electric diesel-electric locomotive

DIESEL LOCOMOTIVES

Class	Axle Arrangement	Transmission	Rated Power hp	Max lb (kg)	Tractive Effort Continuous at lb (kg)	mph (km/h)	Max. Speed mph (km/h)	Wheel Dia. in (mm)	Total Weight Tons	Length ft in (mm)	No. Built	Year first Built	Builders: Mechanical Parts	Engine & Type	Transmission
Dx	Co-Co	Elec	2 750/ 2 600		46 500 (21 090)	17 (27.4)	75 (120)	37 (940)	96	55' 6" (16 916)	15 34	1972 1975	GE (USA)	GE 7FDL12 D3	GE (USA)
Da	A1A-A1A	,,	1 425/ 1 310	32 480 (14 730)	28 000 (12 700)	14.7 (23.6)	60 (96)	Driver 40 (1 016) Idler 30 (762)	76	43' 0" (13 106)	30	1955	GM	GM567C	GM
				,,	,,	,,	,,	,,	78	44' 6" (13 564)	10	1957	Clyde-GM	,,	,,
,,	,,	,,	,,	33 460 (15 180)	30 600 (15 180)	12.0 (19.3)	,,	Driver 40 (1 016) Idler 33 (838)	76	43' 0" (13 106)	72 34	1961/6GM 1967			
Db	A1A-A1A	,,	950/875		22 050 (10 227)	12.0 (19.3)	60 (96)	Driver 40 (1 016) Idler 30 (762)	67.5	43' 0" (13 100)	17	1965	,,	GM567CR	,,
De	Bo-Bo	,,	660/630	28 600 (12 970)	12 700 (5 760)	15.4 (24.8)	55 (88)	36½ (927)	51	35' 0" (10 668)	15	1951	English Electric	English Electric 6SRKT	English Electric
Dg	A1A-A1A	,,	750/682	25 600 (11 600)	20 200 (9 160)	10.1 (16.2)	,,	Driver 37 (950) Idler 37 (940)	69	45' 0" (13 716)	42	1955	,,	English Electric 6SRKT	,,
Di	Co-Co	,,	1 012/ 923	40 000 (18 200)	29 500 (13 400)	9.0 (14.5)	60 (96)	37 (940)	63	45' 3" (13 792)	5	1967	English Electric Australia	English Electric 6CSRKT/Mk 2	,,
Dj	Bo-Bo-Bo	,,	1 050/ 990		28 900 (13 100)	10 (16)	62 (100)	37 (940)	63	46' 3" (14 100)	62	1967	Mitsubishi Heavy Ind.	Caterpillar D 398 TA	Mitsubishi
Ds	C (0-6-0)	Mech	204	14 300 (6 500)	14 300 (6 490)	4.0 (6.4)	30 (48)	39¾ (1 010)	26	22' 0½" (6 718)	16	1949/ 1955	Drewry Car Co	Gardner 8L3	Hyd coupling Type 23 Epycyclic gearbox CA5 Final Drive gearbox RF11.
Dsa	C (0-6-0)	Mech	,,	16 500 (7 500)	16 500 (7 500)	3.47 (5.6)	26.42 (42)	,,	29.5	25' 1" (7 645)	20	1953	,,	,,	,,
,,	,,	Hyd*	304	28 500 (13 000)	13 200 (6 000)	7.2 (11.6)	20 (32)	,,	30	23' 11¼" (7 296)	10	1956	W. G. Bagnall Ltd.	Caterpillar D343	Twin Disc
,,	,,	Mech	250	16 800 (7 620)	16 800 (7 620)	4.75 (7.6)	25.65 (41)	,,	,,	23' 6½" (7 175)	9	1954	Hunslet	National M4AA6	Hunslet clutch and gearbox
,,	,,	Hyd	,,	21 550 (9 770)	12 490 (5 670)	6.38 (10.3)	25.65 (41)	,,	,,	,,	6	1957	,,	,,	Hunslet torque converter & gearbox
,,	,,	,,	315	20 000 (9 100)	17 000 (7 700)	4 (6.4)	35 (56)	39¾" (1 010)	30	27' 10¼" (8 490)	12	1967	Mitsubishi Heavy Ind.	Caterpillar D 343 T	Niigata torque conv DBS 115; Mitsubishi final drive
Dsb	C (0-6-0)	Hyd*	335	26 300 (11 900)	13 200 (6 000)	6.7 (10.8)	20 (32)	,,	36.6	25' 4⅞" (7 744)	25	1954	Drewry Car Co	Caterpillar D343	Twin Disc
,,	v	,,	375	23 000 (10 400)	18 000 (8 200)	4.5 (7.2)	35 (56)	39¾ (1 010)	37.5	27' 10¼" (8 490)	3	1967	Mitsubishi Heavy Ind.	Caterpillar D 343 TA	Niigata torque converter DBS 115
Dsc	Bo-Bo	Elec	420/370	22 700 (10 300)	10 400 (4 720)	8.5 (13.6)	40 (64)	37 (940)	40.5	35' 0" (10 668)	18	1959	A.E.I.	Rolls Royce C6SFL	A.E.I.
,,	,,	,,	,,	,,	,,	,,	,,	,,	,,	,,	52	1963/7NZR†		Leyland 902/903	,,

* Originally provided with National Engines, hydraulic couplings and Self Changing Gear Co's epicyclic gearboxes. They were re-equipped in 1964-66.
† 35 locos re-equipped with Cummins NT-855-L3 engines in 1976.

ELECTRIC LOCOMOTIVES

Class	Axle Arrangement	Line Current	Rated Output hp	Max lb (kg)	Tractive Effort (Full Field) Continuous at lb (kg)	mph (km/hr)	Max. Speed mph (km/hr)	Wheel dia. ins (mm)	Weight tonnes	Length ft in (mm)	No. Built	Year Built	Builders Mechanical Parts	Electrical Equipment
Ea	Bo-Bo	1 500 V dc	1 285	23 000 (10 460)	18 000 (8 200)	22.5 (36)	45 (72)	40 (1 016)	54	38' 0" (11 582)	5	1968	Tokyo Shibaura	Tokyo Shibaura
Ed	2-D-1	,,	1 240	34 300 (15 560)	11 600 (5 260)	29 (46.6)	55 (88)	,,	86	43' 2" (13 157)	2	1937	Eng Elec & NZR	,,
Ew	Bo-Bo-Bo	,,	1 800	42 000 (19 050)	18 600 (8 440)	30 (48.2)	60 (96)	36½ (927)	75	59' 0" (17 983)	7	1952	,,	,,

EQUIPMENT
For many years New Zealand Railways have used containers on their air link between the North and the South Islands. These containers are 2.26 m long × 1.9 m wide × 1.83 m high.

RAILWAY DEVELOPMENTS
Many new wagons were placed in service including "Fm" class guard's vans. These vans were built by Mitsubishi in Japan.

A prototype pedestal suspension system was successfully tested at speed over 120 km/h on a modified "Ks" wagon. This modification led to the building of a four wheeled flat top multipurpose wagon ("Nx"1) carried on the same pedestal suspension.

"Aratika", one of the four rail ferries, was sent to Hong Kong for conversion from a freight to a passenger vessel.

"Hole-through" was achieved in the 9 km Kaimai tunnel, part of a deviation being built under Ministry of Works control, designed to give better access to the Bay of Plenty. Work is still in progress on the 8 km deviation between Mangaweka and Utiku on the North Island main trunk line. This project will, when completed, enable the line to bypass a very difficult section with poor alignment and steep gradients.

NEW LINES PROJECTED
Kaimai Deviation under construction: A 24.9 km line from Waharoa near Matamata in the Waikato through the 8.9 km Kaimai Tunnel to Apata north of Tauranga in the Bay of Plenty.

NEW RAIL LAID
Rail Weights:

Main Line	50 kg/m; 91 lb/yd, 85 lb/yd
Provincial Line	91 lb/yd, 85 lb/yd, 75 lb/yd, 70 lb/yd
Branch Lines	70 lb/yd, 55 lb/yd

Rail Laid:

Total Length	4 745 km
Total Welded	2 100 km
Total CWR	25 km
Longest length CWR	5.2 km
Relaid in New Rail (50 kg) 1976-77	75 km
Relaid in Second Hand Rail (85 & 91 lb)	32 km

Welding Method:
Flash Butt in Depot; Thermit in Field.
New rails are flash butt welded in depots into lengths of 76.8 m and transported to site for laying.
Short Rail in track may be thermit welded into similar lengths.
Continuous welded rail is now being formed on straight track by Thermit process with lapped expansion joints at extremities and epoxy glued insulated joints.

Sleepers:
Types & Use:
Australian hardwoods: All Lines (superseded by Pine)
NZ pinus softwood: All Lines
Concrete: Main lines only
Spacing:
Main line: Timber 600 mm, Concrete 750 mm
Other lines: Timber 650 mm
Fastenings:
Main lines:
Timber: Pandrol Spring fastenings on bed plates with rubber pads and nylon insulators. Clips, screw spikes, spring washers on double shoulder bedplates. Spring clips and screw spikes without bedplates.
Concrete: Pandrol Spring fastenings with rubber pads and nylon insulators.
Branch Lines:
Timber: Elastic Spikes, screws and dog spikes cascaded from higher ranking lines.
Laying Method:
Concrete: By NZR designed and built sleeper laying machine.
Timber: Laid manually either in face or by spotting.

Sleepers (cross ties):
Type: Australian hardwood, 9 inches by 4½ inches. NZ pinus softwood, 8 inches by 6 inches. Prestressed concrete 10 inch base × 7½ inches high all 7 feet (2 134 mm) long.
Sleeper spacing:
Main lines: Timber 600 mm. Concrete: 750 mm.
Branch lines: Timber 675 mm.

Rail fastenings (types used): Pandrol spring fastenings on rolled Pandrol steel bed-plates are the new construction standard for the North Island main trunk line. On new deviations and where face resleepering can be justified, concrete sleepers with Pandrol spring fastenings, rubber pads and nylon insulators are being used. Other current types of fastenings include double shoulder bed-plates with clips, screw spikes and spring washers, and spring clips and screw spikes without bed-plates. Light traffic lines are generally laid with elastic spikes, screws or dog spikes cascaded down from higher ranking lines.

Welded Rail

Total length of track laid at 31 March 1977	2 100 km
Length laid during 1976-77	75 km
Longest individual length of welded rail	1 761.2 m in open
	5.2 km in Otira Tunnel

Standard method of welding: Flash-butt (and Thermit) process.
Standard method of laying: Rails are flash-butt welded at depots into lengths of up to 252 ft *(76.8 m)* (6 × 42 ft) and after laying in open track the ends are fishplated. Joints permit partial expansion and contraction related to a mean temperature of 80 degrees F. In tunnels the ends are Thermit welded to form continuous rail, apart from insulated joints. In the Otira Tunnel a length of 5.2 km is in use. Continuous welded rail is now being adopted on open track by the same method, with lapped expansion joints at the extremities, and epoxy glued insulated track joints.
Rail in use is mostly 91 lb/yd, but small quantities of 100, 90, 85 and 72 lb/yd, have also been laid. 50 kg/m rail is being ordered for future relaying on main lines.
Rails are secured to softwood sleepers, 7 ft × 8 in × 6 in, with double-shoulder bedplates, screw spikes, spring washers, and clips on heavy traffic lines, and screw spikes, with spring clips without bedplates on other lines. Pandrol bedplates and fastenings on softwood sleepers have been adopted for new main line relaying with continuous welded rail. 5 mm. synthetic rubber pads are being added between rail and bedplate.

New Zealand Railways' "UKX" class multi-purpose flat-top bogie wagon, 100 of which were brought into use in year ending 31 March 1976.

Auckland—Wellington "Silver Star" sleeping car express train, headed by a 2 750 hp "Dx" class Co-Co locomotive, arriving at Wellington station at the end of its 423 mile journey.

NIGERIA

NIGERIAN RAILWAY CORPORATION
Ebute Metta

Telephone: Lagos 44302

Chairman: Alhaji I. Dasuki
General Manager: T. I. O. Nzegwu
Assistant General Manager, Staff: F. M. Alade
Assistant General Manager, Works: S. O. Omotsho
Public Relations Officer: J. B. O. Holloway

Mechanical Engineer's Department
  Chief Mechanical Engineer: T. I. Awosika
  Deputy Chief Mechanical Engineers:
  Carriage and Wagon: T. O. Griffin
  Locomotives: M. A. Lawal
  Electrical Engineer: V. E. N. Allanch

Civil Engineer's Department:
  Chief Civil Engineer: S. M. O. Denloye
  Deputy Chief Engineer: A. O. Adewoyin
  Bridge Engineer: C. O. Idowu
  Project Engineer: K. S. Kamlani
  Signal Engineer: S. L. O. Ojekwe

Operating and Commercial Department:
  Chief Superintendent: O. D. Oshosanwo
  Deputy Chief Superintendents:
  Operating: F. O. Onanuga
  Commercial: T. S. Agbabiaka

Accounts Department:
  Chief Accountant: A. Oyelowo
  Deputy Chief Accountant: C. O. A. Smith
  Data Processing Manager: T. O. Keleko

Medical Department:
  Principal Medical Officer: Dr. W. G. Ogunyemi
  Hospital Superintendent: Dr. B. C. Anyakwo

Gauge: 1.067 m.
Route length: 3 523 km.

During the next five years, the Nigeria Railway Corporation is proposing to change the gauge from 1.067 m to standard 1.435 m track, on the major lines of its network. This involves re-laying 3 500 km of lines, some extensions, and replacement of most of the rolling stock.

Two groups signed contracts in Lagos on July 11, 1977, for survey and design of the first two stages of Nigerian Railways' standard-gauge network. Ferronigeria, a consortium of Fougerolle SA (France), Laing International (Britain), Philipp Holzmann (West Germany) and Impresa Astaldi Estero (Italy), has been allotted the Port Harcourt—Makurdi contract, while the Oturkpo—Ajaokuta steelworks line goes to the Italian group Italraco. Survey and design work on the two contracts is expected to take 15 months.

The two sections will make up a 685 km 1 435 mm gauge route linking the new steelworks complex being developed at Ajaokuta with the Enugu coalfields and Port Harcourt; this is the first stage of NR's plan for eventual reconstruction of the entire 1 067 mm gauge network to standard-gauge. The Port Harcourt-Makurdi section is to be double track.

Associated contracts awarded at the same time include a £9 m design and site investigation contract to Hidro-service (Brazil) for the Benue river bridge at Makurdi, while Sofrerail is to carry out a survey of traffic patterns.

Meanwhile, it seemed possible at the end of 1977 that Indian Railways might take over management of the Nigerian system for a five year period. Rail India Technical and Economic Services (RITES) produced a study during 1975/76 and a small team of Indian engineers revisted Nigeria during 1977 to identify actual requirements.

TRAFFIC

	1972	1973
Ton-km ('000s)	1 200 206	1 349 796
Passenger-km ('000s)	955 731	1 024 168

FINANCES	1973/4	Forecast 1974/5
Revenues	N25 799 291	N20 860 000
Expenses	N42 324 970	N52 542 690

MOTIVE POWER
New locomotives taken into service in 1974 included 40 MLW and 22 Brush Diesel Electrics.

Class: 1701
Type: Diesel Electric 1 500 hp
Wheel (or axle) arrangement: 1-Co-Co-1
Max speed: 60 mph (96 km/h)
Dimensions: 58' 6'' Inside Pulling faces, width 9' 11''
Weight: 99 Tons 16 Cwt (101 396.8 kg) Height 12' 10''
Number of units: 40 out of 54
Builders: MLW
Tractive Effort: 46 500 lb (21 227.145 kg)

Class: 921
Type: Diesel Electric
Wheel (or axle) arrangement: 0-6-0
Max speed: 15 mph (24 km/h)
Dimensions:
Weight: 39 Tons 7 cwt (40 00 kg)
Number of Units: 22
Builders: Brush Electric
Tractive Effort: 18 800 lb (8 527.145 kg)

By the end of 1974 the motive power fleet included 133 mainline steam locomotives (43 shunting); 130 mainline diesel electrics (39 shunting); eight mainline diesel-hydraulic locomotives.

ROLLING STOCK
  Number of freight wagons: 5 738.
  Number of passenger coaches: 55.

A Japanese consortium, headed by Nippon Sharyo Seizo Kaisha, Ltd and trader Mitsui & Co, received a Nigerian order for 250 coal freight cars, totalling Y4 500 million, including Y400 million for parts, during 1976. Settlement will be 20 per cent in advance payments and 80 per cent in letters of credit. Delivery will be completed between May and August 1977. The Japanese consortium was also negotiating with Nigeria on its supply of 325 general freight cars and 160 passenger coaches.

NORWAY

NORWEGIAN STATE RAILWAYS
Norges Statsbaner (N.S.B.), Storgt. 33 Oslo

Telephone: 20 95 50

Central Administration
  Chairman of the Board: Ole Haugum
  General Managers: Edvard Heiberg, Robert F. Nordén
  Public Relations: Odd Kjell Skjegstad

Administration and Finance:
  Director, Personnel: Odd Wessel Larsen
  Director, Purchase and Stores: Oddvar Bø
  Director, Finance: B. Egeland-Eriksen

Operation and Commerce:
  Chief Director: Knut Skuland
  Director, Operations: Finn W. Westlie
  Director, Commerce: Martin Killi

Engineering:
  Chief Director: Eivvinn Lovseth
  Director, Way and Works: J. Jarnaes
  Director, Rolling Stock: A. Øhrn
  Director, Electrification: R. Sørvik

District Administration:
  Oslo: Trygve Meinstad
  Drammen: Lorentz H. Aas
  Hamar: Sverre Saetersdal
  Trondheim: Harald K. Henriksen
  Stavanger: Lars Aarrestad
  Bergen: Per Engen
  Kristiansand: Sig. Andreassen
  Narvik: Erik B. Raae

Gauge: 1.435 m.
Route length: 4 241 km.

TRAFFIC	1974	1975	1976
Total freight ton-km (mill)	2 885.5	2 560.8	2 709.4
Total freight tonnage (1 000)	31 329.3	25 061.5	28 755.7
Total passenger-km (mill)	1 883.9	1 948.2	1 997.1
Total passengers carried (mill)	32.6	33.5	32.7

FINANCES	1974	1975	1976
Revenues (mill Norw crowns)	1 125.4	1 251.9	1 443.5
Expenses (mill Norw crowns)	1 360.5	1 570.7	1 895.8

MOTIVE POWER
At the end of 1976 NSB's motive power park consisted of 158 electric train locomotives, 89 diesel train locomotives, 138 electric motor coaches, 48 diesel motor coaches, and 184 shunting engines and maintenance tractors.

Norwegian State Railways has purchased six electric trainsets with a maximum speed of 130 km/h. The six-car trains, each with a capacity of 350 passengers, will be put into service in 1981 between Oslo and Trondheim, reducing journey time from seven to six hours. Average speeds will be raised to about 110 km/h. NSB's plans envisage introduction of tilting trains over the same route about four years later; these would allow up to 40 min to be cut from the 6 hour schedules. In the meantime an intensive test programme to determine the best design of tilting rolling stock will be carried out. Earlier

3 600-hp Bo-Bo electric locomotive built in Norway under licence from Brown Boveri

Class El 16 locomotive delivered in 1977/78 by Strommen and ASEA

this year a rake of Swiss tilting coaches underwent trials on NSB routes.

ROLLING STOCK
Passenger coaches in service total: 920, freight wagons: 8 711.

TRACK
Extensive construction and building work is in progress at the railway tunnel beneath Oslo, scheduled for opening in 1979, and at Oslo new central station.
Rail, types and weights: s. 54 kg/n, s. 49 kg/n, 40 kg/n.
Sleepers (cross ties) type: Concrete 160 000, Wood 60 000.
Thickness: 6.7 in *(17 cm)*; 5.5 in *(14 cm)*
Spacing: 25.6 in *(65 cm)*; 23.6 in.-25.6 in *(60* and *65 cm)*.
Rail fastenings (types used): Pandrol; Hey-Back.
Welded rail:
Total length of track laid 31 December 1974: 112 miles *(180 km)*.
Length laid during 1973: 826 miles *(1 330 km)*.
Standard method of welding: Thermit.

Rail fastenings: On main lines the principal fastenings to wood sleepers are Hey-Back and Deenik. Pandrol fastenings have been adopted as standard fastenings on concrete sleepers. On the new Bergen-Tunestveit line, and in long tunnels where UIC54 and S64 rails are used, the fastening is elastic double-shaft railspikes on hardwood sleepers-without baseplates.
On branch lines the fastenings consist mainly of dog spikes, wedge plates and Hey-Back.

Pads under rails: With Hey-Back fastenings a thin, 0.05 inch *(1.25 mm)* asphalt impregnated pad (Fjeldhammer Brug) is inserted between rail and baseplate.
With "Pandrol" fastenings a 0.19 in *(5 mm.)* thick rubber pad is inserted between rail and concrete sleeper.
As a general rule pads are not used under rails except with Hey-Back fastenings.

Welded rail: At 31 December 1976, the total length of track laid with welded rail was 1 840 km, the length laid during the year being 170 km.
Rails are pre-welded at depot by flash-butt method. Site welding into continuous length is generally thermit.
Continuous welded rail is used in tunnels longer than 500 m, the longest in tunnel being 11 km.
Several continuous welded rails in the open are more than 100 km long and the longest continuous welded rail is more than 200 km.
Sleepers used in welded track are:—

Under rail types	*Material*	*Thickness*	*Width*	*Length*
S35, S49	Soft Wood (fir)	5.5 in *(140 mm)*	9.84 in *(250 mm)*	8 ft 2.4 in *(2 500 mm)*
UIC54, S64	Hardwood (beech)	6.3 in *(160 mm)*	10.24 in *(260 mm)*	8 ft 6.4 in *(2 600 mm)*
UIC54, S64	Concrete	6.3 in *(160 mm)*	11.0 in *(280 mm)*	7 ft 6.6 in *(2 300 mm)*

It is intended to continue the laying of long continuous welded rail in main line track.

ELECTRIFICATION
Total electrified route length on 31 December 1976: 1 516 miles *(2 440 km)*
Total electrified track length on 31 December 1976: 1 954 miles *(3 144 km)*.
System of electrification: 15 kV 1/16 2/3.

SIGNAL AND TRAIN CONTROL INSTALLATIONS
New signal installations (1974):
Type: NSI 63.
Route length: 44 miles *(71 km)*.
Location: Vikersund-Hønefoss and Fredrikstad-Halden.
Supplier: a/s Elektrisk Bureau, Oslo.

ELECTRIC LOCOMOTIVES

Class	*Axle Arrangement*	*Line Current*	*Rated Output hp*	*Max* lb *(kg)*	*Tractive Effort (Full Field) Continuous at* lb *(kg)*	mph *(km/hr)*	*Max Speed* mph *(km/hr)*	*Wheel dia.* ins *(mm)*	*Weight* tonnes	*Length* ft in *(mm)*	*No. Built*	*Year Built*	*Builders: Mechanical Parts*	*Builders: Electrical Equipment*
El-8	1-Do-1	15 kV 1/16⅔ ac	2 830	35 700 *(16 200)*	19 000 *(8 650)*	52 *(83)*	68 *(110)*	43⅞ *(1 350)*	83	45′ 3¼″ *(13 800)*	16	1940-1949	Thunes	Norsk Electrisk; Brown Boveri
El-9	Bo-Bo	15 kV 1/16⅔ ac	970	22 700 *(10 300)*	13 700 *(6 200)*	22 *(36)*	37 *(60)*	39⅜ *(1 000)*	48	33′ 5½″ *(10 200)*	3	1947	Thunes	Norsk Electrisk; Brown Boveri
El-10	C	15 kV 1/16⅔ ac	700	23 400 *(10 600)*	11 700 *(5 300)*	17 *(27)*	28 *(45)*	43¼ *(1 100)*	47	31′ 6″ *(9 600)*	17	1949-1952	A.S.J.	ASEA
El-11	Bo-Bo	15 kV 1/16⅔ ac	2 280	35 280 *(14 300)*	17 640 *(7 800)*	44 *(71)*	62 *(105)*	40⅜ *(1 060)*	62	47′ 5″ *(14 450)*	40	1951-1964	Thunes	Norsk Electrisk; Brown Boveri
El-12	1-D+D-1	15 kV 1/16⅔ ac	6 520	99 200 *(45 000)*	8 157 *(3 700)*	31 *(60)*	47 *(75)*	53⅛ *(1 530)*	180	82′ 4″ *(26 490)*	4	1954-1957	Motala	ASEA
El-13	Bo-Bo	15 kV 1/16⅔ ac	3 600	41 900 *(19 000)*	28 700 *(13 000)*	43 *(69)*	62 *(100)*	53⅛ *(1 350)*	72	49′ 2½″ *(15 000)*	37	1957-1966	Thunes	Norsk Electrisk; Brown Boveri
El-14	Co-Co	15 kV 1/16⅔ ac	6 900	77 200 *(35 000)*	47 619 *(21 700)*	41 *(76)*	75 *(120)*	50 *(1 270)*	105	58′ 5″ *(17 740)*	31	1968-1973	Thunes	Norsk Electrisk; Brown Boveri
El-15	2 (Co-Co)	15 kV 1/16⅔ ac	14 700	171 600 *(78 000)*	111 480 *(53 400)*	44 *(71)*	75 *(120)*	49¼ *(1 250)*	132	130′ 4″ *(19 900 +19 900)*	3	1967	Thunes	ASEA -Per Kure
El-16	Bo-Bo	15 kV 1/16⅔ ac	6 040	72 311 (32 800)	45 194 (20 500)	48 (78)	81 (140)	51 (1 300)	80	(15 520)	6	1977-1978	Strømmen	ASEA

DIESEL LOCOMOTIVES

Class	*Axle Arrangement*	*Transmission*	*Rated Power* hp	*Max* lb *(kg)*	*Tractive Effort Continuous at* lb *(kg)*	mph *(km/h)*	*Max Speed* mph *(km/h)*	*Wheel Dia.* in *(mm)*	*Total Weight* Tons	*Length* ft ins *(mm)*	*No. Built*	*Year first Built*	*Builders: Mechanical Parts*	*Builders: Engine & Type*	*Builders: Transmission*
Di 2	C	Hyd	575 600	30 600 *(13 900)*	26 500 *(12 000)*	3.7 *(6)*	50 *(80)*	49¼ *(1 250)*	45	32′ 10″ *(10 000)*	6 33	1954	Thunes	MaK MS301A BMV-LT6	Voith
Di 3a	Co-Co	Elec	1 900	48 500 *(23 000)*	37 900 *(17 200)*	14 *(23)*	65 *(105)*	40 *(1 016)*	102	61′ 0″ *(18 590)*	32	1954-1969	NOHAB	GM 16-567C	GM-ASEA
Di 3b	(A1A)-	Elec	1 900	37 478 *(17 000)*	30 864 *(14 000)*	11 *(26)*	81 *(143)*	40 *(1 016)*	104	62′ 0″ *(18 900)*	3	1959	NOHAB	GM 16-567C	GM-ASEA

6 930-hp electric locomotive built in Norway by Thunes under SLM license

PAKISTAN

PAKISTAN RAILWAY

Shara-E-Sheikh Abdul Hameed Bin Badees, Lahore

Chairman, Railway Board: A. M. Akhoond
Chief Engineer (Survey and Constructions): S. S. A. Wahidi
Chief Mechanical Engineer: M. A. Aziz
Chief Mechanical Engineer (Carriage Factory Project): M. Rashid
Chief Operating Superintendent: Gul Abdullah
Chief Commercial Manager: A. B. Khan
Chief Controller of Stores: S. A. Hussain
Chief Controller of Purchase: S. M. Danial
Chief Personnel Officer: G. Abdullah
Chief Medical and Health Officer: Dr. A. H. Saeed
Chief Electrical Engineer: S. H. Nawab
Chief Officer (Administration and Budget): M. Siddique
Chief Officer (Research): S. A. Sasheed
Chief Superintendent (Watch and Ward): Rauf Ali
Chief Officer (Organisation and Research): M. A. Kahn
Chief Officer (Traffic): Muhammad Asghar
Financial Adviser and Chief Accounts Officer: A. Ahmed
Divisional Superintendents:
 Rawalpindi: Gul Abdullah
 Lahore: M. Nizamuddin
 Multan: H. M. A. Hakim
 Karachi: Ahmed Raza
 Quetta: S. Khan
 Sukkur: A. A. I. Vohra

A new five-year Rs 8 000 million development plan was announced in December 1977 for the period 1978/82. Major items of expenditure include: purchase of 133 diesel-electric locomotives; rebuilding of 60 locos and 25 diesel railcars; construction of 750 passenger coaches; and extension of the Lahore—Khanewal electrification to Samasatta (117 km). Emphasis has been laid on permanent way upgrading and renewal—some 1 200 km of track is to be relaid with heavier section rail and sleeper renewal carried out over 1 800 km. Five concrete sleeper plants are to be set up to reduce dependence on imported timber.

Construction of two important links is to be undertaken: The connection from Rawalpindi to Islamabad, is to be completed by March 1979 at a cost of Rs40 million. Major task, however, will be a 99 km line connecting Chishtian, on the Samasatta—Bahawalnagar branch, with both the Lodhran—Raiwaind line at Mandi Burewala, and the Karachi—Lahore main line at Chichawatni Road. Cost of construction is put at Rs240 million. Final location surveys have been completed and the line could open in 1983. Another essential project is provision of modern telecommunications to replace the existing open-line network. Core of the system will be a microwave link between Karachi and Rawalpindi, with branches to Quetta, Multan and Lahore. Outlying areas will be served by UHF links, while VHF radio will be provided at about 200 base stations and in 500 locomotives, giving voice communication between controllers and moving trains. Automatic block signalling will be installed between Hyderabad and Lodhran and tokenless block between Lodhran and Wazirabad. Total cost will be Rs372 million. Other important works will include strengthening or renewal of bridges; further expansion of marshalling yard capacity; and modernisation of rolling stock works and maintenance procedures.

The total expenditure of Rs8 000 million is more than double the figure originally budgetted for the period up to 1982-83. Foreign exchange element of the total is Rs4 800 million, for which further loans will have to be sought.

FINANCIAL

Pakistan Railways expects to earn Rs2 144.4 million from passenger and freight business during fiscal 1977/78—an increase of Rs451.4 million on the revised estimates for 1976/77. The improvement is due to growth in the level of business and increases in fares and freight charges. Passenger fare increases should yield Rs70 million in extra revenue while traffic growth is expected to add Rs74.1 million. Increased freight rates should realise Rs 135 million while expansion of business in line with national economic growth is expected to yield an extra Rs172.3 million.

MOTIVE POWER AND ROLLING STOCK

Pakistan Railways is to recondition 47 life-expired diesel locomotives following a pilot project in which four locomotives were reconditioned for half the cost of equivalent new units. The work will be carried out over the next two years and will provide the locomotives with a further 20 years of useful life.

An ambitious programme for the building of 750 passenger coaches in the Islamabad coach factory has been outlined by Pakistan Railways. Of the total, 58 will be supplied to Bangladesh under a recently-signed contract. The scheme would involve building 150 coaches a year for five years, at a cost of Rs. 1 120 million with a foreign exchange component of Rs. 300 million. Major imports would include steel sheet, train lighting equipment, axle boxes, roller bearings and other components. The Islamabad plant delivered 55 all-welded steel coaches during the last financial year (1975-76). Pakistan Railways expects to require 1 032 new coaches during the next five years if traffic projections prove correct.

NEW CONSTRUCTION

Engineering surveys and traffic forecasts for a Pakistan Railways' link between Fort Sandeman and Manzai were due to be completed by the end of 1977. The link would allow through running of narrow-gauge services from Boston along the Zhob river valley to Tank and Lakki Marwat. Pakistan Railways is also planning in the long term to convert the whole of the route to broad gauge to allow an alternative link from Baluchistan province to Northwest Frontier province other than the existing main line up the Indus valley. Economic viability of the scheme rests on opening up of magnesite and other mineral deposits along the route.

A new railway line is to be built between Dadu and Larkana, the then Prime Minister Mr Zuffikar Ali Bhutto announced in 1977. The line will run via Johi, Khairpur, Nathan Shah, Mehar, Nasirabad and Kambar.

Work began in May 1977 on a new railway passenger terminal in Karachi, Pakistan. Cost is estimated at Rs. 60 million ($US 6 100 000). The terminal will have nine new passenger platforms, a terminal building with modern facilities, and an administrative block. Once the terminal comes into operation, the existing cantonment and city station will handle only freight trains and suburban passenger traffic.

The Federal Communications Ministry has proposed a double-track rapid transit system costing Rs 1.3 billion as the solution to Karachi's transport problems. Called the Integrated Mass Rapid Transit System, the underground line will link Mereweather Tower with North Karachi via Saddar, Liaquatabad and North Nazimabad— the route with the highest traffic density. It will also be linked with the Karachi Circular Railway which will be improved and extended to North Karachi. According to the Ministry study, the present population of Karachi (4.5 million) will increase to 6.9 million by 1985 and 12.6 million by 2000. Peak hour traffic is expected to rise to between 30 000 and 40 000 an hour each way, on the route of the proposed rapid transit railway alone, by 1985. The annual recurring losses resulting from the lack of such a system are estimated at Rs86 million in 1985. The study recommended against increasing the number of buses in the city on the grounds that this would aggravate air pollution and result in more accidents.

Work started in 1978 on construction of a new rail link between Chichawatni—Mandi Burewala—Chishtian at an estimated cost of Rs234 million.

ELECTRIFICATION

A feasibility study for extension of electrification between Lahore and Samasatta was completed in 1975. Cost of the final project would be around Rs 80 million.

MARSHALLING YARDS

Pakistan Railways (PR) has signed a contract worth about $3.5 million with L M Ericsson of Sweden for the supply and installation of the signalling and tele-communications network for the new Pipri marshalling yard near Karachi. The agreement also provides for the training of PR personnel in Pakistan and Sweden. Delivery of equipment is due to begin shortly and installation is due for completion by the end of 1978. The Pipri Marshalling Yard is the first of its kind in the country.

Pakistan Railways (PR) proposes to lay two additional railway tracks between Pipri and the Karachi Port area. The proposal envisages that the existing two rail tracks will be reserved for fast traffic while the new tracks will be used exclusively for slow traffic. The proposal is being studied by a team of visiting French consultants who are studying rail freight and passenger problems and anticipated traffic growth up to the year 2000.

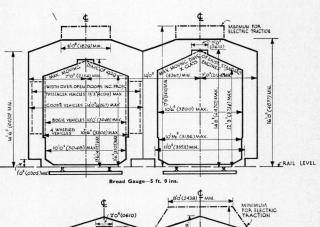

Broad Gauge—5 ft. 0 ins.

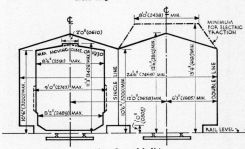

Metre Gauge—3 ft. 3⅜ in.

PARAGUAY

FERROCARRIL PRESIDENTE CARLOS ANTONIO LOPEZ
Mejico 145, CC 453 Asuncion

Chairman of the Board of Directors of the Railway: Ricardo Garay
Director: Dr. Bader Rachid Lichi
Director: Arq. Miguel Angel Barrios Arce
Manager: Dr. Modesto Alí
Chief Accountant: Juan Manuel Arnella
Director of Planning: Dr. Héctor Benítez P.
Chief of the Statistic & Costing Dept.: Dr. Aníbal R. Gamarra
Chief of the Warehouse Dept.: Eduardo Perinetti
Chief of the Traffic Dept.: Julio Rodríguez P.
Chief of the Workshop & Traction Dept.: Carlos A. Bavera
Chief of the Track & Work Dept.: Eng. Julio C. Zucchini
General Superintendent: Palmiro Rojas
General Secretary: Aníbal Maidana
Chief of the Personnel Dept.: Alipio Ovando
Chief of Public Relations: Lic. Armando César Arguello
Supervisor Bridges Buildings: Cap. Carlos Royg Ferreira
Treasurer: Jorge R. Esquivel

Gauge: 1.435 m.
Route length: 440 km.

Paraguay is a landlocked country, 164 100 sq miles *(425 000 km²)* in area, divided into two parts by the Paraguay River which is navigable, for vessels drawing twelve feet of water, as far as Asuncion, the capital. There are four separate railways, only one being common carrier, the F.C. Presidente Carlos Antonio Lopez, the others being industrial lines in western Paraguay and the Chaco.

The F.C. Presidente C.A. Lopez is the longest in the country, extending from Asuncion southeast to Encarnacion and Pacú-Cua, 234 miles *(376 km)* with a branch from San Salvador to Abai 40 miles *(65 km)* long. At Encarnacion a train ferry across the River Alto Parana connects at Posadas with the Argentine State Railways (F.C. General Urquiza).

The present name was adopted when the former F.C. Central was acquired by the Paraguan Government at the end of 1961.

Plans were announced in 1977 to modernise the railway at a cost of about $US 70 million, covering electrification, track renewal, replacement of motive power and rolling stock. The plan would be carried out in two stages: 1) track renewal—rail and sleeper changing, realignment of some gradients and ballasting over the 376 km between Asunción and Pacúa Cúa on the Argentina border. The first stage would also include purchase of new locomotives, freight wagons and passenger coaches, as well as new signalling and communications; 2) electrification.

TRAFFIC	1973	1974	1975	1976
Total freight ton-km	30 024 081	32 503 998	20 382 000	16 123 000
Total freight tonnage	131 713	144 367	—	—
Total passenger-km	26 465 887	26 980 764	23 550 000	16 086 000
Total passengers carried	217 640	207 619	—	—

FINANCES	1973	1974	1975	1976
Revenues (Guaranies)	196 892 894	247 669 357	—	—
Expenses (Guaranies)	169 198 962	209 056 949	—	—

MOTIVE POWER
Last motive power and rolling stock purchases were made in 1971 which increased the railway's locomotive fleet to: 20 steam locomotives.

ROLLING STOCK
Passenger coaches in service total 10; freight wagons 96.

DEVELOPMENT
In 1974 the Government of Japan arranged for a technical team to make a feasibility study of electrification and modernisation of the Paraguyan State Railways. The Paraguayan Government now possesses the report and is in favour of carrying out the project, at a cost of 68 million dollars.

ELECTRIFICATION
Electrification is projected on the 376 km Asunción-Encarnación line for completion by 1983.

PERU

ENAFER
Empresa Nacional de Ferrocarriles del Peru, Ancash 207, Lima

General Manager: Sr. Edmundo Montagne
Assistant General Manager: Ing. Carlos Meneses
Technical Adviser: C. I. Mercer
Finance: P. Grados
Treasurer: G. Winder

Enafer-Perú was formed in 1972 with the nationalisation of The Peruvian Corporation railways, a private company who ran most of Perú's railways and the Lake Titicaca services. The system now comprises the Central and Southern Railways with headquarters in Lima and Arequipa respectively.

CENTRAL RAILWAY
Ferrocarril del Centro del Perú
Offices: Ancash 201, Lima
Manager: Ing. J. Baigorria
Operations: Ing. G. Corrales
Traffic: P. O'Brien
Way and Works: Ing. C. Zolezzi
Mechanical: J. Wright
Purchasing: A. H. Davis

Gauge: 1 435 m, 0.914 m
Route length: 384 km, 129 km

ROLLING STOCK
50 locomotives (14 oil, 31 diesel electric, 5 diesel mechanical). 1 188 freight cars, 68 passenger cars, 10 rail motor, 124 miscellaneous.

The total route length with branches is 240 miles *(384 kms)* of standard gauge and 80 miles *(129 kms)* of narrow gauge. The standard gauge main line runs 216 miles *(346 kms)* from Callao to Huancayo where it connects with the 80 mile *(129 kms)* 3 ft 0 in *(0.914 m)* gauge line to Huancavelica.

There are 66 tunnels with aggregate length of 5.3 miles *(8.9 km)*, 59 bridges and 9 zig-zags (reversing stations) on the standard gauge section and 38 tunnels on the narrow gauge line.

The main line climbs from sea level to its highest point 15,688 ft *(4 782 m)* in the Galera Tunnel in 106 miles *(171 kms)* from Callao on an average gradient of 1 in 25 (4 per cent). The highest point on the system is 15 844 ft *(4 829 m)* at a siding at La Cima on the Ticlio-Morococha branch. This makes it the highest standard gauge line in the world. The steepest gradients occur in the first 138 miles *(222 kms)* from Callao, at sea level to Oroya at 12 222 ft *(3 726 m)* above sea level.

SOUTHERN RAILWAY
Ferrocarril del Sur
Offices: Tacna—Arica No 200, Arequipa

Manager: V. Foulkes
Traffic: E. Bedoya
Way and Works: R. Ricketts
Mechanical: D. Russell

Gauge: 1 435 m, 0.914 m
Route length: 923 kms, 151 kms

ROLLING STOCK
57 locos (10 oil, 43 diesel-electric, 4 diesel mechanical). 900 freight cars, 122 passenger cars, 30 rail motor cars, 133 miscellaneous.

STEAMSHIP SERVICE
Lake Titicaca 204 kms from Puno, Peru to Guaqui, Bolivia.
Ships comprise of 1 train ferry, 5 passenger-freight vessels, 1 dryer and two launches.

Tacna-Arica Railway
(Administered by Southern Railway)
Offices: A. Aldarracin 484, Tacna, Perú

Gauge: 1 435 m
Route length: 62 kms

ROLLING STOCK
1 steam locomotive, 40 freight cars, 1 passenger car, 9 rail motor car.

The total route length with branches is 576 miles *(923 kms)* of standard gauge and 94 miles *(151 kms)* of narrow gauge. The standard gauge main line runs from Mollendo to Juliaca 297 miles *(476 kms)* where the line divides. To the right to Puno 29 miles *(47 kms)* distant for connection with the Lake Titicaca steamer service to Bolivia and to the left to Cuzco 211 miles *(338 km)* where it connects with the 94 mile *(151 kms)* 3 ft 0 in *(0.914 m)* gauge line to Chaullay.

The main line climbs from sea level to its highest point at Crucero Alto 14 688 ft *(4 477 m)* in 224 miles *(359 km)* from Mollendo on an average gradient of 1 in 33 (3 per cent). The steamer service on Lake Titicaca at 12 526 ft *(3 818 m)* is the highest in the world. The Cuzco-Chaullay narrow gauge passes Machupicchu, site of an Inca township, discovered in 1911 and which thousands of tourists visit yearly.

DEVELOPMENTS
The military government has recently made several announcements on new lines to be built in the near future such as Chimbote-Lima-Nazca; a coastal line that would link the iron ore deposits of Nazca with the steel making complex in Chimbote. The joining of the Central and Southern Railways by standard gauge track between Huancayo and Cuzco which would then give, via the Lake Titicaca service, rail connection from Lima to the capitals of Bolivia, Chile, Argentine and Brazil. Also a line from La Oroya on the Central Railway to Pucallpa on the River Ucayali which would give access to the unexploited rich agricultural and forest lands on the eastern slopes of the Andes and the upper Amazon basin.

Authority has been given to extend the Cuzco-Chaullay narrow gauge line to Quillabamba some 13 miles *(21 kms)*. Works on this extension to commence soon.

Plans for the development of the railways is in the hands of the Ministry of Transport; Enafer-Peru acts solely in an operational role. As regards plans for reorganisation, the Canadian Government has been approached to give technical assistance on the following points:

(a) Data processing and statistics
(b) Operating procedures
(c) Costs and their relation to tariffs.
(d) Containerisation

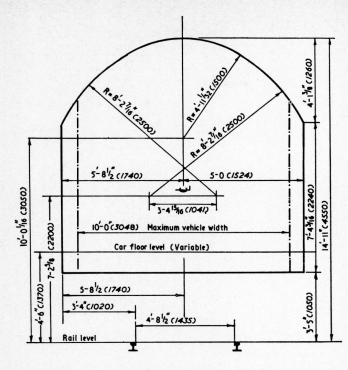

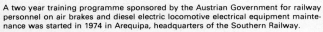

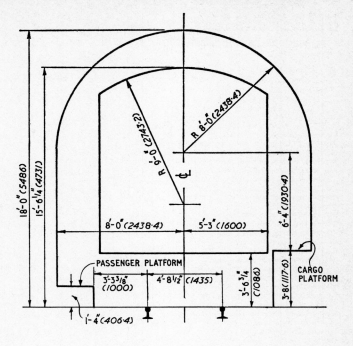

A two year training programme sponsored by the Austrian Government for railway personnel on air brakes and diesel electric locomotive electrical equipment maintenance was started in 1974 in Arequipa, headquarters of the Southern Railway.

ROLLING STOCK
New rolling stock were received from Mecanoexport-Import of Romania in 1974/75: 32 light weight coaches; 305 wagons.

MOTIVE POWER
Locomotives delivered in 1974:

Class:	600	430	400
Type: Diesel Electric:	DL-560	DL-535	DL-532
Wheel (or axle) arrangement:	Co-Co	Co-Co	Bo-Bo
Max speed:	80 km/h	80 km/h	80 km/h
Dimensions	15.89 m	13.81 m	12.8 m
	4.14 m	3.87 m	3.65 m
	2.94 m	2.91 m	2.74 m
Weight:	102 541 kg	74 000 kg	62 600 kg
Number of units:	15	5	5
Builders:	MLW	MLW	MLW
Tractive effort:	38 228 kg	21 460 kg	15 268 kg

TRACK
Standard rail:
80 lb per yd *(39.7 kg/m)* BS(R)
75 lb per yd *(37.2 kg/m)* BSS
75 lb per yd *(37.2 kg/m)* ASCE
70 lb per yd *(34.7 kg/m)* ASCE
70 lb per yd *(34.7 kg/m)* Livesey

Lengths: 24, 30, 33, 39 and 46 ft
Joints: 4-hole angle fishplates and bolts.
Cross ties (sleepers): Peruvian hardwood 8 in × 6in × 8 ft 0 in—1 435 mm track, 8 in × 6 in × 6 ft—914 mm track.
Made-up sleepers consisting of 2 blocks of reinforced concrete joined by a piece of used rail have been used in sidings and on straight stretches of main line.
Spacing:
Main line: 2 575-2 735 per mile *(1 600-1 700 per km)*
Branch line: 2 195-2 735 per mile *(1 365-1 700 per km)*
Rail fastenings:
Soleplates and ⅞ in coachscrews: 80% of track.
Soleplates and ⅝ in dogspikes: 20% of track.
Filling: 2 in to 4 in broken stone ballast; 6 in under tie on main lines and 3 in on branch lines.
Max curvature: 17.5° = min rad of 328 ft *(100 m)*.
Max gradient: 4.4% = 1 in 22.7 uncompensated.
Worst combination of curve and grade: 512 ft *(156 m)* curve on 4.22% (1 in 23.7) grade for 771 ft *(235 m)*
Gauge widening on sharpest curve: ½ in *(12.7 mm)*
Super-elevation on sharpest curve: 4 in *(101.6 mm)* speed limited.
Rate of slope of super-elevation: 1 in 360.
Max altitude: 15 844 ft *(4 829 m)*. On the Central Railway at La Cima siding on Ticlio-Morococha Branch, 107 miles *(173 km)* from Callao. On main line; 15 690 ft *(4 782 m)* inside Galera Tunnel, 107 miles *(172 km)* from Callao.
Max axle loading: 18.52 tons.
Bridge loading: Coopers E-40.
Max permitted speed:
50 mph *(80 km/h)* on level and low gradient section.
31 mph *(50 km/h)* on high gradient sections.

Alco diesel-electric locomotive hauling new rail sections through the Andes.

PHILIPPINES

PHILIPPINE NATIONAL RAILWAYS

943 Claro M. Recto Avenue, Manila

Chairman: Col. Salvador T. Villa
Vice-Chairman: Col. Nicanor T. Jimenez
Members: Roberto V. Reyes
         Alfredo Pio de Roda, Jr.
         Aber P. Canlas
         Victor G. Nituda
         Antonio M. Locsin
General Manager: Nicanor T. Jimenez
Asst. Gen. Manager on Admin.: Benjamin C. Garcia
AGM on Civil Engineering: Pio G. Valle
AGM on Finance: Benito P. Isip
AGM on Development: Dionisio Figueroa
AGM on Rolling Stock: Jesus Remotigue
AGM on Trans-Mark: Juan N. de Castro Jr.
Corporation Auditor: Amancio Garcia
Corporate Secretary: Rodolfo G. Flores
Director, PEG: Cesar Poblete
Chief, Executive Dept.: Salvacion Bundoc
Personnel Manager: Dominador F. Macaranas
Chief, Corp. Legal Counsel: Jose B. Calimlim
Chief, Actg. Dept.: Francisco V. Silva
Chief, Const. Engineer: Jose Bonuel
Chief, Engineer Dept.: Ramon Mariano
Mech. Supt.: Jacinto Oller
Medical Director: Felicisimo Manalese
Purchasing Agent: Simeon dela Cruz
Real Estate Manager: Recaredo Lagula
Manager, Motor Service: Cesar Diaz
Supt. Transport: Jose G. Nuguid
Marketing Manager: Delfin E. Reyes
Treasurer: Julita G. Vida
Manager Commuter, Service Management Body: Ramon Jimenez

Gauge: 1.00 m.
Route length: 1 060 km.

PNR is carrying out extensive modernisation and track upgrading with the aid of Asian Development Bank loans. During 1977 a consultancy contract valued at $US 1 million was awarded to Rail India Technical and Economic Services using proceeds of the loan. Future patterns were indicated in the Asian Development Bank mission report which said: "In the long term, total transport demand is expected to grow at around 8 per cent per annum in Southern Luzon. For some years after 1980 it is expected that the rate may be rather faster, particularly for freight traffic, as the process of easing the severe transport supply restraint of recent years will not yet have been completed."
The report also recalls, "Freight tonnage remained within, or very close to, the range 1.1 to 1.3 million tons per annum for some years before a persistent decline set in after 1960.
"From 1964 the decline accelerated, with tonnage falling by 74 per cent from 1.09 million tons in that year to 0.29 million tons in 1972. A further heavy fall in 1973 was caused partly by the severe typhoons of that year, but with results beginning to be achieved from the mechanical rehabilitation programme, there was a rise to 0.35 million tons in 1974. This traffic was, however, still only 30 per cent of the average annual tonnage in the period 1959-63."
A major project for the total rehabilitation of Philippine National Railways 474 km Southern Lines, from Manila to Legaspi, got underway in January 1977 following the granting of the $US 24 million loan from the Asian Development Bank. PNR general manager Col. Nicanor T. Jimenez said in Manila that work sould be completed within four years. The work will involve spreading 367 000 m³ of new ballast and 383 000 m³ of earthworks; and laying 604 800 new sleepers. New and recovered steel rails will be welded to 60 m lengths. New rail fastenings will also be used between Manila and Naga City—a distance of 378 km. In addition, PNR will continue its track doubling on the Manila suburban network. Track is to be doubled out to San Pedro, Laguna, a distance of 35 km, to make it possible to improve commuter train frequencies. Cost is estimated at $162 000 per km.

TRAFFIC

Year	Passenger Journeys	Passenger km
1971-2	4 477 598	691 787 743
1972-3	3 754 489	725 668 539
1973-4	4 451 127	932 336 690
1974-5	5 395 699	979 641 127
1975-6	4 893 995	905 435 877

	Freight/Express Tonnage	Freight/Express ton-km
1971-72	353 336	93 710 361
1972-73	275 707	69 252 158
1973-74	449 531	108 512 268
1974-75	398 940	91 849 300
1975-76	309 620	70 199 188

MOTIVE POWER

Twenty new 1 050 hp GE diesels were delivered in 1976 as part of PNR's aim to revitalise the system.

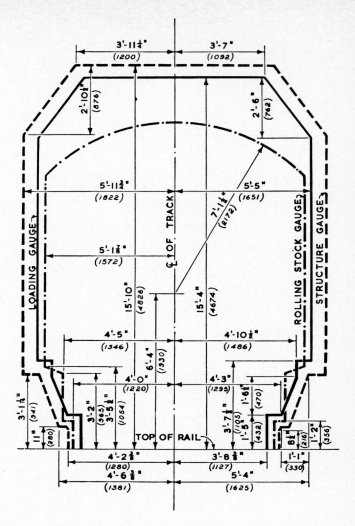

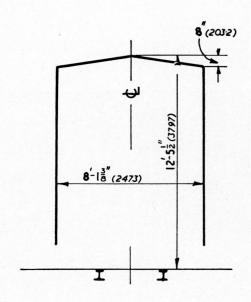

MOTIVE POWER

Traction fleet includes

Particulars	901-905	1001-1010	2001-2020	1501-1510	2501-2513	3001-3010	4001-4010
Class	Streamliner	Streamliner	Streamliner	Streamliner	Streamliner	Road Switcher	Road Switcher
Type (Road No.)	900 type	1000 type	2000 type	1500 type	2500 type	3000 type	4000 type
Wheel (or axle) arrangement	C-C	C-C	C-C	B-B-B	B-B	B-B	B-B
Max Speed	82 mph	60 mph	60 mph	60 mph	60 mph	60 mph	40 mph
Dimension							
Width	2 717 mm	2 821 mm	2 821 mm	2 749 mm	2 749 mm	2 743 mm	2 921 mm
Height	3 732 mm	3 683 mm	3 683 mm	3 372 mm	3 687 mm	3 687 mm	3 687 mm
Weight	180 000 lb	182 000 lb	192 000 lb	60.5 tons	120 000 lb	120 000 lb	104 000 lb
Number of units	5	10	20	10	13	10	10
Builders	General Electric	General Electric	General Electric	Alsthom	General Electric	General Electric	General Electric
Tractive Effort	54 000 lb	37 400 lb	37 400 lb	38 000 lb	26 400 lb	32 200 lb	16 500 lb

NEW LINES

The Philippines government has approved in principle a proposal to establish a 1 321 million pesos ($US 178 million) railway system in Mindanao to link productive areas in the south with coastal towns in the north. Implementation, however, will depend on whether Philippine National Railways officers give the project priority over the previously approved railway extension to Cagayan Valley. PNR cannot undertake both projects simultaneously because of the huge financial requirement. The proposed Mindanao system would have two main routes. The first would run 330 km from Koronadal, South Cotabato, through Carmen and Malaybalay to Cagayan de Oro City. Cost of the line would be about 620 million pesos. The second line would run 232 km from Magonoy, North Cotabato, to Iligan City passing through Datu Piang, Pigawayan and Molundo.

A new 344 km railway system on Panay Island in the Philippines has also been proposed by General Salvador Abcede, manager of Philippine National Railway services on Panay. The new system, now being studied by the Negros Occidental provincial government, calls for construction of new rail lines between Hinobaan in the south and San Carlos in the north.

A track doubling programme has progressed 11.5 km from Paco to Food Terminal, Inc. junction. The project will reach San Pedro, Laguna, covering 35 km to speed up movement of trains to and from the south and to maximise commuter train frequencies between Manila and Laguna.

TRACK

Standard rail:

Main line:

65 lb per yd *(32.2 kg/m)* in 30 and 33 ft lengths.

75 lb per yd *(37.2 kg/m)* in 33 ft lengths.

Branch lines:

65 lb per yd *(32.2 kg/m)* in 30 ft lengths.

54 lb per yd *(26.8 kg/m)* in 30 ft lengths.

45 lb per yd *(22.3 kg/m)* in 23 ft lengths.

Type of rail joints: Angle bars with slots for spikes.

Cross ties (sleepers):

Main line: "Molave" wood, 5 in × 8 in × 7 ft *(127 × 203 × 2 133 mm)*, spaced at 22 in *(558 mm)*.

Branch line: "Molave"wood, 5 in × 8 in × 7 ft *(127 × 203 × 2 133 mm)*, spaced at 24 in *(610 mm)*.

Bridge ties: "Yacal" wood, 8 in × 8 in × 8 ft *(203 × 203 × 2 438 mm)*, spaced at 16 in *(406 mm)*.

A limited number of steel ties are also used.

Rail fastenings: Track spikes; bolts with square nuts; "Hipower" nutlock washer; "elastic Rail Spikes".

Filling: Volcanic slag; river gravel with 15% sand; some crushed rock.

Max curvature:

Main line: 9.2° = min rad of 623 ft *(190 m)*

Branch line: 11½° = min rad of 492 ft *(150 m)*

Max gradient: Compensated, 2.6% = 1 in 38½.

Max gradient: Uncompensated, 1.2% × 1 in 38.

Max axle load: 35 000 lb.

Max permitted speed: 37.5 mph *(60 km/h)*

Signalling: In the Manila terminal area 13.6 km. of double track line with semaphore signals controlled from interlocker cabins. On single track lines elsewhere trains operated on English "Staff" system or by telegraph or telephone communication from station to station.

POLAND

POLISH STATE RAILWAYS

Polskie Koleje Panstwowe (P.K.P.) ul. Chalubinskiego 4, 00-928 Warsaw

Telephone: Warsaw 21 08

Minister of Transport: Tadeusz Bejm
Director, Economic Department: K. Ratajczak
Director, Financial Department: J. Stokowiec
Director, Chief of Investments: E. Kopciński
Director, Commercial: R. Pajak
Director, Way and Works: A. Golaszewski
Director, Movements: K. Sankowski
Director, Rolling Stock: S. Krychniak
Director, Traction: J. Skonjecki
Director, Telecommunications: Z. Mościcki

Gauge: 1 435 m.
Route length: 23 816 km.

Polish State Railways (PKP), which carried more rail freight than the combined total for France, Britain and Italy last year, hoped to expand its business by 19 million tonnes to 474 million tonnes in 1977. Investment has doubled during the past ten years and more than 1 200 km of new line is to be built between 1976/80. Most important project is the metal and sulphur line from Hrubieszow and the Katowice steelworks. The first section from Zawiercie to Radzice has already been completed. The second section from Idzikowice to Warsaw is being built and electrified and the third section to Plock with a branch line to Modlin will be completed later, PKP plans to specialise more in long-haul bulk transport with shuttle services carrying coal, building materials, ore and farm produce. Electrification is to be increased from 6 000 km to 8 000 km by 1980. Main problems at the moment seem to be inadequate capacity of track and stations, shortage of rolling stock and a slow turn-round of wagons.

In 1976, the first year of the 1976-82 transport development programme, rail transport fell short of its planned tasks. Only a modest increase in goods traffic was achieved of 2 million tons; the target for total goods traffic in 1977 is 47 million tons. In February 1977, the Minister of Transport assured a national transport conference that rail investment would be increased during the year. In Katowice the railway directorate is to speed wagon turnround in marshalling yards, electrify the Kochlowice-Gliwice line and rebuild Gliwice station where a container terminal is being built. At least one station in each Silesian railway directorate is to be developed for the mechanical handling of coal. In 1977 Silesia's railways were expected to carry 215 million tons of freight—mainly coal—an increase of 7 million tons on 1976. Despite adverse weather conditions and a shortage of heavy construction plant, especially bulldozers, construction of the 250 mile line between Hrubieszow to Katowice steel works is being speeded up, according to a programme on Warsaw television in 1977. The line will be used for the direct transfer of Soviet ore to Katowice and Polish sulphur to the USSR. Wagon shortages continue. In 1976 it is estimated that the railways lost the use of 1 700 wagons a day because of customers' lack of discipline—equivalent to a reduction in capacity of 4 million tons for the year. In addition to delay, damage to wagons is becoming more frequent. The railways handle 460 000 tons of coal from the Upper Silesian Basin every day, but nearly a quarter of the wagons arriving in Silesia for this traffic are unusable and have to be sent away for repair. Warsaw TV also reported the case of the modernisation of a station near Kielce where the rebuilding of the track requires about 150 000 tons of stone ballast a year. All this could be supplied from nearby quarries, but, the construction combine is allocated 70 per cent of its ballast from a quarry 150 miles away tying up 4 000 wagons a year.

TRAFFIC

PKP carries a high proportion of national freight. In 1965 this amounted to 85.9 per cent of all traffic, 79.7 per cent in 1970 and about 73.6 per cent in 1975. By 1980 the railway

Class SP-47 locomotive delivered in 1977/78 by Cegielski: rated output 3 000 hp.

Emu EW-58 which first entered service in 1976.

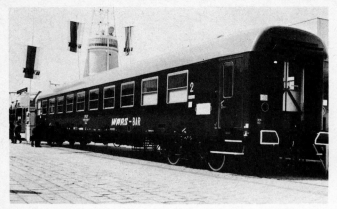

New type Wars dining car

Six axle type 601 freight wagon

ELECTRIC LOCOMOTIVES

Class	Axle Arrange-ment	Line Current V Type	Rated Power hp	Max kg	Tractive Effort	Continuous at	Max Speed km/h	Wheel Dia mm	Total Weight tonnes	Length mm	No. built	Year First Built	Mechanical Parts	Electrical Equipment
					kg	km/h							*Builders*	
EP02	BoBo	3 000 dc	1 840				100	1 220	81.0	15 000		1953	Pafawag	Pafawag
EP03	BoBo	3 000 dc	2 500				100	1 220	81.2	14 170		1951	AS	ASEA
EU04	BoBo	3 000 dc	2 900	23 000	1 700	45.5	110	1 350	86.0	16 370		1954	LEW	LEW
EU05	BoBo	3 000 dc	2 820	24 800	11 400	63.0	125	1 250	82.5	16 140		1960	Skoda Pilzno	Skoda Pilzno
EU06	BoBo	3 000 dc	2 720	26 500	14 400	49.0	125	1 250	80.0	15 915		1961	Vulcan Fdry.	AEI/EE
EU07	BoBo	3 000 dc	2 720	26 500	14 400	49.0	125	1 250	80.0	15 915		1963	Pafawag	Dolmel
EP05	Bo-Bo	3 000 dc	2 280	24 800	8 820	82.7	140/160	1 250	80.0	16 140		1973	Skoda Pilzno	Skoda Pilzno
EP08	BoBo	3 000 dc	2 720	25 500	10 600	63.0	140/160	1 250	82.0	15 915		1973	Pafawag	Dolmel
EU20	CoCo	3 000 dc	4 340	32 000	2 300	50.0	110	1 350	120.0	18 500		1955	LEW	LEW
ET21	CoCo	3 000 dc	3 270	32 000	14 900	49.6	100	1 250	121.0	16 500		1957	Pafawag	Dolmel
EU22	CoCo	3 000 dc	4 080	35 000	21 600	50.0	125	1 250	120.0	19 240		1971	Pafawag	Dolmel
ET40	BoBo + BoBo	3 000 dc	5 660	50 000	31 500	46.4	100	1 250	1 640	34 420		1975	Skoda Pilzno	Skoda Pilzno
ET41	BoBo + BoBo	3 000 dc	5 440	50 000	28 300	50.6	100	1 250	166.0	31 880		1977	Legielski	Dolmel
ET42	BoBo + BoBo	3 000 dc	5 830	50 000	29 360	52.1	125	1 250	164.0	31 000		1978	Nowoczerkask	Nowoczerkask

DIESEL LOCOMOTIVES

Class	Axle Arrange-ment	Trans-mission	Rated Power hp	Max kg	Tractive Effort	Continuous at	Max Speed km/h	Wheel Dia mm	Axle Load Tons	Total Weight Tons	Length mm	No. Built	Year first Built	Mechanical Parts	Engine	Transmission
					kg	km/h								*Builders*		
SM02	B	Mech	44	4 000			12	850	8.0	16.0	6 000		1955	Chrzanow	Nowotki	Dolmel
SM03	B	Mech	150	5 043			45	950	12.0	24.0	7 000		1960	Chrzanow	Nowotki	Dolmel
SM25	C	Hyd	350	12 700			60	1 100	12.5	37.4	8 600		1961	Chrzanow	Nowotki	Voith
SM30	BoBo	Elec	300	7 500	3 200	15.0	60	850	9.0	36.0	9 440		1956	Chrzanow	Nowotki	Dolmel
SM31	CoCo	Elec	1 200	36 000	16 500	12.3	80	1 100	20.0	120.0	17 000		1976	Chrzanow	Cegielski	Dolmel
SM40	BoBo	Elec	600	18 600	10 400	9.6	80	1 040	15.44	61.76	11 290		1958	Ganz-Mavag	Ganz-Mavag	Ganz
SM41	BoBo	Elec	600	18 600	10 400	9.6	80	1 040	15.44	61.76	11 290		1958	Ganz-Mavag	Ganz-Mavag	Ganz
SM42	BoBo	Elec	800	22 300	11 460	12.5	90	1 100	18.0	72.0	14 240		1967	Chrzanow	Chrzanow	Dolmel
SP42	BoBo	Elec	800	23 500	11 400	12.5	90	1 100	17.0	68.0	14 240		1971	Chrzanow	Cegielski	Dolmel
ST43	CoCo	Elec	2 100	32 000	20 000	21.5	100	1 100	19.4	116.4	17 000		1965	EpCr	Resica	EpCr
ST44	CoCo	Elec	2 000	35 000	20 000	20.0	100	1 050	19.4	116.5	17 550		1966	Horoszyiougrad	Kolomna	Charków
SP45	CoCo	Elec	1 700	30 800	13 350	24.8	120	1 100	17.0	102.0	18 990		1968	Cegielski	Cegielski	Dolmel
SU46	CoCo	Elec	2 250	31 700	16 350	28.75	120	1 100	17.5	105.0	18 990		1976	Cegielski	Cegielski	Dolmel
SP47	CoCo	Elec	3 000	38 130/3 597	18 580/15 930	31.8/37.3	120/140	1 100	19.0		20 180		1978	Cegielski	Cegielski	Domel

expects to be carrying about 68 per cent. Freight carried over the highways in 1970 totalled 862.5 million tons, increasing to more than 1 700 million tons in 1975. By 1980 truckers expect to be carrying around 2 700 million tons. Passenger traffic on the highways increased from 1 400 million passenger journeys in 1970 to 2 200 million in 1975. About 3 400 million passengers will be travelling by road in 1980.

	1975	1976
Freight tonne-km (millions)	129 230	130 857
Freight tonnage ('000)	464 248	465 200
Passenger-km ('000)	42 819	42 799
Passenger journeys	1 117 959	1 109 760

The PKP expect to be able to convey 590 million tonnes of freight in 1980 and 750 million in 1990.

FINANCES

	1975	1976
	(Zlotys)	
Revenues ('000)	43 253 044	64 779 839

MOTIVE POWER

During the five-year 1971-75 plan, deliveries of 1 270 diesel locomotives were completed. Diesel traction now operates about 43 per cent of train km.

ROLLING STOCK

In order to handle a forecast freight traffic increase of 15 to 18 million tonnes annually during the present 1976-82 improvement programme, PKP is to purchase 72,000 wagons during the next six years.

ELECTRIFICATION

Electrification of about 1 700 km during the 1971-75 plan brought the length of electrified lines to about 5 588 route-km, 24 per cent of the PKP network. During this period, electrification was completed over the following lines:
Kalety/Silesia-Kluczbork-Olesnica-Wroclaw; Kluczbork-Ostrow Wielkopolski-Poznan; Kielce-Czestochowa; Krakow-Zakopane; Lodz-Ostrow Wielkopolski-Wroclaw. Also completed was the first section of the new central trunk line from Zawiercie to Radzice. The electrification programme plans for electric traction over 10 000 to 11 000 km, i.e. 40 per cent of the network, by 1985. 2 500 km will be electrified as part of the 1976-1980 Five-Year Plan; at the same time, the PKP is continuing the work of providing the network with electric locomotives.
By the end of 1976 electrified route length totalled 5 988.

TRACKWORK

In the five years up to 1971 only 160 km of new line was laid. During the last plan (1971-75) about 1 200 km was laid. Most important new line was the central trunk line from Silesia to Warsaw with the first 143 km section between Zawiercie and Radzice entering service in 1974. Though the line will be used initially for movement of heavy coal trains from Silesia to Warsaw and Bialystock, and for feeding power stations in Ostroleka and Kozienice, it is being built to parameters which will make it possible to operate passenger trains of up to 5 000 tons at speeds of 200-250 km/h. Minimum curve radius is 4 000 m, and clearance between tracks is 4.5 m. The line will be laid with continuous-welded S60 rails.
Hardwood sleepers are being used throughout.
To ensure maximum security, the new line will have no grade crossings. Modern signalling will make it possible to operate trains in each direction on both tracks. Fifty viaducts, 17 bridges and more than 120 culverts are under construction. All are being built from standardised, prefabricated elements.

Sleepers: These are of both wood type INBK4 and concrete type INBK3 5¾ in *(15 cm)* and 7⁷/₁₆ in *(19 cm)* in thickness respectively. Wooden pads 7 mm. thick are used under the rails.

Welded rail: At the end of 1973 the total length of track with welded rail was 2 548 miles *(4 874.5 km)* of which 491 miles *(790 km)* were laid during the year. The longest length of continuous welded rail is 4.3 miles *(7.0 km.)*
Rails used are Type S 49, Type S 42, and Type S 60 in 98 ft 5 in *(30 m)* lengths, flash butt welded in workshop and thermit welded at site. Rails are secured to either wood or concrete sleepers (cross ties) by "K" type fastenings, and are laid by means of mobile cranes.

PORTUGAL
PORTUGUESE RAILWAYS
Companhia Dos Caminhos De Ferro Portugueses (C.P.),
Calçada Do Duque 20, Lisbon

Telephone: 33181

Management Council:
Chairman: Eng. Amilcar Marques
Members: Eng. Almeida e Castro
Eng. Gonçalves Ferreira
Dr. Pestana Bastos
Dr. Manuel Moura

Administration Main Officers:
Planning: Dr. José Aleluia
Organisation: Eng. Victor Biscaia
Information: Dr. Pereira dos Santos
Legal Office: Dr. Tinoco de Faria
Public Relations and Press: Dr. Américo Ramalho
Design: Scp. Santa Bárbara
Administration Secretary: Dr. Chaves Brilante

Operations
Director: Eng. Martins Pinheiro
Assistant Directors: Eng. Eduardo Zúquete
Eng. Abilio Rodrigues
Technical Secretary: Eng. Luis Antunes
Commercial Department: Eng. Álvaro Campelo
Transports Department: Eng. Azevedo Batalha
Fixed Installations Department: Engo. Vilaça e Moure
Northern Region: Eng. Fernando Ávila
Central Region: Eng. Feio Borges
Southern Region: Eng. Oliveira Santos
Cascais Line: Eng. Felizardo Brazão

Equipment
Director: Eng. Antunes da Cunha
Assistant Directors: Eng. Moreira Andrade
Eng. Fernando Salvado

Industrial
Director: Eng. Matos Torres
Assistant Director: Eng. Francisco Carapinha

Financial
Director: Dr. Gonçalves Henriques

Personnel
Director: Eng. Luis Areias
Assistant Directors: Dr. Carlos Gaspar
Dr. Tomás de Aquino

Purchasing & Supplying Division
Manager: Eng. Camarate de Campos
Assistant Manager: Eng. Abilio Lopes

Gauge: 1.665 m; 1.00 m.
Route length: 2 807 km; 759 km

The following transport companies were nationalised on 11 March, 1975:
—Companhia dos Caminhos de Ferro Portugueses—or Portuguese Railway Company (CP);
—Companhia Nacional de Navegacao (CNN);
—Companhia Portuguesa de Transportes Maritimos (CTM);
—Companhia Nacional de Transportes Aerios.

MOTIVE POWER

Portuguese Railways (CP) placed orders, in 1975, with domestic suppliers for 17 three-car electric suburban trainsets and 20 two-car diesel sets for broad-gauge operation.
Traction equipment and bogies will be delivered by French, German and Swiss suppliers.
Schindler Waggon, Switzerland, has an order for 38 complete electric motor bogies and other parts worth SFr 4 million.

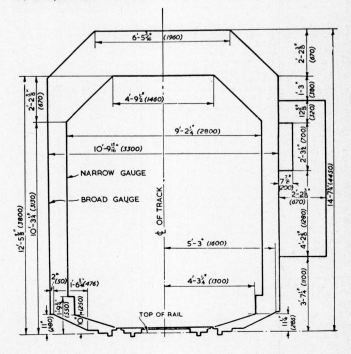

Suburban three-car stainless-steel trainset for 25 kV 50 Hz electrification built by Soreframe under Budd license.

Santa Apolonia station, Lisbon.

LINE CONSTRUCTION

CP is to construct an 80 km cut-off route to cater for industrial expansion at the port of Sines in southern Portugal. Plans for the scheme were finalised and bridge and earth-works contracts let in 1977.

The route leaves the existing CP southern main line at Poceirão and runs south on a double-track alignment to cross the Setúbal-Alcacer do Sal line north of the river Sado at Pinheiro. A spur will be provided as a link to Aguas de Moura. The line then becomes single track and continues south following the coast, passing just to the west of the Grandola hills. It finally sweeps round to cross the existing line to Sines a short distance east of the port.

The line will include four major civil engineering projects: a 450 m long viaduct at Melides, an 840 m long bridge across the Marateca river, a viaduct almost 2 km long crossing the Sado river and a 550 m bridge at Cascalheira. All four are to be constructed in prestressed reinforced concrete.

Track will be laid with 54 kg/m welded rail on concrete sleepers with profile and curve radii suitable for running. Modern signalling and telecommunications will allow maximum operating flexibility and high throughput.

Main traffic on the line will be fuel and other oil products from the new refinery at Sines; a tender for manufacture of 80-tonne tank wagons has been awarded to Metalsines. Other freight traffic will build up as industrial development as Sines progresses.

CP's plans call for eventual future extension of the route further south to serve the Algarve.

TRACK WORK

A plan for renewing track on 497 miles *(800 km)* of route with 54 kg rail has been initiated.

Routes affected are:
- Lisbon—Campanhã
- Campolide—Braço de Prata
- Campolide—Sintra
- Ermezinde—Marco
- Contumil—Nine
- Alfarelos—Figueirada Foz
- Cacéin—Caldas da Rainha

248 miles *(400 km.)* of track will be reballasted so average train speeds should increase.

TRACK DETAILS

Standard rail:
Broad gauge: 60.5 to 111 lb/yd *(30.5 kg/m)* in 8 to 18 lengths.
Narrow gauge: 40.4 to 72.6 lb/yd *(20.36 kg/m)* in 8 and 12 m length.
Cross ties (sleepers):
Broad gauge: 10¼ in × 5⅛ in × 8 ft 6⅜ in *(260 × 130 × 2 600 mm)*, spacing 23⅞ in *(605 mm)*.
Narrow gauge: 9 in × 4½ in × 5 ft 11 in *(230 × 120 × 1 800 mm)*, spacing 32¼ to 32½ in *(820-850 mm)*.
Rail fastening: Screw spikes or bolts. "RN" flexible fastenings used with welded rail.
Filling: Broken stone gravel or earth.
Max curvature:
Broad gauge: 5.9° = min rad of 984 ft *(300 m)*
Narrow gauge: 29° = min rad of 197 ft *(60 m)*
Max gradient:
Broad gauge: 1.8% = 1 in 55½.
Narrow gauge: 2.5% = 1 in 40.
Longest continuous gradient:
Broad gauge: 5.2 miles *(8.3 km)* of 1.4% grade with curves varying from 1 936 to 4 924 ft *(590 to 1 501 m)* in radius.
Narrow gauge: 4.4 miles *(7.2 km)* of 2.5% grade with curves varying from 246 to 1 640 ft *(75 to 500 m)* in radius.
Gauge widening on sharpest curve: 0.984 in *(25 mm)* for both gauges.
Super-elevation on sharpest curve:
Broad gauge: 7.874 in *(200 mm)*
Narrow gauge: 4.724 in *(120 mm)*
Rate of slope of super-elevation: 1 in 2 000 to 1 in 333.
Max altitude:
Broad gauge: 2 666 ft *(812.7 m)*
Narrow gauge: 2 878 ft *(849.7 m)*
Max axle loading:
Broad gauge: 19 tons.
Narrow gauge: 11 tons.
Max permitted speed:
Broad gauge: 62 mph *(100 km/h)*
Narrow gauge: 50 mph *(80 km/h)*

Welded rail: The total length of track laid with welded rail is 282 miles *(455 km)*. Thermit process is used. Rail used weighs 109, 101, 90, 80 lb per yd *(54, 50, 45, 40 kg/m)* in 18 m and 24 m lengths. The length of continuous welded rail is usually 2 756 ft *(840 m)* but occasionally 3 150 ft *(960 m)*. Rails are secured to sleepers by RN flexible clips.

ELECTRIFICATION

50 cycles, 25 000 V OH electrification has been completed between Sintra and Porto and is in process of completion between Esmoriz and Villa Norade Gala in the north. Modern block signalling and signal cabin installations have been constructed on this route. The 406 km Lisbon—Oporto line is electrified at 25 kV 50 Hz.

RHODESIA

RHODESIA RAILWAYS
Metcalfe Square, PO Box 596, Bulawayo

Telephone: Bulawayo 72211

Chairman, Railway Board: W. N. Wells
Deputy Chairman: J. R. Hedley
Members: A. T. Mills
  J. A. Mcdonald
  T. A. Wright
Secretary: P. J. Murray
General Manager: T. A. Wright
Deputy General Manager: W. F. Sievwright
Asst. General Manager: F. C. Viljoen
Chief Medical Officer: Dr. L. B. Thompson
Chief Mechanical Engineer: G. H. Patterson
Chief Civil Engineer: R. F. Maclean
Chief Personnel Officer: J. Henderson
Chief Accountant: J. E. Bolton
Chief Superintendent Operating: N. Lea-Cox
Area Manager (Eastern): C. A. S. Thorn
Area Manager (Southern): D. H. Constable
Chief Electrical Engineer: P. L. Overbury
Chief Signal Engineer: A. L. Rutherford-Jones
Chief Commercial Manager: B. Dardagan
Chief Planning Officer: J. F. Carlisle
Supplies Manager: A. J. K. Innes
Manager, Computer Services: J. F. Carlisle
Manager, Road Services: A. Ferguson
Catering Manager: T. W. E. Boulter
Chief Security Officer: J. L. Dunbar
Chief Internal Auditor: G. G. Fraser

Gauge: 1.673 m.
Route length: 3 239 km.

TRAFFIC
The newly proposed Botswana Railway Corp is due to take over RR's main line between Plumtree and Ramatlhabama on January 1, 1980. The route was transferred to RR from South African Railways when Botswana became independent in 1966. A five-man team from Transmark arrived in Gabarone in January 1978 to spend a year sorting out administration problems for the new Botswana Railway and advise on maintenance facilities, as well as study rolling stock and motive power requirements.

1976 AT A GLANCE

RAIL SERVICES	Unit	1975	1976
Operating revenue	$000's	71 666	78 754
Operating expenditure	$000's	63 183	72 736
Operating surplus	$000's	8 483	6 018
Revenue earning tonnes	000's	12 018	12 845
Free haul tonnes*	000's	782	778
Total tonnes hauled	000's	12 800	13 623
Train engine km	000's	20 212	20 391
Operating revenue per train engine km	$	3 546	3 862
Operating expenditure per train engine km	$	3 126	3 567
Gross tonne km	Millions	14 686	14 670
Net tonne km	Millions	6 141	6 358
Steam-locomotive km	000's	5 571	5 343
Diesel locomotive km	000's	17 551	17 808
1st class passengers carried	000's	43	48
2nd class passengers carried	000's	216	239
3rd class passengers carried	000's	240	242
4th class passengers carried	000's	2 628	2 576
Total passengers	000's	3 127	3 105

ALL SERVICES			
Gross revenue	$000's	76 607	84 291
Gross expenditure	$000's	97 833	113 410
Net deficit	$000's	21 226	29 119
Total staff employed at 30th June	Nos.	21 247	
Total salaries and wages paid including related costs	$000's	63 565	70 996

*The haulage of Railway stores and materials for which no revenue is earned.

Freight train hauled by an English Electric diesel-electric locomotive negotiates a curve on the run to Umtali.

DIESEL LOCOMOTIVES

Class	Axle Arrangement	Transmission	Rated Power hp	Max lb (kg)	Tractive Effort Continuous at lb (kg)	Tractive Effort Continuous at mph (km/h)	Max Speed mph (km/h)	Wheel Dia. in (mm)	Total Weight Tons	Length ft in (mm)	No. Built	Year first Built	Builders: Mechanical Parts	Builders: Engine & Type	Builders: Transmission
DEI	Co-Co	Elec	720	51 000 (23 150)	17 500 (7 940)	15 (24)	60 (96)	36 (914)	75.8	46' 8'' (14 224)	6	1952	Davenport Bessler Corporation	Caterpillar D 397 (2 per Loco)	Westinghouse
DE2	1 Co-Co 1	Elec	1 710	60 500 (27 440)	36 000 (16 330)	13.6 (22.0)	55 (88)	Driven 37½ (952) Carrier 28½ (724)	113	56' 0'' (17 069)	33	1955	English Electric	English Electric 16 SVT	English Electric
DE3	1 Co-Co 1	Elec	1 850	59 000 (26 760)	40 000 (18 140)	13 (20.9)	66 (106)	Driven 37½ (952) Carrier 28½ (724)	110	51' 1'' (15 570)	16	1962	English Electric	English Electric 12 CVST	English Electric
DE4	Co-Co	Elec	1 730	50 000 (22 680)	37 400 (16 920)	13.5 (21.9)	60 (96)	40 (1 016)	90	51' 1'' (15 570)	14	1963	Brush Electric	Mirrlees JVSS12T	Brush Electric
DE6	Co-Co	Elec	2 090	—	59 880 (27 160)	13 (20.9)	72 (116)	38 (965)	89	52' 0'' (15 850)	10	1966	GE (USA)	GE FoL-12	GE

SAUDI ARABIA
SAUDI GOVERNMENT RAILROAD ORGANISATION
Dammam

Telephone: 3001

Director General: Faysal M. Shehail
Deputy Director General: A. M. A. Badhawri
Assistant Director General Financial Affairs: M. A. Bubshait
Assistant Director General Administration: F. Z. Al-Hazmi
Assistant Director General Engineering: A. S. Afandi
Superintendent Motive Power & Equipment: A. Ali
Superintendent of Police: Khalid Jarabzooni
Chief Civil Engineer: C. A. Veli

Gauge: 1.435 m
Route length: 572.28 km

The Saudi Government Railroad Organisation's track is standard gauge with a route length of 572.28 km. The mainline connects the Port of Dammam with Riyadh, the capital of Saudi Arabia.

There is a daily passenger train service to and from Riyadh. A daily freight train is also scheduled as required, and certain trains are run daily between intermediate points to serve the needs of private business companies.

In addition to operating the railroad, the Organisation is responsible for managing the Port of Dammam which is considered one of the largest ports on the Gulf. A large proportion of imported cargo is brought to the shore on rail and is off-loaded in public off-loading lines which have recently been extended while a new rail serving warehousing area is being developed.

The track consists mainly of 80 lb/yd *(39.7 kg/m)* ASCE rail on timber sleepers, but relaying is being carried out with UIC-54 rail weighing 110 lb/yd *(54.55 kg/m)*.

The line is served throughout by a VHF Radio Link and all traffic is radio controlled from a Central Control Room in Dammam by direct contact with the driver of each locomotive. A VHF Tele-Communication link is also maintained.

The port of Dammam is owned and operated by the railway. The deep water berths are equipped with portal cranes; tug boats, barges, lighterage facilities and storage are available.

TRAFFIC	1973	1974	1975	1976
Total freight ton-km (000's)	229 627	191 887	188 214	163 238
Total freight tonnage (000's)	1 584	1 307	1 618	3 638
Total passenger km (000's)	53 334	69 216	68 080	79 705
Total passenger journeys (000's)	156	351	200	235

FINANCIAL	1973	1974	1975	1976
		(in '000 SR)		
Revenues	47 334	44 541	56 187	153 123
Expenses	47 049	53 281	68 941	122 096

MOTIVE POWER
Number of diesel-electric locomotives 26.

ROLLING STOCK
Number of passenger coaches	36
Number of freight wagons	1 502

TRACK WORK
Some 25 km of new track is being built in connection with the port extension. 2 km of track was built in siding during 1973 and a further 5 km is being added to the classification yard.

Rail, types and weights: 80 lb ASCE, UIC-54, AREA 100 lb and AREA 115 lb.
Sleepers (cross ties) type: Wooden Length 8 ft, Width 8 in.
 Thickness: 6 in.
 Spacing: 1 850 per km.
Rail fastenings (types used): Base plate and spikes and elastic spikes.

LEVEL CROSSINGS
The Saudi Government Railroad awarded a contract for solar-powered level crossing equipment to Wabco Westinghouse SpA of Turin during 1977. Increasing traffic on the Damman-Riyadh line, and on the country's limited road network, has made it necessary to protect level crossings on the route. The major problem was the lack of efficient electricity supply in remote areas, so solar power, already being tried out in Canada and elsewhere, was chosen as a solution.

The system developed for Saudi Arabia by Wabco uses silicon solar cells rather than copper sulphide or gallium arsenide. Each cell generates 0.4 to 0.5 V. Batteries are made up from a number of cells and connected to a conventional lead-acid storage battery. In this way, power is available even during periods of solar inactivity.

A typical crossing installation will comprise road and rail signals, automatic half-barriers, track circuits and power supply from a number of solar batteries. Operation of flashing lights, bells and the half-barriers at the crossing are initiated by train occupancy of the track circuits in the usual way. A rail signal is also provided to inform the driver that the barriers are properly closed.

Three batteries are required, one each at a distance of about 1 000 m from the crossing, and one at the crossing itself. This major installation of solar batteries will provide an excellent proving ground for equipment that is now being considered widely for similar installations in areas remote from mains electricity supply.

NEW YARDS
The Dammam railway yard has been rebuilt; capacity is now 500 wagons in the classification yard and 400 in the tie yard. There are now 13 tracks in the classification yard and 28 in the tie yard.

HEDJAZ RAILWAY
Rebuilding work is in hand on the derelict portion of the Hedjaz Railway from Ma'an in Jordan to Medina in Saudi Arabia with a connecting line through to Aqaba for phosphate traffic. The total length of this railway from Damascus to Medina is 809 miles *(1 303 km)*, gauge 3 ft 5⅜ in *(1.050 m)* and originally it was built with 21.5 kg rails on steel sleepers. The new line is being built of 30.1 kg and 34.8 kg rail and Jarrah sleepers. Nearly 1 800 bridges and culverts have to be rebuilt with local stone, and the work progresses from both ends of the line.

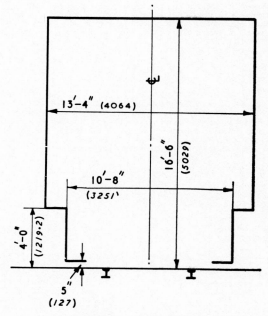

Saudi Government Railway

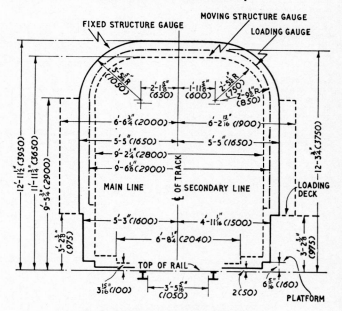

Reconstructed Hedjaz Railway

SENEGAL

REGIE DES CHEMINS DE FER DU SENEGAL
Cité Ballabey, Thies

Telephone: 317.46

Director General: Papa Malick Mbengue
General Manager: Khalilou Sall
Deputy General Manager: Marcel Gioan
Heads of Departments:
  Administration and Personnel: Jean Hombert
  Operations: Adama Diagne
  Motive Power and Rolling Stock: Souleye Diop
  Way and Works: Mamadou Basse
  Purchases and Supplies: Raymond Alaux
  Chief Accountant: Malick Tine

Gauge: 1.00 m
Route length: 1 034 km

The 800 mile principal line formerly known as C.F. Dakar-Niger, runs through Senegal into Mali. It extends from km 0 at Dakar in Senegal to km. 1 286 at Koulikoro, the terminus of the railway in Mali. Fortunately the frontier station of Kildiri is exactly halfway along this line at km 643.
In Senegal the rail system is administered by the *Regie des Chemins de Fer Sénégal.* It has a total route length of 642 miles *(1 033 km)* and consists of:—

	miles	km.
Dakar to Kidiri	400	643
Dioubel-Touba branch	29	47
Guinguinéo-Koalack branch	13	21
Thiès to St. Louis du Sénégal	120	193
Louga to Linguère	80	129
	642	1 033

TRAFFIC	1975/76
Total freight tonne-km (000's)	326 240
Total freight tonnage (000's)	1 613
Total passenger-km (000's)	186 214
Total passenger journeys (000's)	1 850

MOTIVE POWER
The railway took delivery in 1977 of three Class AD 18B diesel-electrics from Alsthom-Atlantique of France. The railway now operates 33 diesel electrics, 26 loco-tractors and 11 rail cars.

ROLLING STOCK
Number of passenger coaches total 65, railcar trailers 28, baggage vans 23, freight wagons 911, service vehicles 233.

RAILWAY DEVELOPMENTS
The International Development Association provided a loan of US$9 million for improving the railway. The money is being spent on upgrading heavy traffic lines, welding rail, building second track, and acquiring locomotives, railcars, wagons, highway trucks and trailers, machine tools, etc.

FUTURE PROSPECTS
An increase of about 2 per cent per year in passenger traffic is envisaged. It is proposed to use diesel trainsets in place of locomotive-hauled trains and this will require a further 6 railcars and 8 trailer cars. It is also intended to increase train speeds, particularly between Dakar and Thiès where road competition is active.
An increase of 5 per cent per year on average for the present internal traffic would bring the tonne-km figure up to 400 million by the end of 1972. Additional traffic is foreseen from the growth of other products:— sugar for a further refinery at St. Louis; cotton fibre and cotton seeds; grains.

INVESTMENTS
During 1974 the railway spent Frs (CFA) 1 667 million on new equipment and facilities, including:
Locomotives:

Shunting, diesel-electric—2	135 000 000
New line construction (370 km)	715 651 474
Major track improvements	123 500 000
Bridges and buildings	17 500 000
Shops or repair facilities	170 000 000

SOUTH AFRICA

SOUTH AFRICAN RAILWAYS
South African Railways and Harbours Administration
Paul Kruger Building, Wolmarans Street, Johannesburg

Administration:
Minister of Transport: The Hon. S. L. Muller, M.P.
Administrative Secretary to the Ministry of Transport: G. Basson
Private Secretary to the Ministry of Transport: F. Potgieter
Railway Commissioners: C. V. de Villiers
          A. S. D. Erasmus
          P. L. S. Aucamp

Management (Johannesburg):
Director General: J. G. H. Loubser
Deputy General Manager: Dr. D. J. Coetsee
Deputy General Manager: H. J. L. du Toit
Assistant General Manager (Harbours and Pipelines): P. J. Conradie
Assistant General Manager (Staff): J. P. Verster
Assistant General Manager (Technical): E. A. Fenske
Assistant General Manager (Operating): H. A. Loots
Assistant General Manager (Commercial): L. M. Engelbrecht
Assistant General Manager (Planning): J. C. de Waal
Financial Manager: Dr. E. L. Grove
Assistant General Manager (Airways): M. E. Smuts

Chief Engineers:
Chief Civil Engineer (Johannesburg): J. G. Holahan
Chief Electrical Engineer (Johannesburg): A. H. Winchester
Chief Mechanical Engineer (Pretoria): P. A. Marais
Chief Engineer (Signals and Telecommunication) (Johannesburg): C. F. B. Fourie

Other Departmental Heads (Johannesburg):
Chief Stores Superintendent: Dr. B. D. Botha
Chief Accountant: D. L. Pheiffer
Manager, Publicity and Travel Department: P. L. Strydom
Commissioner of S.A. Railways Police: Maj. Gen. J. J. Jansen van Vuuren
Catering Manager: H. A. Crouse

Systems Managers:
Durban: J. C. B. Irving
Cape Town: C. P. van Coller
Johannesburg: D. K. Morkel
Pretoria: Dr. G. T. Eureira
Bloemfontein: C. E. Lubbe
Kimberley: D. Fourie
Windhoek: D. W. Ackermann
East London: D. M. J. Butler
Port Elizabeth: B. J. Lessing
Saldanha: A. S. le Roux

Assistant System Managers:
Johannesburg: A. J. Jonker
Cape Town: B. Heckroodt
Durban: J. P. Radyn
Port Elizabeth: M. M. C. Crous
Pretoria: G. D. Engelbrecht

Gauge: 1.065 m; 610 mm.
Route length: 21 767 km; 706 km.

Although economic activity in the country as a whole continued in recession during 1975-76, business was maintained at a high level for South African Railways as both import and export traffic increased. However, the increased revenue produced by this upsurge in traffic was entirely swamped by the effects of the continuing high rate of inflation. Freight tonnage rose by 4.5 per cent to 130 million tons, with increased hauls being recorded for many commodities including coal and other minerals for export, petroleum products and foodstuffs. Revenue-earning ton-km rose by 5 per cent to 65 060 million. Income from the three main categories of traffic—general freight, coal and livestock—rose by 10, 24 and 29 per cent respectively to produce a combined figure of R 988 million.
While first and second class passenger-journeys declined by 5 and 11 per cent respectively, third-class traffic was up by 6 per cent. Overall increase in passenger-journeys was 3.7 per cent to 643 million. Income was up by 8.5 per cent to R 116 m. Long-distance journeys declined by 5 per cent, but suburban journeys hit the record figure of 606.8 million, a 4 per cent increase over the previous year's result. Within this total, third-class journeys were up by 7 per cent.

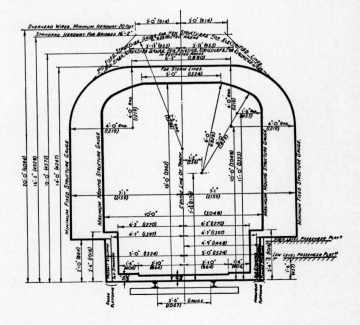

Income from all rail operations totalled R 1 375 m, an increase of R 158.5 m or 13 per cent. This was accounted for by tariff adjustments made in November 1974 and by the increased traffic; improvements were recorded under all principal headings. Expenditure, too, showed substantial increases, with administrative charges up by 30 per cent, and those for motive power and rolling stock running by 30 and 25 per cent respectively. Total rail expenditure was up by almost 20 per cent to R 1 498 m, producing a deficit of R 123 m on the year's operations. This was R 89 m or 261 per cent greater than in the previous year.

The year was marked by several technical developments, and extensive track upgrading and doubling schemes were begun. By the end of the year, work on the Vryheid-Richards Bay coal railway was practically complete. A further 180 km of electrified railway was commissioned during the year.

TRAFFIC

	1975	1976
Total freight tonne-km (millions)	68 100.7	72 076.5
Total freight tonnage ('000)	128 012	137 788
Total passenger journeys	632 888 799	644 130 688

FINANCIAL

The operation of the Railways, Harbours, Airways and Pipelines during the calender year 1976 resulted in a net loss of R 39 818 885, representing a deterioration of R 31 031 243 when compared with the net deficit of R 8 787 642 reflected in the results of working for 1975.

Although the downswing in the general economic activity continued in 1976, earnings derived from the operation of all the Administration's services reached the record level of R 2 147 420 959 which exceeded the figure of R 1 831 068 938 for the previous year by R 316 352 021, or 17.28 pet cent. This improvement is attributable mainly to the tariff adjustments operative from 1 April and 1 September 1976, as well as a higher volume of traffic conveyed by rail and air and increased tonnages of general and bulk cargo shipped through the harbours.

Expenditure (including appropriations from Net Revenue Account) increased by R 347 383 264 or 18.88 per cent, from R 1 839 856 580 in 1975 to R 2 187 239 844 in 1976. This steep rise in expenditure is largely due to rises in the cost of oil, coal, electricity and steel; the general salary improvements granted to the staff with effect from the July 1976 paymonth; the higher rate at which the Administration has contributed to the Superannuation Fund with effect from 1 October 1976; an increase in the volume of traffic conveyed, and the higher payments made in respect of interest on capital owing to more assets being placed in service. The results of working the four main services over two calendar years are reflected in the appended statement:—

	1976	1975
Revenue:—	R	R
Railways	1 601 805 633	1 353 778 040
Harbours	131 853 936	117 425 622
Airways	309 305 992	263 020 644
Pipelines	104 455 398	96 844 632
	2 147 420 959	1 831 068 938
Expenditures:—		
Railways	1 700 745 476	1 443 322 461
Harbours	75 235 464	57 543 979
Airways	310 015 275	253 784 486
Pipelines	14 609 988	13 851 154
	2 100 606 203	1 768 502 080
Surplus/Deficit:—		
Railways	(98 939 843)	(89 544 421)
Harbours	56 618 472	59 881 643
Airways	(709 283)	9 236 158
Pipelines	89 845 410	82 993 478
	46 814 756	62 566 858
All Services		
Less—		
Net Revenue Appropriations—		
Deficiency in Superannuation Fund	237 103	197 352
Contribution to Level Crossing Elimination Fund	2 500 002	2 500 000
Contribution to Betterment Fund	77 500 002	62 500 000
Contribution to Sinking Fund Redemption and Reserve Account	6 396 534	6 157 148
Total Appropriations	86 633 641	71 354 500
Net Deficit	39 818 885	8 787 642

Class 6E/1 electric locomotive; tractive force: 185 kN, number in service, 498

Class 34 diesel electric from General Motors

Total railway expenditure for the calendar year under review amounting to R 1 700 745 476 and reflecting an increase of R 257 423 015 or 17.84 per cent, compared with the figure of R 1 443 322 461 for 1975 is subjoined in detail:

	1976	1975	Increase or Decrease	
	R	R	R	%
Transportation Services:–				
Administration and general charges	70 560 041	60 345 458	(I) 10 214 583	16.93
Maintenance of permanent way and works	244 010 109	202 546 406	(I) 41 463 703	20.47
Maintenance of rolling stock	207 822 037	180 388 094	(I) 27 433 943	15.21
Motive power operating expenses	250 119 662	205 130 072	(I) 44 989 590	21.93
Traffic and vehicle running expenses	363 388 896	323 459 770	(I) 39 929 126	12.34
Cartage services	25 282 021	22 985 808	(I) 2 296 213	9.99
Superannuation	—	11 281 242	(D) 11 281 242	100.00
Ordinary working expenditure	1 161 182 766	1 006 136 850	(I) 155 045 916	15.41
Depreciation	124 637 621	113 762 428	(I) 10 875 193	9.56
Total: Transportation Services	1 285 820 387	1 119 899 278	(I) 165 921 109	14.82
Subsidiary Services:–				
Catering and bedding services	17 165 084	14 559 357	(I) 2 605 727	17.90
Publicity and advertising	320 599	259 346	(I) 61 253	23.62
Grain elevators	2 127 341	2 148 119	(D) 20 778	0.97
Pre-cooling services	10 552 157	9 452 871	(I) 1 099 286	11.63
Road transport service	53 530 792	47 296 561	(I) 6 234 231	13.18
Tourist service	16 966 594	15 359 512	(I) 1 607 082	10.46
Net Revenue Account:–				
Interest on funds	1 535 565	1 515 347	(I) 20 218	1.33
Interest on capital	262 909 893	201 252 141	(I) 61 657 752	30.64
Miscellaneous expenditure	49 817 064	31 579 929	(I) 18 237 135	57.75
Total:	1 700 745 476	1 443 322 461	(I) 257 423 015	17.84

Electric Motor Coaches

Class	1st Reserved and Van	3rd	1st	1st and Van
Type	N-15-CM	S-4-M	L-2-M	N-26-M
Wheel (or axle)	9' 0'' wheel base 41' bogie centres	9' 0'' wheel base 41' bogie centres	9' 0'' wheel base 41' bogie centres	9' 0'' wheel base 41' bogie centres
Max speed	60 mph	60 mph	60 mph	60 mph
Weight (Imperial)	136 000 lbs	136 600 lbs	136 500 lbs	139 500 lbs
Number of units	31	34	5	9
Builders	Union Carriage and Wagon Co. Ltd, South Africa		Union Carriage and Wagon Co. Ltd, South Africa	

Electric Plain Trailer Coaches

Class	3rd	1st reserved
Type	S-11-T	L-52-CT
Wheel (or axle)	2 057,5 mm wheelbase	6' 9'' wheelbase
Arrangement	13 563 mm bogie centres	44' 6'' bogie centres
Max speed	—	—
Weight (Imperial)	72 000 lb	72 000 lb
Number of units	170	20
Builders	Union Carriage and Wagon Co. Ltd, South Africa	

Special bogie wagons for the conveyance of sugar in bulk

SAR has taken over control of the 880 km Sishen-Saldanha line built by South African Iron and Steel Corporation (Iscor) and brought into operation in May 1976. SAR's ownership of the line—bought from Iscor at a cost of R 650 million—became effective on April 1, 1977. The line was built to transport iron ore from the mines at Sishen in the Northern Cape down to the port of Saldanha on the west coast. At present, three ore trains a day run down to Saldanha, giving the line an annual haul of 16.5 million tonnes. When a fourth train comes into operation soon, capacity will reach an annual 22 million tonnes. In just under a year since the line has been operating—at first experimentally—about 4 million tonnes of ore has been railed, 2.5 million tonnes for export. Following the SAR take-over, iron ore will continue to be the basic traffic. But other mining commodities are also to be carried, and SAR expects to develop other types of traffic to take up spare capacity.

In two phases, SAR's forward planning policy is aimed first at increasing the annual load of the line to 40 million tonnes. This means that more crossings will have to be built. At the moment there are nine in all: SAR plans to lay 10 more. Seven are already under construction. So far no date has been set for phase two of the plan—aimed at raising the annual load to 68 million tonnes.

For the first two years SAR expects the line will require a subsidy of R 15 million. For the third year, R 5 million should be sufficient. After that cost and operating figures should break even. Already operating on the line are 992 gondola ore wagons, and 758 more are on order. Trains are made up with 202 wagons, headed by three 2 600 hp diesel locomotives to give a total length of 2.2 km. Axle loading is 25 tonnes (100 tonnes gross mass). A total of 36 diesels have so far been delivered, and four more are on order.

Bogie wagon with rotary couplers for coal shipments

Construction and installation of overhead equipment on the 1 065 mm gauge route is proceeding at a rate of 2.5 to 4 km per day. With up to three diesel-hauled trains daily in each direction as well as inspection and maintenance traffic, installation is handled on tight schedules and follows an established procedure developed between the construction crews and the engineering support teams. All catenary work, augerable foundation holes, foundation setting, mast setting and wire stringing is carried out from railborne equipment.

As far as possible components are prefabricated and installed to close construction tolerances.

Built by South African Iron & Steel Industrial Corporation Ltd (Iscor), the line links iron ore mines at Sishen with the deep-water port at Saldanha Bay. It was transferred from Iscor ownership to SAR on April 1 this year.

Ore traffic now moving over it is hauled by rakes of five General Electric U26C diesel locomotives. When electric operations commence in mid-1978 three 50 kV 50 Hz GEC-Union Carriage Co-Co locomotives working in multiple will haul 204-wagon trains carrying 17 000 tonnes of ore at speeds up to 72 km/h. A loaded train weighs 21 000 tonnes and this demands an hourly rating for the three locomotives of 11 360 kW. At the design stage Iscor considered several voltage levels before it became apparent that the advantages of a 50 kV system made it the optimum choice for such a sparsely-populated region without convenient electrical transmission systems.

New Lines Opened During 1976

Broodsnyersplaas—Ermelo	89 km
Ermelo—Sikame (Existing Line Reconstructed on New Location)	204 km
Beestekraal—Atlanta (Extension of Existing Line)	12 km

Bogie wagon for fruit movements

Lines Projected
(i) Lines Under Construction
Arnot—Wonderfontein (Extension)	22 km
Table Bay—Kensington—Bellville (Avoiding Line)	18 km
Winternest—Mabopane (Double Line)	19 km

(ii) Additional Tracks Under Construction
Elandsfontein—Knights (Quadrupling)	4 km
Newcastle—Volksrust (Doubling)	53 km
De Wildt—Brits (Doubling)	18 km
Houtheuwel—Potchefstroom (Doubling)	70 km
Durban—Umgeni (Sextupling)	5 km

TRACKWORK
New lines: The capital amount spent on the construction of new lines during the year under review was R 91.3 million and that in respect of existing lines R127 million. Of the 204 km line under construction between Vryheid and Empangeni to serve the new Richards Bay Harbour, 22 per cent of the project as a whole still remained to be completed. 81.9 per cent of the scheme for the Richards Bay Development Harbour area and the layout of the marshalling yard, is completed and in use.

ELECTRIFICATION
An additional 411,35 km of track were electrified in 1977, bringing the total length of electrified track in the Republic to 10 969.17 km which means that 33.0 per cent of the total track network is now energised. This affected the route distance which increased by 244.67 km and brought the total distance to 5 079.10 route km. At the close of the year 3 645 track km (1 827 route km) were still under construction or authorised.

Lines electrified during 1976
	Route km	Completion Date
Welverdiend—Lichtenburg	103.02	July 1976
Springs—Kaydale	31.303	February 1976
Kroonstad—Hamilton	220.82	December 1975
Empangeni—Richards Bay	18.00	December 1976

Lines now under electrification 1977
	Route km	Anticipated Completion Date
Brits—Thabazimbi }	289	December 1978
Brits—Beestekraal—Atlanta }		
Derwent—Roossenekal	96.74	March 1977
Phalaborwa—Kaapmuiden	210.00	December 1977
Kensington—Bellville	14.12	1979/1980
Table Bay Harbour to point on Kensington—Chempet line	8.45	1977/78
Kensington—Chempet	8.13	1980/81
Vryheid (Sikame) to point on Empangeni—Richards Bay Line	160.00	December 1977
Broodsnyersplaas—Arnot Power Station	54.00	July 1978
Arnot Power Station—Wonderfontein	20.00	January 1978
Broodsnyersplaas—Ermelo	82.69	November 1977
Ermelo—Vryheid (Sikame)	205.00	June 1978
Witbank—Eerste Fabrieke	37.00	1977
Nyanga—Strandfontein	17.70	1979
Thabazimbi—Ellisras	120.00	Not available

Electrification projected
	Route km	Anticipated Completion Date
Beaufort West—De Aar	260	1988
Hamilton (Bloemfontein)— Beaconsfield (Kimberley)	163.312	1984

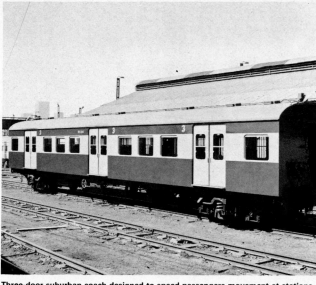
Three-door suburban coach designed to speed passengers movement at stations

Beaconsfield—De Aar	244.52	1983
Port Elizabeth—De Aar	526	1999
Hamilton—Noupoort	289.19	1990
Bloemfontein—Bethlehem	434.95	1993
Springs—Hamelfontein	153.83	1982
Krugersdorp—Mafeking	272	1987
Pretoria North—Pyramid	10.42	1986
Pyramid—Pietersburg	261.45	1992
New Central Yard (Bapsfontein) Stage 1	23	1982
New Central Yard (Bapsfontein) Stage 2	19	Not available
Winternest—Mobapane	44	December 1982
Richards Bay—Golela		Not available 1986
Connecting lines to Central Yard (Bapsfontein) Stage 1	23	Not available
Connecting lines to Central Yard (Bapsfontein) Stage 2	23	Not available 1981/82
Connecting lines to Central Yard (Bapsfontein) Stage 3	112	Not available 1982
Connecting lines to Central Yard (Bapsfontein) Stage 4	77	Not available

Due to urgency and financial position which has resulted in numerous deferments of projects, full particulars of target dates, etc. are not available.

NEW SIGNALLING INSTALLATIONS

POWER SIGNALLING INSTALLATION. Individual Geographic Circuit Interlockings.

Route Length in km	Location	System	Engineered by	Main Equipment Suppliers
	Dover, Wolwehoek, Kalkvlakte, Holfontein, Hennenman, Whites	Orange Free State	GEC Engineering	WESTINGHOUSE BELLAMBIE: CTC Supervisory equipment and point machines.
	Welkom			SIEMENS:
	Geneva, Norvalspont	Orange Free State	SAR	Interlocking equipment, control panels and axle counters.
				WESTERN INDUSTRIES:
	Kroonstad	Orange Free Satate	Siemens	Track circuit equipment, control panels, Axle counters. GEC ENGINEERING: Colourlight signals.
	Cambridge, East London, Arnoldton	Cape Eastern	SAR	
	Wellington, Beaufort West	Cape Western	Western Industries	
	Eerste Rivier	Cape Western	SAR	
	New Brighton South, Redhouse	Cape Midland	SAR	
	Gingindlovu	Natal	SAR	
	Paulpietersburg, Sikame	Natal	Siemens	
	Komatipoort, Broodsnyersplaas	Eastern Transvaal	SAR	
	Ermelo, Piet Retief	Eastern Transvaal	Westinghouse Bellambie	
	Ogies, Maraisburg	Western Transvaal	SAR	

POWER SIGNALLING INSTALLATION. Individual route relay Interlockings.
	Paarlshoop, Randfontein	Western Transvaal	SAR

CENTRALISED TRAFFIC CONTROL. Geographic relay Interlocking.
Route Length in km	Location	System	Engineered by
78	Queenstown—Burgersdorp Controlling station at Queenstown. Section lower incline—Burgersdorp completed.	Cape Eastern	Westinghouse Bellambie
120	Wellington—Touwsrivier Controlling station at Worcester. Completed up to Orchard.	Cape Western	Western Industries
15	Richard's Bay Central, Richard's Bay North Richard's Bay South, Richard's Bay Junction Richard's Bay Coal Terminal	Natal SAR	
47	Potchefstroom—Klerksdorp.	Western Transvaal	Siemens
108	Nelspruit—Komatipoort	Eastern Transvaal	SAR
82	Broodsnyersplaas—Ermelo	Eastern Transvaal	Westinghouse Bellambie
Will be 96	Eerste—Fabrieke—Witbank Balmoral, Wakefield and Clewer only under Witbank control so far.	Eastern Transvaal	Western Industries
205	Kamfersdam—Postmasburg Loop lengthening to accommodate long ore trains. This necessitated the provision and three additional relay rooms.	Cape Northern	Siemens

Class	Axle Arrange-ment	Line Current	Rated Output hp	Max. lbs (kg)	Tractive Effort (Full Field) Continuous at		Max. Speed mph (km/hr)	Wheel dia. ins (mm)	Weight tonnes	Length ft in (mm)	No. Built	Year Built	Builders	
					lb (kg)	mph (km/hr)							Mechanical Parts	Electrical Equipment

REMOTE CONTROLLED INSTALLATIONS. Power signalling. Geographic relay interlocking except where RC equipment is specified otherwise.

Mooiveld interloop, Kaalvlei interloop, Mothusi intersiding,	Orange Free	GEC Engineering
Gunhill North Station, Gunhill South Station	State	Siemens
Ruiterskop—Interloop, Antjieskraal—Interloop,	Cape Western	SAR
Botesland—Interloop, Power—Interloop	Cape Midlands	SAR
Vlakdrif—Interloop, Battery—Interloop, Florida—Station,	Western Transvaal	SAR
Cachet—Station, Minaar—Blackhill West—Station,		
Ogies—Minnaar—Station, Ogies—Saaiwater—Station		
Sitebe—Station, Clove—Station, Hudley—Station,	Natal	SAR
Dassenhoek—Nshongweni A—Station, Dassenhoek—		
Nshongweni B—Station, Tembalihle—Station,		
Ginnery—Station		
Lebombo—Station, Gelukplaas—Station	Eastern Transvaal	SAR

Reclaimed WBS RC equipment plus above.

Reclaimed GRS RC equipment plus above.

LOCOMOTIVES AND RAILCARS

DIESEL LOCOMOTIVES

Class	Axle Arrange-ment	Transmission	Rated Power hp	Tractive Effort Continuius at Start kN	Hauling kN	Max Speed kmlh	Wheel Dia. mm	Total Weight kg (Average)	Length mm	No Built During 1976	Year First Built	Builders
34-600	Co-Co	Six dc 4 pole axle hung EMD type D29B	One 16 Cylinder 2 Stroke Turbocharged and aftercooled EMD type 16-645E3	272	218	100	1 016	111 000	19 202	37	1974	General Motors South Africa (Pty) Ltd South Africa
35-200	Co-Co	Six dc 4 axle hung EMD type D29CCBT	One 4 stroke V-8 Turbocharged aftercooled EMD type 8-645E3	201	161	100	915	82 000	16 485	55	1974	General Motors South Africa (Pty) Ltd South Africa
35-600	Co-Co	Six dc 4 pole axle hung EMD type D29CCBT	One 2 stroke V-8 Turbocharged and aftercooled EMD type 8-645E3	201	161	100	915	82 000	16 485	26	1976	General Motors South Africa (Pty)Ltd South Africa
36-000	Bo-Bo	Four dc 4 pole axle hung GE type 5GE761A13	One 4 stroke V-8 Turbocharged aftercooled GE type 7FDL8	177	141	100	915	72 000	15 151	26	1975	General Motors Co. Dorman Long Loco Group South Africa
35-400	Co-Co	Six dc 4 pole axle hung GE type 5GE 764-Cl	One 4 stroke V-8 Turbocharged aftercooled GE type 7FDL8	201	161	100	915	82 000	15 152	50	1976	General Electric Co. Dorman Long Loco Group South Africa

ELECTRIC LOCOMOTIVES

Class	Axle Arrange-ment	Transmission	Rated Output kW	Tractive Effort Continuous at Start kN	Hauling kN	Max Speed kmlh	Wheel Dia. mm	Total Weight kg (Average)	Length mm	No Built During 1976	Year First Built	Builders
6-El	Bo-Bo	Four-AEI 283 AZ motors	2 252 Continuous 2 492 One Hour	311	193	113	1 219	88 904	15 494	96	1969	Union Carriage and Wagon Co. Ltd. South Africa

SPAIN

SPANISH NATIONAL RAILWAYS

**Red National de Los Ferrocarriles Españoles (RENFE),
Plaza Sagrados Corazones 7, Madrid (16)**

Telephone: 4.57.14.00
Telex: 23420

President: Placido Alvarez
Vice-president: Alfredo Moreno
Consellor-Director: Antonio Carbonell
Consellors: Antoni O Cores
　　　　　　　Vicente Diez-Corral
　　　　　　　Alberto Oliart
　　　　　　　Carlos Roa
　　　　　　　Carlos Ferrer
　　　　　　　Jaime Badillo
　　　　　　　Jorge Hernando
　　　　　　　Luis Llubia
Secretary: Jesus de Ledesma

Administration

Director General: Antonio Carbonell
Deputy Director General: Antonio Debesa
　　　　　　　　　　　Jose Luis Santiago
Secretary General: Antonio de Juan
Inspector General: Emilio Magdalena
Director Way and Works: Jose Escolano
Director of Material: Angel Gomez
Director of Transport: Pelayo Martinez-Regidor
Commercial Director: Jose Augustin Dominguez
Director of Planning: Fernando Oliveros
Director of Finances: Francisco Donate
Social Director: Antonio Pinazo
Director of Strategy: Antonio Dionis
Director of Information: Miguel Angel Eced

Zonal Managers

Zone One:	Eloy Gutierrez
Zone Two:	Antonio Crespi
Zone Three:	Jorge Santamaria
Zone Four:	Rafael Montalt
Zone Five:	Jose M. Fortuny
Zone Six:	Jose Maria Silvan
Zone Seven:	Manuel Contreras

Gauge: 1.676 m.
Route length: 13 509 km.

RENFE's management is preparing a major step forward under a plan to follow completion of the 1972-75 plan.
By 1975, total rail traffic was 10 693 million net ton-km, and was expected to rise to 26.1 million by 1977 and to 37.5 million in 1980. However, total ton-km in 1976 was only 10 766 million—far short of anticipated totals, but nevertheless up on the 10 693 million tonne-km carried in 1975.
Passenger traffic, already on the increase, is also likely to grow at a much faster rate as services improve. In 1975 the system recorded 16 146 million passenger-km, compared with a Plan forecast of 14 020 million. By 1976 the total was 16 686 passenger-km.

TRAFFIC

While many European railways suffered traffic losses of up to 20 per cent RENFE's traffic fell by less than 8 per cent.
An important factor leading to the railways relative success in attracting and keeping freight traffic has been a campaign of rationalisation over the past five years, which has led to a speed up in deliveries and important improvements in reliability.
Container traffic has been growing steadily in spite of the recession. During 1972, a total of 2 500 containers were moved. Increasing to 7 000 in 1973, 9 500 in 1974 and 11 600 in 1975—7 000 of them with a total of 98 000 tonnes loaded.
Further big increases in bulk traffic are expected as a result of a 5 000 million peseta investment in the Asturias network, completed in 1976.

	1975	1976
	(millions)	
Total freight tonne-km	10 693	10 766
Total freight tonnage	37.7	36.0
Total passenger-km	16 146	16 686
Total passenger journeys	199.6	206.3

FINANCES	1975	1976
	(Pesetas' millions)	
Revenues	38 156	47 689
Expenses	44 227	57 095

TRACK WORK

Development of the important Asturias mineral region, where almost all the coal, iron ore and limestone production is shipped by rail, is already increasing traffic to and from the region. Coal traffic reached 7 940 000 tons in 1976, more than double the 1971 tonnage.
Iron ore traffic rose to 2 220 000 tons, compared with 1 040 000 tons in 1971. Siderurgical products are expected to increase from 1 180 000 tons (1971) to 3 460 000 tons. Total traffic to and from the region rose from the 1971 figure of 6 990 000 tons to almost 16 million tons.
To increase capacity over the single-track line from Leon to Gijon, RENFE launched a massive improvement programme in 1970. The first phase, included track renewal, improvements and track extensions in 27 stations, and installation of ctc.
The second phase of the programme, completed in 1976, included:
—Track doubling on the line from Pola de Lena to Serin
—Construction of a new siding on the section from Villabona to Nubledo
—Elimination of the grade crossing at Abono
—Restructuring of tracks and yards in the Verina, Abono, Musel and Gijon port region
—Construction of a south access in RENFE gauge to the port of Musel
—Construction of a double-track variant between Serin and Gijon, via Sotiello, or doubling the Serin-Verina-Gijon section.
Total cost of the second phase was 2 784 million pesetas, of which 2 400 million pesetas were for track doubling projects.

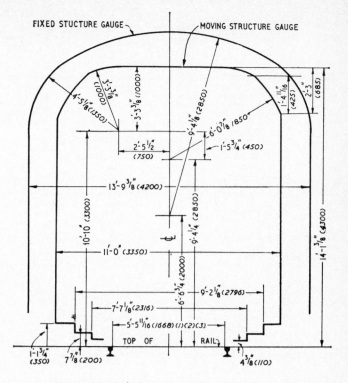

General Motors/Macos-built diesel electric locomotive hauls a mainline passenger train over the Tortosa bridge.

ELECTRIFICATION

At the end of 1976 RENFE had a total electrified route length of 4 328 km.
New electrification put into service during 1975/76 included the Madrid-Guadalajara (57 km) section the coastal line from Malaga to Fuengirola (30.5 km) and short sections from Sants (Barcelona) to Prat airport, Chamartin (Madrid) to Cantoblanco and from Manzanares to Puertollano—a total of 148 km of single track and 58 km of double track lines.
Since 1975 major electrification projects have been completed between Cordoba and Seville (137 km) and along the Miranda-Zaragoza-Lerida-Roda-Reus line (543 km). An impressive list of lines now being converted includes:
—Guadalajara-Baides-Torralba (99 km)
—Zaragoza-Ricla-Calatayud (96 km)
—Espeluy-Jaen (32 km)
—Valencia-Jativa (56 km)
—Seville-Cadiz (153 km)
—Seville-Huelva (110 km)
—Cordoba-Malaga (193 km)
—Zaragoza-Mora (191 km)
—Alcazar-Chinchilla (149 km)
RENFE began electrified services over the 141 km Alsasua—Pamplona—Castejon line in the northeast on November 28, 1977. The line is electrified at 3 000 kW dc.

TRACK

Standard rail main lines: 109 lb/yd *(54.4 kg/m)* for all relaying. 90.8 lb/yd *(45 kg/m)* and U.I.C. 91 lb/yd *(54.1 kg/m)* in 12 and 18 m lengths.
Branch lines: 85.6 lb/yd *(42.5 kg/m)* in 12.4 m lengths.
Rails weighing 57 lb to 81.7 lb *(28.3 to 40.5 kg)* are being replaced on secondary lines, and 91.8 lb *(45.5 kg)* rail on main lines is also being replaced.
Rail joints: Suspended; 4- or 6-hole fishplates and welding.
Wooden sleepers: Mainly creosoted oak, pine, and sometimes beech. *Sizes:* 2.60 × 0.24 × 0.14 for ordinary track. For points, crossings etc. 3.00, 3.50, 4.00 and 4.50 m of the same width and thickness (the centre crossing sleeper being 4.50 × 0.30 × 0.14), and for expansion joints, 2.60 × 0.35 × 0.14 m. Special sleepers of up to 6.20 m are used for diagonals on double track.
Reinforced concrete sleepers: Type R.S. for 54 and 45 kg rail with a thickness of 22 cms. They are made in Torrejón, Venta de Baños and Alcázar de San Juan.
Spacing for 45 kg rail: 20 for 12 m lengths; giving 25⅛ in *(640 mm)* spacing for inner sleepers.
30 for 18 m lengths; 24½ in *(620 mm)*
Rail fastenings: Screw spikes on wood sleepers and elastic clamps on reinforced concrete sleepers. Elastic fastenings for wood sleepers are also being tested.
Filling: Crushed limestone or quartz ore: 1½ to 3 in *(40-80 mm)*
11⅞ in *(300 mm)* under sleepers on main lines.
7⅞ in *(200 mm)* under sleepers on secondary lines.
Max curvature: Generally 5.85° = min rad of 984 ft *(300 m)* except 7.6° = min rad of 754 ft *(230 m)* on Ripoll-Puigcerdá line and 8.75° = min rad of 656 ft *(200 m)* on Cordoba-Almorchón line.
Max gradient: 4.1% = 1 in 24½ on Ripoll-Puigcerdá line.
Longest continuous gradient: 5.15 miles *(8.27 m)* of 2% (1 in 50) grade, with 5.85° curves (984 ft *(300 m)* radius) on 3 miles *(4.84 km)*.

Gauge widening on curves:	Radius of curve	Widening
	Larger than 1 312 ft *(400 m)*	None
	1 230-1 312 ft *(375-400 m)*	0.20 in *(5 mm)*
	984-1 230 ft *(300-375 m)*	0.40 in *(10 mm)*
	656-984 ft *(200-300 m)*	0.79 in *(20 mm)*

Super-elevation on sharpest curve (8.75°): 6.89 in *(175 mm)*
Max altitude: 4 901 ft *(1 494 m)* on Ripoll-Puigcerdá line.
Max axle load: 22 tons
Max permitted speed:

Talgo trains	87 mph *(140 km/h)*
Diesel trainsets (TAF)	68 mph *(110 km/h)*
Other trains	62 mph *(100 km/h)*

ROLLING STOCK

Purchases during 1976 included 3 500 freight wagons, 100 passenger coaches, 55 sleeping cars, 50 TALGO cars, 15 TALGO baggage vans and 30 vans for other trains.
In 1974, two trains of the TALGO sleeping car type inaugurated a regular service between Barcelona and Paris, under the designation of "Barcelona-TALGO". The distance between the two cities of 1 144 km is covered in 11 hours and 50 minutes, corresponding to an average speed of 97 km/h, the highest average speed yet attained in Europe on a regular night train service.
This train incorporates the most up-to-date technical improvements in railway rolling stock design, whilst retaining the main design features of its predecessors. It is thought that this represents the first sleeping car in service anywhere in the world with an all-aluminium alloy structure and a carriage tare of only 11 tonnes.
The main dimensions of the sleeping car correspond to those of the TALGO III, with the exception of the overall width, which amounts to 3 018 mm. The interior arrangement of the basic car types was designed in two versions, viz. single/twin bed compartments with 10 beds in all per coach, and tourist sleeper accommodation with 4 beds per compartment and 16 beds in all per coach.
The axles have automatic zero degree run-up angle guidance, independent wheel suspension, with an 880 mm wheel diameter and an automatic track width adjustment mechanism, enabling the carriages to operate as required on Spanish and international railway networks. During the trial runs of the TALGO prototype sleeping car train carried out in May 1972, a maximum speed of 222 km/h was attained, a world speed record at that time for a diesel driven train.
The vertical suspension consists basically of two diaphragm-type air cushions. The car bodies are connected to these air cushions via a number of inclined swing arms which take care of the transverse suspension. Tests of travel comfort were carried out in July 1973 for the Rolling Stock Division of the French Railways (SNCF), in accordance with ORE B6, RP1, annex No 5, and these tests resulted in the following calculated travel comfort values, expressed in hours:
(a) Curved stretch of track between Brive and Cahors stations, with radii of bends of the order of 500 m and non-compensated superelevations of rails of 130 to 150 mm:
  Transverse comfort: 11.4 to 11.75
  Vertical comfort: 25 to 37
(b) Straight stretch of track between Les Aubrais and Vierzon, at speeds between 160 and 170 km/h:
  Transverse comfort: 15.4 to 17.2
  Vertical comfort: 27.8 to 55
The disc brakes, which are equipped with an antilock device, are capable of achieving a 1 m/s² deceleration rate of the train.
The couplings between adjoining cars are of the same basic design as on previous TALGO types, making it impossible for an individual car to tip over sideways.
The monocoque or tubular structure of the car body embodies extruded and folded aluminium alloy sections and rolled sheets, mainly of 7 075, 2 014, 5 052 and 6 351 alloys.

TER trainset built by CAF runs over the single-track line in Ciudad Real y Jaen.

The compartment partition walls are flexibly attached to the car body side walls and roof, and rigidly attached to the floating floor.
The compartments are arranged at an oblique angle (a unique and original design), which makes optimal use of the available space, both in the corridors, where the partition walls are offset in saw-tooth formation to facilitate the movement of passengers walking in opposite directions, and within the compartments themselves, where a toilet and washroom compartment, which also includes a wardrobe and small cupboard, can be shut off from the remainder of the compartment. The floor and walls are carpeted with moquette, which, apart from giving a very pleasing appearance, improves the soundproofing of the interior of the compartments. The noise level at speeds of 180 m/h fluctuates between 60 and 62 dBA.
The luxury electric trains on the Madrid-Valladolid and Barcelona-Cerbèrl services have been replaced with fast diesel railcars. This follows the poor load factors being achieved which did not justify the electric stock. The replacements run to the same timings but are second class only.

DIESEL LOCOMOTIVES

Class	Axle Arrangement	Transmission	Rated Power hp	Max lb (kg)	Tractive Effort Continuous at lb (kg)	mph (km/h)	Max. Speed mph (km/h)	Wheel Dia. in (mm)	Total Weight Tons	Length ft in (mm)	No. Built	Year first Built	Builders: Mechanical Parts	Engine & Type	Transmission
1600	Co-Co	Elec	1 790	57 000 (26 000)	45 900 (20 800)	11 (17)	65 (105)	40 (1 016)	109	58' 11'' (17 960)	17	1955	Alco	Alco 244-G 244-H	
Talgo	Bo-Bo	Elec	810	13 300 (6 000)			87 (140)	34 (840)	66	39' 4½'' (11 989)	4	1950	A.C.F.	Maybach MD-320	
10300 11300	C	Elec	350	26 400 (12 000)	14 500 (6 500)	6.8 (11)	28 (45)	47¼ (1 200)	48	32' 2'' (9 800)	160 100	1953 1961	La Maquinista Terrestre y Maritima; Babcock & Wilcox (Spain)	Sulzer 6 LD 22A	
1800	Co-Co	Elec	1 980	57 000 (26 000)	45 900 (20 800)	11 (17.5)	65 (105)	40 (1 016)	110	59' (17 986)	24	1958	Alco	Alco 251-B	
10500	D	Hyd	550	39 670 (18 000)	28 650 (13 000)		6 (60)	45 (1 150)	60		20	1957	Henschel	Sulzer	Voith
10700	Bo-Bo	Elec	725	36 322 (16 480)	24 244 (11 000)		50 (80)	39½'' (1 016)	66	48' 9'' (14 680)	10	1962	Sulzer	6LD-22/E	
1900	Co-Co	Elec	1 977	57 855 (26 250)	40 664 (18 450)	13.5 (21.6)	75 (120)	42 (1 067)	105	55' 7'' (18 472)	90	1965- 1972	GM; Macosa	G16-567/C	GM
2100	Co-Co	Elec	2 180	60 610 (27 500)	42 590 (19 325)	14 (22.5)	75 (120)	39½'' (1 016)	111	55' 11'' (18 567)	69	1964- 1970	Alco; A.E.	Alco 251-C	GE (USA)
4000	B-B	Hyd		57 880 (26 400)	53 116 (24 100)		80 (130)	39½'' (1 016)	88		13	1966	Maybach	M-184BT	
10800	Bo-Bo	Elec.	1 000	35 214 (16 000)	29 320 (13 300)		71 (114)	39½'' (1 016)	64	42' 5'' (12 935)	16	1969	Babcock & Wilcox	Caterpillar D398	GT 601 B.I.
3000	B-B	Hyd	3 000	58 422 (26 500)			112 (180)	46'' (1 170)	88	62' 4'' (19 000)	5	1969	Krauss Maffei	Maybach Mercedes MD 6557	Mekydro 18H-U

ELECTRIC LOCOMOTIVES

Class	Axle Arrangement	Line Current	Rated Output hp	Max lb (kg)	Tractive Effort (Full Field) Continuous at lb (kg)	mph (km/hr)	Max Speed mph (km/hr)	Wheel dia. ins (mm)	Weight tonnes	Length ft in (mm)	No. Built	Year Built	Builders Mechanical Parts	Electrical Equipment
7200	2-Co-Co-2	1 500 V dc OH	2 860	34 400 (15 600)	28 600 (13 000)	37 (59.5)	68 (110)	61⅜ (1 560)	145	78' 9'' (24 000)	12	1928	Babcock & Wilcox	Brown Boveri
7400	Co-Co	1 500 V dc OH	2 400	37 700 (17 100)	27 400 (12 450)	32 (51.5)	62 (100)	51⅛ (1 300)	99	50' 10½'' (17 030)	24	1944 to 1947	Devis	Secheron
7600 8600	Co-Co	3 000 V dc OH	3 000	40 000 (18 150)	36 375 (16 500)	30 (49)	75 (120)	49 (1 250)	120	62' 1¾'' (18 940)	136	1952 to 1965	Alsthom; C.A.F.; MACOSA; Maquinista Euskalduna; Babcock & Wilcox (Spain)	Alsthom; Cenemes; General Eléctrica Española, SICE; Oerlikon
7700	Co-Co	3 000 V dc OH	3 000	38 360 (17 400)	30 500 (13 850)	36 (58)	68 (110)	55 (1 397)	120	67' 9½'' (20 660)	75	1952 to 1955	Vulcan Foundry	English Electric
7500	2-Co-Co-2	1 500 V dc	3 410	40 125 (18 200)	31 300 (14 200)	40 (65)	68 (110)	62 (1 560)	147	79' 10¾'' (24 000)	12	1944 to 1945	Compañia Auxiliar de Ferrocarriles	Brown Boveri; Oerlikon
7800	Bo-Bo-Bo	3 000 V dc	3 000	42 400 (19 250)	36 900 (16 800)	29 (47.4)	81 (130)	44 (1 120)	120	67' 7½'' (20 610)	29	1953 to 1960	S.E. do Constr. Naval; Westinghouse	Westinghouse
10000 (2-current) (2-gear Ratio)	B-B	1 500 V and 3 000 V dc	3 000	28 540 (12 950) 48 930 (22 200)	26 665 (12 100) 45 620 (20 700)	(67) (39)	75 (120) 43 (70)	49 (1 250)	80	52' 9'' (17 600)	4	1963	Alsthom	Alsthom
8900 (2-current) (2-gear Ratio)	Bo-Bo	1 500 V and 3 000 V dc	4 150	(3 100)	38 500 (17 000) High gear 60 000 (27 200) Low Gear		87 (140)		83	56' 8'' (17 270)	36	1969- 1970	Cenemesa C.A.F. Mitsubishi	Cenemesa; Mitsubishi

SRI LANKA

SRI LANKA RAILWAYS
PO Box No. 355, Colombo 10

General Manager: V. T. Navaratne, C.A.S.
Additional General Manager (Technical): P. Rajagopal
Additional General Manager (Administration): B. Polwatta, C.A.S.
Office Assistant to General Manager: M. Supramaniam, C.A.S.
Transportation Superintendents:—
  Operating: A. Chanmugarajah
  Motive Power: B. D. A. J. Fernando
  Administrative: A. G. L. Serpanchy
District Superintendents:—
  Nawalapitiya: I. S. Fernando
  Anuradhapura: H. D. Jinadasa
Commercial Superintendent: S. J. V. Weeraratne
Chief Engineer, Way and Works: J. P. Senaratne
Deputy Chief Engineer, Way and Works: C. Kalidasan
Chief Engineer, Construction: L. S. de Silva
Assistant Chief Engineer, Way and Works: S. Amarasuriya
Superintending Engineer (South): A. B. E. Seneviratne
Superintending Engineer (North): R. Ratnasingham
District Engineers: M. S. A. Farook
                 S. Panchacharavel
                 D. C. Lelwela
                 T. D. S. Pieris
Signal Engineer, Way and Works: T. W. U. Seneviratne
Chief Mechanical Engineer: E. Rasakulasurier
Deputy Mechanical Engineer: H. M. Jayawardham
Chief Accountant: E. S. P. Seneviratne
Deputy Chief Accountant: S. Nagamani
Chief Security Officer: Major O. C. de Alwis
Deputy Chief Security Officer: V. D. K. Wijeratne
Superintendent, Railway Stores: M. Zareen

Gauge: 1.435
Route length: 1 496 km

The Sri Lanka Government Railways completed a Rs 202 million three-year (1975-77) improvement programme last year. Most of the investments were allocated for major track improvements, with Rs 31.6 million spent on rehabilitation of the system and Rs 45.5 million on conversion of the narrow-gauge Colobo—Homagama line to broad-gauge operation. Remainder of the budget was allocated for purchase of 16 diesel-electric locomotives from MLW (Rs 50 million) and construction of new plant for production of freight wagons (Rs 38.9 million).

TRAFFIC
The railway believes that future freight demand will grow by about 5 per cent annually after rising to an estimated 390, 461,000 tonne-km by 1977. This will mean a require-ment by 1978 of 3200 covered wagons alone and at present the railway has only 1564 covered units fit for operation.

MOTIVE POWER AND ROLLING STOCK
During 1977, the railway announced its intention to purchase 16 diesel-electric locomo-tives. The MLW 1500 hp diesel-electric locomotives were delivered in 1975, following closely the arrival of ten new power cars from Hitachi. Acquisition of this new stock went a long way to improving SLGR operations in 1975.
Main motive power problem has been the shortage of spares, necessitating withdrawal from service of a high percentage of the system's 142 diesel locomotives. To supple-ment the fleet of diesels still in service, a number of the railway's 39 broad-gauge steam locomotives—originally withdrawn entirely from service—have been converted to oil firing and put back to work.
The average age of the present motive power stock is more than 25 years, and if a

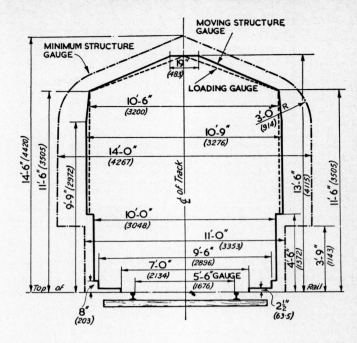

satisfactory service is to be maintained new stocks of vehicles will have to be ordered soon, says SLGRO.
The same is true of passenger coaches and freight wagons. SLGR at present operates 823 broad-gauge coaches. Out of this total, 528 coaches are over 20 years old while nearly 400 are not far short of fifty years old. The railway estimates that more than 50 per cent of the present stock is ready for replacement. A limited programme to rebuild coaches was started in 1973 and up to the end of 1975 about 100 rehabilitated coaches had been returned to service.
In addition an order was placed for 140 new coaches from Romania for delivery by 1977.
Average of the wagon fleet is not so critical as that of the coaching stock. Of the 3703 broad-gauge wagons in operation at present nearly 2500 are less than 30 years old. Biggest wagon problem is the high percentage of four-wheelers still in operation—77 per cent of the park, all of which have a very short wheel base of only 2.8194 m. Permissable speed for these units is only 64 km/h; a handicap for speedy operation. Faced with fast rising prices for imported stock (up from about Rs 90 000 in 1970 to Rs 240 000 in 1975) SLGR hopes to increase production of locally-built wagons under a three-phase programme for development of a new wagon plant. Under stage one of the programme—put in hand during 1977—a total of 100 wagons are to be built using imported components. Under stage two, certain types of components would be manu-factured locally either by SLGR workshops or by local manufacturers. Under stage three, 100 wagons annually, using 100 per cent locally-built components, would be turned out. The railway calculates that local freight wagon manufacture will result in a saving of foreign exchange on 100 wagons of Rs 2.6 million (at 1974 prices).
Once the wagon building project is fully underway it is hoped to expand construction activities to production of passenger coaches. Plans are even being laid for eventual manufacture of both wagons and coaches for export.

DIESEL LOCOMOTIVES

Class	Axle Arrange- ment	Trans- mission	Rated Power hp	Max lb (kg)	Tractive Effort Continuous at lb (kg)	mph (kmlh)	Max Speed mph (kmlh)	Wheel Dia. in (mm)	Total Weight Tons	Length ft in (mm)	No. Built	Year first Built	Builders: Mechanical Parts	Engine & Type	Transmission
M1	A1A-A1A	Elec	1 000	33 700 (15 300)	24 600 (11 160)	11.7 (18.8)	55	43	88	50' 9'' (15 469)	25	1953	Brush	Mirrlees JS12VT	Brush
M2	A1A-A1A	Elec	1 425	35 840 (16 250)			55	40	79	46' 9'' (14 250)	10	1954	GM	GM 567C	GM
M2C	A1A-A1A	Elec	1 425	44 240 (20 070)			55	40	79	43' 0'' (13 106)	2	1961	GM	GM	GM
G2	Bo-Bo	Elec	625	35 000 (15 875)	15 000 (6 800)		20	43	54	37' 9'' (11 506)	8	1951	North British Loco Co	Paxman 12RPHXL	GEC
S2	Bo-Bo	Hyd	789				56	43	55	55' 0'' (16 764)	15	1959		Maybach MD 435	Maybach Mekydro K104U
S3 S4	Bo-Bo	Hyd	880				56	36	47	55' 0¾'' (16 780)	30	1959		MAN L12V 18/21	Maybach Mekydro K104U
N1	1-C-1	Hyd	492	20 150 (9 040)			30	36	41	28' 0¾'' (8 550)	5	1953		Deutz T8 M233	Krupp
P1	C (0-6-0)	Jack Shaft & Coupl- ing Rod Drive	132	9 000 (4 080)			19.5	33	20	20' 2¾'' (6 165)	4	1950	Hunslet	Ruston Hornsby	Hunslet Patent
T1	Bo	Elec	180					34	37	61' 0'' (18 593)	24	1947		English Electric Type 6H	English Electric
Y	C (0-6-0)	Hyd	550	29 900	1 900 (5 700)	6.0 (20)	26 (42)				28	1967	Hunslet	Rolls-Royce DV8T	Twin Disc CF 12800
W1		Hyd					50 (80)						Henschel		
W2		Hyd					50 (80)						VEB		

IMPROVEMENTS

A long-term plan has been drawn up to carry out a number of major improvements throughout the system. These projects include:
Expansion of the principal carriage yard at Colombo to accommodate the increased passenger stock;
Remodelling of the former steam shed at Dematagoda to accommodate multiple-units;
Extension and provision of additional lines to the main marshalling yard at Colombo;
Construction of additional platforms at key stations;
Provision of additional crossing facilities at Taple on the coast line and Gatambe on the main line;
Extension of centralised traffic control to Chilaw, Polgahawela and Alutgama, and other improvements to signalling;
Provision of a radio communication network between main stations on the island, and the extension of the telephone links to the terminal stations of Badulla and Matale. Public address systems will also be installed at all junctions and terminals, together with intercommunication systems at Colombo marshalling yard and Anuradhapura Junction to facilitate better train and traffic control.
Proposals for the electrification of suburban lines and construction of a central workshop to manufacture spare parts, components and accessories are under consideration by the government.
Action has already been taken to place orders for 14 main line locomotives and 10 multiple-unit sets and these are expected to arrive on the island this year. It is also proposed to purchase 140 carriages for main line passenger service during the year.

TRACK

Up to 1975 the railway was operating a 1496 route-km broad-gauge system and a 140 route-km narrow-gauge system. Following mounting losses from narrow-gauge operations the Government agreed to close down all 762-mm gauge services—with the exception of commuter operations over a short section between Maradana and Homagama—as from early 1976.
SLGR is still faced with the generally poor condition of remaining broad-gauge lines which have not been kept in a good state of repair due to the inadequate supply of essential track materials.
Railway builders in Ceylon used mainly 32.6 kg/m section rails, with sleepers 9144 mm apart and an additional two sleepers on the incline for every 6.4 m of rail. With experience it was later found that closer spacing of the sleepers had little effect in reducing stresses on the rail, but that an increase of the weight of rail permitted a higher load-carrying capacity. Since 1957, therfore, the railway has been gradually replacing existing track with 36 kg/m and 40 kg/m rail sections with sleepers spaced at 6 604 mm. Under the last three-year programme the railway purchased and installed 154 km of 40 kg/m rail and 233 km of 36 kg/m sections. Cost of the rail was Rs 10.6 million.
Recent improvement and strengthening of the track with the introduction of steel sole plates has been very successful, reports the railway. It has not only increased the life of the sleepers by transmitting the load through an increased area, but has also provided a better seat for the rail bottom. Provision of additional dog spikes and introduction of elastic spikes has also helped improve the permanent way.
At present imported sleepers mainly of keruing and kempas timber varieties are used on the track along with local varieties of timber. Normal annual replacement requirement is in the region of 150,000 to 200,000 sleepers. With the shortfall in supplies in recent years, by 1975 the railway needed 400 000 sleepers for normal maintenance work.
The sole local supplier—the State Timber Corporation—is able to supply SLGR with about 100 000 timber sleepers annually. The remainder will have to be purchased from abroad and to supplement these a new concrete sleeper plant is planned to produce about 200 000 units annually.
The length of rail sections used has been increased from 6.4 m to 13.7, reducing the number of rail joints needed. Thermit welding has been introduced to weld rails, applied at site for welded panels of about 68.5 m.
Following the decision to close down narrow-gauge services it was decided to convert the 54 km line between Colombo and Opanaide (via Homagama) to broad gauge. The Rs 45.5 million estimated for the complete project includes a foreign exchange component of Rs 11.75 million. Work will include: installation of new 36 kg/m rail with new fastenings and sleepers; construction of 122 m long platforms at the 12 stations on the line; alterations to station buildings; construction of new bridges and culverts; installation of new signalling apparatus.

SIGNALLING

Although the list and morse system of interlocking is still in operation in the northern parts of Ceylon, majority of the SLGR network is signalled by type A6 equipment. Work started during the 1975-77 programme on installation of a route interlocking panel and centralised Traffic Control system. The route interlocking is at Maradana and Fort, connecting the yards in Colombo. Buttons are mounted on a geographically laid out panel and all points are moved by electrical motors. Miniature light indications on the panel give necessary information on train movements and position of switches and signals. The CTC system at present covers south of Colombo as far as Kalutara (40.2 km), north up to Alawwa (64.3 km), and northwest to Katunayaka (28.9 km). Double line tracks operated by CTC are signalled with automatic block signals with a minimum headway of three minutes at an average speed of 48 km/h.

SUDAN

SUDAN RAILWAYS
Atbara

General Manager: Mohamed Abdel Rahman Wasfi
Deputy General Manager for Traffic, Civil, Mechanical & Electric Engineering: Abbas Ali Ragi
Deputy General Manager for Training, Personnel, Financial & Economic Affairs: Ibrahim Hag Ali
Director of Civil Engineering: Yahiya Shams El Deen
Director of Traffic: Abdel Ghafour Tewfik
Director of Mechanical & Electric Engineering: Saleh Mohamed El Tayeb
Director of Personnel: El Sir A Alla
Director of Supplies and Stores: Khawad Ibrahim
Director of Accounts and Finance: Mohamed El Hassan Osman
Assistant Director of Planning and Economic Research: Abdel Rahman Mohamed Fahmi

Route length: 4 780.8 km

The International Development Association, two Arab investment banks, and the European Development Fund are to lend $US68 m to Sudan for modernisation and development of Sudan Railways during the country's current six-year plan. Principal items of expenditure will be a batch of new diesel-electrics and track-doubling between Port Sudan and Haiya Junction (203 km). Other work will include track upgrading and relating with heavier rail, improvements to signalling and telecommunications, and establishment of a staff training college at Atbara.
Further aid came during 1977 from the World Bank, when a loan of $US20 million was granted for the railways' three-year investment programme.
Sudan's single-track rail network is currently under strain. It was designed to carry 3 million tonnes of goods and 2.5 million passengers a year but at the moment it is having to cope with about 4.5 million tonnes of freight and an increasing number of passengers. In 1974-75 petroleum products accounted for 25 per cent of all freight movements followed by grain (11 per cent) and cotton, fertilisers, cement and sugar (5 per cent to 7 per cent).

MOTIVE POWER

1976 witnessed the introduction of 50 new line diesel locomotives: 20 heavy units from Henschel of Germany. 20 heavy units from General Electric of USA. 10 light units from General Electric of USA. In addition 20 new diesel shunting locomotives were introduced into service in 1976 completing dieselisation and increasing transport capacity.

FINANCES

The earnings of the corporation showed a remarkable increase in 1974-75 compared to the previous year's results due to the introduction of the new tariff since February 1974. Goods transport earnings increased by 23.41 per cent from Ls14 875 318 in 1973-74 to Ls18 358 749 in 1974-75. Livestock transport earnings increased by 1.73 per cent from Ls196 991 in 1973-74 to Ls200 403 in 1974-75. Passenger traffic earnings increased by 21.27 per cent from Ls4 432 326 in 1973-74 to Ls5 375 076 in 1974-75.
Tons carried declined by 6.4 per cent from 2 552 207 to 2 389 336 in 1974-75. The corresponding decline in net ton kms was 6.3 per cent from 2 305 million ton kms in 1973-74 to 2 160 million ton kms in 1974-75.
Revenue from catering services also showed a noticeable increase from Ls232 828 in 1973-74 to Ls294 499 in 1974-75.
To sum up, the total receipts for all services increased by Ls4 682 128 from Ls20 758 910 in 1973-74 to Ls25 441 038 in 1974-75.
Working expenses for all services increased by Ls5 080 950 from Ls22 448 499 in 1973-74 to Ls27 529 449 in 1974-75 (excluding Port Sudan which had been separated from Sudan Railways as from 1 July 1974). The increase of Ls607 738 in staff costs was mainly due to the increase in wages and salaries since 1 July 1974. The increase of Ls319 924 in stores is attributed to the consequent increase in rolling stock maintenance. Fuel costs increased by Ls1 943 342 as a result of the rise in prices of pet-

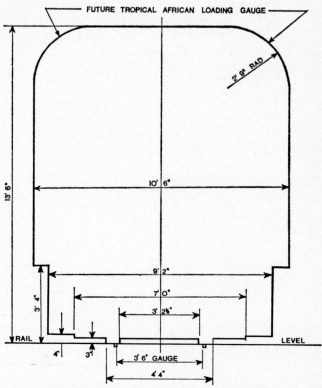

LOADING GAUGE ADOPTED FOR ROLLING STOCK AFTER 1957

roleums. Depreciation account decreased by Ls136 470 due to the elimination of Port Assests.
The deficit for all services amounted to Ls2 088 411 compared with deficit of Ls1 689 589 in 1973-74. After deduction of interest charges, appropriation of net revenue in respect of redemption of loans and grants-in-aid to local Government Councils, the deficit amounting to Ls7 572 545 was deducted from the general reserve account.
Interest charges paid to the International Bank for Reconstruction and development in respect of loan 202 SU was Ls282 298; the total amount redeemed up to 30 June 1975 was Ls10 166 422 out of which the sum of Ls993 780 was in respect of the year 1974-75.
Interest charges paid to the International Bank for Reconstruction and Development in respect of the second loan 440 SU amounted to Ls597 511. Total amount redeemed up to 30 June 1975 was Ls1 582 380 out of which the sum of Ls380 029 was in respect of 1974-75.
Interest charges paid to Kuwait Fund for Arab Economic Development amounted to Ls114 420. Total amount redeemed up to 30 June 1975 was Ls4 594 846 out of which the sum of Ls779 200 was redeemed in 1974-75.

TRACK WORK

A joint Sudanese/Egyptian engineering team has begun surveys in the border area of the proposed 410 km Wadi Halfa—Aswan link between the two countries' networks.

Maintenance Cost: The cost per kilometre for normal maintenance was Ls453 613 in 1974-75 compared with Ls321 600 in 1973-74. On the other hand the total cost per km for normal maintenance, renewals and washouts was Ls470 300 in 1974-75 against Ls510 686 in 1973-74.

Resleepering: A total number of 67 231 sleepers were renewed in sections Khartoum, Kosti Babanousa and Kassala.

Relaying and Renewal of Rails: Rerailing of 204 rails was completed at Atbara District.

Broken Rails: The total number of rails which were replaced is 60 compared with 120 in the previous year.

Washouts: The main line was washed out at various locations in Kassala, Kosti and Babanousa districts.

Standard Rail: Flat bottom, weighing 50 lb/yd *(24.7 kg/m)* in lengths of 30 ft *(9.14 m)*; and 75 lb/yd *(37.2 kg/m)* in lengths of 36 ft *(10.97 m)*; joined by fishplates and bolts. 90 lb B.S. rail for relaying Khartoum-Port Sudan Line.
Sleepers (ties): Steel; and wood impregnated under pressure in mixture of creosote and oil (½ and ½), 9 in × 5 in × 6 ft 6 in. Concrete has been used in a few cases as an experiment.
Spacing: 1 275/km under 36 ft long 75 lb rail, and 1 311/km under 30 ft long 50 lb rail. This is 12 per rail.
Rail fastenings: 50 and 75 lb rails: screw spikes and elastic spikes. 90 lb rail: clips and screw spikes. Pandrol fastenings are in service under test. Steel sleepers: steel keys are being replaced by clips with bolts and nuts.
Filling: Generally earth is used, but in some stretches of line quarry spoil and ballast.
Max curvature: (Main line) 4.5° except few at 5.0°.
Max gradient: 0.66% (1 in 150) except on section in Red Sea Hills between Summit and Port Sudan, where 1% (1 in 100) occurs. Gradient compensation for curves is 0.04% per 1° curvature.
Longest continuous gradient: The overall gradient from Port Sudan to Summit, a distance of 80 miles *(3.75 129 km)*, is 0.7%, with a continuous 2.3 miles *(3.75 km)* of 0.98%. There are only five short level sections, three of which are stations, in the whole 80 miles.
Worst combination of gradient and curvature: 1% grade with 4½° curve-radius of 1 274 ft *(388 m)*.
Gauge widening on curves: ¼ in *(6.4 mm)* on curves of 4° and over.
Super-elevation on sharpest-curve: 3 in *(76 mm)* max.
Rate of slope of super-elevation:
⅙ in *(4.2 mm)* per rail length for curves under 3° = radius of 1 910 ft *(582 m)*.
⅓ in *(8.4 mm)* per rail length for curves of 3° and over.
Max axle loading:
16½ tons for 75 lb track.
12½ tons for 50 lb track.
Max bridge loading: 17 units B.S.
Max speed:
31 mph *(50 km/h)* on 50 lb track.
37 mph *(60 km/h)* on 75 lb track.
Max altitude: 3 013 ft *(918.5 m)* at Summit Station on Port Sudan line.

Future building: A line is to be built from Abu Zabad to the Nuba Mountains; and the Western Line is to be extended from Nyala to Geneina, near the border with Chad. Other planned extensions include the line from Wau to Juba in Southern Sudan, and rail connections with Chad and with the Central African Republic.

DIESEL LOCOMOTIVES

Engine Class	Axle Arrange-ment	Trans-mission	Rated Power hp	Total Weight tons	*Tractive Effort* Max lb *(kg)*	*Continuous at* lb *(kg)*	mph *(km/h)*	*Max Speed* mph *(km/h)*	*Length* ft in *(mm)*	*Wheel Dia* in *(mm)*	*No. Built*	*Year first Built*	*Builders:* *Mechanical Parts*	*Engine & Type*	*Transmission and Type*
100	B (0-4-0)	Hyd	340	32					23′ 8″ *(7 213)*	40 *(1 016)*	6	1962	Robert Stephen-son&Hawthorns Ltd. & W. G. Bagnall Ltd. Also Clayton Dewandre-England	Rolls Royce C8TEL	Robert Stephen-son Torque convertor-twin disc, 11 500. Final drive gearbox-Wiseman 15 RLBG.
403	C (0-6-0)	Elec	350	43½					30′ 1⅛″ *(9 173)*	48 *(1 219)*	5	1952	English Electric	English Electric type 6 KT	English Electric
450	C (0-6-0)	Hyd	350	46.26	30 852 *(13 770)*				32′ 5³⁄₁₆″ *(9 885)*	48 *(1 219)*	4	1958	Henschel & Sohn-Kassal	English Electric type 6 KT	Voith; Turbo-transmission
460-466 467-480	C (0-6-0)	Hyd	500	46.5	34 400 *(15 360)* at 33% adhesion			37.5-18.7 *(60-30)*	28′ 11¼″ *(8 820)*	45 *(1 143)*	21	1962/3	Henschel Werke-GMBH	Rheinstahl Henschel AG 12-cylinder 4-stroke type 12 V1416A	Voith Turbo-Trans-mission Type L37Vb
1000	Co-Co	Elec	1 850	99	55 000 *(24 900)*	48 000 *(21 770)*		45 *(72)*	55′ 0″ *(16 764)*	36 *(914)*	25 30	1960 1963 1969	English Electric	English Electric 12 CSVT	English Electric
1200	Co-Co	Elec	1 850	99	55 440 *(25 146)* at 25% adhesion 66 528 *(30 175)* at 30% adhesion	35 700 *(16 200)*		52.8 *(85)*	57′ 7¾″ *(17 570)*	36 *(914)*	15	1961	Gregg Cockerill Ougree	Cockerill Ougree-BLH model 608A	A.C.E.C.
1400	AIA-AIA	Elec	1 500	75	33 600 *(15 230)* at 30% adhesion			50 *(80)*	48′ 6⅝″ *(14 800)*	36 *(914)*	2 20	1964 1969	Hitachi	Hitachi-M.A.N. Model V6V 22/30 MAul	Hitachi
1600	B-B	Hyd	1 500	52.8	38 976 *(17 400)*	35 168 *(15 700)*	9 375 *(15)*	56.25 *(90)*	43′ 6¹⁄₁₆″ *(13 260)*	36 *(914)*	1	1965	Henschel Werke AG	Maybach MD 654	Voith L 630 r U2 with hydro dy-namic brake and built in reverse gear.

SWAZILAND

SWAZILAND RAILWAY

Swaziland Railway Building, Johnstone Street, PO Box 475, Mbabane

Chairman: D. H. Stewart
Chief Executive Officer: A. L. Weidemann
Financial Controller: P. Barnes
Chief Operating Executive: C. J. Hubinger
Chief Civil Engineer: R. N. Scott
Chief Mechanical Engineer: C. G. Aitkenhead
Acting Chief of Administrative Services: Prince Nqaba Dlamini
Management Services Officer: C. R. Carter
Chief of Personnel and Labour Relations: B. N. Fakudze

Gauge: 1.067 mm
Route length: 219 km

For the year ended March 31 1976 1 983 000 tons of iron ore were moved for shipment to Japan. The Swaziland Iron Ore Development Company Limited, owners of the iron ore mine, will cease mining operations in October 1977 whereupon it will take the Railway until mid-1979 to transport the ore remaining in stockpile to Maputo. Construction has started on a rail link to join with the South African Railways system at Colela. The route chosen is from Phuzumoya via the sugar and citrus estates in the area of Big Bend. It is hoped that the link will be operational in approximately 18 months. For the year ended March 31 1976 the Working Account showed a deficit of E71 512-96. The tonnage of iron ore moved declined from 2 088 409 in the 1975 financial year to 1 983 614.

TRAFFIC	1975	1976
Freight tonne-km	529 394 00	489 513 000
Freight tonnage	2 735 675	2 613 472

FINANCES	1973	1974	1975	1976
Revenue	4 206 000	4 307 000	4 865 000	5 429 000
Expenses	4 666 000	4 370 000	4 669 000	5 561 000

MOTIVE POWER & ROLLING STOCK

All locomotives are hired from the Caminhos de Ferro de Mocambique. No passenger coaches are operated; the railway owns 713 freight wagons.

TRACK

A new 102 km line is projected from Phuzumoya to Golela; to be laid on concrete sleepers using 40 kg/m rail. The route leaves Swaziland Railway's Ka Dake-Mlawula (-Mozambique) line at Phuzumoya and runs almost due south past the Mtambama mountain range to Lavumisa and the border at Golela, linking up with South African Railways. At the moment Swaziland Railway moves iron ore from Ka Dake to the Mozambique port of Maputo. Completion of the Phuzumoya-Golela link in about two years will open up a second iron ore export route with trains running to South Africa's deep-water port at Richard's Bay.

Rail—types and weights:
  40 kg/m FB Mainline
  30 kg/m FB Sidings
Sleepers (Cross ties) type: Hardwood
  Thickness: 127 mm
  Spacing: up to 814 mm
Rail Fastenings (types used): Soleplates and Coachscrews
Welded Rail: Total length of track laid 31 December 1975: 126 km

SWEDEN

SWEDISH STATE RAILWAYS

Statens Järnvägar (S.J.), S-105 50 Stockholm C.

General Manager: Lars Peterson
Chief Officers:
  Operating Department: G. Rosqvist
  Commercial Department: E. Sunden
  Fixed Installations Department: R. Enberg
  Mechanical and Workshops Dept.: B. Larsson
  Department of Finance and Economics: M. J. G. Högberg
  Administrative Department: B. L. Ulf
  Department of Development and Research: P. G. Andersson
  Legal Department: C. Nordström
Commercial Department:
  International Freight Manager: O. Johannesson
Container Services:
  Freight Manager: A. Plyme
  Assistant Chief Operating Manager: P. Eije

Gauge: 1.435 m; 891 mm
Route length: 11 179 km; 182 km

Policy control of the SJ is exercised by a Board consisting of eight members under the chairmanship of the Director General. Seven members are appointed by the Government.
The heads of the eight departments and the Director General constitute the Directorate (consultative function).
Operating and Fixed Installations regions coincide with regional centres at Malmö, Göteborg, Norrköping, Stockholm, Örebro, Gävle, Sundsvall and Lulea.
Swedish State Railways (SJ) operate a total of 7 059 miles (11 361 km) of route, made up as follows:—

Gauge	4 ft 8½ in (1.435 m)		2 ft 11 in (0.891 m)		Total	
	miles	km	miles	km	miles	km
Route length	6 946	11 179	113	182	7 059	11 361
Electrified route length	4 324	6 959	—	—	4 234	6 959
System of electrification	16 kV 16⅔ Hz		—			

The line from Trelleborg, the ferry port on the south coast, northward to Narvik, Norway, is one of the longest continuous electrified lines in the world. It is 1 373 miles (2 210 km) long, of which the last 24 miles (39 km) section is in Norway.

TRAFFIC

The annual report for Swedish State Railways for the financial year 1975/76 shows that passenger traffic remained virtually constant while freight traffic declined considerably compared with the previous year. While the number of passenger journeys fell by 3 per cent to 63.6 million, passenger miles rose by 2 per cent. Average load factor remained constant at 37 per cent. Freight traffic fell by 17 per cent in terms of total tonnage and 15 per cent on ton-miles. Of the Kr4093million total turnover 52 per cent came from freight and 31 per cent from passenger traffic. State compensation for non-profitable rail traffic contributed 13 per cent. Profit after depreciation fell from Kr134 million to Kr49 million.
Freight traffic handled by Swedish State Railways (SJ) increased by 1 per cent to 54.2 million tonnes and 15 100 million tonne-km in fiscal 1976-77. Number of passenger journeys remained unchanged at 65 million. Seat utilisation was 36 per cent and passenger-km amounted to 5 500 million. At the end of June 1977 the Swedish railway network comprised 11 400 km of track. A total of 45 200 wagons were in service. Half of the total income of Kr4 552 million ($US 945.8 million) related to freight and 31 per cent to passenger traffic. SJ ferries carried 5.2 million tonnes of railway freight during 1976-77.

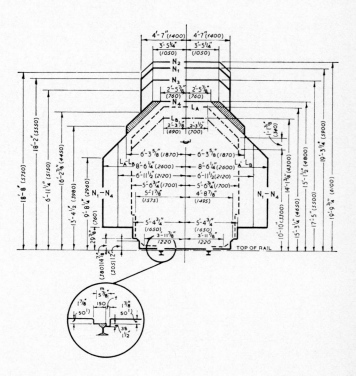

	1974	1975	1976
		Million	
Total freight ton-km	18 500	15 200	14 762
Total freight tonnage	69	55	53.5
Total passenger-km	5 400	5 700	5 570
Total passengers carried	70	69	63.6

FINANCES	*1972-73*	*1973-74*	*1974-75*
		Million Skr	
Revenues[1]	2 799	3 257	3 657
Expenses[2]	2 775	3 107	3 540

[1] Railway operating revenue
[2] Operating charges, including depreciation

MOTIVE POWER AND ROLLING STOCK

ASEA won its largest order yet in 1977 for electric locos to be supplied to Swedish State Railways. SJ has ordered 40 Class Rc4 thyristor-controlled locomotives at a cost of SwKr190m. Delivery will start in 1979.

The first of six Class Rm thyristor locomotives continuously rated at 3 600 kW were delivered by ASEA to Swedish State Railways (SJ) for use on the Lulea-Kiruna-Narvik iron ore haul, during 1977. They are a modified version of SJ's numerous Bo-Bo Class Rc4, the main differences being that the Rm has rheostatic braking and is ballasted to give an axleload of 23 tonnes. For this reason the bogies are a heavy-duty design similar to those developed by ASEA for its Bo-Bo-Bo locomotives.

Trains of around 6 000 tonnes gross are hauled up 1 per cent gradients on this route—which is electrified at 15 kV 16⅔ Hz and crosses the Arctic Circle— by SJ's triple-articulated Class Dm locos continuously rated at 7 200 kW. These will now be supplemented by the six Class Rm locos, which will normally be used in two groups of three working in multiple. Automatic couplers of Type SA3 are fitted to cope with the high tractive effort, which will exceed 90 tonnes at starting. Among the modifications to the standard Rc4 is extra heating in the cab to cope with Arctic weather, and a new static converter replacing the motor-generator set previously used to produce 50 Hz power from the 16⅔ Hz traction supply. This static converter will be standard on all future deliveries of Class Rc4.

Number of locomotives in service	*Line haul*	*Shunting*
Number of locomotives in Electric	628	134
Number of locomotives in Diesel-electric	125	—
Number of locomotives in Diesel-hydraulic	88	417
Number of locomotives in Diesel-mechanical	—	21

Number of railcars, electric	42
Number of railcars, diesel	176
Number of trailer cars, electric	56
Number of trailer cars, diesel	111
Number of multicar trains, electric	132
Number of multicar trains, diesel	6
Number of passenger train coaches	1 683
Number of freight train cars	46 349

Class Rc4 locomotives are being built by ASEA, Nohab and KVAB; rated output 4 900 hp, maximum speed 135 km/h, weight 78 tonnes.

Class T44 diesel-electric locomotives, built by Nohab, are rated at 1 670 hp. A total of 73 units are now in service. More are being delivered.

ELECTRIC LOCOMTIVES

Class	*Axle Arrange-ment*	*Line Current*	*Rated Output* hp	*Max* lb *(kg)*	*Tractive Effort (Full Field) Continuous at* lb *(kg)*	mph *(km/hr)*	*Max. Speed* mph *(km/hr)*	*Wheel dia.* ins *(mm)*	*Weight* *tonnes*	*Length* ft in *(mm)*	*No. Built*	*Year Built*	*Builders: Mechanical Parts*	*Builders: Electrical Equipment*
Da	1-C-1	15 kV 1/16⅔	2 500	45 200 *(20 500)*	21 200 *(9 600)*	43.2 *(69.5)*	62 *(100)*	60¼ *(1 530)*	75	42′ 8″ *(13 000)*	92	1952	Nohab; ASJ; Motala	ASEA
Du	1-C-1	15 kV 1/16⅔	2 500	34 600 *(15 700)*	21 100 *(9 600)*	43.2 *(69.5)*	62 *(100)*	60¼ *(1 530)*	80.4	42′ 8″ *(13 000)*	237	1925	Nohab; ASJ; Motala	ASEA
Dm	1-D+D-1	15 kV 1/16⅔	5 600 6 500	137 000 *(62 000)* 137 000 *(62 000)*	63 500 *(28 800)* 63 500 *(28 800)*	32.4 *(51.8)* 37.0 *(59)*	47 *(75)* 47 *(75)*	60¼ *(1 530)* 60¼ *(1 530)*	180.0- 186.4 190.0	82′ 3¾″ *(25 100)*	19 1	1953 1971	Nohab; ASJ Motala	ASEA
Dm3	1-D+D+ D-1	15 kV	8 400 1/16⅔	205 000 *(93 000)*	96 000 *(43 500)*	32.4 *(51.8)*	47 *(75)*	60¼ *(1 530)*	258.4	115′ 8″ *(32 250)*	3	1960	Nohab; ASJ Motala	ASEA
Dm3	1-D+D+ D-1	15 kV	9 750 1/16⅔	205 000 *(93 000)*	96 000 *(43 500)*	37.0 *(59)*	47 *(75)*	60¼ *(1 530)*	273.2	115′ 8″ *(35 250)*	15(1)	1967	Nohab; ASJ; Motala	ASEA
F	1-Do-1	15 kV 1/16⅔	3 500	44 500 *(20 200)*	20 000 *(9 100)*	58.7 *(94.5)*	84 *(135)*	60¼ *(1 530)*	102	49′ 11¾″ *(15 230)*	23	1942	Nohab; ASJ; Motala	ASEA
Hc	Bo-Bo	15 kV 1/16⅔	1 600	37 400 *(17 000)*	17 200 *(7 800)*	33.6 *(54.1)*	50 *(80)*	43¼ *(1 100)*	59.8	41′ 0″ *(12 500)*	13	1942	Nohab; ASJ Motala	ASEA
Hg	Bo-Bo	15 kV 1/16⅔	1 760	40 200 *(18 300)*	18 500 *(8 400)*	34.1 *(54.9)*	50 *(80)*	43¼ *(1 100)*	64.8	41′ 0″ *(12 500)*	55	1942	Nohab; ASJ; Motala	ASEA
Ma	Co-Co	15 kV 1/16⅔	4 500	82 500 *(37 400)*	36 800 *(16 700)*	44.4 *(71.5)*	63 *(100)*	51⅛ *(1 300)*	105	55′ 1½″ *(16 800)*	32	1953	Nohab: ASJ; Motala	ASEA
Mg	Co-Co	15 kV 1/16⅔	3 600	65 200 *(39 600)*	32 400 *(14 700)*	36 *(58)*	50 *(80)*	43¼ *(1 100)*	102	55′ 1½″ *(16 800)*	16	1944	Nohab; ASJ; Motala	ASEA
Ra	Bo-Bo	15 kV 1/16⅔	3 600	43 200 *(19 600)*	20 000 *(9 100)*	65.5 *(104.5)*	93 *(150)*	51⅛ *(1 300)*	64.0	49′ 6½″ *(15 100)*	10	1955	Nohab; ASJ; Motala	ASEA
Rc4	Bo-Bo	15 kV 1/16⅔	4 900	61 700 *(28 000)*	34 600 *(15 700)*	48.5 *(78)*	84 *(135)*	51⅛ *(1 300)*	78.0	50′ 9″ *(15 470)*	41	1975	Nohab; KVAB	ASEA
Rm	Bo-Bo	15 kV 1/16⅔	3 600 kW	65 000 *(31 400)*			63 *(100)*		92	50′ 11″ *(15 570)*	6	1977	ASEA	ASEA
Ub	C	15 kV 1/16⅔	700	29 800 *(13 500)*	16 700 *(7 600)*	15.5 *(25)*	28 *(45)*	43¼ *(1 100)*	47.4	31′ 6″ *(9 600)*	90	1930	Nohab; Motala	ASEA
Uc	C	15 kV 1/16⅔	700	29 800 *(13 500)*	16 700 *(7 600)*	15.5 *(25)*	28 *(45)*	43¼ *(1 100)*	49.2	31′ 6″ *(9 600)*	1	1933	Nohab	ASEA
Ud	C	15 kV 1/16⅔	840	28 600 *(13 000)*	15 200 *(6 900)*	20 *(32)*	37 *(60)*	43¼ *(1 100)*	50.4	31′ 6″ *(9 600)*	25	1955	Nohab; ASJ; Motala	ASEA

Notes: Class Dg2, rebuilt from Dg in 1950. Class Du, rebuilt from Dg, Dk and Ds.
Class Rb1, Silicon rectifier. Class Rc, thyristor control.
(1) Rebuilt from Class Dm to Dm3

New experimental wagon. Two were built by Talbot, Western Germany, in 1976. Weight 15.9 tonnes, loading capacity 24.0 tonnes. The covers (each covering half of the wagon) slide easily to the side, leaving half of the car easy to load or unload from the side or from above.

Artist's impression is of a future high-speed passenger train to be developed for SJ. Meanwhile, a multiple unit class X5 trainset built by ASEA in 1948 was modified for high-speed tests in 1975.

DIESEL LOCOMOTIVES

Class	Axle Arrangement	Trans- mission	Rated Power hp	Max lb. (kg)	Tractive Effort Continuous at lb (kg)	mph (km/h)	Max. Speed mph (km/h)	Wheel Dia max (mm)	Axle load tonnes	Total Weight Tons	Length ft in (mm)	No. Built	Year first Built	Mechanical Parts	Engine & Type	Transmission
T21	D	Hyd	800	41 200 (18 700)	26 500 (12 000)	7.5 (12)	50 (80)	49⅜ (1 255)	14.2	57	37' 1" (11 300)	51 3	1955 1956	MAK ASJ	MAK MA 301A	Voith and MAK
T23	D	Hyd	750	26 000 (11 800)			47 (75)	40 (1 015)	13.0	52	35' 9" (10 900)	11 4	1954 1954	MAK AJS	MAK MA301A	Voith and MAK
T41	(A1A)- (A1A)	Elec	1 445	42 300 (19 200)	25 300 (11 500)	14.3 (23)	62 (100)	40 (1 015)	16.0	84	50' 6¼" (15 400)	5	1956	Nohab	GM 12-567C	Asea (GM licence) and GM
T42	Bo-Bo	Elec	1 445	47 600 (21 600)	25 300 (11 500)	14.3 (23)	62 (100)	40 (1 015)	18.0	72	47' 3" (14 400)	1	1954	GM	GM 12-567C	GM
T43	Bo-Bo	Elec	1 445	47 600 (21 600)	28 200 (12 800)	14.3 (23)	59 (95)	40 (1 015)	18.0	72	46' 8¾" (14 240)	50	1961	Nohab	GM 12-567 D1	Asea (GM licence)
T44	Bo-Bo	Elec	1 670	48 600 (22 100)	36 000 (16 500)	11 (17)	56 (90)	40½ (1 030)	19	76	50' 6¼" (15 400)	35	1968-70	Nohab	GM 12-645E	GM
Tb snow- plough	Bo-Bo	Elec	1 670	48 600 (22 100)	36 000 (16 500)	11 (17)	59 (95)	40½ (1 030)	18	72	50' 6½" (15 400)	10	1969	Nohab	GM 12-645E	GM
Tc snow- plough	B	Hyd	625	19 400 (8 800)	13 700 (6 200)	8 (13)	56 (90)	38¾ (985)	16	32	46' 8¾" (14 200)	20	1969	Nohab	KHD BF 12M 716	Voith and Gmeinder
Tp	1-C-1	Hyd	750	23 800 (10 800)	18 700 (8 500)	7.5 (12)	40 (65)	43¼ (1 100)	10.0	46	35' 1¼" (10 700)	10	1954	MAK	MAK MA 301A	Voith and MAK
V3	C	Hyd	450	36 400 (16 500)	15 400 (7 000)	6.8 (11)	31 (50)	43¼ (1 100)	16.7	50	31' 10" (9 700)	50	1952	Esslingen	Deutz V6M536	Voith
V4	C	Hyd	265	34 800 (15 800)	30 400 (13 800)	3.1 (5)	43 (70)	38¾ (985)	16	48	33' 9½" (10 300)	10	1972	Henschel	Deutz BF12M717	Voith and Gmeinder
V5	C	Hyd	265	34 800 (15 800)	30 400 (13 800)	3.1 (5)	43 (70)	38¾ (985)	16	48	34' 11" (10 640)	30	1975	Henschel	Deutz BF12M717	Voith and Gmeinder
Z3	B	Hyd	130	14 500 (6 600)			34 (55)	33½ (850)	10	20	24' 10" (7 570)	10	1953	Klöckner Humboldt Deutz AG, Köln	Deutz A8L 614	Voith and Klöckner Humboldt Deutz
Z4p	B	Hyd	160	10 300 (4 700)			25 (40)	30 (760)	7	14	21' 0" (6 400)	25 14	1950 1956	Kalmar Verkstad	Scania Vabis D812	Atlas Diesel and Kalmar Verkstada AB
Z43	B	Hyd	160	14 500 (6 600)			34 (55)	38⅛ (970)	10	20	28' 10½" (8 800)	52 64	1951 1958	Kockums Mek Kalmar Verkstad	Scania Vabis D812	Atlas Diesel and Kalmar Verkstads AB
Z49	B	Hyd	150	13 000 (5 900)			28 (45)	38⅛ (970)	9	18	25' 11" (7 900)	10	1939	Kockums Mek	Wisconsin EO-2A	Atlas Diesel and Kockum
Z49	B	Mech	160	14 500 (6 600)			37 (60)	38⅛ (970)	10	20	28' 10½" (8 800)	11 10	1941 1941	Kockums Mek Kalmar Verkstad	Scania Vabis D802/812	Friedrichs
Z49	B	Hyd	160	14 500 (6 600)			28 (45)	38⅛ (970)	10	20	28' 10½" (8 800)	22	1944	Kockums Mek	Scania Vabis D802/812	Atlas Diesel and Kockum
Z61	B	Hyd	295	20 500 (9 300)			37 (60)	38¾ (985)	14	28	28' 6½" (8 700)	10	1957	Kockums Mek	M./.N. AC W6V 17.5/22A	Krupp
Z62	B	Hyd	295	20 500 (9 300)			37 (60)	38½ (980)	14	28	28' 10½" (8 800)	10	1957	AB Hägglund & Söner	Scania Vabis D643/632	Ulvsunda Verkstads AB and Hägglund & Söner
Z63	B	Hyd	295	20 500 (9 300)			37 (60)	38¾ (985)	14	28	27' 2¾" (8 300)	12	1956	Nydqvist & Holm	General Motors Twin Six	General Motors and Deutsche Getriebe Gesellschaft
Z64	B	Hyd	240	20 500 (9 300)			33 (53)	33½ (850)	14	28	24' 2¼" (7 370)	35	1953	Klöckner Humboldt Deutz	Deutz T4M 625	Voith and KHD
Z65	B	Hyd	295	20 500 (9 300)			37 (60)	38¾ (985)	14	28	30' 3¾" (9 240)	102	1962	Kalmar Verkstad	Rolls Royce C8TFL MK IV	Twin Disc and Deutsche Getriebe Gesellschaft
Z66	B	Hyd	295	21 160 (9 600)			43 (70)	38¾ (985)		32	33' 9½" (10 300)	30	1971	Kalmar Verkstad	KHD F12 M 716	Voith and Gmeinder

Note: Class Tp, Z4p 2 ft 11 in *(0.891 m)* gauge. Class T23 rebuilt from Tp.

Class V5 diesel locomotives are being built by Henschel; hydraulic transmission: rated output 265 hp.

Class Tb is a special diesel-electric snowplough locomotive built by Nohab.

TRACK

Standard rail: The only rail sections now being bought and installed are:
Type SJ 43: 87 lb per yd *(43.2 kg|m)*
Type SJ 50: 101 lb per yd *(50.0 kg|m)*

Sleepers (cross ties):
Wooden sleepers:
Type 1: 9 ½ in × 6 ⅛ in × 8 ft 6 ¾ in *(240 × 155 × 2 600 mm)*
Type 2: 8⅜ in × 6⅛ in × 8 ft 6¾ in *(220 × 155 ×2 600 mm)*
Concrete sleepers:
Type B10: 12½ in × 8¾ in × 8 ft ⅜ in *(320 × 222 × 2 500 mm)*
Type S3: 12½ in × 8¾ in × 8 ft ⅜ in *(320 × 220 × 2 500 mm)*

Rail fastenings: With wooden sleepers the Hey-Back fastening is used. With concrete sleepers the FIST, PANDROL and HAMBO types are used with a rubber or plastic pad under the rail.

Sleeper spacing:
Main lines: 25½ in *(650 mm)*
Secondary lines: 29½ in *(750 mm)*
On the ore line Kiruna-Riksgränsen spacing being reduced to 19⅝ in *(500 mm)*.

Welded rail: Total length of track 31 December, 1976: 3 700 km. The rail bars are flash butt welded in workshop into 360 m lengths which are carried on a train of flat cars to site. After laying in a position, the rails lengths are Thermit welded to form continous rail.

SIGNALLING

An order worth Kr140 m placed by Swedish State Railways with L M Ericsson and Standard Radio & Telephone AB provides for an automatic warning system to be installed system-wide by 1982. Basically this is a track-to-train communications system using pairs of beacons located between the rails adjacent to signals and on-board transmitters and a microprocessor. If a train driver fails to apply the brakes in response to an adverse signal aspect an optical warning is shown in the cab; if this does not provoke a response from the drive an acoustic signal is sounded, and if this is unheeded the brakes are automatically applied.

Ferry Link: A new railway ferry went into operation on the Sassnitz (German Democratic Republic)-Trelleborg (Sweden) route in July 1977 following completion of the 158 m long MV *Rostock* by Bergens Mekaniske Versteder of Norway. The *Rostock* carries 49 rail wagons on 605 m of rails and be able to operate at a top speed of 20.5 knots. The new ferry joined three German-owned and four Swedish ships already plying over the route. In 1976, freight totalling 3.22 million tonnes was carried between the two ports. The crossing takes three hours 40 minutes.

SWITZERLAND
SWISS FEDERAL RAILWAYS

Schweizerische Bundesbahnen (SBB)
Chemins de fer Fédéraux Suisses (CFF)
Ferrovie Federali Svizzere (FFS)
Hochschulstr 6, CH-300 Bern

Telephone: Berne 60 11 11

Railways Board of Administration:
Chairman: Dr h.c. Rudolf Meier
Members: Werner Meier   Dr Willie Joerin
Franco Robbiani   Jean-Pierre Pradervand
Dr Pierre Glasson   Ernst von Roten
Dr Hans Herold   Dr Gion Willi
Jean Badel   Dr Roger Perret
Franz Muheim   Kurt Schweizer
Dr Ernst Jaggi   Arthur Schmid
Secretary: Dr Arnold Schärer
President and Manager of Financial and Staff Dept.: Ing. Roger Desponds
Departmental Managers:
Traffic Department: Dr Karl Wellinger
Technical Department: Dr Werner Latscha
Heads of Divisions:
Secretariat: Dr Arnold Schärer
Organisation and Planning: Hans Walter
Financial: Heinz Diemant
Personnel: Dr Ernst Moor
Medical: Dr Antonio Serati
Legal: Dr Matthias Sulser
Passenger Traffic: Samuel Ed. Berthoud
Freight Traffic: Dr Franz Hegner
Traffic control: Jean-P. Berthouzoz
Stores (at Basle): Réné Auberson
Operating: Ing Arthur Borer
Traction and Workshops: Ing Paul Winter
Electric power stations: Ing Peter Schaaf

Regional Management:
Region I, Lausanne
Manager: Ing André Brocard
Heads of Divisions:
Administration: Dr François X. Savoy
Way and Works: Pierre Cavaleri
Operations: Réné Emery
Traction: Ing Roland Berberout

Region II, Lucerne
Manager: Ing Rolf Zollikofer
Heads of Divisions:
Administration: Dr Richard Felber
Way and Works: Ing Alfred Etterlin
Operations: Dr Ernst Schneider
Traction: Ing Robert Zwinggi

Region III, Zürich
Manager: Dr Max Strauss
Heads of Divisions:
Administration: Dr Hermann Büchel
Way and Works: Ing Hansrudolf Wachter
Operations: Adolf Peter
Traction: Ing Jakob Rutschmann

Gauge: 1 435 m; 1.00 m.
Route length: 2 853 km; 74 km.

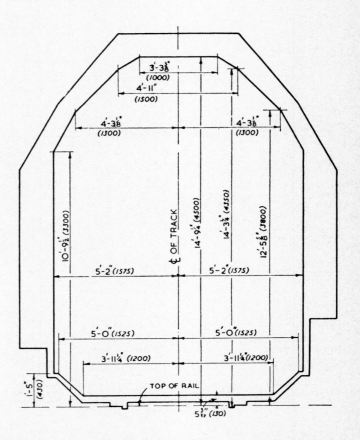

Swiss Federal Railways reported worsening losses in 1976. However, the worst-ever deficit of approximately £165 million, some £19.8 million higher than in 1975 was less than expected thanks to economies during the year. The SBB also points out that about £6.8 million was spent exceptionally on initial steps towards automatic coupler adoption. Passenger traffic again fell, but by a marginal 1.1 per cent compared with the 4.1 per cent decline in 1975, largely through a continuing fall-off in international business; nevertheless, fare increases helped to push revenue above budget. On the freight side, tonnage was improved by 8.4 per cent, the biggest rise coming in international transit traffic, but revenue was slightly below budget because of the fierce competition created by excess trans

TRAFFIC

Swiss Federal Railways (SBB) reports that, compared with 1975, freight tonnage improved by 11.1 per cent in 1976 with an increase in freight train mileage of 5.6 per cent. The carriage of road vehicles through the three Alpine tunnels dropped: through the St Gotthard by 16 per cent; through the Lötschberg by 2 per cent; and through the Simplon by 19 per cent. Overall there was also a decline in trans-Alpine car-sleeper traffic although there was an improvement on some individual routes: Calais-Lyss, 19 per cent down; Belgium-Brig 5 per cent down; Boulogne-Milan 15 per cent down; Paris-Milan, 4 per cent down; Belgium-Milan, 2 per cent up; Holland-Milan — via St Gotthard, 14 per cent up, — via Simplon, 20 per cent down; West Germany-Milan, 15 per cent down.

SBB was one of the last European systems to slide into major deficit, losses rising in the last three years to SwFr708 m in 1976 against revenue of SwFr2 370 m. Although SBB is tightly run, the 25 per cent drop in freight traffic in 1975 due to the recession could not be matched by cost savings; carryings remain well below the 1974 figure although there was some improvement during 1977.

Switzerland's economic health is to a considerable extent dictated by the industrial vicissitudes of its European neighbours. Germany and Italy in particular suffered severely from recession in 1975 and this fact is strongly reflected in Swiss Federal Railways' (SBB) performance for that year, with transit freight over the Alpine passes substantially less than in the previous year. Total freight traffic slid by about 25 per cent from 7 004 million tonne-km in 1974 to 5 141 million tonne-km in 1975.

Passenger-km in 1975 totalled 7 984 million, a drop of 3.7 per cent compared with 1974. First-class travel declined as more people became cost conscious and only receipts for accompanied motor vehicles showed an increase, principally because the Alpine roads passed were closed for longer periods than usual in the spring.

SBB's performance in 1975 confirms the susceptibility of rail transport to industrial performance; during the year relentless competition from road hauliers took a severe toll of rail carryings and up to 10 000 freight wagons were stored out of use at one time. The net result was a deficit of SwFr623m, an increase of SwFr389 m compared with the previous year.

In the first eight months of 1977 goods traffic increased by 1.4 million tonnes, or 5.8 per cent. There was only a slight fall (1.1 per cent) in the number of passengers from January to August 1977. Receipts from passenger traffic in the first eight months of 1977 were 8.4 per cent higher. Total passenger receipts for 1977 have been estimated at SwFr855 million and on this basis the figure budgeted for 1978 is SwFr877 million. The improvement is expected to come from a small growth in season ticket and party travel, assisted by increases in certain season ticket rates. Total operating receipts are placed at SwFr2 003 million, SwFr148 million more than the expected final figure for 1977. The subsidy payable to the railways is reviewed every two years. For 1978 and 1979 it would have been based on the expenditure in 1976, taking 1974 as the reference year. The extent to which the general financial situation has worsened since, then, however, would have made a calculation on this basis unsatisfactory and the railways have therefore proposed a figure of SwFr250 million, an increase of SwFr55 million on the calculated figure.

Wages and salaries are still the largest item on the expenditure side, accounting for 60.5 per cent of the total. The budget assumes a staff of 38 970 in 1978, or 1 302 fewer than in 1976 but no change on 1977. Provision has been made for cost-of-living increases of 6 per cent, compared with 4 per cent in 1977. If the index rises further it is estimated that each 1 per cent would require a further SwFr17 million in the budget. Other expenditure is placed at SwFr525.1 million, 8.1 per cent above the anticipated figure for 1977 and SwFr10.3 million more than the final figure for 1976. The principal causes are increases in hire charges for rolling stock, in the cost of electricity purchased from other suppliers, and in the price of equipment necessary for operating the railways. On the other hand less will be spent on new construction and renewals. Expenditure is being reduced to the practicable minimum and concentrated on completing work already in hand.

In percentage terms, the forecasts for 1978 show increases of 10.1 per cent in passenger and 7 per cent in freight receipts over the last full accounting year, 1976, but the freight result 1976, depends on economic factors which are difficult to predict in the short-term. The administration cannot feel optimistic about the future, pointing out that even a moderate increase in prices would cause the situation to worsen rapidly. Significant increases in receipts in the medium term cannot be counted on because of the limited scope for raising rates and fares which is open to the railways in the next few years.

TRACK

Early in 1977, the SBB Board allocated 69.5 million Swiss francs for the construction of a direct line between Olten and Rothrist; this line will enable the Basle-Olten-Lucerne and Zurich-Olten-Berne traffic flows to be kept separate. At present there are 250 traffic movements a day over the Olten-Aarburg section. The construction of this line will increase the Swiss network's capacity considerably and cut running times appreciably.

FINANCIAL

The CFF have recieved a grant for improving the Saint Gotthard line: enlarging the tunnel cross-section to take road vehicles on wagon traffic, modernisation of stations and replacement of Gotthard Station in the middle of the tunnel. The total cost will be SFr50 million. Other expenditure authorised includes SFr10 million on the station at Schwyz, including modernisation of signalling, and SFr43 million for the replacement of the block post in the middle of the St Gotthare Tunnel by the provision of two diamond crossings and the installation of signalling for two-way working. Meanwhile SBB is still hoping to get approval for the new 49km St Gotthard base tunnel which would short-circuit the existing line between Erstfeld and Biasca. It would consist of a double-track tunnel and a parallel pilot tunnel, as well as two intermediate underground service stations. It would give a capacity of 18 million net tons of goods per year through the Saint Gotthard.

The new line would take 13 to 14 years to build.

DIESEL LOCOMOTIVES

Class	Axle Arrangement	Transmission	Rated Power hp	Max lb (kg)	Tractive Effort Continuous at lb (kg)	mph (km/h)	Max. Speed mph (km/h)	Wheel Dia. in (mm)	Total Weight Tons	Length ft in (mm)	No. Built	Year first Built	Builders: Mechanical Parts	Builders: Engine & Type	Builders: Transmission
Bm 4/4 II (18451-52)	Bo-Bo	Elec	830	22 000 (10 000)	9 700 (4 400)	31.4 (50.6)	68 (110)	41 (1 040)	65	48' 10¾'' (14 900)	2	1939	SLM	Sulzer	Brown Boveri
Bm 4/4 (18401-26) (18427-46)	Bo-Bo ,,	Elec ,,	842 ,,	48 500 (22 000) ,,	28 700 (13 000) ,,	10.9 (17.5) ,,	47 (75) ,,	41 (1 040) ,,	72 ,,	41' 6'' (12 650) 43' 1¾'' (13 150)	26 20	1960-65 1968-70	SLM ,,	SLM ,,	Secheron ,,
Bm 6/6 (18501-14)	Co-Co	Elec	1 300	75 000 (34 000)	41 900 (19 000)	11.5 (18.5)	46 (75)	41 (1 040)	106	55' 9½'' (17 000)	4 10	1954-55 1960-61	SLM	Sulzer	Brown Boveri Secheron
Em 3/3 (18801-06) (18807-41)	C	Elec Elec	440 ,,	26 500 (12 000) 27 800 (12 600)	15 400 (7 000) 15 400 (7 000)	10.5 (17)	40 (65) 40 (65)	41 (1 040) 41 (1 040)	50.5 50.5	32' 7¾'' (9 950) 32' 10½'' (10 020)	6 35	1959-60 1963-64	SLM SLM	SLM SLM	Secheron Brown Boveri Secheron
Am 6/6 (18521-26)	Co-Co	Elec	1 950	(40 000)	(40 000)	(13.2)	(85)	(1 260)	111	(17 400)	6	1976	Thyssen-Industrie AG Henschel	Chantiers de l'Atlantique	Brown Boveri

ELECTRIC LOCOMOTIVES

Class	Axle Arrangement	Line Current	Rated Output hp	Max. lb (kg)	Tractive Effort (Full Field) Continuous at lb (kg)	mph (km/hr)	Max. Speed mph (km/hr)	Wheel dia. ins (mm)	Weight tonnes	Length ft in (mm)	No. Built	Year Built	Builders Mechanical Parts	Builders Electrical Equipment
Re 4/4 (10001-26) (10027-50)	Bo-Bo	15 000 V 1/16⅔	2 480 2 520	31 000 (14 000) 31 000 (14 000)	17 800 (8 100) 18 000 (8 200)	51.5 (83) 51.5 (83)	78 (125) ,,	41 (1 040) ,,	57 58	48' 2¾'' (14 700) 48' 10¾'' (14 900)	26 24	1946-48 1950-51	SLM	Brown-Boveri; Oerlikon; Secheron
Re 4/4 II (11101-106) (11107-155) (11156-304) (11351-11370)	Bo-Bo ,, ,, ,, Re 4/4 III	,, ,, ,, ,,	5 450 6 320 ,, ,,	,, 57 300 (26 000) ,, (20 000)	32 400 (14 700) 37 500 (17 000) ,, ,,	,, 62 (100) ,, ,,	,, 87 (140) 78 78 (125)	,, 49⅝ (1 260) ,, ,,	,, 80 ,, ,,	48' 6¾'' (14 800) 48' 10¾'' (14 900) 50' 6¾'' (15 410) ,,	6 49 149 20	1964 1967-68 1969-74 1971	SLM ,, ,, ,,	Brown Boveri Oerlikon; Secheron ,, ,,
Re 6/6 (11601-689)	Bo-Bo-Bo	,,	10 600	88 600 (40 200)			87 (140)		120		36(+53 on order)	1972-78	SLM	Brown Boveri
Ae 3/5 (10201-24) (10225-26)	1-Co-1	,,	1 800 ,,	31 000 (14 000) ,,	17 000 (7 700) ,,	39 (63) ,,	56 (90) ,,	63⅜ (1 610) ,,	81 85	40' 5'' (12 320) ,,	24 2	1922-25 1925	SLM	Secheron
Ae 3/6 III (10261-71)	2-Co-1	,,	1 800	31 000 (14 000)	17 000 (7 700)	39 (63)	56 (90)	63⅜ (1 610)	89	45' 1¾'' (13 760)	11	1925-26	SLM	Secheron

Class	Axle Arrangement	Line Current	Rated Output hp	Max. lbs (kg)	Tractive Effort (Full Field) Continuous at lb (kg)	mph (km/hr)	Max. Speed mph (km/hr)	Wheel dia. ins (mm)	Weight tonnes	Length ft in (mm)	No. Built	Year Built	Builders Mechanical Parts	Electrical Equipment
Ae 3/6 II (10401-20)	2-C-1	,,	2 000	33 000 (15 000)	18 300 (8 300)	40 (65)	62 (100)	63⅜ (1 610)	99	46' 5" (14 150)	20	1924	SLM	Oerlikon
(10421-60)		,,	,,	,,	,,	,,	,,	,,	97	,,	40	1925-26		
(10439 = historical locomotive, other scrapped)														
Ae 3/6 I (10601-36)	2-Co-1	,,	1 920	31 000 (14 000)	18 500 (8 400)	38.5 (62)	62 (100)	63⅜ (1 610)	92	48' 5" (14 760)	36	1921-25	SLM	Brown Boveri
(10637-86)			2 100	33 000 (15 000)	19 400 (8 800)	40 (65)	68 (110)	,,	95	,,	50	1925-27		
(10687-712)		,,	,,	,,	,,	,,	,,	,,	94	,,	26	1927-28	,,	Oerlikon
(10713-14)		,,	,,	,,	,,	,,	,,	,,	95	,,	2	1929	,,	Secheron
Ae 4/6 (10801-12)	IA+Bo+AI	,,	5 540	49 000 (22 200)	38 800 (17 600)	53 (85)	78 (125)	53⅛ (1 350)	105	56' 7" (17 250)	12	1941-45 rebuilt 1961-63	SLM	Brown Boveri; Oerlikon; Secheron
Ae 4/6 III (10851)	IA+Bo+AI	,,	2 300	32 600 (14 800)	17 400 (7 900)	49 (79)	68 (110)	49⅝ (1 260)	80	53' 7¾" (16 350)	1	1941 (1961)	SLM; Swiss Fed Rlys	Brown Boveri
Ae 4/7 (10901-72)	2-Do-1	,,	3 120	44 000 (20 000)	28 700 (13 000)	40 (65)	62 (100)	63⅜ (1 610)	118	54' 11½" (16 750)	72	1927-31		Brown Boveri (53); Oerlikon (52); Secheron (22)
(10973-002)		,,	,,	,,	,,	,,	,,	,,	123	56' 1¼" (17 100)	30	1931-34	SLM	
(11003-27)		,,	,,	,,	,,	,,	,,	,,	118	54' 11½" (16 750)	25	1931-34		
Ae 6/6 (11401-02)	Co-Co	,,	6 000	80 160 (40 000)	48 400 (22 000)	46 (74)	78 (125)	49⅝ (1 260)	124	60' 4½" (18 400)	2	1952-53	SLM	Brown Boveri
(11403-50)		,,	,,	,,	,,	,,	,,	,,	120	,,	48	1955-60		Oerlikon
(11451-11520)		,,	,,	,,	,,	,,	,,	,,	,,	,,	70	1962-66	,,	,,
Ae 8/14 (11801)	IA-AIA-AI+ IA-AIA-AI	,,	7 000	110 000 (50 000)	57 300 (26 000)	40 (65)	62 (100)	63⅜ (1 610)	240	111' 7" (34 000)	1	1931	SLM	Brown Boveri historical locomotive
Be 4/6 (12303-12)	IB-BI	,,	1 760	39 700 (18 000)	20 300 (9 200)	32 (52)	47 (75)	60¼ (1 530)	107	54' 4" (16 260)	30	1920	SLM	Brown Boveri
(12313-42)			2 040	39 700 (18 000)	23 400 (10 600)	32 (52)	,,	,,	110	,,	30	1921-23		
(12320 = historical locomotive, other scrapped)														
Be 4/7 (12501-06)	(1-Bo-1)- (Bo-1)	,,	2 400	44 000 (20 000)	25 600 (11 600)	35 (56)	50 (80)	63⅜ (1 610)	111	53' 5¾" (16 300)	6	1922	SLM	Secheron
(12504 = historical locomotive, other scrapped)														
Be 6/8 II (13251-59, 61, 63-65)	IC-CI	,,	3 640	66 000 (30 000)	48 000 (21 800)	28 (45)	47 (75)	53⅛ (1 350)	126	63' 9¾" (19 450)	13	1920-21 (1942-47)	SLM	Oerlikon
(13253 = historical locomotive, Ce 6/8 II 14253)														
Be 6/8 III (13301-18)	IC-CI	,,	2 460	66 000 (30 000)	41 900 (19 000)	22 (35)	47 (75)	53⅛ (1 350)	131	65' 9¾" (20 060)	11	1926-27	SLM	Oerlikon
Ce 6/8 I (14201)	IC-CI	,,	2 370	57 300 (26 000)	34 400 (15 600)	25 (41)	40 (65)	53⅛ (1 350)	118	63' 2" (19 250)	1	1920	SLM	Brown Boveri historical locomotive
Ce 6/8 II (14266-85)	IC-CI	,,	2 240	57 300 (26 000)	37 000 (16 800)	22 (36)	40 (65)	53⅛ (1 350)	128	63' 9¾" (19 450)	20	1920-22	SLM	Oerlikon
De 6/6 (15301-03)	C+C	,,	1 170	39 700 (18 000)	25 400 (11 500)	17 (27.5)	31 (50)	41 (1 040)	73	45' 11" (14 000)	3	1926	SLM	Brown Boveri
Ee 3/4 (16301-02)	I-C	,,	585	19 900 (9 000)	12 800 (5 800)	17 (27.5)	25 (40)	41 (1 040)	49	32' 2" (9 800)	2	1923	SLM	Brown Boveri
Ee 3/3 (16311-26)	C	,,	585	19 900 (9 000)	12 800 (5 800)	17 (27.5)	25 (40)	41 (1 040)	45	29' 6¼" (9 000)	16	1928		
(16331-50)			,,	,,	,,	,,	,,	,,	,,	29' 10½" (9 100)	20	1930-31	SLM	Brown Boveri
16351-76			,,	,,	,,	,,	,,	,,	11	31' 10" (9 700)	26	1932-42		
16381-414			680	22 000 (10 000)	14 330 (6 200)	18.4 (29.6)	31 (50)	,,	39	31' 2" (9 500)	34	1944-47		
(16421-24)			,,	26 500 (12 000)	15 400 (7 000)	16.5 (26.5)	28 (45)	,,	45	,,	4	1951	SLM	Brown Boveri
(16425-30)											6	1956		Oerlikon;
(16431-36)			,,	,,	,,	,,	,,	,,	,,	,,	6	1961		Secheron
(16437-40)											4	1962		
(16441-60)			,,	,,	,,	,,	,,	,,	44	,,	20	1966	SLM	,,
Ee 3/3 II (16501-02)	C	2-current	685	29 800 (13 500)	15 400 (7 000)	16.5 (26.5)	28 (45)	41 (1 040)	46	31' 2" (9 500)	2	1957	SLM	Brown Boveri
(16503-04)	f	730	28 700	15 650 (13 000)	16.8 (7 100)	28 (27)	,, (45)		46	,, 2		1957	,,	Oerlikon
(16505-16511-1g)			685	29 800 (13 500)	15 400 (7 000)	16.5 (26.5)	28 (45)	,,	46	,,	11	1958, 62-63)	SLM	Secheron
Ee 3/3 IV (16551-60)	C	4-current	529	26 500 (12 000)	13 250 (6 000)	14.8 (23.8)	37 (60)	41 (1 040)	48	32' 8" (10 020)	10	1962-63	SLM	Secheron
Ee 6/6 (16801-803)	C+C	15 000 V 1/16⅔	1 370	53 000 (24 000)	30 900 (14 000)	16.5 (26.5)	28 (45)	41 (1 040)	90	48' 8¾" (14 850)	2	1952	SLM	Brown Boveri; Secheron
Eem 6/6 (17001-17006)	C+C	2-current	1 045	53 000 (24 000)	26 500 (12 000)	14.8 (23.8)	40 (65)	41 (1 040)	104	58' 7" (17 850)	5	1970-71	SLM	Secheron
			533	,,	,,	7.5 (12.0)								

Note— Series Ae 4/7. Nos. 10939-51 and 11009/17 weight 120 T.
Series Ee 3/3 II operate on 15 kv 1/16⅔ and 25 kv, 1/50.
Series Ee 3/3 IV operate on 15 kv 1/16⅔ and 25 kv, 1/50 and on 1 500 V and 3 000 V dc.

SYRIA

CHEMINS DE FER SYRIENS

BP 182, Aleppo

Telephone: 13900/2030

Members: Ing. Abdulkader Moulayess
Ing. Vartkès Mardirossian
Ing. Farès Sahhar
Ing. Omar Sultan
Ing. Khaled Dada

Officials
President General Manager: Abdeljabber Koundakji
Assistant General Manager: Abdulhamid El-Hassan
Assistant General Manager: Abdulkader Moulayess
Director, Development Division: Ing Vartkès Mardirossian
Director, Construction Division: Ing Farès Sahhar

Directors
Technical Development Division: Ing Naoufal Kassouha
Goods and Traction: Ing Mourhaf Sabouni
Movement and Traffic: Ing. Zafer Attar
Fixed Installations: Dr. Ing. Adnan Elias
Returns: Fouad Attar
Communications and Signalling: Ing. Tarek Bourhan
Judicial Affairs: Dhémil Sayem El-Dahr
Financial Affairs: Omar Sultan
Stores and Purchasing: Adib Meymeh
Medical: Dr. Sabet Issa
Planning and Statistics: Ing. Laurent Khayat
Technical and Construction Division: Ing. Jean Didos
Tracklaying: Ing. Abdulaziz Koundakji
Steamworks: Ing. Safouan Rihaoui
Bridging works: Ing. Bechir Nasser
Engines and Vehicles: Ing. Abdulghafour Nached
Signalling and Electrification: Ing. Abdulrahman Abou-Saleh

All standard gauge lines in Syria, are operated by the Chemins de fer Syriens, and comprise the lines from the Lebanese border via Homs and Aleppo to the Turkish border and in the northeast, the connecting line between the Turkish and Iraqi borders. A 26 mile *(42 km)* line between Tartous and Akkari was recently completed.
A new standard gauge line 461 miles *(742 km)* is under construction from the port of Latakia to Aleppo and then following roughly the line of the River Euphrates to Kamechli.
Two sections of this new line, Aleppo-Ragga and Aleppo-Sisr El Choughour, 176 miles *(283 km)*, have been completed and were opened to traffic on 1 January 1972. The whole of the new line is laid with Soviet rails 25 km long on prestressed concrete sleepers.
The service between Lattaquié and Kamychly 750 km became fully operational in 1974, providing a direct outlet to the Mediterranean for the oilfields of Central Syria. This line was built with the technical and financial support of the Soviet Union.
Work on the final section of the 750 km line from the port of Latakia to the oil centre of Damascus.
Work on the final section of the 750-km line from the port of Latakia to the oil centre of Kamyshly is now completed. The line was built with Soviet technical and financial assistance, and Soviet diesel locomotives are operating.
Syria is to lay 6 000 km of new lines during its 1976-80 development plan. The target—more than four times that set under the Third Five-Year Plan—stresses Syria's continuing emphasis on the development of its railway network.
Two important new lines, between Qamishli and Latakia (750 km) and Damascus and Homs (208 km) are now under construction. Both lines will carry a total of about 5.5 million tonnes of freight annually.

TRAFFIC	1975	1976
Freight tonne-km ('000)	149 505	303 229
Freight tonnage ('000)	992.6	1 315
Passenger-km ('000)	127 500	150 000
Passenger journeys ('000)	841	772

CHEMIN DE FER DU HEDJAZ

BP 134, Damascus

General Manager: Fahmi Kosara
Chief Engineer: Mohamad el Bizen
Manager, Traffic Department: Fayez Hafez
Manager, Accounts Department: Tayssir Kari

Gauge: 3 ft 5⅜ in *(1.05 m)*
Route length operated: 192 miles *(307 km)*

In addition to its own 150 miles *(240 km)*, route length, the CF du Hedjaz also operates the 42 mile *(67 km)* long narrow gauge Damascus-Zerghaya line on behalf of the Syrian Government.
The 3 ft 5⅜ in *(1.05 m)* gauge Hedjaz Railway originally extended 809 miles *(1 303 km)* from Damascus to Medina to carry pilgrims to the Holy Cities of Mecca and Medina. During the 1914-18 war the southern portion was severely damaged and the 524 miles *(844 km)* section from Maan in Jordan to Medina in Saudi Arabia was left derelict.
In October 1977 the Syrian and Jordanian transport ministers met in Amman to decide in principle to make a second attempt to revive the Hedjaz Railway. Built originally for pilgrim traffic between Damascus and Medina, the portion of the line passing through Saudi Arabia has not operated since 1917 following collapse of a scheme to reopen the section during the 1960s. Under latest proposals it is hoped to reconstruct the 1 300 km line as a high-quality standard-gauge freight line with 60 kg/m rail and an axle loading of 25 or 30 tonnes.
Because the Hedjaz at present is 1 050 mm gauge the project will entail extensive gauge conversion including the new branch line to Aqaba (116 km) opened in 1975.
Construction teams are already approaching Damascus from the north laying new standard gauge track.

TAIWAN

TAIWAN RAILWAY ADMINISTRATION

2 Yen-Ping Road, Taipei

Telephone: 551113
Telex: 21837

Managing Director: J. Fan
Deputy Managing Directors: W. J. Shan
T. Y. Chen
J. Wang
Chief Engineering: S. T. Su
Chief Secretary: Y. L. Po
Superintendents:
Transportation Department: S. S. Lai
Civil Engineering Department: C. T. Wang
Mechanical Engineering Department: K. M. Lee
Signal and Communications Department: Y. C. Loh
Purchase and Stores Department: S. C. Lee
Planning Department: C. Y. Liu
Hualien Office: C. C. Huang
General Affairs Department: J. Y. Feng
Accounting Department: J. C. Shen
Chief, Finance Control Office: H. Chiang
Chief, Personnel Office: Henry Lei
Chief, Electronic Data Processing Department: M. T. Yang
General Manager, Railway Freight Service Office: C. P. Wu
General Manager, Catering Service Dept.: W. Y. Chang
Chief, Employees Training Academy: Y. C. Cheng
Manager, Taipei Railway Workshop:
Manager, Kaohsiung Railway Workshop: H. S. Wan
Director, Railway Police Bureau: C. Y. Chen

Gauge: 1.067 (West); 0.762 m (East)
Route length: 1 926 km; 240 km

TRAFFIC

The Taiwan Railway is the principal artery of transportation on the island of Taiwan. It consists of three lines—the West Line with its branches, the East Line—totalling 1 007.5 km and the new 82.3 km North Link Line from Nanshenghu to Trenpu.
The West Line, a double-tracked railway system, 831.8 km in length, and 1 067 mm in gauge, stretches from north to south along the West Plain Area of the Island, linking the two big seaports of Keelung, and Kaohsiung with the intermediate cities of Taipei, Hsinchu, Tai-chung, Chang-hua, Chia-i and Tai-nan. In the middle section of the system there are two routes from Chu-nan to Chang-hua: The Coast Line runs along the West Coast while the Mountain Line 91.4 km in length, runs through the cities of Miao-li, Feng-yuan, and Tai-chung joining again with the Coast Line at Chang-hua.
Construction work on the North Link Line commenced on December 25, 1973: 5 km at the northern end and 26 km at the southern end (including 5.8 km branch to Hualien Harbour). Construction of the middle section which amounts to 57 km was started in early 1974. Tunnel construction forms the most important works on the North Link Line, the expenses of which amount to some 65 per cent of the total cost of the whole project. By the end of 1976, 29.57 per cent of the project was completed, including 2 370 000 m³ of earthwork, 12 major bridges, 62 minor bridges, 18 grade separation bridges, 180 culverts, 7 tunnels totalling 1 454 m, 6 250 m² of buildings and 26.6 km of track laying.
As to the branches, the I-Lan and Chung-ho branches pass through the coalmine districts in north Taiwan; the Tam-shui branch is mainly for transporting commuters in the suburban of Tai-pei area; both the Nei-wan and Tung-shih branches are intended to develop the natural resources in the mountain areas; the Chi-chi branch threading through the forest area in central Taiwan has timber as its principal freight commodity. The Pin-tung branch plays an important role in the transport of grains and marine products; the Ping-hsi, Shen-Kang- Shen-ao and Linkou branches were constructed to keep up with the economic development and traffic demand; the Tai-chung Kang branch was intended to assist the construction of Taichung Harbour.
Along a narrow valley area of the East Coast, the single-tracked 0.762 m gauge East Line (Hualien-Taitung) runs for 175.7 km in length and is responsible for the passenger and freight transportation.
The daily averages of passenger and freight traffic are 400 000 persons and 45 000 tons respectively. With the existing route and equipment, the transportation capacity has already reached saturation point. According to the statistical figures, the passenger and freight traffic of 1976 was as follows:
Passenger traffic: The total number of passenger person in 1976 was 140 030 000: its

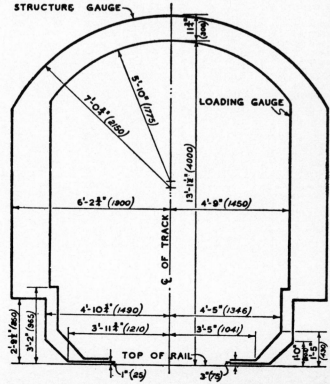

daily average was 382 602 which is 9 513 (2.43 per cent) less than that of the year 1975.
The total number of passenger kilometers of 1976 was 8 511 660 000: its daily average was 22 982 680 which is 457 547 (2.03 per cent) more that that of the year 1975.
The total revenue of passenger traffic in 1976 was NT$ 4 118 330 000: its daily average was 11 252 269 which is 557 058 (5.21 per cent) more than that of the year 1975.

Freight traffic: The total tonnage in 1976 was 17 000 000 tons: its daily average was 46 449 which is 1 150 (2.54 per cent) more than that of the year 1975.
The total number of ton kilometer was 2·700 080 000: its daily average was 7 377 269 which is 451 152 (6.51 per cent) more than that of the year 1975.
The total revenue of freight traffic is NT$ 1 185 680 000: its daily average was 3 239 568 which is 176 584 (5.77 per cent) more than that of the year 1975.

		1974	1975	1976
Total freight ton-km		2 649 448 110	2 528 032 814	2 700 080 323
Total freight tonnage		16 634 022	16 534 024	17 000 403
Total passenger-km		8 276 596 558	8 221 673 529	8 411 660 857
Total passengers carried		145 442 911	143 122 163	140 032 528
Finances		1974	1975	1976
Revenues	US$	156 022 368.42	161 412 421.08	171 280 736.08
Expenses	US$	133 770 052.63	135 588 736.84	151 287 868.42

MOTIVE POWER AND ROLLING STOCK
During 1976 the following stock improvements were carried out:
(a) Ten locomotives purchased under an Eximbank loan.
(b) Six engines of GM electrical cars have been purchased under the same loan while out -of -use Hitachi locomotives have been reconstructed.
(c) 36 Chu-kuang passenger cars and 4 dining cars have been constructed by Tang Jung.
(d) 180 flat cars for containers have been purchased by the railway.
Delivered during 1977 to Taiwan Railway Administration were 13 five-car 25 kV 60 Hz multiple-unit train-sets built in British Rail Engineering's York Workshops. Overall design of the complete trainsets was by Traction which delivered 20 Bo .Bo 2 100 kW locos to Taiwan in 1975-76. All 13 of the units will be used on fast services over the 400 km main north-south route linking Taipei and Kaohsiung. Traction motor current is thyristor-controlled and preselection speed control and rheostatic braking are fitted.
For newly electrified lines, TRA ordered 74 electric locomotives from GE (USA) and 20 locomotives and 13 five-car electric trainsets from GEC Transportation Projects (UK). The 74 Model E42C units from GE are 96-tonne thyristor-controlled Co-Co rectifier locomotives. The 20 thyristor controlled Bo-Bo locomotives supplied by GEC, weigh only 72 tonnes.

Number of locomotives in service:
Number of locomotives in Steam	125
Number of locomotives in Diesel-electric	161
Number of railcars, diesel	61
Number of trailer cars, diesel	10
Number of passenger train coaches	1 180
Number of freight train cars	6 922

ELECTRIFICATION
As part of the national economic development programme, TRA is at present engaged in electrification of the West Trunk Line.
The project covers the electrification of the 495.4 km between Keelung and Kaohsiung and was approved by the Executive Yuan in October 1971. The planning stage was concluded when the supply contracts and foreign loan agreements were signed in June 1974. An Electrification Unit was established in June 1974 to carry out all necessary planning and engineering studies and construction work. Actual work on site was started in March 1975.
Electrification, at 25 kV 60 Hz, over the initial 107-km Keelung—Hsinchu section was switched on December 1977. Electrification over the entire line is expected to be completed by 1979.

Anticipated advantages of electrification of the line include:
1. Economic benefit: benefit/cost ratio = 1.95:1
2. Increase of line capacity and train tonnage: to 50 per cent.
3. Increase of train speed:
   Taipei-Taichung: 2 hours
   Taipei-Kaohsiung: 4 hours
4. Lowering of operating cost: fuel cost reduced ½, maintenance cost ⅔.
5. Safer and more comfortable travelling: free of smoke, noise, and pollution; smooth running of trains; the introduction of automatic train warning and stop system to ensure safe operation.
6. In accordance with the national economic development: making full use of natural resources and ensuring social welfare.
The construction work has been divided into three major sections: Electrical engineering includes overhead contact system 1 153 km, 11 substations and two remote control centers underground cables 520 km and carrier system, improvement of signalling system.
Civil engineering includes track upgrading, installation of 50 kg long-welded rail, reballasting, replacing with PC sleepers, clearance modification of tunnels, easing sharp curves in 17 curves in 17 places, track improvement and realignment of stations and yards.
Mechanical engineering includes the purchase of 94 electrical locomotives and 13 emu's, installation of automatic train warning and stop system (ATW/ATS), new equipment for Nankang and Kaohsiung Car Inspection and Locomotive Section and Taipei Workshop.
The electrification project is being carried out in three stages: The first: from Keelung to Chunan, completed in December 1977.
The second construction period: from Chunan to Changhua, scheduled to be completed in December 1978, including both the Mountain and Coast lines.
The third construction period: from Changhua to Kaohsiung, scheduled to be completed in August 1979.

FUTURE PROJECTS
The isolated East Line (Hualien-Taitung) is 176 km in length with branches of 72 km. The guage is 0.762 m. After the completion of the North Link Line the gauge has to be widened to 1.067 m so as to meet the same standard of the West Line.
This project has been proposed to be carried out in the later part of the 6-year construction plan. The general schedule has been drawn up and more detailed specification is now under consideration. The construction work may be carried out in several sections. When most of the construction work of the North Link Line is completed and the governmental funds are available, widening of the gauge will begin.

South Link Line
With the completion of the South Link Line, Taiwan Railways will go completely round the island. National economy, people's livelihood, national defence, etc. will benefit greatly. Since 1974 surveying teams had been organised to survey the land and route. In 1958, four routes were proposed. In 1963 new surveys were made and it was found that two of the routes were geologically unsound and too many bridges and long tunnels would be required.
Therefore, another team was organised to find new routes. The construction of North link line proves that long tunnels can be excavated by new mechanical equipment; therefore in January 1976, new routes were proposed. Brand-new plans for South Link Line have been drafted and they are now under overall consideration and estimation. After the Ggovernment makes the final choice, more detailed and improved plans will be made.

TANZANIA
TANZANIA RAILWAY CORPORATION
PO Box 2834, Dar es Salaam

General Manager: A. Janguo

Since the formal break up of the East African Railways Corporation, Tanzania has set up a separate railway administration to operate all railways in the country, including the Tanzania-Zambia Railway Authority (TAZARA) which was set up to administrate the new 1 860 km line between Dar-es-Salaam and Kapiri Mposhi, Zambia.
During 1977, Canada agreed to grant Tanzania Shs 110 million towards the first phase of its five-year railway development plan. Under the first part of an agreement Canada will supply 205 petrol tanks, cold storage and cattle wagons worth about Shs 96 million. In the second part the Canadian International Development Agency (CIDA) will provide locomotive spares worth about Shillings 12 million for maintenance of the 120 locomotives bought from Canada in 1972. Future agreements will cover construction and equipping of a locomotive overhaul facility at Morogoro; provision of additional motive power and rolling stock and expansion of railway training facilities at Tabora.

TAZARA
Agreement was signed in 1968, between the Governments of Tanzania, Zambia, and the People's Republic of China to provide finance and technical services for a rail link of approximately 1 860 km from Dar es Salaam, Tanzania, to Kapiri Mposhi, Zambia, at a cost of K230 million together with new workshops at Kabwe costing K12.6 million. Construction was officially inaugurated at the end of October 1970. Of the total length, 970 km is in Tanzania and 890 km in Zambia. The line has 147 stations, as well as the workshops at Kawbe. The construction of TAZARA was completed in June 1975.Trial running of freight and passenger services commenced on 22 October, 1975, and the hand-over of the railway line to the Zambian and Tanzanian Governments by the Chinese Government took place on 14 July, 1976.
During the first six months of full operations (July-December 1976) the Tanzan Railway (Tazara) earned a total of Shillings 151.5 million. During the period, 530 200 tonnes of freight were carried, earning Shillings 142.6 million. In passenger service the railway carried over 412 000 passengers providing revenues of Shillings 7.9 million. Catering and cabin services earned over Shillings 947 000.
In 11 months from the official opening of the Chinese-built line in July 1976 to the end of May 1977, Tazara handled 780 000 passengers and more than one million tonnes of freight, says a report from the Chinese *Hsinhau* News Agency. Monthly volume of freight traffic was 132 per cent up on the best month of trial operations, the report claims. The railway now employs about 6 000 workers in administration and operations. "At all levels workers and staff have constantly striven to improve efficiency," says *Hsinhau*. Monthly and three-monthly schedules are drawn up to ensure operations keep to the timetable, to improve methods of track maintenance, and to ensure rolling stock and other equipment is kept in good condition.
Twelve hours have been cut off the previous 48-hour passenger journey from Dar es Salaam to Kapiri Mposhi. New scheduled freight trains and passenger services have been added to last year's timetable.
Hsinhua reports that at the Dar es Salaam terminal, which handles the bulk of imports and exports to and from Tanzania and Zambia, "lines of loaded lorries stream into the station, where there are depots for machinery, grain and other commodities. Loading goes on around the clock." Workers load up to 60 wagons a day moving 2 000 tonnes of freight. In the 11 months to the end of May this year staff at the station loaded 5 500 wagons (190 000 freight tonnes) and discharged 2 500 wagons.
With the aid of Chinese technicians says *Hsinhua*, staff have introduced new loading methods which have significantly increased loading capacity at the station. The small Kalonje station in Zambia has been awarded the title "outstanding station" for handling 495 passenger trains and 3 230 freight trains "without a hitch" in the 967 days since the station first opened in September 1974 to the end of April 1977.

Chinese-built diesel hydraulic locomotives under inspection in Tazara's locomotive sheds near Dar es Salaam. In all, China supplied 102 locomotives for the line; some 1 000 hp and others 2 000 hp (Courtesy, National Council for US—China Trade)

THAILAND
STATE RAILWAY OF THAILAND (RSR)
Krung Kassem Road, Bangkok

BOARD OF COMMISSIONERS
Chairman: General Kriangsak Chomanan
Members: General Yose Davahasdin na Ayudhya
Lt Cdr Arree Satayamana R.T.N.
Krit Sombatsiri
Nukul Prachuabmoh
Major General Pat Urailert

MANAGEMENT
General Manager: Sanga Navicharern
Deputy General Managers:
  Administrative: Dhawat Sangpradab
  Operating: Banyong Saralamp
Chief of Department attached to the General Manager: Smer Sakhakorn
Chief, Administration Department: Ploen Sootarsukorn
Comptroller: Hiran Radeesri
Assistant Comptroller: Monthien Boonyaprasop
Traffic Manager: Samai Sanguanvongs
Deputy Traffic Manager: Prasith Singhapundu
Chief Mechanical Engineer: Somsak Prabhavasit
Deputy Chief Mechanical Engineers:
  Workshop: Sombongese Charubhumi
  Motive Power: Chalor Siricharoen
Chief Civil Engineer: Prachoom Annavadhana
Deputy Chief Civil Engineers:
  Construction: Siri Fookiart
  Permanent Way: Chamras Ukachoke
Marketing Manager: Pojana Nagavajara
Chief Legal Officer: Sammieng Kongkabej
Chief Medical Officer: Prabhandha Viravatana M.D.
Medical Director, Railway Hospital: Dr Kasem Isarankura na Ayudhya
Stores Superintendent: Chird Boonyaratavej
Chief, Railway Police Bureau: Pol. Major Gen. Nipat Soranarak
Chief, Railway Training Centre: Chawarn Boonyawat
Chief Development Coordinating Bureau: Somchai Chulacharitta

Gauge: 1.00 m
Route Length: 3 830 km

TRAFFIC

	1974	1975	1976
Total freight ton-km	2 363 520 665	2 353 264 337	2 504 583 616
Total freight tonnage	5 116 760	5 052 496	5 351 379
Total passenger-km	5 375 622 336	5 693 513 580	5 627 955 444
Total passengers carried	61 408 517	61 566 800	57 206 995

FINANCES

	1975	1976
Revenues	1 171 022 203	1 395 308 251
Expenses	1 398 417 396	1 486 690 750

Number of locomtives in service

	Line Haul		Shunting (Switching)	
	1975	1976	1975	1976
Number of locomotives in Steam	60	39	9	1
Diesel-electric	158	151	12	25
Diesel-hydraulic	67	67	2	—

Number of railbuses, 2-axle

	1975	1976
Number of railcars, diesel	45	45
Number of trailer cars, diesel	45	45

Rolling stock in service

	4-wheeled bogie		8-wheeled bogie	
	1975	1976	1975	1976
Number of passenger train coaches	7	7	954	974
Number of freight train cars	6 937	6 138	2 427	2 537

TRACK WORK 1976
New lines projected (length, location): Surveying on a 160 km new line project from Chachoengsao to Laem Cha Bang and Aatlahip was completed and fixed alignment established. Construction is now being considered by the government. In addition, there will be two spur lines, one running to the site of the future deep-sea port at Laem Chabang (12 km) and the second extending to a secondary port near Sattahip (15 km). Cost of the project will be about $US 26.3 million will be required for the purchase of rolling stock, warehouses and associated facilities. The line has been under consideration for a number of years as a necessary stimulus to the economic development of Thailand's east coast.

Rail, types and weights: Flat-bottom 50 (BS), 60 (BS, ASCE), 70 (BS, ASCE), 80 (BS) pounds per yard.

Sleepers (cross ties) type:

	Untreated hardwood	Creosote-treated softwood	2-block concrete (R.S. type)
Thickness:	15 cm	12.5-15 cm	20 cm
Spacing:	65-70 cm	65-70 cm	65 cm
Rail fastenings (types used):	Dörken elastic spikes	Dog spikes	R.N. elastic clips

Welded rail:
Total length of track laid 31 December 1974: 2 244 km
Length laid during 1974: Standard method of welding: 55 km

NEW SIGNAL INSTALLATIONS 1975/6
Type: (1) All-relay interlocking. (2) Route storaged retarder. (3) Mechanical fully interlocking with colour-light signal. (4) Mechanical fully interlocking. (5) Mechanical semi-interlocking. (6) Tokenless block working instrument for single track. (7) Grade crossing barrier.
Route length: (1)-(2)-(3) 82 km. (4)-(5)-(6) 242 km (7)

Location: (1) Bangkok & Bang Sue station yards. (2) Bang Sue marshalling yard. (3) On double-track section from Bang Khen to Ban Phachi, 13 stations totally. (4) 30 stations. (5) 8 stations. (6) From Nakhon Sawan to Phitsanulok, 35 stations totally. (7) 35 grade crossings.
Suppliers: (1) Siemens & Halske (Germany). (2) Kyosan Electric, Co. (Japan). (3)—(7) locally made.
Fare and rate system: By the State Railway of Thailand Act B.E. 2494, the setting up of the standard rate for passemger fares and freight charges is subject to the sanction of the Council of Ministers. RSR is, however, authorised to make at its own discretion an increase of not greater than 25 per cent or a reduction of not more than 50 per cent from the standard rates provided that such an action is not "Inconsistent with the general economic and financial policies of the Council of Ministers." Consequently, RSR has never made any tariff increase without an approval of the Government.
During the fiscal year 1975, after the oil crisis and worldwide inflation, RSR submitted a request for an increase in standard rates for freight charges and passenger fares which had been in use since 1 June, 1952 and 15 February, 1955 respectively.
The new freight rates were finally introduced on October 1, 1975 and passenger fares on 20 November, 1975.
The freight rates now comprise six classes of commodities as compared to the old nine classes. Class 1 which has two sub-classes and special classes for daily newspapers and other printed matter, is for less-than-carload traffic and the rest are for carload traffic. Class 4 is still the predominant class under which 56 per cent of total tonnage was carried in 1976.
The magnitude of the increase is shown below by Class 4 rate at various distances:

Distance	Rate per ton (in Baht)		
km	present rate	old rate	% increase
50	14.00	13.80	1.4
100	28.00	27.50	1.8
150	39.50	37.50	5.3
200	51.00	47.50	7.4
300	69.50	60.00	15.8
500	102.50	82.50	24.2
700	131.00	101.50	29.1
1 000	173.00	128.50	34.6

The relationship between different classes of the present carload rates can be seen from the following table:

Distance	Rate per ton (in Baht)				
km	Class 2	Class 3	Class 4	Class 5	Class 6
50	19.00	17.50	14.00	12.50	12.00
100	38.00	35.00	28.00	25.00	24.00
150	53.50	49.50	39.50	35.30	33.80
200	69.00	64.00	51.00	45.50	43.50
300	94.00	87.00	69.50	62.00	59.00
500	138.50	128.00	102.50	91.50	87.00
700	177.00	163.50	131.00	117.00	111.50
1 000	234.00	216.00	173.00	154.50	147.50

Specimen list of commodities and their classes are as follows:
Class 2: Electrical appliance, motor car, tin, aviation fuel
Class 3: steel coil, log, timber, tile, gasoline
Class 4: fresh fish, rice, maize, rubber, jute, kenaf, cement, lignite, fluorspar, manganese, gypsum, chemical fertilizer, kerozene, diesel oil.
Class 5: fresh fruits, paddy, bran, salt, marl, sand, gravel, asphalt.
Class 6: vegetables, cocnuts, eggs, charcoal, organic fertilizer.

RSR also set up concession and contract rates for some commodities and customers in order to attract large volume of shipments and better utilise wagons during certain periods of the year. About 400 000 tons were carried under concession and contract rates in 1976.
The structure of the new standard rate for passenger fares per kilometres is as follows:

	Fares per km (in Stang)		
km	First Class	Second Class	Third Class
1-10	45	26	15
101-200	41	23	12
201-300	38	20	10
301 and over	36	18	9

The actual fares as well as the percentage increase over the old fares at various distances are as follows:

	First Class		Second Class		Third Class	
km	Baht	%	Baht	%	Baht	%
100	45.00	12.5	26.00	30.0	15.00	50.0
150	65.50	9.2	37.50	25.0	21.00	40.0
200	86.00	7.5	49.00	22.5	27.00	35.0
300	124.00	5.1	69.00	16.9	37.00	25.4
400	160.00	3.9	87.00	13.0	46.00	19.5
500	196.00	3.2	105.00	10.5	55.00	15.8
700	268.00	5.5	141.00	11.0	73.00	15.0
900	340.00	6.9	177.00	11.3	91.00	14.5

Discounts of between 10-20 per cent are given on roundtrip tickets and group travels are entitled to a slightly greater reduction. Point-to-point special fares are also set up attract more passengers especially on the Northern and Northeastern lines where competition is exceptionally keen.

HISTORY
The State Railway of Thailand, is a government owned enterprise. It came into being as a department of the government in 1890, until it was made an autonomous organisation on 1 July, 1951 by the State Railway of Thailand Act B.E. 2494 (1951).The first line was commenced in 1892 and reached Nakhon Ratchasima in 1900, a distance of 264 kms. All the earlier line was 4 ft 8½ in gauge, but the construction of southern main line, from 1900 onwards, brought into being a metre gauge system for it was intended that this line should eventually be linked with Malaysia and Burma. Conversion of other line to metre gauge was decided upon in 1919, and completed by April 1930. At the close of the fiscal year 1976 (30 September, 1976) RSR had a total of 3 765 route kilometres (excluding Mae Klong line) open to traffic. The system radiates from Bangkok, and connects with the Malayan Railway at Padang Besar and at Sungai Kolok in the South. The formulation of policies and the supervision of the general affairs of RSR are entrusted to the Board of Commissioners consisting of a chairman and other four to six members appointed by the Council of Ministers. The General Manager, chief executive of RSR, is also in his capacity a member of a Board. The Minister of Communications has general supervisory power and may call upon RSR to give a statement or an opinion or to submit or suspend RSR's actions.

DIESEL LOCOMOTIVES

Class	Wheel Arrangement	Transmission	Rated Power (hp)	Max Tractive Effort at wheel rim kgs @ % Adhesion Weight	Minimum Continuous Tractive Effort kgs @ km/h	Max Speed (km/h)	Wheel Dia (mm)	Service Weight (tons)	Length (mm)	No on book	Year in service	Builders Mechanical Parts	Engine & Type	Transmission
Sulzer	Bo-Bo	Elec	735	10 000 @ 21.5%	4 600 @ 27.5	65	914	46.5	12 100	4	1947	Sulzer Bros, Switzerland	Sulzer, 6 LDA 25	Oerlikon, Switzerland
Davenport	Bo-Bo	Elec	500	14 770 @ 30%	5 700 @ 16	82	914	48.12	9 893.2	30	1952	Davenport, USA	Caterpillar D.397	Westinghouse, USA
Davenport	Co-Co	Elec	1 000	24 000 @ 30%	11 370 @ 16	92	914	80	16 954.4	15	1955	Davenport, USA	Caterpillar D.397	Westinghouse, USA
Hitachi	Co-Co	Elec	1 040	21 600 @ 30%	14 580 @ 11.74	70	914	72	14 300	4	1958	Hitachi, Japan	M.A.N., W 8 V 22/ 30 m A.U.L.	Hitachi, Japan
Hitachi	Co-Co	Elec	1 040	21 600 @ 30%	13 140 @ 12.76	70	914	72	14 300	23	1961-1962	Hitachi, Japan	M.A.N., W 8 V 22/ 30 m A.U.L.	Hitachi, Japan
GE	Co-Co	Elec	1 320	22 500 @ 30%	17 963 @ 13	103	914	75	16 288	50	1965-1966	General Electric, USA	Cummins, VT 12-825 B1, VTA-1710-L	General Electric, USA
Alsthom	Co-Co	Elec	2 400	24 800 @ 30%	20 600 @ 21	95	914	82.5	16 258	54	1975	Alsthom, France	S.E.M.T. PIELSTICK, 16PA 4V.185	Alsthom, France
Kraus-Maffei	C	Hydr	440	12 000 @ 33.33%	7 450 @ 7.55	27	1 106	36	8 350	5	1955	Krauss-Maffei, Germany	M.A.N. W 8 V 17.5/ 22A	Voith, Germany
Hunslet	C	Hydr	1 240	19 100 @ 33%	2 430 @ 12.1	19.5	1 106	30	7 658	5	1964	Hunslet, England	GARDNER, 8L 3B	Voith, Germany
Henschel	B'-B'	Hydr	1 200	17 160 @ 33%	14 900 @ 11	90	914	52	12 800	27	1965	Henschel, Germany	MAYBACH, MB.12V 493 TY 10	Voith, Germany
Krupp	B'-B'	Hydr	1 500	18 150 @ 33%	15 250 @ 14.5	90	914	55	12 800	30	1969	Krupp, Germany	MAYBACH, MB.12V 652 TB 10	Voith, Germany

DIESEL RAILCARS

Class	Wheel Arrangement	Transmission	Rated Power (hp)	Max Tractive Effort at wheel rim kgs @ % Adhesion Weight	Minimum Continuous Tractive Effort kgs @ km/h	Max Speed (km/h)	Wheel Dia (mm)	Service Weight (tons)	Length (mm)	No on book	Year in service	Builders Mechanical Parts	Engine & Type	Transmission
Niigata	2-4 wheel bogie Driving Trailer	Hydr-mech	320	4 460		85	851	Power Type A. 31.0 Type B. 31.0 Trailer 33.75	20 800	3	1962	Niigata Japan	Cummins NHHRS-6-B	Niigata Japan
Tokyu	2-4 wheel bogie Driving Trailer	Hydr-mech	440	4 560	2 260 @ 25	85	851	Power Type A. 36.8 Type B. 37.0 Trailer 26.9	20 800	7	1965	Tokyu Japan	Cummins NHH-220-B-1	Niigata Japan
Hitachi	2-4 wheel bogie Driving Trailer	Hydr-mech	440	4 560	2 310 @ 27	85	851	Power Type A 37.5 Type B. 37.3 Trailer 27.5	20 800	10	1967	Hitachi Japan	Cummins NHH-220-B-1	Niigata Japan
Hitachi	2-4 wheel bogie Driving Trailer	Hydr-mech	440	4 380	2 340 @ 25	90	851	Power Type A. 38.5 Type B. 38.3 Trailer 28.6	20 800	28	1971	Nippon Sharyo & Hitachi Japan	Cummins NHH-220-B-1	Niigata Japan
Tokyu (stainless)	2-4 wheel bogie Driving Trailer	Hydr-mech	220	5 400	2 175 @ 30	70	851	Power Type A. 33.6 Type B. 32.2 Trailer 27.8	20 800	4	1971*	Tokyu Japan	Cummins NHH-220-B-1	Niigata Japan
Teikeku	1-4 wheel bogie Driving Trailer	Hydr-mech	300			60	851	Power 25.9 Trailer (1) 16.0 (2) 17.5	17 000	6	1961	Teikokucar Japan	Cummins NHHRBS-600	Niigata Japan

TUNISIA

TUNISIAN NATIONAL RAILWAYS

Société Nationale des Chemins de fer Tunisiens (SNCFT)
67 Avenue Farhat Hached, Tunis

President/Managing Director: M. A. Souissi
Assistant Managing Director: N. Fékih
Administrative Director: A. Bellil
Financial Director: L. Soussi
Operations Director: M. Mehiri
Equipment and Rolling Stock Director: M. Chéour
Permanent Way and Works Director: H. Tounsi

Gauge: 1.435 m; 1.00 m.
Route length: 489 km; 1 516 km.

The railway includes 5 489 km of standard gauge lines in the north and 1 516 km of metre-gauge lines in the centre and south.

FUTURE PLANS

SNCFT plans to purchase 20 locomotives at a cost of TD 4 million ($9.5 million) and 40 passenger carriages at a cost of TD 6 million ($14.3 million) over the period of the Fifth Five-Year Plan (1977-81). SNCFT expects the number of travellers using its services to increase from the present 21.6 million annually to 30.6 million in 1981.

TRAFFIC

Passenger traffic, which had been declining steadily since 1945 has, since 1965, resumed its progress; in 1975 the SNCFT carried 20 million passengers for 558 million passenger-kms while the lines served by the "Blue Arrows" have increased their traffic by 50 per cent in a single year.

The economic development of the last fifteen years and the industrialisation of the country have considerably increased freight traffic without noticeably changing its general pattern; 70 per cent for ore transports, 30 per cent for sundry goods.

In order to increase the capacity of transport from the Matlaui phosphate fields, the SNCFT has undertaken the construction of new routes; the reconstruction of the Haidra-Kasserine line was due for completion early in 1977 and the Gafsa-M'Dilla branch will be extended to Sehib.

Moreover the lay-out of Tunis Station is being entirely modernised and the improvement to modern standards of the so-called "TGM" suburban line is now under way; finally a long-term scheme is at present under study for the construction of a 500-km standard gauge line from Gabes to Tripoli; this will entail the reconstruction on the standard gauge of the metre gauge line from Tunis to Gabes.

	1973	1974
Total freight ton-km	1 391 678 564	1 521 783 960
Total freight tonnage	6 852 758	7 367 485
Total passenger-km	526 412 954	534 096 461
Total passengers carried	17 986 932	18 783 558

FINANCES	1973	1974
Revenues	DT13 406 915	DT16 541 570
Expenses	DT15 003 734	DT17 964 955

MOTIVE POWER AND ROLLING STOCK

Dieselisation, which had begun as early as 1922, was completed in 1965. Locomotive-hauled trains have been replaced by railcars and self-propelled multiple-unit trains, particularly the 1 050 hp "Blue Arrows" built by Alsthom and introduced in 1975. This modern rolling stock has a top speed of 130 km/h and has made possible an increase in train occupation on the Tunis-Algeria, Tunis-Bizerte and Tunis-Sfax lines. The diesel-electric locomotives which haul freight trains are more and more powerful; those supplied in 1973-75 by Canada and the USA have 2 000 hp engines.

Carriages and wagons have also been modernised in recent years; modern stainless steel carriages built by Francorail-MTE have been introduced on the "Atlas" Transmaghreb service which connects Tunis and Algiers in eighteen hours instead of thirty-three previously. Over thirty metal carriages have recently been ordered from Macosa in Spain.

As regards freight rolling stock, the SNCFT has purchased in Belgium and Spain prefabricated elements for 950 wagons which are being assembled in the Sidi Fath Allah workshops, near Tunis. These workshops are to be reorganised so as to become able to undertake the full construction of wagons. Moreover, 60 containers have been ordered from SNAV.

TRACK

The Hungarian consultancy Uvaterv's has completed initial proposals for a 300-mile rail link between Sfax and Tripoli. The $1.1 million cost of the proposals is being met by the Tunisian government with assistance from Libya. If the proposals are accepted by both governments they will be expanded into firm engineering plans. Uvaterv is also undertaking the planning of signal safety devices, stations and bridges in connection with the track. If approved by the Tunisian and Libyan Governments, the plan was to be elaborated into a construction plan by October 1977.

MOTIVE POWER

A total of 28 new electric railcars were delivered by MAN and Siemens during 1977 for operation over the electrified (750 V continuous, third rail) line between Tunis and La Marsa.

TRACK

Standard rail:
   Standard gauge: Flat bottom, 72.6 to 92.8 lb per yd *(36 to 46 kg/m)* in lengths of 39.4 to 59 ft *(12 to 18 m)*.
   Meter gauge: Flat bottom, 50.3 to 72.6 lb per yd *(25 to 36 kg/m)* in lengths of 25.6 to 39.4 ft *(7.8 to 12 m)*.
Welded joints: Thermit welding of rail joints (see below).
Cross ties (sleepers): Oak impregnated with creosote; metal; concrete R.S. type.
   Standard gauge: 4¾ in × 8⅝ × 8 ft 4⅜ in *(120 × 220 × 2 600 mm)*.
   Meter gauge: 4¾ in × 8⅝ × 6 ft 6¾ in *(120 × 220 × 2 000 mm)*.
Spacing: 2 400 per mile *(1 500 km)*.
Rail fastenings: To wood sleepers: spikes. To metal sleepers: clips and bolts. To concrete sleepers: special resilient fittings.
Filling: Broken stone.
Gauge widening:
   1.435 m gauge: 1⅜ in *(35 mm)*.
   1.000 m gauge: 1 in *(25 mm)*.
Max. curvature:
   1.435 m gauge: 7° = min. radius of 820 ft *(250 m)*.
   1.000 m gauge: 11.6° = min. radius of 492 ft *(150 m)*.
Max. gradient: 2% = 1 in 50.
Gradients:

	1.435 m	1.000 m
Level	29%	22%
Up to 0.5% (1 in 200)	37%	26%
0.5 to 1.0% (1 in 200 to 1 in 100)	20%	26%
1.0 to 2.5% (1 in 100 to 1 in 40)	14%	26%
	100%	100%

Max. altitude: 3 124 ft *(952 m)* on line Haidra to Kasserine.
Max speed:
   Standard gauge:
      Railcars: 62 mph *(100 km/h)*.
      Diesel trains: 56 mph *(90 km/h)*.
   Metre gauge:
      Railcars: 62 mph *(100 km/h)*.
      Diesel trains: 43 mph *(70 km/h)*.
Max. axle load:
   Standard gauge: 21 metric tons.
   Metre gauge: 18 metric tons.

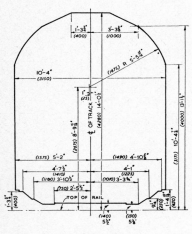

Standard gauge
All vehicles

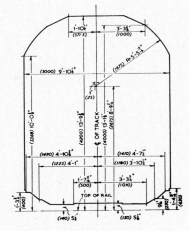

Metre gauge
Locomotives and passenger cars

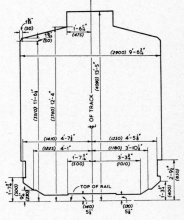

Metre gauge
Freight cars

TURKEY

TURKISH STATE RAILWAYS

Türkiye Cumhuriyeti Devlet Demiryollari, (TCDD)
TCDD Isletmesi, Genel Müoürlügü, Ankara

General Director: Orhan Acarlar
Member of Board of Management: Necdet Kalfa
Assistants: Salih Kaya Sagin
        Ender Çetinkaya
        Dogan Aydin
        Nahit Ozşahin
Department Director, General Inspection: Veli Gültekin
President of the Track Department: Şükrü Karaçali
Assistants: Tarik Kozanoglu
        Feridun Kumbasar
President of the Traction Department: Haşim Saltik
Assistants: Bülent Köksal
        Necdet Kocabay
        Ahmet Kaya Sarp
President of the Commercial Department: Hilmi Gözen
Assistants: Ihsan Kunday
        Osman Dinçer
        Eşref Cengiz
President of the Accounting Department: Niyazi Şahin
Assistants: Ayhan Kuter
        Ismail Gültekin
        Mehmet Degirmencioglu
President of the Operating Department: Lütfi Uskan
Assistants: Hayri Ipekeşen
        Necdet Özdamar
        Turgut Bayraktar
President of the Health Department: Ismet Ülgen
Assistant: Münim Yücel
President of the Exterior Relations and Administrative Affairs Department:
        Hüsnü Kayaoglu
Assistants: Abdurrahman Togay
        Turan Ersayin
President of the Staff Department: Ibrahim Erişen
Assistants: Yüksel Özmalkoç
        Ziya Seval
        Nazmi Ökten
President of the Supply Department: Ismail Hakki Akyüz
Assistants: Yasar Erdem
        Süreyya Mergen
        Özdemir Ataman
Presidnet of the Ports Department: Vacant
Assistants: Ziya Ülkü
        Fahamettin Akçay
President of the Construction Department: Ibrahim Çubukçu
Assistants: Erdogan Ortaç
        Mustafa Kargi
        Orhan Togay
President of the Research, Planning and Coordination Department: Rifat Serdaroglu
Assistants: Kudret Baykan
        Cumhur Yener
President of the Installation Department: Erdal Dikmen
Assistants: Oktay Bilkay
        M. Metin Karaman
Legal Advisers: Bülent Kandiyali
        Adnan Duruari

Gauge: 1.435 m.
Route length: 5 128 km.

A new five-year (1978-82) plan for Turkish State Railways (TCDD) was announced in 1977 as part of the country's Fourth Five-Year Economic Plan. Investment level, now being considered by the "High Planning Council," is TL 23 000 million ($US 1 373 million). The modernisation plan will include the construction of new workshops for the building of locomotives and rolling stock. Foreign credits or capital participation will be required for more than half the planned investment. About TL 10 000 million will be spent on the new manufacturing plants, to be built close to Eskisehir, where TCDD already has a rolling stock plant. Capacity of the new plants would be designed for 250 coaches, 100 diesel locomotives, 80 electric locomotives, 4 000 freight wagons, 10 000 flanged wheels and 100 trainsets annually. Most of the investment would be between 1978 and 1980.

A total investment of TL 7 500 million was planned for 1973-77, with assistance from the World Bank, although a number of projects were not completed. The objective of the plan was to expedite modernisation of the railway as a whole—replace steam locomotives with diesel and electric traction; renew passenger and freight rolling stock; install modern signalling, train control, and telecommunications systems; renew and strengthen track—so providing faster and more convenient services, passenger and freight, to meet the expected traffic growth.

The targets of TCDD's overall development plan are to obtain greater efficiency and economic viability, and to meet the country's rapidly increasing transport demands. The main features of the plan are expected to be:
Renewal of about 1 740 km of track and upgrading of a further 410 km; 1 475 new switches will be installed and more mechanised track maintenance equipment will be purchased:
Detailed studies are to be made of the signalling and telecommunications requirements on the busiest lines, and much new equipment will be ordered;
270 diesel-electric locomotives of 2 400 hp are to be built in TCCD workshops, as well as 60 shunters, 300 passenger coaches, and over 5 400 wagons;
Modernisation of works and maintenance facilities is to be carried out by installation of up-to-date machinery;
Improvement of staff training facilities; a large new training centre is to be built in Ankara, and training schemes will be set up both at home and abroad;
Conversion of steam locomotive maintenance depots to handle diesel units will continue as diesel fleet expands.
Furthermore, consulting services are to be included in the project. Experienced and selected consultants will study, in close co-operation with TCCD's engineers and economists, important questions such as uneconomic lines, management reorganisation, and feasibility of new lines. A new traffic costing system is to be established and there will also be tariff reforms.
Several other important works are to be included in the plan. Completion of electrification schemes already in hand will have immediate priority, as will modernisation of important stations. TCCD also plan to transfer the railway works in Ankara and the city's present scattered freight stations to a combined terminal at Behicbey on the outskirts of the city.

TRAFFIC

	1975	1976
Ton/km ('000)	7 354 745	7 932 271
Tonnage ('000)	14 676	14 726
Passenger/km ('000)	4 735 723	4 615 344
Passengers carried ('000)	109 710	107 267

FINANCES

	1975	1976
	TL ('000)	
Revenues	4 931 788	7 004 039
Expenses	6 004 950	7 197 462

TRACK

The Turkish Government has approved the construction of the new 279-km line to connect Adapazari with Ankara via Arifiye and Esenkent, thus eliminating the detour by Bilecik-Eskisehir; this new line, which is expected to cost 11 600 million Turkish pounds, will be double-tracked, electrified, and will run through 56 km of tunnels. Contract for engineering design went to Hoffmeier of the Federal Republic of Germany during 1977.
Construction work is underway on a new line between Tecer and Kengal on the main Sives-Malatya route. Work Total cost is expected to reach about 375 million Turkish lira. The new line will replace the old line which is considered unsafe for the much greater loads now being carried on the section by TCDD. Further development of iron ore transports between the central and eastern parts of Anatolia will be possible.
Total lengths of the new line, will be about 47.5 km (69 km with sidings). Grades will be kept to a maximum of 11 per cent, compared with a 22 per cent maximum on the old line. Minimum curve radius has been raised to 1 000 m, so that much higher speeds will be possible.
Rails on the new line will be 49.05 kg/m. They will be laid mainly on reinforced concrete sleepers (though timber sleepers may be used on some sections) manufactured at TCDD's own sleeper plant at Afyon.
Work will include construction of many long bridge sections and 7 500 m of tunnel. The Turkish Government is considering establishing a rail link across the Bosphorus. Either a railway line across the new Bosphorous road bridge or a tunnel is envisaged. Rail traffic across the Hellespont is increasing and the present transhipment by rail ferry is proving increasingly unsatisfactory.

MOTIVE POWER

Number of locomotives in service:

	Line	Shunting
Steam	533	100
Electric	18	—
Diesel-electric	243	—
Diesel-hydraulic	9	72

Number of railcars in service:

Diesel	23
Emu's	30
Dmu's	27

2 400-hp Co-Co mainline diesel-electric locomotive powered by a Pielstick 16PA4-185 engine; weight 112.8 tonnes; maximum speed 119 km/h. Supplied by TCDD's own Eskisehir Locomotive and Motor Plant.

A 2 400-hp locomotive about to leave the Eskisehir plant.

SIGNAL AND TRAIN CONTROL INSTALLATIONS

Work is in hand on the installation of Centralised Traffic Control (CTC) on the 365 mile *(585 km)* Haydar Pasa-Adapazari- Arifiye-Ankara line, with control Units located at Haydar Pasa, Eskisehir, and Ankara. Equipment is being supplied by the Westinghouse Air Brake Co.

Automatic telephone communications are also being provided on this route.

Future Dispatching and Telecommunication Works (1973-77)

Location:	Length of route	
	miles	km
Malatya-Elazig-Tatvan	441	459
Yolcati-Diyarbakir-Kurtalan	198	318
Afyon-Konya-Adana	213	643
Izmir-Balikesir-Eskisehir, Balikesir-Bandirma	514	672
Narli-Karkamiş-Nusaybin	326	500
Total	1 692	2 592

Future Electrical Signalisation Works (1973-77)

Kalin-Sivas-Divrigi	124	200
Basmane-Çigli	11	17
Toprakkale-Fevzipaşa-Narli	81	132
Hisarönü-Zonguldak	17	25
Total	233	374

Future Renewal of Track Works (1973-77)

Yenice-Mersin	27	43
Toprakkale-Yeşilkent	15	11
Toprakkale-Narli	79	132
Sivas-Çetinkaya	69	112
Yolçati-Erhani	58	103
Malatya-Çetinkaya	87	140
Alayunt-Balikesir	163	262
Adana-Taşkale	49	78
Kayseri-Sivas	139	222
Total	686	1 103

MOTIVE POWER

ELECTRIC LOCOMOTIVES

Class	Axle Arrangement	Line Current	Rated Output hp	Max lb (kg)	Tractive Effort (Full Field) Continuous at lb (kg)	mph (km/hr)	Max. Speed mph (km/hr)	Wheel dia. in (mm)	Weight tonnes	Length ft in (mm)	No. Built	Year Built	Builders Mechanical Parts	Electrical Equipment
4001-4003	Bo-Bo	25 kV 1/50	2 200	41 900 (19 000)	23 150 (10 500)	39 (62.5)	56 (90)	51⅛ (1 300)	80	52' 11⅜" (16 138)		1955	SFAC Alsthom	Alsthom-Jeumont-SW
40001-40008	B-B	,,	4 000	69 500 (31 500)	47 130 (21 350)	30.6 (49.0)	81 (130)	43¼ (1 100)	77	49' 3" (15 010)	8	1971	Groupement 50 Hz	

DIESEL LOCOMOTIVES

Class	Axle Arrangement	Trans-mission	Rated Power hp	Max lb (kg)	Tractive Effort Continuous at lbs (kg)	mph (km/h)	Max. Speed mph (km/h)	Wheel Dia. in (mm)	Total Weight Tons	Length ft in (mm)	No. Built	Year first Built	Builders: Mechanical Parts	Engine & Type	Transmission
U18C	Co-Co	Elec	1 980	60 900 (27 620)	51 000 (23 134)	18 (29)	60 (97)	38 (965)	102	56' 6" (17 220)	4	1957	GE (USA)	Cooper-Bessemer FV-12	GE
ML2700	C-C	Hyd	2 700	73 400 (33 300)	65 150 (29 550)	10.5 (17)	62 (100)	39⅜ (1 000)	111	64' 6½" (19 670)	3	1961	Krauss-Maffei	Maybach MD655	Voith
DH 33100	C	Hyd	360	18 200 (8 250) 29 300 (13 300)	2 650 (1 200) 5 950 (2 700)	2.5 (4)	31 (50) 25 (40)	43¼ (1 100)	40.5	30' 4¼" (9 250)	38	1953	Mak	Mak MS-304	Voith
DH 44100	D	Hyd	800	24 900 (11 300) 40 560 (18 400)	4 000 (1 800) 7 300 (3 300)	3.7 (6)	50 (80) 30 (48)	49¼ (1 250)	58	37' 1" (11 300)	6	1953-54	Mak	Mak MA-301 A	Voith
DH6500	C	Hyd	650	29 000 (13 150) 35 500 (16 100)	4 400 (2 000) 8 800 (4 000)	5 (8) 18 (30)	37 (60)	49¼ (1 250)	48.8	34' 5¾" (10 510)	13	1960	Krupp-Eslingen	Maybach GTO 6 A	Voith
Dh4101	C	Hyd.	400	15 750 (7 150) 30 650 (13 900)	1 870 (850) 4 630 (2 100)	5 (8) 2.5 (4)	37 (60) 18 (30)	37⅜ (950)	42	30' 5¼" (9 280)	1	1960	Jenbach	Jenbach Werke JW 400	Voith
DH6001	C	Hyd	600	24 800 (11 250) 35 000 (15 900)	3 850 (1 750) 7 780 (3 500)	5 (8) 2.5 (4)	37 (60) 18 (30)	97⅜ (950)	48	30' 8" (9 350)	1	1959	Jenbach	Jenbach Werke JW 600	Voith
U20C	Co-Co	Elec	2 150	82 700 (37 500)	76 100 (34 500)	10 (16)	71 (114)	40 (1 016)	111	56' 6" (17 220)	40	1956	GE (USA)	GE FDL12	GE
DE 24000	Co-Co	Elec	2 400	86 650 (39 300)	46 300 (21 000)	14.6 (24.2)	74 (119)	43¼ (1 100)	112.8	62' 6" (19 040)	14	1971	ELMS	Pielstick 16PA4-185	Jeumont-Schneider
DE 18000	Bo-Bo	Elec	1 800	57 760 (26 200)	30 850 (14 000)	44.5 (27.8)	74 (119)	43¼ (1 100)	80	54' 0" (16 440)	3	1971	ELMS	Pielstick 12PA4-185	Jeumont-Schneider
DH 3600	C	Hyd	360	18 210 (8 260) 29 300 (13 300)	2 650 (1 200) 5 950 (2 700)	2.5 (4.0)	15.5 (25) 31 (50)	43¼ (1 100)	40.5	30' 4¼" (9 250)	8	1971	ELMS	ELMS 360	Voith

UNION OF SOVIET SOCIALIST REPUBLICS

SOVIET UNION RAILWAYS

Ministry of Communications, Moscow 107174, Novo Basmannaya, 2

Administration
Minister of Communications: Boris Pavlovich Beschev
First Assistant of the Minister of Communications: Nikolai Aleksievich Gundobin
Department for International Communications: Anatoli Andreyevich Chernych

Gauge: 1.520 m; 0.60 to 1.00 m; 1.435 m.
Route length: 135 324 km; 2 863 km; 73 km.

The general management of railways throughout the whole territory of the Soviet Union is vested in the Ministry of Communications, which has its headquarters in Moscow. The Ministry has several main departments, each of which is responsible for a separate branch of the railway industry: operating; traction; passenger and freight traffic; construction and maintenance of track and buildings; signalling and telecommunications; electrification and power supply; planning and economic problems; finance; personnel, etc.
The whole railway system is divided into 26 railways each of which is independent from the point of view of day-to-day operating and finance. The management of each railway has an administrative structure similar to that of the Ministry.
The 26 railways are named as follows:—

Azerbaidzhan	Kazakh	Central Asian
Bielorussian	Kuibyshevsk	Northern
East Siberian	Lvov	North Caucasian
Gorkov	Moscow	Sverdlovsk
Donetz	Odessa-Kishinev	South-Eastern
Far East	October Commeration	South-Western
Trans-Caucasian	Baltic	Southern
Trans-Baikal	Dnieper	South Ural
West Siberian	Volga	

ELECTRIFICATION

By the end of 1975 the length of electrified lines amounted to 38 900 km (38.9 thousand kms), comprising 28.1 per cent of the total length of railway lines in use.
Power system: dc 3 kV, ac 25 kV 50 Hz.
Additional 771 km of track were electrified in 1975, including the following routes: Korshunikha-Lena; Kamensk Ural'sky-Bogdanovich; Miniral'niye Vody-Prokhladnaya; Magnitogorsk-Novo Abzakovo; Minsk-Stol'btsy, and others.
At present there are several electrified main lines in the USSR totalling several thousand kms; Moscow-Zabaikal (6 500 km); Leningrad-Leninakan (3 400 km); Moscow-Chop and Moscow-Sverdlovsk, each of approx 2 000 km in length. All larger railway junctions are now electrified, and electric traction occupies the leading place in town-to-town traffic.

TRAFFIC	*1974*	*1975*	*1976*
Freight turnover (milliard ton/kms)	3 097.7	3 236.5	3 295.4
Dispatached freight (million tons)	3 496.8	3 621.1	—
Passenger turnover (milliard passenger/kms)	306.3	312.5	315.1
Dispatched passengers (million people)	3 388.7	3 470.5	—

FINANCIAL

Income from transportation	15.6 milliard roubles
Expenditure on transportation	8.8 milliard roubles
Profit from transportation	6.8 milliard roubles

MOTIVE POWER AND ROLLING STOCK

During 1975 a total of 389 electric, 622 main line diesel and 486 shunting diesel locomotives joined the Soviet railways. Among the delivered main line locomotives were dc-powered VL 10 (5 200 kW) and ac-powered VL 80T (6 520 kW) locomotives for freight transportation and ChS 4 (5 100 kW) for passenger transportation. Introduced were also diesel-powered 2 TE 10L (6 000 hp) and 2 TE 116 (6 000 hp) locomotives for freight, and TEP 60 (3 000 hp) for passenger transportation. The fleet of shunting locomotives was augmented by diesel-powered TEM 2 and ChME 3 locomotives of 1 200 and 1 350 hp respectively. 1975 also saw the introduction for test purposes of the experimental series AC-powered VL 80R locomotives developing 6 520 kW; these units have a recuperating braking system. Also under operational tests are experimental diesel-powered TEP 70 passenger locomotives of 4 000 hp, with designed maximum speed of 160 km/h. This new locomotive uses a novel four-stroke diesel engine and other progressive technicalities, such as electric transmission of ac-dc power, 'jaw-bone' bogies, electrodynamic brakes, etc.
Main characteristics of the diesel-powered TEP 70 locomotive are as follows:

Axle formula (arrangement)	So-So (30-30)
Transmission	Electric ac-dc current
Designed speed:	160 km/h
Load from axle to rails:	21.5 tons
Functional weight with ⅔ of fuel and sand:	129 tons ±3%
Output:	4 000 hp
Pulling power at continuous rate:	17 000 kg (tractive effort)
Speed at continuous rate:	50 km/h
Wheel diam:	1 220 mm
Distance between axles of automatic coupling:	20 470 mm
Year of construction:	1973
Manufacturer:	Kolomensk Diesel Locomotive Works

The electric locomotives were supplied in two main series: ER 2 running on dc current of 3 kW, and ER 9P running on ac current of 25 kW. Operational tests are going on with the high-speed electric train ER-200 capable of 200 km/h. The electric train ER/200 has a power rating of 10 320 kWt, weighs 738 tons, and can accommodate 1 224 passengers. The bodies of carriages are made of lightweight aluminium alloys and the bogies have pneumatic suspension and are fitted with disc brakes. The ER-200 was built at Riga Carriage Works, Latvian SSR. During 1975 the Soviet railways received 3 200 all-metal passenger carriages, part of which are equipped with air conditioning devices. Tests are going on with passenger carriages suitable the RT 200 ('Russkaya Troika') locomotive traction, developing a speed of 200 km/h.
Main technical characteristics of passenger carriages for the RT 200 train are as follows:

Length of carriage:	26 384 mm
Width:	3 050 mm
Tare weight:	43 tons
Number of seats:	76
Gabarit (size):	O-T
Designed speed:	200 km/h
Manufacturer:	Kalinin Carriage Works

The fleet of freight-carrying wagons was supplemented by 76.6 thousand four-axle units. In addition to these the industry has also started delivering 8-axle semi-wagons with a freight-carrying capacity of 125 tons and volume capacity of 137.5 m³, and 8-axle tank-cars with a freight-carring capacity of 120 tons and volume capacity of 134.8 m³.

Among the delivered freight wagons was an increased number of specialised units for the transportation of concrete, fertilisers, bitumen, hot AGLOMERAT, automobiles, gas, milk, acids, live fish, etc. The fleet of refrigerator cars was considerably augmented, particulary units with mechanically-operated cooling and electric heating equipped with automatic controls. The specific weight of freight wagons on roller bearings was also increased.

TRACKWORK

In 1975 an additional 788 km of new track was introduced into service, of which the most important were the lines between Mikun-Koslan-Yertom (197 km), Orel-Mikhailovsky Rudnik (71 km), Pobedino-Nysh (175 km), and others. The material used to lay down these tracks comprised the following:
Rails: Standard type R 75, R 65 and R 50 weighing respectively 75.1; 64.6 and 51.6 kg/m.
Sleepers: Of impregnated wood, length 2 750 mm, thickness 160-180 mm, width of lower bed (on main tracks) 250 mm (remainder) 230 mm. Ferro-concrete type: pre-stressed; length 2 700 mm, width 30 mm, thickness (under rails) 193 mm. Number of sleepers on 1 km, 1 840; distance between ferro-concrete sleepers 550 mm.
Rail fastenings: Wooden sleepers and standard length sleepers—spikes with two-flanged underlay (sole) plates. Welded rails—split attachments on reinforced concrete sleepers, with rigid terminals (Type KB) and spring terminals (Type ZhB).
During 1975 railway sleepers were laid for a total of 4.5 thousand km of track, plus welded track of another 4.5 thousand km. The rails were joined by means of contact welding and gas-pressure welding. A total of 5.7 thousand km of track was put on heavier ballast.

SIGNALS AND BLOCK SYSTEMS (TRAIN CONTROL)

The introduction of automatic systems and remote-control mechanisation is continuing at an intensive rate. Likewise the installation of 'Neva' centralised movement control, automatic blocking with automatic locomotive signalling (multi-frequency for high-speed traffic) and centralised frequency control. Installation work is also proceeding on route-relay centralisation with programmed control operations and inter-station radio communications as well as electric centralisation for smaller stations on single-track lines, and units for axle-box control of train in motion. During 1975 a total of 3.2 thousand km of railway lines were equipped with centralised traffic controls and automatic block systems; and about 8.4 thousand km were provided with centralised electric controls.

MARSHALLING STATIONS (YARDS)

A whole complex of systems has been created for the marshalling yards: automatic regulation of rolling speed of rakes from the hump (ARS-TsNII); automatic centralised hump control of the block type (GATs-TsNII); automatic assignment (task-setting) of variable increased speed of carriage uncoupling (train division) (AZSR-TsNII). These systems are functionally connected with each other. The industry has also produced additional programmed automatic centralised control installations for hump lines (GPZU) which implement direct contact between the sources of information regarding the composition of any given train, the master control device at the hump, and the control-register installation (KRUG) which checks the fulfilment of programmed tasks allocated by GPZU and takes stock of accumulated wagons (carriages) on each line below the hump.
Important significance have the installation of automatic hump locomotive signalisation (ALS) which responds to the specific conditions of work of locomotives pulling trains up into hump. For spaced-out and intended slowing-down of uncoupling on humps the marshalling yards use pneumatically-operated retarders of the following types:
'Pincer-pressure' T-50 (KLESHCHEVIDNO-NAZHMIMNIYE)
'Pincer-weight' KV-62M and KV-72 (KLESHCHEVIDNO-VESOVIYE)
'Pincer-pressure and lifting' KNP-73 (KLESHCHEVIDNO-NAZHIMNIYE i PODYOMNIYE)
The KNP-5-73 retarders ('delay elements') are structurally similar to T-50, except that they are 1.5 times more powerful and intended to replace the latter. The KV-72 and KNP-5-74 retarders are intended for installation mainly on the launching sides of very powerful humps. A special hydraulically-operated retarder TsNII-3V has been introduced for use on rolling-stock lines of automated humps, launching sides (tracks) of smaller capacity humps, and extraction of individual carriages or groups of carriages while shunting. Its braking effort changes automatically according to the weight of wagons. This retarder is made up four track shoes linked together.

CONTAINER TRANSPORTATION

In 1975 more than 35.4 million tons of various freight were carried in containers. The Soviet railways use mainly universal containers.
Principal Soviet container types and their technical characteristics

Type	*Tare weight (kg)*	*Freight capacity (kg)*	*Dimensions (mm)* External	
IA	3 200	26 800	12 192×2 438×2 438	11 998×2 299×2 030
IS	2 100	17 900	6 058×2 438×2 438	5 867×2 299×2 030
ID	1 300	8 700	2 991×2 438×2 438	2 802×2 299×2 030
3A	950	4 050	2 650×2 100×2 400	2 510×1 950×2 090
3V	650	4 350	1 325×2 100×2 400	1 225×1 980×2 090
3S	500	2 000	1 325×2 100×2 400	1 225×1 980×2 090

The dimensions of containers of gross weight 3.5 and 20 tons correspond to international standards.
The railways network of the USSR features 1 280 container transfer points, established, first and foremost, at all large industrial centres and sea and river ports. The loading and unloading at these transfer points is carried out by suitable lifting transportation technology. In container areas use is made chiefly of electric twin-cantilever travelling cranes of 5, 10 and 30 ton lifting capacity. All are equipped with spreaders. The container transport on the Soviet railways is carried out the 'door-to-door' system. To transport universal medium- and large-tonnage containers the Soviet railways use a fleet of specialised carriages. In 1975 the Soviet industry produced 84.9 thousand containers.

DEVELOPMENTS

The Tenth Five-Year Plan (1976-80) of Soviet economic development envisages a further improvement of transit and transport means of Soviet railways, with emphasis on higher freight capacity and increased efficiency, as well as better use of marshalling yard and goods station technology, and reduced goods turn-over time. Apart from that, it is intended to speed up the movement of freight and passenger trains, increase the amount of freight carried along regular routes and average weight of freight trains. The planned increase in Soviet railway transport would amount to an estimated 22 per cent in freight and 14-15 per cent in passenger turnover. On the more overloaded routes of the Soviet railway network it is intended to construct 2.8 thousand km of secondary lines to electrify 2.5 thousand km, and to equip with automatic block systems and movement centralisation some 16-17 thousand km of railways.
It is planned to construct approximately 3 thousand km of new railway track, to continue the construction of Baikal-Amur main line and its access lines. During the period of this Five-Year plan it is planned to supply the Soviet railway transport with 2.2 thousand electric locomotives, 6.4 thousand main line and 2.5 thousand marshalling diesel locomotives, 386 thousand freight and 16.6 thousand passenger carriages. It is also intended to raise the level of mechanisation of loading and unloading work on railway transport to 93 per cent. Likewise, it is planned to realise certain measures to improve the organisation of passenger transport. Work will also continue on the electrification of railway lines and larger junctions, particularly near towns. It is also planned to raise the productivity level of work on railway transport by 18-20 per cent.

Type TEM2 diesel shunting locomotive (1 200 hp).

DIESEL LOCOMOTIVES

Class	Axle Arrange-ment	Trans-mission	Rated Power hp	Max lb (kg)	Tractive Effort Continuous at lb (kg)	mph (km/h)	Max. Speed mph (km/h)	Wheel Dia. in (mm)	Total Weight Tons	Length ft in (mm)	No. Built	Year first Built	Builders: Mechanical Parts	Engine & Type	Transmission
TE-3	2 (Co-Co)	Elec	4 000	128 000 (58 200)	95 200 (43 200)	12.4 (20)	62 (100)	41⅜ (1 050)	252	111' 4'' (33 940)		1953	Voroshilovgrad	2 × 2D 100	Elektrotyazh-masch
TE-7	2 (Co-Co)	Elec	4 000	73 800 (33 500)	34 000 (15 400)	34.8 (56)	87 (140)	41⅜ (1 050)	252	111' 4'' (33 940)		1957	Transmasch Works	2 × 2D 100	Elektrotyazh-masch
TE-10	Co-Co	Elec	3 000	92 600 (42 000)	59 500 (27 000)	14.3 (23)	62 (100)	41⅜ (1 050)	129	61' 1'' (18 610)		1958	Transmach Works	10 D 100	Elektrotyazh-masch
TE-109	Co-Co	Elec	3 000	83 800 (38 000)	38 800 (17 600)	22 (35.5)	87 (140)	41⅜ (1 050)	120	67' 8'' (20 620)		1969	Voroshilovgrad	5 D 49-V16	Elektrotyazh-masch
2TE-10	2 (Co-Co)	Elec	6 000	185 200 (84 000)	119 000 (54 000)	14.3 (23)	62 (100)	41⅜ (1 050)	258	122' 2'' (37 220)		1960		2 × 10 D 100	Elektrotyazh-masch
2TE-10L	2 (Co-Co)	Elec	6 000	185 200 (84 000)	114 600 (52 000)	14.9 (24)	62 (100)	41⅜ (1 050)	258.6	111' 4'' (33 940)		1961	Voroshilovgrad	10 D 100	CKD Prague
2TE-40	2 (Co-Co)	Elec	6 000	256 850 (116 500)	119 000 (54 000)	14.9 (24)	62 (100)	41⅜ (1 050)	252	122' 2'' (2 × 18 610)		1964	Kharkov Works	D70	Elektrotyazh-masch
TEP-10	Co-Co	Elec	3 000	66 350 (30 100)	38 100 (17 300)	22.4 (36)	87 (140)	41⅜ (1 050)	129	61' 1'' (18 610)		1960	Transmasch Works	10 D 100	Elektrotyazh-masch
TEP-60	Co-Co	Elec	3 000	55 750 (25 300)	27 500 (12 500)	31.1 (50)	100 (160)	41⅜ (1 050)	127	63' 2'' (19 250)		1960	Kolomna Works	D 45 A	Elektrotyazh-masch
TEM-1	Co-Co	Elec	1 000	79 400 (36 000)	44 000 (20 000)	5.6 (9)	56 (90)	41⅜ (1 050)	123	55' 8'' (16 970)		1959	Bryansk Works	2 D 50	Elektrotyazh-masch
TEM-2	Co-Co	Elec	1 200	79 400 (36 000)	46 300 (21 000)	8.7 (14)	62 (100)	41⅜ (1 050)	120	55' 8'' (16 970)		1960	Bryansk Works	PD-IM	Elektrotyazh-masch
VME-1	Bo-Bo	Elec	600	39 700 (18 000)	20 300 (9 300)	7.1 (11.5)	50 (80)	41⅜ (1 050)	69	42' 2'' (12 850)		1958	Ganz Mavag	XVIIV 170/240	Ganz Mavag
ChME-2	Bo-Bo	Elec	750	48 500 (22 000)	22 900 (10 400)	8.7 (14)	43 (70)	41⅜ (1 050)	64	40' 10½'' (12 460)		1959	CKD Prague	6S310-DE	CKD Prague
ChME-3	Co-Co	Elec	1 350	81 350 (36 900)	50 700 (23 000)	7.1 (11.4)	59 (95)	41⅜ (1 050)	123	56' 9'' (17 000)		1964	CKD Prague	K6S310 DK	CKD Prague
TG 16	2 (B-B)	Hyd	3 280	99 200 (45 000)	83 800 (38 000)	12.4 (20)	53 (85)	41⅜ (1 050)	136	101' 4½'' (30 900)		1966	Lyudinovsk Works	M 756AC	
TG-102	2 (B-B)	Hyd	4 000	119 300 (54 100)	72 000 (39 400)	12.2 (19.5)	75 (120)	41⅜ (1 050)	160	96' 8'' (29 460)		1960	Leningrad Works	4 × M 756A	
TGM-1	C	Hyd	400	30 800 (14 000)	24 700 (11 200) 12 350 (5 600)	3.1 (5) 6.2 (10)	19 (30) 37 (60)	41⅜ (1 050)	48	32' 8½'' (9 970)		1956	Murom Works	ID12-400	Murom Works
TGM-3	B-B	Hyd	750	49 470 (22 440)	43 000 (19 500) 19 850 (9 000)	4.3 (7) 9.3 (15)	19 (30) 37 (60)	41⅜ (1 050)	68	41' 4'' (12 600)		1958	Lyudinovsk Works	M 753B	Lyudinovsk Works
TGM-6	B-B	Hyd	1 200	52 470 (23 800)	30 860 (14 000)	9.3 (15)	25 (40) 50 (80)	41⅜ (1 050)	80	46' 11'' (14 300)					
TGM-10	C/C	Hyd	1 200	79 400 (36 000)	67 000 (30 400) 33 500 (15 200)	42 (6.8) 8.4 (13.6)	25 (40) 50 (80)	41⅜ (1 050)	121	55' 8'' (16 970)		1961	Bryansk Works	PD-2	Kaluga Works

GAS TURBINE

Class	Axle Arrange-ment	Trans-mission	Rated Power hp	Max lb (kg)	Tractive Effort Continuous at lb (kg)	mph (km/h)	Max. Speed mph (km/h)	Wheel Dia. in (mm)	Total Weight Tons	Length ft in (mm)	No. Built	Year first Built	Builders: Mechanical Parts	Engine & Type	Transmission
G-1	Co-Co	Elec	3 300	92 600 (42 000)	55 100 (25 000)	15.5 (25)	62 (100)	41⅜ (1 050)	140	65' 7'' (19 980)		1959	Kolomna Works	GTU-4	Elektrotyazh-masch

* Class TGM-3 has fluid-mechanical transmission.

ELECTRIC LOCOMOTIVES

Class	Axle Arrange-ment	Line Current	Rated Output hp	Max lb (kg)	Tractive Effort (Full Field) Continuous at lb (kg)	mph (km/hr)	Max. Speed mph (km/hr)	Wheel dia. ins (mm)	Weight tonnes	Length ft in (mm)	No. Built	Year Built	Builders Mechanical Parts	Electrical Equipment
VL 8	Bo+Bo+ Bo+Bo	3 000 V dc	4 200	77 800 (35 300)	66 800 (30 300)	27.5 (44.3)	62 (100)	47¼ (1 200)	184	90′ 3½″ (27 520)		1955	Novocherkassk Works	Novocherkassk Works
VL 10	Bo-Bo-Bo-Bo	3 000 V dc	5 200	88 000 (40 000)	72 750 (33 000)	32.3 (52.0)	62 (100)	49¼ (1 250)	184	99′ 10½″ (30 440)		1961	Tiflis Works	Tiflis Works
VL 22 m	Co-Co	3 000 V dc	2 400	53 800 (24 400)	38 600 (17 500)	23.7 (38.1)	46 (75)	47¼ (1 200)	132	53′ 9¼″ (16 390)		1947	Novocherkassk Works	Novocherkassk Works
VL 23	Co-Co	3 000 V dc	3 150	58 200 (26 400)	50 000 (22 700)	27.5 (44.3)	62 (100)	47¼ (1 200)	138	55′ 10″ (17 020)		1956	Novocherkassk Works	Novocherkassk Works
ChS 1	Bo-Bo	3 000 V dc	2 344	30 900 (13 800)	25 100 (11 400)	39.1 (63)	75 (120)	49¼ (1 250)	85	56′ 0½″ (17 080)	100	1957	Skoda Works Czechoslovakia	Skoda Works Czechoslovakia
ChS 2	Co-Co	3 000 V dc	4 200	37 500 (17 000)	31 100 (14 100)	57.8 (93.0)	100 (160)	49¼ (1 250)	120	62′ 1″ (18 920)	944	1958	Skoda Works Czechoslovakia	Skoda Works Czechoslovakia
ChS 3	Bo-Bo	3 000 V dc	2 800	32 600 (14 800)	27 550 (12 500)	45.0 (72.5)	75 (120)	49¼ (1 250)	85	56′ 0½″ (17 080)	87	1960	Skoda Works Czechoslovakia	Skoda Works Czechoslovakia
ChS 4	Co-Co	25 kV 1/50	5 100	38 400 (17 400)	37 000 (16 800)	67 (108)	100 (160)	49¼ (1 250)	123	65′ 7″ (19 980)	230	1965	Skoda Works Czechoslovakia	Skoda Works Czechoslovakia
VL 40 Monomotor bogies	B-B	25 kV 1/150	3 170	30 900 (14 000)	26 450 (12 000)	54 (87)	100 (160)	49¼ (1 250)	88	59′ 1½″ (18 020)		1969	V.I. Lenin Works Tbilisi	Lugansk Works
VL 60	Co-Co	25 kV 1/50	4 140	70 100 (31 800)	58 000 (26 300)	34.2 (55.1)	62 (100)	49¼ (1 250)	138	68′ 3″ (20 800)		1963	Novocherkassk Works	Novocherkassk Works
VL 60k	Co-Co	25 kV 1/50	4 650	70 500 (32 000)	58 200 (26 400)	34.5 (55.6)	62 (100)	49¼ (1 250)	138	68′ 3″ (20 800)		1962	Novocherkassk Works	Novocherkassk Works
VL 80k	2(Bo-Bo)	25 kV 1/50	6 520	99 400 (45 100)	90 200 (40 900)	33.3 (53.6)	68 (110)	49¼ (1 250)	184	107′ 9″ (32 840)		1963	Novocherkassk Works	Novocherkassk Works
VL 80T	2(Bo-Bo)	25 kV 1/50	6 520	99 400 (45 100)	90 200 (40 900)	33.3 (53.6)	68 (110)	49¼ (1 250)	184	107′ 9″ (32 840)		1966	Novocherkassk Works	Novocherkassk Works
VL 82 Dual-current	2(Bo-Bo)	25 kV and 3 kV dc	5 600	86 400 (39 200)	76 200 (34 560)	32.7 (52.7)	68 (110)	49½ (1 250)	184	107′ 9″ (32 840)		1966	Novocherkassk Works	Novocherkassk Works

Type VL 10 dc electric freight locomotive (5 200 kW) with regenerative braking.

Type TEP 60, diesel locomotive (6 000 hp) designed for passenger train service.

UNITED KINGDOM

BRITISH RAIL

British Railways Board, 222 Marylebone Road, London NW1

Telephone: 01-262 3232

MEMBERS OF THE BOARD
Chairman: Peter Parker, MVO
Deputy Chairman: J. M. W. Bosworth, CBE
Vice Chairman: R. L. E. Lawrence, CBE, ERD
Full-time Members: H. L. Farrimond
　　　　　　　　　　Derek Fowler
　　　　　　　　　　David Bowick
Part-time Members: David McKenna
　　　　　　　　　　Sir Alastair Pilkington
　　　　　　　　　　Sir David Serpell, KCB, CMG, OBE
　　　　　　　　　　Lord Taylor of Gryfe
　　　　　　　　　　Sir Alan Walker

BRITISH RAIL HEADQUARTERS
Chief Executive Railways: David Bowick
Finance Controller: D. H. Jones
Executive Director Freight: D. S. Binnie
Executive Director Passenger: H. C. Sanderson, ERD
Executive Director Personnel: C. A. Rose
Executive Director System and Operations: I. M. Campbell

BRITISH RAIL REGIONS
Eastern Region General Manager: D. J. Cobbett, ERD, TD
London Midland Region General Manager: J. G. Urquhart
Scottish Region General Manager: J. Palette
Southern Region General Manager: R. B. Reid
Western Region General Manager: L. Lloyd

1976 was described as a hard going year full of change and achievement in which British Rail more than met the financial objectives agreed with the Government. The first objective was to operate within the cash limits set in advance for the Public Service Obligation Passenger Services. The Contract price was set at £385 m; British Rail provided the services required for £319 m.

The second objective was to contain the short term grant for losses on freight and parcels operation within a limit of £60 m. BR actually required £35 m.

British Railways Board described 1976 as a year in which headway was made and despite the eroding effects of inflation and recession, a year in which forecasts were held and at the end of the year there was an improvement of £42 m over 1975 in terms of operating surplus. The success was however described as short term, being bought at a calculated cost in terms of the future.

1977 saw the publication of the Government's Transport Policy Proposals which were cautiously welcomed by British Rail. The proposals included comments such as:-
—"There is no question of the National Transport System being without a railway".
—"The Government rules out any notion of imposing major cuts in the railway network."
—Railways "to continue as the major public transport carrier of long distance passenger travel of a network of services connecting all the major centres of population".
—Railways "to continue and develop their function, which is essential to the industrial strategy, in carrying large flows of freight traffic from siding to siding".
—Railways "to continue as a major carrier of people to and from work in London".
—Railways "to continue to provide local stopping services in many parts of the country" where local judgement requires them.
—Large scale financial support for passenger business will continue, "but support from public funds should be directed not only towards meeting needs but also towards adapting the system to changing needs so that it will meet them more efficiently. Support should be provided in such a way that there is a discipline upon management to make the best use of it, looking not only to their present situation, but to the future as well".

The Policy Paper does not accept any losses in the Freight business after 1978 nor any rise in the level of support for passenger operations. In fact it stipulates a reduction in the level of support by the end of the decade. The Board sees this as posing tough and challenging problems.

Commenting on the Policy Proposals the Board said:-
　　"The Paper itself does not claim to be 'the last word' on transport policy and if, after analyses, the key strategic options are seen to be left open, the Board take some encouragement for the long term. However, the central problem that railways should reconcile their conflicting social and financial objectives remains undefined and unresolved.
　　The most welcome aspect of the Paper is its recognition of the continuing role of railways and that railways will be put at the heart of the nation's industrial strategy."

The Board also welcomed the Government's proposals for a rolling programme of investment but, whilst recognising the arguments for a more 'devolved' policy for transport services, considers the Government's proposals too drastic. These might lead to handing of responsibility for the future of provincial and rural services to shire counties, leading to a fragmentation of the national railway system.

Manpower was reduced in 1976 by 8 151 staff, a cut of over 3 per cent.

More freight was carried than in 1975 and the downward trend in passenger volume was reversed despite manpower reductions and fewer locomotives (171), passenger vehicles (670), and freight vehicles (29 000).

British Rail Engineering worked on overseas orders worth over £9 million and Transmark, the Board's consultancy subsidiary, had overseas earnings of over £2 million. Subsidiary businesses made progress with a higher surplus from property, hotels and harbours while shipping losses were halved and hovercraft services broke even.

FREIGHT

Although the level of industrial activity in the country was low, Railfreight achieved a marginal increase of 1 m tonnes over 1975 to a total of 176 m tonnes and gross revenue rose by £62 m to £307 m.

Bulk Traffic in Trainloads:
The proportion of trainload to wagonload traffic has risen over the years as British Rail consolidated its position as the mover of those bulk traffics— coal, iron and steel, and petroleum— which form the hard core of the business. In 1968, only 32 per cent of BR freight traffic was conveyed in trainloads. By 1976, the figure was 83 per cent.

Coal:
Coal traffic totalled 97 m tonnes, the same as 1975, with a higher intake of power station coal (55 m tonnes) compensating for a decline in other sectors of the market.
A revised long term contract was signed with the Central Electricity Generating Board for the delivery of coal to power stations, most of it by "merry-go-round" services—trains with automatic loading and discharge wagons which enable coal to be loaded at the pit and discharged at the power station without bringing the train to a halt.

Iron and Steel:
Although iron and steel consumption rose only marginally, movement of raw materials (imported ore and scrap and inter-works semi-finished steel) helped to boost rail

Class 47 diesel locomotive and Speedlink train
A new British Rail service for freight in less-than-trainload quantities is being promoted under the brand name "Speedlink" with the slogan: "Speedlink; the freight name for reliability". The Speedlink wagonload services, using new high capacity vehicles running to a strict timetable at up to 75 mph, have been developed from a pilot scheme in 1972 between Bristol and Glasgow. Now a national network linking main centres of industry in Britain, with European connections through the Ferry Train ports of Dover and Harwich, is being expanded. Speedlink is complementary to Railfreight's main business of bulk freight traffics in trainloads and the Freightliner system of door-to-door movements for containers.

carryings by more than 14 per cent to 29 m tonnes.
Ten-year agreements were signed with the British Steel Corporation for the movement of imported ore between Port Talbot and Llanwern and between Redcar and Workington. The Llanwern trains with a gross weight of 3 000 tonnes, are the heaviest ever run in Britain.

Other Traffic:
Three major cusomers agreed terms for new 10-year contracts for carrying petroleum products by rail and BR's market share was maintained in 1976 with carryings of 16.7 m tonnes.
The other main bulk traffics, chemicals (4 m tonnes), and building materials (5 m tonnes) held up well despite reduced demands nationally, and Railfreight's share of the market in the movement of finished vehicles for the motor industry went up by 7 per cent to 20 per cent (412 000 vehicles).

High Speed Freight:
Freight customers requiring a 'less than trainload' service are now being offered a new high speed wagon service called Speedlink.
Following a successful trial between Bristol and Glasgow in 1972, a network of 29 daily Speedlink trains has been phased in, linking main centres of industrial production and demand in Britain and including connections with Europe through the ferry train ports of Dover and Harwich. Feeder services connect at key points to cover much of Britain. These Speedlink trains operate on lines similar to Inter-City passenger services. The trains, with spacious high-capacity open, covered and specialised wagons capable of speeds of up to 75 mph operate to strict timetables. Most services are overnight, generally arriving for start-of-work next day. Covered vans, twice the size of traditional wagons, have strengthened floors for fork-lift operations. Speedlink trains also haul privately-owned wagons- including tankers and other vehicles available for hire.

Loading ships at Dunkerque
A campaign to increase railway freight traffic to Europe has been launched by British Rail, following introduction of improved Ferry Train services. Journey times to the Continent have been reduced significantly, extra trains and shorter Channel crossings have been added to the timetables, and new, larger wagons are being introduced on the services which are being marketed under the slogan, "Speed Your Exports by Ferry Train—its like the Channel wasn't there". The Ferry Trains have scope for great expansion of business because of the introduction last month of additional express services on Britain's Railfreight network with new shipping links from Dover to Dunkerque, where the French have invested massively in the new port of Dunkerque West, speeding turnround and journey times for the Sealink ships which carry the rail wagons across the Channel. At Dunkerque, the wagons are shunted straight on to high speed European freight trains. In addition to the Dover/Dunkerque route, which is the most important with up to six journeys a day, there are also train-carrying ferries to Dunkerque and Zeebrugge from Harwich.

Speedlink trains, unlike previous wagonload services, do not get shunted in marshalling yards during their journey, but instead call briefly at key junctions to attach or detach groups of wagons in much the same way as some passenger trains convey portions for different destinations.

Already 1 250 new wagons are in use on Speedlink trains and a further thousand started rolling-off the production lines at British Rail Engineering Ltd's works in late 1977. During the next four to five years, 3 400 further wagons—2 000 open wagons, 1 100 steel carriers and 300 vans—should be available for Speedlink, in addition to new vehicles planned for other Railfreight operations. Total capital investment outlay in Speedlink wagons amounts to £67 million.

By the end of next year, it is expected the number of daily Speedlink trains will be stepped up from the present 29 to about 50, with double the present tonnage. Within four years, today's Speedlink services and tonnages are expected to at least quadruple. A quarter of the annual two million plus tonnes of traffic already with Speedlink is new to rail. For the rest, much of this tonnage might have switched to road if BR had not introduced Speedlink, with its new standards of reliability.

Private Sidings:
Under the 1974 Transport Act, grants can be made to customers for up to half the cost of providing private sidings, wagons and associated equipment for loading and unloading railbourne freight where these are considered to be in the interests of the local environment and worthwhile to rail. By the end of 1977 a total of 37 grants valued at £6.79 million had been approved.

TOPS:
The nationwide wagon monitoring system TOPS (Total Operations Processing System) developed and installed in under four years, completed its first full year of operation and was a principal factor in the movement of a slightly higher tonnage in 1976 with 29 000 (13 per cent) fewer wagons than in 1975.

Through TOPS, rail managers can pin-point any wagon on the the system at any time of the day or night ensuring efficient use, supervision and distribution of the fleet.

The data from TOPS is used to provide greater flexibility in the response to changes in customer demand and thus to improve the use of movement resources.

The system provides real time information to customers and also monitors the movements of the 18 400 privately-owned wagons which go to make up most of the 4 000 company trains which run on BR every week.

PASSENGERS:
During 1976 the rail passenger business earned £505 m, an increase over 1975 of 18 per cent, or about 2 per cent in real terms.

The sequence of rapid price rises to make up for a period of restraint at a time of continuing inflation ended, after a 12 per cent increase in March, with a voluntary freeze on general fares for the rest of the year.

The loss of business due to pricing, together with the factors of inflation and shortage of disposable income, was very much as forecast by the Board, with passenger journeys (708 m) down by 3 per cent and passenger miles (17 800 m) down by 5 per cent on 1975.

Higher prices, however, brought in higher revenue—an extra £205 m in the two years (1975-76)—to meet the government objective of reducing support.

Active marketing and selling, especially of reduced fare offers, helped by the announcement of the freeze, resulted in a recovery in passenger business by the end of the year, when volume was some 6 per cent up on the low point just after the March increase.

Inter-City volume showed an even more buoyant trend being 8 per cent up at the end of the year over the March low point preliminary figures for the early part of 1977 indicated that the recovery is continuing and strengthening despite a further increase in fares to keep pace with inflation.

Inter-City has become big business with current turnover of £220 m and generating about 8 800 m passenger miles of travel annually (about 110 m journeys).

About 1 800 expresses, electric or diesel, run every weekday on the Inter-City network, which comprises about 6 000 route miles and serves about 200 cities. Many trains average well over 70 mph and have top speeds of 100 mph. A new breed of High Speed Train (HST) with a top speed of 125 mph is being introduced.

Inter-City 125: The world's fastest diesel rail service, operating on Western Region's London (Paddington) to Bristol and South Wales routes, is claimed by BR as Europe's fastest form of land transport and among the world's most frequent high speed rail services. The services are operated with the 125 mph High Speed Trains.

On Mondays to Fridays 82 daily services are operated by Inter-City 125 trains with faster than ever journey times. Similar services are run on Saturdays.

Ten trains a day, Mondays to Fridays, reach the world's's fastest average start-to-stop speed for diesel traction when they cover the 36 miles from Paddington to Reading in 22 minutes at an average speed of 98.2 mph. Another train averages about 96 mph from Paddington to Bristol Parkway, and five take only 86 minutes to cover the 133 miles from Paddington to Newport—an average speed in excess of 93 mph.

27 High Speed Trains have been delivered to the Western Region already, 32 are being built for the London to Edinburgh services in 1979 and 14 sets will be built for the line from London to the South West of England via Plymouth.

In line with British Rail's declared policy for Inter-City services the 125 mph trains are not restricted to passengers paying first class fares with supplements but are the standard train freely available to passengers using BR's range of reduced fares and special travel offers.

By the end of 1976 the new fast services with their substantial cuts in journey time and higher standards of passenger comfort had produced a 20% increase in passenger volume.

Inter-City Sleepers: Complementary to conventional Inter-City expresses, Inter-City Sleeper Business now handles well over 800 000 passengers annually. Turnover is £12 m annually. Services operate over 100 destinations in main business and holiday areas on 19 routes with 51 trains a night.

Rail Catering: Over the last few years reconstruction or refurbishment of almost all station catering facilities has been carried out and is planned to continue up to 1981. Service quality is being promoted through improvements of design, presentation, equipment, and staff attitude. BR accepts that train catering cannot be profitable at present but is a necessary part of overall passenger package. Costs are being kept to a minimum as a result of changes to the type and level of train catering during 1976. A new style of "grill" service is being introduced, which allows a simpler meal service to be offered, continuously throughout the day, using fewer staff.

Motorail: Started in 1955, BR's Motorail service has become a £2.8 m-a-year business with car spaces totalling 103 000 a year.

Trains are made up of Inter-City coaches, day trains with buffet cars, and sleeping cars for overnight travel. Passengers' cars are carried on flat wagons or covered vans attached to ordinary Sleeper services. A typical train carries 100-150 passengers and 30-48 cars. most services accommodate vehicles up to 7 ft high.

St. Pancras Moorgate/Bedford: A further 10 000 commuters will benefit from electrification of the line between Bedford and St Pancras/Moorgate, a distance of 53 route miles. Government authorisation of the £80 m scheme was received in November, for completion in 1982.

Passenger Transport Executive: The establishment of a new approach to payments by Passenger Transport Executives for rail services compatible with the PSO (Public

High Speed Train at the new HST maintenance depot at Old Oak Common
British Rail's 125 mph *(200 km/h)* passenger services started on 4 October 1976, when the first of 27 High Speed Trains began daily "Inter-City 125" services between London-Bristol and South Wales. 82 services now run each day. British Rail Engineering Limited are now building 32 trains for the London to Edinburgh services starting in 1978, followed by 14 sets for the London to West of England line. The prototype High

Speed Train holds the world speed record for diesel trains at 143 mph *(229 km/h)*. The trains comprise two power cars each containing a 2 250 hp diesel engine and seven coaches, including catering vehicles. The coaches are airconditioned, carpeted, extensively sound insulated and double-glazed. Air springing and improved bogie design ensures smooth, comfortable riding. The catering vehicles provide both full restaurant style meals and a buffet service of simple hot dishes.

Service Obligation) payments by central government continued in 1976, with two agreements signed and five accepted in principle.
In 1976, the Board received £25 m for the provision of rail services from the PTEs in Greater Manchester, Merseyside, West Midlands, Tyne and Wear, Greater Glasgow and West Yorkshire. Increasing financial pressures on PTEs have led to their raising fares to meet increased costs and also to a critical examination of the services currently being supported.

Birmingham International: Birmingham International, officially opened in September, was the first new station of major international importance to be built in Britain this century. Five years ago the site was open farmland.
The £6 m station was purpose-built to serve the new National Exhibition Centre with frequent Inter-City and local train services providing easy access to the central piazza within the Centre. In 1976 it was used by 35 per cent of all visitors to the Centre.

TRACK

Major results of BRs policy to continuously improve track are one steady spread of continuous welded rail (9 000 miles by mid 1977) which gives passengers a quieter ride, and reduces maintenance costs, rolling stock wear and risks of rail breaks, and replacement of traditional timber sleepers by prestressed concrete sleepers. The planned amount of renewal for 1977 was held back to 550 miles due to the financial situation but the aim is to increase this to 610 miles a year subsequently. £157 m was spent on track maintenance and track renewals during 1977.
Periodic measurement of track geometry and assessment of its ride qaulity is the key to the optimum economic use of maintenance resources. British Rail has developed a track recording vehicle capable of much more accurate measurements than previously possible and at the same time able to operate at speeds up to 125 mph (200 km/h).
The vehicle, known as the High Speed Track Recording Coach, runs behind any scheduled passenger train and measures the quality of the track during the journey. It will run over 80 000 miles each year checking most of BR's 21 000 miles of track, and can even be used with the 125 mph High Speed Trains—probably the only test coach of its kind in the world capable of working at these speeds.
Designed to supplement the regular patrolling of track by trained inspection staff, the coach's high speed capability overcomes the problems experienced when trying to fit existing recording vehicles, some of which can only run at 20 mph, in between normal passenger and freight trains.
The on-board electronic systems measure and record during the journey twelve different factors which indicate the condition of the track.
If the computer system detects any major irregularity, it fires a paint gun which marks the location on the track for attention by the local maintenance team.
At the end of each run, the measurements recorded are analysed so that the quality of the track can be assessed and maintenance programmes planned to ensure that the best possible use is made of the maintenance resources available.
The High Speed Track Recording Coach, together with its sister vehicle, the Ultrasonic Test Train, demonstrate British Rail's expertise in the field of automated track inspection systems.
In parallel with the development of the Track Recording Coach, the performance of the Ultrasonic Test Train is being greatly enhanced by the addition of automatic analysis equipment.
The train uses ultrasonic techniques to examine rails for hidden defects, with data from the sensors being recorded on photographic film for subsequent development and analysis. Until recently, this analysis has been carried out by trained evaluators visually scanning the processed film. A joint programme of work with the Nondestructive Testing Centre of the Harwell Laboratory of the United Kingdom Atomic Energy Authority has resulted in the development of an automated defect analysis system which exploits Harwell's expertise in computerised data analysis.
Further technical improvement and economies are expected to be made in the defect inspection system by placing the analysis computer actually on board the Ultrasonic Test Train to provide an automatic real time film-free system which will not only record and process data directly from the ultrasonic probes, but will also operate a track-marking system to pinpoint certain defects. Work on this is proceeding.

MOTIVE POWER

In 4 October (1976) Britain became the third country in the world to operate 125 mph (200 km/h) passenger services when the first of 27 High Speed Trains started carrying passengers from London to South Wales and the important commercial and industrial area around the city of Bristol.
The trains have been designed to provide top quality service on Britain's non-electrified Inter-City routes and attract more customers by considerably reducing journey times.
Most important, as far as British Rail's marketing policy is concerned, is that the trains are standard Inter-City trains available to all passengers with first or second class tickets or any of the wide range of special excursion or cut-price tickets which British Rail offers.
Passengers in both second and first class sections enjoy air conditioning, wall-to-wall carpeting, individual seats, double glazing to cut down noise and automatic draught free sliding doors at the end of each saloon. New catering vehicles have been designed and built to provide freshly cooked meals which can be ordered by and served to passengers at their seats, or simple hot dishes which passengers may collect from the buffet and take back to their seats.
The High Speed Trains are powered by two 2 250 hp diesel engines located behind a driving cab at each end of the train. The design of the train has been developed from the highly successful prototype train which, on 12 June 1973, became the fastest diesel train in the world when it ran at 152 mph *(229 km/h)* during engineering trials.
Each train consists of two power cars and seven passenger coaches. Advanced technology and design has enabled train weight to be reduced from the 466 tonnes of a conventional train to 383 tonnes. Each train can carry 318 passengers and consumes about 3.75 litres of fuel per kilometre at the 125 mph *(200 km/h)* cruising speed. An important factor when energy costs are continually rising.
Particularly important is the High Speed Train's ability to stop within the same distances as conventional trains thus eliminating the need to modify signalling systems. A wheel slide protection device has been specially developed to ensure that the wheels do not lock during braking, eliminating the risk of skidding.
In addition to the 27 train sets already in service a further 59 have been ordered.

ADVANCED PASSENGER TRAINS

The APT project is designed to provide a cost effective solution to the problem of providing fast inter-urban transport on existing tracks, in both financial and energy consumption terms.
APTs have developed from a programme of research into the dynamics of rail vehicles—passenger and freight—which was started in 1964 at the then newly established Railway Technical Centre, Derby.
The cost of the research and development phase of the programme, including building and running the experimental train APT-E has been £10m.
During the development phase, the experimental train not only became the fastest train ever to run in Britain, running at 152 mph *(243 km/h)* on 10 August 1975, but even more significantly, two months later it covered the 99 miles *(159 km)* between London and Leicester in 58½ minutes. It was this demonstration which showed just how effectively APTs can improve on the performance of present day trains. The fastest scheduled Inter-City trains are timed to cover the London-Leicester distance in 1 hour 24 minutes, an average speed of 70.7 mph *(112 km/h)*, APT-E cut the journey time by nearly one-third, averaging just over 100 mph *(160 km/h)*.
The project has now moved from the experimental stage. In October 1974, with Government approval, British Railways Board authorised the building of three prototype electrically propelled passenger carrying APTs at a cost of £9.9m.
The total cost of the APT prototype programme is about £25m, including the three trains, production line and other development costs which will not recur, and major items such as maintenance depots which will be required for subsequent trains. £11.6m has been loaned to the project by the European Investment Bank.
When APT-Ps enter experimental commercial service, the maximum speed will be limited to 125 mph *(200 km/h)* giving a possible journey time of 3 hours 57 mins from London to Glasgow with one intermediate stop. This compares with the best present day timing for the 401 mile *(640 km)* journey of 5 hours. Each train will have accommodation for 592 passengers.
Early 1978 will see the first test runs of a power car with three APT trailer vehicles, to be followed quickly by the first proving runs of a complete APT-P train. For these trials, the train will be based in the Glasgow area.
Later in 1978, driver training runs will start with a second APT-P and, when the equipment has been proved and sufficient crews trained, an ATP-P will be substituted for one of the standard 100 mph London to Glasgow trains in daily passenger service.
Because of more efficient use of energy by APTs and better utilisation of trains due to higher average speeds, overall cost per seat mile will be similar to that of existing trains.

Class 56 Freight Locomotive: Late in 1973, BR identified a potential significant increase in freight traffic available for railway haulage. In order to handle this traffic, 60 Class 56 locomotives were ordered in September 1974 from Brush Electrical Machines and British Rail Engineering Ltd (Doncaster)—each manufacturer to supply 30 locomotives.
A subsequent follow-on order of 30 additional locomotives was placed on BREL Doncaster in December 1975.
The Class 56 locomotive is the first BR locomotive to be specifically designed with the operation of Merry-go-round trains in mind, it having been identified that, following the severe increase in oil prices during 1973/74, a major portion of the increase in freight traffic would be attributable to bulk transportation of coal from colliery to power station. This involves hauling a gross load of up to 1 400 tonnes, a payload of 1 000 tonnes, and it is essential that during loading and unloading operations a constant slow speed is maintained even with the continuously varying trailing load. The Class 56 locomotive achieves this without driver intervention being required.

Class 56 Locomotive

BR Rating	2 424 kW
Max speed	130 km/h
Engine	GEC/EE.16RK 3CT
Traction Motor	Brush TM 73-62
Gauge	1 435 mm
Wheel arrangement	Co-Co
Length over buffers	19 355 mm
Total wheelbase	14 580 mm
Distance between bogie centres	11 480 mm
Max height	3 896 mm
Width over bodysides	2 686 mm
Wheel diam (new)	1 143 mm
Weight (with full supplies)	128 tonnes
Max axle load	21.3 tonnes

Class 313 Inner Suburban Electrical Multiple Units: The Class 313 units are specifically designed to provide smooth, comfortable travel for passengers on the shorter distance inner suburban commuter services.

One of the first Class 56 locomotives to be built undergoing trials with a train of 'Merry-go-Round' hoppers

Rated at 3 250 hp, the Class 56 locomotives are the most powerful freight only diesel engines working on British Rail. Designed to cope with heavy freight trains up to a maximum speed of around 70 mph *(130 km/h)*, the locomotives also have special control systems to enable them to haul 'Merry-go-Round' trains at a constant speed of about ½ mph *(1 km/h)* whilst they are being automatically loaded or unloaded. The locomotives are 63 ft long *(19.3 m)* and weigh 85 tonnes. 60 Class 56 locomotives were ordered in September 1974, 30 from Brush Electrical Machines Limited and 30 from British Rail Engineering Limited. An additional 30 locomotives were ordered from British Rail Engineering in 1976.

One of 64 three-car units for operation on the inner suburban services of the Great Northern Suburban Electrification

Specifically designed to provide smooth comfortable travel for passengers on the shorter distance inner suburban commuter services are a new generation of trains designed by the Chief Mechanical & Electrical Engineer of British Railways Board. The train design is based on experience gained after extensive passenger and engineering evaluation trials with prototype units. Each three car set has a seating capacity of 232 and a maximum speed of 75 mph *(120 km/h)*. The train doors are power-operated with passengers initiating the opening at stations. The trains can work from third rail electrified systems or 25 kV overhead lines or both. They are being constructed at the York Works of British Rail Engineering Ltd.

The train design is based on experience gained after extensive passenger and engineering evaluation trials with prototype units on the Southern Region.

The first order was for 64 three-car units for operation on the inner Suburban services between Welwyn Garden City, Hertford North and London (Moorgate) of the Great Northern Suburban Electrification.

Each three car set has a seating capacity of 232 and a maximum speed of 75 mph *(120 km/h)*. The train doors are power-operated with passengers initiating the opening at stations.

The trains can work from third rail electrified systems or 25 kV overhead lines or both. They are being constructed at the York Works of British Rail Engineering Ltd.

Variations to the basic design of the 313 units are being built for local services in the Clydside, Liverpool and Southern Region commuter areas.

Class 312 Outer Suburban Electric Multiple Units: The Class 312 trains are the latest generation of electric multiple units to enter service on British Rail. They are specifically designed to provide fast, comfortable travel on long distance commuter services.

Nineteen four-car units are currently under construction for service on the Eastern Region lines from Liverpool Street to Shenfield, Chelmsford, Colchester and Clacton. Further units are to be built to operate the services between King's Cross and Royston when the Great Northern Suburban Electrification works are completed. Another four units will operate local services for the West Midlands Passenger Transport Executive running between Birmingham and Coventry on the London Midland Region, serving the new railway station constructed alongside the National Exhibition Centre.

Each unit comprises four cars and the design is based on the earlier Class 310 trains introduced in 1967 to operate the suburban services from Euston. A number of improvements have been incorporated in the designs for the latest trains which include raising the maximum speed of 90 mph *(145 km/h)*, 15 mph *(24 km/h)* faster than the Class 310 and the provision of inter-vehicle gangway connection throughout each set, unlike the 310 stock which does not have a corridor connection between the middle two vehicles.

The vehicles are being built in the York Works of British Rail Engineering Limited. Each unit provides 297 second and 25 first class seats and up to three units can be operated in multiple.

The brake system is non-automatic, electro-pneumatic for all service brake applications and a classic automatic air brake for emergency applications.

The Class 312 design enables traction equipment to be fitted for operation with 25 kV overhead electric line supply or, as appropriate on the Great Eastern units, dual 25 kV/6.25 kV systems.

EXPORTS

British Rail's increasing success in world export markets is spearheaded by the manufacturing capability of BR Engineering Ltd (B.R.E.L.) and the transport expertise offered through Transmark, the Board's consultancy subsidiary.

In 1976, Transmark undertook work on 36 projects in 22 countries, covering most aspects of railway and transport activity, and were active in a further 14 countries. Close co-operation was maintained with consultancy organisations in the other nationalised industries and in the private sector.

Steady progress was made with design of the Tehran/Tabriz railway in Iran. Design work was completed on electrification of the Dublin and Brisbane suburban services, and there were negotiations for further Transmark participation in later stages of both projects.

A contract worth £250 000 was placed by the Hong Kong Government for a feasibility study on modernisation and expansion of the British section of the Kowloon-Canton railway.

A new company, Gulf Transmark is being formed with local interests in Dubai to promote railway and training developments in the Arabian Gulf area. Some success was achieved with the sale of BRB licenses, including bogie design to the United States, computer programmes to South Africa and overhead electrification in Australia.

Transmark increased its overseas earnings from £195 000 in 1973 to £2.2m in 1976, with prospects that this rate of growth will be exceeded in ensuing years.

In 1976 BREL was engaged on export orders to a value of over £9m and, following a substantial reinforcement of the marketing and sales staff to promote sales of locomotives and rolling stock, laid the groundwork for orders worth at least another £40m.

Designed for fast, comfortable travel on long distance commuter services, 26 of these **Class 312 electric multiple units** are soon to be introduced on the **Great Northern Outer-Suburban route between King's Cross and Royston**

New power signal box at London's King's Cross station showing the control room

SIGNALLING

There has been much care and expenditure by BR to improve control of traffic and promote maximum safety and efficiency. Major feature of the policy is extension of colour-light signalling with control concentrated in large centres.

The National Signalling Plan envisages that the majority of Inter-City, commuter and important freight routes will ultimately be controlled from about 75 major signalling sentres. So far 43 centres have been established, with the remainder of the system controlled from about 2 945 manual signal boxes.

By the end of 1976 about 10 100 single track mile *(16 400 km)* had been equipped with continuous colour-light signalling.

Edinburgh— First stages of the Edinburgh resignalling scheme were authorised at total coast of £14.8 m in June 1976, and the work is now well advanced. Total area covered by these stages amounts to 106 route miles *(170 km)* from Berwick to Polmont. Further authority of £12.3 m has been given for phase 3 (stages VI & VII) which will extend control area by 115 route miles *(195 km)* northwards to Ladybank and southwards to Carstairs.

Doncaster—Current estimate is £40.6 m for a resignalling scheme covering 180 route miles *(290 km)*; one control centre is to replace 61 signal boxes. Completion is due 1978.

Peterborough Stages 2 and 3— A £6.2 m scheme covering 44 route miles *(77.3 km)* of East Coast Main line which will eliminate 20 signalboxes is nearing completion.

King's Cross-Hitchin/Sandy Royston— Associated with new electrification, the scheme covers signalling and route improvement over 83 route miles *(134 km)*.
One control centre at King's Cross replaced 54 signal boxes. The scheme was completed before the introduction of electric services in 1977. Project authorised at estimated coast of £35 m.

St Pancras-Bedford— New signalling extending from Sharnbrook to St Pancras/Moorgate, a total of 70 route miles, *(110km)* will be controlled from control centre at West Hampstead resulting in abolition of 30 existing signalboxes. Estimated completion 1982

Reading Extension— Section of line from Theale to Heywood Road Junction controlled at present by 16 signalboxes, will be resignalled and controlled from Reading control centre, extending control area of this centre by 53 route miles *(84 km)*. Authority granted: £4.09 m. Completion expected 1979.

Victoria— Rationalisation of track and renewal of signalling authorised at estimated cost of £32.3 m. Work is due to be completed 1982. Signalling provides for centralised control of 103 route miles *(170 km)* at present operated from 36 signalboxes.

P. T. E. Projects— Signalling works to a total value £3.1 m are in progress in connection with projects promoted by Passenger Transport Executives at Glasgow, Liverpool, Manchester, West Midlands and Tyne & Wear.

Automatic Warning System— More than 4 138 route miles *(6 650 km)* have now been equipped with AWS. High speed equipment has been developed and is now undergoing service trials.

National Telecommunication Plan—Provides extension-to-extension dialling between approximately 200 railway telephone exchanges; planning is proceeding to connect remaining exchanges to the network. Provision has also been made for a National Radio Plan to be integrated into the network. The network carries the equivalent of £60 000 worth of trunk telephone calls each working day and provides the base system for TOPS, MANIS and many other data transmission systems, effecting large savings on Post Office leased lines.

National Radio Plan— Plan aims to provide two-way radio contact between lineside and traffic staff and a control base. National scheme will have 32 control centres and about 250 static transmitting points. Pilot schemes now cover routes between London-High Wycombe, Northampton and Bedford also Carlisle-Glasgow including Greater Glasgow area. Authority is being sought for Liverpool Street scheme, which would include Fenchurch Street-Southend and Liverpool Street-Clacton and Bishops Stortford. Scheme in progress providing signalbox to train communication on GN inner suburban lines.

National Data Plan— To meet growing need for data transfer between computer terminals and computer centres a network of high grade data channels over BR trunk telephone cable network is being provided.
New projects include connection of data communication channels between Nottingham computer centre and 30 data input centres throughout BR. Data channels will also be provided for manpower information, stores accountancy and BREL stock control systems.

National Teleprinter Plan— To meet the continuing need for use of teleprinters in the operating, commercial and administrative areas a project has been authorised for a national teleprinter network. This will include renewal and expansion of existing facilities with greater provision for general correspondence. Account is also being taken of the development of work processing systems and their impact on administrative communication procedures.

ELECTRIFICATION

After completion of the Great Northern suburban schemes currently underway about 45 per cent of all train miles on BR will be electrically operated, but on only 20 per cent of total route mileage.

By 1982 train mileage proportion may have risen to well over 50 per cent and thereafter will continue to increase, even if no further electrification schemes are completed, because of planned concentration and greater growth of traffic on electrified routes.

BR believes that steady long-term programme of electrification would result in maximum efficiency and lower running costs for whatever size of system is considered necessary.

Proposals for next ten years will generally cover the following types of schemes—

1. Extension of existing electrified routes to displace maximum number of diesel locomotives consistent with minimum cost: cross-London link with connections to four regions coupled with some extensions on Eastern Region.
2. Suburban schemes where there is large recognised element of social benefit: St Pancras-Bedford.

Eventually, with advent of higher-speed passenger trains, capacity restrictions may largely force the separation of passenger and freight traffic on to different routes, resulting in further electrification proposals.

St Pancras-Bedford Electrification— Work was started on a scheme to electrify (on 25 kv 50 cycles ac system) 53 route miles *(85 km)*, over 200 track miles *(320 km)*, between Moorgate /St Pancras and Bedford at cost of over £80 m. The scheme received Government authorisation in November 1976 and is due for completion 1982.

BRITISH RAIL RESEARCH

The role of British Rail's Research & Development Division is to generate technological innovations for use in rail transport and to provide technical and scientific advice and information to the British Railways Board.

The programme of research carried out by the Division spans the complete range from invention and assessment of possible future transport systems through the development of specific projects with medium term objectives to the support of current operations by problem-solving on a day-to-day basis.

British Rail's Research & Development budget is approximately £7 million a year. About 25 per cent of the Division's expenditure is on day-to-day or short term support work for railway engineering departments or railway business.

In recent years, British Rail's research has been epitomised by the Advanced Passenger Train project—the train specially developed to make the best possible use of existing railway and energy resources. The key to the performance of this train is that it can take curves much faster than a conventional train.

The Research Division is working on a number of projects which, while arguably less spectacular than the APT, are likely to make a major contribution to the future of British Rail and ensure that the future railway will make the best possible use of manpower and other valuable resources.

Much of the work currently in progress in the Research & Development Division is relevant to the great transport debate initiated in April 1976, when the Government published its Consultation Document as part of the quest for a national transport policy. The work is based on the belief that railways have a greater role to play and, as the work proceeds, even more evidence in support of this belief is being established.

Train Control: Projects in hand include the development of track-to-train communications which can be used not only for speech links between drivers and controllers but, more importantly, to automatically pass data about train speeds, locations and similar information to central control systems.

In the shorter term, advisory systems using similar techniques will be developed and installed. They could then evolve via mandatory control to perform automatic route setting and by linking with track to train communications equipment, comprehensive automatic control systems should become possible. The first step towards these objectives is an experimental advisory system now undergoing trials at Glasgow Central Station.

The first three passenger carrying Advanced Passenger Trains (APTs) will have a basic cab display system providing safe speed information during the journey although the system specially developed for these trains uses "beacons" mounted between the rails at intervals along the track and not a continuous exchange of data throughout the journey.

Work is also well advanced on a system to automate the passage of merry-go-round coal trains through unloading plants at power stations. At the moment, trains are driven through the unloading bays at about 0.5 mph. If this can be done automatically while the train crew takes a rest or meal break, it would be possible to achieve even greater productivity from an operation which is already highly efficient. A pilot scheme has already been demonstrated and the technique has considerable potential for use at new coalfields such as Selby.

Radio Communication: Considerable development work has been undertaken to engineer a radio system which can link key personnel and maintenance staff into the railway telephone system wherever they happen to be working. Work on the use of radio systems to provide signalling functions on branch lines—eliminating the need to install or renew fixed trackside equipment—is at an early stage, but if an absolutely reliable system can be developed, considerable financial savings should be achieved.

New Tracks: A major project at Derby for a number of years has been the development of new forms of track construction.

Track maintenance costs are a major item of expenditure for British Rail amounting to well over £100 million each year. Even before the recent cash limits imposed on ER support grants, there was considerable incentive to reduce maintenance costs whilst at the same time providing the new generations of faster passenger and heavier freight trains with smooth, accurate tracks.

British Rail has in service over 6 mile *(10 km)* of track laid on solid concrete slab usually put down in the form of a continuous ribbon. More is being laid, not only in tunnels where access for maintenance can be difficult, but also as part of the new or extended local rail systems being built by the Passenger Transport Executives on Merseyside and in Glasgow. Engineers from Derby are also involved in installing BR's slab track in Spain and New Zealand.

In all cases, subsequent maintenance costs have been practically zero and the tracks have remained in perfect shape.

Concrete slab takes some days to harden before the rails can be installed and trains run. The designers at Derby have investigated the possibilities of using rapidly hardening asphalt as a base on to which pre-cast concrete units can be placed ready to take the rails. This technique is still under evaluation, but initial results show that the resultant systems can easily handle traffic at today's level with little, if any, maintenance.

The use of lightweight electric batteries would offer considerable advantages to BR if suitable cells can be developed providing high enough energy outputs from reasonably sized batteries. If suitable batteries could be built into electric locomotives or commuter trains for example, operation along non-electrified branch lines or in sidings would be possible without having to provide a diesel unit or install expensive overhead supply equipment. Derby is one of the centres working on the development of the Sodium-Sulphur cell under a government sponsored and co-ordinated programme involving a number of UK organisations. These batteries have, applications in modes of transport other than railways.

Electrification: British Rail quite firmly believes in the advantages of electric railways. Different teams at Derby are working on projects to improve the performance of existing electrical equipment and components and develop designs of overhead electrification systems which are cheaper or can perform at higher speeds than existing designs or both.

Considerable interest is being shown both at home and overseas in the development of the Tubular Axle Induction Motor.

This motor actually fits into the vehicle axle which is made larger for the purpose and eliminates much of the complicated gearing and electrical equipment associated with conventional motors. In effect, the motor is "inside-out" with the case of the motor—and axle tube—revolving around the main part of the motor which stays still. The first two prototype motors are under test in the laboratories and at a later stage a test vehicle will be built for track running. The system is of particular application to commuter trains where every wheel could be powered right down the train. This particular motor also provides a very good braking action, another important advantage.

BRITISH RAIL STATISTICAL SUMMARY

Railways		*1973*	*1974*	*1975*	*1976*
Passenger receipts and traffic					
Receipts	£m	297.3	328.8	428.8	505.1
Passenger journeys	millions	728	733	730	708
Passenger miles (estimated)	millions	18 500	19 200	18 800	17 800
Freight receipts and traffic					
Freight train traffic					
Receipts	£m	198.5	205.5	244.8	307.0
Traffic	tonnes, m	197	177	175	176
Net tonne miles (trainload and wagonload)	millions	14 268	13 442	13 040	12 706
Coaching train traffic					
Receipts	£m	73.8	75.3	87.7	98.2
Traffic	tonnes, m	1.9	1.8	1.7	1.4
Operations					
Loaded train miles					
Coaching	millions	195	198	204	202
Freight	millions	54	51	47	43
Traction hours in traffic					
Coaching	millions	9.5	9.4	9.6	9.5
Freight	millions	8.4	7.8	7.3	6.9
Loaded wagons forwarded	millions	9.7	8.6	8.1	7.8
Loaded wagon miles	millions	887	839	769	716
Assets—at end of year					
Standard gauge					
Locomotives					
Diesel		3 639	3 619	3 508	3 338
Electric		333	352	352	351
High Speed Trains					
Power cars				2	42
Passenger carriages				8	151
Coaching vehicles		23 344	23 238	22 892	22 222
Freight vehicles (excluding brake vans)		248 682	241 429	216 367	187 000
Total stations		2 735	2 790	2 873	2 865
Route open for traffic—standard gauge	miles	11 326	11 289	11 258	11 189
Staff—at end of year		190 874	194 891	189 931	182 695
Ships					
Passenger receipts					
Passenger	£m	15.2	19.2	25.8	29.5
Passenger—accompanied vehicles	£m	6.9	7.9	10.7	13.1
Passenger journeys	millions	15.7	16.1	16.9	16.5
Freight receipts	£m	14.8	18.9	24.1	29.6
Ships owned—at end of year		48	45	43	40

Notes: *Railways—Passenger* and *Freight receipts* for year 1973 have not been amended to take account of changes in classification and allocation. Rolling Stock includes vehicles hired or leased.

FINANCIAL SUMMARY

Profit and Loss Account	*1972* *£m*	*1973* *£m*	*1974* *£m*	*1975* *£m*	*1976* *£m*
Income					
Rail					
Passenger fares and charges	273.7	297.6	328.5	428.5	504.7
Grants/Support	68.2	91.4	154.3	324.1	319.1
Freight	182.6	197.7	204.7	243.7	305.4
Parcels and PO mails	68.5	72.7	75.1	87.5	97.9
Miscellaneous	38.2	11.9	11.9	12.8	14.4
Rail Workshops	6.7	4.8	8.8	7.5	4.7
Ships	38.3	44.1	54.6	72.7	89.0
Hovercraft	2.5	3.0	2.8	3.7	5.2
Harbours	4.8	6.0	8.1	9.8	12.3
Hotels	16.5	17.6	18.9	21.5	24.5
Rail Catering	23.6	24.8	28.8	35.3	37.3
Non-operational Property	6.6	7.2	7.5	8.1	9.2
Operational Property (Letting)	9.6	10.4	10.9	13.3	16.0
Total Turnover	739.8	789.2	914.9	1 268.5	1 439.7
Other income (less Taxation)	1.5	5.8	11.6	18.5	12.7
Total income	741.3	795.0	926.5	1 287.0	1 452.4
Expenditure (before depreciation amortisation and interest)	665.1	734.7	959.0	1 288.2	1 407.9
	76.2	60.3	32.5	1.2	44.5
Provision for depreciation and amortisation	51.3	54.6	53.4	27.1	31.0
Operating surplus/loss after depreciation and amortisation but before charging interest	24.9	5.7	85.9	28.3	13.5
Interest and other financing charges	51.1	57.3	71.9	32.5	43.4
Loss before extraordinary item	26.2	51.6	157.8	60.8	29.9
Extraordinary item				66.3	35.2
Balance				5.5	5.3
Balance sheet and financing					
Financing					
Capital liabilities	404.0	404.0	438.27	313.3	339.6
Special Grants	32.0	52.4	109.6	—	—
Reserves and Provisions	100.5	115.1	125.3	139.7	198.5
Liabilities to staff superannuation funds	355.7	357.8	317.9	438.6	531.9
Loans and deposits by staff savings bank	55.3	59.7	62.1	63.6	98.2
	947.5	989.0	1 053.6	955.2	1 168.2

	1972 £m	1973 £m	1974 £m	1975 £m	1976 £m
Assets					
Fixed assets	884.6	924.3	1 005.5	569.8	670.6
Other net assets	62.9	64.7	48.1	385.4	497.6
	947.5	989.0	1 053.6	955.2	1 168.2
Source of funds during year					
Loans—from Secretary of State	—	—	34.7	63.3	26.3
—other	6.7	6.1	3.6	2.2	35.5
Special grants	32.0	20.4	57.2	—	—
Grants for repayment of staff superannuation funds deposits				34.7	34.7
Internally generated					
Scrap proceeds	23.7	21.6	17.2	18.7	28.9
Surplus/loss	25.4	—	—	5.5	5.3
Adjustment for items not involving the movement of funds					
Depreciation and amortisation	52.3	55.0	56.8	28.4	31.6
Other items	4.1	5.4	5.2	0.3	0.3
	85.2	97.7	164.3	153.1	162.6
Application of funds during year					
Purchase of fixed assests	99.6	101.5	129.0	110.6	143.1
Repayment of staff superannuation funds deposits			34.7	34.7	34.7
Working capital	14.4	3.8	0.6	7.8	15.2
	85.2	97.7	164.3	153.1	162.6

FREIGHTLINERS LIMITED

**National Freight Corporation
43 Cardington Street, London NW1 2LR**

Chairman: P. A. Thompson
Managing Director: C. Bleasdale
Assistant Managing Director: G. V. Burks
Directors: D. D. Kirby   D. H. White
A. D. Mundy   H. R. Wilkinson
F. Paterson

OFFICERS AND HEADQUARTERS STAFF

Secretary: I. R. C. Johnson
Director of Marketing: J. R. Burnham
Chief Engineer: M. K. Filsell
Personnel Manager: D. Watson
Chief Accountant: G. F. E. Mitchell
Chief Officer: (Development): S. G. Howard
Operations Manager (Rail and Terminals): M. B. Marsden
Road Services Manager: A. C. Dust
Regional Operations Manager (South): K. F. Bonwick
Regional Operations Manager (North): R. W. Hall
Communications Manager: J. M. Meara

Freightliners Limited operate a network of road/rail container services. Containers are carried on the trunk haul by high-speed rail, with road vehicles on hand at either end of the journey to provide a complete door-to-door capability.
Main principle of the Freightliner operation is that the trains run direct and in fixed formation between specially equipped road/rail transfer terminals. The wagons are designed specifically for containers and are capable of high-speed (75 mph) movement; trains run to a laid-down timetable and space is reservable in advance, as with a passenger service. The Company has a fleet of 8 000 containers for customers to load their products into, and it also carries on its trains containers belonging to other organisations. Shipping companies come into this category; indeed, with the recent spread of maritime containerisation, this has been a rapidly increasing facet of the business and now accounts for something like 40 per cent of the total carryings.
The Freightliner service came into being in 1965 and since then the picture has been one of steady expansion. Currently, Freightliner owns 26 terminals and serves a further 11 belonging to other organisations—chiefly port authorities. Some 190 train services operate each day and last year the company carried almost 720 000 containers with a turnover of almost £40m. The road fleet numbers 600 vehicles and 1 600 trailers, and staff total 2 350.
Freightliners Limited operates as a jointly-owned subsidiary of the National Freight Corporation and the British Railways Board, with N.F.C. holding the majority (51 per cent) shareholding.
In addition to regular services between main centres in this country, services operate daily to the ports of Felixstowe, Greenock, Harwich, Southampton and Tilbury for the short sea routes to Europe and deep sea to all parts of the world. The container port at Holyhead has a number of services connecting inland centres with British Railways container ships for Belfast and Dublin and there are also links with Ireland through other terminals.

Terminal	Name of Manager	Address and Telephone Number
Aberdeen	T. Burke	120 Market Street, Aberdeen AB9 2EZ Telephone: (0224) 54817/8
Barking	S. F. C. Smith	Box Lane, Renwick Rd. Barking, Essex IG11 0SE Telephone: (01) 595 1131
Birmingham (Landor St.)	R. W. Howlett	Landor Street, Birmingham B8 1BT Telephone: (021) 359 1985
Bristol	R. A. Hatton	South Liberty Lane, Bedminster, Bristol 3 Telephone: (0272) 632762
Cardiff	S. Jones	Rover Way, Pengam, Cardiff CF2 2YS Telephone: (0222) 497314
Coatbridge	J. H. McCall	Gartsherrie Rd., Coatbridge, Lanarkshire ML5 2DS Telephone: (0698) 69116
Coventry	A. Dawson	46 Binley Rd, Gosford Green, Coventry, West Midlands CV3 1JQ Telephone: (0203) 21330
Dudley	W. Banks	Castle Hill Road, Dudley, Worcs. DY1 4QG Telephone: (0384) 53754.
Dundee	T. Burke	88 Marketgait, Dundee, Angus Telephone: (0382) 23935
Edinburgh	W. H. Nicol	St. Marks Place, Edinburgh EH15 2QA Telephone: (031) 557 2646
Glasgow	A. McFadyen	100 Cathcart Road, Glasgow G42 7BG Telephone: (041) 332 9876. Extension 2018
Hull	W. A. Reed	Clyde Terrace, Brighton Street, Hessle Road, Hull, Humberside HU3 4UW Telephone: (0482) 561121/4
Leeds	H. N. Hall	Wakefield Road, Stourton, Leeds LS10 1SD Telephone: (0532) 31137
Liverpool (Garston)	F. G. Plumb	Dock Road, Garston, Liverpool L19 2JN Telephone: (051) 427 7941
London (Kings Cross)	C. MacDonald	Goods Way, London NW1 1UR Telephone: (01) 837 4200. Extension 4417
London (Stratford)	A. Chapman	Temple Mills Lane, London E15 2EN Telephone: (01) 534 4500
London (Willesden)	W. G. Lapham	Stephenson Street, Willesden, London NW10 6TY Telephone: (01) 965 8541.
Manchester (Longsight)	R. T. Dunn	New Bank Street, Manchester M12 4HD Telephone: (061) 273 2631
Manchester (Trafford Park)	R. Smith	Westinghouse Road, Trafford Park, Manchester M17 1FA Telephone: (061) 872 3072
Newcastle	A. MacDonald	Follingsby Lane, Wardley, Gateshead, Tyne & Wear NE10 8YA Telephone: (0632) 693741
Nottingham	H. W. Cross	Beacon Road, Beeston, Notts NG9 2FP Telephone: (0602) 48531 Extension 2400
Sheffield	E. Earnshaw	The Ickles, Sheffield Road, Rotherham S60 1DN Telephone: (0709) 63294
Southampton (Millbrook)	S. E. Scarley	Millbrook Road, Southampton, Hampshire SO1 0ST Telephone: (0703) 30223 Extension 2487
Southampton (Maritime)	S. E. Scarley	Weston Docks Extension Telephone: (0703) 30223 Extension 2251
Stockton	D. M. Carter	Haverton Hill Road, Stockton-on-Tees, Cleveland TS18 2NX Telephone: (0642) 612731
Swansea	M. H. Rees	Crymlyn Burrows, Swansea, West Glamorgan SA1 8SH Telephone: (0792) 41704

OTHER TERMINALS SERVED BY FREIGHTLINER SERVICES

BRB TERMINALS
Harwich (Shipping Division)   Telephone: (02555) 4670
Freightliner Agent: R. W. Meredith
Holyhead (Shipping Division)   Telephone: (0407) 2852
FELIXSTOWE DOCKS & RAILWAY CO
Felixstowe   Telephone: (03942) 70551
Freightliner Agent: R. Riddell
IPSWICH PORT AUTHORITY
Ipswich West Bank Terminal   Telephone: (0473)
Freightliner Agent: D. A. Spiller
PORT OF LONDON AUTHORITY
Tilbury Rail Container Terminal   Telephone: (0473) 3165
Freightliner Agent: N. L. Thompson
CLYDE PORT AUTHORITY
Greenock Container Terminal   Telephone (0475) 26484

CONTROL OF CONTAINER MOVEMENT

The immediate control and allocation of containers is exercised at the terminals, with overall balancing throughout the system directed from Headquarters.
A reservation system operates on all Freightliner services, and space is booked very simply by contacting the originating terminal for the service it is desired to use. Full 'consist' details of all trains are telexed through from originating to destination terminal as they depart, ensuring that resources will be promptly available at the other end to meet the workload.
Charges on the Freightliner system are generously on a per container basis.

FREIGHTLINER/CONTAINER CODE NUMBERS

Numbering system is alpha-numeric using 2 digits, one letter and 2 digits in that order—eg 01G00 and 69Y80. The four digits make up the fleet number as such within the overall range 0100. The letter denotes the type of container and is interposed so as to ensure accurate reporting and transcription of container stock and movement data. During 1978 a full real-time computer control system will go into operation covering all Freightliner containers as well as those of other operators which may be in the network at any one time.

UNITED STATES OF AMERICA

NATIONAL RAILROAD PASSENGER CORPORATION (AMTRAK)

400 North Capitol St, Washington DC 20024

President: Paul Reistrup
Executive Vice-President: J. R. Tomlinson
Vice-President, Public Relations: E. E. Edel
Director, News: B. Duff
Director, Plans and Projects: L. F. Prouty
Vice-President, Marketing: H. L. Graham
Director, Services: D. Ensz
Director, Reservations and Communications: R. J. Dooley
Director, Programme Development: J. V. Lombardi
Director, Advertising: J. Mariner
Director, Sales: R. W. Brown
Vice-President, Personnel and Admin.: K. A. Housman
Office Manager: L. Battley
Director, Personnel: J. Lewis
Vice-President, Operations: F. S. King
Chief Mechanical Officer: G. M. Beischer
Manager, Terminal Planning: A. L. Clark
Director, Transportation: D. Folsom
General Manager, Operations: R. Hopkins
Chief Engineer: H. Longhelt
Vice-President, General Counsel and Secretary: R. S. Medvecky
Vice-President, Public and Government Affairs: R. C. Moot
Director, Federal Affairs: J. G. Mathews
Vice-President, Finance: R. C. Moot
Controller: S. S. Sterns
Manager, Budgets: J. L. Ashbrook
Manager, General Accounting: R. R. Yetter
Manager, Taxes: W. E. Missert

Electric-powered Metroliner trainset
The sets operate hourly between New York, Philadelphia and Washington.

In 1929 United States' railroads, operating some 20 000 passenger trains, carried 77 per cent of intercity passenger traffic. By 1950, more than half the passenger trains had disappeared, and the railroads' share of the intercity passenger traffic had declined to 46.3 per cent. In the meantime, traffic on buses increased to 37.7 per cent and the airlines' share had grown to 14.3 per cent.
Twenty years later, in 1970, railroad passenger traffic dropped to 7.2 per cent of the commercial share and the number of trains still operating was less than 450. Of these, about 100 were in the process of being discontinued. Airlines dominated the public carrier market with 73 per cent, while buses, still in second place, held on to barely 16 per cent.
By this time, it was increasingly recognised that the country's excessive reliance during the past four decades on the private automobile and the airplane for intercity travel had left the nation with a serious imbalance in its transportation network.
The formation of Amtrak was proposed as it became evident that the United States could not rely solely upon further massive construction of highways and airports to meet its transportation needs. Creation of a national rail passenger system was viewed as a method to save an alternate form of transportation that possessed a priceless asset—existing tracks and rights-of-way into the major population centres of the nation.
Amtrak was created when the Rail Passenger Service Act was enacted on 30 October 1970. A Board of Incorporators was formed to organise the Corporation. On Amtrak's first day of operation, 1 May 1971, it inherited a dying business. Not one railroad operated a computerised reservations system. The majority of the rail passenger cars were old, and many were in disrepair. Too many of the stations and maintenance facilities had been neglected and were inefficient and unslightly.
On its first day, Amtrak did not own any railroad tracks, any stations, any terminals, any yards or repair facilities, any locomotives, any passenger cars or other railroad equipment; and there was not one manufacturer in the US building intercity rail passenger equipment.
For the first two years, Amtrak was almost totally dependent on the railroads, leasing equipment from them and using their facilities. An Amtrak customer could make a reservation, buy a ticket and complete his journey without ever coming into contact with an Amtrak employee. Congress had given Amtrak only a two-year experimental period of life, with no fixed route structure beyond that time, and planning future improvements was excruciatingly difficult.
Meanwhile, even Amtrak supporters were in disagreement about what Amtrak should become. Some wanted 150 mph corridor "trains of the future" while others called for the restoration of great long-distance "name" trains of the past.
The underlying thrust of Amtrak's first efforts was to revitalise gradually public confidence in rail passenger service through service improvements and thereby attract the travelling public back to the trains. Amtrak viewed its first few years as a building period.
The Corporation began with some specific goals: To increase the consideration with which railroad employees served the public; to offer reliable performance and well maintained equipment, and to issue accurate information to travellers.
Most of all, Amtrak developed positive programmes to entice an increasing share of the travel market to train travel. The principal target: the 87 per cent of intercity travellers who use private automobiles.

MEMBER RAILROADS

Beginning 1 May 1971, Amtrak assumed the responsibility of managing the operation of 23,000 route-miles of intercity passenger trains between the 21 city-pairs designated by the Secretary of Transportation.
The 13 railroads that signed contracts with Amtrak and immediately began operating Amtrak service were: The Santa Fe; Burlington Northern; Baltimore & Ohio-Chesapeake & Ohio (now Chessie System); Milwaukee Road; Louisville & Nashville and Seaboard Coast Line (now The Family Lines). Also included were: Missouri Pacific; Penn Central (now part of Conrail); Richmond, Fredericksburg & Potomac; Southern Pacific; Union Pacific; Gulf, Mobile & Ohio and Illinois Central (now the Illinois Central Gulf).
Because of route expansions, Amtrak later signed contracts with the Boston & Maine; Central of Vermont; Canadian National; Grand Trunk Western; Norfolk & Western; and Delaware & Hudson.
Three railroads—the Denver & Rio Grande Western, the Rock Island, and the Southern—were offered contracts by the Amtrak Incorporators in 1971, but they chose not to operate under the Amtrak system. Since 1 January 1975, these companies have been free to petition appropriate regulatory bodies to discontinue service, and this has been done in some instances.

SERVICES

By law, Amtrak is permitted to experiment with service outside the Basic System at any time. An amendment in 1973 authorised the Secretary of Transportation to designate at least one experimental route each year to be added to the Amtrak system. After two years of operation, the Secretary would determine if the route is to be operated permanently or discontinued. The Act was further amended in 1975 shifting the responsibility for selection of new services to Amtrak's Board of Directors. Under current law, Amtrak is no longer required to start one new experimental route per year, but may do so if resources permit.
Experimental services and dates instituted include:
North Coast Hiawatha—Chicago-Seattle via Billings, Mont., 14 June 1971.
Blue Ridge—Washington, DC-Parkersburg, W. Va., 7 September 1971. Modified to Washington-Cumberland, Md., 7 May 1973, because of poor patronage. Modified to Washington-Martinsburg, W. Va., 31 October 1976, when the Shenandoah began operating between Washington, Cumberland and Cincinnati.
San Joaquin—San Francisco/Oakland-Fresno-Bakersfield, Cal., 6 March 1974.
Inter-American—St. Louis-Dallas-Laredo, 13 March 1974. (Extension of Fort Worth-Laredo International service that began on 27 January 1973.)
Mountaineer—Norfolk-Roanoke-Cincinnati, 24 March 1975. Route discontinued on 2 June 1977, per direction of the Secretary of Transportation.
Lake Shore Limited—Boston-Buffalo-Cleveland-Chicago with a New York section joined at Albany, 31 October 1975.
Shenandoah—Washington, DC-Cumberland, Md.-Cincinnati, 31 October, 1976.
Pioneer—Salt Lake City-Boise-Portland-Seattle, 7 June 1977.
The Secretary of Transportation had designated the Lake Shore Limited and Mountaineer routes, both on 27 June 1974.
On 22 June 1972, Congress authorised International services to Canada at Vancouver and Montreal, and to Mexico via Nuevo Laredo. Such service was inaugurated as follows:
Pacific International—Seattle-Vancouver, BC, 17 July 1972.
Montrealer—Washington, DC-Montreal, PQ via Vermont, 29 September 1972.
Inter-American—Fort Worth-Laredo, 27 January 1973.
Two trains operate with state assistance and serve Canadian points: the Adirondack, New York-Albany-Montreal, and the Niagara Rainbow, Buffalo-Detroit through Southern Ontario.
The Act provides for states or regional agencies to obtain service not included in the Basic System. To do so the local unit must assume 50 per cent of the solely related losses of operating the service, plus capital expenses for equipment, facilities or track repair. Prior to 1 October 1976, other formulas were in effect at different times, depending upon the language of the Act. Such service in operation and their start dates are:
Illinois Zephyr—Chicago-Quincy, Ill, 4 November 1971.
Philadelphia-Harrisburg—Additional frequency, 29 October 1972.
State House—Additional train, Chicago-Springfield, Ill, 1 October 1973.
Illini—Additional frequency, Chicago-Champaign/Urbana, Ill, 19 December 1973.
Black Hawk—Chicago-Dubuque via Rockford, 14 February 1974.
Adirondack—New York City-Montreal via Albany, 6 August 1974.
Blue Water Limited—Chicago-Lansing-Port Huron, Mich, 15 September 1974.
Empire Service—Additional frequency, New York-Albany, 27 October 1974.
Niagara Rainbow—Detroit-Buffalo with through cars to New York City, 30 October 1974.
Michigan Executive—Additional frequency, Detroit-Jackson, Mich, 20 January 1975.
Arrowhead—Minneapolis-Duluth/Superior, 15 April 1975.
San Diegan Service—Additional frequency, Los Angeles-San Diego, 1 September 1976. Second state-assisted frequency, 24 April 1977, bringing route total to five daily trains in each direction.
Amtrak has increased frequency on some of its routes, bringing about increased passenger usage. Added trains on the New York-Washington, Chicago-Detroit and Los Angeles-San Diego routes has brought about significant increases in revenues and ridership.
A gain in ridership was also experienced on a long-distance route with added frequency. On 15 June 1976, Amtrak began operating its first daytime train in the Carolinas on the heavily travelled New York-Florida route. This New York-Savannah train, the Palmetto, immediately began carrying large numbers of passengers while patronage continued at high levels on the New York-Florida trains. Amtrak will continue to evaluate frequency increases in an attempt to strengthen route ridership.
The Rail Passeger Service Act, enacted on 30 October 1970, created Amtrak to manage the basic national passenger network and be responsible for the operation of all intercity passenger trains under contracts with the railroads.
The legislation identifies three underlying purposes and objectives of the Corporation: (1) Provide modern, efficient intercity rail passenger service within the basic rail system of the nation; (2) Employ innovative operating and marketing concepts to develop fully the potential of modern rail service in meeting intercity transportation needs; and (3) Strive for operation on a "for profit" basis.
This fundamental philosophy has remained, but the Act has been amended in several respects since. The Amtrak Improvement Act of 1973 continued Amtrak's authority beyond the original two-year experimental stage and locked into law for a minimum of one year all of the routes which Amtrak was operating at the end of 1973. The new Act also stated that quality of service should be a major factor in determining compensation to the railroads for the services they provide.
The Amtrak Improvement Act of 1974 expanded Amtrak's scope of responsibilities. It required the Corporation to directly perform its own maintenance and repairs, and directed Amtrak, the US Railway Association and the Secretary of Transportation to cooperate in a project to improve service in the Northeast Corridor.

The Amtrak Improvement Act of 1975 authorised, for the first time, funding for Amtrak for more than a one-year period, and authorised cash grants for capital improvements rather than federally guaranteed loans. The Act also directed Amtrak, the Secretary of Transportation and the Interstate Commerce Commission to submit to Congress proposals setting forth criteria and procedures under which Amtrak would be authorised to add or discontinue routes.

The Amtrak Improvement Act of 1976 mandated that the president of Amtrak shall automatically become an ex-officio member of the Board of Directors. This Act also amended the Railroad Revitalization and Regulatory Reform Act to permit Amtrak to purchase the Northeast Corridor railroad line.

FUNDING
The Corporation is financed by a combination of earned revenues from passenger service operations and Federal Government assistance. The one exception is a $197 million "entry fee" paid by the railroads over a three year period as compensation for Amtrak assumption of rail passenger service. The fee was equivalent to one half of the participating railroads' passenger service operating losses for 1969. These funds were used by Amtrak to cover operating expenses.

Government assistance has been provided in terms of cash appropriations to cover operating expenses and a mixture of guaranteed loan authority and direct grants for capital improvements.

Support provided through Fiscal Year (FY) 1977 has been:

	($ millions)		
	Operating Grants	Guaranteed Loan Authority	Direct Capital Grants
Initial Funding FY 1971	40.0	100.0	—
FY 1972-73	179.1	100.0	—
FY 1974	140.0	300.0	—
FY 1975	278.0	400.0	—
FY 1976	357.0	—	114.2
Transition Quarter	105.0	—	25.0
FY 1977	482.6	—	93.1
	$1 581.7	$900.0	$232.3

Federal funding to Amtrak is a multi-step process. Funds must be authorised by legislation originating in both House and Senate by Commerce Committees. Funds must also be appropriated by legislation from House and Senate Appropriations Committees. After the bills have been signed into law by the President, the money is then released to the Department of Transportation. These funds are apportioned to Amtrak on a quarterly basis for operating and capital purposes.

Amtrak funding should be viewed in the context of government assistance to other forms of transportation. From 1921 to 1976, all levels of government provided $457 000 million to build and maintain the nation's highways and streets. About $302 000 million was covered by receipts of Federal, state and local highway user imposts and toll receipts and $155 000 million from general fund revenues. Since 1925, government assistance in the development of airways and airports has totalled $40.9 000 million.

BOARD ORGANISATION
The Rail Passenger Service Act, as amended, states that the Board of Directors shall consist of 17 members, as follows:
8 Appointed by the President of the United States
2 Ex-officio members
3 Representing Common Stockholders
4 Representing Preferred Stockholders (vacant)

The President of the United States nominates and the Senate confirms eight members of the Board, of whom not more than five shall be from the same political party. Of these eight, not less than three shall be designated consumer representatives; further, not more than two consumer representatives shall be from the same political party. The two ex-officio Board members are the Secretary of Transportation and the President of Amtrak.

Three Board members are elected annually by the common stockholders of the Corporation. Shareholders were created by a provision of the Act that permitted railroads to take stock instead of tax write-offs when Amtrak was organised. Four railroads are shareholders— Burlington Northern, Milwaukee Road, Grand Trunk Western, and Trustees of the former Penn Central.

Four Board members to be elected by preferred shareholders. To date, no preferred shares have been issued and these seats remain vacant.

Because Amtrak is a large and widespread corporation, it is organised into 12 departments, each charged with specific objectives as follows:

Name of Department	Primary Functions
Executive	Overall Direction of Corporation
Computer Systems	Computer & Telecommunication Support Services
Executive Planning	Planning & Evaluation
Finance	Financial Management & Reporting
Government Affairs	Liaison with Government on National, State & Local Levels
National Operations	Directs Train Operations, Services, Routine Maintenance
Marketing	Advertising, Sales, Market Research, Tour Development
Northeast Corridor Operations	Operates Amtrak-owned Lines In Northeast Area Only
Operations Support	Heavy Overhaul of Equipment, Procurement, Engineering, Real Estate, Safety
Public Affairs	Communications with Public and Employees
Legal	Claims, Representation before Regulatory Bodies and Courts
Personnel & Administration	Employment, Benefits, Labour Relations, EEOP, Security, Training, General Administration

THE AMTRAK FLEET
By 1977, more than three out of every four passengers on short-distance trains and about half of all passengers were riding in new equipment purchased by Amtrak within the last 3½ years.

Amtrak started operations with 286 diesel and 40 electric locomotives, and 1 275 cars, all purchased or leased from the railroads. As ridership increased, Amtrak bought more equipment as needed. The last major addition to the fleet of old cars was precipitated by the energy crisis in the Winter and Spring of 1973-74 when Amtrak found 113 usable cars after an extensive nationwide search. Slightly over $114 million was spent in the first three years to purchase and repair this equipment.

Amtrak began operating French Turboliners beginning in the Summer of 1973 from Chicago to St Louis, and later to Detroit and Milwaukee. In each instance the new equipment brought ridership gains. Amtrak began service with two of the French trains, but ultimately purchased four more. Amtrak also ordered seven Americanised versions of the Turboliners and placed them in service on the New York-Albany-Buffalo line in the Fall of 1976, and on the Adirondack route to Montreal in the Spring, 1977, once again sparkling increases in patronage.

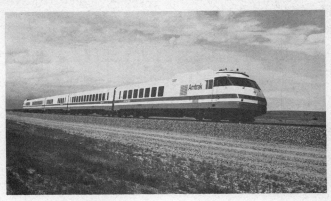

Amtrak's newest Turboliner
A blend of US and French design with modern lines and comfortable, all-electric interiors. Seven of the red, white and blue turbos, built by Rohr Industries in California, are operating Amtrak intercity rail services.

New F40PH four-axle diesel locomotive
A total of 30 of the lightweight 3000hp F40PH were ordered from General Motors in 1975 at a cost of $16.3 million; a further 10 were ordered in 1977.

Beginning in October, 1973, Amtrak placed a series of orders, totalling 492 Amfleet cars, with the Budd Company at a total cost of $206.3 million. The cars have an improved suspension system, public address system, attractive and carpeted interiors and seating that may be increased or decreased depending on the market served. The first Amfleet train operated in test revenue service on 7 August 1975, from Washington DC to Boston.

For long-distance service between Chicago and the West Coast, Amtrak placed on order 284 bi-level cars at a cost of $206.2 million. The first of several orders was placed with the Pullman Standard Company of Chicago, in April, 1975. The first cars entered service by late 1977. This bi-level equipment, named the Superliners, have stairways, double-levels and generous lounge and dining areas, improved air-cushioned suspension systems give a smoother ride, and sound-absorbing materials isolate the passengers from exterior noise and mute sounds within the train. Standardisation of components makes the cars considerably easier to maintain than Amtrak's aged fleet of long-distance cars.

In an effort to further improve the sophistication and reliability of its passenger equipment, Amtrak has extensively tested electric locomotives leased from Sweden and France. The Corporation also has leased two high-speed Canadian-built LRC (Light, Rapid, Comfortable) trains for test operations between Vancouver, Seattle and Portland.

Amtrak has spent or committed $582.7 million in capital funds over six years to buy a variety of new equipment, as follows:
40 diesel 3 000 hp locomotives (SDP40F) from General Motors; 2 November 1972; $18 million.
15 electric 6 000 hp locomotives (E60CP) from General Electric; 26 March 1973; $10.8 million.
57 Amfleet cars from Budd Co; 12 October 1973; $24 million.
110 diesel 3 000 hp locomotives (SDP40F) from General Motors; 12 October 1973; $50 million.
11 electric 6 000 hp locomotives (E60CP) from General Electric; 12 October 1973; $7.6 million.
200 Amfleet cars from Budd Co; 5 June 1974; $82 million.
6 five-car Turboliners (including two under lease and already in service) from ANF-Frangeco; 21 June 1974; $18 million.
25 diesel 3 000 hp locomotives (P30CH) from General Electric; 24 June 1974; $12.2 million.
7 five-car Turboliners based on French design from Rohr Co; 26 July 1974; $30.3 million.
35 Amfleet cars from Budd Co; 25 October 1974; $14.6 million.
235 bi-level Superliner cars from Pullman Standard Co; Divison of Pullman, Inc; 2 April 1975; $167 million.
200 Amfleet cars from Budd Co; 2 April 1975; $85.7 million.
30 lightweight 3 000 hp diesel locomotives (F40PH) from General Motors; 8 May 1975; $16.3 million.
14 Superliner cars from Pullman Standard Co, and reconfigure 42 previously ordered cars; 29 July 1973; $12.3 million.
35 Superliner cars from Pullman Standard Co, including 25 sightseer/lounge cars; 24 November 1976; $26.9 million.
10 lightweight 3 000 hp diesel locomotives; May 1977; $7 million.

MAINTENANCE
The Corporation owns and operates various types of maintenance and servicing facilities, located in Beech Grove (Indianapolis), Boston, Buffalo, Chicago, Dallas, Detroit, Harrisburg, Houston, Jacksonville, Kansas City, Long Island City, Los Angeles, New Haven, New York, Newark; Philadelphia, Rensselaer (Albany), Savannah, St Louis and Wilmington, Del.

Amtrak has built one new maintenance base, Brighton Park, in Chicago, for repair and servicing the Midwest Turboliners, and a $14.8 million Turboliner maintenance facility north of the Albany-Rensselaer, NY station with two turbo service tracks, a diesel repair track, an all-weather car washer, auxiliary shops, storeroom, employee facilities and offices.

Improvements are underway to several facilities purchased from the railroads. On 24 February 1977, Amtrak announced the start of a $6.8 million programme to begin modernising the 12th Street maintenance yard and 16th Street locomotive shop in Chicago. It is the first phase of a $38 million modernisation programme scheduled for completion by 1981.

On 1 April 1975, Amtrak purchased from Penn Central the rail car overhaul and repair shops at Beech Grove, Ind, for $3.8 million. It is Amtrak's primary heavy overhaul and car modernisation facility and it, too, is undergoing renovation.

NORTHEAST CORRIDOR

With the acquisition of the Northeast Corridor from the Consolidated Railroad Corp. (Conrail) on 1 April 1976, Amtrak became a full-fledged operating railroad. The property acquired comprised 456 route-miles from Boston to Washington, 62 miles from New Haven to Springfield, Mass, and 103 miles from Philadelphia to Harrisburg, for a total of 621 route-miles.

The properties, along with selected equipment, were conveyed to Amtrak from bankrupt railroads through Conrail under terms of the Regional Rail Reorganisation Act of 1973, as amended by the Railroad Revitalisation and Regulatory Reform Act of 1975. Operating on Northeast Corridor lines is an average of 960 trains a day, including over 120 Amtrak trains, nearly 660 commuter trains under contract with transportation authorities, and more than 170 Conrail freight trains.

Amtrak has been negotiating labour agreements in the region, and by 31 December 1976, an estimated 7 600 people were employed by Amtrak in the Northeast Corridor.

In addition to trackage, Amtrak purchased 107 railroad stations and numerous maintenance shops and yards at key points along the route. The purchase price for Northeast Corridor facilities was about $86 million, the net liquidation value certified by the United States Railway Association. The purchase agreement between Amtrak and Conrail calls for payment over an eight-year period, with an option for accelerated payment.

The Boston-Washington route will undergo improvements in a programme enacted into law on 5 February 1976. The $1 600 000 000 programme calls for upgrading of the Corridor within five years. An additional $150 million in federal money, to be matched by state funds, has been authorised for improvements to non-operational aspects of stations and installation of right-of-way fences.

The project includes: installing 420 track-miles of continuous welded rail, replacing 900 000 ties, cleaning the ballast, improving drainage, realigning approximately 50 curves, rebuilding the tunnels at New York and Baltimore, replacing or rebuilding over 600 bridges, modernising the electrification from Washington to New York and electrifying the line from New Haven to Boston.

When completed, electric-powered trains will run at speeds up to 120 mph, and will move travellers between New York and Washington in 2 hours 40 minutes, including intermediate stops, and between Boston and New York in 3 hours 40 minutes also with stops. The programme is funded and administered by the US Department of Transportation, Federal Railroad Administration, in cooperation with Amtrak.

The laws that authorised the Northeast Corridor purchase also permitted Amtrak to buy properties elsewhere. Included are 83 miles of line between Kalamazoo, Mich, and Michigan City, Ind; stations at selected points such as Battle Creek, Mich, Syracuse, NY, Lima, Ohio and Johnstown, Pa; several maintenance facilities, and 50 per cent stock ownership in both Chicago Union Station and Washington Terminal Company. The purchase price for off-corridor properties was nearly $3.9 million.

TRACK AND ROADBED

Outside of the Northeast Corridor, Amtrak routes depend on track improvement on privately owned railroads. In May 1975, before Amtrak purchased the Northeast Corridor, it began a $15 million programme to improve track conditions between New York and Boston. That August, Amtrak and Michigan jointly began a $958 000 project to improve portions of the Chicago-Detroit line. In April 1976, Amtrak committed another $2.7 million for additional work on this route, with another $2.3 million available from the State.

A time-consuming back-up operation in Fort Worth for the Inter-American was eliminated in 1976 after certain tracks were improved in a $350 000 project. This train also benefited that year from a $1.8 million track improvement project between Temple and Taylor, Tex, that eliminated a round-about routing.

Amtrak has also funded track improvements in terminal areas or when required in conjuction with new services. Included is work in Chicago Union Station, Little Rock, Kenova, Ky, Cincinnati, and between Springfield, Mass, and White River Jct, Vt, after inauguration of the Montrealer.

STATIONS AND TERMINALS

Over the past six years, 12 new stations have been constructed where previous stations were unavailable, unacceptable for passenger use or presented serious operational problems. Almost 300 stations have received some degree of repair or improvement. The station programme generally falls into the following seven categories:

1) **New Stations**— Work has been completed and new stations are in use in Cincinnati (1973), Jacksonville (1974), Port Huron, Mich (1975), Catlettsburg, Ky. (1975), Richmond, Va. (1975), Roanoke, Va. (1975), Bluefield, W. Va. (1975), Worcester, Mass. (1976), Cumberland, Md. (1976), Cleveland (1977), Duluth (1977) and Parkersburg, W. Va. (1977). Locations where new stations are under construction or in the advanced design stage include: Rochester, NY; Richmond, Cal.; Miami; Canton, Ohio; New Carrollton, Md.; and Minneapolis/St. Paul. Amtrak operates out of a new station in Louisville as a result of a 1976 contract with the Auto-Train Corporation, owner of the terminal.

2) **General Improvements**— Major rehabilitation has been completed in Nashville, Laredo, New York, Houston, Chicago and Springfield, Mass., and is underway in Oakland, Cal., Detroit and North Philadelphia. In many instances, station efforts have coincided with inauguration of service over a new route. For example, Amtrak has spent nearly $500 000 to upgrade 13 stations in Utah, Idaho and Oregon in preparation for the Salt Lake City-Boise-Seattle train, the Pioneer.

3) **Northeast Corridor Improvement Plan**— Under this project, $115 million in federal funds is available to improve the operationally essential parts of the primary intercity passenger stations between Boston and Washington. This includes some structural work, new or lengthened high-level platforms, and utilities necessary for passenger safety, train operations and train information systems. The major stations are: Boston, Providence, New Haven, Stamford, New York, Newark, Philadelphia, Wilmington, Baltimore and Washington DC. Not included in that sum is $150 million authorised for 50/50 state/federal programmes to improve certain portions of stations such as waiting rooms and ticket offices.

4) **State & Local Government Participation**— Amtrak co-operates with various levels of government to share station modernisation costs. In joint programmes with Michigan, a new station was built in Port Huron and seven other stations were upgraded. Amtrak and New York have renovated nine stations and the new Rochester station is being built in conjunction with the city and state. In Texas, Dallas purchased and modernised the station for Amtrak use; Lima, Ohio, helped to refurbish and landscape its station; and Bridgeport, Conn., served by many commuter and Amtrak trains, built an entirely new station. Duluth, Minn., constructed a new station and leases it to Amtrak, and a joint project is also underway in Minneapolis/St. Paul.

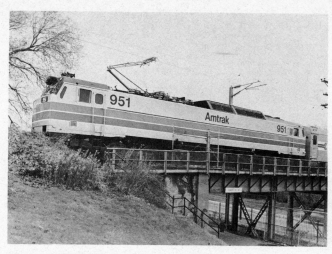

Electric type E60CP locomotive on the Northeast Corridor
A total of 11 electric 6000 hp locomotives were purchased from General Electric in 1973 at a cost of $7.3.

Amtrak has also participated in the construction or remodeling of facilities to be used jointly with transit authorities. Included are the Back Bay Station in Boston, a new station in New Carrollton, Md., and another in Richmond, Cal.

In a programme announced on 29 November 1976, Amtrak committed $1 million to be used as matching funds in a one-year project aimed at encouraging a broad upgrading of stations in smaller communites where current levels of ridership do not permit early improvements by Amtrak acting on its own.

5) **Railroad Contracts**— New passenger stations were built in Catlettsburg, Ky., and Cumberland, Md., as a result of Amtrak's contract with the operating railroads that requires station construction when the old station property is sold, converted to other uses or otherwise unavailable for Amtrak use.

6) **Private Developers**— Because of urban renewal concerns and opportunities, private developers saved and completely renewed the historic station in New London, Conn., and another developer is building a new station as part of a convention centre in Columbus, Ohio. Similar plans have been formulated to varying degrees in Indianapolis, Kansas City and San Diego.

7) **Citizen Help**— Citizens' organisations staffed with volunteers have helped to repair and remodel stations in White River Jct., Vt.; Kingston, RI; Windsor Locks, Conn.; Chelsea, Mich., Kirkwood, Mo., and other communities.

Amtrak succeeded in doing on 6 March 1972, what the individual railroads could not do for many years — it consolidated passenger operations in one terminal in Chicago instead of three. Later, Amtrak consolidated its operations into one terminal in Houston and one station in Richmond, Va.

RESERVATIONS

Amtrak's new nationwide, computerised reservation system has brought order to the previously fragmented railroad information and ticketing procedures. Now, reservation and information clerks at five major locations—Bensalem, Pa., New York City, Chicago, Los Angeles and Jacksonville— give schedule and fare information and take reservations for Amtrak and Southern Railway trains.

Incoming call volume during 1976 averaged 50 000 calls daily, significantly higher than the average of 32 000 calls per day handled during the peak summer months of 1973. This computerised reservations system is also used by station agents to automatically print tickets. The automatic ticket printing devices are located in busy stations and 65 per cent of all Amtrak ticketing is now done in such a manner. A new reservations service was installed in 1976 that permits deaf persons who have access to teletypewriters to communicate with specially trained Amtrak agents using similar machines. "Talking" is done through the keyboard.

AMTRAK PROFILE

General	1972	1973	1974	1975	1976
System Route Miles (thousands)	23	22	24	26	26
Stations Served	440	451	473	484	512
Train Miles Operated (millions)	26	27	29	30	31
No. of Employees (thousands)	1.5	5.3	8.3	8.7	18.4
Ridership					
Passengers (millions)	16.6	16.9	18.8	17.4	18.6
Passenger Miles (millions)	3 038	3 806	4 258	3 939	4 221
Total Revenue (millions)	$162.6	$202.1	$256.9	$252.7	$287.2
On-Time Performance					
Systemwide	75%	60%	75%	77%	73%
Short-Distance	82%	70%	80%	80%	75%
Long-Distance	53%	30%	63%	72%	67%
Revenue Cars					
Operating Fleet (thousands)	1 569	1 717	1 881	1 882	1 932
Out of Service (daily avg.)	NA	NA	18.0%	17.5%	15.4%
Average Age (years)	22.0	23.1	24.3	24.7	20.3
Number Overhauled	177	410	458	490	496
New Deliveries	0	0	0	115	241
Locomotive Units					
Operating Fleet (Dec 31)	185	337	442	362	353
Out of Service (daily avg.)	NA	NA	23.5%	13.0%	17.1%
Average Age (years)	22.3	18.7	13.6	14.4	10.7
Number Rebuilt	0	15	24	11	38
New Deliveries	0	40	110	30	51
Turbo-Powered Trains/Units					
Operating Fleet (Dec 31)	3	5	5	9	13
Out of Service (daily avg.)	NA	NA	9.0%	10.0%	14.0%
Average Age (years)	7.0	4.8	5.8	3.7	1.3
New Deliveries	0	2	0	4	7
Metroliners					
Operating Fleet (Dec 31)	61	61	61	61	61
Out of Service (daily avg.)	NA	NA	28.7%	27.3%	25.6%
Average Age (years)	6	7	8	9	10

NA—Not Available

THE ALASKA RAILROAD

US Department of Transportation,
Federal Railroad Administration,
PO Box No 7-2111 Anchorage, Alaska 99510

General Manager: W. L. Dorcy
Assistant General Manager: D. L. Allen
Comptroller: E. E. Callihan
Supply Officer: L. D. Parmenter
Acting Chief Counsel: T. E. Williams
Assistant to the General Manager, (Wash DC): William E. Fravel
Personnel Officer: R. W. Krueger
Real Estate Officer: Merle Akers
Operating Department:
  Operations Officer: W. C. Davidson
  Chief Engineer: T. C. Fuglestad
  Chief Mechanical Officer: G. V. Randall
  Chief Communications Officer: Andrew J. Clark, Jr.
Traffic Division:
  Traffic Officer: F. W. Hoefler
  Traffic Manager:
  General Agent, Fairbanks: R. G. Fendenheim
  General Agent, Seattle: R. W. Clegg

LINES AND TERRITORIES

The Alaska Railroad runs from the ports of Seward on the Gulf of Alaska, and Whittier, on Prince William Sound, northward through Anchorage and McKinley National Park to Fairbanks, and eastward to Eielson, with branches serving Palmer and Suntrana. Total route length with branches, 522 miles *(840 km)*.

PIGGYBACK AND CONTAINER OPERATIONS

There are 315 containers for door-to-door service. Terminal handling equipment used by the Alaska Railroad includes gantry cranes at Seaward and Fairbanks for train to ship movement, and an 'American' bridge-type gantry crane at Anchorage for train to road transport movements. The railroad has 134 trailers.

LOCOMOTIVES AND CARS

In service with the Alaska Railroad are 54 diesel electric locomotives (32 road haul and 22 switcher units); 1 765 freight train cars of these 38 are passenger coaches.

DEVELOPMENTS

In recent years Alaska Railroad completed the laying of a 10 mile *(16 km)* spur track to Fairbanks International Airport on a subgrade that was the result of a unique community enterprise involving Federal, State and Municipal agencies, the military and the private sector.

Although a spur track to the airport had been under discussion for several years, it really began in 1970 when a group of private individuals, known as the Metro Consortium, initiated discussions with the Railroad and other groups which culminated in the decision to begin actual construction.

The route mutually agreed upon departed from the Eielson Branch at Mile Post 5.9. It proceeded south and then westerly through a potential industrial area near the Tanana River, to a terminus at Mile Post 10 on the west side of Fairbanks International Airport. Since the Railroad announced that it could fund not more than the $1 million necessary for the construction of the track alone, it was agreed that the various landholders would be responsible for the placing of the subgrade on their respective properties. Under this arrangement, the US Army, Fort Wainwright, constructed the first 1.75 miles of sub-grade, plus a revision of the Eielson Branch. The next mile was placed by private landowners, the Rahoi Brothers, who were then followed by the Metro Consortium for the next four miles. The State Department of Public Works, Division of Aviation, completed the remaining 3.25 miles lying in the Airport Reserve. Other agencies participated in providing right-of-way, sources of borrow material, the relocation of utility lines, etc.

Due to the shortness of the construction season remaining to the Railroad, it was decided to use the panel method of laying track. Panels were assembled by a production line method, trucked to the railroad subgrade where they were laid end to end. Using this method it was possible to lay as much as 0.5 miles of completed track in one day.

With the link to Fairbanks International Airport now in operation, aviation fuel can be moved directly to bulk storage yards and dry cargo destined for the North Slope can be offloaded into waiting aircraft.

ATCHISON, TOPEKA AND SANTE FE RAILWAY SYSTEM

80 East Jackson Boulevard, Chicago, Ill 60604

Chairman, President and Chief Executive Officer: John S. Reed
Executive Department:
Vice-President, Executive Department: John C. Davis
Vice-President, Executive Representative, (San Francisco): R. W. Walker
Vice-President, Washington: F. N. Grossman
Operating Department:
Vice-President: L. Cena
Chief Mechanical Officer: M. B. Adams
Assistant Chief Mechanical Officer: K. A. Wolfe
Assistant General Manager, Mechanical Department, Topeka, Kansas: H. L. Hawkins
Assistant General Manager, Mechanical Department, Amarillo: V. G. Nail
Assistant General Manager, Mechanical Department, Los Angeles: R. T. Dennisen
Superintendent Car Service, Topeka: R. F. Kelly
Assistant Chief Engineer—Signals: B. J. Hutton
Assistant Chief Engineer—Communications: C. A. Crouch
Superintendent of Safety, System: R. D. Shaver
Director, Technical Research and Development, Topeka: C. R. Kaelin
General Manager, Topeka, Eastern Lines: H. J. Briscoe
General Manager, Amarillo, Western Lines: J. R. Fitzgerald
General Manager, Los Angeles, Coast Lines: H. D. Fish
Chief Engineer, System: W. S. Autrey
Assistant Chief Engineer: H. G. Webb
Assistant General Manager, Engineering, Topeka: C. L. Holman
Assistant General Manager, Engineering, Amarillo: E. C. Honath
Assistant General Manager, Engineering, Los Angeles: J. G. Fry
Finance Department:
Vice-President: R. W. Harper
Traffic Department:
Vice-President: L. C. Hudson
Assistant Vice-President: F. J. Wright
Assistant to Vice-President, Traffic: J. A. Stevenson
Freight:
Assistant Vice-President—Sales: A. A. Moser
Assistant Vice-President—Pricing: J. A. Grygiel
Market Research:
General Manager, Market Development and Research: A. J. Lawson
Manager, Market Development and Research: S. F. Baca
Advertising:
General Manager, Advertising: F. A. Tipple
Real Estate and Industrial Development Department:
Vice-President, Real Estate and Industrial Equipment: J. R. Scott
Informations Systems Department:
Vice-President, Information Systems: R. M. Champion, Jr
Purchasing and Stores Department:
Director of Purchasing and Materials, Topeka: C. C. Glover
Manager of Materials System: B. T. Randolph
Public Relations:
Vice-President: W. C. Burk
Assistant to Vice-President: R. E. Gehrt
Special Representative: J. W. Tilsch

LINES AND TERRITORIES

Santa Fe operates 12 569 route-miles *(20 228 route-km)* extending from Lake Michigan to the Gulf of Mexico and the Pacific Coast. Authority was granted 31 December 1972 to abandon 369 miles *(594 km)* of uneconomic branch lines and applications have been made to abandon additional lines totalling about 446 miles *(718 km)*.

On 15 February 1973 the Interstate Commerce Commission approved the Union Pacific-Rock Island merger and sale of Rock Island's lines south of Kansas City to

In track welding for Santa Fe
Santa Fe became the first US railroad to adopt in-track electric welding on a four-mile *(6.4 km)* section near Princeville, Illinois.

Southern Pacific. Under the proposal, Sante Fe would acquire trackage rights over Rock Island's line between Kansas City and St. Louis and purchase the line between Amarillo and Memphis. Further wide-sweeping recommendations would result in a total realignment of western railroads into four systems built around Santa Fe, Burlington Northern, Union Pacific and Southern Pacific. Santa Fe would acquire the Missouri Pacific system, the Western Pacific, the Denver and Rio Grand Western, and a Southern Pacific line into Oregon.

FINANCIAL RESULTS

The company's largest business activity, slipped to the position of contributing only 28% of consolidated pre-tax income. In some ways, however, the Railway's performance was an improvement over 1975. Revenue ton miles exceeded 1975 levels, and its operating revenues increased by 10.6%.

These higher revenues were more than offset by expenses, and the net result was a pre-tax contribution from rail operations of $47.5 million versus $51.2 million in 1975. Part of the increased expenses resulted from expanded rail and tie renewal programmes, which reflected the policy of maintaining high track and equipment standards even during business downturns.

In order for rail operations to regain the role held every year until 1974 as the largest single contributor to Industries' income, the Santa Fe Railway must have both regular growth and a regulatory and competitive environment permitting timely rate adjustments. The sluggish recovery of the general economy in 1976 produced volume increases below expectations. This situation was worsened throughout the year by unusually low grain shipments.

FIVE YEAR FINANCIAL SUMMARY

RESULTS FOR THE YEAR	1976	1975	1974	1973	1972
	(Dollar amounts in thousands)				
Operating revenues					
Freight	1 126 155	1 017 762	1 046 621	923 297	815 217
Other	23 093	21 297	25 372	24 446	16 478
Total operating revenues	1 149 248	1 039 059	1 071 993	947 743	831 695
Operating expenses					
Maintenance of way and structures	194 150	161 492	157 262	146 657	130 975
Maintenance of equipment	209 824	192 652	202 301	176 725	164 046
Traffic	27 300	25 280	23 760	21 690	19 179
Transportation	448 307	414 053	432 218	361 344	293 412
Other	62 688	51 886	47 756	42 417	37 685
Total operating expenses	942 269	845 363	863 297	748 833	645 297
Net revenue from operations	206 979	193 696	208 696	198 910	186 398
Taxes, other than federal income tax	101 142	93 383	97 915	75 069	64 255
Equipment and joint facility rents—net	34 291	24 923	19 175	24 579	19 140

RESULTS	1976	1975	1974	1973	1972
		(Dollar amounts in thousands)			
Operating income	71 546	75 390	91 606	99 262	103 003
Interest and other income—net	19 612	13 713	22 481	27 490	13 161
Interest expense	30 908	28 316	20 904	20 075	18 846
Income before federal income tax	60 250	60 787	93 183	106 677	97 318
Federal income tax					
Currently payable	6 622	4 667	9 449	15 543	13 361
Deferred	(1 535)	(124)	19 106	17 207	20 646
Total federal income tax	5 087	4 543	28 555	32 750	34 007
Net income	55 163	56 244	64 628	73 297	63 311

Revenue ton miles of 52 200 million were up a modest 1.8% from 1975, reflecting a somewhat less vigorous improvement in the general economy than expected. However, freight revenues advanced 10.7% due to approximately $78 million from rate increases and a more favourable traffic mix.

The total number of carloads handled during the year was virtually unchanged from 1975, although the first half of 1976 was slightly stronger and the second half a bit weaker than the corresponding periods of the prior year. To a great extent, this variation resulted from a 16% reduction in wheat movements from 1975. With lessened export demand for wheat and farmers' reluctance to sell in expectation of achieving higher prices, grain transportation demand was sharply reduced from the relatively high levels experienced in the latter half of 1975.

Significant year-to-year increases occurred in a number of diverse sectors. The number of trailers and containers moved in piggyback service grew 32%. Carloadings of motor vehicles rebounded 30%, despite a strike in the industry late in the year. Shipments of forest products rose more than 14%. Freight forwarder, shipper association and shipper agent carloads increased 18%. Declines were experienced in refrigerated carloads, 18%; non-metallic minerals, 20%; iron and steel, 18%; and mail, 58%. This latter decline—reflected the Postal Service's decision not to renew certain mail shipment contracts.

Sustained economic growth through 1977 should produce continued improvements in freight traffic. Furthermore, the decline in grain shipments experienced in 1976 coincided with a wheat crop which, contrary to initial indications, resulted in the third largest harvest ever in Santa Fe Railway's territory. Consequently, substantial amounts of grain remain in storage awaiting future movement. Wheat acreage planted in the autumn declined about 3% from the prior year.

Contractual arrangements with Amtrak for providing passenger services were unchanged, and it is likely that compensation for such services in 1977 will be in accordance with existing arrangements. During 1976, Amtrak leased its 21st Street Coach Yard in Chicago and the service facility at Fort Worth. In January 1977, the Los Angeles 8th Street Coach Yard and Redondo Junction mechanical facilities were sold to Amtrak for $8.1 million, resulting in a pre-tax gain of $7.1 million. Amtrak has assumed the passenger train mechanical services previously performed at these four locations by Santa Fe Railway under contract.

Financial assistance from the State of California enabled Amtrak to inaugurate one

Six-Pack cars for trailers

additional train in intercity service between Los Angeles and San Diego. Similar financial assistance to effect line improvements shortening schedules between these two cities is under study.

Capital expenditures in 1976 totalled $102.4 million, comprising $63.9 million for equipment and $38.5 million for roadway and structures. During the year, 1 510 new freight cars were acquired. Equipment improvements included conversion of 207 cars for various purposes and rebuilding of 24 locomotives in the railway's shops.

Improvements to roadway and structures included installation of 382 track miles of new and reconditioned continuous welded rail, with most of the cost charged to operating expense. The Railway now has 5 806 track miles of welded rail. The programme for replacement of timber trestle bridges with those constructed of fireproof components was continued. The Railway's $50 million automated classification yard at Barstow, California became operational in February 1976. The yard is a key facility in West Coast operations and has increased train operating efficiency into and out of northern and southern California.

Crossing protection was improved with the installation of 84 sets of automatic gates and 23 flashing warning light systems at rail-highway intersections. Sytems were also expanded for centralised traffic control and for automatic detection of dangerous operating conditions.

Curve reduction were undertaken at various locations, including a major project between Williams Junction and Phoenix, Arizona which will reduce the running time of freight trains into and out of Phoenix by an hour.

Automobile unloading facilities were constructed at Houston and Los Angeles. Modernisation of locomotives maintenance shops at Cleburne, Texas and of the westbound classification facility at Argentine Yard in Kansas City continued. Near Fort Worth, the new Saginaw Yard was finished, and piggy back facilities near Denver were substantially completed.

1977 Improvement Programme

The railway anticipates capital expenditures of $150 million during 1977. Of this amount, $46 million will be for the purchase of 1 175 new freight cars, $24 million for rebuilding locomotives, $24 million for other equipment improvements, and $56 million for work on roadway and structures.

The planned rail programme for 1977 includes 391 track miles of new and reconditioned continuous welded rail, and the bridge renewal programme will continue throughout the system.

Major communications projects planned for the year are replacement of the microwave system between Topeka and Wellington, Kansas, and addition of supplementary channels to the telephone system. Traffic control signalling will be installed at additional locations, as will track-side detection systems for oveheated wheel bearings, high water, dragging equipment and shifted cargo. Automatic gate protection systems will be installed at 112 rail-highway crossings, and flashing light systems will be applied at 38 crossings.

Other projects include completion of improvements to the westbound classification yard at Argentine, continuation of work on the locomotive rebuilding and hopper car cleansing facilities at Cleburne, relocation of repair shops for refrigerated cars and trailers at Argentine, completion of the new Denver piggyback facility and expansion to handle automobile unloading, expansion and improvement of piggyback facility at Los Angeles and Chicago, and construction of a new piggyback facility at Lubbock, Texas. Locomotive painting facilities at San Bernardino, California will be completed.

A new Santa Fe Railway subsidiary, Star Lake Railroad Company, was incorporated in 1976 and has filed an application with the Interstate Commerce Commission for authority to construct a common carrier railroad to serve the San Juan Basin of north-west New Mexico. This area is the location of substantial undeveloped coal reserves owned by a Santa Fe subsidiary and others. The new line would leave the Railway's existing line near Baca, New Mexico and continue northward for about 60 miles to Pueblo Pintado, from which it would extend eastward 10 miles to Star Lake and westward 10 miles to Gallo Wash. It is anticipated that the line will ultimately be extended northwest from Gallo Wash to serve other coal deposits. Star Lake Railroad has filed applications concerning the line with various other government and Navajo tribal agencies. A preliminary draft of a regional environmental impact study has been filed with the Bureau of Land Management.

BOSTON AND MAINE CORPORATION

Iron Horse Park, North Billerica, Mass 01862

LINES AND TERRITORIES

The principal lines of the Boston & Maine run north and west from Boston through the states of Maine, New Hampshire, Vermont, Massachusetts, and in eastern New York State where it makes connections at Albany and Schenectady with other lines.

Essentially a freight operating railway, the company is under contract with the Massachusetts Bay Transportation Authority to continue passenger service within a twenty mile radius of Boston, with some reimbursement of excess expenses by the Authority. Total length of the B & M network totals 1 400 miles.

This company was formed in 1969 to take over the railroad, Boston & Maine Corporation, and to facilitate the acquisition of business enterprises in fields other than the railroad industry.

The plan to establish two major railroads in the eastern states proposed the Penn Central as one, and the Norfolk and Western and C & O/B & O as the second; with the latter group required to include five smaller railroads, of which the Boston and Maine was one.

Norfolk and Western made an offer to the B & M, but this was not accepted. In March 1971 the N & W and the C & O/B & O railroads announced that their proposals to merge were abandoned due to changed circumstances—presumably partly the Penn Central bankruptcy. Subsequently Trustees were appointed for the B & M.

TRAFFIC

During 1976 Boston and Maine's total freight tonnage was 5 393 057 ton miles. The 1975 figure was 5 331 246; 1976 total freight tonnage was 12 748 397 (12 884 754 for 1975). Total passenger miles during 1976 totalled 68 721 904, down on the 1975 figure of 77 840 898. Also total passengers carried during 1976 at 42 48 457 was down on the 1975 figure of 4 766 038.

FINANCIAL

The 1976 revenue figures were $99 977 000 (1975 $88 582 000); expenses during 1976 stood at $86 095 000 (1975 $81 575 000).

LOCOMOTIVES AND CARS

B & M's total rolling stock and motive power fleet have been reduced to; locomotives in 1976 totalling 94 diesel-electric line haul and 67 shunting diesel electric; 84 diesel railcars; 3 543, freight train cars; 850 containers for door to door service.

BURLINGTON NORTHERN

176, E Fifth St, St. Paul, Minn 55101

OFFICERS

Chairman of the Board and Chief Executive Officer: Louis W. Menk
Vice-Chairman and Chief Operating Officer: Robert W. Downing
President, Transportation Division: Norman M. Lorentzsen
President, Resources Division: C. Robert Binger
Executive Vice-President: Thomas J. Lamphier
Executive Vice-President, Finance: Frank H. Coyne
Vice-President, Law: Frank S. Farrell
Vice-President and Secretary: John C. Ashton
Treasurer: Leo N. Assell
Regional Vice-President, Twin Cities: Wilburn R. Allen
Regional Vice-President, Seattle: Richard A. Beulke
Vice-President, Executive Department: Wilbur K. Bush
Vice-President and Regional Counsel, Portland: Roger J. Crosby
Regional Vice-President, Billings: John O. Davies
Vice-President, Labour Relations: Thomas C. DeButts
Vice-President, Sales & Service: Fred E. Deines
Vice-President, Purchasing and Material: Guy M. deLambert
Vice-President—Eastern Counsel Washington, DC: Lloyd L. Duxbury, Jr.
Vice-President and Controller: William N. Ernzen
Senior Vice-President Marketing: Ivan C. Ethington
Vice-President, Operations: John H. Hertog
Vice-President, Market Development: Curtis J. Hockaday
Vice-President, Industrial Development and Property Management: James C. Kenady
Regional Vice-President, Chicago: Donald H. King
Vice-President, Energy and Minerals, Billings: Thomas C. Kryzer
Vice-President, Western Region, San Francisco: Clarence E. Larsen
Regional Vice-President, Denver: Ralph L. Merklin
Vice-President, Timber and Land, Seattle: Somers G. Merryman
Vice-President, Intermodal Sales: James D. Nankivell
Vice-President, Public Relations and Advertising: Albert M. Rung
Regional Vice-President, Portland: Robert H. Shober
Chief Medical Officer: Abbott Skinner, MD
Vice-President, Executive Department, International Commerce, Seattle: Taul Watanabe

LINES AND TERRITORIES

Territory served embraces 17 states and two Canadian provinces, and reaches from the Great Lakes and the Ohio river to California and the seaports of the Pacific Northwest. Operations and services on the 22 987 miles network are directly supervised from six regional headquarters: Chicago, Twin Cities, Omaha, Billings, Portland and Seattle. Total track length is 33 877.9 miles.

The opening of new low-sulphur coal mines continues to require construction of new trackage. A 37-mile line was recently completed to Westmoreland Resources Company's Sarpy Creek mine in southeastern Montana, expected to commence operations this year. An 18.2-mile spur was built to the Amax mine near Gillette, Wyoming, which began operations in 1973.

BN also owns the Colorado and Southern Railway Company, Fort Worth and Denver Railway Company and the Oregon Electric Railway Company.

Burlington Northern is the name for the merger of the Chicago, Burlington & Quincy Railroad, the Great Northern, the Northern Pacific Railway, Pacific Coast Railroad and the Spokane, Portland and Seattle Railway. The merger became effective on 2 March 1970, nine years after the application was originally filed.

Burlington Northern in its continuing pursuit to build a modern, efficient and profitable rail system increased its originally budgeted capital spending programme from $165 million to $194.6 million in 1974. Thus Burlington Northern's investment for capital improvements for road and equipment has totalled $890.8 million since merger. These capital expenditures are in addition to heavy maintenance expenses incurred for construction and roadway improvement programmes that were necessary to put the railroad's roadway in its best overall condition since merger. Likewise equipment maintenance programmes emphasised both regular and preventive maintenance. In 1974 these maintenance expenditures amounted to $439.7 million raising the total expended by Burlington Northern since merger to $1 800 million.

Capital expenditures are expected to continue at a high level and Burlington Northern believes that increased profitability and a rate of return of at least 10% after taxes is required to attract the large amounts of new capital necessary for financing such programmes. The debt/equity per cent for 1974 was 37% debt and 63% equity.

RESULTS OF OPERATIONS

	(In thousands of dollars)		
	1975	1974	1973
Operating Revenues and Sales			
Transportation	1 474 325	1 431 915	1 222 544
Natural Resources:			
Forest products	61 240	68 267	69 290
Oil and gas	20 839	18 981	10 773
Coal and minerals	8 112	4 275	5 650
Other, including land and real estate	30 702	28 077	23 267
Total	1 595 218	1 551 515	1 331 524
Net Operating Income			
Transportation	73 108	92 678	54 987
Natural Resources:			
Forest products	13 812	23 624	29 754
Oil and gas	11 474	14 034	6 505
Coal and minerals	7 006	3 392	4 878
Other, including land and real estate	16 442	15 798	11 907
Total	121 842	149 526	108 031
Other Income (Charges)	7 395	12 120	2 290

FREIGHT TRAFFIC

Coal volume rose from 26.7 million tons carried in 1973 to an estimated 31.4 million tons. Coal-hauling revenues escalated from $91 million to $143 million, an increase of 57%.

However, grain remained the railroad's top revenue producer. The amount carried receded to 27.9 million tons, from the record 32.1 million tons of 1973, but grain revenues went up 4% to $231 million.

The importance of timely rate increases was confirmed anew in 1974 in a number of commodity areas, but most emphatically in forest products. Although carloadings declined about 9% as lumber and plywood movements were sharply depressed by the fall-off in activity in the housing industry, revenues from forest products traffic rose 6% over 1973.

The 10 commodity groups that account for more than 78% of rail freight revenues each produced increases last year. Other gainers in addition to coal, grain and timber, were food and kindred products, chemicals and allied products, primary metals, pulp and paper.

Burlington Northern 100-car unit coal train being loaded in motion at Peabody Company's Big Sky mine in Montana for Midwest destination.
(Burlington Northern photo courtesy Pullman-Standard).

PASSENGER TRAFFIC

Since 1971 BN has been under contract to Amtrak to operate intercity passenger services.

During 1972, the entire fleet of equipment used for the railroad's suburban commuter services in the Chicago area was sold to the West Suburban Mass Transit District. Proceeds from the sale were contributed to WSMTD, to be used, along with Federal and State grants, to rebuild and modernise the existing fleet and purchase 25 new cars. All equipment is being leased back to Burlington Northern for continued operation.

LOCOMOTIVES AND CARS

Each week an average of 8 820 freight cars received repairs ranging from minor securing of a hand rail to work requiring many man hours. Another 4 649 cars received heavy repairs during the year (at least 20 man hours of work) and 526 were rebuilt. Outlays for maintenance of rail equipment were 8.2% higher, to $233.3 million, largely due to higher labour and material costs. The bad-order ratio (equipment undergoing or awaiting repairs as a percentage of total ownership) for the year averaged 7.5% for locomotives and 8.9% for cars. (Comparable national average for cars was 7.7%. A similar national average for locomotives is not available.)

With demand for rail transportation down, some of the car fleet was put in storage, particularly older, smaller cars. At year's end the percentage of Burlington Northern's cars out of service for repairs had risen to 10.4, from 1974's 5.6%. (Comparable national averages were 8.6% and 6.4%, respectively.) A total of 3 304 cars needing repairs are small-capacity, 40 ft box cars held for stand-by use and will not be repaired, but retired. Subtracting these from the total number of bad-order cars reduces the bad-order ratio to 7.48%.

During the year, 17 locomotives were rebuilt and 272 given heavy repairs. The year-end locomotive bad-order ratio rose to 8.6% from 5.6% in 1974.

Last year, 3 515 new freight cars and 30 locomotives were delivered; in 1976, 1 090 cars and 75 locomotives are expected to be added. Average age of the 2 329-unit locomotive fleet is 14.7 years; the average age of Burlington Northern's 118 653 freight cars is 19.4 years.

OTHER DEVELOPMENTS

The Northtown locomotive maintenance shop was completed in the Twin Cities. It replaces three older shops and can be expanded to handle a larger locomotive fleet. Burlington Northern's maintenance policy is to maintain its physical plant, including track structure, at a level which will allow it to carry out its obligations as a common carrier and to upgrade and modernise its plant and facilities to enable it to meet competition and provide for future traffic requirements. Since merger, the railroad has expanded in excess of $1 000 million on maintenance and improvement of its track structure and physical plant. These expenditures increased 9% in 1975, to $241.4 million or about 17 cents of each revenue dollar, compared with $221.7 million in 1974. The condition of Burlington Northern's plant today is better than at any time since merger and continues to improve.

At year's end, 2 369 miles of track were subject to slow orders (speed restrictions), a figure not significantly different from last year. This represents 8.8% of total system mileage of over 26 800 miles.

To accommodate more coal trains, and to speed their movement, 10 sidings were extended along primary unit coal train routes, an additional 3 are nearing completion and 14 more are scheduled for 1976.

Construction began at Superior, Wisconsin on a $57.9 million taconite storage and shiploading facility which, with land and construction financing costs will total $70 million.

Line up of Bicentennial locomotives.

A Burlington Northern transcontinental freight train, powered by four 3 000 hp diesels, glides across the Columbia River, east of Wenatchee, Washington.

Burlington Northern piggyback/container lifting equipment comprises:—

Location	Equipment	Used for
Chicago, Illinois	1-Side-Porter	Containers
	2-Straddle-Port Cranes	Piggyback trailers and containers
	1-Overhead Crane	Containers
Kansas City, Missouri	1-Piggypacker	Piggyback trailers and containers
Seattle, Washington	2-Piggypackers	Piggyback trailers and containers
Denver, Colorado	1-Piggypacker	Piggyback trailers and containers
Minneapolis, Minnesota	1-Piggypacker	Piggyback trailers and containers
Pasco, Washington	1-Piggypacker	Piggyback trailers and containers

BURLINGTON NORTHERN INC. Through the Burlington Truck Lines Inc., Burlington Northern Motor Lines and the Northern Pacific Transport Company, along with various truck line common carriers, the Burlington Northern provides direct TOFC/COFC service from the Great Lakes and the Ohio River to California and the Pacific Northwest, from the Canadian Border to the Gulf Coast, operating over 26 000 miles of track. TOFC/COFC service is provided through the use of the following owned or leased equipment; 3 480 semi-trailers, 200 containers, and 406 railroad flats designed for TOFC/COFC service. Ramp facilities exist at over 200 towns of which the following are largest:

Aberdeen, S.D.	Dubuque, Ia.	Klamath Falls, Ore.	Portland, Ore.
Aberdeen, Wash.	Duluth, Minn.	Lewiston, Idaho	Prairie du Chien, Wis.
Abiline, Tex.	Everett, Wash.	Lewiston, Mont.	Pueblo, Colo.
Alliance, Neb.	Fargo, N.D.	Lincoln, Neb.	Quincy, Ill.
Amarillo, Tex.	Fort Benton, Mont.	Little Falls, Minn.	Renton, Wash.
Astoria, Ore.	Fort Collins, Colo.	Livingston, Mont.	Rochelle, Ill.
Aurora, Ill.	Fort Madison, Ia.	Loveland, Colo.	Rockford, Ill.
Bellingham, Wash.	Fort Morgan, Colo.	Lubbock, Tex.	St. Cloud, Minn.
Bemidji, Minn.	Fort Worth, Tex.	McCook, Neb.	St. Joseph, Mo.
Billings, Mont.	Fremont, Neb.	Macomb, Ill.	St. Louis, Mo.
Bismark, N.D.	Galesburg, Ill.	Minneapolis, Minn.	St. Paul, Minn.
Boulder, Colo.	Galveston, Tex.	Minot, N.D.	Savanna, Ill.
Brainerd, Minn.	Glasgow, Mont.	Missoula, Mont.	Seattle, Wash.
Burlington, Ia.	Glendive, Mont.	Moline, Ill.	Sheridan, Wyo.
Butte, Mont.	Glenwood, Ia.	Moorhead, Minn.	Sioux City, Ia.
Casper, Wyo.	Golden, Colo.	Morris, Minn.	Sioux Falls, S.D.
Centralia, Ill.	Grand Forks, N.D.	Mt. Morris, Ill.	Skykomish, Wash.
Centralia, Wash.	Grand Island, Neb.	Newcastle, Wyo.	Spokane, Wash.
Cheyenne, Wyo.	Grand Rapids, Minn.	New Rockford, N.D.	Sterling, Colo.
Chicago, Ill.	Great Falls, Mont.	North La Crosse, Wis.	Superior, Wis.
Clinton, Ia.	Greeley, Colo.	North St. Louis, Mo.	Tacoma, Wash.
Coeur d'Alene, Idaho.	Hannibal, Mo.	Olympia, Wash.	Vancouver, B.C.
Colorado Springs, Colo.	Hastings, Neb.	Omaha, Neb.	Walla Walla, Wash.
Corsicana, Tex.	Havre, Mont.	Oroville, Wash.	Wenatchee, Wash.
Council Bluffs, Ia.	Helena, Mont.	Ottumwa, Ia.	West Quincy, Mo.
Creston, Ia.	Hibbing, Minn.	Paducah, Ky.	Whitefish, Mont.
Cut Bank, Mont.	Houston, Tex.	Pasco, Wash.	Wichita Falls, Tex.
Dallas, Tex.	Kalispell, Mont.	Pendleton, Ore.	Williston, N.D.
Denver, Colo.	Kansas City, Mo.	Peoria, Ill.	Winnipeg, Man.
Des Moines, Ia.	Kewanee, Ill.	Plainview, Tex.	Winona, Minn.

CHESSIE SYSTEM
(Affiliated Chesapeake and Ohio and Baltimore and Ohio Railways and Western Maryland Railroads)
Terminal Tower, Cleveland, Ohio 44101

Chairman of the Board and President: Hays T. Watkins
Executive Vice-President, Commercial: Norman G. Halpern
Vice-President, Law: Roland W. Donnem
President, Western Maryland: William P. Coliton
Executive Vice-President, Operations: John T. Collinson
Vice-President, Taxes: John P. Ganley
Senior Vice-President: Norman G. Halpern
Vice-President, Merchandise Pricing: Charles J. Henry Jr
Senior Vice-President, Coal: H. Preston Henshaw
Vice-President, Finance: Robert L. Hintz
Senior Vice-President, Casualty Prevention: William F. Howes Jr
Senior Vice-President, Merchandise: James B. McCahey Jr
Vice-President, Administration: Robert C. McGowan
Vice-President, Public Relations and Advertising: Howard Skidmore
Assistant Vice-President and General Counsel: Doyle S. Morris
Secretary and General Solicitor: Garth E. Griffith
Assistant Vice-President Finance: Carl C. Hawk
Assistant Vice-President, Finance and Comptroller: Bruce G. Lawler
Assistant Vice-President, Finance and Treasurer: L. C. Roig Jr
Vice-President Coal Traffic: Jerry E. Gobrecht

LINES AND TERRITORIES
On 31 August 1972 the affiliated Chesapeake and Ohio Railway and the Baltimore and Ohio Railroad unveiled a new short name for the 11 000-mile *(17 700-km)* transportation network—"Chessie System". The two carriers continue to publish separate annual financial and statistical reports. While the C&O company controls the B&O company through stock ownership, the two railroads have unified management in all major areas.
C&O total mileage owned: 4 086 miles *(6 576 km);* total mileage leased: 231 miles *(372 km);* used jointly: 684 miles *(1 101 km)* total 5 002 miles *(8 050 km).* Territories: Canada, 338 miles *(543 km);* District of Columbia, 3 miles *(4.8 km);* Illinois, 43 miles *(69 km);* Indiana, 309 miles *(497 km);* Kentucky, 696 miles *(1 115 km);* Michigan, 1 436 miles *(2 300 km);* New York, 34 miles *(55 km);* Ohio, 425 miles *(684 km);* Virginia, 700 miles *(1 126 km);* West Virginia, 1 017 miles *(1 627 km).*
B&O total mileage owned 3 625 miles *(5 820 km);* total mileage leased 1 637 miles *(2 260 km)* used jointly: 234 miles *(376 km);* total 5 396 miles *(8 820 km);* Territories: New York, 175 miles *(282 km);* Delaware, 34 miles *(55 km);* Pennsylvania, 909 miles *(1 462 km);* Maryland, 317 miles *(510 km);* District of Columbia, 21 miles *(32 km);* Virginia, 33 miles *(53 km);* West Virginia, 1 276 miles *(2 205 km);* Ohio, 1 661 miles *(2 267 km);* Indiana, 533 miles *(858 km);* Illinois, 519 miles *(835 km);* Kentucky, 3 miles *(4.8 km);* Missouri, 4 miles *(6.4 km).*
The Chessie System also owns majority stock in the Western Maryland Railway, and the South Shore Line.

FINANCIAL RESULTS
For the first time in its history, Chessie earned over $100 million ($102 million), an increase of 12 per cent over 1975 earnings and up seven per cent from the previous record of $5.33 in 1974.
Chessie reported record second quarter results, with earnings of $37.3 million. Because of the fast recovery of coal traffic the third quarter was excellent. Earnings were $22.2 million. The fourth quarter is usually a strong business period for Chessie but 1976 differed in this respect. The economy remained dormant, and carloadings slackened.

EARNINGS
(Thousands of Dollars)

Operating Revenues	1976	1975	1974	1973	1972
Merchandise	295 977	266 004	277 868	267 687	239 196
Coal, coke and iron ore—US and Canada	226 553	190 973	194 799	164 805	158 640
Coal and coke—overseas export	71 823	85 762	68 578	35 375	37 062
Other freight services	27 999	26 471	25 080	20 011	14 366
Passenger services	2 301	2 290	2 505	2 184	2 066
Total Operating Revenues	624 653	571 600	568 830	490 062	451 330
Operating Expenses					
Maintenance of way and structures	83 426	71 568	61 618	56 886	52 414
Maintenance of equipment	107 811	103 244	96 263	87 641	80 679
Traffic	9 611	9 153	10 145	10 057	10 128
Transportation	236 141	222 149	212 306	190 667	171 124
Miscellaneous and general	36 820	34 692	35 318	32 024	29 299
Total Operating Expenses	473 809	440 806	415 650	377 275	343 644
Net Revenue from Railway Operations	150 844	130 794	153 180	112 787	107 686
Other Income—Net	12 655	22 212	10 216	9 409	8 467
Total	163 499	153 006	163 396	122 196	116 153

Chessie Traffic	1976	1975	1974	1973	1972
Freight revenue (thousands)	1 332 380	1 211 867	1 244 409	1 059 648	974 364
Per cent of total operating revenues	95.6%	95.3%	95.4%	95.3%	96.1%
Revenue ton miles (millions)	53 896	54 166	63 083	61 612	56 853
Average revenue per	.0247	.0224	.0197	.0172	.0171
Tons of coal exported at tidewater (thousands)	14 950	17 890	15 979	10 527	10 418
Per cent of US exports	35.3%	36.5%	34.6%	27.1%	27.6%
Tons of coal originated (thousands)	77 520	78 903	82 752	81 096	84 426
Percent of national production	11.7%	12.3%	14.0%	13.8%	14.6%

Chessie Operations	1976	1975	1974	1973	1972
Freight revenue per mile of road	120 360	109 661	110 770	94 109	85 524
Freight train miles per mile of road	2 165	2 112	2 378	2 565	2 397
Average number of cars per train					
Loaded	40.7	42.1	43.6	40.2	40.8
Empty	31.0	33.5	33.1	31.1	33.3
Total	71.7	75.6	76.7	71.3	74.1

EARNINGS
(Thousands of Dollars)

	1976	1975	1974	1973	1972
Average revenue tons per loaded car	61.4	59.9	58.3	56.6	56.6
Average revenue tons per train	2 251	2 304	2 345	2 119	2 070
Average revenue tons hauled per locomotive unit	811	824	846	782	706

FREIGHT TRAFFIC—C & O	1976	1975
Total miles of road operated	4 885	4 899
Total miles of track operated	9 763	9 857
Freight revenue (thousands)	594 353	542 738
Per cent of total operating revenues	95.1%	95.0%
Revenue tons carried (thousands)—		
Coal and coke—		
Tidewater	11 439	13 797
Lake	10 656	10 248
Other	37 455	35 811
Total	59 550	59 856
Merchandise freight	41 224	39 659
Total	100 774	99 515
Tons of coal originated (thousands)	48 150	48 068
Per cent of national production	7.2%	7.5%
Tons of coal exported at tidewater (thousands)	8 574	11 291
Per cent of US exports	20.3%	23.0%
Revenue ton miles (millions)	26 227	26 850
Average miles each revenue ton was carried	260.3	269.8
Revenue tons carried per mile of road	20 630	20 313
Revenue ton miles per mile of road (thousands)	5 369	5 481
Freight revenue per mile of road	121 676	110 785

FREIGHT	1976	1975
Average revenue per ton—		
Coal and coke	4.75	4.41
Merchandise freight	7.55	7.03
All freight	5.90	5.45
Average revenue per ton mile—		
Coal and coke	.0181	.0160
Merchandise freight	.0295	.0270
All freight	.0227	.0202
Average revenue tons per loaded car	63.3	62.3
Average revenue tons per train	2 472	2 627
Average tons per train, including company's freight	2 500	2 657
Average revenue tons hauled per locomotive unit	988	999
Average tons hauled per locomotive unit, including company's freight	1 000	1 011
Average number of cars per train—		
Loaded	40.4	43.1
Empty	33.7	37.1
Total	74.1	80.2
Freight train mileage per mile of road	2 172	2 087
Freight revenue per freight train mile	56.02	53.09

PASSENGER OPERATIONS
On 1 May 1971 all C&O long-distance passenger trains were discontinued, except for the train between Washington and Newport News in the East and Cincinnati in the West which is operated under contract for Amtrak. C&O continues to transport passengers and their automobiles on Lake Michigan trainferries.

EQUIPMENT (Excluding Service Equipment)

Locomotives	Multiple Purpose	Switching	Total
Number owned and used	693a	90	783
Number leased from others	191	1	192
Average age—years	15.2	26.4	16.2

Freight Train Cars	Box	Flat	Gondola	Hopper	Cov. Hopper	Other	Total
Number owned and used	11 408	1 368b	5 801c	39 555d	2 444	536	61 112
Number leased from others	1 978	—	784	6 474	287	224	9 747
Average age—years	15.9	29.1	17.0	17.9	15.0	23.4	17.6

Floating Equipment	Tugboats	Lake Michigan Carferries	Car Floats	Other	Total
Number owned and used	5	3	5	1	14
Average age—years	18.2	26.3	36.0	49.0	28.5

a Does not include 6 units leased to Chicago South Shore and South Bend Railroad
b Does not include 1 car leased to Nuclear Fuel.
c Does not include 50 cars leased to B&O
d Does not include 2 005 cars leased to B&O

CAPITAL EXPENDITURES
(Thousands of Dollars)

Expenditures—Road	1966-1975	1975	1974
Additions and betterments to existing track and roadbed	42 463	4 429	5 053
Erecting and modernising stations and offices	7 527	1 115	270
Constructing and improving shop buildings, enginehouses and fuel stations	4 428	897	971
Building and improving, wharves and docks	1 358	67	15
Erecting and strengthening bridges	5 807	394	240
Installing centralised traffic control and modernising interlockers and communication systems	10 214	2 362	356
Installing modern roadway and shop machinery	13 089	2 874	678
Other additions and improvements to the roadway	765	208	50
Total road expenditures	85 651	12 346	7 633

Expenditures—Equipment	1966-1975	1975	1974
Locomotives	73 591	3 256	39
Freight-train cars	459 934	56 021	14 129
Passenger-train cars	15	—	—
Trainferries and other floating equipment	1 994	120	769
Other equipment	5 954	1 714	230
Total equipment expenditures	541 488	61 111	15 167
Total Capital Expenditures	627 139	73 457	22 800

EARNINGS

Operating Revenues	1975	1974
Merchandise	400 162	441 444
Coal, coke and iron ore	158 740	153 418
Coal and coke—overseas export	34 816	29 600
Other freight services	20 290	23 315
Passenger services	398	606
Total Operating Revenues	614 406	648 383

Operating Expenses		
Maintenance of way and structures	94 605	73 765
Maintenance of equipment	90 326	83 766
Traffic	10 702	10 770
Transportation	232 160	236 634
Miscellaneous and general	35 767	39 726
Total Operating Expenses	463 560	444 661
Net Revenue from Railway Operations	150 846	203 722

TRAFFIC AND OPERATING STATISTICS—B&O

FREIGHT	1976	1975
Total miles of road operated	5 412	5 412
Total miles of track operated	10 156	10 146
Freight revenue (thousands)	$661 864	$593 718
Per cent of total operating revenues	96.7%	96.6%
Revenue tons carried (thousands)—		
Coal and coke—		
Tidewater	7 476	8 164
Lake	3 147	3 076
Other	35 204	34 611
Total	45 827	45 851
Merchandise freight	54 980	52 407
Total	100 807	98 258
Tons of coal originated (thousands)	23 203	25 397
Per cent of national production	3.5%	4.0%
Tons of coal exported at tidewater (thousands)	6 376	6 423
Per cent of US exports	15.1%	13.1%
Revenue ton miles (millions)	24 941	24 708
Average miles each revenue ton was carried	247.4	251.5
Revenue tons carried per mile of road	18 627	18 156
Revenue ton miles per mile of road (thousands)	4 609	4 565
Freight revenue per mile of road	$122 296	$109 704
Average revenue per ton—		
Coal and coke	$4.34	$3.78
Merchandise freight	$8.42	$8.02
All freight	$6.57	$6.04
Average revenue per ton mile—		
Coal and coke	$.0212	$.0183
Merchandise freight	$.0297	$.0276
All freight	$.0265	$.0240
Average revenue tons per loaded car	59.4	57.9
Average revenue tons per train	2 076	2 076
Average tons per train, including company's freight	2 098	2 098
Average revenue tons hauled per locomotive unit	689	711
Average tons hauled per locomotive unit, including company's freight	697	719
Average number of cars per train—		
Loaded	41.8	42.1
Empty	30.0	31.7
Total	71.8	73.8
Freight train mileage per mile of road	2 219	2 199
Freight revenue per freight train mile	$55.10	$49.88

PASSENGER OPERATIONS

On 1 May 1971, all B&O long-distance passenger trains were discontinued. Subsequently, under a contract with Amtrak, a train was added which now operates between Washington DC and Martinsburg, West Virginia. A second train operated for Amtrak started in October, 1976 providing service between Washington DC and Cincinnati, Ohio. The company continues operation of a limited commuter service at Washington and Pittsburgh.

EQUIPMENT (Excluding Service Equipment)

Locomotives	Multiple Purpose	Switching	Total
Number owned and used	375	160abc	535
Number leased from others	425	11	436
Average age—years	12.2	26.3	15

Freight Train Cars	Box	Flat	Gondola	Hopper	Cov. Hopper	Other	Total
Number owned and used	6 525d	709	3 567e	16 632f	1 893	542	29 868
Number leased from others	5 650	68	6 097g	7 256	1 919	209	21 199
Average age—years	14.2	20.4	11.3	15.5	11.0	20.6	14.2

Floating Equipment	Tugboats	Deck Scows	Car Floats	Other	Total
Number owned and used	1	5	11	2	19
Average age—years	22	19.6	21.5	26.0	22.3

a Does not include 1 unit leased to C&O
b Does not include 34 units leased to B&OCT
c Includes 35 units held awaiting disposition
d Does not include 1 car leased to C&O
e Does not include 39 cars leased to Dearborn Leasing Co
f Does not include 240 cars leased to CNJ
g Does not include 113 cars subleased to Dearborn Leasing Co

Western Maryland Railway Company

EARNINGS	1976	1975
Operating Revenues	(Thousands of Dollars)	
Merchandise	$41 709	$41 074
Coal, coke and iron ore	25 085	24 748
Other freight services	4 123	5 028
Total Operating Revenues	70 917	70 850

Operating Expenses		
Maintenance of way and structures	8 090	9 047
Maintenance of equipment	14 164	12 015
Traffic	1 815	1 725
Transportation	24 168	25 509
Miscellaneous and general	4 825	4 580
Total Operating Expenses	53 062	52 876
Net Revenue from Railway Operations	17 855	17 974
Other Income Net	2 502	3 141
Total	20 357	21 115

CHICAGO SOUTH SHORE AND SOUTH BEND R.R.

Michigan City, Ind 46360

President and General Manager: Albert W. Dudley
Vice-President, Sales: Carlton A. Ernst
Vice-President and Comptroller: Raymond J. McGee
Secretary: Garth E. Griffith
Treasurer: Henry J. Konda
Auditor and Assistant Secretary: Clarence D. Moore

Total electrified route length: 88 miles

DIESEL LOCOMOTIVES

Class	Axle Arrangement	Transmission	Rated Power hp	Max. lb (kg)	Tractive Effort Continuous at lb (kg)	mph (km/h)	Max. Speed mph (km/h)	Wheel Dia. in (mm)	Total Weight Tons	Length ft in (mm)	No. Built	Year first Built	Builders: Mechanical Parts	Engine & Type	Transmission
GB-7	B-B	Elec.	1 500	44 000	10	65	40	124	65				EMB	567 BC	Electric

ELECTRIC LOCOMOTIVES

Class	Axle Arrangement	Line Current	Rated Output hp	Max. lb (kg)	Tractive Effort (Full Field) Continuous at lb (kg)	mph (km/hr)	Max. Speed mph (km/hr)	Wheel dia. in (mm)	Weight tonnes	Length ft in (mm)	No. Built	Year Built	Builders Mechanical Parts	Electrical Equipment
—	2-D+D—L	1 500 V dc	5 400		101 500	11	65	48	273	87 10		1948		General Electric

CHICAGO, MILWAUKEE, ST. PAUL AND PACIFIC RAILROAD COMPANY
(The Milwaukee Road)
516 West Jackson Boulevard, Chicago, Ill 60606

Chairman of the Board and Chief Executive Officer: William J. Quinn
President: Worthington L. Smith
Vice-President, Operations and Maintenance: Paul F. Cruikshank
Vice-President, Law: Raymond K. Merrill
Vice-President, Finance and Accounting: Richard F. Kratochwill
Vice-President, Traffic: George H. Kronberg
Vice-President, Executive Department: L. Vincent Anderson
Vice-President, Executive Department: P. Laurin Cowling
Vice-President, Executive Department (Seattle, Wash): Warren H. Ploeger
Vice-President, Chief Engineer: Burton J. Worley
Vice-President, Real Estate, Economic and Resource Development: Edward J. Stoll
Vice-President, Corporate Services: Gaylord A. Kellow
Vice-President, Market Development and Pricing: Glenn F. Reynolds
Vice-President, Sales and Service: Donald M. Wiseman
Vice-President, Labour Relations and Personnel: Lawrence W. Harrington
General Solicitor: Joseph J. Nagle
Comptroller: Fritz T. Miller
Secretary: James T. Taussig
Assistant Secretary: George G. Grudnowski
Treasurer: Charles L. Schiffer
Assistant Treasurer: Frederick H. Voss
Assistant Treasurer (Seattle, Wash): Robert A. Brinkley

Operations and Maintenance:
Vice-President, Operations and Maintenance: Paul F. Cruikshank
Vice-President, Operations: M. Garelick
General Manager, Operations Planning: William F. Plattenberger
General Manager, Lines East: Delbert O. Burke
General Manager, Lines West (Seattle, Wash.): Quentin W. Torpin
General Superintendent of Transportation: Robert E. Beck
Assistant Vice-President, Mechanical: Frank A. Upton
Vice-President, Chief Engineer: Burton J. Worley
Assistant Chief Engineer, Staff: Walter E. Fuhr
Assistant Chief Engineer, Maintenance: Nathan E. Smith
Assistant Chief Engineer, Signals and Communications: Donald L. Wylie
Assistant Chief Engineer, Structures: Kenneth E. Hornung
Assistant Chief Engineer, Planning: Robert H. Michaels

Traffic:
Vice-President: George H. Kronberg
Vice-President, Sales and Service: Donald M. Wiseman
Assistant Vice-President, Sales (New York, NY): George V. Valley
Assistant Vice-President, Sales (Chicago, Ill): Douglas C. Workman
Assistant Vice-President, Sales (Seattle, Wash): Douglas A. Keller

Labour Relations and Personnel:
Vice-President: Lawrence W. Harrington
Assistant Vice-President, Labour Relations: V. Wayne Merritt
Assistant Vice-President, Personnel: Earle D. Adamson

Real Estate:
Vice-President: Edward J. Stoll
Assistant Vice-President, Real Estate, Economic and Resource Development: Bill H. Bobbitt

Corporate Services:
Vice-President: Gaylord A. Kellow
Director, Data Systems and Operations: Leslie S. Imbery
Director, Corporate Planning: Thomas F. Power, Jr.
Assistant Vice-President, Purchases and Materials: Howard H. Melzer

Corporate Communications:
Director: Wallace W. Abbey

The Milwaukee Motor Transportation Company:
President: P. Laurin Cowling
Vice-President: Robert F. Munsell
Assistant Vice-President, Operation: Clarence E. Goldsmith
Assistant Vice-President, Administration: Thomas S. Hartnett
Assistant Vice-President, Marketing and Sales: Eugene A. Solvie
Assistant Vice-President, Maintenance: Donald J. Kinsfather

Market Development and Pricing:
Vice-President: Glenn F. Reynolds
Assistant Vice-President (Grain and Food Products): Jens C. Jensen
Assistant Vice-President (Lumber and Paper Products): Peter C. White
Assistant Vice-President (Automotive Mfg. and Misc. Products): Robert E. Bennett
Assistant Vice-President (Chemicals, Fuels and Metal Products): Gene B. Beckman

Commuter and Passenger Services:
Director of Passenger Services and NRPC Operations Officer: Stephen J. Barry

Law:
Vice-President: Raymond K. Merrill
General Solictor: Joseph J. Nagle
Assistant Vice-President, Legal Administration: Kenneth D. French
General Adjuster: Robert W. Centen
Director of Property Tax: Leonard R. Norberg

Finance and Accounting:
Vice-President: Richard F. Kratochwill
Comptroller: Fritz H. Miller
Assistant Comptroller: George W. Corbett
Assistant Comptroller: David C. Young
Assistant Comptroller: Paul S. Patterson

LINES AND TERRITORIES
The Milwaukee Road operates 10 200 route miles of railroad, the line extending from Louisville, Kentucky, to the Pacific North Coast ports of Seattle, Tacoma and Longview, Washington, and Portland, Oregon. The line also extends west and southwest from Chicago to Omaha, Nebraska and Kansas City, Missouri.
The railroad's wholly owned subsidiary companies are Milwaukee Land Company, The Milwaukee Motor Transportation Company and the Washington, Idaho and Montana Railway Company.

FINANCIAL RESULTS
Consolidated operating revenues in 1975 totalled $392 842 000 compared with $410 984 000 in 1974. Expenses totalled $416 487 000 ($402 233 000 in 1974).

FREIGHT TRAFFIC
With a diminished demand for freight service brought about by a generally depressed economy, and therefore with reduced funds available to it, the Milwaukee Road placed itself in the position of maintaining the best service it could with the limited funds. To the degree that it could, consistent with safety, efficiency and service, the railroad postponed some planned improvements until a better year. Projects and activities which would both increase efficiency and reduce operating expenses received priority. Throughout 1975 the generally depressed economy resulted in a reduced movement of the commodities most important to the railroad's revenue posture. Grain and forest products, especially, registered marked declines as compared to 1974 levels. Freight traffic, however, did improve in each succeeding quarter of 1975 and this trend continued into 1976.
There were several major marketing achievements during the year.
In import traffic, a new schedule of rates significantly increased the volume which moves in containers and trailers inland from ports on the Pacific North Coast.
Unit-train movements of coal recorded steady gains during the year. An operation inaugurated in 1975 delivers coal to a power plant in eastern South Dakota from a mine in western North Dakota.
Mail became an important traffic element as a result of contracts with the US Postal Service. The mail is moved out of various concentration points "piggyback" on freight cars.
The Milwaukee Road reintroduced its seasonal "mini-unit" trains for certain portions of the grain trade. Market conditions were such, however, that the trains were needed for only a few weeks. The railroad expects to operate these trains again in 1976.

PASSENGER TRAFFIC
The Milwaukee Road operates four passenger trains for Amtrak daily, from Monday to Saturday, in each direction between Chicago and Milwaukee, and five on Sunday. Two Amtrak trains are also operated daily in each direction between Chicago and Minneapolis.
On 12 March 1976 the Milwaukee Road was the first Chicago-area commuter railroad to enter into a purchase of service agreement with the Regional Transportation Authority. Under this contract the railroad will function as a supplier of transportation services in much the same manner as it does with Amtrak. The RTA contract provides for fixed price annual payments to the railroad and for incentive payments based on superior on-time performance and increased ridership.

LOCOMOTIVES AND CARS
During 1975 the Milwaukee Road acquired, through lease, 32 new 1 500 hp diesel-electric locomotives. These locomotives along with 32 more ordered during 1975 and delivered in the early part of 1976, will replace approximately 100 older locomotives. In 1975 the Milwaukee Road placed in service, through lease, 683 freight cars of six types and, through purchase, 100 tri-level cars for the transportation of automobiles and two specially equipped cabooses. Additionally, 105 existing cars were rebuilt and returned to service. Planned major rebuild work on additional cars and some locomotives was postponed.

OTHER DEVELOPMENTS
Several departments were partially or wholly restructured during the year with greater internal effectiveness in mind. The field sales force of the Traffic Department was reorganised as was the Corporate Communications Department.
The number of operating divisions was reduced by one in the first phase of a comprehensive reorganisation of the Operating Department which continued in 1976.
Physical improvements were confined to those which were essential and to those which consumed few operating-expensive dollars. Additions and improvements to property totalled $13.8 million, down from $14.2 million in 1974.
Notable among the fixed-property improvement projects in 1975 was the start of construction on a new locomotive maintenance facility at St. Paul, Minnesota. The facility, which became operational early in 1976, represents the transfer of a principal maintenance base to a more natural point of concentration of locomotives and thus will increase the over-all efficiency of the locomotive maintenance process.
Early in 1975, the Interstate Commerce Commission approved the Milwaukee Road's application to acquire and operate the Port Townsend Railroad, a 12-mile line between Discovery Junction and Port Townsend, Washington. The line provides a link between the Milwaukee Road's own Port Angeles, Washington branch and the remainder of the system.
The railroad was successful in obtaining during 1975 the permission of the Interstate Commerce Commission to eliminate 63 miles of branch-line track no longer necessary to provide service to the company's customers.

PIGGYBACK AND CONTAINER HANDLING FACILITIES
The Milwaukee Road has Piggyback facilities at 66 locations: Aberdeen, S.D.; Appleton, Wis.; Austin, Minn.; Bellingham, Wash.; Billings, Mont.; Bozeman, Mont.; Butte, Mont.; Cedar Rapids, Iowa; Chamberlain, S.D.; Chehalis, Wash.; Chicago (Franklin Park), Ill.; Cloquet, Minn.; Coeur d'Alene, Idaho; Council Bluffs, Iowa; Davenport, Iowa; Deer Lodge, Mont.; Des Moines, Iowa; Dubuque, Iowa; Duluth, Minn.; Everett, Wash.; Fargo, N.D.; Great Falls, Mont.; Green Bay, Wis.; Harlowton, Mont.; Iron Mountain, Mich.; Kansas City, Mo.; LaCrosse, Wis.; Lewistown, Mont.; Longview, Wash.; Louisville, Ky.; Madison, Wis.; Mankato, Minn.; Marion, Iowa; Mason City, Iowa; Menasha, Wis.; Metaline Falls, Wash.; Miles City, Mont.; Milwaukee, Wis.; Missoula, Mont.; Mitchell, S.D.; Mobridge, S.D.; Moses Lake, Wash.; Neenah, Wis.; New Holstein, Wis.; Omaha, Neb.; Oshkosh, Wis.; Othello, Wash.; Ottumwa, Iowa; Perry, Iowa; Portage, Wis.; Portland, Ore.; Postville, Iowa; Rapid City, S.D.; Ripon, Wis.; St. Paul, Minn.; Seattle, Wash.; Sioux City, Iowa; Sioux Falls, S.D.; Spencer, Iowa; Spokane, Wash.; Tacoma, Wash.; Terre Haute, Ind.; Warden, Wash.; Wausau, Wis.; Winona, Minn.; Wisconsin Rapids, Wis.

CHICAGO AND NORTH WESTERN TRANSPORTATION COMPANY

400,West Madison Street, Chicago, Ill 60606

President: Larry S. Provo
President and Chief Executive Officer: James R. Wolfe
Vice-President, Sales and Marketing: W. E. Braun
Vice-President, Law: Richard M. Freeman
Vice-President, Finance: John M. Butler
Vice-President, System and Corp. Ind. Engr.: R. D. Leach
Vice-President, Materials and Real Estate: I. R. Ballin
Vice-President, Personnel and Labour Relations: R. W. Russell
Comptroller: G. R. Carr
Treasurer: J. W. Conlon
Secretary: R. D. Smith
Director of Public Relations: J. R. Macdonald
Director of Commuter Services: H. A. Lenske

Sales and Marketing Department:
Vice-President, Sales and Marketing: W. E. Braun

Labour Relations Department:
Vice-President, Labour Relations: R. W. Russell
Assistant to Vice-President, Labour Relations: W. H. Clark

Operating:
Director of Labour Relations: M. Humphrey
Director, Labour Relations: J. D. Crawford

Non Operating:
Director of Labour Relations: W. J. Fremon

Personnel and Labour Relations:
Vice-President: R. W. Russell

Operating Department:
Vice-President, Operations: J. A. Zito
Assistant Chief Engineer: D. E. Oakleaf
Assistant Vice-President & General Manager: J. W. Alsop
Assistant Vice-President, Transportation: E. A. Burkhardt
Superintendent of Intermodal Operation: R. B. Gordon
Assistant Vice-President & Chief Engineer: J. A. Barnes
Assistant Chief Engineer, Administration: M. S. Reid
Assistant Chief Engineer, Construction: J. F. Brower
Assistant Chief Engineer, Maintenance: J. A. Zito
Assistant Vice-President, Motive Power: J. D. O'Neill
Assistant Vice-President, Car Department: F. E. Cunningham
Signal Engineer: V. S. Mitchell
Director of Communications: T. M. Evans

Law Department:
Vice-President, Law: Richard M. Freeman

Systems and Corporate Industrial Engineering:
120 South Riverside Plaza, Chicago, Ill 60606
Vice-President: R. D. Leach
Vice-President, Systems and Information Services: R. D. Leach
Assistant Vice-President, Data Processing Services: D. J. Fliss
Assistant Vice-President, Systems Design and Installation: W. A. Zimmerman
Assistant to Vice-President, Systems and Information Services: R. C. Zogg

Passenger Traffic:
Director, Commuter Services: H. A. Lenske
Manager, Commuter Services: R. W. Coakley

The Railroad was acquired, from the parent company, Northwest Industries Inc, by the employees on 1 June 1972.
Around 3 500 of the Road's employees have now purchased stock in the company. 1973 was the company's first full year under employee-ownership.

LINES AND TERRITORIES

Chicago North Western operates some 9 990 miles of route mainly in the states of Illinois, Wisconsin and Iowa, but with routes extending to Minneapolis and Duluth in Minnesota; Rapid City in S. Dakota; St. Louis and Kansas City in Missouri, Omaha in Nebraska and Riverton, Wyoming.

FINANCIAL RESULTS

The Chicago and North Western Transportation Company had net income of $5 252 000, or $1.18 per share in the fourth quarter of 1975 compared with net income of $2 656 000, or 60 cents per share in the 1974 fourth quarter. Fourth quarter operating revenues were $123 939 000 in 1975 compared with $123 347 000 in the fourth quarter of 1974. For the full year ended December 31, 1975, the company had a net loss of $8 301 000, compared with net income of $14 400 000, or $3.24 per share in 1974. Full year operating revenues in 1975 were $458 990 000, compared with $484 901 000 in 1974.
January 1976, results marked a $3 800 000 improvement over January 1975 (a loss of $600 000 in January which compared with a loss of $4 400 000 in January, 1975) 'and we expect to be profitable in the first quarter, traditionally the weakest of the year'. In the first quarter of 1975, the Company had a net loss of $8 541 000.

LOCOMOTIVES AND CAR

The locomotive fleet totals 920 units: 677 freight, 59 passenger, and 184 switch. Passenger units are all EMD, mostly recently rebuilt F-7 and E-8, including six former E-8B units with a cab added. Units in freight service include: 39 GP-35, 139 GP-7, 62 GP-9, 22 GP-30, 61 SD-45, 30 SD-40, and 125 SD-40-2. The 125 SD-40-2 units were acquired between 1973 and 1975. 10 SD-38-2 and 15 MP-15 engines were delivered from EMD in early 1975. Cars received in 1975 include 164 all-enclosed auto-racks and 200 open top hoppers equipped with rotary couplers. Maintenance-of-way equipment delivered included two ultrasonic rail-testing trucks, 23 boom-equipped trucks, six Hydra spikers, 10 spike pullers, and two brush cutters. The BUC, the $500 000 ballast undercutter cleaner delivered in 1975 from Plasser-Theurer of Austria, continues to upgrade track across the system.

DEVELOPMENT

The Wood Street Falcon, the all-intermodal transcontinental express train, continues to better its performance. Operated with the Union Pacific and Southern Pacific railroads, the Falcon departs 10 times weekly from Chicago for major West Coast Cities. It offers 50-hour service to San Francisco and 26-hour service to Denver. A third "Piggypacker", which can lift 90 000 lb, has been added to Wood Street to load and unload trailers and containers.

CHICAGO, ROCK ISLAND AND PACIFIC RAILROAD COMPANY

139 West Van Buren Street, Chicago, Ill 60605

Trustee: William M. Gibbons
Counsel for the Trustee: Nicholas G. Manos
Assistant to the Trustee: Bruce Clinton
Officers for the Trustee:
Executive Vice-President: Dr. Paul H. Banner
Comptroller: Victor C. Bohne
Vice-President—Purchases and Stores: John A. Burnett
General Counsel: Martin L. Cassell
Chief Operating Officer: William C. Hoenig
Vice-President: Christopher Knapton
Vice-President—Staff: John D. Mitros

On March 17 1975, when the Rock filed its reorganisation proceedings in the Federal District Court of Northern Illinois, its credit was exhausted. It was unable even to order diesel fuel without paying cash in advance. It was predicting only $200 000 in the cash drawer. It had millions upon millions in unpaid bills.
Yet, a short nine months later, the Rock Island had $20 million in its cash drawer; its 6 million gallon fuel storage tanks were full of diesel fuel (all paid for); it is currently on its post-reorganisation bills; it is processing pre-petition claims against the railroad, and turned in profitable months in September, October and in November. The Rock Island is also handling its business better, safer and more reliably.
The Rock rebuilt 27 locomotives in 1975, rebuilt 1 213 40-ft boxcars, and 169 50-ft boxcars, added 650 100-ton covered hoppers and 24 airslide cars to its fleet. It also bought 80 miles of new rail an 676 765 new ties. The Rock also surfaced 575 miles of mainline, rebuilt 38 235 feet of bridges and installed 355 153 new ties and 495 692 tons of ballast. In 1976 pending court approval, the Rock planned to add 56 new locomotives to the fleet and rebuild 93 more.
What happened to the Rock in 1974 was a revealing prelude to what was in store for the railroad in the first quarter of 1975, when carloads fell 20%, bringing on the cash crisis that led to the railroad's request for reorganisation.
The softening economy led to a 4.7% decline in carloads in 1974. The Interstate Commerce Commission approved nominal rate increases to offset the retirement tax increase and to neutralise higher fuel costs. The railroads were able to raise rates on export grain 10% and on all commodities by 14%, but inflation put the cost of running the railroad beyond the scope of these rate increases. Expenses, particularly fuel costs, rose dramatically. The familiar "too little, too late" pattern of rate adjustments is perpetuating the Rock's imbalance between revenues and expenses.
Increased movements of farm implements and grains in the Rock's territory were the result of record acreages under cultivation.
Fertiliser moved from the Gulf area to the Rock's mid-continent farm belt in covered hoppers which were then used for southbound grain movements. In 1974, 228 unit grain trains operated from the railroad's northern lines to Gulf ports.
In November, the Rock began operating fast turn-around mini-trains of 20 cars shuttling corn and soybeans from Iowa country stations to barge transfer facilities on the Mississippi near Davenport.
During 1974, 119 new industries were located along the Rock and 47 firms were expanded. Investment in new plant and equipment is estimated at $119.1 million. 975 acres of surplus land were sold for $900 000. Rents from Company property totalled $1 489 993.
Private industrial developers and investors acquired 589 acres of land adjacent to the right-of-way. Warehouse space was increased by 2.2 million ft². Grain storage firms raised their capacity by 3.2 million bushels.
A levee failure on the old I & M Canal at Bureau, Illinois on January 27, 1974, severely damaged a sizable section of roadbed. Restoring the line cost $191 313, a sum the Railroad is suing to recover from the State of Illinois. In May, floods in the Bureau Creek Basin caused roadbed and bridge damage of $212 220. Federal and State agencies are now studying ways to prevent future flooding in the area.
Removal began of the Railroad's bridge across the Illinois River at Pekin. Constructed in 1900, the 679-foot long bridge had been battered repeatedly by barge tows. In January 1973 it was taken out of service when a barge damaged the swing span. Pekin customers are now served by the Rock over another railroad.
The Rock laid approximately 15 miles of new continuous welded rail, 65 miles of second hand continuous welded rail and 10 miles of second hand conventional jointed rail. 500 000 cross ties were installed. This is far short of the massive upgrading needed to make the Rock competitive and only emphasises the capital starvation of the Railroad.
The Rock's two intercity passenger trains ran at a deficit of $2 million. Revenues dropped 1.5% despite a 15% fare hike in July.
Commuter revenues were up 7% but the service still produced deficits of $2.7 million. The newly created Regional Transportation Authority is scheduled to take over the operation of all mass transit facilities, including the Rock's commuter service, in the six counties of northeastern Illinois on July 1, 1975. Subsidies from the State of Illinois for intercity and suburban passenger service during 1974 totalled $2 320 000.
Maintenance projects included improving engine repair facilities at Silvis and installing high-capacity fuel storage tanks at six key points on the system. Locomotive parts worth almost $3 million were ordered and 281 locomotives received heavy maintenance ranging from engine rebuilding to turbocharger changeouts. The Federal Department of Transportation made 1 314 locomotive inspections on the Rock and ordered 25 units out of service temporarily for correction of defects.
1 601 freight cars received heavy repairs or conversion work.
Rock Island Motor Transit, the Rock's trucking subsidiary, grossed $18.3 million in 1974, a 6.2% increase over 1973. Net was $239 000 as against $291 000 in 1973. RIMT acquired 82 new tractors, 8 pick-up trucks and 20 single axle trailers. A through-trailer co-ordinated service to the west coast was started March 1.
The Company By-Laws were amended July 15 by reducing the Board of Directors membership from 18 to 16.
Lewis B. Harder, Chairman and Chief Executive Officer of International Mining Corporation was elected Chairman of the Rock on November 1, succeeding Theodore E. Desch who continued as a Director.
John W. Ingram, former Federal Railroad Administor, and an experienced railway executive, was elected President, Chief Executive Officer and a Director November 1. He replaced William J. Dixon, who resigned.
Frederick M. Mayer resigned from the Board in November and Harry A. Darby resigned in February 1975.
On December 16 the Board elected: Dr. Paul H. Banner, Executive Vice-President; John D. Mitros, Vice-President-Staff and Christopher Knapton, Vice-President. Dr. Banner has jurisdiction over sales and marketing, intermodal services, passenger services and Rock Island Motor Transit. Mr. Mitros overseas personnel, public relations, technical services and insurance. Mr. Knapton serves as the Rock's legislative representative in Washington and the 13 States served by the Railroad.
On March 17, 1975, the Rock filed a petition in the District Court of the United States for the Northern District of Illinois, Eastern Division, under Section 77, of Chapter VIII, of the Acts of Congress relating to bankruptcy. The Honorable Frank J. McGarr, District Judge, on the same day, issued an order approving of the petition and ordering the railroad to run until April 12. On March 28, the Court appointed William M. Gibbons trustee of all railroads, lands, properties, estates, rights and franchises of the Chicago, Rock Island and Pacific Railroad Company and subsidiary companies. On April 4, the Interstate Commerce Commission affirmed Mr. Gibbons as trustee. Thus ended a

decade-long decline, during which the railroad's plant was increasingly neglected, and during which it lost more than $100 million as it waited, in vain as it proved, for approval by the Interstate Commerce Commission of a merger to which Union Pacific and Rock Island had agreed in 1963.

On April 6, Trustee Gibbons affirmed Mr. Ingram as Preisdent and Chief Executive Officer of the railroad. On April 15, the Trustee asked the District Court to lift the May 15 date which the Court had set to determine if Rock Island should continue to operate. The Court lifted the date and has, in Trustee Gibbons' words, "made it possible for Rock Island to continue its operations as it seeks access to capital and attempts to bootstrap its way back".

Plans and programmes to help offset Rock Island's reduced business and liquidity crisis were either in effect or being implemented at the time of filing for reorganisation. From January 1 to April 21, 1975, train miles were reduced 24.4% compared with a year earlier. Yard engine hours were reduced 13.3% in the same period.

In mid April, a painful but necessary internal restructuring of management followed reductions in the railroad's work force. 200 management positions were eliminated. Six operating divisions were consolidated into four.

LINES AND TERRITORIES

The Rock Island operates in the middle west states a total route mileage of 6 595 miles *(10 605 km)*, and has important traffic both west from Chicago and north and south, but has severe competition since its lines parallel other railroads.

During 1973, 210 miles of money-losing branch lines were abandoned. Of this 120 miles were sold to newly established short line railroad companies in Iowa and Texas. The Interstate Commerce Commission issued its order on December 3, 1974 in the proceeding which has been pending since 1963 whereby various railroads are seeking to acquire all or part of the Rock Island. This order authorised the merger of the properties of the Rock Island into the Union Pacific subject to numerous conditions which include the sale of the southern lines of the Rock Island to the Southern Pacific. In addition, Southern Pacific must offer to sell to the Santa Fe the Rock Island line between Amarillo, Texas and Memphis, Tennessee. In the event that Santa Fe accepts this offer, it must purchase the Missouri-Kansas-Texas Railroad Company and include it within the Santa Fe system. The Commission imposed certain protective conditions for the benefit of Frisco and certain other railroads which would be in effect for a period of five years.

FINANCIAL RESULTS

Rock Island operations in 1973 resulted in a consolidated net loss of $14 944 000 compared with a loss of $6 128 000 the preceding year. Consolidated operating revenues amounted to $344 899 000 in 1973, a 7.4% increase over the 1972 revenues of $321 003 000. Freight revenues were $324 128 000 compared with $303 243 000 in 1972. The improvement in revenues was generated very largely by increases in freight rates and somewhat by a more profitable product mix and longer average hauls. Passenger revenues totalled $5 130 000 compared with $4 823 000 in 1972. Consolidated operating expenses totalled $282 693 000 in 1973, an increase of 9.7% over the 1972 expense figure of $257 647 000. Transportation expenses totalled $156 590 000, up $21 332 000 or 15.8% over 1972. Maintenance expenses, involving track, roadway, freight cars, locomotives and other equipment, were $100 991 000 in 1973 and $97 192 000 in 1972. These large increases were caused by the inflationary trend of labour costs, both wages and fringe benefits, and material prices, along with startling increases in fuel charges. Congressional amendments to the Railroad Retirement Tax Act in the summer of 1973 substantially raised the amount of railroad retirement taxes to be paid by the Company. This tax figure is now $22 million a year, an increase of $7 million.

OPERATING REVENUES	(Thousands of Dollars) Year ended Dec 31	
	1974	1973
Freight	361 851	324 128
Passenger	5 470	5 129
Other	17 514	15 642
Total operating revenues	384 835	344 899
Operating Expenses		
Maintenance of way and structures:		
Exclusive of depreciation	42 657	38 423
Depreciation	3 339	3 306
Maintenance of equipment:		
Exclusive of depreciation	60 163	52 264
Depreciation	6 898	6 998
Traffic	8 711	8 739
Transportation	179 937	156 590
Other	17 470	16 373
Total operating expenses	319 175	282 693
Net revenue from operations	65 660	62 206
Other Expenses		
Taxes	33 035	26 011
Equipment and joint facility rents	54 444	54 211
Total other expenses	87 479	80 222

	(Thousands of Dollars) Year ended Dec 31	
Net operating loss	21 819	18 016
Non-Operating Income, Net	1 193	5 538
	20 626	12 478
Fixed Charges (principally interest on funded debt)	2 471	2 466
Net loss for the Year	23 097	14 944
Retained Income at beginning of Year	77 573	92 517
Retained Income at end of Year	54 476	77 573
Net Loss per share of Common Stock	7.91	5.12

FREIGHT TRAFFIC

The predominant factor in the year's traffic and operating picture for the Rock Island was the tremendous demand for transportation to move export grain, which was shipped in unprecedented quantities. This created a capacity requirement which could not be accommodated even with a large increase both in new jumbo covered hopper cars, and in boxcars specially leased from other railroads, resulting in an equipment shortage throughout the year. The situation was further aggravated by recurrent delays at port unloading terminals. Export grain continues to move in heavy volume, and forecasts are for an even larger movement in the years ahead as American farmers feed the world. While Rock Island is particularly well situated to participate in this movement, serving, as it does, the major producing areas of all four of the principal cash grain crops (wheat, corn, milo, and soya beans), it also faces a problem in revamping its plant to handle the increased load. Branch lines which for many years handled only a few cars a week are now moving solid grain trains day after day. Freight revenues were up on last year's figures $324 128 000. Compared with the 1972 figure $303 243 000.

In conjunction with the Southern Pacific, and the Chessie System, the Rock Island began offering Auto-trans service to move personal and company-owned automobiles between the Chicago area, eastern points, and Los Angeles or San Francisco.

Freight loss and damage expenses dropped 16% in 1972.

LOCOMOTIVES AND CARS

The Rock Island locomotive fleet consists of 609 units—452 road units and 158 switchers. Of the total, 394 are owned by the railroad, and 215 operate on lease.

Rock Island still owns 132 passenger cars.

The freight car fleet totals 25 818. Late 1973 the Rock Island took delivery of 28 new six-axle, high horsepower locomotives, valued at $9 million. 1 255 new freight cars valued at $23 million were received under lease agreements during 1973. Included were 450 50-ft general purpose box cars of 70-ton capacity; 150 52-ft gondolas of 100-ton capacity, of which 50 are covered for carrying coiled steel; 100 60-ft specialised box cars for transporting commodities such as synthetic rubber products and paper; 40 86-ft "hi-cube" box cars used for auto parts; 15 60-ft "hi-cube" cars for appliances; and 500 jumbo covered hopper cars of 100-ton rating for hauling grain. The Rock Island now has more than 4 500 of these jumbo grain cars.

To sustain maximum availability of the car fleet, major repairs were made to 46 jumbo covered hopper cars, 337 special box cars and 256 miscellaneous cars. 65 flat cars were converted for use in pulpwood service. Light repairs were given to 1 325 cars for use in carrying grain and for other service. However, with inadequate freight rate increases granted in recent years, and the extremely adverse impact of incentive per diem payments on the Company's car hire costs, the Company has been unable to maintain the degree of serviceability in its fleet that it would have liked.

OTHER DEVELOPMENTS

A quality-control section was added to the Kansas City Transportation Control Centre to direct and measure the handling of cars. Sophisticated electronic equipment enables central staff to monitor train service effectively so that problems can be spotted in the development stage. The new feature is especially helpful in keeping tabs on special movements to maintain stricter adherence to schedules. To enhance the efficiency of the system, a new train numbering system went into effect late 1972 which identifies trains by territory, date and consist.

Two new IBM system 360-50 computers were installed in 1972, replacing three model 40 units. Computer reports continue to be expanded for the benefits of all departments. Of particular value are those provided to improve operating efficiency. One report now produced, for example, shows average length of time for loads and empties in terminals, as well as average per diem figures for the equipment involved. Another report is transmitted daily to each mechanised yard and to certain key officers, listing cars on hand in excess of 24 hours.

During 1972, 123 new industries located on the Rock Island and 52 companies expanded operations. It is estimated that these companies will invest $100.5 million for plant and equipment.

TOFC/COFC

Rock Island piggyback service offers plans I, II, II¼, II½, III, IV and V, and operates 3 704 trailers. Flat cars as required are available from its own fleet and by lease from TrailerTrain Company.

Ramps are provided at Chicago, Peoria, Davenport, Des Moines, Minneapolis, Sioux Falls, Omaha, Denver, Colorado Springs, Topeka, Kansas City, St. Louis, Wichita, Amarillo, Tucumcari, Little Rock, Memphis, and Galveston. Iowa Falls, Iowa; Ottawa, Illinois; ManKato, Kansas; and Belle Missouri, Houston and Fort Worth and at Liberal, Kansas and Mason City Iowa.

CONSOLIDATED RAIL CORPORATION (CONRAIL)
Transportation Center, Six Penn Center Plaza, Philadelphia, Pa 19104

Chairman and Chief Executive Officer: Edward G. Jordan
President and Chief Operating Officer: Richard D. Spence
Secretary and Assistant to the Chairman: Richard C. Sullivan
Vice-Presidents:
  Vice-President, Law: Ronald M. Dietrich
  Senior Vice-President, Strategic Planning: Leo F. Mullin
  Vice-President and Controller: Robert Wadden
  Vice-President, Public Affairs and Advertising: Donald J. Martin
  Vice-President, Government Affairs: John L. Sweeney
  Assistant Vice-President, Executive Development and Organisation Planning: David R. McCarthy
  Vice-President, Operations: Richard B. Hasselman
  Assistant Vice-President, Transportation: Hershel E. Ring
  Vice-President, Operations Planning and Control: Carl N. Taylor
  Acting Vice-President, Sales: Ralph N. Cramer
  Vice-President, Labour Relations: Alvin E. Egbers
Executive Vice-President, Finance and Administration: Robert H. Platt
Senior Vice-President, Marketing and Sales: James A. Hagen
Vice-President and Treasurer: Richard T. Fox
Vice President, Materials and Purchasing: Wesley A. LaCourt
Vice-President, Marketing: Richard H. Steiner
Assistant Vice-Presidents:
  Assistant Vice-President, Integration and Consolidation: Robert H. Clement
  Assistant Vice-President, Intermodal: Hugh L. Randall
  Assistant Vice-President, Systems: Michael D. Sims
  Assistant Vice-President, Market Analysis and Special Projects: M. F. Coffman
  Assistant Vice-President, Intermodal: R. L. Hayes
  Assistant Vice-President, Coal and Ore: C. H. Wolfinger
  Assistant Vice-President, Automotive: M. S. Sanders
  Assistant Vice-President, Pricing: J. E. Musselwhite
  Assistant Vice-President, System Equipment and Service: D. A. Washburn
  Senior Assistant Vice-President, Strategic Planning: James R. Sullivan
  Assistant Vice-President, Government Affairs: Alvin J. Arnett
  Assistant Vice-President, Strategic Planning: Edward P. Frasher
  Assistant Vice-President, Subsidised Services and Public Policy: Ralph R. Mueller
  Assistant Vice-President, Strategic Planning: Warren G. Barber
  Assistant Vice-President, Auditing: Ralph P. Wille
  Assistant Vice-President, Financial Analysis: John J. Dawson
  Assistant Vice-President, Agency Administration: James W. McDonnell
    Assistant Vice-President, Executive Development and Organisation Planning: David R. McCarthy
  Assistant Vice-President, Contracts: Robert W. Orr
  Assistant Vice-President, Real Estate: Lawrence A. Huff
  Assistant Vice-President, Sales (East): C. Philip O'Rourke, Jr
  Assistant Vice-President, Sales (Central): Herbert E. Simpson
  Assistant Vice-President, Sales (West): Joseph B. DiCarlo
  Assistant Vice-President, Industrial Development: Vincent J. Floyd
General Managers:
  Metropolitan Region: Kenneth E. Smith
  Northeast Region: C. R. McKenna
  Eastern Region: W. C. Wieters
  Central Region: C. W. Owens
  Northern Region: B. L. Strohl
  Western Region:
  Southern Region: J. G. Robins
  Atlantic Region: D. A. Swanson

Consolidated Rail Corporation—ConRail—a private, for-profit corporation established by the Regional Rail Reorganisation Act of 1973, as amended, began operations on April 1, 1976.
Representing the largest corporate reorganisation in American history, Conrail is composed of most of the rail properties of six bankrupt railroads: Central of New

New logo is being adopted by ConRail member railroads as motive power and rolling stock get their new system face lift.

Jersey; Erie Lackawanna; Lehigh Valley; Lehigh and Hudson River; Penn Central; and the Reading. Primarily a freight railroad, Conrail provides transportation service to 16 states, two Canadian provinces and Washington, DC over 17 000 route miles of track. The Corporation also provides, under contract to various commuter and transportation authorities, daily passenger service for more than 360 000 commuters in major metropolitan areas of the Northeast and Midwest.
In terms of employees, equipment and revenues Conrail is the largest railroad in America. Its fleet includes some 148 000 freight cars and more than 4 460 locomotives.
Conrail was the result of extensive planning by the United States Railway Association (USRA), an agency created under the Rail Act of 1973 and chartered by Congress to develop a private sector solution to the rail crisis precipitated by the financial collapse of the Penn Central and other railroads serving the region.
The Corporation is well into its planned 10-year, multi-billion dollar plant and equipment rehabilitation programme aimed at eliminating more than two decades of deferred maintenance and at the same time achieving the mandate of Congress—service excellence, at a profit, in the private sector.

FINANCE
Consolidated Rail Corporation—United States Railway Association holds $1 000 million of 7.5% debentures and $1 100 million of Series A Preferred Stock.
Under the Regional Rail Reorganisation Act of 1973, as amended and the terms of the Financing Agreement between USRA and the Corporation, USRA may invest up to $1 000 million in 7.5% debentures at any time and thereafter up to $1 100 million in Series A preferred stock.

A pair of General Motors GP38 locomotives in ConRail livery.

THE DENVER AND RIO GRANDE WESTERN RAILROAD COMPANY

1515 Arapahoe St, Denver, Co 80202
P.O. Box 5482, Denver, Co 80217

Chairman of the Board and Chief Executive Officer: G. B. Aydelott
President: W. J. Holtman
General Manager: A. H. Nance
Vice-President, Traffic: Clarence R. Lennig
Vice-President, Finance and Comptroller: H. W. Bushacher
Vice-President and General Counsel: S. R. Freeman
Secretary and Treasurer: R. C. Schulte
Assistant Treasurer: W. F. Downes
Director, Industrial Development: A. R. Fjeldsted
Director of Personnel: J. W. Lovett
Assistant to the Chairman: J. B. Love
Executive Assistant to the President: C. O. Penney
Director, Economic Management and Controls: C. H. Smith
Director of Security and General Claims: A. A. Capps
Passenger Traffic Manager: L. J. Bernstein
Director, Public Relations: E. L. Main
Assistant Vice-President, Market Development: C. D. Brainard
Superintendent of Communications: M. F. Black
Chief Transportation Officer: D. J. Butters
Chief mechanical Officer: J. E. Clancy
Chief Engineer: E. H. Waring
Signal Engineer: F. A. Dunham
Director, Transportation research: R. L. Jacobsen
Director, Rules and Training: R. S. Eno
Purchasing Agent: S. A. Silverman
Director, Budget and Controls: R. W. Hambrick
Director, Unit Train Operations: J. E. Timberlake

The Denver and Rio Grande Western Railroad Company is now 105 years old. The Rio Grande Railroad operates over 1 850 miles of mainline track from Denver and Pueblo, Colorado, on the east, to Salt Lake City and Ogden, Utah, on the west. The company has over 255 locomotives and 11 000 freight cars of various types. Virtually all its revenue is derived from hauling freight with major items being coal, food products, lumber, steel, and autos and auto parts. Approximately 60% of its revenue comes from originating, terminating and local traffic, while 40% results from being an intermediate carrier between other railroads.

Rio Grande Industries, Inc (Denver) was established in 1969 as a holding company to control Denver and Rio Grande Western Railroad, and to permit diversification. Although the railroad continues to be its most important activity, diversification has been made into real estate development (Leavell Development Co, El Paso, Tex); people-moving systems (Arrow Development Co); information industries (Computer Sharing Services); and Rio Grande Motor Way.

TRAFFIC RESULTS

For the ninth consecutive year, the Rio Grande Railroad achieved record freight revenues. In 1976, freight revenues were 13% above those of 1975. Freight ton-miles increased 4%, and average revenue per ton mile increased 9%. Coal represented 26% of total freight revenues in 1976, and were up 19% over 1975, accounting for about one-third of the year-to-year increase.

Passenger revenues were up slightly in 1976 with almost all of the increase coming from the Durango-Silverton narrow gauge tourist train.

FINANCIAL RESULTS
Financial Summary

	1976 $	1975
Gross Operating Revenue	206 793 000	186 307 000
Income Tax	9 084 000	7 091 000
Net Income	16 387 000	14 290 000
Net Income per common and common equivalent		
share before conversion of Series A Preferred	2.90	2.39
assuming conversion of Series A Preferred	2.36	2.06
Depreciation	11 919 000	11 245 000

Operating expenses increased 14% in 1976.
Following 1975's record capital improvement expenditure, equipment purchases in 1976 were $1.3 million, with the only major purchase being ten cabooses.

LOCOMOTIVES AND CARS

The present fleet of diesel electric locomotives totals 254 units, of which 234 are road units and 20 are switchers.
The passenger fleet comprises 19 cars. Total freight car fleet as of January 1977 was 8 433.

DEVELOPMENT

Installation of Centralised Traffic Control system on the Craig Branch in Northwestern Colorado was completed during 1976, as was the installation of CTC between Springville and Gilluly in Utah.
Additional expenditures involved expansion of fuel handling facilities, terminal expansion and modernisation, machines for roadway and track maintenance, safety and security improvements, including hot box detectors, dragging equipment detectors, rock slide detector fences, etc.
Rio Grande also initiated an extensive programme for modernisation of bridges, installation of new equipment for repair facilities, and construction of industrial spur tracks.
Thirty-six track miles of new and heavier rail, and 192 000 crossties were installed in 1976.

ILLINOIS CENTRAL GULF RAILROAD

An IC Industries Company

233 N Michigan Ave, Chicago, Ill 60601

Chairman and Chief Executive Officer: Stanley E. G. Hillman
President and Chief Operating Officer: William J. Taylor
Vice-Chairman: Alan S. Boyd
Senior Vice-President—Administration: Glenn E. Konker
Senior Vice-President—Operating: Henry F. Davenport
Senior Vice-President—Marketing: Harry J. Bruce
Senior Vice-President—Maintenance and Manufacturing: Jack C. Humbert
Vice-President—Law: Percy W. Johnston
Vice-President—Materials Management: Harry C. Miller
Vice-President & Chief Engineer: Lee F. Fox
Vice-President and Chief Transportation Officer: I. B. Hall
Vice-President—Real Estate: Rixon A. Irvine
Vice-President—Personnel: Martin J. Fingerhut
Secretary-Treasurer: John B. Goodrich
Vice-President Communications & Computer Services: Paul F. Deady
Vice-President Manufacturing & Sales: Bryan D. Venable
Vice-President—Subsidiary Activities: Frank J. Lott
Comptroller: D. R. Montgomery

The Illinois Central Gulf Railroad was formed by the merger in 1972 of the Illinois Central and Gulf, Mobile & Ohio Railroads. It also operates the Chicago & Illinois Western Railroad, a small Chicago switching line. Additionally, the Illinois Central Gulf Railroad owns the Waterloo Railroad Company, a small line providing rail service in and near Waterloo, Iowa, holds a controlling interest in the Peoria, and Pekin Union Railway Company, terminal and connecting carrier, and owns Gulf Transport Company, a charter and scheduled bus line operator which also has trucking rights along lines of the former GM&O Railroad.
The Illinois Central Gulf is a strong and profitable line operating in 13 states in the heartland of America and runs from the Great Lakes to the Gulf of Mexico, providing a vital rail connection between some 2 000 communities that include Chicago, St. Louis, Memphis, New Orleans, Birmingham, Nashville, Louisville, Indianapolis, Omaha, Kansas City, Montgomery and Mobile.

FINANCIAL	1975 $	1976 $
Revenue	554 370 000	626 878 000
Expenses	574 118 000	633 330 000

ICG serves vital areas: Today the ICG is a strong 9 200-mile carrier serving a territory with a unique combination of favourable characteristics. The ICG's territory contains the highly industrialised Chicago Metropolitan Area; the agricultural centre of the country; one of the nation's largest proven coal reserves; and the rapidly growing South Central States of Alabama, Louisiana and Mississippi. The inherent ability of the railroads to move large volume of freight, their energy, efficiency—four times that of highway carriers and relatively low level of environment pollution are other factors which should favour long term growth for ICG.
Improved service with connections was the focal point of Illinois Central Gulf service improvements during the last two years. The Central Link established in 1975 was improved a number of times attracting over twice the original volume through the Effingham gateway. Early in 1977 a similar operation was inaugurated with the Norfolk and Western at Tolono, Illinois. This service, called the Delta Cannonball, like the Central Link, has improved service between the south and north-east carriers.
A number of improvements was made to connections at the Chicago gateway. Arrangements were made for the Soo Line to operate a run-through train from Stevens Points, Wisconsin into ICG's Markham Yard at Chicago. This connection permitted traffic to by-pass former yards in the Chicago terminal, greatly speeding up traffic. Also, in Chicago, the ICG began pre-blocking Grand Trunk traffic to by-pass intermediate yards on their system, reducing turnaround on large volumes of service-sensitive business.
A run-through train was established between Chicago and Pine Bluff, Arkansas over the East St Louis gateway with the Southern Pacific-Cotton Belt. This new run-through train connects the south-west and upper mid-west markets. A new service with the Rock Island, the Sun Belt connection, over the Memphis gateway brought together some previously designed run-through connections. The Central Link and Delta Cannonball are reached quickly in overhead service between the new Sun Belt connection off the Rock Island.
Additionally the ICG initiated its Truck-Rail-Truck operation between Markham and East St Louis. This concept combined local truck deliveries and pickups of palletised steel with fast overnight rail movement between Chicago and East St Louis. The system has worked well and has expanded to include Kansas City and soon will include Iowa. Bulk transfer facilities have also begun operating throughout the system, allowing shippers to combine the economies of all rail service with local trunk delivery.
A major activity conducted by the Illinois Central Gulf Railroad at its Paducah, Kentucky shops is the remanufacture of diesel electric locomotives for itself and other roads. Incorporating over 35 major modifications over the original locomotive, the ICG remanufactured locomotive performs as good as new locomotives.
The decision to remanufacture locomotives in 1967 was made because the majority of ICG power at that time was of the GP-7 and GP-9 configuration and was getting old.
The railway has found remanufacturing costs half as much as buying new locomotives. Once the decision was made to remanufacture the fleet and to do the same for other railroads the railway began an extensive retooling and retraining programme. After a $12 million improvement at ICG's major locomotive facility, Paducah (nearly 1 million square feet under roof) became the largest US plant devoted to the remanufacture of locomotives.
Railroad's statistics covering reliability and maintenance costs (14 per cent reduction in maintenance costs) (ICG's availability of remanufactured locomotives is over 90 per cent) proves remanufacturing is the intelligent alternative to purchasing new. Railroads who come to ICG for remanufacturing enjoy new locomotive financing and a one-year warranty.

KANSAS CITY SOUTHERN RAILWAY COMPANY
114 West 11th Street, Kansas City, Mo 64105

President: Thomas S. Carter
Chairman of the Board and Chief Executive Officer: W. N. Deramus
Vice-President Marketing and Assistant to the Chairman: M. F. McClain
Senior Vice-President, and Secretary: G. E. Kellogg
Vice-President and Comptroller: T. A. Giltner
Treasurer: V. C. Pragman

Law Department:
Vice-President-Law: Robert E. Zimmerman

Purchasing and Stores Department:
Assistant General Manager, Mechanical: T. T. Souter
Director of Purchasing: J. B. Dehner

Operating Department:
General Manager: J. E. Gregg

Personnel Department:
Vice-President, Personnel: J. L. Deveney

Traffic Department:
Freight Traffic:
Vice-President: L. J. Tamisiea

Kansas City Southern Railway is a member of the Kansas City Southern Industries group of companies. In addition to road and rail transportation, KCSI owns television and radio stations, a plant manufacturing specialised industrial vehicles, coal mines and financial services companies. While transport services continued to contribute the largest share of KCSI's earnings in 1972, transport share fell from 77.6% in 1971 to 61.4% in 1972, whereas contributions from other sources increased to 38.6% in 1972 compared with 22.4% in 1971.
The Louisianna and Arkansas Railway is controlled by KCS but is separately operated.

LINES AND TERRITORY
The main line runs direct from Kansas City to the Gulf ports of New Orleans, Louisiana and Port Arthur, Texas. A line runs west from Shreveport to Dallas.
Total route: Approximately 1 600 miles *(2 575 km)*.
Woodpulp, paper, and petroleum and port expansion are activities which are expanding in the KCS territories.
All passenger train operation has ceased.
KCS seeks protection from adverse effects of the merger of Union Pacific/Rock Island now under review by ICC.

FREIGHT TRAFFIC
Despite the downturn in business and reduced volume in the second half of 1976, gross tons of revenue freight handled during 1976 increased 6.2 per cent to 24 980 000 compared with 23 523 000 in 1975.
Net ton miles of revenue freight handled in 1976 totalled 6 773 million, up 7.2 per cent from the 6 316 million handled in 1975. The average revenue per net ton mile hauled was 2.036 cents in 1976 compared with 1.914 cents in 1975, and the average revenue per carload handled increased to $351 per car, up 10 per cent above the $319 per car in 1975.

CAPITAL IMPROVEMENTS
Capital additions and Improvements during 1976 amounted to $4 305 000 primarily for roadway improvements.

LOCOMOTIVES AND CARS
Kansas City received 450 Box Cars in May 1977 at the cost of $14·5 million.

LONG ISLAND RAIL ROAD COMPANY
Jamaica Station, Jamaica, NY 11435

President: Walter L. Schlager, Jr
Vice-President, General Counsel & Secretary: George M. Onken
Vice-President, Operations: Jeremy Taylor
Treasurer-Controller: Thomas P. Moore
Chief Engineer: John D. Woodward
Superintendent-Transportation: Joseph C. Valder
Director, Planning and Development: Donald O. Eisele
Director, Public Relations and Community Affairs: George O. Thune

LINES AND TERRITORIES
The LIRR operates the whole 100 mile length of Long Island, New York with the inner suburban lines electrified (103 route miles and 294 single track miles) and operated by electric multiple unit stock, and the outer, sparser traffic operated by diesel electric locomotives. Total mileage including electrified lines, is 321 miles route 740 miles single track.
LIRR operates both diesel and electric trains. Electric territory (third rail) adds up to 121 miles, diesel-only territory to 207.
Extension of electrification for 23 miles from Huntington to Port Jefferson and for 24 miles from Hicksville to Ronkonkoma is under active study. A consultant's report has been completed and further review and evaluation are underway, although necessary funds are not yet available. The last major extension of electrification on the Long Island Rail Road was completed from Mineola to Huntington in 1970.
The LIRR is a wholly-owned subsidiary of the Metropolitan Transportation Authority, and agency of the State of New York, whose members constitute the railroad's Board of Directors.

FINANCIAL RESULTS

Revenues:	1974	$	1973
Passenger	92 964 051		80 584 964
Freight	14 020 348		9 509 250
Food and beverage	1 957 415		1 657 454
Rents and sundry	2 852 542		2 988 064
	111 794 356		94 739 732
Expenses:			
Transportation	91 875 756		72 080 425
Maintenance of equipment	53 165 353		41 258 120
Maintenance of way	37 781 969		27 222 278
Administration	24 103 794		19 959 224
	206 926 872		160 520 047

FREIGHT TRAFFIC
Total freight tonnage for 1975 (latest available figures) was 2 408 479; Total freight ton-miles 30 871 000. In sharp contrast to other US railroads, freight accounts for less than one-sixth of gross revenue on the LIRR, Freight volume is at present about 3.8 million tons a year. Three-quarters of freight is inbound to Long Island; only one quarter is moved westward off the island. LIRR has direct interchange with all trunk line railroads serving the New York area.
Several freight improvements have been put in hand to streamline and improve service provided by the LIRR. A computer record keeping service, for instance has been installed to provide for greater effectiveness and more efficient means of keeping track of the nearly 100 000 wagons handled each year.
Regular transfer of freight cars to and from Penn Central has been accomplished by direct rail routing over the Hellhate Bridge rather than by slower, and expensive, floating of cars through New York Harbour. This new routing involves direct delivery each day of the complete trains which have been classified into three major delivery area groups. Then the LIRR receives these "blocks" of cars at the freshpond interchange and moves them directly to three points for final distribution to individual consignee of the cars. Annual operational savings using this method are estimated to be approximately $750 000 as compared to the more costly car float system. Negotiations are under way to expand this system to include other linehaul railroads.

PASSENGER TRAFFIC
Passengers carried during 1975 were 67 172 598 and total passenger miles 1 851 429 814. LIRR operates about 800 scheduled trains a day—670 passenger trains and 130 deadheads (empties moving to terminals to begin runs or to yards after runs). About 425 scheduled trains are run on Saturdays and Sundays.
Equipment for the diesel-hauled service continues to be improved. With the conversion to all-Metropolitan service in the electrified zone in 1973, a programme was begun to convert late-model electric cars of older design into coaches for use in diesel service. By the end of 1974, 90 coaches and 19 power cars had been adapted for "push-pull" trains. An additional 33 coaches (including 4 generator cars) have been authorised for conversion and funds from the 1974 Transportation Bond Issue are being sought for the remaining 38 coaches (including 5 generator cars) to be converted for use in diesel service.
The system is in fact the nation's busiest passenger railroad. Total annual journeys are approximately 69.6 million passengers a year. An average of 260 000 passengers a day are carried, which breaks down to 90 000 commuters who make two trips a day and 80 000 single-fare passengers.
There are 147 stations for the railroad, plus 26 "road-and-rail" bus-stops in Suffolk County. The average distance between stations is slightly over one mile.

One of the 22 new General Motors class GP-38 Type 2 diesel-electric locomotives Long Island has in service.

ROLLING STOCK

Passenger cars operated by LIRR number 1 067. The Company has 60 line haul diesel electric locomotives and 23 switching locomotives. Electric railcars number 766 and 301 diesel trailer cars.

TRACK IMPROVEMENTS

With the arrival of the 770 new high performance M-1 electric multiple-unit cars and the upgrading of the electric power system which will permit these cars to operate at their designed capability, it was determined that the condition of the Long Island Rail Road's track required improvement to standards consistent with 100 mph operation of this new equipment.

The improvement programme involves the installation on 50 miles of track of all new heavier weight (119 lb) continuous welded rail, new ties and stone ballast, and new heavier weight switches, many of which will have improved turnout angles for higher train speeds and greater riding comfort. Highway grade crossings in the improvement programme areas will be surfaced with modern rubber crossing panels to eliminate the traditional noise and shock normally experienced by vehicles passing over railroad tracks. All salvageable material removed during the programme will be rehabilitated and utilised to upgrade other portions of the railroad.

The programme focuses on two categories of the railroad's track: first, heavily-used, presently-electrified trackage, and second, heavily-used, non-electrified track which is slated for electrification in the future. As a part of the improvement of track in the second category, third rail ties will be installed in preparation for eventual electrification.

The improvement of the Main Line trackage for high speed operation between Harold Interlocking (Sunnyside) and Jay Interlocking (Jamaica), and between Hall Interlocking (Jamaica) and Nassau Interlocking (Mineola) falls into the first of the above categories. The improvement of Main Line trackage between Divide Interlocking (Hicksville) and PW Interlocking (Pinelawn), and Port Jefferson Branch trackage between Huntington and Northport, is in the second category.

As of the end of December 1974, 85% of a 50-mile track improvement programme had been completed.

All tie renewals in the programme are completed and all highway crossings have been completed. Continuous welded rail installation is complete with the exception of approximately 9 800 ft still remaining to be installed on Main Line track No 4 between Hall and Queens. Interlocking renewals have also been completed at Bellerose and PW. Completion of the switch work at Queens, Nassau, Metropolitan Avenue and "B" Interlocking were accomplished in 1975.

MAINE CENTRAL RAILROAD COMPANY

242, St. John St, Portland, Maine 04102

President and Chairman of the Board: E. Spencer Miller
Vice-President: John F. Gerity
Clerk of the Corporation: Stanley W. Watson
Assistant to President: Bradley L. Peters
Mechanical and Labour Relations Department:
Vice-President: Arnold J. Travis
Operating:
General Superintendent: A. N. Tupper
Chief Mechanical Officer: S. P. Park Jr
Engineering:
Chief Engineer: J. O. Born
Assistant to Chief Engineer: Stanley L. Jordan
Superintendent, Signals and Communications: P. C. Lentz
Accounting and Finance Department:
Vice-President: John F. Gerity
Comptroller: John Michaels
Treasurer: S. W. Watson
Assistant Treasurer, Director Cost Analysis: Eric P. Smith
Purchases—Stores Department:
Manager, Purchases and Stores: K. W. Phillips
Purchasing Agent: E. R. Russell
General Storekeeper: H. F. Flynn
Law Department:
General Counsel and Clerk of Corporation: S. W. Scully
Marketing Department:
Vice-President, Marketing and Traffic: G. H . Ellis
Asst. Vice-President, Sales and Service: W. J. Berry
Director of Pricing: Forest C. Ryder

LINES AND TERRITORIES

Maine Central Railroad Company is a freight-only railroad and operates 908 miles of road; 765 miles in Maine, 114 in New Hampshire, 24 miles in Vermont and 5 miles in New Brunswick. Maine Central serves all of the large population centres and with two exceptions the industrial centres of the State of Maine. The primary commodities carried are the raw materials and finished products of the pulp and paper industry with over 50% of Maine Central's traffic generated by this industry. Other major sources of freight revenue are: petroleum products, feed and mill products, corn, clay, chemicals fibreboard and pulpboard, canned food, cement and potatoes.

FINANCIAL RESULTS

The company earned an income of $269 609 000 in 1976 compared with $232 961 000 the previous year.

	1976	1975
Operating Revenues	$37 209 888	$32 556 318
Operating Expenses	33 039 358	29 555 112
Operating Ratio	88.79%	90.78%
Net from Railway Operations	4 170 530	3 001 206

A record high $37.2 million railway operating revenue was recorded in 1976, a 14 per cent increase over $32.6 million for 1975, despite a gain of only 4 per cent in revenue ton miles. Anticipated improvement in traffic, which had actually increased in the last quarter of 1975 and first quarter of 1976, did not result, as paper mill expansion was delayed and a depressed economy continued in most areas of Maine. The improvement in 1976 dollar revenue is attributable to the availability during the full year 1976 of ICC rate increases previously allowed at three different dates during the year 1975 and to a general freight rate increase allowed by the ICC in two stages in 1976. Ex Parte 318, granted March 21, 1976, produced a 4.7 per cent increase to Maine Central, based on 7 per cent selective general rate increase, and Ex Parte 330, allowed October 7, 1976, provided an additional 0.3 per cent yield to Maine Central.

As stated in prior annual reports, revenues generated under the 10 per cent freight rate increase granted under ICC proceeding Ex Parte 305 have, since June 20, 1974, been restricted to use for deferred maintenance and delayed capital improvements after deduction to allow for increased cost of materials (except fuel). By further order of the Commission on December 21, 1976, the same restrictions on use were retained and the expiration date was extended to January 1, 1978. During 1976, Maine Central's revenue yield from Ex Parte 305 after deductions for such increased material costs was $1.9 million while $1.1 million was used for deferred maintenance and delayed capital improvements, as compared with a revenue yield of $1.8 million and application of $.6 million for the year 1975.

Operating expenses also reached a new high of $33 039 358, an 11.8 per cent increase over $29 555 112 in 1975. Despite continuing restrictions on spending, the needs to maintain plant and equipment and provide adequate customer service resulted in substantially higher maintenance and operating costs. Wage increases, pursuant to existing national agreements, of 5 per cent on October 1, 1975, 2 per cent on January 1, 1976, 3 per cent on April 1, 1976, 2 per cent on July 1, 1976, and increased employee benefit plans, amounted to over $1 750 000 in 1976, or approximately half of the increase over 1975 operating expenses. Higher expenses for ties, rails, ballast, and maintenance to machines and significantly higher derailment costs in 1976 accounted for another $975 000 of the increase.

Diesel fuel costs increased by $175 000, or 9 per cent, on top of an increase in 1975 of almost $100 000, even though consumption of diesel fuel oil was reduced again in 1976.

General Motors Bo-Bo 253 being turned on the turntable ready for stabling in the roundhouse at Bangor Maine, Maine Central RR

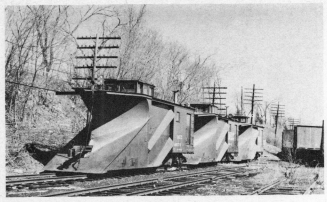

Bangor Maine USA line-up at Snowploughs in Maine Central yard MWS75, MWS80, MWS72

Two GE U18B 1800 hp Independence Class diesel electrics of Maine Central RR runs light into Bangor station yard after uncoupling from a freight they had just brought from Vanceboro. N0400 "General Henry Knox" and No 408" Battle of the Bagaduce"

LOCOMOTIVES AND CARS

Late in 1976, Maine Central acquired, by 15-year nonequity leases, 500 new 50-foot box cars having a value of about $14 700 000. It is estimated that the time/mileage per diam income, at levels now applicable, from these box cars, without consideration of incentive per diem, will more than meet accruals for annual lease payments of about $1 643 000. It is anticipated that such per diem levels will be substantially increased in the near future.

As of December 31, 1976, Maine Central held under lease 1 961 units having an aggregate value when new of about $35 000 000. Rental payments for these leased cars are charged against income and accounted for under equipment rents on the income statement.

PRINCIPAL SOURCES OF FREIGHT TONNAGE AND REVENUE

	Number of Carloads		Percent of Total Carloads		Tons		Percent of Total Tons		Gross Freight Revenue		Percent of Total Freight Revenue	
	1976	1975	1976	1975	1976	1975	1976	1975	1976	1975	1976	1975
Paper Products	42 849	41 801	31.0	30.3	1 918 266	1 833 971	26.8	26.2	$11 893 602	$10 579 681	32.4	32.9
Woodpulp	10 937	10 646	7.9	7.7	650 929	630 782	9.1	9.0	3 909 058	3 497 472	10.7	10.9
Petroleum Products	19 080	19 197	13.8	13.9	1 106 465	1 080 708	15.4	15.5	3 351 740	1 901 292	9.1	9.0
Feed and Mill Products	7 223	7 519	5.2	5.5	298 771	312 998	4.2	4.5	1 910 330	1 688 785	5.2	5.2
Pulpwood	12 757	11 965	9.2	8.7	599 137	563 597	8.3	8.1	1 897 219	1 572 999	5.2	4.9
Corn	4 133	3 676	3.0	2.7	385 759	333 293	5.4	4.8	1 649 685	1 195 412	4.5	3.7
Clay	3 307	2 948	2.4	2.1	281 978	251 437	3.9	3.6	1 034 278	883 943	2.8	2.7
Caustic Soda	2 126	1 821	1.6	1.3	144 181	123 368	2.0	1.8	934 171	736 353	2.5	2.3
Canned Food (Not Frozen)	2 517	2 362	1.8	1.7	156 385	149 893	2.2	2.1	805 334	663 552	2.2	2.1
Fiberboard and Pulpboard	2 129	1 926	1.5	1.4	122 938	110 886	1.7	1.6	752 088	653 300	2.1	2.0
Chlorine	1 051	979	.8	.7	63 574	57 113	.9	.8	740 133	591 000	2.0	1.8
Lumber	2 324	2 074	1.7	1.5	104 674	89 877	1.5	1.3	589 961	419 608	1.6	1.3
Salt	1 801	2 064	1.3	1.5	129 896	141 596	1.8	2.0	440 657	404 005	1.2	1.3
Wastepaper	1 792	1 958	1.3	1.4	71 777	76 972	1.0	1.1	404 137	376 278	1.1	1.2
Cement	1 530	1 832	1.1	1.3	103 884	129 129	1.4	1.8	357 160	399 386	1.0	1.2
All Other Carloads	22 678	25 140	16.4	18.3	1 027 977	1 100 238	14.3	15.7	5 988 293	5 628 136	16.3	17.4
Less Carloads	—	—	—	—	815	1 170	.1	.1	12 735	11 988	.1	.1
TOTAL	138 234	137 908	100.0	100.0	7 167 406	6 987 028	100.0	100.0	$36 670 581	$32 203 190	100.0	100.0

FREIGHT TRAIN OPERATION

	System		Portland Division		Mountain Subdivision		Eastern Subdivision	
	1976	1975	1976	1975	1976	1975	1976	1975
Gross Ton Miles (000)	1 740 245	1 691 390	1 279 573	1 235 152	228 211	221 386	232 461	234 852
Net Ton Miles (000)	821 333	790 983	601 678	572 089	111 382	110 396	108 273	108 498
Train Miles	744 932	771 895	477 284	475 663	114 325	112 728	153 323	183 504
Train Hours	50 632	53 037	30 786	32 537	7 991	7 598	11 855	12 902
Average Train Load	2 336	2 191	2 681	2 597	1 996	1 964	1 516	1 280
Average Train Speed	14.7	14.6	15.5	14.6	14.3	14.8	12.9	14.2
Average GTM per Train Hour	34 370	31 891	41 563	37 961	28 559	29 137	19 609	18 203
Average Cars per Train	36.3	36.3	40.2	40.9	33.5	31.9	28.7	28.4

MISSOURI PACIFIC RAILROAD
210 N 13th St, St. Louis, Mo 63103

Executive Department (St. Louis)
Chairman of the Board: D. B. Jenks
President and Chief Executive Officer: J. H. Lloyd
Vice-President: J. E. Angst
Vice-President and General Counsel: M. M. Hennelly
Vice-President, Traffic: R. K. Davidson
Vice-President, Operations: J. W. Gessner
Vice-President, Engineering: J. G. German
Vice-President, Transportation: J. M. Toler
Vice-President, Administration: D. L. Manion
Vice-President and Controller: T. D. Rodman

LINES AND TERRITORIES
Total length of the MoPac system is 11 679 miles *(18 788 km)*. Supplementing the rail lines is a network of approximately 17 000 miles *(27 400 km)* of truck routes operated by Missouri Pacific Truck Lines. Most of the highway mileage parallels the rail lines but many routes provide scheduled freight service to places not reached by the railroads. The highway subsidiary also performs all terminal and piggy back ramp loading and unloading for Missouri Pacific Railroad traffic and over-the-highway service for piggy back traffic.

FINANCIAL RESULTS
Consolidated net income for the Missouri Pacific System in 1976 totalled $68.7 million on consolidated revenues of $1 013.7 million. In comparison, consolidated net income in the record year of 1974 was $49.7 million on revenues of $889.9 million.

	Fourth Quarter	$	Twelve Months	
	1976	1975	1976	1975
Operating Revenues				
Freight	251 729 482	237 759 931	981 004 789	858 676 505
Switching	4 459 198	4 274 346	18 879 140	15 520 002
Other	3 568 363	3 068 011	13 784 177	14 349 767
Total Operating Revenues	259 757 043	245 102 288	1 013 668 106	888 546 274
Operating Expenses:				
Maintenance of Roadway and Structures	29 775 610	30 610 696	140 098 384	121 210 955
Maintenance of Equipment	41 856 836	35 176 677	159 337 953	137 530 584
Traffic	5 046 439	4 488 461	19 668 583	18 122 844
Transportation	98 242 016	97 172 398	390 354 651	357 324 376
General	9 601 480	9 045 070	37 782 022	33 504 864
Total Operating Expenses	184 522 381	176 493 302	747 241 593	667 693 623

FREIGHT TRAFFIC
The economic recession of 1975 did not affect MoPac as severely as it did the railroad industry nationally. Missouri Pacific operating revenues were less than 0.2% below the all-time record level of 1974. Nationally, railroad operating revenues declined 4%. MoPac increased its share of the rail freight market in the Central-Western districts from 16.6% to 17.3%.
MoPac freight revenues increased slightly as a result of freight rate increases but revenue ton-miles declined by more than 12% from 1974. The decrease in ton-miles was due primarily to lower levels of business in several major markets served by MoPac. However, changes in traffic patterns also played a significant role in some commodity areas. For example, much of the heavy grain harvest moved only from country elevators to interior terminal elevators without the subsequent movement to Gulf ports which was experienced in 1973 and 1974. Metal ore traffic also moved shorter distances in 1975 than in previous years. Lumber revenue ton-miles declined more sharply than lumber revenue largely as a result of lower production levels along the Pacific Coast with a subsequent loss of long-haul lumber movements.
Coal traffic, both from on-line mines and coal fields in the Western United States, represents a rapidly-growing market for MoPac as the nation rushes to utilise this form of energy in the face of gas and oil shortages. MoPac coal revenue ton-miles increased 32% in 1975 while coal revenue soared more than 33% above the level of 1974.
Automobile and auto parts traffic recorded an increase of 3% in revenue ton-miles while revenues increased 13%. Chemicals, sharply depressed during the first three quarters, strengthened in the fourth quarter but still registered a decrease of 16% in revenue ton-miles and 4.6% in revenues. Food products, metal ores and aggregates, while showing declines in revenue ton-miles ranging from 5 to 17%, posted gains in revenues of from 4 to 6%.
International traffic continued to provide a significant share of revenue. Continued gains were made in traffic moving between Canada and Mexico over the Missouri Pacific single-system route between Chicago and the Texas gateways to Mexico.

ROADWAY AND EQUIPMENT
Missouri Pacific invested $104 million in capital improvements during 1975. This included the acquisition of 2 591 freight cars and 80 diesel locomotives—38 of the locomotives being leased.
Track upgrading included laying 290 miles of rail, most of it welded; insertion of 954 000 cross ties; application of 1 215 000 yds³ of ballast, and the resurfacing of 5 900 miles of track. In addition 33 new bridges totalling 3 484 lineal feet were constructed and hot box and dragging equipment detectors were installed at 23 additional locations.
The 1976 Capital Expenditure will again top $100 million. Since 1962 MoPac has invested $1 100 million in modernisation.

COFC/TOFC
MoPac increased its share of the national piggyback market in 1975, From 6.8% in 1974 to 7%. Overall, MoPac piggyback loadings declined about 16% compared to a decrease nationally of more than 19%. It should be noted, however, that MoPac expanded its piggyback base substantially in 1974 with an increase of more than 20% in trailerloadings at a time the industry as a whole was experiencing a slight decline. Traffic was stronger during the fourth quarter of 1975.
New piggyback ramps were constructed at Hesston, Kansas and Freeport, Texas. Piggyback facilities at Chicago were expanded.
The Chicago & Eastern Illinois piggyback traffic increased slightly from 1974. The C&EI benefited from additional traffic attracted through inauguration of the new run-through service between Chicago and Southeast points.
Container cargo decreased 14.9% in 1975 from 1974 due to some loss of mini-bridge traffic. Despite the decrease, the base was broadened to include many more individual shippers and receivers. This is reflected in a 32% increase in our non-mini-bridge cargo.

MISSOURI-KANSAS-TEXAS RAILROAD COMPANY
Katy Building, Dallas, Tex 75202

Chairman of Board and President: R. N. Whitman
Vice-President: B. R. Bishop
Vice-President, Sales and Service: H. T. Dimmerman
Vice-President, Secretary and Treasurer: K. R. Ziebarth
Vice-President, Operation: H. L. Gastler
Assistant to the President: F. J. Heiling
Vice-President, Marketing: T. F. Steiniger
Assistant Vice-President: W. H. Zeidel
General Counsel: W. A. Thie
Comptroller: K. R. Langford
Manager of Personnel: H. M. Hacker

Operating Department:
Vice-President, Operation: H. L. Gastler
General Manager: T. G. Todd
Assistant General Manager: M. L. Janovec
Superintendent Transportation: D. D. Doyle
Superintendent: B. R. Musick
Superintendent: R. L. Clarkson
Superintendent: M. L. Janovec
Chief Engineer: J. H. Hughes
Assistant Chief Engineer: R. N. Wagnon
Assistant Chief Engineer: O. W. Smith
Engineer, Communications and Signals: B. D. Phillips
Assistant Engineer, Communications and Signals: E. G. Bowdre
Assistant Vice-President, Mechanical: M. F. Rister
Superintendent Cars and Locomotives: D. S. Kukull
Superintendent Motive Power: P. W. Larery
Superintendent Air Equipment and Diesel Operation: M. D. Woodroof
Superintendent of Rules: J. M. O'Brien
Superintendent of Safety: W. T. Grier
Assistant to Vice-President, Operation: O. C. Putsche

Piggyback and Highway Services
(Co-ordinated & Katy Transportation Companies)
Vice-President and General Manager: W. H. Wiley
Assistant to Vice-President: G. E. Aronhalt

Purchasing Department:
Director of Purchases and Stores: J. D. Hemperley
Purchasing Agent: B. M. Gilliam

Freight Claim and Prevention:
Director of Freight Claim and Prevention: R. O. Bothun
Assistant Director, Freight Claims: L. C. Susler
Assistant Director, Damage Prevention: B. G. Shulter

LINES AND TERRITORY
The Missouri-Kansas-Texas Railroad—familiarly known as the "Katy"—operates 2 223 miles of route from Kansas City and St. Louis in the north, to Altus in western Oklahoma, and south to San Antonio and Galveston in Texas.
Principal traffic is in the movement south to port of wheat, lumber, steel products, coal and minerals and automobiles and trucks.

FINANCIAL RESULTS
1976 revenue was $101.1 million. Revenue from freight sources totalled $96.5 million. The unexpectedly sharp downturn in 4th quarter business coupled with the heavy maintenance of way and equipment programmes created a slight decline in working capital during 1976. Debt due within one year, exclusive of maturing collateral trust notes which were extended, increased about $1.2 million as a result of an USRA loan.

TRAFFIC
The M-K-T's freight revenue rose 11.7% in 1976 as compared to the year 1975. The revenue ton miles increase of 4% compared favourably with the rail industry's gain, and the 3.6% carloading increase doubled the national average. This superior result was due to the M-K-T's conscious efforts to solicit more profitable types of traffic, to make appropriate rate adjustments, to attract new industries to its lines, and to the effects of service improvements resulting from the rehabilitation of the road.
Several commodities showed substantial gains during 1976. Sorghum grains were up 21% due to heavy export demands. Crushed stone movements increased 8% due to a new limestone facility at Stonetown, Texas. The increased demand for silica sand at Ford Glass and PPG accounted for an increase of 20% in industrial sand loadings. Cement was up 48% due to the continued increase in the movement of clinkers from Longhorn, Texas. Increased home building caused a 28% rise in wood products, and heavy demand for fertiliser resulted in chemical shipments rising over 22%. Though total volume is small, higher production levels coupled with extensive marketing and pricing efforts caused a 70% increase in flat glass loadings. Other commodities such as metallic ores, plastics, glass products, fabricated metals, and scrap paper also showed slight increases. Of course, some commodities such as metal products, soybeans, corn and superphosphate showed declines, mostly as a result of reduced production or termination of contracts. Carloadings for 1976 were 257 662 compared with 248 765 for 1975, an increase of 8 897.
Coal traffic in 1976 increased 7% as a result of the location of new coal mining operations in Oklahoma. The Grand River Dam Authority announced plans to construct a large generating station at Pryor, Oklahoma, with a target date of 1981.

Line up of MoPac diesel locomotives 1976

TOFC PIGGYBACK

TOFC traffic handled by the M-K-T increased 30% in 1976. With the average revenue per trailer up 5%, net piggyback revenue rose 36% ($8 630 966). This gain is substantially higher than the national average of 13%.

LOCOMOTIVES AND CARS

Total locomotive fleet in 1976 consisted of 168 road freight units including 37 switching units. They presently have 61 GP 40, 18 GP 38, 3 U 23B, totalling 82 units or 66% of fleet hp. Fleet of freight cars totals 8 570.

DIESEL-ELECTRIC LOCOMOTIVE FLEET

Builder	Class	No. Units	hp	Total hp
EMD	Freight F-3 & F-7	3	1 500	4 500
EMD	Freight FP-7	1	1 500	1 500
EMD	Freight F-9	2	1 750	3 500
EMD	Road Switch GP-40	61	3 000	183 000
EMD	Road Switch GP-38	4	2 000	8 000
EMD	Road Switch GP-38-2	18	2 000	36 000
EMD	Road Switch GP-7	33	1 500	49 500
EMD	Switch	19	1 200	22 800
EMD	Switch	6	1 500	9 000
EMD	Switch (Slug)	1	—	—
	Total	148		317 800
GE	Road Switch U23B	3	2 250	6 750
	Total	3		6 750
Baldwin	Switch (Repowered)	8	1 000	8 000
Baldwin	Switch (Repowered)	3	1 200	3 600
	Total	11		11 600
Alco	Road Switch	6	1 500	9 000
	Total	6		9 000
	Grand Total All	168		345 150

DIESEL LOCOMOTIVES

Class	Axle Arrangement	Transmission	Rated Power hp	Max lb (kg)	Tractive Effort Continuous at lb (kg)	mph (km/h)	Max Speed mph (km/h)	Wheel Dia in (mm)	Total Weight Tons⅛	Length ft in (mm)	No. Built	Year first Built	Builders: Mechanical Parts	Builders: Engine & Type	Builders: Transmission
GP-7	Bo-Bo	Elec	1 600	63 750 (28 920)	41 000 (18 600)	12.0 (19.3)	65 (105)	40'' (1 016)	127.5	55' 11'' (17 040)	174	1950	EMD	EMD 16-567-B	EMD
GP-9	''	''	1 800	62 710 (28 450)	46 200 (20 960)	12.0 (19.3)	''	''	125.4	56' 2'' (17 200)	54	1955	''	END 16-567-C	''
GP15-1	''	''	1 500	65 270 (29 610)	46 800 (21 230)	9.3 (14.9)	''	''	130.5	54' 11'' (16 740)	60	1976	''	END 12-645-E	''
MP-15	''	''	1 500	66 700 (30 260)	46 800 (21 230)	9.6 (15.4)	''	''	133.4	47' 8'' (14 530)	25	1974	''	''	''
GP-18	''	''	1 800	64 235 (29 140)	46 200 (20 960)	12.0 (19.3)	''	''	128.5	56' 2'' (17 200)	138	1960	''	EMD 16-567D1	''
GP-28	''	''	2 000	65 825 (29 860)	51 300 (23 270)	12.0 (19.3)	''	''	131.6	56' 2'' (17 200)	2	1964	''	EMD 16-645-E	''
GP-35	''	''	2 500	64 700 (29 350)	51 300 (23 270)	12.0 (19.3)	''	''	129.4	56' 2'' (17 200)	64	1964	''	EMD 16-567D3A	''
GP-38	''	''	2 000	65 780 (29 840)	51 300 (23 270)	12.0 (19.3)	''	''	131.5	59' 2'' (18 100)	7	1965	''	EMD 16-645-E	''
GP38-2	''	''	2 000	67 240 (30 500)	51 300 (23 270)	12.0 (19.3)	''	''	134.5	59' 2'' (18 100)	149	1975	''	''	''
U23B	''	''	2 250	67 400 (30 570)	60 400 (27 400)	10.8 (17.3)	''	''	134.8	60' 2'' (18 340)	39	1973	G.E.	G.E.7 FDL-12	G.E.
U30C	Co-Co	''	3 000	98 510 (44 680)	90 600 (41 100)	9.6 (15.4)	''	''	197.0	67' 3'' (20 500)	35	1968	G.E.	G.E.7 FDL-16	G.E.
SD40	''	''	3 000	98 130 (44 510)	77 000 (34 930)	12.0 (19.3)	''	''	196.2	65' 8'' (20 050)	90	1967	EMD	EMD16-645E3	EMD
SD40-2	''	''	3 000	98 100 (44 500)	77 000 (34 930)	12.0 (19.3)	''	''	196.2	68' 10'' (20 980)	146	1973	''	''	''
SW7	Bo-Bo	''	1 200	62 025 (28 130)	36 000 (16 330)	9.0 (14.5)	55 (88.5)	''	124.0	44' 5'' (13 540)	9	1950	''	EMD12-567-A	''
SW8	''	''	900	58 500 (26 540)	24 640 (11 180)	9.0 (14.5)	''	''	117.0	''	8	1952	''	EMD8-567-B	''
SW9	''	''	1 200	62 390 (28 300)	36 000 (16 330)	9.0 (14.5)	''	''	124.8	''	36	1951	''	EMD12-567-B	''
SW12	''	''	1 200	62 390 (28 300)	36 000 (16 330)	9.0 (14.5)	''	''	124.8	''	139	1954	''	EMD12-567-E	''
SW15	''	''	1 500	65 290 (29 620)	43 000 (19 500)	10.7 (17.2)	''	''	130.6	44' 8'' (13 700)	4	1972	''	EMD12-645-E	''

*Weight shown in Short Tons

NORFOLK AND WESTERN RAILWAY COMPANY
8 North Jefferson St, Roanoke, Virginia 24042

President and Chief Executive Officer: John P. Fishwick
Executive Vice-President: Robert B. Claytor
Senior Vice-President: Richard F. Dunlap
Vice-President, Finance: John R. Turbyfill
Vice-President, Merchandise Traffic: John R. McMichael
Vice-President, Coal and Ore Traffic: T. C. Hamill
Vice-President, Law: John S. Shannon
Vice-President, Administration: Joseph R. Neikirk
Vice-President, Public Affairs: Walter S. Clement
Vice-President, Taxation: D. L. Kiley
Vice-President, Material Management: E. G. Gentsch
Secretary: Donald A. Middleton
Vice-President and Comptroller: Jean Jones
Treasurer: John M. Fricke
Director, Public Relations and Advertising: Lewis M. Phelps
Chief Engineer: L. A. Durham, Jr
Assistant Chief Engineer: P. P. Dunavant, Jr
Assistant Chief Engineer, S and C: J. E. Hartfield
Assistant Chief Engineer, Maintenance: Don E. Turney, Jr
General Manager, Transportation: Leon Atkinson, Jr
General Manager, Motive Power and Equipment: H. L. Scott, Jr
General Manager, Safety: G. W. Gearhart

The Norfolk and Western Railway, with a predecessor dating back to 1838, was organised under its present name in 1896, after another predecessor had opened the rich coal fields of western Virginia and southern West Virginia. By the early 1900's, it was a six-state system with a main line connecting Norfolk, Va. and Cincinnati-Columbus, Ohio. The road has paid dividends on its common stock each year since 1901.

The first of all modern mergers between independent rail lines was consummated 1 December 1959, when the Virginian Railway, also connecting the coal fields with Norfolk, became part of the NW.

A project which took over four years was realised on 16 October 1964, when the largest completed railroad consolidation in history became operative. The new 7 800 mile *(12 550 km)* 14-state NW system was created through merger with the Nickel Plate Road, lease and planned purchase of the Wabash Railroad, purchase of the Columbus-Sandusky line of the Pennsylvania Railroad, and acquisition of the Akron, Canton and Youngstown and the Pittsburgh and West Virginia roads. Operation of the NW system was integrated with headquarters in Roanoke, Va.

The new Jersey, Indiana and Illinois Railroad and the Lake Erie and Fort Wayne Railroad are also part of the NW System.

LINES AND TERRITORIES
The Norfolk and Western operates from Norfolk Va. and Buffalo, N.Y., in the east, through 14 states and one province of Canada, to St. Louis, Kansas City and Omaha, Neb., in the west. The NW system, which spans 7 659 miles *(12 325 km)* with a route length of 14 858 miles *(23 910 km)* serves the rich coal fields of West Virginia, southern Ohio and eastern Kentucky, as well as the industrial centres of Cleveland, Pittsburg, Chicago, Detroit, Columbus and Cincinnati.

FINANCIAL RESULTS
Railway operating revenues for 1976 totalled $1 200 million. Railway operating expenses grew to $845.0 million, from the 1975 level of $765.3 million.

FREIGHT TRAFFIC
Merchandise traffic levels rebounded in 1976 from the depressed levels of 1975, rising 3.1 per cent to 62.4 million tons from 60.5 million tons a year earlier. Rate increases approved by the Interstate Commerce Commission effective in April and October helped boost merchandise revenues by 16.2 per cent in 1976 to $601.6 million from $517.8 million in 1975.

For the second year running, coal traffic fell disappointingly short of expectations. NW originated on its own lines slightly less coal in 1976 than the year before, and coal received from connections dropped more than 21 per cent. While the long-term outlook for coal remains bright, continued lack of a clear-cut national energy policy, coupled with conflicts between environmental and energy interests, has inhibited expansion of coal use in this country.

During 1976, a total of 12 new or reactivated mines began operations on NW lines. When these mines reach full production, they are expected to produce about 5.2 million tons of coal annually. An additional 10 new mines and a number of reactivated operations will begin in 1977, adding another 7.7 million tons annually when they reach full production levels.

TOFC/COFC Ramps

Illinois	Iowa	Ohio	Virginia
Chicago (Calumet)	Des Moines	Bellevue	Bristol
Danville	**Michigan**	Brewster	Norfolk
Decatur	Adrian	Cincinnati	Roanoke
Peoria	Detroit	Cleveland	**Canada**
Indiana	**Missouri**	Columbus	Welland, Ont.
Fort Wayne	Kansas City	Lima	
Lafayette	Moberly	Montpelier	
Marion	St. Louis	Toledo	
Muncie	**New York**		
	Buffalo		
	North Carolina		
	Winston-Salem		

PENN CENTRAL TRANSPORTATION COMPANY
Six, Penn Center Plaza, Philadelphia, Pa 19104

This company is now included in the ConRail system.

READING RAILWAY COMPANY
Reading Terminal, Philadelphia, Pa 19107

This company is now included in the ConRail system.

RICHMOND, FREDERICKSBURG AND POTOMAC
Broad Street Station, Richmond Va. 23220

President: Stuart Shumate
Vice-President, Administration: John J. Newbauer, Jr
Director of Real Estate and Marketing: Richard L. Beadles
Director of Personnel: Thomas B. Choate
Comptroller: Frank A. Crovo, Jr
General Superintendent Transportation: James D. Doswell
General Counsel: Urchie B. Ellis
Chief Engineer: James C. Hobbs
Chief Mechanical Officer: Hartwell T. Rainey, Jr
General Traffic Manager: Rupert H. Rose
Chief Medical Director: Adney K. Sutphin, MD
Treasurer: Eugene A. Byrd
Corporate Secretary and Assistant Treasurer: Edward A. Wallace
Assistant Secretary: Carolyn K. Fleming

LINES AND TERRITORIES
The RF & P is an important "bridge", 113 miles *(182 km)* long from Washington DC in the north to Richmond, Virginia in the south.
At Washington it connects to the B & O and Penn Central, and at Richmond to the Seaboard Coast Line.

FINANCIAL RESULTS

	1975	1974	1973
Operating revenues	$28 558 677	$32 262 050	$28 079 512
Operating expenses	$16 581 269	$17 679 634	$15 869 066
Operating ratio (per cent)	58.06	54.80	56.51
Freight revenue	$26 467 349	$29 607 886	$26 021 115
Revenue freight tonnage	9 695 000	12 212 000	12 185 000

FREIGHT TRAFFIC
The recessionary nature of the economy was fully evident in the transportation of freight traffic. Sharp decreases in all principal commodity categories, which began in 1974, continued well into the third quarter of 1975 before there were some signs that the bottom had possibly been reached. There were a few indications during the last quarter of slight improvement in comparison with the traffic declines experienced in the earlier months. Encouragingly, by year end several principal commodities, including paper products, trailer-on-flatcar traffic and food and kindred products, were showing signs of return to previous years' levels. Nevertheless, as result of the heavy monthly traffic declines during the majority of the year, total loaded cars handled in 1975 decreased 22% and revenue freight tonnage was down 21%.

Even with the rate increases, freight revenue of $26 467 349 in 1975 was 11% below the prior year due to the significant decline in traffic volume.

	1975	1974	1973
Revenue ton miles (thousands)	956 034	1 194 130	1 200 803
Revenue per ton mile	2.77¢	2.48¢	2.17¢
Total loaded cars	220 947	282 371	291 875

LOCOMOTIVES AND CARS
The Company has 40 diesel-electric locomotives—26 line haul and 14 shunting. Freight train cars total is 1 708.

During 1975 the Company purchased 50 new 100-ton gondola cars; purchased 12 vehicles for automotive fleet to replace older and less efficient equipment and 8 new machines for improving production in the track maintenance programme.

BUSINESS
The nationwide downturn in business activity which was in evidence during the last quarter of 1974 continued at a severely depressed level generally throughout the year 1975. It was a year which saw a higher than usual number of production plants shutting down or drastically curtailing operations for extended periods of time due to lack of orders. Unemployment was a national concern. At the same time, costs of doing business, particularly wages, were moving upward.

The effects of the significant retrenchment on the part of the economy, together with inflation in labour and material costs, are reflected in the Company's financial resuts for the year. Consolidated earnings of RF&P and its wholly-owned subsidiary, Richmond Land Corporation, in 1975 amounted to $7 185 210, or $19.95 per share, down 14% from the $23.12 per share recorded in the prior year. (Richmond Land Corporation is the surviving company of the merger on September 1, 1975, primarily for administrative purposes, of the three separate and wholly-owned subsidiaries—Richmond Land Corporation, Richmond Holding Corporation and South Washington Land Corporation).

Railway operating revenues were $28 558 677, some $3.7 million, or 11%, below 1974. Practically the entire decrease was in freight revenues, reflecting the 21% reduction in revenue tonnage handled in 1975, partially offset by various freight rate increases authorised during the year.

OTHER DEVELOPMENTS
During 1975 the computer capabilities at Potomac yard were improved—old equipment was replaced by two new Model 151 NCR computers. Also at this yard 69 sodium vapor lamps replaced the 101 incandescent type lights in the floodlight towers, providing improved lighting at reduced electrical and maintenance costs.

SEABOARD COAST LINE INDUSTRIES INC.
THE FAMILY LINES SYSTEM
500 Water Street, Jacksonville, Fla 32202

Chairman of the Board and Chief Executive Officer, Richmond, Va: W. Thomas Rice
President and Chief Operating and Administrative Officer, Jacksonville, Fla: Prime F. Osborn
Executive Vice-President, Jacksonville, Fla: David C. Hastings
Vice-President, Management Information Services, Jacksonville, Fla: Samuel A. Alward
Vice-President and Treasurer, Richmond, Va: Leonard G. Anderson
Vice-President, Sales, Jacksonville, Fla: James D. Bozard
Vice-President, Operations, Jacksonville, Fla: James B. Clark
Vice-President, Phosphate and Paper Products, Jacksonville, Fla: Aubrey M. Daniel
Vice-President, Staff, Jacksonville, Fla: Nelson S. DeMuth
Vice-President, Passenger Traffic, Richmond, Va: James R. Getty
Vice-President, Marketing, Jacksonville, Fla: James W. Hoeland
Vice-President, Industrial Development, Jacksonville, Fla: J. Ross LeGrand
Vice-President, Freight Traffic, Louisville, Ky: Douglas McKellar
Vice-President and Secretary, Richmond, Va: Robert E. Northrup
Resident Vice-President, Atlanta, Ga: Hershel W. Parmer
Vice-President and Comptroller, Jacksonville, Fla: Josiah A. Stanley, Jr
Vice-President, Law, Jacksonville, Fla: John W. Weldon
General Counsel, Richmond, Va: Richard A. Hollander
Assistant Vice-President, Personnel and Labour Relations, Jacksonville, Fla: William B. Seymour

1968 was the first full year of operation of this railroad, formed by merger of the Seaboard Air Line Railroad Company (with head office at Richmond, Virginia) and the Atlantic Coast Line Railroad Company (with head office at Jacksonville, Florida).
SCL maintains two general offices, with the Chairman of the Board at 3600 West Broad Street, Richmond, Virginia 23213 and the President at 500 Water Street, Jacksonville, Fla. 32202.
SCL owns the Louisville and Nashville Railroad (into which the Monon was merged in July 1971); has a holding in the RF & P, and leases, equally with L & N, the Clinchfield and Georgia Railroads.
L & N continues to operate as a separate company. Operating results are consolidated, and reproduced under Seaboard Coast Line Railroad Company, including subsidiaries Clinchfield Railroad Company and Georgia Railroad Company.
Combining the SCL and L & N, with their subsidiary Rail Carriers, has created a system of some 16 500 miles, serving 13 states. Together they are known as The Family Lines.

LINES AND TERRITORIES
With 9 300 miles of route, SCL constitutes the major railway system in Florida and in the coastal states to the north of Florida ie. Georgia, South and North Carolina, as well as Virginia and Alabama; and through the L & N lines to Tennessee, Kentucky, Indiana and Illinois (Chicago).
The Northern headquarters at Richmond Va. connect to the RF & P and the North East Corridor to Washington and New York.

FINANCIAL RESULTS
Total operating revenues for the company were 5·2% lower than they were in the previous year.

	1974 ('000$)	1975 ('000$)
Transportation Operating Revenues	$1 357 090	$1 290 777
Transportation Expenses		
Transportation	519 545	508 322
Maintenance of way and structures	176 436	171 549
Maintenance of equipment	223 542	224 651
Traffic, general and other	77 418	77 223
Total operating expenses	996 941	981 745
Taxes other than income	115 789	115 003
Long-term equipment lease rentals	42 508	50 089
Other equipment and joint facility rents	35 739	33 480
Total transportation expenses	1 190 977	1 180 317

FREIGHT TRAFFIC
With the exception of construction materials, there is now a very gradual improvement in practically all freight categories. Carloadings of coal, paper, automobiles, chemicals, foodstuffs and grain have increased—some not so much as others—but the improvement is apparent in all. Confidence in the advancement of the company's financial stability in 1976 is based largely on the essentiality of several commodities hauled in great quantities. Two of the most important are coal and phosphate.
On the Family Lines, coal traffic is the most important. In 1975, more coal was hauled than in any previous year. The companies together moved a total of nearly 90 million tons, with revenues of $246.5 million. Demand for high-quality, low-sulphur coal—available in abundance on both the L & N and Clinchfield—continues to increase. The outlook is especially bright, both for the short range and the long term.

Seaboard is optimistic about the future of the phosphate industry. Along its lines in Florida, that industry is committed to an investment of about 500 million dollars for enlarging its capability. The Company is confident that the long-range demand for fertiliser will continue to grow, for America's pre-eminence as a major supplier of grain for the world should continue unabated, and other applications of fertiliser will remain high.
Because of reduced traffic volume, some of the long-range capital improvement programmes have been delayed where the decline in business level had reduced the urgent necessity for early completion.

LOCOMOTIVES AND CARS
SCL owns 2 268 road locomotive units and 407 switchers for a total fleet of 2 675. During 1972, 144 new road and switcher diesel locomotives were placed in service along with 18 MATE (Motors for Additional Tractive Effort) units.
The railway owns 140 000 freight cars. New cars put into service during 1972 totalled 2 018, including 50 automobile racks and 20 Vert-A-Pac automobile cars.
During 1975 40 new locomotives were acquired and 5 500 new and rebuilt freight cars; 3 100 were coal hoppers. All equipment obtained by the company involved a capital expenditure of approximately $135 million.

TOFC/COFC PIGGYBACK
Piggyback trailer loads were down 20·7% and revenues were off 17·0%. However, the company has faith in the continuing growth of long-term piggyback traffic.

OTHER DEVELOPMENTS
Some of the more notable improvements to the physical plant of the Family Lines accomplished in 1975 included:
installation of microwave communication along 168 additional miles of the System. This modern and efficient way of handling communication has now been installed over a total of 382 miles of Family Lines routes:
completion of three major bridges—one near Franklinton, NC, another near Georgiana, Alabama, and a third near Grandy, Va:
opening of a new transportation centre at Atlanta—locating in one facility the operating and sales functions of the five railroads which comprise the Family Lines. More than 200 employees—formerly housed in nine different locations—staff the facility; similar facilities have been put into use at Evansville, Ind:
yard improvements, including completion of expansion of Baldwin Yard, near Jacksonville:
continued construction work on the classification yards at Louisville and at Waycross, Georgia.

SCL Ramps
Alabama. Birmingham, Dothan, Elba, Enterprise, Montgomery.
Florida. Arcadia, Auburndale, Avon Park, Bartow, Bell, Bradenton, Brooksville, Clearwater, Clewiston, Dade City, Duda, Fort Lauderdale, Forest City, Fort Myers, Gainesville, Groveland, Haines City, High Springs, Homestead, Immokalee, Jacksonville, Jasper, Lakeland, Lake Wales, Leesburg, Live Oak, Miami, Ocala, Orlando, Oviedo, Palatka, Plant City, Plymouth, Pompano Beach, St. Petersburg, Sanford, Sarasota, Tallahassee, Tampa, Trenton, Umatilla, West Palm Beach, Winter Garden, Winter Haven, Yulee.
Georgia. Albany, Americus, Athens, Atlanta, Augusta, Bainbridge, Brunswick, Cedartown, Columbus, Cordele, Fitzgerald, Gainsville, Jesup, LaGrange, Macon, Manchester, Moultrie, Oglethorpe, Savannah, Thomasville, Tifton, Tucker, Valdosta, Vidalia, Waycross, Woodbine.
North Carolina. Aberdeen, Ahoskie, Charlotte, Durham, Fayetteville, Goldsboro, Greenville, Hamlet, Henderson, Jacksonville, Lumberton, Maxton, Raleigh, Rocky Mount, Roanoke Rapids, Smithfield, Wilmington, Wilson.
South Carolina. Anderson, Barnwell, Camden, Charleston, Chester, Columbia, Conway, Denmark, Estill, Florence, Georgetown, Greenville, Greenwood, Hampton, Inness, Lobeco, Orangeburg, Port Royal, Spartanburg, Stono, Sumter.
Virginia. Franklin, Jarratt, Portsmouth (Norfolk), Petersburg, Richmond, Suffolk.

L & N Ramps
Alabama. Anniston, Birmingham Bridgeport, Florence, Gadsden, Decatur, Huntsville, Mobile, Montgomery, Bylacanga, Tuscaloosa.
Florida. Chipley, Pensacola.
Georgia. Atlanta, Cartersville, Dalton, Ringgold, Tate.
Illinois. Chicago, Danville, Dalton, E. St. Louis.
Indiana. Bloomington, Crawfordsville, Evansville, Hammond (Chicago and District), Indianapolis, Lafayette, Terre Haute.
Kentucky. Bardstown, Bowling Green, Frankfort, Franklin, Glasgow, Hawesville (Stillman Yard), Hopkinsville, Lexington, Louisville, Owensboro, Paducah, Richmond, Williamsburg.
Louisianna. New Orleans.
Mississippi. Gulfport, Pascagoula.
Ohio. Cincinnati.
Tennessee. Alcoa, Athens, Bruceton, Calhoun, Chattanooga, Clarkesville, Columbia, Cookeville, Crossville, Fayetteville, Humboldt, Jackson, Knoxville, Lawrenceburg, Lebanon, Lewisburg, Lexington, Memphis, Morrison, Murfreesburg, Nashville, New Johnsonville, Oak Ridge, Old Hickory, Paris, Pulaski, Sparta, Springfield, Tallahoma.

SOO LINE RAILROAD

500 Line Building, Minneapolis, Minn 55440

Executive:
President: Leonard H. Murray
Executive Vice-President: Thomas R. Klingel
Vice-President, Staff and Secretary: Thomas M. Beckley
Vice-President and General Counsel: Fordyce W. Crouch
Vice-President, Traffic: Ray H. Smith
Vice-President, Accounting: Richard L. Marlowski
Assistant to the President: C. H. Chlay
Director of Industrial Engineering: Lloyd L. Wasnick
Director of Corporate Planning: George W. Guthrie
Manager of Employment: Paul H. Pfeiffer
Director of Real Estate: George T. Bergren
Manager Highway Vehicles: Arthur C. Bahls
Director of Personnel: Donald L. Borchert
Treasurer: Rollin J. Baker

Operations and Maintenance:
Executive Vice-President: Thomas R. Klingel
Assistant Vice-President, Transportation Group: Gilbert A. Gillette
Assistant Vice-President, Maintenance Group: Lloyd L. Waswick
Assistant Vice-President, Operations: Kent P. Shoemaker

Transportation Department:
General Manager, Transportation: Gilbert A. Gillette
Assistant to the General Manager, Transportation: Harry A. Peterson
Director of Transportation Operations: George W. Carr
Director of Transportation Administration: Donald L. Hart
Director of Transportation Equipment: Thomas Kopriva
Director of Transportation Planning: Joseph D. Darling
Division Superintendent, Stevens Point, Wis: Harry W. Ellefson
Division Superintendent, Enderlin, ND: Douglas F. Kemmer
Division Superintendent, Minneapolis, Minn: Edward A. Hamerski

Mechanical Department:
Chief Mechanical Officer: Thomas F. Kearney
Manager, Fond Du Lac Shops: Edward W. Beyer
Manager, Shoreham Shops: Eugene H. Henkel
Assistant to Chief Mechanical Engineer: Wayne O. Ayers

Engineering Department:
Chief Engineer: Bert E. Pearson
Assistant Chief Engineer: Bernard R. Prusak
Assistant Chief Engineer, Bridges and Structures: Donald I. Kjellman
Assistant Chief Engineer, Signals and Communications: James H. Tone
Assistant Chief Engineer, Maintenance of Way: Warren B. Peterson
Assistant Chief Engineer, Staff: Raymond C. Postels
Regional Engineer, Stevens Point: John P. Gannon
Regional Engineer, Minneapolis: William J. Egan

Law and Claims Department:
Vice-President and General Counsel: Fordyce W. Crouch
General Solicitor: Robert G. Gehrz
General Attorney: C. Harold Peterson
Attorney: Patrick J. McPartland
Attorney: Wayne C. Serkland
General Claim Attorney: Ernest A. Jensen
General Freight Claim Agent: Herbert F. Schumacher

Data Systems Department:
Director, Data Systems: Robert R. Dickinson

Purchasing Department:
Manager, Purchasing and Materials: Thomas C. Roth

Traffic Department:
Vice-President, Traffic: Ray H. Smith
Assistant Vice-President, Traffic: James T. Hartnett

Sales and Service:
General Freight Traffic Manager, System: Douglas T. Walen

Pricing and Market Development:
General Freight Traffic Manager: Charles H. Clay

Intermodal Services:
Director, Intermodal Services: James A. Welton

FINANCIAL RESULTS

Increased traffic in 1976, higher freight rates and control of expenses produced record revenues and the second highest net income in the Company's history.

REVENUES

Railway revenues increased by $28.1 million to $189.3 million. Revenues were higher for most major groups of commodities handled except farm products, which decreased $2.4 million or 7 per cent. Revenues from the lumber and wood products group increased 42 per cent or $8.3 million. Chemicals were up 33 per cent or $9.4 million and pulp and paper revenues increased 20 per cent or $3.9 million.
Potash, of the chemical group, was again the largest revenue producer, bringing in revenues of $28 million. Lumber shipments came back strongly due to increased construction activity and produced revenues of $17.4 million.

100-ton covered hoppers received in 1973
Part of Soo's fleet of nearly 1 800 jumbo hoppers used extensively for grain and other bulk loading demands.

Freight rate increases of 7 per cent and 5 per cent were approved by the Interstate Commerce Commission during the year. These increases could not be applied on all traffic, however, because of competitive conditions and certain exemptions specified by the Commission. The Commission also approved a further increase of 4 per cent effective 7 January 1977.

EXPENSES

Total railway expenses increased $22 million because of increased traffic volume, an expanded track maintenance programme and higher material prices, wage rates and payroll taxes. The vital transportation ratio decreased from 35.3 per cent to 33.6 per cent. The ratio of total working expenses to revenues decreased from 92.0 per cent to 90.4 per cent principally due to improved productivity and increased traffic volume. Approximately 50 per cent of every dollar of operating revenue was paid for wages, fringe benefits and payroll taxes. Soo's payroll of $76 million in 1976 was up 11 per cent from 1975 with increased wage rates accounting for approximately 9 per cent of this increase. Payroll taxes increased 17 per cent. Total hours paid for increased 1 per cent compared with the increase in revenue freight ton-miles of 11 per cent.

MAINTENANCE OF TRACK AND EQUIPMENT

Expenditures for maintenance of way and structures increased $5.4 million over 1975 to $32.4 million. 273 000 new crossties were installed compared to 207 000 in 1975. 409 000 yd³ of crushed rock ballast were applied on approximately 235 miles of track compared to 424 000 yd³ applied on approximately 242 miles of track in 1975. New rail relays increased to 49 miles from 25 miles. Second hand relays amounted to 22 miles compared to 9 miles the previous year. The maintenance of way ratio, the per cent of railway revenues spent for maintenance of fixed facilities, was 17.1 per cent compared to 16.7 per cent in 1975.
The maintenance of equipment ratio for 1976 was 11.9 per cent compared to 12.1 per cent in 1975. Total expenditures for maintenance of equipment were up $3.1 million, however, because of increased traffic and higher costs.
At the end of the year, 13 per cent of Soo's revenue freight cars were undergoing repairs or awaiting repairs. This number included approximately 600 cars which have now been sold for scrap. During the year a substantial number of serviceable freight cars were in storage from time to time due to lack of demand for rail transportation and cars not required for immediate service were not repaired. Because of anticipated increased traffic in 1977, an accelerated car repair programme has now been initiated.

CAPITAL AND OTHER IMPROVEMENT PROGRAMMES

Soo took delivery during 1976 of 700 new freight cars having a value of $19.7 million. The new equipment included 100 cars ordered in 1975 and delivered in 1976 along with an additional 600 cars approved for acquisition during the year by the Board of Directors. Acquired during the year were 300, 100-ton covered hoppers, 200 high side gondolas, 100 insulated box cars built by Soo employees in the Fond du Lac shops and 100, 100-ton open top hopper cars.
Industrial expansion along the Soo in 1976 included location of 37 new industries on line. An additional 25 industries already on line expanded their facilities. The new industries include a metal fabricating plant, a fertiliser warehouse, and a farm service center.

FINANCIAL

Working capital increased 23 per cent in 1976 to $34.7 million. The current ratio at year end of 1.72 to 1 was unchanged from 1975. During the year, the Company sold $13.9 million in equipment trust certificates to finance the purchase of 600 freight cars.
The Minneapolis, St Paul & Sault Ste. Marie First Mortgage Refunding Loan in the amount of $5 655 000 was refinanced in January 1977. The loan matures on 1 January 1980, and bears an interest rate of one half of one per cent over the prime rate.
The number of times fixed charges were earned before income taxes increased from 4.7 in 1975 to 5.8 in 1976. The times fixed and contingent charges were earned before income taxes was 3.7 in 1975 and 4.6 in 1976. Return on stockholders' equity was 10.5 per cent in 1975.

SOUTHERN RAILWAY SYSTEM
920 15th Street, NW, Washington DC 20005

List of Officers:
President and Chief Executive: L. S. Crane
Executive Vice-President, Marketing and Planning: R. S. Hamilton
Executive Vice-President, Administration: G. S. Paul
Senior Vice-President, Operations: H. H. Hall
Senior Vice-President, Law & Accounting: A. B. McKinnon

Marketing and Planning:
Executive Vice-President, Marketing and Planning: R. S. Hamilton
Vice-President, Marketing: E. G. Kreyling Jr
Assistant Vice-President, Market Management: E. A. Evers
Vice-President, Sales: E. L. Dearhart
Assistant Vice-President, Agri-Business Service: J. P. Duncan, Jr
Assistant Vice-President, Industrial Development: R. S. Geer
Assistant Vice-President, Corporate Planning: P. D. Dieffenbach
General Manager, Services Industries: N. G. Heller

Law and Accounting:
Senior Vice-President, Law and Accounting: A. B. McKinnon
Vice-President and Comptroller: D. R. McArdle
Vice-President and Chief Financial Officer: K. A. Stoecker
Assistant Vice-President and Treasurer: G. M. Williams
Assistant Vice-President, Taxation: W. G. Handfield
Vice-President, Law: J. L. Tapley
Secretary: M. M. Davenport
Vice-President, Public Affairs: E. T. Breathitt
Vice-President, Real Estate and Insurance: W. D. McLean

Administration:
Executive Vice-President, Administration: G. S. Paul
Vice-President, Management Information Services: J. L. Jones
Assistant Vice-President, Labour Relations: R. E. Loomis
Assistant Vice-President, Personnel Administration: R. D. Hedberg
Assistant Vice-President, Public Relations and Advertising: W. F. Geeslin
Assistant Vice-President, Purchasing and Materials Management: N. B. Coggons, Jr
General Manager, Passenger Sales and Services: L. G. Sak

Operations:
Senior Vice-President, Operations: H. H. Hall
Vice-President, Transportation: H. H. Bradley
General Manager, Eastern Lines: H. R. Moore
General Manager, Western Lines: E. B. Burwell
General Manager, Intermodal Transportation Services: B. R. Osborne
Assistant Vice-President, Transportation Planning: J. R. Martin
Assistant Vice-President, Police and Special Services: J. O. Greenwood
Assistant Vice-Preisdent, Safety and Freight Claim Prevention: F. M. Kaylor
Vice-President, Engineering: W. W. Simpson
Assistant Vice-Prrsident, Engineering and Research: C. E. Webb
Assistant Vice-President, Mechanical: J. G. Moore
Assistant Vice-President, Communications and Signals: J. T. Hudson
Assistant Vice-President, MW and S: H. L. Rose
Assistant Vice-President, Stations and Terminals: J. R. Tipton

The consolidated figures for Southern Railway Company include many subsidiaries. There are four class 1 subsidiary railroads:—
Alabama Great Southern
Cincinnati, New Orleans and Texas Pacific
Norfolk Southern
Georgia Southern and Florida
Central of Georgia
and there are several Class II railroads and terminals and other companies—railroads, terminals, motor transport, pipelines and real estates.
Other companies in which SR have some ownership are treated as investments income.

LINES AND TERRITORY
The Southern Railways operates 10 494 miles of route and a total track length of 17 282 miles.
Northern limits are St. Louis, Cincinnati, and Washington, and operation is mainly in the States of Kentucky, Tennessee, Virginia, North Carolina, South Carolina, Alabama and Georgia.

COMPOSITION OF THE SYSTEM
The Southern Railway system comprises the following companies:—
Class I
The Alabama Great Southern Railroad Company
Central of Georgia Railroad Company
The Cincinnati, New Orleans and Texas Pacific Railway Company
Georgia Southern and Florida Railway Company
Norfolk Southern Railway Company
Class II
Atlantic and East Carolina Railway Company
Birmingham Terminal Company (67%)
Camp Lejeune Railroad Company
The Georgia Northern Railway Company
Interstate Railroad Company
Live Oak, Perry and South Georgia Railway Company
Louisiana Southern Railway Company
New Orleans Terminal Company
St. Johns River Terminal Company
State University Railroad Company (54%)
Tennessee, Alabama & Georgia Railway Company
Tennessee Railway Company

FINANCIAL RESULTS
In revenues and earnings 1976 was the best year, in the Company's history. Capital improvements continued at a historically high rate and industrial development along the System's lines maintained near record levels.

	1976	1975
Railway operating revenues:		
Freight	$1 002 186	$839 651
Demurrage	10 484	8 976
Passenger	5 566	5 484
Other	9 756	9 579
	1 027 992	863 690
Other income:		
Interest	7 175	7 507
Gain on sale of properties	5 120	5 662
Other	12 498	9 799
Total income	1 052 785	886 658

Piggyback Traffic
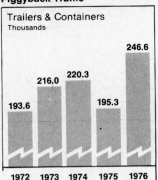
Trailers & Containers
Thousands
193.6 (1972) 216.0 (1973) 220.3 (1974) 195.3 (1975) 246.6 (1976)

Freight Revenue
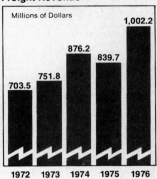
Millions of Dollars
703.5 (1972) 751.8 (1973) 876.2 (1974) 839.7 (1975) 1,002.2 (1976)

Revenue
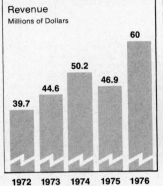
Millions of Dollars
39.7 (1972) 44.6 (1973) 50.2 (1974) 46.9 (1975) 60 (1976)

Revenue Ton Miles
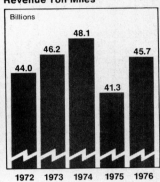
Billions
44.0 (1972) 46.2 (1973) 48.1 (1974) 41.3 (1975) 45.7 (1976)

Capital Expenditures
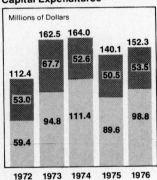
Millions of Dollars
1972: 112.4 (Road Property 53.0, Equipment 59.4)
1973: 162.5 (67.7, 94.8)
1974: 164.0 (52.6, 111.4)
1975: 140.1 (50.5, 89.6)
1976: 152.3 (53.5, 98.8)
Road Property
Equipment

1976 Freight Revenue (Quarters)
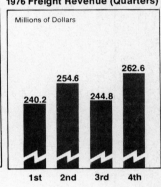
Millions of Dollars
240.2 (1st) 254.6 (2nd) 244.8 (3rd) 262.6 (4th)

	1976	1975
Railway operating expenses:		
Maintenance of way and structures	175 185	138 449
Maintenance of equipment	177 977	141 237
Transportation	325 997	286 731
Other	66 504	56 250
	745 663	622 667
State and local taxes, principally property	24 965	25 245
Payroll taxes	55 712	45 979
Net freight car rent (income) based on time and mileage	(14 817)	(12 836)
Other equipment rent expense	40 314	30 748
Joint facility rent expense	1 012	771
Miscellaneous deductions from income	7 373	4 821
Fixed charges, principally interest	54 383	49 629
Total expenses	914 605	767 024
Income before income taxes	138 180	119 634
Federal and state income taxes:		
Current	25 754	18 267
Deferred	23 185	23 042
Total income taxes	48 939	41 309
Net consolidated income for the year	$89 241	$78 325
Per average share of common stock outstanding	$5.85	$5.12

Certain 1975 data have been changed for comparability

FREIGHT TRAFFIC

Run-through trains operated by Southern in conjunction with other railroads, using pooled motive power and avoiding intermediate yards and the terminals interchange of freight wagons, continued to increase the speed and efficiency of through freight service during the year.

The usefulness of Southern's unit coal trains is clearly reflected in the growing volume of coal traffic and revenues. Eleven such trains are now shuttling between mines, steel mills and power-generating plants and a number of others are in the planning stages. Total freight ton-miles was 41 339 978 000 during 1975 (48 058 484 000 in the record year of 1974).

CAPITAL EXPENDITURE

Souther System's expenditures for capital improvements in 1976 amounted to $152.3 million, up by $12.2 million or 8.7% from 1975. Expenditures by category were as follows:

	1976	1975
	(Thousands)	
Equipment	$ 98 779	$ 89 610
Roadway	53 533	50 507
	$152 312	$140 117

Total capital expenditures over the last ten years have amounted to $1 300 million—$900 million for equipment and the remaining $400 million for roadway improvements. These high levels of expenditures serve to keep Southern's physical plant strong and efficient and the fleet of locomotives and freight cars among the most modern in the country.

LOCOMOTIVES AND CARS

Total Southern System locomotive fleet at the end of 1975 consisted of 1 160 line haul diesel-electric locomotives and 193 switchers—a total of 1 353 units.
The railroad placed in service 20 new diesel locomotives in 1975.
The railroad has a total of 75 855 freight train cars and a total of 167 passenger cars.

TOFC-COFC

Intermodal traffic handled during 1976 was 246 636 up from 199 304 in 1975
Containers and trailers are handled at the following points:

Direct freight train services: Run-through freight train service using pooled locomotive power of the participating railroads and by-passing intermediate terminals of part of a growing pattern in providing better and faster service for Southern's customers.

SOUTHERN PACIFIC COMPANY

Southern Pacific Building
One Market Plaza, San Francisco, Cal 94105

Chairman, President and Chief Executive Officer: B. F. Biaggini
President, Southern Pacific Transportation Co: D. K. McNear
Executive Vice, President-Traffic: F. E. Kriebel
Executive Vice, President-Finance: R. J. McLean
Executive Vice, President-Law: A. C. Furth
Vice-President, Operations: R. L. King
Vice-President: A. D. DeMoss
Vice-President, Industrial Relations: W. R. Denton
Vice-President, Engineering and Research: W. M.Jaekle
Vice-President: L. E. Hoyt
Vice-President, Sales: R. C. Hudson
Vice-President, Management Services: J. W. Germany
Vice-President and Controller: D. L. Praeger
Vice-President, Public Relations: J. G. Shea
Secretary: A. E. Hill
Assistant Vice-President and Treasurer: B. G. McPhee
General Purchasing Manager: D. K. Rose
Assistant Vice-President and General Manager, Intermodal Traffic Department: T. A. Fante
Chief Mechanical Officer: W. O. Brown
Assistant Vice-President, Research: P. V. Garin
Chief Engineer: W. J. Jones

LINES AND TERRITORY

Southern Pacific operates 13 483 miles *(21 761 km)* of railway route in the west and southwest and is one of the largest systems in the US. Additional main track is 1 076 miles *(1 513 km)*; yards and sidings 6 641 miles *(10 548 km)* for a total of 21 170 miles *(34 016 km)* of single track.
Western Lines run from San Francisco north to Portland, Oregon, east to Ogden, Utah, and south to Los Angeles.
From Los Angeles the line runs east, roughly parallel to the Mexican border, through Phoenix and El Paso where it connects to a line northeast to Tucumcari in New Mexico making connections to Kansas City and Chicago, East from El Paso the line—known as the Sunset Route—continues to Galveston, New Orleans and to Fort Worth and Dallas—which are also important traffic feed points.
The Northwestern Pacific Railroad Company is operated as part of the overall Southern Pacific Organisation.
SP highway truck service follows roughly the route of the railway lines—a system of 27 048 route miles *(43 253 km)*.
Pacific Motor Trucking operates west of El Paso, Southern Pacific Transport in Texas and Louisiana, and South Western Transportation Company along St. Louis Southwestern lines.
Pipelines run 2 752 miles *(4 402 km)* from San Francisco, Los Angeles, San Diego and El Paso.

DIVERSIFICATION

Southern Pacific Company has pursued a policy of diversification for many years.
In addition to holdings in other railways, it owns trucking companies, and a marine transport company which handles containerised freight shipments at the many ports it serves; is active as an air freight forwarder; owns pipelines distributing petroleum products in California, Nevada and Arizona from sources in Texas and California.
SP owns land (over 3 million acres); extensive mineral and oil rights; timber lands; and real estate including terminal buildings, and plans to intensify development of its non-railway real-estate.
It is active in leasing through its wholly-owned subsidiary Banker's Leasing Corporation, and operates a 275 mile *(443 km)* coal slurry pipeline to bring coal from Arizona to a steam-powered electric plant in Nevada.

FINANCIAL

Total Southern Pacific 1976 operating revenues were $1 883 095 000 up from $1 647 317 000 in 1975.
Net income during 1976 was $119 550 000 compared with 1975 figure of $74 932 000.

FREIGHT TRAFFIC

Revenue freight tons handled were 1.23 million, from 1.18 million in 1975; ton miles totaled 73 472 000 up from 69 235 000.
Freight revenues of Southern Pacific Transportation Company and its railroad subsidiaries totaled $1.60 1 000 million in 1976 compared with $1.42 1 000 million the previous year. More carloadings, heavier loadings per car and freight rate increases contributed to the 12.7 per cent growth in revenues. Revenues from transportation equipment (including motor vehicles and parts), miscellaneous manufactures and forest products showed especially strong gains over 1975. Shipments of paper products, chemicals, processed food products, ores, minerals and fuels also improved. Revenues were lower from shipments of petroleum products, metal products and most farm products.

Southern Pacific container train north of Santa Barbara. Containers were loaded in the Far East

Piggy Packers off loading Southern Pacific Trailers

PASSENGER TRAFFIC
Amtrak operates all inter-city passenger services in Southern Pacific territory. SP maintains commuter service between San Francisco and San Jose, California.

LOCOMOTIVES AND CARS
Railway equipment owned or leased at December 1976 consisted of 2 476 diesel locomotives, 84 332 freight cars; 84 passenger train cars and 2 156 company service units and cabooses.
New equipment acquired during 1975—
Freight cars

Box	310
Flat	602
Gondola	36
Open top hoppers	350
Total freight cars	1 298

Southern Pacific Communications Company has been offering a wide range of specialised voice and data communications services to private line customers since 1973. At the close of 1976, S.P.C.C. had virtually completed its coast-to-coast microwave system and was serving more than 750 individual customers. The airline industry represented one of the largest user groups.

TOFC/COFC PIGGYBACK
Southern Pacific's piggyback volume in 1976 increased significantly. Growth in volume was 17 per cent, with a record 321 000 units handled. Minibridge traffic growth continued very strong in 1976 with new steamship lines and ports adopting this concept of intermodalisation which includes a rail segment as part of the total trip.
Southern Pacific was able to increase their share of the mini-bridge container growth with newly expanded terminals at Houston, Texas and New Orleans (Avondale) La. to serve the Gulf of Mexico.

LOADING RAMPS
Loading ramps are located at the following points on the Southern Pacific:
Austin, Tex.; Avondale, La.; Bakersfield, Ca.; Beaumont, Tex.; Brooklyn, Ore.; Brownsville, Tex.; Chico, Ca.; Colton, Ca.; Corpus Christi, Tex.; Dallas, Tex.; Del Rio, Tex.; Edinburg, Tex.; El Centro, Ca.; El Paso, Tex.; Ennis, Tex.; Eugene, Ore.; Ft. Worth, Tex.; Fresno, Ca.; Flatonia, Tex.; Harlington, Tex.; Gregory, Tex.; Guadalupe, Ca.; Hearne, Tex.; Houston, Tex.; Klamath Falls, Ore.; Lafayette, La.; Lake Charles, La.; Los Angeles, Ca.; Lufkin, Tex.; New Orleans, La.; Nogales, Ariz.; Oakland, Ca.; Ogden, Utah.; Oxnard, Ca.; Phoenix, Ariz.; Redding, Ca.; Roseville, Ca.; Salem, Ore.; Salinas, Ca.; San Antonio, Ca.; San Diego, Ca.; San Francisco, Ca.; San Jose, Ca.; Shreveport, La.; Sparks, Nev.; Stockton, Ca.; Tuscon, Ariz.; Victoria, Tex.; Waco, Tex.; Yuma, Ariz, Schriever, La.
Additional loading ramps are located on SP subsidiary, St. Louis Southwestern Railway Co:
Arkansas: Brinkley, Camden, Jonesboro, North Little Rock, Pine Bluff.
Illinois: East St. Louis.
Louisiana: Shreveport.
Tennessee: Memphis.
Texas: Corsicana, Dallas, Fort Worth, Lufkin, Texarkana, Tyler, Waco.

LIFTING EQUIPMENT
Piggypacker units are located at Oakland (2), Los Angeles (3), Phoenix (1), Houston (2), and St. Louis (2). Overhead cranes are in use at Oakland, Los Angeles and Dallas and New Orleans.

CONTAINERS
Containers move daily in expedited Piggyback trains and trans-continental manifest trains on 85 ft and 89 ft cars.
The great majority of containers in rail-water carrier intermodal service, to and from points in the United States, are furnished by water carriers or container leasing companies on a per diem charge basis.

CONTAINER TERMINALS
Oakland, Ca.; San Francisco, Ca.; Los Angeles, Ca.; Houston, Texas; New Orleans, La.; Dallas, Texas; St. Louis, Mo.; Phoenix, Ariz.
These connect with all US and foreign flag ocean carriers calling at Pacific Coast and Gulf Ports. They participate in routes with all transcontinental rail carriers.

SCHEDULED NATIONAL SERVICES
Between United States and Hawaii through Pacific Coast ports.

SCHEDULED INTERNATIONAL SERVICES
Between United States and Japan, Hong Kong, Australia, Singapore and other Far Eastern ports as well as Europe.
Land-bridge movement—From Far East ports to Pacific Coast thence rail to Atlantic Coast and by ship to Europe as well as to Gulf points for destination delivery or further ship movement to Europe.

ST. LOUIS—SAN FRANCISCO RAILWAY COMPANY
906 Olive St, St. Louis, Mo 63101

Chairman of Board and President: R. C. Grayson
Senior Vice-President, Marketing: E. D. Grinnell
Senior Vice-President, Operationa: W. F. Thompson
Vice-President, General Counsel: D. E. Engle
Vice-President, Corporate Affairs: J. H. Brown
Vice-President, Finance and Treasurer: H. B. Parker
Vice-President, and Secretary: G. E. Bailey
Vice-President, Administration: P. E. Odom
Vice-President, Personnel: J. K. Beshears
Asst. Vice-President, Intermodal Services: L. A. Thomas
Controller: C. C. Roberts
General Manager: H. C. Bitner
Chief Engineer: G. E. Warfel
Chief Mechanical Officer, Equipment: J. P. Knox
Chief Mechanical Officer, Motive Power: O. H. Summers
Gen. Supt. Communications and Signals: J. S. Downs

LINES AND TERRITORIES
The "Frisco" operates 4 741 miles *(7 800 km)* of route in the midwestern and southern states, from Kansas City and St. Louis in the north to Dallas, Texas; Mobile, Alabama; and Pensacola, Florida in the south.
Its central, in-between location makes it an important link in trans-continental and north-south routing.

FINANCIAL RESULTS
1975 revenues decreased to $276 257 791 down from $285 853 549 in 1974.
All passenger operation has ceased.

FREIGHT TRAFFIC
Average ton-miles for 1975 was 1 489.17 up on the previous year's figure of 1 463.96.
Revenue to miles were 13 492 838 000 for 1975 (15 012 069 000 1974).

LOCOMOTIVES
At 31 December 1975, Frisco owned 390 road locomotives unit and 92 switchers for a total of 462 units. Locomotives and rolling stock put into service 1975 included 5-GP-38-2 and 5-U-30-BRX freight and 5-MP-15 switch.

FREIGHT CARS
At 31 December 1975 Frisco owned 18 708 freight cars.
Freight Car Equipment Acquired 1975:

15	100-ton 60' High Cube Box Cars;
25	100-ton Covered Gondolas For Coil Steel Loading;
**200	100-ton Open Hopper Cars;
**200	100-ton Plain Gondolas;
20	All-Steel Cabooses (Company Shops);
50	100-ton Ballast Hopper Cars (Company Shops).

**Leased

CAPITAL EXPENDITURE
In the past five years, the Frisco has been spending in the neighbourhood of $36.4 million annually on capital improvements, including major leasing. In 1975, capital expenditures with major leasing totalled $37.7 million, reflecting not only the need for modern equipment and facilities but also the continued inflationary effect of constantly escalating unit costs.
Included in Frisco's 1975 capital spending programme was the acquisition of 22 locomotives and 767 freight cars. All of the locomotives and 367 of the freight cars were purchased under Conditional Sale Agreements; the remaining freight cars were financed through leveraged leasing.
Frisco's 1975 capital expenditures included $9.4 million for roadway and structures and $16.7 million for other additions and improvements to its property.

OTHER DEVELOPMENTS
To meet the expanding Company demand for electronic technology, the Frisco has completed a 1 000-mile microwave system to replace the telephone circuits it previously leased from the Bell System. As greater capacity becomes necessary, the present 300-voice channel capacity can be expanded to as many as 600 channels.
Presently, the microwave system consists of 38 sites, with towers ranging in height from 70 feet at Valley Park, Missouri, to a 460-ft tower at Turrell, Arkansas. Microwave signals are received and transmitted from tower to tower via an electromagnetic beam.
Aside from voice transmission, the system also transmits important data to and from the Frisco's computer center at Springfield, Missouri, and is an important adjunct to the Centralised Traffic Control system used in monitoring and directing the movement of trains over the railroad. The microwave system also permits direct dialling to many of its more important wayside stations and affords two-way radio communications between dispatchers and train crews.

UNION PACIFIC CORPORATION
345 Park Ave, New York, NY 10022

In 1969—the Centenary Year of the Golden Spike Ceremony—a new holding company was formed, named the **Union Pacific Corporation.** The Union Pacific Railroad Company is now a corporate subsidiary of the Corporation.

In 1971 the basic business activities of the parent Corporation were realigned into operating groups;

Transportation
Union Pacific Railroad Company, 1416 Dodge Street, Omaha, Nebraska 68179

Oil and Gas
Champlin Petroleum Company, 5301 Camp Bowie Blvd., Fort Worth, Texas 76107.

Land
Upland Industries Corporation, 110 North Fourteenth St., Omaha, Nebraska 68102.

Coal and other minerals
Rocky Mountain Energy Company, 4704 Harlan Street, Denver, Colorado 80212.

The Corporations' principal officers are:—
Chairman, Board of Directors and Chief Executive Officer: Frank E. Barnett
President: James H. Evans
Chairman of the Executive Committee: E. T. Gerry
Executive Vice-President: W. S. Cook
Senior Vice-President-Law: W. J. McDonald
Vice-President, Corporate Relations: W. P. Raines
Secretary: C. N. Olsen
Treasurer: H. B. Shuttleworth
Controller: C. A. Rose
Vice-President-Finance: William F. Surette
Vice-President-Employee Relations: John P. Halan
Vice-President: Richard N. Little
General Counsel: Paul J. Coughlin, Jr.

UNION PACIFIC RAILROAD COMPANY
1416 Dodge St, Omaha, Nebr 68179

President: John C. Kenefick
Vice-President, Operation: Robert L. Richmond
Vice-President, Traffic: Walter P. Barrett
Vice-President, Executive Department: C. Howard Burnett
Vice-President, Labour Relations: Glen L. Farr
Vice-President and Western General Counsel: C. Barry Schaefer
Controller: John P. Deasey
Vice-President, Finance and Administration: Robert L. Richmond
Assistant Vice-President, Sales: Fred L. Morgan
Assistant Vice-President, Marketing: Robert L. Godfrey

LINES AND TERRITORIES
The Union Pacific operates an average 9 700 miles *(15 253 km)* of route.

The system extends from Council Bluffs, Iowa and Kansas City, Missouri in the east, to the Pacific Coast ports including Portland, Oregon, Vancouver, Longview, Tacoma and Seattle, Washington, Los Angeles Harbor and Long Beach, California.

The Union Pacific has a reciprocal arrangement with other railroads to avoid breaking up trains and switching at intermediate points.

Union Pacific owns 1 500 dry trailers of various types plus several hundred of various types under lease. Flat cars of 89 ft are used for transportation of these vehicles.

FINANCIAL
Consolidated 1976 revenues and sales of $2.02 1 000 million reached an all-time high for Union Pacific Corporation with an increase of $269 million or 15 per cent over 1975. Net income for 1976, including an extraordinary credit of $7.5 million, also achieved a new high of $195.2 million or $4.18 per share after giving effect to a two-for-one common stock split effective 27 January 1977. Earnings in 1976 of $187.7 million before the extraordinary credit were up $39.1 million or 26 per cent over 1975 net income of $148.6 million. Earnings per share in 1976 before the special credit were $4.02 compared with a restated $3.21 for 1975. The extraordinary credit represents an adjustment of an accrued liability established in 1971 relating to Amtrak's assumption of the Railroad's intercity passenger service.

Union Pacific Railroad Company earnings for 1976, before the $7.5 million Amtrak related extraordinary credit, were $98.7 million, an increase of $14.8 million or 18 per cent over 1975 results. Revenue growth of $170.2 million or 17 per cent reflected higher freight volume and the effect of incremental increases in freight rates. Carloadings increased by 7 per cent and revenue ton-miles grew from 52.2 to 56.8 1 000 million or 9 per cent. Traffic gains in motor vehicles and parts, intermodal trailer traffic, soda ash, coal, paper products and lumber products were the major contributors to higher freight volume.

An increase of $137.7 million in Railroad operating costs partially offset the 1976 revenue improvement. Labour costs rose by $64.5 million, reflecting increases in wage rates and higher payroll taxes and other employee benefit costs. The cost of materials and supplies increased by $44.4 million as a result of higher prices and expanded track and equipment maintenance programmes, as well as greater diesel fuel costs due to higher prices and additional freight volume.

FREIGHT OPERATIONS
Union Pacific achieved a record level in revenue ton-miles in 1976 as a result of the improving economy and the Railroad's aggressive marketing strategy. Revenue ton-miles increased 9 per cent to 56 800 million, compared to 52.2 billion in 1975.

Carloadings in 1976 were up 7 per cent over the 1975 volume. The difference in the rates of increase between revenue ton-miles and carloadings reflects the increasing number of higher-capacity freight cars and a greater proportion of heavy commodities hauled by the Railroad.

The Railroad's operating expenses were up $137.7 million or 16 per cent in 1976. Labour expenses escalated 12 per cent as a result of nationwide wage agreements negotiated in 1975, and, though inflation abated somewhat, the prices paid for fuel, materials and supplies increased steadily throughout the year. In the face of these inflationary pressures, the Railroad intensified its campaign to increase productivity and reduce costs.

LOCOMOTIVES AND CARS
Union Pacific acquired 73 locomotives for $35.3 million compared with 49 units for $19.6 million in 1975. It also acquired or constructed 2 597 freight cars and 249 bi- and tri-level auto racks at a total cost of $74.7 million.

During 1976, Union Pacific initiated a programme to construct open-top hopper cars at its Albina, Oregon shops, and completed 1 000 of these units during the year. This approach results in a substantial saving to the Railroad and assures the availability of this critically needed rolling stock. The Railroad also purchased 1 217 covered hopper cars from outside manufacturers.

EMD SD40-2 300 ohp locomotive of the Union Pacifics fleet

OTHER DEVELOPMENTS

Union Pacific Railroad planned the largest capital spending programme in the company's history for 1977.

The railroad programmed $246.7 million for capital improvements in 1977, up more than $91 million from the 1976 figure of $155.1 million.

The programme includes a previously announced $160 million for new rolling stock consisting of 90 locomotives, 3 079 freight cars, 200 ballast cars and 315 auto racks; plus another $10 million for miscellaneous work equipment and $76 million for road and fixed plant improvements.

Major items in UP's road and fixed plant schedule for 1977 included laying 350 miles of new continuous welded rail, installation of 875 000 cross ties, construction of 115 miles of centralised traffic control signalling on mainline trackage and continued construction of a major new 32-track automated freight classification yard at Hinkle, Oreg.

TOFC/COFC PIGGYBACK

W. R. Davis *(General Manager Intermodal Services)*

In 1976, Union Pacific run-through trains, connecting with nine different railroads, completed more than 7 000 separate trips to points throughout the country. The Railroad scheduled additional daily, high-speed, all-van trains between Midwest gateway cities and West Coast points.

The Railroad was successful in increasing its trailer and container traffic to an all-time high in 1976. Last spring, it began to handle an estimated 40 000 trailer loads of mail a year for the US Postal Service under a four-year agreement. This traffic is being hauled between bulk mail centres in Chicago, Denver, Oakland, Seattle and Los Angeles.

Union Pacific continued to increase its shipments of United Parcel Service trailers throughout its territory. During 1976, the Railroad handled several thousand United Parcel trailers by special high-speed service from Chicago to Denver, Salt Lake City and Portland; and from Los Angeles and Salt Lake City to Denver.

3 000 hp GE 430-C, UP 2852 and two helpers with westbound trains 25 miles west of Salina, Kansas

EMD DDA-40X 6 600 hp Centennial locomotives

WESTERN PACIFIC RAILROAD
526 Mission St, San Francisco, Cal 94105

Officers:
President: R. G. Flannery
Chairman of the Board: Alfred E. Perlman
Chairman of the Executive Committee: Howard E. Newman
Vice-President, Operations: Robert C. Marquis
Vice-President, Marketing: R. G. Meldahl
Vice-President, Finance: Richard W. Stumbo, Jr
Vice-President, Administration: F. A. Tegeler
Vice-President, Law: Walter G. Treanor
Vice-President, Industrial: Alexis P. Victors
Treasurer: H. W. Klebahn
Corporate Secretary: William D. Brew

LINES AND TERRITORIES
Twenty-five track miles of rail have been renewed with heavier rail. A programme of upgrading bridges to handle heavier loadings, was continued. Work also progressed on reinforcing of steel bridges.

Western Pacific is a wholly owned subsidiary of Western Pacific Industries Inc. It operates in the Western portion of the United States, providing Freight service from the San Francisco Bay area through California and Nevada to Salt Lake City, Utah. The railroad also provides service North and South between Bay Area and the Oregon Line. During the year the Company acquired 200 box cars; and 20 diesel-electric locomotive units.

FINANCIAL RESULTS
Transportation revenues of the Western Pacific Railroad Company in 1975 were $102 932 000 which was $4 472 000 below the 1974 level. Carloadings were down 17 per cent. During 1975, railroads were granted three general freight rate increases which generated incremental revenues of about $6.2 million. Increased costs of salaries, fringe benefits and higher material costs aggregated $10.9 million for the year.

LOCOMOTIVES AND CARS
WP locomotive fleet consists of 141 units of road power (EMD and GE) and 17 switchers.

Delivery was taken during 1975 on 200 new insulated box cars equipped with air bag bulkheads for damage free movement of canned goods, beverages and other packaged products; 65 new 100-ton open hopper cars for crude barites; 35 100-ton covered hopper cars for ground barites, potash, rice and grain; 17 high cube damage free box cars for appliances and 10 enclosed tri-level "safe pak" cars for automobiles.

OTHER DEVELOPMENTS
Arrangements were concluded with Burlington Northern and Canadian Pacific for establishment early in 1976 of new routes via Bieber to and from Western Canada which will open up significant new traffic potentials for Western Pacific. A sales programme aimed at hauling materials used in constructing the Alaska Pipeline was implemented and produced new revenue. Market development and planning efforts were continued to promote future movements of bulk commodities.

The Safety Programme in 1975 showed further improvements. Total personal injuries were 398, down 25 per cent from 533 in 1974.

Cathode Ray Tubes were placed in service in the Customer Service Center in San Francisco in December 1975 providing instantaneous car and train inquiry response from the newly implemented Advanced Transportation System. Twenty one track miles of new and reconditioned rail and 85 000 new mainline hardwood ties were installed in continuance of our improvement programme. Street and highway grade crossing protection was newly installed or improved at 18 locations.

A "one-spot" car repair facility was constructed at Stockton. This facility features a roof over two tracks, 3 "in floor" hydraulic jacks, 2 sets of jib cranes for truck repairs and centrally located material racks, all of which will double the productivity of the repair facility. New office facilities were built at the Milpitas repair track facilities along with a new wheel storage area. An air compressor was also installed for the yard air system. A new wheel crane was built at the Sacramento Shops including 4 new wheel storage tracks, improving handling and efficiency.

TOFC/COFC PIGGYBACK
TOFC/COFC revenue increased 7 per cent.

Intermodal (COFC and TOFC) services were expanded and improved. The Intermodal and International Sales Group was restructured to provide the resources for specific concentration on this important growing segment of the business. Sales territories and manpower requirements were analised to make the most effective use of field sales personnel.

New Western Pacific U23B diesel locomotive
A WP freight heads east behind a new GE U23B diesel locomotive as a Bay Area Rapid Transit (BART) commuter train crosses WP's mainline on elevated tracks near San Leandro, California.

ABERDEEN & ROCKFISH RAILROAD CO
PO Box 917, Aberdeen, NC 28315

President: W. Formyduval
Vice-President: R. Veasey
Secretary: D. C. Russell
Treasurer: Juanita Baker
Vice-President, Traffic: W. F. Hilliard
Vice-President, Engineering, Construction, Roadway & Equipment: Charles Monroe
Vice-President, Finance. C. C. Parker

47 route miles; 3 locomotives; 1 freight car.

THE AKRON, CANTON AND YOUNGSTOWN RAILROAD COMPANY
8 N. Jefferson St, Roanoke, Vir 24011

President and Chief Executive Officer: J. L. Cowan
Comptroller and Secretary: D. K. Heidish
Traffic Manager: C. Engelo
Superintendent of Equipment: E. H. Davidson, Jr

171 route miles; 16 locomotives.

ALIQUIPPA AND SOUTHERN RAILROAD CO

General Superintendent: T. T. Deyak
Assistant Treasurer: H. W. Uber
Superintendent, Transportation: P. O. Wynkoop
Superintendent, Equipment: S. T. Pile
Superintendent, M/W & Engineering: R. F. Duffy

48 route miles; 19 locomotives; 891 freight cars.

ANN ARBOR RAILROAD CO
One Parkland Blvd, Dearborn, Mich 48126

President: K. P. Shoemaker
Vice-President, Operations: A. C. Robinson
Vice-President, Traffic: R. B. Wright
Secretary: N. A. Wallen

299 route miles; 15 locomotives; 386 freight cars.

THE APACHE RAILWAY COMPANY
PO Drawer E, Snowflake, Ariz 85937

President and Chief Executive: Flake Willis
Vice-President: P. C. Gaffney
Secretary: R. A. Miller
Treasurer: R. W. Rehfeld
Manager-Purchases and Equipment: D. M. Ramsey
Supervisor: S. Selby
Supervisor-Track and Construction: H. W. Teel

84 route miles; 8 locomotives; 613 freight cars.

APALACHICOLA NORTHERN RAILROAD CO.
803 Florida National Bank Building, Jacksonville, Fla 32201

President: E. Ball
Vice-President: B. R. Gibson
Auditor: J. R. Alligood
Superintendent and General Traffic Manager: R. H. Ellzey

96 route miles; 11 locomotives; 106 freight cars.

ASHLEY, DREW AND NORTHERN RAILWAY COMPANY
PO Box 757, Crossett, Ark 71635

President: E. A. Temple
Vice-President: G. W. Kincheloe
Manager of Engineering, Mechanical, Communications and Signals: R. G. McManus
General Manager: P. H. Schveth
Superintendent of Operations: J. H. Richards
Assistant to President: E. B. Chesser
Supervisor of Track: F. M. Thompson

41 route miles; 5 locomotives; 558 freight cars.

ATLANTA AND ST. ANDREWS BAY
514 E. Main St, Dothan, Ala 36301

Chairman and Chief Financial Officer: R. A. Givan
Vice-President Operations: J. W. Cunningham
Resident Vice-President: J. A. Smith
Chief Traffic Officer: Q. D. Bruner
Secretary-Treasurer: H. B. Davis
Assistant Secretary: B. E. Goodman
Auitor and Assistant Treasurer: A. A. Taylor
Traffic Manager, Sales: D. P. Clark, Jr.
Chief Engineer: D. R. Davis
Chief Mechanical Officer: T. L. Edwards
Director of Safety and Public Relations: M. B. Holloway

88 route miles; 12 locomotives; 365 freight cars.

BALTIMORE & EASTERN RAILROAD CO
6 Penn Center, Philadelphia, Pa 19104

President: A. M. Schofield
Vice-President: E. L. Claypole
Vice-President: F. J. Gasparini
Secretary: R. W. Carroll
Treasurer: R. C. Lepley

73 route miles.

BALTIMORE & OHIO CHICAGO TERMINAL RAILROAD
2 N Charles St, Baltimore, Md 21201

President: H. T. Watkins
Executive Vice-Presidents: J. T. Ford
J. T. Collinson
Vice-Presidents: R. W. Donnem
J. P. Ganley
R. C. McGowan
Secretary: G. E. Griffith
Treasurer: R. C. Roig
Real Estate Agent: J. R. Hickman
General Superintendent, Transportation: M. O. Benson
Chief Engineer: J. W. Brent

62.02 route miles.

BANGOR AND AROOSTOOK RAILROAD COMPANY
Northern Maine Junction Park, R.R.2, Bangor, Maine 04401

Chairman of the Executive Committee and Chief Executive Officer:
Frederick C. Dumaine, Jr
Chairman: W. J. Strout
President: W. E. Travis
Vice-President, Operations: L. W. Littlefield
Vice-President and General Counsel: W. M. Houston
Vice-President, Marketing: H. L. Cousins, Jr
Vice-President Finance: O. H. Bridgham
Treasurer: D. B. Annis
Vice-President, Public Relations: R. W. Sprague
Manager, Personnel: L. F. Lewis
Assistant Vice-President, Operating Transportation: R. P. Groves
Manager, Highway Division: S. F. Corey
Controller: O. J. Gould
General Auditor: R. L. Condon
Manager, Data Processing: H. W. Oliver
General Freight Traffic Manager: H. G. Goodness
Chief Mechanical Officer: H. W. Hanson
Chief Engineer: V. J. Welch
Manager, Purchasing and Stores: H. F. Bell

543 route miles; 45 locomotives; 4 808 freight cars; 19 containers.

BELFAST AND MOOSEHEAD LAKE RAILROAD
11 Water St, Belfast, Maine 04915

President: H. H. Hutchings Jr
Vice-President: James F. Murphy
General Manager and Auditor: W. I. Hall
Treasurer: E. G. Elwell
Master Mechanic: Gerard Simoneau

33 route miles; 4 locomotives; 4 freight cars; 1 snow plough.

BELT RAILWAY COMPANY OF CHICAGO
6900 South Central Ave, Chicago, Ill 80538

President and General Manager: R. E. Dowdy
Vice-President and Assistant General Manager: D. R. Turner
Vice-President and Controller: R. G. Rubino
Secretary and Treasurer: G. D. Moriarty
Director of Personnel: C. M. Crawford
Chief Engineer: A. B. Hillman
Superintendent of Transportation Department: J. Overbey
Chief of Motive Power and Purchasing Agent: V. L. Smith

The Belt Railway Company of Chicago was built by the Chicago and Western Indiana Railroad as the Belt Division of the C & WI under a separate charter. The purpose of the Belt Line was to intersect and connect all Chicago trunk lines for interchange of traffic. Construction of the Belt Division was completed in 1883. In 1882 prior to the completion of Belt Division Mr. J. B. Brown, private developer of the C & WI and Belt Division received an offer from the C & WI's five using railroads for purchase of the Belt Division. In October, 1882 the Belt Division was reincorporated as the Belt Railway Company of Chicago with five owners the C & EI, Erie, Monon, GTW and Wabash.
For a number of years the Belt Railway was not utilised intensively, however, in August, 1911 the Lowrey Agreement covering application of uniform switching charges was put into effect in the Chicago Terminal. The outcome of this agreement, which made Belt Line operations more advantageous was the Belt Operating Agreement of 1912. This agreement brought the ATSF, Rock Island, Illinois Central, PRR, CB & Q, C & O and Soo Line into the BRC as owners.
The Belt Railway Company at Clearing built and utilises one of the largest hump yards in the world for classification of freight traffic. Clearing Yard has a working capacity of 12 600 cars and has the ability to hump four trains simultaneously during classification. The principle functions of the Belt Railway are to:
1. Provide classification and interchange of freight cars for its twelve owners and for other non-owner roads. In connection with this classification the Belt provides blocked train service for the benefit of many of its owners in connection with their run through train connections.
2. Provide excellent location and switching service for over 325 industries, giving industries access to all Chicago truck lines for movement of their freight.

27 route miles; 48 diesel electric locomotives.

BESSEMER AND LAKE ERIE RAILROAD COMPANY
Gateway 4, 600 Grant St, PO Box 536, Pittsburgh, Pa 15230

President: M. S. Toon
Vice-President: R. D. Lake
Vice-President, Finance: V. W. Kraetsch
General Counsel and Secretary: J. D. Morrison
Treasurer: J. E. Ralph Jr.
Director, Purchases and Stores: F. T. Brandt
General Manager, Greenville, Pa.: J. W. Read
Superintendent, Transportation: J. A. Magner, Jr
Chief Engineer: M. Rougas

221 route miles; 66 locomotives; 8 579 freight cars.

BIRMINGHAM SOUTHERN RAILROAD CO
PO Box 579, Fairfield, Ala 35064

President: C. D. Cotten
Secretary and Treasurer: T. F. Driscoll
Vice-President: G. W. Parker
Superintendent, Transportation: J. W. Greene

89 route miles; 17 locomotives; 1 003 freight cars.

BUTTE, ANACONDA AND PACIFIC RAILROAD COMPANY
Box 1421, 300 West Commercial Ave, Anaconda, Mont 59711

President: L. V. Kelly
Vice-President: G. W. Parker
Secretary and Treasurer: T. F. Driscoll
Superintendent of M.W. & S.: J. F. Young
Superintendent of Transportation: J. W. Greene
Shop Superintendent: G. Kurtz
Material Controls Supervisor: E. J. Hamill
System Freight Agent: J. T. McNay

56 route miles; 8 locomotives; 750 freight cars.

CALIFORNIA WESTERN RAILROAD
Foot of Laurel St, Fort Bragg, Cal 95437

President: R. H. Schwarz
Vice-President, and General Manager: F. H. Sturges Jr
Vice-President, and Treasurer: E. W. Cleary
Vice-President, Secretary and General Counsel: J. E. Clute
Assistant General Manager and Auditor: R. A. Regalia
Roadmaster: Vernon Petrick
Superintendent, Transporation: L. M. Weller
Traffic Manager: Henry A. Foltz

40 route miles; 6 locomotives; 2 railcars-diesel; 8 passenger train coaches.

CAMAS PRAIRIE RAILROAD CO
PO Box 815, Lewiston, Ida 83501

President: T. P. Rogers
Vice-President: J. W. Wicks
Agent-Auditor: R. F. Jones
Trainmaster: J. W. Clem
Manager: J. H. Harwood

256.7 route miles; 20 locomotives.

CEDAR RAPIDS AND IOWA CITY RAILWAY CO
PO Box 351, Cedar Rapids, Iowa 52406

President and General Manager: Duane Arnold
Vice-President and Secretary: Stevan B. Smith
General Superintendent: O. R. Woods

25 route miles; 6 locomotives; 35 freight cars.
Executive Department includes all of the above people.

O. R. Woods, General Superintendent, has charge of Operating, Mechanical, Engineering, Track Signal, Communications Departments.

THE CENTRAL RAILROAD COMPANY OF NEW JERSEY
1100 Raymond Blvd, Newark, NJ 07102

Trustee: R. D. Timpany

CENTRAL OF GEORGIA RAILROAD CO
Chairman and Chief Executive Officer: W. G. Claytor, Jr
President: R. E. Franklin
Vice-President, Operating: L. S. Crane
Secretary: M. M. Davenport
Assistant Vice-President and Treasurer: G. M. Williams

2 207 route miles; 132 locomotives; 5 606 freight cars.

CHICAGO AND ILLINOIS MIDLAND RAILWAY CO
PO Box 139, Springfield, Ill 62705

President: Carl D. Forth
Vice-President and General Manager: William G. Harvey
Auditor: Leo J. Povse
Treasurer: Raymond Bachert
Assistant Secretary: Robert Bresemann
Superintendent: A. S. Alstott
Chief Engineer: R. E. Pearson
Manager of Personnel: A. E. Brockschmidt
General Traffic Manager, Purchasing Agent and General Storekeeper:
  Joe Mosteika
Chief of Police: T. J. Wright

121 Route miles; 21 locomotives; 837 freight cars.

CHICAGO SOUTH SHORE AND SOUTH BEND RAILROAD (ELECTRIC)
Carroll Avenue, Michigan City, Ind 46360

President and General Manager: A. W. Dudley
Vice-President, Sales and Industrial Development: C. A. Ernst
Vice-President, Comptroller: R. J. McGee
Treasurer: H. J. Konda
Superintendent of Transportation: R. D. Shipley
Chief Engineer: C. F. Mulrenan
Superintendent, Mechanical Department: J. R. Dukehart

75 miles; 3 electric locomotives; 8 diesel locomotives; 48 electric motor cars; 60 freight cars.

CINCINNATI UNION TERMINAL

President: T. L. Hintz
Vice-President: R. B. Hasselmann
Manager: G. S. Gray
Treasurer: F. D. Dziech

45 route miles; 2 locomotives.

CLINCHFIELD RAILROAD CO
229 Nolichucky Ave, Erwin, Tenn 37650

General Manager: T. D. Moore
Assistant General Manager: J. H. Bolden
Treasurer: J. C. Blackwell
General Auditor: W. J. Beals
Freight Traffic Manager: C. E. Bond
Chief Mechanical Officer: P. O. Likens
Chief Engineer: J. A. Goforth

295 route miles; 87 locomotives; 5 345 freight cars.

THE CORINTH AND COUNCE RAILROAD COMPANY
Box 128, Counce, Tenn 38326

President: C. W. Byrd
Secretary and Treasurer: J. H. Burton
Vice-President: W. C. Wells, III
Assistant Secretary: John Ross, Jr
Transportation Co-ordinator: A. A. Mann

26 route miles; 3 locomotives.

Connects at Corinth, Miss. with GM & O, IC and SR.

COLORADO AND SOUTHERN RAILWAY CO
1405 Curtis St, Denver, Colo 80202

President: George F. Difiel
Vice-President, Operations: John H. Hertog
Secretary and Treasurer: W. P. Healey

695 route miles; 95 locomotives; 2 910 freight cars.

COLUMBIA, NEWBERRY & LAURENS RAILROAD CO
500 Water St, Jacksonville, Fla 32202

President: P. F. Osborn
Chairman: W. T. Rice
Executive Vice-President: D. C. Hastings
Vice-President and General Manager: James L. Williams
Secretary: J. L. Williams
Treasurer: L. G. Anderson

75 route miles; 5 locomotives; 41 freight cars.

COLUMBUS AND GREENVILLE RAILWAY CO
Box 591, Columbus, Miss 39701

President: H. L. Morrison
Vice-President and General Counsel: R. C. Stovall, Jr.
Vice-President, Traffic and Assistant to the President: J. B. Swanzey
Treasurer and Assistant Secretary: W. B. Webb
Traffic Manager: Donald Z. Woolbright
Auditor: T. E. Eastburn
General Manager: C. A. Arnett
Car Accountant: M. K. McLemore
Superintendent, Motive Power and Equipment: W. A. Trayler, Jr
Superintendent of Telegraph: Bennie Ivey
Storekeeper: J. B. Kellum

168 route miles; 10 locomotives; 229 freight cars.

DETROIT, TOLEDO AND IRONTON RAILROAD CO
One Parkland Blvd, Dearborn, Mich 48126

President: K. P. Shoemaker
Vice-President, Marketing: M. J. Barron
Vice-President, Operations: A. C. Robinson
Vice-President, Finance: R. Guregian
Purchasing Agent: C. H. Leidholdt
Director Corporate Planning: M. H. Weisman
Vice-President, Accounting: W. S. Aaron, Jr
Vice-President, Data Processing: G. Sabo
Secretary Treasurer: N. A. Wallen
Director, Multi-Level and Trailerferry Service: M. J. Newbourne
Superintendent: J. E. Schlosser
Chief Mechanical Officer: R. G. Lipmyer
Superintendent, Car Department: D. W. Brammer
Personnel Manager: R. J. O'Brien
Superintendent, Signals and Communications: L. W. Olsen

476 route miles; 74 locomotives; 4 130 freight cars.

DULUTH, MISSABE AND IRON RANGE RAILWAY COMPANY
Missabe Building, Duluth, Minn 55802

President: M. S. Toon
Vice-President and General Manager: D. B. Shank
General Superintendent: M. G. Alderink
Vice-President, Finance: V. W. Kraetsch
Comptroller: W. J. Pritz
Manager, Freight Revenue and Car Accounting: R. W. Haver
General Counsel and Secretary: J. D. Morrison
Assistant Treasurer: W. E. Bester
Superintendent, Motive Power and Cars: B. E. Lewis
Director of Labour Relations: C. L. Signorelli
Superintendent: E. W. Anderson
Director of Safety and Plant Protection: C. W. Bailey
Chief Engineer: R. B. Rhode
Director of Purchases and Stores: F. T. Brandt

Locomotives 98; freight cars 9 736.

This railway of 462 miles *(743 km)* connects the Mesabi Range iron ore deposits with the ports of Duluth and Two Harbours on Lake Superior from where the ore is shipped to the steel centres throughout the Midwest.

DURHAM AND SOUTHERN RAILWAY CO
904 Ramseur St, PO Box 451, Durham, NC 27702

President: G. W. Hill
Executive Vice-President: R. D. Teer
General Manager: E. H. Tart
Treasurer: B. F. Coble
Secretary: C. B. Nye
General Traffic Manager: O. F. Asbury

59 route miles; 4 locomotives.

EAST CAMDEN & HIGHLAND RAILROAD CO
PO Box 3180, East Camden, Ark 71701

President: R. S. O'Connor
Vice-President and General Manager: D. E. Ghent
Secretary: J. L. Bianchi
Treasurer: R. B. Walton
Auditor: J. E. O'Neal
Superintendent: J. T. Wagnon

43 route miles; 3 locomotives.

ELGIN JOLIET AND EASTERN RAILWAY
208 S Lasalle St, Chicago, Ill 60690

President: M. S. Toon
Vice-President, Operating: F. A. Fitzpatrick
Vice-President, Finance: V. W. Kraetsch
Secretary and Treasurer: R. B. Hood
Director, Labour Relations: N. W. Kopp
General Operating Superintendent: V. M. Christensen
Chief Mechanical Officer: M. R. Seipler
Director of Purchasing and Stores: F. T. Brandt

199 route miles; 110 locomotives; 10 442 freight cars.

ERIE LACKAWANNA RAILWAY CO
Buffalo, NY 14206

Trustee: T. F. Patton
President and Chief Executive Officer: G. W. Maxwell
Senior Vice-President: J. R. Neikirk
Treasurer: H. A. Zilli
Manager, Transportation: T. E. McGinnis
Chief Engineer, M/W: R. F. Bush
Chief Mechanical Officer: R. A. Carroll

3 029 route miles; 523 locomotives; 20 309 freight cars.

As of April 1st 1976 this company became part of ConRail.

ESCANABA AND LAKE SUPERIOR RAILROAD
Wells, Mich. 49894

President: F. H. Lee
Treasurer: J. F. Walbeck
Secretary and General Counsel: N. A. Lemke
Assistant Secretary and Assistant Treasurer: R. E. Beal
Vice-President and General Manager: L. L. Hamilton
Traffic Manager: H. C. Pierson
Car Accountant: F. H. Flagstadt

64 route miles; 4 locomotives; 12 freight cars.

FLORIDA EAST COAST RAILWAY COMPANY
1 Malaga St, St. Augustine, Fla 32084

Chairman: E. Ball
President: W. L. Thornton
Vice-President, Traffic: J. E. Corbett
Vice-President, Engineering: H. E. Hales
Vice-President, Transportation: R. W. Wyckoff
Vice-President, Accounting, Data Processing and Secretary: J. T. Rice
Comptroller: G. S. Meserve
Assistant Vice-President: C. D. Meitin
Assistant Vice-President: R. J. Barreto
General Superintendent: B. D. Vlasin
General Mechanical Superintendent: S. D. Smith

554 route miles; 59 locomotives; 942 freight cars.

FORDYCE AND PRINCETON RAILROAD COMPANY
Fordyce, Ark

President: E. A. Temple
Director: F. E. Woods
Director: Philip McClendon
Director: E. A. Temple
Director and Secretary: W. E. Hastings
Superintendent (Fordyce, Arkansas): Tom Branch

FORT WORTH AND DENVER RAILWAY CO
Union Station Building, Denver, Colo 80217

President: P. F. Cruikshank
Vice-President, Operating: L. C. Ethington
Secretary and Treasurer: W. L. Kirkpatrick
General Superintendent: A. D. Powers
Superintendent, Transportation: C. N. Parker

1 343 route miles; 20 locomotives; 1 505 freight cars.

GAINESVILLE MIDLAND RAILROAD CO
3600 W. Broad St, Richmond, VA 23230

President: W. T. Rice
Vice-President: P. F. Osborn
Vice-President, Operations: D. C. Hastings
Assistant Secretary: J. L. Williams
Treasurer: L. G. Anderson

40 route miles; 1 locomotive; 1 freight car.

GALVESTON WHARVES
PO Box 328, Galveston, Tex 77553

Chairman, Board of Trustees: Sam G. Tramonte
Executive Director and General Manager: C. S. Devoy
Deputy Executive Director: O. L. Selig
Director of Engineering: Ron Surovik
Deputy Port Director, Operations and Sales: L. B. Prino, Jr
Traffic Manager: Carl S. Parker, Jr
Treasurer and Personnel Director: F. R. Macik
General Counsellors: McLeod, Alexander, Powel and Apffel
Supt., Construction and Maintenance: Carl Meier
Supt., Loading/Unloading: H. G. Miller
Supt., Railroad Operations: Paul Attanasio

44 route miles; 6 shunting diesel-electric.

GENESEE AND WYOMING RAILROAD COMPANY
3846 Retsof Rd, Retsof, NY 14539

Chairman of the Board: M. B. Fuller Jr
President: M. B. Fuller III
Administrative Vice-President: J. N. Kiefer, Jr
Vice-President, General Counsel: G. R. Williams
Vice-President: W. B. Putney, IV
Secretary: L. S. Fuller
Treasurer and Assistant Secretary: J. M. Fuller
General Manager and Assistant Secretary: G. E. Johnson
Director of Finance: A. F. Radesi
Chief Engineer: F. R. Matthews
Traffic Manager: P. J. Crowley
Administrative Assistant: P. A. Mastralio
Superintendent of Equipment: F. J. Pascuzzo
Superintendent of Track, Bridges and Culverts: G. N. Brown

12 route miles; 6 locomotives; 208 freight cars; 1 passenger train coach.

GEORGIA NORTHERN RAILWAY CO
PO Box 152, Moultrie, Ga 31768

Chairman: W. G. Claytor
President and General Manager: W. L. Pippin

68 route miles; 1 locomotive.

GEORGIA RAILROAD
1590 Marietta Blvd, NW Atlanta, Ga 30318

General Manager: M. S. Jones Jr
Treasurer: C. H. Edwards
Chief Traffic Officer: H. M. Emmerson
Chief Engineer: Jack Cherry Jr

331 route miles; 35 locomotives; 1 251 freight cars.

GRAND TRUNK WESTERN RAILROAD CO
131 West Lafayette, Detroit, Mich 48226

President: J. H. Burdakin
Executive Assistant and Corporate Secretary: E. G. Fontaine
General Manager: W. Glavin
Vice-President, Finance and Administration: P. E. Tatro
Controller: W. V. Steeves
Treasurer: R. L. Ritchie

1 235 route miles; 195 locomotives; 10 183 freight cars; 640 piggyback trailers.

GREAT WESTERN RAILWAY CO
PO Box 5308, Denver, Colo 80217

Executive Vice-President: R. E. Munroe
Vice-President: J. M. Holt
Treasurer: M. E. Rebhan
Assistant Treasurer: J. T. Gray
Secretary: J. R. Parish
Assistant Secretary: S. C. Metzger
General Manager: J. W. Kelly
Manager of Accounting and Traffic: D. F. Rauer
Director Legal Affairs: P. J. Adolph
Director Labour Relations: R. A. Brenimer

58 route miles; 5 locomotives; 234 freight cars.

GREEN BAY AND WESTERN RAILROAD
PO Box 2507, Green Bay, Wisc 54306

President: H. Weldon McGee
Vice-President, Traffic: L. J. Kelly
Vice-President, Operations: C. H. Halvorson
Secretary and Treasurer: Robert Goethe
General Superintendent: L. J. Knutson
Supervisor, Locomotive Dept.: R. C. Stutleen

256 route miles; 17 locomotives and 1 400 freight cars.

GREEN MOUNTAIN RAILROAD CORP
Box 57, Chester Depot, Vt 05144

President and Superintendent: R. W. Adams
Vice-President: R. Ashcroft
Treasurer: R. W. Nimke
General Counsel: George W. Nostrand
General Freight Agent, Car Accountant: R. C. Ellis
Supervisor, Maintenance of Way: R. Pingrey
Chief Mechanical Officer: Peter L. Read
Signal Supervisor: T. J. Hancock

52 route miles; 6 locomotives; 114 freight cars.

HELENA SOUTHWESTERN RAILROAD COMPANY
Box 2517, West Helena, Ark 72390

President: J. B. Wiseman
Vice-President and General Manager: R. Rich
Secretary: W. D. Carlson
Treasurer: C. S. Caruthers
Assistant Secretary-Treasurer: R. M. McCarty, Jr
Assistant Secretary-Treasurer: J. R. Shipley
Director: J. B. Wiseman
Director: C. S. Caruthers
Director: W. D. Carlson
Director: R. Rich
Director: J. Sallis

4 route miles; 1 locomotive.

HOUSTON BELT & TERMINAL RAILWAY CO
202 Union Sta. Building, Houston, Tex 77002

President and General Manager: L. B. Griffin
Vice-President: J. G. Sheppard
Assistant to President: P. L. Broussard
Vice-President, Operations: L. B. Griffin
Secretary and Treasurer: R. L. Robertson
Chief Engineer: J. H. Robertson

53 route miles; 23 locomotives

LAKE ERIE, FRANKLIN AND CLARION RAILROAD
East Wood St, Clarion, Pa 16214

President and Chairman of the Board: J. F. Miller
Vice-President, Operations: J. L. Hartle
General Counsel: H. R. Pope, Jr

15 route miles; 3 locomotives.

ILLINOIS TERMINAL RAILROAD CO.
PO Box 72821, 710N 12th Blvd, St. Louis, Mo. 63177

President: E. B. Wilson
Vice-President and General Manager: D. E. Visney
Vice-President, Traffic: W. A. Nelson Jr
Secretary and Treasurer: H. D. Johnson
Chief Engineer: W. O. Pearson
Chief Mech. Officer: R. L. Bain
Controller: L. B. Rudloff

442 route miles; 32 locomotives; 2 508 freight cars.

INDIANA HARBOR BELT RAILROAD CO
Union Station, Chicago, Ill 60606

President: J. B. Addington
Vice-President, Operations: R. B. Hasselmann
Secretary: R. W. Carroll
Treasurer: B. D. Wellmon

114 route miles; 109 locomotives; 143 freight cars.

KENTUCKY & INDIANA TERMINAL RAILROAD
2910 North Western Parkway, Louisville, KY 40212

President and General Manager: J. J. Gaynor
Secretary and Treasurer: K. I. Williams

131 route miles; 21 locomotives.

LAKE SUPERIOR TERMINAL AND TRANSFER RAILWAY COMPANY
17, Washington ave, North, Minneapolis, Minn 55401

Superintendent (Highpost Operating Office): K. V. Marthe
President and Director: W. S. Byrne
Vice-President and Director: C. R. Hussey
Director: W. K. Bush
Director: W. S. Johnstone
Director: W. R. Allen
Director: T. R. Klingel

Owns and operates depot at Superior, Wis.

LAURINBURG AND SOUTHERN RAILROAD CO
Box 546, Laurinburg, NC 28352

President: Murphy Evans
Vice-President and General Manager: W. S. Jones
Secretary and Treasurer: C. E. Beman

28 route miles; 7 locomotives; 31 freight cars.

LEHIGH VALLEY RAILROAD COMPANY
415-425 Brighton St, Bethlehem, Pa 18015

Trustee: Robert C. Haldeman
Senior Vice-President, Chief Ops Officer: W. C. Wieters
Director, Labour Relations: M. W. Midgley
Superintendent, Safety: R. Tauber
Chief Mechanical Officer: D. G. Merrill
Chief Engineer: B. J. Murphy
Engineer, Maintenance of Way: A. W. Grimes
Engineer, Signals and Communications: W. J. Varner
Manager, Freight Claims: A. J. Wago
Superintendent, Stores: G. A. Rundquist
Division Superintendent: A. G. Lageman III
Superintendent, Terminal Operations: W. J. Nocitra
Superintendent, New York: G. F. Bresser
Superintendent, Transportation: F. J. Jackson
Supervisor, Train Movement: R. W. Whitehead
Supervisor, Car Distribution: J. Pecora
Superintendent, Stations: J. P. Duffy
Supervisor, Buffalo: Gerald Lorsong
General Counsel: R. D. Lalanne
Vice-President, Assistant to Trustee: H. M. Rafner

506 route miles; 147 locomotives; 3 966 freight cars.

MANITOU AND PIKE'S PEAK RAILWAY COMPANY
PO Box 1329, Colorado Springs, Colo 80901

President: Wm. Thayer Tutt
Vice-President: Russell T. Tutt
Vice-President: Gunnar Alenius
Vice-President and General Manager: Martin R. Frick
Secretary, Treasurer: Jerry Roblewski
Traffic Manager: Wayne E. Harry
Auditor: Zola M. Lyons

9 route miles; 4 diesel electric cars; 2 diesel-hydraulic twin-cars; 3 diesel-electric locomotives; 3 passenger coaches; 1 freight car; 1 diesel hydraulic rotary snow plough.

MANUFACTURERS RAILWAY CO
2850 South Broadway, St. Louis, Mo 63118

President: R. W. Schmidt
Secretary: M. L. Laskowski
Treasurer: R. W. Chapman

42 route miles; 9 locomotives.

MARYLAND AND PENNSYLVANIA RAILROAD CO.
490, East Market St, York, Penn 17403

Chairman of the Board: Harold Grossman
President: H. Lazarus
Vice-President and Secretary: Robert Grossman
Vice-President and Treasurer: Joseph Marino
General Manager: William Partington
Mechanical Supervisor: Robert Cook
Supervisor, Maintenance of Way: Ronald Flaharty

90 route miles; 6 locomotives.

McCLOUD RIVER RAILROAD COMPANY
PO Drawer A, McCloud, Cal 96057

President: C. T. Hester
Vice-President, Operations: S. Muma
Vice-President, Secretary and Treasurer: Guido Cottini
Claims Accounts Officer: Bob Ferraris
Traffic Manager: G. Holmquist
Chief Mechanical Officer: Ken Bogard

78 route miles; 4 locomotives; 7 freight train cars.

MINNESOTA TRANSFER RAILWAY COMPANY
2071 University Ave, St. Paul, Minn 55104

President: M. Garelick
Vice-President and General Manager: J. A. Lehn
Superintendent: W. S. Hammond
Chief Engineer: John L. Jensen
Secretary—Comptroller: M. A. Schensted
Assistant Superintendent: E. V. Devine

13 route miles; 5 locomotives.

MONONGAHELA RAILWAY COMPANY
53 Market St, Brownsville, Pa 15417

President: H. G. Allyn, Jr
Vice-President: C. W. Owens
Vice-President: H. P. Henshaw, Jr
Secretary: R. W. Carroll
Treasurer: R. W. Packer
General Counsel: G. E. Neuenschwander
Assistant General Counsel: G. E. Yurcon
Comptroller: R. P. McConnell
Manager, Real Estate: A. R. Brunner
Director, Labour Relations and Personnel: P. N. Mansfield
Supervisor, Labour Relations and Personnel: J. K. Emery
Manager, Freight Claims: L. F. Battaglia
Chief Claim Agent: M. D. Devecka
Superintendent: D. E. Gratz
Train Master: J. C. Murphy
Train Master: G. L. Staggers
Supervisor, Freight Transport: A. J. Yuhas
Chief of Police: R. L. Moore
Director, Purchasing & Materials: C. E. LeSuer
Chief Mechanical Officer: F. H. McHenry
Master Mechanic: A. H. Kovac
Chief Engineer: W. M. McCracken
Division Engineer: A. D. Grueser, Jr
Supervisor, MW & S: J. M. Fata
Supervisor Signals and Communications: J. F. Smith

171 route miles; 11 locomotives.

MONTANA WESTERN RAILWAY COMPANY
Valier, Mont 59486

President: W. Duncan MacMillan
General Manager, Secretary and Treasurer: H. E. Lovcik
Vice-President: Art Jardine
Associated with BN.

MORRISTOWN AND ERIE RAILROAD COMPANY
PO Box 2206R, Morristown, NJ 07960

Chairman of the Board: Ralph L. Monroe
President and Treasurer: Andrew L. Cobb, III
Chief Executive Officer: Byron F. Andrews
Executive Vice-President and Secretary: Daniel T. Lindo
Vice-President, Finance & Development: Ralph L. Monroe
Vice-President, Administration: William E. Anderson
Vice-President, Traffic: Edward H. Tobey
Vice-President, Chief Mechanical Officer: Edward Sinclair
Chief Accounting Officer: Byron F. Andrews, Sr.
Assistant Treasurer and Auditor: Thomas G. Peterson
Assistant Secretary: Allen Wolfson
Freight Agent: Thomas B. Peterson
Public Relations Officer: Michael Allen

11 route miles; 2 locomotives.
Connects ConRail
This branch is controlled by Midland Holding Corporation of Washington DC. It also operates the Caldwell branch of the former Erie Lackawanna railroad.

NEVADA NORTHERN RAILWAY CO
East Ely, Nev 89315

President: J. C. Kinnear Jr
Vice-President and General Superintendent: H. M. Peterson
Traffic Manager: J. Piccinini
Auditor: M. Fondi
Trainmaster: J. H. Marsh
Roadmaster: C. R. Smith
General Shop Foreman: J. P. Whitmore, Jr
General Car Foreman: F. V. Workman
Purchasing Agent: R. A. Evans

162 route miles; 2 locomotives.

NEW YORK & LONG BRANCH RR CO
1100 Raymond Blvd, Newark, NJ 07102

President and General Counsel: R. B. Wachenfeld
Vice-President: R. F. Lawson
Vice-President and General Manager: M. C. Jacobs
Secretary: J. W. Leppington
Property Manager and Assistant Secretary: F. V. Petraitis
Treasurer: J. H. Schaffer
Comptroller: C. S. Hill

Associated with Central RR of New Jersey.
40 route miles: No equipment owned.

NEW YORK, SUSQUEHANNA AND WESTERN RAILROAD
One River Road, Edgewater, NJ 07020

Trustee: W. Scott
President: I. Maidman
Chief Executive Officer: T. J. Smith
Comptroller: Len Burrell
Vice-President: H. Hohrst
Secretary and Treasurer: Catherine A. Lyons

65 route miles; 15 locomotives and 75 freight train cars.

NORFOLK FRANKLIN AND DANVILLE RAILWAY CO
181 S. Main St, Suffolk, Va 23434

President: Richard F. Dunlap
General Manager: L. G. Grace
Treasurer: F. R. McCartney
Chief Engineer: L. A. Durham, Jr
Superintendent: L. C. Capps, Jr

Associated with Norfolk & Western.

205 route miles; 6 locomotives; 247 freight cars.

OREGON & NORTHWESTERN RAILROAD CO
PO Box 557, Hines, Oreg 97738

President: H. H. Howard
Executive Vice-President: J. J. Fitzgerald
Vice-President: F. N. Blagen
Secretary: R. F. Brodl
Local Auditor: R. R. Shaffer
Vice-President: F. W. Feekin
Superintendent: R. L. Roy
Purchasing Agent: R. H. Van Houten

51 route miles; 4 locomotives; 146 freight cars.

PENNSYLVANIA-READING SEASHORE LINES
Camden, NJ 08103

President: J. B. Abbington
Secretary, Treasurer: A. M. Arnold
Legal Counsel: B. E. Capehart
General Claim Agent: W. D. Erdman Jr
Freight Claim Agent: L. J. Hauer
Manager, Real Estate: J. J. Sweeney
Comptroller: C. S. Hill
General Manager and Traffic Manager: R. E. Blosser
Industrial Agent: D. C. Gotschall
Superintendent, Transportation: C. L. Ryan
Supervisor, Track: H. D. Miller
Supervisor, Communications and Signals: J. W. Durst
Manager, Car Service Records: A. C. Weamer
Purchasing Agent: J. A. Smith
Master Mechanic: G. J. Huemmrich
Chief Engineer: C. E. Diefendorf

318 miles; 26 locomotives.
Associated with ConRail.

PITTSBURG AND SHAWMUT RAILROAD
R.D. 2 Middle St, Brookville, Pa 15825

President: W. R. Weaver
General Counsel: T. D. Stauffer
Purchasing Agent: P. J. Marshall
Vice-President, Traffic and Transportation: John Reale

100 route miles; 9 locomotives; 2 200 freight cars.

PORTLAND TERMINAL RAILROAD CO.
242 St. John St, Portland, Maine 04102

President: E. Spencer Miller
Vice-President: John F. Gerity
Assistant to President: Bradley L. Peters
Treasurer: Stanley W. Watson

23 route miles.
The Company is wholly-owned by Maine Central as one of its subsidiaries.

ROSCOE, SNYDER & PACIFIC RAILWAY CO
PO Box 68, Roscoe, Tex 79545

President: Wm. L. Bailey
Chairman of the Board: D. Wooten
Vice-President: Glen E. Pitts
Secretary and Treasurer: J. Collins

30 route miles; 2 locomotives; 766 freight cars.

ST. JOHNSBURY AND LAMOILLE COUNTY RAILROAD
Stafford Street, Morrisville, Vt 05661

President: Bruno A. Loati
General Manager: Robert H. Vincelette
General Sales Manager: Francis Emmons
Vice-President and General Manager: B. S. Sloboda
Senior Mechanical Engineer: William Flanders

98 route miles; 2 locomotives; 4 freight cars.

THE ST. PAUL UNION DEPOT COMPANY
2071 University ave, St. Paul, Minn 55104

President: F. W. Crouch
Secretary and Comptroller: M. Schensted
Chief Engineer: John L. Jensen

1.54 route miles.
C. R. Hussey, C. & N.W. Transp. Co, Chicago, Ill; F. W. Crouch, Soo Line RR Co, Minneapolis, Minn; F. S. Farrell, Burlington Northern Inc, St Paul, Minn; M. Garelick, C.M. St P. & P. RR Co, Chicago, Ill; C. R. Grogan, C.R.I. & P. RR Co, Chicago, Ill.

SAN FRANCISCO BELT RAILROAD
Ferry Building, San Francisco, Cal 94111

Superintendent: J. B. Silva
Master Mechanic: J. J. Quinn
Traffic Manager: T. Grinstead
Chief Engineer: E. L. Sembler

Operated by City of San Francisco.
58 route miles; 4 locomotives.

SANTA MARIA VALLEY RAILROAD COMPANY
PO Box 340, Santa Maria, Cal 93454

President: Marian Hancock Barry
Vice-President and Manager: Sue J. Sword
Secretary and Treasurer: J. E. Barry
Superintendent, Transportation: E. E. Estes
Superintendent, Shops: Cal McDonald
General Freight Agent: R. W. Van Orsdel
Auditor: D. H. Blackie

18 route miles; 8 locomotives.

SIOUX CITY TERMINAL RAILWAY COMPANY
Exchange Building, Sioux City, Iowa 51107

President and General Manager: Ray A. Rodeen
Vice-President: L. V. Kuhl
Secretary, Treasurer: Rodney A. Livings
Auditor: Fred Heuy

Loading and unloading rail-borne livestock only. Roadbed leased. No rolling stock.

SIERRA RAILROAD COMPANY
781 S. Washington St, Sonora, Cal 95370

President: Charles Crocker
General Manager: D. J. Franco
Treasurer: H. B. L. McClung
Master Mechanic: C. K. Logan

57 route miles; 5 locomotives.

SOUTH CAROLINA STATE PORTS AUTHORITY
Charleston, Georgetown, Port Royal, SC

Executive Director: W. Don Welch
Director of Operations: Joseph P. D'Amaral
Director of Trade Development: Charles A. Marsh
Director of Finance: G. Luther Rosebrock
Director of Management Studies: Larry E. Beldner

UPPER MERION AND PLYMOUTH RAILROAD CO
Box 112, Conshohocken, Penn 19428

President and Treasurer: Joseph I. Hallman
Secretary and Comptroller: Donald F. Riley
Manager, Traffic and Car Service: Frank E. Schuman
General Superintendent: V. P. Perone

16 route miles; 8 locomotives; 174 freight cars.

VENTURA COUNTY RAILWAY COMPANY
Box 432, Oxnard, Cal 93030

President: M. V. Smith
Vice-President: R. G. Barnard
Vice-President and General Manager: C. C. O'Hara
Secretary and Treasurer: Mrs. M. E. Garlock
Controller: Walter Graf

11 route miles; 2 locomotives.

VIRGINIA BLUE RIDGE RAILWAY
Piney River, Va 22964

Chairman of the Board: Roy C. Lytle
President: John W. Cobb
Secretary and Assistant Treasurer: Mrs. J. W. Spencer
General Superintendent: E. T. Drumheller

10 route miles; 2 locomotives; 3 freight cars.

VIRGINIA CENTRAL RAILWAY
Box 239, Fredericksburg, Va 22401

General Manager: F. Freeman Funk

Connects with R F & P. 1 mile; 2 locomotives.

WARREN AND OUACHITA VALLEY RAILWAY COMPANY
PO Box 150, Warren, Ark 71671

President: R. J. Lane
Vice-President: C. R. Grogan
Assistant Treasurer: J. J. Magruder
Comptroller: V. C. Bohne
Auditor: L. C. Hedger
General Manager: L. Williams, Jr
Assistant Secretary: R. S. Lindsey
Assistant Secretary: R. A. Weise
Director Tax Administration: L. J. Kuntze

Associated with CRI & P.
16 route miles; 1 locomotive.

WINCHESTER & WESTERN RAILROAD CO
Box 264, Winchester, Va 22601

President, and Treasurer: Betty L. Hughes
Vice-President, Secretary: Lanny J. Hughes
Secretary: Leslie J. Hughes

18 route miles; 1 locomotive.
Connects to B & O.

YAKIMA VALLEY TRANSPORTATION CO.
Yakima, Wash 98902

President: G. H. Baker
Vice-President and Secretary: J. W. Jack
Manager: J. L. Price
Superintendent, Operating and Traffic: R. B. Hardin
Chief Engineer, Engineering: G. W. McDonald

21 route miles; electric; 2 locomotives.

URUGUAY

STATE RAILWAYS ADMINISTRATION

Administración de Ferrocarriles del Estado (AFE),
La Paz 1095, Montevideo

President: Cnel. Iván Paulós
Vice-President: Cnel. Oscar Maciá
Director: Cnel. Carlos Poladura
Secretary General: Sr. Carlos Baldomir
Chief, Publishing: C/C (R) Edison Iglesias
General Manager: Cr. Carlos M. Lázaro
Deputy General Manager: Ing. Julio Ader
Office Manager: Cr. Máximo Dellacasa
Manager, Developments: Ing. Martin Zorrilla
Manager, Traction: Ing. Humberto Preziosi
Manager, Works: Ing. José Rinaldi
Chief Signalling and Communications: Ing. Francisco Puppo
Chief, Medical Dept: Dr. Héctor Bazzano
Chief, Stores Dept: C/N (R) Inocencio Feijoo
Chief, Personnel Dept: Sr. Lorenzo Pena

Gauge: 1.435 m
Route length: 2 987 km

New rail links with Argentina are major features of a five-year (1977-81) railway modernisation and expansion plan in Uruguay. The plan includes development of the Litoral line and continued extension of the central line northwards from km 329. Now under construction is a new 27 km section between Mercedes and Ombucito which is due for completion in 1980 providing a cut-off for the existing Chamberlain-Duraznolink with Argentina. Also due for completion by 1980 is a new international rail connection across the hydro-electric dam at Salto Grande.

TRAFFIC	1975	1976
Total freight tcn-km	302 438 000	352 218 000
Total freight tonnage	1 424 000	1 570 000
Total passenger-km	362 308 000	371 600 000
Total passengers carried	6 074 000	6 078 000

FINANCES	1973 N$	1974 N$	1975 N$	1976 N$
Revenues	5 100 886.47	11 229 886.79	25 244 000	43 077 000
Expenses	13 943 132.27	20 273 731.21	47 667 000	76 654 000
	19 044 018.74	31 053 018.00		

MOTIVE POWER

Improvements to the motive power fleet in 1974 included installation of two reconditioned Alco diesel engines and purchase of 12 further reconditioned power units financed with proceeds of a $US 800 000 World Bank loan.
During the year 13 General Electric and Alco diesel locomotives were repaired in AFE shops and 14 Alsthom locomotives received extensive renovation using spare parts supplied from France at a cost of $US 500 000. The railway now plans to overhaul eight more locomotives at a cost of about $US 850 000 which will enable them to be returned to service.
Purchases during the year included four diesel shunting units from General Electric and 500 40-ton freight wagons. Orders have now been placed for 543 wagons with the United States department of defence.
Other motive power introduced in 1977 includes 15 diesel trainsets (power car plus second-class intermediate trailer and first-class trailer with driving cab and bar), one railcar, six first-class trailers, and spare parts from Ganz-Mavag, Hungary, at a cost of $US 8 539 231.

TRACK

Work began in 1977 on the Mercedes-Ombucito cut-off in western Uruguay. Completion of the cut-off will provide a direct link between Montevideo and the Fray Bentos—Algorta line and reduce transit times for north-south freight which has previously used the circuitous route via Tres Arboles and Molles. The Mercedes—Ombucito cut-off is 27 km long and includes a major bridge across the River Negro. Together with the planned Bellaco—Paysandu cut-off further north, it will greatly improve access to northwestern areas; in the long term it will also form part of the route from Montevideo to Argentina across the Salto Grande dam, due for completion in 1980, thus completing the Coast Railway project along the River Uruguay.
Three new lines are planned:
(1) Litorial line, running from Bellaco to Paysandú, and forming the first section of a new projected link with Argentine State Railways (FA) and Ferrocarril Presidente Carlos Antonio Lopez of Paraguay;
(2) Construction of a new rail bridge across the Rio Negro river and extension of the present line running from Sarandí del Yí to km 329, and subsequently to km 347;
(3) 13-km ore line from Valentines on the Florida-Melo line as far as new mine deposits.
The Litorial line project is designed to stimulate economic development around Paysandú which is now Uruguay's second most important industrial city. Construction will also speed rail transport into and out of both Fray Bentos and Salto which are expected to grow in importance within the next ten years or so.
Construction will, in fact, involve three new lines: Bellaco to Paysandú, Mercedes to Ombucito, and a 14 km extension just north of Salto towards new dam works and the frontier with Argentina.
Toughest construction project is likely to be between Mercedes and Obucito which passes through difficult terrain. Materials required include: 1 500 tons of 18-m length 40 kg/m rails; 2 000 pairs of fishplates; 30 000 sleepers (either timber or steel); 120 000 rail spikes; 22 000 m³ of ballast.
The projected new bridge across the river Rio Negro was, in fact, started in 1948 when work was halted south of km 329 on an extension constructed from Blanquillo. The final bridge will be 2 080-m long and materials required are: 1 450 tons of 18-m lengths of 40 kg/m rails; 28 200 timber or steel sleepers; 2 000 pairs of fishplates; 116 000 rail spikes; 20 000 m³ of ballast.

VENEZUELA

VENEZUELA STATE RAILWAYS

Instituto Autónomo Administración de Ferrocarriles Del Estado, ave Principal los Ruices, Edif Stemo, Pisos 1, 2, 3, Caracas

General Manager: Ing. Roberto Agostini C.
General Secretary: Ing. Antonio Lyon Luchessi
Director: Ing. Lucio Baldó Soules
Director: Ing. Italo Chaparro
Director: Arq. Samuel Benchimol
Director: Ing. José González Lander
Director: Gral. Brig. Humberto Blanco
Director: Ing. Olegario Briceño
Director: Sr. Carlos Andrade
Legal Adviser: Dr. Rafael A. Ron
Technical Adviser: Ing. Antonio Ornés R.
Development and Operations Manager: Ing. Antonio Ascanio
Administration and Finance Manager: Econ. Carlos Villegas
Manager, Planning and Costing Office: Econ. Hugo Padilla
Manager, Public Relations Office: Dr. Luis Montagne R.
Manager, Personnel Office: Prof. Carlos Padilla L.

Gauge: 1.435 m.
Route length: 175 km.
Track length: 264 km.
Proposed route length: 777 km.

TRAFFIC	1974	1975	1976
Ton-km	10 279 536	14 230 388	13 652 109
Tonnage	97 924	117 577	116 266
Passenger-km	43 046 081	39 798 862	41 895 666
Passenger journeys	392 118	300 554	381 763

FINANCES	1974	1975	1976
		(Bolivars)	
Income	9 581 428	8 230 744	8 812 100
Expenses	12 471 406	15 666 759	19 864 000

MOTIVE POWER

Number of locomotives in service (1975): 1 diesel-electric 1 500 hp; 6 diesel-electrics 1 750 hp; 3 diesel-electric shunters 700 hp.

ROLLING STOCK

In operation: 200 freight wagons; 22 passenger coaches.

TRACK WORK

A new plan recommends construction of a rail system measuring 3 700 km by 1990. Work will commence starting on the existing line from Puerto Cabello to Barquisimeto line at Yaritagua and proceed towards Acarigua, Villa Bruzual, Guanare and Barinas. Extensions will then be constructed to San Juan de los Morros, Valle La Pascua, Anaco, El Tigre, Ciudad Bolivar and Ciudad Bolivar. A branchline to Tuy Medio is at present under consideration.
In addition to these lines which are due for completion by 1979, new sections between Moron, Yaracol and Riecito which will carry a million tons of phosphates annually from the mines of Riecito for processing at the petrochemical plant at Moron are being constructed at present.
By 1979, therefore, a total of 1 160 km under the plan will be completed and 90 km under construction. To which must be added the 178 km already in operation. Cost of construction by the year 1979 will be 2 403 million Bolivars. The lines planned will give rail access to the Altos Llanos Occidentales area of the Andina region, connecting with the central-western region and uniting the two with the sea and providing outlets for petrochemical plants which will supply fertilisers to agricultural regions under development.
Finally, the planned network will establish a freight corridor by 1980 able to serve the north-eastern and Guayana regions. In particular the railway will provide a new transport mode for the region of Sidor which is planned to generate 2.65 million tons of freight annually by 1980.
Second stage of the plan is to be carried out between the years 1979 and 1985. The following lines will be built:
—North-eastern region: Anaco—Barcelona—Cumana; Anaco—Maturin—Carupano
—Central region: San Juan de Los Morros—Calabozo—San Fernando de Apure; Vaijencia—Puerto Cabello
—Andean region: Barinas—San Antonio de Caparo; San Christobal—La Fria.
By the end of phase two, 1 088 new km of railway lines will have been built, bringing the total in operation to 2 513 km. Investments by 1985 will have totalled 4 055 million Bolivars.
Third and final stage of the mainline network will be completed between the years 1985 and 1990 with completion of the following lines: Barquisimeto—Carora—Sabana de mendoza—Mene Grande—Santa Rita—Maracalbo—Machiques—Orope; La Fria—El Vigia—Sabana de Mendoza; Yaracal—Coro—Punto Pijo.
Infrastructure investment during the third stage of the plan will total 1 920 million Bolivars and track constructed will total 1 114 km. So, by the end of the plan, 5 593 million Bolivars will have been spent on construction and it is forecast that 1 473 million Bolivars will have been invested in rolling stock.

Shunting operations at Cabello-Barquisimeto, centre of much of the railway's new plans for massive railway development.

VIET-NAM

VIET-NAM RAILWAYS SYSTEM
Regie des Chemins de fer du Vietnam
2, Cong-Truong Diên Hông, Ho Chi Minh City

The VRS metre-gauge system has an owned route length of 873 miles *(1 405 km)*. During 1977 Vietnamese government officials in Hanoi requested the World Bank for assistance to construct a railway passenger coach and freight wagon factory together with workshop facilities for maintenance of railway equipment. The request was made during a visit by a World Bank mission to Viet-Nam. Government officials who met the Bank economists stressed the nation's need to integrate the northern and southern regions by 1980, the end of the present Five-Year Plan period.

TRACK
The last metre of track on the 1 730 km trans-Viet-Nam railway, linking Hanoi with Ho Chi Minh city (formerly Saigon) was laid on 4 December 1976 and two trains started on experimental runs, one from Hanoi and the other from Ho Chi Minh city. The final track was laid on the Vinh Cith to Minh Cam portion, between Chu Le and Minh Cam. In the preceding month the Da Nang—Tien An section of the Thong Nhat railway, over 190 km long, had been opened to traffic, as had the 169 km Hoi-Hue section crossing the Bne Hai river.
But the key development was completion of the 11 km Chau Lau bridge on the Phu My—Da Nang railway section in Quang Nam-Da Nang Province. Because of its remoteness it was necessary to built a 30 km road to bring materials and equipment to the construction site and, despite flooding last October, the workers and cadres strengthened the old piers by means of 460 m³ of ferroconcentrate before assembling the main 180-ton girder bridge.
A total of 725 bridges with an aggregate length of 20 000 m have been built or repaired on the Thong Nhat railway. Among the 475 new bridges are the Yen Xuan bridge across the Lam river in Hghe Tinh Province, 420 m; the Ky Lam bridge over the Thu Bon river in Quang Nam-Da Nang Province, 500 m; and the Tra Khuc bridge spanning the Tra Khuc river in Nghia Binh Province, 550 m. To ensure the success of this bridge-building programme, dozens of engineering works, in co-operation with many mechanical co-operatives of various provinces, manufactured 20 000 tons of girders and tens of thousands of other bridge sections.
VR also completed in 1977 an 80 km link between Kep, north of Hanoi, and coal mines at Uong Bi.

FINANCIAL	1967	1968	1970	1971	1972
Revenue ($VN) (000's)	268 769	272 392	530 066	542 041	389 910
Expenses ($VN) (000's)	470 262	548 378	801 567	925 585	1 075 222
Operating ratio	174	201	151	170	275

TRAFFIC
Total freight traffic is expected to grow by 27.3% annually over the next five years. Rail freight is expected to increase by 30% a year over the same period.

	1971	1972	1973
Total tonne-kms (000's)	38 273.7	6 626.3	1 971.6
Total freight carried (000's)	554.6	136.9	38 116
Number of passengers carried	2 846.6	1 851.7	3 945 738
Total passenger-km		65 672 409	172 777 173

MOTIVE POWER TREND
Proportion of total train-kms operated by:—

		1965	1966	1967	1970	1971	1972
Steam traction	(%)	28.9	20.2	10.6	7.1	7.8	2.2
Diesel Traction	(%)	71.1	79.8	89.4	92.9	92.2	97.8

Number of locomotives in service include: seven line haul steam; three steam shunters; 35 line haul diesel-electric units; ten diesel-hydraulic shunters; two diesel-mechanical shunters.
Number of passenger coaches total 106; freight wagons, 660; and containers, 1 230.

YUGOSLAVIA

YUGOSLAV RAILWAYS
ZAJEDNICA JUGOSLOVENSKIH ZELEZNICA (JZ)
(Community of Yugoslav Railways)
Nemanjina 6, Belgrade

General Manager: Nicola Filipovic
Director Generals:
  Belgrade: Dipl. ecc. Djordje Strizak
  Sarajevo: Dipl. ing. Dane Maljković
  Zagreb: Directeur Principal Dipl. jur. et Dipl. ecc. Joakim Crnosija
  Skopje: Directeur Dipl. ing. Risto Petrovski
  Ljubljana: Dipl. ing. Joze Slokar

Gauge: 1.435 m
Route length: 9 993 km

Yugoslav Railways (JZ) drew up a medium term expansion plan in 1977; it involves 10 300 million dinars (£310 million) and covers the years 1977 to 1980.
A number of project guidelines have been drawn up for rail development up to 1985. These include:
—after the completion of the programme in hand, and after the completion of the new line from Belgrade to Bar, the modernisation programme in the narrower sense and the reconstruction of the principal main lines should be concluded;
—electric traction should be extended to another 1 200 km of key sections so that, by 1985, a total of 3 500 km will be electrified, and steam traction will have completely disappeared by 1980;
—modern signalling and telecommunication installations are to be introduced, in keeping with the traffic demands on the different lines;
—the axle loads will be increased so that all principal main lines will be able to take axle loads of at least 20 t; at the same time, these lines are to be remodelled for higher speeds (up to 160 km/h during the first phase);
—where necessary, the capacity of existing lines is to be increased through reconstruction or the addition of another track; these works should, by 1985, cover some 600 route kilometres;
—the railway junctions are to be re-modelled for automatic operation, and the automatic coupling will be introduced;
—motive power units and rolling stock as well as the equipment for integral transport, mechanical handling of goods, cybernetics and automatic data processing are to be modernised;
—the fleet of goods wagons is to be modernised with the aim of increasing the share of modern four-axled wagons, suitable for speeds above 100 km/h, to 80% of the fleet: similarly, there will be a substantial increase in the number of modern passenger vehicles with greatly improved technical and technological characteristics.

Croatian Railways (division of JZ) is to spend about £450 million in its 1975-85 modernisation programme. Work includes completion of main line electrification, upgrading of most lines for 160 km/h running, and expansion of the freight and passenger rolling stock fleets. Track-doubling will also be carried out between Zagreb and Novska, and Zagreb and Rijeka.

TRAFFIC

	1974	1975
Total freight ton-km (millions)	23 081	21 638
Total freight tonnage (millions)	81	78
Total passenger-km (millions)	10 429	10 284
Total passengers carried (millions)	135	129

MOTIVE POWER AND ROLLING STOCK
Delivery of 402 Diesel locomotives, 227 electric locomotives, 111 motor coach trains and railcars and 11 940 wagons to the Yugoslav Railways between 1969 and 1973 has contributed significantly to the renewal of the rolling stock fleet. Total fleet now includes 556 steam locomotives; 321 electric locomotives; 794 diesel-electric locomotives. Number of two-axle rail cars in service in 1976 was 526; passenger coaches total 3 396; freight wagons 52 350.

TRACK WORK
Following completion of the new Belgrade-Bar mainline, Yugoslav Railways (JZ) is to build seven new lines during the period 1975-85.
Lines planned include: Prahovo-Kladovo-Danube; Pec-Matesevo; Sarajevo-Priboj; Kavadarci-Mrezicko; Kicevo-Ohrid-Kanfanas; Seljakovci-Kriva Palanka-Guesevo; Rijeka-Karlovac.
During the same period three lines are to be double-tracked: Tabanovci-Sjopje-Titov Veles; Zagreb-Novska-Sisak; and Karlovac-Zagreb.
JZ has started double-tracking part of its Ploce line between Doboj Novi and Zenica *(93 km)* to raise capacity in 1977. Completion is scheduled for November 1978.
ELECTRIFICATION
Total electrified length is 2 647 km. It was announced during 1977 that the Belgrade ZTP is to electrify the newly opened Belgrade—Bar rail line using the proceeds of a 75 million Dirham loan from the United Arab Emirates.

SIGNALLING AND COMMUNICATIONS
JZ is to equip the main lines between Jesenice, Ljubljana, Belgrade and Skopje with high-frequency train radio. The system adopted is the same as that used on the German Federal Railway and supplied by AEG-Telefunken. A DM30 m contract has been signed.

DIESEL LOCOMOTIVES

Class	Axle Arrangement	Trans-Mission	Rated Power hp	Max kg	Tractive Effort Continuous at		Max Speed km/h	Wheel Dia mm	Axle Load Tons	Total Weight Tons	Length mm	No Built	Year First Built	Builders: Mechanical Parts	Engine	Transmission
					kg	km/h										
644	BoBo	Elec	600	16 650	12 030	8.5	80	1 040	15.4	61.7	12 290	80	1960	MAVAG	Ganz	Ganz
642	BoBo	Elec	825	16 000	10 950	14.5	80	1 100	16.8	67.2	14 740	104	1961	Dj. Djakovic	MGO/Dj.Dj.	Br&L/RK
643	BoBo	Elec	925	16 800	10 800	16.5	80	1 100	16.8	67.2	14 740	22	1967	Br&L/Dj.Dj.	MGO/Dj.Dj.	Br&L
644	A1AA1A	Elec	1 650		26 400		100	1 016	14.9	96.0	14 173		1975	Macosa	GM	GM
661	CoCo	Elec	1 950	21 200			120	1 016	18.0	108.0	17 272	218	1960	GM	GM	GM
662	CoCo	Elec	1 650	22 000	10 600	28.4	120	1 100	16.0	96.0	17 740	17	1965	Dj. Djakovic	MGO/Dj.Dj.	RK/Sever
663	CoCo	Elec	3 300		30 490		124	1 016	19.8	118.0	19 520	14	1972	GM	GM	GM
664	CoCo	Elec	2 200		26 290		124	1 016	16.3	108.0	15 764	58	1972	GM	GM	GM
665	CoCo	Elec	2 750				127			127.0		20	1972	MLW	MLW/Alco	GE
731	C	Hyd	400	12 500	3 600	17.0	60	950	14.0	42.0	10 500	44	1958	Jenbach/Dj.Dj.	Jenbach	Voith
732	C	Hyd	600	13 100	6 000	17.0	80	950	14.5	43.5	10 500	77	1969	Dj.Djakovic	Jenbach	Voith
733	C	Hyd	600	15 800	5 000	18.0	60	1 250	16.0	48.0	10 180	37	1968	Dj. Djakovic	MGO/Dj.Dj.	Voith
740	B B	Hyd	600	10 900	3 100	33.0	50	850	8.0	32.0	11 600	40	1968	Dj. Djakovic	MGO/Dj.Dj.	Voith
741	BB	Hyd	1 500	21 300	17 750	14.0	120	920	16.0	64.0	14 000	3	1966	MIN	Maybach	Maybach
742	BB	Hyd	1 650	19 200	16 800	12.0	120	1 000	17.0	68.0	14 400	60	1972	MIN	Pielstick	CKD-SRM
743	BB	Hyd	1 600				120	950	16.0	65.0	15 340	1	1975	Dj. Djakovic	MGO/Dj.Dj.	Voith
761	CC	Hyd	1 950	24 000			120	950	16.5	97.8	20 270	3	1957	Krauss-Maffei	Maybach	Maybach

740: 760 mm Gauge
RK: Rade Koncar
Zagreb
Br&L: Brissonneau & Lotz

ELECTRIC LOCOMOTIVES

Class	Axle Arrangement	Line Current KV	Type	Rated Power hp	Max kg	Tractive Effort Continuous at		Max Speed km/h	Wheel Dia mm	Total Weight tonnes	Length mm	No built	Year First built	Builders Mechanical Parts	Electrical Equipment
						kg	km/h								
341	BoBo	3	dc	2 130	19 000	13 800	53.0	95	1 250	78.0	16 024	1	1954	Alsthom	Alsthom
342	BoBo	3	dc	3 060		14 700		120	1 250	76.0	15 800	40	1968	ASGEN	OMFP
361	BoBoBo	3	dc	2 810	26 200	13 700	45.0	95	1 250	93.0	14 950	17	1930	Diff Italian	manufacturers
362	BoBoBo	3	dc	4 550	33 000	26 400	45.0	120	1 250	110.0	18 400	40	1960	ASGEN	OMFP
363	Coco	3	dc	3 750	25 000	15 400	63.0	125	1 100	114.0	20 190	40	1976	Alsthom	Alsthom
441	BoBo	25	5oac	5 550	28 000	17 700	65.0	120	1 250	78.0	15 470	190	1967	SGP/RK	Traction Union
461	CoCo	25	5oac	6 840	42 000	26 500	69.5	120	1 250	126.0	19 800	45	1972	Electroputere	Electroputere

ZAÏRE

SOCIETE NATIONALE DES CHEMINS DE FER ZAIROIS (SNCZ)

PO Box 297, Lubumbashi, Shaba Region

Director General: Gaston Goor
Secretary General: Citoyen Kasongo Nyamrie
Director of Operations: Robert Baudour

Gauge: 1.067 m; 1.00 m; 6.00 m
Route length: 3 573 km; 125 km; 1 025 km

The Republic du Zaire (name changed on 27 October 1971 from Republique Democ-ratique du Congo) has a superficial area of 904 600 square miles *(2 343 000 km²)*. With Kinshasa as its capital, the country is divided into eight regions: Bas-Zaire, Bandundu, Equateur, Haut-Zaire, Kivu, Shaba, Kasai Oriental, and Kasai Occidental. It is rich in minerals—copper, manganese and zinc concentrates being the main mineral exports. Agricultural exports include bananas, coconuts, cotton, rubber, and hardwoods.
The 3 ft 6 in *(1.067 m)* gauge KDL has a route length of 1 628 miles *(2 620 km)* of which 533 miles *(858 km)* is electrified. It is mainly single track with passing sidings, protected by Webb-Thompson electric token block system.
SNCZ was created in December 1974 with the merger of three former railways: La Compagnie des Chemins de Fer Kinshasa—Dilolo—Lubumbashi (KDL); Les Chemins de Fer des Grands Lacs (CFL); Les Chemins de Fer Vicinaux (CVZ). SNCZ is state owned. A total of 858 km are electrified.
The former KDL railway serves the important mining centres of the Shaba—Lubum-bashi, Likasi, Kolwezi and Mososhi—and other important mining and industrial areas such as the manganese mine at Kisenge, cement works at Lubudi, collieries at Luena, diamond mines at Mbuji-Mayi, etc. Expanding agricultural and forest product indus-tries have developed along the line of its route.
It connects at Ilebo (ex-Port Francqui) with the ONATRA inland waterway services; and at Kabongo with the CF des Grands Lacs (CFL).
Internationally, KDL has through connections at Dilolo with the CF du Benguela (CFB) in Angola to the Atlantic port of Lobito; and at Sakania with Zambia Railways and, further on, Rhodesian Railways, CF du Moçambique, and South African Railways.
Based on the continuing improvement in the economic situation, further increases in traffic movement are anticipated for the future. Production of copper from GECAMIN is scheduled to reach 450 000 tonnes in 1973 and 500 000 tonnes in 1976, and SODIMIZA will produce 1 200 tonnes of copper concentrates by the end of 1972.

RAILWAY DEVELOPMENTS

Steam traction ceased on the KDL in 1972 with the arrival of 15 more Class 1300 diesel-electric locomotives from General Electric (USA) and 10 Class 2500 electric locomotives built by Hitachi (Japan).
The position on the whole KDL system is as follows:
Electric traction   Lubumbashi—Kamina
Tenke—Mutshatsha
Diesel Traction   Kamina—Kabongo (connects with CFL)
Kamina—Ilebo (connects with ONATRA water services)

Mutshatsha—Dilolo (connects with CFB, Angola)
Lubumbashi—Sakania (connects with Zambia Rly.)

The work on the extension of the railway-operated Port at Ilebo has been temporarily suspended awaiting the results of a study of the stability of the quays. The work involves increasing the length of the quays from 1 640 ft *(500 m)* to 2 625 ft *(800 m)* and improving the lifting and handling equipment.
Special facilities are provided for mooring ONATRA barges and pumping oil to bulk storage tanks for distribution.
The port of Ilebo is the hinge of the National Transport Route, joining the KDL rail traffic and the ONATRA waterborne traffic streams.

TRAFFIC

Closure of the lines of Angola and Mozambique during 1975 resulted in SNCZ losing 900 wagons in the ports of Lobito and Beia—seriously affecting traffic loadings.

	1972	1973	1975	1976
Total freight tonnes (000's)	5 250	5 920	5 585	4 605
Freight tonne-kms (000's)	2 004 546	2 645 087	2 471 068	1 795 505
Total passengers carried (000's)	1 335	1 927	3 011	2 616
Passenger-kms (000's)	283 420	309 396	609 924	602 642

FINANCES

	1975	1976
	£Z	
Revenues	56 227 585	66 209 798
Expenses	67 245 884	92 880 877

MOTIVE POWER AND ROLLING STOCK

Number of locomotives in service 1976:

	Line	Shunting
Steam	—	3
Electric	56	5
Diesel electric	59	62
Diesel hydraulic	32	

Number of diesel railcars: 17
Number of passenger coaches: 234
Number of freight wagons: 5 405

ELECTRIFICATION

The heaviest traffic lines, in the Lubumbashi area, have been electrified at 25 000 V, single phase, 50 cycles.

	Route length		Completion
Route	Miles	Km	Date
Likasi-Tenke	65	105	1952
Tenke-Kolwezi	65	104	1954
Likasi-Lubumbashi	85	137	1956
Tenke-Luena	114	184	1959
Kolwezi-Mutshatsha	93	149	1963
Luena-Kamina	111	179	1970
Total	533	858	

DIESEL LOCOMOTIVES

Class	Axle Arrangement	Trans-mission	Rated Power hp	Max. lb (kg)	Tractive Effort Continuous at lb (kg)	mph (km/h)	Max. Speed mph (km/h)	Wheel Dia. in (mm)	Total Weight Tons	Length ft in (mm)	No. Built	Year first Built	Builders: Mechanical Parts	Engine & Type	Transmission
1300	Co-Co	Elec	1 650	48 000* *(21 750)* 57 750† *(26 190)*	55 500 *(25 200)*	6.8 *(11.0)*	37 *(60)*	36 *(914)*	87.3	46′ 4½″ *(14 134)*	38	1971-72	GE (USA)	GE FDL8	GE 76/A.10
1250 m	Co-Co	Elec	1 350 *(2×675)*	34 700* *(15 700)* 41 500† *(18 850)*	27 000 *(12 250)*	13.0 *(20.9)*	47 *(75)*	42 *(1 067)*	96	52′ 6″ *(16 000)*	2	1948	Whitcomb Loco Co	Caterpillar D 398A	Westinghouse
1260	Co-Co	Elec	1 500	33 000* *(15 000)* 39 700† *(18 000)*	29 750 *(13 400)*	13.6 *(21.8)*	45 *(72)*	42 *(1 067)*	80	51′ 6″ *(15 700)*	12	1969-70	Hitachi	MAN V22/30ATL	
1200 v	B-B	Hyd	550	24 800* *(11 250)* 29 800† *(13 500)*	22 300 *(10 120)*	4.0 *(6.4)*	20.5 *(33)*	36.6 *(880)*	45	37′ 9″ *(11 500)*	25	1968	Hitachi	Cummins VT-1710L	Twin-Disc
1160	B (0-4-0)	Hyd	320	19 800 *(8 970)*	16 500 *(7 500)*	3.1 *(5)*	19 *(30)*	33 *(840)*	30	17′ 1¾″ *(5 225)*	13	1965	Cockerill	Cummins NHRS-6	Twin-Disc
1100	C (0-6-0)	Mech	260	21 000 *(9 500)*	13 000 *(5 900)*	3.9 *(6.2)*	19 *(30)*	38 *(838)*	30	25′ 8¾″ *(7 842)*	2	1947	Fare-Root-Heath	Hercules DFXH	Twin-Disc
1900	B (0-4-0)	Mech	145	10 900 *(4 906)*	9 900 *(4 500)*	2.5 *(4.0)*	19 *(30)*	24 *(610)*	18	18′ 5¼″ *(5 620)*	1	1948	Fare-Root-Heath	Caterpillar D 13000	F-R-H

* 25% adhesion.   † 30% adhesion, using sand.

ELECTRIC LOCOMOTIVES

Class	Axle Arrange-ment	Line Current	Rated Output hp	Max. lb (kg)	Tractive Effort (Full Field) Continuous at lb (kg)	mph (km/hr)	Max. Speed mph (km/hr)	Wheel dia. in (mm)	Weight tonnes	Length ft in (mm)	No. Built	Year Built	Builders Mechanical Parts	Electrical Equipment
2100	Bo-Bo	25kV 1/50 ac OH	1 680	39 700 *(18 000)*	20 500 *(9 300)*	29.5 *(47.5)*	43 *(1 150)*	45¼	78 *(15 065)*	49′ 5″	10	1952	Brugeoise et Nivelles	ACEC
2200	Bo-Bo	,,	2 200	41 900 *(19 000)*	28 200 *(12 800)*	28.3 *(45.5)*	40 *(65)*	51⅛ *(1 300)*	76	50′ 1″ *(15 260)*	9	1956	,,	,,
2300	Bo-Bo	,,	2 040	48 500 *(22 000)*	36 800 *(16 700)*	19.5 *(31.5)*	40 *(65)*	43⅜ *(1 100)*	75	53′ 4″ *(16 260)*	11	1958	,,	,,
2400	Bo-Bo	,,	2 000	39 700 *(18 000)*	26 500 *(12 000)*	28 *(45)*	43 *(70)*	40 *(1 016)*	60	44′ 8¾″ *(13 630)*	2 9	1960 1964	,,	,,
2500	Bo-Bo	,,	2 150	41 000 *(18 600)*	33 770 *(15 320)*	23.2 *(37.3)*	43 *(70)*	40 *(1 016)*	64	47′ 1″ *(14 360)*	15	1968-72	Hitachi	
200	Bo-Bo	,,	640	46 300 *(21 000)*	17 200 *(7 800)*	13.7 *(22)*	28 *(45)*	36 *(914)*	62	45′ 9½″ *(13 960)*	5	1970	Hitachi	

Proportion of total train-miles operated by:—

		1961	1964	1966	1967	1969	1970	1971	1973
Steam traction	(%)	60.93	60.36	60.05	60.69	55.6	47.8	23	1
Diesel traction	(%)	0.20	0.32	1.59	1.18	4.7	12.2	28	51
Electric traction	(%)	38.87	39.32	38.36	38.13	39.7	40.0	49	48

TRACK CONSTRUCTION DETAILS

Standard rail: Vignole 59 and 80.6 lb/yd *(29.3* and *40 kg/m)* in length of *10 m* and *12 m.*

Joints: Fishplates and bolts.

Welding: See paragraph below.

Cross ties (sleepers): Steel: T.2243 (MI) weighing 112 lb *(51 kg)* each, under *37* and *40 kg* rail. T.3376C weighing 93 lb *(42 kg)* each, under *29.3 kg* rail. RS type prestressed concrete sleepers and T.3401A wooden sleepers under long welded rail.

Spacing: 2 400 per mile *(1 500 per km).*

Rail fastening; By lugs or clips and bolts to steel sleepers. RN flexible fastenings to concrete sleepers.

Filling: Broken stone.

Gauge widening:
   Nil: Tangent to 2.9° curve; rad. of 1 968 ft *(600 m).*
   0.35 in *(9mm):* 2.9°-4.3° curvature; min. rad. of 1 968-1 312 ft *(600-400 m).*
   0.7 in *(18 mm):* Curves sharper than 4.3°; min. rad. of 1 312 ft *(400 m).*

Max Curvature: 8.75° = radius of 656 ft *(200 m).*

Max gradient: 1.25% (1 in 80) except between Tenke and Bukama 2% (1 in 50).

Max altitude: 5 295 ft *(1 614 m)* at Dilongo-Yulu near Tenke on Bukama line.

Max permitted speed:
   Electrified lines: 32 mph *(52 km/h).*
   All other lines: 28 mph *(45 km/h).*

Max axle load: 15 tons nominal: 20 tons in special cases.

WELDED RAIL

At the end of 1973 the length of track laid with welded rail was 652 miles *(1 055 km)* of which 1.8 miles *(3 km)* were laid during the year.

Rail weighing 59.2 and 80.6 lb/yd *(29.3* and *40 kg/m)* in workshops. These are carried to site and thermit welded into long welded rail. The longest individual length of continuous welded rail is 10 miles *(16 km).*

SIGNALLING AND TRAIN CONTROL

Traffic in the industrial zone is increasing so rapidly that the Likasi-Tenke section in particular could become saturated. Accordingly, centralised Traffic Control (CTC) is to be installed on the sections Likasi-Tenke-Kolwezi.

The control centre will be at Likasi and will eventually control all traffic movement on the sections Lubumbashi-Likasi-Tenke-Kolwezi, a total route length of about 190 miles *(310 km).*

ZAMBIA
ZAMBIA RAILWAYS
PO Box 935, Kabwe

RAILWAY BOARD
Chairman: B. M. Monze
Members: Senior Chief Mushili
   D. A. R. Phiri
   A. B. Munyama
   A. M. Misiya

MANAGEMENT
General Manager: H. J. Soko
Deputy General Manager: A. K. Mazoka
Assistant General Manager: S. S. Wier
Director of Research: M. S. Shankaya
Chief Accountant: C. Sengebwila
Manager Administration & Company Secretary: L. Y. Kalumba
Commercial Manager: P. C. Nkonkomalimba
Operations Manager: K. Mason
Personnel Manager: F. Mulenga
Chief Civil Engineer: N. K. Sikka
Chief Mechanical Engineer: J. Zulu
Chief Signal and Telecommunication Engineer: Y. U. Hussain
Chief Supplies Officer: B. M. Kunda
Chief of Transportation: D. Mwape
Chief of Transportation (Development): G. Dollis
Commandant ZR Police: B. Mwale
Customer Services Manager: G. Mungaila
Manager Passenger Sales and Services: F. B. Munkasu
Manager Industrial Participation: A. S. Lubinda
Manager Information Service: Mr. Wark
Chief Internal Auditor: G. Panek

Gauge: 1.067 mm
Route length: 1 104 km

TRAFFIC	1973	1974	1975
Total freight ton-km	1 323 414 434	1 105 514 929	919 401 000
Total freight tonnage	6 557 083	6 996 930	26 486 000
Total passenger-km	2 169 123 250	1 735 298 600	200 000 000
Total passengers carried	1 510 846	1 238 176	10 140 000

LOCOMOTIVES PUT INTO SERVICE 1975-1976
   Class: U-20-C
   Type: Diesel Electric
      Wheel (or Axle) Arrangement: Co-Co
      Max speed: 103 km/h
      Dimensions: Length over Frames: 15 846 mm
      Weight: 89.2 tonnes
      Number of Units: 12
   Builders: GEC, USA
   Tractive Effort: Continuous 22 800 kg
                  At 30% Adhesion 26 800 kg
      Number of Locomotives in Service: 89
      Line Haul: 59
      Shunting (Switching): 30

1 200-hp Zambesi class diesel-electric locomotive, supplied by General Electric Traction.

RAPID TRANSIT, UNDERGROUND
AND SURFACE RAILWAYS

AMSTERDAM

Authority:
Gemeentevervoerbedrijf Amsterdam (GUBA)
Stadhouderskade 1 (West), Amsterdam, Netherlands
Telephone: (20) 16 01 28
Cables: TRAMWAYS/AMSTERDAM

Type of system: Full-metro.

History: Amsterdam began operation on line 1 during
1977. A decision to proceed with the project, taken by
the City Council in 1968, was endorsed by the Government in 1970, when financial support of 195 million
guilders (approximately £23 million in 1969) was
promised, contributing about half the construction
cost of an 11 miles *(18 km)* line that will be the initial
line of a planned 48.5 mile *(78 km)* network. This first
line will start at Central Station, Netherlands Railways,
and run south-east for about 4.4 miles *(7 km)* before
dividing into two, one route of 3.7 miles *(6 km)* to East
Bijlmer and the other route of 3.1 miles *(5 km)* to
Bijlmermeer. The growing Bijlmermeer community is
expected to develop into a new town with 100 000
inhabitants by 1978.
The decision to provide Amsterdam with a Metro system was motivated by the need for sophisticated mass
transportation between Amsterdam's centre and its
suburbs. The bicycle, once predominant as a commuting conveyance, is disappearing as peripheral
development increases commuter distances to
roughly three times that of the pre-war average of 2.5

miles *(4 km)*. There are growing business and industrial areas (in the Schiphol Airport district, for example) to which the Metro network will eventually
extend. It will comprise three radial lines and one line
circling the central district. Under central Amsterdam,
a densely built up area of narrow streets, all Metro
lines will descend into tunnels. About 17.4 miles *(28
km)* of the network will be underground.

Technical Data:
Gauge: 1.435 m
Projected new lines (in construction): 18 km (3.5 km in
tunnel)
Number of lines: one under construction
Number of stations (total): 20
    (in tunnel): 5
Average distance between stations: 0.8 km
Stations:
    platform length (minimum): 150 m

Type of tunnel: In order to keep out ground-water, sections of the underground portions have to be built by
the pneumatic caisson method, which involves building pre-fabricated rectangular tunnel segments on the
surface and sinking them into their final positions
(with the tunnel roof 14 ft 9 in *(4.5 m)* below surface
level). Some 820 ft *(250 m)* will be of cut and cover
construction. The outer stretches of the initial line will
all be built on viaduct or embankment, except for a
short southern section, to be built in shallow concrete
trench about 6 ft 6 in *(2 m)* deep. The tunnels, 13 ft 6 in
(4.10 m) high above rail level and 27 ft 3 in *(8.30 m)*
wide, carry two tracks.

Gradient (max): 3.2%
Curvature (max): 300 m
Speed (design max): 80 km/h
    (average commercial): 35 km/h
Electric system: Third rail; 750 V
Type of rails: 49 kg/m

Rolling Stock: Rolling stock, built by Linke-Hofmann-
Busch, is made up of twin-coupled car units resting on
four bogies.

Car type:	MI.1	MI.2
Number of units:	33	33
Car dimensions (length):	18.27 m	18.67 m
(width):	3.01 m	3.01 m
(height):	3.54 m	3.54 m
Passenger capacity:		
per car (total):	150	153
(seated):	49	—
Rating:	180 kWh	—
Brakes (type):	Rheostatic	
Weight (tonnes): Motorcar:	26	26

Traffic Data:
Trains/track/hour (planned): 20
Train capacity (passengers): 1 200
Total passengers/track/hour (peak): 24 000
Train headways design: 2 minutes

Signalling: ATO is planned together with two-way radio
communications.

ANKARA

Authority:
Ankara City Transit
Mayor's Office, Ankara City Administration, Ankara,
Turkey

Type of system: Full-metro.

History: New City Transit Authority has been set up to
plan and design an 11.4 km transit system.

General: With a city area of 48 km² and a population of
1 270 000 Ankara has decided to plan for a future
transit system.

Technical Data:
Gauge: 1.435 m
Projected new lines (in design): 11.4 km
Number of lines: 2
Number of stations (total): 18

Speed (design max): 80 km/h
Electric system: Third rail; 750 dc

Rolling Stock:
Car type: proposed
Number of units: 130
Car dimensions (length): 15 m
    (width): 2.6 m

ANTWERP

Authority:
**Maatschappij Voor Het Intercommunaal Vervoer te
Antwerpen (MIVA)**
Grote Hondstraat 58, 2 000 Antwerp, Belgium
Telephone: (031) 30 99 15

Provisional pre-metro access ramp at De Keyzerlei.

General: Antwerp at present operates a 79.3 km light-rail
tram system: those sections at present operated in
tunnel are being upgraded to full-metro standards.
Following the start of operations on the 2.6 km section
of Antwerp's first 2.67 km pre-Metro line in 1975, city
authorities plan to have another 3.07 km of the line
open by mid-1979. Construction is now underway on
the Centraal station-Mercatorstraat section, with a
short spur to Belgiëlei. All concrete construction over
the section was completed by 1977. Work on the interchange station at Astrid began March 1976, although
work on the remainder of the line between Centraal
station and Schijnpoortweg will not start until after
completion of the second line: Frankrijklei-Zuid — Fr
Rooseveltplaats — Carnotstraat — Turnhoutsebaan —
Foorplein — Stenebrug. Work on this line started 1976.
Length of the final system has still to be decided, but it
is known that an initial two line system with a track
length of 20.7 km with 16 stations is planned for construction.

Interior view of the new Meir pre-metro station.

Construction:
**First section: Groenplaats—Centraal Station (oper-
ative):**
    The construction of this section started on January
    5, 1970. It became officially operative on March 25,
    1975. The present route length in use is 1 300 m, or
    2 600 m of single track.

**Second pre-metro section: Centraal Station—Bel-
giëlei—Mercatorstraat:**
    The construction of this section started on October
    22, 1973 at Station Diamant. It includes a total length
    of 3 070 m single track.
    The raw work was finished by early 1977 and the
    section will possibly be in full operation by mid
    1979.

**Third section: Centraal Station—St. Elisabeth-
straat—Onderwijsstraat:**
    Construction of the interchange station Astrid
    started on March 15, 1976 and will take 45 months
    for the raw work. Tunnelling has been adapted in
    order to lessen considerably the effects of the works
    on the local traffic and business, in the centre of the
    city. The remaining construction of this section, with
    a route length of 1 815 m or 3 630 m single track, will
    be undertaken after those of the second axis are
    completed.

**Second Axis: Frankrijklei Zuid—Fr Roosevelt-
plaats—Carnotstraat—Turnhoutsebaan — Foorplein
with branchline to Stenenbrug:**
    The route length of the Second Axis will be 4 520 m
    (9 040 m single track).Construction of the first sec-
    tion Turnhoutsebaan—Stevenbrug started March
    21, 1977.

ATHENS

Authority:
Athens/Piraeus Electric Railway Co Ltd (ISAP)
67 Athenas St, Athens, Greece
Telephone: (21) 3248 311
Cables: RYP Athens

History: The line between Athens and its port of Piraeus
was the first railway to be built in Greece. It was electrified in 1904 and in 1930 its northern end was carried
under the centre of Athens by means of a tunnel, of
"cut-and-cover" construction, extending from the
south end of Athenas Street to Attiki Station, and from
there to Kifissia in open way track.

General: Piraeus being the principal port of Greece,
there is naturally a heavy passenger traffic between it
and Athens; much of this traffic is carried by the Hellenic Electric Railways line. There are two lines of
buses between Athens and Piraeus and three lines of
buses within Piraeus. Further underground lines in
Athens have been proposed.

Technical Data:
Gauge: 1.435 m
Route length: 25.7 km

In tunnel: 2.9 km
Projected new lines (in construction):
    (in design): 21 m
Number of lines: 1
Number of stations (total): 20
    (in tunnel): 3
Average distance between stations: 1.35 km
Stations:
    platform length (max): 110 m

Type of tunnel: Double track, cut-and-cover, tunnel of
rectangular section, 24 ft 1 in *(7.34 m)* wide by 13 ft 9
in *(4.2 m)* high, with centre supports.
Gradient (max): 3%
Curvature (max): 160 m
Speed (design max): 80 km/h
    (average commercial): 35 km/h
Electric system: Third rail; 600 V
Type of rails: Flat bottomed

Car type (year introduced):	1925	1952-58-68
Number of units:	61	74
Car dimensions (length):	13.8 m	17.8 m
(width):	2.70 m	2.86 m
(height):	3.66 m	3.60 m

Passenger capacity:		
per car (total):	120	180
(seated):	36	56
Motors per car:	4	4
Train composition (minimum):	2	2
(max):	5	4
Brakes (type):	Air	Regener-ative and Air
Body material:	wood	steel
Motor rating:	95 k/wh	120 k/wh

Traffic Data:
Trains/track/hour: 16
Train capacity (passengers): 900
Total passengers/track/hour (peak): 14 400
Train headways
    design: 3.5 minutes
    existing: 3.5 minutes
Passengers carried (weekday): 235 000
    (annually): 86 010 000
Average journey length: 7.6 km
Vehicle-km operated annually: 13 150 000 km

Signalling: Wayside signals incorporated with non-
computerised central traffic control office.

ATLANTA

Authority:
Metropolitan Atlanta Rapid Transit Authority (MARTA)
2200 Peachtree Summit, 401 West Peachtree St, NE
Atlanta, Ga 30308, USA
Telephone: 1-404-586-5000

Board Chairman: John E. Wright
Board Vice-Chairman: William R. Probst
General Manager: Alan F. Kiepper
AGM Transit Operations: Donald Valtman
Transit System Development AGM: William D. Alexander
AGM Planning and Public Affairs: Morris J. Dillard
AGM Finance and Administration: Robert Duvall
Legal Counsel: Jeff Trattner

History: From 1962 onward the Atlanta authorities put forward successive proposals for a massive rail rapid transit system to serve the city and metropolitan area. In 1971, after a public referendum, the go-ahead was finally approved.

General: The Metropolitan Atlanta Rapid Transit Authority (MARTA) has begun work on construction of an 85-km rapid rail transit system that is eventually to be operated in conjunction with the existing fleet of 735 buses and a new 12.8-km rapid busway system.
MARTA estimates that the total new rapid transit system of 98.2 km will cost about $2 100 million, of which $800 million will come from federal funds.
The Phase A System will consist basically of two lines—one running east to west from Avondale to High Tower Road (to include 13 stations), and the other running south-north from Garnett Street to North Avenue.
The eastern section of the first line is expected to go into service by December 1978, the western section by the end of 1979, and the north-south line by the end of 1980.
Meanwhile, MARTA has taken delivery from Franco-Belge of France of the system's first 100 transit cars. Value of the order is $54.2 million. Franco-Belge negotiated a sub-contract for electric traction equipment with Garrett Corporation of the United States. A fully-regenerative solid-state chopper system will be used.

Technical Data:
Number of lines: 4
Number of stations (total): 38
Gauge: 1 435 mm

Total route length (Planned): 85.3 km
Total track length (Planned): 170.6 km
Average speed: 0.89 km/sec (Designed)
Max speed: 1.88 km/sec (Designed)
Couplers: Ohio Brass Transit Coupler with Walton Electric Heads.
Height above rail (mm): 10 couplers center line, 558.8 (22″)
Braking: Pneumatic over hydraulic tread brakes; Westinghouse Air Brake Servotrol
Rails: 119 RE
Weight (kg/m): 119 lb/yd (52.12)
Sleepers:
Type: Concrete
Thickness (mm): 152.40 min/194.45 max
Number per km: 1 312
Track:
Minimum curvature: 228.60 m (main line); 106.68 m (yard and secondary)
Max gradient: ±3%
Max altitude: 333.19 m present design

Axle load:
Max 13 834.8 kg (Standard)
$$0\frac{122\ 000\#}{4} = 30\ 500\#/\text{axle}$$

AUCKLAND

Authority:
Passenger Transport Division
Auckland Regional Authority, 121 Hobson Street, Auckland 1, New Zealand
Telephone: 364 420
Cables: TRANSBOARD/AUCKLAND

General: A report on the city's comprehensive transportation needs was released by the regional authority in 1976 after a three-year study. This report indicates that an original scheme—consisting of a 5-km underground inner city loop and a 26-km surface line from Auckland central to Papakura in the south—will no longer provide sufficient benefits to justify its costs. The latest transit proposals recommend scrapping the underground inner city loop scheme and achieving cost effectiveness through upgrading services on the existing rail line between Auckland and Papakura.

BAKU

Authority:
Bakinski Metropolten
Baku City Soviet, Baku, USSR

Type of System: Full-metro

History: Baku, situated on the west coast of the Caspian Sea, is the capital of Azerbaidjan and in 1973 had a population of 1 337 000. Construction has been in progress for some time on an underground railway for the city. During excavation for the tunnels and station structures, variations in the ground from rock to water-bearing subsoil were encountered. Tunnel lining methods made use of concrete rather than iron segments, and take the form of ring elements of ferro-concrete blocks, which are said to have had a considerable saving effect on construction costs.
Prior to the recent line extensions the annual total of passengers carried on the Baku Metro was approximately 42 millions, including 62.9 million in 1972.
In late 1967 the first section of line 6.3 miles *(10.1 km)* was opened, with six stations: Narimanov, Gyandzhlyk, 28 April, Shaumyan 26 Baky Commisars, Baku Sovety, four of which lie at deep level and are served by high-speed escalators. This line connects three main districts, the western administrative, the eastern residential, and the central industrial. Ulduz station was opened in 1970. A further 8.5 km of route serving 4 more stations planned over the next 3 years, is nearing completion. During 1973 extensions to the east and west were opened, to Neftchila and Nizami respectively.

Technical Data:
Gauge: 1.524 m
Route length: 10.5 km
In tunnel: 10.5 km
Projected new lines (in construction): 8.1 km
Number of lines: 2
Number of stations (total): 7
(in tunnel): 6
Average distance between stations: 1.4 km
Stations
platform length (max): 100 m

Type of tunnel:
Speed (design max): 75 km/h
(average commercial): 42 km/h
Electric system: Third rail; 825 V
Type of rails: 50 kg/m

Welded joints: 320 m

Rolling Stock:
Car type (year introduced): 1960

Car dimensions (length): 18.8 m
(width): 2.7 m
Passenger capacity:
per car (total): 170
(seated): 40
Motors per car: 4
Train composition (minimum): 5
(max): 5
Brakes (type): Regenerative and electro/magnetic
Body material: Steel
Weight (tonnes) motorcar; 32
Motor rating: 68 kW/h

Traffic Data:
Trains/track/hour: 20
Train capacity (passengers): 850
Total passengers/track/hour (peak): 17 000
Train headways:
design: 3 minutes
existing: 3 minutes
Passengers carried (weekday): 172 000
(annually): 40 800 000
Average journey length: 4.9 km
Vehicle-km operated annually: 5 500 000

Signalling: Cab signals with non-computerised central traffic control office; ATS and ATC systems are utilised.

BALTIMORE

Authority:
Mass Transit Administration of Maryland
1515 Washington Blvd, Baltimore, Md 21230, USA
Telephone: (301) 539 6281

Type of system: Full metro

Section A of the Baltimore Region Rapid Transit System, a distance of 12.8 km, is scheduled to be operating in 1982.
Initial funding of Section A was approved by the Maryland General Assembly in 1976. Construction began in late 1976 on the Bolton Hill Tunnel segment and is now progressing on two additional tunnel segments and the first subway station.
Section A extends from the Charles Center Station in the retail-business district of Baltimore City to the Baltimore City-Baltimore County line at Reisterstown Plaza. It includes nine stations, six subway and three aerial; 4.5 miles in subway, less than one mile at grade, and 2.5 miles of aerial structure.
Although funding is only available at this time for Section A, under Phase II planning by the Maryland Department of Transportation, several other lines are being evaluated for future expansions. The primary considerations are an extension of the Northwest Line (Section A) to Owings Mills, a South Line and a Northern Central Line to Cockeysville.
A feeder bus system, now being designed, will integrate the city's bus network with the rapid transit system, providing fast and efficient access to the outlying stations. The three aerial stations will also be serviced by parking lots and Kiss N' Ride facilities (special lanes for dropping off people by car).
Section A is a dual-track system, high-speed (up to 75 mph) line, with steel-on-steel trains propelled by 650 V dc collected from a third rail. Six-car trains will be composed of married pairs, and 56 cars will be required for Section A. MTA engineers are evaluating several cars and plan to select a car which is generally proven and available at the time they are ready to order.
The Baltimore system will have a computer-equipped operations centre at the Lexington Market Station, but it is not a computerised central command system. The Baltimore command centre will have information on train performance and scheduling, but it will be up to dispatchers to handle irregularities. This system has the capability for manual operation if necessary, and it could be upgraded to full computerised control if desired in the future.
Automatic fare collection, using encoded cards similar to credit cards, may be installed in the Baltimore system at a later date but initially a form of semi-automation, based either on coins or cards, is preferable. Fares are expected to be compatible with MTA bus fares with free transfers from one system to another.
The cost of Section A is estimated to be $721 million, with almost 80 per cent, or $573 million, coming from the Urban Mass Transportation Administration, and 20 per cent, or $148, from the State of Maryland through its Consolidated Transportation Trust Fund.
It is expected that approximately 83 000 persons will ride the system daily.

Technical Data:
Route length (planned): 12.8 km
Projected new lines (in design): 45 km with 11.8 km in tunnel
Number of stations (total): 9
Speed (design max): 120 km/h
Electrical system: Third rail; 650 V

Rolling Stock:
Car type: proposed
Car dimensions (length): 22.9 m
(width): 3.35 m
(height): 3.00 m
Passenger capacity per car (seated): 75

BANGKOK

Authority:
Expressway and Rapid Transit Authority of Thailand
Bangkok, Thailand

Type of system: Full-metro

General: The Expressway and Rapid Authority of Thailand, formed in 1975, has proposed a three-line initial mass transit rail system for Bangkok for projected opening by 1983. The lines include: Pra Kanong-Bangsue (18 km); Wong Wiang Yai-Lard Prao (17 km); Dao Kanong-Makkasan (13 km). It is hoped that construction will start in 1978. The estimated cost of $US 150 million.

BARCELONA

Authority:

F.C. Metropolitano de Barcelona SA (FMB)
Ronda de San Pablo, 41, Barcelona 15, Spain
Telephone: (03) 241 00 07

Chief Executive: D. Roberto Cortadas Arbat
Director of Operations: D. Manuel Conde Cabeza
Director of Reserves and Development: D. José Piñol Vidal
Director of Administration: D. Joaquin Buguñá Forcat
Sub-Director, Chief of Operations: D. Juan Maria Mascort Corominas
Sub-Director, Chief of Rolling Stock: D. Fernando Coello Goyri
Sub-Director, Chief of Infra-structures: D. Guillermo Yenes Villafáñez
Sub-Director, Secretary General: D. José R. Fanés Sans
Sub-Director, Chief of Research and Development: D. Guillermo Virgili Rodón
Sub-Director, Chief of Personnel: D. Pedro Cuxart Bartoli
Chief of General Affairs: D. Agusti Masagué Petit

Type of system: Full-metro

History: First sections of each line were opened:—
Line No. 1: June, 1926.
Line No. 2: July, 1959.
Line No. 3: December, 1924.
Line No. 4: February, 1973.
Line No. 5: November, 1969.

General: There are now six underground railway lines in Barcelona, five are operated by *FC Metropolitano de Barcelona SA,* and the other by *FC de Sarria a Barcelona SA.* The lines operated by FCMBSA were once named but are now numbered.
The whole system is underground, except the Mercado-Sta. Eulalia section of Line 1.
Considerable expansion has been carried out in two stages. The Metropolitano has extended north, east, south, west and central, including construction of an entirely new line.
Line 2 (Sagrera-Horta) provisionally operated for Line 5, is currently being extended 4.31 km southwestward across the city to Pueblo Seco, to serve an additional 7 stations.

Technical Data:
Gauge: 1.674 m/1.435 m.
Route length: 44.1 km with 33 km in tunnel.
Projected new lines (in construction or projected): 77 km
Number of lines: 5, all double track.
Average station spacing:
Lines 1 and 3: 0.37 miles *(0.59 km).*
Line 2: 0.34 miles *(0.55 km).*
Lines 4 and 5: 0.43 miles *(0.70 km).*
Passengers per annum: 257 120 000
Number of cars per train: 4 motor cars, or 2 motor cars with 1 or 2 trailers.
Track gauge:
Line 1: 5 ft 6 in *(1.674 m).*
Lines 2, 3, 4, 5: 4 ft 8½ in *(1.435 m).*
Weight and type of rails:
Lines 1 and 3: 101 lb/yd *(50 kg/m).*
Line 2: 91 lb/yd *(45 kg/m).*
Lines 4 and 5: 109 lb/yd *(54 kg/m).*
All flat bottom rail.
Type of tunnel:
Line 1:   Double track tunnel 26 ft 3 in *(8 m)* wide and 18 ft 0 in *(5.5 m)* high above rail level.
Line 2:   Double track tunnel 23 ft *(7 m)* wide and 19 ft 3 in *(5.85 m)* high above rail level.
Line 3:   All as Line 2.
Line 4:   Double track tunnel 24 ft 1 in *(7.35 m)* wide and 18 ft 3 in *(5.55 m)* high above rail level.
Line 5:   As Line 2, except height 18 ft 5 in *(5.65 m)* above rail level.
Method and voltage of current supply:
Line 1:   Third rail; 37 kg/m; 1 500 V dc Sub-stations situated at tunnel mouth (Bordeta) and near the stations Triumfo Norte and Sagrera.
Line 2:   Overhead line, 1 200 V dc Sub-station situated near Sagrera common to this line and to remainder of Line 1.
Line 3:   Overhead line, 1 200 V dc Sub-station situated near Lesseps.
Line 4:   Aluminium steel third rail 6.75 kg/m. 1 200 V dc sub-station at Verdaguer.
Line 5:   As Line 2 with extra substation at Roma.
Rolling Stock:
Line 1:   Class "100": Built 1926. Body length 21.7 m, width 3.2 m. Three sets of sliding passenger doors on each side. Weight per car 55.7 tonnes. Number of cars: 12 (all motor cars). Class "200-A". Built 1944. Body length 16.5 m. Three sets of sliding doors on each side. Weight per car 34.5 tonnes. Number of cars: 4 (all motor cars). Class "200 B". Similar to Class "200-A" but with four sets of doors on each side. Built by Maquinista Terrestre y Maritima. Number of cars: 20 (10 motor cars, 10 trailers). Class "400"; similar to Class "200 B". Number of cars: 80 (60 motor cars, 20 trailers). Weight per car 40 tonnes.
Line 2:   Class 600. Built 1959. Body length 21.7 m, width 2.5 m. Four sets of sliding passenger doors on each side. Weight per car 40 tonnes. Number of cars: 14 (all motor cars). Built by "Material y Construcciones" (MACOSA).
Line 3:   Class "R" built 1923. Body length 14.604 m, width 2.52 m. Three sets of sliding doors on each side. Weight per car: 17.7 tonnes (motor car) 3.8 tonnes (trailer). Number of cars: 20 (12 motor cars, 8 trailers). Class "S" built 1943. Body length 14.852 m, width 2.348 m. Four sets of sliding doors on each side. Weight per car: 13.7 tonnes (motor car) 9.8

Four car trainset (class 600), built by Macosa, pulls into Sagrada Familia station on Line 2

Construction work underway at present:

Line	Route	Length km.	Stations	Date scheduled for completion
1	Sta. Eulalia—Hospitalet Centro	3.2	4	1979
1	Torras y Bages—Sta. Coloma	1.9	2	1980-81
2	Pueblo Seco—Sagrada Familia	4.3	7	1978
3	Lesseps—Montbau	3.2	4	1979
4V	Barceloneta—Selva de Mar	4.1	5	1976
4	Selva de Mar—La Paz	3.2	3	1977
4	Guinardó—Les Roquetes	3.8	3	1977
5	Pubilla Casas—San Ildefonso	2.5	3	1976
5	La Paz—Pep Ventura	3.9	6	1980-81
	Total	30.1	37	

Estimated costs in million Pts.

Line	Route	Infrastructure	Superstructure	Total route
1	Sta. Eulalia—Hospitalet Centro	650	575	1.225
1	Torras y Bages—Sta. Coloma	480	373	853
2	Pueblo Seco—Sagrada Familia	1.069	498	1.567
3	Lesseps—Montbau	890	573	1.463
4	Barceloneta—Selva de Mar	956	519	1.475
4	Selva de Mar—La Paz	557	500	1.057
4	Guinardó—Les Roquetes	599	473	1.072
5	Pubilla Casas—San Ildefonso	489	461	950
5	La Paz—Pep Ventura	1.080	765	1.845
	Total	6.770	4.737	11.507

tonnes (trailer). Number of cars: 4 (2 motor cars, 2 trailers). Class "B" built 1948 trailers, 1958 motor cars. Body length 14.852 m, width 2.510 m. Four sets of sliding doors on each side. Weight per car: 16 tonnes (motor car) 12.1 tonnes (trailer). Number of cars: 10 (6 motor cars, 4 trailers). Class "C" built 1962. Body length 14.872 m, width 2 560 m. Four sets of sliding doors on each side. Weight per car: 16 tonnes (motor cars), 12.1 tonnes (trailers). Number of Cars: 14 (4 motor cars, 10 trailers).
Line 4:   Class "C" as Line 2. Number of cars 18 (12 motor cars, 6 trailers).
Line 5:   Class "1000" motor cars delivered 1973/74. Built 1970-1-2. Body length 16.5 m, width 2.52 m. Three sets of sliding doors on each side. weight per car, 17.7 tonnes. Number of cars 66 (all motored). At present this line is also being serviced by 17 "C" class cars formerly on Line 3.
Signalling: Automatic block, with ac track circuits, and colour-light signals. Central Traffic Control is being introduced for Line 4.
Station layout: Station platform lengths vary from 88 m on Lines 1 and 2, to 96 m on Line 5, (75 to 90 m on Line 3). Their arrangements are various, adapted as the system grew (from formerly individual lines) for interconnection. Cataluna and Triunfo stations are common with the Spanish National Railways, which parallel the Metro Transversal on that section.

Authority:

FC de Sarria a Barcelona SA
1, Plaza de Cataluna, Barcelona, Spain
Telephone: (03) 2.21.14.90

Type of system: Full-metro

General: This line was originally wholly on the surface, and steam-operated. It has since been electrified, and its intown section (under the Calle de Balmes) has been rebuilt in tunnel. The Tibidabo line was opened in 1954. The line runs underground from Cataluna to Tibidabo and to Sarria. At the latter point it connects with the surface system of the associated Cataluna Railway Company, which has the same gauge, running on to Tarrasa and Sabadell.

Technical Data:
Gauge: 1.435 m
Route length: 7.1 km to Sarria and Tibidabo
In tunnel: 4.4 km

Projected new lines (in construction): 0.9 km
Number of lines: 2 (radial)
Number of stations (total): 12
(in tunnel): 11
Average distance between stations: 0.790 m
Stations:
platform length (max): 85
(minimum): 68

Gradient (max): 4%
Curvature (max): 150 m
Speed (design max): 60 km/h
(average commercial): 30 km/h
Electric system: Catenary; 1 300 V
Type of rails: Flat-bottomed

Rolling Stock:
Car type (year introduced): 1959
Number of units: 26 (all motor cars)
Car dimensions (length): 19.0 m
(width): 2.70 m
Passenger capacity:
per car (total): 116
(seated): 56
Motors per car: 4
Ratings: 92 kWh
Train composition (minimum): 1
(max): 2

Traffic Data:
Trains/hour/track: 24
Trains capacity (passenger): 232
Total passengers/track/hour (peak): 5 570
Train headways: 2.5 minutes
Passengers carried (annually): 26 500 000

Line	Route	Length km	Stations
1	Sta. Eulalia—Torras y Bages	12.2	20
2	Sagrada Familia—Horta	5.3	8
3	Zona Universitaria—Lesseps	10.9	17
4	Barceloneta—Guinardó	6.0	9
5	Pubilla Casas—Sagrada Familia	7.3	10
	Total in service	41.7	64

BERLIN (EAST)

Authority:
V.E. Kombinat Berliner Verkehrs-Betriebe (VEB)
Rosa-Luxemburg-Str 2, 102 Berlin, German Democratic
Republic
Telephone: (02) 51 03 11

Type of system: Full-metro

General: Line A, Pankow-Thalmannplatz, small profile,
4.66 miles *(7.49 km)*, including 3.32 miles *(5.32 km)* in
tunnel. Line E, Alexanderplatz-Friedrichfeld, large profile, 4.41 miles *(7.095 km)* all in tunnel.

Technical Data:
Gauge: 1.435 m
Route length: 14.6 km
In tunnel: 12.4 km
Projected new lines (in design): 56 km by 1995
Number of lines: 2

Number of stations (total): 22
Average distance between stations: 0.772 m

Gradient (max): 4%
Curvature (max): 74 m
Speed (design max): 50 km/h
  (average commercial): 25 km/h
Electric system: Third rail; 750 V

Rolling Stock:

Car type	A1	A2	E3
Number of units:	165[1]	89[2]	52[3]
Car dimensions			
(length):	12.1 m	12.4 m	18 m
(width):	2.3 m	2.3 m	2.6 m
(height):	3.2 m	3.2 m	3.4 m
Passenger capacity			
per car (total):	129	122	163
(seated):	27	26 motor cars	38
		34 trailers	

Motors per car: 4 4 4
Rating: 60 kWh 60 kWh 60 kWh
Train composition
  (minimum): 4 4 4
  (max): 8 8 8
Acceleration (max): 1.2 m/sec²
Deceleration (emergency): 1.2 m/sec²
Brakes (type): Electro-pneumatic

[1] 92 motor cars; 73 trailers
[2] 45 motor cars; 44 trailers
[3] 26 motor cars; 26 trailers

Traffic Data:
Trains/track/hour: 30
Train capacity (passengers): 1 200
Total passengers/track/hour (peak): 36 000
Train headways: 2 minutes
Passengers carried (annually): 61 000 000
Vehicle-km operated (annually): 11 200 000

BERLIN (WEST)

Authority:
Berliner Verkehrs-Betriebe (BVG)
Berlin (West) Eigenbetrieb von Berlin,
Potsdamer Str 188, 1 Berlin 30, German Federal Republic
Telephone: (0311) 2561
Cables: BEVAUGE BERLIN WEST

Type of system: Full-metro.
Route length: 93 km, including 75.8 km in tunnel.
Number of lines: 9 all double track.
Number of stations served: 100, including 15 interchange stations.
Average station spacing: 0.48 miles *(0.77 km)*.
History: Before the political division of Berlin in 1961, its
U Bahn system, one of the oldest on the Continent,
served the whole city. Today there are two systems
(that part in the German Democratic Republic is
referred to in the Berlin (East) entry) operating under
their own organisations. The BVG Authority operates
bus services in the western sector of Berlin in addition
to its U Bahn.
The first section of the present systems was opened in
1902, an 11.2 km stretch of line (now Line 1), of which
most was on viaduct and only 2.3 km in tunnel, from
Warschauer Brücke westward through central Berlin.
There has been progressive building of new lines and
extensions to existing lines in Berlin's western sector
since World War II, the last extension being on Line 8,
Osloer Str.—Gesundbrunnen.
The BVG transport network covers 8 underground
lines of a total length of 93.0 km of track and 100
stations, 15 of them interchange stations, as well as 83
bus lines having a total length of 1 046 km and 4 317

stops.
In 1975, the Underground carried 282 million passengers, the buses 400.6 million.
To perform this service a rolling stock of 914 transit
cars and 1 619 buses is available. In 1975 the buses
travelled a distance of 81 million km, the underground
59 million km.
U Bahn sections under construction: West Berlin is at
present building a 12.7 km extension of line 7 from
Fehrbelliner Platz to Rathans Spandau. The first 3.1 km
extension to Richard Wagner Platz will be opened in
April 1978. An additional 15 km is planned.
Passengers per annum: 285 010 000
**Passengers carried per annum on the whole of the BVG
system (Bus, U Bahn) (1976):** 685 650 000.
Max number of cars per train: "Large profile" lines 6;
"small profile" 8.
Max line density: about 40 000 passengers per hour
(Line 7).
Average scheduled speed (including stops): "Large pro-
file" lines 33.5 km/h.
Average scheduled speed (including stops): "Small pro-
file" lines: 28.8 km/h.
Track gauge: 4 ft 8½ in *(1.435 m)*.
Weight and type of rails: 82.8 lb/yd *(41 kg/m)*, flat-
bottomed, laid in *18 m* lengths.
Max gradient: 1 in 25 (4%).
Minimum radius of curves: 285 ft *(74 m)* on running
lines; 164 ft *(50 m)* on sidings.
Type of tunnel: There are two sizes of tunnel—"large
profile", on the former North-South Company lines
(now lines 6, 7, 8, 9 and E), and "small profile" on the
former Elevated and Underground Company lines
(now lines 1, 2, 3, 4 and 5). All are double-track rectan-

gular tunnels, with and without centre supports; the
large profile tunnels are 22 ft 8 in *(6.9 m)* wide and 11 ft
10 in *(3.6 m)* high from rail level, while the small profile
tunnels are 20 ft 6 in *(6.24 m)* wide and 11 ft 2 in *(3.4 m)*
high. Construction was mostly by cut-and-cover
method, the tunnels being generally just below surface level. Tunnel linings are of concrete.
Method and voltage of current supply: Third rail; 780 V
dc. Bottom contact current collection on large profile
lines.
Rolling Stock: Number of cars owned: 774 motor cars,
25 trailer cars (in three western sectors of Berlin only).
Details: Cars on the large-profile lines are 50 ft 10 in
(15.5 m) long and 8 ft 8 in *(2.65 m)* wide, with 3 double-
leaf doors on each side, and are made up in 2-car units.
The latest (1960-66) small profile cars are 12.5 m long
(body) and 2.30 m wide, with Scharfenberg coupling.
They are made up in 2-car units.
Signalling: Automatic block, with colour-light signals
and train stops.
Station layouts: Stations on the older sections of line
were built with platforms 262 ft 6 in *(80 m)* long. Later
stations had platforms 360 ft 10 in and 393 ft 8 in *(110
and 120 m)* long.
With the exception of stations on the oldest sections of
the small profile lines, which have separate side-
platforms, the standard station layout is of island type.
There are additional platforms at some of the terminal
stations. There is a variety of ticket hall layouts, many
being sub-surface, with stairwells from the street.
Interchange passages are provided at stations where
lines intersect, and where connection is made with the
electric suburban system of the main line railways (the
"Stadtbahn").

BOCHUM

Authority:
Bochum-gelsenkirchener Strassenbahnen AG
Universitatsstrasse 50/54—Postfach 349, 4630 Bochum,
German Federal Republic
Telephone: (02321) 37481

Type of system: Pre-metro

General: Bochum began construction in 1970 on a planned 42-km network with 2.1 km of tunnel to Hattingen
nearing completion. Future pre-U-Bahn lines are
planned to Herne/Witten, Castrop-Rauxel and Wat-
tenschied. Some of the existing 126.4 km of tramway

lines are to be incorporated. Details listed below
record facts on the existing tramway system.

Technical Data:
Gauge: 1.00 m
Route length: 109 km of which 34.7 km is over exclu-
sive right-of-way
Projected new lines (in construction): 2.1 km
  (in design): 42 km
Number of lines: 13

Speed (average commercial): 18.1 km/h

Rolling Stock:

Car type	ART4	6XDE	6XSE
Number of units:	5	33	proposed
Car dimensions (length):	21.2 m	21.2 m	21.2 m
(width):	2.2 m	2.2 m	2.2 m
Passenger capacity:			
per car (total):	176	180	190
(seated):	41	44	50
Rating:	163 hp	190 hp	190 hp
Train composition			
(minimum):	1	1	1
(max):	4	4	4

Traffic Data:
Passengers carried (1975): 42 000 000
Passenger-km (1975): 188 000 000

BOMBAY

Authority:
Metropolitan Transport Project (Railways).
Churchgate Station Bldg, (Annexe) 2nd Floor, Bombay
  400 020, India

General: The HTP, working under the Ministry of Railways, has recommended construction of two rail
transit corridors: 6 and 7. Proposed corridor 6 would
comprise a 33.7 km double-track line costing Rs 1 590
million (at 1972 values). The line would be mainly

surface except at the Fort Market south end terminal.
Corridor 7 would run 26.4 km and cost an estimated Rs
4 484 million; the line would run 1 km on the surface; 7
km elevated and 18 km underground.

BOSTON

Authority:
Massachusetts Bay Transportation Authority (MBTA)
50 High St, Boston, Mass 02110, USA
Telephone: (617) 722 5000

Type of system: Full-metro

General: The Massachusetts Bay Transportation Authority is seeking federal approval of a plan to reconstruct five miles of existing railway line at a total cost
of $476 million. The federal share would be $380.8
million. The project involves relocation of the existing
elevated Orange Line as well as improvements to the
railroad line, which is used for MBTA-sponsored
commuter service and is also part of Amtrak's intercity
network. Eight new rapid-transit stations will be constructed; three of them—Back Bay, Massachusetts
Avenue and Ruggles Street—will accommodate inter-
city passengers as well as Orange Line riders.

Technical Data:
Gauge: 1.435 m
Route length: 48 km
In tunnel: 15 km
Projected new lines: 15 km
Number of lines: 3
Number of stations (total): 49

(in tunnel): 21
Average distance between stations: 1.2 km
Stations:
  platform length (max): 146 m
  (minimum): 76 m

Gradient (max): 5%
Curvature (max): 122 m
Speed (design max): 80 km/h
  (average commercial): 31 km/h
Electric system: 6.5 km operated with catenary; all
remaining is third rail, 600 V dc
Type of rails: 42-57 kg/m

Rolling Stock:

Car type (year introduced)*:	1957	1963	1968
Number of units:	50 × 2	46 × 2	76
Car dimensions:			
(length):	16.77 m	21.18 m	21.18 m
(width):	2.84 m	3.15 m	3.05 m
(height):	3.63 m	3.80 m	3.77 m
Passenger capacity			
per car (total):	240	308	228 (motors)/ 239 (trailers)
(seated):	48	54	60/64

Motors per car: 4 4 4
Rating: 75 kWh 75 kWh 75 kWh
Train composition
  (minimum: 1
  (max): 8
Acceleration
  (max): 1.12 1.12 1.12
Deceleration
  (emergency): 1.56 1.55 1.45
Brakes (type): Regenerative
Weight (tonnes)
  Motorcar: 26.3 32.0 29.1
  Trailer: 27.6
* Additionally pre-metro operated on five lines using
230 PCC vehicles, and 38 light rail vehicles.

Traffic Data:
Trains/track/hour: 27
Train capacity (passengers): 1 060
Total passengers/track/hour (peak): 29 000
Train headways: 2.5 minutes
Passengers carried (weekday): 580 000
  (annually): 145 740 000
Annual vehicle operation: 11 037 765 revenue miles

Signalling: One line is operated via cab signal and the
other two by ATS, ATC and Train/Car Identification.

BRUSSELS

Authority:
Societe Des Transports Intercommunaux de Bruxelles (STIB)
Avenue de la Toison d'Or 15, 1060 Brussels, Belgium
Telephone: (02) 512 17 90
Cables: STIB-Bruxelles

Type of system: Full-metro/Pre-metro

General: Public urban transportation in Brussels includes buses, trolley-buses and trams. Over the 196 kms of bus routes and the 173 kms of tram routes, some 175 million passengers were carried during 1970. But in common with other comparable European cities, Brussels tram services suffer increasingly from delays wherever they operate in traffic-congested streets. To obviate such delays it was deemed necessary to segregate trams from other traffic in effected areas, and a project now being implemented will accomplish this by providing trams with their own underground rights of way, in the central area. Tramway tunnels and stations are being constructed, in design and proportion, for adaption to accommodate conventional Metro trains. The new system, named "Pre-Metro", will eventually extend over about 40 km of route; but conventional Metro trains will not be introduced until the tunnel system is sufficiently extensive to justify their use.

The first section of tunnel, 2¼ miles *(3.5 km)* long, on an East-West axis, became operative in 1969, with six stations. Full-scale Metro operations on the 7.8 km St. Catherine—Schumann line in 1976. By the end of 1977 other pre-Metro lines were being prepared for full-Metro Running. These included the 3.2 km inner ring, the 3 km outer ring, and the 2.5 km north-south line. By 1986 full metro operations are planned over 45 km. Trams in single and articulated units at first will operate through the tunnels; but a system of automatic signalling and braking will permit service frequencies of 45 seconds. The cars will provide from 105 to 160 seats. Running tunnels are rectangular (apart from a short section of circular tunnel) internally 24 ft *(7.40 m)* wide and 13 ft *(4.0 m)* high from rail level. Station platforms are 13 ft *(4.0 m)* wide and 311 ft *(95 m)* long, sufficient to accommodate conventional Metro trains of five cars.

Technical Data:
Gauge: 1.435 m
Route length: 7.8 km full-metro
Projected new lines (in construction): 13.4 km
(in design): 30 km
Number of lines: 1 Full-metro; 3 Pre-metro
Number of stations (total): 18
(in tunnel): 14
Average distance between stations: 600 m
Stations:
platform length (minimum): 95 m
Gradient (max): 6.2%
Curvature (max): 100 m
Speed (design max): 72 km/h
(average commercial): 30 km/h
Electric system: third rail; 750 V

Rolling Stock:
Car type (year introduced): 1976
Number of units: 55
Car dimensions (length): 18.2 m
(width): 2.7 m
(height): 3.55 m
Passenger capacity
per car (total): 210
(seated): 40
Motors per car: 2
Rating: 280 kWh
Train composition (minimum): 2
(max): 5
Acceleration (max): 1.16
Deceleration (emergency): 1.70
Brakes (type): regenerative/pneumatic
Body material: alloy
Weight (tonnes) Motorcar: 31

Traffic Data:
Trains/track/hour: 30
Train capacity (passengers): 850
Total passengers/track/hour (peak): 25 500

BUDAPEST

Authority:
Metro Budapesti Foldalatti Vasut
Hungaria Krt. 46, Budapest XIV, Hungary

Type of system: Full-metro.

General: First 3.7 km subway line opened in 1896. It was subsequently lengthened by 1.2 km, modernised and capacity increased to 9 000 passengers hourly in 1973.
First of the modern Metro lines (running 10.1 km east-west) was opened in 1972 and at present operates five-car trainsets carrying about 530 000 passengers daily on headways of 135 seconds in peak periods.
Now under construction is the 20.7-km north-south line, with the first 3.7 km section between Nagyvarad Square and Deak Square opened at the end of 1976. The complete line is scheduled to go into operation by the end of 1985.
Construction is to start on a planned southwest-northeast 20-km line in 1980 and should be completed by about 1990.
Final planned Metro line will run from Obuda in the northwest to Varga J. Ter in the south and is expected to be built by the year 2000 when the Metro will total a length of about 75.6 km.

Technical Data:
Gauge: 1.435 m
Route length: 13.8 km
In tunnel: 8.6 km
Projected new lines (in construction): 20.7 km
(in design): 75.6
Number of lines: 2
Number of stations (total): 11
(in tunnel): 9
Average distance between stations: 1.08 km
Stations:
platform length (minimum): 120 m

Type of tunnel: Bored single-track tunnels are 16 ft 8 in (5.1 m) inside diameter, lined in part with cast iron, part cast-in-situ concrete; and for later construction, hinged 20 cm thick concrete blocks with cavity grouting. There is approximately 1.3 m of cut and cover construction where the line ascends from deep level to the surface at its eastern end. Maximum tunnel depth is 120 ft approx. (36.5 m).

Gradient (max): 3%
Curvature (max): 400 m
Speed (design max): 70 km/h; (average commercial): 34 km/h
Electric system: third rail; 825 V supplied through 10 kV underground cables from the city supply
Type of rails: 48 kg/m

Rolling Stock:
Car type (year introduced): 1970
Number of units: 100
Car dimensions (length): 19.2 m
(width): 2.67 m
(height): 3.66 m
Passenger capacity
per car (total): 270
(seated): 42
Motors per car: 4
Rating: 66 kWh
Train composition (minimum): 2
(max): 4
Acceleration (max): 1.15
Deceleration (emergency): 1.20
Brakes (type): electro-pneumatic
Weight (tonnes) Motorcar: 32.5

Traffic Data:
Trains/track/hour: 40
Train capacity (passengers): 1 080
Total passengers/track/hour (peak): 26 000
Train headways
existing: 2.5 minutes
Passengers carried (weekdays): 252 000
(annually): 31 000 000
Average journey length: 3.8 km

Signalling: Hungarian built Swiss Integra type signalling with colour-light signals and train stops permits train intervals of 90 seconds with 30 seconds station stops. Reversing of trains is automatic. Radio telephone communication between traffic control at Deak Square and motormen. Automatic train operation is under consideration.

Authority:
Budapesti Közlekedesi Vallat (BKV)
Akacfa u 15, Budapest VII

Type of system: Full-metro

General: The east-west line passes under the busiest axial thoroughfare of the town, the Kerepesi and Rákóczi Street and the inner town and passing under the bed of the Danube, it leads to two important junctions of Buda, the Moszkva Square and the Magyar Jakobinusok Square and also touches the Keleti and Déli Railway terminals (Budapest East and South). Passengers may change trains directly at Örs Vezër Square and Batthyäny Square for Gödöllo, resp. Szentendre (suburban trains). There are eleven stations along the line, including two surface stations (at Fehér út and Pillangó utca), one subsurface station (at the Népstadion) and eight deep-level stations (Keleti pályaudvar, Blaha Lujza tér, Astoria, Deák Ferenc tér, Kossuth tér, Batthyány tér, Moszkva tér, Déli pályaudvar). Access to four of the underground stations is provided via subsurface pedestrian subways which offer opportunities for easy changing for other means of mass communication.
Two separate round-section tunnels of 5.1 m inside diameter are built for the underground railway track. Corresponding to the soil conditions and to the method of construction, the walls of the various tunnel sections are built from cast iron segments, cast-in-situ concrete and in the recently built sections, from reinforced concrete members. The 20 cm thick concrete blocks are hinged, no bolted joints are used. After assembling the members, the cavities behind them are filled with grouted concrete. The concrete rings so built form a stiff wall of high load bearing capacity. The railway tracks are secured to reinforced concrete sleepers let into concrete; bedding into concrete reduces the maintenance works and enables a smaller vertical clearance. The trains are supplied with current from a live rail run along the railway track, via current collectors.
A length of 1.3 km of the line is layed on the surface; the subsurface section is equally 1.3 km long and the length of the underground section is 7.5 km. The underground construction of the line enabled application of radius of curve exceeding 350 m and the construction work could proceed without interfering with the surface traffic. Most of the tunnels were built in clayey soil. However, since from the sandy gravel layer above the clayey bed, water might seep through sand streaks towards the tunnel, adequate waterproofing withstanding water pressures of 2 to 2.5 atm gauge had to be provided. In tunnel sections consisting of segments and concrete members, the joints were sealed with expanding cement, whereas the path of seeping water in cast-in-situ concrete structures was blocked by gunite coating on the inside wall and by steel sheets. Ventilation of the tunnels and stations was provided by heavy-duty axial fans sucking in fresh air via the stations and discharging the exhaust air via the line shafts during the summer and inversely in winter.
The stations at Baross Square, Blaha Lujza Square, Deák Ferenc Square, Moszkva Square and Budapest South comprise three tunnels. The inside diameter of each station tunnel is 7.8 m. The track and platform of approximately 3 m width are located in the external tunnel. The height above rail top level of platforms is 1.1 m so embarkation and disembarkation may take place at the carriage floor level. The passenger distribution space is arranged in the middle hall and the escalators carry the passengers from this hall to the surface. (30 escalators are operated along the whole line; at a speed of 0.9 m/sec, each escalator is capable of transporting 8 000 passengers per hour). Five-tube column-supported stations are built at the Astoria, under the Kossuth Lajos Square and the Batthyány Square where the two external tunnels are formed by the line tunnels led through the stations. This solution results in a better utilisation of the available space and construction is more economical, too. The interior design of stations reflects the general idea whereby in addition to serving communication purposes and being well usable, the underground railway should offer an interesting aesthetic experience to passengers. It is also important that the lining materials employed should be durable and easy to keep clean. Wear-resistant granite is used for floor covering, the side walls are lined with marble, hard limestone or small mosaic tiles; the ceiling is lined with Luxaflex aluminium sheets. A 80 cm wide rubber safety band is run along the platform edges.
The full capacity of the east-west underground line is 42 000 passengers hour direction. Trains comprising 6 cars may follow each other every 90 seconds along the line. Up-to-date signalling and Integra-type railway safety appliances ensure traffic safety. All equipment is automatic. Turning of trains takes place similarly automatically, according to a predetermined programme. The electrically driven Autostop system with mechanical strikers ensures enhanced safety; when the train runs past the stop-block the equipment switches on the brake systems. The maximum speed that can be achieved is 70 km/h; when dwelling times on stations are taken into consideration, the average travelling speed may amount to 32.8 km/h. The cars are designed to accommodate 178 passengers (42 seats and 136 standing-places). Swift embarkation and disembarkation is provided by the four double-sash sliding doors, each of 1.2 m width mounted on each car.
The underground railway is supplied with electrical power from the remote-controlled traction and branch-work transformer stations built at the main points of consumer load; the transformer stations are supplied by 10 kV underground cables of the Budapest Electricity Works. The 825 V rated voltage direct current used for traction is rectified by semi-conductor silicon diode rectifiers. The escalators, ventilating equipment, pumps, lighting and safety systems are supplied from two 630 kVA transformers installed into substations. Water supply to workers and plant equipment (eg transformers) is provided from a water-pressure system connected to the water supply system of the town. Sewage and water seeping into the tunnels from the ground are collected by open water gangs and enclosed sewage ducts connected to the sumps of lifting plants. From the sumps, the sewage and water are pumped into the public sewerage system.
The central traffic manager stationed at Deák Ferenc Square keeps the traffic of trains under observation and his duty is to ensure undisturbed traffic. All important traffic data are displayed on his control desk. All communication and other means enabling immediate action are available to the traffic manager. Motorcar drivers and the traffic superintendant may talk to each other via a radio-telephone communications system. Type Em motorcars made by the Soviet Union are well-proved. Each unit of the train comprising exclusively motorcars incorporates an independent electrical drive and when coupled into a train, all motors can be controlled from one driver's cabin. The automatic coupling devices enable rapid coupling and discoupling of trains. The rubber inserts incorporated in the underframe and the running gear reduce the travelling noise, decrease wear by damping the dynamical efforts and provide quiet, uniform running. The rolling stock of the Budapest Underground Railway is completed by a considerable number of special service vehicles like tunnel scrubbers, rail, scaffold and per-

sonnel transport carriages. The central car depot at Fehér Street was built for storing and maintaining motorcars; the depot is capable of accommodating 22 four-car-trains. The depot includes a shed, a maintenance workshop, an office and social building and storing facilities.

Technical Data:
Gauge: 1.435 m
Route length: 3.9 km
In tunnel: 3.28 km
Projected new lines (in construction): 0.8
Number of lines: 1
Number of stations (total): 11
(in tunnel): 9
Average distance between stations: 360 m

Stations:
platform length (minimum): 24 m

BUENOS AIRES

Authority:
Subterraneos de Buenos Aires (SBA)
Bartolomé Mitre 3342 513, Buenos Aires, D.F. Argentina
Cables: SUBTEBA, Buenos Aires

Type of system: Full-metro

History: The present day Buenos Aires Subway system is not more than 30 years old, but its earliest line (Plaza Mayo-Primera Junta) has been running more than 55 years, being opened partially in December 1913 and fully in July 1914. It was operated by the Anglo-Argentine Tramways Company; it is now known as Line A.

The second line (Leandro N. Alem-Federico Lacroze) was opened in October 1930, and was operated by the Buenos Aires Central Terminal Railway; it is now Line B. The remaining three lines (Retiro-Plaza Constitucion Catedral-Palermo, and Plaza Constitucion-Boedo) were opened between 1930 and 1944, and were operated by a Spanish Company with interests in Argentina (CHADOPYF); they are now respectively Lines C, D and E. The Buenos Aires Transport Corporation was formed by law in October 1939 for the co-ordination of passenger transport (including the underground railways) in Greater Buenos Aires. A consortium ran the principal services until 1952 when the Corporation was dissolved and its authority transferred to the Ministry of Transport. In June 1963 a new State entity, the "Subterráneos de Buenos Aires" was formed under Government decree to operate the City's underground system.

In April, 1966, two extensions of Line E were opened simultaneously, the westward extension to Avenida La Plata being ½ mile (1 km) and the northward extension from San José Station to Plaza de Mayo (Bolivar Street) being 1.25 miles (2 km) long. Work is being carried out to extend lines B and D (from F. Lacroze and Palermo) northwestwards for approximately 2¼

Gradient (max): 3%
Curvature (max): 40 m
Speed (design max): 40 km/h
(average commercial): 19 km/h
Electric system: catenary; 550 V

Rolling Stock:

Car type	OLD	OLD	Ganz-Mavag
Number of units:	17 (motors)	16 (trailers)	21 sets
Car dimensions:			
(length):	11.1	9.6	30.4
(width):	2.35	2.30	—
(height):	2.67	2.62	—
Passenger capacity			
per car (total):	60	64	171
(seated):	14	12	48

and 4 miles respectively. The planning and design work for the Line B extension involves 2.24 miles (3.6 km) of route, all in tunnel, four additional stations and an underground car depot to accommodate 75 cars. Additionally, feasibility studies have been carried out for a new Line F, from Avellaneda (south of Buenos Aires) via Constitucion and Entre Rios to Callao, a distance of 3.1 miles (5.0 km).
Track gauge: 4 ft 8½ in (1.435 m).

Technical Data:
Gauge: 1.435 m
Route length: 64.9 km
In tunnel: 34.7 km
Projected new lines (in construction): 10.2 km
(in design): 5 km
Number of lines: 5
Number of stations (total): 57
(in tunnel): 57
Average distance between stations: 600 m
Stations:
platform length (minimum): 106 m

Type of tunnel: The tunnels are double track, of cut-and-cover construction only in Line A and some of the stations in Lines B, C and D. The other lines and stations were constructed by tunneling. The Line A tunnel is 25 ft 3 in (7.7 m) wide, and 14 ft 7 in (4.45 m) high from rail level; it is of rectangular section without centre supports. Line B runs partly in tunnel of rectangular section. 27 ft 9 in (8.45 m) wide by 15 ft 3 in (4.65 m) high, with centre supports, and partly in tunnel with arches over each track.

Gradient (max): 4%
Curvature (max): 80 m
Speed (design max): 10 km/h
(average commercial): 18.26 km/h

Electric system: On Line A, overhead wire distribution;

Motors per car: 2   —   4
Rating: 44 kWh   —   61 kWh
Body material: steel/wood
Weight (tonnes) Motorcar: 16.5

Traffic Data:
Trains/track/hour: 30
Train capacity (passengers): 171
Total passeengers/track/hour (peak): 5 130
Train headways
existing: two minutes
Passengers carried (annually): 21 000 000
Average journey length: 3.3 km
Vehicle-km operated annually: 2 200 000

1 100 V dc. On Line B, third rail distribution; 550/600 V dc. On Lines C, D and E, overhead wire distribution: 1 600 V dc.

Type of rails: Track is chaired, (except on Line B, which has spiked flat-bottom rails), with timber sleepers and stone ballast; rails weigh 88 lb/yd (49.6 kg/m) on Line B, and 91 lb/yard (45.93 kg/m) on other lines. Heavier rail at 50.5 kg/m is laid on concrete sleepers on new sections of Line E.

Rolling Stock:

Car type:	CDE/67	CDE/33	A/26
Number of units:	80	108	124
Car dimensions			
(length):	17 m	17 m	15 m
(width):	2.6 m	2.6 m	2.6 m
(height):	2.52 m	2.34 m	3.41 m
Passenger capacity			
per car (total):	150	150	140
seated):	42	40	42
Motors per car:	4	—	2
Rating:	116 kWh	—	115 kWh
Train composition (minimum): 2 (max): 5			
Body material:	steel	steel	steel/wood
Weight (tonnes):			
Motorcar:	27.2		28
Trailer:	—	20	—

Traffic Data:
Trains/track/hour: 30
Train capacity (passengers): 750
Total passengers/track/hour (peak): 22 500
Train headways
existing: 2 minutes
Passengers carried (annually): 242 100 000
Vehicle-km operated (annually): 23 400 000

BUFFALO

Authority:
Niagara Frontier Transportation Authority
181 Elliott St, Buffalo, NY 14203, USA
Telephone: (716) 856 6524

Chairman of the Board: Chester R. Hardt
Executive Director: James E. Kelly
General Counsel: William E. Straub
Authority Engineer: Col. Loren W. Olmstead
Comptroller: Robert M. Dracup
Purchasing Director: Roman S. Bernacki
Manager of Airports: Richard F. Rebadow
General Manager, Marine Division: Arthur Lancaster
Trade Development Manager: Richard H. Van Derzee
Executive Vice-President, Metro Bus: Robert G. Decker
Urban Transportation Planner: David A. Casciotti

Metro Construction Division
(Light Rail Rapid Transit Project)
General Manager: Kenneth G. Knight
Office of Systems Development: Eugene C. Lepp
Director, Office of Contracts & Programme Control: Theodore Beck
Director, Office of Community Services: John R. Winston
Director, Office of Architecture & Engineering Design:

Erik Collette

Type of system: Full-metro

An in-depth Mass Transit Study in 1971 recommended a 12.5 mile, 19-station heavy rail rapid transit line, extending from downtown Buffalo to a vast, new university complex in suburban Amherst. In 1972, NFTA received a $1.8 million grant (80 per cent Federal—20 per cent State) for preliminary engineering design. A shorter, 11.6 mile heavy rail line was then proposed. Following a Public Hearing in 1974, at which strong community support was evidenced for this project, the Federal government requested, because of the $476 million price tag, in-depth alternatives analysis to the heavy rail concept. NFTA studied an all-bus solution and a light rail mode, weighing these against the heavy rail proposal. The light rail concept proved the most cost-effective and the Authority scaled its line down further to a 6.4 mile initial segment. A Public Hearing was held in 1976 on an application for $336 million grant to fund this system, which will run on street surface for 1.2 miles in the central business district and 5.2 miles in subway. About one mile of the surface section will incorporate a transit pedestrian, auto-free mall in the downtown sector and will utilise floor-level, platform boarding stations. A total of 14 stations are planned, six of which will be at street surface and eight underground. In June 1976, the NFTA

received "a commitment in principle" for the Federal government for the project. In October 1976, it was awarded a $10 million grant (80 per cent Federal—20 per cent State) for General Engineering and Architectural Design Activity. Present plans call for start of construction in late 1978 and revenue service operation in late 1982.

Technical Data:
Projected new lines (in design): 17.7 km with 13.5 km in tunnel
Number of Stations (total): 15
(in tunnel): 11

Type of tunnel: —
Gradient (max): 3%
Curvature (max): 305 m
Speed (design max): 89 km/h
Electric system: third rail/650 V

Rolling Stock:
Car type: Proposed
Car dimensions (length): 20.4 m
(width): 2.9 m
(height): 3.4 m
Passenger capacity
per car (total): 200
(seated): 60

CALCUTTA

Authority:
Metropolitan Transport Project (Railways)
Calcutta City Government, 14-16 Government Place East
Calcutta, India

Type of system: Full-metro

General: Work on 1.9-km of Calcutta's planned 16.3-km first Metro line between Dum Dum and Tollyganj in the city's north-south corridor is nearing completion. The first section includes an elevated line running alongside the existing suburban railway line and the initial tunnel section between surface and underground construction.

Work has also begun on the second, 1.8-km section while feasibility studies are underway on expanding the system by construction of an east-west line and a second north-south link. The final Metro programme of highway and commuter railway improvements in the area.

Metro authorities have drawn up a tentative revised plan calling for completion of a 139-km system by 1990. This would entail construction of three additional lines and a short extension to Tucuruvi on the north-south line.

Technical Data:
Gauge: 1.676 m
Projected new lines (in construction): 3.7 km

(in design): 139 km
Number of lines: 1 (under construction)
Number of Stations (total): 17
(in tunnel): 16
Speed (design max): 80 km/h
Electric system: third rail; 750 V

Traffic Data (estimated):
Trains/track/hour: 24
Train capacity (passengers): 2 560
Total passengers/track/hour (peak): 61 440
Train headways design: 2 minutes
Passengers carried (weekday): 1 320 000 (1979)
(annually): 442 000 000
Vehicle-km operated annually: 27 300 000

CALGARY

Authority:
The City of Calgary Transportation Department
PO Box 2100 Calgary, Alberta T2P 2M5, Canada

Director: W. C. Kuyt
General Manager: R. H. Wray
Project Engineer: J. D. Hemstock

General: A network of almost 13 km of grade-separated routes has been devised in an attempt to incorporate a standard of rapid service which is the highest prospective transit development for the area. Consideration is given to the provision of exclusive grade-separated rights-of-way for high-speed vehicles.
Several corridors of movement to down-town justify consideration for grade-separated transit. It is evident that any system of rapid routes should focus on the CBD and provide radial spokes to the northwest serving the rapidly growing University of Calgary and residential sectors. A route to the south provides the opportunity to serve the stampede grounds (which includes potential for a major park-ride facility, 11 months of the year), Chinook Center and the rapidly expanding residential section south of 82nd Avenue. The Killarney-26th Avenue area south and west of downtown is a third sector for consideration of grade-separated transit. Major traffic flows to downtown are generated along Center Street in the north sector—consideration must be given to this dense area for improved transit facilities.
The Calgary area is laced with a number of existing rail rights-of-way. Careful consideration has been given to these in the development of possible routings for high-speed service to the corridors mentioned above. However, comparison with the locations of these rights-of-way and the locations of population (and, therefore, travel demand) indicate a disparity between available right-of-way and convenient travel for workers and shoppers. Canadian Pacific tracks to the west of downtown follow the Bow River and are relatively inaccessible. The north line crossing the Bow River at Nose Creek and following the valley past the airport is also circuitous and inacessible. The CPR line running south from the CBD is better situated than other routes but still bypasses most of the major travel generators to the south.

Technical Data:
Gauge: 1.676 m
Route length (proposed): 13 km

CARACAS

Authority:
Oficina Ministerial Del Transporte (OMT)
Ministerio de Obras Publicas, Edificio Camejo 5 Piso, Esquina de Camejo, Caracas, Venezuela
Telephone: 426651
Cables: METROMOP-CARACAS

Type of system: Full-metro

General: Following approval of a 2 000 million bolivars loan in 1975, work has started on tunnelling and station construction over the projected 19.8-km first line of the city underground rail system. The line is to run east-west from Petare to Catia and will include 22 stations. First section of the line is due to go into operation in 1980 and the entire line is expected to be in service by 1982. Cost will be about 3 200 million bolivars.
Generally, the line is located under the most important urban arterials; from west to east: Avenidas España and Sucre in Catia, Avenida Universidad in the centre, Calle Real de Sabana Grande (Avenida Lincoln) and Avenida Miranda in the eastern part of the city.
The line has been divided into three construction and operating divisions: Catia-Silencio, Silencio-Chacaito and Chacaito-Petare described below.
Storage yard and maintenance shops will be located at the extreme western end of the line, north of the first station in Pro-Patria. The yard will occupy land presently being used by the "Cuartel Urdaneta" (armoury) and a part of that being used by "Banco Obrero" (public housing). The underground line starts at the Pro-Patria Station and runs east a short distance before curving northward underneath Avenida España. The line then curves to the east, continues under Avenida Sucre, and surfaces near Manicomio Station after passing over "Quebrada Caroata" (drainage ravine). The line then proceeds towards Avenida Universidad, passing through Caño Amarillo on an aerial structure over the block presently occupied by "Loss Bultos Postales" (Customs Warehouse) and continues below Avenida Universidad to La Hoyada Station.
The Catia-Petare line crosses the Central Business District of the city from the west to east underneath Avenida Universidad until it reaches the end of Avenida Mexico, where it turns toward Avenida Libertador. It contines below Avenida Libertador, turning south towards Plaza Venezuela, and then proceeds under Avenida Lincoln in Sabana Grande, until Chacaito.
From Chacaito, the line continues toward the east under Avenida Miranda. This entire section is underground up to a point 400 m west of the terminal station at Petare, where it emerges to the north of Avenida Mirande and rises on an aerial structure until it reaches the last station.
The Catia-Petare Line will have 22 stations, 19 of which will be underground. Of the remaining three, one will be at grade (Manicomio) and two will be on aerial structure (Caño Amarillo and Petare). The stations have been located in areas where there are major concentrations of employment and population. The distances from centre-to-centre of stations are shown in the table. It can be seen that in the centre of the city (Silencio to Morelos) the stations are closely spaced, the maximum distance between any two stations being 630 m. Outside the CBD, however, the distance between stations is greater, with a maximum of 1 640 m (La California to Petare).
The number and location of stations have been selected not only on the basis of logical sites and reasonable costs but also to provide adequate operating characteristics and good service. The distance between stations has been kept relatively short—almost 1 km on the average—because the people of Caracas are not accustomed to walking distances greater than 400 m. The distances between stations permit the development of a minimum commercial speed of 35 km/h. This speed produces satisfactory travel times, in relation to the average trip length in Caracas which is relatively short.
The line follows the alignment of existing major arteries for most of its route except in the following places: in Catia where the two curves pass under residential development, to the south of Avenida Sucre, where the line is at grade alongside the channelised Quebrada Caroata (drainage ravine), in Caño Amarillo where it runs on aerial structure, between Santa Rosa and Plaza Venezuela, and at the end of the line at Petare. Since the streets of Caracas are fairly narrow in many parts of the city (the Avenidas España, Universidad and Lincoln are only 18.5 to 20 m wide on the average), the edges of the stations and the line sections often encroach upon existing buildings, and it will be frequently necessary to expropriate or underpin structures in these areas of the city.
In general the line descends from the west to the east. The top of rail elevations in the Pro-Patria and Petare terminals are at 971 m and 838 m above sea level, respectively—a difference in elevation of 133 m in 20 km. As could be expected, the profile does not descend uniformly but adapts itself to the topography and fixed obstacles that cross the line in numerous places. These obstacles are generally drainage ravines, avenues and overpasses. Among the major drainage ravines affecting the profile of the Catia-Petare Line are: Caroata in the west and in the center of the city, Catuche and Anauco in the center, La Florida and Chacaito in Sabana Grande and Seca and Tócome in the east. The major overpasses and crossings are: the Caracas-La Guaira Autopista under Avenida Sucre, Avenida Fuerzas Armadas under Avenida Universidad, and the Avenida Libertador under Avenida Miranda.
Nowhere does the resulting depth of the line exceed reasonable limits. The maximum depth of 20 m occurs in the centre of the city but the average depth of the line varies between 14 and 15 m. Similarly, the grades achieved are moderate, never exceeding 3.8 per cent.
At present, 31 per cent of the total population and 44 per cent of the total employment of Caracas is located within walking distance of the line; even though the area so defined by this distance constitutes only 25 per cent of the total developed area. It is estimated that because of the expansion of the city by 1990, the area within walking distance of the line will constitute only 14 per cent of the total developed area, but it will still contain 24 per cent of the total population and 40 per cent of the total employment for that year.
According to the results of the 1975 patronage demand study, 34.8 per cent of the total daily trips made by potential bus users and 38.0 per cent of potential "jitney" taxi users will be diverted to the Catia-Petare Line for at least a part of their trip. That is, 36 per cent of the estimated 1 785 000 total daily trips to be made by public transportation in 1975 will use the Metro for all or part of the trip.
It is hoped to have a total of 49.7 km of underground rail transit lines in service by the year 2000, serving approximately 50 stations. Other lines planned include: Antimano-Morelos (together with a branch to El Silencio), 15 km; La Rinconada-Panteon, 11.8 km; La Bandera-Plaza Venezuela, 3.2 km.

Principal Characteristics of the Metro System Lines (1990)

Line	*Operating Length (km)*	*Number of Stations*	*Passenger Volumes (1000's)*	*Cost (Millions of Bolivars)*
1 Catia-Petare	19.7	22	1 151.4	1 260
2 Caricuao-Center	13.9	11*	505.2	700**
3 La Rinconada-El Valle Center-Panteón	11.6	12*	446.2	750**
4 El Valle-Plaza Venezuela	3.0	3*	56.5	120**
Totals	48.2	48	2 159.3	2 830

* Assumed for the purposes of estimating patronage.
** Derived by an extension of the costs estimated for the Catia-Petare Line.

General Characteristics of the Catia-Petare Line

Stage	*Operating Length (km)*	*Number of Stations*	*Volume of Passengers (Daily)**
Catia-Silencio	6.7	8	245 150 (1973)
Catia-Chacaito	11.9	14	465 200 (1974)
Catia-Petare	19.7	22	642 700 (1975)

* For the first year of operation.

Technical Data:
Gauge: 1.435 m
Projected new lines (in construction): 19.8 km
(in design): 49.7 km (2000)
Number of lines: 4
Number of stations (total): 22 (first line)
(in tunnel): 19
Average distance between stations: 0.9 km
Stations:
platform length (minimum): 150 m

Gradient (max): 3.5%
Curvature (max): 225 m
Speed (design max): 80 km/h
(average commercial): 37 km/h
Electric system: Third rail; 750 V

Rolling Stock:
Car type: Proposed
Number of units: 210
Car dimensions (length): 21.35 m
(width): 3.05 m
(height): 3.20 m
Passenger capacity per car (total): 180
(seated): 60
Motors per car: 4
Rating: 75 kWh
Train composition (max): 7
Acceleration (max): 1.48
Deceleration (emergency): 1.35
Weight (tonnes) Motorcar: 33

Traffic Data (estimated):
Train/track/hour: 40
Train capacity (passengers): 1 260
Total passengers/track/hour (peak): 40 000
Train headways
design: 1.5 minutes
Passengers carried (weekday): 650 000
(annually): 200 000 000

CHARLEROI

Authority:
Société des Transports Intercommunaux (STIC)
Chaussée de Namur 28 Montignies sur Sambre, 6080, Charleroi, Belgium
Telephone: (071) 32 05 70

Type of system: Pre-metro

General: At Charleroi—a large area but with a relatively low density of population—the first section of a new pre-metro system was opened for operation in 1976. Existing tramway routes were diverted into tunnels or over viaducts. The system will consist of a circular central section with a series of branches on their own right of way. By 1985 the central section plus five branches should be in operation. Branches will be short but designed for intensive exploitation. There will be a network of bus feeder routes.
A new series of wide articulated cars with capacity for 160 passengers and all doors at the sides are to be delivered for Charleroi. Builders will be CFC and Brugeoise et Nivelles.

Technical Data (Existing system):
Gauge: 1.00 m
Route length: 19.4 km
Number of lines: 3
Rolling Stock:
Car type: 2x
Number of units: 23
Car dimensions (length): 10.2 m
(width): 2.2 m
Passenger capacity
per car: (total): 75
(seated): 22

CHICAGO

Authority:
Chicago Transit Authority
Merchandise Mart Plaza, PO Box 3555 Chicago, Ill 60654, USA
Telephone: (312) 664 7200

Acting Transit Board Chairman: Clair M. Roddewig
General Manager: T. B. O'Connor
Operating Manager: G. Krambles
Director of Public Information: C. W. Baxa
Finance Manager: P. J. Meinardi

History: Prior to 1943 Chicago had a system of urban elevated railways (including the famous "loop"), but no underground passenger railways. In that year, the first passenger "subway" line—The State Street Line—was opened: 4.6 miles *(7.4 km)* long. It provides an in-town underground link between the North Side Elevated Lines near Armitage Avenue and the South Side Elevated Lines near Sixteenth Street. The second passenger "subway" line—the Milwaukee-Dearborn-Congress Line—was opened in 1951.

In April, 1964, CTA began operating a rail rapid transit service on the Skokie Swift line, non-stop between the terminals at Howard Street, Chicago and Dempster Street, Skokie. The five-mile line was purchased from the former North Shore Line. Standard CTA cars were equipped with remote-control overhead current collection devices for this line.

Completed in September, 1969, the Dan Ryan extension connects with the elevated structure at 18th Street and operates south via expressway median between 26th and 95th Streets. Average riding to and from the 9 new stations is 120 000 passengers daily. Lake-Dan Ryan trains operate a distance of 20.75 miles between the Harlem and 95th terminals.

An extension of the Milwaukee branch of the West-Northwest route completed in February, 1970, operates through a 1.2 mile Subway and then for 3.9 miles in the median of the Kennedy Expressway to Jefferson Park terminal. About 63 000 passengers use the 6 new stations daily.

During 1977 it was announced that federal officials had authorised grants giving the green light for extending the Kennedy rapid transit route to O'Hare International Airport. The project will cost $135.7 million.

The city's Public Works Department was granted $5 million in federal funding to begin engineering work, and there was assurance that the US Department of Transportation will provide the full federal contribution of $108.5 million which will represent 80 per cent of the project cost. The remaining 20 per cent will be provided by the state and city governments.

The O'Hare rapid transit extension will cover a distance of 12.8 km between the airport and the CTA's Jefferson Park terminal to provide for fast trips to and from Chicago's downtown. It also will serve as a connecting link with O'Hare for the CTA's entire rapid transit and surface systems, serving not only air travellers, but also thousands of airport workers and employees in the hotel, commercial and industrial area near the airport. It is estimated that more than 36 500 riders a day will use the O'Hare rapid transit extension. The project is expected to be completed within 30 to 36 months, which means that trains can be rolling to and from the airport by 1980.

This two-track extension will be constructed in the median strip of the Kennedy expressway from the present end of the tracks near Foster Avenue to a point just west of East River road. There, it will continue westward in the median strip of the Airport access road. About 100 m west of the airport taxiway bridge, the line will enter a tunnel, and curve in a south-westerly direction to an O'Hare Airport station beneath the main parking garage.

Intermediate stations are to be built at Harlem Avenue, Cumberland road, and River road. Parking facilities for more than 2 500 cars will be provided at these stations.

The running time of the CTA's trains between the airport and the downtown Dearborn subway stations will be about 35 minutes.

Technical Data:

Route length: The route length of the whole "rapid transit" system of the Chicago Transit Authority totals 89.4 miles *(143.9 km)*, including seven elevated lines. The two lines which include tunnel sections have a combined route length of 50.6 miles *(80.9 km)*, while the route length of the tunnel sections themselves is 10.1 miles *(16.3 km)*. the length of sections of each of the 3 lines operating in expressway medians is:

Eisenhower Expressway	9.0 miles
Dan Ryan Expressway	9.1 miles
Kennedy Expressway	3.9 miles

Number of lines: 2 underground lines (radial); double track.
Average station spacing: 0.7 miles *(1.1 km)*.
Passengers per annum: On the whole CTA system including road services (1975): 612 546 778.
Rapid Transit system: (1975): 89 476 235.
Max number of trains per hour in both directions: 66 (This refers to the "Loop" at the centre of the network).
Max number of cars per train: 8.
Estimated capacity per car: 100 passengers (including 48 seated).
Average schedule speed (including stops): State Street Line, 23.4 mph *(38.7 km/h)*. Milwaukee-Dearborn-Congress Line, 25.4 mph *(40.9 km/h)*.
Track gauge: 4 ft 8½ in *(1.435 m)*.
Weight and type of rail: 100 lb/yd flat-bottomed *(49.6 kg/m)*.
Max gradient: 1 in 28.6 *(3.5%)*.
Minimum radius of curves: 90 ft *(27.4 m)*.
Type of tunnel: The underground sections are generally about 40-50 ft *(12.2-15.3 m)* below surface level. Some portions of the lines are in tube tunnels, others are of "cut and cover" construction. The tube tunnels have an internal diameter of 20 ft 5 in *(6.2 m)*, the top of the tunnel being 16 ft 10½ in *(5.1 m)* from sleeper level.
Method and voltage of current supply: Third rail system-wide, except trolley wire on two miles of the Skokie line; 600 V dc.
Rolling Stock: Number of vehicles owned (1975): 1 079 on the whole "rapid transit" system; ie including those on both elevated and underground lines. Of these 765 are PCC-type vehicles with two sets of folding doors on each side.
Included in the fleet are 150 air-conditioned stainless steel cars manufactured by Budd in 1969-70 and 180 air-conditioned aluminium cars manufactured by Pullman Standard in 1964. Both types are designed for rapid acceleration and speeds up to 65 mph. They are each equipped with 4 × 100 hp traction motors, as compared with 4 × 55 hp motors on the standard PCC-type cars. All three types have a length over couplers of 48 ft 3 in; maximum width of 9 ft 4 in, and a height of 12 ft 0 in.
Signalling: Automatic block, with three-aspect colour-light signals, and train stops. The Lake route and the 1969-70 extensions are equipped with in-cab signalling and speed control system using audio-frequency circuits.

CLEVELAND

Authority:
Greater Cleveland Regional Transit Authority
1404 East 9th St, Cleveland 44114, Ohio, USA

Manager of Operations: Thomas A. Nooner
General Counsel: John W. Kellogg
Comptroller: William E. Deckman
General Manager: Leonard Ronis
Manager of Marketing and Communications: Gregory N. Fern

History: The most important event on this rapid transit railway since its opening in 1955, was the line's extension in 1968 to the city's Airport. As this Airport-city direct rapid transit link is the first in the USA, keen interest is being shown in the future of Cleveland's air-rapid transit traffic trend.

General: In addition to the Cleveland Transit System, there is the Shaker Heights (high-speed PCC streetcar) line which runs eastward from Union Terminal Station, parallel to Norfolk and Western RR Mainline tracks are entirely on private right of way. At Shaker Square, six miles out, the line divides one branch continuing eastwards for four miles along Shaker Boulevard to Shaker Heights, the other runs for three miles along Van Aken Boulevard to Warrensville Heights.

The Shaker Heights line was built in the early 1920s to develop the community bearing that name. On its 13 mile *(21 km)* of route in 1972 it carried 3 893 664 passengers.

For 2.55 miles *(4.1 km)* between Union Terminal and East 55th Street the Shaker Heights and the Cleveland rapid transit lines share the same tracks and the same overhead traction current supply. Campus station was opened here in March, 1971.

Route length: 19 miles *(30.6 km)*.
Number of Stations: 18.
Passengers per annum: (1972): 12 702 206. (1974): 11 348 244. (1975): 14 496 698.
Number of cars: 116 heavy high platform cars and 55 PCC cars. Bids have been taken for 60 new light rail cars for Shaker and it is planned to purchase 20 high platform cars for the RTA high platform system.
Car details: Length of 87 older-type cars is 48 ft 6 in *(14.7 m)*. Length of 30 newer-type cars is 70 ft *(21.3 m)*. All have two double sliding doors on each side.
Capacity per car: Seats for 52 passengers in single units (older-type cars), 54 per car in the double units (older-type) and 80 per car in the newer-type cars. Three new transit cars, on test in service on the Airport line, features a new WABCO power system with pulse width modulation (PWM) propulsion. The effect of this system is to convert the dc traction current to variable voltage, variable frequency 3-phase power for delivery to the induction motors. Advantages claimed for the new system include improved propulsion control and lower maintenance.
Average scheduled speed: 30 mph *(48 km/h)*.
Station details: Platforms of 300 ft minimum length are of island type at all but two stations. Escalators at eight stations.
Type of rail: Continuous welded rail on wood sleepers.
Current supply: 600 V dc with overhead equipment.
Signalling: Automatic block with train stops, three colour light signals. The new four-mile extension has an audio frequency "in-cab" signal system.

COLOGNE

On 11 October 1968, the first 0.9 mile *(1.4 km)* east-west section of the new underground tramway (street-car) system for Cologne opened, between Cathedral-Hauptbahnof and Friesenplatz. The ultimate object of this large project is to provide segregated rights of way for some 75 miles *(120 km)* of Cologne's tramway system, by the construction of cutting and embankment, and by tunnelling. The work is divided into phases and sub-divided into stages. The new town of Chorweiler on the northern outskirts will typically be served by tram route partly in tunnel, partly in cutting and partly on embankment. There are now 4.1 miles *(6.6 km)* of underground route operative served by sub-surface stations. The most recently operative stretches of tunnel-line are those extending north from Hauptbahnhof U Bahn stations and south from Zueghaus U Bahn station, the latter tunnel dividing into two just beyond Postrasse station.

The project will accelerate travel by tramcar and relieve congestion in the city centre. Main north-south thoroughfares in Cologne are semi-circular following the course of the River Rhine. The Underground network will first be built along a north-south axis across the city centre, with radiating spurs. These will link with inner radial thoroughfares and in three instances will project to outer radial thoroughfares. Long-term planning envisages some outer stretches of tram-route being in part placed in tunnel, or where remaining at surface level, being made crossing-free of other traffic. Of the 93 miles *(150 km)* (approximate) of Cologne's tram-route, some 25 per cent may additionally be replaced by bus services.

The double-track tunnel of rectangular section is internally 15 ft 3 in *(4.65 m)* high and 23 ft 11 in *(7.30 m)* wide. Tunnel height above rail level *(4.09 m)* allows clearance for the cars' overhead pantograph system. There are no centre supports. The tunnels are sufficiently large to accommodate conventional underground trains should this system be required later.

Stations, with platforms 80 m long, accommodate two trains of twin-articulated tramcars (or later one conventional underground train). They are spaced in inner areas 600 m apart on average, and 800 m apart on average in the outer areas, allowing for average service speeds, including stops, of 24 km/h and 30 km/h respectively. The passage of trams automatically actuates fixed visual signals.

Since 1968 a total of 20.4 km with 21 stations—with 11.1 km and 15 stations in tunnel—have been opened on the four-track Ebertplatz-Hauptbahnhof-Appelhof cross-city line and on an unconnected 1 km stretch in the north-west from Longerich to Chorweiler where a later connection with the S-Bahn is planned.

Plans have been made up to 1990, with total system of 120 km expected to take 70 to 80 years. Public transport demand is expected to be 2.65 million passengers yearly by 1980. Park-and-ride facilities with space for 12 500 automobiles are planned for 35 stations.

Construction costs since 1963 have totalled around DM 500 million.

Track over 14 km has been laid on rubber-cushion beds with concrete sleepers. Although the method was tested in Munich several years ago and eventually turned down, it has now proved entirely satisfactory. The new rail bed means 20 cm shallower tunnels, less maintenance and longer rail life, according to Cologne officials.

DORTMUND

Authority:
Stadtbahn Dortmund
Stadtverwaltung Dortmund—Stadtbahnbauamt—Viktoriastrasse 15, 4600, Dortmund, German Federal Republic

General: On September 22, 1969 the Dortmund City Council decided to go ahead on the Inner City underground extension. The new section begins at the present terminus Mallinckrodt-Str or Münsterstr, crosses the Inner City and ends at the Ruhr High Speed Railway (B1) with branches to Hörde and Hacheney. The overall length is 10.5 km.

DUSSELDORF

Authority:
Stadt Düsseldorf
Dusseldorf, German Federal Republic

ESSEN

Authority:
Stadt Essen
Essen, German Federal Republic

FRANKFURT AM MAIN

Authority:
Stadtwerke Frankfurt am Main
6 Frankfurt am Main, Dominikaner Platz 3, German Federal Republic.

Managing Director: Reinhard Brunk
Operating Manager: Helmut Oesterling

General: The U Bahn system being developed in Frankfurt am Main is part of a 5-year road-rail redevelopment project for the city and its environs. Segregation of the city's street-car traffic from general road traffic became necessary in certain busy thoroughfares and at junctions in order to relieve street congestion, and this is being accomplished by diverting street cars into sub-surface tunnels under the thoroughfares. Ordinary street cars are routed thus, together with a newly-developed, conventional underground type of vehicle to operate both in tunnel and at street surface. Trains of this type of vehicle comprise four twin-car articulated units, with greater acceleration and overall capacity than the ordinary street cars, which themselves are normally coupled to form trains of cars. The latter will be phased out over a period of years as the system develops and more conventional underground-type cars come into service.

Trams and U-Bahn trainsets, built by Duwag, now share rights-of-way over 36.2 km of rapid transit tracks. Line A has 9.75 km and 16 stations in operation between the suburb of Nordwestzentrum and Theaterplatz. The line is due to be extended across the Main river to Sachsenhausen by 1985.

Line B (5.22 km) runs from Theaterplatz to Giessner Strasse with an extension to the thickly-populated Bornheim district in the northeast due for completion by 1980.

The U Bahn was extended southward from Hauptwache to Theaterplatz in 1974. Future development plans include: (1) Continued construction of the S Bahn (Federal Railway), in a four track tunnel which will be common to both S Bahn and U Bahn trains, between Hauptwache and Konstabler Wache. (2) Construction of a new U Bahn line in tunnel running from

General: Dusseldorf will open the city's first stretch of pre-U-Bahn track north of Heinrich Heine Allee in 1979 with another 1.7 km tunnel running south to Hauptbahnhof due to come into operation in 1983. Goal for

General: Essen has a 5 km U-Bahn line in service, as part of a 15-km system, due by 1985. Total planned network is 58 km with 20 km underground. The first line,

Type U2 light rail trainset, built by Uerdingen (under license from Duwag) for Frankfurt with electrical control and switching equipment from Siemens.

North-East (Bornheim) to Central Station (Hauptbahnhof) with 8 stations including a junction station with the existing North-South-U Bahn line at Theaterplatz and one cross-station with the S Bahn (Hauptbahnhof). This line will be started in 1978. The ultimate U Bahn network extending north and south of the River Main will comprise 123 km of tunnel and segregated surface route.

Stations: Tunnel stations have side platforms minimally 640 ft (95 m) long. On the segregated stretch of surface line, halts have raised platforms and are approached by pedestrian tunnels from the sidewalks.

1990 is an 11.4-km line—with 6 km in tunnel—linking Hauptbahnhof with the northern Stadtbahn line. Costs by 1990 are expected to total DM 1 000 million.

opened in 1977, runs from the new Wiener Platz station to Essen Hauptbahnhof and Bismarck Platz.

Tunnels: Depth below street level varies between 39 ft and 46 ft (12₃14 m) of box section, they are double-tracked (track gauge 1.453 m), 23 ft 4 in (7.10 m) wide internally and 15 ft 9 in (4.80 m) high, providing clearance for current-collecting pantographs, with which both streetcars and U Bahn cars are equipped.

Rolling Stock: Type U 2 articulated units, 75 ft 5½ in (23.0 m) long and 8 ft 8½ in (2.65 m) wide, are powered by two 150 kW motors. Doors: Four double-leafed, automatically operated. Passenger capacity: 230 per unit (including 64 seats). Max speed 80 km/h. 65 articulated units are at present operative.

GLASGOW

Authority:
Greater Glasgow Passenger Transport Executive
48 St. Vincent Street, Glasgow C2 5TS, Scotland.
Telephone: (041) 248 5971

Chief Engineer: W. Kirkland
Underground Engineer: J. Wright

History: The line was opened in December 1896 as a cable railway. From 1923 to 1973 it was owned by the Glasgow Corporation, but in June of that year it was transferred to the Greater Glasgow Passenger Transport Executive. It was converted to electric traction in 1936.

General: In 1974, the Secretary of State for Scotland announced approval of a 75 per cent Government Grant towards the £12m project by the Greater Glasgow Passenger Transport Executive for the modernisation of the Glasgow Underground.

The project, work on which began in 1974 and is planned to be completed by 1978, involves the rebuilding of stations with the provision of escalators; the complete replacement of rolling stock and new facilities for its repair and maintenance; and new signalling and track.

The permanent way and signalling will be replaced and the first of the new rolling stock was delivered in 1977.

The Argyle Line is the first part of a series of additions to the central core of Glasgow's conventional rail network. This series of additions, called Clyderail, is a combined venture between British Rail and the Greater Glasgow Passenger Transport Executive forming part of an overall rail improvement scheme within the Greater Glasgow area.

The complete Clyderail Scheme involves the following physical works:

1. The re-opening and electrification of the former Central Low Level Line, 4.77 miles in length (Kelvinhaugh/Rutherglen section—now called the Argyle Line). Work on this is now under way.
2. The opening of the two new electrified link lines at Bridgeton and St. John's (0.90 route miles in total).
3. The electrification of 2.39 route miles from Shields Junction to Bellgrove currently used for freight traffic only.

The three miles of tunnel from Stobcross to Dalmarnock on the Argyle Line are being provided with concrete slab track with the remainder conventional sleepered track. The disused tunnel is fortunately in

good condition and requires only minimal attention. Stations are being re-opened at Rutherglen (resited), Dalmarnock, Bridgeton, Anderston, Stobcross and Central Low Level with a completely new station at Argyle Street (adjacent to some of Glasgow's largest department stores). On the existing North Bank electric system (with which Clyderail connects at its western extremity by a burrowing junction at Kelvinhaugh), Partickhill Station will be resited to give a direct interchange with the Underground.

These new lines will provide direct rail links between the following sectors of the city—northwest with a population of 272 000 served by 17 stations; northeast with a population of 318 500 served by 14 stations; southeast with a population of 320 000 served by 14 stations and southwest with a population of 429 000 served by 13 stations.

Coupled with the modernisation of the Underground, full implementation of the Clyderail package will mean that an average of 94 per cent of all retail businesses and central area employment will be within five minutes of a rail station.

It is estimated that forty 3-car emu sets will be required to operate the new Clyderail services and these will be similar to the high density electric multiple units currently on order for a BR London suburban electrification scheme in the Eastern Region. These have a capacity of 232 seated and 324 standing passengers. The cars will have automatic couplings. Sixteen 3-car sets have been ordered for the Argyle Line.

The off-peak train service pattern on the North Bank electric system will be transformed with 15 trains per hour plus additional trains at the peak operating over the busiest sector of the line between Hyndland and Kelvinhaugh. (It is this frequency of service which determines the need for a burrowing junction at Kelvinhaugh).

At present eight trains per hour are run over the Hyndland/Kelvinhaugh section to which will be added two additional trains from Hamilton via Bridgeton and five new trains via the Central Low Level Line. With the opening of the Tron Line and High Street Link a further two eastbound and two westbound trains would operate on the system.

The new signalling system will be of modern design and be compatible with the systems operating on the present rail network with which Clyderail will connect. The system allows for a 3-minute headway for trains making an average 30 second stop at each station and running at a maximum of 40 mph between stations. Other new equipment of significance will be a public

address system capable of both local and central control and also train indicators at more important stations. Argyle Line expenditure of £18.63 million (November 1974 prices) will be financed 75 per cent by Government grant and 25 per cent by British Rail through normal borrowing sources for capital investment in PTE areas. The capital charges will be taken into account by British Rail in computing the charge for operating the service on behalf of the PTE when the Argyle Line commences operation in 1978.

(The equivalent cost of providing an express bus service of commensurate speed additional car parking facilities including improvements to radial routes has been computed to be £37.65 million).

Route length: 6.6 miles (10.4 km)
Number of lines: 1 (circular line); double track.
Number of stations served: 15. Average station spacing: 0.44 miles (0.71 km).
Passengers per annum: 13 924 000.
Train miles per annum: 1 252 753.
Trains/track/hour: 17.
Max number of cars per train: 2.
Estimated capacity per car: 80-100 passengers (including 42 seated).
Average schedule speed (including stops): 13.76 mph (22.14 km/h).
Track gauge: 4 ft 0 in (1.219 m).
Weight and type of rails: 80 lb/yd (39.7 kg/m), flat-bottomed, continuously welded.
Max gradient: 1 in 16 (6.25%).
Minimum radius of curves: 660 ft (201 m).
Type of tunnel: Double tubes, each of 11 ft (3.35 m) nominal diameter. Tunnelling was by means of shields. Depth of the tunnel top ranges from 7 ft to 115 ft (2 to 35 m) below surface; average depth is 29 ft (8.84 m).
Method and voltage of current supply: Third rail; 600 V dc.
Rolling Stock: Number of cars: 43 (22 motor cars, 21 trailer cars). Of these 32 are in service at peak hours. Details: Each car is 42 ft long, with end doors on one side. Fluorescent lighting installed in some cars is to be standard for the whole fleet.
Signalling: Colour light signalling, with train stops.
Station layout: Stations have island platforms, 15 ft 0 in (4.572 m) wide and 120 ft (36.576 m) long. Access is by stairway from surface ticket halls.
Workshops: The rolling stock is stabled on the running lines, and cars must be lifted by crane to the surface for overhaul.

GUADALAJARA

Authority:
Comision Inter-Departmental Para El Estudio del Transporte Masivo en la Cuidad de Guadalajara
Guadalajara, Mexico

Type of system: Projected full-metro

History: The transit authority was set up in 1967 and work has begun on construction of the first line.

Technical Data:
Gauge: 1.435 m
Projected new lines (in design): 33 km
Number of lines: 3
Number of stations: (total): 34 planned
Speed (design max): 35 km/h
Electric system: Third rail; 1 500 V
Type of rails: 48 kg/m

Rolling Stock:
Car type: Proposed
Passenger capacity
per car: (total): 210 m
(seated): 76 m
Rating: 500 hp
Train composition (minimum): 4
(max): 6

Cut and cover work in progress on the first line section.

Tunnelling complete on the first section of the north-south line.

Traffic Data:
Trains/track/hour: 20
Train capacity (passengers): 1 260
Total passengers/track/hour (peak): 15 000
Train headways design: 1.5 minutes
Passengers carried (weekday): 1 000 000 estimated

HAIFA

Authority:
Municipal Corporation of Haifa
City Engineers Dept, Haifa
122 Hanassi Ave, Haifa, Israel.
Telephone: (4) 83765

Type of system: Funicular subway.

General: An underground railway of unusual character has been in operation since 1959. It commences about ¼ mile from the harbour at Paris station, in the downtown district, and runs in a straight line for 1.12 miles *(1 800 m)* to its other terminus, Gan Haem, in the Carmel district. In that distance it ascends nearly 900 ft *(274 m)*. Before its inception there was increasing traffic on the steep winding roads between the downtown business district, the shopping and entertainment district on the lower slopes of Mount Carmel, and the large residential area higher up the mountain. To provide a better public transport system between the districts a tunnel railway was constructed, but because of the steep gradient it was necessary for the trains to be cable hauled.

This funicular railway is built wholly in rock tunnel. The roof is of concrete bearing directly on the rock sides, except where the rock is unsound. At these points reinforced concrete walls have been constructed. The tunnel depth below surface varies from 112 ft *(35 m)* to 20 ft *(6 m)*. It was designed by the French *Societe d'Etudes des Transports et de Communications* and built by the Municipality jointly with

the *Cie. Dunkerquoise d'Entreprises* and a local building firm, *Solel Boneh*. The cars also were built by the *Cie. Dunkerquoise.*
The railway is single track throughout except for a passing point where two trains cross. The track is of concrete strips on which the pneumatic tyred cars run, guided by steel rails. At intermediate stations, "up" passengers use one platform and "down" passengers the other. All platforms are 100 ft long, conforming to the train's length, but because of the slope of the tunnel and track they are built as a series of level sections stepped to follow the line of the slope. When a train stops, its doors are opposite a platform section. The cars, 49 ft long and 7 ft 9 in wide, coupled two to a train have multi-level floors like the platforms. A stepped gangway with seats either side connects the level floor vestibules. There are four sets of air-operated doors on each side of each car, and a cab at each end for the train attendant who operates the doors and, if necessary, can apply a service brake or emergency brake on the train.
The trains normally are braked by the cable, which is wound by two 675 hp electric motors in the machine room, situated at the highest station. The motors are geared to an 8 ft diameter cable pulley. This railway, which was opened on October 6, 1959, has six stations and a train every six minutes. It has a capacity of 4 000 passengers per hour. The normal capacity per car is 160 passengers, but a maximum of 200 can be carried. Escalators working in the upward direction are provided at five stations. Fares are paid for tokens that operate mechanical turnstiles.

Technical Data:
Gauge: 1.980 m
Route length: 1.75
In tunnel: 1.75
Number of lines: 1
Number of stations (total): 6
(in tunnel): 6
Average distance between stations: 350 m
Stations:
platform length (minimum): 30.5 m
Gradient (max): 15.5%
Curvature (max): 0
Speed (average commercial): 30 km/h
Electric system: 1 200 V
Rolling Stock:
Car type (year introduced): 1959
Number of units: 4
Car dimensions (length): 15 m
(width): 2.4 m
(height): 3.8 m
Passenger capacity
per car (total): 160
(seated): 24
Train composition (minimum): 2
(max): 2
Brakes (type): Cable
Traffic Data:
Total passengers/track/hour (peak): 2 000
Train headways existing: 6 minutes
Passengers carried (weekday): 45 000
(annually): 6 000 000
Vehicle-km operated annually: 250 000

HAMBURG

Authority:
Hamburger Hochbahn Aktiengellschaft
Steinstr 20, Postfach 6146, 2000 Hamburg, German Federal Republic
Telephone: (0411) 321041
Cables: HOCHBAHN-HAMBURG

Type of system: Full metro

History: The Hamburger Hochbahn AG, a public company 90 per cent of whose shares are held by the city and state, has since 1918 operated the city's underground, street-car, bus and water-borne public transport. Of the present U Bahn system, the first operative line was the circular line running beneath the inner city. Work on it began in 1906 and it was opened in stages, fully operating in 1912. By 1914 two spur lines, to Hellkamp and Ohlsdorf, were opened, and between 1921-27 the Wolddorfer Railway's two lines to Ohlstedt and Gross Hansdorf had been incorporated.
To the basic network there have been periodic extensions but the most important addition to the system, is a new inner-city transverse underground line. Fully opened in June 1973, this links the Central Station North with Schlump to the west. It has involved both cut and cover and deep-level shield-driven methods of tunnelling (beneath Alster Lake). There are below-ground interconnection facilities with Hamburg's S Bahn at Ballindamm, Hamburg's first U Bahn deep station built in tube construction. The U Bahn system as a whole runs partly in tunnel, but mainly in open cutting, at surface or on viaduct.
Further plans provide for a new line between the northern business district and the city centre.
Of considerable importance in this period of world-wide urban traffic problems, the foundation in 1967 of the Hochbahn AG's subsidiary, the traffic advisory and technological company Gesellschaft für Verkehrsberatung und Verfahrenstechniken mbH, offers its expertise to city authorities both at home and abroad.

Benefitting from its long experience of public transport, service integration (U and S Bahn, buses and ships) with common tariff and ticket systems, this Hamburg company offers advice on technological and operational procedures ranging widely through one-man operation of underground trains, buses and trams, automatic traffic control and workshop design, to fare structuring and efficient passenger handling.

Technical Data:
Gauge: 1.435 m
Route length: 89.5 km
In tunnel: 32 km
Number of lines: 3
Number of stations (total): 80
(in tunnel): 36
Average distance between stations: 1.052 km
Stations:
platform length (max): 125 m
(minimum): 90 m

Type of tunnel: Rectangular section. Construction in town was by cut and cover method. On the Ochsenzoll line extension, apart from a short section of twin circular tunnel, prefabricated "concrete box" sections of tunnel, each 6 ft 6 in long, 24 ft wide and 13 ft 9 in high, supported by centre columns, were lowered into open cut. This method speeded the work and minimised the period during which streets along the railway route were rendered unusable. The new transverse line is in part in shield-driven tunnel under the city centre (Schlump-Hauptbahnhof).

Gradient (max): 5%
Curvature (max): 68 m
Speed (design max): 70-80 km/h
(average commercial): 31 km/h
Electric system: Third rail; 750 V
Type of rails: 37 kg/m

Rolling Stock:

Car type:	DT 1	DT 2	DT 3
Number of Units:	50 × 2	184 × 2	127 × 3
Car dimensions:			
(length):	28.44 m	28.44 m	39.52 m
(width):	2.50 m	2.56 m	2.56 m
(height):	3.34 m	3.37 m	3.35 m
Passenger capacity			
per car (total):	260	256	364
(seated):	82	82	116
Motors per car:	8	4	8
Rating:	74 kWh	80 kWh	80 kWh
Train composition (minimum): 2			
(max): 9			
Acceleration			
(max):	1.0	0.9	1.2
Deceleration			
(emergency):	1.25	1.3	
Brakes (types): Regenerative			
Weight (tonnes):			
Motorcar:	50.5	39.1	45.5

Traffic Data:
Trains/track/hour: 24
Train capacity (passengers): 1 092
Total passengers/track/hour (peak): 25 000
Train headways existing: 2 minutes
Passengers carried (weekday): 540 000
(annually): 178 300 000
Average journey length: 5.6 km
Vehicle-km operated annually: 55 100 000

Signalling: Automatic block, with colour-light signals. An automatic train guidance system was introduced during 1972 to a passenger carrying section of line. In 1974, the Hamburger Hochbahn began to install train telephones linking U-Bahn train drivers with a central control room. By mid-year, twelve power cars had been fitted with cab telephones. During the year track cables for the system were laid on the 33 km Wandsbek Markt-Ohlsdorf line (UI). Other lines will be equipped by 1976.

HANOVER

Authority:
Hannoversche Verkehrsbetriebe (USTRA)
Hanover, German Federal Republic

Type of system: Pre-metro.

General: The first 7 km of Hanover's projected 90-km pre-U-Bahn system opened to traffic between Oberricklingen and the Hauptbahnhof on Line A in September 1975. By spring, 1976, construction had been completed over a further 7 km and trains are now operating the full 14 km (3.9 km in tunnel; 10.1 km at grade) on Line A between Oberricklingen in the southwest and Lahe in the northeast.
A new tunnel extension from Oberricklingen to Wettbergen, went into operation by the end of 1977. Also underway is 1.8 km in tunnel on Line B northwards from Weissekruzplatz to Vahrenwald, for completion in 1978. Also under way is construction work on the Kropcke-Georgstrasse/Hildesheimer Strasse section of Line B.
Work on Line C will be started in 1978 and completed between Herrenhausen in the west and Kleefeld in the east by 1985. No construction timetable has yet been drawn up for Line D which would run 4.4 km from Bismarckstrasse to Limmer.
Most of Line A is being constructed using cut-and-cover methods at an average depth of 13 m beneath

Pre-metro trainset shown operating on the underground section of Line A and on the surface.

the surface. After excavation the tunnel is shored with 30-m-long shell elements and treated with bituminous coating or impervious concrete. Shield driving is to be adopted for Lines B, C and D.
Costs for the first 2-km tunnel section built on Line A between Gustav-Bratke-Allee and Podbielskistrasse amounted to DM 430 million. The entire 14-km line between Oberricklingen to Lahe is expected to cost around DM 780 million.

Track has been built using Wiener Oberbau polyurethane sleepers originally developed by Voest-Alpine for the new Vienna subway. The sleepers are embedded in recesses precast in two parallel concrete slabs—leaving the centre of each sleeper unsupported.
Duwag-built eight-axle cars are to be operated over the new line. Deliveries are at present underway and should be completed by 1978.

HELSINKI

Authority:
Helsingin Kaupungin Metrotoimisto
PO Box 53242
Toinen Linja 7, 00531 Helsinki 53, Finland
Telephone: 71 83 21

Type of system: Full-metro.

General: Helsinki's first metro line from Kamppi to Puotinharju is scheduled for opening in 1981 as the first stage in a plan to build about 35 km of new rapid transit rail lines within the city by the year 2000.
Length of the Kamppi-Puotinharju line will be 11.5 km including 4 km double tunnels. Five of the nine stations shall be underground, all the others surface stations. A small section of the tunnel will be built below the ground water level using a freezing method. By the end of 1977 all the tunnels and platforms of the underground stations were blasted but the ticket halls are still under construction. The active freezing of the soil is now completed and the installation of cast iron lining is under work.
Total cost of the line including stations, bridges, via-

ducts, 7.5 km surface— and 4 km underground double track, depot, electrical supply system, ATO and ATC systems, relay interlocking system and rolling stock will work out at about FM 1040 million. Tunnel stations are expected to take about FM 300 million; surface stations about FM 70; track FM 110 million; yard and workshop about FM 80 million; rolling stock FM 310 million and miscellaneous equipment (such as power supply, safety equipment) about FM 170 million.
Trials have been carried out with a six-car prototype train since 1972 on a 2.8 km track section.
The rolling stock—42 two-car sets—for the first line are now under construction and the three first two-car sets have been delivered in 1977.

Technical Data:
Gauge: 1.524 m
Projected new lines (in construction): 11 km
Number of lines: 2
Number of stations (total): 9
        (in tunnel): 5
Average distance between stations: 1.1 km
Speed (design max): 80 km/h
  (Average commercial): 40 km/h

Electric system: third rail, 750 V

Rolling stock:
Car type (year introduced): pre-series 1977
Number of units: paired
Car dimensions (length): 22.1 × 2
  (width): 3,20 m
  (height): 3,60 m
Passenger capacity
  per car (total): 200
  seated: 67 (2 + 2 seating)
Motors per car: 4
Rating: 125 kW
Train composition (minimum): 2
  (max): 6
Acceleration (max): 1,2 m/s²
Deceleration (emergency): 1,2 m/s²
Brakes (type): rheostatic/disc brake
Body material: Aluminium
Weight (tonnes) Motorcar: 31.6 × 2

Traffic Data:
Passengers carried (weekday): 130 000 (1980)

HONG KONG

Authority:
Hong Kong Mass Transit Railway Corporation
PO Box 9916
General Post Office, Hong Kong

Name of Railway: Mass Transit Railway

Type of system: Full Metro

Chairman: N. S. Thompson
Managing Director: Dr T. M. Ridley
Project Director: R. J. Mead
Engineering Director: P. H. F. Andrew
Operations Director: A. R. Cotton
Administration Director: J. A. Glover
Finance Director: W. S. Lau

Following ten years of planning, Hong Kong started work on a 15 stations, 15.6 km Metro line in September 1975.
The cost estimate for completion of the line by 1979-80 is $5 800 m (HK). The line will run from Chater Station in the Central District of Hong Kong Island via immersed tube beneath Hong Kong Harbour through Kowloon to Kwun Tong in the north-east. The line will run in twin-tunnels, partly bored and partly constructed using cut-and-cover.
Trains will be equipped with conventional steel wheels running on standard gaged steel track. Four-car trains are planned initially. There will be standing room for 327 people with 48 seated in each car. The number of cars will be increased to six and by the mid 1980s, eight cars.
In July 1977, the Government gave the Corporation approval to construct a line extension to Tsuen Wan. Work on the 10.7 km extension is expected to begin during the middle of 1978 and be completed in 1982. There will be 11 stations on the extension. The estimated construction cost of the extension is HK$4 100.

Technical Data
  Construction Period: November 1975—December 1979
  Inauguration Date:
    Choi Hung-Shek Kip Mei: September 1979
    Chater-Kwun Tong: March 1980
  Number of Lines: 1
  Length of Line:
    Total: 15.6 km
    Overhead: 2.8 km
    Underground: 12.8 km
    including a Cross Harbour Tunnel of: 1.4 km
  Stations:
    Total: 15
    Overhead: 3

ROLLING STOCK	Car type A	Car type C
Year of manufacture	1977-78	1977-78
Dimensions:		
Length, m	22 750	22 000
Width, m	3 096	3 096
Height, m	3 700	3 700
(powered cars with and without driver's cab)	Powered cars with driver's cab	Powered cars without driver's cab
Tare weight (powered and trailer cars), tonnes	39	39
Body material	Aluminium	Same as for Car type A
Bogie material	Steel	"
Materials for interior trim	Melamine faced aluminium	"
Total carrying capacity, persons	375	"
including seating capacity, persons	48	"
Arrangements of seats: longitudinal, transverse, mixed	Longitudinal	"
Number and dimensions of doors	10@ 1 400 mm × 1 800 mm	"
Method of door operation	Electropneumatic	"
Noise level in driver's cab	75 dBA max	"
passenger compartment	75 dBA	"
Ventilation	AC driven A/C Units	"
Lighting	Fluorescent 250 lux	"
Specific electric power consumption, KWh/1 000 tonne-km	50	"
Design speed, km/h	90	"
Operating speed, km/h	Max 80 km/h. Overall mean including 30s station dwell time 33 km/h	"
Type of body suspension	Primary suspension rubber chevron; secondary air springs	"
Bogie wheelbase, mm	Nose suspended, axle hung	"
Distance between bogie centres	2 500 mm	"
	15 600 mm	"
Type of automatic coupling	BSI Automatic and BSI Semi-Permanent Splittable type	
Wheel dia, mm, and type	@850 mm new, Ø775 mm fully worn; Steel monobloc type	
Number and power of motors	4 × 90 kW	Same as for Car type A
Weight of one motor (without gear train), kg	1 020 kg	"
Armature rotating speed, rpm	2 900 rpm	"
Commutator dia, mm	Ø235 mm	"
Braking—service	Rheostatic/Air	"
—emergency	Air	"
Time required for an empty car to accelerate on level track to 80 km/h	54.2s	"
	17s	"
Time required for braking an empty car on level track from 80 km/h	22s	"
Ditto from 50 km/h	14s	"
Time required for emergency braking of an empty car on level track from 80 km/h	16s	"
Ditto from 50 km/h	10s	"
Degree of automation (automatic train operation, automatic speed control, train radio communication, etc.).	Automatic Train, Operation and Protection, Communication, channels, Driver to Control, Driver to Passengers, Control to passengers	

Underground: 12
Depth: 17-25 m
Length: Chater: 380 m
others: up to 270 m
Platform length: 182 m
Mean Spacing between stations: 1.1 km
Facilities: Escalators, Automatic Fare Collection, Public Address, CCTV, No Smoking, Air Conditioned (underground only)
Security: Royal Hong Kong Police Force

Trains
Car Builder: Metro-Cammell Ltd, Birmingham, England
Car length over headstock:
A cars: 22 750 mm (including cab)
C cars: 22 000 mm (no driving cab)
Car width: 3 096 mm
Car height: 3 700 mm
Height of floor above rail: 1 110 mm
Car Weight: Tare—A car: 39 f
C car: 39 f
Gross—A car: 60.5 f
C car: 60.5 f
Headroom, floor to ceiling: 2 060 mm
Number of doors per side: 5
Doorway width: 1 400 mm
Doorway height: 1 800 mm
Bogie centres: 15 600 mm
Wheel base: 2 500 mm
Wheel dia (new): 850 mm
(Fully worn): 775 mm

ISTANBUL
Authority:
Istanbul Elektrik, Tramvay re Tünel Isletmeleri (IETT)
BP 2175, Umum Müdürlügü, Istanbul, Turkey

Type of system: Underground electric incline railway

History: Prior to 1970 the cable-operated subterranean incline line was steam powered but has since been converted to electric operation. The line first began operating in 1875.

Technical Data:
Gauge: 1.510 m

JAKARTA
Authority:
Municipal Authorities,
Jakarta, Indonesia

General: A new rapid transit rail system is bring planned

KHARKOV
Authority:
Kharkov City Transport
Kharkov, USSR

Type of system: Full-metro

General: The first stage of an underground railway system is under construction in Kharkov. With a population of 1 223 000 in 1970, Kharkov is the second city of the Ukraine. There are more than 1 000 factories. The city's extensive bus, tram and trolleybus services are now inadequate to meet demands and an urban underground railway system is projected.
The underground tunnels are to be built 18 ft in diameter to accommodate Soviet underground rolling stock. The Riga coach building works are building the cars. They will be capable of speeds of 56 mph (90 km/h). Car seats will be arranged transversely and the car capacity will be 240-250 passengers.
The underground lines will be transverse, crossing the city east-west and north-south via the Southern Railway Terminal. The first underground line will be 6.2 miles (9.8 km) long and have two deep-level stations

KIEV
Authority:
Kievski Metropolitan Railway
Kievski City Soviet, Brest Litovsku Prospect 37A, Kiev 55, USSR

Type of system: Full-metro

General: The third metropolitan railway in the USSR came into operation in 1960 in Kiev—capital of the Ukranian SSR (population 1 827 000 in 1973). The first section of 3.2 miles (5.2 km) served 5 stations: Terminus, University, Kretschatik (also the city's principal street) Arsenal and Dnieper.
In 1963 the line was extended 2.1 miles (3.3 km) to Zavod Bolshevik, in 1965 a further 2.7 miles (4.4 km) to Darnitsa, and in 1968 to Konsomolskaya via the Metro bridge crossing of the Dnieper River. In the north-west two further stations. Oktyabrskaya and Zavodskaya, were opened in 1973.
A new transverse line from Priorka, south east, south and south-west to Teremky, crossing the existing line at Kreshchatic, now also under construction, will add 16 more stations to the system.

Technical Data:
Gauge: 1.524 m

Motors: 4 per car 90 kW GEC
Motor Suspension: Nose suspended, axle hung
Motor voltage: 350V dc
Gear ratio: 82 : 15
Gear drive: Parallel Helical
Brake system: service: Rheostatic/air
emergency: Air
No of passengers:
Total (Max load): 375
Seated: 48
Standing: 327
Train Configuration:
4 car: A – C + C – A
6 car*: A – C + B – C + C – A
8 car*: A – C + B – C + B – C + C – A
Facilities: Load control acceleration and braking rates, Public address, Air conditioning, automatic train operation and protection, No smoking, Air operated doors, vestibules between cars
Operation:
Frequency of trains: 2 mins at peak
Journey time overall: 28 min
Station dwell time: 30s
Mean speed including stops: 33 km/h
Max service speed: 80 km/h
Service hours: 0600-0100 daily (ie 19h/day)
Passenger volume per day: 1 million by mid 1980's
Fare: HK$1.00 minimum, HK$1.25 mean

Vehicle Performance & Data
Design speed: 90 km/h
Service speed (max): 80 km/h

Route length: 570 m
In tunnel: 570 m
Number of lines: 1
Number of stations (total): 2
(in tunnel): 2
Average distance between stations: 570 m
Stations:
platform length (minimum): 30 m

Gradient (max): 14.9%
Speed (design max): 30 km/h
(average commercial): 30 km/h
Electric system: 440 V

for Indonesia's capital city. Basically, the scheme consists of four cross-city routes and a central area circle line.
The proposals are being based on recommendations made by engineers from Orge Intertraffic-Lenzconsult of the Federal Republic of Germany which prepared a

and six of cut and cover type. Stations will be from 0.9 km to 1.7 km apart, and will have platforms 328 ft (100 m) long. They will be: Sverdlova Street, Yuzhny Vokzal, Rynok (Market), Centre, Levada Stadium, Zavod Malysheva, Turbinni Zavod. During peak hours it is expected that 15 trains each made up of two pairs of 4-car units will serve the line initially. Construction of the second stage will add 11¾ miles (7.3 km).

Technical Data:
Gauge: 1.524 m
Projected new lines (in construction): 10.6 km with 8.9 km in tunnel
(in design): 27 km
Number of lines: 2
Number of stations (total): 14
(in tunnel): 6
Average distance between stations: 13 km
Stations:
Platform length (minimum): 100 m
Gradient (max): 4%
Speed (design max): 90-120 km/h
Electric system: Catenary; 3 000 V

Route length: 18.2 km
In tunnel: 14.0
Projected new lines (in construction): 10.7 km
Number of lines: 1
Number of stations (total): 15
(in tunnel): 10
Average distance between stations: 1.4 km
Stations:
platform length (minimum): 100 m

Gradient (max): 4%
Curvature (max): 400 m
Speed (design max): 75 km/h
(average commercial): 38 km/h
Electric system: Third rail; 825 V
Type of rails: 50 kg/m

Rolling Stock:

Car type	Diesel	Electric
Number of units:		194
Car dimensions (length):	18.8 m	18.8 m
(width):	2.7 m	2.7 m
(height):	3.7 m	3.7 m
Passenger capacity per car: (total):	210	220

Service acceleration rate: 1.3 m/s²
Service retardation rate: 1.0 m/s²—1.35 m/s²
Emergency retardation rate: 1.4 m/s²
Max jerk rate: 0.8 m/s³

Electrical & Control System
Line voltage: 1 500V dc
Current collection: Pantograph on C car
Exterior lights: Incandescent heavy duty head lamp
Saloon lights: Fluorescent
Train control: Automatic Train Operation (Manual Control Available)

Body Specification
Frame: Aluminium extrusion—monocoque
Exterior cladding: Rivetted aluminium alloy panels
Interior cladding: Epoxy powder aluminium alloy
Ceiling cladding: Nylon faced aluminium alloy
Floor: Vinyl faced plywood on aluminium troughing
Windows: Tinted high strength safety glass
Air conditioning: 80 kW heat load per car 2 roof mounted package units
Air conditioning drive: 1 package driven from own car, other from adjacent car, 440 V 60 Hz
Noise—Inside: 75 dBA max

* B Cars will be identical with C cars in structure, but have identical equipment to A cars, and no driving cab.

Rolling Stock:
Car type (year introduced): 1970
Number of units: 2
Car dimensions (length): 16.0 m
(width): 2.5 m
Passenger capacity per car (total): 200

Traffic Data:
Train capacity (passengers): 200
Total passengers/track/hour (peak): 6 000
Train headways, existing: 2 minutes
Passengers carried (1976): 6 097 800
Vehicle-km operated (1976): 67 980

study on future city transport needs in 1974. Motive power and vehicles to be used are expected to consist of five sets of four-car electric trainsets and 12 sets of two-car diesel trains. Maximum speeds will be limited to 40 km/h and trains are expected to operate at 20 minute intervals.

Rolling Stock:
Car type: proposed
Car dimensions (length): 19.60 m
(width): 2.70 m
(height): 3.70 m
Passenger capacity per car (total): 260
(seated): 40
Motors per car: 4
Rating: 68 kWh
Train composition (max): 8
Acceleration (max): 1.0
Deceleration (emergency): 1.2
Brakes (type): Rheostatic
Body material: Steel
Weight (tonnes) Motorcar: 30

Traffic Data:
Trains/track/hour: 30 (estimated)
Train capacity (passengers): 2 080
Total passengers/track/hour (peak): 62 400
Train headways
design: 2 minutes

(seated):	44	40
Motors per car:	4	4
Rating:	73 kWh	68 kWh
Train composition:		
(minimum): 3		
(max): 3		
Acceleration (max):	1.3	
Deceleration (emergency):		
Brakes (type):	Rheostatic / Electro-pneumatic	

Body material: Steel
Weight (tonnes) Motorcar: 32

Traffic Data:
Trains/track/hour: 30
Train capacity (passengers): 750
Total passengers/track/hour (peak): 22 500
Train headways
existing: 2 minutes
Passengers carried (weekday): 486 900
(annually): 177 700 000
Average journey length: 5.6 km
Vehicle-km operated annually: 23 200 000

KOBE
Kobe City, Japan

General: This important port has four surface railways (besides the Japanese National Railway) whose terminal stations were until 1968 unconnected by rail with each other. The underground-elevated Kobe Rapid Railway provides this rail connection and permits interworking of three of the surface railways' services. The linking railway begins in the west at the Sanyo Electric Railway's Nishidai station and runs for 3.5 km to Kosoku-kobe central station. There it forks, one branch running for 2.2 km to the Hankyu Electric Railway's Sannomiya station and the other for 1.5 km to the Hanshin Electric Railway's Motomachi station, both in the east. Additionally, from an intermediate underground Shinkaichi station, a short 0.4 km spur

runs north to the Kobe Electric Railway's Minatogawa station.

This heavily used railway, built by the Kobe Rapid Railway Co Ltd at a cost of Y16 000 000 000 (about £16m at that time) carries 1 500 trains daily. The first 5.6 km section of an east-west traverse line from Naya to Shin-Nagata has been under construction by the Municipal Authority since 25 November 1972, and was opened in December 1975. It will be extended from the city centre eastward to Nunobiki to complete a total route length of 13.4 km.

Details: Route length, east-west line, 7.2 km; north-south line 0.4 km; east-west traverse line 5.6 km. Of the total 7.6 km; 0.6 km is elevated and the remainder in tunnel.

Tunnels: Double-tracked sub-surface Box-Rahmen type.
Gauge: 1.435 m (standard) east-west line, 1.067 m north-south line.
Station lengths: 120-160 m.
Motive power: Current is collected from overhead compound catenary wires (part rigid type) at 1 500 V dc, supplied initially at 33 000 V.
Signalling: Automatic block with lineside signals and train stops. A control centre is equipped with a train position indicator and train classifying equipment.
Rolling Stock: The Kobe Rapid Railway owns no stock. The Sanyo, Hankyu and Hanshin Electric Railways interwork their own stock over the east-west line, and the Kobe Electric Railway over the narrow-gauge north-south line.

KYOTO
Authority:
Municipal Transportation Bureau
Kyoto, Japan

Type of system: Full-metro

General: Kyoto, situated about 25 miles north-east of Osaka, has no underground railway system as such at present, (although there are plans for a north-south 11 km rapid transit line). It is connected to Osaka and Tokyo by the Japanese National Railway's Tokaido trunk line, and with Osaka also by the Keihan and Keihanshin Kyuko private electric railways. The latter railway approaches the city from the west and con-

tinues underground to terminate at its centre.
In 1963 the original underground portion of this line, opened in 1931, was extended to its present length of 2.2 miles *(3.6 km)*. It runs beneath a main thoroughfare, in rectangular tunnel for the most part, with sufficient headroom for overhead current collection by pantograph. A sub-surface continuous concourse provides connection with the railway below, and entry from street level is by stairways situated at a number of points along the main thoroughfare. There are four stations.
Construction of the city's first 12 km subway line—began in 1974 and reached completion in 1976—is now underway and the first 6.9 km of the Karasuma line—between Kitaoji and Kyoto station—is

due to open in 1980.
Technical Data:
Projected new lines (in design): 21 km system

Speed (design max): 30 km/h

Rolling Stock:
Car type: proposed
Number of units: 112
Passenger capacity per car (total): 130

Traffic Data:
Passengers carried (weekday): 430 000 (estimated for 1985)

LENINGRAD
Authority:
Leningradski Metropoliten Imeni V.I. Lenina
Moskovskit Prospekt 28, Leningrad LI3, USSR

Type of system: Full-metro.

General: Leningrad's population in 1973 was 4 133 000 and of these over a million use the Metro every working day. Its two busiest stations are Park Pobedy and Moscovskaya in the southern residential districts.
The Leningrad Metro was the second underground system in the USSR. The first line 6.7 miles *(10.8 km)* long from Avtovo in the south to Ploshchad Vosstania was opened in November 1955, and extended to Ploshchad Lenina in June 1958. It connected five main-line stations.
In 1961 the first 3.5 mile *(5.6 km)* section of the Moscovsko-Petrogradskaya was opened, crossing the existing line at Technical Institute and connecting the city's southern district with the right side of the River Neva. In 1963 it was extended north four stations to Petrogradskaya.
Construction began also in 1963 of the Nevsko-Vasiliostrovskaya line and four stations of this line were opened in 1967, in which year the Avtovo-Ploshchad Lenina was extended south to Dachnoe. In 1969 the Moscovsko-Petrogradskaya line was extended south to Moscovskaya Station.
The original underground line, last extended to Ploshchad Lenina in 1958, is being extended considerably in the north and also extended southward. Under a four-year plan, it is scheduled for completion north to Kalininskaya and south to Vitebskaya by 1974. In 1972 the Vasiliostrovskaya line was extended two

stations, serving a new Leningrad district of Obokho-va, and the Moskovskaya line was extended southward two stations to Kupchino.
Plans call for an eventual network totalling 240 km. By 1980 a system of 116 km and 72 stations is planned.

Technical Data:
Gauge: 1.524 m
Route length: 45 km
In tunnel: 44.4 km
Projected new lines (in construction): 10+km
(in design): 71 km
Number of lines: 3
Number of stations (total): 29
(in tunnel): 28
Average distance between stations: 1.44 km
Stations:
platform length (minimum): 80 m

Type of tunnel: The line is of deep-level tube construction, and depending on the cambresian clay formation, is at places nearly 200 ft (over *60 m*) below surface level. Each single-track tunnel is of metal and ferro-concrete tube construction and has an internal diameter of 5.1 m.

Gradient (max): 4%
Curvature (max): 400 m
Speed (design max): 65 km/h
(average commercial): 40 km/h
Electric system: Third rail; 825 V

Rolling Stock:
Car type: Diesel Electric
Car dimensions (length): 18.77 m 18.77 m

(width):	2.70 m	2.70 m
(height):	3.70 m	3.70 m
Passenger capacity		
per car (total):	250	250
(seated):	44	40
Motors per car:	4	4
Rating:	73 kWh	68 kWh
Train composition		
(minimum): 2		
(max): 6		
Acceleration (max):	1.2	1.3
Deceleration (emergency):	1.1	
Brakes (type): Rheostatic/Electro magnetic		
Body material: steel		
Weight (tonnes)		
Motorcar:	36.2	32

Traffic Data:
Trains/track/hour: 30
Train capacity (passengers): 1 500
Total passengers/track/hour (peak): 45 000
Train headways
existing: 2 minutes
Passengers carried (weekday): 1 321 000
(annually): 399 000 000
Average journey length: 6.8 km
Vehicle-km operated annually: 70 100 000

Signalling: Automatic operation of trains is being introduced progressively on the system. On the first line, full automatic control in operation includes programmed traffic interlocking control and automatic train operation, thus dispensing with assistant motormen and limiting the motormen's duties to train supervision.

LILLE
Authority:
Lille Rapid Transit
Lille, France

Type of system: Automated light-rail

General: The French Government finally gave its approval to the construction of the Lille light-rail automated Metro (VAL) system in June 1975. The first line will be 11.5-km long, comprising cut-and-cover and bored tunnel sections in the town centre and viaduct sections east of Helemmes and on the approach

to the terminal at the Regional Hospital. Total cost of the project—which is scheduled for completion by 1980/81—will be about Frs 1 200 million.
The VAL system, developed for Lille by Matra, has undergone a number of modifications since trials started on a 1.6-km oval test track at Lille-Est. While it was initially planned to use two-car sets, the system is now to be adapted for eventual introduction of four-car consists made up of two articulated units. Designed to run at 60 seconds intervals, capacity will be 15 000 passengers an hour.
To meet this requirement, station platforms are to be

just over 50 m long and it has been decided to provide three wide double doors on the side of each car instead of four narrow doors. Also modified is the automatic control system which was to have been supervised from a central control cabin. Now that the length of the line is to be increased from the original 8.5 km to 11.5 km, separate control desks are to be located at approximately every 4 km.
Construction on the line has now begun and a preliminary order for six two-car trainsets has been placed with Matra. It is eventually intended to operate up to 50 two-car units on the line.

LISBON
Authority:
Metropolitano de Lisboa SARL (ML)
28 Ave Fontes Pereira de Meto Lisbon, Portugal
Telephone: 58 171
Cables: METROPOLITANO-LISBOA

Type of system: Full-metro

General: The owning and operating authority of the Lisbon Metro is a private company, the majority of whose shares are held by the Municipality. The Metro was built between 1955 and 1959 to provide a fast mass transit facility between Lisbon's northern districts and the centre. The first section was opened on 30 December 1959, the extension to the city's commercial centre at Rossio in January 1963 and two extensions, to Anjos and then to Alvalade, in 1966 and 1972 respectively. Target is an eventual route length of 40 km; studies on projected new lines are now underway.

Technical Data:
Gauge: 1.435 m
Route length: 12.0 km
In tunnel: 12.0 km
Projected new lines:
(in design): 7 km
Number of lines: 1
Number of stations (total): 20
(in tunnel): 20
Average distance between stations: 630 m
Stations:
platform length (minimum): 40 m

Type of tunnel: Arched roof on vertical side walls, and straight or arched inverts. Minimum dimensions on alignments are:—double track 16 ft 3 in *(4.95 m)* high, 24 ft 1½ in *(7.35 m)* wide; single track 14 ft 3 in *(4.35 m)* high, 14 ft 9 in *(4.5 m)* wide.
Built by the "cut and cover method", except on two

short sections tunnelled or built by the "Belgian method", and on part of the central area where both underpinning of 18th Century buildings and temporary decking under roadways was necessary. Linings are of concrete and, at stations, of reinforced concrete.

Gradient: (max): 4%
Curvature (max): 150 m
Speed (design max): 60
(average commercial): 28
Electric system: Third rail; 750 V
Type of rails: 50 kg/m
Welded joints: 18 m lengths

Rolling Stock:
	1959	1970
Car type (year introduced):	1959	1970
Number of units:	38	32
Car dimensions: (length):	16.4 m	16.5 m
(width):	2.7 m	2.7 m

(height):	3.45 m	—
Passenger capacity		
per car: (total):	200	200
(seated):	36	36
Motors per car:	4	4
Rating:	90 kWh	100 kWh
Train composition:		
(minimum): 2		

(max): 2		
Acceleration (max):	0.9	—
Deceleration (emergency):	1.2	—
Brakes (types): Rheostatic/Electro-magnetic		
Body material: Steel		
Weight (tonnes)		
Motorcar:	36.5	—

Traffic Data:
Trains/track/hour: 24
Train headways existing: 2 minutes
Passengers carried (annually): 70 400 000
Average journey length: 3.9 km
Vehicle-km operated annually: 4 400 000

LIVERPOOL

Authority:
British Railways (London Midland Region)
Euston House, London, NW1, England

General: Liverpool lies on the east side of the estuary of the River Mersey, while Birkenhead lies opposite on the west side, in the Wirral Peninsula. The Mersey Railway Company was incorporated in June 1866 to construct a railway tunnel under the river to join the two cities, but it was not until January 1886 that the line was opened, with steam operation. Electrification was introduced in May 1903. In March 1938, the local Wirral (surface) lines of the London Midland and Scottish Railway were electrified, and through-running between them and the Mersey Railway began. Since 1948, the Mersey Railway has been incorporated in the London Midland Region of the nationalised British Railways system. Through trains to the Wirral run from Liverpool to New Brighton and West Kirby via Birkenhead Park and to Rock Ferry via Birkenhead Central.

The length of the under-river section of the Mersey Railway tunnel between James Street and Hamilton Square is 1 mile 350 yards *(1 930 m)*. The total length of the tunnels, extending from Liverpool Central to Birkenhead Central and Park is 3¼ miles. The line runs from Liverpool (Central) southwestwards under the river to Hamilton Square, on the Birkenhead side, where it splits, one branch running northwestwards to Park, and the other southwards to Rock Ferry. The line is double track throughout.

Current supply on the Mersey Railway is at 650 V dc, and until 1955 (when it was converted to third-rail, as on the Wirral lines), four-rail distribution was used.

Trains consist of multiple unit stock. Before its incorporation into British Railways, the Mersey Railway Company owned about 80 cars. The last rolling stock replacement programme was completed in 1957. The Company's system had a route length of 4.8 miles *(7.7 km)*.

On March 5, 1970 the recently-formed Merseyside Passenger Transport Authority agreed that detailed drawings should be made, at a cost of about £240 000, for a new underground railway line for Liverpool. This would form a 2-mile terminal loop running beneath the city centre, connecting at James Street station with the Mersey Railway, and extending the latter to link with Exchange, Lime Street and Central Stations and back to James Street.

Construction work on the Loop scheme started in January 1972, with completion estimated at a cost of approximately £23·6 million. Platforms are designed to accommodate six-car trains. Lime Street underground station is sited under St. George's Plateau with a subway connection to the mainline station.

Including station tunnels, the single track has been formed using Dosco Roadheader machines which are crawler mounted and have a cylindrical cutting head.

On the Liverpool side of the Mersey it is between 55 and 124 ft *(16.8 and 37.8 m)* in depth. As part of the project a new burrowing junction at Hamilton Square station, which will eliminate the present double-line junction and allow for greater train frequencies, is approximately 113 ft deep.

A further proposal was for another underground line (the Link scheme) 1⅛ miles long, to extend the Southport and Ormskirk lines from Exchange to Central Station. Trains would then use Moorfields Station enabling Exchange Station to be closed.

As presently envisaged, the system will continue to be operated by British Railways, but the Passenger Transport Executive will be responsible for service frequency and fare structure.

Main Contractors

	Loop	*Link*
Signalling	ML Engineering (Plymouth) Ltd	(Work to be carried out by BRLM Region)
Telecommunications		
Cables	BICC (Telephone Cables Division) Prescot	BICC (Telephone Cables Division) Prescot
Public Address Equipment	Planned Equipment Ltd, Northolt	Planned Equipment Ltd, Northolt
CCTV	Rediffusion Ltd, Surbiton	Rediffusion Ltd, Surbiton
Train describers	AP Electronics Ltd, Wembley	AP Electronics Ltd, Wembley
Platform Indicators	Telesign Ltd, London	Telesign Ltd, London

James Street PSB

	Loop	*Link*
Route miles	4¾	4
Track miles	7¼	8
Controlled running signals	16	22
Repeater signals	9	11
Automatic signals	15	5
Position light ground signals	4	3
Number of routes	40	41
Number of point ends	12	24

The following "Fringe" signalboxes work to James Street PSB:

Loop	*Link*
Birkenhead Park	Kirkdale East
Birkenhead Central	Bootle Junction
James St (Link)	James St (Loop)
	Hunts Cross West

Rail Types and Weights:
In new tunnel section: 113A (56 kg/m) Flat Bottom UIC Class B
In other sections: 113A Flat bottom or as existing

Conductor Rail:
In new tunnel section: 150 lb (74 kg/m)
Elsewhere: 106 lb/150 lb mixture

Sleepers:
In new single bore tunnels: Short lengths, 2 m long concrete. 152 mm thick spaced at 750 centres
Outside tunnels: Standard timber or concrete sleepers for third rail electrified lines

Slab Track: Thers are 7 130 m lengths of slab track situated in station platform areas, with rail laid in modified cast iron base plates.

Rail Fastenings:
In single bore tunnel: Malleable cast iron shoulders with pandrol clips or pandrol clips in modified base plate
Elsewhere: Timber sleepers with chairs on base plates or concrete sleeper with built-in shoulder.

Signalling: The proposed signalling between Exchange Junction and Brunswick is three aspect colour light with continuous track circuiting and is arranged for a two minute headway service with 30 second station stops. Train stops are to be provided at all running stop signals in the tunnel section.

This signalling, together with the existing signalling, installed in the Sandhills area in December 1973, and at present controlled by Liverpool Exchange No 1 signal box, is to be controlled from a new power signal box at James Street.

Four digit train describers will be provided working to fringe boxes at Kirkdale East, Bootle Junction and Hunts Cross. Telephone services, public address and train indicators will be provided at Sandhills, Moorfields and Central stations and telephones for communications will be provided at all running stop signals.

The proposed signalling for the Liverpool loop section is two aspect colour light, with train stops fitted at all running signals and continuous track circuiting. The signals are designed to cater for a headway of 95 seconds, allowing a station stop of 30 seconds duration.

The scheme will be controlled from the new station box at James Street. Four figure train describers will be provided, working to fringe signal boxes at Birkenhead Park and Birkenhead Central.

Telephone services, public address and train indicators will be provided at all stations.

An emergency telephone circuit will be provided in the tunnels which will enable the train driver to isolate the section of track he is occupying and/or communicate with the Electrical Controller. Telephones for communication to the signalbox will be provided at all running signals.

LONDON

Authority:
London Transport Executive
55 Broadway, Westminster, London SW1H 0BD, England
Telephone: (01) 222 5600
Cables: PASSENGERS-LONDON

History: On 1 January 1970, the Greater London Council became the statutory planning authority for London, with responsibilities which include the effective integration of its transport, including that of London Transport. The London Transport Executive is responsible for the operation of London Buses and the Underground. During 37 years previous to 1970, all London urban public transport services were under the control of a single Authority, known successively over the period as the London Passenger Transport Board, the London Transport Executive, and latterly the London Transport Board.

The first sub-surface steam railway, opened by the Metropolitan Railway Company on 10 January 1863, was a development of an idea of Charles Pearson, a London City solicitor, who foresaw the possibility of underground travel to overcome the increasing street congestion in the mid-19th Century. The first section of the line opened was nearly four miles in length between Paddington (Bishops Road) and Farringdon Street.

The opening of this railway was followed by another sub-surface enterprise, the Metropolitan District Railway Company which, by the end of 1868, had opened a length of line between Gloucester Road and Westminster, joining up with the Metropolitan Railway which by then had been extended from Edgware Road to South Kensington. By 1871, the Metropolitan District had been extended to Mansion House and by 1876 the Metropolitan to Aldgate. A line joining these stations was opened in 1884 thus completing the railway which became known as the Inner Circle and is today the Circle Line.

These lines were mainly built by the 'cut and cover' method.

The first 'tube' railway in the world was a subway between Tower Hill and Bermondsey through which passengers were carried by a cable-operated car. It was opened in August 1870 but was not a success and after only a few months, the car was withdrawn and the subway converted for pedestrian use until 1896 by which time Tower Bridge was opened.

The first tube railway proper, the City and South London Railway, was opened on 18 December 1890 running from King William Street in the City of London to Stockwell, south of Thames, a distance of three and a quarter miles. This railway employed electricity as its motive power.

The next tube railway, the Central London, popularly known as the "Twopenny Tube", was opened from Shepherd's Bush to the Bank in the centre of the City of London, a distance of nearly six miles, on July 30, 1900. It derived its popular title from the fact that when it first opened a uniform fare of 2d was charged whatever the distance travelled. By 1907, the Baker Street and Waterloo, the Great Northern, Piccadilly and Brompton and the Hampstead tube railways had been added to the map so that in a matter of less than fifty years there had grown from the embryo of the Metropolitan Railway a network of underground railways reaching out to many parts of London and its suburbs. All these railways were started by individual companies and—except for the Metropolitan—became amalgamated into the Underground group in 1915. The Metropolitan remained a separate company until 1933 when the London Passenger Transport Board was formed.

During the blitz on London in the second world war, 'tube' stations were used as shelters, a practice started in the first war during the Zeppelin raids of September, 1917. No fewer than 177 000 people were recorded as having taken shelter from the blitz in the tubes on 27 September 1940. Thereafter the average number of shelterers dwindled until they were temporarily stabilised at about 60 000 per night. A refreshment service was operated and as much as seven tons of food and 2 400 gallons of liquid such as tea, cocoa and milk were sold nightly. Seventy-nine stations were used by shelterers in Greater London. In addition some miles of tube tunnel, either temporarily disused (such as the Aldwych branch) or not yet used, as in the case of the newly constructed but incomplete eastern extension of the Central Line through Bethnal Green, Mile End and Stratford, also provided protection. Lavatory accommodation and medical-aid posts were installed, together with bunks to accommodate over 22 000 people. The total length of platforms and subways, together with the length of tunnel east of Liverpool Street and the Aldwych branch, used by shelterers reached a figure of fifteen miles. Between Leytonstone and Gants Hill, a total of five miles of tunnel on the uncompleted extension of the Central Line was used as an underground aircraft component factory, while the temporarily disused section of the Aldwych branch of the Piccadilly Line was used to house British Museum treasures.

In 1949, far-reaching plans for the improvement of railway facilities in the London area were put forward which at that time were estimated to cost some £340 million. They proposed the construction of several new tube lines as well as further electrification and improvement works on certain suburban lines of British Railways. However, owing to economic conditions, it was only in the summer of 1955 that powers were sought by the British Transport Commission for the carrying out of the first and most urgently needed of these works. This was a tube known to the planners as "Route C" since named the Victoria Line. Government approval for the construction of the first ten-mile section of this line—linking Victoria and the West End with the main line railway termini at Euston, King's Cross and St. Pancras and with the densely populated north east suburbs of Tottenham and Walthamstow—was given in August, 1962. Within a few weeks construction work had been started and on September 1, 1968 the first section of the line—between Walthamstow Central and Highbury & Islington—was opened for passenger traffic. The second section—from Highbury & Islington to Warren Street came into operation on 1 December, and the third section—through the West End to Victoria—was officially opened by Her Majesty the Queen on 7 March 1969.

The 3½-mile southern extension of the Victoria Line from Victoria to Brixton, on which work started in August 1967, was officially opened by HRH Princess Alexandra on July 23, 1971. Except for Pimlico station, which was opened by the Lord Mayor of Westminster on 14 September 1972, this extension marked the completion of the Victoria Line between Walthamstow and Brixton.

As well as opening up new cross-town and cross-river links, the Victoria Line relieves the heavy strain placed on other Underground lines and eases street congestion. Of the sixteen stations on the Victoria Line—all of which are in tube—fifteen provide interchange facilities with other underground or British Railways lines. Incorporating automatic train operation, automatic ticket issue and control and closed circuit television, the Victoria Line is one of the most highly-automated and technically advanced underground railways in the world.

Work commenced in April 1971 on the construction of the first section of the extension of the Piccadilly Line beyond Hounslow West to Heathrow Airport (for which Parliamentary Powers were obtained in 1967). The first section from Hounslow West to Hatton Cross was opened on 19 July 1975, and as far as Heathrow Central Station by December 1977. Another railway project is a completely new line—the Jubilee Line—which will take over the Stanmore-Baker Street branch of the Bakerloo Line and continue through the West End to a new terminus at Charing Cross. Work commenced early in 1972 on the construction of this new line. Parliamentary powers have been obtained for the construction of the second stage from Charing Cross to Fenchurch Street and powers will be sought shortly for a proposed extension through Docklands to Thamesmead.

There are today eight lines making up the London Transport system of Underground railways, these are:

Metropolitan: Covering 55 route miles and serving 61 stations, the Metropolitan is the longest line in the system and is operated in three sections:

Main section: Baker Street (Aldgate in peak hours) to Amersham, with branches to Chesham, Watford and Uxbridge.

Hammersmith and City section: Hammersmith to Whitechapel, with a peak hour extension to Barking.

East London section: Whitechapel (Shoreditch in peak hours) to New Cross or New Cross Gate.

District: Between Upminster and Ealing Broadway with branches to Richmond, Wimbledon, Edgware Road and Olympia, covers 40 route miles and serves 60 stations.

Circle: The Circle Line is basically a combination of the central sections of the Metropolitan and District lines. Thirteen miles in length and serving 27 stations, it connects most of London's main line railway termini.

Bakerloo: From Elephant & Castle to Stanmore, or Queens Park, with a peak hour extension to Watford Junction, Covers 18 miles (32 in peak hours) and serves 29 stations (44 in peak hours).

Central: Ealing or West Ruislip to Hainault or Epping with a branch to Ongar and a loop from Woodford to Hainault. It covers 52 miles and serves 52 stations.

Northern: Morden to Edgware, Mill Hill East or High Barnet via Bank or Charing Cross; serves fifty stations. Within its 36 route miles is the longest continuous railway tunnel in the world—the 17¼ miles from East Finchley to Morden via Bank.

Piccadilly: Cockfosters to Hounslow West or Uxbridge, with a peak hour shuttle branch from Holborn to Aldwych, covers 38 miles and serves 49 stations. An extension from Hounslow West to Heathrow Central was commenced in 1971 and opened in December 1977.

Victoria: Walthamstow Central to Brixton; serves sixteen stations and is fourteen miles in length.

The first three lines listed above are of the 'cut and cover' or sub-surface type, the other five being tube lines. A sixth tube is the Waterloo & City Line which runs from Waterloo main line station to Bank. This line is owned and operated by The Southern Region of British Rail and has never been part of the London Transport Underground system.

Route length: (January 1976): Served by London Transport trains 254 miles of which 237 miles are administrated by London Transport, the remainder being British Railways lines over which London Transport trains run. Of the whole system, 97 route miles are underground, 74 miles in small-diameter deep-level tube tunnels, and 23 miles in sub-surface tunnels of larger section.

Rolling Stock: Broadly speaking there are two types of Underground rolling stock—'surface' and 'tube', the first identifying the stock on the Metropolitan, District and Circle lines (the tunnels on which are of the 'cut and cover' type) which is larger than the stock on the 'tube' lines. All Underground cars are of the saloon type with seating for 32-40 passengers (54-58 in the Metropolitan Line stock) and standing room for about 100. The length of trains is mainly six, seven or eight cars, although shorter units of four cars are used in off-peak hours on the Metropolitan Main Line and all day on certain sections. In the peak hours so intense is the service that trains run at intervals as short as 90-120 seconds in the central area and the average length of time a train stops at a station is only 20-25 seconds. High speed trains are not generally practicable because of the frequency of the service and the short distance between stations, but acceleration is high; 20 mph is reached in about 15 seconds (10 seconds on the Victoria Line and slightly less on the H & C and Circle Stock) and 40 mph in the open in about one minute. On the Metropolitan Main Line, some trains cover quite long distances between stops, and speeds of 60 mph are sustained over a number of sections. All cars are fitted with air-operated sliding doors, which, except on automatically-driven trains, are under the control of the guard. A 'pilot light' is illuminated when all doors are closed and not until he gets this light can the guard give the bell signal for the driver to start. On the automatically-driven trains of the Victoria Line and the Woodford-Hainault section of the Central Line, which have no guard, the pilot light is situated in the driving cab and the starting and door circuits are inter-locked to ensure that a train cannot start unless the doors are closed.

Railway cars with light alloys instead of steel in body construction have been in use since 1952, the reduced weight affecting a substantial saving in running costs. The first of these trains, on the District Line, was painted red to match the rest of the fleet, but subsequent light alloy stock has been left unpainted and, for uniformity, those which were painted red have now been painted silver. All the Metropolitan, Central, Picadilly and Victoria Line trains and the majority of the trains on the Northern Line and an increasing percentage of trains on the Bakerloo Line, are composed of unpainted aluminium stock. Entrance doors on some of the new 'silver' trains now entering service have red doors to make the entrance more conspicuous and to provide a flash of colour.

Although the Victoria Line trains were the first to be designed and built for automatic operation on the Underground, four trains, specially converted, have been driven automatically on the Woodford-Hainault branch of the Central Line since 1964. Delivery was completed in 1971 of new unpainted aluminium 'surface' stock for the Circle and Hammersmith and City Lines. Although the stock is initially for two-man operation, conversion to one-man operation can be undertaken by means of minor modifications. Thirty new trains ordered for the Northern Line entered service in the summer of 1972 and delivery was completed in the first part of 1973. These are similar to those on the Victoria Line, but have a two-man crew, as the layout of stations on the Northern Line makes the future conversion of the line to ATO (with consequential one-man operation) difficult. A second batch of 33 similar trains (known as 1972 Mk 11 Stock) has entered service, also on the Northern Line, but these trains are destined eventually for use on Stage 1 of the Jubilee Line when this opens and in consequence have been delivered with provision for conversion to one-man operation. New Stock (1973 Stock) is now operating on the Picadilly Line and the displaced stock is being transferred to the Northern Line. The new 6-car Piccadilly line trains feature a new electrical braking system and more space for luggage.

New trains, designated D78 stock, have been ordered for the District line. They will feature passenger-activated doors; the crew will retain overall control, but doors will only open on demand. This will help to keep trains warm in outlying sections where passenger traffic is small.

Maintenance: Repairs and day-to-day maintenance of Underground trains are carried out at rolling stock depots and car sheds. There are eleven passenger depots, basically two per line except that Hammersmith Depot caters for the Hammersmith and City and Circle Lines and Neasden deals with two lines—the Metropolitan and, at present, the Bakerloo. A new depot for Bakerloo trains is being built at Starebridge Park, and Neasden will then serve the Metropolitan and Jubilee lines. There is one depot—at Northumberland Park—for the Victoria Line. There are also a number of minor depots at some of which minor repairs and inspections are carried out—for example New Cross for the East London Line.

All major overhauls are carried out at Acton Works, the older rolling stock being overhauled every five years and the newer at varying periods up to 10 years.

Trains operate daily from 05.00 to 01.00 hours and it is only during the intervening four hours that maintenance of tracks and signals can be carried out. In this comparatively short period every yard of tunnel is inspected.

Signalling: The signalling on the Underground has two vital functions to perform: to ensure complete safety of operation and to enable maximum possible use to be made of the available line capacity. It is based on a system of track circuiting whereby individual sections of track are isolated from each other electrically. The passage of each train over one section automatically sets the coloured light signals behind it at danger, the signals clearing automatically once the train has proceeded a safe distance. All sections of the Underground which are free of junctions are automatically signalled in this way. A safety device, known as the 'trainstop', is installed to halt a train automatically should it pass a signal at danger.

The signalling of junctions is semi-automatic but under the supervision of a signalman; again special safety interlocking devices are fitted to guard against any element of human error. The gradual development of a system of 'route control signalling'—under which one manual act in the signal cabin clears the signals and sets the points for a complete route—and remote control have enabled cabins to control train movements over much wider areas.

On London Transport railways, 'programme machines' are employed—a system pioneered by London Transport in the fifties which automatically signals a complete day's train service. This is done by means of a plastic roll, with coded information about each train's origin, destination, route and time, passing through a machine which sets the signals and points for each train in the timetable.

Programme machine signalling, which needs no human intervention unless the service is seriously dislocated, is now installed on the Northern and parts of other Underground lines and is the basis of junction signalling on the new Victoria Line, where the safety signalling is otherwise carried out by a system of coded impulses in the rail.

Automatic Train Operation: The system of automatic train operation employed on the Victoria Line was designed and developed by London Transport. Following initial tests on a short section of the District Line in 1962, full-scale trials were started in 1964 on the Woodford-Hainault branch of the Central Line using four specially converted trains, the branch being worked as a self-contained automatic railway.

Each train responds to safety codes which are transmitted through the running rails and high frequency driving commands that are injected at predetermined intervals on short sections of the track, these signals are picked up by coils mounted in front of the leading wheels. The train cannot run unless safety code is being picked up and these codes ensure that the speed of the train is being controlled to keep it a safe distance from the train in front. If this safety factor is infringed for any reason, the safety codes will automatically stop the train.

The driving commands control the motors and brakes so that the train, once the Train Operator has pressed the twin starting buttons, will accelerate, coast and brake to a stop in the right position at the next station without further intervention from the Operator. They will also cause the train to observe any speed restrictions and to stop and restart as required by the traffic conditions on the way.

The Victoria Line employs no Signalmen, all junctions are set automatically by a programme machine and the whole line is supervised from one central control point at Euston.

Power Supply: Until 1890 all the sections of the Underground railway opened had been steam operated but the City and South London introduced electric traction which was employed by all subsequent tube developments. The Metropolitan and the Metropolitan District railways started experiments in 1900 which led them to convert their lines to electric traction, starting in 1903.

The electric power for operating the Underground services today comes mainly from London Transport's own generating stations at Lots Road (Chelsea), and Greenwich. In addition, a bulk supply is taken from the central Electricity Generating Board at Neasden, Heathway and Old Oak Common to feed sections of the surface lines in those areas, leaving Lots Road and Greenwich Generating stations to supply power to the deep level tubes, and certain other areas.

The modernisation and re-equipment of Lots Road Generating station, to convert it from coal-fired to oil-fired boilers was completed at the end of 1968, and modernisation of Greenwich, the smaller of the two stations, was completed in December 1972; the coal-fired boilers, and steam driven turbo-alternators previously installed have now been replaced by eight turbo-alternators each driven by the exhaust gas of a Rolls Royce 'Avon' jet engine, to produce the electrical power. Greenwich is remotely-controlled from Lots Road and operates in parallel with Lots Road through a 22 kv cable distribution network. Only 20 to 25 staff are needed to operate the station compared with about 350 staff previously employed. The two generating stations, which have a total installed capacity of 300 megawatts, are being converted to use natural gas as an alternative to oil if desired. It is intended that natural gas will normally be used as it should be cheaper and reduce atmospheric pollution, but the ability to use either fuel will give greater flexibility and enable the electricity supply for about 70 per cent of the Underground system to be maintained even if the supply of one of these fuels is interrupted.

Lifts and Escalators: From the outset, the deep level stations on the tube lines were equipped with lifts to convey passengers to and from platforms. The first escalators were introduced in 1911 at Earl's Court Station. Today, 248 escalators with capacities to move 9 000 passengers an hour in either direction and travelling speeds of 92 to 145 feet a minute are installed at 70 stations. The longest is at Leicester Square and has a vertical rise of 80 feet 9 inches.

There are 69 station passenger lifts in service at 25 stations, the average rise being 68 feet and the longest 181 feet at Hampstead. The majority of these lifts travel at 180 feet per minute with a maximum load of 50 passengers in the car, but in more recent years a number of high speed lifts with modern equipment have been installed at Goodge Street, Hampstead and Queensway. These travel at speeds varying between

300 feet and 800 feet per minute according to the rise and are arranged for completely automatic control, no lift operator being required, although provision is made for operator control if traffic conditions require this. Automatic control has also been added to some of the older lifts.

Fare Collection: For many years, passengers' tickets on the Underground have been issued from machines. Apart from those inside the booking offices themselves, modern 'self-service' coin operated machines which print, cut and issue a ticket in three seconds are provided for the convenience of passengers.

On the Victoria Line a system of automatic fare collection—under which automation will eventually largely replace manual control of ticket checks and sales at stations—was introduced on a large scale.

The system has been developed as a deterrent to fraudulent travel and to reduce costs. Passengers entering Underground stations have their tickets checked by automatic gates in the booking halls. Two types are being used—the four-door and the tripod gates. They are operated by yellow tickets with magnetic oxide backing—like that of a recording tape—on which journey details are magnetically encoded. When a passenger inserts his ticket into a slot in the gate these details are "read" by electronic equipment, and the doors open or the tripod arm is released if the ticket is valid. Both types of gate return tickets to ingoing passengers. All passengers leaving stations at present use ticket collectors' barriers, but London Transport has proposed a completely closed

system, with a check on all tickets both entering and leaving the system. The proposed system will be able to handle all tickets, including seasons, and will be compatible with a system being developed by British Rail, so that through tickets will also be accepted.

Station Car Parks: At a number of suburban stations, London Transport provides car parking facilities for its railway passengers and has been engaged on a programme of expansion in this field in recent years—both by providing completely new parks at certain stations and by extending existing ones. At present nearly 11 500 car spaces are provided at 66 stations.

Some car parks are equipped with automatic barrier control. At most of these the control is in the form of a 'rising kerb', which lowers on the approach of a car to allow the motorist to drive in. A counting device is incorporated in the mechanism which illuminates a "Full" sign on the approach once all car spaces have been taken. The barrier will not then reopen until at least one car has left. On leaving the park, a motorist drives up to the exit and, without having to leave his car, inserts a coin equivalent to the parking fee—or a special token—into the mechanism which lowers the kerb for him. This form of 'rising kerb' control is being introduced at many of the larger station car parks.

Tunnel Cooling and Draught Relief: More than 100 fans handling nearly 2 400 m/sec of air per sec, are in operation on the system. This means the temperature underground is kept at an annual average in the region of 23°C. (73°F.)

To reduce draughts created by movement of trains in

the tube tunnels, special relief shafts are provided at some 31 stations to by pass some of the 'train-moved' air from the escalator shafts and passageways, directly to the open air.

The Victoria Line is equipped with 16 fans handling 531 m³ of air per sec with draught relief at every station. The average annual temperature on this line does not exceed 21°C (70°F).

Radio and Television Communications: A closed-circuit television system is installed throughout the Victoria Line. Cameras located on platforms and at other key points in stations transmit pictures to station operations rooms and to the line's control centre at Cobourg Street, Euston, enabling the control staff to see what conditions are like at any time and to take any action that may be necessary. A two-way sound system enables the staff to hear as well as see what is going on and to make announcements over the public address systems. Coupled with this equipment at certain stations, are push-button enquiry booths, provided to enable passengers to obtain travel information from the operations room.

Closed-circuit television has been introduced at a number of other stations to combat hooliganism.

By means of a carrier wave system fed through the current rails the staff at Cobourg Street can speak to any train operator, whether or not the train is moving. Similar systems, using radio, are being developed on other lines. On all modern rolling stock, the train operator can make announcements to passengers on the train through loudspeakers in each car.

LOS ANGELES
Southern California Rapid Transit District

In December 1976, UMTA committed funds for the Southern California Rapid Transit District to proceed with refinement of plans for a 24 km rapid transit starter segment. It is anticipated that an application for funding the preliminary engineering will follow in mid-1978.

The District is committed to the development of a high-capacity modern rapid transit system while improving and expanding existing bus services—the backbone for a future rapid transit feeder network.

On 23 July 1973, the RTD Board of Directors received the Consultants' Recommendations for a rapid transit sys-

tem in the Los Angeles Basin. At that time, the Board directed District staff to take the report to the field and elicit public response.

The regional plan for rapid transit presented by the consultants on 26 March 1974, is the result of that directive. The plan was submitted to the voters of Los Angeles County in November, 1974, and duly approved.

The aforementioned effort is exclusive of the El Monte Busway Project, the first seven miles of which went into operation in January 1973. The 11-mile route, which takes railroad rights of way as well as central and side strips of the highway route, will permit a trip of 15

minutes, less than half that of the corresponding automobile trip. The Express Busway, it has been stated, preserves a vital artery for transit—for buses now, and for any form of transit which may be feasible at a later date.

In the meantime, a study has been made of existing railroad rights of way in the Los Angeles area for interim rail commuter services. Three such lines, now largely used for freight services, are being further evaluated to consider whether commuter-transit benefit would justify the large capital cost of re-equipping and up-grading such lines.

LYON
Authority:
Societe d'Economie Mixte du Metropolitain de l'Agglomeration Lyonnaise (SEMALY)
Grand Palais de la Foire, Galerie 309, 69459, Lyon, France
Telephone: (78) 52 90 09

Type of system: Full-metro.

General: The city of Lyon is completing construction of a new 11.4 km Metro system and extending the existing rack railway. City municipal authorities first started Metro studies in 1968 when the Societe d'Economie Mixte du Metropolitain de l'Agglomeration Lyonnaise (SEMALY) was set up to prepare a city transport programme for the years up to 1985. SEMALY's plan, first published in 1970 and given Government backing in 1971, calls for immediate construction of two rubber-tyred Metro routes—Lines A and B—and an 0.3 km extension to the existing 0.6 km rack railway. By April 1975 a 1.6 km section of line A between the new workshop depot and Cusset was completed and tests had begun with a prototype two-car trainset built by Alsthom. The complete initial system was ready for commercial operation in May 1978.

First line section runs 9.4 km—with 8 km running underground—from Perrache station (the interchange with French National suburban and intercity trains) to the city outskirts in the east. There are 13 stations, with Charpennes providing interchange with Line B. The entire 1.4 km Line B (with three stations) is constructed underground.

Cut-and-cover construction is being used for both lines—a method made necessary by the poor soil conditions and exceptionally high water table, says SEMALY.

Phase two of the Metro programme calls for construction to start on a 2.5 km extension of Line B at a cost of Frs 295 million. Phase three is to be started with work on projected Line D which will connect with Line B. Completion of this line is due in 1985. No date has yet been given for commencement of the final stage of construction which calls for a 9 km extension to Line D and 3 km extension to line A, giving a complete system totalling 50 km with 57 stations.

Technical Data:
Gauge: 1.995/1.435 m (rubber/steel)
Projected new lines:
(in construction): 9.2 all in tunnel
(in design): 30.8 all in tunnel
Number of lines: 4
Number of stations:
(total): 16
(in tunnel): 15

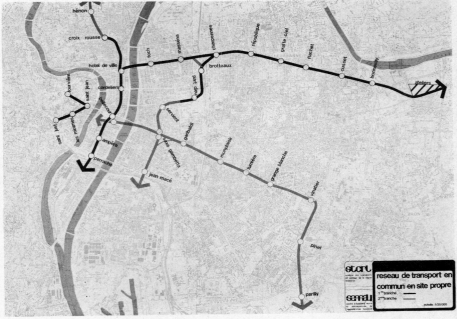

First line of the planned Lyon metro network will run from Perrache to the new workshops in the south.

Stations:
platform length (minimum): 70 m
(max): 100 m
Gradient (max): 7
Curvature (max): 150 m
Speed (design max): 90 km/h
(average commercial): 30 km/h
Electric system: Two-side guide bar; 750 V
Welded joints: Yes

Rolling Stock:

Car type (year introduced):	1975 (proto- type)	1977	
		(motor cars)	(trailers)
Number of units:	—	42	21
Car dimensions:			
(length):	16.5 m	17.9 m	18.6 m

(width):	2.9 m	2.9 m	2.9 m
(height):	3.2 m	3.4 m	3.4 m
Passenger capacity		M	R
per car (total):	—	126	132
(seated):	50	52	56
Rating:	—	2	4
Train composition			
(minimum):	3		
Acceleration			
(max):	1.3	1.2	—
Deceleration			
(emergency):	2.6	1.6	—

Traffic Data:
Trains/track/hour (planned): 20
Total passengers/track/hour (peak): 7 700
Train headways design: 1.5 minutes

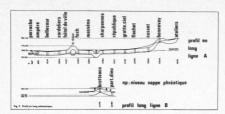

Profiles of Lines A and B.

Prototype of the new Alsthom trainset *(above)* and line drawing *(below)*.

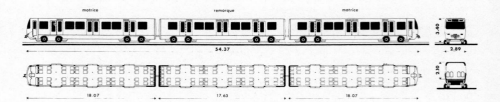

MADRID

Authority:
Cia. Metropolitano de Madrid
Cavanilles, 58, Madrid, Spain
Telephone: (01) 252 49 00

Type of system: Full-metro

Chairman: Carlos Mendoza
Delegate Director: José F. Otamendi
Manager: Adolfo Pool
Asst. Manager: Eduardo Nuez
Asst. Manager (Operating): Ramón Mancisidor
Schemes and Planning: Javier Valero
Rolling Stock: Ricardo Tejero

History: Madrid's growth in recent years has been largely due to a consistently planned expansion of its Metro network, facilitating urban travel and encouraging the growth of industry. The city's population of 3.4 millions is expected to increase to a total of 4.5 millions in ten years (1980). To meet transportation needs the city expects then to be served by a 100 km network of Metro lines (besides suburban lines). The Metro was first opened in 1919 with a line from Sol at the centre northwards to Caminos. There have been regular additions and extensions to the system since then, and at the time of writing, known extensions under construction total 12.3 miles *(19.8 km)* of route.

General: Two new line extensions were opened in 1977, extending the present 60 km system length by 5 km. Now under construction is a 2-km extension to existing Line 4 and a 3-km extension to Line 5. New lines being built at present include: Line 6 between Pacifico and Oporto; Line 8 between Fuencarral and Ministerios; Line 9 between Herrera Oria and Pavones. First section of the new Line 6 between C. Caminos and Pacifico was opened by the middle of 1977 and the entire line should be in operation by 1978. Lines 8 and 9 will be opened in 1979 and 1978 respectively.
Automatic train operation is under trial on Line 7 and it is hoped to introduce full automation by the end of this year.
Madrid authorities are planning for the future and it is expected that tenders will be called soon for construction of 35 km of new lines and extensions. Completion of a total network comprising 130 km was authorised by the government for construction by 1985.
Route length: Metro: 60.4 km with 54.9 km in tunnel.

Exterior of new type 5000 two-car trainset built by CAF-Wesa equipped with MTE-supplied Sumiride air suspension bogies, Krupp-Bochum resilient wheels and 210 kW fully-suspended Jeumont motors. Electrical power regulator is by AEG; air brakes by Knorr.

Interior of the new type 5000 car able to seat 80 passengers; crush capacity is 360 standing plus 80 seated.

Number of lines: 5 Metro, 1 Suburban (4 transverse and 2 radial), double track.
Number of stations served: 90; 85 underground.
Average station spacing: 550 m.
Passengers per annum: 547 000 000.
Average length of journey: 5.2 km.
Car km per annum: 60 800 000.
Number of cars per train: 6 on Lines 1 and 6; 4 on Lines 2, 3 and 4; 3 on Suburban.
Track gauge: 4 ft 8⅞ in *(1.445 m)*.
Weight and type of rails: 90.9 lb per yd *(45 kg/m),* flat-bottomed; laid in 18 m lengths on oak sleepers, with quartz ballast.
Max gradient: 1 in 20 (5%).
Minimum radius of curves: 295 ft *(90 m)*.
Type of tunnel: Double track tunnel 22 ft 6 in *(6.86 m)* wide. The height above rail level is 14 ft 7 in *(4.45 m)* on sections of cut-and-cover construction and 15 ft 5 in *(4.70 m)* on sections tunnelled by the Belgian (gallery) method. Tunnel linings are of concrete, masonry or brick.
Method and voltage of current supply: Overhead wire, with collection trolleys on the car roofs. 600 V dc (transformed by 9 sub-stations from the three-phase

15 000-V supply of the public grid).
Signalling: Automatic block, with ac track circuits and colour-light signals. There are electric interlocking installations at Goya, Sol, and Cuatro Caminos stations. Lines 3 and 5 have centralised traffic control (CTC) and Line 5 automatic train control (ATC) with cab signals.
Station layout: Some stations have separate side platforms, 197 ft *(60 m)* long, in a single elliptical station tunnel 45 ft 11 in *(14 m)* wide. The platforms themselves are 13 ft 1 in *(4 m)* wide at main stations, and 9 ft 10 in *(3 m)* wide at others. Terminal and junction stations have additional platforms.
Sub-surface ticket halls are favoured, with stairwell entrances at street corners. The most important individual station is Sol (Puerto del Sol), where three lines cross. There is a large central sub-surface ticket-hall and concourse, with pedestrian subways to and between the three lines.
Workshops: The main workshops and depot facilities are at Cuatro Caminos. At Ventas, Aluche and P. de Castilla there are smaller workshops and depot facilities, and at Arguelles and Moncloa there are underground depots.

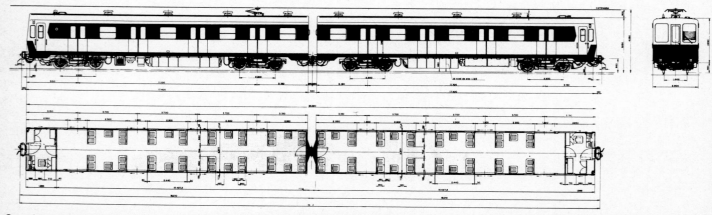

General arrangement drawing of the type 5000 trainset. Length over carbody 35,320 mm; Width 2,800 mm; Height rail to floor 1,125 mm; Empty weight 64,000 kg; Gross weight 100,000 kg; Inside width 2,577 mm; Headroom, centre aisle 2,182 mm; Width, centre aisle 724 mm; Doorway width 1,200 mm; Doorway height 1,900 mm.

MANCHESTER

Authority:
Greater Manchester Passenger Transport Executive
PTE Peterhouse, Oxford Street, Manchester M1 5AW, England
Telephone: (061) 236 4707
Cables: CIVICBUSES-MANCHESTER

Type of system: Metro link line

General: The South-East Lancashire and North-East Cheshire Passenger Transport Executive (SELNEC) was formed in April 1969 to take over the bus operations of 11 former municipal authorities. From 1972 it has been financially responsible for local railway services operated by British Rail and now, as Greater Manchester Passenger Transport Executive, is responsible on behalf of the Metropolitan County of Greater Manchester for promotion and operation of an efficient public passenger transport service within the county which comprises an area of 524 miles² and contains a population of approximately 2.8 million.
GMPTE's Long Term Plan for Transport in the conurbation has as its objective development of an integrated bus/rail public transport system which will be able to compete with the private car.
The Picc/Vic Tunnel Scheme is Stage 1 of the Long Term Plan. It provides a tunnel with five central area stations to bring people into the commercial heart of the City. Associated works involve up-grading the rail network to link four services in the south of the city with two in the north.
In December 1974 the DoE indicated that at the time the scheme could not be financed and would have to

be deferred. It was, therefore, decided that Greater Manchester Council, DoE and BR should co-operate in developing a package of rail up-gradings compatible with future provision of a tunnel. The package which was developed concentrated on up-grading the Northern Radial Lines, being those routes in the conurbation in most urgent need of attention. The object was to provide a cross-conurbation electric service affecting three main radial routes centring on two northern Manchester stations, Victoria and Salford. Bus/rail interchange was planned at several locations. However, further announcements indicated that the level of Government grant under the Transport Policies and Programmes would be insufficient to fund these proposals. In the present economic situation, £15 million (at November 1974 price levels) was the most that could be made available over the next four to five years for rail up-gradings and there is no prospect of investment on the scale required for Picc/Vic for some years.
The PTE assisted by BR have, therefore, developed a package of rail improvements which will be carried out over the next five years. The aim has been to spread the investment to give benefits to each area of the conurbation. DoE are encouraging the provision of park-and-ride and bus/rail interchange facilities at selected locations; the main objective being to significantly increase rail ridership over the next five years. It has been accepted that the provision of new stations and track and signalling alterations to improve capacity is compatible with the overall policy. Greater Manchester have not abandoned their Long Term Plan for Transport although it now appears that major investment may not be forthcoming for up to

ten years. All works being carried out to suburban railways within the conurbation have the long term plan in mind and, as far as possible, are compatible with eventual implementation of the Picc/Vic scheme.

Technical Data:
Gauge: 1.435 m
Projected new lines (in design): 17.7 km
Number of lines: 1
Number of stations (total): 15
Electric system: Third rail; 750 V
Type of rails: 113 lb/yd

Rolling Stock:
Car type: Proposed
Number of units: two-car sets
Car dimensions (length): 23.3 m
  (width): 3.05 m
  (height): 3.66 m
Passenger capacity per car:
  (total): 200
  (seated): 80
Motors per car: 4
Train composition (minimum): 2
  (max): 6
Acceleration (max): 1.3
Deceleration (emergency): 1.6
Weight (tonnes) Motorcar: 29.0

Traffic Data:
Train capacity (passengers): 800 (planned)
Total passengers/track/hour (peak): 24 000 (planned)
Train headways design: 1.5 minutes

MARSEILLE

Authority:
Ville de Marseilles
Hotel de Ville, 13, Marseille, France

General: Operations began in November 1977 on Marseille's first 6 km section of the new 9 km Metro line on a route running beneath the city centre to the north-east suburbs. Construction comprised 6 km of tunnelling, a 690 m viaduct at the north-east terminal of the line, 1 300 m of track running on the median strip of a new motorway, and 800 m of open cutting. A prototype three-car trainset was delivered in July 1976 with bodies by CIMT, bogies by ANF, motors by STCO and electrical equipment by MTE. Capacity of the set under normal load will be 352 passengers, with 136 seated. By the addition of a fourth car the capacity could be increased to 472 passengers with 184 seated. Overall length of the three car set is 49.070 m, width 2.6 m,

height above rail 3.55m, tare weight about 70 tonnes. Installed power for the three-car set is 1 400 kW giving a top speed of 80 km/h and an acceleration on the level of 1.3 m/s². At the start of operations, 21 three-car sets had been delivered.

Technical Data:
Gauge: 1.990/1.435 m (rubber/steel)
Projected new lines:
  (in construction): 9 (6 km in tunnel)
  (in design): 20 (17 km in tunnel)
Number of lines: 2
Number of stations (total): 12 (first line),
  26 (second line)
  (in tunnel): 9/22
Average distance between stations: 760 m
Stations:
  platform length (minimum): 100 m
Gradient (max): 7

Curvature (max): 150 m
Speed (design max): 80 km/h
  (average commercial): 30-35 km/h

Rolling Stock:

Car type (year introduced):	Motors	Trailers
	Prototype	
Car dimensions (length):	16.0 m	15.3 m
(width):	2.65 m	2.65 m
(height):	—	—
Passenger capacity		
per car (total):	225	225
(seated):	44	48
Motors per car:	2	—
Rating:	120 kWh	—
Train composition (max): 6		

Traffic Data:
Train capacity (passengers): 1 350

MELBOURNE

Authority:
City Transit Office
Melbourne, Australia

General: Melbourne (Victoria) transport facilities comprise an electric railway system and a network of roads on which trams, buses, private cars and commercial vehicles compete with one another for right of way. The railway system makes a major contribution to the transportation needs of the commuters of this metropolis. The number of commuters and others using the railway for travel between the suburbs and the city is increasing, and peak hour services must be expanded to cope.
Planning provides for duplication of existing single track sections, the construction of a third track or double track sections and the provision of four tracks on the inner sections of heavy traffic lines, together with improved signalling throughout the system.
The increased route capacity resulting from these works will mean an increase in the number of peak hour trains arriving and departing the central terminal, Flinders Street Station, where additional capacity must likewise be provided. Provision must also be made to relieve the increasing commuter congestion at Flinders Street Station.
This will be relieved by the building of the Underground Loop and dispensing the city's work force through a number of stations around the central business district instead of concentrating them at one. Linking these stations to the existing rail tracks to form a loop will improve the train capacity of Flinders Street Station.
The underground will comprise four single track tunnels connecting with the four major groups of suburban lines as follows:
1. The Eastern group, passing through Burnley;
2. The South-eastern group, passing through Caulfield;
3. The North-eastern group, passing through Clifton Hill;
4. The Northern and Western groups, passing through North Melbourne.
There will be three new city stations on the underground part of the system and all the trains passing round the loops will also pass through Flinders and Spencer Street stations, so that passengers will have the choice of five stations in the city area. In order to operate the loop trains in the direction of the predominant traffic flow in each peak period, signalling will be reversible. Each of the loops will have an effective capacity of 24 trains an hour and, in addition to the loop trains, at least another 60 trains an hour will, as a

Surface construction works underway on the Melbourne loop.

result of overall improvements to the suburban system, be able to operate to and from Flinders Street station. It is estimated that a total comfortable capacity of 130 000 passengers an hour will be reached. The modern seven-car suburban train has a comfortable capacity of 850 and a peak load capacity of 1 300 passengers.
The Metropolitan Planning Authority estimates that when the city's population reaches 3 700 000 in 1985, from its present figure of just over 2 250 000, planned improvements to the rail system will be adequate to meet the maximum forseeable demands made upon them. It is also anticipated that the new underground loop will attract more passengers to the suburban railway system and so reduce road congestion.
In 1970, the Melbourne Underground Tail Loop Authority was constituted by Act of Parliament to finance and build the Underground Rail Loop. The first 'sod' of this multi-million project was turned by the Minister of Transport, the Honorable Vernon Wilcox,

Work underway at Parliament underground station.

on 22 June 1971, and work on building access tunnels, under-passes and ramps for the four line tunnels is progressing.
The Melbourne Underground Rail Loop will expand the operations of the suburban railway system by providing three new stations underground supplementing two existing surface stations. All will be linked by rail tracks forming a loop around the central core of the city. The three underground stations will be known as Parliament, Museum and Flagstaff. Together with Flinders Street-Princes Bridge and Spencer Street Stations, the five city stations will serve passengers to and from 191 suburban stations and beyond. The stations will be linked by four tracks, part underground, part surface, part elevated. Running underground, the tracks will traverse Spring Street and La Trobe Street. They will surface near Spencer Street Station or North Melbourne Station at one end and between Flinders Street and either Jolimont or Richmond Stations at the other, connecting there with existing tracks.
The only fixed rail transport in Melbourne other than the Victorian Railways lines, is the Melbourne and Metropolitan Tramways street car system. Although the city's streets are wide, a policy of surface traffic separation by putting the tramway underground is favoured. In addition to the actual underground railway project. It would take the form of tram subways leading into and traversing the city within the rectangular central area bounded by the proposed underground railway loop. Where practicable, convenient passenger interchange between the underground railway and tramway systems is visualised.

MEXICO CITY

Authority:
Sistema de Transporte Colectivo (STC)
Delicias 67, Mexico 1, D.F., Mexico
Telephone: 521 86 20

Type of system: Rubber-tyred metro

General: The Mexico City Metro system is closely modelled on the Paris Metro, its architecture and pneumatic-tyred rolling stock particularly reflecting French influence. The latter country's interest extended to a 15-year loan to assist construction, besides consultancy as to its construction. The Metro operates under a computerised electronic system of traffic control.

While work continues on extending the Mexico City Metro, the Mexican National Railways has completed studies on a new suburban rapid transit system calling for construction of six new lines. The aim of the plan is to encourage development of nearby towns and relieve the population strain on the metropolitan area. Line 1 would run from San Lazaro in the eastern part of the city southeast to Los Reyes (17 km), and could eventually be extended north to Texcoco and south to Chalco. Line 2 would connect Tacuda with Tlanepantla (9 km), and could be continued on to Zumpango—proposed future site for a new international airport. Line 3 would run from La Villa de Guadalupe east to Ecatepec (19 km), and could be extended to Teotihuacan. Line 4 would run along the Periferico (95 km), using two lanes of the existing freeway for the double-track line. Line 5 is planned as a suburban link between the Benito Juarez international airport, and the projected new one at Zumpango (45 km). Line 6 would run from Calzada Ignacio Zaragoza to Texcoco (26 km).

Technical Data:
Gauge: 1.995/1.435 (rubber/steel)
Route length: 40 km
In tunnel: 30.9
Projected new lines (in design): 45 km
Number of lines: 3
Number of stations (total): 48
  (in tunnel): 37
Average distance between stations: 830 m
Stations:
  platform length (minimum): 150 m

Gradient (max): 7%
Curvature (max): 105 m
Speed (design max): 80 km/h
  (average commercial): 34.6 km/h
Electric system: Two-side guide bar; 750 V
Type of rails: 35 kg/m

Rolling Stock:

	Motors	Trailers
Car dimensions (length):	17.2 m	16.2 m
(width):	2.5 m	2.5 m
(height):	3.7 m	3.7 m
Passenger capacity per car		
(total):	162	165
(seated):	38	39
Motors per car:	4	
Rating:	110 kWh	
Train composition (minimum):	6	
(max): 9		

Acceleration (max): 1.35
Deceleration (emergency): 2.25
Brakes (type): Rheostatic/pneumatic
Weight (tonnes) Motorcar: 24.6
  Trailer: 16.9

Traffic Data:
Trains/track/hour: 20
Trains capacity (passengers): 1 530
Total passengers/track/hour (peak): 30 600
Train headways
  design: 1.5 minutes
  existing: 3 minutes
Passengers carried (weekday): 1 200 000
  (annually): 390 000 000
Average journey length: 7.6 km
Vehicle-km operated annually: 60 800 000

MILAN

Authority:
Azienda Trasporti Municipali
Foro Buonaparte 61, 20121 Milan, Italy.

General: The system is designed for the operation by one man for each train (driver) and one man for each station, who controls the entry barriers of passengers and, by means of TV, the platforms at the lower floor. In 1974 Milan city authorities approved a Lire 35 000 000 million loan to the Milan Metro for construction of 20.5 km of new lines. Aim of the plan is a 51.570 km underground railway network with 67 stations by 1984. The project calls for construction of four new lines. First to be completed will be an 8.5 km extension of the red line from the newly-built QT8 station to the boroughs of Pero and Rho in the northwest of the city. Work is now in hand on a 1.9 km extension of the red line from the present railhead at Lotto to QT8. Tunnelling and station construction has been completed and work is now underway on installation of an electrical sub-station and automatic control system. Completion of the third and fourth rail electrification system is planned for early next year and operation as far as QT8 should start by next summer.

The planned 8.5 km extension from QT8 will run through the Gallaratese suburbs area to a new terminal station which will have drive-and-park facilities for motorists joining the underground from the Turin motorway.

At the eastern end of the red line, a 4 km extension is planned from Sesto Marelli to Sesto San Giovanni where it will connect with the mainline station services to Como, Chiasso, Lecco, Sondrio and Bergamo. A total of five stations will be built along the extension. On the green line—now in operation from Cascina Gobba to Piazza to Garibaldi (8.5 km with 11 stations)—a 2.19 km section with three stations is already under construction from Garibaldi to Piazza Cadorna. Under latest plans, the line is to be eventually extended 1.3 km as far as Piazza to Genova where it will join Italian State Railway (FS) tracks until reaching a new terminal to be built at the Barona San Cristoforo station.

Finally a brand new line—designated the blue line—is to be constructed from the Garibaldi station in the north of the city to Piazza Romana in the south. A total of seven new stations will be built along the 5.7 km line.

Latest plans for the Milan metro include construction of park-and-ride facilities throughout the system.

A total of 15 280 car parking spaces are to be provided with eight new car parks projected for the red line, four for the green line and one for the blue line. Largest will be at Lampugnano where space will be available for 4 500 cars. Others are planned for Pagano (1 500 parking spaces), Amendola-Fiera di Milano (1 500 spaces), Cascina Gobba (2 000 spaces), Pero, Cimiano and Garibaldi (1 000 spaces each). Others will be smaller with space for 300 to 580 cars.

During construction of the park-and-ride facilities—many of which are to be built underground—city residents affected by construction are to be temporarily rehoused by the metro authorities in a new apartment building in the centre of Milan. The same building—purchased for the purpose by the subway company—will be used for rehousing residents affected by subway construction under the city.

Metro route length: Line 1, 8.8 miles *(16.9 km)* all in tunnel; Line 2, 12.6 miles *(20.28 km)* of which 3.8 miles *(6.1 km)* is in tunnel.
Number of lines: 2 transverse, double track, with branch.
Number of stations: 43.
Average station spacing: 0.37 miles *(0.59 km)*, (Line 1). 0.52 miles *(0.83 km)* (Line 2).
Passengers per annum: (1972): 104 000 000. (1973): 112 000 000. (1974): 147 000 000.
Passengers per annum carried by the whole system of Azienda Trasporti Municipali (includes metro, trams, buses, trolleybuses and ATM suburban services): (1972): 488 979 253.
Max number of cars per train: 6.
Estimated capacity per car: 213 passengers (including seating for 27) in the first 60 motor cars; 200 including seating for 30 in the second batch of 24 motor cars, and 208 and 228 in the latest motor cars and trailers, including seating for 32 and 40 respectively.
Average schedule speed: 18.6 mph *(30 km/h)* including stops.
Journey time on line: (Marelli-Lotto) 24 minutes, (Marelli-Gambara) 24 minutes. (Garibaldi-Gorgonzola) 30 minutes.
Type of tunnel: Large profile, double track tunnels 24 ft 7 in *(7.50 m)* in width and 12 ft 9½ in *(3.9 m)* in height (above rail level).
Tunnelling was by the "Milan" method of cut and cover which permitted the resumption of surface wheeled traffic, after a minimum period of interruption, over temporary surfaces whilst excavation proceeded below ground. Tunnel roofs are generally 10 ft *(3 m)* below street level, allowing space between tunnel extrados and street level for pedestrian subways and public utility services. The actual tunnel is of rectangular section in cast concrete. Part of Line 2 has been built in shield-driven tunnel to minimise surface traffic interference.

Method and voltage of current supply: 750 V dc on Line 1. Traction current is collected by shoes contracting 3rd outside rail on a vertical plane, and returns via 4th rail. 1 500 V dc on Line 2, via overhead wire system, with current return through insulated track rail. There are 8 sub-stations, all unmanned, on Line 1 and 4 on Line 2.

Rolling Stock: Number of cars owned as at 1 April 1974: 164 motor cars and 55 trailers, total 219. The motor cars, each with single control cab are 17.50 m long, 3.50 m high and 2.85 m wide. Weight 33 tons. Each car has four sets of air operated doors on each side. Motive power is supplied by four 90 kW *(120 hp)* motors to each car. Braking is electro-regenerative and pneumatic, incorporating electro-magnetic and mechanical standby braking equipment. Trailer cars, unladen weight 27.5 tons, are of the same dimensions as motor cars. Delivery continued through 1972 of a batch of 54 motor cars and 27 trailer cars, in light alloy, for Line 2. Details are:
Car dimensions (length): 17.5 m
  (width): 2.85 m
  (height): 3.47 m
Doors: 3 per side.
Passenger capacity: 200, including 46 seated
Motors: 4
Max speed: 90 km/h
Train make up: 3-car units (M-T-M)
Signalling: Automatic block, with signal aspects repeated in control cabs and automatic speed control. Automatic train stops. Differing colour signals indicate permissive train speeds; green 50 mph *(80 km/h)*; yellow 31 mph *(50 km/h)*; red-yellow 18.6 mph *(30 km/h)*; permissive red 9.3 mph *(15 km/h)*; red stop. Train movement is under remote central control with monitoring installations for each switch.
Station lay-out: All stations have side platforms 347 ft 9 in *(106 m)* long. Stations have ticket halls which are located between railway and street level and are equipped with escalators, of which there are 88 on Line 1 and 26 on Line 2. Admission to platform is via ticket-actuated electronic turnstiles (with magnetic checking of ticket) placed across ticket halls. Basic fare is 100 lire, but a tariff introduced in 1970 permits, on an hourly basis, travel on municipal surface transport with the same ticket. Closed circuit television equipment is installed.

MONTREAL

Authority:
Montreal Urban Community Transit Commission
159 St. Antoine Street West, Montreal 126, Quebec, Canada
Telephone: (514) 877 6300

Chairman and General Manager: Lawrence Hanigan
Commissioners: Robert Hainault, M.C.
  Armand Lambert, C.A.
Secretary: Yvon Clermont, Q.C.
Treasurer: Jacques Bouvrette, C.A.
Director of Transportation: Guy Blain, Eng.
Director of Engineering: Georges Donato, Eng.
Director of Vehicle Maintenance: Gaston Beauchamp, Eng.
Director of Planning: Henri Bessette, Eng.

General: Montreal's Metro system is a comparatively modern concept, as reflected in its enlightened architecture and operational performance. Serving as it does the second largest French-speaking city, the Metro understandably reflects French influence in both its stations and rolling stock. It was originally planned, constructed and financed by the City of Montreal. Actual construction began on 23 May 1962. On 6 August 1963, the City Council approved extensions of Line 2 at both ends and construction of Line 4 to serve the communities on the south shore of the St. Lawrence river, and also the 1967 World Exhibition. The major portions of Lines 1 and 2 were put into operation on 14 October 1966, and all three lines were in full operation on 1 April 1967.

On 12 February 1971, the Montreal Urban Community Council voted a loan Bye-law for the borrowing of $430 m to be used to extend the Metro system a further 28.5 miles. Lines 1 and 2 would be extended east, west, and north-west. A new north-east line would be built and connected midway by a cross-city line to lines 1 and 2, the whole being served by an additional 50 stations. Extension work eastward on line No 1, started on 14 October 1971.

In mid-June 1976 Montreal opened a 7.6-km extension to the existing 6.1-km line one—in time to cope with big traffic increases expected in conjunction with the Olympic Games in the city. When completed sometime in 1984, the entire Metro system will total 74.3 km and include 85 stations.

Route length: 36.1 km
Number of lines: 3.
Number of stations: 35.
Average Station spacing: 0.544 mile *(0.875 km)*.
Passengers per annum (Rapid Transit): Annual figures approximately 125 million passengers. Approx. 400 000 revenue and transfer passengers use RT on typical weekday.
Total passengers per annum (Bus and Rapid Transit): 304 394 301.
Car km per annum, estimate: 34 000 000.
Max number of trains per hour: Line 1: 20; Line 2: 24; Line 4: 3.
Number of cars per train: 9.
Passenger capacity per car: 160.
Average schedule speed: Line 1: 20 mph *(32.2 km/h)* Line 2: 23 mph *(37.1 km/h)*; Line 4: 32 mph *(51.1 km/h)*.
Track gauge and weight and type of rails: Pneumatic tyred traction system is used, requiring standard gauge, 4 ft 8½ in *(1.435 m)* steel security rails (70 lb/yd), flanked by 10 in wide concrete running tracks, and lateral guide bars.
Max gradient: 6.3%.
Minimum radius of curves: Main line 460 ft *(140 m)*.
Type of tunnel: All lines in single tunnel 23 ft 4 in wide, containing both tracks. Generally through rock, they are concrete lined, with vertical walls and arched roof 16 ft high at centre. About 30 per cent of tunnels were constructed by cut and cover method using single rectangular concrete section. Depth of tunnels varies from 20 ft, to 180 ft below ground level. In the downtown area the lines are located beneath streets closely paralleling those carrying heavy traffic.

Method and voltage of current supply: Traction current is at 750 V dc delivered to the guide bars from 26 rectifying stations. Primary supply is at 12 000 V ac from Quebec Hydro power distribution system.

Rolling Stock: 233 motor cars, 56 ft 5 in *(17.2 m)* long. 124 trailer cars, 53 ft 10 in *(16.5 m)* long. All cars are 8 ft 3 in *(2.5 m)* wide.

The cars were manufactured by Canadian-Vickers Ltd, Montreal and Bombardier (for the new rolling stock). They are semi-permanently coupled in three-car sets, comprising two motor cars with trailer in the centre. Each of the car's two bogies rest on four pneumatic-tyred wheels, each doubled by an auxiliary flanged steel wheel mounted on the same axle. The latter wheels in normal service conditions do not touch the steel security rail, but act as standbys in the event of a pneumatic tyre failure. There are also four horizontally-mounted pneumatic-tyred guide wheels per bogie. Maximum length of train, comprising three 3-car sets (9 cars) is 500 ft. Each motor car has four 150 hp motors. Braking is electro-pneumatic, with wood shoes acting on the steel security wheels. Each car has four double doors on each side. Maximum speed is 47 mph *(75.2 km/h)*.

Signalling: Conventional block system with line-side indications.

Station layout: All stations are of the side platform type with concourse above. Platforms are 500 ft long and 13 ft wide. Except in three cases the entire two-level station structures are below street level. At Berri-de-Montigny station where the three lines intersect there are four levels below ground. There are no sidewalk entrances to stations. Accesses are through small off-street structures and through commercial buildings. Escalators are provided wherever the difference in level is 12 ft or more.

Rubber-tyred trainset, supplied by Canadian Vickers, enters Bonaventure terminal station.

MOSCOW

Authority:
Moskovski Metropolitena Imeni V.I. Lenina
5 Kolokolnikov Street, Moscow 103045, USSR
Telephone: 222 10 01

Route length: (1977): 164.5 km.

Number of lines: 7 (6 transverse and 1 circular); all double track.

Number of stations served: 103.

Average station spacing: 1.69 km.

History: Russian theory and practice in underground railway engineering has changed radically since Moscow's first underground line was built (1933-35). Excavation then was accomplished partly with pneumatic tools, but largely with pick and shovel, and the spoil removed by light railways much implemented by wheelbarrows. Slow progress then can be compared with a recently reported 440 yard tunnel excavation in a day, accomplished by massive mechanical excavators and earth movers.

Moscow's urban street transport at the end of the 19th century consisted of tramways and thousands of cabs. River ferries, tramways extensions and bus services developed from the 1920s, and trolleybuses in 1935. An expansion of the city boundaries and siting of large projects away from the centre, besides a concentration of railway terminals in the north and commercial and social activities at the centre, involved increasingly long journeys for the Muscovites which were expedited by the construction of Moscow's Metro system. It serves a population (1976) of 7.7 millions.

The first 7.2 mile *(11.6 km)* section between Sokolniki and Park Cultury, crossing the city, was opened on 15 May 1935. The second section of underground completed in 1938 was from Smolenskaya to Kiev Station, and two other lines were built at the time to Kursk Station and towards Sokol in the north-west, thus developing a small network of radial lines about 16 miles *(26 km)* in route length. Underground building continued during the World War (1941-1945) for economic and cultural reasons and to provide shelters from enemy air raids. By the war's end 25 miles *(40 km)* of Metro linked the city's area with 7 railway stations, and by 1954 all main railway stations were connected by Metro. The first major stage of Metro building concluded with the merging of the several radial lines with the circular underground route.

New sections were added to the system as large-scale building projects were launched in 1954 in areas of new developments.

Arbat underground section was originally built at shallow depth in 1933-38, crossing the Moscow river by bridge. Closed down in 1953 and retubed under the river, the Orbat-Fili line six years later was linked to a newly-built Kutusovskaya-Kiev Railway Station line, which was extended in stages westward to the developing areas reaching to Molodezhnaya in 1966. In 1966 a further addition to the system, the eastern rapid Zhdanovskaya line, became operative. There are seven stations, with the inner terminus at Taganskaya (for interconnection with the Ring Line). The line at its inner end is at deep level in twin tube, and afterwards runs at sub-surface and surface levels.

In August 1969 the extension of the line from Avtozavodskaya to Kakhovskaya with 4 stations came into operation. This line will have a spur from Kashirskaya to Lenino. On 5 January 1972, a new 1.9 mile *(3 km)* north-south tube across central Moscow was opened, linking existing north and south lines between Prospect Mira and Ploshchad Nogina, enabling the through north-south Moscow run to be reduced to 31.5 minutes.

Also being extended are the lines Taganskaya-Novogireevo towards the east, and Krasnopresnenskaya-Planernaya, a large new development area to the west of the capital. The latter extension, from Tanganskaya in east-central Moscow, westward across the city to Planernaya, will be 14.2 miles *(22.8 km)* in length.

At present building work is in hand on extension of Moscow's Kaluga-Riga line from the VDNCh station to Medvedkovo (8.2 km) with four new stations.

Also underway is the new Kalinin radial line from Marksistskaya to Novogireyevo—a distance of 11.1 km.

Future plans call for completion of a new Sserpukhov radial line from Dobryninskaya to Dniepropetrovskaya (12.8 km with eight stations).

Cost of construction work is at present estimated at between 10 and 17 million Roubles per km.

In the more distant future there is to be a Timiryazev line from Novoslobodskaya to the Academy of Agriculture, via the Savyolovo Railway Station, and an extension of the radial lines, from the VDNKh to Medvedkovo. There is the choice either of building a new large circular underground route to include new areas, or of linking up the radial lines' terminal stations, in elliptical loops, to ease the congestion of passengers on the central stations while improving communications in the outlying areas. Running towards the centre and by-passing the Kremlin area in semi-circles these new radial lines would become diametrical and greatly ease passenger traffic in the old central area. By 1980 a network of 196 route-km and 113 stations is planned.

Average daily passenger total: (1976): 5.5 millions.

Passengers per annum: (1976): 2 030 millions.

Max line capacity (one way): 88 600 passengers.

Max number of trains per hour each way: 45.

Max number of cars per train: 7.

Estimated capacity per car: 170 (including 40 seated).

Average schedule speed (peak periods, including stops): 25.2 mph *(78.09 km*/3h).

Track gauge: 5 ft *(1.524 m)*.

Type of rails: 101 lb per yard *(50 kg/m)*. Flat-bottomed: welded up to 1 066 ft *(325 m)*.

Max gradient: 40%.

Minimum radius of curves: 655 ft *(200 m)*.

Type of tunnel: The earlier sections were partly of cut-and-cover construction, the tunnels being double-track and of rectangular section, 25 ft 0 in *(7.6 m)* wide by 12 ft 10 in *(3.9 m)* high from rail level. Subsequent lines (including the ring line recently built) have been largely of deep-level tube construction, each single-track tube tunnel having an internal diameter of 17 ft 11 in *(5.46 m)*. Tube lines are as much as 131 ft *(40 m)* below surface level (for example, at Dynamo Station).

Method and voltage of current supply: Third rail; 825 V dc; contact on underside of current rail. A centrally controlled unmanned transformer substation system was completed in 1960.

Rolling Stock: Length of car over couplers 61 ft 5 in *(18.7 m)*; external width 8 ft 10 in *(2.7 m)*: tare weight 31.7 metric tons. Each car has four sets of automatic double doors on each side. Seating is longitudinal. Automatic centre buffer couplers. All motored axles. The cars are manufactured at the Mytishchi Engineering Plant, near Moscow.

Signalling: Automatic block, with colour-light signals, speed control, and train stops. Over the next six years it is planned that all rolling stock will be converted to an automatic driving system with automatic speed control.

Station layouts: Stations are of island type, often embodying a vast circulating concourse between the two platforms. The surface buildings of the Moscow Metro are palatial and the whole system has the reputation of a show-piece. As an example of station dimensions, the concourse of Komsomolskaya Station is 538 ft *(164 m)* long, 59 ft *(18 m)* wide, and 37 ft 9 in *(11.5 m)* high. Escalators are widely used. The ring line alone has 82 escalators out of a system total of 338. Reversing at termini is carried out on sidings beyond the stations. Platforms are 510 ft *(155 m)* long. The busiest stations include Ploshchad Sverdlova, Prospekt Marksa, Belorusskaya and Sokol.

Experiments being carried out on the shunting of trains at terminal stations using automatic control equipment are reducing the number of teams of shunters now employed.

MUNICH

Authority:
Stadtwerke München-Verkehrsbetriebe (MVB)
Einsteinstr 28, 8-Nünchen 80, Postfach 801860, German Federal Republic
Telephone: (089) 2 19 11

Type of system: Full-metro

General: Since construction began on the Munich U Bahn 11 years ago, a total of 35 km of lines have been put into operation.

Under the city's medium-term plan further new lines totalling 15.5 km are to be built by 1985: the 3.3-km west line from Hauptbahnhof to Rotkreuzplatz, and the 10.2-km Laim-Bogenhausen line, to run via Ostbahnhof.

Construction costs since work began on the system in 1965 have totalled DM 1 200 million. To complete the medium-term programme U Bahn authorities estimate that a further DM 1 000 million will be needed.

On 19 October 1971, 6½ years after the start of construction, the first 12 km of the north-south subway line were opened, running from the service depot at Freimann to Goetheplatz in the south-west of the city centre. This was followed soon afterwards, on 8 May 1972, by the opening of another 4 km section. The volume of traffic was unexpectedly high from the very beginning and has increased steadily since then. The total of some 230,000 passengers on working days is about 27 per cent above the altogether optimistic forecasts made before service started. The fact that the subway is used by such large numbers in the central urban area guarantees a relatively favourable cost-benefit ratio (figures for 1973: at 38 million DM operating costs and 60 million passengers carried, 0.63 DM per passenger). The priority given to the inner network in the city's development and transportation policies is thus justified from the point of view of business economics also.

Construction of the route section between Goetheplatz and Harras—the southern branch of line U 6—began in August 1971. The section is about 2.7 km long and runs from the previous terminus at Goetheplatz, under Lindwurmstrasse and Implerstrasse to Implerplatz, and from there in a wide curve in a westerly direction to the new terminus at Harras. The construction work was divided into four project sections and cost some 208 million DM.

The construction work was accompanied by a number of problems which made exceptional demands upon all people involved. Engineers, geologists and tunnellers were repeatedly forced by extremely unfavourable geological and hydrogeological conditions to find solutions and make decisions that were not in any "textbooks". The tunnels were driven under the protection of a very carefully planned pre-drainage system which, in the interests of safety, was always given trial runs to check its efficiency. Whenever there was an adequate covering of marl above the apex of the tunnel, the tunnel was driven below the upper ground water stratum, so that it was possible for the groundwater lowering activities to be directed at the lower ground water strata only. Over long sections, considerable difficulties were caused by an unusually thick "Flinz" marl with a tendency to cave in, which, in conjunction with the driving conditions, initially led to

surface subsidence and caused the shield to deviate from its course.
The subway station at Harras was the first station building in the Munich subway system to be constructed entirely of waterproof concrete. This is cheaper than the conventional method (no bituminous insulation) and, above all, safer (no fire risk). On the other hand, it requires experience in the difficult process of making large concrete areas.
The platform hall and service rooms in the subway station at Poccistrasse were built by underground means between the tunnels which had already been driven. The underground hall was made by driving 31 cross tunnels, about 10 m long, between the main tubes, and by subsequent step-by-step construction of floors, columns, and vaults in exposed concrete and waterproof concrete.
The next line to be tackled in the Munich subway network was the line 8/1, in June 1971. This line is 16 km long and runs from the existing junction station at Scheidplatz (U 3), via Schwabing-West through Augustenstrasse and Luisenstrasse, to Munich Central station and on to Sendlinger Tor Platz. From the station at Sendlinger Tor (intersection with line U/3) it runs via the Isarvorstadt, Au, Giesing, Ramersdorf and Perlach districts to the planned joint station on the Kreuzstrasse rapid-transit route.
The overall project is divided into 29 sections.
Since 1974, the construction of subway line 8/1 has involved some impressive new developments which have already achieved cost reductions in comparison with conventional methods. In this way it has been possible to keep the overall subway costs at a stable level in the last few years, in spite of the general rise in prices.
For project section 7.1 (Isar underpassing) a subway tunnel in a water-bearing foundation was, for the first time in Germany, lined with a single shell of rubber-sealed precast reinforced-concrete segments. The tunnel was driven with a fully-mechanical shield driving machine using compressed air, without sheet piling at the working face. This type of tunnel lining has proven more economical than the cast-iron segmental lining often used. There is considerable interest in this new development, both at home and abroad.

Plans: In the past 10 years the Subway Department has concentrated its planning activities on continuous management of the network as a whole and, at the same time, firstly on the north-south subway line and the Olympia line, then on line U 8/1 and finally, since 1973, on lines U 1 and U 5/9. In the course of this work the technical data required for the corresponding route authorisation procedures and designation orders were established. These planning data largely determine the quality of the later operations and the transportation service. They serve as a basis for critical assessments when the plans are discussed with the relevent administrative departments and with the authoritative political bodies in the city of Munich, the State of Bavaria, and the Federal Republic. They are also a basis for the information supplied to the interested public and for medium-and long-term financial planning. Lastly, they are an essential foundation for all further subway construction.
In the first years of subway construction the main points of concentration were more in the technical sector: execution of construction work, track laying, technical equipment and the service concept were in the foreground. To cope with the special circumstances in Munich it was necessary to develop new methods on the basis of the relevant experience of other towns with subway systems. The way in which the problems were tackled, their scope, and the rapid progress of the subway construction met with widespread interest among the public and even aroused enthusiasm.
Today, the main focus is clearly on the planning work and the organic integration of the technically necessary buildings in a historical city structure; apart from technical perfection priority is also given to the manifold needs of the users and to the understandable interests of the residents along the route. The wealth of experience gathered in the past years guarantees a virtually "perfect" subway as far as construction and service principles are concerned.
Of course, there is a constant inflow of technical innovations, and these are studied and applied primarily from aspects such as economy of operation, rationalisation, and protection of the environment. The growing number of organisations, pressure groups and citizens intervening in the subway planning work with their own interests, and often seeking to prevent necessary measures and their consequences, are today turning the practicability of a planning concept into a major problem. In lengthy proceedings the objections are investigated and weighed up, and plans are modified and revised in an effort to guarantee their practicability. this "open planning" principle means that tough battles are often fought over details.
The situation is likely to be equally problematic when it comes to the completion of the subway network—extending into the outlying areas as well. Here again, topical technical questions that affect the public, such as whether the subway should run above-ground or underground, will arouse interest on all sides and may well lead to some heated discussions.

Route length: 11.9 miles *(18.5 km).*
Number of stations: 17.
Passengers carried: 180 000 per working week average.
Max line capacity: 40 000 passengers per hour in each direction.
Max Number of cars per train: 3 twin-car units.
Capacity per 6-car train: Max 1 158 persons, including 294 seated.
Average scheduled speed: 22 mph *(35 km/h).*
Max speed: 50 mph *(80 km/h).*
Track gauge: 4 ft 4½ in *(1 432 mm).*
Type of tunnel: Shield-driven circular tunnel 18 ft 10 in *(5.74 m)* diameter; rectangular cross-section cut and cover tunnel, and vaulted cross-section where built by tunnelling method.
Method and voltage of current supply: 3rd rail underside contact, 750 V dc.
Rolling Stock: No of cars owned: 54 double motor coaches (built by a consortium of German manufacturers), powered by four 180 kW traction motors. Car width 9 ft 6 in *(2.90 m)*, single car length 59 ft 1 in *(18.00 m).* Three sets of sliding doors on each side. Aluminium-alloy carbodies.
Signalling: The continuous automatic train control system, incorporating line control cables carrying variable-speed, braking and stopping instructions, permits minimum headways of 90 seconds. Train starting is by driver-push-button control.

NAGOYA

Authority:
Nagoya Municipal Transportation Bureau
1-1 Sannomaru 3 Chome, Naka-ku, Nagoya, Japan

General Manager: Shigeyuki Tani
R.T. Construction Manager: Sunao Miura
R.T. Division Manager: Tomoji Shimogaki
Engineering Manager: Yukihiko Kawai

General: Nagoya, located roughly midway between Tokyo and Kobe on the populous Pacific coastal belt, has become a centre of industry, commerce and culture. In order to cope with increasing population, and travel demands which could no longer be met by private railway, street-car and bus services, the city embarked on an extensive municipal Subway system programme, which began soon after World War II. Line 1 from Nagoya main-line station east to Sakaemachi was opened for passenger traffic in 1957. The north-south Lie 2 was initially opened in 1967, and the Subway network has developed in regular stages of extensions or new lines over the last 15 years.
By 1980 a network of 77.4 km in 5 lines is planned. Nagoya's 1972 population of 2 millions is expected to increase to 3½ millions by 1985. Based on this assumption Nagoya plans a rail rapid transit network totalling 5 lines and 48.1 miles *(77.4 km)* route length, all within the city limits.
Construction work on No. 4 line proceeding at a cost of approx. Y 25.2 billions (£38m), is that from Kanayama to Aratamabashi 3.5 miles *(5.6 km).* Together with No. 2 line, No. 4 line will eventually form a 16 mile *(26 km)* circular line. The 8.2 mile *(13.6 km)* section between Fushimi and Akaike on Line No. 3 is now under construction at a cost of Y 73 billions (£110 m).
Public transportation within the city area includes three JNR trunk lines and two private railways, the Nagoya Electric and the Kinki Nippon, totalling 53.5 miles *(86 km).*

Operative route length: 32.4 km.
Number of lines: 2 Transverse.
Number of stations served: 36 (33 in tunnel).
Average station spacing: 0.59 miles *(0.95 km).*

Passengers per annum:
(1971): approx 143 millions.
(1972): approx 179 millions.
(1975): approx 235 millions.
Max number of trains per hour each way: 30.
Number of cars per train: 4 to 5.
Estimated capacity per car: 115.
Average scheduled speed: 20.4 mph *(32.8 km/h).*

Track gauge: 4 ft 8½ in *(1.435 m).*
Weight and type of rails: 101 lb/yd *(50 kg/m);* flat-bottomed.
Max gradient: 1in 28 (3.5%).
Minimum radius of curves: 410 ft *(125 m).*
Type of tunnel: Double track rectangular tunnel, of cut-and-cover construction, with centre supports except where the tunnel is circular, shield driven.
Method and voltage of current supply: Third rail; 600 V dc.
Rolling Stock: The cars are all motored, with each axle motor driven. They are 51 ft 1½ in *(15.58 m)* long overall, 8 ft 3 in *(2.50 m)* wide and 11 ft 3 in *(3.43 m)* high from rail level. The wheels are resilient to reduce noise in tunnels. There are three double-leaf doors on each side of each car. Weight of cars, 24 tonnes.
Signalling: Automatic block, with colour-light signals. On Line 2 a system of cab signalling and Automatic Train Control is employed.
Station layouts: Stations have an extensive sub-surface (mezzanine) concourse, flanked by shops, from which stairs lead down to side or island type platforms 341-656 ft *(104-200 m)* long and 11 ft 6 in-37 ft 0 in *(3.5-11.3 m)* wide.
Workshops: At Fujigaoko, Meijo and Meiko, with capacity for 330 cars, 28 cars and 96 cars respectively.

NAPLES

Authority:
Naples Rapid Transit
Direzione Comple F.S., Campania, Naples, Italy

General: In 1925, while the original Rome-Naples "Direttissima" line was under construction, an underground railway was opened in Naples, running westwards from the Central Station to Mergellina, a suburb four miles away. This underground section was intended to provide an alternative approach for the "Direttissima" into Naples from the west, and at the same time form the nucleus of a local underground system for Naples itself. The actual length of the tunnel between Mergellina and Naples Central is 3.4 miles *(5.5 km).* Mergellina is an open station, but there are three intermediate stations on the tunnel section—Piazza Amedeo, Montesanto, and Piazza Cavour—connected with the surface by escalators. The tunnel is at places 98 ft 6 in *(30 m)* below street level. Both main line (non-stop) and local (stopping) trains operate electrically through the tunnel section.
Plans have been put in hand for a new 8-km underground line with 15 stations; 1 500 V dc overhead electrification.
Naples is also served by the 140 km long Circumvesuviana Railway, which is being up-graded and equipped with new rolling stock. The line's gauge is only 2 ft 5½ in, but the new stock is being built wider than the old (2.7 m as against 2.35 m). The vehicles will be formed into 3-car articulated units resting on 4 bogies. The modernised railway has been described as a metropolitan-suburban line.

NEWCASTLE

Authority:
Tyne and Wear Passenger Transport Executive
Cuthbert House, All Saints, Newcastle-Upon-Tyne NE12OA, England
Telephone: (0632) 610431

Type of system: Full-metro

General: Britain's first light-rail rapid transit in the Newcastle area of north-east England could be ready for full operation by 1980. The Tyneside Rapid Transit system will consist of a 55.6-km network comprising 14.8-km of new line construction and 40.8-km of existing railway at present operated by BR. A joint company is to be formed with BR to own the existing track with Tyneside having majority control. BR will continue to operate limited freight services over parts of the route.
The transit system first got official approval in 1973, following announcement of a 75 per cent grant towards the project cost of £143 million by the Government.
By early 1976 the first tunnel sections were well advanced and two prototype trainsets, built by Metro-Cammell, were running evaluation trials on a 2.5 km test track in North Tyneside. Route-km of new underground construction will total 5.5 km, and length of new—or substantially new—surface routes about 9.3 km.
New construction work includes twin north-south tunnels under Newcastle town centre and neighbouring Gateshead. There are to be six new underground stations at Jesmond, Haymarket, Monument, Central Station, St. James Park and Gateshead. The north-western section will be the first to open in 1978, connecting Haymarket with Benton and Kenton Bank Foot, followed by an extension south to Heworth and Benton-Manors section of the main circle route. The entire network is scheduled to begin operating in 1980 when four services will provide peak hour frequency interval operation of 2 to 2.5 minutes. It is expected to carry up to 30 million passengers annually, compared with six-million a year now handled by existing BR commuter services in the area. According to Tyneside authorities the present rail system—needing a subsidy of £2.5 million a year from the Tyneside Passenger Transport Executive—is far more expensive to run compared with operating estimates for the forthcoming transit system.
Possible extensions to the basic system are already being examined, including lines southwards to Sunderland, westwards from St. James and Kenton to the Tyneside airport, and a link across the mouth of the Tyne river between North and South Shields.

Technical Data:
Gauge: 1.435 m
Projected new lines (in construction): 1.8 km
(in design): 53.8 km (3.65 km in tunnel)

Number of stations (total): 43
(in tunnel): 7
Average distance between stations: 1.3 km
Stations:
platform length: 95 m

Gradient (max): 1/30
Curvature (max): 210 m
Speed (design max): 80 km/h
(average commercial): 34 km/h
Electric system: Overhead; 1 500 V dc
Type of rails: 50 kg/m
Welded joints: Yes

Rolling Stock: Two prototype twincar articulated sets have been on test since June 1975 and orders are in hand for 95 units. They are to be supplied by Metro-Cammell with electrical equipment by GEC Traction, Duwag mono-motor bogies, Westinghouse Westcode system disc brakes, Kiekert (German Federal Republic) plug-type doors, and Scharfenberg automatic couplers.

Car type: Articulated
Car dimensions (length): 28.4 m
(width): 2.65 m
(height): 3.15 m

Passenger capacity per car (total): 272
(seated): 84
Motors per car: 2
Rating: 205 × 2 continuous
Train composition (minimum): 1
(max): 3
Acceleration (max): 1.0
Deceleration (emergency): 2.0
Brakes (type): Disc and magnetic track
Body material: Aluminium
Weight (tonnes) Motorcar: 39

NEW YORK

Authority:
Staten Island Rapid Transit Operating Authority (SIRTOA)
25 Hyatt Street, Staten Island, NY 10301, USA
Telephone: (212) 447 1581

Type of system: Transit line

History: A subsidiary of the Metropolitan Transportation Authority.

Technical Data:
Gauge: 1.435 km
Route Length: 23 km
Number of Stations (total): 22

Stations:
platform length (max): 91 m

Gradient (max): 1.9%
Speed (average commercial): 32 km/h
Electric system: Third rail. 600 V
Type of rails: 49.6 kg/m

Rolling Stock:
Car type (year introduced): 1975/76
Number of units: 52
Car dimensions (length): 22.87 m
(width): 3.05 m
(height): 3.66 m
Passenger capacity per car (total): 300
(seated): 74

Motors per car: 4
Rating: 86 kWh
Train composition (minimum): 2
(max): 4
Acceleration (max): 1.12
Weight (tonnes) Trailer: 38.6
Traffic Data:
Trains/track/hour: 15
Train capacity (passengers): 900
Total passengers/track/hour (peak): 13 500
Train headways
existing: 4 minutes
Passengers carried (weekday): 22 000
(annually): 4 800 000
Average journey length: 10.6 km
Vehicle-km operated annually: 3 030 000

NEW YORK—NYCTA

Authority:
New York City Transit Authority
370 Jay Street, Brooklyn 1, NY, USA
Telephone: (212) 852 5000

Chairman and Chief Executive Officer:
Harold L. Fischer
Senior Executive Officer—Operations Management:
John G. de Roos
Executive Officer—Construction Administration and Chief Engineer: John T. O'Neill
Executive Officer—Labour Relations and Personnel:
Wilbur B. McLaren
Executive Officer—Controller:
Andrew T. O'Rourke
Executive Officer—Rapid Transit:
Steven K. Kauffman
Executive Officer—Surface: Frederick D. Wilkinson, Jr
General Counsel: Alphouse E. D. Ambrose
History: The history of New York's rapid transit railways began in the 1870s with the first of what was to become a network of elevated railways. The "Elevated" has all disappeared (except for the subway extensions in outlying areas) and the ubiquitous Subway, dating from 1904, now covers the New York and district areas with a dense network of lines. Until recent years the network was subdivided into three groups of lines, the Interborough Rapid Transit, the Brooklyn-Manhattan Transit and the Independent (IRT; BMT; IND), which developed historically in that order. The first two were Company concerns and the last was owned by the City from the outset. In the year 1940 and those immediately following, the New York City Board of Transportation, already controlling the IND group, acquired the undertakings of the first two, together with several street-car, bus and trolley-bus system. In 1953 the New York City Transit Authority was created, enpowered to lease, operate, improve and extend the city's passenger facilities.
In March, 1968, the NYCTA came under the jurisdiction of the Metropolitan Transportation Authority, which is an agency created by the New York State Legislature.
General: Construction work is now underway to add 28.2-km of new lines to that basic system. The following projects are now under construction: East 63rd Street line (4.8 km; cost $750 million); Remodified super-express line (9.3 km; cost $450 million); South-east Queens line (7.3 km; cost $650 million).
The New York subway system carries more passengers per annum than any other underground railway system in the world. On the other hand, the total number of passengers on all public transport (underground and road services) is less in New York than London, a much larger proportion of the total in London using buses.
Many of the New York City Transit lines have parallel fast (limited-stop) and local (all-stations) services in each direction. Such services are worked either on four tracks (with one fast and one slow track in each direction) or on three tracks (with one slow track in each direction) and the third track is used for fast trains in the direction of passenger traffic during peak hours. A flat-rate fare operates over most of the NYCTA System.
In addition to the Port Authority Trans Hudson System (dealt with separately) two railway systems in the vicinity of New Yok are designated as self-contained Rapid Transit railways.
One is the Newark Subway which acts in part as a feeder to the Hudson Bay Tube. It runs south for three miles on the surface and one mile underground to terminate in Newark City beneath the Pennsylvania Railroad Station and the Hudson Bay Terminal. It operates with 30 PCC-type cars drawing power at 600 V dc from overhead wires.
The Staten Island Rapid Transit Railway Company was turned over to the Metropolitan Transportation Authority on 1 July 1971 and is now operated by the Staten Island Rapid Transit Operating Authority, a subsidiary of the MTA. The line runs the length of an island that is politically the Richmond Borough of New York. Its multiple-unit stock matches the latest equipment of the BMT Division of the NYCTA, but a contemplated connection with that System never materialised. Power is at 600 V dc through third rail top contact.
Work was completed in 1974 on the $69 480 000 contract for the East River Tunnel, which was started in November 1969. Construction began in 1971 of the tunnel under part of Central Park which will connect the existing lines in Manhattan with those in Queens. The tunnel will be double-decked with two tracks being built for Subway use and two tracks for Long Island Railroad trains. Construction began also in 1972 on the 14 mile Second Avenue Subway in Manhattan and the Jamaica Line Subway extension on Archer Avenue, Queens. This work is being done with the assistance of a $2 500 million transportation bond issue approved by the governor, the legislature and the voters of New York State, which will finance the biggest expansion in the history of the New York City Subway system.
During 1974 1.13 miles of the Culver Shuttle line was closed.
Route length: 231.73 miles *(372.2 km)*, including 137.05 miles *(220.1 km)* in tunnel and 71.80 miles *(114.8 km)* on elevated structures.
Number of lines: 3 major systems (IND, IRT and BMT), and comprising a total of 30 lines and branches. The lines are all of a transverse or radial type. The whole system is double-, treble-, quadrupled-tracked.
Number of stations served: 462.
Average station spacing: Approx ½ mile between local stations and 1-4 miles between "Express stop" stations.
Passengers per annum: 1 096 006 529.
Passengers per annum carried by New York City Transit system (including road services as well as railways): 1 559 030 395.
Max number of trains per hour each way: 34.
Max number of cars per train: 10 local, 11 express.
Estimated capacity per car: 54 seated, 146 standing.
Average schedule speed (including stops): Express trains 22 mph *(35 km/h)*; Local trains 20 mph *(32 km/h)*.
Track gauge: 4 ft 8½ in *(1.435 m)*.
Weight and type of rails: 100 lb/yd *(49.6 kg/m)*, flat-bottomed.
Minimum radius of curves: 52 m.
Type of tunnel: Many of the underground railway tunnels in New York are of "cut-and-cover" construction, being of rectangular section and double or multiple-track width. The double-track tunnels of the first subway line, opened in 1904, were 25 ft 3 in *(7.96 m)* wide and 12 ft 9 in *(3.886 m)* high (from rail level), and had centre supports. There are, however, several sections of tube construction (particularly under the East River) where concrete tunnel linings were used.
Method and voltage of current supply: Third rail; 600 V dc, The New York City Transit Authority has sold its 3 power generating stations to the Consolidated Edison Co, from whom power is now being purchased. There are about 150 sub-stations, which are being retained by the Transit Authority. Modernisation of the power distribution system to meet requirements of high-acceleration cars, and an increase in the total number of cars, includes the building of additional sub-stations, and replacement of some now manually opperted by centrally-operated sub-stations.
Rolling Stock: Number of cars owned: about 6 800. This includes 1 000 cars manufactured by the Pullman Car Company for service on the former BMT and IND Divisions and for the Staten Island Railroad, mentioned subsequently. These cars are being used to replace older equipment and are of an entirely new design with an overall length of 75 ft.
Details: Cars introduced since the war on the BMT and IND Divisions are 60 ft *(18.3 m)* long, 10 ft *(3.05 m)* wide and 12 ft *(3.66 m)* high. The latest model (R-44) is 75 ft long in four-car units, made of low alloy, high tensile steel and fibreglass with stainless steel exteriors and aluminium roofs. They are capable of increased acceleration and of reaching a speed of 70 mph.
Signalling: Automatic block, with colour light signals and train stops. An "Indentra" train operating system, similar to the electronic "programmes" train operating system used on London Transport, is in use on the IRT-Flushing line.
Station layout: Ticket halls at underground stations are at sub-surface (mezzanine) level, and are reached by stairwells from the street. There is a variety of platform layouts. On double-track lines, separate side platforms are usual. At "express stop" stations on four-track lines, island platforms for cross-platform interchange are provided between the fast and slow tracks in each direction. Escalators and lifts are installed at some stations between the ticket hall (mezzanine) and platform levels.

NEW YORK—NEW JERSEY—PATH

Authority:
Port Authority Trans-Hudson Corporation
One World Trade Center, New York, NY 10048, USA

New York
President: A. G. Kuhbach
Vice President and General Manager:
L. G. Gambaccini
Counsel: P. J. Falvey
Director Public Affairs: J. Tillman
Supv. Passenger and Community Services:
M. L. Hurnitz
Claims Agent: M. Lynch
Purchasing Agent: A. Koplik

Jersey City
General Superintendent: A. Rubbert
Assistant General Superintendent: T. C. Rutmayer
Superintendent Transport: P. N. Scaturro
Superintendent Car Equipment: W. H. Miller
Superintendent Power, Signals & Communications: R. Schiff
Superintendent Track and Structures: L. Pelton

General: Construction of the former Hudson and Manhattan (H & M) Railroad began in 1874. Upon completion of the two uptown under-river tunnels, first operations began from Hoboken, New Jersey to 19th Street and Sixth Avenue in Manhattan in early 1908, and were extended up Sixth Avenue to 23rd and 33rd Streets by 1910.
In 1909 Hudson Terminal-Jersey City service began, upon completion of the downtown tunnels. By 1911, service was extended to Newark by agreement with the Pennsylvania Railroad. A north-south tunnel linked Hoboken and Jersey City in 1909.
The system reached its highest levels of daily passenger volumes in the late 1920's. However, while the formal banckruptcy proceedings did not begin until 1954, the H & M as a commercial enterprise was insolvent from the early 1930's.
In 1962, following passage of legislation by the States of New Jersey and New York, the Port Authority Trans-Hudson Corporation (PATH) was created to acquire, operate and modernise the bankrupt inter-state rapid transit system, which faced the prospect of abandonment.
PATH began operations on 1 September 1962, and initiated a long range, multi-million dollar rehabilitation and modernisation programme. PATH has now invested over $258 million in acquisition, rehabilita-

tion and modernisation of the 14-mile rail system. Cumulative operating deficits, calculated in accordance with Interstate Commerce Commission regulations, have totalled nearly $262 million since 1962. The PATH modernisation programme includes the design and purchase of a fleet of 251 new air-conditioned cars, completed in 1972; completion of a new World Trade Center terminal in lower Manhattan in 1971; and completion and dedication of a new PATH Journal Square Transportation Center in Jersey City, New Jersey, in October 1975. Other modernisation work includes the rehabilitation and rebuilding of the signal system and replacement of the electric traction power system, and rehabilitation of track, tunnel drainage, station, and communications systems.

In November, 1972, the Governors of the States of New York and New Jersey proposed a new 17.6 mile PATH service to Newark International Airport and Plainfield, New Jersey, as part of an extensive programme of rail transportation improvements to be undertaken by the Port Authority of New York and New Jersey. This project is now awaiting federal funding. Other elements of the proposed bi-state rail improvement programme would provide direct service to Penn Station, New York for many ConRail riders, and direct rail service between Penn Staion, New York and Kennedy International Airport via the Long Island Rail Road.

Passengers per annum: (1971): 38 877 360.
                    (1972): 40 282 283.
                    (1974): 37 774 199.

Method and voltage of current supply: Third rail, 650 V dc. A new traction power system employing ultra-modern silicon rectifiers, has been installed at PATH's New York and New Jersey sub-stations, at cost of over $8 m, to replace the old rotary converter system.

Rolling Stock: Number of cars owned 298. At present, the fully air-conditioned passenger car fleet consists of 47 cars acquired in 1958 and 205 cars acquired in 1965-67, all of which were manufactured by the St. Louis Car Division of General Steel Industries, Inc. There are also 38 various pieces of work equipment. The 1965-67 stock comprises 123 driving cars and 82 motored trailer cars. Bodies are aluminium with capacities of about 140 (41 seated and 42 seated respectively). Two automatic double doors on both sides of each car. All the cars are 51 ft 3 in *(15.62 m)* long, 9 ft 4½ in *(2.86 m)* wide, 11 ft 8½ in *(3.56 m)* high. Braking is dynamic down to 10 mph *(16 km/h)* and then electro-pneumatic. They can be in trains of from 2 to 10 cars. During 1972, 46 air-conditioned cars, type PA-3 manufactured by Hawker Siddeley Canada, Ltd. were delivered. They permit longer trains to be operated on PATH's services between Newark, Harrison, Jersey City, Hoboken and the World Trade Center terminal in lower Manhattan.

Other aspects of PATH's extensive modernisation

Interior of a PA-3n car.

programme includes improvement of stations, rebuilding of the signal system; rehabilitation of track; tunnel drainage, and utility systems, installation of a two-way train-to-wayside radio communication system, and the implementation of a new exact change fare collection system.

A major new addition to the PATH system is the new World Trade Center terminal which opened in 1971 replacing the obsolete Hudson Terminal in downtown Manhattan. It lies beneath the twin 110-storey office and Trade Center towers. In addition, PATH has constructed the PATH Journal Square Transportation Center, in Jersey City. This co-ordinated rail, bus and parking facility accommodates more than 56 000 PATH and bus passengers each weekday. It opened in stages from late 1973, with completion of the entire project in October 1975. Both the World Trade Center terminal and the PATH Journal Square Transportation Center will better equip PATH to meet the increased peak hour traffic demands which are expected in the years ahead.

On November 15, 1972, the Governors of the States of New Jersey and New York announced plans for a $650 million programme of rail transportation improvements to be undertaken by the Port Authority. Plans for the first of three elements, the proposed new 18-mile PATH service to Newark International Airport and Plainfield, call for construction of a completely new PATH rail line between Newark and Elizabeth serving the Airport, and construction of a new PATH airport station, as well as improvements along the Central Railroad of New Jersey mainline between Elizabeth and Plainfield. The second major element would provide direct rail service to Penn Station, New York, for some 20 000 ConRail riders via direct track connections in Kearny and Secaucus, New Jersey. The third element, in which the Port Authority is co-operating with the Metropolitan Transportation Authority (MTA), is the planned direct rail Long Island Railroad

One of the air-conditioned PA-3 cars delivered to PATH in 1972.

One of the platforms at PATH's new World Trade Center Terminal.

service to John F. Kennedy International Airport via Long Island Railroad tracks. Legislation authorising the Port Authority to do this work has been adopted by the State of New Jersey. Identical legislation was submitted to the New York Legislature in January, 1973, and subsequently adopted.

NUREMBERG

VAG Verkehrs Aktiengesellschaft
Hochhaus am Plärrer, 85 Nüremberg, German Federal Republic
Telephone: (0911) 2711
Cables: VAG-NURNBERG

General: By early 1978 a total of 9.3 km of the city's new U Bahn system had been opened with the completion of Line 1 as far as Bahnhof Turm. The complete line should be finished not before 1982 when trains will be running from Langwasser in the south to Furth in the north. A final U Bahn system of 43.9 km is planned at a cost of around DM 1 700 million with annual construction costs amounting to about DM 70 million.

Technical Data:
Gauge: 1.435 km
Route length: 8.5 km
In tunnel: 6.2 km
Projected new lines (in construction): 2.0 km
  (in design): 5.4 km
Number of stations (total): 14 existing; 13 planned
  (in tunnel): 10; 10
Stations:
  platform length (minimum): 90 m
Gradient (max): 4%

Curvature (max): 100 m
Speed (design max): 80 km/h
  (average commercial): 30.9 km/h
Electric systems: Third rail; 750 V

Rolling Stock:
Car type (year introduced): 1971
Number of units: 24 Doppeltriebwagen
Car dimensions (length): 18.6 m
  (width): 2.90 m
  (height): 3.55 m
Passenger capacity per car (total): 290
  (seated): 98
Motors per car: 4
Rating: 180 kW
Train composition (mimimum): 2 cars = 1 unit
  (max): 4 cars = 2 units
Brakes (type): Rheostatic
Body material: Aluminium
Weight (car) 26 tons unloaded

Traffic Data:
Trains/track/hour: 16
Train capacity (passengers): 580
Total passengers/track/hour (peak): 9 280
Train headways existing: 3¾ minutes

A MAN-built trainset at Langwasser Sud terminal station.

OSAKA

Authority:
Osaka Municipal Transportation Bureau
Kujo Minami-I, Nishi-ku, Osaka 550, Japan
General Manager: Maseya Nishio
Superintendents:
  Management & Planning: Megumu Yamamoto
  General Management: Tomio Morita
  Subway Transportation: Masataka Sawaoka
  Automobile: Junichi Michiba
  Engineering: Yoshio Akamatsu
  Rapid Transit: Yasunori Hayaki
  R.T. Planning: Tsunehisa Miura
  R.T. Construction: Takeshi Oura

General: Japanese commerce centres largely on Osaka, Japan's second city. The city proper has 2.79 million inhabitants but its day-time population is 1.21 millions more. Numerous rapid transit lines of both national railways and 5 private railways bring incoming passengers from the suburbs and other cities, to be distributed by Osaka's municipal public transport and the 13.5 mile *(21.7 km)* Osaka Loop Line.

The efforts being made to improve travel conditions include reserved bus lanes and implementation of suburban and subway extensions, recommended by the Ministry of Transport, to deal with an expected daily inflow of 1.8 millions in 1990.

Osaka's first underground railway opened in May, 1933 with two miles of line. Extensions were made in subsequent years and resumed after World War II despite financial difficulties. Expansion has been particularly rapid since 1964, when Line 1 was extended to provide interconnection with the JNR New Tokaido Line at Shin Osaka.

Osaka's Emergency Subway Construction Project was completed in 1970, but rapid expansion has continued, with a 2.8 km extension of Line 3 in 1972, and a 3.1 km extension of Line 2 in 1973.

With a present route length of 75.6 km the Osaka Municipal Transportation Bureau intends to construct a total of 20 km new subway lines by 1985.

Already under construction are two new sections: Tennoji to Yao-Minami (10.4 km; estimated cost Yen 135 336 million); Shin-Fukae to Minamitatsumi (3 km; estimated cost Yen 39 252 million).

In 1977 work started on other two lines; Fukaebashi to Nagata (3 km; estimated cost Yen 45 675 million) and Moriguchi to Dainichi (0.6 km; estimated cost Yen 12 530 million).

The Transportation Bureau also operates the city's buses. With the considerable increase in Subway patronage, and in general surface traffic, the city's trams were withdrawn in 1969, and the trolley-buses in June 1970.

The metropolitan transport area of Osaka is served by a network of electrified lines, comprising the JNR Osaka Loop Line and 9 private railways, 5 of which have their terminals in the downtown area. Between Lines 1 and 6, and the Hanku and Osaka North Express railways, there is reciprocal working of trains.

The extension on Line 2, 5.4 km from Miyakojima northeast to Moriguchi was opened to traffic on 6 April 1977 and 10.4 km from Tennoji to Yao-Minami will be completed in 1980.

Route length: 75.6 km, mostly in tunnel, partly on elevated track.
Number of lines: 6 (5 transverse, 1 radial); double track.
Number of stations served: 61.

Average station spacing: 0.70 miles *(1.10 km)*.
Average length of journey: 4.15 km.
Total passengers per annum carried by Osaka Municipal Transit System (including road services): (1976): 715 million passengers.
Car kms per annum on underground system: 58 167 647.
Number of cars per train: Line 1, 8; Line 2, 6; Lines 3 and 6, 5; Lines 4 and 5, 4.
Max number of trains per hour each way: 27 (Line 1).
Track gauge: 4 ft 8½ in *(1.435 m)*.
Type of rail: Flat-bottomed, 100.8 lb/yd *(50 kg/m)*.
Max gradient: 1 in 28.6 (3.5%).
Minimum radius of curves: 393 ft *(120 m)*.
Type of tunnel: Generally double-track, cut and cover tunnel, rectangular section, mostly in re-inforced concrete with centre supports. At the city centre, parts of Lines 2 and 4 are at deep level in twin, single-track tube, internal diameter 18 ft 8 in *(5.7 m)*. The depth of rectangular tunnel below surface varies from 75 ft *(23 m)* to 25 ft *(7.5 m)*.
Method and voltage of current supply: Third rail, at 750 V dc and on Line 6, overhead wire at 1 500 V dc.
Rolling Stock: Number of cars owned: 692.
Details of latest cars: Series 30 (1973): Length 18.70 m 4 double-leaf doors on each side. Passenger capacity 130-140. Designed for short in-town passenger journeys, with rapid acceleration and deceleration characteristics.
Series 10 (1973): Length 18.9 m 4 double-leaf doors on either side. Aluminium construction. Provided with current chopper.

Most trains carry inductive radio equipment.

Signalling: Automatic block, with colour-light signals and train stops. In addition, protection is afforded by continuous Automatic Train Control (ATC) and Centralised Traffic Control (CTC).

Station layout: Some stations have an island platform (eg Shinsaibashi), others have separate side platforms (eg Showacho). Platform lengths vary from 120 m to 180 m. (10-car train length).
Daikokucho Station's two island platforms permit cross-platform interchange between Line 1 and Line 3 in each direction.
Most stations have mezzanine space for ticket halls and passenger circulation.

OSLO

Authority:
A/S Oslo Sporveier
Post Box 2857 Kampen, Oslo 5, Norway
Administrative Director: Ove Skaug

General: Prior to 1966, Oslo's rapid transit system comprised a group of electrified light railway or tramway lines serving its western outskirts, and inter-urban tramways serving the east and south-east suburbs. The western groups, until 1928, had a common terminal at Majorstua, but a double-track underground line 1.25 miles *(2.0 km)* long, opened in that year, extended the group's services to the city centre at National Theatre.
There was no such facility for the east and south-east Oslo suburbs, where there has been considerable industrial and residential development since 1950. A new "Tunnelbane" system has therefore been constructed to link this area with the business centre. The whole scheme, the "Oslo Eastern Rapid Transit System", will include 21.75 miles *(35.0 km)*, double-track line. Of this 18.1 miles *(29.2 km)* is now operative.
As part of the scheme, two new lines, the Grorud and Lambertseter Lines, have been constructed, and, together with the newly constructed common line (Tøyen-Jernbanetorget) linking them with the city centre, they were opened for traffic in 1966. The old tramway line, the Ostensjø line to Oppsal Station, has been re-constructed to rapid transit standards and extended to Skullerud. A fourth line, the Furuset, was opened for traffic in November, 1970, for a distance of 2.4 km serving two new stations. Work is proceeding with an extension northeast from Grorud, of 2.5 km, and construction is under way on a cross-city extension westward from Jernbanetörget. Interconnection facilities between the south east rapid transit system and the western system will be provided at a new Slotts Bakken station near National Theatre.
The downtown tunnel project, running 0.74 km between Jernbanetorget station and National Theatre is expected to be completed by 1979. Most of the tunnel will pass through along rock necessitating construction using a resistant membrane subsequently concreted with sulphate-resistant cement. The line will include one station at Sentrum. Expected to cost about Nkr 90 million, the line should be completed by the end of this year.
It is planned to eventually extend the section as far as Slottsparken, enabling interconnection with the western suburban branchline service. The alignment to Slottsparken passes mainly through rock, but as the rockroof has proved too weak cut-and-cover construction is to be adopted. Work on this section was started in 1977 and due to be completed by 1980 at a cost of Nkr 90 million.

Biggest project at present under construction is the 2.28 km Furuset branchline being built through clay and rock using open cut methods. Estimated cost of the line is Nkr 65 million.
A future extension is planned from Furuset to Ellingsrud, via Ellingsrudasen—a length of approximately 1 km, with half in tunnel and half on the surface. The extension could be opened by 1979 at a cost of Nkr 45 million.
Details of the system in operation are as follows:
Number of stations: 42.
Average station spacing: 0.51 miles *(815 m)*.
Minimum radius of curves: 656 ft *(200 m)*.
Gauge: 1 435 mm
Main line curves (radius minimum): 200 m
In the workshop area (radius minimum): 50 m
Max gradient, main line: 50%
Max gradient, stations: 3%
Platform length: 110 m
Platform width: 4—8 m
Platform level above rail: 1.00—1.07 m
Ballast, main line: 0.45 m
Ballast, concrete tunnels: 0.35 m
Switches, main line: 1 : 9
Switches, workshop area and sidings: 1 : 7
Number of cars per train: 6.
Estimated capacity per car: 150 (incl. 63 seats).
Average scheduled speed: 19.8 mph *(32 km/h)*.
Method and voltage of current supply: 3rd rail, underside contact, from Oslo Electricity Supply Commission at 5 000 V ac transformed to 750 V dc through 14 rectifier stations. Total installation 55 000 kW.
Signalling: Cab signal system, actuated by coded signal impulses through track, controls the following speeds: 70-50-30-15 km/h. Train services operate under Central Traffic Control at Traffic Centre building at Tøyen. Trains' communication equipment includes radio and telephone.
Power Supply: 14 Rectifier stations 750 V dc. Third rail, weight 40 kg/m. Underside contact. Total installation 71 900 A.
Signal and security equipment:
Cab-signals based on: Max speed on level straight line: 70 km/h
Train interval: Joint tunnel 90 sec
Branches 120 sec
Following speeds are controlled:
H—70 km/h: High
M—50 km/h: Middle
L—30 km/h: Low
K—15 km/h: Crawl
In the joint tunnel 50—30—15 km/h are controlled, on the branch lines 70—50—15 km/h.
Telecommunications:
A Two-way telephone communications, incl. Oslo

Telephone and special internal lines.
B One-way telecommunication installations, loudspeaker and amplifier, alarm for fire and assault clocks, thermometers and indicators for ground water levels.
C Radio communication between traffic control centre and trains.
D Miscellaneous installations for tunnel lighting, tunnel ventilation, tunnel gates and electric heating of switches.
Stations: Five inner stations are underground. Grønland station is built on two levels, with circulating area, ticket offices and shops over platforms and tracks. Side platforms, 110 m long, are sufficient for 6-car trains.

Rolling Stock: 155 cars, all motored and of steel construction, are 17.0 m long overall, 3.20 m wide, and have 3 double doors, opening to 1.25 m on each side. Four 98 kW motors per car. Dynamic, air and hand-braking equipment is installed.
Distance between couplings: 17.50 m
Length of body: 17.00 m
Max external width: 3.20 m
Max height above rail: 3.67 m
Floor level above rail: 1.14 m
Dia. of wheels, new tyres: 0.82 m
Max wear on tyres: 60 mm
Distance between bogie centres: 11.00 m
Weight, unladen type 1₁: 28.8 t
type 1₂: 29.8 t
Weight, laden, 170 pass. type 1₁: 40.8 t
type 1₂: 41.8 t
Number of motors in each car: 4
Capacity of motor, 1 hour, 1 540 R/M: 98 kW
Capacity of motor, lasting: 86 kW
Voltage: 375 V dc
Gear ratio: 6.73 : 1
Double sliding doors on each side: 3
Clearance of door openings: 1.25 m
Seats for passengers, type 1₁ = 60
type 1₂ = 63
Standing passengers (allowed): 107
Max speed: 70 km/h
Acceleration (0-40 km/h): 1.0 m/sec²
Middle retardation from 50 km/h to standstill: emergency brakes 0.9 m/sec²
dynamic brakes max 1.35 m/sec²
Load dependent dynamic brakes and compressed air brakes. Hand-brake
Current collectors, on each bogie: 2
Car Dept: Near Ryen station on Lambertseter line. Capacity 120 cars, but equipped for maintenance of 150 cars. Extra capacity of workshop is used for tram-car bogie maintenance during winding-up period of Oslo's tramway system.

PARIS

Authority:
Régie Autonome des Transports Parisiens (RATP)
53 ter Quai des Grands Augustins, Paris (6e), France

Chairman: Roger Belin
General Manager: Jacques Deschamps
Railways Manager: Philippe Essig

General: The present Paris Metro system originated as a short cross-city line of some 6¼ miles serving 18 stations, which were opened for passenger traffic on 19 July 1900. Over subsequent years it developed rapidly into a closely-meshed urban underground railway system, confined until 1934 within the Paris city boundaries. From that year onward it extended into the suburbs and now operates over 258.25 miles of route (including Regional Express system) serving 330 named stations corresponding to 405 stopping stations.
The main characteristics of the Paris Metro system (with the exception of the Regional Express system) are the close proximity of its stations one with the other and the general shallowness of its tunnels and stations. It has in consequence the advantages both of accessibility and convenience which, coupled with most intensive train service, accounts for the fact that the Metro carries more than half of all the passengers conveyed by the Paris Transport Authority. Like most other extensive urban systems the present Metro is a product of formerly separate transport undertakings. In 1942 it was joined with the Paris bus organisation, and in 1949 the present Authority, the Régie Autonome des Transports Parisiens (a public corporation) came into being.
The Paris Metro system carries much short-distance traffic, and although the number of passengers carried exceeds that on the London Transport rail system, the average distance travelled is much less. Of the 21 urban lines, 15 are wholly underground, the remaining 6 having short sections on the surface or on viaduct. Unlike the French main-line railways, the urban system (but not the Regional Express system) has right-hand running throughout its urban system.
Already operating 183.4 km of urban Metro lines and 74.86 km of regional Metro routes, the Regie Autonome des Transports Parisiens (RATP) has a number of lines at present under construction in Paris and several projected for years up to 1986.
Route length (1976): 154.1 miles *(248 km)* including the Sceaux line, 22.2 miles *(35.8 km)* long, the Boissy-St Léger line 12.0 miles *(19.3 km)* and the Germain-en-Laye line 12.3 miles *(19.8 km)*.
Number of lines: 13 radial, 2 circumferential, and the Regional Express System (the Sceaux line, the Boissy-St Léger line and the St-Germain-en-Laye line) 3.
Number of stations served: Urban system 353: Sceaux Line 29, Boissy-St-Léger Line 11, St Germain-en-Laye Line 11.
Average station spacing: Urban system 0.33 miles *(0.54 km)*; Sceaux line 0.8 miles *(1.3 km)*; Boissy-St Léger line 1.2 miles *(1.9 km)*; St Germain-en-Laye 1.4 miles *(2.2 km)*.

Lines recently completed or under construction	Length (km)	Cost (Frs millions)	Scheduled completion date
Regional Metro:			
Auber—Nation	5.6	1 360	1977
Luxembourg—Chatelet	2.0	615	1977
Fontenay-sous-Bois—			
Noisy I	8.5	662	1977

Urban Metro:			
Porte de la Villette—			
Les quatre chemins	0.9	150	1979
Porte d'Auteuil—			
Bologne Jean Jaures	1.7	171	1980
Carrefour Pleyel—			
Saint-Denis Basilique	2.4	203.5	1976
Porte de Clichy—Asnieres	3.0	365	1980
Champs Elysees—Invalides	0.8	130	1976
Porte de Vanves—			
Chatillon I	2.3	170	1976
Chatillon I—Chatillon II	1.7	111	1980

Lines projected			
Regional Metro:			
Sceaux line			
Chatelet—Gare du Nord	2.6	580	1981/82
Orly branch	4.2	170	1981/82
Marne-la-Vallee line			
Noisy I—Torcy	8.1	360	1980/81
Saint-Germain-en-Laye line			
Interconnection to Cergy	1.1	140	1983/84
Urban Metro:			
Porte d'Orleans—			
Montrouge	1.5	120	1982/83
Eglise de Pantin—Prefecture			
de Bobigny	3.3	270	1980/82
Gare de Lyon deviation	1.7	220	1984/85
Porte d'Italie—Villejuif III	3.0	490	1980/83
Quatre chemins—			
Quatre routes	2.2	210	1979/82
Creteil Prefecture—			
Parc regional	0.9	30	1981/82
Mairie de Montreuil—			
Roisny-sous-Bois	3.8	250	1985/86

Boulogne Jean Jaures—Boulogne Rhine et Danube	0.9	90	1980/81
Extension in the XIII district	3.0	420	1985/86
Marie des Lilas—Romainville	1.3	170	1983/84
Saint Denis Basilique—Stains	1.5	320	1984/85
Asnieres Gennevilliers I—Asnieres Gennevilliers III	2.5	150	1981/83
Chatillon II—Velizy	9.3	640	1984/85

Passengers per annum: Urban system, 186 000 000 Sceaux line, 14 100 000, Boissy-St-Léger line 8 700 000, St. Germain-en-Laye, 12 000 000.

Total passengers per annum carried by Paris Transport Authority (including road services and Montmartre cable-railway as well as Metro and Regional Express (1976)): 1 867 200 000.

Car-km per annum (1972): Urban System, 186 000 000; Sceaux line, 14 100 000, Boissy-St-Léger line, 8 700 000, St. Germain-en-Laye 12 000 000.

Number of trains operated on each line at peak hours: 4 (Line 3) to 66 (Line 9).

Number of cars per train: Metro; 4, 5 or 6; Reg. Express 3 to 9.

Average scheduled speed (including stops):
Metro: 23.6 km/h to 26.1 km/h.
Sceaux:
(all stations), 29.9 km/h.
(semi-direct), 40.4 km/h.
Boissy-St-Léger:
(all stations), 44.7 km/h.
(semi-direct), 52.7 km/h.
St. Germain-en-Laye: 49.4 km/h.

Track gauge: 4 ft $8\frac{11}{16}$ in *(1.44 m)*.

Weight and type of rails: 105 lb/yd *(52 kg/m)*. Flat-bottomed in 18 m lengths. Sceaux line 93 and 111 lb *(46* and *55 kg)* in 16.5 or 18 m lengths; Boissy-St-Léger and St. Germain-en-Laye: flat-bottomed, 60 kg/m, 144 m lengths welded in situ on underground sections; surface sections in 36 m lengths are fish-plated.

Minimum radius of curves: Urban systems 246 ft *(75 m)* and exceptionally 131 ft *(40 m)*, Sceaux line 722 ft *(220 m)* Boissy-St-Léger line 1 312 ft *(400 m)*, St Germain-en-Laye 479 ft *(146 m)*.

Max gradient: Urban system 40 mm/n; Sceaux line 30 mm/n. Boissy-St-Léger line 30 mm/n. St. Germain-en-Laye, 36 mm/n.

Type of tunnel: Double-track tunnel of eliptical section, 23 ft 3½ in *(7.1 m)* wide and 17 ft 1 in *(5.2 m)* high. On Regional Express system, tunnels are either rectangular (8.70 m × 6.30 m) or circular (8.70 m internal diameter). Various construction methods used include cut and cover on suburban sections especially, and shield coupled to boring machine. Tunnel linings are generally of concrete and masonry.

Method and voltage of current supply: Initially, the power for traction, lighting and signalling is received at 63 000 V ac, 225 000 V ac or exceptionally 20 000 V ac then stepped down to 15 000 V.
—Metro at 750 V dc through 109 automatic rectifier stations.
—through 26 automatic rectifier stations.

Rolling Stock: Number of cars owned: Urban system, 1 957 motor cars (including 614 pneumatic-tyred cars, 788 new conventional cars on Lines 3, 7, and 13 (9 and 8 partially) and 40 motored units of the articulated sets operating on Line 10; 1 528 trailers (including 316 pneumatic-tyred cars, 503 modern conventional cars). Sceaux Line has 148 cars of older type. Three-car trains ordered for the East-West transverse line are now operated on the Sceaux line, the Boissy-St-Léger line and the St. Germain-en-Laye line. By the end of 1976, the number of cars of this new stock was 321 (216 motor cars and 105 trailers).
The new motored cars on the urban system are 49 ft 8¼ in *(15.145 m)* long with driving cab and 47 ft 2½ in *(14.390 m)* long without driving cab. The overall length of a Regional Express train 3-car unit is 239 ft 2 in *(72.900 m)*.

Signalling: Generally automatic block, with ac track circuits, and three-aspect colour-light signals. No train stops are used. Sceaux line: 4-aspect colour-light signals with instantaneous repetition of overrun signal inside drivers cab. Boissy-St-Léger and St. Germain-en-Laye; French National Railways signalling; signals repeated in cab on console showing aspect which train passes and of signal approaching.

PEKING

Authority:
Metropolitan Railway Department
Peking Municipal Council City Administration Building, Peking, China

Type of system: Full-metro.

General: Reports on the Peking Underground Railway to date detail the following: the railway now in operation runs at shallow level for 23 km in a straight east-west line from the Peking main railway terminus westward to Shi Ching on the outskirts. There are 16 stations. It was opened on October 1, 1969 (although this presumably refers to the completion of the infrastructure and not to passenger operation). The stations, varying in size, are all interiorly clad with marble. The line is air-conditioned.
Four-car trains travel at a maximum speed of 46-49 mph *(75-80 km/h)*. Each car has a normal capacity of 186 passengers including 60 seated. The cars were built at the Chang Chan Locomotive Works. Operationally the line is controlled by a system of telecommunication. There is a flat fare of 10 sen (about 5 US cents or 2p). There are plans for an eventual network of radial lines linking Peking's centre to a circle line, reported to be under construction.
Since 1949, Peking's public transport vehicles have increased from 164 to more than 2 000, to serve the city's built-up area which has also greatly increased (nearly tenfold) since that year. The population of Peking City and its metropolitan area is now estimated at 7 millions.

Technical Data:
Route length: 23 km
In tunnel: 23 km
Projected new lines (in construction): 20 km
Number of lines: 1
Number of stations (total): 16
(in tunnel): 16
Speed (design): 80 km/h

Traffic Data:
Train capacity (passengers): 1 200
Train headways
design: 2.5 minutes
existing: 15 minutes
Passengers carried (annually): 20 400 000

PHILADELPHIA

Authority:
Southeastern Pennsylvania Transportation Authority
200, W. Wyoming Avenue, Philadelphia, USA

Chairman: James C. McConnon
General Manager: William R. Eaton

General: Philadelphia and District present another example of large-scale co-ordination of different transport concerns serving a region, integrated under a single Authority. In 1963 the Southeastern Pennsylvania Transportation Authority was created by legislature to co-ordinate and improve transportation in the five-county area of Philadelphia, Bucks, Chester, Delaware and Montgomery Counties. Previously these services were operated separately by public and privately owned concerns.
Progressive amalgamation or acquisition over the years culminated in the creation of SEPTA, which variously owns and operates, leases (or renders financial aid to) the services formerly individually operated. The last acquisition was the Norristown rapid transit railway and a suburban bus system from the Philadelphia Suburban Transportation Company in January 1970.
The oldest underground-elevated line in Philadelphia is the east-west Market Street Line, completed in 1908. Alongside its in-town tunnel tracks for part of their length run also the tracks of local street cars. The "Frankford Elevated" to Bridge in the north-east followed in 1922; the wholly-underground north-south Broad Street Line in 1928, and a spur off this line to the 8th Avenue shopping district in 1932. The Camden Line from 16th Street to Camden, across the Benjamin Franklin Bridge over the Delaware River, was opened initially in 1936. It now forms part of the Lindenwold Line mentioned below.
Interworking of the Market Street-Frankford Line on one hand and the Broad Street, and Ridge-Eighth, on the other hand, is impossible because of the different gauges. In addition to its underground system, the Authority subsidises suburban Penn-Central and Reading Railroads' Philadelphia commuter services through annual purchase of service contracts. It also operates an extensive network of bus, trolleybus, and tramway services.
Planned is a 6.4 mile *(10.3 km)* extension of the same line at its northern end, branching out north-east from Erie Station. The extensions form part of a $1 400 m Capital Programme announced under a comprehensive Plan for the whole of Philadelphia and its Regions' mass transit systems.
A basic cash fare system operates on any of the Transportation Company's vehicles for any distance within the City limits, plus a small charge for first and for subsequent transfers.

Route length: 29 miles *(47 km)* including 18 miles *(29 km)* in tunnel.

Number of lines: 4 (2 transverse, 1 radial, and 1 in-town); all double or quadruple track.

Number of stations served: 52.

Average station spacing: 0.58 miles *(0.93 km)*.

Passengers per annum (subway-elevated system only): (1975): 58 000 000. The authority now records only revenue passengers. The stated total thus excludes transferees from other services.

Average journey (subway elevated system): 3.5 miles.

Max number of trains per hour each way: Broad St. Line 25, Market St. Line 26.

Max number of cars per train: 6.

Estimated capacity per car: Broad Street cars: 190 (including 67 seats). Market-Frankford: 150 (including 56 seats).

Average schedule speed (including stops): Broad St. Line, local: 17.2 mph *(27.7 km/h)*. Market St. Line: 20.2 mph *(32.5 km/h)*. (Broad St. Line carries both local and express trains).

Track gauge: Market Street-Frankford Line 5 ft 2¼ in *(1.581 m)*; Broad Street, Ridge-Eighth and Camden Lines 4 ft 8½ in *(1.435 m)*.

Weight and type of rails: 100 lb/yd *(49.6 kg/m)*. All flat-bottomed.

Max gradient: 1 in 20 (5%).

Minimum radius of curves: Market Street-Frankford Line, 105 ft *(32 m)*: Broad Street and Ridge-Eighth Lines, 160 ft *(49 m)*.

Type of tunnel: Double or multiple track tunnel, of rectangular section.

Method and voltage of current supply: Third rail (top and bottom contact, according to line); 600 V dc

Rolling Stock: Number of cars owned: 466. Stainless steel cars have now replaced the older stock on the Market-Frankford Line. They were manufactured by the Budd Company of Philadelphia and are 55 ft long and 9 ft 1 in wide. 46 single cars seat 54 passengers per car; 112 coupled pairs seat 56 passengers per car. There are four driving motors per car. The single cars have controls at each end and can be operated in combination with the coupled cars. On the latter there is only one control position, and these cars cannot be operated singly. Braking is dynamic and/or pneumatic.

Signalling: Automatic block, with colour-light signals.

Station layout: Many of the stations have direct entrance from buildings and shops. Around the City Hall, there is a vast complex of passageways and concourses, providing undercover connection between eight underground stations, the Pennsylvania and Reading Railroad terminals, and numerous offices and shops.

Other railways: Philadelphia is also served by a system of suburban lines including a self-contained rapid transit railway, the Norristown High-speed Line, also operated by SEPTA. This electrified line runs from 69th Street Terminus of the Market Street Line north-west for 13½ miles *(8.4 km)* to Norristown. Track gauge is 4 ft 8½ in *(1.435 m)* and current supply is by top contact third rail. There are 19 cars run as single units or 2-car sets, and two former "Electroliner" trains.

Authority:
Port Authority Transit Corporation (PATCO)
Benjamin Franklin Bridge Plaza, Camden, NJ 08101, USA

General: Additional to the SEPTA networks, a Rapid Transit surface-underground railway to serve Philadelphia was opened on 15 February 1969 to passenger traffic. The surface portion together with the former Locust Street Subway and Delaware Bridge line comprises the new Lindenwold Line whose in-town end is at 16th Street. It is operated by PATCO a subsidiary of the Delaware River Port Authority. The services are operated by 6-car commuter type trains, the stock of 75 cars, built by the Budd Company, being powered by four dc traction motors giving train speeds of up to 75 mph *(121 km/h)*. The Westinghouse system of signalling includes cab signalling devices automatically governing train speeds from start to stop.
A renewal of interest in expanding the PATCO system has arisen since the encouraging growth in ridership, from 6.1 millions in 1969 to 8.6 millions in 1970, and approximately 10.5 millions in 1972. The expansion plan endorsed by the Delaware Valley Regional Planning Commission proposed that first priority be given to a four-station extension east from Broadway (Camden) to Moorestown Mall, and further expansion is planned.
Present route length of the Philadelphia rapid transit line operated by PATCO is 22.6 km. Of that length about 18 per cent is in subway and the remainder either depressed below grade in open cut or elevated on embankments or viaducts.
Since it opened in 1969 the line has carried over 70 million passengers and present daily average is about 42 000. There are 14 passenger stations, each equipped with television surveillance and automatic fare dispensing equipment.
While there is no construction work under way at present, approval and funds have been provided for residual requirements and a new station on the existing line.
Future line projects are in the planning stage and an extensive study for expanding the system is now nearing completion. Projects under study include:
—extension of the existing line from Lindenwold, 11.1 km to Atco at an estimated cost of $95 million.
—construction of a new branchline extending south from Camden, 29.7 km to Glassboro at an estimated cost of $308 million.
—construction of a branchline from Camden, 22.9 km to Mount Laurel at an estimated cost of $267 million.

Technical Data:
Gauge: 1.435 m
Route length: 22.6 km
In tunnel: 4.6 km
Number of lines: 1
Number of stations (total): 12
(in tunnel): 6
Average distance between stations: 2.12 km
Electric system: Third rail; 600 V

Rolling Stock:

Car type (year introduced):	1968(1)	1968(2)
Number of units:	25	50
Car dimensions (length):	20.57 m	20.57 m
(width):	3.05 m	3.05 m
(height):	3.76 m	3.76 m
Passenger capacity per car		
(total):	120	120
(seated):	72	80

PITTSBURG

Authority:
Port Authority of Allegheny County (PAT)
121 Seventh Street, Box 1918, Pittsburg, Pa 15230, USA
Telephone: (412) 471 7458

Type of system: Proposed PTS.

General: A test facility with 2.8 km of track has been in operation since September 1965. The authority hopes to start work on first line construction in 1978.

Technical Data:
Gauge: 2.033 m
Route length: 2.8 km
Projected new lines (in design): 16.9 with 3.2 km in tunnel

PRAGUE

Authority:
Dopravni Podnik Hlavniho Mesta Prahy (DP)
Bubenska 1, Praha 7, Czechoslovakia
Telephone: 37 25 41

Type of system: Full-metro.

General: With 6.5 km of subway in operation since 1974 Prague authorities are now constructing 11 km of new lines which are due to go into operation by 1978. Total length of the planned underground rail system is 90 km.

Under an agreement signed April 1975 the Soviet Union is to send 16 specialists to Czechoslovakia in 1977 to help with underground construction and 37 Czechoslovak engineers are to receive construction and operating training in the Soviet Union. In addition, the Soviet Union is to supply Prague with 50 type Ecs transit cars, six escalators, earthmoving machinery, and spares for drilling and construction equipment. The ultimate underground network will consist of three transverse lines A, B, C laid with 4 ft 8½ in *(1.435 m)* gauge track, which will form a triangle of lines at the centre supplemented by Line D. The first stage until 1983-1985 comprises a network of three surface and underground lines of a total projected length of 21 miles *(34 km)*. The ultimate network will be about 58 miles *(93 km)* in total route length, serving 104 stations.

RIO DE JANEIRO

Authority:
Metro Company de Rio de Janeiro
Rio de Janeiro, Brazil

Type of system: Full-metro.

General: Following a slow start on Rio de Janeiro's first 12.8 km subway line—with only 1.4 km completed between 1969 and 1975—work is now being stepped up and it is hoped to have the section between Botafogo and Saens Pena in operation by March 1979. Construction costs for the line are expected to total Crs 6320.7 million.

By the end of 1977 work was scheduled to start on the first section of line 2, between Estacio de Sa and Maria da Graca, and on a light-rail line to be built between Maria da Graca and Sao Mateus.

Line 2 will be 7.8 km long and include five stations—two of them interchange stations with line 1 (at Estacio de Sa and Maria da Graca). Cost of the line will be about Crs 1978.4 million.

The light-rail line will run 17.4 km, with 11 stations, and cost approximately Crs 1472.8 million.

Basically, Rio's conventional Metro lines 1 and 2 are to be constructed to the same technical standards as those adopted for Sao Paulo: track construction will be to the same standards; energy will come from a 750 V dc third-rail system; trains will be to the same design.

Cut-and-cover construction is being used, with diaphragm walls used as the retaining structure together with steel profiles, wooden plates, struts and connecting rods.

ROME

Authority:
Societa delle Tramvie e Ferrovie Elettriche di Roma (STEFER)
Piazzale Ostrense 6 00154, Roma, Italy
Telephone: (06) 57 98
Cables: STEFER-ROMA

General: Construction of Line A of a new Metro network for Rome is nearing completion, after delays due to avoidance of destruction of historic buildings and

---

Motors per car:	4	4
Rating:	116 kWh	116 kWh
Train composition (minimum): 1		
(max): 8		
Acceleration (max):	1.34	1.34
Deceleration (emergency):	1.43	1.43
Brakes (type): Rheostatic		
Body material: Steel		
Weight (tonnes) Motorcar:	36.1	33.9

Number of lines: 1
Number of stations (total): 10
(in tunnel): 2
Stations:
platform length (minimum): 64 m
(max): 107 m
Gradient (max): 10%
Curvature (max): 45.7 m
Speed (design commercial): 88 km/h
Electric system: Third/fourth rail; 600 V
Type of rails: Concrete

Rolling Stock:
Car type: Motocars
Number of units: paired
Car dimensions (length): 9.3 m
(width): 2.6 m

The work actually in progress is that on the first 4.2 miles *(6.8 km)* of Line C, which is all in tunnel except for the Botic River and valley crossing by the 480 m Klement-Gottwald Bridge. 2.9 km of this section is being built in rectangular tunnel by the cut and cover method, which employs the 'Milan' method of wall construction. The remaining 3.4 km will be in circular tunnel 18 ft 8 in *(5.10 m)* internal diameter, lined with concrete segments except where iron lining is assumed necessary in water-bearing or disturbed soil. Excavation is by Soviet-built shield.

Stations on Line C will include the island type and side platform type. There will be eight underground stations and one built in the abutment of the Klement-Gottwald Bridge.

Technical Data:
Gauge: 1.435 m
Route length: 6.5 km
In tunnel: 6.5 km
Projected new lines (in construction): 11 km
(in design): 78.2 km
Number of lines: 1
Number of stations (total): 9
(in tunnel): 8
Average distance between stations: 850 m
Stations:
platform length (minimum): 100 m
Gradient (max): 4%
Curvature (max): 300 m

Line 1 is to serve as a city feeder system for surface rail services calling at Central railway station. Theoretical capacity of the line will be 80 000 passengers hourly, based on six-car trainsets operating on a 90-seconds headway.

Line 2 is designed as a basic link-up system between Line 1 and the projected light rail line which will operate transit services to the crowded northern suburbs of the city.

For the future Rio de Janeiro transit authorities are studying a three-point programme:
1. to extend Line 1 by a 7.2 km extension from Botafogo and NS da Paz using shield drive and cut-and-cover techniques;
2. construction of a light rail Line 2 between Niteroi and Alcantra—a distance of about 17.41 km; estimated cost is Crs 778.6 million;
3. to extend the conventional Metro Line 2 between Estacio de Sa and Castelo.

Under a programme first drawn up in 1968 it is hoped that the final city rapid transit system will total 67 km.

Technical Data:
Gauge: 1.6 km
Projected new lines (in construction): 12.8 km
(in design): 54.2 km
Number of lines: 1
Number of stations (total): 22
(in tunnel): 22
Average distance between stations: 860 m
Stations:
platform length (minimum): 136 m
Gradient (max): 4%
Curvature (max): 500 m

remains of archeological importance. The line's infrastructure has been completed from Termini eastward to Ostaria del Curato *(10.3 km)* and from Termini westward to Piazzale Flamingo *(2.2 km)*. Line A, when complete, will extend from Via Ottaviano in the west for some 9 miles *(15 km)* to Ostaria del Curato.

The existing Metro serves a less populated area than will the proposed new lines. It was planned in connection with the World Exhibition which was to have been held in the Italian capital in 1942. The work was sus-

---

(height): 3.05 m
Passenger capacity
per car (total): 66
(seated): 28
Motors per car: 2
Rating: 60 hp
Train composition (minimum): 2
(max): 6
Acceleration (max): 1.3
Brakes (type): Rheostatic
Body material: Steel
Weight (tonnes) Motocar: 11.34

Traffic Data:
Train headways
design: 1.5 minutes
existing: 2 minutes under test

Speed (average commercial): 35 km/h
Electric system: Third rail; 750 V

Rolling Stock:

Car type (year introduced):	Proposed	Type Ecs Production
Number of units:	8	50
Car dimensions (length):	15.84 m	19.21 m
(width):	2.90 m	2.71 m
(height):	3.70	3.70
Passenger capacity		
per car (total):	192	220
(seated):	44	42
Motors per car:	4	4
Rating:	84 kWh	84 kWh
Train composition (minimum): 3		
(max): 6		
Acceleration (max):	1.0	1.15
Deceleration (emergency):	1.2	1.2
Brakes (type): Rheostatic/Electro pneumatic		
Body material: Steel		
Weight (tonnes) Motorcar:	23.0	32.5

Traffic Data:
Trains/track/hour: 40 (planned)
Train capacity (passengers): 1 000
Total passengers/track/hour (peak): 40 000 (planned)
Train headways
design: 1.5 minutes
existing: 3 minutes

Speed (average commercial): 34 km/h
Electric system: Third rail; 750 V
Type of rails: 56.9 kg/m
Welded joints: Yes

Rolling Stock:

Car type (year introduced):	Proposed (motorcars)	Proposed (trailers)
Car dimensions (length):	21.75 m	21.75 m
(width):	3.17 m	3.17 m
(height):	3.65 m	3.65 m
Passenger capacity		
per car (total):	349	360
(seated):	61	70
Motors per car:	4	4
Rating:	135 kWh	135 kWh
Train composition (minimum): 3		
(max): 8		
Acceleration (max):	1.35	1.35
Deceleration (emergency):	1.5	1.5
Brakes (type): Rheostatic		
Body material: Aluminium		
Weight (tonnes) Motorcar:	42.8	33.9

Traffic Data:
Trains/track/hour: 40 (planned)
Train capacity (passengers): 2 100 (planned)
Total passengers/track/hour (peak): 80 000 (planned)
Train headways
design: 1.5 minutes
Passengers carried (weekday): 1 593 000 (planned)
(annually): 496 000 000 (planned)
Average journey length: 4.2 km (estimated)
Vehicle-km operated annually: 36 000 000 (planned)

pended during World War II and resumed soon afterwards. The whole line was opened to public traffic on 10 February 1955. The Metro was built wholly at State expense, but is at present being operated (with its own rolling stock) by STEFER, a private company also operating the Rome-Ostia line, over whose tracks some Metro trains operate via a connection at Magliana.

Route length: 6.8 miles *(11.03 km)*, including 3.7 miles *(6.1 km)* in tunnel.
Number of lines: 1 (radial); double track.

Traffic Data:
Trains/track/hour: 12
Train capacity (passengers): 960
Total passengers/track/hour (peak): 11 520
Train headways
existing: 5 minutes
Passengers carried (weekday): 38 000
(annually): 9 500 000

Number of stations served: 11.
Average station spacing: 0.6 miles *(1.1 km)*.
Passengers per annum: 25 300 000.
Passengers per annum on whole Rome Public Transport (including buses, trams, trolley buses): 718 177 700.
Average length of journey: 3.9 miles *(6.2 km)*.
Number of cars per train: 6 (Termini-Lido); 3 (Termini-Laurentina).
Estimated capacity per car: 240 (including 48 seated).
Track gauge: 4 ft 8½ in *(1.435 m)*.
Weight and type of rails: 93.8 lb/yd *(46.5 kg/m)*, flat-bottomed.
Minimum radius of curves: 640 ft *(195 m)*.
Max gradient: 1 in 28.6 *(3.5%)*.
Type of tunnel: Double-track, elliptical tunnel, 26 ft 4 in *(8.02 m)* wide and 18 ft 1 in *(5.5 m)* high from rail level.
Method and voltage of current supply: Overhead wire; 1 500 V dc There are four sub-stations, drawing their power from the public electricity supply.
Rolling Stock:

Car type:	1954	1956
Number of units	18	22
Car dimensions (length):	19.10 m	19.10 m
(width):	3.04 m	3.04 m
(height):	3.61 m	3.61 m
Total floor area (m^2):	57	57
Doors per side;	4	4
Door (width):	1.25 m	1.25 m
Passages per side:	8	8
Passengers		
per car: (total):	243	247
(seated):	48	52
Motors per car:	4	4
Motor rating:	117 kWh	117 kWh
	161 hp	161 hp
Power per train		
(minimum):	1 404	1 404
(max):	1 404	1 404
Acceleration (max):	—	1.25
Deceleration		
(normal service):	—	0.84
Speed (max):	100	—
Bogie truck rigid base:	2.8	—
Distance between bogie Pivot:	11.0	—

Brakes (type): Rheostatic/Electro-magnetic
Equipment used:

speed recorders		
dead man control	Yes	Yes
air conditioning		
cushion seats		
doors other than sliding type		

Body material: Aluminium
Weight-empty (tons): 40.5
Tare/floor area (kg/m^2): 711
Tare/length (kg/m): 2 120
Tare/passenger (kg/pass): 167

Signalling: Automatic block, with track circuiting. Cab signalling is contemplated, with a signalling capacity of 40 trains per hour.

Station layout: Stations have side platforms. Some ticket offices are underground, others on the surface.

ROTTERDAM

Authority:
Rotterdam Electric Tramways
Kleiweg 244, Rotterdam-12, Netherlands.

General: The Rotterdam Metro follows a main traffic route connecting southern dock and residental areas with the city centre north of the River Maas. The Metro was 8 years in building, from 1960 to its opening for traffic in February 1968. After a settling down period following its opening, the line appears to have attracted considerable regular patronage, carrying about the same passenger load per mile of route as the Paris Metro.

It connects at Central station with the Netherlands Railways, and along the Metro route with more than 30 bus and tram routes, including an express tram route. South-west the line has been extended from Slinge to Hoogvliet.

The Metro's relatively long construction period was due to the complexities of projecting a railway under a wide river, and building it partly within a city that lies below river level. Prefabricated tunnel sections, built in excavated dry dock and excavated trenches, were sealed, the dock or trench flooded, and the sections floated wholly or partially submerged to their respective sites and sunk into position.

Construction work is underway to add a new 13-km centre-east city line (5-km in tunnel) by 1981. An 0.6-km link between the line is now in operation and the new city line is completed. Under study are two possible extensions: a 1.5-km underground extension to the existing line, and a new branchline to Marconiplein (1 km).

Tickets are available covering Metro, bus and tram journeys.

Operative route length: Approx 10.5 miles *(17 km)* of which 2.7 miles *(5.3 km)* is on viaduct, 3 km underground or underwater tunnel.
Number of lines: 1 transverse, double track.
Number of stations served: 12.
Passengers per annum: 34 million.
Passengers per annum on the whole Rotterdam public transport system, including buses, trams and Metro, (all operated by RET): 152 millions.
Number of coach-units per train: 4 (articulated) maximum.
Estimated capacity per articulated unit: 290 passengers, included 80 seated.
Max number of trains per hour: 20 in each direction.
Line capacity: 35 000 passengers per hour.
Track gauge: 4 ft 8½ in *(1.435 m)*.
Track detail: Welded rail is fixed by spring clamps direct on to longitudinal concrete supports. There are no cross-ties.
Minimum radius of curves: 650 ft 6 in *(192.7 m)*.
Max gradient: 1 in 26.
Type of tunnel and viaduct: Rectangular twin-track underground tunnel with supporting web, 32 ft 2 in by 18 ft 4½ in externally, lies at maximum depth of 31 ft 6 in (underwater tunnel's maximum depth is 58 ft 1 in). The viaduct, carrying tracks approximately 30 ft above ground, is basically longitudinal concrete beams resting on recessed transverse beams, carried on single piers at 150 ft intervals.
Current supply: Third rail underside contact, 750 V dc, rectified from 10 000 V main supply through 7 sub-stations.
Rolling Stock: Number of coach-units owned: 71. The articulated units 95 ft 3 in long overall and 8 ft 9⅝ in wide, rest on three bogies, each of the unit's six axles being motored. Braking is electro-dynamic with electro-pneumatic disc wheel brakes.
Signalling: A visual signals system in the driving cab operates under Automatic Train Control from the control centre at Hilledijk car depot.
Station lay-out: Mostly side platforms, 393 ft 8 in *(120 m)* long, equipped with close-circuit television for surveillance. Below-ground concourses at underground stations and intermediate level concourses at elevated stations are reached by escalators, further escalators at latter stations rising to platform levels.

SAN FRANCISCO

Authority:
Bay Area Rapid Transit District
800 Madison St, Oakland, Cal 94607, USA
Telephone: 465 4100

Type of system: Full-metro.

BART construction officially began on June 19, 1964, with ground-breaking ceremonies for the 4.4-mile Diablo Test Track between Concord and Walnut Creek in Contra Costa County. Setting off the first charge of dynamite was President Lyndon Johnson, who declared to a large assembly, "Those who believe the frontiers of America are closed should be here today." Completed 10 months later, the test track was used to develop and evaluate new and sophisticated design concepts for BART's transit cars and automatic train control system.

In charge of construction management, overall design of system facilities and equipment, and monitoring of BART's major contractors were the District's General Engineering consultants, Parsons-Brinckerhoff-Tudor-Bechtel, or most commonly known as "PB-T-B." A joint venture enterprise formed to manage all technical, as well as construction aspects of the BART project, PB-T-B was comprised of three well known engineering consultant firms: Parsons-Brinckerhoff-Quade & Douglas of New York (who had done the original BART transportation plan); Tudor Engineering Company of San Francisco; and Bechtel Corporation of San Francisco.

Through this joint venture, the firms supplied (or recruited from the US and abroad) the most impressive array of engineering talent ever assembled for a single public works project. The basis of the joint venture concept was that engineering specialists could be supplied as needed, moving on to other projects when their respective BART assignments were completed. This was considered less costly and more permanent than building up a large District staff.

Construction began on the Oakland subway in January, 1966. November of that year saw the first of 57 giant steel and concrete sections of the 3.8-mile transbay tube lowered to the bottom of the Bay by a small navy of construction barges and boats.

The 3.2-mile bore through the hard rock of the Berkeley hills was completed in February, 1967, after 466 work days, to become the fourth longest vehicular tunnel in the US.

In July, 1967, work began on the Market Street subway and stations. Carried out 80-100 ft below heavy downtown traffic, against the combined pressure of mud and Bay water, the work required one of the greatest concentrations of tunneling crews and equipment in construction history. Construction of the giant five-story-high stations beneath Market Street, and the tunnels themselves, was accomplished under extremely difficult conditions imposed by the high water table in down-town San Francisco, plus an incredible maze of underground utilities installed over the last 100 years. The first tunneling in the western US done entirely under compressed air conditions, the project produced a succession of "firsts" in constructing the subway and stations in a difficult mud and water environment.

The BART construction effort reached its peak in 1969 with a contractor force of 5,000 working on the San Francisco subway and other parts of the system, earning a weekly payroll of more than $1 million.

The final tunnel bore was "holed through" into the west end of the Montgomery Street Station on 27 January 1971. It marked the completion of tunneling work in the huge, two-level Market Street subway and climaxed six years of tunneling underground.

Tunneling under compressed air required a special medical center with equipment specialists for close monitoring of the "sandhog" construction force. Despite the complex problems of sandhogging, the BART project was completed with one of the best safety records in heavy construction. Its overall accident rate of one per 28.13 million man hours worked was 25-30 per cent below the norm, and there were no fatalities from the sandhog operation.

Meanwhile, a truly great chapter was written in the history of civil engineering with the completion of the transbay tube structure in August, 1969. Constructed in 57 sections, and reposing on the Bay floor as deep as 135 ft beneath the surface, the remarkable $180 million structure took six years of soil and seismic studies to design, and less than three years to construct. Before it was closed to visitors for installation of tracks and electrification, many thousands of adventurous people had walked, jogged, and bicycled through the tube. It received a dozen major engineering awards and rapidly became famous, seeming to capture the imagination of visitors from all over the world.

The San Francisco line between Montgomery Street and Daly City stations was opened for revenue service on 5 November 1973. Service would remain a shuttle operation on that eight-mile, eight-station line, however, until the District could obtain State approval of its operating procedures to open the seven-and-a-half mile transbay line. Daily patronage (which had quickly recovered to 35 000 after the summer strike) doubled with San Francisco service. Four trains were operating on the line, in addition to the 18 trains on the three East Bay lines. Train lengths ranged from five to seven cars.

In technical areas, meanwhile, major programmes were going forward to improve the overall reliability of the vehicle fleet and also improve margins of train safety under automatic train operation, as desired by both the District and the California Public Utilities Commission (CPUC). Equipment modifications were keyed to an analysis of the system's technical problems by a State-appointed three-man panel of electronic experts, who reported their recommendations to the State Senate Public Utilities and Corporations Committee early in 1973.

In December, Westinghouse was directed to install a new train detection system, called SOR (for Sequential Occupancy Release), as an added safety back-up to the basis ATC detection system. After careful analysis, engineers with the CPUC, the District and its engineering consultants, agreed that a back-up detection system would become desirable when train headways were reduced below five minutes (or approximately one-station separation) as they eventually would have to be to provide a high level of service.

Thus, as the District moved into 1974, its immediate goal was the startup of transbay service—the only segment not yet in operation, but the most vital link in the 71-mile system.

Early 1974 was marked by a severe gasoline shortage in the Bay Area, which boosted daily system patronage from 70 000-plus to more than 80 000 for a two-month period. Patronage then settled back to the 70 000 level. The eight San Francisco stations were shut down from 11-15 March by BART management owing to picketing by San Francisco municipal employees as part of a city-wide strike.

But 1974 was to see more change and conflict within the District. Its continued operation threatened by a spiralling budget deficit, BART called on State legislators to provide an operating subsidy as the only means of budgeting a widening cost-revenue gap without unreasonably raising fares and lowering service levels. Although rising deficits were what the whole transit industry was experiencing, BART's unique founding legislation required it to operate strictly on fare revenue. Solvency through the fare box appeared increasingly remote. The Director of Finance warned that, without a direct subsidy, the District would be insolvent by the coming November. The system might have to be shut down as early as September to conserve funds needed to pay its bills. General Manager B. R. Stokes and other officials called for a temporary extension of the half-cent sales tax authorised in 1969 to complete construction of the system. The tax was seen as a temporary means of meeting the unfunded deficit until the legislature could identify and enact more permanent sources of an operating subsidy.

In repsonse, Senator James Mills (D. San Diego) introduced SB1966 extending the sales tax for two years as a temporary operating subsidy. The bill subsequently became State law in September.

On 30 June, Governor Ronald Reagan signed into law AB3043, which established voting districts from which a nine-man BART Board of Directors would be popularly elected for the first time in November, 1974 supplanting the long-standing 12-man appointive Board. The nine voting districts were marked out on the criteria of equal population, community of interests, and "geographical cohesiveness".

Also on 30 June, the resignation of General Manager B. R. Stokes became effective. Stokes, who had become a controversial figure among the BART Directors, was succeeded by Acting General Manager Lawrence D. Dahms until the incoming elective Board could make a permanent appointment to the post. Meanwhile, the major effort toward transbay service continued. By July, one-station separation in train operations had been accomplished system-wide. This was the vital step toward transbay operation, as the San Francisco line had to handle trains on closer headways due to the convergence of two East Bay lines through the tube.

On Monday, 16 September—passenger-bearing BART trains began travelling at 80 mph through the tube. Opening at the same time was the Oakland West Station, at the tube's eastern end, leaving only the Embarcadero Station to open in mid-1976. The Monday opening was preceded on Saturday by appropriate ceremonies and introductory train rides through the tube for the public.

Patronage, which had been 73 000 prior to opening of the tube, jumped to 118 000 within the first week. The number of trains operating increased from 22 to 30. Having linked its East Bay and West Bay lines, the District's next objective was to improve the reliability of both the cars and the train control system. Once this was accomplished, the District could address the question of extending service hours to nights and weekends—an issue of increasing concern to the public.

As a District marketing analyst has stated, "BART has, beyond a doubt, demonstrated that a strong demand for rapid transit exists in the Bay Area".

"BART's technical and financial problems—and certainly its limited service hours—have thus far kept it from achieving full ridership potential. Despite this, we know from surveys that at least 52 per cent of our patrons have left their automobiles to ride BART".

"Besides the quality of BART's own service", the analyst emphasised, "an important factor in its ridership will be how well feeder bus service can be improved to all BART stations".

The District has worked out BART-to-bus transfer systems with both ac Transit (which operates buses in the East Bay) and the San Francisco Municipal Railway (which operates buses in that city). The District is also working to help get local bus service to all on-line communities where none yet exists.

On 2 December, BART activated five express feeder bus routes to outlying communities in the District which are not directly served by the train system. The bus lines are operated by ac Transit under contract to BART.

On 4 December, the nine men comprising the first elective Board of Directors in the history of the District were formally installed. By lot, some were installed for initial two-year terms, and others for regular four-year terms, in order to stagger subsequent four-year terms of office. Thus, BART entered 1975 with the full system in revenue operation and governed by a Board elected directly by the District residents.

Technical Data:
Gauge: 1.676 m
Route length: 121 km
In tunnel: 32.5 km
Number of lines: 1
Number of stations (total): 34
(in tunnel): 14
Average distance between stations: 3.7 km
Stations:
platform length (minimum): 244 m
Gradient (max): 4%
Curvature (max): 150 m
Speed (design max): 128 km/h
(average commercial): 80 km/h
Electric system: Third rail; 1 000 V

Rolling Stock:

Car type:	1969A	1969B
Units:	150	100
Car dimensions (length):	22.84 m	21.36 m
(width):	3.20 m	3.20 m
(height):	3.20 m	3.20 m
Total floor area (m²):	71.3	66.6
Doors per side:	2	2
Door (width):	1.37 m	1.37 m
Passages per side:	4	4
Passengers		
per car: (total):	216	228
(seated):	72	72
Motors per car:	4	4
Motor rating:	112 kWh	112 kWh
	150 hp	150 hp
Power per train:		
(minimum):	896	896
(max):	4 480	4 480
Acceleration (max):	1.34	1.34
Deceleration:		
(normal service):	1.34	1.34
(emergency):	1.34	1.34
Speed (max):	80	80
Bogie truck rigid base:	2.13	2.13
Distance between bogie pivot:	15.2	15.2
Brakes (type): Rheostatic/Electro-magnetic		
Equipment used:		
speed recorders		
dead man control		
air conditioning	Yes	Yes
cushion seats	Yes	Yes
doors, other than sliding type		
Body material: Aluminium		
Weight-empty (tons):	25.6	25.0
Tare/floor area (kg/m²):	359	375
Tare/length (kg/m):	1 121	1 170
Tare/passenger (kg/pass):	119	110

The initial contract for the production and delivery of the revolutionary BART electric transit car was signed with Rohr Industries, Inc, of Chula Vista, California, in July, 1969. The contract called for delivery of 250 cars, with the first 10 vehicles to serve as test prototypes. The first prototype car was delivered at the Hayward Shop in August, 1970. The prototype cars were run many thousands of miles day and night over the next 16 months to ferret out as many design and manufacturing problems as possible before Rohr began full-scale work on the production cars.

The taxpayers' suits which literally halted the project before it could begin cost the District $12 million in lost time. Moreover, it presaged a decade of many such costly delays. These delays, plus improvements or changes made to the system, substantially increased the cost, or value, of the system. But the largest cost-increasing factor was, of course, inflation.

Unhappily, with the heavy construction years for BART in the 1960's came 7 per cent average annual inflation—more than double the rate anticipated by economists and allowed for in the project cost estimates. In this climate, and before substantial federal grants were available, BART's financial history was a troubled one.

While delay and inflation factors were sapping capital reserves, pressures from public and governmental groups resulted in the relocation of 15 miles of right-of-way and 15 stations, as well as a general upgrading of station plans. Stations were also substantially altered after construction to include elevators and other facilities for the handicapped and elderly at an added cost of $10 million. The cost of the transbay tube rose to $180 million from the originally estimated $133 million.

Prime examples of how public pressures escalated the cost of the system are the Berkeley subway and the Ashby Station. After originally approving a combination aerial and subway line through Berkeley, that city later came to oppose the plan in favour of a subway-only line, which was much more expensive. The new plan necessitated redesign of the Ashby Station from an aerial to a subway facility. Extensive controversy and hearings ensued for the next two and a half years, finally to be resolved by Berkeley residents voting to tax themselves additionally to finance the changes they wanted. Next, a Berkeley City Councilman filed a successful suit to redesign the Ashby Station, a second time, asserting the use of skylights in the original plans was not a true subway design.

The Berkeley situation resulted in a two and a half year delay in subway construction, a 17-month delay in starting Ashby Station construction, and combined increased costs of $18 million.

During 1966 it became clear the District would fall $150 million short of funds to complete the system. The only apparent solutions were a fresh infusion of more funds, or a drastic scaling-down of system track miles to fit the original budget. Major construction contracts were rewritten and readvertised in anticipation of the threatened cutbacks.

But, BART Directors and management stood firm during the crisis, refusing to compromise the planned 71.5-mile system until every possible alternative could be explored. Finally, in April, 1969, after three years of debate, the State Legislature granted the District's request for aid by authorising the levying of half-cent sales tax in the BART counties. The needed $150 million thus came from the sale of bonds pledged against the sales tax revenues.

With funds to complete the system assured, construction contracts were returned to their original scope and work quickly reached peak level in 1969. But three years of financial uncertainty had taken their toll on work schedules. The shortage of funds had also held up ordering the transit cars. When the first 250 cars were finally ordered from low bidder Rohr Industries, Inc, of Chula Vista, California, the cost was $80 million—$8 million more than the original cost estimate for the entire 450-car fleet. (Subsequently, 200 more transit cars were ordered for another $80 million. Delivery of the total 450-car fleet was completed by July 30, 1975).

On the bright side, federal monies began flowing into the project at an increasing rate, making possible a wide range of improvements over the original system plans. BART's widely-known "linear park", for example, was constructed under the aerial right-of-way through Albany and El Cerrito to demonstrate how function could combine with aesthetics to enhance community environments. A $7.5 million programme for systemwide landscaping and right-of-way beautification was partly funded by several of the largest federal grants ever made for this purpose. Of the $160 million base cost of BART's 450-car fleet, 64 per cent was funded by federal grants.

Included in the construction contract for the lower Market Street subway, awarded in the busy year of 1969, was the basic "box" structure for the Embarcadero Station. Not in the original plans, the system's 34th station was added as a result of increasing development of the lower Market Street area. Station funding was co-operative, with the San Francisco business community raising money for design, and BART spending $25 million on construction. (Of the latter figure, $16 million was raised by curtailing construction of the Muni subway at the west portal station instead of St. Francis Circle as originally planned.) The station, opened in mid-1976, is certain to become another vital transportation hub in down-town San Francisco. It will serve as the turnaround terminal for the Muni streetcar subway, as well as the first BART train stop west of the transbay tube.

A total of $315 million has been received to date in federal capital grants. While these monies are an important factor in upgrading the system from original plans, they nonetheless total only 20 per cent of the total $1 600 million investment in the system. If BART were being built today, 80 per cent of its capital costs could be federally funded under the US Urban Mass Transportation Assistance Act of 1974.

SAN JUAN

Authority:
Department of Transport and Public Works
San Juan, Puerto Rico

Type of system: Proposed metro.

General: Planning for a rapid transit system in Puerto Rico's capital, San Juan, began in 1967 when an in-depth investigation of future transport needs and land use plans was considered.

A number of studies have been carried out since. The city's Department of Transportation and Public Works is now studying a number of alternatives which include: heavy rail, light rail, extended bus system.

The heavy rail alternative is based on a two-line system covering the Metropolitan area. A north-south (20 km line with 17 stations) would intersect an east-west line (34.7 km with 19 stations) and a bus feeder service provided at all 36 stations.

The complete system could be in operation by 1987 at an estimated cost of $US 810.2 million.

SANTIAGO

Authority:
Ministry of Works
Morande 71, Santiago, Chile

Type of system: Full-metro (rubber-tyred).

General: Santiago, Chilean capital with a population exceeding two millions, is now operating the first section of Line 1 of an eventual 5-line Metro system (La Red de Transporte Colectivo Independiento o Metro de Santiago). The decision to construct a Metro is welcomed by city authorities, who estimate that average vehicle speeds in the Santiago central area are down to 7½ mph *(12 km/h)* during busy periods owing to street congestion.

The total length of the proposed 5-line system will be approximately 37 miles *(59.3 km)*, consisting of Line 1, 14.5 km; Line 2, 11.5 km; Line 3, 8.3 km; Line 4, 17.0 km; Line 5, 8.0 km. The main characteristic of the system is its division into surban and suburban portions, using two different types of rolling stock. The urban portion will carry fast and frequent services over a network of 1.435 m gauge track. The suburban portion will carry less frequent services, linking existing State Railway stations but running on independent tracks; which will be of the same wide gauge *(1.676 m)* as the State Railways. The passenger, however, will not be affected by the Metro's two physical divisions as he will be offered interchange facilities over the whole system. The main features of the east-west Line 1 are as follows: double tracks in vaulted reinforced concrete tunnel, approx 7-9 m below street level, throughout, (except the westernmost portion which temporarily is in open cut); straight tunnels are 32.5 m section (slightly larger at curves).

Technical Data:
Gauge: 1.995 m/1.435 m
Projected new lines (in construction): 26.3 km (20.5 km in tunnel)
(in design): 31.2 km
Number of lines: 1/5
Number of stations (total): 35
(in tunnel): 26
Average distance between stations: 740 m
Stations:
platform length (minimum): 135 m
Gradient (max): 4.5%
Curvature (max): 260 m
Speed (design max): 80 km/h
(average commercial): 30 km/h
Electric system: 2 side guide bars

Rolling Stock:
Car type: Motocars
Units: 137 (ordered)
Car dimensions (length): 17.18 m
(width): 2.60 m
(height): 3.62 m
Total floor area (m²): 43.6
Doors per side: 4
Doors (width): 1.3 m
Passages per side: 8
Passengers
per car (total): 169

(seated): 38
Motors per car: 2
Motor rating: 120 kWh; 165 hp
Power per train

(minimum): 720
(max): 720
Distance between bogie pivot: 11.0
Brakes (type): Rheostatic

Weight-empty (tons): 25
Tare/length (kg/m): 1 455
Tare/passenger (kg/pass): 148

SÃO PAULO

Authority:
Companhia Do Metropolitano de São Paulo
Rua Augusta 1626, São Paulo, Brazil.

Type of system: Full-metro

General: Construction work under way since 1969 on a Metro system for São Paulo, had by 1974 reached completion of the entire 17.2 km which went into revenue service in September 1975. São Paulo has been described as the most rapidly growing, eighth city in the world. Whilst Brazilia is the future administration capital city of Brazil, São Paulo has attracted the country's greatest concentration of industry and commerce and is still doing so. Its population of nearly 6 millions (over 7 millions in Greater São Paulo) is expected to increase to 10 millions by 1980, and 15 millions by the year 2000.

To provide mass urban transit commensurate with a city of this size and potential, it aims to have a conventional Metro system of four lines, totalling 66.2 km, to which extensions may later be made. Line 1, cross-city, links the northern suburb of Santana with Jabaquara in the south, with a branch to Moema, totals 21 km. Line 2, crossing the city east-westward from Vila Maria for 13.3 km to Casa Verde; Line 3, crossing the city from the south-west to the south-east, from Pinheiros to Via Anchieta, branch to Vila Bertioga (total 23.8 km), and Line 4, running from Madalena in the north-west, southeast for 8 km to join Line 1 at Paraiso, will complete the primary network. The outer stretches of Line 1 leading to Santana and Meoma is at elevated level. Nearly all the remainder of this line, that is the main north-south line to Jabaquara, is in cut and cover tunnel. The exceptions are short inner stretches of the main and branch lines totalling 920 m, which are in driven tunnel excavated by the shield method. In cut and cover the tunnels are double-tracked, 29 ft 10 in (9.1 m) wide and 11 ft 6 in (3.5 m) high. The single-track driven tunnel is 18 ft 8 in (5.7 m) in diameter. These larger than normal dimensions allow for more generously proportioned rolling stock running on wide gauge track, in this case 5 ft 3 in (1.60 m).

Line 2. east-west, will link all districts between Itaquera and Lapa. The east segment of this line begins at Sé Station, then crosses Parque Dom Pedro II, passes over the railway tracks at Brás Station, and then continues parallel to the railway line until Artur Alvim in the Itaquera District, after crossing the districts Brás, Belezinho, Tatuapé, Vila Matilde, Vila Guilhermina

and Patriarca. After Artur Alvim the Line will leave the railway and run towards the yard in Itaquera.
The east segment will be constructed prevailingly on surface, with some minor sections in aerial structure or underground. Between Arouche and Sé it will be in tunnels to be bored by the shield method. From Arouche Square, already at the west side, the Line will follow to the districts Santa Cecilia, Pacaembu, Perdizes, Pompéia up to Lapa.
Line 2, east-west, will form with Line 1 north-south, a large cross, the centre of which will be located at Sé Station. This station is approximately 12 000 m² and four levels. The lowest floor, at 21 m depth, is designed for Line 1, north-south; the level immediately above serves Line 2, east-west and the remaining ones are for the distribution and circulation of passengers. With the unification of Sé and Clóvis Bevilaqua squares, an area is planned for this location, totalling some 45 000 m².
Work on civil construction at Sé, the main station of Line 2, east-west, and which provides connection with Line 1, continued during 1975, with a work force of over 1 000 men. Structure work of Sé Station is partially complete and has already reached its various under ground levels.
With the erection of the first job-site in the Anhangabaú Valley near Ladeira de Memória, in March 1975, work was started for the installation of the shaft for the shield equipment, which will bore the tunnels between Arouche and Sé Squares. Buildings already expropriated were demolished to enlarge the Anhangabaú Valley job-site. Utilities have been relocated in the Valley, ground water has been lowered and the shaft for the shield equipment is complete. The first such equipment has been installed and will bore the tunnel towards Arouche Square.
Real estate expropriation procedures relating to downtown area between Anhangabau and Sé, required for the development of work have been concluded and are under way with respect to remaining sections of the line towards Itaquera.
Late in December 1975 a contract was awarded for the first work phase of the Yard and Repair Shops of Line 2, east-west, which will be located in a 780 000 m² area, including an area reserved for Metrô's future Technological Training Center. In size and capacity, the Yard of Line 2 will be three times as large as that of Line 1, north-south. The Itaquera yard will have a road access system through a large avenue. To provide possibility for future extension of Line 2, farther to east towards Moji das Cruzes, the location chosen is parallel to the Metró line and not at its end.

Technical Data:
Gauge: 1.60 m
Route length: 17.2 km
In tunnel: 17.2 km
Projected new lines (in construction): 4.2 km
(in design): 44.8 km
Number of lines: 1
Number of stations (total): 23
(in tunnel): 16
Average distance between stations: 900 m
Stations:
platform length (minimum): 136 km
Gradient (max): 4%
Curvature (max): 300 m
Speed (design max): 100 km/h
(average commercial): 35 km/h
Electric system: Third rail; 750 V
Type of rails: 57 kg/m

Rolling Stock:
Number of units: 99 × 2
Car dimensions (length): 21.20 m
(width): 3.17 m
(height): 3.55 m
Total floor area (m²): 65.5
Doors per side: 4
Door (width): 1.30 m
Passages per side: 8
Passengers per car (total): 354
(seated): 34
Motors per car: 4
Motor rating: 75 kWh
103 hp
Power per train
(max): 1 800
Acceleration (max): 1.35
Deceleration
(normal service): 1.20
Bogie truck rigid base: 2.1
Distance between bogie pivot: 15.6
Brakes (type): Rheostatic
Weight-empty (tons)
(Motors): 32.4

Traffic Data:
Trains/track/hour: 40
Train capacity (passengers): 2 000
Total passengers/track/hour (peak): 80 000
Train headways existing: 1.5 minutes

SAPPORO

Authority:
Sapporo Municipal Transportation Bureau
Sapporo, Japan

History: The Sapporo Municipal Transportation Bureau embarked an improvement plan of the city transit network in 1962. The city council introduced a demand on realisation of the new rapid transit plan, and the test line of centre-guide pneumatic-tyred system and car were prepared in 1964.
The third test car, propelled by two gasoline engines, was completed in 1965.
The fourth test car, twin-coupled and propelled by electric motors, succeeded its test run in 1967.
The first line, so called Nan-boku (south-north) line, between Kita 24 Jo (North 24th Street) and Makomanai, distance of 12.625 km was prepared as one of the major projects for the 1972's Sapporo Olympic Winter Games to transport visitors, and its construction work was started on 7 February 1969. This line was opened on 16 December 1971, and a train run in 23 minutes to cover whole line.
In order to serve a densely populated area in the northern part of Sapporo city, the northern extension of Line 1 between Kits 24 Jo and Azabu-cho, distance of 2.500 km was constructed in 1977.
The construction work of Line 2, so called To-zai (east-west) line, between Shiroishi and Kotoni, distance of 10.670 km, was started in 1973, and completed in 1976.

Route length: Line 1: 12.625 km (underground 7.950 km; elevated 4.675 km)
Line 1 extension: 2.500 km (underground)
Line 2: 10.670 km (underground)
Total: 25.795 km, including 21.120 km tunnel
Number of lines: 2 transverse lines
Number of stations served: Line 1: 14, Line 1 extension: 2
Line 2: 11
Total: 27
Average station spacing: Line 1: 0.92 km, Line 1 extension: 1.10 km
Line 2: 0.97 km

Passengers per annum (1973): Line 1: 70 996 000
Average length of journey: Line 1: 3.6 km

Number of cars per train: Line 1: 6, Line 2: 8
Max number of trains per hour: Line 1: 11
Track gauge and type of rails: Line 1: pneumatic-tyred car 2.180 m in width. Centre-guide rail steel I-beam (310 × 446 mm). Running tracks paved with epoxy-resin plastics.
Line 2: pneumatic-tyred car 2.190 mm in width. Centre-guide rail steel I-beam. Running tracks paved with steel plates.
Passenger capacity
per car: Line 1: 96 and 90
Line 2: 126 and 116
Average schedule speed: Line 1: 31.6 km/h
Line 2: 38.0 km/h
Max gradient: Line 1: 4.3%
Line 2: 3.5%
Minimum radius of curve: Line 1: 205 m
Line 2: 205 m
Type of tunnel: Generally double-tracks, cut and cover tunnel, rectangular section, mostly reinforced concrete with centre supports. Under the Toyohira-river, the sections were constructed by caisson-method. Elevated section has circular aluminium shelter to avoid heavy snowfalls.
Method and voltage of current supply: Line 1: Third rail 750 V dc
Line 2: Overhead rigid body rail 1 500 V dc

Rolling Stock:
Number of cars
Line 1: 84
Line 2: 80
These cars were manufactured by the Kawasaki Heavy Industry Co Ltd. Kobe
Class 1 000: Passenger capacity 96 (44 seats, 52 standings)
90 (38 seats, 52 standings)
Length overall: 27 m
Width: 3.05 m
Height: 3.7 m
Motors per car: Four 90 kW 375 V dc
Fluorescent lighting. Cars have four sets of double,leaf sliding doors in each side.
Car Type (year introduced): 1971
Units: 56
Car dimensions (length): 27.6 m
(width): 3.08 m
(height): 3.7 m
Doors per side: 4

Door (width): 1.40 m
Passages per side: 8
Passengers per car (total): 180
(seated): 60
Motors per car: 4
Motor rating: 90 kWh
125 hp
Acceleration (max): 1.1
Deceleration (normal service: 1.1
(emergency): 1.4
Speed (max): 75
Bogie truck rigid base: 1.15
Distance between bogie pivot: 5.5
Brakes (type): E1Pn
Equipment used:
speed recorders
dead man control: Yes
air conditioning: No
cushion seats: Yes
doors other than sliding type: No
Body material: Aluminium
Weight-empty (tons): 33.0
Tare/length (kg/m): 1 100

1 Rolling stock composed of 2 car sets permanently coupled on 7 axles.

Signalling: Full Automatic Train Control (ATC) and Centralised Traffic Control (CTC) devices were installed, moreover, tyre-puncture detecting device and automatic announcement system were synchronized in Line 1, and Automatic Train Operating (ATO) system shall be introduced in Line 2.

Station layout:
Island platform stations : Line 1: 5
Line 1 extension: 1
Line 2: 5
Separate side stations: Line 1: 9, Line 1 extension 1
Line 2: 6
Platform length; Line 1 extension : 120 m (to take 8-car train)
Line 2: 170 m (to take 9-car train)

Workshops:
Line 1: There is a train depot and workshop at Jieitaimae, elevated level.
Line 2: There is a train depot and workshop at 24 Ken, underground.

SEOUL

Authority:
Seoul Metropolitan Rapid Transit Bureau
Seoul Metropolitan Government
Seoul, Korea

Type of system: Full-metro.

General: Thers has been a population explosion in Seoul, the capital city, which in 1935 housed ½ million people. In 1972 after a decade of expansion at the expense of the rural areas, the population of Seoul's metropolitan area had reached six millions, and there are now proposals for a decentralisation programme. The need for a city mass transit rail system has been met by the construction of a 10.31 km line initially, and by a proposed extensive regional network in the long term. Korean manufacture of equipment using Japanese technology, plus Japanese financial aid, are enabling features.

Future subway construction will be on a radial alignment in ten directions from the central area of Seoul, taking into consideration current transport conditions, prospective regional development, and linking with other transport facilities. Total length of the five subways to be constructed is 133 kms, of which the underground portion will be 61 kms:
in the direction of Suyuri
in the direction of Bulgwangdong
in the direction of Seoul Station
in the direction of Cheonhodong
in the direction of Gurodong
in the direction of Cheongryangri
in the direction of Jamsilri
in the direction of Yeongdong
in the direction of Yeoyido
in the direction of Yonhidong

Technical Data:
Gauge: 1.435 m
Route length: 10.31 km
In tunnel: 8.60 km
Projected new lines (in design): 18 km
Number of lines: 1
Number of stations (total): 9
(in tunnel): 9
Average distance between stations: 975 m
Stations:
platform length (minimum): 120 m
Gradient (max): 3.5%
Curvature (max): 120 m
Speed (design max): 80 km/h
(average commercial): 35 km/h
Electric system: Catenary; 1 500 V dc
Type of rails: 50 kg/m

Rolling Stock:

Car type:	Motocars	Trailers
Units:	124	62
Car dimensions (length):	20.1 m	20.1 m
(width):	3.18 m	3.18 m
(height):	3.8 m	3.8 m
Total floor area (m²):	60.5	55.2
Doors per side:	4	4
Door (width):	1.3 m	1.3 m
Passages per side:	8	8
Passengers per car: (total):	160*	148*
(seated):	54	48

Motors per car:	4	—
Motor rating:	120 kWh	
	165 hp	
Power per train		
(minimum):	1 920	—
(max):	2 880	—
Acceleration (max):	0.7	—
Deceleration		
(normal service):	1.0	—
(emergency):	1.2	—
Speed (max):	111	—
Bogie truck rigid base:	2.1	2.1
Distance between bogie		
pivot:	13.8	13.8
Brakes (type): Electro-pneumatic		
Equipment used:		
speed recorders:		
dead man control:	Yes	Yes
air conditioning:	No	No
Cushion seats:	Yes	Yes
Doors other sliding type:	No	No
Body material:	Steel	Steel
Weight-empty (tons):	43.5	34.5
Tare/Floor area (kg/m²):		
Tare/length (kg/m):	2 164	—
Tare/passenger (kg/Pass):	272	—

*peak crush load equals 360 persons

Traffic Data:
Trains/track/hour: 12
Train headways existing: 5 minutes
Passengers carried (weekday): 560 000 (1974)

STOCKHOLM

Authority:
AB Storstockholms Lokaltrafik
Tegnérgaten 2A, Stockholm, Sweden

General Manager: Ingemar Bäckström
Vice General Manager: Bengt Gustafson
Operating Manager: Karl-Erik Rapp

General: Greater Stockholm's public transport organisation has since 1971 been fully established under the administration of Storstockholms Lokaltrafik, a compay whose shares are held by the County Council and whose responsibilities include the operation of the Underground, buses, and commuter train services of the State Railways. The Stockholm T-Bana (tunnel railway) system is modern, all construction (including conversion in 1949-50 of about 1 mile of tunnel tramway south of Slussen to conventional Underground standards) having taken place since World War II. The T-Bana was built to meet the transportation needs of a fast expanding city, Stockholm having more than doubled its population since 1920.

Nearly one-half of the system is in tunnel, but construction posed problems, including underwater crossings involving new methods of tunnelling, since about one-half of the area within the boundaries of Greater Stockholm is open water. Extensions and new T-Bana lines have periodically added to the system since 1951, and the process is continuing as Stockholm's suburban areas develop. The third line was Vårberg over Vårby Gård-Masmo to Fittja was opened in October 1972, inaugurated in August 1975.

Route length: (1975): 206.5 km.
Number of lines: 3 (transverse), with branches; double track.
Number of stations served: 89.
Average station spacing: 0.43 miles *(0.7 km)* in tunnel; 0.56 miles *(0.9 km)* in open.
Passengers per annum: (1975) 175 million.
Passenger km: 1 050 million.
Max number of trains per hour: T-Bana 1, 42; T-Bana 2, 30; T-Bana 3, 9.
Max number of cars per train: 8.
Estimated capacity per car, latest type: 156 (including 48 seated).
Average schedule speed (including stops): 19.8 mph *(31 km/h)*.
Track gauge: 4 ft 8½ in *(1.435 m)*.
Weight and type of rails: 86.6 and 101.1 lb/yd *(43 and 50 kg/m)*, flat-bottomed.
Max gradient: 1 in 25 (4%).
Minimum radius of curves: 656 ft *(200 m)*.
Type of tunnel: Double track tunnel, of rectangular section, 24 ft 11 in *(7.6 m)* wide. At some points, the roof of the tunnel is as much as 49 ft 3 in *(15 m)* below ground level.
Method and voltage of current supply: Third rail; 650 V dc; sub-stations are about 1.5 km apart an are fed by alternating current at 30 000 V.
Rolling Stock (1971): Number of cars owned: 659. Details: The cars were built by the Svenska Järnvägverkstäderna of Linköping, in collaboration with ASEA. Each car has an overall length of 57 ft 1 in *(17.4 m)*, a body length of 55 ft 10 in *(17.0 m)*, and a width of 9 ft 2 in *(2.8 m)*. Each car has three double-leaf automatic sliding doors on each side, and is equipped with centre-buffer couplers. The latest types C4, C5 and C6 have rubber suspension, and have driving and guard's cab at one end only. Type C5 were built by

Hägglund Söner; Type C6 by ASJ, ASEA and Hägglund

Signalling: The signalling provides for 1½-minute train intervals, and 30-second station stops. Cab-signalling is employed, with two speed ranges, up to 9.3 and 31 mph *(15 and 50 km/h)* and a third for higher speed. Fixed lineside signals are installed only at junctions. Central Control office is linked to all trains through radio-communication.

Planned expansion of the system includes the following extensions: T-Bana 3 in the northwest, from Hallonbergen to Akalla (4 stations, length 6.2 km) and in the City from T-Centralen to Kungsträdgården (1 station, length 0.7 km) opening 1977. T-Bana 2 from Universitetet to Mörby Centrum (3 stations, length 4.2 km) opening 1978. T-Bana 3 Västra Skogen-Rinkeby, (5 stations, length 7.0 km) opening 1982-1985 and T-Bana 2 Mörby Centrum-Täby Centrum (3 stations, length 6.2 km) also opening 1982-1985.

Fare structure: As from February 1973 a common fare system operated over all undertakings controlled by the Stockholm County Council. These include underground, buses, tramways and railways within the county region. The fare system is zonal, the region being divided into 43 zones. Payment, is for travel coupons, minimally two for travel within one zone adding one coupon for each additional zone, maximum 10 for unlimited travel within a time limit. Monthly and annual tickets valid within the county region are issued and there are a number of concessional fares. For the six months ended 30 June 1975 the monthly and annual ticket held a share of 68.7 per cent, pre-sale coupons 12.6 per cent, cash-pay coupons 15.9 per cent and the concessional fares 2.8 per cent.

STUTTGART

Authority:
Stuttgarter Strassenbahnen AG
Postfach 499, 7 Stuttgart 1, German Federal Republic

General: Stuttgart, with a population of about 650 000, is engaged on projects similar to those being undertaken in Frankfurt and in other German cities. Much of Stuttgart's tramway (street-car) system will be diverted into tunnel beneath the central area, in order to relieve street congestion and to accelerate services. The work is being completed in sections. Section 1, comprising 0.75 miles *(1.2 km)* of tunnel line crossing beneath the busy road junction at Charlottenstrasse, together with an undergroundtram station, has been in operation since 1966. Section 2, 1.6 miles *(2.5 km)* of tunnel line from Charlottenstrasse south-west to

Marienplatz, became operative in September 1971, and Section 3, 0.9 miles *(1.5 km)* of tunnel line northeast from Charlottenstrasse to Neckartor, became operative in May 1972. There are six sub-surface stations. Work on Section 4, a tunnel line running north from Hauptbahnhof beneath Heilbronnerstrasse and beyond, is scheduled for completion in 1976. Stuttgart's future plans envisage altogether a total of 59 miles *(95 km)* of double-track U Bahn Line. The tunnels of "cut and cover" construction, are approx 14½ ft *(4.7 m)* high, and approx 23 ft *(7.5 m)* wide, in rectangular section. The present tramcars are equipped with pantographs for overhead power supply, and sufficient tunnel headroom has been allowed for these. The overall dimensions are also sufficient to allow for possible future adaptation for larger-profile, conventional

subway cars. The underground tramway system has been named the U Bahn.

The second project is the building of Stuttgart's S Bahn. A 6.2 km section of line is proposed to run, partly in deep-level tunnel, to connect the state railways (DB) Central Station with the south-western railway system. At two points, beneath Bahnhofsplatz (Central Station) and Stadtmitte, it will also provide interchange with the underground tramway network. This project will eventually provide an underground south-western extension for electrified suburban railway services from the north, and lessen the amount of cross-city surface traffic. Work on this project is under way, involving difficult excavation under the many tracks at Central Station, and involving also excavation beneath a canal.

SYDNEY

Authority:
Public Transport Commission of New South Wales

Head office: 11-31 York St, Sydney, Australia

General: The Public Transport Commission of NSW operates all NSW rail and government bus services and the Sydney Harbour ferry services.

The urban and suburban electrified rail system in the Sydney area includes an underground City Railway in the form of a loop that is linked with the suburban railway systems at Central and Wynyard. The length of the loop is 3½ miles *(5.6 km)* approximately three-quarters of it being underground. Four of the six stations (Town Hall, Wynyard, St James and Museum) are underground. Central is at ground level and Circular Quay is elevated and forms an open break in the

tunnel loop. The City railway is all double-track with trains operating in both directions. As with the suburban railway system the City railway is electrified with power being supplied through single overhead wiring at 1 500 V dc.

Automatic block signalling (with five aspect colour-light signals, and a system of speed signalling with electro-pneumatic train stops) is provided.

Extensions: Work is now nearing completion on the Eastern Suburbs Railway, a 10 km underground extension which will provide a rapid transit service to the densley populated eastern suburbs of Sydney. The ESR will connect with the existing metropolitan network at Erskineville and will follow a route, completely underground (except for two viaducts) via Redfern, Central, Town Hall, Martin Place, Kings Cross, Edgecliff to Bondi Junction. New underground stations are being built at all these locations except Town Hall

which is being extended to accommodate additional platforms.

The Eastern Suburbs Railway will be double-track and will use the same 1 500 V overhead wiring method as the present electric network. The line is expected to be completed in 1979.

Trains: Sydney urban and suburban electric trains comprise double-deck and single-deck rolling stock, at 30 June 1977 364 of the total of 1 195 suburban and interurban electric carriages, were double-deck and a further 230 double-deck cars are being manufactured. The Sydney suburban and Outer Metropolitan (interurban) electrified route distance is 446 km and extends West to Lithgow 154 km and North to Gosford 80 km from Sydney. On an average weekday over 1 400 'train runs' operate on this network and during one year electric trains travel over 16 million km—passenger journeys total over 500 000 each working day.

TASHKENT

Authority:
Tashkent Metropolitan Railways Authority
Tashkent, USSR

Type of system: Full-metro.

General: Tashkent, capital city of the Uzbek Soviet Socialist Republic announced plans for a new 'Metro' system in 1967. In 1973 it had a population of 1 504 000, and as the centre of the Tashkent region. The project for a metropolitan railway for Tashkent was begun in 1968. The first line, now completed, is transverse, from the south-west to the city centre and then to the north-east to serve a region of mass hous-ing construction. It was 12.5 miles (20.2 km) of route with 14 stations and runs from Dustlik in the south-west to Lenin Square in central Tashkent.

Technical Data:
Gauge: 1.524 m
Route length: 20.1 km
  (in design): 28 km
Number of lines: 1
Number of stations (total): 14
Average distance between stations: 1.5 km
Stations:
  platform length (minimum): 100 m
Gradient (max): 4.0%
Speed (deign max): 90

Electric system: 825 V

Rolling Stock:
Car type: proposed
Car dimensions (length): 19.2 m
  (width): 2.7 m
Doors per side: 4
Passages per side: 8
Passengers
  per car: (total): 170
  (seated): 44
Motors per car: 4
Motor rating: 66 kWh
Brakes (type): Rheostatic

TBILISI

Authority:
Tbilisski Metropolitena
Tbilisi, USSR

Type of system: Full-metro.

General: Tbilisi is the capital of the Georgian republic, with a population in 1973 of 946 000. Public transport in Tbilisi includes trains, buses and trolleybuses. In 1946 design work for an underground railway was carried out by the Caucasus Design and Survey Institute, for an underground railway that would provide means of mass rapid transit between the city's large industrial and residential areas and its centre. The lines' geography was dictated by the lay-out of Tbilisi along the River Kura, with the industrial and residential areas at either end. The planned lay-out of the railway system centres on the city's main throughfare, Rustaveli Prospekt.
Construction of tunnels, and excavation for station structures, was undertaken from the surface. Both solid rock and ground impregnated with water from mineral springs were encountered, the latter neces-sitating heavy machinery to pump out subsoil waters. The first 3.9 mile (6.3 km) section of the underground came into operation in 1966. The line then had six stations, two of which, Didube and Electrodepovskaya were surface stations. In 1967 the line was extended eastwards 2.4 miles (3.9 km) to 300 Aragvintsev and further extended in 1971 for 1.5 miles (2.4 km) to Samgory. A further westward extension with two more stations is under construction.
Planned for the second construction phase is a ring line with four stations; Saburtalo, Vokzalnaya, Rustaveli. The name for the fourth station has not yet been decided.

Technical Data:
Gauge: 1.524 m
Route length: 12.9 km
In tunnel: 11.4 km
Projected new lines (in construction): 6.0 km
Number of lines: 1
Number of stations (total): 11
  (in tunnel): 9
Average distance between stations: 1.17 km
Speed (average commercial): 38.1 km/h

Electric system: Third rail; 825 V

Rolling Stock:
Car type: E-1960
Car dimensions: (length): 18.8 m
  (width): 2.70 m
  (height): 3.70 m
Doors per side: 4
Door (width): 1.28 m
Passages per side: 8
Passengers
  per car: (total): 170
  (seated): 40
Motors per car: 4
Motor rating: 68 kWh (94 hp)
Power per train:
  (max): 816
Brakes (type): Rheostatic/Electro-pneumatic

Traffic Data:
Passengers carried (weekday): 256 000
  (annually): 68 000 000
Average journey length: 3.7 km
Vehicle-km operated annually: 9 300 000

TOKYO

The population of the Tokyo Metropolitan Area and of the Metropolitan Traffic Zone (50 km radius of Tokyo Station) has increased dramatically in recent years. The traffic Zone area now has a population of approximately 25 million. The daily average of commuters, in 1955 amounting to 467 000, is today nearing 2 million.
The commercial development in central Tokyo, and population growth in suburban areas has resulted in exceptional increases in public transport commuter traffic. However, private car use has also increased and a greatly expanded underground network is required, to handle future commuter traffic which it is hoped will include most of the present day car commuters.
In addition to the JNR main and suburban lines there are 7 private railways feeding Tokyo. Until recent years none of these private lines' services entered the city centre almost all of them terminating on the JNR loop line to which many passengers transferred.
The basis of the underground network plan now being implemented is to improve commuter travel conditions by inter-working the converging suburban trains over the underground tracks, to enable them to discharge and pick up their passengers at stations in the central area of the city. Subway trains are also at times reciprocally run over suburban tracks; and additionally, two of the surface railways are being projected in deep level tunnels to the city centre. These measures will relieve pressure on the heavily loaded JNR loop line.
The present underground railway rapid transit network comprises 7 lines of which 5 (Nos. 2, 3, 4, 5 and 9) are operated by the Teito Rapid Transit Authority (TRTA) and 2 (Nos. 1 and 6) by the Transportation Bureau of the Tokyo Metropolitan Government (TBTMG).
Lines recently completed include 20.7 km of Line 8 and 10.7 km of Line 11 completed by TRTA in 1975. 7.6 km of Line 9 (presently partly operative) also by TRTA in 1974; and 14.5 km of Line 10 completed by TBTMG in 1975.

Line	Name	Gauge	Route km	Total km
1	—	4' 8½''	19.5	*20.0
2	Hibiya	3' 6''	20.3	21.1
3	Ginza	4' 8½''	14.3	17.5
4	Marunouchi	4' 8½''	27.4	28.2
5	Tozai	3' 6''	30.8	31.7
6	—	3' 6''	13.1	30.5
7	—	—	—	20.7
8	Narimasu	—	—	33.2
9	Chiyoda	3' 6''	14.7	32.7
10	—	—	—	31.2
11	—	—	—	19.4

*Of which 1.2 km from Sengakuji to Shinagawas is operated by the Keihinkyuko Railway Co.

Authority:
Teito Rapid Transit Authority (TRTA)
19-6 Higashi Ueno 3-Chome, Teito Ku, Tokyo, Japan
Telephone: (03) 832 2111

Type of system: Full-metro.

History: The first section of Line 1 from Oshiage southward to Asakusa was opened in 1960, and extended in stages southward to its present terminus at Nishimagome. The TBTMG subsequently assumed operation of Line 6 Nishtakashimadaira to Mita.

General: Line 1 connects with private railways at each end, and thus provides the latter's suburban trains access to the city centre. At present (1976) Lines 1 and 6 are carrying about 810 000 passengers daily on average.

Technical Data:
Gauge: 1.067/1.435 m
Route length: 40.8 km
In tunnel: 35.7 km
Projected new lines (in construction): 14.5 km
Number of lines: 2
Number of stations (total): 44
  (in tunnel): 38
Stations:
  platform length (max): 165 km
Gradient (max): 3.5%
Curvature (max): 164 m
Speed (design max): 100 km/h
  (average commercial): 30.9-31.4 km/h
Electric system: Overhead; 1 500 V

Rolling Stock:

Car type:	Line 1	Line 6
Units:	164*	168*
Car dimensions: (length):	18.0 m	20.0 m
(width):	2.80 m	2.79 m
(height):	3.65 m	3.65 m
Total floor area (m²):	44.6	49.8
Doors per side:	3	4
Door (width):	1.3 m	1.3 m
Passages per side	6	8
Passengers per car:		
(total):	145	160
(seated):	50	54
Motors per car:	4	4
Motor rating:	85 kWh 117 hp	100 kWh 137 hp
Power per train:		
(max):	2 040	2 400
Brakes (type):	Rheostatic	

*Motorcars

Authority:
Transportation Bureau of the Tokyo Metropolitan Government (TBTMG)
10-1, 2-Chome, Yurakucho, Chiyoda-Ku, Tokyo, Japan
Telephone: (03) 216 1411

Type of system: Full-metro.

History: Operations began on the 14.3 km Ginza line (now Line 3) in 1927.

General: Teito operates 4 lines (Hibiya—20.3 km; Ginza 14.3 km; Maranouchi 27.4 km; Tozai 30.8 km) and is constructing two others: the 20.9 km Chiyodaline and the 10.2 km Yurakucholine.

Technical Data:
Gauge: 1.067/1.435 m
Route length: 123.9
Projected new lines (in construction): 31.1 km
Number of lines: 4
Number of stations (total): 115
Average distance between stations: 1.1 km
Gradient max: 4%
Curvature (max): 200 m
Speed (average commercial): 44.9 km/h
Electric system: Third rail and overhead
Type of rails: 50/60 kg/m

Rolling Stock:

Car type:	Line 2	Line 5	Line 9
Units:	304	246	178
Car dimensions:			
(length):	18.0 m	20.0 m	20.0 m
(width):	2.79 m	2.80 m	2.80 m
(height):	3.65 m	3.90 m	3.69 m
Total floor area (m²):	49.0	54.6	54.6
Doors per side:	3	4	4
Passengers per car:			
(total):	124	140	140
(seated):	52	54	51
Motors per car:	4	4	4
Motor rating:	75 kWh 103 hp	100 kWh 137 hp	145 kWh 200 hp
Power			
per train: (minimum):	600	800	—
(max):	3 000	—	—
Acceleration (max):	0.98	—	1.4
Deceleration:			
(normal service):	0.98	—	1.6
(emergency):	—	—	2.1
Bogie truck rigid base:	2.1	—	2.2
Distance between pivot	bogie 13.8	—	13.6
Brakes (type):	Rh/Pn	Rh/Pn	Rh/Pn
Weight-empty (tons):			
M:	31.5	32.0	30.2
R:	—	—	34.5
Tare/floor area (kg/m²):	643	586	553
Tare/length (kg/m):	1 750	1 600	1 510
Tare/passenger (kg/pass):	216	254	229

Traffic Data:
Passengers carried (weekday): 3 896 000
Average journey length: 7.2 km

TORONTO

Authority:
Toronto Transit Commission
1900 Yonge Street, Toronto, Ontario M4S 1Z2, Canada

History: This urban underground railway was the first "subway" to be built in Canada, materialising after many years of consideration, to relieve surface congestion on the streets of downtown Toronto. The first line, on a north-south axis (opened in 1954) and the second line on an east-west axis (opened fully in 1968) follow the course of the two main traffic arteries, Yonge Street, and Bloor Street and Danforth Avenue. A 2.68 mile section of the Yonge northerly extension opened 31 March 1973 and a further 2.73 miles opened on 30 March 1974.

Construction has been completed on a total of 8.65 miles of new subway. The Spadina subway runs 6.17 miles from a terminal station at Wilson Avenue to St. George Station. The line includes eight stations at an estimated cost of $220 million with the Province of Ontario and Metropolitan Toronto sharing the cost 75 per cent and 25 per cent respectively.

Construction is also in progress on a one-mile westerly extension and a 1.6 mile easterly extension of the Bloor-Danforth subway. Target date for opening 1980. The Commission also operates the City's 690-mile surface transit system of street cars, electric trolley buses and diesel buses.

Approval has been given to build a 4.3-mile light rail line—exclusive right-of-way—to connect the Scarborough Town Centre—a large Metro sub-centre—to the Bloor—Danforth subway at Kennedy subway station. Target date for opening—1982.

A total of 134 new subway cars worth $C65.7 million—the largest subway car purchase in the history of the Toronto Transit Commission—have been delivered from Hawker-Siddeley Canada for operation on the Spadina line and to meet additional service demands on the existing 50-km subway system.

General: Total cost of the 8 miles of new Bloor-Danforth Line was $C160 m. A further $77 m was expanded on the recent east and west extensions. The western extension from Keele to Islington, 3.49 miles *(5.6 km)*, includes 5 intermediate stations. The eastern extension from Woodbine to Warden, 2.77 miles *(4.8 km)* includes two intermediate stations. Total cost of the Yonge subway extension $140 million.

Route length: 26.55 miles *(38.3 km)* including 5.01 miles in shield-driven tunnel. Remainder in cut and cover or open cut.

Number of lines: 2 (radial); double track.

Number of stations served: 49.

Average station spacing: 0.66 miles *(1.1 km)*.

Passengers per annum: (1976): 199 million.

Max number of trains per hour each way: 26-27.

Max line capacity, one way: 40 000 passengers per hour on each line.

Number of cars per train: Old stock: 2-car units coupled to form 4, 6, or 8-car trains. New stock: 2 to 6 cars.

Capacity per car: Old stock: 230 (including 62 seated). New stock: 310 (including 83 seated).

Average schedule speed: 20 mph *(32 km/h)*.

Track gauge: 4 ft 10⅞ in *(1.5 m)*.

Type of rails: Flat-bottomed, 100 lb/yd *(49.6 kg/m)*.

Max gradient: 1 in 29 *(3.45%)*.

Type of Tunnel: Double-tracked 13 ft 9 in *(4.06 m)* high, 29 ft 2 in *(8.87 m)* wide between stations, 56 ft 4 in *(16.10 m)* wide at stations. They are at least 8 ft *(2.44 m)* below ground level to give frost protection and were built by the cut and cover and shield method. Tunnel linings are partly in cast iron and partly in concrete.

Method and voltage of current supply: Third rail; 600 V dc.

Rolling Stock: Number of cars owned December 1976, 494. Old stock: 136 cars built by the Glocester Carriage and Wagon Co, England. Overall length 57 ft 1½ in *(17.4 m)* and external body width 10 ft 4 in *(3.15 m)*.

Three sets of automatic double-doors each side of car. Weight per car 27 tons. Automatic centre-buffer couplers and British Thomson-Houston control equipment. 6 cars are of aluminium construction. 28 cars delivered 1957 are non-driving steel motor cars similar to the original 100 steel cars. 6 other steel cars have dynamic braking and rubber bogie suspension.

Other characteristics include: Fluorescent lighting; winter warmth from waste heat generated from the dynamic braking; voice transmission between crew and control and control and passengers.

New stock: The first subway cars to be built in Canada, 36 in number, by Montreal Locomotive Works, are 74 ft 5⅜ in long (17 ft longer than the older stock), 10 ft 3 in wide, and are of aluminium construction. There are 4 sliding doors on each side of each car. The passenger seating capacity of a 6-car train of this stock (at 84 per car) is equivalent to that of an 8-car train of the older stock. 164 cars were built by Hawker Siddeley Canada Ltd. for the new Bloor-Danforth Line. Similar to the previous 36 cars, they are driven by four 125 hp motors to each car. 76 Hawker Siddeley cars for the Yonge extension are similar to the previous Hawker Siddeley order with the exception of 6 cars which are equipped with solid-state (chopper) traction controls. 88 car order from Hawker Siddeley received during 1975 to meet additional service demands on existing subway systems.

Signalling: Automatic lock, with three-aspect colour-light signals and train stops.

Station layout: A number of stations have subsurface ticket halls. All platforms are 500 ft *(152.4 m)* long. There are both sides and centre platform stations on the system, the deeper being equipped with escalators to the total number of 152. Of these, 87 are on the Bloor-Danforth Line. Closed circuit television is installed at some stations.

Workshops: There is a car depot and workshops at Davisville and a new one at Greenwood.

VIENNA

Authority:
Wiener Stadtwerke-Verkehrsbetriebe
Favoritenstrasse 9, 1041 Vienna, Austria

Director:
Dr. Dipl.-Kfm., Ing. Mauric Carl

Vice Directors (Technical):
Dipl. Ing. Cabana Rudolf
Dr. techn. Dipl.-Ing. Körber Erich

History: The Stadtbahn system was opened, with steam traction, in June 1898. Electric traction was introduced between June, and October 1925.

General: Vienna's tramway system is the most extensive and the largest of Vienna's carriers, with 296.0 km (55 per cent) of the city's total 541 km of bus, tram and Stadtbahn route, and 67 per cent of the passenger total. As part of the declared policy to separate public transport from other traffic, some central tram routes are being diverted underground. In 1966 a semi-circular tunnel line was put into operation near the Ring (city centre) and in January 1969, additional tunnels for 4 tram routes, comprising 2 tunnel branches with 6 underground halts, became operational. Designated Phase Two in the tram-tunnel project, this section is situated on the South Belt, near the Süd-bahnhof. The tram tunnels are suitable for, and may form part of a 3-line U Bahn network, U1, U2, U4 for Vienna. In November, 1969, work commenced on Line 1 of this network and first section of the line completed at the end of 1973.

Line 1 begins at Praterstern near the North Schnellbahn station and runs for about 6 km southward, under the city centre and via Favoritentrasse to Reumannplatz, just beyhond the Gürtel (outer Ring Road). Tunnel construction is by the cut and cover method and shield-driven tunnel. Conventional underground trains will carry approximately 382 passengers per two-car unit. Line 1 was partly operational by 1977, and should be completed by 1980. It is proposed that Line 2 will incorporate the tram tunnels mentioned earlier, and Line 4 part of the existing Stadtbahn.

Another separate, but later, project is the proposed spur for the existing Stadtbahn, to link Vienna's growing north-eastern suburbs by rail with the city centre. This link would take the form of a tunnel beneath the river Danube, joining the present Stadtbahn at Nuss-dorferstrasse.

Vienna is also served by a surface rapid transit railway, the Austrian Federal Railway's "Schnellbahn". This line has recently been extended and now runs from Strebersdorf and Sussenbrunn, south-west to Liesing, a total route length of about 20.0 miles *(32 km)*. A common fare tariff applies to Vienna's Stadtbahn and Schnellbahn system.

Stadtbahn route length: 16.65 miles *(26.8 km)* (including 3.9 miles *(6.3 km)* in tunnels).

Number of lines: 4 lines (DG, GD, WD, G), which are physically connected to form a single operating system; all double track.

Number of stations served: 25.

Average station spacing: 0.6 miles *(1 km)*.

Stadtbahn passengers per annum: (1973) 73 500 000; (1974) 70 000 000. (1975): 75 000 000.

Number of cars per train: 3-9 cars.

Estimated capacity per car: Driving car, 20 seated, 52 standing; trailing car, 20 seated, 62 standing.

Track gauge: 4 ft 8½ in *(1.435 m)*.

Weight and type of rails: 35.8, 48.3 and 59.7 kg/m; flat-bottomed.

Max gradient: 1 in 35.

Minimum radius of curves: 426½ ft *(130 m)*, on running lines.

Type of tunnel: Tunnels are double track. On some sections they are 33 ft *(10 m)* wide, with vertical walls and an elliptical roof with a maximum height of 19½ ft *(5.93 m)*. On other stretches of line, they have a circular cross-section with a diameter of 29 ft 6 in *(9 m)*.

Method and voltage of current supply: Overhead; 750 V dc Power is supplied by the Vienna Electricity Works partly at 5 000 V ac and partly at 10 000 V ac and is transformed to 750 V dc at seven substations:— Hutteldorf; Unter St. Veit; Sechshaus; Thury; Kaunitz; Hauptzollamt; and Heilgenstadt.

Rolling Stock: Cars are two-axled. Simmering-Graz-Pauker have in recent years delivered 128 motor cars and 200 trailer cars with a length over buffers of 39 ft 1 in *(11.9 m)*, width 7 ft 4 in *(2.24 m)* and height 10 ft 6 in *(3.2 m)*. Motor cars weigh 17.25 tonnes, trailer cars 10.25 tonnes. Each car has two sets of doors on each side. Motor cars are equipped with single pantographs. All cars fitted with automatic central buffer-couplers.

Signalling: Automatic block, with ac track circuits and two-aspect colour-light signals.

Station layout: Mostly side-platforms.

WARSAW

Authority:
Biuro Planowainia Rozwoju
ul. Senatorska 36, Warsaw, Poland
Telephone: 27 37 35

Type of system: Full-metro.

General: The electrified suburban lines of the Polish State Railways in the Warsaw area include an underground section running through the centre of the city in an east-west direction. The tunnel which is 2.8 miles *(4.5 km)* long, four-tracked, and of "cut-and-cover" construction, lies on the so-called "Warsaw Through Line" between Warszawa Sródmiescie and the River Vistula, and passes for most of its length beneath main roads. Power is supplied at 3 000 V dc by overhead conductor wires. Electrification was carried out between 1936 and 1938 by British contractors, and the multiple-unit rolling stock supplied consisted of 3-car trainsets (one motor car and two articulated trailers), with automatic air-worked doors and Scharfenberg couplers. Severe damage was done to the Warsaw electrified lines during the Second World War, but reconstruction took place after 1945, and the electrification has since been further extended outwards from Warsaw along the main lines. New multiple-unit stock purchased from Sweden or built in Poland since the war for the Warsaw suburban lines is similar to the pre-war stock; the new cars have automatic doors (3 double-leaf doors on each side) and automatic centre-buffer couplers, and are coupled to form 3-car trainsets.

At present the Greater Warsaw area, about 166 m² *(430 km²)* is served by about 43 miles *(70 km)* of conventional railways with more than 20 stations linked with the countrywide Polish Railways network. These lines are used for suburban traffic and also link the outskirts with the town centre. Detail includes: 3-car traction units produced by PAFAWAG Wroclaw. Continuous hp of traction motors type Lkc-450 is 580 kW; dead load 125 tons; maximum speed 68 mph *(110 km/h)*, number of seats 228, standing room for 372 passengers; Knorr braking system. The economic speed of trains of 3-car units in the Warsaw district is 27 mph *(45 km/h)*.

There is also a separated segment about 5 miles *(8 km)* long of normal track line to Grodzisk Mazowiecki handled by Different rolling stock, 600 V dc, produced by PAFAWAG Wroclaw. The electrification of the Warsaw railway and all its suburban sections was completed in 1972. At present the electrified lines carry suburban passenger traffic in seven directions radially from Warsaw.

Final design studies are being completed on Warsaw's first rapid transit line to run 24 km between the southern and northern districts via the city centre. The entire line will run in tunnel at an average depth of 10 m below the surface. At present 23 stations are planned to be spaced at approximately 600 to 700 m intervals through the centre of the city and at 1 200 m intervals on the outskirts. Track gauge is to be 1.435 m and planned power supply, third rail 825 V dc. The line is expected to operate with six-car trainsets on a 90 second headway. The line is to form the first stage of a projected 130 km subway system serving about 130 stations. Following construction of the first line a second is to be built between the two banks of the Vistula river.

Technical Data:
Gauge: 1.435
Projected new lines (in design): 24 km
Number of lines: 1
Number of stations (total): 23
Average distance between stations: 650 m
Electric system: Third rail; 825 V dc

WUPPERTAL

Authority:
Wuppertal Stadtwerke AG-Schwebebahn
Bromberger St 39-41, 56 Wuppertal 2, German Federal
Republic
Telephone: (0202) 5691
Cables: STADTWERKE-WPT

Type of system: Suspended monorail.

History: Operations commenced 1901.

Technical Data:
  Gauge: Monorail
  Route length: 13.3
  Number of lines: 1
  Number of stations (total): 18

Speed (design max): 80 km/h
  (average commercial): 25.1 km/h
Electric system: Third rail; 600 V

Rolling Stock:

Car type:	B-50	GTW
Units:	16	28
Car dimensions: (length):	11.83 m	24.1 m
(width):	2.2 m	2.2 m
(height):	—	4.2 m
Total floor area (m²):	26.4	53.0
Doors per side:	3	4
Door (width):	1.3 m	1.3 m
Passages per side:	6	8
Passengers		
per car: (total):	90	200
(seated):	31	48

Motors per car:	2	4
Motor rating:	45 kWh	—
	62 hp	50 hp
Power per train:		
(minimum):	90	—
(max):	180	—
Bogie truck rigid base:	1.5	1.28
Distance between bogie pivot:	8.0	7.65
Brakes (type):	E1 Disc	E1 Disc
Equipment used:		
speed recorders		
dead man control		
air conditioning		
cushion seats		
doors other than sliding type		
Body material:	Steel	Steel
Weight-empty (tons) M:	11	—
Tare/floor area (kg/m²):	11	

YOKOHAMA

Authority:
Municipal Transportation Bureau
3-31 Chome Honmachi, Nakaku 231, Yokohama, Japan

Type of system: Full Metro.

General: Construction work on Yokohama's new underground railway system has been in progress since 1970.

Recent mushrooming population increase in Yokohama has caused excessive congestion of road traffic as well as transportation facilities. In order to modernise the latter to cope with the aggravated traffic situation, the City of Yokohama decided to discontinue street car services and construct rapid transit railways instead.

In 1966, a plan for the construction of an extensive rapid transit system including subway lines linking the suburban and downtown areas was approved by the Municipal Transportation Council. It was agreed that the subway system should be completed by 1985.

This rapid transit project calls for the construction of four lines with a total length of 46.3 miles (64.5 km) costing Y155 000 million which will be raised by floating bonds.

The following four lines are planned:
Line 1: Shonandai (Fufisawa City) — Totsuka — Kamiooka — Isezaki-cho; 11.4 miles (18.6 km).
Line 2: Byobugaura — Yoshinocho — Yokohama Station — Kanagawa Shinmachi; 7 miles (11.4 km).

Line 3: Honmoku — Yamashitacho — Isezakicho — Yokohama Station — Shin Yokohama Station — Katsuda; 11.8 miles (19.2 km).
Line 4: Tsurumi — Sueyoshibashi — Katsuda — Moto Ishikawa; 9.4 miles (15.3 km).

Priority is being given to the important rapid transit routes 1 and 3 passing through the city's central area. The section of Line 1 from Kami-Ohoka to Isezakichoja-machi (5.3 km) was opened to traffic on December 16, 1972, and a 2.7 km southward extension to Kami-Nagaya was due to open in 1974.

On Line 3, construction work from Yokohama Central, south to Onoe-Cho 1.71 miles (2.75 km), was started in February 1972.

The network will consist of sub-surface lines in box-type tunnel under urban Yokohama, rising to elevated tracks in the suburbs. The trains, drawing power at 750 v dc from a current rail, will initially comprise three-car units, increasing to six-car units ultimately. They will operate under a system of automatic train control. The track gauge of 14 ft 8½ in (1.435 m) will be similar to that adopted in most of the recent Japanese rapid transit railway construction.

Technical Data:
Gauge: 1.435 m
Route length: 5.7 km
In tunnel: 5.7 km
Projected new lines (in construction): 8.5 km
  (in design): 50.3 km
Number of lines: 1
Number of stations (total): 6

(in tunnel): 6
Stations:
platform length (minimum): 120 m
Speed (design maximum): 90 km/h
Electric system: Third rail; 750 V

Rolling stock:
Car type (year introduced): 1971
Units: 21
Car dimensions:
  (length): 18.0 m
  (width): 2.78 m
  (height): 3.54 m
Total floor area (m²): 50.0
Door per side: 3
Door (width): 1.30 m
Passages per side: 6
Passengers per car:
  (total): 145
  (seated): 52
Motors per car: 4
Motor rating: 120 kWh
  165 hp
Power per train:
  (maximum): 1 440

Traffic Data:
Train/hours/track: 12
Train capacity (passengers): 435
Total passengers/track/hour (peak): 5 220
Train headways existing: 5 minutes

INDEX OF MANUFACTURERS

INDEX OF ASSOCIATIONS AND AGENCIES

INDEX OF CONSULTANTS

GENERAL INDEX OF RAILWAYS

Printed in England by Netherwood Dalton & Co. Ltd., Huddersfield

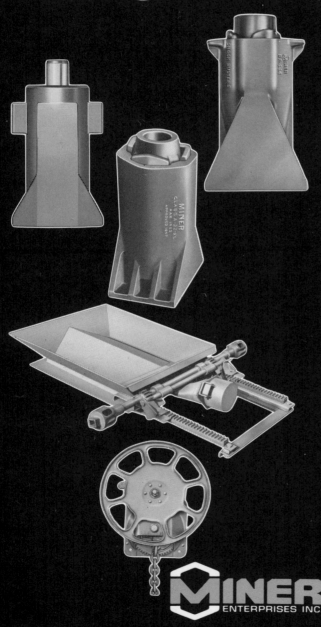